$\frac{|b}{|g}$

McClane's
New
Standard

Encyclopedia

AND INTERNATIONAL ANGLING GUIDE

ENLARGED AND REVISED EDITION

Edited by A. J. McCLANE

Illustrated by RICHARD E. YOUNGER
and FRANCES WATKINS

HENRY HOLT AND COMPANY
NEW YORK

**Enlarged and Revised
Second Edition
of McCLANE'S
STANDARD
FISHING ENCYCLOPEDIA**

Pictures on the following pages are credited to: p. 51, photo by Arizona Game & Fish Dept.; pp. 53, 593, photos by Tom McNally; p. 170, FPG-photo by H. Rowed; p. 192, Photo Researchers, Inc.; pp. 249, 250, photos by Vernon Ogilvie, C.G. Maxwell; p. 286, photo by John Tarlton, AIBP, ARPS; pp. 315, 319, 325, 327, 330, photos by Arie de Zanger; p. 409, photo by J. Clegg, England; p. 426, photo by Bob Smallman, DPI; p. 575, photo by Manitoba Department of Industry & Commerce; pp. 580, 587, photos by D.P. Wilson, F.R.P.S.; p. 595, photo by A. Upitis from Shostal; p. 600, photos by Stanley G. Jewett, Jr.; p. 668, photo by Russ Kinne, Photo Researchers, Inc.; p. 679, photo by Richard Younger; p. 747, photo by Photo Researchers, Inc.; p. 810, photo by P.M. McClane; pp. 868, 869, photos by Gilbert Drake, Jr.; p. 1132, photo by FPG Photo.

Published by Henry Holt and Company, Inc.,
115 West 18th Street, New York, New York 10011.
Published in Canada by Fitzhenry & Whiteside Limited,
195 Allstate Parkway, Markham, Ontario L3R 4T8.

Library of Congress Cataloging-in-Publication Data
McClane, Albert Jules, 1922–   ed.
    McClane's new standard fishing encyclopedia and international angling guide.
    First ed. published in 1965 under title: McClane's standard fishing encyclopedia and international angling guide.
    1. Fishing—Dictionaries. I. Title. II. Title: New standard fishing encyclopedia and international angling guide.
SH411.M18   1974   799.1'03   74-6108
ISBN 0-8050-1117-X

Designer: Marion Needham Krupp
5   7   9   10   8   6   4
Printed in the United States of America

Articles on Louis Agassiz, Van Campen Heilner and Henry W. Herbert are condensed from *Profiles in Salt Water Angling* by George Reiger. © 1973 by George Reiger. Published by Prentice-Hall, Inc., Englewood Cliffs, New Jersey. The article "Algae: 'Grass' of Many Waters" and the accompanying art are from *Maine Fish and Game*, Summer, 1968, copyright 1968, Maine Dept. of Inland Fisheries and Game.

Contributors

Initials and names of contributors to McCLANE'S NEW STANDARD FISHING ENCYCLOPEDIA AND INTERNATIONAL ANGLING GUIDE with the principal subjects written by them. The arrangement is *alphabetical by initials*.

A.C.H.   SOUTH AFRICA
A. CECIL HARRISON, Secretary, The Cape Piscatorial Society, Westminster House, Capetown, South Africa; editor of *Piscator*

A.C.N.   TROUT UNLIMITED
ARTHUR C. NEUMAN, former Executive Secretary, Trout Unlimited, Saginaw, Michigan

A.D.B.   STRIPED BASS
ARTHUR D. BRADFORD, Jr., Chief, Fisheries Division, Pennsylvania Fish Commission, Benner Spring Fish Research Station, Bellefonte, Pennsylvania

A.E.N.   SUNAPEE TROUT
ARTHUR E. NEWELL, Supervisor, Fisheries Management and Research, Fish and Game Department, Concord, New Hampshire

A.G.   ANGLING LITERATURE
ARNOLD GINGRICH, Publisher, *Esquire*, New York, N.Y.; Author of *The Well-Tempered Angler*, Editor of the *Gordon Garland*

A.H.   CHILE (part)
ALFRED HEUSSER, Angling Guide, Pucon, Chile

A.H.G.   ALGAE
ALTON H. GUSTAFSON, Chairman, Department of Biology, Bowdoin College, Brunswick, Maine

A.J.B.   AFTMA
ANDREW J. BOEHM, Executive Director, American Fishing Tackle Manufacturers Association, Chicago, Illinois

A.J.McC.   EDITOR
A. J. McCLANE, Executive Editor, *Field & Stream*, New York, N.Y.; Author of *The Practical Fly Fisherman, The American Angler, Spinning for Fresh and Salt Water Fish of North America, 100 Best Fishing Spots in the World*

A.L.R.   WYOMING
ANDREW L. RUSKANEN, Information Assistant, Game and Fish Commission, Cheyenne, Wyoming

A.M.B.   LONGFINNED/SHORTFINNED EELS
A. M. BURNETT, Fisheries Research Division, New Zealand Marine Department, Christchurch, New Zealand

A.P.   ROD-BUILDING
ALAN PRATT, Seattle *Times*, Washington

B.B.C.   FISH SPECIES
BRUCE B. COLLETTE, Ph.D., Assistant Director, Bureau of Commercial Fisheries Ichthyological Laboratory, U. S. National Museum, Washington, D. C.

B.McC.   GREAT LAKES FISHING
BINGHAM McCLELLAN, President, Burke-Flexo Products Company, Traverse City, Michigan

B.O.F.   MISSISSIPPI
BARRY O. FREEMAN, Chief, Fisheries Division, Game & Fish Commission, Jackson, Mississippi

B.S.   INDIANA
BILL SCIFRES, Outdoor Editor, *The Indianapolis Star*, Indianapolis, Indiana

B.Sr.   ARIZONA
BILL SIZER, Chief of Information and Education Division, Game & Fish Department, Phoenix, Arizona

B.W.   SALTWATER FISHING METHODS
BILL WISNER, former Managing Editor, *Sportsmen's Life*, Roosevelt, New York; Author of *How to Catch Salt Water Fish*

C.A.P.   MISSOURI
CHARLES A. PURKETT, Jr., Chief of Fisheries, Missouri Conservation Commission, Jefferson City, Missouri

C.C.L.   LAKE TROUT
C. C. LINDSEY, Institute of Fisheries and Department of Zoology, University of British Columbia, Vancouver, British Columbia

C.Cy.   IDAHO
CLARE CONLEY, former Editor, *Field & Stream*, New York, N. Y.

C.J.K.   NEW BRUNSWICK
C. JAMES KERSWILL, Ph.D., Assistant Director, St. Andrews Biological Station, Fisheries Research Board of Canada, New Brunswick

C.K.   MANITOBA
CORY KILVERT, Assistant Director, Travel & Publicity, Province of Manitoba, Winnipeg, Manitoba

C.M.K.   ROD-BUILDING (part)
CLAUDE M. KREIDER (Deceased), former Angling Editor, *Western Outdoors*, Newport Beach, California; Author of *The Bamboo Rod and How to Build It*

C.R.M.   SHARK FISHING
CHARLES R. MEYER, Patchogue, New York; Author of *Fishing America*

C.S.W.   SOUTHERN SMELTS
C. S. WOODS, Ph.D., Zoology Department, Canterbury University, Christchurch, New Zealand

D.A.W.   THERMAL STRATIFICATION
DWIGHT A. WEBSTER, Ph.D., Professor, Fishery Biology, Department of Conservation, New York State College of Agriculture, Cornell University, Ithaca, New York

D.B.   MONTANA
DAN BAILEY, Dan Bailey's Fly Shop, Livingston, Montana

D.deS.   FISH SPECIES
DONALD P. de SYLVA, Ph.D., Marine Biologist, The Marine Laboratory, University of Miami, Miami, Florida

D.F.R.   NORTH CAROLINA
DUANE F. RAVER, Jr., Managing Editor, *Wildlife in North Carolina*, Wildlife Resources Commission, Raleigh, North Carolina

D.Gr.   ROD-BUILDING
DON A. GREEN, Vice President, Fenwick Rod Company, Bainbridge Island, Washington

D.H.S.   NEBRASKA
DICK H. SCHAFFER, Chief, Information-Tourism, Nebraska Game Commission, Lincoln, Nebraska

D.K.C.   FISH SPECIES
DAVID K. CALDWELL, Curator of Ichthyology, Los Angeles County Museum, Los Angeles, California

D.L.   FISH SPECIES
DARREL LOUDER, Fishery Biologist, Division of Inland Fisheries, North Carolina Resources Commission, Raleigh, North Carolina

D.M.   FISH SPECIES
DAVID MARLBOROUGH, Fishery Biologist, London Branch Section, British Ichthyological Society, Associate, Institute of Biology, British Ecological Society

D.McC.   BAHAMAS
DON McCARTHY, Director, Bahamas Fishing Bureau, Nassau, Bahamas; Author of *Fisherman's Guide to the Bahamas*

D.P.B.   JAMAICA / NORTH CAROLINA (part)
DOUGLAS P. BOURNIQUE, Palm Beach, Florida; Angling Association of Jamaica; Cape Hatteras Billfish Club

D.S.O'B.   NORTHWEST TERRITORIES
D. S. O'BRIEN, Tourist Development Officer, N.W.T. Tourist Office, 150 Kent Street, Ottawa, Canada

D.W.   FLY-TYING
DAVID WHITLOCK, Fly-tyer, Bartlesville, Oklahoma

E.A.B.   PUERTO RICO
ESTEBAN A. BIRD, Banco Crédito y Ahorro Ponceño, San Juan, Puerto Rico; Author of *Fishing off Puerto Rico*

E.A.S.   AMERICAN FISHERIES SOCIETY
ELWOOD A. SEAMAN, former Secretary and Treasurer, American Fisheries Society, Washington, D. C.

E.B.   NEW MEXICO
ELLIOTT BARKER, Executive Secretary, New Mexico Wildlife and Conservation Association, Santa Fe, New Mexico; author of *Beatty's Cabin*

E.Br.   WASHINGTON
ENOS BRADNER, Outdoor Editor, *The Seattle Times*, Seattle, Washington; Author of *Northwest Angling*

E.C.   TENNESSEE
ERNEST CONNER, Jr., former Education Supervisor, Tennessee Game and Fish Commission, Cordell Hull Building, Nashville, Tennessee

E.C.B.   SALTWATER FISHING METHODS
EDWIN C. BUCKOW, Outdoor Editor, *Palm Beach Post-Times*, West Palm Beach, Florida

E.C.M.   TAXIDERMY
EDWARD C. MIGDALSKI, Ichthyologist, The Bingham Oceanographic Laboratory, Yale University, New Haven, Conn.; Author of *How to Make Fish Mounts, Angler's Guide to the Salt Water Game Fishes, Fresh Water Sport Fishes of North America, Boys' Book of Fishes*

E.F.   SOUTH CAROLINA
EDDIE FINLAY, Secretary, South Carolina, Wildlife Resources Commission, Columbia, South Carolina

E.H.R.   FLY-TYING
E. H. ROSBOROUGH, Fly-tyer, Chiloquin, Oregon

E.M.B.   MARYLAND
EDWIN M. BARRY, Chief, Inland Fish Management, Game and Inland Fish Commission, Annapolis, Maryland

E.M.L.   FRESHWATER ECOLOGY
EDWARD M. LOWRY, Ph.D., Professor of Zoology, Stout State College, Menomonie, Wisconsin

E.T.W.   LOUISIANA
EDNARD TRIST WALDO, Wildlife and Fisheries Commission, New Orleans, Louisiana

F.C.   UTAH
FRANK CALKINS, Etna, Wyoming; Associate Editor, *Fishes of Utah*

F.C.O.   OREGON (part)
FLY FISHER'S CLUB OF OREGON, Portland, Oregon

F.H.B. FISH SPECIES
FREDERICK H. BERRY, Systematic Zoologist (Fishes), United States Department of the Interior, Fish and Wildlife Service, Bureau of Commercial Fisheries, Brunswick, Georgia

F.J.M. VIRGIN ISLANDS / BLUEFIN TUNA
FRANK J. MATHER III, Associate Scientist, Woods Hole Oceanographic Institution, Woods Hole, Massachusetts

F.K. LONG ISLAND
FRANK KEATING, Outdoor Editor, *Long Island Daily Press,* Jamaica, New York

F.M.P. OUTBOARD MOTORS / NAUTICAL TERMS
F. M. PAULSON, Boating Editor, *Field & Stream,* New York, N. Y.

F.W. SURF CASTING
FRANK WOOLNER, Editor, *The Salt Water Sportsman,* Boston, Massachusetts; Outdoor Editor, *The Worcester Evening Gazette;* Co-author, *The Complete Book of Striped Bass Fishing* and *The Complete Book of Weakfishing*

F.W.B. SARGASSUM FISH
FREDERICK W. BROCKMAN, Fishery Biologist, U. S. Fish & Wildlife Service, Florida State University, Tallahassee

G.A.B. BLUEFIN TUNA (part)
GEORGE A. BASS (Deceased), Chairman, Board of Governors, Annual Bahamas International Tuna Match, Nassau, Bahamas

G.B.G. VERMONT
GEORGE B. GORDON, Jamaica, Vermont

G.D.O. HOOK
GUNNAR DAHL, O. Mustad & Son, Oslo, Norway

G.E.C. SASKATCHEWAN
G. E. COULDWELL, Director of Fisheries, Department of Natural Resources, Province of Saskatchewan, Prince Albert, Saskatchewan

G.H.C. OKLAHOMA
GEORGE H. CROUSE, Editor, *Oklahoma Wildlife,* Department of Wildlife Conservation, Oklahoma City, Oklahoma

G.S. ARGENTINA (part)
GUSTAVO SCHWED, Angling Guide, San Carlos de Bariloche, Argentina

G.V. KANSAS
GEORGE VALYER, Forestry, Fish and Game Commission, Pratt, Kansas

G.V.F. PRINCE EDWARD ISLAND
GEORGE V. FRASER, Director, Prince Edward Island Travel Bureau, Charlottetown, Prince Edward Island, Canada

G.W.R. ANGLING LITERATURE
GEORGE W. REIGER, Washington Editor, National Wildlife Foundation; Associate Editor, *Field & Stream;* author of *Profiles in Salt Water Angling;* editor of *The Zane Grey Outdoorsman*

H.A. OHIO
HANK ANDREWS, Outdoor Editor, *The Cleveland Press,* Cleveland, Ohio

H.A.D. FLY-TYING
HARRY A. DARBEE, Chairman, Conservation Commission of BEAMOC, Roscoe, New York

H.A.M. ROD-BUILDING
HORACE A. MARTIN, Director of Production, Fenwick Rod Company, Westminster, California

H.B.M. MARINE ECOLOGY
HILARY B. MOORE, Ph.D., Professor of Marine Biology, The Marine Laboratory, Virginia Key, Miami, Florida; Author of *Marine Ecology*

H.D.Z. GEORGIA
HOWARD D. ZELLER, Chief, Fisheries Division, State Game & Fish Commission, Atlanta, Georgia

H.F.B. ICE FISHING
HAROLD F. BLAISDELL, Pittsford, Vermont; Author of *Tricks That Take Fish*

H.G.M. OPALEYE
H. GEOFFREY MOSER, Research Assistant, Allan Hancock Foundation, University of Southern California at Los Angeles

H.L. BLUEFISH
HENRY LYMAN, Commander USNR (Ret.); Publisher, *Saltwater Sportsman,* Boston, Massachusetts; Co-author of *The Complete Book of Striped Bass Fishing* and *The Complete Book of Weakfishing;* Author of *Bluefishing*

H.S. FLY-TYING
HELEN SHAW, Fly-tyer, New York, N. Y.; Author of *Fly-Tying*

H.T. KENTUCKY
HARRY TOWLES, Director, Division of Public Relations, Department of Fish and Wildlife Resources, Frankfort, Kentucky

H.V.L. FIRST AID
HAROLD V. LIDDLE, M.D., Thoracic & Cardiovascular Surgery, Rumel Chest Clinic, Salt Lake City, Utah

H.V.R.P. WOODS HOLE OCEANOGRAPHIC INST.
H. V. R. PALMER, Jr., Public Affairs Officers, Woods Hole Oceanographic Institution, Woods Hole, Massachusetts

I.B.B. ALABAMA
I. B. BYRD, Chief Biologist, Fisheries Section, Department of Conservation, Montgomery, Alabama

J.B.M. MINNESOTA
JOHN B. MOYLE, Research Supervisor, Minnesota Division of Game and Fish, St. Paul, Minnesota

J.C. AUSTRIA
JACK CORNELIUS, Director of The American Heritage Foundation; Member, Minnesota Natural Resources Council, Minneapolis, Minnesota

J.C.B. FISH SPECIES
JOHN C. BRIGGS, Ph.D., Professor and Chairman, Department of Zoology, University of South Florida, Tampa, Florida

J.E.M. FISH SPECIES
JAMES E. MORROW, Associate Professor, Fisheries, Department of Wildlife Management, University of Alaska, College, Alaska

J.E.R. FISH SPECIES
JOHN E. RANDALL, Ph.D., Director, Institute of Marine Biology, University of Puerto Rico, Mayagüez, Puerto Rico; author of *Caribbean Reef Fishes*

J.F. CALIFORNIA
JIM FREEMAN, Outdoor Editor, *Oakland Tribune*, Oakland, California

J.F.McI. VIRGINIA
JAMES F. McINTEER, Jr., Chief, Education Division, Commission of Game and Inland Fisheries, Richmond, Virginia

J.G. CONNECTICUT/SEA TROUT
JAMES GALLIGAN (*Deceased*), former Chief of Fisheries, Board of Fisheries & Game, Hartford, Connecticut

J.Gr. FIBERGLASS/ROD-BUILDING
JIM GREEN, Research and Development, Fenwick Rod Company, Bainbridge, Washington

J.K. NEW BRUNSWICK
JAMES KERSWILL, Ph.D., former Assistant Director, Fisheries Research Board of Canada, St. Andrews, New Brunswick; Director, Research and Development, Fisheries and Marine Service, Ottawa, Ontario

J.McD. DAME JULIANA BERNERS/ THEODORE GORDON
JOHN McDONALD, Member, Board of Editors, *Fortune*, New York, N. Y.; Author of *The Origins of Angling*, *The Complete Fly Fisherman*, *The Notes & Letters of Theodore Gordon*

J.McM.U. BRITISH ISLES
JAMES MacMILLAN URE, Secretary General, British Ichthyological Society; Editor, *British Ichthyological Journal;* Member, The Anglers' Research Group

J.R. FISH SPECIES
JOHN RAYNER, Ph.D., Chief, Division of Wildlife Research, Oregon State Game Commission, Corvallis, Oregon

J.Ry. SPORTFISHERMAN
JOHN RYBOVICH, Jr., Rybovich & Sons Boat Works, Inc., West Palm Beach, Florida

J.S. BIG-GAME FISHING
JACK SAMSON, Editor, *Field & Stream*, New York, New York; author of *Line Down*

J.T.S. FISH SPECIES
JAMES T. SHIELDS, former Director, Division of Game and Fish, Department of Conservation, Saint Paul, Minnesota

J.W.A. CRAYFISH
JAMES W. AVAULT, Jr., Ph.D., Associate Professor of Fisheries, Louisiana State University, Baton Rouge, Louisiana

J.W.B. SALTWATER FLY-FISHING
JOSEPH W. BROOKS, Richmond, Virginia; Author of *The Complete Book of Fly Fishing*, *Greatest Fishing* and *A World of Fishing*

J.W.L. AQUATIC INSECTS
JUSTIN W. LEONARD, Ph.D., Professor of Natural Resources and Acting Chairman, Department of Fisheries, School of Natural Resources, The University of Michigan, Ann Arbor, Michigan; Author of *Mayflies of Michigan Trout Streams*

J.W.S. NORTH DAKOTA
JAMES W. SPRAGUE, Fisheries Biologist, Fish and Game Department, Riverdale, North Dakota

K.B. FISH SPECIES/FISH CULTURE
KEEN BUSS, former Chief Aquatic Biologist, Benner Spring Fish Research Station, Bellefonte, Pennsylvania

K.D.C. IOWA
KENNETH D. CARLANDER, Ph.D., Professor of Zoology, Iowa State University of Science and Technology; Leader, Iowa Cooperative Fishery Research Unit; Author of *Handbook of Freshwater Fishery Biology*

K.M.M. POLLUTION
KENNETH M. MACKENTHUN, former Public Health Biologist of the Committee on Water Pollution Control for the State of Wisconsin; presently associated with Department of Health, Education, and Welfare, Robert A. Taft Sanitary Engineering Center, Cincinnati, Ohio; Author of *Limnological Aspects of Recreational Lakes*

L.A.W. TEXAS
L. A. WILKE, Texas Game and Fish Commission, Austin, Texas; Author of *Lakes and Streams of Texas*

L.B.F.   ROD-BUILDING
LOUIS B. FEIERABEND, Consulting Engineer, IBM, Poughkeepsie, New York

L.E.M.   SWORDFISH (part)
LOUIS E. MARRON (Deceased), Palm Beach, Florida; Brielle Marlin and Tuna Club, Brielle, New Jersey; I.G.F.A.

L.J.P.   NEW ZEALAND SNAPPER/KAHAWAI
L. J. PAUL, Fisheries Research Division, New Zealand Marine Department, Wellington, New Zealand

L.L.M.   FLY LINE MANUFACTURE
LEON L. MARTUCH, President, Scientific Anglers Inc., Midland, Michigan

L.R.   FISH SPECIES
LUIS RIVAS, Professor, Department of Zoology, Ichthyological Laboratory & Museum, University of Miami, Coral Gables, Florida

M.F.B.   SOUTH DAKOTA
MARVIN F. BOUSSU, Superintendent of Fisheries, Department of Game, Fish and Parks, Pierre, South Dakota

M.J.P.   ALBERTA
MARTIN J. PAETZ, Ph.D., Chief Fishery Biologist, Alberta Department of Lands and Forests, Edmonton, Alberta

M.K.B.   CAVIAR
MALCOLM K. BEYER, Brig. General USMCR (Ret.); President, Iron Gate Products, New York, N.Y.

M.K.McK.   TARAKIHI
MARGARET K. McKENZIE, Fisheries Research Division, New Zealand Marine Department, Wellington, New Zealand

M.W.S.   NEW BRUNSWICK
MORDEN W. SMITH, Ph.D., Fishery Biologist, Fisheries Research Board of Canada, St. Andrews, New Brunswick

N.E.C.   TEXAS
NEIL E. CARTER, Texas Parks and Wildlife Department, Austin, Texas

O.K.   HOTEL FISHING
OLIVER KITE (Deceased), Netheravon, Salisbury, Wilts., England; Author of Nymph Fishing in Practise, Grayling

P.C.   FIBERGLASS/ROD-BUILDING
PHILIP T. CLOCK, President, Sevenstrand Tackle Manufacturing Company, and Fenwick Rod Company, Westminster, California

P.E.H.   NEW JERSEY (part)
PAUL E. HAMER, Senior Fisheries Biologist, Marine Fisheries Laboratory, Seaside Park, New Jersey

P.H.   QUEBEC (part)
PIERRE HEBERT, Assistant Director of Information, Department of Game and Fisheries, Quebec City, Quebec

P.I.T.   MICHIGAN
P. I. TACK, Ph.D., Professor and Chairman, Department of Fisheries and Wildlife, Michigan State University, East Lansing, Michigan

P.N.J.   AMERICAN CASTING ASSOCIATION
PAUL N. JONES, Executive Secretary, American Casting Association, Nashville, Tennessee

P.O.R.   ONTARIO
P. O. RHYNAS, Chief, Operations Branch, Ontario Department of Lands and Forests, Toronto, Ontario

P.S.F.   HAWAII (part)
PETER S. FITHIAN, Director, Pacific Fishing Unlimited, Honolulu, Hawaii

R.A.J.   FISH SPECIES
ROBERT A. JONES, former Supervisor, Fisheries Management, Connecticut Board of Fisheries and Game, Hartford, Connecticut

R.B.R.   LOBSTERETTES
RICHARD B. ROE, Fishery Biologist, Bureau of Commercial Fisheries, Pascagoula, Mississippi

R.C.   BAJA CALIFORNIA
RAY CANNON, Fishing Editor, Western Outdoor News, Los Angeles, California

R.C.W.   SPIN-CASTING REEL (part)
RICHARD C. WOLFF, Vice President, The Garcia Corporation, Teaneck, New Jersey; Author of Fishing Tackle and Techniques

R.E.   MAINE
ROBERT ELLIOT, former Director, Recreational Promotion, Department of Economic Development; State House, Augusta, Maine; Author of The Eastern Brook Trout, New England Bass Fishing

R.F.S.   NEW JERSEY (part)
ROLAND F. SMITH, Ph.D., Assistant Chief, Branch Marine Fisheries Division of Biological Research, Bureau of Commercial Fisheries, Washington, D. C.

R.H.G.   FISH SPECIES
ROBERT H. GIBBS, Jr., Ph.D., Associate Curator, Division of Fishes, U. S. National Museum, Washington, D. C.

R.H.S.   SPORT FISHING INSTITUTE
RICHARD H. STROUD, M.Sc., Executive Vice President, Sport Fishing Institute, Washington, D. C.

R.M.   VIRGINIA
ROBERT MARTIN, Chief, Fish Division, Commission of Game and Inland Fisheries, Richmond, Virginia

R.P.   FLY-TYING
ROY PATRICK, Patrick's Fly Shop, Seattle, Washington; Author of *Tie Your Own Flies* and *The Pacific Northwest Fly Patterns*

R.S.L.   ALASKA/YUKON
RICHARD S. LEE, M.Sc., University of Alaska, College, Alaska

R.S.McC.   MASSACHUSETTS
ROBERT S. McCAIG, Assistant Biologist, Division of Fisheries and Game, Westboro, Massachusetts

R.T.J.   NEW ZEALAND
R. T. JACKA, Secretary, New Zealand Angling and Casting Association, Auckland, New Zealand

S.G.J.   AQUATIC INSECTS
STANLEY G. JEWETT, Jr., Fishery Biologist, U. S. Bureau of Commercial Fisheries, Portland, Oregon

S.J.   WEST VIRGINIA
SKIP JOHNSON, Outdoor Editor, *The Charleston Gazette*, Charleston, West Virginia

S.L.P.   BERMUDA
S. L. PERINCHIEF, Director, The Bermuda Fishing Information Bureau, Hamilton, Bermuda

S.N.   ZANE GREY
STEVE NETHERBY, Camping Editor, *Field & Stream*, New York, N.Y., Editor of *The Experts Book of Freshwater Fishing*

S.R.   ROD-BUILDING
STEVE RAYMOND, Seattle *Times*, Washington, and Editor of *Fly Fishing Magazine*, official publication of the Federation of Fly Fishermen

S.W.   ARKANSAS (part)
SAM WELCH, Editor and Publisher, *The Ozark Fisherman*, Bull Shoals, Arkansas

T.B.T.   BRITISH ISLES (part)
T. B. THOMAS, Captain (Ret.), Milward's Fishing Tackle Ltd., Redditch, England

T.D.W.   FISH SPECIES
THOMAS D. WHITE (Deceased), General USAF; former Air Force Chief of Staff; Military Editor, *Newsweek*; American Society of Ichthyologists and Herpetologists

T.H.H.   ARKANSAS
T. H. HOLDER, Chief, Environmental Preservation Division, Arkansas Game and Fish Commission, Little Rock, Arkansas

T.J.W.   RHODE ISLAND
THOMAS J. WRIGHT, Chief, Division of Fish and Game, Department of Agriculture & Conservation, Providence, Rhode Island

T.L.W.   WISCONSIN
THOMAS L. WIRTH, Fishery Biologist, Conservation Department, Madison, Wisconsin

T.McN.   ILLINOIS
TOM McNALLY, Outdoor Editor, *Chicago Tribune*, Chicago, Illinois; Editor, *Fishermen's Digest*, Chicago, Illinois

V.O.   FISH SPECIES
VERNON OGILVIE, Fishery Biologist, Florida Game and Fish Commission, West Palm Beach, Florida

V.W.   OARFISH
VLADIMIR WALTERS, Ph.D., Assistant Professor, Department of Zoology, University of California

W.A.R.   DISEASES AND PARASITES
WILLIAM A. ROGERS, Ph.D., Associate Professor, Department of Fisheries and Allied Aquacultures, Auburn University, Auburn, Alabama

W.B.   STEELHEAD FISHING
WAYNE BUSZEK (*Deceased*), Buz's Fly and Tackle Shop, Visalia, California

W.B.H.   FIRST AID
WALTER B. HOOVER, Jr., M.D., General Surgeon, John F. Kennedy Hospital, Lake Worth, Florida

W.E.H.   BRITISH COLUMBIA
W. E. HAWKINS, Jr., Commissioner, The Victoria & Island Publicity Bureau, Victoria, British Columbia

W.G.   NOVA SCOTIA
WILLIAM GREENAWAY, Major (Ret.), Vice-President, Nova Scotia Salmon Anglers Association, Halifax, Nova Scotia; Author of *The Way to Better Angling*

W.H.K.   NEW YORK
WILLIAM H. KELLY, Fishery Biologist, New York State Fish Laboratory, Livingston Manor, New York

W.J.   ROD-BUILDING (part)
WEST JORDAN, Vice President, Charles F. Orvis Co., Manchester, Vermont

W.M.I.   POLLUTION
WILLIAM M. INGRAM, Ph.D., In charge, Biological, Chemical & Oceanographic Activities; Technical Advisory and Investigations Section, Technical Services Branch, WSPC; Director, Robert A. Taft Sanitary Engineering Center, Public Health Service, Department of Health, Education, and Welfare

W.M.S.   SCUBA DIVING
WILLIAM M. STEPHENS, The Marine Laboratory, University of Miami, Florida; Author of *Our World Underwater*

W.R.S.   COLORADO
WAYNE R. SEAMAN, Chief of Fisheries Research, Fort Collins, Colorado

McClane's

New
Standard
Fishing
Encyclopedia

Acknowledgments

Aside from the authors themselves, many individuals and institutions gave time and assistance in the compilation of McClane's New Standard Fishing Encyclopedia. In this connection special thanks go to staff members of the Miami Marine Laboratory, the Woods Hole Oceanographic Institution, the Fisheries Research Board of Canada, the Oregon State Game Commission, the Bureau of Commercial Fisheries of the United States Fish and Wildlife Service, the British Ichthyological Society in Glasgow, Scotland, and the Department of Conservation at Cornell University in New York.

For assistance in collecting uncommon saltwater specimens I am most grateful to Dr. Donald P. deSylva of the Miami Marine Laboratory; Burton Clark and Warren Zeiler of the Miami Seaquarium; Al Pfluger, Jr., of Miami; Joseph Reese of Fort Lauderdale; James Paterson of Port Antonio, Jamaica; and Gilbert Drake at Deep Water Cay in the Bahamas. For obtaining uncommon freshwater specimens I want also to thank Edward Schneberger, Superintendent of the Fish Management Division, State of Wisconsin Conservation Department; Keen Buss, Chief Aquatic Biologist at the Benner Spring Fish Research Station of the Pennsylvania Fish Commission; Charles and Raymond Williams of the Green Walk Hatchery at Bangor, Pennsylvania; Herbert Wyatt, Fisheries Biologist of the Georgia State Game and Fish Commission; Ted Trueblood of Nampa, Idaho; Dr. U. B. Stone, Regional Fisheries Manager of the New York State Conservation Department; Vernon Ogilvie, Fisheries Biologist of the Florida Game and Fresh Water Fish Commission; Dr. W. Harry Everhart, Chief, Fishery Division of the Maine Department of Inland Fisheries and Game; Eric Swan and Lennart Borgstrom, Jr., of Svangsta, Sweden; and Stanley Leen of Bangor, Maine. I also want to thank A. F. Wechsler for the research facilities provided by the Eden Brook Trout Hatchery of Forestburg, New York.

For technical assistance in treating certain subjects I am especially indebted to Reg Ellis and Jim Barhydt of E. I. duPont de Nemours & Company, Wilmington, Delaware; Elsie and Harry Darbee of Livingston Manor, New York; Francis Davis of Roscoe, New York; Helen Shaw of New York, New York; E. H. Rosborough of Chiloquin, Oregon; Dan Bailey of Livingston, Montana; Alan Palmer of Brooklyn, New York; Lou Feierabend of Woodstock, New York; Bill Gallasch of Richmond, Virginia; George Forrest, editor of the *Pennsylvania Angler;* and West Jordan of Manchester, Vermont. The illustrations for the black bass of North America are by Ned Smith, courtesy of *Field & Stream.*

I want also to thank Michael J. O'Neill, Publisher, and Jack Samson, Editor, of *Field & Stream* for permission to use parts of certain articles which appeared in my columns in slightly different form.

And, finally, my deepest appreciation is extended to Louise Waller of Holt, Rinehart and Winston for her unflagging devotion in seeing this project to its conclusion.

—A. J. McCLANE
Executive Editor
Field & Stream

A

AAWA The Hawaiian name for the black-spot wrasse *Bodianus bilunulatus*. This is a valuable food fish in the islands but of no angling importance. *See also* Hawaii

ABAFT A relative term at sea used to describe location of one object in relationship to another in which the object described is farther aft than the other. For example: The helmsman's seat is abaft the windshield.

ABALONE A large marine snail common to California. There are a number of species, but the most common one in western United States markets is the red abalone, *Haliotis rufescens*, which is taken chiefly between Monterey and Point Conception. The abalone has been heavily exploited in the past both as food and for the iridescent shells, which went to the jewelry trade. Abalones are also a popular food on the west coast of South America.

ABDOMEN The lower region of a fish's body between the pectoral fins and the anal fin. *See* Anatomy

ABEAM Refers to an object outside the boat, amidships to either side of the boat, and at right angles to the fore and aft line of the boat.

ABERDEEN A hook pattern featuring a round bend and a wide gap between point and shank. The Aberdeen is most often used in fishing that requires live minnow baits. *See also* Hook

ABOARD Within or on board the boat.

ABYSSAL The ocean depths from about 8,000-19,000 feet where the temperature does not exceed 39°F (4°C). It usually describes marine organisms especially adapted to the extreme pressures, low temperatures, and lack of light at these depths. Abyssal fishes may be blind or luminescent.

ACHIGAN The French name for black bass which may be specifically the *achigan à petite bouche* (smallmouth bass) or the *achigan à grande bouche* (largemouth bass). The nonrelated white bass is the *bar blanc*.

ADIRONDACK GUIDEBOAT A famous double-ended lightweight sportsman's rowboat of the past that once crowded the landings of upper New York state resorts.

Great strength and extreme lightness were coupled in the handcrafted guideboat through the use of the finest-grain northern white pine planking, ³⁄₁₆ of an inch thick, which was fastened to red spruce ribs cut to the natural grain of root crooks from selected stumps. Fifty to sixty ribs were not uncommon in a sixteen-foot model, and thousands of small brass screws and tiny copper tacks were used to join the parts together. Built in a shape not unlike the famous Grand Banks dory, but light enough to be carried on your back, the guideboat's high stem and stern also casually resembled a canoe. The traditional wood guideboat is no longer in commercial production anywhere, but the history of the boat is well-documented at the Adirondack Museum at Blue Mountain Lake, New York, where a representative collection of guideboats is on exhibit. The clean-cut shape of the traditional guideboat, however, is now available in fiberglass models built by Thomas T. Bissell of Long Lake, New York. —F.M.P.

AFRICA *See* Kenya, Mozambique, Rhodesia, South Africa, Uganda

AFRICAN POMPANO *Alectis crinitus* Also called Atlantic threadfin (when young) and Cuban jack, this Atlantic species is not a true pompano. It is closely related to the Indo-Pacific species, Pacific threadfin, *Alectis ciliaris*. These species have also been listed or described under the generic names of *Blepharis*, *Scyris*, *Blepharichthys*, *Gallus*, *Gallichthys*, and *Hynnis*. The first five of these names pose no problem; they are merely nomenclatorial derivatives of *Alectis*. The name *Hynnis*, however, is more firmly and more incorrectly entrenched in fish literature. *Hynnis cubensis* is the adult of *Alectis crinitus*. The body shape and fin structure of the small juveniles are so different from those of the large adults that, in the absence of intermediate sizes, the two extremes were previously considered to be entirely different genera and species.

The body of the African pompano is deep and thin but becomes less deep in large specimens. The head profile, in fish larger than about 14 inches long, is blunt and nearly vertical, with the large eyes located anteriorly in the profile. The first 4–6 softrays of the dorsal fin are elongated in small specimens; the first two rays may be

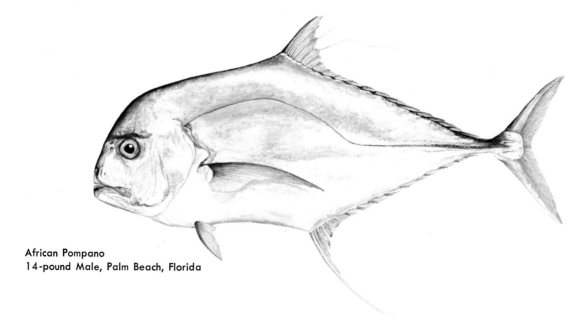

African Pompano
14-pound Male, Palm Beach, Florida

four times as long as the fish; these rays become shorter with growth and may be shorter than the pectoral fin in very large specimens.

The seven spines in the first dorsal fin are of nearly equal length in small specimens but are completely covered by skin and molded into the body profile by a body length of about 4–5 inches. The second dorsal fin has one short spine and 18–19 softrays. The two separated spines of the anal fin disappear in fish of about 4–8 inches long; the remainder of the anal fin consists of one spine and 15–16 softrays. The first gill arch has 4–5 gillrakers on the upper limb and 14–16 gillrakers on the lower limb. There are about 24–38 relatively weak scutes in the straight lateral line. Scales on the body are minute, embedded in the skin, and difficult to see. Young specimens have 5–6 bars on the body. Larger specimens are light bluish-green on the back and silvery over most of the remainder of the body.

The African pompano occurs on both sides of the Atlantic Ocean. In the western Atlantic it is recorded from Santos, Brazil, to Massachusetts and the West Indies.

This species probably grows to a length of more than 3 feet; specimens weighing 25–35 pounds have frequently been caught off Florida. The size of these larger specimens should be adequately documented.

LIFE HISTORY

The life history of this interesting fish needs to be studied. The smallest young have been taken in offshore waters from about July to September. The size at which metamorphosis occurs—the change in form from the deep-bodied, filamentous-finned young to the shallower-bodied, relatively short-finned adult—appears to be quite variable, for a deep-bodied, long-finned specimen with dark bars on the body has been taken that was 24 inches long.

ANGLING VALUE

The African pompano is a fairly strong-fighting gamefish, usually taken by trolling in tropical waters. It reportedly has been considered as a fine food fish in Cuba and the Florida Keys. *See also* Carangidae, Threadfins   —F.H.B.

AFT Indicates location of object as being toward the stern of the boat or behind the boat, dependent upon where the speaker is standing.

AGASSIZ, LOUIS American (1807–1873) Born on May 28th in the village of Motier-en-Vuly on the shores of Lake Morat, Switzerland, Agassiz was the first of five children in a pastor's family who survived babyhood. As a result, his parents indulged their son's early, extraordinary activities. At an early age he was permitted to keep all kinds of wildlife in his bedroom, while a spring pool in the backyard—some say a watering trough in his front yard—held his ever-changing collection of fishes. In addition, he spent countless hours on the lake with local anglers learning all he could about the fish they caught and the techniques they used to catch them. Before he was 8 he knew the name, classification, and habits of every freshwater fish in Switzerland. Years later he advised his students to "study nature; not books"; and never to be afraid to say "I don't know."

Agassiz was born in an age when man's faith in the future was firmly linked to his faith in science. The oceans in particular were attracting thoughtful minds.

His early schooling included a boarding school at Bienne, where he studied English, Greek, and Latin. As a Swiss he already knew French, and was familiar with German and Italian. Entering the College of Lausanne to study for a business career, he was persuaded by an uncle to enroll in Zurich's medical school in 1824 to study medicine and natural history. After two years in Zurich he took advanced studies at Heidelberg and Munich.

Among his closest friends during his college years were Karl Schimper, Arnold Guyot, and Alexander Braun, who introduced Agassiz to his parents in a letter as "one who knows every fish which passes under the bridge." The two students spent the holiday collecting specimens, dissecting them, and with the aid of Alexander's artistic sister, Cecile, drawing them.

By November 1827 Braun and Agassiz set off for the University of Munich to finish their medical studies. Agassiz's primary pleasure in visiting new cities was to make a beeline for the central fish market to see what different species he could find. He soon came to the attention of Professors von Martius and von Spix, just back from an expedition to Brazil. Eager to examine the fish Von Spix had in his collection, Agassiz volunteered to help him classify the specimens. At first this was occasional after-school work, with Agassiz's medical studies dominating his routine. But gradually his greater interest in Von Spix's collection caused Agassiz to spend increasing amounts of time in the laboratory. When Von Spix suddenly died, Von Martius asked Agassiz to continue the classification and prepare the results for publication—a rare opportunity for any young scientist. The Martius-Spix expedition was famous throughout Europe. Would Agassiz diminish the value of the forthcoming publication because of his youth and lack of accreditation? In the midst of his medical studies, and while continuing the work of classifying the South American fishes, he commuted to the neighboring university town of Erlangen to earn a Doctor of Philosophy degree in 1829, just so he would have a title on the cover page of *Brazilian Fishes*, which was published that summer in Latin.

Agassiz was now a young man in a hurry. He received his medical degree on April 3, 1830, when he was not yet 23 years of age, and soon set off for Paris. Though medicine was his apparent career, Agassiz knew in his heart he wanted to be what he called a "traveling naturalist." He lived on the Left Bank with an artist-friend, Joseph Dinkel, just 200 steps from the Botanical Garden.

Agassiz' stay in Paris also made possible his first visit to the sea. Alexander Braun came on a holiday and persuaded Agassiz and Dinkel to make a short trip to the Norman coast with him. "At last," he wrote, "I have looked upon the sea and its riches!"

In the fall of 1832, incomprehensibly to his French and German friends, Agassiz decided to leave Paris and return to Neuchatel in Switzerland. Agassiz tried to explain his decision in a letter in which he said: ". . . in a quiet retired place like Neuchatel, whatever may be growing up within me will have a more independent and individual development than in this restless Paris . . ." Another reason for returning to Switzerland was Agassiz'

The Swiss-born naturalist, Louis Agassiz, from an 1873 steel engraving (*The Granger Collection.*)

of fossil fishes (with a Neuchatel dateline), and converted the entire community into students of natural history. Merchants took up rock collecting; bankers became butterfly collectors; and lawyers saved any odd fish they caught in their seines along the lake front.

One of Agassiz' teaching techniques was to leave a student alone with a given specimen for many minutes—even hours. When he returned, Agassiz would ask the student to tell him all he had learned in the interim. If the student recited the fish's name and classification Agassiz would say, "Wrong, wrong. You have not learned that since I left you; you knew that before you came in. Look at the fish as though you have never seen one before." Then he would leave the room for an even longer period of time. Sometimes several such sessions were necessary before the student began to perceive details in the fish's fins, tail, or mouth, and to ask himself how this fish differed from others and why. Forced to concentrate on a single specimen, the student became an observer of all fish, which to Agassiz was the first step in becoming a naturalist.

Another technique consisted of presenting a student with a box full of the jumbled skeletons of half-a-dozen unrelated fishes, and then asking the student to reassemble them. A month or more went into such work, but lessons learned in this manner were not easily forgotten. The students most capable of reassembling skeletons were given new fish, frequently all of the same genera. As the students worked they began to see the similarities in this new batch and to comprehend the differences between these and the fish previously assembled. Thus their understanding of what they were about was built on experience.

Agassiz' five volumes on fossil fishes (the last one finished in 1834) has many lessons for the layman. Previous to Agassiz' writing, the only major division of fishes was between the *cartilaginous* and *osseous* types. While most early nineteenth-century natural histories correctly put the sharks and rays into the cartilaginous category, they often mistakenly included bony fishes like the eel or sturgeon for no other reason than that eels looked like lampreys and sturgeon had bottom-hugging habits like a dogfish. Agassiz suggested that a more realistic classification could be made after comparing internal structure, organs, and scales. He drew examples of different scale types and explained that toothlike placoid scales were found on very primitive sharks, skates, and rays; diamond or rhomboid-shaped ganoid scales identify the ancient gars and sturgeons; round, smooth cycloid scales represent other relatively old fish like the salmon; and saw or spine-edged ctenoid scales are found on the more recently evolved sea bass and perch.

Agassiz also adopted Ernst von Baer's theory that the evolution of a species could be seen in the development of a single egg, and illustrated how a modern fish embryo goes through stages that resemble various ancient forms. In fact, Agassiz made Baer's theory so widely known that even today he's popularly credited with it.

Agassiz did not spend all his time at Neuchatel. He made a couple of trips to Great Britain to examine fossil fish forms foreign to central Europe. In England he learned of his great popularity in America and first conceived the idea of going there. Harvard, Yale, and the Boston Natural History Society were among the

hope that his practice as a country doctor would yield sufficient income and leisure to allow him to finish the giant study of fossil fishes initiated by Georges Cuvier, the zoologist and creator of the science of paleontology, who had asked Agassiz to finish the study when Cuvier was on his deathbed. Agassiz was determined to leave *Recherches sur les Poissons Fossiles* as a memento to Cuvier; at the same time it would represent his most substantial bid for fame in the science world.

Within a year of his arrival in Neuchatel Agassiz had founded the Society of Natural Sciences, a Museum of Natural History, produced the first volume of his study many subscribers to his *Research on Fossil Fishes*, and Agassiz was intrigued by the many natural history organizations he heard were multiplying throughout the United States. "Every educated American is a naturalist," he was told, and in the cities as many tradesmen attend science lectures as professionals. Through the assistance of the British geologist Sir Charles Lyell, who had already made an American tour, Agassiz was commissioned to give a lecture series at the Lowell Institute in Boston.

In a matter of weeks after his arrival in Boston Agassiz was convinced he had found a new home. He was most impressed by the nature of the audiences he spoke to. The rumor that a genuine cross-section of America existed in the lecture hall was true. Since tickets to the Lowell lectures were obtained in drawings, there were as many shopkeepers and street cleaners in his audience as students and fellow scientists. The faith that education was the key to social betterment was part and parcel of nineteenth-century man's faith in science.

Some European colleagues viewed this popular approach to education with alarm, even contempt, but Agassiz loved it. He rented a three-story brick house at water's edge in East Boston from which he went out into the harbor every morning to dredge or seine, bringing back specimens for his house tanks and worktables mere hours before he would give a lecture on the results of that day's outing before a Standing Room Only audience at the Institute. As soon as one lecture series was completed, another subscription was quickly raised. Bostonians wouldn't let him go. As many visitors came to Agassiz' home as went to his lectures, and regardless of what other work he was doing at the time, Agassiz was always eager to show the curious around, commenting on something unique about this fish or that, treating each visitor as though he were a scientific colleague. Soon all kinds of little boats were seen in Boston harbor, their occupants noting sea creatures for the first time as objects of wonder rather than merely as something "good to eat" or "not good to eat."

Familiar with European fishes and now confronted by an entirely different spectrum of American species, one of the first observations Agassiz made on behalf of American marine science was to suggest that there were considerably more fish in the world than the thousand or so species claimed in natural histories up to that time. While Agassiz found some fishes overclassified (for example some ichthyologists thought the young Atlantic sea bass or "pin bass" found in the bays and inlets were different from the large "humpback" adult males found offshore) he more often found American naturalists parochial or timid in not recognizing the possibility of species beyond their experience.

When Bostonians heard there was a ray in southern waters that reached a width of 20 feet from wing tip to wing tip, they could only suppose this was a tropical variety of their local skate or sting ray. Many naturalists wrote that all catfish were the same; saltwater varieties in the south were merely sea-run hornpout, and stories of huge eels in coral seas with toothy mouths that would put a shark to shame were either false (if the local naturalist's experience with eels went no further than what was found in New England bays and rivers) or true (if the Northern naturalist was familiar with the conger). In neither case did they imagine the moray.

Agassiz' Boston audiences respected his education and experience, and his descriptions of fish and animals in faraway places excited their awe.

However, spellbinding wasn't Agassiz' intention. Basically, he wanted people to examine nature, and, where possible, to dispel mythology, comprehending that function derives from form. For example, it was nonsense to claim that eels are the boa constrictors of the sea simply because neither the eel's body structure, nor its victim's reliance on gills (not lungs), give this fish the smothering or crushing capabilities of a constricting snake. It was also absurd to suggest that sturgeon are great predators which rush through the water, seizing and tearing prey nearly their own size, for even a cursory examination of this fish's vacuum-cleaner type of mouth would inform any thoughtful naturalist that he is dealing with a scavenger. The examples, and therefore the lessons, were endless.

Agassiz was practical about any surplus specimens brought his way. Always short of money and generally overstocked with common varieties of local fishes, he converted many of them into meals when a day's work was done. He once crowned an exhaustive study of a live giant sea turtle by turning the animal into a series of soups, steaks, and potpies that lasted his household of 20 visiting and resident naturalists for days.

Dr. Alexander Bache, great grandson of Benjamin Franklin and Superintendent of the U.S. Coast Survey, urged Agassiz to use the local Survey steamer whenever he wanted. By this means, Agassiz was soon out and about Cape Cod, Nantucket Island, Martha's Vineyard, and the Elizabeth Isles fishing, collecting, dissecting, preserving, studying. He recruited assistants on the basis of willingness, and such was the enthusiasm engendered by this Pied Piper of the Seas that he was soon changing fishmongers into naturalists and commercial fishermen into marine scientists.

He wasn't always successful. On his first visit to New York City Agassiz postponed all official presentation of letters until he had made a tour of the Fulton Fish Market, the leading commercial fish center of America. Fish were brought here from all up and down the Atlantic seaboard and the Caribbean islands, and many were kept alive in display aquaria built into the stalls. While most of the fishmongers were intrigued by Agassiz' presence and countless questions, and charmed by his curious accent, one fellow is reported to have remarked: "The more worthless the fish is, the more he likes it. He's daft, I'm thinking."

Agassiz often depended on anglers for his saltwater specimens. And sometimes in that great age of discovery, the specimen was of more than passing laboratory interest. For instance, A. C. Jackson set the scientific world on its ear in 1852 with a pair of perch he caught in San Salita [Sausalito] Bay, San Francisco, California. Not only were the fish a new species (which Agassiz acknowledged by naming them after Jackson) they represented a wholly new concept in marine biology: a sea perch that bears its young alive!

Agassiz designated a new family for these viviparous sea perch and called it *Holconoti* or *Embiotocoidae*. The first specimens Jackson sent from California Agassiz titled *Embiotoca Jacksoni*, which still stands as the scientific name. However, most West Coast anglers know the fish more commonly as the blackperch, and most are unaware that these remarkable spiny-rayed sea fishes are unusual in their live-bearing characteristics.

Agassiz' lectures took him to Philadelphia (where he first met Spencer Fullerton Baird, America's leading native-born naturalist); Washington, D.C. (where he visited the recently-founded Smithsonian Institution); and Charleston, South Carolina (where he met English novelist William Makepeace Thackeray, also on a tour of American cities). In the winter of 1850 Agassiz traveled south to the Florida Keys and there studied the reefs and reef fishes. So widespread was Agassiz' fame that in 1854, when he needed only 500 subscribers to launch a 10-volume study of the natural history of the United States at $12 a volume, he received over 2,500 orders in the first few weeks. His enthusiasm for America was so great that Agassiz became a United States citizen in January 1865.

Gradually Agassiz began to attract wealthy patrons who not only freed him from the pesky worries of rent, travel expenses, and equipment costs but provided him with considerable sums to do precisely the kinds of things he'd always dreamed of doing. Thomas Cary presented him with a summer cottage and laboratory on the northeast shore of Nahant, a rocky peninsula just north of Boston where Agassiz spent afternoons with fellow naturalist, Dr. Joseph B. Holder, collecting fishes from Lynn Bay. Francis C. Gray left $50,000 in his will for the purchase of specimens for a museum of comparative zoology to be established at Harvard College. Agassiz took on the task of acquiring money for the building and, through personal persuasion and influence, got $100,000 from the Massachusetts state legislature and raised $71,000 in private donations. This biological facility is still one of the nation's finest. Classification of the many collections bought for the museum took years and was carried on by countless volunteers.

Perhaps, the most wonderful conversion of a monetary gift to the natural history education of the New World occurred when millionaire John Anderson offered Agassiz little Penikese Island in the Elizabeth Chain south of Cape Cod in 1873, plus $50,000 to operate a summer school of natural history.

Within recent years Agassiz had made a number of long sea voyages, including one to Brazil and another, completed only the year before, around Cape Horn to San Francisco, during which he had personally collected 265 barrels and countless cases of specimens. All these needed sorting and organization. But the urge to teach was too strong. He accepted Anderson's gift and set about recruiting the best possible staff and processing the applications of hundreds of eager students.

That winter Agassiz' energy ran out. Suffering from heartache and general fatigue, he spent much of his time in bed. One day, after a lecture in Fitchburg, Massachusetts, he returned to Cambridge, made out his will, and died soon after on December 14, 1873, at the age of 67.

Agassiz organized and added to our knowledge of the oceans; he turned fishermen into students, and students into teachers. He built bridges between men of leisure and men of science, so that in the century since his death few men of wealth have undertaken a major angling expedition without recruiting men of science to share their experiences. The spirit of Agassiz is part of any angler who wants to know more about the fish he pursues and who wonders about the wriggling catch in his net or on the gaff. —G.W.R.

AHI The Hawaiian name for the yellowfin tuna. *See also* Hawaii

AIR BOAT The air boat, a flat-bottomed, aluminum-hulled craft powered by an aircraft engine, is in wide use for traversing the inundated sawgrass country of South Florida's Everglades. Originally developed by commercial frog giggers who hunted at night in the Everglades, the air boat is now used principally by sportsmen for fishing and hunting.

Prior to World War II, Everglades frog hunters poled a craft similar to a pram or river punt through the Sea of Grass as they sought out the oversize frogs with a head lamp. Today's remarkably engineered air boat was invented when a frogger mounted an automobile engine on one of these flat-bottomed craft and fitted it with an aircraft propeller and an aircraft-type rudder at the rear. It was only natural that lighter and faster aluminum hulls and more powerful and lighter airplane engines would soon follow the crude original. According to records available, the development of the air boat took place in the Everglades country in Palm Beach County.

The average air-boat hull of today is a rectangular, open, aluminum hull built around a frame similar to that of a snub-nosed skiff. The forward part of the craft slopes gradually upward like the front of a sled. Most sawgrass-country-type air boats are powered by 125 hp and 145 hp opposed light aircraft engines. The engines are mounted on frames of aircraft structural tubing. The framing of propeller guards is of aluminum tubing.

Single or double rudders are mounted behind the aircraft engine. The controls are very similar to those of a light plane. A small aircraft bucket seat is mounted ahead of the engine or on the bow of the craft in an elevated position. The pilot controls the rudder with either a stick or pedals . . . or both. This is the basic air boat, but there have been refinements. The "sawgrass air boat," for instance, could be termed the sports-car version of the line.

SAWGRASS AIR BOAT

This air boat has been designed especially for travel through the heavy, high stands of sawgrass in the southern regions of the Everglades. Instead of the square chines of air boats used in deeper water and in inundated areas where the grass is sparse, the sawgrass model has far less flat-bottom area. The sawgrass air boat has what might be termed a round chine. The sides of the

Sawgrass Air Boat

craft flare outward instead of rising almost straight up. This gives a pilot much greater maneuverability in the heavy grass country. When a pilot finds his boat stuck, he can actually "rock it" around with the rudder and head back out the way he came. These sawgrass boats can hit 40 to 50 mph on the flat.

There are many other variations of the basic air boat. The family air boat and the guide boat are often much larger and not quite so fast as the sawgrass sports model. Extra seating capacity is a standard feature of the craft in this class. Often the pilot seat will be mounted on a deck on the bow, and a thwart will be built just forward of the engine running from gunwale to gunwale. However, construction for extra seating varies.

AIR FOIL HULL

One of the most radical advancements in air-boat construction came about late in 1962 with the Florida Game and Fresh Water Fish Commission's development of the air-foil hull. From bow to stern, this decked-over air-boat hull from the side view is very similar to the cross section of an aircraft wing. Purpose of the design was greater stability at high speeds. One of three such craft, built at West Palm Beach, was powered by a 175 hp aircraft engine and reportedly is capable of a speed of about 100 mph. The craft were built for game law enforcement work in the Everglades.

VERSATILITY OF AIR BOATS

Air boats, especially the fast sawgrass-country boats, are capable of almost unbelievable things. An air boat can go faster on wet grass than on open water due to the buoyancy provided by the grass. During periods of drought in the Everglades, more than one deer hunter has operated his craft early in the morning, running only on the night's dew remaining on the grass. Some air boatmen test their boats on the lawns of their homes.

Because much of the Everglades country has been partitioned by flood-control levees and canals, running from one area to another by air boat posed something of a problem. The ingenious air boatmen solved the problem with more power and by adding galvanized sheeting to the bottom of the hull. They can actually run down a dry road atop a levee. Even more remarkable, when confronted by a levee in their path of travel they think nothing of running their air boat up and over the levee to the other side, even though the levee may be several feet high.

Air boatman use their craft to get into isolated fishing waters. These may be canals or deep basins in the Everglades that can be highly productive for bass and panfish when water levels are up.

—E.C.B.

AIR EMBOLISM *See* Skin and Scuba Diving Dangers *under* First Aid

AIR TANK A metal, airtight tank built into a boat to provide flotation should the boat be swamped.

ALABAMA Water is one of Alabama's greatest resources, and sport fishing is one of its most important assets. An average rainfall of 53 inches provides an abundance of water for Alabama's 50 rivers, 250 creeks, 25 large reservoirs, and 21,000 ponds and small lakes. In addition, there are numerous brackish bays and bayous along the state's 60-mile Gulf Coast.

The winters in Alabama are mild. The mean annual temperature for the state is 64° F. This provides a long growing season for the fish and year-round sport for the fisherman. Since 1971 trout have been successfully introduced in several lakes, notably Lewis Smith and Inland Lake. However, fishing for bass and other warmwater species is some of the best found anywhere. Forests, grasslands, and improved pastures cover most of the state, and its topography includes mountains, hills, and plains. The Appalachian Mountain Range extends through the northeastern portion of the state and as far south as Birmingham. Much of the central portion is hilly with some plains, and the coastal plains are found in the southernmost part of the state.

Alabama's important freshwater sport fish are largemouth, smallmouth, spotted, and redeye bass; striped, white, and yellow bass; rock and warmouth bass; walleye, sauger, crappie, bluegill, redear sunfish; flathead, blue and channel catfish; and pickerel. The important saltwater and brackish-water sport fish are spotted seatrout, cobia, channel bass, tarpon, sailfish, king and Spanish mackerel, red snapper, and grouper. There are no size limits or closed seasons for any species of fish taken in Alabama's public waters by anglers and the creel limits are most liberal. The spring months of March, April, and May and the autumn months of September and October normally provide the best fishing. Studies by fishery biologists of the Department of Conservation have shown that the average catch per fisherman-trip is slightly higher during the winter than it is during the warmer months of the year.

Alabama probably has the finest river system in the nation. The state has more than 1,700 miles of rivers classified as navigable by the U. S. Corps of Engineers. Of this total mileage, 858 miles already offer improved nine-foot navigation channels. An angler could travel by boat (including a large cabin cruiser) for some 350 miles and fish in the Black Warrior, Tombigbee, and Mobile rivers. He could cover 200 miles on the Tennessee River and fish its 180,000 acres of impoundments and 150 miles on the Chattahoochee and fish the river and its 50,000 acres of impoundments from Florida to Phenix City. More than 30 impoundments have been constructed on the larger rivers and streams of Alabama (*see* table). These reservoirs contain 433,595 surface acres of water, and all of them are open to the public and provide a variety of sport fishing. This is excluding 45,000-acre Lake Walter F. George (also known as Lake Eufaula) on the Alabama-Georgia border.

TENNESSEE RIVER

The Tennessee River enters Alabama near the northeastern corner of Alabama, flows southwest for about 60 miles to Guntersville and then northwest for about 140 miles before re-entering the state of Tennessee. Its four large reservoirs—Guntersville, Wheeler, Wilson, and Pickwick—contain a total of 180,000 surface acres of water. These impoundments provide some of the best fishing found in the state. Excellent smallmouth-bass fishing is found in Wheeler, Wilson, and Pickwick lakes while a lesser number are taken from Guntersville Lake. Probably as many, or more, trophy smallmouths come from Wilson and Pickwick lakes as are caught in any other waters in America. Six- to 8-pound bass are not uncommon. One smallmouth weighing 10½ pounds, taken from Wilson Lake immediately below Wheeler Dam in 1950, held the world record for smallmouth for several years.

Largemouth and smallmouth bass, white bass, crappie, sauger, catfish, and bluegill are the most sought after species in the Tennessee River and its impoundments in Alabama. The tailwaters of the four large dams attract thousands of fishermen annually. However, most of the species of gamefish indigenous to the state are found in this river. More than fifty fishing camps and resort motels are found along this 200-mile stretch of the river.

Bait-casting, fly-fishing, and spinning are all effective methods for catching largemouth and smallmouth bass along the weed beds. Live gizzard shad (*which see*) are a popular bait for largemouth and smallmouth bass in the tailwaters. Cut shad and shad entrails are good baits that are used by many fishermen in the area for channel and blue catfish. Fly-fishing is very effective for taking of bluegills along the deep ledges and weedy banks of all four lakes during the spring, summer, and fall.

Little Mountain State Park at Guntersville provides improved camping areas for the fishermen using Guntersville Lake. Also, Wheeler State Park at Wheeler Dam has cabins available for rental at a very reasonable fee. This park is convenient for those fishing Wheeler, Wilson, and Pickwick lakes.

CHATTAHOOCHEE RIVER

The Chattahoochee River serves as the boundary between Georgia and Alabama and flows in Alabama from Lanett, Alabama, to the Florida state line, a distance of about 150 miles. A series of five hydroelectric dams—Bartlett's Ferry, Goat Rock, Oliver, Fort Gaines, and Columbia—impound about 56,300 surface acres of water. Fort Gaines Dam impounds about 46,000 acres and creates backwater from Fort Gaines to Phenix City, Alabama. The other impoundments range from 1,000 to 5,500 acres in size. Largemouth bass, crappie, and channel catfish are the most abundant sport species found in this river and its impoundments. However, large redeye bass (*which see*) weighing in excess of 4 pounds have been taken from this river and its tributaries. Redeye bass up to three pounds are not too uncommon. Striped bass "runs" occur up to the Columbus Dam. Specimens of twenty-five pounds have been reported by fishermen at Phenix City.

This river is navigable with a nine-foot channel from Phenix City to the Florida state line. Approximately one-half of the entire acreage of the impoundments on the Chattahoochee is in Alabama. A reciprocal agreement between the states of Alabama and Georgia makes it possible for anglers to fish any part of the impoundments with either an Alabama or Georgia license.

TALLAPOOSA RIVER

The Tallapoosa River originates in central Alabama near the Georgia line. It flows for about 125 miles southwest and connects with the Coosa River near Montgomery to form the Alabama River. The Tallapoosa and its three impoundments—Martin, Yates, and Thurlow—offer a variety of sport fishing. Largemouth

LARGE IMPOUNDMENTS IN ALABAMA

Impoundments	Nearby Cities and Towns	Size (Acres)
Alabama River		
Clairborne's Lake	Grove Hill, Monroeville	5,850
William Dannelly Reservoir	Selma	17,200
Jones Bluff	Selma, Benton	12,200
Big Creek	Mobile, Tanner	
Big Creek Lake	Williams	3,700
Cahaba River (Little Cahaba)		
Lake Purdy	Birmingham, Leeds	1,000
Chattahoochee River		
Bartlett's Ferry Lake	Fairfax, Opelika	5,500
Goat Rock Lake	Phenix City	1,000
Oliver Lake	Phenix City	3,000
Fort Gaines Lake (Lake George)	Eufaula, Phenix City	45,200
Columbia Lake	Columbia, Fort Gaines	1,600
Conecuh River		
Gantt Lake	Andalusia	1,600
Point A Lake	Andalusia	600
Coosa River		
Weiss Lake	Centre, Cedar Bluff	30,000
Lay Lake	Clanton, Columbiana	6,000
Mitchell Lake	Clanton	5,850
Jordan Lake	Wetumpka	4,900
Sipsey River		
Lewis Smith Lake	Jasper, Double Springs	21,000
Sougahatchee Creek		
Opelika City Lake	Opelika	560
Tallapoosa River		
Martin Lake	Alexander City, Dadeville	40,000
Yates Lake	Tallassee	2,000
Thurlow Lake	Tallassee	575
Tennessee River		
Guntersville Lake	Guntersville, Scottsboro	69,100
Wheeler Lake	Decatur, Athens	67,100
Wilson Lake	Florence, Killen	15,800
Pickwick Lake	Florence, Sheffield	28,000
Tombigbee River		
Demopolis Lake	Demopolis	10,000
Jackson Lake	Jackson	8,800
Black Warrior River		
Bankhead Lake	Hueytown, Gorgas	9,100
New Holt Lake	Tuscaloosa, Holt	3,160
Oliver Lake	Tuscaloosa	1,100
Warrior Lock and Dam Lake	Eutaw	7,100
Black Warrior River (Blackburn Fork)		
Inland Lake	Remlap, Oneonta	5,000
TOTAL SURFACE ACRES		433,595

bass, spotted bass, crappie, bluegill, and white bass are plentiful. Fishermen also enjoy good catches of channel catfish on this river.

The most prolific runs of striped bass in Alabama are found in the Tallapoosa below the dam near Tallassee. The peak of this resulting striped-bass fishery occurs during the month of June and usually extends from mid May to mid July. Specimens up to fifty-five pounds have been taken. Baits used range from live herring and shad to large artificial lures. Fishing for stripers is most productive in the early morning between daylight and 7:00 A.M. while the power turbines are cut off. This is difficult fishing done off the rocks below the dam, and normally only for the more ardent fishermen.

COOSA RIVER

The Coosa River flows for about 175 miles in Alabama and connects with the Tallapoosa near Montgomery to form the Alabama River. The Alabama Power Company has created a series of four large impoundments—Weiss, Lay, Mitchell, and Jordan—that contain 45,750 acres of water that is used for the generation of hydroelectric power. Two other impoundments that will contain approximately 25,000 acres are presently under construction. This river contains practically all the species of fish that are found in the state. Largemouth, spotted, and redeye bass, along with crappie, white bass, bluegill, and channel and blue catfish are most abundant. All the tailwaters of these four dams provide excellent fishing. Some striped bass are taken in the tailwaters of Jordan Dam during May, June, and July. Walleyes are frequently caught by fishermen in the tailwaters as well as the impoundments and their tributaries.

BLACK WARRIOR RIVER

The Black Warrior River is formed by a series of smaller rivers, large creeks, and tributaries that drain the north central portion of the state from the Tennessee River to Demopolis. Blackburn Fork, Mulberry Fork, and the Sipsey River are the primary rivers that join to form the Black Warrior. Lewis Smith Lake, a 21,000-acre impoundment, is found on the Sipsey, and Inland Lake (5,000 acres) is located on Blackburn Fork. Bankhead, New Holt, Oliver, and Black Warrior lakes, representing 20,460 acres, are located on the main body of the Black Warrior River. All of these streams and impoundments offer good fishing for largemouth bass, spotted bass, redeye bass, crappie, white bass, walleye, rock bass, catfish, and a variety of other species. Stocked with rainbows, Lewis Smith Lake produced trout up to 13 pounds in 1973.

TOMBIGBEE RIVER

The Little Tombigbee River enters Alabama from Mississippi and joins with the Black Warrior at Demopolis to form the Tombigbee River. The Tombigbee flows for about 200 miles in the state and has been developed for navigation by the U. S. Corps of Engineers. Locks and dams at Demopolis and Jackson create 18,800 acres of backwaters. This is a very productive river, and it provides an excellent sport fishery for catfish plus good largemouth bass, spotted bass, crappie, white bass, and walleye fishing. Fish population studies by biologists of the Department of Conservation have revealed that

some areas of the river contained more than 1,000 pounds of blue, flathead, and channel catfish per acre. Blue and channel catfish are the most abundant and specimens of the former weighing more than 100 pounds have been taken by sport fishermen on this river.

MOBILE RIVER DELTA

The Mobile River Delta includes the Mobile and Tensaw rivers and hundreds of natural lakes that are formed following the merger of the Tombigbee and Alabama rivers. This vast acreage of water extends for about forty miles above the Mobile Causeway that separates the Delta from Mobile Bay. This area is heavily covered with gum, cypress, and other water-tolerant trees that are laden with Spanish moss. The fishermen who enjoy the wild, unmolested swamps and beautiful scenery will enjoy fishing this area of Alabama. Largemouth bass, bluegill, redear sunfish, and crappie are plentiful. Bass weighing four pounds or more and bluegill and redear sunfish of more than one pound are commonly caught. Many fish camps exist along the lower Delta, and guides are available.

ALABAMA RIVER

The Alabama River has three major impoundments: Claiborne's Lake, William Dannelly Reservoir (locally known as Miller's Ferry Lake), and Jones Bluff. Initially, these waters provided excellent striped bass fishing with a state record of 55 pounds. Although the striper fishing has since leveled off, occasionally large specimens are still taken. All three are noted for excellent largemouth and spotted bass angling. The Alabama River and its impoundments extend for about 225 miles from Wetumpka to Baldwin County where it connects with the Tombigbee River to form the Mobile River Delta System. It offers good bass, crappie, bluegill, and catfish fishing, particularly in the mouths of its numerous tributaries. Large blue catfish weighing in excess of 40 pounds are commonly caught from the Alabama River.

BAY AREAS

Mobile, Grand, Porterville, Bon Secour, and Perdido bays comprise about 500,000 acres of brackish waters. These waters provide excellent sport fishing for tarpon, spotted seatrout, channel bass and many other brackish-water species. Good catches of largemouth bass, crappie, bluegill, redear sunfish, and catfish are also often taken in these brackish waters. These areas are highly developed, and there are ample motels, hotels, fishing camps, boats, and guides for the sport fishermen in these bay areas.

SALTWATER FISHING

Excellent sport fishing is found in the Gulf of Mexico adjacent to Alabama's Gulf Coast. Dauphin Island is headquarters for the Mobile Deep Sea Rodeo that is held during late August each year. Party boats are available for fishing trips in the Gulf throughout the year. This area of the Gulf is famous for its tarpon, red snapper, cobia, king and Spanish mackerel, little tunny, dolphin, bluefish, and sailfish. The Game and Fish Division of the Alabama Department of Conservation has developed artificial reefs by using old car bodies, barges, and concrete culverts in several areas in 60–90 feet of water about 8–12 miles from the coast. These areas provide excellent fishing for red snapper and other marine game species that congregate near them.

SMALL STREAMS

In addition to its large rivers, Alabama has about 7,000 miles of minor rivers and major creeks and 15,000 miles of minor creeks. These streams provide a variety of fishing, particularly for largemouth, spotted, and redeye bass, pickerel, bluegill, and catfish. The shorelines of portions of many of these streams are posted. However, a state law provides that all waters that flow across more than one person's or corporation's property are considered public.

Several of these smaller rivers and creeks offer exceptional float-fishing such as Cahaba River, Little River, and the Conecuh River for largemouth and spotted bass, bluegill, chain pickerel, and walleye. Probably the best walleye fishing in Alabama is found on the Cahaba.

STATE-OWNED PUBLIC FISHING LAKES

The Alabama Department of Conservation is providing excellent fishing through its state-owned and -managed public fishing lake program. The Department has constructed twenty lakes ranging in size from 32 to 250 acres and comprising a total of 1,733 acres. These lakes were constructed in those areas of the state having insufficient public fishing waters. They were stocked with bluegills, redear sunfish, and largemouth bass. The lakes are fertilized and managed by fishery biologists of the Department. Complete creel records on these lakes reveal that sport fishermen catch a total of about one million fish weighing approximately 300,000 pounds annually from these twenty lakes. Largemouth bass weighing up to thirteen pounds and bluegill and redear sunfish weighing up to two pounds have been recorded from these lakes. The lakes were constructed on selected sites with drainage areas of woodlands and/or improved pastures. In addition to fishing, facilities for picnicking and boating are available at each of these lakes.

SMALL PONDS AND LAKES

There are more than 21,000 artificial ponds and small lakes in Alabama containing about 100,000 acres of water. Most of these lakes provide good to excellent largemouth-bass, bluegill, and redear-sunfish fishing. Many of these are open to public fishing for a nominal daily fee. Boats are usually provided at an additional small charge.

Bass ranging to ten pounds and bluegill and redear sunfish up to two pounds are frequently taken from these small ponds and lakes although larger specimens are occasionally taken. The world-record bluegill, which weighed 4¾ pounds, was taken from Lake Ketona, a forty-five-acre lake, near Birmingham in 1950. A former record redear sunfish, which weighed 4¼ pounds, was caught from Chattahoochee State Park Lake (40 acres) near Dothan in 1962.   —I.B.B.

ALABAMA SPOTTED BASS *Micropterus punctulatus henshalli* A subspecies of the spotted bass found in the Alabama River system in Mississippi, Alabama, and Georgia. *See also* Black Bass, Spotted Bass

ALASKA The 49th State covers approximately 586,000 square miles making it one-fifth the size of the continental United States. Much of the area is wilderness as its population density is about one-half a person per square mile. Inevitably, some excellent angling exists in Alaska, but quality waters are found well away from the main cities such as Anchorage, Juneau, and Fairbanks. Few spots can be reached by road; most tourist sportsmen use bush pilots to reach primitive areas. The principal species of fish sought are the rainbow trout, chinook salmon, coho salmon, Dolly Varden, Arctic char, sockeye salmon, grayling, whitefish, northern pike, inconnu, and white halibut. Many waters in Alaska have been overexploited, and others are barren at certain times of the year; so it requires a sound local knowledge to enjoy what is generally considered the Last Frontier.

THE PANHANDLE

In order to classify Alaskan fishing it is necessary to divide the state into several regions. Each has its own characteristics and climate, but all have in common some unusual and exciting fishing. The most southerly of these sections is referred to as the "Panhandle," and is the long strip of land that runs from the Kenai Peninsula along the edge of British Columbia. This area is a maze of islands and canals and is one of the least-known and most beautiful areas of North America. Huge forests of spruce, nurtured by a heavy rainfall and mild winters, follow the mountain sites right down to the saltwater. The streams are crystal clear (with the exception of the larger glacial runoffs) and cold. In the saltwater of the coastal inlets and channels, trolling for salmon and halibut provides sport and nourishment for native and tourist alike, while the freshwater lakes and streams abound in cutthroat and rainbow trout, with salmon and steelhead as seasonal migrants.

The Panhandle is true wilderness. There are no roads, and villages are few and far between. It is the land of the light plane, the backpacker, and the man who wants to get as far away from civilization as possible. Paradoxically, the area is very easily reached by commercial airlines or by boat. The best move, for the average person who wants to fish in this section, would be to get in touch with one of the many local guides. These men usually spend the winter in the major towns such as Juneau, Ketchikan, and Sitka.

KENAI PENINSULA

The second area for consideration is the Kenai Peninsula. The Kenai is one of the best-known and most visited areas of the Forty-ninth state. Its fishing is varied and wonderful. Salmon, steelhead, and rainbow trout make up its principal freshwater gamefish. In saltwater, the coho and chinook salmon, halibut (one hundred pounders and better have been taken on sport gear), and the occasional shark provide excellent sport for the angler. Those interested in an entirely different type of fishing should try scooping up the little eulachon (*which see*) or "hooligan" as they enter freshwater in early spring. This fish is not only a delicacy on the menu, but it also serves a very utilitarian purpose in the native cultures; when threaded with a wick it can be lit and will burn like a candle. The Kenai is also one of the centers of Alaska's vast crab industry and features the huge king crab, as well as the Dungeness variety. Crab fishing in coastal waters off southern Alaska is an all-year industry, and

Playing a big sea-run cutthroat in the Pavlof Bay area in a spectacular setting of mountains and forest

the tourist can enjoy some of the finest eating in the world near the Kenai town of Homer. Still in the realm of shellfish, digging for razor and butter clams on the tidal flats of the Kenai area, as well as in other southern Alaskan waters, is considered a fascinating sport.

Moving inland, the Kenai River is the main river of the peninsula. The lower reaches are estuarine for a fair distance inland and provide accessible and varied sport fishing. Here the sportsman can catch a mixed bag consisting of most of Alaska's important anadromous species. The first to arrive in the spring are the "hooligans," which are greeted by crowds of natives and tourists, all armed with scoop nets and looking forward to a delectable smelt meal.

There is a cannery located at the mouth of the river which, in years of good runs, provides excellent and easy pink-salmon fishing early in the summer. Farther up the river, yet still within the reaches of the tidal effects, spring brings large runs of sockeye salmon and chinooks. The king-salmon run continues at a lower rate during the summer, and then is followed in the fall by a run of sporty coho salmon and Dolly Varden. During the early winter, the Kenai gets a run of steelhead trout, considered by some to be the greatest sport fish of all. Five-pound trout are not unusual, but fish of ten pounds and better are often taken. The salmon vary in size with the pink or "humpback" running in the neighborhood of five pounds, the coho around eleven pounds. The kings, however, are the champions. Commercial fishermen have taken chinooks near the hundred-pound mark, but because of their tremendous strength and the magnitudes of the currents, fish over forty pounds are very difficult to subdue in the river. Although large salmon are frequently hooked, they are rarely brought to shore.

Farther upstream Beaver Creek joins the Kenai River, and there is a landing here where tourists can rent a boat. From here the tourist can sample the Kenai itself or fish in Beaver Creek which yields good trout fishing for rainbows and some fair salmon fishing. Farther upstream is Eagle Rock, a well-known fishing site, which is usually very productive during the salmon runs. Two miles farther up, the Kenai turns a right-angle corner, forming an eddy which is famous for the number of chinook salmon that congregate in the slack water.

The Kenai is not the only good river on this peninsula.

The Ninilchik, the Anchor, and the Moose rivers are all accessible from the road and offer fishing similar to the Kenai. The fisherman is better equipped on all of these rivers with a boat and a reliable motor. If the angler does not bring his own, there are numerous places where they can be rented. However, a word of caution should be injected here; these rivers are all swift, rocky, and very cold. For the person not familiar with boating on such water, it is strongly recommended that the services of a guide be enlisted.

There are several large lakes on the Kenai Peninsula. They offer wonderful rainbow trout and Dolly Varden fishing. Accessible from the road are Siklak Lake, Kenai Lake, Russian Lake (a three-mile hike), Hidden Lake, Jean Lake, and many others. The Russian River is about a mile from the road on a good trail and is one of the outstanding rainbow-trout streams in the country.

WESTERN ALASKA

The third major division in regard to Alaskan fishing lies west of Anchorage, bounded to the north by the Alaska Range and Bristol Bay and to the south by Shelikof Strait and the Pacific Ocean. The Alaskan Peninsula strings on and into the Aleutian Chain. It encloses the Katmai National Monument and the world-famous Brooks River. The Brooks is accessible only by air, but there are several fine fishing camps in the area. The river offers excellent rainbow, grayling, lake trout, Dolly Varden, northern pike, sockeye, and coho salmon.

Bristol Bay is another popular area. The saltwater yields excellent chinook and coho salmon by trolling. While inland, one finds rainbow trout, steelhead, Dolly Varden, sockeye, chinook, and coho salmon, as well as whitefish. Running into Bristol Bay are drainages which are very important to the Alaskan fishing scene. The Kuichak River drains Iliamna Lake, and the Wood River drains the Tikchik lakes.

Further out on the Alaskan Peninsula dollies, sockeye and coho salmon are to be found in the major lakes and rivers. This is a wild and beautiful country, full of game, relatively untouched by man. Again accessible only by plane, a fishing jaunt to this area is likely to be a unique and rewarding experience.

Just north of Bristol Bay lies the Kuskokwim watershed. Here again is a completely roadless wilderness, accessible only by air. However, there are several villages such as Bethel, Sleetmute, Stony River, and McGrath where guide service may be obtained. The Kuskokwim River is a silty stream like many of Alaska's big rivers, and the finest fishing may be found where the tributaries meet the main current, forming an interface of clear and muddy waters. Here two of Alaska's favorite sport fish are found in abundance. The grayling is a flyfisherman's delight, with its huge sail-like dorsal fin and its dramatic way of engulfing a dry fly, then arching out of the water in a frantic jump before it dives for the safety of the bottom. The other species is the lantern-jawed pugnacious sheefish or inconnu (*see inconnu*). The shee is a migratory species entering saltwater, but its life history is rather complex. The natives start catching these fish in March, through the ice, and fish for them until late into the fall. One of the many legends that has grown around the shee is that it never eats while in freshwater and therefore only strikes out of anger. Stomach examinations of this species show that this is false and that the inconnu is a voracious feeder on chubs, salmon fry, small grayling, sculpins, and any other small fish. With this in mind, the prospective angler should arm himself with a spinning rod and a collection of wobbling spoons and spinners. Eight pounders are common, but individuals of fifty pounds have been taken and the largest recorded is approximately eighty pounds. Sheefish justly earn their reputation of "Arctic tarpon" by putting on fantastic aerial shows and shoulder-jarring runs.

Some of the important waters of this drainage are the Holitna, the Hoholitna, the Stony, and the Aniak rivers. The latter contains the only native population of rainbow trout north of the Alaska range. All these waters also have superlative grayling fishing, and the slack waters of the sloughs of the lower reaches of all these rivers harbor large northern pike.

YUKON-TANANA DRAINAGE

Our next subdivision would take a lifetime to fish. The Yukon-Tanana drainage stretches east and west from the Canadian border to the Bering Sea and from the Alaska Range to the south to the remote Brooks Range in the north. Much of the good water in the eastern section is accessible by road, but the area from Nenana west can only be reached by float plane or by river boat. The main species are grayling, sheefish, salmon, and pike.

There are three ways to fish Alaska's vast interior, by float plane, by riverboat, or by car and foot. The plane is of course the most mobile and convenient, but while ferrying the fisherman to and from the remoter hinterlands it is also the most expensive. For the man with time the riverboat is one of the best ways to explore the wilderness of this section.

The Tanana and Yukon Rivers, with their tributaries, form an extensive watershed, thousands of miles long. One of the best short trips by riverboat can be made from Circle to Eagle near the Canadian border. The Yukon River itself is not good fishing water, although it harbors large chinook, coho, and sockeye salmon, as well as sheefish, grayling, and pike. Due to the eroding action of the river the water is too silty and opaque. The tributaries are crystal clear and provide fast and exciting fishing for trophy-size fish. The first of these is the Charley River, which drains the hills south of the Yukon. It is navigable for many miles with a small riverboat, and its headwaters lie in some of Alaska's finest Dall sheep and caribou country. It is primarily a grayling stream, but salmon, sheefish, and pike may be encountered. The next stream upriver is the Kandik, draining the northern and eastern hills. At the mouth of this stream is a beautiful sandbar, which forms a perfect campground. The Kandik is an excellent kayak stream, being fairly fast and too shallow for the river boat. The mouth of the river is a deep bay, connected by a narrow channel to a series of beaver ponds. This channel and the bay provide some excellent fishing for pike. Due to the shallowness of the water these fish are forced to display all their aerial acrobatic ability, and they are worthy of the most enthusiastic user of light tackle. Further up the Kandik, grayling are abundant in ideal dry-fly water.

The Nation River is the next on the list on our journey up the Yukon. This is one of the most renowned grayling streams in Alaska. It might easily hold a fish of the world-record class. These grayling are at their best on light dry-fly tackle but are also sporty for the spinfisher-

man. As with the Kandik, the Nation is also an excellent kayak stream, and both are in the heart of bountiful big game and fur country. Wolves are common (though not often seen), and bears are abundant, as are the magnificent Alaskan moose.

The Tatonduk River is the next upstream and features grayling and sheefish, as well as pike in the sloughs and backwaters. For the late-summer fisherman, the sheefish is tops. These voracious whitefish migrate into the clear streams to spawn and strike at spoons, plugs, and wet flies with a terrifying abandon. The shee is the most acrobatic of Alaska's gamefish, and although they do not seem to run large in size in the Yukon streams, five pounds of sheefish on light tackle will thrill the most jaded angler.

The whole trip from Circle to Eagle takes about a week, with time out to sample each tributary. It covers about 175 miles of true wilderness. However, the Yukon, like the Tanana, is a dangerous and tricky river. It is a mile wide at points but is very shallow in many places. The navigable channels are constantly shifting, and shoals present a continual hazard to the boatman. It is not a river for the novice in a runabout or power cruiser. The Alaskan riverboat is a piece of equipment designed especially for these waters, and it is advisable that guide services be secured for at least the first trip on the rivers of the interior.

The Circle-to-Eagle trip is only one of the many that may be undertaken. Another one can be started at Fairbanks, down the Chena River and into the Tanana, past the natives' fish wheels which scoop salmon from the river. Five miles down and across the river, Salchaket Slough, a fast, deep cut-off from the mainstream enters. The fisherman follows up the slough for several miles and comes to a small clear stream entering from the right. This is Clear Creek and is one of the prettiest streams of the interior. Winding through vast stands of paper birches, it seems to be of another world. It features grayling and, after July, sheefish. It is a wonderful stream for the fly-fisherman and for the spin enthusiast, as well as the nonfishing bird watcher, for the area is populated with ducks, mergansers, and kingfishers, as well as all kinds of small songbirds. The Clear Creek trip is an all-day affair, and again a guide is needed, as threading one's way across the Tanana is a tricky business at best.

HIGHWAY FISHING

The roadbound fisherman need not despair. Although Alaska's highways are few and far between and heavily traveled, there is still good fishing to be had. However, to be successful, a knowledge of local areas is necessary. The Sport Fish Division of the Alaska Department of Fish and Game puts out an excellent guide to the roadside fishing of the state, and this guide may be obtained by writing to the Sport Fish Division in Juneau. This manual leaves out one important road, the Taylor Highway, which joins Eagle, on the Yukon, to the Alaska Highway near the Canadian border at Tetlin Junction. This road crosses and parallels for some distance the brawling Fortymile River which offers wonderful grayling fishing over its length. At the last bridge there is a deep pool which yields an occasional sheefish and quite a few lingcod (which see). The latter species deserves recognition as not only a fair sport fish, but as the finest eating fish found in Alaskan waters. It is a member of the cod family and quite ugly in appearance. Its meat, however, is white and flaky, with a truly fine flavor. The natives prize the liver which they eat raw or fried.

Briefly looking at some of the fishing hot spots along the highways of the interior, we find excellent rainbow-trout fishing in some of the lakes between the border and Delta Junction on the Alaska Highway. These are planted trout, and have done very well. The first is Deadman Lake at Mile 1251. The next and best known is Jan Lake at Mile 1324. The lake lies three-quarters of a mile off the road, but there is an excellent bulldozed trail to it. A third one is just south of Delta on the Richardson Highway. This is Bolio Lake and is also easily accessible from the road.

Further on the Richardson, on the other side of Black Rapids Pass, lies a series of lakes which offer year-round lake trout fishing. These lakes consist of Summit Lake, Paxon Lake, and then on the Denali Highway, Tangle Lakes. The best fishing for these lakers is right after ice goes out in June or July, when they are feeding on the surface near the shores.

Driving north from Fairbanks the fisherman can travel on either the Steese Highway or the Livengood road, both good gravel roads. The Livengood fork crosses many good fly-fishing streams, such as the Chatanika River, Washington Creek, the Tatalina River, and the Tolovana. All these are heavily fished near the road, and the angler would be well advised to walk about a mile or so to get away from the traffic. Near the end of the highway the traveler crosses the Hutlinana River which features good grayling, salmon, and Dolly Varden fishing in the spring and fall. The terminus of the highway is at Manley Hot Springs, where boats may be rented to take in the excellent pike fishing in the sloughs.

The Steese Highway parallels the upper Chantanika for almost seventy miles. The whole stream is beautiful grayling water and is the site of the University of Alaska's investigation on grayling biology. The Chatanika also has some feeder creeks on both sides of the river which harbor grayling. The Steese passes the headwaters of Chatanika and then rises over Twelve-Mile Summit and drops into the Birch Creek drainage. This marks the site of another week-long (or more) float trip, this time by kayak or canoe. Birch Creek is crossed by the Steese fifty miles further on, but in the meantime the stream travels 120 miles through the wilderness. Birch Creek offers near record-size grayling, whitefish, and pike, as well as sheefish in September. After leaving the headwaters of Birch Creek, the Steese again climbs over another summit, passing through the caribou country. From this summit to Circle City the traveler passes over several small clear streams, which all offer fair to good fishing for small grayling.

ARCTIC CIRCLE REGION

Moving north and west the next subdivision lies entirely within the Arctic Circle. There are three major rivers in this section, the Kobuk, the Selawik, and the Noatak, all with their mouths in the Kotzebue area. Sheefish are the prize, and it is here that they reach their maximum size. Again it is a totally roadless area, and the only practical means of transportation is by float plane. There are several towns that one can use for a base of operations, depending upon what kind of fishing is

planned. The largest town is Kotzebue, on the coast, from which the angler can reach the lower sections of all three rivers, as well as Hotham Inlet and the huge inland lake which abound in sheefish up to sixty pounds and better. The Kobuk and Noatak fan into a delta, which holds pike of great size in all its sloughs.

Further inland, the town of Kiana lies on the Kobuk. There is a lodge here that caters primarily to anglers seeking sheefish. During the summer months a huge run of spawning sheefish passes through the Kiana area.

From the towns of Alatna, Allakaket, or Bettles (on the Koyukuk River) one can fly to the headwater lakes of the Kobuk-Walker and Shelby Lakes, which hold good populations of lake trout.

The Noatak is prized for its Dolly Vardens and its beautiful and virgin scenery. The Selawik is a slow stream with large sheefish and pike. The native village of the same name is a good place to look for local guide service, or your pilot from Kotzebue will act as your guide in your quest for the inconnu.

Our final subdivision is the vast Arctic slope from the Bering Sea to the Arctic Wildlife Refuge and the Canadian border. Again the only practical transportation is by plane. In this area lie hundreds of lakes probably untouched by the white man. What fish do they hold? Grayling, pike, whitefish, probably sheefish, perhaps Dollies or Arctic char, lake trout, ling, and coho salmon. This is the last frontier for the adventurous fisherman. No one knows really what lies in these waters, and many of them are yet unnamed. The principal known rivers are the Meade, the Colville, the Ikpikpuk, the Canning, and the Sagavanirktok.

The touring fisherman needs to remember that Alaska is apt to be cool in the evenings and often quite hot during the summer days. The temperature can drop from 114° to 30° in a twelve-hour span on the Fortymile River. Thus the fisherman should select his wardrobe accordingly. One should be prepared for Alaska's most dangerous big-game animal, the mosquito, which is abundant through the early summer. A headnet is always a welcome haven, as are light gloves.　　　　—R.S.L.

Angler Bing Crosby fishing an Alaskan lake

KATMAI NATIONAL MONUMENT

There are a number of camps located in the Katmai National Monument and surrounding area. The angling here consists of grayling, rainbow trout, lake trout, northern pike, Dolly Varden, sockeye salmon, and chinook silver salmon as well as Arctic char. The base camp is easily reached by daily flights from King Salmon or Kulik. Accommodations are mostly log cabins with modern facilities, as well as some tent houses. Huge brown bears, majestic moose, migrating salmon, and snow-splotched mountain peaks provide colorful subjects for the amateur photographer. Much of the wildlife footage in Walt Disney's now classic nature films was made in the Katmai region.

The fishing is done in a rugged, mountainous landscape not far from the volcanic peaks of the Valley of Ten Thousand Smokes. Although there is some lake casting, the peninsula is drained by crystalline, gravel-bottomed rivers, which are easy to wade. Generally, you can get along with a pair of hip boots. Rainbow trout from 1½–5 pounds are numerous, and fish of 10 pounds or more are a daily possibility. The grayling usually run 1–2 pounds and provide excellent dry-fly fishing. More unique perhaps is the sockeye salmon, which in other parts of the Northwest rarely strikes artificial lures, but at Brooks River this species readily hits a streamer fly. The sockeyes vary from 5–10 pounds, while the acrobatic silver salmon are in the 6–12-pound class. Alaskan pike and lake trout are normally smaller than those found in the Canadian provinces, but they are numerous.

To reach the Brooks River, travel to Anchorage and then via airline to King Salmon or Kulik.

Tackle should include at least one fly rod and one bait-casting or spinning outfit. Inasmuch as these waters are open and readily covered by moderate-range casts, the gear can be from medium to light in weight. Fly-fishermen rely on standard stateside patterns in wet, dry, and streamer types. For spinning or bait-casting, a variety of wobbling spoons and spinners in the ¼–½-ounce class are effective. Tackle is stocked at the camps, as are cigarettes, liquor, insect repellant, and other sundries.

Brooks camp is located on Naknek Lake, which is forty miles long and approximately fifteen miles wide, dotted with beautiful islands with many small streams and rivers that empty into the lake and the Naknek River, some twenty miles long, that empties into the Bering Sea.

Grosvenor camp is located in a spit between Coville Lake and Grosvenor Lake. These two lakes combined have a total length of some twenty-eight miles with the fifty-mile-long American River feeding these lakes from the high lakes that abound in the Katmai area. Grosvenor and Coville lakes empty into the Savanoski River, which in turn empties into Naknek Lake. These three lakes and their feeding and discharge rivers comprise some 163 miles of continuous waterway, most of which is excellent fishing.

The Ugashik Lakes, (about 90 miles south of King Salmon) produce the best grayling fishing in Alaska, particularly in The Narrows between the two main lakes. Fish of over 4 pounds are fairly common. —A.J.McC.

ALBACORE *Thunnus alalunga* Also called longfin tuna. A fish of the mackerel family that has longer pectoral fins than other tunas although it may be difficult to distinguish from small individuals of bigeye tuna. There

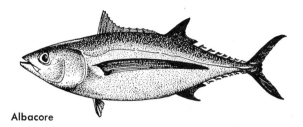

Albacore

is a narrow white margin on the caudal fin that is absent in the other tunas. The deepest part of the albacore's body is near the second dorsal fin rather than near the middle of the first dorsal fin as in other species of tunas. There are 25–32 gillrakers on the first branchial arch, and the ventral surface of the liver is covered with fine striations. The hook-and-line record is a fish taken from the island of St. Helena that was 3½ feet long and weighed 69 pounds. Commercially caught fish from near Hawaii have weighed as much as 93 pounds.

The Atlantic and Pacific forms of albacore, once believed to be separate species, are now known to be a single species, found in tropical, subtropical, and temperate waters around the world. Tagging has shown that the albacore in the North Pacific migrate annually between the American and Japanese fisheries. The food consists of fishes, squids, and crustaceans. Spawning occurs in the summer in the North Pacific and in the southern summer in the South Pacific. A single female may shed one to three million eggs.

ANGLING VALUE

Albacore are strong gamefish and are eagerly sought by anglers when the runs occur (from July through October along the west coast of North America). Water temperature plays a key role in locating albacore, with the fish commonly found at 60°-66°F. Colder or warmer currents tend to divert the schools farther offshore, and both sportfishing boats and commercials may operate from several up to 100 miles from land in clear blue water at various points along the coast. When the schools are beyond a practical distance for a one-day trip some large party boats go out for 2 or 3 days. A standard procedure on the fishing grounds is to locate the albacore by fast trolling with feathered jigs; when contact is made, these tuna are more readily caught with live bait such as anchovies, herring, sauries, and sardines on No. 1/0 and 2/0 hooks. As a rule 20–40-pound test tackle is used and a 3–4 foot wire leader (30-pound test).

FOOD VALUE

Albacore are sought by sport fishermen and by commercial fishermen using longline or live-bait methods. They are the most valuable of the tunas for canning and the only species that can be labeled as "white-meat tuna." —B.B.C.
—R.H.G.

ALBERTA The province of Alberta comprises a land mass of about 255,285 square miles lying immediately to the east of the Continental Divide. From this divide the province slopes in easterly and northeasterly directions, from altitudes of nearly 13,000 feet to 2,100 feet at its eastern boundary and 500 feet at its northern boundary. Located within the provincial boundaries are 6,485 square miles of permanent lakes and between 12,000 and 13,000 linear miles of streams. The lakes vary in size from several acres to over 800 square miles and vary in nature from the deep, cold types found in mountainous regions to the expansive, productive bodies of water of the prairies. The streams are divided into seven drainage systems, five of which have their headwaters in the steep slopes of the Rocky Mountains. It has been calculated that about 40 per cent of the total stream mileage (5,000–6,000 miles) is capable of supporting such coldwater species as trout, mountain whitefish, and grayling, while the remaining 60 per cent may be classified as warmwater fish habitat frequented by northern pike, walleye, goldeye, sauger, and numerous nongame species.

The lakes of Alberta support a commercial fishing industry as well as providing tremendous recreational opportunities for the province's 140,000 licensed anglers. Most of the 175 commercially fished lakes lie in the Great Plains region, and, due to the fertility of the area, these waters are among the most productive in the northern part of the continent. Annual commercial yields of some twelve million pounds of fish are being harvested, and yields from individual lakes in the southern parts of the province have been in excess of fifty pounds per acre. In order of their importance, whitefish, tullibee, walleye, northern pike, perch, lake trout, and goldeye are the species which are harvested commercially. Other species such as burbot and suckers are taken for animal food in lesser quantities. Alberta whitefish have been well known for their excellent quality and have enjoyed wide distribution in United States markets. Continued construction of large irrigation reservoirs on the prairies is increasing the commercial fishery potential of the province, especially with regard to whitefish.

Sport fishermen in Alberta are able to pursue their quarry on a year-round basis except in certain trout streams where closure on alternate years is effected to provide for adequate natural reproduction. Traditional "fishing seasons," extending from May or June until September, were abandoned on all game species early in the 1950's, thereby increasing the recreational opportunities provided by the many streams and lakes in the province. While the more accessible trout streams on the east slopes of the Rockies are quite heavily fished, some of the headwater streams of the Peace River and Athabasca River systems still offer virgin fishing conditions for native char, trout, and grayling. In addition, many lakes in the northeastern regions of the province have a much greater angling potential for pike, walleye, and perch than is now being utilized.

An important addition to the sport fishery has developed as a result of the stocking of a large number of pothole-type lakes with fast-growing strains of rainbow trout. These lakes, generally under two hundred surface acres in area, are scattered throughout the prairie, parkland, and foothill regions. They are readily accessible to anglers from urban centers. For the most part they have no well-defined inlet or outlet streams, and are often in sheltered locations—factors which sometimes combine to make them susceptible to winter-kill. Their waters teem with the smaller aquatic forms of life but usually do not contain fish other than a few minnow species and sticklebacks. The first experimental introductions of

rainbow trout in these lakes were made in 1949, and the outstanding fisheries which resulted led to rapid expansion of "pothole-lake" investigation and stocking program. The growth rate of trout in these lakes is so rapid (up to 5 pounds in 2 years) that anglers have difficulty in securing an adequate harvest before the trout become large and difficult to catch. The lack of permanent inlet streams or suitable beach spawning sites prevents natural reproduction of trout. Fisheries, therefore, must be maintained by stocking with hatchery fish. This use of the hatchery product has produced gratifying results, especially to anglers who otherwise would have to travel many miles to the waters of the mountains and foothills for their trout fishing.

FISHERIES RESEARCH AND MANAGEMENT

Fisheries research in Alberta was initiated by the late Dr. R. B. Miller of the Zoology Department, University of Alberta, in 1940. The first area of investigation was the life cycle of the pike-whitefish tapeworm, *Triaenophorus crassus*. The presence of this parasite in fish flesh posed one of the major problems of inland commercial fisheries. Although experiments to control the tapeworm proved largely unsuccessful, a great deal of scientific information was obtained through these studies, and this information has formed the basis of a number of subsequent control experiments. During these early years of research, investigations were also carried out on the causes of fluctuations in abundance of whitefish in selected commercial lakes of the province. It was generally thought by fishermen that these fluctuations were due to overfishing and that the stocking of whitefish eyed eggs from hatcheries would be an effective method of restoring normal populations. Miller's investigations showed that the fluctuations were due to the failure of certain year classes and that the planting of whitefish eggs in Alberta lakes, as practiced at the time, was not contributing to the commercial fishery in future years.

Research in sport fisheries has been carried out since 1946. This began with basic surveys on trout streams of the eastern slopes and on many of the smaller lakes throughout the province. A number of significant facts concerning streams and their fish populations were brought to light through these surveys, and major changes in stream-management policies were effected. In order that fishery research pertaining to streams might be carried out more efficiently, the Alberta Biological Station was established at Gorge Creek, southwest of Calgary, in 1950. Various studies have been carried out at this station, but much of the work has been centered around the survival of hatchery trout in streams and the causes of mortality in stream-stocked trout. The homing behavior of stream trout, the effects of stocking densities on survival of the trout, and parasite studies are some additional research projects being conducted at the Alberta Biological Station.

Much investigational work which does not belong in the category of basic research is also being conducted in the province. This includes inventories of lakes and streams, sampling fish populations to determine growth rates and species distribution, conducting creel census to determine rate of harvest, observations on winter-kill, and many similar projects. Data are accumulated which are useful in modifying management practices, as well as serving as a basis for future study.

CUTTHROAT TROUT

The cutthroat trout is native to headwater lakes and streams from the International boundary northward to and including the Bow River system. This species has supplied a great deal of the stream-trout fishing in Alberta in the past, but unfortunately few pure strains of native cutthroat remain due to hybridization with rainbow trout which were extensively stocked in cutthroat waters between 1930 and 1950. To preserve cutthroat fishing, this species was introduced into the Ram River in the North Saskatchewan drainage in 1955. This river contained no other trout due to several impassable falls and its relative inaccessibility to man. The introduction was a decided success, and the Ram River system is now providing fine cutthroat fishing. Other streams in the southwestern part of the province which have remained essentially cutthroat streams are the west and south branches of the Castle River, Daisy Creek, Vicary Creek, Dutch Creek, Racehorse Creek, and the northwest branch of the Oldman River and the Livingstone River.

The native cutthroat of the province is often more colorfully marked than the species tends to be near the southern parts of its range. The black spotting is somewhat more profuse, and the red-orange streaks beneath the lower jaw are very distinct. It is not generally considered a difficult fish to catch, and takes wet or dry flies readily from May through October.

RAINBOW TROUT

The rainbow is probably the best-known and most widely publicized of the trout group in Alberta. As in other areas of the continent, it has received a great deal of attention in fish-culture work due primarily to the ease with which it can be raised in hatcheries and its ready acceptance by the angling public. A fact that is not well-known, however, is that rainbow trout are native to the Athabasca River system in Alberta from headwater streams near the Jasper Park boundary to the south slopes of the Swan Hills. Many "oldtime" fishermen attest to good catches of rainbows from streams of the Athabasca system years before fish-cultural activities and introductions were carried on in this province.

As previously mentioned, rainbows have provided excellent fishing in pothole lakes and reservoirs in which they have been stocked. Among those which have become well-known are Strubel Lake, Mitchell Lake, Star Lake, Chickako Lake, Two Lakes, Reesor Lake, Beauvais Lake, Wildhorse Lake, Beaverdam Lake, Police Lake, and, more recently, Henderson Lake, Tyrrell Lake, and Schuman Lake have been added to the list of popular rainbow-trout waters. The rehabilitation of selected small lakes which have contained undesirable species or species incompatible with trout introductions is gradually increasing the number of lakes being managed for rainbow fishing.

The best stream fishing for rainbow trout in Alberta is to be found in the Bow River for approximately twenty-five miles downstream from the city of Calgary and in the Oldman River as it winds through the foothills northwest of the town of Pincher Creek. The Bow River,

throughout the aforementioned stretch, is probably one of the most productive trout streams on the continent, and catches of rainbows varying from two to six pounds are not uncommon. Trout of this size, taken on light tackle in this swiftly flowing river, provide excellent sport for the fisherman.

BROWN TROUT

The introduction of the brown trout into a number of streams on the eastern fringe of the foothills has given great satisfaction to those fly-fishermen who choose to pit their skill against this wariest member of the trout clan. The brown trout has been most successful in streams with gentle flow rates, moderately cool temperatures, and abundant cover in the form of overhanging banks, sunken logs, and tangles of tree roots. These favorable environments are provided by streams such as the Raven River, Beaver Creek, Stauffer Creek, Fallen Timber Creek, Alford Creek, Dogpound Creek, and Shunda Creek in the west-central parts of the province. Recent introductions in selected streams of the Athabasca River, Peace River, and Waterton River systems have been made with a view to extending the range of this desirable species.

Brown trout may be taken by those skilled in the art of fly-casting on either wet or dry flies especially during late evenings in the months of July and August.

GOLDEN TROUT

This colorful native of the Sierra mountain region was introduced to three alpine lakes southwest of Pincher Creek in 1959. Several additional plantings followed, and reproducing populations now exist in five lakes (1974). Although golden trout up to 4 pounds have been caught, they provide a very limited fishery.

BROOK TROUT

This member of the char group was generously stocked in streams and lakes during the early history of fish culture in Alberta. It has become very abundant in a number of small tributary streams, particularly those on which beaver impoundments occur. Attempts to establish the species in some cutthroat waters met with only limited success. The brook trout has, however, been a welcome addition to the sport fishery in waters where spawning conditions are not favorable for other trout species. Streams which have consistently provided good brook-trout fishing are the north and south forks of Prairie Creek, Upper Stony Creek, Williams Creek, Alford Creek, and Lookout Creek. A number of lakes also have become well-known as brook-trout producers. They are Bovin (Blue) Lake, Elbow Lake, Rat Lake, and Muskiki Lake, the latter having yielded specimens up to seven pounds.

DOLLY VARDEN

Dolly Varden are common in headwater streams and lakes from the Peace River to the southern extremities of the South Saskatchewan River system. Although they provide many hours of recreational fishing, they are not regarded as highly by anglers as the other trout species. Dolly Varden are taken through a wide range of sizes—

from specimens of a few ounces in weight in tiny headwater tributaries to large fish of fifteen pounds or more in the larger rivers. In some of the more inaccessible areas of the province, the Dolly Varden is the only member of the trout group present in the streams. The Berland, Wildhay, Muskeg, and Cardinal rivers are some of the more popular producers of large Dolly Varden.

LAKE TROUT

Lake trout are somewhat sparsely distributed in the province due to the shallow nature of most of our lakes. They are most abundant in the extreme northeastern section in the deep, cold lakes of the Precambrian Shield. These lakes are accessible only by air at the present time so that the sport fishery is in a relatively undeveloped state. Other waters in the province which provide lake-trout fishing are Cold Lake, Grist Lake, Namur Lake, Margaret Lake, Wentzel Lake, Peerless Lake, Swan Lake, and Rock Lake. Lake-trout introductions into two hydro impoundments, Spray Reservoir and Ghost Reservoir, have been successful, and moderately good fisheries have developed in these reservoirs.

Fishing for this species is most rewarding immediately after spring break-up and again in the fall when the fish are found in relatively shallow water. Trolling with spoons or large flashing lures is the most common method of taking lake trout.

AMERICAN GRAYLING

This fine gamefish is found mainly in streams of the Athabasca River and Peace River drainages. Many of the tributary waters of the middle and lower reaches of the Athabasca River, as well as the headwaters of the Wapiti and Smoky rivers, have grayling populations which have rarely been fished by man. Recent road-building programs are, however, creating access to these areas, and in a short time much of this water will provide a sport fishery for one of Canada's best native gamefish. Although the grayling is typically found in the riffle or rapid portions of streams, the species has been introduced into a limited number of pothole-type lakes with fair to excellent success. In either situation, grayling from the ¾–3-pound class are a dry-fly fisherman's delight.

A number of the more popular waters for grayling fishing are the Swan River, Freeman River, Wapiti River, Kakwa River, Cutbank River, certain portions of the McLeod River, Berland River, Marten River, Christina River, Christmas Creek, Two Creek, Marsh Head Creek, Pinto Creek, Pembina River, Trout Creek, Sunday Creek, and Kinky Lake.

MOUNTAIN WHITEFISH

Mountain whitefish (*which see*) are among the most numerous of the coldwater gamefishes in the province, being widely distributed throughout the upper and middle reaches of all the major river systems. They are generally not resident in the smaller tributary streams on the east slopes of the Rockies, apparently preferring the larger creeks and rivers. They also inhabit a considerable number of mountain lakes and the hydro impoundments of the Bow River system.

Mountain whitefish are often erroneously referred to as "grayling" in Alberta, especially in areas where Arctic grayling do not occur. They may, however, be easily distinguished from the latter species by their much smaller mouth and smaller dorsal fin, as well as by the lack of dark spots on the anterior portions of the body.

As a gamefish, the species is generally considered by anglers to be somewhat inferior to the trouts, chars, and Arctic grayling, but in spite of this many fishermen-hours are spent annually in pursuit of this fish, and its contribution to the over-all sport fishery resource of the province is quite substantial.

These fish are most often taken by using small morsels of bait on the hooks of artificial flies, but wet flies fished near the stream bottom are also very effective.

The Castle River, Crowsnest River, Oldman River, Highwood River, Upper Bow River, Red Deer River, and Athabasca River are choice streams for mountain whitefish. While the average catch may consist of fish slightly under 1 pound, specimens up to 2 pounds are not uncommon, and fish of 5 pounds have been recorded from Alberta waters.

LAKE WHITEFISH

The lake whitefish has until very recently been considered exclusively a commercial species in Alberta. However, anglers have now begun to realize its potential as a gamefish and have developed methods of taking this species with hook and line, especially during the winter months. During the past two years Lake Wabamun has developed a flourishing sport fishery for lake whitefish. Several hundreds of anglers frequently have taken part in this fishery on weekends. Other waters which are beginning to attract whitefish anglers are Pigeon Lake, Hanmore Lake, Buck Lake, and Moose Lake.

NORTHERN PIKE

Northern pike are the most abundant and widely distributed of the province's warmwater gamefish. They occur in streams, lakes, and reservoirs throughout the prairies and forested regions, but rarely in mountain waters. Undoubtedly Alberta anglers take more pike than any other species because of the accessibility of pike waters and the relative ease with which this fish can be caught. There is a growing interest in trophy-sized pike and a considerable number between 20 and 32 pounds have been reported in recent years. Seibert Lake, near Lac la Biche, has been famous over the years for its large pike with 15–25 pounders commonly being taken. A brief list of other lakes which support major pike fisheries would include Pinehurst Lake, Moose Lake, Fort Lake, Skeleton Lake, Lac la Biche, Beaver Lake, Calling Lake, Cold Lake, Sturgeon Lake, Winagami Lake, Wabamun Lake, Lac la Nonne, Buck Lake, Chestermere Lake, Lake Newell, Lake McGregor, Park Lake, Keho Lake, and St. Mary's Reservoir.

WALLEYE

This member of the perch family is the most prized of our warmwater gamefishes because of its excellent table qualities. While not as widely distributed as the pike, the province has a good number of lakes and large rivers which provide walleye fishing. Walleyes tend to be localized in distribution within a given lake or stream, showing a preference for rocky or sandy bars. Anglers have found it advantageous to locate these areas when fishing for this species.

The better-known lakes for walleyes are Fawcett Lake, Sturgeon Lake, Smoke Lake, Wolf Lake, Moose Lake, Helena Lake, Elinor Lake, Seibert Lake, Ironwood Lake, Touchwood Lake, Baptiste Lake, and Buck Lake. The lower regions of the large rivers also yield excellent catches of walleyes. The Athabasca, Peace, Pembina, Beaver, Red Deer, and South Saskatchewan rivers contribute significantly to the walleye sport fishery. Six-to-8-pound fish of this species are not uncommon in the Red Deer and South Saskatchewan rivers, and specimens up to 12 and 14 pounds have been taken in the Athabasca and Pembina rivers.

The sauger, a close relative of the walleye, is also taken in rivers of the Saskatchewan drainage system. Most anglers do not distinguish between the two species so that the sauger is more often than not thought to be a walleye. Owing to its restricted distribution and small size, the sauger does not assume a position of importance in the province's sport fishery.

YELLOW PERCH

This colorful little panfish is almost as widely distributed as the northern pike and frequents essentially the same habitat in lakes. It is not, however, a fish of the flowing waters of the province. In many lakes perch are so prolific and underharvested that populations have become stunted. Lakes which are noteworthy for their large perch are Sturgeon Lake, Kehiwin Lake, Moose Lake, Beaver Lake, and Elkwater Lake. Perch of two pounds are not unusual in Beaver Lake.

GOLDEYE

The goldeye is probably the best of the province's warmwater gamefish as far as sporting qualities are concerned. It is not unusual for this fish to leap out of the water in troutlike fashion when hooked on light tackle.

The distribution of the goldeye is limited to the warm, silty sections of the large rivers, such as the lower Peace River, Athabasca River, North and South Saskatchewan Rivers, and Red Deer River. Its occurrence in lakes is limited to Lake Claire, in Wood Buffalo Park, and Lake Athabasca where it is taken for commercial purposes but not as a gamefish.

In the streams previously mentioned, goldeye are taken on wet flies, small spinners, and natural bait. —M.J.P.

ALDERFLIES *Sialis spp.* So similar are the species of alderflies that a general description of the genus will suffice for all of them. The larva of the alderfly is similar in structure to that of the hellgrammite but is, of course, very much smaller, being less than an inch in length and differing most noticeably in possessing a long, slender tip to the end of the abdomen.

Adult alderflies have uniform gray or blackish wings and are not much more than half an inch in length. They look very much like a medium-sized caddisfly. There are no tails, and the antennae are about two-thirds as long as the forewing. They are robust insects without functional mouthparts in the adult stage, so far as known. They are often seen actively flying among bushes or sedges at the edge of lakes and streams during sunny late spring days.

Several artificial flies are designed to imitate the alderfly and one, the Alder, is a popular early season trout pattern. *See also* Dobsonflies —S.G.J.

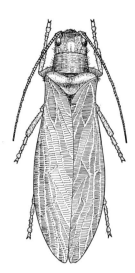

Alderfly

ALEWIFE *Alosa pseudoharengus* The alewife differs, along with the blueback herring and shad, from the skipjack herring and hickory shad, in its lower jaw, which does not project noticeably beyond the upper. It has a deep notch in the upper jaw, as in the shad, from which it differs by the presence of a small patch of teeth on the tongue and a relatively low number of gillrakers (33–40) on the lower part of the first gill arch in the adult. The eye is larger than in other species of the genus. It is bluish above with silvery sides, with faint dark stripes along the sides.

In saltwater, this species grows to a length of over a foot, but the landlocked or freshwater form only reaches 3–6 inches. It is found along the Atlantic Coast from Florida to Labrador, throughout the St. Lawrence River drainage, recently occurring in Lakes Huron and Michigan through the Welland Canal. In saltwater forms, the species begins its migration in February and April, returning to the sea in May. Some may stay in the shallow waters of the estuaries as late as early winter, but most disappear in the fall. In freshwater, migrations occur upstream in April and May. Following this, they return to the larger bodies of water, where they spend the fall and winter in deepwater. During the summer, the landlocked form is subject to mass mortalities, when large numbers of alewives die and float up on the beaches creating considerable nuisance to property owners. This mortality is believed to be related to changes in water temperature. The alewife feeds primarily on plankton, including shrimps, small fishes, diatoms, and copepods.

ECONOMIC VALUE

The marine form of the alewife was formerly of commercial importance, with a landing of over 15 million pounds reported in 1960. Most are canned, salted, or

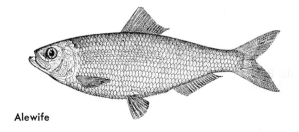

Alewife

smoked, although the flesh is bony and of poor quality. The roes are excellent. The alewife is also used as bait for various fishes, as well as for chum.　　　—D.dS.

ALGAE Man and his domestic animals, and many populations of terrestrial animals are largely dependent on members of the grass family for their food, either directly or indirectly. Similarly the animal life of aquatic environments is dependent for food on several groups of photosynthetic plants collectively known as the *algae*. Although 25,000 species of algae have been described and given scientific names, relatively few have common names. One may refer to such conspicuous examples as rockweeds, kelps, Irish moss, pond scums, mermaid's tresses, and a few others, but the remainder have not been called sharply to the attention of laymen. Their important place in the natural world has not been generally recognized. These numerous, abundant, diverse, ubiquitous, and fascinating organisms are well worth study for many reasons. Perhaps the recent concern with problems of pollution will serve to direct proper attention to them.

Terrestrial plants possess roots, leaves, stems, and reproductive structures such as cones and flowers; and we utilize these as recognition marks for the various groups included among the 350,000 species known the world around. The algae do *not* possess any of these organs. Although they carry on the same fundamental processes as the terrestrial vegetation, they are organized in a wholly different manner. Their forms range from simple, single cells, to colonial aggregates, to simple and branched filaments, to structures resembling higher plants, and some are very complex. They include some of the tiniest plants as well as some of the largest, such as the giant kelps. Their sexual organs are unicellular in contrast to those of the terrestrial types which are always multicellular. They lack the vascular systems by which land plants transport materials from one part of the plant to another. Finally, they do not have embryos, although all land plants do.

The cells making up the bodies of both land plants and the algae are very similar in general features, but they differ from one another in a number of distinct ways. The major differences lie in the nature of the photosynthetic pigments, the cell walls, and the food reserves which they produce. These features are useful in distinguishing the 8 recognized groups of algae.

CHARACTERISTICS

Algae are essentially aquatic organisms, growing in all our natural bodies of water from the smallest to the largest, the coldest to the warmest supporting any kind of life, the freshest to the supersaline, and surface to hundreds of feet in depth. A large number of kinds grow on moist surfaces such as the soil. Others grow on or in other types of plants and animals. Some species grow in close association with certain fungi to form those numerous, varied, and widespread growths known as *lichens*.

Spirogyra

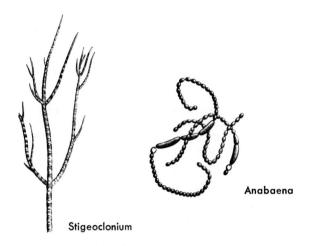

Stigeoclonium

Anabaena

Many single-celled and some colonial representatives of green algae, yellow-green algae, euglenoids, and dinoflagellates are motile; they can move about by means of hairlike structures called *flagellae* which are normal cellular features. The reproductive cells of many algae are also motile.

Most species of algae are not motile, and thousands of kinds spend most of their lives attached to solid objects of great variety. Intertidal algae, such as the rockweeds, are excellent examples. Some of the larger algae, such as the *Sargassum*, float about and pass most of their lives in this state. Indeed, the Sargasso Sea, an area as large as Texas, is named for and characterized by the presence of great floating masses of gulfweeds.

Of special interest are thousands of small species whose members float about at the mercy of winds, waves, tides, and currents. Collectively known as the phytoplankton, they are extremely important as primary producers. In oceanic waters, two groups of unicellular algae, the diatoms and the dinoflagellates, carry on most of the photosynthesis essential to all nongreen organisms. The products of this process serve to feed small herbivorous animals, these in turn are consumed by larger animals, and these in turn furnish food for still larger forms. The algae are the starting points for many of the food chains and food webs which have been recognized. When one considers the vastness of the oceans as compared to the land surfaces of the earth, the idea that these tiny algae carry on more photosynthesis than does the terrestrial flora is not unreasonable.

In addition to their extremely critical role as primary producers, the algae are important to animal life in other ways. As a by-product of photosynthesis, they release oxygen and, thus, aerate the waters to the benefit of the animal life which requires it in its respiratory activities. The plants provide protection and shelter for the many small animals which live among them. They provide breeding grounds in which eggs may be laid, the young produced, and the juvenile stages developed until they seek wider horizons for their activities. In light of these considerations, the necessity for obtaining algae in aquatic life becomes very apparent.

REPRODUCTION

Asexual reproduction takes several forms in the various groups of algae. A common method is by *fragmentation*. A portion of a plant simply separates from its parent and becomes a new plant which may grow to normal size. *Cell division* is characteristic of most algae. Here an original cell produces another, identical to itself, by a rather complicated division of the cellular components. Both cells grow back to normal size, and the process may be repeated several times in the course of a day.

Most algae produce one or more types of *asexual spores*. Here a cell may divide its contents into several or many parts. Each one becomes a spore capable of growing into an entire new plant. Spores may be motile or non-motile, produced in vegetation cells or in cells specialized for the purpose. In any event, the process may lead to the production of very large numbers of new individuals.

Some spores are *resting stages*. They are resistant to adverse environmental circumstances, and they tide the organism over until more favorable conditions prevail, at which time they germinate to produce a new alga. Many algae winter over by means of resistant resting spores.

Sexual reproduction occurs in most groups of the algae. Indeed, this form of reproduction may have originated among primitive algae. The ramifications of the phenomena associated with sexual reproduction in the algae are beyond the scope of this short article, and we touch upon the subject lightly. Suffice it to say that, in general principles, the fundamentals of the process are the same as in animals. Special cells called *gametes* or sex cells unite with one another, as is the case with the sperm and the egg in higher animals. The product of the union, the *zygote*, may grow into a new plant or it may divide first and give rise to several new individuals. Sometimes special sex organs and highly differentiated gametes are produced. In some cases, male and female plants occur, and in others, both males and female structures appear on the same plant. Further, since many sex organs may occur on one plant, the opportunities for increasing the number of organisms is very great.

In summary, reproductive devices in the algae have the potential for yielding very large numbers of offspring and account for some of the phenomena to be mentioned later.

SPREAD OF ALGAE

Algae may spread rapidly from one region to another, and if the proper conditions prevail in the newly invaded territory, the distribution may be increased. They may be carried by water movement to every portion of the body of water in which they grow. They may be transported inadvertently by many other agencies. Birds, water-inhabiting animals, man, boats, and winds are prime agents for carrying entire plants or spores to new regions.

Under certain combinations of environmental circumstances, such as high temperatures, adequate light, and favorable concentrations of mineral substances, some types of algae reproduce at a rapid rate causing *algal blooms*. Diatoms, dinoflagellates, blue-green algae, euglenoids, and some types of green algae are notorious bloom producers. Whole ponds, lakes, streams, and even hundreds of square miles of oceanic waters have been recorded in bloom states over a long period of time. The widely publicized "red tides" are blooms of certain dinoflagellates.

The release of huge quantities of the wastes of civilization into streams, rivers, ponds, lakes, and even arms of the ocean have stimulated the development of such blooms. This phenomenon has become more noticeable in recent years as our population has increased and more and more pollutants have been poured into our waters from industrial plants, paper-pulp mills, sewage outlets, and others. The condition of some of the Great Lakes has been called to our attention dramatically in the last few years.

These wastes contain materials ideally suited for algal growth, and they flourish. The growths become so thick they prevent light from reaching deeper waters. The algae in this lower region cannot carry on photosynthesis, and thus they and the animal life suffer from depletion of oxygen. Bacteria and fungi attack the vegetation, but they, too, utilize oxygen, and the bodies of water become stinking masses of half-decayed vegetation and dead animals. Thus, under the circumstances described, the algae which normally tend to purify the waters simply add to the unwholesome condition.

Civilization is in serious trouble, which will increase unless man takes the necessary steps to adjust the balance which once prevailed.

RESEARCH

Algae are almost ideal organisms for many kinds of research and have long been used to simplify study of fundamental problems in biology. This use has accelerated in the last few decades coincidentally with our increasing ability to grow many kinds of pure culture. Upward of a thousand species of algae are now being grown in this manner and may be obtained from depositories in several countries.

Studies of productivity—both in natural waters and under controlled experimental conditions—occupy many algologists, for, as basic members of the food chains and food webs occurring in aquatic surroundings, their contribution is of fundamental significance. We have become

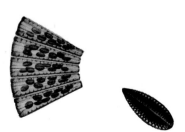

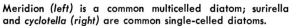

Meridion (*left*) is a common multicelled diatom; surirella and *cyclotella* (*right*) are common single-celled diatoms.

Draparnaldia

Tolypothrix

Euglena

more conscious of this as the problems associated with water pollution have come to the fore.

Lichens, those curious mixed growths of algae and fungi, have attracted the attention of naturalists for more than two centuries. Only recently have they been grown in pure culture, and attempts to ascertain the relative roles of the two components show some hope of realization.

USES OF ALGAE

A number of kinds of algae have been used directly as a source of food by man. Oriental peoples have been more appreciative of their value in this respect than have people of the Western world, although there is now world-wide interest in the potentialities. Japanese people cultivate a number of species as food sources. Certain red algae are sources of agar, a gelatinous substance used as a basis for making the culture media used in growing microorganisms for study in medicine and commercial applications. The Irish moss (*Chondrus crispus*) is widely used as a basis for blanc-mange and other confections. Colloids extracted from this species have come into prominence in making ice cream, puddings, and chocolate milk. Alginic acid derived from the cell walls of certain brown algae is used in foods and in various capacities in the textile industry.

Coastal dwellers in various parts of the world have made fairly extensive use of algal material as a vegetable manure, which adds humus to the soil as well as such important scarce elements as potassium, phosphorus, and nitrogen that are released as they rot away in the soil.

The *diatoms* so useful to aquatic animals as food have some direct economic benefits for man. Their silicon walls are very durable. When a diatom dies, its shell sinks to the bottom of the body of water in which it grows. Over long periods of time, vast quantities may accumulate as fossils on ocean bottoms. Great deposits of "diatomaceous earth" laid down in various earth geological strata have become exposed in later times. Found in many places on our globe, such deposits may be hundreds of feet thick and run for many miles, thus testifying to the enormous numbers which inhabited ancient seas as they now inhabit modern waters. They are mined and used in many ways in industry.

Many algae, especially green and red algae, precipitate large quantities of calcium carbonate in carrying out their metabolic activities, and this becomes converted to limestone rock in the course of time. Prominent ancient deposits are known from many parts of the world, and the same activity is being carried on currently. This may be observed in the great coral reefs of the tropical and semitropical seas of the world. Coral animals and the algae seem to contribute about equally to the making of coral reefs. Some members of the blue-green algae also precipitate limestone now as they did in ancient times. They also form travertine rocks in hot springs where they live at temperatures as high as 85°C as shown so colorfully in the springs in Yellowstone National Park.

Interestingly enough, the blue-green algae have long been known from ancient fossil-bearing rocks in North America and recognized as some of the oldest fossils, with an estimated age of at least 500 million years. A few years ago in the Lake Superior region, additional beds of fossiliferous blue-greens were found whose age has been put at approximately 1.5 billion years, and even more recently beds discovered in Australia have been estimated to be about 3.5 billion years old. These relatively primitive plants have been in existence for a longer period of time than any other known organisms.

Scientists believe that the early atmosphere of the earth did not contain free oxygen as it now does. When photosynthetic algae evolved, they released free oxygen into the atmosphere as a by-product of the chemical reactions involved in the manufacture of carbohydrates. The earth's atmosphere contained oxygen from this remote period on, until now about 20 percent of the atmosphere is oxygen. This great event made it possible for many oxygen-utilizing animals to evolve.

DANGERS OF ALGAE

Algae, along with many other plants, are known to release chemicals into their surroundings which are antagonistic, irritating, antibiotic, deleterious, or poisonous to other organisms. By this means, the distribution of some organisms is controlled, thus providing an explanation for the observed fact that certain organisms are not compatible and cannot occupy the same territory. An outstanding and much studied case of this kind is the famous "red tide" brought about by the prodigious growths of some types of dinoflagellates. We are only beginning to sense the extent to which such phenomena may be involved in the ecological picture.

Further, there is good evidence pointing to the possibility of deriving chemical substances useful in medicine from these versatile plants. —A.H.G.

ALLIGATORFISH *See* Sea Poachers

ALLIGATOR GAR *Lepisosteus spatula* The alligator gar is one of the monsters of inland waters. It often attains a weight of 100 pounds or more. The largest reported was 10 feet long and weighed 302 pounds. No other gar attains a size near this. When it is young, it can be distinguished from other gars by the double rows of large teeth on each side of the upper jaw; others have only one row. Otherwise the snout is similar to that of the shortnose gar. Other distinguishing characteristics are the lateral-line scales; 62 usually are present. The body is long, slender, and olive- or greenish-brown above and lighter below. Sides are mottled toward the head with large black spots toward the rear and on the rear fins.

Its range extends from northeastern Mexico, up the Mississippi River basin to near St. Louis and up the Ohio River to Louisville, Kentucky.

Alligator Gar

Possessing a modified gas-bladder, used in part for breathing air, gars can thrive in very stagnant water. The alligator gar prefers the backwaters, lakes, oxbows, and bayous along the large Southern rivers. In some areas it is sought by fishermen because of the obvious sporting qualities of the huge adults. Fishes are the principal food. The roe of all gars is very toxic to humans if used as food. —C.A.P.

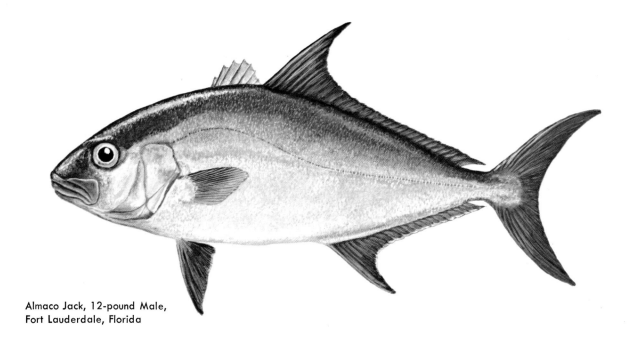

Almaco Jack, 12-pound Male,
Fort Lauderdale, Florida

ALLISON TUNA *See* Yellowfin Tuna
ALMACO JACK *Seriola rivoliana* This Atlantic species
has also been called falcate amberjack and, much less
appropriately, bonito, and has previously been recorded
by the scientific name of *Seriola falcata.*

The nuchal band of the Almaco jack extends from the
eye to the origin of the first dorsal fin. The five bars on
the body of young fish are split and irregular and disappear at lengths larger than eight inches. The body is relatively deep, but the depth decreases proportionally with
growth. The greatest body depth goes into the standard
length about 2.7–2.85 times in specimens up to 16 inches
in standard length, about 2.85–3.1 times in specimens
16–24 inches, and about 3.1–3.3 times in larger specimens
(standard length is measured from the tip of the snout to
the end of the bony plate of the tail). The dorsal-fin lobe
is relatively long; its length goes about 4.6 times into the
standard length, but there is considerable variation in the
lobe length. The total number of gillrakers on both limbs
of the first arch is relatively high, and this number decreases with growth of the fish; there are about 24–28
total gillrakers in fish up to 16 inches in standard length,
and about 21–25 in fishes larger than this size, and sometimes as few as 18 gillrakers in very large individuals.

The first dorsal fin has 7 spines (but rarely 8). The
second dorsal fin has one spine and 27–33 softrays (usually 28–32). The anal fin has two detached spines (which
may be covered by skin at large sizes), followed by one
spine and 19–22 softrays. There appear to be several color
variations in the adults. The nuchal band is usually olivaceous with golden reflections, but the basic body color
may be predominantly dusky or brownish, or more steely-
blue, or olivaceous. Frequently the sides also have a
lavender tint.

This species occurs on both sides of the Atlantic and in
the Mediterranean. In the western Atlantic it extends
from Buenos Aires, Argentina, to Cape Hatteras and
northward to the offing of New Jersey, in the West
Indies, and at Bermuda. Fish up to about 32 inches in
length and 14 pounds have been recorded.

ANGLING VALUE
The almaco jack is of some interest to sport fishermen,
particularly in the Bahamas, in the West Indies, and at
Bermuda. There is no large commercial fishery of this
species. *See also* Amberjacks, Carangidae.
—F.H.B.
AMA-AMA The Hawaiian name for mullet (*which see*).
AMBERJACKS Twelve species of four genera are listed
for amberjacks occurring in American waters.

They are distinguished from other carangids by having
elongated, usually thickened bodies; no scutes in the
lateral line; usually 7–8 spines in the first dorsal fin; and
the anal fin is appreciably shorter than the dorsal fin (the
dorsal fin has 7–19 more rays than the anal fin). *See also*
Carangidae, Greater Amberjack, Lesser Amberjack,
Pacific Amberjack.
—F.H.B.
AMERICAN CASTING ASSOCIATION (ACA) A national nonprofit organization composed of affiliated
clubs, regional (state and district) associations, and individual members, which lists among its objectives the promotion of casting and angling as a recreational activity,
co-operation with and assistance to groups desiring to
initiate classes in casting, training of casting instructors,
research and experimental work in the development of
improved angling and casting equipment, and the prom-
ulgation of standard rules governing tournament fly- and
bait-casting in the United States. ACA is affiliated with
the Amateur Athletic Union and is recognized by that
organization as the sole governing body of all tournament
casting in the United States.

HISTORY
ACA was originally formed in 1906 under the name
"National Association of Scientific Angling Clubs"
(NASAC), although at least two other national organiza-
tions had preceded it (National Rod and Reel Associa-
tion, 1882–1890, and American Fly Caster's Association
1891–1906). Another national organization, the National
Amateur Casting Association, was organized in 1913 with

a limited membership, and subsequently merged with NASAC in 1922. In 1939 the NASAC was renamed the National Association of Angling and Casting Clubs and was so designated until 1961 when the present name was adopted.

MEMBERSHIP

Membership varies from year to year, with clubs and individuals from twenty-two states and two Canadian provinces represented. All bona fide members of an affiliated club are extended ACA recognition, and the total of such membership is an estimated 2,000. The governing body of ACA is its executive committee, consisting of president, four vice presidents, treasurer, recording secretary, and the immediate past president. They in turn appoint an executive secretary through whom all administrative affairs are handled.

TOURNAMENT CASTING

ACA does not assume jurisdiction over any form of fishing or fishing contests. It is the philosophy of this organization that competitive fly- and bait-casting under uniform regulations simply provides an effective approach to its other aims. Tournament fly- and bait-casting, both in accuracy and distance, can be regarded as a proving ground for tackle and a course in training for the fisherman. The serious caster can get a sound evaluation of his equipment and its limitations or potential when using it over a measured course at specific targets and can test his own abilities while either practicing or competing. Experience on the tournament course also gives the neophyte an opportunity to become better acquainted with the functions of various tackle components.

CERTIFIED CASTING INSTRUCTORS

ACA includes, as part of its education program, a Casting Instructor Certification Program. Individuals desiring to be certified as Casting Instructors are required to give proof of their qualifications by posting a minimum score under ACA tournament conditions in the casting category applied for. It is deemed that this evidence of skill in use of tackle is sufficient proof of the candidate's familiarity with it and ability to teach others to use similar tackle satisfactorily in fishing. The prescribed course calls for a minimum of six hours of instruction of the candidate, with at least one hour devoted to lecture and demonstration and the remaining five to practice. Three Casting Instructor categories are provided: Bait, using level-wind reel; Spinning, using fixed-spool reel; and Fly. Persons qualifying in less than all three are certified as to category; those qualifying in all are known as Certified Casting Instructors. A number of colleges now include casting in their curricula, with emphasis on instructor certification of the students.

Research and experimental work in tackle is not on a scheduled program basis but is done instead on an individual or committee basis. The tournament caster is constantly seeking ways to improve his equipment, to modify it in some way so that it will give a better score than his competitor's. This may result in a different rod action, a new reel principle, or the design of a fly line or leader. It has been found that most of such modifications successful in tournaments have been adaptable in principle to practical fishing tackle.

REGISTERED TOURNAMENTS

Fly- and bait-casting tournaments sanctioned by ACA are almost entirely an amateur activity, although in isolated cases some few professionals participate. However, amateurs and professionals may not compete against each other, and professionals may not receive official recognition of scores of ACA awards on basis of achievement. One outdoor annual national tournament is held each year for the determination of national championships in each recognized event; heretofore no national indoor tournament had been authorized, but this annual event was approved by the 1962 convention and was held for the first time in 1963 in Chicago. In addition, member clubs may hold tournaments locally and register them with ACA for recording of scores and ACA awards to those qualifying; in addition, registered tournaments are held annually by state and district associations for determination of championships in those areas. All registered tournaments are required to be conducted under ACA regulations governing the events scheduled.

Competition in the national tournaments is divided into separate divisions for Men, Ladies, Intermediates (13–16 years of age), Juniors (12 and under), and Professionals. Events and championships are in two categories—ACA Official and Skish, making it in effect two separate tournaments run concurrently.

Both ACA Official and Skish events are divided equally into accuracy and distance events. Official events are:

⅝-oz Bait Distance	⅜-oz Bait Accuracy
⅜-oz Bait Distance	⅝-oz Bait Accuracy
Trout Fly Distance	Dry Fly Accuracy
Salmon Fly Distance	Wet Fly Accuracy

Skish events are:

Skish Bait Distance and Accuracy
(revolving-spool reel, ⅝-oz wt)
Skish Spinning Distance and Accuracy
(fixed-spool reel, ⅜-oz wt)
Skish Fly Distance and Accuracy

In addition, special events may be held on a trial basis to determine popularity or feasibility of adopting them into the competitive program annually. All tournament games require the use of special tournament weights or flies; no hooks are allowed.

Tournament accuracy events are related to some form of actual fishing, either in type of tackle used or the form of casting required. Most of the distance events are purely competitive in nature and have little relation to actual fishing, except through ultra refinement of some principle involved. Exceptions are the Trout and Skish Fly distance events which can be related to steelhead fishing. Salmon Fly Distance requires the use of a two-handed rod, and it and the Trout Fly Distance game both require the services of a line tender for the caster. No reel is used in these games.

SKISH EVENTS

The Skish events are intended to simulate actual fishing style more closely than the Official games, with regulations requiring that all primary tackle be of standard manufacture with no home alterations. This principle carried considerably more weight in the earlier days of the game, when the serious tournament caster used more specialized equipment. In later years, however, the improved tackle available over the counter has been equal to the maximum demands of the accuracy games, and in most cases casters use the same "store-bought" tackle for both Skish and Official games.

A widespread misconception is that all tournament casters use special tackle. Not more than an estimated 10 per cent of the total male tournament casters take part in the distance events, which is the only area where special tackle is of value. In the accuracy events there is no need for special equipment—only for careful selection. It is true, however, that the tournament caster does as a rule have *better* tackle, properly balanced for its intended purpose. —P.N.J.

AMERICAN EEL *Anguilla rostrata* The common American eel, sometimes called silver eel, is a catadromous freshwater fish and is closely related to the European eel *Anguilla vulgaris*. The American eel is elongate, almost snakelike in appearance, and the dorsal fin originates far behind the pectorals; this characteristic distinguishes it from the conger eel on which the dorsal originates slightly behind the tip of the pectorals. The eel has a pointed snout, a large mouth which extends as far back as the midpoint of the eye or past it, and its gill slits are arranged vertically, the upper corners opposite the base of the pectorals.

EEL MIGRATIONS

From the time of Aristotle (384–322 B.C.), people have pondered the problem of the genesis of the eel. Because no ripe roe was found in these fish, it was believed they came into existence in some mysterious manner. Aristotle declared that eels arose spontaneously from the mud, both in freshwater and in the sea, while others held their origin to be small worms or horsehair dropped in water.

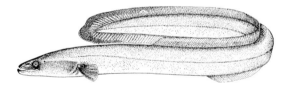

American Eel

In the first century after Christ, the Roman scholar Pliny the Elder (Gaius Plinius Secundus, A.D. 23–79, author of *Naturalis Historia*) ventured the belief that young eels were produced from fragments rubbed off by the adults against the rocks, a different version of the abiogenetic myth.

When the facts were discovered by Dr. Johannes Schmidt in 1905–1922, they were as remarkable as the ancient beliefs were fantastic. Eels are born in the southwest part of the North Atlantic (this has been given as the Sargasso Sea but is not precisely established). The young eel is ribbonlike and so transparent that print may be read through its body. In this stage it is called a *leptocephalus*, and in about a year it changes to a more eel-like form called an elver. During all this time the young eels have been working shoreward, and it is only when they near the coast that coloration begins to develop in the transparent bodies or that they begin to feed. Elvers 2–3½ inches long appear along our shores in spring, entering tidal marshes and estuaries in tremendous numbers along the coast from the Gulf of St. Lawrence to the Gulf of

Mexico. It is believed that the males remain in tidewater, while the females ascend the rivers, clambering over falls, up dams, and even over damp rocks if necessary. Eels can live out of water so long as to give rise to the story that they often travel overland, but there is no positive evidence for this. Although a gluttonous feeder, the eel grows slowly, and full-grown adults may be 5–20 years old. When fully grown, the female eels, traveling mostly at night, drop downstream. They and the maturing males that have been living in the river mouths cease feeding, change from an olive to a black color, and move out to sea. Once they leave the shore, the eels drop wholly out of sight. Only the discovery of newly hatched larvae over the deep parts of the oceanic basin, south of Bermuda and one thousand miles east of Florida, shows where their destination lies. Evidently the eels die after this single spawning, for no spent eels have been found and no large eels ever run upstream again. On their spawning grounds, American eels mingle with the European species which have made the longer westward journey. Although the breeding grounds overlap, the larvae of the American species always work back to the west side of the Atlantic and the European to the eastern side. This trip takes about a year for the American eel, which approaches a length of 6 inches by the time it reaches the brackish waters along our Atlantic Coast. The European eel, however, takes three years to make its longer journey, which may be as much as five thousand miles.

REPRODUCTIVE SYSTEM

There are several logical reasons why this problem eluded solution for the over two thousand years since, for the first time of which we have record, it was considered by Aristotle. The general structure of the organs contributed much to the difficulty. The reproductive organs resemble those of some fishes, the salmons and sturgeons for example, but are unlike those of the majority. The spermatic organs are made up of two rows of very tiny lobes, about fifty on each side, connected by *vasa deferentia* running almost the whole length of the body cavity. In young eels of 8–12 inches or less the testes have not yet attained the lobulated form and are similar to the ovaries of the female. The greatest length of the male specimens revealed the males to be smaller than the females. The fact that the testes are easy to identify only in specimens of 16–17 inches is one reason why they were not identified for so long.

FOOD VALUE

The eel is an exceptionally good food fish. It can be fried, baked, sautéed, jellied, made into a chowder, smoked, and served with a variety of sauces. The demand for eels in Europe often exceeds the supply. In the United States, particularly among families of Old World origin, no Christmas is complete without live eels during the preholiday fast. The tradition of fresh eels in December creates a large market for the product in many cities. This winter specialty keeps thousands of commercial fishermen at work in the principal supply points at the St. Lawrence River in Canada; Cape Charles, Virginia; and Chesapeake Bay. Weather watching is important among commercial men as winds from the right quarter will usually drive the eels into shallow water where they are netted by the tons. The eels are shipped by aerated trucks (a single truck may carry ten thousand pounds in its tanks) to such places as Chicago, Boston, and New York City.

HOW TO SKIN AN EEL

To remove the skin, tie a stout string around the head, tie the string to a secure nail, cut the skin around the fish just below the head, peel back the skin a little, and then quickly jerk the skin back the length of the fish.

Remove the head, cut the fish open and clean it thoroughly, and remove the fins with a pair of scissors. If fillets are desired, just cut down through the flesh on both sides of the backbone.

—A.J.McC.

AMERICAN FISHING TACKLE MANUFACTURERS ASSOCIATION (AFTMA) Organized as the Associated Fishing Tackle Manufacturers in 1933, the association adopted its present name in 1961. The basic objective of AFTMA is to educate, guide, and assist the members of the association in any and all matters so that the members shall maintain a high standard of conduct, efficiency, and usefulness to the industry, to the government, and to the public. Regular membership is open to all reputable firms and individuals engaged in the domestic manufacture of fishing tackle and accessories. Associate membership is open to all reputable firms and individuals engaged in the importation of fishing tackle and domestic manufacture of closely related products and accessories other than fishing tackle.

AFTMA is governed by an executive committee, which includes the four officers elected annually by the regular membership and the nine product-division chairmen elected annually by regular members who manufacture one or more of the products in the following nine categories: rods, reels, lines (braided), hooks, baits, floats, monofilament, containers, sundries. The immediate past president is chairman of the executive committee. Specialized activities are assigned to standing committees appointed by the president.

In 1949, association members organized Sport Fishing Institute, a fish-conservation agency with a three-point program of research, education, and service dedicated to improve sport fishing. Ever since the institute's inception, AFTMA has provided financial and promotional support of efforts "to shorten the time between bites" for millions of fishermen.

In 1956, in co-operation with the firearms industry, AFTMA helped to organize the Outdoor Education Project of the American Association for Health, Physical Education, and Recreation—a department of the National Education Association. The project's nationwide workshops and clinics have helped thousands of schools and colleges to add casting and fishing instruction to physical education curricula.

Since 1958, AFTMA has owned and operated a Fishing Tackle Trade Show for the industry's buyers at all levels of distribution. The four-day show (not open to the public), held each August in Chicago, offers the world's largest selection of tackle, accessories, and allied merchandise in advance of the industry's selling season.

Aside from the fact that it caters to the country's largest single group of outdoor sportsmen, the fishing tackle industry enjoys another distinction; it is one of only two industries that have endorsed an excise tax on their products at the manufacturer's level. Producers of rods, reels, creels, and artificial baits not only opposed a move to repeal the 10 per cent excise tax on these items but also supported a bill which would make these monies available for the improvement of sport fishing. Since 1952, under the Dingell-Johnson Act, the tackle manufacturer's excise tax has provided more than $69,000,000 for allocation to the states and territories as "Federal Aid in Fish Restoration Apportionments." The states are required to help finance their various projects with one dollar for every three they receive. (The other industry with a similar setup is sporting arms and ammunition under the Pittman-Robertson Act.)

In recognition of the physical, mental, and moral recreation values of sport fishing, the American Fishing Tackle Manufacturers Association is financing a program to explain the fun and fascination of sport fishing to millions of men, women, and children, as individuals and as members of families, who have more leisure time than ever before. In behalf of more than 60 million Americans who go fishing every year, AFTMA has approved the following statement of policy:

Sport fishing is the natural heritage of millions of American men, women, and children—more persons than participate in any other outdoor sports activity.

Members of the American Fishing Tackle Manufacturers Association (AFTMA), in appreciation of the physical, mental, and moral recreation values of sport fishing, acknowledge their responsibilities to these millions of Americans as follows:

1. To support all legislative and organizational activities which protect, improve, or expand sport fishing facilities;

2. To oppose any law, regulation, ordinance, or activity which adversely affects sport fishing, directly or indirectly, provided such opposition is not detrimental to the general welfare of the United States;

3. To produce equipment which creates confidence in craftsmanship and pride of ownership as well as increases sport fishing skill and pleasure.

Increasing pressures on existing waters imperil the sport fishing pleasure of millions of Americans. Since their natural heritage depends on this natural resource, AFTMA endorses all efforts to protect fresh and salt waters from pollution, diversion, or other infringement; to improve the capabilities of existing waters to support a sport fishery; to expand sport fishing facilities by acquisition of, and access to, presently unavailable waters.

Multiple use of a natural resource inevitably develops a varying degree of governmental supervision for the greatest good to the greatest number. However, AFTMA opposes any type of legislation or practice which unnecessarily restricts or is detrimental to sport fishing in violation of sound principles of fish, water, or land conservation and management.

—A.J.B.

AMERICAN FISHERIES SOCIETY Founded in New York City on December 20, 1870, under the name "American Fish Culturists' Association," the primary objective was to promote the cause of fish culture. On February 28, 1878, the organization modified its name to "American Fish Cultural Association" and broadened its scope to include all questions of a scientific and economic character that pertained to fish. On May 14, 1884, the name was changed to "The American Fisheries Society," and on December 16, 1910, the society was incorporated under that name in the District of Columbia.

The society antedates practically all of the specialized groups interested in some particular aspect of natural science, conservation, or fisheries. Although there were many outstanding scientists active in society affairs in early years, these names stand out as key leaders who influenced the thinking in the field of fisheries: Dr. George C. Embody, Dr. H. S. Davis, Dr. E. A. Birge, James A. Henshall, Dr. Barton W. Evermann, Dr. Jacob Reighard, Dr. R. W. Eschmeyer, Thaddeus Surber, Dr. Hugh M. Smith, Dr. J. G. Needham, Dr. Raymond C. Osborn, Dr. A. G. Huntsman, Percy Viosca, and E. C. Fearnow.

PURPOSE

The present-day objectives of the society, which have broadened from time to time, are as follows: (a) to promote the conservation, development, and wise utilization of the fisheries, both recreational and commercial; (b) to promote and advance the development and application of all branches of fishery science and practice, including aquatic and fishery biology, engineering, economics, fish culture, limnology, oceanography, fish parasitology, ichthyology, and related fields such as nutrition; (c) to gather and disseminate technical and other information on fishes, fisheries, fishing, and all phases of fishery biology and practice; (d) to hold meetings for the presentation, exchange, and discussion of information, findings, and experience on all subjects and techniques related to fisheries and all phases of fishery science and practice; and (e) by such other means as may be appropriate to unite and encourage those interested in fisheries and all other phases of fishery science and practice.

MEMBERSHIP

The American Fisheries Society has expanded into an international association which draws its membership from the United States, Canada, Mexico, and over thirty-five other countries throughout the world. Its scope now covers every interest and activity related to fish and fisheries. Although membership is not limited to professional biologists and the allied fields associated with the field of fisheries, 80 per cent of the membership consists of the professional type. Lay conservationists interested in maintaining an adequate knowledge of the field hold membership.

The society meets once a year, usually in September in conjunction with the International Association of Game, Fish, and Conservation Commissioners. The places of the meetings are rotated among the different sections of the North American continent. Seven annual meetings have been held in Canada, one in Mexico, while the remainder have been in the United States. The society is an affiliate member of The American Institute of Biological Sciences and a member of the Natural Resources Council of America and supports in various ways the Watershed Congress and Boy Scouts of America.

Four regional meetings of the society are held each year, namely, the Northeastern, the Southern, the North Central, and the Western Divisions. Several "chapters" of the society meet throughout the year, principally local and state groups. The divisions include the Canadian provinces.

OFFICERS

Annually the society elects at its annual meeting a president, a first vice president, a second vice president, a secretary-treasurer and a finance committee. The editor of the society is appointed by the president. Major decisions of the American Fisheries Society are made by an executive committee.

PUBLICATIONS

The official scientific journal of the American Fisheries Society, the *Transactions*, has been published without a break since 1870. It is one of the oldest scientific publications in the nation, indeed the oldest in the field of conservation. This quarterly is the principal reference source for scientific reports on various subjects on fisheries and aquatic resources of North America and elsewhere in the world. A wide range of subjects is covered, such as pollution, limnology, ichthyology, fish culture, fish nutrition, and fish parasitology.

At 10-year intervals *A List of Common and Scientific Names of Fishes from the United States and Canada* is published by the society. This reference is the only publication of its kind available and is in wide demand.

A newsletter for the membership is published six times a year. The society has available a brochure entitled *Fisheries as a Profession* which serves as a career guide for students interested in entering the field of fisheries. This publication is made available to all high schools or individuals seeking information on this career field.

The society issues Professional Certificates to its members qualified by academic study and/or experience in the field of fishery biology.

—E.A.S.

AMERICAN GRAYLING *Thymallus arcticus* To United States anglers a comparatively rare freshwater gamefish, highly prized for its beauty. This is the only species of grayling found in the western hemisphere where it is endemic to North America and Siberia. The most productive grayling fishing in the United States today exists in Alaska (*which see*). Token populations occur in Montana, Wyoming, and Utah. Outside of the United States, grayling are an important quarry in the Yukon Territory, Northwest Territories, northern Alberta, northern Saskatchewan, and to a lesser extent in northern British Columbia. Nearly all the large oligotrophic lakes of this region, such as Great Slave, Great Bear, Athabasca, Reindeer, and Careen, also contain grayling. The species is both a lake and river fish in North America.

The American grayling is readily distinguished from other genera of the Salmonidae by the large sail-like dorsal fin which has more than 17 rays and a lateral-line scale count of 90–100. In coloration, grayling differ widely, not only within a region but within a single watershed; it may be gray, brown, or silvery on the back and sides with X- or V-shaped spots on the forepart of the body with zigzag horizontal lines between the rows of scales, which, like the spots, may be vivid or indistinct. But when seen at certain angles of light it may reflect lilac or gold, and at times the entire fish has a silvery or brassy sheen as though wearing an ancient suit of mail.

The tail, pectoral, and anal fins are usually a dusky yellowish-green color, but the pelvic fins commonly have lengthwise stripes of pink and black, which again can be

American Grayling, 3¾-pound Male, Great Bear Lake, Northwest Territories

more or less obscure. However, it's the dorsal fin of the grayling which is unique. The dorsal of the male is the larger; the female's dorsal is not only shorter, but it is high in front and low in the back. The male's dorsal is reversed, starting low and sweeping high in the rear. This disproportionate fin has irregular but distinct rows of dark spots; it is often tinged with pink or white on the upper edge.

LIFE HISTORY

Grayling feed on insects and aquatic forms of other groups such as worms and crustaceans. Large numbers of grayling are often seen cruising along rocky points and shorelines while feeding in the evening or early morning hours.

The species produces 1,000–13,000 eggs from March to June and usually reaches maturity at 3 years of age. It spawns in small, rapidly flowing streams and does not build a nest. Males establish a territory and defend it against other males. One function of its large dorsal fin can be observed at this time; the male holds it erect when repelling invaders.

Male grayling grow larger than female grayling, and the present world's record, a 21-inch, 5-pound fish from Great Slave Lake, is probably fairly close to its maximum growth. In most waters, even in the Arctic, a 2-pound grayling is considered a nice catch, although fish of 3–3½ pounds are not uncommon in the North Country. South of Canada, American grayling seldom will exceed 1½ pounds.

For all practical purposes this colorful gamefish became extinct south of the Canadian border shortly after the turn of the century. Until that time one could easily pursue grayling on the Jackson, Lansing and Saginaw Railroad. In the halcyon years, when *Forest and Stream* was the fly fisherman's Baedeker, articles about the Manistee and Au Sable rivers attracted anglers from all over the United States to Michigan. Then suddenly the fish disappeared. The devastating loss of forest cover through lumbering, which greatly diminished the water quality of lower peninsula streams, is certainly one reason for its demise, but the unprecedented slaughter that took place between 1870 and 1880, when the fish were stacked like cordwood along the riverbanks and hauled out by the wagonload to be sold in Detroit and Chicago restaurants,

was no less a factor. Thousands of grayling were left to rot when no transportation appeared—which was all too frequent. From what little we know about the Michigan grayling (*Thymallus tricolor*), first described by Cope in 1865, this species did not reach a large size. An average catch was between 6 and 10 ounces and the exceptional fish weighed 1½ pounds. Nevertheless, its willingness to take the fly and its singular beauty caused the citizens of Crawford to change the name of their town to Grayling, a distinction which few fish achieve.

The graylings consist of a single genus composed of at least 4 species and several subspecies. On the basis of diversity of forms it has been postulated that the origin of this group of fishes was in the mountains of southern Siberia and northern Mongolia, and from here the fish migrated through the foothill lakes and rivers to Europe and across the Bering Sea land mass to North America. Its postglacial distribution to the west which extended its range to Britain (which was still part of the mainland of Europe) was via a river which flowed through what is now the North Sea and its two major tributaries, the Rhine and the Thames. Today, the European grayling (*Thymallus thymallus*) is found throughout the Continent except in southern France, Portugal, Spain, southern Italy, and Ireland. It also inhabits the basin of the Arctic Ocean. It is distributed in the east as far as the Ural Range in the Soviet Union, and may be encountered in the upper reaches of the Volga and Ural rivers. This wide distribution is somewhat deceptive because the grayling's habitat preferences within its range are narrow. It is a fish of fast-flowing, cold, clear streams. Although trout can thrive in any grayling river, grayling will not thrive in *all* trout rivers. Generally speaking, trout can exist where conditions are less than perfect, but this is not true of the grayling.

Beyond the Ural Range two distinct species occur in Mongolia, the Kosogol grayling (*Thymallus nigrescens*), which differs from the American grayling in having more gillrakers (26-33 as compared to 14-22), and the Mongolian grayling (*Thymallus brevirostris*), which is the "largemouth" of its tribe as the lower jaw extends beyond the posterior margin of its eye; American grayling by comparison have a very small mouth with the maxilla ending at the anterior margin of the eye. Soviet ichthyologists recognize a number of subspecies and racial stocks such as the Baikal white grayling, Angara black grayling, and West Siberian grayling, which are more or less isolated to single watersheds from Siberia across northern Asia and into North America; the American grayling (*Thymallus arcticus*) has the widest range of any member of the family. Apparently the postglacial distribution in North America was south of what is now the Great Lakes and of the vast sea that once extended over the Rocky Mountains which isolated several geographic stocks not only in Michigan but in the Big Hole and Green river watersheds of Montana and Wyoming. It was later introduced (1899) to the Unita Mountain district of Utah where it still exists today. There may have been yet another species which Jordan and Evermann recognized as the Ontario grayling (*Thymallus ontarionsis*), but the only clue left is two old museum specimens.

The only significant grayling fishing in the United States exists in Alaska. The Holtina, Stony, Aniak, Kandik, Birch, Forty-mile, Tatonduk, and Nation rivers are some of our more important streams. But the Ugashik Lakes in the Bristol Bay area are probably most productive of large fish. Ugashik grayling average about 18 inches in length. To prevent their depletion the Alaska Board of Fish and Game established a creel limit of 2 fish per day in that watershed, which is enough for the hungriest angler. The Alaskan record for grayling is just 4 pounds; the species doesn't grow fast here. Anything over 3 pounds is at least a 7-year-old. Nevertheless, Ugashik produces consistently large grayling to the fly.

The Northwest Territories of Canada has the distinction of providing the heaviest grayling in North America with a 5-pound, 15-ounce specimen from the Katseyedie River as the present record. A number of fish in the 5-pound class have been caught both in the Great Bear Lake and Great Slave Lake areas. In common with other grayling waters the world over, these lakes have an abundance of invertebrate food in the form of amphipods and copepods. The so-called opossum shrimp (*Mysis relicta*) thrive at depths to over 1,000 feet, while two species of scuds (both *Gammarus* and *Pontoporeia*) are abundant along the shore areas. These marine glacial relicts are circumpolar in distribution and are more important in the grayling's diet than insects. Although stoneflies and mayflies emerge in Great Bear and are consumed by the grayling, shrimplike animals are their basic food. The abundance of grayling in the Baltic Sea (which was once so great that they were fished commercially by Sweden and Finland) is correlated to an amphipod diet. Like all Arctic fauna, grayling grow slowly in lakes like Great Bear. A 2-pound fish is about 9 years old. Even their population is numerically limited, as they are unable to maintain an annual breeding cycle; although some proportion of the population does spawn each year reproduction of any individual fish occurs at two- or three-year intervals. The trophy lake trout which earned Great Bear its reputation are 30-40 years old when they reach the 30-pound class, so it would be relatively simple to "fish out" this fourth largest lake on the North American continent.

Elsewhere in Canada grayling are found in the Yukon Territory where they can literally be caught by the motorist along the Alaska Highway. This road follows mile after mile of grayling streams as it crosses the lake district. In northern Alberta popular waters are the Swan River, Freeman River, Wapiti River, Kakwa River, Cut-

bank River, certain portions of the McLeod River, Berland River, Marten River, Christina River, Christmas Creek, Two Creek, Marsh Head Creek, Pinto Creek, Pembina River, Trout Creek, Sunday Creek, and Kinky Lake. In Saskatchewan grayling fishing is available in Athabaska Lake, Black Lake, Careen Lake, Cree Lake, Cree River, Fond du Lac River, Geikie River, Hatchet Lake, Reindeer Lake, Tazin Lake, Wapata Lake, Waterbury Lake, and Wallaston Lake. Generally speaking, nearly all the large oligotrophic lakes and their tributaries in this northern region contain grayling.

FLY-FISHING TECHNIQUE

A fallacy about the grayling probably began with Walton when he wrote that "he [the grayling] has so tender a mouth, that he is oftener lost after an angler has hooked him, than any other fish." This has been endorsed in angling literature for centuries. Actually, the grayling has a *small* mouth which is somewhat difficult to get a hook attached to, but once the barb is sunk, there's little chance of losing the fish. Its mouth is somewhat leathery and offers a firm hold. There is a tendency not to strike forcefully enough, simply because of the peculiar way a grayling takes the fly in a half-roll, which requires an almost perceptible pause before it actually has the fly inside. When grayling are lost it's usually due to only getting the tip of the point stuck.

Unlike the trout, grayling rove about in schools. It is a gregarious species, and where you find one there is certain to be more. In lakes, the schools are frequently seen cruising near the shore, particularly in early morning and evening as they search for food. The tactic then is to paddle or row quietly parallel to the bank and about fifty feet out, watching for moving fish. They may appear as mere shadows or reveal their locations with dimpling rises. Grayling can hold any place in a river, but you'll often find that they favor one type of water in a particular stream; in some the deeper main channels might be their concourse, or, as is so often the case in the Arctic, they may crowd into the deeper pockets wherever you find an obstruction that deflects the current. It is not unusual to look down into a lie and see twenty or thirty grayling arranged along the bottom.

Depending on the depth at which they rest and the speed of the surface current, the fish may dart upward and take the fly with a splash. Grayling often leap over the surface and hit a floating pattern on the way down. As a rule, the strike occurs *behind* the fish's position; they tend to take a fly several feet to the rear, rather than go forward or to either side of the feeding lane. European grayling (*which see*) are perhaps more precise in so far as the drift is concerned and will frequently ignore a neatly cast artificial which is a foot or two off. Although they are more critical than trout with respect to presentation, grayling have an insatiable curiosity and may rise again and again to examine an offering and finally accept it. As a rule, they are less wary than trout with respect to the angler's presence, but the mere hint of a coarse leader tippet can put the fish down completely. You may come face to face with a grayling and be ignored; yet it will study every fly as though trying to help you find the right one.

The main difference between trout and grayling fly-fishing is that for the latter, downstream casting is usually more effective than casting upstream. Because the fish can be extremely leader-shy in rivers which get any amount of angling pressure, the grayling expert tries to wade into a position where he can drift the fly over the fish, showing the fly first. This is accomplished with a slack line cast by aiming the fly a yard or so short of the target. When the maneuver is done correctly, the fly falls as light as thistledown on the surface and drifts down into the grayling's feeding lane without drag. The knack of downstream casting with a slack line is easily learned with a little practice. Of course, you can work in a cross-stream direction, too, if the fish is in an awkward position.

Leader shyness is probably not the only reason for the higher scores made by fishing downstream. When working with the current, the angler can cover more water with less effort and at a slower pace. This combination of factors is important when you realize that grayling usually take their stations on the bottom and require a bit more time to get to the top than a trout. They also have a common tendency to follow a fly before taking it; there's a bit of time lag involved, and the upstream fly which floats back so quickly often moves but does not earn fish. Of course, the same can be said of the wet fly or nymph. Ordinarily, it's best to fish them across and downstream, minimizing drag as much as possible so that the fly sweeps around below. However, be ready for a strike at the moment the line has straightened out directly downstream. The grayling, as noted, has a habit of pursuing the fly for a distance, and many strikes occur just as you are ready to pick up for a new cast.

The grayling is prominently a fly-angler's fish. Appropriate tackle consists of a 7–8-foot fly rod with suitable line and leaders tapered from 3X to 6X. There is no real need for long casts in grayling waters as the fish can be approached quite closely, and in their season in most locations winds do not pose any real threat. As a rule grayling prefer dark flies in black, gray, or brown. Some good patterns are the Black Gnat, March Brown, Black Ant, Gray Hackle, Brown Hackle, Stone Fly, Quill Gordon, and Dark Cahill on Nos. 10, 12, and 14 hooks. It is also advisable to bring along some tiny black patterns such as ant, midge, or gnat imitations on Nos. 18 and 20 hooks, as grayling often show a definite preference for the minutae.

Grayling are easily caught on a large variety of spinning lures but ⅛-to-¼-ounce wobbling spoons, and 1/16-to-¼-ounce spinners in brass, gold, silver, and red-and-white finishes are the most popular baits. The angling techniques are substantially the same as those used for trout. *See also* Spinning, Ultralight Spinning

FOOD VALUE

American grayling are an excellent food fish and may be prepared in a variety of ways. The flesh is firm and white, with a very delicate flavor. Although they are ordinarily panfried outdoors, they are ideal for poaching in a court bouillon with herbs, and can be broiled or smoked. *See also* European Grayling —J.R.
—A.J.McC.

AMERICAN JOHN DORY *Zenopsis ocellata* This species belongs to a family (Zeidae) of primitive spiny-rayed fishes that are typical of the upper continental slope at depths of 100 to about 500 fathoms. All are compressed, deep-bodied fishes with large mouths and projecting lower jaws. The species is restricted to the western North Atlantic and is found from Nova Scotia to Cape Hatteras. It has been taken up to a length of 24 inches and a weight of 7 pounds.

Its color is silvery all over. The young up to about 10 inches are marked on each side with about 12-24 vaguely outlined dark spots, irregularly arranged. Most of these spots disappear with growth, for the larger specimens that are more than 16 inches in length have only one spot on each side a short distance behind the gill opening.

Other distinguishing characteristics of the American John Dory are body very deep, much flattened, depth ½ length. First dorsal fin with 9-10 spines, the first 3 prolonged, their length about equal to body depth, remainder progressively shorter; second dorsal fin with 25–27 softrays, low, extending almost to caudal peduncle; anal fin with 3 spines and 24–26 softrays, spines stout; pectorals small, inserted below and behind eye, tips of rays free; pelvics larger than pectorals, ventral to and in front of pectorals; caudal small, brush-shaped.

Head with lower jaw projecting, large mouth set very obliquely, dorsal profile of head concave; eye 5 in head. Scaleless but with bony bucklers, each with one or more hooked thorns, arranged near dorsal and ventral edges; 2–3 along base of spiny dorsal, 4 along base of soft dorsal, 2 in midline in front of pelvic fins, 1 in midline behind pelvics, 6 pairs along belly to the anal fin, and 5 along base of anal fin.

FOOD VALUE

This species is good eating and its relative, the European John Dory, has been esteemed as a table fish since Roman times. However, the American species is not abundant enough to have commercial value. The John Dory is a classic ingredient of bouillabaisse. —J.C.B.

AMERICAN LOBSTER *Homarus americanus* A large marine crustacean which ranges from the Maritime Provinces of Canada (as far north as Belle Isle) to the coast of North Carolina. It is most abundant in the waters of Maine, Nova Scotia, and Newfoundland. In 1963 more than five thousand commercial men were operating a half-million traps along Maine shores alone. The United States industry has grown from $500,000 in 1880, when lobsters sold for a penny apiece, to nearly $10,000,000 in 1963. Like caviar, the lobster has had a history of plenty and scarcity. The American lobster is one of three true lobsters, a second species being found throughout Europe, and a third on the coast of Norway. The lobster that made Maine famous usually weighs 1–5 pounds, but they grow up to 45 pounds. One might imagine that so large a lobster would be tough and tasteless, but there is no loss of quality in these giant crustaceans. The big ones, however, are usually taken for canning rather than boiling as few kitchens are equipped to handle a twenty-pounder. Within its range, the lobster is trapped at depths from 10 to 200 feet, but New Jersey draggers get the monsters at depths over 600 feet in the canyons ninety miles off the coast.

DESCRIPTION

Except for minor details, the lobster is very much like its freshwater relative, the crayfish. The upper part of the body is covered by a hard shell, or carapace, which has a free edge on each side projecting down to cover the gills.

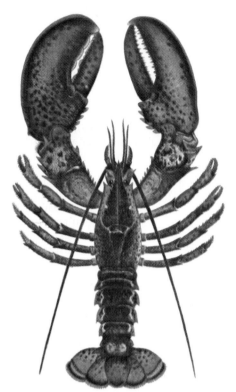

American Lobster

Nineteen pairs of appendages project from the under surface of the body. These are the small feelers, which are continually whipping the water and in which the sense of smell resides; the long feelers concerned with touch; the hard jaws on each side of the mouth which grind up the food; the five pairs of mouthparts serving to hold the food; the pair of large claws for capturing food; the four pairs of walking legs; the five pairs of swimmerets, one pair projecting from each segment of the tail, and the last segment of the tail which has the tail fan with a central portion called the telson.

The color of the adult varies from greenish-blue to reddish-brown. Generally the upper surface of the body is speckled with greenish-black spots. Contrary to popular belief its shell is red only after boiling.

The large claws of these crustaceans are usually different, a heavy crusher claw and a lighter biting claw or "quick" claw, the latter so-called because the lobster is much quicker in reaching out and snapping with this claw. In both the males and females about 50 per cent have crusher claws on either the right or the left side. Sometimes both claws are biting claws and occasionally, though more rarely, both are crusher claws.

HABITS AND MOVEMENTS

The adult lives and feeds on the bottom of the sea. By means of its tail fan, its swimmerets, and its walking legs, it can move rapidly from place to place. However, numerous tagging experiments have shown that populations are essentially local, migration being limited to random movements along shore. The lobster shuns the light and in shallow water spends the daylight hours hidden in holes among the rocks or in other shady spots.

FOOD AND FEEDING

The lobster is a scavenger and lives chiefly on fish, dead or alive, and on the invertebrates which inhabit the bottom. In very cold water, just above freezing point, very little if any feeding occurs. As the water warms up during the spring and summer months, feeding increases. All the fixed or slow-moving animals on the bottom, such as shellfish like the mussels or clams, the sea urchins and starfish, worms and crabs, serve as food. Small fish may also be captured and eaten. Seaweed is often found in the stomach. In seeking food the lobster uses its senses of smell and touch, more than its sense of sight. Adult as well as small ones are cannibalistic and when crowded together in captivity would quickly destroy each other if the claws were not plugged or banded.

REPRODUCTION

Due to the different water temperatures along the Atlantic Coast, lobsters reach sexual maturity at different sizes. In the warmwaters of the southern Gulf of St. Lawrence and the south and west coasts of Newfoundland females as small as 7–8 inches in length, 3–4 years old and weighing 7 ounces, may occasionally be found carrying eggs. Near the mouth of the Bay of Fundy where the waters are cold, lobsters take much longer to mature, and the smallest carrying eggs are about 14 inches long, weigh about 44 ounces, and are about 8–9 years old.

Lobsters mate usually within a few hours after the female has cast her shell. This is when the female is in the new, soft-shelled, and helpless condition. The male has, at this time, a hard shell. Sperm is deposited and may be retained by the female in sperm receptacles until the eggs are laid from a month to a year after mating. The mature females as a rule lay eggs only once every two years. As the eggs are laid, they pass over the sperm receptacle and are fertilized and drawn into a pocket formed by the curve of the tail. The eggs are covered by a sticky cement which hardens and holds the eggs firmly attached to the female. The number of eggs laid varies according to the size of the female. An 8-inch female carries about 5,000 eggs while one 16 inches carries about 60,000 eggs.

The eggs are carried and protected by the female for 11–12 months, and by the latter part of June or in July or August or, in the case of a few lobsters in the colder areas, September of the following year, the eggs are ready to hatch. The eggs are small and very dark green in color when first laid but become lighter in color as the young develop.

Hatching of the eggs is accomplished by the female who, over a period of 1–2 weeks, shakes the young out of the egg shells.

The young, which are about one-third of an inch long, then rise to the surface and drift on the water at the mercy of the wind and water currents.

GROWTH

To grow, the lobster casts off its shell. This process is called "molting" or "shedding." Molting begins on the second day after hatching and lasts throughout life or at least as long as there is growth. On hatching, the larvae continue to swim near the surface for 3–5 weeks or until after the fourth molt, when they sink to the bottom and pass the remainder of their life essentially like adults.

These small lobsters live under stones and submerged rocks and have been found along the rocky shores of bays and small inlets where they are out of reach of most of their enemies. At a later period, when from 3½–5 inches long they grow bolder and go out further into the deeper waters but never lose their timid habits.

Growth is faster in warmer waters. In general, the young lobster reaches the 6-inch size in about 3 years and the 9-inch size in about 4½ years after molting about 22 times. After it becomes mature, at an average length of about 9 inches in warmer waters, the female grows more slowly than the male since many females molt one year, lay eggs the next, and cannot molt again until the eggs are hatched 11–12 months later. Thus a 15-inch male is about 10 years old, while a 15-inch female is over 16 years old. As lobsters grow older the number of molts per year decreases.

METHOD OF CAPTURE

Lobsters are captured in traps called pots which may vary in shape but which operate on the same principle. In general they are oblong, wood boxes with one or more funnel-shaped openings through which the lobsters pass in their efforts to get at the bait. Pots are weighted down with stones or bricks to keep them on the bottom. Almost any kind of fresh, salted, or stale fish is used as bait depending on the custom and the kind of bait available. [Most of the information on this species was obtained from Information Services, Department of Fisheries, Ottawa] *See also* Lobsterettes, Spiny Lobster

AMERICAN PLAICE *Hippoglossoides platessoides* Also called the Canadian plaice, plaice, dab, sand dab, and blackback, this species, which is broadly distributed on both sides of the North Atlantic, is related to the Bering flounder and the flathead sole of the Pacific coast. It ranges from southern Labrador and the Grand Bank south to Rhode Island. In the eastern Atlantic it is found from west Greenland, Iceland, and Spitzbergen south to the English Channel.

Its color is reddish to grayish-brown on the eyed side, blind side white or bluish-white, tips of dorsal and anal fins white; the young are usually marked with dark spots along the edge of the body.

Other distinguishing characteristics of the plaice are body oblong, compressed, lying on left side; greatest width 2⅖ in total length at tip of pectoral fins; caudal peduncle moderate. Head 4½ in total length; mouth large, front angle of lower jaw projecting slightly, angle of mouth under middle of pupil; one row of small, conical teeth in each jaw, no teeth on vomer or palatines. Eyes 6 in head, a low interorbital ridge between them.

Dorsal fin with 76–96 softrays originating just in front of left eye and terminating on caudal peduncle; caudal well rounded; anal fin with 64–77 softrays beginning just behind vent and under posterior gill opening, ending under posterior end of dorsal, a prominent preanal bony spine; pectorals on midside behind gill opening, fin on eyed side slightly the larger and equal to ⅖ length of head; pelvics 6-rayed on ventral edge in front of pectorals. Lateral line straight except for a very slight arch above pectoral. Head and body covered with small scales; those on eyed side with rough serrations; those on blind side mostly smooth.

LIFE HISTORY

The plaice lives at various depths from 20–390 fathoms on bottoms with fine sand or soft mud. It prefers cool to cold water, not over 55°F. The males become mature at about 10 inches in length and the females at about 18 inches. The females produce 30,000–60,000 eggs, spherical in shape, and 1/10–1/12 inch in diameter. The eggs have a large perivitelline space and float near the surface. Spawning takes place in the spring in the southern part of the range and about midsummer in the northern part.

The growth rate varies depending on water temperature. On the Grand Bank plaice reach a length of 12 inches in 5 years. Growth is slower in later years, and 20-inch fish from the Grand Banks may be up to 26 years old. One plaice 32½ inches long and weighing 14 pounds was caught at Sable Island. The pelagic fry eat diatoms and small copepods. Young on the bottom eat amphipods, caprellids, mysids, decapods, and other small crustaceans. Adults eat sand dollars, sea urchins, brittle stars, mollusks, shrimp, and worms.

FOOD VALUE

This is an important commercial species being taken by other trawls, Danish seines, and sometimes by longline. *See also* Plaice   —J.C.B.

AMERICAN SAND LANCE *Ammodytes americanus* Commonly called the sand launce, sand eel, and launce-fish. It is a small, slender, round-bodied marine species which superficially resembles an eel. The family Ammondytidae includes two other North American species, the northern sand lance (*A. dubius*) and the Pacific sand lance (*A. hexapterus*). The sand lance can be distinguished from a young eel by its separate rather than continuous dorsal and anal fins, and by the rounded caudal fin of the eel. The sand lance grows to a length of about 6 inches and is important as a food for many gamefish such as the Arctic char, coho salmon, mackerel, and striped bass.

Schools of sand lance are often abundant in shallow water along sandy shores. For protection the fish can quickly burrow into the sand, snout first, to a depth of about 6 inches. Quantities of sand lance are often dug up in the intertidal zone by people seeking clams.

FOOD VALUE

Sand lances are excellent to eat when prepared in the style of whitebait (*which see*).   —A.J.McC.

AMERICAN SHAD *Alosa sapidissima* The American or white shad is an anadromous fish, and like the salmon it ascends coastal rivers to spawn. Two species of shad are of angling interest—the American shad and the hickory shad (*which see*). The former is generally distributed along the entire Atlantic Coast as far south as Florida, but the hickory is more dominantly a Southern species straying north to the Gulf of Maine. Physically, the fish are easy to separate in that the hickory has a long, projecting lower jaw; the lower jaw of the American shad is entirely enclosed within the upper when the two are pressed together. The American shad is a larger fish, generally ranging 1½–8 pounds, with a maximum weight of about 12 pounds. The hickory runs 1–3 pounds, with a maximum weight of about 6 pounds. In habitat, American shad prefer the main rivers, whereas the hickory seeks smaller tributary streams for spawning. The Sus- quehanna, for example, attracts both species, but only the hickory enters its feeder brooks. Some rivers, such as the Potomac, have lost the bulk of their American shad to commercial fishing but still maintain a heavy inventory of hickories which are snagged and spooned a few miles northwest of the Capitol building in Washington. Other rivers such as the St. Johns provide 90 per cent of their harvest in whites, and the annual yield to anglers runs to 55,000–65,000 fish.

ATLANTIC DISTRIBUTION

Although shad are found as far north as the Gulf of St. Lawrence, the sport really has its roots in Connecticut. The Salmon River at Leesville and the Connecticut River north of Hartford are the meccas of shaddom. The Scantic, Eight Mile, and East rivers are also good spots in the Nutmeg State. All of the fishing is for American shad, and the yearly harvest to angling exceeds 25,000 fish. Connecticut has a daily limit of six fish. It's esti- mated that the actual number caught, including those released, is three times as great. In comparison, neigh- boring Massachusetts produces about 10,000 shad on a no-limit basis. Down the coast, New York's Hudson River and the interstate Delaware attract shad.

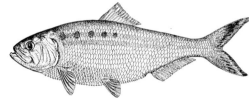

American Shad

The first real spread of shad streams occurs in Mary- land in her Chesapeake drainage system. The Susque- hanna is the largest and perhaps best-known. Migrating fish encounter the Conowingo Dam above Havre de Grace and either turn north into Octararo Creek or south into Deer Creek. The Octararo usually draws more fish and fishermen. South of the Susquehanna there are other shad waters such as Winters Run, the Gun Powder, Patuxent, and Middle rivers. Across the bay in Virginia there are many productive shad streams south of the Potomac such as the Pamunkey, Mattaponi, York, Chickahominy, James, Appomattox, and Rappahannock. Although the James and York are extremely large, turbid rivers, the shad spawn up the branch streams, where they are caught with sporting gear. The Carolinas support many shad waters, but the main arteries in North Caro- lina are the Neuse, Pee Dee, and Roanoke rivers. South Carolina has the Cooper, Edisto, and Combahee. In Georgia, the Ogeechee, Satilla, and Altamaha draw major runs. The triggering factor in shad migrations is water temperature. The difference from South to North is that shad spawn earlier in the swamp belt; the peak of the St. Johns run is in March, whereas the peak of the Connecti- cut River run is in May. Shad begin entering Florida waters from the St. Marys south in late November or December. The St. Johns, which is the southernmost limit of the shad, is one of the top producers in the nation. According to the U.S. Bureau of Commercial Fisheries, the average is five shad per fisherman-trip, which is very

high when one considers the thousands of anglers who visit that river from December to April. Limit catches are common after mid January. Popular spots to fish are near Deland at Crows Bluff, upriver past Blue Spring, and near Lake Monroe. But Lemon Bluff out from Osteen and the Lake Harney reaches are also productive.

PACIFIC DISTRIBUTION

Originally native only to the Atlantic (various species are called *alose* in France, *ceppa* in Italy, *finte* in Ger- many, *finta* in Russia, and *stamsild* in Scandinavia), these members of the herring family are also found in the Pacific. The man responsible for introducing shad to the West Coast was a pioneer fish culturist, Seth Green. In 1871, Mr. Green transported eight cans of newly hatched Hudson River fry from Rochester, New York, to Te- hama, California. The trip took seven days, but more than 66 percent of the fry survived to be liberated on the Sacramento River. The fish spread rapidly from Cali- fornia; nine years later they were caught in Oregon's Umpqua and Coos rivers, then the Columbia, and shortly thereafter into Puget Sound and the Fraser River in British Columbia. Today American shad range from San Diego to southern Alaska, but the chief points of distribution in California are the San Francisco Bay area and the San Joaquin and Sacramento River watersheds. On the Amer- ican, Russian, and Feather rivers, shad fishing with cast- ing gear has become an important game to the Western angler.

LIFE HISTORY

Shad enter the sport fishery during their spawning runs. South of North Carolina shad reproduce only once, but a large percentage of the northern populations spawn two or more times. Tagging studies indicate that some adults return to their parent stream, but a significant number have no migratory pattern. Shad tagged in the Hudson River have been recaptured in the Bay of Fundy, and shad tagged in Maine have been found in different river systems from the Connecticut to the Altamaha in Georgia. Migrations begin in November at the southern- most limit of their range in the St. Johns of Florida and end in June on the Gulf of St. Lawrence. Except for the southern populations where there is a recognized mor- tality after spawning, shad generally return to the sea. The newly hatched fish remain in the river until fall, then spend 2–5 years in saltwater before returning to repeat the cycle. Little is known of their marine existence, but American shad are almost entirely plankton feeders. Evidently ocean feeding encompasses a broad coastal area, as shad have been trawled 110 miles from shore and to depths of over 60 fathoms.

TROLLING

Trolling with spinning or bait-casting tackle is the most popular method of catching shad throughout their range. The standard procedure is to troll a small silver spoon, such as the No. 00 Drone type, and work it close to the bottom, manipulating the blade with short, snappy jerks. However, casting is just as effective, provided you know where the fish are located, and it has the advantage of allowing more erratic rod work than when the bait travels at a fixed speed. Naturally, much depends on the water conditions and the number of shad available, but generally speaking, almost any small spinning lure is going to connect. In swifter, Northern streams, such as the Connecticut River, many anglers prefer to let their spoons hang in the current with only an occasional jerk of the rod to vary the lure action. One noticeable difference between shad in the North and those in the South is that Florida fish strike freely in bright sunlight while New England shad are more active in gloomy weather. Usually, early morning and the period before sunset are most productive in Northern locales.

FLY-FISHING

Fly-fishing is the ideal method for catching shad. It's not the most popular method because many Southern rivers in particular are much too deep for effective rod work. Ideally, the fly angler wants a comparatively shallow, swift stream where the shad are concentrated in large schools. With rare dry fly exceptions such as the Delaware River in New York (*which see*) wet flies are the rule. The prime requisite is that the fly be weighted. A vast collection of special shad streamers has grown from the old Enfield pattern, the Silver Yank, but essentially any white wing and tinsel body will take fish provided the lure swims deep. The sizes you'll need are limited to Nos. 2, 4, and 6 Sproat or O'Shaughnessy. Actually, shad are caught on yellow, orange, and even black flies—with or without the traditional red beads. Glass beads were once considered a necessary adjunct to all patterns. Perhaps the chief reason beaded flies scored so well was simply due to the fact that they sank more quickly. However, if you want to add more flash to your lure, string three or four 1/8-inch or 1/4-inch diameter beads on your leader just above the fly; orange, orange-red, red, pink, and yellow glass baubles are all acceptable. Even beads and a bare hook will take shad in clear water, but in the usual turbid flow that white wing helps to locate shad. Ordinarily, anglers favor streamers with copper wire wrapped under the body material, and to cover all bets they also use a weighted fly line. The idea is to toss the lure up and across stream and let it swing around along the pebbles with short, quick jerks. Because shad fishing is usually done in high, roily water with heavy flies, you'll need a rod comparable to a bass bugging stick—8½–9 feet long with a fairly powerful action. Remember also that shad are relatively large fish and extremely strong gamefish.

SPINNING AND BAIT-CASTING

There are no definite tackle requirements for taking shad. Standard tools consist of a 5-foot bait-casting rod and a reel spooled with 12-pound-test braided line, or 6-pound monofilament. If you use the braid, add a 20-inch monofilament leader. Spin-casters favor 6–7-foot medium-action glass sticks and 6-pound monofilament on the reel. Small silver wobbling spoons and jigs in the 1/4-ounce class are by far the most popular baits. A great variety of jigs will take shad, but the white or yellow bucktail is preferred. The guiding principle here is that your lure be small and flashy. It is advisable, however, that you take along a large landing net as the shad's mouth structure is frail and many fish are lost when snubbed tight at the boat.   —A.J.McC.

AMERICAN SMELT   Synonomized with Arctic Smelt (1963); but neither accepted as common name (1970). *See* Rainbow Smelt

AMERICAN SOLE   *See* Hogchoker

AMIDSHIPS   In the center portion of the boat with reference to the line of the keel and the width of the boat, midway between bow and stern.

AMPHIDROMOUS   Any fish which moves freely between the sea and freshwater rivers or lagoons, but not for the purpose of spawning. Some amphidromous species are the snook, tarpon, and milkfish.

ANADROMOUS   Any fish which migrates from the sea into freshwater rivers for the purpose of spawning. Some anadromous species are the Atlantic salmon, striped bass, alewife, and shad. Fishes which migrate in the reverse direction from freshwater rivers into the sea for their spawning are *catadromous*.

ANAL FIN   The unpaired or single fin on the ventral surface of the body. *See* Anatomy

ANATOMY   A fish is a cold-blooded vertebrate having a backbone, permanent gills, and fins. It is estimated that there are from 15,000–17,000 living species of fish known to science, and new ones are being discovered each year. Fossils are known from over 400 million years ago, but a real explosion in numbers of species has only occurred in about the last 100 million years. Fishes may grow to only an inch (a goby) or over seventy feet (whale shark). Fishes occur in a variety of aquatic habitats, from frigid polar waters to the hot, stagnant pools of the Equator, and from depths of a few inches to 20,000 or more feet. This diversity of environments is associated with extreme variations in body structure as well as specialized organs and functions, such as poison glands, light-producing organs, coats of mail-like scales, internal fertilization, live-bearing, egg-laying, teeth located in the throat, electric "shock" organs, air breathing, parasitic reproduction, and many other unusual features.

FORM AND LOCOMOTION

The forms of fishes reflect great plasticity of adaptation according to the type of environment. Fast-swimming species are sleek and torpedo-shaped, while sedentary, sluggish species are apt to be far from streamlined. The ideal streamlined form is the tuna, whose fusiform body is hydrodynamically almost frictionless. Bonitos, mackerels, trouts, some sharks, and other fast-swimming fishes fall into this category. A reduction in the size of the scales usually occurs in these swift forms which increases swimming speed, Eels, lampreys, and blennies have terete, or circular, bodies in cross section and swim with a serpentine or anguilliform motion. Many species which habitually live on the bottom are flattened or depressed, including skates and rays, goosefish, catfishes, batfishes, and sculpins. Fishes flattened from side to side are compressed. Angelfish, freshwater sunfish, pompanos, and flatfish are such examples. Truncated, or squarish bodies in side view characterize triggerfish and ocean sunfish. Globular shapes are those of cowfish, trunkfish, porcupinefish, and puffers, the latter particularly when they are inflated. Needlefish, pipefish, and some eels are filiform or attenuated. Others, which are elongated but also compressed, and ribbonlike, include eel larvae, ribbonfish, and oarfish.

BODY COVERING

The body covering, quite different from that of mammals, is made up of living cells as far as the outermost layer. There is a coating of slime over-all, which forms a wall against disease and parasite attack, reduces friction,

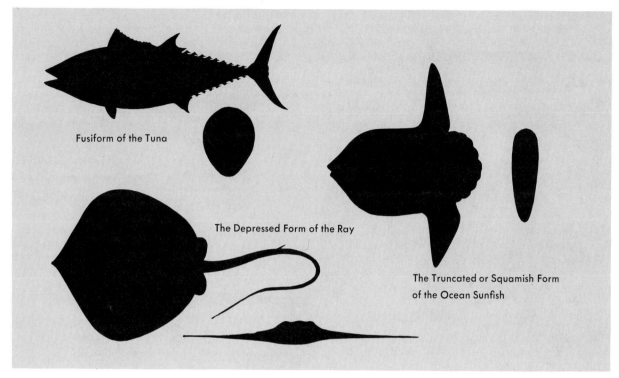

Fusiform of the Tuna

The Depressed Form of the Ray

The Truncated or Squamish Form
of the Ocean Sunfish

and aids in making the fish watertight, for without it liquids would move through the body wall uncontrollably. It also has respiratory and excretory functions. The skin contains chromatophores, or color cells, which control color, shades, and pattern. Electric organs, venom glands, and mucous glands are also in the skin. Photophores in the skin of some fishes give off bioluminescence. Light-producing bacteria sometimes occur in pockets of the skin. Under the tough body covering of most bony fishes lie scales which are made up of nonliving tissue. Lampreys, hagfishes, some catfishes, morays, and a few other fishes lack scales, while others (paddlefish, sticklebacks, and darters) are partly naked. In some cases, the bases of the fins are covered with scales. Scales as covering have evolved into many shapes having other functions, among which are the spine of the stingray, armor plates in pipefish, catfish, cowfish, and searobins, spines in porcupinefish, scutes (bony plates) in jacks, and tubercles in batfish and some flounders.

The number of scales on a fish is relatively constant and does not change with growth, although there is some variation in the number depending on the habitat, and the number is an important taxonomic tool to identify and classify fishes.

There are many scale shapes, grading from circular and diamond-shaped to rhomboid and hexagonal. There is a logical relationship between habitat and mode of living and the development of scales. Generally, species with large or unusually developed scales rely on them for protection and are relatively inactive. Fishes with small scales are generally fast swimmers, although there are many exceptions, such as the sedentary eels.

Scales are divided among four general types. In sharks, skates, and rays, the small scales, called denticles, are placoid, or toothlike, and project backward, forming shagreen, the roughened skin. Thorns of skates, sharks' teeth, dogfish spines, and sawfish teeth are all modified

placoid scales. Cosmoid scales are found in the "living fossil," the coelacanth. Gars, sturgeons, and paddlefishes possess a hard, platelike ganoid scale, which differs structurally and chemically from placoid and cosmoid scales. Most bony fishes have bony-ridged scales which are either smooth cycloid, or round, or roughened ctenoid, or comblike. Cycloid scales have rings, as in a tree, and are characteristic of minnows, herrings, trouts, salmons, and suckers. Ctenoid scales have rings as well, though of different form. These scales have the anterior section truncate, and there are radial furrows along the anterior field. The bony ridges, or circuli, are deposited regularly, depending on temperature and other environmental factors (see also *Age and Growth* at the end of this section).

COLORATION

Various types of skin pigments are responsible for the color of fishes. Some fishes are nearly transparent (larvae, some pelagic fishes, young herrings, anchovies), while coral-reef fishes and some fresh-water darters reach extreme combinations of all conceivable colors. Bottom-dwelling fishes are generally dark with concealing mottlings, while deepsea (abyssal) fishes are black. The fishes of moderate depths are often such colors as red, pink, or pale.

Color comes from chromatophores, located in the skin, including red, orange, yellow, and black, various combinations of these colors resulting in hues of pigments. Iridocytes are also responsible for color, and these, derived from excretory products, produce the reflective substance characteristic of most fishes. Some deepsea fishes have photophores, or light organs, which are derived from the skin. These may be simple or complex, and are present on the body, fins, and various parts of the head. They are used in schooling and for camouflage against predators.

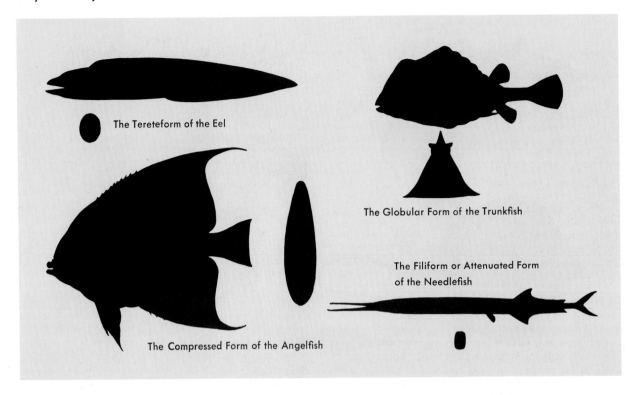

The Tereteform of the Eel

The Globular Form of the Trunkfish

The Filiform or Attenuated Form
of the Needlefish

The Compressed Form of the Angelfish

Color and color patterns are used in concealing behavior, aggressive behavior, and reproductive behavior. In many freshwater fishes, bright spawning colors are apparent only during the reproductive period, and are involved in courtship, nest-building, and care of the young. Intensity of color and patterns are important in marine fishes. The color of most fishes changes with growth, the young being colored differently from the adults, and, for example, in the bluehead wrasse the male and the female are very differently colored, both being distinct from the juvenile.

SKELETAL STRUCTURE

The body of a fish has a supporting framework of connective tissue which holds the body parts together and supplies a place for muscle attachment. The skeleton may be considered to be modified connective tissue.

The elements of the skull are of diverse origin. Sharks have a cartilaginous "skull" (chondrocranium) and branchial or throat arches (branchiocranium). In bony fishes, the neurocranium, or brain case, consists of a membranous covering strengthened by cartilages to protect the brain, and the branchiocranium comprises the jaw and associated bones. The three paired organs of sense are enclosed in cartilaginous capsules. The parts, together with the jaws, tongue, and gill arches, form the skull. This can be seen in at least the embryos of all vertebrates above the lampreys. The lampreys and hagfishes are fishes without jaws. Their skull, as well as the rest of the skeleton, is cartilaginous as in the sharks and rays. In bony fishes, the cartilaginous portions of the skull are more or less ossified and strengthened by outside dermal bony plates making a complex structure.

The vertebral column is flexible and covers the notochord, the dorsal neural canal, and, in the caudal region, the ventral hemal, or blood-carrying, canal. Fibrous rings and tissue connect the parts or vertebrae. In addition, interlocking spines assist the fast swimmers by providing a solid axis on compression and a unit more loosely held together in an opposite bend. Ribs help give strength to the fish's swimming and hold the viscera in place, as well as being a site for muscle attachment.

In all fishes the longitudinal notochord persists as a definite feature. It is a stiff flexible rod or beadlike structure occurring beneath the central nervous system. It is the main skeletal axis in the more primitive forms. In higher animals it forms the basis for the vertebral column. More than other skeletal features, it probably serves most strongly as a basis for the development of the form of body in fishes and for the genesis and continuance of the lateral movement as a propulsion method in early vertebrates.

The dorsal and anal fins are also known as the vertical or median fins, and are important in maintaining balance. There may be a single soft dorsal fin, containing no spines, as in minnows, herrings, and tarpon. Perchlike fishes, such as bass, groupers, and snappers, have two dorsal fins, a spinous, or first dorsal fin, as well as a soft dorsal fin. Sometimes these are united (groupers, grunts, snappers) or are separate (barracuda, snook, striped bass). In some of the cods, there may be three dorsal fins. In freshwater trout and chars, and in deepsea relatives of these salmonlike fishes, a small, fleshy adipose fin is present between the dorsal fin and the tail. It contains no bony supporting rays or spines.

The anal fin is behind the vent or anus, on the lower surface of the body, and may be soft or spinous. In the cods and marlins there may be two anal fins. In some pelagic fishes, a series of small detached fins called finlets follow the dorsal and anal fins. These are found in tunas and their relatives, snake mackerels, some jacks, and sauries.

The tail or caudal fin is also a median fin and appears as three major types. In the diphycercal type, the body axis divides the fin into an apparent dorsal and ventral part as in the lampreys. The heterocercal type as in the sharks has the body axis upturned to form a longer dorsal lobe. The lower lobe is smaller and composed of rays only. The homocercal tail has a platelike fusion of bones from which the fin rays radiate as in the more highly developed bony fishes.

In shape, a caudal fin may be lunate, or crescent-shaped, as in the tunas. If it is only slightly crescent-shaped, or not definitely forked, it is then emarginate as in some trouts. A sickle-shaped tail, or one that is deeply concave with short middle rays and long exterior rays, is said to be forked or falcate. A tail with a perfectly straight rear edge is truncate. Eels and morays have pointed tails, with no apparent caudal fin, and seahorses and snake eels lack a caudal fin entirely. Some tails (seahorse) are prehensile.

The pectoral and pelvic (or ventral) fins, which correspond to arms and legs of higher vertebrates, are supported by girdles except in the lampreys and hagfishes. The unpaired fins of bony fishes are supported by cartilage or bone. In the lampreys, there is membranous support only for the cartilaginous fin rays. The chief function of the paired fins is for steering, and the pelvic fins are also used by some fishes for balancing on the bottom. The pectoral fins are usually placed in front of the pelvic fins. Pelvic fins are placed far to the rear in primitive fishes (gars, needlefish, and herrings), moving forward in evolutionary progression, with some "advanced" forms having the pelvic fins under the throat (cods, blennies, cusk-eels). In some forms the pelvic fins may be missing entirely (swordfish and eels). The pelvic fins show great diversity, and in gobies and clingfishes they are modified to form a sucking disk for holding onto rocks. In sharks and their relatives, the claspers of the male are modifications of the pelvic fins for copulation. Pectoral fins may be greatly modified as in skates and rays, or specialized for walking (batfish, mudskippers, and searobins), gliding (flying fishes, flying gurnards), or grasping (sargassum-fishes).

MUSCULAR STRUCTURE

As in other vertebrates there are three types of muscle—smooth muscle as found in involuntary gut muscle, skeletal as in the large body muscles, and cardiac as found in the heart. Instead of having many specialized muscles, such as those which activate the limbs of higher vertebrates, fishes have only a few. The entire body from the back of the head to the tail is a mass of muscle which constitutes the principal motive force for swimming. Each muscle mass, or myotome, is divided into an upper and lower section. These body muscles become specialized in the embryo to form muscles which move the eyes, gill arches and associated structures, jaws, and fins. Muscles are sometimes specialized into electric organs which are capable of stunning or killing prey, and can give a man a sizable shock. Torpedo rays, electric eels, electric catfish, and stargazers produce a strong current which paralyzes, while elephantfish and their relatives produce pulses which are used for echo sounding of obstacles or prey.

Types of Caudal Fins: *(top to bottom)* Diphycercal Fin (Lampreys), Heterocercal Fin (Sharks), Homocercal Fin (Sunfishes), Lunate Fin (Tunas), Emarginate Fin (Trout), Falcate Fin (Jacks), Truncate Fin (Groupers)

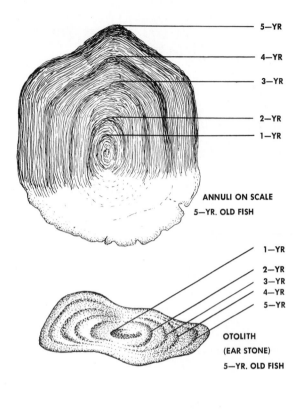

ANNULI ON SCALE
5—YR. OLD FISH

OTOLITH
(EAR STONE)
5—YR. OLD FISH

BONY GILL COVER
5—YR. OLD FISH

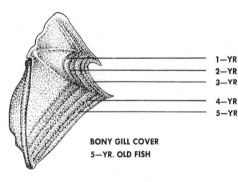

FIN RAY SECTION
3—YR. OLD FISH

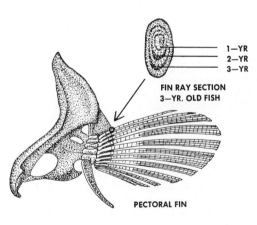

PECTORAL FIN

Four Methods of Aging Fish

LOCOMOTION

Fishes swim mainly by an undulating movement of the body. This is achieved by the successive contraction of the muscle segments, first along one side of the body and then the other. In effect, the fish pushes against the water laterally.

Vertical fins are largely used in balance, and paired fins are mostly used in steering. Fins are used in various ways in the swimming process, depending on the habits of the fish and its body shape. The caudal fin is most important, and is used in sudden bursts of speed (jacks, tunas, barracuda, needlefish). In some species (bowfin, filefish, electric eel) the dorsal or anal fin is important in locomotion, moving front to back in a progressive "S," or sine wave. The sine wave is also used in flattened fishes such as flounders, skates, and rays. Some species, such as wrasses and parrotfishes, rely almost exclusively on the pectoral fins for locomotion. The caudal peduncle is also important in locomotion and, with the tail, is responsible in large part for movement. Cowfish, trunkfish, and puffers use the peduncle or caudal fin to propel themselves in a sculling fashion. The anglerfishes and their relatives use jet propulsion, expelling water from the gills to carry them forward in short bursts. Most species use water jets in this fashion to assist in quick turns, in conjunction with the use of body movements and fins. Mackerels, tunas, marlins, swordfish, and some sharks (mako, white, porbeagle) have one or two lateral keels along the caudal peduncle which give strength to the peduncle and also keep the fish stabilized, since with the streamlined bony fishes the fins which are important for balance and steering are usually retracted into grooves or depressions at high speeds to reduce friction. It is thought that the hammer of the hammerhead sharks also may be used for sudden turning in pursuit of prey.

Some fishes are not active swimmers but float passively with the currents. Among these are the ocean sunfish (*Mola*), tripletail (*Lobotes*), and the larvae of many fishes. Following hatching of the eggs, the helpless larvae are affected by winds, tides, and storms, and have virtually no swimming ability of their own.

Swimming Speed The ordinary travel rate of fishes, the highest sustainable speed, and top speed can vary widely. With some variance, according to experiments at Cambridge University, some small fishes can travel in a short burst of speed the equivalent of ten times their own length in a second. Speed is proportional to length up to about 1 foot and is less so beyond in direct proportion to length. The length of the fish and the frequency of tail oscillation determine the speed.

Most estimates by anglers of swimming speeds are vastly overrated, and such estimates as 60–70 miles per hour for sailfish are without experimental evidence. One of the fastest fishes in the sea, at least for short bursts, is the great barracuda, which has been experimentally clocked at 27 mph. Probably other fast species such as wahoo, marlin, and tuna do not greatly exceed this speed. Flounders swim about 1½ mph, brown trout a little over 5 mph, and mackerel nearly 7. In short bursts, striped bass have been clocked at 12 and mackerel over 20. Under conditions in which a prey must escape its captor, or where a predator must ensnare its prey extreme speeds are possible, but such high speeds are exceptions.

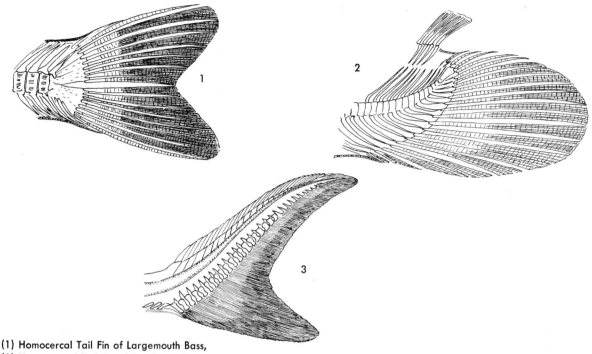

(1) Homocercal Tail Fin of Largemouth Bass,
(2) Heterocercal Tail Fin of Bowfin, and
(3) Heterocercal Tail Fin of Sturgeon

FEEDING

Fishes are commonly predators, and most are active pursuers of all organisms. Depending on form and habitat, a wealth of structural modifications exists for food getting. Primitive fishes (hagfish and lamprey) lack fins and obtain food by rasping or burrowing into the parasitized host. Most sharks have well-developed teeth which can bite and tear, while skates and rays have plates for crushing snails and clams. Bony fishes reflect a wide diversity of herbivores (plant eaters), carnivores (flesh eaters), and omnivores (fishes which feed on both). Mouths and teeth are so modified to the environment that the position of the mouth and its size and the size and shape of the teeth are usually sufficient to tell something about the species' way of life.

Typically, fishes may have teeth in the jaws, mouth, and throat, including the roof of the mouth, the tongue, and the gill arches. Anglerfish, pike, groupers, and snappers have numerous, conical canine teeth. Usually those at the front are much larger than those at the sides. In some families they are curved inward and depressible so that the prey goes one way only. Tropical mackerels, wahoo, bluefish, barracuda, and piranhas have canines, incisors, and palatine teeth well-developed into cutting or shearing teeth.

Fishes feeding on attached algae, mollusks, or barnacles are adapted for nibbling or grazing, and usually have incisor teeth. These include porgies, sheepshead, surgeonfish, and parrotfishes, which are grazers. Their teeth are flattened, thin, and sharp. Porgies have specialized crushing teeth (molariform) on the sides for crushing and grinding shellfish.

Fishes which pick up mud or detritus from the bottom or surface film are suckers and usually lack teeth or have only much-reduced teeth which are cardiform or bristlelike. These include mullet, sturgeons, suckers, and some minnows.

Plankton feeders are strainers, and filter small organisms from the water, collect them on gillrakers or branchial sieves, and swallow them. Plankton feeders usually have reduced teeth and numerous well-developed gillrakers on the first gill arch. Anchovies, herrings, paddlefish, the basking shark, and the whale shark are such examples.

DIGESTIVE TRACT

Fish have a mouth, gullet, stomach, intestines, pancreas, and liver. The development of the mouth depends on the feeding habits of the fish. Food is temporarily held in the mouth during the swallowing process. The stomach varies in shape and length, and, generally, carnivorous fishes have a short stomach, while herbivores have a long stomach. In mullets, sturgeons, gizzard shads, and butterfishes a gizzard grinds the ingested food. The intestine is short in carnivores, and is long and highly convoluted in plant eaters, and in some plant eaters there is no obvious demarcation between the stomach and intestine. Sharks and their relatives as well as some primitive bony fish have a corkscrewlike spiral valve which increases surface area for food absorption.

Digestion occurs all along the tract of the stomach. Blind, fingerlike pouches, called pyloric caeca, are attached near the anterior part of the stomach and are involved in enzyme production and fat absorption. The typical fish stomach is very acid, and food contents as well as hooks are dissolved rather quickly. The liver acts in digestion and stores fats and sugar, as well as other metabolic functions. The gall bladder, usually a greenish organ, temporarily stores liver secretions. The pancreas, which produces enzymes, is also involved in digestion.

RESPIRATION

Gills The body cells of fishes require a continual supply of oxygen for their vital processes. One of the end products of the chemical changes occurring in the cells is carbon dioxide which must be constantly eliminated. The exchange of these gases, or respiration, occurs in the gills of a fish. The blood conveys oxygen from the gills to the cells and returns laden with carbon dioxide. Because the fish obtains oxygen from a liquid, the blood in its gills must have close contact with the water to make an exchange of gases possible.

There are four pairs of gills in bony fishes. From five to seven pairs occur in sharks, in addition to the spiracle, a small opening in front of the gill cleft. The gills of bony fishes are covered by the gill cover or operculum. The gill arch is supported by central gill bars, behind which are the feathery, red gill filaments. Inside these filaments is a network of tiny branchial capillaries and carbon dioxide is discharged from the blood into the water. The gill arches have fingerlike projections called gillrakers on the side toward the throat.

The gill slits are closed with the operculum, and water is drawn into the open mouth. The mouth is then closed, the gill arches contract, and the rear edge of the operculum is raised forcing the water over the gill filaments, through the slits, and out of the gill chamber. Water flow can be regulated by oral valves located behind the lips on the inside of the mouth. The amount of oxygen required depends upon adaptation, metabolic activity, and temperature. The trout, for example, does well in swift-flowing streams with a high oxygen content, whereas carp can thrive in muddy stillwaters with a low oxygen content.

The gills have the additional functions of excretion of certain nitrogenous wastes and the regulation of internal salt concentration. Tolerance of freshwater fishes to saltwater can differ within a species and vary with age and size.

Respiration in fishes also occurs through the lining of the mouth and the skin, and specialized modifications occur in some embryos and larval forms to facilitate respiration.

A false gill or pseudobranch is often to be found on the inside of the gill cover. It regulates the gas supply to the eye and functions as an enzyme-producing gland.

The Gas Bladder A structure occurring in most fishes is the gas bladder (swim or air bladder), which lies under the kidney. It is an air-breathing device in some fishes, both ancient and modern. It can serve as a noise-producing or hydrostatic organ and acts as a resonator in hearing. The gas bladder is richly supplied with blood vessels and is used as a temporary respiratory organ by fishes living in conditions of low oxygen content. Gars, bowfin, elephantfish, and tarpon are obligatory air breathers, having to surface periodically to gulp air.

Sound conduction of the gas bladder is particularly good, and in some species (cods and porgies) an anterior extension of the bladder connects with the inner ear. In minnows, characins, and catfishes, an elaborate specialization of the first four vertebrae into a Weberian apparatus connects the inner ear with the gas bladder. Its function appears to be in detection of water movements or pressure waves and thus in hearing. Sound conduction also occurs in triggerfish and squirrelfish.

Sound production is widespread in fishes, and is associated with the gas bladder resonating from bones or muscles. Among those fishes which produce sound in this manner are grunts, groupers, porgies, squirrelfish, triggerfish, drums, searobins, jacks, and toadfish.

The gas bladder also acts as a hydrostatic or flotation organ to adjust the weight of the fish to equalize its water displacement so that it neither rises nor sinks. This membranous sac is inflated with oxygen, nitrogen, and carbon dioxide, which pass into it from the blood. Fish which normally inhabit deepwater, such as the lake trout, deepwater snappers, and certain groupers, are often killed when rapidly drawn to the surface; the gas bladder expands and pushes the esophagus into the mouth. Species which do not possess, or have only a rudimentary, gas bladder, such as the darters, sink to the bottom if they stop swimming.

Air Breathing Air breathing occurs in some fishes as a temporary measure to allow the fish to leave the water (climbing perches) or to survive stranding when water dries up or becomes low in oxygen. The gars, tarpon, bowfin, and others have a much-modified gas-bladder lining allowing the use of air in breathing.

Gas-bladder lungs have evolved in lungfish, similar to the gas bladder of most fishes. This highly specialized device enables the fish to breathe while encased in a mud cocoon for three or four months.

Other modifications for air breathing include the specialized wall of blood vessels on the inside of the operculum and gill chamber in the mudskipper, while the climbing perch has a convoluted structure in the gill cavity. In loaches and some other fishes, part of the intestine serves as an air-breathing apparatus. Branchial cavity enlargement into a long sac reaching the tail occurs in an Asian catfish. Many species habitually living in areas of low oxygen content or those which burrow into mud bottoms are able to live for many hours out of water, such as some soles, eels, catfish, and stargazers.

CIRCULATION

The circulation of blood in fishes is much simpler than in higher vertebrates. A single circulation occurs rather than a double one as found in mammals, and is effected by a simple two-part heart. The blood is pumped forward toward the gills, where respiration, or exchange of oxygen and carbon dioxide, occurs with the surrounding water. Oxygenated blood then traverses the large arteries to the smaller arteries and capillaries of tissues and organs, where oxygen is dispersed and carbon dioxide is picked up. Carbon-dioxide-laden blood then returns by way of the liver system in the veins toward the heart.

Circulation functions in transporting gases, metabolic wastes, minerals, and nutrients to and from tissues and organs. Tissue fluids in fishes are plasma, a clear liquid carrying minerals, metabolic byproducts, enzymes, and gases. Blood cells contain hemoglobin and occur in the plasma, and although they are usually red, eel larvae and some Antarctic fishes lack the red coloration. Blood is manufactured in bone marrow, the spleen, and the lymphatic system, a supplementary, open circulatory complex.

EXCRETION

The kidneys of a fish, which excrete urinary wastes, lie under the backbone. In freshwater fishes they are seen as

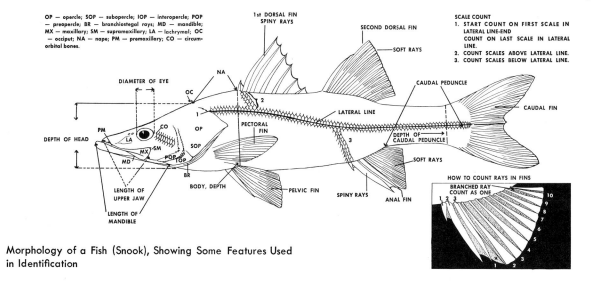

Morphology of a Fish (Snook), Showing Some Features Used in Identification

slender, reddish masses which look like coagulated blood. In saltwater fishes the kidney is less developed and usually covered by heavy connective tissue, making it less visible.

Their structure consists of numerous tubules supplied with many blood capillaries which remove waste products and poisons such as urea from the blood. Collected wastes empty into two excretory ducts along the kidneys' length, usually joining a common duct known as the urinary bladder in freshwater bony fishes or the urogenital sinus in sharks and their relatives.

Because salts tend to diffuse (by osmosis) from an area of high concentration to low concentration of salts, freshwater fishes lose body salts, and water tends to diffuse into the body across the gills and the linings of the mouth and intestine. In freshwater fishes, the kidney produces a concentrated urine, and thus the kidney is larger and more conspicuous than in marine fishes, and the main function of the kidney of the freshwater fish is to get rid of water and to retain salts. Important in retaining salts are the chloride cells, or salt-saving glands, believed to be primarily on the gills. The endocrine system and the brain are also involved in salt retention.

Marine fishes lose water because their environment is saltier, and must therefore drink water to compensate for water loss. Excess salts are eliminated from the body through the gills, the gut, and some through the urine. Chloride cells are present on the gills and lining of the mouth in some marine fishes. Fishes that go from saltwater to freshwater, such as salmons, compensate for a loss of sea salt by the development of chloride cells and calcium salts. Eels, moving downstream from freshwater to saltwater, use chloride cells alternately to produce and get rid of salts depending on their surroundings. Endocrine activity also closely governs those physiological changes.

Sharks and their relatives have slightly higher salt concentration in their blood than the water in which they live as a result of the deposition of urea in the blood. The urea in the flesh and blood is responsible for the smell of ammonia in fresh and, particularly, decomposing shark meat.

ENDOCRINE ORGANS

Even the lowest forms of fishes contain the basics of endocrine systems. Fishes, in general, differ from the higher vertebrates in having endocrine systems which permit adaption of color cells to backgrounds; promotion of body-length growth; balancing extrarenal water; adaptation to salinity, light, and temperature; diadromous migration (free movement between saltwater and freshwater); calcium metabolism; stimulation of the sympathetic nervous system; and pancreatic secretion.

The endocrine glands are intricately tied up with all bodily functions, and are roughly comparable biochemically with those in mammals, although the functions are different. Among the most important, the pituitary gland is responsible for growth, color changes, reproduction, and possibly proper gill function. The thyroid controls metabolic rates, and the ultimobranchial regulates the uptake and release of calcium within the body. Various other glands regulate heartbeat and blood pressure, digestion, sexual development, and reproduction.

REPRODUCTIVE SYSTEM

The reproductive and urinary systems of fishes are intimately related and may be described as the urinogenital system. The reproductive organs are the gonads. Individually, the female reproductive system consists of two ovaries suspended dorsally in the body cavity, in which the ova, or eggs, are formed. The ripe ovary may comprise up to 25 per cent of the fish's weight at spawning time. The ovaries are saclike, round in cross section, and covered with connective tissue. A central passage, or lumen, is usually visible, along which the eggs pass at spawning time. Unripe, small eggs, or oöcytes, can usually be seen in the ovary. A pair of oviducts conveys the ripe ova to the vent where they are discharged, but some fish do not possess oviducts. Salmonids, for example, pass the ripe ova into the body cavity.

The testes of the male occupy a position corresponding to the ovaries of the female. When mature they appear as a pair of long, white sacs in which the spermatozoa are formed. The testes are smaller than the ovaries, sometimes reaching 12 per cent of the total body weight. The spermatozoa are conveyed from each testis by a number of fine tubes called the vasa efferentia into a larger tube or vas deferens. The latter joins its opposite to form a single receptacle which opens into the vent.

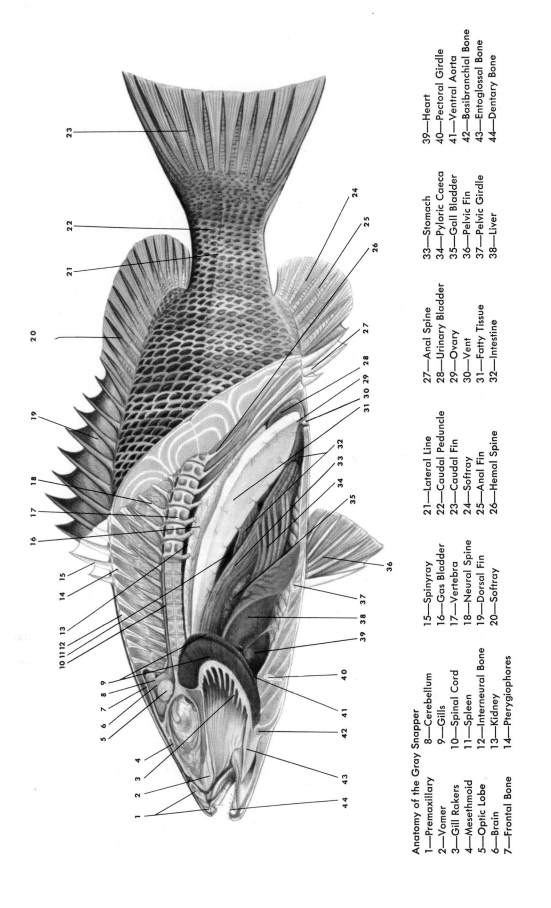

Anatomy of the Gray Snapper

1—Premaxillary
2—Vomer
3—Gill Rakers
4—Mesethmoid
5—Optic Lobe
6—Brain
7—Frontal Bone

8—Cerebellum
9—Gills
10—Spinal Cord
11—Spleen
12—Interneural Bone
13—Kidney
14—Pterygiophores

15—Spinyray
16—Gas Bladder
17—Vertebra
18—Neural Spine
19—Dorsal Fin
20—Softray

21—Lateral Line
22—Caudal Peduncle
23—Caudal Fin
24—Softray
25—Anal Fin
26—Hemal Spine

27—Anal Spine
28—Urinary Bladder
29—Ovary
30—Vent
31—Fatty Tissue
32—Intestine

33—Stomach
34—Pyloric Caeca
35—Gall Bladder
36—Pelvic Fin
37—Pelvic Girdle
38—Liver

39—Heart
40—Pectoral Girdle
41—Ventral Aorta
42—Basibranchial Bone
43—Entoglossal Bone
44—Dentary Bone

Most fishes are bisexual, requiring a male and a female to produce eggs and sperm. A few are hermaphroditic, where both sexes regularly occur in the same individual (some sea basses), and occasionally a hermaphroditic individual will occur in a number of groups (perch, salmon, darters, bass). Black sea bass (*Centropristis*) are males first and become females as they grow older.

It is usually possible to identify the sex of a fish only by opening it and examining the gonads. But in some fishes, particularly in freshwater forms, the males clearly differ from the females. In dragonets and flounders, the dorsal or pectoral fins may be longer in the male, the position of the eyes in the sexes of some flounders may differ, and in some catfish the barbels are much longer in the male. Male livebearers may have the first few anal rays greatly elongated. The male dolphin (*Coryphaena*) has a square head, while that of the female is rounded. Sexual dimorphism is seen in the elongate claspers of sharks and their relatives, which are modifications of the pelvic fins and are found only in the male. They are used in copulation for sperm transference. The sexes of freshwater fishes generally differ in outward appearance only at spawning time. Darters become highly colored, the male becoming the brighter, while male minnows and suckers become covered with horny breeding tubercles which are used to drive other males from the nest. Trout and, particularly, salmon show a well-developed hook, or kype, on the lower jaw and usually the upper, and the male salmon may develop a bizarre dorsal hump. Most male trout and salmon also have intensified coloration at spawning time. A genital papilla is developed near the anus of the male in some fishes such as darters, white bass, and lampreys.

Fishes usually lay eggs (oviparity), while others are livebearers (viviparity), as in mosquitofish, surfperch, and some sharks. In many sharks and rays, the eggs are hatched within the mother and remain there during development (ovoviviparity).

Usually, oviparous fishes lay many eggs, and viviparous fishes produce relatively few young. Ocean sunfish produce over 28 million eggs and cods about 3 million, but nest-building fishes, such as sunfish, bass, and sticklebacks, may lay only a few hundred. Generally, the greater the parental care, the fewer eggs or young produced. Nest building and parental care may be highly developed, as in the darters, sunfish, cichlids, and sticklebacks. The lumpsucker may spend months faithfully guarding the nest, carefully guarding the developing eggs from predators, and fanning and cleaning the nest from silt and fouling organisms. Where eggs are spread over the surface or bottom, reproduction usually involves a simple bumping of the male and female with a simultaneous release of the eggs and sperm. Fertilized eggs subsequently drift at the surface or sink to the bottom to develop.

Sexual maturity is generally related to size, and fishes which are small and have a short life span usually mature younger. Mosquitofish mature at one year, while sturgeons do not mature until fifteen years or more. The cause of reproduction in fishes is not well understood, but seems to be tied up with light, temperature, and the endocrine system. Some species breed once a year (trout), others according to the tide (grunion), while some (surgeonfish) spawn with every full moon. Salmon spawn once every 2–5 years, while eels spawn every 10–14 years.

EGGS AND LARVAL DEVELOPMENT

Fertilization occurs when the sperm unites with the egg. Subsequently, the embryo divides in half, and these and subsequent cells subdivide to form the prelarva and its specialized organs. During the egg and prelarval stage, the embryo absorbs food from its yolk sac and possibly directly from the environment. Following hatching, the larva, or postlarva, is capable of feeble swimming movements but is largely subject to winds, currents, and tides. In pelagic or deepsea fishes the young are characterized by grotesque-looking adaptations for feeding and floating, with long fins, spines, and membranes in various stages of specialization. Often a developmental metamorphosis occurs in which these specialized features are suddenly lost and the characters of the adult are assumed. This usually occurs when they drop to the bottom or otherwise change from the drifting, pelagic habitat. Among the fishes which have unusual larvae are eels, bonefish, tarpon, herrings, flounders, oarfish, goosefish, snake mackerels, and marlin. Freshwater fishes usually do not undergo marked metamorphosis but are heavily pigmented and often resemble the adults at an early stage. Fishes pass from the postlarval to juvenile to adult stages, the period from the juvenile to adult usually being accompanied by changes in color, pigmentation, and the size of the gonads.

AGE AND GROWTH

Some fishes are annual, such as some minnows and gobies, living only a year or so. Salmon, pike, and sturgeon are credited with long life spans. Fishes have a life span which they usually attain, but in captivity, where problems of predation and competition do not occur, fishes may far exceed their life expectancy. For example, brown trout usually live six or eight years; yet in captivity individuals have lived over eighteen years, and goldfish, usually dying after seven years, have lived to thirty. Eels, which usually live to be from seven to eleven years old, have been kept in captivity up to sixty years.

Theoretically, fishes are capable of indefinite growth, although the rate of growth decreases with age. Age and growth of fishes can be studied by (1) maintaining fishes in captivity; (2) studying bones and other hard parts which show growth rings; (3) tagging and recapture of marked fish; and (4) experiments with radioactive chemicals. Items (2) and (3) are most widely used, either separately or, preferably, conjointly.

Growth checks are deposited in scales, bones, and other hard parts, similar to the rings of a tree. The scales of a fish grow at about the same rate as the body. Consequently, the number of scales remains constant throughout life. The growth of a scale is achieved by the addition of new material on its outer margin. A fish scale develops several circuli, or growth rings, each year. During periods when food is abundant and growth rapid these rings are widely spaced. During the spawning season, or in winter when growth is slow, the circuli occur close together. A group of winter rings actually appears as a dark band because of their proximity to each other, and such a band is known as an annual check or annulus. A trained biologist can determine the age of the fish from the number of annuli. The scales may also reveal how many times the fish has spawned or, in the case of an anadromous fish, how many years it has spent in the sea. It is usually also possible to determine the length of the fish at different periods in its life because the ratio between the present length of the fish scale and its length at any previous annulus equals the ratio between the present length of the fish and its length at the time of the same annual check.

As already indicated, some fish do not have scales, and others have scales which are difficult to analyze. According to the species, the researcher may use other parts of the fish such as a cross section of the vertebrae or the bones of the gill cover to determine its age. It is also possible to use the ear stone, or otolith. The otolith, which is composed largely of calcium, develops concentrically, and variations in its density provide bandlike markings similar to those found on a scale.

The growth of a single species of fish is not constant because different populations are products of different environments; there may be an abundant food supply in one area, where the fish grow exceptionally large in a short period, and a poor food supply in a nearby region where the same species averages very much smaller or even becomes stunted.

Variations in temperature result in different rates of growth, and generally fishes grow faster during warm weather than during cold periods. Chemical composition of the water, storms, water-level changes (in reservoirs), and the presence or absence of food, competitors, other members of the species, and predators (biotic factors) all influence rate of growth.

A knowledge of the age of fish is important to their conservation; their maximum life span, age at the time of spawning, and time spent in a marine environment are but a few factors which help to establish practical fishing regulations. Fish which are short-lived can be harvested early, while those which have a long life span may not become mature until they are quite old and will thus require protection for a greater period.

SENSES

The brain, spinal cord, nerves, and sense organs are coordinated into a unit which controls the nervous sensory and motor actions of the body. Compared to that of higher vertebrates, the nervous system is poorly developed.

Brain The fish brain, which is essentially a specialized enlargement of the spinal cord, is divided into an anterior forebrain, a connecting 'tweenbrain, the midbrain, and the hindbrain. All are contained within the bony cranium of the skull, and the spinal cord runs posteriorly within the vertebrae. The forebrain is responsible primarily for smell reception. In sharks and those bony fishes which feed largely by scent, this portion may be quite enlarged and specialized. The 'tweenbrain is sensitive to light stimuli through the pineal organ, and is variously developed in different species. Part of the 'tweenbrain is involved in endocrine control and in the complex reception and transmission of different stimuli. The midbrain is responsible for vision, and is composed of the paired optic lobes, which are well-developed in most fishes. The hindbrain contains the cerebellum, which controls equilibrium, orientation, and swimming in general. The other major component of the hindbrain is the medulla oblongata, which receives all sensory nerves except those of sight and smell, the main function of the medulla being as a relay between the spinal cord and the well-developed complexes of the brain. Breathing, salt balance, and color changes are also controlled through the medulla.

The spinal cord is relatively unspecialized in structure and contains two types of nerves, spinal and cranial, the former originating along the spinal cord and the latter confluent with the brain. These nerves control the senses of smell, vision, motor responses, hearing, respiration, and heartbeat, among other functions.

Fishes respond well to conditioning and display a reasonable amount of intelligence for such a low group on the evolutionary scale. Fishes learn to distinguish colors and associate certain sounds or signals with punishments and rewards. Memory is developed to a certain extent, and salmons are able to "memorize" odors of their parent stream for 2–6 years. Gobies are able to learn and remember with amazing accuracy paths between tidepools. Snappers, barracuda, trout, and bass seem to display an undue amount of wariness at times in taking a hook, and it is likely that some species are more intelligent than others. Even within the same school, wide variations in learning ability are displayed among individuals.

Touch Fishes can detect touch through small nerve-containing pits scattered over the body, as well as on the lips and barbels. Barbels are elongate fleshy feelers on the mouth, on the head, and sometimes on the pectoral and pelvic fins. Barbels are particularly important to species feeding where the water is muddy or light is poor. Probably barbels are also used in a sensory function, picking up swimming vibrations of approaching fishes.

Physical changes, such as temperature and touch, are detected by the skin, and it is highly developed in some species, gobies being able to detect a temperature change of 0.03° C.

Pain in fishes is probably not experienced in the same manner as in higher vertebrates. Evidence points to fishes not being particularly sensitive to pain. Sharks notoriously return to the bait after being severely mutilated or even eviscerated, and fishes repeatedly take a hook again after being caught shortly before. Possibly hunger is a stronger sense than pain.

Taste A sense of taste enables a fish to detect food, dissolved chemicals, acidity or alkalinity, and saltiness of the water. Generally, specialized taste organs are present on the epidermis of the mouth area, including the lips and throat. Fishes depending largely on taste for food detection may have additional taste buds on various parts of the body, including the skin. Catfishes and sturgeons have taste buds on their barbels, while searobins and hake contain taste receptors in the paired fins which are especially receptive during locomotion of the fish along the bottom. In some cods and catfishes, taste buds extend to the base of the fins and over the entire body including the tail. Coupled with this increase is an enlargement of that segment of the facial nerve concerned with taste and of its brain centers.

Smell In most fishes the organ of smell occurs as a blind pouch which is lined with sensory epithelium. It is open to the water through two nares, or nostrils, on either side of the head and connects with the brain through the olfactory nerve. The sense of smell is highly developed in most fishes, and some species, such as sharks and catfishes, depend on it to a larger degree than on sight when feeding. It has also been established that anadromous fishes such as the salmon can detect "odors" in the water which probably reveal the location of their parent stream.

Sight Eyes of fishes are generally similar to those of other vertebrates except that they are modified for an aquatic life. A fish eye has an eyeball, a transparent cornea, an iris, a lens, a retina, and a horny capsule, or sclerotic capsule, and eye muscles. Only higher bony fishes have an iris capable of regulation of size. The eye's outer surface is flattened and fits smoothly in the head. Occasionally a layer of fatty tissue (the adipose "eyelid") is developed, as in herrings and mullet, for streamlining. Except in some sharks which have a nictitating (winking) membrane, the eyes of fishes are lidless.

The lens is round in side view, unlike the ellipse of mammals, and focus is effected by changing the position of the lens with the muscles rather than by changing its shape. Many species are farsighted, while others are nearsighted. Some, like the brown trout, have clear vision over a wide range and can focus clearly on distant and nearby objects simultaneously. Generally, a fish's vision is adapted to its particular habits and environment. Most fishes have only monocular vision and can focus each eye on separate objects, but seahorses and sea bass can focus with both eyes at once.

Odd modifications often occur in deepsea fishes, some of their eyes being telescopic, barrel-shaped, or on the ends of long stalks. Hammerhead sharks have the eyes placed on either end of the hammer. The four-eyed fish of Central and South America has the eye partitioned into two equal parts by a horizontal band at the level of the water and can see in air and water simultaneously. Some species have adapted to total darkness, living in caves and subterranean wells. Often the absence of light has been associated with a reduction or loss of vision and body pigment. Usually there is a corresponding increase in the sensitivity of these fishes to sound, taste, and smell.

The retina of fish eyes contains cones, which function in bright light, and rods, which function in dim light. Deepsea fishes and those which live in dim-lit areas contain many rods, while predators active in the day have a large number of cones.

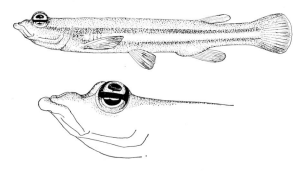

Four-eyed Fish or Anableps

Fishes see color well, distinguishing 24 different shades of the spectrum, and in some cases they can see colors (violets) which man cannot. They can also experience color contrasts and brightness and can differentiate between shades. Apparently, well-developed color vision is only present in shallow-water species, for only a few colors (blues and greens) are visible in deeper water.

Hearing and Balance Most fishes probably do not detect high-frequency sounds, for their hearing apparatus is geared primarily to low-frequency vibrations. Detection of sounds is accomplished through the lateral-line system, through the inner ear, and reception and detection of pressure changes on the gas-bladder. The lateral-line system, which may be highly branched over the body in some species, is essentially a canal along the head and sides of the body lined with sense organs. It is sensitive to temperature, low-frequency sound, and water currents and assists in maintaining balance. It is also utilized as a "sonar" system, and some fishes are able to detect objects from reflected vibrations induced through their own swimming movements. Elephantfishes and their relatives set up a small electrical field with their electric organs, and any organism entering this field of continuous pulses can be detected by the lateral-line system.

Fishes possess only an inner ear, which consists of a membranous sac containing fluid. Receptors within the organ receive vibrations and stimuli for hearing and balance. Within the inner ear is a series of canals, and connecting pockets containing ear stones (otoliths) which function in maintaining balance.

In some fishes, the gas bladder is connected to the inner ear, so that vibrations are passed on from the body tissues and gas bladder to the brain. In herrings and elephantfish the posterior part of the inner ear is open and contacted by extensions of the gas bladder. The Weberian apparatus occurs in dominant freshwater groups, the minnows, catfish, suckers, and characins, and is a series of modified vertebrae which intricately connects the inner ear to the gas bladder. It appears to intensify sound waves, but probably is not important in detecting changes in pressure. It is still debatable if fishes hear sounds in the way higher animals do. However, outboard motors, banging of sticks and rocks, and changes in frequency of sounds all apparently attract fish to the angler, and, unfortunately, some of these same sounds evidently attract sharks to boats and swimmers.
　　　　　　　　　　　　　　　　　　　　　　—J.R.
　　　　　　　　　　　　　　　　　　　　　　—D.dS.

ANCHOVY *See* Northern Anchovy, Striped Anchovy
ANEMONE A soft-bodied, complex polyp resembling a flower and belonging to the coelenterate class Anthozoa. Anemones are usually large, brightly colored, solitary animals. Slow-moving carnivores, they catch their prey with stinging tentacles which surround the mouth in the center of the oral disc, the flattened upper portion of an anemone's body. *See* Coelenterate
ANGELFISH *See* Queen Angelfish
ANGEL SHARK *See* Atlantic Angel Shark, Pacific Angel Shark
ANGLER In modern usage one who fishes for sport; specifically, with rod, reel, line, and hook or lure. The word *angler* is used interchangeably with *fisherman* although the latter may imply fishing for nonsporting purposes (commercial fishing) or fishing with nonsporting tackle such as a handline.

The word *ânka*, meaning bend or angle, or to fish with a bend or angle, comes from sanskrit, one of the oldest of man's written languages. It is the root from which the words *angler* and *angling* stem. In many countries of the world, hooks are still better known as *bends* or *angles*.

ANGLERFISH A common name for the goosefish (*which see*), also called bellyfish, monkfish, frogfish, and sea devil.

ANGLEWORM A common earthworm used as bait in angling. *See also* Live Bait

ANGOLA (PORTUGUESE WEST AFRICA) There are few facilities for anglers fishing the coast of Angola. Some accommodations and boats may be found at Luanda. The offshore fishing is primarily for sailfish, tarpon, dolphin, barracuda, tunas, and various jacks.

ANOXIA *See* Skin and Scuba Diving Dangers *under* First Aid

ANTERIOR Forward, before, or ahead of.

ANTIFOULING PAINT The coat of paint applied to a boat's bottom to prevent buildup of marine growths, algae, barnacles, etc. Contains poisons so formulated that they will leach out over a period of time to provide an ever-present discouragement to marine organisms.

ANUS Or vent. The external opening at the posterior end of the alimentary canal; located on the ventral surface of the body at the anterior base of the anal fin. *See* Anatomy

APACHE TROUT *Salmo apache* Also called Arizona trout, this species has in years past been confused with the Gila trout (*which see*). In most characters the Gila and Apache trouts resemble the cutthroat species more than the rainbow, but in the absence of basibranchial (hyoid) teeth they are similar to rainbows. Both the Apache and Gila are chunky, deep-bodied fish with long heads and jaws, long fins with the origin of the dorsal slightly more posterior than ½ the standard length. The obvious distinction between the two, however, is the smaller, more profuse spots found on the Gila trout, especially on the dorsal and caudal fins.

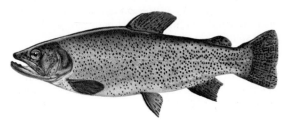

Apache Trout

In the 1960's the Apache trout's range had been reduced to only a few streams on the Fort Apache Indian Reservation in the White Mountains of Arizona. To save the trout from extinction the Arizona Game & Fish Department implemented an artificial propagation program from a brood stock of a pure-strain wild population. The recovery program has been very successful, with some 20,000 fish released in public waters during 1971.

APHOTIC ZONE The region of the ocean below the dysphotic zone where no light exists at all. Herbivorous marine animals are totally absent. Most life forms in the aphotic zone possess luminescent organs. Many are without eyes, or the eyes are reduced in size. *See also* Marine Ecology

AQUATIC Living in the water, or pertaining to water, such as aquatic birds, aquatic insects, or aquatic vegetation.

ARCTIC CHAR *Salvelinus alpinus* A salmonid found in coldwaters of the northern hemisphere. Anadromous and landlocked char are common to parts of northern Canada, Baffin Island, Greenland, Iceland, northern Norway, northern Siberia, and Alaska. In addition the landlocked form occurs south of this range in the lakes of southern Norway, Sweden, Finland, England, Ireland, Scotland, westcentral Europe, and the USSR.

The char is similar to the brook trout in appearance but without the wormlike markings (vermiculations) on its back. The dorsal surface is usually olive-green or blue or sometimes brown; the sides may be pale or bright red or orange. The fish is not heavily spotted like a trout and sometimes may not be spotted at all, but when present these are large, cream, pale pink, or orange markings. Sea-run char are almost entirely silver when they first arrive in the river, but gradually the freshwater colors suffuse, then replace the saltwater disguise. The Arctic char has a slightly forked tail and a more rounded body than the brook trout, but its pectoral, pelvic, and anal fins often have the same cream-trimmed leading edges as well as the bright carmine color similar to the adult male squaretail. Arctic char usually weigh 2–8 pounds; however, there are dwarf landlocked and nonmigratory populations as well as giants among the sea-run fish, and the maximum size is over 25 pounds.

To separate the Arctic char from a brook trout the key points in field identification are:

(1) Absence of vermiculations on the back; faint markings may be suggested on a char, but they are not developed.

(2) Absence of any markings on the dorsal fin. Brook trout have irregular dark or blackish markings.

(3) Absence of red spots surrounded by bluish halos. Char often have red spots, but lack the blue halos.

(4) Absence of any markings on the caudal fin. Nearly all brook trout have irregular black markings or spotting on the tail.

ISOLATED FORMS

The Arctic char is one of a number of salmonids which apparently evolved from a common ancestor in the Pleistocene Age when the Pacific Ocean was separated from the Arctic Ocean by a land bridge. It has been speculated that the "bridge" isolated a population of char to the south, which we know today as the Dolly Varden, and another population to the north, which followed a circumpolar path across Asia, Europe, and North America and which became the Arctic char. In many waters the Dolly Varden is so similar to the char that it's difficult to separate them. Their range overlaps in Alaska, but the Dolly Varden or bull trout is distributed as far south as northern California and inland to Idaho and Montana. Both the lake trout and the brook trout evolved from the same char genotype as did the Sunapee trout, blueback trout, and Marston trout. Whether the three latter fish qualify as distinct species or subspecies has not been established; most taxonomists consider them as isolated populations of Arctic char. These char were left segregated from others of their kind since the Ice Age, and they have developed individual morphological characteristics caused by their landlocked environment. Elsewhere, char continued to migrate to sea and return to lakes for spawning. As a result, a variety of names [The

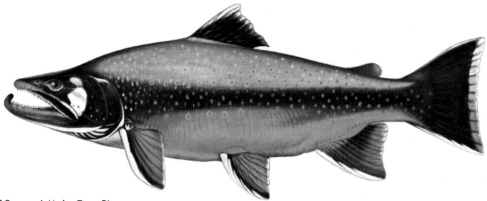

Arctic Char, 19-pound Male, Tree River,
Northwest Territories

Eskimo names (commonly "ilkalupik") are variable, depending on the maturity and sexual differences of the fish. The Arctic char is known as *röye* in Norway, *bleikja* in Iceland, *röding* in Sweden, Windermere char in England, *omble chevalier* in France, *der Seesaibling* in Germany, and *paliya* in the USSR.] has been given to the Arctic char in different parts of its range, and in many cases the distinctions upon which different specific and subspecific names have been based is obscure. Dymond and Vladykov (1933) have included in the *Salvelinus alpinus* group the forms found in northern North America and Asia to which the following subspecific names have been given: *alpinus, malma, leucomaenis, erythrinus, kundscha, spectabilis, pluvius, imbrius, arcturus, naresi, alipes, stagnalis, aureolus, oquassa, marstoni,* and *fontinalis* (the latter an Asiatic subspecies of *alpinus,* not to be confused with the American brook trout).

MIGRATIONS

The migrations of Arctic char conform to a general pattern throughout the north country. They descend to saltwater about the time the ice breaks in the rivers during late spring or early summer, and the ascent into freshwater to spawn takes place in the late summer or early fall. The fish usually begin their nomadic existence when 5–7 years old and make most of their growth during these initial visits to the sea even though they have a known life span of twenty-four years. Char apparently summer near the river mouths where they feed heavily before wintering inland again. It is doubtful whether any char ever remains in saltwater. The Eskimos around Ungava Bay, Frobisher Bay, and the Arctic Ocean say not. But this fish is at its angling best when it first comes into the river. Like salmon, they show themselves frequently by jumping and rolling with the incoming tide. They remain in large schools, a habit which is apparent even far upstream. A mile of river may be full of Arctic char when there are few if any above or below. As a result one must do considerable prospecting to locate a shoal of fish. These schools are often composed of char of the same age group so that if one is caught of, say, four pounds, all the rest of the fish will be about the same weight.

FLY-FISHING FOR ARCTIC CHAR

The Arctic char feeds chiefly on capelin, the lance or sand eel, the sculpin, and various crustaceans. Insects are a relatively minor part of its diet in tidewater or for that matter during the initial days of its upstream journey. At

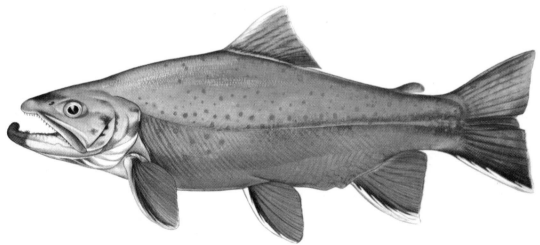

Arctic Char, 18-pound Male in Breeding Colors,
Tree River, Northwest Territories

Arctic Char, 6½-pound Male (Sea Run), George River, New Quebec

this point fly-fishing is generally limited to techniques which imitate forage fish or shrimp. But as the school moves inland, insects become an increasingly important food item. Occasional good dry-fly-fishing can be had on the rivers of Iceland. Here the fish rise to hatches of grayish-colored caddisflies. The char cruise near the surface and along the deep banks making a typical bow wave as they approach the drifting fly. This wave is always out of proportion to the size of the fish. Obviously, it requires a great amount of insect life to trigger a rise, and one may not often find the same conditions of weather and water in other regions. The dry fly is certainly a possibility on anadromous char, but sunk patterns are effective 99 per cent of the time.

When Arctic char are not visible, the best place to look for them is in fast, shallow water. They usually school near the mouths of tributary streams or in the riffles adjacent to gravelbars where the water is 2–4 feet deep. The fish are not particularly shy; in fact when you do locate them the action may come so fast that the angling pales. For this reason, it is preferable to use a very light fly rod and give the char every opportunity to put on a show. In common with the Dolly Varden, they have a rather typical way of taking a lure. Both fish tend to swim slowly and deliberately behind a fly or spoon and snatch it after a prolonged stalk—even as you lift the lure from the water. Char frequently hit a fly after following it for twenty or thirty feet.

In many rivers Arctic char, even very large ones, can be disappointing. It would appear that they deteriorate rapidly in flesh and enthusiasm during their long journey, which in some rivers is over one hundred miles from tidewater. In other streams, however, they may arrive still fresh with sea lice, and prime char are every bit as strong as a grilse pound for pound. Typically, the fish moves with rapierlike speed for about one hundred feet, then leaps clear of the water and runs again. A four- or five-pound fish jumps a half-dozen times in swift currents and goes well down into the backing before it can be turned.

The trick in taking Arctic char consistently with flies is to use brightly colored patterns worked slow and deep with short twitches. Even if the water is quite shallow the fly should swim as close to the river stones as possible. Although you can catch fish in tidewater with streamers such as the Supervisor, Light Tiger, Nine-Three, and Gray Ghost, the ideal flies are European sea-trout patterns which are liberally garnished with gold and silver tinsel such as the Teal and Yellow, Bloody Butcher, Blue Zulu, Teal and Green, and the Mallard and Claret. You can also use some of the steelhead standards like the Thor, Golden Demon, Railbird, or the Carson tied on No. 4 and No. 6 hooks.

SPINNING FOR CHAR

Because of the char's carnivorous appetite, it is probably one of the easiest fish to catch with a spinning rod. Few other species strike a flashing blade with more enthusiasm. However, char do not fight as well when hooked on spoons (they seldom jump), and large fish may act almost paralyzed by a treble hook. Big fish are apt to take a lure deep, and they bleed profusely. They are accustomed to gulping their capelin and can commit suicide on hardware. The choice is up to the angler; you may use heavy gear and lose the opportunity of some first-rate sport, or go to light calibers such as 2- and 3-ounce spinning rods equipped with 4- to 6-pound-test lines. With small ¼ to ½-ounce spinners or wobblers and icetong-style double hooks the char will cavort in fine fettle. The little blades and small hooks are far less damaging.

WHERE TO GO

There are many productive Arctic-char waters which the modern angler can conveniently reach. Baffin Island, Greenland, Alaska and the whole northern tier of the Canadian provinces extending from the Yukon to Labrador are open to travel. However, it is important to learn when planning a trip for char if you will be fishing for the anadromous kind down near the river mouth, because the run will pass through rather quickly and your sport may be limited to anywhere from one to two weeks. You would have to hit their arrival with great accuracy. Arctic char do not linger in one area very long until they are well upriver where you will find them in source lakes, at the mouths of small tributary streams, or, as it so often happens in many northern rivers, below the first impassable waterfall. Landlocked char also exist in the lakelike portions of Arctic streams as well as in bodies of water not connected to the sea. Nonmigratory populations are seldom interesting to catch as they invariably range from ten to fifteen inches long and are inclined to frequent very deep water. Do not confuse these, however, with migratory char which also occur in lakes such as Naknek in Alaska when they come up from the Bering Sea to spawn.

FOOD VALUE

The Arctic char is an excellent food fish. The color of the flesh is variable from yellowish-white to fiery red. Fresh char are largely consumed by the Eskimos, but great quantities are smoked by Canadians, who ship the product to United States gourmet markets, and by the Scandinavians. In barren polar regions they are smoked over sheep dung (Iceland).   —A.J.McC.

ARCTIC GRAYLING *See* American Grayling

ARCTIC SMELT Synonymous with Rainbow Smelt (*which see*).

ARGENTINA This southernmost South American country is one of the finest trout-fishing areas in the world. Being long (2,300 miles), it provides a range of habitat from tropical in the north to subarctic in the south. However, the salmonids are distributed along the Andean Ridge which roughly parallels the Chilean border. Although trout and landlocked salmon are not endemic to Argentina, a fish hatchery built in 1903 at San Carlos de Bariloche has been responsible for their widespread introduction throughout the country. The initial stocking of trout was an ecologist's dream. No predator fish existed, and few native species of any size occurred in freshwater, other than the trucha criolla and the pejerrey. The trucha criolla, which translates to "native trout," is not a trout nor is it a perch (as it is often described) but a member of the family Percichthyidae more closely allied to the drums. There are five species in Argentinian rivers and they are a valuable market fish. The pejerrey is a member of the family Atherinidae, or silversides; three species occur in freshwater, and sea-run forms exist. Pejerrey are also important commercial fish. The only common forage species is the puyen, represented by five species in the family Galaxiidae (this is the same galaxias found in New Zealand and Australian waters). Galaxias are easy to identify, as they are scaleless and have a single small dorsal and anal fin positioned close to the tail. Fortunately, the colorful Argentinian sea lamprey has never found access to Patagonian streams, and barring human error in future hydroelectric projects it may never become a dangerous parasite. Thus trout were planted in a comparative vacuum shortly after the turn of the century. The rainbow, brown, and brook trout and the landlocked salmon are the four principal species sought by angling. The success of their establishment is due to the thousands of miles of cold, clearwater rivers and lakes which exist in Argentina and the sparse human population in the fishing areas.

SAN CARLOS DE BARILOCHE

The city of Bariloche, located 850 miles southwest of Buenos Aires, is the chief angling center. Although angling in the immediate vicinity of this popular summer and winter resort can be excellent, Bariloche is the natural jumpoff point for visitors traveling north or south. Here guides and ground transportation may be obtained for the fishing in either direction. One aspect of the local scene that has changed dramatically is the fishing in Lake Nahuel Haupí. This 330-square-mile body of water is probably the most productive spot in South America today. It drops to 1,600 feet in depth, and is divided into many branches which vary in character biologically. Twenty years ago the lake was primarily a brown-trout fishery (record 36 pounds), but, as is typical of brown

Some beautiful fly fishing can be found in Argentina, with trout and salmon up to 12 pounds or more

trout in an ocean-sized environment, it produced little for the fly-fisherman. Rainbows were in the minority then, and, like the brownie, were taken mainly by deep trolling. A stopover in Bariloche was merely a pause between flying and driving. Despite the creature comforts of a resort town, serious anglers either headed north or south another 200 dusty miles and stayed at a *hosteria* or camped out.

Today, rainbows not only dominate the lake but you can wade knee deep and cast to risers within sight of town. Some idea of the angling quality is reflected in these facts: In the 1973 season 398 trout of over 7 pounds were registered at the Nahuel Haupí Fishing and Hunting Association. Bear in mind that this is a small local club and doesn't reflect the tourist catch. Of these, 123 weighed over 12 pounds and the two largest were a 24-pound brown trout and a 26-pound rainbow trout. Among the qualifying fish were 22 brook trout exceeding 7 pounds. The majority fell to spoons and spinning lures, but a good percentage were taken on flies. The 24-pound brownie was caught on a fly in the lake's outlet river, the Limay, in one of the big pools about 6 miles downstream.

On the way from Bariloche the road crosses another two rivers. The first one is the River Traful, the original home of the landlocked salmon in the Argentine. The initial shipment of landlocked salmon from Lake Sebago in Maine met with a number of difficulties which delayed the transport, which was done by mule cart, the nearest railway station being about four hundred miles away, and in the end to avoid total loss of the shipment due to the lack of cooling material, the whole load was dumped into this river, being the nearest one.

Historically, the Traful River, from its confluence with the Limay River upstream to its source at Lake Traful, provided exceptional salmon fishing until about 1950. The stream average then was eight pounds, and fifteen such fish in a day were quite ordinary. Due to heavy fishing pressure the catch from these waters now is quite modest. In the spring month of November, anglers still hook sizable landlocks as well as trout in the lake and at the mouths of tributary streams, but the summer fishery has declined all along the Traful River. The best stretch is the first five miles immediately below Lake Traful. A few large salmon from 8–12 pounds with the uncommon large rainbow are taken early or late in the season.

The other river crossed by the road to Junín de los Andes is the Caleufú, and, because this river is almost inaccessible during the greater part of its course, it yields trout of considerable size. Nearing Junín de los Andes the road passes Lake Meliquina, which is famous for its number of fish caught there yearly during the fishing season. According to the log of the Club de Pesca Norysur, which has the fishing rights in this lake, an average of over six thousand fish is the rule, mostly rainbows but with a good sprinkling of brook trout and landlocked salmon. However, the average weight has shown a decrease over the last four or five years. Next the road passes through the town of San Martin de los Andes on the eastern end at Lake Lacar, which empties into the Pacific through the River Huahun, another excellent trout stream. San Martin has excellent hotels, and the fishermen who appreciate their comfort are advised to make this place their headquarters, though it means an additional forty-minute drive to some of the rivers mentioned above.

NORTH OF BARILOCHE

From the standpoint of accessibility and quality of angling, the village of Junín de los Andes is the ideal headquarters for visiting anglers. It is approximately 125 miles north of San Carlos de Bariloche. In Junín de los Andes the place to stay is the Hostería Chimehuin, a scant few yards from the shores of the river of the same name. This hostelry is the meeting place of an international brotherhood of fly-fishermen, and during the height of the season almost every civilized tongue can be heard around the dinner tables—though English is the prevailing language. The only problem which confronts the fisherman is the lack of transport, and he would be well-advised to engage the services of a guide with car, though in an emergency he can always get a helping hand from fellow anglers. From the village one can fish the Malleo, Quilquihue, Collon-Curá, Chimehuin, and Aluminé. These are all large streams and ideal for fly-fishing. Rainbow trout predominate, but brown trout are abundant. The best fishing period depends on the amount of snow melt. In a year when the snowfall has been normal, the season, which begins on the first day of November and lasts until the third week of April, can be divided according to the preference the angler has in his fishing methods. During the first two months the rivers are full of water with the runoff from the melting snows in the mountains. This is the best time for spinning and bait-casting in the rivers and trolling in the lakes. During the next two months, the midseason, this type of sport declines somewhat, and the fly-fisherman has an ever-increasing chance through the rest of the season when the rivers carry less and less water and the fish become more concentrated in the pools and deeper runs. An outstanding fishing spot in this area is the *boca* or the outlet of the river Chimehuin from the lake Huetchalafquen, where brown trout up to twenty-

The wading angler can catch large trout within the city of Bariloche around the mouths of tributary rivers

four pounds have been caught. Another excellent place is the confluence of the Malleo River with the Aluminé River, a tremendous pool, which toward evening produces big brown trout and during the day rainbow trout of considerable size. For quantity (trout between 2 and 2¼ pounds) it would be hard to beat the Collon-Curá River, and the experienced angler should have no trouble in getting one or two rather large fish during a day's outing.

West of Lake Huetchalafquen and directly connected with it are two more lakes, Paimun and Epulafquen, both good fishing grounds. North of Junín, in a stretch of 150 miles, are several more lakes, the most important of which are Lake Quillen with the river of the same name flowing into the Aluminé River, and Lake Aluminé, the most northern of the Argentine lake district giving birth to the river of the same name. The fishing in Quillen yields a surprisingly great number of rainbow trout of ½–1 pound, and for some reason insect life along this stream is more abundant than in other parts, and dry-fly-fishing is much more successful. Most of the better fishing in Lake Aluminé takes place on the western end, and the average weight is considerably higher than caught in lake and river Quillen.

SOUTH OF BARILOCHE

South of Bariloche the chain of lakes continues for many hundreds of miles to the southernmost point of the continent, most of the waters emptying into the Pacific Ocean. Because of the dispute about the border location between Argentina and Chile, the Argentine thesis of "high points" against the Chilean claim of "watershed" was adopted with the result that in many places the watersheds are deep in either Argentine or Chilean territory. From an angler's point of view it is interesting to observe that, due to the absence of streams on the Argentine side of the Andes, fly-fishing becomes almost impossible only a few hundred miles south of Bariloche and even bait-casting and trolling are unsuccessful in many lakes. However, there are brook trout in these waters, caught generally with live bait. The first lakes to the south, Mascardi, Hess, Fonck, and Roca, belong to the Manso system and are good fishing grounds. The Manso River, from which the system derives its name, after passing through lakes Stefen and Martin, crosses the border into Chile forming several cascades up to sixty feet high, before emptying into the Pacific Ocean. Due to the migratory habits of the rainbow trout very few, if any, large fish are ever caught in these waters. However, brown trout of over fifteen pounds are no rarity and are generally found close to the *boca* or river outlets of the aforementioned lakes. This same observation holds true, with certain reservations mentioned before about the fruitlessness of sporting methods in a great number of lakes farther south, for all the rest of the lake district. After a series of isolated lakes, all emptying into the Pacific—the more important ones being Lake Puelo near El Bolson, a small town with good hotels, and Lake Epuyen, which produces reasonably good fishing by trolling—we come to the next bigger system of Futalafquen, which comprises Lakes Cholila, Rivadavia, Menendez, Verde, Kruger, Futalafquen, and Situación.

SOUTH OF FUTALAFQUEN

Southernmost Argentina is difficult of access and variable in quality. The most outstanding rivers are the Gallegos, Santa Cruz, and Penitente for brown and rainbow trout and a late-season run of sea trout. There are no central headquarters in this region. Ordinarily, one would have to plan on driving and camping out. Of the lakes in southern Patagonia, Lake General Paz, Lake Fontana, and Lake Cardiel are excellent fisheries. General Paz is remarkable for its production of big brook trout (3–8 pounds), but it's a vast, wind-swept body of water with the better locations on the Chilean side. Lake Fontana is the only watershed which drains into the Argentine through the Alto Senguerr River; although Fontana also produces large brook trout and the river supports good rainbows, it is eventually absorbed in the dry sandy soil of Patagonia. This is the last body of water which maintains rainbow trout for many hundreds of miles, although there are a great number of huge lakes to the south. At about two hundred miles from the end of the continent you again find fish-bearing rivers, such as the aforementioned Gallegos, Santa Cruz, and Penitente. Here, the weather has an important bearing on the angling possibilities as the infamous Patagonian winds lash these open streams almost continually. However, large sea trout (brown trout) occur in all the major watersheds, and fish up to fifteen pounds are occasionally caught.

FLY-FISHING METHODS

In the selection of trout flies for fishing in Argentina, it should be realized that mayfly hatches are the exception rather than the rule. Although there is an abundance of aquatic insects in many streams, the larger fish rarely seek their food at the surface. The main item of trout diet in Argentinian streams is the "cangrejo," a small freshwater crab (*Aegla*) which is ordinarily 1–1½ inches in diameter. There are true crayfish present also, but the more abundant crab is consumed in such quantities

that the stomach of a big trout sometimes feels like a sack of gravel. As a result, the flesh of Argentinian trout is a brilliant red, the coloration deriving from dietary fat-soluble carotenoids found in crustaceans. A dark Woolly Worm is about as effective an imitation of the crab as any, particularly when the hackle is given a pumping action in short, quick jerks on the retrieve. Streamer flies in black, brown, tan, and dull green probably score for the same reason, as one seldom finds fish remains in the stomachs of river trout. The concept of fly-fishing, therefore, must be modified to be effective. This change of tactics becomes even more apparent when one observes the surface of an Andean river rushing down the valley, presenting a succession of rapids and white water and only rarely developing into placid pools on its way to the ocean. Ideally, these are wet-fly and streamer-fly rivers. It is not implied that a dry fly, given the appropriate circumstances, cannot be used to good advantage, but it is always limited by prevailing wind and water conditions whereas a sunken fly will give results at all times, if properly handled. Although the importance of shape and size of the fly cannot be denied, its success or failure depends mainly on the way the fly is worked in the water to attract the fish. As a rule the darker flies are the more effective ones. The range of size gives plenty of latitude to the preferences of the individual angler but is, to some extent, dictated by the characteristics of the water to be fished. Barring certain exceptions, the larger the body of water the bigger the fly required. Popular sizes range from No. 8 to No. 4 with a No. 6 hook probably the most universal selection. There are also many opportunities to use outsized (1/0 to 3/0) streamers, especially when fishing for big brown trout toward evening.

The local fly-tying industry produces a great variety of wet flies and streamers which are appropriate for the different conditions prevailing in the lakes and streams in this country. Many popular United States patterns give excellent results also.

DORADO FISHING

The best and most accessible place in Argentina for dorado fishing is the Parana River. Flowing for 2,796 miles, the Parana begins in Brazil and forms the international boundary between Brazil, Paraguay, and Argentina. The river heads generally southwest and finally joins the Rio de la Plata in Argentina. Dorado in this river system exceed 70 pounds (the present rod-and-reel record is 75 pounds). A 20-pounder is very ordinary, and when conditions are right it's not unusual to catch three or four fish of 30 pounds or more in one day. Dorado were taken commercially for years, but Argentinian sportsmen finally succeeded in elevating the dorado to gamefish status. It is the official national fish symbolically, and market fishing is strictly controlled.

The season for dorado fishing in Argentina is from the beginning of August until late in October. Although it is true that some fish may be caught during the summer months after November 1st, as a rule the Parana floods in the warm rainy season and it would be only by some freak weather condition that you would find any angling.

The tipoff to the best period are the many dorado "fiestas." Each year some thirty-odd fishing clubs along the Parana River in Argentina hold their annual Fiesta Nacional del Dorado—a dorado fishing contest that lasts for several days. The various Clubes des Pescadores are partisan bands representing townships on the river. Most have a clubhouse, marina, restaurant, and other facilities. Their competition is fierce; from 100-200 anglers divided into teams sally forth and give the golden one a fit. It's as much a social event as a contest, ending in a great dorado *asado* with split fish sputtering over the coals and the *vino* flowing like Niagara.

August and September are winter months at this latitude. The weather is cool with temperatures ranging from 45°–65°F.; and one is well advised to bring along a heavy sweater and rain gear as strong, chilling winds are common. By Christmas the air temperatures from Posados north run above 100°, and insects make life impossible. Stock a repellent even for your winter trip, as this is not only mosquito country but the happy hunting ground of the black-fly-like jejen. *See also* Dorado

—A.J.McC.
—G.S.

ARIZONA A good portion of Arizona is not ideally suited to fishing. There is considerable semiarid desert country, and in many places where stream beds do exist they only hold water after an infrequent thundershower. However, Arizona is the sixth largest state, and within its boundaries are a thousand miles of trout streams running amid beautiful mountains and numerous artificial lakes which produce excellent fishing. Although tourists are familiar with the Grand Canyon, Boulder Dam, the Painted Desert, the petrified forests, and the Navajo Indian Reservation, travelers might also investigate the trout fishing, which produced the state-record rainbow trout of 18 pounds taken at Willow Beach.

TROUT FISHING

Arizona's trout fishing exists in the northern and eastern portions of the state and along the Colorado River in those areas immediately below major power dams. The foremost trout fishery in the state is Big Lake, which is located at the extreme eastern edge of the state amid the spruce-fir forests of the White Mountains. Big Lake features rainbow and brook-trout fishing and is the pride and joy of many Arizona residents. This White Mountain region generally produces the best trout fishing in the state. In addition to Big Lake, it includes Luna Lake, Becker Lake, Nelson Reservoir, Lyman Reservoir, and Lee Valley Lake. All of these contain rainbows with the exception of Lee Valley, which is strictly a brook-trout fishery. Because the elevation ranges from seven to nine thousand feet, most of these waters are subject to freezing during the winter time. In the eastern portion of the White Mountains, Rainbow Lake, Show Low Lake, Fool's Hollow Lake, and several smaller lakes provide top-quality rainbow-trout fishing.

The White Mountain area also offers stream fishing, and among the top streams are White River, Black River, and the Little Colorado River, along with their smaller tributaries. None of Arizona's trout streams is large enough to maintain its own trout; so while there are carry-overs in all of them, the volume of the fishing consists of hatchery-planted rainbows.

Another popular trout-fishing area is that part of the White Mountain area which is located on the Fort Apache Indian Reservation. The Apache tribe, with the help of the U.S. Fish and Wildlife Service, keeps its streams and lakes well-stocked with rainbows. The White River flows through a major portion of the reservation and forms most of the stream fishing there. Among reservation lakes which offer good trout fishing are Hawley, Drift Fence, Tonto, and Pacheta. Indian Reservation permits are required to fish in these waters in addition to regular Arizona state fishing licenses.

Northcentral Trout Fishing Second in importance to trout fishermen is the northcentral portion of the state. Here again, the big producers of trout fishing are the lakes, and among the most popular are Ashurst, Kinnikinick, Woods Canyon, and White Horse. A number of small lakes also dot the region, but the bulk of the fishing effort is directed at these waters.

The two major stream drainages which provide trout fishing in northcentral Arizona are Oak Creek and Tonto Creek. Each of these, along with their tributaries, is stocked regularly with rainbow trout. While the rainbow is the most common trout in Arizona, browns occur in varying quantities in all of the streams and quite a few of the lakes. Brown trout are not stocked as frequently, however, since rainbows are much easier to raise in the hatcheries and so much easier to catch once they are planted. Fishing for brown trout is usually better during the early spring and fall months.

Another salmonid which can be found in Arizona is the kokanee. This fish has been planted in Ashurst Lake and in Luna Lake. Arizona also has its own native trout, the Gila trout (*which see*). This species has hybridized with the rainbow in most of its natural range, but it can still be found as a pure strain near the headwaters of some of the smaller White Mountain streams. The native exists throughout Grant Creek, which is located atop Mount Graham in the southeastern part of the state. Grant Creek was selected for maintaining the species because it is a complete drainage in itself with no source of access by other fish species.

Colorado River Trout Fishing The other major trout fishing in Arizona is found on the Colorado River in those areas immediately below Hoover Dam and Davis Dam. These are both good producers of large rainbows and are managed cooperatively by the Game and Fish Departments of Arizona and Nevada and the U. S. Fish and Wildlife Service. The Fish and Wildlife Service has recently completed a new hatchery at Willow Beach just below Hoover Dam; prospects for the future seem to indicate even better trout fishing in these waters.

Further upstream on the Colorado River several small streams at the bottom of the canyon offer primitive trout fishing for the angler who is willing to hike or ride a mule to the bottom of the Grand Canyon. However, the newest trout fishery on the river is located immediately below Glen Canyon Dam near the Arizona-Utah border. This portion of stream was stocked in the spring of 1963. It is excellent trout habitat amid unsurpassed scenery. Entrance to this area is limited, with Lee's Ferry being the only major access point at this time.

Lake Powell, which is formed behind Glen Canyon Dam, is stocked with rainbow trout as well as with largemouth bass. Fishery biologists who have studied the drainage cannot accurately predict what the future water conditions will be in Lake Powell; so they have prepared for any eventuality by stocking both coldwater and warmwater species.

THE COLORADO RIVER LAKES

The major warmwater area of Arizona is the Colorado River and its chain of lakes. Beginning at Glen Canyon (most of which is in Utah) the river offers large-mouth bass as the leading warmwater species. Few bass are found in the river itself below Glen Canyon Dam, although the Lee's Ferry area has been providing excellent fishing for channel catfish. Once the river reaches Lake Mead, however, it offers warmwater fishing ranging from modest to excellent. The upper end of Lake Mead near Pierce's Ferry is the favorite grounds of most cat-fish anglers, but over the bulk of the lake the large-mouth bass reigns supreme. The year-round, average fisherman-catch on largemouth bass from Lake Mead is ½ fish per hour. This figure includes not only the expert but also the dude who has just picked up a fishing rod for the first time. During the spring months the crappie moves into the limelight, and excellent fishing can be found somewhere on Lake Mead from the first of February through the end of May.

Below Mead, on the Colorado, is Lake Mohave. In its upper reaches (the Willow Beach area), Mohave is primarily trout water, but further south the water warms up sufficiently to produce some real lunker largemouths. Mohave also contains crappie, catfish, and panfish, but the trout and the bass are the main attractions there. During the winter months large rainbows can often be taken from deeper water near the lower end of the lake. Apparently these fish move downstream following the cold currents in the old river bed. Until recently, very few fishermen were aware of this, but during the winter some limit catches of 3-4-pound rainbows are caught by bass fishermen. Cutthroat trout have also been planted in Lake Mohave.

Immediately below Davis Dam, which forms Lake Mohave, is the Bullhead City fishery, Rainbows in the 12–15-pound class have been taken here on numerous occasions. Further downstream the river slows and broadens to form Lake Havasu, which is characteristi-cally a sporadic lake as far as fishing is concerned. Hava-su frequently offers excellent fishing for crappies, bass, and catfish, but success there sometimes jumps from high to low within a relatively short period of time. Havasu has been stocked with striped bass. After investigating the Santee-Cooper project in South Carolina, Arizona fisheries biologists decided the conditions there were similar to those in Lake Havasu. As a result, Arizona and California co-operated in planting stripers in the lake.

Below Parker Dam, which forms Lake Havasu, the Colorado River winds for a hundred miles or so in a leisurely fashion and throughout this length generally provides good fishing for bass and catfish. Striped bass have also been planted here by the California Department of Fish and Game, and some very good catches have been made in the Palo Verde area of the river. By the time the river reaches Lake Martinez it has broad-ened out to provide a number of highly exciting fingers, channels, coves, and hidden bays which are practically untouched by fishermen. In addition to fine angling for bass and catfish, this portion of the river provides the

A fly fisherman enjoys the magic of the evening rise in the mountain country of Arizona

panfisherman with large quantities of overgrown blue-gills as well as seasonal catches of large crappies during the spring months. This area of the Colorado River is probably one of the most untapped fishing resources in the continental United States. Except for local anglers, very few fishermen try their luck there. The regional personnel of the Arizona Game and Fish Department insist that the area could stand many times the fishing pressure it presently receives.

CENTRAL ARIZONA FISHING

With the exception of the Colorado River and its lakes, Arizona's finest warmwater fishing is found within a hundred-mile radius of the state's population center. This fishing is provided by the Salt River chain of lakes and four individual lakes.

Beginning at Phoenix and working eastward along the Salt River, the first lake on the chain is Saguaro. This lake is a week-end haven for water skiers, speedboaters, and other water enthusiasts, but it still manages to provide some excellent fishing. Fishery managers claim Saguaro's bass population is underharvested. Saguaro also provides some lunker catfish for the nighttime angler, plus excellent panfishing for the angler who locates a school of yellow bass. These fish only average ten inches or so, but they can be caught by the boatload, and in addition to being one of the scrappiest fish in the lake, they are unsurpassed in the frying pan. Just above Saguaro Lake is Canyon Lake, which suffers from the same week-end congestion of water-sports enthusiasts. It still manages, though, to provide bass, catfish, and yellow-bass fishing and occasionally produces large catches of kingsize bluegills to the fly-rod man.

The next lake in the chain is Apache, which contains a hodgepodge of fish species. The three that offer the most fishing, though, are bass, catfish, and crappies—in that order. Apache Lake does not have abundant numbers of bass, but the odds of catching a lunker are better on this lake than on most of the others in the area. Some very large channel catfish are also taken from Apache Lake, and when the crappie cycle is high, fishermen frequently take strings of seventy-five to one hundred.

At the top of the Salt River chain is the granddaddy of them all, Roosevelt Lake. This is one of the most productive bass lakes in the Southwest and is a favorite of most Central Arizona fishermen. In addition to the bass, Roosevelt offers excellent catfishing and crappie fishing. While Apache Lake is not subject to heavy weekend use by water skiers and power boaters because of its inaccessibility, Roosevelt is accessible but suffers no congestion because of its size. At average water level, Roosevelt is about 18 miles long and 1–4 miles wide.

Another high-producing bass lake in Central Arizona is San Carlos Reservoir, located about thirty miles east of Globe on the Gila River. San Carlos produces bass much faster than fishermen can remove them. The only problem is that the lake is sucked dry for irrigation purposes almost every summer. The engineers who planned the dam overestimated the amount of runoff it would receive. When the lake goes dry, the Game and Fish Department restocks it with spawners, but fishing has to wait for about a year to recover.

Lake Carl Pleasant, northwest of Phoenix, is a highly productive bass fishery, but it too suffers from low water most of the time. The bass there are always numerous, though, and they weigh more per inch of length than any other bass in the state. The lake also contains white crappies and channel catfish, along with bluegills and other panfish.

The Verde River, which flows southward through central Arizona, provides some bass fishing, including a few smallmouths, and good catfishing over most of its length. Two dams block its progress as it nears the Salt River Valley. These are Horseshoe, which is nearly always dry, and Bartlett. Horseshoe itself has not provided real fishing in recent years, but the river immediately below it produces bass and catfish. Bartlett Lake is an excellent bass and catfish fishery, and has recently been stocked with black crappies.

The only other warmwater lake worth particular notice is Peña Blanca Lake, which was constructed in 1956 by the Game and Fish Department. Peña Blanca has turned out to be an excellent fishery for bass, catfish, and crappies, but its small size of fifty acres prevents it from being a major fishery. Peña Blanca also provides put-and-take trout fishing during the winter months.

Arizona bass fishermen follow the same general rules bass fishermen follow anywhere else during the spring and summer months, but in the Southwest the "bottom scratching" techniques are the rule during the winter. These skirted, jig-type lures and rubber-worm lures are fished very slowly along the bottom and, when presented properly, will result in some excellent catches. In most waters, the larger bass are taken near the bottom. Bait-fishermen use waterdogs and minnows to fill their stringers. —B.Sr.

ARIZONA TROUT *See* Apache Trout

ARKANSAS The Land of Opportunity offers a wide variety of fishing from swift mountain streams to flatland bayous. The ascendancy of Arkansas as a leading angling state is largely due to a vast program of reservoir construction. Historically, warmwater fishing, particularly for black bass, has been most significant, but through water-resources development coldwater habitats were also created which provide unusual trout fishing. With the great increase of total surface acreage available to the public both the quality and the quantity of the annual game and panfish harvest far exceeds that of years past.

CORPS OF ENGINEERS IMPOUNDMENTS

Arkansas has always had its share of natural lakes, sloughs, bayous, and streams, but the addition of man-made reservoirs and public fishing lakes are what has pushed the state into prominence. Although fishing is incidental to the primary purpose for constructing most of these impoundments, practically all are open to public fishing. The large flood-control and hydroelectric reservoirs have played a major part in placing the state near the top in the number of nonresident fishing licenses purchased. The oldest lakes of this kind are the 1,600-acre Lake Catherine, constructed in 1924, and the 4,000-acre Lake Hamilton, constructed in 1931. Both of these lakes are located near Hot Springs and were constructed by the Arkansas Power and Light Company.

The U.S. Corps of Engineers began its lake construction in connection with flood control and development of electric power by constructing the 3,600-acre Nimrod Reservoir near Plainview in 1942. Its type of soil, depth of water, and other habitat conditions must be close to ideal for crappie because Nimrod soon became, and has remained, one of the best places to fish for crappie in the whole state. Nimrod, like all other large impoundments, also supports good populations of largemouth bass, bream, catfish, and other varieties of warmwater fish. The second lake constructed by the Corps of Engineers is the 22,000-acre Norfork Reservoir near Mountain Home which was completed in 1944. The corps then completed the 2,900-acre Blue Mountain Reservoir near Booneville in 1947 and in 1950 completed the 7,260-acre Lake Greeson near Murfreesboro. Bull Shoals, with its Arkansas portion covering 35,000 acres near Mountain Home, Flippin, and Lead Hill, was completed in 1952. The largest impoundment which is entirely within the state is the 40,100-acre Lake Ouachita near Hot Springs and Mount Ida which was completed in 1953. Most of the Table Rock Reservoir, which was completed in 1958, is in Missouri, but the upper 4,000 acres are in Arkansas near Eureka Springs. The 31,500-acre Greer's Ferry Reservoir near Heber Springs was completed in 1962. Beaver Reservoir, which will flood 28,000 acres near Rogers and Fayetteville, is almost completed. Other corps projects under construction are De Gray Dam on the Caddo River near Arkadelphia and the Millwood Dam on Little River near Ashdown.

The Corps of Engineers is also well on the way toward providing a tremendous addition in good places to fish by the multipurpose development of the Arkansas River. The Dardanelle Dam is nearing completion and will soon impound water on 37,000 acres. Construction is also beginning on the navigation locks and dams on the lower portion of the river. The river development will transform the entire river into a series of lakes. The 3,000-acre impoundment near the junction of the Arkansas and White Rivers is expected to have all the habitat conditions necessary for highly productive fishing water.

This impoundment will be adjacent to the newly created Arkansas Post National Monument, which is the site of the first white settlement west of the Mississippi River. Plans are being made to provide adequate public access to all of the Arkansas River impoundments.

STATE LAKES

The aggressive program of the Arkansas Game and Fish Commission for public fishing lake construction has put fishing water in portions of the state where it was most needed. Lake Conway, twenty miles north of Little Rock, has a surface area of 6,700 acres and was constructed by the commission in 1948. It not only is by far the largest lake of its kind in the entire nation but also is one of the best for bream, bass, and crappie. Eighteen commercial boat docks, with free launching for privately owned boats, help supply boat rentals, bait, tackle, and other needs for sportsmen. Modern fisheries management techniques, such as complete or partial periodic drainage, use of chemicals, and the corrective stocking of fish following other practices, are employed at Lake Conway and all other commission-owned lakes without having to take into consideration anything except what is best for angling. No license is required for fishermen under sixteen years of age, and the regular resident or nonresident fishing license is all that is required for adults to fish on these lakes. There is no special fee or special regulations of any kind. Local and nonresident fishermen alike seem especially to appreciate the fact that water skiing and speedboating are prohibited on all commission-owned lakes.

The next largest commission-constructed lake is the 2,700-acre White Oak Lake completed in 1958 near Camden. This lake is a two-level lake with water in the lower lake backing up against the dam for the upper lake. This feature facilitates manipulation of water levels for fisheries management. The 1,305-acre Harris Brake Lake near Perryville and the 752-acre Lake Atkins near Atkins were constructed in 1956. The 720-acre Bois d'Arc Lake near Hope was constructed in 1961, and the 620-acre Halowell Reservoir near Stuttgart was constructed in 1959. The 560-acre Distress Creek Lake near Harrisburg, the 500-acre Lake Pine Bluff, located at the back door of the County Court House, and the 320-acre Lake Greenlee near Brinkley were constructed in 1962. The 530-acre Seven Devils Lake near Monticello and the 324-acre Sugar Loaf Lake near Fort Smith were constructed in 1954. The 300-acre Lake Wilhelmina near Mena was constructed in 1958. All of these lakes, except Seven Devils, have commercial boat docks. Some of the smaller commission-constructed lakes not listed also have commercial boat docks.

The Soil Conservation Service has completed the construction of the 720-acre Lake Charles near Walnut Ridge. This lake is part of a small watershed flood-control project. The Arkansas Game and Fish Commission has paid the additional costs which were necessary to make this lake large enough to serve as a public fishing lake. There are other small lakes on this same watershed, and the Soil Conservation Service has also constructed other small lakes in various parts of the state.

Two other important artificial lakes are the 625-acre Bear Creek Lake near Marianna and the 600-acre Storm Creek Lake near Helena. Both of these lakes are on Crow-

leys Ridge inside the beautiful St. Francis National Forest. They are especially popular with people living in Memphis. Still another important artificial lake is Grand Marie Lake near Huttig. This lake is part of the old navigation system on the lower Ouachita River. It is best known to the sportsmen in southern Arkansas and northern Louisiana, however, as a wonderful place in which to fish.

OVERFLOW LAKES

All the natural lakes in Arkansas are old oxbows resulting from a change in location of a river or stream. The best natural lake fishing is to be had in those lakes which are still subject to the overflow of rivers and bayous and some distance from areas where agricultural chemicals are being used extensively. Many lakes of this kind still exist in the overflow bottoms of White River, particularly in and around the 117,000-acre White River National Wildlife Refuge near St. Charles. Good overflow bottom lakes also are found elsewhere along White River from the mouth to above Newport. The bottom lands adjacent to the Cache, Black, Ouachita, Arkansas, and Mississippi Rivers also contain lakes and sloughs which provide excellent bass, bream, crappie, and catfish fishing. Fishing success in the overflow lakes is highly dependent upon water conditions. Fishing is usually best shortly after the overflow water has receded within the banks of the river. Local sportsmen keep a close watch on river gauges. When the White River recedes to seventeen feet on the Clarendon gauge they know that most of the lakes on the lower White are ready. This usually occurs in May or June. These lakes are most famous for bass, but the brief period when pecan worms are falling or when the willow bugs are hatching can afford some fabulous bream fishing. It is not too unusual to see bream jump clear out of the water after a falling worm or bug. On rare occasions bream have been caught above the surface of the water by fishermen who accidentally get their bait or lure hung in a bush a couple of inches above the water.

Norfolk Lake is one of the more popular spots for largemouth, smallmouth, and spotted bass

Some lakes which are no longer subjected to overflow water are also very good. These lakes, which are inside the levee, like the protected farm land, are likely to be in fishing condition during the time that the overflow lakes are unsuitable. Lake Chicot adjacent to Lake Village and Grand Lake near Eudora are two of the best crappie lakes in the state. Both are protected from Mississippi River overflow by the levee, but both are subjected to considerable interior drainage. The commission constructed a dam across the upper third of Chicot just above where the drainage water enters. Water above this dam is usually at a higher level and is clear most of the year. Another good lake in this same (southeast) part of the state is beautiful Lake Enterprise, near Wilmot, with its moss-covered cypress trees. Boat docks are on all three of these lakes and also on some of the other similar lakes in other parts of the state.

Gravel roads on top of some portions of the levees on the Mississippi River (near Eudora), or the White River (near Elaine), or the Arkansas River (near Reydel) lead to some fine fishing in borrow pits as well as isolated lakes and sloughs. Some of the other bottomland fishing lakes are difficult to get to, except with a jeep, unless the ground is unusually dry. Fall fishing in the overflow lakes is usually excellent, and the weather in the fall is frequently dry enough to permit driving to many of the lakes and sloughs. Many lakes can also be reached by going up or down the river from the public boat-launching facilities located at Clarendon, DeValls Bluff, Des Arc, and some of the other river towns.

RIVER FISHING

The rivers and streams are the preferred fishing places of many sportsmen. There are numerous small streams all through the northern and western portions of the state which provide smallmouth bass, Kentucky bass, rock bass, longear sunfish, and green sunfish for the fly-, spin-, or bait-caster. Many of these isolated, clear, rock-bottom streams can be waded, especially on the shoals. A boat is required on the lower portions of some of these same streams as well as on all of the larger streams and rivers. West Fork and Middle Fork near Fayetteville, War Eagle near Huntsville, Kings River and Osage near Berryville, Crooked Creek near Harrison, North and South Sylamore near Mountain View, Mulberry River near Cass, Illinois Bayou near Russelville, Archies Fork near Clinton, Spring River near Hardy, Ouachita River near Pine Ridge, Strawberry River near Poughkeepsie, Eleven Point and Current Rivers near Pocahontas, Cossatot near De Queen, Caddo near Caddo Gap, North, Alum, and Middle Fork of Saline River near Benton, and another Saline River near Dierks are just a few of the more appealing streams. In addition to these streams in the mountainous or hilly portions of the state there are also streams in eastern and southern Arkansas which are excellent. Cache River near De Valls Bluff is recognized as being one of the best in eastern Arkansas. Boats are available for rent on the Cache and on some of the other more important streams and bayous but not on the smaller streams.

The most picturesque of all streams is the Buffalo. All who have ever float-fished the Buffalo have been impressed by its spectacular bluffs and by its unspoiled wilderness beauty. Float-fishing is a popular method of fishing by floating with the current from one access point to another one located farther down the stream. Arrangements have to be made to have someone either move your vehicle or meet you in another one at the take-out point. Many of the streams can be float-fished, but guide service is now almost limited to the Buffalo and other nearby streams.

The construction, by the Corps of Engineers, of the big dams has increased manyfold the production of fish and attraction of fishermen. At the same time, however, it has eliminated float- and other fishing on large portions of some of the streams. It has also changed the temperature of water below the dams, and this change has resulted in the establishment of a remarkable trout fishery. The U.S. Bureau of Sports Fisheries and Wildlife operates a large trout hatchery below Norfolk Dam, and the commission assists in distributing the fish along the more than one hundred miles of trout water. Approximately 175,000 pounds of trout, mostly 6 to 11 inches long, are placed in Arkansas trout waters every year. An abundant food supply enables rapid growth. Rainbows and brownies have been caught which exceed 15 pounds. Excellent facilities and guide service are available to serve both trout and lake fishermen in the Bull Shoals-Norfolk area. The bureau is also going to operate a trout hatchery at Greer's Ferry to maintain trout fishing below the dam in Little Red River. Trout also are stocked in the Little Missouri below Greeson Reservoir, in the Ouachita River below Lake Ouachita, in Blanchard Springs Creek near Mountain View, and in a few other streams.

Alligator gar fishing is perhaps the most unique fishing that the state has to offer. It takes saltwater tackle to land a medium-size one, and some of the large ones exceed 200 pounds. Gar fishing is most popular on the lower White River, but the big fish can also be found in the Arkansas, Red River near Texarkana, and in the lower Ouachita. Guide service is available at Stuttgart and at De Witt.

The fisheries production and management program of the commission plays a major part in making fishing good. The commission's Lonoke Hatchery has long been recognized as the largest of its kind. In all probability, however, the smallest of the three warmwater hatcheries is larger than any outside the state. Of more importance is the fact that practically all of the tremendous hatchery production is now being utilized in new impoundments or in waters which have received special fisheries management treatment. More than a million gamefish, including six tons of adult bass, were placed in Greer's Ferry Lake when it first started filling with water. This all-important initial stocking assures that gamefish will not be suppressed by the more prolific rough fish. Another million gamefish were placed in Lake Hamilton following a partial drawdown and a chemical application to eradicate most of the existing fish population.

—T.H.H.

BULL SHOALS LAKE

The Bull Shoals impoundment was created in 1951. It was formed by backing up the waters of the White River of the Arkansas-Missouri Ozarks behind the fifth largest concrete dam in the country. The project required four years and seven months to complete. The lake is eighty-seven miles long, the major portion of which, including the dam, is located in northcentral Arkansas. But the upper reaches of the impoundment extend across the border into the southern Missouri Ozarks.

There are twelve commercial boat docks with adjacent picnic and camping areas where anglers may obtain rental boats, motors, tackle, and guide service. Some 250 overnight establishments are located in the vicinity of the reservoir with accommodations for more than 5,865 guests per day. Some of these resorts and motels also have docking facilities for guests. Motel and resort accommodations are reasonably priced. Paved or all-weather roads lead off the main highways into the resort communities. A number of small towns are within a few miles of the lake, among them being Mountain Home, Bull Shoals, and Lakeview, Arkansas, and Gainesville and Forsyth, Missouri.

There is no closed season on fishing in Bull Shoals Lake, and the water never freezes over. It is an ultra-clear lake, due to the rocky, forested terrain and the fact that White River (its feeder source) has always been one of the clearest streams in the Ozarks.

Bull Shoals Lake is nationally famous for the largemouth bass it produces. During a reporting period of 228 weeks over 25,000 bass in the 4–13-pound class were recorded. These fish were caught on jigs and eels, spinner-type baits, live bait, underwater and surface plugs, and plastic worms. Other species of fish for which the impoundment is noted are spotted (Kentucky) bass, smallmouth bass, white bass, crappies, walleyes, bluegills, and channel catfish.

Due to its hilly confines, Bull Shoals is not spread out over wide, flat areas. Its greatest width approximates three miles and is much narrower in other portions. The lake is over 200 feet deep in the vicinity of the dam, and the length of the shoreline at normal power-pool level is 740 miles. It is a federal project, formed primarily for flood-control and electric-power development, but has bloomed into great popularity as a major recreational area.

WHITE RIVER

White River, which was dammed to form Bull Shoals Lake late in 1951 and Table Rock Lake several years later, has long been regarded as one of the finest fishing streams in the nation, having been especially noted for the smallmouth-bass fishing it produced prior to construction of the dams. The species now furnishing the sport that has attracted anglers from all over the nation is trout, rather than smallmouth bass. The flow of water from under the dams is much colder than formerly (approximately 52°F. the year around) and, as a consequence, has become an excellent habitat for rainbow and brown trout. The stream has been stocked with great numbers of these fish, rainbows in particular, since the completion of Bull Shoals Dam, and prior thereto behind Norfolk Dam, the latter having been completed in 1944. The Norfolk Dam is on the North Fork of the White, which runs into the latter stream approximately four miles distant.

During a reporting period of 261 weeks a total of 4,253 trout in the 4–17-pound weight class was recorded

Float fishing the White River is a family affair. Trips that combine camping with trout fishing are very popular

from catch reports. A North American record for brown trout (31½ pounds) was taken here in 1971. Limit strings of smaller trout are commonplace. Float-trip operators are located on the White from Bull Shoals Dam downstream sixty miles or more. They conduct trips lasting from one to several days and nights, depending on the desires of the anglers. The scenic appeal of the Ozarks as well as the excellence of the fishing has made these trips very popular in recent years. Guides and commissary men attend to all the details of setting up camps on the gravelbars and preparing meals.

White River is an ultraclear stream. It is several hundred feet wide in places, but narrower in most stretches. The current normally is not overly swift, nor is it very deep except in some of the larger, longer pools. The bottom can be seen in many places. Float-fishermen catch trout over a distance in excess of seventy miles below Bull Shoals Dam; however, most of the fishing is done over a forty-mile stretch below the dam.

There is no closed season on the White, but artificial lures only are permitted during the months of November, December, January, and February. During the other eight months the most commonly used lures are earthworms, crayfish tails, minnows, plastic worms, small spinners and flies, spoons, and plugs. Spinning and baitcasting equipment are most popular.

The Buffalo River, a major tributary of the White, is now the principal smallmouth-bass stream. White River operators conduct float trips on the Buffalo as well as the White. Both streams can be float-fished on a daily or overnight basis.

There are good camping areas in Bull Shoals State Park and on White River a mile or so below Bull Shoals Dam, and points downstream.   —S.W.

ARMORED CATFISH Family Loricariidae A large family of catfishes indigenous to northern and central South America. There are many genera, some of which have bony plates covering the body including the ventral surface; others are naked on the lower side. The first group also has an adipose fin, while the second does not.

Armored Catfish

The armored catfish was accidentally introduced to Florida and its present range is unknown. Numerous specimens have been caught in creeks, rock pits, and canals north of the Miami area and in the Tampa Bay area, notably 6-mile Creek; these locations coincide with major tropical fish farms. There are many armored catfishes weighing up to 100 pounds, but the genus present in the United States (*Plecostomus*) is apparently one of the smaller members of the family. Like the walking catfish, its distribution has been limited by water temperature. Armored catfish have powerful pectoral spines which serve for locomotion when working forward along the bottom against swift currents. Caught on all the usual catfish baits, it is edible but virtually impossible to clean. Amazonian Indians toss the fish in the fire whole and crack the "shell" to pry loose the meat. —A.J.McC.

ARUANÁ *Osteoglossum bicirrhosum* A freshwater gamefish found in the Amazon watershed from eastern Peru through Brazil and the Guianas. The name (Portuguese) is also given as arahuaná (Spanish) and arowana (the Guianas). The aruaná is a member of the Osteoglossidae, which are represented in South America by one genus, *Osteoglossum*. A second genus, *Heterotis*, is found in tropical Africa; and a third, *Scleropages*, occurs in the Malay Archipelago, New Guinea, and Australia. The latter includes *Scleropages formosus* or the barramundi, a popular Australian gamefish. The aruaná attains a length of 3 feet and a weight of 6–7 pounds. It has an elongate and compressed body; the back is rounded, but the ventral surface is trenchant or bladelike; mouth very large and oblique with small teeth; a pair of soft barbels on the lower jaw (lacking in all other scaled Brazilian freshwater fishes); opercle with a broad membranous edge. The aruaná has large, vertical cycloid scales which decrease in size toward the anal region. The origin of the dorsal fin is nearer to the caudal fin than to the eyes; the anterior rays are feeble. The origin of the anal fin is nearer to the snout than to its last ray. The caudal fin is small and rounded. The ventral fins reach past the origin of the anal, while the pectorals are large, nearly reaching the anal. The fins of the aruaná are pink; the body is a dull silver, each scale with a dark bar bordered with pink. The dorsal fin has 45–48 rays; anal fin 53–57 rays; there are 31–35 scales along the lateral line with 3 rows above and 2.5 rows below. There are 13 gillrakers on the lower gill arch.

LIFE HISTORY

The aruaná inhabits weedy stagnant river backwaters and shallow lakes. Typically, it is found in schools near the surface. At the beginning of the rainy season in the Amazon basin (October) a male and female select a spawning site. When the eggs are fertilized, the female gathers the eggs in its mouth 6–8 days prior to hatching. The larvae receive parental care, returning to the mouth through the branchial openings when disturbed by other predatory species. The coloration of the young is much brighter than that of the adult; the head and body is rose while behind the opercle there is a quadrangular spot bicolored with blue and scarlet. The tail and pelvic fins of immature fish are much longer than in the adult, and the former curves down so that its rays are parallel with the anal rays. Aruaná are piscivorous, although some invertebrates are consumed.

ANGLING VALUE

Due to its size and food value (usually treated as a salted product) the aruaná is eagerly sought by many Amazonian Indian tribes. It is an easy target for the bow and arrow or spear. Aruaná take a variety of artificial lures such as spoons, plugs, and jigs. The aruaná is a strong gamefish, usually making long runs and frequent jumps. Schools are seen cruising slowly at the surface, and casting ahead of the fish brings a fast strike. However, because of its bony mouth the aruaná is difficult to hook and the ratio of strikes to fish landed is extreme. The flattened, elongate body of the aruaná gives the impression of a much heavier fish in the water, but typically a 30-inch specimen weighs about 5½ pounds. —A.J.McC.

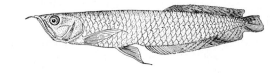

Aruaná

ASTERN Any area behind a given boat, but not in the boat; on a bearing 180 degrees from ahead.

ATLANTIC ANGEL SHARK *Squatina dumerili* A distinctively flattened shark, it has the pectoral fins expanded into winglike structures similar to those of skates. The gill openings are mostly ventrally placed, rather than on the sides as in other sharks. The head is broad and blunt, and the dorsal and caudal fins are small, with the caudal peduncle flattened and expanded. The teeth in both jaws are the same and are thin and pointed, with the conelike cusp on a rounded base. Fresh specimens are bluish-gray or ashy-gray above to brown, with hues of red or purple on the head and fins. The lower parts are white, with a reddish spot on the throat, the belly, and just behind the anal opening. The pelvics are irregularly banded with red. Specimens of 5 feet are reported, and a 4-foot fish weighed about 60 pounds. Its European relative grows to 8 feet and a weight of 170 pounds.

It is a western Atlantic species, known only from southern New England to southern Florida, the northern Gulf of Mexico, and Jamaica, being most abundant between Virginia and Delaware. Specimens have been taken mostly from shallow water, but several have been captured in depths of about 100 and 700 fathoms. It enters brackish water at times, and is commonly found in the lower reaches of estuaries. Apparently it moves into deeper water in the winter, returning in the spring. The angel shark often buries itself in the sand or mud, where it preys on fishes, crustaceans, and gastropod mollusks. The young are presumably born during the summer, in shallow water. The eggs are held within the female until hatching, and 13–25 embryos have been taken. Although a related species is eaten in Europe, there is no commercial use for the western Atlantic species.

DANGER TO MAN

It is a pugnacious species, which, when caught by fishermen, often attempts to bite them, and there is a report of a skin diver being bitten by one after he had speared it. *See* Pacific Angel Shark —D.DS.

ATLANTIC BLUNTNOSE JACK *Hemicaranx amblyrhynchus* This species occurs only in the western Atlantic. A similar form in the eastern Atlantic from off West Africa is considered to be a distinct species, *Hemicaranx bicolor*.

The second dorsal fin of the Atlantic bluntnose jack has one spine and 27–29 softrays. The anal fin has two detached spines followed by one spine and 22–25 softrays. The first gill arch has 8–10 gillrakers on the upper limb and 19–23 gillrakers on the lower limb. The arch or curved part of the lateral line is relatively short; the straight lateral line is about 2½ times as long as the curved lateral line. The straight lateral line has about 45–55 pointed scutes.

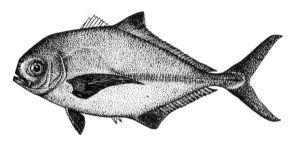

Atlantic Bluntnose Jack

The body is moderately deep and thin, the head short and rounded in anterior profile, and the mouth small. The lobes of the dorsal and anal fin are not elongated. At about 1½–6 inches in length there are four bars on the body and one on the nape. Above six inches in length the body is usually golden yellow with a small dark opercular spot.

This species ranges from Santos, Brazil, northward at least to North Carolina. The largest known specimen is fourteen inches long.

LIFE HISTORY

The life history is not known. The smallest known specimen, just under one inch in total length, was taken in early March at the surface near the sea buoy off Beaufort, North Carolina—near the northern extreme of the known range of the species. The banded young have been reported using jellyfish for shelter. Larger fish are most frequently taken by bottom trawls in moderately shallow water.

There are two species of bluntnose jacks in the eastern Pacific, and both range from about Peru to Magdalena Bay, Baja California. The scientific names of these two are confusing. Studies in progress indicate that they should be *Hemicaranx leucurus*, the Pacific bluntnose jack, and *Hemicaranx atrimanus*, the longfin bluntnose jack. At sizes larger than 6½ inches total length they can be separated by the length of the pelvic fin. In *Hemicaranx leucurus* the pectoral fin is only slightly longer than the head; in *Hemicaranx atrimanus* the pectoral fin is almost 1½ times as long as the head. At smaller sizes *H. leucurus* has only 4–5 bars on the body, and *H. atrimanus* has 6–8 (usually 7). These bars may persist to the larger sizes in certain individuals, but they usually fade out at about 4–5 inches in length, making many intermediate-sized specimens difficult to identify in the field.

ANGLING VALUE

The bluntnose jacks are seldom caught by sport fishermen, but when taken on small jigs or small baited hooks on light tackle, they are very scrappy fighters. *See also* Carangidae, Jacks —F.H.B.

ATLANTIC BONITO *See* Bonito

ATLANTIC BUMPER *Chloroscombrus chrysurus* This Atlantic species is very closely related to the Pacific bumper, *Chloroscombrus orqueta*.

The ventral body contour is much more curved and deeper than the dorsal contour, and the body is very thin. The scutes in the straight lateral line are very weakly developed, only about 7–12 scutes developed out of a total of 61–68 scales in the straight lateral line. The second dorsal fin has one spine and 26–28 softrays. The anal fin has two detached spines followed by a spine and 25–27 softrays. The first gill arch has 9–11 gillrakers on the upper limb and 31–35 gillrakers on the lower limb. There is a black spot on the upper part of the base of the caudal fin; the body is dark above, light silvery or golden below; a faint black opercular spot is usually present.

LIFE HISTORY

The life history is inadequately known. Ripe females were reported in June and running ripe males and females were taken together in August from Texas. Very small fish are frequently found in offshore waters, specimens larger than one inch in length are abundant along sandy beaches, and large fish are common in schools around pilings. The young often occur swimming in association with jellyfish. When caught, the bumper frequently emits a grunting noise by pharyngeal stridulation.

In the western Atlantic this species ranges from Massachusetts to Uruguay. It occurs at Bermuda and in the eastern Atlantic from at least Senegal to Angola. In the western Atlantic it reaches a length of 10 inches. In the eastern Atlantic, specimens 12 inches long have been recorded, but the species is reported to grow much larger.

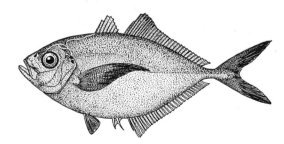

Atlantic Bumper

ANGLING VALUE

This fish is occasionally caught still-fishing or trolling. It is generally not valued as food; the flesh has been described as thin and dry with large bones.

The very similar Pacific bumper, *Chloroscombrus orqueta*, also called *xurel de castilla*, is recorded from Chilca, Peru, to San Pedro, California, and at Cocos Island. Limited amounts are sold for food in Mexico. *See also* Carangidae, Jacks —F.H.B.

ATLANTIC COD *Gadus morhua* This important member of the cod family Gadidae is a heavy-bodied fish, recognized by its three dorsal fins and two anal fins, in combination with the pale lateral line, and a single, large barbel at the tip of the chin. As in other members of the cod family, the mouth is large and contains many small teeth in both jaws.

It differs from the haddock in its pale lateral line, and can be readily separated from the pollock by the large barbel and the projection of the upper jaw beyond the lower. It resembles the tomcod (*which see*), which has small, narrow pelvic fins which are prolonged as feelers and in which the outline of the caudal fin is broadly rounded, whereas in the cod it is square to slightly concave.

The color is variable, there being two color phases, the red and the gray. The red phase varies from reddish-brown to orange to brick-red, while the gray ranges from black to brownish-gray to greenish. The sides are covered with numerous dark spots.

Most fish taken in the New England area range 6–12 pounds, although 50–60 pounders are not at all unusual. The largest cod on record weighed over 210 pounds and was over 6 feet long, although any fish taken now over 100 pounds is unusual. This species is taken in the North Atlantic, from West Greenland and the Hudson Strait, south to Cape Hatteras, North Carolina, where they occur in deepwater. In the eastern Atlantic, they are found throughout the Baltic Sea and the northern part of Scandinavia, eastward to Novaya Zemlya, USSR, south to the Bay of Biscay.

This common New England species occurs from the surface to a depth of more than 1,500 feet, the young being found in shallow water, while the large cod are generally found in depths exceeding 60 feet. During the winter, many come into the shallow water, and during the summer they are found in deeper water.

LIFE HISTORY

Some cod populations participate in fairly extensive migrations, while others are relatively sedentary. Spawning occurs from December to late March in about twenty fathoms of water in the Gulf of Maine area. The cod, in general, lays great quantities of eggs, and a 75 pounder was estimated to contain over 9,000,000 eggs. Its eggs are

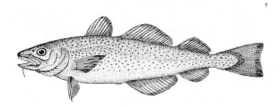

Atlantic Cod

floating, being at the mercy of the winds and currents, as well as numerous predators. The very young cod feed upon copepods and other small crustaceans while they are found in the surface layers, after which they drop to the bottom and feed upon shrimps, barnacles, and small worms. Adults feed upon clams, snails, mussels, crabs, lobsters, worms, squid, and various small fishes.

ANGLING VALUE

The cod is a popular sport fish in the New England area, being taken by anglers using clams, herring, and squid. Party boats are the mainstay of the sport fishery, although small boats and jetty-fishing account for large numbers of cod taken.

The commercial fishery has always been extremely important historically, the 1960 catch accounting for nearly 40,000,000 pounds in the United States. In 1945, about 71,000,000 pounds were taken, but over the years, for example, fluctuations in the Gulf of Maine have not varied greatly. —D.DS.

FISHING METHODS

Cod are cold-weather fish, a detail which imposes limits on the angling season throughout much of their range. In three of their most important sport-fishing regions—southern New England, New York, and New Jersey—the season begins in autumn and continues through the winter on into early spring. Depending to a great extent upon the water temperatures involved, the cod season may begin as early as mid October and last on into April. In general, the season starts in November and ends sometime in March. Exceptions are certain deepwater areas in the vicinity of Montauk Point, New York, and Block Island, Rhode Island. Here an apparent combination of coldwater and good food supply makes for a cod sport-fishing season which lasts to some degree the year around. This Montauk-Block Island region has runs of cod in the winter, spring, summer, and fall, and in that respect is unique on the Atlantic Coast. One ground in particular—located southeast of Block Island and known variously as Cox Ledge, Cox's Ledge, Coxe Ledge, and Coxe's Ledge—regularly produces excellent codfish catches of up to 40 or 50 pounds.

Although cod may be encountered at different levels in the sea, they are mainly a bottom fish, prowling on or near the ocean floor. Angling techniques, therefore, are planned accordingly. Most cod taken by anglers are caught when bottom-fishing at anchor. Sometimes, if winds and currents are not too strong and the nature of the ground permits, bottom-angling can be done while the boat drifts slowly. Drifting has certain advantages over fishing at anchor in that it covers more territory and imparts an attractive motion to the bait.

Jigging is another method. In this technique, a diamond jig is allowed to drop to the sea floor; it is then reeled upward for 10–20 feet, lowered to the bottom again, then reeled upward—all in a continuous, fairly fast process.

TACKLE

There is no need for "purism" so far as codfishing tackle is concerned. The latitude is quite wide, but the recommended selection is confined to conventional equipment and does not include spinning gear. The latter is impractical because (1) the angling is done in fairly deep-water, (2) the weight potential of the fish is 30–40 pounds or more, and (3) generally strong tidal currents prevail in cod areas, necessitating heavy sinkers. However, tackle specifications are flexible. Almost any fiberglass boat rod with a tip section 5–6 feet in length is adequate. Some anglers use surf rods in codfishing, the reasons being that the longer tip section keeps their lines clear of the boat and those of neighboring fishermen alongside them and also makes it easier to handle the long terminal rigs often employed in this sport. The main requirement of a cod-fishing rod is that it be sturdy and have enough rigidity to handle heavy terminal tackle, as well as fish of appreciable weight.

The reel should be a saltwater model equipped with a star drag; in shoal water and when lighter lines can be used, a 1/0 reel will suffice. For other conditions—deeper water, stronger currents, heavier lines, and larger fish, a 2/0 or 3/0 may be preferable. As a general requirement, the reel should have a 150–200-yard capacity of 36-pound test. Helpful in retrieving, particularly in deepwater and in jigging, is a reel with a wide-diameter spool and an oversize crank handle that has a 3:1 or 3½:1 gear ratio.

Codfishing lines can be of linen or one of the modern synthetics such as Dacron or braided nylon. Today more and more fishermen are using nylon monofilament because of its durability in saltwater and low percentage of water absorption. This second characteristic has special value in cold-weather angling. A line that is almost impermeable to water cannot freeze on the reel. Excessive stretch, a drawback among early monofilament lines, has been corrected to a great extent. Also in monofilament's favor is that great strength is incorporated in a small diameter. This decreases water drag on the line in areas where currents are strong, and it enables an angler to use a lighter sinker.

Since the cod has a large mouth, hook sizes are not a matter of precision, although there is some gradation upward to conform with an increase in weights of the fish. Hooks, therefore, range from 5/0 to 9/0. This range will handle cod of just about any size, from the smallest fish up to real heavyweights. Different designs are popular. One is the so-called standard codfish hook, intended for setline use, which is mounted with a tarred-line snell. Other patterns include the Sproat, O'Shaughnessy, and Eagle Claw.

The most common sinker used in codfishing is the bank type. Also employed is a diamond-shaped lead. There can be no set rule as to its weight, since that detail is governed by depths and the strength of tidal currents. In shoal areas or where currents are weak, 5–6 ounces may keep the rig on the bottom. In other places where currents are strong or swift, it may be necessary to use 8- to 12-ounce sinkers. In certain areas, such as some of those in the Montauk-Block Island sector, the tide's race can be too great for a 12-ounce lead. This necessitates repeatedly paying out of line to enable the sinker to hit bottom and to compensate in part for the current's powerful upward thrust against the rig.

Some codfishing is done in the vicinity of wrecks and in rocky areas; and the toll of terminal tackle is considerable because the rigs foul in obstructions. It is wise to carry extra hooks and sinkers. Loss of terminal tackle can be reduced somewhat by the use of a simple device.

Instead of a metal sinker, the angler ties on a small bag, fashioned from any kind of cloth and filled with sand to the desired weight (keeping in mind that the sand will be a bit heavier when wet). The sandbag sinker is attached to the line with string which will break under strain. If this sinker becomes fouled in an obstruction and cannot be freed by pulling, the string will break and the fisherman can retrieve his hooks. The device can also be used in wreck- and rock-angling for tautogs and black sea bass.

BAITS AND RIGS

Cod are predatory feeders, with a varied diet to match their voraciousness. Numerous baits are employed to catch them, including strips of fresh and frozen squid, hard and soft clams, razor clams, pieces of conch, a whole small herring (and, to a much lesser extent, the frozen and salted forms), and pieces or strips cut from the undersides of silver hake, cunners, and mackerel. Cod also feed on crabs of different kinds, such as the calico. A trick used by some oldtime codfishermen is to open the first fish or two they hook, then use any crabs they find in the stomach as bait. In the more northerly part of the species' range small fishes such as sand eels and capelin have accounted for cod catches. However, the bait used most extensively in sport fishing for cod (and in commercial setlining in some areas), notably in the New York-New Jersey region, is the ocean clam or skimmer. This rather large, plump-bodied mollusk is a proven cod-attractor. In areas where other fish are found simultaneously with cod, skimmer baits also will draw haddock, pollock, tautogs, and winter flounders. Skimmer clams also can be used as chum for cod and these bottom fishes. The shells are cracked to release body fluids and bits of meat into the water and dropped overboard a few at a time. Just the shells can be used in chumming, too. After the clams have been shucked for bait, small pieces of meat cling to the shells, which can be dropped overboard in the boat's vicinity.

Although natural baits are used most extensively in this sport, chrome diamond jigs weighing 4–10 ounces take fish, notably in wreck-angling and when cod are feeding on small bait fish which the jig resembles. It is this lure's shape and the flash of its chrome finish, together with the action imparted by the angler, which comprise its attraction.

Fishermen with an experimental bent might try trolling artificials. Small cod in shoal water have been hooked on bucktails and on spinners baited with a piece of pork rind. Tinned squids occasionally take cod in the surf. Deep trolling accounts for cod. The lure should be a shiny spoon or a metal squid with a bright finish. Its hook is baited with a strip of natural squid. This terminal rig must be trolled deep, near the ocean floor. The weight of the baited lure may accomplish that; or it may be necessary to use a wire line, such as that employed in deep trolling for pollock and striped bass, or a drail or trolling sinker, such as that used in deep trolling for large bluefish.

The basic cod rig consists of a single hook, on a long snell or on a nylon or monofilament leader about twenty-four inches long, tied into the line at varying distances above the sinker. As personal preference and experience dictate, attachment can be made anywhere from right above the sinker to 12–18 inches above it. A second or high hook can also be added on a snell or leader of similar length, attaching it in the same fashion about three feet above the first hook. A variation of this rig is to attach both hooks farther down on the line, closer to the sinker and just far enough apart to keep from tangling. (If a third hook is added it is secured to the line just far enough above the second to keep the two from tangling.) Circumstances can alter these arrangements, and an angler might do well to experiment, varying the distances of his hooks above the sinker, but preferably rigging his topmost hook so that it will be within 6 feet of the bottom.

Many anglers are content with a single-hook rig, and in fishing wrecks or rocky places it has that much less chance of getting caught on an obstruction. A two- or three-hook rig does have an advantage, however, in that it stands ready to attract cod traveling at different levels above the sea floor.

An old anglers' saying advises, "Large fish, large baits." In many instances that is true. But in the case of cod it is not necessary to use a large bait—or at least an oversize one, despite the spaciousness of their mouth. Some fishermen take that big-bait saying too literally, thinking that the more skimmer clams they impale on a hook, the better their chances of catching cod. In such cases it is not uncommon to see three or four clams on the same hook. This actually can be a handicap, losing fish instead of catching them. One fair-size skimmer on a hook (some anglers use half the body of a large clam) usually is enough. Even for the largest cod two whole clams, at the most, should suffice.

If cunners (bergalls), those bait-stealing pests which frequently are found in company with tautogs, are present in numbers they will strip hooks of clam bait. At such times the angler might try a combination bait for cod. First on the hook goes a tough, theft-resisting strip of squid; next is impaled a skimmer clam. The idea is that if cunners denude the hook of clam there still will be an acceptable bait—the squid strip—for cod.

STRIKING AND PLAYING THE FISH

Cod can be as individualistic as other species in their approach to a bait. One type of strike is aggressive, with the fish readily seizing the offering. Other cod may appear timid. The fish first will investigate the bait, perhaps pull on it once or twice, then really mouth it and swallow it. This procedure is translated at the angler's end by a series of tugs, followed by a steady pull when the cod finally has swallowed the bait. Or the bait might be taken more subtly—so much so that the fisherman does not realize that he has a fish. What happens here is that the cod accepts the bait but does not move away with it; and what little movement there may be is absorbed by the terminal tackle and line, especially when fishing in deep-water with a heavy sinker.

It is wise, therefore, to lift the rig off the bottom a little at intervals. This serves a threefold purpose: It imparts motion to the bait, adding to its attraction; it will reveal whether or not a cod has taken the bait and is lying immobile; and it checks to determine if the sinker is right on the ocean floor (as indicated by a dulled thud of the lead hitting bottom after lifting) where it should be.

Once a cod is hooked, its resistance can take the form of a few power surges on short, deep runs. Among the larger fish these can be strong. The hook is not likely to tear out at this stage, unless it is set only superficially in the jaw; but it is best to let the fish have its way until its activity lessens. Then the cod can be reeled toward the surface. In deep water an angler sometimes can extract the most action from his quarry by reeling fairly slowly. This enables the cod to adjust, more or less, to decreasing water pressures as it ascends and so keeps the fish alive and uninjured as long as possible.

If, during nibbling or toying with the bait, the tugs cease and are not followed by signs of further activity, the fisherman might leave his rig on bottom for a few minutes to see if the fish will return. Then, if there is no further action, the angler might do well to check his hook for bait.

A gaff is a handy accessory in codfishing, especially when heavy specimens are common. Remember to aim the gaff into the forward part of the body for a firm hold.

CODFISHING GROUNDS

Cod are ocean fish. In the main they are the target of deepsea boat fishermen. In some areas and/or in certain seasons they can be caught in the littoral (shore) zone not far off the beach. That frequently is true of young cod. Along the south shore of New York State's Long Island, for example, an autumn cod run can begin with the fish appearing quite close inshore in October, after which they shift to locations farther out for their winter stay. At times, in some places, cod are so close to shore that surf-fishermen, jetty-anglers and even pier-fishermen can catch them.

Theoretically, any ocean bottom, from shoal inshore waters to offshore depths of one hundred feet or more, is potential cod-producing ground. But there are certain expanses of sea floor which are more likely to yield codfish than others. Pebbly and rock-strewn regions are among those. Cod also are encountered over sand, mud, and patches of bottom well-studded with broken shells; and sometimes the fish are located in places containing gardens of marine plants. As noted elsewhere here, wrecks have codfishing potential too.

Although not accompanied by a guarantee, a general rule is that the larger cod tend to prowl for food closer to the bottom than their smaller, younger brethren. A sequel to this rule, therefore, is that the closer to the sea floor an angler fishes, the better his chances of catching cod in the upperweight brackets.

FOOD VALUE

Cod have been an important American market fish for generations. One reason is that they can be sold fresh, frozen, salted, and in a dried form in cans. Another reason is that they are a good table fish and can be served in a variety of ways which include fillets, steaks, frying, and as the principal ingredient of fishcakes and fish chowder.

Smaller cod, to about 6–7 pounds, can be cleaned, dressed, and baked whole. Cod also can be filleted. Filleting produces two solid slabs of white meat which can be fried or boiled and flaked for use in fishcakes. Large fillets can be baked if desired. The heavier cod—those weighing more than, say, fifteen pounds—can be steaked. First the fish are dressed, then the body is cut into steaks of desired thickness. When baked, these steaks are delicious. *See also* Fish Cookery   —B.W.

ATLANTIC CROAKER *Micropogon undulatus* This species is most closely related to *M. furnieri*, a tropical form that extends from the West Indies and the southwestern Gulf of Mexico to Argentina. The Atlantic croaker has a temperate distribution ordinarily extending from Rhode Island to Cape Kennedy and, in the Gulf of Mexico, from Tampa Bay across to the southern Gulf of Campeche. There are records from southern Florida, but these are probably the result of occasional southward migrations under the stress of unusually cold winter conditions.

Atlantic Croaker

Its color is a very light silvery gray above with a vertical pattern of interrupted bars giving a faintly spotted effect. The lower one-third of the body is white. During the spawning season, the fish becomes a distinct bronze or yellow color and, for this reason, is occasionally called the golden croaker. The iris becomes golden on the dorsal margin, the pelvic fins yellow, and the pectorals blackish at their bases. The inside of the mouth becomes a pinkish-red, the anal fin a bronze-yellow, the caudal a faint yellow, and the preopercle bronze.

Other distinguishing characteristics of the Atlantic croaker are 28 dorsal rays (26–30); gillrakers 15 (14–16) on lower limb of first arch; scales above lateral line 8 (7–9); orbit 22 (15–27) percent of head length; without conspicuous black lines along the back.

Anal rays 8; pectoral rays 18 (17–20). Pored lateral-line scales 50 (47–50); scales below the lateral line 8 (8–9). In percent of standard length: head length 32 (30–34), head depth 21 (19–25), body depth 30 (26–35), dorsal base 59 (52–62), predorsal length 38 (33–42), and length of caudal peduncle 23 (20–25). In percent of head length: snout 32 (28–36), postorbital length 48 (44-54), cheek length 42 (37–47), interorbital 28 (24–32), anal base 33 (24–42), and depth of caudal peduncle 28 (25–31). The otoliths (sagitta) of this species are also characteristic.

LIFE HISTORY

The life history of this important food and sport fish is still incompletely known. To the north in the Chesapeake Bay area, the postlarval and juvenile stages migrate into the estuaries and return to the ocean as yearlings. Adults have been observed to move into the bays in the spring and leave in the fall. In the winter, the adults move out to the deeper, warmer waters of the shelf and may also migrate to the south. Along the Texas coast, adults in spawning color appear in the passes and bays from mid October into November. Apparently, the spawning takes place in the open Gulf near the passes.

Along the Gulf Coast, most Atlantic croaker spawn and die at the end of their second year. The adults seldom reach more than two pounds being considerably smaller than the 4–5 pound fish of the Chesapeake Bay area.

This species is a bottom feeder existing mainly on shrimp, mollusks, worms, and crabs. [Most of the information on this species from a 1963 University of Texas M.A. thesis by Robert S. Jones.] *See also* Drums
—J.C.B.

ATLANTIC CUTLASSFISH *Trichiurus lepturus* Also called the ribbonfish, it is found in the Atlantic, Indian, and western Pacific oceans. In the western Atlantic, it ranges from Massachusetts to Argentina and throughout the Gulf of Mexico. Its only close relative in the Western Hemisphere is the Pacific cutlassfish found on the west coast from southern California to northern Peru.

The general appearance is striking, especially the long, silvery body; the tapering, filamentous tail; and the large mouth with sharp, arrow-shaped teeth. Head enters 7.2–8.2 times in total length; depth 13.0–14.5; 133–140 dorsal fin rays; anal fin contains 97–108 short spines. The body is extremely elongate, strongly compressed, band-like; head long, compressed; snout long, pointed, its length 2.75–2.9 in head; eye 6.1–7.45; interorbital 7.05–7.8; mouth large, lower jaw strongly projecting; maxillary concealed under preorbital, reaching to about anterior margin of pupil, 2.2–2.7 in head; teeth in jaws strong and unequal, compressed, the largest with distinct barbs on posterior edges; gillrakers poorly developed and of unequal length, from 5–15 more or less developed on lower limb of first arch; dorsal fin extremely long, beginning over preopercular margin and occupying the whole length of the back; caudal and ventral fins wanting.

Color plain silvery; tips of jaws blackish; dorsal plain, with dusky margin; pectorals plain but with dusky punctulations.

LIFE HISTORY

The cutlassfish is a voracious eater of small fish and is found in large numbers in the bays and the shallow parts of the open ocean. It is particularly numerous along the Texas coast, and, there, it is extensively utilized as bait for the large species of gamefish.

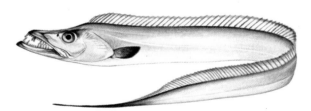

Atlantic Cutlassfish

The adults attain a length of about 38 inches and a weight of about 2 pounds. They are readily caught on shrimp or cut bait and will also take small artificial lures.

The cutlassfish is a valued food species in other countries (Japan), but Americans are not accustomed to eating it. Virtually nothing is known about its life history except that sexually mature individuals have been caught in the spring.
—J.C.B.

ATLANTIC GUITARFISH *Rhinobatos lentiginosus* This saltwater ray is characterized by its long, flattened body and its lance-shaped snout, which is shaped like an elongated triangle. The dorsal fins are well-developed, and the pectoral fins are rounded at their posterior edge.

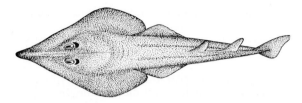

Atlantic Guitarfish

It is brown or olivaceous above with numerous light dots and the lower parts are pale. The area on either side of the midline of the snout is translucent. Maximum size seems to be 2½ feet, and sexual maturity is reached at about 19–20 inches, at least in the male.

LIFE HISTORY

This guitarfish is found along the Atlantic Coast from North Carolina to Yucatan, being relatively common about Florida. A limited northward migration of at least a few individuals occurs in the spring and early summer. Inshore habitats are preferred whenever shallow waters are found, but they have been found as deep as sixty feet. They are taken in quiet waters or in regions of moderate surf, where they prod for food, predominately amphipods and mole crabs. —D.dS.

ATLANTIC HAGFISH *Myxine glutinosa* An eel-like marine scavenger distinguished from the lampreys by three pairs of short barbels on the head, lack of eyes, and a single finfold (a fold of skin rather than a true fin) which runs around the posterior end and forward on the lower surface of the body without division into dorsal, caudal, and anal fins. The hagfish is sometimes called "slime eel" because of the great quantities of mucus which it exudes from a series of glands located on either side of the abdomen. Hagfish commonly grow 1½–2 feet long. They do not have bones; they are completely cartilaginous, the mouth is jawless, the eversible tongue is studded with rasplike teeth, and the skin is without scales. Although blind, the hagfish finds its food through a sensitive olfactory apparatus. Hagfish vary in color from a mottled gray-brown to a reddish-gray above, and whitish- or pale gray on the ventral surface.

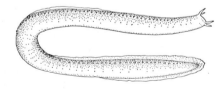

Atlantic Hagfish

HABITS

Hagfish feed chiefly on dead or injured fish which they attack by boring into the body cavity or entering through the mouth. The hagfish literally consumes its host from the inside out leaving nothing but an empty skin. This is most frequently observed by commercial fishermen using longlines or gillnets for haddock, cod, hake, and various other ground fishes; the hagfish is hauled aboard while attached to its disabled prey. Hagfish are largely nocturnal and spend most of the day partially buried in soft mud bottoms with the tip of their snouts projecting. They prefer coldwater and are most common in the North Atlantic banks where they are found at depths of 20–300 fathoms or more. Unlike the lamprey, hagfish do not enter freshwater to spawn; the horny shelled eggs are dropped at random and at all seasons of the year throughout their range.

ANGLING VALUE

Hagfish are infrequently caught on live bait. However, they have no angling value. —D.dS.

—A.J.McC.

ATLANTIC HALIBUT *Hippoglossus hippoglossus* Similar in general shape to the Pacific halibut (*which see*), this large member of the righteye-flounder family has a concave tail, and the dorsal and anal fins have their middle rays pointed. The large mouth extends to the middle of the eyes, and a distinct arch occurs over the pectoral fin. The color on the eyed side is chocolate to olive to grayish-brown, occasionally becoming almost black in large fish. Irregular dark markings sometimes enclose a lighter center region. The blind side is white in small individuals but may be blotched in large specimens. One of the largest of marine bony fishes, the Atlantic halibut grows to a weight of 600–700 pounds and a length in excess of 9 feet, although fish over 300 pounds are rare. Females are generally larger; males run 50–200 pounds.

It occurs in the cooler waters of the North Atlantic from New Jersey, and occasionally to Virginia, to Greenland and along the northern European coast southward to the English Channel. A coldwater species, it is found in relatively deep water over sand, gravel, or clay, rather than on soft mud or on rock. It is not an arctic form, generally being taken in waters from about 40° to 50° F, although it may be found either in cooler or somewhat warmer waters. A deepwater species, it seldom enters water shallower than about two hundred feet deep and frequents waters as deep as three thousand feet. It feeds primarily on fishes, including cods and their relatives, ocean perch, herring, skates, mackerel, and other flounders. Crabs, mussels, lobsters, and clams are also eaten; in turn, halibut are eaten by seals and the Greenland shark.

LIFE HISTORY

Spawning is thought to occur on the bottom, in depths perhaps in excess of two thousand feet. The spawning season is from late winter to early September. The eastern Atlantic form spawns from March to May, with a peak in April. The eggs float at subsurface depths, at least as deep as three hundred feet. The eggs are unusually large, about 3–4 millimeters in diameter, and a 200-pound female may produce 2,000,000 of these eggs. Transformation of the left eye to the right side of the transparent larva begins when the fish is about an inch long, after which the young takes on dark pigmentation and a bottom existence. Growth is slow; a 3-year-old fish is only 13 inches long. Females grow more rapidly; a 400-pound halibut measuring about 68 inches long was 20 years.

Sexual maturity in the female occurs in 9–10 years, at lengths of about 34–37 inches. Males mature younger and at a smaller size.

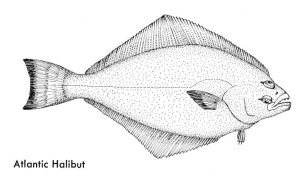

Atlantic Halibut

ANGLING VALUE

Formerly, the Atlantic halibut was an extremely important commercial species, but overfishing and perhaps other factors have reduced it from its former strength. A few are taken in trawls, but the commonest method is by longline fishing on the bottom. Some are taken by anglers drift-fishing, and the species is an excellent fighter. Its flesh is highly desired, particularly the specimens less than twenty pounds, called "chicken halibut." The liver produces a vitamin-rich oil. —D.dS.

ATLANTIC HERRING *Clupea harengus harengus* This typical member of the herring family has a compressed body which is more elongate and less compressed than most other members of the family. It has a large mouth and a projecting lower jaw which is not notched, as in the shads, from which it also differs in the presence of a patch of teeth on the roof of the mouth. Its back is a deep steel-blue to greenish-blue with silver sides and belly. Fresh specimens are iridescent with shades of blue-green and violet, these colors fading shortly after death. It reaches the length of about 18 inches, although the average is less than 12 inches. Maximum weight is about 1½ pounds.

The Atlantic herring is found on both sides of the North Atlantic, from Greenland to North Carolina, and from the Straits of Gibraltar to the Bay of Murmansk and Novaya Zemyla, USSR. The species dwells in the surface waters of the open ocean, traveling in huge schools.

LIFE HISTORY

Spawning may occur in the spring, summer, or autumn, depending on the locality. Spawning occurs in the open ocean over rocky or gravel bottoms generally, from between two or three to about thirty fathoms, although in the eastern Atlantic, they may spawn as deep as one hundred fathoms. The slender, almost transparent larvae grow to about 3½–5 inches during their first year of life. The young feed on copepods, small shrimps, and crustacean larvae. Adults are also plankton feeders, although a

few fish have been found in their stomachs. Herring are preyed upon by cod and their relatives, striped bass, mackerel and tuna, salmon, sharks, and squids.

ECONOMIC VALUE

Young herring, sometimes known as sardines, are important commercially, while the adults form the basis of one of the world's largest commercial fisheries. Some are canned, smoked, and sold fresh or salted. They are extremely popular as bait in hook-and-line fisheries, and are also used as chum. A portion of the catch is used to obtain oil and fishmeal and for the essence-of-pearl industry. *See also* Blueback Herring, Pacific Herring

—D.dS.

ATLANTIC HORSE-EYE JACK *Caranx latus* Also called goggle-eye jack, this western Atlantic jack crevalle is closely related to the Pacific horse-eye jack, *Caranx marginatus*, of the eastern Pacific. A species named *Caranx sexfasciatus* which ranges in the Indo-Pacific from Hawaii to the eastern coast of South Africa is very similar to these two, and they constitute a nearly circumtropical species complex.

The chest in front of the pelvic fins of the Atlantic horse-eye jack is completely covered with scales. The second dorsal fin has one spine and 19–22 softrays; the anal fin has two detached spines followed by one spine and 16–18 softrays. Gillrakers on the first arch number 6–7 on the upper limb and 16–18 on the lower limb. The body and fins are never entirely black or dark brown. The tip of the dorsal fin lobe is usually black.

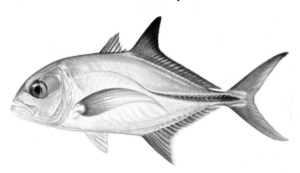

Atlantic Horse-eye Jack

The body is moderately deep; the head profile is convex; and the relatively large eyes with their thick adipose eyelids are located well forward in the profile. The dorsal and anal fin lobes are moderately elongated. The straight lateral line is about 1.5–1.8 times as long as the curved part. There are about 32–39 scutes in the straight lateral line. Some of the gillrakers on the anterior parts of the upper and lower limbs become very short or rudimentary with growth. It is generally dark blue to blue-gray above and silvery white or sometimes golden on the sides and below, and the tip of the dorsal fin lobe is black in smaller specimens. The caudal fin is yellow. A small black spot may be present on the upper edge of the operculum. Schools of this fish have been seen to change their coloration, as from dark to light, to blend with their immediate surroundings. The young, up to about seven inches long, have 5 (rarely 4 or 6) bars on the body plus one on the nape; these may persist in larger sizes in live fish.

Atlantic Herring

The Atlantic horse-eye jack ranges from Rio de Janeiro, Brazil, to the Manasquan River, New Jersey, throughout the West Indies, and at Bermuda. The maximum recorded total length is 22 inches, but it very possibly grows larger. A suggestion of its attaining 35 pounds may be excessive.

LIFE HISTORY

Little is known of the life history. Off the southeastern United States the spawning season has been estimated to extend from about March to July. Specimens from Puerto Rico were reported to be in spawning condition during June. The smallest recorded specimen, ¾ inch long, was taken on the east coast of Florida during June. It is suspected that spawning occurs in offshore waters. The very young of this species, smaller than ¾ inch long, have not been distinguished from the young of the crevalle, *Caranx hippos;* and small specimens representing either or both of these species have been taken well off-shore in the Florida Current. The horse-eye jack, as with the crevalle, is at least temporarily euryhaline, and has been caught and seen in coastal freshwater rivers and streams. It is more often found, however, in small schools around islands and offshore islands and along sandy beaches in the tropics. The main food is fish as well as shrimp and crabs.

ANGLING VALUE

The horse-eye jack is edible, although not a delicacy. Its flesh has been under suspicion of being poisonous in Cuba and the West Indies. Once, when its sale was banned, specimens were seen in the Havana market with the characteristic black-tipped dorsal-fin lobe broken off, as if to conceal the identity.

Larger specimens of the horse-eye jack and the crevalle have sometimes been confused, both in oral and published reports. When specimens of both species can be compared, the larger eye of the horse-eye jack and the blunter profile of the crevalle are very obviously distinguishing. However, these two species can always be separated by the scales on the chest (in specimens over 1 inch long). The horse-eye has a completely scaled chest. The crevalle has a small, circular patch of scales on an otherwise scaleless chest—this is the type of character that is very obvious if one knows what to look for.

ANGLING VALUE

The horse-eye is a very strong gamefish especially on light tackle. These jacks occur in blue holes and in the channels adjacent to flats where they travel in schools. Horse-eyes are taken on a great variety of lures including plugs, jigs, spoons and flies as well as live bait. They are very common in the Florida Keys and Bahamas where fish of 2–6 pounds are average. Their maximum size is not really known due to its similarity to the crevalle and frequent misidentification. Horse-eyes have been authenticated to 12 pounds in weight, however, and it's probable that the fish will exceed that size. As with most jacks, the successful angler will operate his lure at a fairly rapid speed. See also Carangidae, Jacks —F.H.B.

ATLANTIC LOOKDOWN *See* Lookdowns
ATLANTIC MACKEREL *See* Mackerels
ATLANTIC MANTA *Manta birostris* This member of the ray family is easily distinguished by the two hornlike, projecting appendages on the front of the head, the large disk which is about twice as wide as long, and the very long tail. The large eyes are placed on the sides of the distinct head. Its closest Atlantic relative, the devil ray (*which see*), has a mouth which is located beneath the head, while the mouth of the manta is at the tip of the head. Usually a serrated spine is present just behind the dorsal fin. The skin, which is roughened with numerous small tubercles, grades from reddish to olive-brown, to black in older specimens. The lower parts are white or white with gray or black blotches. White markings are sometimes present in various patterns on the shoulder, on the posterior part of the disk, behind the eye, or on the outer surface of the hornlike fins. It grows to a known width of 22 feet and a length of 17 feet, at which size it approaches 2 tons.

LIFE HISTORY

The manta is known from Brazil to the Carolinas, drifting northward to New England and Georges Bank and Bermuda. In the eastern Atlantic it is known from Madeira and the tropical waters of West Africa. Closely related, if not identical, species occur in the western Pacific and Indo-Pacific region and in the tropical waters of the eastern Pacific Ocean. These huge, batlike rays are encountered at the surface as they swim or bask there, but they probably rest on the bottom as well. They are seen in pairs or in groups of as many as thirty, splashing and somersaulting about the surface, with a resounding splash that can be heard quite distantly. The head fins are used to channel food into its large mouth, and in this respect its food and feeding habits differ from other rays.

Adults eat small shrimps, mullets, and plankton, and juveniles eat anchovies, shrimps, and copepods. Sexual maturity evidently does not occur before a width of 14 or 15 feet, and the young are hatched from eggs, and the young subsequently develop within the mother's body. Free-swimming individuals of 4 feet wide have been observed, but some unborn mantas are 50 inches wide and 20 or more pounds. Birth has been described as occurring during the somersaulting activities of the mother.

Small mantas can be eaten, and the flesh of larger ones is used for fishmeal, while the skin is used as an abrasive and oil is extracted from the liver. Sport fishermen hook them occasionally but seldom land them. The chief danger of mantas lies in their potential to overturn a small boat with a flip of the fin. See also Pacific Manta   —D.dS.

ATLANTIC MENHADEN *Brevoortia tyrannus* This deep-bodied member of the herring family is characterized by a large head and comblike edges to the rear portions of the scales, which are straight rather than being rounded as in other herrings. It is dark blue to green or dark gray above with shades of brown, with the sides, belly, and fins with a brassy sheen. A definite large spot on the shoulder is generally followed by a number of small, dark spots on the upper sides. Its numerous, long, slender gillrakers differ in their structure from other members of this family. It reaches a length of 18 inches and a weight of nearly 4 pounds, although most taken are less than 15 inches long.

This species is restricted to the western Atlantic Ocean, occurring from Nova Scotia to northern Florida and the Gulf of Mexico. Three other species are also taken,

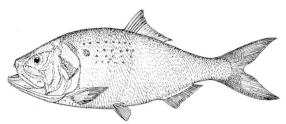

Atlantic Menhaden

being present predominantly in the southern part of the Atlantic Coast and in the Gulf of Mexico. This species travels in huge, compact schools which occasionally jump from the water during their wanderings.

Little is known about the habits of the Atlantic menhaden during the life of the adult, but its history has been marked by tremendous fluctuations in abundance and availability. It is a warmwater species, being available in late spring and throughout the summer, but disappearing usually in mid October. Breeding habits are virtually unknown except that it spawns at sea in the spring and summer to the north, but it may spawn late in the summer and fall in the Chesapeake Bay region. Larger specimens are found at the mouths of the estuaries and offshore. The young are found in the lower part of the estuaries, and the juveniles usually spend the summer in the upper parts of the estuaries in brackish water. During the fall, they move offshore again to spend the winter.

Young and adults are plankton feeders, sifting large quantities of water with their comblike gillrakers. They eat diatoms, small worms, crustaceans, and shrimp larvae, although the small plants are the most important. Menhaden themselves are eaten by whales, porpoises, sharks, cods and their relatives, as well as bluefish, swordfish, tuna, and striped bass and other predatory fishes. Small menhaden are excellent bait, and the larger ones are cut up for chum. Occasionally they are used as bait in tuna fishing.

ECONOMIC VALUE

This is the most important commercial finfish in the United States, accounting for over 2 billion pounds in 1960 from the fishery. Most of the catch is taken with purse seines, and the catch is almost entirely used in the production of animal and poultry feeds, while some is used in making paints and oil. A small portion is sold commercially for chum and bait. The oily consistency of the manhaden flesh which makes it so desirable for chum for bluefish and weakfish detracts from its value for human food. —D.dS.

ATLANTIC MOONFISH *See* Lookdowns

ATLANTIC PERMIT *Trachinotus falcatus* This is also called great pompano and, when young, round pompano. Large specimens of this western Atlantic species for many years were recorded as *Trachinotus goodei*, but that name cannot apply. *Trachinotus goodei* was named from two specimens slightly over 1 inch long from Florida waters, and these specimens are the same species that has the name *Trachinotus glaucus*, the palometa. "Permit" has been used to describe any large pompano of medium depth and with fin lobes of medium length, and at times all three species of pompano that occur in Florida have

been called permit. But permit is actually only the species described below. The Pacific permit, *Trachinotus kennedyi*, is a very closely related species.

The first dorsal fin of the Atlantic permit has 6 spines; the second dorsal fin has one spine and 17–21 softrays; the anal fin has two short, detached spines followed by one spine and 16–19 softrays. There are no black bars or spots on the sides. Young (less than 6 inches long) have the body about half as deep as the total length.

Body and fin proportions change appreciably with growth, and these are very variable. The body is almost half as deep as the total length in specimens of less than 6 inches long; the body depth is progressively less in large specimens. The dorsal-and anal-fin lobes are more elongated in smaller specimens; the dorsal-fin lobe extends back to the caudal peduncle in specimens about fifteen inches long and becomes progressively shorter in larger specimens. Coloration is variable. The small, deepbodied young may be almost entirely black, or largely silvery, or black and silvery with a dark red tinge; and they can alternate these colors rapidly. Larger fish are usually bluish or grayish on the back, with the remainder of the body silvery, the dorsal fin bluish or black along its anterior margin and lobe, the anterior margin and lobe of the anal fin and the pelvic fins frequently orange, and the caudal fin dusky. Very large permit may have the body almost entirely silvery, with a greenish-blue tinge, and all the fins dark or dusky.

The Atlantic permit ranges from Brazil to Massachusetts, in the West Indies, and presumably at Bermuda. It is supposed to be most abundant and to reach its maximum size off southern Florida. It has been reported to occur in the eastern Atlantic. The maximum size is in excess of 50 pounds, although rod-and-reel catches are ordinarily in the 20–30-pound class.

LIFE HISTORY

Life history data, on a species of this importance, are disappointingly meager. A 32-inch total-length female, apparently with very large ovaries, and a 29½-inch male were taken in July at Tortugas, Florida. Spawning may extend from December to September, probably concentrated around May. Spawning apparently occurs in association with waters of the Florida Current, for the smallest known young, about ¼–½ inch long, have been taken in the Florida Current and the Gulf Stream (one of these 360 miles east of Virginia). At a length of about ½–2 inches the young apparently move inshore. The young are usually found inshore over sandy beaches, while the adults may occur in the surf and have also been taken on the edge of the Florida Current. Adults are more solitary; the young move in small schools. The young feed on a variety of small invertebrates, and larger specimens eat mainly bottom-living invertebrates and some small fish.

—F.H.B.

FISHING TECHNIQUE

The range of the permit is loosely defined as various parts of the tropical Atlantic, but nowhere does the species *appear* to be abundant. To a large degree it's a fish that is present but seldom seen—and more often seen than caught. There are more permit in southern Florida and the Bahamas than most people realize. Permit tend to stay in channels and holes, but they come up on the flats like bonefish when the tide floods. The difference is that they wait a bit longer than bonefish because permit are deep-bodied and twice their size, so they need more water to get over the banks. They rarely make a "mud" like the bonefish. Occasionally you might see a little puff of sand or marl as an individual fish roots in the bottom, but a school will never cloud the water by their feeding. The experienced angler looks for the movements of schools disturbing the surface and, of course, their tails and dorsals when actively feeding.

Although individual fish will be seen from time to time, permit usually travel in schools of ten or more fish. This game demands 20/20 vision, polaroids, and chrome-plated nerves. The permit first appear as dim shapes, and, ghosting along at a distance of thirty yards, they can barely be distinguished against patches of grass. The fish might easily weigh 10–40 pounds or more; 20 pounders are common. As in bonefishing, the school will suddenly

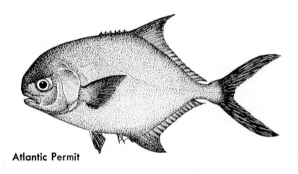

Atlantic Permit

stop, as though poised for flight; then abruptly they tip down to root for crabs, and their forked tails seesaw upward. On an average day in the Content Key area of Florida it is not unusual to sight a hundred fish. On rare occasions, professional guides have reported seeing 1,000–2,000 permit in a single day. But for all the fish sighted, comparatively few are hooked and boated. Bear in mind that it requires from thirty minutes to three hours to land a large permit on light tackle; the fish doesn't quit easily. When hooked, a permit has that initial burst of speed in the style of a bonefish. But the permit continues running long after the bonefish would quit. It will pause to twist its body or bang its head on the bottom to see if it can get the hook loose—then take off again. The angler might boat a permit miles from his starting point. Instinctively, a permit when hooked on a shallow bank will head for deep-water. There's a zone of transition between the grassy flats and offshore where the bottom is covered with sea fans, sponges, coral heads, and all sorts of vertical snags around which the permit can wrap a line. Getting over this obstacle course is tricky, and it takes some luck.

Standard permit tackle consists of a medium-action 6½-foot spinning rod, a large-capacity freshwater spinning reel with a reliable drag, and 8-pound-test monofilament line. The experts do not use a leader but prefer instead three feet of double line at the terminal end, which is spliced very carefully. The double line is then tied to a 2/0 Eagle Claw hook—a size and pattern which is perfect. At least 90 per cent of permit fishing is done with live bait using a small blue crab or spider crab.

The permit is a sight feeder. So it will hit artificials also. Unfortunately, when a permit gets its head down to

look for food, and that's the way they are found most of the time, the fish concentrates on a few square inches of bottom under its nose and ignores everything else. Anglers may cast more than twenty times to a tailing permit, and the fish will pay no attention to the lure at all. When a little finney crab plops on the water, often as not the fish will stop rooting and go for it. However, not just *any* splash will attract permit. The sound has to be just right. Permit spook easily, and knowing what they will tolerate or accept is something the angler must learn for himself. A crab of 2–2½ inches across the shell is perfect.

The ideal situation for a permit to take an artificial lure is in a competitive position. A lone, tailing permit is a lot tougher to interest than a fish which is feeding with a school. When an artificial drops among a number of fish the competitive instinct prevails. The permit may grab it out of sheer gluttony whether the lure looks right or not. Permit have a mouth with the texture of an automobile tire. It is difficult to set the hook properly, and for that reason it's necessary to strike hard (within the limits of the tackle) and keep on striking six, seven, or eight times. It is also important to keep a tight line. Often the hook will drop out after a fish is boated. The only reason the point stays in a permit's mouth is because the angler has kept his line tight. When given slack, the point will invariably come free. Permit have a habit of running a long distance, then diving for the bottom where they bury and rub their mouths in the sand to get rid of the hook. You can't allow slack for a second. Of course, some fish are hooked well with the barb in deep, but you can never tell until the permit is in the boat—and that's not easy in any case.

Permit are also caught on flies. However, the number of anglers who succeed in taking them with the fly rod are in the minority. Basically, the same techniques used in catching bonefish are applicable to permit. *See also* Carangidae, Pacific Permit, Saltwater Fly-Fishing

—A.J.McC.

ATLANTIC POACHER *See* Sea Poachers
ATLANTIC SAILFISH *Istiophorus platyperus* A marine species of little commercial value, it is highly prized by anglers because of its outstanding sporting characteristics. Although present taxonomy suggests that the Atlantic and Pacific sailfishes are the same species, it is probable that there are at least three, including an Indo-Pacific form. For practical purposes the Atlantic and Pacific sailfishes are treated separately.

The outstanding characteristic of the sailfish is the enormous dorsal fin, which is much higher than the greatest depth of the body. This height is maintained for almost the entire length of the fin. The longest ray is usually about the twentieth, counting from the anterior end, and the length of this ray is usually about 150 per cent or more of the greatest depth of the body. In addition, the pelvic fins of the sailfish are much longer than those of other istiophorids, reaching nearly to the anal fin. These fins also have a wide membrane attached to them, missing in other forms, which is quite noticeable in the freshly caught fish. If allowed to dry, however, the membrane sticks tightly to the fin rays and is not at all obvious.

The body of the sailfish is long, slender, and compressed, resulting in a slab-sided appearance. The lateral

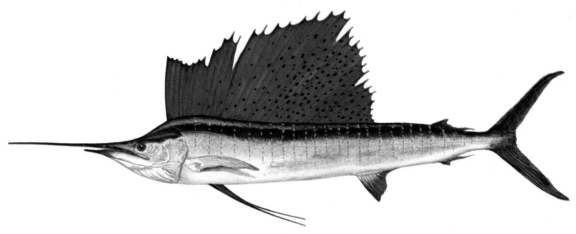

Atlantic Sailfish, 62-pound Female, Palm Beach, Florida

line is single and quite prominent. The vent is just in front of the anal fin. The spear is long and slender, often slightly curved, with the upper jaw generally a little more than twice as long as the lower. In color, the sailfish is dark steely-blue dorsally, fading to white or silvery on the ventral side. On the sides of the body, a number of pale vertical bars, often made up of rows of pale spots, may be present and may or may not persist after death. The vertical fins are bright cobalt-blue in life, and the dorsal fin, especially in its posterior part, may be more or less liberally sprinkled with round or oval black spots. Sometimes the fish are a deep bronze color when brought into the boat, but this color does not persist after death.

The pectoral fins are moderately long, and the pelvics are the longest of any istiophorid and are provided with a broad membrane.

The Atlantic sailfish is one of the smaller members of the family. The average weight of angler-caught fish in Florida waters is somewhere around 40 pounds, although the largest on record weighed 141 pounds. The length averages about 7 feet, but larger ones, up to about 8½ feet, are not too uncommon.

HABITS

Spawning of the sailfish occurs chiefly in the summer, but may begin as early as April and extend well into the fall. The eggs are about 0.85 millimeters in diameter, and a large female may produce more than 4,500,000 eggs. Development appears to be very rapid, with the result that young sailfish may reach a weight of about six pounds in as many months. At this weight, they are about 4½ feet long. Subsequently, growth in length slows down, while the weight continues to increase. Along the Florida coast, young sailfish one foot or so in length are not uncommon from August to October. Presumably, these are the young of the year which have hatched from the eggs of the previous summer.

The very young sailfish bears but little resemblance to its parents. Just out of the egg, the little sailfish is scarcely more than ⅛ inch long. It is a stubby little fish, with a large head, short jaws, and large spines above and behind the eye and at the lower corner of the gill cover. A third, smaller spine is found between the two large ones. At about ¼ inch, the jaws, both upper and lower, begin to

elongate. By the time the little fish is one inch long, however, the upper jaw is much longer than the lower. All this time, the jaws are armed with rather prominent teeth. The sail-like dorsal fin is well-developed at one inch. By the time the young fish is almost 3 inches long, it is quite clearly a proper sailfish, although the spines are still present on the head, teeth are still in the jaws, and the first and second dorsal and anal fins are joined together. At 8 inches, these larval characteristics have all disappeared, and except for some of the body proportions, the young fish has all the characteristics of the adults.

Along the Atlantic Coast of the United States, sailfish undertake regular seasonal movements. There appears to be a center of abundance off the coast of Florida, where some fish remain the year around. But in the spring, large numbers of them tend to move northward from this area, possibly following the northward movement of their food as the water warms. But as soon as the cold north winds start to blow in the fall, the sailfish school up and swim southward again.

The list of the foods of the sailfish is a long one. This does not mean that the sailfish has a more varied diet than other istiophorids, merely that it has been better investigated. Squid and octopuses, especially the paper nautilus, form about 17 per cent of the total diet in the Florida area, with various fishes making up the remaining 83 per cent. Among the fishes, the mackerels and tunas seem to be the most important, followed by jacks, half-beaks (ballyhoo), and needlefish. Also included in significant numbers are herrings, cutlassfish, and porgies. Oddly enough, two fish that are commonly supposed to be staple items with the sailfish, mullet and flying fish, apparently are eaten only rarely. The relative numbers and the known habits of the animals eaten by sailfish indicate that a good share of their feeding is done in midwater, along the edge of reefs, or close to the bottom. They are by no means exclusively surface feeders.

In the Atlantic, the sailfish has been taken regularly from Cape Hatteras to Venezuela, including such spots as Bermuda, Puerto Rico, the Windward Islands, and the Gulf of Mexico, It may stray as far north as Cape Cod, perhaps even into the Gulf of Maine (unconfirmed reports), in warm summers, and a few have been recorded from as far south as Brazil. On the eastern side of the

Atlantic, locality records include the coast of Devon, England; France; the African coast at least as far south as Ghana; and the Mediterranean.

FISHING METHODS

Most Atlantic sailfish are caught by angling. The favorite method is trolling, using a strip of tuna belly, or a whole mullet, or ballyhoo for bait. Sometimes sailfish will take feathers or spoons. A few sailfish may be caught incidental to tuna fishing operations, but the meat tends to be tough, although tasty, and is of little commercial value except when smoked. —J.E.M.

TACKLE FOR SAILFISH

Light-tackle anglers (10–30-pound-test class) generally prefer a revolving-spool trolling reel with star-drag in the No. 3/0 size. The standard No. 3/0 reel has a capacity of about five hundred yards of 20-pound-test line. In most cases, however, three hundred yards of the desired fishing line are spooled over backing as an economy measure. A 20-pound-test Dacron or monofilament is probably the favorite line size of light-tackle sailfish anglers. Many feel that 30-pound line is heavier than needed. Except among experts the use of 10-pound-test is not popular because so much help is necessary by way of boat maneuvering when a large fish is hooked. With 20-pound test, an angler can handle his fish with a minimum of assistance from the boat, engines, and the captain. The matching rod is a regulation 5½-foot fiberglass tip of approximately 6 ounces; this total length includes the rod butt.

Heavier tackle, using a No. 4/0 reel, is still widely used for sailfish. Such outfits are often found aboard charter craft which fish a great many novice anglers. The No. 4/0 is spooled with 50-pound-test line, which is more than adequate for beginners.

Spinning tackle is of limited interest for sailfishing. It is largely restricted to private craft—not charter boats. The fixed-spool reel is, however, standard gear aboard large party boats which specialize in reef-fishing for king mackerel and other of the small offshore and reef gamefish.

Popular leader-wire sizes range from No. 7 to No. 9, depending on the time of year along the sailfish sector. In the summer, No. 9 is preferred because of the increased possibility of hooking a blue marlin while sailfishing. In the winter, No. 7 is used widely—especially aboard boats on which the practice is to release a sail by a quick snap, breaking the leader wire, rather than cutting the wire. A fifteen-foot length of leader is used, with a length of double line above the swivel. Guides and anglers make it a point to adhere to International Game Fish Association rules, including the terminal tackle requirements and restrictions.

The size of the hooks used usually runs from No. 7/0 to 9/0 for sailfish, depending upon the size of the bait used.

Trolling skipping, whole, dead-bait fish and slow trolling with live baits below the surface are the two major sailfishing methods. More and more live-bait trolling is being done with each passing year; it has become increasingly difficult to lure sails to a dead, skipping bait. It has been suggested that in heavily fished areas, at least, sailfish can develop a shyness toward this type of bait.

BAITS FOR SAILFISH

The two main surface-trolling baits are whole mullet and whole balao (the latter commonly called ballyhoo). Whole mullet are easier to obtain and for that reason alone are in the widest use.

Silver mullet of only five or six inches are preferred. A slit is made the length of the body on either side of the backbone and the bone and innards removed. A small slit is then made in its belly. The hook shank is placed through this slit and pushed forward until the eye of the shank is in the mullet's mouth. A tiny hole is pierced in the exact center of the bait's head. The end of the leader wire is run through this hole and thence through the eye of the hook and out through the center segment of the mullet's throat. With the hook intact in the mullet, the point protruding from its belly, the bait is wrapped tightly on the end of the leader. Make as small a loop as possible, with the twist of the wire snug against the bait's lips. The tighter the wrap, the better it will skip and behave on the surface.

The balao is left with backbone intact. A hook is placed inside this bait the same as the mullet, but the eye is shoved all the way through the fish's mouth from the inside. This fish has a long protruding lower jaw like a tiny sailfish bill. The shank of the hook is wired tightly to its bill with a short length of light wire. Then the hook eye is wrapped to the end of the leader.

Strip baits and "Palm Beach baits" consist of the tail portion and underside of a mullet. Neither of the latter two baits is used to any extent anymore.

The blue runner (*which see*), a small baitfish, is the most popular live bait for sailfish. Sailfish boats usually pick up a small supply of runners before they head offshore; using a light spinning rod and a small jig or shrimp for bait, they catch the runners around sea buoys and on rocky reefs close in to the beaches. Runners are either hooked in the shoulder directly behind the head or are sewed on the hook with cord, leaving the hook fully exposed. Some gamefish guides believe the exposed rig results in a higher percentage of hooked fish because the bare hook has a better chance of getting a good hold in the jaw of a sailfish.

Live-baitfishing may raise more fish, but it also results in a higher percentage of lost fish as compared to trolling. For one thing, the baits are usually big as compared to a trolling bait, and a dead mullet or balao is a good deal less elusive than a darting blue runner. Some anglers do not care for subsurface blue-runner trolling because they enjoy seeing a sailfish appear behind a skipping surface bait, sometimes with the forward part of its dorsal cutting through the water.

On the other hand, there are anglers who enjoy the sustained excitement that goes with live-baitfishing. Often when a sailfish discovers a trolled runner, the baitfish will become panicky, thus telegraphing to the angler the presence of his quarry. The fishing line will jerk as the runner darts evasively, and the baitfish may even pop to the surface at times. This is a game of suspenseful waiting.

TROLLING TECHNIQUE

In trolling, four lines are fished as a general practice. Two are suspended away from the boat in clothespins at the tip of long outriggers. When a fish hits, the line pulls free of the 'rigger. The other two lines are trolled from the stern. These stern lines are commonly called "flatlines." An angler may either hold a stern rod or keep it in a rod socket on the gunwale. When the rod is placed in a gunwale socket, the reel is sometimes set on light drag or ratchet and the line placed in a clothespin or similar device. This practice not only prevents broken tips due to explosive strikes but allows the bait a momentary dropback and relatively light resistance in the event of a sailfish strike.

Fighting chairs have gimbals mounted in the forward edge of the seat in the center. A pin running through the gimbal fits inside a slot in the butt of a trolling rod. An angler sitting in the swivel chair with the butt resting in the gimbal finds that he can move the rod tip up and down and sideways with ease. The pin in the slot of the butt also prevents the reel from moving from side to side.

Most experienced sailfishermen fight their fish from a standing position in the cockpit. They may use a rod belt with a small gimbal mounted on it or use only a leather fighting belt with a round receiver for the butt. Actually, standing up is the most efficient way to battle a gamefish of the size of a sailfish. An angler has greater mobility and control over the rod.

The Atlantic sailfish probably averages a bit over 7 feet and about 40 pounds. One exceeding 8 feet and weighing over 60 pounds is considered quite outstanding and a special trophy. Pacific sailfish run somewhat larger, but the technique remains the same.

How long it might take an angler to whip an average-size fish would depend completely upon his skill, tackle, and the boat. A boat provides maneuverability and the opportunity, if he wishes, to back down on or even run down the fish. Most anglers, however, prefer a good fight and a minimum of assistance from boat and skipper. If you feel this way, too, make certain you apprise a charter captain of this upon stepping aboard his boat. Otherwise, you might hook a sail and find yourself reeling in slack line and have the fish aboard in five minutes flat.

HOW TO HOOK SAILFISH

The basic hooking technique is simple. When the sailfish strikes the bait with its bill, throw the reel in free-spool, and count to ten as line is released to the fish. At the end of the ten count, brake the reel and set the hook. As a technique, this advice is probably as good as any for the beginner. It works rather well, provided the sailfish is of "average" size. But if you spend any amount of time on the Gulf Stream, you will soon learn that you have to treat each sailfish individually and adopt various techniques to counter each situation.

Contrary to a widely accepted bit of sailfish lore, a sail does not always strike a bait with its bill to kill it before eating it. There are times when a sail will surface and gulp a bait with no preliminary tap with its bill. On these occasions it may seem that the sail is slashing at the bait with its bill because to get a surface bait in its mouth the bill has to appear above water. Some veteran gamefish guides theorize that a sailfish is more likely to use its bill on an elusive live bait or a surface bait that is skipping on a choppy sea, rather than a bait that is moving along on a straight and steady course.

Experienced billfish anglers depend upon their thumb to tell them how much line should be released before

setting the hook. Unless a sail actually crashes a bait, the angler will free-spool and "feel" the revolving spool. They can often tell if the bait has been dropped by the fish and is merely drifting astern at the speed of the moving craft. If this is the case they will usually brake, reel the bait across the surface for a short distance, and hold it there on the chance the fish will return to it.

If a fish has taken the bait in its mouth following the strike, the speed of the spool usually indicates this. If the spool suddenly speeds up, however, this almost always is the tip-off that the sail has felt the hook and is accelerating for a leap. In this case, an angler wastes no time in setting the hook.

There are days when the efforts of the most experienced anglers at hooking sailfish will be frustrated. Perhaps due to weather conditions or an abundance of available food, sailfish will do little more than play with the bait that is offered them. This may take different forms. Gamefish guides apply the term "window shopper" to a sailfish that goes from bait to bait and, after a close inspection of the offerings, meanders off. Another kind of fish that is rough on an angler's nervous system is one that repeatedly hits a bait and drops it.

In striking a sail it is extremely important to allow the line to become taut before sinking the hook. When an angler engages the brake and immediately raises the rod tip to strike the fish, there is usually too much slack in the line to sink the hook point. After braking, an angler should keep the rod tip pointed at the fish until the line comes taut. Then, before the fish has a chance to react to the hook, the tip should be raised sharply. The average sail will make a long, scorching run after being hooked, spicing this with a variety of leaps. If an angler is lucky his fish will tail-walk, which is a thrilling sight. But the sail has a variety of surface maneuvers. It might stand on its bill or bolt straight out of the water and come down on its belly. There are novice fishermen who become so engrossed with the speeding reel spool on one of these runs that they actually miss the aerial performance. Often a beginner will reel feverishly while the sail is taking line. This is fruitless and serves only to weary the individual on the rod.

When a sail is making a run the best thing to do is relax and watch its acrobatics guarding against slack in the line. If the fish suddenly reverses its field, the skipper of the fishing boat will gun the engines in an attempt to prevent the fish from shaking the hook. Eventually, a running sail will slow down. That's the time to retrieve line with a pumping motion of the rod tip. This is done by slowly raising the tip, and then lowering it smoothly while picking up line with the crank. Dropping the rod tip too quickly can result in slack line and a lost fish.

SAILFISH ON THE FLY ROD

Catching a billfish on fly does not just happen; it is made to happen, using a very specialized technique originally developed by Dr. Webster Robinson of Miami, Florida. The fishing is difficult, but most certainly rewarding for those who want to spend the time becoming accomplished in the ultimate of light-tackle sailfishing.

Tackle and rigging are of prime importance, and care and attention to detail often spell the difference between success and failure. Generally a rod capable of handling at least a No. 10 line is sufficient. The reel must be able to carry a minimum of 200 yards of 27-pound test backing plus flyline. Dacron is important, since it has little stretch and the chances of popping a spool after retrieving a couple of hundred yards of line under pressure are slight. A big plus for any reel is a good cork drag. Tension can be applied critically, without fear that a sudden bit of unexpected resistance will cause a break-off. The leader is kept short and simple. Six feet of 60-pound-test monofilament is connected to the flyline with a nail knot. The knot itself is covered with a fast-drying glue (pliobond). This enables it to slip easily through the guides which becomes particularly important during the final stages of the battle. Tippet strength is up to the individual angler, though most fishermen prefer 12-pound test. To qualify for a record or to catch the fish in the true spirit of the game the tippet must measure at least 12 inches in length with an additional shock tippet of no more than 12 inches. The tippet is fastened to the rest of the leader and to the shock tippet with a 100 percent knot; that is, a knot as strong as any part of the line. The improved blood knot is particularly effective when joining monofilaments of greatly dissimilar size, or a Bimini twist may be used in conjunction with an Albright Knot for joining the monofilament tippet to a wire shock tippet. The shock tippet is usually made of a hard monofilament testing 100 pounds or a piece of No. 5 leader wire.

Both Atlantic and Pacific sails have been caught on a wide variety of flies ranging from tandem-hooked 8-inch streamers down to the size used for bonefish. Color seems to matter little. The fly which has accounted for the most fish, however, is a simple white streamer constructed of 6-inch saddle hackles with a few strips of mylar. It is tied on a 5/0 hook. Care should be taken to sharpen the hook properly; that is, filed to a three-edged razor-fine point.

Sailfish may be found almost worldwide in tropical waters, but there are only a relatively few practical places in which the average angler may hope for success. South Florida during the winter is the best bet for Atlantic sails, particularly during December and January in the Palm Beach, Jupiter, Stuart area. The Pacific sail, which averages about three times the size of its Atlantic variety, is found in good supply from the tip of the Baja peninsula all the way to Ecuador.

The actual fishing is best accomplished from a small, open boat with an unobstructed cockpit. Generally two assistants are required—one to operate the boat, the other to work the teaser. The teasing equipment may be any standard offshore rod or heavy plug rod equipped with at least 30-pound-test line. The teaser itself is usually a hookless rubber squid about 10 inches long. This is more durable than a natural bait. Generally two teasers are pulled at one time. When a sail rises behind one of the teasers the man running the boat grabs the alternate rod and pulls that squid from the water. The boat continues to run at its normal trolling speed. The angler stands in the stern with 30 or 40 feet of line stripped out ready to shoot. The sailfish will usually begin by batting the teaser with its bill. Soon its tactics change and it will attempt to swallow the teaser. Instead of letting the teaser be taken, it must be jerked away each time, but with short jerks just enough to keep it out of the fish's mouth. Invariably the sail becomes frustrated to the point of charging the squid with great lunges. At this point the man operating the teaser signals the captain to put the boat in neutral. The angler

must make one quick last check to be certain that his flyline is free of any obstructions. The teaser is retrieved just ahead of the onrushing sail to a point 30–35 feet from the boat. Then the man with the teaser yanks back hard pulling the lure clear of the water as the angler shoots his fly at a spot slightly ahead of where the teaser departed. Timed correctly, the fish will be under the fly and there is no need to retrieve; otherwise, the fly is stripped back rapidly toward the boat. When the fly is taken, the hook should be set solidly three times, and the sailfish begins a series of magnificent leaps starting almost at boatside. The angler must concentrate on getting his loose flyline off the deck and smoothly through the guides. As soon as the fish has indicated its course the captain must have the boat headed in that direction—fast enough for the angler to gain line back on his reel under slight tension. The idea is to keep the boat as close to the fish as possible in order to cut the odds of a long, uninteresting battle. Within the first 10–20 minutes the average Pacific sail, weighing about 100 pounds, will begin to tire. This is an almost crucial period. The pressure has to be maintained to within ounces of breaking point, so all knots must test 100 percent. Under relentless pressure the sail will come to the surface and roll on its side, a sure sign the fish is exhausted. If the boatman is experienced, the fish will only be a few short jumps away. On the other hand, if the angler has missed his chance to bill the fish quickly, he will spend much of the next hour or two, or even three, standing in a backbreaking position doing little more than holding the rod while the fish slowly regains its strength, in which case it's better to break the fish off and start over again.

BOATING THE SAILFISH

The handling of a sailfish after it has been brought to the boat is not something that should be taken lightly. The bill of a sailfish is a weapon, and can wound through intent or chance. On charter boats and most of the larger private fishing cruisers, the boating or releasing of a sailfish is done by an experienced crewman. Wearing cotton gloves, the crewman grasps the leader wire and carefully works the sail beside the boat. If the fish is going to be killed, he will grasp the sail's bill and lift it aboard headfirst. However, most sailfish are released alive unless the angler wants the fish for a trophy mount. An easy way to release a sail is to cut the leader wire near its mouth. The hook in a sail's jaws disintegrates quickly in saltwater.

The angler who intends to start off sailfishing on his own should remember to take along gloves. Not only can the wire cut deeply into a fisherman's hand, but the surface of a sailfish bill is like a rasp. You can run your hand down the bill toward a sail's body, but not the other way.

Sailfish incidentally should never be gaffed. It is not wise to bring a sailfish aboard a boat with its dangerous bill swinging free. *See also* Big-Game Fishing, Billfish, Pacific Sailfish
—E.C.B.

ATLANTIC SALMON *Salmo salar* This best-known member of the family Salmonidae is found in the northern part of the Atlantic Ocean. Along North American shores it occurs from Greenland to Cape Cod. In Europe it is found from Russia to Portugal. The species is migratory for the most part but some lakes in Maine, southeastern Canada, and Argentina contain resident races where they

Atlantic Salmon 28-pound Male, Laerdal River, Norway

are known as Sebago Salmon, ouananiche, or landlocked salmon (*which see*). Unlike the Pacific salmon, the Atlantic salmon can spawn more than once.

The body of the Atlantic salmon is five times as long as it is deep. It has 8–10 rays in the anal fin. The dentaries become large and sharp in the spawning season and the lower jaw of the male develops a cartilaginous protuberance in the form of a hook known as a kype. Teeth are also present on the vomer. The scales are large and there are 120–130 on the lateral line. The body color is variable; stream dwelling fish are brownish-olive, the young with red spots on sides, 2 rarely 3 dark spots on the operculum, and parr marked, look very similar to young brown trout; sea run fish are blue-black dorsally and bright silver on the sides. During the long journey to their spawning grounds the silvery flanks of the male become a dirty red and those of the female black. Although weights to 100 pounds have been reported, the average is probably closer to 12 pounds. Many attempts have been made to transplant Atlantic salmon to the Pacific, but without success. Fish of sea-run origin have been stocked in Oregon lakes with no outlet to the sea and this landlocked form does provide a token fishery in the western United States.

SPAWNING

The salmon spawns in the fall in the upper reaches of streams and the young remain in freshwater from 1 to 4 or 5 years, migrating then to sea and reaching maturity at 3–5 years of age or more. They may spawn two or three times, but usually less than 10 per cent of adults entering freshwater have spawned before. The nest or redd is dug by the female in gravel that has been carefully selected. Powerful strokes of the tail when she is on her side move the gravel by means of the resulting hydraulic action of water currents and a pocket is formed. After the eggs are deposited in the pocket and fertilized, the female covers them and in doing so may instantly cut another depression and deposit eggs in it also. Each spawning act is accompanied by the male lying at her side who fertilizes the ova with a cloud of milt. Sometimes a redd is several yards in length and as much as 18 inches deep—depending on the size of the female. Parr may also assist in fertilization by lying in close proximity to the redd and releasing milt at the same time as the adult male. The periods of rest between several ovipositions varies considerably, as does the number of ovipositions. The total

number of eggs deposited by one female may be roughly calculated at 700–800 per pound of her body weight.

GROWTH

Wherever their river of origin, the parr disguise their first fragile years under silvery scales and start off to the ocean when 5 or 6 inches in length. They are now called smolts. The age at which smolts migrate depends on how fast they have grown; some begin their journey at 3 years, but the largest 2-year-olds migrate also; while still others, the smallest of their year group, will remain in freshwater until they are 4 years old. With this apparent attempt at a somewhat uniform beginning, one would expect Atlantic salmon to reach a common weight before returning to their rivers. But eventual size may be a hereditary trait, and geographically the fish divide themselves into two, three or four different age classes who may return at independent seasons. The smallest of these is the grilse which is ordinarily 3–5 years old. Grilse live through just one winter in the ocean, during which time they grow from the 6-inch smolt size to 4 pounds or more (this includes prewinter and postwinter growth). Most rivers have grilse runs, but some regions like the east coast of the Province of Newfoundland are dominated by grilse, while other regions have runs of both grilse and older salmon. Older salmon, having passed two winters at sea, return as small adults of 4 or 5 years in age, weighing from 9–12 pounds. The third group consists of large adult fish of 5 and 6 years old with three winters of ocean feeding, which weigh in the 18–30 pound class. The fourth and least common group consists of very large fish who have passed four, five, or even six winters in the ocean and weigh from 35–45 pounds. In this same age class and endemic to certain areas are really big salmon weighing from 50–70

Atlantic Salmon, Male Head, Showing Kype

pounds. These trophy fish are more common to Europe and appear most often in the rivers of Norway. The world's record rod-caught Atlantic salmon, a Norwegian fish, weighed 79½ pounds.

MIGRATIONS

With rare exceptions, all salmon return to their parent rivers for spawning. To what extent they travel in the ocean or what determines the pattern of their marine existence is not known. There is some evidence that salmon from both sides of the Atlantic share a common feeding ground near Greenland. On October 10, 1960, an Atlantic salmon 71 cm. total length, weighing 3.7 kgm. (8.2 pounds), and carrying Fisheries Research Board of Canada tag No. 1,616, was caught in the sea off Tassiussaq (65° 06′ N., 52° 08′ W.), near Napossok to the south of Sukkertoppen, Greenland. The fish was tagged on May 22, 1959, in the estuary of the Miramichi River near Chatham, New Brunswick (47° 04′ N., 65° 28′ W.), as a smolt 17.5 cm. in total length. It was one of 3,500 smolts tagged there in May and June, 1959, with tags patterned after those used by Dr. Borje Carlin in Sweden, but had printed laminated plastic pendants supplied by a commercial firm.

Scales from the recaptured fish show three years of river life typical of Miramichi River smolts, followed by a first sea year of moderate growth and a relatively wide winter band. The second sea year includes a period of fast growth followed by a summer check, then a period of fast growth continuing to the time of capture in October.

This recapture represents one of the longest migrations recorded (about 1,500 miles) for Canadian Atlantic salmon, the river of origin of which is known through fin-clipping or tagging. Many fin-clipped salmon from Quebec, New Brunswick, and Nova Scotia rivers have been recaptured, however, in sea fisheries as far away as Newfoundland and Labrador. The first direct evidence of Scottish salmon reaching Greenland waters was provided by the recapture in October, 1956, near Sukkertoppen, Greenland, of a fish tagged as a kelt in November, 1955, at Loch na Croic, Ross-shire. Similar recaptures of tagged salmon known to be of North American and European origin have been made off Greenland in recent years.

A marked salmon from the Northeast Margaree River of Nova Scotia was captured two years later off the coast of Newfoundland (over 500 miles from home), then tagged, and released again. Three months afterward the fish was caught by an angler—in the Northeast Margaree River. It had returned to spawn. This ability of salmon to travel around countless miles of ocean and return to their natal watershed is constant. Despite painstaking efforts to isolate the homing mechanism, there is no simple explanation as to how orientation is achieved in the sea.

The olfactory senses are apparently responsible for the ability to discriminate between one watershed and another. Pure water does not exist in nature. There are various substances dissolved in it which come from the soil, air, and the metabolism of its organisms. The composition of organic communities is highly varied, and changes in the chemical state of water are caused by the withdrawal of nutrients on one hand and the release of metabolic products on the other. Thus, water is not a consistently flavored liquid. Parenthetically, the sense of smell in fish is keen. They will respond to concentrations of organic materials below the odor threshold of man. Their nostrils are represented by conventional holes in the snout, but instead of connecting with the throat passage as in man, they lead into small sacs which are sensitive olfactory organs. Odor-carrying water is delivered into these tissues by muscles or hairlike cilia. The discriminatory ability of salmon is embodied in the principle that each river has a distinctive aroma, and individual salmon react differently to that odor depending on their familiarity with it. One might suppose that after two or three years in the ocean a fish would no longer recognize its parent stream. However, laboratory extinction tests have demonstrated that fish will react to different stream odors after a "forgetting" period and the ability to remember was keener among fish who were trained when young than among those who learned later in life.

COMMERCIAL VALUE

The Atlantic salmon has great value as a market fish the world over. The bulk of these salmon are not caught by sport fishermen. On the Canadian coast the gear comprises surface drift nets operated offshore, inshore fixed trap nets and a few floating gillnets, while some salmon are taken incidentally in gear set for other species. Traditionally, the nets have been set to take adult fish as they apparently move from the feeding areas, which are often

Fly fishing for salmon is great sport, made even more exciting with light tackle on big rivers such as the Spey in Scotland

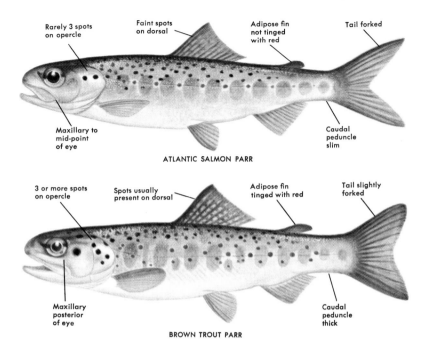

Characteristics of the Atlantic Salmon Parr and Brown Trout Parr (5 inches in length)

far away in the sea, toward the native streams to spawn. Reliable information on the capture of adult salmon of known river origin by such gear over a wide area of the coast has come from a marking program involving smolts produced in the Miramichi and Pollett Rivers, New Brunswick, the Port Daniel River, Quebec, and the Little Codroy River, Newfoundland. It has been found, for example, that many salmon produced in maritime streams are taken far away in commercial nets, particularly around the east coast of Newfoundland. Also, they may wander into the estuaries of other maritime rivers and be caught there by commercial gear. Of course, many are also taken by the gear set in the estuary of their native river.

There are fishery regulations covering the opening and closing date of the seasons which are different for different areas of the coast, mesh regulations aimed at protecting small salmon (grilse), weekly closed periods to allow fish to escape the nets completely for a couple of days each week, but no quota systems. Most of the catch consists of two-sea-year fish, except around Newfoundland where in some limited areas grilse can still be caught for market in commercial nets. Each year the run of fish into many estuaries is marked by two peaks, one early in the summer and one in the autumn. In some rivers like the Miramichi the late run has by far the most fish, which come in after the commercial season is over. Only early run fish are desired by most commercial fishermen, and at present there is no demand for a fall fishery. As the spawning season approaches, salmon are not considered to be in good condition for the gourmet market.

ANGLING VALUE

The Atlantic salmon is one of the most prized trophies among freshwater anglers. Individual fish will sometimes run up to 50 pounds or more, but 15–20-pound Atlantic

salmon are fairly common. The fish is very active when hooked and invariably jumps from the water. When compared to other outstanding gamefish, the salmon will not run as swiftly as the bonefish, nor will it leap to the dizzy heights of a tarpon, and it lacks the acquired caution of a brown trout. And no fish in the world can match a white or blue marlin for sheer aerial tenacity. But the decathlon salmon has part of all these talents to a large degree. Some idea of its spirit can be realized in seeing the fish leap five or six feet in the air to hit a torrential waterfall, then with powerful body contortions, it literally swims upward through the flow. But the other part is the unique quarry adult salmon become; they leave the ocean with enough stored energy to survive with no food for many months. The paradox of angling for them is that the fish are not actively feeding in freshwater. The fact that they strike a lure is believed to be more of a conditioned reflex than any particular desire to eat.

Although the Atlantic salmon may legally be taken with spoons, plugs, and live baits in some countries, its chief angling value is to the fly fisher. However, the quality of the sport varies with the location and the season. All salmon rivers do not fish well to the fly because of their size or turbulence or the prevailing weather conditions. Thus, a premium is placed on first-class water and the cost of angling is often expensive. In the United States only the state of Maine provides Atlantic salmon fishing so the angler must travel long distances in the known periods that correspond with a run of fish.

PLANNING A SALMON TRIP

The world of the salmon angler is in Norway, Sweden, Quebec, the British Isles, Spain, France, Iceland, Greenland, the Maritime Provinces of Canada, and the state of Maine. At its satisfying and productive best, salmon fishing is probably the most exclusive sport in the world. One must have leisure time to visit the famous streams because there's no guarantee of success on any particular day or week. In fact, if you can average one salmon per day in a ten-day period the fishing would be rated quite good. If you average two or three salmon per day in the same time —it's exceptional. The recorded average on the legendary Alta River is four fish per ten rod-days. So abundant moments notwithstanding, the game is qualitative and unpredictable. When planning a trip, allow one month to be on the safe side, and expect two weeks of quality fishing. Weather and water conditions must be favorable, not only at the time of your arrival, but in the critical months preceding it. The region might have heavy snowfalls followed by drenching spring rains that swell the rivers into yellow arteries, thus triggering an early migration. The salmon dash upstream quickly, and before you can unpack your tackle, the fishing is nearly done on the lower beats. Or a prolonged drought could make the run late, and you are left fishless on the upper beats. There is no way of anticipating the quality of the angling that is to be found on even the best rivers in a brief visit.

FLY-FISHING TACKLE

There is no one fly rod perfectly suited to all salmon fishing. The variable factor is the conditions under which your fishing must be done. At the extremes, let's suppose that you are going to the Aaro River in Norway for big salmon. The Aaro is a chaos of white water that shoots into the head of Sognfjord. Near its mouth the stream gradient is 90 feet within a 200-yard distance. The biggest Aaro salmon weighed 76 pounds (4 feet 8 inches long), but 40- and 50-pound fish are an everyday possibility. On the Aaro you must stop your fish at the very first run. This requires heavy tackle. Even with 14-foot rods and 60-pound-test leader tippets, Aaro anglers break off frequently. There is little point in working such a flow with finely calibered rods. On the other hand, if you are planning a trip to Iceland, don't hesitate to sample the delights of those miniature 7½-foot, 2½-ounce wands. There is very little opportunity of hooking a large fish in the treeless barrens, and the island is fissured by sparkling watercourses of an ideal size for light tackle. The average Icelandic salmon weighs about 6 pounds, and a 20-pound fish would be out of the ordinary. Although some of the Canadian rivers are still fished with big two-handed rods, the general trend today is toward 8½- and 9-foot lengths on most streams. Fortunately, maritime rivers lend themselves to the use of fairly light tackle and under normal conditions in the summer and fall low water and small flies are the rule. As a general gauge, rods which handle No. 8 or No. 9 (floating) lines are best adapted for Canadian salmon fishing. It requires 220 to 246 grains of line to push large flies through the air comfortably. The line should float both for clean pickups and easier handling of the fly.

The fly reel (*which see*) for Atlantic salmon fishing should be ample enough to hold whatever fly line your rod requires plus 150 yards of backing. For the most part, reels in the 3½–4-inch diameters are suitable.

The fly leader (*which see*) for Atlantic salmon fishing should test 6–12 pounds in the tippet section; it should be in the 9–12-foot lengths. For dry-fly-fishing in the summer you will also need fly leaders tapered down to 3X or approximately 5-pound test.

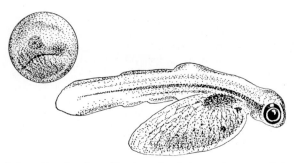

Salmon Egg Ready to Hatch, and a Salmon Alevin with Yolk Sac Attached

FLY SIZE IMPORTANT

The Atlantic salmon is among the heaviest fishes to be caught on artificial flies in freshwater streams, and as such, the angling represents, with few perceptible changes, a projection of the caster's art on a larger scale. Ordinary trout patterns may provoke salmon when the stream is low and clear, but, traditionally, the angler presents feathered extravagances which vary from thumbnail size to highwater patterns big enough to fill a man's palm. These are divided into two main types: wet flies, which sink and are fished below the surface; and dry flies, which float on top of the water. In his fasting, *salar* becomes a whimsical Nero; so the size of the fly, its presentation, and to a lesser degree the color of the fly are critical factors in drawing a strike. Generally speaking, a well-rounded assortment should include all sizes from hooks No. 8 to No. 6/0 in the Silver Wilkinson, Silver Grey, Jock Scott, Durham Ranger, Dusty Miller, Green Highlander, Blue Doctor, Blue Charm, March Brown, Black Dose, Brown Bomber, Lady Amherst, Silver Rat, Red Abbey, and Nepisquit Gray wet patterns.

The choice of a wet fly on the stream depends on the stage of the water. Broadly speaking, the lower and clearer the river, the smaller the fly should be. A popular preference for summer conditions is a sparse low water dressing on either a No. 6, 8, or 10 hook. The low water fly is actually a small fly tied on an oversize hook. A No. 6 low-water pattern is about the same size as a standard No. 10. This hook has the advantage of greater hooking and holding power on big fish when a small fly is the only thing that will seem to interest the salmon.

In contrast, for early-season fishing, when the river is at flood stage, the most popular sizes are No. 1/0 to 5/0 hooks. These larger flies are more visible to the fish in discolored water.

THE LIE

Salmon differ from trout in their choice of stations in the river. A salmon will make its temporary residence in some of the most unlikely looking places. This "lie" may be nothing more than a slight depression in the bottom along the shallow edge of the stream—a spot where the trout fisherman would wade. Or it may be in a narrow slick at the tail of an empty pool. Most of the pretty water used by trout (which are conscious of feeding lanes) is meaningless to the Atlantic salmon. Furthermore, a salmon will not hold just anywhere in the stream. Comparatively long stretches are ignored. A mile of beautiful but fishless water may exist between one lie and the next. The salmon may stop to rest in certain pools for a short period in its upstream journey, but these are not the "taking" lies where it will rise to a fly. And as the water level drops with the approach of summer the salmon will change its position once more to compensate for some deficiency in the current. Wherever it moves the most productive lies are apt to be fairly shallow. Three or four feet is the average depth. Salmon utilize the same lies year after year, and unless you are familiar with the river, it's important to seek the counsel of a competent guide. Blind casting is seldom productive without some knowledge of the fish's location.

WET-FLY-FISHING

The main difference between trout and salmon angling is that when we seek the former we are dealing primarily with feeding fish; our intent is to imitate their food. Salmon on the other hand do not feed at this time, or they feed so sporadically that for all practical purposes there's no reason why they should take a fly. In the endless debate, irritation, natural ferocity, memories of parr life, and various other theories have won some favor. So the artificial flies we use can be extremely fanciful as well as lifelike. The size and type to select depend on several factors, but its presentation is of prime importance. It's generally agreed that the sunk fly should come to the fish sideways so to speak, rather than hanging in a nose upstream position. This doesn't mean a salmon won't hit the feathers at any angle, but the broadside fly usually draws more strikes and because of his position he almost automatically travels at the right speed. Whereas trout are sought by casting upstream with the dry fly, nymph, and often the wet fly, the search for salmon is almost wholly in a cross and downstream path. This is not a rigid rule, but the trout fisher and the salmon angler commonly travel in opposite directions.

Classically, Wood's greased-line method, which boils down to fishing a fly close to the surface without any pull from the line or other movement except that imparted by the currents, has as its antithesis Crosfield's system in which the fly is always dragging. Both methods require the fly to be fished high in the water—a position which is usually most effective. Where Wood prescribes casting a slack line and fishing it downriver quite loose and unrestrained, Crosfield recommends casting a tight line across stream, then pulling it along with the left hand to make the salmon dash for the fly. Both were skillful anglers, and their methods are effective with small wet flies in a bright, clear stream. Most anglers try some part of each technique or use them interchangeably in all levels of water.

Ordinarily, the salmon angler casts the wet fly across and slightly downstream. Whether the line is perfectly straight or slightly slack as it touches the water doesn't matter too much. The important thing is to keep the fly from lagging behind the line and leader. By mending, or rolling the line so that it makes a curve upstream over intervening fast currents, he prevents the fly from dragging. How this can best be done varies with almost every cast. The experienced caster fishes with his mind as well as his hands. In slow water, for example, it may be necessary to lift the rod and strip line to put the fly under tension and keep it swimming at the correct speed. Conversely, the quick spots may require lowering the rod or paying out a few coils of line to decrease it. The thing to avoid is

accelerating drag which ends with the fly whipping around like a cow's tail. Crosfield sought to control its speed by stripping slow or fast according to the pull of the current. In flat water many anglers are inclined to lean on his system entirely. They cast straight across then with an extended rod, and the leader and fly under tension retrieve fast while the rod tip follows the downward path of the line. At the end of any drift, the fly is left to hang in the current for a few moments and then carefully lead out of the apparent holding water before making a new cast. This is the merest outline, as we have endless possibilities within the basic presentation. Regional schools of technique differ as greatly as the choice of flies.

DRY-FLY-FISHING

The time to use a dry fly for salmon is in stale water under a blazing sky. All salmon regions do not provide consistent dry-fly-fishing. Most European rivers are deficient in this respect. But in Maine and Canada the Atlantic salmon displays a keen interest in floating patterns. An angler could probably go through a whole summer season on Anticosti Island, for example, using nothing but the dry fly—an addiction which a Norwegian angler would never find practical. Fjord streams are bucketed with ice water right through August. To be ideal, the water temperature should be over 60° F and its level somewhat on the droughty side. Under these conditions the dry fly is often superior to any of the sunk patterns. Occasionally, salmon are caught on floaters early in the season; however, it is the exception rather than the rule. Unlike the trout technique, which requires casting in an upstream direction, the dry fly for salmon is a more relaxed method. For the most part we work across quartering downstream. Salmon are not as easily disturbed by the sight of a man flailing the air; in fact, they often regard him with disdain. So the advantage of sneaking up behind the fish is unimportant. True, we use the longest casts possible and try to remain inconspicuous, but what we really want is to *see* the salmon. Knowing exactly where the fish is holding and what his reactions are to our presentation is the key to earning strikes. This doesn't imply that the salmon should be visible at all times; a flash, a stirring of the water, or some faint sign of its presence is all that we need to justify any series of casts. If a trout is hungry and the fly is presented nicely the first time, it will invariably rise to it. But the chance of taking that trout after a great number of casts decreases proportionately, This is not true of a salmon. It may rise to the first cast or the one hundred and first. Perhaps the chief mental hurdle an experienced trout angler must overcome is the fact that in dealing with *salar* we must often coax him into a strike.

THE SALMON STRIKE

Trout and salmon also differ in their strike. Typically, a trout grabs the wet fly and ejects it almost instantly. We may see nothing more than a wink of bright color in the water or a stopping of the leader. Whatever the sign, it is brief, and our reaction must be fast. By contrast, a salmon takes with a heavy, almost dead pull. It often flashes under the fly and creates a commotion even before the feathers have been touched. Here a reflexive snap of the rod will simply pull the fly away. It's possible to let a salmon mouth the fly and turn downward before striking.

We simply lift the rod to increase line tension enough to set the hook in the fish's jaw. When using the dry fly, it may require a bit more force to drive the barb home if there is any length of slack line on the surface. This requires some judgment.

The dry-fly rise is usually more spectacular and perhaps for that reason easier to miss. In a playful mood the fish may roll under the fly like a surfacing porpoise and lift it out of the water or even slap it with its tail. Such a fish can often be interested in some other fly at some other moment. But as a rule the false riser is not ready to be caught. Grilse will also leap over the fly and snatch it on the way down. Big fish may come straight from below or in a roll half out of the water or like a skilled gymnast a fish will do a flip at the surface and nail the feathers within inches of his own tail. Visually, it's difficult for an angler to control trout-trained reflexes and adopt the deliberate strike. The important thing is to give the salmon time to get the fly in his mouth and close his jaws.

BLACK-SALMON FISHING

From an angling standpoint, the best salmon fishing occurs when the fish are "bright" or coming into freshwater still wearing their sea lice. As the river months pass, *salar* gradually deteriorates in flesh and spirit, and after spawning it is little more than a ghost of itself. At this stage it becomes a "black" salmon—the spent fish which drifts back to the sea after wintering under the ice of wilderness pools. These ragged kelts shorn of their beautiful coloration are not universally legal game. In New Brunswick alone, black salmon are fished in the spring months—a play in which performance lags behind conviction. The special circumstance which makes black-salmon fishing possible is because over 90 per cent of the fish entering these provincial waters are spawning for the first time; about 6 per cent are repeat spawners, and thus a limited amount of angling represents a minute depletion of the total population.

CANADIAN SALMON FISHING

(Quebec and New Brunswick)

Quebec and New Brunswick both afford excellent Atlantic salmon fishing for the American angler, whereas the revival of Maine's once splendid salmon fisheries has not yet progressed to the state where it provides much more than enough sport to go round for the local fishermen. Salmon are to be taken by the score in Quebec and by the hundreds in New Brunswick for every dozen to be taken at this stage of the game in Maine.

In general, the Quebec waters are deeper and the average salmon is larger than in New Brunswick. While fishing from canoes and wading are both done in both places, the former predominates in Quebec and the latter in New Brunswick. And—again to generalize—the average cost per day's fishing in Quebec is apt to be just about as much higher as the fish are larger, in comparison to New Brunswick. Similarly, the size of tackle required is proportionately heavier in Quebec. Guides are required by law, for nonresident anglers, in both provinces. But in Quebec they tend to behave like servants and do things for the visiting angler, whereas in New Brunswick they tend rather to do things with their "sport" than for him and to show him the ropes by example rather than by suggestions, as would be the case in Quebec. There are excep-

tions, of course, in both provinces, but the generalization is as accurate as any generalization can be.

The fishing in Quebec tends to be more leisurely, more luxurious, more sedate, and less demanding than in New Brunswick, where roughing it is more likely to be the rule than the exception. And whereas public fishing, such as in the Matane River, is very unusual in Quebec, where most waters are privately held by individuals or clubs, the opposite is the case in New Brunswick, where only a small portion of the water is leased or otherwise restricted. For the trout fisherman who simply wants to do some postgraduate work with larger members of the *Salmo* group, the change from his native streams and the alteration of his present tackle and fishing habits would be much less abrupt if he were to go after salmon in New Brunswick than in Quebec.

In general, and again with exceptions in both places, the best fishing is early in Quebec and late in New Brunswick. There are successive runs in both instances, but the Quebec rivers usually start earlier—June 5th, say, for Quebec, as opposed to June 25th for New Brunswick—and while the bigger fish come early in Quebec, the opposite is the case in New Brunswick. A twenty-five pounder is average in June in Quebec, for instance, whereas a fish of that size would be exceptional in New Brunswick before September, and unusual even then. Rivers like the Matapedia and Restigouche average about twenty pounds over the entire season, while the entire season average on the Miramichi is just under ten pounds. Another contrast —and again subject to exceptions in both places—is that the best taking time in the Quebec rivers is late morning— say, 10:30 A.M. to noon—whereas it's early evening—say, 6 to 8 P.M.—in New Brunswick.

The angler in Quebec will need at least an 8-foot rod, with a 3½-inch reel, to take a No. 8 or No. 9 line and 200 yards of backing as an absolute minimum. He will be unhappy with lighter tackle than this, first because he's very apt to find it difficult to get adequate casts from a canoe with a shorter rod or a lighter line and second because in the heavy water he is very likely to need 1/0-size flies, or even larger, to get down to where the fish may be under given water conditions. Favored flies are Silver Rat, Green Highlander, and Jock Scott. Sizes should run 1/0, 1, 2, and 4, with little likelihood of needing more than an occasional and exceptional fly either larger or smaller than that range.

The guide anchors the canoe, in successive "drops," from the head of the pool to its tail, and the angler casts alternately across to the right and left, letting the line swing the fly, from both directions, to a point directly below the canoe. The great majority of the takes are directly downstream from the angler, in line with the bow of the anchored canoe, and most often within twenty to thirty feet below the canoe. Once fast to a fish, the angler contents himself with keeping the rod tip up and confines his playing of the fish to the irreducible minimum until the guide has had a chance to raise the anchor and start getting the canoe toward shore, where the angler will then make an earnest effort to regain his backing and his line and to bring the fish within range of the enormous net that the guide has by now taken out of the canoe.

In contrast, the angler in New Brunswick will wade out within casting range, raise his rod tip when the fish takes, stumble and scramble back toward shore as best he can, meanwhile letting the fish run until the angler can get out of the water and chase after him along the river bank, trying to get below the fish and head him back upstream, where the current will help to play him out, then finally beaching him. The chances are better than equal that the guide will not even be in sight at this point. He will be either somewhere else along the same beach, chasing after another fish (because when salmon take they're very apt to take in sudden flurries), or he will be off at some other pool on the presumed pretext of casing another "hot spot" for the benefit of the fisherman he is guiding.

The angler accustomed to the use of a short, light rod will find it no more of a handicap fishing for salmon in New Brunswick than it has ever been on his own trouting haunts. Nor will he need a heavier line. What he will need is at least two hundred yards of backing. Even a four-pound grilse will be as likely as not to run into the second hundred yards of backing before the angler gets to a position where he can start regaining it.

Black Dose and Jock Scott are the two most effective flies among the standard patterns. The former will bring strikes from both grilse and salmon, whereas the latter seems to exercise a slight degree of selectivity, being a bit more likely to be taken by salmon than by grilse. The latter, however, seem especially devoted to the Conrad, a black-bodied, silver-ribbed, black-hair wing fly with a bright green butt. The butt is of Gantron vividness and appears to be visible to an extraordinary degree. This fly can be murderous when the grilse are in a taking mood. In general, hair-wing flies have been increasingly favored in New Brunswick in recent years, although such staple standard patterns as Silver Doctor, Silver Grey, Silver Wilkinson, Silver Blue, and Blue Charm still take fish when the fish are taking. So, for that matter, do trout flies, including streamers and bucktails. In New Brunswick it is very rare to need any fly larger than No. 6, and after the first week in July, No. 8 and smaller can be used effectively. In the September fishing, when the dry fly comes into its own, spiders down to No. 16 have been used successfully. In both provinces guides are prone to try to get the angler to use heavier terminal tackle than he needs. They will try to get you to use tippets of 20-pound test in Quebec, and 10-pound-test in New Brunswick. Ten is heavy enough for the former and 6-pound-test for the latter. You will lose a measurable percentage of fish hooked in both places, and rather more in New Brunswick than in Quebec, but the fly will come back to you almost every time.

The angler should not go to either New Brunswick or Quebec without being reminded that money spent in pursuit of Atlantic salmon ranks midway between money invested in backing a Broadway show and money invested in an Irish Sweepstakes ticket. The rewards are glorious in all three cases, but no crying towels are provided in the event of failure to cash in. General experience has been that there will never be more than one good week out of every four spent fishing for salmon, and there is no way that anybody can know in advance which one of the four it will be. So unless you have four weeks to devote to it, the odds are three to one against you that it will be either the week before you get there or the week after you leave. Par for the course, the world over, is a fish a day, but very rare is the salmon angler who consistently breaks par. *See also* England, Finland, Iceland, Ireland, Labrador, Landlocked Salmon, Maine, New Brunswick, Newfoundland, Norway, Quebec, Scotland, Spain, Sweden, Wales

—A.G.
—C.J.K.
—A.J.McC.

ATLANTIC SAURY *Scomberesox saurus* A small saltwater species found in the North Atlantic which somewhat resembles the needlefish. It has no angling value. The saury appears sporadically along eastern shores during the summer months when it travels in dense schools.

Atlantic Saury

For this reason commercial men seldom catch them, and there is no market for an otherwise good table fish. There is also a Pacific saury (*Cololabis saira*), which ranges from Japan to California. The Japanese freeze, can, and ship part of their catch to the United States during peak periods. —A.J.McC.

ATLANTIC SHARPNOSE SHARK *Rhizoprionodon terraenovae* This small shark is distinguished by the labial furrows at the corners of its mouth. It is a slender species with a pointed, narrow snout and a high dorsal fin, which is placed relatively far forward. Its slanting teeth are smooth save for a notch on the outer edge. The body is brownish to olive-gray above, with a white belly and white along the rear edge of the pectoral fins, and the dorsal and caudal fins are dark-edged.

LIFE HISTORY

It grows to about 3 feet. A 20-inch specimen weighed about 3 pounds. It is known from both sides of the Atlantic Ocean, being found from Uruguay to North Carolina and also as an accidental visitor as far north as the Bay of Fundy. In the eastern Atlantic it is known from Morocco to the Cameroons and the Cape Verde Islands. Its reproductive habits are poorly known, except that the young are born alive. Probably this occurs in late spring and summer in the northern part of its range. It is a fairly common species, occurring in rather shallow waters of bays, beaches, and estuaries, with reports of this species entering brackish and tidal freshwater. Small fish are eaten, including menhaden, and invertebrates (shrimps and mollusks), depending on locality of capture. It is known to sportsmen as a bait snatcher, and in the Caribbean it is sometimes used for food. —D.dS.

ATLANTIC SILVERSIDE *Menidia menidia* This species is one of a group of small, silvery fishes that inhabit both marine and fresh waters in the eastern United States and Canada. Its closest relatives are the Waccamaw silverside, key silverside, tidewater silverside, Mississippi silverside, and the brook silverside (*which see*). The Atlantic silverside is found along the shore and in estuaries from the southern Gulf of St. Lawrence to Cape May.

Its color is transparent green above; belly white; a silver band, edged above with a narrow black streak, runs from the upper part of the base of the pectoral fin to the base of the caudal fin. Each scale is outlined with a series of brownish or greenish dots.

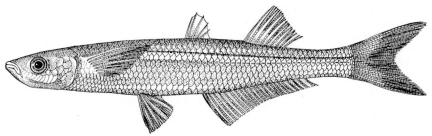

Atlantic Silverside

Other distinguishing characteristics of the Atlantic silverside are body slender, belly rounded, depth 7½ in total length; caudal peduncle slender. Head 5½ in total length, slightly compressed; mouth terminal, small, each jaw with a band of slender teeth. Eye 4 in head, 1¼ times its own diameter from snout. Two dorsal fins, first with 3–7 spines, origin slightly in front of middle of body; second with 7–10 softrays, height almost twice that of first dorsal; caudal fin large, moderately forked; anal fin with 1 spine and 22–25 softrays, beginning under middle of first dorsal; pectorals inserted high on sides, ⁴/₅ length of head; pelvics inserted on ventral edge of body under tips of pectorals. Scales moderate, cycloid, covering body and head behind eye.

LIFE HISTORY

Although the Atlantic silverside is a small species, seldom growing larger than 3½ inches in length, it often occurs in large schools. They eat copepods, mysids, shrimp, small squid, and marine worms. In turn, they are preyed upon by larger fishes, such as the striped bass and bluefish. They spawn in shallow water in May, June, and early July. The eggs are about 1/20th of an inch in diameter, and each is supplied with sticky filaments for attachment to weeds or the bottom. Hatching takes place in about 10 days.

FOOD VALUE

While the Atlantic silverside serves as an important link in the marine food chain, it has little commercial or sports value. Easily netted in shallow water, it is occasionally used as bait and is excellent eating when fried as "whitebait" (which see). —J.C.B.

ATLANTIC SPADEFISH *Chaetodopterus faber* This deep-bodied fish belongs to the spadefish family, Ephippidae, and is related to the angelfish.

The body is almost as deep as it is long. The back is high and strongly arched; the ventral outline of the body is somewhat less arched. The color varies from grayish to greenish and yellowish, and the sides bear 4–6 vertical bars. The first bar is on the head and passes through the eye; the last is on the caudal peduncle. These bars are apt to be somewhat obscure in large adults. The small mouth is equipped with terminal jaws and with bands of slender, movable teeth. The preopercle is finely serrate or saw-toothed.

There are 2 distinct dorsal fins. The first has 8–11 spines; the second is somewhat longer, and the anterior rays of the second are elongated as are those of the anal fin. The caudal fin is broad and concave at the tip and bears a blackish bar at the base. The fins are mostly gray, greenish, or dusky.

The spadefish grows to about 3 feet and attains a maximum weight of about 20 pounds; average specimens are usually less than 1 foot in length. A 16-inch spadefish weighs between 3 and 4 pounds.

LIFE HISTORY

The spadefish is widely distributed from Cape Cod to Brazil, but it is rare north of Chesapeake Bay. Throughout the summer and fall the spadefish is found in the southern part of its range in places where crustaceans are abundant—in bays, about wharves, rockpiles, and old wrecks. In the fall large schools are found along the sea beaches, evidently preparing to depart for deeper waters.

Spawning occurs during the summer. The eggs are buoyant, nonadhesive, and slightly over 1 mm. in diameter. They hatch in 24 hours at a temperature of 78°F. By late August the young fish reach a length of close to 3 inches.

ANGLING VALUE

Spadefish are excellent food fish. They are taken commercially in pound nets and haul seines and occasionally on hook and line. Anglers catch them when using shrimp as bait and fishing near the bottom around wrecks or on rocky shores. —A.J.McC.

ATLANTIC STINGRAY *Dasyatis sabina* A prominent, triangularly pointed snout sets this stingray off from its relatives. The disk is rhomboid, and the outer corners are broadly rounded, a character which it shares with the bluntnose stingray (which see). But the distance from the snout to the eyes is much greater than the distance between the spiracles, or dorsal gill openings, in the Atlantic stingray. Further, the anterior margin of the disk is slightly indented along either side of the snout. There is a well-developed skinfold along the dorsal and ventral tail surfaces, and a row of thorny tubercles along the dorsal midline extends about one-quarter of the way onto the tail. Otherwise, the skin is smooth. The upper parts are brown to yellowish-brown, with light edgings along the margin, and the ventral surface is whitish. It is a small species, growing only to a length of about two feet.

LIFE HISTORY

Largely a tropical species, it occurs predominantly about Florida and the Gulf of Mexico. It is known from Chesapeake Bay and is questionably reported from Surinam and Brazil. Most records are from shallow, coastal waters, from only a few inches to 7–8 feet deep. It tolerates warmwaters and penetrates estuaries, being taken in water that is completely fresh, as well as full-strength ocean water. In the Gulf of Mexico this stingray occurs in the shallows during spring and summer and moves off into deeper water during the late fall. Young are produced from spring through fall, in shallow, coastal waters, at which time they are only about 6–7 inches wide. Adults eat amphipod crustaceans and worms. There is no commercial use for this species but in the Gulf Coast it is a nuisance to fishermen because it entangles their nets.

—D.dS.

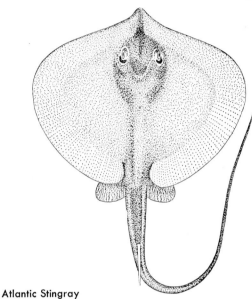

Atlantic Stingray

ATLANTIC THREADFIN *See* African Pompano

ATLANTIC TOMCOD *Microgadus tomcod* This small member of the cod family Gadidae resembles the Atlantic cod in general body shape and the presence of three dorsal fins and two anal fins, with a heavy body tipped with a large, subterminal mouth. It differs from the Atlantic cod in the long ventral fins which taper into the shape of a filament. The posterior margin of the tail of the tomcod is rounded rather than being straight or slightly concave. In addition, the eyes on the tomcod are quite small in comparison. In coloration, instead of being spotted as in the Atlantic cod, it is olive- or muddy green above with dark spots or blotches forming a mottled pattern on the sides. Unlike the plain fins of the cod, those of the tomcod have wavy or mottled markings. This small species grows to 15 inches and a little over 1 pound, but most are 6–12 inches long.

The tomcod is found along the North American coast from Labrador and the Gulf of St. Lawrence south to Virginia, and is common locally from Long Island northward. This inshore fish seldom is taken deeper than 2–3 fathoms. It may be commonly taken in brackish water and occasionally in freshwater during winter. This hardy species is also resistant to changes to salinity and sudden cold spells.

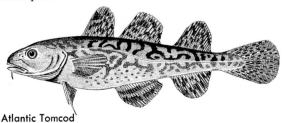

Atlantic Tomcod

LIFE HISTORY

It spawns in either brackish or saltwater from November to February, the eggs sinking to the bottom and attaching to algae and rocks.

The tomcod lives close to the bottom, utilizing the chin barbel and ventral fins as sensory organs to detect food. Small shrimps, amphipods, worms, clams, squid, and small fish are eaten.

ANGLING VALUE

This small but delicious fish is taken by anglers in large quantities during the colder months in the spawning season. It is also caught commercially in small numbers using bagnets, traps, and weirs. —D.dS.

ATLANTIC TORPEDO *Torpedo nobiliana* This relatively large ray differs from its relative, the lesser electric ray (*which see*), in its size, the straight anterior margin of the disk, and the dark chocolate color which is either uniform or with a few vague, darker spots. The disk is not quite as circular as that of the lesser electric ray. Its skin is smooth, and two well-developed dorsal fins and a large caudal fin are set on a muscular tail. A maximum weight of 200 pounds has been reported, but any torpedo of over 100 pounds is rare, and most are about 30 pounds. It grows to 5–6 feet long.

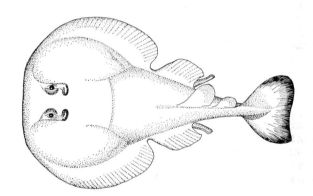

Atlantic Torpedo

LIFE HISTORY

This is strictly an Atlantic species, occurring from Nova Scotia to Cuba and from Scotland to West Africa and the Azores. It appears to be more common in the cooler parts of its range. Most records have been from shallow water, but they are believed to be most common in waters 10–40 fathoms deep. Some specimens have been taken off New York in depths of 50–60 fathoms. It lives on the bottom, capturing fishes such as flounders and eels, but it is apparently able to obtain fast-swimming prey, for torpedoes taken in England have contained sharks and salmon. This species, like others of the family, can give a considerable electric shock, the power for which is generated through specialized cells in the disk. This shock is used in stunning its prey, and voltages of 170–220 have been recorded for the species.

Reproduction apparently occurs in the deeper waters in the warmer parts of its range, and the young are born alive. There is no commercial value for the species.

—D.dS.

ATLANTIC WOLFFISH *Anarhichas lupus* The wolffishes are large blennylike fishes occurring in the cold waters of the North Atlantic and North Pacific. They have well-developed canine teeth and large molars on the vomer and palatine bones. Thus, they are well adapted to feeding on mollusks. The Atlantic wolffish is sometimes called the striped wolffish or loup (France). It is found on both sides of the North Atlantic; in the west it occurs from southern Labrador to Cape Cod and occasionally as far south as New Jersey; in the east it has been taken at western Greenland, Iceland, Faroes, Spitzbergen, and from the White Sea to the west coast of France.

Its color varies from slaty blue to dull olive-green to purplish-brown. Usually 10 or more dark transverse bars on the anterior two-thirds of the body, some of these extending on the dorsal fin; underside of head and belly to vent dirty white, tinged with general tint of upper parts.

Other distinguishing characteristics of the Atlantic wolffish are body compressed and elongate, greatest depth 5½ in total length, occurring about middle of pectoral fin; body then tapering to a small caudal peduncle. Head 5 in total length, heavy, blunt, profile rounded; mouth terminal, oblique, angle somewhat behind posterior edge of eye; a row of about 6 large, stout, conical teeth at front of upper jaw with a group of 5 or 6 smaller canine teeth behind them; these opposed by 4–6 large tusks at the front of the lower jaw, 3 series of crushing teeth in roof of mouth, 2 rows of rounded molars in lower jaws, small scattered teeth in throat. Eye small, 7½ in head.

Dorsal fin with 69–77 spines, fin begins over posterior part of head and extends to base of caudal; caudal fin small, very slightly rounded; anal fin with 42–48 softrays, a little more than half length of dorsal and ending under posterior tip of dorsal. Pectorals heavy, rounded, base low in sides, a short distance behind gill openings; pelvics absent. Lateral line absent. Head scaleless, body covered with poorly developed scales.

This species lives in moderately deep water (10–85 fathoms) over hard bottom. Individuals are apparently solitary and are caught in the same areas at all times of the year. Their food consists primarily of whelks, mussels, clams, and other mollusks. Crabs, hermit crabs, sea urchins, and starfish have also been found in their stomachs. The eggs are about 3/16 inches in diameter and are attached to the bottom in large, loose clumps.

FOOD VALUE

The Atlantic wolffish is a good food fish and catches of about 1½ million pounds per year are made in the Gulf of Maine and on the Georges Bank. It is popular table fare in Denmark and Spain. It grows to a length of about 5 feet and a weight of about 40 pounds. *See also* Spotted Wolffish

—J.C.B.

AUFWUCHS *See* Freshwater Ecology

AUSTRALIA The most arid continent on earth, Australia nevertheless has claim to some of the world's best fishing in its surrounding oceans and its island state of Tasmania. While Australia appears to be small, a mere spot on the underbelly of the globe surrounded by the Pacific and Indian oceans, the country is immense. In general shape and total land area (approximately 3 million square miles) Australia is comparable to the United

An over-thousand-pound black marlin comes out of the sea off Cairns. No other area produces such large billfish today

States. Despite the kangaroo and Outback image, it is one of the most urbanized nations in the world, with two-thirds of its population living in cities. But sports-minded Aussies are well aware of their outdoor heritage. Numerous black marlin of over 1,000 pounds have been caught in North Queensland, which fronts the Great Barrier Reef. The boats working out of Cairns have made the area one of the most important fishing centers in the Pacific. Blue marlin, striped marlin, sailfish, swordfish, yellowfin and bluefin tuna, wahoo, and dolphin are also seasonally abundant in Australian waters. Shark fishing, which has always been an Aussie preoccupation, is popular among local anglers, and some exceptional white, mako, gray nurse, bronze whaler, and hammerhead sharks have been boated. The estuaries and tropical rivers of Australia also produce excellent angling to the light-tackle caster for barramundi, ox-eye, jungle perch, black grunter, riflefish, mangrove jack, flathead, Australian bass, and Murray cod.

Australia is south of the equator; summer begins in November, autumn in April, winter in June, and spring in September. Climates vary greatly, but in general you can expect mild weather with temperatures in the 60's and 70's. The trout season runs from January to the end of April, with February a prime month.

NEW SOUTH WALES

Sydney, the major port-of-entry for most travelers, is a big city with a kaleidoscopic population (2½ million) drawn from all over the world. Aside from the usual tourist offerings Sydney also provides some offshore fishing for striped marlin and yellowfin tuna just outside North and South Heads, the massive rock bluffs guarding its harbor. Down the coast toward Victoria, the offshore grounds at Bermagui are where big-game fishing began in Australia, and this popular port still draws a faithful coterie of anglers from Sydney; striped marlin, kingfish, and yellowfin tuna are the principal species sought here, with wahoo, dolphin, and the occasional black marlin in season.

The visiting angler might prefer to try the trout fishing, which, in New South Wales, is the best the mainland has to offer. One of the most popular locations is in the Great Snowy Mountains south of Canberra. There are a number of fine rivers in the area including the Snowy, Murrumbidgee, Eucumbene, Thredbo, Geehi, and Tumut. Famous, but not as productive as it was during the initial years of impoundment, is Lake Eucumbene. Due to an abundance of forage the trout display a rapid rate of growth. When conditions are right even the largest trout rise at times in the shallows near shore. Both browns and rainbows in excess of 10 pounds have been taken on large dry flies such as the Muddler. Nearby Tantangara Reservoir, a feeder lake of Eucumbene, also provides some wonderful flyfishing.

There are seven main angling centers which give access to the Snowy Mountains trout streams; these have hotels or motels and other facilities for the tourist:

Dalgety Gives access to the Snowy River below Jindabyne, Bobundara Creek, and the MacLaughlin River.

Jindabyne Mowamba River (fly only), Thredbo or Crackenback River, Spencers Creek and Island Bend, Upper Snowy River, Gungarlin River, and lower Eucumbene River.

Thredbo Alpine Village Upper Murray River and Thredbo or Crackenback River. Local guides are available together with hire of all equipment.

Khancoban Geehi River, Bogong Creek, Swampy Plain River (partly closed), Swampy Plain Creek and Upper Murray River, Khancoban Dam, Geehi Dam.

Adaminaby Eucumbene River, Swamp Creek and Hughes Creek (tributaries of Lake Eucumbene, and fly only), Nungar Creek at Tantangara Dam, Goorudee Rivulet, Murrumbidgee River, Yaourk Creek, Bradley's Creek, and Sam's River.

Kiandra Headwaters of Eucumbene River, Chance Creek, Racecourse Creek, Bullock's Head Creek, and Three-mile Dam near the town. Tantangara Creek, Upper Murrumbidgee River, and Mosquito Creek flowing into Tantangara Dam. Yarrangobilly River and Wallace's Creek at Ravine. Tumut River at Hares. Tumut River and Happy Jacks Creek through Cabramurra.

Bombala Bombala River (joins Snowy to northwest), Cambalong River (flows into the Bombala at Cambalong), MacLaughlin River (enters Snowy at Merriangah), Delegate River (joins Bombala at Quidong), Bendoc River (runs into Little Plains and Delegate Rivers). The Mila Bog (enters Little Plains River) and Saucy Creek (joins Bombala River).

North of Sydney, in the New England Range of mountains, there are some good trout streams, such as Jock's Water and the Styx River. Rainbows predominate, although they do not rise to a fly as readily as the brown trout, and wet flies, nymphs, and small streamers fished from rapid mountain streams to slowly meandering, meadow-type of streams. Every year rainbows up to 8 or

10 pounds are taken. The center of the district is Armidale, and many streams are within 40 miles. There is an active trout fishing club here.

SOUTH AUSTRALIA

The main attraction in this state is saltwater fishing out of Kangaroo Island, St. Vincent's Gulf, and Streaky Bay. South Australia is popular among shark specialists, and whites of over 1 ton have been boated here. Makos and hammerheads occur well offshore, as do small bluefin tuna which appear seasonally in vast schools. Australian salmon (*see* Kahawai) are very abundant in South Australia's waters, and attract light-tackle anglers using spinning and fly-rod equipment.

There is little freshwater fishing in South Australia. Streams such as Myponga Creek, Gawler and Finis Creek, and Onkaparinga Creek provide some sport for anglers living in Adelaide. These are mainly brushy overgrown streams. Consistent with this type of water, beetle and grasshopper imitations are more effective than caddis or mayfly patterns.

WESTERN AUSTRALIA

This is the largest state in the Commonwealth, with an area of nearly 1 million square miles. Its coastline is about 4,000 miles in length, and while saltwater fishing is extremely productive, particularly along the northern perimeter, facilities are very limited and much of the angling is still exploratory in nature. Bluefin and yellowfin tuna, sailfish, blue and black marlin, wahoo, dolphin, amberjack, and many other game species occur in Western Australia's waters. The northwest Cape area, Rosemary Island, Montebello Island, and Albany in the southwest portion show great promise for future development. There is considerable fishing around Rottnest Island offshore from Freemantle not far from Perth.

Aborigines in northern Australia haul a giant grouper aboard

There are no major river systems in Western Australia as far as the trout angler is concerned, although there is some sport to be had from Ginhin north of Perth to Albany in the south. Two of the best-known streams are Warren River and Big Brook.

NORTH QUEENSLAND

The reefs extending for 1,200 miles north and south of Cairns (collectively the Great Barrier Reef) form one of the most prolific big-game fishing grounds in the Pacific. Black marlin fishing exists in such quality and quantity that it has attracted anglers from all over the world. Sailfish, wahoo, yellowfin tuna, dogtooth tuna, kingfish, and a variety of other species are seasonally abundant. Cairns is serviced by daily flights from Sydney via Brisbane.

The town has ample motel accommodations; however, the number of boats in the local charter fleet is minimal and advance bookings are essential. The marlin season runs from September through December, with some blacks present the year round. This area was pioneered by an American charter-boat skipper, George Bransford, a former Floridian.

West of Cairns on the opposite side of the Cape York Peninsula is the Gulf of Carpentaria. This is largely unexplored from an angling point of view. The rivers emptying in the Gulf offer good to excellent barramundi and Australian salmon fishing.

TASMANIA

The island of Tasmania is a trout angler's paradise. Practically all its rivers provide suitable habitat for browns and rainbows from their uppermost reaches to where they enter the sea. While caddis larvae are the dominant food item of trout on the mainland, in Tasmania the mayflies are most important. Hatches are not only prolific but much more predictable on the island, and consequently some wonderful dry-fly-fishing is possible. Good angling can be found close to every town and village. Some of the more famous trout waters are Great Lake, Penstock Lagoon, Macquarie River, Derwent River, Shannon River, South Esk, and the Break O'Day. There is superlative fishing everywhere. Many rivers have fine runs of sea trout. Generally, the best season is from September to about mid-December, and again in March and April. Nymphs and wet flies can be used, and streamer flies are often productive in highwater.

Besides having the best trout fishing in Australia, Tasmania offers some saltwater fishing. Boats for offshore work are available out of Hobart. This capital city nestles in the shadow of Mt. Wellington, the summit of which is about 12 miles from the center of town. The principal big-game fish here is the southern bluefin tuna. School fish run 20–40 pounds with the occasional fish from 100–200 pounds. Striped tuna, albacore, mako, and white shark are also common. Although striped marlin and swordfish have been caught on the east coast, this is not considered a billfish area.   —A.J.McC.

AUSTRALIAN SALMON *See* Kahawai

AUSTRIA This comparatively small central European country offers some excellent freshwater fishing. Its crystal-clear rivers are very productive of trout and grayling. Pollution is almost nonexistent due to strict regulations, and all waters are kept well stocked. Although spinning and bait-fishing are practiced here as elsewhere, many Austrian streams are restricted to fly-fishing only, and, as a result, the fishing is carefully maintained. Fishing with lures other than flies is, in the main, reserved for larger species such as the northern pike, huchen, pikeperch, sheatfish, and the chars. The huchen (*which see*) is a large Eurasian member of the salmon family which is distributed all along the Danube River in Germany, Czechoslovakia, and Yugoslavia. The pikeperch (*Lucioperca sandra*) is very similar to the North American walleye. The sheatfish (*Silurus glanis*) is an endemic catfish. With the exception of the brown trout, which is native to Austria, the brook, rainbow, and lake trout have been introduced. Austrian grayling are the native European grayling (*which see*).

Austria possesses numerous alpine streams of indescribable beauty which are easily reached by auto. Experienced, accurate advice is available everywhere in all localities and is willingly and enthusiastically given, for every traveler is a welcome guest—particularly fishermen.

A visiting angler in Austria needs two kinds of licenses or permits. The first is known as "The Official Fishers License"—a document with a photograph, valid for the calendar year in the province where it is secured and issued at the local government office. The fee is minimal, but varies according to the province being fished. Most provinces also have temporary licenses for a specific preserve which replaces the official license and is issued by the private waters being fished.

The second kind of license required is the "Private Fishing Permit" and is obtained from the local owner. Price varies according to the type of fish and the quality of the supply and the waters. Half-day, weekly, and monthly permits are most often available at lower rates.

There are differences in the various Austrian fishing preserves as to size and daily limit. The owner of the local fishing rights, the local government office, or tourist office will advise. In a few cases where particularly outstanding fishing is available only a limited number of licenses are issued. In these cases, advance reservation at the place you have chosen to visit is advisable.

The rivers of Austria seldom produce large trout but their crystalline waters delight the flyfisher in Alpine settings

Grayling attain good size in Austrian rivers. Fish of 18–20 inches in length are average in waters such as the Traun

Austria has done a particularly fine job of making readily available clear, concise, and informative information and material. For each locality one may easily find the altitude, name of the fishing preserve, and approximate distance from any locality. The kind of fish available to be caught is plainly and accurately indicated along with type of fishing permitted, the bait and tackle that may be used. Figures and information are also shown with regard to seasons, licenses, and prices.

The most important trout stream in Austria is the Traun, followed by the Salza, the Mur, the Lammer, the Enns, and the Alm rivers. The best fly fishing occurs in July and August and small patterns (No. 14–20) on fine leaders are the rule. Chest-high waders are advisable, as the better waters are quite deep.

Besides the many rivers, streams, and lakes mentioned in the available fishing booklets on Austrian fishing are a great many more excellent preserves which are controlled by Austria's two fishing associations. These are the Austrian Fishing Association and the Association of Austrian Workers Fishing Clubs. Rights to fish their waters may readily and easily be obtained at a reasonable rate.

The Austrian Fishing Association controls some very good fishing and fishing waters in Vienna and Lower Austria, including some particularly outstanding trout fishing. It issues yearly permits for a single preserve, several preserves, or all of its fishing preserves, as well as daily permits. Temporary licenses for Lower Austria as well as any sort of information desired may be obtained from the offices of the Austrian Fishing Association at Elisabethstrasse 22, Vienna 1, Austria.

The Austrian Workers Fishing Clubs has its headquarters in Vienna with branches in Graz, Linz, and Salzburg, Upper Austria, and in Carinthia. Information including daily, weekly, and weekend permits may be secured from the Association at Lenaugasse 14, Vienna VIII, Austria. —J.C.

AWA The Hawaiian name for the milkfish (*which see*).

AWNING Temporary canvas canopy erected over boat's cockpit as a sunshade or protection from rain.

B

BACHELOR PERCH A regional name for the white crappie (*which see*)

BACKING In fly fishing, a line put on the reel under the casting line to fill up the reel. When spliced to the line, it is available as reserve line for playing large fish such as steelhead, salmon, and saltwater fish which make long runs.

BACKING DOWN The maneuver executed when a boatman reverses the boat for some distance, always keeping the stern exactly lined up with the fishing line, thereby assisting the angler in retrieving line quickly under reduced tension. Also termed "backing down the line."

BACKING STAY An extra or temporary stay of wire or rope to ease unusual strain on a mast. It is usually hastily rigged to a gin pole before loading an especially heavy fish aboard a boat that is heaving in rough water. *See* Gin Pole

BACKLASH A term in casting which means an overrun of the reel spool resulting in a tangled line. Specifically, a backlash occurs with revolving-spool reels when the spool spins at a speed greater than the pull of the outgoing weight (lure or sinker), creating an excess of loose line on the reel. A backlash may be caused by casting with too much force, or by casting against a strong wind, or by laying the line too loose or unevenly when retrieving, or by improper thumb control of the spool. Most casting reels have a level-winding mechanism as well as some form of antibacklash device to correct these problems to some degree. Although fixed-spool reels (spinning or spin-casting) do not backlash they can tangle occasionally through other causes. *See also* Bait-Casting, Spinning, Spin-Casting

BAHAMAS The islands, islets, cays, rocks, sand ridges (exposed at certain tides), and reefs that make up the Bahama Archipelago extend through more than six degrees of latitude and almost seven degrees of longitude. The group starts with the Little Bahama Bank, the northwest extremity of which lies about fifty-four miles east of Fort Pierce, Florida, and extends southward to the Cay Sal Bank, which is a mere thirty miles from Cuba. The islands sprawl eastward and southeastward to Great Inagua Island, which is fifty-five miles from the coast of Haiti. There are two other island complexes and banks— Caicos and Turks Islands and Mouchoir and Silver banks —lying farther to the east that are geographically and geologically part of the Bahama chain. *See* Caicos Islands

The Bahamas are flattened peaks of an extensive mountain range, but nowhere is there an elevation greater than four hundred feet. The usual height above highwater is probably 5–10 feet. The channels and passages, Exuma Sound, the Tongue of the Ocean, and the Straits of Florida are the "valleys" of the range. In some places they drop away to great depths—2,500 fathoms or more. Geologically the Bahamas are formed of loose coral sand on beaches and weathered limestone rock on a limestone formation. Sample borings made some time ago show this limestone deposit to be thousands of feet deep.

What the Bahamas do have is an ideal year around climate, a maximum rainfall of 50–60 inches, waters that are gin-clear and run the gamut of every shade of green and blue interspersed with white, brown, and yellow, and gamefishing that leaves little to be desired. The coldest temperature ever recorded was a cool 49°F. The average winter temperature is about 70°F. The summer months vary from 80°–90°F. and the highest recorded was 94°F. The Bahamas have twenty-one of the fifty recognized marine gamefish in the world. Some of the fish are quite plentiful, some are purely seasonal, and a few—such as the broadbill and mako—wander in and out of Bahamian waters without rhyme or reason.

As might be expected of an island group so blessed with good fishing—both commercial and sport—it is enjoyed every month in the year. Unlike Florida, there is no conflict between commercial and sport fishermen, principally because each group pursues different fish. Goggle-eye, grouper, jack, small mackerel, various members of the snapper family, conch, spiny lobster, and turtle make up the bulk of commercial fishing. On the other hand the fish hunted by the rod-and-reel angler are amberjack, barracuda, bonefish, bonito, dolphin, both species of Atlantic marlin, permit, sailfish, tarpon, three species of tuna, and wahoo—nearly all edible fish, of course, but impractical to catch commercially.

DEVELOPMENT OF BAHAMIAN FISHING

In the early days of Bahamas' sport fishing, anglers believed that only the islands facing the Gulf Stream had the major gamefish. To these places—Bimini-Cat Cay (50 miles east of Miami Beach), West End on Grand Bahama (60 miles from Palm Beach), and Walker Cay (northernmost of the inhabited islands)—flocked the big-name, big-game anglers. On March 9, 1919, B. F. Peek, fishing at Bimini, landed a bonefish weighing 13¾ pounds. It stood as an all-tackle world record from that date until 1948 and as a 9-thread-line record until 1952. In 1932, C. E. Benet caught a huge barracuda of 103¼ pounds off West End that is still on the record charts. The

One of the most sought-after prizes among Bahamian flats anglers is the permit. They are exceptionally difficult to catch

late Ernest Hemingway landed the first unmutilated bluefin tuna brought into Bimini during the 1935 season, and Mrs. Marion Stevens boated a world-record 152-pound white marlin off Bimini in 1936.

It was not until after the end of World War II that the central and eastern parts of the Bahamas attracted fishermen. A lot of the interest came about through the efforts of K. L. "Snake" Ames who in April 1943 had caught a world-record wahoo weighing 133½ pounds in the Northeast Providence Channel off Green Cay. But there were no places to stay on most of the Out Islands; so a great deal of the fishing had to be done out of Nassau. The first indication that there were heavy blue marlin in places other than Bimini, Cat Cay, West End, or Walker Cay came in April of 1952 when C. J. Maxson of Buffalo, New York, raised, hooked, and boated a blue marlin of 485¼ pounds off Fresh Creek, Andros. This established a world record in the 50-pound-test class. Marlin, both blue and white, were later caught off Green Turtle Cay and Hope Town, Abaco; Grassy Cay, at the south end of Andros; Northwest Channel Light, Berry Islands; Powell, Bamboo, and Southeastern points, Eleuthera; along the drop-off of the 10-fathom passage between Eleuthera and Little Cat Island; and in the Exuma Sound (east) off Hawk's Nest, Cat Island, and (west) off Wide Opening in Exuma Cays.

Since then blue marlin, white marlin, yellowfin tuna, record-sized oceanic bonito, kingfish, and wahoo have been boated all over the central and eastern Bahamas. Although most of the sixty-odd world records are still held by anglers who caught their heavy fish in the western Bahamas, there are twelve credited to the islands farther east.

BONEFISHING

The Great and Little Bahama banks offer wide expanses of shallow water ranging in depth from a few inches to twelve feet. Over these banks the currents sweep back and forth with the tides, carrying enormous quantities of crustaceans and small fry to the deepwater along the dropoffs of the Straits of Florida, Northwest and Northeast Providence channels, Tongue of the Ocean, Exuma Sound, and Atlantic Ocean.

Although bonefish are widely distributed throughout this area, only specific locations on certain islands contain the flats so necessary to this type of angling. Some of the most outstanding flats are found along the coast of Andros Island, the Berry Islands, Green Turtle Cay, Bimini, Abaco, and the east end of Grand Bahama; here it becomes a series of creeks and small cays, stretching from Rummer Creek at the end of the Freeport road to Jacob's Cay some 15 miles away to the southeast. The tides ebb and flow from the deep ocean water of New Providence Channel, through a dozen or more of these creeks, to the large shallow-water sound known as the Bight of Abaco. Using Jacob's Cay as an eastern boundary, and the Cross Cays which connect Grand Bahama to Little Abaco as a western boundary, we have a vast area that offers what is probably the finest bonefishing in the Bahamas. The flats vary from pure white ocean sand, through the many sheltered creeks, to the thick turtle-grass and mangrove shoots of the bays and small sounds, making it possible to wade for tailing fish and to cast to the "muds" in the deeper channels. This entire area can be fished from Deep Water Cay located at the junction of Rummer Creek and Big Harbor Creek (known as Carrion Crow Harbor).

RECOMMENDED TACKLE FOR THE BAHAMAS

There is fishing to suit all kinds of tackle in the Bahamas, starting with the fly rod for shallow-water species and calibered up to the 130-pound-test-class gear for giant bluefin tuna. Although individual skill and experience determine to a large extent the final selection of equipment, the following should serve as a general guide for the first-time visitor.

Fly-Fishing Tackle *Rod:* a bamboo or glass rod of medium to heavy action, 8½–9½ feet in length, 6–8 ounces in weight. *Reel:* a large saltwater model with sturdy drag mechanism that can carry tapered or level lines in orthodox length backed with 6-thread line or 15–20-pound nylon line. Full capacity of reel should be not less than about 200 yards. *Line:* to match rod action. Tapered line is to be preferred over level line. *Leader:* in 9-foot length tapered to 10–12-pound test tippits. *Lures:* multiwinged or bucktail streamer flies with size 1/0 hooks. Yellow, yellow-and-white, pink, and black patterns will give best results. For bonefish use hook sizes 2, 4, or 6.

Plug-Casting Tackle *Rod:* a 5½–6-foot, stiff-action bamboo or glass rod for most fishing conditions. *Reel:* any quality level-winding reel, preferably with a cub or star drag, that is corrosion resistant (extra pawls and worm gears are advisable). *Line:* most Bahamian fish can be taken on 10–15-pound-test nylon line. When casting for larger fish such as barracuda and sharks, or casting in a blue hole (*which see*) heavier tests are recommended. *Leaders:* optional. Very light piano wire fastened with snaps and swivels has proved satisfactory. Monofilament leaders also give good results. If using wire an 8–10-inch leader is long enough for the ordinary fish and will not affect the action of the lure. *Lures:* blue, silver-and-blue, or black plugs over shallow sandy bottom or close to mangrove points will raise fish. In medium-deep or deep cuts and over reefs, try sinking lures, bucktails, or feather jigs 1½–2 ounces in weight in red-and-white, black-and-white, yellow, brown, or gray colors.

Spinning Tackle *Rod:* a bamboo or glass rod of 6½–7½ feet in length, medium to heavy action, with screw-locking reel seat. *Reel:* any quality fixed-spool reel which has a 200-yard or more line capacity (of 8-pound test) which has been anodized to protect it from saltwater. *Line:* 6–10-pound test monofilament. *Lures:* Bucktails, feathers, sinking baits in yellow, yellow-and-white, or black will work better than the regular surface or semi-surface plugs.

Twenty-Pound-Test Tackle *Rod:* bamboo or glass tip weighing 4–6 ounces with fittings. Tip not less than 5 feet when fully seated in the butt. Roller tip-top recommended. *Butt:* this light tackle is best handled when the rod is fished from a belt rest rather than from a chair gimbal. *Reel:* any good-quality reel with a substantial drag in 3/0 to 4/0 size. Some anglers like the 4/0 size on which they wind some backing then seal it off with adhesive tape. The larger reel permits faster retrieving of line. *Line:* a 20-pound-test Dacron or monofilament should be used. Synthetics have replaced linen in this class. *Lures:* cut bait, whole bait (balao, small mullet, or

Chief target of the fly fisher in the Bahamas is the bonefish. A sturdy reel is most important as the fish make sustained runs

jack), feathers, or large pork rind. Feathers, strip baits, and pork rind can be trolled "flat"; whole baits or large strips will work best from outriggers.

Thirty-Pound-Test Tackle This is the most popular and satisfactory tackle for the average run of fish to be taken trolling. If the gear is well cared for and properly handled, an angler can hold almost any fish that he will encounter with the exception of the bluefin tuna, blue marlin, and mako. *Rod:* bamboo or glass, 6–9 ounces in weight, with a tip measuring not less than 5 feet when fully seated in the butt. A roller tip-top is recommended. *Butt:* may be 14–15 inches in length if the angler fishes from a rod belt; 18–21 inches if the rod is to be fished from a chair gimbal. Slotted butt caps are recommended. *Lures:* same as noted for 20-pound-test tackle. *Reel:* any good-quality reel with a smooth drag in 6/0 size. *Line:* a 9-thread linen line of 50 lead weight or a synthetic line (Dacron, monofilament, or braided nylon) with a breaking strain of not more than 30 pounds.

Fifty-and Eighty-Pound-Test Tackle These two classes are for the person who wants to get the "feel" of Bahamian fishing before launching into lighter trolling gear. The following specified tackle will handle anything from grouper and amberjack to big kingfish, white marlin, and wahoo. *Rod:* good-grade trolling rod with tip weighing 12–16 ounces and a butt of 18–21 inches made to fit in chair gimbal. Roller tip is recommended. Stiffness in rod a desirable factor. *Harness:* a belt harness is used when standing, a seat harness when using a fighting chair. *Line:* 15–24-thread linen or Dacron in similar weight line. Monofilament line can be used in 45–70-pound tests, but the stretch may prevent the solid setting of the hook. *Lures:* Large feathers, whole fingerling mullet, balao, jack, small mackerel, or blue runner or strips from barracuda, bonito, or dolphin.

130-Pound-Test-Tackle Charter boatmen specializing in blue marlin and giant tuna usually carry all of the tackle needed for big-game fishing. However, the angler who plans to fish from his own boat or likes to have his own gear will do well to consult with experienced dealers who carry a full line of big-game tackle. *Rod:* very heavy, exceedingly stiff fiberglass rod with a tip that measures not less than 5 feet from shoulder of ferrule to tip-top. Tip-top and intermediate guides should be of roller type. *Butt:* there are two types of butts in use today; one is the conventional straight butt, the other is offset. Exponents of the offset butt claim to get better leverage with it. *Harness:* this is a matter of choice; some fishermen use a kidney harness, others a standard seat harness. *Line:* for light-tackle big-game fishing a good-quality, 24-thread line or 80-pound-test Dacron line will take the average blue marlin or big tuna that the angler will encounter. Standard line for this fishing, however, is 39-thread linen line or 130-pound-test Dacron. *Leaders:* Cable leaders are used for blue marlin; heavy piano wire for tuna. *Hooks:* heavy wire 12/0 to 14/0 hooks of the so-called Sobey type. *Baits:* whole mullet are most popular in tuna fishing; bonefish, bonito, dolphin, mackerel, and tuna of 2–3 pounds make fine baits for blue marlin.

—D.McC.

BAIT *See* Live Bait

BAIT-CASTING The art of casting an artificial lure with a revolving-spool reel. The tackle was originally developed in the nineteenth century solely for the purpose of casting live minnows, and thus the reference to "bait"

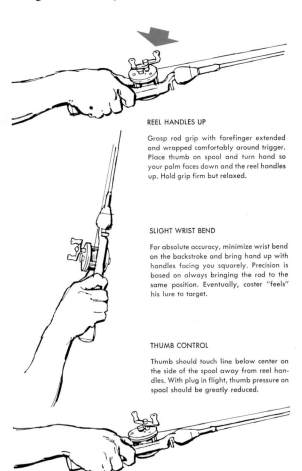

REEL HANDLES UP

Grasp rod grip with forefinger extended and wrapped comfortably around trigger. Place thumb on spool and turn hand so your palm faces down and the reel handles up. Hold grip firm but relaxed.

SLIGHT WRIST BEND

For absolute accuracy, minimize wrist bend on the backstroke and bring hand up with handles facing you squarely. Precision is based on always bringing the rod to the same position. Eventually, caster "feels" his lure to target.

THUMB CONTROL

Thumb should touch line below center on the side of the spool away from reel handles. With plug in flight, thumb pressure on spool should be greatly reduced.

casting. The plug (*which see*) is the most common lure used in bait-casting, and consequently it is sometimes referred to as "plugcasting." Bait-casting encompasses many kinds of fishing in both fresh- and saltwater; it is especially popular for black bass, northern pike, and tarpon. The revolving-spool reel is more difficult to operate than the fixed-spool reel used in spinning and spin-casting because of its tendency to overrun or backlash (*which see*). However, bait-casting reels are preferred by many anglers for a number of reasons.

HOW TO BAIT-CAST

A fairly flexible rod in the 4½–5-foot lengths is easiest for the beginner to use in his first practice sessions. Longer rods or fast tip-action rods can feel awkward at the start. For lawn or indoor casting use a ⅜–⅝-ounce rubber practice plug. The line should be a 9–12-pound-test braided nylon. There are two general types of bait-casting reels, the free-spool and the level-wind. The free-spool reel requires some skill to cast without backlashes; a quality levelwind reel is simpler to operate.

Thumb Control The value of an antibacklash mechanism on a bait-casting reel is considerable; however, to get consistent results under adverse winds you must learn the correct thumb control. Some manual dexterity is required. Thumb pressure is applied in varying degrees, and only experience can teach you how much to use. The thumb is also used as a brake against running fish (unless the reel is equipped with a mechanical drag), and when the reel is palmed for retrieving, the thumb can apply tension to the line for tight, smooth spooling.

Holding the Rod Grasp the rod grip without squeezing it tightly. Your forefinger should be extended and wrapped comfortably around the trigger. Place your thumb on the spool, and turn your hand so your palm faces *down* and the reel handles are up. The up-handle position allows complete wrist freedom. A ⅝-ounce casting weight should be ½–1 inch below the top guide; the ⅜-ounce weight should be about 3 inches below the top guide. The position of the weight (lure) is important in bait-casting; as you use lures of less and less weight, they should be suspended progressively further away. For absolute accuracy remember to minimize your wrist bend on the backstroke and to bring your rod and reel up with the handles facing you squarely. Precision is achieved by always bringing the rod to the same position. Eventually, you will "feel" the lure to the target.

The Overhead Cast Face the target directly; then take a quarter turn to the left so that your right shoulder is now pointed toward the target and your left foot is slightly to the rear of your right foot. (A left-handed caster simply reverses the procedure by quartering to the right.) Of course this position will be assumed naturally as you progress. Most of your body weight is now on the right foot. Hold the rod at about a thirty-five-degree angle so that the tip is slightly above head level and the rod handle above hip level. Your elbow should not touch the body, and your outstretched forearm should parallel the angle of the rod. The rod shaft should be "splitting" the target.

Start the backward phase of your cast by lifting the forearm and pivoting slightly on your elbow until your hand comes smoothly to eye level. The rod should stop at the vertical position where the lure weight will develop a

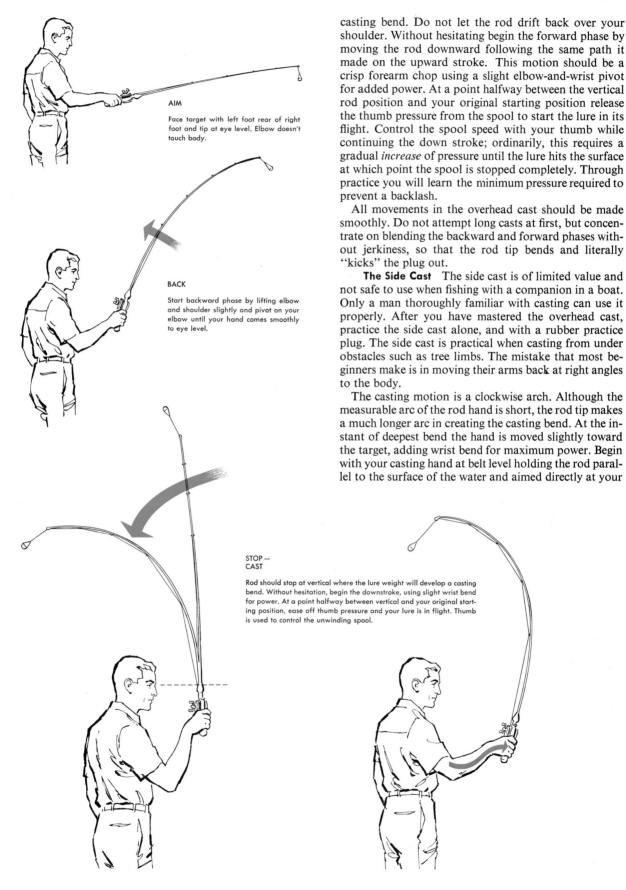

AIM

Face target with left foot rear of right foot and tip at eye level. Elbow doesn't touch body.

BACK

Start backward phase by lifting elbow and shoulder slightly and pivot on your elbow until your hand comes smoothly to eye level.

STOP — CAST

Rod should stop at vertical where the lure weight will develop a casting bend. Without hesitation, begin the downstroke, using slight wrist bend for power. At a point halfway between vertical and your original starting position, ease off thumb pressure and your lure is in flight. Thumb is used to control the unwinding spool.

casting bend. Do not let the rod drift back over your shoulder. Without hesitating begin the forward phase by moving the rod downward following the same path it made on the upward stroke. This motion should be a crisp forearm chop using a slight elbow-and-wrist pivot for added power. At a point halfway between the vertical rod position and your original starting position release the thumb pressure from the spool to start the lure in its flight. Control the spool speed with your thumb while continuing the down stroke; ordinarily, this requires a gradual *increase* of pressure until the lure hits the surface at which point the spool is stopped completely. Through practice you will learn the minimum pressure required to prevent a backlash.

All movements in the overhead cast should be made smoothly. Do not attempt long casts at first, but concentrate on blending the backward and forward phases without jerkiness, so that the rod tip bends and literally "kicks" the plug out.

The Side Cast The side cast is of limited value and not safe to use when fishing with a companion in a boat. Only a man thoroughly familiar with casting can use it properly. After you have mastered the overhead cast, practice the side cast alone, and with a rubber practice plug. The side cast is practical when casting from under obstacles such as tree limbs. The mistake that most beginners make is in moving their arms back at right angles to the body.

The casting motion is a clockwise arch. Although the measurable arc of the rod hand is short, the rod tip makes a much longer arc in creating the casting bend. At the instant of deepest bend the hand is moved slightly toward the target, adding wrist bend for maximum power. Begin with your casting hand at belt level holding the rod parallel to the surface of the water and aimed directly at your

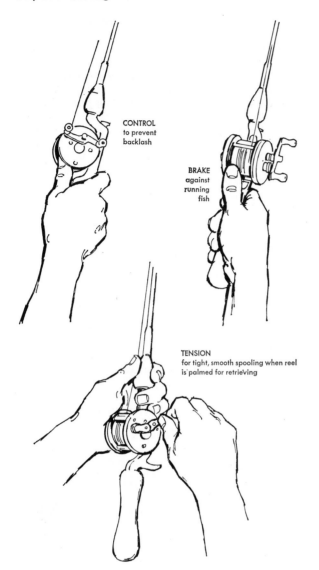

CONTROL
to prevent
backlash

BRAKE
against
running
fish

TENSION
for tight, smooth spooling when reel
is palmed for retrieving

target. Grip the rod with your palm facing left and the reel handles to the right. Your left foot should be slightly in front of your right foot with the left side of your body angled toward target. Distribute your body weight on both feet. With a crisp movement bring your rod back, and stop at a right-angle position to your body. At the instant of deepest bend, move the rod forward with wrist and forearm emphasis, releasing thumb pressure from the spool at the forward impulse. It is important to get the correct release point which "feels" early, or the lure will swing to the left. The tendency to angle casts away from target is due solely to improper release and follow-through. Once mastered the side cast is easy, accurate, and safe.

The Underhand Cast The underhand cast serves the same purpose as the side cast in working under obstacles, although it is safer to use and a great deal more accurate. It does have a limited range, but properly executed it can deliver a plug to practical fishing distances. As in the overhead cast the rod grip should be grasped palm down with the reel handle in the up position. However, unlike the overhead stance, quarter your body to the right so that your left shoulder is pointed toward the target and your weight is shifted to the *left* foot. There is a natural and perhaps effective tendency to lean toward the target when casting in this position. Your casting hand should be held forward at hip level, so that the rod is parallel with the surface of the water and both rod and forearm form a straight line.

Begin the underhand cast by making an upward lift with the rod, keeping a stiff wrist and forearm and pivoting on the elbow. When the tip reaches shoulder level, reverse the direction immediately with a crisp downward push so that the rod returns to its starting position and stops abruptly. The weight of the lure will cause the rod tip to flex down and in toward your feet. As the rod recovers from its bend and begins upward, release your thumb pressure from the spool. The lure will snap outward in a low arc. Do not attempt to push the rod forward. When the underhand cast is executed properly by the angler, then the casting bend of the rod itself will provide sufficient velocity to the lure.

STOP

Stop the rod at original position and, as lure nears target, increase thumb pressure. When lure hits the water, stop spool completely. Keep arc of outgoing line as flat as you can, because wind spoils accuracy.

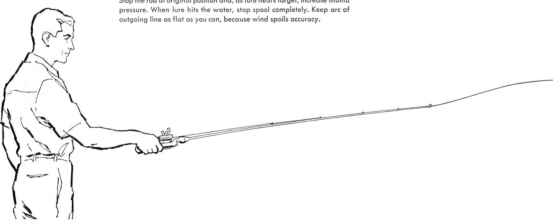

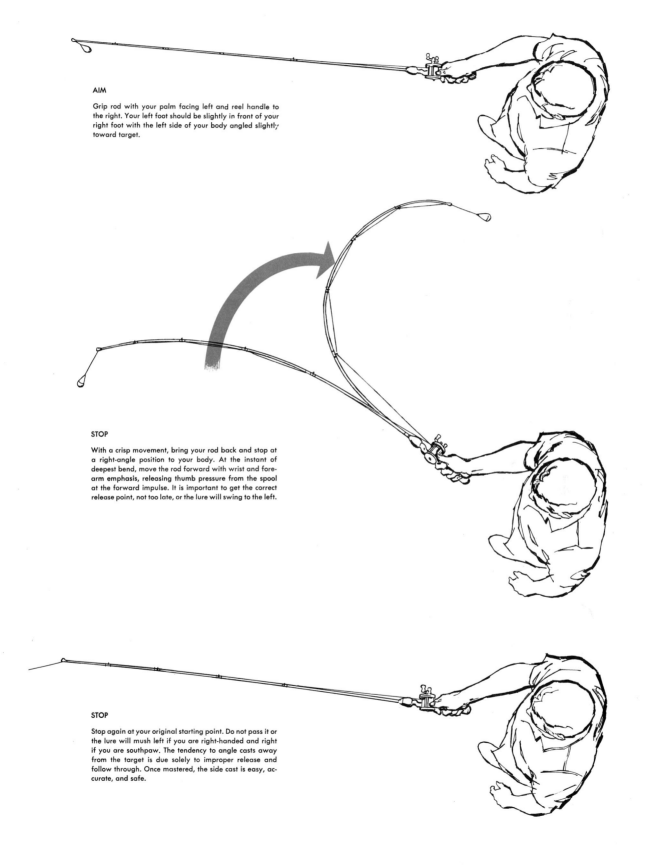

AIM

Grip rod with your palm facing left and reel handle to the right. Your left foot should be slightly in front of your right foot with the left side of your body angled slightly toward target.

STOP

With a crisp movement, bring your rod back and stop at a right-angle position to your body. At the instant of deepest bend, move the rod forward with wrist and fore-arm emphasis, releasing thumb pressure from the spool at the forward impulse. It is important to get the correct release point, not too late, or the lure will swing to the left.

STOP

Stop again at your original starting point. Do not pass it or the lure will mush left if you are right-handed and right if you are southpaw. The tendency to angle casts away from the target is due solely to improper release and follow through. Once mastered, the side cast is easy, accurate, and safe.

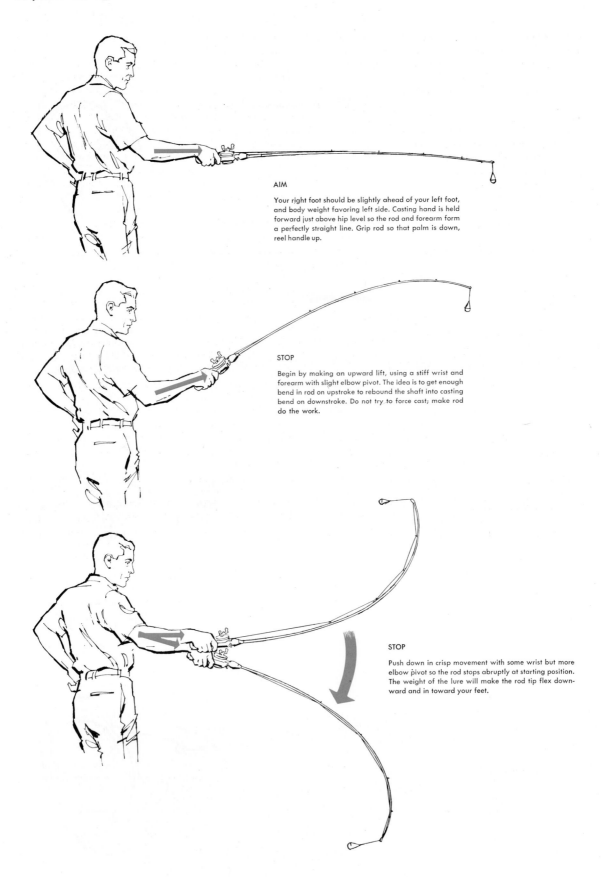

AIM

Your right foot should be slightly ahead of your left foot, and body weight favoring left side. Casting hand is held forward just above hip level so the rod and forearm form a perfectly straight line. Grip rod so that palm is down, reel handle up.

STOP

Begin by making an upward lift, using a stiff wrist and forearm with slight elbow pivot. The idea is to get enough bend in rod on upstroke to rebound the shaft into casting bend on downstroke. Do not try to force cast; make rod do the work.

STOP

Push down in crisp movement with some wrist but more elbow pivot so the rod stops abruptly at starting position. The weight of the lure will make the rod tip flex downward and in toward your feet.

TACKLE

Extra-Light Outfit This outfit is matched for lures of less than ⅜ ounce. Functionally, it encompasses much of the hardware used by spinfishermen, and for that reason only a small number of experts favor extra-light gear. Rods in this class are 6–6½ feet in length, and their ability to flex smoothly with the minimum lure weights is resolved by their taper. A tournament type or narrow-frame free-spool with level-wind reel, spooled with 4–8-pound-test line, completes the outfit. The chief distinction between these two types of reels is that the tournament type has no level-wind mechanism. In both models the handle is disengaged before casting, and only the spool turns. The strictly tournament reel has almost disappeared from angling as most fishermen find it awkward to spool incoming line evenly without a level wind. Actually, this tackle class is a refinement of the next heavier one, and the size of its components overlap. Experts make a distinction, however, because the extra-light rod is tapered for maximum flection with weights from a low of 60 grains, or ⅛ ounce, to a high of 140 grains, or slightly more than ¼ ounce.

Light Outfit The light bait-casting outfit is matched primarily for tossing lures from 120 grains or ¼ ounce to 240 grains or ½ ounce. This also implies clearwater conditions and educated fish. Northeastern bass specialists are the leading exponents of light gear. The light outfit is seldom used in the Deep South largely because the most efficient lures in this region are in the 300-grain or ⅝-ounce class. Suitable rods vary from 5½–6½ feet in length, but a 6-foot shaft is most popular. Reels may be tournament type, or narrow-frame level-wind with or without free spool; there are many precision-built level winders, notably those developed for Skish accuracy work, which are sensitive enough to cast light baits even though the handle turns. The lines suitable for light bait-casting range are 6–12-pound test. Be especially careful, however, that the end plates of the reel spool fit snugly against the frame. Fine monofilaments can easily get tangled inside the reel.

Medium Outfit This tackle class is the most popular all-around gear for freshwater casting. It's also used to some extent for saltwater work. The lure weight range is from 300 grains or ⅝ ounces to 360 grains or ¾ ounces. Rod lengths are 4–6½ feet, depending primarily on the fishing. Some anglers prefer very short rods in regions where casting is commonly done on heavily wooded creeks. They want a flat trajectory to avoid overhanging branches. Although longer rods deliver a high-arc flight, this is preferred by anglers who seek delicacy in presentation. Generally speaking, the 5-foot and 5½-foot lengths are most popular, and the beginner should buy one that is fairly flexible. Reels for the medium outfit can be narrow-frame level-wind with or without free spool, or the standard wide frame with or without free spool. Most casters are partial to heavier lines in this class and, consequently, wide-frame reels are favored. Besides being sturdier, these reels spool more yardage in the 10-20-pound-test range. It's not uncommon to use an 18-pound-test line with medium tackle when casting for bass, pike, muskies, lake trout, or any husky gamefish living in snag-filled waters.

Heavy Outfit The heavy outfit is matched chiefly for saltwater casting. But the gear is also popular regionally, among muskie, steelhead, and salmon anglers using lures from 360 grains or ¾ ounces, to 600 grains or 1¼ ounces. A heavy rod is required not only for casting but to set the hooks when using large baits on big fish. Frequently, such angling is a part-time trolling proposition, which requires heavy-caliber sticks. Rod lengths are 4½–7½ feet; however, over 5½ feet we enter the realm of two-handed casting rods in popping, mooching, and surf fishing. The average heavy-bait rod is 15 feet long. Few wrists can comfortably support more than 480 grains or a 1-ounce casting load; so the length and weight factors more or less stop at this point. With the five-foot heavy rod, you would need the standard wide-frame reel, with or without free spool. Lines in this class range 18–25 pounds. For big game like tarpon, salmon, or muskies, select tackle on the heavy side of medium, and try to keep the lure weights in the 300–360-grain range. A 14-pound-test monofilament is perfectly adequate, even for tarpon in the up to 150-pound class—provided, of course, you select a quality reel with a smooth drag.

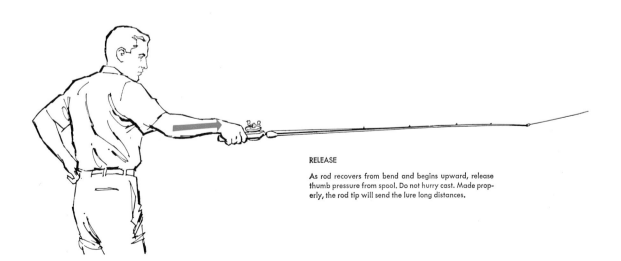

RELEASE

As rod recovers from bend and begins upward, release thumb pressure from spool. Do not hurry cast. Made properly, the rod tip will send the lure long distances.

Bait-Casting Reels: (*left to right, top row*) True Temper 944F, Garcia Ambassadeur 8000, Shakespeare Sportcast 1982, (*second row*) Garcia Ambassadeur 5000, Heddon Mark III, South Bend 50, Pflueger Supreme 1573, (*third row*) Pflueger Nobby 1960, Bronson Coronet 25C, H-I Admiral 1840, (*bottom row*) Zebco Streamlite 310, and Shakespeare President 1971

Reels supplied by True Temper Corp., Abercrombie & Fitch, Shakespeare Co., Heddon & Sons, South Bend Tackle Co., the Pflueger Corp., and the Harrocks-Ibbotson Co.

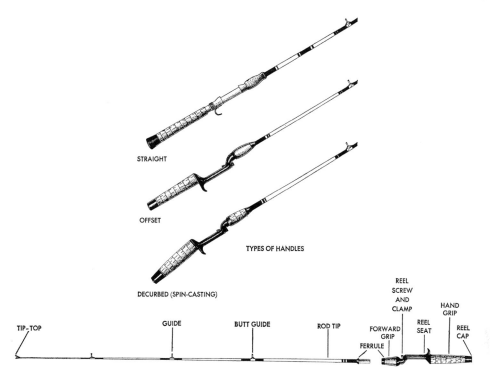

STRAIGHT

OFFSET

TYPES OF HANDLES

DECURBED (SPIN-CASTING)

REEL
SCREW
AND
CLAMP

HAND
GRIP

FORWARD
GRIP

REEL
SEAT

REEL
CAP

TIP-TOP

GUIDE

BUTT GUIDE

ROD TIP

FERRULE

Bait-Casting Rod Nomenclature

DEVELOPMENT OF BAIT-CASTING REELS

The Kentucky Reel The bait-casting reel prior to 1880 was entirely a handmade mechanism. Yet every one of them was crafted with painstaking exactness. No two screws were alike, and as a result every screw had to be put back in its proper place after the reel was taken apart. The lathe work, fitting, and filing were truly perfect. Reel handles were chopped out of sheet metal with a cold chisel and then filed to shape. The gears were slotted on Swiss cutting engines and then filed by hand. The main gear wheel was always made of brass casting or a section of brass rod that was hammered on an anvil, while the small wheel or pinion gear was made of the very best tempered tool steel. This resulted in a gearing that was almost indestructible. However, considering the labor involved, the average monthly production for a skilled builder was about seven reels, and these would sometimes bring $60–$70 apiece. Customers didn't ask the price—they ordered and were charged what the builder throught it was worth. The best a sporting goods dealer could hope for was a 10 per cent discount, and the order was filled when the "manufacturer" was in the mood. Oddly enough, fully 90 per cent of all bait-casting reels made came from the state of Kentucky. These were great reels. While none of them is made now, the modern bait-casting reel owes its existence to the craftsmen of Frankfort, Paris, and Louisville. Many of their original reels, now over one hundred years old, are still in use today.

George Snyder The modern bait-casting reel was developed in the nineteenth century by a group of Kentucky watchmakers. Foremost among these was George

Snyder, who made the first multiplying reel in 1810. Until that year, there were only two kinds of casting reels available—the English single-action reel made of brass or the domestic wooden kind made from a discarded sewing spool mounted on a frame by the local tinsmith. The rods used by these pioneer bass fishermen were native woods such as bethabara, Osage orange, and hickory; they were nearly 10 feet long but comparatively light, weighing 5–8 ounces. This was nearly one hundred years before James Heddon was to manufacture the first bass plug; so Snyder's customers were actually looking for a very sensitive spool with which to cast live baits. The inertia of a heavy single-action brass spool or the crude wooden type was too much for a bait to overcome. With a fine raw-silk line they could cast live minnows about 50–60 feet, provided the wind was right. The "cast" was what we know today as strip-casting. The angler would lay coils of line in the bottom of the boat or, if he was adept, hold the loops in his hand and propel the bait with a sideswiping motion.

Having a watchmaker's knowledge of gearing, George Snyder was able to make not only a delicate spool but one that revolved several times for every turn of the crank handle. In his reel the steel ends of the spool shaft were beveled to points, which in turn fitted in beveled recesses of pivots that screwed into the center caps of the outer disk plates of the reel. This compensating measure would take up any wear, and the running of the reel could be regulated by a turn of these screw pivots. How sound Snyder's methods were is best shown in the reel he made for the Honorable Brutus Clay in 1821. Seventy years later the same reel was being used by Clay's son. This, like all of his reels, had its pillars riveted to the backplate and projecting through the inner frontplate, where they were secured with wire keys. Snyder reels were also quite narrow in spool diameter and long, in accordance with the belief that a long narrow spool runs more rapidly than a short one of greater diameter—all things being equal. On some of his reels he built an oddly shaped flat lever to operate the click spring with a pin working in a curved slot.

Jonathan F. Meek There was no such thing as mass production in the early 1800's, so even though he won local acclaim in creating a revolutionary reel, Snyder could build very few of them. However, other watchmakers saw reel building as a profitable hobby. A Judge Mason Brown of Frankfort, Kentucky, lost his reel, and finding Snyder too busy to make a new one, he went to another watchmaker by the name of Jonathan F. Meek. Although Meek was later to be credited with inventing the bait-casting reel, his work was really an improvement on the Snyder. Meek built his with a collar around the crankshaft; the ends of the spool did not project, and the click and drag springs were operated by sliding buttons, as in the modern reel. He made the reel for Judge Brown in 1832 and continued making reels along until 1840, when he formed a partnership with his brother, Benjamin F. Meek, who was, of course, a watchmaker. Ben Meek proved so good at building reels that for a while he made all of their production, stamping the side plates "J. F. & B. F. Meek." Sport fishing was on the march, or at least under motion, for railroad-riding General W. W. Shriver caught some bass in the Ohio River drainage which he dumped in a perforated pail that hung in the water tank of a locomotive tender. The fish rode over the Alleghenies on the Baltimore and Ohio Railroad and were released in the Potomac basin. Thus the black bass came out of its native haunts, and as the fishing spread eastward, there was a fantastic demand for Meek reels.

John Hardman At about this time, still another maker of watches turned to reels, a man named John W. Hardman of Louisville, Kentucky. His reels were a great improvement on the Snyders and the Meeks. Instead of the 3 : 1 and 3½ : 1 gear ratio popularized by Snyder, Hardman used a 4 : 1 gearing—and as a result he is credited with making the first quadruple multiplying reel. However, George Snyder had been using the quadruple gearing in his personal reels several years before Hardman began building. Hardman did make a more modern-looking reel; he shortened the spool and increased the diameter, affixed the pillars to the disk plates by screws instead of riveting, and added some ornamentation. The use of screws, incidentally, makes the Hardman reel the first one having a "takedown" feature. The Hardman reel of 1845 was made of German silver with gold-plated click buttons and screws.

Benjamin C. Milam Benjamin C. Milam of Frankfort, Kentucky, joined the Meeks as an apprentice in 1840. After the retirement of Jonathan Meek, the firm became known as Meek and Milam, which was in turn dissolved after a 5-year period. The partners continued to occupy the same store, Milam devoting himself to making reels while Ben Meek re-established his watchmaking and jewelry business. All reels made by Mr. Milam continued to be stamped "Meek and Milam"

until 1878. Having trained his son to the trade, Milam took him into the business under the firm name of B. C. Milam & Son. How well they succeeded may be seen in the fact that a Milam reel won the international first prize in Chicago in 1893 at the World's Fair. Actually, this model was of 1844 vintage; the pillars were still of the Snyder plan, as was the narrow spool. The improvements were a collar on the crank, sliding buttons for the click and drag, and a bent or U-shaped click spring formed from a piece of watch spring. With exception of the ornamentation, this reel closely resembled the Hardman in general form. B. C. Milam & Son also won first prize at the Fisheries Exposition in Bergen, Norway, in 1898, and at the World's Exposition in Paris, France, in 1904. President Grover Cleveland wrote Milam letters of appreciation for the workmanship in his reels.

The Spiral Gear Benjamin F. Meek wearied of his watch trade and in 1883 once again turned to the reel business. His indecision can probably be explained by the fact that he was never an angler. Of all the Kentucky reel makers, this autocratic master had no interest in fishing. He formed a partnership with his two sons, and together they created a new departure in the gearing of reels, which is called the "spiral gear." This consisted of cutting the teeth of the wheel and pinion diagonally instead of horizontally. The space between the teeth at their base was rounded instead of being made flat or square. But even more significant was the fact that the Meeks started building reels in an organized fashion. Here is what the *Tri-Weekly Kentucky Yeoman* of November 21, 1882, had to say in an article on Benjamin F. Meek: "He proposes, we learn, to make his reels entirely of wrought metal, no casting or drawn wire being used, and the machinery will be as perfect as that of an astronomical instrument. For this purpose he has provided himself with machinery of the most improved pattern, most of it being invented by himself, and made under his immediate direction at Waltham, Massachusetts, by the American Watch Tool Company. This will run by a gas engine, which he is now engaged in putting up. But such is the nature of the works that the greater part has to be done by hand, and Mr. Meek says that there will not be a piece that will not receive his touch. . . . He will not be able to turn out reels before the first of February, but after that time he will endeavor to supply the demands. We commend Mr. Meek as in every respect worthy of the respect and confidence of the people of Louisville, and as to his reels, they will commend themselves."

Meek made reels for the next sixteen years, and by the time he died in 1901, he had made some of the most important contributions toward the development of modern bait-casting reels. His use of spiral gears instead of spur gears and the introduction of jeweled pivot bearings reduced wear, resulting in a practical mechanism. E. J. Martin of Rockville, Connecticut, started making braided silk casting lines in 1884; so the delicate sensitivity of Meek reels was brought to full flower. Ben cashed in his chips just as the game ended; bait-casting rods had been growing shorter all the time—now they used 5-foot bamboo sticks and cast Dowagiac minnows in "Kalamazoo" style. The overhead, or Kalamazoo, cast was the dawn of a new era and the end of the Kentucky reel-maker. Bait-casting became immensely popular, and mass production methods became absolutely essential.

The Level-Wind Mechanism Although Snyder, Hardman, the Meeks, and the Milams did most to perfect the bait-casting reel other itinerant watchmakers such as Talbot, Noel, Sage, and Gayle were in business during the nineteenth century. However, it remained for a Wisconsin firm (Wheeler & McGregor) to make a device for level-winding the line on the spool. This mechanism was a great boon in preventing backlashes, and their original design is still embodied in our modern reel.

HOW TO SELECT A CASTING LINE

There are several things to be considered in selecting a casting line, but the fundamental point is that a heavy line will not function with a light lure—nor will a light line work with a heavy lure. A delicate bait won't create enough velocity to pull the heavy line any distance, and, conversely, a spidery line will break under the load of a heavy lure when the rod is snapped into a casting bend. There is a definite relationship between the strength and/or diameter of a line and the weight to be thrown. In a sense, the line must act as a shock absorber when the rod gives the lure its backward momentum, and then the line must follow the weight through the air with a minimum resistance to the lure's velocity. These two demands are in opposition to each other. The ideal is maximum strength with minimum diameter in any casting line. So the factor to consider is what the weight range of the lures will be in a day's fishing.

This doesn't present much of a problem for the practical angler. With the standard lure-weight range of $\frac{3}{8}$–$\frac{5}{8}$ ounce a 10-pound-test line is usually adequate. If the fishing requires small baits of $\frac{1}{8}$–$\frac{1}{4}$ ounce, then it would require something less than 8-pound test to get any distance. At the other extreme when casting lures of $\frac{5}{8}$–$\frac{3}{4}$ ounce a 12-pound test is about right. This, of course, is a rule of thumb.

HOW TO RETRIEVE A PLUG

There are two skills which distinguish the expert angler from the beginner. The first is his ability to cast accurately at all distances within the limits of his tackle, and the second is how he handles the retrieve. By angling definition, retrieving simply means recovery of the lure through reeling. But in actual practice it's the final touch of success —your sword point in the delicate art of catching fish off their guard. Although technical advances have spawned a variety of nearly automatic baits, there are qualities of action which cannot be built into a plug or spoon.

Anybody who has fished very often is aware of that classic angling paradox: two men cast from the same boat, using the same lure, and one angler hooks fish to the point of monotony, while his companion feels like a charity case. A casual observer might say it's "luck," but it doesn't take a genius to realize that there is unending variation and novelty within a task which to a duller eye might seem mechanical. The successful angler knew *how* to work his bait. Retrieving is the practice of innocent deceptions to make fish believe that metal and plastic are edible—a kind of artful storytelling in which the plug plays the role of a tired frog, a leaping mullet, or whatever seems appropriate at the moment. The mere reeling of a lure is not enough. There are many retrieves which might be classified one from another on the basis of distinctive

movements, but most anglers use four which vary in speed and emphasis.

The Correct Speed Different reels have different rates of line recovery. How many inches will be spooled with one turn of the handle depends on (1) how much line is on the reel, (2) the gear ratio, (3) the cranking radius of the handle, and (4) the spool diameter. A very small reel, with, say, a 2 : 1 gear ratio, is going to recover much less line than a large reel with a 4 : 1 ratio. It's possible, therefore, for a man to crank rapidly with the smaller reel and believe that he is making a fast retrieve, but his actual lure speed may be less than half of what it would be with the larger reel. Thus, we have a considerable degree of variation in what constitutes fast and slow—mechanically speaking. The most workable definition of a slow retrieve is the minimum speed at which the inherent action of a bait will function. If it's designed to wobble, it should wobble; if it's built to flap a pair of aluminum arms, it should flap. By the same token, a fast retrieve must imply the maximum speed at which these devices operate. If the plug is "straight" or completely without mechanical action of any kind, then we might define a slow retrieve as the minimum speed at which you can activate the bait and a fast retrieve as the maximum speed at which you can reel. In the latter case, this usually means the plug will skip over the water.

To determine the correct reeling speed on any particular day, it's a good idea to vary the retrieve every fifteen minutes, until you catch a fish or at least see one. On a fast retrieve, for instance, if a fish follows the lure for a long distance without striking, you can stop reeling and let the plug sit motionless on the water. There is a reasonable chance that he will strike when the plug is at rest or when it starts to move again. On subsequent casts if more fish continue to follow without striking until the plug stops, it would indicate that reeling at a slower speed with pauses is going to be more effective. Conversely, you may get the same response to a slow retrieve; if the fish swims along behind the bait without hitting, then a sudden increase in reeling speed might trigger a strike. Of course, you don't have much chance of seeing fish when casting deep-running lures, but in this connection it's worth remembering that we all tend to work at a neutral speed, and it's usually the very slow or very fast retrieves that pay off when bottom scratching.

The Popping Retrieve Popping is probably the most universal method of working a plug in both freshwater and saltwater. It's based on the fact that fish can be attracted by sound—not necessarily a loud noise, but a convincing one. Popping is particularly effective when fish are hiding under bank brush where they can't be reached. They will hear the bait and come out for it. Or if they're loafing in a submerged weed bed in 5–10 feet of water, the sound of a popper is often enough to bring them up. Popping is also the easiest way to get strikes in muddy water when the visual search for food is limited by turbidity. Still another situation for popping plugs is when schooling fish such as white, black, or striped bass are foraging on concentrations of baitfish. The sound commands their attention if you have to compete with a melée of panicky minnows.

A plug's ability to pop is a matter of design. The lure should have a slanting concave face. When sitting on the water, most poppers float in a head-up position with tail submerged. A slight stroke of the rod tip lifts the plug to a horizontal position which causes the face to scoop water, creating a large bubble which breaks with that tantalizing sound. However, it must be worked correctly. The retrieve is a slow one with long pauses. There is a tendency for beginners to pop themselves out of business. Frequently, too much noise will spook gamefish rather than attract them. A good rule of thumb is to wait until the disturbance made by a popped plug has completely vanished—then count off ten seconds before popping again. Mild pops can be made with the rod tip moving upward and loud ones by using a sharp downward jerk. If the plug simply flips out of the water, then you are not holding the rod correctly in relation to distance you have cast. The correct rod position for any type of retrieve depends on the lure itself (its design and weight) and the length of line extended on the water. For example, a surface bait built to skip over the water is going to require your holding the rod very high. A darter on the other hand will require your pointing the tip downward to keep it weaving under the surface. And while you can begin all retrieves with a high rod on a long cast, the tip will have to be gradually lowered to work many baits; it becomes increasingly difficult, for instance, to pop a surface plug when the extended line length is shortened because the lure is eventually pulled over, rather than under the water. An experienced angler gauges the correct rod position with each cast. He tries to keep the tip at an angle 45–60 degrees in relation to the line, whether he's working with tip up, down, or to the side. As much rod as possible should absorb the shock of a strike; yet it must never be so close to ninety degrees that he is unable to set the hooks.

The Whip Retrieve Essentially, this is a rod performance which counts on the fact that your plug has little, if any, incorporated action. The whip is most commonly used in saltwater and in the South, but it's effective on many occasions in freshwater also. Starting with the rod tip at horizontal and pointed in the direction of the lure, pull the rod fast and forcefully in a ninety degree arc to the side of your body. The instant the rod stops, crank very fast to take up slack as you move the rod back to its original position. When pointed in the direction of the lure again, whip the rod once more, repeating the process of reeling and whipping so that the plug achieves a rhythm of darting in a curved path over and below the surface. Saltwater gamefish can be extremely selective in the matter of lure action and speed. Anybody who fishes for tarpon or snook regularly is usually a master of both popping and the whip retrieve.

The Nodding Retrieve This is the manual opposite to whipping, and vastly different from popping. While the pop artist creates sounds and bubbles to draw the fish's attention to his lure, the nodder assumes that a fish is nearby, already watching the silent plug. The best time to nod is when you have located the lair of a big fish—or on those dreary days when the popper is left talking to itself. Although you can do it with almost any kind of surface plug, the chances of a strike are greatly improved if you use the right kind; the ideal is one with a propeller in the rear and a weighted tail section. The face of the plug should poke out of water so that it assumes the posture of a free-swimming frog resting on the surface. The idea is to tip the plug every few minutes so that it seesaws without any forward motion. After a reasonable

length of time, you can retrieve very slowly with frequent pauses to let the plug nod again. This is a painfully patient method of bringing a bait back, but it pays off on smart fish. It worries them into striking. Most, if not all kinds of fish, can be intrigued by a lure that literally sits and does nothing. This is by far the most difficult technique to learn because it demands that one quality anglers are famous for, patience.

The Skipping Retrieve This is a refinement of spoon skittering. It's faster than a fast retrieve. The plug should actually skip over the surface. Several things are required to do it right. The lure must have enough body length so it doesn't flip over your line. The rod must be long —or else you will have to stand on a boat seat or high bank to keep a maximum length of line elevated from the water. And your reel must have a rapid rate of retrieve. The idea is to make the fish think that something good to eat is hightailing out of sight. While the days of a slowly worked plug outnumber effective periods for a fast playback, this retrieve brings some of the most explosive strikes from reluctant fish. Invariably, it stirs them to full speed with dorsal out, humping water behind the wildly skipping plug as though it were a last meal. It doesn't matter whether your quarry is a chain pickerel or a 200-pound tarpon.

The art of retrieving a plug is equally as important as casting skill. In fact anybody who can toss a bait twenty yards (and that's not difficult with modern enclosed spool reels or spinning reels) may be reasonably certain of catching fish, provided he doesn't become addicted to automatic reeling. If the lake or a particular kind of fishing is new to you, it's worth the effort to ask the local experts how they manipulate their lures. Get the exact details. Most guides, dock operators, tackle dealers, and game protectors are reliable and generous sources of information.　　　　　　　　　　　　　—A.J.McC.

BAIT-CASTING REEL *See* Bait-Casting

BALAO Family Hemiramphidae Also known as bally-hoo and halfbeak, a number of species comprise this unique family. One species, *Hemiramphus balao*, is specifically given the common name of balao, but almost all members of the family are also known under that name. The body is slender and elongate, somewhat flattened from side to side, and the lower jaw projects noticeably, equivalent to the length of the head, the upper jaw being very short. The dorsal and anal fins are set far back on

Balao

the body, close to the caudal fin, the lower lobe of which is the longer. These beautifully hued fish are generally a translucent green on the back, with blue or gold reflections and a silvery band along the sides, becoming pale below. In some species the lower jaw is tipped with red in fresh specimens, and, depending on the species, the tip of the lower lobe of the caudal fin may be tipped with yellow or the upper lobe may be tipped with red or orange. Some Pacific species reach 2 feet long, but most species grow to less than a foot.

LIFE HISTORY

Balao are found in all tropical seas, some drifting poleward during the warmer months. All are coastal species, generally found over reefs, but some occur over shallow grass flats. They are easily attracted by a light at night and leap from the water when frightened. They travel in vast schools, skimming over the surface and feeding on green algae, bits of turtle grass, surface detritus, small fishes, and plankton. In turn, they are eaten by barracuda, jacks, groupers, cero mackerel, and other inshore, predatory fishes. When sailfish occur over shallow reefs, they feed heavily upon them, bunching them into tight schools. Several sailfish will work together concentrating the balao, then they will slash at the "ball," feeding on the stunned or dead balao.

The spawning season is believed to be in late spring and early summer. Young are found over deep reefs but in "green" coastal water. They resemble the adults except that they lack a beak.

Balao are a most important baitfish, and they are primarily trolled for sailfish, marlin, kingfish, wahoo, dolphin, king mackerel, and tuna. They are taken in seines, cast nets, lift nets, hoopnets, and with underwater lights and dipnets.

FOOD VALUE

Although not widely eaten in the United States they are popular in Caribbean countries, and their flesh is excellent. —D.dS.

BALLAST Heavy material such as lead, stone, iron, carried in the bottom of the boat or fastened to the keel to increase stability by lowering center of gravity.

BALLYHOO A common name for the balao (*which see*) widely used as a trolling bait in big-game fishing.

BAMBOO ROD *See* Rod-Building, Tonkin Cane

BANDED BUTTERFLY FISH *See* Butterflyfishes

BANDED DRUM *See* Drums

BANDED KILLIFISH *Fundulus diaphanus* This species superficially resembles males of the mummichog (*which see*) but is very slender, with a depressed head and an elongate snout. The tail is usually square-edged or slightly concave. The scales are smaller than in the mummichog, and, in addition, the numerous light and dark bars distinguish it from the striped killifish (*which see*). The banded killifish is green to olive-green above, to white below and on the lower sides. The young resemble the female in coloration, assuming the adult pattern at a length of about 2 inches. It reaches a length of about 4 inches.

Banded Killifish

This is a common freshwater species which also inhabits slightly brackish water. It is found from the area of the St. Lawrence River to South Carolina. A subspecies occurs to the west, extending through the Great Lakes and the Dakotas. Found generally in quiet waters, the banded killifish is common in large lakes, rivers, estuaries, small bodies of water.

LIFE HISTORY

Spawning occurs in large schools from April to September. The large eggs are laid on a sand bottom where they stick to sand or weed by adhesive threads. This killifish eats small crustaceans, mollusks, worms, and plant material. In turn, it is eaten by predatory fishes, and in this respect plays an important role in the economy of shallow-water environments.

ANGLING VALUE

The banded killifish is frequently used as bait. It is not as hardy on a hook as the mummichog but, nevertheless, is of some value because of its abundance and ease of capture. —D.dS.

BANDED PYGMY SUNFISH *Elassoma zonatum* This tiny perchlike fish has an olive-greenish color and about ten vertical dark bars on each side. There is a dark spot on each side below the origin of the dorsal fin. The lateral line is absent, the dorsal fin is shallowly notched, and the tail fin is rounded. The maximum length is about 1½ inches.

This little fish is distributed from southern Illinois to Texas and east to western Florida. It is considered a swampwater fish living in these waters and bayous under mats of heavy surface vegetation.

LIFE HISTORY

The pygmy sunfish starts breeding in the middle of March when the water temperatures reach 62°–68°F. Spawning continues to the first part of May. It is believed that they do not build a nest. The spawning takes place 7–11 inches from the bottom, and the eggs are dropped 40–60 at a time in submerged vegetation for protection. One female less than 1½ inches produced 970 eggs. Maturity in these fish may be reached before they are one year old. One male in its third summer was ⅓ inch long.

These tiny fish live on small crustaceans, aquatic insects, and small mollusks.

ANGLING VALUE

Because of its small size the banded pygmy sunfish has no value to the angler. —K.B.

BANDED RUDDERFISH *Seriola zonata* Also called slender amberjack, this western Atlantic species has previously been confused with *Seriola lalandi*, a distinct species in the South Atlantic Ocean.

Fish of less than about eleven inches long have a dark nuchal band extending from the eye to the origin of the first dorsal fin and six prominent bars on the body. The anal-fin base (excluding the two detached spines) is relatively short; the second dorsal-fin base is about twice as long as the anal-fin base (about 1½–1⅔ times as long as the anal-fin base in other Atlantic amberjacks).

The body is relatively slender. The second dorsal-fin lobe is relatively short. The first dorsal fin usually has eight spines. The second dorsal fin has a spine and 33–40 softrays. The anal fin has two detached spines (which may be overgrown by skin in large individuals) followed by a spine and 19–21 softrays. The anterior gillrakers tend to become rudimentary with growth; the first gill arch has a maximum total of 25 gillrakers at small sizes; that decreases to a range of 15–20 total gillrakers in 5–9-inch

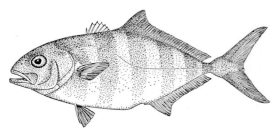

Banded Rudderfish

fish, and 12–16 in still larger specimens. In smaller specimens, the bars and nuchal band are solid black, the lower part of the body silvery, and the body between the bars is light brown, with a faint golden or bronze stripe along the sides. The larger, unbarred fish are mostly brownish, darker above and lighter below.

The banded rudderfish ranges from Santos, Brazil, to Nova Scotia. Its reported occurrence at Bermuda has been questioned. A specimen slightly less than 25 inches long is the maximum size that has been recorded, and one unsubstantiated account stated that the maximum length was about 3 feet.

LIFE HISTORY

This is apparently an inshore species, but the life history has not been investigated. The very young are often found under jellyfish and drifting weed, and slightly older fish have habits similar to the pilotfish in following sharks and other large fish.

ANGLING VALUE

This species is sometimes caught by sport fishermen, and occasionally large numbers are taken in traps, but there is no significant commercial fishery. *See also* Amberjacks, Carangidae   —F.H.B.

BANDED SUNFISH *Enneacanthus obesus* A small, chubby sunfish with a rounded tail. The banded sunfish has 5–8 dark vertical bars (which may be indistinct) on its sides. It has a dark opercular spot on the gill flap (more than one-half the size of the eye), which is usually velvet black in color bordered with purple.

The banded sunfish is most often found in sluggish streams of the Atlantic drainage from southeastern New Hampshire to central Florida.

ANGLING VALUE

The banded sunfish seldom reaches 3 inches in length and has no angling value. It is utilized as forage by larger gamefish.   —K.B.

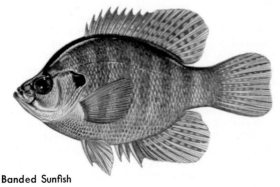

Banded Sunfish

BANKS DORY The banks dory, or Grand Banker as it is also known, is the most famous type of all the dories originated and used by New England's commercial fishermen. Normally made of pine planking fastened to oak ribs, the banks dory runs 14–18 feet long. It is a high-standing and seaworthy rowboat with flaring sides, a narrow transom, a sharp-pointed prow, and a flat bottom. Capable of being rowed, sculled, sailed, or powered by inboard and outboard motors the banks dory was designed for use on the Grand Banks and other exposed fishing waters offshore from the Maritime provinces of Canada and the New England coast. Used as a tender or working rowboat in conjunction with a deepwater vessel, the dory was built so that a number of them could be carried on the deck of the mother ship by stacking them in nest fashion one inside the other. This is made possible by removing the thwarts or seats.   —F.M.P.

BANTAM SUNFISH *Lepomis symmetricus* This small sunfish with the rounded, deep body is characterized by its extremely large scales along the incomplete lateral line. Many of the lateral-line scales lack pores. The gill flap has a light margin, and the pectoral fins are rounded. Maximum length does not exceed 3 inches.

Bantam Sunfish

The bantam sunfish is found in the Mississippi drainage from southern Illinois to Louisiana.

It feeds mostly on insect larvae such as dragonfly nymphs and midge larvae.

ANGLING VALUE

Because of its small size the bantam sunfish has no value to the angler.   —K.B.

BARBEL (1) A fleshy projection or process usually attached to the maxillary, such as the barbels of a catfish. *See* Anatomy

(2) **Barbus barbus** A large member of the carp family sought after by many European anglers in the fast rivers which it prefers. The barbel has a characteristic shape. The only fish closely resembling it is the gudgeon (*Cottus gobio*), which frequently occurs in the same streams as barbel; and the semling (*Barbus petenyi*), which is restricted to the Danube basin and replaces the barbel in that watershed.

The body of the barbel is long, but thick and "chunky" in cross-section. The ratio of length to width is over 5 : 1; and the caudal peduncle is extremely thick and muscular. The shape of the head is most characteristic: The upper surface slopes sharply down from behind to a snout level with the line of the belly. It has been suggested that this acts as a concave surface which keeps the barbel's head down when it faces into a strong current. The mouth is inferior and subterminal; that is, it is on the lower side of the head and behind the snout. This mouth is diagnostic: it has extremely thick and fleshy lips with four barbules hanging down from it. The gudgeon has a similar, though smaller and more delicate, nose and mouth; but gudgeon bear only 2 barbules. A mouth such as the barbel's is plainly adapted for feeling food and taking it off the bottom.

Of the fins the dorsal is single and almost at the midpoint of the body length. It has 3 unbranched hardrays (the first extremely tough and saw-edged) and 8–9 branched softrays. Other fin ray counts are:

Pectoral	1 unbranched /15–17 branched
Pelvic	2 unbranched /8–9 branched
Tail	19 branched
Anal	3 unbranched /5–6 branched

The lateral line scale count is 58–60.

Barbel are normally green to gray on the back, with a whitish belly and golden flanks. The fins usually have red tints, especially on their margins, and in some specimens may be extremely red. Occasionally barbel of ornamental colors occur, usually an all-yellow type. This is not unknown in other members of the carp family—the carp itself, the goldfish, and the tench—even in wild populations.

The body and mouth shape show barbel to be fish highly adapted to a specific habitat and mode of life. They are normally found where the river in its course has reached lowlands, but retains much of the faster flow nearer its source. Such a river stretch is clear, gravel, sand, or pebble-bedded, and with only a few marginal weeds. Well-known examples are the English rivers Kennet, Thames, Hampshire Avon, and Dorset Stour. So characteristic indeed is the barbel of this type of water that it is called "the barbel reach" by Continental European fishery writers.

Though this is their preferred habitat, they will penetrate into others. They are quite frequently found farther down the river's course in the slower reaches, at the points where man has made weirs which speed up the current locally. The river can be quite small in width and still contain them so long as depth, clarity, and current speed are present. They are even found in canalized water courses quite close to towns—for example, the River Lea near London, England. It is even rumored that they can survive in drinking water reservoirs fed from barbel-containing rivers. This should by no means be discounted, as other fish liking the same sort of habitat as barbel are definitely found therein; that is, trout, chub, and dace.

Normally, however, "the barbel reach" is where to expect barbel, as they seem more sensitive than most members of the carp family to pollution, which perhaps indicates a great need for the oxygen which also goes with fast clear water. Certainly effluents have been known to kill barbel selectively in a mixed fish population.

Barbel habits seem to vary from one river to the next, and this lack of precision is reflected by the lack of basic research upon them in the wild. Within the general area of their preferred habitat, however, they seem to have daytime haunts, where they lie and do some feeding, and nighttime haunts, which are visited for serious feeding. Usually the latter outnumber the former, so barbel can

be located by day but with more difficulty by night, when they would be most receptive to baits.

In some localities they will feed during daylight hours: weir pools are the best-known places. Also there is some evidence that the larger barbel are more nocturnal, or more difficult to track to their feeding areas, than are smaller barbel.

The diet of barbel is catholic, mostly all types of bottom-living freshwater invertebrates. Soon after the spawning period is over, when they must rebuild protein, they chase fish fry.

Barbel distribution may be described as temperate European; their extreme westerly limit is England (not Scotland or Ireland) and thence eastward across Europe north of the Pyrenees. At the Danube watershed in central Europe the closely related semling takes over. As more anglers come to appreciate the sporting qualities of barbel, this range is extended. In England especially anglers have been responsible for its introduction into several river systems where it was not native.

Barbel growth rates have been comparatively little studied, but they appear to grow slowly and steadily to a maximum weight, depending on feeding potential, of 16–20 pounds. The energy expended in the fast-flowing rivers of its habitat must be considerable, and feeding slows down considerably, or even stops, in winter. Normal specimens taken by anglers range from 2–5 pounds; anything over 10 pounds is a real specimen.

LIFE HISTORY

Barbel spawn in late spring, but if the weather is cold then the act may be delayed until midsummer. Legal protection normally lasts only to mid-June, so anglers may be frustrated by fishing at still spawning fish early on in the season.

Before mating barbel come together in shoals, the spawning shoal being larger than the small groups in which they are normally found. The spawning shoals then migrate upstream to fast gravelly shallows. Males have by this time assumed the normal carp-family breeding dress of white spots or tubercles on the head.

The sexes pair off and drop the eggs onto the gravel of the riverbed, where they will adhere to the stones by their stickiness. They are not laid in a "redd" as are the eggs of many other gravel spawners. The eggs themselves are 2 mm in diameter and the yolk is yellowish rather than orange (hence distinguishable from salmonid eggs). The sexual act must be performed quickly, as the sperm are viable for only 2 minutes after being shed from the male.

Larvae-bearing yolk sacs are hatched from the eggs in the usual manner of the carp family. They hide amongst stones and weeds until the yolk sac is lost, and then the fry emerge as shoals and begin hunting for food. The shoaling habit persists during the whole life of the barbel, though the shoals get smaller with maturity; very large and old barbel are found in pairs or threes.

One black mark against the young and actively rooting barbel is that they will unearth salmonid redds and eat the eggs. Barbel are normally active far enough into the winter or late fall to be able to take these eggs. Hibernation is not normal at this early stage in a mild climate, though feeding and metabolism do slow up.

Sexual maturity is gained in the fourth spring of life, when by this time the young barbel have habits and haunts like their parents.

ANGLING VALUE

Barbel have long been a favorite of discriminating anglers interested in a dour, hard-fighting fish. The fight is not spectacular, but it is dogged and immensely powerful; they get great help from the fast current. One trick they can play, even when exhausted, is to open their pectoral fins and "kite" on the current, making them very hard to bring to the net.

In the last century wealthy sportsmen went to fish for barbel on the Thames near London, especially at the tail of the larger weirs. They would first arrange for servants to dig and put thousands—literally—of worms into the swim. Massive prebaiting on this scale brought the fish into the swim and concentrated them there, changing the barbels' habits by sheer abundance of food.

Then these sportsmen would settle in on a punt moored upstream of the baited swim and run float tackles baited with worms through it, using the current to do so. With the barbel concentrated in this way they could hardly put a hand wrong—and they rarely did, for great bags were made this way.

Those days are past. Hardly anybody has the inclination—or the money—to hire bait-diggers and feed a swim on that scale. So, with the passing of the holocausts of worms, this method passed into limbo also. Modern barbel fishing is more selective, more dependent on observation in finding where barbel will feed rather than creating such abundance to change the fish's feeding areas.

Concurrent with this change has come a change in tackle. Float tackles are less in evidence, the usual method being a leaded ledger rig, which rolls slowly through the swim, bites being indicated by touch on the line or by watching the rod tip. This is an extremely skillful use of tackle, as the angler has to know the contour of the swim bottom and also be versed in the nuances of line feel which indicate stones, a bite, vegetation washed down with the current, and so on.

Barbel rods are nowadays a compromise between the sturdiness necessary to fight the fish and the sensitivity of the tip to indicate bites. Such a rod usually has a test curve of 1–1½ pounds, and is 8–11 feet long with line to match on a fixed-spool reel.

Barbel bites are almost as varied in their form as the "false alarms" found with this tackle. They may vary from a most positive pull, which deflects the rod hard round, to a mere "buzzing" on the line.

The baits for this modern style of fishing are worms, balls of soft cheese, small doughballs, sausage meat, and other concoctions.

As barbel will eat fry, spinning has occasionally taken them—and sometimes very large specimens at that. But such captures are accidental and often the result of salmon-spinners out of the barbel legal season.

A few waters, especially in southern England, have been heavily fished with much lighter tackle for smaller species, using the very popular blowfly maggot (or "gentle") as bait. These may be put into the water at the rate of a gallon measure per day per head in extreme cases. It is not difficult to imagine that this will have the same effect on barbel as the old-fashioned worming marathons, even though the maggots were not put in for barbel in the first place.

In many ways this is a disadvantage compared with the older worm prebaiting. At least worms were large enough to hide stout hooks capable of holding powerful fish. In the maggot-baited waters it has meant a guarantee of finding feeding barbel and a known certain bait, but one so small that only light tackle can be used. Many are therefore hooked, but also lost.

COMMERCIAL VALUE

Barbel are practically unknown on English tables today; there was, however, a limited market in the last century when they were taken on baited lines. In Germany and other parts they are still sold and are taken for sale in nets, especially in the breeding season when they congregate.

Barbel flesh is said to be delicious, though rather bony. Barbel roes are poisonous, and if eaten will cause severe alimentary upsets. On no account should roes or eggs be used for food.　　　　　　　　　　—D.M.

BARBLESS HOOK　A type of hook made without a barb. Although barbless hooks have the virtue of being easy for the angler to remove from the mouth of a fish, they have never gained widespread popularity. Most sportsmen prefer to cut the barb from a regular fish hook or flatten the barb with pliers when releasing the fish unharmed is of prime importance. *See also* Hook

BAR JACK *Caranx ruber*　Also called cibi mancho or skip jack, this species is endemic to the western Atlantic.

The gillrakers on the first gill arch of the bar jack number 31–35 on the lower limb (more than any other jack crevalle in the western Atlantic) and 10–14 on the upper limb. The second dorsal fin has one spine and 26–30 softrays. The anal fin has two detached spines followed by one spine and 23–26 softrays. Specimens larger than about four inches in length have a dark band over most of the lower lobe of the caudal fin, contrasting with the relatively unpigmented upper lobe.

The body is moderately deep. The dorsal and anal fin lobes are only slightly produced. There are about 23–29 pointed scutes in the straight lateral line. The straight lateral line is only very slightly longer than the curved part. The body is blue-gray above and lighter or whitish below. In live or fresh fish, a dark blue or black stripe continues forward from the band on the lower caudal lobe along the back to the nape. The color is changeable, depending upon the background. The young up to about 5 inches in length have 6 (rarely 5 or 7) dark bars on the body plus one at the nape.

The bar jack has been questionably reported as far south as Rio de Janeiro, Brazil. It is known to range along the continent from Caledonia Bay, Panama, to Cape

Bar Jack

Hatteras, North Carolina. It has been taken in the West Indies from as far south as Union Island and northward to the northern Bahamas. The young have been taken well offshore in the Gulf Stream east of New Jersey, and the adults are common at Bermuda. The maximum size and weight attained are not known. Bar jacks of 12–15 pounds have been reported in the Bahamas.

LIFE HISTORY

Very little is known of the life history. Although this species does occur inshore in the United States, it appears to have more offshore or insular habits than the other four common jack crevalles in the western Atlantic. It has been described as a fish of the open water, swift and restless, and a terror to smaller fishes. Spawning probably occurs in offshore waters, because most of the developing young are found there. The spawning season has been estimated to extend from February to August off the Southeastern United States.

ANGLING VALUE

The bar jack is an active gamefish and will strike a variety of natural baits and artificial lures, including plugs, jigs, streamers, and popping bugs. Unlike most other jacks it occasionally jumps when hooked. Bar jacks are usually found in large schools in channels, blue holes, and deep flats. This species has firm white flesh and is a highly regarded food in the Bahamas and the Caribbean. It is excellent when smoked. *See also* Carangidae, Jacks

—F.H.B.

—A.J.McC.

BARNACLES Subclass Cirripedia Barnacles are crustaceans, related to crabs, shrimps, and lobsters. Most species have a hard, limy shell and live attached to rocks, logs, seaweeds, turtles, manatees, whales, crabs, or various mollusks. They fasten themselves tenaciously to their substrate by root-like projections. They feed by continuously waving filamentous legs through the water and straining out the minute plankton organisms. The male and female sex organs occur in the same animal, and the young are expelled from the calcareous barnacle body, thence undergoing a short larval life which is characterized by a preshelled stage when they attach themselves. Although most species are marine, they do tolerate brackish water and one species penetrates freshwater. They occur from the tropics to subpolar waters.

Most barnacles are the "acorn" type, with a flat base and a cylindrical or paraboloid body. These are commonly observed encrusting boats, wharves, pilings, hawsers, and the like, especially between tide lines, and the rate at which the young colonize a smooth area is amazing. They prefer areas of moderate currents, especially where nutrients are high and much food occurs in the water. Another group, the stalked barnacles, are characterized by the leathery "neck" at the end of which is the flattened animal. These are pelagic, attaching themselves to floating objects such as logs, seaweed, and other flotsam. The term "goose barnacle" is still used for this group, for the ancient naturalists believed that young geese were brought forth from these crustaceans. Today, the only remaining myth is that the saltwater boatman can easily keep his ship's bottom clean of barnacles. Although a good many antifouling paints are on the market, barnacles are a nuisance to boatmen and an expense.

FOOD VALUE

The goose barnacles have some food value. They can be steamed, and, after peeling away the rind-like skin, there is a small amount of edible meat which has a crab-like flavor. Barnacles are best prepared in Newburg style or in any of the methods used for cooking squid.—D.dS.

BARNDOOR SKATE Raja laevis One of the largest of the skates, it reaches a length of 5–6 feet. Its size, coupled with the pointed snout, smooth skin, the pigmented mucous pores on the lower parts, and the presence of spines on the tail only, distinguish it from its relatives. The teeth are large (32–36 in each jaw). Round, dark spots or blotches cover the dorsal surface which is reddish-brown to brown. Each pectoral fin generally has an oval blotch at its base. These skates grow to nearly 40 pounds, and most taken are over 2 feet long, the very small ones being rarely seen.

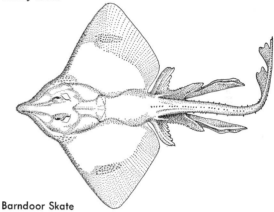

Barndoor Skate

LIFE HISTORY

Known only from the western North Atlantic Ocean, it is recorded from the Newfoundland Banks to South Carolina, but it is most common in the New England-Middle Atlantic region. To the north it is taken the year round generally over sand or gravel bottom. It has been taken from the surf zone down to 235 fathoms, but is most abundant from 5–80 fathoms. Although a cool-water species, it has been taken in warmwaters. Similarly, this saltwater skate occasionally enters brackish water or water that is nearly fresh.

Spawning occurs throughout the barndoor's latitudinal range and over its depth range. The eggs are laid in the winter, and the young are hatched the following spring to early summer. Adults eat large crustaceans such as lobsters, crabs, and shrimps. Mollusks are taken, and the barndoor skate is an active predator on fishes, including spiny dogfish and various species of herrings.

FOOD VALUE

This species is not commonly landed, but because of its large size, its "wings" are valuable for food and are often sold as scallops. —D.dS.

BARRACUDA *See* Great Barracuda, Guaguanche, Pacific Barracudas, Northern Sennet

BARRED SURFPERCH Amphistichus argenteus The species is the most important surf fish taken by anglers in California, and more is known of its life history than that of any other surfperch (*which see*).

There is a row of scales along the posterior half of the base of the anal fin; a broad frenum interrupts the posterior groove of the lower lip; the lower jaw is somewhat shorter than the general height of the soft dorsal; a series of olivaceous brassy vertical bars alternating with spots usually on sides, softrays in dorsal 23–27, in anal 25–28;

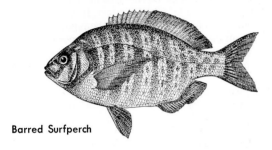

Barred Surfperch

length to 16 inches; weight to 4¼ pounds. Its color is silvery to white, with blue or gray above and plain white along the belly and sides. Sometimes it is brassy-olive above and silvery below. Taken in the surf and to depths of forty fathoms, its range is from central Baja California to central California.

LIFE HISTORY

The California Department of Fish and Game conducted an intensive study of the species determining that the young at birth were 42–53 millimeters (about 1⅝–2⅛ inches) long; the number of embryos per female were 4–113, with an average of 33.4; the young are dropped from mid March at least through July; they mature at the end of their second year at about 130 millimeters (about 5⅛ inches); females reached 9 years of age, and no males were found older than 6 years. Sandcrabs were found in 90 per cent of 479 stomachs examined and made up over 90 per cent of the food by volume. The December-January period usually provided the best fishing, and in that period the best return to the angler was found in the Oceanside region where fishermen averaged twenty minutes per perch. Tag-recovery data indicated that some mixing occurs between areas studied. The longest distance traveled was 31 miles in 48 days out; the longest time at liberty was 242 days, and the fish was recaptured 2 miles from the release point.

There is no commercial season for the species in California. —J.R.

BARREL KNOT A knot used chiefly in leader making for joining two strands of gut or monofilament together. It is sometimes used to join a line to the leader. *See also* Knots, Fly Leader

BASE OF FIN That portion of a fin attached to the body. *See* Anatomy

BASKING SHARK *Cetorhinus maximus* A giant shark exceeded in size only by the whale shark (*which see*), it has a streamlined shape similar to the white shark and the mako shark (*which see*). With these sharks it shares the pointed snout, small second dorsal fin, and nearly symmetrical caudal fin. But the huge gill openings which extend completely around the neck, nearly meeting at the middorsal surface, distinguish it from all other sharks. Further, the unique, peculiar teeth are reduced to conical protuberances, their length being only ⅛ inch in a 12-foot specimen. Long, comblike filaments, like gillrakers

of bony fishes, are present on the first gill arch. The mouth is huge, and in the young the snout is particularly long and rather bizarre in shape compared to other sharks. The body varies from gray-brown to nearly black, sometimes grading to lighter shadings or even white beneath. This large shark grows to 40–50 feet, and a small free-swimming specimen of about 5½ feet has been taken. California specimens of 28 feet and 30 feet weighed 6,580 pounds and 8,600 pounds, respectively.

LIFE HISTORY

Although predominantly an Arctic species, it regularly occurs as far southward as Newfoundland and Norway, straying farther south to Morocco and North Carolina. Closely related, or possibly identical, species occur in the cooler waters of the South Atlantic and off Peru and Ecuador, California to British Columbia, Australia, New Zealand, China, and Japan. The basking shark is sluggish in habits and, as the name implies, is often seen floating at the surface, occasionally on its back, or lazily swimming open-mouthed, ingesting quantities of plankton. The comblike gillrakers sieve out the tiny organisms, which are converted into several tons of shark. Occasionally small crustaceans are eaten.

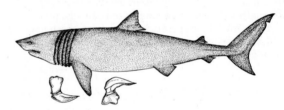

Basking Shark, showing teeth of upper (*left*) and lower jaws

This species is seen during the warmer months. Usually a solitary species, schools of 60–100 have been seen floating at the surface. It is not easily frightened by man, and can be easily approached by boats. They apparently move northward during the summer, possibly retreating southward into deeper water with the onset of cool weather. The breeding season is unknown, but the young are 5–6 feet long at birth, and sexual maturity may occur at 15–20 feet.

ECONOMIC VALUE

During past whaling days, basking sharks were often hunted for the oil in their livers, which compared favorably with sperm-whale oil for lamps. Some are still taken in various parts of the world, both for the low-vitamin oil and for fishmeal. From 80 to 600 gallons of oil can be recovered from a single individual.

MYTHOLOGY

A number of sea-serpent stories can be traced to the skeletons of basking sharks, for, in various stages of decomposition, the carcass affords a peculiar sight with its jaws and gill arches, the long vertebral column, and the fin supports. Such a sight on a beach has been sufficient to provoke the imagination of many people thus giving rise to innumerable sea-serpent reports. *See also* Oarfish —D.dS.

BASS (1) A common name applied to a variety of freshwater and marine species which may or may not be related to the true sea basses of the family Serranidae. The earlier form of the word (*barse*) is from the Teutonic root *bars* or "bristle," which is descriptive of spiny-rayed fishes in general. The European species, *Morone labrax* (*see below*), is the only fish with this singular common name; the collective name black bass (*which see*) indicates any of the larger sunfishes of the family Centrachidae.

(2) **Morone labrax** This is probably the most highly prized of European marine gamefish. The bass is a member of the Percichthyidae, a diverse family which includes the striped bass, groupers, and some freshwater species such as the white bass, yellow bass, and white perch. Local names include gray bass, sea bass, salmon bass, and loupe der mer (French).

The bass has a long but thick body, covered with ctenoid scales; the fine teeth on the outer scale margins gives the fish a rough texture when handled. The scales extend on the sides of the head and gill covers. More sharp points are found around the head—a serrated pre-opercular bone and two sharp spiny processes of bone from the gill covers.

The mouth is extremely large in proportion to the head. Inside, the mouth is studded with many fine teeth—on the jaws, the roof of the mouth (vomer and palate), the tongue, and the entrance to the gullet.

Like others of its family, the bass has both spiny and soft-fin rays. The fin-ray counts are:

Pectoral	16 soft
Pelvic	1 spiny, 5 soft
Dorsal I	8 or 9 spiny
Dorsal II	1 spiny, 12 or 13 soft
Anal	3 spiny, 10 or 11 soft
Caudal or Tail	17 soft. This fin is also strongly forked.

The lateral-line scale count is 72.

Bass have simple and handsome colors. A mature fish has a bluish-gray back, silver flanks, and a white-silver belly. In older fish there may also be a hint of gold or brown. The lateral line is made prominent by dark markings; there is a black spot on each gill cover; and the eye is dark with gold. The fins are a deep gray, growing darker still with age; only the anal fin retains an edge of white.

When younger ("school-bass" or "schoolies"), bass are lighter in overall color and often there is a touch of olive on the back. Some very young specimens may be slightly spotted.

Bass are characteristically very much inshore fish, ranging into less than a foot of water in strong surf. Certainly the normal place anglers seek them is between tide levels on surf-washed beaches. Below the low-tide mark scuba divers say that they have observed bass defending nonbreeding territories amongst rocks. They normally gather their food, however, over beaches of mixed rock and sand. A mixture of fresh with sea water is said to attract them, and the beaches with streams running across them are often good bass spots. In addition they may enter estuaries and range up into completely fresh water.

The shore-hugging habit is found in the warmer months; bass are very much summer fish. At other times they are far out to sea, the date of return to the beaches varying from place to place. Generally it is between February and May, going out to sea again in October or November. It has been stated that some school-bass do not always leave the inshore waters, especially near river estuaries. School-bass certainly tend to be the first to return inshore in spring.

The offshore migration appears to be due to the cooling of the shallow waters; certainly the sea is warmest in September-October, and declines rapidly in temperature after that.

Bass food covers a wide variety of different items—shore and hermit crabs, shrimps, prawns, razor clams, squids, and small fish. The younger or school-bass feed on smaller crustaceans or fish fry. This can sometimes be seen when bass intervene in a mackerel shoal attacking a shoal of "brit" (small herring and other fry). The mackerel slashing into the shoal create great disturbance; the school-bass may join them, and the older bass may join in chasing the mackerel rather than the brit. An average-sized mackerel is only a mouthful for a large bass.

It has been claimed that thundery weather may put them off feed, which is a possibility in very shallow water, though bass are extremely disturbed by surf. Certainly one of the bass's preferences is for turbulent and well-oxygenated shallow water. Even in aquaria they delight in bubbles arising from an aerator. In shallow waters, too, they may frequently be nocturnal; high tides on dark nights being a favorite time for bass fishing. They are also sensitive to disturbance other than the surf, and are said to desert beaches which become popular for swimmers.

As has been said, bass move offshore when the sea cools; it is not therefore surprising to find that they are essentially warm- and temperate-water fish. Their range in the Atlantic is from Madeira to southern Britain. They do not come farther into the Irish or North seas than south of a line from Wales through Lincolnshire (England) to Holland. Some authorities state *M. labrax* enters the Mediterranean; others claim that a similar species, *M. punctata*, is present there.

Bass reach good sporting weights. Normal rod-caught specimens range from 2–10 pounds, anything over this is a real specimen. Fish over 20 pounds exist, and 30-pound fish are by no means impossible.

LIFE HISTORY

Much of the life history of the bass is a partly-solved mystery. The matter of the offshore fall migration has been well known. What is not so clear is where the majority of bass go in winter. Winter bass are a rarity, and very few records of catches of winter bass out to sea are recorded. The most notable is one of a large shoal taken by a trawler off Wexford, Ireland, near a 20-fathom channel by the Lucifer Bank; these fish were different from summer bass; the silvery color was brighter, and their stomachs were empty.

It has been suggested on the strength of this catch and smaller ones that winter bass go into the deeper Continental Shelf water, though this is not over 300 feet deep in areas where the evidence has been taken. It is further suggested that they gather into large shoals in midwater, and hence are not taken by conventional methods. The formation of a large shoal in itself is unusual; the inshore summer bass of fair size are not schooling fish.

Evidence of the early spawning and egg stages of Atlantic bass is almost equally rare. In the Mediterranean spawning is much better described, and this is used as a pointer to what happens in the Atlantic.

It was once thought that bass spawned *in*shore; that is, that the inshore run was both a feeding and spawning migration. To back this view older workers pointed to the bass' United States counterpart, the striped bass (*Morone saxatilis*), which does run inshore for this reason. However, this view may be contradicted by the facts. Records of bass kept by Kennedy from Youghal, Ireland, show a wide variation in sexual maturity, especially in females, and a wide variation in the eggs they were carrying. Some were arriving inshore fully spent, so plainly the inshore migration could not be to spawn as these fish at least had already done so.

Some of Kennedy's fish, however, had not spawned. While this does not wholly support the older view of an inshore spawning run, it does suggest that bass eggs are not necessarily shed at one predetermined spawning time. It is suggested that they may be shed in installments or over a period in the offshore waters where bass migrate in winter. A similar pattern has been noted in mackerel (*Scomber scomber*).

Based on this negative evidence and upon behavior observed in the Mediterranean, the broad outlines of bass spawning may be described. Little evidence indeed is available from the Atlantic; the best being the capture of 4–8 mm-long larvae at a depth of 60 feet off the coast of Cornwall, England. Such larvae in such a place do, however, seem to corroborate that Mediterranean and Atlantic patterns are similar.

The eggs are laid offshore and are pelagic but not remarkably buoyant. Their density is only a little less than that of sea water; if put into freshwater they would sink. They are 1–1.5 mm in diameter, with an undivided yolk and a single 0.3 mm-diameter oil globule at one end. It has been suggested that this oil drop provides not so much overall buoyancy as it serves to insure that the egg floats the right way up. It is easy to see how the older view, of an inshore spawning often in an estuary with bottom-laid eggs, grew up—they would indeed sink in such conditions.

The bass larva hatch within 4 days, emerging tail first as a small black-and-yellow creature with a prominent yolk sac and a special "pre-anal" fin, which vanishes in later development. Growth is very rapid at this state; it has been said the larva doubles its length in 6 days after hatching.

At a time up to 16 days after hatching the young bass has absorbed the last of its yolk sac and is a uniformly-colored little pelagic fish. This stage is the one comparable to those taken off Cornwall (*see above*) in the Atlantic.

By the time it is 2 inches in length the bass is ready to come inshore and assume "school" and later adult life.

In the adult the bass is extremely slow-growing: fortunately the large square scales can be reliably read. An approximate set of figures for British Atlantic bass can be deduced from published tables. They have a length of 9 inches at 2 years, 13–18 inches at 5 years, 18–20 inches at between 7 and 9 years, and 30 inches or so at 20 years. The large size reached by bass, therefore, seems to be a reflection of their long life expectancy rather than their growth rate. Some see in this the result of an active life in a turbulent environment in summer and a winter fast, meaning most of the food is used as energy rather than as bone and flesh increments.

Bass are slow to mature, as well as to grow. The majority of females are mature around the sixth year and a length of 12–14 inches; some exceptional ones mature at the fifth year. Males usually mature at this latter age. One thing is certain, the majority of bass over 3 pounds are females, even though a few males to 6 pounds have been taken. The sexual difference is well marked in other sea fish as well; for example, in conger eels, a totally different fish in almost all other respects. Male bass, therefore, appear to have an even slower growth rate and a shorter life expectancy than the females. The figures given above were for females and their growth rate.

The onset of maturity may vary from place to place, probably depending on sea temperature. In the Mediterranean the mature length is 12 inches or less; whereas in the Atlantic it is a full inch or more longer.

COMMERCIAL VALUE

Bass are excellent on the table. Their flesh is delicious and they are easy to skin and bone. But because they inhabit the shore line in summer and are inaccessible offshore in winter (or rather, are rarely caught in colder months), there is little commercial exploitation of them.

Hence they are rarely offered for sale in Atlantic countries, even though the flesh compares favorably with mackerel or other rich sea fish. They are more used in the Mediterranean, as are inshore fish in general; there the consumer prefers the young school bass, the older fish being regarded as less of a delicacy. From the author's experience of Atlantic bass, this is not true.

In short, bass are only eaten and appreciated by their captors—spearfishermen and anglers. This is perhaps just as well as the slow growth rate and late maturity would make them particularly vulnerable to overfishing. There have even been doubts raised on some British coasts that the intensity of surf fishing in a few areas may be harmful—and surf angling is a lot less efficient at catching fish than commercial gear.
—D.M.

BASS BUG A fly-rod lure designed to imitate a variety of aquatic and terrestrial foods consumed by bass such as moths, mice, frogs, bees, and dragonflies. Although a bass bug floats on the water, it is distinguished from a dry fly in having a bulky body made of cork, plastic, or natural hair; it almost always lacks a hackle, although hackle feathers may be used in making the wing or tail, and the wings are usually turned down over the body or at horizontal angles. Bass bugs are usually tied on large hooks (No. 4 to No. 2/0); however, smaller and very similar versions are made for panfish. They may also be tied of durable materials for saltwater fishing, in which case the lures are identified as saltwater bugs. In concept, therefore, the bass bug is not limited to bass fishing but may be used for such widely diversified species as tarpon, striped bass, bluegills, white bass, chain pickerel, snook, and Spanish mackerel. Almost any surface-feeding gamefish can be caught on a bass bug, the lure being more or less effective according to the species and water conditions.

CORK-BODIED BASS BUGS

The first cork-bodied bass bug, and the progenitor of the modern type, was made by Ernest H. Peckinpaugh of

Chattanooga, Tennessee. In a letter written just before his death in 1947 he explains why he made the lure and why bass bugs were originally tied on double hooks:

"I discovered that late in the afternoon, and at dusk, if I could keep a bucktail fly on top of the water, I would catch more fish. This gave me the idea of putting a cork on a hook, and tying the bucktail hair to the lure, and in that way making it stay on the surface. A little experimenting quickly showed me that a single hook could not be securely fastened to the cork, but I did find that by using a double hook, I could make a very solid bug. Therefore all the first bass bugs I made were on double hooks. These bugs were designed for taking bream [bluegill]. I found that just before dark the bream would strike on the surface and I could catch them by using one of these little cork body bugs.

"There was practically no further development in these bugs until 1910 or 1911. I am uncertain about which year. Anyway, at this particular time, my work as a contractor kept me pretty busy and the jobs were always so far away from home that they interfered considerably with my usual periods of fishing. By the time I arrived at one of the lakes or ponds where I usually fished, it would be just about dark, so I was compelled to fish at night. I then discovered that bass would strike the same bugs which I had been using for bream. But the hook was small and I lost most of the fish. This inspired me to make a larger edition of the double hook bugs, and inasmuch as they were developed for night fishing, I called them 'Night Bugs.' I made these bass bugs in many colors of feathers and bucktail hair. Naturally they all had double hooks. If I remember correctly, you will find these listed in the 1913 or 1914 catalog of the John J. Hilderbrandt Company under the name of 'Night Bug.' This firm and as mentioned before, the old concern of Abbie & Embry of New York were among the first to market my lures. I continued making the double hook bugs until around 1914, when the European war started. The double hooks I had been using were made in England, and I was not able to secure any more hooks similar to those I had been using, and therefore, I turned my attention to the building of the bugs on single hooks.

"In the early days, Chattanooga was a tourist stopover for all Florida-bound travellers, and they would stop to see the historical points of interest. Many of these tourists were fishermen. They bought my bass bugs, which they found in local stores. These lures were carried to Florida, and later on, back North. In this way, they became distributed in many sections of the country. When I made the first cork-bodied bug, fly-tying and lure building was a hobby. It wasn't until quite a number of years after I made the first bass bug that I actually sold any. The few I disposed of at first were traded to local stores for items of fishing tackle that I was unable to make myself, such as reels, lines, hooks etcetera. Like all amateur fly-tyers I gave away to friends and fishermen many more bugs than I used myself, and in that way they also became widely known. Mr. Wilder, I believe his initials are B. F., who was the Butterick Pattern designer, obtained some of these bugs and used them in the East. He passed some along to Will H. Dilg of Chicago. Mr. Dilg secured the services of a Chicago fly-tyer named Cal McCarthy. Together, they worked out a number of patterns with feather and hair wings on a single hook, which later became known as the

Mississippi River patterns. To Will H. Dilg should go the credit of popularizing the cork-bodied bass bug, as it was due almost entirely to his writing about them in the magazines that made them quickly accepted."

BASS-BUG TACKLE AND TECHNIQUE

The standard bamboo bugging rod is 8½–9 feet long and weighs approximately 6 ounces. These dimensions are comparative, however, as many fiberglass rods in lesser weights and shorter lengths will cast air-resistant lures provided the line is a WF-6-F (or HCF old-scale) size or larger. The important thing is to keep some sense of proportion among rod, line, and bug. A light outfit, such as an eight-foot, five-ounce rod with the WF-6-F line is suitable for small bugs in the No. 6 and No. 4 dressings. But it would not function smoothly with the larger No. 2/0 bugs which are virtually standard in big-bass country. Therefore, the ideal rod is somewhat heavier than usual, and the most popular line a WF-8-F (or GAF old-scale). Bugging tackle must be powerful to overcome the air resistance of a bulky lure.

It's also important to use the correct leader with a bass bug. If you do not make your own, buy some of the tapered synthetics in 9-foot lengths. A practical range would be from 1X to 7/5. Although a 7/5 leader tests about 12 pounds, which is much heavier than you need to handle a bass, it requires considerable terminal rigidity on the part of the leader to turn over a big No. 2/0 bug. Bass are not leader shy to the extent that trout are; so tippets in the 8–12-pound class may be used successfully. The diameters should be selected according to the lure size; a No. 6 or smaller bass bug handles nicely on 1X, while a No. 4 or larger requires a proportionate increase in diameter. If the bug falls back on the leader on your forward cast it's either too long or too light. If the bug slaps the water, your leader is too short or too heavy. A little experimenting with various leader diameters will usually solve most casting problems. Bear in mind that tossing a bug is bound to be awkward at first, particularly if you've been practicing with little No. 10 dry flies.

Casting a bug differs in its rhythm from casting an ordinary fly. The strokes must be made slower to match the speed of the wind-resistant lure as it travels back and forth. You must wait until the line loop is properly straightened by allowing a longer pause between rod movements. Beginners should try short distances first and watch the back cast instead of the forward cast, observing just how long it takes the lure to complete its rearward flight. On the forward stroke, start slowly, and gradually accelerate the forward speed of your rod. Successful bugging doesn't require extreme casting distances. A 30–40-foot cast is good enough for nearly all fishing conditions. Whether you cast from the bank or a boat, or by wading, the knowledge of where bass feed is most important.

Importance of Retrieve The largest percentage of bass taken on bugs are caught within 20–30 feet of the shoreline among rocks, weed patches, downed timber, and lily pads. In fact, it's a good general rule to make your first few casts in knee-deep water. Bass hunt frogs, mice, and minnows along the marginal areas of a lake, and most insect life is blown there from the trees and bank brush. There are several ways of fishing a bug in these places, but the best tactic is to work slowly. The slower you fish

Bass bugs are made in a variety of shapes and colors but all are designed to fish on the surface

shallow water where bass are easily frightened at the sight or shadow of a lure passing overhead. On a bright sunny day, particularly, the angler will often see the surface swirls of fleeing bass. The same thing applies to an unrolling fly line or a splashy presentation; more bass are frightened by the actual process of casting than by the appearance of any lure. For this reason it's a sound tactic to start with short casts and fish each one out, gradually extending your range, until the bug is presented at your maximum comfortable distance. For example, if you see a stump 40 feet away which looks like a good bet, make one or two short casts between your position and the real target. The bass may *not* be under the stump, but wandering around looking for something to eat. If you put the line over it and the bug beyond it, there's very little chance of getting a strike. This progressive casting technique earns big bass. It's particularly valuable when you're working pocketwater among lily pads; often the most insignificant spot within a short distance of the boat will hold fish, while the stump is empty. By working short casts first, you will achieve clean presentation all the way out to the target. There's nothing that makes an angler feel more foolish than laying out a long cast and a pretty bug, only to have a hog-sized bass boil off for deepwater not ten feet from the boat. So keeping your target in mind, show as little line or leader as possible both in the air and on the water. It's much better to undercast than overcast.

The same approach applies to bugging in rivers. Old log jams, leaning tree limbs, and boulders are the prime targets in a bass creek. Fish get under these objects to look for food, and when an attractive lure comes bobbling down with the current or drops on the surface nearby, a hungry bass seldom questions its edibility. Pay particular attention to places along the river where you can present the bug in a truly lifelike fashion by dropping it on the bank grass or on top of a log, then twitching it into the water. You can even cast the bug directly into a low-hanging tree limb and hop it loose to drop on the surface. You will get hung once in awhile, but not nearly as often as you would expect.

Types of Bass Bugs   There are many kinds of bass bugs, and you should have a collection of at least three different types. Most experts use popping bugs about 50 percent of the time. A good popper has a hollow, dished-out face, so that when you give the rod an upward pull, the bug buries its nose under the surface and makes a hearty *gerblub* sound. If you get nothing but splash or if the lure skids over the surface, then either you are not doing it right, or the bug is no good. The great advantage of the popper is that even when a bass is snoozing in its hole, a noisy bug will bring it out. It may not see a quiet moth-type bug, but his sensitive lateral line will "hear" a deftly worked popper. However, this type of bug is not always effective. If you are casting in heavy weed mats or pads, the broad bug face will get hung and pick up grass constantly. You can buy weedless poppers, but bullet-head bugs are much better. Bulletheads have a collar of hackle and a skirt of streamer feathers. Actually, you can get some noise out of a lure of this type by pulling downward with the rod. But the long tail feathers dangling under the surface make it easy for the bass to locate a bullethead in thick pad cover, and the streamlined head doesn't hang up.

a bug, the more bass you will catch. Covering a small section of the shoreline thoroughly will usually produce more strikes than trying to scattershot the whole pond fast. This means you should allow 20–40 seconds for each retrieve. Working too fast is the most common reason for poor results. Ordinarily, you just want to animate the lure enough so that it looks like a water-stuck moth. A bass will generally swim up to within a few feet for a closer look. While the bug rests motionless, the bass's appetite or curiosity should be sufficiently aroused to strike the next time it moves. There are times when a fast retrieve or a change of pace will get strikes from otherwise indifferent fish. This happens more often in rivers, and especially with smallmouths which have been regularly worked over.

Presentation of the Bug   Presentation is important in bass bugging. This type of fishing is generally done in

Besides the popper and the bullethead you should stock a moth-type bug. There are a thousand variations of the old Calmac Moth on the market today, made with soft deer-hair bodies as well as wood and plastic ones. The virtue of this type of bug is that it's a lifelike suggestion of a large insect which moves quietly over the surface. On bright days in clearwater where there are no emergent plants, a bottom-hiding bass or a cruising fish is apt to stay away from noisemakers, but it will be attracted by faint movements, ripples, or the silhouette of a quiet swimmer. Good examples of this type are the Faulkner Bug, Whisker Bug, Tuttle's Devil Bug, Prior Hair Bug, and Dragon Bug.

You must make certain when buying bass bugs that they are tied on quality hooks. A needle-sharp hollow-point hook will stick no matter which way the fish hits it. A dull hook, and it needn't *look* dull to be unsuitable, is going to cause missed strikes no matter how fast you react. Don't use bugs that are mounted on heavy wire spear points; the spear-point hook has the virtue of strength in a tough, bony mouth, but that's not the problem in bass fishing. The bug should also have a straight eye. If the hook eye is turned up or turned down, a sunken leader will pull the bug deep when you work it. This is important with popping-type bugs which have to scoop the surface to do their tricks. —A.J.McC.

BATFISH *See* Longnose Batfish

BAT RAY *Myliobatis californica* This is a member of the eagle ray family, a group characterized by having a conspicuous head set off from the pectoral fins. The disk is much wider than long, and its tapering tips have the outer corners rounded. The tail is much longer than the body, and one or more sharp spines are near the tail base. A small dorsal fin is located on the tail base next to the pelvic fins. The large eyes protrude on either side of the head, and the teeth are arranged in a flat series. Its skin is smooth, and it is dark brown to olive or even black above, and white below. Maximum size is just over 200 pounds and about 5 feet wide.

LIFE HISTORY

They range from Oregon to the Gulf of California along sandy bottoms of bays and quiet lagoons, although they are taken on occasion in rocky areas where sand patches are interspersed. Bat rays occur singly or in schools where they are sometimes seen jumping about the surface, or they may be seen along the bottom cruising in search of clams, oysters, and shrimps, which they dig by flapping their "wings" to create turbulence. In more open areas they eat snails and abalones which they easily crush with their flat, pavementlike teeth. They are so predaceous on clam beds in San Francisco Bay that sport fishermen especially try to fish them out.

Mating occurs in summer, the young being born about a year later at a width of 12–14 inches, more young being produced in larger females. Sexual maturity occurs at about 50 pounds in the female and about 10 pounds in the male. —D.dS.

BEACH BUGGY A motor vehicle which has been customized and rigged to transport anglers and their equipment over soft-sand beaches; often an elaborately appointed camp-on-wheels featuring bunks for passengers, a galley with propane gas range and refrigerator, head, shower bath, and other creature comforts.

BASIC VEHICLES

Four general types of motor vehicles lend themselves to practical conversion as beach buggies. They are:

1. The small, compact machine which is designed to provide fast transportation to and from the fishing areas and to carry a minimum of fishing tackle.

2. The small station wagon, fitted to carry more equipment and to provide emergency shelter for anglers in foul weather.

3. Panel or carryall trucks, which are roomy enough to sleep two anglers and to tote all basic equipment.

4. The pickup truck with coach-camper unit attached, and the walk-in truck. These are the roomy camps-on-wheels which usually boast bunks for four persons, plus living accommodations and adequate duffel space.

Modern stock pleasure cars do not make good beach buggies, primarily because they are too lowslung for sand driving. However, by fitting larger wheels than the standard 14's and by employing air lifts, one can use late-model station wagons.

Model-A Fords, vintage 1928–1931, were the first of the highly successful beach buggies. These old Fords still serve the purpose on many beaches, but they are passing into the category of collectors' items.

Many light cars of the period 1930 to 1950, plus a majority of late-model pickup trucks, panels, and carryalls are well-suited to conversion. Walk-in trucks make excellent family beach buggies.

Thousands of two-wheel-drive buggies serve anglers along America's coasts, but the four-wheel-drive models offer far superior performance. Where dunes are sugar-soft, a two-wheel-drive machine should always be fitted with a four-speed transmission.

Automatic transmissions can be used, but the stick shift is considered more reliable for rough work. Clutch and cooling system must be mechanically perfect.

WHEELS AND TIRES

Perhaps most important of all beach-buggy components are properly matched wheels and tires. The tires must be oversized, in order to insure traction, and they must be resilient to perform well at ultra-low pressures.

Nylon shoes are favored over those of rayon construction, because nylons will absorb more heat and flexing before the sidewalls break down. Ideally, the beach tire should lack tread, but the necessity to drive over public highways to and from beaches dictates a safe margin of rubber. Actually, there is small loss of performance caused by new tires which have plenty of tread. Tubes should always be used for low-pressure beach work.

Generally, there is no necessity to install extra-wide rims. Standard wheels are adequate on most of the smaller vehicles, and they are readily available. Walk-in trucks, in some cases, must have wheels custom-built to take the proper tires.

Beach buggies in the Jeep- to panel-truck- and carryall-size range will perform well with 820 x 15 four-ply tires. However, performance of heavier panels and carryalls will be improved by the use of 900 or 950 four-plies. Coach-camper and walk-in units, due to their bulk, usually require a six-ply shoe. The 890 x 15 and the 900 x 15 are quite popular.

Tires must be deflated on a soft-sand beach, with pressure determined by the weight of the machine and the texture of the sand. On a very soft beach, it may be necessary to deflate the tires of a small vehicle to 10–12 pounds; heavier cars and four-wheel-drive models to 15–20. To insure proper traction, pressures should be equal. If one front tire is deflated to twelve pounds and the other to fifteen, the tendency to dig in will be apparent. An accurate tire gauge is a necessity. Once off the beach, tires should be inflated to road pressures as quickly as possible. Spark-plug compressors are employed by a majority of beach drivers.

RIGGING FOR THE BEACH

Small, light cars, such as the famous military Jeep, lack sufficient space for elaborate rigging or carrying capacity. Nonetheless, they can be fitted with tubular rod racks bolted vertically to front bumpers and with built-in tackleboxes and duffel compartments.

Depending on the size and headroom in station wagons, panel trucks, and carryall trucks, conversion may include one or two bunks, an inset propane gas camp stove, a small refrigerator or foam plastic icebox, and considerable enclosed duffel space.

Carryalls and panels usually are designed to take two bunks, with a walk-through area between them. In some cases a third and even a fourth bunk will be suspended on chains from the roof. Foam rubber or air mattresses are used.

Most of the station wagons, panels, and carryalls are fitted with roof-top boxes designed to tote duffel and serve as boat and rod racks. An aluminum planing boat in the 12–14-foot-size bracket can be snugged down over such a box. Rods are racked on vertical stringers and are held in place by steel tool clips, available at any hardware shop.

An outboard motor is often carried on an angle-iron bracket bolted to the front bumper.

Coach-camper and walk-in trucks offer the ultimate in living room, and most of them feature a complete galley—propane gas lights, stoves, refrigerators, chemical toilets, and running water. Skiffs may be racked on top, but because most of these machines are high-sided, trailers are more practical.

The object in designing interior furnishings is to make use of all available space.

Beach-buggy veterans always carry a heavy-duty jack, plus a hardwood plank to use as a base; a shovel and a length of heavy chain or Manila tow line. These are required items of equipment on beaches where permits are issued by local or federal authorities.

Binoculars, usually 8 x 50's, are basic, as is a well-stocked first-aid kit.

OPERATION ON THE BEACH

Sand driving is an art and a science, particularly where beaches are soft and badly cut up by other vehicles.

Initially, tires must be deflated to ideal pressures, and the driver must understand that he will "track," rather than use power, to grind out of a soft spot.

Whenever possible it is wise to follow existing tracks. These have been used by other buggies, and therefore offer more support and traction than surrounding sand areas.

From a halt, the sand driver must accelerate slowly to prevent "spinning in." Any attempt to power out of difficulty usually results in immediate bogging down. The proper procedure is to back slowly and then move forward again to "make a track."

On some of the harder beaches it is possible, although not always the course of wisdom, to run the waterline. In most cases it is wise to remain well above the high tide mark, so that a breakdown will not result in loss of the vehicle to an incoming tide.

A sharply sloping beach may be negotiated by small, light buggies, but will defeat heavier machines which have a tendency to sideslip toward the water.

Beach-buggy associations have been organized in many coastal areas, and members invariably observe the good neighbor policy. Sand drivers who get into trouble usually find help near at hand.

Most of the associations pattern their regulations after those written by organizers of the Massachusetts Beach Buggy Association in 1949. MBBA is the oldest of existing beach-buggy groups, and its Code of Ethics constitutes law for a majority of mechanized anglers. The code:

"1. To enter and leave beaches in prescribed ways.

"2. To eliminate speeding and reckless driving.

"3. To respect local ordinances and the rights of property owners, particularly in regards to camping.

"4. To offer aid to any fisherman or buggy owner in trouble on the beach.

"5. To respect picnicking and bathing groups by avoiding them whenever possible and slowing to minimum speed when passing picnicking or bathing groups.

"6. To avoid littering the beach with trash, by using disposal barrels when available, or by burning paper wrappers and burying other rubbish. [In many areas beach buggy associations now require members to carry all cans, bottles, and similar refuse off the beach to the nearest trash cans.]

"7. To leave no dead fish or bait of any kind above the high water mark. Throw dead fish, bait and trash back into the surf where they will be found by gulls and other scavengers.

"8. To use public toilets when available and, when not available, to respect the beach for others by digging latrine trenches behind the dunes and by filling these trenches after use.

"9. To avoid overcrowding any one area and elbowing other fishermen out of their chosen spots. This is particularly important where surfmen without buggies are concentrated.

"10. To leave the track when a halt is made, so that other buggies will not be forced to detour.

"11. To fill in holes after getting stuck, and to avoid indiscriminately criss-crossing tracks.

"12. To observe the rules of common courtesy on the beach.

"13. To simplify passing of vehicles meeting head-on on a single track: the driver who has the dunes on his right will be required to turn out of the track to the right. This rule to be tempered by common sense in difficult circumstances."

Permits are now required to run many coastal beaches. These are issued by local, state, or federal government agencies, and regulations vary. The National Park Service does not charge for permits to drive on seashore areas, but there is no standard applicable to local and state permits.

—F.W.

BEACH SEINE A beach seine is a wall of webbing suspended vertically in the water by means of floats on the top line and leads on the bottom line. The set is usually made from one point on the shoreline around the fish to another point farther down the shore line. Then the seine is slowly pulled to the beach, enclosing the fish in a decreasing semicircle. A conical-shaped bag is usually attached at the center of the net to capture the fish.

BEACON Navigational mark placed on or near a danger. It may be a simple framework of white slats set high for visibility, or may be more elaborate including a light.

BEAM Width of a boat at its widest point.

BEAR An object "bears" in the direction the person calling the bearing sees it. A bearing is the direction of an object from the person observing it expressed in terms of compass points or degrees. To bear down upon a boat is to approach a boat. To bear a hand is to hurry and give help.

BELL BUOY A buoy rigged with a bell which sounds out as the waves move the buoy.

BENGUELA CURRENT *See* Currents

BENTHIC Referring to the ocean's bottom, generally applied to marine organisms that live on the ocean floor.

BENTHOS The bottom of the sea (fr. Greek *benthos*, depth of the sea). Biologically, the flora and fauna of the sea bottom or bottom-dwelling organisms of deep freshwater lakes; hence benthic organisms. *See* Freshwater Ecology, Marine Ecology

BERGMAN, RAY American (1891–1967) The Dr. Spock to a whole generation of American fishermen who were literally brought up by the book—the most widely read book on trout by a wide margin is Ray Bergman's, first published in 1938 by Penn Publishing Company, New York. It was reissued by Alfred A. Knopf, New York (1944), and unlike the vast majority of angling books of this century has been kept in print ever since. A revised and enlarged edition was published by Knopf in 1952, and has been reprinted at frequent intervals since then. Second in size only to the English Eric Taverner's *Trout Fishing from All Angles*, Bergman's *Trout* is the largest (451 pages) ever devoted to one fish in American publishing history. Many anglers, obviously feeling that there's nothing that you can learn from a book that you can't learn better from a fish, consider their libraries complete once they've bought their copy of Bergman's *Trout*. They don't expect or want a fishing book as a birthday or Father's Day present on the perfectly logical grounds of "What do I want with a book? I've already got a book." Nobody would ever argue, beginning with Bergman himself, that this is the best fishing book ever written, but its continuing sale seems to indicate that it must be the most satisfying. Many of the best fishing books are like Chinese food in that they very quickly make you want to come back again for more soon after you've read them, whereas Bergman's *Trout* must stimulate the appetite to go fishing rather than wanting to read any more about fish.

Bergman was for many years fishing editor of *Outdoor Life*, and his books reflect the professional's wide acquaintance with all aspects of the subject. In a lifetime of listening to and appraising the passionate advocacy of many specialists for their theories and techniques, Bergman's position can be likened to that of the old-fashioned general practitioner—he had some sympathy and understanding for all the many schools of modern angling, but largely felt that nature should be allowed to take its course, and that the element of luck might possibly be abetted but never supplanted. His other books were *Just Fishing* (1932), *Bass* (1942), and *With Fly Plug and Bait* (1947). Since his death, his one-time associate, Edward C. Janes, has compiled a book of his magazine writings, *Fishing with Ray Bergman*, but it is as the author of *Trout* that Bergman will go on being read. Certainly worse things could be said of a fishing book than that it makes you want to stop reading and start fishing. —A.G.

BERMUDA The compact and miniature group of British islands which comprise Bermuda thrust through the surface of the Atlantic 578 nautical miles (665½ statute miles) south 72° east of Cape Hatteras Lighthouse, North Carolina. This location makes the Bermuda islands unique in that they are the most northerly coral islands. The total land area, inclusive of all the islands, is 20.41 square miles. Prophetically, a map will reveal that the islands combine to form a rough but unmistakable outline of a fish hook.

Shallow reefs completely surround Bermuda; the reefs on the south are quite close inshore, some as near as half a mile. To the north, they extend outward for as much as nine miles, then curve sharply around to meet the eastern and western ends of the main island. To give an indication of the area of these reefs if they were pushed upwards and exposed, Bermuda would be ten times its present size. Submerged, they provide two hundred square miles of excellent reef fishing.

Unwary mariners of yachts, freighters, submarines, and ocean liners, even in this age of modern navigational equipment, learn with regret that Bermuda's coral reefs are treacherous and worthy of the utmost respect. Only one main ship channel, to the east, gives safe access to the harbors, sounds, and bays.

From the foregoing it will be evident that Bermuda is a plateau which, upon reaching the thirty-five fathom mark and within a matter of a very few yards, drops away sharply to depths measured in hundreds of fathoms. Fifteen miles to the southwest lies the twenty-six-fathom-

One of the most popular spots in Bermuda for flats feeding bonefish is located at Whale Bay from July to October

deep Challenger Bank; an additional 10 miles, in the same direction and approximately the same depth of water, brings one over Plantagenet Bank. This latter bank is more popularly known as Argus Bank, upon which is erected one of the famous "Texas Towers," which is named "Argus Island." As might be expected both banks are prime fishing locations, and the combined areas of the two banks form one hundred square miles of fishing grounds.

Bermuda has long been famed as a tourist resort, but it is only in comparatively recent years that the islands have begun to assume their rightful place among the angling centers of the world, and in this respect are becoming famous as a mecca for light-tackle fishermen. A factor of vital importance to visiting anglers is that Bermuda does not promote its fishing as being excellent throughout the year. In keeping with this policy and for the record, it should be remembered that good fishing begins to get under way in mid April. By the middle or end of May it is excellent and continues until the latter part of November. Weatherwise, December is an uncertain month. If the weather continues fair and without strong winds, the fishing picture holds as for November. January to the end of March cannot be relied upon, although the fishing may be quite good at times. By the middle of April the weather has generally settled down, and the cycle commences once more.

INSHORE FISHING

Bonefish are found throughout the year with the best months being May through October. Bait, rather than artificial lures, will take more fish in May and June. No satisfactory explanation has been put forward as to why this should be, but the fish are extremely skittish when confronted with an artificial lure of any type during these two months. From July through October the bonefish are impartial and will take bait or lures, particularly small feather and bucktail jigs.

Five of the top bonefish spots are Whitney's Bay (more often referred to locally as Whale Bay) in the parish of Southampton; Long Bay in Somerset; Shelly Bay in Hamilton Parish; The Causeway, connecting Hamilton Parish and St. George's; and Castle Point in St. George's. The latter location is accessible by boat only, since, in order to reach it from shore, one would have to cross private property. The first three named locations are wonderful for the experienced bonefisherman, for he can wade, search, and cast to the fish. Falling tide does not bother local bonefish, and the best time for wading anglers is 2–2½ hours before low tide and the first 2–2½ hours of the rising tide; this gives waders a minimum of 4 hours' fishing.

Palometa or "pompano" favor the south shore beaches from April through November, and are also found in harbors, bays, and around bridges. Lightest of spin tackle will give the greatest amount of sport. They are commonly taken at ¾–1 pound. Two and three pounders are trophies for the species. Anglers can give themselves an assist of real value by chumming with white bread broken in chunks about the size of a thumbnail and mixed with a generous portion of canned sardines and the oil in which they are packed.

The gray snapper, better known as "mangrove snapper," appear inshore when the water temperature reaches

70° F. (about mid April) and depart again about the end of October. These wary fish are one of the most difficult to take on artificial lures, but a persistent angler will achieve a measure of success by going after them at night. There is no substitute for bait (alive or dead) for those who really wish to catch the timid mangrove snapper. White grunt, bigeye scad, seaworms, mussels, anchovy, and fry are all good baits.

The sennet (*see* Northern Sennet), a small member of the barracuda family, is found along the shore, in bays and inlets, and, at night, around wharves and bridges, particularly where a strong electric light or lantern casts its rays on the water. Small and medium-size plugs, streamer flies, and jigs are made to order for these voracious little fighters. Bait is used at times but is seldom necessary if a supply of lures is at hand. A short wire leader is essential for sennet. November to April are the best months with peak angling from January to March. Fish of one pound are average. A three-pounder is exceptional.

Barracuda also frequent the shallow inshore waters during the summer months and are caught from skiffs and by wading fishermen. Fly-casting and spinning equipment give the ultimate in action. Bucktail and feather streamer flies, weighted jigs, and shallow diving plugs are best lures.

REEF-FISHING

Chumming with a bucket full of small minnowlike fish (called fry) mixed with fine sand is standard practice on all well-organized reef-fishing expeditions. This chum acts like a magnet and attracts such species as the yellowtail snapper, little tuna, mangrove snapper, amberjack, the Bermuda amberjack, and the Bermuda chub. On or near bottom, various rock-dwelling species are numerous, and although delicious in the pan they can hardly be classified as gamefish.

For the angler who takes his sport seriously, artificial lures will attract all the reef species mentioned, even, on rare occasions, the mangrove snapper. However, due to the clarity of the water, it is not an easy task to fool these fish with any degree of consistency, and knowledgeable fishermen keep an open mind and switch to live bait when conditions demand.

Spinning equipment is the favored tackle for the reef-fisherman, with rods 6½–7½ feet in length. Line is 10–20-pound test with monofilament being the top choice of material. Reels of sturdy construction, and capable of holding 200–300 yards of line, balance the outfit.

OFFSHORE FISHING

Trolling, drift-fishing, and still-fishing with the boat at anchor are the three effective procedures for offshore fishing. The productive areas lie at the 35–50-fathom depths at the edge of the plateau, beyond which the dropoff plunges to several hundred fathoms. An echo sounder (depth finder) of either the recording type or flashing-light variety is of great assistance, particularly when trolling, for a boat working too far inside or outside of the depths mentioned is unlikely to encounter the major concentration of gamefish.

With the possible exception of that used by neophyte anglers, the tackle most used by fishermen is 12-, 20-, or 30-pound-test line matched to appropriate rods. Reels range from No. 3/0 to No. 6/0. Leader material is either light cable or straight (piano) wire 60–100-pound test, and its length varies from 15 feet (the maximum allowed for light tackle) to not less than 8 feet. The hooks used are No. 5/0 to No. 10/0.

Wahoo are taken year around, but the best angling is from May until the end of October. It is during May and into the first week or ten days of June that a minor run of wahoo takes place. The word "minor" is used because compared with the run in September and October, it is less significant. For the remainder of the summer and until the major run commences, wahoo are taken regularly. The trolling speed is important, and it has been established that 6½–7 mph will result in more wahoo strikes than any other speed. The favorite baits are balao (locally called garfish), flying fish, and strip baits which are trolled from an outrigger or on a flatline. Feather jigs and spoons are not generally used.

Yellowfin-tuna fishing is popular on the Challenger and Argus banks. Although trolling accounts for a considerable number of fish each year, the best results are obtained by chumming. With the tide running from the banks toward the deep, two methods can be used. Anchor in 28–30 fathoms, and drift back until the boat is directly over the edge of the bank; then secure the anchor rope and commence chumming. Or run in over the bank until the boat is 400–500 yards from the edge, and drift back, letting out a steady stream of chum until the echo sounder indicates that the boat has passed over the edge. If no fish are hooked or brought in sight, return to starting point and repeat as often as necessary. It is seldom that fish fail to put in an appearance within the first hour. Anchovies or fry are most effective both for chumming and as bait. The yellowfin tuna is here throughout the year, but the best months are mid April to the end of November.

Blackfin tuna have produced more world records than any other fish in Bermuda waters. Skip baits and feather jigs work equally well. Like all members of the tuna family, the blackfin is a stubborn fighter, and a fish cannot be considered whipped until it is in the boat. Rainbow runners frequently flash into the chum line when fishing for tuna. There is little trouble in identifying this fish when it comes in sight—the tail is brilliant yellow and shows up clearly in the water. If a spinning rod with 12–15-pound-test line is aboard, tie a No. 3/0 or No. 4/0 hook to 3 feet of 20-pound-test monofilament leader. Secure a single anchovy or several fry to the hook, cast out, and get set for action. The runner is one of the marine world's most beautiful fish, and it always gives a rousing account of itself on light tackle. If no spinning tackle is available, try for the runners on 12–20-pound-test trolling rods.

Amberjack commonly reach a weight of 70–100 pounds in Bermuda waters and go to as much as 180 pounds. They are taken near the edge of the plateau and also the edge of the banks. Fishing from an anchored boat is usual, and the preferred baits are live bream, yellowtail, mackerel scad (locally called ocean robin), and red hind. An exception to live bait is a large squid, and it is practically impossible for an amberjack to pass up this hors d'oeuvre. The best angling for amberjack is September to April. The related horse-eye amberjack (*Seriola rivoliana*) is taken by the same methods as described for the amberjack except that the best months are April to October, with May producing the largest fish. The top weight is 50–55 pounds.

A 74-pound yellowfin tuna comes aboard. This tuna is a very strong gamefish and is taken here primarily by chumming

Frequently barracuda tear into trolled baits, feather jigs, and spoons when boats move over depths of less than twenty-eight fathoms. Beyond twenty-eight fathoms there is rarely any action from the species. A barracuda on light tackle is worthy of any serious fisherman's attention, and often during the fight it will put on an aerial display of no mean proportions.

The dolphin in Bermuda do not appear to have a definite season since they can be taken throughout the year. However, it has been established that they are most numerous from May to December. Also, when prevailing winds blow from the northeast or southeast, huge quantities of sargassum weed appear, and dolphin generally accompany it. Dolphin are just about the most obliging of all fish as far as anglers are concerned—just show them a fast-moving bait or lure, and let it be smaller than the fish—they will climb all over it, and if they miss on the first pass they will reverse and try again.

MARLIN FISHING

Blue marlin and white marlin are caught each year, but these are not species which can be deliberately sought. Their appearance behind a bait is sudden and unexpected, and it invariably happens when trolling for other species. The white marlin is one of the finest light-tackle fish that an angler can hope to catch, and the tackle used is apt to be entirely suitable for the task at hand. However, the picture is somewhat different when a big blue begins to stalk a skipping outrigger bait and the tackle is thirty-pound test or lighter.

There are two approaches open to the fisherman. Go out ready for any emergency and use heavy gear, or adopt the philosophical attitude of the light-tackle angler and take your chances. In the former instance you may be lucky and raise a blue marlin. But it is far more likely that fish suitable to light gear will be caught, and these will provide little sport on heavy tackle.

July and August are the best months for blue marlin. The white marlin is taken in small numbers throughout the year. As is usual in the case of members of the billfish family, baits skipped from an outrigger are the top producers, and the following are used: balao, flyingfish, little tuna, and strip bait. —S.L.P.

BERMUDA CHUB *Kyphosus sectatrix* The sea chubs or rudderfishes (family Kyphosidae) are ovate fishes with somewhat compressed bodies, forked tails, small heads, and relatively small mouths with incisiform outer teeth but no molariform teeth. They are herbivorous, in general, and have long digestive tracts. Two species are recognized in the western Atlantic, the Bermuda chub (*Kyphosus sectatrix*) and the closely related *K. incisor*. The dorsal fins of both nearly always have 11 dorsal spines, but the number of softrays differs. *K. sectatrix* has 12 dorsal rays (rarely 11–13), and *incisor* usually has 14 (sometimes 13 and rarely 15). Similarly, *sectatrix* has 11 (rarely 12) anal softrays and *incisor* 13 (sometimes 12). Specimens falling within the small zone of overlap in finray counts may be differentiated by gillraker counts. *K. sectatrix* usually has 17–18 rakers on the lower limb of the first gill arch, and *incisor* 19–22.

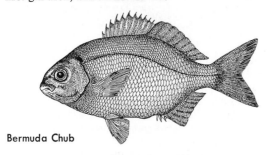

Bermuda Chub

At first glance the Bermuda chub seems to be a drab gray fish, but closer inspection reveals that it has lengthwise brassy bands on the body following the scale rows and two horizontal yellowish bands on the head which are confluent on the snout. One color phase shows pale spots on the body as large as the eye.

The young are often found hiding beneath floating masses of *Sargassum natans*. In the spotted juvenile phase, the spots are yellowish-brown like the bladders of the *Sargassum*.

The Bermuda chub is known from Brazil to Cape Cod, the West Indies, and Bermuda. It is also reported from the Mediterranean, the Canary Islands, Madeira Islands, and Azores. Fully grown adults are not known along the Atlantic Coast of the United States north of Florida. The occurrence of the species in the more northern localities is probably the result of transport of the young in the Gulf Stream.

ANGLING VALUE

The Bermuda chub reaches a length of nearly 30 inches and has been reported to weights of 20 pounds. It is a powerful fish and fights vigorously on hook and line. Although feeding most of the time on algae, particularly *Sargassum* (both floating and attached), it will accept animal food such as cut bait, and is known to feed on offal. Although often reported as a good food fish, some individuals have undesirable flavor. —J.E.R.

BERNERS, DAME JULIANA (also Barnes and Bernes) **English** A hunting writer and compiler of the fifteenth century, by legend a nun and noblewoman, to whom the first known essay on sport fishing, *The Treatise of Fishing with an Angle*, has long been attributed.

That Dame Juliana was a real person there is no doubt; her name is attached to the didactic poem on hunting in the *Book of St. Albans* (1486), the first and most famous sporting book printed in English. But the legend that she was of noble rank and Lady Prioress of Sopwell, a nunnery near St. Albans in the Abbey of that name, is without any direct evidence; it has been furiously disputed among antiquarians for centuries. Her connection with fishing is even more nebulous; but *The Treatise of Fishing with an Angle* has wanted an author, and as her name has been the only convenient one, it was adopted for the treatise by fishing writers and librarians, and has outlasted the protest of historians. Her legend is intriguing and in part will perhaps remain forever a mystery.

The thread of connection between Dame Juliana and the *Treatise of Fishing* is the fact that the fishing treatise was first printed in the second *Book of St. Albans* in 1496. The first *Book of St. Albans*—its title conferred, by tradition, from the town where the book was printed—contains treatises on hunting, hawking, and heraldry. When Wynken de Worde reprinted the book ten years later in London, he added the fishing treatise, anonymously, to the collection. The only author's name that appears in either edition is Dame Juliana's, at the end of the book of hunting (the first edition calls her "Dam Julyans Barnes"; the second, "dame Julyans Bernes). Nothing in the styles of the hunting and fishing treatises suggests that they came from the same author; but the whole *Book of St. Albans* in time was attributed to the "author" of the hunting treatise. Her unquestioned authorship of the hunting treatise needs this qualification, that the work, like many in the Middle Ages, was compiled and versified in large part out of earlier hunting treatises.

No earlier evidence of Dame Juliana's existence is known. During several centuries after her name appeared in print, her legend was created by a number of noted English antiquaries. A gap was made in the records of English history in the first half of the Sixteenth century when Henry VIII abolished the monasteries without making provision to save their libraries. Antiquaries attempted to close the gap and restore old glories with a combination of research and imagination. One of these, John Bale, in 1559 described Dame Juliana, without evidence, as an illustrious female who regarded the sports of the field as a source of virtue, honor, and nobility. He stated that she flourished in 1460, and "is said to have edited a small work on Fishing." Raphael Holinshed in his *Chronicles* (1577) said she was "a gentlewoman endowed with excellent gifts both of body and mind." John Pits (1611) described her as a manlike woman of noble rank, "a Minerva in her studies and a Diana in hunting." But the most important statement in the history of the legend was made by William Burton (1575–1645), antiquary and brother of Robert Burton. In his copy of the *Book of St. Albans*, he wrote in longhand that the book was made by Lady Julian Berners of a noted Berners family, giving some details, and said that she was Lady Prioress of Sopwell and that the book was printed in the Abbey of St. Albans. Similar observations were made by a county historian, Sir Henry Chauncy, in his book on

Nolb to speke of balkhys. firste Nterlbarde they bene disclosed balkhys been disclosed. as sone as the mote tymeli after the contre is of be And be shall say that balkhis m the lboodes. And be shall say tho they bene tymbering to their nestes. ke ther nestes And m the tyme of th kauke. And be shall say that they And lbhen they bene enclosed ar thyng of lengthe Anoon be kynde t of the nest: and drab to tolbis. and

Part of First Page of the *Book of St. Albans*, 1496

Hertfordshire in 1700. All subsequent writing on Dame Juliana derived from these sources.

Controversy raged among antiquaries during the Eighteenth and Nineteenth centuries as to whether it was possible to conceive of a woman who was both nun and sportswoman. In his great facsimile edition of the second *Book of St. Albans*, in 1810, Joseph Haslewood undertook to resolve the difficulty by supposing that she might have been first one and then the other; at court in her youth engaging in field sports and keeping a commonplace book; afterward retired to a convent, perhaps "from disappointment," there passing the time versifying the rules of sport. Trying thus only to reconcile reasonably the roles of nun and sportswoman, Haslewood put the seal on the legend.

Along with other antiquaries of the Eighteenth and Nineteenth centuries, Haslewood explicitly denied the possibility that Dame Juliana could have written the *Treatise of Fishing*, but their view could not prevail. The legend of the noble nun, which they and not fishermen had created, was brought into the fishing world for the first time in 1760 by John Hawkins in his introduction to the eighth edition of *The Compleat Angler*. Hawkins appears to have relied on Bale and Pits for his belief in her association with the fishing treatise, and, for the rest, he picked up the assertions of Burton as they had been restated by later antiquaries. Despite the strong efforts of the antiquaries to scotch the attribution Dame Juliana Berners, nun and noblewoman, was established as the first fishing writer and so became famous for the wrong reasons. Her hunting treatise is seldom read and had no great influence on hunting; it was in fact a treatise on the language of hunting rather than on the sport itself. The fame of *Treatise of Fishing* shone on her name.

The appearance of the *Treatise of Fishing* is a remarkable event in the history of fishing. It was written in the early Fifteenth century and appears to be original. Before the treatise there is little sign of fishing as a sport. Its codification of the sport dominated the angling world for two centuries, the Fifteenth and Sixteenth; it was a major influence on Walton and other early fishing writers. As the

sole progenitor of the literature of the sport, it thereafter formed the main line of angling tradition. It remains one of the best essays ever written on the sport. The only surviving manuscript version, copied by a scribe around 1450, is in the Yale library, thanks to the late American angling collector, David Wagstaff. —J.McD.

BETHUNE, GEORGE WASHINGTON American (1805–1862) A Doctor of Divinity who styled himself only "The American Editor" out of deference to the feelings of parishioners who might be scandalized at the thought of an angling work by a minister, the Reverend G.W. Bethune was America's foremost angling scholar and first angling book collector. In 1847 he edited for publication both here and in London the first American edition of Walton and Cotton's *Compleat Angler*, changing the spelling of the title work to *Complete* and old Izaak's spelling to Isaac. At a time when the English were still saying that nobody reads an American book the impact of this scholarly work was sensational. Bethune not only provided copious notes of irrefutable authority but also a "Bibliographical Preface" that was an account of fishing and fishing books from the earliest antiquity to the time of Walton, together with a notice of Cotton and his writings. There was also an appendix that was monumental, including, as advertised on the title page, "illustrative ballads, music, papers on American fishing, and the most complete catalogue of books on angling, etc., ever printed." It was, and remains, one of the very best of the nearly 400 editions of Walton and Cotton to date. Bethune's only previous publication was *A Plea for Study* (1845), an oration before the Literary Societies of Yale College, and his only other book was *Lays of Love and Faith, with Other Fugitive Poems*. A minor literary figure, Bethune is of major stature in the eyes of anglers, who have developed an affection for him reflecting his own for the *Compleat Angler*, which he termed "this darling book." Bethune's own love of books was too great to let him give his 600 angling volumes the "affront" of a bookplate or any other mark of his ownership. This detail caused anguish to subsequent collectors avid for "association" with his books when his collection was sold at Sotheby's after his death. —A.G.

BIFURCATED Divided into two branches as in a fin. *See also* Anatomy

BIGEYE SCAD *Selar crumenophthalmus* The tropical, worldwide species is also known as the goggle-eye scad, goggle-eye jack, and goggler. It at times has been recorded under the generic name of *Trachurops*.

The shoulder girdle of the bigeye scad has two papillae on the vertical limb with a furrow, or groove, below the lower. There are no detached finlets at the back of the dorsal and anal fins and no scutes in the curved lateral line. The eyes and the thick adipose eyelids are noticeably large.

The second dorsal fin has 1 spine and 24–26 softrays. The anal fin has 2 detached spines followed by a spine and 21–23 softrays. The first gill arch has 9–12 gillrakers on

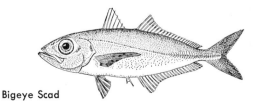

Bigeye Scad

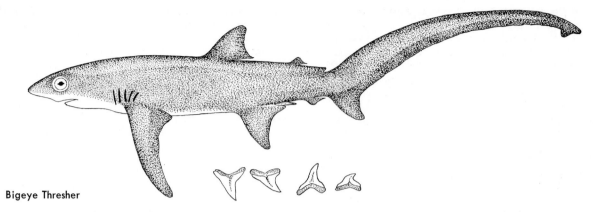

Bigeye Thresher

the upper limb and 27–30 on the lower limb. The anterior curved part of the lateral line has a very shallow arch; there are 30–41 pointed scutes in the straight lateral line. The body and head are silvery or golden, almost uniformly colored, with the upper parts usually darker. A faint elongated opercular spot is usually present.

The bigeye scad occurs in tropical and subtropical waters around the world. In the western Atlantic it is known from Rio de Janeiro, Brazil, to Nova Scotia, in the West Indies, and at Bermuda. In the eastern Pacific it is known from Cabo Blanco, Peru, to Cape San Lucas and Muertos Bay, Baja California, and at the Galápagos Islands. This species has been reported to grow to two feet in length in tropical waters.

LIFE HISTORY

The life history is inadequately known. Males and females in breeding condition were taken in June from Tortugas, Florida. Eggs and newly hatched larvae attributed to this species were described from India and the Java Sea.

ANGLING VALUE

This species is rarely fished for, and it has no significant commercial use in the United States; but it has been reported to be excellent as live bait for other fish. It is fished commercially in some areas of the Indo-Pacific. *See also* Carangidae, Scads   —F.H.B.

Bigeye Shiner

BIGEYE SHINER *Notropis boops* A small olivaceous minnow with dusky sides and a very dark lateral band which passes through the eye and over the snout. The lateral line has 34–38 scales. The mouth is terminal and large, with the upper jaw about as long as the distinctively large eye. The eye is ⅓-½ as long as the head. Adults are 2.0-3.0 inches with the largest about 3.5 inches.

LIFE HISTORY

This shiner is found in clearwater streams of the Ohio River drainage and southwestward into Oklahoma and Arkansas. It is a sight feeder. Most feeding is on animal

food from the surface and at middepths. It often will jump into the air to feed on small insects hovering above the surface. Spawning occurs in midsummer.

The bigeye shiner serves as forage for large fishes and as an excellent bait minnow.   —C.A.P.

BIGEYE THRESHER *Alopias superciliosus* This distinctly shaped shark is closely related to the thresher shark (*which see*), from which it differs in the much larger eye and longer snout. The tip of the first dorsal fin reaches past the base of the pelvic fins of the bigeye but falls far short of the base in the thresher. The bigeye's second dorsal fin is well in advance of the anal, while in the thresher the second dorsal tip reaches the anal-fin base. The bigeye thresher has far fewer teeth (10–11) than the thresher (about 20) on each side of the jaw.

Its caudal fin, as in the thresher, is enormously long, about half of the total length. The pectoral fins are long and are less curved than those of the thresher. Its color is nearly uniformly slate-gray, with dusky edgings to the first dorsal, pectoral, and pelvic fins. It reaches a length of 18 feet.

The bigeye thresher is known from Florida, Cuba, Madeira and California. Its habits are unknown, although it is believed to occupy deeper waters than its relative, the thresher shark. Hake, squids, and lancetfish have been found in stomachs of bigeye threshers.   —D.dS.

BIGEYE TUNA *Thunnus obesus* A fish of the mackerel family, it is difficult to distinguish from some individuals of the four other tunas in American waters. The length of its pectoral fin is greater than 80 per cent of the head length; the dorsal and anal fins are never greatly elongated; the finlets behind the dorsal and anal fins are yellow with black margins; and there is no white margin on the caudal fin. There are 23–31 gillrakers, and the ventral surface of the liver is striated. The largest fish taken by hook and line, from Cabo Blanco, Peru, was 7 feet 9 inches long and weighed 435 pounds.

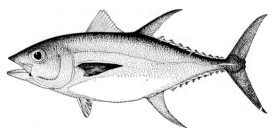

Bigeye Tuna

The Atlantic and Pacific forms of bigeye tuna, once called separate species, are now considered to be a single species, found in tropical and subtropical waters around the world. The food consists of fishes, squids, and crustaceans. In equatorial regions, spawning occurs throughout the year, but farther from the equator spawning is concentrated in the summer months. A single female may shed several million eggs.

Bigeye tuna are taken mainly by commercial fishermen using Japanese longlines.

—B.B.C.
—R.H.G.

BIG-GAME FISHING A general term covering a number of large marine game species. Specifically, big-game fishing encompasses the black, blue, white, and striped marlin; swordfish; wahoo; sailfish; bluefin and yellowfin tuna; tarpon; and the more active sharks, such as the mako, hammerhead, tiger, white, and bronze whaler shark. Other species usually of smaller size (less than 100 pounds), and often caught incidental to the quarry sought, such as dolphin, African pompano, amberjack, king mackerel, tanguigue, albacore, and great barracuda are included in the general definition. In common all are taken by trolling or drift fishing and to a lesser extent by kite fishing.

Big-game fishing as a recognized sport in America had its beginnings off the California coast near the turn of this century. A bluefin tuna weighing 183 pounds was caught off Catalina Island on June 1, 1898, by Charles Frederick Holder. He formed a tuna club later that same month and by the end of July 24 members had caught fish weighing more than 100 pounds.

Though there were tarpon caught on rod-and-reel in the 1870's, the first widely publicized catch, which set off a stampede of anglers south to Florida on the Atlantic coast, occurred on March 25, 1885. Two fish—one weighing 93 pounds, the other weighing 81 pounds—were caught by W.H. Wood of New York. This is generally considered as the beginning of interest in big-game fishing on the East Coast.

In 1924 Zane Grey caught the first "giant," a 758-pound bluefin tuna off Yarmouth, Nova Scotia, and from that time on interest in big-game fishing mushroomed. Other early pioneers were Michael Lerner, who battled bluefin tuna from a dory off Nova Scotia; Van Campen Heilner, long-time associate editor of *Field & Stream;* S. Kip Farrington, generally credited with the discovery and development of the big-game fishing grounds off Chile; and later Alfred Glassel, who is credited with the promotion and development of Pacific black marlin off Cabo Blanco, Peru.

Until the 1950's the sport was limited to anglers who had the time and money to travel and charter the expensive craft that typifies big-game fishing. With the development of fiberglass hulls, collapsible outriggers, inboard-outboard engines, and modern trailers capable of transporting and launching boats up to 30 feet in length became financially feasible for the average man. Today there are thousands of avid sportsmen prowling the Gulf Stream off Florida, the Bahamas, the Gulf of Mexico, the Caribbean, the Pacific Coast, and the Montauk-Block Island area with well-equipped craft in the 19–28-foot class and capable of subduing almost any big-game fish. The mobility of these boats, plus the development of more sophisticated rods and reels (minia-

turized electronic gear) have resulted in a whole new breed of ocean anglers.

There are factors which do not change—innovations in boats and gear notwithstanding—and that is the nature of big-game fish. They react the same today as they did 100 years ago and require the same intelligent stalking and the same careful handling, once hooked, to land today as they did in the days of the first wood boats designed to fish for them.

While the gear has been refined somewhat the basic equipment and techniques remain the same. Most big-game species sought are migratory and feed not only by established migratory patterns but on the same available food. Giant bluefin tuna cross the same flats at Cat Cay and Bimini in the Bahamas each year in the spring within a few weeks of the same dates and are caught off Newfoundland within the same time framework in late September. White and blue marlin continue to hit off the Bahamas in May and June each year, and the whites continue to show up off Ocean City, Maryland, and in the Baltimore Trench off New Jersey in July and August. The same holds true for blue marlin in the Gulf of Mexico, black marlin off Peru on the west coast of South America, striped marlin in Panama, sailfish off Guymas on the west coast of Mexico, black marlin off the east coast of Africa in the vicinity of Mozambique, and black marlin off Hawaii and Cairns (Australia).

Big-game fish are predators. Their food consists of baitfish of many species—depending upon the part of the world in which they are feeding. Whether it is a sailfish "balling" pilchard off Florida's east coast or a black marlin pursuing a school of bonito off Panama, the technique is the same. Big-game fish have voracious appetites and will chase almost any number of species of baitfish, from cruising singles to schools of hundreds. It is enough to know that they are vitally interested in rigged baits skipped on the surface or trolled just below or allowed to swim alive and close to the surface while kite fishing.

There are a number of methods of rigging baits for trolling. From slices of small baitfish such as mullet—called strip baits—to the rigging of large mackerel or bonito there are only slight variations. The speed of trolling depends on the species of fish sought, but generally trolling is done at a rather rapid rate, enough to keep a rigged bait of a pound or so skipping on the surface. The trolling speed of the boat depends on the current, wind direction, and wave action. Fishing the Gulf Stream off Florida or the Bahamas, for instance, might require a speed of 10 knots while traveling north to keep a mullet bait skipping correctly. This is because the Stream moves in a northerly direction at about 5–6 knots and the boat is moving with the current. Heading south, however, would be against the same current and would require less speed to keep the bait in proper action. Professional charterboat captains learn the correct combination of speed and engine revolutions in various sea conditions that produce strikes.

THE BOAT

Basically a boat for big-game fishing should meet certain requirements. It should be seaworthy enough to withstand fairly high seas. It must have enough power to get to the fishing grounds—regardless of how far out—

A sportfisherman equipped with tuna tower. The tower offers a great advantage in spotting billfish as well as tuna

be able to cruise while trolling all day, and return to port at night. It should be maneuverable enough to speed up when necessary or to make tight turns. Preferably it should allow the skipper some altitude to spot fish ahead of the boat, feeding sea birds, and gamefish coming up from below the baits. In addition, it should be equipped with a fighting chair if possible, although many big-game fish are fought with a rod belt. Fighting chairs may come in all shapes and sizes, from the folding, lightweight chairs used on small boats to the intricate and sophisticated fighting chairs on the big sportfishing boats. Ideally the chair should contain a gimbal or socket in which to place the butt end of the big-game rod. The best chairs provide a foot rest so that the angler can utilize the strength of his legs in battling a fish, armrests, an adjustable backrest, provisions for a fighting harness, and should be capable of swiveling in a 360° turn upon a pedestal mounted solidly on the cockpit deck.

The adequately-equipped sportfisherman should also carry two outriggers. The smaller boats can mount collapsible fiberglass or aluminum outriggers, which extend out about 15–25 feet, while the larger boats generally mount more sophisticated outriggers of aluminum, capable of extending out 45 feet from the port and starboard gunwales. Obviously the farther out the baits can be trolled on either side of the wake of the boat, the better the chances are for attracting the attention of cruising gamefish. The boat should have at least four solidly mounted rod holders—preferably two in each gunwale at the sides of the cockpit—in order to run two outrigger lines and two "flat lines." The two flat lines are positioned at different distances behind the boat in the wake, but closer to the boat than the outrigger baits.

A fish box is necessary, and the larger boats usually have no trouble installing one across the inside of the transom or below deck in the cockpit area. Smaller boats may have to improvise, but many fish boxes today are built into the hull of small sportfishermen. The tuna tower of the large sportfisherman provides a place from which the captain can run the boat high above deck level. Small sportfishermen do not provide as high a platform, although lightweight towers may be installed on small

boats. In many of the smaller boats the center console-steering system enables the angler to get considerably higher over the surface of the water than older steering methods. A transom door which swings open close to water level is ideal for sliding large fish into the cockpit. Many of the large sportfishermen are equipped with these. On smaller boats anglers must rely on hauling the catch over the transom or gunwales after it has been brought to the boat and subdued. A gin pole may be mounted on both small and large boats, and provides the best method for raising large fish above the water surface with a system of pulleys. Many gin poles today are made of lightweight aluminum and can be mounted in smaller sportfishing boats. Baitboxes can be and usually are portable ice chests where both rigged and unrigged baits are kept cold to be used when ready. There should be stowage room for big-game rods and reels while underway.

Equipment considered absolutely necessary on a big-game sportfishing boat consists of a long-handled gaff and a wooden billy club, preferably weighted, and a tail rope. In addition, a flying gaff can prove invaluable for larger fish. The gaff is necessary for every species of big-game fish. Billfish, in addition to being gaffed and hopefully tail-roped, can be killed quickly and cleanly, if wanted for mounting purposes, by a solid whack between the eyes with the billy club. Cloth gloves are also advisable for grasping not only the wire leader used in big-game fishing but in grasping the rasplike bills of marlin, sailfish, and broadbill.

Communication equipment on the larger boats may include sophisticated marine radios, ship-to-shore radio telephones, radar gear, and Loran for bad weather and long-distance navigation. Somewhat more refined depth-finding and fish-finding equipment can be carried on the bigger boats, but—with the miniaturization of equipment prevalent in the space age—many small sportfishing boats today carry excellent small marine radios, including citizens band sets and depth and fishfinders.

TACKLE

There is considerable leeway in this day and age for selection of big-game tackle. Fifty years ago most big-game anglers had to rely on the huge, stout wooden rods, such as those built by Hardy, and heavy, big reels such as the Vom Hoff. But today, with the excellent hollow, tubular glass rods and precision, lightweight reels with excellent braking systems an experienced angler can subdue a big fish with relatively light tackle. The advent of spinning tackle has also made it possible to wear down battling big-game fish with limber rods and adjustable drags of saltwater spinning reels.

With big-game fish on spinning tackle it is important to remember that the greatest danger of losing a fish is breaking the line. It is for this reason that considerable care should be taken to watch the drag setting on a spinning reel. The most common mistake made by the novice using spinning reels on big-game fish is tightening the drag during a long run. The reaction should be just the opposite. As a big-game fish takes off several hundred yards of line, the tension on the line increases as it nears the center of the spool. The drag should be loosened rather than tightened. Many don't realize that the more line a big fish has out, the easier it is for the angler and

1 Main purpose of fighting chair is to let fisherman use powerful muscles of legs and back against fish. Here, boat's mate adjusts length and tilt of footrest.

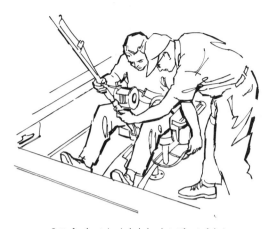

2 Butt of rod rests in gimbaled socket at front of chair, main harness goes around angler at small of back. Thongs around thighs complete harness rig.

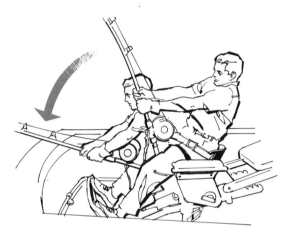

3 Action of pumping, with fish on, consists of quick drop of rod from vertical to horizontal, and swift reeling in of slack gained. Then, using legs and back . . .

4 . . . fisherman pulls rod upward toward vertical once more, to drop rod and gain line again. This is critical maneuver against big fish with drag set high.

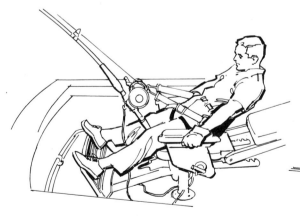

5 When fish makes run, as after first strike, angler reduces drag and waits. There is no way of stopping him, and too much pressure will only break tackle.

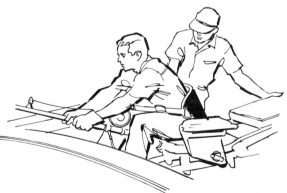

6 Throughout playing of fish, rod must be kept pointed in same direction as line leading from it. Boat's mate swings chair as necessary, relays advice from captain.

Fighting Chair Technique

the harder it is on the fish. Line being pulled through the water creates tremendous resistance and this not only punishes the fish but the line itself. So the standard procedure is to loosen the drag and raise the rod tip high when the fish is making a run. It will cause the bend of the rod and the drag of the line through the water to tire the fish. It also relieves the line of a tremendous strain close to the center of the spool. Lines for big-game fishing are now manufactured in various classes in order to conform to International Game Fish Association regulations. These classes are 12, 20, 30, 50, 80, and 130 pound maximum breaking test line.

Conventional saltwater rods differ from freshwater rods only in size and ability to handle large fish. Conventional tackle is generally considered to be the relatively shorter rod used with the level-winding reel. However, spinning tackle, using monofilament lines in the 20–30 pound class, have been used with some success in taking big-game fish. Salt-water flyrods are also used on big-game fish in many areas—such as on tarpon—but it is unlikely they will become popular for the taking of extremely heavy ocean gamefish for the majority of anglers.

Decades ago, the most popular of the big-game rods were made of split bamboo, but fiberglass is now generally accepted as the best material for these rods. It makes an extremely strong and yet light rod which will not take a "set" and is almost impervious to salt water and corrosion. Roller guides are used almost exclusively now on the best big-game rods and perform the important function of reducing friction between the line and guide. Corrosion-proof guides and those made from stainless steel or Carboloy are preferable for big fish. Among the features to look for in a preferred big-game rod are: a wooden butt section of excellent wood with a strongly made end ferrule to fit a fighting chair gimbal or a "Bimini Belt" socket; an equally corrosion-proof reel seat with strong locking rings to allow the rod tip to be locked into position and to keep the reel from working loose from the seat during action.

The following chart gives the generally recommended weights in ounces for big-game rods. It also shows the suggested reel size and line test (in pounds) for various species of big-game fish. Rod weights are given at the tip of modern glass rods.

BAIT AND RIGGING BAIT

The mullet is found over much of the world and it is one of the best all-around trolling baits. Although the mullet rarely enters the actual diet of big-game species (during an extensive study of sailfish stomach contents, for example, the only mullet remains found were "split" for baits) it has the durability required for ocean trolling. In areas where mullet are not abundant or do not occur at all, there are a number of good surface baits available. In the Florida, Bahamas, and Caribbean areas the balao is an excellent bait for sailfish, white marlin, and small blue marlin. It can be purchased in fresh and frozen form and is easily stored. However, it is not effective in taking the larger blue and black marlin and that is where the bonito, bonefish, mackerel, and even small dolphin come in. Also, live or frozen squid can be used, as well as artificial squid lures. In addition, many other baits are manufactured today (herring eels, for example) as artificials. There are as many ways to rig bait as there are methods to use them (*see* illustrations) on the commonly accepted methods of rigging baits for trolling. Strip baits are popular for some of the smaller billfish.

LEADERS AND HOOKS

Wire leader comes in shiny and dull finish and it is a matter of choice which one uses. The main thing to remember is that any kink in wire leader can weaken it to the point where it will easily break. As far as test strength is concerned, each roll of wire gives the breaking test on the package, and it is wise to base the size of wire leader you are going to use on the size and species of the fish sought. It is best to overguess your fish's weight when deciding on the wire leader. Many a big fish has been lost because it hit a bait being trolled on leader meant for a smaller fish.

Big-game hooks must take a tremendous strain, so it is wise to purchase good hooks if one is to succeed in taking fish of several hundred pounds or more. The best hooks

BIG-GAME FISHING TACKLE
Light

Species	Reel Size	Line Test (Pounds)	Rod Weight* (Ounces)
Atlantic Sailfish	2/0–4/0	12–20	6–9
Pacific Sailfish	2/0–4/0	12–20	6–9
White Marlin	2/0–4/0	12–20	6–9
Striped Marlin	4/0	12–20	6–9
Blue Marlin	6/0	20–50	9–16
Black Marlin	6/0	30–50	12–16
Swordfish	6/0	30–50	12–16
Bluefin Tuna (Giant)	9/0	50	16–20

Medium

Species	Reel Size	Line Test (Pounds)	Rod Weight* (Ounces)
Atlantic Sailfish	4/0–6/0	20–30	9–12
Pacific Sailfish	4/0–6/0	20–30	9–12
White Marlin	4/0–6/0	20–30	9–12
Striped Marlin	7/0	30–50	9–12
Blue Marlin	9/0	50–80	16–24
Black Marlin	9/0	50–80	16–24
Swordfish	9/0	50–80	16–24
Bluefin Tuna (Giant)	9/0	80	16–24

Heavy

Species	Reel Size	Line Test (Pounds)	Rod Weight* (Ounces)
Atlantic Sailfish	6/0	30–50	16–18
Pacific Sailfish	6/0	30–50	16–18
White Marlin	6/0	30–50	16–18
Striped Marlin	9/0	80	18–20
Blue Marlin	12/0	130	24–30
Black Marlin	12/0	130	24–30
Swordfish	12/0	130	24–30
Bluefin Tuna (Giant)	12/0	130	24–30

*The rod weight as given is for the tip only in tubular glass construction. When using monofilaments the heavier rod weights are suggested, due to the elasticity of the line.

are made of high carbon steel alloy wire and are plated with cadmium or tin to prevent rusting. The wire is hardened at 1550°F and tempered at 750°F; the ring at the eye is formed by cold swagging which reduces bulk at the eye. All large saltwater hooks today are forged; that is, after the hook has been made, it is hammered flat along both sides of the bend, while still hot, to give it additional strength. The appropriate hook size and pattern depends not only on the fish but the type of bait or rigging used. The following is a general guide:

TERMINAL TACKLE

Fish	Hook Size	Pattern	Leader Wire Size	Mono (pounds)
Atlantic Sailfish	7/0-8/0	O'Shaughnessy	No. 5–No. 7	50
White Marlin	7/0-9/0	O'Shaughnessy	No. 8–No. 9	80
Pacific Sailfish	8/0-9/0	O'Shaughnessy	No. 8–No. 9	80
Striped Marlin	8/0-9/0	O'Shaughnessy	No. 8–No. 10	80
Blue Marlin	9/0-10/0	Sobey	No. 11–No. 13	
Swordfish	8/0-12/0	Sobey	No. 11–No. 13	100–180
Black Marlin	9/0-12/0	Sobey	No. 11–No. 13	
Bluefin Tuna	10/0-12/0	O'Shaughnessy / Sobey	No. 14–No. 15	

THE STRIKE

Perhaps the most crucial instant in all of big-game fishing is when the fish strikes the bait. Many times the fish will hit with such force—brought on either by hunger or anger—that it will hook itself. In that case it removes any problem of whether to drop back or speed up the bait. The angler in this case is simply concerned with handling the fish properly, now that it is hooked. But all fish do not strike the trolled baits instantly, preferring to inspect them closely before deciding to take one. It is this situation which can cause problems. The angler may choose to free-spool the reel, allowing the bait to drop behind the boat and sink, and the fish will swallow it "dead" in the water. On the other hand, when a fish can't seem to make up its mind to hit one of the baits, either speeding up the boat slightly or rapidly cranking the handle of the reel will excite the fish, causing it to strike. Sometimes neither method works and the fish simply departs without striking at all.

One thing is certain on the strike. It is wise for the angler to be watching the baits and preferably either seated in the chair or standing close to it when the strike comes. In this way the fisherman can either grab whichever rod contains the line the fish hits and get ready to strike the fish himself—in order to set the hook properly—or a mate may hand the angler the proper rod and the butt can be quickly fitted into the chair gimbal. Many big-game fish are missed because the angler is too far away

from the rods or chair when the strike comes. Big-game fish do not occur numerically as often as smaller species and an angler may go many hours or even days and not get a strike. But when a big-game fish does strike, there is very little time in which to make the correct moves. It is best to be ready.

If the crew is certain the fish has taken the bait there are several options open to the angler. If he is inexperienced, it is best to take the advice of the skipper or mate. In many cases, knowing their own waters and the habits of the fish, they will slow the boat down almost to idle, and allow the fish to take the bait and circle down to a depth where it will turn the bait around and swallow it. It is an unnerving experience for a novice to have a crew tell him to wait for a 10–15 second count before striking, but occasionally this is best. Big-game fishing crews in many parts of the world use this system, particularly off the west coast of Mexico. At the end of the count the skipper will gun the engines of the boat to take up slack. The angler then lowers his rod tip almost horizontally and strikes once, or twice, hard; by bringing the rod up sharply to the vertical position he sets the hook.

In other areas of the world crews may use a different system. For example, some Bahamian skippers seem to prefer to speed up the boat as soon as the slashing bill of the fish has struck the bait and the line has fallen to the surface of the water from the outrigger clips. Many of them feel this will succeed in hooking the fish at the instant it swallows the bait. In contrast, many sportsmen prefer to see the skipper put the engine in neutral as soon as the fish is hooked, feeling that an angler should fight his fish on more equal terms. This is somewhat academic, but is the method required in the Palm Beach Masters' Tournament, for example. At any rate, most conventional techniques of fighting big-game fish today include the use of the boat as much as the rod-and-reel. It has been said by many of the "pros" that more big-game fish are caught by the man at the wheel of a sportfisherman than by the angler in the chair. There is no arguing that a good combination of skipper, mate, and angler is hard to beat when it comes to landing big-game fish.

The revolving-spool reel for saltwater big-game fishing has undergone some major changes in recent years until the two most widely used reels fall into these categories: the older of the two uses what is referred to as a "star drag," while the newer reels utilize a quadrant lever to achieve drag tension. Unlike the star drag, the quadrant lever is separate from and does not rotate with the spool drive shaft. The star drag reel is still widely used, but more of the newer reels are being found on sportfishing craft today. The advantage of the lever action drag is that the striking drag can be preset, giving the modern angler a distinct advantage in that the exact striking drag can be set or reset instantly under a number of varying conditions. Drag tension is of great importance in fighting large, fast-moving big-game fish—whether in setting the striking drag just before a strike, resetting it after changing damaged baits, or upon bringing a heavy fish to the boat.

Many skippers and mates have their own opinions about the preferred striking drag for different reels, lines, and species of fish, but a rough chart can be made up that will serve generally for most cases. A general rule could be that the striking drag should not be set to less than 20

A striped marlin hooked off the coast of Ecuador puts on an aerial display. This is a spectacular fish on light tackle

percent of the line's maximum test strength or more than 40 percent of that same breaking strain. A simple pocket-sized fish-weighing scale can be used to measure the pound test of the line at the tip, after the rod has been set in a gunwale rod holder. The chart would look approximately like this:

Rod Class	Line test (pounds)	Reel	Capacity (yards)	Species	Striking drag (pounds)
Very light	12	2/0	475	Atlantic Sails	4
	20	3/0	500	Atlantic Sails	5
Light	30	4/0	500	White Marlin	7
Medium	50	6/0	575	Blue Marlin	20
Heavy	80	9/0	600	Black Marlin Swordfish	25-30
Very Heavy	130	12/0	750	Giant Tuna	40

Terminal Tackle That tackle which exists between the snap swivel at the end of the line and the hook—is of the utmost importance in fighting large ocean fish. Considerable importance should be attached to the selection of good swivels, for a cheap, weak, or defective swivel has caused the loss of many a fine fish. The ideal swivels are those made of stainless steel and operating on small bearings. They are slightly more expensive than the conventional brass or black swivel, but hold up better and prevent line twist.

Double Line Just above the leader, this should be constructed and tied with a Bimini Twist knot, allowing approximately 10–15 feet of double line for lines of 50-pound test and under and up to 30 feet of double line for the heavier line tests, such as 80- and 130-pound. It should be tied every 24–36 inches with a few twists of dental floss which will keep it together so that it can easily pass through rod guides. Wire leaders come in both braided cable and stainless steel. Both are about equal in strength for the length and weight. What the braided wire makes up for, in less tendency to kink over stainless steel, is lost in its tendency to rust more easily, especially in salt water. It is up to individual skippers to choose. A simple guide can be followed as to which wire size should be used with classes of rods and line tests. It also gives the suggested monofilament leader and its breaking test.

Tackle Class	Species	IGFA Line Class (pounds)	Mono test (pounds)	Stainless Steel (pounds)
Very light	Atlantic Sailfish	12–20	30–50	#3 (32)
Light	White Marlin	30	80	#8 (86)
Medium	Blue Marlin	50	120	#10 (128)
Heavy	Black Marlin Swordfish	80	200	#12 (176)
Very heavy	Giant Tuna	130	300	#15 (272)

Using stainless steel leaders or nylon monofilament is optional. Wire leaders have a tendency to kink and break at that spot where monofilament does not. Yet the wire has advantages, such as being almost impervious to cutting by sharp teeth. Mono is made in so many grades and sizes that tables of diameters and breaking strains mean little. The breaking strain of monofilament leaders is marked on the packages, as is also the case with steel leaders.

PLAYING THE FISH

Big-game fish, almost without exception, will make their most frantic and longest run right after being hooked. Depending on the size and condition of the fish, it may take out anywhere from several hundred to more than a thousand yards of line in a matter of minutes. With marlin or sailfish one can expect a heart-stopping series of acrobatic jumps as the fish clears the surface repeatedly in an effort to get rid of the hook. In the case of the bluefin tuna there will be no jumping but a tremendous burst of strength as the fish streaks away and downward. In both these cases the angler is advised to keep the rod tip up to let the bending rod absorb the shock and—as the fish gets farther out from the boat, still speeding—slightly reduce the drag to prevent the line from breaking. This is the moment, as the pressure on the line increases progressively when more of it leaves the spool rapidly, where most fish are lost. They are lost because the lines break from too much strain alone or the angler becomes too worried about his fast-disappearing line and increases the drag, hoping to slow it down. It is better to have a lot of line out. The drag of the line being pulled through the water will do more than anything else at this time to slow down the fish. When the fish has stopped its initial run and begins to swim, then

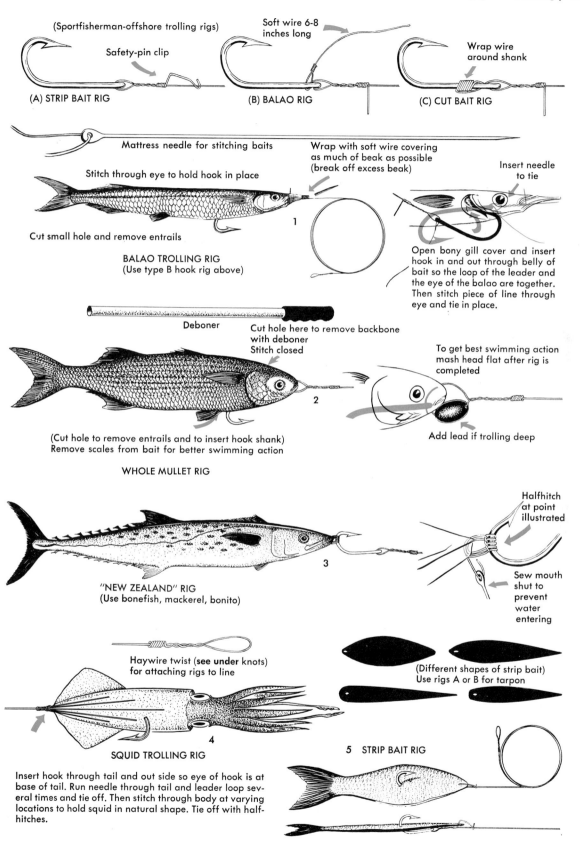

(Sportfisherman-offshore trolling rigs)

Safety-pin clip

(A) STRIP BAIT RIG

Soft wire 6-8 inches long

(B) BALAO RIG

Wrap wire around shank

(C) CUT BAIT RIG

Mattress needle for stitching baits

Stitch through eye to hold hook in place

Wrap with soft wire covering as much of beak as possible (break off excess beak)

Insert needle to tie

Cut small hole and remove entrails

BALAO TROLLING RIG
(Use type B hook rig above)

1

Open bony gill cover and insert hook in and out through belly of bait so the loop of the leader and the eye of the balao are together. Then stitch piece of line through eye and tie in place.

Deboner

Cut hole here to remove backbone with deboner
Stitch closed

To get best swimming action mash head flat after rig is completed

2

(Cut hole to remove entrails and to insert hook shank)
Remove scales from bait for better swimming action

Add lead if trolling deep

WHOLE MULLET RIG

Halfhitch at point illustrated

3

"NEW ZEALAND" RIG
(Use bonefish, mackerel, bonito)

Sew mouth shut to prevent water entering

Haywire twist (**see under** knots) for attaching rigs to line

(Different shapes of strip bait)
Use rigs A or B for tarpon

4

SQUID TROLLING RIG

5   **STRIP BAIT RIG**

Insert hook through tail and out side so eye of hook is at base of tail. Run needle through tail and leader loop several times and tie off. Then stitch through body at varying locations to hold squid in natural shape. Tie off with half-hitches.

Offshore Trolling Rigs

Rod holders serve a two-fold purpose—for storage when not in use and providing a mount when lines are attached to outriggers. This also permits multiple use when trolling

the angler can begin to regain lost line. The fish may jump any number of times after that, but always remember that the slight decrease in drag as it makes its runs will lessen the chances of losing a fish. Regaining line on a fish is a matter of pumping properly. The rod is raised or pumped when the slack is taken up. It is quickly lowered while the reel handle is pumped to gain slack, then pumped or raised again. The reel handle should not be turned while the rod is being raised to regain line. It will simply cause the drag to slip unnecessarily, losing rather than gaining line.

The mate will have reeled in the other three lines to give the angler room to fight the fish without becoming entangled in other lines. The advantage of the swiveling chair becomes apparent to a novice big-game fisherman when he feels the mate constantly turning the chair so that the angler is facing the direction where the line slants out to the fish at all times. This permits the equal distribution of weight on the part of the angler fighting the fish. It is during this time that the captain of the boat can help or hinder a fisherman by the way he handles the boat. If the angler is tiring and the fish is either swimming down and away from the boat or sounding, the skipper may ''back down'' on the fish by putting the boat into reverse, thus taking considerable strain off the back and arms of the angler and allowing him time to gain line

on the fish. Other skippers follow a different battle plan and may turn the boat and run parallel to the swimming fish allowing the angler to slightly reduce the drag and causing a billow to form in the line between the boat and the fish. This exerts tremendous pressure on the fish, causing it to tire far more rapidly than the backing-down method, which is really more to spare the angler than to tire the fish.

It is at this stage, particularly if an angler is a novice at the game and is feeling the strain in his back and arms, where a harness can ease the pressure. Slipped under the angler, it fits snugly around the lower back in the kidney region. It has canvas or leather straps which can be snapped to rings on both sides of the reel. This allows the angler to absorb the powerful pull of the big fish with the back and leg muscles rather than taking all the pressure on the back and arms alone (note illustrations).

As the fish gets closer and closer to the boat, the angler can roughly judge its depth by the angle of line slanting from the rod tip to the fish. As the angle (from the vertical) lessens quickly, one can expect the fish to surface and jump. It is then that the rod tip should be held high to absorb the strain of the thrashing jump and also to prevent slack from forming, allowing the fish to throw the hook.

Usually big-game fish will sound toward the end of a battle, going as deep as the thousand-foot level or more. They may even die down there from exertion or from pressure or the combination of both. There are two options for the angler: He can have the boat move directly over the fish and try to pump it up, depending on the angler's physical condition, the size of the fish, the length of the fight. This can and many times does require hours of very difficult work, particularly if the fish is large and dead. This often attracts sharks, particularly if the fish is bleeding. The only alternative is to move the boat several hundred yards ahead of the fish, preferably with the drag reduced to avoid putting any additional stress on the line. Then the angler resets his drag higher and begins to pump the fish up again. The new angle of the line (rather than straight down) tilts the head of the fish up as it is pulled, planing it up rather than pulling it. Many sportfishing skippers utilize this method.

If the fish is not dead, or if it did not sound for long, and is now obviously tired and coming into the boat, a series of things can take place which will greatly affect the angler's chance of boating it. Most billfish are extremely strong fighters and will make last-minute jumps quite close to the boat when the novice angler least expects it. This is the time when most billfish are lost because the angler allowed slack to form in the line and the fish was able to throw the hook. At this point the rod tip should be held as high as possible. A fish jumping close to the boat is also more likely to get itself tail-wrapped by the wire leader.

The snap swivel marking the place on the single line where it joins a short length of double line, which is in turn fastened to the wire leader, will finally appear. This is the signal for the boating process to begin because the snap swivel cannot pass through the roller guides at the rod tip. That is as close to the boat as the angler can bring the fish with the rod. It is then up to the mate to reach out, preferably with gloved hands, take the double line or leader, and lead the tired fish close to the side of the boat near the stern. There he will grasp the bill or use his gaff. If the fish is very large and/or it is wanted for mounting, the skipper or another member of the crew will either whack it across the forehead with a weighted wooden billy club or stun it temporarily while a tail rope is passed around the head, snapped closed, and slid down the length of the body until it is pulled tight at the slender area at the base of the tail of the billfish or tuna. The skipper or other crew member may also have gaffed the fish to prevent it wrenching itself free from the man holding the bill. If the fish is to be tagged for migration studies or is not wanted for mounting, it will be released. In that case it is not gaffed or struck with the club nor is a tail rope fastened to it. The tag is inserted in the musculature at the base of the dorsal fin and the wire leader is snipped off close to the eye of the hook. A combination of salt water and stomach acids will erode the hook in time and give some other big-game angler a chance to battle the fish another day.

If the fish is to be boated, it is either taken aboard through the transom door; pulled over the gunwales if it is small enough; or the tail rope fastened to the snap of the gin pole and the fish hoisted, tail first, above the surface.

The moments of boating a big-game fish can be very dangerous for anglers and crew members who are not experienced. The slash of the bill or the swipe of a large sickle-shaped tail can seriously injure people. It is better for the angler to stay in the chair—even if he is experienced—while the crew is going about the business of boating the fish. Crew members and anglers in the cockpit should be extremely careful not to step into any coils of the line or leader while the fish is being held alongside. Serious injuries can occur if a big fish breaks loose from the man holding the bill or the gaff. It is for that reason that an angler should set his drag on the very light position during this time. If the fish does get loose and make a last-ditch run, it will have less chance of snapping the line than if the drag is on full position.

RECORDING THE CATCH

If the fish is to be entered in a tournament there are several factors to remember. No one on the boat was to have assisted the angler during the fight by touching him in any way or helping with the rod-or-reel. The mate may turn the chair for the angler and other persons may hand him the objects if he asks for them, such as a cold drink or a seat harness or rod belt. These rules have been long established by the IGFA. The angler is to fight the fish alone until the mate reaches out to take the double line or leader wire.

Also, upon reaching the dock or marina, the fish should be weighed by an official weighmaster or dockmaster. The proper forms should be filled out and signed by the weighmaster and a witness. The fish should also be measured for length and girth to insure proper mounting. The test of the line should also be recorded and the type of bait used. It would not be too bad an idea to have a few pictures taken during that moment. It may not happen many times in an angler's lifetime.

Use of the Rod Belt

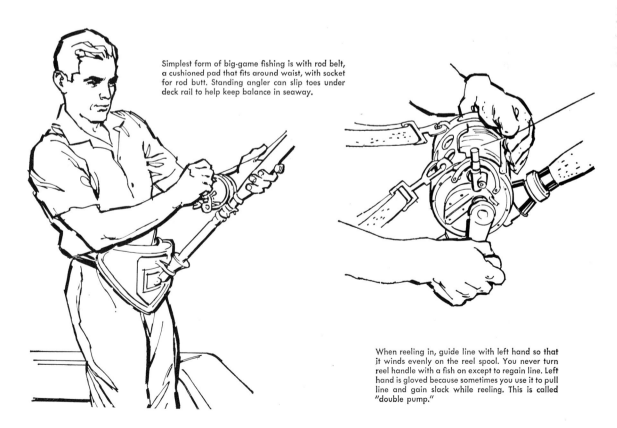

Simplest form of big-game fishing is with rod belt, a cushioned pad that fits around waist, with socket for rod butt. Standing angler can slip toes under deck rail to help keep balance in seaway.

When reeling in, guide line with left hand so that it winds evenly on the reel spool. You never turn reel handle with a fish on except to regain line. Left hand is gloved because sometimes you use it to pull line and gain slack while reeling. This is called "double pump."

The kite acts as an outrigger from a stationary or drifting boat. A helium balloon is added on windless days to keep it aloft

KITE FISHING

The use of a kite for big-game fishing dates back to South Pacific cultures of the Procto-Malayan period in 2,000 B.C. Its modern adaptation began in 1912 when Captain George Farnsworth tried the system off Catalina Island, California, for bluefin tuna. Farnsworth was extremely successful and in the season of 1913 one of his anglers, William Boschen, succeeded in landing the first swordfish ever taken on rod-and-reel while baiting with a kite. Subsequently, Captain Tommy Gifford utilized the kite off Florida and the Bahamas. However, it was not until Captain Bob Lewis of Kendall, Florida, began producing kites commercially that the method became popular.

Kite fishing is a complete departure from the traditional and very successful method of taking big-game fish be trolling. It incorporates fishing with live bait with the use of an outrigger—the outrigger in this case being the kite itself. The boat is not kept in motion as it is while trolling; however, the engines are left to idle in many cases so that it can get underway when a fish hits the bait.

The theory of kite fishing is to use a system of surface angling for big-game fish where there is no line in the water or on the surface between the boat and the bait. Also, devotees of the sport feel that live bait—allowed to swim naturally on or just below the surface—attract gamefish better than dead trolled baits. Live bait fishing has been done for as long as man has fished, but it has always been difficult to keep a bait on the surface where

the strike can be seen by the angler in time to strike back at the attacking fish. Live bait fished deep also takes gamefish, but the angler does not know the fish has struck until he feels the strike as a tightening of the line, sometimes too late to set the hook.

The billfish is a surface or close to the surface feeder, as are many species of gamefish. Kite fishermen have noticed that baitfish hooked through the meaty part of the body, so as not to injure the backbone, send out distress signals when swimming on or just below the surface. These signals are picked up for considerable distances by predators and result in slashing strikes which are truly spectacular.

Kingfish, wahoo, barracuda, and dolphin take swimming surface kite baits at full speed, sometimes shooting high into the air as they take the live fish. Billfish and tuna hit these baits without the careful scrutiny they sometimes use on trolled baits—hooking themselves solidly. The slack line, from the rod tip to the clip on the kite line and down to the swimming live bait, apparently allows just enough room for the fish to hook themselves before the line is taken up by the reel. If a boat is allowed to drift with the engine or motor off there is no sound or vibration to alert gamefish to the presence of a fishing boat.

There is the problem of keeping bait alive, which is not present in the trolled-bait system and which may be the reason many charter-boat skippers do not specialize in kite fishing. But those professionals who have managed to solve the problem of keeping the bait alive have done so with not too much trouble. There are a number of inexpensive oxygen-supplying pumps which work off regular boat batteries or even flashlight batteries and can supply a bucket or box of live bait with enough air to live for days. Live bait boxes can be built at the stern of any inboard-engine boat which will circulate sea water to fish.

The choice of small bait fish is up to the individual, but those who have practiced the sport for years tend to lean toward the pilchard, the pinfish, and the blue runner in Florida, Bahama, and Caribbean waters, although many other small fish will serve as well. In northern waters the porgy is a favorite. Live eels can be used in the surf when kites are used to fish off a beach rather than from a boat. An offshore wind, however, is necessary for this system to work.

The same basic tackle is used in kite fishing as in conventional trolling. If big-game fish are being sought—and any species of big-game fish may be taken with kites—the same rod weights, reel sizes, and line test should be used. Saltwater spinning tackle can be adapted well to kite fishing. Rods may be held in the hand or rested in rod holders, but drag should be set fairly light to prevent the rods from being jerked from the rod holders in case of a sudden and unexpected strike by a large fish. The angler or a crew member should man the large reel holding the kite line at all times. This is because the baits should be kept swimming on or just below the surface and any sudden gust of wind can elevate the kite and raise the bait fish high above the water where it will wriggle in the air and attract nothing. A few turns of the kite spool will lower it back into the water. The opposite is true when the wind dies down and the bait swims too deep. A few turns of the spool will bring it back up to the surface.

When the wind dies down to calm or almost to calm there is not much one can do about flying a kite by itself.

One method of using the kites in no-wind conditions is to troll with them as outriggers. The kite may be flown on the downwind side of the boat out to as much distance as the kite line will allow. Dead trolled baits may be skipped across the surface—much the same way as with the conventional outrigger—but they can be run much farther from the boat wake. Many kite fishermen troll rigged mullet and balao baits as much as 100 yards off the side of a trolling boat providing a surface bait far away from the boat. Another system of keeping kites aloft on calm days has been refined by such skippers as Captain Allen Self of North Key Largo, Florida. He uses helium balloons fastened to the kites on no-wind days or days with not enough wind to keep a regular kite aloft.

CONSTRUCTION

The construction of the kite reel spool is self-explanatory to any mechanically inclined angler. The crude reel, about a foot in diameter, can be constructed from two circular plates of plywood glued or nailed to a smaller wooden plate inside. It can be turned by crank and should be able to carry a minimum of 150 feet of heavy braided line—braided is best, although mono can be used. The reel is mounted on a broomstick handle one part protruding below to fit into a rod holder and the other sticking up above the reel with a screw eye or rod guide at the end to let the line run out.

Made of light silk or nylon, the kite dries fast in wind, after rain, or a dunking. The crosspieces are made of either new or used sections of fiberglass fishing rods. The cloth is fastened to the hollow ends of the rod blanks by sewing a regular dress hook at the corners of the silk so that it hooks into the hollow end of the rod blanks. The kite should be about 3×3 feet and the kiteline should be fastened to it by a harness from all four corners and by a line connected to the crosspieces in the very center (tied to a fishing swivel to keep it stable). The kiteline should be fairly heavy, at least 50-pound thread.

Two regular swivels, one smaller than the other, should be inserted in the kiteline—one 50 feet from the kite and one at 100 feet. There should be at least another 50 feet of kiteline between the last swivel and the spool to allow the last swivel to move out to about 50 feet from the boat.

Two regular wooden clothespins should slide along the kiteline. The clothespin nearest the kite should have a small hole bored through it so neither swivel will pass through it. This means that the first swivel to hit it, the one 50 feet from the kite, will carry the clothespin with it. Then the ordinary U-shaped staple or half paper clip should be clamped in the jaws of the clothespin and the line from the first fishing rod passed through the staple so that it moves freely back and forth. If a fish strikes, the staple will pull from the jaws of the clothespin and the line will fall free to the surface.

The second clothespin should have a larger hole drilled through it so that the first swivel is allowed to pass through but not the larger second swivel. Thus, the second swivel will stop this clothespin 100 feet from the tip of the line. The second staple and the next fishing line is fastened to this one. Then the reel is allowed to let out about 50 feet more of kiteline until two lines dangle from it, running freely through the clothespin-held staples 50 and 100 feet from the boat.

TECHNIQUE

There are times when the kites will get dunked by a sudden drop in the breeze, before the boat can be speeded up enough to keep it aloft. It is for this reason that having several kites along is a good idea, because it takes time for the light silk or nylon to dry even in the hot sun.

The rod holder or seat for the kite should be strong because the strain on the kite reel shaft is considerable; the wind pushing the kite exerts more pressure than is commonly realized, particularly when used in trolling.

It is not necessary for the angler or another crew member to reel in the second fishing line in case a fish strikes the first bait. Since there is no line in the water there is no way the line can be fouled. *See also* Sportfisherman

—J.S.

BIGMOUTH BUFFALO *Ictiobus cyprinellus* The bigmouth buffalo is the largest member of the sucker family and the most important from an economic standpoint. However, it is seldom caught by sport fishermen. Found principally in the plains states, it ranges from North Dakota and southern Saskatchewan east to Ohio and Pennsylvania and south to the Gulf. Large rivers and shallow lakes provide ideal habitat for the bigmouth buffalo. It often becomes extremely abundant in the shallow, fertile lakes of the Central Plains and sometimes reaches population levels of several hundred pounds per acre.

The body of the bigmouth buffalo is robust and elliptical in shape. The mouth is large, wide, oblique, and terminal, with the upper lip almost on a level with the eye. There are no teeth in the mouth. The dorsal fin begins about midway along the back and extends nearly to the tail. There are no spines on any of the fins. The tail is moderately forked, and there are 35–43 scales along the lateral line. The color is a coppery olive-brown or slate-blue above, gradually fading to white on the belly.

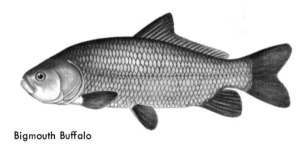
Bigmouth Buffalo

The bigmouth buffalo seldom is referred to by its correct name, usually being called buffalo, buffalo-fish, common buffalo, lake buffalo, or blue buffalo.

The most common size of the bigmouth buffalo taken by commercial fishermen usually is 3–12 pounds. Occasionally specimens reach 20–30 pounds, and one weighing over 80 pounds has been reported from Iowa.

LIFE HISTORY

Spawning takes place in April or May when water temperature reaches 60 to 65°F. Adult buffalo school in shallow, weedy areas and scatter their eggs randomly in water up to 2–3 feet deep. A ten-pound female may spawn as many as a half-million eggs. The eggs adhere to vegetation or debris and hatch in 10–14 days. No parental care is given the eggs or the young. The young fish remain in relatively shallow water most of the summer feeding on small animal and plant forms of plankton. By the end of their first summer they will measure 4–6 inches. In subsequent years under average conditions they will measure about 11, 15, 18, 20, and 21 inches. Weight will approximate 2 pounds at 15 inches, 5 pounds at 20 inches, and 10 pounds at 25 inches. Only under ideal conditions will many individuals live longer than 6–8 years and attain weights of over 20 pounds. Adulthood can be expected to occur at three years of age. Schooling tendencies prevail throughout their life, aiding in harvest by commercial fishermen.

Feeding habits were long thought to be similar to carp and other bottom feeders. However, studies in recent years have revealed that buffalo feed primarily on animal plankton. Entomostraca (small crustaceans) comprise about 90 per cent of the diet, while plant material (mostly algae) rounds out the menu. Insect larvae and other bottom organisms comprise only a minute portion of the diet.

As with most warmwater species, natural mortality takes a heavy toll each year. Unfavorable conditions during spawning and hatching may obliterate an entire year class. Thus in most lakes and rivers the buffalo population is comprised of one or two strong and several very weak year classes. Generally speaking, years of ample precipitation in the spring and early summer will produce strong year classes, while low waters depress reproduction and survival. After age 1 is attained, natural mortality can be expected to be 60–70 per cent annually.

ANGLING VALUE

Very little angling value can be associated with the bigmouth buffalo. Since their food consists primarily of plankton, they seldom are tempted by an angler's bait. Occasionally one will be taken on a worm or doughball or snagged by an artificial lure.

COMMERCIAL VALUE

The bigmouth buffalo is placed high on the list of freshwater commercial species. Usually considered a "coarse fish" by anglers, conservation agencies are free to and do encourage elimination of the species. This public demand added to the fact that the flesh of the buffalo is white and delicious creates an ideal situation for commercial harvest. Prices paid to the fisherman may range from five to twelve cents a pound, depending upon size and quality of the fish. On the retail market, dressed buffalo have brought prices upwards of fifty cents a pound.

Seines, traps, and gillnets are the primary methods of harvest. In large, shallow lakes where the species may commonly weigh 5–10 pounds it is possible to harvest well over one hundred pounds per acre.

The abundance and commercial value of the bigmouth buffalo is reflected by the wholesale commercial fish market in Chicago. In 1961, buffalo (including black and smallmouth buffalo) shipped to this market totaled over five million pounds and were exceeded in total poundage only by whitefish. Even with this heavy catch the buffalo maintains large populations throughout the plains states, thus substantiating the fact that heavy fishing pressure usually harvests nature's surplus but seldom controls or eliminates a species. —J.T.S.

BIGMOUTH SCULPIN *Hemitripterus bolini* A sculpin (*which see*) of large size, reaching 27 inches in length, it is found from northern British Columbia to the Bering Sea at depths of at least 400–700 feet. The bigmouth sculpin is distinguished by its enormous, obliquely placed mouth; large, high, blunt, bony head spines; a deeply incised dorsal fin with filamentous rays on tips of spines. Color gray, brown, and white. —J.R.

BIGMOUTH SHINER *Notropis dorsalis* An olive or straw-colored shiner with a large, horizontal mouth. Its scales are narrowly dark-edged, with 36–39 in the complete lateral line. The sides are silvery, and the ventral surfaces are silvery and milkwhite. The length of the upper jaw

Bigmouth Shiner

is longer than the diameter of the eye. The head is flattened on its upper surface. The range of this species is from North Dakota and Missouri eastward through the Great Lakes drainage to New York.

HABITS

A fish of many habitats, the bigmouth shiner is reported in small streams with sandy bottoms and some current; in muddy streams; off sandy beaches; and in larger, warm tributaries. The food of this species consists of midge larvae, fragments of aquatic insects, and diatoms. The bigmouth shiner seldom exceeds 3 inches in length.

ECONOMIC VALUE

A common forage species, this shiner is undoubtedly used as bait although it may be unrecognized due to its similarity to other species. —R.A.J.

BIGMOUTH SLEEPER *See* Sleepers

BIG SKATE *Raja binoculata* This is the Pacific relative of the barndoor skate of the Atlantic (*which see*). The upper surface of the skin is prickly, and the outer margin of the pelvic fins is slightly concave, in contrast to that of the California skate (*which see*), which has the margin slightly convex. It is brown above, covered with numerous light spots scattered about the body. Each "wing" is characterized by a dark ocellus or eyespot, which is dark with a white rim. The underparts are pure white with black spots on the mucous pores. It grows to 8 feet in length.

LIFE HISTORY

Found from northwestern Alaska to southern California, it is most common south of central California, where it is one of the most abundant of the California skates. Eggs are laid, and the egg cases are large for skates, being about 1 foot long and lacking the filaments characteristic of the little skate (*which see*) and its relatives. These cases have 2–7 eggs, and hatching is believed to occur the year round. Adults eat crustaceans and fishes. Its flesh is good, and the wings are valued as food. —D.dS.

BILGE (1) The turn of the bottom of a boat's hull from the keel upward toward the waterline. A *hard* bilge is one that turns sharply upward.

(2) The deepest area of the hull along the keelson.

(3) Water that has stood in the bilge so long that it develops a vile odor.

BILGE KEEL The keel fitted on the outside of a boat at junction of sides and bottom to keep a boat from flipping on a turn. Also serves to throw spray away from the boat and passengers, and protects the hull from collision damage.

BILLFISH In arbitrary use as an angling term it may refer to any of a number of billfishes (family Istiophoridae) and usually includes the swordfish which, however, is the sole member of a separate family (Xiphiidae). The term "billfish" is sometimes also used to describe members of the family Belonidae (needlefishes) and the family Lepisosteidae (gars).

Taxonomically, the billfish family comprises the spearfishes, sailfish, and marlins. These are marine species of moderate to extremely large size. Characteristically, the adults of all the members of this family have the upper jaw more or less prolonged into a spear or bill, which is fairly round in cross section and is covered with small prickles. The dorsal fin is elevated, at least in its forward part, and a small second dorsal and second anal fin, each with an elongate terminal ray, appear at some distance behind the main fins. There are two small keels on each side of the caudal peduncle at the base of the tail fin.

The fishes belonging to this family are divided into three groups. The first of these composes the spearfishes (genus *Tetrapturus*). These fishes are generally rather slender, with the anterior part of the dorsal fin about as high as the greatest depth of the body, or a little higher. The air bladder is made up of a single layer of compartments, the pectoral fin folds freely back against the sides, and there are 12 abdominal and 12 caudal vertebrae in the backbone. The lateral line is simple. Within this genus, there is a progressive development of the length of the snout or spear. In the shortbill spearfish of the Pacific, the snout of the adults is scarcely longer than the lower jaw. In the longbill spearfish, an Atlantic species, the snout is somewhat longer, and in the white marlin and striped marlin (both of which are really spearfishes), the snout is very much longer than the lower jaw, forming the typical spear.

The sailfish (genus *Istiophorus*) seems to represent an offshoot from the basic spearfish line. In almost all respects, it is a typical spearfish, but the bill is rather longer and more slender, and the dorsal fin is enormously developed into the "sail" from which the species gets its name. The fin of the adult is almost twice as high as the greatest depth of the body, and the height is maintained for almost the entire length of the fin.

In the blue marlin (genus *Makaira*), the body is rather heavy the sides rounded rather than more or less flat. The dorsal fin is generally lower than the body depth. The air bladder is a single layer of compartments, the pectoral fins fold freely, but the backbone is composed of 11 abdominal and 13 caudal vertebrae. The lateral line is extremely complex, covering the whole body in a chainlike network, but is almost invariably invisible in adults.

The black marlin (genus *Istiompax*, but sometimes included in the genus *Makaira*) also has a deep-heavy body, but is slab-sided. The forward part of the dorsal fin seldom exceeds about 75 per cent of the body depth and averages about 60 per cent, thus is much lower than in the other species. The air bladder is composed of a double layer of compartments, and the pectoral fins are rigid, at right angles to the body, and cannot be folded flat without breaking the joint. As in the blue marlin, the backbone is made up of 11 abdominal and 13 caudal vertebrae, but the lateral line is simple and is generally invisible.

As far as is known, the members of this family are mostly summer spawners, with eggs about 0.85 millimeter (about $1/30$ of an inch) in diameter. Presumably, the eggs are shed in the open seas and left to their own devices. Each female may produce as many as four or five million eggs.

All the members of this group are good food fishes, although the shortbill and longbill spearfishes and the sailfish are not as good as the marlins. Smoked and eaten as hors d'oeuvres, cooked in almost any manner, or eaten raw with a good sauce, the marlins make a real treat. Spearfish and sailfish are also tasty dishes, but they do tend to be tough. *See also* Atlantic Sailfish, Black Marlin, Blue Marlin, Longbill Spearfish, Pacific Sailfish, Shortbill Spearfish, Swordfish, Striped Marlin, White Marlin.

—J.E.M.

BILL WRAPPED The condition when the leader wire has a turn or more around the spear or bill of a fish being fought by an angler. This may occur when the fish jumps or rolls, even when striking the bait. *See also* Big-Game Fishing

BLACK-AND-YELLOW ROCKFISH *Sebastodes chrysomelas* The species is one of the most highly esteemed rockfish (*which see*) of central California. It is a favorite of the angler as well as the commercial fisherman.

The black-and-yellow rockfish is characterized by strong spines on the top of its head; lower jaw not projecting; interorbital space concave; and a broad pectoral fin with thick rays. The general coloration is olive-brown to black tinged with yellow; several large, irregular yellow blotches on body; indistinct dark stripes radiate from the eye. It reaches a length of 15 inches. It is found from northern Baja California to northern California. —J.R.

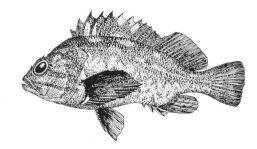

Black-and-Yellow Rockfish

BLACKBACK FLOUNDER A common name for the winter flounder (*which see*)

BLACKBANDED SUNFISH *Enneacanthus chaetodon* This diminutive, handsome sunfish has 6–8 sharply defined black bars across the straw-colored body and fins, the first bar passing through the eye. The mouth is very small, the fins are high, the scales are very large, and the tail fin is rounded. This is considered one of the handsomest of sunfish, and the Latin name means literally the "butterfly" fish.

It ranges in coastal streams from New Jersey to Florida. In New Jersey, this sunfish lives in strongly acid waters of the pine barrens with pH's of 4.0–5.0. The pH value is an index from zero to 14 of acidity and alkalinity. A pH approaching zero is highly acid, while a pH approaching 14 is highly alkaline; a pH of 7 indicates neutrality. It was found that they failed to thrive in aquaria in pH above 6.5.

LIFE HISTORY

Blackbanded sunfish build disk-shaped nests in sand in a foot of water or less. Spawning takes place in May. One pair spawned in an aquarium, and in two days the eggs hatched. Spawning again took place the following

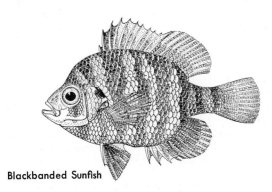

Blackbanded Sunfish

day. As in most other sunfish species, the male guards the nest. The maximum length of this fish rarely exceeds more than 2½ inches, and 4 years of age seems to be about maximum in the wild, although aquarium fish have lived up to 6 years. This secretive fish apparently feeds at night in weedy environments on bottom insect larvae and plants.

ANGLING VALUE

Because of its small size it has no angling value. —K.B.

BLACK BASS *Micropterus* **spp.** A collective, popular name for any of 6 species and 4 subspecies of the larger members of the sunfish family (Centrarchidae). Black bass are indigenous to North America but have been transplanted to other parts of the world including Europe, Africa, and Central and South America. They are all warmwater fishes, occurring in both lakes and streams, although there are distinct individual preferences in habitat. Black bass are not related to the true basses (Serranidae), which they superficially resemble. Due to widespread introductions of several black bass species, which formerly had a limited range, the problem of identification has become important to both the biologist and angler.

FIELD IDENTIFICATION

The length of the jaw or maxillary is a popular method for separating a largemouth from other bass species. If the jaw extends beyond the posterior margin of the eye (as opposed to the midpoint of the pupil in the smallmouth) the fish is generally assumed to be a largemouth. But jaw length is not always reliable. It is not unique for a largemouth to have a short maxillary and other species to have a long one. Fish, like humans, are subject to physical variations. When in doubt it requires a combination of characteristics to make an identification. The apparent separation between the spinous dorsal and fins, as well as the presence or absence of scales on the interradial membranes at the base of the soft dorsal, anal, and caudal fins will at least establish whether the fish is a largemouth or some other species.

Body coloration and the pattern of pigmentation is of local value in separating the various black bass. One can generally say that the largemouth is a dark green above fading to white below, with a dark lateral band on its sides; the smallmouth, on the other hand, has a bronze or brownish cast with dark olivaceous vertical bars. However, these generalizations do not apply to fish of all age groups in either species, nor to every locality, and color can change radically after the fish is put in a live well or killed. If you are fishing in an area where spotted and redeye bass are present also the similarities become

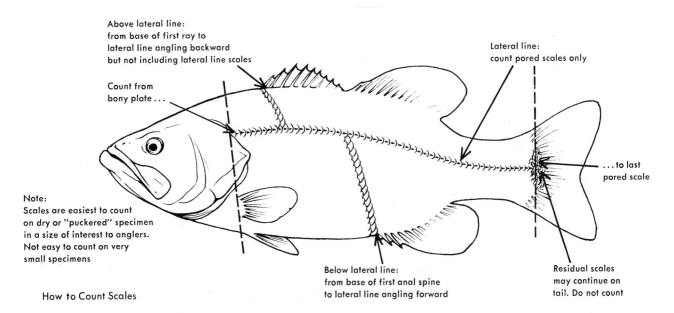

Above lateral line:
from base of first ray to
lateral line angling backward
but not including lateral line scales

Count from
bony plate . . .

Lateral line:
count pored scales only

. . . to last
pored scale

Note:
Scales are easiest to count
on dry or "puckered" specimen
in a size of interest to anglers.
Not easy to count on very
small specimens

Below lateral line:
from base of first anal spine
to lateral line angling forward

Residual scales
may continue on
tail. Do not count

How to Count Scales

more confusing, as the former has a dark lateral band and the latter a bronze body coloration and dark vertical bars. In this case it's a simple matter to rub your forefinger over the tongue of the fish and if you feel a patch of bristlelike teeth, it's a spotted bass. If the teeth are absent then it's almost certainly a largemouth (assuming that the dark lateral band is present). If it has vertical bars and no glossohyal teeth it is either a redeye or a smallmouth. If the jaw extends to the posterior margin of the pupil and the fish has bluish spots on the dorsal surface and red pectoral and caudal fins, or if the blue spots are lacking and the bass has a very prominent dark spot at the base of its tail and white pectoral and anal fins, it is one of the two forms or races of redeye. If the bass has none of these characteristics it's a smallmouth—unless you are fishing in West Texas or on Florida's Suwanee River, which narrows the choice down to a Guadalupe bass or a Suwanee bass. The Suwanee bass is distinctive not only in its robust shape and comparatively small head but in having a dusky blue-green (more nearly turquoise) coloration which extends from the underside of its lower jaw across the opercles and stomach.

If you are still in doubt the only external features left to evaluate are the number of fin-rays and scales. These counts are fairly easy to make. The spiny portion of the dorsal and anal fins can be felt quite readily with your fingertips. All species invariably have 3 anal spines and most bass have 10 dorsal spines, although a fair percentage will have 9 and a smaller percentage 11. The important thing is *not* to count the rigid, pointed spines as softrays, which are flexible and segmented or branched at their tips. There is enough variation in the number of softrays to make this a useful character. You can count the softrays just by running a pointed instrument such as a pencil along the base of the fins and actually feeling each "bump." The last ray of the dorsal and anal fins is always a double ray divided at the base and should be counted as 1. Although there is some duplicity in the number of softrays—this character wouldn't separate the

Guadalupe bass from the redeye or the Alabama spotted bass—again it's a question of geography; to be certain you can resort to scale counts. It takes a little patience to make the scale counts suggested on our chart; there are additional counts used by taxonomists, such as the number of scale rows in the cheek and the number of scales around the caudal peduncle, but these are not as easy to make (cheek scales are often embedded for example). As supplementary characters, however, the number of scales in the lateral line, as well as above and below it, can help make a final identification. While the number is seldom exact, it usually fluctuates within a definite range. In any population of northern spotted bass, for example, the lateral line count varies from 60–68 scales. A small percentage will have 59 or 69 lateral line scales and the rare individual will have less or more, but the great majority of northern spotted bass fall within the 60–68 range. This would separate the species from the more finely-scaled smallmouth with 69–77. One bass whose scale counts overlap the northern spotted is the northern largemouth, but if you look at the chart these are readily separated by the fin-ray counts as well as the absence of scales on the interradial membrane at the base of the tail, second dorsal, and anal fins on the largemouth.

Scale counts should be made on a dry specimen. If the bass is large it's fairly easy to count the pored scales in the lateral line while it's still fresh. The above and below lateral line scale counts run on an angle with the first dorsal and first anal spines as reference points. To make certain that you follow the body contours use the edge of a sheet of paper as a guide in paralleling the correct sequence from the spines to the lateral line. It helps to raise or move each scale as you count and this can be done with a thin-bladed pen knife; however, don't "pick" at the scales too much or they will pop out and confuse any recounting. The scales on the interradial membranes of the fins are often very hard to see, as these are frequently imbedded and it may require considerable picking under a magnifying glass to establish their presence. —A.J.McC.

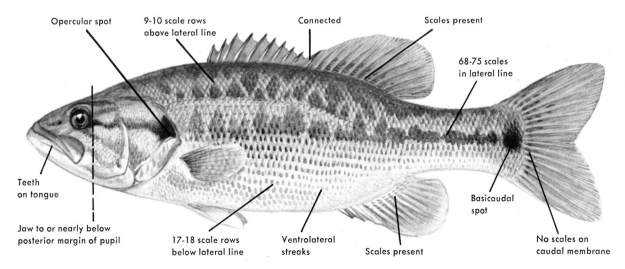

Alabama Spotted Bass

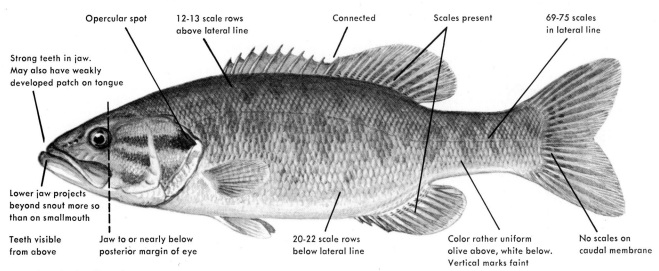

Opercular spot

12-13 scale rows
above lateral line

Connected

Scales present

69-75 scales
in lateral line

Strong teeth in jaw.
May also have weakly
developed patch on tongue

Lower jaw projects
beyond snout more so
than on smallmouth

Teeth visible
from above

Jaw to or nearly below
posterior margin of eye

20-22 scale rows
below lateral line

Color rather uniform
olive above, white below.
Vertical marks faint

No scales on
caudal membrane

Neosho Smallmouth

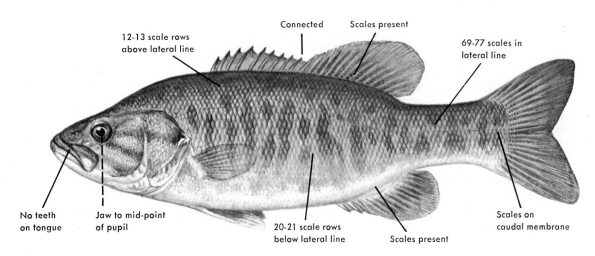

12-13 scale rows
above lateral line

Connected

Scales present

69-77 scales in
lateral line

No teeth
on tongue

Jaw to mid-point
of pupil

20-21 scale rows
below lateral line

Scales present

Scales on
caudal membrane

Northern Smallmouth Bass

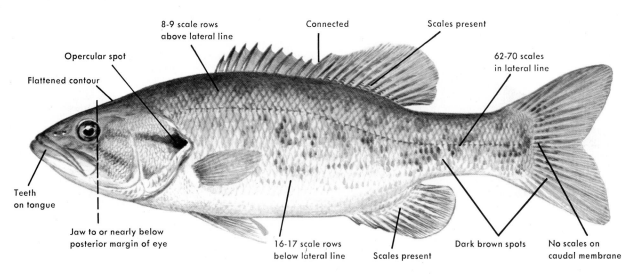

Opercular spot

Flattened contour

8-9 scale rows
above lateral line

Connected

Scales present

62-70 scales
in lateral line

Teeth
on tongue

Jaw to or nearly below
posterior margin of eye

16-17 scale rows
below lateral line

Scales present

Dark brown spots

No scales on
caudal membrane

Wichita Spotted Bass

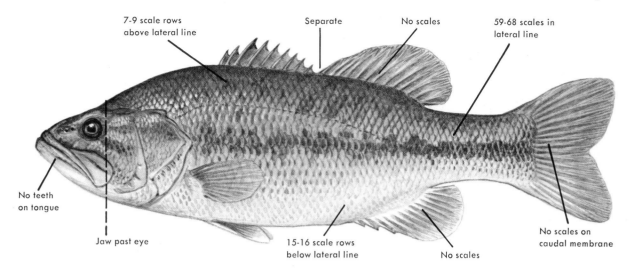

7-9 scale rows
above lateral line

Separate

No scales

59-68 scales in
lateral line

No teeth
on tongue

Jaw past eye

15-16 scale rows
below lateral line

No scales

No scales on
caudal membrane

Northern Largemouth Bass

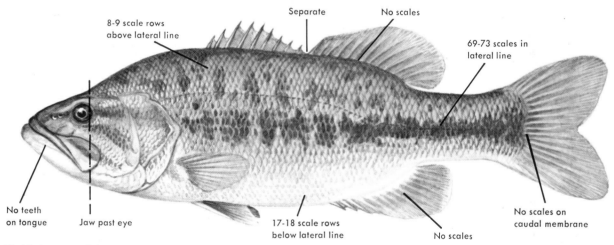

8-9 scale rows
above lateral line

Separate

No scales

69-73 scales in
lateral line

No teeth
on tongue

Jaw past eye

17-18 scale rows
below lateral line

No scales

No scales on
caudal membrane

Florida Largemouth Bass

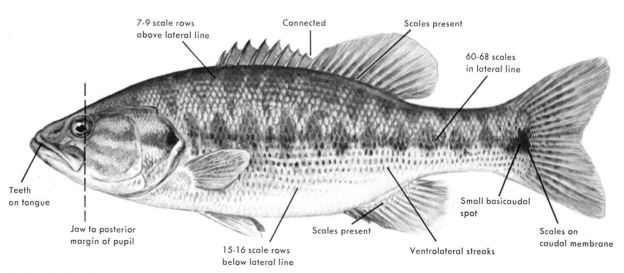

7-9 scale rows
above lateral line

Connected

Scales present

60-68 scales
in lateral line

Teeth
on tongue

Jaw to posterior
margin of pupil

15-16 scale rows
below lateral line

Scales present

Ventrolateral streaks

Small basicaudal
spot

Scales on
caudal membrane

Northern Spotted Bass

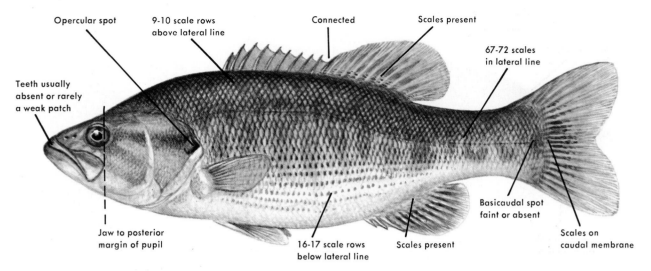

Opercular spot

9-10 scale rows above lateral line

Connected

Scales present

67-72 scales in lateral line

Teeth usually absent or rarely a weak patch

Jaw to posterior margin of pupil

16-17 scale rows below lateral line

Scales present

Scales present

Basicaudal spot faint or absent

Scales on caudal membrane

Redeye Bass (Alabama River Form)

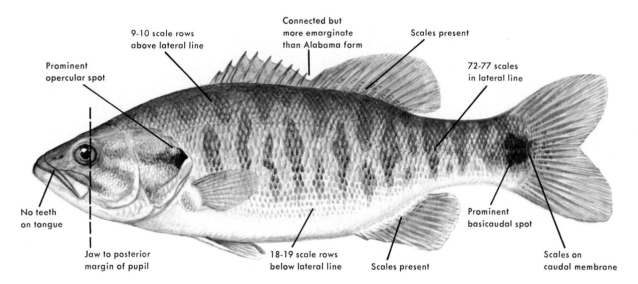

9-10 scale rows above lateral line

Connected but more emarginate than Alabama form

Scales present

72-77 scales in lateral line

Prominent opercular spot

No teeth on tongue

Jaw to posterior margin of pupil

18-19 scale rows below lateral line

Scales present

Prominent basicaudal spot

Scales on caudal membrane

Redeye Bass (Apalachicola Form)

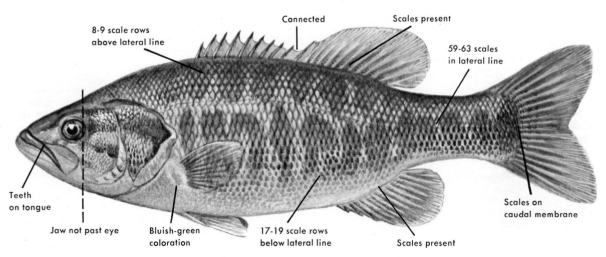

8-9 scale rows above lateral line

Connected

Scales present

59-63 scales in lateral line

Teeth on tongue

Jaw not past eye

Bluish-green coloration

17-19 scale rows below lateral line

Scales present

Scales on caudal membrane

Suwannee Bass

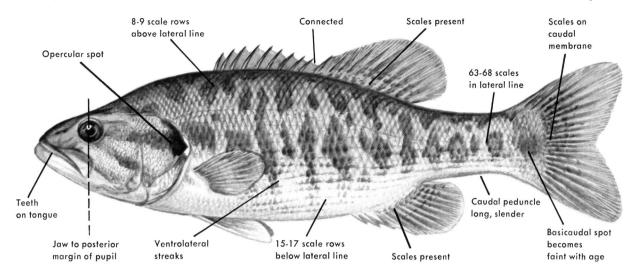

8-9 scale rows
above lateral line

Connected

Scales present

Scales on
caudal
membrane

Opercular spot

63-68 scales
in lateral line

Teeth
on tongue

Caudal peduncle
long, slender

Jaw to posterior
margin of pupil

Ventrolateral
streaks

15-17 scale rows
below lateral line

Scales present

Basicaudal spot
becomes
faint with age

Guadalupe Bass

For many years the bass angler
thought there were only two species
of black bass. Now the experts
present at least eleven varieties

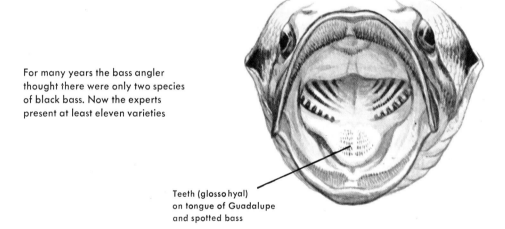

Teeth (glosso hyal)
on tongue of Guadalupe
and spotted bass

BLACK BULLHEAD *Ictalurus melas* The black bullhead, similar in appearance to the yellow and brown bullheads, is distinguished by its dark-colored or spotted chin barbels and its pectoral spines without serrations. Color dorsally is black, dark green, or yellowish-green; sides yellower or whiter; underparts bright yellow, yellow, or milk-white. Body chubby and deep at dorsal origin; angle steep from dorsal to snout. Adipose prominent with free lobe. The range of the black bullhead is from New York and North Dakota to Texas. It has been widely introduced elsewhere.

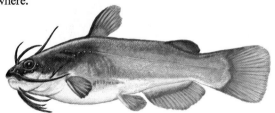

Black Bullhead

HABITS

This catfish seems to prefer silty water with soft mud bottoms. It is highly tolerant of many types of industrial and domestic pollutants and warmwater. It appears to be happy in all but cool, clear, deep water.

Spawning takes place in spring when eggs are laid in nests or depressions or sometimes attached to plants and debris. As is the habit of others of the catfish family, the black bullhead guards the nest and young for some time. A mostly carnivorous species, it subsists on insects, small fishes, and mollusks. The black bullhead is a smaller member of the catfish family and seldom reaches more than 2 pounds.

ECONOMIC VALUE

The "horned pout" of the central states, the black bullhead, is a commonly stocked farm-pond species which is well-adapted to most water conditions, easily raised, and an excellent table fish. It affords considerable sport to the young angler. —R.A.J.

BLACKCHIN SHINER *Notropis heterodon* A silvery, small shiner with a dark bank extending from chin to tail. The lateral line is incomplete with 34–35 scales in the lateral series. Scales are large everywhere on the body. The anterior edge of the lower jaw is bordered with black, and scales of the back are dark-edged. The range of the blackchin extends from southern Canada to Maine and south to Iowa and the Ohio River drainage.

Blackchin Shiner

HABITS

The blackchin shiner prefers weedy lakes over bottoms of mud and sand. Omnivorous in its food habits, the blackchin eats algae, fragments of aquatic insects, midge larvae, fish eggs, and small crustaceans. The spawning time of this species appears to be in late spring. A small minnow, this fish seldom reaches more than 2½ inches long.

ECONOMIC VALUE

Used to some extent as a bait species, the blackchin contributes greatly to the diet of lake-dwelling predatory species. —R.A.J.

BLACK COD *See* Sablefish

BLACK CRAPPIE *Pomoxis nigromaculatus* A popular freshwater panfish in the United States, like the closely related white crappie, it may grow to a fairly large size in suitable environments. The black crappie is flattened in appearance with silvery sides grading to dark olive or black on the back. Spots or blotches are scattered irregularly on the sides and on the dorsal, anal, and caudal

fins. There are 6 anal spines, and 7–8 dorsal spines. It differs from the white crappie in this respect since the white crappie has only 6 dorsal spines.

The range is from southern Manitoba to the upper St. Lawrence River in Quebec and then south through eastern Nebraska and western Pennsylvania to northern Texas and southern Florida, then north along the Atlantic Coast to North Carolina, but introduced farther north along the Atlantic drainage. Introductions have also occurred in the west and as far north as British Columbia.

The black crappie is a fish of quiet waters which seeks more vegetated areas than the white crappie. It also prefers less turbid waters than the white crappie. It is gregarious and often travels in schools. This species does not seem to reach the abundance so characteristic of the white crappie.

The black crappie is strictly carnivorous, feeding on small fishes, aquatic insects, and crustaceans.

LIFE HISTORY

The spawning takes place in late spring or early summer in saucer-shaped nests excavated amidst aquatic vegetation. The nests are crowded together in colonies in 3-6 feet of water. A half-pound female will produce 20,000–50,000 eggs, and one large female contained 158,000 eggs. Maturity is reached at two years. The average growth rate is 1–3½ inches the first year and 3½–8 inches the second year. It usually requires four years to reach 12 inches.

The best fishing for the black crappie is in the spring in the prespawning periods when the fish are congregated in large schools. Trolling with small minnows or a spinner-fly combination is very productive. Flies or poppers at dusk will also take fish. In still-fishing for crappies, small minnows about two inches make the best bait. With a bobber on the line and a good spinning or casting rod, anyone can catch his share. —K.B.

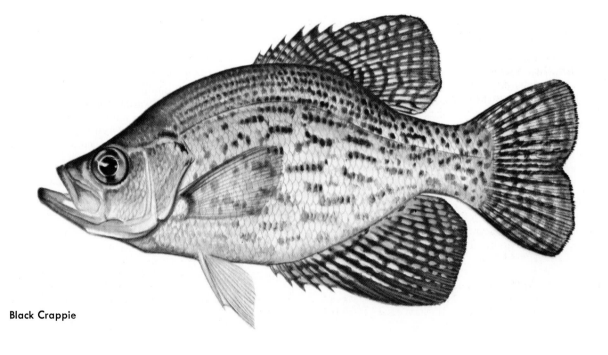

Black Crappie

BLACK CROAKER *See* Drums

BLACK DRUM *Pogonias cromis* This fish occurs along the Atlantic Coast of the Americas from southern New England to Argentina. It is common from New York southward. The species is known to reach a weight of 146 pounds. Most of the specimens caught weigh 20–40 pounds. The rod-and-reel record, a specimen 4 feet and 3 inches long, weighed 94 pounds and 4 ounces and was caught at Cape Charles, Virginia.

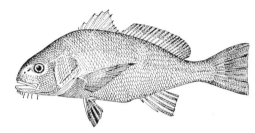

Black Drum

The black drum has a short, deep body (less than three times as long as it is deep to the base of the caudal fin). Its back is high-arched, and the ventral surface is somewhat flattened in appearance. The mouth is low and horizontal, the upper jaw projecting beyond the lower. The maxillary does not reach to the posterior margin of the orbit. Chin barbels are present. The throat of the black drum is armed with large pavementlike teeth with which it crushes shellfish. In life the body coloration is silvery with a brassy sheen, which turns to a dark gray after death. The fins are blackish. There is no black spot at the base of the caudal fin as in the case of the red drum. The black drum has 11 dorsal spines; 20–22 dorsal rays; 2 anal spines; 6–7 anal rays, and 41–45 scales along the lateral line. There are 14–16 gillrakers on the lower limb of the first arch.

ANGLING VALUE

A bottomfish which feeds on crustaceans and mollusks, the black drum is usually taken with a fishfinder (*which see*) using clams, mussels, crabs, or shrimp for bait. Although its strike is slow, the fish puts up a strong fight. Basically a shoreline fish, the black drum is caught from party boats, piers, skiffs, and in the surf. In the Gulf states it is most commonly caught in bays and lagoons; a spring run along the lower mid-Atlantic coast (from Delaware to the Carolinas) produces large specimens to the surf caster.

FOOD VALUE

The flesh of large black drum is coarse and poorly flavored. Small drum (up to 15 pounds) are quite good eating but frequently infested with parasites. These parasites, so far as known, are not injurious to man and thorough cooking would eliminate all possibility of infection. *See also* Surf-Casting   —L.R.
—A.J.McC.

BLACKFIN LOOKDOWN *See* Lookdowns

BLACKFIN SNAPPER *Lutjanus buccanella* This species occurs around southern Florida and throughout the tropical American Atlantic. A medium-sized snapper it may reach a weight of 30 pounds and over 2 feet in total length.

The blackfin snapper has 10 dorsal spines, 14 dorsal rays, and 8 anal rays. Pectoral rays normally number 17. There are 11–13 gillrakers on the lower limb of the first arch, not counting rudiments. Rows of scales around caudal peduncle 24–27, usually 25–26. Cheek scales in 6, rarely 7 rows. Upper jaw reaching to or beyond vertical from anterior margin of orbit. Pectoral fin not reaching to vertical from origin of anal fin. Anal fin rounded, not angulate posteriorly. General coloration crimson-red, silver below. Pelvic and anal fins yellow. Dorsal fin

Blackfin Snapper

crimson-red, margined with scarlet. Pectoral fin pink, its base and axil jet-black. Caudal fin orange-yellow. Black spot on sides of body absent. Eye orange.

The jet-black base and axil of the pectoral fins distinguish this species from all the other snappers.

HABITS

A bottom feeder occurring in waters of medium depth, usually at 20–60 fathoms, small individuals may occur in shallower water. It takes live or dead bait but is not known to have been taken on artificial lures.

ANGLING VALUE

Although a good fighter, specimens taken on rod and reel in shallow water are usually small. Like the silk snapper (*which see*), larger individuals may be taken in deepwater with electric reels and wire lines.

FOOD VALUE

Good eating, this commercial snapper is usually marketed as "red snapper."   —L.R.

BLACKFIN TUNA *Thunnus atlanticus* A fish of the mackerel family, it is a small, dark-colored species, with fewer gillrakers (20–24) than any other tuna, and with the finlets behind the second dorsal and anal fins which are uniformly dark, not partly yellow. An occasional fish may reach 35 pounds, but most are less than 10 pounds.

This species is found only in the western Atlantic from Cape Cod to Brazil. Its food includes fishes, squids, and crustaceans. It is one of the commonest items in the diet of blue marlin. Spawning occurs off southern Florida from April to November.

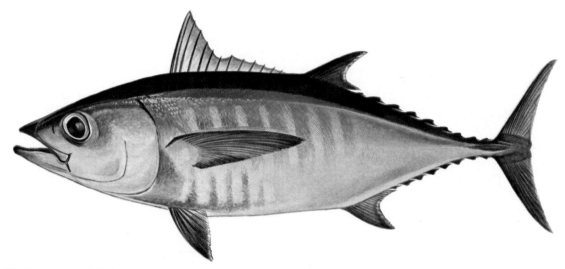

Blackfin Tuna, 6-pound Male

Blackfin tuna are taken in the commercial fishery in Cuba and are commonly caught by anglers in Florida and the West Indies. Its flesh is delicious.   —B.B.C.
    —R.H.G.

BLACKFISH   A regional name in the Gulf states for the tripletail (*which see*). Also a common name in the eastern Atlantic for the tautog (*which see*).

BLACK GROUPER *Mycteroperca bonaci*   A common grouper in southern Florida and throughout the tropical American Atlantic. It may reach 50 pounds in weight and a total length of over 3 feet.

The black grouper has 11 dorsal spines; dorsal rays 16–18, usually 17; anal rays 11–13, usually 12; and pectoral rays usually 17. Posterior nostril about as large as the anterior. Insertion of pelvic fin under or somewhat behind lower end of pectoral base. Posterior margin of caudal fin straight or somewhat convex. Sides of body with rows of rectangular dark blotches or with irregular pale lines forming a chainlike or reticulate pattern.

This grouper is distinguished from the others by the color pattern. The gag (*which see*) is commonly called "black grouper" in Florida waters, but the latter can be separated by its plain coloration and lunate caudal fin.

Young individuals may occur close to shore, but the larger adults are found on rocky bottom in deeper water.

ANGLING VALUE

A good fighter, especially when taken by trolling with natural bait, or plugs, spinners, or spoons. Very good eating. A grouper of some commercial importance.
    —L.R.

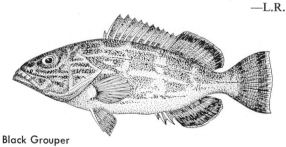

Black Grouper

BLACK JACK *Caranx lugubris*   Also called brown jack and caranx le garbage, this is primarily an insular species of almost worldwide occurrence in tropical waters.

The body and head of the black jack are very dark brown or black, and the fins and the scutes in the straight lateral line are black. Its second dorsal fin has one spine and 20–23 softrays; anal fin has two detached spines followed by one spine and 17–20 softrays. Gillrakers on the first gill arch are 6–9 on the upper limb and 19–22 on the lower limb.

The head and body are deep and moderately compressed. The head is blunt, and the profile is rounded on top with a slight concavity in front of and slightly above the eyes. The dorsal and anal fin lobes are elongated, and the dorsal-fin lobe is usually longer than the head, although these lobes are proportionally shorter on very large specimens. A few of the gillrakers on the anterior portions of the upper and lower limbs become rudimentary with growth of the fish. There are about 24–33 pointed scutes in the straight lateral line. The body and head are colored, almost uniformly, dark brown or black, and the fins and the scutes in the straight lateral line are black. The pigmentation of young specimens is unknown.

The black jack has been reported from many tropical waters of the world, principally from around offshore or isolated islands. It may be almost circumtropical in occurrence, and gaps in its known range may only be a reflection of inadequate fishing and collecting in its chosen habitats. In the western Atlantic, this species has been recorded from Bermuda, the Bahamas, Cuba, Puerto Rico, Trinidad, well offshore in the Gulf of Mexico, and from Santos, Brazil—all records of its occurrence in inshore, continental waters of the United States that have been possible to trace proved to have been of some other species. In the eastern Pacific, it has been taken at the Galápagos, Clipperton, and Revillagigedo islands, and at Los Frailes in southern Baja California. Maximum reported sizes are about 39 inches in total length and 15½ pounds (length and weight from different fish). One report from Hawaii alleged that this species grew to be 3–4 feet in length.

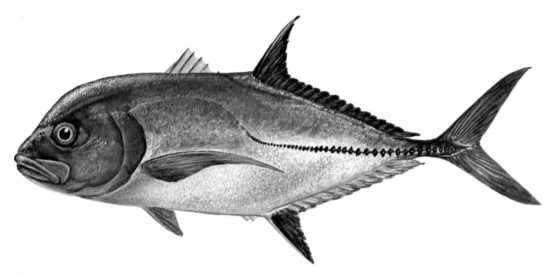

Black Jack

LIFE HISTORY

Knowledge of the life history of the black jack is essentially nil, and its early life history is an intriguing mystery. The smallest specimen that has ever been recorded is a relatively large ten inches long. Because the known specimens are taken around offshore islands, spawning should be in oceanic waters. Specimens with microscopic eggs have been taken from Clipperton Island in October and from the Revillagigedo Islands in March and April. A number of specimens from the western Atlantic were taken in deepwater (about fifty fathoms). At the Revillagigedo Islands, however, small schools rose to the surface to scramble for the ship's garbage.

ANGLING VALUE

The black jack is not accessible to most sport and commercial fishing interests. But when one is caught, it should be appreciated and appropriately recorded to further the quest for knowledge of this unusual jack. In the mid 1800's its sale was prohibited in Cuban markets because its flesh was suspected to be poisonous. A few records of its toxicity from the Indo-Pacific indicate that the larger fish are the more toxic. *See also* Carangidae, Jacks   —F.H.B.

BLACK MADTOM *Noturus funebris* Found along the Gulf Coast from western Florida to Louisiana. Anal fin with 20–25 rays. An inhabitant of springs and small creeks with a moderate current and some aquatic vegetation. Maximum length about 4 inches. Seldom used as bait, but has some value as a foragefish for bass.

Black Madtom

BLACK MARLIN *Makaira indicus* A marine species found almost entirely in the Indian and Pacific oceans, of considerable value commercially and much prized by sport fishermen. The outstanding identifying character of the black marlin is the rigid nature of the pectoral fins. In contrast to all other istiophorids, the pectoral fins of this species are held out rigidly, at right angles to the body, and cannot be folded flat without breaking the joint. This characteristic holds, even in the smallest specimens known.

The body of the black marlin is a little deeper than in other species, though closely rivaled in this respect by the blue marlin. The black, however, seems to have a more prominent shoulder hump so that it looks deeper. The sides of the body are quite flat, and this feature is emphasized in the really big ones. The lateral line is an inconspicuous double row of pores and is generally not visible in any but the smallest fish. Its vent is found just in front of the anal fin. The spear of the black marlin gives the appearance of being heavier and more robust than that of other species.

In color, the black marlin is highly variable. Most specimens are dark slate-blue above, changing more or less abruptly to silvery white below the lateral line. Occasionally, pale blue stripes may be seen on the sides when the fish are alive, but these seldom if ever persist after death. Sometimes the fish are milky-white, hence the Japanese name, *shirokajiki* or white marlin, and Chinese *pu-pi*, white skin. But the white color seldom persists long after the fish is out of the water. Sometimes a black marlin will turn an almost uniform bronze color as it comes out of the water, but this seldom lasts long. All the fins are dark.

The pelvic fins of the black marlin are shorter than in other marlins, almost always less than a foot long, regardless of the size of the fish. In all other marlins, a mature fish with unbroken pelvic fins only a foot long is a rarity.

The black marlin rivals the blue in size, being reported by commercial fishermen up to about 2,000 pounds. However, the rod-and-reel record of 1,560 pounds from Cabo Blanco, Peru, is considerably larger than the

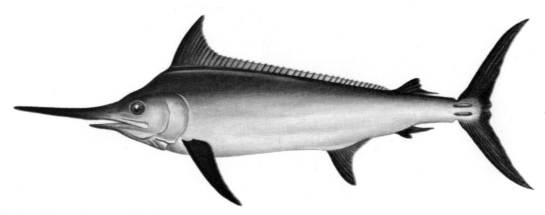

Black Marlin, 365-pound Female, Piñas Bay, Panama

corresponding record for the blue. Most of the fish over one thousand pounds seem to come from the commercial fishing areas of the central Pacific, but at Cabo Blanco fish of this size, or close to it, are not uncommon. By contrast, in other areas, such as northern New Zealand or the east coast of Africa, a fish half this size is an unusually big one. On the Atlantic side of Capetown, South Africa, ten fish taken by longline in the spring of 1961 weighed 1,082 pounds.

HABITS

The spawning season seems to be in the summer, or at least the warmer months of the year. Fish with running roe and milt have been recorded from the western Pacific from July to October. But from early November to late spring, the fish are not ready to breed. The females are larger than the males, the relative sizes being similar to those of the blue marlin. The males seldom, if ever, exceed 300 pounds. Relatively little is known of the early development. Young fish of 20–30 pounds are already typical black marlin.

The migrations of the black marlin are poorly known. All the evidence that exists indicates that they do not undertake migrations of any extent. More or less discrete local populations exist, some of them so well-defined that they can be identified and distinguished from one another. This certainly indicates that the groups do not mix to any great extent, and hence probably do not move far from home. Intensive fishing pressure in one region may influence their local abundance.

No specific studies of the food of the black marlin have appeared, but casual observation indicates that fish and squid are the chief items in the diet. They have also been reported to eat the stinging jelly fish, the Portuguese Man-of-War. That they can and occasionally do eat rather large fishes is shown by the reports of tunas up to 158 pounds in the stomachs of large black marlins. If the marlin can capture fish of this size and nature, it would seem as though there would be few animals in the sea fast enough to escape them.

DISTRIBUTION

The black marlin is primarily a fish of the Pacific and Indian oceans, although it has recently been discovered

that the species penetrates the Atlantic around the Cape of Good Hope, in the water of the Agulhas Current. As yet, however, there have been no reports of the black marlin from elsewhere in the Atlantic. Within the Indo-Pacific region, the black marlin is found from Mexico to Peru, with unverified rumors of occasional occurrences as far north as southern California. It is well-known from the central Pacific, although apparently rather scarce around Hawaii. Along the western side of the Pacific, the range extends from Japan in the north to Australia and New Zealand in the south. It is reported to be the most numerous marlin around Taiwan. In the Indian Ocean, it has been recorded all the way from Sumatra to Africa, north to the Muscat coast and south to Mauritius and South Africa.

FISHING METHODS

Longlining and sport fishing are the most important methods for catching black marlin, although a few are taken with harpoons. The fine white meat is delicious either raw or cooked, and is highly esteemed in Japan as a component of "fish sausage." About a million pounds a year of black marlin meet this fate. For the sport fisherman, trolling is the favored method of fishing, but in some areas still-fishing with live bait is practiced with good results. The smaller individuals are known to take feathers and other artificial lures. *See also* Panama, Peru, Sportfisherman   —J.E.M.

BLACKMOUTH SALMON A regional name in the northwestern United States for an immature chinook salmon (*which see*).

BLACK MULLET *See* Striped Mullet

BLACKNOSE DACE *Rhinichthys atratulus* A small, silvery minnow with a distinct, dark, lateral band, this species has the tip of the upper lip about on a level with the lower edge of the eye. Scales in the complete lateral line number 56–70. The snout projects just beyond the oblique and subterminal mouth. The blacknose dace ranges from North Dakota to the St. Lawrence drainage and south to Nebraska and North Carolina.

HABITS

The blacknose dace is abundant in small, rapid streams with clearwater. They are known to be able to withstand

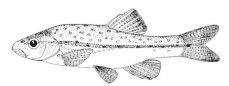

Blacknose Dace

the stagnant conditions of summer pools but prefer moving water. This dace feeds on small aquatic forms including midge larvae, mayfly nymphs, and crustaceans. Little is known of the breeding habits of this fish. It apparently spawns in spring and early summer in shallow, gravelly riffles. A small minnow, the blacknose dace seldom reaches 4 inches in length.

ECONOMIC VALUE

Of no food value, the blacknose dace provides food for trout and salmon, and is considered an excellent bait species due to its size and hardiness.　　—R.A.J.

BLACKNOSE SHARK *Carcharhinus acronotus* A small member of the requiem shark family (Carcharhinidae), it lacks a dermal ridge between the dorsal fins, and the snout is relatively long. The upper teeth are asymmetrical, and their outer margins are deeply indented, in contrast to the symmetrical teeth of the closely related blacktip and spinner sharks (*which see*). The gill slits are short, the first gill slit being only one and one-half times the horizontal eye diameter. It varies from brown to pale brown to yellowish-gray. The fins lack markings, but the snout tip is dusky in the young, becoming less distinct in adults. It grows to not more than 5–6 feet long. It is known only from the western Atlantic between Rio de Janeiro and North Carolina and the Gulf of Mexico, but it is more common in the Caribbean, although it is never really common anywhere.

LIFE HISTORY

Ripening females with near-term young have been taken off southwestern Florida, but nothing else is known of its habits. Blacknose sharks are commonly eaten by other sharks.　　—D.dS.

BLACKNOSE SHINER *Notropis heterolepis* A silvery shiner closely resembling the blackchin shiner. The black lateral band, however, does not touch the chin. A distinctive characteristic of this species is the dark posterior borders of the scales in and immediately below the lateral band expanding to form black, crescent-shaped bars. Lateral line incomplete, 34–38 scales in the lateral series. Anal rays 8, seldom 7. The range of the blacknose shiner is from southern Canada to Maine and south to Iowa and the Ohio River drainage.

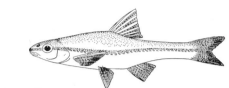

Blacknose Shiner

HABITS

The blacknose shiner is found in clear lakes and streams in association with aquatic vegetation and overall bottom types except silt. The food of this species consists of midge larvae, other aquatic insects, and microscopic plant life. The blacknose shiner apparently spawns in early summer. A small minnow, this fish averages 2½ inches in length.

ECONOMIC VALUE

Although small, this fish is used for bait for yellow perch and bass.　　—R.A.J.

BLACK PERCH *Embiotoca jacksoni* Often taken by sportsmen around pilings, in bays, and along rocky coasts. The over-all color varies from brown to being tinged with blue, yellow, orange, green, or red; anal and pelvic fins may be orange to red; anal sometimes barred with blue; lips vary from brown to orange and yellow. Length goes to 14 inches. Its range is from Bodega Lagoon, California, to Abreojos Point in Baja California. A cluster of large scales occurs between pectoral and pelvic fins; a broad frenum interrupts the posterior groove of the lower lip; a row of small scales along the anal fin base; softrays

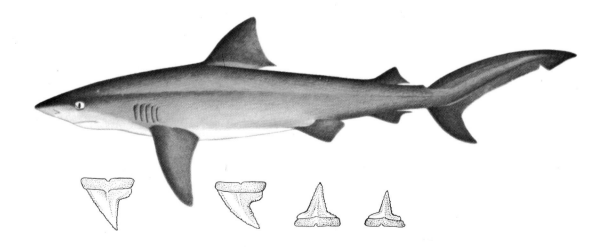

Blacknose Shark, showing teeth of upper (*left*) and lower jaws

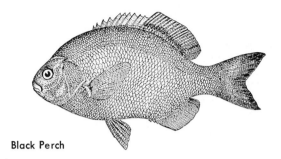

Black Perch

in anal 24–27; softrays in dorsal 19–22; dorsal softrays longer than dorsal spines; lips somewhat thick.

Life history, food, and angling similar to all surf-perch (*which see*) in general.

COMMERCIAL VALUE

Forms a minor part of the catch of "perch" in California. —J.R.

BLACK ROCKFISH Sebastodes melanops This rockfish (*which see*) is common inshore in shallow water from Pt. Conception, California, to the Gulf of Alaska. It reaches a length of 20 inches. An important food fish in northern California.

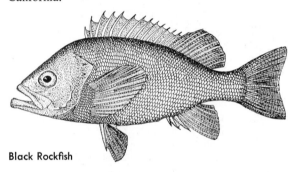

Black Rockfish

The black rockfish has a broad and strongly convex interorbital space; anal softrays usually eight, rarely 7–9; maxillary to hind border of eye; eyes large; peritoneum white. The body color is very dark, almost black shading to dirty white on belly; fins dark; lower portion of spinous dorsal membrane black spotted.

The flesh of this fish must not be allowed to stand long without refrigeration for the fats become rancid most rapidly. —J.R.

BLACK SEA BASS Centropristis striata One of the most popular bottomfish species of the northeast Atlantic Coast. The sea bass ranges from southern Massachusetts to northern Florida, with its chief center of abundance from New York (Long Island) to North Carolina. Sea bass are exclusively marine fish and, in contrast to the related striped bass, never venture into rivers. They are found in bays, sounds, and along the inshore and off-shore zones. The sea bass can readily be identified by its moderately stout body which is three times as long (not counting the caudal fin) as it is deep. It has a high back but a flat-topped head, moderately pointed snout, and one sharp spine near the apex of each gill cover. The dorsal fin contains 10 spiny rays and 11 softrays, and the caudal fin is rounded. Like many fish which inhabit rocky bottoms the color of the sea bass is variable. It ranges from smoky gray to dusky brown to a blue-black

or indigo. The color is sometimes mottled, or has the appearance of being barred with longitudinal spots of a lighter shade because the bases of the exposed parts of the scales are paler than the margins.

Sea bass are not large fish. The smallest, sometimes called "pin bass," range from a few ounces to a pound or so. The average is about 1½ pounds, and they are seldom heavier than 5 pounds. A few have been recorded at a weight of 7 pounds. The larger males are nicknamed "humpbacks" because of a pronounced rise just in back of the head.

REGIONS AND SEASONS

Sea-bass sport-fishing regions include the Cape Cod area of Massachusetts, Long Island Sound, both shores and the eastern section of Long Island (New York), and the coastal waters of New Jersey, Delaware, and North Carolina. In the New York–New Jersey region, sea bass are an important component of the warm-weather sport fishery.

Sea bass live offshore in the winter (where they are commercially netted in Virginia and North Carolina waters). In the spring, populations of them move inshore. Some remain in the ocean while others forage in sounds and bays. This spring sport-fishing run usually begins in May and lasts throughout the summer, reaching its zenith in the warmer months. When autumn chills the water they swim offshore to spend the winter. Depending upon water temperatures, the seaward journey can occur as late as October or even early November.

These fish are essentially bottom dwellers, spending most of their time on, or a short distance above, the sea floor. They favor hard bottoms in water that is clear and fairly deep. In the ocean they are caught down to depths of one hundred feet. In bays and sounds they often show a preference for water that is 20–50 feet deep. They may seek food in channels, including those with briskly moving currents, or in creeks containing at least 15–20 feet of water which are flanked by steep sod banks (they forage beneath the undercuts). Like the tautog, or blackfish, they also frequent wrecks, dock pilings, piers, and trestles which have accumulated barnacles or mussels. Sea bass are commonly found on bottoms which contain rocks or broken stone or which have shellfish beds.

The largest specimens are those hooked by deep-sea anglers. The usual weight range is 1½–3 pounds, but at the height of a run the occasional sea bass will weigh up to 4–5 pounds. In bays and other confined waters the general run of fish is smaller, with sizes up to two pounds.

METHODS AND TACKLE

The bulk of the sport-fishing catch is made by bottom-fishing from a boat at anchor. Some are also caught by jigging and by fishing from docks and piers. Any kind of light tackle, including spinning gear, will handle sea bass. The outfit used for the large ocean fish, however, should be sturdier than the tackle employed in bay angling, since the bass are heavier, depths are greater, and larger sinkers are required. Here the angler can use a light, all-purpose rod of glass or other material, about 5½–6 feet long overall, with a 1/0 reel. The reel need not have a star-drag.

For ocean bass the tackle depends upon the size of the fish running, depths and tidal currents, and the weight of the sinker required to keep the rig on the bottom. A medium spinning rod and reel comprise one outfit. A light or medium all-purpose boat rod and a 1/0 or 2/0 reel, with or without star-drag, are another. Whichever type of gear is used, the rod should have flexibility, yet possess enough "backbone" to handle fairly heavy terminal rigs and fighting fish hooked in 50–100 feet of water. A light line can be used—15-pound test is the maximum necessary. Although linen lines are employed, monofilament is most popular, particularly among spin-fishermen.

BAITS AND RIGS

Baits for the ocean-run fish include the sea clam or skimmer, hardshell clam, and a piece of shedder crab. The first-named is one of the most common baits. Fairly large baits can be used since sea bass have mouths of rather generous dimensions. Baits for the smaller bay-inhabiting sea bass include bloodworm, sandworm, shrimp, a piece of clam, squid, or shedder crab. Also employed effectively is a large mummichog, hooked carefully through the lips to keep it alive on the hook and presented in as natural a fashion as possible. Artificial lures, as a general rule, are not productive of bay-run sea bass although trolling small spoons just off the bottom has produced results.

Sea bass have rather large mouths, so hook sizes are less critical than in some other kinds of angling. A 1/0 will do for the smaller bay fish, a 2/0 for the larger sea bass. Fine wire hooks are recommended if live killifish are used. For ocean bass, sizes are matched more or less to the weights of the fish currently running, and range from 2/0 to 3/0 up to 5/0 or 6/0 for humpbacks. The popular hook patterns include the Sproat, O'Shaughnessy, Carlisle, and Eagle Claw.

A sinker completes the terminal tackle. Most commonly used in sea-bass fishing is the bank type, but more important than its design is its weight. The sinker must be heavy enough to keep the baited rig on a bay bottom or ocean floor. This weight will be determined by current strength in the area fished. A 3-ounce lead might be sufficient in a bay. In deep oceanwater, where there are fairly strong tidal currents, the required weight might be up to 8 ounces or even more. The angler will have to experiment. He can tell if his rig is where it should be by lifting it, letting it drop back, and feeling for the dull "thud" as the sinker bounces on bottom. If there is no contact the rig is being pushed up off the bottom by currents, and more weight is indicated. The rig should not be over-weighted, however, because there will be just that much more lead to tire the fish and detract from its fight.

Because some sea-bass fishing is done around wrecks and other underwater obstructions, there can be losses of terminal tackle as rigs become snagged. Sometimes a firm, steady pull will free the rig. At other times the line breaks or has to be cut. It is wise, therefore, to carry spare hooks and sinkers. A simple device helps to minimize losses of rigs in snagging. It consists of a little bag, made from cloth, which is filled with sand to the desired weight and tied to the rig with ordinary string which will break under strain. This sand bag serves as a sinker.

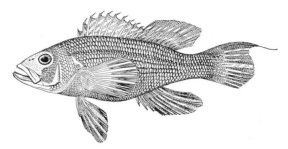

Black Sea Bass

If it fouls in an obstruction the string will break, and the angler retrieves his hooks.

BOTTOM-FISHING

For bottom-fishing one or two hooks may be used. Each is secured to the line, with or without a swivel, by its snell. One hook is tied into the line immediately above the sinker. The second, if used, is tied into the line just far enough above the first to keep the two from tangling. No leaders are needed in this rig.

The same arrangement is used for bay bass. Ordinarily no leaders are needed, but there are times when the larger fish are coy about taking a hook. The angler then might try a 2–3-foot leader on the lowest hook, securing it directly or through a swivel immediately above the sinker. If a second hook is used it can be given a 2-foot leader and attached to the line in similar fashion about 12–16 inches above the first.

Although sea bass generally are bottom feeders, there are occasions, notably in the vicinity of wrecks, when they venture a few feet above the ocean floor. For these higher-swimming fish the second hook can be rigged by its snell, without a leader, 2–3 feet above the first hook.

Another variation of the two-hook rig often is used when there are porgies (scup) in the area, too. Both hooks are attached, with or without swivels, to the line by 10-inch snells—no leaders. The bottom hook, for sea bass, is secured close to the sinker. The second hook, a smaller size to match the porgy's smaller mouth, is tied about a foot above the snell of the low hook and baited with a piece of ocean clam, squid, or other porgy bait.

JIGGING

This technique has proved effective in deep-sea angling, at anchor and drifting. The lure is a 3–4-ounce diamond jig with a bright finish (chrome is good because the flash is attractive in the water) and armed with a 3/0 or 4/0 fixed hook. This jig is tied directly to the line and serves as both lure and sinker. It need not be baited. Its movement and flash are sufficient attraction. Jigging consists simply of letting the lure drop to the bottom, then reeling it upward, imparting a little extra action to the jig with the rod tip en route. This lowering and raising process is repeated continuously, and it has accounted for good catches of ocean-run sea bass.

FISHING TECHNIQUE

Possibly because of the varying feeding habits at different ages, pin bass and their ocean-run elders often approach baits in different ways. The latter usually hit with enthusiasm, dispensing with any preliminary nibbling, and the strike frequently sets the hook. The same is true of pin bass, especially when they are hungry and when a live killifish is used. In the latter instance the strike is energetic because the bass must capture a moving bait. In any event, if the fish has not hooked itself a tightening of the line or a short upward lift of the rod will accomplish it.

Bay bass can test an angler's patience by toying with the bait. The fish might nibble on it or seize it gently and move away a few feet, "ticking" at it all the while. There will be no real pull on the rod at such times, but the angler will feel a series of twitches at the line. The procedure is to keep the line fairly taut, paying out a few feet as needed and constantly feeling for the bass's weight. When the fish finally mouths the bait and feels the hook it begins its resistance. A short upward lift of the rod tip will set the hook.

Sea bass resist capture with lively movements. There is nothing sluggish about them. They fight with spirit. The larger fish especially provide good action, even though the battle is neither spectacular nor acrobatic.

FOOD VALUE

The angler should handle a live sea bass with caution. The dorsal fin has stiff, sharp spines which can inflict painful punctures. These spines are erectile while the bass is still alive. When the fish is dead they lie flat against the back, but even then can be a menace if the handler is not careful.

Sea bass are excellent eating. Their flesh is white, firm, and delicately flavored. The smaller fish are beheaded, gutted, and scaled or skinned. Any blood pockets in the body cavity should be removed with a knife point. The tail and lesser fins are removed easily. The dorsal fin can be eliminated by "running"—making an incision on either side of it and lifting it out. Fish cooked whole should be either scaled or skinned. Larger sea bass can be dressed in a similar manner and baked, or they can be filleted, skinned, and cooked by various methods. It is particularly tasty when deep fried and served in the Chinese style of sweet-and-sour fish. —B.W.

BLACK SKIPJACK *See* Bonito

BLACKSMITH *See* Opaleye

BLACK SNAPPER *Apsilus dentatus* This is a distinctive, deep-water snapper that is placed in a genus of its own. It belongs to the family Lutjanidae, a huge group consisting of about 25 genera and 250 species. The family is worldwide in distribution and most of the species inhabit the shallow waters of the tropics. The black snapper is found only in the Western Atlantic from southern Florida to the West Indies. It is quite rare in most of its range, but is reported to be common in Cuban waters.

The color of the black snapper is dusky violet above and paler on the sides. The inside of the mouth and fins are the same violet or brownish color, except that the anal and ventral fins have blackish tips and the soft dorsal has some olive shades.

Other distinguishing characters of the black snapper are dorsal fin spines 10, softrays 10; anal fin spines 3, softrays 8; scales above lateral line 7, along lateral line 60, below 16; other scales in rows running parallel to lateral line, 7 rows on cheek, 2 rows on interopercle,

1½ on subopercle, and 4 on temporal region. Gillrakers numerous; the longest $^2/_5$ diameter of eye; about 17 on lower half of gill arch.

Head length about 3 and body depth about $2^5/_7$ in standard length. Body rather deep, oblong, elliptical, compressed; profile from snout to nape a little convex; snout relatively short and blunt, about 3½ in head length; eye large, $3^5/_6$ in head; interorbital space convex, $3^4/_5$ in head. Mouth small; maxillary broad, almost reaching pupil, 2½ in head. Upper jaw with a narrow band of villiform teeth, outside of which is a series of larger, caninelike teeth; lower jaw with a single series of small teeth, about six of those in front larger, similar to the larger teeth of upper jaw; inside of this series a comparatively wide band of villiform teeth in front of jaw only; tongue without teeth; vomer with an A-shaped patch of teeth.

LIFE HISTORY

Nothing is known of the life history of the black snapper at present. It attains a length of about 1 foot and apparently prefers a depth of 100 feet or more. It is sometimes caught by handlines incidental to some other commercial fishery. —J.C.B.

BLACK SNOOK *Centropomus nigrescens* This species occurs on the Pacific side of tropical America, from Baja California southward to northern Peru. It is known to reach a total length of 30 inches, but is reportedly larger. This snook is called *robalo prieto* in Mexico and is closely related to the snook (*which see*).

The black snook has 67–75 lateral scales. Gillrakers 9–11 on lower limb of first arch, not including rudiments. Anal rays 6. Pectoral rays 14–16, usually 15. Second anal spine not reaching to vertical from caudal base. Pectoral fin not reaching to vertical from tip of pelvic. Pelvic fin not reaching to anus. Maxillary reaching to or beyond vertical from center of eye.

This species is distinguished from the other Pacific snooks by the number of dorsal rays which is 9, rarely 10, instead of nearly always 10.

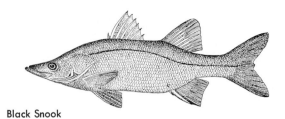

Black Snook

The black snook occurs along the coast in saltwater, in addition to bays, estuaries, canals, and the lower course of streams. It takes live bait and artificial lures.

ANGLING VALUE

Fights well, like other species of snook. Live shrimp, top-minnows, and finger mullet are the best natural baits. Good sport on spinning, fly, or plug tackle.

Should be skinned, especially large specimens. Good for baking or broiling. This snook is commercially important throughout most of its range. —L.R.

BLACKSPOTTED PIKE *See under* Northern Pike

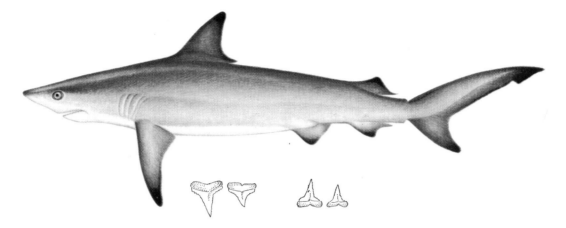

Blacktip Shark, showing teeth of upper, *left*, and lower *right*, jaws

BLACKTIP SHARK *Carcharhinus limbatus* A widespread tropical shark, the blacktip shares the characteristic black tips of the pectoral fins with several other species, including its close relative the spinner shark (*which see*), and the lack of a dermal ridge between the dorsal fins. It resembles the spinner shark but has a shorter, less pointed snout and larger eyes. The eye of the blacktip is about one-fifth the snout distance compared to about one-ninth that of the spinner, and the gill slits of the blacktip are relatively short, the first being about two-thirds of the distance between the nostrils. The teeth are regularly serrated from their bases to their tips. The body is dark gray grading through yellowish to gray-blue above, with white to yellowish-white beneath. A dark band extends along the side up to about the pelvic region. The pectoral fins are black-tipped, as are the dorsal and anal fins and the lower lobe of the caudal fin, especially in young.

LIFE HISTORY

This small shark seldom grows to more than about 6 feet. An individual 5½ feet long weighs only about 68 pounds. It occurs through the tropical Atlantic from Madeira to the Cape Verde Islands and from southern Brazil to Cape Cod. The blacktip is also reported from lower California to Peru. Although it is also recorded from the Indian Ocean area, it is not definitely known if this is the same as the Atlantic species. Like the spinner shark, it is an active, strong-swimming shark which is frequently seen leaping from the water. It occurs both inshore and off, where it pursues small fishes such as menhaden, sardines, butterfish, and stingrays.

ANGLING VALUE

In the Gulf and Caribbean, it is one of the most common sharks, and is often caught by commercial fishermen. It readily takes a bait and puts up a determined fight. The blacktip is one of few sharks which will strike artificial lures with any consistency; large bucktail flies, jigs, and plugs are effective. This shark can be stalked on the flats or taken at the edges of channels and banks. *See also* Saltwater Fly-Fishing, Shark Fishing —D.dS.

BLEEDING SHINER *Notropis zonatus* One of the most beautiful minnows. As it moves, it flashes like bright silver, and when ready for spawning the males become bright red on the lower part of the body and head and the fins become orange-red except on the borders. It has a broad black mid-dorsal stripe and a distinct lateral stripe, with a secondary stripe above which is separated from both the lateral and dorsal stripes. In the young there is a pair of blackish crescents between the nostrils. Its large dorsal fin is submedian; there are usually 9 anal rays; the lining of the peritoneal cavity is blackish; the pharyngeal tooth count is 2, 4-4, 2. The eye is ⅓–¼ as long as the head. The maxillary does not reach the eye. Mature specimens attain a length of about 5 inches.

LIFE HISTORY

The bleeding shiner is one of the most characteristic fishes of the Ozark region of Missouri and Arkansas and is very abundant in the clear streams of the Ozarks, where it prefers pools with moving water. It is found less frequently in fast riffles or quiet waters. It spawns from mid-April to mid-June in gravel-bottomed riffles.

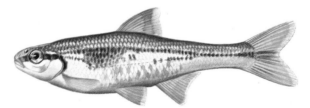

Bleeding Shiner, 4-inch Breeding Male

The unusual red and black coloration of the males at this time and the fact that large numbers spawn together makes the observation of their spawning one of the most memorable activities to be seen during a spring visit to an Ozark stream.

This is a good bait species which is readily trapped or seined. Its abundance in the pools of Ozarks streams makes it one of the more frequently used bait fishes.

—C.A.P.

BLIND CASTING An expression used in both fresh- and saltwater fishing which means casting without seeing fish. The angler relies on his knowledge of the water and probable locations or "lies" of fish.

BLOOD WORM *See under* Live Bait

BLOWFISH A regional name for the puffer in north-eastern United States. *See also* Northern Puffer, Smooth Puffer, Southern Puffer

BLUE ANGELFISH *See* Queen Angelfish

BLUEBACK HERRING *Alosa aestivalis* Like the other members of the herring family, it is a slab-sided, silvery species with a small, terminal mouth. It differs from the other herrings in having a black peritoneum (intestinal lining) and a darker, more slender body. A weight of almost 1 pound and a length of about 15 inches have been

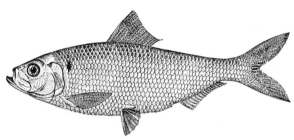

Blueback Herring

reported. It is found along the Atlantic Coast from Maine to Florida, being more common in the southern part of its range. Like the other species of the genus *Alosa*, it ascends tributaries in the spring for spawning. The young feed on plankton, while the adults eat fish and small crustaceans. It is not particularly important commercially, most of the catch being reported in the catch for the alewife (*which see*). The flesh has little value commercially. —D.dS.

BLUEBACK TROUT *Salvelinus alpinus* The blueback trout is very similar to the Marston trout, and the Sunapee trout, and the three are presently considered a landlocked population of Arctic char (*which see*). Blueback trout were once common to the Rangely Lakes of Maine, but they became extinct here in the early 1900's. Their distribution today is limited to less than a dozen ponds in Maine.

Despite its present taxonomic status the blueback trout (formerly *S. oquassa*) has very specific habitat and food requirements which are distinct from the ordinary Arctic char and its natural associate the brook trout. In Maine lakes the upper limit of the blueback's depth distribution is correlated with the cold waters of the hypolimnion, where it feeds on benthic organisms, mainly plankton.

ANGLING VALUE

Due to its relatively small size (6–12 inch average) and limited distribution the blueback trout has little angling value. However, this discrete population is of biological interest and efforts are being made to preserve the stock. This char occupies an ecological niche not utilized by the brook trout. Bluebacks can be caught by deep jigging with very light spinning tackle using small spoons and on occasion with natural baits. —A.J.McC.

BLUE CATFISH *Ictalurus furcatus* A pale blue catfish with a deeply forked tail, its anal fin contains 30–36 rays and is straight on its rear edge. The eyes appear to be located in the lower half of the head. The color is silvery pale blue above, lighter on the sides, and silvery or milk-white below. The blue catfish is distributed in large rivers from Minnesota and Ohio southward into Mexico, and has been introduced into Atlantic Coast streams.

Less fond of turbid waters than the other catfish, the blue catfish prefers the clearer, swifter streams. In its natural range it was apparently more abundant prior to extensive impoundment of streams. It is found over stream bottoms of bedrock, boulders, gravel, or sand. Feeding in swiftly flowing rapids or chutes, the blue catfish prefers fish and crayfish in its diet. Spawning in the manner of others of its family, the blue catfish builds its

Blue Catfish

nest in sheltered areas under rocks or logs where both male and female assist in rearing the young. The blue catfish is the largest of the catfish family, sometimes reaching over 100 pounds, although the average is less than 50 pounds.

ANGLING VALUE

Due to its large size and strong fighting qualities as well as its fine flavor the blue catfish is a favorite of many anglers. It is considered one of the best gamefish of its family. "Jugging" has been a popular method of capturing this fish. A large jug is tied to 9–10 feet of heavy

Blueback Trout

twine and a large hook. Baited with a pound or so of meat or fish, the whole rig is floated down a chute in fastwater with the angler following in a boat.   —R.A.J.

BLUE CORVINA   *See* Shortfin Corvina

BLUE CRAB *Callinectes sapidus*   The common crab of the Atlantic, this is the most important crustacean commercially in the United States following shrimp and lobsters. Although many species of crabs are eaten in the United States, this species is best-known among seafood lovers. Also known as the hardshell or softshell crab, it belongs to the family of swimming crabs (Portunidae), which includes the green crab (*which see*), and which is generally characterized by having the last pair of legs flattened into paddles for swimming. The claws are long and pointed, and the anterior part of the shell, or carapace, has numerous sharp teeth. The shell is oval and about twice as wide as it is long, with the lateral tips of the shell elongated into sharp spines. The shell varies from a dark blue or blue-green to brownish with mottlings of blue and cream, with scarlet markings and whitish or cream below. It grows to about 8 inches across.

LIFE HISTORY

The blue crab is found from Cape Cod to Florida and the Gulf of Mexico, straying occasionally to Nova Scotia and Uruguay, and into France, Holland, and Denmark. A closely related species (*C. ornatus*) is commoner in warm waters. The recent abundance of the crab in Israel is possibly due to its transport there in ship ballast. It inhabits saltwater, as well as freshwater where chlorides exist, but its center of abundance is in brackish water, in muddy bays, and in estuaries.

Blue crabs occur inshore during warm weather, but during the winter they move into deeper water, entering a state of semihibernation, although they are active throughout the year. It is an active swimmer and can move readily between the sand, into which it can burrow, and the upper water layers.

The spawning season is May to October in middle Atlantic waters, with a peak in late August and early September. Crabs move inshore, and the mating process occurs in brackish water. Eggs are laid in June, July, and August, two to nine months following mating, depending on which time of the year the first mating occurs. The egg-carrying females are referred to as sponge crabs, cushion crabs, or berry crabs, and the eggs when first laid are bright orange. Males may mate with several females, and some females may spawn twice or more. From ¾ of a million to more than 2 million eggs are carried by a female, and only a few survive to adulthood, the predation on young crabs by fishes and invertebrates and other factors being high.

The larval crabs pass through several marked changes in shape, as is the case with many saltwater crustaceans, which superficially resemble shrimp. Survival of the young stages is closely related to favorable water temperatures, salinity, and the availability of suitable food. The young stages reach the adult form in about a month, following several moults, and begin migrating inshore in midsummer, moving upstream to continue their development and to seek a ready supply of food. Crabs grow rapidly through the young and juvenile stages, and within a year to a year and a half, adult size may be reached. They may live to an age of 3½ years, but most live less than a year.

Blue crabs migrate downstream in the fall, preparatory to a semihibernation in deeper water during the winter, while an additional downriver migration, during May, comprises recently mated females from spring and the previous fall.

They are pugnacious and will eat almost anything, from fresh and dead meat to plants, including roots, leaves, seaweed, and decomposing grasses and seaweeds. They are eaten by a number of fishes during various parts of their life cycle, and one fish, the cobia (*which see*), regularly feeds on them.

Blue Crab

ECONOMIC VALUE

Commercially, the blue crab is of great importance and is the principal source of supply for softshell crabs. It is taken in dredges, trawls, nets, pots, seines, trotlines, and dipnets, amounting to a value of about $10,000,000 a year to the fisherman. The lucrative hardshell and softshell crab industry is supplanted by limited use of crabs for chum and for fishpots. The product for human consumption is sold fresh, frozen, and canned, being used in fresh cocktails, salads, soups, and barbecue dinners.

—D.dS.

BLUEFIN TUNA *Thunnus thynnus*   One of the largest marine gamefish, the bluefin tuna is a member of the mackerel family. It has shorter pectoral fins (less than 80 per cent of head length) than the other American tunas. It also has more gillrakers on the first branchial arch (31–43) than any other species of *Thunnus*. The ventral surface of the liver is covered with striations as in the albacore and bigeye tuna. The body of the bluefin is robust, tapering to a pointed snout. Its color is generally dark steel-blue above with green reflections, blending to a silvery-gray on the ventral surface. Small bluefins have white spots and streaks forming vertical lines on the lower sides. The bluefin has two dorsal fins, the first retractable and the second fixed. There are 9–10 yellow finlets with black edges behind the second dorsal fin, and 8–10 finlets behind the anal fin. The tail is lunate.

Until recently, some researchers believed that one or two species of bluefin existed in the Atlantic Ocean and two or three more in the Pacific and Indian Oceans. It now seems fairly certain that the bluefin tuna is a single worldwide species, but subspecific variation is still in need of further study.

The body temperature of a large bluefin tuna may be as much as 3°C. or more above that of the seawater. This is because the heat generated internally cannot be dissipated rapidly through the thick body muscles. The midlateral strip of dark red meat (called *chiai* by the Japanese) is caused by an abundance of blood vessels together with an accumulation of myoglobin (muscle hemoglobin). This dark meat is rich in stored carbohydrates and may be an energy reserve.

Bluefin tuna grow to a large size; although the rod-caught record is a 977-pound fish, taken off Nova Scotia (St. Ann Bay), they are known to exceed 1,100 pounds, and there are unconfirmed reports of 1,500-pound fish.

DISTRIBUTION

Bluefin tuna are worldwide in distribution, being caught chiefly in temperate and subtropical waters. In the western Atlantic concentrations of tuna appear inshore seasonally in the Bahamas and as far north as the Labrador Current. For a number of years, the late spring run of large bluefin in the Bahamas was thought to be part of a yearly migration to New England and as far north as Newfoundland. However, fish tagged in the Bahamas have been recaptured off Norway, proving that at least some individuals undertake a transatlantic migration. Other smaller fish have been tagged off New England and recaptured in various European areas. Thus the exact migration pattern is not yet certain.

SPAWNING AND GROWTH

The spawning grounds of western Atlantic bluefin tuna have not been well-defined. Large fish in or near spawning condition have been reported from Windward Passage in the Antilles, Straits of Florida, and the northern Bahamas from late April until early June, and medium-sized fish in breeding condition have been caught off the continental shelf south of New England in June. A female may shed from one to several million eggs. The young apparently grow very rapidly at first, reaching a size of about 8½ inches by early July. By the next July they have attained a length of nearly 2 feet. A 7-foot bluefin is about 10 years old.

FOOD

Bluefin tuna feed on a variety of fishes, squids, and crustaceans. Whatever is available seems to be eaten. Thus stomachs of bluefins feeding near land may be filled with herring, sand lance, or hake, while those offshore will often contain, among other items, luminous deepsea fishes.

COMMERCIAL VALUE

Bluefin tuna have been taken commercially for centuries in the Mediterranean and eastern Atlantic using set nets and hook and line. They are taken in pound nets and purse seines in New England and mainly by purse seines in the eastern Pacific. The total world catch of all tunas is in excess of 800,000 tons. Japan has the leading fishery in annually taking about 50 percent of the total. Long lining, a method in which one boat may set fifty miles of lines with two thousand hooks, is practiced throughout the world. The Japanese prize the flesh of the bluefin even more than that of other tunas.

ANGLING VALUE

The bluefin is considered one of the strongest and most active gamefish. There are many famous tournaments held each year for giant bluefins at such locations as the Bahamas, Rhode Island, and Nova Scotia. —B.B.C.
—R.H.G.

DISTRIBUTION AND MIGRATIONS OF NORTH ATLANTIC BLUEFIN TUNA

The bluefin tuna, an important food and gamefish, is noted for its size, speed, and strength, its schooling habits, its abundance and wide distribution, and its dramatic and little-known migrations. It is by far the most abundant teleostean fish which commonly reaches weights of over 500 pounds. Its distribution is apparently circumglobal in temperate and subtropical waters, extending into the tropics in the winter and, in one area at least, above the Arctic Circle in summer.

North Atlantic bluefin differ slightly from those of the Pacific and Indian Oceans, and the subspecific names *T. thynnus* and *T. thynnus saliens* have been tentatively assigned. Bluefin tuna have been taken by Japanese longline fishermen in the South Atlantic, but few data on them are available for comparative studies. Individuals resembling the North Atlantic form and others resembling the Indo-Pacific variety have been taken in South African waters.

Bluefin-tuna fisheries of great antiquity exist over much of the Mediterranean Sea and its Atlantic approaches, and the species also occurs in the Bosporus and Black Sea. Additional commercial fishing takes place in the Bay of Biscay, in the North Sea, and along the coasts of Norway. Sport fishing for bluefin is very popular along the north coast of Spain and is also practiced in the Öre Sund between Denmark and Sweden. The species has been recorded from the North Atlantic islands of Madeira, the Azores, Iceland, and Bermuda.

Exploratory longline fishing has shown that the bluefin occurs over vast areas of the northwestern Atlantic, the Gulf of Mexico, and the northern Caribbean in winter and spring. In North American waters, it is seasonally important to sport fisheries from Cape Hatteras to Newfoundland and off the northwestern Bahamas, often being the most abundant gamefish of its size available. Commercial fishing for this tuna in the northwestern Atlantic has been on a modest scale, but now appears to be on the increase.

Western North Atlantic The range of the bluefin tuna extends over vast areas of the western North Atlantic, but its occurrences vary drastically with the time of year and with the size of fish. In analyzing the temporal distribution of the species, we have found it convenient to divide the year arbitrarily into periods somewhat different from the seasons. These are July through October, a summering period corresponding roughly to the period of maximum water temperature; November and December, apparently a migratory period for the bluefin; January through April, a wintering period corresponding roughly to the lowest water temperatures; and May and June, another period of migration.

There are three major size groups in the fishery, each with a distinct distributional pattern. These we have called small (5–69 pounds, 1–4 years old), medium (70–269 pounds, 4–9 years old), and large or giant (270 pounds and over, 9 years old or older). The cycles of these groups overlap during parts of the year, and of course individuals of nearly marginal sizes may be found with one group or the other. There are also some differences in the cycles of the respective ages comprising the small group and possibly of those comprising the medium one also, but the major changes usually occur at about the sizes indicated.

The summer occurrence of bluefin tuna in coastal waters from New Jersey to Nova Scotia has long been known to commercial fishermen, and the first Atlantic sport fisheries for the species developed in this area. The spread of the big-game and commercial fisheries and exploratory efforts have shown that this summer habitat extends from Cape Hatteras to southern Labrador, including the Continental Shelf at least as far northeast as the Nova Scotia banks.

In this area, the first bluefin are usually taken in late May or early June, frequently in Cape Cod Bay or near Gloucester, and they are generally large fish. The small individuals usually appear next, in late June or early July. This may occur anywhere from Cape Cod to just north of Cape Hatteras. The medium-sized bluefin generally enter the coastal fishery last. They are sometimes numerous off northern New Jersey or eastern Long Island in July, but do not ordinarily appear in the Gulf of Maine, where they are more usually abundant, until August, or in Nova Scotia waters until September. This size group also tends to be the last to depart in the fall, being available to the fishery well into October and sometimes into November, after the larger and smaller individuals have disappeared.

The geographical distribution of the respective size groups also varies in this season. In coastal waters most of the small bluefin are usually found south and west of

Cape Cod, and the larger ones north and east of eastern Long Island. The small fish are also found far to the eastward on the shoals and banks, however, while the medium and large ones are sometimes abundant in the New York Bight and even further south. Occurrences of bluefin tuna in this season are extremely erratic. Some long-term trends have been discernible, as well as changes from year to year and within seasons. Possibly the long-term changes are related to similar changes in water temperature, while the more sudden ones may be caused by local changes in water conditions or in the availability of food. Within these limitations, however, there are certain areas where bluefin tuna tend to concentrate and furnish good fishing. For the larger fish, these include the "Mud Hole" off New York Harbor, the Rhode Island-Block Island area, Cape Cod Bay, the northern edge of Stellwagen Bank, Ipswich and Casco bays in United States waters, Trinity Ledge, the Tusket Islands (Wedgeport) and St. Margaret's Bay in Nova Scotia, and Conception Bay, Newfoundland. The smaller fish are usually found over larger areas and further offshore, anywhere from the Chesapeake capes to Cape Cod. In the latter area, they have sometimes been very abundant close to shore in Cape Cod Bay and off Chatham. Commercial fishermen have repeatedly taken extremely heavy catches of small to medium bluefin in the South Channel area 40 to 50 miles east of Chatham in late summer and early fall. Remarkable longline catches in the fall at Hydrographer and Veatch canyons at the southern end of South Channel indicate that at least a great many of the bluefin tuna leave the Gulf of Maine through this passage. Observations of offshore swordfishermen and spotting-plane pilots, as well as some longline fishing, suggest that bluefin enter the Gulf of Maine in quantity by the same route in June.

Four recaptures of small tagged bluefin tuna show movements or shifts of habitat within the summering area. Three of these were marked off Martha's Vineyard. One was caught off Block Island a year later weighing 23 pounds, a 35-pounder was recaptured at Provincetown within six weeks of its release, and the last was recaptured in the latter locality after a year at large, having attained a weight of 84 pounds. A 65-pound bluefin

Bluefin Tuna, 502-pound Female, Conception Bay, Newfoundland

tagged off Chatham was recaptured two years later off Gloucester, having doubled its weight in this period.

Longline fishing has indicated the almost complete absence of the bluefin tuna from the oceanic waters of the northwest Atlantic during the July–October period. Nearly all the catches have been made at or very near the edge of the shelf early in July or late in October, probably representing the end of the migration into the summering area and the beginning of the one away from it respectively.

During the late fall, the bluefin tuna move from their summer feeding grounds to their wintering areas, which are much more extensive. Exploratory longline fishing has revealed dense concentrations of medium-sized individuals, sometimes with considerable admixtures of smaller ones, in the canyons along the edge of the Continental Shelf, from Hudson Canyon off New York to Lydonia Canyon off the southeast part of Georges Bank, in late October and November. Lesser numbers were taken along or near the one thousand-fathom curve eastward to Browns Bank, and also at Norfolk Canyon, but the bluefin were apparently still absent from the area southward toward the Gulf Stream. In December, however, a few individuals have been taken by longline about 350 miles east of the Bahamas, and by rod and reel off southeastern Florida.

In the period of minimum water temperature, January through April, medium-sized bluefin tuna have been taken over a large area from the edge of the Continental Shelf to 50° W., and from 36° to 42° N. A few small and large individuals were caught with them, but the giants range south to the Bahamas and the Greater Antilles and into the Gulf of Mexico and the Caribbean Sea. Concentrations of them have been found in the northern Gulf of Mexico and the Windward Passage. The smaller individuals, with the exception of larvae and very small juveniles, are rarely found south of 35° N. In fact very little is known about the distribution of the small bluefin in this period, beyond scattered oceanic longline catches and a few by sport fishermen off Cape Hatteras. The eastward limit of this wintering area has not been determined.

The northward run of giant bluefin along the edge of the shelf off Cat Cay in the northwestern Bahamas from early May to mid-June is the most dramatic evidence of the general spring migration of the species. Recent explorations suggest a connection through the Old Bahama and Santaren channels between this run and the April concentration in the Windward Passage. However, large bluefin have also been taken in the northern Gulf of Mexico into June, and these probably also contribute to this run. The fish are very rarely encountered on the west side of the Straits of Florida, and the available evidence indicates that most of them remain east of the Gulf Stream to a point beyond Cape Hatteras. It has been generally supposed that the giant tuna passing Cat Cay migrate to the northwestern Atlantic coastal waters, but recent tagging results raise some doubts about this theory. Our longline fishing has also revealed the presence of giant bluefin tuna over a great area east of the Bahamas, extending from San Salvador to Walker Cay and about one hundred miles to the eastward.

In May the medium-sized bluefin are found in the same areas as during the winter, but tend to be more concentrated. These concentrations, some of them comparable to those found along the one thousand-fathom curve in the fall, have been discovered just north of the Gulf Stream. On one occasion many of these fish were tagged, and one was recaptured in Cape Cod Bay three months later. In June, most of the small and medium-sized bluefin are on or closer to the Continental Shelf, and more large individuals are taken near the northern edge of the Gulf Stream. On one occasion, large numbers of small individuals were caught by longlining just south of the South Channel in early June. At this time schools of them have also been observed off the eastern channel between Georges Bank and the Nova Scotia banks, and many sport-fishing catches have been reported from the Hatteras area. The movement of the bluefin tuna from the oceanic waters onto the Continental Shelf by late June or early July completes their year cycle.

In the above discussion we have not considered the very small bluefin tuna weighing less than 5 pounds, which, although they must be extremely numerous, are little-known and are not significant in the fisheries. The indications are that the bluefin spawn over wide areas and a considerable period of time in the western Atlantic. The giants evidently spawn in the southern areas in April and May, while the medium-sized ones apparently spawn north of the Gulf Stream somewhat later. Ripe or nearly ripe giant bluefin have been taken east of the Bahamas and in the Windward Passage area in April, and in the Gulf of Mexico in May. Juveniles less than 3 inches long have been collected in the Windward Passage area in late April, in the western Gulf of Mexico in late May and early June, and off the Carolinas in early June. In the northern area, ripe or nearly ripe medium-sized fish have been caught along the edge of the Shelf and toward the Gulf Stream off southern New England and the banks in June, and juveniles less than 3 inches long have been collected near the edge of the Continental Shelf off the middle Atlantic states late in July.

In some years, large numbers of larger juveniles, about 12–15 inches long, are caught or observed passing northward through the Straits of Florida in July. Similar fish have been caught there, at gradually increasing sizes and in lesser numbers, through the remainder of the summer and the fall into early winter. Others have been taken in the Gulf of Mexico in September and December. All these were evidently spawned by the giant bluefin in the southern areas. Very small bluefin have also been taken by trolling off South Carolina in September, and off Hatteras in October, January, and March. Considerable runs of these fish have occurred in occasional years at various areas from the Chesapeake capes to Cape Cod, from late July into October. They are usually most abundant in September, and in the New Jersey area. It is uncertain whether these fish are the results of the spawning of the giant bluefin in southern waters or of the medium-sized ones in the northern areas. The wide size range of those taken off New Jersey suggests that both spawning groups may be represented, or that the 12–18-inch fish may actually be slightly more than a year old rather than young of the year.

Western North Atlantic Summary From the end of June through October, bluefin tuna have been found almost exclusively on the Continental Shelf between Cape

Hatteras and Newfoundland and southern Labrador. In general, the smaller individuals occupy the southwestern part of this range and the larger ones the northeastern part. By November, most of the bluefin have left the coastal waters, and large concentrations of medium-sized and small individuals have been found along the edge of the Shelf off southern New England. They evidently migrate to their wintering grounds during this month and possibly December, but information on their distribution in the latter month is meager. During the period January–April, the species is spread over a vast area, probably extending from the Continental Shelf to a line from the southeastern corner of the Grand Banks to Puerto Rico, and including the Gulf of Mexico and northern Caribbean. The bluefin are with rare exceptions absent from the Shelf north of Hatteras in this period, but the eastward limit of distribution has not been established. In this extensive wintering habitat, only very large individuals and very small juveniles are often found south of 36° N., while medium-sized individuals are predominant north of that parallel with a scattering of larger and smaller fish. During May and June, the giant bluefin leave the southern areas with large numbers of them passing through the Straits of Florida. In late May, medium-sized individuals tend to concentrate in the Gulf Stream frontal area, but in June the large ones become more abundant there and the medium-sized ones, as well as smaller individuals, are found closer to the Shelf. By the first of July, the southern and oceanic areas are virtually devoid of bluefin over 5 pounds, and the summering area begins to fill up.

Eastern Atlantic Although information on their winter whereabouts in the area is meager, the distributional pattern for bluefin tuna in eastern North Atlantic seems rather similar to that in the western part of the ocean. In the summer, small and medium individuals are abundant in the Bay of Biscay, which is somewhat analogous to our New Jersey-Cape Cod area, while large- and medium-sized bluefin are found along the coasts of Norway and in the North Sea, which in some ways resemble the Nova Scotia and Gulf of Maine area. In the spring and early summer there are regular runs of these tuna in the approaches to the Mediterranean, which are comparable in some ways to the spring run in the Straits of Florida. Four large bluefin marked during the summer fishery off the Norwegian coast have been recaptured, each after about nine months at large, near Cádiz, Spain. A smaller tuna marked in the latter locality was recaptured off the Mediterranean coast of France, proving for the first time an interchange between the Atlantic and Mediterranean populations.

POPULATIONS

The distributional cycles for bluefin tuna on the respective sides of the North Atlantic, and the apparent absence of the species from the western oceanic waters in summer, strongly suggest two separate populations. On the other hand, 39 tag returns have proved migrations of both large and small bluefin from the western Atlantic to European waters. Of the giant bluefin tagged off the Bahamas a substantial number have been recaptured off Norway and in the Bay of Biscay. From local taggings, 2,223 have been recaptured in American waters

(to 1973). Even allowing for the greater productivity of the Norwegian tuna fishery, which is probably about double the western Atlantic effort, these prove an important transatlantic movement of giant bluefin. Further tagging will be required to determine the regularity and extent of this movement.

GROWTH RATE

Bluefin tuna grow very rapidly. The following table is an average age-length-weight relationship for western North Atlantic tuna, and considerable variation may occur. Tuna are aged by their otoliths rather than by the scale method as the annuli on the scales become obscure as the fish becomes larger.

Age (Years)	Length (Inches)	Weight (Pounds)
0–3 months	13	1.5
1	23	8.5
2	31	22
3	39	40
4	47	69
5	55	100
6	61	140
7	67	185
8	73	240
9	79	300
10	85	360
11	91	430
12	96	510
13	101	600
14	105	690

The otolith or cross section of the vertebrae bear concentric depressions which may be counted on the face of the vertebral centra; each represents one year of the tuna's life.

FISHING TECHNIQUE

Bluefin tuna are caught chumming at anchor, chumming while drifting, and trolling. The chumming-at-anchor method is most often employed on the Northeastern coast at such locations as Rosie's Ledge, Nebraska Shoals, and Charlestown Breachway. The comparatively shallow water makes anchoring feasible. At open-sea locations such as Block Island and Shark Ledge, the chumming is necessarily done while drifting. Menhaden "soup" and cut mossbunkers are most effective for attracting and holding tuna. However, live baits are used, the most effective being whiting, mackerel, small codfish, and ling. The baits are obtained on the fishing grounds by jigging.

In the chumming method, the angler ordinarily strikes his tuna by hand. The rod is placed in a holder in the fighting chair, and the reel is left in free spool with the click engaged. Generally, two lines are fished, one with a bait about thirty feet below the surface and the other on the bottom. When a tuna is felt, the angler strikes his fish with the line, then takes his place in the fighting chair. The reel brake is engaged to the correct drag, while the crew hauls anchor.

Trolling is employed when tuna are plentiful. Schools are sighted in the clear Bahamian waters, for example, while migrating north. They may also be visually located in the Maritimes as they "fin" or "push water." For trolling, live or dead mackerel, mullet, and squid are commonly used baits. In the trolling method, the angler does not hold the line but strikes with the rod. The angler holds the rod, while seated in the fighting chair. The bait is dropped back a considerable distance (approximately one hundred yards) so the boat wake will not spook the fish. The brake is on, set at about 45–50-pound drag. The strike and hook-up are instantaneous. There is no dropback as with the sailfish.

TUNA TACKLE

For giant bluefins the standard outfit for deep-water fishing is a heavy-duty 39-thread or 130-pound-test-class rod, and 550 yards of 130-pound-test Dacron spooled on a 12/0 reel. In fishing the shallow water of the Bahamas it is possible to use a lighter 24-thread outfit; the rod should be an 80-pound-test-class fiberglass, with 550 yards of 80-pound-test Dacron or 24-thread linen spooled on a 9/0 reel. Although the heavy-duty outfit can be used with some degree of certainty, the 80-pound-test outfit requires expert teamwork between the angler and his crew. The tactics of a tuna in shallow water are more erratic and violent when hooked, and the captain must provide skilled assistance with the boat. *For details on tackle see also* Bahamas, Big-game Fishing, Sportfisherman

—F.J.M.

BLUEFISH *Pomatomus saltatrix* A popular marine game-fish found in nearly all warm seas, the bluefish is the only member of the family Pomatomidae. The bluefish has a moderately stout body, and the belly is flat-sided but blunt-edged on the ventral surface. The "snapper" or young bluefish of 7–9 inches is relatively deeper and more flattened in appearance than the adult fish. The bluefish has a moderately pointed snout and a large oblique mouth with a projecting lower jaw and prominent canine teeth. Its caudal fin is broad and forked, and the first dorsal fin (7–8 spines) originates over the middle of the pectorals; the second dorsal is more than twice as long as the first (23–27 rays) and tapers toward the tail. The coloration is generally a blue-green above shading to silvery white on the belly. Its fins are of the same general body color but the pectorals usually have a black blotch at the base.

Bluefish are found along the Atlantic Coast of the United States, ranging from Cape Cod Bay off Massachusetts down through Argentina. When a population cycle is at a peak, stragglers may even travel as far east and north as Nova Scotia. Huge specimens swim off the northwest coast of Africa, the Azores, Portugal, and southern Spain. The species is found throughout the Mediterranean and commonly occurs in the Black Sea. Research on bluefish spawning activities, about which very little is known, has been more complete in the Black Sea area than anywhere else in its range. Both coasts of South Africa, the eastern Indian Ocean, the shores of the Malay Peninsula, southern Australia and New Zealand also support large populations of blues. Although the fish will often be found in tidal estuaries, it is basically a deep-water species.

MIGRATORY HABITS

Migrations of bluefish along the coasts of the United States follow a similar general pattern from year to year when the fish are plentiful. Formerly it was believed that the schools worked up along the coast from south to north. From recent investigations, it is apparent that the major movements are from east to west, although there is some south to north migration also as coastal waters warm up.

Individual fish in any given school tend to be of approximately the same size. Their cannibalistic tendencies make the reason for this fairly obvious. Tiny snappers, which are the young of the year, will be densely packed and will venture well into tidal rivers, although never in entirely freshwater. Larger fish feed in more open waters, and the very large specimens rarely move into the shallows. In general, the bigger the fish, the smaller the school will be.

Bluefish first appear offshore along the southern Florida coast in midwinter, and, by late March, catches inshore are good along most of the peninsula. During March and April, schools migrate in quantity past Georgia and the Carolinas to appear off Virginia and Delaware during late April. Some blues break off from the main body and remain in various areas to form what might be termed resident populations. First catches off New Jersey and New York are well offshore at the end of April or in early May, and fishing in that section improves steadily well into September. New England commercial fishermen take the species starting in mid May, but rod-and-reel angling is not good until June at the earliest. Note that the first fish to appear in any area during the spring run are swimming deep, and an angler therefore should fish at or near the ocean floor for them. These early bluefish usually are filled with eggs or milt, are fussy feeders, and are difficult to catch. During this period, natural bottom baits such as small live crabs are particularly effective. Once the blues have spawned, their appetites are immense, and angling results improve spectacularly.

With the coming of autumn, bluefish leave New England around mid-October, generally after a major northeaster. As elsewhere, just before their departure, fishing is at its peak. Approximately two weeks later, blues forsake the coasts of New York and northern New Jersey —and so on, southward down the coast. Weather can change this pattern, and a sudden, cold storm may speed the fish on their way ahead of schedule. December and early January fishing can be excellent off the Florida shore. Some blues are taken in that state throughout the winter until the spring migrations start again.

Unfortunately for the angler, bluefish are cyclic in their periods of abundance—that is, they may vanish from whole sections of the coast for years at a time. No one has been able to determine the reasons for these cycles nor to predict when they will occur despite many tales to the contrary.

Words cannot describe the basic savagery of bluefish on a feeding rampage when they maim or kill all other creatures in their path, including their own kind. Nature equipped the bluefish with a formidable set of teeth, and the fish uses these to great effect from the time it is a tiny snapper a few inches long until it reaches maximum size. This maximum is close to 45 pounds—a specimen recorded off the coast of North Africa. However, the world record on rod-and-reel is 31 pounds, 12 ounces taken at Hatteras Inlet, North Carolina (1972). As many anglers

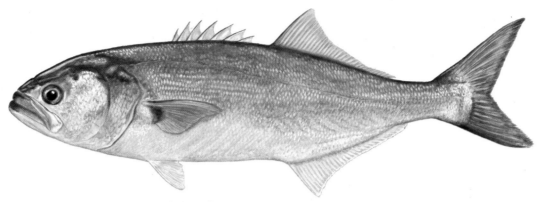

Bluefish, 8-pound Female, Atlantic Highlands, New Jersey

have learned, those teeth can inflict wicked wounds on human flesh. The species is one of the few which apparently can see almost as well out of water as in it, with the result that any bite is accurately aimed. This fact should never be forgotten by the angler. Quite naturally, the bloodthirsty qualities of the blue make it an ideal fighting fish when taken on rod-and-reel. Although the strike may vary from a gentle nip on a bottom bait to a savage slash at a surface plug, the ensuing battle is remarkable and may include everything from headshaking jumps to powerful, surging runs.

HOW TO LOCATE BLUEFISH

Locating bluefish is not difficult if the school is surfaced and feeding. Often there will be an oily slick in the vicinity even when the school is deep underwater, and those who "sniff out" blues will detect an odor similar to that of freshly cut melon or cucumber. Surfaced, they can be readily distinguished from other species because of the wild showers of spray and frantically leaping bait fish. The school is more tightly packed than is the case with fish such as bonito or striped bass. Terns and gulls wheel overhead, and the smaller birds will dip down to pick up bits of torn flesh. Almost never will they dive completely underwater because, if they do so, they may never emerge again as the blues attack.

Locating bluefish when they cannot be seen is a more difficult task. Both boat and shore fishermen should look for tide rips and other spots where currents clash. The fish like to lie a few yards down current from the actual visible rip, where they can gobble up unfortunate bait that is being tumbled about by the current. Although blues may chase bait into smooth water, chances are that the choppers will not stay there for long. They lead turbulent lives, and turbulent water suits them well. During the early part of the season and when hot weather sets in, best results come from fishing deep. At other times, all depths should be tried until a strike results. Once the first fish has been taken, chances are good that there will be others in the area.

ANGLING METHODS

Practically every known method of angling from handline to fly rod is successful in taking bluefish. Because of their voracity, the fish at all times will strike at anything and everything. However, they can also be extremely selective in their feeding habits. Most anglers who fish

regularly for blues use a wire leader of some sort because of their quarry's wicked teeth. When they are playing hard to get, bluefish may be scared from the lure because of this wire. Then the fisherman must be prepared to shift to nylon leader material. With a small lure, loss of both fish and lures will be high under these circumstances. If the lure is of sufficient size to prevent contact of teeth with the leader, such losses can be kept to a minimum.

One of the most common mistakes made by the neophyte when bluefishing is to cast across or troll through the center of a surfaced school. Chances are better than even that the fish will sound immediately if such tactics are used. If casting, the lure should land either just ahead of the line of movement of the school or on the side of the school nearest the angler. If trolling, the boat should be maneuvered so that the lure passes through the edge or just ahead of the sighted fish. When boat fishermen are heavily concentrated, blues in any given area may become extremely boat shy and will sound before the angler gets within casting range. For this reason, the habit of chasing surfaced schools will often ruin chances not only for the chasers, but also for all others in the vicinity. It is far better either to drift and cast or to troll at a steady rate.

Although every method can be used by the angler after bluefish, there are certain modifications to these methods that apply to this species in particular. Thus when trolling, as mentioned above, the best water in a tide rip lies a few yards down current from the rip's edge. The craft should be kept well clear of this area and only the lures themselves allowed to swing through the payoff spot. Experienced skippers often can be seen playing a sort of follow-the-leader game along such rips. When the end of the turbulent current is reached, the leading boat will swing wide, circle, and join the procession once more, this time in the stern position.

For most trolling, speeds of 5–8 knots are the best, but note that this indicates the speed of the lure moving through the water, not the actual speed of the boat. If operating in swift rips, this makes a considerable difference. A rough rule of thumb for distance astern at which the lure should be trolled is five times the length of the boat itself.

Boat fishermen off the New Jersey coast have developed the method of chumming for blues down to a fine art. Ground menhaden is used primarily for this work because these oily bait fish make a fine slick in the water. To catch the blues themselves from such a slick, it is a good plan to use a bait which is not menhaden in the chum line. Chumming, for some reason best known to fishermen, is not commonly practiced in other areas where blues are found, but it is highly successful anywhere.

Drift-fishing is another specialized method which takes bluefish both with and without use of a chum line. If chum is used, the rate of drift should be controlled to keep the boat in the slick at all times. If it is not, lures or baits may be either cast or allowed to stream off the craft much as they would do when trolling. This method is particularly deadly when the blues are deep. Often wire, lead-core, or heavily weighted lines are used to good advantage for this type of fishing. Live-lining and even still-fishing of a sort may be done while drifting.

The shore fisherman, whether he is on a pier, bridge, or beach, has almost as many choices as the boatman when it comes to taking bluefish. Still-fishing, live-lining, and casting are all included. It is even possible to chum by using a chum pot or chum sinker. With the exception of still-fishing, either artificial or natural baits may be used. The main point to remember is that bluefish prefer a moving lure to one that is still. Whether that motion is imparted by current, as is the case when a small cork is placed at the eye of a hook when bait-fishing, or by speedy retrieve of a metal squid makes little difference. Keep the lure moving, and chances of success are improved.

As far as the caster is concerned, whether he is tossing a 4-ounce block tin with a surf rod or a streamer fly with a split bamboo wand, varying the speed of retrieve is just as important as changing the lure from time to time. Every now and then, bluefish will not touch anything that is not moving rapidly the moment it hits the water. There are other times when it is necessary to let the lure sink well below the surface before starting its shoreward journey. When the quarry is being selective, try all speeds of retrieve in the same way as the boatman should try all speeds of trolling.

Casters of artificials actually have an advantage over other types of bluefishermen. Blues lying in a rip often will ignore a lure the first time it passes near them. The second time it appears, they will note its passage. The third time, brace your feet! This characteristic of the species means that an angler should cast to a likely looking spot at least three times before moving on.

Under normal circumstances, shore anglers will have best luck in the early hours of the morning and at dusk. In the heat of the day, small forage species of all kinds tend to work into deepwater, and bluefish follow them there. When the sun is low, bait moves into the shallows. In some areas, excellent bluefishing prevails in the dead of night, but it is also true that blues vanish from other sections after dark for unknown reasons. As with any other fishing, the exceptions to the general rule are almost as common as examples of the rule itself.

TACKLE FOR BLUEFISH

As far as tackle for bluefishing is concerned, the choice depends almost entirely upon the method being used and the size of fish expected. The Floridian spinning for small blues at an inlet will not use the same outfit as the Nantucket surf caster tossing a heavy drail into the eye of a raging northeaster. The gear selected should suit the circumstances. Thus a fly rod is not welcome on a New Jersey party boat because the angler cannot control his catch sufficiently to keep it clear of the lines of other patrons aboard. By the same token, a stubby boat rod and wire line is something less than ideal for live-lining a bait fish off the edge of a shallow tidal flat. Tackle should be properly balanced for the task at hand.

Whatever tackle is used, the bluefisherman should follow one basic rule after the fish has been hooked—keep it coming! If any slack line is allowed during the course of the battle, the fish will shake the hook almost instantly. Salmon fishermen are taught to drop their rod tip when their fish jumps. Bluefishermen are taught to heave back on the rod and to try to break the jumper's neck in mid-air. One nasty habit of the blue is to jump, with a great shaking of the head, just as it is about to be beached or boated. A slack line at this point means a lost fish.

HOW TO SELECT LURES

Blues continue to chomp on a lure throughout their whole fight for freedom. Often, when they are hooked with a hard metal jig, their teeth will be completely worn down when they finally surrender. This characteristic of the species should be kept in mind when selecting lures. For example, a rigged eel makes an excellent bluefish bait, but it can be used only once because it will be shredded to pieces by the first catch. Feather, bucktail, nylon, and Saran trolling lures probably account for as many bluefish during the course of a season as any other types; yet damage and loss of these lures are high. Shore casters favor metal squids and similar designs. Oddly enough, trollers rarely use spoons—which are the boat fisherman's equivalent of these—even though such spoons, particularly when tipped with a strip of pork rind, are very effective. Plugs, both surface and underwater models, account for many big blues every year. However, because of the bluefish habit of chewing while it fights, many tear free when this type of lure is used. Those who concentrate on the species find they have better luck when they re-rig plugs with one or two single hooks rather than with the sets of trebles found in most production models.

When it comes to natural bait, bluefish will gobble almost anything presented when they are in a feeding mood. However, live bait will out-fish dead consistently. If the live article is not obtainable, the next best thing is to impart motion to the dead. "Working" the bait by raising and lowering the rod tip at regular intervals will improve results. In the early season, natural bait often will produce when lures do not. During the rest of the bluefishing year, artificials are far more effective.

No matter what lures, tackle, or methods are used, the angler seeking bluefish faces a challenge from this wolf of the sea. If the species grew to the size of the bluefin tuna, nothing could stand before it in the oceans of the world. *See also* Saltwater Fly-Fishing, Surf-Fishing   —H.L.

BLUEGILL *Lepomis macrochirus*   One of the most popular panfish in United States waters, the bluegill is regionally known as bream (Southeast), sun perch, blue sunfish, and copperbelly.

The bluegill will vary in color probably more than any other sunfish. The basic body color ranges from yellow to dark blue, and those coming from sterile quarry holes will often appear transparent. The sides are usually marked by 6–8 vertical, irregular bars. The distinguishing features of the adult are a broad, black gill flap with no trim, a black blotch on the posterior of the dorsal fin, and

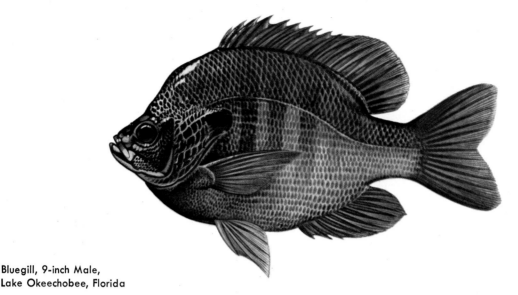

Bluegill, 9-inch Male,
Lake Okeechobee, Florida

a long pointed pectoral fin. The mouth does not extend beyond the eye. The maximum size is about 15 inches, and rare specimens may weigh up to 4½ pounds.

The original distribution was from Minnesota through the Great Lakes region to Lake Champlain on the east, south to Georgia, and west to Arkansas. Because of its use in farm ponds, it has now been introduced and is thriving in most states.

LIFE HISTORY

Bluegills prefer quiet, weedy waters where they can hide and feed. In the daytime the smaller fish are close to shore in coves under an overhanging limb or under a dock. The larger fish prefer the adjacent deeper waters in the daytime but move into shallow areas in the morning and evening to feed.

This sunfish spawns in late May when the water temperature reaches about 67° F. Spawning may continue until early August. Shallow, saucerlike nests are excavated in the sand and gravel and are vigorously guarded by the male. One female may deposit as many as 38,000 eggs which, under normal weather conditions, will hatch in 2–5 days. The young are protected by the male for a few days and then must fend for themselves.

In the North, the young grow a little over an inch a year and reach 4–6 inches in 3 years if the competition with others of its kind is not too heavy. A 9-inch specimen may be 6–8 years old. In the southern part of their range the growth is much faster. Sizes of over four inches in the first summer have been recorded.

The food of the bluegill consists of insects and some vegetation. As they grow they take the larger forms of insects and crustaceans. Mayflies, damselflies, and crustaceans make up a large part of their diet. In the summer when aquatic animal life is scarce, they consume more plant food. They feed only in daytime and preferably in the mornings and evenings.

ANGLING VALUE

The bluegill, along with perch and bullheads, is the most sought-after panfish (*which see*). It is a widely used species in farm ponds, but tends to become stunted as the population increases. This panfish provides excellent sport on the fly rod. It is not spectacular but resists vigorously by swimming at right angles to the pull of the line. The bluegill takes most any kind of small bait, either artificial or natural, floating or sinking. Some of the best fishing in the North can be obtained in the spring when water temperatures go into the 60's. At this time, wet flies and dry flies are particularly effective. In winter they can be caught through the ice in or near weed beds. Baits such as grubs, worms, or jigs are most often used.

—K.B.

BLUEHEAD CHUB *Hybopsis leptocephala* A large minnow reaching a total length up to 12 inches, the bluehead chub is found from the York River in Virginia southward to the Savannah River system in South Carolina. The body of this minnow is cylindrical in shape and is only little compressed; the mouth is rather large, almost horizontal to somewhat oblique, and subterminal. The depth of this minnow is contained 4.25 times in its total length, and the head is large and broad, being found 0.25 times in the total length. The lower jaw is slightly shorter than the upper. The barbel is well developed. The pharyngeal teeth vary from 4-4 in a single row to 1, 4-4, 1 in two rows. The scales are large, and there are 40 scales in the lateral line with 10 in the transverse series and 18 before the dorsal fin. The lateral line is decurved and the dorsal fin is located slightly posterior to the pelvic fins. Dorsal and anal fin rays number 8 and 7, respectively. This fish is similar to the river chub, *Hybopsis micropogan*, the difference being that the river chub has no caudal spot whereas the bluehead chub has a distinct, small, round caudal spot. The color of this large minnow is blueish-green above; scales dark-ended with coppery and green reflections on the sides, and white below. The fins are pale orange with the breeding males having a red spot on each side of the head with the lower part rosy in color. The top of the adult's head is swollen into a high crest, which is covered with breeding tubercles. Local fishermen refer to this minnow when it is breeding as the "horny head." The nuptial tubercles are located on the internasal and interorbital areas, sometimes extending to the sides of the head and front of the snout, and number about 40.

Bluehead Chub

LIFE HISTORY

The bluehead chub is the most ubiquitous nongame fish in the Piedmont watersheds. It appears in a wide variety of habitats ranging from small to medium size—clearwater streams having sand, gravel, and rubble bottoms to large, muddy rivers. The bluehead chub spawns from April-July, at which time the tubercles are the most pronounced. The average length of the fish is 5 inches, but specimens up to 12 inches have been collected. The fish serves as a major host for the Tremetoda parasite, *Neascus sp.* (black-spot). These parasites appear as small cysts about the size of pinheads, and are located below the scales creating a black-spotted appearance.

The smaller bluehead chubs serve as forage for the largemouth bass, smallmouth bass, bluegill, redbreast sunfish, and green sunfish. The larger specimens (9–12 inches) are caught on hook and line and eaten by local fishermen. —D.E.L.

BLUEHEAD SUCKER *Pantosteus delphinus* A grayish-blue sucker with a large mouth and broad snout. Body slender. Upper lip large, forming a fleshy hood over the mouth. Lips notched at each side of the mouth. Caudal peduncle long and slender. Scales small, more than 90 in the lateral line. This species is limited to the upper Colorado River drainage.

Bluehead Sucker

HABITS

This species is found in great abundance in mountain streams. It prefers riffle areas among the stones. The bluehead spawns in summer, when the males become colored with orange and pink. The food consists of mostly algae although some aquatic insects are eaten. The maximum size of this species is about 12 inches.

ECONOMIC VALUE

The bluehead sucker is considered one of the more important sources of food for trout within its range.

—R.A.J.

BLUEHEAD WRASSE *Thalassoma bifasciatum* A member of the family Labridae, it is closely related to the tautog, cunner, and hogfish (*which see*). This beautifully colored coral-reef fish has a smooth, elongate body, with a pointed head ending in a small mouth from which protrude canine teeth. The dorsal fin is long and low, and the anal fin is low and about half the dorsal-fin length. In small specimens the tail is rounded, the outer rays becoming some-

what produced with growth, reaching an elongation equal to about the length of the tail in large males. The scales are small, and the body is slippery and hard to grasp. The adult males are brilliantly colored, with the head and throat to the pectoral-fin base grading from blue or green to violet. Two black bars appear on the back, one just ahead of the dorsal fin, the other on the anterior rays, both partially encircling the body. The space behind the first is blue, and that behind the second greenish. Dark bars occur on the upper and lower caudal lobes of the tail. Young and immature fish may be pale greenish or bright yellow or whitish, with the dorsal fin having a light blue rim. Females display the white or yellow phase. The young have a brown or black lateral stripe, which may be solid or broken into six squarish blotches in the female. The striped phase is seen in the swimming fish, while the resting fish displays the blotched phase. Color variation is marked, and coloration of all is pale at night. It grows to about 6 inches long.

This colorful reef species is found from Colombia and the southwestern Gulf of Mexico throughout the West Indies north to southern Florida and Bermuda. They occur at depths up to about one hundred feet but are most abundant at less than fifty feet, about rock or coral. Males hover over the tops of sea fans, while females and young travel in loose schools in depressions below. While more than three or four males are seldom seen together, the females occur in groups of a dozen or more, and young travel in rather large aggregations. It is active during the day, hiding in burrows or crevices at night. Spawning takes place throughout the year, either through mass spawning by a group of individuals or pair spawning. They feed on planktonic crustaceans, such as copepods, and bottom organisms, including worms.

PARASITE PICKER

This species in the yellow phase is a "parasite picker," like many small wrasses, searching the skin of other fishes for parasitic isopods and other small crustaceans which are attached to the hosts' skin. Fishes which are "cleaned" include surgeonfish, jacks, damselfishes, and snappers. —D.dS.

BLUE-HOLE FISHING Blue holes exist in many tropical marine habitats. These circular pits, resembling submerged pot holes, attract many fish species, such as grunts, porgies, triggerfish, snappers, jacks, and occasionally tarpon. In appearance these holes are a deeper blue color than the surrounding shallow water because of their great depth. They may be many yards in diameter, and are lined with coral growths. Usually, there is a submarine connection with other "holes" and often with the open sea outside the reef.

Landlocked blue holes are like ponds in low porous rock of an island. These may also contain a wide variety of fish species which enter only by a submarine passage. The landlocked type has a corresponding submerged blue hole in the shallow water outside the island. When the tide is flowing, it is sucked into the outer holes and rises in the landlocked pools. When it is ebbing, the water level drops in the landlocked pool and rises turbulently out of the submerged hole (sometimes called a "boiling" hole) offshore. These blue holes were probably formed by rain erosion when they were elevated above sea level, and have been enlarged by wave and current action.

FISHING TECHNIQUE

Because of the confined area and sharp coral typical of a blue hole, fairly strong tackle and wire leaders are essential. Although the fish are likely to be shy, chumming will usually stir them into feeding; it is standard procedure for this type of fishing. —A.J.McC.

BLUE MARLIN *Makaira nigricans* This is a marine species of worldwide distribution in warm and temperate seas. Highly valued by sports fishermen because of its size and the spectacular fight that it puts up when hooked, it is sought in many parts of the world by commercial fishermen also because of the fine quality of its meat. It is reported to be the largest of the istiophorid fishes. The distinguishing characters of the blue marlin are the relatively low dorsal fin and relatively high anal fin, the latter averaging about 86 per cent of the height of the former, which in turn averages about 79 per cent of the body depth in adults; the round, rather than flat, sides; and the nearly cylindrical form of the anterior part of the body before the first anal fin.

The body of the blue marlin is, as just noted, nearly cylindrical in the forward part, so that the fish is not at all slab-sided, and carries its weight further back than do most members of the family. The lateral line is most peculiar. Generally not visible from the outside of the fish, the lateral line is extremely complex, showing a chainlike pattern of irregular hexagons on the inside of the skin. Rarely, usually in small specimens, a fish will be found in which the lateral line is visible on the surface, or sometimes it can be made visible by scraping off the scales. The vent is just in front of the anal fin. The spear is generally more nearly a smooth oval in cross section than in most other marlins, and in very large blue marlins it appears to be much longer. This is because of a peculiar growth relationship between the upper and lower jaws in this species. The lower jaw, in mature fish, does not grow as fast as the upper; hence the spear seems to be much longer than in other species.

In general, the blue marlin is colored like the striped marlin; that is, dark steely-blue on the dorsal areas, fading to silvery-white on the ventral side. The sides of the body are usually marked with a series of lighter-colored vertical bars, but these are never as prominent as they are in the striped marlin, and they tend to fade out rather quickly after the fish is boated. Sometimes a blue marlin will turn a beautiful bronze color when it dies, which fades in a few minutes to a few hours, leaving the skin a nearly uniform

dark slate-blue. The dorsal fin, and often the anal as well, is cobalt- or purplish-blue, sometimes marked with dark spots or blotches.

The blue marlin is reported by Japanese longliners to be the largest of the marlins, reaching weights of over 2,000 pounds. This has not been the experience of anglers, however; a blue of 1,805 pounds was caught in 1972 by rod and reel, although it was disqualified for record due to more than one angler handling the tackle. This fish came from Hawaii. The giants of the blue marlin, though, appear to be mainly creatures of the high seas, for the longliners claim they get these big ones only far offshore. This suggests that the really large blue marlin are probably not common in the areas accessible to sport fishermen. The biggest blue marlin are always females. The males seldom get much heavier than 300 pounds, and any blue much over this weight is almost certainly a female. In the Pacific, the males are reported to be 200–255 pounds. Parenthetically, this is the region from which come the biggest females.

HABITS

The spawning habits of the blue marlin are poorly known, but enough information is at hand to make some educated guesses. As with other marlins, and the sailfishes, the blue produces 2–5 million eggs per spawning. Ripe females have been found north of Cuba in July, but at Cape Hatteras, North Carolina, the fish are not nearly ready to spawn in late June. On the other hand, fish in breeding condition have been taken in the central Pacific from February through October. It is probable that the blue marlin spawns more or less all year 'round over rather vast areas of ocean, but that various local populations have more restricted breeding periods.

A few larval stages of blue marlin have been described. The very smallest rather resemble the young of the sailfish, apparently a typical form for the early developmental stages of istiophorid fishes in general. However, the young blue marlin do not take on the adult shape as early as do the young sailfish. At about 2 inches in length, the young blue marlin show quite plainly the reticulated, chainlike pattern of the lateral line. When they are 8 inches long, the pattern of the lateral line is perhaps even more clearly visible, the dorsal fin is uniformly high throughout its length, the upper and lower jaws are almost equal in length, and the pectoral fins are quite short. By the time the young blue marlin has reached a length of about 3 feet and a weight of about 5 pounds, it looks very much like a shortbill spearfish. The jaws are somewhat elongate and pointed, but the snout is only a little longer than the lower jaw. The dorsal fin has a small peak anteriorly, but the rest of the fin is still nearly as high as the peak. The pectoral fins are short. The complex lateral line is obvious, making it certain that the specimen is really a blue marlin. At a length of 4–5 feet and a weight of about 30 pounds, the young fish looks like a proper blue marlin, although the pectoral fins are still relatively short. Again, the complex lateral line is visible.

The blue marlin appears to undertake regular north-south migrations according to the season of the year, moving away from the equator in the warmer times and back again in the cooler months. This holds true in both the Atlantic and the Pacific oceans.

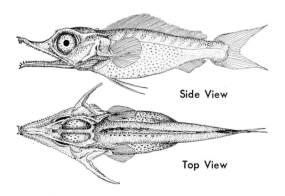

Side View

Top View

Blue Marlin Larva, 12 mm. long

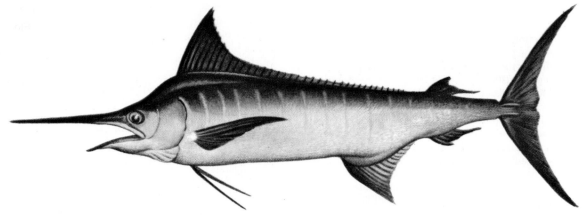

Blue Marlin, 420-pound Female, Bimini, Bahamas

All reports indicate that the blue marlin is broadly carnivorous on fish and cephalopods, with fish perhaps favored over the squid and octopuses in most areas. Particularly among the larger blues, tuna and bonito are favored foods. And some blues have been found with young broadbill swordfish in their stomachs.

The blue marlin is a fish of worldwide occurrence in warm and temperate seas. Off the Atlantic Coast of the Americas, it has been found commonly as far north as Cape Cod, even straying occasionally into the Gulf of Maine and to Georges Bank. The principal center of abundance is much further south, however, apparently off North Carolina in the summer and even further south in winter. The range extends southward at least as far as Uruguay. On the other side of the Atlantic, blue marlin have been found from the coast of France to Capetown, South Africa. In the Pacific, blues seem not to occur regularly north of Mexico (Acapulco), although a few have been found as far north as southern California. They have been recorded as far south as Mancora, Peru, and from Japan in the north to Australia and New Zealand in the south on the other side of that ocean. There seems to be a pretty good-sized population around the Hawaiian Islands, too, as well as throughout the central Pacific in general. The blue also ranges pretty well all through the Indian Ocean, as there are recorded catches from Ceylon, west of the Maldive Islands, at Mauritius, and off the coast of Africa.

FISHING METHODS

The vast majority of all blue marlin caught are taken on commercial longlines. Additional numbers come to sport fishermen, who generally troll for them. Favorite baits are ballyhoo, mullet, flying fish, and strip baits, but they will also take, on occasion, feather jigs and other artificial lures. A few fish are taken, in some parts of the world, by hand lining and harpooning. —J.E.M.

BLUE PIKE *Stizostedion vitreum glaucum* A subspecies of the walleye (*which see*) which is found only in Lake Erie. Within this lake it frequents deeper and cooler waters than does the walleye. There are other so-called "blue pikes" in Lake Ontario, the Lake Huron and St. Lawrence River drainages in Ontario, and Lake Winnipeg in Manitoba. However, it is not certain whether or not these can be properly identified as the same subspecies.

Blue pike can be distinguished from walleyes by their grayish-blue cast and the absence of the brassy yellow mottlings of the walleye. The pectoral and pelvic fins are bluish-white rather than clear or yellowish as in the walleye. The blue pike's eyes are larger and set closer together than are those of the walleye. —J.T.S.

BLUE ROCKFISH *Sebastodes mystinus* The species resembles the black rockfish (*which see*). It is found usually in shallow water from the Bering Sea to southern California. It reaches a length of 20 inches. The blue rockfish has a broad, strongly convex interorbital space; maxillary bone extends to middle of eye; small prefrontal spines; spinous portion of dorsal fin lower than softrays; eyes small; peritoneum black, but sometimes white in specimens exceeding 14 inches. The color is a slaty-blue shading to white on belly; the lateral and upper portions blotched light and dark; fins blackish. The young are brick-red to about 6 inches in length.

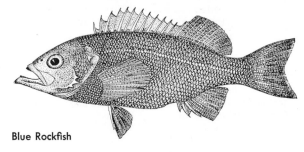

Blue Rockfish

LIFE HISTORY

According to J. H. Wales in *California Fish and Game*, Vol. 38, No. 4, males mature at four years, females at five. Spawning occurs in winter. In excess of 500,000 embryos were found in one female. The species inhabits water to a depth of three hundred feet. The young are often found in tide pools. —J.R.

BLUE RUNNER *Caranx crysos* Also called hard-tailed jack, this is one of the more common species of jack crevalles in the western Atlantic. A very similar species, the green jack (*Caranx caballus*) occurs in the eastern Pacific. Another species (*Caranx fusus*) in the Mediterranean and eastern Atlantic is also very similar to *Caranx crysos* and is thought to be the same species; it has been reported as such, but this has not been adequately studied.

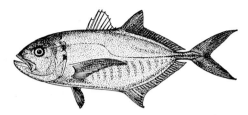

Blue Runner

The second dorsal fin of the blue runner has one spine and 22–25 softrays; the anal fin has 2 detached spines followed by a single spine and 19–21 softrays. Gillrakers on the first arch are 10–14 on the upper limb and 23–28 on the lower limb. Pointed scutes in the straight lateral line number about 46–56, and the straight lateral line is about twice as long as the curved portion.

The body shape is more slender in profile and more rounded in cross section than in most other jack crevalles. The dorsal- and anal-fin lobes are only moderately produced, and the spines of the first dorsal fin are shorter than the length of the dorsal-fin lobe. The chest is completely scaled. The coloration is dark black to bluish-green to olive-green on the back, and dark gray to golden to silvery on the belly, with a black opercular spot, and the fins colorless to blackish. In small specimens there are usually 7 broad bars (rarely 6 or 8) on the body, plus 1 on the head; these bars may be present on live fish up to a foot in length, but they fade rapidly after leaving the water. Specimens that are sexually ripe or nearly ripe are probably generally darker in color, with ripe males having almost black bodies and fins.

The blue runner ranges from Cananeia in São Paulo, Brazil, to Herring Cove, Nova Scotia, in the West Indies, and at Bermuda. The young are frequently found well offshore in the Gulf Stream and the Gulf of Mexico. The average size is about a foot long or less, the maximum recorded length is 28 inches, and the maximum weight recorded is 4 pounds, and suggested to occasionally attain 6 pounds.

LIFE HISTORY

More is known of the life history of the blue runner than of any other American species of jack crevalle, and the sum of this knowledge is very small. Spawning off the Southeastern United States is apparently concentrated around May through August, although it may occur throughout the year in warmer waters. The place of spawning appears to be in offshore waters, as in the Florida Current, for the smallest juveniles have been found there. The young of about 1–5 inches long begin to move inshore, and some have been observed within the bell of jellyfish. Larger fish occur in schools, at times in large numbers, in moderately shallow waters around beaches or bays or even around offshore reefs. The young feed on small plankton, and adults eat smaller fish, shrimp, and other invertebrates. They may reach a size of about 7–10 inches by the end of their first year of life. There is a northward migration of young and, to a lesser extent, of adults along the Eastern states during the summer.

ANGLING VALUE

The blue runner is frequently caught trolling, casting, or still-fishing with bait. Its taste is good, and the flavor is improved if the tail is cut and fish allowed to bleed immediately after capture. It is fished for and sold commercially, either fresh or frozen, and is a very important live bait for large gamefish. The great bulk of the commercial catch comes from Florida, where it is the most important commercial jack, in volume and in price, and where it is taken primarily in haul-seines and runaround gillnets. *See also* Carangidae, Jacks —F.H.B.

BLUE SAC DISEASE *See* Diseases and Parasites

BLUE SHARK *Prionace glauca* This distinctive, beautifully colored shark is recognized by its very long pectoral fins, the bright cobalt coloration of the back, the snowy-white belly, and the long snout. It is a slender, elongate species, with the first dorsal fin set relatively far back, at about the middle of the body. The teeth are nearly triangular, and are serrated along the edge. Although reported to grow to 20 feet, the blue shark averages less than 10 feet.

LIFE HISTORY

The blue shark ranges throughout the temperate and tropical waters of the world, being one of the most common of the oceanic sharks. On the Pacific Coast, it is frequently seen in shallow waters. In the western Atlantic Ocean, it is more common in northern waters, and although blue sharks are not often caught by anglers fishing on the surface in tropic waters, deepline or nighttime fishing may produce results. Blue sharks are commonly seen at the surface in northern waters. They rove in packs at times, and at other times are seen singly or in pairs.

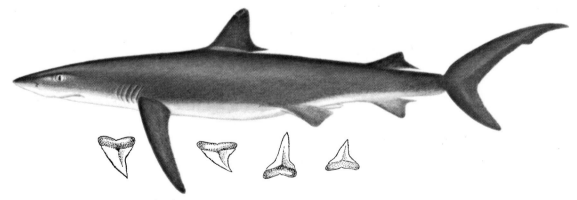

Blue Shark, showing teeth of upper (*left*) and lower jaws

They also school by sex, with more males being found in some areas (more often the northern and the western parts of the North Atlantic) and the females in others (the more southern and eastern parts of the North Atlantic). This species makes extensive seasonal north-south migrations in the Caribbean from New England to tropical waters. The fastest rate of travel was 27 miles per day for a blue shark tagged near Block Canyon in September and recaptured off Venezuela in December (1,720 miles in 64 days).

Maturity occurs at 7–8 feet, and as many as 54 young are born at one time, the young being about 1½–2 feet. Food taken includes mackerel, herring, squid, and other sharks, and in California it takes flying fish and anchovies as well. Sea birds resting at the sea surface are eaten, and blue sharks commonly feed on garbage dumped at sea. These sharks proverbially followed the old whaling ships for long periods, feeding on the carcasses of sperm whales that were thrown overboard.

DANGER TO MAN

The blue shark has been implicated in attacks on swimmers, and is believed responsible for attacks on military personnel involved in ship accidents or torpedoings during World War II. Although a voracious species, it puts up a poor fight on hook and line, and its flesh is poor and strong in ammonia. —D.dS.

BLUESPOTTED CORNETFISH *See* Cornetfish

BLUESPOTTED SUNFISH *Enneacanthus gloriosus* This attractive little sunfish has a basic body coloration ranging from light olive to almost black. The light green to dark blue spots on the body are arranged to form a definite lateral pattern. The gill flap is short and black; the unpaired fins are heavily spotted; and the tail is rounded.

The bluespotted sunfish is found in the Atlantic drainage from southern New York to Florida. It is found in shallow, weedy, acid waters and often in situations where the oxygen concentration is too low for survival of companion species.

LIFE HISTORY

The 5–12-inch circular nest is built among the aquatic plants, but is not necessarily excavated through to the bottom algae. The eggs adhere to the plant particles and rootlets.

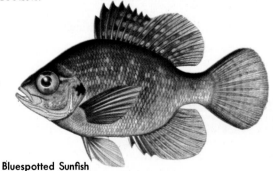

Bluespotted Sunfish

ANGLING VALUE

This sunfish is too small (maximum length about 4 inches) to be considered an angler's quarry. It does serve as forage for larger gamefish, however, and has ecological value in mosquito control. —K.B.

BLUESTRIPED GRUNT *Haemulon sciurus* This grunt is rather common in southern Florida and throughout the rest of its range, which extends southward throughout the West Indies and along the coast of Central and South America to Brazil. The average total length of mature adults is about 10 inches, but larger individuals are sometimes taken. This grunt is distinguished from all others by the color pattern which consists of continuous blue horizontal stripes over a yellow or brassy-yellow body color. The inside of its mouth is blood-red or carmine in color. The bluestriped grunt has 12 dorsal spines; dorsal rays 16–17, usually 16; 9 anal rays; pectoral rays 16–17, usually 16. Pored lateral-line scales 48–51. Gillrakers 27–31, usually 29. Its pectoral fins are naked.

The bluestriped grunt is a bottom feeder. Abundant in relatively shallow water close to the shore, it forms schools along reefs in deeper water.

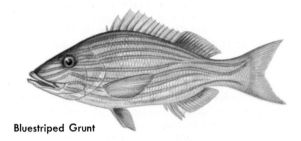

Bluestriped Grunt

ANGLING VALUE

This species is easy to catch on natural bait such as cut mullet, cut pilchard, or dead shrimp. Bluestriped grunts will also strike flies, jigs, and small plugs. This grunt is excellent eating. A panfish highly appreciated in the Florida Keys, it is a commercial fish of some importance in Florida, the Bahamas, and the West Indies. —L.R.

BLUE TANG *Acanthurus coeruleus* The blue tang is known from the entire Caribbean area south to Brazil. It is found occasionally along the eastern seaboard of the United States as far north as New York and is common in Bermuda. The blue tang is one of the surgeonfishes (family Acanthuridae), which are characterized by relatively high, compressed bodies and scalpel-like spines at the base of the tail with which they can inflict deep gashes. The species of *Acanthurus* (and the related Indo-Pacific genera *Ctenochaetus* and *Zebrasoma*) have a single folding spine that fits into a lengthwise groove on the caudal peduncle. Species of *Naso*, another Indo-Pacific genus, have a pair of fixed, keel-like spines that project laterally from each side of the caudal peduncle. Some species of *Naso* have a bony rostral prominence that extends forward from the forehead, a characteristic that has earned them the name of unicornfishes.

The blue tang is one of four surgeonfishes from the western Atlantic. All are species of *Acanthurus*. As implied by the name, *A. coeruleus* is blue as an adult and is most easily distinguished by color. It is not a uniform blue, however, but has numerous lengthwise, irregular dark lines on the body. It may also be identified by its great body depth (about 1.7 in standard length) and the high number of dorsal and anal softrays (26–28 dorsal rays and 24–26 anal rays). The young are bright yellow. The size at which the yellow color is replaced by the blue is variable. Yellow specimens as large as 77 millimeters in

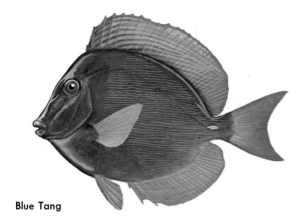

Blue Tang

standard length and blue ones as small as 31 millimeters have been collected. The last yellow to disappear is that of the tail; thus an occasional individual may be seen which is blue with a yellow tail. The blue tang reaches a maximum length of about one foot.

FEEDING HABITS

The teeth of species of *Acanthurus* are close-set and denticulate on the edges, thus ideally adapted for feeding on filamentous algae which forms the main part of the diet. The word *tang* means seaweed in German, and the use of this name for various of the surgeonfishes is probably based on knowledge of their plant-feeding habits.

Whereas the other western Atlantic species of *Acanthurus* have a thick-walled, gizzardlike stomach and usually ingest sand with their algal food, which is presumably ground in the stomach, *A. coeruleus* has a thin-walled stomach and ingests relatively little inorganic material.

ACRONURUS

The late postlarval stage of species of *Acanthurus* is called the acronurus. It is orbicular and transparent with silver over the abdomen. This stage of *coeruleus* is about an inch long, and it is attracted to a light at night and may be caught with a dipnet. The pelvic, second dorsal, and second anal spines of at least some of these late larval stages are venomous, and if one is stuck with them, an unpleasant stinging sensation not unlike a bee sting is experienced. The venomous quality of the spines is lost when the acronuri transform to the juvenile stage.—J.E.R.

BLUE WATER A saltwater fishing term referring to the blue ocean water offshore. This *apparent* color is because the clearer the water the greater is the average depth from which dispersed light reaches the human eye. As a result of extensive light filtering in deepwater, the color appears to be more saturated and darker; the adjacent inshore area, for example, may appear pale green due to the smaller depth of reflection and because dissolved and suspended plant pigments lend a yellow hue to the coastal water. The blue color is particularly intense in tropical seas where there is a low production of colored materials such as plankton in suspension. The term "blue water" implies to the angler the presence of large marine species such as the tuna, dolphin, and blue marlin. The term "blue-water angling" is synonymous with big-game fishing. –A.J.McC.

BLUE WHALE *See* Whales

BLUNTNOSE JACK *See* Atlantic Bluntnose Jack

BLUNTNOSE MINNOW *Pimephales notatus* A silvery minnow with a cross-hatched appearance and a dark black caudal spot. A dusky band is found around the snout and extending to the spot on the tail. Dorsal fin with dusky blotch on forward portion. Back flattened predorsally and with scales crowded. Lateral line complete. Mouth subterminal. The bluntnose is found widespread from North Dakota through the Great Lakes and southward.

HABITS

A rather plastic species, the bluntnose is found in a variety of habitats. It is able to withstand high degrees of turbidity and pollutants. Found in the smaller brooks and the larger lakes, it appears to prefer moderate-sized lakes and streams rich in organic matter and high in phytoplankton populations. The food of the bluntnose consists

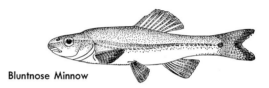

Bluntnose Minnow

of microscopic plant and animal life along with midge larvae and other aquatic insects. It is also accused of eating eggs of other species. Spawning over an extended period from midspring to early fall, the bluntnose male develops three rows of sharp-pointed tubercles across the snout. The eggs are deposited on the underside of logs, stones, or other objects. The egg masses are cleaned by the male with the spongy growth which develops on the nape. A small species, the bluntnose seldom exceeds 3½ inches in length.

ECONOMIC VALUE

Considered an important bait species, the bluntnose undoubtedly contributes heavily to the diet of gamefish and panfish. There is some question that its spawn-eating and competitive food habits may be detrimental to other fish populations.

The bluntnose minnow has been the subject of various artificial flies but no standard pattern copying it has evolved. Many streamers dressed with barred rock and badger hackle wings are thought to represent the species and regionally these are effective. The striped badger feather is probably a reasonable suggestion, especially when combined with a silver body. Such a fly is usually effective in waters where the bluntnose is common and suitable for taking smallmouth bass and trout. —R.A.J.

BLUNTNOSE STINGRAY *Dasyatis sayi* A small member of the stingray family, it is characterized by the subcircular shape of the disk with broadly rounded outer corners of the pectoral fins. Both the anterior and posterior margins of the disk are slightly convex. The tail is long, with a sharp spine about one-quarter of the distance from the base of the tail to the tip. Conspicuous folds are present along the upper and lower surfaces of the tail, and there are no rough thorns along the tail. Except for a row of small thorns along the midline just behind the head and supplementary thorns on either side of the midline, the skin is smooth. Small specimens are yellowish to light brown above, while adults are gray to brown or red-brown to greenish. The tip of the tail is black, and the lower surface of the disk is white. Although the average size from the United States mainland is probably about 1 foot wide, individuals from French Guiana are reported to average about 3 feet, which is about the maximum size reported for North America.

LIFE HISTORY

It is known from Brazil to Massachusetts and throughout the Caribbean area. In certain places, notably North Carolina, Florida, and French Guiana, it is extremely common in shallow-water situations, where schools roam in search of food. When resting, they remain partially buried in sand, occasionally stirring up their surroundings with the edges of the muscular disk. They eat worms, clams, small shrimps, crabs, and snails. In turn they are eaten by sharks and large groupers. During the summer, extensive coastwise migrations take place in shallow coastal waters from southerly waters to the north, with movement offshore during the cooler months. Specimens have been taken from twenty feet to only a few inches of water. The feeding activities are accompanied by vigorous swimming, so that groups of feeding stingrays can often be spotted from a distance because of the commotion.

Mating is believed to occur the year round in the tropics. The young remain within the mother until birth where they receive nutrition from hairlike projections which secrete milklike food, in addition to the food obtained during yolk-sac resorption. Two to four young are produced at a time, and they are about 6–7 inches wide at birth.

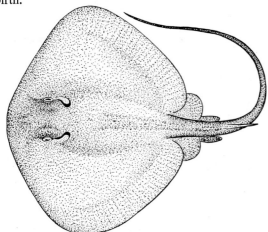

Bluntnose Stingray

DANGER TO MAN

Since this is a very common stingray, it offers a real danger to bathers and fishermen, and causes damage to the fishermen's nets. Treatment for a bluntnose stingray wound is the same as for that of the round stingray (*which see*). —D.dS.

BOAT *As used in fishing, see* Adirondack Guide Boat, Airboat, Canoe, Charter Boat, Johnboat, Inboard-Outboard, Oregon Surf Dory, Outboard, Party Boat, Rowboat, Sea Skiff, Skiff, Sportfisherman

BOAT HOOK A wood, aluminum, or steel pole with a hook on it. Of varying lengths, some are telescopic for easier storage. Used to pick up a mooring line or fend off or hold on to a dock or other boat.

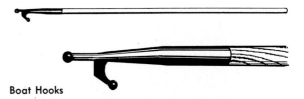

Boat Hooks

BOBBER A float used in still-fishing. The bobber indicates when a fish has taken a baited hook by its bobbing movements, and also suspends the bait at a predetermined depth below the surface. It is most effectively used where a live bait such as a minnow, crab, or crayfish might hide among weeds or rocks on a free-sinking line. Bobbers are made of many materials, but the traditional cork and quill bobbers have been largely replaced by plastics. *See also* Live Bait

BOCACCIO *Sebastodes paucispinis* This rockfish (*which see*) is common from northern Baja California to central British Columbia in Canada. It reaches a length of 3 feet and a weight of 21 pounds. On the bocaccio the interorbital space is strongly convex; lower jaw projects greatly; large mouth; pectoral fin with 15–16 rays; dorsal fin deeply notched; anal softrays normally 9. Color, olivaceous or brown above; orange or reddish laterally; pink to white ventrally; a red tinge throughout.

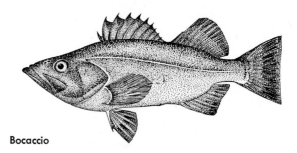

Bocaccio

The bocaccio is usually found at depths below 240 feet. It is one of the most important commercially taken rockfishes in California, occurring in greatest numbers on the central and southern coast. —J.R.

BOLLARD An upright wooden or iron post on a dock to which mooring lines can be secured.

BONEFISH *Albula vulpes* An inshore marine gamefish which is highly prized by light-tackle anglers. Also called banana, ikondo, and kpole (Africa), macabi (West Indies), and raton (South America), this distinctive species, the only living member of its genus, belongs to a family (Albulidae) of very primitive bony fishes which date back to the Cretaceous Period (125 million years ago). Like the tarpon and the ladyfish, it possesses an eel-like, leptocephalus larval stage. It has a worldwide distribution in tropical and warm waters; on the Atlantic coast of the New World it has been taken as far north as Woods Hole, Massachusetts, but generally does not extend north of Cape Hatteras, and occurs as far south as Rio de Janeiro; on the Pacific coast it has been taken from San Francisco Bay, California, south to Talara, Peru. One other species of bonefish is presently recognized, *Dixonina nemoptera*, or longfin bonefish (*which see*) occuring spottily from Florida to Central America. However, it is probable that several species exist on a world basis.

The color of large bonefish is bluish above; bright silvery on both sides and below; dark streaks between rows of scales, at least on dorsal half of side; dorsal and caudal fins with dusky margins. Very young adults with a double series of dark spots on the back, each just off the median line; these spots soon uniting to form about 9 dark crossbands on the back, extending down nearly or quite to lateral line; the third band crossing back at origin of dorsal; next two situated posteriorly under base of dorsal; bands persisting until a length of about 75 mm. The dark longitudinal streaks of the adult appear shortly before crossbands become obscure.

Other distinguishing characteristics are body slender, rounder, and less compressed in large specimens than in young adults; its dorsal profile more convex than ventral profile; its depth at dorsal origin 4.35–4.9 in standard length in large specimens. Scales firm with crenulate membranous edges; 65–71 in lateral series. Head low, flat above, its depth exceeding its width at middle of eye by about diameter of pupil. 3.0–3.8 in standard length. Snout rather long conical, projecting about a third of its length beyond mandible, 2.2–2.5 in head. Eye moderately small, 4.4–5.5 in head; its center nearer to margin of opercle than to tip of snout. Maxillary not quite reaching to eye in large specimens.

Dorsal fin somewhat elevated anteriorly, its origin a little nearer to tip of snout than to base of caudal; 17–18, rarely 19 softrays. Caudal fin deeply forked, the upper lobe somewhat longer than the lower. Anal fin very small, its origin nearer to base of caudal than to base of pelvic; 8 or 9 softrays. Pelvic fin somewhat smaller than pectoral, inserted under or slightly behind middle of dorsal base. Pectoral fin with rounded margin reaching less than half-way to pelvic; 16–17, rarely 15 softrays; axillary scale about half as long as fin, adherent to body. Gillrakers 7–8 + 9–10.

Bonefish attain weights of over 20 pounds. The average fish taken by angling in popular Florida and Bahamian locations is from 4–6 pounds and somewhat smaller in Central American and Mexican waters. Fish of 8 pounds or more are considered large and the rod-and-reel record of 19 pounds was caught off Zululand, South Africa. Bonefish in excess of 20 pounds occasionally enter the commercial markets in Mozambique, Africa, where large individuals are caught by handline in deep water.

LIFE HISTORY

Although the eel-like, leptocephalus larval stage is well known, the spawning season and spawning grounds remain undescribed. Ripe fish and larvae are taken at various times of the year, which indicates a prolonged breeding period. Exceptionally large schools (densely formed and covering an acre or more) are sometimes seen in the Bahamas from mid-February to April, "milling" in protected shallow bays behind reefs. Both small and very large adults occur together, and these concentrations may be prespawning or spawning bonefish. Metamorphosis to the fry stage involves a profound alteration in body form. The eel-like leptocephalus grows to a length of about 2½ inches before it starts to develop fins, then it commences shrinking. It continues to shrink for 10–12 days until it is about half of its original length. It next metamorphoses into a bonefish form before starting to grow again.

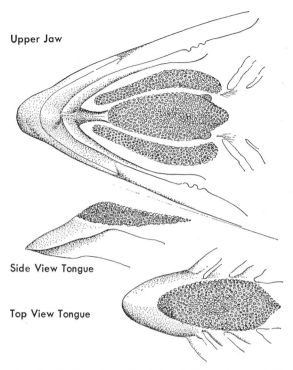

Upper Jaw

Side View Tongue

Top View Tongue

Granular Teeth or Specialized Dental Plates of Bonefish Can Grind Mollusks and Crustaceans

The adult bonefish usually digs for its food in the bottom with its snout, and sometimes turns somersaults in the process. In the West Indies and Florida it may be seen by day along shallow sandbanks and among underwater grasses. It feeds on marine worms, mollusks, crabs, squids, small fish, shrimp, and sea urchins.

FOOD VALUE

Despite an abundance of fine bones this fish is not only edible but highly esteemed by many seafood fanciers. The flesh is firm and nutlike in flavor. It is prepared in a variety of ways. A popular island method is to kite the fish and marinate it for several hours in lemon or lime juice. The flesh side is then wiped with a tomato based sauce seasoned with onion, black pepper, crushed red pepper, and bay leaves; it is wrapped in foil and baked at a low heat for several hours. Bonefish roe is also excellent eating and is usually pan sautéed in the manner of shad roe. Smoked bonefish (kited rather than in the round) is a taste treat seldom experienced by the average angler.

ANGLING VALUE

The bonefish is often difficult to catch on artificial lures, and some study must be given to mastering the game. Although a bonefish rarely jumps from the water when hooked, it usually makes an incredibly swift run of 50–100 yards or more, and even a small fish has power out of proportion to its size. Bonefish live in a constant state of alarm. Sometimes it would seem that if you breathe too hard the whole flat erupts in fleeing schools. They are usually flushed when a skiff or wading angler comes too close, but often just the faintest *plop* of a lure on the surface or the sight of a fly line unrolling in the air will send them running. And when they accelerate in a foot of water, leaving a trail of bursting bubbles, you are not likely to see them again. This is probably the only fly-fishing game in which the angler can scare a hundred fish with one bad cast. Fortunately, the bonefish is not always alert. With a proper amount of caution in the stalk and presentation of the lure, you can expect to catch a few or, on rare occasions, many fish. One of the enigmas of the game is that bonefish will not respond to a bait for awhile; then on the next tide in the same place with identical conditions of wind and sunlight they will hit nine casts out of ten. They may snatch the lure right at the boat. Such erratic behavior cannot be speculated on in terms of angling technique. Bonefish have lusty appetites plus a powerful set of grinders located in the throat which accommodates anything that passes their pig-like snouts. There is reason to believe that what we are sometimes coping with is the immediate previous experience of a particular school. Fish are much less cautious when they aren't being exposed to predators including man, and the frequency at which new schools move into an area that is either heavily angled or not being fished at all makes a considerable difference in results.

DISTRIBUTION

Bonefish forage in all tropical seas. You can fish them in such widely separated places as Brazil, Palmyra Island, or Portuguese West Africa. However, the best angling occurs in the Florida Keys and in the Bahamas. It would be hard to match the south end of Exuma, the east end of Grand Bahama, and the middle bight of Andros for numerical abundance of schools. For convenience and suitable fly-fishing conditions the Key Largo and Islamorada areas of Florida provide excellent fishing when the weather is normal.

In Africa the bonefish is known as *banana*, *ikondo*, and *kpole*, depending on which coast you fish. From Cuba to Mexico it's called *macabí*, but further down along the South American coast it's known as the *raton* or ratfish due to the nibbling posture at a bait. In Hawaii, which has the largest bonefish, but no suitable flats for the fly rod, it's called *o'io*.

Paradoxically, very little is known about the life cycle of the bonefish. It metamorphoses from a 3-inch transparent eel-like larva which gradually shrinks in size. When this reverse growth is completed, a tiny bonefish is formed. From that day on, it wears chrome-plated scales and grows to a probable weight of 20 pounds or more. Their average size varies according to the area, but 4–6 pounds is the general run of fish, with anything over 8 pounds being considered above average.

BONEFISH FLATS

The bonefish is primarily a shallow-water species, and its habitat for angling purposes is the flats or intertidal areas adjacent to sand and coral islands or mainland beaches. Bonefish generally enter the flats on a flood tide and drop back to deeper water on the ebb. It requires some local knowledge to determine which flat the schools favor. A beginning angler may lose his sense of dimension

in an endless calm stretching to a far horizon, but gradually the grass beds and urchins, sand dollars, and sponges covering the undulating marl plain become as familiar as the bottom of any trout stream. There are small but important differences in each flat. Some are much more productive than others; crabs, shrimp, squid, and all the mollusks which bonefish eat can be abundant on one flat and almost absent from the next. However, the angling is invariably done for visible fish which are stalked by wading or with a skiff.

TAILING AND MUDDING

When actively feeding, bonefish reveal their location in two ways. The first, and most desirable situation for the fly-rod angler, is the "tailing" fish; this means that the fish is grubbing nose down in water so shallow that its tail in part or whole breaks the surface. You may only see the very tip of one lobe, but usually the work is boldly fluttering in the air as the fish roots for crabs and mollusks. With a quiet stalk this is the easiest fish to catch. On deeper parts of the flat an individual, group, or school of bonefish will plow the bottom and raise little puffs of marl; these are "mudding" fish. When you learn what to look for, the muds are visible from considerable distances. Actually, marl creates a kind of pasty-white color when in suspension, although it becomes extremely dense and large in diameter if a school is at work. Mudding bonefish are not quite as easy to take with the fly because it's difficult to spot targets. However, they present much less of a problem than cruising fish which swim along in a level path.

SCHOOL BEHAVIOR

Fundamentally, the responses of school-oriented fish are integrated. They turn right or left, maintaining a precise distance from each other and traveling at identical speeds. When feeding, bonefish scatter to some extent just as individual cows graze away from the herd. But each bonefish is oriented to the group as a whole. If frightened, they will respond by coming together again in the synchronized movement of a unit rather than that of an individual.

Frequently, you find that large bonefish appear as singles, or in pairs, or groups of perhaps 4–6 fish. A trophy might be feeding in a large school, but as a general rule the big fish keep to themselves. A school of any species is generally composed of fish which are similar in size. This is undoubtedly part of the behavior pattern starting from early life when fish of equal size join a group whose speed and responses to maneuvering are identical. As adults, bonefish weights may vary somewhat, but a school is likely to consist of 2–5-pound fish, or 5–8-pound fish, while the much less common 8–10 pounders appear as groups or individuals.

STALKING THE BONEFISH

Stalking bonefish requires some experience. The beginner fishing without a guide will invariably mistake the tails of ground sharks and the wing tips of small rays for bonefish signs. Too, the technique of poling a skiff is too much for the novice to master on a short vacation. Wad-

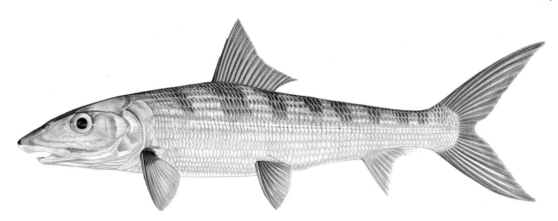

Bonefish, 7-pound Male, Deep Water Cay, Bahamas

ing is often the most desirable method for both economic and physical reasons. Theoretically, the wading angler can get closer to a bonefish as his silhouette is less obvious, and it's certainly the easiest way to work when you are alone. However, a correctly designed skiff with topsides sheered to minimize freeboard and a suitable casting platform is hard to beat when poled by a competent guide. You can cover far more water in a day's fishing and present your lure to many more bonefish. When fishing alone, you can pole to within fifty yards of the school then slip over the side and wade quietly into casting range. It's awkward to manage a skiff and the rod too. With any luck you can get within 30 feet of a bonefish by wading, but 40–50 feet would be a safe distance even from the platform. So the difference is negligible. Beginners are well-advised to start with a guided craft. It takes time to learn to spot bonefish on sun-blasted flats, and if the man with the pushpole knows his business, you'll get a lot more fishing than you'd find by mucking in the marl. An experienced guide is half the job, and he earns his fee. Many of the top guides are booked months, and sometimes as much as a year, in advance.

SPINNING FOR BONEFISH

Spinning tackle is the most popular gear for bonefish. It is used chiefly for casting leadhead jigs or live bait such as shrimp or crabs. You might prefer a regular fixed-spool reel or one of the enclosed-spool reels, but in either case, make certain that it has a smooth drag. A jerky drag will pop the line. Bonefish clip along at 25–30 mph, and if the spool freezes, the line will break instantly. An 8-pound test is the standard one. You can use a 6-pound test with very light jigs, but keep several extra spools on hand. Check your line for abrasions frequently. Spinning rods should be medium action in the 6½–7-foot length. Don't use a very short rod because it helps to be able to hold line high off the water when hooked up. Bonefish are not selective; so you don't have to carry a large variety of lures. Actually, you can get along with a few shallow-running leadheads, but camps and tackle shops sell the correct sizes and patterns. The chief problem in casting artificials is to judge the correct distance at which the lure should be presented to the fish. Although experience quickly dictates the range (usually about twenty yards), it's often difficult to estimate the safe target area. You can cast a small leadhead quite close to tailing or mudding fish. As a rule of thumb, try to put the lure about three feet from your target. But when the school is moving or fidgeting in a steady, level swim, the lure must be presented well ahead of them, say 20–30 feet, and retrieved very slowly. When casting spinning lures, the disparity between one tide or one school and the next is sometimes great. There are times when you can't toss a small leadhead within ten feet of a tailer without its busting for the deep. So the three-foot rule doesn't always apply. If you are using ⅛-ounce leadheads, it generally works. A ¼-ounce leadhead is best placed about 5 feet from target. Anything heavier than ¼-ounce is not often suitable for bonefish. *See also* Saltwater Fly Fishing, Spinning, Longfin Bonefish

—A.J.McC.

BONITO Three species of the genus *Sarda* are likely to be taken by the American angler although only two occur in American waters. These are *Sarda sarda*, the Atlantic bonito; *Sarda chiliensis*, the Pacific or California bonito; and *Sarda orientalis*, the striped bonito. These are fishes of the mackerel family which have prominent longitudinal or oblique stripes on the back, large conical teeth, and numerous spines in the first dorsal fin (17–22).

The species are somewhat difficult to distinguish. *S. sarda* is found only in the Atlantic Ocean and Mediterranean and Black seas. It differs from the other two species in having 20–23 spines in the first dorsal fin (compared to 17–19 in the other two). It has 17–23 gillrakers on the first branchial arch, overlapping *S. chiliensis* which has 20–27, while *S. orientalis* has only 8–13. *S. chiliensis* is found along the Pacific coast of the Americas, but its range is divided into a northern portion, from British Columbia to southern Baja California, and a southern portion, from Peru to Chile. Between these two areas, *S. orientalis* occurs from Baja California to Peru. All are medium-sized fishes. *S. sarda* may reach a length of 3 feet and a weight of 12 pounds, *S. orientalis* attains at least 2 feet 8 inches and 7 pounds.

The food of bonitos consists mostly of smaller schooling fishes. The spawning season for *S. sarda* is the spring and early summer. A female may shed 700,000 to 6 million eggs. Bluefin, little tuna, swordfish, and sharks feed on *S. sarda*.

Bonito

The importance of bonito as a sport or commercial fish varies with the species and the geographical area. *S. sarda* is a valued food fish in the eastern Atlantic, and there is an extensive commercial fishery for it. The same fish is much less important in the western Atlantic. A large number of *S. chiliensis* are canned on the Pacific Coast, but they are considered the least valuable of the tunalike fishes and legally cannot be labelled as "tuna." *See also* Little Tunny, Skipjack Tuna

—B.B.C.
—R.H.G.

BONITO SHARK *Isurus glaucus* This Pacific species was long thought to be identical to the mako (*which see*) of Atlantic waters, but the bonito shark differs from it in its lower dorsal fin and shorter head. The streamlined shape of the mako is also characteristic of the bonito shark, as are its slender, recurved teeth, the pointed snout, and the nearly symmetrical tail. It differs from the salmon shark in its shallower body depth and in having the first dorsal fin set entirely behind the pectoral fins, and in having the second dorsal fin somewhat in advance of the anal fin. They are dark blue above, with an abrupt change to white on the sides and on the lower parts. The bonito shark reaches a weight of 1,000 pounds and a length of at least 12 feet.

It is found from southern California to Chile, Hawaii, Japan, and the Indo-Pacific. A closely related species is reported from India. Like the mako, it is a swift-swimming species of the open sea which feeds actively on schools of tuna, bonito, mackerel, and sardines.

ANGLING VALUE

Highly prized for its sporting qualities, it is a recognized gamefish in Australia and New Zealand. But its sportiness also makes it a potential danger to men, and it

has attacked boats. Its flesh is valued, being similar in flavor to the mako.

—D.dS.

BONNETHEAD *Sphyrna tiburo* This member of the hammerhead shark family (Sphyrnidae) has a broadly widened head which is shaped in the form of a shovel, with the eyes at the ends of the expanded head. The distinctive head is more broadly rounded in front than in the great hammerhead (*which see*) and its relatives, and there is no deep indentation in its margin opposite each nostril. The pectoral fins are large and broad, and the high dorsal fin, characteristic of this family, is equal to the depth of the body. A slightly indented anal fin also separates this species from the other hammerhead types which have the anal fin deeply indented. Its color is grayish-brown or gray above on the body and fins, grading to light gray beneath. Occasionally individuals have round, dark spots along the sides. Adults are about 3½ feet long when sexual maturity occurs. It is reported to grow to 6 feet, but even 5 feet is large.

LIFE HISTORY

In the western Atlantic it strays as far north as southern New England, but it occurs most commonly between southern North Carolina and Brazil and throughout the Caribbean Sea and the Gulf of Mexico. It probably also occurs in the warmer parts of the eastern Atlantic and eastern Pacific oceans. In the warmer parts of its range, it is a year-round resident, but to the north it occurs only during the warm, summer months as far as Cape Hatteras. It is one of the commonest shore-dwelling sharks, occurring in less than a foot of water out to at least several fathoms. Young are born alive following a direct connection between the mother and the young through the yolk sac. Newborn are about 1 foot long, and 6–9 are produced at a time.

Among the hammerhead family, it is relatively sluggish, and it is of no danger to man. Crabs, mantis shrimp, shrimps, mollusks, and small fish are eaten.

ANGLING VALUE

Occasionally this species is caught on artificial lures and baits, and, despite its small size, it offers a fair fight on light tackle.

—D.dS.

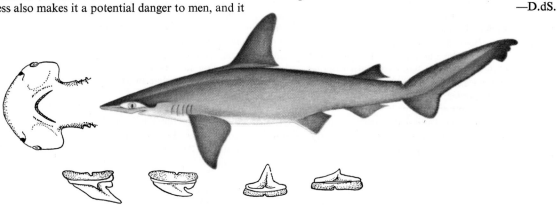

Bonnethead, showing ventral view of head and teeth of upper jaw (*left*) and lower jaw (*right*)

BONYTAIL *Gila robusta* A finely speckled silvery minnow with a dusky or light green back. Area around lower fins is yellowish to orange. Body slender. Eye small. Caudal fin long, broad, and deeply forked. Ventral parts and middorsal region often incompletely scaled or naked. Origin of dorsal fin slightly behind origin of ventral fins. The bonytail is found only in the Colorado River basin.

HABITS

The bonytail is found in rivers, streams, and lakes in the Colorado basin. It is carnivorous, feeding on insects and crustaceans. However, filamentous algae are often found in stomachs of this fish. At spawning time the sides of the head of males becomes slightly reddish. The bonytail reaches a length of 15 inches but averages about 9 inches.

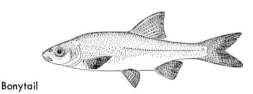

Bonytail

Although quite bony and unsuitable for food, the bonytail is a favorite of young anglers. —R.A.J.

BOOTS *See* Waders

BOSTON MACKEREL A market name for the Atlantic mackerel (*which see*).

BOTTLENOSE DOLPHIN *See* Porpoises

BOUILLABAISSE A saffron-flavored fish soup of the Mediterranean region from Marseilles to Toulon. Bouillabaisse has been glorified by numerous poets and writers since the eighteenth century, and is one of the classic dishes in seafood cookery. The soup cannot be exactly duplicated elsewhere in the world because most of the fish used in it are endemic to the Mediterranean such as the *rascasse*, *chapon*, *rouquier*, and *saint-pierre*. However, very satisfactory substitutes may be prepared in the bouillabaisse manner. In its Marseilles form the soup is made with fish and some crustaceans (crab, shrimp, and spiny lobster), but no mollusks are used. When mollusks are added the dish is identified as an Ocean Bouillabaisse or a Parisian Bouillabaisse. (*See* Snapper Bouillabaisse *under* Fish Cookery.) —A.J.McC.

BOW The forward part of a boat.

BOW CHINE The junction between sides of the bow and hull, designed to funnel spray, water, and air downward, outward, and aft. The bow chine is easily visible in vee- and semivee-bottom boats, and it also provides lift to the bow. Sometimes called "spray chine." *See also* Chine

BOWFIN *Amia calva* Also known as dogfish, grindle, grinnel, and cypress trout, the bowfin has a stout olive-colored body, a long dorsal fin, and a rounded tail. The top of the head is flattened; the mouth is large and filled with strong, sharp teeth. On the underside of the head is a distinctive gular plate. The sexes of the adults can be differentiated by a spot at the upper base of the tail. The male's spot is rimmed with orange-yellow; on the female the rim is lacking, or the spot is absent. A feature of the bowfin's unique structure is an air bladder connected to the throat and used as a lung, enabling them to live in waters unsuitable for other fish. They attain lengths up to 3 feet and weights in excess of 20 pounds.

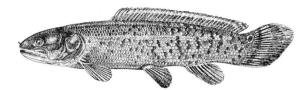

Bowfin

This primitive fish is the lone survivor of a large family now found only as fossils in the rocks of Europe and the United States. It is found in most parts of this country from the Mississippi River drainage eastward to the St. Lawrence River and south from Texas to Florida. It usually inhabits shallow, weedy lakes and sluggish streams and is seldom found in fast currents.

LIFE HISTORY

Spawning occurs in the spring, April through June, depending on the water temperature of the locality, in quiet bays or inlets containing vegetation. The male builds a nest by biting off the vegetation in a small area and brushing it away with its tail and fins. When it has cleared away the weeds, a bed of soft rootlets, sand, or gravel remains for the eggs. Spawning takes place at night. After one or more females have spawned in the nest the male guards the eggs for the 8–10 days required for hatching. As soon as the larvae hatch, they attach themselves to rootlets by an adhesive organ on the snout or lie on their sides in the bottom of the nest until they are about ½ inch long. The male continues to stand guard; it hovers in a runway to the nest, its head projecting over it. When an unwelcome visitor approaches, it makes a noisy escape, probably to decoy the intruder away from the nest.

At about nine days the larvae can swim and begin feeding. The adhesive organ ceases to be used, and the young follow the male in a close school. If one becomes separated from the parent, the young fish swims in close circles until its protector reappears. When about 1½ inch long, the adult colors appear, and they begin to protect themselves by seeking cover individually. When 4 inches or so, they cease to gather in schools.

Because the bowfin is a poor food fish and because it feeds extensively on other fish, it usually is considered as undesirable. But since the areas it prefers are likely to be overpopulated by stunted panfish or rough fish, the bowfin is often really an asset. It can be quite effective in holding fish populations in check.

Fish compose upward of 80 per cent of this voracious feeder's diet, with crayfish comprising much of the remainder. Many other items are taken when they can be had easily.

ANGLING VALUE

Most bowfin are caught while the angler is fishing for other species. It is then that he discovers that this fish is a rugged fighter that strikes hard and fights better than some highly rated gamefish and is worth seeking for angling fun. Some sportsmen regularly travel long distances in search of bowfin. —C.A.P.

BOW LINE A mooring or dock line led forward through a bow chock and making an angle less than 45 degrees with the fore and aft line of the boat.

BRAZIL This largest South American country has tremendous fishery resources which are not readily available to the tourist angler due to the lack of accommodations and boats in virtually all areas. Brazil occupies almost half of South America and all but two of the twelve other countries on the continent border it. From its northwest to its southeast corner Brazil extends the same distance as a line drawn from the Arctic Circle to the middle of the Sahara Desert. Beyond the lush forested mountains that surround Rio de Janeiro the land is brown and folded and the low barren hills extend for countless hundreds of miles before giving way to a scrubby flood plain pocked by giant mud termite nests. There is no real sign of jungle until you reach the southern tributaries of the Amazon, which run their northerly courses in serpentine fashion and then, abruptly, the solid mass of green begins. Over half of Brazil is contained in the Amazon basin; the 3,915-mile length of it pumps out one-fifth of all the freshwater in the world; scores of isolated, nomadic, and occasionally hostile Indian tribes exist in an almost 6 million-acre rain forest. The future development of Amazonia depends on the Transamazon Road which connects Brazil's easternmost city, Joao Pessoa, with Peru. Paved roads radiate from Rio de Janeiro and Sao Paulo heading north along the coast, south into the farmlands, and west to Brasilia, the capital city; there they terminate.

Winter here is from June to September. Generally speaking, this is the best period for freshwater fishing, with the peak month in August. The rainy season on the Amazon begins in November and extends to June. Saltwater fishing, on the other hand, is best in spring and summer, which extends from October to March. In the interior the weather is hot and humid, with the cooler part of a day beginning about 3 A.M. and extending to about 10 A.M. It's always warm in Rio, with average temperatures between 78° and 80° F. During the summer season it is also humid.

SALTWATER FISHING

Brazil has 5,589 miles of shoreline including all the large indentations of its coast, with its extreme limits at Cabo Orange (latitude 4°20′45″N) and Arroio Chui (latitude 33°45′10″S). Being situated in the Western South

A rayado or striped catfish taken in the Rio São Laurenço of the Mato Grasso. Rayado are popular food fish in Brazil

Atlantic it encompasses tropical, subtropical, and temperate waters. Extensive oceanic formations—such as São Pedro and São Paulo Reefs, Fernando de Noronha Archipelago, Roccas Reefs, Trinadade Island, and Martin Vaz Archipelago—create diversified habitat conditions reflecting the distribution and abundance of marine fishes. The most common species of angling interest are sailfish, blue marlin, white marlin, yellowfin tuna, swordfish, wahoo, king mackerel, albacore, tarpon, dolphin, barracuda, cero mackerel, snook, great and southern amberjack (*Seriola lalandi*), bluefish, cobia, and various groupers. Mako, tiger, hammerhead, and blacktip sharks are also frequently caught.

Offshore fishing is popular near several coastal cities. However, there are no boats for charter and, for the present at least, it's necessary to be invited by a Brazilian angler to sample what is available. The luxurious Rio de Janeiro Yacht Club (Iate Club do Rio de Janeiro) harbors some 600 craft of assorted types, including a large fleet of modern sport fishermen. A few boats work out of Cabo Frio and Salvador. As a rule of thumb big-game fishing is found closer to land in the north (7–8 miles offshore at Salvador) and at greater distances as you proceed south.

Billfish are very abundant off Brazil. There is some fishing for sailfish throughout the year in the vicinity of the continental shelf off the north and northeast coasts, as well as in the Archipelago of Fernando de Noronha. But the active sport fishery is around Cabo Frio and Rio de Janeiro during the summer season. Sailfish are both numerous and of good average size (about 60 pounds). The productive big-game season is from November through February, with blue marlin peaking in late November and December and sailfish becoming abundant in January. The fishing grounds out of Rio are 25 miles or more offshore; Brazilian anglers seek blue water with a surface temperature of about 76°F to locate concentrations of gamefish, and this condition varies from day to day occurring sometimes at 35–45 miles from the coast. Blue marlin are taken in the same area, and fish of over 1,000 pounds are a real possibility, although the present Rio Yacht Club record is 680 pounds. White marlin are numerically less abundant than the blue, but they appear earlier (September) and remain in the south of Brazil until April. Swordfish are frequently sighted, particularly in the Fernando do Noronha Archipelago, in the vicinity of Cabo São Roque, and in the Abrolhos Archipelago. Few swordfish are hooked, although a great many are baited.

Small bluefin tuna (less than 200 pounds) are occasionally caught off the Brazilian coast, but not in great number. Yellowfin tuna are more abundant and occur in three different areas: the Fernando de Noronha Archipelago in the vicinity of Cabo São Roque (Rio Grande de Norte State), in the Abrolhos Archipelago (Bahia State), and during the summer in the area of Cabo Frio (Rio de Janeiro State). Fish of 140–150 pounds are common. Another but smaller tuna, the albacore, also enters the sport fishery. The albacore, with rare exceptions, in the tropical region of the Atlantic is an infrathermoclinal species, where the larger known concentrations are situated southwest of a diagonal line oriented in a northwest-southeast direction dividing the zone in half. Albacore fishing in Brazil occurs in two different areas: in the Abrolhos Archipelago throughout the year and in Cabo Frio during summer.

Wahoo and king mackerel are also important Brazilian gamefish. Both occur in the same general areas during the summer months along the continental shelf and oceanic islands from Amapa Territory to Rio de Janeiro State. These species are of good size, with the wahoo running to 100 pounds and the king mackerel to 60 pounds. Dolphin are very abundant along the entire coast of Brazil, but only during the summer months in the southern zone; this colorful acrobat is caught in large numbers out of Rio in weights up to 40 pounds and often somewhat closer to shore (6–7 miles) than other marine gamefish. Barracuda, by contrast, are neither abundant nor large in the southern zone, being distributed mainly along the reefs and oceanic islands of the north and east.

Tarpon form migratory schools in Brazilian coastal waters, penetrating into estuaries of large rivers as far as tidal influence reaches. It is a regionally important species for sport fishing, reaching 150 pounds or more in weight. Tarpon are caught in large numbers throughout the year along the coast of Maranhao, Piaui, and Ceara states, where it concentrates, and to a lesser extent farther north as far as São Paulo State. Two popular locations for tarpon fishing are the Rio Dolce and Cabedelo Harbor. Typically, snook occur in the same habitats as the tarpon, although it is believed that the former has declined somewhat due to unrestricted spear-fishing, which is a popular method in Brazil.

The great amberjack has a wide distribution in the Western Atlantic. It measures up to 6 feet in length and over 100 pounds in weight. Amberjacks are caught along the coast of Brazil throughout the year. However, the best fishing occurs during May and June in the area of Cabo Frio. The southern amberjack known locally as "yellowtail" or oeillete is a popular foodfish.

FRESHWATER FISHING

The freshwater rivers of Brazil have a great variety of endemic species such as the pavón (locally tucunaré), dorado, aruaná, pacu, payara (locally peixe-cachorro), and numerous large catfishes. Considerable stocking has been done with the pavón and dorado (which was successfully introduced in the Paraiba River not far from Rio) in new impoundments and farm ponds, but the quality fishing is found in clearwater tributaries of the upper Amazon watershed and major river systems to the south, which are difficult of access. Two large species of dorado occur in Brazil, *Salminus brevidens*, in the São Francisco River, and *S. maxillosus*, in the Parana and Paraguai River systems which rise in the Mato Grosso. Although extremely fertile and containing a great variety of fishes, the two latter rivers are muddy even in the dry season and of little interest to sport fishermen until they reach rock substrate—the Parana below Iguassu Falls and the Paraguai below its junction with the Apa River. Some of the better dorado waters in this area are the Piquiri, Taquari, Aquidauana, and Apa rivers. The Apa forms the border between Brazil and Paraguay. During a *piracema* or spawning run, which generally begins with the early rains in October, the Apa literally boils with dorado from 20–40 pounds in size. However, all these rivers are difficult of access; the mosquito problem is bad; and there are no functional facilities.

Many Amazon tributaries provide excellent pavón fishing. Pavón are very strong for their size and offer excellent sport

Bananal Island This National Park and Indian reservation is formed by the bifurcation of the Araguaia River, which divides the states of Matto Grasso and Goias in central Brazil. This river island, largest in the world (480 miles long and 136 miles in width), is dotted with countless lakes and lagoons which contain gamefish such as the pavón, aruaná, and picua. Some of the more remote lakes hold an abundance of pavón, and it is possible to catch 50 or 60 in a day averaging about 2 pounds, with the occasional 6 or 7 pounder. There are at least 2 species of pavón indigenous to the area which are separate and distinct from those found in the Orinoco watershed; the Indian name tucunaré is applied to both. These are cichlids of standing rather than moving water and not common to the main rivers. Easily caught, these pavón will take almost any plug, spoon, jig, streamer fly, or bass bug.

The best option, from the standpoint of services and fishing potential, is a houseboat operation based at the northern end of Bananal Island. The houseboat cruises about 100 miles on the Araguaia River and its tributaries; it provides aluminum John-boats with guides for actual fishing. The houseboat departs four times a month beginning in June until mid-November. August would be the prime month.

Iguassu Falls On the Argentine border this is one of the unique sights of the world. The falls can be reached in about 2 hours by plane from São Paulo. Higher than Niagara, they are also 2½ miles wide. More than thirty rivers pour into the Iguassu basin. Eight miles away are the falls of Sete Quedas. There are two modern hotels near Iguassu which arrange dorado fishing. —A.J.McC.

BREACHING When an unhooked fish is seen jumping, it is "breaching." Fish breach for various reasons; sometimes to get rid of annoying parasites (remoras or sucker fish); and sometimes when they are feeding, traveling, or about to start a migration. This is strictly a big-game fishing term. *See also* Big-Game Fishing

BREAK (1) The offshore line parallel to the beach where peaking ocean swells cap over and fall into rollers is the *break*, and the wave then is a *breaker*.

(2) An anchor is *broken out* when hauled sufficiently free of the bottom so that a fluke no longer can get a bite; and the same term is applied to any other equipment aboard a ship when taken from its normal storing place.

(3) An order to *break off* means to cease operations.

BREAM A regional colloquialism (Southern United States) for various sunfishes, usually pronounced as "brim." Also the common name for a European cyprinid. *See* Bronze Bream

BRIDLE SHINER *Notropis bifrenatus* A small, straw-colored minnow with a prominent, shining, lateral black band. Body slender, lateral line incomplete with thirteen scales before dorsal fin. Similar to blackchin shiner and blacknose shiner but with more black pigment on the chin. A small but handsome species. The range of the bridle shiner is from Maine to Virginia in the Atlantic drainage.

Bridle Shiner

HABITS

The bridle shiner is found in clear, quiet water of lakes and streams, preferring shallow water with abundant vegetation over sand and mud bottom. Little is known of the food habits of this species. It apparently spawns in May and June when gravid females can be distinguished from the males by their deeper bodies. A diminutive minnow, this fish has a maximum size of 2 inches.

Although small the bridle shiner is an attractive bait for bass and is taken greedily by yellow perch and other panfish.   —R.A.J.

BRILL *Rhombus laevis* The brill is closely related to another European flatfish, the turbot (*which see*). Both fish lie on their *right* sides. The brill differs in being more oval in outline, with small embedded cycloid scales on both sides and no tubercles on the back. The mature brill resembles the young turbot, but brill lack the turbot's characteristic head spines.

The left or upper side of the brill is variable, gray-brown to green with darker and lighter patches. The patches may be varied by special changing-pigment cells; the colors fade after death. The underside (right) is an opaque white. Fin-ray counts are: dorsal 76–85; anal 53–65.

Brill are normally found at depths of about 100 feet, but they do range up to three times this depth. Geographically, they are found in the Mediterranean and eastern Atlantic, though absent from truly Arctic waters.

Brill feed dominantly on small fish—the sand-eel (*Ammodytes* spp.), sprats (*Clupea sprattus*), and pout-whiting or "blynn" (*Gadus luscus*).

Brill are smaller than turbot, reaching about 10 pounds in weight with a record of 16 pounds.

LIFE HISTORY

The brill spawns between March and August at its living depth, the female discharging 100,000 eggs per pound of weight. The eggs, as with those of other flatfish, are pelagic (that is, they float) and are dispersed by surface currents. The eggs are 1–1½ mm. in diameter with a single pale-colored oil globule. Little is known of the early life of the brill. The male reaches maturity at 10 inches, the females at 13 inches.

COMMERCIAL VALUE

Brill are taken in trawls along with turbot, but they do not command such a good market price as the turbot does. However, it is bought when available and eaten in many parts of Europe.

ANGLING VALUE

Anglers catch brill while turbot fishing, but brill are not normally sought on their own, nor do they occur with enough regularity to justify doing so.

The tackle on which they are caught is therefore normally too heavy to bring out any fighting qualities they have for two reasons: first, it is designed for the heavier turbot; second, the preferred ground of both is a shallow sand or gravel bank scoured by a fast tide race. Fishing

Brill

from a boat, this means heavy sinkers and correspondingly heavy rods and lines. Although English boat parties (particularly from the Channel ports) seek brill with natural baits, there is every reason to experiment with leaded jigs and other lures.   —D.M.

BRINDLED MADTOM *Noturus miurus* A small, mottled catfish with poisonous pectoral spines. Color grayish with dorsal blotches. Pectoral spine with 4–8 sharp teeth on rear edge. Tail rounded. Adipose with no free lobe and separated from caudal by a slight notch. Upper jaw longer than lower jaw. Eye rather large. It ranges from Illinois to southern Ontario and to Mississippi and Oklahoma.

LIFE HISTORY

This species appears to prefer quiet, clear streams over sand bottoms and organic debris. A secretive fish, it hides by day under stones, roots, or logs. Little is known of its breeding habits, but it appears to spawn much in the manner of others of its genus. An omnivorous feeder, the brindled madtom subsists on various aquatic organisms found in the organic debris in which it lives. This species is quite small, averaging less than 4 inches in length.

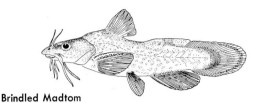

Brindled Madtom

ECONOMIC VALUE

The brindled madtom is too small and rare to be of much value. However, it is said to make a good aquarium species. —R.A.J.

BRITISH COLUMBIA This westernmost province of Canada encompasses 366,266 square miles with a variety of geographical terrain which includes everything from heavily forested areas of fir and spruce and agricultural valleys to desert areas. Located in this vast region are innumerable lakes, rivers, and streams, many of them accessible only by pack train, where unfished waters still exist. British Columbia has a coastline extending for some 16,900 miles from the state of Washington to the state of Alaska, with innumerable fjords and islands, and offers unlimited fishing for those who prefer their fishing in saltwater.

Climatic conditions are such that it can be safely said that in some part of this vast province fishing is available during all seasons of the year. A very active Provincial Fish and Game Department has in recent years engaged in a most successful replanting of sport fish in many of the lakes so abundant throughout the province, and the results of this program have been most satisfactory. Lakes that were stocked three years ago with fingerling rainbow trout are now producing fish weighing from 8–12 pounds. In most instances, these lakes are readily accessible to the motorist who visits British Columbia.

In the freshwater areas the steelhead is one of the great trophies available, followed closely by the resident rainbow or Kamloops trout, while in the saltwater the chinook salmon, reaching weights of as high as 80 pounds, is surpassed by the very active coho salmon as a light tackle fish.

STEELHEAD FISHING

The steelhead is distinct from the resident rainbow or Kamloops trout of British Columbia, in so far as angling is concerned. Generally, steelhead live in freshwater for 1½–2 years after hatching, then migrate to the sea. About a year and a half is spent in the ocean, and it is during this period that growth is rapid. Most steelhead return to the streams to spawn from November to March, although there are some rivers which support summer runs. Thus the steelhead is most often fished in the winter months, after the rivers have swollen from the fall and winter rains.

Vancouver Island The island provides excellent steelheading on both coasts. On the west coast some of the better streams are the Ash River near Alberni, with summer and winter runs from June to October and from December to March, and the Stamp River near Alberni, with summer and winter runs from July to September and from December to March. Of the many steelhead streams on the east coast the following are outstanding: the Cowichan River near Duncan, with a good winter run; the Nanaimo, Little Qualicum, and Puntledge rivers with runs from December to April; Campbell River with a winter run from December to March and possibly a small summer run; and much farther up the island, Nimpkish River with a winter run from November to March.

Lower Mainland The Vedder, by far the best steelhead river in the lower mainland, has an excellent run from December to April. On the north side of the Fraser River, the Chehalis, Coquitlam, and the Alouette are good steelhead rivers with runs from December until March. Elsewhere in the lower mainland several streams provide fair steelheading. The Capilano and Seymour, both on the north side of Burrard Inlet, near Vancouver, have runs from December to April and in June and July. However, steelhead are in these two streams at other times of the year. The Nicomekl and the Campbell, both near the International border, produce light winter runs from December until March. The Coquihalla and Silver, near Hope, support summer runs that reach their peak in July.

Southern Interior The Thompson River is the only important steelhead river in the southern interior and has become recognized as one of the finest in the province. Running through the dry country of the interior from the Rocky Mountains, it is a clean, swift-flowing river that joins the Fraser at Lytton. For 65 miles upstream, from Lytton to Savona, the fishing is excellent, and the auto road shadows the river all the way, at times virtually on the bank. Though fish are taken from September until May, the better months are from October until March. The steelhead in this river are usually much larger than those in coastal streams and average 16 pounds.

A few other rivers in this area should be mentioned. The Nahatlach (Salmon), a tributary of the Fraser that enters near Boston Bar, has a fairly good run in April and May. Steelhead of 20 pounds have been taken in this stream. Near Alexis Creek in the Chilcotin district, the Chilko and Chilcotin rivers also have late spring runs.

Prince Rupert Area Several important steelhead rivers lie northeast of Prince Rupert in the Skeena River drainage, among them the Kispiox, Morice, Telkwa, Copper, and the Bulkley. The Kispiox is justly famous because it was from this river, in October 1954, that a record steelhead of 36 pounds was taken. Easily fished, the Kispiox can be reached by road from Prince George via Hazelton or from Prince Rupert. The Morice, Copper, and Telkwa rivers are tributaries of the Bulkley, and all three offer excellent fishing.

Queen Charlotte Islands Excellent steelhead fishing is available, particularly in the Copper, Tlell, and Yakoun rivers, with air transportation to and on the islands.

Coastal The Bella Coola River, with an excellent steelhead run from November to April, has miles of easily fished water. The Brem and Dean rivers, fine steelhead streams but not easily reached, have winter and summer runs. Squamish and Powell River areas also offer good steelheading.

RAINBOW-TROUT FISHING

The rainbow trout is native to British Columbia. Within the last fifty years, thousands of lakes have been planted with fry or eggs. Ideally suited to British Columbia lakes and streams, this species is the most important freshwater sport fish in the province. A strong fish, it has firm, salmon-like flesh that provides excellent eating either fresh or smoked. The rainbow exists in a variety of fishing conditions. Lakes such as the Lightning Lakes in Manning Park might be called family lakes; the fish are small (a 10-inch fish would be a big one) but so plentiful that no one leaves disappointed. However, in the larger lakes, such as Shuswap and Kootenay, trout may tip the scales at 25 pounds. In 1913 two huge rainbows, one weighing 56 pounds and the other 48 pounds, were taken from Jewel Lake in the Kootenay district. Giants like these (they were not caught by rod-and-reel) are extremely rare, and today the average size of a Kamloops or rainbow trout is about 1½ pounds.

Although there is no closed season for fishing in British Columbia lakes, fishing is largely carried out after the ice is gone. Generally, lakes are ice free in May. Lower altitude lakes, in the South Okanagan for example, may be open in early April, whereas those at higher levels, regardless of latitude, may not be open until June.

The Kootenays and Okanagan Fishing in these areas is best from May until September or October. In Okanagan and Kootenay lakes, which rarely freeze over, fishing may last from early spring until late fall. In the Kootenay district Kootenay, Upper and Lower Arrow, Christina, and Jewel are some of the better-known lakes. A great many small lakes lie in the hills on either side of Okanagan Lake in the Oliver, Penticton, Kelowna, and Vernon areas. Okanagan and Kalamalka lakes have produced some large rainbow trout.

Kamloops District The City of Kamloops is truly the heart of the rainbow-trout country and provides the regional name of the trout in that district. Shuswap, the biggest lake in the area, produces some large Kamloops. The mouth of the Adams River, which flows into Shuswap, is an excellent spot in May and June. Innumerable small lakes in the Merritt and Princeton areas and between Clinton and Lac La Hache offer really fine trout fishing. The fish in these smaller lakes will not usually be as heavy as those in the larger lakes, but they are plentiful and provide good sport.

Quesnel-Chilcoton District Several rainbow-trout lakes lie east of Quesnel, among them Horsefly and Quesnel. The Chilcotin is a relatively new area containing many little-known lakes. The western portions of this district, toward Bella Coola, Anahim, and Nimpo, have only recently been found to contain many excellent trout lakes. These waters can be reached by road from Williams Lake via Alexis Creek or also from Bella Coola on the west coast.

Burns Lake About 140 miles west of Prince George, this area is relatively unexploited. Between Burns Lake and Tweedsmuir Park lie a number of excellent lakes, some large like François and Ootsa and many smaller such as Burns, Tchesinkut, Uncha, and Binta. Tweedsmuir Park, liberally endowed with lakes and rivers, offers many opportunities for trout enthusiasts. North of Burns Lake several large lakes such as Babine, Stuart, Trembleur, and Takla offer not only rainbow trout but lake trout and Dolly Varden as well.

Vancouver Island Rainbow trout occur in most lakes on the island and are found in all lakes which have access to the sea and in many streams and rivers.

CUTTHROAT-TROUT FISHING

This trout occurs in virtually all lakes and streams along the entire coast of British Columbia. Like the rainbow, the cutthroat may be either anadromous or nonmigratory in freshwater. The sea-run cutthroat enters spawning streams in late November, and both it and the resident cutthroat spawn from February until May. The anadro-

The westernmost province of British Columbia is veined with picturesque rainbow trout streams

mous form is smaller than the steelhead but will run 1½–4 pounds. The resident cutthroat shows a greater weight range. Those in streams are usually small while those in lakes vary from a few ounces to as high as 17 pounds. The cutthroat is a popular fly fisherman's quarry.

Lower Mainland Cutthroat fishing in this area is mainly for the sea-run variety. The Nicomekl, Campbell, and Serpentine rivers are heavily fished in January and February. The Nicomekl is the best of the three. From Hope to the coast, bar-fishermen on the Fraser River enjoy good cutthroat fishing from August to late fall. Butzen Lake, on the north of Burrard Inlet, Alouette, Stave, and Harrison lakes on the north side of the Fraser all provide resident cutthroat fishing. Somewhat surprising, perhaps, is the fact that resident cutthroat inhabit Big Bar, a lake in the interior of the province, about twenty miles northwest of Clinton.

Upper Coast Bella Coola, Brem, and Dean rivers support both sea-run and resident cutthroat trout.

Queen Charlotte Islands The rivers here are excellent cutthroat rivers. The Tlell and Yakoun in particular provide fishing of the highest quality.

Vancouver Island Apparently sea-run cutthroat do not roam far from freshwater during their saltwater life. They move in and out of larger streams throughout the year, preying on salmon eggs in the fall, or salmon fry in the spring. Many such streams drain both coasts of the island. The larger lakes, particularly Nimpkish, Campbell, Buttle, Sproat, Great Centraland, and Cowichan produce fine resident cutthroat.

BROWN-TROUT FISHING

The brown trout was introduced in the Cowichan and Little Qualicum rivers in 1932 and is now well established in these two river systems as well as Niagara Creek on the east coast of Vancouver Island. In the upper reaches of the Cowichan, brown trout up to 5 pounds have been taken. As in the case of sea-run cutthroat the brown trout may migrate to saltwater but does not seem to stray far from its native stream. The brown trout is highly valued by fly-fishermen because of its extreme wariness.

CHINOOK-SALMON FISHING

The coastal waters of British Columbia support five species of salmon—chinook, coho, pink, sockeye, and chum. All are important commercial species, but only the chinook and the coho are of interest to the saltwater angler. The pink salmon, although caught in fair numbers, is not highly rated as a sport fish when compared to either the coho or the chinook. There are size variations of chinook and coho entering the sport fishery; early maturing males in freshwater are known as *jacks;* 2-year-old coho are known as *grilse;* and *blueback* are young coho in their final year of sea growth.

A boat, powered if possible, is generally required for saltwater salmon fishing. Trolling and stripcasting are the two most popular angling methods. Coho, however, are good sport and in excellent condition for some time after they have entered freshwater, and here methods vary. Generally, fly-fishing and bait-casting are preferable. The chinook is also called tyee, king, blackmouth, and spring salmon. Locally tyee applies only to chinook over 30 pounds. A world record was set in 1959 when a giant 92-pounder was rod-caught in the Skeena River near Terrace. Since it it continually searching for food (largely for needlefish and herring), this salmon is found in all coastal waters and can be caught the year round. The best chinook fishing is in July and August and September. Normally, the run reaches its peak in the first half of August.

Vancouver Island Favored places on the island are Port Alberni, Bamfield, Campbell River, Cowichan, and Comox. However, as springs migrate from northern waters toward the rivers and larger streams, they are found in most inshore areas along both coasts of the island.

The Mainland Out of the maze of inlets, channels, and islands from Vancouver to Prince Rupert several areas stand out as fishing localities: Howe Sound (by boat and road), Powell River (by road), Phillips Arm (by boat), Rivers Inlet (by boat), and Bella Coola (by boat and road), all in the lower coastal area. In the upper coastal area, the estuary of the Skeena River, the channels and inlets in the Prince Rupert area (by boat, road, rail, or air), and off Prince Rupert, the rivers of Queen Charlotte Islands (by boat or air).

Gulf Islands The climate in this region is ideal. Temperatures are moderate throughout the entire year, rainfall is low (about 25 inches annually), and sunshine is the rule. The waters surrounding the Gulf Islands are well sheltered and, combined with the gentle climate, make fishing pleasant in any season. Both chinook and coho are found in abundance in this area. The majority of this group lies off the southeastern coast of Vancouver Island. Gabriola, Galiano, Salt Spring, and Pender (North and South) are the biggest islands, and all are accessible by air or boat from either Vancouver or Vancouver Island.

COHO-SALMON FISHING

Coho are not as large as chinook salmon. However, because they occur in greater numbers they provide more fishing. Coho will spawn in practically any running water where suitable gravel is available. They are found in almost all coastal streams of the British Columbia coast. In their last year of sea growth coho will weigh about 5 pounds in May and up to as much as 15 pounds in late September. Strong fish and highly prized by anglers, they put up a tremendous, leaping fight, particularly if hooked on light tackle. Unlike other salmon, coho provide good fishing after entering the spawning streams.

August and September are usually the best months for coho fishing in most coastal waters. Coho are still feeding extensively, and their movement toward the spawning streams has begun. However, June and July are also good months. Late in the season, in October, when coho congregate near stream estuaries waiting for fall rain freshets, they can still be taken on the fly. After they have entered the streams—and some will arrive as early as August—they are fishable until they begin to darken. Coho spawn late, sometimes as late as January.

Vancouver Island Good coho fishing may be enjoyed in most of the sheltered bays and inlets on either coast. On the west coast, Barclay Sound is the main fishing area at present, and on the east coast two famous places are Cowichan Bay and, further up the coast, Duncan Bay near Campbell River. Several other places on the east coast of Vancouver Island also provide excellent coho fishing. A few of them are Comox, Nanaimo, and Oyster Bay.

The Mainland Because of their spawning habits, coho are found in practically all inlets and bays. Some of the better-known areas on the lower coast are Howe Sound (road), Sechelt (road), Jervis Inlet (boat), Powell River (boat and road), and Toba Inlet (boat). In the upper coastal area, Bella Coola and Prince Rupert are the principal centers.

Queen Charlotte Islands West of Prince Rupert, these islands have for years had a reputation as being ideal fishing and hunting grounds. Although air and boat services from Vancouver are good, few tourists visit the Queen Charlottes. Copper River and Bay on Moresby Island is probably the best coho region in British Columbia. The Tlell and the Yakoun rivers also provide excellent coho fishing.

KOKANEE FISHING

The kokanee (*which see*), variously known as little red fish, kokininee, or silver trout, usually spawns in its third or fourth year of life, and, like the anadromous sockeye, it dies after spawning. The average size of the kokanee is about a pound in Lac La Hache on the Cariboo Highway or Woods Lake near Kelowna, but the species can attain a weight of 9 pounds, as a kokanee of this size was caught in Echo Lake near Okanagan.

The kokanee has deep red flesh and is probably the finest eating fish, either smoked or cooked, in British Columbia. There is no closed season in lakes for kokanee, nor are there catch or bag limits. With the exception of northern British Columbia, kokanee occur in most of the larger lakes, both on the mainland and on Vancouver Island. The Bowron Lake chain produces some excellent fly-fishing for kokanee during June and July.

LAKE-TROUT FISHING

Also called the gray trout, the lake trout is found in all the larger lakes from Shuswap Lake north to lakes of the Yukon River drainage. This species prefers deep coldwater lakes, and has been recorded in the province to 60 pounds. However, 5–25 pounds would be more within the range of those generally caught. Larger lake trout subsist almost entirely on other fish.

Although some fishing is done through the ice, late spring and summer are the best seasons for lake-trout fishing. A few of the char lakes from Shuswap northward are Adams, the larger lakes in the Lac La Hache-Quesnel area, Fraser, Stuart, François, Babine, and Morrison of central British Columbia. Lake trout are not found in the Columbia River system.

DOLLY VARDEN FISHING

The Dolly Varden is much more widespread than the lake trout. It occurs in lakes and streams throughout British Columbia with the exception of the Okanagan drainage. Like the coastal cutthroat and rainbow, the Dolly Varden may spend its entire life in a lake or stream or may migrate to sea.

Vancouver Island Dolly Varden inhabit a few of the rivers and lakes of the island. The Campbell River system, and Comox and Cowichan Lakes, at least, support both the sea-going and resident type.

Lower Mainland Dolly Varden are found in most of the lakes and streams which connect, or have connected, with the Fraser River. In Alouette and Stave lakes on the north side of the Fraser, Dolly Varden up to 4 pounds have been taken. Sea-run Dolly Varden probably enter the streams in July and August.

Upper Coastal Though the Dolly Varden is spread throughout a large part of the province, the sea-run form is more abundant toward the northern coastal section. Dolly Varden occur in the Bella Coola, in the Skeena, and in many other rivers in this section.

Interior Dolly Varden inhabit the main Thompson (a 20-pounder was caught at Savona) and the North Thompson rivers.

Southeastern British Columbia The Dolly Varden is present in most of the streams and larger lakes open to the Columbia drainage except the Okanagan River drainage. Kootenay Lake is the most abundant source in this region, and Dolly Varden up to 22 pounds have been caught there. However, the usual weight of the species in the Columbia drainage is generally 3–4 pounds.

BROOK-TROUT FISHING

The brook trout (*which see*) was introduced into British Columbia in 1908, and is now found in waters of south and southeastern British Columbia and Vancouver Island. It is generally a small fish but runs occasionally to about 5 pounds. The brook trout does not compare with the rainbow as a sport fish. However, in some streams in the Kootenay area, it seems to be well suited to the new habitat and provides angling of high quality.

Vancouver Island Brook trout occur in tributaries of the upper reaches of the Cowichan River, Spectacle Lake in the Malahat District, and in Round and Semenos lakes near Duncan.

The Mainland Eastern brook trout are found in many lakes and streams in the southeastern part of the province as well as in lakes and streams of the Princeton and lower Okanagan regions.

WARMWATER FISHES

The warmwater fishes, notably smallmouth bass and perch have been introduced to British Columbia from the United States. In their native waters they are highly valued as sport fish but in British Columbia are of little interest to anglers. The smallmouth is the most important of the

warmwater fishes and is better suited to local habitats than the largemouth. Introduced into a few lakes of Vancouver Island and the mainland in 1901, the smallmouth is now found in Christina and Boldue lakes and Kettle River below Cascade Falls, all in the Grand Forks area; it is reportedly found in Moyie Lake south of Cranbrook; several lakes on southern Vancouver Island including Florence, Langford, Beaver, Durrance, and Spider lakes. The bronzeback also became established at St. Mary and Rosemergey lakes on Salt Spring Island in Georgia Strait.

The largemouth bass is believed to have entered British Columbia from Idaho some time before 1920. It is found only in lakes of the Columbia River drainage system: Vaseux, Osoyoos, Shannon, Christina lakes near Grand Forks; Duck and Kootenay lakes; Mirror Lake near Kaslo; and Wasa Lake near Cranbrook. Yellow perch inhabit a few lakes of the southern Okanagan Valley, including Osoyoos Lake, and occur in Duck Lake and Kootenay River sloughs.　　　　　　—W.E.H.

BRITISH HONDURAS Extending south of the Quintana Roo Territory of Mexico, British Honduras offers a variety of saltwater angling with the seasonal emphasis on tarpon and snook. Fishing may be divided between the mainland—with its numerous rivers, lagoons, and mangrove-bordered bays—and the Turneffe Islands, which are located within a 190-mile-long barrier reef that parallels the mainland about 15 miles offshore.

The northern half of British Honduras is low (less than 200 feet above sea level); the southern half consists in part of a plateau and the Maya Mountains. The climate is subtropical, with a dry season that lasts from February to April and a wet season from June to October. The mean annual temperature varies from 74°F in December to 83°F in July. The coolest weather is from October to December. Trade winds prevail through most of the year.

THE MAINLAND

The mainland of British Honduras offers snook and tarpon fishing in the many lagoons and rivers north and south of Belize City. Some of the better locations are the Northern River, Belize River and its tributaries, Sibun River, Manatee River, Stann Creek, Southern Stann Creek, Sapodillia Lagoon, Monkey River, Goldstream, Rio Grande River, and Moho River. The fishing is usually done in comfortable outboard-powered skiffs, but one resort in Belize also charters houseboats for extended trips to more remote rivers. The houseboat, which has functional sleeping quarters and dining facilities, accommodates four anglers.

On the average, snook in these waters weigh from 5–20 pounds (the local record is 47 pounds), and the tarpon from 20–50 pounds, with the occasional possibility of fish in the 100-pound class. Although some tarpon are present the year round, with large individuals occurring far inland in the headwater sections, the major run extends from late April through June. The best snook fishing is in December. Bonefish, snappers, groupers, jacks, and some permit are found in suitable habitats along the 120-mile coast. An endemic species unfamiliar to tourist anglers is the so-called "bay snook" (*Petenia splendida*), which occurs in fresh and brackish water. Known also in Honduras as the blanco, this species averages from 1–4 pounds in weight and provides some sport on a light fly or spinning rod.

Remote Lighthouse Reef off the coast of British Honduras. This area produces fishing for small tarpon and bonefish

There are few all-weather roads so most of the coastal fishing areas are inaccessible except by boat.

TURNEFFE ISLANDS

These islands are a complex of low mangrove-covered cays lying within a barrier reef about 20 miles due east of Belize City. This reef extends 36 miles on a north-south axis. The fishing consists primarily of bonefish, great barracuda, mutton snapper, yellowtail snapper, mangrove snapper, dog snapper (locally reef snapper), yellow jack, horse-eye jack, cero mackerel, dolphin, and king mackerel. There is also tarpon here beginning in April, with fish running from 20–60 pounds which provide good sport on light tackle into July. Reef fishing for various groupers (the Nassau and black grouper are most common), snappers, cobia, jacks, ocean and queen triggerfish, and mackerels is excellent.

Turneffe Island bonefish flats exist on the easterly shores inside the barrier reef. These have a hard bottom of coral, sand, and extensive turtle grass beds. They are easily waded. Due to the extreme tides on this type of flat much of the fishing is done in ankle to knee deep water. Fly fishermen should include buoyant patterns (light wire hooks and bushy hair wings) or weedless keel hook flies to avoid snagging in the bottom. During low tide periods bonefish gather in deep holes on or adjacent to the reef, where they can be caught on artificial lures and natural baits in large number. Fish of all sizes may be present, and while the average is probably less than 3 pounds, fish of 6–9 pounds have been taken. Occasional permit may be sighted as singles or in schools. Both trunkfish and parrotfish forage on the reef flats and at a distance are often mistaken for bonefish by their tailing and grubbing behavior.

Lighthouse Reef (locally Half-Moon Reef), lying about 12 miles east of the Turneffe Islands, is a vast shoal over 25 miles in length with only a few widely scattered cays; of these, Long Cay on the southern perimeter provides fishing similar to that around Turneffe.

TACKLE

A heavy-duty spinning or bait-casting rod is standard in these waters. Much of the fishing is done close to mangrove shores in narrow rivers. A 12-pound-test line should be the minimum. Wire leaders are essential (No. 5 piano wire), as there are many sharp-toothed species and numerous snags in the form of coral heads and mangrove roots. Surface plugs are usually effective as are 1–3-ounce jigs for shore casting and deep fishing.

There are good possibilities for fly rodding both on the bonefish flats and in the rivers for tarpon and snook. A 9-foot saltwater fly rod with a floating line is adequate for British Honduras waters.

There are no tackle shops in Belize City, but some replacement items such as lines and lures may be obtained in the fishing camps.

CLOTHING

The climate throughout British Honduras is warm to hot, so lightweight clothing is advisable. For wading on bonefish flats an old pair of slacks and topsiders or similar foot gear affords the best protection from sunburn and coral cuts. Be sure to include an insect repellent, as sandflies and mosquitoes become active when the wind abates. Rain gear should always be carried. —A.J.McC.

BRITTLE STAR A starfishlike echinoderm belonging to the class Ophiuroidea. Unlike the true starfish, it has long, slender, jointed arms distinctly separated from its small, disc-shaped body. These flexible limbs have a remarkable power of regeneration.

BROACH TO To be caught broadside in the trough of a heavy sea or surf.

BROADBILL SWORDFISH *See* Swordfish

BROAD FISH TAPEWORM *Diphyllobothrium latum* A fish parasite which also infects man, at one time it was estimated that over ten million people in the world are hosts to this tapeworm, which is the largest (a mature length of 20–30 feet) found in humans. The tapeworm can live in man for twenty years or more and causes a severe type of anemia. Carnivorous mammals such as mink, otter, and bear may also become infected. The parasite develops in pike and other freshwater fishes that have consumed "water fleas" (copepods) containing the larva of the worm. Cooking invariably destroys the parasite, but in parts of South America, Europe, and the Orient fish are commonly eaten raw and the ingested larva continues its growth in the human host. *See also* Diseases and Parasites. —A.J.McC.

BROCHET The French name for northern pike and sometimes called *grande brochet*. In Quebec the chain pickerel is *brochet maillé*, the grass pickerel is *brochet vermiculé*, and the redfin pickerel is *brochet d'Amérique*.

BROKEN BACK A vitamin-C deficiency in catfish. *See* Diseases and Parasites

BRONZE BREAM *Abramis brama* Bream are cyprinid fishes of European still- or sluggish freshwaters. Because of their large individual size and the great numbers of their shoals, they are a popular quarry of European anglers; successful bream outings have sometimes bagged over a hundred pounds of fish on rod-and-reel.

The bronze bream is found in nearly all shallow eutrophic lakes or slow streams of Europe north of the Alps, except Scotland. In most suitable habitats, it occurs naturally, but because of its great favor with anglers it is regularly transplanted and introduced into new waters. So typical is it of the lower, sluggish reaches of major rivers that this area is classified by French ecologists as the *zone à brême*. It is also abundant in canals and lakes over an acre in extent, provided they have extensive muddy shallows. It does not fare so well in smaller stillwaters except when cultivated (which it rarely is).

The bream has a strongly laterally compressed body, with a very pronounced obtuse angle where the head joins the back. The lateral compression is probably an adaptation for moving through extensive weed beds and rush growths or other vertical water plants. The tail is deeply forked; the back is black or brown, fading to a grayish-white belly. The fins are uniformly dull gray or brown. One of its most characteristic and unendearing features is the mass of easily shed slime covering the flanks.

What has been described is the adult coloration; it is much lighter in its first and second years of life. Then it may be confused with the silver bream, *Blicca bjørnka*. This often shoals with the bronze bream; so misidentification is common. However, the silver bream is much smaller (usual weight ½–1 pound) and the fins more delicate and translucent. Its over-all color is aptly described in England as "tinplate." One distinguishing character is that the eye of the silver bream is wider than the length of its snout (measured from the anterior edge of the eye to the tip of the nose), whereas the eye of the bronze bream is smaller in diameter than the snout length. Another is that the bronze bream has 50–57 scales in the lateral line, while the silver bream 44–48. Scale counts from the lateral line to the leading edge of the dorsal fin are 12–15 for bronze bream and 9–10 for silver bream. As in all the minnow family, there is only one dorsal fin.

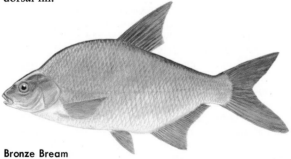

Bronze Bream

The mature adult bronze bream reaches 13–15 pounds; anything over 10 pounds is very unusual, anything over 5 pounds a good fish. The usual size caught by anglers is 1–3 pounds.

LIFE HISTORY

Bream spawn from May to July in warm shallows, draping their eggs on weeds. Investigators vary in their accounts of the breeding dress, which may itself be variable. Certainly little change is seen on fish observed in the water. The actual mating ritual is most obvious, as it is accompanied by rolling and splashing in very shallow water, often barely deep enough to cover their backs.

The fry from their adherent eggs are as terete as the fry of other fish; the deep shape and lateral compression develop during the first year. At the end of that time they are near the adult shape, three times as long as they are deep.

As the bream area of rivers is frequently used for navigation, spawning shallows may suffer great damage from intermittent dredging. In such rivers whole crops of spawn are destroyed, and whole year classes are missing. Besides, spawning success may vary without actual damage to the beds. In a population studied by Leeming on the English river Welland, 3-year-old fish formed no less than 93 per cent of the bream present. Success or failure may depend upon many factors, but chiefly temperature. Lengthening daylight speeds the maturation of the gonads, but a certain minimum temperature is probably needed to initiate the spawning act. In southern England, this is not reached until mid June or later, and a hard winter will delay it further.

First-year bream are about 3 inches long, growing in their second year to 6½ inches; the weight increases eightfold in this time, due to the deepening of the body. In the next few years it puts on ¼–½ pound per annum. The life expectancy is about 20 years, but 8–10 years is a normal age. From this it may be deduced that double-figure fish are quite old, unless in a really exceptional water.

One reason for a relatively slow growth rate is their dependence upon optimum temperature while feeding. They will feed actively during the summer at water temperatures of between about 50° and 70°F.; a drop of below 45°F. puts them off feed. In winter, except on some mild days, they cease to feed altogether. They are less subject to this in rivers than in lakes. With the onset of low temperatures, their gut fills with mucus, and a fatty reserve is built up in the abdominal cavity to last them until early spring.

The most notable habits of the bream stem from its shoaling behavior. The schools consist of size ranges, each one being homogeneous within limits. The size range is in inverse relation to the numbers of the shoal; thus shoals of 10-pound fish will be very small, while shoals of one-pound fish may consist of hundreds of individuals. A typical bream shoal moves in a strict path across the bottom of a river or lake, each path peculiar to a particular shoal although different shoals' paths criss-cross each other. In passing a given observation point, a shoal displays a definite order. Ahead of the main bulk come the smallest members, increasing in size toward the rear until the majority of the shoal, of modal size, passes. The largest fish are to the rear of the majority; bringing up the rear are a few smaller fish. This is very typical of shoals of the 1½–4-pound-size range; smaller fish tend to be more homogeneous and not so ordered; larger fish are very much fewer in number, and the size range is narrower, so no order is discernible. The largest fish are in groups, often only five or less in number. Presumably these are the survivors of formerly larger shoals of smaller individuals, thinned by predation and normal mortality.

The paths of the shoals are concentrated in areas with muddy bottoms shallow enough to bear rooted plants. Very often the routine journey is diurnal, for fishermen often take bream from the same swims at the same time of day for several weeks. The path of a shoal in shallow water is easy to follow from the roiling caused by feeding fish. Another good sign of feeding bream is the occasional appearance of a member of the shoal rolling on top; fish from the majority seem to do this more often than fish from the van- or rearguards. Except in spawning time, the shoals prefer water 4–15 feet deep; so rolling on the surface demands a departure from the shoal. What causes this is unknown. The departure is only temporary, for at all times bream are in shoals (except the very largest ones); it is not known whether members can move from one shoal to another, but possibly not. The order of size within a shoal in motion indicates a hierarchy or order of precedence, but this is not yet a proven fact.

While this pattern holds true during daylight hours, observations in large tanks indicate that the shoal splits up into smaller units at dusk, and is reunited at daybreak. This has been explained by the fish not being able to maintain visual contact with each other. Whether shoals mix when they reunite has not been settled, nor how far such units move apart in the wild.

Bream show peaks of activity at dawn and dusk, and sport is most productive throughout the night. The two hours after dawn and after dusk seem optimal, but this does vary with temperature and oxygen content.

Although bream are fish of eutrophic waters, and one would expect them to be adapted against oxygen deficits, nonetheless a small percentage of the bream population in many waters dies every summer. The loss is not great, and well within the population's ability to bear. The water is thus "over-stocked" when the oxygen capacity falls below certain limits. Bream are very prolific, and soon reach a size too great for the average predator to take; so this may be a natural check on the population.

ANGLING VALUE

A fish of impressive appearance and average size occurring in large shoals is of great value to anglers. Bream are taken regularly by fishing with baits such as worms, blowfly maggots, or bread lying on the bottom. Lines of 3–6 pound test are commonly used because the bream is not a hard fighter unless a river current plays on its broad flank. The best sport is on dull days, twilight, or at night. The fish is big for its weight; so bream anglers use large landing nets and keep nets.

Feeding bream have voracious appetites; so large baits and hooks are commonly used. However, the actual bite is circumspect, and the angler must wait until it is definite. As the shoal moves along slowly but surely, groundbait must be put in the swim to keep them from leaving; large quantities are used where many bream are expected. Despite its appetite, it has a relatively small stomach, so it is easily filled by groundbait; the large quantities used are necessary because of the *numbers* of fish to be satisfied when a shoal is contacted.

As bream grow larger and more solitary, it is believed that they become increasingly predatory. Although like all members of the minnow family it has no teeth in the mouth, it does take small fish. In Holland, bream have been taken by spinning with ultra-light tackle, and a definite technique has been successfully evolved.

ECONOMIC VALUE

Bream are not eaten much in places where there is access to sea-fish markets, but inland, and where preserving difficulties make sea fish scarce, it is a common article of diet. Its flesh is firm and quite edible. Germans compare it to carp. They take it on a commercial scale for local consumption, in seine-nets or traps, or on nightlines. It is also appreciated in communities living near bream waters, such as some parts of Norfolk, England, and among the rural poor of Ireland. However, it is only consumed locally, and few efforts are made to cultivate it or sell it further afield.

Apart from economic value as a food fish, the bream is valuable to some communities for revenue from anglers seeking it. In the English angling contests, contacting a shoal of bream ensures the best weight of the day and a prize; most "match-fishing" rivers are also bream-fishing rivers, and considerable sums of money in betting, accommodation and catering, or license fees come the way of communities fortunately placed.

Ireland's largest industry next to agriculture is tourism, and many of the tourists are anglers seeking the large bream of the Irish lakes and rivers. The bream was originally an introduction to Ireland (which has a poor indigenous fauna), but its attraction provides important revenue to the Irish people and the Irish authorities, especially in the catchment area of the river Shannon in Eire. A similar case is the English Norfolk Broads, a maze of ideal bream waters, whose attractions are the boating and breaming facilities.

—D.M.

BROOKS, JOSEPH American(1902–1972) One of America's great anglers, Joe Brooks was an outstanding writer and Fishing Editor for *Outdoor Life*. He also appeared in many TV films, notably the *American Sportsman*. His last book, *Trout Fishing*, published shortly before his death from a heart ailment, was probably his most significant work. The previous nine books were all good, straight workmanlike jobs of doing simply what he set out to do and doing it without fuss or feathers. There's always been an irreducible minimum of every sort of ostentatious pretense down to an almost vacuumlike absence from every Joe Brooks book. Though the titles—*Saltwater Game Fishing*, *Bass Bug Fishing*, and *Saltwater Fly Fishing*—were as straight as his last one, it is always felt they could have been preceded by such a phrase as "*The Common Sense of.*" One did not look to Joe Brooks for any such fancy-pants trappings as *The Mystique of Trout Fishing*. But that's exactly what the old fooler tossed into his tenth volume, along with all the factual material that the jacket promises and Joe duly delivers. Along with the facts, which are all here and admirably organized and presented, he tells the truth, the bright blinding revelation that makes the trout rise above the status of a fish to achieve almost that of a religion. This is the part of the Brooks story that, in his foreword to the book, Charles K. Fox characterizes as "the magic of trout fishing" and that the author in his preface terms "the universal charisma of the trout."

Beginning with the first chapter, a history of trout fishing that has to be the best job of condensation since H.G. Wells wrote *The Outline of History* in one volume, and continuing with the next, "The Trout We Fish For," which is so good it makes you almost start feeling for fins, the master fisherman puts his reader through the best short course of trout appreciation and understanding that our day affords.

Born in Baltimore, Maryland, Joe Brooks is buried in Livingston, Montana, where he spent 50 years angling for trout. —A.G.

BROOK SILVERSIDE *Labidesthes sicculus* A slender streamlined little fish, it is nearly transparent when alive. It has 2 well-separated dorsal fins, the first of which contains 4–6 weak flexible spines and a large anal fin having 1 spine and 20–25 rays. Its color is pale olive above; it has a distinct silvery stripe along the sides. The large eyes occupy most of the small slender head. Jaws are blunt and beaklike, and the lower jaw projects slightly beyond the upper. The larger adults attain a length of 3–4 inches.

This member of the silverside family, most of which are found in the oceans, is distributed through the central part of the United States from Minnesota to western New York in the north, and its range extends south through Florida and westward into eastern Texas. It is common in clearwater lakes and in the quieter parts of streams. Silversides often swim in schools at the surface and may skip short distances out of the water, thus earning the local name "skipjack." They are extensively used as a forage fish by predator species and are a good baitfish. However, they die quickly.

Brook Silversides

LIFE HISTORY

Brook silversides spawn in the spring and produce a unique egg that has a sticky thread which enables the egg to float until it attaches to some object where it will remain until the larva hatches. Growth is rapid, and they spawn at the age of 1 year. They eat small animal food including crustaceans and insects and their larvaes. Few live through the second winter. Thus, they have basically a 1-year life cycle. *See also* Atlantic Silverside —C.A.P.

BROOK STICKLEBACK *Culaea inconstans* This is a strictly freshwater member of the family Gasterosteidae, characterized by its naked body, a lack of a caudal keel, and the number of spines, which may be either 5 or 6. The pelvic fins are greatly reduced in size, and the caudal fin is rounded. Color is variable, but it is usually green to olive above, and white to cream colored below. Breeding color of the male is more intense. Maximum size is about 3 inches.

It is found throughout the north central drainages of North America, from British Columbia to Hudson and James bays and New Brunswick to western New York and Pennsylvania, west to the Missouri River in Kansas, and throughout the Great Lakes. It occurs in clearwater, the coldwaters of weedy spring holes, boggy lakes, and streams, and in cold streams and springs.

LIFE HISTORY

Spawning takes place in April and May, and the nest is built and guarded by the male. As with other sticklebacks,

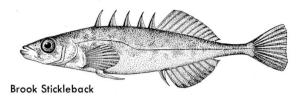

Brook Stickleback

this is a very aggressive species, driving away others from its territory. It eats small crustaceans and insects. In recent years, man-made alterations of the environment, such as dredging, filling, and pollution, have reduced its habitat, resulting in a disappearance of the species in many areas. —D.dS.

BROOK TROUT *Salvelinus fontinalis* This beautiful gamefish is distinguished by red spots with blue aureoles on the sides, dark wavy lines (vermiculations) on the back and dorsal fin, pink or reddish lower fins edged with white on leading edge, and teeth on the head of the vomer. Males at spawning time often have orange on the belly and black on the lower sides. In its native range there are brilliantly colored races with cadmium-colored sides and belly. The body is about five times as long as it is deep. The caudal fin is only slightly forked or square; thus the name "squaretail" is often applied. All fins are softrayed; the dorsal has 10 rays; the anal fin 9 rays. Teeth are well-developed on the maxillary, premaxillary, and on the vomerine bone. Although the record weight of the brook trout is 14½ pounds, and the length 31½ inches, fish of over 5 pounds may be considered exceptional.

The brook trout is native to northeastern North America from Georgia to the Arctic Circle. It has been introduced to the remainder of the United States, Canada, South America, and Europe where suited to the habitat.

In the eastern United States the brook trout has figured prominently in the development of fly fishing as it was the species sought before the introduction of the brown trout in the 1880's. Despite its dwindling habitat the native is still regarded as the principal gamefish in many parts of New England and management programs are designed to favor it over other trouts.

LIFE HISTORY

Brook trout spawn from September in the northernmost part of their range until early December in the southernmost regions. Egg production is determined largely by size; the number of eggs may vary from 100 in a 6-inch female to 1,200 in a 14-inch fish. As with salmon this char constructs a redd in gravel in the fall, but its stream-spawning habitat requirements are more specific in that it prefers cold, spring-fed water and will enter very small brooks. In lakes, the requirements are not as rigid, for it will spawn over bark, twigs, or other material along shores or in deeper water. Incubation depends on water temperature which at 35° F would require 144 days, while at 55° F would take 35 days; these are mean incubating periods since stream temperatures are rarely constant and all the eggs do not hatch at once, but sometimes continue hatching over a period of a week. Egg loss is greater at temperatures below 39° F than in the upper range (below 53° F). The ability to spawn successfully in lakes has been its undoing in that bodies of water have become overpopulated in western Canada and in the

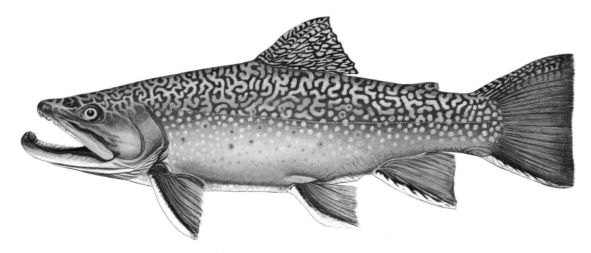

Brook Trout, 5½-pound Male, God's River, Manitoba

Western United States. In the Wallows Mountains of eastern Oregon a daily bag limit of thirty brook trout in force in sixty lakes for fifteen years had no measurable effect in diminishing the populations, which were made up of brook trout averaging 7 inches in length.

Large brook trout occur in the same regions where they existed millions of years ago—with very few exceptions. Unlike the more cosmopolitan brown trout and rainbow trout which have thrived in many parts of the world through man's distribution, the squaretail is not as adaptable. Good brook trout water has definite chemical and physical properties, and perhaps a few characteristics with respect to size, associated species, and food supply. It is also remote.

In the Eastern United States, Maine still provides some relatively inaccessible brook-trout fishing on such streams as the Allagash, Spencer, Kennebago, Moose, and upper Kennebec rivers. Official records kept at the turn of the century indicate that quite a few squaretails approaching world-record size (9–11 pounds) were caught in Rangeley lakes and Moosehead, but today, 2–3-pound trout are considered exceptional, and a 5 pounder is unusual. Elsewhere in Northeastern United States, brook trout

become progressively smaller as one goes south; the southernmost part of the range is in the highland streams of north Georgia where trout still exist in naturally reproducing populations. A large native here, as well as in the Midwestern United States, would be a two pounder. The typical fishery consists of small spring-fed stream and headwater populations in the 7–10-inch class. There are some outstanding brook-trout fisheries in the Rocky Mountain region, but this is the stronghold of the native rainbow and cutthroat. Montana, Idaho, and Wyoming produce a 5–6-pound squaretail now and then, but for every such fish caught here, a score are caught in the Hudson-Ungava Bay region, and probably a hundred in Labrador and the Argentine.

Several factors conspire against the widespread success of brook-trout populations. The fish require cold water; the lethal limit is about 77° F, which is less than any other trout, although acclimatized fish can survive for short periods at temperatures in the low 80's. However, they are never really abundant in habitats where water temperatures exceed 68° F for any prolonged period. Their preferred temperature range is 57.2°–60.8° F. In rivers having a mixed-trout population the brookie is most often

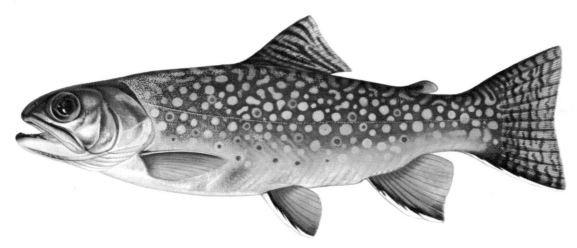

Brook Trout, 9-inch Female, Beaverkill River (headwaters), New York

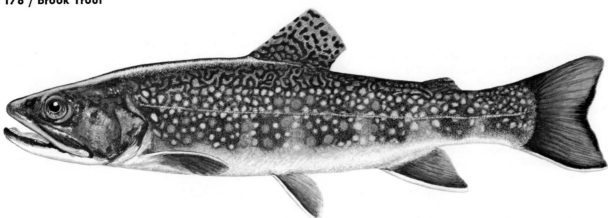

Brook Trout, 10-inch Male, Beaverkill River (Headwaters), New York

found in the headwater section and around cold tributary streams. Spring seepage in a comparatively small area is often enough to hold a number of brook trout in otherwise warm streams where brown and rainbow dominate. It has been observed that wild strains survive better at low temperatures (streams with ice cover during winter) than domestic stocks. They can also become acclimated to low oxygen concentrations, and the fingerling at least are better adapted in this respect than the brown or rainbow. Their tolerance to both acid and alkaline waters is also greater, with a range from pH 4.0–pH 9.8. The lumber industry, land development, poor farming practices, road building, and pollution contributed greatly to the elimination of many native trout habitats early in United States history. Too, the fish is relatively easy to catch (in small sizes), and being a short-lived species in comparison to brown or rainbow trout, few fish ever attain large sizes except in isolated areas.

Recent investigations indicate that brook trout in some of the more productive Canadian watersheds are long-lived populations (up to 10 years). Elsewhere, however, 4-year-old brook trout are uncommon. Ordinarily, allowing for all the problems a civilized trout must face, for every ten thousand which emerge from the egg, five hundred live to be one year old. There is only one chance in twenty of surviving the first year. About three hundred of the five hundred will become 2-year-olds, and less than half of these will survive the third year. About twenty-five will reach age 4, and five will attain age 5. One brook trout out of the original ten thousand will be a 6-year-old. The rate of growth in that period depends, of course, on its habitat. Brook trout in low fertility environments may never grow over 7–8 inches long, particularly if there's a high population density. It follows that lakes with little stocking produce larger fish than those that are heavily stocked unless the angling pressure is not efficient and the population becomes dense. It also seems apparent that brook trout thrive best where there is predation or competition to keep their numbers down. Either northern pike or walleye, or both species, inhabit the same waters as the squaretail in almost every trophy river or pond in the North Country. Where these two predators are absent, Arctic char or lake trout are present.

The biggest brook trout today occur in Labrador, northern Quebec, northern Manitoba, and southern Argentina. There are probably hundreds of lakes which

will be tapped during the next decade in Labrador alone which are still unfished and hold an abundance of squaretails in the 4-pound-and-over class. Labrador is probably the center of the brook trout's original habitat, which extended from as far south as Georgia to the Maritimes, north through Ungava and into Hudson Bay. The water conditions are right, food is surprisingly abundant, and there's little rod pressure as yet. Argentina produces some heavy squaretails in several rather unique watersheds, notably Lago General Paz, where it's literally easier to catch a 5-pounder than a 5-incher, and God's River in Manitoba has a stream average of about 4 pounds. In Quebec, Broadback River, the Rupert, Nemiscau, and Assinica Lake have all produced squaretails of over 10 pounds; the Broadback has come closer to the record (11½ pounds) than any other stream.

One feature that trophy brook-trout waters have in common is that they are *big* streams. The Broadback watershed, for example, is several hundred miles long. The same thing applies to God's, Limestone, and Forteau. These are heavy rivers, wholly unlike the tinkling upland rills we associate with "native" trout fishing in the United States. Some of the better pools on God's River are a half-mile wide. It's also a general rule that the trout are not numerous. In other words, you can't expect to catch one after another—you have to do a lot of searching and experimenting with lures to find the right combination in most trophy waters. This may be because of predation, which keeps their numbers down, and the size up. On God's River, for example, you can't reasonably expect to take more than a half-dozen fish a day, although with any luck you might exceed that number sometimes.

Another anomaly of the brook trout's life history is the fact that sea-run populations, while often larger in their average size than freshwater residents, seldom attain the heavy weights of apparently nonmigratory fish. Brown trout and rainbows achieve remarkable growth in saltwater, but the sea-run brookie or salter (*which see*) seldom exceeds 4 pounds. It is possible that some of the larger brook trout in Labrador streams, for example, have some past history in a marine environment. However, a salter cannot be identified in freshwater with any accuracy unless the fish has recently migrated (within two weeks) at which time the dorsal surface is a dark greenish-blue in color and the sides very silvery.

—A.J.McC.

DOMESTIC VERSUS WILD STRAINS

The diminishing number of brook trout and generally poorer angling during the mid-nineteenth century was responsible, in part, for the development of trout hatcheries in this country. In 1864, Seth Green built a trout hatchery near Mumford, New York, to raise fish to supplement the wild trout populations. Since that time trout hatcheries have been erected from coast to coast for that same purpose. Even though the role of the early and modern hatcheries is still the same there is a major difference between the brook trout of Seth Green's era and the brook trout found in a modern trout-cultural station. The trout that stock these present-day hatcheries are domestic strains many generations removed from the wild trout which made up the early hatchery fish. The development of the so-called domestic strain of brook trout was necessary because wild trout were not readily adaptable to the unnatural environment of a hatchery. Although wild brook trout had the potential growth rate, they were nervous and scary and did not feed readily in a rearing pond. While domestic strains come quickly to the feeder, wild fish scurry for cover at the approach of a human being. The wild strains did not readily accept man's substitute for their natural diet, and consequently many perished before they learned to take artificial food. The stresses placed on wild trout by crowding, exposure to diseases, lack of cover, and poor chemical conditions were decimating factors with which they were unable to cope.

In order to rear trout economically and efficiently in a hatchery, it was necessary to domesticate some of the best of these wild strains. The present domestic stocks of brook trout which are now in hatcheries throughout the country are a result of some very elementary selective breeding—propagating those which survived the stresses, resisted the diseases, and grew the fastest. This was a simple case of survival both for the fish and fish-culturist. Undoubtedly in the development of the domestic strains something has been lost or changed from the original wild fish. Without question, constant in-breeding, unless it is controlled, contributes to many abnormalities. In lots of inbred trout, albinism, short gill covers, turned-down jaw, and even two- and three-headed monsters are more evident. This is a result of undisciplined breeding rather than a stringent, scientific selection which is practiced in most domestic animals. Comparatively, modern fishery genetics is still in its infancy, but some states have established or are constructing laboratories to improve the

stocks of domestic trout. Research in these laboratories is aimed not only at developing traits of trout which fit the hatchery program but also those qualities which are needed for survival in the wild.

The albino brook trout is not uncommon in some trout hatcheries. Often a cross of normal-colored fish will produce not only natural pigmented fish but also some albino progeny. Normal-colored fish may have the dominant gene for natural coloration, masking the recessive gene which produces albinism. Since the genes for albinism are always recessive, the cross of two albinos results in all albino young.

This albino form, which lacks the dark pigmentation, is rarely, if ever, encountered in the wild. Because it lacks protective coloration, it is an obvious target for fish predators and is soon destroyed. For this same reason albino hatchery trout are not usually stocked, but instead are held in hatchery ponds as exhibits.

Albino animals are usually pictured as having pink eyes. Albino trout are a novel genetic situation in which the eyes may be pink, black, or shades between the two. Geneticists believe that this variation in eye pigment is due to two different forms of albinos, one having black and one having pink eyes, which produces the variation in eye color.

Survival Experiments Some tests have been made to test the difference in survival of hatchery-reared trout and wild trout. Some of these tests were conclusive for the species and the environment where the research was conducted. In a small mountain stream in Alberta, Canada, two sections of stream were fenced to study the difference in survival of stocked cutthroat trout and wild trout of the same species. After forty days all of the stocked trout had lost weight, but after a hundred days all survivors had regained the lost weight. The survivors consisted of one-third of the 3-year-old fish and none of the 2-year-olds. The mortalities were believed to have been caused by shock and the inability to compete with the native population present in the section. The wild trout present in the section with stocked trout gained the same amount of weight as the native population in the section without hatchery trout. The results of this study indicate that hatchery trout could not compete in the wild as well as their native counterpart.

In another test in British Columbia, wild trout from the same source were split and reared in different environments. One group was reared under hatchery conditions and the other under natural conditions for the first year.

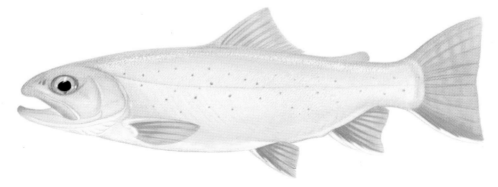

Brook Trout, 9-inch Albino Male, Benner Spring Fish Research Station, Pennsylvania

Three years after stocking there was no significant difference in survival. The inference drawn from such results is that previous history was not as important as the trout strain.

An elaborate experiment was conducted at Cornell University to study the difference between the strains of wild and domestic brook trout. A wild strain from an isolated Adirondack lake and a hatchery strain which had been domesticated for ninety years were the two stocks used in this experiment. These were reared in troughs side by side for one year. At the end of this time the domestic trout averaged 5.2 inches and the wild strain averaged only 3.6 inches. The biologists noted great differences in the behavior of these two stocks of trout. In contrast to the wild strain the domestic trout did not hunt for concealment, act wary, or stay close to the bottom. Further tests showed that the wild trout also had more stamina.

Seventy-three days after these two brook-trout stocks were planted in a small stream, 80 per cent of the domestic strain, but only 67 per cent of the wild fish, had perished. During this time the wild trout grew .48 of an inch while the domestic strain grew only .34 of an inch. The same experiment conducted in a pond showed that survival favored the wild trout 65–43 per cent. After four months of being on their own in the wild, the domestic strain never did become very wary.

Unquestionably the results of any tests such as these depend on the source of the wild and domestic strains and the conditions under which they were tested. There never will be entirely uniform results, but it is quite possible that future trout hatcheries will have two strains of fish—one for the market or quick put-and-take fishing where fish survival is no problem and the other for stocking situations where survival and growth are required to support the fisheries. The ideal, of course, is to have one trout which will fit both situations. —K.B.

ANGLING METHODS

Brook trout are caught with live bait, spinning lures, and by trolling and even plug-casting according to local conditions. However, they are preeminently a fly-fisher's quarry. Brook trout feed on insects, crustaceans, mollusks, and fish. They occasionally forage on leeches, and on shrews and other mammals. One would expect the large trout to have a decidedly piscivorous appetite; however, this is not always the case, as they often show a preference for insects: stoneflies, mayflies, caddisflies, and terrestrials such as ants, beetles, and grasshoppers are important items in the squaretail's diet. The largest brook trout are caught on spoons and spinners chiefly because more people favor the method and inevitably more fish are taken on hardware. Contrary to a widely accepted belief that the brookie is more of a subsurface feeder than other trout, it rises readily to the dry fly under the proper conditions when water temperatures are cool and bug life is on the move. The safe rule, of course, is to match the hatch. At other times a wet fly or nymph will score nicely, and in this respect don't neglect trying both dark and bright patterns; squaretails often favor the extremes in flies such as the Black Gnat, Black Moose, Conrad, Royal Coachman, Silver Doctor, Parmachenee Belle, and Montreal. For strictly trophy squaretails, don't miss trying big, roughlooking wet flies such as the Burlap, Fledermaus, or Silver Shrimp on No. 2 to No. 6 hooks. The latter are often better than streamer flies. However, streamers are virtually standard in the Northeast, and the Black Ghost, Light Tiger, Dark Tiger, Supervisor, Mickey Finn, and Nine-Three are favorite patterns.

FOOD VALUE

The flesh of the brook trout is of excellent flavor. It varies in color from white in fish of recent hatchery origin to a bright orange in wild populations, according to their diet. The fish may be panfried, baked, broiled, poached, made into chowders, and smoked. *See also* Fish Culture, Fly-Fishing, Spinning, Ultralight Spinning

—J.R.

—A.J.McC.

BROWN BULLHEAD *Ictalurus nebulosus* A medium-sized, slender-bodied catfish with dark chin barbels. Anal fin has 20–24 rays, and the tail is slightly emarginate. Rear edges of the pectoral spines are endowed with many sharp teeth. The color is yellow-brown to light chocolate-brown with vague, darker mottlings above, lighter sides,

Brown Bullhead

and yellow or milk-white below. The natural range of the brown bullhead is from Maine and the Great Lakes south to Florida and Mexico. It has been widely introduced elsewhere. The brown bullhead prefers weedy, deeper waters of lakes and sluggish streams. Although not commonly found in turbid waters, it is associated with mud or deep muck as well as sand- and gravel-bottom types.

LIFE HISTORY

An omnivorous feeder, the bullhead may be found eating anything from plant material to fish. Due to its bottom-feeding habits, however, insect larvae and mollusks form a major portion of its diet. The bullhead feeds mostly at night, feeling for its prey with its sensitive barbels.

Like others of the catfish family, the bullhead is very tenacious of life and, if kept moist, will remain alive many hours out of water. Its ability to breathe atmospheric air allows it to live for long periods in warm waters with little oxygen.

Reproducing in the manner of other catfish, the bullhead spawns in a nest consisting of a shallow depression or cleared spot usually sheltered by logs, rocks, or vegetation. Adhesive eggs are laid in cream-colored clusters. One or both parents guard the nest and young, and, as incredible as it seems, have been observed cleaning eggs and fry by taking them into their mouths and then blowing them gently back into the nest. The adults stay with the young until they are swimming freely, sometimes until they are an inch in length.

The brown bullhead adult is commonly 6–16 inches in length and seldom exceeds 3 pounds.

ECONOMIC VALUE

The brown bullhead is a very popular panfish among young and old alike. Using worms, scraps of meat, or bits of fish by still-fishing, bullhead anglers are legion during summer evenings.   —R.A.J.

BROWN SMOOTHHOUND *Mustelus henlei* A member of the requiem shark family (Carcharhinidae), this California species is closely related to the smooth dogfish (*which see*), from which it differs mainly in the presence of compressed teeth having several pointed cusps. The body is elongate, the head pointed, and the fins rather long. The anal fin is relatively small. The body is reddish-brown to bronze above, with a white belly, and sides which are sometimes silvery. It reaches a length of slightly over 3 feet. Very common in San Francisco Bay, its range is from northern California to the Gulf of California. The young are born alive.

ANGLING VALUE

The flesh has some value, but its chief attraction is to anglers, who catch it on light tackle.   —D.dS.

BROWN TROUT *Salmo trutta* The native trout of Europe, found in streams from the Mediterranean basin to the Black Sea and north to Arctic Norway and Siberia. Widely introduced to North America beginning in 1883, and subsequently to New Zealand, parts of Asia, South America, and Africa, the brown trout has become a favorite of fly-fishermen the world over. The species is less tolerant of warm water than the rainbow trout, but, because it persists in streams more than native species, where the habitat is favorable it enjoys a reputation for being able to resist environmental change. It is ordinarily a difficult fish to catch when compared to the brook and rainbow trout. Streams have been known to have an abundance of browns and to produce only a few for the angler. Where equal numbers were stocked experimentally in the Deschutes River in Oregon with rainbows there was one brown taken for every four rainbows caught by anglers. In Maine, the ratio was one brown to every five brook trout. Probably because the fish is difficult to catch, some individuals live to become quite large and to prey upon smaller trout.

The body of the brown trout is usually 4½–5 times as long as it is deep. All fins are soft rayed; the dorsal has 10–13 rays; the anal fin has 9 or 10 rays. This trout is generally a golden brown in color with large brown or black spots on its sides, back, and dorsal fin. These spots are usually surrounded by faint halos of a lighter shade than the body. A lesser number of red or orange spots are generally evident along the lateral surface; the dorsal and adipose fins are often fringed or spotted with bright orange or red. The belly color is dusky yellow but may be creamy-white on small stream-born trout. The tail, which is slightly forked in young fish, is more nearly square in old trout; it is yellowish-brown and may be indistinctly spotted near its borders. The pectorals, ventrals, and anal fin are usually yellowish-brown and without markings. The vomerine teeth are the most useful character for distinguishing the brown trout from the landlocked salmon, the only other salmonid with which it might be confused in United States waters; in brown trout these teeth are well developed in the form of a double zigzag row on the vomer. The vomerine teeth of the salmon are poorly developed and exist as a single row, or the shaft may be without teeth as these are deciduous in a salmon and easily broken off. Brown trout found in large lakes (notably in the Great Lakes, New York, New Hampshire, and Maine) as well as sea-run populations, may otherwise resemble landlocked salmon in that they become very silvery in color and are spotted black.

The brown trout is slightly less tolerant of warm water (with lethal limits at 84°–86° F) than the rainbow. However, there are frequent exceptions to the rule for both species, depending on the strain of fish and the rate of temperature change. By comparison, sensitivity to heat is more marked in the brook trout and other chars with the lethal limits normally given at 77° F. Their preferred temperature range is 54.3–63.6° F. Brown trout can survive a considerable pH range from 4.5–9.8, but in acid or moderately acid waters the fish tend to be quite small; while those in highly alkaline water (pH 8.2 or more) display the best growth. This species has been known to reach a weight of 40 pounds, although fish over 10 pounds are considered exceptional in most waters. The brown trout caught in most United States streams weighs less than a pound; however, some of the better eastern and western fisheries produce a substantially higher average

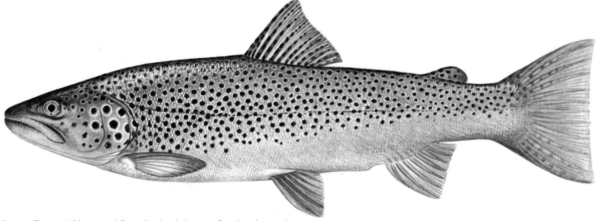

Brown Trout, 4 ½ pound Female, Loch Leven, Scotland

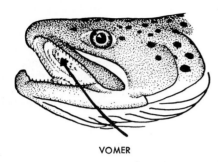

VOMER

Vomerine Teeth of the (2) Landlocked Salmon and of the (3) Brown Trout

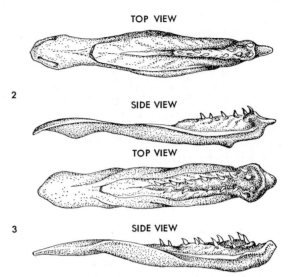

TOP VIEW

2

SIDE VIEW

TOP VIEW

3

SIDE VIEW

than this to the skilled angler. The record on rod-and-reel for the United States is 31½ pounds from the White River in Arkansas (1972).

FOOD

The brown trout feeds on both aquatic and terrestrial insects. It also eats mollusks, crayfish, and other fish. Large trout will occasionally feed on frogs, birds, and on mice and other small mammals; however, these food forms are not part of its ordinary diet. The brown trout forages freely on the surface when mayflies, caddisflies, and stoneflies are emerging and thus becomes a significant quarry of the fly-fisherman. It is very active at night, and some of the largest brown trout are caught after dark, particularly in the summer months. This preference for nocturnal feeding is universal and is more highly developed in the sea-run brown trout than in the nonmigratory strains. One race of brown trout, known as the gillaroo in Ireland, is almost entirely a snail feeder; the name is derived from two Gaelic words *giolla* and *ruadh* meaning "red fellow." Gillaroo are not only red-fleshed but more heavily spotted in red than the normal brown trout which occur in the same lakes.

SPAWNING HABITS

Brown trout may spawn in the fall or early winter (from October through February) depending on the location. The eggs are deposited in shallow redds in the gravel of the stream bottom. In lake habitats, the trout will seek a tributary stream for breeding; however, if none is present the fish will spawn in the coarse rubble near the shores. The number of eggs varies with the size of the female but may be 600–3,000 in the case of a large fish. After fertilization, the female covers the eggs with fine gravel; the redd is so constructed that a current is created inside which holds the eggs and milt in place. Under natural conditions, the young hatch out the following spring. In a hatchery, the time required is 48–54 days at a water temperature of 50 F.

Among sea-run populations the young brown trout (smolt) migrates downstream in the spring after 2 to as much as 6 years in freshwater. Sea trout normally spend 3 summers in saltwater before reaching maturity and returning to spawn. Maturation is partially a function of total age; thus the older smolts of 5 or 6 years (a fraction of the population) may return after only 1 or 2 sea summers.

Brown trout generally mature at the end of their second or third years and live from 7–12 years; the oldest on record was aged at 18 years.

FLY-FISHING FOR BROWN TROUT

The brown is acknowledged as the most difficult trout to take on the fly. It is pre-eminently a quarry of the experienced angler who seeks the species with dry flies. Owing to the fact that brown trout commonly

Brown Trout, 6½-pound Male, Missouri River, Montana

Brown Trout, 1½-pound Male,
Loyalsock Creek, Pennsylvania

feed in the relatively quiet pools and runs of clear rivers and are inherently cautious, the fly-fisher must be skillful and gain an understanding of the trout before he can catch the brown with any consistency.

On visible rises, the dry fly is presented to the fish, which may of course take fright at once and rush off to its shelter; short of this the trout may drop slowly downstream to inspect a drifting fly before quietly going away. Or it may just sink to the bottom and cease feeding. However, if the trout ignores the fly and makes no movement away from it, or makes some movement toward it, the fish is a worth-while target. Sometimes a change of pattern but more often a change of size will encourage the brown to take the floater in a confident rise. We all tend to fish with flies that are too large because they are easier to see. Comparatively few naturals in the trout's larder are equal to the popular No. 10 dressing. As a rule of thumb on clearwater pools the expert will favor No. 14's and frequently use 16's and 18's before trying larger sizes. Generally speaking, "low impact" dressings, such as the variants and spider-type dry flies, or sparsely dressed winged patterns which drop to the surface without creating a disturbance are most effective. On flatwater or slick water the fly must float upright, buoyantly, as if it were unattached to a comparatively heavy line just a few yards away. Some of the most famous brown-trout fly patterns are the Quill Gordon, March Brown, Blue Dun Spider, Cream Variant, Hendrickson, Adams, Royal Coachman, and Light Cahill and Dark Cahill; these dressings will take brook and rainbow trout as well, but they are especially effective on browns.

Wet fly fishing (*see* Fly-Fishing) and the somewhat related form of nymph fishing (*see* Nymph) are effective methods of seasonal importance. Due to the tendency of large brown trout to become almost wholly piscivorous, the streamer fly and bucktail are of regional value. Night-crawlers, angleworms, minnows, and insect baits such as the grasshopper and hellgrammite are widely used in streams and lakes. Spinners, spoons, occasional small plugs are used in casting and trolling with good results.

SUBSPECIES AND RELATED SPECIES

There are four recognized subspecies of brown trout. The taxonomic position of one, the Caspian trout, is not sufficiently clear, as it may possibly be related to the At-

lantic salmon (L.S. Berg and A.N. Derzhavin). However, in present taxonomy the four are:

Black Sea trout	*Salmo trutta labrax*
Caspian trout	*Salmo trutta caspius*
North African trout	*Salmo trutta macrostigma*
Aral trout	*Salmo trutta aralensis*

From fossil remains it has been concluded by Soviet icthyologists that the sea trout was more widely distributed before the last glacial epoch, and that those brown trout subspecies found in the Black, Caspian, and Aral seas are like other central European and Eurasian salmonids evolved through isolation. The Kura strain of the Caspian trout spawns only once in its lifetime, between the ages of 5–9 years. This is the largest member of the genus *Salmo* (record 112 pounds) and its fecundity is phenomenal, with females bearing up to 30,000 eggs, which may account for its singular spawning behavior. Although the Caspian Sea has undergone a great ecological change in recent times due to dams and pollution, during its ancient period of fertility this sea trout was a formidable predator. But like the Black Sea trout it is no longer numerous. The Aral trout may be synonymous with the Turkish form "Allah Balik" (God's Fish). Turkey has large stocks of brown trout and a subgenus in a recently recognized species *Salmo (Platysalmo) platysephalus*.

There are 5 other species of trout which greatly resemble the brown and probably evolved from a common ancestor:

Sevan trout	*Salmo ischchan*
Ohrid trout	*Salmo letnica*
Garda trout	*Salmo carpio*
Softmouth trout	*Salmo obtusirostris*
Marble trout	*Salmo mormoratus*

The softmouth trout is unique in having the general shape and coloration of a typical brown trout but the inferior mouth of a sucker. Despite the location of its mouth this trout hits the fly without fumbling. Softmouths are very common in the Neretva River watershed of Yugoslavia, where they attain weights up to 10 pounds. Sevan trout found in Lake Sevan, U.S.S.R., and the Garda trout found in Lake Garda, Italy, differ morphologically from *Salmo trutta*, but at first glance they appear to be

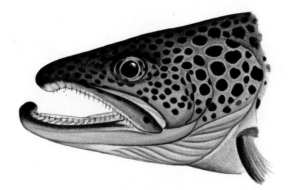

Brown Trout, 19-pound Male, Showing Kype

lightly-spotted brown trout. Ohrid trout, which are limited to Lake Ohrid in Yugoslavia, were introduced in Minnesota on a test basis, but found to be slow-growing and late-maturing. Marble trout, another Yugoslavian exotic, grow to more than 40 pounds, but are more predacious than brown trout and only occur in Dalmatian rivers having an abundance of forage fish. There are several reasons why these 5 species of trout probably came from a common brown trout ancestor, but the most significant characteristic is in their sexual dimorphism. Generally speaking, the development of a "kype" or hooked lower jaw of an old male will separate it from the female. However, there is a constant feature in the brown trout, its subspecies, and its close relatives; the anal fin is falcate (curves inward) in females and convex or rounded in the males. While it is not as obvious in very small fish, it is easily seen on any specimen over 7 or 8 inches long.

—J.R.

—A.J.McC.

BRYCONS *Brycon* spp. Also known as piracanjuba and piabanha (Brazil); dorado (Colombia); sardinita (Venezuela); machaca (Nicaragua). A fine freshwater gamefish of tropical Central and South America. There are many species, including some which grow only to aquarium size and others reaching 15 or more pounds. This fish varies a great deal in characteristics and coloring, depending on its species.

The piracanjuba of Brazil is often found with the dorado in the same waters, such as the Parana and Tiete rivers; however, here it is not the great jumper but fights doggedly underwater. There are at least two kinds in the Orinoco: one a bright silver color and the other having a broad black stripe (sardinita) its entire length. The fish are shaped and often colored somewhat like a North American shad with fairly large scales. Some varieties have golden or reddish fins and are known in parts of Colombia as dorado. Relatively easy-to-reach fishing places for large brycon are in Lake Nicaragua and its tributaries, Gatun and Madden lakes and tributary rivers in the Panama Canal Zone.

In most localities this fish is a leaper and a strong fighter. It can be caught on spoons, plugs, topwater lures, spinners, poppers, and streamer and dry flies.

—T.D.W.

BUCKTAIL An artificial fly made with a long hair wing and designed to imitate a minnow or other forage fish. The name is derived from the common use of hair from the tail of a deer for making the wing. Bucktails are used in both fresh- and salt-water fishing. Unlike the streamer fly which is very similar in design and function, a bucktail is durable, and for that reason it is preferred by many anglers who fish where large or sharp-toothed species are common. Most bucktails feature a two-color wing, with a dark or bright shade on top and a contrasting light color below. A simple brown-and-white or black-and-white wing tied over a silver tinsel body can suggest many brook minnows; it broadly imitates the dark back and light underbelly of a natural baitfish. There are also bucktails tied with single color and multicolor wings. As a general angling term "bucktail" has become synonymous with the streamer fly (*which see*), and regionally in the Southern United States it is often identified with the leadhead jig. *See also* Fly-Tying, Jig, Saltwater Fly-Fishing

BUFFALOFISH *See* Bigmouth Buffalo, Smallmouth Buffalo

BULLNOSE RAY *Myliobatis freminvillei* The broad disk, slender tail, and the peculiar-shaped head readily identify this relative of the stingrays. The teeth are in seven series in each jaw and are platelike in structure. The snout projects noticeably from the disk, unlike the stingrays, and the sides of the snout are partially attached to the pectoral fins. One or two spines are located near the base of the tail. It resembles the spotted eagle ray (*which see*) but lacks the spots, the upper surface of the disk being plain reddish-brown to gray-brown, with the margin of the disk pale and the tail dusky to black. Its ventral surface is white or whitish with dark hues. It is a small ray, growing only to about 3 feet wide.

LIFE HISTORY

A western Atlantic species, it is known from Brazil and from North Carolina to Cape Cod, being most abundant from Virginia to New Jersey. It should be expected to occur in the Gulf and Caribbean from where it has not yet been recorded but where a closely related species, *M. goodei*, separable from the bullnose ray in several proportional characters, is more common in western South Atlantic waters.

It is found in quiet bays and sloughs, where it searches the sandy and muddy flats for crabs, clams, snails, and lobsters. It visits the north from June to October, thereafter disappearing in the cooler months. Although reportedly common in Brazilian waters, it is common along the temperate northeast coast of the United States only in certain places and at certain times.

The young, which closely resemble the adult, are about 10 inches wide at birth.

—D.dS.

BULL SHARK *Carcharhinus leucas* The bull shark is easily recognized by its short, broadly rounded snout, the large dorsal fin placed well in advance over the pectoral fins, the absence of the dermal ridge between the dorsal fins, a small eye, and the subtriangular, serrated teeth. It is gray to gray-brown above and white below, with dusky markings on the pectoral fins only in the young. A weight of 400 pounds and a length of 10 feet have been reported for this chunky shark, but most seen are less than 8 feet.

LIFE HISTORY

It occurs in the western Atlantic from Brazil to North Carolina, straying north to New York. Records of the bull shark are from most of the Caribbean islands, the

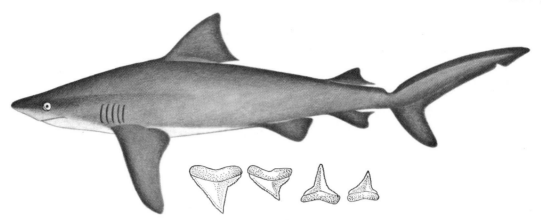

Bull Shark (upper teeth left, lower teeth right)

Gulf of Mexico, and Bermuda. It freely enters fresh-waters and occurs in both lakes and rivers in Guatemala and Nicaragua. Throughout its range it is abundant in shallow waters, particularly around harbors, bays, and estuaries. Young are born from May to July in brackish waters, and these same waters are an unusually popular place for the adults to congregate. Feeding is correlated with tidal movements, and this normally sluggish shark becomes a vigorous feeder on other sharks, stingrays, and bony fishes such as mackerel and shad, as well as garbage, which it scavenges actively.

DANGER TO MAN

It is a vicious shark under some circumstances, and it has attacked bathers and skin divers. The migratory form which enters Lake Nicaragua is responsible for attacks on a number of swimmers. —D.dS.

BUOY A floating mark moored to the bottom which, by shape and color, conveys navigational information. Buoys are used to mark channels, wrecks, shoals, etc.

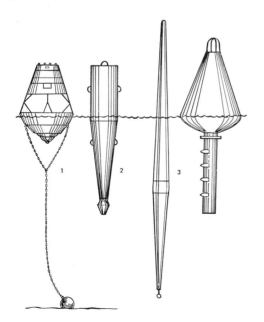

From Left to Right, Bell, Can, Spar, and Whistling Buoys

The many types of buoys include bell, can, flashing, whistle, nun, and spar, and are used to serve different navigational needs. Boatmen have an axiom regarding buoys that says: "Red right returning." When returning to a port from the sea, keep the red, even-numbered nun buoys on your right. Black, odd-numbered can buoys will be on your left as you pass upstream. Midchannel buoys are painted black and white in vertical stripes, and you may pass to either side. Black and red horizontal stripes on a buoy indicate an obstruction; pass on the side indicated by the topmost color. A buoy may also be a floating drum or piece of wood attached by rope to an anchor to show its position. When it is used in this manner it's called a mooring buoy. —F.M.P.

BUOY BASS *See* Tripletail

BURBOT *Lota lota* Also called cusk, ling, or lawyer, this is the only member of the codfish family found in freshwater in North America, Europe, and Asia.

The body is elongate, somewhat eel-shaped, with a barbel on each anterior nostril and one longer one in the middle of the chin. The small first dorsal fin is followed by a long second dorsal fin which is similar in shape to the anal fin. The small, numerous scales are imbedded in the heavy skin which is colored dark olive above with chainlike blackish or yellowish markings on the sides. This coloration is more marked in the young of the species. The burbot occasionally exceeds 30 inches, although the average size is less than 1½ feet. While the average weight of the Great Lakes form is about a pound, the subspecies found in Alaska and Siberia may attain a length of 5 feet and a weight of 60 pounds. The common form is distributed from New England and the Susquehanna River system in the East, throughout the Hudson Bay drainage, and in the Columbia River. This is a coldwater species, occurring in lakes; it seeks deepwater in the summer, and it has been caught to depths of seven hundred feet.

Although it is not normally found in streams, it is abundant when present and is most often taken by the angler around large boulders and other shelter. The burbot occurs in both sluggish and swift streams.

LIFE HISTORY

Reproduction occurs under the ice, usually over sand or gravel bottom. During February, burbots enter shallow water 1–4 feet deep, where they spawn at night.

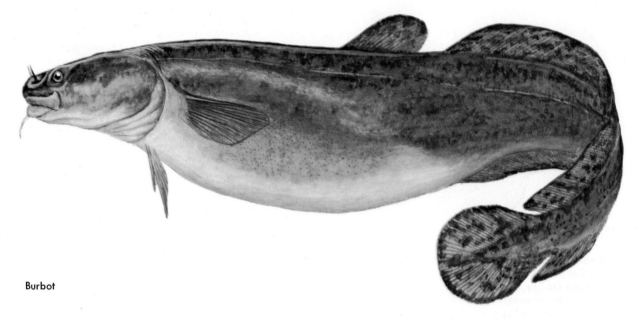

Burbot

voracious feeder, the burbot takes fish, crayfish, and other animals, the feeding being carried on essentially at night. It competes with lake trout for food and eats large numbers of whitefish and ciscos. Although its flesh is good, the burbot is not utilized to any extent, nor is its vitamin-rich liver. —D.dS.

BURGEE A pennant, sometimes swallow-tailed. A club burgee is used to identify membership in a specific boat club or organization.

BURRFISH *See* Porcupinefish

BUTANE Liquefied petroleum gas, bottled under pressure and used for cooking in small boats. Also used for portable refrigerators. It is heavier than air and must be used with caution. If allowed to escape and gather in the bilge or below decks it becomes a potential explosion hazard.

BUTTERFISH *Peprilus triacanthus* A finely flavored saltwater fish common to the Northeast coast. Butterfish are fat, tending to be oily, but this in no way detracts from their table value. They are best known to the smoked-fish trade, with only small amounts getting to the local market. The butterfish has a very thin, deep body and seldom attains a weight of over one pound. They have little or no angling value.

Butterfish

BUTTERFLYFISHES **Chaetodontidae** The chaetodontids are among the most beautifully colored and graceful

fishes of the sea. They are high-bodied and compressed. Their mouths are small and their teeth brush-like. Two sub-families are grouped in the family, the butterflyfishes (Chaetodontidae) and the angelfishes (Pomacanthinae). Butterflyfishes lack the stout spines of the preopercle which are characteristic of angelfishes.

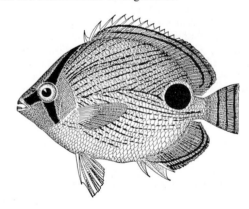

Foureye Butterflyfish

Chaetodon is the largest butterflyfish genus. In the tropical western Atlantic there are six species. Most are small, rarely exceeding 7 inches in length. Usually there is at least some yellow coloration. Perhaps the best known is the foureye butterflyfish (*Chaetodon capistratus*), the most common species of the family on West Indian reefs. Its name is derived from two pale-edged, eye-like spots posteriorly on the body, one on each side, hence giving a total of four "eyes." The true eyes are obliterated by a vertical black bar, thus a predator might mistake the posterior part of this fish for the front.

Another feature which affords protection is their deep body, coupled with formidable dorsal and anal spines. Also, their narrow width enables them to hide in crevices.

Banded Butterflyfish

Another common shallow-water species is the banded butterflyfish (*Chaetodon striatus*). In addition to a black bar through the eye, it has two broad bars on the body and another in the posterior part of the dorsal fin, which extends on to the caudal peduncle. The spotfin butterflyfish (*Chaetodon ocellatus*) has only the ocular black bar, a nonocellated round dark spot basally in the soft portion of the dorsal fin, and a small black spot at the posterior edge of the fin. Less frequently seen are the reef butterflyfish (*Chaetodon sedentarius*), which has a dark ocular bar and a broad posterior dark bar that extends into the dorsal and anal fins; the bank butterflyfish (*Chaetodon aya*); the Caribbean butterflyfish (*Chaetodon guyanensis*); and the longsnouted butterflyfish (*Prognathodes aculeatus*)—all of which tend to occur in deeper water than the preceding species.

Species of *Chaetodon* feed primarily on small crustaceans and polyps from various coelenterates.　—J.E.R.

BUTTERFLY PAVÓN *Cichla ocellaris* One of the most beautiful native gamefish found in tropical South American waters. Also called pavón mariposa (Spanish) and tucunaré-pinima or lukanani (Indian). The butterfly pavón is generally basslike in body shape; breeding males, however, develop a prominent hump on the posterior portion of their heads. The body coloration is blue-green on the dorsal surface blending to bright yellow on the sides, which are accentuated by three black spots along the midline of the body and a narrow black border on the posterior edge of each scale. The eye is bright red; and the pelvic, anal, and lower half of the caudal fin is orange to brick red. The gold-rimmed black ocellus on the base of the caudal fin also helps to identify this fish.

The butterfly pavón, much like the North American largemouth bass, prefers still waters. Fish collected during February and March in Orinoco tributaries were found to be maturing sexually, and it is probable that they spawn during April and May, the start of the Venezuelan rainy season.

ANGLING VALUE

The butterfly pavón is a fair gamefish, easily caught on spinning, bait-casting, or fly-rod tackle. It strikes more readily, but is not nearly as game as the peacock pavón (*which see*). Its fight is characterized by vicious strikes, short head-shaking runs, and occasional jumps. It rarely exceeds 5 pounds, but occasionally grows to 11 pounds; the average weight is 2–3 pounds. *See also* Colombia, Peacock Pavón, Venezuela

BUTTERFLY RAY *See* Smooth Butterfly Ray, Spiny Butterfly Ray

BUTTER SOLE *Isopsetta isolepis* Rough scales and, usually, yellow-edged dorsal and anal fins distinguish this Pacific member of the righteye flounder family. A slight arch of the lateral line over the pectoral fin, an accessory dorsal branch to the lateral line, and scales which extend onto the fins also help to identify this species. It is brownish to gray, irregularly blotched with yellow or light green spots on the eyed side, occasionally with darker markings. It reaches a length of 18 inches, and is found from southern California to northwestern Alaska, being more common in its northern range. Found usually over a soft, silty bottom, it is a shallow-water form. A spring spawner, it is of importance to both commercial and sport fisheries.

Its excellent flesh finds a ready market as fresh and frozen fillets.　—D.dS.

BYSSAL THREADS Long, strong, adhesive threads secreted by the byssus gland found in the foot of some bivalve mollusks, such as the mussel; these mollusks attach themselves to rocks or other objects by using the threads.

BY-THE-WIND SAILOR *See under* Portuguese Man-of-War

Butterfly Pavón

C

CABEZON *See under* Drums

CABEZONE *Scorpaenichthys marmoratus* The species is one of the largest sculpins (*which see*) on the Pacific Coast, reaching a length of 30 inches and a weight of 25 pounds. Even though the flesh is of varied colors, it is an excellent food fish with the exception of the roe which is poisonous. It is found from central Baja California to northern British Columbia.

The cabezone has a large head and high, closely set eyes. The skin is smooth and thick; the snout has a prominent flap (cirrus); the spined portion of the dorsal

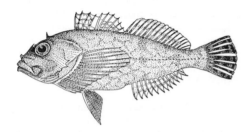

Cabezone

fin is notched; there are large marbled pale areas on dorsal and caudal fins and body, and a spine and five rays in the pelvic fins. Body color may be from green to cherry-red, and changes with the environment.

LIFE HISTORY

The fish carries as many as 100,000 greenish eggs and spawns from the fall to March, depositing the ova in a mass. Its food consists largely of crabs, but other crustaceans and fish are taken. It is found on many types of bottom and in kelp beds in shallow inshore waters to depths of about two hundred feet. Maturity in the males is at 2–3 years of age and in the females at 3–5. It has been known to reach 13 years of age. The young are pelagic, and are blue and silver in color. It does not move rapidly unless in pursuit of food.

ANGLING VALUE

An important sport fish, it is but little used except in California near Santa Barbara and Monterey. In 1960 only 3,000 pounds valued at less than $500 were landed by commercial fishermen of the Pacific Coast states including Alaska. The sport catch is much greater.

It can be caught throughout the year by jigging or with whole or cut bait.   —J.R.

CADDISFLIES Trichoptera More than 800 different species of caddisflies occur in the United States and Canada. They vary in body length from the so-called "micros," some of which are less than ⅛ inch long, to forms exceeding 2 inches. Representatives occupy almost every type of freshwater habitat; and, while adults of most species emerge in spring and summer, even in the Northern states adults may be found in every month of the year.

Caddis larvae are important dietary items for many kinds of fish. Adults are of less frequent occurrence than larvae in trout stomachs which have been examined.

With the notable exception of the Adams, the Grannom, and the White Miller, few artificial flies patterned after caddisflies have won wide acceptance.

LIFE HISTORY

Eggs deposited in or near water hatch into the worm- or grublike larva which, after completion of growth, enters a resting stage or pupa from which, usually after 10–14 days, the winged adult emerges.

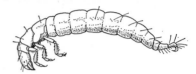

Caddisfly Larva

Caddisfly Adult

Larvae of many caddis species build a protective case. Cases may be constructed of plant fragments or sand held together by silken threads secreted by the larva, and are often of characteristic pattern in a given species. Examples are the familiar "log cabin" and "snail shell" cases. Some larvae do not make cases but move freely through chinks and interstices of stream- or lake-bed material. Others construct a partial case faced with a silken net behind which the larva lurks to feed on tiny aquatic organisms trapped in the net. Caddisfly larvae tend to be omnivorous. Some of the larger species popular as live bait may exhibit cannibalism if kept together in a small container.

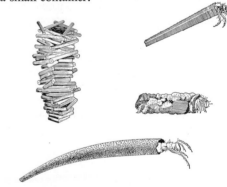

Types of Caddisfly Larva Cases

Caddisfly adults bear a superficial resemblance to moths, but, among other differences, lack the latter's coiled sucking tube for feeding. They have long, threadlike antennae but no tails. At rest the wings are folded like a tent over the back. Expanded, the hind wings are broader than the fore wings. In most species the wings are clothed with tiny, hairlike scales. Varying widely in size and coloration, most caddisflies are rather drab in appearance. A few species show striking color patterns. The white species of the genus *Leptocella* are models for the White Miller dry fly.   —J.W.L.

AMERICAN SEDGE

Brachycentrus americanus This is a widespread North American member of a genus with many American and European species, the British forms giving rise to the common name, sedge. They frequent moderate-size streams and at times during the spring season fairly swarm among shrubs and sedge plants along stream margins. Females deposit their large, gray egg masses in flight at water's surface shortly after midday mating. Along with the somewhat larger *Hydropsyche* which also "dance" in groups the sedges are among the most frequently seen caddisflies along Western trout streams. Adults are eagerly sought by trout and other gamefish on many Western streams.

The larvae of the sedge usually construct long, four-sided, chimney-shaped cases of small bits of dead plant, but occasionally round cases are made. Larvae frequent fast riffle areas, and there is but one generation a year.

The adult sedge is about ½ inch in length, gray in color, and robust in general appearance. The sides of the body proper are occupied by a wide, light stripe. The compound eyes are very large and there are no ocelli.

The Sedge is a well-known artificial fly pattern that is effective during a hatch.

AUTUMN PHANTOM

Dicosmoecus atripes Large, darkish caddisflies emerge late in the season on many of our Pacific Coast streams and fly rapidly and erratically over streams and along highways bordering rivers and creeks. There are several species, brown, grayish, or blackish in color. All are of large size.

Atripes has dark gray, black-veined, elongate wings about 1¼ inches in length. Antennae are nearly an inch long, and the long legs and body are orange-tinted. In addition to the pair of large, compound eyes, there are three ocelli, shiny and black, on the bristly head.

The larva of this species constructs a cylindrical case of small bits of gravel and is often used as a bait for trout. The larvae are especially tempting to the lake-frequenting kokanee, or landlocked sockeye salmon. Cases of this species occur abundantly in riffles of clear mountain and coastal streams. They are incorrectly called periwinkles by uninformed anglers.

The artificial fly pattern called Caddis can be tied to resemble this species. —S.G.J.

BLACK DANCER

Mystacides alafimbriata A blackish caddisfly of moderate size but with enormously long, dark antennae, several times the length of the body, *Mystacides* occurs abundantly on Northern lakes and slow-moving streams. The adults dance in loose assemblages, usually all males, from a few to perhaps two dozen individuals over the water's edge during most any time of day and in shadow as well as in sunlight. There is evidently a single generation, but adults often emerge over a long time from early spring to early autumn.

The larvae construct long, cylindrical cases adorned with available bits of material, pieces of plant debris, or bits of gravel or sand. They crawl about detritus on the bottom of ponds or muckbottom streams.

The Sedge can be tied to resemble this insect. It is also suggested that a small, blackish, artificial nymph be employed beneath the water surface at the margins of blue-gill or trout ponds when a hatch of the Black Dancer is on the wing. —S.G.J.

WHITE MILLER

Leptocella albida and some of its closely related species are almost certainly the insects after which the White Miller pattern was developed. Related to the insects known to British anglers as silverhorns, these caddis-flies are predominantly white in color and, since they are most commonly on the wing during and after dusk, stand out prominently from their darkened surroundings.

The slender, wormlike larvae are less than ½ inch long when fully grown and construct a protective case of tiny sand grains which is slender, tapering, and slightly curved.

Adults are on the wing from early June to mid September. Their habit is to fly in swarms of varying size, rising and falling very little but circling back and forth very rapidly at a height of 2–6 inches above the water.

The body length is about ⅝ inch, but the slender antennae are more than twice as long. Head and thorax dark, but clothed with white hair. Wings almost entirely white, faint gray markings along the front margin of the forewing visible on close inspection. Legs and abdomen white to grayish white.

Because of the flight habits of this caddisfly, fish must jump clear of the water to capture one, and on the basis of stomach examinations the fish are not often successful.

While it may be heresy to suggest it, the possibility remains that a well-tied White Miller might be a fair imitation of almost any predominantly white insect, including some mayflies and a variety of moths. Further, it is an easier fly for the angler to control after he has been overtaken by darkness. Whatever the explanation, the artificial generally proves more successful than the habits of the natural would lead one to expect. —J.W.L.

CAESAR GRUNT *Haemulon carbonarium* This grunt occurs in the Florida Keys and the Bahamas southward throughout the West Indies, and along the coast of Central and South America to Brazil. The average total length of mature adults is about 10 inches, but larger individuals are sometimes taken. This species resembles the Spanish grunt (*which see*), from which it is distinguished by the number of pectoral rays, anal rays, lateral-line scales, and gillrakers. The sides of the body have longitudinal, bronze to bright yellow stripes. The mouth is light red. The Caesar grunt has 12 dorsal spines; dorsal rays 15–16, usually 15; anal rays 8; and

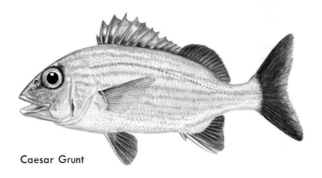

Caesar Grunt

pectoral rays 16–17, usually 17. Pored lateral-line scales 49–50. Gillrakers 23–25. Its pectoral fins are naked.

ANGLING VALUE

The Caesar grunt is a bottom feeder and prefers clearwater. It enters tidal creeks and boat basins along the Florida Keys. It fights well on very light tackle. This grunt is taken on dead shrimp, cut mullet, and cut pilchard. It is good eating and is frequently seen in West Indian markets. —L.R.

CALCUTTA CANE *See* Tonkin Cane

CALICO BASS A regional name for the black crappie (*which see*).

CALICO GROUPER *See* Speckled Hind

CALICO SALMON A local name for the chum salmon (*which see*).

CALICO SURFPERCH *Amphistichus koelzi* Similar to the redtail and barred surfperches; frenum is usually absent but is narrow when present; lower jaw projects slightly; dorsal spines similar in height to softrayed portion; 17–20 scales between lateral line and anterior end of vent; 24–

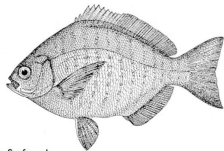

Calico Surfperch

48 dorsal softrays, 26–32 softrays in the anal fin. Found in the surf from northern California to northern Baja California. *See also* Surfperch —J.R.

CALIFORNIA One of the most popular and productive states for the United States angler. Its freshwater rivers and lakes provide more than twenty game and pan species. Rainbow, brown, brook, lake, and cutthroat trout are the dominant coldwater fishes, while largemouth and smallmouth bass, bluegill, catfish, redeared perch, Sacramento perch, and crappie are common in the warmwater fishery.

Along California's thousand-mile coastline there is an even larger variety of fish to choose from ranging from striped marlin and broadbill swordfish down to the diminutive grunion (*see* California Grunion) of the far southern portion of the state around San Diego and Los Angeles which are scooped off the tideline with bare hands as a wave recedes. And many of the species that the California fishermen prize are anadromous, like the salmon, steelhead, striped bass, shad, and sea-run cutthroat trout in the far north.

Within the borders of California there are many mountain ranges. The Sierra Mountains are the mightiest of this group, and they form a trout and black-bass haven near the Nevada border in the north. The coastal mountain ranges are bunkered up against the Pacific Ocean, and they are cut and chopped up into series of mountain ranges that provide ample watershed for numerous streams which empty into the ocean every few miles. The

streams in the far north of the state are host to most of the migratory species, and those to the south are seasonal in the extreme. The mountains of California are literally dotted with man-made impoundments. Virtually every major stream in the entire state has some form of dam on it. These man-made lakes have changed the character of freshwater fishing in California. When the Forty-niners settled California the rainbow trout and its migratory form, the steelhead, shared the mountain streams with very few other species. Most of these were anadromous, such as the king and silver salmon. But now the lakes tucked into every fold in these mountains provide the angler with phenomenal black bass, bluegill, crappie, and other kinds of warmwater fishing. And yet trout and some of the salmon still find good habitat in the depths of these same lakes.

The central portion of California running from north to south is divided by a massive system of valleys which are among the most fertile in the world. This Central Valley area separates the two major mountain systems and runs from the Mexican border to within a hundred miles of the Oregon border. These valleys were formed by the two primary river systems—the Sacramento, which drains from the north, and the San Joaquin River, which flows from the south. Both of these rivers join and empty into San Francisco Bay.

The delta area formed by the meeting of these two rivers is the wellspring for a tremendous fishery which tempts roughly half of California's million and a half license-carrying anglers. The striped bass and shad were introduced into this fertile spawning ground in the late nineteenth century, and they have come to dominate the fishing attention of most of the immigrant fishermen. Both the shad and the striper are immigrants, too. They were imported from New Jersey waters.

The Pacific coast of California is rugged and rocky for most of its length. Here and there are sandy beaches where the saltwater surf-fisherman can catch everything from the numerous perch species to the striped bass. Saltwater anglers who specialize in rock-fishing have thousands of inlets and rock-studded indentations to choose from, and they will find that this type of fishing is virtually untouched by the trout- and salmon-minded California anglers.

If the saltwater fisherman likes to take his fish from a boat, he can catch salmon and bottom fish, such as the halibut and lingcod in almost the same area as he takes his striped bass, throughout the waters from Monterey Bay to Humboldt Bay in the far north. Southern California deepwater fishermen can go for albacore and bonito; sea bass, which run up to several hundred pounds; and he can take barracuda, kelp bass, opaleye, and a dozen other species just about any time he feels like it.

The long-time California fisherman is usually a trout- and salmon-man if he fishes primarily in freshwater. But with the influx of people from other areas of the country, black bass and panfish became equally interesting to the average fisherman. Some of the bass and panfish available in California are very respectable indeed. In the far north Lake Shasta and Trinity Lake can produce specimens that weigh up to 10 pounds. Some of the reservoirs in the San Diego and Los Angeles areas, as well as those near the sizable city of Fresno, have consistently yielded large fish and abundant limits. But the salmon is still king among the majority of California anglers. In fact, its accepted name is "king salmon" in this area of the Pacific Coast range. The steelhead, which runs in most of the same streams, is considered the ultimate in fly-fishing by most serious anglers.

Dam building and pollution of streams cut into the gamefish supply during the first fifty years of this century in California. And, while these problems are being conquered slowly at the present time, there are still serious threats to spawning migrations of gamefish such as the striper, salmon, steelhead, and shad. The chief culprits are chemical fertilizers, sand and gravel removal, and poor lumbering practices, especially in the far northern tier of the state. City pollution from sewage and industrial wastes is currently under control in most cases, and authorities have made a remarkable improvement since the industrial explosion during World War II. The Fish and Game Department, along with various antipollution agencies, can depend on strict laws to back them up when they discover new sources of pollution. When a new dam is constructed in California the builder is required to provide hatchery facilities to replace at least the number of fish that have been cut off from their spawning grounds when that dam blocks the stream.

The current population increase in California is causing very serious pressure on the state's available water supply and the fish using these waters. However, new lakes are rising behind more and more dams. Large dam-building programs are being approved at an accelerated pace. It's almost a certainty that the fishing character of the state will continue to change, but it is also very doubtful that a state with as much water, and newly planned water supplies, will ever be fished to exhaustion.

CENTRAL VALLEY RIVERS

The Sacramento and San Joaquin River drainages are perfect examples of the effect of public ignorance of fish requirements. The Sacramento River is fast becoming a prize example of how a modern-day river should be used.

Before Shasta Dam was built the Sacramento was a flooding monster in the winter and a tepid and unreliable stream in the summer. There were fair supplies of steelhead and salmon in the mountain streams which fed into the drainage, and everything depended on the weather cycle. But now that Shasta Dam has tamed this once destructive stream, the river proper has a reliably even flow for nine months of the year. The Coleman Hatchery for salmon and steelheads at Battle Creek, a few miles south of Red Bluff, is one of the largest in the world, and it is supported from power revenues. The water is reasonably cool throughout the entire year, and there is a salmon or steelhead run in progress for twelve months of the year.

The San Joaquin, on the other hand, has been virtually dammed out of existence. This once great river has been diverted and irrigated to such an extent that it is little more than a creek where it flows into the tide backup of the Delta area in the vicinity of Tracy and Stockton. The great runs of fish have disappeared completely, where they once ran and spawned south almost as far as Fresno and into the mountains to the east. Some of the lakes formed by the dams on the San Joaquin and its tributary streams range from fair to excellent, but if there

had been a policy of replacing the spawners when these streams were denied to the migrants, at least the lower river could still host a population of migratory fish.

THE DELTA

The Pacific Ocean backs up through San Francisco's Golden Gate and affects the water level of the Sacramento River to a point close to the state capital at Sacramento, roughly one hundred miles upstream. This Delta area was originally a vast swamp, but now it has been lined with dikes and drained so that there are about a thousand miles of sloughs and river in an area of about fifty square miles. This fertile water hosts an amazing selection of fish. Black bass, steelhead, bluegill, crappie, salmon, catfish, shad, perch, sturgeon, and rough fish, such as carp and the remains of wayward goldfish hordes, can be taken by any angler who wishes to use the accommodations in over a hundred resorts and fishing camps. The striped bass, salmon, and steelhead share the limelight with large catfish as the main attractions for most of the local angler population.

FAR NORTH STREAMS

The Klamath River is the most dominant stream that flows from the mountain systems in the far north near the Oregon border. The Klamath originates in Oregon and is at present controlled by two dams, COPCO (California-Oregon Power Company) and Iron Gate Dam, which originally was intended as a water-control dam but which will undoubtedly soon become another major power-producing operation.

The Klamath steelhead and salmon fishing is a modern legend. Such names as Seiad Valley, Happy Camp, Somesbar, Orleans, and Weitchpec in the upper and middle river and Klamath Glen or Blue Creek in the lower river are famous throughout the entire world wherever steelhead fishermen come together and talk.

The Klamath River is a big, turbulent stream that flows over large boulders for most of its length. Other

A favorite among steelheaders is the Klamath River in northern California. It produces both winter and summer-run fish

famous steelhead and salmon waters that are far more sedate, and often just as productive for the fishermen in far northern California, are the Eel River, noted for the large size of the steelheads taken, and the Smith, which produces the largest average salmon in the state. Lesser streams such as the Mattole, Trinity, Scott, Salmon, Van Duzen, Mad, and half a hundred other rivers and creeks are primarily salmon and steelhead waters, and they can absorb a lot of fishing pressure.

THE INLAND STREAMS

While the vast majority of good fishing streams flow toward the Pacific, a few notable streams also flow toward the east of the Sierra Mountains and Nevada's desert country. The Truckee River, emptying from the north end of volcanic Lake Tahoe, is a picturesque stream that skirts the fringe of Highway 40. This unfortunate nearness to the main east-west highway link has put extreme pressure on the trout population of the Truckee. The original Lahontan cutthroat is virtually extinct, but sizable rainbow trout are still stocked by the Fish and Game Department, and record brown trout have been taken from this stream in the past.

South of Lake Tahoe, east-flowing streams that will yield good trout to fishermen are the Walker and Carson River systems. But the jewels of these high-altitude streams are the Owens River and Crowley Lake, which year after year withstand tremendous pressure from the burgeoning California angling population. A private stream which ranks among the top ten streams in the nation for rainbow trout is Hot Creek, a classic dry-fly stream that flows cold and clear across a desert of sage brush and rocks. The crystal clarity of these high mountain streams demands the ultimate in angling technique, and here the size No. 16 to No. 22 fly is a common sight among the talented fishermen.

The Colorado River actually flows into the Gulf of California, but it does skirt the backbone of the lower

The well-stocked Merced River in California's Yosemite Park is popular among trout anglers

southern mountain chain. The Colorado, since it was dammed at Boulder City by massive Hoover Dam (originally Boulder Dam), now provides the far-south California angler with some of his best sport. The black bass are very respectable in the lower portion of the Colorado, with the largemouth having already taken root. But in the middle and upper portions of the Colorado the trouts are making a comeback with the help of stocking programs between states. Also, the smallmouth black bass have a foothold in Colorado River waters from recent California plants.

LAKE FISHING

It is possible here to mention only a few of the lakes in California. Lake Tahoe, the original home of giant Lahontan cutthroat, is a 1,600-foot deep volcano. It still yields good rainbow trout to over 10 pounds and lake trout of all sizes to deep-trolled lines. Fishing Tahoe is a challenge to any fisherman because the water is so crystal clear than an angler can see pebbles on the bottom at fifty-foot depths.

Shasta Lake, near the sizable city of Redding, has just about every freshwater gamefish. The large black bass are the main attraction in Shasta Lake, but Kamloops rainbow, rainbow, and brown trout are also abundant. The bluegill population is under-harvested—as it is in most California lakes—and the kokanee-salmon fishing during May and June is superb if the angler hits it right.

Clear Lake, one of California's few large natural lakes, is a low-altitude lake with shallow depth. The warmwater species such as largemouth bass, bluegill, and crappie vie for space with catfish which run to well over 10 pounds. This extremely fertile lake is one of the few in California that is open to day and night fishing.

There are over a hundred "average" lakes in California. These irrigation-flood-control lakes have black bass, bluegill, crappie, catfish, and carp in them. If they are deep enough they also support a fair to good trout population, normally rainbow trout, but often some brown-trout fishing. Good examples of these lakes are Lake Berryessa and Folsum Lake in central California. Further south, Millerton Lake, Pine Flat Reservoir, Isabella Reservoir, and in the coast range such examples as Twitchell Reservoir and Cachuma Reservoir will always yield good limits of warmwater fish to a diligent angler.

A distinctive group of lakes that is continuing to provide good fishing for far southern California anglers is the waters of the San Diego Utilities. These are experiments that have proved that anglers can safely use municipal water-supply lakes.

OCEAN AND BAY

Residents of southern California are among the nation's top boating sportsmen. This has led to a popularity in bay and ocean fishing that demands traffic control on at least bay waters. And fishing is usually the prime excuse for owning a boat in California.

San Francisco Bay is a major sport-fishing center for both the private boater and the commercial party boat. The prime target inside San Francisco Bay is the striped bass. Every year the bag of stripers climbs. Roughly three million stripers are netted or gaffed out of bay and the nearby Delta waters each year. Party boats often split a day's charter with a morning and afternoon schedule and 5–20 anglers on each boat. During peak seasons limits within an hour are relatively common because the striper limit is now set at three fish of 16 inches or better.

Outside San Francisco Bay party boats with an average of ten anglers troll "cannon-ball" weights of 3 pounds on a sinker-dropping rig for king and occasionally silver salmon. This outside salmon fishing is the most certain way to take a king on the whole coast, but the heavy gear needed to tow the cannon balls around does keep the kings from showing what they can do. Private and commercial fleets as well as party boats work out of all the ports from Monterey Bay north for salmon when they can be found and for bottom fish when the salmon don't cooperate. Bodega Bay, Point Arena, Albion, Fort Bragg, Humboldt Bay, and many other small inlets and ports along the coast offer good access for private boats and have charter-boat accommodations.

In southern California the bay and ocean sport is handled about the same as it is in northern California. The main interest in the Santa Barbara to Long Beach area is the often fantastic fishing near the Channel Islands and Santa Catalina in particular. The Channel Islands National Monument, a federally owned and privately operated group of larger islands just off the southern coast, offers some of the best saltwater sport in the state. These islands, San Miguel, Santa Rosa, Santa Cruz, and Anacapa, have no sportsman accommodations or facilities; their main industry is cattle raising. But they are serviced with regular party-boat trips out of Port Hueneme Sportfishing Landing during the spring and summer months, generally. And special bass- and bottom-fishing runs are made by party boats out of Santa Barbara to the island of Santa Cruz.

Anacapa is particularly noted for its population of giant black sea bass. These fish can come in large economy sizes, even for the small-craft fisherman, and they've been taken to 400 pounds. Common tackle for these mammoth fish are: a 22-ounce tip, double-built swordfish rod fitted with 72-pound-test line and No. 14/0 hooks with a 500-yard-capacity reel—plus all the muscle the angler can spare.

The channel has some fair to good albacore fishing in irregular years as these fish make their northern migration. But the queen of these islands is Santa Catalina. Catalina is a large, twenty-one-mile by eight-mile island that has been built up as a major resort and sport-fishing center. The only accommodations for the fisherman are out of the city of Avalon, where charter-boat and small-boat rentals are numerous. The isthmus has restaurants, a pier, moorings, and housing facilities as well as gas and motor-repair facilities, and it is a major yachting center—it is about fourteen miles from Avalon. Some catches of marlin are taken near Catalina, but the main fisheries are for sea bass, the kelp bass, yellowtail, and barracuda.

San Diego tuna fishing is world famous, and during the summer a huge fleet works out of San Diego harbor with the commercial fleet based in the city of San Diego and a sizable private fleet working from exclusive Coronado.

Beach-, cove-, and rock-fishing on the California coast is in its infancy. With so many other forms of angling to choose from, it has been pretty much overlooked. At present, a flurry of interest along the beaches from Santa Barbara to San Diego yields good catches of corbina and a variety of perch. The beaches of San Francisco, even in the city limits, are lined with striped-bass fishermen from May to September because Western anglers have finally become convinced that lure-fishing is productive in Western waters for the imported striper. North and south of the Golden Gate the catches of rockfish can range into the realm of fantasy because these fish rarely ever see a bait. Part of this is due to the fact that accessibility is often difficult, and the techniques of working a bait or lure in the massive belt of kelp beds, which lies close in to shore from the Oregon border to the Los Angeles area, are not generally understood.—J.F.

CALIFORNIA BONITO *See* Bonito

CALIFORNIA CORBINA *See* Drums

CALIFORNIA GRUNION *Leuresthes tenuis* A small, silvery fish, somewhat like a smelt in general appearance, found chiefly between Point Conception in southern California and Punta Areojos in Baja California. At times they may stray as far north as Monterey Bay. Unlike other fish, the grunion come completely out of the water to spawn in moist beach sand at which time they are caught by hand. Grunion spawn at night shortly after high tide, but only for three or four nights following each full or new moon. The run only lasts a few hours, but thousands of fish may be on the beach at one time. The reason why the moon plays a role in their

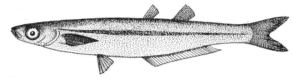

California Grunion

spawning run is because the highest tides occur when the moon is full or new. Since wave action erodes sand from the beach as the tide rises and deposits sand as the tide falls the grunion unerringly times their arrival for the falling tide. The female deposits its eggs about two inches below the sand, and they are buried deeper by the outgoing tide. The eggs remain buried for about ten days at which time the next series of high tides erodes the beach, and minutes after they are free the baby grunion hatch.   —A.J.McC.

CALIFORNIA HALIBUT *Paralichthys californicus* Although a member of the lefteye flounder family, it is righteyed nearly half the time. The species is somewhat similar in body shape to the Pacific halibut (*which see*) which, however, has the eyes generally on the right side and which

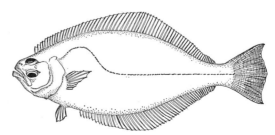

California Halibut

has numerous sharp teeth and a smaller mouth. The unbranched lateral line is arched over the pectoral fin, there is a wide, flat area between the eyes, and the scales are small. It is greenish to gray-brown, and occasionally mottled, the young often with small whitish spots. The species reaches a length of 5 feet and up to 60 pounds, although unofficially reported to 72 pounds.

Found from central California to within the Gulf of California, they occur generally in water less than ten fathoms deep. Sandy bottoms are their favorite haunt, although they may be taken in channels or even in heavy surf, along sandy or rocky beaches.

LIFE HISTORY

Migrations are not extensive, particularly in young. Spawning occurs from April through July in rather shallow water. A 30-pound halibut was found to be 15 years old, growth being fairly slow. Maturity occurs at an age of 2–3 years (male) to 4–5 years (female), at a length of about 11–17 inches. Anchovies and other small fishes are eaten in abundance, and halibut themselves are eaten by angel sharks, rays, sea lions, and porpoises.

ANGLING VALUE

Important commercially, about a third of the catch is taken in Mexico, the rest in California, most being sold as fresh fillets. The valuable sport fishery is most successful utilizing drift-fishing methods with live anchovies, queenfish, and shrimp, although slow trolling accounts for some of the catch.

FOOD VALUE

As in other members of this genus, the flesh is excellent.
—D.dS.

CALIFORNIA SHEEPHEAD *Pimelometopon pulchrum* The unique color and shape distinguish this Pacific member of the wrasse family Labridae. A deep body and a slight hump on the head readily separate it from other California wrasses. The head bluntly slopes to the thick lips, and the large canine teeth protrude forward from the heavy jaw. During the breeding season, the male develops

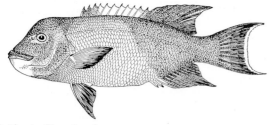

California Sheephead

a distinct hump over the eyes. The tips of the caudal and spinous dorsal and anal fins are pointed. Coloration of the sexes is distinct. The male has the head, fins, and posterior part of the body purple or black, with the rest of the body red to purple-black; the lower jaw is white. The female is uniformly reddish to rose color, occasionally with black blotches. A weight of 30 pounds and a length of 3 feet are the maximum size.

It ranges from the Gulf of California to Monterey Bay, California, about kelp beds or near rocky bottoms and shores, most commonly in depths of 20–100 feet.

LIFE HISTORY

It is believed to reach an age of at least 20 years and to mature at 4–5 years, spawning apparently occurring during the summer. Adults defend a given section of territory and are pugnacious, driving away others from their lair. Examination of stomachs of the sheephead have revealed lobster, abalones, and other types of shellfish.

ANGLING VALUE

Of some importance to sport fishermen in southern California, it is taken on cut bait such as abalone, lobster, or fish and is also a chief target for spearfishermen. The largest landings are in the winter, the smallest in the summer, although the species is caught throughout the year.
—D.dS.

CALIFORNIA SKATE *Raja inornata* The relatively long snout is produced into a tip but not so much as in the longnose skate (*which see*). The front margin of the disk is convex, and there is no eyespot on either side of the disk

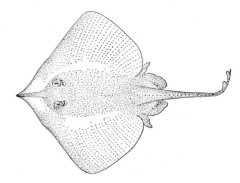

California Skate

as in the big skate (*which see*). It is dark olive-brown above with a dark ring at the base of each pectoral fin, and the belly is pale to dusky with irregular mottlings. It grows to 2½ feet, and occurs from Washington to southern California in deepwater. Taken by trawlers, it is common enough to enter the commercial catch, and its wings are valued as food.
—D.dS.

CALIFORNIA YELLOWTAIL *Seriola dorsalis* This is a very well-known amberjack from the Pacific Coast of the United States and northern Mexico, where it is usually known simply as yellowtail—by which undistinguished common name it can be confused with many other kinds of fish bearing the same name (the rainbow runner, a snapper, the pinfish, two flounders, a drum, etc.). References to this species from Panama, the Galápagos Islands, and South America are now thought to refer to another species.

The first dorsal fin of the California yellowtail usually has 6–7 short spines, although only as few as 3 spines may be visible in some large fish. The second dorsal fin has 1 spine and 31–37 softrays. The anal fin has two detached spines followed by one spine and 19–23 softrays. The first gill arch has 4–9 gillrakers on the upper limb and

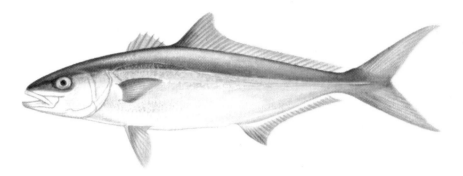

California Yellowtail

14–22 gillrakers on the lower limb, with the anterior gill-rakers becoming rudimentary with growth of the fish. A dark or brassy stripe extends horizontally through the eye to the tail in fish of about 10 inches and longer. The dorsal- and anal-fin lobes are only moderately elongated; the dorsal lobe is only about $1/7$–$1/10$ as long as the head and body (without the tail).

The body is elongate and moderately compressed, tapering to a rather sharp snout. When caught, the yellowtail is bright metallic blue to green above the stripe and silvery below. The fins are a dusky greenish-yellow except for the bright yellow caudal fin. Young, up to about 7 inches long, have about 9–10 bars on the body, with many of the bars having a median lighter area.

The yellowtail has been taken from Mazatlán, Mexico, into the Gulf of California at Los Angeles Bay on eastern Baja California, and northward to the coast of southern Washington. It is usually only common, however, from Los Angeles County to the tip of Baja California.

The two largest recorded fish were just under 4 feet 10 inches in total length. The larger weighed 80 pounds, the smaller, 63 pounds.

The record-size amberjack that has been recorded as *Seriola dorsalis* from New Zealand, weighing 111 pounds and 5 feet 2 inches in length, should be distinguished by another name, possibly *Seriola grandis* both for purposes of classification and gamefish records, until its relationship to the California yellowtail has been adequately studied.

LIFE HISTORY

Because of popular interest in the yellowtail, its life history has been studied in some detail. By analyzing the annuli on the scales, it was found that this species lives to an age of more than 12 years and that fish in their second year of life attain an average length of 23 inches, 5–6-year-old fish average about 36 inches, and 10–11-year-old fish average about 45 inches. The length at any particular age and the weight at any particular length are variable, but a 23-inch fish weighs about 4 pounds, a 36-inch fish about 16 pounds, and a 45-inch fish about 27 pounds.

The California yellowtail has been described as an op-portunistic feeder, implying that it feeds upon whatever is available. It feeds upon schooling fishes and in-vertebrates, primarily sardines, anchovies, Pacific jack mackerel, Pacific mackerel, squid, and the pelagic red crab. Feeding is predominantly during the daytime Spawning has been observed at least one time, at an off-shore bank west of southern Baja California. Spawning generally begins in July and continues until October, al-though the ovarian eggs usually begin to develop in March and the females do not reach maturity until late June. Larger fish apparently spawn a little at a time over a three month period. Fish may first begin spawning when about $1\frac{1}{2}$ years old, and all have begun spawning by their third summer of life. Larger fish have more eggs than smaller fish; the number of eggs per female may range from almost one-half to four million. Yellowtail larvae have been identified from plankton-net collections, but their descriptions have not been published. Tagging experiments have shown some interesting patterns of movement of large fish. They normally move from central Baja California into southern California during early spring and south again during late summer and fall. Fish 3–8 years old appear to school with others of similar size and to migrate greater distance than older fish, which seem to be more sedentary and solitary.

ANGLING VALUE

The yellowtail is a strong, fast swimmer and provides a very popular sport fishery. This is largely concentrated between Los Angeles and Ensenada and at the channel islands, with the Coronado Islands being the most pro-ductive. Most fishing is done by casting with live sardines or anchovies for bait. Cast and trolled artificial lures are also used. Most of the fish caught by sport fishermen is eaten fresh or frozen; some is smoked or canned. Indi-vidual opinions of the taste range from fair to delicious. Commercial fishing for yellowtail is very limited and has been declining. Round haul nets, entangling nets, and hook and line are used. *See also* Carangidae   —F.H.B.

CANARY ROCKFISH *Sebastodes pinniger* The species is probably the most important rockfish (*which see*) on the Pacific Coast, dominating the commercial catch of rock-fish in California. It is prized by the angler and the com-mercial fisherman alike for its palatability. It is found from northern British Columbia to northern Baja Cali-fornia and is common all along the coast.

The canary rockfish has small spines on top of head, lower jaw slightly projecting, a knob on the lower tip, lower jaw smooth to touch. The general body coloration is orange with three bright orange stripes across head;

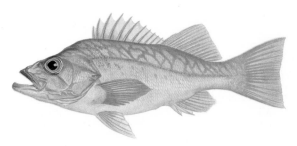

Canary Rockfish

lining of mouth pale red with dusky mottling; fins usually bright orange. Length to 30 inches.

Older fish are usually found in deeper waters to at least 600 feet, young inshore. As many as 600,000 ova may be carried by large females.   —J.R.

CANDIRU *Vandellia cirrhosa* A miniature tropical South American catfish which is a vertebrate parasite to man. The eel-like fish enters the human body through the sex

Candiru

organs of bathers who may urinate in the water where the candiru abound. The candiru become lodged in the host by means of erectile spines. These parasites can only be removed through an operation.

Little is known of the life history of candiru. They usually burrow in mud or sand bottoms of tropical streams and normally avoid sunlight. They may reach a length of about 3 inches.   —T.D.W.

CANDLEFISH *See* Eulachon

CANE POLE A long bamboo pole which is used in still-fishing. The cane pole is not equipped with guides or reel seat although a ferrule is sometimes added for convenience in transportation. The line is tied directly to the pole tip, and the bait is lowered to the water. This crude tackle is inexpensive and often very effective in taking pan species such as the bluegill, catfish, and crappie. A variant of cane-pole fishing is the skittering method, which utilizes a large spinner, spoon, or pork rind rather than a live bait; the operator swings his lure out among lily pads or other vegetation and skitters it rapidly over the surface. Skittering with the cane pole was popular in the early 1900's in catching pike, pickerel, and bass.
                                    —A.J.McC.

CAPELIN *Mallotus villosus* This smelt (*which see*) is almost circumpolar in distribution and is found in the North Atlantic and Pacific Oceans south to Maine, Juan de Fuca Straits, Korea, and Norway.

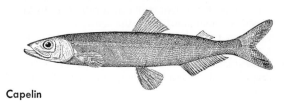

Capelin

Males are larger and have deeper bodies and a larger anal fin than the female; they have filamentous processes on the lateral-line scales in the breeding season. Scales are small, 175–209 on lateral line; adipose fin large; opercles rough. Eggs deposited on sandy beaches at high tide, though there are some that spawn at depths to 1,000 feet; 3–56 thousand eggs per female; incubation period 2–3 weeks; spawns more than once. It feeds on plankton and is an important link in the food chain of northern seas. Salmon and cod feed on it extensively.

ANGLING VALUE

Capelin have no angling value. They are utilized as food in the areas where they are caught, and only a small poundage is exported. Like the California grunion capelin come in with the breakers and spawn on the beach where they are easily caught with dipnets, seines, and castnets. Identical to smelt in size, flavor, and texture, they are deepfried, smoked, and dry salted.   —J.R.

CARANGIDAE This family of marine fishes includes the jacks, scads, pompanos, amberjacks, threadfins, lookdowns, leatherjackets, and roosterfish. This large and diverse family of fishes is represented in all tropical and subtropical marine waters of the world; some species occur in colder, temperate waters. Most of the members of this family are strong, fast swimmers and are excellent gamefish, especially on light tackle. Many species are important to commercial fisheries. The palatability for the various species ranges from excellent to poor, although many that are taken by sports fishermen are not eaten, and the flesh of a few species (especially from tropical Indo-Pacific waters) has been reported to be poisonous at some times in some areas.

The relationships within this family, in many instances, are very inadequately known. There are three principal reasons for this. (1) Many of the species undergo very great changes in body shape and fin structure and coloration as they grow—many of these changes are completed while certain species are small (at less than 6 inches long), but in other species they continue to occur after the fish is over 1–2 feet long. (2) Many of the species or species complexes occur around the world or in different and isolated waters, and slight differences in form have been variously interpreted. Different names, both common or popular names and scientific names, have been applied to similar carangids in different areas. The names used here are those that are most commonly accepted at this time. (3) The carangids have not been adequately studied. More specimens, both very large and very small, need to be saved and preserved in our museums, so that detailed studies can be made.

The 67 species in this list are known to occur in the western Atlantic and in the eastern Pacific oceans. These are divided into 8 groups, and each group is discussed elsewhere in the book under the heading of its common name. While these groups express close relationships and similarities of shape, certain of them are for convenience in reference only. The species marked by an asterisk are the most important or the most abundant, and these species are detailed under their common names. (A = western Atlantic; P = eastern Pacific)

Descriptions and life histories are given under the common name of the species marked with an asterisk and under the names of the eight different groups of carangids.
                                    —F.H.B.

JACKS

*Socorro jack	*Carangoides orthogrammus* (P)
*Yellow jack	*Caranx bartholomaei* (A)
*Green jack	*Caranx caballus* (P)
Juan Fernandez jack	*Caranx georgianus* (P)
*Blue runner	*Caranx crysos* (A)
Gwelly	*Caranx dentex* (AP)
*Crevalle jack	*Caranx hippos* (AP)
*Atlantic horse-eye jack	*Caranx latus* (A)
*Black jack	*Caranx lugubris* (AP)
*Pacific horse-eye jack	*Caranx marginatus* (P)
*Spotted jack	*Caranx melampygus* (P)
Bar jack	*Caranx ruber* (A)
*Mazatlán jack	*Caranx vinctus* (P)
*Atlantic bumper	*Chloroscombrus chrysurus* (A)
Pacific bumper	*Chloroscombrus orqueta* (P)
*Dorade	*Gnathanodon speciosus* (P)
*Atlantic bluntnose jack	*Hemicaranx amblyrhynchus* (A)
Longfin bluntnose jack	*Hemicaranx atrimanus* (P)
Pacific bluntnose jack	*Hemicaranx leucurus* (P)
Milkymouth crevalle	*Uraspis helvola* (P)
*Cottonmouth jack	*Uraspis secunda* (AP)

SCADS

Jurel fino	*Decapterus afuerae* (P)
*Mexican scad	*Decapterus hypodus* (P)
Mackerel scad	*Decapterus macarellus* (A)
*Round scad	*Decapterus punctatus* (A)
Galápagos scad	*Decapterus scombrinus* (P)
*Bigeye scad	*Selar crumenophthalmus* (AP)
*Rough scad	*Trachurus lathami* (A)
Peruvian scad	*Trachurus murphyi* (P)
*Jack mackerel	*Trachurus symmetricus* (P)
Chicharro	*Trachurus trachurus* (A)

THREADFINS

*Pacific threadfin	*Alectis ciliaris* (P)
*African pompano	*Alectis crinitus* (A)
*Threadfin jack	*Citula otrynter* (P)

LOOKDOWNS

Blackfin lookdown	*Selene brevoorti* (P)
Pacific lookdown	*Selene oerstedi* (P)
Atlantic lookdown	*Selene vomer* (A)
Pacific moonfish	*Vomer declivifrons* (P)
Atlantic moonfish	*Vomer setapinnis* (A)

POMPANOS

Argentine pompano	*Parona signata* (A)
	Trachinotus blochii (WP)
*Pompano	*Trachinotus carolinus* (AP)
Cayenne pompano	*Trachinotus cayennensis* (A)
*Atlantic permit	*Trachinotus falcatus* (WA)
*Palometa	*Trachinotus goodei* (A)
*Pacific permit	*Trachinotus kennedyi* (EP)
Spotted Pompano	*Trachinotus marginatus* (A)
	Trachinotus maxillosus (EA)
	Trachinotus mookalee (WP)
*Paloma pompano	*Trachinotus paitensis* (P)
*Gafftopsail pompano	*Trachinotus rhodopus* (P)
Clarion pompano	*Zalocys stilbe* (P)

AMBERJACKS

*Rainbow runner	*Elagatis bipinnulatus* (AP)
*Pilotfish	*Naucrates ductor* (AP)
*Pacific amberjack	*Seriola colburni* (P)
*Yellowtail	*Seriola dorsalis* (P)
*Greater amberjack	*Seriola dumerili* (A)
*Lesser amberjack	*Seriola fasciata* (A)
Southern amberjack	*Sericla lalandi* (A)
Little amberjack	*Seriola mazatlana* (P)
Peruvian amberjack	*Seriola peruana* (P)
*Almaco jack	*Seriola rivoliana* (A)
*Banded rudderfish	*Seriola zonata* (A)

LEATHERJACKETS

Panama leatherjacket	*Oligoplites altus* (P)
Pacific leatherjacket	*Oligoplites inornatus* (P)
Deepbodied leatherjacket	*Oligoplites mundus* (P)
Maracaibo leatherjacket	*Oligoplites palometa* (A)
Slender leatherjacket	*Oligoplites refulgens* (P)
Sauteur	*Oligoplites saliens* (A)
Atlantic leatherjacket	*Oligoplites saurus* (A)

ROOSTERFISH

*Roosterfish	*Nematistius pectoralis* (P)

CARIBE *See* Piranhas

CARITE The Spanish name for king mackerel or Spanish mackerel (*which see*).

CARP *Cyprinus carpio* This Old World minnow was first successfully introduced into this country from Germany by the United States Fish Commission in 1876. Indigenous to Asia, carp were so abundant on the European continent that they were mentioned by Aristotle as early as 350 B.C. The carp reached Britain from the continent at the end of the medieval period, about 1450. There is no evidence to suggest an earlier date, despite persistent legends of carp in British monastery ponds. Carp are not mentioned in the Domesday Book of 1086, nor in the Feudal Aids Records to 1272. The earliest reference to British carp is 1462, as a stockfish. The first angling reference is from Dame Julia Berners in 1496. The introduction, well investigated by an English writer, John Nixon, is said to have been done by one of two men, a certain Mascall or John Howard, First Duke of Norfolk.

The carp has a single, serrated spinous ray in its dorsal fin along with 16–22 softrays. The lateral line contains 32–38 scales, except in the partly scaled or scaleless varieties known as "mirror" and "leather" carp. The upper jaw has two fleshy barbels on each side, the rearmost of which is the larger. The carp is golden-olive-colored above, with sides becoming lighter and golden-yellow to yellowish-white below. Each scale has a dark spot at its base and is darker around its outer edge, giving the fish a cross-hatched appearance.

Since its introduction into this country the carp has become widely distributed. Common in eastern North America, it is found from coast to coast. Although the carp is known to survive under a wide range of conditions it prefers warm streams, lakes, and shallows with an abundance of organic matter. Carp are tolerant of all bottom types and clear or turbid waters and are not normally seen in clear, cold waters or streams of high gradient.

The carp is widely cultivated and highly regarded as a gamefish in the Old World. Historically, it was an unwise introduction to North American waters and is a textbook example of the problems encountered with exotic species. The carp is not only a prolific breeder, but due to its grubbing in the bottom which muddies the water, thereby destroying aquatic plants and the habitat of native gamefish, it does not hold a position of high esteem. No study was made of the carp in 1876; the United States Fish Commission received 345 adults which were placed in breeding ponds at Druid Hill Park in Baltimore, Maryland. In the following year some of these fish were shipped to Washington, D.C., and from that politically oriented environment a scheme arose to create a demand for carp. The fish were multiplying so rapidly that any Congressman wishing to collect a few votes could pass out some carp to his constituents. This scheme was so well organized that the fish were transported according to congressional districts on special railroad refrigeration cars. Within five years hundred of thousands of carp were being "gifted" annually. But soon the fish found their way through broken dams and by indiscriminate stocking to waters that held bountiful supplies of trout, pike, and bass. The adaptable carp took over. Eradication of carp populations through netting and eventually chemical treatment became more important than carp production. The use of spears and bow-and-arrows was encouraged as additional controls.

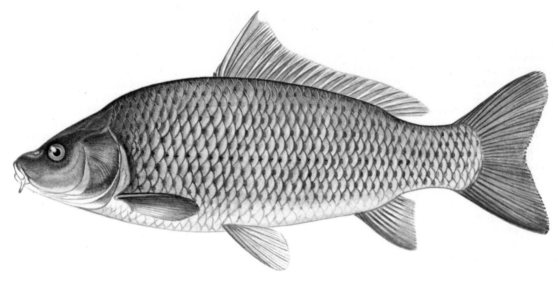

Carp

The adverse publicity the carp received inevitably created myths which haven't died to this day. The story is still told how carp have been found in a pond that has been previously drained dry for many months, because they are able to burrow under the mud and remain alive. They will sometimes lie dormant partially or wholly buried in a lake or stream bottom during the winter months in a state of hibernation and revive as the spring water temperatures stir the spawning urge. But water is still essential to their existence.

Another story that remains is that carp gorge themselves on the eggs of gamefish, but in a study made by the New York Conservation Department over a five-year period not a single egg was found in 600 stomach analyses. Occasionally, an egg is found in a carp stomach, as the fish is a wandering bottom feeder; but the bluegill sunfish, for example, is a nest raider, which the omnivorous carp is not.

LIFE HISTORY

In the wild carp spawn from April to July depending on the latitude beginning at a water temperature of about 60°F. Like the northern pike, the male and female carp pair off in weedy shallows and losing their natural caution spawn with a great deal of splashing. The small (1½–2 mm) grayish-white eggs are broadcast over a wide area and adhere in masses to plants and debris where they are left unguarded. Female carp are prolific; 150,000 eggs per pound of body weight is the average; a fish of 20 pounds may drop over 2 million eggs. Such numbers indicate a high mortality among eggs and fry. But the eggs eye rapidly and hatch within 4–8 days, at which time the quarter-inch-long fry bear a large pear-shaped yolk sac. The fry sink to the bottom grasping it or grasping plant stems with an adhesive organ on the way down. On the second day they struggle to the surface to gulp air for their gas bladders. Once this has been done, they swim actively, absorbing the yolk sac first, then feeding on algae and plankton. As adults their food will also include small crustaceans, insect larvae (particularly midges), and mollusks. The protractile mouth, which extends into a leathery tube, is adapted for sucking food from the bottom.

Young carp grow rapidly, under exceptional conditions gaining 3 pounds per year; 1 pound per year is a good average increment. The major reason for this fast growth is the very sufficient conversion of food into flesh, one of the best in the animal kingdom. In temperate climates males mature by their third year, females up to a year later. In the tropics maturity can be reached by the second year or, exceptionally, in the first. The size attained varies according to feeding opportunity and climate. A 10-pound fish is a good angling catch; a 20-pound fish a real trophy. The maximum size is, however, much greater. In Britain and Holland the rod-caught records stand at over 40 pounds, with much larger fish known to exist. A United States rod-caught carp was 55 pounds, 5 ounces (Clearwater Lake, Minnesota); the heaviest carp on record was 83 pounds, 8 ounces taken in a net in Pretoria, South Africa.

Long lived (20–25 years in the wild and to 47 years in captivity), tolerant of high temperatures (to 96°F. for a 24-hour period), yet equally tolerant of low temperatures to the point of withstanding temporary freezing, able to utilize atmospheric oxygen and thus the last to expire in a drying pond, and, above all, smart—this shrewd Oriental remains an enigma to most anglers. The carp has most attributes except good public relations.

SELECTIVE BREEDING

The carp offers many advantages to the fish culturist. It has been farmed intensively in Europe since probably the tenth or eleventh centuries A.D. Selective breeding is nearly as old, and many varieties or strains exist, distinguished principally by body form and scale pattern. Variations in these have become stabilized as an accidental by-product of the search for a fast-growing pond fish. The typical wild carp is three times as long as deep in the body and fully scaled. However, it is relatively slow-growing. In the German-derived vocabulary of the carp breeder selectively-bred varieties are known as "king" carp to distinguish these from the wild strains. King carp are found in all variations of body form and scale pattern, although they will regress to the typical carp after several generations in the wild. In body form two main groups of king shapes are recognized: the longer, thick-bodied Lausitz, Bohemian, and French strains; and the short, deep-bodied Galician and Israeli strains. These king carp may be scaled in three ways: fully scaled as the wild fish and indistinguishable except for their faster growth rate; partially scaled or "mirror" carp which may be a line mirror with its scales distributed along the lateral line; and the scattered mirror with scales spread haphazardly over the body. The line mirror is the commonest and is often called the Israeli carp. Scalation in the third type is completely absent, which makes it a "leather" carp. These scaling patterns are controlled by a complex of genes in which certain combinations for the leather type are believed to be. Thus, the leather carp is most unusual and does not always breed true.

Selective breeding has been done for many reasons. The Russians have produced cold-resistant "king" strains for stocking Arctic waters, and in Asia the "golden carp" or Hi-goi is an ornamental variety showing nearly the same range of colors as the goldfish. It is widely introduced to stock ornamental ponds, and interbreeds with other carp strains. Chiefly, however, the carp has been a cheap source of protein, and United Nations agencies have promoted the fish among underfed peoples throughout the temperate and tropical zones. From a pond without fertilizer or supplementary foods, 300 pounds of carp per acre is a fair yield. With intensive fertilization, yields can be three or four times this figure. So the yield of protein per unit area, unit cost, and unit effort is superior to that from cattle on prime pasture. It is small wonder that carp culture is extensively carried out on marginal land too poor for other crops. Bear in mind that large fish are not needed for the table; European practice is to cull the fish by nets or pond drainage at up to 3 years old, a certain proportion being set aside for breeding the next year.

ANGLING VALUE

Few topics separate European and American anglers so much as the question of the carp's sporting value. In the Old World the carp has always been within ecological balance with other native species. Climatic and competitive or predatory checks have operated effectively. While it roils water and uproots weeds, it seldom if ever displaces the native fauna. And because fewer European fishes are amenable to spin- or fly-fishing its roiling activities are tolerated. It has therefore achieved a desirable status. It is almost invariably caught and released, few angler-caught carp being eaten. Next to the northern pike and the salmon, it is the largest European angler's fish, difficult to lure, a hard fighter, and satisfying to catch.

The mystique of carp angling reads like a cookbook with advice on proportions of water to flour in making dough balls, methods of kneading, the use of canned whole-kernel corn, cooked potatoes, and even gumdrops and jelly beans. The fact that carp will take flies at times, especially in the spring of the year when midges and nymphs fished near the bottom in reasonably clear water have their moments of success, does not substantially alter the approach to carp trickery. Bread dough is the basic carp bait. It is the simplest and easiest to make, and the most efficient if molded properly around the hook point.

To make dough from bread, break a few slices into a cloth or handkerchief and place it in the water, but do not knead it there. After it has soaked, squeeze the water out, open the cloth and knead the dough, working in cornmeal as you do. Too much of the latter, however, will make the dough too brittle. You need no cotton batting or any other binder, just bread and cornmeal. The doughball should just cover the barb of a No. 2 sproat. The key to the carp's character is that he enjoys taste sensations similar to mammals. A carp can distinguish between salty, bitter, sweet, and acid stimuli. Thus, a dollop of sugar or cheese in a dough ball could make the difference in angling success. Though alien to normal diet, the carp makes prolonged inspections of a bait, oftentimes picking it up and expelling it until the taste is established in its suspicious barbuled mouth.

The popularity carp finds among European (especially British, Dutch, and French) anglers is of recent origin. The change of attitude dates from about 1950 and stems from the activities of the present English carp record-holder, Richard Walker. The tackle, as evolved by Walker and his associates, is specialized but widely used. The rod is a 10-foot progressive action 1½-pound-test curve type, not unlike some salmon spinning rods. The lines are from 8–10 pounds breaking strain, carried on a large fixed spool reel. The terminal tackle is almost invariably a single large hook tied direct to the running line; fished over baited swims or places where carp are known to frequent, being cast out and left for several hours at a time. American carp specialists use a medium-weight spinning or spincasting outfit. Monofilament lines from 8–12 pound test are standard here also, although in the spring period, when big carp are numerous and greedy and fishing can be accomplished at short ranges, many anglers use 15–18 pound test braided lines. In summer, when the carp are scattered in deep water and biting lightly, the strike must be made the instant the float shakes or tips the slightest bit. It is late, the carp will have spit the bait out. Long rods are especially valuable then because with them there is a minimum of line between the rod tip and the float. There is no time to gather up line sagging in the water before striking.

FOOD VALUE

The carp is a good fish to eat when properly prepared. It's important to skin them and trim out the dark flesh. This mass of "dark meat" has fibers which differ biochemically from other muscles and has different contractile properties which make it both unappetizing and tough. Carp is excellent when smoked, and the roe is edible and often sold in canned form. Carp flesh is an important ingredient in making gefilte fish (*which see*).

—A.J.McC.

CARVEL BUILT Boat planked so that the edges of the planking lie parallel and flush to each other. Achieves a smooth and unbroken hull, and is made watertight by caulking.

CAST The British term for a leader (fly-fishing).

CASTER One who practices casting.

CASTING The act of throwing an artificial lure or bait. Skill at casting is achieved in distance and accuracy as well as the execution of difficult casts. Although casting is the basic art of angling, it is also practiced as a game or contest. *See also* Bait-Casting, Fly-Casting, Spinning, Surf-Casting, Tournament Casting

CATADROMOUS Any fish which migrates from freshwater to the sea for the purpose of spawning, as does the American eel. It is the opposite condition to anadromous (*which see*).

CATAMARAN In its simplest form it consists of a platform that rides above but joins two floats or twin hulls. It's a centuries-old design popular with the Polynesians who perfected use of twin canoes joined by a platform for use in the South Pacific. The modern outboard "cat" also consists of twin hulls held together by a wing-deck but sometimes doesn't look much different from an extrawide conventional outboard until it is hoisted out of the water when you can see a fore-and-aft tunnel where most boats carry a keel.

CATFISH There are 15 or more families of catfish in world distribution, with the greatest number of species found in South America. Many of these families are highly specialized; there are walking catfish, talking catfish, blind catfish, toothless catfish, armored catfish, electric catfish, climbing catfish, and parasitic catfish. The largest catfish are found in the Amazon Basin and European rivers east of the Rhine, where specimens of over 400 pounds (*Siluris glanis*) have been recorded. There are 28 species in United States' waters, varying in size from the inch-long least madtom to the giant blue catfish which may weigh up to 120 pounds. Until the 1960's all North American species could be divided into 2 families, the Ictaluridae, or fresh water catfishes, and the Ariidae, or marine catfishes; since then both the Asiatic walking catfish and the South American armored catfish have become established in Florida waters, bringing the present total to 4 families.

Except for the armored catfish, which has overlapping bony plates on its body much like tiles on a roof, all catfish are scaleless. All of the North American species have barbels or "whiskers" around their mouths. The barbels, as well as the general surface of their skin, enable the fish to taste, touch, and smell—a combination of senses necessary to foraging at night and in turbid water, although a few species, notably the channel catfish, are also keen sight feeders. The barbels are arranged in a definite pattern; the freshwater catfishes have 4 under their jaws, 2 nasal barbels above, and 1 each at the tip of the maxillary for a total of 8. Marine catfishes commonly enter southern United States coastal rivers, and at times may be caught among typical freshwater species; these can be recognized by the absence of nasal barbels, with a total of 4 barbels on the gafftopsail and a total of 6 on the sea catfish. It's not uncommon for catfish to grow Y-shaped barbels, which appear as a branch near the tip. This variation is consistent among armored catfishes which always have multibranched barbels. At least one South American species lacks barbels completely, and on the walking catfish, which tends to dehydrate after prolonged periods out of water, the barbels will slough off at the base. However, the walking catfish has rapid regenerative powers and can grow new barbels or even fins in a relatively short time.

FIELD IDENTIFICATION

In the field bullheads can be quickly separated from other catfishes on the basis of caudal fin shape. All bullheads have emarginate or rounded tails. The only major catfish with a rounded tail is the flathead, but it also has an extremely large free-moving adipose fin which differs from the small adipose of the bullhead. The miniature madtoms can be separated from both catfish and bullheads by their adnate adipose fins, which give the impression of a continuous fin with a slight notch on the upper posterior half of the body. There are a dozen madtom species (including the stonecat) whose principal value to the angler is as live bait for river smallmouths and walleye. When positioning on a hook they should be grasped from the rear, with fingers at the base of their pectoral and dorsal fins to avoid getting "stung." The sharp spinous ray at the leading edge of the pectoral fin has a locking structure which enables the catfish to hold it erect as a defensive weapon. In the madtoms and sea catfish this needlepoint ray has a poison gland at its base. When the spine punctures flesh the toxin is injected and produces a paralyzing sensation much like a severe bee sting. Although the pain usually disappears in a few hours the wound may continue to hurt for weeks. Both the sea and walking catfishes can maneuver their pectoral fins and literally seek an unwary finger, so these must be handled with extra caution. Their sting is almost electric on contact and may require medical treatment.

There is some color variation in catfishes from one region to the next, and juveniles usually differ from the adults. The green bullhead, for example, starts life as a "brown cat" (hence the latin name *brunneus*) before turning an olive green; the channel catfish is both slender and spotted when young, but with age the spots disappear as the fish becomes jet black and its body conformation changes radically. Another species that may be caught in a widely divergent coloration is the walking catfish. When this bizarre form first arrived in Florida it was dominantly an albino; the vast majority were white to yellowish in color; the mutation is in demand by tropical fish dealers and under hatchery conditions albinos can be culled and reared. In the wild, however, genetic law soon prevailed and it reverted to the dark camouflage of a nocturnal animal. Albino channel catfish or "golden cats" are popular in the restaurant trade because of their appeal to the eye, but they are rare in nature. Other than color, the key features to examine are tail shape, anal fin-ray count, head shape, the presence or absence of serrations or barbs on the pectoral spines, jaw length, and the number or color of the barbels.

ANGLING VALUE

Literally millions of catfish are caught in the United States each year. With the exception of the channel catfish, and to some extent the blue, the majority are taken on natural baits ranging from doughballs to whole suckers. The channel cat is attracted to artificial lures with consistency, particularly deep running spoons, jigs, and plugs; 25–30 percent of all the prize winners in *Field & Stream*'s Fishing Contest fall to artificials. Bullheads will also take a lure, such as wet flies, tiny jigs, and spinners. Marine catfish are caught on a great variety of artificial baits. However, canepoles, trotlines, bushhooks, snag-hooks, jugs, slat-traps, basket-traps, trammel, and gill nets account for the most and biggest. During the breeding season huge catfish are captured by "noodling," an art form that requires grabbing the nest-defending male by the jaw or gills while he hides in a hollow log or bank. This game is not without its difficult moments, and experienced noodlers submerge with a rope tied to their waists as old channel cats have beartrap mouths, and it may require an assistant noodler to pull them both out.

In the swift tailwaters of Southern impounds over 50-pound catfish are taken on heavy tackle. The big blues of Tennessee's Pickwick Dam require what amounts to deep-sea gear, with lines of 100-pound test or more and 4–8 ounces of lead sinker to bounce a bait on the bottom. The mystique of catfish baits is in its own fashion as diversified as artificial flies for trout; astute commercial fishermen, for example, use soap (and not just any soap, as there are distinctions between Camay, Palmolive, and Lifebuoy) as bait in one location and grass shrimp in the next. Crayfish, minnows, frogs, salamanders, hellgrammites, suckers, mullet, gizzard shad, worms, leeches, sweet and sour freshwater clams, mussels, rabbit liver, pig liver, beef liver, chicken-blood bait, flavored-sponge baits, soybean meal cakes, and cheese balls barely reveal the whole galaxy of "specials" used to lure the taste-sensitive catfish in specific waters in certain seasons.

ECONOMIC VALUE

The commercial catfish industry is a significant economic factor involving hundreds of thousands of acres of farm ponds in 34 states, the research facilities of 15 universities, and the leadership of the Catfish Farmers of America. A profitable wetcrop, with yields up to 2,000 pounds per acre, the blue, channel, and white catfishes are inventively marketed through modern processing plants under rigid state and federal controls (*see* Propagation of Catfish *under* Fish Culture). Some of the larger operations purvey 10,000 pounds of fresh and frozen catfish per week. The major buyers include supermarkets, restaurants, and over-the-counter dealers. While the prime sales have been, for obvious reasons, below the Mason-Dixon Line, the demand in the North now exceeds the supply. Such disparate enclaves as San Francisco, Chicago, and New York have discovered that catfish are a gastronomic delight.

When it is poorly prepared the fault is seldom a matter of flesh quality but too often the inability of the chef to cook a catfish. The most popular method of preparation is deep frying, an art form that requires careful attention to detail. In sophisticated Southern cities large catfish are more popular than small ones. The reason is that a city like Atlanta, for example, is conditioned to steaked and filleted saltwater fish. Thus, the crosscuts taken from a large channel or blue catfish find a more receptive audience than the little half-pounders that country boys skillfully crisp and eat like corn on the cob. Unlike trout addicts, who disdain whitefleshed fish, a catfish with red flesh, such as the brown bullhead or "red cat," has few admirers among catfish fanciers. Firm, white, and moist is the rule. *See also* Armored Catfish, Black Bullhead, Blue Catfish, Brown Bullhead, Channel Catfish, Flat Bullhead, Flathead Catfish, Gafftopsail Catfish, Green Bullhead, Headwater Catfish, Sea Catfish, Spotted Bullhead, Stonecat, Tadpole Madtom, Walking Catfish, White Catfish, Yaqui Catfish, Yellow Bullhead   —A.J.McC.

CAUDAL   Toward the tail or pertaining to the tail; the tail. *See* Anatomy

CAUDAL FIN   The tail fin or tail. *See* Anatomy

CAUDAL PEDUNCLE   That portion of a fish's body immediately preceding the tail. *See* Anatomy

CAVALLA   *See* King Mackerel

CAVIAR   A lightly salted sturgeon roe. The word is from the Turkish *khavyah* However, the Soviet Union is the largest producer and consumer of caviar in the world. There this delicacy is known as *ikra*. In many European countries caviar is preserved with borax, but this is prohibited in the United States. The grading of caviar is determined by the size and color of the eggs. The names of the various types of caviar derive from the name of the sturgeon from which it comes.

Beluga is the largest egg, and is taken from the beluga sturgeon (*Acipenser huso*). This species often reaches a weight of 2,000 pounds and attains an age of one hundred years or more. The beluga produces the most highly regarded of the world's caviars.

Osietr is the Russian word for sturgeon, but it represents the species (*Acipenser sturio*) most sought for its eating qualities. The flesh is particularly delicious when smoked. Specimens have been caught as large as 700 pounds. The osietr produces a caviar (often preferred by European gourmets) sometimes golden-brown in color similar to that of sterlet and has a delightful nutlike flavor.

Sevruga is the smallest yet most prolific species (*Acipenser sevru*). It may reach a weight of 100 pounds, but usually enters the fishery at 35–50 pounds. The eggs of its roe are small, but of exceptionally fine flavor.

Sterlet This is an almost extinct species (*Acipenser ruthenus*), relatively small, but highly esteemed for its roe. Sterlet is the legendary "gold" caviar of the Czars and is rarely seen outside the Soviet Union.

Ship This is a hybrid sturgeon resulting from a cross between the osietr and the sevruga. It is seldom found in areas other than the deltas of the rivers near Baku on the Caspian Sea. The roe is particularly firm and produces an excellent caviar but is always in short supply.

THE STORY OF CAVIAR

Until 1961, any fish roe that was black was called caviar in the United States, even when artificially colored. However, only sturgeon roe may now be called caviar, while the origin of the others must be properly defined as, for instance, whitefish roe with artificial coloring added, lumpfish roe, etc. But even within the limitation of sturgeon roe there is a wide field for misapprehension, since any number of different kinds of sturgeon contribute to the annual caviar production.

The most highly regarded caviar is prepared from the roe of the yellow-bellied sterlet. Unfortunately, only a few mortals, not even some of the greatest connoisseurs, have ever made the acquaintance of this apogee of the Russian delight. Before World War I, sterlet-roe caviar was reserved for the Russian Imperial court and other dignitaries of the Muscovite Empire and was never exported, at least legally. Not even the great restaurants of Paris and London ever saw this delicacy.

The most expensive grade of caviar exported from Russia in sufficient amounts to supply restaurants and the connoisseurs of the world is the one made of the roe of the beluga (the white sturgeon). And of the belugas, the ones caught in the Azov Sea are preferred as a source of caviar to those caught in the estuaries of the rivers that flow into the Caspian Sea. In all likelihood, good salesmanship also had something to do with the fame of beluga caviar, because the beluga sturgeon is the largest of this family of fish, having been recorded to a weight of 2,500 pounds. Hence, the beluga roe produces the largest egg, so dear to the eye of the gourmet, and usually commands the highest price. As first quality, it is always packed as malosol but, contrary to some belief, is never prepared without any salt. The salt is what transforms raw roe into delectable caviar.

The term malosol, usually found coupled with the word beluga, simply translated from the Russian, means "little salt." In other words, malosol is not a brand of caviar, but do note that only malosol caviar is entitled to the term *fresh*. (All types are prepared malosol.) With the small amount of salt used, constant refrigeration during transport is essential (all types today are expensive). To explain in plain figures: for malosol, one pound of salt is used for each pud of caviar; pud is a Russian weight representing approximately 41 American pounds.

Occasionally—but very occasionally—the beluga will feed on small, live fish. Normally, however, like the osietr and sevruga, it is a vegetarian feeding on aquatic plant life. Usually these fish are netted with heavy seines, though sometimes grappled by dangling unbarbed hooks placed across the well-traveled runways leading from the sea into the rivers, the Volga particularly.

When the roe is taken from the fish to make the caviar, it is processed manually. First, the connective tissue, which encloses the eggs, is broken by whipping it with a birch switch. The freed roe is passed over screens with varying-sized mesh to grade the eggs—washed, drained, and the salt added. Packed into slip-lid tins, never sealed, it is now malosol caviar.

Most caviar connoisseurs misguidedly choose their caviar first by the size and then by the color of the individual "berries" as the eggs are called in the American trade. Gourmets today love to reminisce over the great gray berries that were served in profusion on the trans-Atlantic liners before World War I and often wonder why this quality of caviar—although it is more a type than a quality—was never available in the United States. The explanation for this is that the United States government only allows caviar to be imported that is either processed, i.e., canned, or preserved solely with salt.

The great gray berries, however, contain a preservative permitting less salt, hence less shrinkage in their size, and the retention of their original grayish-black color. The preservative, a minute quantity of borax, is forbidden in the United States though accepted by health authorities of many other countries.

But if the size of the berries and their color are no criteria of quality in caviar, what is? The most important characteristic of first-quality, whole-grain caviar is that each berry must be whole, uncrushed, and well-coated with its own glistening fat. Considering these two prime requisites of good caviar, the caviar buyer, before he pays a small fortune per pound, should make sure that the fattest part of the caviar did not rise to the surface of the

can during transport and was then scooped off by the vendor for some favorite customer, thus leaving the less fat berries for other and later buyers. It is for that reason that the conscientious caviar merchant assures that the caviar tins in the refrigerator are turned frequently to keep the fatty substance well distributed.

The word *refrigeration* in connection with caviar also calls for explanation. The modern refrigerator with its compartments for below-freezing-point storage presents many dangers to the preservation of caviar, for once caviar is frozen and then thawed, the berries will have burst, the product becomes mushy, and the quality deteriorated. The proper temperature for long storage is 26° F., or 6° below the freezing point of water. The salt content of the caviar permits this lower temperature. When so stored caviar will retain its delicacy for many months.

With so many operations involved, each calling for meticulous care, it must be obvious that the Russian caviar industry is no new enterprise. Caviar has been most appreciated by the Russians since approximately the thirteenth century. Due to poor methods of trade and transport, other countries only learned about this delicacy considerably later. But as early as 1520, Pope Julius II spoke highly of this most famous Russian product. And less than a hundred years later, Shakespeare uses the word caviar to define a play as too exquisite for the masses: " 'Twas caviare for the general." (*Hamlet*, Act II.)

To return to the renowned beluga, not all of its roe is packed as whole grain, whether malosol or not. The smaller damaged or less firm eggs, of all types of caviar that are sieved out during the grading, are prepared as *pausnaya*, literally "pressed caviar." This pressed caviar is usually packed in small barrels of one hundred pounds each though sometimes in the same type of tins as the whole-grain caviar. When available for export, it is lightly salted and of excellent flavor. It resembles in its final state a gooey mass similar to a thick marmalade. The Russians, who may be considered the original connoisseurs, in many cases prefer pressed caviar to the whole-grain variety. However, it should be added at this point that Russians—in Russia—eat caviar much more frequently even today than the wealthiest patron of the most expensive restaurant in New York.

Considering the variations under which it may be sold, only one foolproof test for caviar can be suggested. Good caviar should have no fishy odor whatever; if it has, it has been treated in any one of innumerable ways, and chances are that an attempt is being made to pass off an inferior quality. When the term *inferior quality* is used, no implication is intended that caviars that do not spring from the beluga or, by some lucky chance, the sterlet, are not fit to eat or not worth the considerable price they bring. Foremost and always foremost, the quality of caviar depends on the handling it has received. A well-treated caviar made from the roe of members of the sturgeon family other than beluga or sterlet may be just as good, if not better, than a poorly handled beluga roe. So don't be misguided and consider a caviar to be of inferior quality that does not carry the magic word beluga.

It would be difficult to say which of the other sturgeons produces the next best caviar. In most cases if the roe was treated in the proper manner, the choice is a matter of taste. However, the confused state of the nomenclature of the other sturgeons adds considerably to the puzzle of which is which. The sevruga sturgeon produces a fine roe and a fine caviar (also spelled sevriouga or chivrouga). This holds true for another caviar that is called osietr. These two are often exported, and, as said before, their quality depends entirely on the care with which they have been handled. Again, in these two products, the firmness and lack of fishy smell are the most important tests.

Caviar from still another member of the sturgeon group is rarely exported, that of the ship—actually a hybrid resulting from a cross between a sevruga and an osietr. An excellent caviar, incidentally—rather a small egg but firm and delicious. Quite scarce so usually used in the Caspian Sea area.

There are seven species of sturgeon (*which see*) in American waters, and while the commercial production of caviar is almost nonexistent due to the scarcity of large fish, anglers frequently capture the white, lake, and Atlantic sturgeons, all of which provide a quality homemade product. The flesh of these species is excellent, either fresh or smoked. The Canadian lake sturgeon in smoked form is considered the standard-bearer of the world. As with caviar, the method of preparation is of prime importance.

HOW TO SERVE CAVIAR

The best caviar is generally eaten as is, *au natural*, on a piece of thin, freshly made toast, with or without butter; though the caviar itself should be fat enough not to require butter. Caviar that is more heavily salted than the malosol grade can stand a few drops of lemon juice, or it may be sprinkled lightly with some finely chopped egg white, egg yolk, onions, or chives. Then there is the famous Russian manner (usually using pressed caviar) of serving this delicacy heaped high on blinis (small thin pancakes), sprinkled with onions and chopped eggs to taste and generously anointed with thick, very thick, sour cream. The crowning achievement in serving caviar is probably the one which originated with the Nobles' Club in Riga, an association peculiarly named Die Schwartzenhäupter. For this service the breast meat of cold roast pheasant is minced extremely fine but not ground. It must be knife-chopped. Each guest heaped as much caviar as he wanted on a piece of dry toast or very thin black bread and then sprinkled the minced pheasant meat over the caviar. The meat was not heaped on the caviar but only as much was kept on as would adhere to the surface.

Naturally many chefs have tried to incorporate caviar into various dishes, but once cooked or mixed with other ingredients, the true caviar flavor is lost, although a plain French dressing made with very little and very fine wine vinegar and the best of olive oil reaches new heights when a generous amount of caviar is stirred in it. This dressing, however, is to be used only with plain greens and not in the stronger-flavored, mixed-green salads.

HOW TO MAKE CAVIAR

Caviar can be made at home from the roe of any freshly caught sturgeon. It's important to remove the roe from the fish as soon as it is killed. The eggs should be washed on a fine screen (with a mesh size larger than the indi-

vidual eggs), permitting the eggs to fall into a tub or bowl, placed beneath the screen. This is done by *gently* stirring the roe to separate the eggs from the tissue and sac. They are then tenderly washed in coldwater (changing the water 3–4 times) and drained for not more than 10 minutes, removing any froth. After draining, the eggs should be salted, using five ounces of very fine-grained salt to each ten pounds of eggs (approximately 3 per cent). Immediately after this is done, the caviar should be placed in a slip-lid tin or a jar, with *no* air left in the container. The caviar must be held under refrigeration at a temperature of 26° F. to 30° F. It will reach its peak of delicacy in one week, and should be served before six months have elapsed, for after that it may lose its delicacy and eye appeal very rapidly.

Be sure all utensils and containers are spotlessly clean, preferably sterilized in boiling water. It is recommended that a gauze mask, similar to that used in hospitals be worn by the preparer to avoid contamination. —M.K.B.

CAYMAN ISLANDS These islands are located 480 miles south of Miami. Consisting of three islands—Grand Cayman, the largest; Cayman Brac, 86 miles to the east; and Little Cayman, 74 miles to the east-northeast—this Caribbean paradise rapidly developed as an angling resort. The islands are projecting peaks of the Cayman Ridge, a range of submarine mountains extending from the Maestra of Cuba and running west to the Misteriosa Bank toward British Honduras. Geologically, Grand Cayman is a flat-topped mountain of about 22 miles in length (east to west) and from 1–8 miles in width. Cayman Brac, which is 12 miles long and a mile wide, rises 140 feet above sea level at one point. Little Cayman is 10 miles long and 1 mile wide, but is surrounded by reefs and extensive flats. Known among amateur beachcombers as a place to vegetate among the sea grapes and cocoanut palms, the Caymans remain unspoiled. Nevertheless interisland transportation is a reality and the essential facilities for fishing, such as boats and accommodations, are now more readily available than before.

Fishing in the Caymans is typical of the Caribbean area, with an abundance of offshore, reef, and flats species with the emphasis on bonefish around Little Cayman and Cayman Brac, and the winter run of wahoo, which is spectacular at times. A half-mile offshore the water is 3,600 feet deep. Ten miles west of Grand Cayman are the Cayman Banks, a shoal area 15 miles long and about a half-mile wide. The depth varies from about 60–110 feet with sharp dropoffs where wahoo, blue marlin, and dolphin concentrate. Wahoo are ordinarily caught by anglers who are seeking other species, such as sailfish, marlin, or tuna. In Grand Cayman, where the wahoo school (December is the peak month), fantastic fishing is often had just off the beach from 16-foot outboards as well as from larger sportfishermen. —A.J.McC.

CENTERBOARD A wooden or metal board which can be lowered from its position in the slot of a fore-and-aft trunk to overcome the leeway of a boat sailing on the wind.

CEPHALAPOD A member of the class Cephalapoda, which includes the most highly evolved of the mollusks. Cephalapods have large well-developed heads with complex eyes similar to the vertebrate eye, and long muscular arms or tentacles usually bearing suckers. Nautiluses, cuttlefish, squids, and octopuses are all cephalapods.

Cero, 5-pound Male, Deep Water Cay, Bahamas

CERO *Scomberomorus regalis* Also called cero mackerel and pintada it is a fish of the mackerel family that differs from the king mackerel and Spanish mackerel in having a pattern of both spots and stripes on the sides of the body. The first dorsal fin is black anteriorly, and there are 17–18 spines in the first dorsal fin as in the Spanish mackerel. The pectoral fin is covered with scales as in the king mackerel. There are 15–18 gillrakers on the first branchial arch. Cero may reach a weight of as much as 35 pounds, but the average is 5–10 pounds.

Cero are found from Cape Cod to Brazil and are abundant around southern Florida and the West Indies.
—B.B.C.
—R.H.G.

CEYLON In the Indian Ocean, separated from the southeastern tip of India by the 20-mile-wide Palk Strait, Ceylon was occupied by the Portuguese and Dutch for almost three centuries and ruled by the British until 1948. This independent Asian nation has many tourist attractions derived from its polyglot culture. It is 270 miles long and 140 miles wide, and encompasses a variety of landscapes. It also has extreme climatic differences. Around the palm-fringed coast and in the wide alluvial plains of the south and west it is hot and humid with temperatures in the 90's; in the jungle plains of the southeast and the central-north (the unique Tank Country) it is hot and generally dry. In the mountains at the island's center, where elevations reach a peak of 8,298 feet, temperatures vary from cool (average 55° F) to cold, and the weather from wet to dry. Rivers cascade down the wooded hills creating a number of waterfalls including Diyaluma Falls, the sixth highest in the world. Distinct from the southern portion of the island is the hot and dry northern peninsula, which ranges from sandy desert to thick forest in a few watered areas. Rainfall throughout Ceylon is equally extreme, with 25–250 inches annually according to altitude.

OFFSHORE FISHING

There are several types of fishing available in Ceylon. Foremost of these is big-game fishing, which as a sport is not yet fully developed. There is a good run of sailfish off the west coast near Colombo from August through October. Blue marlin and yellowfin tuna also occur during this period. Striped marlin and some blacks appear from October to March, with the peak beginning in January on the north, south, and west coasts. On the east coast off Trincomalee and Batticaloa the peak fishing period is from February through May. Wahoo, dolphin, barracuda, jacks, and smaller oceanic species are in evidence most of the year. Charter craft and on-location accommodations can be obtained through the Ceylon Sea Angler's Club at Clappenburg, Trincomalee.

SURF FISHING

Surf fishing offers unusual possibilities. The lagoons along the southeast coast open up during the flood season (from November to January) which triggers mullet runs into the sea; these baitfish are attacked by many species of gamefish including huge jacks (*Caranax ignobolis*) up to 100 pounds in weight. This type of fishing is most productive at Arugam Bay, Panama, Pottuvil, Yala, Kirinda, and Bundala. Two species of Pacific permit (*Trachinotus blochii* and *T. mookalee*), which also attain large size, are common along the coastal beaches. In addition there are two unusual species of spotted pompano (*Trachinotus russellii* and *T. bailloni*). For information and rental of small craft for surf and inshore fishing, contact the Ceylon Angler's Club at Galle Buck, Fort Colombo.

FRESHWATER FISHING

Freshwater fishing consists principally of rainbow trout in the higher altitude streams between Nuwara Elyia and Adam's Peak. The streams are stocked by the Ceylon Fishing Club at Nuwara Elyia and their quality is modest; the average catch is less than a pound and 5-pound fish are exceptional. At lower elevations the rivers contain small mahseer (*Barbus tor*), which average about 5 pounds but occasionally range up to 20 pounds in weight.
—A.J.McC.

CHAFING GEAR A guard of canvas, line, or plastic tubing around spars, chocks, rigging, or fishing nets to prevent chafing.

CHAIN PICKEREL *Esox niger* A popular gamefish in the Eastern and Southern portions of the United States. The chain pickerel is elongate and bears black chainlike, vermiculated markings on the sides. The body color varies from green to bronze. It can be distinguished from its nearest relatives, the grass pickerel and the redfin pickerel (*which see*), by the number of branchiostegals, which in the chain pickerel are 14–16. The chain pickerel also has a slimmer snout, with the length of the snout being longer than the distance between the back edge of the eye and the edge of the opercle.

The natural distribution of chain pickerel is in regions where the larger pikes are either rare or absent. This range extends from Maine to east Texas and north to the Great Lakes. The center of abundance is east of the Alleghenies in New Jersey, southern New York, Connecticut, Rhode Island, Massachusetts, and southern Maine. These Atlantic states produce some big pickerel, particularly in coastal ponds and brackish creeks. Although not too common in most of the South, chain pickerel grow to large sizes in Georgia and Florida. They are easy to catch and grow to sporty lengths rather quickly. The chain pickerel will reach 14 inches in 3 years; it takes about 6 years to attain a stout 20 inches, and if it survives to the probable maximum of 10 years, it should be 36 inches long and weigh approximately 9 pounds.

ANGLING VALUE

Chain pickerel provide a year-round fishery. They are taken by ice fishermen on minnow baits, and in productive lakes the shanty set finds plenty of action. Old chainsides doesn't lose his appetite when the snow flies. But even if the lakes don't freeze, or until the time they do, you can enjoy wonderful fishing on those cold, gray days of early winter. They can be caught in ice-bordered ponds and creeks, using streamer flies and spinners.

Chain Pickerel

Chain pickerel eat other fish. They also eat crayfish, insects, frogs, mice, newts, and just about every living creature which invades their sanctuary, including other pickerel. There's hardly a surface within its mouth which isn't armed with recurved, needlelike teeth. One would imagine that the pickerel never ceases eating, but chainsides has periods of hunger and fasting as many a disappointed angler has discovered. At times it will rest quietly in the weeds while schools of minnows swim by its nose with immunity. The pickerel can totally abstain from feeding after an orgy which found him swallowing a spoon while the nether part of a shiner will still be protruding from his mouth. After an inactive period he may choke to death while trying to ingest a fish as big as himself. The wacky king of the Weed Empire is, to say the least, unpredictable. You can work a pond to a lather one day and catch so few fish that you'd swear they had vanished. The next day they'll chew the paint off every wobbler in the box. But the angler who catches pickerel consistently is a specialist who varies his methods according to the conditions and the mood of the fish.

Comparatively few anglers fish solely for pickerel. The major harvest is made by bass and walleye fishermen who are casting spoons and plugs which happen to appeal to chainsides also. To get the most out of this scrappy gamefish, however, it's worth the effort to use suitable tackle and baits. The theme is refinement. Even if you lose a few fish with light gear, you still have a

numerical advantage in their abundance. The pickerel's lackluster reputation originates with the use of rug-beater rods and multi-gang hook plugs which are heavy enough to dismantle a tarpon. The proper bait-casting tackle for pickerel is the 5½–6-foot rods designed for ¼–⅜-ounce lures, mounted with small, fast reels and light lines. Skish or tournament-accuracy tools are perfect. The same thing applies to spin-bait-casting or enclosed-spool reels which differ in their mechanics but are equally capable of delivering midget baits. From a sporting standpoint, the size of your lure is important. Big baits are out. Chainsides has the unfortunate habit of swallowing a lure right up to the swivel. This results in an understandably listless struggle when six or nine barbs lock its jaws shut. By comparison, when taken on a single-hook fly-rod lure or small spinning bait, the pickerel becomes a formidable foe.

Hairline tackle, which means any of the 4–5½-foot ultralight spinning rods and a small reel spooled with 3-pound-test line, is ideal for pickerel fishing. The 3-pound-test line permits long casts with tiny lures and makes the capture of even a modest pickerel a sporting proposition. When hooking a strong pickerel with hairline equipment, the tricky part of the play after leading it away from the weeds and snags occurs when you are ready to net it. Chainsides puts up a terrific fuss at the sight of the meshes or your hand. When you think the fish is played out, it will invariably thresh the water to a boil as you draw it close. With a light line you must play pickerel to a standstill; otherwise you will lose one after another. At all times keep a reasonable length of line between yourself and the fish. Pump it very gently until its energies are sapped. Naturally, you will have your antireverse in the "on" position, and the dragbrake set low as the elasticity of hairline is almost nothing when a fish has been led within reach. Otherwise, ultralight gear is easy to use even in places where the fish are hefty.

Another good method of fishing is with the fly rod. Almost any minnowlike pattern will attract pickerel. The standards are a red-and-white bucktail with silver body, Mickey Finn, Yellow Marabou, and White Marabou. Use No. 4 dressings, but it pays to try larger and smaller sizes as well. Streamers can also be combined with a 2/0, 3/0, or 4/0 spinner for added flash. The hair nature lures, such as bucktail frogs and mice, are real killers early and late in the day. Some mouse and frog imitations have sufficient weight to be used interchangeably with the fly rod and hairline spinning outfit.

The pickerel's habitat overlaps that of the largemouth bass. Ordinarily you will find it around lily pads, in beds of muskgrass, pondweed, or parrot feather. Weeds are important to its method of feeding. Unlike the bass, it doesn't often roam about unless food is scarce; the pickerel invariably waits for its meal to swim by, rather than going out to look for it. So it's important to cover plenty of water in searching for a lunker. You might also remember that if you miss a good fish the chances are excellent that it will be hiding in the same spot tomorrow, next week, or possibly a month from now. Where the marginal areas of a pond are free of heavy vegetation, the pickerel will face shoreward from the nearest weed bed. If the shallows are choked with grass, it will assume the opposite position, facing deepwater. Nature designed chainsides for inshore foraging, and even a lunker will wait motionless in a foot or two of water for some opportune target. As a general rule, the best fishing area extends from the shore to a depth of about seven feet. During the summer months, or periods of drought when the shore areas of a lake shrink from the bank covers, pickerel may move out to depths of 12–15 feet where forage is more abundant. Under normal conditions, however, pickerel stay as close to the banks as possible. Two other productive locations are the shallow "necks" between ponds and backwater sloughs. In rivers pickerel inhabit all grassy slow water sections and display the same tendency to hole up in a suitable weed bed or brush pile. Again, pay particular attention to backwaters leading off the main stream. More lunkers are caught in these quiet, out-of-the-way places than in the obvious river covers.

There are two points about pickerel technique worth stressing. You can generally get more strikes by casting parallel to the weed or lily beds. The fish hide just inside the grass where they can keep an eye on open water. With the lure passing the length of the bed, more than one pickerel will be tempted to strike. Also, large fish are not as likely to follow a bait drawn away from their weed sanctuary across open water. When fishing from a boat, work close to the bank casting parallel to it, rather than standing offshore and casting into the bank. Much depends of course on the contour of the weed bed. The other thing to remember is that contrary to standard bass technique, which consists of slow- to medium-speed retrieves, pickerel are more susceptible to a moderately fast retrieve. This is especially noticeable if you get many follow-ups or close strikes right under your rod tip. As a rule, most casters quickly crank out the last few yards of a retrieve. A pickerel which has been following the lure is often excited by its accelerated motion and hits just as the angler lifts it from the water. If you see fish stalking the lure without striking, increase your reeling speed. With the standard wobbling spoon, the correct pace may be described as a fast flutter.

Surface lures on the other hand are often taken when they are perfectly motionless. This is probably because floating baits seem to work best on days when there's little activity; a hair frog popped within easy reach isn't likely to be spurned even if chainsides has a full stomach. But topwater baits are not always effective when fished slowly. Much depends on what the lure looks like; an orthodox popping plug might be completely ignored because it doesn't suggest anything the duckbilled gourmand understands. The success of spoon skittering, for example, is largely due to the speed and disturbance created by a lure which is drawn rapidly across the surface. Move it slowly and you get nothing but follow-ups. As executed with the old cane pole a big spinner or pork chunk is skimmed over the pad beds in a rhythmic swinging motion similar to cutting hay with a scythe. Retrieving speed is the key to taking lunkers and that applies to all methods of casting.   —A.J.McC.

CHANNEL BASS *See* Red Drum

CHANNEL CATFISH *Ictalurus punctatus*   The only spotted catfish with a deeply forked tail. Like all members of the North American catfish family, the channel catfish possesses long barbels about the mouth, 4 under the jaw, 2 above, and one on the tip of each maxillary. The anal fin contains 24–30 rays. It is most easily separated from the blue catfish and white catfish by the number of anal rays and the presence of black spots.

This catfish varies in color from bluish or olivaceous silvery above and silver-white below in young individuals to dark steel-blue above and whitish below in older specimens. The black spots are small and irregular, and may be few or many in different individuals.

The range of the channel catfish extends from the Great Lakes and Saskatchewan River southward to the Gulf of Mexico and into Mexico. It has been introduced with varied success both east and west of its natural range.

LIFE HISTORY

The channel catfish inhabits lakes and larger rivers which have clean bottoms of sand, gravel, or boulders. It is not often found in association with dense weed beds. The adults are highly migratory, ascending small streams to spawn. Yearlings and subadults apparently are more tolerant to fast currents than adults. This catfish feeds, as others of its family, on nearly all aquatic forms including fish, insects, and crustacea. They feed chiefly at night, sometimes in rather swiftly flowing water.

Channel-catfish males attain a darker blue-black coloration during the spawning season. The eggs are deposited in a nest below undercut stream banks or under logs or stones. The nest is guarded by the male for some time after the fry have hatched.

Channel Catfish, 57-pounds,
Lake Moultrie, South Carolina

Among the larger species of the catfish family, the channel catfish is most commonly taken at 11–30 inches in length and up to 15 pounds in weight. Commercial fishermen have reported their maximum weights to be about 60 pounds.

Channel Catfish, 2 pounds,
Lake Okeechobee, Florida

ANGLING VALUE

The channel catfish is considered by some to be superior to other members of its family because of its excellent food and sport-fishing value. Reared commercially, this catfish is transported to all parts of the country. Channel catfish are taken readily on set lines and also by floating bait (strips of fish flesh cut from the belly of another fish) downstream in fastwater. Favored angling spots are below power dams where currents are rapid.

—R.A.J.

CHANNEL CATFISH VIRUS DISEASE *See* Diseases and Parasites

CHARLEY NOBLE The galley smokestack.

CHARS *Salvelinus* **spp.** A holarctic genus of salmonids which fall into three distinct groups—*S. namaycush*, *S. fontinalis* and *S. alpinus*. Nearly all taxonomists consider each of the first two groups as single species (the lake trout and brook trout). The *S. alpinus* group, however, is circumpolar in distribution and contains a yet undetermined number of species. This group is represented by the Arctic char (*which see*). The Dolly Varden is closely related to the *S. alpinus* group, and some taxonomists consider it a subspecific member *S. alpinus malma*. Others consider the Dolly Varden (*which see*) a distinct species, *S. malma*. Chars are distinguished from trout by their mouth structure; the vomerine bone in the center of a trout's mouth has teeth all along it, while the vomer of the char has only a few teeth on the front end of the bone.

CHARTER BOAT A boat available for rent on an exclusive basis for the use of an individual or a group of anglers. Charter boats are engaged complete with crew by the day, week, or month. The licensed operator in charge is the *charter boatman* or *charter captain*, who, for purposes of big-game angling, will have a mate aboard, sometimes known as the *striker*. Charter boats are generally twin-engine craft, 36–45 feet in length, and are equipped to fish four anglers simultaneously at the flatlines and outriggers; however, two anglers are preferred. The charter boatman supplies the necessary tackle and bait. *See also* Sportfisherman

CHEST SQUEEZE *See* Skin and Scuba Diving Dangers *under* First Aid

CHICKEN HADDIE A canned fishery product common to the east coast of Canada. It consists of hake, cod, haddock and cusk which are combined in a brine solution to firm and salt the fish. The brined fish are then steamed, and the meat is separated from the bones and drained on a perforated tray. The flakes of fish are again steamed in parchment-lined cans. The result is a composite of all members of the cod family.

CHILE Famed for both its freshwater and saltwater fishing, Chile encompasses a wide range of climates from its arid north to its subarctic south. Here, as in Argentina (*which see*), trout are not endemic to the lakes and rivers but were first introduced from Germany in 1905. Habitat and food conditions were so ideal that the fish quickly became established in all the major watersheds south of Santiago. This system of rivers for a distance of over one thousand miles can be divided into three sections.

The first section extends from Santiago to Temuco. From the tourists' point of view the waters are little-known with the exception of Laguna de Maule, the Laja River, and the Bío Bío Alto which are internationally famous for their large trout.

The second section between Temuco and Puerto Montt is called the Chilean Lake District, and includes all the better-known places like Villarrica, Pucón, Chan-Chan, Llifén, Riñinahue, Puerto Nuevo, Puyehue, and Petrohué. The rivers here are big and inaccessible, and are therefore fished from a boat.

The third section, the vast river and lake system between Puerto Montt and Punta Arenas (which is the southernmost city in the world), is primitive and little explored except for the Puelo, Manso, and Palena rivers which are very big and hold plenty of large rainbows and browns. These rivers rise in Argentina and empty into the Pacific. Further to the south is the province of Aysen with its Aysen and Simpson rivers. The Simpson has fine brown-trout fishing, and the principal road from Puerto Aysen to Coihaique runs near the river. Boats are used on its lower reaches after the Manihuales River joins the Simpson and forms the huge Aysen River. Near Punta Arenas the most notable river is the Serrano which produces trout of 4–5 pounds. Toward the Antarctic is Tierra del Fuego, which is perhaps most famous for its large sea trout. Unfortunately the climate is very severe in the "Land of Fire," and most of the time a gale is blowing which makes fly-fishing difficult. Off the continent, a short distance south of Puerto Montt, is the island of Chiloe. Chiloe has some lakes and rivers, and all hold trout, mostly browns. Its important streams are the Puntra and Putalcura. The color of their waters is like strong tea, created by decaying vegetation. After they join, the river is called Chepu, and empties into the Pacific. There is an airfield for small planes located here, and the river offers interesting fishing.

When trout were first introduced from Germany to the rivers south of Santiago, the food conditions were ideal and the fish became rapidly established. In common with Argentina, Chilean rivers contain a freshwater crab (locally *pancora*), which is the staple food of the trout. Besides the *pancora* there are native forage fish like the *peladilla* (now practically extinct), *pejerey*, *cauques*, and a small minnow called the *puye*, which, incidentally, is delicious when eaten in the form of an omelette. So food is plentiful in lakes and rivers. Although there has been a

The sight of rising trout on Chilean rivers is counterpointed with rugged mountain scenery. This is the Toltén River

noticeable decline in angling in some watersheds due to natural catastrophes such as volcanic eruption and earthquakes, mismanagement of forest lands, and inadequate law enforcement, Chilean waters continue to produce some very large trout each season. Trout of over 20 pounds have been recorded, and fish of 8–15 pounds are taken in considerable number each season. A trout of 2–3 pounds is common in Chile. Nevertheless, including all the small fish caught, the angler's average is often lower. Much depends on where the fishing is done and at what time of the season. The rainbow and brown trout are the two principal species. There are some brook trout in the Laguna de Inca at Portillo, a famous ski resort 6,000 feet up in the Andes mountains. A predominant brook-trout fishery exists only in the Negro River, at Peulla, an overnight stop en route from Puerto Varas to Bariloche, Argentina. This river was privately stocked in 1932. Some brooks have crossed Todos los Santos Lake, and are caught in the Petrohue River. Brooks are also found in the Manso and Puelo rivers, which flow from Argentina where the species is widespread.

All trout waters in the lake district, which attracts most foreign anglers, are boat streams. A great deal of time must be spent running rapids and floating from pool to pool. As a rule the *botero* (boatman) will cover about ten miles in a day as access roads are widely separated. The boats are comfortable, and the fisherman is seated and facing downstream. He can troll or cast, or, when the river is low in summer, he can wade. Actually, the *botero*, seated behind the fisherman and skillfully holding his craft in the current, does the fishing. He guides the lure or fly over the best places at the correct speed. Float-fishing is a delightful form of angling if you want to see a lot of country and enjoy a wonderful *asado* with delicious Chilean wines. This cookout alone is worth the journey. But the greater part of the boat streams is heavily fished, and the quality of the sport is not comparable to wilderness waters. Experts may prefer the wading rivers like the Laja, Bío Bío Alto, or the Petrohue. These flow too fast and broken for float trips, but they can be negotiated with felts or chains.

TEMUCO, VILLARRICA, PUCÓN

Temuco is the gateway to the lake district and lies about 400 miles south of Santiago. Here is the great Cautin River flowing right through the town. Some fifteen miles north is the main hatchery at the town of Lautaro, which is a good place to start a float trip down the Cautin. Or you can start at the village of Pillanlelbun. The float can be extended below Temuco to the town of Nueva Imperial where the Quepe joins the Cautin. The Quepe was once a fine river with good-size trout, but intensive fishing ruined it, and the yield now is mostly small fish. The lower part of the Toltén river, from Pitrufquen flowing toward the Pacific, is fished from Temuco. Here the Toltén is a very big river, but it divides in many arms and is ideal for fly-fishing. A good two-day float trip can be made as far as Cumuy, leaving the boats at Los Galpones returning for the night to Temuco and proceeding next day to Cumuy. Trout of 3–7 pounds can be expected. This trip has one disadvantage. At times the river is not clear from volcanic ash which comes from a feeder stream on the Llaima Volcano. The best time is before January 15 and again at the end of March. Temuco is also the starting point to fish Lake Gualletue and Lake Icalma, near the Argentine border. By road it's about an 80-mile trip. There is an airstrip near Icalma, at 3,500 feet. Most lakes in the district are between 700–1,000 feet. Out of Gualletue flows the Bío Bío River, and for miles and miles there is fine trout fishing amid beautiful scenery. In the central valley, a long distance away, the Bío Bío is most likely the largest river in Chile. A lake worthy of mention is Concillo, behind the Llaima Volcano. Not too long ago the lake was full of 3–8-pound trout, but the fishing today is moderate.

The most concentrated fishing is about five hundred miles south of Santiago, at Villarrica, a small town at the west end of Lake Villarrica or Pucón which lies at the east end. The Toltén River, which empties from the lake, is the most beautiful of all the float streams, winding at the beginning between high banks heavily overgrown with thick vegetation and wild flowers. The water is crystal clear, flows rapidly between large pools and many rapids. The Toltén is fished as far as Allipen, where the river of same name enters the Toltén. Access roads between are at Prado Verde, Catrico, and Coipue, leaving boats there and returning next morning to proceed. The float from Coipue to Allipen is quite different as the river divides in many smaller arms, forming islands. In the last mile or so, the river again flows in one bed, and large fish are caught here. The Toltén holds rainbows and brown trout. Heavy fishing, especially during the summer months, made it less productive as in former years, and many small fish of a pound or so are among a daily catch of larger-size trout. The best is at the beginning of the season and again at the end.

Pucón is the best-known trout center in Chile, and its fame dates many years back when fish were plentiful and of large size. But the eruption of Villarrica Volcano in 1948 and again in 1964 has done some damage to the fishing. In spite of this it is amazing to see how productive the lake is—a natural hatchery, the water temperature just right and plenty of food. Consequently the Trancura River entering the lake produces exceptionally well at times. To float the Liucura river is the most intriguing fishing trip in Chile. At the starting point, the bridge, the river is small for several miles and then gets bigger after the Carvello joins the Liucura. The river has a regular speed as far as below Mata Quila. From then on it is all shooting rapids between great pools. Just below the point where the Liucura enters the Trancura is famous Martinez Pool which usually holds good-size trout. There are still a few more rapids not without danger, but the *boteros* are real experts. The Liucura is always clear whereas the Trancura runs very muddy after the end of January due to volcanic ash brought down by the Turbio River. In such cases the Trancura can be fished further up, from Curarrehue downstream. Lots of small trout, all rainbows, but plenty of action all day which makes fun-fishing.

The next lake south is Calafquen, and in years past it was *the* place in Chile. Trophy fish of 20 and more pounds were caught in the Huanehue River, the outlet of Calafquen, and in Lake Pullingue. Farmers came on horseback to Villarrica with trout hanging on their saddles, the tails dragging in the dusty road. This is gone. A hydraulic plant was built at Pullingue which contributed to its decline. There are still trout in the lake, and at Conaripe, at the mouth of the river of same name, good fishing can be had. This small village was partly destroyed by the eruption of Villarrica Volcano in 1964.

CHAN-CHAN, LAGO RANCO, PUYEHUE, PETROHUÉ

Chan-Chan at the west end of Lake Panguipulli is where the Enco leaves the lake to join Lake Riñihue. It is a short link of only about 4–5 miles, and mile for mile it was the best fishing water in all Chile before the earthquake in 1961. The stream gradient was over ninety feet, but after the quake it literally disappeared. Nearby at Kankahuasi is the club house of the Rainbow Fly Fishing Club of Chile formed by a group of American sportsmen. The large house was built by a Mr. Gundelach, an ardent angler who spent his last years on the river. In the good old days there wasn't an angler coming to Chile who didn't pay a visit to Kankahuasi. The Enco is still a fine river, and it may come back again as it is the main link of an enormous lake system. The Fui River is another water to fish at the Rainbow Club. It is a lovely, fast, and broken river coming out of Pireihueico Lake and entering Panguipulli Lake a few miles away from the club house. The river is floated in part, but some stretches can be waded. The largest fish, of 4–8 pounds, are caught mostly at the *barra* or in the pools directly above it. The river flowing out of Riñihue Lake is the San Pedro, one of the great rivers in Chile. This river suffered most in the 1961 earthquake. However, it recovered rather quickly as a fish of 27 pounds was taken several years later. A very fine piece of water is the stretch from the Malihue bridge down to the small town of Los Lagos and should produce good-size rainbows and browns.

Continuing south comes Lake Ranco, the second largest lake in Chile. At the east end is Llifén, at the west end Puerto Nuevo, and to the south Riñinahue. All three have a good reputation in Chilean fishing. The principal river at Llifén is the Calcurrupe, coming out of Lake Maihue, about fifteen miles to the east. The float trip is usually made in two days. Start at Maihue, leave the boats at *medio río*, and return next morning to continue down to the lake. Down to *medio río* the water is perfect, and most trophy fish are caught in this part of the river. There is an award for the largest trout caught each season, and generally it is a brown trout of about 16 pounds or so with several more runner-ups. It is worth while to be on the water at daybreak near the *barra* as this hour is most productive. North of Llifén a small river enters the lake, called the Cauenahue. The *barra* still yields good-size trout, but unfortunately the former lava pools about a mile above have filled with sand and gravel and hold only small trout. The Cauenahue can be waded about ten miles or more following a road to a sawmill. It's ideal water for the angler who is content to work a dry fly over 1–3-pound fish. There are several smaller rivers emptying Maihue Lake, and one worth visiting is the Blanco River. It can be reached by road or with an outboard from the outlet of the lake. Where the Blanco River enters the lake many trout of 4–8 pounds or more are caught. There is good wading water above this point.

The Riñinahue River has been in the past twenty years the most astonishing river for its continuous and constant fishing of large-size trout. There was nothing comparable in Chile or Argentina. The river is rather a small one, and its water extremely cold. This is noticeable in summer when the temperature of the lake is considerably higher. Most large fish are caught at the mouth or immediately above it. Fishable water extends only for about a mile to where a high waterfall forms a barrier to upstream migration. The Riñinahue has been under heavy pressure in recent years, but the fishing is as good as before. The average trout is 4–5 pounds. From the Trahuilcho Farm one can fish a beautiful mountain lake called Encanto or Pichi (*pichi* in Indian language is small). This lake is full of rainbow trout of 2–3 pounds. A daily catch of 20–30 trout is ordinary. This is a horseback trip of under two hours. The fishing is done from boats. At the west end of Lake Ranco the great Bueno River leaves the lake. The Bueno plunges out of the lake with a roar into white water through a canyon for a half a mile. This is perhaps the most beautiful outlet in Chile. The view looking over the lake toward the Cordillera and the many islands is very scenic. Most of the fishing is done at this outlet, and trout of over 20 pounds have been caught here. A boat is necessary, but there is on both sides a short stretch of water for wading. The best fishing occurs very early and again in the evening with preference to the morning. A recommended excursion is from Puerto Nuevo to Huapi Island inhabited by Indians. A steamer can be chartered which brings the anglers and their boats to the island. The fishing is done by trolling around the island which produces very good results; trout of 4–10 pounds are not unusual. It is also productive to cast with spinning equipment toward shore from the boat. A half-day float trip can be arranged from Puerto Nuevo to Puerto Lapiz.

Due to the steep banks and swift currents of many Chilean rivers, float-fishing is the only practical method of angling

From here the Bueno River can be floated in two days to the town of Río Bueno, and boatmen can be hired there at the Hotel Plaza. This float trip is delightful; the river is fast and has two difficult rapids which the *boteros* go through alone. The river is flanked by high banks of the type of the Toltén but still more spectacular. This water is lightly fished by local anglers, and therefore it produces more trout and of larger size. Rainbows and brown trout of 4–8 pounds are common. It is advisable to leave the boats first day at the Ramirez Farm and stay overnight at Río Bueno if not camping. Fine float trips are on Pilmaiquen River which is a short distance from Río Bueno. The Pilmaiquen comes out of Lake Puyehue. One day float is from the Lumaco Farm to the bridge of Trafun, where the Chirre joins the Pilmaiquen. The Pilmaiquen is a much smaller river than the Bueno River, and it produces good fishing for 1–5-pound trout.

At the town of Osorno is another large river, the Rahue. The boats are owned by local fishermen, and it's advisable to make reservations through the Gran Hotel Osorno. There are several floats to be made on the Rahue, but the best is from the outlet at Lago Rupanco down to the village of Cancura. The Rupanco is a big, long lake and well-known for large trout. There are two small rivers entering the lake, the Pulelfú coming from north, and the Caviota, larger, at the very end of the lake.

The village of Puyehue is a hot spring settled over a hundred years ago by Indians. The principal river nearby is the Golgol. It can be floated starting at the sawmill and down to the lake. The largest fish are generally caught at the inlet. During the earthquake of 1961 the otherwise dead Puyehue Volcano came to life for about twenty-four hours and did considerable damage, especially to the river bed of the Golgol. The inlet is not as good as it was before. A few large trout are still caught there. From here, on the road to Antillanca, a ski resort, are several lovely mountain lakes to fish such as the Espejo, Encanto, Torito, and Toro. Toro Lake is the best, and rainbows of 2–6 pounds are common. Virgin forests surround all these small lakes, and the fishing must be done from a boat.

Petrohué is best known as an access point for tourists crossing the lakes from Chile through the lakes to Bariloche, Argentina. The Petrohué River flows out of Todos los Santos Lake. It is a large river, and it runs very calmly for about ½ mile to where a cable crosses the river to measure the outflow of water. Below the cable the river gains momentum and behaves like a wild horse—a turbulent river with occasional pools at intervals. The largest trout are caught just above and below the cable, and a fish of 15 pounds is not at all rare—mostly rainbows and browns and an occasional brook trout. Downstream the trout are much smaller (1–5 pounds) but nevertheless hard-fighting fish. An interesting place to visit is at the big waterfalls several miles below the lake. At the sightseeing bridge, leading to the falls, a small arm of the Petrohué is formed which is fed by a big, cold spring. This section looks like an English chalk stream and at times, generally early season, offers fine fishing. Where the arm again enters the main river, the pool is called Ultima Esperanza (Last Hope), and it is seldom disappointing. All this fishing below the cable is by wading, above it from a boat. A boat is used again further down where the river calms down, at the ferry, and from there to Ralún. Some large fish are caught in this part of the river as this stretch is not often fished.

Puerto Montt is an important seaport and at the same time the end station of the Chilean Railroad and of the road system. The vast continent to the south can only be reached by sea or by air. For the fisherman is a good river near town, the Chamiza. For best results the tide has to be taken in consideration. The river comes out of Chapo Lake, and from there down to the sea there are many fine places to fish. There are no organized facilities, and it is advisable to get in touch with the Club de Pesca through the various hotels. Puerto Montt is also the starting point to fish one of the very best trout rivers in Chile, the Puelo. There is a steamer service several times a week to the village of Puelo where the river empties into the Estuario de Reloncaví, a long, narrow branch of the sea. Rainbow, brown, and brook trout can be caught in the brackish water. The Puelo comes a long way from Argentina and enters Tagua Tagua Lake about 7–8 miles above the village. The outlet is called El Baraco where record fish are caught. On the way down are great fishing pools like El Salto, Quita Calzones, Pangal, Urupa, La Carrera Vacilio, and others. Fish of 4–8 pounds can be expected. Probably the best place to fish the Puelo is at the Argentine border. The Chilean air force maintains an airfield at Segundo Corral in the Distrito Llano Grande. A small plane can be chartered at Puerto Montt to reach the river.
—A.H.

SALTWATER FISHING

Chilean saltwater fishing is exceptionally productive because of the upwelling of nutrient-rich waters as the Peru current flows northward along Chile (*see* Currents). The multitudes of plankton offer a rich food supply for bait species such as anchovies, sardines, sauries, and squid, which abound off the coast and which in turn attract and hold the large game fishes along Chile's 2,600-mile coastline.

Tops in Chile's saltwater gamesters is the swordfish, known locally as *albacora* or *pez espada*, and a record 1,182-pound fish has been taken at Iquique, the prime angling port. The usual catch is from 300 to 900 pounds, but commercial fishermen have harpooned broadbill swordfish in these waters weighing over 1,500 pounds, and reliable persons have sighted fish that would probably exceed 2,000 pounds. Swordfish prefer warmer waters, and are thus concentrated in the northern waters of Chile, although they occur at least as far south as Valdivia. The chief commercial fishing ports are Iquique, Tocopilla, Coquimbo, and Antofagasta, so good sport fishing should be expected there. The best months are March, April, and May. Swordfish are not fished blind, but are spotted from the crow's nest and then the bait (usually a bonito or small tuna) is presented.

Striped marlin (*marlin*) run large off Chile, with 300-pound fish fairly common and specimens of over 400 pounds being caught each season. The fishing is from January through October with a peak in March and April.

Black marlin (*pezzuncho*) are occasionally taken in the north parts from Arica to Mejillones, but only when a thin surface layer of warmer water from the north flows southward, as occasionally happens in April. Similarly, occasional sailfish (*pezvela*) are taken in the north.

Among the tunas, the bigeye tuna (*atún*) is perhaps the largest of the Chilean tuna, but is not always distinguished from the yellowfin tuna (*atún de aleta amarilla*).

The bigeye approaches 400 pounds, but fish of 100–150 are the rule. They are usually caught in the deeper strata by commercial drift or longliners, or by anglers deep-trolling. The bigeye apparently occurs at least as far south as Valparaiso, running northward and becoming rather common off Peru. It apparently swims in the deeper strata toward the north and shallow levels in the south, following its food and preferred temperature.

Yellowfin tuna are occasionally taken in large numbers by commercial fleets, but these prefer slightly warmer water than the bigeye and are more readily taken at the surface under the right conditions. They reach at least 150 pounds, and although they are reported to reach 330 pounds, it is likely that these big ones are really bigeye tuna. Although it is taken occasionally off Valparaiso, the yellowfin's center of abundance is from Antofagasta to Arica. The main commercial fishing center is from Iquique to Arica, so sport fishing should be similarly productive. Like the swordfish and marlin, this and the other tunas eat anchovies, sardines, sauries, and squids. It also feeds on shrimps and lobsters (langostinos), the latter are especially popular commercial food items.

Albacore (atún de aleta larga) are taken in good quantity by commercial fishermen, chiefly from the central coast (approximately Valdivia to Antofagasta). Like the bigeye tuna, they prefer cooler waters, and are usually taken in the deeper levels on longline gear, although they may be taken by anglers deep-fishing. Otherwise its habits are generally similar to the yellowfin and bigeye tunas. The excellent quality of this white-meat tuna affords it a high price in local markets.

The skipjack tuna (barrilete or cachurreta) can be extremely common in the warmer waters of northern Chile. It grows to about 10 pounds, and feeds avidly on anchovies, sardines, and small squids. It is taken commercially in purse seines for canning, although its meat is darker and its flavor stronger than other tunas. Easily taken in small jigs, it is a popular bait of local anglers for swordfish and large marlin. It is usually drifted just under the surface, and hooked in a "New Zealand" rig.

The bonito (bonito) is similar to the Atlantic bonito (which see). It is extremely common along the coast and is one of the mainstays of the commercial purse-seine industry between Antofagasta and Arica, where it is canned and sold fresh. It occurs in huge schools in these areas from October to May and is known southward to Taltal, about 200 miles south of Antofagasta. Like the barrilete, it is an important trolled bait for swordfish and marlin.

Dolphin (Coryphaena hippurus) are taken occasionally in the northern part of Chile, as far south as Antofagasta. Blue sharks, bonito sharks, and soupfin sharks are occasionally taken by anglers along the coast, but only the bonito shark puts up a good fight. One of the amberjacks, Seriola mazatlana, known locally as vidriola, is taken from Arica to Taltal and around the islands of Juan Fernández, San Abrosio, and San Féliz, and in other relatively warm waters. It is not known definitely which species this is, or if there is more than one species involved (e.g., mazatlana, lalandi, peruana).

Along shore and about the offshore islands, several species of groupers (locally apañado, cabrilla común, and bacalao de Juan Fernández) can be taken about rocky areas by bottom fishing. The latter species exceeds 200 pounds, and the flesh of all is excellent. Several species of grunts and croakers (families Pomadasyidae and Sciaenidae) are taken from sandy beaches and quiet bays. Locally known as ayanques, cabinzas, corvinillas, and corvinas, their flesh is excellent. Small lures or live baits are productive for bottom fishing. Unfortunately, the cabinza, because it is a scavenger in heavily populated areas, is regarded with suspicion as a food.

Several species of cusk eels (family Ophidiidae), locally called congrios, occur in Chile, all of which have excellent flesh and are prized locally. The most highly prized table fish in Chile is the congrio colorado (Genypterus chilensis), which grows to nearly 5 feet. It occurs from Cape Horn to Arica and into Peru. Its wide range and abundance makes it the target of an intense commercial hook-and-line fishery. Found around rocky areas, it hides among the rocks feeding on lobsters and other crustaceans. It is not a particularly hard fighter but clings to its burrow when hooked.

Several species of rockfish (which see) are of considerable importance because of their flesh. Known as pejediablos, they occur around rocky areas along the bottom and can be taken on small pieces of cut or live bait.

One of the most important species, both commercial and sport, is the lenguado. This flounder, Paralichthys microps, grows to about 1½ feet long, although specimens of over 3 feet have been taken. Like that of other flatfishes, the flesh is delicious and highly esteemed locally. They occur from Iquique to Patagonia, from the shore to waters of moderate depths, but especially along the coastline. Quiet bays of sandy and muddy bottom are preferred. Only light tackle should be used, and small jigs, feathers, or bucktails can be used, tipped with a piece of squid. Clams, mussels, and, especially, bits of squid are good cut bait, while anchovies and sardines are very effective if used alive.　　—D.dS.

CHILIPEPPER *Sebastodes goodei* The species is, with the bocaccio, the most important rockfish (which see) landed commercially in California. It is found from central lower California to northern California. On the

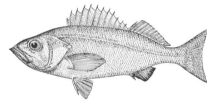

Chilipepper

chilipepper the interorbital space is convex, broad; lower jaw projecting but not as much as the bocaccio; scattered small white dots on white peritoneum; normally 8 anal softrays. Color, brownish-red above, pink below, with a distinct, narrow pink stripe along the lateral line.　　—J.R.

CHINA ROCKFISH *Sebastodes nebulosus* This distinctive rockfish (which see) has a broad, irregular, bright yellow stripe on each side of a blue-black body, beginning between the third and fourth dorsal spines, dropping to the lateral line, and extending to the base of the tail fin. Except on the stripe, the body is covered with small yellow or white spots sometimes tinged with blue.

It is a desirable species and commands a good price on the fresh-fish markets although it is of minor impor-

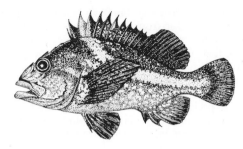

China Rockfish

tance. It is found from northern Baja California to southeastern Alaska.

It reaches a length of 16 inches. —J.R.

CHINE (1) A structural member of a boat hull; that part of the framing on which sides and bottom are fixed. (2) The area on the outside of the hull where the sides and bottom meet. Most commonly refers to the edge at the junction of the side of a boat hull and the bottom of the hull. The exact amount of angle, ranging from very sharp or hard chine to round or soft chine, often evokes controversy among boatmen and boat builders. The question is involved and related to types of materials as well as use.

HARD-CHINED HULL

A hard-chined hull is one that has a semi-vee bottom in the bow and is flat aft. The junction of sides and bottom make a sharp or hard angle. These make excellent outboard boats because they require minimum power, provide maximum range for the fuel consumed, have a shallow draft, and leap on plane. They do pound in choppy seas. Hard-chine designs are more stable and able to take turns faster.

SOFT-CHINED HULL

A soft-chined hull or round-bilge boat has a pronounced curve section where the sides and bottom meet. Soft-chined hulls set lower in the water and so increase hull drag in comparison to hard chine. The complexities of the curved sides make soft-chine boats more difficult to build, but they are favored for displacement boats which must push their way through the water. Due to the nature of the material, most molded plywood or veneer hulls have a round or soft chine. Planked plywood designs feature a hard chine.

NONTRIP OR RELIEF CHINE

The nontrip or relief chine is a modification of a hard chine which provides greater safety on fast turns but reduces speed in a planing hull. It pertains mainly to high-speed outboard boats. —F.M.P.

CHINOOK SALMON *Oncorhynchus tshawytscha* The species is the largest of the Pacific salmon (*which see*), reaching 126 pounds, but rarely does it exceed 60, and the average is about 18. The chinook salmon has irregular black spots on back, dorsal fin, and both lobes of caudal fin; black pigment at teeth bases and loose conical teeth characterize mature specimens. Parr marks on the young are large and well-defined.

LIFE HISTORY

There are several races, distinguishable by the time of river entrance which varies from January to late fall. The fish are thus termed spring, summer, or fall chinook. The chinook salmon often travels great distances from the sea, as much as 2,000 miles in the Yukon, and seems to prefer large rivers. It spawns in June to November of each year. In the Columbia the spring race has little tendency to spawn in the main river, entering side streams from near the mouth to the headwaters. The fall fish spawned almost entirely in the main-river system, but the advent of multiple dams has created slackwater, eliminating most of the available spawning area. The race is rapidly declining in the river system.

The species matures at 1 (males only) –8 years of age. The 1-year-old mature males become ripe before going to saltwater, and some, at least, recover to reach saltwater and return. The young chinook emerge from the gravel and may go to the sea immediately; others may not migrate for a considerable period. As a rule, the fall chinook goes to sea at 3–4 months of age while the spring chinook usually remains in freshwater for approximately eighteen months. At spawning time the fish is less emaciated than other species of Pacific salmon, and especially is this so of the female which may be plump and clean five hundred miles from the sea. The male gets progressively blacker with the passage of time spent in the spawning area while the female may take on a rich brassy color.

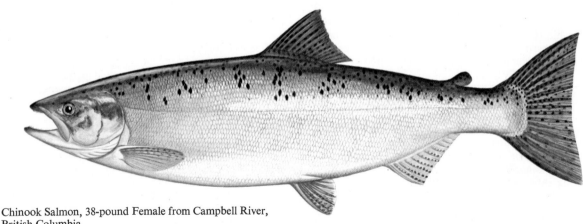

Chinook Salmon, 38-pound Female from Campbell River, British Columbia

ANGLING VALUE

The estimated ocean sport catch for Oregon, Washington, and California has reached 659,000 fish and has been close to 20 per cent of total chinook landings for the three states in recent years. It is the species most often caught by the sport angler, exceeding in numbers and pounds the catch of any other Pacific salmon.

TROLLING FOR PACIFIC SALMON

Chinook and silver salmon are most commonly caught by trolling. The standard tackle consists of a conventional trolling rod or boat rod, with a star-drag reel and 20–45 pound-test line; a saltwater spinning rod 6½–7½ feet in length may also be used with a sturdy reel. The line capacity in either case should not be less than 150 yards. Dacron, nylon, and monofilament are popular line materials, but many anglers prefer wire (.016–.024-inch diameter); wire lines should be spooled on oversize frame reels made for that purpose.

Salmon trolling is practiced in the ocean near shore, in large protected straits or sounds, or in river estuaries. Ordinarily, more fish over a longer period will be taken in the ocean, but there are local exceptions. Ocean trolling can be done with large plugs or spoons, but these are not as popular as bait. Nearly all Pacific salmon are taken on herring, anchovy, candlefish, or, when available, the Pacific sardine. The herring or other baitfish must be presented to the salmon in a particular way, dependent upon the method of bait attachment or use. In trolling, two hooks are ordinarily used. They are small, about No. 2/0, the upper one being free to slide on the line but not so free as to lose the position at which it may be set. Usually both hooks pass through the snout and down through the "chin," the upper hook remaining in that position and the other passed through and inserted near the tail in such a manner as to bend the body of the herring slightly. The bend will cause the fish to gyrate slowly as the lure is trolled if the hooks are properly positioned.

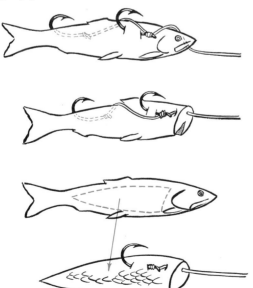

Herring Hook-ups (*top to bottom*) whole hook-up, plug-cut, cut spinner

How to Rig Herring There are three methods in common use for rigging herring and other baitfish for salmon trolling.

1. Using a treble hook with wire or monofilament leader attached, thread the leader through the herring with a large needle so that it passes from the mouth and out the vent; the hook should be drawn tight so that one prong can be inserted in the body and the other two prongs are exposed at the vent. The mouth of the herring is tied closed with a short string or length of leader material.

2. Using both a treble and a single hook on monofilament leader, secure the treble hook in herring just forward of the tail, and put the single hook through its mouth.

3. Using two single hooks on monofilament leader, secure one hook in the side of the herring on the lateral surface just forward of the tail and the other hook through its mouth.

The Herring Dodger As a variation a Herring Dodger or large shiny metal flasher may be placed between the sinker and bait. The attractive, side-to-side gyrations of the dodger will in part be transmitted to the bait, and with such a rig the bend in the body of the herring is not as critical. However, the baitfish must be at the correct distance from the dodger, and the dodger at the correct distance from the sinker. Most anglers prefer to use small baitfish, usually not over five inches in length, for coho or silver salmon, although chinooks can be taken on larger baits. The trolling speed differs with location and sometimes species. The coho will often take a bait at speeds of 4–8 miles per hour. The chinook will usually be picked up at a speed of 1–2 miles per hour. In the early part of the day a 2–6-ounce crescent sinker should be tried, and larger weights later in the day. For deep chinooks a 3–5 pound sinker or "cannon ball" is sometimes used which releases at the strike, thus permitting the fish to be fought without hindrance. In river estuaries, salmon will take a herring in much the same manner as in the ocean. They are more prone to strike at a spinner, such as a brass Bear Valley No. 2 to No. 4 or other similar types with a 3/0 to 5/0 hook, a single Siwash or treble. The trolling speed is slowed to 1–2 mph. For silvers the weight is attached to a 6–8-inch dropper line which is about 4 feet above the lure, and the smaller blades are used. For chinooks use larger spinners.

Terminal Rigging With medium- or small-size herring the following leader lengths are best:

LEADER LENGTH

Herring Dodger Size	Distance Sinker to Dodger (Inches)	Distance Dodger to Bait (Inches)
No. 3/0	20	12
No. 0/0	24	16
No. 0	26	20
No. 1	30	22
No. 2	36	26

Any variation from suggested leader lengths should be on the short side. Longer bait leader cuts down action to bait; longer sinker leader prevents Herring Dodger from having snappy action; shorter sinker leader tends to prevent the Herring Dodger from spinning. Shorten the bait leader when using extra-small herring or baitfish.

The amount of line to let out will vary with the weight of the sinker and the depth at which the angler wants the herring to be. For cohos the bait can often be trolled with success 8–10 feet behind the boat in the propeller wash. The depth at which the fish are caught can vary considerably. As a rule chinooks can be found at depths of 50–100 feet, while cohos can be caught in the upper 40 feet. At times both species are at the surface and can be seen breaking the surface in feeding activity.

How to Locate Salmon Locating the fish can sometimes be difficult. Often the success of other anglers can be noted. Birds may work on small fish at the surface to give an indication of the possible presence of salmon nearby. The surfacing, feeding fish may be obvious. There may be a traditional trolling "slot" that seems to have fish in it consistently. The mouths of rivers are usually most productive. Tide-rips are also favored fishing spots. They are easily located by the floating eelgrass or other debris which strings out in a narrow line over the surface. Sometimes a rip is marked by foam on the surface. Under the worst conditions the angler may have to prospect for fish with no signs to offer help, and this may be particularly true of chinook which are deep-running.

The time of day can be significant. The early angler who is on the water at daybreak will be usually the most successful in taking salmon. At that time and until the sun has been up for a while the wind may be at its lowest activity, providing more pleasant fishing conditions.

In a seaway the angler with a tendency to *mal de mer* will find it advantageous to keep his eyes at horizon level and to avoid stopping the forward motion of the boat. On the Pacific Coast, ocean fishing is safest when the winds are below twenty miles per hour. The double-ended, wide-bottomed, 20-foot dory of the Oregon coast is probably the best all-around craft for the salmon angler. With a 5–10-horsepower outboard engine in the well, the design will handle beautifully in a difficult situation. *See also* Pacific Salmon　　　　—J.R.
　　　　　　　　　　　　　　　　　　　—A.J.McC.

CHINOOK SALMON DISEASE *See* Diseases and Parasites

CHINQUAPIN A regional (Louisiana) name for the redear sunfish (*which see*)

CHIPOLA BASS A regional name (Florida) for the redeye bass (*which see*)

CHOCK A metal or wood guide fastened to decks and gunwales through which mooring and anchoring lines are run.

CHOP A disturbed condition of the sea or large inland lakes which shows irregular white caps. A chop is created by the tide meeting a surface current or by moderate winds.

CHUB (1.) A regional colloquialism (Eastern United States) for the fallfish (*which see*). Also a common name for a large number of fishes of the family Cyprinidae, e.g., Utah chub, blue chub, lake chub, and flathead chub. Among marine species a common name for two members of the family Kyphosidae, the yellow chub and Bermuda chub. As a species name it may refer to a European cyprinid.

(2.) *Squalius cephalus* One of the most sporting of Europe's cyprinids. The chub is found all over central Europe and Asia Minor, but is absent from the fringes of the continent in Denmark, Sicily, northern Scotland, and Ireland.

It is primarily a river fish, especially of those with a moderate flow and depths over 2–3 feet. Its typical habitat, and the one it thrives in, is the upper reaches of rivers where the flow is still brisk and the water not yet turbid. The width of the river makes no difference; chub grow equally well in streams six feet wide or twenty yards wide, provided the conditions of flow, clarity, and oxygenation are met. A few introductions of chub into clear, spring-fed or oligotrophic lakes have been successful—an interesting British experiment which promises better fisheries in a country where river fisheries are getting scarce. As long as the chub has the necessary clarity and oxygen it appears to thrive.

The chub has a terete body four to five times longer than it is broad, a shallowly forked tail fin, a prominent and erect single dorsal fin, and a characteristic broad, massive head with prominent white lips, which are visible in the water. Young chub are often mistaken for the much smaller dace, *Leuciscus leuciscus*, but always the chub dorsal fin is straight along its upper edge, the dace's being concave.

Chub

The chub's coloration is black or brown on the back, silver on the sides (with very prominent scales on the flank), and fins gray or pale pink.

Chub grow to 10 pounds or more, but any fish over half this weight is an excellent catch. The usual size caught by anglers varies from 1–3 pounds.

LIFE HISTORY

Chub breed from April to June, laying sticky eggs on plants and stones in gravelly shallows. The male displays a breeding dress of sexual tubercles on the head. Chub are mature by their third year, females by their fourth.

The young when hatched are gregarious, moving in shoals over the entire river bed and taking food at most levels. They are most voracious scavengers at this stage of life, which persists until the first or second year after hatching. By this time they have achieved about a pound or so in weight.

The scavenging shoals break up near the time of sexual maturity, never to re-form. From then on the chub takes up a solitary life in selected territories. Favored areas are runs between streamers of weed over gravel bottoms, around old piles and jetties, under overhanging trees and bushes, or downstream of dense beds of reeds, if the water is deep enough. The preferred depth appears to be 2–6 feet. All likely territories have the following in common:

1.　A bolt hole, usually right in under the bank where

the current has gouged it out. The chub retreats into it at the first sign of danger.

2. A clear run in the main stream, where the fish can hold station and snap up food drifting downstream.

3. Safety from bankside predators. In a wide river, such territories are generally some distance out or on the unfrequented bank. In narrow rivers, chub lies are frequently in deep cuttings with steep, unapproachable banks or under dense bushes. Artificial walls and cover are used where the above is absent, especially near mills.

Although adult chub seek favorable localities in a given stretch of river, they cannot be said to be territorial in the same way trout are. A likely territory may be shared by several fish, though rarely more than five. Only the very large chub are solitary or live in pairs. Even though they share a lie, there appears no evidence of a hierarchical structure within the group nor of individual aggressiveness. Indeed, many such groups are composed of fish of differing sizes and ages, the younger and smaller ones appearing to act as "scouts" in exploring new foods. When danger threatens, they all enter their bolt hole simultaneously without jostling—though the smaller ones are the first out, after all is safe. Anglers indeed claim that chub take "ten minutes to the pound to unscare."

The territory extends up and downstream of the hiding place, but usually further up than down, so that they do not swim against the current to retreat. They cover the whole territory regularly, swimming up against the flow, then letting it take them backwards diagonally across the current. This involves a minimum expenditure of energy; yet they are always facing upstream ready for food and never turn so that the current flows through their gills the wrong way.

Chub are perhaps the most omnivorous of European river fish, taking anything living in, or falling in, the water. They accept food at any level. Chub eat quantities of vegetable matter, varying this with crustaceans, mollusks, and insects. In calcareous streams, the crayfish *Astacus fluviatilis* is a common and appreciated delicacy. Other fish form an appreciable article of diet; Leeming found that the larger chub of the English river Welland were in the main either vegetarian or piscivorous. Of twenty-three piscivorous chub examined, twelve contained small eels. The descending order of preference was found to be eels, gudgeon, dace, and roach. In other streams, minnows form a part of this diet as well.

Although like other cyprinids the chub lacks teeth in the mouth, the pharyngeal teeth are exceptionally able to substitute for them. They are particularly vicious, with the cutting surfaces shaped like the chopping carnassial teeth of land carnivores—quite unlike the molars of the others of the carp family. The pharyngeal teeth will cut a 5-inch fish or crayfish clean in half, despite the latter's lobsterlike exoskeleton; they will do the same for an incautious finger poked down the throat.

The chub is very tolerant of wide ranges of temperature and light intensity, feeding just as vigorously on blazing summer days as in icebound rivers in the depths of winter. It gives sport on days when other fish will not, but it will not tolerate disturbance. Izaak Walton called it "the fearfullest of fishes" with good reason.

No extensive investigations have been performed on the growth rate of the chub, but judging from their weight at the onset of maturity and the breakup of the

immature shoals, a fair annual increment would be ½ pound per year, slightly less before maturity though more proportionally. Most predation is concentrated in the immature stages, when large shoals move in the open; later, retiring habits and increasing size make it less vulnerable. The only enemy of large solitary chub besides man is the otter, and this animal is no longer common in Britain.

ANGLING VALUE

Chub are favorites among anglers who like to stalk their fish. Unfortunately the larger chub-bearing rivers are very popular for other species as well, and are heavily overfished. Consequently stalking is only practiced on lesser-known waters, where passers-by will not inadvertently spoil one's chances. Tactics on large rivers mainly center around exploring the bottom thoroughly with a bait allowed to run downstream with the current, on a variety of tackle.

On smaller rivers, the fish must first be found (usually by observation) before they are fished for. Stealth is far more necessary, and a wider variety of tackles and baits can be used.

Soft cheese is a widely used bait, but worms, grubs, and bread are also favored. Extensive prebaiting is not essential, and many natural baits are employed without preparation. Foremost among these are black slugs, caterpillars, whole crayfish, and small fish. Spinning produces a few piscivorous chub, though plugs are not as effective as simple, silver rotating lures. They also take dry flies.

The chub bites boldly but does not fight exceptionally well, the major tactic being a dash back to its lair once it feels the hook.

COMMERCIAL VALUE

Chub flesh has been described as "cotton wool stuffed with needles," so they have no direct economic value. As a strictly sporting fish, there is revenue from the more famous chub fisheries, such as the English Wye, Hampshire Avon, and Dorset Stour. Otherwise most chub fishing is practiced in smaller rivers, and the over-all revenue from their pursuit is not high. In many waters where they occur, more desirable fishes such as salmonids are preferred, the chub being classed as vermin and actively destroyed. Stocks are not threatened, however, because they are almost impossible to eradicate once established.
—D.M.

CHUB MACKEREL *See* Mackerels

CHUCKLEHEAD A regional name for the blue catfish (*which see*).

CHUM A living substance, such as minnows or mollusks, chopped or ground into pieces or a mash; or grain or vegetable such as rice or corn; or processed food such as cooked macaroni, dog food, or cat food, which is distributed in the water to attract gamefish to the angler's bait. The act of chumming is most common to saltwater fishing, although it has a broad application to freshwater angling in various parts of the world. Chum is particularly valuable for bringing fish up from deepwater to a bait (bluefin tuna) or for locating fish in the open ocean (mako shark) or for stimulating less gregarious species into striking (gray snapper) or for locating bottom feeders in water of moderate depths (flounder).   A.J.McC.

CHUMMING The act of using chum to attract fish to a baited hook. *See* Chum

Chum Salmon, 15-pound Male (in breeding color)

CHUM SALMON *Oncorhynchus keta* This Pacific salmon (*which see*) is distinguished by having no large black spots on fins or body, a slender caudal peduncle, black-tinged fins (except dorsal), dark bars or streaks on body at or near spawning time, 140–160 pyloric ceca, and 19–26 smooth gillrakers on the first arch. The green back and the slender parr marks reaching below the lateral line distinguish the young.

LIFE HISTORY

Runs of chums are marked by wide yearly fluctuation in numbers. It matures at 4–5 years of age. In part of its range it is represented by two forms, a summer and a fall fish. The summer fish enters the river earlier, reaches maturity earlier, is smaller, and does not travel up the river as far. Entrance to the river takes place from July to December.

Though the species is usually given to spawning in the lower reaches of rivers, it is to be found near the head of the Yukon River in Teslin Lake, which is approximately two thousand miles from the sea. It spawns in November and December. The egg of the chum is large, approaching $\frac{5}{16}$ inch. Its range is from northern California to Korea and Japan. Its food consists largely of fish and crustaceans. Only rarely is it ever taken by the sport fisherman. It is third in value of Pacific salmons, exceeded by the sockeye and pink. In 1960 the United States pack was valued at over $14,000,000.

Reaches a weight of 33 pounds but is usually taken in sizes from 8–18 pounds.

ANGLING VALUE

Due to the fact that chum salmon usually arrive at the mouths of freshwater streams late in the year (November and December) very little angling is done for this species over much of its range. However, this salmon provides good light-tackle fishing in saltwater in the Queen Charlotte Islands (British Columbia) from September until mid-October. The chum is partial to small wobbling spoons and spinners, and especially blades with some red or fluorescent red on them. First introduced in the Barents Sea in 1956 by the U.S.S.R., chum salmon have become established in Soviet streams and in northern Norway. Anglers have reported taking chums on flies and spinning lures in this area. *See also* Pacific Salmon   —J.R.

CIGUATERA A type of poisoning, which can be fatal, produced by eating a large variety of tropical marine fishes. The name *ciguatera* (Spanish) was applied by early settlers in the Caribbean. It is not caused by "spoiled" fish, but may exist in perfectly fresh and otherwise edible species. The exact origin of ciguatera has not been established. The enigmatic feature of this toxicity is that it can occur in a species which was previously known to be edible in a specific locality or in a species which is commonly eaten in other regions with no history of ciguatera intoxications. In all, more than three hundred different fishes have been known to cause ciguatera, primarily in the West Indies and the central and South Pacific Ocean. For many years it has been believed that tropical species became poisonous because of their feeding habits. The toxic substance was thought to originate in marine plants. However, recent researchers indicate that the theory may be more complex than originally believed. There is no way of determining the toxicity of a fish by its appearance. However, the most common ciguatera-producing fishes around North American shores are the great barracuda, the yellowfin grouper, and the amberjack. Under most circumstances the viscera of tropical marine fishes should not be used as food.

SYMPTOMS AND TREATMENT

A tingling sensation on the lips, tongue, and throat may occur at any time within twenty-four hours of ingesting the fish. It most often occurs within 2–3 hours. There is usually a feeling of numbness accompanied by nausea, abdominal cramps, vomiting, and diarrhea. The muscles of the mouth may become drawn and spastic. There is a feeling of weakness which becomes progressively worse, accompanied by muscular pains in the arms and legs. Vision may also be affected through either blurring, temporary blindness, or extreme sensitivity to light. Skin eruptions consisting of a red papular rash, blisters, or simply intense itching are common. In severe cases the victim has difficulty in walking and may lose muscular co-ordination or suffer paralysis. The mortality rate among ciguatera victims is low (less than 10 percent); however, recovery is very slow in severe cases and may require many months. *See also* First Aid   —A.J.McC.

CISCO *Coregonus spp.* There are eight North American species in this group of lake-inhabiting members of the Salmonidae. The ciscoes are sometimes called grayback, tullibee, or lake herring because they superficially resemble a herring in outward appearance. They all have large scales, usually less than 120 in the lateral line; silvery bodies, somewhat darker on the back; the eggs are smaller than those of trout or salmon; there are no teeth on the tongue in North American species; the snout does not markedly extend over the lower jaw. They usually vary in length from 6–20 inches, but in some species a weight of 7 pounds has been recorded. All ciscoes are coldwater fishes, occurring from New England through the Great Lakes into Canada.

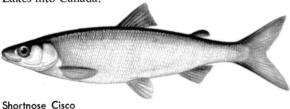

Shortnose Cisco

Little is known of the species ecology of the ciscoes. Some of them are schooling types with pelagic habits, staying near the surface or swimming to depths of several hundred feet. They move near shore in July and August

Deepwater Cisco

and spawn over hard bottom in November in depths from shallow water to somewhat over one hundred feet. They feed on planktonic crustacea and bottom-dwelling insects.

The eight species are as follows:

Cisco	*Coregonus artedii*
Deepwater Cisco	*Coregonus johannae*
Longjaw Cisco	*Coregonus alpenae*
Shortjaw Cisco	*Coregonus zenithicus*
Shortnose Cisco	*Coregonus reighardi*
Blackfin Cisco	*Coregonus nigripinnis*
Kiyi	*Coregonus kiyi*
Bloater	*Coregonus hoyi*

ANGLING VALUE

Ciscoes are fine gamefish, although the periods during which they can be taken are limited. During large summer mayfly hatches they often come to the top where they can be taken on dry flies. In the annual hatch which occurs on Owasco Lake in mid-June, New York anglers turn out en masse to catch ciscoes on every type of tackle imaginable. Fly-casters derive great sport with fish averaging 16 inches in length and running up to 2 pounds. The fun begins just at sundown and continues until dark, by which time the adjacent highways look like Times Square. However, there are substantial populations of ciscoes in many other lakes, and there's reason to believe that the fish can be caught when anglers become aware of them and learn the techniques. Some jumbos exist in Lake Champlain, Hatch Lake, and at the mouth of the Niagara River at the place where it enters Lake Ontario.

Ciscoes are most susceptible to angling in the winter months, however, and they are often taken in 30–40 feet of water with handlines and short ice rods by jigging small spoons, beads, buttons, spinners, and leadheads. Ciscoes shun bright daylight even under the ice, and as a rule the best fishing for them is from dawn until about nine o'clock in the morning and again in the evening. Many Michigan and Wisconsin lakes have excellent cisco fishing; yet even here the fishing pressure is not intensive. Good spots to try in Wisconsin are the Lucerne Lakes in Forest County, Green Lake in Green County, and Tomahawk Lake in Oneida County. Michigan's outstanding cisco and whitefish waters are South Manistique and Whitefish Lake in Mackinac County, Crystal Lake in Benzie County, and Higgins Lake in Roscommon County. The June and July mayfly hatches also trigger surface fishing in various parts of Lake Huron. —J.R.
A.J.McC.

CLAMS A large number of bivalved mollusks, which are sought as food or bait. Clams are an important item in the restaurant trade and are collected in great quantities by people along both coasts of the United States. Nearly all clams are delicious to eat, although the meats of some species are bitter. Depending on the environment, clams can be toxic or deadly to humans, depending on either (1) the occurrence of noxious plankton blooms (*see* Red Tide) or (2) the presence of pollution (*which see*) from untreated sewage. It is advisable to check with local health authorities in all areas where these bivalves are taken as food. Some forms of hepatitis may originate from eating raw clams. Commercial stocks must pass rigid inspection.

In the United States one of the best known clams is the softshell clam *Mya arenaria*. Along the Atlantic coast it occurs from the Arctic Ocean to Cape Hatteras, and it has been introduced into western Florida where it has done exceptionally well. It has also been introduced into Europe, although it is not especially sought there as food. It also occurs in central California. Found on mud flats and under stones, generally in the intertidal zone, it is avidly sought by gourmets and beachcombers. The hardshell clam, *Mercenaria mercenaria* or quahog (pronounced có-hog) is equally delicious and is avidly sought, being eaten more often cooked and in chowder than the softshell, which is considered a delicacy raw as well as cooked. Usually found from 1–6 fathoms deep, hardshells can be obtained commercially by clam rakes operated by hand or using hydraulic dredge boats, which utilize high-pressure jets of water that unearth the clams from their burrows. These are then picked up with large rakes or dredged; such operations usually being carried out from medium-sized boats. A related form, the surf or skimmer clam, *Polynyma solidissima* is also highly esteemed for use in chowder. It is found in water deeper than the soft- or hardshell clams. Along the Pacific coast of the United States, the geoduck (pronounced gooey-duck), *Panomya generosa* has a large, delicious siphon, which may be up to six or seven times as long, when protruded, as the shell, which grows to about 7 inches. Other delicious clams are the bean clam (*Donax spp.*), a small, colorful clam found in the intertidal zone, and which is delicious in soup; and the cockles, which are especially prized in Europe, both as fresh food and in stews and chowders. One large clam, the granddaddy clam, *Tridacna gigas*, occurs throughout Oceania and is especially sought as a souvenir. Its shell is white with pink, orange, or blue tints, and is delicately sculptured. Large individuals reach 500 pounds. Although it is alleged that native divers have been trapped in the powerful jaws, there is no record to authenticate this report.

FRESHWATER CLAMS

Several species of freshwater bivalves are called "clams," but these are really mussels which belong to the family Unionidae. They are important in the pearl button industry and for making essence of pearl. *See also* Fish Cookery —D.DS.

CLEARNOSE SKATE *Raja eglanteria* The combination of the distinctive, subquadrate disk with its markings of bars and dots, the translucent snout on either side of the midline, and the single row of thorns along the midline identify this species. It resembles the barndoor skate (*which see*) in many respects, but the barndoor has the midrow of thorns only on the tail. The dorsal fins are separate, and there are no large circular markings on either wing as in the roundel skate (*which see*). It is reddish-brown to light brown above with numerous dark, broken bars interspersed with dark spots. In some cases darker and lighter spots and bars occur together. The underparts are white. It grows to about 37 inches, but most seen are less than 30 inches, at which size it weighs about 6 pounds.

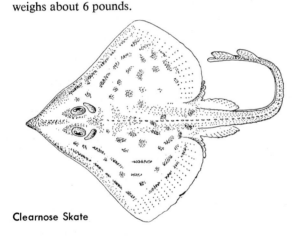

Clearnose Skate

LIFE HISTORY

The clearnose ranges from Cape Cod to middle Florida, most commonly between the Carolinas and Long Island. It is a shallow-water species, usually taken in less than ten fathoms, but it has been taken from depths of sixty-five fathoms. It breeds inshore, during the spring, and the young are hatched from the horny cases after three months or more. A springtime, inshore migration occurs with a converse offshore movement in the fall, the time of movement depending on temperature and latitude. They feed on mud shrimp, crabs, squid, anchovies and other small fishes, and small mollusks. In turn, it is occasionally eaten by the sand shark (*which see*).

ANGLING VALUE

Although a few are used as food, there is no commercial market for them, but they are taken during the summer, sometimes in large numbers, by anglers fishing in inshore waters. —D.dS.

CLEAT A fitting of wood or metal with horns, used for securing lines. Types include an open base, square base, and hollow base.

CLINKER A type of boat construction in which the successive strakes lap each other, with the lower edge of each plank lapping the upper edge of the plank immediately below it, as viewed from the outside of the hull. Clinker-built boats are extremely seaworthy and range from small outboards to sportfishermen. The clinker is also called lapstrake. *See* Sportfisherman —F.M.P.

COALFISH (1.) A common name for the sablefish (*which see*).

   (2.) Also a common name for the Pollock (*which see*).

COAMING Raised framework about deck openings and cockpits of open boats. Provides protection against splash and weather.

COASTAL SHINER *Notropis petersoni* The coastal shiner is a graceful little minnow having a dark stripe down each side and seldom exceeding $2\frac{1}{2}$ inches in total length. Its distinguishing characteristics are: a dorsal and anal fin-ray count of 8 and 7, respectively; 35–36 scales in the lateral line, with 5 scale rows above the lateral line and 3 rows below; 15 scale rows from the back of the head to the origin of the dorsal fin; a pharyngeal tooth formula of 2, 4-4, 2; a dark lateral band extending from the head to the tail, but poorly developed posteriad; anterior lateral line scales not elongated; scales below the lateral line without pigment; a terminal mouth with the lower jaw being included and the snout slightly overhanging; a large eye about $\frac{1}{3}$ the length of the head; and a body depth of about $4\frac{1}{2}$ times the standard length. The color of the coastal shiner can best be described by stating that above it is olivaceous, lighter below, tip of the chin black, ventral fins rosy, and a black stripe down each side from the snout to the base of the caudal fin. The anal rays are edged with scattered melanophores and the basicaudal spot is wedge-shaped and separated somewhat by a light area. Two large dark crescents appear on the internarial area. The geographical range of the coastal shiner is along the Coastal Plain from the Escambia River eastward to peninsular Florida and northward to the Neuse River watershed in North Carolina.

LIFE HISTORY

Very little is known about the life history of the coastal shiner and only brief comments have been published about it. It prefers the swift coastal streams, and is found over gravel, sand, and silt bottoms. The principal foods of the coastal shiners are Ostracods, Copepods, Isopods, and small aquatic insects. Prior to the breeding season the males develop one or two rows of large tubercles on their snouts.

It provides forage for the largemouth bass, chain pickerel, redfin pickerel, redbreast sunfish, and warmouth. It is sold locally as bait, being taken from natural lakes and streams. —D.E.L.

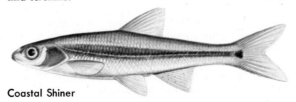

Coastal Shiner

COASTER A regional name for migratory brook trout (*which see*) found in Lake Superior. The fish descend from tributary streams and live in the lake waters where they often grow 3–5 pounds in weight.

COBIA *Rachycentron canadum* Also called the crabeater or ling, this species has a worldwide distribution in tropical and warm-temperate waters. In the western Atlantic it is found from Bermuda and Massachusetts to Argentina (35° S.) and is widespread in the Gulf of Mexico. This species has no close relatives and is placed in a family by itself (Rachycentridae).

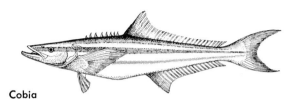

Cobia

The cobia is distinguished as follows: head 4.05–5.3 in standard length; depth 5.55–8.1; dorsal spines 8–10; dorsal rays 28–33; anal fin with one spine and 23–26 rays; body elongate, fusiform; head very long, much depressed; snout broad, its length 2.45–2.85 in head; eye 4.85–6.35; mouth moderate, the lower jaw projecting; maxillary reaching anterior margin of eye, 2.3–2.6 in head; teeth small, in bands on both jaws, vomer, palatines, and tongue; gillrakers short, 7–9 on lower limb of first arch; lateral line continuous, more or less wavy; scales minute, covering entire body; first dorsal comprised of very short, stiff spines; second dorsal long, slightly elevated anteriorly; anal similar to second dorsal; caudal truncate in young, slightly forked in adult; ventrals moderate, as long as post-orbital length of head; pectorals large, 1.1–1.3 in head length.

Color dark brown above, a paler brown on sides and below; a black lateral band, wider than eye, extending from snout to base of caudal; ventral surface of head pale; fins mostly black. The black lateral band is very conspicuous in the young but tends to become obscured in the adult.

The cobia feeds on crabs, shrimp, and small fish of all kinds. The young are frequently caught in bays and inlets, but the adults prefer the shallow parts of the open ocean. They are attracted to floating objects of any kind, being found close to buoys, anchored vessels, and floating debris. Small, live fish are very attractive bait. The largest cobia ever caught with hook and line was taken by J. E. Stansbury off Cape Charles, Virginia, on July 3, 1938. It weighed 102 pounds and was 5 feet, 10 inches in length.

The cobia is an exceptionally good food fish. It is occasionally found in the market, but the commercial catch is very small. Adults of 30–50 pounds are commonly seen.

In the summer, this species migrates north as far as Chesapeake Bay and Cape Cod. In the fall, it apparently moves south to tropical waters.   —J.C.B.

ANGLING VALUE

Cobia are caught from boats, piers, and beaches. The most popular tackle for cobia fishing is heavy spinning gear designed to cast 15–25-pound test monofilament lines. Large plugs, similar to those used for striped bass in blue scale or silver-flash finishes, and 1½–3-ounce jigs with white or yellow skirts are standard baits. A 3-foot wire leader (No. 7–No. 9) or a 60–80-pound test monofilament shock tippet is necessary. Cobia are usually sighted near the surface, along the coast, often quite close to shore, and the ability to spot fish at long distances is an advantage. A beach buggy (*which see*) or a boat equipped with a tower is employed by cobia specialists.

Cobia are large, strong gamefish which make determined runs and occasional jumps. The fish has good food value; it is usually skinned and deep fried in fingers or chunks. Cobia are excellent when smoked.   A.J.McC.

CODS AND HAKES Family Gadidae These are marine fishes of cold-temperate and arctic waters mainly confined to the Northern Hemisphere. Most of the species are found in shallow waters of the continental shelves, but a few have penetrated into deeper waters. Almost all are bottom fishes; two species in arctic waters and one in the North Pacific are found in the epipelagic environment.

The cods are softrayed fishes; the first dorsal and pelvic fins sometimes filamentous; caudal usually distinct but sometimes joined to dorsal and anal fins; scales small and cycloid; mouth usually large and gill openings wide; a single chin barbel is usually present, and sometimes barbels are present on the snout.

The family contains about 60 species. Many of them are of considerable commercial value, being taken mostly by otter trawls and baited hooks. *See also* Atlantic Cod, Atlantic Tomcod, Burbot, Haddock, Pacific Hake, Pacific Tomcod, Pollock, Silver Hake, Southern Hake, Squirrel Hake, Walleye Pollock, White Hake

COELACANTHS The coelacanths belong to a group of fishes (Coelacanthidae, Order Coelacanthiformes) which was believed to be extinct for about 60 million years. Coelacanths were once very successful and remained virtually unchanged for over 200 million years. They are characterized by curious, long fins on wristlike stalks which are believed to be used for creeping about the bottom and which probably give the fish marked mobility in swimming. The caudal fin is pointed with fanlike, shortened lobes. The body is robust and heavy, and is covered with large, roughened scales. Closely related to the lungfish, living coelacanths have a large lung which is degenerate but which is believed to have been functional in fossil forms. A specialized heart, a simple, tubelike backbone composed of cartilage, an intestine which is similar to that of sharks, the pituitary of the brain (*see* Anatomy) which connects to the roof of the mouth, and hollow, cartilaginous fin spines are peculiar to the order.

LIVING FOSSIL

The first living coelacanth taken, in 1938 off South Africa, is named *Latimeria chalumnae*, and is a true "living fossil." It was 5 feet long and weighed about 127 pounds. Since then, about a dozen more have been taken in South African waters, the largest of which was about 160 pounds. The body of this coelacanth varies from bright blue to brownish, and the scales and body give off a great deal of slime and oil, respectively. They apparently live along moderately deep slopes in areas about 500–900 feet deep, although two specimens have been taken at about 220–240 feet. Coelacanths are taken over very rocky bottoms and in rather cool water. Nothing is known about their mode of life except that they are active

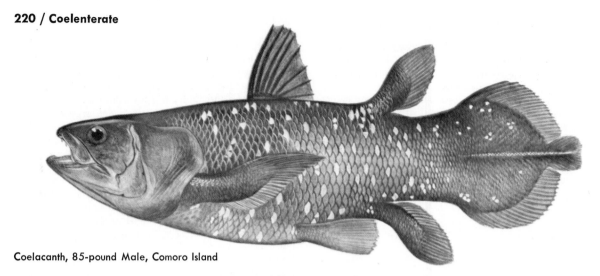

Coelacanth, 85-pound Male, Comoro Island

and believed to be voracious. The presence of recognizable young in fossil forms indicates that the young are born alive.

The discovery of living coelacanths permits scientists to study the anatomy and function of a very important group of animals whose close relatives gave rise to amphibians, reptiles, birds, and mammals. Coupled with studies of living relatives, such as the lungfish, and fossil coelacanths, the history of life on earth can now be studied in greater detail, and the discovery of living coelacanths has been called by some the greatest find of the twentieth century.

FOOD VALUE

Natives in the Comoro Islands, off the Malagasy Republic, have long been familiar with coelacanths, which they call "kombessa," and they use the meat dried and salted but not fresh. —D.dS.

COELENTERATE A member of primitive aquatic phylum which may take one of two basic forms: the jellyfishlike medusa or the stalked sedentary polyp which is attached to a solid object at one end of its body and has tentacles at the other end. Usually marine animals, coelenterates have stinging cells called nematocysts. Coelenterata include the Portuguese man-of-war, jellyfish, and the polyps

of the class Anthozoa, which resemble flowers and include the corals and anemones (*which see*).

COHO SALMON *Oncorhynchus kisutch* Also called silver salmon and hooknose, the coho is a popular gamefish of the Pacific Northwest and since the year 1967 has provided an immense fishery in the Great Lakes. In saltwater the coho is a strong quarry and often leaps when hooked. Of the Pacific salmon (*which see*) this species occurs in anglers' catches in numbers second only to the chinook. A good year has seen 321,000 fish taken in Oregon, Washington, and California and the catch has exceeded 20 per cent of the total landings of salmon in those states.

The coho salmon is generally silvery in color with black spots; the spotting is confined to the back and upper lobe of the caudal fin; a white gum line occurs at the teeth bases; teeth are needlelike and firm; there are 19–25 gillrakers in the first arch. Young fish have longer rays in the leading edge of the anal fin, and the parr marks are elongate. There have been weights up to 33 pounds, 3 ounces (Little Manistee River, Michigan, 1970) recorded, but 6–12 pounds is usual at maturity.

LIFE HISTORY

The coho can spawn in gravel in the headwaters or near the sea in streams and has no outstanding require-

Coho Salmon, 18-pound Female, Neah Bay, Washington

ment. It enters the rivers beginning in July and spawns from October to February. Most spawning is completed by the end of December. Most young fish migrate to the sea when a year old, but some may go earlier or wait until the third year. Maturity is usually reached at 3 years of age, but some of the males and a few females mature at two and a few come into the river in the fourth year. Its food consists of fishes, squid, and crustaceans. Large numbers of crab larvae are eaten.

The coho is found from California to Japan. The species does not travel far from the parent stream. Its chances for survival or even of enhancement in numbers are good because it spawns in largest numbers in the smaller coastal streams that do not appear to be useful in the production of hydroelectric energy or in irrigation. Unlike the chinook salmon (*which see*) which undertakes long migrations, the coho salmon ranges in a more confined area with populations from one state overlapping into adjacent states. The coho originating in northern California contribute primarily to the fisheries of that state, but also range as far north as Washington. Populations in Oregon streams range from northern Vancouver Island to northern California. Cohos from British Columbia streams mainly concentrate offshore north of Vancouver Island, but these are mixed with salmon from the rivers of Washington. Cohos from Washington rivers travel as far north as the Queen Charlotte Islands and south to northern California. Populations originating in Alaska are predominantly local in movement and contribute principally to the Alaskan fishery.

ANGLING METHODS

Coho salmon are commonly taken in saltwater by trolling with herring and other fishes as well as spoons. They are also caught with spinning lures and artificial flies in both salt and freshwater. Depending on the locale, coho may be taken any time from May through November. The larger fish occur in the Puget Sound area beginning in late August, and around Vancouver Island, British Columbia, in mid-September. Trolling with the streamer fly or a fly-and-spinner combination is a popular and exciting method of catching these salmon and is most effective during the feeding periods. Surface activity generally lasts from one to two hours and begins an hour before the change of tide to an hour after at either high or low stages. Seagulls and other birds frequently reveal the location of feeding coho as they hover over the water catching herring and candlefish. At such times it is easy to see salmon chasing bait at the surface. As a rule the angler can troll the streamer with 30–90 feet of line at a fairly rapid pace and expect strikes. A zigzagging course is suggested and the boat should circle or try to cross ahead of the moving schools. At times the fly alone will work better than the fly-and-spinner combination, however, it pays to try both and also to change to different patterns. The most popular coho streamers are tied on No. 1 to No. 3/0 Siwash hooks and are made of bear hair with tinsel bodies; patterns such as the Coronation, Candlefish, Coho Special, Silver Killer, and Blue and White are very successful. Spinner sizes vary from No. 1/0 to No. 4 in silver or brass blades.

Casting the fly to coho salmon is also successful, provided the angler can handle a long line to cover the fast-moving schools. A 9-foot fly rod designed for a GBF or

A bright coho taken in Alaskan streams is an outstanding gamefish. Fresh from the sea, these salmon are active jumpers

GAF (No. 7 or No. 8) line, and a reel with sufficient capacity to hold 150 yards of backing makes an ideal outfit.

The popular method of fishing for coho in rivers is with spinning tackle and small wobbling spoons or spinners. However, cohos will take a fly in freshwater if worked in a manner similar to that used for steelhead. The coho is a nonfeeding fish on its spawning run, and consequently the quality of the sport varies from river to river. *See also* Pacific Salmon   —J.R.
          —A.J.McC.

COLDKILL A mortality among saltwater fishes which occurs among the cold-sensitive species, such as the spotted seatrout, gafftopsail catfish, snook, and tarpon. A coldkill results from a sudden and sharp drop in water temperature. Some species can tolerate low temperatures provided the change occurs gradually; others retreat to deeper, warmer waters, and therefore are not distributed in the shallows as they would be in normal seasons. *See also* Winterkill

COLOMBIA Bordered by the Pacific and Atlantic oceans (Caribbean Sea), Colombia is the northern terminus of the Andean Ridge, which branches into three principal mountain ranges with peaks reaching over 18,000 feet.

Fishing in the Magdalena River produces a variety of fish including a unique species of dorado which is silver in color

From the arid land of the Guajira Peninsula to the swamps of the Magdalena and from the Llanos or eastern plains to the volcanic western cordilleras and south to the luminous green rain forest of the Amazon is an area of 440,000 square miles. Between these extremes of oceans and altitudes exist an amazing variety of saltwater and freshwater fish. Colombia has thousands of streams which form three major watersheds, those that drain into the Pacific, those that flow into the Caribbean, and those that enter the Atlantic through the Amazon and Orinoco rivers. Because of this diverse habitat, anglers in Colombia can run the gamut from rainbow trout to dorado and blue marlin to peacock pavón.

Much of the country is still undeveloped from a tourist angler's point of view, but facilities in remote areas are growing, and for the adventuresome the Colombian jungles are uniquely rewarding.

Colombia lies almost entirely within the north tropical zone. High temperatures prevail in the lowlands, including the coastal plains and the larger river valleys. Cooler climates prevail at higher altitudes with subtropical weather found at elevations up to 6,000 feet and temperate zone weather from 6,000–10,000 feet. Above 10,000 feet the weather is *cold*. Most of Colombia's major cities are 3,000–9,000 feet above sea level so the temperature in Bogota, for example, will average about 58°F the year round.

Colombia has a wet season (*invierno*) and a dry season (*verano*). The area of highest rainfall is in the Department of Choco, where the annual average exceeds 400 inches and there is no dry season. Generally speaking, the January through March period is the dry season in lowland jungle rivers and is the best time for freshwater fishing. For the high-altitude trout waters the best period is June through September. Along the Atlantic coast April-May and October-November are generally rainy periods.

SALTWATER FISHING

The inshore Atlantic Coast region of Colombia has a great variety of marine species dominated by snook and tarpon because of the many brackish estuaries and bays.

These fish also occur in the lower reaches of the coastal rivers and penetrate quite far inland for at least 250 miles in the swamp regions of the Atrato and Magdalena river systems. The waters of the lower Magdalena are dissipated over a wide area of marsh, lakes, and lagoons; concentrations of tarpon are found around Ayapel and El Banco. The more accessible fishing of this type is at the port cities, such as Barranquilla at the Magdalena River mouth in the Cienaga Grande area. The blue-water species seasonally common to Colombia's north coast are blue and white marlin, sailfish, wahoo, king mackerel, dolphin, barracuda, and yellowfin and blackfin tuna. Presently the Del Rosario Island group is a popular location for boats working out of Cartagena. Charters can be made here through the local Club de Pesca.

The Pacific Coast region of Colombia is largely undeveloped. There are many short, precipitous rivers coming off the Western Cordillera, which is heavily forested and humid. The coastal lowlands are sparsely populated in the Departments of Choco, Valle, Cauca, and Narino. Rainfall exceeds 200 inches per year. Exploratory vessels have reported good fishing along the coast from Cabo Marzo to Isla Gorgona for black marlin, sailfish, amberjack, roosterfish, dolphin, and yellowfin and big-eye tuna, but there are no on-location facilities for visiting anglers. Occasionally boats run down from the Panama Canal Zone to fish the Cabo Marzo area, but this is a two-day trip and requires a long-range craft suitable for living aboard.

FRESHWATER FISHING

The largest family of freshwater fishes found in South America is the Characidae. There are 1,350 known species, which includes the dorados, piranhas, pacus, the trahira, and many pikelike species without common names. The great majority of characins are carnivores and nearly all of the larger species are excellent gamefish.

The local names of fishes in South America are extremely confusing, as they are derived from Spanish and Portuguese and a great many dissimilar Indian dialects. The Spanish word *picuda*, for example, which means "beaked," is applied to at least 30 different species ranging from the saltwater barracuda to the freshwater dorado. The serious angler can profit greatly by learning at least a few of the Latin, as well as the common, names of important native gamefish. With the exception of the well-publicized piranha (Portuguese)—known elsewhere in South America as the caribe (Spanish)—Spanish common names are preferable, as they are more widely used.

There are two dorado (locally picuda, picua, dorada, or rubio) found in Colombia: *Salminus affinis* is confined to the upper Magdalena River and its tributaries (the Cauca system), which flows north into the Atlantic; *Salminus hilarii*, which is distributed in the Orinoco watershed (notably in the Meta and Guaviare rivers) and the upper Amazon. Neither species attains the large size of the Argentine dorado (*Salminus maxillosus*), which has been recorded up to 75 pounds (1971). Colombian dorado in general range from 2–8 pounds; 12-pounders are uncommon. Both Colombian species are more slender than *S. maxillosus* and very silvery rather than gold in color. They are found in fast-flowing, gravel-bottom streams and will take a variety of lures. Spinning and fly tackle provide excellent sport.

Of major importance as a gamefish in tropical South America is the payara (*which see*). This fish is distinguished by a pair of long canine teeth in the lower jaw which project through the snout. Payara are large (to 30 pounds or more), powerful fish. They make strong runs and frequent leaps. Their sharp mouths also make them difficult to hook solidly. Almost any artificial lure and especially topwater plugs will attract payara.

Tropical South America has a vast and unknown number of species in the Cichlidae family. Among these in the genus *Cichla* and *Cichlasoma* are some of Colombia's most important gamefish. The cichlids are represented by the pavóns. These fish are generally basslike in appearance with a hump developing on the posterior region of the head in males which becomes most prominent as the April spawning season approaches.

There are two common species of pavón in Colombia and possibly more in isolated streams along the Venezuelan border. The peacock pavón (locally pavón rayado, pavón cinchado, or tucunaré pintado) is indigenous to the Orinoco and upper Amazon watersheds in Colombia, but since 1950 has been widely transplanted by the Ministry of Agriculture to lowland streams and farm ponds. Inland from the Pacific coast on the plateaus and higher river valleys is a well-populated agricultural region extending northward from Popayan. The Popayan to Cali region probably represents the westernmost distribution of the peacock pavón, although this species was stocked rather than native to the area. The second species common to Colombia is the butterfly pavón (locally pavón amarillo, pavón mariposa, or tucunaré comun).

Pavón are caught with essentially the same lures and techniques used for North American black bass. During the dry, low-water season, when both forage and gamefish are concentrated in small areas, the sport can be phenomenal at times. In general, pavón feed sporadically, and in the course of a day there will be bursts of action followed by lulls, although large numbers of fish can be caught during active periods. Pavón are strong fighters, and leap repeatedly from the water when hooked. They are a superior table fish and gourmet travelers rate them among the world's best.

Organized facilities in the primitive fishing regions of Colombia are extremely limited. There is a fishing camp at Miraflores, less than three hours by air from Villavicencio and an additional hour by boat, which offers excellent pavón fishing. This is a modern, fully equipped wilderness camp.

TROUT FISHING

There is some good trout fishing in Colombia. It is not comparable to the angling found in Chile and Argentina, but the quality is above average—and can be uniquely combined with fishing for tropical species on the same trip. The most popular spot for trout is Lake Tota near Bogota. Tota produces fish in the over 10-pound class each season. Big rainbows are also taken in Lake Cocha near Pasto in the Department of Narino and in the streams near Popayan in the Department of Cauca.

TACKLE

There is little tackle available in Colombia, and whether you plan an offshore trip or a safari into the jungle, it is necessary to bring appropriate gear. The usual equipment

popular in United States saltwaters is suitable here. Freshwater anglers, however, are well advised to select somewhat heavier tackle than is ordinarily used in river and lake fishing. Bait-casting and spinning equipment in the 15-pound class should be the minimum. Many tropical species average quite large in size and are caught along densely wooded banks where snags are common. In addition, wire leaders (18-inch stainless steel coated with vinyl in 30-pound test) provide needed protection from the various sharp-toothed gamefish. Bring plenty of lures—floating and sinking plugs, jigs, spoons, spinners, and bucktails, large streamers, and popping bugs for the fly rod.   —A.J.McC.

COLORADO The Centennial State is a land of contrast from the standpoint of climate and geography. The eastern third of the state is mostly rolling, treeless prairie. Rainfall in this area is low, and natural lakes and streams are noticeably absent. The western two-thirds of the state comprise the highest area in the Rocky Mountain chain.

Colorado is almost a perfect rectangle in form with dimensions approximately 387 miles by 276 miles. The area is 104,247 square miles, of which only 350 square miles are in water area. Elevation varies from 3,400 feet to over 14,400 feet. A total of 52 of the 67 highest mountains in the United States occur in Colorado, and 75 per cent of the land area over 10,000-feet elevation in the United States is located here.

Although Colorado has a year-round fishing season for all species including trout, much of the high-country fishing is governed by weather and snow melt. Many high lakes remain frozen until mid-June, and high-country roads are seldom free of snow before the end of May. The weather and snow-melt pattern greatly influence stream fishing. Once the spring runoff starts, most streams are high and roily until late June or early July. Streams are seldom clear enough for fly-fishing until late

A brook trout x lake trout hybrid called the splake has been successfully introduced in some Colorado high mountain lakes

June. Early-season bait- and lure-fishing is usually best in May and June during the runoff. However, little difference is noticed in lakes, and often trout can be taken in high lakes on flies as soon as they are ice free.

The best stream fly-fishing is experienced in September. The days are clear and warm and the nights cool at this time. The streams are low and clear. Fishermen and tourists dwindle rapidly after Labor Day, and you have much more choice and freedom in your fishing. An added attraction is the spectacular coloring of the aspen, willow, and scrub oak at this time of year.

Colorado is blessed with vast tracts of public land, mostly Forest Service and Bureau of Land Management lands. This doesn't mean that all waters are open to the public since much of the early settlement in the mountains was along the stream courses in the valleys. Of the 10,000 miles of trout streams in the state, 4,500 miles are private and 1,700 miles of the private category are posted against trespass. The remainder still leaves considerable area open to fishermen, however. The stranger need but ask directions locally for information on best fishing spots. As elsewhere the better waters are not along the main highway.

The State Game and Fish Department vigorously pursues a program of fishing-lake construction and fishing-easement acquisition as funds permit. Since 1949, 36 fishing lakes totaling over 4,000 surface acres have been constructed. During the same period 37 lakes and reservoirs totaling over 39,000 acres have been acquired by purchase, lease, and management agreement. A large hatchery program insures continued stocking of the state's waters. Approximately 1,300,000 pounds, numbering over 24,000,000 fish, are planted annually.

Several mighty river systems are born in Colorado mountains: the Rio Grande, Arkansas, Platte, and Colorado rivers. There are over 2,000 lakes and 1,400 streams, totaling more than 14,000 miles, but lakes over 100 acres and streams over 200 feet wide are rare. Colorado is usually thought of as a trout-fishing state, and, although basically true, there are also 62 plains-area reservoirs that have fairly creditable warmwater fishing.

The annual creel census indicates species availability accurately. The coldwater catch percentages follow: rainbow (74 per cent), brook (15 per cent), brown (7 per cent), cutthroat (2 per cent), and kokanee salmon and mountain whitefish (1 per cent) each. The warmwater catch in descending order of availability is: yellow perch, bullhead, crappie, largemouth bass, sunfish, walleye, channel catfish, white bass, and drum.

THE HIGH PLAINS

The eastern third of the state is a dry, rolling prairie area. Only two major rivers traverse it: the South Platte River in the north and the Arkansas River in the south. Both rivers are tapped extensively for irrigation, and the streams themselves offer practically nothing in the way of fishing. Many irrigation storage reservoirs occur along both drainages, however, and it is these waters which offer warmwater fisheries.

In the northeast corner are two of the best crappie lakes in the state: Julesburg (Jumbo) Reservoir and North Sterling (Point of Rocks) Reservoir. Two- and 3-pound crappie are not rare in North Sterling, and it is generally considered the best warmwater lake. Besides crappie, large walleye, largemouth bass, white bass, and channel catfish are available.

Moving south into the center of the state near the Kansas border there is one lone, large reservoir, Bonny Dam, on the South Republican River. White bass, walleyes, drum, largemouth bass, and crappies are the principal species here.

The central, eastern part of the state is essentially waterless, so the next lakes are found off the Arkansas River in the south. The best of these are Adobe Creek and Horse Creek Reservoirs. Walleye, white bass, and channel catfish are the main species.

The western portion of this third of the state breaks at the foothills. Near the mountains are numerous small irrigation reservoirs, especially from Denver on north. Most of these contain mixtures of yellow perch, bullheads, crappie, and largemouth bass. Trout are present in some of the lakes, and it is actually a transition zone between the warmwater and coldwater fisheries. Some of the better lakes in this area are clustered near the town of Loveland and consist of Lone Tree, Boyd, Horseshoe, and Loveland reservoirs.

FOOTHILLS AND FRONT RANGE

The central third of the state starts the trout-fishing zone. Many small streams break out of the front range to join the South Platte and the Arkansas rivers. All are suitable trout habitat from the foothills on up to their snowbank sources. Small lakes and reservoirs are scattered throughout the front range.

The only drawback to this area is the fact that 80 per cent of Colorado's human population also live in this zone, and the heaviest fishing and recreation uses are concentrated here. Much of the small-stream trout fishery is dependent upon stocking, and the fishing in some areas becomes somewhat artificial. Rainbow and brown trout are the principal species. Brook trout are found in small, high, cold streams and beaver dams. Cutthroat trout are found only in the high remote timberline and alpine lakes.

Best streams north to south in this area are the Laramie, Poudre, Big Thompson, South Platte, and Arkansas rivers. Best lakes north to south are Dowdy, Parvin, Seaman, Jefferson, Tarryall, Eleven Mile, San Cristobal, and Monument.

THE WESTERN SLOPE

This is the true remaining high-mountain wilderness of Colorado. Human population is scattered as compared to the eastern slope, and more variety in fishing areas allows the fisherman to "get away from it all" and avoid gasoline fumes, Sunday drivers, and picnickers.

Many high, remote lakes are present for those who like to jeep, walk, or ride horseback to their fishing. It is the last stronghold of the colorful native trout, the cutthroat. Streams are larger and offer greater variety of habitat and fishing conditions. Mountain reservoirs are present for those who like to fish from boats by trolling for trout and kokanee salmon.

Best streams going from north to south are the North Platte, Yampa, White, Colorado, Roaring Fork, Frying Pan, Gunnison, and Rio Grande rivers. Best reservoirs

Skilled anglers take a big trout on Colorado's Roaring Fork by float fishing the headwaters in the spring season

north to south are Lake John, Granby, Shadow Mountain, Williams Fork, Vega, Twin Lakes, Taylor, Road Canyon, La Jara, and Vallecito.

Best natural lakes occur in primitive areas. The northernmost are in the Routt National Forest north of Steamboat Springs. South of here start the White River Flattops which have numerous high lakes and generally excellent fishing. Grand Mesa east of Grand Junction has 170 lakes about half of which offer fine fishing. The high country west of Aspen has several excellent high lakes.

Two high lake areas in the southern part of the state complete the grouping. The eastern area is in the Upper Conejos River drainage. The western area takes in the rugged San Juan Mountain region north and east of Durango. The San Juans have been termed "the roughest continuous stretch of mountains in the North American Continent." Only two spectacular automobile passes cross this range, the so-called "Million Dollar Highway" (cost a million dollars a mile) on the west and Wolf Creek Pass on the east. Most fishing in the back country is reached only by foot and horseback. Colorful scenery is an added attraction to fishing in the San Juans.—W.R.S.

COLORADO SQUAWFISH *See* Northern Squawfish
COMELY SHINER *Notropis amoenus* A medium-sized minnow seldom exceeding 4 inches in total length, the geographical range of the comely shiner is from New York southward to North Carolina on the eastern slope of the Alleghenies. The body of the comely shiner is long and compressed, the depth contained 4.7–5.5 times in

its total length. The head is relatively large, being contained 0.25 times in the total length. The mouth is oblique, jaws equal; and the eye is equal to or greater than the length of the snout. The pharyngeal teeth are in two rows 2,4–4,2. The lateral line is decurved, ending in a faint caudal spot. There are from 37–39 scales in the lateral line with 9 scale rows in a crosswide series (6 above lateral line). The origin of the dorsal fin is well behind the insertion of the pelvic fins. The dorsal fin is about ½ the distance from the dorsal origin to the occiput. The number of rays in the dorsal and anal fins are 8 and 10–11, respectively. The color of this minnow is translucent green, sides silvery; and there is a faint lateral band. This minnow is similar to the rosefin shiner (*Notropis ardens*), the difference being that the rosefin shiner has greater than 40 scales in the lateral line, whereas the comely shiner has 39 or less.

LIFE HISTORY

Practically no work has been done on the life history of the comely shiner. This minnow is a common inhabitant of the larger streams throughout its geographical range except for brackish-water areas. It is associated with sand and clay bottom streams, and is tolerant of a pH range of 5.0–7.4. It spawns in early spring.

This minnow serves as forage for the channel catfish, largemouth bass, bluegill, redfin pickerel, and redbreast sunfish. It is also sold as bait. —D.E.L.

COLUMNARIS *See* Diseases and Parasites
COMMON POMPANO *See* Pompano
COMMON SHINER *Notropis cornutus* A large, silvery shiner with a large head, mouth, and eyes. The exposed parts of the lateral scales decidedly deeper than long; body slab-sided; snout rounded. Complete lateral line with 37–40 scales. Dusky dorsal band, but lateral band lacking. It ranges from Colorado eastward to the Appalachians. There are several subspecies.

Common Shiner

LIFE HISTORY

This shiner is a streamfish, preferring pools in clear, rapid water. It may also be found in lakes having tributary streams. The common shiner feeds extensively on both terrestrial and aquatic insects. Vegetable matter in the form of algae is also found in its diet. Spawning in streams in spring and early summer, the common shiner builds a depressed nest in fine gravel about 12 inches in diameter and 1–2 inches deep. Large schools of brilliantly colored spawning adults are found during breeding time. Males become bright blue with rose-colored fins. The common shiner averages 6 inches long and occasionally reaches 8 inches.

ECONOMIC VALUE

This shiner is famous as a bait species. *See also* Propagating Baitfish as a Business *under* Fish Culture—R.A.J.

Comely Shiner

COMPASS ROSE Diagram of the compass card indicating the 360 degrees of the compass; used on charts.

COMPRESSED The body form of a fish when it is thin or flattened from side to side in appearance. A sunfish has a compressed body. *See* Anatomy

CONCHS Conchs are marine snails of the order Mollusca, which contains clams, oysters, chitons, squids, and octopuses. Closely related to slugs, limpets, and freshwater snails, they are soft-bodied animals lacking vertebrae and having more or less of a head, with a pair of eyes, a muscular foot for locomotion, and gills. The shell is spirally coiled, and the animal manufactures the calcium shell through chemical secretions of its body. A horny cover or operculum covers the opening of the shell and protects the animal, and is also used for moving, digging, and sometimes in fighting and obtaining prey. The sexes are in separate animals, and eggs are laid in tough capsules. The necklacelike spirals of flat disks sometimes seen along shore are the egg cases of the whelk, one of the common conchs. Sometimes the egg cases are fan-shaped or flower-shaped. Conchs are often predaceous but may scrape algae from rocks and the bottom, or they may probe the soft bottom muds and sands for food.

One of the commonest snails in the West Indies is the queen conch, *Strombus gigas*, which is widely renowned as a source of food and for its beauty as a souvenir. Its length sometimes exceeds 15 inches and it is one of the largest conchs in the United States. The heavy, flaring lip varies from a pale pink near the edge to a rich rose toward the inner parts. It is commonly found over turtle-grass beds, where it appears camouflaged by dense growths of fouling organisms on the shell. But sharp-eyed natives take large quantities of them in shallow water using glass-bottom buckets and conch hooks or nets, while many conchs are taken while diving. It is certainly one of the important staple seafoods of the West Indies. Bahamians sometimes use them for dinner horns, for baiting lobster and fish traps, and as hook-and-line bait for reef fishes.

Piles of conch shells are common in the Caribbean where Islanders utilize the mollusk as food and bonefish bait

The helmet conch (*Cassis*) is also a snail, somewhat triangular in shape, and having a massive shell. It is more often found on sandy bottoms than the queen conch, and, while edible, it is somewhat bitter and difficult to remove from the shell for food. A species occurs in the Caribbean, and another is found in the Mediterranean, where it is used extensively in making cameos.

The left-handed whelk (*Busycon*) is a common snail along the East Coast of the U.S. and the Gulf of Mexico. Its shell is more delicate than the queen conch or helmet shell and is pale with irregular, brownish-red stripes running lengthwise. Common over mud and sand-mud bottoms, it is a scavenger and predator as well. It is eaten to some extent, and about a half million pounds are sold annually, obtained largely from New England, the middle Atlantic Coast, and Chesapeake Bay. Eaten fried and in chowder, called "scungilli," it is also used for baiting crab traps.

The horse conch (*Fasciolaria gigantea*) is a large, orange-colored snail found in Florida, sometimes growing to nearly 18 inches. It has a long spire at either end and is tapered nearly symetrically. The flesh is bitter and seldom eaten. *See also* Fish Cookery —D.dS.

CONEY *Cephalopholis fulva* This is one of the most common and perhaps the smallest of groupers, it is fairly abundant in southern Florida and much more so in the West Indies. It occurs throughout the tropical American Atlantic. Seldom reaches over 15 inches in total length.

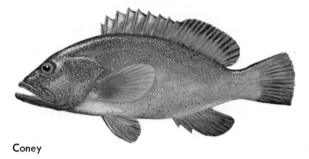

Coney

The coney has 9 dorsal spines; dorsal rays 14–15, usually 15; anal rays usually 9, and pectoral rays usually 18. Posterior nostril about as large as the anterior. Insertion of pelvic fin under or behind lower end of pectoral base. Posterior margin of caudal fin convex. General coloration variable; red, brown, or yellow, usually with small, light blue spots. Two black spots on top of caudal peduncle.

The number of dorsal spines distinguishes this grouper from the others except the graysby (*which see*). It is distinguished from the latter by the more numerous dorsal, anal, and pectoral rays and by the two black spots on top of the caudal peduncle.

ANGLING VALUE

Occurs on rocky bottom in relatively shallow water. Too small and sluggish to be called a gamefish but frequently taken bottom-fishing by anglers using live or dead bait.

An excellent-eating, pan-sized grouper. Highly valued as a food fish in the West Indies. —L.R.

CONGER EEL *Conger oceanicus* This large marine eel is a favorite with anglers in Europe and also finds some commercial sale. It may be confused with two other species in European waters: the freshwater eel (*Anguilla anguilla*) and the moray or murry eel (*Muraena* sp.). The latter is separated at once from conger by having a distinct "step" between head and trunk, whereas in the conger the join is smooth and even; and the moray is a very southern species.

North of the latitude of southern Britain freshwater eels and congers may occur around the coasts, and this will lead to some confusion. The conger has a large (typically "fishy") eye, which separates it at once from the small-eyed "yellow" or immature river eel. However, the "yellow" eel matures into a large-eyed "silver" eel, so more criteria are needed. In the conger the gill opening is large, in the river eel small. In the conger scales are absent altogether; in the river eel they are reduced but present, as small leaf-shaped granules embedded in the skin. Looking at the mouth profile, the river eel's lower jaw projects beyond the upper; in the conger the two are practically equal in length or else the upper jaw slightly projects. Inside the mouth the river eel has patches of small rasping teeth on the jaws and roof of the mouth. The conger's teeth are those of a predator, forming a sharp serrated cutting edge continuous along the margin of the jaws. Reflexive snapping of these jaws will continue long after death, and may cause serious injury to an incautious hand or foot.

Like other eels, conger have the 3 fins dorsal, caudal, and anal in one continuous band around the tail. In the river eel it starts dorsally just above and behind the pectoral fin. In the conger the dorsal edge starts much further back. Also like other eels, both lack pelvic fins.

The front or anterior pair of sensory nostrils in the conger are tubular; the posterior pair are set far back by the front edge of the eye.

The skin of the conger is slimy, and its color somewhat variable. Normally they tend to be black on the back and silver on the belly, but this varies with the bottom over which they are taken. Conger from rocks tend to have a purple-black tinge (so-called "black conger"); while those taken over sand or shingle have a bluish tinge and when grayish are called "white conger." Some of these color phases are similar to the mature or "silver" freshwater eel, but most of these are rarely far advanced in maturity inshore and still have tints of bronze in the back and yellow in the belly. Their scales may appear as gold or cream flecks, which are absent in river eels. Conger fins have a black edge, and the lateral line is picked out with dull gray spots. These are not seen in river eels.

The normal habitat for congers is among rocks or other broken ground, as they habitually get their tails into a crevice and use this as home territory. One of the features of the fight of a hooked conger is the tremendous pull to get back to this "safe" place, and then the immobility of the fish once it has wrapped its powerful tail around some obstacle. Conger range between 400 feet deep and in such shallow water that some can be stranded during low spring tides in rock pools. Sometimes they are found and taken like this by fishermen visiting lobster pots.

They will penetrate a short distance into brackish water and estuaries, especially into a harbor with its wealth of old piers, pilings, and wrecks. Though these, and rocks, are their normal daytime haunt at night they will emerge and forage along beaches, taking both angler's baits and fish on long lines. Conger living in deep-water wrecks are less markedly nocturnal and may be encountered by scuba divers.

The geographical distribution of conger and their close relatives is practically cosmopolitan—in the Atlantic, Pacific, and Indian oceans. In European waters conger are found from the Mediterranean northward to Scandinavia. However, this is the northern part of their range, for they most decidedly prefer warmer waters. Even around Britain they may be killed by cold temperatures. Many, for instance, were killed in the Irish Sea in the exceptionally severe winter of 1947, and further mortality was reported in the winter of 1962–1963.

Active mainly at night, conger hunt by their keen sense of smell. Their diet is mainly small rock fishes (including other congers) and squids or octopus. Conger have few natural enemies beside larger conger; when young some are eaten by birds, and when older some are taken by dolphins. Most natural control must therefore be from high mortality when in the larval state. A large conger is in fact extremely hard to kill by normal means. There is a lymph-heart in the tail, which may be destroyed by a hard blow across the back. This does not stop reflex action, however! The jaws are still dangerous even after death.

Having few natural enemies, conger may grow to a good size. Females are much larger than males; they reach 6–8 feet long as against 2–3 feet for males. Various maximum weights for females are quoted: 130–160 pounds and 9 feet long, for example. Few exceed 60 pounds, and specimens over 80 pounds are extremely rare when taken by angling methods. Females are much more numerous than males, as well as being larger. The majority of conger are over 30 inches, and nearly all these are female. The rod-and-reel record for Britain is 85 pounds.

LIFE HISTORY

The details of the life history of the conger eel predate that of the freshwater eel by relatively few years. Basically it is like that of the freshwater eel. About six months before they will move out to spawn the conger ceases to feed. When this period is up they will leave the inshore waters and migrate out to sea. Unlike the Atlantic freshwater eels of Europe and the United States they do not return to a single spot like the Sargasso. They only go as far as deep water off the coastal Continental Shelf whence they migrated. Thus, Mediterranean conger travel to the deeper parts of that sea rather than, as the freshwater eels of Mediterranean lands do, out through the Straits of Gibraltar and across the Atlantic. The conger from the European Atlantic coast move out to sea, over the Continental Shelf, and spawn in an area about 1,600 fathoms deep between 30° and 40° north latitude.

The maturation of the conger is completed shortly before and during the spawning migration. Like the freshwater eel, these changes in maturity involve degeneration, and it is likely from these that the conger also spawns only once in its life and then dies. The changes from the immature but powerful and malevolently handsome inshore fish and the breeding eel are immense and almost more far-reaching than those of the river eel. The teeth soften and fall out; the bones decalcify and become soft and cheeselike; the muscles atrophy and become feeble; the body fat is lost during the 6-month premigration fast and turns to water. Males especially may become ulcerated; sores appear on the skin and eyes and even blindness may follow. Pérard calls this enfeebled creature a "rubber conger." It is too feeble to recover from migration and the spawning effort if it is this far gone *before* spawning.

These observations are based on captures far out to sea, and upon congers held in aquaria. Males will mature completely even in shallow aquaria; females have never been seen in full mating condition. It has been suggested that sheer bathymetric (water) pressure is essential to complete the maturation of the female from the immediately prespawning "rubber conger" state.

Even this partial knowledge of one sex is more than we have for the freshwater eel, which does not mature in any sort of captivity. Here bathymetric pressure may be the stimulus for both sexes; and conger studies have been much used to suggest the probable events in the less-known story of the maturing of river eels.

The mating of conger, like that of river eels, has never been observed. Eggs stated to be those of conger have, however, been found. They were suspended at a considerable depth over the spawning ground, and 2½–3 mm in diameter.

The post-hatching larvae of conger have been known for a long time to science, but, like those of other eels, were not recognized as such. The willow-leaf-shaped larvae of eels were considered to be a separate type of fish, and called "*Leptocephalus*." The larvae of the conger were called *L. morrisii*; while those of the river eel were called *L. brevirostris*.

Even at this early stage the two may be distinguished. Samples of both at about 1 year old were taken off Gibraltar in 1930 and studied live by Spärck. He found that the conger larvae used at least four times as much oxygen as river eel larvae. This confirms an older observation by Dean in 1912, who found conger larvae extremely active little fish. They also differ from freshwater eels in some physical characters, principally in the number of vertebrae developing and muscle blocks and in the position of the vent or anus. Bertin in 1926 put this difference as a percentage:

$$\frac{\text{Muscle segments before vent}}{\text{Muscle segments after vent}} \times \frac{100}{1}\%.$$

His figures were 45 percent in conger, 30 percent in river eel larvae, and only 5 percent in the larvae of moray eels.

It had been hinted even as far back as the 1860's by United States scientists that "*Leptocephalus morrisii*" was in fact a larval conger eel. Conclusive proof of this assumption was, however, lacking until 1886, when Delage saw the transformation into a young conger; in 1891 Calandruccio and Grassi (the latter famous for his pioneer work on malaria mosquitoes as well) saw various "leptocephalus" larvae turn into young eels, and were able to relate "species" of "leptocephalus" with various eels, including conger and river eels. Today the various leaf-shaped transparent and planktonic larvae are still called "leptocephali," but the terms "*L. morrisii*" and "*L. brevirostris*" are not used.

The slow migration back from the breeding ground to the inshore waters takes 1–2 years. When near the coast the leptocephalus larva of the conger is nearly 5 inches long. It then changes from a laterally flattened larva into a cylindrical transparent young conger (or "glass eel") only 3 inches long. This shrinkage in length at the change-over was one of the main difficulties in the way of an early recognition of the true nature of "*Leptocephalus morrisii*." It did not seem possible to 19th-century scientists that a 5-inch larva could change into a 3-inch eel. But it has since been shown that the leptocephalus larva fed extremely actively and this caused a rapid early growth.

The small transparent conger takes up its position and behaves as it will do in future. The normal colors are assumed at about 12–15 inches long. The growth rate in the wild from this point onward has not been reported. Under aquarium conditions and with intensive feeding they are said to put on 18 pounds in two years, 66 pounds in four years, and 87 pounds in 5½ years.

COMMERCIAL VALUE

Conger "steaks" (transverse slices) are not uncommon in the fish shops of European maritime countries. As such, they are used for feeding pets, especially cats, or for human food. However, they are not nearly so frequently eaten as the river eel, even though the conger is a far cleaner feeder.

Most commercial conger are taken on long lines over rocky ground, though a proportion are taken in trawl nets.

ANGLING VALUE

Size for size the conger is the most powerful adversary encountered off the British coast, attaining weights upwards of 100 pounds (British rod-caught record 84 pounds).

Conger, nocturnal by nature, haunt rocky weed-covered ground, old wrecks, broken harbor walls, and the mouths of deep-water estuaries, where they prey on live fish, squids, and crabs.

The fight of a hooked conger, in its efforts to break free, consists of a strenuous series of back-breaking power dives, and when finally brought thrashing to the surface it often spins furiously, kinks the trace, and escapes. Even when gaffed and brought aboard, the angler's troubles are not over, for great care must be taken to avoid the powerful snapping jaws.

Strong tackle is vital where conger run large, and for offshore fishing over deepwater marks, where they grow to the largest sizes, a powerful but flexible 6-foot rod and a heavy-duty single-action reel containing plenty of 80 pound-test Dacron, together with a reliable harness, are required.

The bait, which must be fresh, as conger are not scavengers and refuse stale offerings, should be presented on a forged steel size 10/0 hook attached to a well-swiveled stainless steel trace. Fresh mackerel, herrings, and squids are the favorite lures.

Large conger eels are encountered all around the British Isles, but particularly dense concentrations are found off the coasts of Devon, Cornwall, Southwest Wales, and Southern Ireland.　　　　　　　—D.M.

CONNECTICUT At first glance Connecticut would appear to offer relatively little in the way of fishing opportunity. It is small, very densely populated (over 2½ million people) and is in the heart of a very intensively industrialized region of the United States. In its favor, however, is its 250-mile coastline on Long Island Sound, about 160 lakes and ponds that range in size from 30 to 5,000 acres, and approximately 300 streams which are stocked annually with trout. There is also a unique type of aquatic habitat that satisfies a wide range of fishing interests existing in two of the major rivers in the state, the Connecticut and Thames. Marine species such as winter flounder, fluke, mackerel, weakfish, "snapper" bluefish, and striped bass can be taken in the lower 15 miles of the Thames. The striped bass also provides a unique winter fishery. The Connecticut River being longer and larger provides an even greater variety of fishing opportunity. In addition to the species found in the Thames there is a run of American shad that results in fabulous sport fishing in May and June. Large numbers of white catfish and a good population of northern pike as well as all other warmwater species found in the state can be caught in the Connecticut River.

It would be impossible to maintain top-quality or even a modest amount of fishing in such a densely populated area as Connecticut without giving these recreational assets proper consideration. An intensive fisheries management program geared to the existing conditions has been successful. Despite the high degree of development of the waters of Connecticut, the Board of Fisheries and Game has constructed some seventy public boat-launching sites on lakes and ponds, ten sites on its major rivers, and ten on Long Island Sound. It has also been able to provide some better-than-average trout fishing in lakes and ponds through reclamation and careful management in a few waters. Another means of providing trout fishing has been the stocking of 1½- and 2-year-old brown trout in selected ponds that have an appreciable volume of good-quality water; brown trout of these sizes can do well in the face of competition from the existing warmwater fish population. This finely tailored stocking policy provides some fairly consistent trout fishing—where the trout survive the fishermen's offerings in spring and summer they return to the surface in fall and again afford some better than average sport.

LONG ISLAND SOUND

Though there are only 98 airline miles between Rhode Island and New York, as mentioned previously, the Connecticut coastline is some 250 miles long. The 1960 population in 24 shoreline towns was just over one million people; so about 35 percent of the state's population reside in these coastal towns year round. In addition, approximately 41,000 summer residents move into the area. This, plus the fact that most any resident in Connecticut can reach the coast and be on the water fishing in under two hours, adds up to a tremendously popular fishery. All public and private boat-launching facilities are very heavily used by fishermen. There is what might be termed exceptional fishing activity in the waters of Long Island Sound for practically nine months of the year. Seasonally, the first and probably most sought-after species is the winter flounder or blackback (*which see*),

which appears in March and April. The army of small-boat or outboard fishermen moves out after an impatient winter to take this tasty bottomfish in astounding numbers. The tautog or blackfish, though an unspectacular-appearing species, is nevertheless high in the category of poundage landed. Along the rocky coast, fishermen commonly measure their catch of blackfish by the bushel or tubful. With the onset of summer conditions in late June, the winter flounder move offshore, and the summer flounder or fluke move in. Being more of a fish eater, the fluke is taken by a wider variety of fishing methods and is considered somewhat a gamier fighter than winter flounder. Also in this late-spring and early-summer period, striped bass move into Connecticut waters on their northern migration from Chesapeake Bay and the Delaware and Hudson rivers. A great amount of effort is spent by striped-bass fishermen in trolling, casting artificials both top and bottom, and throwing whole bait such as squid or eels for this reputable fighter. Even more fishing is done at night by the real bass fishermen. In midsummer, another bottom species, the scup or porgy, is taken in large numbers and poundage when the larger and more colorful species such as the blues and bass are not hitting. Connecticut was formerly a favorite area for weakfish, but, unfortunately, there have not been large, northward migrations of this species for over twenty years. In late summer, the bluefish, believed by many to be the fightingest fish that swims, come into Connecticut waters. The baby "snapper" blues move into the bays, estuaries, and rivers in large schools and provide good fishing on light tackle from bridges, docks, and small boats for young and old, male and female alike. In some years, butterfish or mackerel can be taken in the same areas and by the same methods to add variety and spice to this inshore fishing. The big blues are usually out in the deeper waters, and larger boats and heavier tackle are in order. When a flock of birds starts to work over a school of baitfish which have been driven to the surface by the bluefish, there is

One of the favorite spots to fish for shad is by the spillway at Enfield Dam, Connecticut. Peak fishing is in April

real excitement in such popular fishing grounds as the Race, Plum Gut, or the Bloody Ground. Mixed in with the bluefish in the fall are the striped bass schooled up for their southward migration. This is truly an exciting time for saltwater fishermen in Long Island Sound. Mixed bags of bluefish and trophy-sized bass can add up to fishermen's paradise when the timing is right. In the fall, the bottom fishermen get another period of top-quality sport before the long winter months set in when the blackfish really become active again before moving offshore. Also, the winter flounder return to the inshore waters when temperatures cool down. Another fishery becoming more popular out of Connecticut ports has been the off-shore fishery for school bluefin tuna in Block Island Sound. These school tuna run 15–40 pounds. These same boats also take a considerable number of swordfish each season. For the hearty saltwater enthusiast, there is even offshore fishing for cod all winter.

TROUT FISHING

Though approximately 300 streams are stocked annually with catchable-sized trout, most of these are marginal in so far as water quality. For the most part, the streamfishing can be considered the put-and-take variety. The emphasis in the state's stocking program is on 2-year-old brown trout. Brook trout are stocked in some of the very small streams and in the major streams where they are expected to provide immediate fishing for the not too skillful angler in the early part of the season. The brown trout, however, seem to persist in many of the streams throughout the entire fishing season, and better than average fly-fishing can be had by the more skillful anglers. Streams that have a reputation for being consistent spring, summer, and fall producers are the Housatonic River in Cornwall, Sharon, and Kent; the Saugatuck River in Weston and Westport; the Pequonnock River in Monroe; the Pomperaug River in Woodbury; the West Branch of the Farmington River in Colebrook, Hartland, and Barkhamsted; the East Branch of the Salmon Brook in Granby; the Salmon River in Colchester; the Fenton River in Mansfield; the Mt. Hope River in Ashford; Bigelow Brook in Union; and the Natchaug River in Eastford. In these streams and their tributaries there is also a possibility of catching the occasional wild brook trout that has run down from the tributary system or the occasional brown trout that is rugged enough to carry over from year to year and then indeed becomes a challenge to even the more skillful angler.

As previously mentioned, Connecticut has carefully selected certain ponds having a sufficient layer of cool and well-oxygenated water, which will not only support trout during the critical summer months, but may be of sufficient quality and volume to insure the carry-over of the longer-lived and somewhat hardier brown trout. It is interesting to note that the waters carrying over some trophy-sized browns are for the most part those that have populations of landlocked alewives. The board is making an effort to introduce this desirable forage species (for both trout and warmwater gamefish) in several more impoundments throughout the state. A few ponds are intensively managed for trout via the reclamation technique, and these produce phenomenal yields to fishermen, but, unfortunately, because of the heavy traffic, nontrout species are reintroduced in a disappointingly short time.

Ball Pond Ball Pond is located in the township of New Fairfield. It is 90 acres in size, has a maximum depth of 62 feet and an average depth of 23 feet. This pond has both a public boat-launching site and commercial liveries for the use of fishermen. This pond has been reclaimed, and it is managed for rainbow and brook trout. It is extremely rich, even for a trout pond, and, as a result, it is possible to stock this body of water with 1–2-inch spring fingerling rainbows and have them attain a size of 8 inches by the fall and 10–12 inches the following spring. In addition to stillfishing and trolling for trout in the conventional fashion, a popular method of taking rainbows is under a light at night. It has been estimated that in the neighborhood of 20,000 to 25,000 trout are harvested from this 90-acre lake each season.

Wononscopomuc Lake This beautiful lake of 352 acres in the northeast corner of the state, town of Salisbury, has a reputation for being one of Connecticut's best producers. Its maximum depth is 108 feet. It has an average depth of 36 feet and even its bottomwaters are well-supplied with dissolved oxygen. Although the stocked brown and rainbow trout do not utilize these great depths, a modest lake-trout population prevails, with some fish in the twenty-pound class. Wononscopomuc, or Lakeville Lake as it is commonly known, is controlled by the town of Salisbury, but the "Town Grove," however, boasts an exceptionally fine beach, picnic area, boat livery, and launching ramp. Based on a four-year experimental stocking program involving brook, brown, and rainbow trout in this lake, Connecticut formed the basis of its current trout-stocking policy for lakes and ponds (75 per cent 2-year-old brown trout; 25 per cent 2-year-old rainbow trout) containing warmwater species. In addition to the fine fishing afforded by the annual stocking of brown and rainbow trout, occasional holdover brown trout up to 8–9 pounds are available to the fishermen.

East Twin Lake This body of water is in the same township as Lakeville and has essentially the same physical and chemical characteristics. It is somewhat larger, being 562 acres in size with a maximum depth of 80 feet and an average depth of 32 feet. There is a good boat livery available for fishermen's use. East Twin Lake seems to have assumed even greater popularity than Wononscopomuc Lake for yielding good catches of browns, including the occasional holdover trout. East Twin Lake is receiving attention in a kokanee (*which see*) management program. The kokanee average 16 inches in size and weigh approximately 2 pounds.

Highland Lake Highland Lake, in the township of Winchester, is another good trout pond. It is 444 acres in size and has a maximum depth of 62 feet and an average depth of 20 feet. Here again, there are adequate boat-launching facilities, and good catches of the hatchery-stocked brown and rainbow trout are made. An attempt is also being made to manage kokanee in this body of water.

West Hill Pond West Hill Pond fits in the category of the two above-described waters. Located in the town of New Hartford, it provides fishing for residents in the vicinity of Hartford and the north central part of the state. In addition to commercial liveries, it has a public boat-launching site. It is 238 acres in size, 59 feet deep, and has an average depth of 32 feet.

Lake Saltonstall Lake Saltonstall is a water-supply reservoir for the city of New Haven. It is located in the township of East Haven and Branford, and although close to the coast, it has a maximum depth of 108 feet (lake bottom is 88 feet below sea level). It is 410 acres in size and has an average depth of 41 feet. Unfortunately, fishing opportunity is confined to a limited number of permits obtainable from the New Haven Water Company. Saltonstall is one of the few waters possessing a population of landlocked alewives. Though receiving only a light stocking of trout, due to its semi-private nature, this lake, nevertheless, produces trophy-sized brown trout annually. Five-pound fish are not uncommon, and several 8–12-pound specimens have been recorded.

Crystal Lake Crystal Lake is a 200-acre body of water in the townships of Ellington and Stafford that also has a population of landlocked alewives. Accordingly, this is reflected in the good holdover and growth rate of brown trout. In addition to the trout fishing, it provides a fair number of smallmouth bass. Yellow perch are of good average size, and are heavily fished in both summer and winter. Crystal Lake has a maximum depth of 50 feet and an average depth of about 20 feet. It has both public and commercial boat-launching facilities.

Gardner Lake This lake lies in three towns: Salem, Montville, and Bozrah. It, too, is quite sizable, being 487 acres with a maximum depth of 43 feet and an average depth of 14 feet. There has been good angler success in recent years for stocked brown trout, and occasional holdover individuals appear in the anglers' creels.

WARMWATER FISHING

Strange as it may seem, some of the same waters mentioned above as good trout producers prove to be good warmwater, gamefish and panfish producers. This is particularly true for East Twin Lake, Salisbury, which, in addition to trout, produces an excellent crop of large-mouth bass; the same applies to Lake Saltonstall near New Haven, another exceptional largemouth producer. Despite what might be considered a poor state for fishing, it is in this warmwater category where Connecticut may prove to be rather unusual. A compilation of sportfishing records in Connecticut resulted in the following information:

Mashapaug Lake in Union has yielded a 7-pound 10-ounce smallmouth bass (*Field & Stream* honor award) and also from the same water a 12-pound 14-ounce large-mouth bass (1961 winner of the *Field & Stream* northern division). The state record for northern pike is a 16-pound 11-ounce specimen from the Connecticut River. A white catfish weighing 8½ pounds was caught in Candlewood Lake, and Wononscopomuc Lake has yielded a 7½-pound chain pickerel. Some of these records are exceptional; nevertheless, many other fish approaching these weights have also been creeled. Some of the better warmwater producers are as follows:

East Twin Lake Statistics on this body of water have been mentioned previously; in addition to the fine trout and largemouth-bass fishing in recent seasons, those who have been interested in panfish have had a heyday also. Tremendous strings of 8–12-inch yellow perch and large-sized bluegill sunfish are being recorded routinely.

Bantam Lake Bantam Lake, in the townships of Litchfield and Morris, is one of the bigger impoundments in Litchfield County, being 916 acres in size; it has a maximum depth of 25 feet and an average depth of 14 feet. It is well-supplied with commercial boat liveries. Bantam produces good largemouth bass, but like most heavily fished waters, this species is often taken by the more skillful anglers fishing at night. Yellow perch and largemouth bass are abundant in all age classes and exhibit growth rates well above the state average. White perch appear to be more abundant in Bantam Lake than in most other lakes in the state, and their growth rate in the past 15 years is greatly improved; this could be due to their reduction in numbers by heavy fishing pressure.

Lake Lillinonah Lake Lillinonah is a hydroelectric impoundment on the Housatonic River and is in the townships of Newtown, Brookfield, Bridgewater, and Southbury. It is 1,900 acres in size, 100 feet at its deepest point, and is rather steep-sided throughout its long, narrow length. An attempt to introduce the walleye has apparently been unsuccessful; however, a few individuals of this species are recorded each year from Lake Zoar, the impoundment which lies immediately downstream of Lillinonah. Fishing for largemouth and smallmouth bass has been excellent in Lake Lillinonah. The growth rate is rapid for both species, as it is for yellow perch, white perch, and bluegill sunfish. Good public boat-launching facilities are available at Lillinonah as they are at Lake Zoar.

Wood Creek Pond Wood Creek Pond, situated in the town of Norfolk, is state-controlled and has a public launching site. It is 151 acres in size and has a maximum depth of 8 feet. It is considered a better-than-average largemouth-bass pond, but the growth rate is above average for yellow perch and chain pickerel. Good bullhead fishing is enjoyed in the spring of the year. The state draws the pond each fall as a management method to improve the growth rate of the gamefish and reduce the panfish population which could tend to become overabundant and stunted.

Black Pond Black Pond, in the towns of Meriden and Middlefield, though only 75 acres in size, is an excellent bass producer. It has a 23-foot maximum depth and an average depth of 8.6 feet. A few catchable-sized trout are allotted to this lake each year. Again, one of the reasons for the healthy state of the warmwater fish population is the presence of a landlocked alewife population. The growth rate for both chain pickerel and largemouth bass is good. Yellow perch, though not as abundant as in some waters, are better than average size in Black Pond.

Moodus Reservoir Moodus Reservoir is a rather large shallow impoundment of 451 acres with a maximum depth of only 10 feet. The largemouth bass is the dominant gamefish species here, but yellow perch, bluegill sunfish, and calico bass are abundant. The growth rate of the largemouth bass is about equal to the state average. Until very recently, the pond was drastically drawn by late summer in connection with industrial use. This inadvertently resulted in the healthy largemouth bass population. Now, with more stable water levels, it is expected that the bass will have more competition, and growth rate will drop off somewhat. Both public and commercial launching facilities are available at Moodus Reservoir.

Waumgumbaug Lake This body of water, also known as Coventry Lake, is located in the town of Coventry and is 377 acres in size, has a maximum depth of 40 feet and an average depth of 28 feet. The outstanding gamefish species in Coventry Lake is the smallmouth bass. Although the growth rate for smallmouth bass is slightly below the state average, the bass are very abundant, and hence catchable-sized specimens are available to the angler. Bluegill sunfish and yellow perch are abundant, and both exhibit an excellent growth rate. Both public and private boat-launching facilities are available.

Mashapaug Lake This beautiful lake is located in the town of Union and has a surface area of 297 acres, a maximum depth of 43 feet, and an average depth of 9 feet. It receives a rather liberal stocking of catchable-sized brown and rainbow trout; yet its reputation lies in its ability to produce exceptional-sized largemouth bass, smallmouth bass, and chain pickerel. As previously mentioned, it has produced two record-size bass for the state and some exceptionally large pickerel. The growth rate for both game- and panfish species is at least equal to the Connecticut average for all species. There is indication that recent introductions of landlocked alewives have been quite successful. Public boat-launching facilities are present.

Pachaug Pond Pachaug Pond, in the town of Griswold, is another large, shallow, fertile impoundment with a surface area of 831 acres and an average depth of 6 feet. Much of the wooded shoreline is in the Pachaug State Forest. Pachaug has for years enjoyed the reputation of being one of the state's best largemouth-bass waters. Yellow perch and bullheads are common in abundance, with the bluegill sunfish being very abundant. As with Moodus Reservoir, this pond was a better producer of big largemouth bass when heavily drawn for industrial uses. Though the state now controls the water rights, it is quite impossible to employ drawdown as a fish-management tool until after the summer recreation season ends on September 1.

Connecticut River It is believed that the Connecticut River is just "arriving" as a fishing area. It was long felt that industrial and domestic pollution rendered the fish inhabiting the river worthless for human consumption. Sportsmen are gradually coming to realize that the real reason for a decline in anadromous fish populations has been the large number of dams on the Connecticut and its tributaries and not gross pollution. It is true that there is still some pollution in the river, but the mere fact that it supports a spawning population of American shad (*which see*) is indicative of the fairly good standard of water quality. The Connecticut River, one of New England's largest, slices the state into two nearly equal portions. Its length in Connecticut is approximately 80 miles, and it is within easy driving distance of nearly 2 million persons.

It has been estimated that anglers take between 25,000 and 35,000 shad each year using a wide variety of methods and tackle. One of the most popular spots on the river is the Enfield Rapids Dam where fishermen stand on the abutments of the dam or line the banks on either side of the river for several hundred yards downstream of the dam. Most of these fishermen use spinning tackle and cast a wide variety of small jigs, spinners, or beaded lures. Also popular is the boat fishery in midriver at this same dam. Here again, small jigs, a willowleaf spinner, or colored beads are used on either fly or spinning rods. Other locations are the Windsor Locks Bridge, a boat fishery near the Windsor Locks-Windsor town line, the lower Farmington River in Windsor, and also the Salmon River some miles downstream in the town of East Haddam.

Another fishery increasing in popularity in the Connecticut River is for northern pike. Pike in the 5–15-pound-size class are taken with live bait or conventional pike-fishing lures, such as wobbling spoons, by anglers who have learned something of the habits of this fish. Early spring and late fall are popular times for pike fishing in the vicinity of Wright's Cover, Portland, near the Glastonbury-Rocky Hill ferry slips; the mouth of the Farmington River; and the mouth of the Scantic River.

The white catfish has also become popular in Connecticut. This species is found from the brackish waters in Saybrook throughout the river up to the Enfield Rapids area. They are particularly abundant in the vicinity of Hamburg Cove in Lyme in the fall of the year and near Hartford in the early summer months. Being omnivorous in their feeding habits, white catfish can be taken more readily by fishermen who experiment with a variety of baits. These catfish run as large as 5 pounds in the river with an average size of about 1¾ pounds.

With the existence of nine public boat-launching sites on the river, there is certainly plenty of room for fishing opportunity in this large stretch of water bisecting the middle of the state. —J.G.

COPEPOD Tiny member of the crustacean subclass Copepoda that includes the parasitic sea lice. They are aquatic and may be either free-swimming (providing a rich source of food for fish and other predators) or live on the bodies of larger animals.

COPPER ROCKFISH *Sebastodes caurinus* This rockfish (*which see*) is found from southern California to southeastern Alaska, and is abundant in and near the Strait of Georgia. It is distinguished by the slightly thickened rays in the long, blackish pectoral fins, the coppery brown

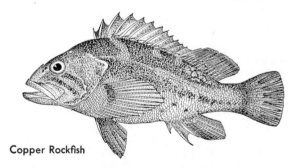

Copper Rockfish

coloration, and the 40–48 scales in oblique rows above the lateral line. It reaches a length of 20 inches. —J.R.

CORAL *See* Coral Reefs *under* Marine Ecology

CORBINA *See* Drums

CORDAGE A general term for rope of all kinds

CORNETFISH *Fistularia tabacaria* Also erroneously called the trumpetfish. (*Aulostomus maculatus* is of a different but very similar family to the Fistulariidae.) Related species occur in the eastern Atlantic, Indo-West Pacific, and the eastern Pacific. It ranges to both sides of the Atlantic. In the western Atlantic it is found from the Gulf of Maine and Bermuda to Rio de Janeiro and throughout the Gulf of Mexico.

The body of the cornetfish is very elongate, much depressed, always broader than deep; head very long, the anterior bones much produced, forming a long tube, terminating in a small mouth; both jaws and usually the vomer and palatines with small teeth; branchiostegals 5–7; gills 4, a slit behind the fourth; scales absent; bony plates on various parts of the body, mostly covered by skin; a single dorsal fin, placed posteriorly; caudal fin forked, the middle ray produced into a long filament; anal fin similar to dorsal and opposite it; ventral fins abdominal, far in advance of dorsal with 1 spine, 4 rays; pectoral fins small, preceded by a smooth area.

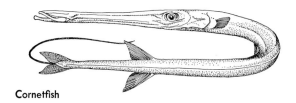

Cornetfish

Head 2.7 to 2.8 in standard length; depth 28 to 37; dorsal 14–15 rays; and 13–15 rays. Head in vicinity of the eye quadrate, slightly broader than deep; snout very long, depressed, its length 1.35–1.4 in head; eye 9.8–11.5; bony interorbital 4.7–5.5 in postorbital part of head; mouth oblique; lower jaw projecting; maxillary broad posteriorly, about 10 in head; skin slightly rough; lateral line posteriorly armed with bony scutes, but these are not evident in the young. The ventral fins are small and are inserted nearer base of caudal than tip of snout; pectoral fins rather small, 9–10 in head.

Color in life greenish-brown above; pale below; sides with a row of blue spots close to vertebral line on back; sides and back with about ten dark crossbars, the spots and bars disappearing in preserved specimens, leaving the back uniform brown; caudal filament deep blue.

LIFE HISTORY

This species is said to reach a length of 6 feet, but most specimens seen are 2–3 feet. It apparently feeds on small fishes and shrimp. Its life history is unknown. —J.C.B.

CORVINAS Cynoscion **spp.** This group is closely related to the weakfishes of the Atlantic Coast, and is in the same genus. It could be said that the weakfishes are Atlantic Coast corvinas or vice versa. Corvinas are found from Alaska to Peru along the Pacific Coast, with the majority of species below the Mexican border. Only the white sea bass is consistently found in the northern part of the range. The shortfin corvina is occasionally taken in southern California waters. They are much sought after by commercial fishermen. Only the totuava and white sea bass are extensively caught by sportsmen in coastal waters. The orangemouth corvina was successfully introduced into the Salton Sea from the Gulf of California and at present supports a large sport fishery.

As a family (The group is well-described in "*Peces de importancia comercial en la costa noroccidental de México*," by Julio Berdegue A.; in California Fish and Game Fish Bulletin 91, "*Common ocean fishes of the California coast*," by Phil M. Roedel; California Fish and Game Fish Bulletin No. 113; and in "*The ecology of the Salton Sea, California, in relation to the sport fishery*," Boyd Walker, Editor.) the corvinas are distinguished by a lateral line which extends out on the tail to the end. There are two spines in the anal fin. In appearance, the corvinas have a metallic iridescence on the body, and the fins are usually orange or yellow. The back is gray, bluish, olive, or bronze, while the belly is generally white. There is no barbel on the lower jaw.

ANGLING VALUE

The corvinas are highly regarded game- and food fishes. They are caught by still-fishing with live bait or trolling and casting with artificial lures such as plugs, spoons, and leadheads. Corvinas can also be caught on the fly rod using large streamer flies. As food fish corvinas are obtained in California, but they are more common in Mexico, Central and South America. The popular South American pickled-fish *seviche* is made from corvina. *See also* Fish Cookery, Gulf Corvina, Orangemouth Corvina, Shortfin Corvina, Striped Corvina, Totuava, White Sea Bass   —J.R.

COSTA RICA This is a new frontier, and though comparatively few facilities exist for the sportsman Costa Rica can provide exceptional Pacific sailfish and tarpon angling. The country is made extremely diverse by its geography; broadly speaking, the Atlantic or Caribbean side of Costa Rica consists of rain forests and mangrove swamps; but inland it varies from deciduous woodlands and savannas to alpine and semiarid (xeroptic) terrain. It can be pleasantly cold on a Costa Rican trout stream, yet tropically hot on a coastal tarpon river just a hundred miles away. This second smallest country in Central America probably has the greatest variety of fishing contained within a land area of 19,652 square miles.

Here you can find the jungle rivers of the Caribbean coastal plain plus an offshore fishery for Atlantic big-game species, high mountain streams cold enough to support trout, and the tidal rivers of the Pacific coast at lower elevation and its offshore fishery.

Although there is no winter or summer season in the Temperate Zone sense, it is important to plan a Costa Rican visit between December and the middle of May. The mountains (one volcanic peak reaches 11,322 feet) in part determine the rainfall, which can make fishing impossible in either Atlantic or Pacific shore rivers. During the wet season they become extremely muddy. However, in offshore fishing where turbidity is not a factor the prevailing winds must be taken into account and the better period for moderate seas is from April through September. The mean annual temperature in Costa Rica varies from 80°F in the low areas to 59°F at 5,000-foot altitude.

ATLANTIC SIDE

The principal gamefish on the Caribbean shore of Costa Rica is the tarpon. All the fishing is done within rivers or their estuaries which flow clear from January through April. Large runs of tarpon enter freshwater during that period, notably in the Parismina River and its tributaries (the Cabo Blanco, Cabo Negro, the California River, and Tarpon Creek). The tarpon range from 20 to over 100 pounds with progressively larger fish entering

Sailfish are extremely abundant in the summer months off Costa Rica's west coast. Fish of 100 pounds are not unusual

the rivers until the peak period in April and May. The average weights are uniformly high, with 50–70-pound tarpon common. The fish are taken primarily by trolling and plug casting or casting leadhead bucktails. Due to the depth of these coastal rivers fly fishing has only sporadic success. Snook also occur in weights exceeding 20 pounds, although not in great numbers except at the river mouths and in the surf, which is generally muddy. However, there is an excellent run of large (25–35 pound) snook in the Colorado River in late September. Other good tarpon rivers are the Colorado River and its tributaries near the border of Nicaragua and the Frio River and its tributaries which drain into Lake Nicaragua. Like the Parismina, these are sparsely settled jungle streams. There are accommodations on the Colorado River at Barra del Colorado, but no facilities on the Frio. The San Juan River, which in part forms the northern border of Costa Rica, offers good tarpon fishing at the rapids near El Castillo in Nicaragua. Although the rapids are 70-odd water miles inland, sharks follow the migrating tarpon right up the San Juan and can "apple-core" a hooked fish if you don't work them fast—or get lucky.

There are several small freshwater gamefish endemic to these same river systems—such as the guapote, mojarra, and machaca. Of these, the machaca is probably the most interesting from the angler's point of view; it feeds to a large extent on seed pods that fall from jungle trees. The pods can be simulated with a small (No. 4) plastic or cork-bodied bass bug by slapping the lure on the surface. School oriented and therefore greedy at the strike, a machaca moves swiftly and hits the lure hard. Machaca seldom weigh more than 4 pounds, but provide wonderful action on a light fly rod or spinning rod. They are usually found in quiet places under overhanging trees along riverbanks.

PACIFIC SIDE

The Pacific coast of Costa Rica offers excellent sailfish, wahoo, and roosterfish, and an abundance of dolphin. Occasional black and striped marlin also occur. Sailfish are numerous, particularly in the Gulf of Papagayo on the northern end of the Pacific coast; here thirty-five strikes per day (in July) is a recorded average. Rustic accommodations exist at Bahia del Coco west of Liberia, which is reached by rental car from San José. Check San José tackle shops on the availability of charter boats in this area. The only established Pacific coast camp is located near Palmar Sur in the southern portion of the coast.

The west coast rivers (which only run clear during March and April), such as the Tarcoles and Terraba, are fished for black snook, corvina, various snappers, jacks, and jewfish. Black snook up to 64½ pounds have been caught. Trolling with deep-running plugs is the commonly used method.

TROUT FISHING

Unknown to most tourists is Costa Rican trout fishing. Both rainbows and browns have been introduced to many rivers flowing at high altitude, and only a very limited angling pressure exists. Fish of 2–4 pounds are fairly common. There is good fishing in the Savegre, Macho, Poas, and Coto Brus rivers. The latter has produced rainbows up to 9 pounds in weight. The closed season for trout is from November through February, with the best period for fly fishing and spinning from April into June.

No license is required for saltwater fishing. A license is required for freshwater (trout) fishing obtainable at the Ministerio de Agricultura, Calle 1, Avenidas Central and First, Marshall Building. You must present a valid passport or tourist card and two passport-sized photos.

TACKLE

A heavy-duty spinning or bait-casting rod is preferred for the tarpon rivers on the Caribbean side of Costa Rica. Trolling with large (1–2 ounce) plugs is the most effective method, and most anglers use 20–30-pound-test monofilament lines and 30–40-pound-test wire leaders. Naturally, more experienced fishermen will go lighter. Leadhead bucktails of 1–2 ounces in white and yellow are frequently effective; the best lure for snook is a yellow darter type of plug. Although these waters, like most inland rivers, are not ideal for fly fishing you may want to try it, in which case a 9-foot fly rod calibered for No. 11 floating and sinking lines is recommended.

The same spinning or bait-casting outfit can be used on the Pacific shore for casting and trolling, but suitable big-game tackle is necessary for offshore work (4/0–6/0 reel, 20–30-pound-test line, and a 9–12-ounce rod).

There is a well-stocked tackle shop in San José where all replacement items can be obtained. Tackle and lures purchased in Costa Rica are approximately 20–30 percent higher than in the U.S. due to high import duties.

The climate in San José (altitude 3,000 feet) is pleasant and mediumweight clothing is comfortable. In the coastal fishing areas the weather is usually hot; here lightweight clothing is more suitable. In the mountains at trout stream elevations it can be cool and a warm sweater or jacket is advisable. Be sure to bring rain gear, as heavy but brief rains are common to the subtropics. —A.J.McC.

COTTONMOUTH JACK *See* Milkymouth Crevalle

COTTONWICK *Haemulon melanurum* This grunt occurs in the Florida Keys and the Bahamas southward throughout the Caribbean area to Brazil. Mature adults average about ten inches in total length, but larger individuals are sometimes taken. It is distinguished from all others by the color pattern; the back, the upper half of the caudal peduncle and the caudal fin are black. The inside of the mouth is pale red. The cottonwick has 12 dorsal spines; dorsal rays 15–17, usually 16; anal rays 8; and pectoral rays 16–18, usually 17. Pored lateral-line scales 49–51. Gillrakers 21–23. Its pectoral fins are naked.

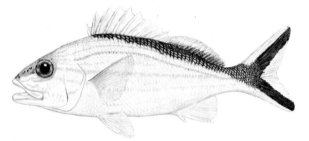

Cottonwick

The cottonwick prefers clearwater and avoids murky inshore waters in Florida where it is usually found about the outer reefs. In the Bahamas, it may be found in the usually clear inshore waters.

ANGLING VALUE

This species is good sport on very light tackle. Like other grunts, the cottonwick is taken on cut bait such as mullet, pilchard, and shrimp. This grunt is good eating. A panfish not taken as frequently as other species of grunt. —L.R.

COWFISH *Acanthostracion quadricornis* The cowfish is one of the trunkfish family (Ostraciidae). The trunkfishes are named because the head and most of the body are enclosed in a hard, boxlike shell composed of polygonal plates. This carapace is so rigid that the fishes are able to move only their caudal peduncle, fins, eyes, and mouth.

In *Acanthostracion* the carapace is more or less triangular in cross section, the ventral surface being essentially flat. There are two preocular spines on the head which are directed anteriorly and another pair projecting posteriorly from the lower rear part of the carapace (hence the specific name *quadricornis*). The cowfish is colored with bright blue or blue-green spots or short lines, those on the cheek usually arranged to form several horizontal bands. The ground color is usually yellowish or olive.

In the western Atlantic there is a second species of cowfish (*A. polygonius*) which is less common than *quadricornis*. It has circular or hexagonal blue markings,

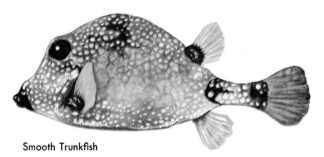

Smooth Trunkfish

one in each of the hexagonal plates except dorsally on the carapace and on the head where there is a reticulum of blue. It has 12 instead of 11 pectoral rays as in *quadricornis*. There seems to be a distinction in habitat in the West Indies, *quadricornis* being found most often on seagrass flats and *polygonius* on reefs.

The cowfish reaches a total length of about 18 inches. It is found in the western Atlantic Ocean from Massachusetts southward to Brazil, including Bermuda, the West Indies, and Gulf of Mexico. It is not common north of the Carolinas. There is one record from South Africa.

Other western Atlantic trunkfishes include the black-spotted *Rhinesomus bicaudalis* which has a single pair of spines extending from the ventroposterior part of the carapace, the common smooth trunkfish (*Rhinesomus triqueter*) which has no spines and is spotted with white, and the large *Lactophrys trigonus* which has the pair of posterior spines, a highly arched sharp dorsal ridge on the carapace, and an isolated small plate dorsally on the caudal peduncle behind the carapace.

Some authors classify all the western Atlantic trunkfishes in the genus *Lactophrys*. —J.E.R.

COWNOSE RAY *Rhinoptera bonasus* It superficially resembles the spotted eagle ray and bullnose ray (*which see*) in its broad disk with pointed pectoral fin tips and a long slender tail, and it is usually included in the same family (Myliobatidae) with them. But the snout is deeply indented to form two lobes. In side view, also, the head is deeply indented along its anterior profile. The eyes are located ahead of the pectoral fin margin, slightly protruding from the disk on the peculiar-shaped head. The skin, which is smooth, is brownish above occasionally with yellow hues, and white or yellow-white beneath. It reaches a width of 7 feet and a weight of perhaps 100 pounds.

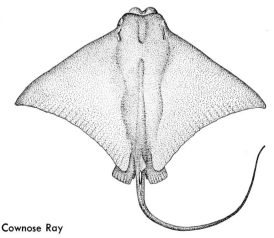

Cownose Ray

LIFE HISTORY

Specimens are known from Brazil to southern New England, with records in the Caribbean only from British Guiana, Venezuela, and northern Cuba, although it should be expected anywhere in the Gulf and Caribbean. It browses across mud- and sandflats in search of food, stirring up food from the bottom with its pectoral fins. It occasionally occurs in very large schools during some years. It eats snails, clams, razor clams, oysters, lobsters, and crabs which are crushed in the pavementlike teeth.

Young are born alive in the spring and summer, and 2–6, measuring 14 inches wide, may be produced each time. Sexual maturity occurs at a width of as small as 2 feet, depending on the latitude. —D.dS.

CRAB The collective name for a large number of marine animals that are related to the lobster and spiny lobster, crabs are classified as jointed-legged animals (*phylum Arthropoda*), and belong to the highly organized crustacea commonly called *Malacostraca*. Within this grouping the true crabs (Brachryura) are characterized by having a flat broad body with the abdomen very short and reflexed in contrast to the long cylindrical body and extended abdomen of lobsters and similar creatures.

Many families are included among the crabs. They are adapted to life in all seas from shallows to great depths. Also some live on land, concealed in rock crevices. Their adaptation to many localities is apparent in their varied structure and coloration. The first pair of walking legs of crabs are fairly large and end in claws or chelae. The remaining 8 legs end in simple points, or, in the swimming crabs, are flattened to form finlets. Most crabs are scavengers and live on plant and animal material found on the bottom.

Small crabs of various species are used as bait by anglers at various times. *See also* Blue Crab, Fiddler Crab, Fish Cookery, Green Crab, Horseshoe Crab, Jonah Crab, Stone Crab

CRAIG FLUKE A common name for the witch flounder (*which see*).

CRANEFLIES Order Diptera Craneflies are the largest of the two-winged flies taken by fish. Resembling overgrown mosquitoes, they are quite numerous along trout streams in the summer months. Craneflies seldom hatch in great quantity and may be considered of minor importance to both the fish and the angler. There are many species of

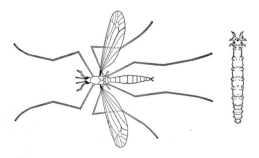

Cranefly Adult and Larva

craneflies. Their wormlike larvae, which are ½–2 inches long, are probably of more interest to gamefish and panfish than the adult insect. These larvae are opaque, and their color is usually pale orange or various shades of

brown. There are numerous imitations of the larval crane fly; spider, skater, and variant-style dry flies represent the winged adult.

CRAPPIE *See* Black Crappie, White Crappie

CRAWFISH (1.) A regional name for the freshwater crayfish (*which see*).

(2.) A regional name for the spiny lobster (*which see*).

CRAYFISH Order Decapoda A small lobsterlike crustacean which inhabits freshwater on all the continents except Africa. In addition to crayfish the order Decapoda includes shrimps, crabs, and lobsters and is so named because all its members have 10 legs. Regionally called mudbug, crawdad, grasscrab, stonecrab, and crawfish in the United States the crayfish is valuable as a food for fish as well as for man. This crustacean is preyed upon by amphibians—such as the bullfrog, reptiles, birds, and mammals (notably the mink and raccoon). Crayfish vary in size from the American dwarf crayfish, which reaches only 1 inch in length, to the Tasmanian crayfish, which attains a weight of 8 pounds. Most crayfish burrow, with a few species living their whole lives underground. Other crayfish never burrow. Some species are restricted to particular types of habitats, while others are able to occupy a variety of waters successfully. Although crayfish all look generally alike, various species differ in their temperature, food, and oxygen needs and in their life cycles.

A crayfish of the genus *Procambarus* or northern crayfish

DESCRIPTION

The body of a crayfish is metameric (segmented) and covered with an exoskeleton of chitin; it has jointed appendages, an open-circulatory system, and a reduced coelom (body cavity). The eyes are compound, stalked, and movable. The body of the adult consists of 19 segments. The first 5 segments form the head; the next 8 form the thorax; and the last 6 form the abdomen. The external demarcation between head and thorax is indistinct. These two regions collectively are known as the cephalothorax, and they are covered by a continuous piece of exoskeleton called the carapace. The serially homologous appendages are modified for a variety of functions. Beginning at the head end are one pair of antennae and one pair of antennules. They are used for balance and sensory perception. The next six pairs of appendages are used chiefly for handling and mincing food. These are followed by five pairs of walking legs, the first pair of which, chelipeds, are greatly enlarged and are used in capturing and crushing food. On the abdomen are found the last five pairs of appendages, swimmerets. The telson, a fanlike tail, forms the posterior part of the abdomen.

Crayfish are versatile animals. More than 300 species are found throughout the world and over 250 species and subspecies are known to occur in North America. There are 29 known species in Louisiana alone. The first crayfish from North America was described in 1798 by Fabricius. Early classification generally included only 2 genera, *Astacus* and *Cambarus*. Today, after many taxonomic revisions, most crayfish in North America can be placed in one of 5 common genera: *Pacifasticus, Procambarus, Cambarus, Orconectes,* and *Cambarellus.* Other genera of limited distribution are: *Faxonella, Hobbseus, Troglocambarus,* and *Fallicambarus.*

The genus *Pacifasticus* includes virtually all crayfish species found from the Pacific Coast landward to the Rocky Mountains and from Canada and Alaska to Mexico. Crayfish in this genus are sometimes called the "European crayfishes" because they are also well represented in Europe and Asia. It is felt by some authorities that these crayfish originated somewhere in Europe or Asia before the Ice Ages, later migrating across the Bering Straits to North America.

The largest genus, *Procambarus,* comprises more than 100 species and subspecies. It is believed that members of this genus originated in the southeastern United States. From here *Procambarus* spread north and eastward, coming up the Mississippi Valley, as well as up the Atlantic Coast. The range today also includes Cuba, Guatemala, Honduras, and Mexico.

The genus *Cambarus,* containing approximately 40 species and subspecies, probably evolved somewhere in the Ozarks of Missouri. Its range presently extends from the Gulf of Mexico northward to Canada. *Cambarus* contains the largest number of cave species (6).

The genus Orconectes, with over 60 species and subspecies, is predominantly found in the Mississippi and Great Lakes drainage systems. It has spread westward to the Rockies, north into Canada, and south to the Gulf of Mexico.

Cambarellus is less widely distributed than the other genera. It probably originated in northern Mexico and moved northeastward through the Southern states. All members of this genus are relatively small, and because of this they are easily overlooked. They are commonly referred to as dwarf crayfish.

Identification of the various species of crayfish is difficult even for the trained eye. Those characteristics most often used to identify a species include the general appearance and form of the cephalothorax, chelae, first-form male pleopod, and the annulus ventralis or sperm receptacle of the female. Of these, the pleopod found on the male is by far the most useful. It is the modified first swimmeret which becomes hardened and assumes a distinctive shape, and is used to clasp the female during mating.

LIFE HISTORY

Life for most crayfish begins, and often ends, in a hole in the ground. This hole is known as a burrow. Burrows vary greatly in complexity. Some may be only a few inches deep, serving as a temporary home, while others are over 40 inches deep. Most burrows have a mud chimney or are capped with a mud plug. Although the time of year for mating varies with the species and the region, the Louisiana red swamp crayfish (*Procambarus clarki*) is fairly typical. Mating occurs in May or June when the female becomes receptive to the advances of the male. The female then digs a burrow which the male enters later. At this time the male crayfish deposits sperm in an external receptacle on the female. The sperm are held until the eggs are laid in late summer or early fall. As the eggs are laid, they are fertilized by the sperm held by the female. After fertilization the eggs are attached to the swimmerets of the female's tail by a sticky substance called glair. The number of eggs laid may vary greatly with the species, from only a dozen to as many as 700 in some red swamp crayfish.

The eggs appear in a cluster on the underside of the female's tail, and she is then said to be "in berry." The eggs usually hatch in two or three weeks. Once hatched, the young stay attached to the female for a week or so, where they usually undergo two molts. Later the young leave the female and begin to forage for themselves. Prior to this the burrow is their nursery and home. Crayfish are omnivorous and will eat a variety of food items. Plant material composes the bulk of the diet along with small organisms (periphyton) that are attached to the plants. When available, however, animal material is preferred. Many crayfish species are nocturnal in habit and most are secretive, usually remaining hidden under rocks and logs. The life span of most species east of the Continental Divide is usually from 1–3 years; some Pacific coast crayfish and the European species reach 6–7 years.

NORTH AMERICAN DISTRIBUTION

Crayfish may be caught in almost any body of water throughout North America. However, in some states this crustacean is more abundant. In Louisiana—and to a lesser extent in Mississippi, Texas, and Alabama—the sport fishery (for food) reaches significant proportions. In the spring, for example, cars are parked all along the 80-mile stretch of Airline Highway from Baton Rouge south to New Orleans. Often the water fished is nothing but an open drainage ditch. There are 29 species of crayfish in Louisiana, but most of those caught in the southern part of the state are the red swamp. Farther north the white river crayfish (*Procambarus blandingi*) becomes more important. In Louisiana there is no limit or closed season. However, these crustaceans are much more active and more easily caught at water temperatures above 55°–66°F. Below this they become sluggish.

In California crayfish are sought by anglers throughout the state. Small lift nets, baited with fish offal, are used. The species *Pacifastacus klamathensis* is the principal one caught. Although utilized as food, this species is also important as bait, especially for large brown trout.

In Oregon crayfish are very abundant, and the state ranks second only to Louisiana as a commercial producer. The most ideal habitat is found in slower-moving streams typical of the flat agricultural valleys of western Oregon. The flood plains of the lower Willamette River and its tributaries and the sloughs of the Willamette and Columbia rivers are scenes of the heaviest harvest. The principal species caught are *Pacifastacus trowbridgii* and

P. leniusculas. Although the season is usually open year round (in the past limits have been set at 144 crayfish per day) the best period for this sport corresponds roughly to the open season for trout.

Washington also has an extensive fishery. A commercial permit is required, and certain regulations must be followed. Crayfish can only be taken from specified waters and only with shellfish pots. A size limit of 3¼ inches in length is also in effect. The legal open seasons vary from April through October, depending on the area fished.

Among the important species in the Eastern states is the northern crayfish (*Orconestes virilis*) which grows to 5–6 inches in length. Its habitat ranges from warmwater streams to large, coldwater lakes. The northern crayfish has some commercial value in Wisconsin; its range extends to Maine. Another Eastern species, the pond crayfish (*Procambarus acutus*) reaches a similar size and appears to have a wide distribution due to transplanting. The mud crayfish (*Orconectes immunis*) is common to shallow, mudbottomed waters with heavy vegetation. It burrows deep into pond and swamp bottoms and can survive drought periods by reaching the lowered water table. This species, incidentally, is in demand among bait dealers because of its relatively thin shell, and may be called "paper-shell crab." Mud crayfish occasionally occur in streams.

Elsewhere in the East a number of crayfish can be found. The stream crayfish (*Cambarus bartoni*) is a very ubiquitous species, seldom growing over 3 inches long; it is well distributed east of the Mississippi River. The stream crayfish prefers cold, small streams having a bottom of rocks or gravel. *Orconectes limosus*, or spring crayfish, is also widely distributed, but is originally found in the Mississippi drainage. It has spread northeast and along the Atlantic coast. This species occurs in ponds, lakes, and streams as far north as Maine. The Allegheny crayfish (*Orconectes obscurus*), a large species, is common to the streams of western Maryland. Its main area of abundance is to the west and north of the Alleghenies in clear streams with gravel bottoms. Another fairly common species is *Orconectes rusticus*, or midwest crayfish, found in Illinois, Michigan, Ohio, and south to Missouri and Alabama.

HOW TO CATCH CRAYFISH

Crayfish may be caught in a number of ways. The casual method is to turn over rocks in a stream and grab the crustacean by hand. To gain an advantage, you might have a long-handled dip net ready to net the crayfish as it scuttles along the bottom. A novel method is with tin cans. In some streams, where hiding places for crayfish are limited, a string of tin cans provides the necessary cover, and one need only inspect the cans periodically. Another method is with a pole, string, and some kind of bait, such as chicken necks or liver. Tied to the string the bait is lowered in the water and the slack is kept out. When you feel one on, slowly raise the bait, and as the crayfish breaks water quickly net it before the crustacean releases its grip.

The most efficient way to catch crayfish is with nets or traps. In waters over 10 feet deep modified crab pots baited with fish heads are used. Floats are tied to the line to mark the trap. In shallow water lift nets and minnow traps with a funnel entrance are used almost exclusively.

To keep a crayfish alive when using it for bait twist a piece of pipe cleaner around its body and run the hook underneath

The bait—usually pieces of fish, beef melt, or fish heads—is tied to the center of the lift net. The net is lowered in the water and raised at suitable intervals. The funnel traps are usually made of ¾-inch mesh wire and are 30 inches long. Baited traps are fished at about 10 per acre. The captured crayfish are emptied via a trapdoor in the top.

CRAYFISH FARMING

A number of states are involved in the commercial fishery. In 1970, for example, approximately 20 fishermen fished in the Sacramento River delta from May 18th through September 10th. Over 83,000 pounds were landed at Courtland, California, for a total of $32,430. Most crayfish caught by commerical fishermen on the West Coast are shipped to Sweden or France. Crayfish farming per se has now begun in Missouri, Texas, Mississippi, and Arkansas. However, the bulk of the United States industry is limited for the most part to Louisiana, and until a few years ago was found almost exclusively in south Louisiana. Even with this limitation, well over 10 million pounds—valued at some $5 million—are harvested annually, and more than 35 processing plants have been licensed by the Louisiana Board of Health.

The bulk of the Louisiana crop is comprised of the red swamp crayfish, with substantial numbers of white river crayfish also being harvested. Until recently most crayfish were taken in the wild, particularly in the Atchafalaya basin, which is the flood plain of the Atchafalaya River, a stream in Louisiana that begins near Simmesport and empties into the Gulf of Mexico near Morgan City.

Levees enclose the basin, which is approximately 17 miles wide and 75 miles long. During years when winters were mild and water was sufficient in the fall the basin produced bumper crops. This could be expected about two years out of five. In 1964 and 1965, for example, wild populations from the Atchafalaya basin were the largest ever. The bumper crops were a result of hurricane "Hilda" in October 1964, which flooded the basin with tidewater and rain.

In the Southern United States crayfish are currently being farmed in three types of ponds: rice-field, wooded, and open ponds. In rice-field ponds crayfish are rotated with the rice. The general procedure followed by rice farmers is to remove water from the rice field about two weeks before harvesting. This permits drying of the field to facilitate harvest. When drying begins, crayfish burrow. The second growth of rice and grasses, along with rice straw, provides food for the crayfish.

Wooded areas are also used, but make poor crayfish ponds. Dense growths of trees and shrubs hinder harvest. Wooded ponds usually have poor wind circulation, resulting in oxygen depletion. Also, water in wooded ponds is often acid, resulting in a low pH and a low total hardness. Neither condition is conducive to good crayfish production. Despite these drawbacks wooded areas are sometimes used for farm ponds because the land is idle and owners feel some production is better than none.

Open ponds are often constructed solely for crayfish farming. The procedure for managing these ponds is generally the same as for farming wooded and rice-field ponds. Crayfish are stocked in the ponds in late May or June. Brood stock, usually bought from a dealer, is planted at rates of 25–50 pounds per acre, depending on the amount of vegetation and the number of native crayfish present. Once stocked, the crayfish burrow. In July the ponds are drained, mainly as a means of predator control, since raccoons and wading birds may make serious inroads on the population. When young crayfish are found in the burrows, generally in September and October, the ponds are flooded to release them. Once the ponds fill, the young forage on native aquatic plants such as alligatorweed, water primrose, and smartweed. If the winter is mild crayfish can be harvested the same year. Some farmers may harvest the first crop as early as Thanksgiving. Typically, it is spring of the next year before the main crop is ready.

Crayfish cultured in ponds are captured in the same manner as in the wild. Both lift nets and funnel traps of chicken wire are used. Chicken-wire baskets or cages are baited with cut shad, beef melt, or fish heads. A trapper usually handles 5–10 traps per acre, depending on accessibility. Lift nets are fished in a similar manner. Most crayfish farmers employ professional fishermen who are paid one-half the live weight market price.

Ponds with good production might yield from 200 pounds to as high as 800 pounds of crayfish per acre. Some report up to 1,000 pounds per acre. The early farm-raised crop brings the best price, and may sell for over 60¢ a pound live weight. Later, when the "wild" crop comes in, the price declines. When it drops below 15¢ a pound many commercials stop trapping. All told, the price generally averages 25¢ a pound. By May the season has peaked and by June the harvest tapers off, and most of the crayfish have become tough.

The future of the industry looks promising and ponds devoted to crayfish farming are increasing annually. In Louisiana over 12,000 acres were devoted to culture in 1969. In 1970 the figure climbed to 25,000; and in 1971 close to 40,000 acres were in crayfish ponds.

Compared with catfish culture little capital is needed to get started with crayfish farming. Levees can be constructed with rice-field equipment or with conventional farm equipment. By setting up a pump for filling ponds from a nearby stream or bayou, or sinking a well, the farmer has his water. No feed is used and harvesting presents no real problem since trapping rights are usually leased. Profits for the pond owner range from $50–$100 per acre.

Research on crayfish farming is being carried out by the Agricultural Experiment Station at Louisiana State University, Baton Rouge, Louisiana.

CRAYFISH DISEASE IN EUROPE

The American crayfish (*Orconectes limosus*) was brought from North America to Poland in 1890 by Max von den Borne and released into a small pond supplied with fresh water from the Hysla River near Barnowek, Zielona Gora province. Since that time, owing to its natural migratory tendency and also with the help of humans, the crayfish has expanded all over the country's lakes and rivers, ranking third after *Astacus astacus* and *Astacus leptodactylus* in the Polish shellfish industry. It received its Polish name "striped crayfish."

The reason for the introduction of *Orconectes limosus* into Poland and France (1894) was the economic consequences of the spread of the parasitic mold *Aphanomyces astaci*. This disease appeared in Italy in 1860, in France in 1876, in Germany in 1878, in Russia in the 1880's, in Finland in 1893, and in Sweden in 1907. It is a most unusual parasite, since the mold kills not only its individual host but, in a short time, the whole population of crayfish. Only rarely, and in small waters, have crayfish populations proved capable of recovery. In Sweden large bodies of water have had crayfish with the disease chronically since 1907. The propagation of the disease in these cases is probably maintained by an intermittent downstream spread of crayfish from lakes situated above dams and streams far away from the infested lakes. No alternative host has been found.

The American species in Europe proved to be resistant to the disease. The size of this American crayfish, however, is comparatively small. The flavor is also considered inferior to that of the *Astacus astacus. Orconectes limosus* proved to be a river-dwelling species, and to be able to stand modestly polluted water; it spread in an uncontrollable way and exterminated *Astacus* within a few years wherever the species commingled.

FOOD VALUE

Crayfish are greatly esteemed among gourmets the world over. Similar to a lobster in texture and flavor the meat differs chemically in that it contains more phosphorus than fish flesh. There are many ways to prepare crayfish (*see* Fish Cookery) but boiling in the Cajun style with herbs, lemons, onions, and salt or in traditional Scandinavian style in great quantities of fresh dillweed and salt are two of the most popular. In Louisiana the crayfish is not only eaten but is honored at festivals and jubilees in "crayfish races." The fierce Houma Indians who once roamed what is now Terrbonne Parish in Louisiana so admired this crustacean that they adopted it as a battle symbol. In Scandinavia the crayfish is the subject of annual ceremonial banquets or *krebfests* in the month of August.   —J.W.A.

CREEK CHUB *Semotilus atromaculatus* A medium-sized, silvery minnow with a single, small barbel near the end of each jaw. This barbel may be hidden between the maxillary and premaxillary. The creek chub has a large mouth, with the upper jaw reaching to or beyond the front of the eye. This fish is bluish above and lighter below, the adults having a dark spot at the base of the dorsal fin. The creek chub is widely distributed from Montana to eastern Canada and south to the Gulf of Mexico. Within its range the ubiquitous creek chub is found in almost all streams capable of supporting fish life. It is a small-brook or creek species throughout the spring after which most fish move downstream to the larger waters. During the spawning season the males acquire a rosy coloration along the sides, and tubercles form on the head. The adult creek chub is usually 3–8 inches in length, and although they have been reported in excess of 11 inches, this size is rare.

ANGLING VALUE

Aside from being a prized bait species and providing forage for stream-resident predator fish, the creek chub has some value as a panfish and has been reported taken in some numbers through the ice in larger waters.—R.A.J.

CREEL A basket or bag used for carrying fish. The creel is slung from the shoulder by a simple strap or harness while the angler is fishing.

CREVALLE *Caranx hippos* Also called common jack, jack crevalle, cavally, cavalla, horse crevalle, and toro. This species is thought to occur almost around the world in tropical and subtropical waters. In the eastern Pacific it has been termed *Caranx caninus* by some writers, but eastern Pacific and western Atlantic specimens are essentially identical. In the Indo-Pacific it has at times been confused with *Caranx ignobilis* and *Caranx sansun*,

with which species it has never up to the present been adequately compared.

The area between the throat and the pelvic fins of the crevalle has a small circular patch of scales (difficult to see in some very small or very large fish) in a scaleless area that extends up the sides toward the pectoral fins (the only jack crevalle in the western Atlantic and eastern Pacific having this character). The second dorsal fin has one spine and 18–21 softrays; the anal fin has two detached spines followed by one single spine and 16–17 softrays. The first gill arch has 6–9 gillrakers on the upper limb and 16–19 gillrakers on the lower limb. There is a prominent black opercular spot, and a rounded spot on the lower rays of the pectoral fins.

The crevalle develops a high, blunt head, with relatively small eyes located near the anterodorsal profile. The posterior 1–4 spines of the first dorsal fin become separated and covered by skin in specimens over 18 inches long. The dorsal-fin and anal-fin lobes are moderately elongated. The straight part of the lateral line is about $1-1\frac{1}{2}$ times as long as the curved part. There are about 26–35 scutes in the straight lateral line in western Atlantic specimens and up to 42 scutes in eastern Pacific specimens. The gillrakers on the anterior ends of the upper and lower limbs become very short or rudimentary with growth (and difficult to distinguish). It is bluish-black or metallic-green above, silvery and sometimes yellowish below; the dorsal fin is dark and the anal fin may be yellowish. The young, smaller than about 7 inches long, have 5 (rarely 4–6) broad bars on the sides plus one on the head.

In the western Atlantic the crevalle has been taken from off Uruguay to Musquodoboit Harbor, Nova Scotia; it is very rare in the West Indies, and reports of its occurrence at Bermuda need to be documented. In the eastern Pacific it ranges from Cape Aguja, Peru, into the northern Gulf of California and up the outer coast of Baja California at least to San Hipolito Bay; there is a single record from the Galápagos Islands which may be questioned, and it is conspicuously absent from the other islands well offshore. A weight of 55 pounds has been

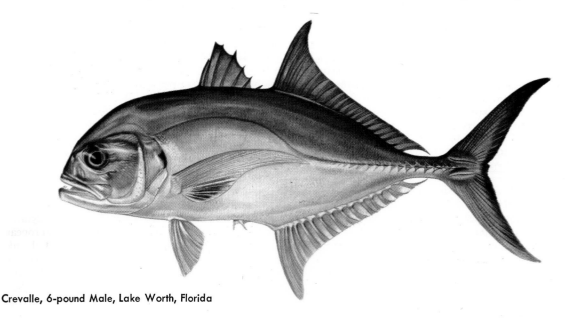

Crevalle, 6-pound Male, Lake Worth, Florida

recorded; but crevalle in the 40–45-pound class are not uncommon in Florida. However, large jacks over 5 feet long and weighing over 70 pounds have been seen and caught, and are probably this species—these larger fish should be adequately documented when caught.

LIFE HISTORY

Life history information is scanty. The crevalle was reported to be in spawning condition in May at Puerto Rico, and specimens with developing eggs were taken in February from Panama and in March from Haiti. Small specimens of the crevalle, less than ½ inch long, have not been distinguished from those of the horse-eye jack (*Caranx latus*). The smallest known specimen, ¾ inch long, was taken in the Gulf of Mexico in May. The spawning season off the eastern United States probably extends from March into September. It is suspected that spawning occurs in offshore waters, for the smallest known specimens were taken there, but the young of 1–2 inches long occur inshore. Early speculation that spawning occurred in saltwater lagoons and bays was based on erroneous interpretations. This species has both very high- and very low-salinity tolerances; it is frequently taken in brackish waters and at times for some distances upstream in coastal rivers. It is probably most common in shallow flats, but very large fish are taken from deeper waters offshore. This is usually a schooling species, but large fish tend to become solitary. Smaller fish seem to be the choice food, but shrimp and other invertebrates are eaten. When taken from the water the crevalle may emit a croaking sound by pharyngeal stridulation. Very large fish develop large, bony growths on many of the median bones, especially in front of the dorsal fin; these are the result of a normal aging, and not caused by parasites or disease, as some have presumed.

ANGLING VALUE

The crevalle is a fierce, stubborn, and dynamic gamefish for trolling, casting, or still-fishing with live or cut bait; and in the late 1800's they were hunted with rifles in shallow water in eastern Florida.

It is frequently sold in Central American markets. The United States commercial catch is concentrated in western Florida, where it is the second most important jack, accounting for less than ½ of 1 per cent of the catch value, and mainly caught by haul seine, runaround gill-nets, and handlines. The taste of smaller fish is good to adequate, but specimens over 1–1½ feet long are reported to be dark and almost tasteless. Cutting off the tail and bleeding immediately after capture improves the taste. In the Indo-Pacific, this species has been considered to be an excellent food fish, although it has been reported there to be moderately toxic when eaten at certain rare times and places. *See also* Carangidae, Jacks, Milky-mouth Crevalle. —F.H.B.

ANGLING TECHNIQUE

One of the several things in the crevalle's favor is the fact that it's a first-class light-tackle fish which can be caught on fly, plug, or spinning gear. Small crevalle up to 6–7 pounds are gregarious and travel in schools. As they become older, big jacks occur in pods, or sometimes you'll see a single or a pair "running" at top speed. Crevalle seldom linger in one spot. When food, such as mullet, is abundant, jacks will chase their prey right up on the sand, against sea walls, or into a boat. In openwater they herd the baitfish into a compact mass, then plow through it from all sides. The individual crevalle takes its feeding seriously. Here and there one mullet will rise above the surface, doing front and back flips, then leaping madly in all directions with a telltale swirl countering each shift. If the hapless baitfish is lucky, it may elude the jack for two or three jumps, but sooner or later the mullet will land in the crevalle's jaws. You can drift through acres of frantic mullet and actually observe this single-minded pursuit.

Ordinarily, jacks are caught on whatever tackle is being used at the time. Plugging is probably the ideal method for most people, and live bait, such as mullet or pinfish, is deadly for the noncaster. Streamer flies tied on No. 2/0 and 3/0 hooks are the usual fly-rod fodder. It is practical to bring along a casting outfit because there are days when fish don't visibly show, and after locating them with a plug, then you can use fly tackle. This is a generally sensible procedure for most types of salt-water fishing. The characteristic feathering slash of a jack at baitfish can be seen a long distance off; so there's usually ample time to decide whether you want the fly rod or not.

The thing to remember about jack fishing is that whatever lure you use should be retrieved progressively faster. A crevalle may slam a plug, for instance, the instant it hits the water, or take it within the first few feet. But if the fish merely boils under it, then speed the plug along. A lure that stops or just doodles along is invariably refused. The faster you pull the bait through the water, the more strikes you'll earn. Also, on a slow retrieve a lot more fish will be missed; this may be due to the jack's relatively tough mouth or the speed with which it raps the lure. When a school is excited, and feeding wildly, the rule is even more inviolable. A whip retrieve is ideal. When fly-fishing you are bound to get in trouble because, as with many otherwise dynamite-charged, salt-water gamefish, such as the dolphin, king mackerel, and the cero to name a few, it's difficult to keep the feathers moving quickly enough to get strikes. With a little practice, however, it's possible (because you have a visible target) to put the fly in front of a jack and strip line in hard pulls.

In common with the permit, large jacks always seem to have an extra ounce of energy in reserve. Their tactics are dogged and unrelenting. It's not uncommon to play a 20-pounder for an hour or more on light tackle. The maximum size of the crevalle isn't really known. Specimens of 35–45 pounds are caught every season in Florida waters, and are not uncommon along the state's southeast coast and down through the Keys. One of the largest crevalle taken in recent years was a 55-pound fish from Lake Worth, Florida. —A.J.McC.

CROAKER *See* Atlantic Croaker, Drums, Spotfin Croaker

CRUCIAN CARP *Carassius carassius* This is a cyprinid fish which has been gaining in popularity with European, and particularly British, anglers over the last decade. It is the closest relative of the common domestic goldfish, *Carassius auratus*. Crucian carp are normally considered to be the European and Asian branches, respectively, of what was once a single common ancestor with a localized habitat. This ancestral home was probably in the region of the Caspian Sea; the Chinese part of the population became isolated, evolving into the well-known goldfish, which is not native west of the Tibetan plateau.

In its turn, the European form, *C. carassius*, has apparently continued a process of evolution; a well-defined variety exists, the Prussian carp. Opinions vary as to whether the Prussian is a variant of the crucian, or a feral goldfish, but the general consensus places it with the crucian as a distinct subspecies, *C. carassius gibelio*. In older texts it was considered a species distinct from either the goldfish or the crucian, as *Carassius gibelio* or (rare and very old) *Cyprinus gibelio*.

Today the true crucian and the Prussian are found together over the same range, which extends over all Europe except Switzerland, Spain, southern Italy, and northern Finland. How native it is over this wide range is not clear; certainly it was introduced into the extremities, especially Britain. The first definite reference to "carrushens" is in 1744; then it was "but lately introduced" to Britain. This is contemporary with the fancy goldfish, which was first kept in Britain during the years 1691–1728. It may have been earlier; Samuel Pepys' diary mentions captive fish which were presumably goldfish in 1665.

It is therefore most likely that both *Carassius* species arrived in Britain simultaneously—and perhaps the crucian was mistaken for goldfish. From whence the crucian first came to Britain is not certain, but scanty evidence suggests north Germany, especially from the port of Hamburg.

The spread of the crucian in Britain since this first introduction in about 1700 is most interesting, poorly documented though it is, as it is one of the few fish observed over many years which has arrived in its place of study within historical times. In the early years, it established itself around London and the River Thames; this is still its main center of population in Britain. Later it spread to East Anglia, and, coincident with the Industrial Revolution of the early nineteenth century, to the Midlands. These areas are still its strongholds, though since then introductions to individual waters have pushed the range just into Wales and into Yorkshire. At present only England has crucian; Ireland and Scotland lack them. It is highly probable that the building of interlocking canal systems during the Industrial Revolution spread the crucian to areas away from London, a reasonable theory on circumstantial evidence.

An adult crucian is a laterally compressed but thickset fish, about 2½–3 times as long as it is broad, with a pronounced humped back. The dorsal fin is long (over 16 scale rows in extent) and its edge convex. The tail fin is barely forked, and very often there is a black spot on the tail root. The back is usually olive-green to muddy brown, the flanks brown-green with "old gold" tints, and the belly yellow-white. Usually the ventral series of fins are tinted with red, and sometimes the tail fin as well. The actual color varies considerably, some populations having a marked brown-silver color scheme, and others with the greens, yellows, and reds more clear. Young fish tend to be much yellower, with bright red fins.

The Prussian carp is similar in color and shows all the crucian characters. It differs in the proportions of the body, being less laterally compressed, or 3½–4 times as long as broad. The scale counts are the same despite their shapes differing. Crucians and Prussians can be distinguished from small common carp by the absence of barbels round the mouth, the common carp having two very prominent ones, and by the convexity of their dorsal fins, the common carp's being concave.

Distinguishing them from goldfish is more difficult. Recently released fancy goldfish may be red, yellow, or patched with several gay colors, but the original wild form, or the coloring they revert to when allowed to run wild for several generations, is identical to the crucian. So recourse must be made to counting fin rays and scales. These are summarized below.

	Crucian	Goldfish
Anal-fin rays	6 to 8	5 to 6
Dorsal-fin rays	14 to 21	15 to 19
Lateral-line scales	28 to 35	29 to 37
Rows of scales from lateral line to front edge of dorsal fin	6½ to 9	5 to 7
Rows of scales from lateral line to pelvic-finbase	5½ to 6	5 to 7
Number of gillrakers	23 to 33	35 to 48

The goldfish generally has the same body proportions as the Prussian variety of crucian. Hybrids between crucian and goldfish are not unknown; those between fancy fish and wild crucian tend to take a crucian body shape and goldfish coloring; but the vice-versa case is met with.

All these fish are typical species of small ponds and sluggish, shallow canals, especially on clay soils. They are rarer in the lower, slow reaches of rivers, and absent from waters of more than very moderate flow.

LIFE HISTORY

Very little is known, and even less accurately investigated, of crucian life histories. They spawn in weedy shallows in their lakes and canals between May and July, the actual spawning date being conditioned by temperature. Large numbers mate in selected areas, but the actual mating act is an affair between only a pair or three fish. Part of the preliminaries is a display dance, swimming in a figure-eight path, rolling at intervals on the surface. This is very evident and can be observed easily when conditions are right.

Crucian Carp

The eggs are small and numerous, as with other carps. Having little yolk, they hatch quickly to small fry, hiding in the weeds from which they were spawned. They feed on animal and plant plankton, together with some epiphytic algae growing on waterweeds. Their diet stays like this throughout life, progressing to larger animals and a higher proportion of algae and plant matter.

Typically, crucians are shoal fish, moving round a lake foraging both by day and by night. In some waters, and with larger fish, the shoals tend to be replaced by small groups of two or three; shoal-splitting is much more likely where common carp inhabit the same water. In such places, the groups tend to aggregate after dark again.

In many waters crucians only feed in summer, but in some their hibernation is intermittent, as they are sometimes caught when the water warms above 40°F. on mild winter days. They are very resistant to high temperatures and oxygen lack and are much more resistant to winter-kill than common carp. These features indeed fit them for a life in small waters prone to dry up almost as well as the tench (which see). In like fashion, they can immure themselves in mud to wait reflooding should the pond dry up.

Crucian are normally rated as bottom-feeding fish, but often they take floating foods and baits. This appears to depend upon the depth of the water, as it is almost unknown in deep clay pits.

Very little is known of crucian growth rates. Their maximum size is perhaps 6 pounds, but fish over 3 pounds are notable specimens. A fish of over 2 pounds is an excellent fish, and the usual caught is ½–1 pound. The actual growth rate appears to vary widely from water to water. One sample shows fish of 2–3 pounds being 6–8 years old; from another water, fish of ¾–1¼ pounds being 7–9 years old. These are extremes, the former water being much better for other species as well. The latter water is interesting in that the common carp also present are even more stunted, fish of one pound being anything up to 10 years old. Plainly in the latter water the common and the crucian occupy ecological niches which do not appreciably overlap, and conditions favor the crucian rather than the common. The life expectancy of the crucian can be taken as similar to the goldfish, about 25 years or more. Predation appears to affect mainly young crucians; so there is a good chance of a fish attaining old age once it exceeds about one pound. The main predator of crucian fry is the European perch, *Perca fluviatilis*.

ANGLING VALUE

Formerly neglected, crucian carp are coming into favor with European pond and canal anglers. Few search for them in rivers, as the shoals are hard to locate. Light bottom-fishing tackle is normally used (though crucians do sometimes take floating crusts), and the best times are summer evenings and nights. The traditional bait is worms, but probably maggots and bread account for more fish. Groundbait is usually employed to attract and keep the roving shoals. The bite is slow and delicate, and the angler should not be impatient to strike. When hooked, the crucian fights hard and doggedly, but without great speed. Hooked in weedy water, they can give a very sporting tussle.

ECONOMIC VALUE

Crucians are not normally eaten for food, except in northern and eastern Germany, although their flesh is good. There they are raised on a commercial scale, especially in flooded quarries and clay pits unsuitable for common carp or other species. On some fish farms which raise pike for the table, crucians are bred in small ponds to feed them. These are small crucians; in the wild the average crucian of ¾ pound is not often taken by pike.

Such small crucians can be used as baitfish, but they are not as attractive as other species, and sluggish unless the water is over 40°F. They travel well in bait cans and are very tenacious of life if carried well-wrapped in wet cloths.

Despite ease of transport, they are not stocked into new waters except by accident. Most responsible organizations and authorities hold the view that they may compete with carp to the latter's detriment, and the crucians themselves overbreed and stunt. Neither of these objections is necessarily true, and some private individuals have continuously stocked small ponds with them. They are attractive fish for ornamental waters.

—D.M.

CRUSTACEAN A member of the Crustacea, the third largest class of the phylum Arthropoda, which also includes the insects. Numbering some 25,000 species, crustaceans are mainly aquatic and range in size from the minuscule water fleas to crabs with leg spans of 9 or 10 feet. Like other arthropods, crustaceans are distinguished by hard external skeletons (often a shell); segmented bodies; and jointed, paired legs. Crustaceans include a major portion of the ocean's plankton, barnacles, shrimp, lobsters, crayfish, crabs, and fish lice.

CUBAN JACK *See* African Pompano

CUBERA SNAPPER *Lutjanus cyanopterus* This fish, also called "Cuban snapper," is by far the largest of snappers. It may exceed a weight of about 100 pounds, and specimens weighing up to 80 pounds have been caught by anglers along the coast of southern Florida. It occurs throughout the tropical American Atlantic.

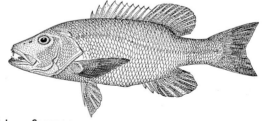

Cubera Snapper

The cubera snapper has 10 dorsal spines, 14 dorsal rays, and 8 anal rays. Pectoral rays 16–17. Gillrakers 5–7 on lower limb of first arch, not counting rudiments. Rows of scales around caudal peduncle 25–26. Cheek scales in 9–10 rows. Upper jaw reaching to vertical from center of eye (young) or from posterior margin of orbit (large adult). Pectoral fin not reaching to vertical from origin of anal fin. Anal fin rounded, not angulate posteriorly. General coloration greenish or dusky gray; paler below; sometimes tinged with red on sides. Black spot on sides of body absent. Eye dark red.

In addition to the large size, this snapper is distinguished from the others by the low number of gillrakers. Anglers sometimes confuse this species with the gray snapper (*which see*).

HABITS

This shallowwater snapper is usually found along ledges in depths of from a few feet to about 20 fathoms. Small- to medium-sized individuals are also known to occur in estuaries and in the tidal zone of the lower course of streams and canals. It takes live or dead bait and artificial lures.

ANGLING VALUE

A very strong fighter, large individuals afford quite a challenge even on fairly heavy tackle. May be taken by trolling close to the bottom in the same way as described under the mutton snapper (*which see*).

FOOD VALUE

Small specimens are good eating, but the large ones are coarse.
—L.R.

CUB SHARK *See* Bull Shark

CUI-UI *Chasmistes cujus* This species (pronounced kweewee) is found only in Pyramid and Winnemueea lakes in Nevada. The sexes differ somewhat in appearance but in general are pale olive, with a dense black lateral stripe in males. The females have a brownish-black back. The head and body are extremely robust, broad, and round; top of head slightly convex. Cheeks puffed out. Eye small. Lips smooth, the lower broad and pendulous.

LIFE HISTORY

Little is known of the habits of this fish since it spends most of its life cycle in deepwater. During mid April it makes a short spawning migration up the Truckee River. It has also been known to spawn over springs along the lake shore. Spawning is suckerlike, and food is not found in the stomachs of migrating fish. Mortality is heavy after spawning. Larger specimens reach 24 inches in length.
—R.A.J.

CULVER'S POMPANO *See* Pacific Permit

CUNNER *Tautogolabrus adspersus* Closely related to the tautog (*which see*), this northern member of the wrasse family is slender, with a long, low dorsal fin, a pointed snout with thick lips, and protruding canine teeth. The gill cover is scaled, and the body scales are larger than in the tautog, there being about 70 lateral scales in the tautog and about 40 in the cunner. It is highly variable in its color, grading from red, or a reddish-brown to bluish, depending on the bottom on which it lives. Uniform brown, with some mottlings, typifies some individuals

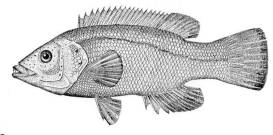

Cunner

while others are olive-green. The young have blotches and dark bars. A small species, it generally only grows to about 10 inches long, although it occasionally reaches 15 inches and a weight of 2½ pounds.

It is the northernmost member of the family Labridae on the East Coast, occurring from Newfoundland to Chesapeake Bay, being most common north of northern New Jersey. Like the tautog, it is a coastal form, being common in nearshore habitats from a few inches deep down to about six hundred feet. But most are taken at 15–100 feet, within 5–6 miles of shore. A bottom dweller, it is very common about rocks, pilings, wharves, ledges, and any place it can find shelter, such as in patches of attached vegetation.

LIFE HISTORY

Spawning takes place in late spring to early August, in deeper water offshore. Young fish move inshore and grow up in shallow waters. During the winter, the cunner may move offshore into deeper water, but it generally stays inshore throughout the year. At the end of 2 years they are 3–4 inches long, and a fish 10–11 inches long is 6–7 years old. Females are larger than males. Cunners eat practically anything, including barnacles, mussels, amphipods, shrimps, lobsters, crabs, clams, and worms.

ANGLING VALUE

They are taken by anglers using clams, crab, or worms. Popular sport fish because of their abundance, the small ones are clever bait stealers. The cunner was formerly important commercially, but despite its fine flesh, it has fallen out of favor in recent years.

CURLFIN SOLE *Pleuronichthys decurrens* A member of the righteye flounders Pleuronectidae, this species is characterized by having the anterior edge of the dorsal fin overlapping onto the blind (eyeless) side extending past the mouth, at least nine rays of the fin occurring on the blind side. The eyes are large and protruding. The body is deep,

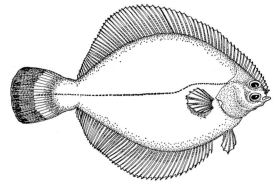

Curlfin Sole

somewhat diamond-shape, but less so than the diamond turbot (*which see*). The small mouth has the teeth chiefly on the blind side, and there is a dorsal, accessory branch to the lateral line which extends posteriorly to about the midpoint of the body. The body is mottled black to yellowish-brown, mottled and with fine spots, and the fins are dark. It reaches a length of 13 inches, and is found from southern California to northwestern Alaska in depths of from 60 to nearly 1,800 feet.

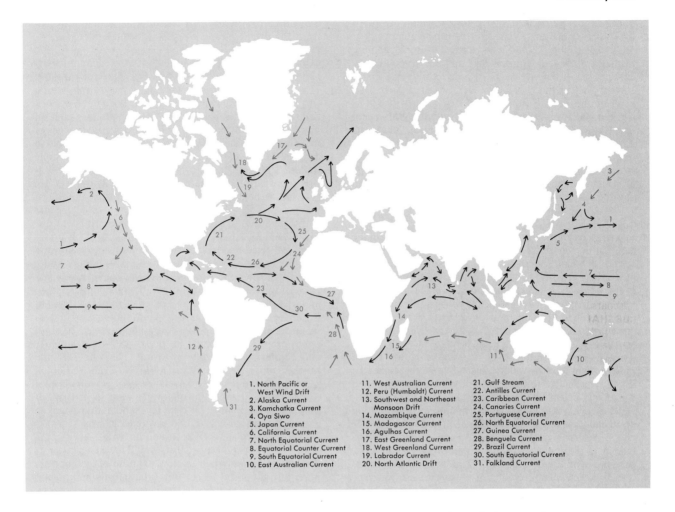

1. North Pacific or West Wind Drift
2. Alaska Current
3. Kamchatka Current
4. Oya Siwo
5. Japan Current
6. California Current
7. North Equatorial Current
8. Equatorial Counter Current
9. South Equatorial Current
10. East Australian Current
11. West Australian Current
12. Peru (Humboldt) Current
13. Southwest and Northeast Monsoon Drift
14. Mozambique Current
15. Madagascar Current
16. Agulhas Current
17. East Greenland Current
18. West Greenland Current
19. Labrador Current
20. North Atlantic Drift
21. Gulf Stream
22. Antilles Current
23. Caribbean Current
24. Canaries Current
25. Portuguese Current
26. North Equatorial Current
27. Guinea Current
28. Benguela Current
29. Brazil Current
30. South Equatorial Current
31. Falkland Current

FOOD VALUE

Although the species is especially desirable for its fine flesh, comparatively few are taken on hook and line. The catch is primarily commercial, with otter trawls, throughout the year. —D.dS.

CURRENTS Currents are more or less permanent bodies of water which usually have motion in one direction. There are four major types of currents: (1) those which exist due to density gradients and which may be maintained by prevailing wind actions; (2) those which result from the effect of the wind on the sea surface; (3) tidal currents; and (4) currents produced by internal waves.

DENSITY-DEPENDENT CURRENTS

Density-dependent currents include the great currents of the world, sometimes known as planetary currents, such as the Gulf Stream or Florida Current, the Kuroshio or Japanese Current, the Equatorial currents, the Benguela Current, off West Africa, and the Peru or Humboldt Current. Where prevailing winds occur, water tends to pile up and must therefore flow somewhere. There are pressure systems within water masses, just as in air masses, and currents run from areas of high pressure to low pressure. Water runs "downhill" from high-pressure regions to low-pressure regions, and slight differences in density of the waters will cause movement of water. Such differences in density can be caused by rain-

fall or by the melting of icebergs, which tends to reduce the density, or by sunlight, which causes evaporation and thus increases density. Similarly, high temperatures make the water lighter and less dense, while low temperatures have the opposite effect, and any combination of temperature and salinity produces variations in density.

Associated with pressure and density gradients is the rotation of the earth which acts on the current. This, then, causes a given body of water to be deflected to its own right in the Northern Hemisphere, and to its own left in the Southern Hemisphere (the Coriolis effect). Thus, density-dependent currents, once initiated through evaporation, rainfall, or temperature, are propelled by prevailing winds, and the location of the current and their relation to land masses determine their direction and fate.

An example of a density-dependent current is the Gulf Stream, which has its origins in the Equatorial Current. Here, a westward drift of high-salinity water is propelled by the trade winds toward the Caribbean Sea, into the Gulf of Mexico, and, to a lesser extent, along the eastern Bahamas. A piling up of water results in the creation of pressure gradients, and as the water flows from the Gulf of Mexico, after having become more dense from evaporation, it flows out through the Florida Straits, where it accelerates up to 4–5 knots from a geographic constriction within the Straits, thence flowing northward. The earth's rotation causes the current to flow to the northeast, and from its offshore movement off the Carolinas it meanders toward Europe, cooling from the Labrador Current and sinking gradually because of the increased density. It is discernible as a major current well to the north, however, and its influence in keeping northern European waters relatively warm is marked. Part of the stream moves into the Norwegian Sea, while the remainder is deflected southward along the African coast, where it subsequently drifts, still moving to its right, joining up with the Equatorial Current once again. All other major currents approximate this type of structure and circulation, according to their location and the shape of the land masses.

DRIFTS

A second type of current is the "drift" resulting from the effect of the wind on the sea surface. Examples are those surface currents found in the North Sea and the Gulf of Mexico. Usually drifts are shallow, but as in the case of the density-dependent current of type (1), the current appears in part to be the result of steady winds. One of the most important types of currents is the vertical current produced by wind drifts, this *upwelling* of water sometimes coming from great depths. In such cases, winds blowing from across land cause water to be blown offshore, and water must move in to replace it, usually vertically from deepwater. Ordinarily, upwelled water is nutrient-rich and, when acted on by sunlight, yields rich plankton supplies, so that areas of upwelling are usually rich in marine life and often support major commercial fisheries. Conversely, drifts moving toward land or a stationary body of water *converge* and sink, carrying with them organisms and warmwater. Occasionally, rich plankton blooms occur in convergence areas, such as are found in red tides (*which see*).

TIDAL CURRENTS

Tidal currents are those generated by the action of tides (*which see*). They involve a relatively small amount of water transport, but in inlets, such as the Bay of Fundy, tidal forces can be strong. In the open sea, due to the Coriolis effect, the tidal currents rotate clockwise in the Northern Hemisphere, counterclockwise in the Southern Hemisphere. Their movement depends on the character of the tide, the depth and type of bottom, and the shape of the coastline.

INTERNAL WAVES

Internal waves are similar to tidal currents in that they too are related to tidal period, but their direction and velocity may vary. Rhythmic variations in density distribution are evidently responsible in part for internal waves.

CURRENT MEASUREMENTS

Currents are studied directly by current meters, by measuring the changes in electrical energy over the earth's magnetic field, and by drift bottles and cards. A wide variety of complex instruments is being developed today to study current direction and speed at various depths. Indirectly, analysis of salinity and temperature reveals the areas of high and low density, so that current direction and speed can be measured accurately through relatively simple means. *See also* Marine Ecology

—D.dS.

CURTIS, BRIAN American (1893–1960) The not very happy life of the author of *The Life Story of the Fish, His Manners and Morals* is a study in frustration, with a surprise ending like an O. Henry plot. Born in New York and Harvard-educated, before settling on a ranch in Northern California, Curtis had every advantage of breeding and money in his background, yet felt unable to achieve his one ambition, which was to be a writer. So he took up ichthyology instead, to give himself some occupation in place of the one for which he felt unfitted. He grew up to be a tall quiet man, anything but the life of the party type, silent as the fish that became his life study; and even in his looks, though his bearing was distinguished, he came to resemble the objects of his attention, with characteristic attributes of strong mouth and receding chin and brow. With a possessive mother and a younger brother on whom he doted, he was relatively late in getting around to any other living companionship and was absorbed in his work. When he married, it was to his opposite, a woman as witty and outgoing as he was taciturn and reserved. They were happy together, until one morning at breakfast he punctuated their laughter and chatter quite simply by dying. His wife sold the ranches, moved to a duplex in a big San Francisco hotel, seemed to be adjusting to a social existence involving a lot of people and travel; but one night went to bed full of pills and never woke up, leaving a note that thanked everybody and said she'd had a wonderful life.

With his own sudden death and his wife's suicide, the annals of Brian and Meta Curtis would have been as short and simple, despite their station, as those of the poor are poetically supposed to be. But Brian Curtis had put on paper all the wit that he had eschewed in social converse, talking shop to himself in a manuscript because he was too well bred to do so in small talk. First published in 1938, *The Life Story of the Fish* was published again in 1949 in a revised edition, and then reissued in 1961 in a Dover reprint. In it, Brian Curtis, the failed writer, achieved one of the rarest forms of writing success, the attainment of a scientifically sound but still wittily and entertainingly comprehensible simplification of one of the most complicated of subjects. It is the story, not of fishing, but of fish; and although the average angler may think, looking at dealers' shelves, that there are a great many books about fishing, the card catalogues of the world's libraries contain ten entries under ichthyology for every one under angling. Most of the ichthyological items are intelligible only to other ichthyologists, but *The Life Story of the Fish* is a felicitous exception. Any angler who can read without moving his lips can follow Brian Curtis through one of the most fascinating life stories ever told; and no angler can be so proficient that he doesn't need to know what this unique little book can tell him.

Most books on fishing seek to persuade the reader to think and act like other fishermen. This one, without presuming to tell the reader how to think like a fish, at least affords him some insight into how and why fish react to certain stimuli in certain ways. It can be debated, indeed, whether fish can really think at all, for thought in the human concept of the process of ratiocination is as alien to all animals as taxation; but fish, like many other members of the animal kingdom, can act as if they could think; and Curtis is brilliant at explaining these actions, and reactions, that to the human observer appear tantamount to thought. In fact, it is that higher strata of fishermen who are concerned with what they regard as "educated" fish, who can read *The Life Story of the Fish* with the most enjoyment and profit.

As the Supervising Fisheries Biologist of the California State Division of Fish and Game, Curtis could track his way with ease through the intricate layers of scientifically established fact and the formidable clouds of learned terminology that make his specialty such an impenetrable thicket of detail. But his mastery of his subject was so consummate that he could, without losing his way or short-circuiting the complicated relationships of the essential facts, strip away all the obfuscations of detail with which scientific pedantry blindfolds the layman. Listening to two biologists talking to each other is about as rewarding to the ordinary angler as listening to two consulting physicians is to the average patient. But listening to Curtis is like hearing the sweet bird of truth through the orchestral din of a jungle of scholarly fact.

One case in point: He describes how "the eel's life-cycle is the reverse of the salmon's. The latter is born in fresh water, goes to sea to live, feed, and grow, returns to fresh water to spawn and die. The former is born in salt water, goes into fresh water to live, feed, and grow, and returns to salt water to spawn and die. It is difficult to conceive how the salmon finds its way back from the sea to its home tributary; but it is even more difficult to conceive how the eel finds its way back across the trackless ocean to the Sargasso Sea.

"A very different kind of spawning migration is that of a little smeltlike fish six inches long called the grunion. The grunion lives along the sandy California beaches, and it has worked out an equation in timing in which the movements of the sun and the moon are the variables.

"The moon, as we all learned in school, is the principal cause of the tides of the sea, but the sun also plays a part. . . .

"In plain words, for the benefit of those not astronomically minded, approximately every two weeks there is a period of two or three days when the high tides are higher than usual. These are called spring tides. At such times, the waves come up on the beaches further than they do at most high tides, and reach points on the sand which, after their subsidence, will remain above water until the next spring tide comes two weeks later to wash over them again . . . [and] the grunion has arranged its whole life-cycle in such a way as to take advantage of it.

"Every two weeks during the spawning season, which lasts from March until July, the grunion mature. . . . At night, in great numbers, the fish congregate in the surf. There they wait, rising and falling in the long Pacific roll, until just after high tide. At the proper moment something gives them the signal, and they begin to come in. Like skillful surf-boarders, they ride the crests of the waves, and they bounce and tumble along with the foam until they land high up on the beach. There each female's tail drills a hole in the dripping sand; into it she pours her eggs, which are fertilized by the nearest male, and the fish, except for the unfortunate few who fail to extricate themselves and are found dead the next morning up to

their armpits, so to speak, in sand, squirm their way back into the next wave and are sucked out to sea. The mating act, including the selection of partners, the digging of the nest, and the deposition of the sex products, takes no more than sixty seconds, and the whole spawning migration sets what must be an all-time record for speed, for from the moment an individual starts in on the crest of a wave until it is back again in deep water cannot be over three minutes.

"The parents, having done what is called their duty, but what in this case must be nothing but a pleasant and exciting excursion, go on their way. The spring tide recedes, next day's sun shines down upon the beach, and there, safely buried three or four inches deep in the warm, moist sand, the eggs develop. Two weeks later the next spring tide scours them from their nest, washes the ready fry out of the egg-membranes, and sweeps them out to sea. . . .

"The eggs take only nine days to develop, but the fry do not emerge until the waves dig them out of the sand. They are thus ready for the appointment ahead of time, in case winds or other circumstances should bring the releasing tide earlier than usual, but they none the less suspend their progress and wait patiently within the egg until the water comes to set them free. If they did not, they would emerge into the almost dry sand, and would perish.

"The whole thing is an equation in timing even more complicated than that of the eel, and, to my mind, even prettier. I would rather be a grunion than an eel.

"There is one fish which has pushed the matter even further. It apparently appreciates the desirable features of the grunion's system, but being an inhabitant of tropical fresh waters it has no tide to help it, and has to take the parts played by the sun and the moon itself. It spawns out of water entirely. Through what feats of acrobatism can only be imagined, the female sticks her eggs to a rock a little above the surface, and the male then goes on duty to keep them wet by splashing water on them until the young hatch. Gilbert and Sullivan could not have thought of anything more nonsensical, nor Alice's White Knight with his

> . . . *plan*
> *To dye one's whiskers green*
> *And always use so large a fan*
> *That they could not be seen*

"The little *Copeina* described above shows a commendable interest in the eggs after they are laid, but there are other fish which go even further. Most touching instance of post-natal care is the so-called 'mouth-breeder.'

"Here we have a fish—a cold, dull, selfish animal in the eyes of most people—going without food for weeks for the sake of its children. This occurs not only among the cichlids, which we mentioned in the preceding chapter as outstanding examples of parental solicitude, but also among the catfish. One of the parents—in some species the mother, in some the father—takes the eggs in the mouth after they are fertilized, and not only holds them there throughout development, but also holds a mouthful of squirming fry until the yolk-sac is absorbed. In spite of all temptations, no food is eaten. And in the case of the cichlids the young, even after they are free-swimming, return to the parental mouth each evening and spend the night there until they are literally too big to get in."

Among the cases of parental solicitude mentioned earlier by Curtis, he cited that of the male bass, who provides and cares for the nest, out of which he chases the female as soon as she has served his purpose by laying eggs for him to fertilize, and then tends it jealously. "His care continues until the yolk-sac is absorbed . . . but as soon as the fry begin to swim he deserts them. Up to this point they have been his joy and pride and the darlings of his heart, but from now on he ceases to recognize them. They are just little fish, and all little fish are good to eat. Parental instinct, at this stage in the evolutionary scale, has made a brave beginning, but it lacks endurance. It breaks down under temptation."

The Life Story of the Fish ends, like a Fourth of July fireworks display, in a bravura demonstration of the ultimate in oddities of adaptation of which fish are capable. After citing the seahorse, which "looks exactly as if the father were giving birth," Curtis trots out his penultimate "believe-it-or-not" exhibit:

"And in a very different species the father, incredible as it may sound, actually does give birth—or, to put it more correctly, the same fish which at one time in its life gives birth later becomes a father. For in one of the live-bearers, Xyphophorus, the sword-tail, authentic records are numerous of complete change of sex. An individual starts life as a female, becomes a mother, and gives birth to numerous offspring. After some years of this she gets tired of males, starts taking up with other females, and before long has fathered numerous offspring. As one ichthyologist described it, 'A mother becomes the father of her own granddaughter.' It seems a happy division of domestic labors," muses Curtis, quietly anticipating Women's Liberation by some three decades, "and one which human beings might well envy. After a youthful probationary period during which she underwent the trials, as well as the joys, of womanhood and motherhood, the individual, instead of becoming barren in middle life, would turn into a man, enjoying thenceforth masculine freedom from physical and domestic woes, and assuming masculine responsibilities. What wise old men we should have! For it is difficult for even the most sensitive of us fully to appreciate situations which we have not personally experienced; but an old man who had been in his earlier days maiden, wife, and mother would be capable of a boundless sympathy for and understanding of all mankind."

Then, with a ringmaster's zest for the spectacular, Brian Curtis introduces the last act in the extravaganza which *The Life Story of the Fish* has by then become: "And now we come to the climax, the ultimate height, the wildest flight of fancy, exemplified by a certain large and quite ugly deep-sea angler-fish. This animal is a perfect Christmas tree of adaptations. Being an angler, it has the dorsal fin modified into a dangling lure. Being a deep-sea fish, it has, as many deep-sea fish do, phosphorescent organs which light up the darkness in which it lives—whether to signal mates or to lure victims is undetermined. And then it goes a step further and stupefies the rest of the animal kingdom by taking unto itself a parasitic mate. Parasitic not in the manner of some human females: here the parasitism is physical, and is practiced by the male . . . The female is forty inches long, her devoted husband four inches long—only one one-thousandth of her weight.

"This species lives at great depths, in complete blackness. Its numbers are few. The chances of a male finding a female are poor, and of his losing her after he has once found her good. What he does, then, if he has the good luck to find a mate, is to make sure that he will never be separated from her. He takes her by the throat or the back, or some other portion of her anatomy. His jaws sink in. And he never lets go again. By and by his skin grows together with her skin. Her blood vessels make connection with his blood vessels. His mouth degenerates and become functionless. He becomes literally one with her.

"In an earlier chapter it was said that no cases of monogamy in the fish world could be proved, and even here, in spite of first appearances to the contrary, true monogamy does not exist, for the female may attach onto herself several males. But of unswerving masculine devotion to a single spouse this is unquestionably the world's outstanding example. Here is conjugal faithfulness carried to the ultimate degree. Here are no puny words about 'till death do us part.' Not even death will part this little fish from his mate. If she dies, he at once dies also. Here is marital fidelity beyond the powers of the most virtuous of the human species.

"Poor fish, indeed!"

These words, with which Brian Curtis concluded *The Life Story of the Fish*, could well leave many readers in the mood for an encore. Their disappointment, in searching out the other writings of this man who thought he had flunked out on his self-imposed tests for authorship, would be as great as Queen Victoria's when she sent for the other writings of Lewis Carroll after reading *Alice in Wonderland* and discovered that they all dealt with mathematics. The only other writings of Brian Curtis lie in the files of the *Bulletin of the American Museum of Natural History* (vol. LXXVI, art. 1, pp. 1–46, 1939) and the *Transactions of the American Fisheries Society* (vol. 64, pp. 259–265, 1934), where they would seem to be beyond what Walton termed "the perusal of most anglers."

But *The Life Story of the Fish, His Manners and Morals* should be read, if not as long as fish still swim, then at least as long as there are still people left who feel like fishing for them. —A.G.

CUSK *See* Burbot

CUSK EEL *See* Spotted Cusk Eel

CUTLASSFISH *See* Atlantic Cutlassfish

CUTLIPS MINNOW *Exoglossum maxillingua* An olivaceous, medium-sized minnow with a distinctive lower jaw. Separated from all other minnows by its three-lobed lower jaw with the center lobe protruding like a tongue. Upper jaw longer than lower. Lateral line complete. The origin of the dorsal fin slightly behind that of ventral fins.

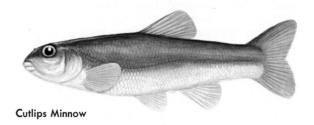

Cutlips Minnow

Cutthroat Trout (Yellowstone River Form) 16-inch Male

The range of this species is from the St. Lawrence and Lake Ontario south into Virginia.

HABITS

The cutlips is found in clear, running streams and seems to prefer clear, rocky pools but not rapids. The distinctive mouth structure of the cutlips enables it to feed on small shellfish which it scrapes from rocks. Although mollusks appear to be its principal food, it also eats insect larvae and diatoms. A nest builder similar to the fallfish, the cutlips male constructs a nest of stones some 18 inches across. Spawning occurs in late spring when the male apparently attempts to herd females over its nest. The cutlips minnow averages 6 inches in length.

ECONOMIC VALUE

The cutlips is not a popular bait species due to its dull coloration but takes a hook readily, and is favored in some areas by youngsters. It is said to be a good panfish.
—R.A.J.

CUTTHROAT TROUT *Salmo clarki* There are many sub-species or races of this species and the various names indicate the areas in which they are found. Endemic to the West, it is the so-called native trout, an appellation also used for the brook trout in Eastern states. The cutthroat is distributed on the coast from Prince William Sound, Alaska, to northern California and inland throughout the western U.S. and Canada, exhibiting varied habits and appearance.

The body of the cutthroat is usually five times as long as it is deep. The tail is slightly forked. All fins are soft rayed; the anal fin has 8–12 rays and there are 9–12 branchiostegals supporting the gill membranes. The red markings which give this trout its common name are visible outside and below the lower jaw. Teeth are located at the base of the tongue. Considerable color variation occurs. The adult inland forms may have cadmium coloring along the sides and belly as in the Piute trout. The Yellowstone cutthroat is a yellowish-green with red on the side of the head and body and sparse but large dark spots which are most numerous in the posterior portion of the body. The Snake River cutthroat is more heavily spotted and this black pigmentation is much

smaller. These two forms do not exist in a pure state in many habitats as there has been a great deal of inter-mingling. The cutthroat trout hybridizes with the rain-bow trout, and on many streams in Wyoming and Montana the cutthroat-rainbow cross is very common. Although the rainbow characteristics remain dominant (including the reddish lateral band), the hybrid is easily recognized by the same bright orange or vivid red "cut" marks under the dentary bone. The cutthroat trout also hybridizes with the golden trout and in areas where these two species are present, such as the high altitude lakes of the Jim Bridger Wilderness in Wyoming, these un-usually colored crosses occur. The anadromous and non-migratory coastal subspecies of the cutthroat trout are usually greenish-blue with numerous, heavy black spots on the head, body, tail, dorsal, and anal fins, as well as with a silvery sheen on the sides.

Cutthroat trout are found in rivers and lakes and the anadromous form enters saltwater. In most instances, the species does not compete well with other fish, and this factor, coupled with its tendency to hybridize, and its inability to withstand heavy fishing pressure has seri-ously depleted many populations. A few attempts have been made to introduce cutthroat trout to Eastern waters but without success.

LIFE HISTORY

All subspecies exhibit the redd-forming habits of most of the Salmonidae, but they spawn in the winter and spring, the majority of the coastal forms in February and March and those inland in April and May. Yellowstone cutthroat trout generally spawn at 4 years of age but usually only in alternate years, rarely every year. The life span of this form is about 6 years and possibly 9 years.

The anadromous fish go to sea as young in the second or third year and return after 1–2 years in saltwater. They can spawn repeatedly, and one tagged, 10-year-old, was caught by an angler in Sand Creek on the Oregon coast. Much of the life of the coastal cutthroat may be spent in the estuarine environment, but some individuals re-main in freshwater for their entire lives. Anadromous races begin to enter freshwater from the ocean in early summer. Food of the young is largely made up of insects but may be fish in larger individuals.

Cutthroat Trout (Snake River Form) 15-inch Male

Although the cutthroat trout has been recorded to a weight of 41 pounds, taken from Pyramid Lake (this race became extinct in 1938), the inland form seldom exceeds 5 pounds. The coastal subspecies has been recorded to 17 pounds, but 4 pounds is considered large for a sea run fish.

Numerous subspecies of cutthroat trout are found from the Rocky Mountains west to the Pacific coast into tidewater, and from northern California to Alaska. Each form, with few exceptions, seems to maintain itself best in its natural habitat. These subspecies probably evolved separately by isolation from the parent type. The largest of these, the Lahontan cutthroat, native to the Lahontan drainage system of Nevada and California, provided an abundance of angling years ago in Lake Tahoe, Pyramid Lake, and the Truckee River. At the turn of the century this big trout was so numerous that it was fished commercially and many thousands were marketed in San Francisco at 50¢ a pound. Yet the Lahontan persisted, and in 1925 a 41-pounder was taken from Pyramid. Before water was diverted from the Truckee River (1938) an average weight of 20 pounds was recorded for 195 trout captured during their spawning run. Today, this cutthroat is maintained by stocking, as native populations have become extinct or nearly so. The Lahontan subspecies is unique in tolerating highly alkaline desert lakes where other trout species fare poorly.

The smallest cutthroat subspecies (maximum length 12 inches), possibly one of the rarest and prettiest salmonids in the United States, native only to upper Silver King Creek in California, has also dwindled to the point where it is on the "endangered species" list, and is totally protected from angling in its native habitat. Transplants of the pure strain have been made to other streams, and these have been most successful in the Cottonwood Creek drainage.

Some of the recognized subspecies of cutthroat trout are:

Lahontan Cutthroat	*Salmo c. henshawi*
Piute Cutthroat	*Salmo c. seleniris*
Yellowstone Cutthroat	*Salmo c. lewisi*
Utah Cutthroat	*Salmo c. utah*
Colorado Cutthroat	*Salmo c. pleuriticus*
Rio Grande Cutthroat	*Salmo c. virginalis*

ANGLING TECHNIQUES

Cutthroat trout feed extensively on freshwater shrimp (Gammarus) and insect larvae. In a study made on Henrys Lake in Idaho, which is unusually productive though fairly typical of native cutthroat waters, it was found that shrimp, damselfly nymphs, and midges composed 90 percent by number of the food utilized by the trout. The larval and pupal forms of the midges amounted to 35 percent (as many as 670 larvae and 730 pupae were taken from a single stomach), while the damselfly provided 28 percent of the food eaten, with one cutthroat gorged on 1,445 nymphs. Shrimp amounted to 27 percent of the number of food items consumed, and one stomach contained 473 shrimp. These figures are interesting as they not only indicate active subsurface feeding but a rather selective diet. Although freshwater snails, for example, only amounted to 3 percent by volume of the cutthroat diet, this kind of food provided 59 percent of the forage for Henrys' numerous rainbow cutthroat hybrids. Only one forage fish, a sculpin, and only three terrestrial insects (ants) were found in the stomach samples.

While in saltwater cutthroats feed on sand launce, shrimp, and various fishes in relatively shallow areas, where they can be caught by trolling or casting small silver spoons close to rocky shores particularly where there is some dropoff. During the spring and early summer, from April until July, sea trout often school along the gravel beaches near river mouths, and if you know the hot spots some good fly-fishing can be had in this period. The tidal stage has a great influence on success, but as a rule the ebb through slack period is more productive than the flood. From late August through October, when the anadromous cutthroats return to the rivers in substantial numbers, all kinds of baits and lures are used, but the thing to remember is that unlike the current-loving steelhead, the "harvest trout" prefer deep slower-moving water around brush piles, stumps, and boulders. Attractor wet flies with yellow, orange, or mixed red-and-white hackles in any of the standard steelhead patterns dressed on No. 6 hooks are most effective. Keep the fly near the bottom and move it in short jerks so that the hackle opens and closes; cutthroats prefer an active lure to a freely drifting one.

The cutthroat trout is not considered as active a game-fish as the rainbow or brown. It seldom jumps when hooked. However, it is an excellent quarry in its native habitat, being both beautiful and shy. The inland forms rise freely to the dry fly and often require fine leaders and small patterns for successful angling. These trout are also taken on nymphs, wet flies, bucktails, spinners, spoons, and live bait, such as worms, crayfish, and minnows. In estuaries the cutthroat usually shows a preference for flies that imitate shrimp or local forage fish. When in saltwater, cutthroats are relatively shallowwater fish, being caught on trolling tackle close to rocky shores, particularly those which drop abruptly into deep water. Medium weight spinning tackle (6-pound test) is very suitable for this kind of angling. Tides and the movement of baitfish play key roles in angling success.

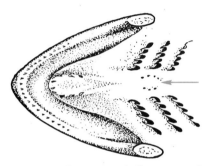

Hyoid teeth at base of tongue in the lower jaw of cutthroat trout separate it from the rainbow, which lacks hyoid teeth

Productive cutthroat trout fishing still exists in the remoter areas of its original range. Wyoming (*which see*) has made a special effort to maintain this salmonid, as it was once the only trout found in the state. Large populations are present in the headwaters of the Snake River and its tributary streams, in 139-square mile Yellowstone Lake and its outlet, the Yellowstone River, and in the tributaries of the Green, Wind, Salt, and Shoshone rivers. Idaho maintains good cutthroat fishing in the Middle Fork of the Salmon River and to a lesser extent in other streams, such as the North Fork of the Snake and North Fork of the Clearwater. Large specimens are also taken in Priest Lake, Henrys Lake, and Lake Pend Oreille. Montana's principal fishery is in the Yellowstone River, but here as elsewhere the better fishing is usually found in small spring-fed streams which receive little angling pressure. The principal Canadian fisheries are in British Columbia, where sea run trout are common both along the mainland coast and on Vancouver and Queen Charlotte Islands.

FOOD VALUE

The cutthroat trout is an excellent table fish. The flesh may vary from white to red and is of fine flavor. This trout can be prepared in a variety of ways including frying, broiling, baking, and smoking. —J.R.
—A.J.McC.

CUTTYHUNK LINE A handlaid, twisted, linen line originally made by Captain Lester Crandall for the Cuttyhunk Fishing Club (1865) on Cuttyhunk Island, Massachusetts. The club, dedicated to striped-bass fishing and gastronomy, was dissolved prior to 1918. *See* Linen Line

D

DAB *See* American Plaice, Pacific Sanddab, Yellowtail Flounder.

DACE *See* Blacknose Dace, Longnose Dace, Southern Redbelly Dace, Speckled Dace

DACRON A Du Pont trademark for a polyester fiber made from dimethyl terephthalate and ethylene glycol. These chemical compounds are derived from familiar sources of most of the polymers used in making synthetic fibers (coal, air, water, and petroleum). Dacron is produced in the same way as nylon by extrusion in one continuous filament. Most Dacron fishing lines are of braided construction. The quality of the construction is an important factor in the over-all physical characteristics of the line.

The strength of Dacron fiber approaches that of nylon. Stretch and elasticity, however, differ quite markedly. Although nylon will stretch 17–30 per cent (depending on prior hot-stretch treatment) before breaking, the maximum elongation of Dacron approximates 10 per cent; most of its elongation occurs during the heavy-stretch phase. Dacron is less affected by water than nylon, and any change in its characteristics from dry to wet is virtually negligible. Dacron also exhibits a high degree of resistance to sunlight deterioration as well as resistance to mildew and rot. Dacron has wide acceptance as a trolling line. —A.J.McC.

DAMSELFLIES *See* Dragonflies.

DANISH LOBSTER One of the lobsterettes (*which see*).

DARTERS Family Percidae The darters, all members of the perch family, are of the subfamily Etheostominae. There are 95 species of darters in the United States and Canada. In range, they occur only east of the Rockies and into southern Canada and northern Mexico.

To most fishermen the darters are recognized as colorful little "minnows" which occasionally are included in their bait buckets. Only close observation will reveal them in their natural habitat, since they are usually only a few inches long and stay hidden among rocks and debris on the bottom. Their name, darters, is derived from the fact that they do not swim in the ordinary fashion but dart from place to place. These movements are so rapid that the eye can scarcely follow them. One second a darter will be seen lying motionless on the bottom, and the next second it has disappeared, only to reappear a foot or so away. They never suspend themselves in the water and have only a rudimentary swim bladder.

Most of the darters do not exceed 3–4 inches in length, and some are even smaller. Only one, the log perch, reaches a length of about 8 inches. They all have the perch family characteristics of two separate dorsal fins, with spines in the first dorsal and anal fins. Their tails, however, are not forked. Their bodies are slender and heads or snouts usually pointed. The pectoral fins are highly developed and are disproportionately large. These fins are used both to propel the fish in their darting movements and to stabilize them as they rest on the bottom. Coloration varies greatly among species, but the one common characteristic is that they all are brilliantly colored. During spawning season the males display the most vivid colors of any freshwater fishes. Pinks, reds, and yellows contrast with the darker colors.

SOME DARTER SPECIES

Common Name	Scientific Name
Brown darter	*Etheostoma edwini*
Arkansas saddled darter	*Etheostoma euzonum*
Iowa darter	*Etheostoma exile*
Fantail darter	*Etheostoma flabellare*
Fountain darter	*Etheostoma fonticola*
Savannah darter	*Etheostoma fricksium*
Swamp darter	*Etheostoma fusiforme*
Slough darter	*Etheostoma gracile*
Rio Grande darter	*Etheostoma grahami*
Tuckasegee darter	*Etheostoma gutselli*
Harlequin darter	*Etheostoma histrio*
Turquoise darter	*Etheostoma inscriptum*
Blueside darter	*Etheostoma jessiae*
Greenbreast darter	*Etheostoma jordani*
Yoke darter	*Etheostoma juliae*
Kanawha darter	*Etheostoma Kanawhae*
Stripetail darter	*Etheostoma Kennicotti*
Greenthroat darter	*Etheostoma lepidum*
Longfin darter	*Etheostoma longimanum*
Redband darter	*Etheostoma luteovinctum*
Spotted darter	*Etheostoma maculatum*
Pinewoods darter	*Etheostoma mariae*
Least darter	*Etheostoma microperca*
Niangua darter	*Etheostoma nianguae*
Johnny darter	*Etheostoma nigrum*
Barcheek darter	*Etheostoma obeyense*
Finescale saddled darter	*Etheostoma osburni*
Goldstripe darter	*Etheostoma parvipinne*
Waccamaw darter	*Etheostoma perlongum*
Riverweed darter	*Etheostoma podostemone*
Cypress darter	*Etheostoma proeliare*
Stippled darter	*Etheostoma punctulatum*
Orangebelly darter	*Etheostoma radiosum*
Redline darter	*Etheostoma rufilineatum*
Rock darter	*Etheostoma rupestre*
Arrow darter	*Etheostoma sagitta*
Saluda darter	*Etheostoma saludae*
Maryland darter	*Etheostoma sellare*
Sawcheek darter	*Etheostoma serriferum*
Tennessee snubnose darter	*Etheostoma simoterum*
Orangethroat darter	*Etheostoma spectabile*
Spottail darter	*Etheostoma squamiceps*
Speckled darter	*Etheostoma stipmaeum*
Gulf darter	*Etheostoma sqaini*
Swannanoa darter	*Etheostoma sqannanoa*
Missouri saddled darter	*Etheostoma tetrazonum*
Seagreen darter	*Etheostoma thalassinum*
Tippecanoe darter	*Etheostoma tippecanoe*
Tuscumbia darter	*Etheostoma tuscumbia*
Variegate darter	*Etheostoma variatum*
Striped darter	*Etheostoma virgatum*
Glassy darter	*Etheostoma vitreum*
Redfin darter	*Etheostoma whipplei*
Banded darter	*Etheostoma zonale*

LIFE HISTORY

The darters generally are found in relatively clear cool-waters. Some species live only in cold streams, while others inhabit the larger rivers and some are found in lakes. Spawning takes place in late spring or early summer. The males select and guard a nesting area, usually in

Johnny Darter

the gravel, and the females dig a shallow depression into which a few hundred eggs are deposited, being fertilized immediately by the male. The eggs are sticky and adhere to the gravel. The male guards the nest until the eggs are hatched.

The darters are primarily carnivorous, eating such foods as small insects and zooplankton. Although they themselves may furnish food for larger fishes, their ability to hide themselves among objects on the bottom and their quick movement make them hard to find and catch. The darters usually are found in fairly shallow water and rather well spread out instead of in schools. Though not much is known about their age and growth, they probably do not live more than a maximum of 5–6 years. Species which reach a maximum length of 4 inches will grow about $1\frac{1}{4}$ inches the first year; they will be $2\frac{1}{4}$ inches the second year; and grow to about 3 inches the third year of life. Maturity should occur in the third year of life if conditions are normal.

Iowa Darter

ANGLING VALUE

The darters are of little or no importance to anglers. Occasionally a few will be used for bait, but their occurrence in the bait bucket is more by accident than by plan. Regionally, however, darters are an important food of gamefish and especially trout. Many streamer-fly patterns are designed to imitate various darters. —J.T.S.

DEAD RECKONING Calculating a boat's position by recording speed and courses since last known position and taking into account current, wind, and compass errors.

DECOMPRESSION SICKNESS *See* The Bends *in* Skin and Scuba Diving Dangers *under* First Aid

DECURVED Curved downward

DEEP-SCATTERING LAYER A layer or layers often present in ocean waters and consisting of stratified groups of organisms which can "scatter" or reflect the pulses from echo-sounding equipment, thus appearing as a "false bottom." The layers move downward during the day and up at night, and may spread horizontally for miles.

DELAWARE The second smallest of the states provides a modest amount of angling for its residents. Delaware only has about fifty freshwater ponds which support largemouth bass, chain pickerel, yellow and white perch, and sunfish. However, some good saltwater fishing can be found from Lewes to the Maryland border. This fronts the ocean, and is indented by Rehoboth and Indian River bays. The fishing here is for flounder, croaker, and white perch. The Delaware River and Bay yield good catches of croaker, weakfish, and porgies. Ocean fishing out of Lewes and Indian River yacht basins is seasonally excellent for black sea bass, bluefish, marlin, and tuna. Complete party-boat facilities are available at Little Creek, near Dover; Bowers Beach; Mispillion Light, south of Milford; Lewes; and Indian River Inlet.

Delaware continues its program of development of new lakes and the development of recently acquired riverfront properties in its endeavor to improve both fresh- and saltwater fishing for the sportsman. Close co-operation between the Game and Fish Commission, interested state agencies, sportsmen, and the state legislature continues to pay off in improved water recreational facilities in the state.

Public-access areas to Delaware's famous flounder fishing in Indian River Bay have been developed at Wuillen's Point and Massey's Landing; one at Dewey Beach on Rehoboth Bay; two inland on Assawoman Bay and one on the ocean shore; one on the Lewes Canal at Lewes. Likewise, public boat-launching facilities are available at Fowler's Beach adjacent to the principal sea-trout grounds in the Delaware Bay.

The commission has purchased frontage on the Delaware River immediately south of Port Penn and including the Augstine Beach Recreational Area. Residents of Wilmington and suburbs are assured an access to the Delaware River in spite of the rapid industrial expansion adjacent to the river.

DEMERSAL An organism which lives close to the bottom of a body of water such as the cod. Demersal species are opposed to fishes of pelagic habits which range close to the surface.

DENMARK Denmark occupies the Jutland peninsula extending north from Germany between Norway and Sweden, and includes a group of nearby islands of which Funen and Zealand (where Copenhagen is located) are the largest. The country encompasses 16,615 square miles, or about half the area of the state of Maine. No part of Denmark is more than 40 miles from the sea.

There are many tourist reasons for visiting the land of Hans Christian Andersen, but its angling is very limited. Several quality rivers are worth a detour if only to relax between other activities. Sea trout, brown trout, rainbow trout, and pike can be caught in the waters of Jutland Province. Sea trout are also taken along many portions of Denmark's coast in the spring and fall seasons. The saltwater fishing is primarily for cod, mackerel, and flounder. In years past there was a fair run of bluefin tuna coming through the Kattegat, but this fishery has virtually disappeared.

TROUT FISHING

Denmark has over 500 trout farms which connect with every fishable river, although these commercial operations are strictly for the export food market. Escapement does occur, however, and hatchery-reared rainbows are in constant supply on rivers such as the Simested, Varde, Sneum, Konge, Omme, and Karup. The two latter streams are probably the best in Denmark from a fly-fishing point of view. The Karup is also an excellent sea-trout river. Being an almost flat country, with little elevation, Danish streams are slow-flowing with silt and sand bottoms and considerable weed growth. They are fertile, nevertheless, and produce an abundance of aquatic insects. Although it's impractical and unnecessary to wade any of these trout streams the banks are usually boggy and waterproofs are recommended.

Literally all worthwhile streams in Denmark are leased by angling associations; a few are restricted to their mem-

A country with little stream gradient, nearly all Denmark waters are slow flowing. This angler is fishing the Omme River

bers only, but most are available on a daily or weekly ticket basis, and many of these through the local hotels.

SEA-TROUT FISHING

Although sea trout are taken in many Danish streams the more popular fishing is in saltwater. In April and May and again in October the sea trout feed actively close to shore over rock-covered bottoms inside the seaweed zone. This shallow fishing is done primarily with spinning and bait-casting tackle using ½–1-ounce wobbling spoons. A lesser number are also taken on flies. Danish sea trout average about 8 pounds, but fish up to 20 pounds are recorded every year. Popular locations for this kind of angling are Isefjorden, Fjellebro, Virksund, Nibe Bredning, Ringkobing, and Korsor.   —A.J.McC.

DETRITUS Organic or inorganic sediment formed from the remains of plants and animals or the disintegration of rocks.

DEVIL RAY *Mobula hypostoma* It resembles the Atlantic manta and Pacific manta (*which see*) by having a broad, diamond-shaped disk and two well-developed fleshy horns on the head. But the mouth of the devil ray is on the underside of the disk and not at the tip of the head. It is much smaller than the other mantas and grows only to about 4 feet wide. The skin of small specimens is smooth while that of larger individuals has fine prickles. The tail base lacks a spine, and the tail is long and whiplike, about as long as the body. The disk is blackish-brown above and yellowish to gray-white beneath, with a dark blotch on the lower parts just behind each eye.

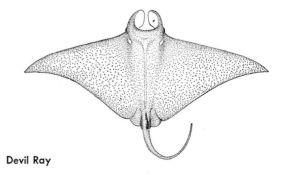

Devil Ray

LIFE HISTORY

The devil ray occurs off Sénégal in the eastern Atlantic, and is known in the western Atlantic at various places between Brazil and North Carolina and western Florida. A few are seen occasionally, but it is never as common as the Atlantic manta. Like other mantas, it leaps from the water.

Its food consists of planktonic crustaceans and small, schooling fishes. Unlike the Atlantic manta, it feeds on the bottom, and has been observed to push itself along the bottom through patches of turtle grass. The head fins are used to funnel the food into its mouth. Young devil rays, which may be produced throughout the range, are about 20 inches wide. —D.dS.

DIAGONAL-BUILT A boat constructed without framing and with double planking running at an angle of 45 degrees with the keel.

DIAMOND STINGRAY *Dasyatis dipterura* This Pacific stingray closely resembles the southern stingray (*which see*) in having the corners of the disk rather sharply rounded and the anterior margin of the "wings" slightly convex. But the bony tubercles which are scattered about the disk of the southern stingray are present only on the midline in a short row. The tail is quite long, about half again that of the disk, and there are one or more long spines near the tail base. The upper parts are bluish-brown, and the ventral surface is dirty white. A length of 6 feet is attained.

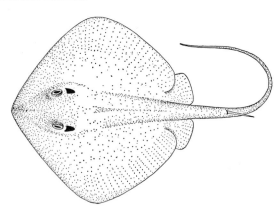

Diamond Stingray

It occurs from southern California to British Columbia; a closely related, if not identical, form occurs southward to Peru. Common in protected bays and off beaches, it eats crabs and mollusks.

DANGER TO MAN

Like other stingrays, it has one or more well-developed tail spines which can inflict serious wounds. —D.dS.

DIAMOND TURBOT *Hypsopsetta guttulata* Occasionally called diamond flounder, this Pacific species is one of the most common flatfish in southern California. A righteyed flounder, it has a yellowish patch on the eyeless side which readily distinguishes it from other California flounders, the colored side being green to green-brown with pale blue spots to mottled greenish-brown. The accessory branch of the lateral line found along the anterior base of the dorsal fin is held in common with the English sole (*which see*); however, the English sole lacks the characteristic diamond shape and has a straight edge to the tail.

The rhomboid, "diamond" shape of the fish is also somewhat similar to the curlfin sole (*which see*), but it differs from this sole in the absence of an extension of the dorsal fin onto the blind side. Reaching a length of 18 inches and a weight of 4 pounds, it is found from northern California to the Gulf of California.

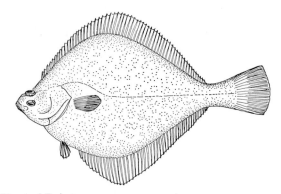

Diamond Turbot

It occurs from the surf to more than 150 feet deep, being most common in less than 60 feet of water in southern California. It is usually found in quiet bays, in sloughs, and in the surf, over mud or sand bottoms.

LIFE HISTORY

Spawning occurs in the early spring. Sexual maturity probably occurs when they are 2–3 years old, the species living to about 8–9 years old. Adults eat worms, crabs, and shrimp.

FOOD VALUE

Taken throughout the year on hook and line and by trawls, it is of minor importance commercially, although the flesh is excellent. Anglers take the diamond turbot using shrimp, clams, and cut bait. —D.dS.

DINGELL-JOHNSON ACT An act passed by Congress in 1950 which provides funds to all states, Puerto Rico, the Virgin Islands, and Guam for the improvement of the nation's sport-fishing facilities and fishery-management programs. The allocation of funds is decided on a formula based on the number of anglers (60 per cent) and the land and water area of each state or territory (40 per cent). The program is financed through a 10-per-cent federal excise tax on sport-fishing tackle, with the states spending at least $1 for each $3 of federal funds. General taxes, either state or federal, are not involved. The angler, through participation in sport fishing, supports the entire cost of the Dingell-Johnson program.

Funds are allocated by the federal Bureau of Sport Fisheries and Wildlife to the state agencies to carry out a wide range of activities as defined by the law. These include fishery research, purchase or lease of lands and waters, improvement of the fish environment, construction of facilities, and other fishery-management activities. State agencies select and develop the type of projects, approvable under the law, that will most benefit sport fishing. The Bureau of Sport Fisheries and Wildlife administers the provisions of the Dingell-Johnson Act through inspection of project proposals and completed work and through audit of project financial records.

DINOFLAGELLATE A single-celled, usually marine organism that may show either plant or animal characteristics (synthesize food material or eat); it generally has two flagella—whiplike appendages—and a cellulose envelope that is often beautifully sculptured. Some dinoflagellates can form thick concentrations of "red tides" which may kill larger marine organisms.

DISEASES AND PARASITES Disease in fishes involves a change or variation in the normal function of cells, tissues, or organs of the animal. Usually there are certain clinical signs or symptoms associated with diseases, and only rarely can certain diseases causing acute mortality eliminate a large population of fish with little or no evidence of the disease.

The nature of a fish kill can often be used to separate "disease-caused kills" from "pollution or adverse environmental factor-caused kills." If a large part of a fish population should die suddenly with no visible lesions—such as swelling, discoloration, or other evidence of disease—a check for such factors as water quality or possible introduction of toxic materials should be made. Disease problems in fish, on the other hand, usually cause a chronic mortality, with fish dying over a period of several days or weeks. Usually there are certain clinical signs associated with these diseases. Common clinical signs are lesions, growths, hemorrhages, abnormal coloration, irritability (such as flashing or twitching) swollen or discolored gills, excess mucous production causing a grayish or bluish film on the skin, distended eyes, swollen or sunken body, loss of appetite, and abnormal swimming or gasping near the surface. Diseases are produced by viruses, bacteria, fungi, parasites (protozoans and higher groups), inadequate nutrition, poor water quality, and a few unknown causes. Certain pathogenic organisms must have a fish host, while others are ubiquitous in the aquatic environment and only become a problem when the host's defenses are weakened and the organism is able to invade the host. For this reason relationships between the host and the pathogen become very complex with environmental factors, food supply, and size and age of host playing important roles in the severity of the disease. Stress-producing factors, such as handling damage, may allow invasion of the fish by bacteria. Antibodies may be produced against bacteria, while host reaction to many parasites is an increase in mucous production and proliferation of tissues.

The most common source of infection is a previously-infected fish. Other animals—such as birds, frogs, and turtles—may be sources of infection. Fish may also take in pathogens with their food. With rare exceptions, the better the condition of the fish, the better his resistance to diseases. An adequate amount of food is necessary for maintenance and growth, and also good water quality is necessary for the host's well being. Overcrowding, which may result in waste build-up and competition for food, should be avoided in any controllable situation. Fish kills that occur in the spring of the year at temperate latitudes are usually caused by bacteria and are related to stress conditions placed on the host. Fish, along with other cold-blooded vertebrates, do not produce antibodies at low temperatures. At the same time most fish spawn during the spring, producing an added stress on the fish. The combination of lack of immunity, inadequate food supply in the winter, and stress of spawning results in greater mortality during this time of the year.

VIRUS DISEASES

Viruses are extremely small particles that depend on living cells for reproduction. Virus particles have a core that is composed of nucleic acid (RNA or DNA), which is surrounded by a protective protein layer; some are surrounded by an envelope. These viruses can be seen only with an electron microscope. A positive diagnosis of virus diseases involves filtering infected material and inoculating the virus-containing filtrate into tissue culture. Viruses reproduce in the cultured cells, causing the cells to rupture and produce a particular type of pathology called Cytopathic Effect (CPE) to the cells. There are no known controls for virus diseases other than avoidance and sanitation.

Infectious Hematopoietic Necrosis (IHN) This disease—along with Chinook Salmon Disease, Sockeye Salmon Disease, and Sacramento River Chinook Disease—affects the blood-forming (hematopoietic) tissues; apparently all of these diseases may be caused by the same virus. It is so far known only from salmonids.

While the signs of the disease in the different species of fish may vary, all fish infected with IHN may show accumulation of fluids in the body cavity, popeyes, anemia, and hemorrhaging. Rainbow trout may have a long opaque wormlike fecal cast extending from the vent. Temperature manipulation may be a means of controlling IHN, since higher temperatures (18°–20° C) adversely affect the disease.

Channel Catfish Virus Disease (CCVD) Channel Catfish Virus Disease affects mainly small channel catfish of usually less than 6 inches in size and only when temperatures are 70° F. and only when temperatures are 70° F. Some stress condition precipitates the disease outbreak most of the time, and a very high percentage of the fry or fingerlings can die in a very short time. CCVD can virtually always be ruled out when larger fish and lower temperatures are involved. Affected fish exhibit distended abdomen and popeyes due to fluid accumulations. The fluid in the abdomen is usually yellowish and mucoid. Small hemorrhagic areas may be present in the skin and fins and in internal organs, and the gills may be pale or hemorrhagic. The fish may swim erratically in small circles and often hang vertically with heads near the surface.

Bacterial infections commonly occur secondarily to CCVD. Both *Aeromonas* and *Columnaris* have been associated with CCVD. There is no known treatment for the disease; so isolation of diseased fish and sterilization of equipment is the best means of preventing its spread. There is no reliable method of detecting carrier fish, but it is suspected that brood fish may transmit the disease through the eggs.

Fingerling catfish infected with Channel Catfish Virus Disease. Note the distended abdomen, popeyes, and hemorraging at base of fins

Infectious Pancreatic Necrosis (IPN) IPN is a virus infection of salmonids causing high mortality mainly in fry and fingerlings. Adult fish can be carriers of the virus, and it is thought that it is passed from adult to young by way of the egg. The IPN virus can be transmitted through the water; it is shed in the feces and other excretions of carrier fish.

Clinical signs of the disease are whirling, protruding abdomen and eyes, darkening of body color, and internal hemorrhaging. Liver and spleen are usually pale and the stomach appears white. An opaque plug of mucous occurs in the stomach and anterior intestine.

Fish infected with IPN virus may die over a period of several weeks. Oddly enough, well-fed rapidly-growing fish seem to be more susceptible to the disease. There is no known control for IPN, so avoidance is the best means of control. Eggs should be obtained from a known disease-free source.

Lymphocystis Disease Lymphocystis is a chronic virus-caused disease that seldom produces deaths, and occurs in both marine and freshwater fishes. Characteristics of the disease are wartlike growths occurring mainly on the fins of perciformid fishes. Individual cells may reach 1 mm in size. The disease may be incorrectly identified as eggs of insects or some parasite, or as Cnidosporidian cysts. The virus particles that cause the disease are transmitted through the water to uninfected fish when the large cells burst and the virus particles are released. Fish infected with lymphocystis are commonly caught on hook and line; the disease does not appear to interfere with the fighting ability of the fish. No treatment is known, but the removal and destruction of infected fish may prevent spreading of the disease.

Bluegill infested with Lymphocystis virus. Granulated appearance is due to greatly enlarged cells. (Courtesy of the Eastern Fish Disease Laboratory)

Carp Pox This disease is characterized by wartlike growths on the skin of carp. Electron micrographs have shown a virus associated with the warts that is their probable cause.

Stomatopapilloma of Eels (Cauliflower Disease) (CPE) This is a disease of eels in which the cells, mainly around the mouth, proliferate causing a large grotesque growth that sometimes prohibits the fish from eating. While a virus has not been shown positively to cause the disease, all indications point toward a virus etiology, with the blood of infected fish containing virus particles that produce a CPE when placed in cell culture.

Infectious Dropsy of Carp (IDC) This disease is now considered to be a complex of diseases with both virus and bacteria being involved in many cases. It was recently established that the acute form of the disease was caused by a virus, and the name "*Spring Viraemia of Carp*" (SVC) proposed for this acute form. A second virus was isolated from IDC fish that produced skin lesions; it was named "Erythrodermatitis." The main symptoms of the complex IDC disease are swollen body, fluid accumulation in the body cavity, lesions on the body and internal organs, and hemorrhaging. There is no treatment for the virus-caused dropsy, but antibiotics may be helpful if bacteria are involved.

Viral Hemorrhagic Septicemia (VHS) VHS, also known as Egtved Disease, affects trout in Europe and has not been reported from the United States or other parts of the world. Epizootics occur most frequently in late winter or early spring. The acute form of VHS is usually found at the beginning of an epizootic, and is characterized by hemorrhaging of eyes and bases of pectoral fins, a dark color, and usually one eye protruding. Heavy mortality is associated with the acute stage. The chronic form is characterized by anemia, dark coloration, and both eyes being distended. Mortality is much less severe in this stage. The third stage is the nervous stage, where the abdomen is shrunken and the fish swim about nervously. There is little mortality associated with this stage.

BACTERIAL DISEASES

Bacterial diseases are usually characterized by the clinical signs that are produced. These signs most commonly include sores or lesions, hemorrhages in muscles or skin, or erosion of fins and tissues. Certain diseases, such as "fin rot," may be caused by a number of different bacteria, while a disease such as furunculosis is caused by a specific bacterium. Many of the fish-pathogenic bacteria are common water bacteria and can live on decaying organic matter, such as vegetation, while others require a fish host in order to live and reproduce.

Bacteria may be constantly entering the tissues and blood of fish, but antimicrobial components of the fishes' body remove them as constantly. It is usually only when some stress-producing factor—such as poor water quality, nutritional deficiency, or adverse temperature—lowers the fishes' resistance that a bacterial disease develops.

Most bacteria-infecting fish are gram-negative (that is, they decolorize when stained with a violet stain). The following is a listing of bacterial diseases, the causative agent, clinical signs, and controls.

Hemorrhagic Septicemia This disease is also known as red mouth disease in trout, red leg disease in frogs, and infectious abdominal dropsy. These are diseases caused by members of the genera *Aeromonas*, *Pseudomonas*, and *Vibrio*. In most cases the name *Aeromonas liquefaciens* is listed as the most common causative agent by American workers, while *Pseudomonas punctata*, *Aeromonas hydrophila*, and *A. punctata* appear frequently in European literature. These latter three are considered synonyms of *A. liquefaciens*. Although *Aeromonas* has been associated with infectious dropsy for years a virus was recently isolated and thought to be the primary cause of that disease (*see* Infectious Dropsy of Carp). The diseases caused by *Aeromonas* and *Pseudomonas* are a problem world wide. They occur most commonly in the spring of the

Hemorrhagic septicemia on channel catfish skin, caused by *Aeromonas hydrophila* (*A. liquefaciens*). This disease is worldwide (Courtesy of the Eastern Fish Disease Laboratory)

Red Sore disease of northern pike caused by *A. hydrophilia* (Courtesy of the Eastern Fish Disease Laboratory)

Dropsy in goldfish, caused by *Pseudomonas* or *Aeromonas*. Note the distended body is filled with fluid (Courtesy of the Eastern Fish Disease Laboratory)

year, apparently when the hosts' resistance is lowest. *Vibrio* usually causes a hemorrhagic septicemia of marine and estuarine fishes that is referred to as red pest, but it also has been reported from freshwater fishes.

The disease caused by these bacteria is characterized by red sores or lesions, eroded tissue—including fins—inflammation around the mouth and bases of fins, and, less commonly, distended abdomen and protruding eyes due to fluid accumulations in the tissues and body cavity.

Bacterial lesions on striped bass fingerlings. These fish were infected with *Aeromonas*, *Chondrococcus*, *Pseudomonas* and a flagellate resembling *Costia*

Control is possible in aquaria or culture systems by feeding or injecting antibiotics, but no practical control is available for epizootics occurring in most natural waters. Terramycin is an antibiotic cleared for use on food fishes by the U.S. Food and Drug Administration. This material is added to the food and fed daily at a rate of 2.5–3.5 gms of active Terramycin per 100 pounds of fish for a period of 10 consecutive days. A 21-day withdrawal period is required before the fish are marketed. Chloromycetin (Chloramphenicol) has been used at the same rates as for Terramycin and some nitrofurans (Furoxone, Furacin) have been used at rates of 10 gms per 100 pounds of fish, but these compounds have not been cleared for use on food fishes.

Injection is feasible when a few fish are involved, such as aquarium fishes or valuable brood fish. Terramycin or Chloromycetin can be injected at a rate of 20 mg per kilogram of body weight with good control of the disease resulting. Carp in Europe have been injected with Chloromycetin prior to being stocked, and mortalities were greatly reduced over noninjected fish.

Myxobacterial Diseases Included in this group of diseases are "columnaris disease," "bacterial gill disease," and "cold-water bacterial disease"—also known as "fin rot," "tail rot," and "peduncle disease." Myxobacteria are a group of gram-negative long rods commonly found in natural waters. They are motile and movement is by means of a flexing or gliding motion. As in the diseases caused by *Aeromonas* and related forms, some predisposing stress factor is usually involved when the outbreaks occur. In culture systems this may be handling, malnutrition, overcrowding, poor water quality, or combinations of these. In natural waters poor water quality, spawning stress, and/or unsuitable temperatures are usually the main factors.

Columnaris Disease This disease is mainly a problem in North America, and is caused by the bacterium *Chondrococcus columnaris*. Clinical signs are grayish to whitish eroded areas of the skin, gills, body, fins, head, or around the mouth. The grayish lesions may look like a fungus infection, and this has led to the name of "cotton mouth," "cotton wool," and "mouth fungus." Another appropriate name is "saddle back," because lesions are commonly produced across the back of the fish in the shape of a saddle.

Disease signs caused by several other organisms may be similar, but columnaris can be diagnosed easily by examining live organisms in a wet-mount scraping from the margin of a lesion under a microscope. The presence of many long, slender flexing rods is usually good enough for a positive diagnosis.

Apparently high water temperatures lower the fishes' resistance to columnaris in culture systems so it is best to avoid handling fish or subjecting them to stress factors during periods when the temperature is high. If it should be found necessary to move or handle fish when water temperature is high, a bacteriostatic compound, such as acriflavin at 4–10 ppm, can be added to the water to help prevent spread of infection.

Bacterial gill disease in sunfish. Large brown necrotic areas on the gills are caused by *Columnaris*

Columnaris disease. Note lesions across backs of catfish and on noses of tadpoles. Bacterial in origin

Control of columnaris is possible in culture systems and aquaria by feeding Terramycin at a rate of 3 gms active material per 100 pounds of fish, the same as for controlling diseases caused by *Aeromonas* and *Pseudomonas*. In aquaria or tanks a Terramycin bath of 20 ppm gives an effective control of columnaris. Other treatments that have been successful are copper sulphate at 1 ppm in ponds or a concentration of 1:2,000 for 1–2 minutes. A new nitrofuran, furpyrionol, has given excellent control as a 1-hour bath at 1 ppm.

Bacterial Gill Disease This disease is characterized by a swelling and fusing of the gill lamellae and filaments. Fish stop feeding and become sluggish.

A related condition, nutritional gill disease, caused by nutritional deficiencies, may be confused with bacterial gill disease. In the latter, however, long slender myxobacteria, similar to those causing columnaris disease, are present on the surface of the gills.

Since the causative bacteria are present in the water supply it is necessary to maintain as clean a water supply as possible. No wild fish, which might serve as a source of infection, should be present.

Several chemicals have been used that give good control of bacterial gill disease. A flushing bath with 5 ppm potassium permanganate has given good results, and a

copper sulphate dip treatment in 1:2,000 copper sulfate for 1 minute also has given good results.

Cold-Water Bacterial Disease (Peduncle Disease) This disease is caused by bacteria similar to those causing columnaris disease, but the former affect fish during periods when water temperature is low. The primary signs of the disease are a darkening of the peduncle and erosion of the caudal fin and peduncle. The disease causes great losses in hatcheries and effects mainly salmonid fry and fingerlings.

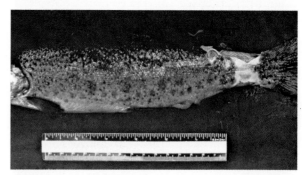

Trout infected with peduncle or cold-water disease, caused by Myxobacteria; sometimes the entire tail will erode away (Courtesy of the Eastern Fish Disease Laboratory)

Cold-water or peduncle disease is mainly systemic, and antibiotic treatment normally must be included in the diet. Terramycin and Sulfisoxazole have given good control of the disease and the nitrofuran, furpyrinol, has given excellent control as a 1 hour bath at 1 ppm because it is readily absorbed into the tissues.

Fin Rot or Tail Rot Although myxobacteria commonly have been found on fish with signs of fin and tail rot there is some doubt as to whether they are the primary cause of this disease. Other pathogenic bacteria, such as *Aeromonas*, will also cause the characteristic fin and tail erosion. Usually the edge of the dorsal fin or tail is infected first and the infection spreads to the other fins. Some factor—such as parasites, handling damage, or nutritional deficiencies—may cause the initial lesion; the bacteria would invade the tissues and be instrumental in the destruction of the fins.

Tail rot in trout, caused by a complex of different bacteria. Note regeneration of tissues in fish at top. (Courtesy of the Eastern Fish Disease Laboratory)

Treatment of fin or tail rot with a disinfectant bath of copper sulfate at a strength of 1:2,000 for 1–2 minutes has been successful. All of the external chemotherapeutic baths are reported to have been used with varying success. Care should be taken to prevent overcrowding in culture systems and to maintain clean tanks and water.

Furunculosis The main signs of this disease are boil-like lesions on the body. In addition to the boils, other common signs are hemorrhages in fins and muscles and a bloody exudate from the vent. This disease is primarily a problem in salmonids in Europe and North America, but other species of fish may become infected. The causative organism of furunculosis is *Aeromonas salmonicida*. Other species of *Aeromonas* are commonly found as saprophytes in water, but *A. salmonicida* is an obligate pathogen that will not live for more than a week or so without a host. The disease is spread from infected fish, and some may be carriers without signs. At low temperatures the disease may be latent without clinical signs or mortalities.

Prevention is possible by eliminating carrier fish and disinfecting the water supply and equipment. Only eggs or fish known to be free of furunculosis should be used. Water low in oxygen may be a predisposing factor in outbreaks of the disease so the O_2 level in water should be maintained above 5 ppm.

Furunculosis of trout. The boil-like furuncule that gives the disease its name is caused by *Aeromonas salmonicida*. It can be controlled by antibiotics (Courtesy of the Eastern Fish Disease Laboratory)

Sulfamerazine at a rate of 10 gms per 100 pounds of fish and fed for 10 days has been widely used with good results to control furunculosis, but kidney damage may result in the fish if it is fed for long periods of time. Also there may be a resistance to sulfa drugs by the bacteria. Antibiotics, such as Terramycin or Chloromycetin, at rates of 3.0 gm per 100 pounds of fish per day for 10 days have also given good control. Some of the nitrofurans have been used to treat furunculosis, and have given excellent results. Furoxone at a rate of 100 mg per kilogram per day for 10 days has been reported to give a better control than Chloromycetin.

Ulcer Disease Ulcer disease is caused by the bacterium *Hemophilus piscium*. Shallow, open sores are the main signs of this disease, and sometimes boils are formed which resemble those of furunculosis. This disease may occur concurrently with furunculosis. Ulcer disease begins as small whitish lesions on the body, fins, or head; they develop into larger reddish lesions. Sometimes the lesions appear similar to those caused by *Aeromonas* and *Pseudomonas*.

Ulcer disease affects brook trout primarily, and has been a problem only in the northeastern United States. It has occurred very rarely during the past decade and is no longer considered to be a major problem. Both chemotherapeutics and preventive measures, such as are used for furunculosis, can be used for ulcer disease.

Pasteurellosis A massive kill of white perch occurred in Chesapeake Bay in the summer of 1963. The causative organism was determined to be a new species of *Pasteurella*, later named *P. piscicida*. Striped bass were killed by the organism, but to a much lesser degree than the white perch were. This was the first time a species of *Pasteurella* was isolated from a fish.

Kidney Disease (Dee Disease) This disease has only been reported from salmonids in the United States, Canada, and the British Isles. A small gram-positive bacterium of the genus *Corynebacterium*, causing white raised areas mainly in the kidneys of diseased fish, is the agent of kidney disease. The disease is much more severe

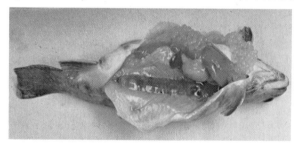

Kidney disease of trout. The grayish patches on the kidney caused by a species of *Corynebacterium*. (Courtesy of the Eastern Fish Disease Laboratory)

in waters of low hardness. Due to the destruction of kidney tissues, a build up of fluids is present in the body cavity and behind the eyes, producing a "popeye" condition. Small unruptured lesions are common on the back of infected fish. Mode of transfer has not been definitely established, but kidney disease may be transmitted on or in the fertilized egg; therefore, eggs should be obtained from parents known to be free of the disease. Treatment of kidney disease is difficult. Erythromycin used at a rate of 9–10 gm per 100 kilograms of fish per day for 3 weeks is recommended.

FUNGUS DISEASES

The most common fungi infecting fishes are the "water molds," such as *Saprolegnia* They are found in most waters living on decaying organic matter, and are considered to be secondary pathogens, usually invading the fish through a wound or after the protective mucous coating of the fish has been disturbed. These same fungi attach fish eggs and are responsible for losses amounting to many thousands of dollars in fish hatcheries around the world.

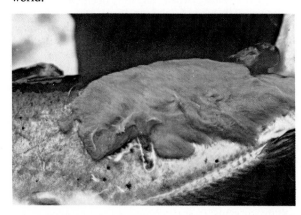

Fungus infection of catfish marked by a large cottony growth caused by the water mold *Saprolegnia*. The reddish color of the fungus is due to iron in the water.

Fungus infections are characterized by a "cottony" growth on the skin of fish or on fish eggs. This cottonlike appearance is due to the thin filaments or hyphae that make up the growth. Most fungi produce spores that are found in waters in great numbers. These spores can only establish a fungus colony on dead tissue or organic matter. In living fish the spores usually attack dead or damaged tissue, and the mycelia start to grow and will kill tissue as it spreads. In eggs the spores usually become established on dead eggs or some organic detritus that has settled on the eggs, and will then spread to live eggs.

Certain fungi will also invade the internal organs of fish. One of particular importance is *Ichthyosporidium*, which attacks both marine and freshwater fishes. Infected fish become thin and sluggish and in many cases cysts and discoloration may occur. Where many cysts are present, normal tissues are replaced by scar tissue, which may . make the affected organs feel hard or granular.

A fungus affecting gills is *Branchiomyces* It blocks the blood vessels and causes the gill tissue to die; therefore the name "gill rot" is given to this disease. Gill rot causes extensive fish mortalities in Europe, and its occurrence has been noted in North America. It is not prevalent enough to be considered much of a threat to North American fisheries, but it is potentially serious. Most of the trouble with gill rot comes when the temperature is high and there is much organic matter in the water.

Several other genera of fungi—such as *Penicellium*, *Alternarie*, and *Fusarium*—have also been reported in the internal organs of fish.

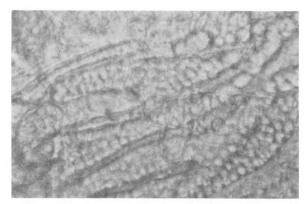

Gill rot caused by *Branchiomyces*. This fungus blocks the blood vessels and finally kills the gill tissues

There are no chemical controls for fungi affecting internal organs, so good sanitation and avoidance is the best course of action for them. The external fungi, such as *Saprolegnia* can be controlled on fish and eggs with malachite green. (*See* Treatment of Fish Diseases.)

PARASITIC DISEASES

Parasites are larger disease-producing organisms affecting fish. These include protozoans, Trematodes (Monogenea and Digenea), cestodes (tapeworms), nematodes, acanthocephalans (spiney-headed worms), Hirudiuea (leeches), and Crustacea (parasitic copepods and fish lice). The following is a key to the major groups of parasites that will aid the reader in determining to which group a parasite belongs.

Protozoan Diseases Protozoans are considered to be the most important group of parasites affecting fish. Fish kills caused by protozoans are reported from all over the world. The condition of the host, environmental factors, food supply, and other such factors affect the hosts' susceptibility to these parasites. Fish population density is important because the more fish present, the easier it is for one of these parasites to find a new host. Many species of protozoans that would not cause problems under less-crowded conditions, therefore, may cause tremendous die-offs of fish where they are densely stocked.

Host reaction to invasion by protozoans is highly variable, with factors such as size, age, immunity, host specificity, and the above-mentioned host condition and environmental factors playing important roles in this reaction. In some cases there are protozoans living on or in fish that show no signs of pathogenicity, and these are classified as commensals. There is a second group that is somewhere between commensalism and parasitism and are potential pathogens, while a third group are true parasites living exclusively at the expense of their hosts. Most host reactions to invasion by protozoans are directed toward expelling or isolating the parasite. Injury to the host is by mechanical damage, secretion of toxic substances, occlusion of blood vessels, obtaining nutrition at the expense of the host, and rendering the host more susceptible to secondary infections by one or more of the above factors. Most recent taxonomic considerations place protozoans in 6 major groups—flagellates, amebas, sporozoans, cnidosporidians, ciliates, and suctorians.

KEY TO MAJOR GROUPS OF PARASITES

1a.	Organism a single cell, microscopic (except for Ich.)	Protozoa
1b.	Organism multicellular, microscopic or not	2
2a.	Microscopic; found on gills, skin, and fins; have anchors, clamps, and hooks for attachment	Monogenetic Trematodes
2b.	Generally seen with unaided eye or located internally if microscopic	3
3a.	Body wormlike or tonguelike, always internal, in cysts in tissues or organs or not encysted in G.I. tract, suckers at front end and near middle of body	Digenetic Trematodes
3b.	Body wormlike or not, no suckers located near middle of body	4
4a.	Parasites internal, in gut or tissues	5
4b.	Parasites external, may be attached to skin	6
5a.	Elongate, flattened, segmented worms located mainly in gut, head (Scolex) attached to gut wall by four suckers	Tapeworms
5b.	Rounded, elongate nonsegmented worms; may be in gut or small capsules in tissues; lacking spiney heads	Nematodes
5c.	Rounded, elongate nonsegmented worms having spiney proboscis, may be in gut or in visceral tissues	Acanthocephalans
6a.	External parasite with elongate segmented body, sucker on each end	Leeches
6b.	Attached to gills, gillrakers, or inside of mouth, or protruding from skin or base of fins and usually with prominent egg sacs attached, or with flat disclike body and no egg sacs	Crustaceans

Flagellates One of the most problematic flagellates parasitizing the gills and external surface of fish is *Costia*. This parasite attaches to and feeds on host cells causing a rather severe host reaction. Discoloration and large amounts of mucous causing a gray to bluish film on the fish are characteristic of *Costia* infestation.

Costia infestations characteristically develop grayish to blue lesions due to excess mucous production. Flagellates are protozoa with motile organs or "flagella"

Several species of dinoflagellates cause diseases in fish. The names "velvet disease," "rust disease," "gold-dust disease," and "coralfish disease" have been applied to diseases caused by species of *Oodinium*.

A dinoflagellate responsible for "red tide" (*which see*) causes massive fish kills in marine water by secretion of toxins. Some related freshwater forms become parasitic on fish and may possibly cause kills by secretion of toxins.

Two genera of blood flagellates, *Trypanosoma* and *Cryptobia*, are commonly found in the blood of both freshwater and marine fishes. The life cycles of these parasites involve an alteration of hosts with leeches being the alternate host and also the means of transfer from fish to fish. A flagellate living in the intestine of salmonids and several other species of fish is *Hexamita*. Pathogenicity of Hexamitiasis is questionable, but most reports indicate injury to the intestinal lining.

Amebas Most reports of amebas in fish indicate that they are not pathogenic; however, "gray crab disease" in blue crabs is caused by an ameba. It appears that most species of amebas in fish are free-living forms and their occurrence in fish is facultative.

Sporozoans This group forms sporozoites; they do not have polar filaments, which separates them from the cnidosporidians. Members of this group have intracellular stages with some living in blood cells in a manner similar to malaria parasites living in mammals. *Eimeria* is a coccidian that usually infects intestinal epithelium. Fish infected with *Eimeria* usually are sluggish, have popeyes and fluid accumulation in the body cavity, and may shed scales. One member of this genus infecting testes of clupeid fishes may cause complete sterility in severe infections. Another species causes serious mortalities in young carp when infections are severe.

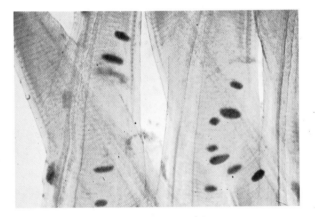

Myxosporidian cysts in gill filaments. These cysts seen under a microscope would appear white to the eye

Cnidosporidians Members of this group form spores with polar filaments and do not have sporozoites. Two main groups occur in the Cnidosporidia. Myxosporea have spores of multicellular origin, while Microsporea have spores of unicellular origin.

Different species of Myxosporea have specific sites of infection; they have been found in virtually all tissues and organs of fish. In freshwater fishes the gills and gall bladder are common sites of infection, while the gall bladder and urinary bladder are most commonly infected in marine fishes. In marine fishes members of the genera *Unicapsula*, *Hexapsula*, and the *Kudoa-Chloromyxum* complex cause destruction of living flesh that has been described as "wormy," "mushy," "milky," and ulcerous.

Whirling Disease of salmonids is caused by the myxosporean *Myxosoma cerebralis*. The most obvious signs are whirling, tail-chasing type of swimming motion, spinal curvature, and cranial deformities in adults, while the young fish may exhibit a black tail. The whirling that gives the disease its name is caused by destruction of cartilaginous tissues and subsequent deformities of the skeleton. The black tail results from pressure on the nerves controlling the pigment cells. Rainbow and brook trout are affected most by the disease, but brown trout and salmon become infected and may act as carriers. No chemotherapy is known for whirling disease. Destruction of infected stock and disinfection of infected waters is recommended.

Whirling disease in rainbow trout, caused by the spore-producing protozoan, *Myxosoma cerebralis*. Cartilege is destroyed in young fish causing spinal deformities (Courtesy of the Eastern Fish Disease Laboratory)

Trout fingerling infected with whirling disease. The black tail is due to pressure nerves controlling pigmentation

A myxosporidian of catfish, *Henneguya*, causes damage to skin and gills, and may cause mortalities in young channel catfish.

A cutaneous form of the Myxosoporidian *Henneguya* in catfish. It damages skin and gills, but may kill young

Microsporea are intracellular parasites causing hypertrophy of affected cells. The microsporidian genera *Nosema* (which now includes the genus *Glugea*) and *Pleistophora* infects both marine and freshwater fishes, often producing large cysts in tissues and organs. *P. ovariae* in golden shiner ovaries may cause sterility in older fish, and *P. hyphessobryconis* that is the cause of "neon tetra disease" destroys the muscle by an apparent chemical histolytic action.

Microsporidian cysts in gizzard shad. This spore-forming protozoan is also responsible for Neon Tetra disease, and will cause sterility in female golden shiners

Ciliates The ciliated protozoans are characterized by having small hairlike cilia as their means of locomotion. Almost all ciliates of fish are ectoparasites living on the skin and gills.

Ichthyophthirius or "Ich" has wiped out many trout hatcheries. Seen as small white spots on this catfish, these parasites can be controlled if observed early

Ichthyophthirius or "Ich" is one of the most devastating parasites of freshwater fishes, and its marine counterpart *Cryptocaryon* is equally as bad. These parasites burrow into the skin of their hosts producing "white spot" disease. They are large enough to be seen with the naked eye, but there are several diseases that have a "white spot" appearance on fish so it is best to have diseases always positively identified, especially before trying to treat them. "Ich" is very nonhost-specific and will attack most species of fishes. An immunity to this parasite is developed, and immune fish may be carriers. This is sometimes evident when new fish are added to an aquarium or pond and a few days later fish start to die. The best treatment for "Ich" is 0.1 ppm malachite green.

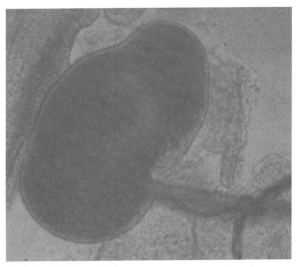

Ichthyophthirius cell. The large C-shaped nucleus is a characteristic of this devastating ciliate

Trichodina is one of the most common external parasites of fish. It often can build up tremendous populations if factors such as temperature and host condition are right. This parasite is one of the easiest to control with almost any recommended treatment giving excellent results. Potassium permanganate at a rate of 2 ppm is one of the best treatments.

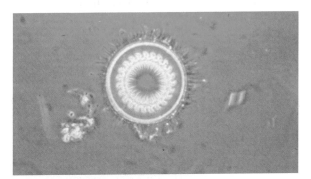

Trichodina is a common ciliate parasite to many species of fish. It is characterized by the denticular ring shown in this phrase-contrast photomicrograph

Chilodonella, *Scyphidia*, and *Glossatella* are some other common ciliates that can be very harmful when abundant on fish. They can all be controlled with potassium permanganate at the 2 ppm rate.

Tilapia heavily infested with the ciliate *Chilodonella*

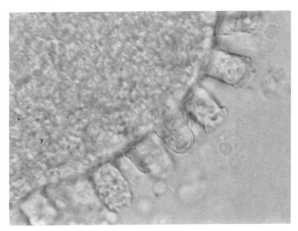

Scyphidia, a ciliated protozoan, is sometimes referred to as commensal, living on but not harming its host. Heavy infestations such as this can cause mortalities

Red sore disease of largemouth bass caused by the ciliate *Epistylis*. Note pitlike lesions where scales have eroded

Epistylis infection of catfish. In this case the spines and portions of the cranium have eroded away

Epistylis is a stalked ciliate that can be especially harmful to fish. A characteristic "red sore disease" with eroded scales is caused by this parasite. Colonies of the parasite also attach to spines and hardrays of fish causing erosion. This parasite is sometimes hard to control. One or more treatments with potassium permanganate appear to be most effective.

Swollen, anemic, clubbed, and eroded gills characteristic of the suctorian parasite, *Trichophrya*. Other disease-producing organisms create the same symptoms

Suctoria Only one suctorian, *Trichophrya*, is found in fish. The early developmental stage is ciliated, but the mature stage is characterized by having tentacles. Heavy infestations of *Trichophrya* cause swollen, clubbed, and anemic gills. Treatment for this parasite may be difficult. One ppm copper sulfate gives a good control.

Monogenea (Gill and Body Flukes) Monogeneans are all obligate parasites that occur mostly on gills or bodies of fishes. They show a high degree of host specificity, with many being so highly specific that the species or subspecies of fish host can be determined by the parasite. They are elongated dorso-ventrally flattened worms without a complete digestive tract.

The worms are divided into 3 main anatomical regions: a head, body, and posterior haptor, the latter usually bearing hooks that are used for attachment to the host. A mouth is located at the front end, and the gut may form a continuous loop or end blindly. Eyespots may or may not be present. All monogeneans are hermaphrodites, with most being egg layers, but some are live bearers. Both larvae that hatch from eggs and those born alive seek a host fish and develop directly into an adult without involving an intermediate host. This accounts for the name Monogenea (single origin), as compared to the digenetic trematodes which have more than one inter-

mediate host. Monogeneans are separated into 2 major groups, the polyopisthocotyleans and the monopisthocotyleans. The haptor (attachment area) of the former consists of modified suckers or valvelike chitinous clamps. The monopisthocotyleans usually have a simple haptor with large hooks in the center and up to 16 marginal hooklets on the margin of the haptor. Monopisthocotyleans are mainly parasites of freshwater fishes, while the polyopisthocotyleans are mainly parasites of marine fishes.

One important genera of monopisthocotyleans is *Dactylogyrus*, which is mainly a parasite of cyprinid fishes. In European and Asian fish culture, where many species of cyprinids are raised under intensive conditions, *Dactylogyrus* can cause serious losses. Probably the most important species of *Dactylogyrus* are those affecting gills of cultured carps. The parasites become very abundant on the gills, causing destruction of gill tissue. Usually the smaller fish are most severely affected, but once they reach several inches in length the effects of the parasites are greatly reduced.

In North America species of *Cleidodiscus* are detrimental in catfish culture and both natural and pond populations of bluegills. Species of *Gyrodactylus* are live bearers and occur mainly on the bodies and fins and less

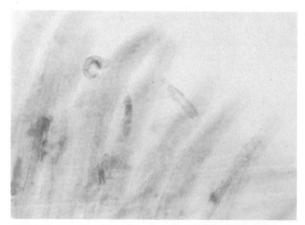

Cleidodiscus, a dactylogyrid monogenean on catfish gills

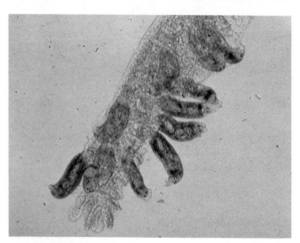

The monogenean *Dactylogyrus* on a gill filament of a carp. This fluke selects that part of the fish's body where the blood is nearest the surface

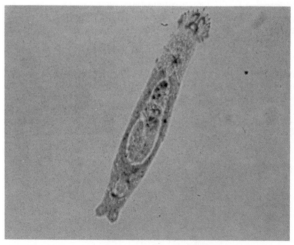

Gyrodactylus, a live-bearing monogenean, occurs mainly on body and fins. Note the embryo inside the body

frequently on gills. Under certain environmental conditions *Gyrodactylus* can develop tremendous populations in a period of a few days. Most fish losses due to *Gyrodactylus* occur during the spring and fall. During an epizootic there is much mucous production and erosion of epithelium that may lead to secondary bacterial and fungal infections.

Important species of Polyopisthocotylea are *Discocotyle*, affecting salmonid fishes, and *Diplozoan*, which occurs on gills of cyprinids. These parasites are bloodsuckers and can cause anemia in severe infestations. Gills also become covered with bleeding ulcers and tumors.

Octomacrum, a polyopisthocotylean monogenean. This parasite has clamps instead of hooks or anchors for attachment. These flukes cause anemia in fishes

Digenea Digenean trematodes also have an elongated dorso-ventrally flattened body. One of the main characteristics are the muscular suckers on these worms. In most cases there is a large oral sucker at the anterior end of the body and a ventral sucker that lies somewhere in the middle of the body. These suckers are rarely missing. The mouth, usually located in the oral sucker, leads to a muscular pharynx and two-branched intestine which ends blindly near the posterior part of the body. Most digeneans are hermaphroditic, but some have separate sexes. The life cycle of digenetic flukes is complex and involves several intermediate hosts. Typically a ciliated larval stage called a miracidium hatches from the egg and swims until it encounters the first intermediate host, which is most often a snail or rarely some other mollusk. In some cases eggs are eaten by the snails and the miracidium will hatch there. The miracidium will turn into a sporocyst, which will then produce a number of new

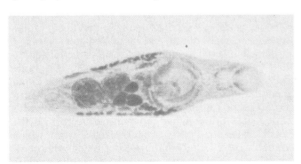

A typical adult digenean, *Triganodistomum*, showing the strong oral and ventral suckers and internal organs

larvae called redia. These in turn produce the next larval generation called cercariae. These emerge from the snail and swim freely in the water until the next intermediate host, such as an insect or commonly a fish, is encountered. Cercarial penetration of man's skin is what causes "swimmer's itch." This is also the way man contracts schistosomiasis. The cercariae encyst in the second intermediate host to become metacercariae. The host bearing the metacercariae is eaten by the final host (a fish, bird, or mammal) to give rise to the adult, thus completing the life cycle.

This life cycle gives us two main groups of digeneans in fish; the immature or metacecariae stages, which live in the tissues, and the adults, which live in the gut or various other organs in fish. The tissue-inhabiting larval forms cause far more problems than the adults. When a cercaria penetrates the skin and migrates into the tissues of a fish, it causes mechanical damage and hemorrhaging and possible toxic damage. If many cercariae penetrate at any one time they can cause death to the fish, but if a few penetrate at a time the fish can tolerate great numbers of them with little apparent damage. Such larval forms as white grubs, yellow grubs, and black grubs or black spot give fish a very unsightly appearance, and they are often rejected by fisherman. One genus, *Nanophyetus*, is a parasite of salmonids that causes serious damage in hatcheries in the northwestern United States. It carries a rickettsia which is the cause of salmon poisoning in dogs.

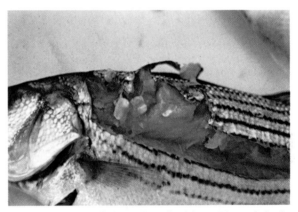

The yellow grub infestation in striped bass. The grub is the larval stage, as the adult worms occur in aquatic birds

White grub infestation in the visceral organs of a bluegill. Aquatic birds are its final host and carrier

Black grub infestation in largemouth bass. As with other "grubs," this larval digenean reaches a final host

Since there is no control for the tissue-inhabiting metacercariae the best approach is to control the snails or the final host, which is often a bird or mammal.

Although adults seldom cause trouble there is one, *Sanguinicola*, that lives in the blood of fish that can cause serious fish mortalities. This parasite moves into the gills to lay its eggs where it blocks the blood vessels.

Cestoda (Tapeworms) The cestodes or tapeworms are flat, elongate worms with bodies usually made up of a series of segments called proglottids, with each segment being capable of independent reproduction. One group has unsegmented bodies. The head of the worm, called a scolex, usually has muscular suckers and/or hooks with which it attaches. There is no digestive tract, and food is absorbed through the cuticle or skin. Eggs are laid containing fully-formed embryos. Tapeworms of fish usually have a life cycle where the eggs are eaten by a microcrustacean, such as a copepod. Inside the copepod the embryo hatches from the egg and develops into a stage called a Procercoid. The crustacean intermediate host is then eaten by a fish, and may either develop into an adult or a second immature stage called a pleurocercoid. As in the digeneans, it is the larval forms that cause most damage to the fish host. Probably the most important tapeworm parasite in North America is the bass tapeworm, in which the pleurocercoid larval stage migrates into the ovaries of bass and causes sterility.

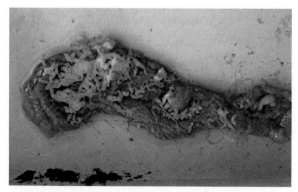

Corallobothrium, a tapeworm in the intestine of catfish

Another important larval tapeworm in fish is the larval broad tapeworm of man, *Diphyllobothrium latum*, which

has been found in smoked fish in the Great Lakes area of the United States. Cooking at the proper temperature or heat smoking at 57° C will kill the larvae and prevent infection. Larval tapeworms occur in many marine species of fish. The common "grub" in spotted seatrout is a tapeworm larva.

Adult tapeworms occurring in fish are not considered to be very detrimental, but some will often build up tremendous numbers in fish. Caryophyllaeid tapeworms are those unsegmented tapeworms parasitizing mostly catostomid fishes. They are often found in pitlike depressions in the intestine.

Nematoda (Round Worms) The nematodes are unsegmented, elongated, cylindrical worms with the adults living mainly in the intestinal tract and larvae living in tissues throughout the fish. Sexes are separate in this group. Most lay eggs, but many are live bearers. The life cycle involves an invertebrate, usually a copepod or an insect, that serves as an intermediate host.

These may be eaten and the worm develops into an adult, or it may use the fish as a second intermediate host and develop in either a fish, bird, or mammal. As is true of the digenetic trematodes and tapeworms, the tissue-inhabiting forms cause the most injury to the host. Larval forms will cause inflammation and hemorrhaging of internal organs and loss of body weight when infections are heavy. The genus *Anisakis* parasitizes the digestive tract of marine mammals and birds, and fish serve as intermediate hosts. Occasional reports have been made that larval migrans of *Anisakis* in man have been quite serious. Larvae of several other genera of ascarid worms are commonly found coiled in mesentaries of fish.

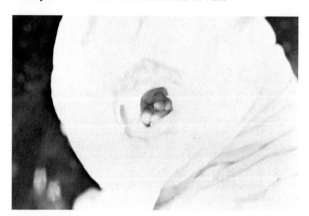

A sometimes fish-fatal nematode, *Goezia*, in large nodule of stomach wall of a Florida largemouth bass

The genus *Goezia* produces nodules and open, pitlike lesions in stomachs of fish, and has caused quite extensive mortalities in certain populations. One tissue-inhabiting adult, *Philometra*, lives behind the eyes, in the body cavity, and in the fins of fish. Another tissue-inhabiting nematode, *Philonema*, migrates through the visceral tissues of fishes causing adhesions and interfering with reproduction. Still another common round worm is the genus *Camallanus*. This is a red, threadlike worm which commonly protrudes from the anus of fishes. Almost all bluegills caught from spawning beds during the summer will have these small red worms protruding from the anus.

The "popeyed" condition of this bluegill is caused by the nematode *Philometra*, which lives behind the eyes

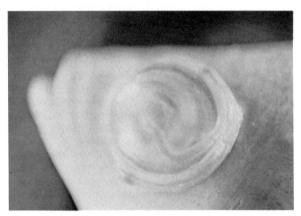

Eye of bluegill showing the coiled nematode *Philometra*

Acanthocephala (Spiney-headed Worms) This group is characterized by having a hook-bearing proboscis, which is attached to the intestinal wall of the host by means of the hooks. These are cylindrical, unsegmented worms that lack a digestive tract. Sexes are separate. The life cycle usually will involve a crustacean eating an embryo-bearing egg. The crustacean is eaten by a final or intermediate host. Final hosts may be fish, birds, or

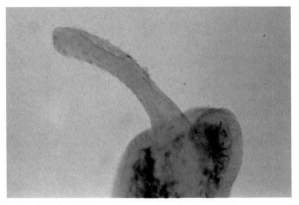

The spiney-headed worm, *Leptorhynchoides*, showing the spines on the proboscis. It can cause mortalities

mammals. Two main groups parasitize fish; these are Neoechinorhynchidea, which has few hooks on the proboscis, usually 3 rows; and the Echinorhynchidea, which has many rows of hooks on the proboscis. Spiney-headed worms occasionally will cause extensive mortalities due to the proboscis penetrating the intestinal wall. One genus, *Pomphorynchus*, has a large bulblike inflated neck that penetrates the intestinal wall and causes severe damage to the host.

Hirudinea (Leeches) Leeches belong to the phylum Annelida of segmented worms and are closely related to the common earthworms. They have a segmented body and a number of rings appearing as secondary annuli. With both an anterior and posterior sucker, many have eyespots at the anterior end of the body. Serrate jaws or plates are present with which the leech pierces the host to suck blood. Leeches are hermaphroditic and lay eggs in cocoons. Many species carry young leeches attached to the body. True fish leeches belong to the family Piscicolidae. These have an elongate, cylindrical body that is sometimes differentiated into neck and trunk.

Leeches will attach to fish, take a blood meal, and then leave the fish for varying lengths of time. Damage done to the host will depend on the number of leeches present and the site of attachment. Many species will attach to the fins and cause little apparent damage other than at the site of attachment. One large leech, *Cystobranchus*, will attach to gills or at the isthmus, where they can feed on gills. They cause much damage to the gills and have been responsible for many mortalities in fish hatcheries.

Leeches serve as vectors for blood parasites of fish, such as *Trypanosoma* and *Cryptobia*, and they are also probably responsible for transfer of blood sporozoans, such as *Haemogregarina*, and fish bacteria and viruses.

Crustacea (Parasitic Copepods and Fish Lice) Crustaceans belong to the phylum Arthropoda (joint-footed animals) and occur in a sometimes bizarre variety of forms. Sexes are separate for the most part, but many times only the female is observed as a parasite. Three main groups occur as parasites of fishes.

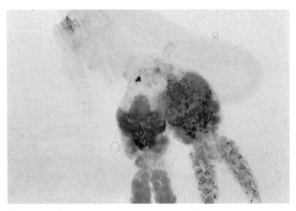

Two parasitic copepods, *Ergasilus*, on gill filament of salmon. One has mature larvae ready to hatch from egg

The first group is the copepods. They live mainly as ectoparasites (outside the body), but some marine species are endoparasitic. Ergasilids are mainly parasites of gills, but bear a striking resemblance to free-living copepods. Usually egg sacs protrude from the small body and make them easily detectable. They destroy the gill epithelium and very often allow invasion of secondary fungus infections. Certain ergasilids occur on fins and body-destroying epithelium.

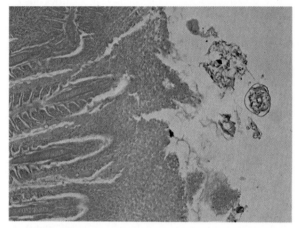

Damage to gills caused by *Ergasilus*. Note the fused gill filaments and cuticlelike layer of epithelium

Lernaeid parasites (anchor worms) attach to the host with branching, rootlike projections that anchor the parasite in the tissues. The long, cylindrical, unsegmented body is all that is seen projecting from the host. Sometimes they penetrate deep into tissues, causing much tissue destruction and providing a site for secondary infections. They have parasitic larval stages which feed on host epithelium and are equally destructive of tissues.

Goldfish infested with the anchor worm *Lernaea*

Lernopodid parasites are copepods having fat rigid bodies and attaching by long armlike processes, which start out as filaments that grow under the host skin and then grow together giving the parasite permanent attachment. They usually attach to gills or in the oral cavity, and have caused extensive fish mortalities. The Branchiura or "gill-tailed" crustaceans include the common fish louse, *Argulus*. The fish louse has a flat oval body, 2 complex eyes, and 2 prehensile discs used to attach to the fish. They have a mouth located adjacent to a preoral sting. The sting is used first to pierce tissues, and then suck the blood of the host. When present in great numbers they can be very destructive to a fish population.

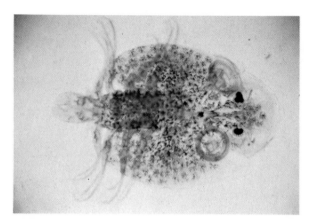

The fish louse, *Argulus*

Isopods are a group of dorso-ventrally flattened crustaceans that are mostly free-living, but some are parasitic. They are mainly marine, and are commonly found as parasites in the gill chambers of clupeid fishes, such as menhaden. Some will burrow into the host at the base of a fin and live an endoparasitic existence. They feed on blood, severely retard growth, and in many cases cause death.

The organophosphate Dylox is the best-known control for most crustacean parasites when used at a rate of 0.25 ppm (active ingredient).

Miscellaneous Parasites A number of various other groups have been found as parasites of fish. Larvae (glochidia) of many freshwater mussels go through a stage where they attach to gills or fins of fish. They have posed a problem when they become very abundant on gills. Mites have been reported as parasites of fishes, but they are not considered to be a threat. Pentastomid larvae (tongue worms) have been reported from several species of fish. Adults of this group live in lungs of reptiles. Coelenterates have caused death of young fish due to stinging, but this is very rare.

MISCELLANEOUS DISEASES

Blue-Sac Disease This is a disease of newly-hatched fry, mainly salmonids, in which the yolk sac shows an abnormal accumulation of bluish fluid. Other signs of the disease are popeye, hemorrhage, white spots in the yolk, and anemia. The fry are sluggish and tend to accumulate in quiet areas of the containers.

A number of causes have been proposed for this disease, but it most likely is a physiological condition brought about by accumulation of wastes in the water while the eggs are incubating. A good flow of well-aerated water past the eggs and prevention of waste build-up is the best method of preventing the disease.

Soft-egg Disease This is a disease of incubating fish eggs, where the eggs become soft and flaccid. Bacteria are known to be associated with a soft-egg condition, and amebas are thought to be a possible cause. Prophylactic treatments of salt, dyes, and antibiotics have reduced losses.

Ulcerative Dermal Necrosis (UDN) This is a disease affecting wild Atlantic salmon and sea trout when they enter fresh water to spawn. So far the disease has not been reported outside the British Isles. Although a virus may be involved, the cause of the disease is not known, and it is thought to affect only wild fish, not cultured fish. Clinical signs of UDN are large skin ulcers that may become secondarily invaded by fungus, in which case it is often fatal. While the primary cause is not known, malachite-green treatments are used to control secondary fungal infections. The skin ulcers usually heal if secondary infections are prevented.

NUTRITIONAL DISEASES

A deficiency of essential components in diets of fishes causes a number of diseases. Also, some commercially-prepared feeds may contain substances, such as aflatoxins, that produce tumors in fish.

A condition known as "*broken-back*" caused by vitamin-C deficiency occurs in cultured fishes that do not have access to sufficient natural foods. Vitamin C (ascorbic acid) is known to be required in the formation of collagen, which forms the organic matrix of bone. Where collagen is not formed properly the backbone becomes weak and breaks just with normal swimming behavior, so that the fish appears deformed. This condition is not reversible, but addition of ascorbic acid to the diet will prevent development of "broken-back."

Nutritional-gill disease resembles bacterial gill disease, and without microscopic confirmation may be mistaken for it. There is not as much epithelial proliferation or fusion of gill filaments in the nutritional gill disease as in bacterial gill disease. A deficiency of pantothenic acid in the diet is believed to be mainly responsible for nutritional gill disease, and fish showing signs of the disease recovered completely when this vitamin was added to the diet.

Blue-Slime disease in trout is caused by a biotin deficiency in which the body is covered by a bluish film. This film begins to slough off after a while, giving the fish a patchy appearance. Brown trout are more susceptible to a biotin deficiency than either brook or rainbow trout, so this disease is mainly a problem in brown trout. It can be easily controlled by feeding beef liver or dried brewers yeast, both of which are high in biotin.

Goiter, an enlargement of the thyroid gland, has been reported in fish. Just as in humans, goiter is caused by a deficiency of iodine. Stress due to overcrowding, poor sanitation, and poor water quality may be contributing factors to the disease.

Hepatoma is a tumor, mainly in the livers of trout, that is commonly caused by a toxin (aflatoxin) produced by a mold (*Aspergillus flavus*). When moldy feeds are fed to fish, even trace amounts may produce hepatoma. Certain other antimetabolites may also cause the tumor. Rainbow trout seem to be most susceptible to the aflatoxin, while other salmonids may be only slightly or not at all susceptible. Prevention of hepatoma is possible by being certain that no moldy feeds or feeds containing other antimetabolites are fed to fish.

Certain other types of growths may occur in fish, but neither causes nor controls are known for them.

TREATMENT OF FISH DISEASES

There are five main ways in which therapeutics are applied to fishes: injection, food additive, short-term bath or dip (usually a few seconds or minutes), long-term bath (usually minutes or hours), and an indefinite prolonged treatment. Treatment by injection is restricted in application to fish that can be easily handled. This type of treatment usually involves antibiotics directed toward controlling bacterial diseases. Food additives may be either

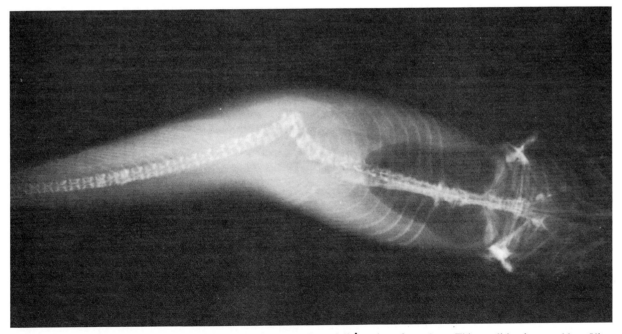

Radiograph of catfish with broken-back disease, showing severe lateral dislocation of vertebrae. This condition is caused by a Vitamin-C deficiency and occurs in artificial environments (Courtesy of Dr. R.T. Lovell, Auburn University)

antibiotics for control of bacteria or antihelminthics. Dips, baths, and indefinite prolonged treatments are aimed at external parasites. The short-term treatments require that the fish be placed into fresh water after the prescribed time in the therapeutic, while the indefinite prolonged treatment does not.

Most treatment levels are expressed as parts per million (ppm) or milligrams per kilogram (mg/kg). One pound of a substance in 1 million pounds of water equals 1 ppm. When treating large bodies of water it is desirable to first calculate the average depth of the water and know the area in surface acres. Average depth times surface acres gives acre-feet of water. One acre-foot is 1 surface acre 1 foot deep. The weight of an acre-foot of water is 2.7 million pounds; therefore, 2.7 pounds of any material in water equals 1 ppm. One mg/liter is equal to 1 ppm, so when working with smaller volumes it is convenient to convert volumes of water to liters for treatment calculation. When treating fish it is best to know something about the quality of the water, because such things as pH and temperature may greatly affect treatment results. Treat a few fish first and see how they react before treating the entire group.

Also, many drugs and chemicals used in treating fish have not been cleared by the FDA for use on food fish. A fish farmer treating food fish with an uncleared chemical runs the risk of having his fish confiscated. Below are some general treatments for specific groups of pathogens:

(a) *Viruses* No treatments are known for virus diseases. Avoidance and prophylactic measures are best for virus-disease prevention.

(b) *Bacteria* As mentioned earlier, bacteria are treated best by injection or food additive of antibiotics. For treatment of bacterial diseases commercially prepared medicated feed pellets may be available, but if they are not a medicated feed can be prepared by adding oxytetracycline, which also goes by the names Terramycin, Liquimycin, and Polyotic. Terramycin is given for 10 days at 2.5 gms per 100 pounds of fish per day. The feed can be prepared by adding Terramycin to a sufficient amount of cod liver or vegetable oil to give a light film of oil on the feed. Then mix in the necessary dosage of antibiotic in the oil and add to the feed, using 82 gms Terramycin per 100 pounds of pellets. Feed the treated food at 3 percent of body weight of the fish. *Example:* A pond stocked with 2,000 fish which average 0.5 pounds each being fed at 3 percent of body weight would have 1,000 pounds of fish. Adding Terramycin at 2.5 gms per 100 pounds of fish would mean adding 25 gms of active ingredient to 30 pounds of feed.

Sulfamerazine, a sulfa drug, is used mainly as a treatment for furunculosis in trout. This drug has been cleared by the FDA. Recommended rate is 10 gms per 100 pounds of fish and fed for 10 days.

Other drugs that are not cleared by the FDA but are very effective against bacterial diseases of fish are Chloromycetin, used in the same manner as Terramycin; Erythromycin, fed at a rate of 4.5 gms per 100 weight for 2 weeks; and several of the nitrofurans (Furozone, Furacin, Furanace) fed at a rate of 10 gms per 100 weight for 10 days.

Potassium permanganate (KMnO₄) used as an indefinite treatment at a rate of 2–3 ppm in ponds has given good results against bacterial infections. This treatment is especially good when the fish are not eating and it is impossible to get an antibiotic into them. It is thought that the effects of the treatment is to reduce numbers of bacteria in the water and also oxidize much of the organic matter that bacteria live on. $KMnO_4$ is not approved by the FDA for use on food fishes.

(c) *External Parasites* The most problematical external parasites are the protozoans, gill flukes, and crustaceans.

Although it is not cleared by the FDA for use on food fishes formalin is one of the best treatments for protozoans and gill flukes. Effective rates are 15–25 ppm as a pond treatment and 100–250 ppm for 1 hour as a prolonged treatment. At temperatures below 60° F fish will tolerate a formalin concentration of 250 ppm for 1 hour, but a rate of 100 ppm for 1 hour should be used at higher temperatures. The fish should be watched during the treatment period, and if they show distress get them back in fresh water. One problem that comes from treating with formalin in ponds is that an oxygen depletion may occur a few days after treatment.

Malachite green used at a rate of 0.1 ppm (0.27 pounds per acre-foot) has been used successfully to treat *Ichthophthirius* or "Ich" which is probably the most damaging parasite of all. A combination of 25 ppm formalin and 0.1 ppm malachite green to treat "Ich" has given excellent results. Malachite green has been used as a dip at a concentration of 1:15,000 to control fungus on both fish and eggs. The zinc-free form of malachite green is used. This material is not cleared by the FDA for use on food fishes.

$KMnO_4$ is used for external protozoans at a rate of 2–4 ppm in ponds, at a rate of 10 ppm for 20–30 minutes, and as a dip at 1:1000 for 30 seconds. This material seems to be especially effective against some of the ciliated protozoans such as *Trichodina*.

Salting fish using common table salt is one of the oldest methods of treating freshwater fish for external parasites, and it is quite effective. A 3 percent solution of salt is made up and the fish are placed in it for a few minutes until they start showing distress and then are placed back in fresh water. Acetic acid at a 1:500 concentration has been used for 1–2 minutes to treat external parasites.

Dylox, an organophosphate insecticide, is not cleared by the FDA but has been experimentally shown to be effective as a control for the anchor worm, *Lernaea*, and other crustaceans. It is also effective as a treatment for gill and body flukes and leeches. The concentration used is 0.25 ppm (active ingredient). Leeches have been controlled with Dylox using 0.5 ppm (active ingredient). Some fish will show symptoms of poisoning, such as muscle spasms and excitability, if treated with Dylox when the pH is above 8.5, so it should be used with caution at high pH levels.

Copper sulfate has been used to treat certain protozoans at a rate of 1 ppm, but the total hardness of the water should be above 25 ppm to be safe.

(d) *Internal parasites* Most of the problems caused by internal parasites are by tissue-inhabiting larval forms. There is no known treatment for these, so preventive measures must be used. Most parasites inhabiting the alimentary canal can be controlled by use of an antihelminthic, Di-N-butyl tin oxide. This compound can be mixed in the food at a rate of 1 percent and then fed at 3 percent of body weight for 3 days. This material is not cleared for use in fish. Experimentally it has shown a control of digenetic trematodes, tapeworms, nematodes, and acanthocephalans.

Certain precautions should be taken when treating fish for disease:

(a) Know the percent active ingredient and toxic levels of the treatment material.

(b) Know recommended treatment levels.

(c) Know volume of water to be treated so accurate treatment levels can be calculated.

(d) If toxicity to species of fish being treated is not known, treat a few fish to see how they react.

CONVERSIONS

---

1 pound (lb) = 16 ounces (oz) = 454 grams (gms)
1 oz = 28.35 gms
1 kilogram (kg) = 2.2 lbs
1 cubic foot (cu ft) = 7.5 gallons water
1 acre-foot = 2,718,000 lbs water = 326,000 gal = 43,560 cu ft
1 gal water = 8.34 lbs = 3,800 gms = 3.785 liters
1 ppm is equal to: 0.0038 gms per gal
       0.0283 gms per cu ft
       2.7 lbs per acre-foot
       1.34 oz per 10,000 gals

—W.A.R.

DISPLACEMENT HULL A boat designed to move through the water as against moving on the surface of the water like its opposite the planing hull. Displacement hulls settle in the water according to their weight. The planing hull operates as a displacement hull when it is operating below planing speed.

DISTRICT OF COLUMBIA The federal district which contains the national capital of the United States represents an area of seventy square miles of which eight square miles are water surface. Due to its limited size and dense population, residents of the district fish in Maryland or Virginia. Seasonally, American shad, hickory shad, and anadromous white perch are caught in the Potomac River (the district lies on the east bank) within sight of the Capitol building. The white-perch run begins in late March, and the shad appear during April and May. Most of the angling is done below the Chain Bridge and below Little Falls. *See also* American Shad, Maryland, Virginia

DIVER'S FLAG The diver's flag should always be displayed on a float in the vicinity of skin- and Scuba-diving operations as a warning to boatmen so they will avoid the area. Many serious and fatal accidents have occurred through neglecting to do so. The flag is red with an oblique, white stripe. *See also* Scuba Diving

DOBSONFLIES and ALDERFLIES Order Megaloptera This is a small order of primitive insects with relatively few species which includes both dobsonflies and alderflies. The latter have long been known as an important trout food, and English anglers have developed several artificial-fly patterns based on them. Superficially, alderflies resemble certain moderately sized caddisflies. There are 16 species of alderflies described from the United States and Canada, and all bear close resemblance. The much larger, gray dobsonflies and somewhat smaller fishflies do not occur in Europe, but are represented in North America by about 15 species. The larvae of the dobson is the hellgrammite so familiar to the smallmouth-bass angler of the Eastern United States.

In the common Eastern dobson, *Corydalis cornutus*, the mandibles of the male are greatly enlarged and elongated. Such tusklike mandibles are not present in the rare dobsonflies of the West Coast. Dobsonflies are large insects with a maximum wing expanse of over 6 inches in Western species.

LIFE HISTORY

The eggs of Megaloptera are laid in patches in a single layer on some object above or near water. The dobsonflies frequent only running water; the alderflies may occur either at streams or at ponds or lakes. Female alderflies often add their eggs to masses already laid by other females. As many as 2–3 thousand eggs are laid by one female. The larvae, upon hatching, immediately search for small invertebrate prey.

The larvae of Megaloptera have paired abdominal appendages on the first seven or eight abdominal segments. Gill tufts occur at the base of these appendages in *Corydalis*. In addition, the larvae of the dobsonflies have a pair of leglike appendages on the terminal abdominal segment. They are most commonly encountered in patches of large-sized gravel in fairly rapid-flowing streams, especially at riffles. Here they carry on a relentless search for hapless lesser creatures, usually immature caddisflies, mayflies, and stoneflies. Alderfly larvae more often occur among detritus, either in streams or ponds and lakes.

When mature the larvae leave the water and construct cells beneath stones, in rotten logs, or in soil above the stream, where they pupate. After an interval of perhaps two weeks the adult insect emerges. Though equipped with biting mouthparts in at least some species, feeding by the adults has not been reported. Alderflies are active fliers during daylight and may occur abundantly during a hatch in and about shoreline vegetation along lake shores. The larger dobsonflies and fishflies fly at dusk or during the night. The adults are most often encountered resting on some object in shade near streams.

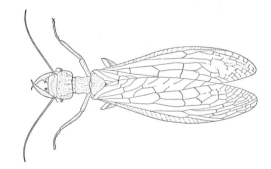

Dobsonfly

Constructing an artificial hellgrammite to fish as a nymph tests the skill of an angler, but such a lure may prove highly successful in fishing for bass and other gamefish. The Duns, artificial flies actually patterned after caddisflies of very similar appearance, strongly suggest an alderfly and prove effective at times for trout on both lakes and streams.

—S.G.J.

DOGFISH Small marine sharks, family Squalidae, found in schools near shore. Although destructive to other fish and fishing equipment, they are a valuable source of oil and fertilizer; they are considered a delicacy in Scandinavia. *See* Smooth Dogfish, Spiny Dogfish

DOG SALMON A local name for the chum salmon (*which see*).

DOG SNAPPER *Lutjanus jocu* This medium-sized snapper is fairly common throughout its range. It occurs around southern Florida and southward throughout the tropical American Atlantic. It may reach a weight of 20 pounds or more, but most of the individuals seen weigh less than 5 pounds. The common name refers to the large anterior fangs.

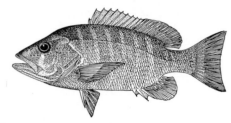

Dog Snapper

The dog snapper has 10 dorsal spines, 14 dorsal rays, and 8 anal rays. Pectoral rays normally 17. Gillrakers 7–9 on lower limb of first arch, not counting rudiments. Rows of scales around caudal peduncle normally 25. Cheek scales in 7–8, usually 8 rows. Upper jaw reaching to or somewhat beyond vertical from anterior margin of orbit. Pectoral fin not reaching to vertical from origin of anal fin. Anal fin rounded, not angulate posteriorly. General coloration olivaceous above, paler below with a reddish tinge. Dorsal, pectoral, and caudal fins orange. Pelvic and anal fins yellow. Black spot on sides of body absent. Eye red.

The large fangs and the color pattern distinguish this snapper from the others.

A shallow-water snapper most frequently found along the shore in rocky areas, it takes live or dead bait and artificial lures.   —L.R.

DOLLAGHAN *See* Ireland

DOLLAR SUNFISH *Lepomis marginatus* The dollar sunfish is a dwarf relative of the longear sunfish, and was once regarded as a Southeastern subspecies of that form. It

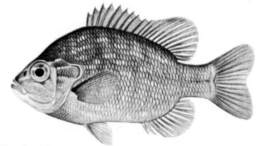

Dollar Sunfish

differs from the longear in having a shorter gill flap with a broader, light margin and larger scales. The lateral-line scales are usually 40 or less, and the rows on the cheek number 4. The longear has 40–45 lateral-line scales, and the cheek scales number 6. The color is olive with orange

spots and many streaks of emerald on the sides and cheeks. The pectoral fin is rounded. Maximum length about 6 inches.   —K.B.

DOLLY VARDEN *Salvelinus malma* This Western char exhibits as much color variation as the degree to which its habitat varies. In saltwater it is silvery; in cold, headwater mountain streams it tends to have bright orange or red spots on the sides; in lakes the spotting is often yellow and only appears on the back. Faint vermiculations on the back occur in the northern part of its range. The ventral and anal fins are whitish on the anterior border. It has small scales and a short vomer. Body conformity varies from slimness in cold mountain streams to very fat, lake-dwelling fish whose diet is of other fishes and particularly so where the kokanee is eaten. Weights to 32 pounds have been recorded.

The Dolly Varden is found from northern California to Alaska and around the northern Pacific to Japan and Korea. It also occurs inland in Idaho, Montana, Utah, and Nevada. Although it inhabits both fresh and saltwater the Dolly Varden enters marine environments only in the northern part of its range.

Named after a character (Miss Dolly Varden) in Charles Dickens' *Barnaby Rudge*, because of her pink-spotted dress, the species is sometimes confused with a similarly appearing Arctic char. In field identification, to separate one from the other, if the spots are smaller than the iris of the eye it is a Dolly Varden; if the spots are larger it is an Arctic char.

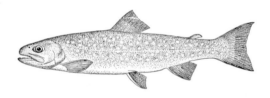

Dolly Varden

LIFE HISTORY

Slow-growing but long-lived (aged to 18+ years) the Dolly Varden usually matures at age 6. A fall spawner it enters streams from September to November. Like other Salmonidae the female digs a redd in the gravel and deposits from 800–3,000 eggs depending on her body size. The eggs hatch in 30–90 days. The fry do not swim up immediately, but wiggle deeper into the gravel where they remain for an additional 60–120 days. Young Dolly Varden are very inactive for the first four years of life, after which the first seaward migration takes place if a marine environment is part of its habitat. This begins a general pattern of migrating to saltwater in the spring and returning to freshwater in the fall. It usually winters in lakes.

The young fish feed largely on insects, but older fish are more piscivorous. Where it is found with Pacific salmon it can in some areas be destructive. An examination of eight Dolly Varden stomachs in the Imnaha River in northeastern Oregon revealed that 5–12 chinook fingerling had been eaten by each char. Generally speaking, however, it has not proved to be a serious predator throughout its range. Other salmonids also consume young salmon and ova.

ANGLING VALUE

Anglers have mixed emotions about the Dolly Varden. In some areas it is condemned as a gamefish, particularly where steelhead, coho, and chinook salmon are considered more important in the catch. Nevertheless it produces fine sport if in prime condition in headwater streams and when returning from the sea. It can be caught on a variety of spinning lures as well as streamer and wet flies, and at times with a dry fly. The firm pink to red flesh is of excellent flavor when prepared as in any of the trout recipes. —J.R.

DOLPHIN *Coryphaena hippurus* Also called dorado. One of two members of its family (Coryphaenidae), the dolphin may usually be distinguished from the pompano dolphin (*which see*) by its slender body; in the dolphin, the greatest depth of the body goes four or more times into the length from snout to fork of tail. It differs further in usually having more than 240 scales in the lateral line and 56 or more rays in the dorsal fin.

In large male dolphins, the front of the head becomes very high and almost vertical, but until this happens, males and females are similar in appearance. In the water, the dolphin is usually a vivid greenish-blue with dark vertical bands that may appear and disappear. When the fish is caught, the color fluctuates rapidly, so that within a few minutes, it may be blue, green, or yellow. After death, these colors fade rapidly to a uniform yellowish or silver.

The usual angler catch is a 5–15-pound dolphin. The largest dolphin on record was caught off Acapulco, Mexico, was 5 feet 3 inches long and weighed 76 pounds.

The dolphin is cosmopolitan in tropical and subtropical waters. On the Atlantic Coast of North America, it is found in areas influenced by the warmwaters of the Gulf Stream, and has been caught as far north as Prince Edward Island. Throughout much of its range, it is a favorite gamefish, and the flesh is a gourmet's delight, often being sold in restaurants under its Hawaiian name, *mahi-mahi*.

In warmer waters, the spawning season appears to be rather long, extending from April to August, whereas further north, as in the Gulf Stream, spawning is concentrated in early summer. The young are commonly found in warm offshore waters, frequently in or near patches of sargassum weed, and are occasionally found inshore. They, like the young of many other fishes, are attracted to lights at night and are easily caught with a dipnet.

The food of the dolphin consists of a variety of fishes, squids, and crustaceans. Flyingfishes are said to form a large portion of the diet in some areas. Well offshore in the Gulf Stream, where flyingfishes are plentiful, dolphins feed mainly on juvenile fishes associated with sargassum such as filefishes, triggerfishes, and jacks.

Certain porpoises are also known as "dolphins," but these are mammals, not fishes. *See also* Pompano Dolphin
—B.B.C.
—R.H.G.

ANGLING METHODS

The riotously colored dolphin follows only the sailfish, marlin, and tuna as a desirable offshore gamefish; it is a spectacular gamefish in many ways. In addition to its brilliant coloration, the dolphin strikes explosively, fights frantically, and performs beautifully in the air. The attack of a dolphin school at a trolled bait is one of the top thrills of Gulf Stream fishing. Often they will streak toward the bait from several hundred feet out, their stubby dorsals knifing through the surface of the water. It is not unusual when two or more baits are being trolled to have a single dolphin hit them all in a racing strike which seems to occur almost instantly.

There are times during the spring and summer when school dolphin may be found concentrated by the thousands in the blue water off the coast. Seaweed rips are their favorite haunts, but they may also be found hovering about almost any drifting object. One southeast Florida skipper made a tremendous catch of dolphin one

Dolphin, 53-pound Male, Boca Raton, Florida

Dolphin, 6-pound Female, Key West, Florida

day by repeatedly circling a discarded ladder that was adrift. When dolphin are in evidence around floating objects, they can be taken on plugs, flies, and spoons. This can be an exciting game in areas such as the west coast of Panama (*which see*) where dolphin are especially numerous.

Although the school-size dolphin offer fine sport on light tackle, it is the big bull dolphin that is highly prized by anglers. Sometimes reaching a weight well in excess of 50 pounds, these heavyweights put up a terrific battle, and on a pound-for-pound basis probably will match the hardest fighting gamefish. Dolphin are most frequently encountered by anglers trolling surface baits for other species. These baits usually are small whole mullet or balao. Dolphin will also take trolled feathers, jigs, and miscellaneous other artificial lures. It is evident that most dolphin are caught by anglers fishing for sailfish (*see* Atlantic Sailfish) or for marlin in the Pacific. Therefore, light sailfish tackle is also common dolphin tackle.

Once dolphin are encountered, however, an angler may switch to lighter, spinning tackle or revolving-spool gear. Sometimes a school of these fish may be kept near the stern of a boat by keeping a hooked fish in the water. The presence of even one fish will hold the school.

There are a number of charter-boat skippers who specialize in "bailing" dolphin. The boat is stopped in a school of fish, and chum is tossed overboard to hold the fish. This can result in scores of dolphin being taken out of one school.

During the warm months, fishermen aboard reef- or drift-fishing headboats get their share of dolphin. They catch them while drifting baits behind the boat or spin-fishing with jigs and other artificials. Fishermen in small private craft search the seaweed rips for dolphin. When they find a school, they stop the boat and cast for them. In keeping with its brawling disposition, the dolphin is voracious and will hit almost anything that moves in the water.   —E.C.B.

DOLPHINS Belonging to the mammalian order of whales (Cetacea). *See under* Porpoises

DORADE *Gnathanodon speciosus* This is a tropical and subtropical Indo-Pacific species. It has been called king trevally. The common dolphin (*Coryphaena hippurus*) is sometimes referred to by the similar names of dourade and dorado.

The dorade has a relatively deep body with about 9–11 bars that persist on most specimens to all sizes. These

may appear as six broader bars, with a narrow bar between each broad pair. There is a less distinct nuchal band through the eye. These bars become less distinct on very large fish. The jaws are toothless in specimens larger than about 4 inches long, the lips becoming wide and fleshy. The second dorsal fin has one spine and 19–20 softrays. The anal fin has two detached spines followed by one spine and 16–17 softrays. The first gill arch has 7–9 gillrakers on the upper limb and about 21 gillrakers on the lower limb. There are about 16–25 weakly developed scutes in the posterior part of the straight lateral line.

This species occurs in the Indian Ocean and eastward to the Hawaiian Islands. In the eastern Pacific it ranges from Panama to Mazatlán, Mexico, and to Santa Maria Bay on the west coast of Baja California. A photograph of a 31-inch specimen has been published, and it has been reported to grow to about 3 feet.

LIFE HISTORY

Life-history information is lacking. A small school of one-inch specimens was taken from beneath a jellyfish. Larger specimens appear to travel in schools of about 6–12 fish.

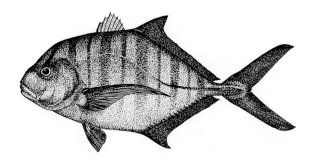

Dorade

ANGLING VALUE

The dorade is a strong and stubborn swimmer. Large specimens have been foul-hooked when trolling near the bottom, and took some time to bring to gaff. This foul-hooking does not seem to be an abnormal occurrence and suggests some unusual behavior characteristics of this species, although some have been hooked normally. This is reported as an excellent or valued food fish. *See also* Carangidae, Jacks   —F.H.B.

DORADO (1) The Spanish name for dolphin (*which see*).

(2) *Salminus maxillosus* One of the outstanding freshwater gamefish native to South America, the dorado is a member of the Characidae family in the genus *Salminus*, which contains 4 species although there are probably more not recognized in present taxonomy. Dorado are distributed from the Magdelena River system of Colombia in the north to as far south as the city of Buenos Aires in Argentina. A fish of the tropics and semitropics, its major waters include the Güejar, Guaviare, and other rivers of the high Orinoco basin, the Caqueta and Orteguazo and other upper tributaries of the Amazon, as well as the São Francisco River system of Brazil. The Paraguay River system of Paraguay and the Uruguay River, which borders Brazil and Argentina, are also important dorado waters. Generally speaking, the smallest dorado species (S. *affinis* and S. *hilarii*) are common to the northern part of its range; a third (S. *brevidens*) is limited to the São Francisco watershed; and the fourth and largest (S. *maxillosus*), though widespread, is more common to the south. The latter has been recorded to 75 pounds. Perhaps the most important watershed today from the standpoint of large dorado and accessibility is the Paraná River of Argentina.

LIFE HISTORY

Dorado are migratory throughout life both for the purpose of feeding and spawning. The chief item of diet is the sábalo (*Prochilodus spp.*), which has a widespread distribution in tropical South American rivers. Sábalo travel in large schools, much like mullet, and are often seen with the top of their heads and upper jaws out of water as they feed in the surface film. The dorado follow the sábalo, which make extensive journeys. As spawning season approaches, the dorado continue upstream. On the Amazon the migration is called a *piracema*. In January and February, when the river is at full flood, great schools of dorado (which are limited to the upper Amazon) migrate toward the headwaters leaping rapids and falls much in the manner of Atlantic salmon.

In the Paraná River dorado spawn in tributary streams. Beginning in January the ripe fish select a shady place over a pebble-and-gravel bottom, and the spawners continue to arrive until March. The female scoops out a redd similar to that of a salmon, while several male dorado fight for the privilege of attending the nuptials; when the eggs are fertilized, the victorious male guards the nest.

However, this paternal devotion is short-lived, because the male soon becomes cannibalistic and the bright-orange-tailed fry escape to shallow water.

For reasons which are not clear some dorado spawn as far south as the Island of Martin Garcia in the Rio de la Plata; here the nest is scooped out of sand, but again only in shaded places. As a result some dorado are caught close to downtown Buenos Aires, yet these are never big fish, rarely exceeding 6 pounds. Apparently the dorado move upstream as they grow larger, and despite easy access to the sea they never venture beyond the low salinities of the river mouth. A similar migration, which occurs during the winter months, also takes place on the Uruguay River. When stocked in lakes reproduction does not take place if there is no inlet or outlet stream.

DORADO ANGLING

In the year 1540 Cabeca de Vaca, a Portuguese explorer, found a dorado or "gilded fish"—from whose head an oil is extracted that cures "all types of leper and itches—" in the headwaters of the Iguazu and Piquiri rivers. Although miracle drug oil has never been celebrated in the annals of civilized medicine, the dorado *is* highly esteemed as a gamefish. It is a great leaper and strong fighter. Breaking water a dozen times is not an unusual performance for a hooked dorado.

The key to a dorado river are its riffles and the presence of rock piles. The latter may consist of nothing more than a few boulders which a steelhead fisherman would have no trouble locating even when their tops are submerged, as the "slick" water is obvious; or the rock pile may be an acre or two in size—large enough to form an island in the mainstream. Nevertheless, running water indicates *where* dorado are in a river because of the way they feed. Although it is true that birds, snakes, mice, and just about every other creature that ventures into the water have been found in dorado stomachs, these items are not selectively sought; the dorado will concentrate solely on eating other fish as long as they are abundant. In the Paraná River, for example, a 2-pound sábalo is a mere hors d'oeuvre to a dorado. Equipped with jaws like a steel trap, bearing double rows of teeth including canines which extend along the outer margin of the maxillary, the dorado bites and swallows its prey in one gulp. Thus, the multitoothed predator favors that strategic position on the upstream face of a rock pile to ambush baitfish schools as they ease through the eddies and slack water—to avoid the strong riffles on either side—before funneling

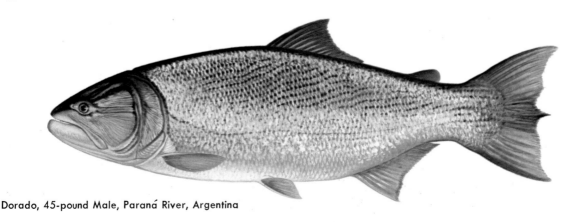

Dorado, 45-pound Male, Paraná River, Argentina

out into the main channel again. Poised among the rocks, a dorado merely waits for the innocent sábalo to appear. As a result the hot-spots change from day to day according to the movements and concentrations of baitfish. For this reason trolling is the most productive method of catching dorado. It's difficult to cast and adequately cover a hot-spot from a drifting boat. Fly-fishing suffers for the same reason. In small streams both plug-casting and fly-fishing are productive, but truly big dorado only venture into the tributaries at the approach of spawning season. For consistent results and a possible trophy the beginner is well advised to troll. The popular sporting tackle is either a 5½- or 6-foot bait-casting rod, or a 7- to 8-foot long spinning rod capable of handling 12–20 pound test line.

The dorado, esteemed as a gamefish, is a great leaper and strong fighter. Fish often run 20-40 pounds

Of great importance are hooks. The vicious smash of a dorado can bust a plastic plug to splinters and flatten out ordinary treble hooks. Single hook lures are by far the best. For this reason large wobbling spoons with fixed hooks are popular. However, jointed plugs with a violent wiggling action produce more dorado. Mount a hook both fore and aft on a wood-bodied plug, of a size that we would use for sailfish or marlin—No. 8/0 to 12/0. A wire leader of 18 inches or more is essential; most anglers prefer the cable kind with strong snaps and swivels. You have to think "big," as dorado are not timid; and if there's a weak link in your terminal gear it will pop in seconds.

Only rarely can dorado be caught on topwater baits. In a big river the great majority of fish are hooked from 5-15 feet below the surface or virtually just over the bottom. Too, the plug should swim fast; slow retrieves or slow trolling is seldom effective.

FOOD VALUE

As a food fish the dorado is not great but it is good, being very similar to the striped bass in texture and flavor. When prepared in asado style—usually split in

half and cooked slowly over a low charcoal fire for 2 or 3 hours and basted with garlic, herbs, and olive oil—it is a mouth-watering dish. The skin is left on, unscaled, to prevent sticking to the fire grate, and the fire bed itself must be at least 18 inches away from the fish, a system that can be applied to literally any other species at a barbecue. The female has immense gray-blue ovaries, much like those of a caviar-bearing sturgeon, and part of its dorsal musculature is supported by fine Y-shaped bones identical to those found in the pikes. *See also* Argentina, Brazil, Colombia, Venezuela   —A.J.McC.

DORE A regional name in the province of Quebec for the walleye (*which see*).

DORSAL Pertaining to the back or the region of the back; the dorsal fin

DORSAL FIN The prominent fin on the back

DORY A type of small boat, generally 16-22 feet in length, and very popular among New England commercial fishermen. A dory is highly seaworthy, even though appearing cranky to men not accustomed to the manner in which dories ride. The typical dory is narrow, flat-bottomed, and has sharply flaring sides. The transom is generally V-shaped and deep. Dories are used extensively on the Grand Banks and in the Pacific Northwest. *See* Banks Dory, Oregon Surf Dory

DOUBLE ENDER Any small craft in which the stern is shaped exactly like the bow, such as the conventional canoe. The identification is most often used in connection with the McKenzie River boat or "double ender" popularized on Western rivers.

DOUBLE HOOK A type of hook which has two separate points and bends joined to a common shank and eye. Double hooks are most commonly used in making Atlantic salmon wet flies. Very small double hooks are also used in making dry flies for soft-mouthed fish, such as grayling and whitefish.

DOUBLE LINE A terminal rigging used by big-game fishermen. A 15-25-foot loop is formed at the end of the line by doubling it back and seizing or splicing it closed. This reinforced section (legal in competitive angling) facilitates snubbing the fish in preparation for boating. A fish is said to be *on the double line* when held close enough to the boat so that the seizing or splice of the loop has passed through the rod tip. *See also* Big-Game Fishing

DOUBLE-TAPERED LINE *See* Fly Line

DOURADO The Portuguese name for the dorado, *Salminus maxillosus*, in Brazil

DOVER SOLE *Microstomus pacificus* Large eyes and a small mouth characterize this righteye flounder. It has a straight, unbranched lateral line and a small gill-cover opening. The slender body has numerous, small scales, and a heavy slime covers the body. Its teeth are found only on the blind side. It is uniformly light to dark brown

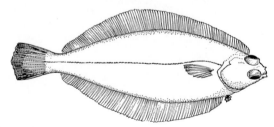

Dover Sole

on the eyed (right) side, sometimes with vague blotches. The dark fins are blackish at the tips of their rays. It reaches 10 pounds and 30 inches. This sole occurs from 100 to more than 3,000 feet, often over mud bottom, being more common in the northern part of its range, which is from southern California to northwestern Alaska.

LIFE HISTORY

A deepwater flatfish, it feeds on invertebrates. It is a winter spawner, and the eggs float at the surface. The young eventually take up a bottom life, as do other flatfishes. The dover sole grows to an age of at least 15 years.

FOOD VALUE

In spite of the heavy slime cover, the flesh is delicious, and recently it has become a major part of the commercial sole catch. —D.dS.

DRAFT The depth of a boat from keel to waterline

DRAG A condition whereby an artificial fly travels through or over the water at a speed faster than the current. This acceleration comes from the line which is extended over currents of several different speeds. Partially caught in a swift flow, that portion of the relatively heavy line pulls ahead of the cast as a whole, thus dragging the sensitive fly along. *See also* Fly Fishing —A.J.McC.

DRAGONFLIES and DAMSELFLIES Order Odonata Among the most conspicuous and showy of aquatic insects, dragonflies and their smaller relatives, the damselflies, are well-known to all anglers. These sunloving insects are most typically inhabitants of marshes and lakes, though many kinds are found in creeks and rivers. The more than 400 species found in North America range in size from small ones with a body length of about an inch to the large varieties with a body length of 4 inches and a wing expanse of more than 5 inches.

The dragonflies are generally larger than damselflies and can be distinguished readily by the position of the wings at rest. These are held horizontally by dragonflies, usually folded vertically in damselflies. The bodies of many dragonflies are conspicuously marked in patterns of black or dark brown against a ground color of red yellow, blue, or green. The eyes are extremely large, covering most of the head and are often glowing green or reddish in life. The bright colors of the eyes and of the body fade rapidly at death and become dull. The wings are strong, with a complex network of veins, and often are with large, colored patches of black, brown, purple, yellow, or red. Anyone who has tried to capture a large, adult dragonfly can attest as to their agility on the wing.

Damselflies generally have more slender bodies; only a few kinds have conspicuously colored patches on the wings, and the wings are not nearly so well developed for flying as in the dragonflies.

The nymphs of dragonflies are rather short and robust, those of damselflies, long and slender. Damselfly nymphs and those of some dragonflies clamber over submerged vegetation in ponds, lakes, and slow-moving streams. Other dragonfly nymphs sprawl among detritus, and one large group includes mostly burrowers. All are predaceous and, when opportunity affords, devour individuals of their own kind as well as a multiplicity of other small aquatic animals. A few of the large species occasionally prey on small fishes.

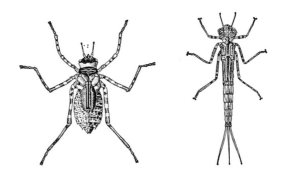

Dragonfly Nymph, *left,* and Damselfly Nymph

Dragonflies and damselflies are eaten by gamefish, both as nymphs and as newly transformed adults. When transformation to the adult stage occurs, the insect is at first very soft and incapable of strong flight. If there is a wind from a reedy shoreline out onto a lake, quantities of the soft adults may afford a bountiful food supply for gamefish. The nymphs of these same species may be important in the diet of large trout as they are in Upper Klamath Lake in southern Oregon.

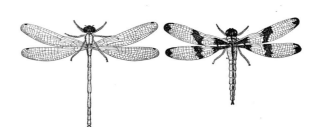

Damselfly Adult, *left,* and Dragonfly Adult

LIFE HISTORY

The Odonata are among those insects that do not undergo complete metamorphosis. Instead of a pupal state as in true flies and beetles, the adult transforms directly from the mature nymph.

The eggs of dragonflies and damselflies are laid in various ways. The simplest egg laying is accomplished in flight over a body of water and by dipping the tip of the abdomen beneath the water surface. A few varieties lay gelatinous strings of eggs among submerged vegetation. The most common method employed is to deposit the eggs in tiny slits in submerged vegetation or occasionally in the stems of bushes or tree limbs overhanging the water surface. As far as is known, the eggs hatch after about two weeks.

The tiny nymphs immediately seek very small aquatic creatures which they devour voraciously. The nymphs are usually dull brown and very hairy. Some forms actively seek prey, but many wait until their victims approach sufficiently close that they may be seized with a rapid forward thrust of the long, scoop-shaped lower lip which has been developed for this purpose. When the nymph has become fully mature, after a single season with some kinds and up to five years with others, the nymph crawls from the water and rests upon a plant stem or other solid support, the skin breaks along the back, and the flabby adult emerges. Gradually, the wings are expanded, and the skin hardens.

Dragonflies are noteworthy fliers, damselflies less so. In some adults regular flight patterns develop along a stream course or along the margin of lakes. These may be of a rather short distance or extend for several miles. Many pond-dwelling species habitually rest on a favorite perch, usually a dead limb or other object in open sunlight.

Mating is usually accomplished in flight soon after transformation from the nymphal stage, and fertilization is of a rather peculiar sort. The male sex organs include terminal claspers at the end of the abdomen and a pair of claspers and a penis on the second abdominal segment, a short distance behind the wings. The sperm must be transferred from an opening near the tip of the abdomen to a hollow space in the tip of the penis, and this is accomplished by bending the tip of the abdomen downward and forward to the second segment. The female genital opening is of the conventional insect sort near the tip of the abdomen.

This rather primitive group of insects contains a great many genera in North America, some typically tropical, others characteristic of northlands. While not among the more important aquatic insects that contribute to the food of gamefish, they are a very conspicuous element along streams and lakes and are therefore of much interest to the angler.

Dragonflies and damselflies are quite harmless insects and are in fact beneficial since both adults and nymphs prey on other insects including nuisance species such as mosquitoes. Called "devil's darning needles" and frequently feared by the uninformed, the adults have no stinger, and most species can inflict only a mild pinch with their mandibles.

DRAGONFLIES

Aeshna verticalis The common name of the species is Blue Darner; it applies equally well to other species of this widespread genus, the members of which are very similar. *Verticalis* is a large dragonfly with clear wings about two inches long and with a slender, graceful abdomen with many markings of blue and some of green or yellow on a generally brownish ground color. The compound eyes are very large and together with the strong wings enable this graceful aerialist to capture countless mosquitoes and other small insects on long, intricate flights sometimes a long distance from water. These are the strong flying dragonflies with blue body markings that often dart past the angler in their constant search for smaller insect prey.

The nymph is among the most streamlined of immature dragonflies. The body is trim and clean, without adhering dirt or detritus, and marked in a pattern of green and brown. The head is flattened and with large compound eyes. An enormous scoop-shaped lower mandible is thrust forward to capture prey. It lives in marshes and among shoreline submerged aquatic vegetation of lakes and quiet streams. The nymphs constantly search for their living food and in turn are eaten by bass, trout, and other gamefish.

Cordulegaster has acquired the common name of flying adder, probably because of a fanciful comparison

of its banded, bright yellow and black body with that of a snake. It is a large insect that flies for miles up small streams in mountainous wooded areas before turning around and flying downstream. Moving swiftly and quietly a few feet above a shaded trout stream in our Western mountains, this dragonfly is apt to startle a fisherman intent on placing his artificial fly on a likely riffle.

Aeshna and allied genera include the abundant, large dragonflies with clear wings and blue-marked bodies that frequent all of the temperate areas of the continent. Often flying far from watercourses, these may sometimes be seen in parks and along streets in the suburbs of metropolitan areas. They feed on many destructive insects and in turn are eaten by gamefish, especially as nymphs or freshly transformed adults.

Somatochlora includes moderate-sized dragonflies with bronzy-green reflections on the body. They are conspicuous among dragonflies flying about northern lakes across the continent. The nymphs are probably consumed in numbers by pickerel, bass, and trout.

Perithemis and *Celithemis* are showy small dragonflies of eastern North America, the former being principally subtropical in distribution. The nymphs of both are climbers and probably contribute to the food supply of gamefish. Both genera include species with showy-colored wing patches.

Libellula species are large, strong fliers typical of ponds and lakes throughout the temperate regions. The wings are often marked with large patches of brown, red, amber, or black. The large, sprawling nymphs contribute to the diet of spiny-ray gamefish. The Ten Spot, *Libellula pulchella*, common across the Northern United States, is a species with ten large black areas on the wings.

Leucorrhinia includes smaller, low-flying species frequently abundant in early summer at northern and Cordilleran lakes. Of the same general size and found in similar places as *Leucorrhinia* are several species of *Sympetrum*, but these emerge later and are most abundant in late summer and early autumn. The nymphs of both are often quite numerous on submerged vegetation and no doubt contribute materially to the diet of northern gamefish.

DAMSELFLIES

Enallagma civile This damselfly is typical of the family, with clear wings and a long abdomen prominently marked with blue in the male. It occurs about lakes, ponds, and slow-moving streams across the continent, and it, or its relatives, are well-known to all who fish pond-fish waters. It is about 1½ inches long, and the wings are about half the body length. Adults are most often found among sedges and other low-growing plants at the water's edge where they rest frequently between forays in search of midges and other very small insects which serve as food. The adults are on the wing from late spring through early autumn.

The graceful nymphs are differentiated quickly from dragonfly nymphs by their much more slender form and by the presence of three relatively large, flat plates which are actually used as fins to propel the nymph through the water. The nymph is buff or greenish in color, quite agile, and preys on small aquatic animals, usually immature insects.

Hetaerina americana is a beautifully marked member of a family of big damselflies the males of which frequently have pigmented areas on the wings. In the male of this species, which occurs in the United States and parts of Canada and Mexico, the base of the wings is brilliant carmine in the male, amber in the female. With a body nearly 2 inches in length and with wings over an inch long, this graceful insect is a strong flier among damselflies and occurs along the margins of gently moving streams.

Lestes includes some of the larger damselflies with clear wings that occur among low vegetation and which are weak fliers. The nymphs occur in stillwater and are climbers.

Species of *Argia* are of moderate size, and the abdomen of the males is marked in blue or violet and black. They occur throughout North America especially among emergent vegetation bordering large streams.

Like the last-mentioned genus, *Enallagma* contains several North American species, some with rather widespread distribution. Of about the same size as *Argia* but differing technically in wing venation and other structural details, the males of these little damselflies have bodies prominently marked with blue and black. They occur commonly among rushes and sedges along the banks of ponds and slow-moving streams.

Generally similar in appearance to the last two genera, *Ischnura* has green markings on the thorax of the males, a blue and black pattern on the abdomen. Oddly, some females of a species are colored and marked like the males while others are dull in coloration like the females of other genera of damselflies. The species are all feeble fliers, spending much of the day resting in a sunny spot after an early morning foray among grasses and sedges in search of small flies. The nymphs clamber among submerged aquatic plants in quiet ponds and stream sections.

—S.G.J.

DRUMS Family Sciaenidae Also known as croakers. They are characterized by the presence of a lateral line which extends onto the caudal fin. Usually there are one or more barbels on the lower jaw. Drums are found worldwide, generally in temperate and tropical waters; and, especially in the western North Atlantic, several of them are of commercial importance. They are fishes of the Continental Shelf, generally being found over shallow, sandy bottom not far from estuaries, and they are relatively seldom taken around oceanic islands or coral reefs. Some species enter brackish water, and it is believed that the young of most species require slightly brackish water for proper growth. Most are invertebrate feeders on small clams, snails, worms, and shrimps, although the larger species are fish eaters.

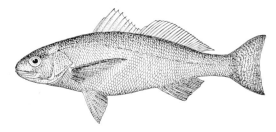

White Croaker

Croakers are so named because of their specialized drumming muscle, usually in the male only, which, through a rapid and repeated contraction with the swimbladder, produces a distinctive drumming sound that can be heard at quite a distance.

Along the Atlantic coast of the United States, the Atlantic croaker, *Micropogon undulatus*, is the most common. Also called hardhead, it has a small, tapered body, with a short, high first dorsal fin and a long, low second dorsal fin. The head is convex and the mouth inferior, and the upper parts of the body are covered with many small, dark specks. It grows to about 4 pounds and 20 inches, but a 2-pound fish is a good catch. This croaker is found from Texas to New Jersey, occasionally northward to Massachusetts, and its center of abundance seems to be from the Carolinas to northeastern Florida and along the northern Gulf of Mexico. Spawning is from late summer to December in the north and somewhat later in the southern part of its range. It eats worms and crustaceans, such as snails and bivalves, as well as any other small invertebrates it can ingest through its inferior mouth.

Historically, the Atlantic croaker has always been an important food and gamefish in the middle Atlantic area and the northern Gulf of Mexico, but in recent years it has dwindled in the northern part of its range. Trawls, gillnets, and pound nets have accounted for vast commercial catches, while anglers have reaped excellent hook-and-line catches using cut bait such as clams, mussels, and squid. As a food fish, it is not spectacular, but its flavor is good, and its abundance in some areas and its usual size of $\frac{1}{2}$–$1\frac{1}{2}$ pounds finds a ready market.

Another important species is the black drum, *Pogonias cromis*, found from Cape Cod to Argentina, with a concentration from Virginia southward through the northern Gulf of Mexico. It has numerous barbels on the lower jaw, and is silvery to brassy black, with the young (sometimes called puppy drum) having distinctive black bars on the sides. It grows to well over 100 pounds, and although it is not a spectacular fighter, it puts up a determined battle. It eats vast quantities of mollusks and crustaceans, and in some areas its depredations on oyster beds has made it a nuisance. Although its flesh is not particularly good, it has considerable commercial value, particularly the smaller individuals.

Other important drums include the banded drum, *Larimus fasciatus*, a small croaker found from Virginia southward to the Gulf of Mexico. Seldom exceeding 10 inches, it has a deep body with flattened sides which have 7–9 black bands. There are no barbels on the mouth, and the distinctive mouth is very oblique when viewed from the side. It occurs in relatively shallow water (1–4 fathoms) over sand or sandy mud, and is of virtually no commercial importance, being taken incidentally in shrimp trawls.

A related species is the cabezon, *Larimus breviceps*, which resembles the banded drum in general shape but lacks the crossbars. It occurs in the Caribbean southward to Brazil.

A beautiful Atlantic croaker is the jackknife-fish, or ribbon fish, *Equetus lanceolatus*, which is characterized by its high first dorsal fin, its long tapering body, which is deepest at the shoulder, and 3 black bands—one passing across the head and backward, a second beneath the first dorsal backward, and a third just beneath the eye. Three other species, variously marked, are found throughout the Caribbean. The jackknife-fish occasionally is found to North Carolina, but is usually restricted to the warmer waters of the Caribbean. It occurs around coral reefs as well as over sand bottom. Like all species of the genus, it is fairly secretive and usually lurks along the bottom under cover of reefs.

The silver perch, *Bairdiella chrysura*, is one of the commonest of Atlantic drums, yet is seldom seen by anglers. Like other drums, its dorsal fins are separated by a deep notch, and the body is high and compressed. The chin lacks barbels. It is bluish-gray to olive and the sides are silvery to white, with yellow to golden fins. Occurring from New York to the Gulf of Mexico, it is most common in bays and quiet lagoons, especially around estuaries. It penetrates brackish and even freshwater, occurring offshore in the winter and coming inshore in the spring to breed. Crustaceans, worms, and small fishes are eaten. Although it only grows to about a foot long, it is easy to catch on shrimp or cut bait, and its flesh is tasty. A related species, the bairdiella, or Gulf croaker, *Bairdiella icistius*, was introduced from the Gulf of California into California's Salton Sea, where it has thrived and grown to a goodly size, affording excellent sport for anglers there.

The star drum, *Stellifer lanceolatus*, has a characteristic, spongy head, with large eyes, an upturned mouth, and no barbels. It is roughly circular in cross section, and it is brown to olive above with silver sides. It reaches only about 7 inches, although its flesh is tasty. Occurring in shallow coastal waters, it is extremely abundant in the southern waters of the United States, especially in the Carolinas and Georgia and along the northern Gulf of Mexico.

The California croakers include nine important species. The queenfish, *Seriphus politus*, is elongate, with 2 widely separated dorsal fins and no chin barbel. Its body is bluish and the fins are yellowish. Growing to about a foot, it occurs from central California to Baja California in shallow water over sandy bottom. Its chief importance is as a baitfish.

The white croaker, *Genyonemus lineatus*, occurs from Vancouver Island to Baja California and grows to about 2½ pounds. Like the queenfish, with which it often schools, it is found in quiet, shallow waters over sandy bottom. The upper jaw projects beyond the lower, and the body is deep and compressed, with a deep notch separating the 2 dorsal fins. Faint, wavy lines appear over the silvery to golden upper parts. Although the flesh is edible, it is not highly prized by anglers.

The California corbina, *Menticirrhus undulatus*, is a member of the whiting group (*which see*). Its convex head profile; a short, high first dorsal; a long, lower second dorsal fin; and barbels at the tip of the lower jaw identify this species. Reported to grow to 8 pounds, it is a prized surf fish, and is caught using small crabs, clams, mussels, or worms. It occurs from Point Conception to the Gulf of California along sandy beaches.

A popular surf fish is the spotfin croaker, *Roncador stearnsi*, which is distinguished by a large black spot at the base of the pectoral fins. Its high, arched body is compressed, and is grayish-silver with a bluish sheen. Growing to over 9 pounds, it is found from Point Conception to Baja California. Also known as golden croaker, it is caught in the surf using crabs, mussels, and clams.

The yellowfin croaker, *Umbrina roncador*, is also a popular sport fish, and occurs from Point Conception to Baja California. It has a small barbel on the chin tip, and 2 strong anal spines, which separate it from other California croakers. It is gray-green on the sides with golden reflections and wavy lines along the sides. The fins are yellowish. Live bait and cut bait take this species.

One of the largest of the drums is a relative of the seatrouts of the east coast. The white seabass, *Cynoscion nobilis*, is the most important drum in California and is reported to reach 80 pounds, but the usual size is 15–20 pounds. The body is elongate, and the 2 dorsal fins touch but are separated by a deep notch. The mouth is large, and the lower jaw, which lacks a barbel, extends beyond the upper. The upper parts are bluish-gray to steely blue with golden tints. It occurs from Alaska to the Gulf of California, being more common in the southern part of its range. It occurs along the coast, often being taken in beds of kelp.

One of the rarer California drums is the black croaker, *Cheilotrema saturnum*, which ranges from Point Conception to the Gulf of California. Its deep, compressed body has a dorsal hump; there is no chin barbel, and the upper jaw overhangs the lower. It is bluish to blackish with a coppery sheen, and is distinguished by the black edge of the opercle. A deepwater species, its flesh is good. *See also* Atlantic Croaker, Black Drum, Weakfish, Whitings (Kingfish), Red Drum, Sand Seatrout, Silver Seatrout, Spot, Spotfin Croaker, Spotted Seatrout, Totuava.

—D.dS.

DRY FLY An artificial fly on which the hackle fibers project at approximate right angles to the hook so that it floats on the surface. The dry fly imitates a floating insect of some kind. An ideal dry fly is made buoyant through its materials, but a chemical paste or liquid is applied for waterproofing. Dry flies are used for a variety of freshwater species, but they are principally designed for trout and salmon; patterns of the latter group are often large and fanciful rather than imitative. *See also* article *The Dry Fly Downstream, The Dry Fly Upstream* under Fly-Fishing; *Dry-Fly-Fishing* under Atlantic Salmon; *How To Tie a Dry Fly* under *Fly Tying*

DUBBING The materials used in making a rough or hairy body on an artificial fly by twisting small bits of fur on a thread. The "dubbed" thread is then wrapped around the hook shank to form the body. This type of body is used chiefly on wet flies because of its translucent appearance in the water. Fox fur, seal fur, and polar bear fur are common dubbing materials. The Light Cahill is a good example of a fly pattern having a dubbed body. *See also* Fly-Tying

DUNNE, J. W. British Wrote *Sunshine and the Dry Fly* (published 1924) which dealt with translucency as a factor in tying imitations of natural flies. Dunne developed a cellulose body over a white, enameled hook shank. This gave the body of the artificial a diaphanous quality, much like the body of the natural. By blending a precise number of strands of different colors to suggest the color required, Dunne designed a series of flies to imitate all the important ephemerids found on British chalk streams. His success inspired a new school of exact imitation in fly-dressing.

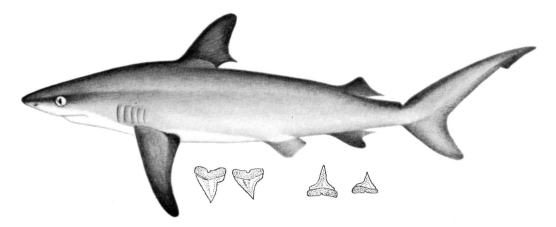

Dusky Shark, showing teeth of upper jaw (*left*) and lower jaw

DUSKY SHARK *Carcharhinus obscurus* One of the inshore members of the requiem sharks, it belongs to the group having a distinct ridge between the dorsal fins. It has a long, pointed snout, somewhat rounded in the dorsal view, with well-developed pectoral fins. The first dorsal fin is high and much larger than the second. It closely resembles the sandbar shark (*which see*) but can be separated from it by the more rearward placement of the first dorsal fin, its origin being over or slightly behind the inner corner of the pectoral fin. The dorsal fin is smaller than that of the sandbar, its height being less than the distance from the eye to the first gill opening. It resembles the sickle shark (*which see*), but its second dorsal and anal fins have their free rear corners much less than twice the height of the fin; in the sickle shark, this rear tip is more than twice as long as the fin is high. The adult is bluish to leaden-gray above and whitish beneath, with a darker coloration of the pectoral tips. It grows to nearly 12 feet long, and embryos 3 feet long have been taken.

LIFE HISTORY

Dusky sharks apparently occur throughout the tropical and subtropical parts of the Atlantic, although it is not certain if this is the same species on both sides of the Atlantic. A closely related species, *Carcharhinus galapagensis*, has been identified from the Atlantic and is distinguished by its more erect and more pointed dorsal fin and the relatively smaller gill slits. In this area, the dusky shark occurs from Massachusetts to Brazil and throughout the Caribbean. Its center of abundance seems to be around Florida. Although found in shallow water at times, it is largely an offshore coastal species which is often taken far from shoalwater. It apparently undertakes spring migrations to the north, and the young are produced over a long season and apparently throughout its range. Fishes are the staple part of its diet.—D.dS.

DUSKY SHINER *Notropis cummingsae* The dusky shiner is a small minnow, seldom exceeding 2 inches in total length. The distinguishing characteristics of this trim minnow are its broad, dark, lateral stripe; a decurved lateral line having a scale count of 38–40, with 6 scale rows above the lateral line and 3 below; a dorsal and anal ray count of 8 and 10–11, respectively; scales from the back of head to the origin of the dorsal fin numbering 18–20; and a pharyngeal tooth formula of 1,4–4,1. The head of this minnow is short and flattened above. The muzzle is rounded. The standard length of the body is 4⅓ to 4⅔ times the length of the head. The fins are large and the fish's body is rather stout. The pelvic fins are abdominal in position. The coloration of the minnow is dark above with a light band of coppery-brown, bordered below by a dull steel-blue lateral stripe. The fins are slightly pigmented, and the tip of the chin is dark. The geographical range of the dusky shiner is from the Neuse River watershed in North Carolina southward to northern and western Florida and westward to eastern Alabama.

LIFE HISTORY

The dusky shiner is associated with black-water acid streams. This species prefers a hard sand bottom and a moderate stream flow. The dusky shiner is a schooling fish and spawns over a sand bottom. The food of this species is small aquatic insects and zooplankton. It reaches maturity in 2 years, with its life span rarely exceeding 3 years.

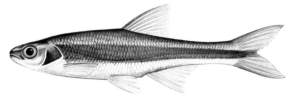

Dusky Shiner

The dusky shiner is one of the principal forage fishes eaten by the chain pickerel, redfin pickerel, warmouth, and redbreast sunfish. It is sometimes used as bait, but is seldom sold commercially.
—D.E.L.

DYSPHOTIC ZONE That region of the ocean from approximately the forty-fathom level where sunlight diminishes to the depth at which it disappears. Light may disappear at the 100–900-fathom level. Herbivorous marine animals become scarce or absent in the dysphotic zone; fish may possess bioluminescence (organs that can emit light). *See also* Marine Ecology

DYSTROPHIC A lake that has been made acid by slowly decaying vegetation. *See also* Types of Lakes under Freshwater Ecology

E

EAGLE RAY *See* Spotted Eagle Ray

EAR SQUEEZE *See* Aerotitis *in* Skin and Suba Diving Dangers *under* First Aid

ECHINODERM A member of a phylum of marine animals which has bilaterally symmetrical, free-swimming larvae and radially symmetrical (generally five-sided) adults. Echinoderms usually have a hard skeleton in the body wall, frequently joined into a shell and often covered by spines. They have a vascular system that circulates seawater to move their suckerlike tube feet. Echinodermata include brittle stars, sea cucumbers, sea lilies, starfish, and urchins.

ECOLOGICAL Pertaining to the relation of animals or plants to their environment

ECUADOR Located on the northwest coast of South America, Ecuador is tropical along the sea coast but cool in its snow-capped mountains. Quito, the City of Eternal Spring at 9,248 feet elevation, is also the second highest capital in the world (next to La Paz, Bolivia) and its temperatures average in the mid-50's. The great banana port of Guayaquil, a key city in Ecuador travel, is about 60 miles inland from the ocean on the Guayas River and is usually hot and humid. The coastal area does not have the distinct wet and dry seasons that one normally expects in the tropics, but there are variations. During December through April the Humboldt Current swings further out from the coast, and the days are usually bright and cloudless. This is summer here. During the remainder of the year this cool current flows closer to shore and frequently produces a cloud cover but no rain.

SALTWATER FISHING

The principal species taken off Ecuador are the black marlin, striped marlin, swordfish, Pacific blue marlin, wahoo, big-eye tuna, sailfish, roosterfish, yellowfin tuna, dolphin, mako shark, sierra mackerel, amberjack, albacore, white sea bass, and corvina. All standard methods of big-game angling are used here. Trolling is fundamental, and the billfish are usually sighted rather than fished blind. The Humboldt Current, which has followed a rather erratic path to the south off Peru in recent years, shows more stability off Ecuador, and the fishing grounds are reached in less than an hour's run. There is a good fleet of 28–34-foot boats at Punta Carnero.

Current and weather conditions being compatible it's commonplace to see 20–30 striped marlin in the 120–160-pound class in a day. The larger black marlin (local record 1,440 pounds) are less abundant, but in hot periods a half-dozen blacks will be seen finning-out just beyond the next set of seas. Swordfish are numerous about 30 miles south of Punta Carnero. Predicting the whims and feeding variations of these billfish becomes an obsession; one local theory is that there is a current reversal approximately every ten days, and when the water is flowing north the fishing peaks.

Black marlin appear to be most plentiful from May through October, but blue and striped marlin are more

A striped marlin comes to boat off Salinas, Ecuador. Good accommodations and ample fleet makes it top big-game spot

numerous from November through April, with the peak on stripes from February through April. Wahoo are taken most frequently in the fall; tuna appear in the winter; and sailfish, swordfish, and dolphin are plentiful at all seasons. If there is an "edge," the December through April period is prime. At this season the sea is very calm; the sun is bright; and marlin are easier to spot. Fishing is always good in these waters, however.

Inshore light-tackle fishing here is typical of the western coast of South America. It is accomplished primarily with skiffs and outboard powered dugouts casting to the rocks and along sandy beaches. Roosterfish, groupers, snappers, jacks, corvina, and snook are the chief targets, and tend to run to larger sizes. Casting with bottom-bouncing feathers and jigs usually produces action.

Despite the glamour of billfishing, one of the stellar attractions in Ecuador is the roosterfish. Roosterfish (locally *papagallo* or *pez de gallo*) range from Cabo Blanco, Peru, north into the Gulf of California and up the western coast of Baja California to Turtle Bay. However, they appear in greatest numbers off the coast of Ecuador. The maximum size recorded is a specimen 5 feet, 2 inches in length, weighing 111 pounds. Roosterfish are exciting gamefish, being strong runners and occasionally jumping when hooked. When swimming at the surface they often "flash the comb" by erecting the long spines of their first dorsal fins out of the water. This species is found along sandy beaches in the surf and offshore to moderate depths. It is a fine light-tackle fish usually taken by trolling with spoons, feathers, and plugs.

FRESHWATER FISHING

There is quality trout fishing in the high lakes of the Andes around Quito. The introduced fish are rainbow cutthroat hybrids which have been planted in waters at 9,000-13,000 feet of altitude.   —A.J.McC.

EEL *See* American Eel, Conger Eel, New Zealand Long-Finned Eel, New Zealand Short-Finned Eel, Snake Eels, Spotted Cusk Eel

ELECTRIC RAY *See* Atlantic Torpedo, Lesser Electric Ray, Pacific Electric Ray

ELEPHANT FISH Family Mormyridae Also called elephant-snout fishes, they are related to minnows, characins, and catfishes. They have a snout which may be only somewhat elongate (*Mormyrops*) to greatly produced and curved (*Gnathonemus*). The elongate, compressed body has dorsal and anal fins set far back, and a narrow caudal peduncle and a deeply forked tail are characteristic of all species. The mormyrid-type *Gymnarchus*, sometimes placed in this family, lacks the caudal and anal fin, and the dorsal fin is elongated for swimming. The eyes are small and often quite degenerate.

About 110 species are in the group, all of which are found in African freshwaters. The elephant-snout fish (*Mormyrops delicious*) grows to 5 feet, and is found throughout the freshwaters of Africa save for Kenya, Tanganyika, and Uganda. Relatives grow to only 6 inches long.

Most are found in slow streams and lakes, usually where the water is deep. Species with modified, elongated snouts or with only the lower lip extended use these structures to locate bottom-type foods including worms, insect larvae, and other small invertebrates. The snout, bearing only a few but relatively large teeth, is inserted

Elephant Fish

into the mud or among rocks in search of food. The lower lip is sensitive and acts as a touch receptor.

Like gars and bowfin, elephant fish can live in stagnant waters. The gas bladder is well-developed and has specialized compartments for oxygen storage, but the fish must rise to the surface to swallow air.

The high development of the cerebellum of the brain in mormyrids is associated with the modification of muscle along the tail tissue into electric organs which can emit low voltages. Such a continuous electrical field is essentially a sonar system, so that predators, prey, mates, or obstacles can be detected through echo-sounding. Electric receptors in the head area receive reflections from distant objects. This specialized development is associated with muddy habitats where the sense of vision is less efficient in obtaining food and avoiding enemies and obstacles.

FOOD VALUE

Mormyrids are eaten in Africa, but the meat is soft and reportedly tasteless, the flavor varying with the species. The flesh of large species is eaten dried.   —D.dS.

EMERALD SHINER *Notropis atherinoides* A small, silvery shiner with emerald reflections. The emerald shiner has a faint lateral band which is emerald-green in color. The dorsal fin is transparent, without spots, and is positioned over or slightly behind the origin of the ventral fins. The body is slab-sided with 36–40 scales in the lateral line, fewer than 22 of which are ahead of the dorsal fin. The emerald shiner and its subspecies are widely distributed throughout Canada and south to Virginia and Texas.

Emerald Shiner

Found in a wide variety of habitats, the emerald shiner appears to prefer clearwater over all bottom types. Remaining at mid-depth during the day and rising to the surface in large schools on summer nights, the emerald shiner feeds on small midges and other flying insects. Large adults are known to migrate into fast-flowing, high-gradient streams during the fall.

ANGLING VALUE

A valuable forage species, the emerald shiner is also a popular baitfish. It has been the subject for many artificial flies although no standard pattern copying this shiner has evolved. Most green-and-white bucktails with silver bodies or variations of the basic theme are thought to represent the species. Such flies are particularly effective for trout, landlocked salmon, and river smallmouths. *See also* Propagating Baitfish as a Business *under* Fish Culture —R.A.J.

ENGLAND England's wealth of angling lore is universally recognized. The birthplace of Izaak Walton is symbolized by centuries of literature pertaining to salmon and trout, and, technically, England still produces some of the finest tackle in the world. The art of fly-fishing was developed here, and ever since the publication of Dame Juliana Berners' *The Book of St. Albans* in 1496, British authors have figured prominently in the establishment of now common practices—dry-fly-fishing, nymph-fishing, and the fixed-spool reel to mention a few.

Angling in England, or at least quality angling, is not easy to find. Yet, the visitor can enjoy excellent sport at times particularly for brown trout and sea trout through many of the country hotels, associations, and private individuals who have rights on the better streams. The system of licensing is somewhat different in England than, say, the United States or Canada. No permit is required for saltwater fishing, but separate licenses are necessary to fish for salmon and migratory trout, and trout and coarse fish. These licenses are issued by each River Board, which is the authority responsible for the administration of a particular river or group of rivers. The cost depends on the quality of the angling, but broadly speaking a season's license is nominal. The funds so provided are used by the River Board for restocking, river improvement, wages of bailiffs (game protectors), and other management expenses. Licenses for shorter periods are available on many rivers. No distinction is made between residents and nonresidents.

ATLANTIC SALMON

The Atlantic salmon distributed in British waters is the same species which ascends the rivers of eastern Canada. The fish occur in most of the faster-flowing streams.

Starting at the northeast border with Scotland, salmon appear in a number of rivers south to the Whitby Esk. However, from this point down to Southampton the rivers are either too slow-flowing and lack the gravel necessary for reproduction, or they are too polluted. From Southampton westward through the West Country (Somerset, Devon, and Cornwall), through Wales and the northwest coast up to the Scottish border, most of the rivers have a salmon run. The most famous in the south are the Avon, Itchen, Test, and Frome. Although these chalk streams are better known as trout rivers, in some places they are dammed to prevent the salmon from ascending too high and therefore maintain separate fisheries. In the west, the Exe, Dart, Teign, Tamar, Tavy, Taw, Torridge, Severn, and Wye are best-known; in the northwest, the Ribble, Lune, Eden, Derwent, and Border Esk are popular. In the northeast, the Tweed, Coquet, and Whitby Esk are major salmon rivers. Boats can be rented on some streams, and the country hotel which offers fishing to its guests is very much a British institution. Most of the hotels are well-run and offer good fishing and the company of fellow anglers. Some clubs and associations issue tickets for days and longer periods.

Salmon vary greatly in size in England. On the Wye and Avon, for example, one or two 40-pound fish are caught each season. In the West Country the fish run much smaller, and a 15-pound salmon is considered a good fish. The season differs slightly from river to river, opening as early as January and ending as late as November. Normally, it extends from mid-February to the end of October. Fly-fishing is, of course, the traditional method of taking salmon. A big wet fly is fished early in the year and a smaller wet fly at season's end. The greased-line method is popular during the warm weeks of summer. The dry fly is little used and is generally conceded to be ineffective, possibly because the water temperature is seldom high enough. Experiments have shown that salmon can be caught on dry flies in Britain but not with consistent results.

Dermot Wilson hooks a fine trout by the old fishing hut on the Test River. This is one of Hampshire's best waters

Unlike Canada, where salmon fishing is restricted to the fly only, any sporting method can be employed in Britain. Spinning (a collective term in England which encompasses bait-casting) is permitted, and the spoon, plug, and devon minnow are commonly used in high cold-water and particularly when the rivers are roily after a rain. The worm, shrimp, and prawn are also legal in some streams.

SEA TROUT

The sea trout is one of the world's great gamefish, and fortunately it's not difficult to obtain good angling for these migratory browns in England. Many hotels and clubs own water where the visiting angler can purchase day or week tickets. Furthermore, the angler is not as dependent on the right water conditions for sea trout as he is for salmon.

Sea trout forage on Britain's coastal waters, and those found in the Irish Sea grow to a very large size. They enter most clean rivers to spawn beginning as early as March. However, the main run commences in June or July and extends to October. Although sea trout are caught in the slow rivers of the south and east, the best fishing is in the West Country on rivers like the Tavy and the Torridge and some of the streams of the northwest. These Irish Sea migrants weigh 3–10 pounds.

Sea trout are caught by all methods but fly-fishing is the more interesting game. These are shy fish, and they feed primarily at night. Consequently, fishing after dark is most effective. A warm night provides the best sport. Sea trout are difficult to catch during daylight hours except in discolored water. They take dry flies and wet flies, as well as spinners and live bait. A medium-weight trout fly rod is perfectly suitable; some anglers fish with a floating line, and others prefer one which sinks. Favorite sea-trout fly patterns are the Black Pennel, Peter Ross, Mallard and Claret, and Silver March Brown. On some rivers the Demons and Terrors (two- and three-hooked feather lures) are very effective. During the day, spinning with a 6–7-foot rod and 4-pound-test line using a small spoon or devon is considered a sporting way of taking these fish.

BROWN TROUT

The native trout of the British Isles is the brown trout. This species is found all over England, and like the salmon and sea trout it prefers fastwater and is most plentiful in the hilly regions. Rainbow trout have been introduced, but apart from a few rivers like the Wye in Derbyshire and the Chess near London this species has only thrived in lakes and reservoirs. Perhaps the most famous brown-trout fishing in England is in the southern chalk streams, particularly in the counties of Hampshire, Wiltshire, Dorset, Berkshire, and parts of East Anglia and Yorkshire. These are extremely clear, spring-fed rivers which originate in chalk hills and are therefore highly alkaline. Their water-plant growth is both fast and dense, and such rivers are very fertile. Under these ideal conditions trout grow rapidly and are free rising. A 2-pound average is not unusual on some streams, and trout of 4 pounds or more remain surface feeders. On a carefully managed river such as the Test big trout come freely to the dry fly. Although the Test fishing of world fame is wholly private (the Houghton Club) it is a classic example of a controlled fishery. The annual catch on the club's

16 miles of stream exceeds 1,000 fish of 1½ pounds or larger. The Test is stocked with both brown and rainbow trout which have been selectively bred for fast growth. As on all productive chalk streams, systematic weed cutting is essential to maintaining a flow through the stream channels which are the important lies of the trout. The vegetation holds vast quantities of insect life as well as freshwater shrimp and snails. The Test managers introduced "fly boards" at an early date to increase mayfly production; the board is anchored in the stream so that mayflies can crawl on the underside for oviposition and thus prevent consumption of mayfly eggs by predator insects (caddis). Chalk-stream fishing has great charm and interest; however the trout lack the gameness of fish found in faster-flowing rivers. A partial list of the best trout streams in England would include the following:

South	— Test, Itchen, Wiltshire, Avon, and Kennet
West Country	— Exe, Otter, and Culm
West Midlands	— Teme, Onny, and Lugg
Derbyshire	— Dove, Wye, and Derwent
Yorkshire	— Wharfe, Aire, Swale, Ure, Derwent, and Driffield Beck
North West	— Ribble, Hodder, Lune, Kent, and Eden
North East	— Till, Coquet, Wansbeck, and Tweed

A type of trout fishing very popular in England is reservoir fishing. Many of the public-utility reservoirs are stocked with browns and rainbows. In such habitats their rate of growth is often rapid, and the condition of the fish is uniformly excellent. At Chew, for example, near Bristol, 3-pound trout are common, and some 5–6-pound trout are caught each season. Reservoir fishing is available in many parts of England on a day-ticket basis.

COARSE FISHING

Apart from the northern pike, which grows to a rather large size in Britain (20 pounders are quite common), coarse fishing in England is very different from most types of American fishing. The season runs from June 16th to March 14th; so much of the fishing is done in winter. Coarse species are usually caught by using very sophisticated still-fishing tackle consisting of a long, very light rod, open-face spinning reel, very fine line, tiny hooks, and a variety of specialized floats or bobbers. The popular baits are maggots, worms, and pastes. Some coarse fish will also take a fly. The species commonly sought are roach *Rutilus rutilus*, European perch *Perca fluviatilis*, chub *Squalius cephalus*, tench *Tinca tinca*, barbel *Barbus barbus*, bream *Abramis brama*, and dace *Leuciscus leuciscus*. The carp *Cyprinus carpio* is also highly esteemed. Carp run over 40 pounds, are difficult to catch, and are extremely game fish. The European grayling *Thymallus thymallus* is a close relative of the Arctic grayling and provides excellent sport on the fly in the autumn and on bait in the winter.

Because in many areas coarse fish are small, and because the British will bet on anything, match-fishing, or fishing in competition to catch the largest weight of fish, is immensely popular. It is not unusual for several thousand anglers to take part in a contest. The prize, together with sweep money and betting wins, may amount to over £1,000 for five hours' fishing. Such

Fishing for sea trout in the pool by the Priory at Christchurch on the Hampshire Avon

competitions are extremely well-organized, and inasmuch as bookmakers are legal in England, they are present at such fishing matches. A high degree of skill is required to be a consistent winner, and successful match-fishermen are known by their form and given short odds by the bookmakers. Coarse fish are never killed in England, but placed in a keepnet then weighed at the end of the match and returned to the water.

Broadly speaking coarse fish are found in the slower rivers and in lakes, and in consequence East Anglia (the counties of Norfolk and Suffolk) is a prime area for this type of fishing. They are also found in some trout and salmon rivers, such as the Hampshire Avon, Severn, Wye, and the Yorkshire rivers particularly in the lower reaches. When gamefish and coarse fish are found together, the water is described as a mixed fishery.

SALTWATER FISHING

Sea fishing in England is similar in its methods and tackle to the Northeastern United States coast. Surf-casting, spinning, and bottom-fishing from rocks, piers, and boats are all popular. While fish are plentiful, they do not run large, and real game species are scarce. The most sporting is probably the bass *Roccus labrax* which is a small relative of the striped bass that attains about 15 pounds in weight. The tope *Galeorhinus galeus*, which is a small European shark running 30–50 pounds, is also much sought. In recent years fishing for blue, mako, and porbeagle sharks has become a popular sport off Cornwall. The blues run to 200 pounds while the mako and porbeagle reach 400 pounds. The common Atlantic mackerel and the gray mullet *Mugil chelo* provide good sport on light tackle. Other angling species of seasonal importance are the whiting, sole, skate, conger eel, cod, and pollack. Bluefin tuna were caught in years past off the Yorkshire coast, but this fishery has diminished. —T.T.

HOTEL FISHING IN ENGLAND AND WALES

Hotel fishing is the principal means available to the tourist for angling in the British Isles. However, the tra-dition and the business of offering fishing rights to guests, or in some cases making day tickets available, are highly satisfactory, and good sport can be obtained for the visitor. Hotel fishing is mainly for brown trout, sea trout, and Atlantic salmon. The cream of English trout fishing in the chalk-stream counties of Hampshire and Wiltshire is virtually all in private hands; however, the Bull Hotel on the Avon at Downton, near Salisbury, yields some good trout fishing during the mayfly season. Although there are many fine establishments for the angler, the following are old favorites which may serve as a general guide for the tourist.

Deer Park Hotel, Honiton, South Devon This hotel, standing in its own spacious grounds, controls both banks of three miles of the River Otter. The beats are all easily accessible, the nearest being only 150 yards from the hotel itself, and car parking is available downstream, just off the busy main road from London to the west. This water has been closely preserved for sixty years as a brown-trout fishery. Dry fly only is the rule, and the number of rods is strictly limited. The river is restocked annually. Detailed records of catches are available for inspection in the fishing register, which shows that baskets average $\frac{3}{4}$ pound and that a number of 2–3-pound trout are taken each season. The basket limit is two brace a day. This weight is much above the usual average for west-country waters. The Otter, indeed, is midway in character between the characteristic rough rivers of the west and the limpid chalk streams of the counties to the east. Both banks are fairly open, and the water is relatively clear. There is some weed growth, and fairly good hatches of mayflies occur, especially in spring and in September. Spent spinners and dusk-hatching caddisflies may give rise to good evening sport. Knee boots are usually adequate for the Otter.

Arundell Arms Hotel, Lifton, West Devon This hotel has 18 miles of fishing divided into 22 individual beats on the Tamar, separating Devon from Cornwall, and its tributaries, the Lyd, Lew, Thrushel, Wolf, and Cary. The Tamar yields some sea-run brown trout and an occasional salmon, but the fishing is mainly for brown trout. Chest waders are desirable for most beats.

For trout the rule is fly only, both dry and wet fly being employed. The hotel issues a handy booklet describing each beat in detail, together with fishing methods recommended for each. The water is not overfished, and on most beats there are plenty of trout of varying size. Fishing begins in mid-March and is usually good right from the start of the season.

Cornwall River Board licenses are available at the hotel. Day tickets may occasionally be available.

Woodford Bridge Hotel, Milton Dameril, North Devon This delightful, thatched hotel, standing in its own beautiful gardens, has five miles of brown-trout fishing on the upper reaches of the River Torridge. Trout are plentiful and fight hard in relation to their size. Fly only is the rule, and the dry fly is generally rewarding. Upstream nymph-fishing pays good dividends during the daytime in summer when fish up to $\frac{3}{4}$ pound or so are taken each year. There are plenty of 9–10-inch fish above and below the bridge. Daily catches are recorded in the fishing register, and it is the custom for good baskets to be displayed in the hotel in the evening.

The upper Torridge valley is rich in bird life, and in spring wildflowers bloom profusely along the river banks. Fishing begins in mid-March and continues to the end of

September, May and June being usually the best months, followed by September when water conditions are suitable. In that month sea trout are sometimes taken. Hip boots are recommended, and a short rod is desirable.

The peaceful Woodford Bridge water is the setting for Chapter 13, "Torridge Interludes," of *Nymph Fishing in Practice* (by Oliver Kite, Herbert Jenkins, London, 1963).

Reservoir fishing is available in the district, and fishing for sea bass can be enjoyed in the Torridge estuary at Bideford about twelve miles away. The hotel is also a good base for fishing other local waters. Devon River Board licenses may be bought from the resident owners.

Gliffaes Country House Hotel, Crickhowell, Breconshire, South Wales This hotel controls 2½ miles of excellent water on the River Usk on the borders of England and Wales. Most of the water adjoins the hotel grounds, but the Red Barn stretch, near Abergavenny in Monmouthshire some miles downstream, is an additional beat.

The water holds many brown trout usually running ½–¾ pound, and there are a number of salmon pools which hold fish in suitable water conditions. The charge for salmon fishing is nominal. Except when the water is high and badly discolored after heavy rains, sport can generally be relied on with the fly. Chest waders are desirable for the Usk is a big river, by British standards.

Visitors are within easy reach of Usk town where the local fishing association holds about two miles of water and issues a limited number of day tickets for trout fishing only. This is some of the finest water, on its day, in the country. Talyboat Reservoir, holding big trout, is seven miles from Gliffaes. Also within reach is Llangorse Lake famous for big northern pike. Usk River Board licenses are available at the hotel.

The Mill, Nether Wallop, Hampshire The Mill is not itself a hotel but rather an angling headquarters which works in cooperation with several hotels, notably the Sheriff House Hotel in Stockbridge. The Mill is the entrée to Test and Itchen trout fishing. Angling author and expert Dermot Wilson makes several excellent beats available to his clients. The idyllic water on the Test is located below Long Parish and provides an abundance of wild brown trout, introduced rainbows, and grayling. Fish up to 4 or 5 pounds are not uncommon.

On the Itchen Mr. Wilson has two stretches of water near Winchester, the cathedral city where Izaak Walton is buried; one section is just above the water Skues fished and just below Lord Grey's fishing cottage. The other stretch is one of the three little streams that form the headwaters of the Itchen. This is all dry-fly water for difficult trout.

Talbot Hotel, Tregaron, Cardiganshire, West Wales This small, inexpensive country inn does not itself control water, but is conveniently situated for visitors who wish to avail themselves of the excellent facilities offered by the local Tregaron Angling Association, which preserves twelve miles of the River Teifi (pronounced "Tie-vee"), together with the upper reaches of the neighboring River Towy and a mountain stream, the Camddwr Mynydd.

A weekly visitor's ticket for salmon and for trout or a season ticket is available from Barclays Bank in the village square near the hotel. A River Board license can be bought from the local drug store. A helpful map issued by the association explains the main Teifi water and designates the salmon pools in which spinning is per-

mitted. Elsewhere, below Glanbrenig Bridge, Tregaron, the rule is fly only. The use of the gaff is prohibited before May 1st.

Night fishing is not allowed, nor is Sunday fishing; dogs may not be taken to the waterside, for this is mainly sheep country. This remote part of Wales is Welsh-speaking, and at night the talk in the hotel bar is in the ancient tongue.

Salmon are not plentiful; their presence is dependent on water conditions, which also govern the sea-trout run in the summer. Brown-trout fishing opens about mid-March and is particularly good in April and May. The size limit is 7 inches, but fish average over ½ pound as a rule, and there are plenty over a pound with an occasional 2-pounder or better.

Above Tregaron the water flows through a Nature Reserve, the desolate, curlew-haunted Tregaron Bog. Below the village there is some most attractive dry-fly water on such reaches as Abercoed, Nantdderwen, and Pont Llanio. Hip boots are desirable.

Local anglers fish mainly on Saturdays, Wednesday afternoons, and in the evenings in summer. The majority fish with a team of wet flies across and downstream in traditional fashion, but dry-fly and upstream nymph-fishing can be very rewarding. The association's water is the setting for Le (Levan) D. Owen's sympathetic study of the old Teifi master, Dai Lewis, who died rod in hand at the riverside in 1945 (*A Fisherman's Saga*, Putnam, London, 1960). —O.K.

ENGLISH SOLE *Parophrys vetulus* Shaped like an elongate diamond, it is sometimes referred to as lemon sole because of the faint odor of lemon of freshly caught fish. The mouth is small, the snout pointed and elongate, and the edge of the upper eye visible from the blind side. The lateral line is nearly straight, arching slightly upward in advance of the pectoral fin and having a dorsal, accessory branch. On the eyed side it is a uniform yellowish-brown, while the blind side is pale yellow to white with reddish-brown tinges. The English sole reaches a length of about 21 inches. It occurs from Baja California to northwestern Alaska, being more common in the northern part of the range. It has been taken in depths of 60–1,000 feet over sandy to muddy bottom. The spawning season is from February to April, and the eggs float at the surface. Small crabs, worms, shrimps, and clams are eaten by the adults.

FOOD VALUE

Despite its small size, the species is desirable because of the delicate flavor of the flesh. It has a high commercial importance, and is also taken by anglers. —D.dS.

EPILIMNION A biological term to describe the warm, upper layer of water in a lake. The epilimnion may extend from the surface to 15–25 feet deep. The water temperature may vary from 75° F. or more at the surface to about 65° F. or slightly less at the lower limit of the epilimnion. *See also* Thermal Stratification

EQUATORIAL CURRENT *See* Currents

ERIOGRAPHID Referring to the members of the family Eriographidae in the Annelida, this is the phylum of segmented worms. They are marine worms with transverse rows of hook-shaped appendages on their abdomens; they do not have eyes on their heads, but possess eyespots on the last segments of their bodies. They live separately in tubes that are massed together within a gelatinous material.

ESTUARY An area where a river or stream meets the ocean; it is characterized by water whose salt content is between that of fresh and marine environments, and by a distinct population of animals and plants.

EULACHON *Thaleichthys pacificus* The common name of this smelt (*which see*) is Chinook jargon, the fish being of much importance to the Indians. The species was known as "candlefish," for it was sometimes dried and fitted with a wick to give light.

In Alaska the eulachon is called "hooligan," and it constitutes a small but important fishery as it is highly esteemed as a food.

The eulachon is a small, slender fish, which seldom exceeds 12 inches in length. It is bluish-brown with a fine black stippling on the back shading to silvery-white on the sides and belly. The striae on the opercles follow the bone contours; pelvic fins are inserted in front of the

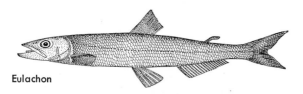

Eulachon

dorsal origin. Its snout is pointed, the head long, mouth large and terminal, and its teeth hooked and small. There are 4–6 gillrakers on the upper half of the arch. The teeth of the eulachon are deciduous at spawning time. The fish enter freshwater streams to spawn from March to May from northern California to the Bering Sea. They mature at 2–3 years, and die after spawning. The eggs, which may reach 25,000 in a single female, are adhesive, sticking to sand or other material and hatching in 2–3 weeks. Eulachon feed on planktonic crustaceans. Most of the commercial catch is by gillnets.

ANGLING VALUE

Although the eulachon has no angling value, it is a forage food for Pacific salmon and the fur seal. Eulachons are also regionally popular as a seafood. All surf smelts are too delicate and soft to stand any preserving process, although some are hard salted and some are sold fresh. The greatest majority are smoked, however, and, having a golden-yellow color coupled with a delicate smelt flavor, they are highly esteemed by coastal Indians from California to Alaska. Sportsmen dip prodigious numbers out of rivers during the spawning runs, but the take is regulated to prevent depletion. *See also* Alaska   —J.R.

EUPHAUSIDS A variety of small, soft-shelled, marine crustaceans that are among the members of the order Euphausiacea. Euphausids consist of shrimplike animals that often possess luminous organs. They are among the most common planktonic animals of the sea, and are a source of food for pelagic fishes such as salmon and steelhead.

EUPHOTIC ZONE The shallow-water zone of the ocean extending from shore outward to a depth of approximately 30–40 fathoms. The maximum depth of the euphotic zone is determined by the water's transparency; it is the area penetrated by sunlight and so the limit depends to some degree on the clarity of the water. The euphotic zone is typified by an abundance of plankton and herbivorous marine animals. *See also* Marine Ecology

EUROPEAN GRAYLING *Thymallus thymallus* The grayling, also known as the "umber" (French *ombre*), is a nontypical freshwater member of the salmon family. It is not so common as the brown trout, nor so large as the salmon; so it takes third place to these in the estimation of most European gamefishers.

The European grayling is found throughout the continent except in southern France, Portugal, Spain, southern Italy, and Ireland. It also inhabits the basin of the Arctic Ocean. It is distributed in the east as far as the Ural Range (USSR), and may be encountered in the upper reaches of the Volga and Ural Rivers. This wide distribution is somewhat deceptive, because the grayling's habitat preferences within its range of distribution are narrow. It is a fish of fast-flowing, clear streams, especially if they are well-oxygenated and cold. Consequently, it is more or less restricted to the headwaters of the river systems in which it does occur. Being sensitive to pollution, industrialization has driven it from some waters it formerly occupied. Even without pollution, changes in the nature of the streams will drive the grayling out; this was apparently the case of the American grayling in Michigan, consequent to deforestation.

It is an elongate fish, six times as long as broad, with a small head and inferior mouth with a narrow gape. Instantly recognizable is the long, high dorsal fin with convex dorsal edge and black stripes running from front to rear. This characteristic fin has 14–17 rays. Behind it is the adipose fin of the salmon family; unlike most salmonids the tail fin is quite deeply forked.

The scales are small and silver, darkening to gray-blue or gray-green on the back. There are 80–88 scales in the lateral line. The silver flanks are dappled with irregular black spots. Often missed but characteristic of the grayling is the pupil of its eye; it is oval, with a pointed "tail" toward the snout.

Grayling are a textbook example of specialized ecological niches in fish—in a group where the overlaps are normally great. French ecologists characterize the cold, clear reaches of a river, below its headwaters, as the "grayling zone" or *zone à l'ombre*. Admittedly in Scandinavia it has thrived in oligotrophic lakes, but streams are its major habitat, especially the "grayling zone" with a typical gradient of 1:250. The terete shape enables it to keep station in the fast currents of such waters; it is said that the optimum current speed is two feet per second.

Preference for coldwater is a most marked characteristic of grayling natural history. Their distribution around the Arctic Circle points to their being part of the freshwater-fish fauna from the earliest postglacial times. An English naturalist-angler, Wilson, has investigated the history of the European grayling in some detail, and the following story emerges.

The ice ages of the Pleistocene wiped out the previous fish fauna of Europe and North America. On the retreat of the ice caps, fish came back from three sources:
1. The sea (e.g., eels and salmon)
2. Central Asia and southern rivers untouched by glaciation (e.g., the carp family of fishes)
3. Original arctic fishes which lived naturally on the fringe of the ice.

The grayling certainly came from source 3. In the postglacial period, Europe was very different from what it is today; Britain was still part of the mainland, and a great

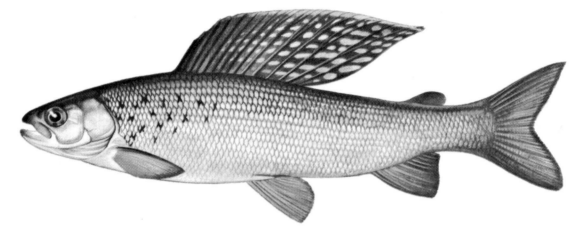

European Grayling, 3-pound Male, Traun River, Austria

river flowed through what is now the North Sea, with its two major tributaries the Rhine and Thames. From this river came the grayling stocks of Britain; even today they are concentrated into the eastward-flowing rivers and those where the headwaters were once continuous with them. Man has spread them further, somewhat masking the original pattern. Introductions have even been made into clearwater lakes and canals, but without much success.

The grayling normally grows to about 4 pounds, but fish up to 6 pounds are reported. A 2-pounder from most rivers is a nice fish, and the average caught by anglers is generally smaller.

LIFE HISTORY

Grayling are unique among salmonids native to Europe in breeding in spring, at the same time as the cyprinid fishes. Males usually mature in their third year, females in their fourth; there is no distinctive breeding dress, and spawning occurs between March and May. The fish pair and mate in fast, gravelly shallows, the female scooping a redd in which she lays 3,000–4,500 eggs per pound of her body weight. The eggs are 3–4 millimeters in diameter. These are fertilized by the males and the redds covered.

The eggs hatch in about 20 days at 50°F., and proportionately less time at higher temperatures. The fry are typically troutlike, with large yolk sacs. This is the only stage where the grayling seeks cover in weeds or among stones; it usually, when adult, lies out into the mainstream and is not so fond of snags as the trout. As soon as the yolk sac is absorbed, it moves out into the current, swimming vigorously for its food. At this stage, and for a long while after, the diet consists of insects and their larvae, crustaceans, and even fish spawn. As the grayling gets older, it becomes increasingly predatory.

Now it is recognizably a fish rather than fry; it forms into schools at selected spots and begins to grow. As it has been spawned and hatched in the spring, it can readily take advantage of the abundance of small foods available in the succeeding summer. The spawning date in this light seems an excellent adaptation to a semi-Arctic existence, taking best advantage of the short summer near the Arctic Circle.

At the end of its first summer the young grayling is about 4 inches long and up to an ounce in weight. It continues to feed each winter, even in the bitterest cold. By the second year, it is 8 inches long and about a $\frac{1}{4}$ pound in weight; in the third and fourth years it attains $\frac{1}{2}$ and 1 pound respectively.

ANGLING VALUE

European grayling usually run small, but it is much admired by fly-fishermen with access to waters where it is present, because it extends the fly-fishing season into winter. Many anglers cease fishing for trout in September and move on with identical tackle to grayling in October; where it is found, fly-fishing is an all-round-the-year sport.

It takes small flies on the surface with a fast dart, showing a very precise estimation of speed, distance, and position. Besides dry flies, it can also be taken well on wet flies and nymphs; some anglers use a traditional bait-fishing method as well, trotting a small round-float tackle downstream baited with worms.

The European grayling fights well for its size, being a very fast-moving fish by nature. Often the fight is more unusual, as it backs away from the angler in a series of sidestepping wriggles.

ECONOMIC VALUE

Grayling flesh is excellent and much esteemed. Its scientific name is supposed to derive from a smell of thyme when the fish is prepared for the table, freshly cut. Although appreciated, the flesh is worth less than trout, and the fish itself is much more difficult to raise in hatcheries. The fry do need live food, whereas trout can be fed on minced meat, and grayling when adult are far more difficult to transport. In consequence grayling for the table is caught from the wild, and its appearance on a menu local.

Grayling hatcheries do exist, in both Germany and Britain—not for food, but for raising fish for stocking rivers. Even this activity is not a widespread commercial proposition, unless only fertilized ova are sold. Transporting the adults requires oxygenated trucks, adding greatly to the cost—quite apart from the cost of raising them to that size on specialized live diets in captivity.   —D.M.

EUROPEAN PERCH *Perca fluviatilis* A panfish very similar to the yellow perch (*which see*) of eastern North America, which is regarded as a subspecies *P. fluviatilis flavescens* by European authors. It is indigenous to Europe, with the exceptions of Spain and southern Italy, and common throughout Asia.

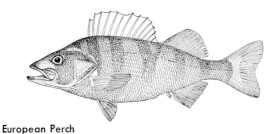

European Perch

The body is somewhat compressed and moderately elongated, tapering posteriorly, with the back more or less humped between the occiput and the dorsal fin. The upper part of the head is smooth and scaleless, while the whole body is covered with small, rough scales. The operculum ends in a characteristically long spine. There are two dorsal fins, a longer anterior one formed of 13–17 spines and a shorter posterior one with 2 spines and 13–15 softrays. There are 58–68 lateral line scales as opposed to 74–88 for the yellow perch.

The coloration of the perch varies somewhat according to locality, age, sex, and season. The color of the back is greenish-yellow; the belly is white. On the side there are five or more dark, vertical bars which are sometimes bifurcated above. The dorsal fin is grayish-black, and the ventral fins are reddish. Sometimes the bars are inconspicuous, and the whole fish appears almost uniformly dark green. In other populations the deep black bars may be in striking contrast to the pale olive background.

In their natural habitat perch are very hardy and inhabit slow-flowing rivers, deep lakes, and ponds, often living in brackish waters where they thrive and grow quite large. They do not usually attain a length of more than 18 inches with a weight of 4–5 pounds; recorded to 8 pounds. An important commercial species in the Baltic Sea. —A.J.McC.

EUTROPHIC *See* Freshwater Ecology

EVERGLADES PYGMY SUNFISH *Elassoma evergladei* This tiny, perchlike sunfish is an inhabitant of the swampy areas of southern Georgia and Florida. It has a rounded tail and large eyes. The color ranges from brown to green, and is often blotched with brilliant blue. The lateral line is obsolete, and there are usually 27–30 scales along side of body.

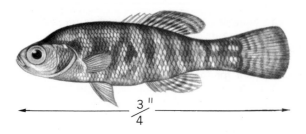

3/4"

Everglades Pygmy Sunfish

The Everglades pygmy sunfish builds a simple nest from bits of plants into which the eggs are placed. The nest is guarded by the male.

ANGLING VALUE

None. The Everglades pygmy sunfish seldom reaches more than 1½ inches. It is utilized as forage by larger gamefish. —K.B.

F

FALLFISH *Semotilus corporalis* A minnow similar to the creek chub in appearance and commonly called "chub" in Eastern United States rivers. It can be distinguished from the creek chub by the absence of the dark spot on the base of the dorsal fin. The fallfish is distributed from eastern Canada into the James Bay drainage, and south on the east side of the Appalachians to Virginia. The fallfish is found in clear streams and lakes, young fish schooling in the shallows and larger adult fish inhabiting the deeper waters. The food of the fallfish consists chiefly of aquatic insects although a variety of other aquatic forms may be consumed.

Fallfish, 5-inch Female

LIFE HISTORY

Spawning in the spring, this minnow, like the creek chub, takes on a rosy coloration, and tubercles form on the upper portions of the head. The fallfish builds a nest of pebbles and stones in the shoal areas of lakes or quiet pools of streams. After the eggs are deposited, additional stones are gathered and placed on the nest by the male, the stones actually being carried in the mouth.

The fallfish grows to a somewhat larger size than the creek chub, some reaching a length of 17 inches or more. In smaller streams, however, they probably attain a maximum size of 10–15 inches.

ANGLING VALUE

Young fallfish provide some forage for gamefish such as bass and pickerel but undoubtedly compete heavily with the more desirable species due to the large number of insects they consume. The fallfish readily takes artificial lures as well as natural baits, and is usually considered a nuisance by anglers in quest of more sporty species. Thoreau has said of its eating qualities, ". . . it tastes like brown paper salted." —R.A.J.

FALSE ALBACORE *See* Little Tunas

FALSE CAST A fly-casting technique in which the angler does not complete his forward cast by letting the fly fall to the water but remakes his back cast in order to lengthen the line or increase its speed. When dry-fly fishing the angler may use a series of false casts to shake the moisture from the fly to achieve a better float. *See also* Fly-Casting

FALSE PILCHARD *Harengula clupeola* Also called the sardina escamuda, sprat, and petit cailleu it is related to the red-ear sardine and the scaled sardine of the Western Atlantic and to two other species in the Eastern Pacific. It is a wide-ranging species found in the Florida Keys, Bahamas and the West Indies, and along the mainland coast from Yucatan to Brazil.

Its general coloration is silvery, especially on the lower half of the head and body; opercular surfaces with iridescent or pearlish reflections; back dark brownish or bluish-gray; body with dark, longitudinal streaks more conspicuous on back; humeral spot faint; tip of snout and mandible dusky; upper sector of iris dusky; fins colorless except caudal, which has some pigment at tips and along inner margin.

Other distinguishing characteristics are inner edge of palatines without a row of pointed teeth anteriorly; predorsal contour evenly and moderately convex, the postdorsal contour more or less straight from origin of dorsal to caudal fin; ventral contour much more convex than dorsal contour, the body axis closer to dorsal than to pelvic fins; dorsal fin originating nearer to tip of snout than to caudal base; pelvic fin inserted nearer to insertion of pectoral than to origin of anal; pectoral fin inserted closer to insertion of pelvic than tip of snout.

Scales adherent, 40–43 transverse rows, 11–14 predorsal; ventral scutes 29–32, usually 30 or 31; gillrakers 28–35, usually 30–32, on lower limb of first arch; anal fin with 17–19, usually 18, rays, its base usually slightly longer than pelvic fin; tip of dorsal fin not blackish.

This is the smallest species of sardine in the Western Atlantic. It seldom reaches a length of more than 100 mm. Its life history is unknown.

This species and its relatives are most abundant in bays and estuaries where they may be captured with beach seines and cast nets. They are utilized for bait and food throughout the West Indies and Caribbean region.

—J.C.B.

FAMILY A group of related genera

FANTAIL MULLET *See under* Silver Mullet

FAN-WING A type of dry fly typified by wings which are made of curved duck breast, throat, or belly feathers. The wings are tied in an upright position and curve outward to either side of the fly. Because of their air resistance, fan-wing dry flies create something of a parachute effect and fall lightly to the water. The most famous fly pattern dressed in this style is the Fan-Wing Royal Coachman. *See also* Fly Tying, Fly-Fishing

FATHEAD MINNOW *Pimephales promelas* A small, olivaceous minnow with a more or less incomplete lateral line. A narrow, dark, vertical bar is often present at the base of the caudal fin. Adults have a horizontal dark bar across the dorsal fin. The fathead, in addition to the 8 developed dorsal rays, has a stout, blunt-tipped half-ray found before the first developed ray. Together with its several subspecies the fathead minnow is widespread from southern Canada, east of the Rocky Mountains to Maine, and southward to the Susquehanna River and to the Gulf States. In addition it has been introduced west of the Rocky Mountains. In Northern waters the fathead prefers boggy lakes, ponds, and streams, while southward

and westward it is found in silty lakes and streams. It is uncommon in fast-flowing streams and larger, deeper impoundments.

LIFE HISTORY

The fathead feeds extensively on microscopic algae as well as other plankton. These minnows deposit their eggs beneath boards or any other flat objects that may be available in the pond or stream bottom. During the spawning season the male develops a thick, spongy predorsal pad on its back with which it cleans the eggs deposited by the female. In addition, the male develops golden-copper bands encircling the body just behind the head and under the dorsal fin. During this time prominent, sharp tubercles also develop on the snout. A small minnow, the fathead seldom exceeds 3 inches.

Fathead Minnow

ECONOMIC VALUE

The fathead is considered a valuable forage and bait species since at its maximum size it is consumed by even young predator fish. An easily propagated species, the fathead is popular with commercial hatchery operators who raise them for bait, as well as forage for bass. It is reported that 400,000 to over a million per acre can be raised under hatchery conditions. *See also* Propagating Baitfish as a Business *under* Fish Culture.   —R.A.J.

FAUNA The composite of animal life of any area or region.

FEATHER To turn the blade of an oar horizontally at the finish of a stroke. Action is accomplished by twisting the wrist. Feathering reduces wind resistance by presenting the sharp edge of the oar to the wind.

FENDER A device hung over the side of a boat to protect it from rubbing against a dock or other boat. Fenders are made of rolls of rope and canvas filled with cork or ground rubber, and, more recently, many are constructed of various plastics.

FERRULE A metal socket and matching plug mounted on the adjacent ends of rod sections, which, when joined together, assemble the sections one to the other. The purpose of a ferrule is to permit a long rod to be dismantled into short lengths for convenient storage and transportation. The socket portion of a ferrule is called the "female ferrule," and the plug portion is called the "male ferrule." Ferrules are usually made of nickel silver or brass; these materials have a high tensile strength, adequate fatigue life, and a resistance to corrosion and are light in weight.

Traditionally, ferrules are manufactured in diametral steps of $\frac{1}{64}$ inch ($\frac{1}{64}$ = .0156) measured on the outside of the male ferrule. The metal to metal fit of the two joining members is very critical, as it must be loose enough to assemble by hand, yet not so loose as to come apart in casting. In practice this means that very close control must be exercised (.0002 inch total diametral tolerance variation). Of equal importance is the configuration of the ferrule opening through which the bamboo or fiberglass section is inserted. The rod section material is flexible, while the metal ferrule sleeve is comparatively rigid and unyielding. This dissimilarity could induce a large concentration of local stress leading to early failure of the rod. To ease the problem, a number of slots or serrations are cut lengthwise (approximate length equal to one or two ferrule diameters), then gradually tapered through this slotted length to a paper-thin wall at the open end. The transition of the flexible rod material to the ferrule metal is no longer concentrated but spread along its length. All fine ferrules are built in this fashion.

A number of substances have been used to cement ferrules to rod sections. These include white lead, shellacrosin mixtures, and, more recently, rubber and epoxy adhesives. Either of the latter two are satisfactory. Epoxy has the advantage of being a good "gap filler" which will not shrink away from voids in a poor metal-to-bamboo fit. If these are used, pinning is unnecessary.

FERRULE SIZES IN 64THS OF AN INCH WITH DECIMAL EQUIVALENTS

64th	thousandths	64th	thousandths	64th	thousandths
1	.0156	22	.344	43	.6719
2	.0312	23	.359	44	.6875
3	.0469	24	.375	45	.7031
4	.0625	25	.391	46	.7187
5	.0781	26	.406	47	.7344
6	.0937	27	.422	48	.750
7	.1094	28	.438	49	.7656
8	.125	29	.453	50	.7812
9	.141	30	.469	51	.7969
10	.156	31	.484	52	.8125
11	.172	32	.500	53	.8281
12	.188	33	.516	54	.8437
13	.203	34	.531	55	.8594
14	.219	35	.547	56	.875
15	.234	36	.563	57	.8906
16	.250	37	.578	58	.9062
17	.266	38	.594	59	.9219
18	.281	39	.609	60	.9375
19	.297	40	.625	61	.9531
20	.312	41	.6406	62	.9687
21	.328	42	.6562	63	.9844
				64	1.000

Fiberglass ferrules were developed in the 1960's for fiberglass rod construction; these are mainly sleeve, slipover, or spigot types. *See also* Rod Building and Fiberglass Rod Construction *under* Rod Building.

—A.J.McC.

FERRULE CEMENT An adhesive bonding material which is used to secure a ferrule to the rod section. There are many different brands of ferrule cement, which are generally made of gutta-percha, rosin, linseed oil, and beeswax; the mixture is sold in stick form and can be softened by holding in a flame. After applying to the rod end, the cement should be reheated, and the ferrule (also warmed) pushed in place. *See also* Rod Repairs

FIBERGLASS ROD Fiberglass is the most important rod-building material in the United States today. Glass rods are not all alike; they vary in the type of raw material used, the type of bonding agent, the proportion of bond to glass, wall thickness, and several other elements which are hidden in the finished product. Broadly speaking, solid glass rods are stronger than the tubular kind be-

cause they contain more glass. But they are also heavier and therefore most suitable in short lengths for casting lures of ½ ounce or more. Tubular rods on the other hand can be adapted to almost any job from ultralight spinning to big-game trolling depending on the quality of the blank. *See also* Fiberglass Rod Construction *under* Rod Building

FIDDLER CRAB Uca spp. These are small crabs distantly related to the stonecrab (*which see*) but belonging to a separate family (Ocypodidae). The shell is short, broad, nearly straight in front, and nearly square (truncate) in outline. There are no teeth on the shell as in the green crab and blue crab (*which see*), and the front and sides of the shell form right angles. The eyestalks are very long, cylindrical, and are easily moved about. The characteristic elongate left claw is developed only in the male and is normally held horizontally in front of the body. Fiddler crabs are small, seldom exceeding an inch across the shell.

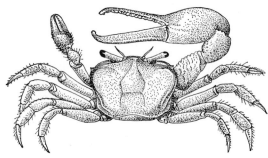

Fiddler Crab

LIFE HISTORY

Fiddler crabs are found in most tropical shore zones where the habitat is suitable, such as sandflats with nearby driftwood, mangrove roots, or debris for shelter. Some species prefer sand, while others prefer sandy mud or mud, but all species have very definite habitat preference. During high tide, they usually plug up the holes and remain in their burrows, emerging on the ebb tide to forage in search of food. Some species live where the water is salty, others where it is quite brackish or nearly fresh. Tidemarshes are a favorite haunt. Fiddler crabs are largely nocturnal, but may be observed to be active during the day. They are incessantly busy, cleaning burrows, scouring sandballs for microscopic particles, and placing small sandballs near their burrow entrance. Feeding involves scooping up mud or sand with the special small claws, which are specially modified into spoon-shaped structures. Food is sifted from the sand and mud, but the manner in which this is done is not known. They also eat garbage, carrion, and detritus of any type.

The breeding cycle is complex, and mating is preceded by courting rituals in which the male, brightened from the usual mottled brown to a rich brown with purples and blues with pinkish iridescence, attracts the female by waving the large claw in the air. Waving of the claw may also occur during nonmating periods to designate territoriality.

Mating evidently occurs within the burrows or at the entrance to the burrows. The eggs are shed into the water after being carried by the female for some time, and the young stages drift about, undergoing development through several planktonic stages to the juvenile. The juveniles grow up side by side with adults on the flats.

ECONOMIC VALUE

Fiddler crabs are preyed on heavily by birds, particularly gulls, herons, and sandpipers. They are excellent bait for bonefish, sheepshead, and other species. Occasionally they are eaten by man. —D.dS.

FIERYBLACK SHINER *Notropis pyrrhomelas* A highly colored minnow seldom exceeding 4 inches in total length. The fieryblack shiner is found in the Santee River Basin in North and South Carolina. The body of this minnow is rather deep, compressed, the depth contained 3.7–4 times in its total length. The head of this minnow is blunt and short, and is contained 0.25 in the body length. The mouth is oblique with the jaws being equal. The eye is large, its length contained 3–3.6 times in the length of the head. The pharyngeal teeth are in two rows 1, 4-4, 1 and are sharp, hooked, and do not have grinding surfaces. The lateral line scale count is usually 34–36 and the crosswise scale series is 9. The dorsal fin is high and longer than the head and contains 8 rays, whereas the anal fin contains 10 rays. The color of the male is steel blue above, milk white below. The snout is reddish with the muzzle, upper lip, and iris being scarlet. The dorsal fin is scarlet anteriorly and has a black spot posteriorly, with a milk white tip. The base of the tail is pale, next to which is a scarlet-and-black band. The females are duller in color. This fish is similar to the whitetail shiner (*which see*) and to the whitefin shiner (*which see*), both of which have 8 anal rays; whereas the fieryblack shiner has 10 rays.

Fieryblack Shiner

LIFE HISTORY

This minnow is usually associated with sand, gravel, and rubble bottom streams. It prefers waters which are relatively clear, are small to moderate in size, and have a pH range near neutral. During the breeding season the male develops four rows of large spines on top of its head, with a single spine on most caudal peduncle scales.

The fieryblack shiner is occasionally seined from the streams by fishermen and used as bait. It also serves as forage for largemouth bass, smallmouth bass, rock bass, and redbreast sunfish. —D.E.L.

FIGHTING CHAIR A type of fishing chair. *For details see* Fishing Chair *under* Sportfisherman

FIJI ISLANDS The Fijis are a group of 250 islands lying 3,000 miles south of Hawaii. Nandi airport, long considered a way-stop for travelers headed to New Zealand or Australia, is now a terminus for big-game anglers seeking the South Pacific's big three—black marlin, sailfish, and wahoo. New hotels and charter craft have created an angling resort complex. The larger islands are volcanic in origin, mountainous (highest peak 4,341 feet), and surrounded by coral reefs; the smallest are coral atolls close to sea level. Dense forests of breadfruit, acacia, Tahitian chestnut, and mulberry trees occur on high ground, with screw pine and ferns on the slopes.

Mangroves and cocoanut palms are common to the shores. Suva, the capital of this British colony, is on the southeast coast of Viti Levu (4,114 square miles). The second largest island, Vanua Levu (2,393 square miles), is about 40 miles to the northeast. The other islands in the Fiji group are considerably smaller.

At present the offshore fishing in the Fijis is limited only by the number of charter craft available. There are good accommodations and potentially excellent fishing grounds, but relatively few boats, and these are in great demand. Although the larger Fiji Islands have some beautiful freshwater rivers flowing through remote gorges, the only native gamefish is a sunfishlike species (*Kulia rupestris*). This genus is widespread in the tropical central Pacific as well as parts of South Africa.

Though Fiji is in the tropics the climate is temperate with a range between 60°F and 90°F. The average annual rainfall on the windward coasts is 120 inches, distributed throughout the year, and 70–90 inches on the leeward coasts; most of the latter occurs in the hot season between December and March, when there are northerly winds. Fiji is in the South Pacific hurricane belt. Although hurricanes may occur from November to April these storms are more common in January and February.

Some offshore fishing is available the year round, but the best period for black marlin and sailfish is from October to April. Yellowfin tuna appear between February and June. Mako and bronze whaler sharks, dolphin, dogtooth tuna, wahoo, barracuda, and various jacks, groupers, and snappers are caught throughout the season. Wahoo are particularly numerous and run to large sizes, with fish of 70 pounds not uncommon (local record 118½ pounds). —A.J.McC.

FILAMENT On a fish, any threadlike structure

FILEFISH *See* Orangespotted Filefish

FIN *See* Ray (Fin)

FIN FORMULA *See* Ray (Fin-Ray)

FINLAND Situated northwest of Russia and east of Norway and Sweden, Finland's 130,085 square miles contain over 60,000 lakes and uncounted streams. Rising as a low plain from the Baltic Sea, it is a country of eroded granites, forested in pine, spruce, alder, and maple. Beyond the Circle dwarf Arctic birch and pygmy willow screen the reindeer herds grazing on the hillsides. The average altitudes in Finland are only 200–400 feet above sea level, but the northwest mountains rise to over 4,000 feet. Due to the topography of Finland its fishing regions are sharply defined. In the vast southern lakes

Salmon fishing on the Teno is done by "harling" with guide rowing boat in a series of drops to cover fish

district the pike is the most common gamefish. Although 4–6 pounds is average, fish exceeding 30 pounds are occasionally caught, especially in the Baltic Sea west of Helsinki to Turku and south to the resort area of Aland Island. The northern third of Finland, which lies within the Arctic Circle, is dominated by grayling and Arctic char; both species tend to run small (½–1 pound average) and only the occasional 2–4-pound fish is taken. Many streams throughout the country contain introduced populations of rainbow and brook trout, as well as the native brown trout. While numerous in some waters the brookies tend to be small also, seldom exceeding a pound. Sea trout (anadromous brown trout) occur only in the Tornio River. Trout streams in general are heavy-flowing, deep "thoroughfares" between lakes which are mostly fished by boat, and the better waters produce browns and rainbows in the 1–1½-pound class with the chance of a 5- or 6-pounder. Rich in insect life, with tremendous mayfly and caddis hatches, these rivers contain fat, red-fleshed trout. Due to the violent nature of the waters, streamers, nymphs, and wet flies are more effective than dry flies.

Unique to Finland is a race of landlocked salmon found only in the Lake Saimaa watershed. The Saimaa salmon (*Salmo salar saimensis*) is distinctively colored and sparsely spotted.

Saimaa Salmon, 8-pound Female

Saimaa Salmon, 7-pound Male

ATLANTIC SALMON FISHING

Atlantic salmon occur in three Finnish rivers—the Tenojoki, the Naatamojoki, and the Tornio. The word *joki* means river, and while attached to most names on local maps it is usually dropped in conversation. Known to neighboring Norwegians as the Tana River, the Teno produces the largest salmon, with yearly records exceeding 45 pounds (the world record of 79 pounds was caught on the Norwegian side and is therefore listed as a Tana River catch). However, including large numbers of small grilse in the 2-pound class which are abundant, a total

would be closer to 10 pounds for the average. You can reasonably expect 20–30-pound salmon in the Teno. The Naatamo on the other hand is a quantity stream, with plenty of small fish to 12 or 15 pounds, and only the rare large salmon. The Tornio, more or less lost to hydro-electric development—which is the history of Finnish rivers—produces few salmon, but a modest run of sea trout. Although the border streams are commercially netted, by international agreement the nets have to be lifted three days a week, which provides a fair number of salmon for the angler. With few exceptions Finnish streams are not wadable. The torrential flows in both trout and salmon waters barely provide a foothold along the stream edges, and a visiting angler can get along with a pair of lightweight hip boots. The Teno River has a number of lies that can be fished by wading in knee-deep water. The Lapp guides, who are commercial fishermen and take their jobs seriously, work the channels and mid-stream riffles. Fish are sometimes hooked by local fishermen on long casts from shore, using spoons and plugs, but the river is ½–1 mile wide, and it would require a perfect knowledge of the stream to know that you are covering a hold. Although casting lures are legally used by the local people, tourists are restricted to fly only. It's customary for the guide to troll two lines, while his client fishes with one or two fly rods. The same "harling" method used on big Norwegian rivers is applied here, with the guide rowing back and forth across the current in a series of drops while the lures and flies are left swimming 50–60 feet downstream.

The peak period for salmon fishing is from late June through July, with a good run of fish sometimes appearing in mid-August. Waters become ice-free about the beginning of May in southern Finland and usually a month later in the north. Air temperatures are ideal in the lakes district, ranging between 60°F and 80°F, sometimes going as high as 90°F. In Lapland, however, the mercury can drop from 80°F to freezing in a 24-hour period, and the fishing hours are normally cold. There are almost 15 hours of sunshine daily during the summer months and no real night in the far north. From about 10 P.M. to 3 A.M., which is considered the most productive time for salmon (guides try to be on the water by 8 P.M. and return at 6 A.M.), the light is best described as a heavy overcast. Long hours of sitting in a boat in 30°F and 40°F temperatures requires warm clothing—thermal underwear, mittens, and a lightweight waterproof parka with hood to deflect spray and neck-chilling breezes. The Teno River is 250 miles north of the Arctic Circle.

Many streams in Finland are bordered by marshlands and swamps where the delectable cloudberries abound, but standing waters also produce literally clouds of mosquitoes. Insect repellent is a must.

TACKLE

There are well-stocked tackle shops in Finland's major cities. Items are mainly of Swedish and American origin, but local plugs are world famous. The Rapala balsa plugs and the Nils Master plugs are made here, and both are exported to the United States.

Any standard 9-foot fly rod calibrated for No. 8–No. 10 lines is adequate for Finnish salmon fishing. Though broad, the rivers are shallow and a floating line, or in

A Lapp guide enjoys his midnight pipe on the Naatamo River after a day of salmon fishing

early season at high water a sinking tip line, is recommended. Tackle need not be as heavy as that used in Norway. Leader tippets should test 15–20 pounds. Fly sizes range from No. 2 to 6/0, with the emphasis on 2/0 and 3/0 dressings. Despite their own preference for plugs, Lapps are extremely critical about the flies used. The fly must be sparsely tied, which eliminates many traditional Norwegian and British dressings. You can buy locally-tied Teno flies, which are not only unique patterns but perfect swimmers. Patterns such as the Peuran yo, Jussin yo, Jarim, Tivri, Tenon Valkea, Lohi suvanto, Teno No. 1, Teno No. 7, Schroderin Special, Eversti, and Kuparinen are works of art designed with slender wings and sparse hackles for perfect balance. How the fly is knotted to the leader is vitally important; there are several popular jams which place the bulk of the knot in back of the hook eye so that the dressing is always upright in the water at all current speeds. There is a ritual testing before each trip. A Lapp will flap your fly in the current for a half-hour or until he is convinced that it's riding true. He will trim, reknot, and go through fifty patterns if necessary. They know what they're doing, so be patient.

LICENSES

The licensing system in Finland is fairly simple. Except for the border rivers between Norway and Finland you need a State Fishing Card, which can be bought at any police station. In some waters local fishing permits are also required, and these cost between 50¢ and $20 per week depending on the quality of the water. Permits can be obtained from the Forestry Board offices, tourist hotels, and local fishing associations. Norway and Finland have a mutual agreement on fishing the border—no card is required and a permit costs about $3.50 per day.

—A.J.McC.

FIN ROT *See* Diseases and Parasites

FINNAN HADDIE The market name for smoked haddock (*which see*). Sometimes erroneously applied to smoked Pacific halibut.

FIRST AID First aid in the field is largely a matter of common sense and adherence to basic concepts of cleanliness and support for injured parts. The need for first aid can usually be avoided entirely by anticipation and by a little precaution. In anticipation of the need for first aid a simple kit can be assembled which will meet most emergencies. The precaution of familiarizing oneself with the local conditions of an unknown area will help the angler avoid an unpleasant experience.

THE FIRST AID KIT

A small plastic bag, which will easily fit in a gear box or fishing jacket, will contain the following list of first-aid gear:

1. One-inch gauze roller bandage
2. Four-inch square gauze pads; cotton balls
3. Rubber bands
4. Roll of 1-inch tape
5. Small plastic freezer bag containing alcohol (70%)-soaked cotton balls, or Zephrine, Ioprep, or Betadine
6. Triangular bandage
7. Chlorinating pills for water
8. Ammonia (smelling salts) sticks
9. Tongue blades
10. Special medication (for diabetics or cardiac patients)
11. Sharp, clean knife
12. Light wire cutters
13. Snake-bite kit
14. Antidiarrheal medication
15. Salt tablets

The roller gauze can be used for binding an injured area; for a tourniquet; for holding splints in place. The gauze pads serve as dressings; padding; and to hold the tongue of an unconscious person. Rubber bands make excellent tourniquets for digits. Adhesive tape has many obvious applications. Alcohol-soaked cotton balls or sponges are better than a bottle of antiseptic since they can apply large amounts of antiseptic; can be used to scrub an area; can be used as continuous, wet, cool dressings. Triangular bandages are excellent slings; are helpful in binding an injured extremity; and are a means of thoroughly washing a dirty wound.

Chlorinating pills are particularly important in semitropical and tropical regions. It is always dangerous to drink water from streams and lakes without knowledge of its character. There are not many diseases which can be contracted from polluted water, but they may be serious illnesses. The dysentery group of diseases, the most serious of which is typhoid fever, is the commonest, and although most of these are readily treatable, they can be most unpleasant. For this reason a few chlorinating pills in one's kit can render most water sources potable and will prevent a serious illness.

Ammonia crystals which can be broken open when needed are helpful in awakening the unconscious when injury is not a major one. The effectiveness of ammonia will often help to determine the seriousness of an injury.

DANGEROUS, POISONOUS, AND INJURIOUS AQUATIC LIFE

Agent	Device	Method	Prevention
Sharks All oceans. Includes white shark, mako, tiger shark, hammerhead sharks, lemon shark, bull shark, gray nurse shark, Ganges River shark, blacktip sharks and possibly blue shark, whitetip shark, sickle shark, dusky shark, and usually any sharks found in rivers.	Teeth and skin.	Bite, scrape, and secondary bacterial infection.	Get out of water if sharks are present. Do not antagonize sharks. Do not splash on surface. If possible, swim away underwater slowly and deliberately. Any shark over 3′ long should be considered potentially dangerous.
Great Barracuda In subtropical and tropical seas. Another large species from West Africa apparently dangerous also.	Teeth.	Bite.	Do not wear bright objects in water which might attract barracuda (bracelets, watches, rings). When large barracuda are present swim slowly and deliberately away. Attacks are rare, but can be provoked by spearing.
Morays Primarily in tropical and subtropical seas. Some in temperate zone.	Teeth.	Bite.	Do not put hands or feet in coral crevasses or holes. Avoid if boated. Do not spear.
Billfish In temperate, tropical, and subtropical seas. Includes marlins, swordfish, sailfish, and needlefishes (houndfish).	Spear.	Intentional or accidental injury by spear. Marlin and swordfish have rammed boats. Injury in boating or by boated fish. Injury by spear of provoked or hooked needlefish or houndfish.	Kill large billfish before boating. Houndfish will leap at light source. When fishing at night have shield between lamp and fishermen.
Dinoflagellates Responsible in part for "red tides" occurring in tropical and subtropical seas.	Possible endotoxin.	Toxin.	No known prevention of occurrence of red tide. Avoid areas of red tide.
Sponges In tropical and subtropical seas. Includes the fire sponge and poison bun sponge.	Chemical irritation.	By handling the surface or especially the broken surface of sponge.	Avoid contact. Wear gloves.
Corals In tropical and subtropical seas. Includes the fire, or stinging, corals.	Nematocysts (stinging cells) and sharp edges.	Toxin from nematocysts and cuts from sharp edges.	Avoid. Wear gloves when handling.
Spiny Dogfish In North Atlantic and Pacific oceans.	Venom apparatus (a dorsal spine anterior to each dorsal fin).	Spines enter flesh.	Avoid spines when handling fish.
Ratfish In Atlantic and Pacific oceans.	Venom apparatus on spine anterior to first dorsal fin; sharp, platelike teeth.	Spines enter flesh; jaws capable of inflicting bite.	Avoid.
Sea Catfishes In subtropical and tropical seas; freshwater relatives in lakes and ponds.	Venom apparatus on dorsal fin spine and pectoral fin spines.	Spines enter flesh; venom produced from skin sheath around spines.	Handle fish with care and avoid spines.
Weeverfish In temperate seas.	Venon apparatus on dorsal and opercular spines.	Spines enter flesh and venom is injected.	Wear wading shoes. Avoid antagonizing fish. Do not handle living or dead fish.

Symptoms	First Aid	Recovery
Bites with loss of flesh and tissue resulting in bleeding, shock, and possible death.	Requires immediate attention. Treat for shock. Apply large compressive dressings (bandages or towels). Keep victim warm, take to hospital at once.	Depends on severity of bites, amount of tissue and blood loss. Often fatal.
Bites with flesh and tissue loss, bleeding and shock.	Compressive bandages. Take to hospital at once.	Depends on severity of bite.
Bites, usually on hands or extremities. Possible secondary infection from slime.	Compressive bandage. Take to hospital at once.	Depends on severity of bite and tissue injury.
Puncture wound by spear.	Compressive dressing. Take to hospital.	Depends on severity of injury. Fatalities have occurred.
Toxic (lethal) effect on fish. Irritation of respiratory tract in man.	Wear mask to prevent inhalation of irritating spray.	Minutes to hours.
Itching and prickling sensation, followed by swelling and discomfort.	Wash with dilute acetic acid or vinegar.	One or two days.
Stinging or burning sensation. Cuts slow to heal	Wash stinging area with alcohol or ammonia. Wash cuts with alcohol or other antiseptics.	Usual prompt recovery from fire coral. Recovery from cuts varies with severity of cut and infection.
Severe stinging pain at site.	Wash and irrigate wound.	Hours to days.
Severe sting; painful bite.	Wash and irrigate wound.	Hours to days.
Painful stings, numbness, and redness; occasional secondary bacterial infection in improperly treated cases.	Remove spine, irrigate wound.	Hours to days; occasionally fatal.
Painful stings described as burning, stabbing, or even crushing; spreads throughout affected extremity; may have general symptoms—sweating, cyanosis, convulsions, respiratory difficulty, death.	No known antidote. Incise wound immediately, aspirate, apply tourniquet between wound and body. Take patient to hospital.	Hours to days. Often fatal.

DANGEROUS, POISONOUS, AND INJURIOUS AQUATIC LIFE (Continued)

Agent	Device	Method	Prevention
Scorpionfishes In temperate, subtropical, and tropical seas. Includes zebrafish, stonefish and some species of scorpionfish.	Venom apparatus on dorsal, anal, and pelvic spines.	Spines enter flesh usually by stepping on fish or by handling and venom is injected.	Avoid. Wear wading shoes. Do not handle fish.
Toadfish In temperate, subtropical, and tropical seas.	Teeth; 2 dorsal and 2 opercular spines with venom apparatus.	May inflict severe bite; spines penetrate skin.	Avoid stepping on or handling. Wear shoes while wading. Do not handle.
Stargazer In temperate and subtropical seas.	Spines with venom apparatus just above pectoral fins.	Spines penetrate skin.	Avoid.
Stargazer, Electric In temperate and subtropical seas.	Optic nerves modified into electric apparatus.	By contact. Stepping on fish concealed in sand; electric organs emit shock.	Avoid. Wear shoes while wading.
Surgeonfishes In tropical seas.	Sharp lancelike spine at base of tail.	Spine cuts flesh.	Avoid.
Rabbitfish (Closely related to surgeonfishes) In Pacific Ocean.	Fin spines (13 dorsal, 4 pelvic, 7 anal) with associated venom apparatus.	Spines penetrate flesh.	Avoid. Handle with gloves.
Stingrays In shallow water of temperate, subtropical, and tropical seas. Some species in tropical freshwater. Includes bat ray, leopard ray, butterfly ray, cownose ray, yellow stingray.	Spine with venom apparatus at base of tail or on tail; venom-producing tissue in fleshy sheath along spine.	By stepping on spine or spine penetrating skin.	Wear shoes while wading; shuffle feet on bottom. Handle with gloves when necessary.
Spoiled Seafood Fish or shellfish from all sources.	Bacterial contamination of seafood. Toxin produced by bacteria or bacterial action on seafood.	Ingestion of spoiled seafood.	Eat only fresh or adequately preserved seafood.
Crustacea Lobster or shrimp in all oceans.	Specific allergy of victim to the particular shellfish. May follow ingestion of spoiled shellfish.	Allergic reaction.	Avoid all foods to which one is allergic.
Mollusk Clams, mussels, oysters, and scallops in all waters where pollution or contamination by dinoflagellates occurs.	Pollution of shellfish by (a) the shellfish ingesting bacteria or (b) dinoflagellates.	By eating (a) polluted or (b) contaminated shellfish.	Do not eat polluted or contaminated shellfish.
Puffers In temperate, subtropical, and tropical seas. Includes blowfish or swellfish, poison puffer (maki-maki of Hawaii), and porcupinefish.	Toxin (tetrodontoxin) in bile, liver, skin, and reproductive organs of all puffers. Occasionally also in flesh.	By eating liver, bile, gonads, flesh contaminated by liver, bile, gonads, or flesh containing tetrodontoxin.	Do not eat puffers or swellfish, particularly from subtropical and tropical seas.

Symptoms	First Aid	Recovery
Immediate severe shocking pain involving entire extremity. Victim frequently thrashes about, might drown in shallow water. Possible convulsions, nausea, vomiting, swelling of extremity, cardiac failure, death.	No known antidote. Incise puncture wound. Aspirate or suck on wound to remove venom. Apply tourniquet between wound and body. Wash wound and take patient to hospital.	Hours to days. May be fatal.
Severe intense pain.	As with scorpionfish.	Hours.
Severe local pain.	As with scorpionfish.	Hours; but venom sometimes fatal.
Electric shock.	No known antidote.	Rapid.
Cut or laceration (no venom produced).	Wash with antiseptic; if severe, go to hospital or consult physician.	Variable.
Severe intense local pain similar to that produced by scorpionfishes.	As with scorpionfish.	Hours.
Instant pain at puncture or laceration stie. May be mild or severe.	Wash with antiseptic, encourage bleeding; take victim to hospital.	Hours to days.
Nausea, vomiting, diarrhea, abdominal pains	Induce vomiting of ingested foods. Consult physician.	Variable.
Nausea, vomiting, diarrhea, rash, hives.	Induce vomiting; consult physician; use antihistamines or adrenalin.	Usually prompt.
Bacterial infection, such as typhoid or paratyphoid fever, nausea, vomiting. Bacterial toxin, i.e., enterotoxin produced by staphylococci. Dinoflagellates produce toxin and cause nausea; vomiting; diarrhea; prickly sensation about mouth, lips; paralysis of arms and legs.	Induce vomiting of ingested food. Consult physician.	Variable; depends upon cause and degree of infection of toxicity. May be fatal.
Tingling about mouth, lips, and tongue. Salivation, weakness, nausea, vomiting, diarrhea, muscular twitching, paralysis, and convulsions.	Induce vomiting of ingested food. Take to hospital at once. No specific antidote for tetrodontoxin.	Variable. May be fatal.

DANGEROUS, POISONOUS, AND INJURIOUS AQUATIC LIFE (Continued)

Agent	Device	Method	Prevention
Ciguatera A type of fish poisoning (*see* Ciguatera in text) in the tropical or coral belt. Many suspected species, but common agents include great barracuda, some species of grouper, snapper, tropical mackerels, triggerfish, jacks, morays.	Toxin inhibits enzyme cholinesterase as with organic phosphate insecticides.	Certain sizes of fish at certain times in certain places may cause severe food poisoning, while at other times may be safely eaten.	Ask local residents regarding edibility of fish.
Spoiled Tunas, including Bonitos, and Skipjack	Bacterial decomposition of flesh produces histamine.	Histamine produces allergy-like reaction.	Eat only properly preserved fish. Do not eat fish which have an unnatural peppery taste.
Sixgill Shark In all subtropical and tropical seas.	Purgative action of flesh.	Unknown.	Do not eat.
Shark Liver; flesh of Greenland Shark In all seas; Greenland Shark in polar waters.	Purgative action of flesh; liver severely toxic.	Suspected excess of vitamins.	Do not eat.
Blue Crab	Claws; sharp edge of shell.	Puncture and cut.	Handle with care; wear heavy gloves.
Portuguese Man-of-War In Atlantic and Pacific oceans and Mediterranean Sea.	Nematocysts, or special stinging cells, containing a toxin or poison in the tentacles.	Tentacles containing the nematocysts are brushed against (in the water) or stepped on (on the beach) or handled.	Avoid tentacles in water or on beach.
Jellyfishes In temperate, subtropical, and tropical seas. Includes moon jellyfish, rocket jellyfish, pinefringed jellyfish, and sea wasp (Indo-Pacific).	Nematocysts, or special stinging cells containing a toxin or poison.	By handling or brushing against jellyfish.	Avoid; wear gloves if handling; wear wet suit if swimming or diving in areas of jellyfish.
Sea Anemones In temperate, subtropical, and tropical seas.	Nematocysts, or special stinging cells containing a toxin or poison.	By handling sea anemones.	Avoid or handle with gloves.
Cone Shells In subtropical and tropical seas.	All cones have a specialized venom apparatus.	By handling cone shells.	Handle all live cones with care; wear heavy gloves and avoid any contact with "soft parts."
Octopuses and Squids In temperate, subtropical, and tropical seas.	Beak; venom produced by salivary glands.	Bite with beak, and venom may be injected. Remote possibility of diver being held under water by octopus.	Avoid animals and caves where they live. Wear gloves and wet suits.
Flatworm (Swimmers Itch) In temperate, subtropical saltwater, and tropical freshwaters.	Penetration of skin by cercaria (a larval stage of parasite).	Cercaria penetrates swimmers' skin.	Do not swim in known areas of infestation.

Symptoms	First Aid	Recovery
Upset stomach; lips and mouth become tingling, numb, or itchy. Nausea and vomiting. Ability to swallow may be lost. Respiratory difficulty, muscle spasms, convulsions.	Induce vomiting of ingested food. Go to hospital	Weeks to months, if not properly treated. Up to 10% of ciguatera type of poisoning may be fatal.
Headache, dizziness, vomiting, diarrhea, abdominal pain, itching, shock.	Vomiting and symptomatic treatment; antihistaminic drugs.	8–12 hours; sometimes fatal.
Diarrhea. (Marketed in Germany for purgative action.)	Induce vomiting of ingested food.	Usually prompt.
Nausea, vomiting, diarrhea, abdominal pain, muscular incoordination leading to paralysis and possibly death.	Induce vomiting of ingested food. Go to hospital at once.	Injury to human liver may be fatal.
Laceration to deep wound and bleeding.	Allow to bleed freely, wash with antiseptic, dress wound. Compressive bandage in severe cases.	Hours to days.
Severe sudden sting, like an electric shock, rash with welts may appear in affected area. If severe, may progress to stomach cramps, dizziness, nausea, numbness, respiratory distress.	Remove adherent tentacles with gloved hand or towel. Wash area with alcohol to neutralize toxin. If severe, take to hospital for further therapy, oxygen, calcium gluconate, and analgesics.	Thirty minutes to several days.
Severe pain and sting. Pain may become very severe and produce shock. Sea wasp stings can lead to muscle cramps, respiratory paralysis, and death in 3–8 minutes.	Wash area with ammonia or alcohol. If severe, support respiration and circulation and take to hospital at once.	Variable, depends on jellyfish and exposure.
Sting. Usually Atlantic sea anemones do not produce painful sting.	Wash with alcohol or ammonia.	Minutes to hours.
Sharp stinging or burning pain at site, followed by numbness and stinging involving entire body, especially about lips and mouth. If severe, paralysis with respiratory and cardiac failure.	No specific treatment. Wash wounds thoroughly with hot water. Local anesthetics and analgesics. Treat shock and cardiac failure. If severe, take to hospital.	Variable. Several species, usually Indo-Pacific, have caused death.
Local burning and discomfort spreading to entire extremity.	Irrigate and wash wound with water. If severe, take to hospital.	Usually prompt, but one fatality reported.
Prickly sensation of skin, followed by itchy papules.	Dry immediately with towel, take shower, rinse with diluted ammonia water. Rash can be treated with cortisone ointment (see physician).	Up to 2 weeks.

DANGEROUS, POISONOUS, AND INJURIOUS AQUATIC LIFE (Continued)

Agent	Device	Method	Prevention
Flatworm (Schistosomiasis) In subtropical and tropical freshwaters. An infestation invading human liver, bladder, intestine. Most common in Asia, the Philippines, the Middle East, Africa, the West Indies, and South America.	Adult worm and ova in infected organ.	Irritation and inflammation. Severe secondary infection from adult worm living in tissues.	Do not drink, swim in, or bathe in infested water. Treatment of clothing and skin with special chemicals may help. Control of host snail required for effective eradication.
Bristleworm In Gulf of Mexico, Caribbean, and Pacific.	Bristles, or setae, develop into stinging organs.	Possible toxin produced by stinging organ.	Avoid bristleworms. Handle with rubber or cotton gloves.
Sea Urchins In subtropical and tropical seas.	Spines and venom organs in certain species.	Sharp brittle spine penetrates skin and breaks off in flesh.	Avoid. Heavy gloves and shoes may not afford adequate protection.
Cottonmouth Water Moccasin In southern United States freshwaters.	Fangs and venom apparatus.	Bite. This snake can bite under water.	Avoid.
Sea Snakes In western Pacific Ocean, Indian Ocean from East Africa to Australia; one species in eastern Pacific from Gulf of California to Ecuador. Unknown in the Atlantic. Includes bonded sea snake and yellow-bellied sea snake.	Fangs and venom apparatus.	Bite. These snakes can bite under water.	Avoid.
Madtom In United States freshwaters.	Pectoral spine with venom apparatus.	By handling fish.	Avoid pectoral spine.
Stonecat In United States freshwaters.	Pectoral spine with venom apparatus.	By handling fish.	Avoid pectoral spine.

The person with head injury, stroke, or heart attack won't respond to this simple device. Tongue blades are also universal tools which can be used to open an airway by depressing the tongue; keep jaws apart in convulsing persons; and act as splints for digits and to secure a tourniquet.

Persons who are receiving special medications such as nitroglycerin, insulin, and allergy medication should always carry an extra supply of these medicaments in case their usual supply is lost or damaged.

A sharp, clean knife is always necessary for a multitude of uses. Lightweight wire cutters are the best means of removing fish hooks which have pierced soft tissue.

CONTACT DERMATITIS

Along with insect bites for which all anglers prepare, the commonest malady encountered is the contact dermatitis produced by poison ivy (*Rhus toxicodendron*), poison oak (*Rhus diversiloba*), and sumac. The antigen is an oleoresin which is volatile when the leaves are burned, and therefore direct contact with the plant is not necessary. Seventy percent of people are sensitive to these antigens, and in some cases it is a serious affliction. This is particularly so when the eyes are involved. The treatment, with exception of the eyes, consists of immediate washing of the area followed by application of an alcohol or an oxidizing agent such as potassium permanganate. In the field, after washing the area, the sap of the jewel weed will often counteract the antigen effectively.

SNAKE BITE

Fear of snake bite is as ancient as man, and with the exception of a few species it is an unrealistic fear. All snakes will make an earnest effort to escape when they encounter man and will only strike when provoked. There are several hundred species of snakes in continental United States, of which only four are potential killers. These four are the rattlesnake, copperhead, water moccasin, and coral snake. Although the physiochemical constituents of venom have not been completely identified, venom is known to be largely a protein substance. Its systemic toxic effects are manifest as neurotoxic, hemolytic, and vasculotoxic or a combination of these three effects.

Despite potential dangers implied, fewer than 2 per cent of poisonous snakebite victims die.

The care of this injury is simple. There are two important considerations: eliminate factors which accelerate

Symptoms	First Aid	Recovery
Transitory itch, as cercaria penetrate through skin. Fever, urticaria, cough, as cercaria pass through lungs, cirrhosis, hematoma, melina later.	Consult physician for specialized treatment.	Variable. Dependent upon adequate medical treatment. Cancer frequent late development.
Painful sting.	Wash area; remove bristles with adhesive tape, and apply ammonia or alcohol.	Prompt.
Needlesharp pain and burning sensation. Venom may cause intense pain, faintness, numbness, respiratory distress. Secondary infection with redness and swelling.	Remove spines and globe-like pedicellariae (venom apparatus), wash wounds and consult physician.	Usually prompt but variable and potentially fatal in severe cases of venom types.
Immediate pain at site.	Avoid exertion of victim, apply tourniquet between bite and body (loosen every 10–20 minutes), cut and aspirate fang punctures. Take victim to physician at once for antivenom.	Variable. Has been fatal.
Pain may be delayed for 20 minutes to several hours. Generalized symptoms: weakness, aching muscles, ascending paralysis, convulsions, respiratory failure.	Apply tourniquet between bite and body. Do not allow victim to exert self. Take to hospital for antivenom. Give general supportive care.	Variable. Sometimes fatal.
Severe pain similar to bee sting, swelling.	Wash and irrigate wound. Apply antiseptic.	Hours to days.
Severe pain similar to bee sting, swelling.	Wash and irrigate wound. Apply antiseptic.	Hours to days.

spread of the venom; obtain antivenom. Local care of the wound should be immediate by first applying a tourniquet above the wound to retard blood transport of venom. Then the area should be lightly washed with cold water; incise the wound with multiple vertical cuts using a razor blade or sharp knife; suck out the venom. The cruciate incision is of no value because it provides inadequate decompression of the area. This procedure must be done within 15–20 minutes of injury, for after that time the venom has already been carried out of the local wound by the blood stream. Immerse the wound area in cold water or preferably in ice to retard blood flow. Finally, obtain antivenom as soon as possible. Antivenom can prevent death no matter how late it is administered. Even without antivenom, most victims will survive the injury. Old-fashioned remedies notwithstanding, liquor, hot applications to the wound, and the excited dash for help will only make the situation worse. It is important to avoid all things which increase the speed with which the venom is disseminated. Don't panic.

BEE STINGS

Bee stings are for most individuals an annoyance and little worse. The venom of a bee or wasp is also a protein substance which produces an antigen-antibody allergic reaction. In most instances this reaction is merely a local hypersensitivity, but occasionally the previously sensitized person will have an anaphylactic reaction to the antigen and may die from it. The local care of the injury is directed at reduction of inflammatory reaction. Therefore, application of cold water or ice will make the wound less irritating. Oral antihistaminic drugs reduce the systemic manifestations. The anaphylactic reaction defies any effective first aid in the field and can only be treated by a medical facility.

BLISTERS

Blisters hardly seem to be a problem requiring first aid. Yet there are many people who enjoy fishing but who have developed arteriosclerotic vascular disease in their lower extremities. For these people a blister can become a serious problem because of poor circulation. The best remedy is obviously prevention, but if a blister forms, it should be protected by a strip of adhesive tape applied directly to the skin, taking care to prevent rupture of the bleb.

HEAT STROKE

Heat stroke is a not uncommon emergency experienced by people who are not accustomed to exposure to the sun for long periods. In any environment where the heat is severe, this problem must be anticipated. The term "heat stroke" is applied to two quite dissimilar situations in both of which the result is loss of consciousness.

Heat exhaustion is the simpler form of this malady and is due to the loss of large amounts of body salts as well as water through perspiration and respiration. The normal adult loses about 1,000–1,500 cubic centimeters (1.0–1.5 quarts) of water via these routes on an ordinary summer day. Should he be exposed to extreme temperatures or very unusual exertion, this loss is greatly increased, and he then becomes very tired, perhaps lightheaded, and may lose consciousness. The treatment is to rest in a shady place with applications of cool water to the skin and gradual water and salt replacement by drinking and the use of salt tablets. If too much or too cold water is given, the individual may become nauseated and by vomiting lose still more body fluid. Therefore, water replacement must be gradual.

Heat stroke, on the other hand, is a very serious problem which is due to heat-induced failure of the brain's heat-regulating mechanism. In this circumstance the body is unable to dissipate heat through the skin, and body temperature very rapidly climbs to 104–106°F. Profound loss of consciousness is the rule, and the only helpful measure is to remove the person to the nearest hospital with all haste.

These two conditions can be distinguished in the field by the profuse perspiration, relatively cool skin, and relatively high level of consciousness in the person with heat exhaustion, and the reverse symptoms in the person with heat stroke.

SEASICKNESS

Seasickness, among minor ills, can perhaps be the most distressing of all. Even the hardiest sailor will occasionally be overcome by the seemingly endless misery of motion sickness. The inner ear is composed of a very complicated series of fluid-filled channels whose walls are lined with sensory nerve endings. The motion of this fluid stimulates the sensory devices which in turn advise the muscular control centers in the brain of the body's position. Constant and rhythmic movement can cause loss of balance and can produce the secondary gastrointestinal disturbance called motion sickness. The deepwater fisherman can prepare for this hazard with any of the several excellent medications which are commercially available to prevent it. Once seasickness starts, however, these medicines rarely help, largely because of the self-perpetuating and suggestive characteristics of the malady.

FISH-HOOK INJURY

A common accident among anglers, and one for which most are ill-prepared, is that of fish-hook injury. Although the novice may become impaled anywhere, the back, scalp, and fingers are the usual sites of injury. These wounds are seldom serious but are always very annoying, and because hooks are often rusty or otherwise contaminated, there is always concern about tetanus or wound infection. The simplest way is to advance the hook until the barb projects beyond the skin surface, cut it off with wire cutters, and then back the wire out of the wound. Following hook removal the wound should be liberally washed with water and then rinsed with alcohol. See your physician for a possible tetanus prophylaxis.

Not uncommonly the angler is impaled by a treble hook, and this circumstance can pose more complications. If possible the remaining free portion of the lure should be removed by cutting the implanted hook from the lure. The latter can then be removed as described above. Occasionally these hooks can become so imbedded that they require surgical removal. In such an event the wound should be rinsed with alcohol, the hook fixed with adhesive to prevent its further movement, and the angler sent to a physician who can remove it surgically. Hook wounds are always a nuisance and may interrupt the day's outing, but rarely do they represent a serious hazard.

PUNCTURE WOUNDS AND LACERATIONS

Puncture wounds and lacerations also have great potential danger if they are inappropriately treated on the scene. Injuries of this kind are best treated by vigorous cleansing of the wound with clean water. They should then be liberally rinsed with alcohol and dressed with gauze or tape. When a doctor can be reached, his advice must be sought about the advisability of further surgical care, antibiotics, and antitetanus shots. The occasional laceration may be accompanied by moderate bleeding, and one must remember that a little bleeding always appears to be a great deal. Point pressure or a tourniquet applied proximal to the injury will usually control bleeding. For those body areas where tourniquets are not practical, pressure applied with dressings over the wound will be quite satisfactory. Once again panic or excitement will make the situation worse, and an otherwise simple injury can be made complicated by unnecessary anxiety. Laceration injuries of the hands and feet are worthy of special attention. These can be very complex, intricate, and dangerous injuries which have the potential of becoming crippling injuries. All digital, hand, or forearm lacerations require immediate professional attention. The hand is a complex machine of muscle, nerve, and vessel, all of which are vital to the continued normal function of the part. Injury to these elements is often difficult to discern and must never be treated lightly. Regardless of the situation, the wound should be seen by a physician when convenient. Tetanus antitoxin is dangerous for some people, but the toxoid is almost universally applicable and should be given for all such wounds.

FRACTURES

Fractures are uncommon field injuries whose long-range treatment will largely depend upon their field management. All fracture injuries which are associated with tear of the skin are immediately contaminated wounds and represent a real emergency. Bones have relatively poor blood supply and therefore lack the privilege of spontaneous healing enjoyed by tissues which are rich in blood vessels. Bone injuries demand infinite attention to cleanliness and to immobilization. The cardinal rules are:

1. Don't move the fractured part.
2. Immobilize the bone with external support.
3. Control bleeding by pressure at appropriate points.
4. Apply cold, ice if possible, to the area of injury.
5. Cleanse an open fracture wound as well as possible with water.

The field care of a fracture requires that the person be left where he lies. Moving such a person may introduce serious but avoidable complications such as paralysis in the man with a fractured spine. After cutting away whatever clothing obscures the injured area, review the injury and determine just how serious it is. For digits or extremities obtain some form of splint to apply externally. A slab of dried bark from a felled tree makes a superb splint for an arm or leg. After laying the bark around the injured area, it can be wrapped with the triangle bandage or the roll of gauze. The tongue blades in one's first-aid kit make excellent finger splints. For fractured toes, the injured toe can be well immobilized by taping it to its normal adjacent neighbor. Obviously, fractures need to be seen by a competent physician as soon as possible. When moving a fracture patient, be certain that the neck and back are normal. This can be done by localizing the site of pain and then determining whether the person can move and detect sensation in all four extremities. Should there be serious concern about neck or back fracture, don't move the patient *at all* until help can be found. These persons must be kept flat, on their backs, immobile and be transported only on a firm, flat surface such as a door or firm canvas stretcher. If need be, leave the person with basic comfort needs, and go to get help rather than risk irreparable, permanent spinal-cord damage. Transportation of people with less hazardous fractures often requires additional support such as a cane or crutch. For this purpose, the striped maple (*Acer compesire*) can be a great help. Its root always forms a right angle with the trunk and if cut off underground will provide a firm handle which will serve either as crutch or cane. Striped maple is a common woodland tree which rarely exceeds twenty feet, is supple but remarkably strong. It can be identified by its occurrence in large groups as trash growth whose bark is pale yellow and green striped. Naturally, all fractures require immediate professional attention.

DROWNING

Resuscitation of stricken anglers whether it be for drowning or some cardiac malady is a true emergency. It consists essentially of artificial support of respiration and of the circulation. Respiratory support can be given by any of a variety of means.

For the victim of drowning, it is essential to effect physical decompression of the lungs by placing the feet high, the head down with the person's face down. In this position excess fluid in the airway can drain out and not be accumulated in the mouth as it would were the person on his back. Respiratory support can be given in the time-honored method of rhythmic, manual chest-wall compression. After the airway has been cleared, which takes no more than a few moments, respiratory support can be continued by mouth-to-mouth breathing. This technique requires that the patient's lower jaw be held upward by pressure against the angle of the jaw with one hand to keep the tongue free of the airway and then direct mouth-to-mouth insufflation of the lung by blowing directly into the patient's mouth. His nostrils should be pinched shut with the other hand. Although this method provides a limited volume of oxygen to the patient, it is better than no oxygen. For those stricken individuals who are not drowning victims, support can be given their respiratory

and vascular systems by direct rhythmic pressure at the rate of 60 times per minute applied to the lower end of their breast bone. With the individual on his back on a firm surface, forceful compression of the lower breast bone will effect respiratory exchange as well as give support to the effective activity of the heart. This can be a dangerous maneuver and cannot be indiscriminately applied. It will rarely revive the person who has suffered a heart attack. The cardinal principles of resuscitation are to:

1. Free the airway
2. Prevent inhalation of fluid from any source (regurgitation)
3. Support the circulation by positioning the head down, feet up and by external compression of the breast bone if indicated.

BURNS

Burns are frequent campsite injuries which are at least very distressing and at worst potentially fatal. The basic principles of burn care are the same as those for any fresh wound. Cleanliness is paramount. The fire (versus hot-liquid) burn requires washing with water to remove dirt and charred debris. The burn wound must then be protected from further contamination until professional help is obtained by applying light, nonconstricting dressings of gauze. Do not try to force fluids by mouth to the point of inducing nausea or vomiting. The burned person needs to conserve all the body fluids he can. Fluid losses by vomiting are wasteful and unnecessary. The injured area should next be immobilized and kept that way. Any but the simplest, limited burns require early professional attention.

GASTROENTERITIS

Gastroenteritis, colloquially known as the G.I.'s, Inca Two Step, Trots, or La Tourista, has ruined many a well-planned fishing trip. This syndrome is more likely to occur in tropical or semitropical countries with poor sanitation, but it may happen anywhere at any time.

The victim in the United States can usually find medical attention within an hour or two for the more severe cases, and consulting your physician is the treatment of choice. This discussion is primarily for the more adventurous sportsman who has traveled many miles from civilization in foreign lands where no doctor is available. When possible, prompt medical attention is far superior to the remedies outlined in the following paragraphs.

The commonest illness is a nonspecific (cause not known) gastroenteritis. It probably originates in the fecal contamination of drinking water or food. It has been shown to be partially preventable by certain antibiotics and sulfa compounds. The disease itself is self-limited. Prevention is better than treatment; so do not drink liquids or eat raw vegetables or fruits of questionable purity. If necessary, boil or treat drinking water with chlorine tablets, and eat only canned or well-cooked foods.

Other causes of gastrointestinal disorders include typhoid and paratyphoid (Salmonellosis and Salmonella food poisoning), bacillary dysentery (Shigellosis), amoebic dysentery, cholera, and staphylococcal food poisoning.

SKIN- AND SCUBA-DIVING DANGERS

Injury	Cause	How
Eye or Face Mask "Squeeze"	A relative decrease (less pressure) within face mask compared to surrounding water pressure.	Diver descends rapidly without exhaling through nose.
Ear Squeeze (Aerotitis)	Increase in pressure on external surface of ear drum (in descent) not equalized in middle ear on internal surface of drum. Obstructed eustachian tubes may prevent clearing ears and equalizing pressure. On ascent, ears should be cleared to allow decrease in pressure in middle ear.	Increasing unequal pressure on drum causes (1) congestion of drum, (2) hemorrhage from drum into middle ear, (3) perforation of drum. Drum ruptures inward on descent and outward on ascent.
Sinus Squeeze (Aerosinusitis)	Obstruction of normal openings of the sinuses prevents air entering to equalize pressure within the air sinuses.	Relative decrease in pressure within obstructed air sinus causes mucosal congestion, then hemorrhage.
Tooth Squeeze	A cavity within a tooth without an adequate opening to mouth is present	Pressure equalization within cavity cannot occur.
Air Embolism	Air being forced through alveoli of lungs into the pulmonary capillaries and veins, then going to heart and systemic circulation to brain, etc.	By too rapid ascent while holding breath or not exhaling adequately or airway obstruction trapping air on ascent.
Mediastinal and Subcutaneous Emphysema	Air being forced through ruptured alveoli to tissues about heart and up to neck.	By too rapid ascent while holding breath or not exhaling adequately.
Pneumothorax	Air being forced through alveoli (or ruptured alveoli) through visceral pleura into chest cavity (space between lungs and inner chest wall).	By too rapid ascent while holding breath or not exhaling adequately. Air is trapped under pressure and will expand further on ascent.
Decompression Sickness ("The Bends")	Nitrogen coming out of solution and forming bubbles in the blood and in the tissues.	By too rapid ascent and inadequate decompression for dissolution of excessive nitrogen to be removed from tissues and blood.
Nitrogen Narcosis ("Rapture of the Deep")	Anesthesia caused by effect of nitrogen on the brain.	As depth increases, concentration of nitrogen in brain tissues increases to amounts necessary to produce anesthesia.
Oxygen Poisoning	Effect caused by breathing oxygen under two atmospheres or more pressure. Mechanism unknown.	Using compressed oxygen or oxygen rebreathers instead of compressed air tank at depths over 25'.
Carbon Monoxide Poisoning	Contaminated air being used by SCUBA diver.	Air from gasoline engine exhaust enters intake of compressor.
Anoxia ("Shallow Water Blackout")	Excessive breath-holding on free dives, ignoring need to breathe until insufficient oxygen is present in blood to sustain consciousness.	Breath holding in prolonged free dives (without SCUBA).
Pseudomonas Intoxication Syndrome	Bacteria growing in dirty or contaminated regulator; source possibly from diver's mouth or contaminated water.	Bacteria or bacterial products (endotoxin) being inhaled and absorbed by lungs of diver. (Possible gram negative bacteremia.)
Chest "Squeeze"	Free diving (without SCUBA) to too great a depth.	During descent, inhaled air in lungs at atmospheric pressure is compressed to extent that rib cage is compressed.

Prevention	Symptoms	Treatment	Recovery
Exhale through nose during descent to equalize pressure inside face mask.	Pain in eyes. Conjunctival hemorrhage.	Equalize pressure in mask. Usually not necessary to treat otherwise. See eye doctor if severe.	Usually prompt on equalizing pressure inside mask.
Clear ears on descent, again on ascent. If difficult to "pop" ears, push mask against nose (or hold nose with fingers, using new types of face mask) and exhale with mouth closed. Stop descent and return toward surface if ears not cleared. Do not wear ear plugs.	Increasing pain in ears as one descends. If one's drum ruptures, cold water entering middle ear may cause dizziness, loss of balance, nausea, or vomiting.	Consult ear specialist and discontinue swimming until ear heals.	Hours to a few weeks, depending on degree of injury to drum. If no secondary infection, recovery usually complete.
Vasoconstrictor nose drops or sprays. Do not dive with active sinusitis or allergies. If pain develops, stop descent and begin ascent.	Pain in face or head around affected sinus and nasal bleeding.	Vasoconstrictor nose drops or sprays. Consult ear, nose, throat specialist.	Variable, depending on degree of injury and possible infection.
Keep teeth in good repair. Stop descent and begin ascent if tooth squeeze occurs.	Pain in tooth or jaw.	See dentist.	Variable, usually prompt when tooth repaired.
Slow ascent while exhaling adequately.	Pain, loss of consciousness, convulsions, paralysis.	Consult physician and take to recompression chamber at once.	Variable, could prove fatal or permanent damage may occur.
Ascend slowly while exhaling adequately.	Pain in chest under breastbone, "crunch" with each heartbeat, swollen neck.	Consult physician and take to recompression chamber.	Variable, depends on degree and amount of damage.
Ascend slowly while exhaling adequately.	Pain in chest, difficulty breathing, cyanosis, irregular pulse.	Consult physician at once to remove air in pleural space.	Variable, should be treated by physician.
Follow standard diving tables when diving to excessive depths. Do not dive multiple tanks multiple times.	Localized pain in areas where bubbles develop (arm or leg). Neurological defects of any type. Respiratory difficulty, "the chokes."	Consult physician and take to recompression chamber.	Variable with prompt adequate treatment usually complete.
Do not dive to excessive depths (100′ or more), use oxygen-helium mixtures for those depths. Avoid air travel immediately after diving.	Euphoria, confusion, finally unconsciousness.	Ascend to shallower depths.	Spontaneous, as the depth decreases, providing one has not made a fatal mistake.
Do not use compressed oxygen or oxygen rebreather apparatus.	Convulsions and unconsciousness.	Ascend to depths less than 25′.	Spontaneous as depth decreases, unless convulsions or unconsciousness cause drowning.
Use pure air.	Respiratory difficulty, "cherry red lips," unconsciousness, death.	Take to hospital at once.	Variable, could prove fatal.
Do not free dive beyond point at which urge to breathe is acute. Avoid excessive hyperventilation before diving.	Loss of desire to breathe just prior to unconsciousness.	Support, artificial respiration if needed, and oxygen.	Usually prompt, if diver does not drown. Possible permanent brain damage, especially from repeated insult.
Use only clean regulators. Clean mouthpiece and low-pressure hoses of regulator after each dive.	Usually begins 1 or 2 hours after dive, fever (up to 104°), respiratory distress, wheeze, chest pains, headache, being "sick all over."	Support, respiration, take to physician for oxygen and antibiotics as necessary.	Usually within 24 hours. Has been fatal.
Do not free dive below 50′. Actual depth varies with individual.	Chest pain.	Ascend.	Usually prompt in minor cases. Could be fatal.

When planning a trip into remote areas consult your physician about two months prior to departure for a smallpox vaccination, typhoid and paratyphoid vaccine, cholera vaccine (if traveling to Africa, the Orient, or Pacific islands), and a tetanus toxoid booster (or the tetanus toxoid series).

The following medicines and drugs are all "prescription type" and must be sanctioned by your physician. Those useful in the prevention and control of acquired gastroenteritis are as follows:

1. A sulfa compound such as Sulfathaladine, Sulfathiazol, or Gantrisin. This can be taken prophylactically on entering endemic areas of gastroenteritis.

2. A broad-spectrum antibiotic for emergency treatment of a febrile gastroenteritis such as tetracycline. This is also effective as a prophylaxis, but should be used with caution as it can produce a diarrhea itself from changing the intestinal flora and is not recommended for use for more than a few days as a preventative.

3. An agent to decrease the motility of the gastrointestinal tract. Lomotil®, paregoric, or codeine are all suitable.

4. An antispasmotic, such as Probanthine® or atropine. These can decrease the spasms and cramps as well as decrease intestinal motility.

5. An antiemetic or antinauseant drug such as Dramamine®, Bonamine®, Sparine®, or Tigan®. Both tablets and suppositories should be taken.

6. A sedative such as phenobarbital to make one's illness more bearable.

The object of treatment is to put the gastrointestinal tract at rest, to replace fluids and electrolytes (salts) lost by vomiting and diarrhea, and to provide symptomatic relief until the illness subsides. Obviously, the severe gastroenteritis which does not respond must be taken to adequate medical facilities.

Diet is reduced to liquids, sips of water or tea, or ginger ale. Only after symptoms have subsided the diet may be gradually increased to jello, cooked cereal, or gruel. Then advance to boiled milk, cooked eggs, cooked vegetables, and well-cooked meats. *Avoid* raw vegetables, fruits, fruit juices, poorly cooked meats, and highly seasoned foods.

If nausea and vomiting prevent retaining medications, Tigan or Sparine suppositories may aid in retaining liquids and other oral medications.

When diarrhea is the primary symptom treat with Lomotil or paregoric or codeine as directed. Adding Probanthine or atropine will decrease the spasms of the intestine and decrease the cramps, as well as aid in further reduction in "transit time" of the intestinal contents. Bed rest and phenobarbital aid in relaxing the patient. Changing from sulfa to tetracycline with onset of symptoms may aid in their more satisfactory subsidence.

A persistent, severe diarrhea (especially combined with vomiting) can cause excessive fluid and salt loss producing dehydration, electrolyte imbalance, shock, renal failure, and even death. The severe complications are more likely to occur in the very young and very old. If one is many miles from civilization, when treatment appears ineffective, do not delay in seeking adequate medical aid.

—H.V.L.
—W.B.H.

FISH (USAGE) Although the plural of fish is fishes, the singular form has long been accepted to mean all fish, or all of a certain kind, as in *the fish in the river are trout*. This is a singular noun used generically, or collectively, and not a true plural. The singular form *fish* may also be used as a mass noun when they are thought of as food, as in *fish market*. These uses of the singular probably gave rise to the belief that *fish* was a plural form. This has, in fact, become standard, and the form *fish* may now be used as a true plural. In contemporary usage we say *five fish* rather than *five fishes*. This also applies to compounds such as *three swordfish* rather than *three swordfishes*.

Scientific literature requires the regular plural *fishes* where it may clarify a relationship, such as a diversity of species, as in *the sample contained juvenile sockeye salmon and associated small fishes*. —A.J.McC.

FISH AND WILDLIFE ACT (1956) Public Law 1024, known as the Fish and Wildlife Act of 1956, provided for reorganization of the U.S. Fish and Wildlife Service into the Bureau of Sport Fisheries and Wildlife and the Bureau of Commercial Fisheries. The act brought increased recognition to fishery research and management activities by the federal agencies and was the basis for several new national programs. It authorized the Secretary of the Interior to conduct continuing investigations to determine the abundance and biological requirements of sport and commercial fishes. It called for the collection of statistics on these resources and authorized education and extension services. The secretary was authorized to "take such steps as may be required for the development, advancement, management, conservation, and protection of the fishery resources."

FISH AND WILDLIFE SERVICE The Fish and Wildlife Service is under the supervision of the Commissioner of Fish and Wildlife. The Commissioner, in turn, is subject to direction from the Assistant Secretary of the Interior for Fish and Wildlife.

The Office of the Commissioner includes his immediate staff and the Offices of Information, International Relations, and Program Review. The Bureau of Commercial Fisheries, under a Director, is responsible for matters relating primarily to the commercial fisheries, whales, seals, and sea-lions. It consists of the Office of the Director and the five Divisions of Biological Research, Industrial Research, Economics, Resource Development and Administration.

The Bureau's field activities, formerly under the direct supervision of the Central Office in Washington, have been decentralized. Regional headquarters are as follows: Pacific Region, Seattle, Washington; Gulf and South Atlantic Region, St. Petersburg Beach, Florida; North Atlantic Region, Gloucester, Massachusetts; Great Lakes and Central Region, Ann Arbor, Michigan; the Alaska Region at Juneau; and the Pacific Southwest Region, Terminal Island, California. An area office comprising the former Pacific Oceanic Fishery Investigations is located in Honolulu, Hawaii. In all, the Bureau operates 177 biological laboratories and field or experimental stations.

Organization of the Bureau of Sport Fisheries and Wildlife includes the Office of the Director, and Divisions of Sport Fisheries, Technical Services, Wildlife, and Administration. It operates 400 wildlife refuges, management areas, fish hatcheries, experiment stations, and field stations; is responsible for conservation and management of migratory waterfowl, including the enforcement of Federal laws relating to fish and wildlife; conducts research on the sport fisheries and on wildlife; engages in the control of pest birds and mammals; carries on specific fish and wildlife management on Federal lands; appraises the effects of Federally-sponsored or licensed water development projects on fish and wildlife; and administers Federal assistance programs for fish and wildlife restoration in the States.

Regional offices of the Bureau, to which considerable authority formerly held in the Washington Office has now been delegated, are located at Boston, Massachusetts; Atlanta, Georgia; Minneapolis, Minnesota; Albuquerque, New Mexico; and Portland, Oregon. Except for the research installations whose officials report directly to the Washington Office, officials of the 400 subordinate field installations report to the Regional Directors.

FISH BOX An integral part of equipment on offshore fishing boats. *For details see* Fish Box *under* Sportfisherman

FISH COOKERY The angler has the best opportunity to enjoy fish as a food because he can obtain choice species in their season and bring them fresh to the table. Too, fishing grounds are often the source of species which are not commercially available, as well as seafoods such as scallops, clams, oysters, lobsters, crayfish, and crabs. Fish cookery is basically simple and the essential principles for preparing fish can be learned quickly.

Any recipe is at best a well-informed suggestion. There is no way of equating the quality of the ingredients nor the skill of the chef. A hatchery trout, for example, seldom has the delicate flavor of a wild fish and would be a poor choice for the subtle poaching method as compared to grilling. Gourmet seafood cookery depends on your knowledge of the raw materials.

FOOD VALUE

From a dietetic standpoint fish shows a slightly higher protein content than meat (19.0 milligrams per 100 grams as opposed to 13.5–16.6 for beef, mutton, and pork). Fish has a lower calorie content than meat (445 calories per pound for fish as opposed to 1,530–1,669 for beef, mutton, and pork). Although fish has the same mineral deficiencies as meat, the calcium, phosphorus, and iron content is higher. Saltwater species also provide a rich source of iodine. The fat content of all fish is low (2.5 milligrams per 100 grams as compared to 30.1–34.1 for beef, mutton, and pork). Fish fat or "oil" is polyunsaturated. The superior digestibility of fish as compared to meat is due to the fact that the connective tissue, binding the muscle fibers together, is composed of collagen, which is easily assimilated by the digestive juices, whereas meat consists of elastin tissues which are less easily digested.

PERISHABILITY

Fish are among the most perishable foods. A fish is adapted to live at low temperatures, and in comparatively warm-air temperatures it deteriorates rapidly from bacterial invasion and autolysis since the high degree of activity of the digestive enzymes is a necessary function in its natural environment. The following check points are characteristic of freshly killed fish:

1. the presence of *rigor mortis*
2. bright red gills
3. clear eyes
4. a fresh odor
5. firm flesh
6. the absence of reddish discoloration on the ventral side of the backbone
7. the fish will float in water

HOW TO KEEP FISH FRESH

To keep a fish in good condition, gut it, and drain off as much blood as possible. Removal of the intestines, liver, heart, and gills means elimination of the largest source of bacterial contamination. Whenever possible, keep an ice chest on board to store your catch. Chips of ice, or flake ice, or scale ice are better than a cake of ice because the smaller pieces have a more intimate contact with all surfaces, thereby increasing the cooling rate which in turn prolongs keeping quality.

On the stream you should use a wicker creel which allows free circulation of air. However, at temperatures over 70°F conditions are most favorable for the growth of spoilage bacteria. Fish should not be kept in a creel for more than 3–4 hours on warm days. Do not put fish in jacket pockets or expose them to the sun. Stringers kept in the water are also of limited value. Hardy species such as bass, walleye, and bluegills may remain alive for hours, but a fish killed instantly will be in better condition than one that dies slowly, struggling and being bruised in the process. At ordinary, warm surface temperatures fish may spoil even before they are removed from the stringer.

FLAVOR OF FISH

The terms most often applied to describing the flavor of a fish are sweet, fishy, bland, mossy, and oily. A fresh fish will taste sweet. Likewise, a correctly frozen product should never taste "fishy." A strong or rancid flavor indicates that the raw material was improperly handled before or during the freezing process or it was kept in protracted storage. Rancidity is caused by an oxidation of the fish oils which produce bitter-tasting carbonyl compounds. This is a more common problem with some species of fish than others. As a rule, aquatic animals containing only a small quantity of oil preserve better than those which have a high oil content. Mackerel, lake trout, flounders, and smelt, for example, are more susceptible to rancidity than walleye, yellow perch, halibut, or lobster. However, there are notable exceptions; of the five species of Pacific salmon, the lean, pink salmon becomes rancid and discolored in less than one-tenth of the time required by the king salmon, which has the highest oil content.

It also is possible that a particular kind of fish may be highly palatable in one geographic location and inferior in another due to environmental conditions; a bluefish from Northern waters, for example, is generally superior to one caught in Southern waters: black bass, pike, and walleye caught in warm, muddy water are inferior to the same species caught in cold clear water. So the source of raw material is important.

BAKING FISH

Baking is ideal for whole, stuffed fish, which are to be cooked with skins on, or very thick cuts of fish, which might dry out under direct heat. Fatty fishes such as large mullet, bluefish, and king mackerel can also be baked. Lean fish and small fillets of fat fish should be braised (baked in stock of some kind similar to poaching) or broiled to retain their best texture and flavor. Baking can be done in a very hot oven for a short period, or a moderate oven (350°F. to 375°F.) for a longer time.

BROILING OR GRILLING

A particularly useful method for treating the fatty fishes, such as bluefish, mullet, shad, and mackerel. Fish to be broiled can be left whole, split, or filleted. Heat the oven and pan before putting in the fish so that it cooks evenly. Small delicate fish, such as snapper, flounder, and trout, can also be broiled, but any lean cut should be cooked at a greater distance from the fire and should be basted with butter, oil, or complimentary sauce. Very thick cuts of fish, such as grouper or large cod, do not broil well as the application of direct heat makes the outside leathery while the inside is barely warmed.

DEEP FRYING

Deep frying is a popular method for treating many kinds of fish. The important part, and the one most neglected, is in bringing the oil or lard to a proper temperature before adding the fish. A thermometer is important in this respect. As a rule, most frying is done from 360°F. to 380°F., with the smaller fish or cuts being fried at the higher temperature. The fish should first be dipped in milk then flour, or dipped in flour then in beaten egg and bread crumbs, or dipped in a batter, or rolled in corn meal, before frying. The oil or lard should be deep so that the pieces of fish are completely submerged. When cooked they will rise to the surface. The fish should be drained on absorbent paper and served immediately.

Fish Batters Batters should only be used on fish for deep frying (390°F or above) to achieve a crisp, greaseless texture. Do not use batters on a fish that is to be panfried or pansautéed. The ingredients of a batter are liquid and flour (eggs contribute to the liquid), which becomes leathery-textured and unappetizing when subjected to low heat. This is a common error in fish cookery. Fish to be panfried should simply be dusted in flour or corn meal after seasoning, then placed in the warm buttered pan.

Tempura Batter This is a generally excellent batter for deep frying fish. It can also be used on shrimp, lobster, crabmeat, and vegetables. The ingredients of this batter must be in proportion, regardless of the amount made. Basically, it requires one part egg, two parts of *ice* water, and three parts of self-rising flour. One raw egg is generally equal to ¼ of a measuring cup; so the formula is as follows: Break one cold *egg* in a mixing bowl, add ½ cup of ice *water*, then ¾ cup of *self-rising flour*. Stir, but do not smooth the mixture. It should remain slightly lumpy. Of paramount importance is to keep the batter absolutely cold (add ice cubes to the water, but do not exceed the proportion given) and the fish cold until the instant it is placed in hot (over 400°) *cooking oil*. It's a good idea to keep the batter and the fish fingers in the freezing compartment of your refrigerator at home until you're ready to cook them. When the oil is bubbling hot, dip each piece in the batter, and drop into the pan. The difference in temperature will prevent the oil from penetrating the batter and cause the fish inside to steam and puff under the golden-brown crust.

PANFRYING OR SAUTÉING

Any small whole fish, such as yellow perch, brook trout, smelt, baby flounder, or sunfish, is ideal panfried. The fish may be sprinkled with salt and pepper, or with seasoned flour, or dipped in a seasoned batter, then placed in a hot skillet where a little butter or margarine has been brought to the foaming stage. It should be cooked over a low flame and turned to brown on both sides. When properly sautéed the skin of the fish should be crispy, not burned, and the flesh moistly succulent. Use a large skillet so the fish are not crowded, and do not in the course of cooking use a lid—either condition will cause steam and the skin will not crisp. If the fish contain too much moisture (which is one reason why they should not be soaked in water before frying), the butter will spatter. To avoid this, invert a colander over the pan. This will keep the butter in and the steam out.

POACHING OR BOILING

Thick steaks (cut in 1½ inch sections) of firm-fleshed fish can be boiled without crumbling by using a Leyse Fish Kettle (Leyse Aluminum Company, Kewaunee, Wisconsin), which is specially designed for this purpose. Poaching is ideal for sections of large, firm-fleshed fish, such as salmon, cod, or halibut. The fish are poached in a court bouillon, which may consist of a fish stock, wine and vegetable liquor, or just plain water and milk. The liquid must submerge the fish completely. Bring the court bouillon to a boil before adding the fish, or much of the flavor will be lost. The problem in poaching is to keep the fish intact. It is not difficult with small cuts, but for whole large fish you should wrap them in cheesecloth or use a regular fish-boiling kettle which has a perforated rack on which to place the fish. When the fish are placed in the kettle, the bouillon will cease bubbling for a minute; but when the boiling point is again reached, reduce the fire. If boiled too rapidly the fish will fall apart.

COURT-BOUILLON

Fish are boiled in a court-bouillon. This liquid may be a simple mixture of salted water with milk and lemon juice to keep the flesh of fish like cod, halibut, walleye, and pollack white during the cooking, or it may be a seasoned liquid made of fish stock and white wine, or a vegetable stock with vinegar to add flavor to the dish. Although small whole fish or sections of fish can be submerged in the court-bouillon and boiled in any suitable pot, a long fish kettle designed for this purpose is superior; this has a perforated rack upon which the fish is placed. To facilitate handling and prevent a whole large fish, such as a salmon, red snapper, or striped bass from breaking while cooking, it should first be wrapped in cheesecloth and secured to the rack. When boiled in this way the fish will remain intact and flat, making it suitable for dinner parties or buffets.

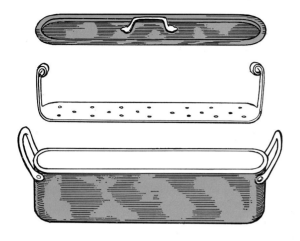

Rectangular pan at top is ideal for poaching or steaming a large whole fish such as salmon. The diamond-shaped pan is designed for fish such as flounder, sole, or turbot, which have a similar form. Fish removed on rack will not break.

In addition to boiled fish, court-bouillon may be used for poached fish (which differs only in that small fillets are just barely covered with the liquid in a shallow pan) and as a stock for fish chowders, stews, or bouillabaisse.

MILK COURT-BOUILLON

To every quart of cold *water* add 1 cup of fresh *milk*, one tablespoon of *salt*, and the juice of half a *lemon*. This liquid is not heated before using; simply submerge the fish in it, bring to a boil, then simmer.

VEGETABLE COURT-BOUILLON

To every 2 quarts of *water* add ½ cup of *vinegar*, 2 stalks of *celery* including the greens, 1 large *onion* quartered, 2 whole *carrots*, a few *lettuce* leaves, 2 *bay leaves*, a handful of *parsley*, 1 teaspoon of *dill* weed, 8 whole *peppercorns*, and a tablespoon of *salt*. Bring to a boil, then simmer slowly for 30–40 minutes and strain.

FISH COURT-BOUILLON

In 2 quarts of *water* add the head, bones, and tail of one fish. These can be obtained from a fish that has been filleted or an extra fish reserved for the stock. To this add 2 stalks of *celery* including the greens, 1 large *onion* quartered, 2 whole *carrots*, a few *lettuce* leaves, 2 *bay leaves*, a handful of *parsley*, 1 teaspoon of *dill* weed, 8 whole *peppercorns*, and a tablespoon of *salt*. Bring to boil, then simmer slowly for 45 minutes.

WHITE WINE COURT-BOUILLON

Follow recipe for *vegetable court-bouillon*, using only 1 quart of water and adding 1 quart of *white wine* and eliminating the vinegar. Or follow recipe for the *fish court-bouillon* using only 1 quart of water and adding 1 quart of white wine.

SAUCES AND BUTTERS

Béchamel Sauce In a saucepan, heat 4 tablespoons *butter* and cook in it over a low flame ½ *onion*, minced finely, until the onion is soft but not brown. Stir in 4 tablespoons *flour*, and cook slowly for a few minutes without letting the flour take on color. Add gradually 3 cups each of scalded *milk* and *fish stock*, stirring vigorously with a wire whip. Add ½ teaspoon *salt*, ½ teaspoon of *white pepper*, a sprig of *parsley*, and a pinch of freshly grated *nutmeg*. Cook slowly, stirring frequently, for about 30 minutes, or until the liquid is reduced by one-third and the sauce has the consistency of very heavy cream. Strain the sauce through a fine sieve, and dot the surface with butter.

Drawn Butter Melt 6 tablespoons *butter* in a saucepan, add 3 tablespoons *flour*, and slowly stir in 3 cups hot *vegetable stock*. Cook the sauce, stirring occasionally, until it is thick. Beat in 6 tablespoons butter, 3 tablespoons *lemon juice*, and *salt* to taste. Serve hot with fish or shellfish.

Maître d'Hôtel Butter Cream ½ cup softened *butter* with 1 tablespoon *lemon juice*, 1½ tablespoons chopped parsley, and ¼ teaspoon each of *salt* and *pepper*. Chill the butter, and serve with fish or shellfish.

Mustard Butter In a saucepan melt ½ cup *butter*. Remove the pan from the heat, and add 1 teaspoon *lemon juice* and ¼ teaspoon *salt*. Beat in gradually 2½ teaspoons prepared *mustard*, and continue beating the sauce until it is thick and cool. Serve slightly chilled with fish or shellfish.

Beurre Blanc In a saucepan combine ¼ cup *wine vinegar*, 1 tablespoon each of finely chopped *shallots* and *parsley*, and a little *salt* and *pepper*. Simmer the mixture until the liquid is reduced by one-half and gradually beat in ½ cup *butter*. Serve hot and foamy with fish or shellfish.

Beurre Noir In a saucepan, over high heat, melt ¾ cup *butter*, and cook it until it begins to brown. Add at

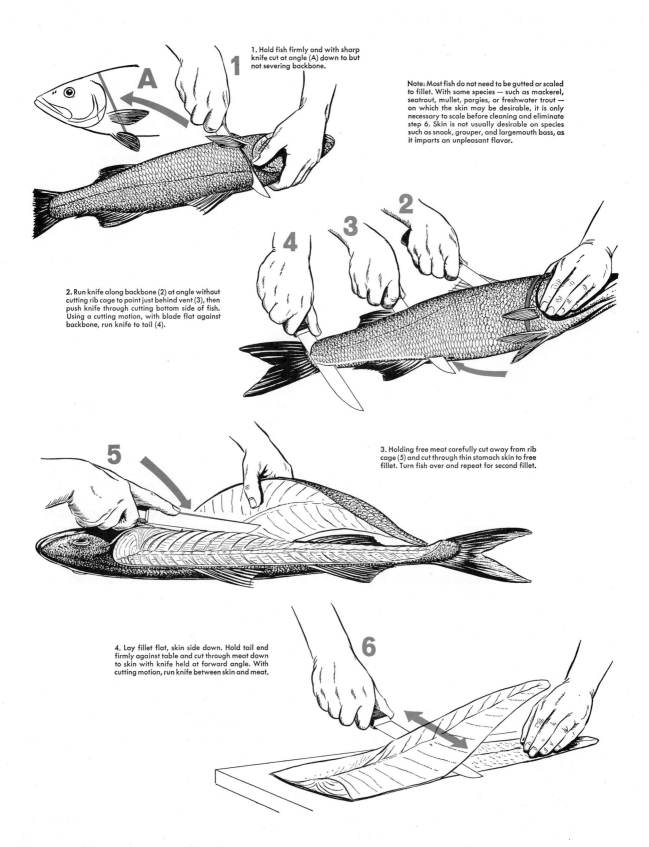

1. Hold fish firmly and with sharp knife cut at angle (A) down to but not severing backbone.

Note: Most fish do not need to be gutted or scaled to fillet. With some species — such as mackerel, seatrout, mullet, porgies, or freshwater trout — on which the skin may be desirable, it is only necessary to scale before cleaning and eliminate step 6. Skin is not usually desirable on species such as snook, grouper, and largemouth bass, as it imparts an unpleasant flavor.

2. Run knife along backbone (2) at angle without cutting rib cage to point just behind vent (3), then push knife through cutting bottom side of fish. Using a cutting motion, with blade flat against backbone, run knife to tail (4).

3. Holding free meat carefully cut away from rib cage (5) and cut through thin stomach skin to free fillet. Turn fish over and repeat for second fillet.

4. Lay fillet flat, skin side down. Hold tail end firmly against table and cut through meat down to skin with knife held at forward angle. With cutting motion, run knife between skin and meat.

Filleting a Fish

once 3 tablespoons each of chopped *parsley* and *capers* and 1 teaspoon *wine vinegar*. Serve with sautéed fish.

Shrimp Butter Shell 1 pound *shrimp*, dry the *shells* in the oven for a few minutes, and pound them in a mortar until they are pulverized as finely as possible. Melt ¼ pound *butter* in the top of a double boiler with 2 tablespoons *water* and the pulverized shells, and cook for 10–12 minutes without allowing the butter to boil. Strain off the liquid. Add a little boiling water to the shells and strain.

Pour the combined liquids through a cloth into a bowl of ice water, and set the bowl in the refrigerator until the butter hardens on the top. Skim off the butter and pack it into a jar. Cover it and store it in the refrigerator.

Tomato Butter Chop 4 ripe *tomatoes*, and stew them until all the surplus moisture is cooked away. Cool the tomatoes, add 4 tablespoons creamed *butter*, and strain the mixture through a fine sieve.

Sauce Espagnole This is a basic brown sauce which has many uses in fish cookery. It can be made up and kept in the refrigerator or deep freeze.

Melt ½ cup beef, veal, or pork *drippings* in a heavy saucepan. Add 1 small *carrot* and 2 *onions*, coarsely chopped, and cook them until the onions just start to turn golden. Add ½ cup *flour* and cook, stirring frequently, until flour, carrots, and onions are a rich brown. Add 3 cups hot *brown gravy* (canned), 1 stalk of *celery*, 3 sprigs of *parsley*, 1 small *bay leaf*, and 1 clove *garlic*, all chopped, and a pinch of *thyme*. Cook, stirring frequently, until the mixture thickens.

Add 3 more cups stock, and simmer slowly over very low heat, stirring occasionally, for 1–1½ hours, or until the mixture is reduced to about 3 cups. As it cooks, skim off the fat which rises to the surface. Add ¼ cup *tomato sauce* or ½ cup *tomato purée*. Cook the sauce for a few minutes longer, and strain it through a fine sieve. Add 2 more cups stock, and continue to cook slowly for about 1 hour, skimming the surface from time to time, until the sauce is reduced to about 4 cups. Cool the sauce, stirring it occasionally.

Hollandaise Sauce In a bowl set in hot water over low heat, beat 4 *egg yolks* with 1 tablespoon each of *light cream* and *tarragon vinegar* or *lemon juice*. Continue beating the eggs with a whisk until they begin to thicken. Add, bit by bit, ½ cup *butter* and continue beating the sauce until it is thick. Add *lemon juice*, *salt*, and *cayenne* to taste. Put the bowl in a pan of lukewarm water until serving time. Serve with any hot or cold poached fish.

Mousseline Sauce To 1 cup *hollandaise sauce* add 4 tablespoons *whipped cream*. Heat gently and serve.

Sauce Colbert Cream 6 tablespoons *butter*, and add 2 tablespoons *chopped parsley*, ⅛ teaspoon *nutmeg*, and a pinch of *cayenne*. In a saucepan dissolve 1 tablespoon *meat extract* in 1½ tablespoons hot *water*, and stir in the seasoned butter, bit by bit, alternately with the juice of 2 small *lemons*. Add 1 teaspoon *Madeira wine* or *sherry*, and serve the sauce hot with fish.

Shrimp Sauce Cook 1 pound *shrimp* in 3 cups boiling water to which have been added a few slices of *onion*, a sprig of *parsley*, a small stalk of *celery* with the leaves, ½ teaspoon *salt*, and 3 *peppercorns*. Simmer the shrimp for 15 minutes, and then strain, reserving the broth. Remove the shells and chop the shrimp coarsely.

Blend 4 tablespoons melted *butter* in a saucepan with 3 tablespoons *flour*. Add the shrimp broth gradually, stirring constantly until the sauce is thick. Add ⅓ cup *light cream*, *salt* and *pepper* to taste, and the shrimp.

Just before serving, remove the sauce from the fire, and stir in 1 *egg yolk* mixed with a little of the hot sauce. Add a few drops of *lemon juice* and serve hot with fish.

Sauce Tartare To 1½ cups *mayonnaise*, add 1 *dill pickle*, 4 *shallots*, and 2 *anchovies*, all finely chopped, 1 tablespoon each of *capers*, *parsley*, *tarragon*, and *chervil*, all chopped, and 1 teaspoon *mustard*. Thin the sauce with *heavy cream*, and season it with ½ teaspoon each of *lemon juice* and *sugar*, and *salt* and *pepper* to taste. Serve with any fried fish or shellfish.

White Sauce Melt 4 tablespoons of *butter* in saucepan. The instant it is melted, remove pan from fire, sprinkle, and stir in 4 tablespoons of *flour* spoon by spoon until it is well-blended. Slowly add 2 cups of room-temperature *milk*, stirring constantly. It will become smooth and faintly yellow. Now, put the pan back on the fire and stir some more. As it starts to bubble, add just a touch of *salt* and *white pepper*. Continue cooking on low flame until it thickens. Have 1 *egg yolk* in a cup. Pour 2 tablespoons of the now hot sauce on yolk, blend them, and slip into mixture. The yolk will hit the pan at proper temperature. Stir to its glorious finish.

FROZEN FISH

Freshly caught fish is superior to the frozen product, particularly when cooked right on the riverbank or at the seashore. However, modern-day freezing units are a boon to the angler who finds his sport miles away from home, and with proper handling he can put in a supply of seasonal species against days of scarcity. Actually, frozen fish often cannot be distinguished by the average person from fresh fish.

The Freezing Process Fish do not have a definitive freezing point. They start freezing on the outside at about 30.3°F., and the process continues to the inside. The center of the fish is the last part to freeze. Most of the water in a fish is frozen at 18°F., but a small part may remain unfrozen at temperatures below 0°F. When large quantities of fish are placed in a freezer, it takes a longer period of time for their temperature to be lowered to the freezing point. If cooling is prolonged, undesirable changes can take place in texture, color, and flavor. It is important therefore to freeze the right amount of fish at any one time.

Amount to Freeze Unless the freezer is specially equipped for quick-freezing, the volume of fish to be frozen in a 24-hour period should not exceed 10 per cent, and preferably 5 per cent, of the total capacity. In a cubic-foot unit (359 pounds) this means about 18 pounds of fish, or 35 pounds in 20 cubic feet (718 pounds). As you increase the amount to be frozen, you will decrease the *rate* of freezing and increase the storage compartment temperature during the cooling process. All freezers have areas which are colder than others; freezing should be done directly on the shelves with coils in an upright, and near the sides or wherever the chest-type freezer coils are located. Fish to be frozen should not be piled one on top of the other nor on top of other frozen foods.

Storage Temperature Fish appear to be frozen solid at 20°F. Actually, their hardness has nothing to do with storage life. Oxidative changes are only retarded. Where economically feasible fish should be stored at 0°F. to 20°F.

Freezer Burn When frozen fish is inadequately protected against moisture loss through its packaging or storage, the surface may become dry, fibrous, and discolored. This is commonly called "freezer burn." The most common cause of desiccation is improper packaging. When a fish, or any cut of fish, is wrapped in such a manner that air spaces are created within the package, moisture is transferred from the surface of the fish to the inner side of the packaging material in the form of frost. This moisture loss will cause a freezer burn.

Packaging Materials The selection of the proper wrap and its application are extremely important to the storage of frozen fish. Air, even freezing air, must be kept away from the fish because oxygen will cause discoloration and rancidity to develop. So the packaging material must eliminate as much air as possible and secondly prevent more air from entering the wrap. As a general rule, papers having a high resistance to moisture-vapor transmission are most efficient. Ordinary waxed paper, for example, is not sufficient; it is not moisture-vapor proof, and it cracks. However, waxed paper can be used with a strong overwrap such as aluminum foil. A good wrapping material must also be strong enough to resist puncture, pliable enough to make a tight wrap, easily sealable, greaseproof, durable at low temperatures, and should impart no odor or flavor of its own.

There are numerous foils, films, resin-coated papers, waxed papers, lacquered papers, and laminated papers on the market. Of these, the most popular for freezing are transparent materials such as cellophane (Gauge Nos. 300 and 450), polyethylene, rubber hydrochloride bliofilm, and vinylidene chloride, which is sold as Saran or Cryovac. Heavy aluminum foil is not transparent, but it is an excellent material for wrapping uneven shaped pieces of fish because it holds tightly against the surface. When properly applied, it eliminates air pockets, and by folding the edges twice or more, it will seal without the use of tape or cord. Vegetable parchment is also a tough wrapping material, and being cheap it's especially suitable for wrapping large chunks of fish. However, it is not as pliable as foil.

Brine Frozen Fish Before freezing lean saltwater fish, such as cod, flounder, fluke, haddock, halibut, pollock, rockfish, or whiting, it's advisable to dip them in a chilled brine made of pure table salt (such as Morton's Iodized) dissolved in water. The brine prevents browning of the hemoglobin and greatly reduces the amount of drip in thawing and cooking. The fish should be immersed for 30 seconds in a 5-percent brine solution (⅔ cup of salt to 1 gallon of water). Oily saltwater species, such as salmon, mackerel, smelt, and mullet, attain maximum storage life (6–9 months) when frozen in airtight containers filled with a 2½-percent brine solution (⅓ cup salt to 1 gallon water).

Ice Glaze When necessary, large, whole, dressed fish can be glazed for maximum storage life. Glazing consists of dipping the fish in cold water to form a protective layer of ice on the outside, which effectively seals it from the air. If it is desirable to employ a glaze, freeze the fish first (wrapped in vegetable parchment), place a pan of water in the freezer, and when the temperature reaches 33°–40°F., remove the wrap and dip the fish in cold water, remove, and let the water film freeze. Dipping should be repeated until a heavy glaze is formed. For storage, the fish should then be wrapped in a moisture-vaporproof material such as aluminum foil.

Freezing in Containers Containers made of plastic or glass, or even glass fruit jars fitted with airtight covers are preferable for all shellfish and bivalve freezing. Containers also provide maximum storage life for various cuts of fish when frozen in a brine solution. Their disadvantage is in the greater utilization of storage space.

To freeze fish in a container, steaks, fillets, small pan-dressed fish, or chunks should be carefully packed to within 1½ inches of the top for quart-size containers and 1 inch of the top for a pint-size. Fill the space around and between the fish with a 2½-percent brine solution (chilled) until the product is covered. Remove entrapped air bubbles with a blunt knife or spatula. The lid should be screwed or pressed tightly in place to assure an airtight seal. The ice that is formed will keep air away from the fish, and the jar seal prevents loss of moisture from the contents. It is also economical and efficient to use quart- or half-gallon-sized milk cartons. Cut off the lid end and place the fish inside. Fill with 2½-percent brine and freeze. When the ice block is formed, reseal the open end tightly with aluminum foil. This method will preserve small pandressed trout up to nine months in storage.

Freezing Fish Steaks Certain species of fish, such as the salmon, kingfish, wahoo, halibut, swordfish, mako, and tuna, are particularly good when steaked and oven broiled or charcoal broiled. The steaks should be cut 1½ inches thick. For convenience, wrap each individual steak in wax paper, then wrap them six to a package in freezer-weight foil. Steaks need not be completely defrosted to cook; merely allow a little longer time on the fire.

How to Freeze Fish Fillets Firm-fleshed fish, such as the striped bass, red snapper, Spanish mackerel, black bass, or walleye, are usually frozen in fillet form with all bones and skin removed. They can be frozen flat in freezer-weight foil by separating each fillet with double thickness wax paper, or single thickness of silicone-treated parchment, or they can be rolled on wax paper and packed in a moisture-vaporproof bag. Cook frozen fillets as you would fresh fillets, allowing a little extra cooking time for complete thawing.

To Freeze Clams or Oysters Shuck raw clams or oysters, and freeze them with their liquor in pint- or quart-sized freezer containers. For easy handling, remove the frozen blocks from the containers, and wrap them in wax paper, then a sheet of foil. When ready for use, thaw frozen clams or oysters overnight in the refrigerator. These bivalves should not be kept in the freezer longer than three months.

To Freeze Scallops Scallops can be frozen in the same manner as clams or oysters; however, they can become tough and lose their delicate flavor if improperly packaged. It is better to cook scallops in court bouillon before freezing (*see recipe*) to retain quality.

How to Freeze Lobsters and Crabs Live crabs and lobsters should be cooked for 10–20 minutes in boiling 2½–5-percent brine. When cool the carapace or top shell, gills, and viscera of the crab are removed and the body meat taken out with a pointed knife. The meat from the claws of crabs and lobsters may be removed by cracking the claws with a small wooden mallet and shaking or picking out the meat. In addition to the claws, the tail of a lobster contains edible meat. The meat in the tail may be removed with a fork; it is then split for removal of the intestinal tract. Crab meat and lobster meat should be packed in jars with 2½-percent brine.

In most cases it is best to use frozen shellfish within a period of 3–4 months; however, a storage life of 6 months may be attained where storage accommodations are especially good and the temperature is as low as 10°F.

Defrosting If possible, defrost the fish on the bottom shelf of your refrigerator 24 hours before using, or in an emergency immerse it in *cold* water. Thawing at room temperature is definitely not recommended. A greater quantity of fluid or "drip" is formed when defrosting in warm air. This fluid consists of dissolved proteins as well as minerals. Aside from the loss of food value, the spoilage process resumes at normal room temperatures. Never defrost frozen fish and then refreeze it.

CLAM COOKERY

There are various kinds of marine clams which commonly come into United States kitchens. Due to differences in size and texture, they are all treated differently. In the East, the most popular one is the quahaug or hard clam. Countless millions of quahaugs are raked, treaded, dredged, and otherwise pried loose from their beds every year. The cherished rite of eating clams on the half shell is made possible by the bivalve, which, depending on its size, is known as a Little Neck (a Long Island town once the center of small clam trade) when about 3–4 years old, then as a Cherrystone (named after Cherrystone Creek in Virginia) when about 5 years old. The name quahaug is a corruption of the Algonkin name for clam. From the age of 6 onward the hard clam ceases to be of half shell interest, but can be used in chowders.

The sea clam or skimmer is similar in appearance but larger than the quahaug (4–6 inches in length), with a smooth, calcerous, elliptical-shaped shell that is covered externally by a yellowish-brown epidermis. The interior of the shell has a slick glistening appearance. Because of its large muscular foot, the sea clam can glide through the water and even skim along the surface for short distances. The skimmer has become of increasing economic importance, because with soft clams in short supply many New England restaurateurs have learned to slice the big yellow muscle into thin strips and fry them, breaded, in deep fat with pleasing results. New York and New Jersey canning companies process skimmers for "chopped clams," which make delicious canapés.

Although quahaugs have been introduced variously in the West, the native delicacy is the versatile butter clam. The butter clam is comparatively smooth-shelled, finely etched with concentric growth lines, and all the inside meat may be eaten. This clam occurs mainly on beaches having a mixture of sand and gravel, at a depth of no more than a foot below the surface from the tidal zone out to thirty feet of water. It is used chiefly in canning, but can be prepared in any manner, including frying, steaming, and in chowders.

Mexican fish stew (*see recipe*) is one of the many artful dishes that can be prepared with a variety of seafoods. Fish trimmings are an important ingredient in making stocks for soups and stews

Both coasts of the United States have the razor clam in common. The razor clam is usually found in very fine sand, free of gravel or clay. It is not found in areas of low salinity (such as river mouths) or where the water temperatures are high. The razor clam is easy to identify as it has a long, thin, narrow shell, which looks much like the old-fashioned straight razor. The shells are almost transparent and are covered with a shiny brown periostracum. Although the razor clam has large creamy-colored meat, it is too chewy to be eaten on the half shell, except when small. It is generally used in fritters. Small razors are also excellent when steamed.

The soft clam or steamer is found from the Arctic Ocean south to Cape Hatteras. Although abundant to the Maryland shore, the bulk of the soft clam crop comes from flats in New England, where tides expose vast areas when the water is low. The long neck or siphon of the soft clam will jet water into the air when you walk near it, making it easy to dig out of its mud burrow. This tasty bivalve has the texture and size ideal for frying and chowders, as well as steaming.

A gourmet treat is Clams Guilford, which is simply the soft clam meats rolled in cracker crumbs and broiled in butter. The most popular method of cooking soft clams, however, is steaming.

The smallest clam used in cooking is the bean clam of the Pacific Coast and the closely related coquina of Atlantic shores. The average specimen is seldom more than ¾-inch long and is often smaller. These clams are extremely abundant within their range, and sufficient amounts can be collected to make an excellent broth or soup. They are too small to be utilized in any other way.

The largest American clam is the Pacific Coast's geoduck. Its shell may be 8 inches long and exceed 5 pounds in weight. The geoduck is nearly rectangular in shape and has such a large neck, or siphon, that it cannot be withdrawn into the shell. The shells always gape and show a brown mantle, which completely hides the body of the clam inside. In a large geoduck, the siphon can be extended three feet or more. This neck pumps hundreds of gallons of water daily to and from the geoduck's digestive apparatus. The meat of this mollusk is sliced into cutlets and fried, and the siphon can be skinned and made into a chowder after grinding it in a food chopper.

The geoduck is not the largest clam ever eaten. Among his other conquests, Alexander the Great managed to extract and consume the giant clam of the Indian Ocean, a Bacchian feat which is still emulated today. The meat of this species may weigh twenty pounds and the shell a quarter ton, which is no easy shuck even by a squad of hungry Macedonians. Latter day navigators, traveling through the tropical Pacific, discovered real giants on the Great Barrier Reef of Australia, where they grow to more than 4 feet in length. A matching pair of these shells were presented to the church of St. Suplice in Paris during the reign of Louis XVI, where they are still in use as holy water basins.

Other clams, or closely related bivalves, which provide an excellent source of food are the cockles (which make good chowders), angel wings, rough piddocks, pismo clam, and the western horse clam, which rivals the geoduck in size.

Deviled Clams Sauté 1 large *onion* and 2 stalks *celery*, both finely chopped, in 4 tablespoons *butter* until the vegetables are golden. Put 20 freshly opened *clams* through a food chopper, and add them to the celery-onion mixture. Add *salt* and *pepper* to taste and 1 cup *cream*, and bring the mixture to a boil. Remove the pan from the fire, and stir in 4 beaten *egg yolks* and ⅓ cup minced *chives*. Fill individual ramekins with the deviled clams, sprinkle with buttered *bread crumbs*, and bake in a moderately hot oven (400°F.) until the topping is brown.

Fried Razor Clams To prepare razor *clams*, first wash them in cold water to remove excess sand, then scald them in hot water to loosen from their shells. Remove the clam, and with a pair of kitchen scissors split the clam lengthwise and directly up the neck. Remove all dark parts from the interior so nothing but the white meat remains. Wash the meats clean, and prepare an *egg batter*. Roll either in *flour* or *cracker crumbs*, and fry in butter until brown.

Clam Fritters Mix 2 cups finely chopped *clams* with 2 well-beaten *egg yolks*, 1 cup *cracker crumbs*, *salt* and *pepper* to taste, a pinch of *cayenne*, 1 tablespoon finely minced *parsley*, and enough *clam juice* to make a heavy batter. Fold in 3 stiffly beaten *egg whites*. Drop the batter by spoonfuls into deep, hot fat at 370°F., the temperature at which a 1-inch cube of bread will brown in 60 seconds. Cook the fritters until they are brown on both sides, turning them once.

Clam Hash In a large iron skillet, melt 6 generous tablespoons of *butter* and sauté finely minced *onion* until it becomes transparent. Now, add 2 cups of finely diced cooked *potatoes* and 2 cups of chopped *clams*. *Salt* and *pepper* to taste. Make sure the mixture is spread evenly around the skillet, then cook over a low flame for 10 minutes. Next add ½ cup of *cream* over the hash-to-be, and continue cooking until browned. It should take about 30 minutes in all. Fold the hash with a spatula, and serve on a heated platter with *lemon* wedges and fresh *parsley*.

Clams Marinière Scrub well six dozen *clams*. Place them in a large kettle with 1 cup *white·wine*, 1 large *onion*, 1 tablespoon chopped *parsley*, 1 *bay leaf*, a pinch of *thyme*, and 4 tablespoons *butter*. Cover and cook over a brisk flame for 6–8 minutes, or until the shells open. Pile the clams on individual serving dishes. Strain the sauce through a fine sieve, taste it for seasoning, reheat it, and add 1 tablespoon butter and 1 tablespoon finely chopped parsley. Pour the sauce over the clams, and serve immediately.

Clams Oreganate Allow one dozen Little Neck *clams* on the half shell per person. Arrange them in pans of salt, and, while the oven is warming, make the sauce as follows: for each dozen clams, combine 1 clove of *garlic*, ¼ teaspoon of *oregano*, ½ teaspoon of chopped fresh *parsley*, and 2 teaspoons of *bread crumbs*. Mix these ingredients and chop fine. Sprinkle equal amounts over each clam, and then pour a few drops of *olive oil* on them. Bake or broil, as you prefer.

Scalloped Clams Mix 1¾ cups coarsely rolled *cracker crumbs* with ¾ cup melted *butter*, *salt* and *pepper* to taste, and a little *paprika*. Reserve ⅓ of the mixture and mix with the rest 3 cups finely minced *clams* and 3 tablespoons each chopped *chives* and *parsley*. Pour the mixture into a buttered baking dish, and top with the remaining butter-crumb mixture. Bake in a moderate oven (350°F.) for 20 minutes, until the clams are heated through and the topping nicely browned.

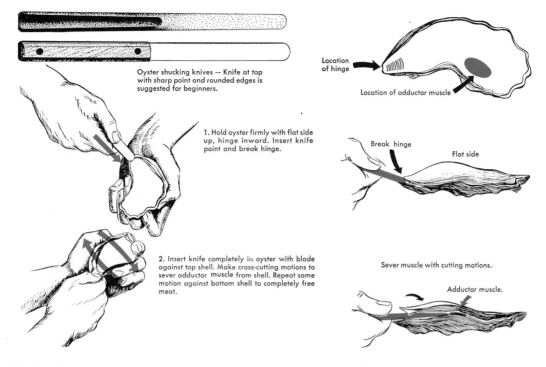

1. Hold oyster firmly with flat side up, hinge inward. Insert knife point and break hinge.

2. Insert knife completely in oyster with blade against top shell. Make cross-cutting motions to sever adductor muscle from shell. Repeat same motion against bottom shell to completely free meat.

Oyster shucking knives — Knife at top with sharp point and rounded edges is suggested for beginners.

Location of hinge

Location of adductor muscle

Break hinge

Flat side

Sever muscle with cutting motions.

Adductor muscle.

How to Shuck an Oyster

Steamed Soft Clams Submerge the *clams* in clear water for at least a half hour to help the bivalve get rid of the grains of sand in its snout. Place the clams in a large kettle in which you have about ½ inch of *salt* water in the bottom. Cover and steam for about 6–10 minutes or until the shells open. Discard any that do not open. Serve in individual dishes smothered in melted *butter*. Strain the broth through several thicknesses of cheesecloth, and season with *salt* and *pepper*. Drink the broth from bouillon cups as you progress with the steamers.

OYSTER AND SCALLOP COOKERY

Oysters are lamentable travelers, and to be palatable they must be perfectly fresh—with the shells firmly closed. If you buy them without shells, the liquor should be clear, If the natural juice is milky in color, do not use them. To open an oyster, hold it firmly with the hinge part of the shell in the palm of your hand. Using a thin, round-nosed oyster knife, push the blade between the shells near the hinge, and run it around until you cut the muscle that holds both valves together. If you shuck the oyster over a strainer placed on a bowl, the liquor that drains through can be used for cooking. The strainer will catch those tiny particles of shell which inevitably break loose. There is a tendency to overcook oysters. Assuming that you start with large, fresh ones, always bear in mind that an oyster is cooked once its edges start to curl. Working from the basic premise that a cooked oyster must have a complementary meat or vegetable to enhance its texture, most recipes are developed primarily around the use of chopped greens and bacon. This can be varied, with the use of chicken, veal, turkey, and chicken livers, but the trick in making any cooked oyster dish on the half shell is to use ordinary round baking tins filled with rock salt and lay the oysters in this bed. It keeps the shells upright so that they retain all juices, and it keeps the shells hot to the moment of eating. Don't trust to luck that some of the juice will stay with the meat.

Oysters Rockefeller Begin with a large handful of fresh green *spinach*, 2 bunches of *green onions*, a few stalks of *celery*, a bunch of *parsley*, and a very small head of *lettuce*. These greens must all be chopped together very finely, preferably in a meat grinder. In a saucepan, melt about a pound of *butter*, and to this add the juice of 1 *lemon*, 3 tablespoons of *Worcestershire sauce*, then *pepper* to taste. To this add the greens, and, assuming that you have 2 dozen large *oysters* sitting on their salt beds, ladle the sauce over each one. Next, sprinkle each oyster with fine *bread crumbs* and some *Parmesan cheese*. Put your pans on the oven rack and slide them in under a very hot fire. Allow 10–15 minutes for the sauce to marry the meats, and when the edges are curling, your oysters are ready. They should be served in the pans and not transferred to plates.

Oysters on Half Shell Raw *oysters* served on the half shell should be packed on crushed *ice* in bowls or oyster plates. They are best when served absolutely cold. Usually a cocktail mixture or dip is used, and this can be made with 2 teaspoons of prepared *horseradish*, 3 tablespoons of *tomato ketchup*, ½ teaspoon of *salt*, 2 tablespoons of *vinegar*, 4 tablespoons of *lemon juice*, and ¼ teaspoon of *tabasco* sauce. Mix all of these various ingredients thoroughly and then serve them in small, shallow glasses.

Oysters à la Czar Nicholas Bed your half-shell *oysters* in dishes of cracked *ice* and put them in the freezer while your grate 3 *onions*. Remove chilled dishes, and sprinkle a bare teaspoon of grated *onion* on each oyster meat, and then a teaspoon of *caviar* over the onion. Garnish each dish with wedges of *lemon* or *lime*, which you will use most sparingly over the caviar. The wine to accompany Czar Nicholas must be that prince of white burgundies, a cold Montrachat. You can serve bubbly for showmanship, but the Montrachat is best.

Fried Scallops Wash *scallops*, and dry them thoroughly. Dip them in *milk*, roll them in *flour*, and shake off the surplus flour. Brown them quickly in very hot *peanut oil*. Drain on paper towels, and season with a little *salt*. Serve very hot with dried *parsley*, a wedge of *lemon* for each serving, and a sauceboat of *sauce tartare*.

Scallops Marinière Wash 1 quart of *scallops*, and put them in a saucepan with 2 tablespoons *butter*, 1 tablespoon finely chopped *shallot*, ½ teaspoon *salt*, a little *white pepper*, and 1 cup dry *white wine*. Bring the liquid to a boil, and simmer the scallops for 6–7 minutes. Remove the scallops to a heated serving platter. Reduce the liquid to one-third original quantity, add 1 cup *cream sauce*, and bring it to a boil. Mix 2 beaten *egg yolks* with ½ cup *light cream* and a little of the hot sauce, and return it to the pan. Bring the sauce gradually to the boiling point, stirring it constantly, but do not allow it to boil. Add 1 tablespoon chopped *parsley* and any scallop juice which may have drained into the bottom of the serving dish, correct the seasoning with salt, and pour the sauce over the scallops.

MUSSEL COOKERY

The rules for preparing mussels are simple. As with other bivalves, discard those with open shells; the live mussel keeps its mouth tightly closed. Each mussel must then be thoroughly scrubbed to remove the mud and grass that clings to the shells. You must trim off the byssus or "beard" either with a blunt knife or with a stiff brush. Mussels are usually served in their shells, either whole or half-shell, and the easiest way to eat them is with a small fish fork. When all the mussels have been consumed you can spoon out the remaining sauce, drink the sauce left in the shells, and wipe the bowl clean with a piece of bread.

Moules Marinière Scrub 36 *mussels* clean, and wash them in running water. Place them in a saucepan with 2 tablespoons finely chopped *shallots* and 1 cup *white wine*. Cover the pan, and cook the bivalves for 6–8 minutes or until they open. Remove one shell from each mussel, leaving the meat attached to the other shell. Put the mussels in a serving dish. Reduce the liquor in the pan to half its original quantity and thicken it with *manié butter* made by creaming together 2 tablespoons *butter* and ½ teaspoon *flour*. Roll the pan to swirl in the butter. Add 1 more tablespoon butter, 1 tablespoon chopped *parsley*, and if desired ½ teaspoon finely chopped *chives*. Correct the seasoning with *salt*, add a little freshly ground *pepper*, and pour the sauce over the mussels.

If a richer sauce is preferred, thicken the sauce with ¼ cup *cream*.

Or, if a very plain sauce is preferred, reduce the cooking liquor to half of the original quantity and then complete the preparation of the sauce with 2 or 3 tablespoons of *butter*. Serve immediately.

Moules Poulette Scrub three dozen *mussels* clean, and wash them in running water. Put them in a saucepan with 2 tablespoons finely chopped *shallots*, 6 mushrooms, thinly sliced, and 1 cup *white wine*. Cover the pan, and cook for about 6–8 minutes, or until the shells open. Remove one shell from each mussel, leaving the meat attached to the other shell, and arrange them in a serving dish. Reduce the liquor in the pan to half its original quantity and add ½ cup *cream sauce*. Bring the sauce to a boil and add 1 *egg yolk* beaten with ¼ cup *cream* and a little of the sauce. Cook slowly, stirring briskly, until the sauce is well blended and slightly thickened, but do not allow it to boil. Correct the seasoning with *salt*, add a little freshly ground *pepper* and 1 tablespoon chopped *parsley*, and, when you are satisfied with the flavor, pour the sauce over the mussels.

TROUT AND SALMON COOKERY

Blue Trout The color of the blue trout comes from the same lubricant that makes a fish slippery—the film that keeps the trout waterproof. Without it he would drown, and without it there can be no blue. Consequently, the idea has existed that the trout must be cooked alive. Something is always lost in translation, but this calculated sadism grew out of the phrase "in a live condition," meaning that the trout should not be washed or scaled before going into the vinegar bath. Actually, your fish should be quite dead, but killed and gutted an instant before bluing. Numerous recipes suggest running a cord through the trout from mouth to tail, or piercing the fish's head with a toothpick and trussing it tail to head. The idea, one would gather, is to serve curved trout, and in a manner of speaking the curve is essential but the methods are contradictory. The final gesture of a freshly killed trout is to curl, and it will do this with no help from the chef. String and toothpicks are necessary only when the fish has been dead for many hours and the muscle tissue will no longer contract.

The ideal-size trout, both from an eating and handling standpoint, are fish of about 10 inches in length. The first step in making *truite au bleu* is to brew a good white wine court bouillon. Bring to a boil 1 quart *water*, 1 quart dry *white wine*, 1 tablespoon *salt*, 2 small *carrots* and 2 medium *onions* thinly sliced, 12 bruised *peppercorns*, 2 *cloves*, and a bouquet garni composed of 2 large *bay leaves*, 4 green *celery tops*, 6 sprigs of *parsley*, and 1 sprig of *thyme*. Simmer the liquid for 30 minutes.

In the meantime dilute some *tarragon vinegar* in another kettle at the ratio of two-thirds vinegar to one-third water and bring to a boil. When the bouillon is fragrant, strain off the vegetables, and you are ready to blue your trout.

Truite au Bleu With large kitchen tongs, grasp each trout firmly by the jaw and lower it in the hot vinegar, and when properly blue, place it in the fast-boiling court bouillon. The bouillon will cease bubbling for a few minutes, but when it comes to a boil again wait another 3 minutes, then remove the pot from the fire and cover. Let this stand for about 15 minutes, and your trout is cooked. The fish should be removed carefully with a spatula and drained. Classically, blue trout are smothered in hollandaise sauce and served with marble-sized new potatoes bathed in butter and garnished with parsley.

Trout for Young Girls Prepare the fish as you would to make blue trout, and set them aside to cool and drain.

Make a sauce Chatillon-Plessis by mixing two-thirds *tomato purée* (thinned and passed through a tammy) and one-third *mayonnaise*, a few shakes of *cayenne* pepper, and the juice of 1 *lemon*. Arrange your serving platter with a bed of *parsley*, garnishing the edges with lemon wedges. Place the fish on platter, and smother with sauce. This must be served very, very cold.

Trout with Grapes Dress a 2–3-pound brook, brown, or rainbow *trout*, and brush the fish with *lemon juice*. Poach in *court bouillon* for 15 minutes (or until done), and remove to a platter. Peel the skin off, leaving the fish whole. Combine ¼ cup of *sugar* with the grated rind of 1 *lemon* and its juice, and 2 *egg yolks*. To this, add 1 cup of the court bouillon and cook until thickened, stirring it to a smooth sauce. Pour the sauce over the trout, and decorate with 1 cup of chilled, halved, seedless *grapes* and a tablespoon of chopped *parsley*.

Trout Sauté à la Meunière This is a good method for cooking small whole trout or yellow perch. After dressing and drying, dip the fish in *milk* seasoned with *salt;* then dredge them in *flour*. Heat ¼ inch of *peanut oil* in a large frying pan, and brown the fish on both sides. Remove the fish to a serving dish, and sprinkle them with *pepper, lemon juice,* and chopped *parsley*. Garnish each piece of fish with a slice of lemon. Pour off the oil in which the fish was browned, and in the same pan melt 1 tablespoon *butter* for each serving. Cook the butter to a rich, hazelnut brown, and pour over the trout.

In sautéing fish, be sure that the pan is large enough so that the fish will not be crowded. Crowding causes the fish to steam, and they will not have the crispy surface that is a distinguishing characteristic of this method of cooking fish. If necessary, use two pans.

Trout Mousse Pass 1½ pounds of brook, brown, or rainbow *trout* fillets through the finest blade of the food chopper three times. Work in the unbeaten whites of 3 *eggs*, and rub the mixture through a sieve. Add gradually 1 cup heavy *cream*, *salt* and *pepper* to taste, and a dash of cayenne. Pour the mixture into a buttered mold, set the mold in a pan of hot water, and bake the mousse for about 20 minutes in a moderate oven (350°F.). The mousse should be set, but not dry. Unmold the mousse on a hot platter, and serve it with *shrimp* sauce (*which see*).

Stuffed Lake Trout in Port Wine For this dish you must have 4–5-pound *lake trout* and an extra trout, or preferably both a trout and a walleye, to make the stuffing. Grind (in blender or food grinder) ¾ pound of trout fillet and ½ pound of walleye fillet with ¼ cup *cold water*. Mix fish with ¼ pound of soft *butter* (use wooden spoon or mixer). Blend slowly with 3 *egg whites*. Blend in 1½ *eggs*. Beat with wooden spoon until fluffy. Add ½ teaspoon *salt*, pinch *white pepper*. Cover; chill mixture until firm. Fill the salted cavity of the trout with stuffing. Tie string 4–5 times around body of fish to hold secure. Cover bottom of roasting pan with ¾ cup each chopped *celery, onions, carrots;* place fish on vegetables. Add to pan 2 cups dry white *wine fish stock*. Bake uncovered 45–50 minutes at 400°F., basting with melted butter. Remove fish to warm platter. Discard string. Strain pan juices into saucepan; bring to boil. Add 1 tablespoon *cornstarch* mixed with little water. Stir in 2 cups *heavy cream*, 5 ounces *port wine, salt* and *pepper* to taste. Serve with slices of fish.

Fish Stock Add to pan bones, heads, and tails of *filleted trout* and *walleye*, 2 cups each *water*, dry white

wine, 1 *bay leaf*, pinch *thyme*, 2 stalks *parsley*, ¼ cup each chopped *carrots, onions, celery*, few pinches *salt, white pepper*. Cover; simmer 30 minutes; strain out fish bones; reserve stock for sauce.

Baked Salmon Use a glass baking dish which must first be rubbed with *butter*. Flake the *salmon* either fresh or leftover into dish and season well with *cayenne* pepper. Add *sour cream* and grated *cheese*, which you must mix thoroughly with the salmon; then sprinkle *bread crumbs* and pats of butter on top. Bake in low oven for about forty minutes.

Cold Poached Salmon Let the *salmon* steaks simmer for about 10 minutes in a court bouillon. Turn just once. Arrange on a serving dish, and place in refrigerator to chill. Cover with green *mayonnaise*, and garnish with fresh, pitted black *cherries*.

Poached Whole Salmon This method can also be used for large trout, cod, striped bass, or halibut as well as salmon. The only limitation is the size of the fish kettle. Begin by wrapping the entire *salmon* in cheese cloth. Lay the fish on a rack in a fish kettle, and add strained vegetable court bouillon to cover. Bring the court bouillon to a boil, and simmer the fish for 40–50 minutes, or about 10–12 minutes per pound. The fish is done when the flesh can be lifted cleanly from the bones. The fish may be allowed to cool in the cooking liquid. In this case, the cooking time should be shortened accordingly. Carefully remove the cheesecloth, and lay the fish on a napkin on a warm platter. The napkin will absorb any excess liquid. Serve hot with *hollandaise sauce*, or chill and serve with *mayonnaise*.

Salmon in Aspic In a saucepan poach chinook, silver, or Atlantic *salmon* steaks, about an inch thick, in white wine court bouillon for about 10 minutes, or until the flesh flakes readily. Put each steak in a shallow, individual serving dish, and garnish it with thin slices of *cucumber* and hard-cooked *egg*, and leaves of fresh *tarragon*.

Make an aspic by soaking 2 tablespoons *gelatin* in ¼ cup cold *water* for 10 minutes and dissolving it in 4 cups hot white wine court bouillon. Cool the aspic, and when it begins to set, brush the decorated fish steaks with the aspic, and set them in the refrigerator to chill. When the glaze is firm, fill the dishes with aspic, and return them to the refrigerator. Serve the jellied fish with *green mayonnaise*.

SHAD COOKERY

Boneless Shad Filleting a shad is so difficult that some people prefer to cook them so that the bones become so soft that they are edible. Clean the *shad*, and brush it inside and out with melted *butter*. Sprinkle the fish thoroughly with *salt* and *pepper*. Wrap several strips of *bacon* around the fish, and place it in a pan lined with oiled brown paper (brush the paper with any *vegetable shortening*). Add two cups of water, and cover the pan. Preheat the oven to 450°F.; then lower to 225°F., put the shad in the oven, and cook it 1½ hours to the pound (a 4-pound shad requires 6 hours). Add more water if necessary.

Shad Cookout The shad cookout is uniquely a New England tradition. Edward T. Bement is the modern-day master. Mr. Bement has been with the Connecticut Board of Fisheries and Game for thirty years, and the annual cookout which he conducts for department personnel is a celebrated event. About the time shad arrive at Enfield

Dam, everybody in the Nutmeg State is trying to wangle an invitation to Bement's festivities.

Preparation The firebox is made of concrete blocks. Bement constructs the box three blocks high, and the length of the box is dependent on the number of shad he has to prepare. The bottom of the box is lined with solid cobblestones, and this bed is approximately six inches high. This provides the proper elevation from his grates to the fire. The width of the firebox is thirty inches to conform with his grating, which is made of concrete reinforcing rods. His broilers, which are laid on the grate, are made of turkey wire using hog rings as hinges. Bement uses 30-by-18-inch broilers so that he can turn several shad at once and avoid having the fillets fall apart. Approximately two hours before he puts the fillets on, he starts the fire on the cobblestone bed and uses hickory or apple wood. Either wood is essential for two reasons. They are hard, close-grained, and slow-burning, which allows him to make one fire and not have to add wood during the cooking process; secondly, either wood imparts just the right smoke flavor to shad.

Cooking the Shad Spread boned *shad fillets* out on aluminum foil skinside down. Paint with *lemon juice*, using a pastry brush to get them evenly covered. Add *salt, pepper,* and *paprika.* Dip in a bath of *Wesson oil*, draining off excess; then place shad on broilers. The broilers are placed on a grate so the shad are skin side up. Broil fish approximately twelve minutes or until light golden-brown. Next turn broilers so the shad fillets are skinside down, and cook for ten minutes on this side.

Cooking the Roe Lay shad *roe* out on aluminum foil. *Salt* and *pepper.* Fry some good country *bacon*, and save the fat in dripping pans. Now place the roe in pans of bacon fat that is ¼ inch deep. Put the pans on the broilers, and cook slowly with flat side of roe down until brown. Turn and brown on the other side. Roe should be served with crisp strips of bacon and *parsley.*

In case you are a beginner at shad fishing and can't distinguish a buck from a roe, then a simple test will dispel any uncertainty. With thumb and forefinger massage the belly toward the vent. If milt (a white substance) is extruded, it's a buck. If tiny red eggs pop out, then it's a roe. With a little experience you can identify the female visually as the vent of a roe is reddish and protrudes slightly, whereas the vent of a buck remains white.

Shad Roe Casserole with Herbs Rinse 4 *shad roe* carefully, and lay them side by side in a shallow, earthenware casserole. Pour over them 2 cups each of dry *white wine* and *fish stock* or *water*, and season with 1 teaspoon *tarragon vinegar* and *salt* and *white pepper* to taste. Bring the stock to a boil, and simmer the roe gently for 12 minutes. Drain them, reserving the cooking stock for another use. Dry the roe on a paper towel, and roll them in warm *olive oil*. Return them to the casserole and pour over them ¼ cup melted *butter*, seasoned with 1 teaspoon each of *chervil, chives, parsley, onion* and *shallots*, all finely minced, a generous pinch each of *rosemary* and *marjoram* and a tiny pinch of powdered *thyme*. Add 6 tablespoons *sherry*, cover casserole, and braise the roe in a moderate oven (350°F.) for 10 minutes. Serve in the casserole.

SOLE COOKERY

This family of flatfishes of which the English sole *Solea solea* is highly esteemed as a food in Europe. The term "sole" has come to encompass any number of flatfishes in North American waters. On our Atlantic Coast both the winter and summer flounders are often marketed as "fillet of sole." On the Pacific Coast the term is more definitely used in the petrale sole, lemon sole, rex sole, and rock sole. These flatfishes are not true soles. Nevertheless they are all widely appreciated as seafood, and sole cookery is one of the classic forms of culinary art. There are probably more than one hundred recipes for preparing sole of which thirty are considered basic.

Methods of Preparation

Grilled	Dipped in plain flour, brushed in butter, and grilled
Fried	Dipped in plain flour, then in egg and milk, then bread crumbs, and fried in deep oil
Duglere	Baked in wine and vegetable sauce
Dieppoise	Poached in fish stock, served in cream sauce with mussels, shrimp, mushrooms, and puff pastry
Meunière	Floured, sprinkled with *fines herbes*, and cooked in *beurre noir*
Mornay	Steamed in white wine; with cheese sauce
Portugaise	Steamed; fresh tomato pulp (seeds and skins removed); shallots; white wine
Colbert	Fried, with the back opened up, and frozen *maître d'hôtel* butter
Bonne Femme	Steamed; with sliced mushrooms, *fines herbes*, and white wine sauce
Florentine	Steamed; lying on crisp leaf spinach, with a cheese sauce covering
Maison	Steamed; with mushrooms, *fines herbes*, shallots, wine, and pulped fresh tomato
Pommery	Sole Meunière, with apples, *beurre noir*
St. Germain	Grilled, with covering of bread crumbs, *maître d'hôtel* butter
Véronique	Steamed; served with muscat grapes, halved, seeded, and skinned; sauterne sauce
Au Goujon	Cut into fine strips and fried; served with *sauce tartare*
Marguéry	Steamed, white wine sauce, with shrimps, oysters, mussels, and mushrooms
Sicilian	Sole Meunière, with anchovy, *beurre noir*
Italian	Steamed, mushrooms chopped fine, cream and butter sauce
Palace	Steamed, sliced mushrooms, *fines herbes*, tomato, asparagus, and white wine sauce
Francaise	Steamed, white wine sauce, asparagus
Dubarry	Steamed, with two separate sauces, white wine sauce and *sauce Américaine*
Pavé	Steamed, sliced mushrooms, *fines herbes*, white wine sauce, and *sauce Américaine*
Maryland	Steamed, white wine sauce, with tomato, asparagus, and truffles
Egyptienne	Poached in fish stock, mushrooms, and truffles, chopped fine on sliced *aubergine* (egg plant), white wine, shallots, chopped parsley sauce and *sauce Américaine*

Note: If paddlefish contains roe, it can be prepared as caviar (see Caviar).

1. Remove head (figure A) and viscera.

2. Cut off dorsal, anal, and ventral fins.

3. Take sharp knife and carefully cut around caudal peduncle (figure B), but do **not** cut through cartilaginous backbone.

4. Hold body of fish firmly and twist tail (figure C) until the cartilaginous backbone breaks. At this point start to pull (figure D); this will remove the long spinal cord. Be very careful not to break it, as its contained fluid imparts undesirable flavor to meat.

5. Lay fish flat on cutting board and split fish through center (figure E), making two large fillets.

6. Take fillets and carefully cut all the cartilage away; make certain none is left or meat will be inedible.

7. Lay fillet skin side down. Using a sharp knife, start at the tail, cutting parallel to the board. Free meat from skin (figure G) after skin is removed. Trim **all** red or dark meat away from fillet and discard. Remaining white meat should be chunked and deep fried.

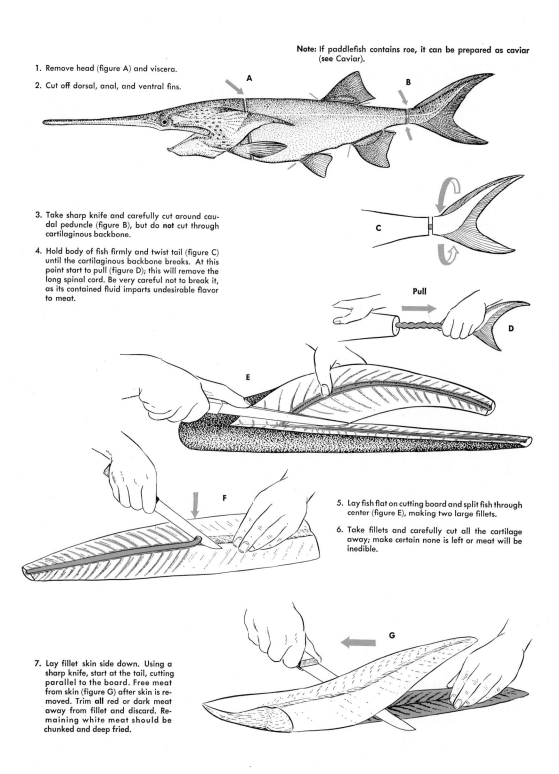

How to Clean a Paddlefish

Normande	Steamed; sauce is white wine, cream, butter, and garnished with fried scampi, button mushrooms, and lobster claw
Walewska	Steamed; with slices of lobster, marsala (or dry sherry) sauce, and grated cheese
Cubat	Steamed; mushrooms and truffles chopped fine, flared in brandy; sherry sauce; grated cheese
Cardinal	Steamed; claw of lobster; button mushrooms; lobster sauce with brandy
Capri	Sole Meunière; with sliced bananas and chutney sauce
Gondu	Steamed; white wine sauce; grated cheese; asparagus tips

Sole Recipes Many sole recipes are difficult to utilize at home because of the difficulty in obtaining all the ingredients. However, the following are noteworthy for their simplicity.

Fillet of Sole Capri (from Wheeler's Seafood Restaurant, London)

One hour before cooking, brush 4 *sole fillets* with *lemon juice;* season lightly with *salt, cayenne pepper,* and a trace of *mace.* Fold each fillet once, lengthwise. Keep cool.

Melt 1 tablespoon *butter* in a pan; blot fish dry, and cook very lightly on both sides, turning with care. Split 4 *bananas* lengthwise, cut them in half, moisten them with lemon juice, roll them heavily in *fine sugar,* then dust them with *powdered clove* and *cinnamon.* Melt ½ stick butter in a second pan, and when butter bubbles put in the bananas; brown lightly on both sides, covered. When the fillets are lightly browned, pour over them ½ cup *dry white wine.* Put a *bay leaf* on each fillet, cover with waxed paper or aluminum foil, and poach in a 350°F. oven for 15 minutes or so. Remove with care, discard bay leaf, arrange on hot platter, and keep warm in open oven. Arrange the spiced bananas all around the fish. To the butter left in the banana pan, add 2 tablespoons *Major Grey's chutney* with the fruit part chopped fine, 2 tablespoons *sherry,* and 2 teaspoons *lemon juice.* Simmer gently, stirring until all is blended into a fairly thick, spicy sauce. Pour over fish; serve immediately.

Fillet de Sole Paysanne Melt ½ tablespoon *butter* in a shallow pan, add 2 medium *carrots* and 2 medium *onions,* both thinly sliced, cover the pan, and cook very slowly until the vegetables are soft, but not at all brown. Add 1 tablespoon butter and arrange the *fish fillets* on the vegetables. Add ½ teaspoon chopped *parsley* and 1 cup *fish stock, white wine,* or *water.* Cover the fish with a circle of buttered paper with a tiny hole in the center, bring the liquid to a boil, cover the pan and simmer for 10–12 minutes, depending upon the thickness of the fillets. Remove the fish to a serving dish, and cook the liquid until it is reduced to ⅓ its original volume. Thicken with *beurre manié,* made by kneading 1 tablespoon butter with 1 teaspoon *flour.* Blend well and correct the seasoning with *salt* and *pepper.* Pour the sauce over the fish, vegetables and all.

RAY AND SKATE COOKERY

Rays and Skates The edible portions of rays and skates are the wings, which are generally similar to sea scallops. Their flavor and texture can be improved if, after cleaning and washing, the wings are covered with cold, slightly salted water and allowed to soak for at least twenty-four hours (in the refrigerator). This preliminary preparation is usually followed by boiling in herbs or a white wine court bouillon.

Raie au Beurre Noir Wash and scrape 1 pair of *skate wings,* weighing about 4 pounds; then cut each into 2 pieces. Place in a large saucepan, add *boiling water* to cover, and drain at once. Now cover with *cold water,* and add a bouquet garni composed of 1 large *bay leaf,* 1 sprig of *thyme,* a handful of fresh *parsley* and a handful of *green celery leaves* (tops), tied with white kitchen thread, also 1 medium-sized *onion,* sliced, a bud of *garlic,* 2 tablespoons of *vinegar,* and 6 *peppercorns,* freshly bruised. Gradually bring to boiling point. Let boil 1 minute or two, lower the flame, and simmer very gently for 20 minutes, or until fish appears to flake, skimming thoroughly. Drain, place in a towel, and remove the skin from both sides and edges of the wings. Return to the cooking broth, and keep hot. When just ready to serve, melt and heat ½ cup of *butter* in a frying pan until foaming; immediately add 1 tablespoon of chopped parsley, 2 tablespoons of *capers,* a few grains of *cayenne* or *tabasco sauce,* and pour sizzling hot over the well-drained skate wings. Garnish with plain boiled *potatoes,* parsley, and *lemon* quarters.

CRAB COOKERY

Oyster Crabs for Poor Young Men Brown 4 chopped *shallots* in *butter.* Add 2 cups of *oyster crabs* with 6 large, fresh, sliced *mushrooms.* Keep the heat low. Next add ½ cup of fresh light *cream,* ½ cup of *brandy,* and ½ cup of *Madeira wine.* Add the yolks of 2 *eggs* which should first be stirred and warmed with a little of the pan juices in a cup. Cook for 15–20 minutes on a low heat, stirring frequently.

Softshell Crabs To clean a softshelled crab, for immediate cooking or freezing, plunge a small knife between the eyes, lift up the pointed parts of the top shell, and pry out the spongy material underneath. Then pull off the apron on the underside. Wash the crabs, dry them thoroughly, and cook them at once. They are generally sautéed, broiled, or fried in deep fat.

Sautéed Softshelled Crabs Clean *softshelled crabs,* wash them, and dry them thoroughly. In a large skillet heat a generous amount of *butter* until it is very hot, add the crabs, and sauté them quickly until they are golden-brown on both sides. Season the crabs with *salt, pepper, lemon juice,* and chopped *parsley,* and pour over them the brown butter from the pan. If there is not enough butter, add more to the pan and cook the butter until it is brown.

Fried Softshelled Crabs Clean *softshelled crabs,* wash them, and dry them thoroughly. Dip them first in *flour,* then in beaten *egg* to which a teaspoon of *water* has been added, and finally in fine, dry *bread crumbs.* Fry the crabs in deep, hot *fat* (375°F.) until they are brown. Serve them with *sauce tartare* and *lemon* wedges.

Crabmeat Creole First prepare the sauce: Sauté 6 *mushrooms,* sliced, in 2 tablespoons *butter* for 5 minutes. Add 1 *shallot* and 1 small *green pepper,* both chopped, and cook them slowly until the green pepper is soft. Add 2 *tomatoes,* peeled, seeded, and chopped, 1 *pimiento,*

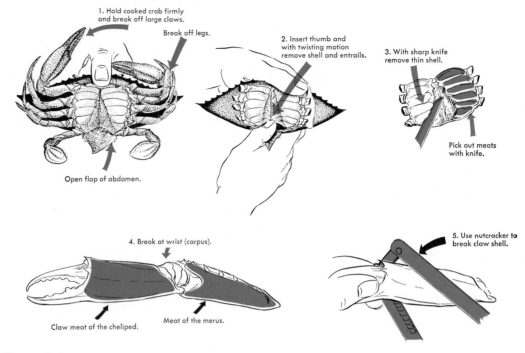

1. Hold cooked crab firmly and break off large claws.

Break off legs.

2. Insert thumb and with twisting motion remove shell and entrails.

3. With sharp knife remove thin shell.

Pick out meats with knife.

Open flap of abdomen.

4. Break at wrist (carpus).

5. Use nutcracker to break claw shell.

Claw meat of the cheliped.

Meat of the merus.

How to Clean a Crab

chopped, and ½ cup *tomato sauce*. Cook all together until the mixture is well-combined, and add ½ cup *cream sauce*.

In another pan, sauté 1½ pounds cooked *crab meat*, flaked and picked over, in 2 tablespoons *butter* for 5 minutes. Combine the crab meat with the sauce, add *salt* and *pepper* to taste, and serve on rice.

King Crab Bordelaise Sauté lightly in *olive oil* 2 *shallots* and 1 clove *garlic*, finely chopped. Add ½ cup *red wine* and a pinch of freshly ground *black pepper*, and reduce the sauce to half its original volume. Add 1 cup *brown sauce* and simmer, stirring it from time to time, for 5 minutes longer. Skim off any excess fat.

Put 1 pound *crab legs* into a flameproof dish fitted with a glass cover. Pour the bordelaise sauce over the crab, and add a few slices of *raw beef marrow*. Cover the dish and simmer the crab legs for about 10 minutes. Serve them piping hot.

PICKLING AND CANNING

Pickled Eels Clean and skin the *eels*, and cut into pieces about ⅝ inch long. Wash, drain, dredge in fine *salt*, and allow to stand for 1 hour. Rinse off the salt, wipe the pieces dry, and rub with a cut clove of *garlic*. Brush with melted *butter* or *salad oil*, and broil until the surface of the pieces is a light brown. Place pieces of cooked eel on absorbent paper. When cool, pack them in layers in a crock with a scattering of *sliced onion, allspice, bay leaves, mustard seed, whole cloves, peppers*, and *mace* between the layers of fish. Then weight the mixture down to keep it compressed. Store the crock for 24 hours. Add 6 percent *acid distilled vinegar* in proportion of 3 parts vinegar to 1 part water sufficient to cover the pieces. Cover the crock tightly, and allow to stand 48 hours

before using. For 10 pounds of eels the ingredients are as follows:

Distilled vinegar	1 quart	Mustard seed	½ ounce
Water	1 pint	Cloves	½ ounce
Allspice	1 ounce	Black peppers	½ ounce
Bay leaves	1 ounce	Mace	½ ounce

Russian Sardines Wash and scale 10 pounds of small *herring* (7–10 inches), remove the gills and as much of the intestines as possible, and pull them out through the gill flap without tearing the throat or belly. Rinse again, drain, and pack in a crock. Cover with 3 parts distilled *vinegar* and 1 part *water*. Allow to stand for 12 hours. Make up a mixture of the following ingredients (the spices should be finely ground and thoroughly blended):

Fine *salt*	2 pounds	*Bay leaves*	½ ounce
Powdered *sugar*	1 pound	*Cloves*	½ ounce
Allspice	1 ounce	*Ginger*	½ ounce
Pepper	1 ounce	*Hops*	½ ounce
Saltpeter	½ ounce	*Nutmeg*	½ ounce

After the fish have drained, dredge them in the mixture, and pack in a crock, belly up. A small additional amount of the mixture may be scattered between each layer. The layers should be packed at right angles to each other, with the top one packed backs up. Scatter the balance of the spice-curing mixture over the top layer, and weight it down so that the fish will be entirely covered when the brine forms. Some people also scatter diced onions, ground or sliced horseradish, and capers between each layer. The amount required for 10 pounds of small herring is ½ pound *onions*, ¼ pound *horseradish*, and a small bottle of *capers* (about 2½ ounces). The fish are allowed to cure for 10 days to 2 weeks before using. Under proper storage conditions they should keep for several months or longer.

HOME CANNING

Tuna Fillet the tuna and carefully slice out the dark meat. Do *not* use dark meat. Cut white meat in chunks, wash well, and soak overnight in saltwater.

The next day, wash well in clear cold water, patting dry the chunks of white meat, and pack into jars. If using pint jars, add ½ teaspoon of *salt* and ½ teaspoon of Wesson or Mazola *oil*; screw jar top tight. If using quart jars, add 1 teaspoon salt and 1 teaspoon oil.

Pack jars in hot water baths, and cook for 3 hours at just boiling point. If using pressure cooker, cook for 1½ hours at 15 pounds pressure. Let cool in pots; test covers for tightness, and then store for future use.

POPULAR FISH RECIPES

Broiled Sea Bass with Fennel Season cavity of dressed 2–3-pound *sea bass* with *salt* and *pepper*. Fill with 1 cup *fennel stalks*, cut into 2-inch pieces, 4 tablespoons melted *butter*, salt, pepper, (or a mixture of 2 stalks celery split lengthwise and cut into 2-inch pieces, ¾ teaspoon ground fennel, butter, salt, pepper). Close with skewers; rub outside of fish well with sweet butter and *ground fennel*. Broil each side 8–9 minutes, or until done, turning once. Flambé with ¼ cup heated *Pernod* or *brandy* (optional). Serve fish with melted butter poured over each serving and with a side dish of boiled potatoes. (This is the recipe for *Loupe de Mer au Fenouil* popular in France. Although the *loupe de mer* (*Roccus labrax*) is not available in United States waters, sea bass, striped bass, and various snappers may be substituted.)

Fillet of Striped Bass, Bonne Femme *Butter* a flat oven dish. Cover the bottom with finely chopped *shallots* and *parsley*; then lay the *bass* fillets in the dish. Allow one ½-pound fillet per person. Season with *salt* and *pepper*, and add some sliced *mushrooms*. Sprinkle the fish with *white wine* and *fish broth*, enough to make a thin layer of liquid in the dish. Bake 10 minutes in a hot oven; when done, the fish will flake with a fork. Remove fish to heated serving platter, and keep hot. Beat 3 *egg yolks* with a little of the sauce; then stir yolk mixture into rest of sauce. Add a piece of butter, and stir over low flame until thickened. Pour sauce over the fish.

Striped Bass with Oyster Stuffing Dress and scale a 6–8-pound *striped bass*. Rub thoroughly inside and out with *allspice, thyme, clove, salt,* and *bayleaf*, all minced very fine. Make a stuffing by taking 1 dozen *oysters;* 1 cup of stale *bread crumbs*, wet and squeezed of all water; one large *onion*, chopped fine; ½ tablespoonful of *salt* and *black pepper* to taste. Mix well, and fry in a pan with a tablespoonful of butter. Stuff the body of the fish, and sew up with soft thread. Lard well, and, after rubbing thoroughly with the *lard*, place in the oven. Pour over immediately 1 cup of warm water, and let the fish bake. In the meantime prepare the following sauce: take 1 large tablespoonful of *butter*, 1 large chopped *onion*, 1 sprig of *thyme*, 1 of *bay leaf*. Brown the onion and butter, being careful not to burn, and put in 3 large *tomatoes*. Add the chopped herbs; brown, and add the pint of oyster water, which has been heated by blanching the oysters. (Blanching means to place the oysters on the fire in their own water and heat thoroughly without boiling.) Season the sauce with pepper and salt to taste. Put the bass in the dish in which it is to be served, and garnish with the oysters, placing them over the fish and adding mushroom caps as desired. After garnishing the fish, pour the sauce over all and set in the oven a few minutes longer and serve hot.

Broiling under the grill or on charcoal is a good method for treating fatty fishes as well as crustaceans. Fish should be basted with butter, oil, or a complimentary sauce while cooking

Deep-Fried Bluegills Although some mighty fancy recipes have been concocted in the past for cooking panfish, the favorite method of preparation is old-fashioned deep-frying. Try making bream chips the next time you get a string of bluegills. Fillet the bream by making a crosscut just above the tail with a sharp flat knife.

The blade should just touch the backbone, then holding the tail with your free hand, run the knife along the backbone toward the gills. Now, with the knife angling in toward the head, make a slice from behind the pectoral fin which lifts that side free. Lay the fillet scaly side down, and, holding it in place at the very end with one finger, cut through the fillet to the skin. Again, run the blade forward, separating the skin from the meat. Although you may waste a smidgin, it helps to trim out the rib cage so you can just forget about the bones. This will leave you with a solid piece of white fillet. Cut the fillet in 2–3-inch strips. While the cooking oil (which is an inch deep in an iron skillet) is reaching a heat just short of smoking, roll the fillets in some good corn meal. Yellow meal is all right, but the white, waterground, unbolted and unsifted, is the kind preferred in the South. Some people drop the fish in a beaten egg before dipping in the meal.

Assuming that you have all the fixings on the table and the guests seated, drop the meal-powdered fillets in the hot oil one by one. With the oil at the correct temperature, the fish will get a crunchy jacket almost immediately, which keeps the oil out and the succulent flavor in. Don't overcook. As soon as one side is golden, flip each piece over and stand by with the spatula. When finished, drop the cooked pieces on a sheet of absorbent paper, and sprinkle them with salt and pepper. Onion salt or, if you prefer, garlic salt adds a point of flavor. Serve immediately. You can also make chips of other panfish, and if there's any trick to getting mouthwatering results, it's frying at the correct temperature. By the thermometer that would be 425°F.

Walleye in White Wine Clean and wash two small fish. If they are larger than 3 pounds, you will have to increase the amount of stuffing which is as follows: 1 tablespoon of finely chopped *parsley*, a clove of *garlic*, and a *shallot*, both finely chopped. For bulk, take 2 cups of *bread crumbs*, and soak them in a little *milk*. Then add ¼ pound of *butter*. Apply the *salt* and *pepper*. When all is mixed, use an *egg yolk* for binding.

Essentially, the walleye is cooked in a shallow baking dish, because the entire fish must rest on a bed of *onions* which you first chop and sauté in butter. The onions should be yellowed and not browned by cooking. Lay the fish on the onions, and cover them with a dry *white wine*. Put the dish in a moderate oven for about 30 minutes; then remove the pan and pour off the juices into a saucepan. The juices must then be reduced and thickened by warming with a lump or two of butter and a tablespoon of *flour*. You might also add another touch of wine at this point to stimulate the sauce. Put the liquid back over the fish and the fish back in a now very hot oven. Another 5–10 minutes should suffice.

Tuna Fish Amandine Blanch and sliver ½ cup *almonds*. Set oven to preheat to 350°F. Empty 2 cans (7 ounces each) *tuna fish* and *juice* of 1 can into baking dish. Separate into large chunks. Add 1 crushed clove *garlic*, 4 tablespoons *lemon juice*, ⅛ teaspoon *pepper*. Combine. Melt 2 tablespoons *butter*, add almonds, brown lightly.

Pour over tuna fish. Bake 15 minutes, or until hot, almonds toasted.

Walleye Fishcakes For each pound of *walleye fillets* use 1 small *onion*, and pass both through a meat grinder twice. Place the fish and onion mixture in a bowl, and add ½ cup *milk*, the yolks of 2 *eggs*, 1½ teaspoons *salt*, and a scant ¼ teaspoon *pepper*. Beat with an electric mixer for 10–15 minutes. Fold in the *egg whites*, beaten to a peak. Take a heaping tablespoon of the mixture, dip it in seasoned *flour*, and shape into small cakes. Sauté the cakes in *butter* until they are golden-brown. When they are nicely browned, transfer them to a heavy aluminum pot, and pour in a cup of *court bouillon* to start. Steam the cakes for half an hour, adding more liquid, as it becomes necessary.

Fried Whitebait Use a deep fryer with basket for *whitebait*. Wash, drain, and pat dry between paper towels, handling the fish as little as possible as they are delicate. Do not remove the heads, tails, and insides; place a few fish at a time in a wire basket; sprinkle over with seasoned *flour*, and shake the basket to remove excess of flour. Just when ready to serve, plunge the basket in hot, clear, deep oil (375°–390°F.), and cook a scant few seconds or until delicately crisp and brown. Drain; serve on a folded napkin, the platter simply garnished with *parsley* and *lemon* quarters.

Chinese Abalone For each pound of *abalone steak*, soak 4–5 large dried *Chinese mushrooms* in hot water for 2 to 3 hours, and cut them into strips. In a skillet heat 1 cup *chicken stock*, add 4 *scallions*, sliced, ½ cup slivered *celery*, 5 *water chestnuts*, sliced, and the mushrooms, and cook for 5 minutes. With a wide knife or cleaver, flatten and tenderize abalone steak. Cut the abalone into strips and add it to the vegetables in the skillet. Add also 1 tablespoon each of *soy sauce* and *sherry*, and 2 teaspoons *potato or corn starch* dissolved in 2 tablespoons water. Cook the sauce, stirring, until it is clear and thickened. Serve with rice.

Abalone Steak Sauté à la Meunière Cut in half 2 large tenderized *abalone* steaks, about ¼ inch thick. Season the steaks with *salt* and *pepper* and dredge them with *flour*. Dip them in beaten *egg*, again in flour, and finally in the egg. Heat well in a shallow skillet ¼ cup sweet *butter* and ⅓ cup *olive oil*, and in it brown the abalone steaks on both sides. Do not overcook the steaks, or they will be tough. Remove the steaks to a serving platter. Pour off the fat, and to the pan add ¼ cup sweet butter. Cook the butter until it turns nut brown and add the juice of ½ *lemon* and 2 tablespoons chopped *parsley*. Pour the sauce over the abalone and serve at once, garnished with fried parsley and lemon wedges.

Black Bass Casserole Fillet a largemouth or smallmouth *bass*, removing all skin. Brush a shallow baking dish with *olive oil*, and rub well with a crushed *garlic clove*. Arrange fillets in dish, and sprinkle with *salt* and *pepper*. In a pan, sauté two large sliced *onions* in *butter* until blond; cover the bass with onion slices and buttered *bread crumbs*. Sprinkle with finely chopped parsley, and bake in a 350°F. oven for fifteen minutes. Crumble crisp bacon bits and additional chopped parsley leaves over the bass.

Channel Bass Vinaigrette Combine 2 quarts *water*, 3 *lemons* cut into quarters, 10 *bay leaves*, 3 stalks of *celery*, and 2 teaspoons *salt*; bring the liquid to a boil, and

Poaching is an ideal method for preparing large sections of firm-fleshed fish or whole small fish and crustaceans. A court bouillon (*see recipe*) is an essential liquid for this method

simmer it for 30 minutes. Wrap a 6–8-pound *bass* in cheesecloth, and poach it in this court bouillon for 45–60 minutes. Drain the fish, cool it slightly, and fillet it. Arrange it on the serving platter in its original form, and chill it for 2–3 hours, or overnight if possible. To 2 cups freshly made *mayonnaise*, thinned if necessary with ½ cup vinegar, add ½ cup each of celery and *green onions*, both finely chopped. Mask the fish with the mayonnaise, and garnish it with 8 hard-cooked sliced eggs, chopped *green pepper* and *parsley, capers*, and *paprika*.

Deep Fried Grouper Instead of meal or flour, use a *cake batter* which seals the fish off immediately upon contact with the hot grease. Actually, the fish will steam in its own juice inside the cake. To 4 cups of batter add 1 fresh *egg*, 2 cups of *milk*, and 1 heaping tablespoon of *sugar* (no salt). Mix well, and roll small squares of grouper in the batter. When your grease or oil is bubbling hot (about 400°F), drop the pieces in one by one, and let them get a crispy golden-brown. Remove to absorbent paper, although this will hardly be necessary.

Mullet in Tomato Mustard Sauce Put 3 tablespoons of *olive oil* in a large skillet, and arrange four *mullet fillets*. Sprinkle with *salt, pepper*, the juice of half a *lemon*, and then add a cup of dry *white wine*. Cover skillet and cook over moderate flame for 15 minutes. Remove fillets, and arrange on serving dish. To the pan juices, add 2 tablespoons of *tomato purée* and 1 tablespoon of *prepared mustard*. Mix well, and simmer for several minutes. Pour sauce over the fish, and serve hot.

Eel Vinaigrette Cut a whole, skinned American *eel*, of about 2 pounds, into 2-inch pieces. Place pieces in buttered pan on layer of 3 tablespoons each diced *onions, carrots*, ½ clove minced *garlic*. Add 1½ cups dry *white wine*, 1 teaspoon *salt*, ⅛ teaspoon *pepper*. Cover; simmer

20–25 minutes, or until eel is tender; set pan aside; let cool. (It tastes a little like firm crabmeat.) Refrigerate until well-chilled. Skin eel pieces; serve with vinaigrette sauce on lettuce bed.

Vinaigrette Sauce Mix together ¾ cup *olive oil*, 7 tablespoons *tarragon vinegar*, 1½ teaspoons *salt*, ¼ teaspoon each *pepper*, dry *mustard*, 3 tablespoons each chopped *fresh chives, parsley, dill*, 1 teaspoon *dry basil, marjoram*. About 1¼ cups.

Poached Flounder In a buttered individual casserole poach a *fillet of flounder* in ¼ cup *white wine* with 2 tablespoons *water*, 2 teaspoons finely chopped *shallot*, 1 tablespoon *lemon juice*, 1 *mushroom cap* sliced, ¼ teaspoon *salt*, and a pinch of *tarragon*, for 12 minutes. Remove the fillet to a heated serving plate, and thicken the liquid remaining in the casserole with 1 teaspoon *butter* kneaded with a scant ½ teaspoon *flour*. Bring the sauce to a boil, and add 2 tablespoons hot light *cream* and 1 beaten *egg yolk*. Mix well, and spoon the sauce over the fish. Garnish the dish with truffle slices.

Tobi-Uo No Kamaboko The flyingfish is a delicacy in many parts of the world, notably in Barbados, British West Indies, and in Japan. They are caught in large, netlike baskets by forming a chum slick which causes them to fly into the traps. As many as ten thousand are taken per boat. West Indians make a very fine flyingfish pie, but the Japanese prefer them as *Tobi-uo no kamaboko*, which is a baked fish paste. To make wash 1½ pounds of *flyingfish* fillets, and mash into a paste. Add one *egg* white, one tablespoon of *cornstarch*, ⅛ teaspoon of *Ajinomoto*, and 1½ teaspoons of *salt*. Mash the mixture once again. Pack the paste into a buttered, shallow baking dish, and sprinkle with Japanese pepper leaves or *crushed red pepper*. Bake in a hot oven for 15 minutes. Serve with a

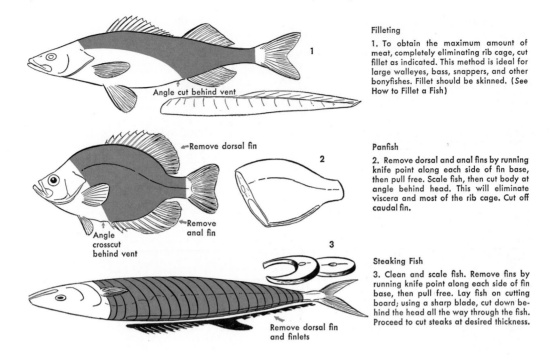

Filleting

1. To obtain the maximum amount of meat, completely eliminating rib cage, cut fillet as indicated. This method is ideal for large walleyes, bass, snappers, and other bonyfishes. Fillet should be skinned. (See How to Fillet a Fish)

Angle cut behind vent

1

Remove dorsal fin

2

Panfish

2. Remove dorsal and anal fins by running knife point along each side of fin base, then pull free. Scale fish, then cut body at angle behind head. This will eliminate viscera and most of the rib cage. Cut off caudal fin.

Angle crosscut behind vent

Remove anal fin

3

Steaking Fish

3. Clean and scale fish. Remove fins by running knife point along each side of fin base, then pull free. Lay fish on cutting board; using a sharp blade, cut down behind the head all the way through the fish. Proceed to cut steaks at desired thickness.

Remove dorsal fin and finlets

Fast Methods of Fish Preparation

shoyu sauce with *grated ginger*, or shoyu sauce with *horseradish*. This amount will serve four.

Frogs Legs Sauté Cut feet off peeled hind legs of medium-sized *frogs*; soak legs in very cold water 20 minutes (allow about ½ pound legs per portion). Dry very thoroughly. *Flour* lightly, dust with *salt* and *pepper*. In *butter* made very hot in heavy frying pan, fry very quickly, first one side, then the other. Remove to hot pan in warm oven 5 minutes to crisp. To serve, arrange legs on hot platter over some previously prepared *maître d'hôtel* butter (*butter* creamed till soft, then blended with *lemon juice* and a good lot of very finely minced *parsley*—to which such fresh chopped herbs as *tarragon*, *chives*, and *shallot* should be aded, if available).

Gefilte Fish Fillet 3½ pounds of *whitefish* and 3½ pounds of *walleye*. Save all bones, heads, and skins. Put the bones, heads, and skins in a large pot, but reserve one piece of skin. Cut into chunk-sized pieces 2 *onions*, 2 stalks of *celery*, and 5 *carrots*, and add these to the pot. Pour in 2 pints of water, and simmer for a half hour. Now grind into a bowl the fillets, passing them through a meat grinder with 2 more onions. When ground, add 2 raw *eggs*, 1 tablespoon of *matzoh meal* and *salt* and *pepper* to taste. This mixture must be chopped. Chopping in this case is a process of getting air into the ground fish and is the secret of the whole thing. It takes about 35 minutes of chopping (during which time you add 1 glass of water bit by bit) to get the texture smooth and fluffy. When correct, roll the mixture into balls which you must lower gently into the reserved broth. The extra piece of skin should now be rolled and added also. Cook slowly for 3 hours, basting the fishballs with broth. Remove fish from pot, and strain the remaining broth. Gefilte fish can be served warm, or if desired the fishballs can be placed in mold and broth poured over them. When chilled, they

will congeal in about 6 hours. Cold gefilte fish is usually served with raw grated carrots, and lemon juice, or horseradish.

Stuffed Fillet of Flounder Wash and dry 2 large skinned *flounder fillets*, of about 1 pound each. Season them with *salt, pepper,* and *lemon juice.* Chop 3 tablespoons *onion* and ¾ cup *celery.* Gently cook onions and celery in 6 tablespoons *butter* until they are soft; then blend in 4 cups *bread crumbs*, 1 teaspoon salt, 1 teaspoon *thyme*, and a pinch of pepper. Spread a casserole with 4 tablespoons butter. Lay in one of the large fillets. Spread it with the crumb stuffing mixture. Lay the other fillet on top, and fasten the fish slices together with skewers. Place 3 strips of *bacon* across the top and bake in a 350°F. oven for 40 minutes. Serve in the casserole, to 4–6.

Spanish Mackerel with Mayonnaise Sauce Cover your broiling pan with aluminum foil, and wipe a little *olive oil* over the paper to prevent the fish from adhering. Side by side, place the *mackerel fillets* skin side down. In a cup make a generous mixture of *mayonnaise* and *dry vermouth*, so that it remains thick but flavored; then spread this over each fillet in a layer about ¼ inch thick. Add *salt* and *pepper* to taste, and then sprinkle each fillet with a pinch of *fennel seed*. Broil the fillets for about 20 minutes in a moderate oven, basting them with the pan juices and a few splashes of vermouth. The mayonnaise will get a golden-brown crust on the outside, but the under liquid will blend with the fish juices and become a creamy sauce.

Squid in Mushroom Sauce Cut 2 pounds of *squid* in small pieces, and wash well. Heat ½ cup of *olive oil* in saucepan; then add a chopped *garlic* clove, 3 chopped *anchovy fillets* and a teaspoon of minced parsley. While this simmers, spill in about ½ cup of dry *white wine* or *dry vermouth*. Next, add 2 tablespoons of *tomato sauce*, a

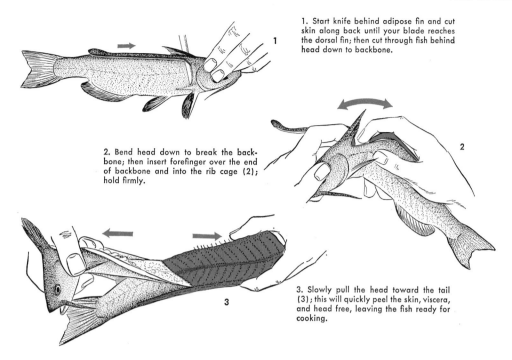

1. Start knife behind adipose fin and cut skin along back until your blade reaches the dorsal fin; then cut through fish behind head down to backbone.

2. Bend head down to break the back-bone; then insert forefinger over the end of backbone and into the rib cage (2); hold firmly.

3. Slowly pull the head toward the tail (3); this will quickly peel the skin, viscera, and head free, leaving the fish ready for cooking.

How to Skin a Catfish

generous dash of *salt* and *pepper*, a small can of mush-rooms including the juice, and then put in the squid. Cover the pan. Cook at a medium heat for about 20 minutes, then turn the flame low for another 30 minutes.

Squid Neapolitan Style Cut 2 pounds of *squid* in small pieces, and wash well. Brown a sliced clove of *garlic* in 3 tablespoons of *butter*. Remove the garlic from sauce-pan and add 1 medium can of peeled *tomatoes*, a generous spray of *salt* and *pepper*, and your squid. Cover the pan, and 10 minutes later, add a dozen chopped *black olives*, 1 tablespoon of seedless *raisins*, 1 tablespoon of chopped *pine nuts*, and a half cup of *water*. Cover the pan, and cook for another 20 minutes, or until the squid are tender. Arrange slices of *toast* in each bowl, and dip the squid and sauce over the toast just before serving.

FISH SOUP RECIPES

Cacciucco Leghorn Style In a large soup pot, place $\frac{1}{2}$ cup of *olive oil*, a clove of garlic, 1 teaspoon of chopped *parsley*, $\frac{1}{2}$ teaspoon of *sage*, and simmer gently until the garlic browns. Add one *lobster* cut in small pieces with shell, and $\frac{1}{2}$ pound of cleaned *squid* which has also been cut small. Salt and pepper, and cover the pot, and let steam for 15 minutes. Now add 2 tablespoons of *tomato paste* and a cup of *water*. To this stock add $\frac{1}{2}$ pound of *haddock* fillet cut in pieces, or $\frac{1}{2}$ pound of *halibut* fillet, and $\frac{1}{2}$ pound of *scallops* cut in quarters. Cover the pot again, and simmer for about 20 minutes, adding water only if needed. It is almost finished, so now add 2 table-spoons of dry *white wine*, and 2 tablespoons of *Marsala* or *sherry wine*, and simmer for a minute longer. Turn off the flame and make one piece of toasted *garlic bread* for each dish, and ladle your soup and fish over the toast.

Conch Chowder The old West Indian song "Conch Ain't Got No Bone" is accurate, but the meat must be pounded to tenderize it, or it can be pressure cooked for about 15 minutes. When tender the conch can be cut in strips, rolled in flour and deep fried, made into fritters, or served in chowder. Purists prefer the liquid version. It requires the meats of 6 dozen *conchs* to make a chowder big enough for eight or ten hungry people. Chop conch in small pieces. Peel a dozen *carrots*, dice them, and add to the stock. In a saucepan, fry $\frac{1}{2}$ pound of diced *salt pork*. When brown, remove pork, and save the fat in a pan. Add pork to stock. Now dice 1 pound of *onions* and several stalks of *celery*, and brown these in the pork fat. When cooked add 1 large can of *tomatoes* and 1 small can of *tomato paste*. Brown the tomatoes, and then add these vegetables to your stock. Cut up 1 clove of *garlic*, and drop in pot. Dice 2 pounds of *potatoes*, but do not put them in the stock until it has reduced by nearly half. When the stock is as thick as a chowder should be, and this takes about 3 hours of simmering, then, and only then, add the potatoes.

Fishball Soup Put $\frac{1}{2}$ pound fillet of raw *whiting* or *flounder* twice through the finest blade of the meat chop-per with 2 ounces lean *pork*. Pound this mixture in a mortar to make a smooth paste, adding as you pound 1 tablespoon each of *cornstarch* and *water* and mixing well. Shape the paste into small balls. Poach the balls in 4 cups simmering *chicken broth* for about 15 minutes. Add 2 whole *scallions* to the soup, finely chopped, 1 teaspoon *salt*, 2 tablespoons *sherry*, 1 tablespoon *vinegar*, and a little *white pepper* to taste. Serve at once.

Italian Fish Soup: Zuppa di Pesce Place in large kettle about 2 pounds of unboned fish (use about $\frac{1}{2}$ pound each *whiting*, *red snapper*, *sea bass*, *porgy*), and *shells* from $\frac{1}{2}$ pound *shrimp*; reserve shrimp. Add 1 quart *water*, 3 chopped *tomatoes*, 3 chopped cloves *garlic*, $1\frac{1}{2}$ teaspoons *salt*, $\frac{1}{4}$ teaspoon *pepper*. Cover; simmer 30 minutes. Strain. Reserve stock; discard fish fragments. Cook ½ pound diced *squid* (or *scallops*) and the reserved shrimp, cut into small pieces, in 1 tablespoon *olive oil*. Season with *salt, pepper;* set aside. Add to a soup pot 4 *leeks* cut into 1½-inch strips, 1 tablespoon *butter;* brown leeks, add 3 chopped, peeled *tomatoes,* pinch powdered *saffron,* ¾ cup *dry white wine,* 2 cups *water,* the fish stock, 2 teaspoons salt, ¼ teaspoon pepper. Cover; simmer 30 minutes. Add the squid, shrimp, stir in 3 tablespoons *heavy cream,* 1 cup cooked *vermicelli* (or *capellini*); heat gently. Serve with *rust sauce* (teaspoon or so to each serving), side dish of grated *Parmesan cheese* and French-bread slices fried in garlic butter (eat bread separately or add to soup, top with cheese). Serves 8. *For rust sauce:* blend in blender 6 cloves *garlic,* 4 *pimentos,* 2 *egg yolks,* 8 drops *Tabasco, salt, pepper;* add ⅓ cup *olive oil,* drop by drop. Stir in 2 tablespoons hot soup.

Mexican Fish Stew Remove skin of 4 lbs. *red snapper fillet;* cut in 3-inch wide pieces. Clean 8 large *shrimp;* leave in shell. Clean 8 *mussels* and 8 *clams.* Cut 2 *lobsters* in 8 pieces. Cut 8 *crab legs* open on white side. Peel and seed 6 *tomatoes;* dice, along with 2 *red* and 2 *green peppers* and 2 *red onions.* Chop 6 *shallots;* place in shallow pan with all the fish. Add ¼ tsp. each *paprika* and *saffron,* 1 tsp. *salt,* and 1 quart *dry white wine.* Cover. Bake in 450° oven for 25 minutes. Sprinkle with small bunch chopped *parsley* and 2 cloves chopped *garlic.* Serve immediately.

New England Clam Chowder In a skillet place several thick slices of *salt pork,* cover with *water,* and cook. At the same time, boil 4 medium-sized *onions* in a small pot and, in another pot, 4 medium-sized new *potatoes* with their jackets. When the salt pork is tender, save the water, then dice and brown the pork in a little fresh butter. These will be the croutons for your chowder. To the salt-pork water add a stick of *butter,* the boiled onions, which you have now ground fine, a dash of *paprika,* and a touch of *Harvey sauce.* Turn the heat low.

Now, separate the clam meats from the rest of the creature. Reserve the meats, and chop or grind the remaining parts fine, adding this plus the clam juice to the salt-pork water. Turn the heat up slightly, and allow the ingredients to thicken. By this stage, the skillet is somewhat full; so transfer the liquid to a large pot in which you have warming a quart of fresh *milk,* a can of *evaporated milk,* and a half-pint of fresh *cream.* Stir the mixture well, and just as it bubbles add the boiled potatoes, the salt pork cubes, and the clam meats.

Allow it to reheat for no more than 3 minutes—so the clams are still bay tender.

Red Snapper Soup à la Bookbinder In a kettle put the *trimmings* of the *red snapper* and some inexpensive fish and trimmings. Add 6 cups *water,* 1 cup dry *white wine,* 1 medium *onion* stuck with a few *cloves,* 6 *peppercorns,* ½ *bay leaf,* 1½ teaspoons *salt,* 2 sprigs of *parsley,* 1 *carrot* cut in thin strips, and a pinch of *thyme:* Simmer the stock for 30 minutes, and strain it. Sauté lightly in 2 tablespoons *butter,* ¼ cup *onions,* ½ cup *celery,* and 1 *green pepper,* all diced. Add the fish stock and bring the soup to a boil. Add 2 cups *sauce espagnole* (*which see*) and bring the soup to a boil again. Add 1 cup diced *red snapper,* and cook the fish until it is tender, about 12 minutes. Just before serving add 1 cup *sherry.*

Snapper Bouillabaisse Prepare a fish stock with the head of a red or mutton *snapper,* 1 sliced *onion,* a little *thyme, bay leaf,* and *parsley* and a quart and a half of *water.* When reduced to 1 pint, remove the head, strain, and set aside to be used later. Mince 3 sprigs of *thyme,* 3 sprigs of *parsley,* 3 *bay leaves,* and 3 cloves of *garlic* very finely, and mix thoroughly with 6 *allspice* finely ground.

Sautéing is done over low heat in foaming butter to crisp the outside while keeping the inside moist. Sauces and appropriate garnish can be added after the food is properly browned

Take 6 fillets of snapper of uniform size, rub well with *salt* and *pepper* and with the herb mixture till every portion is thoroughly covered and permeated. Heat 2 tablespoons of fine *olive oil* in a very large pan, and add 2 *onions* chopped fine. Lay the fish slice by slice in the pan, which must be large enough to prevent them from overlapping, and let brown for 10 minutes, turning over once. Remove fish slices from the pan and set in a dish. Pour a half bottle of *white wine* into the pan, and stir well; then add a pint can of *tomatoes*, or 6 fresh tomatoes finely sliced, and let boil thoroughly. Next add half a *lemon*, thinly sliced, and the pint of liquor in which the head of the snapper was boiled. Season well with *salt, black pepper* and *cayenne*, and let boil till reduced almost one-half, then return the fish slices to the pan, keeping them apart, and let cook 5 minutes. In the meantime chop a pinch of *saffron* exceedingly fine, dissolve well in a little of the sauce in which the fish is boiling, and at the end of the 5 minutes spread over the top of the fish. Take from the pan and lay each slice on toast which has been fried in butter, pour over the sauce, and serve immediately. *See also* Smokehouse Cookery —A.J.McC.

FISH CULTURE The cultivation and breeding of freshwater and marine organisms by artificial means as a means of producing a food crop or to provide stock for angling.

The artificial propagation of fish is not a new science but was established in China at the beginning of recorded history. The ancient Chinese collected the eggs of fish by placing mats in streams or ponds and allowing the fish to spawn on them. The mats with the fertilized eggs were then removed and sometimes used as articles of trade, for they supplied the owner with a source of fish for a pond or a flooded rice field. When the eggs hatched and the young grew to edible size, they were either eaten by the owner or sold on the market. This was simple fish culture under semiartificial conditions.

Another form of fish culture was practiced by the wealthy Roman General Lucullus who lived in the first century B.C. Lucullus could credit some of his wealth to a unique method of fish farming. An old French writer on this subject described the General's techniques, "At his house at Tusculum, on the shores of the Gulf of Naples, he dug canals from his fish ponds to the sea. Into these canals freshwater streams were led, and pure running water thus kept up. Sea fish that breed in freshwater passed through the canals into his ponds, and stocked them with their young. When they attempted to return to the sea, flood-gates barred their egress at the mouths of the canals, and while their progeny were growing the parent fish supplied the market."

After the fall of the Roman Empire there was no mention of fish culture until Dom Pinchon, a monk of the Abbey Rome, discovered, in the fourteenth century, the art of artificially fertilizing fish eggs and then hatching them by burying them in sand in wooden boxes.

Again fish culture lapses until 1763 when Jacobi, a German, repeated Dom Pinchon's experiments, but instead of using sand in boxes, Jacobi used gravel. His work gained renown in the scientific literature of the time.

Between 1763 and 1834 some fish culture was practiced in Norway, and in 1834 it was introduced into the British Isles over a discussion which arose in Scotland as to whether the parr were a distinct species of fish or whether they were the young of salmon. To settle the argument, salmon were hatched in wooden boxes. It was soon learned from these artificially produced fish that the parr were, indeed, the young of salmon, and, further, it was ascertained, that they migrated to the sea in the second and third summer of their life.

In 1857, Dr. Theodatus Garlick described the first attempt at the artificial propagation of fish in the United States. From this initial start, fish culture soon grew in this country including trout, salmon, muskellunge, bass, northern pike, and other species. In Europe and Asia, fish culture was mainly a method to implement the food supply, but in America its aim was generally to better the sports fishery. During the latter half of the nineteenth century the emphasis was on numbers of small fish, but in more recent years, the emphasis has been directed toward producing a better and bigger fish. Although fish farming has not progressed at the same rate as the production of food from land, great strides have been made in recent years in all phases of fish propagation including genetics, pathology, nutrition, mechanization, hybridization, and in general increased production. At the present time almost all states and the federal government have establishments propagating the various species of fish.

PROPAGATING BAITFISH AS A BUSINESS

Although national statistics are not available on the sale of baitfish in the United States, the gross dollar volume may exceed over $2,000,000 in the larger fishing states. Tennessee Game and Fish Commission fish management chief Glenn Gentry reported that 49,000,000 minnows were sold as bait in Tennessee during 1959–1960. During the following year the sales of bait minnows, largely private hatchery production, were up about 10,000,000—to an alltime high of nearly 59,000,000. One dealer reported sales of more than 20,000,000 minnows. Next largest individual sales volume was 5,000,000, then 3,000,000, 2,000,000, and down to as low as 50 minnows. Fathead minnows are the most popular kind, followed in order by goldfish, golden shiners, redfin shiners, and creek minnows. Gentry reports that average retail cost to anglers is 50 cents per dozen minnows; thus total annual expenditure by anglers fishing Tennessee waters totaled over $2,458,000 for this type of bait.

The propagation of baitfish as a business can be financially rewarding. However, in the majority of cases, the operators fail due to the lack of experience in fish-cultural methods. The average person may have kept minnows in captivity either in buckets or spring troughs, but few are qualified to raise baitfish in the proportions which are necessary to make it a profitable proposition. It is easy to raise chickens to supply a few eggs for personal household use, but the countryside is filled with abandoned chicken houses which are memorials to the people who have tried to expand their speculations into a larger and more remunerative employment. The lack of "know-how" and economic pressure had forced them to seek other methods of livelihood. Thus it is with fish propagation. It takes intelligence, foresight, and experience to be successful. Trout hatcheries are examples where experience is necessary. Artificial propagation of trout on a large scale has been carried on in this country since the last half of the nineteenth century. It is not a new business as is found in the baitfish industry, but it is an old, established vocation. Nevertheless, each year many hatcheries are sold or abandoned because the purchaser thought anyone could easily raise such prolific animals in the numbers necessary to make his enterprise pay dividends. This basic ingredient, experience, is not an elusive thing but can be obtained if a prospective propagator of minnows would start on a small scale and build his experience by trial-and-error methods until he has a plausible answer for most of the situations which may arise.

The second important consideration is the property on which the proposed hatchery is to be established. Of course, the limiting factors are the amount of money that is to be invested and the availability of water. As stated above, it is advisable to begin with a small investment. This would mean a comparatively small but practicable water area. Naturally enough, the land should be obtained with a view to expansion in mind.

The Water Supply The available water for artificial ponds should be in excess of the minimum requirements. Springwater has its disadvantages as well as its advantages. The water taken directly from springs into propagating ponds will usually be too cold to be conducive to a high rate of reproduction. This water can be stored in reservoirs to allow the temperature to rise. When the water comes directly from the spring into a very small holding space, such as a trough, it should be aerated in many cases to rid it of gases obnoxious to fishes; otherwise it would not be tenable for fishes. A spring should also be protected from surface runoff to prevent silting and pollution. Springs have their advantages in the fact that the cooler waters are better adapted for holding fish during the warm summer months; they are permanently clear; and they are seldom polluted. In some localities the appearance of the water table on the surface, in the form of a swamp, can be utilized by bulldozing ponds at intervals throughout the area. This forms ponds with dependable water supplies, but often the temperature of the water is low. Water can also be obtained from lakes, ponds, and streams, but conversion dams are imperative to control the flow to prevent flood damage. Often these waters become roily and silt-laden, and this condition can be detrimental to fish life. The temperature of these waters is usually more suitable for minnow reproduction. However, on the other side of the ledger it should be noted that it is almost impossible to eliminate undesirable species of fish. These fish somehow find their way into the ponds and might destroy eggs, fry, and adults in addition to occupying the allotted space which desirable species might use.

Sonic tag for tracking fish during migration studies. The tag emits a constant signal and will operate up to about 12 hours

Pond Construction The choice of a pond site is most important. It has to be on high ground, or at least in a location where there's no danger of a fluctuating water level. Too, the pond shouldn't be on bottomland where storm drainage can wash silt and debris into the pipes and screens. Spring water is the most suitable source for pond culture. However, only enough water is required to maintain a constant level, because an excessive flow will remove natural food and lower the water temperature. For most minnow propagation the water should range from 60° to 80°F. City tapwater, which is chlorinated, can only be used in conjunction with a commercial chemical apparatus that removes chlorine; or the chlorine can be released by using a reserve air-exposed water tank. Either way, chlorinated water is a problem to the amateur because fluctuations in the chemical level may cause sudden mortalities.

The basic baitfish pond is 25 feet wide by 75 feet long—with a 1-foot depth at the shallow end, sloping to a depth of 4–5 feet. Although many professionals use ponds ranging $\frac{1}{4}$–1 acre in area, most feel that $\frac{1}{8}$ acre is the right surface area for a small, one-man business. There is a tendency for beginners to overestimate how much space they need. For the average man with limited space, two ponds are better than one. They needn't be more than 100 feet long and 30 feet wide, if you want to operate on a modest scale.

The actual construction of the ponds would vary according to the location. A competent engineer could lay out the plans for the dam, breastwork, or dikes to meet the specifications provided by law. The main points are to keep the water area small so that it can be easily managed and deep enough to prevent the minnows from freezing in the ice or being winter-killed from lack of oxygen. It is impossible to hold and raise all of the bait in one pond since ponds may have to be drained for various reasons during the season. Plans should be made so that each pond can be drained independently of other ponds.

Selecting the Right Species The ideal minnow would be one which is acceptable to the fishermen because of its attractiveness, hardiness, and keeping qualities. It should also withstand the handling necessary to put it on the market. Also, the ideal minnow should have a rapid rate of growth and high reproductive capacities. Minnows which feed predominantly on plant life are far more desirable, since this trait lowers the losses from cannibalism. The minnows should be of the size that is required most for local needs. The fishermen in areas where the pike family is the predominant gamefish request minnows of larger size, while fishermen in areas where trout and panfish provide the local sport request smaller minnows. Besides this, it should be a species of baitfish which thrives in the ponds available.

The golden shiner (*Notemigonus crysoleucas*) is a minnow which answers most of the above qualifications. The one exception is that when the warm weather arrives and the water becomes warmer, the golden shiner becomes "soft." It is almost impossible to harvest these fish in August without the fish losing their scales. When the scales are missing, the fish soon develop a fungus infection and die in a few days. Fish that are handled in the wintertime appear to weather the roughest handling, but many months later, when spring arrives, they die for no apparent reason. Actually, the cause of death stems from the rough treatment they receive during their "immune" period in the winter. These shiners can be put in cold-water to harden during the summer months, but when they are placed in a fisherman's bucket and lowered in the warmer waters of a lake, they soon die. Certainly it saves the bait for the dealer, but it is not an ethical practice conducive to helping future business. The size of the adult golden shiner is especially well-adapted for larger gamefishes. The smaller shiners are suitable for panfish and trout. Another point in their favor is that the fishermen like this species because of the attractiveness of their coloration.

A great advantage of the golden shiner is that it utilizes almost any kind of available food. It will feed on all kinds of plankton, or introduced foods such as oatmeal, cornmeal, bonemeal, clam meal, bread, ground marine fishes, and probably many other artificial and natural foods.

The fathead minnow (*Pimephales promelas*) is a hardy, prolific fish. It is ideal for panfish and trout. The small size (maximum 3–3½ inches) may be a detriment when trying to sell it in a region where the larger gamefishes are the predominant species which are sought after by the angler.

Almost any small pond the size of the living room rug and upward will produce enough of these minnows to supply the angler and all the neighbors with bait. All that is needed is a few feet of water depth held at a constant level and spawning devices. Bricks, concrete blocks, or boards sunk on the bottom of the pond provide a spawning site. The male fathead takes a position under the devices and coaxes the females to lay their eggs on the bottom side of the sunken object. After the female or females have spawned, the male diligently cares for the eggs until they hatch.

The productivity of the fathead is remarkable, and 400,000 to over a million per acre have been recorded. This fecundity produces problems since more young are often produced than the water area can feed or the area can carry. Growth can be increased by fertilization or by feeding soybean meal at the rate of 10–20 pounds per acre per day. By carefully controlling the number of fish at about 10–20 thousand per acre, the minnows will reach panfish-bait size by August or September. All that is needed to start a pond for a constant angler supply is 500–700 adults per acre stocked in the early spring.

What makes the fathead an ideal minnow is its ability to stand handling and transportation in hot weather. It will also stay alive longer on the hook than most minnows.

The bluntnose minnow with similar spawning habits as the fatheads can be listed in the same category as the fathead—too small for the larger gamefishes.

Other minnows which may form the nucleus for profitable propagation are the emerald shiner (*Notropis atherinoides*), northern redbelly dace (*Chrosomus eos*), fine-scaled dace (*Chrosomus neogaeus*), creek chub (*Semotilus atromaculatus*), pearl dace (*Semotilus margarita*), blacknose dace (*Rhinichthys atratulus*), common shiner (*Notropis cornutus*), spotfin shiner (*Notropis spilopterus*), and brassy minnow (*Hybognathus hankinsoni*). One or more of these baitfish may fit the needs of a culturist or be suited to the particular environment he has provided for his fishes. However, very little experimentation has

been done with these species, and a baitfish hatchery man would have to experiment and start from the proverbial "scratch" to find the possibilities offered by this group. It would also be difficult to locate a source of breeders since they are not propagated by most hatchery men.

The minnows can be harvested by various methods. The baited dropnet (often called umbrella net), seines, and wire or glass traps are most often used. The type to be used depends upon the number of minnows desired and the condition of the bottom of the pond. A system should be developed which best fits the needs of the individual baitman.

Handling the Stock Probably the greatest loss in small fishes results directly or indirectly from handling. The harvesting methods often result in the minnows being crushed in the seine, hurt through careless handling, or dying from too many being confined in too small a space. Often the larger fish will thrash about and knock the scales from the smaller fish, thus leaving them open to different types of infections. In hot weather, the soft minnows suffer a very heavy loss from handling. Live boxes placed in streams or lakes are often too shallow, and only the warmer surface water is available to the fish. Wave action or strong currents may also be hardships on the little fishes. Deeper holding boxes usually provide cooler temperatures and usually have less water motion to harm the fish.

Transportation of the minnows is a problem that has to be arranged to satisfy the dealer's needs. Sudden temperature changes and overcrowding will result in high mortality. Bait can be hauled in various ways from tank trucks to milk cans. If the water is iced, the sudden temperature change when the minnows are put into warmer water is usually fatal. Constant experimentation will show the best methods to transport bait over the distance which is necessary to market them. Transportation of any kind of animal is tricky business, and minnows are no exception.

PROPAGATION OF BLACK BASS

Three species of black basses, the largemouth, smallmouth, and spotted bass, have been propagated in hatcheries. The methods used are very dissimilar to trout and, of course, require warmer water. Although bass can be stripped by hand like trout, it is very impractical since bass reproduce readily in a more natural environment.

Before the spawning season, the retaining ponds are prepared for brood bass. The ponds are usually allowed to remain dry during the winter so that decomposition and oxidation of the bottom material will increase the fertility of the pond. On the bottom where the water will be 2–3 feet deep, wooden boxes of about 2' x 2' x 6" (deep) are filled with gravel and placed 10–15 feet apart. These boxes act as spawning sites and are situated far enough apart so that the males will not fight. Although there is disagreement among fish culturists as to the ideal number of brood fish to use, some fisheries men use two males to three females at the rate of 75–100 per acre. The brood bass will spawn when the water temperatures reach 65°–75°F. and the eggs will hatch 2½–10 days later depending on temperatures. Largemouth-bass fry, as soon as the yolk sac is reabsorbed, swarm to the surface, and the male schools the young fish and protects them for a few days. When the fry are in schools near the surface, they can easily be picked up with a large, fine-mesh net. The fry of the smallmouth react differently, and consequently the critical time for the fish culturist is a matter of a few hours. The nest must be watched very closely, for when the little black fry in the nest begin to rise they come up only once as a swarm, settle back, but soon come up again. It is in the initial rise that haste is necessary to gather them because the next time they come up they rather quickly disperse in little groups with no parental care. Gathering the fry then becomes a difficult task.

At this point, the fish which are dipped off the pond can be reared by either the intensive or extensive method. The intensive method utilizes more complete control of the young bass. The extensive method closely follows the natural processes prevalent in a wild environment.

Extensive Method   If the young bass are reared by the extensive method, they are put into the previously prepared ponds which have been inoculated with daphnia (minute crustaceans often called "water fleas"). This inoculation of daphnia should take place in advance of the introduction of young bass so that the daphnia "bloom" is at its peak when the bass are stocked. The fry will grow quickly on these crustaceans until they reach a length of about 2½–3 inches when their diet begins to include fish. To feed these growing fish, golden shiners, bluntnose minnows, and fathead minnows can be easily reared in ponds. The fathead minnow is the most widely accepted and can be harvested at the rate of over 400,000 per acre. These should be introduced into the bass pond at the right sizes for the young bass to eat.

The most important feature of the extensive method is to be sure that all the young bass at stocking are the same size or else cannibalism among the different-size bass will greatly decrease the production.

Intensive Method   In the intensive method of rearing bass, the fingerlings are placed in tanks and are fed daphnia previously cultured in daphnia ponds. When they are about two inches in size, they are introduced to a diet of liver and marine fish. The young bass do not start to feed on this food immediately, but, with patience, must be taught to take it. The best method is to mix the meat and fish with daphnia and gradually taper the daphnia portion until the diet consists of only liver and marine fish. The response to the artificial diet varies with the individual fish and therefore there is a differentiation in growth. The bass must then be graded according to size to prevent cannibalism. There are always a few individuals which never accept artificial food and must be fed live food or allowed to perish.

The intensive method of bass rearing is a more certain method of guaranteeing a crop, but it is also very expensive. With both methods of rearing, the majority of bass are stocked as fall fingerlings because of the expense and losses incurred during the winter months.

PROPAGATION OF CATFISH

Of the various species of fish cultured, freshwater catfish are the most important commercially. Three species of freshwater catfish are profitable: the blue (*Ictalurus furcatus*), the channel (*Ictalurus punctatus*), and the white (*Ictalurus catus*). The channel catfish is by far the most widely cultured species, with the blue and white playing minor roles. The catfish farmer has four sources of revenue: (1) selling brood fish to other farmers, (2) selling fingerlings, (3) selling food fish either wholesale or retail, or (4) selling stock to private "pay" lakes.

Spawning and Hatching   Each spring in the southeastern United States, when the water temperature reaches 70°F, breeders are selected from fish that are healthy and are a minimum of 3 years old. Fish that range from 3–10 pounds are preferred. The fish are then sexed and readied for stocking into brood ponds. Males have a broader head than females and often are darkly pigmented around the head and lower jaw. A ripe female will show a well-rounded abdomen, indicating eggs. A female usually has 3,000–4,000 eggs per pound of body weight, although this varies. A 3-pound female, therefore, would be expected to have 9,000–12,000 eggs. As a fish ages, the number of eggs per pound of body weight decreases somewhat. Thus the fish farmer can estimate the potential number of young that might be produced.

There are a number of ways to spawn and hatch catfish. The most common way is to stock a pond with about 20 pair of brood fish per acre. Spawning containers, such as milk cans, are placed around the edges of the pond in about 2–3 feet of water. The fish farmer checks his spawning cans every day or two. He does this by wading from one to another and gently poking a stick inside. If eggs are present they can be felt; the sensation is similar to poking a mass of gelatine. Some check cans for eggs by running their hands inside. If so, a fist should be used and not open fingers. After spawning, the male runs the female off and guards the eggs. Some males are so aggressive that an open hand invites a bad bite. When eggs are found, they are noted and the male left to protect them. In about a week the fry can be transferred to another pond for rearing or they may be left, in which case they swim out of the cans into the brood pond. Most catfish farmers remove the eggs and transfer them to a building, where they are hatched artificially. The building usually consists of an open shed over hatching troughs. A typical hatching trough is constructed from 14-gauge metal and is 10 feet long, 20 inches wide, and 10 inches deep. Each trough is supplied with a paddlewheel device. Paddles, 2–3 inches wide, are spaced at intervals along the trough. A small motor moves the paddles into and out of the water at 30 rpm. Water flows through and out of the trough at 3 rpm. Egg masses, held in wire baskets, are placed between the paddles. As the eggs hatch, the fry drop through the wire mesh to the bottom of the trough.

The hatcheryman must maintain a constant water temperature. If the water drops much below 70° F it's too cold and the eggs develop fungus. If too hot, say near 90° F, the embryos develop too fast. A temperature of about 80° F is ideal. Water temperature has an important effect on the number of days required for hatching. At an average water temperature of 83° F eggs hatch in five days; at 81° F six days; and at 79° F in seven days. Generally, a 2° change in water temperature affects the date of hatching by one day. Once the eggs hatch, the fry live off their yolk sacs for several days. They usually stay balled-up in a corner of the tank. As the yolk is absorbed, they begin swimming to the top of the tank in search of food. When the fry surface it is a critical time, because they must be fed immediately. A finely ground high-protein catfish food is broadcast once every hour or two to insure that all fry begin feeding. They are fed whatever they will consume. Once the fry are on feed the number of times they are fed is gradually reduced. During this period the fish culturist must be alert for parasites and diseases. These are best prevented by maintaining sanitary conditions in the troughs. Some parasites, such as *Trichodina*, are a common problem. Dissolved oxygen is also important and should be above 4 ppm at all times.

After the fry have been feeding for about a week they are ready to be moved to the rearing pond. Normally the fish are treated with chemicals to prevent diseases. Following this the fry are stocked in ponds at rates varying from 10,000–150,000 per acre. Fish stocked at lower rates will grow to be 6–8 inches by fall, whereas fish stocked at higher rates will grow to only 3–4 inches. Once stocked, the fish are fed daily with a catfish feed pellet. Periodically the pond is sprayed with a mixture of diesel fuel and a heavier oil, such as cottonseed oil. This forms an oil slick on the surface and helps control fry-eating insects such as the backswimmer. These insects can make serious inroads on young catfish. The insects are killed when their air tubes clog up with oil. After the fish reach 2 inches in length, backswimmers are no longer a problem.

Oxygen Depletion Other problems may occur while the fish are being cultured. One most often encountered is oxygen depletion. The volume of dissolved oxygen may be high one day and low the next, or it may become virtually depleted. Natural sources of oxygen are: (1) diffusion from the air, (2) agitation or wave action, and (3) photosynthesis. By far the most important is photosynthesis. Oxygen is reduced in a pond by: (1) respiration of biomass (except anaerobic forms), (2) decay of organic matter, (3) oxidation reduction, (4) increase in water temperature, (5) bubbling off with other gases, (6) addition of water low in oxygen, and (7) an increase in salinity. Generally, as long as the sun is shining, the dissolved oxygen should be sufficient. Factors leading to oxygen depletion may include one or more of the following conditions: (1) a hot, muggy day with no wind circulation, (2) cloudy or rainy conditions, and (3) a die-off of phytoplankton. There are other factors as well. To increase oxygen content, fresh water saturated with oxygen can be added or water can be recirculated in ponds with pumps.

Harvesting In the fall or spring of the year the fingerlings are harvested. The pond is drained and the fingerlings are seined out and moved to the hatchery again. Here they are held in large concrete tanks of 500 gallons or more, where they are sorted for size. Three-inch fish are put in one tank, 4-inch fish in another, and so on. Once sorted, the fingerlings are ready to be restocked in the ponds again. Stocking rates vary from 1,200–3,000 per acre, but around 1,500–2,000 is best. The fish are then given feed pellets daily at about 3 percent of their body weight per day. For example, a pond with a total of 200 pounds of fish would receive 6 pounds of feed daily.

In about four months the fingerlings will grow to 1–1¼ pounds each, depending on size at stocking. They are ready for harvest. The farmer can now do one of several things. He can sell retail, directly to the consumer, or to local retail outlets, or to regional processing plants. Large catfish are sometimes held and sold later as brood fish.

CATFISH IN PAY LAKES

With an ever-increasing demand for recreation, pay lakes have become significant in the United States. A pond owner stocks sportfish—bass and bluegill and catfish are popular—and charges the public to fish. He might charge a dollar a "pole" and so much a pound for the fish caught. Catfish farmers often supply "stocker" fish to the pond owner. This type of fishing is particularly attractive to the family man. Pay lakes are often within short driving distances from home and one need not make an all-day trip out of it. Some pay-lake operators have a number of ponds. By rotating the use of them, fishing is always good in at least one pond. Some operators stock various combinations of blue, white, and channel catfish in pay lakes. The channel catfish is readily caught in the spring and fall; the white catfish is an active feeder during the hot summer months; and the blue catfish often produces good catches in cold weather.

Catfish are sometimes stocked in combination with largemouth bass and bluegill and redear sunfish. In this case a mixture of bluegill and redear is stocked in the fall at a rate of 1,000–1,500 fingerlings per acre. In the spring bass are stocked at 100 fingerlings per acre. Channel catfish are stocked following this at 100 per acre. This combination works well in the southeast United States. Baits for catfish vary, but catalpa worms are tops. Worms, stink bait, small minnows, and a host of others are also used with success. Sometimes the channel catfish will hit a small spinner or spoon.

As a food fish the channel catfish is one of the best. Most fish fanciers agree that the channel catfish, farm-raised and fed a protein diet of feed pellets, has a delectable taste. There are a number of ways to prepare them (*see* Fish Cookery).

Economics Starting a catfish farm requires a large initial investment. It may cost upward of $1,000 per acre just for pond construction. A well needs to be sunk. Feed and chemicals are required. Feed, for example, costs about $140 a ton, but this varies greatly. If 2,000 pounds of catfish per acre are produced, it might require 3,000 pounds of feed. The cost would be $210. A number of problems face the catfish farmer: an unstable market for a new industry, disease outbreaks, fish kills from low oxygen, harvesting, and many others. In spite of this the catfish farmer can make a profit; $150 net profit per acre per year is not unreasonable.

The bulk of the catfish are farmed in the Mississippi River Delta. The state of Mississippi leads the nation in catfish production with well over 15,000 acres in catfish ponds. Louisiana, Texas, Arkansas, Alabama, Tennessee, Georgia, Kansas, Florida and California are also big on catfish farming. In all there are over 60,000 acres of catfish ponds in the United States (1971).   —J.W.A.

PROPAGATION OF MUSKELLUNGE

There are two methods of propagating the muskellunge. One is the extensive method practiced in most states where the young fry are planted in ponds with established food populations. An excellent account of this method is described in *Pond Culture of Muskellunge in Wisconsin*. The other method of propagating muskellunge is practiced in Pennsylvania. In this intensive method the fish are kept in troughs and fed each day from food brought from outside ponds. When a good survival is obtained, the extensive method will produce more fish, but the number of fish which will survive is not as predictable as when they are reared in tanks under the intensive method. Fish kept in tanks can be more easily treated for disease and can be sorted frequently to prevent cannibalism. Growth is approximately the same with both methods.

Stocking of artificially propagated muskellunge dates back to 1899 in Wisconsin. Ontario started artificial propagation in 1927, New York at Lake Chautauqua in 1887, Pennsylvania and Ohio in 1953, and West Virginia and North Dakota in 1958. Some muskellunge culture was carried on at the Corry Hatchery in Pennsylvania in the 1890's but was discontinued.

In Wisconsin the first muskellunge are taken in nets at 42°F. and very early eggs are collected at 46°F. The best fish and best eggs are taken when the temperature ranges from 48° to 56°F. Muskie eggs are usually taken over a 10-day period.

When a female is stripped, as many as six males are necessary. Each male produces 0.2–0.3 cubic centimeters of sperm, which amounts to only a few drops. The large eggs are preferred to smaller eggs because of the better survival and larger fry. The egg is .100–.130 inch in diameter depending on the size of the adult. This may be more directly correlated to the age, environment, and strain of females. In Wisconsin, egg size varies in the spawners from lake to lake. The number of eggs per quart is 30,000–67,000. The ratio of sexes caught in that state is 61 percent males to 39 percent females.

Muskies in Wisconsin do not ripen when held in small quarters. In Pennsylvania, a pair of large breeders which were green when taken from the net in the early spring were placed in a small hatchery pond of less than ½ acre. This pair of fish successfully reproduced. Ohio has reared and spawned muskellunge held in small ponds. Better results seemed to have been obtained from the Great Lakes muskellunge than had been obtained from the Ohio muskellunge. More eggs were taken in Ohio from pond-reared stock than were taken from wild stock with considerably less time and manpower.

The Wisconsin method of propagating muskellunge is as follows: after the eggs are taken, the eggs are fertilized, and the sperm and eggs are stirred with the fingers. The average time for spawning a female is three minutes; the washing consumes three minutes. The eggs are then allowed to stand and water-harden. A critical time for the eggs is 9–15 minutes, and at this time the eggs should not be disturbed. After one hour the eggs are hardened and will support a 135-gram weight. The eggs are incubated in 4-quart jars, and 1½–2 quarts of eggs are rolled in each jar. Eighty-five to 95 percent hatch results from eggs incubated in water temperatures of 50°–70°F. Thirteen to twenty-one days are required for hatching at these temperatures, but only six days are required at a constant 68°F. temperature with no adverse effects on the fry. Incubation at normal temperatures results in normal fry, whereas in lower temperatures the eggs hatch more slowly and have heavier mortalities. Eggs in 39°F. had 100-percent mortality at the end of thirty-five days. Muskies hatched and reared in water of 48°–50°F. used up yolk-sac material without an increase in size and developed into smaller, weaker fry some of which did not feed. Any temperature below 55°F. is detrimental to the fry. Com-

paratively still water is better for sac-fry since heavy currents use up their energy. The fry are retained in jars an additional 10–14 days until the yolk sac is almost gone and the fry are approximately 0.5 inch long. Then the muskellunge are allowed to swim out of the jars. The swim-up fry are planted in previously prepared outside ponds at the rate of 100,000 per acre. Stocking rates of 150,000–200,000 muskellunge per acre have yielded as much as 30 percent more fish per acre, but the fish were one-third smaller.

An experiment in Wisconsin in 1940 tested the use of hormones on nonspawning muskellunge. These fish, placed in shallow ponds and injected with fresh or acetone-dried pituitary glands of carp, spawned 3–6 days after injection. From 11 fish injected, 9 spawned 3–4 days after injection; the remaining 2 were given a second injection and spawned 6 days after the first injection. A normal hatch was reported.

In Canada it was found that temperatures of 49°–79°F. had no adverse effect on the eggs. One gallon of water per minute was more than sufficient to supply 100,000 eggs and 10,000 fry in troughs. One study noted that fry did better in wooden troughs rather than metal since the fry could cling better to the wooden sides and did not tend to congregate.　　　　　　　　　　　　　　　—K.B.

PROPAGATION OF NORTHERN PIKE

Northern-pike breeders are caught in the spring in trapnets, pound nets, or fyke nets. When pike are caught in the nets, they apparently fight the net and are partially scaled and scarred from this activity. Knotted cotton nets are more prone to injure the fish than are knotless nylon nets. Knotless nylon dipnets are also much easier on fish and produce fewer superficial injuries. Skin abrasions and scaling in nets lead to heavy fungus infection and eventual death of the fish.

When female pike are trapped for brood stock, they are often not ripe. Some will ripen in a few days, but most will remain green. Injections of mammalian hormones and carp pituitaries have been attempted to hasten maturation of the eggs. Mammalian hormones failed to cause the pike to release their eggs; carp pituitary shows some promise, but the techniques need refinement.

Brood stock are sometimes held in ponds or tanks to mature. Care must be taken to be sure the fish are not held in water temperatures below those from which the brood fish were taken as this would inhibit the maturation of the gonads. Breeders can be put in hatchery ponds in the fall along with small coarse fish for food. They can be retained here until spring and then spawned as they become ripe.

The use of anesthetics on brood fish makes the handling and spawning easier for fish and men. When an anesthetic is used the eggs and sperm are more easily taken because the fish are relaxed, it is not necessary to hold the fish tightly to spawn it, and fewer fish are injured by dropping. In Pennsylvania, MS 222 (Tricaine Methanesulfonate) in a concentration of 1:100,000 works satisfactorily. After the fish are anesthetized, they should be dipped in freshwater, wiped, and then spawned.

Stripping Technique Ripe females should be spawned by applying the pressure near the vent and moving forward toward the head as the eggs are extruded. Starting from the front immediately back of the gills and applying heavy pressure toward the rear may not only injure the female but may also break the eggs. Spawning the males by applying pressure on the ventral surface as is done with females is exerting unnecessary pressure. The testes lie in the dorsal region of the abdominal cavity near the kidneys, and the spermatozoa which are ready to be emitted are close to the vent. Therefore, the best method of stripping the male is to use the thumb and forefinger, one on each side of the body in the region where the testes are located. Gentle pressure near the vent in this fashion will remove the available sperm without injuring the fish.

Experiments in Europe revealed that the spermatozoa remain living 60–120 seconds in water of 41°–59°F. Work in Pennsylvania showed activity of the sperm up to two minutes with the peak of activity during the first thirty seconds. When sperm is activated by urine, activity lasts longer than when the sperm is activated by water. However, when sperm is stored for short or long periods, urine has an adverse effect on the motility of the sperm.

Microscopic examination by Bradford revealed that the milt was very viscous and when dropped on eggs the sperm was active only on the periphery of the drop. The unwetted portion or the center of the drop was not active until broken up and exposed to fluid; therefore, thorough mixing of sperm is necessary to obtain maximum efficiency of the milt. Male northern pike in contrast to trout may sometimes produce only one or two drops of sperm, but the northern-pike sperm are smaller than trout sperm. European workers report that only .02 cubic centimeter of milt is required per liter of water, and this small amount contains over 500,000,000 spermatozoa. Bradford's count for ten males was similar.

Removing the ripe testes and squeezing out the sperm through cheesecloth is a good method to produce a large amount of sperm from one male. The sperm count on "squeezed" testes is the same as that produced naturally. There is equal activity from all parts of the testes and good activity even from green males. Testes stored in a dry beaker and refrigerated for five days were still very active.

It was reported from Minnesota that as the water warmed the eggs came more easily and the male sperm was more abundant. The eggs were good to the end of the spawning run, but the sperm became stringy and was not satisfactory.

Results from Ohio indicate that the best results were obtained when the eggs were stripped into $\frac{1}{4}$ inch of water. The milt was then stripped into the eggs, and the two were mixed with the customary swirling. No completely dry method was attempted. In Nebraska, the best fertility was obtained when the male gonads were removed, crushed, and swirled. A hatch of 25.5 percent was obtained by this method as compared to 3.2–8.8 by other methods.

European workers report that best results were obtained when the male and female were wiped in the vicinity of the vent and the eggs and sperm were thoroughly mixed before water was added. Experiments in Pennsylvania using essentially the same techniques resulted in good fertility. Also, testes squeezed through cheesecloth increased the hatchability.

Pike eggs are more adhesive than muskellunge eggs, and for years this has been a problem. To prevent the eggs from sticking, in the past, clay and corn starch were used. However, this is not necessary since the eggs will loosen themselves if allowed to stand in a basin 40–60 minutes. The basin should be floating in a water bath so that the eggs do not become too warm. Experiments in Pennsylvania have shown that eggs allowed to stand in a basin 14 hours showed no adverse effect.

Huet suggests that the eggs should be allowed to stand quietly for only 3 minutes and then washed for 15–30 minutes. This would be in direct contrast to the information from Wisconsin's work on muskellunge which indicated that the eggs from this species go through a critical period for fifteen minutes and should not be moved.

Northern pike eggs are incubated in jars with the water coming from the bottom of the jar and seeping up through the eggs. Europeans use a Zoug jar which is a graduated jar with a water valve at the bottom. Americans use the MacDonald type of jar with the water being carried to the bottom by means of a glass tube centered in the jar. In both cases, enough water is put in to roll the eggs gently. The dead eggs gradually collect on top because of their lower specific gravity and are siphoned off. In Pennsylvania, the jar method of incubating trout eggs was tried. In this method the eggs are stationary and do not roll. This eliminates the possibility of damaging the eggs by excessive rolling.

The eggs were treated for fungus with formaldehyde at a concentration of 1:600 for fifteen minutes daily. Malachite-oxalate at a concentration of 1:200,000 for an hour is used as a fungicide in other states.

Incubation Period The incubation time has been calculated by European workers to be 120 degree-days. The extremes were between 95 and 150 degree-days depending on the incubation temperatures. After 30 degree-days the embryo is visible. A degree-day is 1°C. above 0°C. for 24 hours. In other words, a constant temperature of 10°C. for 10 days would be 100 degree-days. In Pennsylvania records for degree-days necessary for hatching are similar to those stated in the European work.

It has been said that egg mortality is higher at lower temperatures. Temperatures suggested for best incubation are 54°–59°F.

Filtered water is best for incubation. Heavy loads of silt will smother the eggs. Other extraneous material may clog up the incubation system.

Pike eggs under artificial culture do not hatch as well as trout eggs. This has been a perennial problem in many states. Ohio reports a range in hatch of 0–60 percent with an average of 6.6 percent. Pennsylvania using experimental techniques had an average hatch of 43 percent with a range of 9–88 percent. European workers report a hatch of over 80 percent, but it is sometimes lower than 70 percent.

Egg mortalities may occur because of many reasons other than infertility. Ultraviolet light has a strong effect upon eggs and sac-fry. Freshly fertilized eggs are more resistant, but eyed eggs are especially sensitive to light and easily destroyed. Diffused daylight is not harmful to eggs, but direct sunlight is. Strong irradiation of eggs seems to modify the yolk sac and embryo after hatching. An incubation room need not be darkened, but the direct rays of the sun should be kept out. *Vorticella*, a protozoan, will also kill eggs.

How to Ship Eggs Pike eggs, being more delicate than trout eggs, should be handled with the greatest of caution. Eggs should be shipped at 70 degree-days. For shipments of eight hours or less, newly fertilized eggs can be shipped in one part of eggs to three parts of water. Eyed eggs can be shipped in the same manner at temperatures of about 37°–39°F. These temperatures can be maintained by packing moss and ice around the container.

Fry are usually removed from the jar as soon as they hatch. The absorption of the sac takes 160–180 degree-days. From fertilization to swim-up usually takes about 300 degree-days. In Europe, when the sac-fry are placed in tanks, submerged waterplants are usually placed in the tanks with them. This gives the fry more places to attach themselves.

When fry are placed in outside ponds, the pond should be carefully prepared. First, populations of other fish must be completely eradicated. Chlorine, rotenone, or quicklime can be used. Secondly, rooted vegetation and algae should be killed with sodium arsenite or another weedicide. The pond should be filled with water as soon as the first eggs are taken. The pond should be set up so that the water level remains constant. A slight drop in the water will strand many fish. *Daphnia pulex* or *Daphnia magna* should be placed in the ponds immediately so that they have a chance to build up and supply food when the fry are introduced. Fuel oil (or cod liver oil) should be placed in the pond in the evening when there is no wind to blow it up on the shore. The oil will kill the predaceous air-breathing insects.

Fertilizers recommended by various sources are fifty pounds of *Torula yeast* and 25 pounds of 10-10-10 per acre foot, suspended perforated cans of 0-45-0 at 25 pounds per acre, and animal manure.

In ponds, the percentage of loss in fry is mainly due to the relationship of other organisms inhabiting the same area as the fry. There is interspecific competition between the fry and other organisms for food. Whether a predaceous animal eats a fry or an alternate object depends on the choice which is most readily available. A similar choice of food for the pike also determines the amount of cannibalism which occurs.

Cannibalism is comparatively common in ponds but does not occur until after the pike reach 1.8–2.0 inches. Cannibalism depends on variations in the size of the pike, population density, and the available food.

In Europe, fry are stocked in ponds at the end of April at the rate of 200–400 per 100 square meters. In mid June, the fingerlings are taken out at the rate of 50–100 per square meter. The yield surpasses 25 percent.

In Nebraska, 25,000 fry (½–¾ inch) were stocked on April 24; on May 18, 20,000 fry 1.8 inches average size were removed—this was an 80 percent recovery. It was concluded that cropping the fish off at the right time (1.2–2.0 inches) was the secret of high production.

The discarded eggs from a Nebraska hatchery were placed in a fertilized pond. From these eggs, 1,098 fingerlings were harvested.

Mortalities in ponds are usually high. Two causes are, of course, cannibalism and fluctuating water levels. Another cause is predaceous insects such as *Dytiscus*, the the predaceous diving beetle, and *Notonectes*, the back swimmers which suck and kill the fry and fingerlings.

Another method of producing fry and fingerlings is by placing brood fish in ponds to spawn. Ohio was not too successful with this method. Two females and eight males

were placed in each pond. Two ponds were used for the experiment. From the two ponds, 138 fingerlings, 7 inches long, were harvested.

In Nebraska, six males and three females were placed in a two-acre pond. After spawning, all but one adult were removed. When the pond was drained 75,000 fingerlings averaging 1 inch were harvested. This was from an estimated 186,000 eggs.

Adults can be removed by the use of gillnets, and the young can be dipped along the shore since they inhabit only the upper 1 inch or so of the water. Care must be taken when draining a pond. Since northern pike do not like to follow the water current in draining, many will become stranded.

THE ARTIFICIAL PROPAGATION OF TROUT

The artificial propagation of trout goes back to the fourteenth century when a French monk discovered that trout eggs could be artificially impregnated. Between this time and the mid-nineteenth century there were some small individual contributions to the propagation of trout, but trout culture did not gain momentum until 1852 when the first public-owned trout hatchery was constructed in France. The alarming decrease of trout in America soon necessitated their production by artificial methods. In 1864, Seth Green built a hatchery at Mumford, New York, and pioneered most of the basic techniques of trout culture. Within a few years, private and state hatcheries, with Green's help, were established in the New England and Middle Atlantic states. The basic techniques which Green developed were to last until the end of World War II when many states and the federal government hired biologists to do research and modernize the techniques of trout propagation.

Location and Construction The most important requirements for a trout hatchery are a strong flow of clean springwater and a topography which lends itself to the construction of a hatchhouse and raceways. Two of the most common fallacies are that the water must be bitter cold and any farm which has a spring filling a 1–2 inch pipe has sufficient water to start a hatchery. Before building a hatchery, one should find a water supply which has a constant temperature of 45°–55°F. When water temperatures drop below 40°F., egg incubation is very slow, and eggs which would hatch in forty-five days in 50°F. water require as much as ninety days to hatch. When the temperature drops to 35°F., 143 days are required for hatching. Below 40°F. trout feed very little, and growth practically ceases.

The amount of water needed depends on the size of the desired operation. For commercial purposes the volume or flow should be measured in the hundreds of gallons, and for a large operation, at least, 2,000–3,000 gallons per minute are required for good, healthy fish. Sources of the latter size are usually found in limestone regions. Too much constant flow seldom causes problems; too little always does. Spring flows can be supplemented by stream flow as long as the temperatures don't go over 65°F. for any length of time. Temperatures in the 70's over a twenty-four-hour period can be lethal.

Before a water source should be considered as a hatchery site, it should be seen in flood and drought periods, and temperatures should be taken during the different seasons. A chemical analysis of the water should be made by somebody who is familiar with the requirements of trout.

There are three very important requirements in constructing a hatchery so it can be efficiently operated. The first is that a flood drainage is constructed so that highwater can be by-passed without inundating the raceways. Raceways rather than ponds should be constructed in such a manner that the heads are as wide as the raceways so that there are no deadwater areas which accumulate silt and excrement. Raceways should be designed so it is possible to drain each one individually.

The width of raceways is determined by the flow. The faster the exchange of water the cleaner the raceways remain and consequently the healthier the fish will be. All that is required is 9–18 inches deep of water. The length of each section of raceway is partially governed by the topography of land. There should be enough fall between raceways so that the water can be aerated and, if at all possible, the fall should be more than 18 inches in order that automatic, self-cleaning screens can be installed. Dirt or concrete raceways can be constructed, both having their advantages. A dirt raceway is more difficult to clean, harder to catch the fish, and requires more maintenance; but dirt raceways are cheaper to construct, and the fish appear to remain healthier with less fin wear.

Out of necessity, hatchery buildings must be built with the water-supply head at least four feet above the floor of the hatchery building. Pumping water is an expensive procedure. The inside should be laid out in such a fashion that incubating units, which will be discussed later, and concrete tanks can be installed. Wooden and steel troughs and small tanks are as obsolete as Seth Green's original hatchery. Large, double, concrete tanks about twelve feet long and with an over-all width of four feet are far

more efficient. The water supply should be through a $1\frac{1}{2}$ –2-inch perforated pipe running the full length of the bottom of the tank. Since the water enters in this fashion the fish are dispersed rather than huddled near the head of the tank, food is kept in motion, and very little of the excreta is allowed to settle on the floor of the tank but is flushed out. With this method, initial growth is startling as compared to older methods.

One warning in construction of the water supply should be very definitely heeded. Copper, bronze, brass, and galvanized pipes can be very toxic in certain types of water. The first three should never be used for piping, although galvanized after "seasoning" in water or painting can be utilized. Aluminum mesh hardware cloth or perforated aluminum plates should be used for retaining the fish in the tank.

Selection of Brood Trout The most essential item of trout propagation is a good strain of brood trout. Wild trout will not meet the needs because they are not adapted through years of selection for hatchery conditions. In making the initial purchase of eggs for brood trout, it would be wise if the eggs originated from a hatchery that had the same water chemistry as the hatchery for which they are intended. Although eggs from other hatcheries may do as well, there is no way of determining this except through trial and error. A visit to a number of commercial hatcheries of the same water quality would give a lead as to which has the cleanest and fastest-growing fish. More certain results would be obtained if eggs were bought from the hatchery with the best fish.

Spawning and Incubation Brook, brown, and some strains of rainbow trout are fall spawners. As spawning season nears, usually around October 1, all the fish should be tested to see if they are "ripe"—ready to produce eggs or milt. When a light pressure on the abdomen will produce a few eggs from the female and some milt from the male, the trout are ready to spawn. After the first ripe fish are found, the fish should be tested once a week so the eggs can be taken when they are at the peak of maturity. Separating males and females makes it unnecessary to handle the males every time the females need testing. A large number of males are not required because they "recharge" in a week and can be used over and over again.

Females should be stripped of their eggs by putting light pressure on the ventral surface near the vent and gradually working forward until most of the eggs are taken. The milt or sperm is taken from the male by stripping with the thumb and forefinger along the sides of the male toward the vent. The eggs and sperm should be taken in a dry basin, one female to a basin. Broken eggs will curdle sperm and no fertilization will result. If more than one female is stripped in a basin and the first female produces broken eggs, because of rough handling or bad eggs, all the sperm added to the subsequent females' eggs will curdle and hatchability will be greatly decreased.

After the eggs and the sperm have been gently mixed, a little water is added to the basin and the basin slowly rotated. In thirty seconds after the addition of water, the activity of the sperm slows down and fertilization is complete. The eggs from various females can be poured together. Soon they will become very adhesive and stick to each other and the pan. At this time the container is slowly sunk in a trough of running water where the eggs

One of the modern research techniques is the use of an electroshocker in studying fish populations. This Connecticut crew is collecting sea trout from a tidal stream to be tagged and released, then later recaptured for growth data

swell and water-harden. After 30–60 minutes the eggs are loose and ready for the incubating units. The eggs can be incubated in tray incubators or glass jars. One of the newer methods for incubating trout eggs is in 6–7-quart cylindrical jars with rounded bottoms. The jar is set up in such a manner that a galvanized ⅛-inch pipe attached to the water-supply system is centered in the middle of the jar and reaches to within ½ inch of the bottom of the jar. A ⅛-inch screen is cut to fit the bottom of the jar just before the bottom curvature. Gravel is then placed on top of this screen which prevents the gravel from plugging the water supply. On top of the gravel, a similar screen is placed to prevent the eggs and hatching fry from getting into the gravel. About four quarts of eggs are poured in the jar which settle on the top screen. Water is fed through the jar at about two quarts per minute. Since the water comes up from the bottom of the jar, it is dispersed by the gravel and each egg receives a constant flow of water. These jars are attached to a central water supply and are arranged in batteries. About 30,000–50,000 eggs are incubated in each jar. During the time of incubation the eggs must be treated with a fungicide. Fungus develops on white, dead eggs, and if it is not controlled it will spread to the live eggs and kill them. To control the fungus, either malachite green is used at concentration of 1:200,-000 for an hour from a constant-flow syphon, or formalin (a 37-percent solution of formaldehyde) at 1:600 concentration for seventeen minutes is used. Of the two fungicides, formalin is less toxic to eggs and fry and exhibits better fungus control.

Incubation time for trout eggs depends on the water temperature and the species. At 50°F., brook trout hatch in 45 days, rainbow trout in 30 days, brown trout in 41 days, and lake trout in 49 days. These are mean incubating times since all the eggs do not hatch at once, but sometimes the hatching continues over a period of a week.

After the young fish emerge from the egg they are called sac-fry because of the attached yolk sac which will give them a nutrition supply for the first few weeks or months of life. Again this depends on the temperature and species.

The young sac-fry, whose only movement is to try to wiggle into a dark corner, are placed in a basket in flowing water and are allowed to remain there until the yolk sac is resorbed and the fry begin to swim up and look for food. At this time feeding begins.

Nutrition Trout were originally fed meat products, such as liver, lungs, and spleens of beef and horses, either alone or in combination with fish or dry diets. The feeding of meat necessitated freezing, cold storage, and grinding into correct sizes. This was very expensive, not only because of the preparation costs, but also because 5–7 pounds of meat products were required to produce 1 pound of trout. In recent years completely dry diets have been produced which eliminate the expensive meat products, and only approximately 2 pounds are required to grow a pound of trout. However, a word of warning is necessary because not all dry diets are complete diets even though they may be advertised as such. A check with the local conservation department will help determine the best and cheapest diets.

Trout are fed according to their body weight and the temperature of the water. The percentage of food given for amount of body weight decreases as the fish grow larger. The frequency of feeding depends on the size of fish. Young swim-up fish should be fed at least 8 times a day while larger fish may be fed only 2–4 times a day. Trout should be fed every day unless the water temperature drops below 40°F. or the water is very turbid. Dry feeds, particularly pellets, lend themselves to mechanical feeding, and many devices have been developed to mechanically expedite this type of feeding.

Mechanical Aids Mechanical, self-cleaning screens and mechanical graders have also been developed to reduce labor costs. Fish graders are necessary not only at shipping time but during the development of the fish. Graded fish are much easier to feed because they take the same-size feed and are much easier to handle at shipping season.

Transportation Transportation units are many and varied. A good unit is one in which the temperatures and metabolic wastes (carbon dioxide, ammonia) remain low while the concentration of oxygen remains high. There is no one accepted unit, but again a visit to your conservation department will help decide how the first unit should be constructed.

Sources of Information As in all business only the most progressive survive. To keep up with the most modern techniques, a subscription to the *Progressive Fish-Culturist*, published quarterly by the Department of Interior, Fish and Wildlife Service, Washington, D. C., 20025, is very important.   —K.B.

THE ARTIFICIAL PROPAGATION OF HYBRID TROUT

Hybrid trout usually result from man's curiosity rather than a common natural occurrence. If hybridization occurred frequently in nature, species would soon lose their identity. Consequently, nature has provided barriers, or isolating mechanisms, to prevent promiscuous breeding. Under wild conditions very few trout hybridize. There are natural crosses, notably between the rainbow trout and cutthroat trout, and these hybrids are quite common in some Montana and Wyoming rivers. There is such a similarity between the black-spotted parents that progeny are not readily identified. The Gila trout (*which see*) of Arizona also hybridizes with the rainbow to the extent that pure strains of *Salmo gilae* are now very rare. A similar condition exists with the Sunapee trout (*which see*) in hybridizing with other chars. Brook trout and brown trout sometimes hybridize, although these "tiger" trout are most uncommon except as hatchery products.

One of the isolating mechanisms is the length of the egg incubation period. For example, rainbow-trout eggs hatch about thirteen days sooner than do brook trout eggs in 50°F. water. A cross of these two species, if the rainbow egg is used, will result in an immature young since the rainbow egg will release the embryo before it is fully developed. The survival of these premature young is very poor. If the reciprocal cross is made using the brook-trout egg, the embryo dies before hatching because it is not released quickly enough.

Even the size of the egg is very important. When the eggs from a brook trout are fertilized by a lake trout, the embryo is too large for the brook-trout egg and the hatching young are often crippled. This cross is more successful if the cross is made using the larger lake-trout egg. These two species, the lake trout and brook trout, are also examples of isolation due to spawning habits. The lake trout does not build a nest or redd but spreads her eggs over loose stone rubble, but the brook trout excavates a redd, spawns, and then covers the eggs. Consequently, it is very unlikely that these two species would get together over the same area in the spawning season.

The fact that hybrids do originate from different species is a barrier to their creation. The chromosomes which carry the genes, hereditary factors, are often of different number or structure in the various species. Since each contributes a set of chromosomes to the new cell, it is very unlikely that they will be compatible in number or shape. When young do develop they are often "mules," unable to reproduce.

Hybridization of the trout does occur in the wild, but this is usually very infrequent. The bulk of the hybrid studies have been conducted on species crosses which have been produced deliberately in fish-culture establishments or research laboratories. Some of the original hybrids were produced out of curiosity, but in recent years, these hybrids have proven valuable in the study of genetics, taxonomy, and even in the origin of the species. Some have been propagated in an effort to find a fish which is better adapted to certain waters than the parent species. Regardless of the original intent, hybridization is fascinating to both scientists and anglers.

Artificial Trout Hybrids Crossbreeding one species of trout with another was first attempted in the United States in 1877 at the Caledonia Fish Hatchery in Mumford, New York. The Honorable Robert B. Roosevelt (*Procedures of the American Association for the Advancement of Science*, 1884) reported on a number of hybrids made under the New York Fishery Commission. These initial crosses were made between chinook salmon and brook trout, a lake trout and brook trout, and rainbow trout and brook trout. F_1 hybrids (the first generation) from female brook trout and male chinook salmon matured in 1879; but the feature of maturity of hybrid females was that their ova were abnormally large and could not be expressed. However, hybrids between the lake trout and brook trout were successful, and the young were stated to be hardier than those of the parent species, and they matured in 1880. Experiments in back-crossing with brook-trout milt, resulted in F_2 and F_3

hybrids. In 1883, 45,000 F_1 hybrids were distributed in streams, and in 1884, 79,000 F_2 hybrids were released. The hybrids (splake) were stated to grow faster than pure brook trout.

European fish culturists also did considerable work with trout hybrids in the nineteenth century. Francis Day, *British and Irish Salmonidae*, 1887, gave very detailed reports on the experiments conducted at Sir James Maitland's fishfarm, Howietoun, Scotland, (1881–1886). He stated "that hybrids do occur among Salmonidae has been known in this country for upwards of two centuries." He quotes Willoughby (1686) as believing that such hybridizing was possible, and a number of subsequent authors. He also cites Professor Rasch (1867) to have found in hybrid experiments that the ova of European char fertilized with brown-trout milt had 30–40 percent fertility, but great mortality among alevins and fry after hatching; and the reverse cross, trout eggs x char milt, to have only 10-percent hatch and many deformities. Other quotations were: Carl Peyrer, (1876), char x trout hybrids in Upper Austria; Leuchart, (1878), salmon x trout hybrids, and Professor Haack "who showed some lovely fish," char x trout, at the Berlin Fishery Exhibition of 1880.

Day, in the chapter of his book on hybrids, mentions that some could be decidedly recognized by their colors, particularly the brown trout x brook trout (tiger). He had received one specimen in 1882 from a river in Wales, believed to be wild bred; and reports from anglers of wild interbreeding in the Wandle River as well as in the Cardiganshire. He called the Howietoun hybrid male brook trout x female brown trout "zebras," and the reverse cross, using brook-trout ova and brown-trout milt, "leopards."

Day realized that in hybridization a mechanical cause of failure of impregnation would arise if the micropyle of the ovum was too small to admit spermatozoa in the milt used. For instance, when an attempt was made to fertilize the comparatively small eggs of American brook trout with the milt of salmon in November, 1883, all but 21 eggs out of 1,000 appeared to have escaped impregnation.

In two experiments (November, 1882, and November, 1883) when his "zebra" hybrids were produced, "here no mechanical difficulty was present, and the deaths during

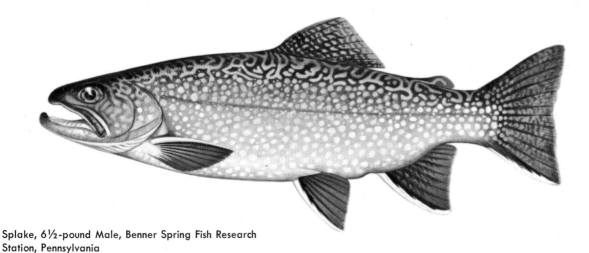

Splake, 6½-pound Male, Benner Spring Fish Research Station, Pennsylvania

Tiger Trout, 11-inch Male, Benner Spring Fish Research Station, Pennsylvania

incubation were from 15% to 17% while comparatively few were lost from want of impregnation."

However, "with two such distinct species as a char and a trout, crossed as described, we find deaths and deformities due to hybridization, in fact due to some physiological not mechanical cause; while as the parents were both pure breeds and no reason existed to suppose that the generative organs of either were affected, this would seem to point out that crossing these two distinct species was calculated to occasion deformities and monstrosities in the resulting offspring."

On the reciprocal cross, brook-trout female x brown-trout male, Day says that the mechanical difficulty would seem to exist (brook-trout eggs being smaller on the average than brown-trout eggs) and the mortality during incubation was about 32 percent, about double that in the preceding cross. The physiologically deleterious cause was likewise present, and deformities were numerous. Subsequent mortality was much greater than in the opposite hybrid.

Splake The splake gets its name from the *sp* in speckled, the Canadian name for brook trout, and the *lake* from lake trout, indicating that this is a cross between the speckled trout and the lake trout.

The splake differs from other hybrids in that it is a fertile cross and able to produce young. In appearance, the body shape is intermediate between the two species, being heavier than the lake trout but slimmer than the brook trout. The body spotting is yellow as in lake trout, with the red spotting of the brook trout being absent. However, when they are placed in a natural environment, they develop the deep red ventral colors of the brook trout.

The first recorded cross of the lake trout and brook trout was made in 1878 by Seth Green, a pioneer fish culturist in New York. In 1886, a cross of these species was recorded at a state fish hatchery in Pennsylvania. The initial interest in these hybrids waned until 1946, when Warden J. E. Stenton of British Columbia experimentally planted some splake in the lakes of Banff National Park. From this introduction and more recent work in New York and Pennsylvania, it was learned: (1) That splake mature sooner than lake trout. Lake trout mature at 4–10

years of age depending on conditions, but a few of these hybrids are sexually mature at 2 years while almost all are mature at 3 years of age; (2) That the maximum size of the splake is greater than any of the present strains of brook trout; (3) That the initial growth of the splake is faster than the lake trout and is intermediate between the parent species; (4) That better hatchability will result when the lake-trout female is crossed with a brook-trout male rather than the reciprocal cross. Young from this reciprocal cross are crippled in the caudal region. This is believed to be due to the cramping of a large embryo into the smaller brook-trout egg; (5) That the viability or capacity to develop of eggs resulting from a splake x splake cross is lower than the original lake trout x brook trout mating; (6) That the splake can be back-crossed with brook trout, and the resulting eggs have a better hatchability than the original lake trout x brook trout cross; (7) That a recurrent back-cross to the brook trout using the progeny of the splake x brook trout back-cross results in still better viability; (8) That the offspring of any generation of these hybrids using splake x splake, splake x brook trout, or (splake x brook trout) x brook trout result in young with varied appearance. Some resemble lake trout, some splake, some brook trout, or any combination thereof.

At the present time, the Canadians are introducing splake into many waters including one of the Great Lakes. It is hoped that early maturing and faster growth will enable them to ward off the lamprey menace which annihilated the indigenous lake trout.

Tiger Trout Tiger trout is a descriptive name not only of the color of this hybrid but of its disposition. The tiger trout is a cross between the female brown trout and the male brook trout. The progeny from this cross have tigerlike markings on their sides and are more aggressive than the parent species. Unfortunately, only about 35 percent of the young are able to develop because of a disease which is inherent in the sac-fry. Occasionally this cross occurs in nature but is unable to reproduce because they are mules of the fish world. Tiger trout have been produced on a small scale in private hatcheries and stocked in various club waters where they are considered a fine gamefish. The tiger is a surface feeder, and is more easily caught than either the brook or brown trout. It is an ideal put-and-take hybrid in that it brings high returns to the creel.

Cutbow The cutbow is a cross between cutthroat and rainbow trout which often occurs in nature. The hybridization of these two species, it is believed, has a tendency to eliminate the native cutthroat population from the streams because of the reported sterility of the progeny. Little work has been done with artificial propagation to learn more about this cross.

Trousal The trousal is a cross between the brown trout and the Atlantic salmon. Poor hatchability results from a cross between the nonmigratory strain of brown trout and salmon producing many weak and immature fry with a high percentage crippled in the region of the dorsal fin. However, large male sea trout (*which see*) have been successfully crossed with small female salmon. The resulting hybrid is fertile and, like the splake, it reproduces naturally. The trousal was initially bred on a large scale in Ireland.

Brownbow When the brown trout female is crossed to the rainbow trout male, none of the eggs hatch; but when the reciprocal cross is made, over half of the eggs hatch, but heavy mortalities result from immature fry. The survivors of this cross are called "brownbow" and have the brownish cast of brown trout with spots extending into the tail similar to the rainbow trout. In a limited experiment in this country, two males and eight females were sterile with both ovaries and testes undeveloped.

However, in New Zealand in the 1920's, three fertile specimens of this cross were found and intercrossed successfully. Large brownbows have been reported caught in New Zealand from time to time.

Sambow The sambow is a hybrid of the Atlantic salmon and rainbow trout. Egg hatchability is poor, and any young which emerge die within 2–3 days.   —K.B.
—A.J.McC.

FISH DISEASES *See* Diseases and Parasites

FISHERY The act, occupation, or season of catching fish. Also a place for catching. In law, the right to take fish at a certain place. In contemporary usage, *fishery* is most often used in a definitive or collective sense, as in *rainbow trout provide the major fishery in the Kamloops area.*

FISHERY BIOLOGIST A scientist capable of recognizing, defining, and investigating problems related to sport and commercial fisheries. The fishery biologist has a knowledge of chemistry, physics, mathematics, zoology, and aquatic biology as well as their practical application to research and management programs. *See also* American Fisheries Society, Sport Fishing Institute

FISHFINDER **1.** A rig used in surf-fishing which features a pyramid sinker with a connecting feed ring, a leather thong, and a barrel swivel. This allows the bait to cover a wide area. Instead of anchoring the bait to the bottom, the fishfinder gives it complete freedom of movement; the bait can be carried by the tide or taken by a fish unhampered by the weight of the sinker. The sliding sinker is placed above the leader swivel so that it does not interfere with the cast. The momentum of the cast keeps the sinker against the leather thong. When the sinker reaches bottom the line runs free through the feed ring. The fishfinder is used chiefly for striped bass, but it is also effective for channel bass, bluefish, weakfish, and other bottom-feeding species. Both blood- and sandworms, as well as clams, cut squids, crabs, strips of whiting, mackerel, or herring belly are effective baits on the fishfinder. *See also* Channel Bass, Striped Bass, Surf-Fishing, Swivel

2. A term used to describe some type of echo-sounder or fathometer, useful in locating schools of fish.
—A.J.McC.

FISH HATCHERY An establishment where fish eggs are hatched and where the young are retained and fed for varying periods, sometimes for several years, until they have matured and been bred for fish-cultural purposes or until they have achieved a size suitable for stocking in angling waters or a size suitable for market in a com-

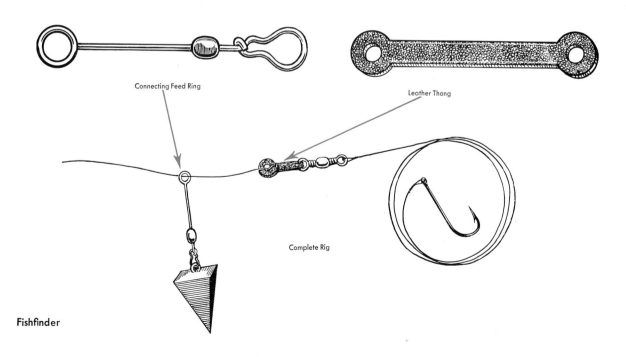

Connecting Feed Ring

Leather Thong

Complete Rig

Fishfinder

mercial operation. The term *fish hatchery* describes the buildings, ponds, and other equipment used in hatching fish eggs and rearing fish. *See also* Fish Culture

FISHING CHAIR An integral part of equipment on offshore fishing boats. *For details see* Fishing Chair *under* Sportfisherman

FISHING GUIDE A person who provides services to anglers for pay and who in nearly all states is required by law to be licensed for the performance of these services. Basically, a fishing guide is responsible for transporting his customer to the fishing area in safety and comfort. The individual guide's moral character, experience, skill, and physical ability are the qualities on which he is judged.

The pay scale for guides is flexible and depends on the additional services required such as making camp and cooking when the trip is longer than one day, and also the amount of equipment the guide must provide in the form of boat, motor, tent, sleeping bags, etc. Within any given region the charges are fairly uniform according to local economic conditions and demand.

FISH PARASITES *See* Diseases and Parasites

FLAG ROCKFISH *Sebastodes rubrivinctus* This colorful rockfish (*which see*) is light pink to white with bright red, vertical crossbars on the head and body. It reaches a length of about 25 inches, and it is found from southern California to southeastern Alaska. It has smooth head scales and a slightly concave interorbital space with moderately strong spines. —J.R.

FLAGFISH *Jordanella floridae* This deep-bodied little fish is a member of the killifish family. It is olive colored, with some yellowish patches and 4–5 diffuse dark cross bars. There is one prominent black spot on the sides. Fins are dusky and may be speckled or barred. Scales are edged in red. The dorsal fin is long, having 16–18 rays, the first of which is a grooved spine. The flagfish is found in coastal swamps and lagoons from Florida to Yucatan.

LIFE HISTORY

Spawning habits are similar to those of the sunfishes. The male fans out a depression with its fins and moves larger particles and debris with his mouth. When the nest is ready he coaxes a female onto it for spawning. The eggs are fertilized and guarded by the male. The young are protected until they can fend for themselves. Food includes both plants and animals, with algae and other plant material apparently preferred. The flagfish is used as an aquarium fish. In the wild it serves as a forage fish for larger species. —C.A.P.

FLANNELMOUTH SUCKER *Catostomus latipinnis* This sucker is distinguished by its unusually large lower lip. It is a slender, fine-scaled sucker with a very long, slender caudal peduncle. The snout is prominent. The sucking

Flannelmouth Sucker

mouth is triangular with very thick, greatly developed lips whose rear margin extends back to a point below the eye. It has a deep cleft in the lower lip which extends two-thirds of the distance to the jaw. The eye is small and high on the head. Its color is olive above and pale below. Fins are orange.

The flannelmouth sucker is found only in the Colorado River Basin of the Western United States.

LIFE HISTORY

This species inhabits creeks and rivers where they feed largely on vegetation. They spawn in the spring and reach a maximum length of 18 inches to 2 feet. It is used as food and can be caught on worms and similar baits. —C.A.P.

FLARE The outward and upward curve built into a boat's bow. Also a temporary blaze made to attract attention, particularly as a distress signal.

FLASHER A common name for the tripletail (*which see*) in the Gulf states.

FLAT A sand, marl, or mud bottom of fairly uniform depth which is exposed partially or wholly at low tide. Some important marine gamefish are sought on flats such as bonefish, permit, and tarpon. Unlike a *bank* the flat cannot be navigated except with specially constructed shallow-draft skiffs under optimum tidal conditions.

FLAT BULLHEAD *Ictalurus platycephalus* Found from the Roanoke River in Virginia southward to the Altamaha River in Georgia. This species has 21–24 anal rays, an emarginate or slightly forked tail, a flattened head, and a narrow black margin on all median fins. In some watersheds the body may have a strong yellowish coloration and is sometimes confused with the yellow bullhead. However, the lower third of its dorsal fin has a prominent black band or blotch. The flat bullhead occurs in streams,

Flat Bullhead

lakes, and ponds with soft muck, mud, or sand bottoms. It feeds principally on vegetation, snails, and mussels. Only a small poundage of this species is taken commercially, but its flesh is comparable to the channel catfish. Maximum size is about 2 pounds, but averages less than 1 pound. The flat bullhead is readily caught on mollusk baits, such as sour clams or mussels, and any of the scent baits. —A.J.McC.

FLATHEAD CATFISH *Pylodictis olivaris* A large, square-tailed catfish with a wide, distinctly flattened head. The flathead catfish has a short anal fin with usually 14–17 rays. Its lower jaw is always longer than the upper. Its general coloration is brown, mottled with darker brown. The upper and lower edges of the caudal fin are white or lighter than the rest of the fin. The flathead catfish is distributed in large rivers in the Mississippi Valley south into Mexico.

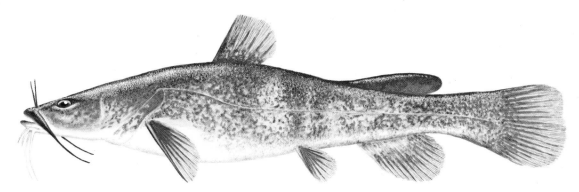

Flathead Catfish

Preferring long, deep, sluggish pools of larger rivers, the flathead catfish is normally found over hard-bottom types. Omnivorous in its food habits, this catfish appears to prefer a fish diet. It has been observed to lie quietly in shallow water with its large mouth wide open. Frightened fish have been seen darting into the open mouth, to be quickly swallowed.

ANGLING VALUE

Like most of its family, the flathead is popular with anglers both because of its excellent flavor and large size. Although 3–4 pound fish are considered average, this species may attain weights up to 100 pounds. Handlines and trotlines are the popular methods, using crayfish or whole or cut fish as bait. Flatheads are also caught by jugging (corked jugs floating on the surface to which a suitable length of line and bait is attached). Both fyke nets and haul seines are employed by the commercial fishery. —R.A.J.

FLATHEAD CHUB *Hybopsis gracilis* A light olive, slender-bodied chub. Sides silver. No lateral band. Head broad, short, and flattened. Mouth large, oblique, and subterminal. Lateral line slightly decurved. This species has 8 dorsal rays and 8 anal rays. All fins have pointed rather than rounded free ends. There is a well-developed barbel at the junction of the jaws. The flathead chub occupies a range from Saskatchewan south to Oklahoma.

Flathead Chub

HABITS

The flathead chub inhabits clear, swift streams with gravelly bottoms. Its ability to withstand turbid and silty flood conditions is notable. This chub is omnivorous, feeding on a variety of vegetation, aquatic insects, and crustaceans. It spawns in early summer and reaches a size of 12 inches.

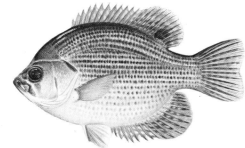

Flier

as a table fish. It will take any bait from worms and flies to popping bugs. —K.B.

FLOAT-FISHING A method of fishing on rivers in which the boat drifts while the angler casts. By implication, a float trip is one that covers greater distances than usual and may extend for several days to a week or more. Float-fishing is a regional specialty which was first organized on a commercial basis in the Ozark Mountains of Missouri and Arkansas; it has since become popular in other areas of the United States. The float-trip operator supplies the boat, guide, motor, fuel, and extras, which may include a commissary boat and cook, cooking utensils, tents, sleeping bags, and other equipment necessary for camping out. The charm of a float trip is in the tranquil atmosphere of journeying down a river and fishing in remote places.

ADVANTAGES OF FLOATING

One thing that makes float-fishing especially productive is that most rivers have a limited number of access points which the man on foot can use. An angler can only walk or wade a limited distance, and as a result long stretches of water are often relatively unfished. Even where a boat livery exists, a one-day angler can't cover too much river. It's also true that while many streams are paralleled by highway there is frequently a considerable mileage that runs away from the road. Such places may provide excellent angling.

Another advantage of float trips lasting two days or more is that you can comfortably be on the water early and late. This makes a big difference in summer angling. Most motorists find it difficult, if not impossible, to arrive on location at dawn or to stay on the river until dark. The leisurely pace of floating not only extends your range but permits you to be on the productive pools at key hours. For nocturnal gamefish like the brown trout, walleye, and largemouth bass, a gravelbar camp is at least half the secret in getting the most out of civilized streams. Some states do not permit night fishing, so check the regulations first.

TACTICAL PROBLEMS

Fly-casting from a freely drifting boat is pleasant. You sit in the bow passing from the shadows of tall timber to a shoring of sand and hardwood where the deer bright in the noon sun come down on sharp-pointed hooves to drink and feed, and around the next bend a great flock of greenheads are waiting to jump and surprise you, but always you watch for the signs of rising trout. The mechanics of fishing are simple. With your shooting line stripped in coils on the floor you can cast quartering downstream, and since the boat is moving at the same speed as the current, the fly will float without drag. In a day's time you can cover an amazing length of river, including places that a wading angler couldn't touch.

When using spinning or bait-casting tackle for trout, bass, or muskellunge, however, you might experience some difficulty in fishing ahead of the boat. Because of the weight of a spoon or plug and the necessity to keep them in motion, the quartering downstream cast can be a handicap. You have to anticipate where your lure is going to work in relation to where the boat will be at the completion of the retrieve. There is a tendency particu-

larly for brown trout, smallmouth bass, and muskellunge to follow a lure long distances; this often results in drawing big fish within sight of the angler and thereby lessening the chance of a strike. Cross- and upstream casting may be more effective, because the boat is always drifting away from the fish. It is also worth while to beach the boat from time to time and cast from the bank or by wading. There are several reasons for this. First, while floating, your fishing speed remains constant. Secondly, you seldom have the opportunity to observe the reactions of your quarry. Third, you will pass a large percentage of good water before you have a chance to cover it or recognize it. A lie can be completely disguised from one direction, and even if you are familiar with the contours of white water, the pocket is invariably hidden from the upstream side looking downriver. Part of your success in this kind of fishing will depend on how accurately you plan your pattern of casting. In a moving boat you are in no position to make corrections in your technique. An experienced guide will anchor or wedge his boat at likely looking places to eliminate some of these problems, but during the greatest part of the trip you are a floating island of unprofitable sanctity—unless you can wade. Obviously, you can't step into five feet of running river, but nearly all rivers have shallow vantage points or banks that offer a stable platform of operation. On Northern and Western rivers with boggy banks, like the Deschutes, Teton, Ausable, and most Southern streams, you can pole your boat up into the bank grass and, after fishing the area within casting distance, move downstream another fifty yards or so.

TACKLE

Naturally, the tackle you favor for any particular kind of fishing is suitable for a float trip. The only difference is that you can take along more than one rod. A basic combination such as the fly rod and a spinning or bait-casting rod is ideal. Sometimes you get combinations of species which do not come readily to one method or the other. If you were floating the Flambeau in Wisconsin, for instance, you would want to bug the riffles for smallmouths and plug the deep pools for muskies. There will also be spots that are out of fly-rod range and sections where the boat is moving so fast that snap shooting a spoon is the only answer. —A.J.McC.

FLORIDA This 447-mile-long peninsula facing the Atlantic Ocean on the east coast and the Gulf of Mexico on the west coast boasts another 58,560 square miles of water surface in the form of lakes and rivers. Florida is uniquely an angler's paradise. Scenically, it is a monotonous state along its major highways but in the back country where live oaks are bearded with Spanish moss and ospreys ride the thermals, you can still hear the grunts of wild pigs and the gobble talk of turkeys. The Everglades region is one of the last great wildernesses remaining in the United States.

The state is flat with its highest point at 345 feet in the panhandle where the average elevation is about 100 feet; however, the altitude quickly drops toward the southern end of the peninsula, and towns in the latitude of Lake Okeechobee are only 6–12 feet above sea level. Nevertheless, there is a definite transition in Florida's flora and fauna beginning with rolling pine lands in the north and semitropical at roughly the midpoint down the state. The pines give way to palmettoes and sawgrass and finally become the wilderness region of the open Everglades. A serpentine series of islands and fills curve away from the very tip of Florida into a limitless horizon of sea toward Cuba. They are given continuity by bridges and causeways all the way to Key West; fishing is a way of life in the Florida Keys, and the tourist can literally stop anywhere to enjoy his sport.

FRESHWATER FISHING

Florida is nationally famous for its bass fishing. The state consistently produces the heaviest largemouths in the United States. A recognized subspecies of the Northern form, the Florida largemouth (*which see*), is frequently caught at weights of 5–10 pounds. A number of 12–16-pound fish are taken annually. There are an estimated 30,000 lakes and temporary sloughs or ponds in the state which may evaporate during the drought periods. These are all bass habitat, but chain pickerel, various sunfishes, catfishes, and gars are natural associates and occur in varying degrees of abundance. The great majority of the lakes are shallow. The maximum depth for nearly all of them is about 20 feet; 700-square-mile Lake Okeechobee has an average depth of 7 feet and a maximum depth of 14 feet.

The lake bottoms range from heavy muck in the Everglades region to the pure white sand in the central part of the state. The water varies from dark brown to perfectly clear, but it's all fertile and the fish grow fast. The bass survive in almost any wet place. Myriads of newly hatched fish are commonly seen in roadside drainage ditches and flooded pastures in the sawgrass country. These plains are level, and consequently, during periods of high-water, large areas of land which are normally dry

Bass fishing in Florida is typically done in heavy vegetation. Weedless lures are essential to success

become inundated from a few inches to several feet or more. Bass are often very abundant in these sloughs, and they remain there until the water level recedes, moving back into the main river, canal, or lake. Thus, natural depressions in the land often become highly productive pot-holes.

There is no closed season on black bass in Florida. Ripe fish are taken during their spawning period, but the practice is basically sound. For one thing, Florida bass spawn every month of the year; they are as likely to bed in November as the more orthodox February to April period. The climatic conditions are constant in comparison to the North where bass predictably reproduce in late spring or early summer depending on the latitude. Secondly, research has demonstrated that Florida bass populations experience a low rate of harvest. The adverse factors in bass production are abnormal conditions, such as drought, pollution, or loss of habitat to land development. In some waters, obnoxious species, such as the spotted gar, and vegetation, such as the water hyacinth, severely limit gamefish production.

Although no list of Florida bass lakes is ever complete, some of the more popular ones in the northern portion of the state near Tallahassee are Lakes Talquin, Jackson, Iamonia, and Miccosukee. Although Talquin is just over twenty-five miles from the capital city, it remains one of the state's most reliable bass lakes. The peak period is rather long, running from October to June of the year. Large striped bass are also caught in the pool below Talquin Dam.

For all its natural bass water, Florida is still creating new fisheries, particularly in the northern portion of the state. Deer Point Lake, a few miles north of Panama City, was designed as a 5,000-acre reservoir and formed by damming the creeks at the upper end of St. Andrew Bay. This resulted in an interesting situation with freshwater species abounding on one side of the dam and spotted seatrout, tarpon, red drum, and the usual bottom species frequenting the saltwater side. Stump-filled Dead Lake, an Apalachicola tributary lying east of Panama City near Wewahitchka, produces big bass, particularly in the spring season. Some exceptional fish have also been caught here on fly-rod poppers in the early summer months.

Heading southeast, there are numerous bigmouth lakes near Palatka and Welaka in the so-called Bass Capital Region such as Lake George, and its southern arm Little Lake George, and Lake Crescent as well as rivers ranging from the mighty St. Johns to smaller streams such as Dunn's Creek and Murphy's Creek. Dropping down to the Leesburg area good bass waters include lakes Tsala Apopka, Griffin, Dora, Panasoffkee, Eustis, Harris, and Little Lake Harris; the lakes in the headwater section of the St. Johns River are extremely productive at times, and these include Lake Hell'n Blazes, Big and Little Sawgrass, and Lake Washington. South of Orlando, the Tahopekaligo lakes are popular as is Lake Kissimmee and the Kissimmee River all the way to its outlet in Lake Okeechobee. In this same general area good fishing can be had at Lake Istokpoga at Lorida, Lake Martin east of Haines City, Lake Lena at Auburndale, and Lake Seminole north of Clearwater. To the east near Vero Beach, Blue Cypress Lake produces very large bass at times as well as big crappies and bluegills, as does Lake

Marianna slightly to the north. The last identifiable lake southwest of Lake Okeechobee is Lake Trafford near the village of Immokalee.

Some bass fishing occurs in Florida's rivers. These are fished primarily by boat, and interesting float trips can be made on several of these rivers. Beginning in the northern part of the state one of the better-known locations is the Chipola River. This stream actually rises in Houston County, Alabama, and flows approximately 100 miles south to its confluence with the Apalachicola River in northern Florida. Principal gamefish are largemouth bass, redeye bass, bluegill, warmouth, and channel catfish, although the river is probably best known for its redeye bass (*which see*), which are caught in the section between Marianna and Clarksville, Florida. However, much of the bigmouth fishing is in the lower blackwater reaches of the Chipola River north of Scott's Ferry.

Sturgeon fishing is popular in northern Florida rivers, and one of the more important fisheries exists on the Apalachicola River below Jim Woodruff Dam. Although the sturgeon enter the river beginning in April, the peak period is from August through September when the water is low. The bait used for these big fish is river moss (algae) which has been toughened by the sun and can be twisted in a ropy mass. This same bait is also used for catching mullet in freshwater. Sturgeon of 80–100 or more pounds are present in the Apalachicola and are highly prized both for their flesh and the roe used in making caviar (*which see*).

Other major Florida bass streams include the Caloosahatchee, Oklawaha, Withlacoochee, Chassahowitza, Suwanee, Homosassa, Crystal, and Rainbow rivers. Those streams which enter saltwater contain mixed fish populations with crevalle, snook, spotted seatrout, ladyfish, snappers, and tarpon occurring as far up as the tidal flow, and as a rule there is some mingling even in areas of very low salinities. The more tolerant snook and tarpon often appear in freshwater habitats with the largemouth bass.

The St. Johns River is Florida's largest stream but not necessarily its best location for bass fishing. The river has a complex ecology with many species of migratory and marine as well as rough species entering the picture. Rough-fish control work, particularly for the gizzard shad, has improved the bass situation to some extent. The upper river from Lake Hell'n Blazes north to Lake Harney is productive when water levels are up. Near Astor, and as far as the south end of Lake George, there are some good spots. The aforementioned Crescent Lake has good fishing periodically, particularly for school bass in the spring season. The mouth of the Oklawaha River is one of the more heavily fished parts of the St. Johns but a fair location at times. The peak season throughout the river is from December through April. Shellcracker (*see* Redear Sunfish) fishing peaks in August when the water temperatures are high.

Perhaps one of the most significant changes in St. Johns angling has been the growing popularity of its American-shad (*which see*) fishery. During the winter season after the water temperatures drop, huge schools enter the river from the Atlantic to spawn. Their main breeding grounds are between Lake Monroe and Lake Harney. In the St. Johns River, American shad die after their spawning run as soon as the water warms again in April.

The methods used to catch Florida bass are the same as in the North; however, the most effective lures are those designed for shallow, weedy water. The three popular artificials are the plastic worm, a wobbling spoon with a plastic skirt, and the pork rind eel. However, to what extent any of these baits is superior may rest solely in their widespread use; topwater, as well as the darter-type plug, and bass bugs are also extremely productive in the hands of a skilled caster. During the general spawning period from January to April, Florida bigmouths are usually found in thick grass bottoms where plug fishing is impractical. Thus, the worm, spoon, and eel have an advantage in being virtually weedless. At other times, and in openwater or in canals the angler has a much wider choice of lures.

Floating bass bugs are often effective particularly in the clear, shallow-water ponds and marshes of the central portion of the state. A great deal depends then on local and seasonal conditions.

The most popular live bait for Florida bass is a large shiner, 6–10 inches long. This big minnow is fished with or without a float and allowed to run just at the edge of deepwater, around lily-pad beds or in the grass patches. Live shiners probably account for more heavy bass through the year than any other bait or lure.

CANAL FISHING

Water conservation and drainage canals constitute an important freshwater sports fishery in Florida, largely due to the vast water impoundment and land reclamation program of the Central and Southern Florida Flood Control District. This canal system is most extensive in south Florida, where thousands of miles of canals and large drainage ditches have been constructed to control the sprawling surface waters of the Everglades south of the great shallow basin of Lake Okeechobee.

There is virtually no man-made waterway in south Florida that is not populated by largemouth bass, panfish, and species such as the undesirable gar and bowfin. However, some of these canals have a much higher rate of production than others due to the nature of their construction. Deep canals, with sheer, nearly perpendicular sides, rarely have a satisfactory rate of freshwater gamefish production due to an almost total lack of shallow areas for spawning. Bass and panfish, such as bluegill, shellcracker, black crappie (locally, speckled perch), and warmouth, require relatively shallow water for nesting purposes. Sunlight is a vital element in the hatching of their eggs on the spawning beds. Deep "channelized" canals that are exceptions to this general condition are those fed by numerous tributary canals that drain shallow sloughs where spawning conditions are favorable. A notable example of this is the West Palm Beach Canal, running between the Atlantic Coast and Lake Okeechobee, which produces bass in excess of 9 pounds.

Canals that have no banks on one or both sides, allowing overflow into inundated lowlands, often produce great numbers of gamefish—to the extent that some become overpopulated with fish during periods of lowwater. Virtually year-around spawning conditions, due to south Florida's semitropical climate, is a principal factor in the overpopulation problem. During peak periods of overpopulation, regular bag limits that are already generous are often relaxed completely in certain south Florida canals so that desirable fish may be harvested rather than allowed to go to waste as they succumb to insufficient oxygen in the water.

The type of construction of the hundreds of miles of canals surrounding the Central and Southern Florida Flood Control District's three huge water conservation areas in South Florida, near the east coast, has resulted in these canals becoming highly productive of gamefish in Florida. It is on these canals, which encircle Conservation Areas 1, 2, and 3, that the Flood Control District, with the cooperation of many state, county, and local agencies, has developed its public outdoor recreation program. This program consists of facilities ranging from simple public access sites consisting of boat launching ramps and parking area to elaborate facilities offering rental boats, sightseeing and fishing by airboat, guides, and the usual fishing-camp services. The first big center, the Loxahatchee Recreation Area, located at the south end of Conservation Area 1 in Palm Beach County, was built in 1962 at a cost exceeding $250,000. Access to these three areas for fishing may be found several miles from the southeast Florida coast in Palm Beach, Broward (Ft. Lauderdale area), and Dade (Miami area) counties. Conservation Area 1, located entirely within the boundaries of Palm Beach County, is administered by the U. S. Department of the Interior and is known as the Loxahatchee Wildlife Refuge. It is encircled by a wide canal of more than fifty miles in circumference. Essentially a refuge for a heavy population of birdlife, the entire perimeter is open to fishing. To the south, Conservation Areas 2 and 3 are administered by the Florida Game and Fresh Water Fish Commission, and are open to both fishing and hunting.

As these large Flood Control District canals are kept clear of noxious vegetation, all types of fishing tackle may be used by the angler. As a matter of fact, fly-rod fishing with bass bugs and smaller panfish bugs is considered by many to be one of the most effective methods of canal angling. Ultralight spinning tackle with 2–4-pound-test lines may also be used by the fisherman. Spinners, tiny plugs, and panfish jigs from ¼ down to 1⁄16 of an ounce and less are recommended for the spinfisherman. Anglers who concentrate on large bass, however, usually use heavier spinning tackle or revolving-spool bait-casting tackle. Surface plugs can be quite productive in these canals, but fishing success usually is in proportion to the number of casts made to within several inches of the canal banks.

Visiting anglers may find it to their advantage to use their own outboard skiffs in the Flood Control canals, but rental boats and guides may also be obtained. Big boats with large-horsepower outboard motors may have an advantage for cruising or ranging long distances, but lighter outboard rigs, which can be controlled with oars, paddles, or light electric motors against wind, are favored by casters who frequently fish the canals.

For maps and printed matter on the location and facilities of canal access areas, write to the Director of Recreation, Central and Southern Florida Flood Control District, Evernia Street, West Palm Beach. For additional information and maps of fishing canals and lakes, write to the Florida Game and Fresh Water Fish Commission, Tallahassee. To make specific inquiries concerning fishing in the freshwaters of south Florida, it is suggested you write to the Regional Manager, Everglades Region Headquarters, Florida Game and Fresh Water Fish Commission, at West Palm Beach.

EAST COAST SALTWATER FISHING

The northernmost section of Florida's east coast is frequently by-passed by visitors heading for the more popular ports such as Palm Beach, Fort Lauderdale, and Miami. However, from Fernandina Beach south to Cocoa Beach there is considerable saltwater fishing in season. This is limited by cooler weather and water during the winter months (the Gulf Stream swings away from the coast about halfway up the state), but surf-casting, jetty-fishing, and bottomfishing for red drum, black drum, whiting, sheepshead, spotted seatrout, and croakers is productive throughout the year. Winter runs of bluefish and Spanish mackerel and tarpon during the summer months can be extremely heavy. Jacksonville, St. Augustine, Daytona, and the beaches of New Smyrna are all popular locations. The latter is the beginning of big trout country; Mosquito Lagoon, which extends about twenty miles between the narrows at Oak Hill and New Smyrna to a point east of Titusville, is a favorite among specialists. This broad (about two miles wide), shallow bay is particularly good in hot weather.

Stalking permit in the Florida Keys requires both wading and casting skills. Peak fishing is usually in the spring season

Some of the largest spotted seatrout in the United States are caught in the vicinity of Cocoa Beach. Although the nearby Cape Kennedy complex has changed the once sleepy fishing village into a busy city, large fish (8–13 pounds) are still taken in the Banana and Indian rivers. From Cocoa Beach south, coastal fishing becomes more semitropical in character. The St. Lucie River at Stuart offers a typical bag of east-coast gamesters including the crevalle, bluefish, spotted seatrout, ladyfish, snook, and tarpon; however, the best fishing occurs in the May through September period. Big snook and tarpon begin to peak in June when the fish move upriver to blast the mullet schools along the mangroves. St. Lucie tarpon average 20–40 pounds, but occasional heavyweights are caught. The snook are above average with 25–30 pounders always in residence. One of the more popular snook spots is from the bridge within the city limits. Bottomfishermen also get sheepshead, drum, and croakers from the span. Actually, the St. Lucie divides above the bridge, with its shorter North Fork retaining some of the back-country flavor that made the stream famous; the South Fork is linked with the Gulf of Mexico, 148 miles to the west, by the Cross-State Waterway, via the St. Lucie Canal and Lake Okeechobee. The river enters the sea seven miles downstream from Stuart at the confluence of the Cross-State and Intracoastal waterways. Thus, the transition from saltwater to freshwater is made a short distance upstream from Stuart, and an angling license is required.

More than a thousand Atlantic sailfish (*which see*) are caught each year in the Gulf Stream between Stuart and Palm Beach. This forty-mile sector also produces kingfish, dolphin, wahoo, amberjack, white and blue marlin, and other marine gamefish in season. The Palm Beach area has more boats, docks, and accommodations than Stuart, but the latter is uniquely an angling town with excellent facilities scaled on a more intimate level. Either port has access to the same fishing.

Due to the proximity of the Gulf Stream, the fishing hours begin almost immediately after leaving the inlet at 8:00 A.M. and continue to a reasonable period after 4:00 P.M., allowing sufficient time for your skipper to make port before dark. Trolling and occasionally drift-fishing are the principal techniques for catching sailfish. Instruction and the correct tackle are supplied by the charter boat. Your chances of raising at least one sailfish per trip are good, and ordinarily you will get several strikes on an average day. During peak periods, notably in mid-December when the fish are schooling and later in February, catches of 5–10 sailfish per boat are not unusual, and a few experts have billed as many as 30 in one day. The fish run 6–8½ feet long and weigh 35–90 pounds. Sailfish are strong light-tackle fish (12-pound test) but are no less acrobatic or powerful against the 20-pound and 30-pound lines spooled by most charter skippers. On occasion both white and blue marlin come to sailfish baits in this area.

You can drive, take a train, or fly to West Palm Beach. Stuart airport doesn't handle large commercial airliners. There are many taxi and car-rental services available in the area, although ground transportation isn't necessary if you stay at a location convenient to the city docks. Florida has two ranges of hotel prices depending on the season. The period from January 1st to April 1st is generally more expensive than the other months, but there are accommodations of all kinds from motels to first-class hotels.

Everything you need is available, including well-stocked tackle shops in Stuart, West Palm Beach, and Palm Beach. You must have tropical clothing including sport shirts, shorts, topsiders for wet decks, and suntan lotion. Also suits and sport jackets for hotel life and a warm sweater for those unseasonable blows. Experienced big-game anglers may want their own tackle, but nothing heavier than thirty-pound test is necessary. It's advisable to include fly, bait-casting, or spinning gear for nearby freshwater bass fishing or the smaller saltwater species, such as ladyfish, snook, bluefish, and Spanish mackerel. The two latter species appear in great numbers at various periods during the sailfish season.

The snook (*which see*) is one of the most popular Florida gamefish. It may grow to weights over 50 pounds and to lengths of 4–5 feet. Although the average snook is much smaller, the state does produce a number of 30–40-pound fish each year. Snook are most abundant in the southern half of Florida, with the biggest fish coming from the inlets and lagoons around Stuart, Palm Beach, and Boynton Beach. However, these east-coast locations are seasonal, and for consistent fishing the lower west coast from Whitewater Bay north to Naples is more reliable. As practiced in Lake Worth, an annual producer of trophy snook, the game consists of plugging on the flats or fishing with live bait from the bridges at night.

Lake Worth, which is really a wide portion of the Intracoastal Waterway, stretching north and south of West Palm Beach, has declined in fish production in so far as the once abundant populations of spotted seatrout, snook, and red drum are concerned due to the destruction of shallow-water habitat in dredging and filling; nevertheless, it maintains a seasonal fishery. Since the ecologically important weed beds and shell bars have been almost entirely eradicated, the angling is more erratic, with migrants such as the bluefish and Spanish mackerel invading the lake during winter months, along with big schools of crevalle, ladyfish, and pompano, followed by snook and the occasional large seatrout beginning in May. Then the action shifts to the inlet and surf in September when the annual mullet migration takes place. This can be sheer bedlam with the snook chopping up city-block-long schools of bait.

But with the first chill north winds the snook specialist looks for his sport in mangrove creeks and bays, particularly in the southwest corner of the state. Many anglers prefer back-country fishing—plugging jungle shorelines where a 10-pound snook or a 20-pound tarpon can bust the next cast. In this kind of water the two fish are frequently found together, and a light-tackle man couldn't hope for a better combination.

The Spanish mackerel appears in Florida waters in vast schools, feeding voraciously upon small baitfish. It is one of the more important commercial species, but has become increasingly popular in recent years as a saltwater gamefish. Contributing considerably to its popularity with anglers is its willingness to take a wide variety of artificial lures and its extremely savage strike. The coastal waters of Florida, both the Atlantic and Gulf sides, constitute an important Spanish mackerel commercial and sport fishery. The big run on the east coast begins in the fall when northerly winds and dropping temperatures prod great schools of mackerel inshore. Commercial fishermen use gillnets a short distance off the beaches to make huge catches. As mackerel run south, anglers score heavily from ocean piers and boats. Surfcasters take mackerel with casting spoons or jigs.

Although mackerel run in and out of ocean inlets on their way southward, they tend to take up extended residence only in tidal bays that have considerable depth.

Lake Worth at West Palm Beach, which has a deep inlet and port turning basin, attracts a tremendous winter Spanish-mackerel run in cold-weather years. The mackerel usually enter Lake Worth some time in late December. It has been noted by observers, year after year, that the fish move into the lake in vast numbers following one or two severe northwesters, which result from cold fronts moving in from the Plains states. The mackerel remain in the lake through March and begin to move out in April, when they begin their return migration northward. At the peak of the midwinter run in the lake, as many as four hundred small boats can be counted over the fishing grounds in a single day.

Although the Miami area has developed into a great metropolis, anglers still find good inshore saltwater fishing in the vicinity of the city, and charter and party boats continue to ply a lively trade in offshore waters. Miami is also an important jumping-off base for anglers who fish the Florida Keys; the myriad bays, rivers, and creeks in the mangrove lowlands on Florida's southwest coast; and the western out islands of the Bahamas.

Biscayne Bay, with its cuts leading to the ocean, is the principal tidal-water fishing area in the Greater Miami region. Bridge and causeway fishermen take a wide variety of bottomfish from the bay the year around, and in some locations they hit ladyfish and Spanish mackerel during the cooler months. Not all the spans and causeways are open to fishing in the bay area; however, an angler may obtain information on available fishing spans from any tackle shop. The inshore fishing territory is so far flung that the purchase of a local fishing-guide publication may be a helpful initial step for the angler.

The 79th Street Causeway and Sunny Isles Draw Bridge are popular nighttime snook-fishing locations, and Government Cut, Miami's main ocean inlet, is productive of tarpon in the cooler months. Kings, mackerel, and blues may be encountered in the vicinity of the Cut in fall and winter, and snook, jacks, and miscellaneous other gamefish take over for the spring and summer. Norris and Bear cuts, south of Government Cut, are considered productive fishing spots. Norris Cut, Virginia Beach, and Cape Florida are noted for their bonefish flats.

Miami, like other fishing centers on the east coast of Florida, is visited by south-bound schools of migratory gamefish beginning in the fall. The quantities of these fish reaching the Miami area each winter season depend upon the number and severity of cold fronts moving down with brisk northerly winds. Anglers at several ocean piers from Miami Beach northward along the Dade County coastline reap a harvest of fish from schools of Spanish mackerel, bluefish, pompano, crevalle, kingfish, and other migrating species. Some of these fish move into the ocean cuts, and mackerel generally enter the bay south of Government Cut. Bridge- and seawall-fishermen get a share of the mackerel, but fishing in the bay from a small skiff is more effective. Trolling, still-fishing, and casting are common ways of taking these fish. Pompano also enter the bay, where they are occasionally taken by fishermen working from skiffs or bridges.

There are a few shell pits and small canals in the vicinity of Miami for the freshwater fisherman, but most angling activity is concentrated along the Tamiami Trail Canal and other canals in Conservation Area 3, west of Miami. The Tamiami Canal offers snook and tarpon action as well as freshwater bass and panfish. Fly-rod fishing is popular all along this canal.

Due to the expanse of tidal inshore waters in the Miami area and the usual complications resulting from urbanization, many year-around residents of this metropolitan area prefer the open spaces and the generally more productive fishing of the Keys and the southwest-coast mangrove country.

Although not considered the equal of Palm Beach and Stuart, Miami is a center of sailfishing activity. Kingfish, wahoo, dolphin, amberjack, and blue and white marlin also occur on this section of the coast. King mackerel, which run about 5–35 pounds, arrive in southeast Florida offshore waters in huge schools during the winter. Fishermen on the reef boats take them drift-fishing and spincasting. Tackle requirements and fishing methods employed in the offshore waters, inshore tidal waters, and freshwaters in the Greater Miami area are little different than elsewhere along the southeast coast.

WEST COAST SALTWATER FISHING

Everglades National Park encompasses 1,400,533 acres in the southwest corner of the state. This includes most of the Ten Thousand Island Region, a vast area of hammocks and creeks bordering the Gulf of Mexico on the west and Florida Bay on the south. It is one of the most unique marine habitats in North America. If you trailer your own boat, there are plenty of launching ramps available, and, by today's standards, inexpensive accommodations, which makes the Park well worth a visit. Despite the encroachments of civilization, the mangrove forests still survive. There is an ecological distinction between the sawgrass and palmetto "open" glades and the estuarine environment of the mangroves, but both are part of the Park. To the casual observer the entire watershed may look like nothing but an endless chain of shallow mud-bottomed ponds connected by meandering creeks; however, the water level fluctuates not only through tide flow but according to rainfall. The amount of rainfall (which affects the salinity) plus the water temperature determines what kind of fish will be found where in any given period. While it's fairly predictable, for example, that red drum are abundant in the fall and tarpon in the spring months, there are almost daily changes in the variety and location of Everglades gamefish. A creek that's empty one day may be full of snook the next.

When Columbus arrived in the New World he found a strange kind of tree growing in shallow saltwater lagoons which he observed in the Santa Maria's log were "so thick a cat couldn't get ashore." The tree was the red mangrove, which is not only capable of building new land by trapping debris among its aerial roots but it also sustains aquatic life by providing cover and food. The mangrove leaf itself is the key to fish production in the Everglades ecosystem. Although a leaf as it falls from the tree is not immediate forage, it soon acquires a growth of microorganisms, and its decay is accompanied by an increase in caloric and protein content. Scavengers such as crabs shred it into smaller and smaller fragments, and in a matter of months the leaf becomes a significant part of the food chain. In effect, bacteria and fungi convert a relatively indigestible product into a forage that can be utilized by the all-important primary consumers, such as shrimp, mysids, amphipods, and omnivorous fishes—the

A successful angler releases his bonefish on the flats near Islamorada. Such fishing is popular throughout the year, the only negative factors being cold spells, which drive the bonefish into deep water, and prolonged winds that make the shallows extremely turbid

mullet and sheepshead minnow among others. In turn these detritus feeders are preyed upon by young gamefish, particularly tarpon, snook, mangrove snapper, and red drum. The chain is long and complex. Suffice it to say, wherever mangroves have been destroyed, fishing has declined, and in some areas whole populations of estuarine dependent species, such as the spotted seatrout, have disappeared. Fortunately, the Everglades watershed remains incredibly fertile at present. As the tide falls, you will see orange-colored "islands" around the higher mangroves which, on close examination, consist of literally millions of fiddler crabs feeding among the aerial roots. The abundance of pink shrimp is so great that the Tortugas commercial fishery is created by juveniles which migrate from south Florida. It has taken man many years even to begin to comprehend the dynamics of this remarkable habitat.

Generally speaking, spring and fall are the best periods for fishing in the Everglades. Heavy summer rains normally begin at the end of June and continue through September. Aside from the storms themselves, which invariably culminate in lightning bolts, prolonged rains create freshwater conditions and most game species remain in the higher salinities of the Gulf. The winter season can be uncertain also; high winds will muddy the creeks, and estuaries and as the water temperature drops below 60°F angling success declines rapidly. Local anglers who really know the back country will head for the nar-

row, deep streams or ditches that are not exposed to the wind. Some of these may remain 10 or more degrees warmer than the broad, shallow rivers during a brief cold spell. If the water temperature drops to 50°F conditions become critical, not only for the angler but the fish as well. In the winter of 1970 a cold-kill extended from the Everglades through the Keys and east into the Bahamas. Thousands of dead tarpon choked the creeks, while windrows of spotted seatrout, snappers, and barracuda covered the flats. Bonefish were hard hit everywhere. Under ordinary conditions these fish would have migrated from the shallows into warmer, deeper waters, but that three-day January blow created a sudden drop into the low 40's while strong winds mixed and chilled the inshore areas so quickly that vast schools never reached safety. Cold-kills do not occur this far south very often. Given a bluebird winter Florida fishing can be exceptional and it is often the best time for baby tarpon.

Tarpon from 10–20 pounds are a real handful on light tackle. Fish of this size concentrate in large schools during the cooler months, usually in a deep bay or backwater off the main rivers. If they are actively feeding you can take them on any surface lure or fly; if the tarpon are simply "rolling," which is more often the case, then a jig or small sinking plug danced just over the bottom will get results. This is great sport with spinning gear using a flashy silver plug of ½ ounce or less. As the weather warms larger tarpon in the 20–40-pound class begin to appear and these can be caught by any method including fly-fishing. By April, tarpon in the 50–100-pound range will be migrating north along the outside bars, but pods of big fish linger to feed in the creek mouths. It comes as a jolt when you are casting the shoreline, anticipating a snook or jack, to feel the tap of a taking fish and suddenly the water explodes as 70 or 80 pounds of hammered silver twists in the air. This often happens in the spring season. In the cycle of estuarine-dependent species young or small fish adapt much more readily to freshwater conditions than the older fish; thus they escape predation. However, after a long period of dry weather the saltier tides draw big fish right up into the mangroves.

Outside bars offer different fishing from the mangrove creeks. Tarpon and snook occur here and in fact the "outside" can produce fast angling, particularly after a spell of rainy or cold weather. But normally this is the area where you'd look for spotted seatrout, red drum, grouper, bluefish, mackerel, cobia, ladyfish, tripletail, pompano, jack crevalle, and numerous other species which trade between the channels and flats. The popular method of fishing the outside is with spinning tackle using a ½ ounce white or yellow jig tipped with a piece of shrimp. Blind casting can produce an incredible variety of fish. If you study the area carefully you'll find that all creeks emerging from the Everglades build up flats on the north or south side of the mouth. These are good spots to watch for cruising snook and red drum. Either species will herd baitfish into the shallows where you have visible targets. The drum or "redfish" are often seen tailing on the flats and can be stalked with the fly rod—just like bonefish. Redfish average 8–12 pounds during peak periods. The thing to remember is that the fish is literally nearsighted and a lure must arrive directly under its nose.

In addition to a standard bait-casting, spinning, and fly rod outfit, which can be used in the larger creeks and outside bars, it's a good idea to bring along abbreviated versions of each. Ordinarily, saltwater casters favor 5½- and 6-foot plug rods, 7-foot spinning rods, and 9-foot fly rods; but if you plan to fish the mangrove canopied back-country stream, where for the most part you can't even turn a boat around, by all means include shorter sticks. Veterans prefer a 4½-foot bait-casting rod, for example, as 12 inches in length can make a world of difference when shooting a plug under limbs. Unless you are out to set a record a 15-pound-test monofilament line spooled on a reel with a strong drag is the advised minimum. It's seldom necessary to cast more than 30 feet, and in many places you won't have to reach half that distance. When a fish is hooked, you must lean back and keep him from burrowing under the mangroves. Even a small snook of 6 or 8 pounds can pull like a mule. For the same reason many casters favor a stiff 7½-foot fly rod when slapping a streamer or bug around the roots. A length of 30-pound-test monofilament will provide the essential shock-tippet no matter what kind of lure you use. If big tarpon are around by all means double the test.

Undeniably, hiring a guide for the first few trips at least is a big asset. If you follow trafficked thoroughfares like Lostman's, Rogers, Broad, Harney, and Shark River you are not likely to get lost. But once you wander away from the channel markers and explore the labyrinth of streams that feed the main rivers, by all means have the proper navigational charts—and a compass. You can also find some locally plotted maps through hotels and marinas.

The Peace River estuary at Punta Gorda and the Myakka River estuary a short distance north at El Jobean produce good tarpon fishing from May through September with the peak period in July. The stocks of smaller fish, such as red drum, spotted seatrout, and snook, are no longer common in either of these shallow-water habitats (even though the snook is classed as a gamefish and not legal in the fishery it does enter the catch in seines and stopnets).

One of the most famous and productive areas for big tarpon in Florida is Boca Grande on the lower west coast of Florida, about thirty miles southwest of Punta Gorda. The tarpon-fishing effort is concentrated in the pass, where the waters of the Peace and Myakka rivers commingle and enter the Gulf of Mexico. The tarpon run is seasonal, beginning in early May and lasting through June into early July. During the peak of the run, a capable angler may strike an average of a half dozen big tarpon a day. The tarpon average roughly 65–85 pounds and reach weights in excess of 100 pounds. Charter craft and guides are available, and these services are recommended for those new to the peculiar type of fishing method used in the pass.

Charter and private boats drift-fish for tarpon in the pass, using live crabs or live baitfish locally known as "mutton minnows." The baits must be fished near the bottom in deepwater, but although lead sinkers up to and exceeding eight ounces are sometimes used, a terminal rig has been devised that will allow the use of light tackle. Sinkers are attached to wire leaders so that they will break away from the leader when a tarpon makes its first violent leap. Small clamp-on leads are used, but when heavier leads are required they are attached to the terminal rigs with light, soft copper wire that will break on the fish's initial jump. With the lead clear of the line, the tarpon is free to run the gamut of his aerial gyrations, and the angler is not handicapped by a wildly flying sinker between rod tip and fish. Experienced Boca Grande anglers consider 20–30-pound test adequate for tarpon fishing in the pass. Twelve-pound-test line is rather an extreme minimum, but has been used by devoted light-tackle anglers and record seekers. A No. 6/0 to 7/0 leader wire of about 7 feet in length and a strong No. 6/0 hook with a needle point complete the terminal rig. During the early morning feeding hour, the angler sometimes hooks a few silver kings trolling in the pass with large spoons. Generally speaking, however, the pass is not fished with artificial lures.

Tarpon fishing can be found along the entire west coast of Florida during some part of the year, with the fish occurring later in the summer as you progress north. One little-known but productive location is near the town of Crystal River, seventy-two miles above Tampa. In May and June the silver kings in weights from 50 pounds to well over 100 pounds are very numerous on shallow St. Martins Reef where they can be taken on casting tackle or by trolling with plugs.

The west coast can be fished along its entire length from piers, bridges, beaches, and by skiff in the bays. The low surf of the Gulf permits a wider use of small boats than on the Atlantic side; so inshore fishing exists almost everywhere. Naples, Fort Myers, Charlotte Harbor,

Sarasota, the Tampa Bay area, Clearwater, Tarpon Springs, Waccasassa Bay—almost every seashore landmark north to Pensacola offers good fishing. The Sunshine Skyway at the mouth of Tampa Bay boasts what is probably the longest fishing bridge in the world; including both sides of the connected causeways between St. Petersburg and Bradenton, as well as the walkways designed solely for angling, there are more than 22 miles of platform to operate from.

The cobia (*which see*), commonly called ling in the Gulf states, is an important west coast migrant. The run from east to west usually begins in April and extends through May. The odd cobia may be caught at any time during the year, but when the fish are schooled, cobia weighing 20–70 pounds are the rule. Party boats operating out of Pensacola make a specialty of ling fishing.

FLORIDA KEYS

The Keys are a 130-mile-long archipelago extending roughly from Key Largo (south of Miami) to Key West. The Keys have been a popular tourist region since 1912 when Henry Flagler completed his railroad which made the islands accessible by land transportation for the first time. Although the railroad no longer exists, the Florida Overseas Highway interconnects the chain of islands direct to Key West, the southernmost community in the continental United States.

Fishing of some kind can be found on virtually every key beginning at Jewfish Creek on Key Largo. The best-known locations are at Tavernier, Islamorada, the Matecumbe keys, Marathon, Bahia Honda Key, Big Pine Key, Little Torch Key, Cudjoe Key, and Key West. From the latter port anglers jump off to the Marquesas and Dry Tortugas by boat. The entire region is more strictly tropical than elsewhere in Florida, and consequently fish which are not common, or commonly caught, in the northern part of the state typify the inshore waters. Tarpon, bonefish, permit, red drum, spotted seatrout, ladyfish, crevalle, barracuda, and various snappers and groupers are most abundant on flats, in channels, and bays. Considerable offshore fishing is also done in the Florida Keys area for sailfish, kingfish, dolphin, amberjack, and several other Gulf Stream species.

Outboard rigs can be rented at all fishing stations and charter boats are available for offshore angling. A great deal of fishing is also done simply by wading from shore. However, tourists in search of bonefish, permit, and tarpon are well advised to use the services of a qualified guide. Their standard equipment is a fast 16–18-foot skiff; though beamy, such a rig has a shallow draft and is poled on the flats. Sighting and casting to inshore gamefish is a two-man job, and for the inexperienced visitor it's worth the cost both from a safety and angling standpoint. *See also* Atlantic Sailfish, Bonefish, Permit, Snook, Tarpon —E.C.B.
—A.J.McC.

FLORIDA GAR *Lepisosteus platyrhincus* Florida gar has been described as the Florida representative of the spotted gar. It is very similar to the spotted gar; the major distinguishing characteristic is the distance from the front of the eye to the back edge of the bony opercle. If it is less than ⅔ the snout length, it is a Florida gar; if this distance is more than ⅔ the snout length, it is a spotted gar. Both species are characterized by the relatively broad snout and the large, round spots on the top of the head.

It is found from South Carolina south through Florida. The spotted gar does not occur in most of its range. The Florida gar inhabits lakes and slow-flowing streams and is notably abundant in the Tamiami and other canals of Florida where removal programs have been used. They are gregarious and can usually be found swimming in groups of 2–10 or more.

LIFE HISTORY

Spawning occurs from May through July in backwaters and sloughs. Normally females average 5,200 eggs. Other habits are similar to those of the shortnose gar.

Fish make up the bulk of its diet, but freshwater shrimp compose 17 per cent; insects, crayfish, and scuds also are taken. In the canals where gar are abundant, largemouth bass have been reported to be adversely affected by its predation and competition. Over 2,000 gar have been taken from a 300-foot long section of canal, and their total production has been estimated at 700–1,000 pounds per acre in some areas. Its lazy habits make it a very efficient utilizer of food: 2½ times as much food is required for the more active bass as for this particular Florida gar. —C.A.P.

FLORIDA LARGEMOUTH BASS *Micropterus salmoides floridanus* A subspecies of the largemouth bass found throughout the peninsula of Florida. It may intergrade with the largemouth bass of southern Georgia. This subspecies differs from the Northern form only in scale counts, however, it grows to a much larger size. Whether heredity is more important than environment has not been determined. In 1959 the city of San Diego, California, began an intensive stocking program in a chain of lakes with the Florida subspecies; this has resulted in doubling the weight of the average bass caught (record 20 pounds, 15 ounces, 1973) as compared to the Northern form which was long established in these same waters. The world's record largemouth of 22 pounds, 4 ounces was taken in Montgomery Lake, Georgia, an area where intergrades are common.

As described by Bailey and Hubbs (1949), the typical Northern form of the largemouth bass found in the Great Lakes drainage area has 59–69 (usually 61–65) scales on the lateral line; 7–9 (usually 8) scale rows above, and 14–17 (usually 15–17) below the lateral line; 9–13 (usually 10 or 11) rows of scales on the cheek; 24–30 (usually 26–28) scale rows around the caudal peduncle.

Florida Gar

Florida Largemouth Bass

In comparison, the Florida largemouth has 65–75 (usually 69–73) lateral line scales; 7–10 (usually 8 or 9) scale rows above, and 16–18 (usually 17 or 18) scale rows below the lateral line; 10–14 (usually 11–13) scale rows on the cheek; 27–32 (usually 28–31) scale rows around the caudal peduncle. *See also* Black Bass, Florida, Largemouth Bass

FLORIDA POMPANO *See* Pompano

FLOUNDERS *Order Pleuronectiformes* Commonly, any one of three families of flatfishes ranging from the small dab to the giant halibut, all having in common a broad,

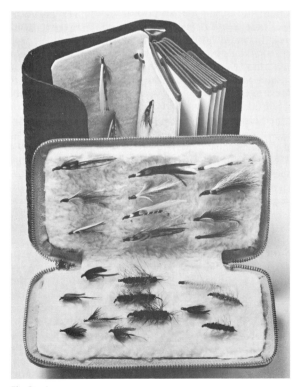

Fly Book

flat body and both eyes on one side of the head. If the eyes are on the right side, the fish is *dextral*, and if on the left side the fish is *sinistral*. There are more than 200 species in both the Atlantic and Pacific oceans. *See also* American Plaice, Blackback Flounder, Brill, Butter Sole, Curlfin Sole, Dover Sole, English Sole, Gulf Flounder, Hogchoker, Petrale Sole, Plaice, Rex Sole, Rock Sole, Sole, Southern Flounder, Starry Flounder, Summer Flounder, Turbot, Windowpane, Winter Flounder, Yellowfin Sole, Yellowtail Flounder.

FLUKE A common name for the summer flounder (*which see*)

FLY BOOK A flat leather or plastic covered wallet containing felt or lamb's wool pages to which artificial flies can be secured. It may also consist of a number of waterproof envelopes in which flies are deposited. A fly book is only suitable for artificials having a flat shape such as streamer flies and wet flies. Because of its light weight and flexibility a fly book is often used in conjunction with the compartmented fly box, particularly in those regions where streamer flies or wet flies are the most popular for anglers.

FLY BOX A box or container usually made of plastic or aluminum in which artificial flies are stored. The box may be divided into any number of compartments with or without individual lids. The most common type is a transparent plastic box in which the cover serves as a single lid to all compartments. The aluminum kind usually has individual transparent lids inside the box which operate on a snap-spring device; these eliminate exposing the entire contents of the box in windy weather when the cover is opened. A box suitable for dry flies must have deep compartments (preferably not less than one inch) to accommodate large-hackled patterns without crushing.

Utility fly boxes are designed to hold different types of flies, and may have in addition to compartments a felt pad inside the cover to hold wet flies, streamers, and other "flat" artificials; or one half of the box may consist of mounted metal snaps under which these same flies can be secured. To be practical all fly boxes should be light in weight, small enough to fit inside a jacket pocket, yet provide ample space to store the minimal number of

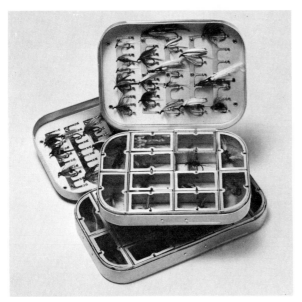

Fly Box

patterns required in fishing. Most anglers prefer to carry two or more fly boxes for the convenience of transport and selection. —A.J.McC.

FLY-CASTING The art of casting an artificial fly either as a sport (fly-fishing) or as a game (tournament casting). Fly-casting differs from all other types of casting in that the weight of the line is propelled through the air rather than the weight of the lure.

BEGINNER'S OUTFIT

Although a serious fly-fisherman will acquire a number of different rods, reels, and lines over a period of time, the beginner only needs one outfit while learning the fundamentals. These need not be expensive.

Rod The first item of equipment you will probably consider buying is the rod. Naturally, the more you spend, the greater the quality of the rod, within limitations. You can find serviceable glass fly rods at very low cost and exquisite models of the craftsman's art in bamboo at over $100. However, you can have just as much fun with one as the other. Except for specialized equipment, there's a point beyond which you are just paying for the window dressing, so to speak, which is a gratifying though not essential indulgence. Bamboo rods are more costly because the material and the number of technicians who still custom-build are both becoming scarce. Regardless of your budget, it is important to select a rod that will be easy to cast with and suitable for the type of fishing you plan to do. There is no absolute rule to follow, but most casting instructors find that an 8–8½-foot rod weighing 4½–5 ounces to be most practical. A short fly rod of 7–7½ feet requires perfect line control to handle smoothly, while long rods of 9 feet or more put a premium on line weight, making it easy to cast but much more difficult to catch fish in an average trout stream. The 8–8½-foot lengths are a good compromise for the beginner. These will take lines weighing 140–170 grains. Your tackle dealer or the rod manufacturer can provide a specific recommendation.

Line In all forms of casting, except with the fly, it is the weight of the lure that is cast. The most efficient casting weight is a compact lead sinker. Artificial flies in themselves have no weight, but the line does, and by propelling it back and forth we achieve enough velocity to shoot it through the air. However, the usable weight of fly line is distributed over 30–40 feet of surface area; thus air friction rapidly absorbs the energy that goes into fly-casting. To utilize that energy to its maximum the weight of a fly line must be arranged in a shape or profile that will maintain velocity for the longest possible time. There are three common profiles among fly lines—a weight-forward (WF), double-taper (DT), and a level (L) distribution. For the beginning flycaster, a double-taper is the easiest to handle. The weights of various lines differ, and you must buy one that is proportionate to the stiffness of your rod—or more precisely to its resistance to bend. Until 1961, line sizes were designated by alphabetical symbols such as HDH or GAF. This never was a very good system because it only related to line diameters and not their weights. Another method was devised which is somewhat better. (*See* Fly-Line Standards) This indicates the profile of the line alphabetically, the weight with a numerical symbol, and the specific gravity by another alphabetical symbol. Thus a DT-5-F is interpreted as a double-taper of approximately 140 grains in the first 30 feet, floating. Or a WF-7-S means a weight-forward line of 185 grains, sinking.

Reel Before the innovation of fly reels, the playing of a fish consisted chiefly in keeping the fish directly under the rod. In Walton's day, and for many years afterward, fly rods were extremely long and supple for this reason. When a trout was hooked, the angler would hold the point of his rod over the fish to prevent it from running too far from the resilient tip. The elasticity of a modern fly rod still means a great deal in handling large fish on fine leaders, but if the pull exceeds its capacity to bend, we simply allow the fish to run more line from the reel. In most kinds of fly-fishing, however, the fly reel isn't as important as the rod and line. You can obtain a lightweight, single-action reel at very little cost. The standard trout reel weighs 3½–5½ ounces and has a 3–3½-inch spool diameter. It should also have a click mechanism, either audible or silent, to prevent overruns. Later in the game, when your fishing expands to strong-running fish like the steelhead, salmon, or bonefish, you will need a large-capacity reel with an adjustable drag. If your line doesn't fill the reel to within ⅜ inch of the cross braces, then use a "backing" line underneath. The usual purpose of backing is to provide extra yardage to handle sprinting fish. However, even though you may not need more than a 30-yard length, the backing also fills the spool and your fly line will have less tendency to kink. Too, a full spool permits more rapid recovery of the line. It's difficult to estimate how much backing to put on a reel before you attach the double-tapered line. Stated reel capacities allow a considerable margin of error because of the variation in line diameters. The accurate way is to wind the fly line on the reel first; then knot a 15-pound-test braided nylon or Dacron to the end and continue reeling until the correct level is reached. When the right amount is on the reel, cut the backing, and run it off on an empty spool. Next, untie the two lines; then remove the double taper from the reel, and rewind the backing on the spool. If you

Fly-Casting Reels: (*left to right, top row*) Walker Salmon Reel, Garcia Beaudex, Fin-Nor No. 3 Tarpon, (*second row*) Ocean City No. 77, Pflueger Medalist, Bogdan Salmon Reel, Hardy St. George, Perrine Auto 88, Martin "Blue Chip," South Bend 1150 Oreno-Matic, (*bottom row*) Hardy Lightweight, H.L. Leonard. Reels supplied by Arthur L. Walker, the Garcia Co., Abercrombie & Fitch, Shakespeare Co., Pflueger Corp., Charles Orvis Co., Perrine Reel Co., Martin Reel Co., South Bend Tackle Co., Arnold Gingrich

do this in a tackle shop it's a simple matter to run the fly line and the backing on a showcase model, then reverse them on the reel you are buying. Remember, the double-tapered line is identical at both ends.

When fly-fishing, the reel is mounted below the rod grip where it won't interfere with the cast. Its only manual function is to play the fish. So you should decide whether it will be more comfortable to seat the reel with the handle to the left or the right. Most anglers prefer to have the handle on the right. Many right-hand casters keep the handle on the left, the idea being that one doesn't have to change hands when a fish is hooked. Some old-timers,

and especially those who use fine bamboo rods, prefer to have their handles to the left with the line running clockwise around the spool. This upside-down arrangement is intended to reverse stresses against the rod by turning it guides-up when playing the fish. Although the average trout or bass won't pull out much line, you should always work them with the reel. Beginners especially benefit by cranking the reel instead of stripping line by hand because the technique of getting yardage back on the spool evenly requires some practice. This will be very important later on when you deal with large fish which must be played directly from the reel.

BALANCED FLY TACKLE STANDARD

Length (feet)	Style (pieces)	Ferrule Size	Approximate Weight (ounces)	Line Recommendations
7	2	11	3⅜	HDH–HDG (6)
7½	2	12	3⅞	HDH–HDG (6)
7½	2	13	4	HCH–HCF (7)
8	2	13	4⅜	HCH–HCF (7)
8½	2	15	5⅛	HCH–GBF (7)
8½	2	16	5½	GEG–GBF (8)
9	2	16	6⅛	GBG–GBF (8)
9	2	17	6¾	GBG–GAF (9)
9½	2	17	7	GBG–GAF (9)
7½	3	15–10	4	HDH–HDG (6)
8	3	16–10	4½	HDH–HDG (6)
8½	3	16–10	4⅝	HDH–HDG (6)
8½	3	17–11	5⅛	HCH–HCF (7)
9	3	18–12	6	HCH–GBF (7)
9	3	19–13	6½	GBG–GBF (8)

Light Salmon

Length (feet)	Style (pieces)	Ferrule Size	Approximate Weight (ounces)	Line Recommendations
8½	2	15	5¼	HCH–GBF (7)
8½	2	16	5⅝	GBG–GBF (8)
9	2	16	5⅞	GBG–GBF (8)
8½	3	17–11	5¼	HCH–GBF (7)
8½	3	18–12	5½	HCH–GBF (7)
9	3	18–12	5⅞	HCH–GBF (7)

Salmon

Length (feet)	Style (pieces)	Ferrule Size	Approximate Weight (ounces)	Line Recommendations
9	3	19–13	6⅞	GBG–GBF (8)
9½	3	19–13	7¼	GBG–GBF (8)
9½	3	20–13	7½	GBG–GBF (8)
10	3	20–13	7⅞	GBG–GBF (8)
10½	3	21–14	8¾	GBG–GAF (9)

Two-Handed Salmon

Length (feet)	Style (pieces)	Ferrule Size	Approximate Weight (ounces)	Line Recommendations
11	3	22–14	10⅞	F2AE Nylon
11½	3	22–14	11¼	F2AE Nylon
12	3	24–15	13	F3AE Nylon
12½	3	24–15	13½	F3AE Nylon
13	3	26–16	16½	E4AD Nylon
13½	3	26–16	17	E4AD Nylon
14	3	28–18	19⅝	E4AD Nylon
14½	3	28–18	20¾	E4AD Nylon

The Fly Leader A long, light leader is necessary, not only because it forms a nearly invisible connection between the line and the fly, but, equally important, it allows the fly to drift and turn like a natural insect. The leader may look very fragile, but the fine end will ordinarily test about three pounds, which is strong enough to hold most trout you will catch. Even if you should hook a fish weighing more than three pounds, the odds on landing him are still in your favor provided you do not attempt to "horse" the trout out of the stream. By all means get *tapered* leaders, as the level kind has very poor casting qualities. There are two facts which you should know about the leader which influence fishing with them: (1) You must select the correct length, or approximate length to suit the water conditions; a 7½-foot leader is standard for small streams where you will be making short casts of 20–30 feet, a 9-foot leader is better for average-size streams that require 30–40-foot casts, and a 12½-foot leader is used during the summer months when the average stream is low and diamond clear. (2) You should also specify the correct tippet size. The tippet is the fine end of the leader where the fly is tied. A leader must have enough rigidity to transmit the energy imparted by the line during the cast. If the fly is too large, or too heavy, for the tippet, you cannot present the fly properly, and the leader will quickly weaken. As a general guide, the following tippet sizes are recommended for various hook sizes:

Tippet	Fly
0X	No. 2 to No. 1/0
1X	No. 4 to No. 8
2X	No. 6 to No. 10
3X	No. 10 to No. 14
4X	No. 12 to No. 16
5X	No. 14 to No. 18
6X	No. 16 to No. 22

So there's really no mystery in leader specifications. When you ask for a 9-foot, 3X tapered leader, you will get one suitable for the average stream, where 30–40-foot casts are the rule, and with a tippet fine enough to handle the average fly sizes of No. 10 to No. 14. If the water is high and roily, you might use a shorter, 7½-foot leader and somewhat larger flies which require a 2X tippet. A 12½-foot, 6X leader would be ideal for extremely clear water when only the tiniest flies are to be used. Don't let long leaders scare you away. When properly made, they are just as easy to cast as short ones if you are working at the distances (forty feet or more) demanded on hot, droughty days when the river flows thin. Occasionally you will hear of somebody using a 15-foot, or even 18-foot leader, but anything over 12½ feet is awkward, and it is doubtful if it serves a practical purpose. By the same token, a very short leader of 3–6 feet is much more likely to frighten fish and cause casting problems.

The Fly Broadly speaking, there are two kinds of flies which you will need at the outset—the wet fly and the dry fly. The wet fly is fished below the surface of the water, and the dry fly is designed to float on top. The purpose of both is to imitate or suggest by shape, color, or action the natural insects upon which fish feed. No phase of angling has had so much esoteric scholarship lavished on it as the tying and selection of trout flies. Yet for all the minute perfection in thousands of patterns the basic standards remain with us year after year. To understand properly the subtleties of fly-fishing you should learn something about entomology; nevertheless, many experts can't tell an emergence table from a grocery list. Again, this is an aspect of the art which you can enjoy and develop as you see fit. All sorts of new subjects are contiguous to fly-fishing, but they should be taken in their proper time. On any ordinary day, during any reasonable weather, there will be a morning rise and an evening rise of trout to the naturals. Occasionally, you may see a midday rise also. These are the periods when dry flies are most effective. Between hatches, or in floodwater or roughwater, the wet fly might be more acceptable. The best way to determine their preference is, of course, to try both. Select a pattern of the size and general coloration of any insects which you see on the river—or, if none is in evidence, use a fly pattern that appeals to you. There are many standard patterns which catch trout most of the time. The following dry and wet flies are used successfully throughout the United States and in many foreign countries:

Dry Flies	Hook
Light Cahill	No. 10 to No. 16
Hendrickson	No. 10 to No. 16
Adams	No. 10 to No. 16
Royal Coachman	No. 10 to No. 14
Quill Gordon	No. 12 to No. 16
Badger Bivisible	No. 10 to No. 14
Muddler	No. 6 to No. 10
Grey Wulff	No. 8 to No. 12
March Brown	No. 10 to No. 14
Blue Dun Spider	No. 12 to No. 16
Irresistible	No. 8 to No. 12
Multi-Color Variant	No. 12 to No. 16
Wet Flies	*Hook*
McGinty	No. 10 to No. 12
Black Gnat	No. 10 to No. 16
Leadwing Coachman	No. 10 to No. 16
Wickham's Fancy	No. 10 to No. 12
Silver Doctor	No. 10 to No. 12
Grizzly King	No. 10 to No. 12
Black Woolly Worm	No. 8 to No. 10
Blue Dun	No. 10 to No. 14
Quill Gordon	No. 10 to No. 16
Dark Cahill	No. 10 to No. 16
Gray Hackle Peacock	No. 10 to No. 14

HOW TO FLY-CAST

As in any other sport you must practice, and the more hours you work, the easier fly-casting becomes. There are only two different casts to learn—the overhead cast and the roll cast. All other casts are movements. To learn fly-casting quickly, it is recommended that you use an 8½-foot rod of 5–5½ ounces. Shorter rods require more experience, and longer rods are too heavy for the average

hand in practice. The rod should be matched with an HCH or DT-6-F line. When practicing use a 7½-foot leader tapered to 1X or 2X. Clip the barb from the fly to prevent accidents. Except for the roll cast all fundamental rod work can be learned on dry land. Whether you are right- or left-handed these instructions should be clear as the terms *rod hand* and *line hand* are used where necessary.

The Rod Hand When you take the rod in your hand you must be relaxed. For average fishing casts up to forty feets the rod is going to perform most of the work. You will simply provide the motion necessary to move the rod back and forth. Hold the cork handle lightly, with your thumb on top of the grip and in direct line with the rod. Most of the squeeze in your grip should be in the lower three fingers as you raise the rod in a backward motion. At vertical, your thumb comes into play to stop the rod. Your forefinger should be so relaxed that it can be moved away from the grip. As you begin the forward cast, thumb pressure should be applied, and the squeeze will be in all fingers momentarily. When you complete the forward cast the rod should stop, again squeezed by the lower three fingers and resting across your forefinger. Your thumb simply follows through after the push.

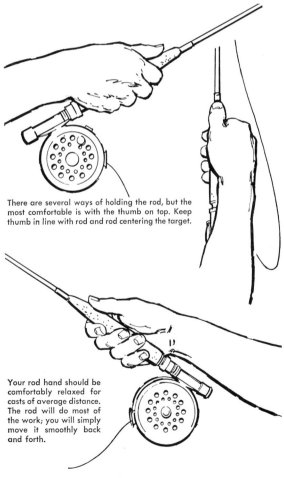

There are several ways of holding the rod, but the most comfortable is with the thumb on top. Keep thumb in line with rod and rod centering the target.

Your rod hand should be comfortably relaxed for casts of average distance. The rod will do most of the work; you will simply move it smoothly back and forth.

The Rod Hand

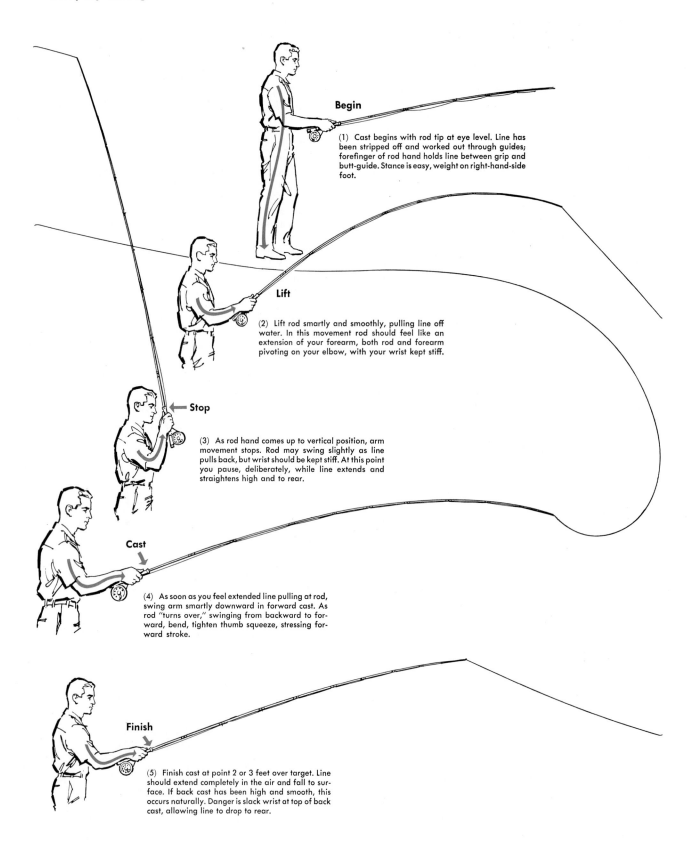

Begin

(1) Cast begins with rod tip at eye level. Line has been stripped off and worked out through guides; forefinger of rod hand holds line between grip and butt-guide. Stance is easy, weight on right-hand-side foot.

Lift

(2) Lift rod smartly and smoothly, pulling line off water. In this movement rod should feel like an extension of your forearm, both rod and forearm pivoting on your elbow, with your wrist kept stiff.

Stop

(3) As rod hand comes up to vertical position, arm movement stops. Rod may swing slightly as line pulls back, but wrist should be kept stiff. At this point you pause, deliberately, while line extends and straightens high and to rear.

Cast

(4) As soon as you feel extended line pulling at rod, swing arm smartly downward in forward cast. As rod "turns over," swinging from backward to forward, bend, tighten thumb squeeze, stressing forward stroke.

Finish

(5) Finish cast at point 2 or 3 feet over target. Line should extend completely in the air and fall to surface. If back cast has been high and smooth, this occurs naturally. Danger is slack wrist at top of back cast, allowing line to drop to rear.

Overhead Cast

The Overhead Cast Every fly-cast consists of several movements blended together in what appears to be one motion. The basic overhead cast is a combination of backward and forward strokes, which can be made at different angles and varying speeds under actual fishing conditions. Of the two parts—back cast and forward cast—the former is most important to the beginner. A proper back cast will automatically create a smooth forward cast. When you begin practice, keep in mind that you cannot make a poor back cast if you block your wrist movement almost completely and pivot on your elbow. A straight upward forearm movement will throw the line high in the air. If your line hits the ground behind you, you are not lifting with enough emphasis or you are bending your wrist.

The Back Cast If you have never held a fly rod before, the first few flexes will feel awkward until you have about 12–15 feet of line out. You are literally casting the weight of the line, and the only usable part is that length extended beyond your rod tip. Strip off about twenty feet of line, and take a comfortable stance. If you are a right-hand caster, your body weight should favor the right foot and vice-versa. You are not going to use your line hand at first; so place the line under your rod-hand forefinger and keep it there; this will prevent throwing slack into your casts. Hold the rod in front of you so the tip is at eye level, with your forearm in a straight line with the rod. Your hand should be relaxed but your wrist somewhat stiff; you should have the feeling that your forearm is an extension of the rod—right down to your elbow. Your elbow should be 1–2 inches from your body and your upper arm a bit closer. Begin the cast by raising the rod smartly, lifting

your hand toward your ear and slightly raising your elbow. The elbow is actually the pivot point. As your rod hand nears eye level, stiffen your wrist even more, and then block all arm movement. The rod should be in a vertical position, and the line unrolling in the rear. There is a definite *pause* at this point, which allows the line to extend and straighten. It is absolutely essential to complete the back cast. Only when the line is actually tugging at the rod and developing its bend can you begin the forward cast.

The Forward Cast With a high, smooth back cast, the forward cast is merely a follow-through phase to the overhead cast. With the rod bending on your back cast, move your forearm down through the same path, applying speed progressively. As the rod begins to turn over, give the grip more thumb squeeze and emphasize that forward stroke. You should have the feeling that you are throwing the rod tip into the cast. Finish your cast at a point 2–3 feet over the target. Do not cast directly on the water—but above it. The line should extend completely in the air and fall to the surface. Pick up the line again and repeat the back cast, allowing each forward cast to be completed. When you have mastered these two phases of the overhead cast, you are ready to blend them in continuous back-and-forth movements—known as false casting. You will use the false cast in fishing to dry the fly and to extend the line.

The Line Hand The work of the line hand becomes increasingly important as you cast longer distances. Its fundamental role, however, is to keep slack out of the line and to maintain constant tension on the line while casting. When fishing, the forefinger of your rod hand

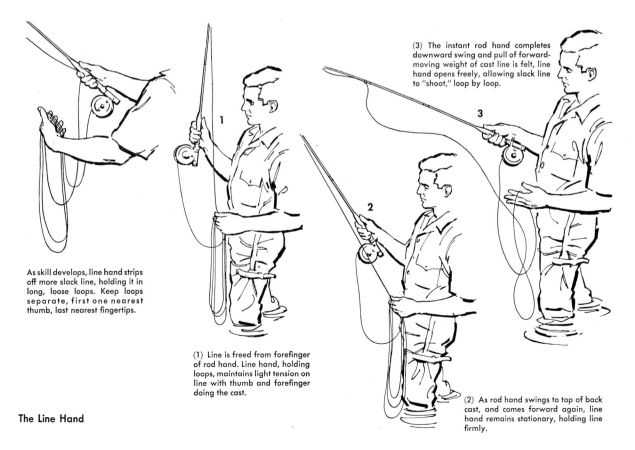

As skill develops, line hand strips off more slack line, holding it in long, loose loops. Keep loops separate, first one nearest thumb, last nearest fingertips.

(1) Line is freed from forefinger of rod hand. Line hand, holding loops, maintains light tension on line with thumb and forefinger doing the cast.

(3) The instant rod hand completes downward swing and pull of forward-moving weight of cast line is felt, line hand opens freely, allowing slack line to "shoot," loop by loop.

(2) As rod hand swings to top of back cast, and comes forward again, line hand remains stationary, holding line firmly.

The Line Hand

acts almost as an additional guide. By running the line over your forefinger the slack between butt guide and rod grip is eliminated. This facilitates the retrieve and striking the fish. Your line hand takes up incoming line and prepares it for shooting the next cast. The easiest system for handling slack is to form loops in your line hand. Simply take the first length of line retrieved (which is the amount you can pull down in a distance from the grip to a straight-arm position), and form a half loop across your hand. Again, reach up to your rod-hand forefinger, and pull the next length of line down. Now drop both, and grasp the line again to form one big loop. Continue your retrieve, looping alternate lengths of line. A large loop is easy to handle in casting, and you can hold more line in your hand without tangling. The last pull should leave your line hand free so that you are ready to cast again. All loops should rest over your hand with each separated from the other, the first loop formed closest to your thumb and the last loop nearest your finger tips.

For the average cast, your line hand maintains constant tension at a position near hip level. After one or two false casts you should have enough line speed to shoot the slack as your rod is approaching a 45-degree angle. Simply open your hand, and the speed of the line traveling through the air is sufficient to pull the slack out.

Casting in Head-Winds The ability to cast against strong winds is a decided advantage, especially in the open country of Western rivers. The chief difference between an ordinary cast and the wind cast is that you exaggerate the forward phase when bucking a head-wind. Make the back cast with your elbow well separated from your body, keeping your forearm stiff. The trick of casting into the wind is to keep your back cast high and your forward cast low. A high back cast is always essential to effortless form, but to buck the wind you have to exaggerate the movement by bringing your hand from near horizontal as the line is lifted from the water to a point above eye level as though you were trying to throw the line straight over your head. Actually, the wind will buffet the line down to a lower level. It also helps to give the line a strong pull on the lift to add speed in straightening because the longer the line is in the air, the more the wind will push it down. The forward cast must be progressive in power. Do not attempt to slam your line against the wind. With your hand held high at the finish of the back cast (which is at about the one o'clock position), begin coming forward with your shoulder, elbow, and forearm just an instant before adding the real power. Keep your forearm and wrist stiff as you pivot at the elbow, and when your rod hand starts down, pull line with the left hand. Put all the emphasis in a forceful wrist and thumb delivery. The rod should almost reach a horizontal position before you release line. In other words you must delay shooting line until the outgoing taper is pulling at maximum. None of the movements is difficult if you remember the cardinal points: exaggerate the height of the back cast; then shoot low over the water, using a sharp line hand pull. Once you have the knack you'll be able to throw a 2/0 bass bug into the teeth of a gale.

Casting in Tail-Winds The fundamental rule of casting with a strong tail-wind is naturally just the opposite of casting against it. Your back cast must be lower than usual and the forward cast high. Now if you work strictly in a vertical plane as you do for an ordinary overhead cast, the only way you can get the line low in the rear is to let it drop or swing the rod horizontally to the rear. Either method is not practical because you lose line speed and at that precise instant the wind will bang your taper on the water. Or on the forward stroke you'll get the whole length of it wrapped around your neck. Remember also, that a tail-wind is going to retard your back cast; so you must maintain maximum velocity. The easiest way is to make a low, fast back cast by moving the rod to the rear at an angle below 45 degrees and bringing it forward in a vertical plane. If the cast is executed correctly, you can reach long distances without losing line control. It has the virtue of two well-separated casting planes and throws a wide loop. Begin by giving the line a brisk left-hand pull, simultaneously making a side cast; then pivot with elbow and shoulder to sweep the rod up into a vertical plane, applying power progressively. The path of your hand should be circular in traveling back and forward. When the line is tugging hard against the rod, finish your forward cast with another left-hand pull as your casting hand comes down with a forceful stroke. The tip should stop at the horizontal position. The line will literally rocket away from the rod.

Casting in Cross-Winds Under normal wind conditions if you are a right-hand caster and the wind comes from your left there's no problem; just keep the rod tip leaning slightly to the right and cast. But if the wind comes from the right side, your line is going to drift toward your body. To some degree this can be neutralized with a forceful side cast on the right side. Experts who can cast with either hand have no trouble even in violent cross-winds. An ambidextrous angler will follow the fundamental cross-wind rule of always keeping the rod on his lee side. The average caster will find use for the backhand cast in a strong cross-wind.

The backhand cast is made by a right-hander with his arm held across the front of his body and the rod pointing to the left. A southpaw makes the cast in the opposite plane, with arm held across the front of his body and the rod pointing to the right. The cast is very simple to execute; with palm facing down and thumb on top of the grip, your rod should be at a 45-degree angle quartering away from and a few inches in front of your body. Pick up the line for a back cast using the full forearm, pivoting at the elbow, and moving your shoulders slightly in the direction of the cast. The rod should stop at a 45-degree angle, quartering away from and to the rear of your body. Start the forward cast by coming closer to the vertical plane on the left side of your body, but do not cast just with your wrist. Lower your forearm slightly, and use the elbow pivot with wrist emphasis. In both the back and forward stroke a slight left-hand pull will add speed to the line and help the turnover. Practice your backhand every chance you get. It's also a good one to use when fishing with a tree-bordered bank on your rod side.

THE DOUBLE-LINE HAUL

Before you are able to cast smoothly to distances of over sixty feet you must learn to understand the brand-new role of your line hand. For a long cast, your rod movements are somewhat exaggerated in that there is more line weight to handle. This means your line hand cannot remain stationary during the actual cast. As you have already seen, your line-hand is responsible for keeping the line under control at all times. Now in distance casting you will actually lift your rod arm in a higher plane; so your line hand must be coordinated with your rod hand. If your line hand remains stationary, the distance between right and left will constantly vary, jerking the line on your back cast and throwing it slack on the forward cast. There must be tension both backward and forward, because with this control you can add speed to the flight of the line whenever needed. When both hands work together, you can correct casts that are affected by the wind, correct your own errors in timing, and get greater distance because the slightest pull on the line will shoot it much further. Although the double haul is applicable to all types of lines, the three-diameter line (GBF for your 8½-foot, 5½-ounce rod) is designed for distance work and is therefore easier to cast.

The reason for the first haul is to make a perfectly straight back cast. It is also axiomatic that a high, straight back cast will result in a perfect forward cast. It's almost impossible to make a bad forward cast if the line has altitude and speed when coming from the rear. By pulling the line toward you as you lift the rod you overcome the resistance of the water, which is variable against the differing diameters of a tapered fly line, and actually slide it off the surface. Secondly, the haul gives greater initial speed to the line, so much so that it's perfectly easy to pick up 35–40 feet and shoot it to 60 feet with one back cast. Under actual fishing conditions you may use a modified line haul even when casting on small streams with light tackle. Just the slightest left-hand pull will break the surface tension, and the fly can be picked off the water cleanly without making a disturbance. This doesn't require raising the rod hand any higher than the normal casting position while the actual movement of the line hand is no more than a tug of 5–6 inches. If the casting range is short it probably won't be necessary to make the second haul. In either case, you will find that very gentle movements do the trick at normal distances.

The reason for the second haul is, again, to increase the line speed. Whatever speed you gained with the first haul in laying out a back cast will be dissipated in sending the line high and straight. So when your left hand starts for your hip pocket you are giving the taper a downhill ride at its maximum velocity (remember the line is a projectile in this case, and momentum only takes over after the line has straightened and lost its forward speed). This movement, which can resemble a man scratching his chin or a man swinging a two-handed axe, depending on his own style and the immediate casting conditions, must be timed perfectly so the rhythmic flow of the line is not broken up. This takes practice.

Grip for Double Haul Although your rod hand should remain in the same position as described for the overhead cast, it cannot be as relaxed because you will be handling greater (i.e., heavier) lengths of line. Distribute your squeeze evenly through all fingers. Some experts with very strong hands and forearms prefer to turn their thumb off center and pinch the grip from opposing sides. This, however, is a matter of individual physique and doesn't necessarily assist all casters.

The Lift for Double Haul Ordinarily, you can lift 15–20 feet of line from the surface by a direct pull from water to back cast without too much disturbance and without

losing line speed. However, if 40–50 feet of taper is extended on the water, a direct lift would splash and because of surface tension against the line, it would travel at about half the speed required for an easy back cast. Therefore, the double haul is always started with a smooth, short pull of your line hand simultaneous with raising the rod. This simple movement will *slide* the line off the water and take the extra burden of weight off your rod.

Presuming that you want to cast 60–70 feet, lay out about 40 feet with an ordinary overhead cast. On nearly all three-diameter lines, this length has the belly extended and the rod tip holding the last foot or so of back taper. Strip off the reel whatever additional yardage you want to shoot. You can let the slack fall on the water or keep it in hand loops. Begin with your left foot (if right-handed) forward, and lean slightly forward at the waist. Then reach out to the butt guide, and grasp the line between thumb and forefinger. Start moving the line toward you an instant before your rod hand begins the upward stroke. Pull the line smoothly to your hip as your rod hand comes to a point opposite your ear. This will throw the line in a high back cast. Your body weight, which was primarily on your left foot, should shift on your right foot as you lean back into the cast.

Role of Line Hand Your hands are now widely separated, but with the back cast unrolling in the rear, move your line hand toward the reel. If executed correctly, the momentum of the back cast will pull the line upward. The instant your back cast is perfectly straight and tugging against the rod, your line hand must start to move down toward your hip again in a smooth, fast pull. Now start the pull a fraction of a second before you begin the forward cast, and follow through with greater emphasis on the rod turnover than ordinarily applied. Your body weight should now come back from the right foot to your left foot. Remember, as you pull and add speed to your line, do it progressively.

At this point you can shoot the line as you would for a regular overhead cast—or continue false casting if you have not achieved sufficient line speed. Usually one or two false casts accompanied by the pull are sufficient to get maximum velocity.

In order to understand fully the double haul, it's a good idea to look over your shoulder while practicing and watch how the line unrolls and how it responds to your left hand. Your back cast should lay out straight without fishtailing, and as the forward motion is applied and you make the second pull, there should be a noticeable increase in its speed. Above all, work to achieve a fluid action throughout the cast. Remember the least bit of jerkiness in your hand and rod movements will destroy the flow of the line.

Handling the slack or shooting line may be a little difficult at first, but you'll soon get the knack of it. During practice sessions you can drop the line at your feet in large, loose coils. When actually fishing you can use the same system if working from a boat or drape the coils around your hand when wading. Some casters use a specially designed "shooting basket" which may be strapped at the waist or suspended from the shoulders. The line is stripped into and shot from the basket. Other anglers drape the coils over clothes pins secured to their wader tops, and the more adept casters prefer to hold a monofilament shoot-

Reach

Pull

Lift

1

2

3

4

Stop

5

Reach

6

Pull

7

(1) With line laid out, reach to butt-guide, grasp line with thumb and forefinger of line hand and pull (2), sliding line off water as rod hand starts upward. Continue pull with line hand (3) as rod hand swings up. As rod hand reaches point about opposite your ear (4), line hand should be about same level as hip. Body weight shifts to rear foot.

As the back cast unrolls, allow line hand to be drawn upward (5), keeping tension on line so that line hand comes opposite reel as back cast straightens. The instant back cast is straight and you feel its weight tugging (6), begin pull with line hand. As line hand moves down, rod hand swings forward and weight shifts (7).

Double Line Haul

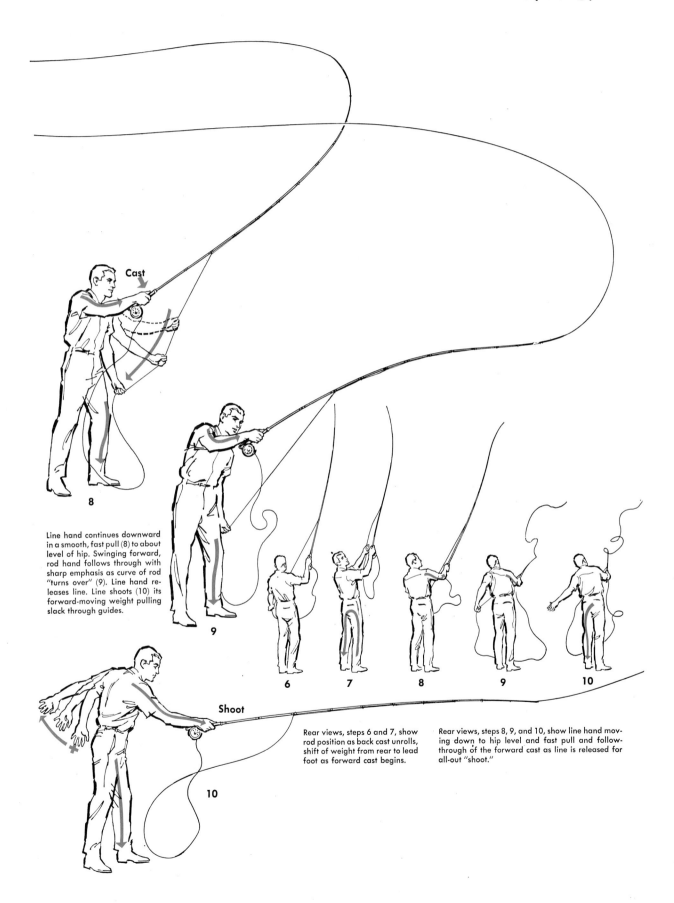

Cast

8

Line hand continues downward in a smooth, fast pull (8) to about level of hip. Swinging forward, rod hand follows through with sharp emphasis as curve of rod "turns over" (9). Line hand releases line. Line shoots (10) its forward-moving weight pulling slack through guides.

9

6

7

8

9

10

Shoot

10

Rear views, steps 6 and 7, show rod position as back cast unrolls, shift of weight from rear to lead foot as forward cast begins.

Rear views, steps 8, 9, and 10, show line hand moving down to hip level and fast pull and follow-through of the forward cast as line is released for all-out "shoot."

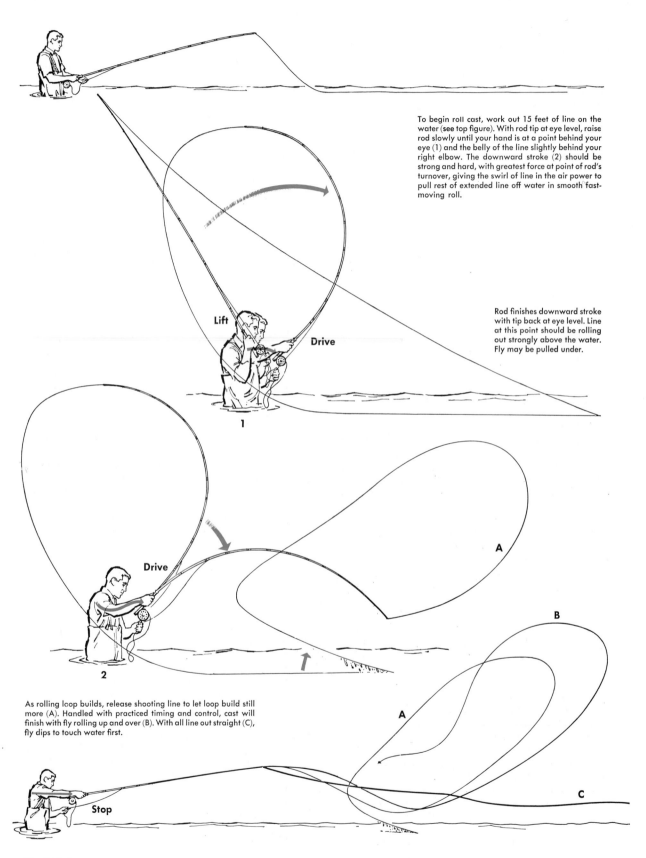

To begin roll cast, work out 15 feet of line on the water (**see** top figure). With rod tip at eye level, raise rod slowly until your hand is at a point behind your eye (1) and the belly of the line slightly behind your right elbow. The downward stroke (2) should be strong and hard, with greatest force at point of rod's turnover, giving the swirl of line in the air power to pull rest of extended line off water in smooth fast-moving roll.

Rod finishes downward stroke with tip back at eye level. Line at this point should be rolling out strongly above the water. Fly may be pulled under.

Lift

Drive

1

Drive

2

A

B

A

C

As rolling loop builds, release shooting line to let loop build still more (A). Handled with practiced timing and control, cast will finish with fly rolling up and over (B). With all line out straight (C), fly dips to touch water first.

Stop

The Roll Cast

ing line between their lips and open their mouths on the forward cast.

There are two things worth mentioning if you use a shooting head rather than a weight-forward line. First, on the pickup you must watch the "overhand," or the distance between the terminal loop of the head and the rod tip. If there's too much monofilament extended it won't support the weight of the line when you lift it and throw it. If you bring the loop too close to the tip you won't get a smooth haul because it will hit the top guide. Secondly, there's a slight difference in trajectory when using a shooting head. The head, which is generally a short 28–32-foot-long single, tapered section of line weighing 275–340 grains attached to 100 feet of .020–.025 monofilament, must be aimed *higher* or released earlier than the regular weight-forward fly line because there is less friction in the guides to retard its flight and it will turn over too fast if aimed low. Shooting heads are not essential except in specialized angling, as anybody can learn to cast the full length of a modern fly line without one. The head has a definite role in steelhead fishing for bottom-bouncing with a wet fly. But the average man can do almost anything, even with a double-taper fly line in all other kinds of fishing, provided he has learned line control.

Although the double haul can look extremely gymnastic, particularly on a casting platform when a man is going for extreme distance, it really doesn't require powerful yanks to get the line going. The haul may consist of nothing more than a gentle tug at the line in either direction, barely perceptible pulls which send the taper over one hundred feet with energy to spare. The trick of course, is in perfect timing and the *smoothness* with which the haul is applied. One thing you'll discover very quickly is that if you jerk at the line and cause it to "snake" or deviate while unrolling toward the perpendicular back path, you'll lose line speed instantly. The best casts are made when the line travels absolutely straight, high, and to the rear, and the increase in speed is applied with gradual emphasis. If you pull just a shade too hard, or at the wrong moment, your haul will create little air-resisting curves which break up the rhythm of the cast, cause the line to sag, and lose momentum. Unless you can cast a high, straight line, it's almost impossible to get the maximum yardage out of a double haul. Of course, under practical fishing conditions, it's often difficult to make a perfect back cast because of gusting winds or your own body position in a balance-rocking current or boat. You can false cast until you feel the line is under perfect control.

The standard procedure is to make two or sometimes three false casts when starting cold with no line extended. When standing in the bow of a boat, for example, drop the shooting line on the deck and leave about 10–15 feet dangling out of the rod tip. The object, of course, is to get the maximum range with a minimum of movement. The first cast, or really a flip skyward, does nothing more than put the line in the air. The second false cast is to extend the line to about forty feet with a double haul to get the belly section completely out of the guides. Very often at this point, the range is already adequate to present the fly. On the third false cast increase the line speed, still using the double haul, and let it go. With a balanced GAF or G2AF, one can easily hit eighty feet, or roughly twice the length of line extended.

If on the second false cast the line is not completely straight, try to correct it with a harder (but smooth) pull. Even though the strokes may be perfect, there's no accounting for the yawing of a 3/0 bucktail fly as it fights the air. Generally it sails overhead die straight, but the slightest puff of wind can grab a hairy wing and cause a chain reaction which finds the line moving faster than the fly, which in turn slows down the leader, which holds back the line point, and then each unit is moving at different speeds. If this occurs, the angler who can apply a sharp haul (in either direction) to regain line speed, altitude, and a straight path backward and forward will pull out of trouble with ease.

The Haul in a Tail-wind Double hauling into a head-wind is simple and needs no explanation. You are driving the line low and forcefully, presenting a minimum surface for the wind to push against. But a strong tail-wind can be more of a barrier to good casting than a head-wind. Inasmuch as the back cast must be made high and straight with an upward sweep of the rod, the first haul does not help much because the wind catches the line along most of its length. Under such a condition it's a simple matter to turn around and face the wind, driving your forward cast into it, and, turning at the hips as you face the water, release shoot on the back cast.

The Roll Cast One of the chief difficulties in fly-casting on small streams, or rivers that are overgrown with trees, is that an overhead cast must extend in the air behind the angler before it can go forward. The roll cast solves this problem. When executed correctly, the line will not travel more than 10–12 inches behind your elbow. Bear in mind that you are not to lift the back cast into the air. Do not practice on dry land, as the roll requires some degree of water-surface tension to complete.

First, work out about fifteen feet of line by using a horizontal cast in any free direction, or even by stripping line from the reel and shaking it out through your tip. Then pull more line off the reel which you can drop on the water for shooting. The rod should be pointed forward as for the overhead cast. Raise the rod slowly until your hand is at a point behind your eye and the rod angled back slightly over your shoulder. When the rod has reached this position, with the belly of the line slightly behind your right elbow, there is a definite pause as in the regular overhead cast. The forward phase of the roll is made by driving the rod sharply downward with stiff wrist and forearm. The impulse given the line causes it to travel forward before the leader and fly have left the water, with the result that they are pulled after the rolling line. To get more distance, shoot your slack as you would in the overhead cast, and repeat the rod movements. Remember, as more line is added, you must put additional emphasis in the forward stroke.

One trick worth learning is to keep the line in slight motion toward you when the forward cast is started. With a long line already on the water, you should gauge the instant between pause and downstroke before the line comes to rest. A practiced roll caster can handle 50–60 feet of line without much difficulty. In fishing a quiet stretch of water, the dry-fly angler can use the roll cast to considerable advantage in retrieving without making a disturbance on the water. However, instead of making a complete roll, snap the rod forward only part way, pick the fly out of the air with a back cast, and then make a regular forward cast. These motions blend smoothly, and when fishing a short line there's little chance of spooking nearby fish.

The Pickup The correct handling of a fly line after a cast is fished out is important. It is sometimes difficult for a beginner to lift the line smoothly from the water and get it in the air for a new cast. If too much line is picked up the ensuing splash is enough to frighten a trout. If too little is lifted from the water, the fly will simply hover over the angler's head until the rod is given more line (weight) for proper flexing. As a general rule, you should have a minimum of 1½ rod lengths of line extended from the tip for an effortless pickup. There are four ways of getting line off the water. You can roll it from the surface, snake it off with a few shakes of the rod, make a snap pickup by throwing slack down the line, or with a smooth left-hand pull, slide the line directly into a back cast.

When dry-fly-fishing, many anglers use the roll pickup. This is nothing more than an unfinished roll cast in which you snap the tip downward to lift the line, then pick the fly out of the air and go into an ordinary back cast. When fishing with a sunken fly line, using nymphs and wet patterns, some anglers make a short, left-hand pull to raise and move the line before making the back cast. Others prefer the pull followed by a straight lift when casting a very long line or in places where there seems to be no likelihood of taking fish close to the rod.

These two methods are the most commonly used. There are two other pickups which are useful to know, however, particularly when fishing fast-water streams where you get varying degrees of slack. They also excel in shallow streams where most of your casting is done in knee-deep water. Frequently you will be working pockets 30–40 feet away while most of your line is drifting around stones, branches, and other obstacles. Making an ordinary pickup or even a roll is difficult, because the line continually snags when drawn *across* the surface. Obviously, any pickup that lifts line upward from the water will escape getting hung.

The Snap Pickup The snap pickup is easy to execute. It literally jumps the line out of any debris or from behind rocks. The snap pickup has the further advantage of permitting you to work the fly right up to your boots. It doesn't make any difference about the slack between tip and fly, even if a fish hits, because one quick wrist movement will set the hook. Essentially, the snap pickup consists of nothing more than moving your rod from a ten to an eleven o'clock position, then snapping the tip back to ten o'clock. The snap motion forms a moving curve that instantly runs down to the leader, lifting line off the water, and *flip* your taper is airborne. Make your normal back cast just at the point when the leader clears the surface. You might be a bit splashy on the first few attempts because there's a tendency to use too much power or use it at the wrong angle. But when done correctly, there is no splash, and the fly is flicked off the water as if by magic.

The Snake Pickup This pickup consists of waving the rod from side to side and forcing a series of S curves into the line. It has the virtue of lifting a heavy front taper off the water, and just as the leader comes free you can flip the bug into a neat back cast without splashing. Naturally, it can be done with trout flies also. Hold your rod at the ten o'clock position, and start shaking the line in a side to side motion, gradually elevating the rod to eleven o'clock. Don't rush it because neat execution depends on getting the S curves running down to the leader to free the line from surface tension. When made correctly, the leader snakes out of the water without so much as a ripple.

—A.J.McC.

FLY-FISHING The art of fly-casting (*which see*) applied to the capture of fish. Using specialized tackle the angler casts an artificial fly to a freshwater or saltwater gamefish. This is one of the oldest and perhaps most artistic forms of sport fishing in the world. The first record of the art of fly-fishing is found in Aelian's *De Natura Animalium* which was written in the third century A.D. Aelian described the subject in some detail in his chapter *De Peculiari Quadam Pisatu in Macedonia.*

"There is a river called Astraeus flowing midway between Berea and Thessalonica, in which are produced certain spotted fish whose food consists of insects which fly about the river. These insects are dissimilar to all other kinds found elsewhere; they are not like wasps, nor would one naturally compare them with the flies called ephemera, nor do they resemble bees. But they are as impudent as flies, as large as the Ant Hedon, of the same colour as wasps and they buzz like bees. The natives call this insect the 'Hippurus.'

"As these flies float on the top of the water in pursuit of food, they attract the notice of the fish, which swim upon them. When the fish spies one of these insects on the top of the water, it swims quietly underneath it, taking care not to agitate the surface, lest it should scare away the prey; so approaching it, as it were, under the shadow it opens its mouth and gulps it down, just as a wolf seizes a sheep, or an eagle a goose, and having done this it swims away beneath the ripple.

"The fishermen are aware of all this; but they do not use these flies for bait because handling would destroy their natural colour, injure the wings and spoil them as a lure. On this account the natural insect is in ill repute with the fishermen, who cannot make use of it. They manage to circumvent the fish, however, by the following clever piscatorial device. They cover a hook with red wool, and upon this they fasten two feathers of a waxy appearance which grow under a cock's wattles, they have a reed six feet long and a fishing line about the same length; they drop this lure upon the water and the fish being attracted by the colour becomes extremely excited, proceeds to meet it, anticipating from its beautiful appearance a most delicious repast; but, as with extended mouth it seizes the lure, it is held fast by the hook, and being captured, meets with a very sorry entertainment."

The "spotted fish" referred to by Aelian was the brown trout. The basic techniques of fly-fishing evolved from trout waters in the centuries following, and while any general discussion of the merits of dry and wet flies cast upstream or down is essentially oriented to the trout angler, these fundamentals are applicable in varying degrees to other freshwater gamefish such as the black bass, Atlantic salmon, grayling, and many panfish species. Saltwater fly-fishing (*which see*) is a comparatively recent development and differs greatly in technique.

THE DRY FLY DOWNSTREAM

Trout always position themselves with heads facing the flow. Thus, the easiest way to stalk them is by coming up from behind where their peripheral vision is limited. It's not only possible to get closer to the fish, but when presented upstream, the fly stands on the water quite naturally, twisting and turning with every subtlety of the current. Although it's difficult for a beginner to manage a cast carried back toward him by the flow, he soon learns to keep the line taut by stripping in slack without pulling the fly. There is also a greater probability of hooking a rising fish because the striking angler draws the fly back into the mouth on an upstream cast and away from it on a downstream cast. Finally, there is much less chance of disturbing the water by fishing upstream. This is most apparent in small pools where a trout hooked at the top will dash down and startle his neighbors with panicky acrobatics. By working up, nearly all hooked fish are drawn down with the current, which leaves the rest of the water undisturbed.

That is the whole argument for upstream fishing, and as a general stream tactic, it can't be beat. There are exceptions to every angling rule, however, and learning to recognize them is a valuable asset to the dry-fly-caster. We know, of course, that on many white water rivers downstream is the only possible direction in which you can work. A floater tossed on the slicks and even skipped over a custardy surface can be amazingly productive. There are rivers like the Thompson, in British Columbia, where the very depth of the water demands going with the current. The Thompson has whirlpools which suck down sawlogs as if they were chips and spits them up again a hundred yards downstream. Pool, in the angler's usual understanding of the term, is nonexistent; the Thompson is more like a giant, wet road that twists along in streaks of froth which dissolve in those quiet places where steelhead lurk on summer evenings. Drag (*which see*) doesn't really matter on its broken surface, and letting the fly work slowly over one spot is the only way you can coax the fish into coming up. He probably has to be convinced that the floater will still be there when he reaches the top. Shallow or calm water, particularly in rivers where brown trout predominate, is another matter, however, and the conditions for downstream fishing are more definitive. The obvious situations like a hat-lifting downstream wind or spots which can't be reached by casting upstream are common enough, but we also have the possibility of earning strikes by presenting the fly directly to a fish without showing line or leader, and adding an action to the floating pattern which puts drag to advantage.

One opportunity for downstream dry-fly work is created by head-winds. A fierce downstream wind creates the conditions to move trout which wouldn't otherwise be caught. It limits their visibility in ruffling the surface for one thing, and it also animates the fly. For best results, a long-hackled fly of the spider or skater type is necessary. Either one will move independently of the current because they stand away from the water without penetrating the surface film. A 10–12-foot leader, tapered to 4X or finer, is equally important, as the flexible length lets the feathers fly freely. If you are on the river with heavier tackle, when a wind starts, it's possible to get some results, but the total score will only be proportionate to your gear; a heavy, three-diameter line won't raise from the surface in anything short of a gale, and a short or heavy leader will only anchor the dry fly in place. And bear in mind

that big floaters tied on small, light wire hooks do the most jumping.

The second opportunity is provided by places which can't be reached any other way except by downstream casting. For the most part, these are awkward spots which anglers habitually avoid or pass by. On all streams, the fisherman should pay particular attention to bridge abutments, sharp bends in the riverbed, rows of boulders, and brush sweepers such as old tree limbs which dangle in the water. These invariably form a blind side to the upstream caster. Brooks also provide a variety of tricky covers, such as tunnels under the willows, footbridges, and fallen timber. Cocked, and floating naturally, a dry fly will invariably take at least one good fish when sent with the current to hidden places.

The third opportunity for downstream casting is one that applies to individual fish—presenting the fly without showing leader or line. As a rule, all downstream casts put the fly in front of the fish before he can see more than a fraction of our terminal gear, but the problem we are solving here isn't concerned with wind or awkward places; the object is to hook a spooky fish in perfectly open, sunlit water. We all have experienced bright summer days when the trout vanish while the line is still hanging in air. Maybe you find one rising in a quiet pool, and before the taper has unrolled it ducks for cover. Even though your cast is long with the line dropping like a cobweb and curved away from his position—the next fish flushes anyhow. This is the kind of day when you can catch trout on the downstream drift, not only because of the fly-first presentation but due to the fact that you don't have to cast into that aerial window.

Correctly executed, the slack line cast is aimed directly down to the position of the fish, but it should float about half that distance. In other words, if the trout is holding 60 feet away, you should drop the fly about 35–40 feet downstream and cover the difference by shaking more nylon out. There are several ways of making slack line deliveries. The oldest and perhaps easiest for most people is to false cast in the usual manner and, on the final stroke forward, stop the rod at a 45-degree angle, and when the line begins to pull shoot, simply wiggle the tip from side to side. This lateral motion will create little curves in the outgoing line. Play with this for a few minutes, and you'll find that you can make narrow or wide elbows of slack with no effort. For our purposes, seven or eight small curves should be enough. When you drift the fly down of a fish, you don't get slack concentrated in one big belly. It will get caught broadside in the current and cause drag. As a tactical advantage, the initial presentation should be made in a perfectly natural float. After the cast is fished out you can begin animating the fly against a dragging line. So the rod wiggling must be timed to distribute the curves through the length of the cast.

The fourth downstream opportunity is, as already indicated, when casting with the wind, a very productive method at times. Of course, a fly can be animated without borrowing the help of a breeze, and there are days, particularly in the late summer and the fall, when a few calculated strokes will produce exceptional fishing. There is a good solid argument for the success of a retrieved dry fly which many casters overlook. Ordinarily, a river surface is freckled with flotsam of various kinds, such as bark, leaves, twigs, weeds, and whatnot. With all these objects coming over the trout's head, the slightest movement from something alive draws its immediate interest. Both dragonflies and stoneflies push their abdomens through the surface when trying to get airborne. They also paddle frantically with their feet, and in the sunlight this movement creates a sparkling trail on the water. The spasmodic kick of a caddisfly is hardly noticeable from above, but at trout level it looks like an explosion. The big mirror is a world of inanimate and animate things, and as the old he-hit-a-cigarette-butt story reveals, the competitive fish must often make immediate decisions.

There is only a shade of difference between a natural and unnatural movement imparted to the fly. On individual rising fishing an effort should be made to get a drag-free drift on the first cast. The fly will reach a point in its float when the trout either accepts or rejects it, and presuming the latter case, the angler must now draw his floater back for a new cast. When working directly down on a fish, this invariably requires pulling it over the fish—a motion which is either going to excite a strike or put the trout down. You will rarely get a second chance as you might in upstream casting when the fly dances away on tippy-toes. The retrieve must begin *before* the line comes near the fish. This is the moment when a fine-line point, long leader, and correctly hackled fly make a critical difference. On calm water in particular, coarse terminal gear is going to create a wake and spoil the whole illusion. Raise the rod slowly, and begin twitching gently, bringing the skater upstream in short, pulsing strokes. If the fly is standing up on its hackles and the fish doesn't respond after it has moved a few feet, lower your rod and let the skater drift near it again. A keen fish sense helps at moments like this, but gradually you will learn to gauge the fly's action according to the response of the trout. A sudden wiggling of the pectorals or a change in the fish's posture may indicate extreme interest. It may make false passes at it. But if nothing else works, try skimming the skater away at a steady speed. As last-cast reeling has repeatedly proven, a positive and continuous flight often triggers blasting strikes. Although mayfly lore more or less conditions our thinking in terms of delicate ephemeral flutters, the fact is that many other aquatic insects disturb the surface greatly.

THE DRY FLY UPSTREAM

Blind casting is a deadly art on nearly all American rivers. Unlike food-rich, silky-faced chalk streams, their turbulent waters do not always, and in some instances only rarely, reveal rising fish. The angler wades along slowly, reading the surface ahead to find pockets and current combinations which previous experience has shown to hold trout. His casting falls into a steady pattern, and often as not, he will catch many fish that way. Some anglers become very adept at the game and instinctively locate trout. However, we also have classic American dry-fly waters such as the upper Deschutes, the Firehole, Green, Salt Creek, upper Madison, the Boardman, Ausable, and some of the limestone streams of Pennsylvania where many fish will be visibly rising. These can be fished blind in their quick parts, but the studied approach is absolutely essential when fish are coming to the mayfly, caddis, and midge in quiet runs. Instead of holding deep and racing up and down like an elevator to grab passing

insects, the flatwater trout has ample time to examine each and every fly. The three basic skills required of the angler for foolproof presentation under these conditions are:

1. correct position of approach
2. completion of cast in the air
3. absolute accuracy

The correct position of approach to a rising trout is from an angle which will reveal only the smallest portion of the leader, no part of the line, and with the fly placed so that it will float without drag. The chief difficulty in blind fishing is that most casters tend to work directly upstream and thus place the leader over the fish. Of course on a rough surface it doesn't matter too much, but on anything from moderate currents to flatwater the best approach is generally quartering from one side of the trout or the other. At times your easiest approach might be almost at right angles to the rise. As a rule aim about four feet above trout, and let the fly pass about one foot away from it. Try to get the fly on target as quickly as possible upon seeing the rise. The chances of a take are very much better if the fly arrives while the fish is still in a feeding posture. If the angle of approach is wrong, maneuver to a better position and *wait* for the next time it comes up.

When a trout has taken a natural and is still at the surface, it is most vulnerable. The vision of a fish is in proportion to its depth, and the deeper a fish rests, the greater its area of sight. Between the disturbance of rising and its limited area of visibility, it's perfectly safe to put the fly on its nose when it's at the top. If the trout is holding several feet down, try to drop a floater at least 4–5 feet upstream, and let it drift into his view. All salmonids will grab the fly from almost any angle in the drift with one exception—the grayling. These fish often strike after the floater has already passed their position. In any event, the ideal moment to present a dry fly is when fish are actually feeding, and the faster you can put the fly over them, the more strikes you will get. If you choose a spot where you can make a drag-free float without showing much of the leader or any part of the line, and preferably remain out of sight yourself, then a third of the problem is solved. Although the wading angler is often less visible than the man on the bank, in very quiet water or in shallow, running water, it's tactically sound to cast from some cover.

The second requirement in good presentation is to complete your cast several feet above the surface. By this time the line and leader have straightened in the air and the fly is dropping. For this reason many experts prefer a very light, somewhat slow dry-fly rod, as the unhurried casting cycle permits "painting" the fly on the water at normal ranges up to fifty feet. With a tip-action rod, you are going to get a different kind of presentation. The casting cycle is faster and less accurate. Casting at the water is almost certain to result in a splashy presentation. If you do make a bad cast on a visible fish, it's advisable to go off looking for other quarry until it's feeding freely again. We can only guess what the "memory" period of a trout might be; generally speaking, fish are ready for business about twenty minutes later. If they've felt the barb, it may be a day or so before you'll have another chance. This is a highly individual circumstance, but except for very large trout with a lot of experience, most fish forget our casting mistakes rather quickly. If you can lay the line on the surface with no forward momentum and place the fly accurately on the first toss, the possibility of a strike is excellent. It diminishes thereafter according to the execution of each succeeding cast.

Besides accuracy or the lack of it, there are three material things which make the job easier. From the instant of turnover, you can achieve a slow, no-splash descent of the fly for these reasons:

1. a balanced leader
2. a fine-line point
3. an air-resistant fly

The balanced leader in basic design consists of 60 percent heavy diameters, 20 percent gradation, and 20 percent tippet. In other words, the butt section should be the longest part of a leader of any given length. This is contrary to the common commercial practice of making short butts, or sections of equal length. Secondly, the fly size must be proportionate to the tippet diameter. With the wrong leader, a tiny No. 20 midge can be as difficult to lay down quietly as an 8/0 salmon fly. Because of its miniscule dressing, the midge offers no air resistance and merely goes along with the leader for a free ride. For this reason, long, fine tippets are necessary for they are air resistant in themselves. In other words, they absorb that final flea power at the turnover instead of whipping around such as a short, heavy tippet does. The tippet length and diameter for proper midge fishing would collapse if you were to use it with No. 10 dry flies. Conversely, the idea of improving your presentation with a No. 10 by using an extra-fine tippet is not often practical. The larger fly is already air resistant. A fine-diameter line point (from .022 to .25) comes gently to the water. There's a wide gap between .022 and the common .037 plastic-coated nylon. Suffice it to say, refinement at the terminal end is going to pay off in more fish. A thick-line point is splashy and creates a broad wake on flatwater, particularly when the fly must be activated with the rod. A thick-line point is less flexible and contributes to drag, and requires the use of extra-heavy leader butts and so on *ad infinitum*. In short, it's a messy thing to throw at a rising trout. If your quarry is a submerged salmon or steelhead which has no intention of looking for mayflies, the heavy diameter won't make a bit of difference. Bear in mind, that in speaking of the line "point" we are actually considering the first 2 feet of a fly line and at least part of the front taper. For delicate fishing the 10 feet nearest the trout must not weigh more than 30 grains, and the diameter should run from .025 to no more than .040 at the 10-foot mark. The first 30 feet must not exceed 120 grains. This more or less approximates an HEH or DT-4-F size. At distances of 50 feet a light fly line almost guarantees lifelike presentation to the fly.

The third material requirement—an air-resistant fly—is seemingly a contradiction to everything we seek of our tackle, as the theorem reads that anything we do to overcome air resistance will increase the length of a cast. However, the rule is a relative one and doesn't apply to presentation of the fly. Remember the cast is gone, the line straightened in the air, and the leader making its dying gasp. Until this instant, the size or type of dry fly (within normal limits) had no influence on the velocity or momentum of the cast. Now in harmony with line point and leader, the feathers may fall in a variety of ways.

At the extremes: a fly with a heavy hook or short, sparse hackles will not glide as smoothly to the water as a spider or variant-type fly. It's almost impossible to make a sloppy presentation with the disproportionately designed spider. At the last impulse when the leader kicks over and the fly starts to drop, the long-hackled floater has all the flight characteristics of a dandelion seed. Not only spiders are conveniently air resistant. The fabled Fan-wing Royal Coachman is another good example of sound design. Although most anglers worship the pattern for its appearance as it dances over a current, the bald truth is that many fan-wing patterns are equally effective because even a poor caster can lay them down quietly. The trouble with fan-wing flies is that they twist and weaken a leader and their life span is brief. After one good trout has mauled the feathers, the wings lose their cocky stance.

For general fishing, many anglers prefer dry flies which are tied slightly oversize for the hook number. So a hackle of standard diameter for a No. 10 dressing can be used on a No. 12 extra-light hook. This produces a modified spider effect with three and preferably no more than four turns of two hackle feathers. It may not look as correct as the stiff, bushy dressing of an orthodox dry fly, but the comparatively smaller hook sits the fibers on their tippy-toes. Of course, there still are periods when wind-blown, meaty, winged foods, such as the grasshopper and stone-fly, are literally whipped into the water and the trout are receptive to the wet *smack* of a natural, but the same rules apply in so far as the leader and line point are concerned. Dumping a fly on the water is easy—it's the neat delivery that earns fish over the greater part of the season.

WET-FLY-FISHING

Wet-fly-fishing is an important early-season method of angling for trout when the rivers are flowing high and cold. There is little surface activity at this time, and the fish forage on larval insect forms which various wet-fly patterns may imitate. While the dry fly is usually fished upstream and allowed to drift in a natural manner, the wet fly is fished in a number of ways, upstream, down, across, and with or without some motion imparted by the rod. As a rule the angler casts diagonally across stream, letting his fly swing down in the current, and when the line starts to drag, he brings the fly to life with his rod tip. The line is retrieved in short pulls, and, ordinarily, a few trout will always find the swimming fly attractive enough to strike. Sometimes more fish respond if your retrieve is very slow, and on other occasions if the return is fast.

The Wet Fly Downstream The wet fly fished downstream is perhaps the easiest method for the beginning angler to use in catching trout. For one thing, you will be wading with the current, which is physically less fatiguing than working upstream, particularly when wearing heavy clothing and waders. And whatever might be gained by getting the fly deeper in upstream casting is invariably lost when the neophyte handles the returning slack line. The role of the line hand is less important in downstream fishing. It won't be necessary to cast more than 30–35 feet. You may see some good-looking water along the far bank, but for the first day concentrate on keeping your back cast high and practice making short casts with a minimum of false casting. Each time a cast is completed, place the line on your rod hand forefinger, so that when you retrieve the line slides over it. You needn't squeeze your forefinger against the corks; keep your hand relaxed and your wrist somewhat stiff. By holding the line close to the rod you will have complete control of the slack between the butt guide and your line hand which makes it easier to hook a fish. If you simply pull line directly from the rings with your left hand, the rod no longer commands the situation. The forefinger hold also expedites handling of the slack with your line hand. When a cast is fished out, drop the line from your finger and cast again.

Presentation Tactically, you should try to modify each cast according to the speed of the current and the depth of the river. In a quiet pool you may be able to cast straight across stream, and when your line begins to sweep around below your position the fly will be bumping bottom. In a swift, deep riffle you will probably have to aim the cast almost directly upstream to get the fly down to the same depth. In any case, you'll know when the fly is not being fished correctly because it will show at the surface. If you come to a place where the currents are varied and the line belly floats too fast, thereby pulling the fly to the top, you can correct the speed with slack. To adjust the drift of a wet fly, release a few yards of line just as the belly part begins to gather speed. If the current isn't strong enough to pull the line from your hand, give the rod a few shakes up and down, and it will slide out of the guides. The addition of slack takes the tension off the line and causes the fly to sink deeper. In time you will learn the many nuances of directing and mending your casts, but all you have to think about at first is putting that fly near a trout.

As you look downstream, you will see slick places in the bouncy water, boulder tops, and perhaps old logs or tree roots, and undercut banks. These all provide cover for the trout. Do not cast at them, however, because the fly won't be swimming deep enough when it passes these lies. Always think in terms of aiming your cast so that (1) the fly has enough time and slack to sink deep and (2) it reaches the fish just as your line completes its swing across the surface. If you are lucky enough actually to see a trout splash, follow the same rule of aiming a proper length of line upstream from its position and let the fly sweep around to it. What really happens when the line tightens in the current after the swing is that the fly comes to life. It rises like an insect from the bottom and moves toward the surface. This is a natural motion for an emerging nymph or larva which has left its gravel home and is swimming toward the top. So even if your wet fly passes several feet under a surfacing trout, it will arc up to the trout's level in a lifelike manner. You may notice, incidentally, that most of your wet-fly strikes occur at the moment your line has completed a swing.

The Strike The strike is the only difficult part of wet-fly-fishing. When a trout strikes the fly, you must hook it. Fish sometimes hook themselves on artificials, but the great majority mouth and eject the fly in a split second. This is countered by raising the rod up and back with enough pressure to sink the barb, yet not so forcefully that the leader might snap. You may miss quite a number of fish in the beginning and probably break off on a few more before a sharp reflex is developed. Eventually, it will become an automatic response to the strike, whether you actually see, feel, or sense the take. Fortunately, early-season trout usually strike hard because of hunger and the strong currents. A fish must act fast to seize its food—and you will feel the impact as a rubbery *pluck* at the fly. If the trout misses and you see its flash or disturbance, don't draw the fly away, but give it a few twitches with the rod tip so that it darts forward a few inches and settles back. If nothing happens in the next minute, pull the fly from the trout's position slowly with continued twitching. Next, repeat the cast to the same place by aiming up or across stream and letting the fly swing around again. If there are no further signs of interest after three or four casts, keep moving downstream. The fish is down for the moment, but mark the spot for later reference. After an hour or so it will probably be feeding freely again.

Fishing Undercut Banks One of the most productive spots for the wet fly is a long undercut bank, particularly one which has a run of white-water at the head of it. Hollow banks are natural food collectors and also provide cover for big trout. Position yourself so the fly can be cast slightly upstream into the ripply flow and left to swing down into the hole. Judging by the conformation of the bank, the stream is probably 6–8 feet deep at this point; so don't hurry the fly along. After making the cast, follow the line around with your rod (the tip should be at eye level), so there's a minimum of drag and you are prepared for a strike. Depending on how the line point reacts, you can do one of several things. If the line twitches or jumps as though it hit a bump, set the hook. You won't often see a fish take in deep or broken water. If the line sweeps around without a bump and stops its arc over deepwater, then just let the fly hang there for a minute or two. Sometimes trout will strike a perfectly motionless fly in the quiet parts of a pool. Actually, the current gives the feathers a slight movement as the fly sinks very slowly toward bottom. Now lift the rod tip, and gently twitch the fly to the surface. That should do the trick. If the current is deceptively fast and the line didn't stop but continued its swing to a point directly below your position in the shallows, then make a new cast and adjust the drift with slack. Devote plenty of time to an undercut because trout are certain to be here. The fundamental technique in exploring hollow banks is to let the fly sink to a level where the fish can see it, before twitching it past their dens.

THE FAST RETRIEVE

The fast retrieve is not always effective, but it's sometimes an excellent technique in heavily fished streams. It is particularly effective for rainbow trout. The basic idea is to work a small wet fly just under the surface in rapid, continuous strokes. The fly must dash about 2–3 feet forward on each pull, with no obvious pause between movements. This is accomplished by brisk line stripping combined with a backward movement of the rod. The rod travels to the rear horizontally, at about half the speed that your line is being retrieved. Unlike the slower, more regular method of wet-fly-fishing, the fast retrieve should be pulsing, unvaried, and preferably swimming away from the fish. You must get the fastest possible movement to the fly in short dashes—without pulling it from the water. The fly might represent a rapidly swimming minnow or some kind of water beetle, but the illusion of something edible escaping is probably its main attraction. The technique is particularly useful when fish are not actively feeding. The success of a fast retrieve depends on your locating the fish and using a long, fine leader and very small wet fly. Dressings on No. 14 and No. 16 hooks are about right. The retrieve is seldom productive if you use larger flies. Remember, this is a technique for silky clear-water streams where large flies are usually poor fish catchers.

FLY FISHING IN LAKES

The techniques used in lakes differ in some respects from fishing in streams. All lakes in which trout live are not necessarily productive to the fly fisher. Some lakes get too warm and the trout remain in deep water during the better part of the season. Others are almost barren of insect life, yet rich in forage fish, and the trout seldom feed near the surface. Practically all the big lakes in South America could be included in the latter category, as can many North American waters, which are so laden with smelt, alewives, or kokanee that fly fishing is restricted almost exclusively to the streamer. This situation is readily identifiable and comparatively easy to exploit within the seasonal limits it suggests. From a purist's standpoint such lakes are marginal at best. However, there are a great many lakes, particularly in the western United States which not only contain an abundance of buglife, that passes its larval development within the water, but are subject to the anemohydrochorus spreading of insects. Actually, terrestrials—such as beetles, grasshoppers, and moths—fall on the surface of all standing bodies of water, but in some regions this wind-dispersed fauna reaches significant proportions. Flying ants in Maine, tortoise shell butterflies in California, or bees in northern New York often bring on a rise which lasts not for hours but days. But whether the source of trout food is from the surrounding land or the lake itself, feeding fish are not always easy to find, particularly on large lakes exposed to the wind.

Extreme differences exist in the gathering capacity of various portions of a lake, depending on the configuration of the shoreline, the prevailing wind direction, and any counter currents that might be present. Thus, some spots are always reliable, while others produce poorly. No small part of your success depends on the ability to read a lake. The calm, glassy water which characterizes mountain lakes in early morning may reveal rising trout everywhere, and in general it's a good time to be fishing. Try to be out at the crack of dawn, as you can expect the best scores of the day on big browns and rainbows before the wind starts to blow. The fish are easy to see, dimpling and rolling in head-and-tail rises. But as soon as the wind begins, ditched insects are gathered in relatively narrow windrows, as they drift toward shore. Although the movement of surface water amounts to about 2 percent of the existing velocity of the wind, the insect mass which protrudes above the surface can move along at a fairly rapid pace. For this reason it's better to cast downwind when fishing a dry fly to avoid drag. If you're casting from a boat, its movement will also add drag to the fly as it drifts before the wind. However, it may be hard to find the feeding areas.

The thing to watch for is a lane of debris between the ruffled places, which usually appears comparatively smooth, while keeping an eye open for rises. If the surface is too choppy for a visible lane to form, then look for little calm spots that interrupt the regular wave pattern, and consider each one a possible rise. Steep banks or cliffs along a windward shore are usually productive, because they can support drifting material offshore until it sinks. Feeder streams also provide a continuous flow of surface fauna, and if a tributary exists on a windward shore, great masses of insects may collect where the dissipating current counters the force of the wind. Of course, in a fertile lake there might be all kinds of insects on the water, which poses the problem of selectivity.

The kind of rise made by trout in a lake will tell you a lot. Adult caddis as well as adult mayflies usually trigger very splashy rises with some fish, particularly the smaller ones, coming clear out of the water. But the sub-imagos or duns of the mayfly, which first pop on the surface after leaving their nymphal shucks, and all terrestrials, create a dimple rise, often accompanied by a sucking sound. If the trout are taking nymphs, you'll generally see bulges in the surface, with the occasional head-and-tail roll. Large aquatics such as the dragonfly, damselfly, and stonefly draw slashing rises, as the trout charge at the strong flying adults.

One way in which lakes differ from streams is that fish often cruise for their meal. Trout feeding in this way are moving right along, picking up insects in a series of successive rises. The idea here is to anticipate the path of the fish, as indicated by its direction after two or three swirls, then present the fly 10–30 feet ahead. It does no good to cast at the fish, because the line will cause a disturbance and, more often than not, the fly will land well to the rear. This is similar to the method used for catching lake whitefish when they're at the surface, and differs only in that whitefish usually move a bit faster than trout. As in scattergun shooting, the tendency is to shoot behind the target, so you have to develop a natural swing to get the proper "lead." The beauty of cruising trout is that when you find an area which is trafficked regularly, it's possible to stand or anchor in one place and let the fish come to you.

Experienced anglers prefer a long rod for lake fishing. For one thing, it minimizes false casts in getting distance and when sitting down in a boat it makes line handling a lot easier. Naturally, the distance you can cast has a bearing on it, and if you are able to hit rises at 60 or 70 feet, it's tactical to stand; but, either way, a rod of 8 feet or longer is a definite advantage. The line should be the lightest possible for the rod, and one that shoots well; however, try not to use heavy forward tapers, because big-bellied lines are splashy. The leader should be as long as you can handle, with 9 feet the minimum, and preferably 12–15 feet in length tapered to the finest tippet practical for the average fish. As a rule, even in waters where trout ordinarily run two pounds or better, a 3X tippet is the norm. It pays to use 4X and sometimes 5X in bright sunlight, and while you will probably lose a few more trout, the number of fish hooked is proportionately greater.

In lake fishing, your leader must sink instantly. If it persists in floating, it will create a wake on the surface when you move the fly, and in glassy water this will spook trout. After rubbing the leader perfectly straight with a piece of rubber, take a cloth and scrub it with a liquid soap or even mud. The very best leader sink is bentonite. This gray, clay-like substance can be found in the banks of some Western trout streams. Bentonite absorbs and holds water better than any sponge. It causes a leader to do the same thing.

Despite the topwater action, that can be enjoyed when conditions are right, the basic method of fly fishing in lakes is with the nymph. In fertile waters trout will take a nymph practically all of the time, provided it's presented at the proper level. Weedy bottomed areas just at the drop-off are a choice location. You might have to get the nymph fifteen or twenty feet down to reach the fish, so by all means carry a spare reel or spare spool with a sinking-type line. This is slow, but often highly productive fishing that requires patience to execute. The trout may strike as the nymph is sinking or take it after the fly has reached bottom or on the retrieve. At the other extreme, when the fish are feeding at the surface, the nymph can be cast with a floating line near the trout and left to sink a foot or two before giving it motion. When the leader has disappeared, give the rod an upward pull to take any slack out of it and cause the nymph to rise toward the surface. Very often you will hook a trout with this first movement.

Fly size is extremely important. Some lakes just don't produce well except to very small patterns or comparatively large ones. The only general rule which might be useful is that high mountain lakes are more likely to demand midge class patterns (No. 18's and No. 20's) and, conversely, the lower the lake elevation the more frequently you will need big artificials. Midge (*which see*), feeding trout, have frustrated many a pack trip. So the ideal is to have something from No. 4 down to No. 18 in wet and dry, plus an assortment of imitations for the periods when beetles, ants, inchworms, grasshoppers, and other terrestrials are abundant. Bear in mind, the trout isn't concerned about the current taking his meal downstream, and he can examine each artificial like a Dutch diamond cutter. This also indicates that in handling the fly, you cannot be in a hurry. Many a fine trout has grabbed a nymph or floater while the angler ate a sandwich or studied a sea gull. On rare occasions, when the fish are running after dragonflies, a rapid retrieve is more effective, but this might happen only once or twice a season.

FISHING BIG POOLS

Big pools on a trout stream differ from most other angling situations in that parts of them will have heavy, conflicting currents which may run clockwise or counterclockwise, as well as extreme depths where the fish will take cover. The classic example of this kind of water is found in a pool which has a waterfall at its head. A waterfall is an extravagance of nature which always holds promise to the angler. No matter how small or how large the stream, its great weight will dig a deep hole and attract elderly trout whose bulk no longer fits the flat river bottoms. Every waterfall hides a trophy. Nevertheless waterfall pools are difficult to work because the main current which begins by churning at the head of the run and flows to the tail also creates clockwise and counterclockwise currents along its edges. These run back into the base of the falls conveying all kinds of insect life to the fish when they are not actively feeding. You will be

able to recognize side currents by a slick surface which usually appears at one side or between paths of freckle-topped water traveling in the opposite direction. To a lesser degree, and depending on the height of the water, these same rotating currents may exist around barrier dams. If the dam is undercut there is bound to be a fine trout under the timbers.

Ideally, we think of a pool as a deep place in a river with a slow, uniform current. At its best with a good hatch of mayflies on the surface the fish rise easily, and one is only concerned with placing the fly a few feet from a visible feeder, then avoiding drag. Particularly at the beginning of a rise when the trout are hungry and off guard we work at the peak of expectation. But most pools are a long way from ideal as they present a complex of currents which a fastidious trout knows in detail. If an insect moves in a direction which is unfamiliar to him, it's instantly suspect. Thus, the angler must have an edge of keenness and patience to raise fish in any normal flow of water. The fly which worked just a few minutes ago in the downstream pockets may be cast on a pool until the angler is weary and draw no response whatever.

Some streams have very few actual pools. A great many trout rivers are dominated by riffles and pocket-water which require a tactical approach that differs in its fine points from fishing the relatively deep flatwater of a pool. Pools are created below waterfalls, log or rock barriers, dams, at river bends, at the foot of any narrow defile such as a gorge, and below any upwelling bottom formed by bedrock or permanent gravelbars. They also occur around bridges although the modern method of sinking pilings in concrete in place of the old-fashioned abutments has made this type of lair less and less common. Invariably, pools will hold the largest fish because their depth offers cover and the current brings an abundance of food into the hold which trout can collect at their leisure. Unlike pocketwater casting, which is characterized by split-second decisions on the part of both angler and quarry, the pool has a slower tempo. It is also trickier in the sense that fish may hold in the most innocent places such as the gravelly shallows at the tail where one is seldom prepared to cast before disturbing them. This is always perplexing. If you flush one, they all disappear. If you hook one, the chances are still very good that the whole community will evaporate in a chain reaction. Look the area over carefully, and if there is a large trout in evidence, cast to it; if the fish are small they generally won't run too far up the pool, as their sanctuaries are invariably near the tail section. This doesn't always succeed of course, but it's a better tactic than wading into the middle of a pool and putting all the trout down.

Fortunately, it's at the head of a pool where one is apt to find the largest trout. Generally, the topwater is fairly deep and turbulent which provides some shelter for big fish, and it's the source of incoming food. Most important aquatic insects originate in the swifter parts of streams, and those trout lying at the top of a pool are in a perfect feeding station. The best holds will be around submerged ledges, log cribbing, downed timber, or along an undercut. What type of fly to use depends naturally on the weather and the posture of the fish. The taking of an insect on the surface is of course unmistakable and indicates a dry pattern. The commotion made by a bulging trout which is seen as a swirl is best attacked with the nymph. Beyond these signs you may have to scratch gravel with a wet fly or bucktail. If the lie looks particularly promising, it may be worth while to change to a sinking-type line.

Most trout streams have submerged ledges formed by granite outcroppings or bedrock. These are real hotspots for cannibal browns who live like hermits in deep pools. If you can locate the open sides of these caves, send a nymph down to the bottom and make it "crawl" near these dens. A sinking fly line is a great boon to deep-fishing. However, it has one idiosyncrasy. Tapered lines do not sink at a uniform rate, and in the very slow currents of a pool the most important part of the line, say the last 6–8 feet, will still be near the surface when the belly portion touches bottom. The length near your rod tip may be on gravel, but for all practical purposes the fly is still in the air. It takes about forty seconds for an H point to sink 8 feet after the heavy portion has already reached the gravel. Using slightly weighted nymphs or wet patterns is no immediate help, as the leader will simply bend in the current because it in itself has no real weight and the fly merely tends to pull the tippet down. Thus, the technique requires great patience to execute successfully.

FLY-FISHING IN SMALL STREAMS

The number of small streams in North America far exceeds the number of rivers. For every stream that we can explore on our feet there are probably twenty which the angler must view like a praying mantis. But these provide a special kind of pleasure. For one thing, we can see almost every fish before it comes to the fly, and a good percentage of the time it will be a brightly colored wild fish. The true native is seldom found near thruways any more, and in most states headwater brooks are literally the last unspoiled habitat left. So miniature streams have their virtues—plus some qualities uniquely their own.

Small-stream fly-fishing requires studied stalks and casts. The angler will often have to hide behind trees, squat below riffles, or kneel on grassy banks. The important thing is to stay out of sight and out of the water wherever possible. It is also necessary to avoid making any noise with your feet. Don't click the gravel together or stumble on a hollow bank; the trout will hear you long before you see them. If the stream is heavily overgrown with trees and you can't get behind one, step quietly into the water and work from under the branches with a side cast. In other words, judge each situation from the standpoint of where the trout must be holding and how you can best cast to that spot without revealing your presence. This means considering every little hole a potential hotspot and choosing a position where you can work it without flashing the rod in bright sunlight or throwing your own shadow over the fish. Although the sun problem isn't easy to resolve, it is apparent that its angle is more important than its position in back of you or in front. A low sun in the rear throws a long leader and line shadow ahead, toward the fish, but if it's high in back of you, or if you quarter the cast (which always seems safest), the odds are against disturbing the trout.

The quality to look for in a small-stream fly rod is its ability to function with a line of 118–146 grains, which for the sake of illustration might be a DT-4-F of 120

grains; the line point should be .030-inch diameter or less and the heavy portion no more than .042 inch. The range of rods catalogued for 120-grain lines runs 6–8 feet in length and 1¼–4 ounces in weight. As a general rule a rod of 7½ feet, weighing approximately 2½ ounces, is a practical choice. What you want is a rod that can hold 20–30 feet of line in the air without the need for excessive casting speed. It should have a slow casting cycle so that you have control of the fly and the line displays no tendency to drop prematurely. These requirements all but eliminate "fast" or tip-action rods. A heavy or stiff rod requires a considerable length of line in the air to kick the fly out. With a proper light outfit you can get on your knees behind a tree and with 9–10 feet of leader and even 5–6 feet of line through the tip-top achieve a neat vest-pocket cast. Before fishing, rub the entire leader through a little square of inner tube to get it perfectly straight and pliable; then tie on a No. 14 spider or variant. A short leader won't stay out of trees any better than a long one, and a balanced ten footer will turn over just as easily provided you have a proper rod.

There are many runs in small streams where the water will narrow to no more than ten feet in width. This water may have to be fished from a distance by casting 20–25 feet across dry gravel and just letting the last 4–5 feet of leader fall on the surface. This results in broken tippets and hooks unless you know the two tricks which every creep-and-crawl artist can put to work. The first is to use a bushy divisible so the hook isn't exposed, or preferably a spider or variant with long, stiff hackles and a tiny hook; in either type the barb won't often contact stones if you lift the line gently. Due to the large diameter of its hackles, the spider is almost impossible to snag or bring down hard on the water. It's a boon to the mediocre caster and, equally important, attractive to the trout. The spider dry doesn't imitate a natural spider, although it may suggest one, but it does have some of the ethereal qualities of many aquatic insects due to the fact that it rides high on the water. A fish probably sees less of it than the angler. It has little tendency to drag on complex currents; it literally bounces over them. Of course, the very similar variant (which is a spider tied with short wings and a body) and the skater (which is a spider without a tail) have these same advantages. Made with stiff hackles and dabbed with flotant, the tiny light-wire hook is defended from snags and can be handled over grass or gravel banks provided you don't try to yank the line off the water. This is the second trick.

When the spider has finished its drift, use the snap pick-up (*see* Fly-Casting) by moving your rod from the ten o'clock position to eleven o'clock, then snapping the tip back to ten o'clock. The snap forms a moving curve that instantly runs down to the leader, lifting your line in the air. The fly will literally jump off the water. You may break leaders occasionally and even get the line caught between rocks, which is a hopeless situation. However, you will also catch some of the best fish of the season in the worst possible places, and the occasional loss of terminal tackle is not so important.

Of course, long, foam-flecked pools and deep, white-water pockets can be fished standing up, provided you don't get too close to them. If you can stay back at least thirty feet from where the trout lie under a broken surface, it won't be necessary to get on your knees. Sometimes, with the stream kinking in every direction you'll have to cast across boulders to drift the fly over a short slick, but these are the payoff spots. However, all bends in the stream are not alike. There may be a sharp, almost right-angle turn, bordered on both banks by hip-high weed. This is a tricky place because the best fish often lie at the narrow throat in the upper arm of the bend. The lower half may be just a series of shallow step-pools which seldom hold anything bigger than 8–9 inches. When you wade to the bend, the larger trout stationed above will usually be flushed. It's often possible to work from the bank by standing 15–20 feet back in the weed and keeping the extended line balanced on top of the plants. You can't see the water, but invariably the first cast will bring a strike. If the line doesn't tangle on the pickup, you may get a second chance.

From the last of the narrow water the stream may flow through open country with no vestige of shelter or the protection of a tree for several miles. Often it will run across a pasture meadow which cows have cropped to the stream edge. Here you may find willow borders of eroded banks with patches of tall grass for cover; however, it's nearly all kneeling country and the fish can be anywhere, in the stream center, or under the other bank. This is a great spot for worm artists in the springtime who can drift their baits deep in the undercuts, but it's difficult to take trout on anything in the flat, transparent water of summer. It may be necessary to rebuild the leader, adding a longer and finer tippet.

If no rises are visible, the telling method in this type of water during midday is often a wet fly or nymph fished in the hollow banks. Trout are accustomed to eating terrestrial insects in breezy, open sections of stream, and unless grasshoppers, ants, leaf rollers, or beetles happen to be particularly numerous and falling in the water, the chances are that you'll have to go deep to get fish. One dry fly stratagem to try first is to work the places where bushes trail in the water because these are natural springboards for high-diving bug life. Start with a terrestrial-type pattern, such as the dry Muddler or Letort Beetle, and stand back in the meadow to work both banks while keeping out of sight. Any rise will be cautious. You may sense the strike before you see it; there's an imperceptible movement below the fly, then a flash of gold, a boil, and instantly the rod is bent like an archer's bow. It's all very different from the snatching rise of the fast-water trout in the forest. However, on days when the fish won't come topside, kneel a bit closer to the bank, and work long, quartering casts with a wet McGinty or Black Ant to the bank opposite, letting the fly sink right down to the bottom and drift naturally with the current. In fishing your own bank, try to keep as much line off the surface as possible by casting upstream and dropping as much of the belly section on the grass border as the situation will allow. Here again we can get in trouble by casting an unwanted curve in the line which throws the fly up on the bank, or getting the line snagged, but for the most part it's possible to drop the leader and maybe 4–5 feet of line on the water ahead. Theoretically, this permits the fly to swim 14–15 feet before the pickup. The main thing in meadow runs is not to stand up and not to throw line scatter-shot fashion up the middle of the stream; either way the trout will spook.

When small-stream fishing you'll cover a lot of mileage in the course of a day. Each spot can tolerate just so many casts; so it isn't unusual to walk several miles. For this reason, and because you shouldn't be wading in the deep spots anyhow, a pair of lightweight hip boots is more practical than waders. Most anglers prefer the kind with fabric tops and cleated rubber soles. Felts wear out much too quickly when taking long walks in the country. You should also bring along sunglasses. Polaroids are a great asset as so much depends on how well you can see the stream bottom ahead. Remember, stalking is a sight game. An insect repellent is also necessary in most headwater streams, and a small bottle or spray can is worth keeping in your jacket. One last item, which you may overlook, is a pair of sharp-nose pliers. Pliers are ideal for slipping the barb out of a baby trout's mouth without even touching the little fellow. Just grab the hook firmly at the exposed part above his lip, and raise the trout slightly from the water turning your wrist in a quick downward circle. The hook will come free and the fish will slip back in the brook.

UNDERWATER OBSERVATIONS

There is no way of conclusively proving exactly how the fish sees an artificial fly from its position in the river. We do know how man sees and understands the trout's environment, largely through the experience of Scuba diving and applying these observations to our knowledge of angling. A laboratory, tank, or prism is without the perspective of an actual river—subject to currents, variable angles of sunlight and shadow, and the clouds of diatoms which decrease visibility. We talk about leader shadow, for instance, from the human viewpoint, which is vertical in the sense that we are looking *down* on a length of gut. But from the trout's position near the stream bottom the view is close to horizontal, the leader wholly or partially invisible, and the shadow distorted or perhaps unseen by the fish. If its cone of vision is primarily upward, and this seems to be the case as trout try to position themselves lower in the water than man (or failing that, they will turn slightly on one side), leader shadow is hardly a factor. Also, in a crystal-clear stream the range of human vision and presumably the trout's is limited according to the position of the sun. If we look toward the sun, details dissolve within a very few feet. In looking with the sun, the stream opens up like a fluorescent tunnel, but once again moving water and suspended matter limit the range of vision. A man standing on the bank can see at least 50 percent further through water than the fish—or, more precisely, an observer in the fish's position. The fish has another disadvantage in having no ability to alter the amount of incoming light, as its retina is fixed, and where man can adjust to changes from dark to bright, the trout is limited to varying degrees of intensity.

Old trout know their visional limits well; they stay in shaded places or in deep holes where the sun has less penetration, and they become nocturnal foragers during the bright summer months. It's interesting to note, when sitting among them on the stream bottom, the fish shuffle back and forth, with the larger ones taking stations directly in the sun once they've figured out which part of the observer's body is the front. This is of no concern to lake fish or fish on reefs in saltwater, as there is no diffusion from current and much less from sunlight when you consider all the inert flotsam that windrows a river surface—bark, twigs, leaves, nymphal shucks, and weeds—the faintest motion in an artificial is enough to draw the trout's interest. Both dragonflies and stoneflies have double images at times because they are heavy-bodied and in attempting to get airborne will push their abdomens through the surface. They are easy to spot from some distance even among large pieces of surface drift because their wings are constantly thrumming, radiating little waves. They also paddle with their feet, making pinpoints of light, and at certain angles in the sun stoneflies leave a whole trail of "sparks" across the surface. Such activity is reasonably imitated by long-bodied dressings which you can activate on the retrieve without causing drag. But the natural mayfly is relatively delicate and moves only spasmodically. There is a very great similarity between the natural and a correctly drifting artificial. However, when the human eye is brought close to a floating fly, the way a trout would approach it, it will see the same thing that must puzzle fish; where the dry fly looked edible from a distance, it invariably has a double image when viewed close at face. Tail, hook, or hackles protrude through the surface film and reflect back against the silvery roof. Only a perfect, high-riding float has the vague silhouette of a natural as it stands on pinpoints of hackle. Flies which are tied with heavy hackles "look" artificial except in bad light or rough-water. When the lower half of the hackle is suspended below the surface film, you get the double-image effect which natural insects do not always have, plus the double image of the hook. It is not hard to understand why we see big trout spiral up to smack a floater, then change their minds in the last instant. Yet, to the fish, reasonable doubt is not wholesale denial, as a properly cocked dry fly with nothing but the faint prints of its feet on the mirrored roof will bring it back with mouth open.

Applying these observations to dry flies—the bulk of our commercial products can be improved with lighter hooks and sparser hackling; there is a tendency among professionals to use three hackles where two would do the trick. While bushy collaring makes a handsome fly and temporarily increases its buoyancy, subsequent floats get lower and lower until only the wings are visible. The fly is soon floating because of its bulk and except in the sodapop screen of moving water the effect is unnatural. Perhaps the chief reason why we often catch trout after knotting on a fresh fly is because it is riding high on the surface, not because it is a different pattern. It is most difficult to distinguish color, form, or even size when the fly is floating. Size would seem to be important in that smaller dry flies are invariably sparse and have the lightest wire hooks, which again results in a better float. Standard patterns such as the Royal Coachman, Quill Gordon, Light Cahill, or whatever you favor locally, can be improved by using extra-light hooks, sparser and longer hackle, and short, sparse wings.

The disturbing factors in fly presentation from the trout's position are faulty casting, especially when the line point slaps the water, leader flash, and an unnatural float of the fly. An underwater observer is most aware of these three things, and sound is undoubtedly a fourth and critical factor to the trout. Surprisingly little can be seen of a floating fly line at ordinary stream depths (say up to your wader tops) because of the angle at which it floats and the length of the leader. If the line slaps the water or penetrates the surface film, again creating the double image, it is immediately apparent. Leader diameters from 4X down are nearly impossible to find when they are floating. All sunken sections are easy to spot due to their double image reflected against the surface.

HOW TO BUY ARTIFICIAL FLIES

In an art form that demands strict adherence to the rules, one would expect all flies of one pattern to be exactly alike. But even with the same ingredients no two fly-dressers achieve exactly the same result. For one thing, it is difficult to tie a pattern correctly from a book description. You must have a model to work from; give one printed description to twenty different tiers, and you have roughly the same fly, but twenty distinct styles. Some fly-dressers use more hackle, longer wings or tails, or fuller bodies, and as a result the angler generally develops a favorite professional according to what he (the angler) feels is ideal. However, quality does count, and the skilled fly-tier will rarely stray from conventional patterns or materials. Naturally, he will dress some originals now and then, but if he runs out of prime hackles he will not substitute say a red-brown for a chocolate-brown even though most people wouldn't know the difference.

Obviously, if you start out buying imitations of all the insects that hatch on American rivers, you will spend a small fortune. Even a basic collection can be an expensive project, and after the investment of several hundred dollars—sometimes an impotent one. For one thing, there's a tendency to collect patterns rather than types, and it's easy to wind up with dozens of flies that were all designed for the same job. Some anglers carry enough feathers to stuff a large mattress, and yet there are many occasions when they lack the right type of fly.

To begin with, regional conditions have a definite influence on your stock. A man coming from New England to fish a Rocky Mountain river, for instance, may not be prepared with the rough hair flies that are so effective in Western rivers. It's a good general rule to buy your flies in the locale you intend to fish. However, if you know a top-notch professional nearby, the chances are that he is aware of those patterns being used in other areas. At least, you can be sure of getting quality flies. You don't want hackle unraveling and wings snapping out, even if the pattern is correct. But no matter where you live, a basic assortment can be acquired that will stand the test of time and travel.

Assuming you want to keep costs to a minimum, begin your inventory with two dozen basic dry flies. Essentially, there are eight types used in American trout streams, and starting with three of each type is a minimum investment with maximum potential. The inevitable loss from trees and snapped leaders may deplete your stock rapidly, but at least you will have some plan for replacement. Never carry many flies when actually on the water, but always make sure that a few of the following are in the box: hair-wings, spiders, divided-wings, bivisibles, fan-wings, midges, hair-bodies, and down-wings. These cover nearly all dry-fly problems no matter where you fish.

For example, you might select the Grey Wulff, the Blue Dun Spider, Brown Bivisible, Light Cahill, Fan-wing Royal Coachman, Black Midge, Irresistible, and Muddler Minnow to represent the basic eight. This is far more practical than the common practice of a dozen divided-wing patterns and a dozen fan-wings because fly types impose a limit on what you can and cannot do.

The Grey Wulff is a hair-wing pattern, and beside being durable, the white, V-shaped wings can be seen in bad light and broken water. It's shaped roughly like a mayfly, and, undeniably, the pattern takes fish. Your second fly, the Blue Dun Spider, is designed for the opposite kind of stream conditions, where you are casting over trout in smoothwater. The long, hackled spider sits down with minimum impact and floats high without drag.

The Brown Bivisible can be used in fast- or slowwater, but it presents a different silhouette from either the hair-wing or the spider-type fly. It works best perhaps when the fish are feeding on insect forms other than the mayfly. Your fourth pattern, the Light Cahill, is a divided-wing with the silhouette of a natural mayfly. It's ideal for rising fish who are going to give the imitation close scrutiny. Don't substitute divided-wing patterns dressed with quill feather wings—they are too heavy and quickly fray. The wood duck or mandarin side feathers in the Cahill wing are suggestively lifelike and stand up to considerable abuse. The fifth fly on your list is a fancy pattern and has the virtue of raising tough, old trout even in bright sunlight. Traditionally, the fan-wing is reserved for those occasions when all else fails. The wings collapse rather quickly after one or two fish have chewed on them, and they also spin in the air, which weakens the leader. Yet, even with these shortcomings, the Fan-wing Royal Coachman is a deadly pattern on brown-trout waters everywhere.

The Black Midge is one of those patterns that doesn't get regular use, but when you need a tiny fly, nothing else can replace it. Dressed on a No. 20 hook, the midge scores on those days when fish are rising for a seemingly invisible insect. Actually, a midge can be fished dry, wet, or, more accurately, in the surface film. The Irresistible is a prototype of a large number of hair-body with hair-wing patterns designed for maximum floatability. It lacks the delicate silhouette of a mayfly, but the intention here is to create a "bug" with real authority. The Irresistible will float in wildwater and take a terrific beating from hard-mouthed fish, which makes it a top Western pattern.

The last fly on your list of floaters is the dry Muddler. The long, low silhouette encompasses many insects that fish feed on; the dragon- and damselflies, stoneflies, caddis, and grasshoppers. Under some conditions this down-wing fly is spectacular.

Except for the midge, which is properly tied on a No. 20 hook, you want the Blue Dun Spider on a No. 14, the Muddler on a No. 10, and the others dressed on No. 12 hooks. Fly size is very important; often, a change from say No. 12 to No. 16 in the same pattern will take fish immediately. This is as true in the West as in the East. Too much emphasis is placed on large flies for the sagebrush country. Besides replacing lost flies and adding a few new patterns, you should concentrate on adding the smaller sizes in the next dozen you buy. Many insects that trout take freely can only be matched with No. 14 and No. 16 dressings.

For sunken patterns, the basic fly box needs four types: the wet fly, nymph, bucktail, and streamer. Here again price may be an obstacle; for the right perspective on your fishing, you can buy a dozen wets, a half dozen nymphs, and the balance in bucktails and streamers. You might get the whole assortment for a $10 bill—or less, if you shop carefully. Once in a while you'll come across a country store or gas station where the local feather merchant turns out creditable flies at a nominal cost. If they are tied with soft, supple hackles, neat varnished heads, and secure matched wings—you've found a bargain. As a rule, the tier is a hobbyist whose work isn't well-known, but that doesn't mean his flies are inferior.

Basically, wet flies take four forms: the divided-wing, hair-wing, feather-wing, and the old-fashioned hackle fly. The divided-wing is made from carefully paired quill feathers with their concave side facing outward. These aren't as rugged as the hair-wing types, which look somewhat like miniature bucktails. Even more durable perhaps are the hackle patterns which are dressed without wings. The feather-wing is made from speckled flank, side, and breast feathers of various ducks, and ranks between the divided-wing and the hair-wing in so far as durability is concerned. Being a highly regional form of fishing, there's a temptation to specialize with wet flies; a Westerner might easily buy all hair-wings, and an Easterner all down-wings, but to keep a good balance, make your first dozen with three each of the four kinds of wet flies.

Starting with the divided-wing, you might buy a Leadwing Coachman, Parmachenee Belle, and Black Gnat. This trio offers a choice of dull, bright, and dark patterns. Modern fly-dressers employ a variety of hairs for making wings, and nearly every standard down-wing pattern can be duplicated with no loss of accuracy. Three effective hair-wing wets are the Royal Coachman, Western Bee or McGinty, and Silver Doctor. Next you have the feather-wing type, which should include the Dark Cahill, Quill Gordon, and Grizzly King. To round out the dozen you might select three hackle patterns: Gray Hackle Yellow, Brown Hackle Peacock, and Black Spider (spiders are made in both wet and dry forms). For a starter get your wet patterns tied on No. 12 hooks if you're an Eastener, and on No. 10 hooks for Western fishing.

Selecting half a dozen nymph patterns that will satisfy everybody isn't easy. Nymphs are even more specialized than wet patterns regionally, but here are six that will produce some fish most of the time: Green Caddis, Breadcrust, Hendrickson, Mossback, Hardback, and Stonefly. These patterns cover a sufficient range of colors and shapes to be effective. Except for the Green Caddis, which is ordinarily dressed on a No. 14 hook, the others should be tied on No. 12's. It's important later on to increase your stock of sizes, particularly for Western trouting, where you'll need some up to No. 6 for imitating the big stonefly nymphs.

Among the flies designed to imitate minnows there are at least twelve different types, but the three basic ones are the plain bucktail, the feather-wing streamer, and the marabou. The most important component here is the wing, and having bought two each of the three kinds, all you need to do is learn how to fish them correctly.

Admittedly, some colors work better than others at times, and eventually you will stock a variety of patterns.

However, there is a tremendous duplication in streamer dressings. For plain bucktail patterns you can start off with a Blacknosed Dace and a Mickey Finn. These two will provide the somber and the bright. In feather-wings you want the advantage of natural markings that don't exist on bucktail. Here a pattern like the Chappie, with barred-rock wings, and the Golden Darter, with a dark center stripe, simulate the appearance of many common minnows.

As for marabous, you can do no wrong with a White Marabou and a Black Marabou. These are attractor-type streamers, and they take fish everywhere. A good size to start your streamer collection off with is the No. 6, 3X Long hook. Later you can get larger ones, and by all means buy some No. 12 streamers for clearwater fishing.

—A.J.McC.

FLYING BRIDGE An integral part of equipment on off-shore fishing boats. *For details see* Flying Bridge *under* Sportfisherman

FLYINGFISHES Family Exocoetidae Swift, pelagic fishes, whose members are found in all tropic seas, generally far from land. Three other groups of fishes have developed the art of flying to a much lesser degree. Two of these types are found in tropical freshwaters in Africa and South America respectively, and the other is a group of marine fishes that includes the gurnards and searobins. One fossil group, now extinct, is also believed to have contained flying members.

THEY DO FLY

Everyone has heard of flyingfishes, but they still come as a surprise to many voyagers visiting tropical seas for the first time. Some people have lumped together in their minds the tales they've heard of flying fishes and flying saucers, of sea horses and sea serpents, and are shocked by the realization that flyingfishes really fly.

The sight of a shoal of small, silvery creatures rocketing out of the blue seas and sailing over the wave tops in brash defiance of gravity is a memorable experience for almost everyone. Especially since the areas that flying-fishes inhabit—the deep, open seas—often appear to the traveler to be relatively devoid of life. For long periods bored passengers on liners may see little but sea and sky. Then, suddenly, flyingfish! Apparently disturbed by the passage of a ship through the water, they skitter along the surface and soar, bank, and ride the air currents like toy airplanes catapulted by rubber slings.

When flyingfish are seen from ships, the inevitable debate arises. Do they or do they not flap their "wings" in flight? For many years this point was argued in scientific circles, but high-speed cameras have resolved the question. The wings, or pectoral fins, do not flap; they are held rigid in flight. The hind wings, or ventral fins, of some species do move somewhat—shifting their planes to provide stability and maneuverability—but the wings are definitely not used for driving power.

This is fairly obvious when a flyingfish is watched carefully during a long, graceful flight of several hundred feet, but not so obvious when a fish makes a series of quick, short flights. When taking off, a rocking motion of the fish's body and a rapid beating of the tail make the wings appear to vibrate independently. Another reason for the confusion is the fact that tiny, immature flyingfish

may move their fins vigorously while swimming and also, reportedly, while making the short practice hops they make before earning their wings.

HOW FLIGHT IS ACHIEVED

Structurally, the "true" flyingfishes are of two basic types: those whose enlarged pectoral fins are their only wings and those whose ventral fins are also enlarged and serve as a second set of wings, lower on the body add farther aft. Writers generally dub the first type the "monoplane" or two-winged flying fishes, and the others the "biplane" or four-winged flying fishes.

In both types the pectoral fins constitute the main lifting surfaces. When swimming underwater, these fins are kept folded against the body and their purpose is obscure. In the four-winged type the ventral fins give added lift

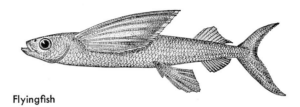

Flyingfish

and also act as ailerons (for banking) and as elevators (for climbing and nosing down). In all species the lower lobe of the tail is elongated, and serves as a sculling oar for taxiing across the surface before take-off; and the tail also serves as a rudder in flight.

As a rule, the four-winged fishes make longer flights than the two-winged fishes and exhibit greater control when aloft. The four-wingeds are usually larger, too—up to 18 inches in length. In fact, it seems to be generally true that the larger the flyingfish, the better it can fly. Since natural selection would therefore seem to favor the larger individuals, we might expect flyingfishes to grow gradually larger. Probably they would if they had stronger propulsion systems. A great deal of speed is required to overcome the water's friction and raise them into the air. A heavier body would require more power. So they are limited in size by the amount of thrust they can produce in water.

Flyingfishes are related to the needlefishes and the halfbeaks, and they clearly descended from similar forms. In their larval stages some flyingfishes strongly resemble halfbeaks, even to the protruding lower jaw. Halfbeaks have elongated, lower tail lobes, like flyingfishes, and use them in a similar sculling motion to skip across the surface for considerable distances.

The flight of the California flyingfish (*Cypselurus californicus*), a large, four-winged species, was first described in detail by Dr. Carl Hubbs in 1918. Dr. C. M. Breder, Jr., later made extensive studies on the aerodynamics of flyingfishes. High-speed photographs made by Professor H. E. Edgerton in 1940 showed that these earlier studies, based almost entirely on visual observations at sea, were remarkably accurate.

Before taking off *Cypselurus* swims just below the surface for some distance, its upper tail lobe often breaking the surface; then it turns upward and spreads its pectoral fins, leaving the water except for the lower lobe of its tail. Now vigorously beating its tail back and forth in a sculling motion, it taxis across the surface to gain flying speed. Finally it extends its ventral fins and rises into the air. Its flight may cover 1,000 feet or more, but the average is much less, perhaps 100–300 feet. Usually it glides no more than 4–5 feet above the water, though it may rise higher in a strong wind, and there are records of flyingfish achieving heights from 25–36 feet. Most flights last for 10 seconds or less, but Hubbs recorded one of 30 seconds, and B. W. Leek, a ship's captain, told Breder of clocking a flight of 42 seconds.

At the end of a flight a fish may close its wings and dive gracefully into the water, or it may plop down with a splash. On occasions it may land awkwardly. Breder saw one flyingfish apparently go out of control and flip upside down before striking the water. In many cases, when flying speed is lost, the fish lowers its tail, begins the sculling motion again, then takes off a second time. Often a fish will fly, scull, and fly again several times in succession. Dr. Leonard P. Schultz recorded a flight of 26 seconds which included ten brief touchdowns.

Sometimes flyingfish may take off without a sculling process, leaping out of waves into the air. This seems to happen more often in windy weather, and Breder's observations indicate that about 75 percent of takeoffs are made into the wind. Whether a fish, swimming underwater, can tell which way the wind is blowing is an interesting question, but Breder points out that the rolling motion of the particles of water within waves would make it easier for the fish to take off against the wind.

It isn't known whether flyingfishes have good aerial vision, but in daylight they seldom strike boats or other obstacles. According to Hubbs, "Sometimes they soar straight toward the side of a vessel, until they seem about to crush themselves. But they suddenly plunge into the water, twist directly backward in their course within a radius of about ten feet, and make away in the opposite direction, either in the water or in the air."

At night flyingfishes are definitely attracted by lights. Frequently they fly aboard lighted boats, landing on deck or coming through open portholes. Fishermen in many areas catch them by suspending a lantern over the water and erecting a net or other barrier to arrest their flights. At Bikini, Schultz placed a 100-watt light just under the surface, and in 1½ hours scooped up 36 flyingfish that congregated around the light.

Many observers say that flyingfishes tend to fly in a curved path, and rarely in a straight line. But some writers suggest that major changes in course are made not in flight but when a fish touches down briefly. Some interesting observations on this point were made by Commander Mason D. Schoolfield. While making patrol flights at 700–800 feet above the Pacific between Hawaii and Wake Island, Schoolfield watched many schools of flyingfish and noticed that most individual fish made flights of about 250 feet, dropped into the water briefly, and then took off again on a course about 70 degrees to the right of the first flight.

If flyingfish do indeed tend to turn to the right in the Northern Hemisphere (*see* Currents) the question naturally arises: Do they turn to the left in the Southern Hemisphere? Or, on the other hand, is the turning action related to winds, waves, feeding habits, or escape from enemies?

THE REASON FOR FLIGHT

There are many unanswered questions about flyingfishes. One of the biggest questions is: Why do they fly at all? From an evolutionary standpoint, the ability to fly almost certainly developed as means for survival, either to help in propagation, in obtaining food, or in escaping enemies.

As far as we know, the function of flying plays no part in finding or selecting mates, and it is hard to imagine how it could aid in feeding. Flyingfishes eat tiny fishes and crustaceans, and there is no evidence that they feed on any kind of airborne organism. (But, strangely, Edgerton's remarkable electronic flash photographs of the California flyingfish, taken at night, show the subjects flying with their mouths open.)

Many writers have suggested that flyingfishes fly mainly to escape from *Coryphaena*, the dolphin, and deepwater anglers can confirm that the dolphin (*which see*) does indeed feed extensively on flyingfishes. In an article in the *London Illustrated News*, Dr. Maurice Burton suggested that the ability to fly does not offer protection from dolphins. According to Burton: "If the function of the flying fishes' wing-like fins is to enable escape from its main enemy, then it seems to have failed dismally. Nothing could emphasize this more than the close correlation between the speeds of the prey and predator: the flying fish travels through the air at an average speed of 35 m.p.h.; its main enemy travels through the water beneath at about 37 m.p.h."

Even assuming that Burton's figures on speed are correct (but all speed estimates for pelagic fishes must be open to question), we would suggest that the top speed of a dolphin swimming through water can be sustained for a much shorter period than the top speed of a flyingfish soaring effortlessly on waves of air. Furthermore, regardless of how fast a flyingfish actually flies, its normal *swimming* speed is undoubtedly much less. Hence, its flight probably has survival value of some indeterminate degree.

SPAWNING HABITS

Flyingfishes spawn in floating rafts of seaweed or other kinds of surface debris. In the Pacific, Schultz found eggs stuck to a whiskey bottle. Some species seem to use sargassum weed almost entirely, building nests by wrapping tightly packed balls of weed with strands of white, elastic material. The eggs are attached to one another and to the nest by thin silken threads. (Breder noted that the eggs are heavier than water so would sink if not attached to floating objects.) The young, when hatched, strongly resemble the round floats of the sargassum. Immature fish are tinted in all colors of the rainbow, prompting William Beebe to dub them "butterflyingfish."

FOOD VALUE

Flyingfish are highly valued as food in many parts of the world. Commercial fisheries have operated off California and Barbados. Generally, fishes are netted at night after attracting them with torches or electric lights. Off India, according to James Hornell, fishermen attach bundles of brush to longlines and drag them behind boats. When flyingfishes congregate around the brush to lay eggs, the bundles are pulled gently over large dip-nets. Flyingfish pie is a famous Caribbean dish.

ANGLING VALUE

It is widely believed that flyingfishes cannot be caught on hook and line. A few light-tackle anglers have taken them in the Gulf Stream with fly rods and very tiny flies. Flyingfishes have also been "hunted" by expert skeet shots using small-gauge shotguns and light loads. The fish will float after being shot and can be collected as food. —W.M.S.

FLYING GAFF A long-handled gaff which features a detachable hook. The hook is bent to a stout running line, which may be up to thirty feet in length, thus enabling the user to hold a large gamefish independent of the shorter, more rigid gaff handle.

FLYING GURNARD *Dactylopterus volitans* The flying gurnard resembles the searobins (*which see*) in general appearance. The head is large and bony, and the pectoral fins are long and winglike. But the first 5–6 pectoral rays are connected to one another yet are separate from the remainder of the pectoral, and the first 2 dorsal spines are free and not connected to the rest of the fin by a membrane. A bony spine projects rearward behind the eye to the middle of the first dorsal, and a second, at the lower level of the opercle, reaches just past the dorsal-fin origin. The body tapers backward gradually, and the dorsal and anal fins are about equal size. The caudal fin has 3 brownish-red bars. The coloration of this brilliant fish is virtually indescribable, but the predominant colors are brown to greenish-olive and paler below. Pink to orange markings variously mottle the body. Intricate vermiculations cover the winglike pectorals with blue streaks, spots, and bars over a reddish-brown background. The young are silvery with cobalt-blue reflections above, and a yellow or pinkish-orange eye. It reaches about 16 inches long.

Flying Gurnard

LIFE HISTORY

Found in the eastern Atlantic and from Brazil to Massachusetts, a stray has been taken in Nova Scotia. But it is largely a warmwater form, where spawning apparently takes place. The silvery young are common at times where bluewater is relatively close to shore. The young can perform repeated, short jumps over the surface but cannot glide as do flyingfish. Adults lie on the bottom with the pectorals spread and can "walk" over the bottom using the ventral fins, rather than the pectoral fins as with searobins.

It reportedly feeds on small crustaceans. Specimens of up to 2 inches are often found in the stomachs of dolphins, and occasionally bonito and tunas, and it is suspected that the pelagic young spend part of their early life associated with sargassum weed. —D.dS.

FLY LEADER A leader used in fly fishing.

THE LEVEL LEADER

The level leader is one that has a uniform diameter throughout its length. It can be made simply by cutting off the desired footage of monofilament and tying a loop at one end. It is used chiefly for bait- and spinner-fishing rather than fly-fishing. The level kind is a poor substitute for a tapered leader, and, considering the low cost of modern synthetics, it is no longer justified even for reasons of economy. Tapered leaders work better no matter what they are made of, and, like a well-designed fly line, each portion will progressively transmit the energy of the cast right down to the fly. Level leaders were in common use before 1940 due to the relatively high cost of Spanish silkworm gut; these level leaders were made of Japanese gut which was the only synthetic material available at that time.

THE IMPORTANCE OF A FLY LEADER

From an angling standpoint, a perfectly presented fly at forty feet is far more effective than an awkward splashing cast at forty yards. Complete mastery of the rod at normal distances from all positions and under varying wind conditions is the ideal most of us seek. However, a large measure of success that one experiences in fly-casting is due to paying careful attention to details like stretching the leader before fishing. This can be done with a small piece of soft rubber. Cut off a 2-inch square from an old inner tube and keep it in your leader pouch. This will earn more fish than a dozen new patterns. Before you begin fishing, rub the leader until it's perfectly straight and pliable. This will get some of the stretch out of it and prevent kinking. It takes only a few seconds to do this, and it will make a big difference in your casting.

It is also frequently necessary to lengthen the butt section or correct the tippet diameter. A leader is not only the connecting link between line and fly, but it also causes the feathers to be delivered softly to the surface. Even when a cast is checked high in the air, the weight of a falling line is sufficient to send out alarming ripples in calm water. To make a perfect presentation the leader must be designed correctly. The length and weight of a leader are a compromise to the fishing conditions, and the taper, which is a vital component, is responsible for the transmission of energy from the line to the fly.

HOW TO DESIGN A TAPERED LEADER

The two main parts of a tapered leader are the *tippet* which is the end section or strand of material to which the fly is tied; its diameter is determined by water or fishing conditions and the size of fly used. At the opposite end is the *butt*, or first strand, to which the line is connected. The butt is the heaviest portion, and generally speaking it should approximate two-thirds the diameter of the line point. Most American double-tapered fly lines are .030 at the end; so a .020 butt is generally correct. If you use any of the modern weight-forward lines made with a plastic coating, their points will measure .033–.037, and for these, a .022 leader butt is necessary. Unless you are certain that the line and leader materials with which you will be working are accurately identified, it is advisable to obtain a micrometer. This is a valuable instrument to have for leader making. It's difficult, if not impossible, to build leaders by pound-test ratings; these can vary so widely in diameter that you might easily tie fine sections behind heavy ones. With the great variety of spooled synthetics available, from both foreign and domestic sources, the materials are not always accurately identified according to size. Of course, the micrometer has many valuable uses in studying tackle, and particularly in rod building.

The most common error in leader design is making too light and too short a butt. Some of the tapers in current fashion start at .014, which was customary in the days when gut leaders were the only kind available. The reason for the light butt was twofold. Finer silk line points were the rule, and only a limited number of gut strands could be used in making leaders commercially. To arrive at a 3X or 4X tippet, the butt had to be light. Natural gut strands longer than 15 inches are almost impossible to find; so the taper consisted of regular gradations just like so many steps of stairs. To maintain its knot strength gut can only be varied by .001 between strands, which means the leader had to drop from .014 to .013 to .012 and so on for eight or nine sections. This made for a very knotty taper. Mechanically, the oldtime leader maker was a conformist because of his material. When making a synthetic leader today, we can jump .002 between sizes without sacrificing strength—and go to 62-inch lengths or longer, if the design requires it. Equally important, synthetics can be produced in finer diameters than gut. Silkworm gut of less than .009 is rare, and it has to be drawn out in a tricky manual operation which is not wholly reliable. Even when properly drawn, gut is not nearly as strong as nylon or platyl in the smallest sizes.

Generally speaking, you will have to do a considerable amount of fishing until you find the leaders with which you can cast best under different conditions. They will vary from line to line, depending on their forward tapers and the length and diameter of their points.

Try to duplicate the proper leader in subsequent purchases. Of course, if you tie your own the chances of learning exactly the right formula are much better. A general design which can be recommended in making leaders is 60 percent butt, 20 percent graduation, and 20 percent tippet. The long, heavy butt turns over perfectly under most wind conditions. Begin by using a bit more than one-half of the total length in heavy diameters, say .020–.018. Following the heavy material, tie in short, graduating strands. These step-down pieces serve the purpose of reducing the diameter rapidly from .018 to the finer tippet sections you would normally use. With synthetics you can skip .002 between each strand and still hold the knots. The tippet section itself should be 20–30 inches long, the exact length depending on how well it turns over. As a rule of thumb, a fly that is proportionately large in relation to the diameter of the tippet will require a shorter length. A 30-inch, .006 (5X) tippet, for instance, will roll over perfectly with No. 16 and No. 18 flies; if you tie on a bushier hackled No. 10, the fly will tend to fall back over the leader. It will also twist in the air and weaken the tippet. This can be improved somewhat by cutting the .006 down to about 8–10 inches, but it's better to replace the tippet with a heavier diameter. For a No. 10 fly, the tippet size should run .008 (3X).

COMPARATIVE RATINGS OF SILKWORM GUT AND NYLON

Classification	Draw-plate gauge size	Diameter inch 1000	Approximate diameter 1/100 mm	Test in lbs.[1] silkworm gut	Test in lbs.[2] synthetics
Hebra	1/5	.021	50/100	24	32.5
Imperial	2/5	.020	48/100	19	29.0
Marana 1st	3/5	.019	45/100	15.5	26.3
Marana 2nd	4/5	.018	43/100	12.5	23.6
Padron 1st	5/5	.017	40/100	10.5	20.5
Padron 2nd	6/5	.016	38/100	8.7	18.5
Regular	7/5	.015	35/100	7	16.8
Regular	8/5	.014	32/100	4.5	14.0
Fina	9/5	.013	30/100	3.5	12.1
Fina	10/5	.012	28/100	3.2	11.0
Refina	0X	.011	26/100	2.8	9.0
Refina	1X	.010	24/100	2.3	7.8
Drawn	2X	.009	22/100	1.8	7.0
Drawn	3X	.008	18/100	1.6	5.3
Drawn	4X	.007	16/100	1.2	3.5
Drawn	5X	.006	15/100	0.8	2.5
Drawn	6X	.005	14/100	0.5	1.8
Drawn	7X	.004	12/100	0.4	1.0

[1] Typical break load of Murcia gut (natural selecta)
[2] Typical break load of DuPont nylon (bulk monofilament)

LENGTH AND WEIGHT

It should be apparent that the length and weight of the leader to be used is dependent on the water conditions and the size of the fish. For instance, when the water is discolored and you're using a large hook like a bucktail, you can safely work with a leader on the heavy side. It doesn't have to be too long either. If you're casting small flies in clearwater, the leader should be light and long; it's impossible to present a tiny fly properly on a short, heavy leader. We usually consider a 7½-foot leader as short, and anything over 9 feet as long. Experts commonly use lengths of 10–12 feet and go up to 15 feet on occasion. For most trout fishing don't be concerned about the pound-test ratings. On the average stream, we seldom hook many fish over 1½ pounds, and while we may break off on the infrequent heavier trout with 5X or 6X, these tippets will hold up to three pounds if handled gently. The fine diameters are a problem if the fish come big, but sometimes it's the only way to move them, and the higher ratio of strikes provides some success. In rivers where 4-pound trout are common (and there are few such waters), try to stay at 3X, but don't hesitate to go down to 5X if the conditions require it. Of course salmon, steelhead, and black bass are going to demand heavy diameters, not merely because of their weight but due to the need for much larger flies and lures.

IMPORTANCE OF BALANCE

The impact a fly makes on the surface often has a great deal to do with its effectiveness. There are days when stoneflies and grasshoppers literally slam the water, and an artificial spanked down in the same fashion will bring furious strikes. This is not the ordinary situation, however, and, by and large, the man who drops his floater quietly is going to raise fish. If you're a beginner, it's a good idea to spend some time on a very quiet pool just studying your line and leader. Make average casts of 30–40 feet, using a 9-foot leader with fly attached. Remember to massage the nylon first with a piece of rubber so that it falls perfectly straight. Watch both the back and forward casts. If the back stroke isn't rolling out straight to begin with, then you have a casting problem. But if the line unrolls without humps and the leader flops around as though unrelated to the cast and falls in a heap on the water, then it's time to start building a new taper. One that is practically foolproof for line points of .025 or a shade heavier: Start with a butt of 42 inches of .018, then add a second, heavy section of 29 inches of .016. This is about 60 percent of a 9-foot leader. Now add three 6-inch graduating strands of .014, .012, and .010. For the tippet tie on 20 inches of .008. This all runs a fraction over 9 feet, but after stretching the leader with a piece of rubber you'll be able to cast it with your bare hand. Any fly from No. 10–14 should sail out, turn over, and sit down as daintily as a mayfly.

Balanced Leader Tapers The following profiles are suitable for all wind conditions. Under normal winds and in clear water, the 20-inch tippet sections may be lengthened to 30 inches, when using small flies.

9 Feet—1X		9 Feet—2X		9 Feet—3X	
Diameter	Length	Diameter	Length	Diameter	Length
.018	41″	.018	41″	.018	41″
.016	35″	.016	29″	.016	29″
.014	6″	.014	6″	.014	6″
.012	6″	.012	6″	.012	6″
.010	20″	.010	6″	.010	6″
		.009	20″	.008	20″

9 Feet—4X		9 Feet—5X		9 Feet—6X*	
Diameter	Length	Diameter	Length	Diameter	Length
.018	34″	.018	54″	.018	48″
.016	30″	.016	12″	.016	12″
.014	6″	.014	6″	.014	6″
.012	6″	.012	6″	.012	6″
.010	6″	.010	6″	.010	6″
.008	6″	.008	6″	.008	6″
.007	20″	.006	20″	.006	6″
				.005	20″

* This taper can be reduced to 7X by substituting a tippet of .004 in place of .005.

For heavy saltwater work when casting to fish that require 80–100-pound test shock tippets in addition to the regulation 12-pound test, or 15-pound-test qualifying tippet, the following profile (by test) in best grade hard finish monofilament for a 9½-foot leader is widely applicable for snook, dolphin, striped bass, sharks, barracuda, tarpon, and sailfish:

	Test	Length
Butt	40 pounds	72 inches
Tippet	12 pounds	30 inches
Shock Tippet	100 pounds	13 inches*

* Shock tippet reduces to 12 inches when the knot is tied.

The butt section must be joined to the fly line with a nail knot. Two coats of Pliobond cement is suggested for extra security and to prevent wear. The butt should be joined to the tippet and the tippet to the shock tippet with a Stu Apte Improved Blood Knot or with suitable Nail Knot variations. The fly is joined to the shock tippet with a Nail Knot Loop or a simple three-turn Clinch Knot (do not use the Improved Clinch Knot). *See also* Knots

Braided nylon or Dacron squidding line in 15–18-pound test makes a good all-purpose backing. From the standpoint of catching fish a 25-yard length is ample insurance for the inland trout and bass angler on the average stream and lake. For steelhead and salmon in large rivers 100 yards is usually adequate. Although bonefish seldom require more than 100 yards if the same reel is to be used for permit, barracuda, and tarpon, 200 yards is more realistic. There are rare situations where a fish will run a mile or even two miles, so obviously the angler must decide on a practical maximum. At the extremes (a 100-pound tarpon on the flats or large salmon in swift rivers) the angler can resort to his boat or to the bank in following a running fish. Thus the amount of backing should only serve for *average* conditions. Oversize fly reels have been made to accommodate 350–400 yards of backing; however, these are of dubious value; such reels are heavy and line breaks from water resistance and snags are inevitable. But regardless of the quarry, some backing should always be added to a fly reel.

The backing line has a dual purpose and on all except the smallest fly reels, which lack the capacity, it should be added in order to fill the reel (to within ⅛–¼ inch of the spool rim). By building up the arbor with this additional line the fly line will be spooled in larger coils. The larger the coil, the less tendency there is for a line to kink, particularly after it has been stored away during the off season. To the angler who is completely familiar with his reel it's possible to guess how much backing is required to bring the fly line to the right level. However, to always get the desired result it's advisable to reel the fly line on the spool first, add the correct amount of backing, and reverse the line. This requires either an identical reel to which the backing can be immediately secured or a spacious lawn where the entire length including the fly line can be pulled gently from the reel and then reversed. Reversing does take a bit more time, but it's worth the effort; just fractions of an inch make a difference in maintaining a supple fly line.

Fly-line maintenance consists of keeping it clean and properly stored. Both algae and salt can make a line "gummy" and cause a floating line to sink. Although it is not usually necessary to clean a fly line after each trip, it should be wiped with a damp sponge or cloth whenever it feels slightly dirty. Naturally, if you are fishing in weedy ponds or in saltwater the line will need a more frequent cleaning. Do not expose a fly line to long hours in a hot sun by leaving the reel uncovered in an open boat. And beware of solvents which damage plastic or silk, such as insect repellents and suntan lotions or the inevitable splash of gasoline from the fuel can in an outboard. Standing on loose coils of slack in the boat or on the bank will chip and crack the plastic finish. All silk fly lines must be thoroughly dried after each trip and rubbed down with a dressing designed for silk, such as Mucilin.

From the fish's point of view the color of a fly line is probably of no significance when it's floating. It is visible as a dark silhouette against sun and sky at least part of the time, and certainly its shadow on the bottom has an adverse effect on timorous species like the brown trout and bonefish. A long leader effectively separates the line from the lure. However, a splashy cast or a line that drags directly over the fish are warning signals that no skittish quarry will ignore. Under bright light in shallow water a great percentage of fish are frightened by the line while it's still unrolling in the air. So the color to choose in a floating fly line is a matter of individual preference— yellow, amber, green, mahogany, and white are the most popular.

THE HISTORY OF THE FLY LINE

The first fly lines were made of braided horse hair. These were in use from Walton's time up until the nineteenth century. During the first half of the nineteenth century, line makers started mixing horse hair and silk. This was followed by the all silk line. It was apparently in the 1870's that the first oil-finished silk lines appeared. This was an American innovation. But even before the advent of the oiled silk line, tapered lines and their advantages were well-known in 1869. As Genio C. Scott says in *Fishing in American Waters* (1869): "Thus, with a finely balanced and finished fly rod, a click reel attached to the rod below the hand, a silk and hair braided line protected from the effect of water by being oiled, varnished, or saturated with some oleaginous substance, braided like a whiplash to taper each way from the middle, a stained gut casting-line tapering from the reel-line to the stretcher, a well selected cast of flies. . . . [From list of equipment to take salmon fishing] Two horse-hair casting-lines, from eighty to one hundred feet long each braided in the form of a whiplash, and nearly one fourth of an inch in diameter in the center. Pritchard Brothers make this upper casting-line to perfection. It is light, and its shape greatly assist casting, while it is not so liable to sink and drown as the silk, or silk and hair line, though protected with varnish."

By 1885, both the weight-forward and double-tapered lines were in use. In this same year the hollow fly line was first introduced to take advantage of its floatability. Although the fundamentals of good fly-line design existed, the material available proved to be the stumbling block. Enameled silk lines were produced, but the oiled silk line remained as the standard until 1948.

After the war years, nylon became available, and the fishing-line manufacturers now had a basic material that would not rot and had very good tensile strength, but many problems remained. The finishes that had been used in the past for silk lines were not satisfactory, and the problem of stretch in the basic nylon had to be solved; so for some period of time the nylon fly line had a very low standing among fly-fishermen.

In 1949, a satisfactory coating material, polyvinyl chloride, became available, and the first successful nylon fly line was produced. This was a hollow fly line, and, while it was much better than lines produced in the past, it had two disadvantages: as they had found out as far back as 1885, the hollow core eventually filled with water, and the method of producing the taper was the same as that used for the first tapered lines made—either by addition or subtraction of threads in the basic core line.

In 1952, the big breakthrough, leading up to the modern fly line, occurred. This was a practical method of automatically making the taper in the coating material, rather than in the core of the line. This not only had a tremendous impact in the cost of producing tapered lines, but also allowed the making of precision lines, one after the other, with a variance of less than .001 of an inch. For the first time, lines could be produced with a uniform weight. This development was followed by a controlled method of altering the specific gravity of the coating material.

PRODUCTION OF MODERN FLY LINES

Revolutionary changes in manufacturing methods make modern fly-line construction and manufacture different from older lines in several important respects. These changes are the use of a level core with a tapered coating, the plastic coatings set by the application of heat, and coatings with controllable density.

The development of heat-cured plastic finishes made possible the first mass production of fly lines. Fly lines are now made continuously, one after the other, in long skeins. This continuous-production method means that lines can be produced that are exact replicas of a standard. The diameters can be controlled to within less than .001 inch, and the weight of the line can be controlled to within 1/500 ounce. The use of dies with a continuously variable orifice, together with the new plastic finishes, allows the tapered coating to be applied over a level core. The result is that the diameter, and hence the weight, can be controlled at any position on the line. This controlled-density coating allows the production of a line that will sink or one that will float indefinitely, since one is heavier than water and the other lighter than water.

Production of the line starts with the core. This core is generally braided from nylon filaments, and has the same appearance as braided nylon casting line. Other core materials such as Dacron and fiberglass can also be used. Although most modern lines have a braided core, a core having twisted filaments, untwisted filaments running parallel to the surface of the line or even a single solid filament can be used. After braiding, the core is singed to remove any fine filaments that extend above the surface, then treated with bonding agents to insure adhesion of the coating.

The treated core is passed through the liquid coating and then through the die, which forms the coating to the desired size. With the application of heat, the liquid coating hardens and fuses to the core to form the line. As the core passes through the die, the taper is formed and, at the end of the line, a marker applied. As it comes from the curing oven, the line is level wound on large spools. When the spool is filled, it is removed and replaced with another.

The final step is the coiling and inspection. The lines are removed from the large spools and wound into individual coils. The marker indicating the end of the line is cut out, and the coil wrapped. After packaging, the lines are ready for shipment. —L.L.M.

HOW TO SELECT A FLY LINE

Design A properly designed fly line will not sag in the air but will extend and turn over smoothly, keeping its weight portion off the water until the cast is completed. Parenthetically, the distribution of that weight is the basic consideration in selecting a fly line.

The most effective casting weights are lead sinkers; therefore any elongation of the projectile, such as a fly line, becomes less and less effective as its length is increased. A 1-ounce sinker is a compact mass, but an equivalent weight of fly line must be arranged over 30–40 feet of surface area; thus air friction rapidly absorbs the energy that goes into fly-casting. To utilize that energy properly the weight of a fly line must be distributed in a shape that will maintain velocity for the longest possible time. Once your cast is released, all parts of the line in the air, from your leader to your rod tip, have an identical velocity, but this speed rapidly decreases as the line rolls over and becomes extended.

There are three profiles or shapes in fly lines, a level, double-taper, and weight-forward distribution. At the extremes, we have the level profile, which is a constant diameter throughout, and the weight-forward or torpedo-taper profile, which is of varying diameter with its weight portion occurring at one end of the line. Theoretically, and from a practical standpoint, the weight-forward profile provides longer and easier casts. In a level line, air friction absorbs the casting energy rapidly, because a diameter of *equal* weight is coming out of the rod guides and therefore adding more burden on the declining momentum of the already extended cast. On the other hand, a torpedo taper with its effective weight in the air is more nearly comparable to the analogous sinker because it can pull a great length of line through the guides before losing momentum from the inertia and weight of the fine-diameter shooting line. Obviously, the slack you hold in your hand has no velocity to contribute to the cast when you make your shoot. It merely waits to be pulled forward. This is made easier by the lightweight shooting line of a torpedo head, but the success of such a line depends on the front taper. It is responsible for completing the turnover of line and leader at the exact instant the line stops shooting, regardless of the speed of the cast. In theory, it is impossible to slap the water with a weight-forward line if the front taper is correctly made.

Although the belly section provides casting weight, the front taper must remain in the unrolling line loop until the last instant, and then deliver the final kick to your leader and fly. If the front taper is too long you'll have great difficulty in unrolling the loop. Your leader will simply fall back next to the line at the finish of a cast. The fly will fall to the right or left or back over the line. With a long front taper you can never turn the leader and fly over against a wind and seldom with it because your back cast will not straighten. Thus, the distance you intend to cast determines the size and length of the belly in a torpedo-head, while the length of the front taper is responsible for pulling and stabilizing that weight until the

shoot is completed. The back taper is unimportant except to provide a reduction in line diameter. So actually you can use several sizes of torpedo-heads on one rod, depending on how far you have to cast. Remember, most trout are caught within a 35–40-foot radius, and the heavier your line, the less chance you have of doing a proper job at short distances. It is fallacious to believe that the more weight you concentrate in a line the better you will cast. There's a law of diminishing returns in this case, because as the belly section is made longer or heavier, the forward taper must be made longer, and there's a limit to how much speed you can apply to turn the taper over. But the longer you can delay complete unrolling of the forward loop, the longer the cast will be, provided the belly of the line maintains its velocity. Although the front taper must be just long enough to hold the weight portion up off the water until the cast is completed, you can, by aiming the rod high on a long cast, delay the turnover and give a more gradual and prolonged flight to the line. The lower you aim your cast, the more rapidly gravity will overtake the belly section, and, thus cause you to lose that extra-long footage which is provided by momentum.

A properly designed weight-forward line promotes the caster from water slapping to perfection. A smooth elbow pivot will suffice for the pickup, then another for the false cast, and away the line goes across the river, turning over in the air, not unrolling on the water. Inasmuch as the function of lines built with all their weight forward is to make that weight immediately available to the cast, you can readily understand that short, stiff rods will throw the same size line as some of the longer and heavier rods. But if the rod is overburdened, the line will touch the water in front and rear when you're making your false cast. The same effect is created with a double-taper or even a level line, in that there's a point beyond which the rod can no longer lift and speed up the weight of the line already extended. You can recognize the difference when a proper casting weight of level or double-taper is extended; the weight of the line that this casting length will have to pull is out of proportion to the created momentum. Instead of pulling a finer, lighter-shooting line such as the weight-forward taper does, the double-taper and level are forced to pull a heavy section of line which quickly retards the speed of the pulling load. Do not underestimate the role of the double-taper, however; any double-taper is better than a poorly balanced torpedo-head line, and they are superior for roll-casting which is important to small-stream anglers. To sum up, if the length of the front taper is too long, the fly goes out of control, falling anywhere, right or left or even on top of the leader and line. If too short, the fly and leader will turn under and slap the water.

Specific Gravity In both wet- and dry-flyfishing as a general rule the line should float. The leader, of course, should sink, and if you want the fly to go down deep, the leader should be long enough to permit you to do so. The reason for the floating line is that it is very difficult to pick up a line which is beneath the surface. The strain on a light fly rod would be too great. Moreover, the floating fly line gives the fisherman more direct contact with the fish when it strikes. A sunken line which is bellied out beneath the water requires some skill to handle correctly. But these are only generalizations which we should examine more closely.

A sinking fly line offers a great advantage to the average fisherman. Simply stated, it brings the fly down to fish level. An ordinary floating line is perfectly all right for wet and nymph patterns on small streams, where you work in knee-deep water, and certainly on lakes, when the fish are foraging close to the surface. Under both conditions, the fly seldom has to sink more than a foot or two to reach paydirt. In fact, a floating line terminated with a 12–15-foot leader is superior to the sinking type in fast, shallow rivers, particularly when using weighted nymphs. You can watch the line point like a bobber—and the slightest nip is signaled by a pull which would otherwise be hard to see. But when fish are feeding 10–20 feet below the surface a floating line is useless.

The original sinking fly line was a metal-cored silk made in England around 1938. The body of the line was simply braided over fine bronze wire and as long as the silk didn't separate from its core, the line sank to reasonable depths. There was, however, the uncomfortable feeling of casting a piece of wire, and the manufacturers didn't find an eager audience for their product. The line also kinked on the reel spool and had a spooky way of landing on the water in hoops. During the 1940's, steelhead anglers working in swollen coastal streams began varnishing silk shooting heads to get their flies down to gravel. Custom-tackle purveyors took 20–25 feet of 3A line and wiped enough varnish on it to bring the weight up well over an ounce. But the sinking coefficient of any line depends on a low ratio of outer area to maximum density, and varnish merely increased the already too large diameter.

In 1958 the first real step toward a strictly sinking fly line was made with the introduction of Dacron, which materially differs from nylon in several respects, and chief among these is its specific gravity. A Dacron line sinks readily. For very deep fishing lead-core fly lines are used in fresh- and saltwater.

—A.J.McC.

FLY-LINE STANDARDS The American Fishing Tackle Manufacturers Association (*which see*) established the fly-line standards now in use in 1961. This numerical system, which replaces the letter system, became necessary due to the various materials which have to a large extent replaced silk. When almost all fly lines were made of silk, they were identified by one or more letters of the alphabet, running from "A" to "I." These letters represented line diameters, ranging from .060 inch (A) to .20 inch (I) and were indicative of line weights. This system served its purpose. The fly-rod fisherman could match his rod with almost any manufacturer's version of an HCH floating line, for example.

When fly lines made of nylon and Dacron were introduced, the manufacturers continued to use the silk-diameter system of letters. However, it soon became apparent that whereas one manufacturer's HCH floating line would work with a particular rod, another similarly labeled line would be too light or too heavy with the particular rod.

The reason is basically simple. Nylon is lighter than silk; Dacron is heavier than silk; thus, each of three lines made to the same diameter specifications performs differently on the same rod.

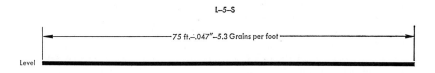

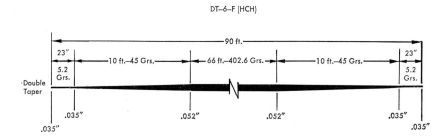

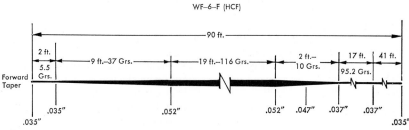

Fly Line Measurements

So line diameter became meaningless as a standard of identification, not only due to the different specific gravities of the basic materials, but also as a result of different types of braids and finishes developed by various manufacturers.

In bait-casting, spinning, and spin-casting, it is the weight of the lure that takes out the line; in fly-casting, it is the weight of the line that takes out the lure. However, a line that is too light, or too heavy, will not "bring out" the rod action that is necessary for efficient casting with almost weightless fly-rod lures.

Working from the basic premise that weight is the all-important factor in the proper matching, or balancing, of line and rod, fly-line manufacturers abandoned the diameter/letter method and adopted a weight/number system of identification.

They were aided and abetted in this decision by officials of the American Casting Association and the International Casting Federation, as well as by outdoor writers protesting in behalf of confused fishermen.

The unit of weight selected for the new standards is the "grain," the smallest unit in the system of weights used in the United States and Great Britain. (One pound avoirdupois equals seven thousand grains.) The numbers 1–12 are assigned to the standard grain weights, ranging from the lightest to the heaviest, regardless of the line's diameter, material, braid, or finish as such.

The segment of a fly line that is weighed to determine its number is the first thirty feet of the "working" portion of the line, exclusive of any tip on a taper, as measured from the very beginning of the taper. The weights of fly lines range from 60 grains (No. 1) to 380 grains (No. 12), plus or minus acceptable manufacturing tolerances.

To return to the example of the HCH double-taper floating line: if the first thirty feet of H to C taper plus "belly" section of the line weigh 160 grains (plus or minus 8 grains), it would be a No. 6. The same standard could apply to an HCF weight-forward line: the first thirty feet of H to C taper plus running section of the line at 152–168 grains would make it a No. 6, too. Since it has no taper, the first thirty feet of a level line at 160 plus or minus 8 grains would be a No. 6.

To identify the various tapers, AFTMA's standards include symbols: "L" denotes a level line; "DT," a double-taper; "WF," weight-forward; "ST," single-taper.

Floating lines are designated by "F"; sinking lines, "S"; intermediate (floating or sinking), "I."

The old HCH double-taper floating line, as used in the example above, is now identified as a DT-6-F line; the HCF becomes a WF-6-F; the level line, L-6-F.

Thus, any rod whose built-in action responds to thirty feet of working line weighing 160 grains will be balanced by any No. 6 line. Other actions will require other weights.

FLY REEL *See* Fly-Casting

FLY ROD A rod used in fly-fishing. Fly rods may be made in 1–3 sections or more, although 2- and 3-section rods are most common. When the sections are joined (*see* Ferrule) the total rod length may vary from 6–14 feet; those of more than 9½ feet long are entirely double-handed salmon rods which are popular among European anglers. The lightest fly rods weigh slightly more than 1 ounce and the heaviest double-handed rods up to 20 ounces. Fiberglass is the most widely accepted rod material; however, many fine fly rods are made of the traditional split bamboo. Bamboo rods, which are entirely hand-made (*see* Rod Building) are generally more expensive, but the "cane" craftsmen have a loyal audience among expert casters.

HISTORY OF THE FLY ROD

The technique of splitting bamboo into strips and gluing them together to obtain the full strength of the cane by eliminating its hollow center is ancient. The art originated in China almost 3,000 years ago, for in the book of *Tchouang-Tseu* (950 B.C.) an explanation is given of how to build a split-cane rod, glue, and bind it. However, the "rod" was used for carrying water pails on one's shoulder and it was centuries before anybody saw its relationship to angling. Izaak Walton fished with a rod which was probably not much different from those used by the Macedonians, who dapped the artificial fly about the time of Christ. The typical fly rod of 1650 was 15–18 feet long and made in 6–8 sections of white ash, hazel, fir, hickory, or willow. There was still no casting involved, as a horsehair line was simply tied to the end of the rod and flailed at the trout (*see* Angling in Walton's Day *under* Walton, Izaak). Despite the nebulous existence of split bamboo as a rod material in 1800 it is evident that cane was limited to tip sections for a long period before complete rods were made from it; ash and hickory were used for the butt and midsections. A complete rod made of split cane seems to have been built in Great Britain between 1830 and 1840 (examples of 3-strip construction were displayed at the Manchester Free Trade Bazaar in 1845 by J.D. Dougall of Glasgow). The earliest mention in angling literature of a split-cane rod is the description of one made by Aldreds (Francis Francis's *A Book on Angling*, 1867). Greenheart, which was imported from British Guiana about 1850, persisted in popularity until the turn of the century. According to chroniclers of that era Greenheart was "stiffer," although it lacked the tensile strength of bamboo. The comparison here was based on 3-strip construction.

The first 6-strip bamboo fly rod was made in America by Samuel Phillippe of Easton, Pennsylvania, in 1846, and during the next hundred years canes were produced in all

AFTMA fly-line standards			AFTMA fly-line symbols
No.	*Wt.*[a]	*Range*[b]	L = Level
1	60	54– 66	DT = Double-taper
2	80	74– 86	WF = Weight-forward
3	100	94–106	ST = Single-taper
4	120	114–126	
5	140	134–146	
6	160	152–168	*AFTMA fly-line types*
7	185	177–193	
8	210	202–218	F = Floating
9	240	230–250	S = Sinking
10	280	270–290	I = Intermediate
11	330	318–342	(Float or Sink)
12	380	368–392	

[a] In grains (437½ gr. = 1 oz.) based on first 30 feet of line exclusive of any taper or tip.
[b] Manufacturing tolerances —A.J.B.

possible exterior shapes, with splines glued in the form of a square, pentagon, septagon, and octagon. The purpose was to find the most efficient distribution of material at a minimum weight. Every cross-section has its proponents, but the 6-strip or hexagonal design satisfied the vast majority of builders and anglers. Nevertheless, all rods are not alike; although the craftsman cuts his splines with a tolerance of .00016 inch or less than 2/100,000 of an inch he must also taper the rod to give it a suitable action. Minute variations in diameter at different points along a rod can radically change its performance. The development of a good original profile may involve months or years of cut-and-try experiments.

With a growing number of American anglers before World War I, manufacturers were seeking a material that could be used in the mass production of rods. In 1913 the Horton Manufacturing Company of Bristol, Connecticut, began selling steel rods. This material did not find a market until a thin-walled steel tube was developed in 1925 (see The Stiffness Factor under Rod Building). Bamboo and steel dominated the industry until 1947, when manufacturers adopted alloys that were developed during World War II. The aluminum alloy (zicral) was much lighter than steel, but it did take a "set" at the slightest stress. Being a malleable material it could be straightened by hand, but the problem was that aluminum rods doglegged so frequently that in time they achieved a corkscrew appearance. Beryllium copper on the other hand was about 3 percent heavier than steel, but it could be stressed to values nearing its yield point without damage and it had an extraordinary fatigue life. Tubular copper rods were never quite successful; in short bait-casting lengths the action was dead, and in the longer fly-rod lengths the material was too whippy. But in 1948 the brief history of alloy rods came to a close when Dr. A.M. Howald invented the first fiberglass (Fiberglas®) rod.

Throughout the search for a rod-building material to compete with bamboo the one factor other than tensile strength that discouraged an experienced caster was the action of the rod (see The Theory of Rod Function in Casting under Rod Building). To a large extent action is a built-in quality dependent on a rod's taper. But this is closely linked with the stiffness factor of the material, or ability to resist bending. Compared to an oak tree bamboo grows to a height out of proportion to its girth, yet it survives because of its unique structure. This tropical grass must bend under the severest winds of hurricane force without breaking, then return to an upright position. So it grows in the form of a tube enclosed in vertical fibers which are stronger than steel; these are cushioned from one another by a corklike pith, and when the bamboo is bent, the fibers compress it; when the stress is relieved or the winds cease, it has the resilience to snap back. This ability to resist bending is the very same quality needed in a fishing rod. The difference is that the rod builder attempts to control the recoil power of his material, so that it bends more or less or at a faster or slower rate under varying stresses. Whether a rod is made of natural cane or any other material the principle is the same.

While the makers of steel and copper could bulkhead their rods by drawing them down like so many steps of stairs to increase the strength of the tube, there was nothing they could do to change their actions radically. More stiffness without more weight means more net recoil power; more weight without more stiffness produces less recoil power, or less casting power. The bamboo maker could hollow-build, double-build, vary the cross section, heat-treat, or impregnate with synthetic resins, but metal rods could only be made heavier or lighter. Steel and copper rods always had the same feeling in the caster's hand. Fiberglass provided the answer; both the strength and stiffness of the rod could be controlled by its bonding agent, or the thermoplastic substance which holds the almost microscopic glass fibers together by varying the amount of glass used and its structure. Due to this method of manufacture the taper or profile of the rod provided degrees of stiffness without seriously altering its weight.

HOW TO SELECT A FLY ROD

There is an understandable preference among experienced anglers to use the lightest fly rod possible. Refined tackle does provide great satisfaction, and in many situations the angler will hook more fish. Under the right conditions, a 2½-ounce fly rod is amply calibered for anything from bluegills to Atlantic salmon. However, in our enthusiasm we might convey the idea that light tackle is appropriate for all occasions—which it definitely is not. There are just as many good reasons for the popularity of heavier gear in taking the same weight range of fish. For example, while bluegills can be readily caught on small wet and dry flies in ponds, if the fishing requires popping bugs, a spinner-and-fly, or any other wind-resistant lure (such as it does in many Southern lakes), you have to follow well-defined requirements and use a 140–170-grain line. By the same token, light salmon rods imply low clearwater and small rivers where you have the opportunity to move fish to small wet and dry flies also. This can be done with a 120-grain line. On big, turbulent rivers, however, where flies from No. 2 to 6/0 must be used, a 220-grain line would be the minimum weight for propelling these heavy dressings. So fly rods cannot be selected simply on the basis of what the angler expects to catch. This is true not only because of the variation in lures but the difference in casting conditions.

WEIGHT AND LENGTH

Rod weight and length are not precise indexes of performance. The amount of material suggests what a rod is capable of doing, while the unseen taper determines exactly how it will perform. However, length and weight are tangible dimensions with a sufficient consistency for evaluation. Some manufacturers list their rod weights as completed sticks with fittings, while others catalogue them in their unfinished weights. Most anglers prefer the final figure as it includes reel seat, hand grasp, ferrules, and guides. Except for the craftsman himself, to whom it's a matter of micrometric accuracy, the unfinished weight doesn't have significance to the average man. A 3-ounce glued cane might evolve into a 4½-ounce rod, or a 6½-ounce rod when fitted and varnished. In either case, it's still going to require the same line size. The weight of the trimmings adds nothing to the taper or strength of the stick. So the basic point to consider when judging rods by their completed weights is how they compare to the line you need. For example, a 4½-ounce rod designed for a 170-grain line (No. 6) is going to be less tiring to swing all day than a 6½-ounce rod which also requires the same line weight. This doesn't mean that the shortest or lightest rod will always be the best choice, but if the job you have in mind demands continuous casting, such as the dry fly on mountain brooks, then it does tell you that the fatigue factor can be reduced. The prerequisite, of course, is to determine what size line will suit your purpose.

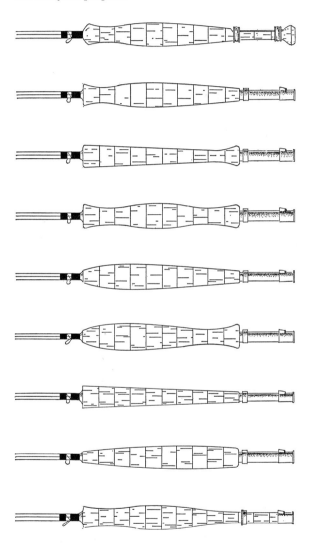

Fly Rod Handles: 1. Thompson, 2. Standard, 3. Ritz, 4. Fishtail, 5. Philippe Cigar, 6. Full Wells, 7. Gordon, 8. Half Wells, 9. Perfectionist

THE FLY ROD FOR SMALL STREAMS

The quality to look for in a small-stream fly rod is its ability to function with a light line (118–146 grains). In the opinion of many experts a No. 4 of approximately 120 grains is the ideal. The line point should be .030-inch diameter or less, and the heavy portion no more than .042-inch diameter. This provides a delicate presentation of the fly in shallow clearwater. Rods catalogued for 120-grain lines run 6–8 feet in length, and 1½–4 ounces in weight. Of course, the shortest rods require absolute precision in timing and are somewhat more difficult for the beginner to master. As a general rule, a 7½-foot rod, weighing approximately 2½ ounces, is a practical choice. The feature to look for in such a rod is its ability to hold 20–40 feet of line in the air without the need for excessive casting speed. The rod should have a slow casting cycle so that you have perfect control over the fly and so that the line displays no tendency to drop prematurely.

THE FLY ROD FOR BIG STREAMS

A trout fisherman who spends his days on sheltered mountain streams where forty-foot casts are rarely made has little in common with another trout fisherman who wades big, wind-whipped rivers where forty feet is closer to average. Perhaps the best fish of the day for either man will be a two pounder; yet the weight and length of their respective rods are essentially different. The former may pleasurably cast a 120-grain line, while the latter needs 170 grains. There is always the temptation to make this a regional distinction of East and West, but the compass needle is no more accurate in determining line size than the weight of an average fish indicates rod size.

A trout angler in California faces the same complex of casting problems as the man in Wyoming, Michigan, or New York. All trout states run the gamut from quiet meadow streams to boisterous rivers. Light, medium, and heavy tackle can be profitably used everywhere. The choice depends on the character of the waters you will regularly fish. Using the common 120-grain (No. 4) and 170-grain (No. 6) line weights as a gauge, the first thing to determine is whether presentation or distance is important. Although one might assume that very little difference exists between line diameters which vary by a mere .010 inch, there is a formidable ⅛ ounce of added weight between a No. 4 and a No. 6. Characteristically, the 120-grain line will fall to the water with less splash, float better with less drag, and therefore earn a margin of advantage in fly presentation. The 170-grain line, however, is capable of making short and long casts easily because more weight is extended at any given length. In a comparative analysis, a No. 6 suggests quick, accurate casting on tumbling mountain streams with the bonus of distance in larger waters.

The kind of river which might be suited to a 120-grain line and a light fly rod is the upper Deschutes in Oregon, the Ausable in Michigan, or the Green River in Wyoming. On the upper Deschutes, for instance, an angler can walk quietly along the bank, watching the water for a rise. A trout may be on the feed and yet rising slowly at long intervals. The light-colored patches of bottom immediately below a sweeper of weed is a favorite hold, and it is often possible to see a fish clearly. Thus, you find targets even when natural flies aren't numerous. The smooth surface requires delicate casting with fine leaders and small nymphs or dry flies. Frequently, a trout will show 50–60 feet away, which is a comfortable distance for 120–140-grain lines when not hindered by large flies.

This "prospecting" differs considerably from blind casting on the rugged headwaters of the Missouri, the canyon runs of the Madison, or the tristate, big Delaware. If most of your fishing is on turbulent rivers with bushy dry flies and streamers, an approximately 170-grain line (DT-6-F or WF-6-F) would be a practical choice. This will probably require an 8-foot, 4–4½-ounce; or 8½-foot, 4½–4¾-ounce rod in top-quality bamboo; it should be capable of 60–70 feet of line with flies up to No. 6 in a normal wind. Tactically speaking, the 170-grain line is a pivotal point; lines below this weight are best suited to casting over wary fish where presentation is all important, while heavier lines are necessary for pushing wind-resistant lures or reaching long distances.

THE HEAVY FLY ROD

For convenience, some manufacturers list their heavy rods as bass action, steelhead-bonefish action, and salmon action. These are a good general guide for the beginner, but before making your choice talk to somebody who knows the fishing. Most tackle salesmen can show you exactly the right rod. Generally speaking, any rod which can be used for steelhead is also suitable for bonefish. However, there is some difference between the ideal rod for each kind of fishing. A popular steelhead rod, for instance, is 8½ feet long and weights 5½ ounces. The stick will send a WF-8-F to 100 feet when necessary. Yet, for bonefishing many casters prefer a longer and heavier rod. The reason for their choice is not predicated on any

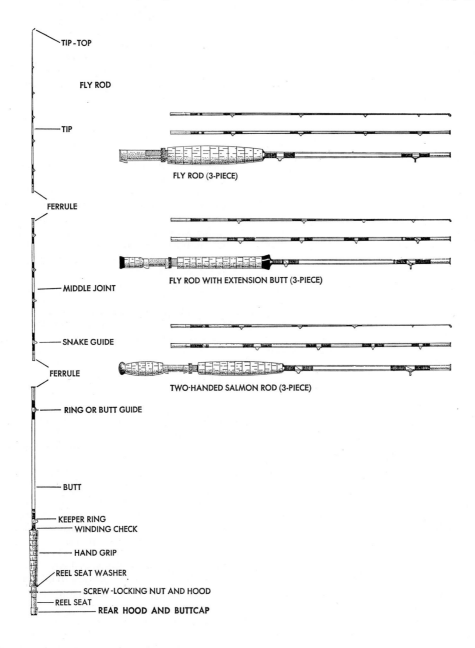

TIP-TOP

FLY ROD

TIP

FLY ROD (3-PIECE)

FERRULE

FLY ROD WITH EXTENSION BUTT (3-PIECE)

MIDDLE JOINT

SNAKE GUIDE

FERRULE

TWO-HANDED SALMON ROD (3-PIECE)

RING OR BUTT GUIDE

BUTT

KEEPER RING
WINDING CHECK

HAND GRIP

REEL SEAT WASHER
SCREW-LOCKING NUT AND HOOD
REEL SEAT
REAR HOOD AND BUTTCAP

Fly Rod Nomenclature

dissimilarity between the size or strength of the two species; it's again based on the conditions under which the casting is done. Most steelhead fishing is blind. The angler combs likely holding water with a large wet fly, searching for fish by repetitive casting. A rod that will swing comfortably, hour after hour, is perfect for the job. You need enough line weight to push No. 4 flies long distances, and that requires either a No. 7 or No. 8 belly. Being a sunken-fly game, the rod must also be powerful enough to pick up lengths of water-soaked taper. To take some of the strain off the rod and achieve a more sensitive contact with the drifting fly, many anglers choose the WF-7-F rather than the next heavier size. Under highwater conditions when the fly must travel deep you can substitute a WF-8-S sinking-type line. Bonefish on the other hand are sought visually, often in fierce winds, and casting is comparatively infrequent. There are more hours of waiting to see bonefish than casting for them. Most of the time you are standing in a skiff watching for muds or tails, and when the time comes to cast, it must be fast to intercept a moving school. You may have to belt a floppy No. 2/0 streamer into the teeth of a fifteen mile per hour blow. Thus a longer and heavier rod can be profitably used on the marl flats without tiring your arm. Inasmuch as the fishing is accomplished in water ranging from 6 inches to 3 feet in depth, a WF-8-F or WF-9-F floater is perfect. It has the weight to propel large flies and to shoot a long distance with one back cast. Such a rod may be 9½ feet long, and weigh 6¾ ounces. It would be overcalibered for steelhead fishing where continuous casting with smaller flies is the basic requirement.

Bass bug rods are generally rated for a No. 8 to No. 10 line. The lures are highly wind resistant, and because of their bulk, one must employ heavy leaders. However, you are always working with a floating line at relatively short ranges when compared to steelhead or bonefish casting, so the pickups are no problem. It's easier to do the job with a long rod because more line can be held from the water when manipulating the lure, plus the fact that a great percentage of bugging is done while sitting in a boat. Thus, you need a long but slow rod to maintain a rhythm with the flight of air-resistant lures and make line handling easier. For many casters a rod similar to the one described for bonefishing is ideal. For other people it's a wrist breaker as the casting is continuous. The majority is inclined toward the steelhead weight and length because a minimum-optimum rod adds more fun to bass fishing. Big sticks are a pleasure to cast with, but the bass is considerably overgunned with 9½ feet of fly rod. For these reasons, plus the fact that a WF-8-F assures better presentation, most casters prefer the No. 8 belly size. Essentially, a bass action is a modification of the so-called steelhead action which is made a shade stiffer to facilitate the pickup with a sunken line. So here again, determining the proper line size leads to the correct rod. —A.J.McC.

FLY-TYING The art of imitating or suggesting insects, minnows, crustaceans, and similar natural foods eaten by fish through the skillful application of feathers, wool, fur, tinsel, and other materials to a hook. Sometimes called "fly-dressing," it requires considerable experience to tie flies suitable for commercial purposes. However, the angler can quickly learn to make flies that will catch fish, and, as such, it has become an important hobby within a hobby; there are an estimated quarter of a million amateur fly-tiers in the United States today. The basic procedures are more or less standardized, although advanced amateurs and professionals may adopt variations in technique to achieve different effects or to improve individual style.

FLY HOOKS

All flies should be tied on hooks made especially for fly-tying. For wet flies and nymphs, a regular-weight hook or one which is 1 or 2X stout, with a turned-down tapered eye, may be used. For the streamer flies, wet-fly hooks may be used as well as hooks with additional length and weight, and eyes best suited for their particular purpose. Dry-fly hooks should be light, 2X fine if possible, and can be obtained with turned-up eyes (T.U.E.); however, in the United States, turned-down eyes (T.D.E.) hooks are used commercially for both wet and dry flies. Made of the finest steel, fly hooks are carefully tempered to be neither brittle nor soft. The eyes are designed so that they will not chafe a leader. The points are needle sharp for quick penetration.

THE TOOLS

The tools necessary to fly-tying are a good vise, preferably a lever-and-cam type, which is easiest to use quickly and efficiently, hackle pliers, and a pair of sharp scissors. In addition to these a thread clip (a rubber bumper with a screw center can be used for this), a stylet, a hook hone, and hackle gauge are most useful. Other tools available are a magnifying mirror, thread bobbin, hackle clip, hackle guards, whip finisher, and magnifying glass.

HOW TO TIE A DRY FLY

For the fly-tier's purpose, exact imitations of the natural aquatic insects are of less importance than something the fish will accept as an attractive suggestion of it. Usually the more accurate in detail the imitation is, the more quickly the fish rejects it as fraudulent. The most successful flies are those which merely suggest something edible, whether it be in the presentation of the fly by the angler, the silhouette of the fly as it rides on the surface, or its behavior in the water.

A dry fly, as the term indicates, is intended to float. For it the lightest weight of hook consistent with strength should be used. Ideally, a dry fly should be tied on a 2X fine, turned-up eye hook with a shank of standard length, or not more than 1X long if for some reason a longer body is necessary. For very small flies, where the standard gap of hook is desired, yet the standard shank length might be too long (as for spiders and variants), a short-shank hook is used.

The *tail* of the average dry fly should be approximately the length of the hook shank and sparse rather than full. It is preferably made from naturally water resistant waterfowl feathers, such as mallard duck, the teal, wood duck, or goose.

The *body*, no matter what material it is made of, should be slim and very firm or tight, to prevent or delay water absorption. Silk or synthetic floss, fur dubbing, and quill are used on a large proportion of dry-fly patterns. Pea-

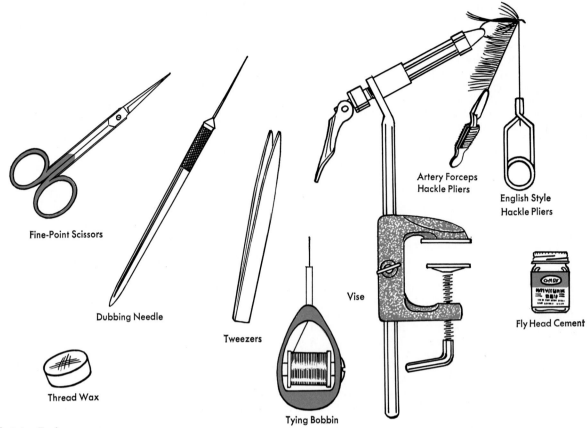

Fine-Point Scissors

Dubbing Needle

Tweezers

Thread Wax

Tying Bobbin

Vise

Artery Forceps
Hackle Pliers

English Style
Hackle Pliers

Fly Head Cement

Fly-tying Tools

cock and ostrich herl and fine chenille are utilized. Very thin cork is sometimes used for dry-fly bodies, and a surprisingly realistic mayfly with body detached from the hook for part of its length can be made of semitransparent latex material. A few dry-fly patterns call for deer-hair bodies, spun and trimmed to shape.

The *ribbing* on dry-fly bodies may be of silk, nylon, or cotton thread; fine tinsel or fine wire; peacock or ostrich herl; or a hackle may be wound over the body in an open spiral for additional wind resistance, which permits a more delicate presentation of the fly during fishing.

The *wings* of a dry fly, like the tails, are made from the feathers of waterfowl wherever possible and are approximately the length of the hook shank. The delicately marked, lemon, flank feathers found on the drake wood duck, mandarin, or summer ducks, of a color so elusive as to be impossible to imitate with dye, are used for the erect, bunched, or divided wings and for tails on many dry-fly patterns. The deep, rich brown scapular or shoulder feathers of the mallard drake, the pale gray and white as well as the darker-barred flank and breast feathers of mallard and teal are also used. Small, whole breast feathers from various ducks are ideal for the delicate and graceful fan-winged flies. Hair from numerous animals may be substituted for the feather wings on dry flies in order to give them greater durability.

The *hackle* of the dry fly not only furnishes wind resistance for a delicate cast but also provides buoyancy

for the fly on the water. Although the prime cocks or roosters from which fine dry-fly hackles are obtained are not aquatic birds, their neck and saddle feathers furnish the bulk of all dry-fly hackles used in fly-tying. Chosen for richness of color, stiffness of barb, and lack of web along a flexible stem or quill, these hackles are wound around the hook so that the barbs stand out in a ruff encircling the hook at right angles and are distributed fairly evenly behind and head of whatever wings are used. The length of the barb or flue of the hackle for a dry fly is approximately one and a half times the width of the gap of the hook on which it will be used. There is no hard and fast rule governing the exact amount of hackle to be tied on a dry fly. It may be sparse, moderately full, or very full. It's a matter of individual preference.

A novel use of hackle created a "parachute" fly, which originally required a special hook having a short, vertical pin centered on the shank. An oversized hackle, wound around the pin instead of the hook, radiated horizontally above the fly body. This type of hackle application can be used with fan-wings by winding the hackle around the stem base of the wings, or the stem of the hackle itself can be used in place of the vertical pin or wings.

Whenever materials that might have a tendency to absorb water are used for body, wings, or hackle of a dry fly, a floatant of light oil made for this purpose can be applied to the fly before it is used for fishing.

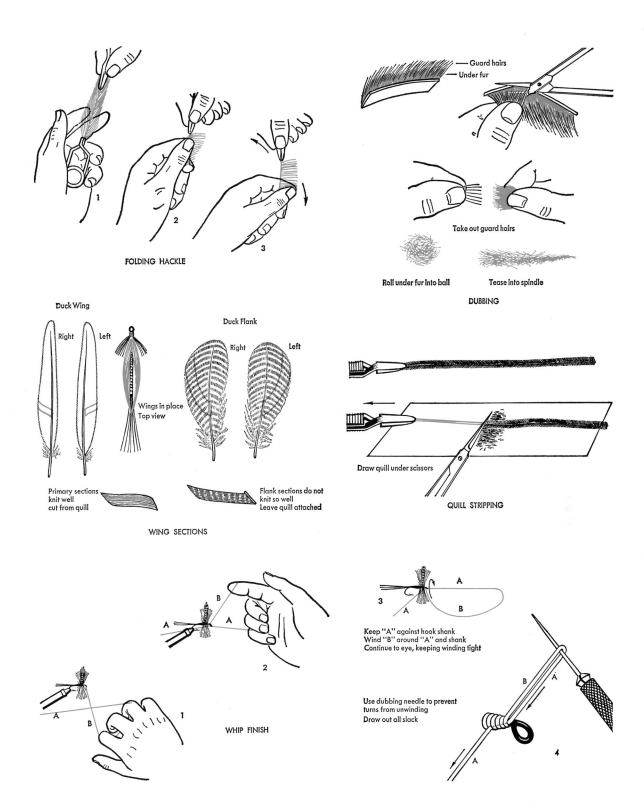

FOLDING HACKLE

Guard hairs
Under fur

Take out guard hairs

Roll under fur into ball   Tease into spindle

DUBBING

Duck Wing

Right   Left

Wings in place
Top view

Duck Flank

Right   Left

Primary sections
knit well
cut from quill

Flank sections do not
knit so well
Leave quill attached

WING SECTIONS

Draw quill under scissors

QUILL STRIPPING

WHIP FINISH

Keep "A" against hook shank
Wind "B" around "A" and shank
Continue to eye, keeping winding tight

Use dubbing needle to prevent
turns from unwinding
Draw out all slack

Fly-tying Techniques

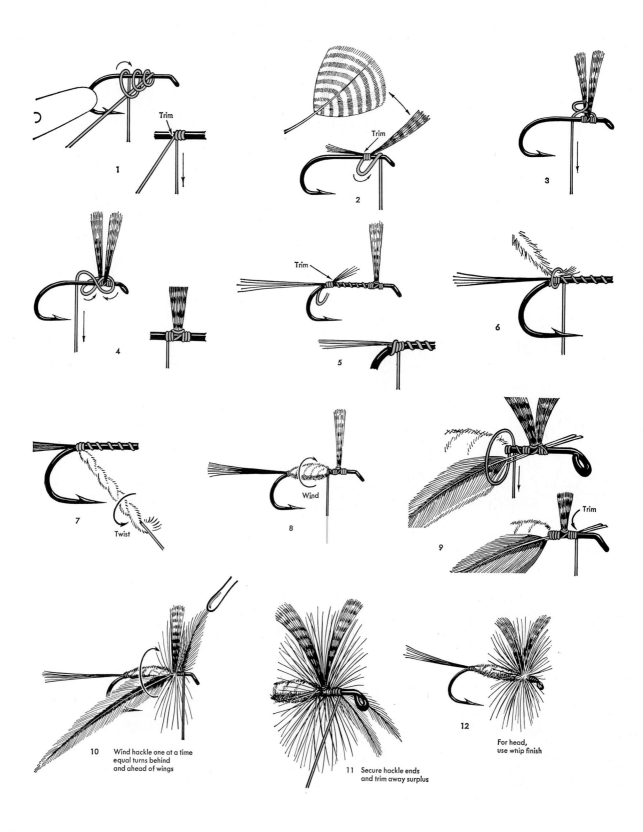

1

2

3

4

5

6

7 Twist

8 Wind

9 Trim

Trim

10 Wind hackle one at a time
equal turns behind
and ahead of wings

11 Secure hackle ends
and trim away surplus

12

For head,
use whip finish

How to Tie a Dry Fly

HOW TO TIE A WET FLY

In any comprehensive list of standard fly patterns most of them will be for wet flies. The wet fly is intended to sink at once and to be fished beneath the surface. It should be tied on a 1 or 2X stout hook which gives added weight for the size required.

A typical wet fly may have a short *tail* of hackle flues, pheasant crest, or pheasant tail, guard hairs from various animals, or none at all. Its *body* may be of tinsel, quill, herl, floss, any one of several furs, or wool yarn, or combinations of the latter two in dubbing, which can be made to absorb water rapidly, thereby aiding the fly to submerge quickly. The combination of wool dubbing with a fur can create a translucent effect which gives the fly a succulent appearance, perhaps more important than having it sink quickly. The body may be ribbed with tinsel, a strand of floss, a thread, a soft wet-fly hackle, or have no rib at all.

The *wings* typical of a wet-fly pattern are slim, made of strips of flight feathers from goose, turkey, or duck. They may be built of narrow feather strips of different colors, making almost any color combination possible. Feathers to be built by strips into wings must be carefully matched and kept together, for a strand from a left-wing feather could not be used with a right feather strip and vice versa. The wet-fly wings may also be made of feather barbs or hair bunched into single wings, or short, paired hackles may be used. Usually the wet-fly wings lie back along the body of the fly, extending very little beyond the bend of the hook, but can also be made to lie flat on top of the body.

The wet-fly *hackle*, chosen for its soft, limp and webby flues, may be applied before the wing is tied on. It may be left with an equal distribution of flues around the hook, or it may be drawn down equally on both sides of the fly body until it is all beneath the hook, forming a throat. This throat may extend halfway from eye to point of hook, or as far as the barb. Or the hackle may be added after the wing is tied on and permitted to sweep back over and around the fly body. This type of hackle will undulate in the current and respond with gentle movement to any twitch of the leader during a retrieve. A few strands of polar-bear hair tied in as a throat and extending back to cover the point and barb of the hook acts as a weed guard in water full of obstructions.

The heads of all flies should be given several coats of lacquer and allowed to dry thoroughly before being used. It will improve their appearance and their wearing qualities.

HOW TO TIE A NYMPH

The nymph is a type of wet or sunken fly representing the larval stage of the aquatic insects which form the bulk of natural food for fish. Many natural nymphs are easy for the fly-tier to simulate, for their form and coloring is simple; it is more difficult to fish them successfully. Nymphs—the silt dwellers, the creepers, the clambering type, the case builders, and so on—differ greatly in their habitat. The artificials must be used in the areas where their natural counterparts are likely to be found. If they are used properly, nymphs are exceptionally effective, and the diligent fisherman is rewarded with success almost in proportion to the time he devotes to mastering this type of fishing.

A nymph has a slim *body*, tapered before the hook barb from a quarter to a half of its length and then swelling out behind the head. This swelling, or *thorax*, may be left in a round bulge at the forward end of the body or may be flattened top and bottom, to bulge only at the sides according to the pattern. Fine chenille as well as dubbings of fur, wool, or the undercoat of polar-bear hair are most commonly used for nymph bodies. The dubbings used separately or combined in various proportions and colors are durable and translucent. Quill, raffia, and hair are also employed.

The basic nymph form may be embellished in several ways. A few short wisps of feather fibers may be added for a minute *tail*, or a pair of fine, stripped feather quills may be used instead. A rib of fine solid wire or fine flat tinsel, or a strand of floss or thread may be added to create a segmented appearance. A feather or silk overlay for the enlarged area behind the head may be inset while the body is being tied and then drawn forward to cover it before the head is formed. The entire body may be given a shellback of silk, quill, or feather strip by tying any one of these in above the tail before the body is made and drawing it forward after the body is completed, tying it off at the head.

Another *back covering* can be made with a sparse tuft of hair such as squirrel or badger, so placed that the dark hair will cover the body and the lighter tips will extend beyond the hook bend for a tail. This back is tied in at the head, after the body is made (the cut ends being covered by the thread which forms the head), and then bound down snugly with a wrap knot behind the nymph body, just above the hook barb. This binding, like all exposed thread windings, should be lacquered. All back coverings should be slightly darker than the body material and can be carefully lacquered to give the back a shiny, shell-like appearance.

Grouse or partridge hackle may be added between the body and head so that the hackle will turn back over the body, and the remaining bit of feather, instead of being cut away, may be allowed to extend forward of the head to represent *feelers*. Very narrow fibers of goose or duck or guinea may be tied on crosswise behind the head and clipped short to represent tiny legs or may be inserted between body and thorax for the same purpose. Small strands of peacock sword feather can be used in place of other material for a tail and also added ahead of the body so that, held in place by the fly head, they will extend forward of the hook eye. Pattern variations are almost infinite.

For the elaborate nymphs, intended to be more accurate representations, the material to be used for *legs* or feelers (such as the fine ends of hackle quills from which the flues have been clipped, or small feathers, from which the flues have been stripped along one side) is easiest to manage when it has been bent into shape and set with varnish before the nymph is tied. The legs can be placed in position while the nymph is being constructed and then cut to the proper length after the fly itself is finished.

The average hook size for a nymph is from a No. 12 to 18, although they may be as large as a No. 6 or 8 and as small as a No. 20. Hooks 1 or 2X stout provide weight without sacrificing size. Additional weight is sometimes required on nymph or wet fly, and when it is, the hook shank can be wound with a soft lead wire approxi-

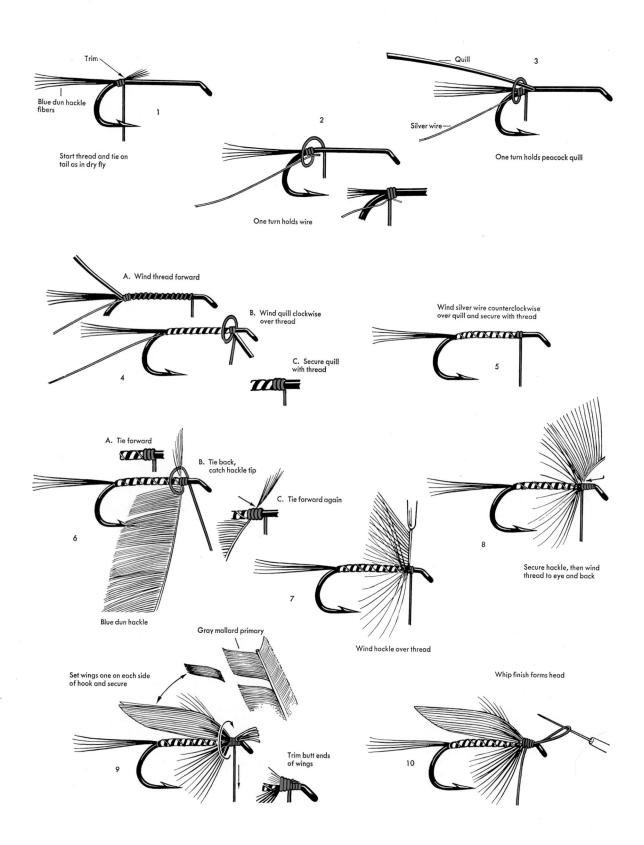

Trim

Blue dun hackle
fibers

1

Start thread and tie on
tail as in dry fly

2

One turn holds wire

3

Quill

Silver wire

One turn holds peacock quill

A. Wind thread forward

B. Wind quill clockwise
over thread

C. Secure quill
with thread

4

Wind silver wire counterclockwise
over quill and secure with thread

5

A. Tie forward

B. Tie back,
catch hackle tip

C. Tie forward again

6

Blue dun hackle

7

Wind hackle over thread

8

Secure hackle, then wind
thread to eye and back

Gray mallard primary

Set wings one on each side
of hook and secure

Trim butt ends
of wings

9

Whip finish forms head

10

How to Tie a Blue Quill Wet Fly

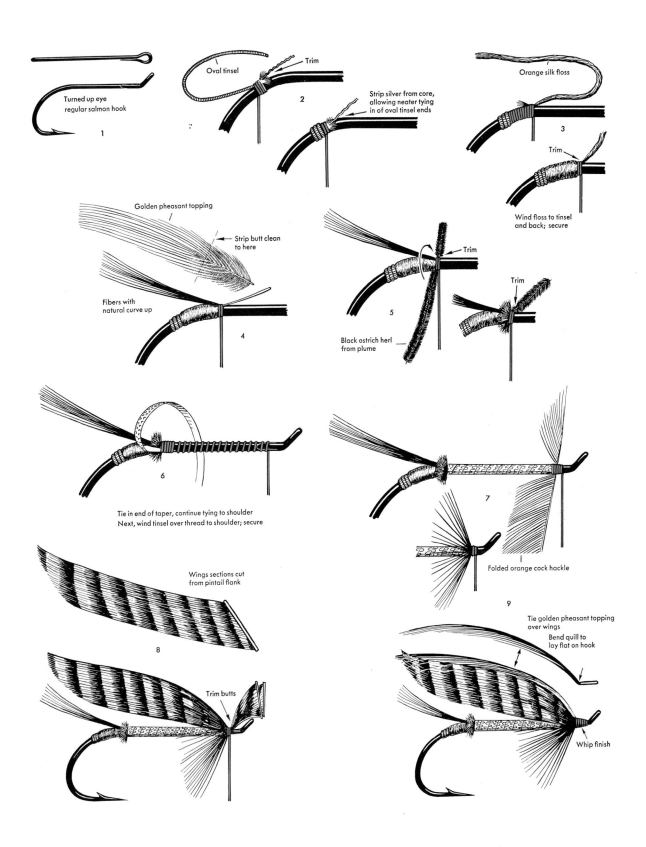

Turned up eye
regular salmon hook

1

Oval tinsel

Trim

2

Strip silver from core,
allowing neater tying
in of oval tinsel ends

Orange silk floss

3

Trim

Wind floss to tinsel
and back; secure

Golden pheasant topping

Strip butt clean
to here

Fibers with
natural curve up

4

Trim

Trim

5

Black ostrich herl
from plume

Tie in end of taper, continue tying to shoulder
Next, wind tinsel over thread to shoulder; secure

6

7

Folded orange cock hackle

9

Wings sections cut
from pintail flank

8

Trim butts

Tie golden pheasant topping
over wings

Bend quill to
lay flat on hook

Whip finish

How to Tie a Blackville Salmon Fly

mately the diameter of the hook. The wire must be securely fastened to the hook and can be done as follows: taper the end of wire, and bind it smoothly to the hook midway between point and barb. Wind the well-waxed tying thread around the hook shank in a close spiral toward the hook eye, stopping about one eighth of the length of the hook from the eye. Apply a coat of lacquer to the thread winding. Before the lacquer has had time to set, wrap the wire over this as closely and tightly as possible, without overlapping. Taper the wire by cutting it diagonally and bind it down at the end of the thread winding with a smooth wrap-knot. Cover the wire with lacquer.

If the weighted hook has been prepared for a nymph which is to be flattened, quickly tie the materials (for whatever pattern you are about to use) onto the weighted base as though you were tying it directly onto the hook, before the lacquer has had time to set. Flatten the finished nymph carefully with smooth-jawed pliers which will not damage the materials, and then permit it to dry out thoroughly. If the lacquered base dries before the pliers are used to flatten the body, there is every possibility of breaking the seal between hook and wire, and the body will turn on the hook.

HOW TO TIE A STREAMER FLY

The streamer fly is also a type of wet fly. These long-winged, sunken flies, intended to represent the slim, streamlined shape of a minnow, may be designated as bucktails or streamers, the major differences between them being one of size and the wing material. Accordingly, the "streamer" should be tied on a hook of standard length, with a feather-wing, and the "bucktail" on a hook of extra length, with a hair-wing. However, the use of feathers and bucktail hair for the streamer type of wing is often found on the regular length of hook as well as on the very long hooks, and the two materials are frequently combined on each type of hook. Other materials such as maribou, polar-bear hair, brown- or black-bear hair, or squirrel hair are also used for the so-called "bucktails" and are not only combined with the actual bucktail hair, but with feathers as well.

There are other flies made of bucktail that could be legitimately referred to as bucktails but not as streamers. It would seem, therefore, that the general term "streamer" covers the long, slim wing that characterizes both the hair-wing and the feather-wing for this elongated type of fly. Within that term, further designation could be "hair-wing streamer" or "feather streamer" to indicate the difference in the major amount of wing material used, the style of tying and the hook sizes being interchangeable.

The main difference between the "Eastern" and "Western" streamer is the angle at which the wing is set—the Eastern method dresses the wing low over the body of the fly, while the Western-style streamer wing is set at an approximate 40-degree angle above the body.

A streamer fly hook may have a return loop eye, a regular turned-down eye, or a ringed (straight) eye. If the streamer is to be fished with a spinner, a ringed eye is best to use since it provides a smooth joining with the spinner which an offset eye would not do.

The *tail* of a streamer fly on a regular length hook should be approximately the length of the hook shank.

On an extra-length hook, about the length of the hook gape. Any of the materials used for wet-fly tails are used for streamer flies also.

The *body* of a streamer fly may be of any one of the ordinary fly-tying materials, or combinations of them, and made with or without a rib. Or, it may be made of a solid brass, or copper, or of silver-colored wire, used alone or covered with floss, wool yarn, or tinsel. Bodies of silk floss or tinsel may be made over a padding of wool in matching color. This underbody should be carefully formed, its contours as smooth as possible.

Hackle may be applied as for the wet flies.

A long hook shank requires a proportionately longer wing which may be made of hair tied sparse, rather than full, or of hackle feathers from necks and saddles. Or, as has been said, hair and feathers may be combined. Hackles should be carefully matched for size and marking, the pairs usually used with the dull sides together, so that the glossy surface is outward on each side of the fly and the wing is balanced. Other materials such as maribou, peacock herl, peacock sword, and the like, may be incorporated in the wing to impart a lifelike quality of movement underwater.

The *wing* is tied in behind the head of the fly and streams back over the hook. Preferably it should not extend much further than the end of the tail beyond the end of the hook, in order to minimize "short" strikes. A *very* long wing has a tendency to catch in the bend, causing the fly to spin and twist leader and line. If an exceptionally long wing is desired, two hooks tandem, joined with gut or strands of a synthetic leader material, are more practical than a single hook. —H.S.

FLY-TYING MATERIALS

Some fly patterns developed many years ago require feathers which are very difficult to obtain at this time. In certain cases the birds are now practically extinct. In other instances government controls prohibit either killing or exporting the birds or feathers from them. A number of substitutes for such scarce feathers have been developed and used successfully in the older or more exotic fly patterns. Many of these are from a different species of bird dyed to resemble a scarce feather. It is true, of course, that the best feathers are ones with natural coloration, but with the aniline dyes that are available today it is possible to match colors very closely and to use dyes that are consistently of the same shade. When a reliable fly-tying material house does its own dyeing, the colors of feathers obtained from such a supplier will be the same from year to year.

Hackle Colors The natural colors, and combinations of colors, found in feathers used for the hackles of artificial flies are many and varied. Some are known by names which are easily identified; others are described in terms which are not so familiar. The natural colors which are most frequently used in fly-tying are as follows:

Badger: The center of the hackle feather is usually brownish-black to black along most of the length of the quill, narrow at the tip, and widening near the base of the feather. The outer portion, from the dark center section to the tips of the fibers, varies in color from ginger, or yellowish-white, to a definite white. Feathers from the neck or saddle of the same bird will usually be the same color. On some badger hackle

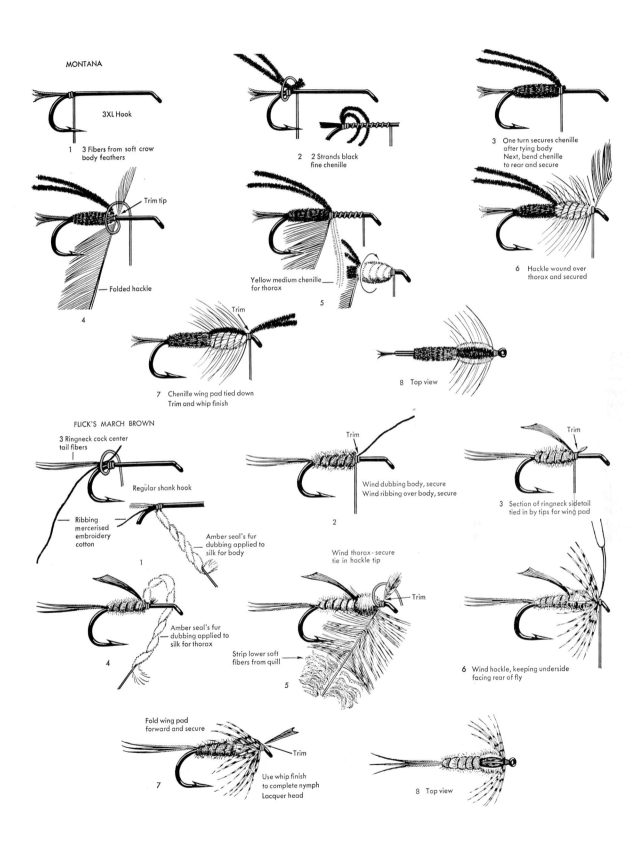

MONTANA

1 3 Fibers from soft crow body feathers

3XL Hook

2 2 Strands black fine chenille

3 One turn secures chenille after tying body Next, bend chenille to rear and secure

Trim tip

Folded hackle

4

6 Hackle wound over thorax and secured

Yellow medium chenille for thorax

5

7 Chenille wing pad tied down Trim and whip finish

Trim

8 Top view

FLICK'S MARCH BROWN

3 Ringneck cock center tail fibers

Regular shank hook

Ribbing mercerised embroidery cotton

Amber seal's fur dubbing applied to silk for body

1

Trim

Wind dubbing body, secure Wind ribbing over body, secure

2

Trim

3 Section of ringneck sidetail tied in by tips for wing pad

Amber seal's fur dubbing applied to silk for thorax

4

Wind thorax - secure tie in hackle tip

Trim

Strip lower soft fibers from quill

5

6 Wind hackle, keeping underside facing rear of fly

Fold wing pad forward and secure

Trim

Use whip finish to complete nymph Lacquer head

7

8 Top view

How to Tie a Nymph

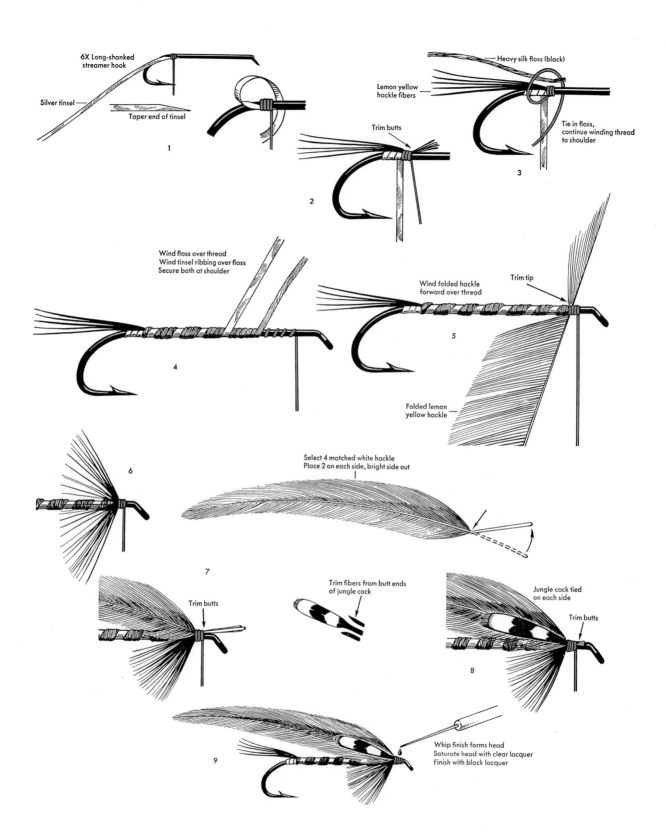

6X Long-shanked streamer hook

Silver tinsel

Taper end of tinsel

Trim butts

1

2

Heavy silk floss (black)

Lemon yellow hackle fibers

Tie in floss, continue winding thread to shoulder

3

Wind floss over thread
Wind tinsel ribbing over floss
Secure both at shoulder

4

Wind folded hackle forward over thread

Trim tip

5

Folded lemon yellow hackle

6

Select 4 matched white hackle
Place 2 on each side, bright side out

7

Trim butts

Trim fibers from butt ends of jungle cock

Jungle cock tied on each side

Trim butts

8

Whip finish forms head
Saturate head with clear lacquer
Finish with black lacquer

9

How to Tie a Black Ghost Streamer Fly

Popular Fly Patterns

DRY FLIES

Spirit of Pittsford Mills
Wings: Light grizzly hackle tips
Tail: Ginger cock hackle fibers
Body: Dubbing from grayish-white duck down ribbed with a clipped ginger hackle
Hackle: Light ginger cock hackles

Atherton # 6
Wings: Dark finely speckled Bali duck flank feathers
Tail: Dark natural rusty dun cock hackle fibers
Body: Mixture of dark muskrat or mole and red-brown fur (dyed) to give a dark reddish-gray brown dubbing ribbed with narrow oval gold tinsel
Hackle: One natural dun and one red-brown hackle tied mixed together

Katterman
Tail: Very small light ginger cock hackle
Body: Peacock with a very dark mahogany brown cock hackle palmered over peacock herl followed by a fine gold wire wound through hackle. Several turns of white hackle at head for visibility

Wickhams Fancy
Wings: Medium light gray tied double divided from slips of duck quill
Tail: Ginger
Body: Flat gold tinsel palmered with ginger hackle
Hackle: (at shoulder) ginger cock

Conover
Tail: Cream badger cock hackle fibers
Body: Dubbing of 1/3 muskrat, 1/3 red dyed wool, 1/3 cream lamb's wool to give creamy gray-red dubbing
Hackle: Brown center cream badger cock hackle slightly longer than regular

Coffin Fly
Wings: Black hackle tips
Tail: Black bear hair or black cock hackle fibers
Body: Clipped white deer hair
Hackle: Badger cock hackles. This pattern should be on 3X or 4X long hook

Female Beaverkill
Wings: Double divided slips from gray duck quill
Tail: Ginger cock hackle fibers; egg sac, yellow wool or fine chenille
Body: Gray muskrat fur dubbing
Hackles: Ginger cock hackles

Pink Lady Bivisible
Tail: Light ginger hackle fibers
Body: Pink silk floss ribbed with flat gold tinsel over which is a light ginger hackle tied palmer followed by one light ginger hackle with a golden-olive cock hackle ahead for visibility

Queen of Waters
Wings: From flank of gray mallard drake
Tail: Ginger cock hackle fibers
Body: Orange silk floss ribbed with flat gold tinsel, a ginger red hackle tied palmer over body
Hackle: (at shoulder) Ginger cock hackle

Brown Bivisible
Hackle: White tied in at head for visibility followed by two stiff brown cocks' hackles palmered to bend of hook
Tail: Formed by the hackle tips

Cross Special
Wings: From flank feathers of drake wood-duck or mandarin
Tail: Light blue dun hackle fibers
Body: Grayish-white fox fur dubbing
Hackles: Light blue dun cock hackle

Greenwell's Glory
Wings: Double divided slips from dark gray duck quill
Tail: Ginger
Body: Medium olive green floss ribbed with gold wire
Hackle: Furnace cock hackles

Dark Hendrickson
Wings: From flank feather of wood-duck or mandarin drake
Tail: Dark rusty dun cock hackles
Body: Brownish gray dubbing from red fox fur
Hackles: Dark rusty dun cock hackles

Gold Ribbed Hare's Ear
Wings: Tied double divided from sections of light gray mallard duck quill
Tail: Furnace hackle fibers
Body: Hare's ear fur dubbing ribbed with flat gold tinsel
Hackles: Furnace or Cochy-bondhu

Woodruff
Wings: Tied spent of grizzly hackle tips
Tail: Medium ginger cock hackle fibers
Body: Chartreuse green wool dubbing
Hackle: Medium ginger cock hackle

Rat Faced McDougal (White Wing)
Tail: Ginger hackle fibers
Body: Clipped tannish gray deer hair
Wings: White calf tail hair
Hackle: Ginger cock hackle

Pale Evening Dun
Wings: Tied double divided from slips of light gray duck quill
Tail: Pale blue dun
Body: Primrose yellow ribbed with fine flat gold tinsel
Hackle: Pale blue dun cock

Whirling Blue Dun
Tail: Blue dun hackle fibers
Body: Light blue-gray muskrat fur ribbed with flat gold tinsel
Hackles: Light blue dun cock hackles

White Wulff
Wings: White calf tail hair or white buck tail
Tail: White calf tail
Body: White wool
Hackle: White badger

Beaverkill Red Fox
Tail: Stiff ginger hackle fibers
Body: Muskrat ribbed with fine flat gold tinsel
Hackles: Ginger tied just ahead of body followed by medium blue dun hackle at head

Male Beaverkill
Wings: Tied double divided from slips of light gray duck quill
Tail: Ginger cock hackle fibers
Body: White floss silk with dark brown cock hackle palmered over body followed by dark brown cock hackle at shoulder

Pink Lady
Wings: Slips of light gray duck quill tied double divided
Tail: Strands of golden pheasant tippet
Body: Pink floss ribbed with flat gold tinsel
Hackle: Ginger cock hackle

Near Enough
Wings: From flank of drake, wood-duck or mandarin
Tail: Two stripped grizzly hackle quills flared and divided, extra long
Body: Two stripped grizzly hackle quills
Hackle: One ginger, one grizzly tied mixed

Boercher
Tail: 2 black whiskers about twice length of hook from fox or other animal muzzle
Body: Dark gray fur dubbing ribbed with black silk thread
Wings: 2 light dun hackle tips
Hackle: 1 gray hackle, 1 medium dark ginger, wound mixed

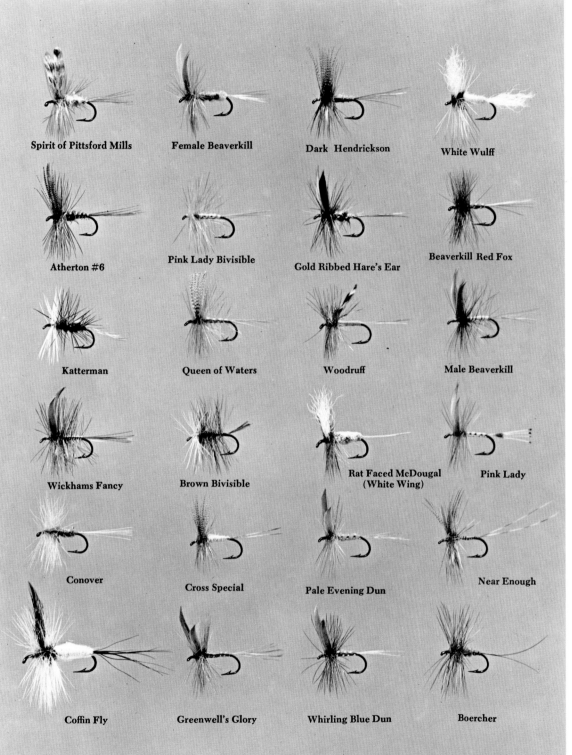

Spirit of Pittsford Mills   Female Beaverkill   Dark Hendrickson   White Wulff

Atherton #6   Pink Lady Bivisible   Gold Ribbed Hare's Ear   Beaverkill Red Fox

Katterman   Queen of Waters   Woodruff   Male Beaverkill

Wickhams Fancy   Brown Bivisible   Rat Faced McDougal (White Wing)   Pink Lady

Conover   Cross Special   Pale Evening Dun   Near Enough

Coffin Fly   Greenwell's Glory   Whirling Blue Dun   Boercher

Tied by Elsie B. Darbee

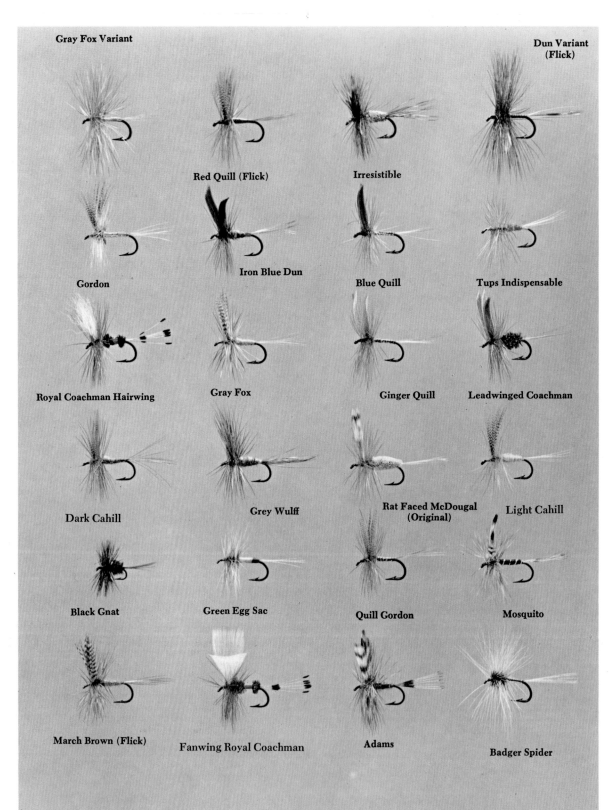

Gray Fox Variant

Dun Variant
(Flick)

Red Quill (Flick)

Irresistible

Gordon

Iron Blue Dun

Blue Quill

Tups Indispensable

Royal Coachman Hairwing

Gray Fox

Ginger Quill

Leadwinged Coachman

Dark Cahill

Grey Wulff

Rat Faced McDougal
(Original)

Light Cahill

Black Gnat

Green Egg Sac

Quill Gordon

Mosquito

March Brown (Flick)

Fanwing Royal Coachman

Adams

Badger Spider

Tied by Elsie B. Darbee

DRY FLIES

Gray Fox Variant
Tail: Ginger cock hackle fibers
Body: Stripped quill from cream hackle (well lacquered)
Hackle: Extra long stiff ginger hackle, dark ginger hackle, and gray grizzly mixed

Gordon
Tail: Cream badger hackle fibers
Body: Old gold silk floss ribbed with fine gold oval tinsel
Wings: Wood-duck flank
Hackle: Cream badger

Royal Coachman Hairwing
Wings: White calf tail hair
Tail: Golden pheasant tippet strands
Body: In three equal parts— 1st third, peacock herl; center third, scarlet silk floss; followed by peacock herl
Hackle: Natural red-brown cock hackles

Dark Cahill
Wings: From flank feather of drake wood-duck or mandarin
Tail: Red-brown cock's hackle fibers
Body: Gray muskrat fur dubbing
Hackle: Natural red-brown cock hackle

Black Gnat
Wings: Tied double divided from slips of medium gray duck quill
Tail: Black cock hackle fibers
Body: Black chenille
Hackle: Black cock hackles

March Brown (Flick)
Wings: Dark heavily marked flank feathers of drake wood-duck or mandarin
Tail: Dark ginger cock hackle fibers
Body: Tan fox fur dubbing mixed with sandy fur from a hare's poll
Hackle: 1 bright red game cock with a gray grizzly cock hackle tied in at the front

Red Quill (Flick)
Wing: From flank of wood-duck or mandarin
Tail: Dark dun cock hackle fibers
Body: Stripped quill from dark brown cock hackle (well lacquered)
Hackle: Dark dun cock hackles

Iron Blue Dun
Tail: Furnace or coch-y-bondhu hackle fibers
Egg Sac: Dark red silk
Body: Dark blue-gray muskrat fur
Wings: Tied double divided from slips of dark gray duck quills
Hackle: Furnace or coch-y-bondhu

Gray Fox
Wings: From flank feather of mallard drake
Tail: Fibers from a ginger cock hackle
Body: Light fawn colored fur dubbing from red fox
Hackle: 1 light grizzly, 1 light ginger wound together

Grey Wulff
Wings: Dark deer hair from white-tail deer
Tail: Dark deer hair same as wings
Body: Dark gray fox or muskrat fur dubbing
Hackle: Medium blue dun cock hackles

Green Egg Sac
Tail: Cream grizzly hackle fibers. Egg sac green wool
Body: Grayish tan fox fur dubbing
Hackle: Cream grizzly showing distinct grayish cast at center

Fanwing Royal Coachman
Wings: Two matched white feathers from breast of drake, wood-duck, mandarin or other wild duck
Tail: Golden pheasant tippet strands
Body: In three equal parts— 1st third, peacock herl; center third, scarlet silk floss; followed by peacock herl
Hackle: Natural red-brown cock hackles

Irresistible
Tail: Dark deer hair from body of white-tail deer
Body: Dark gray clipped deer hair
Wings: From body hair of white tail deer same color as tail
Hackle: Dark rusty dun cock hackles

Blue Quill
Wings: Double divided slips from medium blue-gray duck wing quill
Tail: Medium blue dun cock hackle fibers
Body: Stripped peacock quill; may be reinforced with fine silver wire
Hackle: Medium blue dun cock hackles

Ginger Quill
Wings: Double divided slips from mallard duck quill
Tail: Fibers from ginger hackle
Body: Stripped peacock quill—may be reinforced with fine gold wire
Hackle: Ginger cock hackle

Rat Faced McDougal (Original)
Wings: Cream grizzly hackle tips
Tail: Ginger cock hackle fibers
Body: Clipped tannish-gray deer hair
Hackle: Ginger cock

Quill Gordon
Wings: From flank feather of drake wood-duck or mandarin
Tail: Medium blue dun cock hackle fibers
Body: Stripped peacock quill—may be reinforced with fine silver wire
Hackle: Medium blue dun cock hackles

Adams
Wings: Dark grizzly hackle points
Tail: Golden pheasant tippet fibers
Body: Dark blue dun mole's fur dubbing
Hackle: 1 natural red-brown, 1 dark grizzly cock hackle wound together

Dun Variant (Flick)
Tail: Natural Dun cock hackle fibers
Body: Stripped quill from dark brown cock hackle (well lacquered)
Hackle: Extra long stiff natural dun cock hackles

Tups Indispensable
Tail: Honey dun with primrose yellow tag under
Body: Mixed scarlet and cream lamb's fur dubbing (which should appear creamy pink)
Hackle: Natural honey dun cocks

Leadwinged Coachman
Wings: Slips from dark gray wild duck wing quills (double divided)
Tail: Red-brown cock hackle fibers
Body: Peacock herl
Hackle: Red-brown cock hackles

Light Cahill
Wings: Flank of wood-duck or mandarin drake
Tail: Pale ginger cock hackle fibers
Body: Cream colored fox fur dubbing
Hackle: Pale ginger cock hackle

Mosquito
Wings: Grizzly hackle points
Tail: Grizzly cock hackle fibers
Body: White silk ribbed with black silk or stripped peacock quill
Hackle: Grizzly cock hackles

Badger Spider
Tail: Badger cock hackle fibers
Body: Flat gold tinsel
Hackle: Extra long stiff badger cock hackles

WET FLIES

Professor
Tail: Strip of red duck quill
Body: Yellow silk floss ribbed with flat gold tinsel
Hackle: Dark ginger
Wing: Speckled gray mallard flank

Light Hendrickson
Tail: Lemon wood-duck flank fibers
Body: Fawn colored fox fur dubbing
Hackle: Natural blue dun cock or hen
Wing: Lemon wood-duck flank

Dark Hendrickson
Tail: Lemon wood-duck flank fibers
Body: Brownish-gray fox fur dubbing
Hackle: Dark rusty dun
Wing: Lemon wood duck flank

Mormon Girl
Tail: None
Tag: Red silk floss
Body: Yellow silk floss
Hackle: Gray grizzle tied palmer
Wing: Gray mallard flank feather

Yellow Sally
Tail: Strip from yellow dyed duck quill
Body: Yellow silk floss ribbed with narrow gold tinsel
Hackle: Dyed yellow or natural ginger cock or hen
Wing: From dyed yellow duck quill

Cowdung
Tail: None
Tag: Flat gold tinsel
Body: Olive wool dubbing made by mixing hot orange and medium green wool
Hackle: Dark ginger
Wing: Gray duck quill

Silver Prince
Tail: Three short clipped strands of peacock herl
Body: Solid flat silver tinsel on padding of white floss ribbed with oval silver tinsel
Hackle: Black
Wing: Bronze mallard

Gordon
Tail: Lemon wood-duck fibers
Body: Old gold silk floss ribbed with fine oval gold tinsel
Hackle: Cream tipped badger
Wing: Lemon wood-duck

Black Gnat
Tail: None
Body: Black chenille
Hackle: Black cock or hen
Wing: Gray duck quill

Rube Wood
Tail: Fibers of teal flank or brown hackle
Body: Scarlet floss tip white chenille
Hackle: Brown
Wing: Gray mallard flank

Queen of Waters
Tail: Speckled gray mallard flank
Body: Orange silk floss ribbed with gold tinsel
Hackle: Ginger tied palmer
Wing: Speckled gray mallard flank

Coachman
Tail: None
Tag: Flat gold tinsel
Body: Peacock herl
Hackle: Red-brown cock or hen
Wing: White duck quill

Female Beaverkill
Tail: Fibers from gray mallard flank—egg sac, 1 turn yellow chenille
Body: Muskrat fur dubbing
Hackle: Medium red-brown cock or hen
Wing: Gray duck quill

Dark Cahill
Tail: Lemon wood-duck flank
Body: Blue-gray muskrat dubbing
Hackle: Medium red-brown
Wing: Lemon wood-duck flank

Scarlet Ibis
Tail: Small strip from dyed red duck quill
Body: Scarlet silk floss ribbed with oval gold tinsel
Hackle: Dyed scarlet
Wing: Duck quill dyed scarlet

Mallard Quill
Tail: Bronze mallard fibers
Body: Stripped peacock quill
Hackle: Dark brown cock or hen
Wing: Bronze mallard fibers

Campbells Fancy
Tail: Small golden pheasant crest
Body: Flat gold tinsel ribbed with fine golden wire
Hackle: Ginger furnace
Wing: Dark barred teal flank

California Coachman
Tail: Golden pheasant tippet
Body: In 3 equal parts—first part, peacock herl—second part, yellow silk floss—third part, peacock herl
Hackle: Dyed yellow cock or hen
Wing: White duck quill

Quill Gordon
Tail: Lemon wood-duck flank fibers
Body: Stripped peacock quill ribbed with fine silver wire
Hackle: Natural blue dun
Wing: Lemon wood-duck flank fibers

Rio Grande King
Tail: Yellow hackle fibers
Body: Black chenille with gold tip
Hackle: Yellow
Wing: White duck quill

Ginger Quill
Tail: Fibers from ginger hackle
Body: Stripped peacock quill
Hackle: Ginger cock or hen
Wing: Light gray duck quill

Grizzly King
Tail: Strip from red dyed duck quill
Body: Green silk floss ribbed with narrow flat gold tinsel
Hackle: Light tipped badger
Wing: Speckled gray mallard flank

Stonefly
Tail: 3 or 4 strands of speckled partridge tail or bronze mallard
Body: Light gray fur dubbing ribbed with primrose yellow silk thread
Hackle: Dark gray grizzle
Wing: Hen pheasant quill

Light Cahill
Tail: Lemon wood-duck flank
Body: Cream fox fur dubbing
Hackle: Pale ginger
Wing: Lemon wood-duck flank

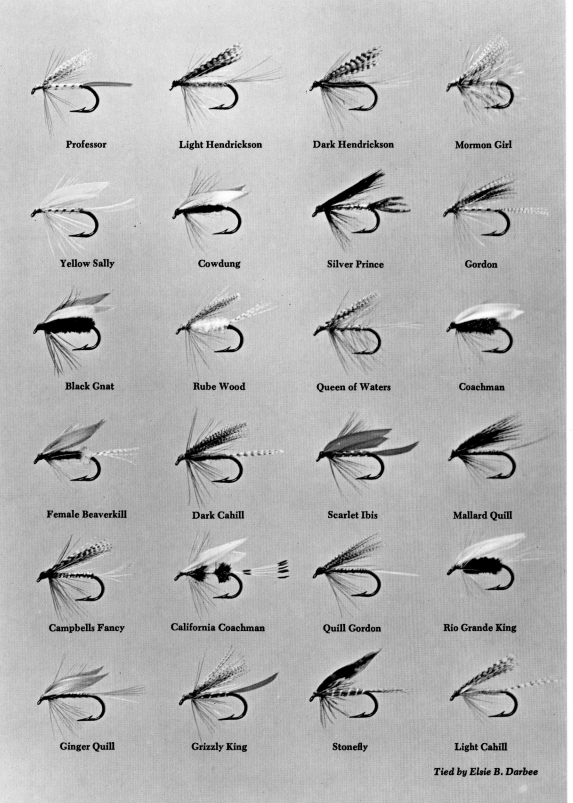

Professor   Light Hendrickson   Dark Hendrickson   Mormon Girl

Yellow Sally   Cowdung   Silver Prince   Gordon

Black Gnat   Rube Wood   Queen of Waters   Coachman

Female Beaverkill   Dark Cahill   Scarlet Ibis   Mallard Quill

Campbells Fancy   California Coachman   Quill Gordon   Rio Grande King

Ginger Quill   Grizzly King   Stonefly   Light Cahill

Tied by Elsie B. Darbee

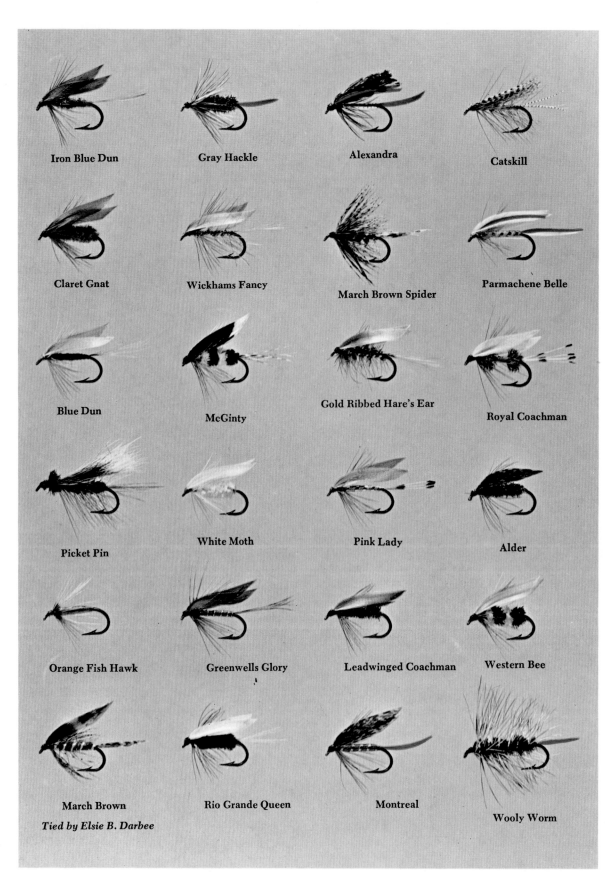

Iron Blue Dun   Gray Hackle   Alexandra   Catskill

Claret Gnat   Wickhams Fancy   March Brown Spider   Parmachene Belle

Blue Dun   McGinty   Gold Ribbed Hare's Ear   Royal Coachman

Picket Pin   White Moth   Pink Lady   Alder

Orange Fish Hawk   Greenwells Glory   Leadwinged Coachman   Western Bee

March Brown   Rio Grande Queen   Montreal   Wooly Worm

Tied by Elsie B. Darbee

WET FLIES

Iron Blue Dun
Tail: Coch-y-bondhu hackle fibers
Tag: (tie in after tail) red silk floss
Body: Mole fur dubbing
Hackle: Coch-y-bondhu cock or hen
Wing: Dark gray duck quill

Gray Hackle
Tail: Fiber from dyed red duck quill
Body: Peacock herl
Hackle: Gray grizzly

Alexandra
Tail: Fibers from dyed red duck quill
Body: Flat silver tinsel
Hackle: Black cock or hen
Wing: Peacock sword herl strands with slips of dyed red duck quill at sides

Catskill
Tail: Lemon wood-duck fibers
Body: Brown silk floss
Hackle: Medium red-brown tied palmer
Wing: Lemon wood-duck

Claret Gnat
Body: Claret chenille
Hackle: Dyed claret cock or hen
Wing: Medium gray duck quill

Wickhams Fancy
Tail: Ginger
Body: Flat gold tinsel, ribbing; gold wire
Hackle: Ginger tied palmer
Wing: Medium gray duck quill

March Brown Spider
Tail: Fibers from speckled partridge tail
Body: Hare's ear fur dubbing, ribbed with narrow gold tinsel
Hackle: Brown partridge

Parmachene Belle
Tail: Married strands of red and white duck quill (red at top)
Tag: Flat gold tinsel
Body: Yellow wool ribbed with flat gold tinsel
Hackle: 1 red, 1 white wound together
Wing: From white duck quill with narrow dyed red duck quill slips at sides

Blue Dun
Tail: Fibers from Blue Dun cock hackle
Body: Muskrat fur dubbing
Hackle: Blue Dun cock or hen
Wing: Medium blue-gray duck quill

McGinty
Tail: Fibers from dyed red hackle and barred teal flank
Body: Alternate bands of black and yellow chenille
Hackle: Medium red-brown cock or hen
Wing: White tipped blue mallard sections or white tipped turkey

Gold Ribbed Hare's Ear
Tail: Brown hackle fibers
Body: Hare's ear fur dubbing ribbed with flat gold tinsel
Hackle: Pick out dubbing at throat to represent hackle
Wing: Light gray duck quill

Royal Coachman
Tail: Fibers from golden pheasant tippet
Body: Divided in equal thirds—first third peacock herl, next red floss, followed by peacock herl
Hackle: Natural red-brown cock or hen
Wing: White duck quill

Picket Pin
Tail: Brown hackle fibers
Body: Peacock herl
Hackle: Brown tied palmer
Wing: From white tipped gray squirrel tail
Head: Peacock herl

White Moth
Tail: None
Tag: Orange silk floss
Body: White chenille
Hackle: White cock or hen
Wing: White duck quill

Pink Lady
Tail: Fibers from golden pheasant tippet
Body: Pink silk floss ribbed with flat gold tinsel
Hackle: Ginger cock or hen
Wing: Gray duck quill

Alder
Tail: None
Tag: Flat gold tinsel
Body: Bronze peacock herl
Hackle: Black cock or hen
Wing: Dark speckled brown hen quill

Orange Fish Hawk
Tail: None
Tag: Flat gold tinsel
Body: Orange silk floss ribbing; flat gold tinsel
Hackle: Light cream badger with gray center, cock or hen

Greenwells Glory
Tail: None
Tag: Flat gold tinsel
Body: Medium olive green silk floss ribbed with fine oval gold tinsel
Hackle: Ginger cock or hen
Wing: Dark gray duck quill

Leadwinged Coachman
Tail: None
Tag: Flat gold tinsel
Body: Peacock herl
Hackle: Dark red-brown
Wing: Dark gray duck quill

Western Bee
Tail: None
Tag: Flat gold tinsel
Body: Alternate bands of black and yellow chenille
Hackle: Ginger
Wing: Gray duck quill

March Brown
Tail: Fibers from speckled partridge tail
Body: Hare's ear fur dubbing, ribbed with primrose yellow thread
Hackle: Speckled brown partridge
Wing: Hen pheasant quill

Rio Grande Queen
Tail: Dyed yellow hackle fibers
Tag: Red floss tied under tail
Body: Black chenille
Hackle: Black cock or hen
Wing: White duck quill

Montreal
Tail: Narrow strip from dyed red duck quill
Body: Claret silk floss ribbed with flat gold tinsel
Hackle: Claret cock or hen
Wing: Speckled hen or turkey quill

Wooly Worm
Tail: Strip from dyed red duck quill
Body: Black chenille ribbed with silver oval tinsel
Hackle: Gray grizzly tied palmer

Badger Bivisible

Head hackle: 2 long stiff fibered white saddle hackles followed by 3 pairs of long stiff badger saddle hackles each a trifle smaller than the preceding pair. These hackles are wound tightly against the white head hackles toward the rear of the fly. The tips of the last pair of hackles used form the tail. The finishing tie off is at the tail of the fly and is finished with colorless or amber head cement

Soldier Palmer

Tail: Stiff ginger red hackle fibers
Body: Red silk floss ribbed with flat gold tinsel
Hackle: Ginger red saddle tied palmer over body to shoulder. 4 extra stiff ginger red saddle hackles at shoulder
Head: Clear cement or black lacquer

MacIntosh

Wing: Tied at center of hook lying flat along hook shank—a bunch of brown bucktail or fox squirrel hair
Hackle: Put on over wing wound very closely to head—stiff brown saddle hackles
Head: Clear cement or black lacquer

Birds' Stonefly (Dry)

Tail: 2 whisks black bear paw
Body: Orange silk floss with bands of furnace hackle clipped short. The latter is not palmered but tied in distinct bands
Hackle: Furnace pressed flat to project at sides only, lacquered and trimmed
Wing: Brown bucktail spread flat over body
Head: Orange tying silk
Feelers: 2 whisks black bear paw

Grey Wulff

Tail: Brown hair from deer tail or calf
Body: Gray fur dubbing
Wings: Brown from deer tail or calf
Hackle: 6 stiff dun saddle hackles
Head: Clear cement or black lacquer

Hairwinged Rat-Faced McDougal

Tail: Stiff white bucktail hair
Body: Creamy gray deer hair clipped to shape
Wings: White calf hair or white bucktail or polar bear tied full and set up ¼–½″ higher than the hackle fibers
Hackles: 3 pairs of bright ginger saddle hackles—fibers should be extra stiff and fairly long
Head: Finish with clear cement or black lacquer may be used

Colonel Monel

Tail: Stiff ginger hackle fibers
Body: Peacock herl ribbed with red silk, stiff grizzly hackle tied palmer over body
Hackles: At shoulder 4 very stiff saddle hackles

Hunt's Wasp

Tail: Stiff dyed red hackle fibers
Body: In 5 equal segments, black at tail, yellow, black, yellow, black, wound to form a taper, using alternate bands of wool yarn
Hackle: 6 saddle hackles, 2 each furnace grizzly and light badger wound mixed to head
Head: Clear cement or black lacquer

Birds' Stonefly (Nymph No. 1)

Tail: Two sections from turkey pointer quill dyed dark gray
Body: Rough gray muskrat fur ribbed with yellow floss silk
Thorax: Peacock herl with clear plastic strip over top
Hackle: Gray through thorax to project at sides only
Head: Yellow tying silk

Salmon Skater Fly

Hook: Size 12 as light as possible consistent with strength
Hackles: Color may vary to suit hackle available but hackle must be extremely long and very stiff—best comes from the throat of old gamecocks or other roosters such as Plymouth Rock, Buff Leghorn. The hackles are wound as closely as possible from just opposite hook point to head. 6 or 8 hackles are often used. The diameter of the fly must be at least that of a silver dollar, larger if possible
Head: Should be finished with clear cement which is thin and put on so as to saturate the butts of the hackles but must not be used so copiously that it runs up into the hackle and causes it to be too stiff to hook fish. The general practice is to apply thin cement sparingly both at head and tail making sure it penetrates thoroughly full length of hook thus cementing hackles in place

Dr. Park Dry Fly

Tail: A bunch of stiff white bucktail hair
Wings: White bucktail hair
Hackles: 3 pairs of very stiff badger saddle hackles several turns tied in front of wings; balance tied full length of hook to tail
Head: Finish with clear cement or black lacquer

Brown Bivisible

Tail: Stiff brown hackle fibers
Body: Entire hook palmered closely with stiff brown saddle hackles at least 6 in number, faced with 2 stiff white saddle hackles at head
Head: Clear cement or black lacquer

Pink Lady Palmer

Tail: Light ginger hackle fibers
Body: Pink floss silk ribbed with flat gold tinsel
Hackle: A stiff ginger saddle hackle tied Palmer over body. Shoulder hackles 4 stiff light ginger saddle hackles faced with 2 chartreuse yellow dyed saddle hackles at head
Head: Clear cement or black lacquer

White Wing Black Gnat

Tail: Stiff black hackle fibers or stiff black bear hair
Body: Dyed black deer hair clipped to shape
Wings: White calf tail or bucktail hair
Hackles: 6 stiff black saddles, the last pair of which are tied ahead of wings
Head: Black lacquer

Birds' Stonefly (Nymph No. 2)

Tail: Two sections from turkey pointer quill dyed dark brown
Body: Rough dark brown fox fur ribbed with orange silk floss
Thorax: Peacock herl with plastic strip over top
Hackle: Brown through thorax to project at sides only
Head: Orange tying silk

Badger Bivisible

Hair Winged Rat-Faced McDougal

Dr. Park Dry Fly

Soldier Palmer

Colonel Monel

Brown Bivisible

MacIntosh

Hunt's Wasp

Pink Lady Palmer

Birds' Stonefly (Dry)

Birds' Stonefly (Nymph No. 1)

White Wing Black Gnat

Grey Wulff

Salmon Skater Fly

Birds' Stonefly (Nymph No. 2)

Dry Salmon Flies Tied by H. A. Darbee,
Stoneflies Tied by Dan Bailey

Humboldt Railbird

Silver Demon

Alaska Mary Ann

Skunk

Improved Governor

Cuming's Special

Kalama Special

Horner's
Silver Shrimp

Copper Demon

Silver Hilton

Royal Coachman

Queen Bess

Orleans Barber

Boss

Orange Optic

Tied by E. H. Rosborough

STEELHEAD FLIES

Humboldt Railbird
Hook: No. 4 or No. 6, 2XS–1XL
Tail: Wine or claret hackle fibers
Body: Wine or claret yarn; palmer with either wine or claret saddle hackle
Hackle: Narrow; shoulder hackle, long bright yellow
Wing: Silver squirrel tail or barred teal; shoulders, medium jungle cock
Head: Black

Skunk
Hook: No. 4 to No. 8, Reg. or 1XL
Tail: Short, thick bunch of red hackle fibers
Body: Black chenille, ribbed with medium to wide oval silver tinsel
Hackle: Black, long and soft
Wing: Fairly short white bucktail somewhat flared
Head: Black

Kalama Special
Hook: No. 4 to No. 8, 2XS–1XL
Tail: Red hackle fibers
Body: Deep or medium yellow yarn
Hackle: Badger palmer tied with another longer one added at shoulder
Wing: White polar bear or impala
Head: Black

Silver Hilton
Hook: No. 4 to No. 8, 2XS–1XL
Tail: Bunch of speckled mallard
Body: Black chenille, ribbed with wide to medium flat silver tinsel
Hackle: Gray grizzly
Wings: Flared out gray hackle tips, almost long enough to reach end of tail
Head: Black

Orleans Barber
Hook: No. 4 to No. 8, 2XS–1XL
Tail: Long matched barred wood-duck
Body: Red chenille
Hackle: Long wide and soft gray grizzly hackle, guinea is also used
Wing: None
Head: Black

Silver Demon
Hook: No. 2 to No. 6, 2XS, 1 or 2XL
Tail: Hot orange hackle fibers
Body: Wide oval silver tinsel over thin floss core
Hackle: Wide hot orange
Wing: Silver squirrel or barred teal, large jungle cock
Head: Black

Improved Governor
Hook: No. 4 to No. 8, 2XS–1XL
Tail: Bunch of red hackle fibers
Body: Rear third, red yarn which is ribbed with narrow oval gold with tip under the tail; front two thirds of body thick peacock herl over core
Hackle: Dark furnace
Wing: Dark brown bucktail or brown turkey; shoulders, medium length jungle cock
Head: Black

Horner's Silver Shrimp
Hook: No. 2 to No. 8, 2XS–1XL
Tail: Thick gray or light brown bucktail body hair
Body: Wide oval silver tinsel over tapered floss core. Space it a bit and palmer between spaces with a long gray grizzly saddle hackle
Hackle: Back of body is tied in on top of tail of thick gray deer hair. Do this before building body. Back is pulled forward and tied down at head. Lacquer heavily on back
Head: Very large, black, with painted white eye

Royal Coachman
Hook: No. 2 to No. 8, 2XS–1XL
Tail: Half dozen golden pheasant tippet fibers
Body: Red or flame fluorescent yarn; red tip under tail; butt and shoulder of heavy peacock flue
Hackle: Dark brown or furnace
Wing: Long white bucktail, impala or polar bear
Head: Black

Boss
Hook: No. 2 to No. 6, 2XS–1 or 2XL
Tail: Long thick bunch of black ringtail
Body: Tapered black yarn, ribbed with wide flat silver tinsel
Hackle: Long extra wide deep hot orange
Wing: None. Eyes of extra large nickeled bead chain cross-whipped in front of hackle
Head: Red or orange

Alaska Mary Ann
Hook: No. 1/0 to No. 6, 2XS & 1 to 3XL
Tail: Red hackle fibers
Body: White or cream yarn, ribbed with wide flat silver tinsel
Hackle: Shoulders, medium jungle cock
Wing: Long white polar bear
Head: Black

Cuming's Special
Hook: No. 4 to No. 8, Reg. or 1XL
Tail: None
Body: Rear third, deep yellow yarn; front two thirds wine or claret yarn, ribbed with narrow oval gold tinsel, full length
Hackle: Claret, long and soft
Wing: Dark brown natural bucktail; shoulders, short jungle cock
Head: Black

Copper Demon
Hook: No. 1/0 to No. 6, 2XS–1XL
Tail: Very short bunch of hot orange maribou
Body: Wide oval copper tinsel over orange floss core
Hackle: Hot orange
Wing: Hot orange polar bear
Head: Black

Queen Bess
Hook: No. 2 to No. 6, 2XS–1XL
Tail: Bunch of black and white barred silver squirrel
Body: Wide oval silver tinsel over thin tapered white floss core
Hackle: None
Wing: Under wing, long bright yellow polar bear or bucktail; top wing, silver squirrel tail; anchored high for fast water
Head: Black

Orange Optic
Hook: 2X stout, 2X short. In general use No. 1 and 1/0 sizes for all optics
Body: Wide oval silver tinsel over a tapered floss core
Hackle: Bright red, heavy and long
Wing: Hot orange polar bear
Head: May be built up of heavy tying thread or a split brass bead clamped over the hook. Enameled black with large eye. White iris with large red pupil

STEELHEAD FLIES

Jock Scott
Hook: No. 2 to No. 6, 2XS–1XL
Tail: Golden pheasant crest
Body: Rear third, bright yellow yarn; front two thirds, black yarn or chenille; ribbed with wide flat silver tinsel
Hackle: Thick bunch of guinea body feather stripped and tied under as a throat. If wound it hides body too much.
Wing: Dark brown bucktail or mallard grand nashua. Top, overdrape, half dozen strands of peacock sword as long as wing. Shoulders, large jungle cock
Head: Black

Badger Hackle Peacock
Hook: No. 4 to No. 8, 2XS–1XL, or Reg.
Tail: Red hackle fibers. Tip under and in front of tail oval gold
Body: Thick peacock herl over green yarn core
Hackle: Long soft badger hackle
Wing: None
Head: Black

Black Gordon
Hook: No. 4 to No. 8, 2XS–1XL
Tail: None
Body: Rear third, red yarn; front two thirds, black yarn; ribbed with narrow oval gold tinsel
Hackle: Long, black, and soft
Wing: Black or very dark brown bucktail
Head: Black

Joe O'Donnell
Hook: No. 4 and No. 6, 2XS–1XL
Tail: Red and yellow mixed hackle fibers
Body: Cream chenille
Hackle: Tied on as a collar in front of wing; red and yellow wound mixed to blend; medium width. Jungle shoulders should be put on alongside of wing prior to hackle
Wing: Splayed, long badger hackle
Head: Red

Umpqua Special
Hook: No. 4 or No. 6, Reg., or 1XL
Tail: White bucktail
Body: Rear third of yellow yarn, front two thirds of red yarn or chenille; rib with wide flat silver tinsel
Hackle: Brown, tied as a collar in front of wing, rather narrow
Wing: White bucktail with smaller bunches of red bucktail on each side
Head: Red

Thunder and Lightning
Hook: No. 4 to No. 8, 2XS–1XL
Tail: Golden pheasant crest
Body: Black yarn, ribbed with wide to medium oval gold tinsel
Hackle: Hot orange, long and soft
Wing: Dark brown bucktail or dark mottled turkey tail feather; shoulders, medium length jungle cock
Head: Black

Al's Special
Hook: No. 2 to No. 6, 2XS–1XL
Tail: Bunch of red hackle fibers
Body: Bright yellow chenille, ribbed with wide flat silver tinsel
Hackle: Bright red, medium width
Wing: Thick bushy polar bear as long as tail; shoulders, medium length jungle cock
Head: Black

Gray Hackle
Hook: No. 4 to No. 8, 2XS–1XL, or Reg.
Tail: Bunch of red hackle fibers
Body: Medium yellow yarn, ribbed with wide to medium gold tinsel, may be oval or flat
Hackle: Long soft gray grizzly
Wing: None
Head: Black

Thor
Hook: No. 2 to No. 8, 2XS–1XL
Tail: Bunch of hot orange hackle fibers
Body: Red or wine chenille
Hackle: Dark furnace
Wing: White bucktail, impala or polar bear
Head: Black

Burlap
Hook: No. 2 to No. 8, 2XS–1XL
Tail: Thick bunch light brown or gray bucktail
Body: From 2 to 5 twisted strands of burlap; twist into piece of tan buttonhole twist; score body heavily with scissor points to make as ragged as possible
Hackle: Gray grizzly, long and soft
Head: Black

Umpqua Red Brat
Hook: No. 4 to No. 8, 2XS–1XL
Tail: Thick bunch of speckled mallard side
Body: Red or claret chenille, ribbed with wide to medium flat silver tinsel
Hackle: Wide speckled mallard side wound tip first and over to make it fold back spider style past hook bend
Wing: Red or claret polar, thick and bushy
Head: Black

Coles Comet
Hook: No. 2 to No. 6, 2XS, 1 or 2XL
Tail: Long thick bunch of orange impala
Body: Wide oval gold tinsel over thin tapered yellow floss core
Hackle: Extra wide of yellow and hot orange mixed
Wing: None
Eyes: Brass colored, pull bead chain tied in front of hackle by cross whipping
Head: Hot orange

Lady Godiva
Hook: No. 1/0 to No. 6, 2XS–1 to 3XL
Tail: Red and yellow mixed hackle fibers; tip under tail flat silver tinsel; butt, red chenille
Body: White yarn, ribbed with wide flat silver tinsel
Hackle: None
Wing: Bright red polar bear
Head: Black

Black Prince
Hook: No. 4 to No. 8, 2XS–1XL
Tail: Red, short thick bunch of red hackle fibers
Body: Rear third, medium yellow wool; front two thirds, black yarn, or chenille; ribbed with wide to medium silver oval tinsel
Hackle: Black, long and soft
Wing: Black bucktail
Head: Black

Golden Demon
Hook: No. 4 to No. 8, Reg. or 1XL
Tail: Golden pheasant crest plume
Body: Wide oval gold tinsel over a thin tapered yellow floss core
Hackle: Hot orange
Wing: Dark brown natural bucktail; shoulders, large jungle cock
Head: Black

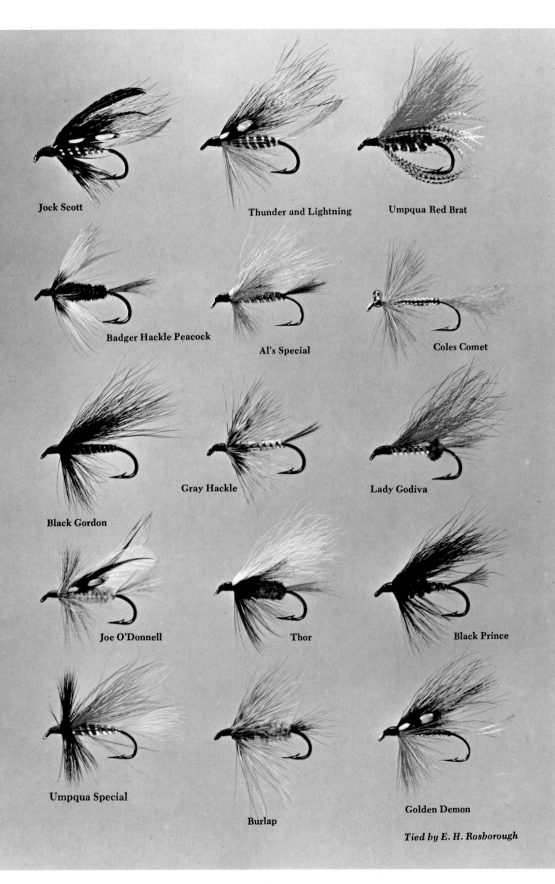

Jock Scott

Thunder and Lightning

Umpqua Red Brat

Badger Hackle Peacock

Al's Special

Coles Comet

Black Gordon

Gray Hackle

Lady Godiva

Joe O'Donnell

Thor

Black Prince

Umpqua Special

Burlap

Golden Demon

Tied by E. H. Rosborough

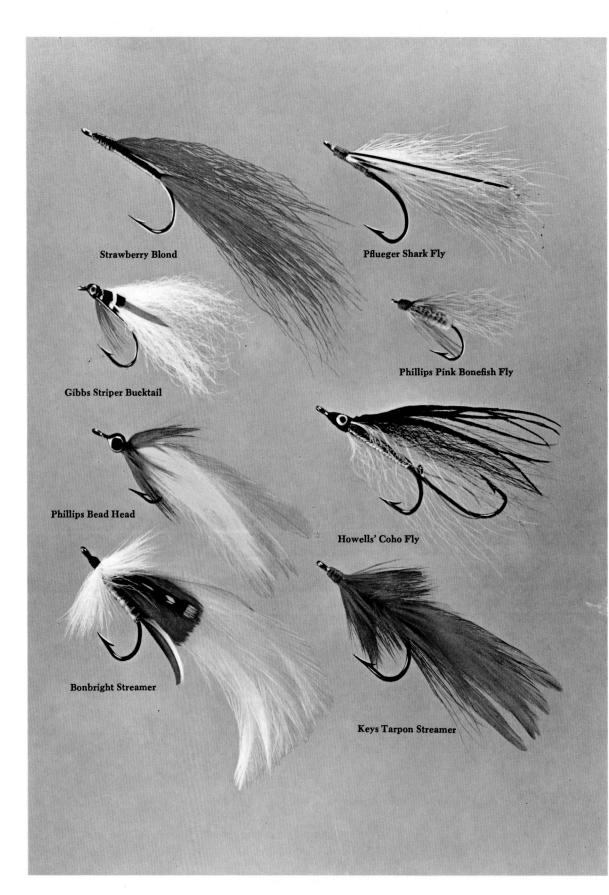

Strawberry Blond

Pflueger Shark Fly

Gibbs Striper Bucktail

Phillips Pink Bonefish Fly

Phillips Bead Head

Howells' Coho Fly

Bonbright Streamer

Keys Tarpon Streamer

SALTWATER FLIES

Strawberry Blond
Wing: Slender wing of dark red bucktail
Tail: Long bright orange bucktail, twice as heavy as wing
Body: Wide gold tinsel
Head: Black

Gibbs Striper Bucktail
Head: Black with little yellow painted eyes with red centers
Body: Narrow flat silver tinsel
Throat: Few strands of red hackle fibers, rather long
Wing: A bunch of Asiatic goat hair with some of the underhair left in
Shoulder: Section of dark blue swan wing feather, half as long as wing, placed to make a stripe down the center of the wing
Cheeks: Short barred bali duck

Phillips Bead Head
Wing: 6 long bright yellow hackles
Body: Yellow chenille
Hackle: Long bright red hackle, extends beyond bend of hook
Bead Head: Lacquered red, with an eye on each side, white iris, black center

Bonbright Streamer
Head: Black
Tail: 2 narrow, rather long sections of red-and-white duck wing feather, married. Crest feather of golden pheasant over
Body: Medium flat silver tinsel, built up slightly near head
Rib: Fine oval silver tinsel
Throat: White hackle fibers, medium length
Wing: 4 long white neck hackles
Shoulders: Red duck breast feather, tied so as not to conceal the body. Golden crest feather nearly as long as wing
Cheeks: Jungle cock, centered

Pflueger Shark Fly
Wing: 3 sections of white polar bear hair tied with red thread on top of hook, first section being placed midway on the hook shank and all sections forming a wing that extends the length of the hook beyond the bend
Body: The red tying thread makes the body
Shoulder: 3 flat strips of medium width tinsel, placed fan-wise on each side, two-thirds the length of the wing
Head: Red

Phillips Pink Bonefish Fly
Wing: Pale pink bucktail extending length of body beyond the hook
Body: Pale pink chenille
Throat: Long pink hackle, a shade darker than body
Head: Bright red

Howells' Coho Fly
Trailer hook attached to main hook with leader material
Wing: Long white polar bear hair above body, overlaid with bright green polar bear hair, topped by six or eight slender strands of peacock herl
Throat: Long white polar bear hair
Body: Heavy oval silver tinsel, lacquered
Head: Black with white eye, black center

Keys Tarpon Streamer
Head: Red
Body: Bright red hackles tied with red thread, in six evenly spaced collars, or tied palmer style
Tail: Long slender bunch of orange bucktail with 3 orange hackles (long) on each side, turned with the dull side outward

STREAMER FLIES

Green Cosseboom
(swift water dressing)
Tag: Flat silver tinsel
Tail: Chartreuse green floss about length of hook shank used
Body: Chartreuse green floss ribbed with flat silver tinsel
Wing: White tipped gray squirrel tail tied at a slight angle above body, should be sparse and slightly longer than tail
Hackle: Yellow, tied sparse after wing and left flaring
Head: Black lacquer

Nine-Three
Body: Flat silver tinsel
Wing: A small bunch of white bucktail extending beyond the bend of the hook. Over the bucktail are 3 medium green saddle hackles tied flat, over which are 4 black saddle hackles tied on edge
Cheeks: Jungle cock
Head: Black lacquer

Red Trude
Tag: Flat silver tinsel
Tail: Scarlet goose quill
Body: Scarlet silk floss ribbed with flat silver tinsel
Wings: Brown fox squirrel tail
Hackle: Brown tied over wing so as to flare
Head: Black lacquer

Muddler Minnow
Tag: Flat gold tinsel
Tail: A strip of speckled brown turkey quill feather
Body: Flat gold tinsel
Wing: Sparse black bear hair with a strip of speckled brown turkey quill feather at either side
Hackle: A bunch of brown deer hair tied about ⅔ hook length, butts cut off to form a bulky head, tie off, finished with orange ambroid cement

Nite Owl
Tag: Flat silver tinsel
Tail: A strip of dyed yellow goose quill as long as the hook
Butt: Scarlet wool or seal's fur
Body: Yellow silk floss ribbed with oval silver tinsel
Wings: Wide white hackles with narrow scarlet hackles at side. The scarlet hackles are about half the length of the white wings
Head: Black lacquer

Cain's River Silver Doctor Streamer
Tail: 2 strips of barred wood-duck
Body: Medium flat silver tinsel
Wing: 2 medium brown saddle hackles with a gray Plymouth Rock saddle hackle on each side
Cheeks: Jungle cock
Hackles: Several turns of French blue saddle hackle with a few turns of Plymouth Rock saddle hackle at head. These hackles are wound so as to flare and are not pulled down close to the body
Head: Black lacquer

Magog Smelt
Tag: Flat silver tinsel
Tail: A small bunch of barred teal flank feather
Body: Flat silver tinsel
Wing: A very small bunch of white bucktail with a very small bunch of yellow bucktail over and a small bunch of violet bucktail topped by 6 strands of green peacock herl
Shoulders: Small barred teal flank feathers about ⅓ as long as wings
Throat: A small bunch of dyed red hackle fibers
Head: Black lacquer with tiny yellow eyes with black centers (eyes are painted on head)

Parson Tom
Body: Flat silver tinsel ribbed with oval silver tinsel
Hackle: A small bunch of white bucktail tied under hook extending about ½" past hook bend
Wing: Above the body 5 strands of green peacock herl over which are tied 4 light blue saddle hackles. A pair of light gray grizzly saddle hackles are tied on each side of the blue hackles
Sides: Silver pheasant feathers
Cheeks: Jungle cock
Head: Black lacquer

Red-and-White Bucktail
(fancy pattern)
Body: Flat silver tinsel ribbed with oval silver tinsel
Wing: A small bunch of white bucktail with a small bunch of red bucktail over, over which is a bunch of green peacock herl as topping
Cheeks: Jungle cock
Head: Black lacquer

Green Ghost
Tag: Flat silver tinsel, 3 or 4 turns
Body: Orange silk floss ribbed with narrow flat silver tinsel
Throat: 5-6 strands peacock herl extending to hook point with white bucktail same length tied underneath
Wing: 6 medium green saddle hackles topped with golden pheasant crest
Sides: Silver pheasant feather
Cheeks: Jungle cock
Head: Black lacquer

Silversides
Tail: Golden pheasant crest
Body: Pale yellow silk floss ribbed with silver oval tinsel wound in 3 or 4 close turns then spiralled up body
Shape: Body thin at tail, thick at thorax
Wings: Mixed bucktail—white, red, green and brown
Hackle: Long blue dun with hackle reaching to point of hook tied on over wing
Head: Black lacquer

Ambrose Bucktail
Tail: A small bunch of scarlet and white bucktail
Body: Yellow chenille ribbed with flat gold tinsel
Hackle: 1 scarlet followed by 1 black hackle tied fairly full
Wing: White bucktail topped with brown bucktail
Head: Black lacquer

Dark Tiger
Tag: Flat gold tinsel
Tail: Tips of 2 very small yellow neck hackles tied back to back
Body: Yellow chenille
Throat: A small bunch of dyed red hackle fibers
Wings: A small bunch of brown bucktail dyed yellow extending just beyond end of hook
Cheeks: Very short jungle cock
Head: Yellow silk thread heavily lacquered with clear lacquer

Warden's Worry
Tail: Narrow section of red goose quill feather moderately long
Body: Orange yellow wool picked out rough ribbed with narrow oval gold tinsel
Throat: 3 or 4 turns of yellow hackle
Wing: A small bunch of light brown bucktail extending just beyond the end of the tail
Head: Black lacquer

Alaska Mary Ann
Tail: A very small bunch of red hackle fibers
Body: Dressed full, of light tan silk floss ribbed with medium flat silver tinsel
Wing: Small bunch of white polar bear extending to end of tail
Cheeks: Jungle cock tied short
Head: Black lacquer

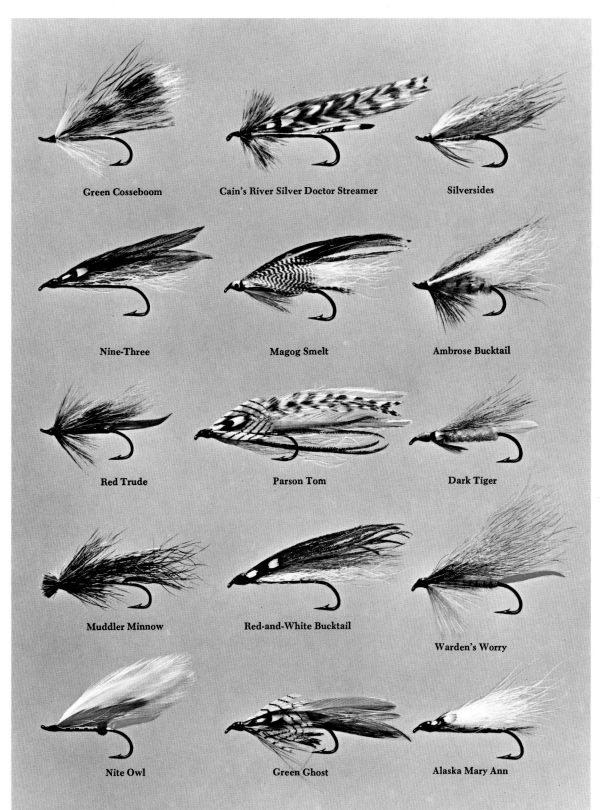

Green Cosseboom

Cain's River Silver Doctor Streamer

Silversides

Nine-Three

Magog Smelt

Ambrose Bucktail

Red Trude

Parson Tom

Dark Tiger

Muddler Minnow

Red-and-White Bucktail

Warden's Worry

Nite Owl

Green Ghost

Alaska Mary Ann

Tied by H. A. Darbee

Cain's River Roaring Rapids Streamer

Golden Witch Streamer

Yellow Butcher Streamer

Black Ghost Streamer

Grey Ghost Streamer

Royal Coachman Streamer

Jim's Gem Streamer

Sky Komish Sunrise Streamer

Black Nosed Dace Streamer

Badger Streamer

Grizzly King Streamer

Jane Craig Streamer

White Maribou Streamer

Brass Hat Bucktail Streamer

Cain's River Black Demon Streamer

Tied by H. A. Darbee

STREAMER FLIES

Cain's River Roaring Rapids Streamer
Tag: Flat silver tinsel
Tail: 2 sections of barred wood-duck feather with a thin section of scarlet goose quill feather between
Body: Flat silver tinsel
Wing: 2 scarlet saddle hackles with a large yellow saddle hackle on each side
Cheeks: Jungle cock
Hackle: Put on over wing several turns of French blue saddle hackle
Head: Black lacquer

Black Ghost Streamer
Tag: Flat silver tinsel
Tail: Lemon yellow hackle fibers
Body: Black silk floss dressed full, ribbed with flat silver tinsel
Wing: 4 white saddle or neck hackles about an inch longer than hook
Sides: Jungle cock about ¼ length of wing
Hackle: Lemon yellow put on before the wing
Head: Black lacquer

Jim's Gem Streamer
Tag: Flat silver tinsel
Tail: Yellow hackle fibers
Body: Black chenille ribbed with flat silver tinsel
Wing: White bucktail—jungle cock shoulders optional
Hackle: Long badger tied over wing
Head: Black lacquer

Golden Witch Streamer
Tag: 4 or 5 turns flat silver tinsel
Body: Dressed very thin with orange silk floss ribbed with flat silver tinsel
Wing: 4 or 5 strands peacock herl as long as the hook over which are 4 barred Plymouth Rock saddle hackles extending about an inch beyond the hook
Shoulders: Each a golden pheasant tippet ⅓ as long as the wing
Cheeks: Jungle cock eyed feathers
Throat: A small bunch of white bucktail tied under body extending to just inside the bend of the hook; under this a small bunch of gray grizzly hackle fibers
Head: Black lacquer

Grey Ghost Streamer
Tag: Flat silver tinsel
Body: Orange silk floss ribbed with flat silver tinsel
Wing: A long golden pheasant crest tied directly over body about 1 inch longer than hook. Over this are 2 dyed gray saddle hackles about an inch and a half longer than hook with short hackles of the same color tied in about ⅓ the length of the first pair of hackles, over which are 5 or 6 strands of green peacock herl about the same length as the longest saddle hackles
Hackle: A small bunch of white bucktail tied under the body extending full length of the wing
Sides: Silver pheasant feather about ⅔ hook length
Cheeks: Jungle cock extending over ½ length of side feathers
Throat: A small golden pheasant crest feather tied about ½ the length of the sides underneath the white bucktail
Head: Black lacquer

Sky Komish Sunrise Streamer
Tag: Flat silver tinsel
Tail: A very small bunch of moderately long red hackle fibers over which is a very small bunch of yellow hackle fibers
Body: Red chenille ribbed with narrow flat silver tinsel
Wing: A small bunch of white polar bear hair extending beyond the tail
Hackle: Put on after wing—several turns of red hackle with several turns of yellow hackle ahead
Head: Black lacquer

Yellow Butcher Streamer
Body: Medium oval silver tinsel wound closely
Wing: Yellow maribou feather about one half inch longer than hook, over which is a bunch of herl from a light brown maribou feather. The brown maribou feather is the same volume and length as the yellow maribou
Sides: 3 heavy strands of peacock herl on each side of the wing tied in along the separation of the 2 colors of wing. Herl should be same length as the maribou
Cheeks: Jungle cock
Throat: The tip of a red hackle or a small bunch of red hackle fibers

Royal Coachman Streamer
Tag: Flat gold tinsel
Tail: A bunch of golden pheasant tippet fibers
Butt: Green peacock herl
Body: Red silk floss with a shoulder of green peacock herl same size as butt
Hackle: Put on before wing—brown saddle hackle dressed sparse
Wings: 4 white neck or saddle hackles about ⅓ longer than hook
Head: Black lacquer

Black Nosed Dace Streamer
Tail: A very short tuft of bright red yarn
Body: Flat silver tinsel ribbed with oval silver tinsel
Wing: A small bunch of white bucktail or polar bear hair over which is a small bunch of black bear hair slightly longer than the white over which is a small bunch of brown bucktail slightly longer than the black. Each bunch of hair should be of about equal volume and should be tied in so all hair is above the silver body and lies in 3 distinct layers of white, black and brown in equal proportions as viewed from the side
Head: Black lacquer

STREAMER FLIES

Badger Streamer
Body: Flat silver tinsel ribbed with oval silver tinsel
Wing: A small bunch of white polar bear hair or bucktail tied fairly long with badger hackles of equal length on either side. Tied underneath the body as hackle is a very sparse bunch of white polar bear extending just beyond the hook bend
Sides: Jungle cock nearly the length of the silver body
Head: Black lacquer

White Maribou Streamer
Tag: Flat silver tinsel
Tail: A bunch of dyed red hackle fibers
Body: Flat silver tinsel ribbed with oval silver tinsel
Wing: Tied full with white maribou extending beyond the tail topped with 5 or 6 strands of peacock herl
Cheeks: Jungle cock
Throat: A medium sized bunch of dyed red hackle fibers
Head: Black lacquer

Grizzly King Streamer
Tag: Flat gold tinsel
Tail: 2 narrow matched sections of red duck quill feather with curve upward
Body: Dressed thin of green silk floss ribbed with narrow flat gold tinsel
Throat: A medium sized bunch of gray grizzly hackle fibers
Wings: 4 gray grizzly saddle hackles
Sides: Barred teal body feathers ⅓ length of wing
Head: Black lacquer

Brass Hat Bucktail Streamer
Tail: A very small bunch of moderately long dyed yellow polar bear or bucktail hair
Butt: Black tying silk wound close against the wire body
Body: Yellow brass wire wound very close and burnished. Body must be heavily lacquered with clear lacquer
Wing: A small bunch of white bucktail over which is a small bunch of dyed yellow bucktail topped with a very few hairs of black bear or skunk. Wing extends about to the end of the tail. The various colored hairs in the wing must be kept separated by a turn of silk around each so they will show up plainly when viewed from the side
Head: Black lacquer

Jane Craig Streamer
Body: Flat silver tinsel
Hackle: Put on before wing—white neck or saddle hackle dressed about ⅓ as long as hook
Wing: 6 white saddle hackles extending beyond hook topped with 7 or 8 strands of green peacock herl as long as the wing
Cheeks: Moderately long jungle cock
Head: Black lacquer

Cain's River Black Demon Streamer
Tail: 2 medium width sections of barred wood duck tied rather long
Body: Flat gold tinsel
Wing: 4 black saddle hackles tied rather long
Sides: Jungle cock about half length of hook
Hackle: Tied on over wing several turns of orange saddle hackle about half length of the silver body
Head: Black lacquer

SALMON FLIES

Red Abbey
Tag: Flat silver tinsel
Tail: A section of scarlet dyed goose quill feather
Body: Red silk floss ribbed with flat silver tinsel
Wing: Brown bucktail
Hackle: Put on over wing several turns of brown cock hackle
Head: Black lacquer

Black Bomber
Tag: 2 turns of fine oval silver tinsel followed by lemon yellow floss
Tail: Golden pheasant crest
Body: Black seal's fur or wool yarn ribbed with silver oval tinsel
Hackle: Put on before wing—sparse black neck hackle
Wing: Black bear hair
Cheeks: Jungle cock
Topping: Golden pheasant crest
Head: Black lacquer

The Rat
Tag: Fine gold oval tinsel
Body: Bronze peacock herl
Wing: Mixed black and white calf tail
Hackle: Put on over wing several turns of badger hackle
Head: Black lacquer

Silver Abbey
Tag: Flat silver tinsel
Tail: A section of red dyed goose quill feather
Body: Flat silver tinsel ribbed with oval silver tinsel
Wing: White tipped gray squirrel tail
Hackle: Put on over wing several turns of gray grizzly hackle
Head: Black lacquer

Rusty Rat
Tag: Flat gold tinsel
Tail: A small bunch of bright green peacock sword herl
Body: Light orange silk floss forms third of body; 2 tags of the body floss are left to form a second tail about ⅔ of the way up the floss from the remaining third of the body which is formed of bronzed peacock herl
Wing: Mixed black and white calf tail
Hackle: Dark badger several turns put on over wing
Head: Black lacquer

Silver Gray
Tag: Fine silver oval tinsel, light yellow floss silk
Tail: Golden pheasant crest
Butt: Black ostrich herl
Body: Flat silver tinsel ribbed with oval silver tinsel
Hackle: Light badger palmered from ⅔ up the body to shoulder
Wing: A few strands of golden pheasant tippet doubled tied low over body extending to butt. Over these are married strands of white, yellow, blue and green goose nazuria or sides. These strands are married and matched. Over these narrow strips of teal and barred wood duck. At sides strips of bronze mallard and a golden pheasant crest topping over all.
Throat hackle: Barred widgeon or pintail fibers
Horns: Yellow and blue macaw
Head: Black lacquer

Copper Killer
Tag: Fine copper tinsel
Tail: A few strands of golden pheasant tippet
Butt: Scarlet wool
Body: Flat copper tinsel, oval copper tinsel, ribbing optional
Wing: Fox squirrel tail
Hackle: Tied sparse at throat only—hot orange hackle
Head: Black lacquer

Jock Scott
Tag: Flat silver tinsel
Tail: A golden pheasant crest, Indian crow over
Butt: Black ostrich herl
Body: First half lemon yellow floss silk ribbed with 4 turns of fine oval silver tinsel and veiled with yellow toucan breast and butted with black ostrich herl. Second half of body black floss silk palmered with black hackle and ribbed with silver oval tinsel
Wing: 2 strips of white tipped turkey tail over which are wings of married strips of yellow, red and blue goose side married to speckled bustard, florican bustard, dark speckled turkey, light speckled turkey. The wing having the lightest feathers at bottom and darkest at top. The mingling of color appears best when the strands of bustard, turkey, etc., are married between the dyed goose side. Over this foundation are side strips of teal, 2 strands of green peacock sword with narrow strips of bronze mallard, topped with a golden pheasant crest, jungle cock at sides
Cheeks: Small blue chatterer or kingfisher feather
Horns: Blue and yellow macaw
Head: Black lacquer

SALMON FLIES

Mitchell
Tag: Fine oval silver tinsel and yellow floss silk
Tail: Golden pheasant crest
Butt: Scarlet wool
Body: Black floss ribbed with oval silver tinsel
Shoulder hackle: Dyed yellow, black hackle at throat
Wings: Strips of black crow quill feather
Sides: Jungle cock
Cheeks: Blue chatter or kingfisher. A golden pheasant topping over all
Horns: Blue and yellow macaw
Head: Black lacquer

Mystery
Tag: 2 turns of fine oval silver tinsel followed by yellow silk floss
Tail: Golden pheasant crest
Butt: Black ostrich herl
Body: Flat silver tinsel ribbed with oval gold tinsel
Hackle: Sparse brown hackle
Wing: Brown bucktail
Cheek: Jungle cock, golden pheasant topping over all
Head: Black lacquer

Night Hawk
Tag: 2 turns of fine oval silver tinsel followed by lemon yellow silk floss
Tail: Golden pheasant crest with a short blue chatterer or kingfisher feather over
Butt: Scarlet wool
Body: Flat silver tinsel ribbed with oval silver tinsel
Hackle: Black at throat only
Wings: 2 strips of crow feather
Sides: Jungle cock
Cheeks: Short blue chatterer or kingfisher
Topping: Golden pheasant crest
Horns: Blue and yellow macaw
Head: Scarlet lacquer

Ross Special
Tag: Flat silver tinsel
Tail: Golden pheasant crest or yellow hackle fibers
Body: Red floss silk ribbed with flat silver tinsel
Wing: Fox squirrel tail
Cheeks: Jungle cock
Hackle: Yellow
Head: Black lacquer

Reduced Black Dose
Tag: Fine oval silver tinsel
Tail: Golden pheasant crest
Body: Black silk floss ribbed with fine oval silver tinsel
Wings: Strips of black crow, jungle cock at sides
Hackle: At throat only—black
Head: Black lacquer

Reduced Silver Gray
Tag: Flat silver tinsel
Tail: Golden pheasant crest
Body: Flat silver tinsel ribbed with oval silver tinsel
Hackle: 2 or 3 turns of light badger hackle at shoulder followed by light widgeon or pintail at throat
Wing: Bunched fibers of lemon wood-duck, jungle cock at sides
Head: Black lacquer

Squirrel Doctor
Tag: Flat silver tinsel
Tail: Golden pheasant crest
Butt: Scarlet wool
Body: Flat silver tinsel ribbed with oval silver tinsel
Hackle: Dyed kingfisher blue with speckled guinea at throat
Wing: White tipped grey squirrel tail with short golden pheasant tippet and a golden pheasant crest topping over all
Head: Scarlet lacquer

Silver Rat
Tag: Flat silver tinsel
Tail: Golden pheasant crest
Body: Flat silver tinsel ribbed with oval silver tinsel
Wing: Mixed black and white calf hair
Hackle: Badger put on over wing
Head: Black lacquer

Squirrel Tail
Tag: Fine oval silver tinsel
Tail: Golden pheasant crest or brown hackle fibers
Body: Black seal's fur ribbed with fine oval silver tinsel
Hackle: Sparse brown hackle at throat only
Wing: Pine squirrel or fox squirrel
Head: Black lacquer

Reduced Dusty Miller
Tag: Embossed silver tinsel
Tail: Golden pheasant crest
Body: Embossed silver tinsel ribbed with oval silver tinsel ⅔ length of body—last third of body orange silk floss ribbed with oval silver tinsel
Hackle: At throat only—gray guinea hackle fibers
Wings: Strips of bronze mallard with jungle cock at sides
Head: Black lacquer

Brown Bomber
Tag: 2 turns of fine oval silver tinsel followed by lemon yellow silk floss
Tail: Golden pheasant crest
Butt: Black ostrich herl
Body: Brown wool yarn ribbed with oval silver tinsel
Hackle: Brown at throat only
Wings: Brown bucktail, jungle cock at sides, golden pheasant topping over all
Head: Black lacquer

Black Dose
Tag: 2 turns fine oval silver tinsel followed by lemon yellow floss
Tail: Golden pheasant crest
Body: 2 turns of black silk floss followed by black seal's fur. The body is ribbed with oval silver tinsel with a black hackle tied Palmer from the black silk floss to the shoulder
Wing: Strips of golden pheasant tippet extending to the tail over which are wings of married yellow goose, florican bustard, red goose, dark speckled turkey, blue goose, sheathed with bronze mallard strips topped with golden pheasant crest; jungle cock at sides
Horns: Blue and yellow macaw
Head: Black lacquer

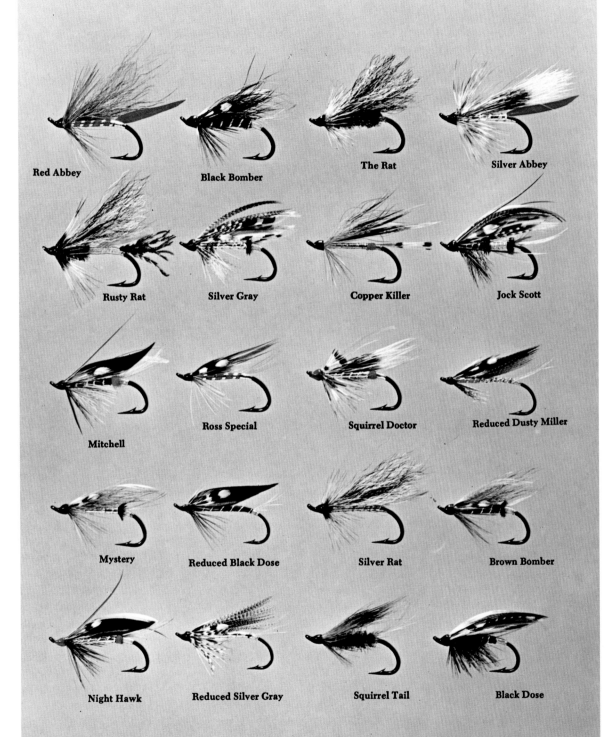

Red Abbey

Black Bomber

The Rat

Silver Abbey

Rusty Rat

Silver Gray

Copper Killer

Jock Scott

Mitchell

Ross Special

Squirrel Doctor

Reduced Dusty Miller

Mystery

Reduced Black Dose

Silver Rat

Brown Bomber

Night Hawk

Reduced Silver Gray

Squirrel Tail

Black Dose

Tied by H. A. Darbee

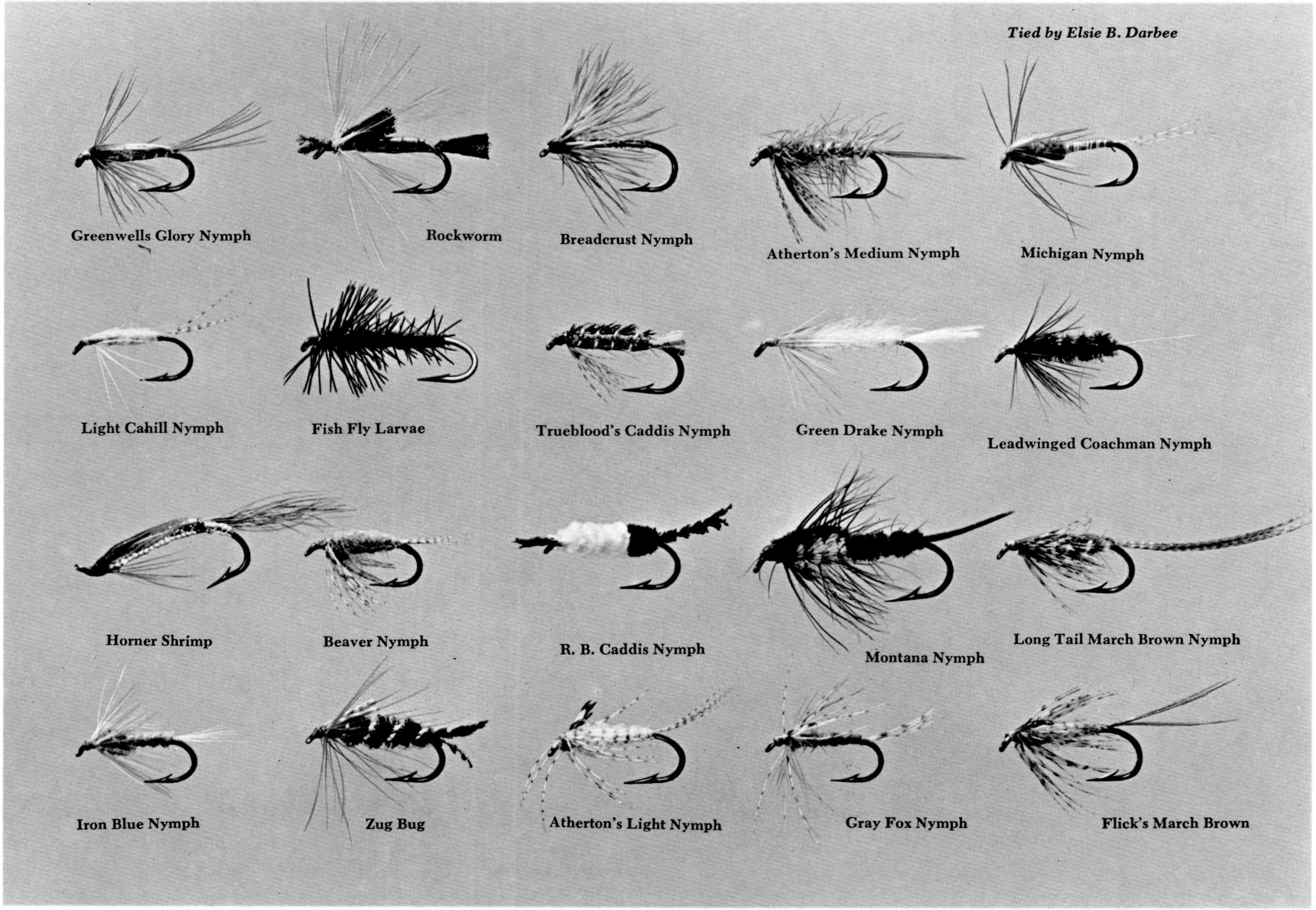

Tied by Elsie B. Darbee

Michigan Nymph

Leadwinged Coachman Nymph

Long Tail March Brown Nymph

Flick's March Brown

Atherton's Medium Nymph

Green Drake Nymph

Montana Nymph

Gray Fox Nymph

Breaderust Nymph

Trueblood's Caddis Nymph

R. B. Caddis Nymph

Atherton's Light Nymph

Rockworm

Fish Fly Larvae

Beaver Nymph

Zug Bug

Greenwells Glory Nymph

Light Cahill Nymph

Horner Shrimp

Iron Blue Nymph

NYMPHS

Greenwells Glory Nymph
Hook: Regular shank
Back: A double slip of light gray mallard quill feather tied in at tail after which a gold wire is tied in to form rib followed by light olive green silk floss
Body: Floss is wound to shoulder followed by 5 turns of gold wire ribbing, next apply 2 or 3 turns of ginger furnace hackle, fold back feather forward and tie down over hackle

Light Cahill Nymph
Hook: Regular shank
Tail: 3 fibers of lemon wood-duck flank
Body: Mixed dubbing of tannish cream fur with a small amount of yellow wool worked in. Tie body moderately rough to shoulder
Hackle: Two turns of pale ginger hackle
Wing pad: Tied on over hackle—pale gray mallard flank feather clipped to shape

Rockworm
Hook: 2XL shank
Tail: 2 or 3 strands peacock herl clipped short
Body: Medium green dyed fox fur or silk floss, ribbed with black silk thread
Wing pads: 4 strands of heavy peacock herl clipped to half length of body tied in as short wings
Hackle: 2 or 3 turns of light green hackle put on over wing
Feelers: 2 strands of short peacock herl

Fish Fly Larvae
Hook: 4XL shank
Body: Skunk under fur ribbed with clipped soft black hackle to shoulder
Hackle: Several turns of long, soft black hackle

Breadcrust Nymph
Hook: Regular shank
Body: The brown quill from the butt of a dark brown saddle hackle. This quill must show a distinct dark line on the shiny side. The quill is flattened and wound to the shoulder
Legs: Several turns of soft gray grizzly hackle

Trueblood's Caddis Nymph
Hook: Regular or 2XL shank
Tail: A short tuft of dark green silk floss
Back: Tie in several strands peacock herl at tail also fine oval gold tinsel for ribbing
Body: Form body of green floss silk
Legs: A few strands of speckled gray mallard. Fold peacock herl forward. Bring ribbing to shoulder and tie down over legs
Head: Generous head of black tying silk well lacquered

Atherton's Medium Nymph
Hook: Regular shank
Tail: 3 short strands from the center tail feather of the ring-necked cock pheasant
Abdomen: A hare's ear dubbing tied rough and ribbed with narrow oval gold tinsel
Thorax: Same dubbing over padding or fuse wire if weight is preferred
Wing pads: Bright blue silk floss or lurex plastic tinsel
Legs: Brown speckled partridge hackle

Green Drake Nymph
Hook: 3XL shank
Tail: 2 soft cream hackle tips
Body: Pale cream fox fur tied very rough
Hackle: Moderately long, 2 turns only of soft cream hackle
Wing pads: A small light marginal wing feather of a hen pheasant clipped to shape and tied down over hackle

Michigan Nymph
Hook: 2XL shank
Tail: Speckled gray mallard flank fibers
Abdomen: Gray quill from a stripped Plymouth rock hackle feather
Thorax: Bluish-gray rabbit fur dubbing slightly flattened
Wing pads: Orange silk floss
Legs: Reddish-brown hackle

Leadwinged Coachman Nymph
Hook: 12 2XL
Tail: Dark brown hackle fibers
Body: Bronze peacock herl ribbed with fine black silk
Hackle: Dark rusty brown
Wing pads: Small dark black duck upper wing covert feathers (cut to shape)
Head: Brown lacquer

NYMPHS

Horner Shrimp

Hook: Regular shank, preferably upturned eye
Tag: Silver oval tinsel which is carried to shoulder, forming body
Hackle: Medium brown. A bunch of brown bucktail is tied over hackle and brought down to the end of the body where it is bound closely over the back with black silk thread which is later heavily lacquered leaving a wisp of bucktail to form the tail
Head: Black tying silk heavily lacquered

Beaver Nymph

Hook: Regular
Tail: Short wood-duck fiber wisps
Body: Beaver fur tied full, ribbed with fine gold wire
Hackle: Gray partridge
Head: Brown lacquer

Iron Blue Nymph

Hook: Regular shank 14 or 16
Tail: Cream or gray hackle wisps
Body: Bluish muskrat fur ribbed with gold wire
Thorax: Bluish muskrat, no rib
Hackle: Grayish cream
Head: Clear lacquer over tying silk

R. B. Caddis Nymph

Hook: 2XL shank
Tail: 2 strands of peacock sword herl
Body: White chenille butted at tail end with black chenille
Feelers: 2 strands of peacock sword herl

Zug Bug

Hook: 14 to size 6 2XL or 3XL
Tail: 3 strands of green peacock sword herl
Body: Heavy peacock herl ribbed with silver oval tinsel. Lead wire may be used if weight is desired
Wing cases: Mallard flank cut short extending over forward one fourth of body
Hackle: Long soft brown
Head: Black lacquer

Montana Nymph

Hook: 3 or 4 XL shank
Tail: A few strands of short black crow feather
Abdomen: Black chenille
Thorax: Yellow chenille ribbed with moderately long soft black hackle
Wing pad: 2 strands of black chenille tied down over thorax and hackle
Head: Moderately large of heavily lacquered black tying thread

Gray Fox Nymph

Hook: Regular shank
Tail: Gray partridge fibers
Body: Gray muskrat fur dubbing ribbed to shoulder with fine gold wire
Hackle: Gray partridge
Wing pads: Tips of two small grizzly hackles tied flat over back

Atherton's Light Nymph

Hook: Regular shank or 2XL, sizes 14 to 10
Tail: 3 strands of wood-duck or mandarin flank feather
Body: Natural Greenland baby seal fur ribbed with narrow oval gold tinsel
Thorax: Built up of same material as body but not ribbed. May be weighted under thorax with lead wire
Wing cases: 2 tiny jungle cock eyes tied over thorax. These must not extend beyond thorax. They should project at a very slight angle at each side
Hackle: Gray partridge
Head: Clear lacquer over light tying silk

Long Tail March Brown Nymph

Hook: Regular shank
Tail: A long strip of bronze mallard
Back: Tied in at tail—strip of hen pheasant quill feather rather dark
Body: Tied rough of hare's ear dubbing ribbed with pale yellow silk thread
Hackle: 2 turns of brown partridge hackle. Bring hen pheasant forward, and tie down over hackle

Flick's March Brown

Hook: Regular #10
Tail: 3 strands from a cock pheasant center tail feather
Body: Seal fur dyed amber mixed with a small amount of tan fur from red fox, ribbed with a single strand of brown embroidery cotton
Thorax: Seal's fur dyed amber mixed with tan red fox tied full
Wing case: From short side feathers of cock pheasant tail (tied over thorax)
Hackle: Brown partridge
Head: Brown lacquer

NYMPHS

Blades' Hackle Nymph

Hook: Regular sizes 10 to 14
Tail: Brown hackle fibers
Body: Yellow and brown hackle wound together and clipped to shape
Thorax: Orange hackle clipped to shape
Wing cases: A section of gray goose wing quill tied over thorax
Hackle: Blue dun at throat only
Head: Brown lacquer

Pink Lady Nymph

Hook: No. 12 2XL; tying silk dark orange
Tail: Cream hackle fibers
Body: Light yellow floss silk twisted tightly to show segmentation
Thorax: Light beige wool dubbing lacquered with thin lacquer and flattened
Wing cases: Gray silk floss tied over thorax
Legs: Gray starling wing fibers
Head: Clear lacquer over tying silk

Blades' Olive Nymph

Hook: 2 or 3XL
Tail: Blue dun hackle fibers
Body: Golden olive seal's fur ribbed with flat gold tinsel
Thorax: Olive seal's fur
Wing cases: Orange silk floss tied over thorax
Hackle: Honey badger
Head: Clear lacquer over tying silk

Martinez Black

Hook: Standard length, any size
Tail: Several strands of single spot guinea hackle
Body: Black seal dubbed loosely, ribbed with oval copper tinsel (flat copper may be substituted)
Thorax: Black chenille
Wing cases: A fold of green raffia tied over thorax
Hackle: Speckled gray partridge
Head: Black lacquer

Darbee's Stonefly Nymph

Hook: 3XL 14 to size 6
Tail: 2 strands from cock pheasant tail center feather
Body: Amber seal's fur ribbed with brown monofilament or brown hackle quill
Wing cases: A split jungle cock eye extending over half of the body
Thorax: Amber seal's fur with second pair of wing cases (a split jungle cock eye) tied over
Head: Amber seal's fur followed by a partridge hackle and brown thread tied full, lacquered with clear lacquer

Dark Hendrickson Nymph

Hook: Sizes 12 3XL; tying silk rusty brown
Tail: Tips of 2 black, 1 brown moose mane hair. Tie in tails; use balance of hair over body
Body: Tied moderately full of tan or brown floss silk. Wind moose mane hair over body to head
Wing pads: English moor hen or black duck wing coverts clipped to shape and tied over upper third or forward third of body
Hackle: Dark rusty dun 2 or 3 turns clipped off at top
Head: Clear lacquer over tying silk

Gray Nymph

Hook: 14 to 6 regular or 2XL
Tail: A few strands of badger hair with white tips
Body: Tied very full and rough of muskrat fur with guard hairs left in. Lead wire underneath if weight is desired
Hackle: Several turns of soft gray grizzle
Head: Black or brown lacquer

Atherton's Dark Nymph

Hook: 16 to 10 regular
Tail: A few strands of dark furnace hackle fibers
Body: Muskrat or mole fur mixed with red brown seal's fur ribbed with narrow oval gold tinsel. Dubbing should be tied rough and picked out between ribs
Thorax: Tied thick and rough but not ribbed
Wing cases: A section of bright blue floss silk tied over thorax and given several coats of clear lacquer
Hackle: Dark furnace clipped off top and bottom leaving a few fibers at either side
Head: Clear lacquer over tying silk

Inch Worm

Hook: 16, 14 or larger 4XL
Body: Green deer hair clipped to shape
Head: Clear lacquer over brown tying silk

Hendrickson Nymph

Hook: Regular length 10, 12 or 14
Tail: Wood-duck or mandarin flank feather fibers
Body: Blend of tan and gray fox fur and claret seal fur ribbed with olive tying silk or fine gold wire
Thorax: Same material as body
Wing cases: A section of blue hen wing quill tied over thorax
Legs: Brown partridge hackle
Head: Clear lacquer over olive tying silk

Strawman Nymph

Hook: Regular or 2XL in sizes to suit
Tail: A few strands of gray mallard or wood-duck flank
Body: Deer hair spun on hook thinly and clipped in a taper from tail to head, ribbed with pale yellow floss silk. May be tied without hackle or, if desired, a turn or two of partridge hackle may be added

Isonychia Nymph

Hook: No. 10 regular or 2XL
Tail: 3 very short pieces of peacock herl about 1/8" long
Body: Dark claret seal's fur mixed with black wool. There is no hump at thorax. Wing cases: None
Hackle: 1 or 2 turns of speckled brown partridge
Head: Dark brown or black lacquer

Brown Nymph

Hook: Regular sizes 16 to 10
Tail: A few fibers of bronze mallard tied short
Body: Dark brown fur dubbing. Ribbing bronze wire or gold oval
Thorax: Tied rather full of tan fur dubbing
Wing cases: A section of speckled brown turkey tied over thorax
Hackle: A few fibers of brown hackle tied as legs at either side
Antennae: 2 fibers of wing case material left extending forward over head
Head: Tan lacquer

Quill Gordon Nymph

Hook: Size 14 regular; tying silk primrose yellow
Tail: 2 or 3 strands of mandarin or wood-duck flank feather about length of hook shank
Body: Light tannish gray muskrat fur tied rough
Hackle: Light honey dun clipped off at top
Wing pad: About one-third length of body trimmed from a dark gray mallard flank feather and tied flat over body
Head: Clear lacquer over tying silk

Carrot Nymph (Rube Cross)

Hook: Regular 12 or 14
Tail: Brown hackle fibers
Body: Carrot colored floss silk or dubbing with black chenille thorax. 2 or 3 turns of soft dun hackle at throat. Top and bottom hackle wisps trimmed off leaving a few fibers at each side as legs
Head: Black or clear lacquer over tying silk

Blue Quill Nymph

Hook: Size 12 to 18 regular
Tail: Soft blue dun hackle fibers
Body: Light peacock quill, varnished
Thorax: Loosely dubbed muskrat fur
Hackle: Several turns of blue dun hen hackle

Black-and-Yellow Hardback

Hook: Size 12 to 18 regular
Tail: Soft black hackle fibers
Body: Yellow dubbing saturated with clear lacquer, pinched flat with pliers, and lacquered black on top only
Legs: Black hackle fibers at sides

Hare's Ear Nymph

Hook: Size 6 to 16
Tail: Brown hackle
Body: Dubbed very rough with fur from European hare's ear, mixed with fur from the hare's face, ribbed with oval gold tinsel
Thorax: Tied very full with wing pad from gray goose or duck tied over
Legs: Dubbing from thorax picked out long and fuzzy; this represents the nymph legs

Tellico Nymph

Hook: Size 6 to 16
Tail: Soft brown hackle fibers
Body: Tied very full with yellow wool or fur dubbing, ribbed with heavy peacock herl
Legs: 3 or 4 turns of soft brown hackle tied on as a collar

Dragonfly Nymph (Gomphus Type)

Hook: No. 6 to No. 10 3X long
Tail: 2 short, stubby fibers from a dark coarse-fibered feather
Body: Tied of olive dubbing rather full tapering from tail to thorax, fat in center. This is saturated with lacquer and a dark quill stripped from a wild goose wing feather or other similar-sized feather is wound over the dubbed body leaving distinct segmented effect. Do not wind quill too closely; let a small amount of dubbing show through
Legs: Tied in at thorax; fibers from a dark-colored wing feather, goose, or similar bird. These are tied in in pairs
Wing pads: From slips of very dark goose, crow, or other bird are tied in over the second pair of legs. The forward pair of legs is then tied in, after which the remainder of the thorax and head are built up of black dubbing saturated with lacquer and pressed more or less flat
Eyes: Black lacquer put on to make shiny black spots in eye position

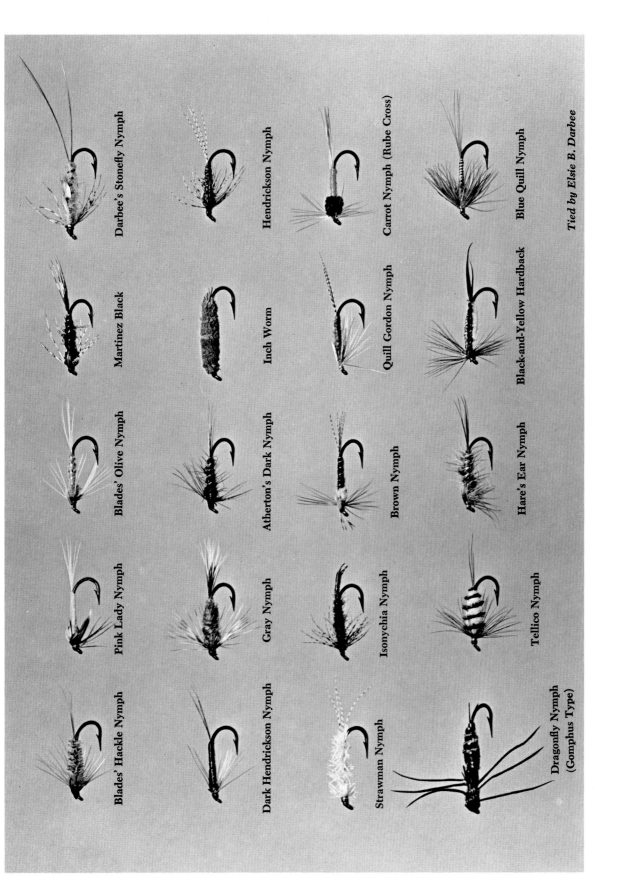

Blades' Hackle Nymph

Pink Lady Nymph

Blades' Olive Nymph

Martinez Black

Darbee's Stonefly Nymph

Dark Hendrickson Nymph

Gray Nymph

Atherton's Dark Nymph

Inch Worm

Hendrickson Nymph

Strawman Nymph

Isonychia Nymph

Brown Nymph

Quill Gordon Nymph

Carrot Nymph (Rube Cross)

Dragonfly Nymph
(Gomphus Type)

Tellico Nymph

Hare's Ear Nymph

Black-and-Yellow Hardback

Blue Quill Nymph

Tied by Elsie B. Darbee

Spuddler

White (Missoulian Spook) Muddler

Troths Bullhead

Whitlock Sculpin

Dan Bailey Muddler Minnow

Dave's Lemon Muddler

Gordon Dean (Yellow) Muddler Minnow

Don Gapen Original Muddler Minnow

Tied by Dave Whitlock

Spuddler

This later version of the Muddler Series was created by Don Williams and Red Monical of Livingston, Montana, and put into production by Dan Bailey. It is a more simplified version of the Whitlock Sculpin and is a hybrid combination of the Muddler and the Dark Spruce streamer.
Hook: Sizes 10 thru 1/0 TDE 3XL (Mustad 9672).
Thread: Yellow nymo.
Tail: None.
Body: Yellow angora rabbit wool.
Wings: 2 or 4 matched grizzly neck hackles dyed brown. Wings should be typical vertical streamer wing style and extend at least ½ length of hook past the bend.
Pectoral Fins or Collar: On right and left sides of body tie on a small bunch of red fox squirrel tail. Bunches should extend out and back to about hook's point. Over hair tiedown wrap a turn or two of red wool.
Head: Spin and flare 2 or 3 bunches of dyed brown antelope or deer hair. Trim head wide and flat; leave a few hair tips extending back to squirrel hair fins.

Troths Bullhead

Al Troth developed this sculpin imitation early in the 1960's. It is an outstanding variation of the Muddler series, but like the Whitlock sculpin and the Marabou Muddlers it represents an extreme departure from the original Muddler Minnow.
Hook: Size 4 thru 3/0 Mustad Salmon hook #36890.
Tying Thread: Black nylon.
Tail: Light-marked skunk tail.
Body: Cream angora yarn.
Back: (Overwing) Black ostrich herl tied in at collar and to tail over body, tied down with herls extending to tail's length.
Collar: Natural dun brown deer body hair, spun and flared around hook just against front of body. Trim collar thin on bottom and top.
Head: Natural dun brown deer hair, spun and flared ahead of collar in at least 2 bunches. Trim head wide and very large.

Dan Bailey Muddler Minnow

(This is the most popular version of the Muddler Minnow)
Hook: Sizes 10 thru 1/0 TDE 3XL (Mustad 9672).
Thread: White nymo.
Tail: Short section of brown speckled turkey quill, about ⅓ length of hook shank.
Body: Flat gold tinsel double-wrapped and finished with 1 coat of clear head cement.
Underwing: Kiptail hair, brown on lower half, white over brown. Length is approximately equal to shank plus tail.
Overwing: Matched right and left sections of brown speckled turkey quill tied directly over kiptails and equal to tail in length.
Collar: Dun brown northern deer hair spun around hook shank in front of wings and flared out with thread pressure. Tips should extend back to hook's point.
Head: Immediately in front of collar hair add another large bunch of deer hair spinning and flaring it also with tying thread. Trim head with scissors to a fat bullet shape about ½-⅓ width of collar.

Gordon Dean (Yellow) Muddler Minnow

This pattern, created by Gordon Dean, is simply a color variation of Dan Bailey's Muddler. However, it is a very effective pattern and deserves recognition. The wing and tail are tied with light brown speckled turkey quill dyed a deep yellow. Otherwise, refer to Bailey's Muddler Minnow for tying instructions. Dean's original variation used yellow chicken feathers, but most tyers now use turkey wing quill sections to better maintain classic muddler outlines.

White (Missoulian Spook) Muddler

This pattern originated in the Threeforks area of Montana's Missouri River. It is most effective for big fall-run browns. Dan Bailey produces the best version of this Muddler.
Hook: Sizes 10 thru 1/0 TDE 3XL (Mustad 9672).
Thread: White nymo.
Tail: Very light section of speckled turkey wing quill.
Butt: Red chenille.
Body: White angora rabbit wool ribbed with flat silver tinsel.
Underwing: White kiptail hair under a few sections of barred teal flank feather.
Wing: Matched pair of very light-speckled turkey wing quills.
Collar: Natural dun brown deer hair spun and flared just in front of body, tips extending back to hook's point.
Head: White deer hair spun and flared. Use 2 or more bunches for a tight head.

Whitlock Sculpin

The Whitlock sculpin is perhaps the best exact imitation of the sculpin minnow, and is truly more imitative than suggestive. This limits its versatility, but when properly fished it is the most successful sculpin imitation.
Hook: Size 1/0 thru 10 3XL/2XS (Buz's Special) weighted with 20 turns of lead wire.
Thread: Yellow or orange nymo.
Tail: None.
Body: Creamish-yellow fur blend of seal fur and orlon wool. Rib with gold oval tinsel.
Underwing: Redfox squirrel tail, ⅓ longer than hook shank.
Wing: Two well-barred wide soft cree neck hackles. Each feather is tied flat over underwing and body. Should be ½ length longer than hook.
Pectoral fins: Two barred breast feathers from mallard hen or prairie chicken tied on either side of body at wing base, flaring right and left.
Gills: Red wool dubbing wrapped over base of wings and pectoral fins.
Collar: Cream-yellow deer hair flared on lower part of hook shank. Golden brown deer hair flared over top of shank. Tips of both should extend back to meet pectoral fins.
Head: Same pattern of light deer hair on bottom, darker shades on top. Use several bunches of deer hair to obtain a very large thick head. Trim head to shape of sculpins that is very wide and flat.

Dave's Lemon Muddler

(for dark days or late evening fishing)
Hook: Size 10 thru 1/0 TDE 3XL (Mustad 9672).
Thread: Yellow nymo.
Tail: Light speckled brown turkey quill section.
Body: Fluorescent yellow nylon tow.
Underwing: Yellow fluorescent kiptail under black kiptail.
Wing: Matched sections of right and left light brown speckled turkey wing quill.
Collar: Natural dun brown deer hair dyed bronze green.
Head: same as collar.

Don Gapen Original Muddler Minnow

Hook: Size 12 thru No. 1 3XL.
Tying Thread: Black or red for weighted.
Tail: Short section of mottled brown turkey quill, about ½ length of hook shank.
Body: Gold flat tinsel double-wrapped over hook shank.
Wing: Gray squirrel tail or wolf guard hair extending up over hook shank and ½ length past hook bend. Mottled turkey quill sections right and left on either side hair wing extending ⅓ length of shank past hook bend.
Shoulder or Collar and Head: A large bunch of natural dun brown northern deer hair spun around hook shank, tips pointing back over wings ½ their length. Trim deer hair butts to form a wide flat shape, widening toward back of head-collar. One or more extra bunches of deer hair added if a larger or more dense head is desired.

Whitlock's Multicolored Marabou Muddler No. 1

Hook: Size 6 thru 1/0 TDE 4XL (Mustad 79580) weighted with 15-20 turns of lead wire about midshank.
Tying Thread: Danvilles (Herb Howard's) 7/0 nylon fluorescent orange.
Tail: None.
Body: Gold mylar piping. Underpad with curon, and paint body with clear lacquer or epoxy to endure wear from fish teeth.
Wing: A small bunch each of yellow, orange, and dark brown turkey marabou extending 1/2 length past hook bend. Top with 8-12 peacock herls.
Collar: Dark brown deer hair spun and flared at wing base. Tips should extend almost to hook's point. Trim most of tips off beneath body, leave sides and tips.
Head: Add 1 or 2 additional bunches of dark brown deer hair, spinning and flaring each. Pack head very tightly. Trim head very wide and flat like toad or sculpin head shape. Darken top of head with black felt-point pen (waterproof ink).

Bailey's Marabou Muddler

The Marabou Muddler was the second fly Dan Bailey improvised from the Gapen Muddler. The wing and body were drastically altered, but the result proved outstanding. Marabou feather action and tensil chenille flash make this a true killer attractor pattern.
Hook: Size 10 thru 1/0 (Mustad 9672).
Thread: White nymo.
Tail: A few red hackle fibers.
Body: Tinsel chenille, gold or silver.
Underwing: White or tan kiptail hair, 1/3 longer than hook shank.
Wing: Two matched turkey marabou feathers flared right and left. Popular colors are white, yellow, black, brown, and gray. These should extend past hook bend at least 1 shank length.
Overwing: 6-10 peacock herl same length as marabou wing and tied directly over wings.
Collar: Natural dun brown northern whitetail deer hair. Spin and flare a large bunch on hook shank directly in front of wing base. Tip should point back just even with hook's point.
Head: Another large bunch or two of deer hair spun and flared tightly against front of collar. Trim head with scissors to a blunt bullet shape approximately same size as Bailey's standard Muddler Minnow. Leave head larger if you wish fly to work on or near surface, smaller for deep fishing.

Whitlock's Midnight Muddler

Hook: Size 10 thru 1/0 TDE 3XL (Mustad 9672).
Thread: Black nymo.
Tail: Section of speckled brown turkey wing quill.
Body: Silver or silver-blue mylar ribbed with size 18 oval tinsel.
Underwing: Black kiptail hair.
Wing: Matched right and left sections of turkey wing quills.
Collar: Natural dun brown deer hair dyed black.
Head: Same.

Whitlock's Scotch-and-Water Muddler

Hook: Size 10 thru 1/0 TDE 3XL (Mustad 9672).
Thread: White nymo.
Tail: Very light speckled turkey wing quill section.
Body: Light amber seal fur dubbed on fuzzy.
Underwing: Guard hair from coyote back or tail.
Wing: Matched sections of very light speckled turkey wing quill.
Collar: Light natural dun brown deer hair.
Head: Same as collar.

Whitlock's Multicolored Marabou Muddler No. 2

Hook: Size 6 thru 1/0 TDE 4XL (Mustad 79580), weighted with 15-20 wraps of lead wire.
Tying Thread: Red Danville (Herb Howard's) 7/0 nylon.
Tail: None.

Body: Silver mylar piping, underpad of curon and painted with 2 coats of clear head cement or epoxy.
Wings: A small bunch of white, yellow, and golden olive turkey marabou. Wings should extend 1/2 times length of body past hook bend. Top wings with 8-12 peacock herl same length as wings.
Collar: Natural dun brown deer hair dyed bronze green (Putnam dye). Spin and flare deer hair just in front of wing base, tips should extend back almost to hook point. Trim off very bottom of collar so that mylar body clearly shows.
Head: Add 1 or 2 large bunches of golden olive deer hair just in front of collar, spinning and flaring each, packing tightly against itself. Trim head very wide and flat like toad or sculpin head.

Whitlock's Salmon Muddler

Hook: Regular or double hook TUE black-finish salmon hook.
Tag: Gold mylar.
Tail: Short section of brown-speckled turkey wing secondary.
Body: Gold mylar ribbed with size 18 silver oval tinsel or silver wire.
Underwing: Black-and-white guard hair from gray fox back or gray squirrel tail hair.
Wing: Short sections of matched right and left speckled turkey wing quills.
Collar: Bunch of natural dun brown white tail deer hair. Spin and flare around hook in front of wing base. Tips should point back and just to hook's point.
Head: Spin and flare 1 or 2 more bunches of coarse deer hair directly in front and against collar to form a large dense head of hair.
Trim head to a blunt shape with scissors. Head should be small if low-water pattern is being tied, rather large for standard salmon muddler. On standard tie, completed fly should be about one size smaller than the hook size it is tied on for best results if fished wet.

Searcy's Muddler

According to Virginia Buszeck, John Searcy's variation of the Muddler Minnow seems to produce better on the West Coast of America than other popular muddler versions. Certainly this hybrid incorporates additional materials and ideas that can be applied to other patterns.
Hook: Size 6, 8, 10 TDE 3XL (Mustad 9672).
Tying Thread: White nymo.
Tail: Small section of black-and-white teal flank, 1/4 shank length.
Body: Light gray otter fur ribbed with size 18 gold oval tinsel. Body should be dubbed very fuzzy.
Underwing: Small bunch of brown bucktail or light brown kiptail. Extend hair 1/4 shank length past hook bend or even with tail tip.
Wing: A pair of well-barred black-and-white teal flank feathers, rather wide and extending over body and even with tail tip.
Collar: A fair-sized bunch of natural dun brown northern or mule deer body hair. Spin and flare just ahead of wings, tips extending to hook point or slightly past.
Head: Butts of collar hair form head. Searcy's muddler has a relatively small simple-shaped head compared to Bailey's and Whitlock's variations. Trim head about twice the thickness of fur body, evenly on all sides.

Whitlock's Brandy Muddler

Hook: Size 10 thru 1/0 TDE 3XL (Mustad 9672).
Thread: Orange nymo.
Tail: Section of very dark speckled turkey wing quill.
Body: Gold mylar ribbed with fine gold wire.
Underwing: Brandy brown kiptail over fluorescent orange kiptail hair.
Wing: Matched right and left sections of very dark brown speckled turkey wing quills.
Collar: Natural dun brown deer hair dyed brandy brown.
Head: Same as collar.

Whitlock's Multicolored
Marabou Muddler No. 1

Whitlock's Multicolored Marabou Muddler No. 2

Bailey's Marabou Muddler

Whitlock's Salmon Muddler

Whitlock's Midnight Muddler

Searcy's Muddler

Whitlock's Scotch-and-Water Muddler

Whitlock's Brandy Muddler

Tied by Dave Whitlock

feathers the tip ends of the fibers are a natural black. This is a desirable feature, as it makes an attractive "foot" pattern on the fly.

Black: Black feathers from a gamecock, Black Minorca, or Black Leghorn rooster are used for the tying of either wet or dry hackles. Feathers from the neck of a black hen may also be used, but only for tying wet flies. As a substitute for natural black hackle, use dyed hackle feathers, either from the bird's neck or saddle.

Blue Dun: The feathers known as blue dun range in color from a fairly light gray or bluish cast to a darker gray which is almost a gun-metal shade. The darker feathers of gun-metal color are more correctly known as "iron blue dun." Any shade within the indicated range may be applicable, but the lighter grays are the ones most commonly used. Natural blue dun necks can be purchased, but are very expensive, and for the beginner it is recommended that dyed feathers of this color be obtained.

Brown (natural): The term "natural brown" means a feather of medium brown shade. The natural brown feather is used whenever the pattern calls for brown hackle, without mention of any particular shade of brown. It is most commonly obtained from a Brown Leghorn cock.

Brown (fiery): Fiery brown is a rich medium brown with a reddish tinge. The feather has a golden glint when it is turned toward the light. This is a color which is very hard to duplicate with dye. Fortunately there is a plentiful supply of feathers of this color, and you can readily obtain the shade you desire. Brown saddle hackle is slightly more golden than neck hackle.

Brown (chestnut): Chestnut hackle is a very dark brown. The underside of the feather is only a shade or two lighter than the outer, or shiny, side. Feathers from the neck of a cock bird are the ones which have this color. These feathers are readily obtainable from fly-tying supply houses.

Furnace: Furnace hackle, like badger hackle, is brownish-black to black along the quill of the feather. The outer ends of the fibers of a furnace hackle feather range from a light brown to a very dark brown. In addition to using this hackle on patterns which specifically call for furnace, you may try an interesting variation by using furnace hackle when tying patterns which call for natural brown hackle. The furnace produces a fly with hackle which is dark near the body of the fly, shading into the brown coloration of the fibers at the outer edges.

Ginger: Ginger hackle feathers vary from a creamy white to a light brown. In patterns which call for ginger hackle, without any indication as to the exact shade, use a feather which is beige with a golden cast or glint. This is likely to be correct, as most fly-tiers prefer to use a medium shade of a natural hackle color for the majority of the flies they tie. However, you may encounter a hatch of natural flies which are either a light ginger or a dark ginger in color. So it is important to have in your fly box a few copies which are tied with the lighter and darker ginger shades. In a ginger neck you will often find variations in color that will provide you with the range of shades. Usually the lighter tint is found in the center of the neck, and the darker shade is on the sides.

Grizzly: Sometimes called Plymouth Rock, barred rock, or dominique. Grizzly hackle varies in color from a black and white combination to a light and dark gray combination. On this hackle the bar pattern is actually V-shaped, tapering down to the quill of the feather rather than crossing in a line perpendicular to the quill. From the standpoint of color, most fly-tiers prefer the extremes of black and white. The width of the dark bars will vary, and here again the individual may prefer a more pronounced or wider black marking. A very light colored grizzly which is only sparsely marked is sometimes called "Chinchilla" and is used principally for mixing with other colors of hackle. All grizzly hackles mix well with contrasting shades such as brown, ginger, or even with blue dun for a buggy effect.

White: Hackle feathers are obtainable in two distinct whites. One is the natural white, which is an off-white. The other is a pure white. Pure white hackle has usually been washed or perhaps bleached lightly. Most of the time the preference is for the pure white tint.

Wing Feathers The pointers, or flight feathers, of a duck are a common source of the material used in making the wings on many patterns of artificial flies. These feathers, which come from the wings of ducks such as the mallard duck, contain the strong fibers (which attach themselves to each other by means of a tongue-and-groove structure) required to make the upright and other types of fly wings.

The pointers, or flight feathers, in the wing of a duck are commonly referred to as primary feathers. There are ten pointer feathers on each wing. One feather from each of the two wings of a duck constitutes a pair of primaries that may be used in making the wings of flies. The feathers in each pair, however, should be matched ones, coming from the same or approximately the same position in the two wings. Each of the feathers in a matched pair of primaries should have approximately the same curve, the same width and be of the same texture. If these differ to any extent, you cannot make a good pair of wings on the fly.

Mallard pointers, or flight feathers, are gray from the base to a point very near the tip of the feather. Each fiber is quite strong. Although the No. 1 pointer is the longest feather in the wing, the fibers are shorter than those of the other primary feathers. The No. 2 pointer is a little shorter than the No. 1 pointer, but the fibers are longer. Progressing to the No. 5 feather you will find that it is not as sharply pointed at the tip as the No. 1 and No. 2, but the fibers of the No. 5 feather are much longer and have more of a curve. Each pointer should be matched with the corresponding flight feather from the other wing in making up matched pairs.

Secondary Feathers: Along a duck wing, after the ten pointer feathers, you will find there are also ten secondary flight feathers. On mallard wings these have white tips and are frequently called McGinty feathers, because they are used in making the wings of the McGinty fly. The outer surfaces of the first two secondary feathers are gray on both sides of the quill. The outer surfaces of the other eight secondary feathers are bluish in color on one side of the quill and gray on the other side of the quill. The white tips of these eight feathers are widest on the outside curve of the feather.

OTHER TYPES OF FEATHERS

Grouse Black Feathers: The feathers from the back of a grouse are used for hackles as well as for wings laid down flat over the top of the fly. Toward the tip there is an abundance of black which changes abruptly to a rich brown. In the center of the tip of the feather there is an oblong spot, much lighter brown in color. At the base of the feather there is a great deal of web.

Grouse Secondary Wing Feathers and Tail Feathers: The secondary wing feathers and the tail feathers of a grouse are a rich, mottled brown. These are used for the wings of very small flies. A matching section is cut from the fibers on each side of the quill of one of these feathers, and then used to make the wings of a wet fly.

Guinea Hackle and Body Feathers: The hackle and body feathers of a guinea fowl are deep gray in color with almost round, white dots. The feathers from the center of the breast and along the flank of the bird are large. Used as hackle on large wet flies, these feathers give a very beautiful pattern of black and white fibers. The feathers on the back of the bird are much smaller and the color pattern more delicate than in breast and flank feathers. Breast, flank, and back feathers of the guinea fowl may be used either as hackle or as wing material. The primary feathers also have the same marking as the hackle and body feathers, and are used in making the wings of wet flies.

Mallard Breast Feathers: A mallard breast feather is whitish-gray, with dark gray, zig-zag bars running across the feather. The dark coloration is not very prominent. All the breast feathers are not the same size, ranging from quite small to fairly large. The coloration is the same on all sizes, but the pattern on the smaller feathers is more delicate.

Mallard Flank Feathers: The flank feathers of a mallard duck are quite similar in color and pattern to the breast feathers of the bird. These feathers are, however, much longer than those on the breast, and the quill is quite heavy by comparison. Although sometimes of value, the flank feather should not be used unless it is specifically called for in the pattern. It is not a substitute for mallard breast feathers.

Mallard Shoulder Feathers: These rich brown feathers are specified as one of the most important wing materials in many salmon patterns.

Partridge Hackle Feathers: Gray partridge hackle is one of the most fragile of all hackles. The feather is miniature in size and gray with small flecks of black dotting its surface. Some feathers have a brown bar at the tip. The brown bar gives a different appearance to the fly. The feather may be used to make an overlay wing. In the Pacific Northwest it is often tied spider style on a fly called the Carot Nymph, which has been proven one of the best for the cutthroat trout of that area.

Peacock Feathers: The multicolored feathers of the peacock provide many different types of materials that are widely used in the tying of flies. The peacock-eye feather is the most important feather of the bird to the fly-tier, and is employed for the body, butt, shoulder, and sometimes the overwing of flies. Each barb of the peacock-eye feather is separate from, and independent of, each other barb. The feather has very fine barbules which stand out perpendicular to the shaft. There are two different kinds of peafowl, and each of these birds has a somewhat different coloration in its tail feathers.

Lemon Wood Duck Feathers: The lemon colored side feathers of the wood duck are highly prized by the fly-tiers. The material is used for wings on many popular patterns such as the Cahill, Hendrickson, and Quill Gordon. These feathers are a delicate, light yellowish-brown with faint black bars. Unfortunately there are not many of these on the market. When they are not obtainable, the side feathers of the mandarin duck is the best substitute. If neither is available, due to heavy demand, or if the price is too high, the next best is mallard breast feathers dyed to match the shade of the wood duck feather. However, it is impossible to duplicate either the color or texture of the lemon wood duck.

Ringneck Pheasant Saddle Feathers: The rump, or saddle feathers, of the ringneck pheasant vary in color depending on the age of the bird. Close to the tail the feathers are a rich chocolate brownish-red; closer to the saddle of the bird they are either greenish or a beautiful blue. These are just in front of the tail, and all the usable feathers of this type cover an area not much larger than a silver dollar. They are used mostly in making flies which imitate the dragonfly nymph.

Ringneck Pheasant Tail Feathers: The long tail feathers of the ringneck pheasant have fibers which are separated at the edges, about half of the fiber being free and the other half (nearest the quill) being attached to the adjoining fibers. The lower half of the tail feather is brownish in color, with wide bars of black, and this portion of the feather is used for the tails or the wings of flies. The upper portion varies from a gray brown to a greenish-brown, depending on the age of the bird, but this part of the feather is not suitable for use on flies. The secondary tail feathers are a much deeper brown color. All of the fibers cling together. These feathers may be used in making wet-fly wings, and many patterns call for them.

Golden Pheasant Neck or Tippet Feathers: The neck or tippet feather is used on many flies. The feather is bright orange with a black edge and a black bar down one quarter of the way from the tip of the feather. From this second bar the orange color fades to a beige at the base of the feather. The size of the feathers will vary; the smallest are next to the crest of the bird while the larger feathers are at the base of the cape or neck.

HAIR AND FUR

Deer Body Hair: The hair from any portion of the body of a deer may be used in making flies. In areas where hair-wings are popular, deer hair is an essential item of fly-tying material. Its primary use is for hair-bodied and hair-wing flies, and it is used extensively in making mouse patterns for bass fishing. The body hair is uniformly gray at the base, but it varies substantially in shade. The tips of the hair may range from a beige to quite a reddish-brown color. The hair of the doe is much more soft in texture than the hair of the buck deer. At the base of the hair of some types of deer there is a small amount of fuzz which is sometimes used for spinning the bodies of flies. For patterns having white hair-wings deer belly hair may be used to make a very attractive dressing.

Badger: The hide of a badger provides both fur and hair which may be used in making flies. The underhair, or fur, may be used for dubbing bodies in colors ranging from dark gray to white. The hair of the badger may be substituted for gray squirrel hair. Both badger and squirrel have the advantage of providing hairs of greatly varying length, making them suitable for use on very small flies as well as on the largest patterns normally tied. Along the lower portions of the body and the belly of the animal the hair color ranges from white to cream, and is usually ¾–1½ inches in length. Near the top of the head the hair is almost black with tips which are white or cream. In length it may be ½–1¼ inches, while on the back the hair is about 1¼–4 inches in length. The base of these longer hairs is light tan. At about the center of the hair fiber its color changes to black; toward the tip it changes again, from black to brown and tan, and the tips of these hairs are white. Some badgers have hairs that vary from a dark brown to almost black on either the shoulder of the forelegs or on the hind legs.

Badger hair is used in making hair-wing flies which are popular in fishing for cutthroat and rainbow trout as well as for steelhead. Flies with badger hair-wings are attractive to fish, but only prime hides, or pieces from prime hides, will provide the badger hair and underfur that is satisfactory.

Beaver Fur: The furs of various animals differ not only in color but also in texture and sheen. The fur of the beaver is brown with very little variation in color from different parts of the body. When wet, beaver fur is a dark brown. The fur is also glossy. Beaver fur may be somewhat difficult to obtain, but it is an excellent material for dubbing brown bodies.

Mole Fur: The whole hide of a mole is about four by six inches, and it is inexpensive. In its natural state it varies from light brown to dark gray. The fur is very short, making it more difficult to use as dubbing material than furs of other animals, but when properly spun on the thread it makes a very good body. As an alternative to spinning the fur, the hide may be cut with a razor in narrow strips and wrapped around the shank of the hook, in spirals, to form the body of the fly. The skins are sometimes dyed, but the natural colors are generally more desirable.

Muskrat Fur: This fur varies at the base from a dark cream to an iron dun. The tips of the fibers are brownish. The longer guard hairs may be mixed with the fur in dubbing to give a more fuzzy appearance to a fly, making it exceedingly attractive to the fish. The fur is somewhat difficult to handle, but it is well worth the time spent in preparing it for use.

Rabbit Fur: There are many natural colors of rabbit fur, ranging from pure white to black. Some rabbit fur has a reddish tinge, which makes it a suitable substitute for fox belly fur. Other rabbit furs are very light gray. Some are iron dun in color. Rabbit fur is used as dubbing material for fly bodies. The fur should be of prime quality, soft and silky, with or without guard hairs. The soft, silky hair makes an ideal streamer wing because the fibers lie closely together. The guard hair is stubby and makes a wing that spreads or fans out over the body of the fly. Either type is good; which to use depends on the effect desired.

Deer Hair (Bucktail): The use of bucktail is never-ending. Every fly-tier should have at least one natural-colored bucktail in his fly-tying kit. Bucktails dyed red, hot-orange, and yellow are also valuable fly-tying materials. The tail of the Eastern or Northern white-tailed buck deer is the best of the bucktails for fly-tying purposes. The snow-white hairs of the tail are 3–7 inches long and some tails may have a slight curl, while others may be very straight. The hairs on the back of the tail vary from a light brown at the tip to gray at the base on some tails, or to a slate gray at the base of others.

Blacktail deer have a small tail, the hairs of which are usually 6–8 inches long. The white hair is coarser than that of the Eastern or Northern deer. The hairs on the back of the tail are almost black.

Mule deer have a tail which is 1–1½ inches in diameter. The hair is short and wiry. There is one bunch of black hair at the tip of the tail which can be used in making hair-wing flies; otherwise the tail of the mule deer is of no use to the fly-tier.

Calf Tail Hair: The hair from a calf tail is used in making many flies. The material is obtained from a very young calf. The tails are 6–12 inches long while the length of the hair is ½–2 inches. Calf tail may be partly straight or curly. It is a solid hair, with a definite sheen or gloss. Calf tails are natural white, light brown, dark brown, and black. The white tails are often colored with dye. Many people prefer calf tail to all other types of hair.

Black-Bear Hair: The hair of the black bear is solid and ranges from a very dark brown to black. This hair has a certain amount of curl, which gives it a lot of action in the water. There is a natural gloss to bear hair which helps to make the fly more attractive. For flies with black hair-wings bear hair meets every requirement. It may be used to make the full wing of the fly, or a few fibers may be used as topping to imitate the back of a minnow. The underfur is used for dubbing the bodies of flies.

Brown-Bear Hair: The hair of the brown bear varies from a seal brown to a dark brown. Like the hair of the black bear it may be used for anything from a caddis pattern to a streamer wing. The hair is solid, has a glossy sheen, and its slight curl helps to give action to the fly. The underfur may also be used for dubbing bodies.

Polar-Bear Hair: Polar-bear hair is a solid hair which helps to sink the fly under the water. It has a translucent sheen which makes it an effective fish attractor. The hair from the back of the animal and from the ruff around its neck is about 1¼–4 inches long. These hairs make very beautiful hair-wing streamer flies. Because the hair is stiff, it requires some practice to tie on a hook securely. The demand for polar-bear hair has increased its cost to the point where many fly-tiers are using substitutes for it, although it is still most popular in making silver salmon, or coho, flies in the Pacific Northwest.

There is a great deal of underfur on the back and ruff of this animal. This may be used for spinning, or dubbing the bodies of flies. The natural sheen of the underfur makes an attractive body. Because of the wiry character of the material, some difficulty may be encountered at the first attempt to use it. Dyed colors as well as the natural color are used for dubbing.

Horse Mane: The hair from the mane of a horse, in black, brown, or white is sometimes used as a body material. In other regions it may or may not prove to be effective. However, most professionals keep a small amount of this hair on hand for wrapping or braiding fly bodies.

Two colors are generally used in making a horse-mane body. A dark color is used on the top of the fly, and a contrasting lighter color is used for the underbody. As an alternative the body may be wrapped with just one color of horse-mane hair with a colored stripe of body floss woven lengthwise under the horse-mane body.

With a tail of either hackle or hair, and a hackle in front of the body, the resulting fly will produce fish at times.

Horse Tail: The hair from the tail of a horse is much more coarse than the hair from its mane. White, brown, and black are the colors most frequently used. This hair is suitable for the hackle of flies. The hair is attached to the hook in the same manner as deer hair. When tied on as hackle each fiber stands out separately. The action of the hair increases as the hairs become saturated in the water.

Moose-Mane Hair: The hair from the mane or the ruff of the neck of a moose is quite long, ranging in length about 3–7 inches. There are two colors of hair, black and white. The black fibers are about one-third less in diameter than the white hair fibers. When both white and black hair fibers are used in making the body a very active fly can be produced. The hair from the mane or ruff of the neck is the only portion used in making flies. The hair on the rest of the body is too short for fly-tying.

Silver-Monkey Hair: On the skin of a silver monkey there are six distinct colors of hair: white, light brown or natural orange, black, dark chocolate brown, and barred (gray and black). Each of the colors is appropriate for use in tying flies, and the glossy sheen of the hair makes an attractive fly. The one most frequently used on flies is the barred hair from the sides of the skin. This ranges in length 1–1½ inches. The hair is gray at the base. From the middle of the hair to the tip it is barred with alternate stripes of black and gray. For hair-type wings the hair of the silver monkey is both attractive and surprising. Bunched over the body it makes a beautiful fly wing and has an insectlike quality which is attractive to fish.

Skunk Hair: The hair of a skunk is black and white. It has a gloss which makes it shine in the sunlight. The short body hair is used in making flies of small size. The underfur may also be used. The popular material from this animal, however, is from the tail. This is a long, coarse hair, 4–8 inches in length, white at the base, ½–⅓ black at the tips. It is used for both wings and bodies by fly-tiers in every locality.

Wolverine Hair: The hair of the wolverine is a very dark brown, glossy and rather stiff. It is highly prized for the making of hair-wings. Some of it is white; other parts of a hide may be orange. The underfur of the animal, not as dark as the guard hairs, can be used for dubbing. The complete skin of a wolverine is very expensive. Small pieces of the hide may be purchased, however.

TYING SILK

Sizes: The silk thread used for the tying of flies varies from size "A," which is the largest, to size 000000 (6/0), which is the smallest used by the average fly-tier. Except for some of the very large, special-purpose flies, such as certain salmon patterns, size "A" is too heavy for tying. For the amateur tier the heaviest silk normally used is 00 (2/0). A small diameter is preferred because it does not add much bulk to the fly and it also makes a smoother head. There is no precise rule to follow with respect to the hook size and the correct size of tying silk. In the larger hook sizes particularly, the silk size depends on the type of fly being made. Generally speaking, a 6/0 can be used for dry flies from No. 24 to No. 10; a 4/0 is appropriate for wet flies from No. 10 to No. 2, while a 5/0 is useful for wet patterns smaller than No. 10.

Colors: Although tying silk is obtainable in a wide variety of colors, black and white are the most commonly used. There is seldom any need for any other than these two colors. Select black or white tying silk, depending on the shade of the fly being tied. Use black silk when tying the dark- to medium-colored flies. Use white tying silk on patterns such as the Ginger Quill, White Moth, White Miller, and very light-colored nymphs.

Body Floss Silk floss is the best material for making the bodies of flies. However, rayon floss is less expensive and therefore more popular. It is durable. It also adheres to the shank of the hook and remains in place. The color does not vary when it is wet. Some materials used in making flies will become from one to three shades darker when wet than they are when dry. Rayon floss may be purchased in various colors, wrapped on small spools convenient for the use of fly-tiers. The floss consists of two strands. The two strands come off the spool together and may be wrapped on together unless the tying instructions are explicitly to the contrary. Popular preference is for the two-strand floss, although it comes in one-, two-, and four-strand spools.

Tinsel Tinsel is a metallic tape. It is a necessary material in fly-tying and comes in several different sizes. The size to be used is determined by the size of the hook upon which the fly is being tied. Whether the tinsel is used in making a solid body on a fly or simply for ribbing, the width of the tinsel is an important factor. Oval tinsel and flat tinsel can be obtained in wide medium, or fine widths. There is also a round or rope tinsel, fine solid wire, and heavier pliable wire tinsel.

Flat tinsel is made in a number of different colors, including red, green, and blue. However, silver and gold tinsel are the most widely used. The surface of tinsel is either smooth or embossed. Embossed tinsel has been "gimped" by running it between two patterned rollers, making its surface uneven. Some professionals like embossed tinsel more than the smooth, or flat, tinsel. Although it is a little more brittle when embossed, theoretically the uneven surface makes a better reflector of light and increases the chances of the fish seeing and being attracted to the fly as it moves through the water. Tinsel has a very definite tendency to tarnish. This tendency is greater when the tinsel is kept in the open and exposed either to sunshine or to damp air. This exposure causes oxidation and eventual tarnish on the surface of the tinsel. A French tinsel called "tarnish-proof" oxidizes less quickly than any other. The best way to protect tinsel from tarnish is to keep it in a dark place (a drawer or box) and away from anything made of rubber which contains sulphur and speeds the tarnishing process. To avoid tarnish on the tinsel on flies, coat the tinsel with lacquer before you use it, by placing a drop of lacquer on your forefinger and drawing the tinsel through, between thumb and forefinger.

Chenille The chenille most commonly used in fly-tying is made of rayon fibers. These fibers are held between two twisted threads of the same color as the chenille. Some chenille is made of silk; this is far superior to rayon chenille. Rayon chenille is a little more wiry than silk, but the fullness of the body remains after it is immersed in water. Rayon chenille is available in a wide variety of colors.

Another type of chenille is made of silver or gold tinsel. This provides a metallic sheen. Still another type of rayon chenille has a ribbing of either silver or gold color. The ribbing is not metal but an acetate tape. When wrapped on the body of a fly small spots of the silver or gold color show in the body. It gives a different effect, which may be quite desirable under some fishing conditions.

The size of the chenille to be used on a fly depends upon the size of the hook upon which it is being tied. Rayon chenille is manufactured in seven different sizes, but the average fly-tier needs only three sizes for the flies he will tie. The following table is a general guide to the size of chenille to be used:

Chenille Number	Maker's Size Number	Common Designation	Hook Sizes
No. 1	00	Small	No. 10–16
No. 2	3	Medium	No. 6–10 Makes a very thin body on No. 6 hook, a very full body on No. 10 hook
No. 3	6	Large	No. 1/0–6 Makes a full body on No. 6 hook, a thin body on No. 1/0 hook

HOOKS

Hook Sizes: Fly hooks vary from No. 10/0 to No. 24, the first being the largest and the last being the smallest size of fly hook made for sale commercially. The "size" of a hook is determined, in accord with a standard gauge of hook sizes, by the over-all length of the hook with a regular shank, measured from the eye to the outside of the bend of the hook. This over-all length varies from ⁹⁄₃₂ inch in size No. 22 to 3¼ inches in size No. 1/0. The over-all length of the hook sizes most commonly used in fly-tying, however, is less than one inch. It is, for example, 1³⁄₁₆ inch in size No. 6, 1¹⁄₁₆ inch in size No. 8, ⁹⁄₁₆ inch in size No. 10, and ⁷⁄₁₆ inch in size No. 12. The gap of the hook—that is, the distance between the point of the barb and the shank—also varies with the size of the hook. But in any particular size the gap is constant whether the shank is extra-long or extra-short.

Wire Thickness: For each size of hook a different gauge, or thickness, of wire is used in the standard or "regular" hook of the size. There may be minute variations, running through the entire line, between the gauges of wire used by different manufacturers of hooks, but such variations are very slight. Hooks of a particular size made of heavier wire than the standard gauge are designated a 2X Stout, 3X Stout, depending upon the relative degree of extra thickness of the wire used one, two, or three sizes larger. Thus a No. 6 hook may be obtained in the standard-gauge wire or a wire which is a size or two heavier than standard. The latter hook would be designated as a size No. 6, 2X Stout (two sizes larger). Dry-fly hooks are also made of smaller-gauge wire (finer diameter) than the standard hook of the same size. The use of smaller-diameter wire in a hook is indicated by adding after the hook size the words Extra Fine, 3X

Fine, or 4X Fine, the latter being the lightest fine-wire hook made. Thus a dry-fly hook made of wire of standard gauge for the size is designated as a No. 12 hook, and a hook of the same size made of the next lighter gauge of wire is known as No. 12 Extra Fine.

Length of Shank: As pointed out there is a standard or regular over-all length for each size of hook. But hooks of each size are also made with shanks which are longer than the standard length. The increased length of the shank is indicated by adding to the hook size the designation 1X Long, 2X Long, 3X Long, depending upon the amount by which such shank length is increased. Thus a hook size No. 10 (gap of regular No. 10 hook) with a shank the length of a regular No. 8 is designated as a No. 10, 2X Long.

From the foregoing you can see that there are a multitude of hooks from which you may choose for use in tying flies. Remember we have been talking only of hooks used for fly-tying and not of hooks designed for use in other types of fishing. A supply house would have to carry virtually millions of hooks if it had an adequate quantity of all of the sizes on hand at all times.

Quality and Price: It is true that you can find fly hooks which are very reasonable in price. But you must remember that those selling at the lower prices must be made of less expensive materials and processed with a minimum outlay of labor and machine time. This means that the cheaper hooks do not have the temper, the sharp point on the barb, or the careful workmanship that the higher-priced hooks have. You must also remember that in fly-tying a correctly tempered hook is the backbone of the fly. So whenever you buy a hook upon which to tie a fly, whether it be a large hook or a very small one, be sure that it is the best quality that you can obtain. If you need some hooks of a certain size and the price of them seems high, buy just the number you will use, whether that is a dozen, or even less. It is more economical to buy a dozen hooks of extra-good quality than to buy a box of one hundred hooks of doubtful quality. It is true that a hook looks about the same whatever its price. Every hook has a shank, a bend, and a barb. But more important is the temper and the quality of the material and workmanship. This doesn't show on the surface. Those qualities are proved only in use. Never buy cheap hooks. Buy from a supplier who will have hooks of the top grade. The best sources are mail order houses that give you personal service and the shop that specializes in fly-tying materials. *See also* Hook
—R.P.
—H.S.

Muddler Minnow Series The Muddler Minnow fly was created by Don Gapen, fishing guide and fly-tier from Nipigon, Ontario, during the 1948 brook-trout season. This unusual-looking bucktail-streamer was designed to imitate the local "cockatush minnow," which is actually a species of sculpin. The sculpin is a favorite food item of Nipigon River brook trout, and Gapen's imitation soon accounted for numerous trophy squaretails. He shared the new pattern with friends and clients. It was introduced to American anglers in a *Field & Stream* article in 1949 by A.J. McClane. The Muddler Minnow became the most versatile and popular fly in this century.

In addition to its almost universal appeal to all species of trout the pattern proved effective on nearly every freshwater and many saltwater gamefish. As the Muddler grew in popularity fly-tyers began to add their own individual styles and materials to the hook. This hybridization proved a mixed blessing. Some merely reduced the pattern's appeal, while other variations of Gapen's dressing were at times more successful than the original. By altering a few materials and the outline Dan Bailey of Livingston, Montana, produced what is considered today the most popular version.

Dave Whitlock designed a series of Marabou Muddlers in the late 1960's for fishing the larger rivers of the West. However, these soon proved effective throughout this country, in Canada, and in South America for very large trout.

Whitlock also worked out a set of Muddlers to extend the useful range of the standard Bailey-style Muddler. The main variation is color change on most, but as a result the Muddler silhouette becomes much more useful over a wide range of water and lighting conditions. Also, in waters where fish see the standard pattern almost daily, these patterns take more fish.

Fishing Methods of the Muddler Series The Muddlers, like another universally effective fly, the woolyworm, are almost impossible to fish incorrectly. They take fish very well when floating, sinking, or swimming deep, or given any type of imparted action. However, the Muddlers will be more effective if more than a single casual approach is given to wetting one over a fish. Here are the three most effective methods of muddlering with a fly rod:

1. Surface Fishing A floating line is used and the head and collar of the Muddler is waterproofed with musclin or silicon. The fly is cast upstream and allowed to alight gently, so it will float. Either let the fly drift naturally or give it a few short quick pulls to cause it to dart under the surface. Near the end of the drift the Muddler is pulled under and retrieved back to the rod with a series of short strips. The greased-line salmon method is also extremely effective for surface fishing Muddlers.

2. Subsurface Fishing The Muddler fly is not treated with any waterproofing and is cast with floating line hard to the water so that it will only float a second or two. It is then quickly pulled under and allowed to follow the action of the currents. This dead-drifting method is extremely effective in most broken-water streams where trout or bass lie waiting for food to be washed with the current to them.

Another exciting subsurface method calls for casting directly across a pool and quickly stripping the Muddler back in fast foot-long pulls. The fly will create a wake just under the surface and attract vicious strikes.

3. Bottom Fishing Using either a sinktip or sinking flyline and also weighting the fly, the Muddler is fished as near the bottom as possible. The cast should angle upstream and across and be given slack so that line and fly drift free and sink. Then the fly is allowed to be carried down and around the angler's side of the stream by current action. Now the Muddler is retrieved slowly and erratically on a tight line, much as a jig would be worked on a spinning outfit. The goal is to sink the fly near the bottom and troll out as much of that area as possible on each cast. Though less glamorous than the other two methods it is most consistently effective for hooking the largest fish.

—A.J.McC.

FORAGE FISH Used in a popular sense to indicate species of no commercial or sport value which provide food for larger predatory fishes, such as darters, silversides, threadfin, shad, sardines, sculpins, chubs, shiners, or minnows. The young of many gamefish are also utilized as food and may be included as forage fish.

FORESTER, FRANK *See* Henry W. Herbert

FORWARD TAPER LINE *See* Fly Line

FOUL Opposite of clear. For example an anchor is fouled when the anchor cable or line has twisted around the flukes.

FOUL-HOOKED That condition when a fish is hooked in any external part of the body, such as the fins, eye, head, or tail. A fish may be foul-hooked when striking at and missing a bait or lure, or by throwing the hook, or simply by crossing ahead of a lure in motion.

FOUR-EYE BUTTERFLYFISH *See* Butterflyfishes

FOURSPINE STICKLEBACK *Apeltes quadracus* This spiny little member of the family Gasterosteidae is identified by the 4 dorsal-fin spines, which may vary from 2-4, and it has another immediately in front of the soft dorsal fin. The body is naked and free from plates, as in threespine stickleback (*which see*), with which it might be confused because of the spine count. A distinct bony ridge occurs on either side of the belly. The soft dorsal and anal fins are almost identical in shape. The caudal fin is long and narrow, and rounded instead of concave as in the threespine stickleback. It is black or brown to olive-brown above, with dark mottlings, grading to paler or silvery below. The pelvic-fin membrane is red, giving the species the sometimes used name of bloody stickleback. It reaches a length of about 2½ inches.

It is known only from the Atlantic Coast, from Nova Scotia to Virginia, in salt-, fresh- or brackish water. During the summer, it frequents freshwater creeks but descends into the lower reaches of the estuaries during the winter into somewhat deeper water. It is able to live in waters of poor quality, as with most other members of this family.

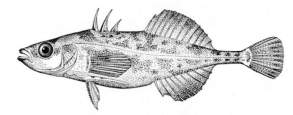

Fourspine Stickleback

LIFE HISTORY

The spawning season is from April to July depending on the location. The male builds a nest from plant fragments, picks up the fertilized eggs, and guards them. Adults frequent quiet stretches of grassy bays and areas wherever there is vegetation. It feeds on amphipods, copepods, and other small crustaceans.

ANGLING VALUE

Because of its abundance in some localities, it may be of importance as a food item for predatory fishes. In some areas, anglers use this and other sticklebacks for bait.

—D.dS.

FOURSPOT FLOUNDER *Paralichthys oblongus* A small flatfish of the family Bothidae or lefteye flounders, which seldom attain 15 inches in length. The fourspot flounder has a limited distribution, occurring from southern New England to New York. It is readily distinguished by the four large oblong black spots edged with pink located two above and two below the lateral line; this dark side is otherwise a mottled gray or gray-brown in color. A spring spawner (May), the fourspot lays buoyant eggs, and about three months after hatching the young, now 2–3 inches long, migrate from the surface to the bottom where the fish live at depths of 50–100 feet. Like most flatfishes it feeds on invertebrates such as shrimp, worms, and crabs and occasionally on small fish.

ANGLING VALUE

Due to its small size the fourspot flounder is of no angling importance. However, the species is taken by bottom fishing, usually incidental to some other quarry.
—A.J.McC.

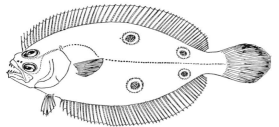

Fourspot Flounder

FRAME The boat's skeleton, including the ribs, the keel, and the stem, all of which give the boat its shape.

FRANCE This European country has comparatively little public freshwater angling to offer the tourist. Nearly all of the better rivers are privately held, although some trout fishing can be obtained through various hotels and associations. Perhaps the most outstanding trout stream is the Loue River in the Province of Franche-Comté. The Allier River in the Province of Auvergne also has some Atlantic salmon fishing, as does the Gaves d'Olloron. There are many small streams, notably in the Pyrenees and the Haute-Savoie, where some trout fishing can be had through contacting local tackle shops. Brown trout and European grayling are most common to France, but rainbow trout and char occur in scattered localities. Northern pike are the dominant warmwater species and inhabit many of the slower flowing rivers as well as lakes. Coarse fish, such as carp, tench, and bream are very popular among French anglers and annual match-fishing events are held in many Provinces.

A limited amount of saltwater fishing can be found along the coast of France, and occasionally some large bluefin tuna and swordfish are caught in the Mediterranean. —A.J.McC.

FREEBOARD That distance or part of the boat that rises above the water line, and runs along from the gunwale, or main deck, to the surface of the water.

FRENCH GRUNT *Haemulon flavolineatum* This is one of the most abundant grunts in southern Florida. It also occurs in the Bahamas, West Indies, and along the coast of Central and South America to Brazil. The average total length of mature adults is about 8 inches. The French grunt is distinguished from others by the color pattern. The sides of the body have dark lines and yellow stripes. The mouth is red. The French grunt has 12 dorsal spines. It has 14–15 dorsal rays, 8 anal rays, and 16–17 pectoral rays, but usually 16. Pored lateral-line scales 47–50, usually 48–49. Gillrakers 22–24, usually 23. Pectoral fins are naked.

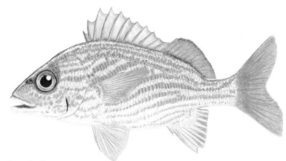

French Grunt

ANGLING VALUE

The French grunt is a bottom feeder occurring in shallow water close to shore and about reefs in deeper water where it is more abundant. It takes natural bait, such as cut pilchard, cut mullet, and dead shrimp. It is good sport on the lightest of tackle. It is a tasty panfish but usually too small to be of commercial value. —L.R.

FRESHWATER DRUM *Aplodinotus grunniens* This is the only member of the drum family found in freshwater. There are over thirty saltwater species. Distributed principally in large rivers and lakes, it ranges from the Hudson Bay drainage of Manitoba and northern Ontario and from the Great Lakes (except Superior) east to Quebec and Lake Champlain, and south to the Gulf and eastern Mexico to Guatemala. The Missouri River drainage forms the western boundary while to the east it extends almost to the Atlantic Coast states. Although the species prefers clearwaters, it is physically equipped to withstand turbid waters better than many species and thus is found in abundance in some of the large, silty lakes and rivers. Industrial and domestic pollution, however, serves to destroy the primary source of food for the species, and thus has depressed populations and limited distribution in some areas.

The freshwater drum has a rather oblong body with the back somewhat humped or elevated. The tail is rounded, the snout blunt, and the long dorsal fin extends from the peak of the humped back almost to the tail. The mouth is subterminal and horizontal and there are small, comblike teeth on the jaws. Close observation reveals that the lateral line extends into the tail fin. The dorsal fin is nearly separated, with the forward part composed of 8–9 spiny rays and the rear portion containing 25–31 softrays. The anal fin has 2 spines, the second of which is long and very stout. The upper portion of the body is pearl-gray and sometimes gives off bronze, blue, and silver reflections. The sides are lighter and more silvery; the belly is milk-white.

Two notable physical features of the freshwater drum deserve special mention. The first of these is the grunting or drumming noise which the fish makes and from which its name probably originated. On calm days or evenings when the fish are near the surface, the weird noise seems to come from everywhere; yet its source cannot be pin-pointed. River fishermen who spend a lot of time on the water are familiar with these noises which are emitted at intervals. It is strongly suspected that the sound is made by rapid contractions of an abdominal muscle which is in contact with the tense air bladder. The other notable feature is the large otoliths (ear bones) which are extremely hard and pearl-like and which bear an L-shaped groove. These are commonly called "lucky bones" and have a long history of superstitious folklore connected with them. The Indians are believed to have used them for wampum, ceremonial purposes, and as neck charms to prevent various sicknesses.

The freshwater drum has a long list of common names, most notable of which are sheepshead, drum, freshwater sheepshead, croaker, crocus, jewelhead, white perch, and grunter. On the commercial market it usually is called white perch or sheepshead.

The usual size of the freshwater drum that are marketed commercially runs 1½–5 pounds. Specimens as large as 20–60 pounds occasionally are reported, and otoliths found in excavated Indian village sites indicate that they may have attained sizes as large as 200 pounds.

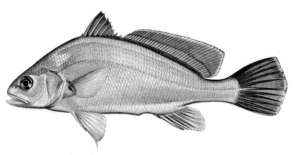

Freshwater Drum

LIFE HISTORY

Freshwater drum spawn over shallow gravel and sandy stretches of shore in April or May when water temperature is about 65°–70°F. The eggs, probably numbering from 10,000 to 100,000 per female, are broadcast and adhere to pebbles. No parental care is given the eggs or young. Hatching may take about two weeks, after which the young stay in the shallows and begin feeding on minute crustaceans. As the summer progresses the young drum begin to supplement their crustacean diet with insects. Through the next year or two, insects and mollusks serve as food until the fish are big enough to start adding small fish to their diet. Depending upon food availability, the diet of adults will consist primarily of mollusks, insects, and fish in various combinations. Mollusks are probably preferred when they are present in sufficient quantity. The species is particularly adept in obtaining and "shelling" mollusks. Searching the bottom mud and debris primarily by touch and taste, mollusks are picked out and then crunched or "shelled" by the large, strong pharyngeal teeth. The shells are spewed out, and the soft bodies are swallowed.

Freshwater drum have some tendency to school in the summer, and usually are found in water 10–40 feet deep. In the winter, the schooling urge is strong, and large concentrations may be located on the bottom in the deeper areas of the lake or river. The species is almost always found very near the bottom.

By the end of their first summer, freshwater drum should be 4–5 inches long. Where food is not seriously limited, they should be 8 inches at age two, 11 inches at three, 13 inches at four, and 15 inches at five years. A 24-inch specimen should be about 10 years old under average conditions. Maximum age attained may be as old as 15–20 years, but most individuals are fortunate to live 6–8 years. Natural mortality accounts for upwards of 60 per cent of the population annually.

A weight of one pound is attained at a length of about 13 inches, 2 pounds at 16 inches, 3 pounds at 18 inches and 5 pounds at 20 inches.

ANGLING VALUE

The freshwater drum is not particularly important as a sport fish. However, it can be taken by casting, trolling, and still-fishing with artificial and live baits. In some localities anglers fish specifically for drum, but in most areas it is taken by fishermen in quest of other species. It is a strong fighter.

COMMERCIAL VALUE

The usual annual commercial harvest of freshwater drum probably varies from 5–10 million pounds. The bulk of this catch comes from Lake Erie, but certain smaller lakes and large rivers throughout the central states contribute to the total. The species is considered a coarse or rough fish wherever it occurs in abundance, so that it is available for commercial harvest with the blessings of most anglers. The quality of the flesh is only fair. Prices paid to commercial fishermen usually amount to 2–3 cents per pound, or about the same as for carp and suckers. The species is quite capable of maintaining population levels even under heavy commercial harvest. Trapnets are the primary method of capture in the Great Lakes, while seines are usually used in the smaller inland lakes. Lake Erie drum average about 1½ pounds, but drum from inland lakes and rivers usually run 2–5 pounds.
—J.T.S.

FRESHWATER ECOLOGY Aquatic ecology is the study of the interrelationships between aquatic organisms and their environments. The environment may include all other organisms except the one under study or all organisms except the species being studied. This is *population ecology*. There may be an aggregate of species living together as a community. This study is *community ecology*. Another science, *limnology*, is concerned with all of the aspects of freshwaters—physical, chemical, geological, and biotic—primarily of lake waters, but usually including streams. Freshwater ecology is based on limnology but is more concerned with aspects primarily biological. *Marine ecology* (*which see*) concerns life in the sea and bears the same relationship to oceanography as freshwater ecology does to limnology. Oceanography is a vast science in itself. The study of streams is sometimes separated into the special science *potamology*.

PHYSICAL CHARACTERISTICS OF WATER

Water, the liquid, is different from air, the gas, as a medium in which to live. In fact, it is different from nearly all other liquids in many respects, similar in others. For instance, as water cools, it contracts until, as it continues to cool below about 4°C (39.2°F), it expands slightly, thereby becoming less dense and lighter. At 0°C (32°F), as it freezes, it adds about $1/11$ to its volume. Consequently ice floats, and the coldest water, that just above freezing temperature, rises to the surface so that only the shallowest lakes will freeze solid, except possibly in the Arctic.

Water has other unusual relationships with heat. It has a high heat capacity; that is, it takes much heat, as distinct from temperature, to warm water enough to be noticeable on the ordinary thermometer. Conversely, water, in cooling, gives off much more heat than an equal mass of almost anything else. Water has a high latent heat of evaporation. Even when water has been raised to 100°C (212°F), its boiling point, it still requires much heat to vaporize it. To change 1 quantity of water at 100°C requires as much heat as it takes to raise 539 equal quantities of water, somewhere below 100°C, 1 degree Centigrade. Water does not have to be boiling to vaporize. As sweat, it evaporates from our bodies taking with it much heat, and it evaporates in the same way from lakes and oceans, thereby cooling the water and the air. When water freezes, changing from water at 0°C to ice at 0°C, it gives off fifty-nine times as much heat as an equal quantity of water would in lowering one degree.

Water is thus a remarkable bank for storage or release of heat. A large amount of heat given off or absorbed produces only a relatively small change in the water temperature. This accounts for the tempering and stabilizing effects of oceans and large lakes on climate.

We tend to think of water as a thin liquid, To a small creature the water provides a great deal of resistance to its movements, and considerable effort must be expended to move about; that is, water is viscous and offers resistance to animal movements. On the other hand, this resistance helps the animal or plant in the matter of maintaining a given depth and in overcoming the tendency to sink. Viscosity changes with temperature, and water is more than twice as viscous at 0°C as it is at 30°C (86°F). Pour some ice water into the sink. Then pour in a kettle of boiling water. The boiling water seems to be, and is, much thinner and splashier than the cold water.

Water is fairly heavy and weighs 62.4 pounds per cubic foot at 4°C (39.2°F), the temperature of water's greatest density. Density as well as viscosity changes with temperature. Because of this density and weight, organisms are subjected to increasing pressure as they descend. In 100 feet of water the pressure at the bottom is about 58 pounds per square inch at sea level. Organisms living at depths must be adapted to the pressures, and those which range (from depth to depth) must be able to adjust rapidly.

Water has a high surface tension so that a film forms on the surface, a film which is easily broken by large organisms such as ourselves. To a tiny creature, the film may provide a barrier that is normally unbreakable, or even a surface to which to attach itself. If the barrier is broken, the organism may be unable to get back to its own side and will either dry up or drown, depending upon its source. Spiders and water striders take advantage of the phenomenon, run across the surface, and never wet their feet.

Light penetrates clear water, but differentially so; that is, red and orange and much of the violet are absorbed near the surface. Much deeper down, the last colors to disappear are blue and yellow-green. In the clearest of freshwaters, just about all light disappears at about 640 feet. Penetration is much less in waters that are turbid. The muddy Missouri River is pitch dark only a few inches below its surface. This factor is important in limiting the depths to which plants can grow.

CHEMICAL CHARACTERISTICS OF WATER

The quest for the universal solvent is old; yet the solvent has always been with us. Water will dissolve almost anything, at least a little bit. Certainly, all the substances that aquatic organisms need are in solution, and indeed must be before they can be taken in by the organism. Furthermore, water does not greatly change the substances dissolved in it, so that they are available to the organisms in the form needed, and the unchanged water can be used over again. Substances in solution tend to ionize; that is, they break up into parts called ions which bear an electrical charge. Recombinations of ions from originally different substances make it possible for the organism to have available many new compounds for its use. Water as a solvent makes possible many chemical

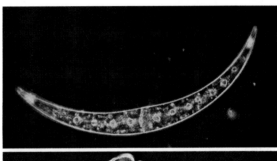

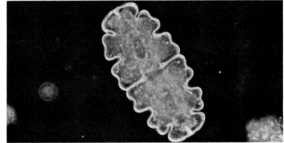

Microscopic plants or algae are important in the food chain for very small consumers such as protozoans to large organisms such as insects

reactions that might not otherwise occur. Dry baking soda and cream of tartar mixed do not react with each other, except very slowly. Yet, this mixture is baking powder, and when water is added the two components almost immediately react together producing gases that cause the biscuits to rise.

Water does combine with some substances. By itself it is neutral, neither acid nor alkaline, but when carbon dioxide (CO_2) is added or is dissolved from the air, water and CO_2 combine to produce the weak carbonic acid (H_2CO_3) which then may react with other substances.

SOURCE OF WATER

The ultimate source of most freshwater is rain or snow, but before it becomes part of a lake or stream, it must first wash the atmosphere, scour the surface, and leach the soil or the rocks. Gases are dissolved from the air, substances are dissolved from the surface by runoff water, and still more are dissolved from the soil or rocks by that water which has penetrated into the soil. There is, therefore, no "pure" natural water.

Some rain, of course, falls directly into already existing waters, but the rest of it must reach the lake or stream as runoff, or, as most of it does, by the underground route, to appear as seepage of groundwater or as springs, emptying directly into the lake or forming the source of a stream or tributary. Runoff water may be charged with material which it has eroded and so may make turbid the water into which it flows. Spring water, on the other hand, tends to be clear but to have much dissolved matter. Its content of dissolved matter depends upon the type of soil or rocks through which the one time rainwater may have been percolating for months, or years, and perhaps many miles. A complete study of water would require a background knowledge of soils and geology. Water from granitic rocks, for example, tends to be slightly on the acid side and soft. Water percolating through limestones is alkaline and hard.

In winter and summer the temperature of deep springs remains much the same since the water comes from such depths as to be unaffected by warm or cold air. This temperature varies only slightly from the mean annual temperature of the region in which the springs exist. Consequently, springs tend to warm lakes and streams in winter and cool them in summer. The water temperature of shallow groundwater springs is more variable but still is more constant than is surface water. Some springs are heated by strata of rock through which they flow before emerging.

Chemically, springs are different from the streams or lakes which they produce. Their water, emerging from depths where pressures are different, contains little oxygen but usually has relatively high concentrations of carbon dioxide. As soon as the springwater tumbles over rocks or flows some distance in a shallow spring run, it takes on oxygen and may give up some of its carbon dioxide, losing some of its minerals as well. The last are deposited as rocks called tufa. Some springs in volcanic regions may contain free acid in their waters.

NATURAL WATERS AS ENVIRONMENTS

Lakes must have a basin in which to exist. The thousands upon thousands of lakes in northern United States, Canada, Siberia, and northern Europe are primarily the result of glacial action. Some, such as the Finger Lakes of New York, were scoured from the surface of the earth. This scouring action is clearly evident in photographs of areas of the Canadian Shield with its hundreds of lakes, much longer than wide, with the axes of all in an area in the same direction. The Great Lakes were formed when depressions, scoured by glaciers out of the course of former stream beds, were further deformed into deep basins by the weight of ice. Sometimes buried ice blocks in moraines melted and formed lakes of the type called kettles. Still others were formed when terminal moraines formed ridges behind which water has been impounded.

Lakes may result from landslides and earthquakes. On August 17, 1959, an earthquake struck about 15 miles northwest of Yellowstone National Park. A landslide blocked the Madison River at this point and formed Earthquake Lake, known for its good fishing. Reelfoot Lake, Tennessee, is the result of the New Madrid earthquakes of 1811–1813. Crater Lake, Oregon, fills the crater of an extinct volcano. Great Salt Lake lies in a basin surrounded by mountains which leave it no outlet. River meanders are often cut off forming oxbow, meander, or "cutoff" lakes. As seepage water dissolves the subsurface rocks, a cavern may be formed. If the roof of this cavern collapses and the hole fills with water, a sinkhole lake or pond is the result.

Lakes change rapidly, geologically speaking. Currents erode materials from one place and deposit them in another, building sandbars, reefs, islands, and sandspits. Waves on larger bodies of water may carve bluffs, only to wear them away again. Ice sheets, as they expand, or are pushed by the wind, may distort the original lake shore. Geologic action may lower or raise the outlet level so that a lake empties more rapidly or may become deeper. Runoff water and streams carry clay, silt, and larger particles into the basin gradually filling it.

MEASURING THE PHYSICAL CHARACTERISTICS OF WATER

It is often sufficient to measure light penetration into a body of water only roughly or to produce an index value for comparison with others. A standard has been developed that serves as an index known as the limit of visibility of a Secchi disk. The disk is a circular metal plate 20 centimeters (13⅞ inches) in diameter, with the surface divided into four equal quadrants, with two opposing quadrants painted black and the intervening two painted white. In use this is lowered into the water until it just disappears from sight and then raised until it just reappears. The average of these two depths is taken as the "Secchi-disk reading." Devices with photoelectric cells something on the order of photographic light meters are used which are exact in their measurements rather than producing only an index figure.

Sometimes the amount of turbidity, that is of suspended matter in the water, is the measurement desired. This would commonly be thought of as muddiness of the water. Turbidities are recorded in parts per million (ppm) with the standard unit designated as that turbidity produced by one part per million of silica (fuller's earth) in distilled water. One of the methods for measuring turbidity is essentially like the Secchi disk except that the object that disappears is a platinum wire. The depth of disappearance and reappearance as the wire is lowered into the water has been calibrated with the same depth in other waters of known turbidities. Turbidities in parts per million are read directly from the scale on the instrument. In another method, the passage of light through a water sample is compared with the passage of light through a standard of known turbidity and the unknown thus determined.

The distribution of organisms is influenced by temperatures so that accurate measurements are essential. In shallow water, temperatures can be measured directly by wading out into the water with a thermometer. Deeper

Turbulence and current are important factors of environment which determine the community of organisms that exists in continuous buffeting

waters present problems. Special sampling bottles have been devised that are lowered, empty, to the desired depth and there filled with water by remote control. This water is brought to the surface and quickly checked with a thermometer. Other samplers pass water through themselves as they are lowered but, when triggered from the surface, close and thus enclose a sample of water which can be analyzed when brought to the surface. A reversing thermometer can be lowered to any desired depth, and, when it is reversed end for end, the mercury column "locks" into place and is not disturbed by its passage through warmer water on its way to the surface. Perhaps the simplest method, once the initial cost is taken care of, is a thermophone (sometimes called a thermistor), essentially an electric thermometer. This acts on the principle that the resistance of metals to passage of an electric current changes with the temperature. The advantages are that a series of temperatures may be taken much more rapidly and without the constant lowering and hauling up of apparatus. Inexpensive instruments of this type have been developed to help anglers find the depths at which fish may be distributed because of the temperature, so that we should see much greater use of the thermophones by ecologists.

Devices of these sorts enable the ecologist to measure temperature in relation to depth and to determine the presence or absence of thermal stratification.

CHEMICAL CHARACTERISTICS OF LAKES

If we were to fill a bottle halfway with distilled water and the remainder with pure oxygen at sea-level atmospheric pressure and 30°C temperature and allowed the bottle to stand quietly, a small amount of the gas would slowly go into solution in the water. If we shook the bottle, the gas would dissolve faster because the splashing would expose more water surface through which the oxygen could pass and expose more water that had only a little oxygen in it. If we then admitted a little more gas

and repeated the shaking and addition of gas until no more gas would go into solution, the water would have become saturated with oxygen. Such situations do not exist naturally, because the atmosphere would be exposed to a body of water not in a bottle. It would not be distilled but would be impure natural water probably with some oxygen already in it, it would be the mixture of gases that is air rather than pure oxygen, the pressure might not be that of sea level, and the temperature would probably be different. The last factor would be important, for the amount of gas that will dissolve in water varies inversely with the temperature. So, differences in pressure, temperature, and concentration all affect the rate at which oxygen, or any other gas, dissolves into water, and indeed, the gas may be going out of solution if the concentration of the gas in the water becomes high enough relative to the air, as it may when photosynthesis results in an excess of oxygen in water. Bubbles of gas can sometimes be seen rising from underwater plants exposed to direct sunlight. Carbon dioxide bubbles out of solution from heavily charged spring water, just as it does when a seltzer bottle is opened.

To return to the bottle, in nature no one is shaking the bottle, but the wind-caused turbulence, whitecaps, the splashing waves upon the rocks all correspond to bottle shaking, so that oxygen and other gases in the air may go into or out of solution faster than if air and water were perfectly still. The amount of gas dissolved in the water is conveniently expressed as parts per million.

Oxygen enters natural waters from the atmosphere and from the photosynthetic activity of plants in the water. During photosynthesis, what happens is that plants take in carbon dioxide and water and produce simple sugar giving off oxygen as a by-product. Since light is necessary for photosynthesis, this source of oxygen is limited to the photic (lighted) zone along the shallow shore region called the littoral zone and to the euphotic zone in the open water of the lake; that is, to the depth that the turbidity will allow light to penetrate to be used in photosynthesis by the small floating plants called algae. Below this depth (the lighted zone), more oxygen is used by the organisms present than is contributed by plants.

In oligotrophic lakes in which the volume of the hypolimnion is greater than the volume of the epilimnion, enough oxygen remains dissolved below the photic zone to allow fish to survive between lake overturns—even such high-oxygen-demand fish as trouts. The epilimnion is usually larger than the hypolimnion in eutrophic lakes, and below the photic zone the processes of decay may lower the oxygen below limits tolerable to fish. This usually happens in summer and results in a temporary desert as far as fish and many other organisms are concerned. Not until the fall overturn is sufficient oxygen restored to make the region habitable.

In shallow lakes and ponds the depleted zone will not exist or will be a thin layer, because in the summer the waters are continually being mixed by wind action. In winter, very shallow lakes and ponds may "winter-kill" because decay of organic material may remove all the oxygen from the water and the ice cover prevents any further addition from the air.

Five parts per million of oxygen will support most warmwater fish in comfort, but trout need about ten parts per million in coolwater.

Carbon dioxide enters natural waters (a) by dissolving in rain as the rain passes through the atmosphere, (b) as a product of decomposition of organic matter in the water, (c) in groundwater which has dissolved carbon dioxide resulting from the process of decay in the soil, (d) as the product of respiration of plants and animals in the water, and (e) from the breakdown of certain chemical compounds already in the water.

Carbon dioxide is essential for plants to carry on photosynthesis, but not all of the carbon dioxide is available as gas. Some CO_2 reacts with water to form carbonic acid (H_2CO_3), which may dissociate to form radicals of HCO_3, carrying a negative charge, and ions of H^+, carrying a positive charge. Carbon dioxide may also be combined with calcium and magnesium to form calcium carbonate and magnesium carbonate ($CaCO_3$, Mg_2CO_3). Carbonic acid may react with carbonates to form bicarbonates, for example, calcium bicarbonate [$Ca(HCO_3)_2$]. With an increase in carbonic acid, more bicarbonates may form.

When CO_2 is removed from the water, some of the carbonic acid breaks up again into CO_2 and water. When this happens, the bicarbonates break up into carbonic acid and the insoluble carbonates. Water heating in a kettle loses CO_2 because hot water will hold less gas in solution. The series of reactions deposits calcium carbonate as "boiler scale" in the kettle. The same thing happens when plants take CO_2 out of the water during photosynthesis, and the carbonate deposit may even be noticeable on the plants. In a "hardwater" lake the carbonates may precipitate out as a marl, a form of limestone ($CaCO_3$). Since the compounds of CO_2 that cause water hardness normally exist as bicarbonates because the carbonates are insoluble, it is easy to see how hardwaters contain reserves of carbon dioxide. The proportions in which the various forms of carbon dioxide or its compounds exist help determine whether natural waters are to be basic, acid, or neutral. When bicarbonates are present, water is alkaline.

As long as the waters of a lake are mixing freely, CO_2 content remains fairly constant, for any excess can readily be given off to the air or a deficit may be made up by solution from the air. When stratification occurs or there is an ice cover with little mixing of water, carbon dioxide may increase and oxygen decrease as organisms carry on their metabolism. If a heavy, light-opaque snow cover prevents photosynthesis with its removal of carbon dioxide and release of oxygen, the situation may become critical, especially in shallow lakes and ponds, and result in winter-kill (*which see*).

Both oxygen content and carbon dioxide content are determined by chemical means and are measured in parts per million. Similar means are used in measuring carbonates and bicarbonates. The value of the carbonates is useful as a means of expressing the hardness of lakes. Carbonate values, expressed as parts per million, higher than 35–40 establish a lake as a hardwater lake. Values between 10 to 35 parts per million define the limits of medium-hardwater, and values below 10 parts per million are softwater lakes. Hardness due to carbonates is called temporary, or carbonate hardness, for it is easily removed by boiling of the water. Sulfates make up the permanent hardness, for such salts as calcium sulfate and magnesium sulfate do not precipitate out when the water is boiled, but such hardness must instead be relieved by chemicals such as washing soda.

DISSOLVED NUTRIENTS

Because water is so general a solute, almost any of the compounds of the earth's surface may be found dissolved in lakes. Some are in exceedingly small proportions although they may be indispensable to the well-being of plant and animal life.

Some of these dissolved substances are organic, but these are usually waste products or the result of the breakdown of dead bodies. These substances are largely sugars, amino acids, or proteins in colloidal form. The degree to which dissolved organic matter may be used by aquatic organisms for food is still open to debate and study, but there seems little doubt that many of the lower forms do use it to some extent as a food source.

The inorganic substances appear primarily as salts, some in relatively considerable quantity. Most lakes total about 100–200 parts per million of dissolved solids. Some of these salts are present in relatively large proportions, but others may appear in amounts detectable only by the most delicate analysis. Calcium is used for bones and for shells, and appears most commonly as calcium bicarbonate. Nitrogen is a necessary constituent of proteins, and must be available to build proteins; it appears as salts of ammonia, as nitrates, and as nitrites. Phosphorus, useful in many proteins and essential in the energy transfer mechanisms in the cells of animals and plants, occurs as phosphate. Silicates supply silicon to the diatoms for their glassy shells. Trace elements, essential for proper cell chemistry and for the formation of chlorophyll and hemoglobin, are indeed present in traces. Manganese, copper, and boron, for example, plus the more abundant iron, sodium, and potassium, are found as salts. If any one of these elements in the form of salts is lacking, the numbers and kinds of animals or plants that may live in the deficient water will be limited. Nitrogen and phosphorus are the elements most likely to be lacking. In smaller bodies of water such as farm ponds or small lakes, these elements may be supplied in commercial fertilizers as nitrates and phosphates so that phosphorus and nitrogen no longer will be limiting factors.

TYPES OF LAKES

A number of attempts have been made to classify lakes. Criteria for classification have been such measurable factors as hardness, whether or not the lake stratifies (*see* Thermal Stratification), whether clear or turbid, the type of bottom fauna, and the primary productivity of the body of water. Sometimes two or more criteria are combined, along with geographic location perhaps, into a complex system. Today, the rate of primary production is most commonly used for classification of the ordinary lakes with which residents of the Northern states and Canada are so familiar. In this classification the category into which a lake is placed reveals the rate in the lake at which energy is stored by the process of photosynthesis in a form in which it can be used as food.

Those in which the productivity is low are called *oligotrophic* ("few foods" or "scant nourishment") lakes. Usually these are deep and clear, and the number of plants and animals is small. Because there is not much decaying organic matter in the deeps and because the hypolimnion is cold and well-oxygenated and is larger than the epilimnion, coldwater fishes such as the lake trout may live here. Such lakes may be old in years but are young in the geological sense. Given time they will mature. Lake basins will fill in, dissolved nutrients will increase, and primary production will increase accordingly.

With this maturity and greater productivity, the waters are said to be *eutrophic* ("good foods," "well-nourished"). Enough organic matter falls to the bottom of the now relatively small hypolimnion so that the process of decomposition may deplete the oxygen to the degree that, in summer, there is a period of stagnation. The coldwater, oxygen-demanding lake trout is eliminated. Most glacier-formed lakes show this tendency toward eutrophication, although it has proceeded slowly in some. Far northern oligotrophic lakes may be much as the glacier left them 10,000 to 15,000 years ago. Toward the south, some waters have gone so far as to have become extinct and are completely filled and covered with forest. Geologically speaking, lakes are ephemeral, being only temporary bodies of water. In many areas in the United States and in Europe man is hastening the eutrophication as the lakes are fertilized with sewage and with fertilizer washed from farms and are filled with eroded topsoil, rich in itself.

There are other kinds of lakes: salt lakes, desert lakes, volcanic lakes, and artificial impoundments. The last category will be considered later since they are not natural. One other type is numerous in some regions. These are the *dystrophic* ("bad food") lakes. These have water that has been made brown and acid by the slowly decaying vegetation. If new vegetation, especially sphagnum mosses, grows and piles up faster than it decays, the lake may become a bog, or at least a lake with a boggy shoreline and accumulations of peat.

Rooted aquatic plants such as the cattail are important to the ecology of a lake, but the floating hyacinth (*foreground*) is detrimental to the habitat

LAKE ZONES

An individual lake basin may be rather naturally divided into regions. The littoral zone includes those areas in the body of water in which rooted plants grow or in which light may penetrate to the bottom. Usually this is a belt around the shore, but may include shoal areas out in the lake. Indeed, in shallow ponds or lakes, this zone may make up the entire lake. A deep lake with an abrupt drop-off from very near the shoreline would have a limited littoral zone. So, too, would a turbid lake into which light could not penetrate, for plants will not grow in the absence of light. Rooted plants will not grow well on a wave-swept sandy shore, but this would still be included in the littoral zone as long as light can penetrate to the bottom. If rooted plants extend across the entire bottom of the pond or lake, it is all considered to be littoral zone.

If the lake is too deep for light to penetrate to the bottom sufficiently to permit the growth of plants, this open, lakeward area is called the limnetic zone and extends to the depth to which the small floating plants, including algae, may flourish. This is about the same as the *trophogenic* ("food-producing") zone. Below the trophogenic is the *tropholytic* ("food-loosening or breaking-down") zone, also called the profundal, and including the lake bottom in which food is used up faster than it can be produced. Organisms living in the profundal must rely on food raining down from above.

STREAMS

Gentle rain may soak into the surface soil only to evaporate when the rain stops. If there is rain over a long enough time, the ground will become saturated with water, and this will seep out into low places to form marshes, ponds, or lakes. After a time, the lake may overflow thus forming a stream of water trickling, flowing, or plunging toward a lower level, and eventually to the sea. If the surface soil is not absorbent, the fallen water will collect in low places and then overflow. Such young streams may be intermittent or permanent depending on the rainfall and the porosity of the soil. Absorbent soils will retain water, releasing it gradually and continuously. As the depressions overflow, the running water erodes a channel deeper and deeper until the lake level is so lowered that it is no longer a lake. In the meantime, other, higher depressions have been filling and overflowing, perhaps into the former lake bed and thence into the stream which drains it. This process may be repeated many times over, and the beginnings of the stream, its headwaters, are moved farther and farther into the highlands. The headwaters are thus young, geologically. It is in this fashion that streams are formed by drainage of fairly level to rolling to mountainous areas, as outlets from depressions, and as seepage from water in the ground.

Gradient, Velocity, and Volume Streams that begin in the mountains fall rapidly in their courses, just as the mountains themselves, over which the streams flow, have steep slopes. The rate of fall, or gradient, is expressed as feet of fall per linear mile of stream. In the mountains the gradient is high, many feet per mile. Farther along its course, the gradient is lower, perhaps 5 to 20 feet per mile, as the stream reaches areas that it has eroded to a lower level in the past or that have always been low. From headwaters to mouth, the gradient becomes less and less until in the lower reaches it may be only 0.5 feet per mile. Obviously, water runs down a steep slope faster than it does down a gentle slope, and this is true of streams. But, as the slope becomes less and less steep, the velocity of the current becomes less, and from a raging torrent the stream becomes a slow-flowing river. Velocity may be measured in linear feet of flow per second. In a given section of stream it is least at the bottom and sides because of the friction between water and the stream bed.

Usually the volume, when the amount of water is measured as cubic feet of water per second, increases with distance from the headwaters, for the stream gains tributaries. Sometimes, however, mountain streams flow into a desert, sink into the sand, and disappear. Nearly always the volume at any one point varies from season to season, even from day to day, with rainfall, output from springs, and rate of evaporation from the surface.

Running waters are capable of transporting solid materials, and the greater the velocity the greater the transport ability. Because the water movement is in one direction only, eroded materials are permanently removed, but may be replaced by other materials from upstream. Thus, erosion, transport, and deposition are factors of the stream environment.

Stream temperatures tend to vary more with the air temperatures than do temperatures of lakes, except those that are completely spring fed. Within the stream, there is little difference from top to bottom, and rarely is there thermal stratification, except in quiet sloughs or extensive pools.

Turbulence and current in the water are important factors of the environment. These may be sources of continuous buffetings for both small and large stream organisms.

Chemistry of Streams Dissolved oxygen and carbon dioxide are nearly always at high levels in streams because of the constant turbulence which exposes and re-exposes all of the water to the air. Only in deep holes, during winter-kill, or in instances of severe pollution does oxygen in streams reach the danger level for aquatic organisms. The solids that are dissolved depend upon the soil over which runoff water has come, and upon the minerals dissolved in springs that may contribute significantly to the stream. Most rivers have waters that are not far from neutrality, neither very acid nor very basic. Occasionally water from coal-mining areas may cause streams to be somewhat acid, and if a strip-mine lake is suddenly drained, the highly acid slug of polluted water may kill fish and other organisms for many miles downstream.

IMPOUNDMENTS

Impoundments present a somewhat specialized instance of standing waters. There are several types. Mainstream reservoirs are usually large, running to thousands of surface acres. Headwaters reservoirs may also be large, but direct runoff or a short stretch of stream is their main source of water rather than that which may have come down from scores or hundreds of miles upstream. Farm ponds such as those found in the Piedmont region of the Southeast are built to retain only runoff water so that they do not dam an existing stream. In Missouri, Illinois, Indiana, and Ohio many small streams, often only intermittent, have been dammed, or a small lake of not more than a few hundred acres has been formed as a drainage area has been damaged.

Impoundments have been built for flood and erosion control, for generation of electrical power, as a source of irrigation water, as reservoirs for urban water supplies, and for recreation. Although most impoundments have been constructed for some primary purpose, they are used in many ways, but the secondary uses often must suffer so that the primary can be more effective.

Certain conditions in impoundments are different from those of natural lakes. If for irrigation, power, or flood control, they are subject to recurrent drawdowns. This affects the shoreline and vegetation thereon, especially in the littoral zone, and may drastically change the volume of water. This may have profound effects on the aquatic life, depending upon the time of year, by trapping organisms in pools that dry up, destroying spawning areas, and changing predator-prey relationships.

Often turbidity and siltation are excessive. If a stream is dammed, there is a constant inflow of silt-bearing water and the consequent outflow. The inflowing water may be warmer or cooler than that in the reservoir and may form a layer on top of or underneath the water already impounded. If the body of water is deep enough to stratify, the incoming water may form a density current at the level at which it is lighter than the water below it and cooler and heavier than the water above it.

Because impoundments are usually in well-dissected terrain, they customarily have a long shoreline in relation to the surface area.

AQUATIC PLANTS AND ANIMALS

Representatives of many of the phyla, the great groupings of organisms with major characteristics in common (Gr. *phylum* tribe; plural *phyla*), are found in freshwater and an even greater diversity in the sea. Thus in the animal kingdom, there are the single-celled Protozoa; the segmented worms, the Annelida, such as aquatic earthworms, leeches, clamworms, and the like; the joint-legged Arthropoda, such as the hard-shelled Crustacea (crabs, crayfish, shrimp, scuds, and many others), the Vertebrata (fishes, turtles, frogs, snakes), and the Insecta (including waterbeetles, mayflies, stoneflies, and so on). Several other minor phyla are represented in freshwater as well. In the plant kingdom are the Algae, some of which are very small, although others, in the ocean, are among the largest of plants, at least in length, for they may be well over 100 feet long. The Fungi include organisms of decay that decompose dead organic matter, but some Fungi attack living things such as the water molds that sometimes infest fish in hatcheries. Many Bryophyta (mosses) grow in water. More conspicuous are the Spermatophyta, the seed plants which include the rushes, sedges, lilies, and all the variety of pond weeds, cresses, and even cypress trees growing in water. Some biologists set aside into a third great kingdom the Protista, certain organisms that have characteristics of both plants and animals, and are very old and perhaps ancestral to most of our present-day plants and animals, although they are not clearly related to modern forms. The bacteria are put here; however, many biologists still consider the bacteria to be Fungi. The blue-green algae are classified with Protista and are considered to resemble the bacteria in many respects. The blue-greens often form "scum" or "moss" on the surface of lakes and ponds, or may become so numerous as to give the appearance of green paint poured on the water. Other Protista are the flagellates, tiny, one-celled creatures, many of which are green, that propel themselves through the water by means of a whiplike flagellum. Some ingest or eat food as animals do, yet are green and manufacture food as the plants do. Both zoologists and botanists claim these. The problems are solved by setting them into the Protista. Some biologists would include all Algae, Fungi, Protozoa, and bacteria in the Protista.

PLANKTON

In the water are many small organisms, mostly confined to the trophogenic zone in both limnetic and littoral areas, that float about at the mercy of wind and current. These make up the plankton (Gr. *plankt* wandering). It is usually subdivided into the animals, or zooplankton, and plants, the phytoplankton. Plankton is collected for study in fine-mesh nets. Some of the organisms are so small that the tiny plants and animals go through the net meshes and must be separated from the water by a high-speed centrifuge. This is the nannoplankton (Gr. *nano* dwarf).

The phytoplankton is made up mostly of algae of all subdivisions, except perhaps the red algae, which are nearly all marine or are attached to the bottom. Bacteria are abundant as are some of the Fungi.

Small animals that feed on the algae are part of the plankton. There are many kinds of protozoans, rotifers, and many of the Crustacea belonging to the orders Cladocera, Copepoda, and Ostracoda. These are the small creatures commonly called waterfleas. The larvae of one of the midges (*Corethra* or *Chaoborus*) are often found.

Upon occasion, almost any aquatic organism that has a form or stage of life small enough to be subject to wind and current action may form part of the plankton. This is especially true in the sea in which many animals, quite large as adults, have larval forms so small that a plankton net is required to secure them. Plankton taken in the littoral zone is usually of many species, although many of them may normally be part of the aufwuchs (organisms living attached to the bottom and bottom debris).

Plankton is primarily a standing-water phenomenon. Streams almost barren of plankton may flow into a lake. In the lake a plankton population flourishes. Later, the same water flows out of the lake carrying with it the lake-developed plankton. Within a few miles downstream of the outlet, most of the lake plankton will be gone if the stream is at all swift-running. If there are large, slow-moving pools, or backwaters, plankton may be abundant, for these are essentially lakes in their environmental features. Large plankton populations may develop in the lower reaches of a large, slow-flowing river.

To a zoologist, plankton is fascinating. In one group, the Cladocera, which are distant relatives of the lobster and crab, individuals are nearly always female, and all the young produced are female as well. This is parthenogenesis (Gr. *partheno* virgin; *genesis* origin). Only when times get hard, as when a pond may be drying up or when winter is approaching or food is becoming scarce, are males hatched. Fertilized eggs called winter or ephippial eggs follow mating, and these eggs are able to withstand cold and dryness, to hatch into females again when spring appears. Other relatives, the Copepoda, have females easily distinguishable from males because they carry egg sacs about with them.

A planktologist becomes familiar with hundreds, perhaps thousands of zooplankters or phytoplankters, depending on his specialty. His skill at remembering the different forms may be almost unbelievable, but a short study by an expert, of the features of an algal cell, for instance, may result in the pronouncement that here "is a new species of desmid." Since there are some thousands of species of desmids, this is indeed a feat.

It is possible for a specialist in plankton to examine a collection of plankton, both animal and plant, and with accuracy state the hardness of the water of the lake from which the collection came, its acidity or alkalinity, and often its geographical location. At the same time small size and resistance to adversity have brought about wide distribution of some species so that certain Cladocera are as likely to appear in a collection from England or Siberia as from the United States.

Within a lake, plankton is not distributed uniformly. Species subject to drift may accumulate where blown by winds to the extent that their innumerable green cells appear as green paint on the water. Bays or coves provide protected situations in which plankton may develop in tremendous quantity. Sometimes conditions are such that the water may be colored by this growth, and it is said that there is a plankton "bloom." Some of the swimming plankton are able to migrate vertically from near the thermocline to the upper waters during the day and to return to the deeper waters at night. Other species may swim toward the surface at night, descending during the day.

Plankton organisms are generally characterized by adaptations for floating, or at least adaptations to reduce drastically the sinking rate.

Throughout the year the standing crop of plankton, that is, the amount of plankton existing at any one time, may vary greatly, increasing or decreasing by several fold. The greatest numbers appear in spring and fall. This is probably due to (a) the upwelling of nutrients at the spring and fall overturns, (b) the water temperature, (c) the amount of radiation from the sun, and (d) the ability of the plankton species to reproduce and multiply rapidly under favorable conditions. Very likely other factors enter in as well, for it seems impossible to relate the upsurge to any single influence.

NEKTON

The larger, free-living organisms, which in lakes are primarily fish, are called nekton.

NEUSTON

Many organisms have become established at the zone of abrupt change from water to air. These make up the neuston and may be on the underside of the surface film and suspended from it, or above the film resting upon it. Those upon the surface are generally more numerous and may be so abundant as to give the appearance of dust on the surface of the water.

BENTHOS

The animals and plants that live on or in the bottom materials of a lake or stream make up the benthos (Gr.

benth the depths of the sea). The rooted plants are not included, but their exclusion is hardly noticed, for the remaining organisms include members of nearly all the phyla of animals and many kinds of plants. There are two major zones of the bottom in lakes: (a) the littoral in which plants are rooted and in which there is generally a high oxygen and low carbon dioxide content in the overlying water and (b) the profundal, which corresponds roughly with the area of the hypolimnion, an area in which there is less light and often low oxygen and high carbon dioxide concentrations in the water. Between these two is a zone of intergradation with characteristics of each, but more or less distinct from either. This is the sublittoral. A fourth zone, the abyssal, out beyond the profundal, is sometimes added to those lakes that are very deep. (There are other systems of classification, but this will suffice here. For example, one system calls the wave-washed area of the shore the eulittoral and the remainder the sublittoral and in no way sets off what we have called the sublittoral.) In shallow ponds there will be no profundal and probably no sublittoral. Only the biggest of rivers would have holes deep enough and still enough to approach the conditions in the profundal of lakes. Of course, the muddy Missouri River would be dark on any part of the bottom more than a few inches deep, but the current and turbulence would keep the water fairly well oxygenated. Other rivers have extensive bottom areas with the physicochemical characteristics of the littoral areas of lakes but with the addition of the continuous but varying factor of the current to which the organisms must adapt.

The influence that the physicochemical factors of light, temperature, oxygen, and carbon dioxide may have is further complicated by the actual nature of the bottom itself. Sand, gravel, pebbles, bedrock, boulders, mud, and plant remains all may be present in lake or stream.

In the course of time suspended clay and silt particles settle to the bottom of a lake, and added to this material is all the organic matter made up of the bodies or parts of bodies of the aquatic organisms, plus whatever may have washed in from the land. Where sufficient oxygen is available, the process of decomposition can be completed, and only inorganic matter remains of what was once complex organic compounds. These inorganic substances may be released into the water as nutrients where they are again taken up and used by plants as raw materials to build new organic compounds into the substance of their bodies. In oligotrophic lakes where oxygen is abundant in the hypolimnion and the rain of dead materials from the sparsely inhabited epilimnion is slight, decay can go to completion. In eutrophic lakes sediments usually accumulate faster than they can be broken down completely, especially in the deeper profundal.

The interface of water and bottom is an important habitat (place to live) for many of the benthic organisms, for here is food of all kinds, from complete, newly dead bodies, to raw materials in all stages of complexity as the breakdown of dead bodies proceeds. Below the interface, however, are zones of diminishing oxygen until finally, only a few inches deep in the ooze, there is no oxygen. Any decomposition at this depth must then be anaerobic (without air). Often the decomposition does not proceed to completion, so that an accumulation perhaps many yards thick of partly decomposed materials will result over a period of time.

In and on the ooze, then, and in and on the sand, gravel, pebbles, and plant remains, the organisms find a place to make a living. In the deep cold water of oligotrophic lakes with abundant oxygen and little carbon dioxide there may be as many as 100–200 different species of animals, not counting the Protozoa, but relatively few individuals of any one species. They are most abundant on a gravelly-pebbly bottom. In the profundal of eutrophic lakes, where there is no light, much carbon dioxide, and little oxygen, there are normally no green plants, and there are fewer species of animals, perhaps in some instances only one. A square foot sample of the bottom deposit may produce many thousands of the larva of the midge *Chaoborus* and nothing else other than the microscopic Protozoa and bacteria. More often there may be some clams, some roundworms, leeches, and a few others. Contrary to the oligotrophic situation, the eutrophic profundal has many individuals of only a few kinds. Both are what can be called dependent situations, inasmuch as all food comes from somewhere else, usually from the water of littoral and limnetic zones.

The littoral benthos has its homemaking affected by the different types of bottom plus the factors of current, waves, and light, and because of food availability, predation by other animals, hiding places, and competition with its own and other species. The rooted plants provide a third dimension as they supply upright structures on which many organisms may climb. Furthermore, many of the littoral benthic organisms are able to swim so that at least part of the time they must be classed with the littoral plankton or with the nekton. Nearly all zones and groups intergrade into each other.

On wave-swept bottoms organisms are scarce. Sand is not a sturdy foundation, and it is abrasive to soft bodies. Large-bodied, hard-shelled clams can exist in sand. Higher populations of larger macroscopic organisms are found in muddy sand, and more especially in sandy mud which may harbor 3,000–4,000 organisms per square yard of bottom. Abundant animals are the sponges, amphipods (scuds), midge larvae of the family Tendipedidae (Chironomidae), snails, the little fingernail clams of the genus *Pisidium*, damselfly and dragonfly naiads, plus a host of microscopic Protozoa, rotifers, roundworms, Cladocera, copepods, mites, and annelids. Insects are most abundant in winter, for then nearly all eggs laid in the water have hatched, predation has not excessively reduced the number, nor have insects begun to emerge in a hatch and fly away, as they will in spring and summer.

AUFWUCHS

We could regard rooted plants, logs, sticks, and trash as outbranchings of the bottom and include any organisms on them as benthos. However, by definition, organisms on these structures are called aufwuchs, and benthos is excluded, and with justice, for the aufwuchs has several characters that set it a bit apart. Some ecologists would exclude any organism not firmly attached to the substrate (the under layer, the surface on which it exists). It is easy to get into difficulties here; so we shall consider the aufwuchs as made up of those organisms that live attached to, or only clinging to, and thereby considered able to move about on (but not penetrating into) an underwater surface projecting above the bottom. Examples of these surfaces are the above mentioned rooted plants, logs, sticks, trash, and rocks except where the bottom is primarily rocks, as in a gravelly stream bed.

The principal producer of food among the aufwuchs is the algae of several kinds. Some of these are single-celled; others are filamentous and form a sort of jungle for the very small consumers such as protozoans, rotifers, and newly hatched annelids, roundworms, and bryozoans (the moss animalcules). To the large forms, such as ostracods, some copepods and cladocerans, and various insects, some of the algae are relatively more nearly the size of grass, and they graze on it, or, if they are carnivores, they may find animal prey among the algal filaments. Still larger insect larvae that attach themselves to the substrate or crawl about on it may be either grazers or predators, or even scavengers. Many of these are organisms ordinarily considered as benthic in nature, but because they are on some projection from the bottom they are classed as aufwuchs. Generally, the aufwuchs organisms are rather specific in their choice of habitat. Some are much more common on broad-leaved plants; others are more often found on the narrow, cut-leaved plants. At least two species of algae are found only on turtle shells, and other organisms may grow among them. Turtles might well be called old algaebacks rather than mossbacks.

The habitat-by-choice is most noticeable when the assemblage of forms on a temporary substrate, such as a leaf, is compared with that on a permanent rock. It takes time to develop a population of algae, diatoms, and insect larvae (larvae of caddisflies and blackflies and mayfly nymphs) such as is found on stones. On the impermanent leaf are the short-lived algae, protozoans, and sometimes hydra and occasional bryozoans.

PSAMMON

Above the water's edge, on sandy beaches, especially those of translucent quartz sand, is an assemblage of organisms called psammon (Gr. *psamm* sand). Very nearly the same organisms are found in sandbars in rivers. In the capillary spaces among sand grains are bacteria, protozoans, rotifers, insect larvae, flatworms, and roundworms. The assemblage of organisms, or the community, is more or less midway between the organisms of the soil and those of the open water of the littoral zone. This band of psammon along the sandy beach may be 10–12 feet wide and up to 2 inches deep. Enough light penetrates the quartz sand so that algae may flourish to color the sand green. This is a source of food for the consumer animals, as is organic detritus washed in by waves. Some ecologists include as a part of the psammon the organisms of the sandy beaches that are normally submerged. These might be called the psammolittoral organisms.

SHORE FLORA

The rooted aquatic plants occupy a specialized place in the ecology of water. Not only may they be producers on a large scale in the littoral zone, but by reason of their extension from the bottom, they vastly increase the substrate for plants and animals. Furthermore, they are late-comers to the water life. Algae, both small and large, and many of the bacteria and fungi have always lived in water or damp places. The rooted, seed-bearing aquatic plants come from ancestors which had made the shift to land and had adapted to it with the production of specialized cells for the conduction of water from roots to leaves, with the production of small openings called stomata

(Gr. *stoma* a mouth) for the transfer of gases to and from the atmosphere, and with the development of adaptations to prevent loss of water. The rooted aquatics, having returned secondarily to the water, still show evidences of their former terrestrial life with the more recent adaptations to the water superimposed upon them. Some stand upright, rooted in the bottom muds with their leaves exposed to the air. These are the cattails and the rushes, marsh plants actually, which can grow out into the lake or pond in shallow water at most a yard deep. Lakeward from these emergent plants are the water lilies and pond weeds with slender, flexible stems and floating leaves. The floating-leaved plants are only partly aquatic; they have snorkels, so to speak, on the dry upper surfaces of the leaves. These are the stomata through which oxygen, carbon dioxide, and water vapor may pass. The floating-leaved plants may extend out to a limit of about 9 or 10 feet of water. Beyond this, it is too difficult to make a land-adapted structure do the proper job in water. There are aeration tubes in water lilies to be sure, but these are not enough. Some plants, such as the water hyacinth or the tiny duckweed, solve the problem by becoming foot-loose to float about on the surface. Others have adapted by becoming completely submerged and truly aquatic, giving up the atmosphere as the source of gases, absorbing oxygen and carbon dioxide directly from the water as well as most of their required nutrients. Examples are some of the waterweeds (potamogetons), milfoil, and hornwort.

The three major types, emergent, floating-leaved, and submerged, typically occur in three zones around the lake shore, with the emergent, of course, nearest the shore. The submerged zone ends at the edge of the profundal zone at the point at which the light becomes insufficient to carry on photosynthesis.

ECOSYSTEM

Organisms cannot exist independent of the non-living portion of the environment. Instead, they interact with it, affecting it physically and taking from it certain substances and returning others to it and being affected by it in turn. The living and nonliving portions of the environment, interacting together, make up an ecosystem. For example, a lake and the organisms within it constitute an ecosystem.

POPULATIONS

A population is a group of organisms in the same area at the same time. Usually a population is considered to consist of one kind or species of organism, but the term is coming to be applied to two or more species with the same ecological requirements in which case it is called a mixed population. Ecologists are much concerned with populations and population dynamics and ask such questions as: What causes a population to increase or decrease? What prevents the unlimited growth of a population? Why are there more of one kind of animal than of another? Why are there more yellow perch than northern pike in a lake, or more largemouth bass than bluegills? How fast can any given population increase under favorable circumstances? What is the greatest density any one species can tolerate?

A population cannot exist by itself, for each organism is dependent upon the environment, which in most cases is affected by other organisms. All organisms do not react alike to stimuli from their surroundings, however. Instead, in response to all the differing environmental situations, organisms adapted to the various habitats in different geographic areas have become grouped into biotic communities.

BIOTIC COMMUNITIES

A community is defined as an aggregate of organisms which form a distinct ecological unit. Put another way, but with the same meaning, a community is "any assemblage of populations living in a prescribed area or physical habitat." (Eugene P. Odum, in collaboration with Howard T. Odum. *Fundamentals of Ecology* [2d ed.; Philadelphia: Saunders, 1959]). Another term for community is biocoenosis. This word indicates the further fact that an assemblage of organisms interacts with the nonliving part of the environment (Gr. *bio* life: *coen* common; L. *osis* a condition of). A community may be as large as a transcontinental forest or as small as a rotting log. Major communities may be as large as the assemblage of living creatures of the ocean, which form a community that is self-sufficient and needs no outside relationships except the sun as a source of energy. Major communities may be smaller, perhaps as small as a farm pond, (or even a puddle) with its benthos, plankton, fish perhaps, and certain plants, just so long as the community is more or less independent of other communities. Within the major are minor communities, which are dependent to some extent on other minor communities. Benthos, nekton, plankton, and aufwuchs are all minor communities.

Biotic communities must have organization. An assemblage of populations of nothing but consumers would soon disappear, for there would be no food produced. The community must be organized so that energy may flow through it from producer to consumer to reducer. This might be called the functional structure. There is also a species structure, for generally in a given habitat certain species are more likely to be found in one kind of habitat than in another. Who would look for trout in a cattle wallow?

The species of a community are not fixed, however, and may change through time or space as the environment changes or as species evolve. The change would be a replacement of one kind by some other organism that performs much the same function. Animals in a present-day swamp are not the same kinds as those that were there 100,000,000 years ago; yet they perform the same functions. The situation in a sandbar island in a river is different from the situation in a sand island in the ocean, and the same species of organisms would not appear in the two places, because of the difference in salinity, if nothing else. Nevertheless in both places there would be producers, algae no doubt; consumers would be present that were small in size and were the prey of larger species; and scavengers and decomposers would be there to dispose of the dead. Species of the two groups that perform the same function would be ecological equivalents of each other. Those on the river bar may even look much like the marine sandflat organisms, for structure and function are interrelated.

ECOLOGICAL NICHE

An organism's habitat is where it lives, but its niche is the way in which it makes a living or its role in the community. This would include its food, its activities, and how it influences other organisms; that is, its effects on the ecosystem. The bluegill is primarily a bottom feeder. So is the bullhead, but the bluegill feeds on insects and the bullhead on almost anything. They occupy different ecological niches. The difference may be greater. The gizzard shad is a plankton feeder, the largemouth bass feeds on the gizzard shad, and the protozoans on bacteria, all in different ecological niches.

POPULATION STUDY

Ecologists are concerned with how many organisms there are, whether it be the total of one species or of several species, over the entire range of the species or in some restricted area. How many bass in this lake? How many deer per square mile in that county? How many of the bluegills per acre of lake surface are of catchable size? How many pheasants per 10 acres in the other county? Many of these questions are argued with great heat by laymen, too. The difference is that the ecologist has devised means to determine populations with a fair degree of accuracy.

How Populations Are Studied Any fisherman worth his salt can say, "This pond is jumping with one-pound bass, but not many are much bigger." Or, "Nobody catches fish of any size in this lake any more. I think it must have winter-killed last year." "Yes, more muskies were caught in Ghost Lake than in Twin Lake last year." This is nature in the raw. In a less natural setting, populations can be observed in the laboratory, in an aquarium. Do the guppies increase in number, or do there always seem to be about as many from month to month? A bowl full of detritus from a small pond can be checked now and then as a little meat, or rice, or barley is dropped among the dead leaves. Even a modest magnification will enlarge the scene enough to see that certain of the organisms have increased, feeding on the bacteria of the decay of the meat. Perhaps the water has turned green because of the upsurge in algae.

The observations may be more qualitative in nature. "Yes, there are bass in this lake." "Yes, we see an eel now and then." "No, there are no trout in Great Salt Lake; at least, I've never seen any."

Such observations may attract the attention of the ecologist, but, if the observations fit in with the work he is doing, he will soon want quantitative information. "How many one-pound bass are there per acre? How old are they? And how fast are the smaller bass becoming one-pound bass? As the number of one-pound bass increases, what happens to the population of bluegills on which the bass feed?" Or, "The water in the lake is green, but which species of algae make or makes it green, and how many grams of dry weight of each kind are there in a liter of lake water?"

Sampling a Population If a pond is properly constructed, it is drainable, and all the fish can be captured and the one-pound bass counted, one by one. On the other hand, it would be impossible to drain Lake Michigan to count the yellow perch, and equally impossible to count the individual algae in a 640-acre lake, nor could this be done for even a small pool. Instead, samples must be taken and counted, and this sampling occupies much of the time of some ecologists, if their research interests happen to lie in this direction. The samples must be representative. If two fish were taken from a pond by angling, one a bass and the other a bluegill, we could justly say that the pond contained both species, or at least it did before we began angling. We would not be justified in saying that the pond contained equal numbers of bass and bluegills. Actually, there may have been one bass and one thousand bluegills.

So, an ecologist's life is made interesting by the necessity of proving that his samples were representative of the organisms present. Consider some of the means of sampling.

Rooted Plants The ecologist must be able to identify the plants, first of all. In a boat, he may then move about over the surface, estimating the area of the bottom that each species covers. If the water is too turbid to see very far into, he will miss plants that nevertheless receive sufficient light to grow. He may drag the bottom with a rake to obtain samples for his estimates. If he wishes to be more exact, he may make quadrant studies. Hollow squares, usually of strap iron and 1 meter on a side, are placed on the bottom in a random pattern and all plants enclosed in the square or quadrant are harvested, identified, and weighed wet, dry, and sometimes even ashed. The weight of plants per square meter gives some indication of how productive a pond or lake may be and how far it may have progressed toward eutrophication. It is impossible to count all the plants of a lake bottom in ordinary ecological work; so this is a sampling method in which the samples, if taken properly, are representative of the bottom as a whole. Sometimes a cord is run from one point to another, usually from shore lakeward, and all plants touched by the cord, or within a specified distance on each side of it, are identified and counted. This is the transect method.

Plankton Plankton organisms are captured in nets made of bolting silk or nylon. This is a very fine-mesh material. A commonly used silk is No. 12 which has 125 meshes to the inch with apertures roughly 0.12 millimeters on a side. Silk as fine as No. 25 with 200 meshes to the inch and apertures of 0.064 millimeters are used in special research projects. Number 6 with 74 meshes to the inch and 0.24-millimeter aperture diameter would be useful for the larger plankton animals. These nets commonly are towed from a boat, although some are designed to be thrown and hauled in by hand. In the ocean it is often enough just to hang them from a pier so that they strain the tide. The nets are conical and the organisms collected are washed into a small bottle and then examined. Seemingly, this should supply qualitative answers to questions about plankton. But what about the organisms that were able to swim out of the way of the net? Was the net always at the same level, or was the catch mixed with organisms of different levels? Quantitatively, the situation is worse, for, in addition, meshes of the net tend to clog and water is pushed aside, as by a sea anchor, rather than being strained, so that many organisms are not caught that should have been. How long a tow was it? Did the meshes of the net shrink? Even more questions may plague the ecologist.

Nets with vanes to keep them at the desired level, nets that close automatically, and nets with narrow mouths have been invented to get around these causes of error.

Frequently, samples of water are taken from whatever depth is desired with special sampling bottles. For surface samples, in a boat, for example, the water can be poured or strained through a net. In this way some of the problems mentioned can be avoided, and a known amount of water can be filtered. Instead of a bottle, a pump can be used with the pipe ending at the desired depth and a known quantity of water pumped and filtered.

Many of the organisms are too small to be captured easily in a net. Instead, a liter or more of water can be centrifuged, thus separating organisms from water. A newer device for capture of this small nannoplankton is a thin cellulose plastic membrane disk with pores so tiny that only water can go through. A known amount of water can be filtered through the disk, and organisms caught on the disk may be counted.

The counting is not always easy. A sample may contain tens of thousands of organisms. So, a sample of the sample is taken, put into a special Sedgewick-Rafter counting cell, which holds 1 cubic centimeter of water, and examined under the microscope. Still there are too many to count; so only a portion of the cell is counted. Suppose we have divided the cell into 100 equal-sized squares, and we have counted the *Daphnia pulex* in 20 squares and find an average of one *Daphnia* per square. Since there are 100 squares, there would be 100 *Daphnia* in the counting cell or in 1 cubic centimeter of water. We have in our sample 20 cubic centimeters. There is, then, a total of 2,000 in the sample. But this was obtained by straining 2 liters of water. Therefore in the lake at the particular time of day, time of year, and depth, perhaps further influenced by our collecting methods and skill, there is an estimated average of 1,000 *Daphnia* per liter of water. The numbers of other organisms can be determined in the same way.

Ecologists have called on mathematicians for help in their distress. Statisticians, and better yet, statisticians who are also biologists, have devised tests to calculate when enough samples have been taken to determine that further collections would not be worthwhile, for nearly all the kinds of animals or plants within the test area had already been captured. Other tests provide answers to the same sorts of questions as to the validity of quantitative samples.

Benthos Almost any means to bring up a sample of the bottom will do for qualitative sampling of the bottom organisms. Rakes, scoops, long-handled dipnets, special scrapers, and wire dipnets may be used to collect bottom materials. Many hours are subsequently spent sorting through the sand, gravel, mud, or detritus with a pair of forceps looking for benthos, especially the animals. The same statistical means are used to decide how many samples are enough to produce a fair representation of benthos. If the study is quantitative, each sample of the bottom that is taken must be of a standard size. Two kinds of dredges are used for this kind of sampling (and also for qualitative work), the Eckman for soft bottoms and the Petersen for firm or pebbly bottoms. Once the organisms are separated from the bottom materials, they must be identified and counted. This analysis appears as a survey count and has some value. The number of organisms in the sample (more probably several samples) multiplied by the proper factors, as was done with the plankton samples, produces a figure that represents the average number of organisms per square meter (or yard) of bottom. This may be a total of all kinds, or the determination may be made by species.

Numbers by themselves mean little, for there may be hundreds of tiny organisms that do not weigh as much as two or three individuals of a larger species. A volumetric analysis helps to overcome the problem. All the organisms, or all of one species, are blotted dry and dropped in a graduated tube containing water. The amount of rise of the displaced water gives the volume of the organisms. This may further be supplemented by a gravimetric (measurement by weight) determination by which the number of grams of organisms per square meter of bottom can be calculated. This figure, grams per square meter, is very useful as a measure of the productivity of lakes or ponds. Other samplers are available or can be made, even to including a length of stovepipe of known cross-sectional area which can be shoved into the bottom thereby delineating a bottom section. With these, fairly accurate determinations can be made. Special samplers have been devised to use in streams to take advantage of the current.

Aufwuchs A qualitative study of aufwuchs is easily made as long as it is possible to reach and harvest plants, or sticks, or to make scrapings of logs, or stones, or boulders in the water. As the sample is being drawn up through the water, any number of organisms may be washed off. To overcome this, and to make an attempt at quantitative study, a collecting trap is used that resembles a lady's purse, except that it is much deeper. This is a long bag with a fine-mesh bottom and a pair of closing jaws. This is slipped over an entire plant. The plant and all organisms on it are then literally in the bag and available for study. The depth range sampled may be increased by the use of diving gear.

Nekton Some animals of the nekton can be qualitatively sampled with dipnets, but a quantitative study of such species as the backswimmers, water-boatmen, and the like might be difficult because of their mobility. Frogs, turtles, salamanders, snakes, and other aquatic animals can be collected quantitatively to see just what species may be present in any environment.

Aquatic ecologists studying nekton are usually concerned with fishes. For instance, what kinds of fish, how many of each kind, what rate of mortality does the population show, how fast do small fish reach a desirable size for angling or for commercial yield, and what is the standing crop? The last question can be asked about almost any organism, and it asks how many pounds (or kilograms) of the species are present at any given time. The weight may be dry weight in the case of smaller organisms, but for fish the weight is that of the fish as caught.

Fish are captured by angling, seining, with hoopnets, trammel nets, electric shocking devices, and by pond poisoning or drainage when that is possible and desirable. In either of the last instances, all fish can be weighed except for a few that inevitably get lost in the mud, and any desired figure can be obtained such as the ratio of pounds of bass to pounds of bluegills. More often the population can only be sampled, and statisticians have de-

veloped means of estimating population sizes from the samples. This is often called the mark-and-recapture method or is named after the originator, C. J. Joh. Petersen, a Danish fisheries biologist. A number of fish are captured, unharmed, and are marked in some way so that they may be recognized if taken again. They are released, allowed to circulate among the free population, and then another harvest is made, this time of both marked and unmarked fish. From the figures at hand, a population estimate can be made.

$$\text{Population} = \frac{\text{number of marked fish}}{\substack{\text{Marked fish recaptured} \times \text{total} \\ \text{marked and} \\ \text{unmarked} \\ \text{fish in sec-} \\ \text{ond catch}}}$$

Calculations based on this formula are subject to error because some fish may be more easily caught than others, the marked fish may not survive as well, the marks may disappear, smaller fish may grow and become part of the population, and the marked fish may not be randomly distributed through the population. A number of modifications have been proposed, and other types of formulae have been developed that partially overcome the difficulties.

INTERRELATIONSHIPS OF THE PHYSICOCHEMICAL ENVIRONMENT

Limiting Factors. No animals or plants live within a fire; yet some animals withstand much higher temperatures than can others. In fact, some can live only in water so warm that it would soon kill most other animals. Thus heat can be a limiting factor. An environment might seem perfectly suited for a species under study in the way of oxygen, carbon dioxide, food, light, cover, nesting space, and area, yet be impossible because the high temperature acts as an environmental factor that limits or prevents its use as a habitat.

High temperatures might, then, prevent occupancy of an otherwise suitable habitat. If the temperatures should change and come to fall within the range of tolerance of a species, the habitat would probably be invaded by this species. If the temperature fell even further, it might still be suitable for the study species, yet outside the range of the other animals which had come to live in the habitat because the latter were only narrowly tolerant. They would then have to adapt, move out, or die. Many would die. In the course of time and with a slow enough temperature change, some organisms that neither moved out nor died would become adapted to the environment, and these adaptations are one form of interrelationship with the environment. The habitat, however, would now approximate the usual temperature range of still other species, which would move in. The newcomers would fill the vacated ecological niches and be the ecological equivalents of the original group of species, for there would still be producers, consumers, and decomposers.

In any environment there are one or more limiting factors for each of the species present. Usually there is at any one time, for any one species, some one factor which, less drastically than fire in the example, limits the size of a population without eliminating it. When it is removed or lessened, the population of the species increases until some other factor such as cover or phosphate becomes limiting. The ability of a species to increase is thus governed in part by physicochemical factors such as the lack of nitrate, light, or oxygen. This effect was described in 1840 by J. von Liebig, so that we speak of Liebig's Law of the Minimum. Sometimes the element that is limiting may actually be present in excess of what is needed, but chemically bound so that it is unavailable. Thus, phosphorus readily combines with iron, so that although present, the phosphorus may be unavailable because it is in an insoluble combination with iron.

Current Current is always a threat, for it may cover the bottom with silt, or scour it out with rocks and gravel, or tear away organisms and carry them into danger. At the same time it is advantageous, for smaller silt and clay particles are carried away leaving gravel, pebbles, and small boulders with crevices among them that serve as shelter.

Algae are held in place with rootlike structures and may appear as mats of green on rocks in swift water. Caddisfly larvae have claws and blackfly larvae have adhesive disks which help to hold them fast. The lamprey has a sucker. Water pennies, the name given to a kind of beetle larva, have become so flattened and hug the rocks so closely that the current has little effect on them. Many animals actively avoid the current. Trout fishermen know that one place to find trout is just on the downstream side of rocks. Tiny creatures avoid current by living in small depressions in rocks or wood. In the depression the water is nearly still; yet even a millimeter away the current is rushing by. Such tiny habitats (microhabitats) are an intersting study in themselves. Trout, in addition to avoidance, have a streamlined form that offers the least possible resistance to the current when the trout must face it. Compare the the shape of a streamlined trout with the more flattened shapes of many pond and lake fishes such as the bluegill and crappie. Bluegills, when in streams, are found in quiet pools that are essentially pondlike.

Current-dwelling organisms nearly always have one or more of these modifications, and are found widely distributed so that we speak of a typical stream biota. Actually the modifications are typical of organisms in moving-water habitats, for they are present in organisms living in wave- or current-swept areas in lakes and are lacking in steam organisms typical of the quiet pools. In slowwaters, where rocks are lacking and the bottom materials are finely divided, the bottom fauna is likely to be made up of burrowing forms.

Some animals take advantage of the current. Certain caddisfly larvae build a funnel-shaped net that filters, from the water passing through it, food that has been torn loose somewhere upstream. Other organisms merely lie in wait for whatever appears. Fishermen take advantage of this behavior, casting their lures so that they will be swept past the retreats of stream fishes. Dissolved oxygen is seldom a problem to current-dwelling animals except in areas of gross pollution. In fact, if an animal can hold its place against the force of the current, it is continually supplied with most of its needs of food and oxygen. Even if oxygen and nutrients are not in high concentrations, the current continually renews the water around organisms so that it never becomes depleted. The severe environment

limits the kinds of organisms, but the plentiful food and hiding places encourage the production of great numbers of those rugged enough to survive these pioneer conditions.

Current influences distribution in other ways. The smallmouth bass is thought of as a swift-water stream fish in the southern portion of its range. In Ohio the smallmouth is seldom found in streams with a gradient less than 3 feet per mile nor more than 17 feet per mile. (Milton Trautman, *Fish Distribution and Abundance Correlated with Stream Gradient as a Consideration in Stocking Programs.* Transcript, Seventh North American Wildlife Conference, 1942, pp. 211–223.) This distribution was borne out in a Missouri study. Large populations of smallmouth bass were observed in streams with gradients of 8 feet per mile and 5 feet per mile. However, one of the more famous Missouri smallmouth streams had a gradient of about 2 feet per mile. (Edward M. Lowry, "The Growth of the Smallmouth Bass (*Micropterus dolomieu* Lacépède) in Certain Ozark Streams of Missouri." Unpublished doctoral dissertation, Graduate School of University of Missouri, 1953.)

Some of the darters, members of the perch family, live in swift water. These little fishes have lost their swim bladders so that they are no longer buoyant. Their pectoral fins are strongly developed, and with these fins they brace themselves on the bottom to hold against the current.

Salinity In both marine and freshwater fishes, adaptations to salinity or its lack are necessary. Marine fishes tend to lose water to the environment by diffusion out of their bodies. Consequently, they actively drink water and get rid of the excess salt by way of special salt-excreting cells. Freshwater fishes, on the other hand, tend to take in water and would swell up like someone with dropsy were it not for very active kidneys which excrete relatively large amounts of urine.

Specific gravity and viscosity Most organisms are heavier than water. For benthos, this is no disadvantage, but others must maintain their position. The familiar gas (swim) bladder of most fishes is a hydrostatic organ that enables the fish to remain at a given depth in the same way that the diving tanks of a submarine operate. The marine sargassum weed has small air bladders that keep it afloat, as have some freshwater aquatic plants as well.

Plankton organisms, in general, are characterized by the extensions of the body. Because of the viscosity of water, the extensions offer resistance to movement through the water and so help prevent sinking. Successive generations of certain kinds of Cladocera change their form with the seasons. In the summer there are prolongations of the head into grotesque shapes that are called the "helmet." Seemingly these extensions are brought about, in some way not clearly understood, in response to warmer water and help to keep the animal afloat in the less viscous, summer water. Some protozoans and rotifers change their shapes, too.

Summer stagnation Oxygen in the hypolimnion of eutrophic lakes may disappear in summer. Some insect larvae move out of the oxygenless area during this period. Some of the copepods form an almost impervious wall about themselves and remain dormant until the fall turnover brings oxygen to the depths again. The larvae of the midge *Chaoborus*, living in the bottom ooze, migrate nightly to the upper waters. They move relatively rapidly, aided by four air bubbles within their body. Near the surface they can replenish the oxygen in their air bubbles and then return to the bottom until the next night.

Winter hardships The winter eggs of Cladocera, a means of meeting the demands of winter, have already been discussed.

Many of the algae form spores capable of lying dormant throughout the winter on the cold, and perhaps dry, bottom of a pond. Sponges form gemmules which both overwinter and distribute sponges. Sometimes the stato-blasts of the Bryozoa are found in tremendous numbers. Not all live through the winter, but enough do to revive the parent species in the spring.

In icebound lakes there is no chance for atmospheric oxygen to dissolve in the water. If light is cut off by a thick snow cover, plants will not carry on photosynthesis to release oxygen into the water in the process. In a shallow lake the oxygen may become so depleted that fish die, or at least the high-oxygen-demand fish will perish. The largemouth bass and bluegills may all, or nearly all, suffocate leaving only the carp, catfish, and goldfish. Thus the species composition in the lake may be changed because the oxygen requirements of carp are less rigid than those of bass and bluegills.

BIOTIC ENVIRONMENT

Food Relationships Food is of prime importance to all living things in the water, partly as a source of materials for growth and repair of body tissues, but also as a source of energy. Ultimately, the source of energy for nearly all organisms is the sun. The green plants can use chlorophyll to capture the radiant sun energy and use the energy to manufacture complex substances such as sugars from carbon dioxide and water. From these sugars, often with the addition of other elements, plants can make fats and proteins and other highly complex compounds. Animals cannot do this, and so are dependent upon the plants, and must eat plants or must be carnivores (L. *carn* flesh; *vor* eat) and eat animals that eat plants. The plants are the primary producers, and the animals that graze or browse upon them are primary consumers, and the carnivores are secondary consumers. The carnivores in turn may be eaten by tertiary consumers and so on. Neither producers nor consumers live forever, and when they die, their bodies are broken down by scavengers and by organisms of decay, the bacteria, and molds and other fungi. These are the reducers or decomposers.

The concept of productivity, as such, can be applied to any aquatic crop, be it insect, fish, or plankton, but the green plants are the original or primary producers of food, so that it is with their rate of production that we are principally concerned. Primary productivity has already been defined as the rate at which food is formed from inorganic materials by the plants. Plants must use some of the food for their own metabolism, so that an index of both the net primary production (the amount of food stored and not used by the plant) and the rate of net primary production is more valuable to the ecologist. The food represented by the net primary production is available to other life forms. The energy in the form of food that is converted by the consumers to the substance of consumer bodies and not dissipated as heat or work is called the secondary production.

Obviously, if the primary producers make more food, more will be available for the consumers, and so more or bigger consumers can exist. This is not a one-to-one relationship, however, for much of the energy stored in the complex compounds that we call food is released in the performance of work or as heat. Thus only a portion of all food consumed at any trophic level (producer, primary consumer, secondary consumer, etc.) is available to be converted into the substance of the next higher level.

The faster that food is converted into substance, that is to say, transferred into bound-up energy at the next level, the smaller is the loss of energy in the form of work, such as that expended in looking for food. Therefore, rate is important in conveying intact energy from the producer level to the higher consumer levels. A merchant's profit is only partly related to the size of his inventory. It is also much affected by the rate of turnover of his stock. A complete plankton crop may be produced in days, rooted aquatics in a year, and a fish crop in two or more years.

Organisms of the higher levels are more efficient at the conversion of food to flesh than are those of the lower levels. An example can be formulated, based on largemouth bass. In a pond, at summer-water temperatures comfortable to bass, let us say that it takes about 2.5–3 pounds of bluegill flesh to produce one pound of bass flesh. It takes about 20 pounds of insects, mostly from the bottom, and about 10 pounds of zooplankton to produce the three pounds of bluegills. It takes about 15 pounds of algae to produce one pound of insects and zooplankton. Therefore, 450 pounds of algae produce one pound of bass. It is not necessary for the 450 pounds of algae to all exist at one time, for the energy transfer from producer to top consumer is not instantaneous anyway. Here again, it is a matter of rate of production, and the faster, the more efficient, within limits.

This is a food chain, from algae to bass, and many such food chains can be uncovered in aquatic environments. Of course, the actual situation is not quite so clear-cut. The bass do not feed exclusively on bluegills. Small bass feed on zooplankton, and the rationale for many of our fishing lures is that bass of all sizes feed to some extent on insects. Other animals than bass feed upon bluegills, and bluegills may feed on bass eggs and fry. Insects themselves may be carnivores and there may be rooted aquatic plants that are not eaten by any animal. Furthermore, nutrients used by plants to build plant material would soon become exhausted were they not returned to the water by decay organisms, the decomposers. In fact, many bluegills die and are decomposed, or are eaten by crayfish or turtles, and never become bass flesh. The food situation thus is not so much a matter of a series of individual food chains as a matter of interlocking chains that form a food web, and the food web does more than just lead to an ultimate carnivore, which in turn may be harvestable by man. At every trophic level organisms die and are decomposed without being eaten. At every level organisms give off wastes that are decomposed so that nutritive substances, the nitrates and phosphates and others, are continually being returned to the plants ready for reuse in building more plant material. Food relationships are, then, a maze of food cycles interlocking with each other.

Since it requires three pounds of bluegills to make one pound of bass in our example, and bluegills live to be several years old and usually are smaller than bass, there cannot normally be more bass than bluegills, either in numbers or in poundage. Also, there is a loss of energy in the conversion from bluegills to bass. There are fewer bluegills than insect larvae on the bottom, and fewer insect larvae than the phytoplankton and phytobenthos organisms on which they feed. The relative numbers of organisms of each level can be visualized as a pyramid with the primary producers in greatest quantity at the base and the top carnivores in very small numbers at the apex. This is called the pyramid of numbers, and holds throughout all kinds of communities besides those of freshwater. The amount of energy bound up in the bodies of organisms varies in the same way, with the smallest amount in the bodies of the top consumer because of the energy losses at each change of level. One would think that a pyramid of weights would also exist, and it does in one sense in that it requires a severalfold quantity of each lower level to produce the level immediately above. However, because of short life cycles resulting in rapid turnover, the weight of the lowest levels at an instant of time may not form the wide, expected base of the pyramid. The number of organisms existing at any one time in a community or ecosystem is the *standing crop*; in a way it is a measure of productivity, but is misleading in that it disregards rate. Two hundred pounds per acre is a higher standing crop than 100 pounds per acre, but it may have taken three years to produce the 200 pounds and only three months to produce the 100 pounds.

This contrast in time required to produce a given standing crop is quite possible, for, except for mammals and birds, the aquatic organisms are cold-blooded and many have indeterminate growth. They grow as long as food is available, although more slowly as they grow older, and the more food, the faster the growth, within limits. When food is scarce, the animal does not often starve, but its growth becomes slower. In a given ecosystem, such as a pond, the maximum possible rate of productivity is fixed, for ultimately all energy to be converted to food comes from the sun and this energy does have limits. Two ponds or two lakes in a geographic area would receive the same amount of radiant energy per square meter for surface. The difference in rate of primary productivity between the two bodies of water will actually depend on supplies of nutrients such as phosphorus, nitrogen, calcium, potassium, and sulfur compounds available to the plants. Lack of any one nutrient may be a limiting factor for production. Limited primary productivity means limited secondary production of insects, fish, and other consumers. In a pond there would be a limited amount of food available for the secondary productivity of fish, but each fish would have its share. With just a little food the fish would not starve but would only grow slowly. If the supply of nutrients is increased, a limiting factor on productivity is removed and there is then more food per fish and consequent faster growth. If the primary productivity remains the same, however, the share of food per fish and therefore rate of growth of fish to catchable size can be increased by removing some of the fish.

Succession Aquatic communities are not static but are subject to change, especially as the environment changes. With the recession of the glaciers, many oligotrophic lakes were left. Through time, eroded soil and plant detritus were washed or blown into the lakes, slowly filling them. As the waters became richer in nutrients, more and more plants came to grow in the water, and detritus from them helped to fill in the lake basin. Eventually some of the lakes became so shallow as to be ponds. Finally some filled in completely and became dry ground which supported a forest. While these changes in the nonliving portion of the environment were occurring, the communities were changing as well. At each stage in the series, different groups of organisms, that is to say, different communities, were to be found. These would be the communities normally associated with oligotrophic lakes, then with eutrophic lakes, then with ponds, with marshes, and finally with dry land. This process of a series of communities following one after the other, grading imperceptibly into each other, is called succession.

As the headwaters of a stream move farther and farther from the mouth, a given section of stream progresses through a succession. First there is a brawling freshet with a high gradient. Then as the headwaters cut back, the stream sections become wider, deeper, slower, with lowered gradient. These changes continue until the stream is a mature river with many pondlike habitats. The stream organisms in the study section change with the stream. Fast-water organisms were to be found when the section was headwaters. By the time the stream reached maturity, the organisms were perhaps more typical of ponds.

APPLIED AQUATIC ECOLOGY

There are many instances of the application of the principles of ecology to the management of some aquatic problem. Drainage of marshes to get rid of mosquitoes is one example. Another, for the same purpose, is the introduction of the little mosquitofish *Gambusia affinis* into ponds and pools to feed on the mosquito larvae and pupae. Most of the applications have been concerned with increasing the yield of fish to the angler or commercial fisherman. Some applications are simple enough, yet in retrospect were a long time in coming. Carp ponds in the old world have long been fertilized to increase yield. Fertilizer increases the nutrients in ponds so that primary production can be increased. In this country, fertilization of ponds to increase sport-fish production is relatively recent but is now quite common in the Southeastern United States. Fertilization of ponds produces unpredictable results sometimes, and often the results are undesirable, so that in other parts of the country fertilization is not recommended as a general measure or is recommended with caution.

Fertilization of ponds and lakes, in effect, speeds eutrophication with its attendant growth of algae. Often these are filamentous algae or some of the undesirable bluegreen algae which make swimming and fishing unpleasant. Unfortunately, in many vacation areas, the addition of fertilizer in the form of organic sewage either directly or by seepage is hastening the eutrophication of lakes. The lakes are shallowing, developing a growth of water weeds, with the production of a muddy bottom, and the species of fish are changing with the succession. The trout and salmon and whitefish and ciscoes of the deep, cold, oligotrophic lakes give way to the largemouth bass, sunfish, bluegill, crappie, and catfish in the warmer, more productive eutrophic lake. These in turn yield to the carp, suckers, and bullheads. The last of the fishes are the bowfin, mudminnow, and perhaps bullheads.

The addition of a small quantity of sewage may actually increase fish production, but the clear, sandy-bottomed lake good for swimming and water sports is not the best for fishing, and if the lake is on the verge of enrichment, it requires the addition of only a relatively small amount of nutrients to cause eutrophication. Nitrogen and phosphorus compounds, both present in domestic sewage, are commonly the limiting factors that prevent the development of large growths of rooted aquatics and blooms of plankton, both of which can lead to eutrophication. Eutrophic lakes are rich in nutrients and are productive, but the aquatics and the algae spoil the swimming.

Fishery management is developing some of the aspects of a precise science, for both commercial and sport fishing. Carp-removal projects in many states produce clearer lakes with increased rates of primary production which tend to increase the higher-level, more desirable consumers such as largemouth bass, northern pike, walleye, and other sport fish. The removal of many restrictions on the size of fish to be taken, on numbers taken, and the season of the year open to fishing have in some instances reduced the number of fish in certain lakes so that the remainder had an increased ration available and could grow faster. This increased the turnover and the rate of harvest possible. There is little point in returning an undersized bluegill to the water to grow to a catchable size; it may already be a grandmother and busy with the contemplation of still another few thousand offspring to share the already meager production.

The manipulation of the environment is notable in trout management. Dredging, straightening, farming up to the stream's edge and the watering of cattle have had disastrous effects on trout streams. Prevention helps, and cure is possible. Installation of dams and wing dams, placement of boulders, stabilization of the banks by plantings, which incidentally shade the stream and cool it, and fencing against cattle have restored many a spoiled trout stream.

Rainbow trout have been stocked in the tail waters below many dams. The rushing water comes from deep in the impoundment, is cold enough for trout, tumbles about and becomes oxygenated, and has provided excellent fishing in regions of the South where trout ordinarily would be unknown.

A knowledge of ecology is basic to successful manipulation of the environment. With human population growth, it is essential knowledge for preserving clean, potable water. —E.M.L.

FRESHWATER MULLET *See under* Striped Mullet
FRESHWATER MUSSEL *See* Glochidia
FRIGATE MACKERELS *Auxis thazard* and *Auxis rochei*
Fishes of the mackerel family with the two dorsal fins separated by a wide space, with 8 free finlets behind the second dorsal fin and 7 behind the anal fin. The body has scales which form a corselet on the anterior portion and

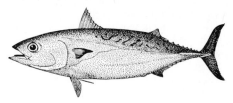

Frigate Mackerel

has no scales on the posterior portion. Between the pelvic fins there is a fleshy flap (the interpelvic process) that is about as long as the pelvic fins.

The two species are difficult to distinguish. In both species an extension of the corselet follows the lateral line posteriorly. In *A. thazard*, this extension is not more than 5 scale rows wide under the second dorsal fin, while in *A. rochei* is is 6–28 scale rows wide.

Frigate mackerels are generally small, seldom reaching a length of 2 feet.

Auxis rochei is found worldwide in tropical and subtropical waters. *Auxis thazard* is found in the Indian and Pacific Oceans and from Florida to the Carolinas in the Atlantic Ocean. They form dense schools of hundreds of individuals.

The food of frigate mackerels consists mainly of fishes, crustaceans, and occasionally squids. They are themselves eaten by larger fishes such as marlins and tunas.
—B.B.C.
—R.H.G.

FROGFISH *See* Sargassum Fish
FROSTFISH *See* Atlantic Tomcod
FUNGUS *See* Diseases and Parasites
FURUNCULOSIS *See* Diseases and Parasites

G

GAFF A hook mounted on a handle which is designed for holding or lifting a fish. Gaff hooks are generally barbless, needle sharp, and curve away from the handle for quick penetration. There are various types of gaffs such as the pick gaff, flying gaff, and long-handled gaff. The size and species of the fish sought are determining factors in selecting the appropriate type.

GAFFTOPSAIL CATFISH *Bagre marinus* The gafftopsail catfish is confined to the western Atlantic and ranges from Cape Cod to Panama and throughout the Gulf of Mexico. Its closest relatives are two species that occur along the Pacific Coast between the Gulf of California and Ecuador.

The body of the gafftopsail catfish is rather robust, its greatest depth a little greater than the width, tapering posteriorly; profile from tip of snout to origin of dorsal straight; body depth 4.05–4.5 in standard length; head depressed, broad, 3.55–3.8 in standard length; dorsal with one spine followed by 7 rays; there are 19–23 anal rays; the snout is short and broad, not much longer than eye; eye 4.6–5.1 in head; mouth broad, cleft reaches or almost reaches anterior margin of eye; teeth small, in villiform bands on jaws, vomer, and palatines, the band on upper jaw continuous, the band on lower jaw interrupted at symphysis; two pairs of barbels present, the maxillary barbel flattened and ribbon-shaped reaching from base of ventrals to opposite anal base, mandibular barbels small, failing to reach opercular margin; gillrakers about five; distance from tip of snout to origin of dorsal 2.95–3.1 in length; dorsal spine 1.1–1.4 in head, its filament reaching to or beyond adipose fin; adipose fin moderate, inserted a little in advance of middle of anal base; caudal fin deeply forked, the upper lobe longer; anal fin anteriorly

Gafftopsail Catfish

elevated, its base 1.5–1.7 in head; ventral fins moderate, inserted a little nearer base of pectorals than to posterior of anal base; pectoral fins moderate, the span 1.1–1.3 in head.

Color uniform steel-blue above, silvery below, with or without dark spots; dorsal fin more or less dusky anteriorly, usually yellowish-green; adipose dusky; caudal with upper lobe somewhat dusky, the lower lobe yellowish-green; the other fins pale with perhaps some dusky markings.

LIFE HISTORY

The gafftopsail catfish prefers intermediate salinities, being usually taken where the salt concentration is 5.0–30.0 parts per thousand. This means that it tends to gather in brackish-water bays and estuaries. However, it is very sensitive to cold and does migrate offshore during the worst part of the winter. Usually, none is reported by fishermen during November, December, and January.

Along the Texas coast, there is a minor commercial fishery. Statistics from this catch indicate that the adults migrate into the bays in the spring and are present in greatest numbers in March, April, and May. Analyses of stomach contents show that blue crab is preferred, but that a variety of other animal foods will be taken.

Breeding takes place in May, and, after the eggs are fertilized, the male carries them in his mouth. It takes about 60–70 days for the eggs to hatch, and, after this, the young are brooded for an additional 2–4 weeks. During this entire period, the male appears to go without food of any kind. As many as 55 eggs or young have been found in the mouth of a single brooding male.

ANGLING VALUE

The maximum length is about 2 feet, and an individual of this size would weigh about 5–6 pounds. Although the gafftopsail catfish is usually caught by bottom-fishing methods with live or cut bait, it will occasionally strike artificial lures such as jigs or plugs. Contrary to popular belief, it is a good food fish.   —J.C.B.

GAFFTOPSAIL POMPANO *Trachinotus rhodopus* Also called pompanito, this eastern Pacific species is closely related to *Trachinotus glaucus*; the palometa (*which see*) from the Atlantic.

The body of the gafftopsail pompano has 4–5 narrow black bars high on the sides. Dorsal- and anal-fin lobes long and falcate; the dorsal lobe extends to or beyond the fork of the caudal fin when the lobe is depressed. The first dorsal fin has 6 short spines. The second dorsal fin has a spine and 19–21 softrays. The anal fin has two anterior spines (which become detached in large fish) followed by a spine and 18–20 softrays.

The range of this species is from Cabo Blanco in northern Peru, into the Gulf of California, and northward to Zumi Beach, California, and at the Galápagos and Tres Marías islands. A specimen 14 inches long appears to be the largest that has been reported.

ANGLING VALUE

Its potential as a light-tackle gamefish has not been stated, although it should be similar to that of the palometa. Large numbers can be caught in beach seines, but its commercial use is not well-known. One account stated that it was not considered very palatable as "table offerings." *See also* Carangidae, Pompano   —F.H.B.

GAG *Mycteroperca microlepis* This species is fairly common along the South Atlantic and Gulf Coast of the United States, from North Carolina to Louisiana. Although reported from as far south as Brazil, it is apparently very rare in the West Indies. This grouper may reach a weight of about 50 pounds and a total length of over 3 feet.

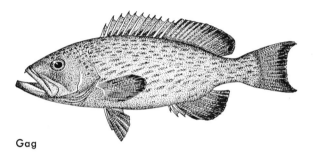

Gag

The gag has 11 dorsal spines, 16–19 dorsal rays, and usually 11 anal rays. Posterior nostril somewhat larger than the anterior. Insertion of pelvic fin under or somewhat behind lower end of pectoral base. Posterior margin of caudal fin concave. Color uniform gray without distinctive markings, or with dark vermiculations tending to group in clusters.

It is distinguished from the other groupers by the plain coloration and the lunate caudal fin.

ANGLING VALUE

Occurs in shallow and medium-depth water. A good fighter, commonly taken by anglers around southern Florida, it strikes trolled artificial lures and live bait.

The gag is a fair food fish of commercial importance in southern United States.   —L.R.

GALLEY The boat's kitchen. Any area or space set aside for cooking.

GAMEFISH In an angling sense any species of fish which can be taken by sporting methods and by reason of its size or vigor prolongs its resistance to capture. In a legal sense any species that under state laws is reserved for angling and prohibited from the commercial catch; however, the status of any species as a gamefish may vary from state to state and in different waters within a state.

GANOID Primitive fishes such as the gar, sturgeon, and paddlefish possessing hard, enameled (ganoid) scales. *See also* Anatomy, Scales

GAR *See* Alligator Gar, Florida Gar, Longnose Gar, Shortnose Gar, Spotted Gar

GARIBALDI *Hypsypops rubicundus* Also called ocean goldfish. A small Pacific reef dweller, the garibaldi has a bright orange body coloration and somewhat resembles a sunfish in shape. It is of no angling importance.

GEFILTE FISH A traditional Jewish holiday dish similar to many European fish-ball preparations. Gefilte fish is difficult to make, and the results are not uniform as there are countless family recipes. The process is tedious and requires the better part of a day to prepare. Although carp is commonly used in making gefilte fish its firm flesh tends to darken and most experts prefer a combination of walleye (often marketed as "yellow pike") and whitefish.

For recipe see Fish Cookery

GENUS A group of related species

GEORGIA An abundant supply of water and an ideal climate combine to make Georgia a haven for fishermen. There are 17 major reservoirs with a combined area of over 300,000 acres. Eighteen major warmwater streams flow 3,500 miles across the state, while their tributaries make up about 700 miles of trout water in north Georgia. An estimated 40,000 small lakes and ponds have been cataloged. And the irregularities of the Georgia coast provide over one thousand miles of saltwater fishing.

One of the greatest assets to fishing in Georgia is the variety in type of fishing and choice of game species. The streams of north Georgia in the southern Appalachian and Blue Ridge mountains support all three common species of trout. Trout exist in naturally reproducing populations, although most streams are supplementally stocked to support fishing pressure. Smallmouth and redeye bass occur in the marginal waters further south. Middle Georgia is the area of large reservoirs, slow turbid streams, and small ponds. Stream fishing becomes much more predominant in the sandy coastal plain. This is the area of black water, stained by naturally occurring tannic acid with high populations of game species in water that rarely gets muddy.

Fishing along the coast is seasonal and tempered by violent tides and climatic conditions. The irregular coast line with the Inland Waterway, sounds, and islands is a rich area for fishing with the right combination of tide and weather. Tarpon, striped bass, and red drum are the species for spring and summer, with spotted seatrout and American shad the mainstay of the winter months.

Geographically speaking, there is some kind of fishing water everywhere in the state. The type and species of fish desired are probably the main factors to be considered by fishermen. The principal gamefish are largemouth bass, crappie, bluegill, redear and redbreast sunfish, white bass, chain pickerel, and trout. Walleye and smallmouth-bass fishing is restricted to a limited area. The largemouth bass is the most popular Georgia gamefish and offers real opportunity for the serious fisherman. It is commonly taken in sizes up to 10 pounds and frequently larger. Crappie and white bass are the dominant species of large impoundments. The latter, a comparative newcomer stocked in the state, monopolizes reservoir fishing during the April and May spawning runs. Crappie fishing is tops during spring and fall and actually holds up well the year round. In Georgia these fish will yield an average size of 1 pound, with 2–3 pounders caught occasionally.

Panfish, collectively called "bream" and including bluegill, redear (shellcracker), and redbreast sunfish, are the main species of artificial ponds and southern Georgia

The Spanish moss-covered Okefenokee Swamp offers fine bass fishing to adventurous Georgia anglers

streams. They are sought with all kinds of tackle, with the cane pole and fly rod heading the list. Bream fishing is real sport, but the choice of time and place is important. The spring spawning season is always the best.

The chain pickerel (locally jack) has been elevated to a new status in Georgia with a world record established from the southern part of the state. Streams and ponds of this section support large populations of this species, which are available the year round but are most common in the spring and during late fall when stream flow is lowest.

Georgia is confronted to a minor degree with the two common threats to fishermen—pollution and the excessive use of water by pleasure boaters. Pollution has definitely made its inroads into fishing waters of the state, but it is difficult to establish the exact degree of damage incurred by pollution. No major fishing water has been totally lost. Pleasure boaters and water skiers cause problems in certain areas, but for the most part there is plenty of water for all interests concerned. Fortunately for the angler, many lakes are not completely cleared of timber which prohibits rapid boat movement.

TROUT FISHING

Trout are confined to the northeast section of the state and the 30-mile tailwater of Lake Lanier near Atlanta. The latter is big water, well suited for float-fishing and highly productive. All fish in this area are stocked as fingerlings. Growth is rapid, however, and the trout, mostly rainbow, have all the qualities of stream-reared fish. The tailrace of Lake Lanier is stocked and regulated by the State Game and Fish Commission. It has a good potential and yields some nice catches. There are some shoal areas suitable for wading, but the best returns come from float-fishermen.

North Georgia streams supply the real trout fishing in the state. The streams are nearly all supplementally stocked, but natural reproduction supports the fishery. Rainbow trout make up about 70 per cent of the total catch, with brook and brown trout about an even split on the balance. Most of the streams are small and heavily wooded. The best fishing is had by wading, using spinning tackle with live or artificial bait. There is also some big water for fly-fishing throughout the mountains.

Fifteen management area streams are heavily stocked and opened according to schedule by the Georgia Game and Fish Commission. These streams all produce excellent fishing throughout the May to September season. Camping facilities are generally available since these areas are in the National Forest. Over-all facilities are good for trout fishing throughout the Georgia mountains. The state stocks around 500,000 trout annually in about 160 streams. The stocking program is carried on throughout the regular trout season. About 350,000 trout are stocked from 9–12 inches in length. Since the stocking is carried on continuously, fishing success is high.

NORTH GEORGIA RESERVOIRS

The important impoundments of north Georgia include the TVA reservoirs of Blue Ridge, Nottely, and Chatuge, and the Georgia Power Company chain of lakes including principally Burton, Seed, and Rabun on the Tallulah River. These are the extreme north impoundments, all clear, deep, and relatively infertile. Fishing is principally for bass and crappie, with big trout frequently taken from Burton, Rabun, and Seed.

Smallmouth-bass fishing is good in the TVA lakes, especially Blue Ridge, which also supports good walleye fishing. These lakes suffer badly from summer drawdown, and the best fishing is always found during the spring months. All of these reservoirs are small, but fishing is excellent, and facilities, including boats, bait, and cabins, are readily available.

Further south, but in the same general area, lakes Lanier, Allatoona, and Hartwell Reservoir support good fishing. Fish populations are definitely warmwater, with largemouth bass, crappie and white bass the main species. White bass and crappie are taken during April and May, but the best bass fishing usually hits in these reservoirs during June and often extends into July. The lakes are generally clear the year around, and fishing pressure is fairly heavy from the metropolitan Atlanta area. Fishing facilities are good for all the lakes.

MIDDLE GEORGIA RESERVOIRS

This is the real heart of reservoir fishing, although turbid water is sometimes a problem in early spring. The principal gamefish of this area are largemouth bass and crappie with white bass, catfish, and bream taken seasonally. The main impoundments in this area include Bartletts Ferry, Goat Rock, and Lake Oliver shared with Alabama on the west, lakes Jackson and Sinclair in middle Georgia, and huge Clark Hill Reservoir on the Georgia-South Carolina line.

Lakes Sinclair and Clark Hill support some of the finest largemouth bass, white bass, and crappie fishing in the state. Crappie begin to hit good in March and continue on through April when largemouth and white bass take over. White-bass fishing on spring spawning runs upstream is tops during April and early May. Spinning tackle, using small, flashy lures, trolling, or casting yields the best results.

Crappie fishing holds up well throughout the summer and hits a peak again in the fall, usually during October and November. Night fishing with a gas lantern is especially popular. Bass fishing usually peaks during April and May and again during the fall months. Largemouth bass are the main game fish for these lakes, and the usual size runs 2–3 pounds. These lakes are not very heavily fished; however fishing facilities are good.

Bartletts Ferry, Goat Rock, and Lake Oliver support fair fishing, but muddy water is sometimes a problem. The real problem for this chain of reservoirs is lack of access and general facilities for fishermen. Bass, crappie, white bass, and catfish are most frequently taken.

SOUTH GEORGIA RESERVOIRS

Lakes Eufaula, Blackshear, Worth, Ft. Gaines, and Seminole provide Deep South fishing at its best. Spanish moss and cypress trees with definite year-round fishing make these reservoirs first choice for many local and visiting anglers. The shallow water of these impoundments brings a slight shift in important game species. The largemouth bass is still king, but bluegill and redear sunfish rank second in importance. Crappie, catfish, and chain pickerel also exist in good numbers.

Walter F. George Reservoir, locally known as "Lake Eufaula," covers over 45,000 acres on the Georgia-Alabama border, extending more than 80 miles along the Chattahoochee River. Bass, sunfish, crappie, and catfish are abundant. The peak bass fishing commences in late March or early April, when the fish begin spawning, and extends to mid-May. However, it produces good fishing throughout the year. Deep running plugs and plastic worms are the popular baits here.

Lake Seminole covers 37,500 acres in the extreme southwest corner of the state. Year-round fishing is good, but the best months are usually October, February, and March. Bass will hit topwater lures all year. The lake produces really big bass, with two fifteen pounders officially recorded during one year. Seminole is full of standing dead timber and cypress trees so heavier tackle comes in handy for landing big bass. Bluegill fishing is good in the lake, and chain pickerel are commonly taken while bass fishing. Crappie fishing is fair but generally seasonal in nature.

Lake Blackshear, with approximately 8,000 acres, is fished mostly for bluegill, white bass, and largemouth bass, probably approximately in that order of importance to fishermen. According to numbers of fish caught, bluegill are most important, but white-bass fishing causes the most excitement. These fish commonly school after shad in the lake, and fishermen follow the schools of white bass, casting small spinning lures or trolling. Largemouth bass rank high in the creel. Success is generally best during peak spring and fall periods. Bass up to and over 10 pounds have been caught in Blackshear.

STREAM FISHING

The rivers and streams of middle and south Georgia support some of the finest warmwater fishing in the United States. This includes the Flint, Alapaha, Satilla, Ocmulgee, Altamaha, Canoochee, Ogeechee, and Suwanee rivers. The reward for a float on one of these fine streams would probably consist of a stringer filled with redbreast and bluegill sunfish, largemouth bass, or chain pickerel, depending on your tackle and method of fishing. The best fishing is usually in the spring or late fall when water is low and the fish are concentrated in pools. Shoals are abundant, but wading is treacherous.

Some good facilities for floats can be found, but over-all access is poor for most of these streams. Fish camps are available on all streams mentioned with bait and boats available.

In addition to the freshwater gamefish, anadromous striped bass and American shad move into the Ogeechee, Canoochee, Altamaha, Satilla, and St. Marys rivers to spawn in freshwater. Both these species hit artificial lures well and supply real sport seasonally. Striped bass up to 50 pounds are taken, although the most common size range is 5–10 pounds. The shad are a real challenge on light tackle.

Weedless lures pay off on inundated waters such as Georgia's Lake Seminole. Plastic worms are favored

SMALL IMPOUNDMENTS

Georgia has an estimated 40,000 small lakes and ponds, but most of these are private and are unavailable for public fishing. There are several small state-owned lakes at state parks for public fishing with good camping and other facilities.

High Falls Lake, 660 acres in size, is owned by the Georgia Game and Fish Commission and intensively managed for fishing. Main species are bass, bluegill, redear, crappie, and channel catfish. Fishing is good, and camping facilities are maintained for fishermen. This area is located in middle Georgia, near the cities of Jackson and Griffin.

Rock Eagle Lake, 110 acres in size, near Eatonton, is also open to public fishing. Bass, bluegill, and redear sunfish supply good fishing as a result of an intensive management program.

SALTWATER FISHING

Georgia's coastline offers a thousand miles of variety and thrills for any fisherman. There is a multitude of tidal rivers, creeks, and sounds, with outlying islands forming a barrier to the mainland. To enhance this natural habitat further, the Georgia Game and Fish Commission has located several artificial fishing reefs within small-boat distance of the coast.

Fishing facilities are fair, with party boats and all the trimmings along the coast. The major problem is usually the unpredictable Atlantic Coast weather and violent tides. The Inland Waterway compensates for this, and protected areas can almost always be found. The principal angling species on the coast are the spotted seatrout, channel bass, tarpon, Spanish mackerel, cobia, and bluefish. Bottom-fishing, especially around cover, is good for sheepshead, drum, flounder, and croakers. Offshore charter boats take sailfish, barracuda, amberjack, and blackfin tuna.

The time and tide are most important in coastal fishing. Speaking in general terms, winter fishing is ideal for spotted seatrout, with spring and fall the best for other species. Tarpon, up to about 100 pounds, move into the sounds during July and August and are most often caught then.   —H.D.Z.

GERMAN CARP *See* Carp

GHOSTFISH A common name for the wrymouth (*which see*).

GIANT SEA BASS A rarely used common name, which persists in literature, for the jewfish (*which see*). *See also* Groupers

GILA TROUT *Salmo gilae* This unique member of the Salmonidae was first described in 1950. Earlier systematists and casual observers had considered it to be a cutthroat trout because of its existence in the headwaters of the Gila River in New Mexico and Arizona, and owing to its general appearance. A closer look discloses attributes which set it aside as unique. It has an extremely long adipose fin; the head and upper jaw are long; there is a high number of scales (usually about 32 above the lateral line); the distance from tip of snout to occiput is great. The Gila trout is dark olive-green along the back, shading to a golden-yellow belly. This yellow-gold color is always found in the pure strains and frequently in hybrid strains. It has small, black spots. Gila trout seldom reach a length of more than 8 inches, although rare fish run to 12 inches.

LIFE HISTORY

This native southwestern trout spawns in March and April, the female laying 150–200 eggs. The eggs are deposited in the redd and covered with gravel. The incubation period is 5–6 weeks. Gila trout are insectivorous, feeding chiefly on the larvae of mayflies, caddisflies, and midges.

HYBRIDIZATION

The Gila trout is of no significance as a gamefish. Its tendency to hybridize with the rainbow trout has reduced the range of the pure strain to a very limited area. Originally the trout was endemic to the Gila River drainage. Subsequently a pure strain was found in Ord Creek of the upper White River drainage. Some of these Gila trout were transferred to Grant Creek in the Graham Mountains where they should not be subject to hybridization.

Gila Trout

A pure strain also exists in Spruce, Diamond, and McKenna creeks in New Mexico. Plans call for stocking them in isolated streams of both states in order to perpetuate the species. At present, the Gila trout is completely protected and not available to angling. *See also* Arizona, New Mexico. —J.R.

GILL ARCH One of the several bony arches which support the gills of fish and amphibians.

GILL, EMLYN American (1862–1918) When Gill wrote *Practical Dry Fly Fishing* (1912) it was the first cis-Atlantic book devoted to the dry fly. Gill ran for immortality as the American Halford, with La Branche as his Marryat. But the aspiration ran afoul of actuality, because while the doughty Captain Marryat never double-crossed his Boswell by writing a book himself, George La Branche within a couple of years (1914) wrote *The Dry Fly and Fast Water* and his fame soon surpassed that of his advance man. In football analogy, La Branche outran his interference.

Gill's one rather tenuous claim to distinction might still have withstood the test of time, since his contemporary, Theodore Gordon, confined his own writing to letters and notes in *The Fishing Gazette* and *Forest and Stream* and had these been allowed to languish in obscurity then today it might be Gill, instead of Gordon, whom we would perforce be celebrating as the American Walton or at least as the father of the dry-fly. But Gill was twice unlucky in that John McDonald in 1947 snatched from limbo the notes and letters of Theodore Gordon and issued them with a scholarly introduction as *The Complete Fly Fisherman*; and the previously neglected Sage of the Neversink, whose hermitlike sojourn in the woods had gone completely unrhymed and unsung, attained instant sanctity, and was enshrined overnight as one of nature's noblemen on the right hand of Thoreau himself, upstaging such venerated figures as Audubon and Agassiz in the process.

The luckless Gill, lacking either the matinee idol charisma of a La Branche or the elfin wispy mystery of a Gordon, has been minimized rather than magnified by the passage of time, and clings today to a sort of mini-eminence, a relatively pygmy position of puny stature among the stalwarts of American angling annals. If his book had been less slavishly devoted to Halford, and if he had at least made the attempt to provide, instead of merely deplore the lack of, an American entomology of stream insects, Gill might have carved out a larger niche for himself, in the gallery of American fishing gods. But he shrugged off

as of undue immensity and complexity, the task of making a start toward a scientific entomological approach to the galaxy of American fly patterns, much as Louis Rhead did only a few years later, and both men missed greater subsequent stature as a result.

But Gill did recognize, more clearly than any American angling writer before him, the necessity for imitation not only of the natural fly upon which rising trout were feeding but equally for imitation of that fly's action on the water, and it is this latter stress that makes him unique in his time.

Even more prophetic of latter-day practice is Gill's anticipation of the "fishing-for-fun" concept: "In these days of depleted streams it is most necessary that the doctrine should be spread broadcast that the one pleasure of trout fishing, apart from the joy of being close to nature, is the matching of one's wits against the cunning of the trout. He alone deserves the title of sportsman who returns carefully to the water all trout that he does not need for food; as soon as the fish is taken into the net, all sport to be had with that particular fish is over, and when killed and put into the creel it has become simply *meat*."

The emphasis on the last word has not been added; it was placed there by Gill himself as long ago as the spring of 1912. So Gill was not only the author of the first American book on dry-fly fishing, but the first American angler to express contempt for meat-fishermen as such. It would be a fair reward to have a local chapter, here and there, named for him in the growing memberships of some of the national organizations devoted to conservation. —A.G.

GILLAROO *See* Ireland

GILL FLUKE *See* Diseases and Parasites

GILLIE A fishing guide (British Isles). The word is ancient Gaelic meaning boy. To be correct, such a person should be called a "fishing gillie."

GILLNET A wall of webbing suspended vertically in the water by means of weights (lead) on the bottom line and corks on the top line. The webbing may be made of cotton, linen, or synthetic material. The mesh size is selected according to the fish which will be captured.

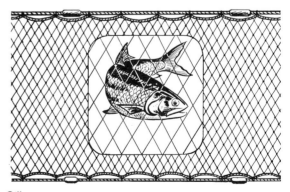

Gillnet

GILLRAKER A series of either short toothlike or long filamentouslike structures along the anterior edge of the gill arches (*which see*). The number on the first arch is ordinarily counted for identification purposes. *See* Anatomy of Fish

GILLS The organs of respiration in a fish. They are found on either side of the head and appear as clefts partially or wholly covered by flaps called the opercula or gill covers.

GIMBALS A pair of rings one within the other and with axles at right angles to one another for supporting the compass and maintaining it horizontal. Galley stoves and lanterns are also sometimes swung in gimbals.

GIN POLE An integral part of equipment on off-shore fishing boats. *For details see* Gin Pole *under* Sportfisherman

GIZZARD SHAD *Dorosoma cepedianum* A member of the herring family, this species is separated from other herrings by the elongated last ray of the dorsal fin, the small mouth which is placed on the lower part of the head, and the gizzardlike stomach. It is a deep-bodied species, generally silver with bluish above and brassy to reddish reflections on the side. The young have a large, dark shoulder spot which may be absent in large adults. This species swims in fresh and brackish water, in bays, lakes, bayous, and large rivers, occurring in clear or turbid water. It is widespread from the Mississippi River and its drainage, from Minnesota south to the Gulf of Mexico, and from New Jersey southward, also occurring to northeastern Mexico.

Unlike most of the shads and herrings, this is not a migratory species, and although it does mill about in large schools it tends to stay in about the same locality throughout the year. This is primarily a fish of lakes and large streams where the flow is sluggish. Spawning occurs during the early summer, the young attaining a length of about 4–5 inches by October. They reach a length of about 1½ feet and a weight of approximately 3 pounds but seldom exceed 12 inches.

ECONOMIC VALUE

Unlike other shads, it is not a plankton feeder, but rather it extracts organisms from the mud from which it strains small organisms with its gillrakers. Most of the food is made up of plant material and organic debris. The food is ground in the gizzard-like stomach and the long

Gizzard Shad

intestine. Because of this almost unique apparatus, this species is extremely important as a forage fish, converting organic matter and plant material directly to fish flesh, which then becomes food for predatory fishes. This important link in the food web which it serves is pertinent to fishermen because such species as striped bass, largemouth bass, and white bass feed upon it heavily. However, in some waters the gizzard shad has created a serious management problem due to its extreme abundance where no large predator population exists. The gizzard shad is a poor live bait because it dies quickly on the hook, although it is used as a dead bait.   —D.dS.

GLASSEYE SNAPPER *Priacanthus cruentatus* This wide-ranging species is believed to occur in the eastern and western Pacific Ocean as well as the Atlantic. In the western Atlantic, it ranges from New Jersey south to Rio de Janeiro and in the Gulf of Mexico. Its close relative in the western Atlantic, *P. arenatus*, has a similar range.

Adult *P. cruentatus* can be distinguished from *P. arenatus* by its truncate instead of forked caudal fin; in having 13 soft dorsal- and 14 soft anal-fin rays, instead of usually 14 and 15 respectively in *P. arenatus*, and by its lower number (54–62 versus 61–72) of lateral-line scales. The adult

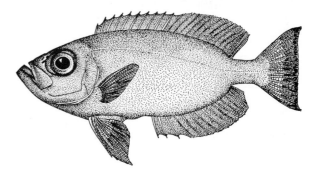

Glasseye Snapper

glasseye snapper is bright red. Pelagic postlarvae are silver with deep blue markings. Both species have large, lustrous eyes, which may be one inch in diameter on a specimen of 8 inches in length. Like the short bigeye (*which see*), the larvae of this species are pelagic, and the carnivorous adults are bottom living, usually over rocks.

ANGLING VALUE

Although they are relatively common over shallow reefs, glasseye snappers usually enter the sport fishery as a deep-water (about 50–100 fathoms) catch. Due to their small size they are not widely sought.   —D.K.C.

GLOCHIDIA In the United States most often the larvae of the pearly or papershell freshwater mussels (family Unionidae), which appear as tiny black spots on the gills, fins, and bodies of fishes. Glochidia are most commonly seen on minnows and sunfishes, but they also attach themselves to the feet of wading birds and larger invertebrates such as crayfish. The glochidia become imbedded in the flesh and are nourished by the host for several weeks. Freshwater mussels achieve wide distribution through this parasitic existence. A few marine deepsea bivalves reproduce in the same way, but the common method is by planktonic larvae. Glochidia-infested fish are not harmful to man when utilized as food, although they have little esthetic value. *See also* Diseases and Parasites

GOATFISH *See* Spotted Goatfish, Yellow Goatfish

GOGGLE-EYE A regional name for the warmouth (*which see*); sometimes called goggle-eye perch

GOLDEN SHINER *Notemigonus crysoleucas* A medium-sized, golden-colored minnow known to bait dealers and sportsmen as the "pond shiner." This minnow has a deep, slab-sided body with a decurved lateral line containing 44–54 scales. Like all others of the minnow family, the golden shiner has all its teeth on its pharyngeal arches, none in its mouth. The midline of the belly from ventral fins to anus is naked, the scales not crossing this strip.

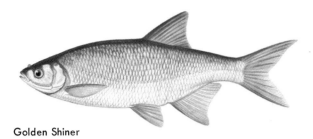

Golden Shiner

Young golden shiners lack the golden color but possess a dusky lateral band which fades with age. They are often silvery in appearance, becoming dark golden in older individuals.

This minnow occupies a wide range in the Eastern half of the United States from Manitoba and Quebec and southward to Florida and Mexico. The golden shiner has also been widely introduced west of the Rocky Mountains.

LIFE HISTORY

The golden shiner is a fish of relatively clear, weedy ponds and quiet streams. Although schools may be found in openwaters, they are not often far from weed beds. The fish exhibits a definite schooling tendency throughout its life, and the young can be found in schools of considerable size. The food of the golden shiner consists largely of planktonic crustaceans. Aquatic insects, mollusks, and algae also appear in its diet.

Spawning in midsummer over an extended period, the golden shiner spreads its adhesive eggs over beds of submerged vegetation. Attended by one or two males, the female sheds her eggs while swimming, and they adhere firmly to whatever they fall upon.

Adults are usually 3–7 inches in length, with specimens seldom exceeding 10 inches.

ANGLING VALUE

The golden shiner is considered to be one of the more important forage species. The young have been observed to provide the first food for juvenile smallmouth bass.

This fish is also rising in popularity with farm-pond owners in the Northeast as a forage species in association with largemouth bass. The fact that the golden shiner breeds over an extended period increases its importance since there is a constant supply of tiny minnows for young gamefish. In addition, the golden shiner is extensively used as a bait minnow. Individuals of large size are edible panfish. The larger shiners can be caught on flies and small spinners. *See also* Fish Culture   —R.A.J.

GOLDEN TROUT *Salmo aguabonita* The most beautiful of the Salmonidae is the golden trout. Those in streams are most brilliantly colored. The species has cadmium along the belly; a carmine stripe along the middle of the side; yellow on the lower side; rosy opercles, about 10 parr marks; an orange-tipped dorsal fin; white-tipped anal and ventrals, spotted caudal, adipose, and dorsal; head and body spotted to the lateral line; caudal peduncle usually wholly spotted. In lakes, older fish develop a carmine stripe along the lateral line and a brassy overall color except for olive on the back. When the species is reared at low altitudes it tends to assume a steely-blue appearance, losing the brilliant coloring.

Originally the fish was found only in headwaters of the Kern River in California. Sustaining populations are to be found in Wyoming, Idaho, and Washington, at least. Its weight is to about 11 pounds, but in streams a weight of one pound is usually maximal.

ANGLING TECHNIQUE

Goldens differ from the common species of trout in being limited to high-altitude lakes and streams, and consequently the techniques of fishing for them are more specialized. In the coldwaters of the Sierra Nevada Mountains, large food forms are scarce or absent. Although the trout are caught on spoons and spinners as well as baits such as worms, salmon eggs, and grubs, their natural forage consists principally of small insects, notably the caddisflies (*which see*) and midges (*which see*). Small crustaceans are also of varying importance, as are terrestrial insects. The fly-fisherman, however, ordinarily achieves good results with flies dressed on hooks from

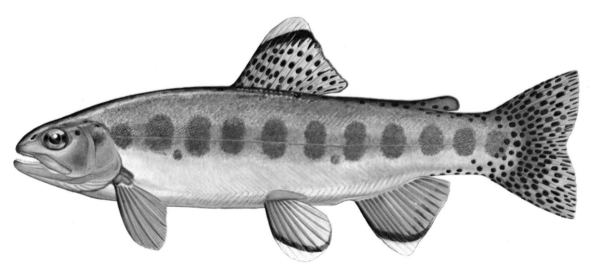

Golden Trout, 10-inch Male from Original Source in Golden Trout Creek (now Volcano Creek), California

No. 12 to No. 20. Perhaps the best of these are No. 18 midge patterns tied on very light leaders (4X to 6X). Dry flies work quite well when the fish are visibly rising, and small bucktails or streamers are effective occasionally. Nymphs on No. 14 and No. 16 hooks which imitate caddis larvae are regularly successful.

FOOD VALUE

The golden trout is a prime food fish. The flesh is firm and finely textured but slightly oilier than other trout. It can be prepared in a variety of ways, but is most often pan sautéed by the waterside. Goldens do not keep well and care must be taken if the fish are to be packed out from remote lakes. It is an excellent fish when smoked. *See also* Mexican Golden Trout —J.R. —A.J.McC.

GOLDEYE *Hiodon alosoides* A freshwater panfish distributed from the Ohio River into southern Canada, the northern limit of its range is not precisely known but it has been taken in the Nelson River. For years the breeding habits of the goldeye were a mystery. Unlike most fish, they do not spawn every year after reaching sexual maturity. A certain proportion of any population will drop their eggs on gravelbars sometime between May and July, but the rest of the goldeyes stubbornly carry immature eggs.

Goldeye

ANGLING VALUE

Being insectivorous in feeding habits, the goldeye provides excellent fly-fishing and like its less distinguished cousin the mooneye, it will hit floating patterns with reckless abandon. They usually average less than a pound or 12 inches in length, but 2 pounders (16 inches) are not uncommon in some lakes.

COMMERCIAL VALUE

Goldeye are less important for angling than they are for food consumption. A large market for smoked goldeye exists in Canada where it is commonly sold as Lake Winnipeg Goldeye. This name no longer identifies the fish with the lake, but rather the city where it is processed. Most of the goldeyes received in Winnipeg are caught in Clair Lake, Alberta, which is in the Wood Buffalo National Park. A smaller amount comes from the Churchill River and Lake Winnipegosis. The ideal goldeye weighs ¾–1 pound on the plate. This requires a live fish of 1½ pounds or so, because it loses 35–40 per cent of its weight in the smoking process. Inevitably, the best goldeyes arrive at Booth's Fisheries in Winnipeg. This venerable institution was originally a Chicago firm established in Manitoba in 1896. Their average production is 150,000 pounds out of the total 200,000 pounds from all Canadian sources. Booth's may ship a hundred pounds or so to United States restaurants, but 98 per cent of the annual harvest is consumed in Canada.

HISTORY OF SMOKED GOLDEYE

Robert Firth was a young butcher who migrated from Hull, England, to Winnipeg in 1886. He did a mediocre business in the meat trade; so relying on a makeshift barrel smokehouse he began curing goldeyes which were plentiful in the Red River. A fresh goldeye is an inferior panfish as the flesh is soft and unattractive. But Firth was getting twenty-five cents a dozen for his cured product. One day he miscalculated the heat of his fire, and the goldeyes came out more cooked than smoked. Experts will identify this as the hot-smoking process, but until that time nobody had tried the high-heat cycle which magically transformed the goldeye from a mere fish to a gastronomical discovery. One nibble and Firth realized that he had found his fortune. To make the fish more appealing, he dipped them in a reddish-colored vegetable dye which remains the hallmark of goldeye to this day. In time President Woodrow Wilson and the Prince of Wales became goldeye fanciers, and business really boomed in the late '20's. Prices went up and up, but the fish population went down to rock bottom. Currently, the inventory of goldeye is limited. The Canadian National Railway no longer lists the Winnipeg Goldeye on its menu, although the die-hard Canadian Pacific Railway still features them—smaller and not as fat as yesteryear but goldeye nevertheless. The decline of *Hiodon alosoides*, in common with caviar and buffalo steaks, is a conservation problem which cannot be solved through large-scale hatchery operations. —A.J.McC.

GOLDFSH *Carassius auratus* Similar to the carp, the goldfish is distinguished from the carp in that it lacks barbels on the jaw, black spots on the scale bases, and prominent cross-hatching. It is separated from others of the minnow family by the presence of a dorsal and anal spine. Of a variety of colors from red to black when bred in captivity, the goldfish in the wild generally reverts to its natural coloration which is brownish-olive with a bronze sheen. Sides lighter and more yellowish; ventrally a yellow-white or white. A native of China, the goldfish, like the carp, presently enjoys a widespread range throughout the United States.

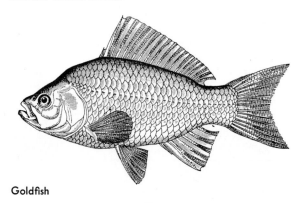

Goldfish

HABITS

The goldfish has nearly the same ecological requirements as the carp except that it is somewhat less tolerant to high gradients, cool water, turbidity, and pollutants. It is somewhat more dependent on dense aquatic vegetation than the carp. The food of the goldfish consists of vegetation, insect larvae, and crustaceans. The spawning habit of the goldfish is similar to that of the carp, and it appears to hybridize freely with the carp. The goldfish may reach a maximum length of 16 inches.

ECONOMIC VALUE

The high economic value of the goldfish as an aquarium fish is obvious; however, when in its wild state it is considered detrimental to gamefish populations. Like the carp in its destructive habits, the goldfish is difficult to eradicate once it has become established. *See also* Carp, Crucian Carp   —R.A.J.

GONADS Reproductive organs of either sex

GOOSEFISH *Lophius americanus* A distinctively shaped species, the goosefish is an inshore relative of a highly specialized group of deepsea anglerfishes. The body is strongly flattened, and the fish appears to be mostly head, with an enormous, toothfilled mouth. The head is very broad, and the small eyes are partially protected by horny protuberances on the top of the head. Modified dorsal spines form a "fishing lure," which is located just behind the upper lip. On the first spine, a flap of skin is used as an attractant to prey. In this species and its relatives, a rapid movement of the lure can be effected, with the resulting attraction of curious prey. The body tapers sharply to a narrow caudal peduncle. The peculiar pectoral fins, modified into footlike structures, are in front of the gill openings, a characteristic typical of the group of anglerfishes. The skin lacks scales and is thin, pliable, and slippery to the touch. The lower jaw is fringed with fleshy flaps. The upper parts are a dark chocolate-brown, with specklings of light and darker hues, while beneath it is a dirty white. Young goosefish are mottled with green and light brown. It has some ability to blend with the coloration of its background. Maximum size is 4 feet and 50 pounds. A specimen slightly over 3 feet weighed 32 pounds.

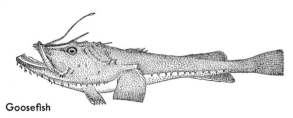

Goosefish

It occurs in the western Atlantic from the Grand Banks (Newfoundland) southward to North Carolina. Records from Barbados, off Yucatan, and Brazil cite this species, but it is not definitely known if these are the same species. The eastern Atlantic form was previously thought to be identical with that in the western Atlantic, but the larvae from the two areas are distinct, even though the adults resemble one another. Found over a wide depth range, it occurs as shoal at the tideline during cool months, retreating to deeper water in the warmer season. They also occur in estuaries but evidently avoid brackish water. A wide range of temperatures can be tolerated, but apparently sudden drops in temperature affect them, for following cold snaps goosefish are sometimes found dead or in a moribund condition in the shore zone.

The appetite of this species is notorious, and perhaps it is simpler to list fishes which it does *not* eat. Flounders,

dogfish, skates, eels, herrings, cod, and sea bass are only a few of the fishes in its diet, and sea birds, including cormorants, gulls, and ducks are part of its regular fare. Lobsters, crabs, squid, and other assorted invertebrates are also taken.

LIFE HISTORY

Spawning occurs from spring to early autumn in shoal- and deepwater, and eggs have been taken from March to September. The eggs are deposited in ribbon-shaped veils of mucus, sometimes 20–30 feet long and 2–3 feet wide. A large female may produce over a million eggs. The young are pelagic up to about 2 inches long, thereafter sinking to lie on the bottom. By the end of their first year, they may reach 6 inches. Maximum age is not known, but a 21-inch specimen is about three years old. It is a good food fish, and while some are eaten locally, the low market for them in the United States hardly compares with the demand in Europe.   —D.dS.

GORDON, THEODORE American (1854–1915), fishing writer, professional fly-tyer, "father" of the American dry fly, and creator of the Quill Gordon and other well-known artificial trout flies.

Theodore Gordon, earliest modern American fishing writer and fly-tier, is a pivotal figure in American angling. He introduced the dry fly in the United States in the 1890's, not long after it was developed in England, and although he made this connection with English tradition, he is distinguished also for breaking the nineteenth century American reliance on English fly patterns. Before Gordon, original American flies were usually fancy. Imitation flies were usually copies of English flies. Gordon developed artificial flies imitative of American water insects and gave them an impressionistic style. "I want to see the fly *on the water*," he wrote, "as well as to have specimens." Gordon was conscious of the historic job to be done in his time but was not doctrinal. The theme of his work is in his statement, "The great charm of fly-fishing is that we are always learning."

That part of Gordon's life which is known to us was a fly-fishing idyll. A consuming passion for the sport and poor health sent him to the life of a near-recluse on the Neversink River in the Catskill Mountains of New York not long after the turn of the century. His keen mind and sure fingers—he tied flies by hand—became wholly absorbed and specialized in fly-fishing. "Anglers should keep a diary," he said, and fortunately he left a record in his "Jottings" and "Little Talks" in *Forest and Stream* (predecessor of *Field & Stream*), beginning in 1903, and in the English journal, *Fishing Gazette*, where his earliest note, in 1891, presents succinctly the state of American fishing and its reliance on the English. He also wrote many letters, especially in his later retirement days. Most of them appear to have been lost, but a cache of them was kept by the incomparable English angling writer, G. E. M. Skues, and smaller bundles by his protégé, Roy Steenrod of Liberty, New York, and Guy Jenkins of New York City. But for these writings and his fly patterns we should know little about Gordon and his work, for almost all else comes from fading memories and legend.

The first substantial record of Gordon curiously marks a turning point in the history of American fly-fishing. It is a letter to him from Frederic M. Halford, the writer in whom the dry-fly revolution centered in England, dated

February 22, 1890, just four years after Halford published his *The Theory and Practice of Dry-Fly Fishing*. Halford clipped into a letter a set of his dry flies (preserved by Steenrod and now at the Anglers' Club of New York) and closed with the request, "kindly let me know the result of your experiments." The result was a new era in American fly-fishing.

Gordon makes it evident in this writing that he had read with intense preoccupation most of the American fishing writers of the nineteenth century, as well as the English, and was able to take so much book learning without harm. From books he tells us he learned to tie flies and to fish upstream. But from the stream itself came his decisive learning. He was one of the most brilliant observers of stream life in recorded fishing history, and in his writing he was a teacher who was master of the fishing anecdote. A photograph shows him small, slender, and elegant, fishing beside the girl of whom he wrote: "The best chum I ever had in fishing was a girl, and she tramped just as hard and fished quite as patiently as any man I ever knew." She is another mystery in his life, for he died a bachelor (May 1, 1915) within sound of a favorite stream. His monument is the Quill Gordon fly.   —J.McD.

GRAPHITE FIBER ROD The first important synthetic material developed since the fiberglass rod, graphite fiber rods were introduced to the U.S. tackle market in 1973 by the Fenwick Rod Company. The material was invented in 1965 by the Royal Aircraft Establishment, Farnborough, England (co-inventor William Watt). Its original application was in aerospace, but in subsequent years it was applied to a number of products in the sporting-goods field.

Technically, graphite fibers are distinguished from carbon fibers on the basis of tensile modulus. Carbon fibers are identified as those materials with a tensile modulus less than 10 million P.S.I. and graphite fibers as those above 10 million P.S.I. Only the high modulus fibers are suitable for rod-building and are identified as H.M.G. (High Modulus Graphite). H.M.G. fibers are made from a synthetic fiber called polyacrylonitrile (PAN). This (PAN) starting material is charred at temperatures up to 2500° C in a special atmosphere without melting. The fiber is stretched during processing and results in a high degree of orientation of the graphite layers parallel to the fiber axis. This results in higher strength-higher modulus (stiffness). Each filament has a diameter of .0003 of an inch, usually 10,000 filaments make up a tow and 3,000 filaments make up a single yarn. The H.M.G. fiber is available in various forms, including continuous yarns and tows, woven construction, straight unwoven tape, and chopped.

DESIGN

H.M.G. fibers are embedded in a homogenous matrix usually epoxy resin. The fibers reinforce the resin system to produce a strong, stiff material. The fibers contribute strength to the composite, while the matrix material maintains the fiber orientation and transfers the loads between fibers. By properly orienting the fibers in the composite matrix, the rod designer can obtain the mechanical properties required, as well as the degree of flexibility and stiffness needed for proper rod action.

PROPERTIES

H.M.G. fibers have a range of 25–80 million P.S.I. tensile modulus. With high strength to weight and high stiffness to weight ratios, H.M.G. fibers are 5–10 times as stiff and 3–9 times as strong as titanium, steel, and aluminum when compared on a weight basis. The specific tensile modulus of H.M.G. fibers exceeds that of all existing structural material. H.M.G. is $\frac{2}{3}$ the weight of glass fibers and can range from 2–7 times the modulus (stiffness). Its corresponding mechanical strengths are about twice that of fiberglass. The high strength and high stiffness, with the low density have a weight saving of 25–50 percent over other materials.

MECHANICAL PROPERTIES

Heat Increase in temperature has no effect on graphite, as graphite fibers maintain their strength and stiffness up to 2,700° F. Any decrease in strength would be due to the resin.

Cold Cycling H.M.G. composites from 0–75 percent of its ultimate strength for 1,000 cycles has virtually no fatiguing effect on the graphite at −319° F.

Moisture Prolonged immersion in water makes virtually no change on the graphite mechanical properties.

Vibration H.M.G. composites have excellent vibration-damping characteristics. The vibrations in graphite dissipate more rapidly than in fiberglass. This means less vibration in a fishing rod, which minimizes friction on the line during casting.

Sensitivity Vibration damping and the lighter weight shaft increases the sensitivity of the rod. With less vibration the tip telegraphs the movement of line down the shaft to the fisherman's hands.

Modulus The speed of recovery from bend is a function of the lighter weight shaft and higher modulus material. The shaft has a higher resistance to bending, which causes an increase in the speed of the rod's recovery. *See also* Rod Building.

GRASSHOPPERS Order Orthoptera A group of terrestrial insects (including the closely related locusts) which are important as food for many freshwater fish. Grasshoppers occur in both migratory and non-migratory forms. Most grasshoppers are winged, but some are wingless. However, they are all similar in appearance, and a few fly patterns suffice to imitate the various species. Grasshoppers are ordinarily skilled fliers, but on a windy day a great many of these insects fall into rivers and lakes, thus causing unusually heavy rises among the fish. The best "hopper" fishing is found on Western meadow streams, but some sport can be had on grassy-banked rivers elsewhere in the United States. This insect does stimulate very large trout into surface feeding, and its appearance is therefore a significant period of the fly-fishing season.

ARTIFICIAL GRASSHOPPERS

Fishing with live grasshoppers is seldom as satisfactory as using an artificial. The insect is fragile and cannot be cast very readily. A live hopper can be drifted with the current, but this method doesn't have the range and flexibility for taking large fish. A long, slim-bodied, buckhair fly tied sparse enough to float high on the water will catch trout and bluegill alike with much less effort. You can buy plastic replicas of the insect, but the most perfect imitation is usually less effective than the impressionistic kind. Patterns like Joe's Hopper, the Muddler, and even the Bucktail Caddis have more fish appeal because they are buoyant and they can be worked on the surface without drag. The correct size depends on the size of the naturals and also on the water conditions. During bright daylight hours it may be possible to take trout with a No. 6 fly, but a No. 8 is generally best. This is a shade small on rivers where large trout are present. You may bend or snap light wire No. 8 hooks in heavy fish. Assuming that you order your hopper patterns on 2X Long, or 3X Long sizes, a No. 8 would be right for trout in streams where the average is less than a pound. The standard for bigwater casting is No. 6, but don't hesitate to use No. 4, if the occasional fish may run over five pounds. Black bass can be safely managed on No. 4 dressings; naturally you can go bigger, but the fly won't float as well. Panfishermen can use No. 10 for bluegills, crappies, yellow perch, and white bass.

An artful grasshopper imitation is especially effective on western American trout streams in the summer season

THE RISE

On a bright day, you can walk quietly along the bank of a meadow stream, and if you watch the water carefully—not out in the main channel but right up against the grass—you may see little wavelets made by hopper-feeding trout. Unless the insects are particularly abundant, there will be comparatively long intervals between rises, but this doesn't mean that your trout are not active. Walk slowly with the sun at your back, and spend a few minutes watching each likely hold. Big fish rest along the grass and can often be spotted if the light is right or if you are wearing Polaroids. Sometimes the trout reveal themselves by moving around to check bits of surface drift. Every twig or piece of bark will be examined and often struck because their surface impressions from the trout's position are similar to that of a grasshopper. Nature designed the insect to camouflage in woodland life, and fish which have been gorging on hoppers frequently swallow debris by mistake. You would expect that almost any fly can take such a fish. It doesn't work that way. For one thing, twigs, bark, and even matchsticks have a more lifelike drift on the surface than a heavy rubber or plastic grasshopper imitation. Regular dry flies float properly, but lack the grasshopper shape; they will take fish occasionally, but a buoyant, long-bodied artificial will raise trout consistently. Patterns such as Joe's Hopper or the dry Muddler are therefore ideal for this kind of fishing.

THE PRESENTATION

Casting straight upstream from the bank you are walking is difficult. You must keep low and use as little rod motion as possible. Even then, you'll frighten many trout because often there are two or three unseen fish holding close to you waiting to feed. The disturbance of a falling line will start a chain reaction of scared fish. As a rule, on smooth, Western meadow streams by casting across and working the bank opposite, you can hook more and larger trout. Obviously, if the steam has a shallow side, you have no problem. Walk or wade along the flat bank, and quarter your casts into the grass along the undercut, twitching your hopper loose just above rising fish. There won't be any line distubance or leader flash as the fly swings down. Essentially, your line point and leader should be extra-light. A 12-foot, 3X leader with a 36-inch tippet is about right. While a few trout will tangle in a root under the bank or bust in a thick bed of weeds, that's a small price for fast fishing in the summer months.

On a very windy day it's a good idea to experiment with your presentation. Although a competent caster will put his dry fly down delicately it often happens that fish respond more readily to the imitation hopper when it's almost slapped on the water. In Western streams big, meaty-winged insects are often whipped into the river. The trout are conditioned to the *splat* of a bug on the surface. This can make a great difference in results. To achieve the right degree of disturbance—without line splash—simply use a larger fly. A No. 6 dry Muddler for example is a size too large for a 3X tippet and will provide the heavy impact needed.

FISHING IN LAKES

In a lake, the hopper rise will invariably occur near shore. Trout, bass, and panfish concentrate in areas where wind-blown food is easiest to find. Deep shorelines with overhanging branches or grassy banks are always productive. Row very quietly parallel to the shore, and cast your hopper back at the water's edge. During an active feeding period your strikes may come instantly. If no fish are in evidence, let the fly float for a minute, then twitch it once or twice. Usually, that's when you'll get a hit. *See also* Live Bait. —A.J.McC.

GRASS PICKEREL *See* Redfin Pickerel

GRAVID Pregnant; specifically among fishes, the condition of a female when the body is swollen by eggs.

GRAYLING *See* American Grayling, European Grayling

GRAYSBY *Petrometopon cruentatum* A small grouper frequently taken in southern Florida but apparently more abundant in the West Indies. It occurs throughout the tropical American Atlantic and seldom reaches over fifteen inches in total length.

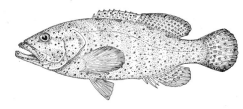

Graysby

The graysby has 9 dorsal spines, usually 14 dorsal rays, usually 8 anal rays, and usually 16 pectoral rays. The posterior nostril is somewhat larger than the anterior nostril. Insertion of the pelvic fin under or slightly in advance of lower end of pectoral base. Posterior margin of caudal fin convex. General coloration reddish or brownish, profusely spotted with red. Several black spots usually present along dorsal fin base.

The number of dorsal spines distinguishes this grouper from the others except the coney (*which see*). It is distinguished from the latter by the fewer dorsal, anal, and pectoral rays, and by the black spots along the dorsal-fin base. —L.R.

GRAY SMOOTHHOUND *Mustelus californicus* Closely related to the leopard shark, this common California shark closely resembles its Atlantic relative, the smooth dogfish (*which see*). The first and second dorsal fins are about the same size, and the first dorsal is about midway between the pectorals and pelvics. Unlike the sharp-pointed teeth of the brown smoothhound (*which see*), those of the gray smoothhound are flat, blunt, and not developed to points. It is dark gray above with a white belly. Maximum length is about 30 inches. It is known only off the coast of California, mostly in shallow waters, being most common in southern California. —D.dS.

GRAY SNAPPER *Lutjanus griseus* This is the most common snapper in the western Atlantic. Its range extends from the middle Atlantic and Gulf coasts of the United States southward to Brazil. It is very common around southern Florida, the Bahamas, and the Caribbean area. Known as gray snapper in the northernmost parts of its range, the common name of mangrove snapper used elsewhere refers to its shallow-water habitat. Seldom reaches a weight of much over 10 pounds.

The gray snapper has 10 dorsal spines, 14 dorsal rays, and 8 anal rays. Pectoral rays 15–17, usually 16. Gillrakers 7–9 on lower limb of first arch, not counting rudiments. Rows of scales around caudal peduncle 21–23, usually 22. Cheek scales in 7–8, usually 8 rows. Upper jaw reaching to or somewhat beyond vertical from

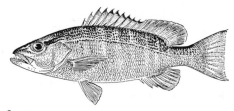

Gray Snapper

anterior margin of orbit. Pectoral fin not reaching to vertical from origin of anal fin. Anal fin rounded, not angulate posteriorly. General coloration grayish above, paler below, with a red tinge on sides. Dorsal and caudal fins grayish. Pectoral, pelvic, and anal fins reddish. Black spot on sides of body absent. Eye red.

In this species, the pectoral fin is shorter than in the other snappers, and it usually does not reach to a vertical from the anus.

ANGLING VALUE

A shallow-water snapper, it is most abundant along the shore in mangrove habitats. Extremely cunning; large individuals are very difficult to catch because of their reluctance to take a baited hook or artificial lure. Only the most enticing of bait (live shrimp), the smallest possible hook, and the most transparent of leaders will induce the big ones to strike. Its accessibility, abundance, and good fighting qualities make this snapper a favorite in the very light-tackle class.

FOOD VALUE

Very good eating. Its small size makes it suitable for panfrying. A common commercial snapper in Southern United States and in the Caribbean. —L.R.

GRAY SOLE A regional name in the northeastern United States for the witch flounder (*which see*).

GREAT BARRACUDA *Sphyraena barracuda* This is one of the largest of the barracudas. It is known to reach a weight of 106 pounds and a probable length of 6 feet. Large specimens are rare, and most of those caught by anglers do not reach 50 pounds. The species is common in the American Atlantic from Florida to Brazil.

The great barracuda is long, slim-bodied, and has a pointed head. In shape it somewhat resembles the pikes. The body coloration is dull to bright silver with a whitish belly, although sooty-black areas occur on many individuals with varying degrees of intensity. There are usually a few irregular, black blotches scattered on the sides of the body, particularly toward the tail. The pectoral fin reaches beyond a vertical from insertion of the pelvic fin. The anterior rays of the second dorsal and anal fins reach to, or beyond, the tip of the last ray when the fin is depressed. The jaws are studded with large, pointed teeth. The posterior teeth of the mandible are not slanted backwards. The great barracuda has 5 dorsal spines; 10 dorsal rays; and 10 anal rays. Its 78–82 scales along the lateral line separate it from other Atlantic species.

BEHAVIOR

Young individuals up to about 3 pounds usually occur close to shore in the shallow water, and may be found in harbors and coastal lagoons. Large adults may occur farther offshore in deeper water, occasionally far out to sea. This aggressive, carnivorous fish frequently attacks flashing objects and other disturbances that presumably appear as prospective prey. Such behavior may account for attacks on humans. Although barracuda display an extreme curiosity toward persons wading or swimming, and will approach quite closely, the known records of attack are comparatively rare. However, the species must be considered potentially dangerous. The bite, unlike the round, jagged wound of a shark, is straight and clean.

ANGLING TECHNIQUE

An underrated gamefish, small individuals are taken from shore, bridge, and boat with spinning, plug, and fly tackle. Larger barracuda are most commonly caught while trolling offshore on fairly heavy tackle. However, when specifically sought on the inshore flats or channel edges with light gear, the great barracuda can be a spectacular gamefish. When hooked in the shallows, the fish makes an incredibly swift run and frequently jumps. Despite its aggressive reputation, the barracuda is often lure-shy and can be difficult to hook on artificials.

Great Barracuda, 10-pound Male, Deep Water Cay, Bahamas

Although barracuda have been taken on live bait at depths of over 200 feet, they are most frequently to be encountered on reefs, flats, and along mangrove shores. These shallow habitats are not wholly the territory of small barracuda; in many regions, notably in the Bahamas, large fish of 20 pounds or more may consistently be found in knee-deep water. There is obviously some migration to the open sea due to temperature and other changes; few fish remain inshore when the water drops under 70°F. But normally, large barracuda appear directly against the bank on a rising tide. The flood- and highwater are the best fishing periods as a rule, and as the water falls the fish retreat to nearby channels. Around small Bahamian islands which are often divided into two types of habitat, with marl and turtle-grass flats on one side and steeper coral shores on the other, you can predictably locate the fish according to the stage of the tide. To some extent this is also true in the Florida Keys, but, elsewhere along the coast, the occurrence of big barracuda inshore is spotty; the reason may be the lack of suitable habitat or the greater variation in water temperature to the north.

Barracuda eat other fishes, and their dietary preferences simply reflect what is available in a particular location. In Florida, barracuda pursue the more numerous mullet. However, everything from the almost sedentary puffers to the swift-moving little tuna are consumed. From an angling standpoint this would seemingly allow a wide choice of lures, but for all practical purposes the selection is rather limited.

Barracuda are ideally a plug-caster's quarry. They can be caught on large bucktails and popping bugs, but two factors work against fly-fishing. As a rule you need to make very long casts, and the fly must be retrieved rapidly. Many curious barracuda will follow a fly without striking. This makes the casting method tedious. Small barracuda strike readily at slow retrieves and short casts, but the trophy fish demand considerable action in a lure. Nevertheless, many anglers prefer bait-casting or spinning tackle, because of the fact that barracuda are partial to topwater plus. This type of bait produces thrilling surface strikes.

The technique favored in the Bahamas is to stalk the fish along mangrove shores by poling slowly, parallel to the islands. Although the fish are big, they can be surprisingly difficult to see. Unlike bonefish, which are almost constantly moving about, barracuda lie motionless and may appear as nothing more than a shadow on the bottom. During high tide, they lay right up among the mangrove roots, and because of their ability to blend into any background, even a four footer is hard to see until you've had some experience. Small sharks, such as the lemon, shovelnose, nurse, and blacktip, are always common in the same areas, but these can easily be distinguished by the undulating movement of their tails. The angler, of course, stands in the bow and watches for targets. It's not enough, however, just to *see* the barracuda but to identify the fish at a distance—the longer the better.

When sight-fishing on the flats never cast near a barracuda. A lure that splashes close to a fish will invariably send it flashing off to deepwater. Too close, by our definition, is within five feet of a visible target. There may be the exceptional cuda who strikes reflexively at anything that falls within reach, but such fish are uncommon. It is far more effective to place your lure ten, even twenty feet ahead or beyond the cuda and retrieve the bait across its line of sight. When a barracuda wants to hit a plug it's impossible to reel fast enough to get it away from it; so the technique is to draw the fish to the lure rather than cast the lure to the fish. This should be accomplished at the greatest practical distance; short casts are not as effective as medium to long ones of 60–100 feet. Large barracuda stalk a bait for some distance; with a short cast you'll quickly get the fish into view of the boat.

The speed of the retrieve appears to be the key in triggering strikes. It must be rapid and erratic. If the lure is retrieved slowly, one or more barracuda will follow the bait but make no attempt to hit it. If the lure is stopped, the barracuda will stop and quickly lose interest. If the lure is worked at a fast pace and the barracuda pursues it without striking, a slight *increase* in its speed will generally bring a flashing hit. As a rule, this is not hard to do because the reaction of the individual barracuda is obvious.

Most accounts of barracuda emphasize that the fish are attracted to flashing objects and that spoons are good lures. Spoons have some value in deepwater trolling, but there are occasions when a wobbler wouldn't attract fish at all, and for casting in shallow water these subsurface baits are impossible to operate because they constantly hang in coral and grass. The ideal lure is a ⅝-ounce, topwater plug 4–5 inches in length. It must not be made of plastic but of wood. Barracuda destroy plastic baits quickly. There are several good wooden plugs on the market which will take a lot of fish before being chewed to splinters.

A wire leader is essential in all methods.

FOOD VALUE

Great barracuda are utilized as food in many tropical areas, but the flesh is sometimes toxic and it is not worth the risk to cook one. The poisoning (*see* Ciguatera) is due to a toxin in the flesh and not from decay or bacterial action. Although several theories have been presented as to the origin of the poison there is no absolute proof that one or another is correct. The most accepted explanation lies in the fact that a very high percentage of the fishes eaten by great barracuda, such as the puffers, are in themselves poisonous and the toxin is thereby ingested. The California barracuda, on the other hand, has never been known to be poisonous, and is, in fact, one of the more popular food fish in California. One reason why the ingestion theory may be valid is because the eastern Pacific does not contain the great variety of the known toxic species which inhabit the coral shores of the Atlantic. There are many beliefs in the Caribbean about how a poisonous barracuda is identified—by its size, the color of its teeth, the rigidity of its scales, the presence of a milky secretion on the body, and the fact that the flesh will turn a silver-coin black—but none of these "tests" is valid.

The dubious food value of the barracuda in no way detracts from its game qualities. Unless the fish is to be kept for mounting, a barracuda should be released after capture. *See also* Saltwater Fly-Fishing   —L.R.
—A.J.McC.

GREAT BRITAIN   *See* England, Northern Ireland *under* Ireland, Scotland, Wales

GREATER AMBERJACK *Seriola dumerili* This is the largest and most important of the Atlantic amberjacks.

The nuchal band of the greater amberjack extends from the eye to the origin of the dorsal fin. The five body bars on young fish are not present in specimens over about eight inches long. The body is relatively slender, and the depth decreases proportionally with growth. The greatest body depth goes into the standard length about 3.0–3.3 times in specimens up to 16 inches in standard length, about 3.3–3.7 times in 16–24-inch specimens, and about 3.7–4.5 times in larger specimens (standard length is measured from the tip of the snout to the end of the bony plate of the tail). The dorsal-fin lobe is relatively short; its length goes about 6.7 times into the standard length. The total number of gillrakers on both limbs of the first gill arch is relatively small, and this number decreases appreciably with the growth of the fish; there are about 18–24 total gillrakers in specimens up to 4 inches in standard length, about 14–20 in specimens 4–8 inches, about 13–16 from 8–16 inches, and about 11–13 in larger specimens.

The first dorsal fin usually has 7 spines. The second dorsal fin has 1 spine and 29–35 softrays (usually 31–33). The anal fin has 2 detached spines (possibly covered by skin in the large individuals), followed by a spine and by 19–22 softrays. In larger fish the nuchal band is olivaceous, the body is dark above, lighter along the sides with lavender and golden tints but sometimes with an amber band from eye to tail, and silvery-white ventrally; the dark area may be brownish, olivaceous, or a dark steely-blue.

The true range of the greater amberjack has been occluded due to its confusion with other, closely related species. Its known range is in the eastern Atlantic from the western coast of Africa to the Mediterranean, and in the western Atlantic from Brazil to Cape Cod, Massachusetts, in the West Indies, and at Bermuda. Another species at Bermuda, known there as horse-eye bonito, has been confused with the name *Seriola dumerili*. All Pacific amberjacks that have been related to this specific name are some other species. A specimen 5 feet 1 inch in length has been examined, and a maximum weight of 177 pounds was reported for a fish from Trinidad.

LIFE HISTORY

The life history has not been adequately studied. Spawning apparently occurs in offshore oceanic waters, because the smallest known young have been found there. Descriptions of larvae and juveniles have been published for specimens from the Mediterranean and from off North Carolina, but the specific identities are uncertain. Most of those from North Carolina were taken from June through September and from offshore waters.

ANGLING VALUE

This species is the most important to sport fishermen of all the Atlantic amberjacks, and is particularly sought by charter-boat fisheries of Florida and the Carolinas. It is edible. It is usually caught trolling near the surface, but has been taken fishing with cutbait on the bottom in 30

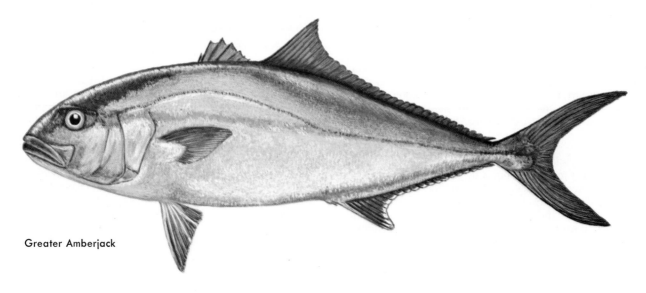

Greater Amberjack

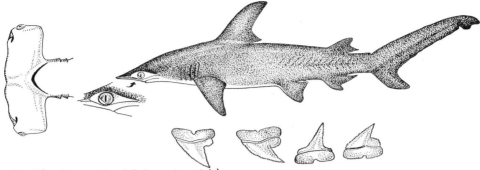

Great Hammerhead (teeth upper jaw *left*, lower jaw *right*)

fathoms. Several large amberjacks, thought to be of this species, were caught on the bottom in 250 fathoms of water off the Bahamas. *See also* Amberjacks, Carangidae

—F.H.B.

GREATER WEEVER *See* Weeverfish
GREAT HAMMERHEAD *Sphyrna mokarran* This species is readily recognized by the hammer-shaped head and the nearly straight profile of the anterior margin with a definite indentation at the center. Its nearly straight anterior margin and the regularly serrated teeth distinguish it from the scalloped hammerhead and smooth hammerhead (*which see*). The pelvic fins are anteriorly convex, and the dorsal fin is less erect than in other Atlantic relatives. Young specimens are brownish-gray to olive above, grading to paler beneath, with dusky shadings on the fin tips. A length of 18 feet is attained, and specimens of 13–14 feet are common.

A warmwater shark, it occurs throughout the tropical and subtropical parts of the Atlantic, the eastern Pacific, and the Indo-Pacific region. It is known in the western Atlantic with certainty from North Carolina to northern Argentina. Apparently it is not as common as some of its relatives, except in southern Florida, where some concentrations have been noted. Sexual maturity occurs at about 10 feet, and the young are born in tropical waters. A large, strong-swimming species, it has been known to attack large tarpon, tuna, and other sharks.

DANGER TO MAN

Because of its size, it is a potential danger to man, and although hammerheads have attacked man, the species involved have not been identified. The hide of this species makes excellent leather, and its liver yields a high grade of oil. —D.dS.

GREAT SCULPIN *Myoxocephalus polyacanthocephalus* A large Pacific sculpin (*which see*) reaching a length of 30 inches, it is common and found from Washington to the Bering Sea at moderate depths.

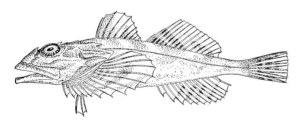

Great Sculpin

The great sculpin has small, fleshy papillae scattered over the body; a large, heavy blunt, short preopercular spine, equal to the eye diameter; a lateral line decurved below the soft dorsal fin. Color dark olive to black dorsally, white to cream ventrally; a pale band across body; black markings on all put pelvic fins. —J.R.

GREEN BULLHEAD *Ictalurus brunneus* Found from Cape Fear, North Carolina, to the St. John's River in Florida, this species has 17–20 anal rays, an emarginate caudal fin, an inferior mouth with decurved snout, and a flattened head. Although the body coloration is generally uniform, it's sometimes spotted and occasionally mottled. The green bullhead occurs in streams and rivers with a moderate to swift current over gravel or rock bottoms. It's usually caught in pools below riffles and dams or in deep channels. Gravid females have been found from February to July, and it's believed that the species spawn throughout the year. Nocturnal and omnivorous, the green bullhead consumes principally vegetation, insects, minnows, and snails.

Green Bullhead

Good eating, it is of little commercial value due to its small size. Maximum weight about 1½ pounds, but averages ¼ pound. Readily caught on scent and natural baits. —A.J.McC.

GREEN CRAB *Carcinides maenas* This small crab is a member of the swimming crab family (Portunidae), having more or less of an oval body and the last pair of legs flattened and with pointed tips. Other members of the family, as the blue crab (*which see*), have the last pair of legs flattened. The shell has sharp teeth on its anterior edge, with rather short claws. The body is dark green or green with yellow mottlings, and it grows to about 3 inches.

It occurs in European waters and in the United States from Maine to New Jersey. The species was apparently introduced into the United States in the early 1800's,

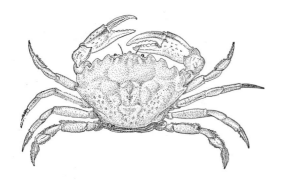

Green Crab

probably into the Cape Cod region. Its present-day distribution is apparently due to colonization by larval crabs of new areas, movement of adults into new niches, and by accidental or deliberate introduction by man. Lobster boats, crates, trucks, and sardine boats are believed responsible for this spread.

LIFE HISTORY

Sexual maturity occurs within a year of hatching at a width of less than an inch. Females carry up to 185,000 eggs. The breeding season occurs from spring to late fall, and the eggs may be laid the following spring.

Although it is found around rocks, the green crab is a sand burrower, as well as a swimmer, and the large claws are used in digging as well as in catching prey. It prefers clayey or silty sand, burrowing to a little over 9 inches deep. During the winter, they burrow into the deep sand, but they are evidently killed during hard winters. Soft clams (*Mya*) are particularly relished, and the shells are easily crushed with the large claws. Vast quantities of soft clams are annually destroyed by green crabs in New England, and their depredations cause great economic losses to the industry.

ECONOMIC VALUE

They are used to a limited extent as bait for tautogs, for chum, and as bait for fishpots. In Europe they are popular as food. —D.dS.

GREENHEAD *See* Striped Bass

GREENHEAD SHINER *Notropis chlorocephalus* A small highly-colored minnow seldom exceeding 2½ inches in total length, the greenhead shiner is not widely distributed, but is found only in the Santee River system of North Carolina, South Carolina, and Georgia. The body of this minnow is rather stout; the caudal peduncle is deep; and the body depth is 0.2 the total length. The head is broad, 0.25 the total length. The orbit of the eye is large, more than 0.33 the length of the head. The interorbital region is wide, exceeding the length of the snout.

Greenhead Shiner

The mouth is oblique, with the end of the maxilla extending beyond the margin of the orbit. The lateral line is slightly decurved, with the number of lateral line scales numbering about 39. The transverse scale series number 8 or 9, with 16 scales before the dorsal fin. There are 8 rays each in the dorsal and anal fins. There is a distinct spot at the base of the caudal peduncle which is round or appears as an intensification of the lateral band. The pharyngeal teeth are in two rows 2,4-4,2. The color of the males is intense during the breeding season. Most of the head and middorsal stripe of breeding males are a metallic green, with the belly, lateral band, dorsal, and caudal bases being crimson. During the breeding season the fins are milk white, occasionally turning light yellow.

LIFE HISTORY

The greenhead shiner is widely distributed in the Santee watershed and is associated with clearwater streams having a sand and gravel bottom. This species is found in large numbers and is usually associated with the bluehead chub, whitetail shiner, and the striped jumprock. It is seldom found in streams having a large number of predator fishes. The greenhead shiner spawns in the gravel during late spring and early summer and prefers water having near neutral pH (6.7-7.2). Its primary food is zooplankton and small invertebrates.

This minnow serves as food for the predator fishes, and on occasion is used locally as bait. —D.E.L.

GREEN JACK *Caranx caballus* This eastern Pacific species is very closely related to the western Atlantic *Caranx crysos*, the blue runner (*which see*).

The second dorsal fin of the green jack has 1 spine and 22-24 softrays; anal fin with 2 detached spines followed by one spine and 19-20 softrays. Gillrakers on the first arch, 13-16 on the upper limb and 28-32 on the lower limb. The vent is located near the first spine of the anal fin and behind the tips of the pelvic fins.

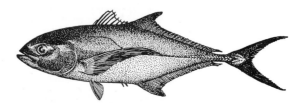

Green Jack

The body is more slender and rounded than any other eastern Pacific jack crevalle. The straight part of the lateral line is about twice as long as the curved part. There are 40-51 pointed scutes in the straight lateral line. The dorsal- and anal-fin lobes are only moderately elongated. It is generally greenish above and silvery to white below with a small black opercular spot that is sometimes indistinct. Specimens nearing spawning condition tend to become melanistic, males more so than females. The young, up to about 6-7 inches long, have seven–eight broad bars on the body plus one on the head; these bars frequently occur in larger living fish but fade out rapidly after capture.

The green jack has been taken from Lobos de Tierra, Peru, to Los Angeles County, California, into the northern Gulf of California, and at the Galápagos, Cocos, and

Revillagigedo islands. The average length is about 1 foot, but a specimen 23¼ inches long has been preserved.

LIFE HISTORY

Life-history data are very meager. Nearly ripe specimens were taken in Banderas Bay, Mexico, during August.

ANGLING VALUE

This is a good gamefish on light tackle and is fairly good to eat. *See also* Carangidae, Jacks —F.H.B.

GREENLAND RIGHT WHALE *See* Whales

GREENLAND SHARK *Somniosus microcephalus* One of the larger species of shark found on both sides of the Atlantic in arctic and subarctic waters and southward as far as the Gulf of Maine. It is very plentiful around Greenland; hence its name. It is normally found near the surface in winter, but in summer it is usually in deeper water and has been recorded at great depths.

The Greenland shark is easily separated from other Atlantic squalid sharks by the lack of spines in the dorsal fin. It is colored brown or black above as well as below, although the color is variable and sometimes individuals are slaty gray all over. The sides and back are crossed by indistinct dark bands, often with whitish spots. It is reported to reach a length of 24 feet and a ton in weight; but the largest specimens found in the Gulf of Maine seldom exceed 17 feet. A specimen 11 feet long weighs about 650 pounds.

This shark feeds on fish, seals, sea birds, and invertebrates; and it regularly gathers around whaling stations to devour the offal.

ANGLING VALUE

A very sluggish shark, it offers no resistance when hooked or harpooned, and may be drawn out of the water very easily. It is sought for by commercial fishermen off Greenland, Iceland, and northern Norway, where it is usually caught on hand lines.

Although the flesh is toxic when fresh, it may be buried and left to decay (*see* Hakarl) or air-dried and made fit for human consumption. —A.J.McC.

GREEN, SETH American (1817–1888) Outstanding fly caster and fish culturist, Seth Green is today best remembered as the first man ever to cast a fly 100 feet. The accomplishment, in an 1864 tournament that was actually won by Robert Barnwell Roosevelt with a cast of 68 feet, was disallowed at the time, but later officially confirmed, and Green's vindication was attested with a certificate. Anticipating later tournament practice, Green was the first to have a rod and line prepared specifically for distance casting.

In 1868 he became New York State's Fish Commissioner. Green served 1 year, then became state fish culturist, and for 18 years was superintendent at the State Hatchery at Caledonia, New York, which he had built and operated personally prior to 1864. His more lasting contribution to today's angling was the introduction of "California trout" (rainbow) to Eastern waters in 1874. This led directly to the subsequent widespread establishment of the rainbow trout throughout the East. Green's first book was *Trout Culture* (1870), followed by *Home Fishing and Home Waters* (1888), and numerous reports on fish and frog culture until the year of his death.

A memorial was erected in Green's honor near Rochester, New York. —A.G.

GREENSTRIPED ROCKFISH *Sebastodes elongatus* This slender rockfish (*which see*) has been taken to depths of about 3,000 feet. It forms only a small part of the com-

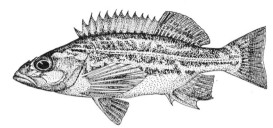

Greenstriped Rockfish

mercial catch. The green-striped rockfish has a slender body; it has a medium-sized eye; four horizontal irregular green bands along the length of the body, joining to form two near the tail; a pale pink stripe along the lateral line; interorbital space narrow, shallowly concave; strong spines on head. Length to 15 inches. —J.R.

GREEN STURGEON *Acipenser medirostris* It has an elongated snout with four barbels midway on its ventral surface and a sucking mouth with extensible lips. The body is covered with bony plates, and the upper lobe of the tail fin is the longer. The skeleton is cartilaginous. It is olive-green with an olive stripe on the median line of the belly and on each side above the bony plates.

Green Sturgeon

The green sturgeon is found in river mouths and along the Pacific Coast from the Gulf of Alaska south to San Francisco.

LIFE HISTORY

This species rarely occurs in freshwater and prefers to spend its time near the mouths of rivers, but it is not numerous even there. The green sturgeon attains lengths up to 7 feet and weighs up to 350 pounds. Its flesh is dark or red and has a disagreeable taste and odor; thus it is not sought as is the white sturgeon.

Feeding is done by feeling along the bottom with the barbels while the mouth extends to suck up bottom organisms. *See also* Sturgeon —C.A.P.

GREEN SUNFISH *Lepomis cyanellus* A short, stocky sunfish usually an olive-green color with a brassy tint on the lower sides and belly. It is sometimes called green perch, sunfish, sand bass, rubber tail, or blue-spotted sunfish. The distinguishing characteristics of this fish are the heavy lips and large mouth extending beyond the front of the eye, 3 spines in the anal fin, and a black blotch on the posterior of the dorsal and anal fins. The gill flap is edged with a light color. The maximum size is about 9 inches.

The original distribution of this fish was west of the Alleghenies through the Great Lakes region and south throughout the Mississippi Valley and west into Colorado and New Mexico. Depending on the area, the green sunfish can be found in large and small lakes, rivers, streams, or artificial impoundments. It is also tolerant to siltation, and can be found where few other species can exist.

LIFE HISTORY

The breeding habits of the green sunfish are similar to those of the bluegill. They spawn in colonies in shallow water. The saucer-shaped nests are built and guarded by the males. Spawning takes place from May through August with the peak, in the Northern states, in June. The

Green Sunfish

number of eggs varies with the size of the fish, but 2,000–10,000 may be deposited from one female. The young grow 1–3 inches the first year. They reach maturity and spawn at 2 years of age at a length of about 3 inches.

The green sunfish feeds on insects, small crustaceans, and small fish.

ANGLING VALUE

The green sunfish is a sporty panfish even though it doesn't attain a large size. Crickets, worms, grasshoppers, and flies are effective baits. It is a popular food fish in some areas. —K.B.

GRENADA This most southerly of the Windward Islands lies about 90 miles north of Trinidad in the eastern Caribbean. The 120-square-mile island is volcanic in origin. A mountain range runs from north to south which reaches its highest point at Mt. Saint Catherine (2,756 feet). A lake, Grand Etang, occupies the crater of an extinct volcano, and another crater lake lies on the northeast shore. There are also several large freshwater streams and many springs which create brackish-water habitat, particularly along the eastern coast where tarpon and snook occur.

Grenada has a tropical marine climate. An average annual range is 76°–79°F at the capital city of St. George's. Temperatures vary with altitude. The rainy season lasts from May to December and the peak fishing season is from December through March.

Grenada is primarily an agricultural island with the emphasis on nutmegs, cocoa, and bananas. Fishing as a tourist attraction is little developed at present. However, it has excellent potential both offshore and inshore, especially for sailfish, blue and white marlin, yellowfin tuna, wahoo, and dolphin. Charter craft suitable for big-game fishing are scarce. Due to the proximity of the 100-fathom curve to Grenada, gamefish migrate through these waters in large numbers within a mile of the coast. —A.J.McC.

GREY, ZANE American (1872–1939) A pioneering fisherman, Grey was the first man to catch a 1,000-pound fish on rod-and-reel; first to explore and popularize some of the world's greatest saltwater fishing grounds; one-time holder of over a dozen saltwater world records; author of eight books and more than fourscore magazine articles on salt- and freshwater angling.

In his foreword to *Zane Grey's Adventures in Fishing* (1952) Ed Zern said of Grey, "No other man . . . has devoted so much of his fortune, nor so large a share of his time and energy, to the catching of fish for the sport of it. In his compulsive quest for bigger and better and rarer gamefish he was almost literally indefatigable, and it is reasonable to assume that no one will ever challenge his right to be known as the greatest fisherman America has ever produced."

Zane Grey was born on January 31, 1872, in Zanesville, Ohio. As a boy he fished for bullhead and bass in the Muskingum River. His first fishing mentor was a gray, tattered man townspeople called "Old Muddy Miser," because he kept to himself and seemed to do nothing but fish. But the old man was well-read and he fired Grey's imagination with tales of trout and salmon and great saltwater fish, which he said no one seemed to go after.

Inspired in part by Old Muddy Miser, Grey himself would be the first man to go after many of those great fish. But first he would win a baseball scholarship to the University of Pennsylvania. He enrolled in Pennsylvania's dental school at the urging of his dentist father. He did well at baseball, poorly at his studies, and barely eked out a diploma in 1896. Zane Grey was an indifferent dentist. In 1905 he quit his practice at 100 West 74th Street in New York City and with his new wife, the former Lina Elise Roth, moved to a cottage in Lackawaxen, Pennsylvania, at the confluence of Lackawaxen Creek and the Delaware River.

After office hours Grey had been writing novels and outdoor stories. He sold two of the stories, "A Day on the Delaware" to *Recreation Magazine* in 1902 and "Camping Out" to *Field & Stream* in 1903, and when his second historical novel, *The Spirit of the Border*, was finally accepted by a publisher after earlier rejections, he decided to become a full-time writer.

Success eluded him for five lean years. Then, in 1910, Harper and Brothers published Grey's *Heritage of the Desert*. In 1912 they published the book that would be called "the greatest Western novel ever written" and would sell over 1,800,000 copies—*Riders of the Purple Sage*. By 1924 the dentist-turned-writer could place his novels in the top-ten bracket of the yearly bestseller list nine times. In one year alone he would earn $575,000.

Grey's Westerns brought him fortune and the freedom to do as he wished. So he went fishing. He left his beloved Delaware and its black bass for tarpon in Tampico, Mexico. He fished Long Key, Florida, becoming president of the famous Long Key Fishing Camp. At the same time he was vice-president of the prestigious Catalina Tuna Club in California. Giant bluefin tuna lured him often to Nova Scotia, where in 1924 he bought his 190-foot-long schooner, *Fisherman*, which he had outfitted with three fishing launches. With *Fisherman* as a base, he fished the Galapagos, Cape San Lucas, New Zealand, and Tahiti. In 1930, having sold *Fisherman*, Grey bought an even grander ship, named it *Fisherman II*, and sailed to Tahiti. His last great trips were two to Australia: the first when he was 63, the second when he was 66. Bracketing all these and slipped between them were his freshwater expeditions to Colorado, Wyoming, California, Washington, Oregon, and the Delaware.

But the log of his fishing journeys is more than a travelog; it's also a record of amazing achievement.

Zern says, "Few men before Zane Grey had fished specifically for the moody, capricious broadbill swordfish.... Before he hung his last swordfish Zane Grey contributed vastly to the knowledge of the species as a gamefish, and to the development of tackle and methods more suited to this specialized sport."

Van Campen Heilner, in his *Salt Water Fishing* (1937), recalls that "Our tackle in those days was too heavy and we had to be educated. Zane Grey, the great pioneer of salt water angling, who really discovered the possibilities of Long Key and made it famous, started a campaign for sailfish on light tackle and the rest followed suit. Soon it was the fish of fishes along the eastern Florida coast and angling for it spread rapidly to other parts of the world." And, "Grey has done more to publicize the world's great marlin centers than anyone else. He's spent his life and his fortune at it."

Ranging out from Long Key, Grey caught snook long before other outdoor writers discovered them. He was one of the earliest bonefishermen and did much to popularize that phantom of the flats. He was the first outdoor writer to recognize the great fighting abilities of the permit. And in 1916 he began showing his Keys fishing companions how to catch sailfish in the fertile blue Gulf Stream.

His remarkable catches, and the stories and books he gained from them, brought fame and fishermen to the fishing grounds of the South Seas, New Zealand, Tahiti, and Australia. In Australia a reef he discovered was officially named Zane Grey Reef.

He brought freshwaters like Oregon's North Umpqua and Rogue rivers to the attention of the fishing world, labeling their steelhead fly-fishing supreme sport.

When his own fame was at its zenith more than a dozen items of fishing tackle were named after him, and several tackle refinements resulted from his prodding.

Among the world records Zane Grey held were bluefin tuna, 758 pounds; yellowtail, 111 pounds; striped marlin, 450 pounds; dolphin, 63 pounds; silver marlin, 618 pounds; tiger shark, 1,036 pounds; Allison tuna, 318 pounds; Pacific sailfish, 171 pounds; broadbill swordfish, 582 pounds; and—Grey's biggest catch—a 1,040-pound Pacific blue marlin; this was the first fish of over 1,000 pounds ever taken on rod-and-reel. (All of these records have been disallowed under modern regulations of the International Game Fish Association.)

Zane Grey was able to become "the greatest fisherman America has ever produced" because he was a blend of all the right attributes. He was an athlete, with an athlete's strength and coordination for fighting world-record fish. He was a dreamer on a grand scale, with the will and durability—and the money—to realize his dreams. (In New Zealand, he caught his world-record 450-pound striped marlin, beating his own previous world record, after 83 fishless days.) He was a talented photographer and fisherman, whose angling companions could back him up with either rod or camera. He was a great student of the fish he

chased. (In Catalina he had a scientist friend dissect his first broadbill swordfish; and he wondered at its strong heart and heavy muscles.) He was one of the early fisherman-conservationists, warning of the dangers of unregulated commercial fishing and advocating the release of healthy fish. He was an adventurer and explorer, with a self-professed fetish for trying new and lonely waters. And he was a writer who could portray his adventures in a way that stirred readers all over the world.

Zane Grey with Umpqua steelhead. As an outdoor writer he pioneered many of the world's fishing grounds

Grey suffered a paralyzing heart attack while trolling the North Umpqua River for steelhead in the summer of 1937. Gradually, he regained the use of most of his muscles and, against the advice of his doctor and family, made his second trip to Australia. After returning home he fished off Catalina and traveled north again for fishing in the Rogue and North Umpqua. On October 23, 1939, at his home in Altadena, California, a second heart attack claimed Zane Grey's life.   —S.N.

GRIBBLE The common name for *Limnoria*, a marine crustacean wood-borer which attacks and undermines dock pilings. *Limnoria* digs a network of shallow tunnels beneath the surface of the wood which breaks away layer by layer creating a typical hour-glass contour to the piling between low tide and the half-tide level. Gribbles are capable of leaving their burrows and swimming to new locations thus destroying pilings along wide areas of coast. *See also* Teredo

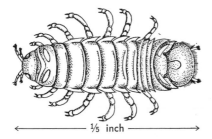

← ⅕ inch →

Gribble (*Limnoria lignorum*)

GRILSE The common name for small or adolescent Atlantic salmon (*which see*) returning from saltwater. The origin of the word "grilse" is thought to be from the Scottish *gralax* which was similarly pronounced.

GROMMET A ring of rope made from a single strand; also iron or brass rings punched into (sometimes sewed) the edge of a hammock, sail, or tarpaulin to make frequent fastening an easier task.

GROUNDFISH In commercial fishing those species that feed on the bottom.

GROUND SWELL (1) At sea, each of a series of long, high swells or waves which have an abnormal distance between their peaks. This condition may be encountered in light air on sea which is otherwise calm, for it may be caused by either a distant storm center or by a seismic disturbance occurring on the bottom a considerable distance away. Ground swells peak higher and may break down upon reaching a shoal area, as when approaching the shore line.

(2) On the beach, each of a series of waves that are larger than usual and that roll in from the sea at regular intervals. The ground swells do not depend on a helping wind and may be present when there is no wind or even move against the wind. They are usually due to an offshore storm, squall, or hurricane.

GROUPERS Family Serranidae Groupers are found all over the world in tropical and temperate, marine, and fresh waters. The family contains over 400 species, and more than 50 are found in Florida waters alone. The name "grouper" is usually applied to the large species of serranid fishes belonging to such genera as *Epinephelus*, *Mycteroperca*, *Paranthias*, *Dermatolepis*, and their relatives.

Groupers are large predatory fishes with usually 8–11 dorsal spines, 3 anal spines, 8–12 anal softrays, and 15 caudal rays; there are 24 vertebrae; the teeth are caniniform, usually largest toward the symphysis of the jaws, and are in two series in each jaw; the preopercle is serrate along the upper limb and at the angle, usually unarmed along its lower limb; there are 3 opercular spines; the body is completely scaled and the scales extend to varying

degrees onto the bases of the pectoral and caudal fins and the membranes of the soft dorsal and anal fins.

Most of the species are found in the shallow marine waters of the tropics. They are important to the economy, for they are excellent food fishes and are sought after by sport fishermen. Some species grow to a very large size. For example, the jewfish of the Western Atlantic is known to scale more than 700 pounds. *See also* Black Grouper, Coney, Gag, Graysby, Jewfish, Marbled Grouper, Misty Grouper, Nassau Grouper, Red Grouper, Red Hind, Rock Hind, Scamp, Snowy Grouper, Speckled Hind, Tiger Grouper, Warsaw Grouper, Yellowedge Grouper, Yellowfin Grouper, Yellowmouth Grouper

GRUNION *See* California Grunion

GRUNTS Family Pomadasyidae A large family of shallow water, tropical-bottom fishes. Many of the species, especially those found in a coral-reef habitat, are very colorful. The common name of the family is derived from the sounds produced by individuals when they are captured. The grinding of the pharyngeal teeth produces an audible noise which is amplified by the air bladder. Some of the subgroups have often been put in separate families (Gaterinidae, Plectorhynchidae, Pristipomidae).

Anatomically, the grunts are a family of advanced, spiny-rayed fishes; the air bladder is separated from the esophagus; the pelvic bones are attached to the pectoral girdle; and the pelvic fins are inserted below the pectoral bases. The grunts are related to the snappers (Lutjanidae), but differ from that family in lacking a subocular shelf, teeth on the vomer, and well-developed canines on the jaws.

The family contains about 20 genera and about 175 species. Most of the species are small, but all are edible and some are of commercial value. *See also* Bluestriped Grunt, Caesar Grunt, Cottonwick, French Grunt, Smallmouth Grunt, Spanish Grunt, Tomtate, White Grunt, White Margate.

GUADALUPE BASS *Micropterus treculi* A distinct, Texas species of black bass (*which see*). It has a striped lateral band, as does the spotted bass, but the stripes are broader and darker and extend up over the midsides. The mouth does not extend beyond the eye and as in the spotted bass it contains glossohyal teeth on the tongue. It also differs from related forms by the number of dorsal spines, anal spines, and soft rays of the dorsal, pectoral, and

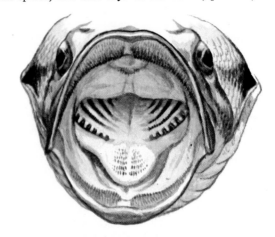

Teeth on tongue of Guadalupe Bass

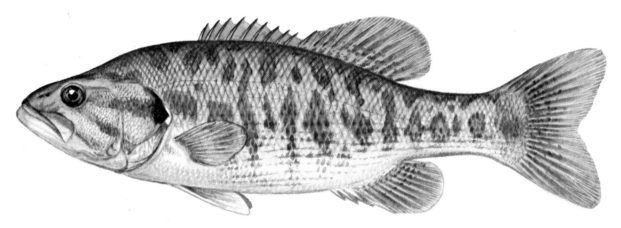

Guadalupe Bass

anal fins. This is a small species, rarely exceeding 12 inches in length.

It is found in the Colorado, San Antonio, and Guadalupe River systems of southcentral Texas.

GUADALUPE PERCH *Micrometrus aletes* This surfperch (*which see*) is confined to Guadalupe Island in the Pacific off the coast of Baja California. Little is known of its habits or appearance in nature since it is a comparatively new species and described from specimens preserved in alcohol. Length of preserved specimens approximately 2½–4 inches. Dorsal softrays 13–14, anal softrays 21–23. —J.R.

GUAGUANCHE *Sphyraena guachancho* This species is much smaller than the great barracuda, but it reaches a somewhat larger size (at least 20 inches) than the northern sennet (*which see*) and the southern sennet. It is most abundant in the tropical Atlantic from Florida southward to Brazil, but it may occur farther north.

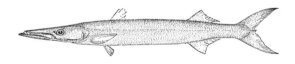

Guaguanche

The body coloration of the guaguanche is an olive-gray on the back and silvery below. There are no black blotches scattered on the sides as on the great barracuda. The maxillary reaches beyond vertical from the posterior nostril. The pectoral fins reach beyond a vertical line from the insertion of the pelvic fin. The anterior rays of second dorsal and anal fins do not reach the tip of last ray when fin is depressed. The posterior teeth of mandible are slanted backwards. The guaguanche has 5 dorsal spines; 10 dorsal rays; 10 anal rays, and 100–120 scales along the lateral line.

ANGLING VALUE

A schooling fish usually occurring along the shore in relatively shallow water. It may be found in clear bays and harbors close to the bottom where it may be taken still-fishing with live or cut bait. This fish also strikes artificial lures and provides good sport on light spinning and fly tackle. Frequently taken in southern Florida but more abundant in the Bahamas and the West Indies.

FOOD VALUE

Probably the best-eating of Atlantic barracudas. Never known to be poisonous and considered a delicacy in the West Indies. An important commercial fish in the Greater Antilles. —L.R.

GUDGEON As a boating term, a fitting with an eye, similar to an eyebolt, secured in the stern post of a small boat in which is mounted the pintle of the rudder.

GUDGEON *Gobio gobio* One of the smaller cyprinid fishes of European rivers and lakes. Despite its size, the gudgeon is very popular among anglers.

It is widely distributed in the Old World from China to south England, but absent from southern Italy, Norway, northern England, Scotland, and Ireland. It is also found in the brackish parts of the Baltic Sea. Originally and still primarily a river fish preferring sandy or gravelly bottoms, it has successfully invaded stillwaters throughout Europe. Gudgeon prefer highly oxygenated water, but they do thrive in habitats having considerably less than would be found in a flowing river. A popular baitfish and very hardy in transit, gudgeon have been extensively and inadvertently spread by anglers. Once established, they breed prolifically, providing food for predators and are somewhat of a nuisance to anglers seeking larger gamefish.

It can be deduced on examination that the gudgeon is a bottom-living fish, essentially at home in rivers of moderate to fast flow, as it has an elongated body with a flattish head and an inferior mouth adorned with sensory barbules. The back is grayish-green to brownish-gold, with prominent dark spots of black or brown. The belly is iridescent silver, and the fins all straw-yellow with irregular brown flecks. The shape is very similar to the much larger European barbel, *Barbus barbus*; but the latter prefers deeper water, and is confined to localized areas within European rivers. As a crucial test, the barbel has four sensory barbules about the mouth, the gudgeon only two.

Gudgeon

The usual size of the gudgeon is 5–8 inches in length; anything larger is a notable fish.

LIFE HISTORY

Gudgeon spawn from May to June or later, the actual time determined by prevailing temperatures. The males develop a breeding dress of tubercles on the head. Whole shoals spawn together, laying their sticky eggs in clumps upon stones and weeds in gravelly shallows. When not in their typical habitat, eggs are laid on weeds in well-oxygenated places.

When hatched, the fry congregate in large shoals eating at first planktonic crustaceans and algae. Later they progress to large crustaceans, small mollusks, insects, and other foods. Although it is commonly believed that small animals form the bulk of their diet, gudgeon do eat large quantities of filamentous algae in the wild (sucking it off stones and embankments), and can be fed on wholly vegetable foods in captivity.

Gudgeon continue to remain in large shoals throughout their life span, which cannot be great on average, as they are much liked by predators. The schools are very compact and orderly, searching up and down a stretch of river bottom for food. There appear to be great differences in the size of this beat, some shoals being more mobile or more sedentary than others. When displaced from their normal beat, they will generally migrate back, thus showing that the schools have a developed territorial instinct.

The shoal characteristic persists in all habitats to which gudgeon have penetrated, and a lingering preference for gravel bottoms still seems apparent. In lakes with mud bottoms and some gravel spits, the latter seem preferred; and in canals, the scoured stony central navigation channel is preferred to the muddier bottom nearer the banks.

In common with many European cyprinids, little has been investigated of gudgeon life histories (apart from the broad outlines) or population growth and dynamics. The scales are difficult to read (40 in the lateral line) on such a small fish, and anglers tend to take them for granted and demand little investigation. All fish on one water are inclined to run the same size, usually 5–6 inches; so either they quickly achieve this size, or spawning is not uniformly successful.

ANGLING VALUE

Gudgeon have two claims to an angler's attention—as a sport fish in their own right and as a baitfish for predators. Northern pike and perch are very fond of gudgeon, mounted on live-bait or spinning rigs.

As a quarry on their own account, they are cooperative and bold-biting to bottom-fishermen using light tackle with baits such as bread, small worms, or grubs. Because gudgeon move in large schools, they are favorites with

small boys. Gudgeon are best sought in swims from 2–5 feet deep, and can be attracted by either baiting with wet bran or else by muddying the water. Often they can be attracted upstream by disturbance of the bottom, such as animals wading across fords. In stillwaters, they are less liable to stay near the bottom; in some ornamental waters, they regularly attack floating breadcrusts meant for domestic ducks.

COMMERCIAL VALUE

Gudgeon are delicious to eat, but except in France they are not widely esteemed by most people. In England during the eighteenth and nineteenth centuries "gudgeon parties" used to be a notable social occasion on the river Thames above London. This practice has long since declined, but some anglers still eat their catches. When a school is in feeding mood (the usual state of affairs), a panful can be caught in a short time.   —D.M.

GUIDES Metal, ringlike devices placed along the length of a fishing rod so that the line follows the action of the rod, and to control the motion of the line from the reel or hand to the lure, and to minimize casting and fish-playing stresses on the rod.

Fly rods are usually fitted with one *ring guide* on the butt section. The usual form is a circular ring of chrome-plated metal mounted to a wire support frame, the base of which is flattened and bound to the rod with silk or nylon. All other guides, except the tip, are of hardened wire (sometimes plated, black, or stainless steel) in the form of a spiral. These are called *snake guides*. The guide ends are flattened for easy wrapping to a rod section.

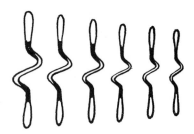

Snake Guides

Their purpose is merely to hold the line closely along the rod without adding excessive weight. Sizes numbered 00 and 0 are "small," 1 and 2 are "medium," 3 and 4 "large." The fly-rod-tip guide or *tip-top* is made of a loop of hardened wire inserted into a small tapered tube and silver-soldered fast. A ferrule adhesive is used to mount it to the rod end. These tubes are also calibrated in increments of $\frac{1}{64}$ inch (.0156 inch) inside diameter, as are ferrules.

The guides on a bait-casting rod are identical to the ring guide of a fly rod. Some have rings of agate or tungsten-carbide metal. Both are extremely hard, but the latter is more shock resistant. Ring guides are used all along the length of casting rods. The tip guide is also equipped with a ring. These are designated by the numbers indicated.

Spinning guides are of larger diameter and lighter construction than casting guides. The first and second butt guides are usually very large (.75–1.25 inch diameter) in order to "funnel" the line from the stationary spool into

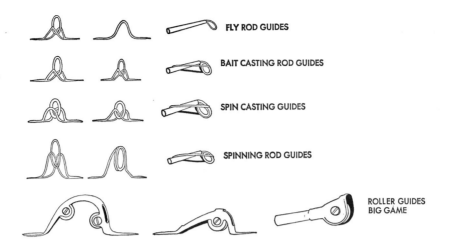

FLY ROD GUIDES

BAIT CASTING ROD GUIDES

SPIN CASTING GUIDES

SPINNING ROD GUIDES

ROLLER GUIDES
BIG GAME

Types of Guides

the guide set. Hard chrome plate or tungsten-carbide rings and top are essential as the fine monofilament lines quickly cut grooves in most other materials.

Guides for light saltwater tackle are usually similar in design and construction as those used on freshwater casting rods although of larger size. Surfcasting guides are rings of agate or tungsten-carbide built somewhat higher than bait-casting guides. The purpose of the additional height is to prevent the line from whipping against the rod during the cast. Ordinarily very few guides are used, one or two and tip-top to reduce friction. Some rods have guides mounted in pairs on opposite sides of the rod. By this means the rod tip may be rotated to balance the casting load if the rod tends to set. The chief asset lies in the "safety factor" in case a guide is broken.

Guides for surf-spinning rods are enormous in size when compared to others. The first guide is sometimes as large as 3 inches diminishing in three or four steps to ⅝ inch (.625 inch) diameter tip-top (which should be tungsten carbide). Construction is strong but light in weight; rings are of ⅛ inch diameter stock, frames $\frac{3}{32}$–$\frac{1}{16}$ inch diameter, all joints are silver-soldered. The assembly is heavily chrome-plated to provide abrasion resistance.

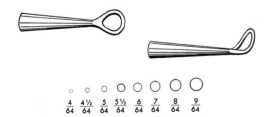

| $\frac{4}{64}$ | $\frac{4\frac{1}{2}}{64}$ | $\frac{5}{64}$ | $\frac{5\frac{1}{2}}{64}$ | $\frac{6}{64}$ | $\frac{7}{64}$ | $\frac{8}{64}$ | $\frac{9}{64}$ |

Tip-top Guides

Guides for big-gamefish trolling rods are almost always of the *grooved-roller* type. Roller-support frames are quite high, exceedingly robust, usually of stainless steel, monel, or nickel alloy material; quality guides are designed to lead the line into the pulley groove. The unbelievable strength and speed of big gamefish requires the

ultimate in frictionless line guiding. Anything less would result in smashed tackle or a lost fish. Some guide rollers are mounted on oilless, porous bronze bushings, others are built upon a greased-sealed ball bearing. Tiptop is also fitted with a ball-bearing roller. *See also* Rod Building
—L.F.

GUITARFISH *See* Atlantic Guitarfish, Rays, Shovelnose Guitarfish

GULAR PLATE A bony plate situated under the chin between the two sides of the lower jaw. It is characteristic of the bowfin (*which see*).

GULF CORVINA *Cynoscion othonopterus* A common corvina (*which see*) in the Gulf of California and ranging probably to Panama.

The caninelike teeth of the Gulf corvina are very small. The caudal fin is semilunate, the upper and lower rays longer than those in the center. All of the fins except the spinous dorsal are covered with small scales which are thickened at the bases. The dorsal fin is sharply pointed. Its body coloration is pale blue dorsally, silvery on the sides and belly. The lower fins are yellowish. Attains a length of about 28 inches.

ANGLING VALUE

The Gulf corvina is imported into the United States. It forms a large part of the sport catch in the upper Gulf of California.
—J.R.

GULF FLOUNDER *Paralichthys albigutta* This close relative of the summer flounder (*which see*) is a member of family Bothidae, which includes a great many flounders of importance to sport and commercial fisheries. Generally, the various flounders are not distinguished from one another in the commercial catch, but the Gulf flounder can readily be distinguished from the summer flounder by the smaller number of gillrakers. In the Gulf flounder and the southern flounder there are less than 12 gillrakers on the lower limb of the first gill arch whereas in the summer flounder there are 13–18. The Gulf flounder generally has 11 pectoral rays and a smaller number of dorsal- and anal-fin rays (71–85, and 53–65, respectively).

This species is a gray-brown in color with a number of round, pale blotches, generally in 5 longitudinal rows, with 3 prominent spots forming a triangular pattern. In general, its coloring is similar to that of other closely related species. Although the usual size is less than 10 inches, it has been reported to attain a length of 15 inches.

Common from Cape Lookout, North Carolina, to Corpus Christi, Texas, the Gulf flounder seems to prefer hard or sandy bottoms, being seldom taken over mud bottoms, whereas the southern flounder (*which see*) prefers a mud bottom. It is more common in the South where it is found together with the southern flounder replacing the summer flounder. It occurs from March to October in the Gulf of Mexico, becoming scarce during the winter.

Spawning apparently occurs in the winter, for fish have been seen in October and November. The young are first found in February and March at a length of 1–2 inches. As in other closely related species, it probably spawns offshore.

The Gulf flounder, being a bottom dweller predominantly, lies on the bottom or buried in the mud where it feeds on crustaceans and other invertebrates of small size. Because of its small size, it is of less economic importance than other commercial flounders.

ECONOMIC VALUE

Since it is seldom distinguished by commercial and sport fishermen from the southern and summer flounder, it is difficult to evaluate its importance.   —D.dS.

GULF KINGFISH *See* Whitings

GULF STREAM *See* Currents

GUNWALE Also called gunnel. Where the deck and side of the boat meet. May be the upper edge of the top plank or the cap that extends over the top plank. Some gunwales are closed, some of open construction, such as is found in wood and canvas dinghies where the ribs extend between an inner and outer gunwale.

H

HACKLE A component part of an artificial fly consisting of small barbules of feather projecting from or extending at angles to the hook. The hackle feather is wound around the hook creating the "legs" in a fly pattern. Hackle is obtained from the neck, upper back, and shoulders of various fowl; the most commonly used feathers are taken from chickens of various colors. The most desirable hackles for dry-fly patterns have a stiff and glossy texture and the best of these are found on gamecocks and old roosters. Wet-fly hackles are preferably soft so as to absorb water and cause the hook to sink; these are found on hens and young roosters. *See also* Fly-Tying

HACKLEBACK STURGEON A common name for the shovelnose sturgeon. *See* Sturgeon

HADDOCK *Melanogrammus aeglefinus* An important member of the cod family, Gadidae, the haddock is characterized by 3 dorsal fins and 2 anal fins, and generally resembles the cod. It is easily distinguished from its close relatives by a black line along the side and the black patch midway between the first dorsal fin and the pectoral fin. Its three dorsal fins distinguish it and its close relatives from the silver hake (*which see*).

Freshly caught haddock have the top of the head, back, and sides a dark purplish-gray, becoming silvery-gray with pinkish reflections below the lateral line, and the belly and the lower sides of the head are white.

The largest haddock on record weighed 37 pounds and was 44 inches long, but the majority of the fish are about 1–2 feet long, and weigh about 1–5 pounds.

Generally, haddock are found in deeper water than cod, most of them being taken in 25–75 fathoms of water. The haddock is found on both sides of the Atlantic, from the North Sea and Iceland to Newfoundland and Nova Scotia, southward to New Jersey, and occasionally in deepwater to Cape Hatteras, North Carolina. It is common on smooth, hard bottom composed of broken shells, sand, and pebbles. It prefers slightly warmer waters than cod, although generally it is a coldwater species. Unlike the Atlantic tomcod (*which see*), it never enters brackish water.

Haddock

LIFE HISTORY

Although there is some seasonal migration to the north in the spring and south in the fall, the haddock is a relatively sluggish species, and, unlike its relatives, it seldon actively feeds upon fishes. Generally, crabs, snails, worms, clams, and sea urchins are eaten by the adults, while young haddock eat copepods as do cod. Fishes and squids are also taken by the adults of the species whenever the opportunity presents itself.

During the spawning season, large concentrations are found at 20–100 fathoms of water, the spawning season occurring between January and June. The young live on the surface for several months after which they move on to live a bottom existence. They grow to an age of about 14 years, but those taken in the commercial fishery are less than 8 years old.

This extremely important commercial species exceeded the catch of cod during 1960, accounting for over 118 million pounds, most of it being taken in the New England ports. The commercial catch is gradually declining during the past thirty years due to overfishing with small-mesh trawlnets. A few are taken with gillnets as well. In smoked form, haddock is called finnan haddie.
    —D.dS.

HAGFISH *See* Atlantic Hagfish, Black Hagfish, Pacific Hagfish

HAIR BUG A type of floating, fly-rod lure used in bass fishing. The hair bug is made entirely of animal hair, the most popular being the hollow body and tail hairs of deer and caribou. Dr. James A. Henshall is credited with having made the original hair bug, a mothlike lure which is popular today. Hair bugs are also designed to imitate frogs, crayfish, and various insects. *See also* Bass Bug

HAKARL In Iceland, one of several species of shark, chiefly hammerhead shark, which has been buried 4–6 months in the ground and then excavated. It is dark pink, thick textured, and served like cheese. Eskimos have a similar preparation called *tipnuk*; however, neither is especially palatable. Presumably, the custom of allowing shark meat to become partly rotten before eating is due to the consumption of Greenland shark (sleeper shark or gurry shark) which is poisonous if eaten fresh but wholesome in an early state of decay.

HAKE *See* Cods and Hakes, Pacific Hake, Silver Hake, Southern Hake, Squirrel Hake, White Hake

HALFBEAK *See* Balao

HALFMOON *See* Opaleye

HALIBUT *See* Atlantic Halibut, California Halibut, Pacific Halibut

HALLOCK CHARLES American (1834–1917) One of the more rewarding of the early American angling authors to read today. His first book, *The Fishing Tourist* (1873), and his last, *An Angler's Reminiscences* (1913), give the best account of nineteenth-century American angling after Thaddeus Norris (*which see*). In 1873 he founded *Forest and Stream*, enlisting the services of a distinguished roster of contributors, including Thaddeus Norris, Robert Barnwell Roosevelt, Seth Green, Reuben Wood, and the famous woman fly tier Sara McBride. Soon tiring of the business side of publishing Hallock turned the weekly publication over to William C. Harris (later to become editor of the *American Angler*), and sold out entirely by 1880, although the publication continued until 1930 when it was incorporated into *Field & Stream*. Afterward, Hallock wrote *The Salmon Fisher* (1890) and two books on Alaska, *Our New Alaska* (1886) and *Peerless Alaska* (1908), as well as his previously mentioned autobiography. He was outstanding in his time as angler, traveler, naturalist, and explorer, and through his magazine, one of the first voices to be heard throughout the land on the then almost unheard of subject of conservation.   —A.G.

HAMMERHEAD SHARK *See* Bonnethead, Great Hammerhead, Scalloped Hammerhead, Smooth Hammerhead

HARDHEAD *See* Croaker

HARDMAN, JOHN *See under* Bait-Casting (Development of Bait-Casting Reels)

HARDWARE A colloquial term for the metal parts of a fishing rod such as guides, ferrules, tip-tops, and reel seats. *Also* a slang term in a collective sense for spoons, spinners, and spinning lures.

HARLING A popular method of fishing for Atlantic salmon in Europe, particularly in the Scandinavian countries. Harling is a form of trolling, except that the boat is allowed to drop down with the current at the same pace as the lure. There is no forward motion involved. Harling accounts for some of the largest salmon caught in Norway, where methods other than fly-fishing are legal. Norwegian anglers use two or three rods, and these are clamped on a harling-board mounted in the stern of the boat. The board is slotted, and has a wooden lock which keeps the rods from being pulled out by a salmon. The guide maneuvers his boat back and forth across the stream, keeping the stern end down so the spoons flutter in fish-holding places. Usually, 3–4-inch silver wobblers are favored. The advantage of harling is obvious, in that the angler presents his baits to fish in very deep, turbulent places on rivers which may be a ¼ mile wide. Casting is a slow process on these broad waters. This same method is popular on the boat streams of Chile in fishing for trout.   —A.J.McC.

HARNESS Gear worn by a deep-sea angler in order to transmit muscular power to the rod or to absorb strain. It is made of canvas or leather and has adjustable straps with snaps that can be fastened to the reel. There are three general types: the shoulder harness, the kidney harness, and the seat harness. *See also* Big-Game Fishing

HATCH As used in fly-fishing a hatch refers to the emergence of the subimago or "dun" stage of the mayfly. At the time of a hatch, the nymph swims to the surface of the water and while floating with the current draws itself free from its shuck. The emerging dun is dull-colored and its wings semi-opaque. While on the surface the dun quickly becomes strong enough for flight and flutters heavily from the water to find a resting place in the vegetation along the river bank to await its next metamorphosis. In that interval from emergence until it leaves the surface very large numbers of subimagoes are taken by the fish. This feeding period is a rise (*which see*). A hatch does not always stimulate a rise, though it will most often do so. *See also* Mayflies   —A.J.McC.

HAWAII Saltwater fishing is of prime interest in the fiftieth state. In general, most of the common species of gamefish can be found almost anywhere in the Hawaiian chain, depending on the individual topography of the bay, channel, or bank. Fishing off the north and northeast sides of all islands tends to be good most of the time. However, the seas, driven by the prevailing trade winds, are often rough. The best plan is to make arrangements locally with charter-boat skippers who are familiar with the immediate fishing and weather conditions.

Cast net fishing is an ancient art form among Hawaiian fishermen. This expert is netting "uouoa" or mullet

The most popular big-gamefishing grounds are out of Honolulu on Oahu Island and at Kailua-Kona on the big island of Hawaii. The boats out of Honolulu range over the Molokai Channel to just offshore of Molokai and Lanai islands, or along leeward Oahu to Kaena Point. Marlin have been caught within one mile of the harbor. The largest blue marlin ever boated, a 15-foot-long fish weighing 1,805 pounds, was taken near Honolulu in June 1970. It did not qualify for a world's record since more than one angler handled the tackle. The Waianae grounds, off the lee coast of Oahu, can also be reached out of Honolulu's Kewalo Basin. A 30-fathom shoal (Penguin Bank), 27 miles southwest of Molokai, is also reached by boat from Honolulu.

The Kona coast of the island of Hawaii is the state's prime marlin ground. Smooth seas and the possibility of record marlin make it a favorite fishing spot. Too far away for a one-day boat trip from Honolulu and back, it is reached by plane either directly from Honolulu or by way of Hilo. The Hawaiian International Billfish Tournament is held in Kona waters early each summer. These grounds are unique in several ways. There's no long run to reach the productive locations as marlin are jumped within two miles of shore, and instead of an endless ocean you can survey at leisure the everchanging panorama of the mountains. The clouds which curdle and thicken behind Kailua at noon are like a giant umbrella—so predictable that the only coffee plantations in Hawaii exist on those slopes. Yet, against the gloomy backdrop, schools of flyingfish zip across the sea like silver bullets in the sun. There is an even greater sense of perspective when Mauna Loa suddenly pokes out of the clouds, sleeping for the moment, but still one of the world's most active volcanoes. The ocean is not silent for long, however. Sometimes the sapphire water is shattered by acres of bonito and screaming birds, then it erupts behind the boat as a pair of *mahi-mahi* slams the dancing baits. These dolphin come heavy in Hawaii; they may easily average 20 pounds and run to 50 or better. The local record is close to 70 pounds. Yellowfin tuna and wahoo also slash at the knuckleheads—the favorite lures of the island skippers. Knuckleheads are made in a variety of designs, but essentially they consist of a large diameter of plastic tubing with a squid-simulating skirt attached. Nine out of ten marlin are caught on the artificial in Hawaiian waters. You may be lucky and go out for one afternoon and take a 700 pounder, or you may troll for several days in succession and never get a tap. But Hawaii offers an opportunity to get hooked up with some immense Pacific blue marlin. Fish over 1,000 pounds have been caught off the Kona coast. Although amateurs may be discouraged by rough seas in some parts of Hawaii, the ocean off Kona is invariably calm and sunny. There is no distinctly wet or dry season, but rather a climatic division between the windward and the leeward sides of the islands. Prevailing northeast trades spill their moisture against the peaks, and the annual rainfall in different locations varies in the extreme. Some leeward areas get no more than 2–3 inches of rain annually, while windward slopes such as Waialeale on Kauai are bucketed under 400 inches. Occasionally, a "Kona" or southerly wind brings muggy weather and heavy rains to the lowlands, but in general the climate is civilized and you can wear an Aloha shirt with comfort. Although the wind is called Kona because of its direction in relation to the other islands, the Kona coast is a millpond.

Lare Point on Oahu is a favorite among "ulua" anglers who take jacks in the surf

Hawaiian charter-boat rates correspond to the prices paid in other ports. Tackle and bait are included in the full charter. Food and drink are supplied by the fisherman, but ice and galley services are available. Some boats run on a per-person basis (split charter) if a full boatload is not available. However, prevacation correspondence is recommended to insure space at the exact time preferred. Hawaiian islanders are avid fishermen, and an unexpected run of any of the big gamefish quickly draws them away from their offices and down to the docks for impromptu trips.

INSHORE FISHING

The light-tackle spinning and fly-rod caster will not find the same potential sport as the big-game man. The most common species of tropical Pacific reef fish are almost entirely absent from local waters. Why there is a gap between small and large carnivorous fishes is not known. The inshore fauna of islands from Tahiti to Japan contains approximately forty different species of groupers and snappers; yet these reef dwellers do not frequent Hawaii. In a rather unique experiment, both groupers and snappers have been introduced into Hawaiian waters by the state Bureau of Fisheries. Bonefish (locally *o'io*) are not absent, however; the islands have produced several world's records, including an 18-pound, 2-ounce all-tackle record taken in Kauai. But here most mainland bonefish anglers will be disappointed, as there are few flats in the Florida sense of the game and no fly-fishing. Most of the coastline drops from volcanic rock cliffs to coral shelves and into deepwater. Where beaches exist, they are subjected to running surfs. Bonefish are caught chiefly by bottom-fishing with live bait in the sand holes between reefs at 20–25-foot depths. They come as a dividend to anglers seeking the popular *ulua* (jacks).

FRESHWATER FISHING

Four important species of freshwater fish have been introduced into Hawaii in recent years, and all have become fairly well established. Regulations and information are available from the State of Hawaii, Division of Fish and Game, Department of Land and Natural Resources in Honolulu.

Rainbow trout have been planted in the mountain streams of Kokee, on the island of Kauai. The season generally opens the first Saturday of August, and for 16 days continuous fishing is permitted; thereafter, fishing is permitted only on weekends and state holidays in the remainder of August and in September. The limit is 10 fish per day, and the minimum size is 6 inches.

The season on largemouth and smallmouth bass is open all year. These can be found in streams, estuaries, and reservoirs on Oahu, Kauai, Hawaii, and Maui.

A fourth introduced fish is the bluegill sunfish. The season is open all year, no daily limit. These inhabit streams, reservoirs, and estuaries on Oahu, Kauai, and Maui, and have recently been introduced on Hawaii and Molokai.
—P.S.F.
—A.J.McC.

HAY-WIRE TWIST A method of forming a strong terminal loop in a single-strand wire leader for use in big-game fishing. The end of the wire leader is bent back to form the loop and to lie parallel to the rest of the leader for a short distance. Both the short and long ends of the leader are then bent or twisted around each other several times. The loop thus formed will not slip in a nooselike manner, as often happens when the short end is twisted around the long end, but the long end is kept straight. *See also* Knots, Leader

HEAD BOAT A boat capable of accommodating large numbers of anglers, which sails on a regular daily schedule to the fishing grounds. A nominal fee is charged on a per-person or "per-head" basis. Head boats specialize in fishing for the smaller varieties of reeffish and bottomfish. These vessels are generally twin-engine craft of 60–100 feet in length and may transport 40–50 anglers. Head boats usually rent the necessary tackle and sell bait on board. *See also* Sportfisherman

HEADWATER CATFISH *Ictalurus lupus* Found from northeastern Mexico to the Pecos River drainage of Texas, little is known of the headwater catfish's life history, as it's rarely identified by commercial or sport anglers. This species greatly resembles a small channel catfish. However, the body lacks spots (present in a channel catfish of comparable size) and the caudal fin is not deeply forked. The base of the anal fin is longer than the head length.
—A.J.McC.

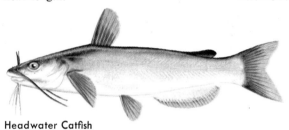

Headwater Catfish

HEE-HEE A wooden lure similar to a shuttlecock in appearance used by the coastal Indians of the Pacific northwest to catch lingcod (*which see*).

HEILNER, VAN CAMPEN American (1899–1961) Nowhere in angling literature is there a finer expression of the pleasures of surf-fishing than in the writings of Heilner. He fished the Atlantic, Gulf, and Pacific coasts of North America, and throughout the Caribbean and South America. He was the first American angler to own a home on Bimini, and he was a member and regular visitor to the Catalina Tuna Club. He caught and wrote about every gamefish from the summer flounder to the broadbill swordfish. Yet the greatest sport he experienced in the sea was surf-fishing. "It is a one-man game from start to finish. You are the one and only factor. Here you are and he is. . . . You must find your quarry yourself; you must rig and bait your hook yourself; you must become proficient in the art of casting so you may reach him; and you must bring him through a line of foaming breakers and singing tides until at last, whipped to a standstill, he lies gasping on the wet sands at your very feet. Then you must let him go because he deserves it."

Heilner was born on July 1st, heir to a Pennsylvania mining fortune. He knew he would never have to grub out a livelihood, and he drifted from school to school, trying to assign a goal to a life that was both prepaid and guaranteed.

Like many wealthy children of the Philadelphia Main Line, he spent his summers at the Jersey shore. In Heilner's youth Atlantic City had already become a kind of oceanside suburb for well-heeled Philadelphians. But it wasn't the boardwalk, swimming, horse racing, or gambling opportunities that drew Heilner back to the coast season after season. It was the memory of the abundance and variety of sea fishes that fell so readily to his surf rod-and-reel, a memory which remained with him during the winter months while he was away at school. In the last analysis it was not the instructors at Phillips Academy or Lake Placid-Florida school who provided Heilner with his direction in life, it was the surf gang down at Corson's Inlet, New Jersey.

Heilner was something of a prodigy in outdoor writing. He began contributing surf-fishing stories and articles to *American Angler, Field & Stream, Motor Boat, National Sportsman,* and *Sports Afield* before he was out of his teens, and by the age of 21 he had written his first book, *The Call of the Surf*—incidentally, the first book ever published devoted exclusively to surf-fishing—with the help of his artist-friend and fellow angler, Frank Stick.

Stick came to New York from the Midwest shortly after the turn of the century to make his reputation as an artist. He had always loved the outdoors and had worked briefly as a guide before coming East. Since the community of outdoor writers and artists was a small one 70 years ago, Stick and Heilner quickly became acquainted and Heilner showed the boy from Wisconsin what surf-casting was all about. Stick became a frequent guest aboard young Heilner's cabin cruiser, the *Nepenthe*, as it moved up and down the Atlantic coast. The artist quickly became as adept with a surf rod as he was with his brush, and it was a most natural outcome of these wanderings that the two young fishermen collaborated on *The Call of the Surf.*

Two years later Heilner did another book, *Adventures in Angling,* using three of Frank Stick's paintings. Derived in large part from a variety of Heilner's articles contributed to *Field & Stream, Motor Boat, National Geographic, Outer's Recreation,* and *Wide World,* this second book of salt-water angling takes the reader from the coast of Monterey for Pacific salmon to Catalina for striped marlin to the Florida Everglades for tarpon then finally to Bimini for sail-fishing. But the most poetic of all chapters is "The Sea Horse," describing a trip to a beautiful and uninhabited barrier island just south of Barnegat Bay. On this expedition, while surf-fishing for that "coppery warrior of the beaches," the channel bass, Heilner found and captured a feral horse, not unlike one of the so-called wild ponies of Assateague Island further south in Virginia. Heilner's horse became a symbol for a forgotten corner of America and an emblem for the wild spirit of the sea. Heilner and his friends realized there was no way for man to take such an animal back to the confines of civilization and at the end of the story they released it.

Following publication of *Adventures in Angling,* Heilner's angling reputation began to soar. He became an associate editor of *Field & Stream* and a field representative in ichthyology for the American Museum of Natural History. On behalf of the museum he participated in ichthyological expeditions to Peru and Ecuador in 1924–1925, to Alaska in 1927, and to Cuba in 1934–1935. After his first trip to Bimini in 1921, during which he took special pains to collect previously unknown fishes from tidal pools in the reefs, his close friend and mentor, Dr. J.T. Nichols of the American Museum of Natural History,

Van Campen Heilner

named two of the new species for Heilner and his boat, *Labrisomus heilneri* and *Eupomacentus nepenthe.*

Following his return from Cuba in 1935 Heilner contributed two chapters on the channel bass and bonefish to *American Big Game Fishing.* Two years later he adapted these chapters and added 24 others, ranging in subject from "Bottom Fish" to "Angling around the World," for his definitive *Salt Water Fishing,* first issued by the Penn Publishing Company in Philadelphia. Feeling that fine-art illustrations of angling scenes do as much to evoke feeling for the sport as good writing, Heilner persuaded his publisher to let him use one of the outstanding outdoor artists of the day, William Goadby Lawrence, to provide 12 paintings for the book. Lawrence spent a year traveling up and down the coast gathering background materials and impressions for his paintings; he even spent time aboard Heilner's boat at Barnegat, New Jersey. The results speak well of the effort. This publication was probably the first bestseller in angling history since Izaak Walton's *The Compleat Angler.* It went through three printings before the end of 1937, six printings by 1940, and by the time Alfred A. Knopf picked it up in 1953 the book had sold tens of thousands of copies. The Knopf edition included changes and developments in saltwater angling during the 15 years during which *Salt Water Fishing* had been in print. The preface for this edition was written by Ernest Hemingway, who cites Heilner as a pioneer who "fished for sport rather than publicity."

Following the first publication of *Salt Water Fishing* there were more honors and expeditions. In 1937 Heilner was decorated with the Order of Carlos Manuel de Céspedes by Cuba, and after World War II he joined the Peabody Museum of Yale expedition to Tierra del Fuego and the straits of Magellan. His publications were known abroad and earned him an honorary membership in the British Sea Anglers Society, fellowship in the Royal

Geographic Society, and association with the Royal Anthropological Institute and the Bombay Natural History Society. At home he was an honorary life member of the American Museum of Natural History, a life member of the Explorers Club, and an associate of the American Society of Ichthyologists and Herpetologists. Finally, for the record, Heilner was a Republican and a 32° Mason!

Salt Water Fishing was the last book on angling Heilner ever wrote. He saw the uninhabited coasts he had explored in the 1910's and 20's settled with countless summer residences, and he lost some of his enthusiasm for angling in general and surf-fishing in particular. But also Heilner was simply growing older and was content to rest on previously-won laurels.

One of the last, and certainly one of the most remarkable, articles he ever published on salt-water angling was for the April 7, 1961, issue of *Life* magazine. The editors asked him for a comprehensive history of the sport—in 1,500 words or less. By touching base with a half-dozen highlights during five centuries of effort, Heilner managed to come up with an amazing summary of what had been accomplished in salt water since Dame Juliana Berners wrote her *Treatyse of fysshynge wyth an Angle* in 1496. Best of all, Heilner was able to work in his preference for inshore angling. For after cataloging some of the achievements of high-seas sport fishermen he concluded his essay by reminding his readers that the largest fish ever taken on rod-and-reel anywhere in the world was caught by a surf-caster!   —G.W.R.

HELLGRAMMITE *Corydalis* **spp.** The larval stage of a dobsonfly. The larva of a large Eastern species *Corydalis cornuta* is an excellent bait for bass and other gamefish. It and the larvae of the dobsonfly's smaller relatives, the fishflies, are often quite numerous in streams even though a paucity of adults attests to heavy loss of the immature stages.

The adult dobsonfly superficially resembles an oversize gray stonefly in having four large wings which are folded slightly tentlike over the abdomen. The wings are mottled or splotched with black dots or patches of pigment. There are no tails, and the antennae are of moderate length. The mandibles or lower jaws of the male are long and tusklike. Adults have a body length of up to 4 inches and a wing expanse of over 4 inches.

A fully mature hellgrammite is a formidable-looking creature with heavy mandibles capable of pinching a fisherman's finger, three pairs of legs, and a pair of lateral, fingerlike appendages on each abdominal segment at the base of each of which is an inconspicuous gill tuft for absorbing dissolved oxygen from the water. *See also* Dobsonflies, Live Bait   —S.G.J.

HELM (1) Any fixed device from a tiller arm to a wheel by which a boat may be steered, but not including a loose oar or paddle used for this purpose. Some commercial boatmen operating a sea skiff steer by means of a rope which is connected to the tiller or rudder quadrant and runs completely around the inside gunnels of the boat, thus permitting boatmen to steer from almost any position aboard. This should not be confused with a *tiller rope* or *tiller cable*, which includes any rope or wire cable used between the quadrant on the rudder post and the wheel forward, and perhaps is more properly called a *rudder control cable*.

(2) Commands to turn a boat are sometimes given in terms of the helm, as *port helm* (to turn left) and *starboard helm* (to turn to the right).

HENSHALL, JAMES ALEXANDER American (1844–1925) Henshall is remembered today as the foremost champion of the black bass, about which he wrote the first complete treatise, the *Book of the Black Bass* (1881), and which reappeared in 1889, 1904, and 1923. Charles M. Wetzel, in *American Fishing Books* (1950) advanced the claim that Dr. Henshall "can also be regarded as the father of the present-day bait casting rods," saying that they were known in those times as "black bass minnow rods, and were manufactured as early as 1875 by C.F. Orvis of Manchester, Vt., from specifications written by Henshall in a *Forest and Stream* article entitled *The Coming Black Bass Rod*. These rods were three-jointed affairs, eight feet three inches long, weighing approximately nine ounces and designed for single-handed casting." With Henshall as the Pied Piper, American anglers went bass-crazy in the 80's and 90's. On the assumption that the brighter the lure the better, trout flies too became increasingly gaudy, a tendency that was general until the turn of the century, after which Theodore Gordon turned the tide back toward the more realistic imitation of natural insects. Henshall's was perhaps the most widely-known angling name in the country in the 90's, but he never wrote anything as colorful as his famous first pronouncement on the black bass ("I consider him, inch for inch and pound for pound, the gamest fish that swims"). Since most of his writings were as sparsely purposive as his prescriptions, they did not outlive him, and he is today one of the most quoted and least read of American angling authors.
                                                —A.G.

HERBERT, HENRY W. American (1807–1858) The story of H.W. Herbert, alias Frank Forester, English remittance man and America's first great outdoor writer, is a book unto itself. Few men who fished or hunted with Herbert knew the reasons for his coming to the United States in 1831. Perhaps even his two closest friends here, Philo Ruggles and Anson Livingston—both of whom later acted as officers for the modest trust established by Herbert's father—never knew the entire story of the young man's precipitous flight from England. Certainly neither has left us a clue to the scandal that drove Herbert abroad and kept him here until his suicide 27 years later.

Henry William Herbert was born in London on April 7, 1807. His father was the Honorable William Herbert, Doctor of Laws, Member of Parliament, and third son of Henry Herbert, Lord Portchester and first Earl of Carnarvon. His mother was Letitia Emily Dorothea, second daughter of Joshua, Fifth Viscount Allen.

Herbert's father was something of a renegade. About the time Henry William was born, the father abandoned a successful political career to begin study for the ministry. This was a less remarkable step in a time when church and state were complementary faces of the same establishment coin. However, Herbert's father pursued his contemplative career as earnestly as he had his political one, and the fact that his family arranged for him upon his ordination to have the lucrative parish of Spofforth in the West Riding of Yorkshire only made his linguistic and literary pursuits a mite more comfortable. With an annual income equivalent to better than $50,000 (and this at 1814 prices), the Reverend Doctor William

Herbert had sufficient funds to dig the ponds and build the greenhouses he needed for his other hobby: botany. William Herbert died before Charles Darwin published *On the Origin of Species* in which he respectfully cites the Reverend Doctor's achievements in botany. Two plant species, *herberta* and *herbertia*, are named for him.

Young Herbert loved Spofforth and spent much of his vacation time from Eton and Cambridge there, learning the ways of guns, dogs, and horses. He knew something of fishing, too, but apparently fished little before coming to America. Less than a year after graduating Cambridge with his Bachelor of Arts degree, however, he had to flee to the cultural backwaters of New York City with the possibility of never seeing home again. Debt was the ostensible cause of Herbert's exile, but since we know that his father paid off the boy's obligations (amounting to some $7,500) within the first year of his going overseas, the evidence suggests that Henry William was guilty of breaking some rigid social taboo. This idea is reinforced when we consider that his father later established a trust for him while still refusing to let him return home. Whatever the reason, Henry William left England, and arrived in a young country to play the remarkable role of being that nation's first sporting conscience and historian.

To read Henry William's descriptions of the wilds of Nassau County, Long Island, or the tranquility of Essex County, New Jersey, makes the sensitive reader who values a good environment weep for this region today. Even Manhattan Island was a not unpleasant setting for men who valued the outdoors. With a bustling population of 200,000 located at the isle's lower end, a man with a day off could wander up to the open country of what is now the east 30's and enjoy the good food and wine of Cato Alexander's roadhouse located at a turning in the Boston Post Road (now Third Avenue).

A little further north, fishermen could cast from shore into the swarming schools of white perch found in the Harlem River throughout the spring and summer, or they could rent boats for trolling at Hellgate where striped bass of 40 and 50 pounds were regularly taken on natural squid baits or tin and pewter facsimiles. If an angler didn't have the whole day off plentiful supplies of squeteague (weakfish) or barb (king whiting) were found in the lower harbor. And sheepshead, for which a bay in Brooklyn was named, was still the pre-eminent food and gamefish of Manhattan Island.

Though Herbert arrived in the New World as an exile, letters of introduction from his father quickly provided him with a number of significant acquaintances. Foremost among them was Anson Livingston, son of Brockholst Livingston of the U.S. Supreme Court and grandson of William Livingston, first Governor of New Jersey under the 1776 Constitution. A mutual respect for antecedents and education, as well as a shared enthusiasm for the outdoors, made a firm base for the friendship. Livingston later became "The Commodore" or "A—" in the Frank Forester stories.

Another good friend was Philo Ruggles, a lawyer who later became a judge, and then, with Livingston, a trustee in the peculiar estate created for his son by Herbert's father. Ruggles' first love was fishing, and much of what Herbert knew about the sport he learned from him. Ruggles instilled such respect for fly tackle in Herbert that when the latter first began saltwater angling he used the fly wherever possible.

Since fly-fishing is in current and growing vogue among salt-water anglers, many modern fishermen find it hard to believe that there were anglers who shared this enthusiasm a century and a quarter ago. However, more than a decade before the outbreak of the Civil War, Frank Forester was advising readers of his *Frank Forester's Fish and Fishing of the United States, and British Provinces of North America* (1849) that "with the sole exception of Salmon fishing, this (striped bass fishing) is the finest of the seaboard varieties of piscatorial sport. . . . The fly will take them brilliantly, and at the end of three hundred yards of Salmon-line, a twelve-pound Bass will be found quite sufficient to keep even the most skilful angler's hands as full as he can possibly desire."

To his contemporary American readers Herbert was something of a revolutionary in suggesting that a given fish species might have some other value beside food or fertilizer. He raised eyebrows by suggesting that herring were fine gamefish simply because they could be taken on a fly tackle. He called for a more sportsmanlike pursuit of shad, another great fly-taking fish, that was more often netted commercially than fished for with rod-and-reel.

In addition to upsetting the assumption that saltwater fly-fishing is of comparatively recent vintage, a thoughtful reading of Herbert's work suggests that the story about Julio Buel inventing the spoon lure in 1834 when he dropped a spoon from his lunch box into a Vermont lake and saw it attacked by fish is more of a pleasant legend than bonafide history. In an essay composed about midcentury for the first edition of *Fishing with Hook and Line*, Herbert refers to the "common pewter spoon" used by "down-east fishermen" to catch bluefish.

Though Herbert arrived in New York with a few hundred dollars in his pocket he quickly spent it on his first Warwick trip and an expedition to Canada that fall. Throughout his life Herbert spent money as quickly as he earned it, but in the winter of '31, he first needed to make it.

Returning to Manhattan he took a job teaching Greek and Latin in the Reverend R. Townsend Huddart's Classical Institute located just off Bowling Green. He worked there eight years before his many publishing activities enabled him to quit teaching in order to give full attention to writing.

That he wrote at all is, perhaps, due to another teacher at the Reverend Huddart's school, an immigrant Scot by the name of Andrew D. Patterson, who taught English but added to his meager salary by contributing articles to a variety of newspapers and magazines. The advent of the steam-powered press and new techniques for producing cheaper paper combined to create the world's first publishing boom. For the first time in history it was less of a problem for an aspirant writer to get something published than for publishers to satisfy the appetites of the reading public. Herbert saw the relative ease with which Patterson picked up money, and he decided to do the same.

Most of Herbert's efforts were elaborate stories and novels about such historical figures as England's Cromwell and Rome's Cataline. He found the work stimulating as well as remunerative, and in March 1833 he and Patterson founded *The American Monthly Magazine*. Though Patterson stayed with the effort but a year, and though Herbert sold his own interest to Park Benjamin the year following Patterson's departure, the creation of *The American Monthly* served to acquaint Herbert with many more of the personalities and possibilities of American publishing than if he had remained a free-lancer throughout his life.

His sales increased tremendously and though his contemporary, Edgar Allen Poe, once remarked that Herbert "has written more trash than any man living with the exception of [Theodore S.] Fay," Herbert nurtured hopes that his American literary fame might provide him with a new reputation in England—one which would eventually enable him to return home.

However, Herbert's everlasting need for money forced him to tap the unprestigious, but lucrative market for tales of horse-racing, hunting, fishing, and other pastimes. He was initially ashamed of these writings and used a pseudonym to hide his real identity, thereby protecting his more "literary" reputation.

William T. Porter, editor of *The American Turf Register*, and his brother George, co-owner with William of *Spirit of the Times*, were the men who first suggested the name "Frank Forester." The Porter brothers also tried to persuade Herbert that there was nothing wrong or "lowbrow" in writing about something he knew and loved. They stressed that the natural, well-informed style of his horse-racing and hunting tales was far more likely to outlive its author than the stiff pomposities of his novels. Herbert listened dubiously, but he did change his pen name from "Harry Archer" to "Frank Forester" in a story, "A Week in the Woodlands; or, Scenes on the Road, or in the Field and Round the Fire," first published in the May/June 1839 issue of *The American Turf Register*. Six years later, when a collection of these *Turf Register* stories was published as The Warwick Woodlands, Herbert found to his surprise and satisfaction that his British readers seemed to prefer the sporting writings of Frank Forester to the novels of Henry William Herbert. He publicly "confessed" that they were one and the same man, and thereafter most of his outdoor writings bore both names.

The year *The Warwick Woodlands* first appeared was also Herbert's first year in a new home. Herbert's young wife had died in Philadelphia the previous March at 23 years of age, and left him with a daughter, Louisa, who died five months after her mother, and a son, William George, who was then 3 years old. Herbert's father, recently appointed Dean of Manchester, was concerned for his grandson's welfare and had doubtless heard of his son's continual shortage of money. Thus, in December 1844, the Dean tactfully suggested that little William George be sent to England for his education and upbringing, while Henry William was to pick a homesite and erect a building of moderate cost against the day that Dean Herbert should visit America. His son could, in the meantime, occupy the home free of expense.

Henry William happily agreed to his father's proposal, and with his friends Livingston and Ruggles acting as trustees bought and began construction of a house in the spring of '45 with the $1,500 sent by his father.

As an alien, Dean Herbert could not own property in New York State. However, the New Jersey state legislature, not many years previous, had removed all such barriers to foreigners in order to enable another exile, Napoleon's brother, Joseph Bonaparte, to settle near Bordentown. Thus, Herbert picked out 1¼ acres over-

looking the Passaic River just a few minutes row upstream from the village of Newark. Gully Road, an old Indian thoroughfare, bordered the north side of this property and led, after a half-hour's stroll, to the town of Belleville.

Despite the fact that there were no cedars about, Herbert planted some as the house was being constructed, and upon its completion christened his new home The Cedars.

From 1845 until his death 13 years later Herbert led an increasingly solitary life. With his wife and family gone, he saw old friends only occasionally, and in the last years hardly at all. He was an excellent cook and handled most of the domestic chores himself. Charles A. Dana of the *New York Tribune* once stopped by for a visit and commented afterward on the outstanding dinner Herbert prepared for him. But in his final decade Herbert had only one regular companion, his handyman or "groom" (as Herbert referred to him), Charlie Holt. It was from Holt that Herbert received his final education in angling.

Holt was a native of Essex County and had spent most of his life fishing and boating on the Passaic River and in Newark Bay. In these early years the Passaic was still a healthy tidal stream which often saw sizeable striped bass take up station in the lees of Green Island just in front of Herbert's home. Holt provided more than one of Herbert's dinners from the river, and Herbert in turn spent considerable time studying Holt's use of the spear, eel pot, and handline. Seeing Charlie's pleasure and proficiency with these instruments caused Herbert to revise his thinking about what constitutes sport. And while he never ranked commercial angling in the same category with sport fishing, Herbert definitely shows greater tolerance for the former in the writing of his final years. Where once he had considered party or head-boat —so named because anglers paid the captain per head rather than chartering the entire boat for the day—fishing as merely a kind of work he later determined that whatever gave people pleasure and provided recreation should be considered sport. He even recommended in *Fishing with Hook and Line*, that in sea bass and porgy angling, an old pair of leather gloves were useful "to preserve your hands from blistering while drawing up your fish."

Though Herbert never quite succumbed to the charms of fundamental fishing, always considering them inferior to "the skill exerted in casting and managing the fly, or the spinning-minnow; much less to the playing, killing and basketing the heaviest kind of fish with the lightest running tackle," unlike all others of his sporting contemporaries he came to honor the skills of the experienced waterman and bottom angler.

Herbert saw in the preparation of natural baits some of the same finesse requisite in the tying of flies. Part of Herbert's extensive writing on natural-bait fishing, like *Fishing with Hook and Line: A Manual for Amateur Anglers*, was a result of demand. Despite his preference for fly tackle and artificial lures, bottom-fishing with handlines remained the Atlantic seaboard's most popular way to catch fish until well after the Civil War. Even in Herbert's day, rods-and-reels were found in increasing use for such species as striped bass and weakfish, and, perhaps, Herbert included special sections on these "shoal water fishes" to encourage the spread of this more sporting tackle. He may also have felt a certain sadness in the gradual decline and disappearance of such Manhattan mainstays as the king whiting and sheepshead. By suggesting that anglers should catch these worthies on rod-and-reel he at least made their departure a more sporting proposition. He once observed that the king whiting, "was formerly very abundant in the waters of New York and vicinity," but is "becoming daily less frequent." Curiously, only once in his writings did Herbert speculate on the reasons for these fishes' disappearance from the New York area. After citing an example of a man and his son who, in six hours of fishing in Jamaica Bay in 1827 took 472 kingfish, Herbert suggests, as others had done, that the kingfish were no longer available in such numbers because of "the persecution of the bluefish." We now know that water temperature changes, pollution, parasites, the dredging and filling of marshlands, and predators, all contribute to the rise and fall of certain littoral species. But even today, we rarely discuss the role overfishing may play in reducing some species whose reproductive capabilities are not equal to man's demand.

But if some species were declining, some seemed to appear almost overnight. In *Fishing with Hook and Line* Herbert comments on the "strange and recent appearance" of the hake in United States waters. Since they were at one time considered to be the dominant offshore species of Ireland, Herbert muses on the possibility that "the hake has followed in the wake of their masters," the Irish immigrants. He says that Bostonians call the new fish "Poor Johns." But considering their Irish ancestry, "Poor Pats would be more appropriate." Actually hake were probably always available over the continental shelves of the North Atlantic, but the Irish immigration to the New World created a market for these fishes in New York and Boston, which meant that offshore fishermen, instead of culling out the hake they caught when after cod or haddock, began to bring them in to the cities for sale.

Herbert is also one of our first sporting writers to note the cycles of abundance and scarcity of certain school fishes, such as the bluefish.

He prided himself on not just being a sporting journalist but a natural historian as well. Thus he was motivated to revise and supplement, particularly in the growing area of saltwater angling, *Frank Forester's Fish and Fishing* in each new edition. However, he sometimes made mistakes. On page 220 of the 1864 printing (copyrighted 1859, the year after his death), Herbert notes that where formerly blackfish ranged "only from the capes of the Chesapeake to Massachusetts Bay, I have recently learned that this fish, as well as the Providence Whiting, is becoming common in Charleston [South Carolina], having, it is believed, escaped from the car of a fishing-boat, and bred there." Unfortunately, Herbert, who never traveled in the South, didn't know that the blackfish his Charleston correspondent, a Mr. King, referred to was actually the sea bass (*Centropristes striatus*) found commonly from Long Island to northern Florida.

Popular names have often confused anglers unfamiliar with local species. And since scientific nomenclature wasn't in good shape until well into this century, tourist-sportsmen have traditionally had to do a little guessing when asking about species in waters new to them. For example, yellowtail in the Pacific is a kind of jack. Yellowtail in the Atlantic is a kind of snapper. Neither should be confused with the yellowtail rockfish or yellow-tail flounder, both sometimes called "yellowtail" for short.

Herbert's error was not in imagining that tautog (or as Virginia fishermen call them, "oysterfish," to distinguish the species from "oyster toads" or just plain "toadfish") couldn't be found off South Carolina—for they will occasionally move that far south in cold winters—but in accepting the name "blackfish" at face value. Similar confusion exists over his second-hand references to "Cavalle" and "Horse Cavalle," also taken from letters with his Charleston angling correspondent. These may be Jack crevalle and amberjack, but since the Spanish in Florida called king mackerel "cavalla," we can't be sure. All these fish range up the Atlantic coast to the Carolinas.

However, Herbert cites one Florida fish he may have known from the fish stalls on Fulton Street. For over a century the exquisite flavor of the pompano has made it a favorite of gourmets. Such fish were sometimes carried north from Florida in the summertime in boats having live wells aboard or towing live fish cars in prerefrigeration days.

Forced into the role of an outsider early in life, Herbert always felt a certain sympathy for other outsiders—fish or men. Perhaps it was this feeling which encouraged him to upgrade the game reputation of the common herring and to disparage the popularity of sea bass and porgy fishing. By midcentury so many steamers were running parties to the offshore banks for bottom-fishing from harbors in New York and New Jersey that what was once sport was fast taking on the aspect of an industry. This alone was sufficient to inspire Herbert's contempt.

He therefore took special pleasure in upgrading a nuisance fish like the cunner or bergall (*Tautogolabrus adspersus*) to sea bass status by allotting similar space for both species in his third revision of *Frank Forester's Fish and Fishing*. He also described the pleasures of shark fishing—a sport that anglers of more "respectable" fish can't comprehend even to the present day. Herbert calls it "stupendous sport resorted to by persons who have a hankering after excitement," and he directs the novitiate first to a ship chandler for the line he'll need, and then to a blacksmith for the proper hook. Herbert's story ends abruptly. On February 16, 1858, he married a woman who soon deserted him, either because of his dangerous temper or because she was disappointed that he wasn't as rich as she had hoped. This desertion seems to have broken his will. On May 15th he invited all his friends to a banquet. However, the invitations were sent out only the day before the dinner, and just one man showed up, a former student from the Classical Institute, Philip Hone Anthon.

Herbert was in a terribly depressed mood, and the two men stayed up most of the night with Anthon doing all he could to distract Herbert from his threats to commit suicide. Just about the time Anthon thought he'd succeeded, Herbert excused himself, went into the next room, and shot himself in the chest. He returned and stood before the stunned young man, saying simply, "I told you I would do it," and fell dead. The Reverend John Shackelford, who had officiated at Herbert's wedding, refused to read the burial service over his grave near The Cedars, and nearly two decades passed before a tombstone was erected to mark the spot.

There's little of Herbert's history left in the Passaic landscape today. For years The Cedars stood abandoned and allegedly haunted. Only schoolboys sneaked near to break windows; and eventually the house burned down.

Yet the legacy of Henry William Herbert survives. His writings were the first to establish guide lines to separate saltwater sports angling from commercial fishing, and he gave ocean anglers pride in their new-found sport. Herbert forever held the Atlantic salmon to be the king of all fishes, but he did so in the name of saltwater sport, not of fresh.

He distinguished gamefish according to their contact with brine, and he once wrote in *Frank Forester's Fish and Fishing* that "those fish which never visit salt-water are unquestionably so much inferior to others of their own family which run periodically to the sea, that they are with great difficulty recognized as belonging to the same order with their roving brethren while of those, none of which are known to leave the fresh-water, but two or three kinds, are worth taking at all; and even these are not to be compared with the migratory, or the pure sea-fish."

—G.W.R.

HERRING *See* Atlantic Herring, Blueback Herring, Pacific Herring, Skipjack Herring

HETEROCERCAL An asymmetrical tail fin with the caudal vertebrae extending into the upper lobe. Sharks, sturgeon, and paddlefish have a heterocercal tail. *See also* Anatomy

HEWITT, EDWARD RINGWOOD American (1866–1957) One of the seminal figures of American angling, Hewitt was to the manor born, both figuratively and literally—he grew up in Ringwood Manor, a northern New Jersey demesne of positively feudal proportions and splendor, and combined the unusual advantages of a pampered background and upbringing (he was a direct descendant of Peter Cooper, the most lordly Mayor of New York since Stuyvesant's time) and the inquisitive nature of a mechanical genius with an inventive flair. With homes in Gramercy Park and on the Neversink, and the means and opportunities for frequent and extensive travels, Hewitt was familiar with the best fishing to be found everywhere throughout the last quarter of the nineteenth century and the first half of the twentieth. In *A Trout and Salmon Fisherman for Seventy-five Years* (1950), published by Scribner's, he summed it up and at the same time pretty well summarized the findings of his nine earlier books, *Secrets of the Salmon* (1922), *Telling On the Trout* (1926), his three Handbooks—*of Flyfishing* (1933), —*of Stream Improvement* (1934), and —*of Trout Raising and Stocking* (1935)—*Nymph Fly Fishing* (1934), *Those Were the Days* (1943), and *Ringwood Manor, The Home of the Hewitts* (1946).

Hewitt must be credited, together with his fishing companions, George La Branche and Colonel Ambrose Monell, with the popularization of dry-fly fishing for salmon. He took a 25-pound salmon on the Upsalquitch before 1925 on his own size 14 Neversink skater, and a 12-pound salmon on a 1½-ounce rod before 1922, both firsts and records that stood for decades until surpassed by Lee Wulff. At the same time he was more influential than any other single figure in the establishment of nymph fishing in America. The Hewitt nymph and the Neversink skater, an extremely long-hackled tailless spider, are still two of the most versatile and de-

pendable attractors and takers of the salmonid species. But the fears he voiced in 1934 that the general use of his nymphs might empty the country's streams of trout were groundless; some of his other dogmatic assertions, such as the attainment of "invisibility" for leaders through use of his patented silver nitrate treatment, have proved to be of less than lasting significance. He was anticipated, notably by Mottram in *Fly Fishing, Some New Arts and Mysteries* (1915), in some of the most perceptive of his pronouncements on the potentialities of light tackle; and despite his pertinacity in lifelong underwater photographic experiments to determine the taking propensities of the salmonid family, his actual findings never exceeded the dilettante level and have since been surpassed by the observations of others, such as J.W. Jones in *The Salmon* (1959).

But Hewitt and La Branche will doubtless live on in angling legend as two of the most colorful figures in the fishing of this century. They dominated such a large part of fishing since both had the luck to fish in the limelight over a span of years as long as that of old Walton himself.

And Hewitt did formulate, as well as anyone ever did before or after him, the three stages in the development of an angler, pointing out that we all begin as fishhogs at heart, with the attitude of little boys who will go to any lengths to get as many fish and as big as we possibly can; and that it's only later that the angler learns, if indeed he ever does, to become selective and discriminating as to the means employed; and, finally, to prize the means above the quarry. He could hardly have made any finding less likely to be superseded than that. —A.G.

HICKORY SHAD *Alosa mediocris* Similar to the skipjack herring (*which see*), this species differs chiefly in the absence of weak teeth and in the presence of faint longitudinal stripes on the sides. The shallow-notched upper jaw, small eye, and strongly projecting lower jaw distinguish it from the skipjack herring. The adults have a row of black spots behind the gill cover. Its body is grayish-green above, with silver sides. The upper rows of scales have well-defined dark lines forming faint lines on the sides of the adult. It has a lower number of gillrakers on the lower part of the first gill arch (19–21) than its relatives, which generally have in excess of 21.

One of the larger of the shads, it attains a length of 2 feet and a weight of 2½ pounds, although specimens of 5 pounds have been reported. The hickory shad occurs along the Atlantic Coast from Florida to the Bay of Fundy. Its habits at sea are poorly known. It enters freshwater tributaries in the spring, which it ascends for spawning, apparently returning to sea during the summer, part of the autumn, and all of the winter.

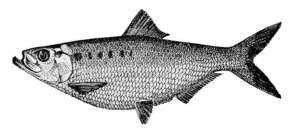

Hickory Shad

ANGLING VALUE

The species is more of a fish eater than other shads and is of considerable importance to sport fishermen who catch it on flies, small spoons, and with live or artificially rigged fish. Its flesh, while not as desirable as that of the shad, is sold fresh, smoked, or pickled. —D.dS.

HIGHFIN CARPSUCKER *See* Quillback

HIGHFIN SHINER *Notropis altipinnis* A small minnow, seldom exceeding 2½ inches in length, found in streams along the Atlantic Coast from the Chowan River system in Virginia southward to the Santee River system in South Carolina. The body of the highfin shiner is rather short and deep, depth contained 3.5 times in its total length. The head is short, not wide, and is contained 4.3 times in the total length. The eye of this minnow is large and enters the head 2.75 times. The lateral line is decurved and contains 36 scales. Other distinguishing characteristics of the highfin shiner are: anal rays 10, very rarely 9; pharyngeal teeth in two rows, 2 teeth in outer row 2, 4-4, 2; caudal base without spot except in very young; width of eye equal to or greater than snout length; no black crescent markings between nostrils; dorsal origin nearer front of eye than base of caudal fin or about midway between these two points; height of dorsal fin more than ½ the distance from the dorsal origin to the occiput; and the snout is marked by a dark preorbital blotch which extends onto the anterior half of the lips and is bordered above by a light streak which passes through the nostrils and around the tip of the snout.

Highfin Shiner

LIFE HISTORY

As breeding time approaches, the male's caudal fin takes on a faint reddish color, the snout turns yellowish, and the lower lip becomes dusky. This species is usually associated with slightly to moderately turbid, lower Piedmont streams having a width of 15–30 feet. The bottom strata of these shallow streams are composed of gravel, sand, rubble, and silt. The highfin shiner is a carnivorous sight feeder, eating small aquatic and terrestrial insects and larger zooplankton. Very little is known about the life history of this species.

The highfin shiner serves as forage for the largemouth bass, bluegill, redbreast sunfish, green sunfish, pumpkinseed, and chain pickerel in the small shallow Piedmont streams of its geographical range. —D.E.L.

HIGH-LOW RIG *See under* Weakfish

HILU The Hawaiian name for the black-banded wrasse (*see* Wrasses). A reef species which is often used as food in Hawaii, the Philippines, and Guam.

HOGCHOKER *Trinectes maculatus* Also known as the American sole, this common species, though seldom taken by anglers, is easily recognized by the lack of pectoral fins. The upper jaw slightly "overhangs" the

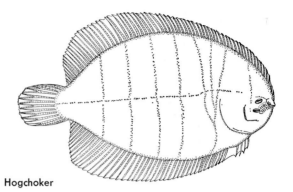

Hogchoker

lower jaw, the head is rounded, and there is no snout, as in other flatfishes. The pelvic fin is united with the anal fin, and the dorsal fin begins well forward on the head. The color is on the right side, the background being a dark brown grading to chocolate or gray, with irregular, wavy bars of darker color. A dark, interrupted stripe is present along the lateral line. Coloration on the blind side varies from creamy to yellow-buff, and dark spots, mottlings, or blotches may occur, the distribution of which is extremely variable from one individual to another, and from one geographic area to another, depending to some extent on the bottom type. Often there are no markings at all on the blind side. It is a small flounder, seldom exceeding 8 inches long and about one-third of a pound.

Found from Massachusetts Bay to Panama, it is a shallow-water species occurring on mud or muddy-sand bottom. It is tolerant of a wide salinity range, and is found from full-strength seawater to freshwater estuaries. It is most often found in brackish water.

LIFE HISTORY

Spawning occurs in waters of high salinity during spring and summer, the young moving toward fresher water as they develop. It reaches an age of at least 7 years and matures sexually at 4. It feeds on worms and small crustaceans.

ANGLING VALUE

Although taken in large quantities over mud or sand-mud bottom by commercial trawlers, it is only occasionally seen by anglers. Its flesh is reportedly good, but the small size and thick hide preclude extensive use of this species. —D.dS.

HOGFISH *Lachnolaimus maximus* Also known as the hog snapper, this member of the wrasse family Labridae is distinctive in shape and coloration. It has a pointed, steep snout, with thick lips and well-developed, protruding canine teeth. The first 3 or 4 dorsal spines are extended into filaments, and the tips of the dorsal and anal fins and the tips of the caudal lobes are pointed. Color is variable from a plain gray-brown phase to red-orange and marbled crimson. There is always a black spot at the base of the posterior rays during these varied phases. Color of the male is more intense than that of the female. The young are mottled red and gray, with a bright red eye. Hogfish are reported to reach 45 pounds, but 25 pounds is very large. The average is about 6 pounds.

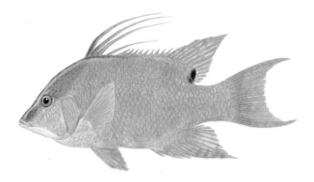

Hogfish

It occurs from Brazil to North Carolina and Bermuda but it is most common throughout the West Indies, in coral regions. The young are found in shallow, grassy areas, while the adults are commonly taken at the edge of coral reefs, particularly around sea fans (gorgonians). Usually it occurs single or in groups of two or three around such areas, but may be seen in larger numbers over sandy bottom in deeper waters.

It feeds on mollusks, crustaceans, and sea urchins. The flesh is excellent, although large specimens are reportedly poisonous in Cuba, or may be poisonous in certain other areas of the Caribbean, apparently resulting from its food habits.

It can be taken by anglers using clams, squid, or small crabs as bait.   —D.dS.

HOG SNAPPER *See* Hogfish

HOMOCERCAL A symmetrical tail fin in which the caudal vertebra does not extend into the upper lobe. This is the type of tail possessed by most fishes. *See also* Anatomy, Heterocercal

HOOK A recurved length of metal wire which terminates in a sharp point for the purpose of catching fish. There are many hundreds of hook patterns which differ in size and shape according to their intended purpose. The parts of a hook are the eye, shank, bend, barb, and point; it is the design and position of these five parts which largely distinguish one pattern from another.

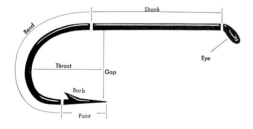

Parts of the Hook

Although not physical parts of a hook, the gap and bite measurements are also important features which further separate the various kinds.

Point: the sharpened end of a hook which penetrates the fish's mouth

Barb: the projection extending backward from the point of a hook. The barb helps to keep the point imbedded by resisting reverse motion

Bend: the bottom or curved portion of a hook

Shank: the upper portion of a hook which extends from the band on the side opposite the point to the eye

Eye: a hole or loop at the end of the shank through which the line or leader is secured

Gap: the distance between point and shank

Bite: the distance from the apex of the bend to its intersection with the gap

DEVELOPMENT OF THE MODERN HOOK

The fish hook is one of man's oldest tools. The first and longest period of human development began about 650,000 years ago and ended about 8000 B.C. During this span of the Paleolithic or Old Stone Age, man invented virtually all the basic tools he was to use in the future. He had partly solved the problem of climate with fire and clothing. He knew nothing about agriculture; so he ate only such fruits, nuts, roots, and other vegetation that he could gather. But he perfected the barbed spear head and the bow and arrow and lived largely on the flesh of the animals he killed. He also caught fish with harpoons and double-ended points or gorges made of stones, shells, antlers, and bones. The gorge was nothing more than a short shaft tapered to a point at both ends to which a line was secured around a groove in its middle. This device could be imbedded lengthwise in a bait, and after it was swallowed a pull on the line would cause the pointed shaft to cross in the fish's gullet. The gorge served man through the Mesolithic or Middle Stone Age, but just before the dawn of the Neolithic or New Stone Age he used recurved, single-pointed fish hooks made of bone.

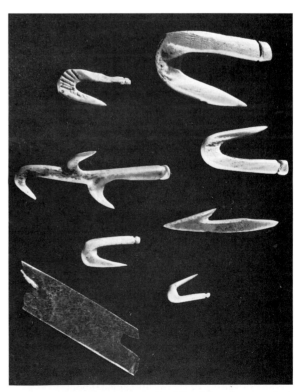

Prehistoric fish hooks unearthed at King Mounds, an ancient burial city in Wichita, Kansas

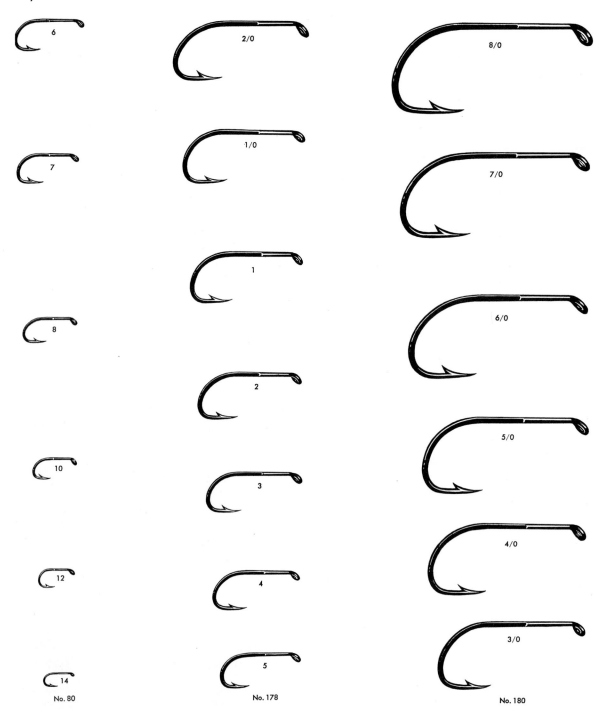

Wright & McGill Eagle Claw Hooks

The Neolithic Age began somewhere in the Near East (Asia Minor, Syria, Palestine, or Egypt), and although the New Stone Age man still made his tools of stone he had discovered how to grind and polish them. Furthermore he began to experiment with metals, notably copper and iron. Thus at the beginning of the Chalcolithic Period, or the era of copper and stone (about 5000 B.C.), among man's initial copper creations were pins for fastening his clothing and hooks for catching fish.

Approximately ten centuries passed before some curious metalsmith discovered that one part of tin melted and mixed with nine parts of copper produces a metal much stronger, more enduring, and easier to work. This marked the beginning of the Age of Bronze about 4000 B.C. The Bronze Age reached its peak on the island of Crete and later spread into Greece and Italy from whence, by way of Switzerland and Spain, it moved into western Europe. In the meantime fishhooks made of

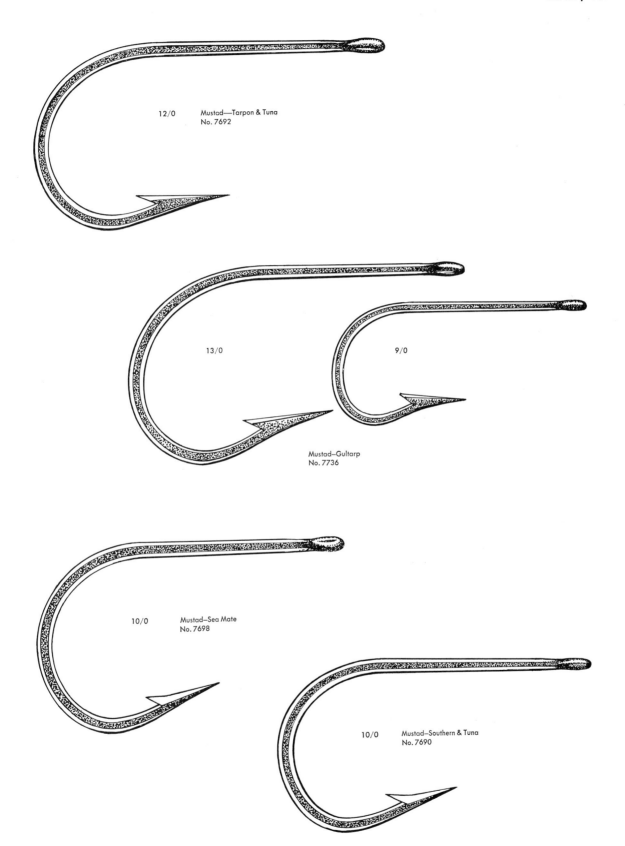

12/0   Mustad—Tarpon & Tuna
        No. 7692

13/0

9/0

Mustad—Gultarp
No. 7736

10/0   Mustad—Sea Mate
        No. 7698

10/0   Mustad—Southern & Tuna
        No. 7690

Mustad Big Game Fish Hooks

bronze with barbed points and turned-down, flatted shank terminals with a hole in the flat were being made and used in Crete and neighboring countries about 3400 B.C.

Man's next great forward stride was the Age of Iron, which is believed to have begun in Egypt about 2000 B.C. The development of steel followed, but just where or when steel was first produced is still a mystery. The Iron Age, however, spread into Europe in two distinct periods. The first occurred about 1000 B.C. The second was dated about 900 B.C.

Thus steel fishhooks with and without barbs were known centuries before the Christian Era, and modern methods of fishhook construction began in Europe near the end of the fourteenth century. However, the industry as such had its origin in the city of London during the seventeenth century. The needlemaking trade was located here, and the manufacture of hooks was an obvious and natural adjunct to it. Foremost among the original hookmakers was Charles Kirby who, in 1651, was producing hooks using the same basic methods that are followed today. Kirby improved the methods for tempering and hardening the metal of the hook and developed the Kirby pattern, which he invented, and which is still in common use all over the world.

The great fire of London in 1666, following the plague which killed so many citizens, caused the disruption of this trade, and surviving members of the industry moved elsewhere to restart the business. By 1730, however, the industry was again becoming centralized—this time on a much larger and a much more permanent basis in the small Worcestershire town of Redditch. The local needlemakers had developed quite advanced machinery which was worked by waterpower. They were quick to see the production similarities between the two items and added the making of hooks to their interests.

By 1810 all of the world's hook trade was centered around the town of Redditch. The Redditch makers were later to lose complete pre-eminence, and while many hooks are still made there, industries now exist in other countries, notably Norway and, to a lesser extent, in France, Japan, and the United States.

It was only natural that Norway with its extensive coastline and many inland waters which contribute to a large commercial fishery would become extremely active in the industry. The firm of O. Mustad & Son established in 1832 at Oslo became a world leader in the manufacture of fish hooks. Today, Mustad markets more than 60,000 items in fish hooks.

HOOK MANUFACTURE

Until quite recently hooks were made entirely by hand. The point was shaped with a file and the barb made by nicking the wire with a chisel or knife and raising a sliver of steel to prevent the hook losing its hold. The other processes of forming the hook and making the eye were likewise performed with hand tools. Such handmade hooks were superbly crafted, with the point and barb literally sculptured for good penetration. However, no two hooks were ever quite the same, and, thus, the quality of the product depended on just how steady was the hand and how keen the eye of the maker.

Modern hooks are made entirely or partly by machine. The material used is 80–85 percent carbon steel, although special hooks are also manufactured for waters where corrosion is a problem from stainless steel and from some of the rustless alloys.

Barbless Hook

The steel wire is first cut into correct lengths and then pointed by grinding at both ends. It is then cut again across the middle to give the right length for one hook. Ground points are now extremely uniform, and while perhaps not quite equaling the perfection of the best hand-filed point, they have an over-all excellence never before attained. The lengths of cut and pointed wire are then fed into a machine which in turn either flattens the non-pointed end (some sport-fishing hooks and many commercial fishing hooks have a flat or hole-eye for attachment rather than a ring) or makes the eye, cuts the barb, sets the point, and finally forms the hook, bending it into one of the established shapes such as the Limerick, Kirby, or Sproat. The eyes are later turned up or down according to pattern.

The hook is now complete but is in a soft state, and the wire requires hardening and tempering. After these heat treatments, which provide both strength and flexibility, the wire is covered with a scale. This scale is removed by scouring or rolling the hooks in a barrel with abrasives so that the scale is worn away. After scouring, the hooks are washed, then plated, japanned, or bronzed according to requirement. The final process is inspection (millions of hooks are inspected visually and by hand each day in Redditch and Oslo alone), counting, and packaging.

These are the basic processes of hookmaking. They will vary according to the firm making the product. Some hooks, particularly smaller and more specialized hooks, are made by semiautomatic methods, and the bending and the forming of the eye especially are accomplished with these hooks by hand-operated tools.

CHARACTERISTICS OF HOOKS

A quality hook is made of steel; it must possess a sharp point, a barb that is not cut so deeply that it threatens to break under pressure, sufficient plating to defeat saltwater rust and corrosion, and a smooth eye with no appreciable gap at the shank. The choice of the most effective hook depends on many factors, such as: tackle used and size of fish sought; how the fish strikes or takes a bait; how the fish's mouth is constructed; and how the gamester wages its resistance.

Unfortunately, there is no all-around hook; so the angler must carry an assortment of types and sizes. Research has proved that a short barb imbeds itself quickly, but is likely to be thrown by an active fish. The long barb doesn't drive home as easily, but is more difficult for the jumping fish to dislodge. Furthermore, hook penetration depends to a large extent upon the balance

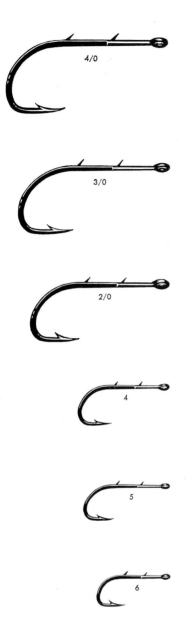

around favorite, with the Siwash or Pacific Salmon and the rolled-point Eagle Claw close behind. The O'Shaughnessy serves anglers who take a host of species, from flounders and cod on up to such medium-sized game as striped bass, sailfish, and tarpon. The Siwash, originally designed for use in Pacific-salmon fishing, is an excellent hook to use on small to medium-sized jumping fish, and especially for those which have soft mouths. It is almost universally favored for chinook and coho salmon fishing, and is a fine hook to use on bluefish. The only fault of the pattern lies in the vulnerability of its long, thin point, which is easily dulled or blunted. Offset, rolled-point patterns like the American Eagle Claw and Mustad Beak hooks are tremendously popular among anglers who fish with bait, and are employed in a wide range of sizes. The Kirby, Carlisle, Sproat, Pacific Bass, Chestertown, and Virginia bends are also employed by saltwater anglers. The long-shanked Carlisle and Chestertown are favored by many winter-flounder fishermen.

Some inexpensive saltwater hooks are blued—as are many of the freshwater models. This finish is never satisfactory. Neither is japanning or the lacquer which

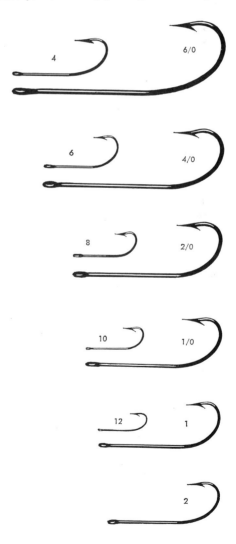

Wright & McGill Eagle Claw Bait Holder

of the hook itself. If a hook is suspended from its point and allowed to hang freely, in theory penetration should improve in direct ratio as the spear becomes more parallel to the pull of the line. This hypothesis becomes questionable when various shank lengths are employed, and specific gamefish upset the equation with hard or soft mouths, methods of taking a bait or lure, and varying degrees of wariness. It is apparent that simple physics and hook design fail to solve all problems. As an example, the tarpon is a fish with an exceptionally hard mouth—requiring a sharp, short-pointed hook which will drive home quickly. Unfortunately for the angler who tries to match the hook to his quarry, the tarpon is also a violent jumper—and this calls for a much longer point on the hook to hold fast. A compromise is necessary.

Fishermen have the choice of hundreds of hook patterns. In saltwater angling, the O'Shaughnessy bend is an all-

Mustad—Sproat Hooks, No. 3365

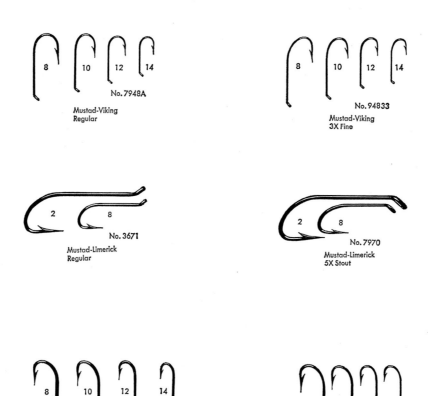

No. 7948A
Mustad-Viking
Regular

No. 94833
Mustad-Viking
3X Fine

No. 3671
Mustad-Limerick
Regular

No. 7970
Mustad-Limerick
5X Stout

No. 3399
Mustad-Sproat
Regular

No. 3399D
Mustad-Sproat
2X Fine Wire

Variation in Wire Size

imparts a bronzed finish; all rust quickly when exposed to salt. Various alloys have been used to defeat rust and corrosion. The most efficient has been nickel alloy; however, it is soft, a deficiency which causes the hook point to become dull or blunt and under heavy stress the hook bend will straighten. The most practical use of nickel alloy is in the fabrication of saltwater flies or small, light tackle jigs. With lures of this type rust is generally a greater problem than actual strength. But alloys have yet to match the all-around excellence of steel. The most popular heavy-duty marine hooks have been made of tempered steel and are heavily plated with cadmium or tin. When correctly tempered, stainless steel is superior, providing almost 100 percent resistance to corrosion, but for years the commercial production of stainless steel hooks was marred by metal that was too soft or too brittle. The first practical hooks of stainless steel material of a kind that were excellent for use by the angler began appearing in 1965.

Hooks, in freshwater or saltwater, may be straight, kirbed, or reversed. A kirbed hook is offset to the right— viewed from the top of the hook with the eye toward you —and a reversed hook is offset to the left. The straight hook is preferred in most instances. However, anglers often feel that a kirbed or reversed hook will not slide out of a fish's mouth without hitting flesh. This may be a decided advantage in baitfishing, but is not always practical where artificial lures are used. Kirbed hooks tend to spin when trolled or cast, and they require somewhat more force to set than do conventional straight models. When a kirbed hook is used to fish a live, small bait which is pierced through the skin of the back fore or aft of the dorsal fin, there is an added handicap. The kirbed hook often embeds its point in the side of the bait, and is subsequently sheathed when the game fish takes hold.

Saltwater gamefish, pound for pound, are far stronger than their inland counterparts. For that reason marine hooks must be designed to take tremendous punishment. One way to increase the tensile strength of a hook is forging. In this process, the hook is not just bent into shape and then tempered. After the bend has been made, the hook wire is hammered along part of the shank and all of the bend so that it is flat on two sides. After tempering, this process gives added strength where it is needed to prevent the bend from straightening under stress. Practically all big-game hooks are forged, and many of the smaller barbs used on medium-sized species are similarly treated to provide additional strength.

WIRE SIZE

The diameter or weight of the wire used in a hook is specified by the letter X and the words Fine or Stout. Thus a 1X Fine hook is made of the standard diameter wire for the next size smaller hook; 2X Fine means that

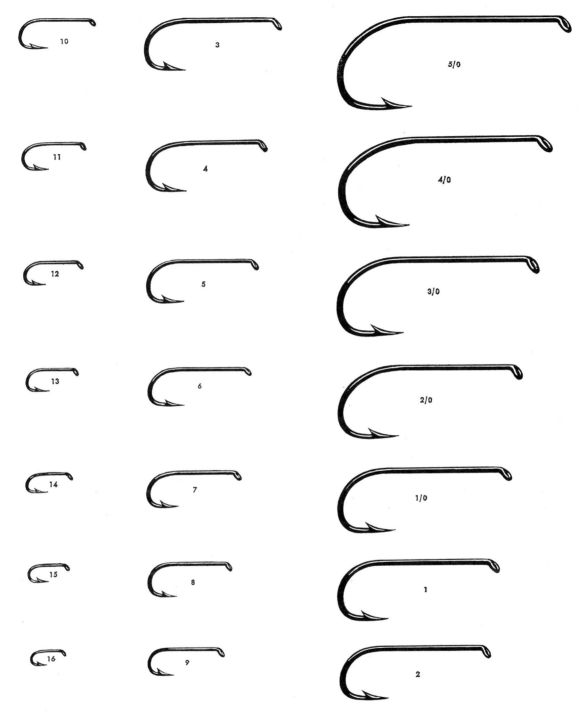

Sproat Redditch Scale

the wire is made of the standard-size wire for a hook two sizes smaller. Wire diameters are seldom made finer than 3X Fine. A heavy-wire hook has a reverse progression with a 1X Stout being the diameter for the size of the standard wire used in the next larger size hook, and a 2X Stout made of the standard diameter for a hook two sizes larger. Hooks are not regularly made with wire diameters greater than 4X Stout.

The qualities of the various weights of wire must be kept in mind when making a selection, for many factors enter the equation. Light-wire hooks, all else being equal, penetrate a fish's mouth more readily than heavy wire but also wear through, or "buttonhole" quickly. Light wire tends to spring and bend. However, when fragile natural baits are used, the light-wire hooks are most practical because they do not tear the bait to pieces. Furthermore, if the bait is small and alive, lightness of the hook permits greater freedom of movement. Light-wire hooks are also important in the making of dry flies, since, because of their lighter weight, the fly floats well. For all practical purposes in this method, the light-wire hook is perfectly adequate for holding even large fish.

Heavy-wire hooks are stronger, do not spring when they strike hard bone or bristle, and do not bend or part under the impact of a strike from sharp-toothed species. Although they do not penetrate as readily, they are apt to hold more securely once they have been driven home. The Stout diameters are most important in saltwater fishing but have broad application to streamers, bucktails, steelhead, and Atlantic-salmon flies as well.

Obviously, the angler must consider his tackle in relation to the hook. Where a light, limber rod can be employed, the hook must be of fine wire and possess a very sharp point if it is to be set. Heavy tackle permits the use of a more rigid, heavy-wire hook.

SHANK LENGTH

The difference in the length of a hook shank from the standard length for its size is specified in X and the words Long or Short. Thus, a hook of 1X Long is one that is as long as the standard length of the next size larger; 2X Long means that the shank is the standard length for a hook two sizes larger. This progression continues to 6X, beyond which length hooks are not ordinarily manu-

factured. In contrast, a hook of 1X Short is one that is as short as the standard length of the hook one size smaller; 2X Short means that the shank is the standard length for a hook two sizes smaller. Hooks are seldom made which have shank lengths shorter than 5X Short.

The advantage of a short-shank hook is that it can be hidden more easily in a small, natural bait, such as a salmon egg. It can also be used for various small flies, such as midges and spiders, to achieve high flotation without adding weight. The short shank has good penetration on soft-mouthed fishes, such as grayling and whitefish.

On the other hand, a long-shank hook defeats the sharp-toothed fish, which may otherwise cut leader or line. In some cases, such as that encountered by winter-flounder fishermen, the long-shank hook is preferred because it facilitates removal of the barb from the small, sucking mouth of the quarry. (One should not confuse the winter flounder and the summer flounder, or fluke. The latter has a large mouth.) Long-shank hooks are equally important to the fly-fisherman in making streamers and bucktails for both freshwater and saltwater fishing.

TYPES OF SHANKS

Hook shanks are manufactured in many shapes, but only six are commonly used.

1. *Straight Shank:* The hook shank is straight from eye to bend.

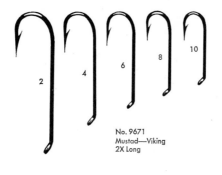

No. 9671
Mustad—Viking
2X Long

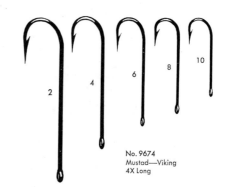

No. 9674
Mustad—Viking
4X Long

Mustad—Viking
5X Short

Mustad—Viking
9X Short

Variation in Shank Length

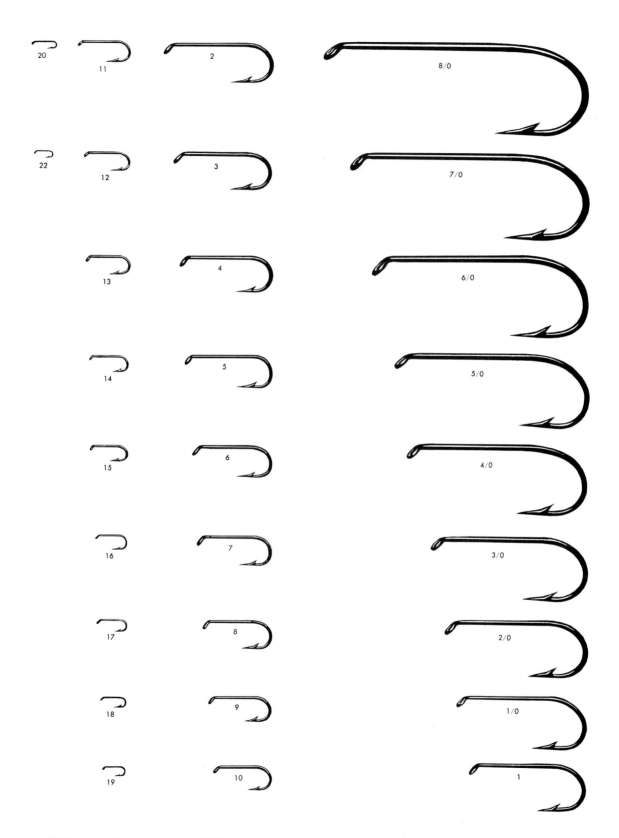

Mustad-Viking Hook Measurements, No. 7958

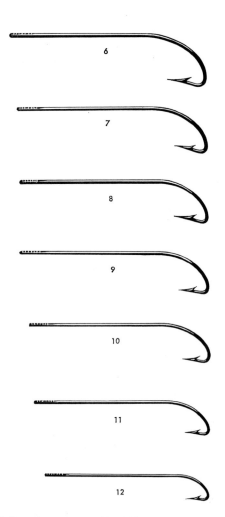

Mustad-Chestertown Hooks, No. 3295

2. *Humped Shank:* A hump or humps are bent into the shank. The purpose of the hump is to prevent cork, plastic, wood, or rubber bodies from turning around the shank. This type of hook is used exclusively in making bass and panfish bugs.

3. *Sliced Shank:* A barb or barbs are cut into the shank. These projections will anchor a soft bait, such as a salmon egg, seaworm, or sand lance.

4. *Curved Down Shank:* This type is designed to bring the line of pull closer to the line of point penetration. Although it takes a shallow bite, it is a good bait hook.

5. *Central Draught Shank:* The shank is bent upward to give the hook a quick, raking penetration.

6. *Step Shank: See* Keel Hook.

TYPES OF EYES

There are six common types of hook eyes which serve different purposes.

1. *Ball Eye:* An eye in which the wire diameter is constant and forms a circle perpendicular to the plane of the hook itself. The ball eye may be closed or open. The closed kind is tempered and therefore stronger; the open eye is usually found on cheap hooks.

2. *Tapered Eye:* In this type the shank of the hook directly behind the eye and the eye itself are tapered. This is done to reduce the weight of the hook and make it effective for dry-fly use.

3. *Looped Eye:* The wire in the eye of the hook runs back along the shank toward the rear of the hook. The end of this wire is usually tapered, although it can also be made untapered. Loop-eye hooks are traditionally used in making salmon wet flies.

4. *Needle Eye:* So called because it has an eye like that found on a needle. One advantage of the needle eye is that it may be easily strung through a natural bait without fouling. It is also strong.

5. *Brazed Eye:* The gap of the eye of this hook is brazed to the hook shank. It makes a very strong eye, and one which will not cut the leader or line. Big-game hooks are usually brazed to insure maximum strength.

6. *Flattened Eye:* In this type the end of the shank is flattened, and a hole is pierced into it. The flattened eye is used for medium-sized species in commercial fishing. Where natural bait, such as a seaworm, is used a hook may possess no eye at all, but simply a flattened end. In this case, a monofilament, steel, or fiber leader is snelled to the hook shank and secured by the flat itself.

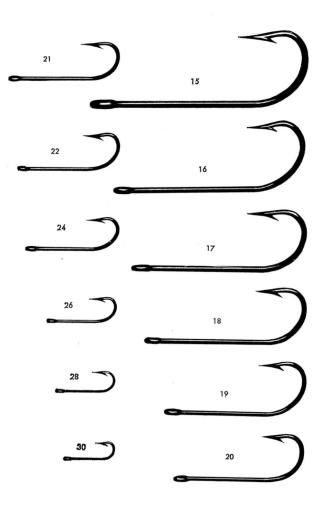

Mustad-Cincinnati Bass Hooks, No. 3306

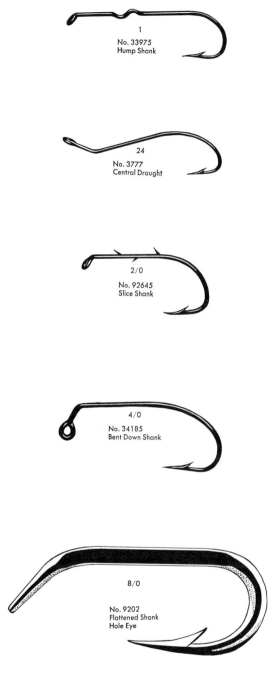

No. 33975
Hump Shank

No. 3777
Central Draught

No. 92645
Slice Shank

No. 34185
Bent Down Shank

No. 9202
Flattened Shank
Hole Eye

Types of Shanks

EYE POSITION

The position of the eye is an important factor in improving the hooking potential of artificial lures. The three most common eye positions are the Ringed Eye (R.E.) in which the eye is parallel to the hook shank, the Turned Up Eye (T.U.E.) in which the eye is turned up from the hook shank, and the Turned Down Eye (T.D.E.) in which the eye is turned down from the shank. The Ringed Eye hook is most often used with lures which are used in tandem with other lures such as a wet fly attached to a

spinner. The Turned Up Eye provides more clearance between the hook shank and the point, which may be an advantage when using fully dressed flies on hooks with short shanks. The Turned Down Eye brings the hook point closer to ideal in the theoretical line of penetration and in most cases is appropriate for hooks with standard or long shanks.

TYPES OF POINTS

There are four types of commercial processes used today in the fashioning of hook points: by upsetting, by forging, by grinding, and by needle grinding. Through any of these methods the following types of points can be made:

1. *Needle Point* (N.P.): The process used in making this high-grade point is not a fast one. The needle point is ground on all sides, and when properly made it has the best penetrating quality, although it easily becomes blunt.

2. *Hollow Point* (H.P.): This type, like the needle point, is designed for fast penetration, being hollowed or rounded out between the tip of the barb and the tip of the point.

3. *Spear Point* (S.P.): As this type of point can be readily manufactured in quantity, it is the least expensive one to make. The precise shape of a spear point varies with different manufacturers. The spear point does not have the quick penetration of a hollow-point hook.

4. *Barbless Point* (B.P.): Although one of the oldest known, this type has never become popular, as the point makes it difficult to hold a fish after it is hooked.

5. *Arrow Point* (A.P.): Shaped like an arrow, this type is rarely used, because the point does not penetrate easily.

6. *Knife Edge Point* (K.E.): This is a very sharp point used mainly for big-game fish. Four sides of the point are ground. The surface of the barb is flat and wider than normal, thus making it difficult for a big fish to throw the hook.

The finest hook loses much of its efficiency if the point is allowed to become dull or blunted. Carborundum stones may suffice to touch up small barbs, but a file is more effective in sharpening a large hook.

POINT POSITION

There are four common hook-point positions given below:

1. *Straight Point:* In this position the point is not bent in or bent out, nor is it rolled. It is in a position parallel to the shank.

2. *Rolled Point:* Sometimes called a rolled-in point, this type has the point bent in toward the shank of the hook. The rolled point is without peer for baitfishing in saltwater.

3. *Bent-in Point:* This differs from the rolled point in that the entire spear is bent toward the hook shank. Although such a point achieves a small bite, it is difficult for a fish to disgorge.

4. *Bent-out Point:* In this position the hook point is bent away from the shank to achieve a quick penetration. A slight degree of out point is sometimes considered desirable in small flies and also on big-game hooks.

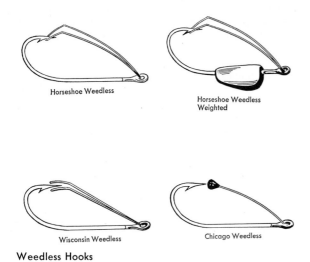

Horseshoe Weedless

Horseshoe Weedless Weighted

Wisconsin Weedless

Chicago Weedless

Weedless Hooks

HOOK MEASUREMENTS

Unfortunately, there is no uniform system of hook measurements. Visual familiarity with the various hook patterns is the only workable gauge for the serious angler. Although attempts have been made to set a standard by measuring the hook in fractions of an inch, the system has never been successful because it merely represents the length of the shank. A hook is really two-dimensional since the gap can vary greatly from one pattern to the next. —A.J.McC.

—T.T.

HORNE, BERNARD SHEA American (1905–1970) Bibliophile and conservationist, compiler of the first comprehensive bibliography of Izaak Walton's *The Compleat Angler* to appear since the publication of *A New Chronicle of the Complete Angler* by Peter Oliver (1936), Horne's *The Complete Angler 1653–1967, A New Bibliography*, was published by the Pittsburgh Bibliophiles, of which he was co-founder and first president, and distributed by the University of Pittsburgh Press, Pittsburgh, Pennsylvania, in late 1970. Soon after completing the final typescript the author was stricken with a cerebral hemorrhage and died at Hyannis Port, Massachusetts, on January 4, 1970.

Horne was born in Keswick, Virginia, on September 6, 1905, and was graduated from Princeton in 1928. A student of angling literature for much of his life, he early became a collector of Walton's *Angler* and Waltonia, and over the years built from a wide variety of sources what was at the time of his death the most complete collection ever assembled, surpassing those of the New York Public Library, the Library of Congress, the Bodleian Library, and the British Museum. He was a fly-fisherman of wide experience, and while studying his seventeenth-century subject he fished the waters recorded by Walton and Cotton and made repeated pilgrimages to their haunts and habitats.

His original intention, in compiling his bibliographical notes, was simply to supplement the Oliver *Chronicle*, which he regarded as definitive. But when the simple annals of his own collecting activities caused him to draw ahead of Oliver—to note, for instance, that what Oliver recorded as the 100th edition turned out to be his own 136th, he began to realize that the pupil had, however unwittingly, surpassed the master. He recorded not only 106 editions and reprints published after Oliver, but 20 editions prior to, and not carried in, the earlier work. Ironically, he also proved, though his avowed admiration for the earlier work never wavered, that a few editions

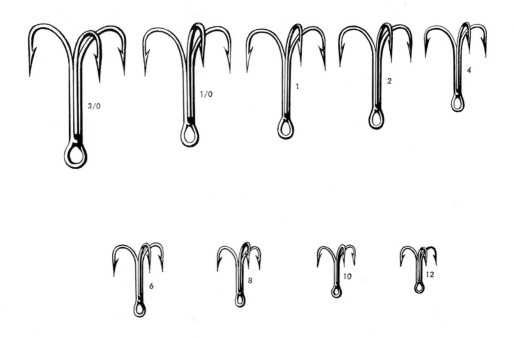

Mustad Treble Hooks, No. 3549

which his predecessors had thought and reported to have existed, had never actually been published.

Horne's bibliographic data was infinitely more detailed than any that had been attempted by Oliver or indeed by Arnold Wood or Westwood and Satchel before him. Yet Horne still stubbornly stood up for Oliver to the last, insisting that nobody could ever equal the original work that Oliver had done on the data of the 5 editions of Walton's lifetime. Even after allowing for the suppression of a number of disproved editions listed by Oliver, Horne's listing for the year 1935, which represented Oliver's ultimate total of 284 editions, still rose to 307; and Horne's last listing, including all the editions published after Oliver, a number of which were translations, surpassed Oliver's by over a hundred.

Horne was also active as an ardent conservationist, serving for many years as a member of the Pennsylvania State Game Commission, culminating in its chairmanship in 1955. For more than a decade he was responsible for the fish hatchery and streams of western Pennsylvania's Rolling Rock Club.

In his dual capacity of angler and scholar Horne was a Fellow of the Pierpont Morgan Library in New York, a member of the Grolier Club, the Anglers' Club of New York, and the Fly Fishers' Club of London.   —A.G.

HORNED POUT   A regional name most often applied to the black bullhead (*which see*), but may indicate any of the smaller catfishes. *See also* Catfish

HORNYHEAD   A common name for the stoneroller (*which see*)

HORNYHEAD CHUB *Nocomis biguttatus*   A slender, bluish-olive minnow with a black spot at the base of

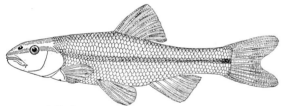
Hornyhead Chub

the caudal fin. A dusky lateral band encircles the snout and ends at the caudal spot. Sides light olive or yellowish. Ventrally pale yellow or white. Eye small. Mouth almost terminal, large, and slightly oblique. Small barbel present sightly above angle of jaws. The hornyhead is found from New York west to Wyoming and Colorado and south to northern Arkansas and Alabama.

HABITS

The hornyhead is found in small and medium-sized streams having clearwater and moderate or sluggish current. It prefers a sandy, gravelly bottom with aquatic vegetation. This chub spawns in the spring when the male develops tubercles over the whole upper part of the head, builds a nest, and guards the eggs. An omnivorous feeder, the hornyhead reaches 8 inches.

The hornyhead chub, due to its larger size, has some food value. Smaller individuals are also used as bait.

—R.A.J.

HORSE-EYE JACK   *See* Atlantic Horse-Eye Jack, Pacific Horse-Eye Jack

HORSE MACKEREL   *See* Bluefin Tuna
HORSESHOE CRAB *Limulus polyphemus*   An Atlantic marine arthropod related to the land spiders and scorpions. The horseshoe "crab" is a remnant of the Paleozoic Period (200,000,000 years ago). Though bathers are

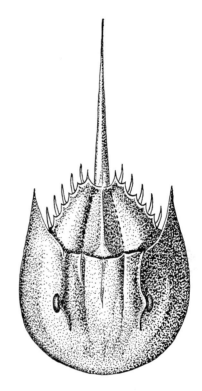
Horseshoe Crab

sometimes frightened by them, horseshoe crabs are harmless; the crab is not aggressive, and its long, pointed tail is simply used for righting itself if turned over by wave action. They feed chiefly on small worms and crustaceans. Horseshoe crabs have three eyes, two on the sides and one centered nearer the fore part of its carapace. The female horseshoe (to 22 inches) is larger than the male. Eggs are deposited close to shore in sand. The young live in deeper water, molting periodically as they grow. Empty shells found washed up on beaches are usually those discarded during the shedding process. Horseshoe crabs are utilized as bait for eel pots when chopped in pieces and are sometimes used for chum.   —A.J.McC.

HUCHEN *Hucho hucho*   The huchen is one of four species in a genus of strictly freshwater Eurasian salmonids which range from the Danube to Siberia and south to Japan. The distribution of the huchen is limited to the Danube basin, both in the main river and also in many of its tributaries. Occasionally, it may be found in freshwater lakes within that range, but it is essentially a river fish. Unfortunately, the species is declining in numbers due to pollution, poaching, and dam building.

The body shape of the huchen is very similar to the related Atlantic salmon, *Salmo salar*. It is, however, rather more cylindrical than the salmon, with a proportionately larger head and adipose fin. The back is colored dark brown to violet, or even gray-green. The sides often have a reddish hue, deepening with age. The belly is white or silver, and the entire body surface is covered with many minute black spots. In contrast with the brown trout, which it generally resembles when small, only black spots are present. The latter species may have orange or red spots as well—the huchen does not.

There are few quantitative differences between the huchen and the salmon or trout. Huchen have by far the smallest scales of these three species, 180–200 in the lateral line. Brown trout in comparison have only 110–120 lateral-line scales, Atlantic salmon 120–130. The huchen has 4–8 hooked teeth in a transverse row along the rear margin of the head of the vomer, with a toothless shaft. The salmon has no teeth on the head of its vomer, but a variable number in a single longitudinal row on the shaft. The trout has teeth on both, 2–6 on the head, and 9–18 on the shaft, in a double row.

Huchen are usually taken 24–48 inches in length. Their growth rate over their entire life is high; 4-pound increments per annum have been quoted, but these are exceptional, and half that is quite acceptable. Their rate of growth is much slower in their earlier years than later in life.

An interesting aspect of the huchen is its status as a landlocked salmon, similar to the landlocked form of Atlantic salmon endemic to Maine. It is believed that the migratory habits of the salmon family arose as a result of the Ice Age. Melting snowwaters kept the salinity of the sea in northern latitudes low, comparable to those of freshwaters. During this period, it is believed that the Salmonidae acquired the habit of ascending rivers to spawn, the young and the spent parents of the Atlantic species returning to the marine feeding grounds to fatten. When the snows ceased melting, the sea became more saline, as it is today. Therefore, only those populations capable of adjusting to a high salinity continued to migrate.

Huchen

LIFE HISTORY

Huchen spawn between March and May, unlike most other European salmonids, which spawn between October and January. The adults migrate upstream into the smaller tributary brooks, but if gravelly shallows are available, they may also spawn in the main river. Breeding dress is shown by an accentuation of color, especially the darkening of reds and blacks. The male develops a special breeding dress of thicker and coarser skin, and a hooked lower jaw, or kype.

Courtship and spawning are similar to the rest of the salmon family. The female scoops a redd in the bottom gravel of a suitable shallow stream with her tail. The eggs are deposited in the redd, and the male fertilizes them by covering them with milt. After fertilization, the eggs are covered up.

The fry hatch as typical salmonid young, bearing large yolk sacs. They commence feeding on small crustaceans as soon as the yolk sac is absorbed. As they get older, the growth rate increases sharply, and so does their appetite for smaller fish. Adult fish cease to move in shoals and will become solitary, taking up station in hollows, weirs, and deep places.

Huchen growth rates are high under good conditions. A 4-year-old fish would weigh about 8 pounds under good feeding conditions, while a 12-year-old would be six times that weight. The maximum size is known to be over 60 pounds.

ANGLING VALUE

As a large landlocked salmonid, the huchen has always been highly regarded by anglers. Huchen are caught primarily by casting spoons and spinners. Playing one is an experience, for the flight consists of long, hard runs at great speed. If these can be turned, the play develops into a series of deep, powerful borings, right up to the moment the huchen is landed.

Numerous attempts have been made to introduce huchen to European rivers which are not suited to Atlantic salmon. Such a river was the Thames in England, where the lower reaches are heavily polluted by the effluent of London. Atlantic salmon have not run up the Thames since the early nineteenth century. It was therefore believed that huchen would provide an excellent salmon fishery above London, and so huchen were planted in large numbers from 1904 to 1914.

These introductions to the Thames are generally regarded as unsuccessful by some authorities; but an English angling writer, Alan Pearson, has collected evidence to show that they seem to be established, albeit in a minority. The last definite report was in the 1930's, when fish up to 35 pounds were seen. Pearson believes that a few of the huchen are caught every year but are not identified as such. The only fish anglers expect in the Thames are large brown trout. Thames trout are solitary and predatory—just like huchen. A male huchen in breeding dress, complete with kype, looks like a senile brown trout. Most trout fishing in the Thames is done by spinning in spring, a time when breeding huchen could be caught. In 1962, a so-called sea trout was captured above London; sea trout are migratory, so it is highly likely that this fish was a huchen.

COMMERCIAL VALUE

Huchen flesh is not as highly prized as other members of the salmon family, nor is it a common article of diet. It is extremely difficult to capture in nets, as its haunts are hard to net fully.

Neither is it particularly easy to rear in hatcheries. The water must be clean, the ova require much oxygen, and the fry need live food. The fish are large by hatchery standards, and so rearing them is not very economical. Nor are they easy to transport. The fry are very sensitive to temperature changes; eyed ova are easier to transport, and the loss is smaller and easier for budgets to bear. Some are bred in hatcheries by European specialists, but a breeding pair takes time and food to rear, because they are generally 2 feet long at maturity. *See also* "Zoogeography of the Lake Trout" *under* Lake Trout   —D.M.

HULL SPEED In a displacement hull this is the speed beyond which it is uneconomical to drive the boat.

HUMBOLDT CURRENT   *See* Currents
HUMPBACK SALMON   *See* Pink Salmon
HUMPBACK SUCKER *Xyrauchen texanus*   A grotesque-appearing sucker with a prominent predorsal hump. Color grayish-silver with white or yellow underparts. Mouth large and ventral. Cleft of lower lip deep, separating the two lower lobes completely. Lateral-line scales 73–95. The range of this species is limited to the lower Colorado River basin.

HABITS

The humpback prefers the slow-moving parts of larger streams and their backwaters. It is a spring

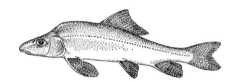

Humpback Sucker

spawner and feeds on mud and algae. It may reach a size of 10 pounds.

ANGLING VALUE

Where abundant the humpback has some food value and can be taken on a baited hook.   —R.A.J.

HUMPED SHANK   A type of fish hook which has an abrupt curve or hump in the shank. The purpose of the hump is to prevent cork, rubber, or plastic lure bodies from rotating around the hook after they have been fastened to the shank. Humped shank hooks are most often used in making bass bugs.

HUMPER LAKE TROUT   *See* Lake Trout
HYBRID   A hybrid is a crossbreed resulting from mixed parentage—the male of one race, species, or genus with the female of another. As long as the two forms of life are closely related, a hybrid can be produced. The laws of genetics follow true right down to flowers, fruits, and grains. Much of the food we eat today is the result of painstaking hybridization. A nineteenth century monk, Gregor Johann Mendel, discovered the principles of modern genetics through plant breeding. Mendel proved that size, color, and other characteristics depend on the presence of genes, which behave as units, and that the second and later generations of crossbreeds exhibit these characters in all possible combinations, each combination in a definite proportion of individuals. Some species of fish can and do hybridize in natural environments, and other hybrid fish are produced artificially, primarily in an attempt to obtain faster growth, greater life span, disease resistance, and similar desirable traits. *See also* "Hybrid Trout" *under* Fish Culture   —A.J.McC.

HYOID   The tongue bone in the floor of the mouth and which in some fishes bears teeth. *See also* Cutthroat Trout

HYPOLIMNION   A biological term to describe the cold, bottom layer of water in a lake. This term is also applied to such a layer in the ocean, but is more properly known as the hypothalassa.

HYPURAL   The expanded last vertebra in a fish which supports the caudal fin. *See also* Anatomy

ICE FISHING   A specialized method of fishing through the ice. As a sport it enjoys widespread popularity, particularly in the Midwestern United States, where "shanty towns" become sizable communities during the winter angling season. The general character of ice fishing differs so greatly from that of conventional forms of angling that the unique qualities which account for its widespread popularity are worthy of identification. Perhaps its greatest single source of fascination is the drastic change in the relationship between man and water brought about by the dramatic appearance of the ice itself. The waters which now lie hidden beneath the frozen surface immediately become a dark, sealed-off mystery and thus pose a tantalizing and compelling challenge to the fisherman. Yet at the same time the latter is suddenly accorded an intriguing advantage; he can walk about boldly on a surface which is normally immune to any such approach.

In all probability, ice fishermen are drawn to their sport not as much by the prospect of hauling fish through the ice, as by the instinctively accepted illusion that to do so is closely akin to achieving the impossible. There is a tense expectancy in watching a line of baited tilts, which has no exact counterpart elsewhere in angling—plus the equally unique thrill experienced when a flag suddenly springs erect. Here again, the actual hauling of the fish comes as an anticlimax; the truly satisfying moment occurs when the activated flat signals actual contact with the alien life of that dark world which lies under the ice.

Like all other forms of angling, ice fishing has its regional variations, but generally speaking it can be divided into two categories. One involves the use of a single line, and is referred to as "jigging." The other centers around the operation of tilts or tip-ups, which comprise a number of single baited lines. There is considerable variation in technique between each.

THE JIGGING METHOD

Jigging through the ice is usually employed when the quarry consists of small fish that the fisherman can reasonably expect to catch in substantial numbers. Included in this list are such species as smelt, yellow perch, bluegills, crappies, and a few other panfish. The jig-fisherman seldom commits himself to a single spot. Instead, he tries various locations and depths until he locates a school of fish, for he knows that it's possible to make a large catch in a short time once he's over such a school.

Jigging equipment is simple. It consists of a jigstick and line, a spud or ice auger, a skimmer, and usually a homemade box on runners to hold lunches, the catch, and any odd items of equipment. The jigstick is essentially what the name implies: a short stick with a scalloped handle upon which the line is wound, and with a single eye or guide at the tip through which line can be paid out and manipulated. Depth is determined by counting the number of turns unwound.

Most fishermen equip their jig-sticks with monofilament, of approximately 10-pound test. Hooks are invariably of small size, but sinker weight depends upon the depths to be fished. Since fish such as smelt and perch are often taken at depths of forty feet or more, sinkers must weigh at least one ounce to take lines down quickly enough for efficient fishing. This is highly important, for retaining the interest of a school often depends on the fisherman's ability to return the bait quickly following each catch.

Many jig-fishermen use sinkers which also serve as fish attractors by virtue of a shiny surface and a shape which produces a flashing action when jigged. Lead sinkers can be given a bright surface by scraping with a knife. Jigging lures and "ice flies" are sometimes used, but these usually prove effective only when employed in conjunction with bait.

Favorite jigging baits vary with the species fished for. Tender, easily stolen baits are generally shunned in deep jigging, even though they may appeal to the fish. Favored are those items which combine toughness with efficiency —baits which bring bites but which don't require frequent replacement. For this reason a single perch eye, on a small hook, is standard among yellow-perch fishermen, while smelt fishermen use a small slice or "slab" cut from the tail section of a smelt. These baits are snapped up eagerly by perch and smelt respectively, but need replacing only infrequently.

Experienced hands at deepwater jigging take the majority of their fish without "feeling" bites. Instead, they employ a jig-and-snatch technique which consists of alternately jigging the bait slightly and then suddenly jerking the bait upward with a quick raise of the arm. The proper jigging interval becomes intuitive with experience, and once the knack is acquired the method is almost incredibly effective. When a school of perch is located, for example, an accomplished jig-fisherman will set the hook solidly in a perch with almost every snatch, yet never dally long enough between snatches to feel a single tug from the biting fish.

Fishermen who jig relatively shallow water for bluegills and crappies rely on natural baits, such as small, live minnows, worms, grubs, maggots, and other insect larvae. They wait for signs of a bite before setting the hook and often rely on a bobber's sensitivity to warn them of the proper time.

Jigging is often done in the comfort of a heated fishing shanty, but the more ardent jig-fishermen usually chafe at this compromise. In all but the most prohibitive conditions they prefer to roam the ice in search of fish, for it is usually only by so doing that large catches can be consistently made.

TILT OR TIP-UP FISHING

The tilt fisherman's aim is not to take a large number of small fish, but to catch much larger ones. Tilt spreads are commonly set for chain pickerel, northern pike, saugers, walleyes, and, where legally permitted, for lake trout, landlocked salmon, and other salmonids.

The tilt fisherman arranges his tilts in a pattern to suit his fancy and limits their number to conform to maximums specified by local fishing regulations. Once he "sets in" he spends the day tending his lines at that location— and the fish either bite or they don't. A warm shanty may help ease the chilly boredom of the inevitable dull days, but the man who strings tilts is usually a fisherman of greater than average patience. He shrugs off the long, cold hours of patient waiting as the price for those exciting periods when flags flip all down the line, and fish after fish comes flopping out on the ice.

Tilts may vary in style, but all are designed to serve the same purpose: to hold the baited line, plus a spool of reserve, and to signal a bite the instant it occurs. The latter may be done by a flag which springs upward, or by a balanced arm, often equipped with a sliding weight,

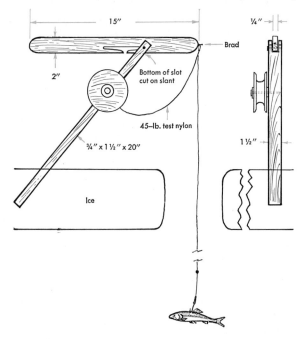

which upends at the first tug. Significant differences in tilt design are limited to two: those in which the line is secured to the flag-tripping trigger above the ice, and so-called "underwater" tilts in which the spool of line rests below the surface where a bite causes it to turn and trip the flag in so doing. Since the line does not come up through the fishing hole, the tilt will function even when the hole is solidly frozen over.

Both styles have their advantages and disadvantages. Above-water tilts require constant hole-skimming on freezing days, but they can be more sensitively adjusted for light biters, and are much easier to tend when bites occur. The underwater design avoids the danger of freeze-up and largely eliminates skimming chores, but underwater tilts are something of a nuisance to tend as they must be lifted from the hole before the fisherman can grasp the line. In general, above-water tilts are preferred by fishermen after walleyes, saugers, and other light-biting fish, while underwater tilts are favored by those who fish for pickerel and northern pike.

Tilt spools should be rigged with sufficient line to provide an ample reserve after the tilt is set. Various kinds of line are used. One of the most economical and satisfactory is twisted nylon seine twine in about 40-pound test, lighter weights having diameters too small for easy handling when fingers may be numb.

Hooks should match the size of the bait, and a small snap-swivel on each line makes hook changing a simple matter. Sinkers should be no heavier than needed to take the bait down, and careful fishermen carry sinkers of various weights for this reason. A short wire or cable leader is recommended when fishing for pickerel and northern pike, as these fish are quite capable of shearing off lines with their sharp teeth.

In setting tilts, depth is first determined by use of a sounding weight, and the line is then adjusted to hold the bait the desired distance above the bottom. This is usually about a foot where the bottom is clear and just high enough to clear the tops of weeds where these exist. When bites aren't forthcoming, fishermen often experiment at different levels and sometimes succeed in stirring up action.

Live baitfish are the standard offering among tilt fishermen. Baits of 6 inches, and longer, are considered best for northern pike and pickerel, and fishermen in search of trophy-size northerns don't hesitate to use foot-long suckers. Minnows 3–4 inches long are commonly used for walleyes, saugers, and trout. Very small minnows, 2 inches long or less, are far more effective for walleyes than is commonly supposed, and these will draw action from any perch in the vicinity as well.

Bites from northern pike and pickerel are usually "waited out," as these fish tend to carry the bait a considerable distance before pausing to swallow it. Line is carefully paid out during this initial run, and no attempt is made to set the hook until the fisherman feels fairly certain the fish has the bait well in its mouth. Walleyes seldom move off with the bait after tripping the flag, and they are inclined to relinquish the bait if given too long a time in which to mouth it. Walleye fishermen therefore usually attempt to set the hook as soon as possible, pausing only to tighten the line gently against the fish before striking.

ACCESSORY EQUIPMENT

Equipment, in addition to the desired number of tilts, includes a spud or ice auger, minnow bucket, sounding weights, long-handled skimmer, and such spare hooks, sinkers, and lines as deemed necessary. A sharp gaff is a wise addition, for really large fish are often lost when the attempt is made to lift them through the hole.

In sharp contrast to fishing equipment in general, that employed in ice fishing has seen few recent improvements save for one exception, the Swedish ice auger. The tool's design seems to belie its unquestionable efficiency, and doubts aroused by its somewhat negative appearance have probably slowed its adoption somewhat. It is steadily gaining in popularity, nevertheless, and promises to replace the time-honored spud. The instrument is by no means self-operating, but it will cut through ice at a remarkable inch-per-second rate, to produce an 8-inch hole (smaller sizes are also available) whose uniform diameter leaves no jagged spurs to interfere with the landing of fish. Although motor-driven augers are available, their relatively high cost makes them a luxury in which few ice fishermen see fit to indulge.

By cutting a strategic pattern of holes the ice fisherman can readily locate schools of fish as they move about the area

Improvement in warm clothing has been far more gratifying. Employment of "insulation" in everything from underwear to boots has virtually assured the ice fisherman of bodily warmth and with minimum weight. Choosing proper clothing for ice fishing is largely a matter of individual taste, the only exception being the matter of proper footwear. All-rubber insulated hunting boots are by far the best choice, for they are both warm and waterproof. The latter is a must, for wet conditions under foot should be anticipated in even the coldest weather. Snow accumulates, adding weight to the ice and causing it to settle. Water comes up through holes and cracks and forms a layer of slush under the snow, making sloppy going even when temperatures may be near zero. Nothing but all-rubber footwear will keep feet dry under such conditions.

PERCH AND SMELT

Although ice fishing is basic hook-and-line fishing which boasts few refinements, success is nevertheless often dependent upon general know-how, plus the fisherman's ability to draw upon the lessons of past experience. For example, in deep water jigging for perch or smelt it is usually much more effective to seek out the fish, rather than wait for them to come to you. Although these two species move about in schools, their movements in any given day are usually restricted to a relatively small general area, and the chance of such a school moving in from any great distance is rather remote. Prolonged fishing in an unproductive spot is therefore likely to prove a waste of time, and it is for this reason that most jig-fishermen spend only a few minutes at a hole which yields no bites before moving on in quest of an area which holds fish.

Once a school is located, it is frequently possible to keep in touch with it, even though the fish may drift from spot to spot. They seldom move far, or rapidly, and relocating them is often only a matter of cutting a strategic pattern of holes in the general area. Once a substantial number of holes has been cut, the movement of the school can frequently be followed by simply shifting from one to the other. Quite often the school will circle, and it is a common experience to make a second good catch through the hole through which the fish were first located.

Although it might seem that little could be done to encourage bites in this form of fishing, this is not the case.

Ice fishing for perch requires patience and warm clothing, but the reward at table deserves three stars

The skillful jig-fisherman constantly manipulates his stick to give his bait just a hint of "action," and it is by this subtle, teasing movement that he sells his wares. The effectiveness of a gentle jigging action is easily demonstrable, for a perch eye promptly becomes a very poor bait when hung from a stationary tilt or bobber.

Reefs and other outcroppings which rise up abruptly from the bottom in deepwater are easily detected when encountered, and these can usually be explored to advantage when located. The experienced fisherman therefore "reads" the bottom as he moves about, and he fixes the position of such bottom irregularities by lining up landmarks on shore. The secret of large catches often consists of little more than the ability to return repeatedly to a productive reef.

When fish must be drawn up from 40–50 feet, or more, hauling becomes a time-consuming process, and fishermen try to speed up operations by gradually luring the school upward. This can be done with perch to a limited extent, but smelt can often be coaxed from very deepwater to directly under the ice simply by winding in a few turns of line every few moments. This, of course, results in much faster fishing whenever it can be accomplished.

Since the tilt fisherman commits himself to a single location, his initial choice of position becomes a matter of critical importance. In general, the best northern pike and pickerel grounds are those with heavy weed growths and a depth of seldom over a dozen feet. Bays and coves usually indicate the shallow, weedy waters which attract these two species, and thus are easily recognized clues to probable good fishing.

NORTHERN PIKE AND PICKEREL

Northern pike and pickerel do not gather in schools, nor do they tend to move about to any great extent. For this reason it is wise to space tilts rather widely apart over a substantial area. Wherever possible it is good strategy to string tilts from the outer edge of the weeds to within a short distance of shore where the water may be no more than three feet deep. This covers all bets, and it should be added that the chance of taking a lunker pike or pickerel on the tilt farthest inshore is fully as great as elsewhere.

As mentioned previously, it is wise to resist the temptation to attempt to set the hook while pike or pickerel are moving off strongly with the bait. Quite often they have the latter clamped crosswise in their jaws, with the hook actually outside their mouths where it cannot possibly engage. A premature yank will only result in a stripped hook—and keen disappointment—while happier results usually occur when the fish is allowed to pause and swallow the bait.

Northern pike and pickerel are essentially bold by nature; yet they become shrewd as they take on age and size. The larger and wiser specimens are likely to "study" a live bait at close range for a considerable period of time, and, conscious of the unnatural circumstance of its tethered state, may eventually decide to pass it up. It is therefore good policy to make frequent trips over the spread of tilts, raising each bait several feet and promptly dropping it back. This has the effect of forcing undecided fish to a decision, for it clearly implies the possibility of the bait's escape. A quick round of the tilts is therefore likely to be followed promptly by one or more sprung flags.

WALLEYE

Unlike pike and pickerel grounds, good spots for walleye fishing are seldom betrayed by visible clues. Picking a likely spot in strange waters is usually a matter of being guided by the advice of local fishermen and noting where the latter make their sets. Walleyes travel in large schools, leisurely following a course which, in large lakes, may cover a range of many miles. These migrations follow an established pattern from winter to winter, and local fishermen are thus able to predict where the fishing is likely to be most productive at any given time.

Because the attention of a school of walleyes is likely to be held longest by a concentration of baits, most walleye fishermen space their tilts at short intervals, usually no more than fifteen feet apart. Since the movement of the fish will be roughly parallel to the shoreline, tilts are usually set in lines at right angles to the latter as most likely to intercept passing schools.

Most walleye fishing is done where the bottom is clear of weeds, and in such locations lines should be adjusted so that the bait hangs no more than a foot above bottom at the most. This is extremely important in walleye fishing; so care should be taken to sound the depth carefully at each hole and to rig lines accordingly.

Walleyes are surprisingly light biters, the largest specimens included, and they are experts at gently working the minnow from the hook without tripping the flag. Tilts should be set as lightly as possible to hold such thievery to a minimum, and holes should be skimmed faithfully for the same reason.

Because walleyes take a bait very deliberately and gingerly, they are extra-sensitive to the presence of large hooks and the drag of heavy sinkers and are quite likely to drop a bait which is unduly encumbered by either, or both. It is therefore best to use the smallest hooks feasible, a matter determined by the size of the bait, and only barely enough sinker to take the latter down.

The stomachs of walleyes are often crammed with tiny minnows hardly an inch long, and this obvious liking for very small bait is a walleye characteristic which is often overlooked. Actually, minnows of the small size normally used for perch fishing make superior walleye bait, and their effectiveness is further enhanced by the small hooks and sinkers which can be employed with their use. Few walleyes become suspicious at the presence of a No. 6 hook—a good choice—nor do they become alarmed by the slight drag of the single buckshot which is all that's necessary for sinker weight.

Walleyes have exceptionally tender mouths, and care should be taken in landing lest the hook tear out at the crucial moment. This becomes especially important when small hooks are used, and, of course, in proportion to the size of the fish hooked. Fish should be drawn through the hole smoothly, and the temptation to give a sudden yank when the fish shows in the hole should be avoided if possible, for it is due to this instinctive yank at the last moment that many good fish are lost.   —H.F.B.

ICELAND Fourth largest island in the North Atlantic, after Greenland, Britain, and Newfoundland. It lies between 63° 24' and 66° 32' N., with its north coast just touching the rim of the Arctic Circle. It is a fifth larger than Ireland, a fifth smaller than Pennsylvania. Iceland's sixty salmon rivers have been building their almost legendary fame among knowing anglers over the past

The Soigdt is one of many excellent salmon and sea trout rivers found throughout Iceland

century, and today there are no waters in the world more jealously held nor more zealously preserved. Since 1945, and after passing from Danish rule to independence, Iceland's law prohibits the ownership of a salmon river by anyone but an Icelandic national, so the one way to assure a more or less permanent beat on one of these idyllic streams would be to marry an Icelandic girl. Major General R. N. Stewart, author of *Rivers of Iceland*, an Englishman who has fished there for more than fifty years, beginning as far back as 1912, said in reference to this then-new ruling, "A single angler could go farther and do worse."

Most people think of Iceland as a remote fastness harboring Eskimos, polar bear, reindeer, seals, and ice floes, and assume that the only proper garb for expeditions there is the type made famous by Admiral Byrd. True, it does lie north of the lower third of Greenland, which is only a couple of hundred miles to the west, and wholly above the Faroe Islands, but the proximity of the Gulf Stream gives it a mild oceanic climate, with a spread of only about twenty degrees between its average winter and summer temperatures. There are both reindeer and seals, but there are no Eskimos, and the only polar bear ever encountered are briefly visiting tourists along the north coast. The average winter temperature is only 30°F., and the summer average is a degree or so above fifty. In the three months of the salmon season, from mid-June to mid-September, the noonday temperature is apt to rise close to seventy, and there is midnight sun, at least over the northern half of the island, for almost all of the season's first month. Even in late August and early September, when the season's end is approaching, there are only a few hours of real darkness, from around eleven at night until around three in the morning. Conversely, in the depth of winter in Reykjavik, the country's one real city, there are only about four hours of actual daylight, from late morning to early afternoon.

Except from the standpoint of his own creature comfort, Icelandic weather need not concern the angler, as the fishing there is as nearly weatherproof as it can ever be anywhere. Since the surroundings of the rivers are volcanic rock, overgrown with tundra, and there are no trees whatsoever, there is also an almost total absence of mud. Hence the clear streams never really muddy up in even the foulest weather. They may "pearl" a bit for a few hours, but they never turn that chocolate color that is so frequently the fly-fisherman's despair almost everywhere else. The one fly in the otherwise serene ointment of Icelandic fishing, however, is that high winds are rather more likely than not to be blowing across the treeless landscape. There are shrubs here and there, standing never higher than about eighteen inches, but the combination of bare rock and tundra is otherwise unrelieved, giving the setting of most rivers the aspect of a scene from the Twilight of the Gods, a bleak and brooding view of surroundings of awesome majesty. Bright intervals between the wind and the rain are frequent, however, and the fish seem to move more briskly at the first emergence of the sun, when the angler's attention is most likely to be distracted by the sight of a rainbow, complete and intact as a croquet hoop, with both of its ends plainly in sight.

Since there are no trees to worry about, it is relatively easy for the angler to maneuver in such a way as to let the wind carry the fly to the fish, even in a gale. Winds of up to Beaufort Force Eight, just short of hurricane velocity, are by no means infrequent, and at such times tossing of the fly up in the air, about the height of a tennis ball for an overhead serve, will be enough to launch it sufficiently, letting the line coiled at the fisherman's feet pay out into the wind, as it will. Regardless of the angry weather, or even perhaps especially in such weather, it is almost a certainty that the angler will ultimately be fast to a fish, when the real worry is to keep one's footing. For the light-tackle man, at least, chest-high waders are thus an absolute necessity.

TACKLE FOR ICELAND

While Icelandic fish don't run as large as those of Arctic Norway, the record salmon for most of Iceland's rivers running about 30–35 pounds, what they lack in size they more than make up in vigor. The average is about 9½ pounds, but since the season is a short one, the odds of encountering a salmon recently in from the sea are proportionally higher, and even a 6–8 pounder, newly arrived, will lead the angler such a merry chase that he's almost certain to be sloshing around in water above the height of hip boots before finally beaching him, unless his tackle is of such stout proportions as to permit horsing the fish in. That, of course, is what the Icelanders do themselves. They use the heaviest rods, derricklike devices of 22–24 ounces, with leaders of around 40-pound test, and their general practice is to fish from the shore, wearing the trawler boots that are sold down by the docks in Reykjavik. At the climactic moment the salmon is tailed by hand and thrown some thirty feet or more from the stream edge, where the odds are overwhelming that it will accommodatingly brain itself on the needle-sharp lava rock. When a visitor shows up with a fly rod of 4 ounces or less, announcing his intention of beaching for himself any fish that he hooks, they laugh themselves into hysterics. Icelanders are outdoors men on a Homeric scale, and as likable a group of people as are to be encountered anywhere, but it has never yet occurred to them to give

a fish anything remotely resembling a sporting chance. Relatively few of them will even fish consistently with a fly, since the matter of terminal tackle is not restricted by law, but will resort to big spoons. Even the visiting English, stout fellows though they are in the matter of suitable tackle, are horrified by the hardware thrown into their rivers by the Icelanders, leading General Stewart to advise giving a good rest to any pool that has been worked over by an Icelander.

The angler going to Iceland will be well advised to take his own rods and leaders, and the rod should not be more than 6 ounces at the very most, since nine out of ten of the salmon hooked will run under 10 pounds. And, since most Icelandic rivers offer a simultaneous chance at two of the five kinds of fish prevalent (that is salmon and sea trout and anadromous char, as well as the nonmigratory strains of both trout and char) almost any salmon pool is equally likely to yield a trout or a char of 2–4 pounds. The latter, of course, are a picnic on rods of from 2–4 ounces, but somewhat anticlimactic if played on heavier tackle. Because of the comparative lack of stream obstructions and the relative ease of finding a bank favorable to beaching the fish, the angler need not feel underequipped with a trout rod and terminal tackle no heavier than 1X.

In Reykjavik there are two excellent tackle shops, where rods can be repaired promptly and well, and all necessary flies obtained. Their own rods and reels and

Icelandic anglers favor heavy tackle for salmon, although large fish, such as this 20-pounder, are scarce

leader material, however, are all likely to be too heavy. As for flies, Silver Doctor, Silver Wilkinson, and Black Doctor are almost a three-way tie for first place as the most dependable all-round fly, with Blue Charm as runner-up, all being taken with enthusiasm not only by the salmon for which they were patterned but also by sea trout, browns, and both migratory and nonmigratory char. The latter are voracious takers of virtually any fly, including dry patterns all the way down to No. 20 midges. Large salmon will play with a White Wulff, or other hair-wing dry, clowning with it and passing it back and forth like hockey players with a puck, but will probably not take until given a wet fly. The Thor steelhead pattern seems to be the best single fly, in No. 6 and No. 4 sizes, after July 10, when the sea trout are in.

WHERE TO GO

The angler who goes to Iceland before July 15 is courting disappointment. The season is open from June 15 to September 15, but the fish are seldom in the rivers in any appreciable numbers much before the first of July. Icelanders generally say that July 15 is the optimum moment, for both salmon and sea trout. But the angler with a choice of dates will do better to take the later one in every possible alternative. Unlike the British Isles, there are no early and late rivers in Iceland, so that in a year when the fish are late in arriving, the angler's disappointment is apt to be as great in the west-coast rivers as it is in those of the northern section. The Big Laxa, near Husavik, has consistently produced some of the largest salmon ever caught in Iceland, and two other very productive north-coast rivers are the Hrutafjardara and the Sika. The suffix —a, pronounced *ow*, means river, and Lax means salmon (Icelandic is basically the Old Norse, or the basic German of the year 1000), hence almost every section has a Laxa, meaning simply Salmon River. The one in the north is usually known as the Laxamyri. The Snaefellsnes section, on the west coast, has three outstanding rivers, the Straumfjardara, the Haffjardara, and the Stadara, the last being exceptionally good as a sea-trout stream. Nearer to Reykjavik are the Grimsa, the Sogid, and the Bruara. All of the mentioned rivers have been fished frequently by Americans, but since there are 60 in all, it is obvious that no one man can have fished them all, nor does the mere naming of them mean that anybody can fish them. The best rivers are on the north, northeast, and west coasts. They are rugged streams, flowing fast and deep. There are a few good rivers in the south, and these are shallow and easily waded. The Laxamyri River probably rates as the best salmon river in Iceland. The fish average 18 pounds, and expert anglers have taken as many as 20–30 such salmon in a single day. Many other rivers provide excellent salmon fishing, and it is a general rule that in large streams the fish range 12–18 pounds; in the smaller ones, 5–7 pounds.

Increasingly, Icelandic rivers are held by syndicates of native owners, and it is by no means axiomatic that permission to fish them can be obtained quickly and easily. However, outdoor travel specialists in New York, Chicago, and London are making more rivers available each season, as salmon angling becomes important to Iceland's economy in the 1970's. For the angler who brings his own gear, bootfoot waders are preferable to the stockingfoot type, since the abrasive action of the omnipresent volcanic rock dust (even the roads are of volcanic rock) will quickly wear through waders at the ankle, where brogues and wading socks make a too convenient catch basin for the diamond-hard particles. The lava river beds, too, are extremely slippery, so hobnailed wading sandals, or at least a set of chains or a pair of wading grips, are a must. As for the rest in the way of stream clothes, it is important that it be both rain-resistant and windproof. A rain jacket, preferably with a hood, should be in the back pocket of whatever tackle pack, vest, or coat the angler normally wears on the stream. It is almost certain to be needed, for protection from wind if not from rain. The winds serve to keep the water temperatures almost always below 50°F., so it is especially important to be warmly clad from the waist down. Ski underwear and heavy socks are indicated, the latter of the insulated or therm-rubber variety for those who tend to be at all cold-footed.

Icelandic Airlines (Loftleidir) has at various times offered salmon fishing to Americans on a package-deal basis, providing about ten days' fishing for those interested. The airline has at such times had access to three of Iceland's best salmon rivers, plus several of the trout-teeming lakes. They can still, in all probability, given sufficient advance notice—a matter of months, that is, rather than weeks—arrange trips on an individual basis. Unless one has an Icelandic friend who owns a salmon river, it could undoubtedly cost a lot more, both in money and in time and trouble, to try to arrange an expedition on one's own. There are no railways in Iceland, and some of the more remote rivers are accessible only by a combination of plane and pack horse. There are buses to put you within reach of the rivers, but those that are within easiest reach physically are the least likely to be within reach financially, in terms of fishing rights.

In general, both food and lodging throughout the land are substantial but not de luxe, the former being more likely to please gourmands than gourmets, since Icelandic portions are of heroic Viking size, and the latter more inclined to comfort than to chic. (Two of the food specialties are smoked mutton, and ptarmigan called *rjupa*, delicious but so tiny as to make squab seem the size of turkey.) In Reykjavik, other than the Hotel Borg, which compares to a good small provincial German hotel, there are at present very few adequate tourist lodgings. Outside the city they are of the farmhouse variety, clean and friendly but strictly potluck all around. The independent angler, setting out from Reykjavik, had better have some of the explorer and pioneer in his makeup.   —A.G.

ICH *See* Diseases and Parasites
ICHTHYOLOGY The study of fishes
IDAHO Idaho is a state with an almost limitless variety of fishing water. It has 10,000-foot-high mountain lakes with unequaled scenery and remote wilderness fishing. It has tiny creeks wandering through forest meadows that challenge dry-fly-fishermen. It is the only inland state that has runs of salmon and true steelhead. And finally Idaho has huge lakes and reservoirs that annually produce some of the largest fish taken in the United States.

Three have been world records for their species. Two of them, a 32-pound Dolly Varden and a 37-pound rainbow trout, came from the famed Pend Oreille Lake in northern Idaho. Even more spectacular is the 360-pound white sturgeon taken from the Snake River in southern Idaho by Willard Cravens in 1956. This huge fish is one of the largest ever officially recorded taken by rod-and-reel from freshwater.

In the coldwaters of the state are seven kinds of trout—rainbow, cutthroat, brook, lake, brown, Dolly Varden, and golden. In addition two kinds of salmon come to the rivers of the state in annual runs. They are chinook and sockeye. Much like salmon are the anadromous rainbow trout, known as steelhead, that also return to the rivers of the Gem State. There is yet another salmon in Idaho—the small landlocked sockeye or kokanee (*which see*) in the large lakes of the state. As a result of the wide variety of terrain, Idaho has an equally large warmwater fishery, which includes largemouth bass, smallmouth bass, crappie, perch, sturgeon, bullheads, sunfish, and channel catfish.

More trout are caught in Idaho than any other fish. Eleven and a half million trout are taken each year, due partly to the state's system of fourteen full-time hatcheries, which supply trout not only of catchable size but also of smaller size for planting in large lakes and reservoirs. Other fish and their annual harvest are 2,000,000 kokanee; 4,000,000 warmwater fish; 400,000 whitefish; 60,000 steelhead; 43,000 salmon; and 1,000 sturgeon.

Idaho's general fishing season opens during the first week of June and extends until October 31. During this time fishing is permitted for all species in all the waters of the state. There are, of course, some waters that open earlier and some that close earlier, but the vast majority are open during the general season. It should be mentioned also that there are a number of fish that may be caught all year long. These include the warmwater species plus steelhead and salmon. Spawning waters for these latter fish are generally closed during the spawning time.

Starting at the northern tip of Idaho there is the Moyie River which enters Idaho from Canada above Bonners Ferry. This is an excellent trout stream especially for fly-fishing in late summer and fall. There are also a number of small lakes and streams in this area that have good cutthroat-, rainbow-, and brook-trout fishing.

Southwest of the Moyie River is the famed Priest Lake, a 23,000-acre body of water that has grown famous because of the huge lake or mackinaw trout it contains. The largest of this species caught in Priest Lake weighed 51 pounds, but many are taken each year in the 20–40-pound range. The principal method of fishing for mackinaws is deep trolling with lead-core or monel lines using a variety of plugs and spoons. Best times for these trophy trout are during May and late October and November. Other gamefish in the lake are Dolly Varden, cutthroat, and kokanee. Dolly Varden, a char often called bull trout in Idaho, run up to 25 pounds in Priest Lake.

PEND OREILLE LAKE

Only a short distance to the south is the famed Pend Oreille Lake, which has achieved wide fame for its large Kamloops trout. Kamloops are a variety of rainbow trout that grow to huge size in lakes where food fish such as kokanee exist. Deep trolling is the method used in taking these fish, and the best times are May, October, and November. Pend Oreille is also without doubt the largest producer of kokanee in Idaho. Each year hundreds of thousands of these fish are caught, not only by sportsmen but by commercial fishermen as well, and although these fish average only about a foot long, they are excellent fresh and smoked. Pend Oreille, which has a 90,000-acre surface, has good cutthroat fishing, too.

Also in the panhandle area of Idaho are Spirit, Twin, Hauser, Haden, and Coeur d'Alene lakes. All these lakes provide trout and bass fishing plus panfish, and Coeur d'Alene has kokanee as well. The Coeur d'Alene River has fine rainbow and cutthroat fishing, particularly in midsummer and fall. Another river, which delivers its water to Coeur d'Alene Lake after running almost across the narrow Idaho panhandle is the St. Joe. This is an excellent trout stream along its whole length, and boat trips on the lower stretches are especially productive.

CLEARWATER RIVER

South of this area is the huge drainage of the Clearwater River, which flows into the Snake River at Lewiston. The Clearwater represents one of the largest and most complex river drainage systems in northern Idaho. Throughout its whole length and that of its tributaries including those of the famed North Fork, the Lochsa River, and the Selway River good rainbow-trout fishing is available. However, the headwaters of the Clearwater River are remote, and access to them is by dirt road; consequently, they may be reached only after the first to the middle of July because of snow on the high-mountain roads. Steelhead fishing is outstanding in the Clearwater in the spring and fall. The annual catch has been as high as 15–20 thousand steelhead; however, the Clearwater River runs through a deep canyon that has long been coveted by Federal dam-building agencies, and it appears certain that at least one dam will be built on the Clearwater, which will threaten the steelhead run there.

SNAKE RIVER

The Snake River, where it is the Idaho-Oregon and Idaho-Washington border south of Lewiston, offers steelhead fishing and, in addition, sturgeon fishing. The river here can be reached only by boat. These trips are arranged in Lewiston. Near Lewiston also are several small, lowland lakes that are fine for late- and early-season trout fishing. They are Waha, Manns, and Blue lakes and the newly built Spring Valley Reservoir, north of Lewiston in Latah County.

SALMON RIVER

An important river of central Idaho is the rugged and beautiful Salmon River. This river, which flows into the Snake River south of Lewiston, has four main tributaries, which are the Little Salmon, the South Fork, the Middle Fork, and the East Fork. This river and all its tributaries have rainbow trout cutthroats, and Dolly Varden. The Salmon River also has excellent fishing for steelhead and chinook salmon. Steelhead may be taken in the spring before the annual runoff and in the fall before the river temperatures drop as a result of high-country snow. Salmon are primarily taken from late June through September along the main Salmon where it can be reached by car on the west side of the state and also in the accessible stretch on the eastern side of the state from the towns of Salmon to Stanley.

The Salmon River in central Idaho can be reached only by airplane, float trip, or pack trip. This is wilderness country and no roads penetrate it. Float trips are generally arranged in Salmon and North Fork, Idaho, and they terminate near Riggins. This exciting trip takes fishermen through the famous stretch known as the River of No Return. Charter flights into the main Salmon and the Middle Fork are made from McCall and the Boise area.

From the mouth of the Salmon River southward (upstream) on the Snake River is a section of river blocked by several hydroelectric dams. Of these the most important to fishermen is Brownlee Dam and its reservoir, which can be reached by driving northeast of Cambridge, Idaho. Built in the middle 50's, Brownlee Reservoir provides average to good smallmouth-bass fishing plus excellent crappie fishing at times. Most of the fishing here is done from small boats with motors.

From the point where the Snake River flows into Brownlee Reservoir on upstream past Weiser, Payette, Homedale, and Marsing to Swan Falls Dam, just east of Murphy, is a section of river that in recent years has become excellent for channel catfish. Many of these handsome catfish are taken from late spring to early fall. Fish in the 5–10-pound range are common, although one almost 20 pounds was taken near Weiser. This section of river also once had reasonably good largemouth and smallmouth fishing, but pollution has taken a heavy toll of these fish so that only fair bass fishing now exists in this stretch. The Weiser River, also once a famous salmon and steelhead river in Idaho, now has closures on both. The construction of Brownlee Dam damaged the runs of salmon and steelhead up the Snake River to the Weiser River so heavily that sport fishing for these species had to be restricted. It was in the section of the Snake River upstream from the point where State Highway 45 crosses the river that the record white sturgeon was caught. Sturgeon fishing is still good in the area and upstream as far as Glenns Ferry, although sturgeon over 6 feet long may no longer be kept.

PAYETTE RIVER

Flowing into the Snake in this section are two more rivers, the Payette and the Boise. Probably the most notable lake fishing in the Payette River drainage is Cascade Reservoir, a 24,000-acre body of water near the town of Cascade on State Highway 15. Trolling with spoons, plugs, and spinners are the primary methods of catching the rainbow trout in this reservoir. The Middle Fork of the Payette River is a beautiful mountain stream ideal for fly-fishing, and even though the trout are not large they are plentiful enough in the area up- and downstream from Boiling Hot Springs to provide interesting fishing. Good wintertime fishing for whitefish is also available on the South Fork of Payette in the area of Garden Valley. These fish are taken on small pieces of bait drifted through slow, deep pools.

BOISE RIVER

The Boise River, which flows through the city of Boise, has been stair-stepped by the construction of three dams—Lucky Peak, Arrowrock, and Anderson Ranch. At the time of the completion of each of these reservoirs, fishing was good for rainbow trout. However, both Anderson Ranch Dam Reservoir and Arrowrock Reservoir are long past their prime for fishing, although a few good trout are taken in each of them by trolling every

year. Lucky Peak, which was completed in the 1950's, still produces good catches of trout, and this lake, only a few miles from Boise, is heavily fished. Probably the most notable stream water on the Boise River is the section of the South Fork of the Boise between Anderson Ranch Dam and the backwaters of Arrowrock Reservoir. Known simply as the South Fork this section of river runs through a rugged canyon, which is known for rattlesnakes, but big rainbows come from this section of river.

Up the Snake River eastward across Idaho there are several good fishing spots for big trout. They are downstream from American Falls Reservoir, below Minidoka Dam, from Twin Falls downstream to Hagerman, and in a few spots downstream such as C. J. Strike Reservoir and the small, seepage lake near this reservoir called Crane Falls Lake.

In the central Idaho drainage of Snake is the famous Silver Creek below Hailey. This stream is famous for its large trout. Once an exceptional stream for fly-fishing, a large section is no longer limited to fly-fishing only as it once was. Big Wood River, also in the Hailey area, is good trout fishing over its entire length and usually is best in September and October. To the east the headwaters of the main branch of the Big Lost River are excellent trout fishing. Mackay Reservoir is especially favored by fishermen for trolling during the early part of the season. Magic Reservoir, north of Shoshone, is a popular rainbow-trout water that has been rehabilitated and restocked under the state's program.

ISLAND PARK AREA

As its eastern limit in Idaho, the Snake River and the area around it are a trout fisherman's paradise, particularly in the Island Park area. Henry's Lake and Island Park Reservoir are fished by trolling; however, this method of fishing may be used only during the early and late parts of the season in Henry's Lake because of the heavy growth of bottom weeds. Fly-fishermen have found that nymph-fishing, with large nymphs imitating dragonfly larvae and small nymphs imitating freshwater shrimp, is very successful for large cutthroat trout and brook trout in Henry's Lake. The north fork of the Snake River is outstanding trout fishing as well, with occasional trout up to 10–12 pounds being taken. This is an outstanding stretch of fly water after early July.

In extreme southeastern Idaho outstanding trout fishing is found in Blackfoot Reservoir and in the river above and below. There are also a number of other reservoirs in this area with fishing success varying from fair to excellent. Portions of the Bear River provide good fishing for trout, especially after midsummer. Bear Lake, which lies partly in Idaho and partly in Utah, provides native cutthroat-trout fishing and fair fishing for mackinaw trout. The Portneuf River, south of Pocatello, provides good trout fishing.

HIGH-MOUNTAIN LAKES

There is one kind of fishing in Idaho that is unlike any other. It is high-mountain lake fishing. Idaho has approximately 2,000 lakes and the vast majority of these are nestled up among the high-mountain peaks. Very few of these lakes can be reached by car. Almost all of them require either backpacking or horsepacking, but they are worth the effort. The fishing may be only moderate or even poor; occasionally it is excellent; but the trip and the alpine scenery in the wilderness country more than make up for it. Some of these lakes do produce large fish and many of them. But the vast majority, because of their altitude, provide only a short growing season for fish and a limited food supply. Because of the many lakes in the high mountains, it is impossible to name all of those that should be visited, but some areas that might be considered for a high-mountain backpack trip are the Selkirk Mountains at the northern tip of the Idaho panhandle; the Powell Area which lies mostly south of the Lochsa River and is bordered on the east by the Montana state line; the Gospel Hill Area, twenty-five miles northeast of Riggins; the Buffalo Hump Area, thirty miles southeast of Grangeville; the Burnt Knob Area located just inside the eastern edge of the Nez Percé National Forest between the Salmon and Selway rivers; the Seven Devils Area lying along Idaho's western border southwest of Riggins; the areas to the east and to the north of McCall; the Big Horn Crags Area located partly in the Salmon River Primitive Area just east of the Middle Fork of the Salmon River; the Sawtooth Wilderness Area and the White Cloud Area, which lie between the Salmon River at Stanley Basin and the upper limit of the South Fork of the Payette River; and the Copper Basin Area bordered by the jagged Pioneer Mountain Range on the west and Craters of the Moon National Monument on the east. Persons who intend to explore Idaho's high-mountain lakes should write to the Idaho Fish and Game Department, Boise, Idaho, for its free booklet, *Mountain Lakes of Idaho*, which gives brief maps of the various areas, hiking distances, elevations, the kind of fish available, and when they were stocked.

Idaho is a state with a wealth of fishing today in spite of itself. Until 1953 it had had huge runs of salmon and steelhead in many of the state's big rivers. But where there is abundance, there is frequently waste. Idaho's runs of anadromous fish have been seriously reduced by the dam builders, and more dams threaten constantly. Unless the Salmon River drainage can be kept free of dams, the great salmon and steelhead fishing Idaho fishermen have known will be a thing of the past. Pollution, too, has taken the fish from many of Idaho's fishing waters, particularly the Snake below the mouth of the Boise River. The much-dammed lower Boise River suffers from heavy pollution both from cities and towns and from industry. Complicating the problem here, almost to the point that it cannot be solved, are the lowwater conditions that occur annually from the holding of water in upstream dams for irrigation purposes. Idaho is a state with a wide variety of fishing, but this variety is narrowing rapidly.   —C.C.

ILLINOIS There are two major reasons why Illinois sport fishing does not compare favorably with that available in most other states; first, there is too little water in Illinois, and, secondly, winters are too severe. Being a plains state, Illinois has no mountains and a few hills to provide extensive underground water supplies which—elsewhere—rise as springs that become rivulets, which grow into creeks, then streams, then rivers. There are too few forested slopes for holding water and channeling it into rivers and lakes.

Illinois winters are long and hard. Consequently, the fish growing season is comparatively short. The fish-food supply is lean in many water bodies. Spawning is often curtailed, or fish spawn is destroyed, by sudden, unseasonable spring freeze-ups. An extensive winter-kill (*which see*) of fish occurs periodically when thick ice and deep snows blanket the shallow lakes. Nevertheless Illinois does provide some angling. In a particular pond on a particular day, one might claim to have enjoyed exceptional sport. The angler's reaction to the day's fishing would depend upon his likes and dislikes, his angling standards, and past experiences.

Illinois' important gamefish are rainbow and brown trout, largemouth and smallmouth black bass, northern pike, white and yellow bass, crappie, bluegill, walleye, bullheads, catfish, yellow perch, suckers, and carp.

For the serious angler, the state offers chiefly largemouth-bass fishing. Trout are stocked in poor streams, and this fishing is short-lived. The smallmouth-bass streams are few, are small, frequently muddy, and their fishing inconsistent. Northern pike are found primarily in the state's upper lakes, near the Wisconsin border. These lakes suffer heavy fisherman pressure, are highly developed, and their pike are neither large nor plentiful.

Geographically, Illinois' fishing opportunities can be quickly summarized. The lower part of Lake Michigan buffets Chicago and two northeast counties. The great Mississippi River forms its entire western boundary. There are two other major rivers, the Illinois and Rock rivers. There are a few lesser rivers, such as the Kankakee, Kishwaukee, Des Plaines, and Fox. There are many meadow-type streams, shallow and usually silted. There is a cluster of small lakes in the northeast. And, scattered throughout the state, are various small lakes and farmponds, but they are not plentiful.

Anyone fishing in Illinois will work water falling within one of the above named categories.

The overall fishing picture changed drastically with the introduction of coho and chinook salmon into Lake Michigan and various tributaries. While Illinois has no rivers emptying into Lake Michigan suitable to serve as natal streams for salmon, both coho and chinook salmon appear along the Illinois shore in early spring and provide an excellent sport fishery.

Some salmon are present in the Illinois portion of Lake Michigan year around, but in the Chicago area the fishing normally is best from late March to mid-May, with most fishing being done from breakwaters and piers or from small boats when weather permits. Salmon of 20 or more pounds may be taken at this time, but these "spring salmon" usually are immature fish commonly ranging from 2–5 pounds.

Illinois' best salmon fishing occurs from about mid-May to mid-July in the Waukegan area. In a normal season great schools of salmon appear in this area (along with numbers of lake trout, some rainbows, and some large brown trout), and limit catches of five salmon per angler daily are not uncommon. The cohos at this time will average 5–8 pounds, but much larger ones, 12–18 pounds, are boated frequently.

The Illinois Department of Conservation has endeavored to establish a "native" stock of salmon that will return when mature to spawn in "home" waters. Both coho and chinook young have been held in pens to "imprint" them with Illinois Lake Michigan water before releasing, and the program appears to have been somewhat successful. In 1972 Garry Vande Vusse caught a 20 pound, 9 ounce coho while trolling off Waukegan; in mid-November of 1972 Ron Hagen landed a 31 pound chinook in Chicago's Diversey Harbor.

The Illinois River is polluted through most of its length and has almost no fishing. Most of Rock River is either polluted or muddy, generally offering only carp, bullhead, and catfish angling.

The Kankakee River has most of the fish species indigenous to Illinois, but is best known for occasional fair walleye fishing. It also is one of the better smallmouth rivers, and catfish can be taken throughout its course. The Kishwaukee River has some smallmouth bass, but when the weather is best for this fishing the river normally is low and muddy. The Des Plaines River suffers from pollution and turbidity. The Fox is turbid and has few game-fish, but it has good white- and yellow-bass fishing during the spring spawning runs, plus consistent summer fishing for channel catfish, bullheads, and carp.

Some of the meadow streams in northcentral and northwest Illinois have modest fishing for smallmouth bass when conditions are ideal. The lakes in the northeast, called the Chain-of-Lakes, have northern pike, largemouth bass, and panfish—as well as murky water, speedboaters, and water skiers. Most other small lakes and ponds around the state are heavily fished and/or turbid.

MISSISSIPPI RIVER

The Mississippi River—at its nearest point more than one hundred miles from Chicago—is overlooked by most Illinois fishermen. A series of locks and dams convert the river into a chain of great pools. Best fishing normally is found just below the dams and in the sloughs and clear, backwater "lakes." In these broad, sleepy waters are found largemouth bass, white and yellow bass, walleye, sauger, crappie, bluegill, and catfish. Largemouth-bass fishing is best from July 15 to mid-October. Prio to July, the backwater areas are frequently flooded and murky. Sauger and walleye fishing is best in autumn. Spring fishing usually is for bluegills and large crappies. White and yellow bass, catfish, carp, and largemouth are taken through the summer.

In general, the Mississippi's major fishing area extends from East Dubuque, on the Wisconsin-Illinois line, down-river to Hamilton, Illinois. In this area are eight dams and pools. The locks, dams, and pools are numbered and identified on most state highway maps. Pool 12 runs from the Wisconsin line to the dam at Bellevue, Iowa. Pool 13 is downstream from Bellevue to the dam at Fulton; Pool 14, Fulton to Hampton; Pool 15, Hampton to Rock Island; Pool 16, Rock Island to Muscatine, Iowa; Pool 17, Muscatine to New Boston; Pool 18, New Boston to Gladstone; and Pool 19, Gladstone to Hamilton.

According to a survey by Illinois fishery biologists, best spring fishing is in Pools 12, 16, and 18. In summer, best pools are 15 and 17, followed by 14 and 18. In autumn, top fishing normally is in pools 14 and 17.

The Andalusia Islands section, off the town of Andalusia, just below Rock Island-Moline, is one of the river's most attractive largemouth fishing areas. The spindly islands split the river, providing sheltered, grass- and weed-filled bays. Surface lures are the rule. Topwater bass fishing here sometimes is exciting, always interesting.

The Mississippi has given up some exceptional fish. In 1947 an unidentified fisherman took a walleye weighing 12 pounds, 7 ounces from Pool 12. Jack Wolfe of Moline, Illinois, got a 10-pound, 1-ounce walleye from Pool 16 in 1953. In 1956, the Alton section of the river produced a 65-pound blue catfish, and in 1947 the same area gave up a flathead catfish weighing 110 pounds.

All along the Mississippi, especially in the upriver areas, are boat docks, boat-rental liveries, bait and tackle shops, public access points, restaurants, and motels.

LITTLE GRASSY LAKE

Little Grassy Lake, in the extreme southern end of the state (southwest of Marion) is Illinois' most consistent big-bass water. Largemouths weighing more than 10 pounds have been caught there. Every few years some of 8–9 pounds are taken, and 7 pounders are annual events.

The lake is man-made, much of it a jungle of underwater trees. Many fishermen have difficulty using lures in this 1,000-acre impoundment; hence nightcrawlers and live minnows account for the bulk of the catch. In skilled hands, leadhead jigs and jig-and-plastic-worm combinations can indeed be deadly.

OTHER BASS LAKES

Also in southern Illinois are Crab Orchard and Horseshoe lakes, and Lake Murphysboro. Crab Orchard and Horseshoe lakes are waterfowl refuges. Lake Murphysboro is a state-built recreational area. Crab Orchard is 6,579 acres. Horseshoe is 1,200 acres. Both Crab Orchard and Horseshoe are shallow lakes, and fishing there has a Deep South atmosphere. Many area farms raise cotton, and the lakes are studded with cypress trees, their "knees" providing good cover for bass. Each of the lakes has produced sizable largemouths, although they are best-known for their crappies, which, in spring, are abundant and large.

Of the three lakes, Murphysboro is the best bass water. It is deeper, although only 165 acres, has an excellent forage-fish population, and the fishing is carefully managed by the Illinois Conservation Department. Fishermen skilled at working deep-going lures often make surprising bass hauls at Murphysboro in May and June.

Another lake, called Devil's Kitchen, has been constructed by the federal government near Crab Orchard Lake. It was opened to public fishing in January 1962. While the early fishing did not come up to expectations, it is likely Devil's Kitchen will develop into a fine largemouth lake.

Crab Orchard Lake is just west of Marion, Horseshoe Lake is near Olive Branch. Lake Murphysboro is in Lake Murphysboro State Park a couple miles west of the town of Murphysboro. The sportsman at Carbondale will be within short driving distance of Lake Murphysboro, Devil's Kitchen, Crab Orchard, and Little Grassy Lake. Horseshoe Lake is about 60 miles south of Carbondale.

Boats can be rented at all of the lakes, but there are restrictions on the use of outboard motors.

ILLINOIS TROUT FISHING

Illinois stocks up to 35,000 trout each April, with the planting normally completed by April 15. There is no closed season on trout, no natural reproduction or carryover of fish worth noting; hence the trout "season" is officially on the day hatchery trucks prime the sluggish and silted streams.

Trout are provided by federal hatcheries. Normally they are rainbows, but brown trout are also stocked. The fish usually range 5–8 inches. Rarely is one better than 9 inches taken. There is no legal minimum size and no "fly-fishing only" streams.

Ordinarily about thirty-five streams in the northern tier of counties, and a couple of small lakes, are stocked with trout. Streams to be stocked vary from year to year. About the best of those planted annually is Apple River, within Apple River Canyon State Park, southwest of Warren. Coleta Pond, a conservation-department-controlled fishing project, receives a heavy stocking of trout. The pond is near Coleta. It is unattractive, shallow, usually murky—its barren shores crowded with anglers for several days following planting of the trout. It is a classic example of put-and-take fishing.

SMALLMOUTH-BASS STREAMS

The Kishwaukee River, in the area around Belvidere and nearby Piscasaw Creek, are among the better places to try for smallmouth bass. Smallmouths are caught in the Kankakee River around Kankakee State Park, and sometimes below a dam within the city limits of Kankakee.

Some Illinois fishermen name the DuPage River, in the vicinity of Plainfield, as one of the state's outstanding smallmouth streams. Other creeks listed by the conservation department as being smallmouth waters include Big Bureau Creek (Bureau County), Plum River (Carroll), Johnson and Elk Horn creeks (Carroll), Wabash River (Clark), and South Branch Kishwaukee River (DeKalb). A 68-acre impoundment built by the Conservation Department in the late 50's is being managed as a smallmouth fishery. Called Siloam Springs Lake and located southwest of Sterling, it has become a good smallmouth bass producer.

The Kishwaukee, Kankakee, DuPage, and other waterways are good float and wading streams. However, many Illinois landowners are sticklers regarding trespass, and a unique state law stipulates that a farmer having river frontage owns "to the center of the stream." Owning the stream bottom, a landowner can prevent fishermen from wading. Even worse, a farmer owning land on both sides of a river can charge floating anglers with trespass.

CHAIN-OF-LAKES

More fish are taken in northeastern Illinois' Chain-of-Lakes by ice fishermen in December and early January than at any other time. Speedboats, swimmers, water skiers, skin divers, and sailing enthusiasts make fair-weather fishing a near impossibility—at least for serious fishermen. Openwater Chain-of-Lakes fishermen do best in very early spring and after Labor Day, times when other recreationists are scarce.

The chain is a series of natural, glacial lakes, fed and drained by the Fox River. Some that are more removed from the main waters are clear, but most of the chain's fishing grounds are wind-swept and muddied. Excluding private lakes, the chain consists of ten major lakes, with Fox Lake being the largest. The lower end of Fox Lake is bridged, just north of the town of Fox Lake. Other

lakes in the chain include Catherine, Channel, Marie, Bluff, Grass, Nippersink, Petite, and Pistakee.

In general these are very shallow lakes, with deepest water being in parts of Fox and Pistakee where, in places, the lake bottom falls away to depths of 60 feet or more. On the average, holes 30–40 feet are considered deep in the chain.

These connected lakes have largemouth bass, northern pike, white and yellow bass, crappie, yellow perch, bluegills, bullheads, catfish, and carp. The bulk of the catch consists of assorted panfish, most of which are very small. Occasionally largemouths of six pounds are taken, but most are small. The panfish bite well early in the ice-fishing season, and even largemouth bass and bullheads are caught.

A change in the state angling laws (1958) protects northern pike during the ice-fishing season. It was learned ice fishing was, surprisingly, seriously depleting the stock of northerns. With wintertime protection, the northern fishery has since improved annually. In 1952, John A. Rahn, a Chicagoan, caught a 38-pound northern pike in the Chain-of-Lakes. Today a 10 pounder, though not uncommon, is an exceptional catch.

Fox, Nippersink, and Pistakee lakes have the best reputation among northern-pike fishermen. For largemouth bass, Grass Lake, Marie, Channel, Fox, and Pistakee are favored. Grass Lake is perhaps the most attractive fishing spot in the chain. Generally shallow, it is very clear in its northwest corner, and is weed and lily-pad filled. One part of Grass Lake has an immense bed of lotus lilies, said to be one of the last large lotus plantings. In bloom, the snow-white lotus flowers spread to diameters of 6–8 inches. Viewed from a distance on a calm day, they look like a million white bowling balls on a green velvet carpet.

Everything a fisherman needs is available at the Chain-of-Lakes. Boats and outboards may be rented, bait and food procured, tackle purchased or rented, and arrangements made for overnight accommodations.   T.McN.

IMPREGNATION (BAMBOO) A patented process whereby the finished rod blanks or joints are subjected to a prepared solution of phenolic resin. The synthetic resin in the joints is then cured with heat in thermostatically controlled ovens. The process waterproofs the rod joints, stiffens them against fatigue and setting, but does not detract from the elastic qualities so necessary when casting or playing a fish. The rod joints are also impervious to temperatures from 40° below zero to 275°F. by actual tests made. However, a fine rod cannot be made from poor material even with the use of this method. It is still necessary to use the best Tonkin cane (*which see*). —W.J.

INBOARD Within or part of a boat's hull. Inboard engines are those permanently installed inside the hull. Also toward boat's center from sides.

INBOARD-OUTBOARD A rig consisting of separate power and propulsion units hooked together to form a drive package adaptable to a variety of hulls ranging from runabouts to houseboats. The inboard-outboard plant is also known as a stern drive and outdrive. Basically the inboard-outboard consists of a gasoline, inboard, marine engine permanently mounted inside the boat and connected through the transom to an outboard-style propeller-drive unit which is detachable. The outdrive principle is available in several systems. Some manufacturers market only the drive unit; others produce marine engines expressly designed for hookup to outdrive units; others produce the complete package—engine and drive unit. Some are sold only to original equipment manufacturers; others are available to anyone for a do-it-yourself installation.

Marine engineers turned to outdrive propulsion in an effort to cancel out the disadvantages of conventional systems—inboard and outboard—while retaining their advantages. The outdrive retains all the steering maneuverability of the outboard engine, which steers with its propeller, and also offers the kick-up feature that safeguards the outboard engine when it strikes an underwater obstacle. Like the inboard, outdrive boats possess a full transom, whereas outboard engines require that the transom be cut down to accommodate the 15–20-inch drive shafts that are standard for outboard engines. On the debit side the outdrive loses the portability of the detachable outboard engine and weighs considerably more per horsepower. It also occupies space inside the cockpit normally available to the outboard boatman. Outdrive power plants are available in conventional four-cycle engines as well as two-cycle motors designed expressly for outdrive use. Some outdrive complexes include diesel power. Horsepower ranges from 40 to 310. —F.M.P.

INCHWORMS Family Geometridae Also called measuring-worms. Inchworms are the larvae of some 1,300 species of geometrid moths occurring in the United States and Canada. Although the adult moths are seldom a significant item of diet among gamefish, the familiar small green caterpillars, which are the larvae of many common species, are eagerly sought by trout, particularly in the northeastern states. Fish may become highly selective when inchworms are abundant, and excellent angling can be obtained with even the simplest imitation. Most artificials are made of bucktail hair dyed light green and tied in a wormlike shape on a No. 12 hook. The fly is most effective along brush banks and tree limbs, where the larvae fall upon the surface. —A.J.McC.

INCISORS Chisel-shaped teeth situated in the anterior or front portion of the mouth.

INCONNU Stenodus leucichthys Also called sheefish, this member of the Salmonidae departs from the usual appearance and habits of the family in having large scales, a late maturity in the female (7–12 years), a migratory habit but only to the freshwater areas in river estuaries, and a period of 3–4 years between spawning periods. It is unique in being the only predatory member of the whitefish group in North America. Migration up the rivers of Alaska and northern Canada occurs in June and July,

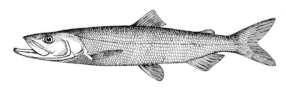

Inconnu

and spawning takes place in the fall. The inconnu travels upstream as much as 1,000 miles. It is sometimes nonmigratory, living in lakes. Egg numbers per female vary from 125,000 to 325,000, and they are broadcast, coming to lie between stones on the bottom where predatory species consume large quantities. Fish to 21 years of age

are not uncommon. It has been known to reach 55 pounds. The young consume plankton, becoming benthos feeders, and later in the second year of life become predatory. The inconnu feeds the year around except during spawning.

ANGLING VALUE

Due to their limited North American distribution, inconnu are prized as gamefish. Although occasionally taken on streamer flies, the inconnu shows a preference for ½–1-ounce wobbling spoons and spinning lures. They are fished for in the manner of trout, and while small inconnu are often very active, larger specimens of over 10 pounds are inclined to make a deep running play. Inconnu have fair food value and are utilized to a large extent by the Eskimos. *See also* Alaska   —J.R.

—A.J.McC.

INDIANA From the land of the jewel-like natural lakes of the northeastern portion of the state to the rockbed streams and stripmine pits of the southwest, and from the Tippecanoe and Kankakee rivers in the northwest to such languid streams as the Muscatatuck River and Graham Creek in the southeast, Indiana has some very good warmwater fishing.

The state's most sought gamefish is undoubtedly the largemouth bass, and angling for this species is very good throughout most of the state. But if the largemouth is most sought, the bluegill and crappie (black and white) are probably most caught; they might well be followed by white perch, white bass, smallmouth bass, channel, blue, bullhead and flathead catfish, rock bass, redear and other sunfish, various suckers, and carp.

Trout fishing in Indiana is strictly a matter of put and take, with the Department of Conservation rearing some 50,000 brook, rainbow, or brown trout each year for release in northeastern streams and lakes. Trout released each spring by the department are of the 7-inch legal size limit or larger. The department also matches the funds provided by the Northeastern Indiana Trout Association, a statewide organization of trout-fishing enthusiasts, to purchase larger trout to add interest to the sport. The open season on trout in streams runs from May through August. However, the trout season remains open year round in lakes. Most of Indiana's trout fishing will be found in lakes and streams of the northeast, but the department is now stocking Flat Rock River in Bartholomew County on an experimental basis. Trout populations, especially rainbows, have carried over well in the northern lakes and streams and 4–6 pounders are fairly common. Most of the streams are in LaGrange and Noble counties, but some Elkhart, Kosciusko, LaPorte, Steuben, St. Joseph, and Whitley county streams are included in addition to a scattering of streams and lakes in other counties.

The Kankakee River in the northwestern portion of Indiana and a good number of the smaller lakes of the northeast provide the state's best fishing, but northerns are taken occasionally from a number of other streams including the Tippecanoe River. Northern pike larger than 10 pounds are not caught very often.

Walleye and sauger are encountered less frequently. Muskellunge are taken now and then from the Little Blue River near English, from the Big Blue River near White Cloud, and less frequently from Leatherwood and Guthrie creeks in Lawrence County.

The northeastern portion of the state is dotted with hundreds of marl, muck, and other natural lakes in which some of the best fishing of the state will be found.

In the southwest, thousands of stripmine pits are attracting more anglers each year and are probably providing the best fishing in the state at this time.

Sprinkled throughout the state are such large bodies of water as Lake Lemon and Bloomington Reservoir; Geist and Morse reservoirs, which provide Indianapolis's water supply; Lake Freeman and Lake Shafer, the state's only lake formed by hydroelectric dams, on the Tippecanoe River at Monticello; Lake Maxinkuckee, Lake Manitou, Lake Wawasee, Tippecanoe Lake, Lake James, and Sylvan Lake—all in the northern portion of the state. Although these lakes are the most popular, hundreds of others provide good fishing but are little known except to anglers living nearby.

Additional fishing water is provided in many cases by State Parks, Forestry, and Fish and Game, the three landholding divisions of the Conservation Department. Yellow Wood Lake in Yellow Wood State Forest (Brown County) each spring yields some of the largest bass taken in the state. Willow Slough, a public hunting and fishing area managed by the Division of Fish and Game in Newton County, has been one of the hot spots in years past. Driftwood Lake, another Forestry property in Jackson County, has also given up big bass, bluegill, and crappie.

Winter-kill is not often a factor in Indiana although the 1962–1963 winter, coldest of the century, thinned fish populations of many of the more shallow lakes. Winters are more severe in the northern-tier counties (where a major portion of the natural lakes are situated) than they are in the south. For this reason the northern lakes do not produce as many large bass and panfish as the strip pits of the Linton, Brazil, and Terre Haute areas, but they probably produce more fish. Limit strings of bluegill in the one-pound class are not uncommon in the strip-pit region. So numerous are the strip pits that even residents of the Linton area aren't familiar with the locations of all the good fishing nearby.

INDIANA RIVERS

Although the rivers and streams of Indiana are not still in their pristine state, they do continue to provide some outstanding catches of largemouth bass, smallmouth bass, white bass (Hoosiers call them silvers), rock bass, white perch, channel catfish, blue catfish, and flathead catfish. In most cases streams and rivers are not as good for bluegill, crappie, and other panfish as are the lakes, pits, and ponds. Indiana is divided into eighteen major watersheds, each providing hundreds of miles of streams and rivers, and nearly all provide some kind of fishing. Streams not large enough for smallmouth or largemouth bass will often support good populations of a number of rock bass, suckers, and other fish.

Pollution is a threat on such rivers and streams as the Wabash, Salamonie, Kankakee, West Fork of White River, Muscatatuck, and the Big Monon Ditch. Some lakes are polluted occasionally. Much progress has been made in the fight against pollution (*which see*), however, and officials of the Indiana Stream Pollution Control Board expect to make even greater strides in the future. Municipalities of Indiana are spending some $30,000,000 per year in pollution-abatement projects.

INDIANA'S BEST

Most popular river of the state is undoubtedly the Tippecanoe River which starts at Tippecanoe Lake in Kosciusko County and flows in a southwesterly course through Marshall, Fulton, Starke, Pulaski, White, and Tippecanoe counties before meeting the Wabash River northeast of the city of Lafayette. Once known as one of the best smallmouth bass streams in the Midwest, the Tippe is a fast-moving, shallow stream that might give up anything from a trophy smallmouth to a huge catfish, with largemouth bass, white bass, rock bass, northern pike, channel, and blue catfish thrown in for good measure at a variety of points along its course.

Boat liveries are not as numerous along the Tippecanoe today as they once were, but one can still find half a dozen places to rent a boat for a float trip. Putting your own boat on the Tippe is not a great problem. The Tippecanoe can also be waded with success.

KANKAKEE RIVER

Flowing from South Bend (St. Joseph County) to the Illinois border (Newton County), the Kankakee is probably Indiana's second-best stream although it does not enjoy the popularity of some of the others. Aside from the fact that the Kankakee provides the state's best northern-pike and walleye fishing, the river is a good producer of smallmouth bass, largemouth bass, channel, blue, and flathead catfish, and the various rough fish.

ST. JOSEPH RIVER

The St. Joseph River flows into Indiana from Michigan through Elkhart and St. Joseph counties before returning to the Wolverine State near South Bend. This shallow, swift stream is known primarily as smallmouth-bass water but also yields largemouth bass, catfish, suckers, and other rough fish.

WABASH RIVER

The Wabash River, Indiana's longest, is underrated by many anglers. Starting in Ohio, the Wabash is first available to Hoosiers in Jay County. From there the Wabash flows westward to Logansport, southwesterly to the town of Covington in Warren County, and then down the western side of the state to its southernmost tip.

The Wabash runs muddy to murky through most of its course and is polluted at several points, but it still gives up good catches of largemouth bass, white perch, crappie, and some real monster flathead catfish. Channel catfish and blue catfish are also taken in good numbers.

WHITE RIVER'S WEST FORK

Starting in Randolph County near the Ohio border, White River's West Fork flows westward to Noblesville before taking a southwesterly course through Indianapolis and downstate to the city of Washington (Daviess County) where it is joined by its east fork.

White River's West Fork is another underrated sport fishery even though it is probably the state's most polluted stream. The West Fork has much to offer, especially when one considers the habitat, for it has deepwater, riffles running over gravelbars, and is lined by trees throughout its course. Between Noblesville and the north side of Indianapolis the West Fork provides good smallmouth and largemouth fishing in the early spring and late fall. Channel and blue catfish and crappie are also taken in good numbers. South of Indianapolis the West Fork provides little fishing before it reaches the town of Spencer in Owens County.

WHITE RIVER'S EAST FORK

Originating at the confluence of Driftwood River, Big Blue River, and Flat Rock River in Bartholomew County, White River's East Fork winds its way through Jackson, Lawrence, and Martin counties before meeting its sister fork in Daviess County and running on to the Wabash.

In contrast to the West Fork, the East Fork of White River is not heavily polluted although some canning-industry wastes find their way into the river. The East Fork provides good fishing for smallmouth bass, largemouth bass, white perch, crappie, channel, blue and flathead catfish, and suckers. Sturgeon are taken now and then from both forks of White River.

The East Fork is most famous for its white-perch runs in the spring, but many Hoosier anglers like its channel cat fishing. White perch congregate below Williams Dam near Bedford and Rockford Dam near Seymour during the month of May. During the remainder of the warm months white perch are taken throughout the course of the river.

MUSCATATUCK RIVER

West (Vernon) Fork of the Muscatatuck, and Graham Creek, also known as the East Fork, originate in Ripley County, but dip through Jennings, Jackson, Washington, and Scott counties before joining White River's East Fork near Sparksville.

East Fork of the Muscatatuck has suffered heavily from industrial pollution in the past at a point west of Austin, but upper portions of this fork and the West Fork provide excellent largemouth-bass fishing in addition to some smallmouth. Both forks of the Muscatatuck also provide good white-perch fishing, plenty of blue, channel, and flathead catfish, crappie, suckers, and other rough fish.

OTHER MAJOR RIVERS

Less known throughout the state but major rivers are the Eel River, Salamonie River, and Mississinewa River, all tributaries of the Wabash; the Patoka River in the southwest; the Whitewater River of the eastern portion of the state; Big and Little Blue rivers of the south. At various points any one of these rivers could provide good largemouth bass and catfish fishing, and some produce smallmouth.

INDIANA'S SMALL STREAMS

While the major rivers listed above absorb a good part of the stream-fishing pressure in Indiana, the smart Hoosier angler has another source of fishing—the small streams. With the great network of rivers and hundreds of lakes, pits, and ponds to choose from, many of the small streams go begging for anglers when they are loaded with smallmouth bass, largemouth bass, and rock bass. Some produce good strings of channel catfish, and almost all are ideal sucker fishing water. Such unheralded streams as Sugar Creek in Montgomery County, Raccoon Creek in Parke County, Deer Creek in Carroll County, Big

Brandywine in Shelby and Hancock counties, and dozens of others provide excellent sport.

Fishing the smaller streams is not an easy task, for one must walk the banks or wade rather than float in most cases. Some of the smaller streams are not open along their entire course because Indiana law provides that landowners own the bottom of the stream to its center—all of the stream bottom if they own land on both sides. Hoosier landowners are much more cooperative with anglers than they are with hunters, though, so the trespass problem is not so great as it could be. Probably the best way for visitors in Indiana to locate a place to fish on the smaller streams is to purchase topographical maps produced by the Conservation Department's Division of Geology in cooperation with the U. S. Geological Survey.

A map describing the various quadrangles to help potential users of the service in ordering can be obtained by writing the Division of Water Resources, Indiana Department of Conservation, Indianapolis, Indiana. The maps include such features as houses, contours, bench marks, and unimproved roads that could hardly be called more than wagon trails. Contour maps at five-foot intervals are also available in several sizes on many of the most popular lakes.

BORDER WATERS

Lake Michigan forms the boundary of Indiana in Lake, Porter, and a portion of LaPorte counties, and the Ohio River forms the boundary between Indiana and Ohio in the southeastern portion of the state and between Indiana and Kentucky from east to west. Neither Lake Michigan nor the Ohio River, however, could be classed as a major fishing water of Indiana.

It is true, of course, that Lake Michigan provides good fishing in the early part of the year for yellow perch and some smelt netting. And the Ohio produces some largemouth bass and channel and flathead catfish. But both the Ohio and Lake Michigan provide more boating than fishing for Hoosiers. —B.S.

INFECTIOUS DROPSY OF CARP (IDC) *See* Diseases and Parasites

INFERIOR Below

INFERIOR MOUTH A mouth located on the lower side of the head

INSECTS Insecta or Hexapoda Of the myriad forms of animal life in our world insects far outnumber all other groups in number and in variety. Among the invertebrates—animals without backbones—there are many groups besides insects which have segmented bodies. Crayfish and scuds (erroneously called freshwater shrimp) resemble insects, but they differ in several ways, an outstanding one being that they have 5 pairs and 7 pairs of legs, respectively, instead of 3. So characteristic of insects is this feature that they are called Hexapoda, which is a Greek word that means six-footed.

The more than half a million kinds of insects are classified into large groups known as orders which in turn are broken down into families. The families are classified into genera and finally into species or specific kinds of insects.

In everyday speech we tend to use terms and names which are understood in our own neighborhood, region, or country. As we venture further afield we may find it increasingly difficult to make ourselves understood. For example, one of our most popular North American gamefishes is known, variously, as walleye, pickerel, pike perch, jack salmon, Ohio salmon, and doré. To scientists the world over, however, it is known as *Stizostedion vitreum*. Insects belonging to the scientific order Odonata may be known familiarly as dragonflies, damselflies, snakefeeders, darning needles, and horsestingers. Scientific names perform the essential function of giving a specific organism a specific name which is the same everywhere (*see* Nomenclature). Therefore, while common names will be used throughout the section on insects, an occasional scientific name will be included as an aid to the angler who may wish to turn to technical publications to learn more about what insects occur where and when.

To most people insects are first and foremost a nuisance, with possible exceptions in favor of the showier butterflies and moths, the honeybee, or, from a practical standpoint, the silkworm, or the lac insect from which shellac is prepared. The informed fisherman, however, recognizes that while some insects may be annoying or even dangerous, almost any of them that live in or blunder into water are potential food for fish. Furthermore, in the hands of the skillful angler, an accurate imitation of an insect may provide unexcelled sport.

CLASSIFICATION OF INSECTS IMPORTANT TO ANGLING

Fish eat a number of different kinds of small invertebrate animals, but insects are almost paramount in importance—particularly for the young of most of our freshwater gamefish. Of the twenty-eight orders into which insects are classified five are wholly aquatic, at least in their immature stages. Like the whales and porpoises, these insects originated as landdwellers and through the ages have evolved toward a life in water. Three more orders have some representatives with aquatic immature stages, and four of the terrestrial orders either venture out on the surface film of water or fall into the water often enough to attract the attention of both fish and fishermen. Each of these twelve orders will be listed and discussed briefly and five given extended treatment. For the remaining sixteen orders, some of whose members might occasionally be found in a fish stomach, the fisherman is referred to a standard textbook on entomology. An excellent book on aquatic insects with general coverage for all of North American and detailed information on the California species is published by the University of California and titled *Aquatic Insects of California*.

Collembola Springtails. Tiny wingless insects, usually black and less than $\frac{1}{32}$ inch in length, sometimes occurring at the edge of streams and ponds. A triggered lever is borne on the abdomen which, when released, throws the insect an inch or more through the air. A swarm of these insects is suggestive of a collection of black pepper grains engaged in violent jumping. They have been found in the stomachs of fry-size trout.

Ephemeroptera Mayflies. So important to the fisherman as to warrant a separate section. *See* Mayflies

Odonata Dragonflies and damselflies. Nearly four hundred species in the United States, ranging from less than one to more than four inches in length. Aquatic immature stages, known as nymphs, characterized by mouthparts modified into a steam-shovellike arrangement which is thrust out to capture prey and return it to the jaws for feeding. Adults with long, slender abdomens and four wings of about equal length, the wings heavily net-veined, usually transparent, sometimes marked to a varying degree with amber, orange, red, or black. Beneficial in that they prey on other insects and are sometimes fed on by fish. Nymphs of large species can capture small fish and may rarely do damage in fish hatcheries. *See* Dragonflies and Damselflies

Orthoptera Crickets, grasshoppers, cockroaches. The first two named groups of this terrestrial order are widely used as live bait and as models for artificial lures. *See* Grasshopper

Plecoptera Stoneflies. Discussed in a separate section. *See* Stoneflies

Hemiptera True bugs. This large order comprises aquatic, semiaquatic, and terrestrial species. Characterized by mouthparts modified to form a sharp, sucking beak and possession of four wings, the hind pair membranous, the fore pair partly membranous and partly horny, members of this order are of only casual interest to the angler. Representatives found in or on water include the water boatman, backswimmer, water scorpion, giant water bug (sometimes called "electric light bug" because it is readily attracted to light), and water strider. Rarely found in fish stomachs, some of the larger forms can inflict painful stings if handled. The giant waterbug can capture and devour small fish.

Megaloptera Dobsonflies, fishflies, alderflies. The immature stage, or larva, of members of this order is aquatic and is well-known to anglers under the name "hellgrammite." Mature larvae of the dobsonfly may exceed three inches in length, those of the fishfly approach two inches, while those of the alderfly rarely exceed one inch in length. The larger larvae are excellent live bait. Adults are seldom abundant enough to warrant imitation by artificial patterns, although some alderfly patterns are used successfully. *See* Alderflies, Dobsonflies

Hymenoptera Ants, bees, and wasps. Members of this terrestrial order come to grief in water often enough to have won a wide variety of artificial imitations. The formic acid secreted by ants and the stings of bees and wasps do not prevent fish from feeding on them.

Coleoptera Beetles. While this order is largely terrestrial, several families are aquatic or semiaquatic, with fully aquatic immature stages or larvae, and adult stages which, while living in water, must return to the surface film periodically to breathe atmospheric oxygen and may be capable of flight from one body of water to another. Familiar examples are the whirligig beetles (sometimes called "mellowbugs" because they give off an applescented odor when handled); marl beetles which, as their name indicates, burrow in submerged marl; water pennies, so called from the nearly circular, coinlike shape of the larvae; and predaceous diving beetles whose larvae, in the larger species, are popularly known as "water tigers" and are capable of preying on small fish. Beetles, including their larval stage, are sometimes a minor source of food for gamefish.

Trichoptera Caddisflies. An important aquatic order given separate treatment. *See* Caddisflies

Lepidoptera Butterflies and moths. This essentially terrestrial order does contain a small number of species whose larvae are aquatic in habit and which rarely occur in fish stomachs. However, some species are regionally important. Occasionally California tortoiseshell butterflies occur in countless hordes in the Sierra-Cascade Mountains of California and Oregon. At such times large numbers fall onto the surface of lakes, and trout gorge themselves on them.

Diptera True flies. This very large order (over fifteen thousand species known from North America) is chiefly terrestrial but contains a number of families whose immature stages are aquatic, such as craneflies, midges, mosquitoes, no-see-ums, blackflies, deerflies, and horseflies. All true flies typically have two wings, hence Diptera (*di* = two, *pteron* = wing), and mouthparts adapted for sucking, as in mosquitoes, or lapping, as in the common housefly. Several of the groups with aquatic immature stages are important enough to fish and fishermen to warrant separate mention by family.

Tipulidae Craneflies. Resembling mosquitoes in appearance but incapable of biting, a fortunate fact since some species have a wing spread in excess of two inches. Other common names are gallinipper and daddy longlegs. Many species have aquatic immature stages utilized by feeding fish. A few artificial patterns have been created to imitate the adults, the most successful, in some views, being tied parachute-style. *See* Craneflies

Chironomidae Nonbiting midges. Aquatic immature stages are characteristic of most of the species of this large family. Adults resemble mosquitoes in size and shape but do not bite. The long, slender aquatic larvae are usually very abundant in both streams and lakes. While small, seldom over ¾ inch in length, their abundance and availability to fish make them one of the most important single items in the diet of many gamefish. Larval color varies with the species and includes olive, green, pale cream, and bright red, larvae of the latter color being known commonly as "blood worms." Adults often emerge in enormous swarms which induce heavy surface feeding by fish. Common species are ¼–½ inch in length, requiring real skill from the angler who wishes to imitate size as well as pattern with his artificials. *See* Midge

Ceratopogonidae Biting midges. The representative best known to anglers is the well-named "no-see-um," which while very tiny (1/32 inch long), attacks in swarms with bites which feel as if one is being pricked with hot needles.

Culicidae Mosquitoes. While mosquito larvae provide some food for fish, the habits of the adult females outweigh such possible benefits and place mosquitoes unequivocally in the category of pest insects. Not only are the bites painful, but many species are capable of transmitting disease, such as malaria, yellow fever, dengue, filariasis, and equine encephalitis. To add to the angler's problems, most present-day methods of mosquito control are hazardous to fish populations inhabiting treated waters.

Simuliidae Blackflies. Other common names are buffalo gnat, humpbacked fly, and white-stockinged fly, all descriptive since most species present a humpbacked profile and many have white bands on the legs. Seldom over ⅛ inch in length, adult blackflies are persistent and insidious biters. Unlike mosquitoes, both sexes feed on blood, and while some blackflies prefer to feed on wild or domestic animals, there are many species which prefer man. The aquatic larvae often occur in large aggregations on the upstream face of large rocks in fast-flowing streams and serve as a principal constituent in the diet of young trout and other gamefish.

Rhagionidae Snipe flies. One common species, *Atherix variegata*, often attracts the attention of the angler by its egg-laying habits. A female may settle on some support crossing a stream, such as the under surface of a bridge. She drops her eggs into the water and dies. Others come to the same site and repeat the performance so that, in time, a mass of dead fly bodies as large as a football may be seen clinging to the support. The green-colored aquatic larvae are often found in fish stomachs. The adults, about half again as large as a housefly, appear much less commonly.

Tabanidae Deerflies. Many deerflies belong to the genus *Chrysops* which means "golden-eyed." The eyes and the conspicuously banded wings are the characteristics most readily seen in these aggressive and persistent tormentors of the would-be contemplative angler. As with the mosquitoes, only the females are bloodsuckers. Larvae, generally whitish in color and typical maggots in form, live in mud near the edge of quiet streams and pools. Almost never venturing into openwater, they almost never appear in fish stomachs. And, since the females deposit their eggs on objects overhanging water rather than in the water, adults are seldom taken by fish.
—J.W.L.

INSTITUTE OF MARINE SCIENCE (UNIVERSITY OF MIAMI) The Institute of Marine Science, University of Miami, was established in 1943 under the name of The Marine Laboratory. Its founder, Dr. F. G. Walton Smith, is still Director of the institute as of now. With a staff of 251 (scientific staff: 185; technical and administrative staff: 66) and over 100 graduate students currently enrolled, it is the second largest graduate school of marine science in the free world and the largest in the field of biological oceanography. The principal offices and laboratories of the institute are located on Virginia Key, near Miami, Florida.

While located geographically at about 26° N., the region surrounding the institute is, from a marine biological standpoint, in the West Indies tropical zone. This is mainly due to the proximity of the Florida Current. The northernmost living coral reefs of the extensive Florida reef tract are only a few miles from the Institute of Marine Science. The Gulf Stream is only a few minutes away by boat, and the Bahama banks are approximately fifty nautical miles due east.

The institute has its own pier and boat docks extending into Bear Cut, an inlet connecting the Atlantic Ocean to Biscayne Bay. A wide variety of typical rocky, sand, and mud bottoms are located nearby. Extensive turtle-grass flats are found within Biscayne Bay and surrounding areas, as well as beds of sponges and alcyonarians. A variety of different shorelines can be easily reached from the institute—unprotected ocean beaches, reef-protected beaches, mangrove shores (with all three species of New World mangrove trees), and typical rocky and rock-platform beaches.

Biscayne Bay and the waters surrounding the keys to the south are still relatively unpolluted and offer opportunities for extensive studies of hundreds of forms of tropical and subtropical animal and plant life. There are approximately six hundred species of marine fishes in the area surrounding the Institute of Marine Science. Excellent collecting for sailfish, dolphin, tarpon, snook, and bonefish—to name only a few—can be had within a few miles of the dock. Skin-diving opportunities are superb throughout the year, with the water temperature rarely dropping below 70°F. Much of the collecting of shallow-water plants and animals for laboratory study is done by diving, and marine biology classes make frequent field trips to nearby coral reefs. For field work the institute has a large selection of boats and ships ranging from outboard-powered skiffs to the 176-foot oceanographic research vessel "John Elliott Pillsbury."

The Institute of Marine Science, University of Miami, is divided into five major departments—the Department of Marine Science (embracing the teaching program for graduate students) and four research divisions—Physical and Biological Sciences, Fishery Sciences, Oceanographic Engineering.

There are over a hundred research projects in operation, ranging from studies of microscopic plankton to giant squid and sharks; from research on hurricanes to an effort to determine the origin and composition of the mysterious abyssal hills on the bottom of the deepsea. For example, during one twelve-month period, members of the staff published 178 scientific papers.

In the Division of Marine Biology studies have included research on the life histories and habits of pelagic fishes, such as sailfish, marlin, dolphin, and flyingfishes. Studies have been made on corals and alcyonarians, turtle grass and associated plants and animals, and on the feeding behavior and color phases of tropical reef fishes. In the latter study scientists have dived on the coral reefs at night, wearing miners' lights on their heads, and observing and photographing the activities of fishes that are rarely seen by daylight.

The institute has set up a department of "fish behavior." This department is housed in the unique marine-life Controlled Environment Building, in which such variables as salinity, temperature, light, and other factors can be controlled at will. From the laboratories of this new building—a "first" in marine science—may come answers to many questions that have always perplexed both anglers and scientists—How and why do fishes migrate? How do they find their way? What controls their feeding habits? Why do they prefer different kinds of baits at different times? What attracts and repels sharks?

The Controlled Environment Building contains 14,000 square feet of working space and is equipped with the latest equipment for studying all kinds of marine organisms from planktonic animals to whales. Special, pressurized tubular tanks forty feet long enable researchers to study marine animals under simulated great-depth conditions. Rooftop tanks provide up to six hundred gallons of saltwater a minute. Live specimens are transferred from the sea to tanks with maximum safety and a minimum of disturbance—in most cases without the necessity to take the fishes from the water.

One of the most important projects in this building has been an extensive study of shark behavior—dealing largely with the vision and hearing of sharks and their response to various stimuli. In addition to the laboratory work with sharks, studies have been made of wild sharks on the coral reefs and in the deep Atlantic. Institute researchers have found that sharks are attracted by certain low-frequency sound waves, such as the sounds produced by a wounded, struggling fish. Transducers are lowered into the water, and different sounds are played through the speakers while scientists in the water observe the reactions of sharks.

Another important program is concerned with the sounds that fishes and other marine animals produce. At Bimini, across the Gulf Stream from Miami, the institute has mounted an underwater television camera on the ocean floor at a depth of 65 feet. Three hydrophones (underwater microphones) are nearby, with another hydrophone located a mile away, at a depth of 1,200 feet. Cables connect the underwater apparatus to a monitor station on shore. Here investigators can listen to the sounds made by marine animals and actually see on the television screen the animals that make the sounds. In addition to the video monitor, the shore station contains a kinescope recorder and sound-recording and -analyzing equipment. Tape recordings are made on a twenty-four-hour basis. Underwater floodlights make night viewing possible. About forty different types of biological sounds have been recorded at the installation. The possibilities of attracting fishes into the camera's range by transmitting certain sounds into the water is being investigated.

Other University of Miami projects include long-range studies on the life history, distribution, and migration of shrimp. Researchers at the institute have succeeded in rearing from egg to adult the commercially valuable pink shrimp, which may eventually make possible the raising of shrimp in "shrimp farms" in certain coastal areas.

The Division of Physical Sciences is making studies of ocean currents, the topography and composition of the sea bottom, and many other aspects of oceanography. In 1963 the Institute's research ship "John Elliott Pillsbury" played a major part in EQUALANT, an eleven-nation international survey of the tropical Atlantic Ocean from South America to Africa. "Pillsbury" has since been used extensively in deepsea coring operations.

The Institute of Marine Science is housed in four permanent buildings and several temporary buildings on a 7½-acre site on Virginia Key, within sight of, and easy access to, the main part of Miami. A carbon-14 laboratory has been installed, as well as a cold-storage building for preserving bottom cores. Modern equipment and instrumentation includes mass spectrometers, X-ray photography equipment, electron microscopes, a photo-processing laboratory, a glass-blowing laboratory, a print shop, and a carpentry shop. A well-stocked scientific library is maintained, and a museum containing a large reference collection of West Indian flora and fauna.

Living accommodations for students and visiting investigators are available at modest rates, both in dormitories at the Institute itself and at the main campus of the University of Miami.   —W.M.S.

INTEGUMENT Outer covering, particularly the skin

INTERCARDINAL POINTS The four points midway between cardinal points of a compass—northeast, southeast, southwest, northwest

INTERNATIONAL GAME FISH ASSOCIATION The IGFA was organized in 1939 for the purpose of maintaining records and collecting information on saltwater gamefish as a potential source of scientific data. The IGFA also established a system of rules and tackle classifications which are observed by its member clubs. The association headquarters is located in Fort Lauderdale, Florida.

INTERNATIONAL OCEANOGRAPHIC FOUNDATION
The International Oceanographic Foundation was founded in 1954 by a group of scientists, anglers, and yachtsmen. A nonprofit organization, its stated aims are: To encourage the extension of human knowledge by scientific study and exploration of the oceans in all their aspects, including the study of game fishes, food fishes, ocean currents, the geology, chemistry, and physics of the sea and the sea floor.

Headquarters for the International Oceanographic Foundation are located on Virginia Key, near Miami, Florida. President of the foundation and Editor of the Foundation's magazine *Sea Frontiers*, is Dr. F. G. Walton Smith. Executive-Secretary is F. May Smith. The more than 20,000 members of the IOF come from many countries and all walks of life. They find a common bond in the enjoyment of, and interest in, the ocean and its life and lore, and in encouraging and developing scientific research and exploration of the sea. Through the foundation's publications, members exchange information about all forms of sea life as well as data on ocean currents and industrial applications of oceanography.

The IOF has two regular publications. *Sea Frontiers* is an illustrated, popular magazine dealing with work being done throughout the world in the marine sciences. Many of the world's leading scientific authorities and science writers are regular contributors. Issued five times a year, *Sea Frontiers* is written and edited for the intelligent layman, and is not highly technical in its treatment.

The other regular publication, *Sea Secrets*, contains news of members and their activities. In it the most provocative letters from foundation members are published, along with authoritative answers to questions on marine science. *Sea Secrets* is issued ten times a year and both it and *Sea Frontiers* go to all members of the IOF.

A number of educational pamphlets and booklets are issued from time to time and in most cases are distributed to members free of charge. One of these booklets, *Training and Careers in Marine Sciences*, has recently gone into its second printing of 20,000 copies.

The International Oceanographic Foundation sponsors each year a meeting of outstanding importance to anglers. The International Game Fish Conference is unique in that scientists, anglers, yachtsmen, skin divers, conservationists, and other interested persons find a common meeting ground for discussion of topics of current interest. During each conference a special Gold Medal Award is made to a nonprofessional who has made outstanding contributions to marine science.

Another function of the IOF is to provide financial aid to research institutions to support studies of gamefishes. Support is also furnished for the training of graduate students in the marine sciences.

Further information about the foundation can be obtained by addressing an inquiry to International Oceanographic Foundation, Virginia Key, Miami, Florida 33149.
—W.M.S.

IOWA Although largely an agricultural state with much of its land under cultivation, it has a rather high proportion of enthusiastic fishermen. The recreational water resources are somewhat limited compared to neighboring Minnesota and Wisconsin, but opportunities for fishing in Iowa provide considerable variety. The fishing waters can be classified as natural lakes, reservoirs, and streams, but each of these can be subdivided. While fishing of some kind is available in almost all areas of the state, the natural lakes are mostly in the northcentral and northwestern third of the state, and the major reservoirs in the southcentral and southeastern third. Only a few vacation-type areas attract fishermen from great distances. Most Iowa fishing is by persons traveling less than twenty-five miles.

As is true most places, the fishermen who catch the most fish are those who fish frequently, learn the best fishing spots, and perfect their fishing techniques, modifying them as fish distribution and feeding habits change during the season. Other fishermen will occasionally have very good luck but may spend many hours with very poor luck at other times. Some Iowa fishermen specialize in catching walleyes, smallmouth bass, or flathead catfish.

There is year-round fishing for trout and all warmwater species except smallmouth bass, walleye, sauger, and northern pike which have a closed season. There is no open season on rock sturgeon (a few of which remain in the Mississippi River). There are no size limits, except a minimum of 5 pounds for paddlefish. Daily and possession limits should be checked for all species.

Iowa lakes and most streams are usually frozen from late November through early April. Many fishermen look forward to the variety of experience provided by fishing through the ice, with or without a shelter house. Water under the ice is usually much clearer than it is during the summer, and the fish can often be watched as they approach the bait.

The state maintains public-access areas on almost all fishing waters. Most of these have boat-launching ramps, some have boat rental, minnows, and other concessions, and several have camping facilities nearby.

NATURAL LAKES

J. R. Harlan and E. B. Speaker, in their fine book on *Iowa Fish and Fishing* (on sale by the Iowa State Conservation Commission), list 52 natural lakes totaling 45,000 acres. Most of these are too shallow to maintain satisfactory fish population through most winters. Bullheads are the only species surviving in many of the lakes. Winter-kills sometimes result in very fast growth by the surviving fish.

The State Conservation Commission has dredged several of the lakes that otherwise would have frequent winter-kills, e.g., Storm Lake (Buena Vista County), North Twin Lake (Calhoun County), Little Wall Lake (Hamilton County), Black Hawk Lake (Sac County). The dredged areas are widely used for boating and other water sports as well as fishing. Fishing has been excellent in a few seasons, but many years it is not very satisfactory in these lakes. Storm Lake (3,080 acres) is a very productive lake which has produced excellent walleye fishing. In some years most of the walleyes caught have been in excess of 5 pounds.

Most of the larger lakes are in Dickinson, Emmet, and Palo Alto counties, the "Iowa Greater Lakes Region." This area is a major vacation center, and is well supplied with resorts, cabins, boating, and other recreational facilities.

Spirit Lake, the largest (5,684 acres), is a glacial lake with many sandy beaches and gravelbars. The lake has a maximum depth of 20–25 feet and is not thermally stratified in the summer. Walleyes, yellow perch, white bass, and bullheads are the principal species, but fishermen also catch many black and white crappies, northern pike, largemouth and smallmouth bass, bluegills, freshwater drum (locally sheepshead), and carp.

West Okoboji Lake (3,939 acres) is clear and remarkably deep (132 feet) for the area. No other lake within 150 miles is over 40 feet deep. Although there is a fairly large volume of deepwater cool enough for trout, this water does not contain enough dissolved oxygen for fish life in most summers, and the surface waters are simply too warm for trout. East Okoboji Lake (1,875 acres) gets the overflow water from Spirit and West Okoboji Lakes and is at the head of a series of shallow lakes draining into the Little Sioux and eventually the Missouri River. East Okoboji has excellent crappie, walleye, bullhead, and sheepshead fishing. Freshwater drum are usually caught from shore or off reefs with crayfish, shrimp, worms, minnows, or cut bait. Occasionally they are taken on wet flies, small plugs, or spinners.

Carp, buffalo, gizzard shad, sheepshead, and bullheads often become excessively abundant in these fertile shallow lakes, and the Conservation Commission annually removes large numbers with seines, traps, and electric shockers. Removal of 1,736 pounds of carp, buffalo, and sheepshead per acre in a four-year period was followed by increased gamefish populations in East Okoboji Lake. Lost Island Lake (1,260 acres), a shallow lake a few miles southeast of the Okoboji lakes, had a very great population of young bullheads in 1941 following a partial winterkill. The population was so abundant that growth was slow and almost stopped by 1946. The Conservation Commission increased carp removal from the lake and removed all limits on bullhead fishing. As a result, in three years over 700 bullheads per acre were removed by anglers, and at the end of the period the bullheads were growing and much larger. The average fisherman caught 5.2 bullheads per hour, and many were catching them at a much higher rate. Bullheads continue to be the principal fish, but walleye and northern-pike fishing is sometimes very good in Lost Island Lake.

Fishermen at Clear Lake (3,643 acres) in northcentral Iowa, catch a wide variety of fish—walleye, northern pike, yellow perch, yellow bass, white bass, largemouth and smallmouth bass, black and white crappies, channel catfish, bluegills, pumpkinseed, bullheads, carp, and occasional suckers. Yellow bass can be caught throughout the summer when walleye fishing usually falls off. In one ten-week period in the summer almost 90,000 yellow bass were caught by anglers, plus almost 50,000 bullheads, 25,000 yellow perch, 9,000 walleyes and northern pike, and about 12,000 species. This was not an unusually good fishing period, but one for which good estimates of the catch are available.

The State Conservation Commission maintains a fish hatchery at both Clear Lake and Spirit Lake, and these fish hatcheries are being expanded to serve as information centers for fishermen. Walleye fry are stocked in several lakes, and research still being continued indicates that the stocked fry contribute significantly to the walleye population and catch.

Oxbow lakes are found along the Mississippi and Missouri rivers, but are here considered with the rivers rather than the natural lakes.

RESERVOIR FISHING

Thousands of ponds ⅛–10 acres in area have been built on Iowa farms for soil and water conservation, stock watering, and other purposes. Fish have been stocked in these, usually largemouth bass and bluegills. They provide fishing, mostly to local people. Winter-kill, particularly in years when water is low, is a serious problem in many of these ponds.

Many larger reservoirs have been built as water supplies for cities and towns in southern Iowa. Most are opened to public fishing. There is only one large Army Engineer reservoir completed in Iowa, the Coralville Dam, near Iowa City, but others are under construction or being planned.

The Iowa Twenty-five Year Conservation Plan in 1933 called for the construction of artificial lakes in the southern part of the state where natural fishing waters were lacking or scarce. The plan, as it developed, provides for an artificial lake within twenty-five miles of any area without other fishing.

The reservoirs provide largemouth bass and panfish for the angler; a few also have bullheads and an occasional large flathead catfish. Most of the reservoirs are thermally stratified and are deficient in dissolved oxygen in the deeper waters in the summer months. Reservoirs in wooded valleys protected from the wind have only the top 6–8 feet of water suitable for fish in mid and late summer. Most of northcentral and northwest Iowa is too flat to be very suitable for construction of artificial lakes. It is much better suited to grow corn. Most reservoirs and farm ponds are therefore in the southern third of the state, which is much more rolling and which has a tight soil capable of holding water.

STREAM FISHING

Streams are found in all parts of Iowa, but many are very turbid and not very productive of good sport fishing. Many of the smaller streams are dry part of the year. Extensive tiling and draining of marshes has eliminated the storage of water which formerly maintained flow in the streams. Hundreds of miles of streams have been straightened, eliminating pools and riffles and creating straight ditches not conducive to fish production nor attractive for angling.

Northeastern Iowa has a section of limestone outcroppings, wooded hills, and deep valleys. In this area many springs create streams quite capable of retaining trout even in Iowa's warm summers. The rugged winters and spring floods do not permit trout to overwinter in many of the streams, but periodic stocking of catchable-sized trout from state fish hatcheries at Decorah and Back Bone State Park and from the federal fish hatchery at Manchester maintains fairly good trout fishing. Rainbow and some brown and brook trout are stocked throughout the season. The scenery, particularly in the spring and fall, is a part of the attraction the area has for the trout fisherman.

Several of the middle-sized streams in the eastern half of the state, particularly those flowing through some limestone outcroppings, are fairly good smallmouth-bass streams. The number of smallmouth-bass enthusiasts is fairly small, but they derive a great deal of sport with fly rods or spinning gear. Bass fishermen should not overlook some of the smaller tributary streams of the Maquoketa, Wapsipinicon, Iowa, and Cedar Rivers.

The Des Moines and Raccoon Rivers and the lower stretches of some other rivers can be classed primarily as catfish habitat. The real catfish fisherman is as much a specialist as the trout-fly enthusiasts. In fact, some ardent trout fishermen transplanted to central Iowa admit that channel catfishing will rank right up with trout for sport. The real specialists are those who go after flathead catfish —many running over 30 pounds.

While the catfish are the prime fish in these rivers, walleye fishing is sometimes excellent in spring or fall, and a variety of other species are taken. Carp comprise a major part of the angler's catch, poundagewise. The carp is not an easy fish to take by angling, and a successful carp fisherman must pay as much attention (perhaps more) to techniques, skills, and equipment (usually not expensive, however) as a trout fisherman.

The Iowa rivers, even though often muddy, support a great deal of fishing. One 7-mile stretch of the Des Moines River, and it was not one of the most heavily fished areas, was found to provide 10,000–13,000 man hours of fishing per mile annually. This amounts to about 400 man hours per acre which is more than many famous lakes are subjected to. The rivers are rich, and it is doubtful that the fishing pressure has seriously depleted the fish population in any Iowa river.

Iowa's eastern and western boundaries are the Mississippi and Missouri Rivers, which probably provide more fishing water than in the rest of the state. Almost every species of fish caught by anglers in the state can be taken from these rivers or their connecting backwaters and associated oxbow lakes. The Missouri River has not been very extensively fished, but development work made it much more attractive for fishing and other recreation. The upstream reservoirs have served as settling basins so that the "Big Muddy" is no longer "too thick to drink and too thin to plow." Channeling of the river for barge traffic has eliminated many of the sandbars and mudflats which discouraged pleasure boating. While straightening and deepening of the channel may not be entirely beneficial for fish production, it is creating some areas for fish concentration and angling near the wing dams. Several of the bends of the river cut off in the straightening are being saved and managed for boating, fishing, and duck hunting.

The Mississippi River along the Iowa border has been converted into a series of pools, which dams to maintain water levels and locks to permit passage of barges and other river traffic. When the first dams were put in there was some evidence of decrease in abundance of some species of fishes, including the paddlefish or spoonbill cat. Recently the paddlefish seems to be somewhat on the increase. In the Mississippi the paddlefish is rarely caught by anglers or sport fishermen. Walleyes, saugers, and northern pike are the prize gamefish in the Mississippi River north of Dubuque, Iowa, and large numbers are caught in a few areas. Largemouth bass, crappies, and other panfish are abundant in the backwaters. Catfish are *the* Mississippi River fish to fishermen along hundreds of miles of the river.

The limestone bluffs, wooded side valleys, and miles of winding side channels and flood-plain lakes to be explored by boat make the picturesque river valley at least as far south as Dubuque, a vacation and week-end recreation area which is just beginning to realize its potential.   —K.D.C.

IOWA DARTER *See* Darters

IRELAND The Emerald Isle provides one of the principal salmon fisheries in the world due to its extreme rainfall and a minimum of industrial pollution. The quality of the sport is usually modest; however, the great beauty of the countryside and the low cost of the angling are incomparable. Ireland has 15 major salmon rivers and 25 minor ones; in the latter group are streams which are fished mostly for trout or pike but in which, under suitable conditions, there is a chance of taking an occasional salmon. The best rivers are held by riparian owners, and these are rented out to local syndicates who exercise their options from year to year; or as is customary in many waters, fishing rights are issued by the day, week, or month. But there is also salmon fishing which is entirely free (except for the license) to visitors staying at various hotels.

Ireland is divided politically into two areas; northern Ireland, or Ulster, and southern Ireland, or Eire. Ulster is a part of Great Britain; Eire is independent. As far as the quality of the fishing is concerned, there is little difference between the two areas, but each country has its own regulations and licenses, and the visitor who intends to tour around should bear in mind the boundary between the two countries.

Ireland is also divided into twenty-one districts—seventeen in the south and four in the north—for the purpose of issuing licenses for fishing for salmon and sea trout. Licenses fall into two categories—those only valid in the district of issue and those valid all over the country. In this way, Ireland combines the merits of free fishing and the system of licenses, for there is revenue for the conservation and restocking of waters, without the disadvantage of anglers' having to buy a separate license for every piece of water which they wish to fish. Furthermore, during the last few years, the Emerald Isle has realized its fine potential as a country which contains almost inexhaustible supplies of good fishing, and has provided many amenities which help make the angler's visit a pleasant one.

There are two major runs of salmon in Ireland—the "spring salmon," which ascend the rivers from January until June, and the grilse (locally peal) that appear with the first rains of June and continue until October. Summer-run salmon are less common, but large fish do come into west-coast waters, such as the Ballynahinch River, and provide fishing until the last day of the season. Spring salmon weigh from 10–30 pounds, with an average of about 5. Prime spring rivers include the Boyne, Suir, Nore, Slaney, and Munster Blackwater. Some of the best summer salmon fishing is found in the large lakes which are physically part of the river systems in Kerry, Connemara, and Donegal. These lake fish are often caught by anglers casting small wet flies for trout, but they are more commonly taken by trolling with a spoon.

Generally speaking, the prices charged for a beat on Irish salmon rivers are inexpensive. A rod license is required to fish for salmon and sea trout. In both Eire and Ulster they are available either for the district of issue or

One of the prettiest salmon rivers in Ireland, the Ballynahinch, fishes best in early summer (June) and again in late September. Stone piers strategically located along the banks are necessary, as most of the stream is too deep for wading

for the whole country. This makes for considerable saving on the part of the fisherman who does not like to limit his sphere of operation to one small area but prefers to sample the sport in other parts of the country.

Only a minority of waters are restricted to flyfishing only; so the visiting angler can be fairly sure of being able to use his favorite method. Wet fly, spinning, and worming are most popular. Many casters find the prawn also makes an admirable bait, especially if used in conjunction with a fixed-spool reel. Worming is rarely used except when other methods have failed to result in a catch, which is generally during the periods of the year when the salmon are not plentiful. Spinning with either artificial lures or natural baits like sprats is the most popular form of fishing for salmon, although fly-fishing still has a good following, especially among the older anglers. Dry-fly fishing for salmon is almost nonexistent and invariably shows poor results.

SEA TROUT

Sea trout are found in almost every small to medium-sized salmon river, and the estuaries of the very long ones, like the Shannon. The majority of Irish sea trout return to the rivers the year after they enter the sea, so that the average weight of the fish is inclined to be low, despite the presence of an occasional large fish. But the Irish sea trout can rival fish from any other part of the British Isles in sporting qualities. A salmon license is required for sea trout, the one license doing for both species. Apart

from this, there may be a local charge for fishing, although there are many rivers and "loughs" where good fishing can be had without charge. Free sea-trout fishing can also be found in saltwater and almost all estuaries, and is particularly good off the southwest coast. In lakes, sea trout will rise to the fly, and a floating pattern can often prove killing. In the rivers, they can be taken by spinning and fly-fishing. The best time for fishing is in the evening, after a flood. They are often difficult to catch when the water is low. The most productive areas for sea trout are all on the west coast, particularly the rivers and streams in Kerry, Mayo, and Donegal.

BROWN TROUT

No license is required for brown-trout fishing in southern Ireland, and only a token fee in the north is required. Since no local charge is made, the brown-trout fishing is virtually free. Of course, it is still necessary to ask permission before fishing in private waters, and in Ireland, all streams belong to somebody. Generally speaking, the browns found in the coastal regions of Cork, Kerry, Connemara, and Donegal are small, with an average of less than 1 pound. These are acid waters with a low pH value in the hill regions or peat bog drainages. The largest trout are found in the clear limestone region of the Central Plain, notably Loughs Sheelin, Derravaragh, Owel, Ennell, Carra, and Arrow. The average weight in these waters is close to 2 pounds and may be as high as 4. Fish of 8 pounds and over are caught on the fly each year. The somewhat less highly alkaline lakes—such as Corrib, Mask, Conn, and Derg—hold fish averaging 1–2 pounds, but these lakes also produce fast-growing, piscivorous brown trout taken chiefly by trolling and spinning, and growing to over 20 pounds.

For trout fishing literally any fly rod is serviceable, as even the light-tackle fancier will find streams where fine lines and tippets can be put to effective use. On the big lakes, however, winds of almost gale force are not uncommon and a 9-foot rod calibered for No. 8 weight forward line is about right; this same outfit is quite adequate for Irish salmon fishing. Ideally you should bring along two outfits: a 7- or 7½-foot rod with No. 4 or No. 5 lines for small-stream fishing, and a 9-foot general-purpose rod. Spinning tackle with lines of 8- or 10-pound-test is suitable for casting and trolling spoons and spinners (¼–½-ounce class).

Local fly patterns are best. Ireland has many expert fly dressers, and in dealing with highly selective trout it's worthwhile to stock imitations of the naturals, particularly when they are emerging in quantities. The Green Drake (*Ephemera dancia*) is the best-known aquatic, which usually begins hatching about mid-May and lasts for a period of about five weeks on various lakes, depending on the weather. The emergence occurs earliest on Lough Derg, a bit later on Lough Corrib, and the latest on Lough Erne, so it's possible to follow the hatches. There are other naturals which bring on good rises: the Blue-Winged Olive (*Ephemerella ignita*), which appears in June and emerges mainly in the evening during warm weather in July and August. Trout may become highly selective during a BWO hatch, taking only the numph, dun, or spinner. The Iron Blue Dun (*Baetis pumilus*) is another mayfly that emerges on cold showery days early in the season, mainly in April and May. The Pale Evening Dun (*Procloen rufulum*) and the Yellow Evening Dun (*Ephemerella notata*) begin to occur in May, the former in slow-flowing rivers and the latter in fast shallow water. Various chironomids or midges also hatch in quantity, creating some angling problems; the Duck Fly (*Chironomus anthracinus*) is a large, dark chironomid that comes on in the latter part of April and early May; again the trout will at times select the winged adult in preference to the pupa or vice-versa. The pupa is taken just below the surface and the activity of the fish may create the impression of a dry-fly rise. Many caddisflies and some stoneflies are locally important, such as the Caperer (*Sericostoma personatum*), Gray Flag Sedge (*Hydropsyche* spp.), Early Brown Stonefly (*Protonemura meyeri*), and the Large Stonefly (*Perla* spp.). Terrestrial insects—such as grasshoppers, beetles, flying ants, and moths—may bring on good rises and the imitations should be fairly obvious.

In Ireland there are two races of brown trout, both noted for their fighting qualities. The first of these is the *gillaroo*, a trout unique in that it has a very hard stomach rather like the gizzard of a bird. This horny stomach is used to aid the digestion of mollusks, which are the main items in the diet of the trout. The name gillaroo is derived from two Gaelic words, *giolla* and *ruadh*, meaning "red fellow" (in reference to its reddish-pink flesh). Gillaroo occur in several lakes, but principally in Lough Melvin.

The other trout is the *dollaghan*. Found in Northern Ireland's Lough Neagh, this fish is a migratory lake-type of brown trout which runs into tributary rivers. Dolla-ghan are the same form as Austria's *Lachforelle* or the lake-type of fish found in many North and South American waters.

The best dollaghan rivers are the Ballinderry, Moyola, Maine, and Blackwater—all of which are within reasonable distance of Belfast. The Ballinderry and Moyola receive the earliest run of fish; the first flood in August usually bringing them up in large numbers. From then until closing day, September 30th, splendid sport may be enjoyed if the water is right. They have been known to run these two rivers as early as the middle of July, but such an early run is exceptional. The Maine and Blackwater do not get a real run of fish until late August or early September, but these are heavier fish and the season has an extra month to run on these rivers, closing day being October 31st.

Another unique feature of Irish trout fishing is the art of dapping. This is practiced during the mayfly hatch from the middle of May until the last week of June. Although very early English angling books do describe dapping, this primitive method has died out in that country, and is now virtually an Irish monopoly, in spite of its obvious advantages. The Irish sport of dapping consists of fishing with a live fly, very light line, and a long rod, the object being to let the fly just touch the water, without any of the line lying on the surface. This fly, which can be of any species but preferably one prevalent in the district, is supposed (in the case of the mayfly) to represent the spent female, during the evening rise. The large lake-dwelling trout rise to feed on the innumerable insects, and are caught by the dozen. This statement would tend to suggest that catching trout in this way is unsporting, while in actual fact the opposite is true. If even an infinitesimal portion of the line is lying on the water, the trout will not take the fly. If the rod is too low, the fly drowns, and the trout will not touch it. If the rod is too high, the fly looks unnatural, and the trout will ignore it. The line must be light, therefore strong-arm tactics will not do, and the fish (which can be very large indeed) must be played well. Dapping is probably one of the most exciting forms of fishing. Although it is definitely best during the mayfly hatch, it can produce good results at other times of the year, when the insect population merits its use.

COARSE FISHING

Ireland does not have the same wide range of coarse fishes as the rest of Britain has, but of those it has, it can be justly proud. European perch, *Perca fluviatilis*, bream, *Abramis brama*, and rudd, *Scardinius erythrophthalmus*, are common throughout the country. Tench, *Tinca tinca*, and carp, *Cyprinus carpio*, are found in a few waters. The roach, *Rutilus rutilus*, and the dace, *Leuciscus leuciscus*, are of limited distribution, but the former is often caught in large numbers. The only areas without good coarse fishing are those in the far west of the country, including Donegal and Kerry.

All Irish coarse fishing is overshadowed by the northern pike which is the heavyweight of Irish fishing. The record Irish pike of 53 pounds is by no means regarded as unattainable, and during every season, anglers catch fish which would shatter the records of countries less well endowed with quality fishing than Ireland. Spinning with very large copper spoons has accounted for many trophy fish, and any bait which contains red is also worth trying. For some obscure reason, however, the Irish pike do not readily take plugs, which are popular in other parts of the British Isles. Live- and dead-bait fishing can produce good catches, the difficulty here being often not the catching of the pike, but procuring the bait. Ireland is not very well endowed with choices of natural baits, but the visitor will find that the omnipresent perch and rudd are very popular with the pike, and, in cases of difficulty, pike up to about 5 pounds in weight can be used to waylay the larger specimens. Noted waters for pike are Lough Conn (where the record was caught), loughs Ree, Derg, and Allen, all on the Shannon Upper and Lower Lough system, Lough Neagh, Erne, and Lough Macrean.

As far as the local Irish anglers are concerned, the pike is the beginning and the end of the list of Irish coarse fish. They take no account of the wonderful perch, bream, and rudd which their country contains, although the visitor can be advised not to follow their example. Perch is found almost everywhere that there is pike, notable waters being Lough Key and the Carnadoe Waters on the Shannon system, and the waters of the Westmeath lakeland. Rudd are similarly scattered over the country, and are particularly popular with English anglers. Oakport Lake near Knockvicar, the Royal Canal, the Grand Canal, and Callough's Lake near Carrigallen in County Leitrim are worth a visit. As far as bream are concerned, good fish will be found in the Grand Canal, Royal Canal, Lough no Glack, near Carrickmacross in County Monaghan, parts of the Dromore River, lower Lough Ree and the river Shannon below Athlone, and Lough Forbes. Whatever species you decide to fish for, there is certainly no lack of waters.

Perhaps the most important feature of coarse fishing in Ireland is its surprisingly low cost. In the south, it is completely free, except for the odd stretch of water where there is a local fee, while in the north, the license required can be had for a very small outlay. The angling visitor should note that there is little difference between the quality of angling in the two political areas in Ireland. It should be remembered, however, that the north covers a very much smaller area, and is very much more highly populated than the south.

SALTWATER FISHING

From the sea angler's point of view, Ireland is perfect. Up until only a few years ago, the saltwater angling in Ireland was virtually unknown; nobody went there, no one thought of going there, nobody wanted to go there. Yet the seas around Ireland, particularly the west coast, are full of fish which by British angling standards are unique. In recent years, Ireland has fully realized this potential and has developed amenities round her coasts which have made her one of the foremost European sea-fishing countries.

Situated on the edge of the Continental Shelf and swept by the Gulf Stream, the west coast of Ireland especially provides a very fine selection of fishes. The gray mullet and the mackerel are common; shile pollack (known in Britain as coalfish) are found in deeper waters off the coast. As has already been mentioned, sea trout and a very occasional salmon can be caught, but a rod license is necessary if you wish to fish for these species. Saltwater fishing in Ireland does not have the same glamor as the

same sport off the coast of, say, Florida, but it can provide plenty of thrills to anyone who is prepared to try for one of the larger species. Among these, the conger, *Conger conger*, which reaches a weight of over 50 pounds, and various species in the shark family, like the porbeagle which can weigh up to 350 pounds, the blue shark, to 200 pounds, and the skate, over 200 pounds, are all worthy of the sea angler's attention.

Almost every town on the coast is an angling center. Boats are freely available for all types of fishing, although those who wish to fish for sharks should visit one of the recognized ports for this type of fishing, like Westport, Kinsale, or Achill Island. Normally, fishing tackle is available for hire in each port, providing a wonderful chance to sample other types of fishing at little cost. Fishing from the beach and rocks is popular and can be rewarding, but there is very little pier-fishing, because there are few piers.

NORTHERN IRELAND (ULSTER)

Salmon fishing in the six counties that comprise Northern Ireland (Tyrone, Fermanagh, Armagh, Down, Antrim, and Londonderry) is largely a summer and autumn activity, and the majority of the fish caught are large grilse returning to the rivers after a single winter in the sea and ranging in weight from 4–10 pounds with an average of about 7 pounds. The level of Ulster's salmon rivers is completely dependent on rainfall; during a dry summer the runs can be held up in the estuaries for weeks. If water conditions are normal, with a reasonable rainfall in July and August, there is scarcely a river that will not carry a large stock of grilse. Naturally some rivers are better than others, and those running into Lough Foyle and Lough Neagh (the largest freshwater lake in the British Isles) receive the most fish.

Ireland's rugged west coast rivers differ from the limestone trout streams of the central plains region

Salmon rivers in Northern Ireland are either completely free of restrictions, and these of modest quality, or in the hands of local clubs and associations; the latter category would include the Strule, Derg, Roe, Glendun, and the Maine River. Club waters are above average. There is also a limited mileage owned by individuals which is either strictly preserved or leased to small syndicates or visiting anglers. The most important private fisheries are the Lower Bann River (where there are no openings for the average visitor, other than those who are personal friends of syndicate members) and in the rivers of the Mourne System, which by contrast offers considerable water to the tourist.

Licenses All salmon anglers in Northern Ireland must be in possession of a license issued either by the Fisheries Conservancy Board, in whose area Lough Melvin lies, or the Foyle Fisheries Commission, which is responsible for the administration and protection of all rivers flowing into Lough Foyle. In the Foyle area the principal rivers are the Roe, the Faughan, the Mourne, and its tributaries—the Derg, the Owenkillew, the Glenelly, the Strule, and the Camowen. In the Northern Ireland Conservancy Board area the best-known rivers are the Glendun, the Bush, and the four main feeders of Lough Neagh—the Moyola, the Ballinderry, the Blackwater, and the Maine.

These licenses only entitle the holder to be in possession of a rod capable of catching salmon. They do not provide access to any stretch of river or lake, and the visitor, who intends to rely on club water for his salmon fishing, can expect to pay a small additional fee.

Lough Melvin The one notable exception to the "summer-autumn" rule is Lough Melvin in County Fermanagh. This lake is divided by the Northern Ireland-Eire border, and angling for spring salmon starts on February 1st in the smaller but productive Northern Ireland section. The village of Garrison is the popular headquarters for anglers wishing to fish Lough Melvin for salmon and brown trout, and local hotels can make all the necessary arrangements for visiting anglers. All the salmon fishing is done from boats, and a ghillie is essential for anyone who does not know the area. In February and March trolling with either a natural gold sprat or a plug is the accepted method; when the water temperature starts to rise salmon are also taken on the fly.

In addition to its spring run Lough Melvin also offers good fishing for brown trout from mid-April to October 15th, when the season closes, and for grilse, which start to run in June.

Mourne River Salmon fishing on the Mourne is available through the Abercorn Estates. Their agent can be contacted at the Baronscourt Estate Office, Omagh, County Tyrone, Northern Ireland. The Baronscourt water consists of a mile-long stretch of the Mourne, which includes the famous Sna Pool at the junction of the Mourne and the River Derg—one of the most important tributaries running into the main river.

Fishing is from both banks for most of the stretch and three rods are available to let during the entire season, which runs from July 1st, when the first grilse and salmon are due, to October 20th. Annual catches in the past have varied between 50 and 200 fish.

The Mourne is an important grilse river and the fish, given suitable water conditions, start to run in late June

and will range in weight from 5–10 pounds, with the very occasional salmon of 12 or 14 pounds. The bulk of the run comes during July and early August, but bright fish can be taken much later in the season, especially after a dry summer. By Northern Ireland standards the Mourne is a large river (the Sna Pool itself is some 50 yards wide) and is fished both from the bank and from a boat. The catchment area for the Mourne is substantial and, while the smaller tributaries drop quickly after a rain, the Mourne remains high for three or four days after a medium spate. The River Derg, which meets the Mourne at the Sna Pool, is an important salmon river in its own right. Further upstream the Mourne is joined by three other well-known rivers, the Glenelly, the Owenkillew, and the Strule.

IRONCOLOR SHINER *Notropis chalybasus* A small minnow having a lustrous, black lateral band from the snout to the caudal base and a light band above the dark band on the snout. Above the dark lateral band the fish is relatively dark, whereas below the band the fish is pale yellow. During the breeding season the males turn bright orange on the lower half. The distinguishing characteristics of this minnow are: 33 scales in the lateral line with 6 rows of scales above and 3 rows below; 16–18 scale rows anterior to the dorsal rays; a lateral line which is moderately

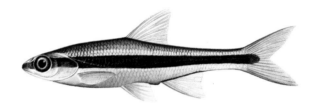

Ironcolor Shiner, 2-inch Breeding Male

to strongly decurved; 8 spines each in the dorsal and anal rays; pharyngeal teeth in two rows, usually 2, 4-4, 2; interior of mouth with much black pigment; and intense black pigment about anus, anal fin base, and caudal peduncle. The body is moderately elongate, the back slightly elevated; and the head is flat above. The head of the ironcolor shiner is contained 3.8 times in the total length of the fish. The muzzle is rather pointed and the mouth is very oblique. The lower jaw is somewhat longer than the upper jaw. The eye is large and the caudal peduncle is slender. The ironcolor shiner is widely distributed on the coastal lowlands from New Jersey to eastern Texas and north in the Mississippi lowlands to Iowa and northern Indiana.

LIFE HISTORY

This minnow prefers small lowland streams and swamps, preferably with a sand bottom. The breeding season is spread over a 5½-month period (mid-April to late September). As the breeding season approaches, the males develop tubercles on the chin and on other limited areas, and the ventral side of the fish takes on an orange appearance. This minnow is a free spawner. The male chases the female during the daylight hours during the breeding season with spawning taking place when the female stops, usually in shallow, quiet water. The eggs hatch in 54 hours at a mean temperature of 62°F. The egg sac disappears after the fifth day, and the young begin feeding on small zooplankton. The larvae swim in large aggregations until they reach a length of 12 mm (70 days), at which time they resemble the adults and join the hetergeneous aggregations of larger ironcolor shiners. This species averages 2 inches in total length.

It is a sight feeder, and even though stomach analysis shows the stomach to contain plant detritus and algae it has been demonstrated that the fish is carnivorous; the plant material being comparatively indigestible, whereas the animal material is macerated.

The ironcolor shiner is used as bait for crappie and bluegill. It also serves as forage for redfin pickerel, warmouth, and mud sunfish. —D.E.L.

ISLAND SEAPERCH *Cymatogaster gracilis* Similar to the shiner perch but more slender and confined to some of the Santa Barbara Channel Islands. *See also* Surfperch
—J.R.

ISOPOD A crustacean of the order Isopoda that includes some 4,000 species, such as water skaters, woodlice, sowbugs, pill bugs, and many parasites. They lack hard outer skeletons and stalked eyes, but do possess oval, usually flattened bodies divided into seven segments, each with a pair of broad, flat abdominal appendages.

ISTHMUS On a fish, the narrow area on the ventral surface of the throat which separates the two gill openings from each other. *See also* Anatomy

J

JACKASS FISH *See* Tarakihi

JACK MACKEREL *See* Pacific Jack Mackerel

JACKS Six genera and 21 species of jacks occur in American waters. These are the jack crevalles *Caranx* and *Carangoides,* the dorade *Gnathanodon,* the whitemouthed jacks *Uraspis,* the bluntnose jacks *Hemicaranx,* and the bumpers *Chloroscombrus.*

The jacks are distinguished by having all or many of the scales in the straight part of the lateral line modified into enlarged pointed scutes; no scutes in the curved lateral line; the body shape ranging from blunt-headed to moderately elongated; usually 8 spines in the first dorsal fin, none of them greatly elongated at any stage; no detached finlets; no furrow or papillae on the shoulder girdle; and the anal fin only slightly shorter than the second dorsal fin. *See also* Carangidae —F.H.B.

JACKKNIFE-FISH *See* Drums

JAMAICA This mountainous Caribbean island is approximately ninety miles south of the eastern end of Cuba. Jamaica is 144 miles long, and 70 miles wide between St. Ann's Bay on the north to Portland Point on the south coast. Anglers flying to Jamaica will either land at Montego Bay on the northwest coast or Kingston on the southeast coast. Both locations offer access to various kinds of fishing.

FRESHWATER FISHING

For the angler who prefers fly or spinning tackle, the mountain mullet offers a special thrill. This small gamefish may be found in most of the larger mountain streams, but two of the popular spots are located in the headwaters of the Rio Grande and the other just below the dam at Bog Walk on the Rio Cobre west of Kingston. To fish the Rio Grande, the angler can travel via chartered aircraft to Port Antonio, some 45 miles from Kingston, or he may motor through the mountains. There are hotels in Port Antonio where information is available on rafts and guides. The Rio Cobre can be reached only by car, via Spanish Town, the old capital of Jamaica. Since it is a forty-five-minute drive, the angler should make certain that he will have transportation back to Kingston as there are no lodgings near Bog Walk. The mountain mullet is usually caught on pieces of avocado pear by the local experts, but it will also strike artificial flies and small spinners. This little mullet lives in fast whitewater, and will run ½–2 pounds in weight.

In the quiet and slow reaches downstream lives another variety of mullet called the hognose. This fish is commonly taken on river shrimp as well as avocado, and will also hit a spinner. The hognose is a tough adversary and grows somewhat larger than the mountain mullet. Several hognose mullet have been taken in the 5–6 pound class.

Even further down the river approaching its mouth lives still another mullet locally called the calopeva. This is the largest of the freshwater mullet and reaches a weight in excess of 10 pounds. Like the hognose it is an excellent fighter, but, once again, the lure needed to take it is most unusual. The calopeva feeds on river moss, and as far as is known will accept nothing else. This fish does not go to sea, but it does find brackish water in which it will spawn. Having done so, it will then return to the quiet pools of freshwater farther upstream.

TARPON AND SNOOK

The two largest rivers in Jamaica are the Black and the Rio Grande. The Black River originates in the Santa Cruz mountain range and terminates at the town of Black River on the southwest coast. The river is naviga-

Jamaica's Black River is the best tarpon and snook stream along the picturesque south coast

ble from its mouth by outboard for some twenty miles upstream. It is perhaps the best river in Jamaica for tarpon up to 100 pounds, snook in the 20–30-pound class, snappers, and jack crevalle. Small boats and guides are locally available, but the angler must bring his own tackle. Accommodations can sometimes be arranged for in Black River. Mandeville, which is an hour's drive from Black River, has accommodations as well. The mouth of the Rio Grande, a few miles west of Port Antonio on the northeast coast, contains some very big snook, tarpon, snappers, and jacks. Good accommodations are available in Port Antonio. Medium to heavy bait-casting or spinning tackle is recommended for fishing the mouths of both the Rio Grande and the Black.

KINGSTON HARBOR

Kingston Harbor is still another area in which the light-tackle angler may find excellent sport. Large schools of tarpon come into the harbor in the late fall with the peak of the run showing best in November. Some tarpon are caught on fast-moving plugs and spoons, but the majority are taken on live minnows, finger mullet, or crabs while driftfishing. Kingston, the largest city in Jamaica, has several good restaurants and hotels. Guides and boats are available, and reliable fishing information may be obtained from personnel at the hotels. In addition to tarpon, jack crevalle, snook, mackerel, kingfish, and snappers may be taken in the harbor during most of the year. Spoons, wobblers, and white feathers are the best artificial lures for both trolling and casting.

BLUE-MARLIN FISHING

The undisputed king of the seas surrounding Jamaica is the blue marlin, and fish may be found there the year round. The average size is small, but they are plentiful. During one International Blue Marlin Tournament held during the first week in October off Port Antonio, 35 boats of all sizes raised 195 marlin in 5 days of fishing and brought to gaff 42. Nine of the boats hooked and caught doubleheaders, and two marlin were taken deep drifting. Most of the marlin are males, and will average 150 pounds per fish. One charter boat operating out of the Blue Water Fishing Club on the southwest coast hung 100 blue marlin in 3 months, the largest of which weighed 323 pounds and the smallest 90 pounds. A few very large female marlin are taken each year by commercial fishermen when using wire lines for kingfish. In the autumn of 1962 one blue marlin over 600 pounds was taken by a local fisherman out of a large canoe. Although sharks are numerous, few marlin are ever mutilated. Some sailfish and white marlin are caught by fishermen, but these fish are not plentiful. Dolphin, wahoo, kingfish, blackfin tuna, common bonito, oceanic bonito, mackerel, as well as rainbow runners will be found to be abundant.

There are four main areas on the coast where at least one charter boat is usually available. Before any extended marlin fishing trip is scheduled, anglers should check on the availability of equipment and boats by writing the Jamaica Tourist Board. In the hands of an experienced angler, 50-pound-test monofilament, Dacron, or linen with matching tip and a 6/0 reel would be sufficient for 90 percent of the marlin; however, most available equipment is either 24- or 39-thread and a 10/0 reel. Fresh bait is usually available and generally consists of bone-

fish, mullet, mackerel, or bonito, and occasionally squid. The four major fishing ports from which marlin fishing is initiated are Port Royal near Kingston, Port Antonio, Montego Bay, and Whitehouse. Jamaica is fortunate in having several good currents and submerged mountain tops off its coast. Many of these banks are within an hour's cruising distance of the port with the exception of Montego Bay, which has a dropoff and currents but no bank within striking distance. Off Kingston and Port Royal, the most famous is California Bank. Two hours run further south and slightly west is Bowditch Bank, larger than California, and the home of thousands of yellowfin tuna. The weather can get a bit testy off Bowditch, usually coming up rather severely in the early forenoon, and the run back to Kingston can be a miserable one quartering into a stiff sea breeze.

WHITEHOUSE

Eighty miles west of Kingston is the small village of Whitehouse where the visiting angler may find some outstanding fishing. A charter boat with experienced skipper and crew is sometimes available at the Blue Water Fishing Club a few miles east of Whitehouse. There are two large banks within an hour's run of the club, Blossom and New Bank. A few small flats occur in this area, and some bonefish can be caught by wading and casting to the schools. Good accommodations are available if arranged for in advance.

MONTEGO BAY

One hour's drive north of Whitehouse is the plush resort city of Montego Bay. Many fine hotels and good food are available here, and there are charter boats for hire. This area is more developed than Whitehouse, and therefore it's easier for the average tourist to arrange his fishing in Montego Bay. Many fine marlin have been taken from this port as well as wahoo, dolphin, small tuna, and bonito. The trade winds prevail around Jamaica; so it is wise to fish east in the morning and when the sea breeze comes up later in the day, a nice easy run with the sea may be made coming back to port.

PORT ANTONIO

Approximately one hundred miles to the east on the north coast we find the town of Port Antonio where an International Blue Marlin Tournament is held every fall. Each succeeding year has found more boats participating and more marlin being taken. This tournament is usually held in September or October. Port Antonio offers excellent accommodations and good food with charter boats stationed there the year round. There is one small bank called Henry Holmes and a larger one named Grappler Bank further offshore. Despite its small size, Henry Holmes Bank attracts countless thousands of fish—yellowfin tuna and rainbow runners gather there each year with the bulk of them congregating during the winter months. Unfortunately there are also swarms of sharks, but it is here that two opposite currents meet and a rip exists. Marlin abound in these waters, and several over 500 pounds have been taken by commercial fishermen.

There are two other outstanding fishing areas near Jamaica; one is the great Pedro Bank lying some forty miles due south of Portland Point and some sixty miles from Kingston, and Morant Cays lying some thirty miles south of Morant Point but sixty miles east southeast from Kingston. Both Morant Cays and Pedro Bank offer coral reefs above high tide and protection from high sea winds, but these expeditions should not be attempted unless a large, fast, well-equipped boat is available.   —D.P.B.

JELLYFISH (Phylum Coelenterata, Class Scyphozoa) Also known as sea jellies, these primitive organisms made up of 99 percent water are related to the Portuguese man-of-war (*which see*), corals, and sea fans. Scientifically they are called medusae. The body, or bell, is umbrella-shaped, with tentacles attached to the main part of the body. The scyphozoan jellyfish are usually large, some attaining a diameter of 7 feet. One of the commonest forms in Atlantic waters is the purple jellyfish (*Aurelia*), growing to about a foot across. It has a circular bell fringed with tentacles, and with four horseshoe-shaped gonads within the transparent disk, from which hang four "arms." It contains stinging cells which paralyze prey, but these cells are usually too weak to be felt by a human.

Jellyfish

LIFE HISTORY

Jellyfish are carnivorous and eat planktonic stages of fishes, crabs, worms, snails, and anything else they can capture. Young purple jellyfish feed more on young fishes and larger creatures, reducing their diet to small plankton with age. They contain balancing organs through which they can detect vibrations of prey. Swimming is accomplished by a pulsing of the bell, and they maintain themselves in the desired water layers in this fashion or can swim at angles if so desired. Some jellyfish have very long tentacles, like the blue or stinger jellyfish (*Cyanea*) whose tentacles may reach thirty feet and are well endowed with powerful stinging cells. *Cyanea* is often accompanied by small fishes swimming beneath it for shelter.

At spawning time, the eggs and sperm are shed from different animals. The young drift inshore to settle on the rocks and stones and can develop into the adult by a succession of growth of young forms. They resemble a trumpet, and as they grow the new ones split off and swim away, resembling the adult. Or the medusa may develop directly into the adult, from the eggs shed by the floating adult, and float about without attaching to rocks on shore. The number of jellyfish which survive depends upon food supply and weather conditions, and the number of jellyfish seen by persons along the coasts depends upon wind and wave conditions. Jellyfish are found singly or in large "schools," usually in the open ocean,

from the surface to depths of 2,000 fathoms. While most of the species swim, a few live on coral reefs or mud banks, where they spend their time resting upside down. Many are phosphorescent and glow intensely when disturbed.

All jellyfish are marine except for a hydrozoan jellyfish (closely related to corals) which inhabits freshwater and grows to nearly an inch across.   —D.dS.

JENNINGS, PRESTON J. American (1893–1962) Nineteen years after Louis Rhead had published *American Trout Stream Insects*, Preston Jennings dismissed the book as being both misguided and inept, and himself undertook to lay the foundation of an American angling entomology with *A Book of Trout Flies* (1935), which was published both as a Derrydale Press limited edition and in a trade edition, offered as a reprint, by Crown Publishers. Within a very short time the Crown reprint was almost as scarce as the Derrydale first edition, and Jennings went into the same eclipse that he had helped to impose upon Rhead. Although Charles Wetzel offered a limited entomology in his *Practical Fly Fishing* (1943), this too was of small circulation (1,395 copies), and it was not until the publication of Art Flick's *Streamside Guide to Naturals and Their Imitations* (1947) that anglers began to become generally aware of the scientific approach to imitation of American stream insects that Jennings had launched a dozen years before. Flick had fished with Jennings and along with a number of others had helped him in the preparation of *A Book of Trout Flies*, as Jennings had acknowledged in the book's preface. That still didn't keep Jennings from feeling, and for the rest of his life saying, that Flick had stolen his thunder. Actually, though Flick's *Streamside Guide* did make more of a stir than any of its three predecessors in the field of fly-fishing entomology, it, too, was something of a seven-day wonder and was soon allowed to go out of print. The same fate overtook the next brilliant contribution to this subject, Vincent Marinaro's *A Modern Dry-Fly Code* (1950), one of the most innovative of American angling books, but within the decade as hard to come by as copies of either Rhead's or Jennings' books. By 1955, when Ernest Schwiebert's *Matching the Hatch* came along it was greeted as if it were a brand-new idea, as if the trail-blazing work of Rhead, Jennings, Wetzel, and even Marinaro had never existed. Their books were, if not out of mind, at least out of sight, and though Schwiebert took pains to point out that he was the last of a long parade, he was still received as if he were first with a new field before him. He was, that is, until *Matching the Hatch* in turn became hard to find. So while Preston Jennings felt unjustly neglected, and indeed was, he didn't lack excellent company in this respect.

With the exception of Ray Bergman's *Trout*, and McClane's *Standard Fishing Encyclopedia*, all the best American angling books of this century have become scarce before they were appreciated, a melancholy fate to which Jennings was simply no exception. Belated justice to the neglected classics has come to some degree since 1970, with the issuance of reprints by Crown Publishers and Freshet Press. The former has already reprinted Jennings, Marinaro, and Flick; and the latter has announced reissuance of such undeservedly obscured works as John Atherton's *The Fly and the Fish* and Alvin R. Grove's *The Lure and the Lore of Trout Fishing.*

Jennings had the classic approach to exactness of imitation, which made him give short shrift to Rhead's attempts at impressionism, considering his flies simply badly-tied. Jennings wrote: "Mr. Rhead was an artist, and the plates in his book are finely drawn, but the flies depicted are not identified, and as Mr. Rhead named the flies himself, it is impossible to check the species, or even to determine whether the flies are actually different species or only different stages of the same species. Mr. Rhead apparently wanted to control the manufacture of what he called Nature Flies, which he designed, and for that reason no dressings of the artificial flies are given in his book. The writer has some of the Rhead flies in his possession and while they are nice to look at, they frankly do not come up to the standards set by the professional fly-tyer of the Catskill regions."

He went on to add that as of 1935, the moment at which he was writing: "Despite the drawbacks of the Rhead flies, the book *American Trout Stream Insects* has its place in the library of the fly-fisher. This is the only book which deals with the fly life of American trout streams."

Jennings had his blind spots and could be dogmatic in his insistence on them. He was convinced, for instance, that salmon do feed in fresh water, not only before they leave it as smolts for their period of growth in the ocean but also when they return to it to spawn, and he spent a great deal of time and trouble trying to prove it. He also was as convinced as E.R. Hewitt that fish could be made to ignore a leader, if you treat it properly before presenting it to them. Hewitt's treatment was silver nitrate, while Jennings applied purple Tintex dye. He maintained that a 2X leader dyed purple would take as many trout as a 5X leader that was not similarly treated. Conclusive proof was never possible, as on every occasion when the experiment was tried, the trout confused the tests by either lunging headlong at flies presented on both leaders or, on other occasions, sniffily shying away from the flies affixed to both of them. Jennings also attributed the success of the *Isonychia bicolor* nymph, when it was successful, to the fact that it represented "the nymph phase of a Royal Coachman," and when it was remonstrated that nobody had ever seen a Royal Coachman, except attached to a hook, he said that was because the fly itself emerged after dark. He was even willing to dignify this argument in print in a magazine article entitled "There IS a Royal Coachman." When taunted with the suggestion that quite possibly this fly constituted the diet of those upstream-feeding salmon, he would only smile forbearingly, as if reminding himself that Columbus, too, was the butt of many jibes.

Deluded, or inspired, as he might have been in some of his personal convictions, Jennings was resolutely disciplined in his scientific approach to the subject of stream entomology. As a result *A Book of Trout Flies* could stand, as Louis Rhead's *American Trout Stream Insects* whether rightly or wrongly did not, as the principal inspiration for all subsequent American books in this field. This has been acknowledged by Schwiebert in his introduction to the 1970 reissue of Flick's *A Book of Trout Flies*, with the added comment, apropos of Flick's work, that the "stream studies that resulted in the *Streamside Guide* had both the book and Jennings himself—who often fished with Flick in the golden years of the Schoharie and its Westkill Tavern—as their wellspring and example."

Jennings would have settled gladly for those two kind words from a peer, after 3½ decades of neglect, for they summarize all he ever wanted to be or seemed to be to other anglers—a wellspring of inspiration and an example of perseverance. —A.G.

JEWFISH *Epinephelus itajara* This is perhaps the largest of the groupers and reaches a weight of 700 pounds. It is fairly common in southern Florida and throughout the tropical American Atlantic. It is also called "spotted grouper" and in Spanish *guasa*.

The jewfish has 11 dorsal spines; 15–16 dorsal rays, usually 16; 8 anal rays, and usually 19 pectoral rays. Posterior nostril about equal to, or somewhat larger than, the anterior. Insertion of pelvic fin under, or somewhat behind, lower end of pectoral base. Posterior margin of caudal fin convex. Irregular dark bars and dark spots on sides of body.

In addition to the large size, the color pattern distinguishes this grouper from the others.

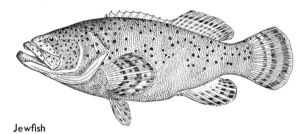

Jewfish

ANGLING VALUE

This is a shallow-water species usually found under ledges not far from shore. Usually, small individuals and often large ones may occur in estuaries and in waterways among keys. It takes live or dead bait and frequently it will also take artificial lures. The very large size it attains makes this fish a spectacular catch although it is not a good fighter. Its habit of swimming into a hole as soon as hooked presents quite a challenge to the angler. Small specimens weighing a few pounds can be taken on fly, spinning, or plug tackle. These are much better fighters than the large adults.

FOOD VALUE

Excellent·eating at any size. In the West Indies, it was salted, dried, and sold as imported salt cod during World War II. —L.R.

JIG Collectively, any artificial lure consisting of a metal head to which a skirt of bucktail, feathers, or nylon is attached. The head of a casting jig is molded to the hook, while the traditional trolling jig or "feather" is threaded on a wire leader to which the hook is fastened. Jigs are made in many sizes from 1/16 ounce to 6 ounces or more. They are designed for nearly all species of fresh- and salt-water fish. Jig heads are made slanted, ball-shaped, oval-shaped, bullet-shaped, coin-shaped, and keeled. It is the shape and weight of the head which functionally distinguish one jig from another. Being a compact mass of lead with very little air resistance, a jig casts easily and sinks readily. It rides hook up in the water and rests nose down, which provides some degree of immunity to snags.

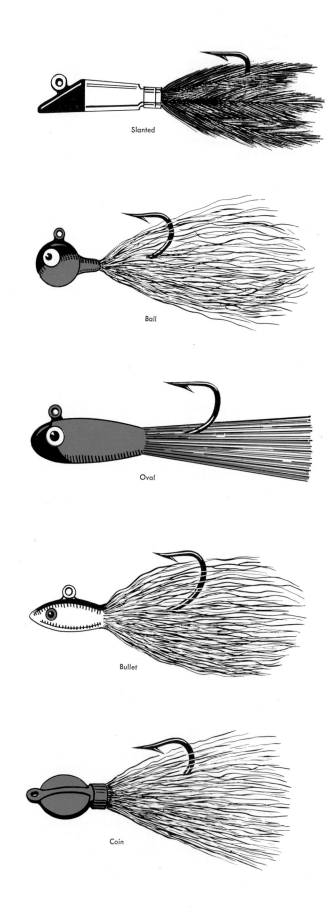

Slanted

Ball

Oval

Bullet

Coin

Jigs

Presumably, jigs can suggest baitfish when moved rapidly through the water, not in the imitative sense of a plug but because of motion and color. Primitive peoples all over the world have used crudely fashioned jigs made of bone or shell for centuries.

HOOK SHARPNESS IMPORTANT

The first, and perhaps most vital, feature of a jig is the hook. On a lure of this type, a dull point just won't penetrate. Because of its hopping and diving action a jig is often struck by the fish when the hook is at a tangent to the direction of the rod. When jigging in deepwater below a boat for instance, the hook bend instead of the point is facing the rod as the lure makes a free fall toward bottom. There is no reeling motion to start penetration such as you have when retrieving a plug through the water—a great percentage of the time. Furthermore, the jig is often grabbed by the fish when it's sitting perfectly still. Consequently the point must be needle sharp. Until 1940, all jigs were made on heavy spearpoint hooks as they were used solely for saltwater clam busters like the striped bass. This didn't make much difference as the heavy casting tackle of that era could drive a blunt nail home. But with the advent of spinning tackle and the adaptation of jigs to freshwater fishing, hook sharpness became a real factor in success. Unfortunately, many lure makers, and anglers for that matter, felt that the flat, thick spearpoint was an integral part of the jig. More so than any other type of lure, the jig requires finely honed hollowpoints on properly tempered wire. The transition to quality hooks made a tremendous difference in both angling results and dealers' sales. A perfectly sharpened hook will "bite" no matter which way the fish hits.

DOUBLE-JIG RIG

Two leadheads are sometimes more effective than a single jig. This is a very popular spinning-rod technique in big Southern reservoirs and the tailwaters when schooling fish are present. Most gamefish are accustomed to chasing schools of bait. In the case of bass, forage such as the threadfin shad, alewives, or smelt are generally attacked collectively. This is epitomized by the "school bass" phenomenon of Dixie impoundments, but it extends to large fertile lakes and rivers everywhere. Bass feed voraciously when clouds of baitfish are available, and it's common at such times to see them disgorge wads of half-digested food upon being hooked. So the appearance of two lures instead of one is not unnatural and may well be, in the case of larger bass particularly, more attractive.

Of course, there is an element of bass psychology which makes the illusion work. Bass are themselves school fish who compete greedily for food. This is evidenced by the fact that plug-fishermen occasionally catch two bass on the same bait. Anglers often observe a second bass attempting to snatch the lure from the mouth of an already hooked fish. There is also reason to believe that the antic movements of a struggling gamefish act as a stimulus because many an angler has hooked a small bass—only to have a larger one swallow it. This even occurs among nonschooling or presumably solitary species such as the northern pike, muskie, and brown trout.

The essence of double-jig technique is to retrieve slowly and deep. The jigs are cast, left to sink to the bottom, then reeled with many variations of pace, using fluttering pauses, sudden, short hops and dashes, everything that would suggest a pair of vulnerable baitfish. To the eye, jigs are stridently unnatural. In the water they are wriggling, swimming, utterly lifelike. When using two jigs, however, it's particularly important to have a strong connection as well as some rigidity to keep the lure away from the leader. The Extension Blood Knot (see Knots) works nicely. Cut the monofilament line at the point where the dropper strand is required, and when tying the knot, merely leave an extra-long length of line extended when forming the knot. The jig will stand out from the leader and seldom tangle. Naturally, if you are using two jigs of different weights, the heavier one should be tied at the end of the leader and the lighter one on the dropper. This distribution of weight is necessary for smooth casting. —A.J.McC.

JIGGING (1) A technique of angling in which an artificial lure is cast, trolled, or simply lowered in the water (as in ice fishing), then manipulated in short, rapid hops. The lure may be allowed to sink to the bottom (as in lake fishing for black bass, walleye, and panfish) or worked just under the surface (as in saltwater fishing for mackerel, bluefish, and striped bass). The fish are attracted by the lure's erratic "jigging" movement. Metal squids, spoons, ice-flies, plastic worms, and various jigs are employed. *See also* Ice Fishing, Jig

(2) Also a frequently illegal method of snagging gamefish, which is sometimes called "snatching." A bare or leaded gang hook, or a series of gang hooks, is cast or lowered among spawning of schooling species and jerked up and down in order to make contact with any part of the fish's body. Although jigging is legally practiced in some states for the sucker and carp in waters where they are undesirable, the method is considered highly unsportsmanlike.

JOHNBOAT This common-type rowboat is known by several names dependent upon the locale. It is a flat-bottomed wooden boat with a square bow and square stern and low, straight sides. Resembling little more than a box on the water, the johnboat runs 18–24 feet in length. It is extremely simple in construction but is a stable, rugged craft that can carry heavy loads in quiet, shallow water. In Arkansas it is known as an Ozark Johnboat; elsewhere it is called the Mississippi River Johnboat, the Ohio River Johnboat. New Englanders call the design a punt or sometimes simply skiff, which, technically, is a name applied to any small rowboat. The efficiency and simplicity of the johnboat design are now available in such modern materials as fiberglass, aluminum, and steel. Several companies make a specialty of producing johnboats for commercial or sport fishing, and one offers twenty different models built on the basic johnboat style. The variations include options on decks, seats, ribs, lengths, weights, and fishing wells.

The original johnboat was designed by Owen Swinney of Winona, Missouri, in 1919. His boat was made of clear pine boards 20 feet long and 18 inches wide. Such wood is rare now, and even plywood lengths must be spliced, which makes the craft heavier and less durable than the hulls of Swinney's era. The sides of his boat had a 130° flare, creating a narrow bottom but a broad beam at the top; the hull tapered fore and aft so that bow and transom were narrow—less than a foot wide at the bottom and less than two feet at the top in Swinney's first boats. Modifications of this design are still popular in the Ozarks where johnboats are paddled or poled on the big streams. A small outboard is usually mounted on the transom for running on long trips. In addition to the guide, most johnboats will seat two anglers comfortably. *See also* Float Fishing

—F.M.P.

JOHN DORY *See* American John Dory
JOHNNY DARTER *See* Darters
JOLTHEAD PORGY *Calamus bajonado* One of the larger members of this wide-ranging genus of the Sparidae. Although common to the western Atlantic, porgies of the genus *Calamus* also occur in the eastern Pacific on the mainland shores of southern North America, Central America, and northern South America, and in the Galápagos Islands. The most frequently encountered species along the coast of the Southeastern United States is the whitebone porgy (*which see*). While primarily a West Indian species, the jolthead porgy is distributed along the Atlantic seaboard as far north as Rhode Island, and in the Gulf of Mexico. It also occurs in Bermuda and as far south as Brazil.

The body color of the jolthead porgy is silvery with violet and blue overtones. Although said to be dull in color, in life it is often beautifully marked with chestnut-brown blotches; these disappear or diminish in intensity when the fish are living on light sand bottoms or when the specimen is dead. The dorsal fin usually contains 12 spines and 12 softrays; there are 3 spines and 10 softrays in the anal fin; and 50–57 scales along the lateral line.

The jolthead porgy, as well as other members of this genus, has conical teeth in the front of the mouth, rather than incisors, and molariform teeth behind. The posterior nostril is slitlike, which distinguishes it from the often confused genus *Pagrus*, the red porgy, which possesses an oval posterior nostril.

LIFE HISTORY

Little is known of the life history of the jolthead porgy. Like many other American sparids it probably spawns offshore in the fall. The fish feed primarily on mollusks and crustaceans. In the Bahamas, where the species is abundant, they are most often observed in deep (over 6 feet) tidal creeks, around blueholes, and inshore reefs. The average size is about one pound, but the jolthead reaches a length of 2 feet and a weight of 8 pounds.

FOOD VALUE

The jolthead porgy readily takes a baited hook (shrimp) when fished on the bottom but seldom strikes artificial lures. It is primarily sought as a table fish rather than a gamefish. The flesh of this porgy is excellent to eat, being firm, moist, and white. Although it has small, sharp bones, if properly fileted these can be mostly eliminated. A good method of preparation is to score (by slashing) a whole, dressed porgy and cook on charcoal. Lift the filets free from the backbone after cooking, and cover with *maître d'hôtel* butter.

See also Red Porgy, Scup, Whitebone Porgy

—D.K.C.

JONAH CRAB *Cancer borealis* A distinctive species; its elliptically shaped, roughened shell is convex and is brick red above and yellowish below. Its larger size, coloration, thicker legs, and scalloped shell distinguish it from the common rock crab, *Cancer irroratus*, of New England. Only abundant in certain areas of the northeast, it occurs between Long Island and Nova Scotia among the rocks about the low-tide level and seasonally in the intertidal zone. It is principally found in clear, open waters rather than inshore, muddy bays as is the blue crab (*which see*). It reaches 6 inches across, and, like other members of this group is delicious to eat. But because it is relatively scarce, it has never been an important commercial item. It is widely used by anglers as bait for blackfish, striped bass, porgies, and black sea bass.

—D.dS.

Jolthead Porgy, 12-inch Male, Deep Water Cay, Bahamas

JURY RIG Any temporary or makeshift rig set up to replace a lost or damaged working part or object.

K

KAHAWAI *Arripis trutta* A pelagic species, kahawai is common in the warm temperate coastal waters of Australasia. It is also known as the Australian salmon, because juvenile kahawai—called salmon trout in Australia and kopapa in New Zealand—are superficially similar in appearance to the true European or Atlantic salmon. In fact the kahawai, together with the less common ruff (*Arripis georgianus*) belong to a family related to the Scianidae (croakers, sea trout, weakfish); and adult kahawai resemble the American weakfish in general appearance and habits.

Kahawai are green above, with numerous blue, green, and bronze spots and markings, shading to a silvery white below. Small juveniles have bronze-colored vertical bands along the flank, while the slightly larger juveniles—kopapa—are conspicuously spotted dorsally. The markings generally become less distinct with age; and the green becomes darker so that large individuals may be almost uniformly blue-green above and white below.

The body is streamlined, well muscled, and broadly oval in cross-section. There are 8 spiny and 14 softrays in the dorsal fin, 3 spiny and 10 softrays in the anal fin. The pectoral fins are small and triangular; the caudal fin is deeply forked. There are several rows of very fine teeth on both jaws.

Adult kahawai average 15–25 inches in length and 3–10 pounds in weight, although regional differences in size and growth occur (*see below*). Large fish up to 32 inches and 16 pounds are sometimes reported by fishermen.

DISTRIBUTION AND ABUNDANCE

Kahawai occur in cool Australian waters (mainly along the southern coast, extending northward to Sydney and Perth), around New Zealand, and at Lord Howe, Norfolk, and Raoul Islands in the southwestern Pacific Ocean. There are probably at least two varieties or races: west Australian and east Australian are one, and New Zealand the other; the two varieties can be distinguished by the number of gillrakers.

Kahawai occur most commonly in inshore coastal waters, large schools often entering harbors and estuaries. They are a schooling, pelagic fish, and their survival is closely linked with water movements and plankton concentrations, so that they may at different times be abundant or scarce in different parts of their range.

LIFE HISTORY AND MIGRATIONS

Because of their commercial importance the two Australian subspecies have been studied for several years, and the outlines of a complex life history involving long migrations of both juveniles and adults are beginning to emerge. The eastern subspecies spawns off the southeast coast of Australia in summer (December–February), and the western subspecies off the southwest coast in autumn (April–May). Both groups of offspring apparently move to nursery grounds in southern Australia and Tasmania,

either by passively drifting as eggs and larvae or by swimming as juvenile fish. They return to their respective spawning grounds when four or five years old. The eastern fish are then 16–22 inches long and weigh 3–6 pounds; the western fish are 22–30 inches long and weigh 6–13 pounds. Although the juveniles share approximately the same southern nursery grounds, the adults of the two subspecies mix to only a limited extent. Subsequent migrations of the adults are not well known. Seasonal movements of the eastern subspecies may be quite variable, probably being influenced by fluctuations in the East Australian Current.

Almost nothing is known of the life history of the New Zealand subspecies. The spawning season varies throughout the country, but occurs mainly in late summer and autumn. There also appears to be a general movement of the larger juvenile and adult fish southward during the warm summer months.

SCHOOLING AND FEEDING

Whatever their migration patterns, kahawai are more conspicuous in summer when they form surface schools up to an acre in area. These appear to be mainly feeding concentrations, for they are usually associated with schools of small fishes (herrings, anchovies), and planktonic crustaceans. The schools are followed by large flocks of sea birds, including terns (called "kahawai birds" by New Zealand fishermen because of their association with the fish), gulls, petrels, and shags. At times the schools are unaccompanied by birds; the kahawai swim with their mouths open, feeding not on small fish but zooplankton, particularly small shrimps or "krill." The spotted juveniles and the blue-green adults school separately. Each school normally contains fish of a similar size.

Other fishes may occur with kahawai schools, the main ones being trevally (*Caranx lutescens*), yellowtail (*Seriola grandis*), and southern mackerel (*Scomber japonicus*).

Schooling kahawai, often recognizable by their circular swirling movements, may spend hours quietly moving with their prey organisms, herding them together at or near the surface and rounding them up again if they disperse. Sometimes they sink quietly from sight to reappear within a few minutes at a new locality; and sometimes they sound rapidly with much splashing, probably as a large predatory fish passes by.

Kahawai are preyed upon by larger pelagic fishes, including tuna and marlin, and because of their abundance, their suitability for trolling, and their acceptance by these fishes they are a favorite bait used by New Zealand big-game fishermen.

ANGLING VALUE

Most kahawai are taken by trolling, some by hand-line bottom-fishing, and some by surfcasting. They will accept almost any spinner or lure and a wide variety of natural baits. Often they are caught incidentally when an angler is fishing for more desirable species (tuna and yellowtail at sea, and true salmon in river mouths). Many are simply hauled in on strong tackle to provide fresh bait for other fishing activities. However, they are the finest light-tackle gamefish in New Zealand waters, and visiting American anglers have likened their fighting performance to that of tarpon. Saltwater-spinning gear is becoming popular for kahawai fishing, with light lines down to 2 pounds b.s.

Almost any lure can be used; it is usually best to try a variety, as the fish may change their preference from day to day. Kopapa are readily taken on small trout flies. Kahawai are strong, very fast swimmers, and frequently broach or "tail-walk" in an effort to throw the hook. They characteristically make a fast initial run, then zigzag or swim toward the angler in wide circles (they are noted for line-tangling), and finally make short rapid dashes in various directions when sighting the boat or nearing the shore.

COMMERCIAL VALUE

Before the main European settlement of New Zealand and the introduction of metal hooks, the Maori people living along the coast caught large quantities of kahawai for local consumption or for barter with inland tribes or with the sealers, whalers, and early settlers. These were beach-seined in nets woven from the tough leaf fiber of flax plants, or trolled from sailed or paddled canoes with flax-leaf lines and wooden hooks inlaid with the iridescent blue paua (abalone) shell. Most of the fish were sun-dried or smoked.

There are at present a few minor and seasonal kahawai fisheries (using a variety of net-fishing methods) in New Zealand. The bulk of the catch is sold as bait or processed into pet food or fertilizer; a small amount is canned for human consumption.

More significant fisheries for kahawai (Australian salmon) exist in Australia, where they are one of the most important commercial species, comprising about 5 or 10 percent of the annual finfish catch. Fishing is done with large beach-seines pulled by hand or by four-wheel-drive vehicles; either the fish are hauled in to the beach or a detachable bag is towed to a "carrier vessel"—a tuna boat or a Danish seiner seasonally engaged in the fishery— waiting offshore. Almost the entire catch is canned; the flesh is dark and rather coarse (it improves with canning) and only limited quantities are sold fresh. Fresh or frozen heads are in considerable demand as crayfish bait.

So far there is no evidence of overfishing in the Australian or New Zealand stocks. Catch fluctuations are probably due to natural variations in abundance on the main fishing grounds and are related to oceanographic conditions.   —L.J.P.

KAMCHATKA TROUT   *See under* Rainbow Trout

KANSAS   This is a state of varied terrain ranging in elevation from a few hundred feet in the eastern sections to over four thousand feet in the extreme west-central border area. The western two-thirds of the state is marked by flat, level plains interspersed by rolling prairies. The eastern third is composed of broad valleys, hilly grasslands, and, in limited areas, wooded hill country. In the extreme south-central part, the plains give way to a rugged area known as the Gyp Hills. The water drainage is separated into two distinct basins composed of rivers feeding into the Kansas River and those which feed the Arkansas River. The separation line is roughly east and west through the center of the state.

Kansas has no natural lakes of any size or depth. What few basins are present contain water only periodically during periods of above average rainfall. But what nature has not provided, man is now building in an extensive reservoir and lake program. This development has greatly improved the fishing possibilities. It would be going overboard to suggest that vast numbers of people would suddenly change their destination and decide to spend their fishing vacation in the center of the nation, but the fact is that more nonresident fishing licenses are being sold in Kansas with each successive year. The trend appears likely to continue with the impounding of a new reservoir almost a yearly feature. These range in size from 2,600 surface acres to nearly 16,000 acres. Additional reservoirs are now in various phases of construction and, when they are completed, will more than double the total water area in such impoundments. Not all of these lakes can be called top fishing waters, but all provide some fishing for the serious angler.

To complete this view of impounded waters, one should not overlook the 38 state lakes created by the Kansas Forestry, Fish and Game Commission especially for fishing. Their sizes range from 337 acres to 24 surface acres. Although not as impressive as the larger reservoirs, some smaller lakes provide excellent fishing and are free from the intrusion of water skiers and motor-boat cruisers.

Cities and county units have also constructed smaller lakes and water-supply reservoirs. The vast majority have been managed for fish production and provide angling opportunities of varying quality.

Stream and river fishing can be called very good in some areas while generally poor in others. For the most part, angling in the watercourses in the western part of the state is confined to the larger rivers. Rainfall in this section is normally too light to maintain flow in the smaller creeks and tributaries. In the eastern part of Kansas, the converse is generally true. The Flint Hills section spawns many spring-fed creeks which run clear because vast tracts of these hills have never seen a plow. In the central part of the state are many sand-bottomed creeks which normally run clear, except during times of heavy rainfall when they carry a load of silt.

In the southeastern portion of Kansas are located some unique fishing waters. Stripmining for coal has left hundreds of long, narrow pits ranging from ½ acre up to 30 acres in size and averaging around 3 acres. Many of these strip pits have been stocked and managed, and some of the better ones are now owned by the state. Others, although still under coal-company ownership, are open to the public. Add to this literally thousands of farm ponds and private lakes, and the fishing potential within the Sunflower State is greater than generally realized.

Due to its lack of mountains and the presence of high summer temperatures, Kansas has no trout fishing. However, nearly all warmwater species are found in the state. These include largemouth and spotted bass, crappie, walleyes, white bass, bluegill, channel catfish, drum, flathead catfish, and bullheads. The introduction of northern pike into Tuttle Creek Reservoir gives promise of another species to challenge the fisherman. Of course, the ever-present carp is common in the more turbid waters of rivers and lakes, and most watercourses in the eastern part of the state contain gar and buffalo.

CATFISH CAPITAL OF THE WORLD

At least two towns located on the Neosho River in southeast Kansas have proclaimed themselves as the "Catfish Capital of the World" because this river annually produces flathead catfish of up to 70 pounds, good strings of the channel catfish, and large bullheads. The Neosho also has good crappie runs at certain seasons of the year. In its upper reaches (the Flint Hills area) largemouth bass can be taken when the waters are low and clear. The Neosho River is the site of two reservoirs. One is located just above Burlington and the other to the north of Council Grove.

RIVER FISHING

Many of the better fishing rivers in Kansas have their start in the Flint Hills region. Besides the Neosho, there are the Cottonwood River, Marais des Cygnes River, Verdigris River, Fall River, Elk River, Caney River, and the Walnut River. The upper portions and feeder creeks in these watersheds are known for the spotted-bass fishing, with some largemouths thrown in for good measure. Smallmouth bass are rare in Kansas, and have been known to have been taken only in the extreme southeast part of the state, principally from Shoal Creek and Spring River.

The rivers in the western part of the state generally produce only fair numbers of catfish. There are exceptions to this, mostly below the reservoirs, where walleyes, crappie, and white bass occasionally show up on the stringers. The Solomon, Saline, and Smokey Hill rivers fall into this category. Other larger streams in central and western Kansas produce mainly catfish and carp. Notable among them are the Arkansas, Pawnee, Medicine Lodge, Ninnescah, and Chikaskia rivers and Rattlesnake Creek.

Beaver dams along many of the streams are helping to stabilize water flows. Beaver have been growing more numerous in the state during recent years, and the effect of their engineering efforts is beginning to pay off with a greater fishing potential. Although siltation is a major problem on most rivers and streams in the vastly cultivated areas, the development of conservation practices on a watershed basis is beginning to be noticed in a lessened silt load. Municipal and industrial pollution, although troublesome at times, is not the problem in Kansas that it is in some other states.

FALL RIVER RESERVOIR

This 2,600-acre lake in southeast Kansas is located on the river of the same name. It was one of the first reservoirs in the state to be stocked with white bass, and it is noted for the spring run of this species. During the spawning period in April, huge numbers of white bass (sometimes called sand bass, particularly in Oklahoma and Texas) swim upstream from the head of the reservoir and can be readily taken in the river. Specimens weighing over 4 pounds have been reported.

Largemouth bass also do relatively well in this reservoir, and channel catfish and flatheads are taken with regularity. Crappie produce lively action during the spring and fall, and two heated fishing docks provide fishing for this species during the colder months. Boats, bait, and limited food service are available.

TORONTO RESERVOIR

This reservoir is located on the Verdigris River near the town of Toronto. It has been a disappointment to some fishermen since the water has been turbid since impoundment. Should this condition be corrected, the lake should be productive of good bass, crappie, bluegill,

and channel-catfish fishing. It has also been stocked with walleyes. An excellent marina, heated fishing dock, and campground are located at Toronto Point on the east side of the reservoir.

KANOPOLIS RESERVOIR

Excellent facilities for fishermen are available at this centralized Kansas impoundment. Kanopolis Lake is best known for its large crappie and walleyes. A state-record walleye, weighing just over 10 pounds, was taken from Kanopolis, and this lake will probably produce the next record since it has been stocked with walleyes longer than any other reservoir. The crappie run in the spring attracts anglers from a wide area, and limit catches of thirty pounds are common during the peak of this activity. Other species to be taken are white bass, largemouth bass, channels, flatheads, bluegill, and drum. Its 3,550 surface acres of water are popular with water skiers during the summer months; night fishing seems most productive at this season.

LOVEWELL RESERVOIR

This three thousand acres of water is located near the northern border of Kansas, about midway. The upper end of the reservoir is characterized by shallow flats which are quite attractive to waterfowl but are also spawning beds for rough fish. Lovewell contains fair to good populations of walleyes, channel catfish, black and white bass, and bullheads. Good catches of catfish may be had near the inlet canal at the north end of the dam during the periods when there is water running into the reservoir. A café, boat rental, and bait station are located on the north shore of the lake.

KIRWIN RESERVOIR

A dam across the Solomon River southeast of Phillipsburg backs up five thousand acres of water to form this reservoir. Under the management of the U. S. Fish and Wildlife Service as a waterfowl refuge, it also provides anglers with some of the best fishing in northwest Kansas. Use of the reservoir is governed by zoning regulations— one-third next to the dam is for water sports, the next third may be entered by boats but only at reduced speeds. The upper third of the impoundment is off limits for any boat use, and anglers must fish from the shore. Largemouth black bass of up to 7 pounds keep fishermen coming back again and again to this favored water. Walleyes, large crappie, and channel catfish are also taken in good numbers at various times. The marina is located at the south end of the dam and offers boats, bait, and food.

WEBSTER RESERVOIR

This is another good northwest Kansas reservoir. Located west of Stockton, its four thousand acres of water provide good walleye and bass habitat. Webster is best-known for its good walleye catches, although most other species are present in good numbers. Minnows fished in deepwater and deeprunning plugs account for most of the success with the walleye with the accent on the live bait. Good fishermen also claim many limit strings of largemouths each year from these waters; bank-fishermen are most successful during the summer while fishing the shallows with surface plugs. A good café is in operation along with the marina and bait shop.

CEDAR BLUFF RESERVOIR

The largest body of water in the western part of the state, Cedar Bluff, is a disappointment to some fishermen. Its 6,600 acres of crystal-clear water seem to be deficient in nutrients, and the growth rate of most fish is relatively slow. The Kansas Fish and Game Commission introduced hickory shad in the hopes that they will provide forage for the walleye, black and white bass, as well as other gamefish. Continuation of the management work by the conservation agencies may, in time, produce the desired results. In the meantime, most fishermen at this reservoir will have to be content with an occasional good catch. White bass provide the bulk of the catch for most anglers. Facilities include the usual café, rental boats, and bait.

TUTTLE CREEK RESERVOIR

This is one of the largest reservoirs in Kansas. The first year for fishing this impoundment was 1963. Good populations of large crappie, channel catfish, and bullheads were present the first season with the walleye, northern pike, and largemouth bass generally too small in size and numbers to provide many fishing opportunities. Additional stockings of some species were made in the spring of 1963. Facilities at this lake are being developed and promise to be the best available in the state. The 16,000-acre lake has over 100 miles of shoreline and is located a short distance north of the city of Manhattan.

POMONA RESERVOIR

Pomona Reservoir warrants mention because of its potential as a good fishing lake. Four thousand acres of water are impounded on the upper reaches of the Marais des Cygnes River west of Ottawa and east of Lyndon. The streams which feed this lake are known as good fishing waters for bass, crappie, bluegill, and catfish. The reservoir should get off to a good start with stockings of walleyes.

STATE LAKES

It is quite easy to determine the general location of the state lakes in Kansas becuase they are named for the counties in which they are constructed. All are man-made lakes built by the Kansas Forestry, Fish and Game Commission and managed by them specifically for fish production. Many of these lakes produce good to excellent fishing while others, located in less than ideal spots, yield only an occasional fair catch. Most of the lakes are stocked with four species—largemouth black bass, crappie, bluegill, and channel catfish. Other fish species seem to make their way into most state lakes; these include bullheads, green sunfish, and, in some cases, carp.

The fact that these lakes can be drained whenever desirable is a great aid to fish management. Should they become overstocked with undesirable species, it is a small matter to open the valve in the dam and clean out the lake. This rehabilitation process is used extensively by Kansas fishery biologists to maintain good, catchable populations in the better lakes.

Rooks County State Lake Located southwest of Stockton, the 67 acres of good fishing water produce largemouth bass and bluegill in satisfactory numbers. The lake has a boat ramp, shelter house, and picnic facilities.

Pottawatomie County State Lake #2 Clearwater and a scenic, wooded shoreline mark this as one of the more desirable fishing lakes. A concession provides bait, boats, and food. Location is northeast of Manhattan.

Leavenworth County State Lake Fishing pressure is heavy at this lake because of its nearness to the population centers of Lawrence, Topeka, and Kansas City. The 175 acres of water seem to produce the best in early spring and fall. Large bass (to 6 pounds) and channel catfish are to be taken. Boats, bait, and limited food service are available.

Hamilton County State Lake This western Kansas lake is conveniently located near U. S. Highway 50 west of Syracuse. The springfed waters provide good fish habitat. Summer night-fishing with surface lures has proved to be productive.

Clark County State Lake The largest and deepest of the state lakes is located off the beaten path but is available from U. S. 54 by means of an all-weather road. Rehabilitation of the lake was accomplished in 1961.

Cowley County State Lake Located in the Flint Hills east of Arkansas City, these eighty acres of water provide good bass, crappie, and bluegill fishing. Boats may be rented, fishing tackle and food are available.

Chase County State Lake Big channel catfish and bass are available at this clear lake, located three miles west of Cottonwood Falls, amid the Flint Hills.

Bourbon County State Lake One of the most scenic lakes in the state, Bourbon Lake is found nineteen miles west of Fort Scott. This is the most rugged section of eastern Kansas, but access is dependable on all-weather roads. Facilities include boat ramps, camping areas, and bait available nearby.

Woodson County State Lake Another picturesque lake, this 179-acre impoundment is famous for large crappie and bass. A state-record black crappie, 4 pounds, 10 ounces, was caught here in 1957. Good facilities are present including café, boat dock and rental, bait house, and day-use areas.

Montgomery County State Lake This heavily used water area is found near Independence. Rowboats, sailboats, and swimmers are found in large numbers on weekends during the summer. Although motorboats may be used only for fishing purposes, as at all other state lakes, the congestion is sometimes objectionable. Best fishing will usually be found during the week in the summer time, and then mostly at night. Good facilities available.

Crawford County State Lake #2 Largemouth bass weighing up to 9 pounds have been taken from this lake, and it is a popular crappie spot for spring and fall fishing. A restaurant, heated fishing dock, boat rental, and café are all provided for the angler. This fertile lake of 150 acres is located northeast of Farlington. A federal fish hatchery is located below the dam.

Other State Lakes Other state-owned and managed fishing lakes are located in the following counties: Scott, Logan, Decatur, Nemaha, Brown, Atchison, Washington, Shawnee, Geary, Douglas, Ottawa, Jewell, Meade, Kearny, Hodgeman, Barber, Kingman, Butler, Lyon, Osage, Wilson, Neosho, McPherson, and Miami.

CITY AND COUNTY LAKES

Some of the larger city and county lakes bear individual mention. Most of these charge an extra fee for fishing. Council Grove City Lake produces some large bass up to 9 pounds and good channel catfish; the size is 434 acres. The 410-acre Lake Shawnee near Topeka has good channel-catfish, bass, and drum fishing. Lake Bluestem near El Dorado contains good fish populations in 870 acres of water. The largest, 980-acre Parsons City Lake, shows promise of being a good bass lake. —G.V.

KEDGE An old anchor design originally used by sailing vessels.

KEEL This is a boat's backbone. Running fore and aft, it supports the balance of the framework of the boat. May be made of 2 or more sections bolted together, or, in smaller boats, laminated from strips.

KEEL HOOK The keel hook makes it possible to tie flies which are virtually snagless. The hook is only snagless when tied into flies, and it may be tied into many styles, including streamer flies, wet and dry flies, bass bugs, and nymphs. The major feature of the hook is the step-shank. This feature causes the shank of the hook to act somewhat like the keel of a boat, which in turn causes the hook point to ride upward. The keel slides over sticks, rocks, and weeds. The hook point is further protected from snagging by the fly dressing. The dressing covers the point and deflects twigs and grasses, but the dressing is easily pushed aside by the strike of the fish.

The snagless feature makes it possible to fish in very difficult spots, such as log jams, weed beds, and around fallen branches. It lends itself well to deep-sinking techniques, bottom-nymphing, and deep-fly trolling. Weighted flies tied on this hook are especially effective, as they can be "crawled" along the bottom without fouling, and the action is enhanced by the weight.

Almost any standard fly pattern may be adapted to this hook, but there are a few important points of caution to be observed. First, the keel or shank portion must be wrapped with dense, tightly-wound, or weighted materials to make the keel sink. The shank must in no way be buoyed up or surrounded by the dressing, or the hook point will not ride upward. Second, the fly dressing must not impede the hooking action by being too heavy or being allowed to mat around the hook point.

KEELSON A wood member bolted or otherwise made fast to the top of a regular keel in a boat to strengthen the structure.

KEEPER RING A small wire·ring fastened to the rod butt just above the hand grasp. The keeper ring is used when the outfit is assembled and being transported from one place to another. The lure is inserted in the ring, and the line is wound tight, so that no slack hangs loose.

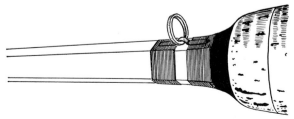

Keeper Ring

KELP PERCH *Brachyistius frenatus* A handsome surf-perch (*which see*) usually found along rocky coasts in kelp. Rosy to copper-brown overlaid with olive above, becoming copper-red below. Fins are plain to reddish. A frenum interrupts the posterior groove to the lower lip; the upper jaw is slightly the shorter; no black triangle in axilla; soft portion of dorsal slightly lower than spinous; 13–16 soft dorsal rays; 21–24 soft anal rays. Length to about 8 inches. The kelp perch is of little importance to the angler. —J.R.

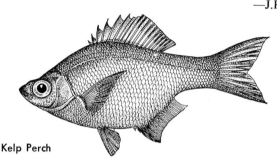

Kelp Perch

KENNEBEC SALMON A market name for the Atlantic salmon. Although the Kennebec River in Maine no longer supports a salmon fishery, this historic name is still used in the northeastern United States restaurant trade.

KENTUCKY The Blue Grass State has a wide range of topography. From the rugged highlands of the Cumberland Mountains in the east, to rolling hills and broad pasturelands in the central part of the state, and the plains of the western section with swampy lowlands bordering the Ohio and Mississippi rivers. Although coal mining has resulted in acid wastes polluting several eastern streams, and farming in the heavily cultivated central and western sections is responsible for erosion and the consequent muddying of a number of rivers, Kentucky still maintains an enviable position in the fishing available to the public. There are more than 13,000 miles of running, fishable water; there are 28 state-owned lakes, more than 50,000 farm ponds, and 10 major impoundments. Historically, Kentucky has been important in the development of American bass fishing. It was here that the first multiplying reels were perfected for bait-casting (*which see*) by the craftsmen of Frankfort, Paris, and Louisville. The state is still most famous for its bass waters, although panfish of all kinds are generally plentiful and a trout fishery has also been established in a number of tail-water reservoirs.

SMALLMOUTH BASS RIVERS

Streams of the commonwealth offer some excellent smallmouth-bass fishing. Elkhorn Creek in central Kentucky has been widely known for over a century. This is a gravel-bottomed river with big pools which can be floated or waded. The Elkhorn has always been a favorite of fly-fishermen. Slate Creek at the edge of the blue-grass region in the east-central part of the state in a limestone drainage area is another popular bronzeback (smallmouth bass) stream. From the standpoint of mileage offered, perhaps the largest is the Ohio River.

Commercial fishermen as well as sportfishermen have reaped great harvests from the Ohio, 700 miles of which form the northern and western boundary of Kentucky. This stream, although running among Kentucky, Ohio, Indiana, and Illinois, is Kentucky's own. The commonwealth owns and controls the fishing to the low-water mark on the opposite shore, and a Kentucky fishing license, or a special license designed for residents of Ohio, Indiana, and Illinois, must be purchased in Kentucky before a nonresident may fish it. Besides the Ohio there's the Kentucky River, lying totally in the state; the long, deep, and narrow Green River that rises in the foothills of southern Kentucky and meanders through the flatlands to the Ohio; the Tennessee, which originates in the state of Tennessee but which flows across the southwestern tip of Kentucky and on into the Ohio; the Cumberland, which originates in the mountains of eastern Kentucky and flows along the southern border of the state, dips into Tennessee, then erupts again into Kentucky to follow its path into the Ohio River. These are the big rivers of which Kentucky fishermen boast. But there are others. Famous Salt River in central Kentucky, with its big bass pools; Licking River in northeastern Kentucky, which flows into the Ohio River near Cincinnati; the Rough River, Nolin River, Barren River, Little Kentucky, and many other streams that are famous wherever the word fishing is mentioned.

Most of the streams provide smallmouth-bass fishing. But they also have other species. For instance, sauger are found in the Kentucky River, and so are white bass. There are also crappie, catfish, and bluegill. Most of the streams support these and other species of fish, but some afford a special type of fishing. Trophy muskellunge may be taken from Red River, Barren, and Green rivers, Tygart and Kinniconick Creeks. And some of these streams, the headwaters of the Cumberland, Licking, and Green rivers as well as others, present good float-fishing with put-and-take spots strategically located along their courses. In the mountainous Cumberland, a fisherman may float for miles without the sight of man or animal and while so doing may fish some of the most fertile waters for the smallmouth bass. Other streams also feature float-fishing, and all, with the exception of a few mountain streams that have been ruined by coal dust and other forms of pollution, support good fish populations.

KENTUCKY LAKE

Heading the list, as far as size is concerned, is mammoth Kentucky Lake lying in far western Kentucky with its 2,380 miles of shoreline that surrounds 134,000 surface acres of water. This huge impoundment was made by a TVA dam across the Tennessee River at Gilbertsville, Kentucky, and the water from this relatively low-level dam is pushed back across the state of Tennessee and actually into the tip of Alabama. This is one of the largest man-made lakes in the world. It is famous for its all-around fishing, but the crappie run in the spring probably is the highlight. During this spawning run literally thousands of fishermen daily visit this lake to take home limits of crappie. But black bass (largemouth) also thrive in this lake as do white or striped bass, bluegill, and catfish as well as sauger and rough fishes. Below the dam in the Tennessee year-round fishing is available in the swift-waters of the Tennessee River where monstrous catfish are taken.

CUMBERLAND LAKE

Second largest lake is Cumberland, which is an impoundment of the waters of the cool, mountain-fed Cumberland River. This lake, lying wholly in Kentucky, is 101 miles long, with a shoreline of 1,250 miles and a surface acreage of 50,250. Black bass (smallmouth, largemouth, and spotted) abound in this lake where biologists once found the largest population of black bass of any lake in the nation. These mostly are caught in the spring and fall months, with some being taken by jig-fishing in the dead of winter. Lake Cumberland has a good population of walleye, which are harvested in its headwaters in the early spring spawning run and also are caught throughout the summer by trollers and casters. White-bass fishing is at its peak in this lake during the spawning run, and the crappie population is above average. Also to be found are bluegill and catfish. Below this dam, where the water emerging from beneath the dam never reaches more than 65° F, is a good rainbow-trout fishery. The trout are stocked in this area each spring and are harvested by fishermen throughout the year for a distance of 28 miles below the dam to Burkesville.

Coming down from Louisville, you can stop at Somerset, Burnside, Monticello, Albany, or Jamestown, and you'll also find camps directly on the lake. The same modest prices prevail here as elsewhere, and the fishing is comparable to the more famous Dale Hollow except that Cumberland is primarily a bigmouth- and spotted-bass impoundment. Cumberland has rocky and wooded cliff shores and plenty of coves where big bass like to poke around, and if you can give any credence to the theory, you'll find the really heavy fish along the old river bed under the lake. Surface plugging is effective in the spring and fall, preferably with some flashy shad or minnow imitation.

DALE HOLLOW RESERVOIR

A large segment of Dale Hollow Reservoir which was impounded by a dam in Tennessee extends into Kentucky. It was from this lake that a world-record smallmouth bass (11 pounds, 13 ounces) was caught in 1958. Dale Hollow is ideal bass habitat; its 850-mile shoreline contains coves, shale banks, stumps, bushes, down-timber, and abrupt dropoffs. The best fishing is from mid-March until early July, and from mid-September through mid-January. The summer fishing (July and August) can be productive at dawn, dusk, and after dark. The spring period is usually best for topwater lures, while the hot-weather smallmouths are taken by deep trolling with plugs and live baits. Jigs and spinners are reliable and particularly effective in the fall.

On the Kentucky side you can reach Dale Hollow from Albany or Burkesville. Accommodations are plentiful. There are modern fishing camps and cabins, and boats, motors, and guides are also available.

HERRINGTON LAKE

Herrington Lake, in the blue-grass region of Kentucky, is the oldest of the man-made lakes. It is located off the Kentucky River, and the extremely high dam backs up water for a distance of thirty miles. The dam was constructed in 1925, and the lake has been one of the better ones down through the years. This impoundment covers

2,940 acres and has an average depth of 73 feet. The fish population boasts the three kinds of black bass, walleyes, and some northern pike also, but it is famous for its white bass and its lunker largemouths. The crappie fishing is above average, and some good bluegill are found there. This lake is highly developed as a recreational area, and the only fault that fishermen may find with it is the interference encountered from motorboat operators and water skiers.

The white-bass spawning run in Dix River, headwaters of Lake Herrington, provides some of the best early-spring fishing in Kentucky. The whites have voracious appetites during this migration and are harvested by the thousands. They are taken on live minnows, or small lures resembling the shad, and during the height of the run fishermen often line the bank shoulder to shoulder to catch these hard-hitting little fish. The run usually starts around mid-April and continues intermittently for three weeks.

DEWEY LAKE

Dewey Lake is a small mountain lake in eastern Kentucky and has an abundance of largemouth bass. Although small in size, about 1,300 acres, it is heavily fished. In addition to largemouths the lake produces good crops of crappie and bluegill, plus a better than average yield of white bass. During the winter months, when muddy water prevails, some heavy bass are caught from Dewey Lake by jig-fishing. The catch in numbers is not phenomenal, but 6–8 pounders are common. The bass may also be caught during the summer months by trolling; the bluegill catch in this comparatively shallow lake peaks during the summer period. One good feature of Dewey Lake is that the water level is held steady throughout the season, except when disturbed by floodwaters, and therefore the fishing potential is uninterrupted.

ROUGH RIVER RESERVOIR

Rough River Reservoir is located a short distance from Louisville. It contains 1,600 surface acres of water and is 27 miles long. The dominant gamefish are largemouth bass, white bass, and crappie. This highly developed lake attracts great numbers of fishermen. There is a vast population of catfish in Rough River, and trotline fishing throughout the summer attracts a big audience. Early-spring fishing yields black and white bass and crappie in great numbers. The fall bass fishing is excellent. Rainbows are stocked below the dam in the swift parts of Rough River, and year-round fishing is furnished by these trout.

During midsummer the bluegill is the most readily caught fish, and it grows to good size in the reservoir. They are popular among family groups with the simplest fishing rigs.

BUCKHORN RESERVOIR

Fourteen-mile-long Buckhorn Reservoir is located in the mountains of eastern Kentucky a few miles from Hazard. It holds great potential for the muskellunge which inhabited the Middle Fork of the Kentucky River which was impounded to form the lake. It has a good population of smallmouth bass, and the crappie and bluegill density is high. This small lake is surrounded by mountains and forests and is a popular tourist attraction. The tailwaters of Buckhorn Reservoir produce good rainbow trout fishing.

NOLIN RESERVOIR

Completed in 1963 this lake of almost 6,000 surface acres lies within a few miles of famous Mammoth Cave National Park. The reservoir may be regarded as one of the better smallmouth black bass lakes of the state. The cool waters of the Nolin River have been impounded and along with this impoundment went a good crop of smallmouth bass for which Nolin River was famous. In addition, largemouth bass have been stocked and it is possible that some of the muskellunge which inhabited Green River, into which the Nolin flowed, could be present in this impoundment. Crappie, catfish, bluegill, and white bass are numerous. The Nolin tailwaters produce rainbow trout.

BARREN RIVER RESERVOIR

This lake of almost 10,000 surface acres was completed in 1964 and its fishing potential has not been established. However, biologists, in pre-impoundment studies, found an abundance of black bass, crappie, bluegill, and catfish. A comparatively shallow lake, Barren River Reservoir is located in south-central Kentucky near the Tennessee border and was created by a dam across Barren River, a tributary of the Green River, which offers, perhaps, Kentucky's best muskie fishing. A state park is to be erected on this lake.

LAKE BARKLEY

Located alongside Kentucky Lake in far western Kentucky, the surface acres in Barkley total 45,000 which is only 3,000 acres smaller than famous Kentucky Lake. Between these two lakes is the huge 170,000-acre Land-Between-the-Lakes Area which is developed as a national recreational area by TVA. Over 10 million dollars was appropriated by Congress for initial work on this project. The lake is formed by a huge dam across the Cumberland River. This dam is a few miles from Kentucky Dam and the two lakes are connected by a canal. Fishing is similar to that of Kentucky Lake. A state park is established on Lake Barkley.
—H.T.
—A.J.McC.

KENTUCKY BASS A regional name for the spotted bass (*which see*)

KENYA This independent East African state bordering the Indian Ocean offers excellent saltwater fishing in season for black marlin, striped marlin, blue marlin, and sailfish, and considerable freshwater fishing for Nile perch and tigerfish. Modest trout angling is also available in high-altitude streams, and largemouth bass provide some sport in Lake Naivasha. Kenya has a total area of 224,960 square miles, but only about 3 percent of this is inland waters; its largest lake, lying almost entirely within the country, is Lake Rudolf in the northwest at the border of Ethiopia. The easterly shore of Lake Victoria indents Kenya at its western border with Uganda and Tanzania. Many sportsmen combine some angling with a hunting or camera safari. Kenya has numerous national parks—all easily reached by good roads—where lions, elephants, hippos, and other free-roaming game can be viewed or photographed at close range.

Extensive areas in Kenya have a mean annual rainfall of less than 30 inches. A large portion of northern Kenya has a mean of less than 10 inches. Low rainfall, high temperatures, and rapid evaporation create much aridity countrywide. Rains come as sudden heavy downpours usually from March to May, while lesser rains occur from October through December. The best months weatherwise are from June through September, with July and August the coolest months. Kenya is on the equator, and the greater temperature differences come with altitude. The coastal region is hot and humid with temperatures from 75°–90°F. The inland plateaus to 4,000 feet altitude are dry and hot, with temperatures often exceeding 100°F. The highland region and Lake Victoria Basin (over 4,000 feet) usually have cool nights and warm days. The temperature range is from 45°–85°F.

FRESHWATER FISHING

Modest quality trout fishing exists in Kenya. In the lakes around Kericho rainbows will average about 1½ pounds with 5- and 6-pounders a possibility. In nearby streams, such as the Kipsanoi and Itari, the fish average about ¾ of a pound, with the occasional large trout going 3 or 4 pounds. Kericho is the comfortable headquarters for trout anglers in this area. Other popular trout rivers are the Chania, Gura, and the Sagana. Most of the fishing for rainbow and brown trout is in cold waters at about 5,000 feet altitude in wild and beautiful surroundings. A number of hotels cater to anglers at distances from Nairobi varying between 56 and 230 miles.

There is no closed season, but during the heavy rains from April through June the high run-off precludes these as fishing months.

Largemouth bass were introduced to Kenya some years ago and have thrived particularly well in Lake Naivasha, only 54 miles from Nairobi. In general the bass average about 1½ pounds, although 5- and 6-pounders are not uncommon. The same methods used in the United States are popular here.

Kenya's principal freshwater gamefish are the tigerfish and Nile perch in Lake Rudolf. The population of big perch is a subspecies (*Lates niloticus rudolfianus*). The rod-and-reel record here for Nile perch is 251 pounds (1971). Although Lake Rudolf is readily accessible by air from Nairobi, it lies in a desolate and otherwise waterless area, the home of the Turkana people, and it has hardly changed in a physical sense in a thousand years. The isolation coupled with the scenery and spectacular sunsets make for a rewarding visit. A popular fishing spot for both Nile perch and tigerfish is Ferguson's

Gulf. Central Island, about an hour by boat from Ferguson's Gulf, is one of the main breeding grounds of crocodiles on the lake and worth a side trip.

SALTWATER FISHING

Kenya offers excellent big-game angling from Lamu in the north, through Malindi, Kilifi, Momasa, and Shimoni to Mafia Island in the south. This section of the western Indian Ocean has more than 700 species of fish. Striped marlin is the principal gamefish along Kenya's Coral Coast. The fish usually arrive about mid-November and continue until mid-March, with the peak in January. Sailfish may appear somewhat earlier in the northbound current, but the best fishing occurs during the same period as the striped marlin run. Black and blue marlin are less abundant, but some large fish are hooked, particularly in the waters off Shimoni. Other gamefish include the yellowfin tuna, dolphin, king mackerel, wahoo, barracuda, mako, cobia, and the occasional swordfish. Light-tackle casters can find plenty of inshore action with bonefish, jacks, ladyfish, barracuda, and the miniature Indo-Pacific tarpon (ox-eye).

TACKLE

All the necessary tackle for saltwater big-game fishing is available on Kenya's charter boats. Naturally, specialists will bring their own. Resorts that cater to Nile perch anglers usually have suitable gear available. The standard tackle consists of a 9- to 10-foot-long surf-spinning rod with a large capacity reel spooling 20- to 30-pound-test monofilament. The most popular lures are 6-inch-long plugs; jointed subsurface models are ideal. For tigerfish, bring along a freshwater spinning rod or fly rod, lightweight but with a fairly stiff tip, to facilitate hooking these toothy gamesters. The trout streams are not generally large and a 7- or 7½-foot fly rod calibered for a No. 5 line will prove adequate. —A.J.McC.

KILLER WHALE *See* Porpoises

KILLIFISH *See* Banded Killifish, Mummichog, Sheepshead Minnow, Striped Killifish

KING CARP *See* Carp

KINGFISH A regional and common name in the Southern United States for the king mackerel (*which see*). Also a regional and common name for the northern whiting (*see* Whitings)

KING MACKEREL *Scomberomorus cavalla* Also called kingfish and cavalla. A fish of the mackerel family that differs from the other two western Atlantic species of Spanish mackerels in lacking any black pigment in the anterior part of the first dorsal fin and in having fewer (15–16) spines in the first dorsal fin. Like the cero, the

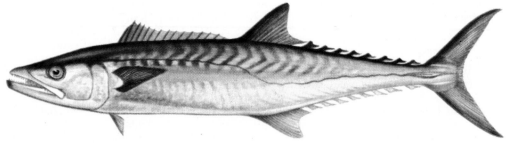

King Mackerel, 34-pound Female, Palm Beach, Florida

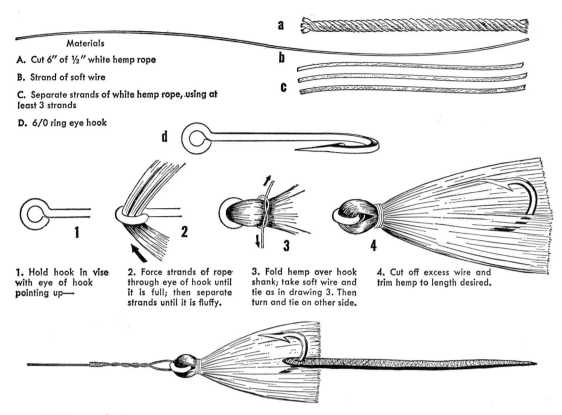

Materials

A. Cut 6″ of ½″ white hemp rope

B. Strand of soft wire

C. Separate strands of white hemp rope, using at least 3 strands

D. 6/0 ring eye hook

1. Hold hook in vise with eye of hook pointing up—

2. Force strands of rope through eye of hook until it is full; then separate strands until it is fluffy.

3. Fold hemp over hook shank; take soft wire and tie as in drawing 3. Then turn and tie on other side.

4. Cut off excess wire and trim hemp to length desired.

King Mackerel O'Bannon Cut Bait Rig

king mackerel has the pectoral fin covered with scales. There are 8–9 gillrakers on the first branchial arch. King mackerel reach a much larger size than any other American Spanish mackerels, 5 feet and 100 pounds. In the summer, they are found regularly from Brazil on, north to North Carolina and occasionally to Cape Cod.

—B.B.C.
—R.H.G.

FISHING METHODS

A wide variety of methods is used to take king mackerel, and the method employed may depend on the size of the kings that are available.

Medium- and heavy-duty spinning tackle is now in wide use for king mackerel of the size usually found offshore in large schools. These "school fish" may range about 7–25 pounds. The advent of saltwater spinning tackle was actually a key development in the king mackerel becoming an important saltwater gamefish. For many years the king mackerel was primarily a commercial species. But when spinning tackle came into use along the kingfish belt it presented anglers with a new, sporty method of taking these fish. Since 1948, the king mackerel has become the foundation of Florida's growing drift or "headboat" fleet. Spinning tackle is standard equipment aboard a very large percentage of these craft. The other method of kingfishing on head boats is drift-fishing with revolving-spool tackle. Both methods used on the head boats are also widely employed on private fishing craft, including outboard skiffs.

In the Gulf area, particularly off the coasts of Texas and Louisiana, many charter-boat skippers work near the shrimp-boat fleet. When the shrimp boats cull out their catch each day the remaining trash fish are dumped overboard. This concentration of food acts as a chum and attracts large schools of king mackerel. Chumming is, of course, a good method for attracting these gamefish and when kings move into a chum-slick they can be caught on everything from jigs to surface plugs. King mackerel will also strike streamer flies; however, fly-fishing per se is a difficult method because the lure must be retrieved rapidly both to attract and hook the fish. For most enthusiasts it is tiresome, and consequently trolling with the fly is more commonly practiced.

DRIFT-FISHING

On Florida's east coast, where tremendous schools arrive in late fall, kingfish anglers cut the engines and allow their boats to drift over schools of king mackerel. Spinfishermen usually use a 1–2-ounce nylon jig. The lure may be all yellow, all white, or a combination of yellow leadhead with white nylon streamer. Common practice is to add a thin strip bait to the lure. Fishermen have found that a second hook added to the one on the lure will result in a much higher percentage of hooked fish. With this lure and strip-bait combination, a spinfisherman will cast ahead of the drifting boat. In other words, if the boat is drifting with the current in a northerly direction, the cast is made to the north. After the lure strikes the water the bail of the spinning reel is left open and the lure allowed to sink to the bottom. Then the angler closes the bail, picks up any slack in the line, and speedily retrieves the lure with a vigorous whipping motion of the rod tip. Kings strike solidly, and the long first run of the fish is the top thrill to be found in spinfishing for this species.

The size of the hook used will depend upon the average size of the fish available, and an angler may use his own judgment in this matter. Two hooks in tandem are popular with drift-fishermen. The method consists of merely letting a bait out behind the drifting boat. A strip cut from any common baitfish will do, but many anglers prefer a strip cut from the belly of a king-mackerel. If the current happens to be strong, a small sinker is sometimes added to the leader just above the eye of the hook. Since kings have razor-sharp teeth, wire leader material is essential in fishing for this species. A No. 5 piano wire is minimum.

Kings often feed more heavily at night than during the day. Natural bait rather than artificial lures is best in the hours of darkness.

TROLLING

There are many other methods of taking kingfish. There are areas in which live shrimp are in wide use as bait. Anglers sometimes plug-cast for the species or troll a large subsurface plug. Trollers also use small baitfish, such as mullet and balao. A great many kings are taken by anglers trolling sailfish baits.

When the kings are sulking deep, offshore anglers may troll for them with a Monel steel wire line that is weighted further by a heavy trolling lead. A whole mullet or balao is the usual bait.

For large kingfish running from 30 to more than 40 pounds, which are often scattered rather than schooled up, live-bait trolling is often employed. The baitfish most often used on the Florida east coast is the blue runner. The fish is hooked through the head above the eyes.

Commercial fishermen troll for kings with handlines consisting of an entire coil of stainless-steel wire leader material. Most of the time—when the boat traffic permits—they will circle their boats above a school of kings, jerking or jigging the lure or bait. Some commercial men have manually operated or electrically operated reels for bringing in the fish. During peak winter runs on the Florida east coast, commercial boats may return to port with up to several thousand pounds of king mackerel per boat.

One of the most spectacular sights off the southeast coast of Florida results from the invasions of the tremendous schools of king mackerel. There are times when more than 100 boats of every size and description may be found concentrated over a school of king mackerel.

The drift-fishing head boats locate schools of fish for everyone. With modern depth-recording equipment of various types, an experienced skipper seldom fails to find the large concentrations. Some veterans become so adept at reading fish signs recorded by a fathometer that they can even estimate the average size of the fish in a school. The head boats serve as fishfinders for private, charter, and even the commercial boats. Catches aboard one craft often run 75–125 king mackerel per half-day trip.

Size of tackle for kings is a matter of personal preference. For school-size kings, medium saltwater spinning tackle or light revolving-spool saltwater casting tackle is suggested for casters. For drift-fishing, No. 2/0 to 4/0 reels are popular sizes. The No. 2/0 may be cutting it a bit thin, however, for a drifting bait may attract sailfish, big amberjack, and even bigger sharks.

Most spinfishermen use monofilament lines of from 10–20-pound-test strength. For light saltwater revolving-spool reels, 20-pound-test line is usually sufficient. Few anglers who drift-fish use line of less than 30-pound-test.

—E.C.B.

KING SALMON A common name for the chinook salmon (*which see*)

KING SPOKE The upper spoke of a boat's wheel that lies in vertical position when the rudder is amidships, usually marked with a knot, a carving, or mark of some kind that can be seen or felt in the dark.

KITE FISHING A method of offshore angling wherein a kite is employed to troll a skipping bait or hold a live bait at the surface of the water. Kites are also used for carrying a bait far away from shore. Fishing kites are made of silk mounted on an X frame of light tubular glass supports, and vary in size according to the velocity of the prevailing wind and the weight of the bait used. The kite line may be wrapped around a section of broom handle or stored on a simple wood or metal reel. The terminal tackle is secured with a clothespin snap as on an outrigger (*see under* Sportfisherman) and releases at the strike. Kite fishing is most often practiced on sailfish and tunas, but it is an effective method for any surface feeding saltwater gamefish over reefs or bluewater. *See also* Big-Game Fishing —A.J.McC.

KNOT In nautical use, a unit of speed equal to one nautical mile (6,080 feet) per hour. The reference in primitive days of navigation was to a knot in a rope. To learn the speed of a ship a log line was trailed astern which was divided into sections and knotted at intervals of such a length that they bore the same relationship to a nautical mile as the time the line was allowed to run free. The sections and time were scaled 1 to 120. Thus approximate 50-foot divisions each represented 1 sea mile (2,026⅔ yards) or $1/120$ part of that distance. Thirty seconds is $1/120$ of an hour; so by counting the knots unwound from the log reel the navigator could estimate how many sea miles his craft was moving over the water, which he referred to as "knots."

The device used by modern boats is more complicated, consisting of a spinning log (similar to the angler's spinner), which causes the hands of dials to indicate distance and speed. Consulting these dials is called "reading the log." —F.M.P.

KNOTS A means of fastening together the parts of one or more flexible materials such as rope, line, or leader, or of fastening such material to a stanchion, mast, or cleat. Knots include bends, hitches, and splices. The average angler should know how to tie at least three knots. In some methods of fishing, such as with fly tackle or big-game tackle, it is necessary to learn six or more for various terminal rigs.

The important thing about tying knots is to form and secure them correctly. They must be pulled slowly,

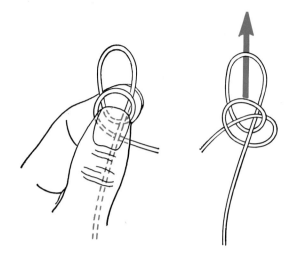

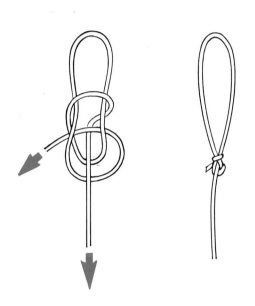

Perfection Leader End Loop Knot

steadily, and tight. You might practice with heavy cord, or even rope, so you can more readily see how the parts are formed and joined. All knots reduce the strength of any material to a greater or lesser degree; therefore you should learn the ones which provide maximum security rather than easy or less efficient knots. Any knot which retains 85 percent or more of the breaking strength of the material is generally useful, although some of the better knots are rated at 90 percent and higher in efficiency. However, due to the specialized requirements of angling and tackle, it is not always possible to employ the best knot for a particular purpose because of its bulk, rigidity, or tendency to slip when tied in various materials.

PERFECTION LOOP KNOT

The Perfection Loop Knot is used to tie a loop at the end of a synthetic leader, such as a nylon leader used in fly-fishing. The loop serves the purpose of joining the line and leader together. Hold the nylon between thumb and forefinger with about 4–5 inches extending upward. With the other hand form a loop behind the stem and hold the crossing part between the fingers. Make a second loop in front of the first loop, and bring the end around between the two thus formed. Holding it with slight pressure at the base, bring the second or front loop through the first loop with the fingers of your other hand. Continue pulling this second loop slowly upward while holding the free end of the nylon and simultaneously drawing the knot portion closed.

IMPROVED END LOOP

The Improved End Loop is used for making loops in leaders or heavy lines. It is stronger than the Perfection Loop Knot but bulkier, and is used to best advantage when security is of prime importance. The knot is easy

Improved End Loop

to make. Form a double strand of 4–6 inches in length by folding the end of material back parallel to itself. Next, turn the double strand around itself five times, and insert the end through the first loop formed. Pull the knot as tight as possible.

BLOOD KNOT

The Blood Knot is used for joining two strands of material together, such as sections of nylon in making tapered leaders. The Blood Knot is efficient provided the diameters of both strands are reasonably comparable. If the variation is great (more than .015 inch) the Stu Apte Improved Blood Knot or an Offset Nail Knot would be more suitable. For most leader-making purposes, however, the Blood Knot is practical.

To form the knot cross the two strands and hold between thumb and forefinger with about three inches of each section extended. Take the near-strand extension (whether right- or left-handed), and twist around the standing part of the opposite strand five times. Poke the end through the loop formed by the two strands, shifting the knot to the other thumb and forefinger to hold the crossing parts firmly together. Twist the other strand extension around the standing part five times in the opposite direction, and return the free end through the formed loop so that it enters from the opposite side. By holding both free ends between each thumb and forefinger, draw the knot together slowly by pulling on all four parts. When the knot is correctly formed, the strands can be pulled tight and excess material clipped from the ends.

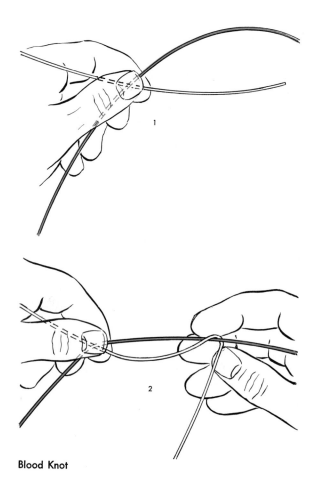

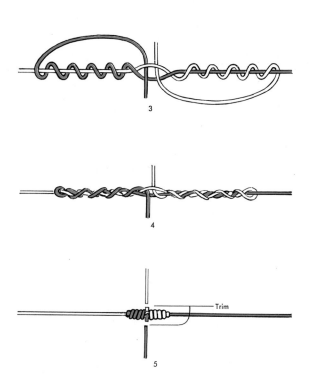

Blood Knot

EXTENSION BLOOD KNOT

This is used for tying dropper strands to a leader. A great many anglers use two or more flies at one time, so it may be necessary to create a dropper strand extending from the leader on which to attach the extra fly. For this

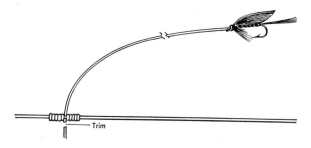

Extension Blood Knot

purpose, the Extension Blood Knot, which is tied in the same fashion as the Blood Knot, is ideal. The only difference between the two is that in forming the dropper you pull one end out 6–8 inches. You have to allow an extra-long overlap when you start tying the knot in order to get the proper length. This extension forms the dropper strand and is a permanent, strong tie.

STU APTE IMPROVED BLOOD KNOT

This is an excellent knot for joining two greatly unequal diameters of monofilament such as a 12-pound-test tippet to a 100-pound test shock tippet. Begin by doubling a sufficient length of the smaller diameter so that it can be wrapped around the standing part of the larger diameter with at least five turns or more, depending on the difference in diameters. Place the doubled end down between the strands.

Hold the looped material between thumb and fore-finger to keep it from unwinding. Wind the larger diameter around the standing part of the doubled line three times, but in the opposite direction. Insert the end up through the loop at the same point.

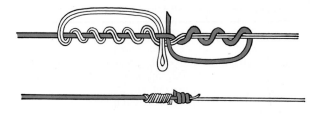

Stu Apte Improved Blood Knot

Pull the knot up slowly, and try to keep it from slipping. Use your fingernails to push the loops together if necessary. To trim, cut off the ends of the double loop and the end of the shock tippet, both about ¼ inch from the knot. Cut off the end of the doubled line ¼ inch from the knot.

DOUBLE TURLE KNOT

The age of synthetics has changed the lore of knot tying drastically. In the days of silkworm gut, it was perfectly satisfactory to use a Single Turle Knot or a Return Jam Knot for attaching flies to leaders. Now, with platyl and nylon completely dominating the angling scene, these knots are practically useless. The synthetics not only differ greatly in tensile strength and elongation, but they are extruded with a smooth as glass finish which causes the traditional knots to "creep out." The modern angler will find that a Double Turle Knot is adequate with synthetics on large flies or tippets down to say 3X, and that an Improved Clinch Knot, with the end passed twice through the hook eye before forming the knot, is better yet when using small flies and 6X or 7X tippets. This provides the impact strength necessary for barbing large fish. From a practical standpoint, no single knot serves all purposes with all materials.

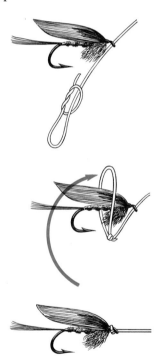

Turle Knot

The Double Turle Knot is compact, strong, and comes out straight through the eye of the fly. To make it, pass the end of your leader through the hook eye from the front and slide the fly up the leader and out of the way. Make a slip knot in the end of the leader bringing the end around twice (one turn would make a Single Turle Knot). Pass the end through both turns so that the extension is parallel to the standing part. Draw tight, and pass the loop thus formed over the fly so that it closes snug around the head of the fly and not in the eye or on the leader itself.

IMPROVED CLINCH KNOT

The Improved Clinch Knot has many applications in tying flies, lures, bait hooks, and swivels to leader or line, or to tie a line to a reel spool. It is preferred by some fly-fishermen to the Double Turle, particularly when using straight-eye or ringed-eye hooks or when using very small artificials. In fine diameters it is more secure than the ordinary Clinch Knot (in which the free end is not drawn through the second loop) and will not slip. There

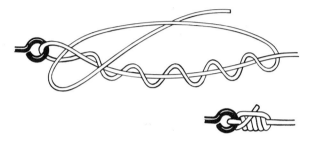

Improved Clinch Knot

are two things worth remembering about it; use five turns instead of the customary three, and when fishing with delicate tippets below 4X, pass the monofilament through the hook eye *twice* before forming the knot. This is important if you have to use midges and tiny nymphs for big trout.

To make an Improved Clinch Knot, pass the leader material through the hook eye (once or twice), and make five turns with the free end around the standing part. Next, pass the end between the eye and the first loop formed. Bring the end through the second loop formed, and slowly pull tight while still holding the free end between thumb and forefinger to prevent its slipping out. Pressure should be applied gradually so the knot is partially closed before securing against the eye.

NAIL KNOT

The development of plastic-coated fly lines has also been responsible for the acceptance of knots which would have had little value to anglers 20 years ago. A Nail Knot, for example, simply cuts through a vacuum-finished silk line; yet it is eminently practical with a tough-coated modern plastic. Actually, the harder you pull the knot, the better it "bites" and holds. So it's no longer necessary to knot a fly line to a leader loop. A knotted loop makes a bulky and not perfectly secure connection which always catches in the rod guides. The smooth Nail Knot on the other hand easily passes in and out, and you can leave the appropriate butt section joined to the line even if you want to change the leader's taper from time to time. By the same token you can eliminate splicing a loop in the end of a line unless you are using a silk line. A loop is not only bulky but prone to come apart under heavy fishing pressure. The Nail Knot, and its variations, are derived from the Hangman's Knot, and it can tolerate a high impact without slipping.

A Nail Knot can also be used for tying an extremely large-diameter section of leader to a small one, as in the

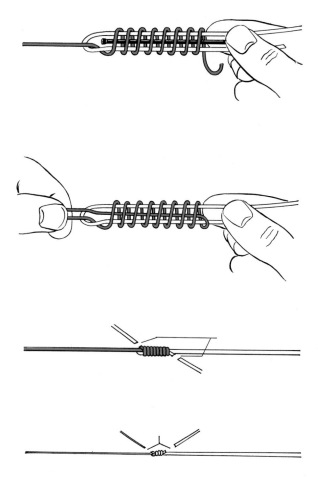

Nail Knot

leader shy so the thick strand is more practical than using wire. With the 60-pound material turned back, pass the 15-pound tippet through the bend it has formed, and lay both parts against the nail. Pinch the free part in place with your thumb against the nail, near the base of the bend, and commence winding. Make eight turns; then pass the free end back through the center, so that it comes out the same side it entered the loop. Do not *cross* the free end and the standing part. Remove the nail, and holding the four ends between thumbs and forefingers, pull the knot tight. Trim off the excess ends.

When making a Nail Knot to join a fly line to a leader butt, follow the same procedure, but it isn't necessary to use eight turns. Three or four turns will do the trick. The tip of a fly line and the diameter of a leader butt are so similar that the material gets a solid bite with only a minimum of winding.

NAIL KNOT (ALTERNATE)

An alternate method of tying the Nail Knot which is practical for all kinds of fly-fishing short of the very large saltwater species is easily tied with the aid of any slender tube such as a pump needle with the tip filed off, or a short section of hollow curtain rod. Start by holding the line, tube, and monofilament parallel, with the end

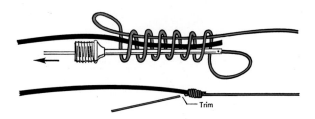

Nail Knot (Alternate)

of the tube and line even, and the leader material extending about six inches beyond to the left. Hold all three firmly; then double the monofilament back to the right and wind it six times around itself, the line, and the tube. Push the end of the leader material through the tube while holding the wraps in position between your fingers. Transfer the tube to your right hand, holding the wraps in place between thumb and forefinger, and slowly withdraw the tube. Pull alternately on short end and leader while turns are still held in position between fingers. When all slack is out, tighten the knot with strong, steady tension on the monofilament, then on line and monofilament. Trim ends close.

DOUBLE NAIL KNOT

Another variation of the Nail Knot is the Double Nail Knot. The difference between the familiar Blood Knot and the Double Nail Knot is that the latter is less bulky when using heavy leader material of 20–60-pound-test. In these large diameters, it is difficult to form and secure a Blood Knot properly because the free ends must be passed back through the loop first formed. The Double Nail Knot is of prime importance in saltwater fly-fishing; however, it can be useful in making heavy salmon leaders or trout leaders.

case of a shock tippet, or to join two heavy sections of material without creating a big lump or a dog's leg in the leader, and to attach a shooting head to a monofilament line. Although a carpenter's nail is commonly used in forming the knot, some anglers carry an ice pick, a piece of metal coat hanger, or a section of hollow tube to wrap the material around. It doesn't matter, as long as the surface is smooth, so the monofilament will slide off easily. The reason you will need something to work *around* is that all nail knots are finished by passing the free end through the center of the turns formed. This is awkward unless you can hold the shape of the knot until the tie is finally completed.

To make the basic Nail Knot, the heavier material, which may be either the fly line or a shock tippet, is first turned or bent back along itself for about two inches. Let's say you want to join a foot-long, 60-pound-test shock tippet to the final 15-pound-test tippet of a 9-foot leader. This will still qualify you for the *Field & Stream* Saltwater Fishing Contest, or for any other contest which would include a fly division, because the 15-pound portion is the actual test of the leader. A short, heavy-diameter shock tippet merely absorbs the abrasion of a hard-mouthed fish like the tarpon or big striped bass; you wouldn't have to use one for bonefish or red-fish. Fortunately, large saltwater gamesters are not

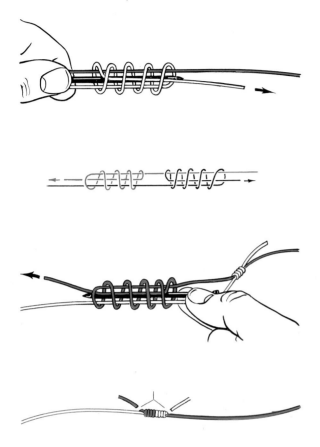

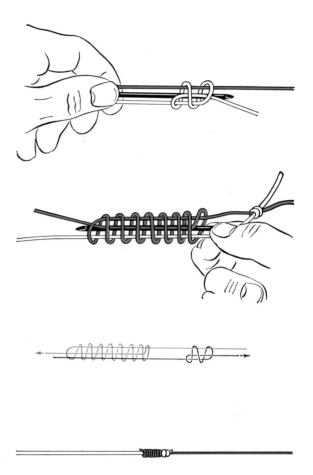

To make the Offset Nail Knot, form the heavy part first by making two turns around the nail and the leader section; then pass the end through the center. Remove the nail, and partially close the knot. Form the light material by making eight turns around the nail; then pass the end through the center. Remove the nail, and close the knot. To close, pull the four ends tight; then pull on the long ends until the knot is secure.

Double Nail Knot

The Double Nail Knot is used to join leader sections of the same or slightly different diameters, i.e., a normal progression such as 20-pound-test to 25-pound-test to 30-pound-test, etc. If the diameters to be joined vary widely an Offset Nail Knot is superior. The Double Nail Knot is made in two parts; the first end is formed with four turns around the nail, and the leader section is then passed through the center as illustrated. The nail is removed, and the knot formed is partially tightened. Form the other end in the same fashion, remove the nail, and tighten the knot. Slowly draw both ends together and pull secure.

OFFSET NAIL KNOT

One of the problems in leader building is that we can't always progress smoothly with little variation in diameter between one section and the next. If you are making abrupt tapers for casting in the wind, for instance, or to help turn over a big-bellied fly line, it may be necessary to jump as much as twenty pounds in rated test between two strands. To tie light leader material to a heavy diameter use the Offset Nail Knot. While the Double Nail is perfectly secure on ordinary tapers, it won't hold well if you are going from 20 to 40 to 60 pounds, for example, which is often necessary in a saltwater leader. To maintain a straight leader without the danger of a slipped knot, the bulk of one part of the double nail offsets the bulk of the other part.

Offset Nail Knot

NAIL KNOT LOOP

It is not always practical to attach a lure directly to heavy (60–90-pound-test) monofilament when using shock tippets. A regular Clinch Knot consisting of just three turns is sometimes used and is perfectly secure in 80–100-pound tests. However, with plugs having a built-in action or with large streamer flies, when a knot is drawn tight against the hook eye the lure will not swing freely. The rigidity of the heavy material will destroy their action. This is particularly important when fishing for striped bass, tarpon, snook, bluefish, and other large gamefish. Thus, a loop is often desirable. This one can be used for fish up to one hundred pounds or more with perfect safety.

The Nail Knot Loop will slip under heavy pressure. However, when tied properly, it rarely does, and if it

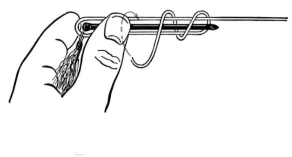

Run short end back through eye—remaining leader

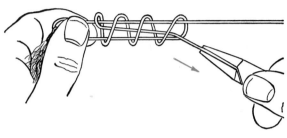

Bring over cut side of hook eye—make loop

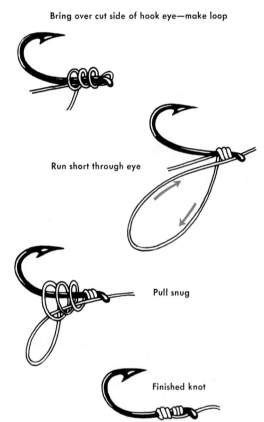

Run short through eye

Pull snug

Finished knot

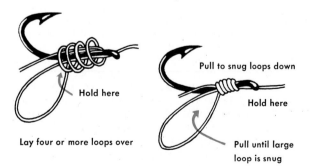

Nail Loop

should, the knot merely jams against the hook eye and will not break. The important thing is that its purpose is served; even a big 5/0 bucktail will dance and flutter in a lifelike fashion when secured to a loop.

To make the Nail Knot Loop, pass the shock tippet through the hook eye and turn the monofilament back parallel to the nail. Make three turns around the nail and standing part, and pass through the center. Remove the nail. Hold one finger in the loop formed, and with a pair of pliers pull the knot as tight as you can. Trim off the excess.

Bumper Tie

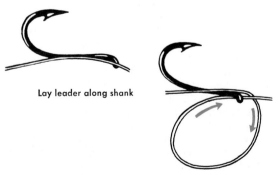

Lay leader along shank

Bring loop around and insert through eye whole length of leader

Lay four or more loops over

Hold here

Pull to snug loops down

Hold here

Pull until large loop is snug

Salmon Hook Knot

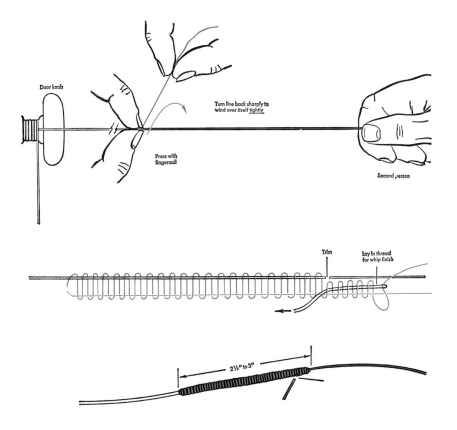

Rolling Splice

SALMON HOOK KNOT AND BUMPER TIE

These two knots are popular among West Coast salmon and steelhead fishermen. The hook knot is used for snelling and permanently securing monofilament to the shank for whole and cut-bait rigs. Generally, this requires two hooks, tied in with the same knot on the same leader and spaced to fit the bait. In the bumper tie the large adjustable loop is snugged down to hold the bait in place.

ROLLING SPLICE

The Rolling Splice follows the same principle of the material being wound back over itself. This is one of the easiest and most secure methods for attaching a braided backing line to a fly line. To make the Rolling Splice tie your fly line to a door knob, about two feet from the end. Although you can become skilled at it, the job can be done more easily if somebody holds the other end of the line. This connection must be made tightly. Lay the backing line parallel to the fly line, and, starting 2½– 3 inches from the end, pinch the backing to the fly line with your finger nail, and make the first turn as close to that end as possible. Continue winding, making as many tight turns as required (usually 30–40) to reach the end of the fly line. Now, when you reach the backing, lay in a piece of thread, and complete with a whip finish, drawing the backing back out in the reverse direction.

The tighter you pull a Rolling Splice, the deeper it will bite into the fly line.

BIMINI TWIST

A difficult but useful knot used to create a double line with the full strength of an unknotted line. A long loop takes two people, but a short loop—placed over spread knees to keep the line apart—will work. First double the line to form a loop somewhat longer than what you want to finish with and, holding the loop at one end, twist the loop twenty times, keeping the index finger in the loop and making circular motions with the wrist. Tighten the twist by separating the two strands of the loop at one end and working back to the other end, which should also be firmly held apart. Bring the loose end of the line toward the loop while placing a forefinger on the twist, continuing to open the loop. Now the twist begins to rotate. As it rotates, the open end is automatically wound around it. Be careful that the open end does not wrap over itself. Continue wrapping until you reach the end of the twist. Stop the rotation by holding the wrap carefully and at the same time make a half hitch around the right base of the loop. Continue to keep the two lines of the loop separated. Then tie another half hitch around the left base of the loop. You can let go of the wrap at this point and finish the knot off with a little clinch knot tied around both lines of the loop at the base. To do this place the lines of the loop together while taking three or four wraps around both lines and coming through, as in the illustration on the next page. Pull the knot up tight and clip it.

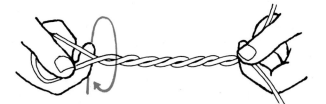

Double the line and form a loop longer than the one you want to end up with. One person holds the end of the line, the other holds the loop end and proceeds to twist the loop 20 times by keeping his index finger in the loop and making circular wrist motions

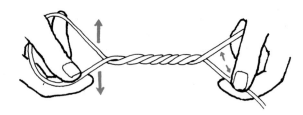

Next separate the two strands of the loop and work back toward the open end to tighten the twist. The person holding the loose ends then pulls the line apart

The person holding the loose ends puts his forefinger on the twist and brings the running end of the line toward the loop, as the first person at the looped end continues to open the loop. The twist begins to rotate

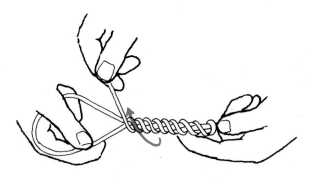

As the twist rotates, the running end automatically winds around it. Be careful not to let the running end wrap over itself. The wrap should continue until the end of the twist is reached

Bimini Twist

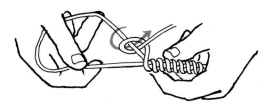

Stop the rotation by holding the wrap carefully and at the same time make a half hitch around the right base of the loop, while the two lines of the loop are kept separated

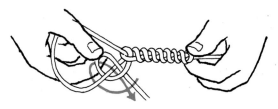

Tie another half hitch about the left base of the loop. You can now let go of the wrap

Finish the knot with a clinch knot tied about both lines of the loop at the base. Do this by placing the lines of the loop together while taking 3 or 4 wraps around both lines and coming through the line. Pull the knot tight

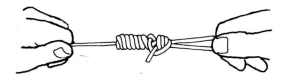

The knot is completed when the clinch knot is pulled tight and clipped

HAYWIRE TWIST

To make a secure loop in a wire leader, twist both ends of the loop several turns. Then, by holding the loop thus formed steady, wind the free end tightly, and uniformly, around the standing part six or seven times. Do not cut the free end with pliers; bend the section to be removed at a right angle, and rotate it in a circular motion. The wire will break cleanly at the base where the winding is completed.

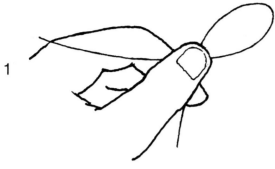

1

Make a loop of piano wire and hold it as shown...

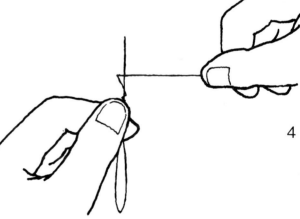

2

...then twist it at least 5 turns (7 for large fish). Make each twist separate, but tight

3

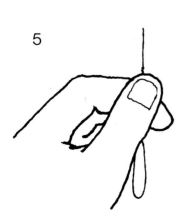

90°

After the last twist, turn the wire out straight
Make 4 turns on the leader and bend wire

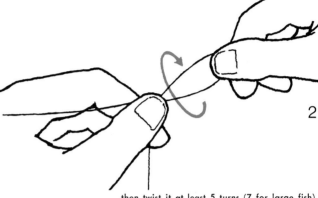

4

Lastly, break the wire off cleanly at leader. Hold leader firmly as shown, then twist or bend wire up and down...

5

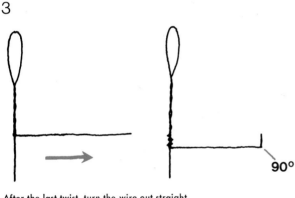

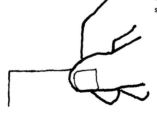

...until it breaks. You'll need no tools for this loop

DOUBLE HALF-HITCH

The half-hitch is a basic part of many more complicated knots, but in itself the half-hitch has numerous uses. The Double Half-Hitch shown here is secure enough for the small boater. To make a half-hitch, single or multiple, bend the line around the piling or through the ring, and then pass its end over or under the standing part and up through the loop formed by the turn. Do this twice to make a Double Half-Hitch.

SPIDER HITCH

Much simpler than the Bimini Twist, the Spider Hitch also is used in the preparation of a terminal line. First double the line and form a loop toward one end. Hold the base of the loop between your thumb and forefinger. Then thread the closed end of the line through the loop and wind it around the thumb. Do this five or six times. Pull both ends of the line until the knot is tight.

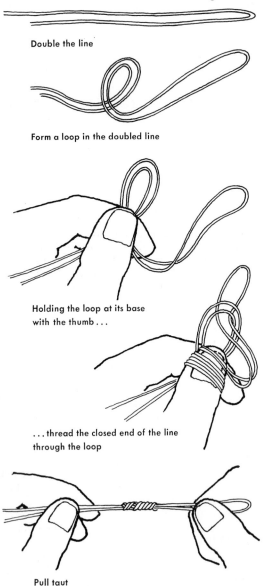

Double the line

Form a loop in the doubled line

Holding the loop at its base with the thumb . . .

. . . thread the closed end of the line through the loop

Pull taut

Spider Hitch

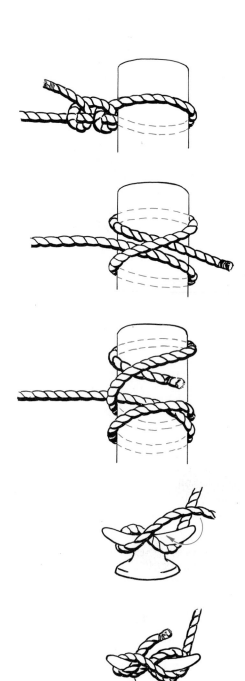

Hitches

CLOVE HITCH

The Clove Hitch binds fast to any surface. It is ideal when you need a quick hitch for making your bumpers fast to a railing, take a log in tow, or tie to a square, round, rough, or smooth piling. A clove hitch is easily formed by dropping two half-hitches over or around the object to which the line is being secured.

ROLLING HITCH

The Rolling Hitch is very similar to the Clove Hitch, except that an extra turn is taken ahead of one of the half-hitches; i.e., one of the two half-hitches is made with two turns or loops of the line instead of only one as in the

Clove Hitch. A Rolling Hitch generally will not slip and is easily unbent. It is often used to make one line fast to a heavier line, as in bridling a boat at a desired angle to the current or wind.

CLEAT HITCH

When tying up a boat to a wedge-shaped cleat, simply pass the line around the arms in a figure 8; then partially form another turn, closing it by making a loop and pulling taut. —A.J.McC.

KNOTTYHEAD *See* Stoneroller

KOKANEE *Oncorhynchus nerka* A landlocked dwarf form of the anadromous sockeye salmon. The kokanee is extremely popular as a sport and food fish in many Western states and is becoming distributed elsewhere in the United States. Although kokanee is the accepted name, it is known locally by a large variety of other names such as little redfish, Kennerly's salmon, silver trout, blueback, landlocked sockeye, kickaninny, yank, walla, red salmon, sockeye, redfish, silver, silversides, landlocked red salmon, kokanee salmon, Kennerly's trout, silver salmon, landlocked salmon, little red, and landlocked sockeye salmon. The Indians called them *Kokos* and in Japan they are called *Benimasa*.

The kokanee was originally found in Oregon, Idaho, Washington, British Columbia, and northward into Alaska to the Bristol Bay region west of the coast range. In Japan, it is found in Lake Akan in northern Hokkaido. It has been introduced in recent years into Maine, California, Montana, Colorado, Connecticut, New York, Vermont, North Dakota, Nevada, Utah, and Wyoming. The kokanee has been transplanted into many other lakes and reservoirs in the states where it is an indigenous species.

DESCRIPTION

Morphologically the kokanee and sockeye are identical. Prior to spawning, these fish have silvery sides and bellies, but during the spawning season, the sides become red on the males and slate-gray on the females. Simon

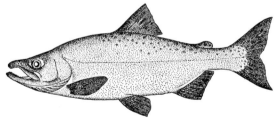

Kokanee

describes the kokanee as a fish with a slender body, moderately deep in breeding males, compressed, eyes moderate, head long, teeth small; dorsal rays 11; anal rays 13–16, usually 14; scales not easily loosened, 19–22 scales above lateral line, 125–140 scales in lateral line, and 19–21 scales below lateral line. Males develop a hooked jaw during the spawning season. Kokanee resemble trout but can be distinguished from them by the fact that they have more than 12 rays in the anal fin and 30–40 long, slender gillrakers.

The size differences at maturity between landlocked populations and sea-run populations are determined by environmental conditions. Generally, kokanee mature at 8–9 inches, with the record weight about 4 pounds. In Lake Pend Oreille, Idaho, kokanee reach a length of 2–3 inches during the first year, 7–8 inches during the second year, 8–9 inches in the third year, and 10–12 inches in the fourth year. Most of the growth is from July until October which coincides with the period of zooplankton abundance. There is little growth in winter. In Lake Granby, Colorado, females average 14.5 inches and males 15.0 inches. Donner Lake, California, kokanee average 18.5 inches with an average weight of 2 pounds. Fry planted in Skaguay Reservoir, Colorado, in 1951, were found to average 5–7 inches in 1952, 7.9 inches in May, 1953, and 8.6 inches in October, 1953. In northern British Columbia lakes, the usual size of the kokanee is 8–9 inches, while in southern British Columbia they average 12–15 inches. In Vermont, eggs from the same source produced kokanee up to 21 inches in one lake while in other lakes they never exceed 11 inches. Kokanee planted in Maine never exceed 10 inches.

HABITS

The food of the kokanee is almost entirely plankton. Crustaceans of the genera *Daphnia*, *Cyclops*, and *Diaptomus* are the prevalent forms. Biologists working on the Skaguay Reservoir in Colorado found the food of kokanee to be almost entirely entomostracans with but few adult insects. Cladocerans were present in 94 percent of the stomachs and amounted to 88 percent of the measurable food. Copepods were in 57 percent of the samples and amounted to 10 percent of the total food. Diptera amounted to 2 percent of the total food and occurred in 20 percent of the stomachs. Studies on this reservoir revealed that the order Hymenoptera was the most important food by volume and occurrence in trout. No hymenopteran was found in kokanee stomachs which were taken the same day. *Volvox* also provided food for kokanee in early spring but was not in evidence after entomostracans had increased. In Idaho it was found that kokanee ate principally copepods and cladocerans.

The kokanee is the only Pacific salmon which matures in freshwater, but like other Pacific salmon, both males and females die after spawning. Kokanee generally reach sexual maturity at 3–4 years of age. Populations in different lakes seem to mature at different ages. Kokanee may spawn in lakes or in the tributaries. They spawn in streams similar to trout. One male and one female spawn in gravel riffles where the nest building is done mostly by the female while the male chases intruders. Saucerlike depressions (redds) with small mounds of sand and gravel on the downstream side 2–4 inches deep are formed. Eggs may be deposited in more than one redd with the female moving upstream as she constructs the nest. In this fashion, the lower redds are buried deeper by the loosened gravel. Spawning takes place in lakes on gravelly shoals very often where there is seepage. Spawning in lakes resembles those of stream spawners with such differences in detail as might be attributable to lake spawners. Kokanee may spawn from August to February, the peak being in December in Lake Pend Oreille, Idaho; November in Flathead Lake, Montana; and October and November in Oregon.

ANGLING VALUE

Because kokanee are plankton feeders, they are generally regarded as difficult to harvest on hook and line. Returns get better as fishermen learn to catch this type of fish. The fish are taken by trolling, still-fishing, and fly-casting. Trolling rigs usually consist of a metal wobbler or flasher with red beads followed by a small hook with a small piece of worm attached. The line should be very tight in trolling so that the fish will hook itself. Bait-fishermen prefer worms, salmon eggs, maggots, and corn. Creel-census reports show that 99 percent of the kokanee catch taken in Lake Pend Oreille in 1955 were taken by handlining with maggots and corn. Kokanee constantly jump on the surface in cool weather, and are sometimes taken on small artificial flies. This, however, is a difficult manner of catching them. Kokanee are vigorous fighters and have a tender and soft mouth; therefore, limber rods are recommended. These fish are not usually caught until their third or fourth year of life, and then they are found in schools which move into deeper water in the summer.

FOOD VALUE

This species is excellent eating. Like most plankton feeders, they build up a reserve of fats and oils. Light smoking or kippering converts the kokanee into the finest of smoked fish. Care should be taken with these fish because they spoil easily. —K.B.

KUROSHIO CURRENT *See* Currents

KYPE A cartilaginous protuberance extending from the lower jaw of a salmonid and roughly in the shape of a hook. The kype is most typical of males at spawning time and at an advanced stage may develop to the point that the fish is unable to close its mouth. *See also* Arctic Char, Atlantic Salmon, Brown Trout, Pacific Salmon

L

LABRADOR CURRENT *See* Currents

LA BRANCHE, GEORGE MICHEL LUCIEN American (1875–1961) Author of *The Dry Fly and Fast Water* (1914) and *The Salmon and the Dry Fly* (1924) (both books reissued as a single volume by Charles Scribner's Sons, New York, in 1951), La Branche was the outstanding exponent and advocate of the dry fly at the height of its vogue in America. With his fishing partners, E.R. Hewitt and Ambrose Monell, he established the possibility and popularized the practice of taking salmon on the dry fly, going on, almost by accident, to a further discovery that has since been put to use by many more anglers than the comparative handful who fish for salmon. His great contribution was the invention of a deadly method for taking almost any fish that refuses to be taken by conventional offerings, the creation of "the artificial hatch," whereby repeated casts are floated over the same spot often enough to convince even the most skeptical fish that a hatch is on and that he'd better take before it's over. It was a demonstration of this method in England, where he was more widely acclaimed and feted than any American angler had ever been before, that elicited this encomium in Britain's oldest fishing weekly, the *Fishing Gazette*: "This remarkable caster cast the dry fly in places in which it would be extremely difficult to drop a worm, under overhanging alders and blackberry bushes, around trunks of trees, casting at will on to particular leaves that the fly might drop thence like a caterpillar from an oak leaf. His fishing is smooth and entirely effortless . . . his flies go where he wishes them to go and act as he directs them when they get there. Briefly, Mr. La Branche is a very beautiful fisherman."

It may be a shock by today's journalistic attitudes to suggest that the last sentence of this tribute was intended to be taken both literally and figuratively, but George La Branche was the Beau Brummel of angling annals; and the grace of his casting was matched by his garb, manner, and personal appearance. Slight and slender, but seeming taller than he actually was because of his erect posture, La Branche was a dandy both on and off stream, wearing vest, collar and tie, and a Sherlock Holmes-like fishing helmet. The delicacy and control of his powerful casting was often likened to a mailed fist in a velvet glove. Convinced that accuracy and finesse in presentation was much more important than color or type of fly, he was known more than once to go through an entire season using for all his fishing, both for salmon and trout, only the single fly with which his name was most closely identified, the Pink Lady. Using tackle that was considered extremely light in the teens and 20's, an 8-foot, 3½-ounce rod, his 60-foot casts in adverse winds astonished the English anglers with whom he fished on the Test, the Itchen, and the Kennet, where he leased some three miles of the stream at Ramsbury in Wiltshire.

A successful New York stockbroker, La Branche never permitted business to cause more than minimal interference with his sporting activities. Almost as ardent for guns as for rods, he allotted a good deal of time to shooting and to the raising of pheasants, and was also devoted to golf and yachting, his 30-foot sloop the *Wee Betty* winning the championship in her class in 1927 and placing second the following year.

Asked in an interview by the feature writer Marguerite Ives whether he considered fishing an art or a science, and whether he thought of himself as what is termed a purist, La Branche answered the first question: "Distinctly an art. Fly fishing is closely allied in my mind with music. I think that to cast a fly properly one must possess a sense of rhythm. The cast should be made in time to a rhythmic beat and the fly could easily be allowed to float on the water for the length of certain notes, withdrawn and the line straightened out and cast again all to musical measure and cadence."

And as to being a purist, he replied: "Not in the broad sense of the term. I consider that the real purist wastes countless joyous and active hours waiting, according to theory, for the rise of the fish before he casts." —A.G.

LADYFISH *Elops saurus* A fairly common fish occurring in the Atlantic, Indian, and western Pacific oceans. It is most abundant in the warmer parts of its range. Very common around southern Florida and in the Caribbean. Despite the various names applied to this species such as chiro and ten-pounder, ladyfish seems to be the most acceptable, although the name ten-pounder is misleading since this fish seldom reaches a weight of much over 5–6 pounds. Large ladyfish of 8–9 pounds are reported from the southern end of Andros Island in the Bahamas.

Ladyfish

The ladyfish is slender, finely scaled, and generally silver in color with a blue-green back. Dorsal rays 20. Anal rays 13. Pectoral rays 16–19. Pelvic rays 13–15. Scales very small, about 100–120 along lateral line. Body quite elongate. Pectoral fins inserted low on body. Dorsal fin single, on middle of back, the last ray not produced into a whiplike filament as in the tarpon. Pelvic fins slightly in advance of dorsal fin, about midway between pectoral and caudal fins. Caudal fin deeply forked. Upper jaw reaching well beyond vertical from posterior margin of orbit.

The ladyfish occurs in shallow water close to shore over sandy and muddy bottom. It is usually taken in bays, estuaries, and passes. Accessible from shore, piers, and bridges.

ANGLING VALUE

The ladyfish is an excellent light tackle quarry. It readily strikes artificial lures and leaps frequently when hooked. Its attack is so swift that a great many fish are missed, although when present, ladyfish generally occur in large schools and obtaining two or more strikes on the same retrieve is common.

Most ladyfish are caught with spinning and bait-casting equipment, using small jigs, spoons, and plugs. At times, deep running, or bottom bouncing, lures are preferred, but ordinarily they can be taken on surface baits while using the whip retrieve (*see under* Bait Casting). Silver and silver scale finish plugs in the ¼–½-ounce class are generally effective. It is advisable to use a light wire leader, as the body of this active gamefish quickly abrades the line.

Ladyfish provide exciting angling on fly tackle and will take both streamer flies and saltwater bugs. As a rule, a fairly rapid retrieve is necessary to draw strikes. The initial run of a 2–4-pound ladyfish against the fly rod is often all out of proportion to its size; it may display the power of a bonefish, but end its surge abruptly in an arcing leap. The fly leader should be reinforced with a shock tippet to prevent abrasion. *See also* Florida

FOOD VALUE

Edible but not often utilized as a food fish because of numerous, fine bones. —L.R.
—A.J.McC.

LAHONTAN REDSIDE *Richardsonius egregius* A brilliantly colored minnow with a broad, deeply forked tail. The color is variable and more intense during the spawning season. The males are usually deep olive-green above, lighter on the sides and silver beneath. Brassy and silvery metallic reflections are seen on various parts of the body. Two rather distinct brassy stripes extend from snout to caudal. Brilliant iridescence is seen along the head and upper body. Below the lower stripe, the sides are strongly suffused with pink. Lateral-line scales 52–61. The edges of the dorsal and anal fins are straight or slightly concave. This species is native to Lahontan Basin and related waters of Nevada and California.

HABITS

The Lahontan redside is a river species found in large numbers in slow ripples and quiet, shallow pools. When found in lakes, it is over submerged logs or around fallen trees or wharves. This species spawns in late spring and early summer when it migrates up the smaller tributaries, chiefly at night. They attain the spawning colors described above and develop small whitish nodules over most of the body. The food of the Lahontan redside is mostly aquatic larvae and winged insects. It also has been observed consuming large numbers of sucker eggs during the spawning of this species. This is a small minnow, the largest reaching 5½ inches.

ECONOMIC VALUE

The Lahontan redside is a favorite bait species due to its size and brilliant coloration. —R.A.J.

LAHONTAN SUCKER *Pantosteus lahontan* A small brownish-olive sucker. Ventral surfaces lighter to whitish. Lips pendulous and provided with many sharp papillae. Pectoral fins pointed and somewhat falcate. Anal fin may extend to the base of the caudal. The range of this species is confined to the Lahontan Basin, Nevada.

HABITS

The Lahontan sucker prefers the swift areas of streams and is not known in lakes. An upstream spawning migration takes place in early summer. There is no information on the food habits of this species. It reaches a length of 6 inches.

ECONOMIC VALUE

This sucker undoubtedly provides excellent forage for stream-resident sport fish. —R.A.J.

LAKE CHUB *Couesius plumbeus* A bluish-silver minnow with a lead-colored lateral band. The body is moderately slender. Eye large. Dorsal rays 8. Anal rays are 7. A small barbel is present slightly above the angle of the jaws. The lake chub ranges from southern Canada and Northern United States, east of the Continental Divide to Iowa and Michigan.

HABITS

This chub inhabits cold lakes and smaller streams. It is carnivorous, feeding almost entirely on insect larvae. Spawning takes place during summer in the small streams. Adults reach a size of 6 inches but average 3 inches.

ECONOMIC VALUE

As the lake chub is quite hardy it is a favorite bait species. —R.A.J.

LAKE CHUBSUCKER *Erimyzon sucetta* A small, greenish sucker without a lateral line. There are usually 11–12 dorsal rays and usually 35–37 lateral scale rows. The young are often mistaken for minnows or shiners. Young chubsuckers have an intense black band from the tip of the snout to the tail. This fish has an over-all bronze cast, and the dark scale edges give a cross-hatched appearance. The range of this sucker is from eastern Minnesota to New England and south to Florida and Texas.

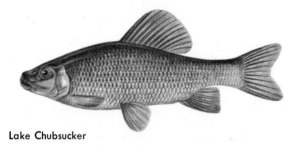

Lake Chubsucker

The lake chubsucker inhabits lakes and larger streams where turbidity and siltation are minimal. They are apparently found in association with much aquatic vegetation. Largely a bottom feeder, the chubsucker's diet consists of insect larvae, aquatic plants, and minute crustaceans. Spawning migrations occur to the smaller tributaries. The lake chubsucker rarely exceeds 10 inches in length.

ANGLING VALUE

Of no food value, the chubsucker undoubtedly contributes to the forage of predator species. —R.A.J.

LAKE STURGEON *Acipenser fulvescens* The lake sturgeon is one of a family of primitive fishes distinguished by the body covering of bony plates and a cartilaginous skeleton. It has a snout which is conical and sharp and not flattened as in some other sturgeons and a pair of spiracles in the head opening anterior to the gills. Beneath the snout is a protractile mouth with thickened lips which is extended for sucking up food. Four barbels are present in a row just ahead of the mouth. It has no teeth except when very young. The upper lobe of the tail is much longer than the lower. The caudal peduncle is distinctive because it is not completely covered by bony plates as is that of other sturgeons.

The lake sturgeon is found from Hudson Bay and the St. Lawrence River through central Canada in the north through Minnesota, Nebraska, Missouri, and southeast to northern Alabama. Formerly abundant, it is becoming scarce because of overfishing and dams which prevent movement to spawning areas.

LIFE HISTORY

It occurs in both lakes and streams of its range and prefers comparatively shallow waters. It ascends streams to spawn in the spring from April to June, but has been reported spawning in lakes. The eggs are adhesive and adhere to gravel and debris. The young feed on plankton organisms until they are 7–8 inches. The protractile mouth is used to suck insect larvae, mollusks, crayfish, and plants from the bottom. It feeds by taste and uses its four barbels to feel its way along and detect food.

It reaches a length of 8 feet and a weight of over 300 pounds, but its usual weight is 2–60 pounds. In the Lake Winnebago region of Wisconsin and three lakes in the Cheboygan River drainage of Michigan it is speared by sport fishermen through holes in the ice. Small decoys are used to lure it near the hole. It also is taken by set lines. It grows slowly and requires 14–22 years to reach maturity, attaining a length of 8 inches the first year; 50 inches and 29 pounds at 20 years; and 65 inches and 69 pounds in 35 years in Lake Winnebago, Wisconsin. Females live longer than males and grow larger. Formerly abundant it now is scarce in many parts of its range. In 1894 Mississippi River commercial fishermen reported catching 249,000 pounds but by 1931 the catch had declined to almost nothing. —C.A.P.

LAKE TROUT *Salvelinus namaycush* The lake trout, also called togue (Eastern United States), mackinaw (Western United States), and gray trout (Canada), is a large char. It almost always inhabits deep, clear lakes, although stream-dwelling populations sometimes occur where the rivers are connected to lakes; the latter situation is most common in Labrador, northern Quebec, and Alaska. The fish is distributed across Canada, and southward in cold-waters of the United States, notably in New England, the Finger Lakes region, the Great Lakes, and scattered

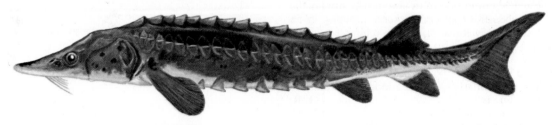

Lake Sturgeon

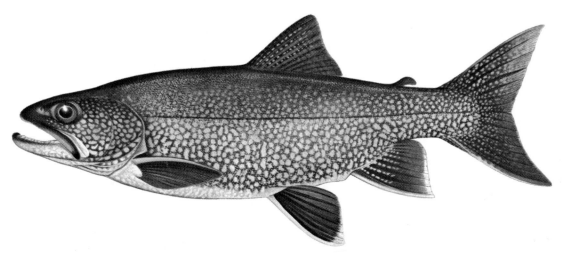

Lake Trout, 18-pound Male, Great Bear Lake, Northwest Territories

Western lakes where it has been introduced. In the southern portion of its range the lake trout is largely restricted to waters which exhibit thermal stratification (*which see*) and have an adequate supply of oxygen in their deeper areas.

The lake trout is distinguished by a raised tooth crest on the head of the vomer; the tail is strongly forked (unlike the splake hybrid which is more nearly square). There is considerable variation in color, but the body is generally blue-gray or bronze-green, with pale spots on sides and back and with pale spots on the dorsal, adipose, and caudal fins. There are 11 rays in the anal fin. The flesh color varies from almost white to red. Lake trout are known to reach a weight over 100 pounds, but they seldom exceed 40 pounds in the sport fishery.

The siscowet, a deep-bodied lake trout found in the Great Lakes region, has been given specific status (1970) *Salvelinus siscowet*; this species recognized by commercial fishermen as a "fat" (Lake Superior) is noted for its extremely oily flesh. Siscowets are ordinarily caught at depths from 300–600 feet, or deeper than the lake trout, however, their vertical distribution overlaps as both are sometimes taken in shallow or deep water. Presently identified as a race resembling the siscowet in its external appearance is the humper lake trout, which is known to the commercial fishermen as the "paperbelly" or "bank trout." The humper lake trout inhabits isolated offshore reefs (banks) surrounded by deep water.

LIFE HISTORY

Lake trout breed in the fall over gravel or rocky bottoms in depths varying from 100 feet or more in the Great Lakes and Finger Lakes of New York, to shoalwater in more shallow lakes. No nest or redd is built by the female as is the case with members of the trout group. The area is "swept" clean by the fish before spawning. Spawning time varies widely between lakes, occurring from September into December. The act of spawning is attended by groups of one or more females and several males, the eggs being scattered over suitable bottom. The eggs are about $1/5$ inch in diameter and settle among the interstices of rocks. Many are eaten by small lake trout, suckers, bullheads, eels, yellow perch, and other fish. The incuba-

tion period is 166 days at 37°F., and 49 days at 50°. The young fish remain in deepwater. They tend to develop cataracts when held in shallow water in direct sunlight as under hatchery conditions. The food of the young is made up of insects and crustaceans. Adults feed on fish such as the kokanee, whitefish, cisco, ling, and sculpin.

During the late fall, winter, and early spring when the water is cold, the lake trout may inhabit shallows, but at other times it lives in deepwater—often at depths of several hundred feet. In the northernmost portions of its range it is not so restricted by temperature since surface waters remain cold throughout the summer.

PROBLEMS IN ZOOGEOGRAPHY OF THE LAKE TROUT, SALVELINUS NAMAYCUSH

The lake trout, *Salvelinus namaycush*, poses a distributional problem unique among North American fishes. It is the only freshwater species that ranges into the far north of Canada and Alaska, but that does *not* extend westward across Bering Strait into Siberia. Since every other freshwater fish whose range approaches Bering Strait has succeeded in crossing over, why has the lake trout failed?

There is complete disagreement in the literature as to the late Pleistocene glacial refugium of the lake trout.

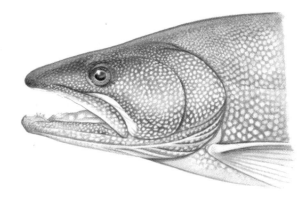

Lake Trout, 44-pound Male, Lake Athabaska, Saskatchewan

Radforth believed the lake trout survived the last glaciation north of the ice sheet in Alaska, and has since spread south. Walters concluded that the lake trout did not survive in Alaska, but has spread from a refugium in the Mississippi valley. Wynne-Edwards believed in a southern refugium, with the possibility of a second refugium in the Yukon River basin.

This article assembles the available evidence concerning lake trout zoogeography, and attempts to assess the conflicting hypotheses concerning where the lake trout originated and why it is confined to its present range.

PRESENT LAKE TROUT DISTRIBUTION

The distribution map with this article indicates distributional limits of the lake trout.

The present natural range of lake trout lies almost entirely within the limits of Pleistocene glaciation. South of the St. Lawrence-Great Lakes and Hudson Bay drainages they occur in Nova Scotia, New Brunswick, some headwater lakes of Atlantic drainages as far south as the Hudson River, in some Wisconsin and Minnesota lakes a few miles south of the Mississippi-Great Lakes divide and in the extreme northwestern headwaters of the Missouri River in Montana. West of the continental divide they are in the upper Fraser but not the Columbia, and in Pacific drainages north to Cook Inlet. They occur in Bristol Bay drainages. In the Yukon River they are present in headwater lakes but are apparently absent from the unglaciated middle and lower portions of the drainage basin. In northern Alaska they are also in higher ground along the Brooks Range, but not in coastal lowlands. Along the Canadian Arctic coast they extend out onto several islands of the Archipelago, and range eastward to Ungava and Labrador but do not reach Newfoundland.

South of their natural range, lake trout have been successfully planted (to establish self-sustaining populations) in New England and westward, including the Canadian prairie provinces, and in high lakes of some western states as far south as Nevada, California, and Colorado.

Lake trout are confined at their southern limits to deep cool lakes, but toward the north they occur also in shallower lakes and even in rivers. Although they are primarily lake spawners, stream spawning occurs in some tributaries to Lake Superior and may be commoner toward the north.

There are no records of lake trout from salt or brackish water in the southern portion of their range. However, like several other species ordinarily considered to be purely freshwater (e.g., grayling, Thymallus arcticus) they are sometimes encountered in brackish water in colder regions. Indeed, they must have crossed sea water to reach lakes on King William Island in the Canadian Arctic, for this island has risen from the sea only since disappearance of local glaciation.

No geographically consistent divergence in morphology of lake trout is known. Local "races" may be recognized, based on color differences, fatness, or growth rate, but these are sporadic in their distribution and have not provided evidence of genetically divergent stocks arising from separate glacial refugia. However, careful study on adequate material from over the range of the species has not yet been attempted.

REFUGIA OF OTHER WIDE-RANGING SPECIES

The glacial refugia for many northern fishes are evident from their present distributions. Some species, to judge by their absence from the Yukon River system today, obviously came from the south, others obviously came from the north. A few (including the grayling, and the Arctic chars, Salvelinus alpinus subspp.) survived both north and south of the ice sheet and have not rejoined their ranges since.

There remains a number of species widely distributed from the Great Lakes to Alaska and, except for the lake trout, across Bering Strait into Siberia. It is notable that every one of these species whose range surpasses that of the lake trout gives evidence of having survived in two or more glacial refugia, at least one south and one north of the ice sheet. Over the North American range of each, there occurs one large area repopulated by fish which have spread northward from south by glaciation, a second large area repopulated by a morphologically distinguishable type which has spread east and south from Alaska, and a zone of intergradation where the two types have met. Such a picture emerges for the slimy sculpin, Cottus cognatus, the ninespine stickleback, Pungitius pungitius, perhaps the humpback whitefishes, Coregonus spp., and probably for at least four other species.

Evidently no other freshwater fish which came from a single North American glacial refugium has achieved a postglacial distribution as wide as that now occupied by the lake trout. Therefore, to suppose that lake trout have reached New England, the upper Mississippi and upper Missouri from Alaska since glaciation, or else have reached Bristol Bay drainages and the Arctic slope of Alaska from south of the ice, is to credit the lake trout with a unique feat of dispersal. Such a possibility cannot be altogether discounted, as the lake trout is well-adapted to capitalize on temporary lakes along the ice face as an avenue for rapid dispersal in waning glaciation.

HAD LAKE TROUT A SOUTHERN REFUGIUM?

The only recorded fossil lake trout comes from Wisconsin close to the southern edge of glaciation within the present Mississippi drainage, a short distance south of the present natural range of the species in the area (see first distribution map). The surrounding clay also contains elephant, mastodon, and caribou remains. It was assigned to the interglacial period between the second and third Pleistocene glaciations by Hussakof. Recently, however, radio carbon techniques give a much later date to the surrounding beds (12,500 to 16,000 B.P.), corresponding to the closing stages of the last or Wisconsin glaciation (R. F. Black, in correspondence to J. D. McPhail). If the later dating be accepted, it offers direct evidence of the presence of lake trout in a southern refugium during Wisconsin glaciation.

Lake trout now occur naturally in some lakes around the northern margin of the Mississippi watershed in Wisconsin and Minnesota. These records do not, however, constitute proof of a Mississippi refugium, because some of the divides between the Great Lakes and Mississippi basins in Wisconsin are low and swampy, and several species of fish have evidently crossed them comparatively recently. Such routes would be less suitable to lake trout than to warmer water species.

Elsewhere in the Mississippi basin, natural populations of lake trout inhabit mountain lakes at the extreme headwaters of the Missouri River in northern Montana. These lakes lie immediately south of the Saskatchewan River basin, and might have received fishes from the north via drainage diversions associated with ice retreat. However, this area lies at the southern margin of continental glaciation. To suppose that lake trout entered the lakes in question from the Yukon basin, one must postulate that they did so by an ice-free corridor which would have had to connect the Yukon and present Saskatchewan River basins *before* drainage disruptions in Montana were complete. Such a corridor could conceivably have opened during a temporary drawing apart of the Cordilleran and Keewatin ice sheets; available geological evidence cannot decide this question.

A much simpler hypothesis is that lake trout existed throughout Wisconsin glaciation in Montana waters and elsewhere in the Mississippi basin, and moved northward following the retreating ice. The refugium in this area may have extended northward some distance into Alberta, where the edges of the Cordilleran and Keewatin ice sheets probably failed to meet.

Regardless of possible origin of lake trout now in Montana, the presence of natural populations as far east as New England and Nova Scotia, coupled with the fossil of probably late Wisconsin age, strongly suggest one or several southern refugia. These may well have existed east as well as west of the Appalachians, wherever suitable lakes lay.

An objection to the foregoing hypothesis rises from the absence of natural lake trout populations in many lakes just south of their present range. Lake trout have been successfully established by artificial introductions in lakes

north of the limits of glaciation but south of natural populations of the region (*e.g.*, in New England and southwestern Manitoba). If lake trout moved north following glaciation they must have passed across the lakes in question. Why then are they absent from these lakes, which we know to be capable of supporting lake trout?

The answer may lie in the "hypsithermal," or "altithermal," a period of thermal maximum which occurred between about 7000 and 4500 B.P.—that is, after retreat of the last glaciation. During the hypsithermal, temperatures were higher than at present (about 1 C° yearly average), with accompanying northward shift of isotherms. After glacial retreat but before the hypsithermal, lake trout probably persisted farther south than at present, in many lakes including those into which they have recently been re-introduced. Their southern limit of distribution was probably determined largely by the combination of water temperature, depth, and bottom type required for successful reproduction. When temperatures rose during the hypsithermal, the ranges of many species shifted north; for example, pollen analysis shows that several species of trees extended their ranges farther north then than at present. It is suggested that lake trout then died out in a number of marginal habitats along their southern limits. Since the hypsithermal, a somewhat cooler climate has rendered some of these waters again habitable, as demonstrated by successful southward introductions by man.

The absence of lake trout from Newfoundland is puzzling; if they persisted south of the ice sheet, they might be expected to have crossed from the lower St. Lawrence River to Newfoundland during ice retreat, when temperatures and salinities were low. Such sea crossings have been accomplished in the Canadian Arctic (for example

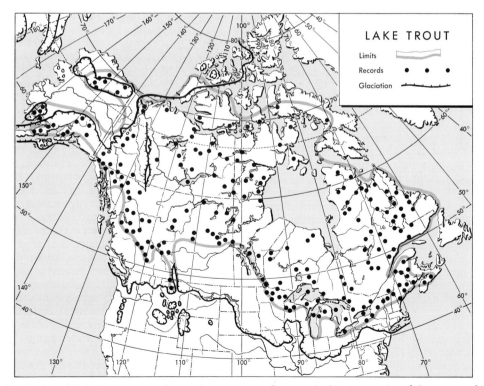

Distribution of *Salvelinus namaycush;* complete coverage for records close to margins of the range only

to King William Island, which has emerged from the sea only comparatively recently). Perhaps lake trout did not reach the Gulf of St. Lawrence until after higher salinity and temperature obstructed the crossing. Postglacially an arm of the sea extended up the St. Lawrence Valley to Lake Ontario, and during that time an ice cap may have persisted in central Maine perhaps blocking the northeastward spread of freshwater fishes. Lampreys may also have checked their eastward dispersal, as is discussed later.

Although lake trout probably had one or several southern refugia, they were almost certainly absent from the Pacific slope south of the ice sheet. None occur naturally in the Columbia River basin today. They have apparently reached the upper Fraser River and Pacific drainages farther north, by crossover from the east or north. One probable route was via postglacial Miette Lake, which lay across the continental divide and connected Moose Lake at the head of the Fraser River to the Athabasca River basin which then drained south.

HAD LAKE TROUT A NORTHERN REFUGIUM?

Lake trout are now distributed in a crescent bordering three sides of the unglaciated basin of the Yukon River (*see* first distribution map). They very probably survived the last glaciation in one or more areas of this Yukon refugium (as well as south of the ice sheet). Presumably lake trout were widespread in northern North America during the preceding interglacial period, particularly in cold regions, and it is difficult to postulate any sequence of events during the development of the last glaciation which would fail to leave populations somewhere in one or more northern refugia. Evidence has been presented above that several other species, probably no better adapted, survived in the north.

Apart from the unlikelihood of lake trout having been excluded from a northern refugium, the species is now distributed in parts of Alaska too remote to suggest postglacial dispersal from the Mississippi basin. It occurs in tributaries to Bristol Bay, in remote lakes tributary to the Kuskokwim River in the Kilbuck mountains, and in lakes on north and south slopes of the Brooks Range in northern Alaska. The possibility of lake trout having reached these places postglacially from a southern refugium cannot be ruled out, but it requires a feat of dispersal not accomplished by any other southern species. The two known southern invaders of the Yukon River system are the lake chub, *Couesius plumbea*, and the trout-perch, *Percopsis omiscomaycus*. The former have been taken downstream on the Yukon River only as far as Nulato (BC 60–367), and the latter at Andreafsky (BC 60–390); both are apparently absent from all Alaskan drainages other than the Yukon River. Present Alaskan lake trout distribution suggests not a recent and expanding invasion from the south but rather the somewhat disjunct and almost relict distribution of a long-established species.

The discontinuity of the lake trout in Alaska is striking. It results at least in part from the discontinuity of suitable habitats. No records exist of lake trout in or near almost the whole of the muddy mainstem of the Yukon River in Alaska, although the species abounds in large clear lakes in the Canadian headwaters. Precipitation in this area is low (presumably a cause of nonglaciation during the Pleistocene) and much of the region traversed by the river is quite dry. More important, deep or moderate lakes are abundant in glaciated areas, but are strikingly rare in unglaciated portions of the Yukon basin. Apparently suitable waters of the Seward Peninsula adjoining Bering Strait probably do not contain the species; these are separated from the nearest lake trout populations to the east by lowland tundra areas.

A strong argument has been put forward by Walters against lake trout having been present in the Yukon refugium during glaciation, in that had the species been there it would have crossed the Bering land bridge into Siberia. During the maximum glaciation so much water was locked up in ice sheets that the sea level dropped, and a strip of land over 1,000 miles from north to south was exposed, connecting Alaska and Siberia. Every freshwater fish species which now reaches Bering Strait from either side has crossed over. Direct evidence of at least three of these having used the land bridge is found on St. Lawrence Island, which lies south of Bering Strait and represents the highest part of the drowned bridge. On it now occur the Arctic grayling, the Alaska blackfish, *Dallia pectoralis*, and the slimy sculpin, *Cottus cognatus*. All are freshwater forms which, although they may venture into brackish water, have not likely crossed 40 miles of sea to the nearest land in Siberia. These and other fish must have passed along from watercourse to watercourse which drained the land bridge during its emergence.

However, unlike these other species, lake trout do not now reach the Bering Strait. Their closest known approach is in the Kobuk River some 400 miles to the east. Whatever combination of factors now checks their westward expansion may very well have checked them also during emergence of the land bridge. If failure of lake trout to cross to Siberia be attributed solely to their absence from Alaska during the last glaciation, then one must suppose that they were also absent during every one of the preceding glaciations, when bridges existed. More probably, lake trout have survived in the Yukon River basin throughout several glacial and interglacial periods, but have rarely or never ranged westward as far as Bering Strait. Absence of suitable waters, particularly for reproduction, would be no less effective a barrier during glacial times than they are now.

If lake trout did occasionally reach the land bridge, they would probably have found it unsuitable for reproduction although perhaps not for survival. The whole of the drowned bridge is now very flat, and presumably it carried no deep lakes, but only meandering streams with gentle gradients and muddy bottoms. The bridge supported no forest, only tundra. On the Siberian side, the Chukotsk Peninsula contains terrain and lakes which might be considered as suitable lake trout habitat. However, almost all of this was covered by an ice cap during the maximum (Illinoian?) glaciation, and at least part of the Chukotsk highlands were glaciated during the Wisconsin (*see* first distribution map). In the south, spawning lake trout require clean gravel or rubble bottom free of sand or mud, in lakes of suitable depths. Little is known of their spawning requirements in the north, but it may be surmised that conditions along the bridge, while allowing passage of suckers, graylings, etc., were less favorable for the spread of trout.

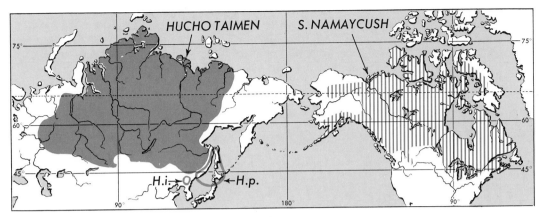

Distribution of *Salvelinus namaycush* and the genus *Hucho*

Lake trout may have survived in northern refugia other than the Yukon River basin. Portions of the Bristol Bay drainage, and also the Arctic slope of Alaska north of the Brooks Range, were unglaciated. Several areas bordering the Gulf of Alaska may have escaped Wisconsin glaciation and could have served as refugia. The northwestern half of Banks Island in the Canadian Archipelago was unglaciated. These areas now contain lake trout, and all might have contained them during Wisconsin times. Nunataks existed between the Cordilleran and Keewatin ice sheets in the Northwest Territories and perhaps farther south; these were possibly refugia for some hardy plants and animals, but probably not for fishes.

ASIAN COUNTERPARTS

The lake trout is the most distinctive of the chars (genus *Salvelinus*), both in habits and structure, so much so that strong arguments have been advanced for its placement in a separate genus *Cristivomer*. Since no obviously close relative of *S. namaycush* survives, it may be profitable to look outside the genus for clues as to its ancestry, and hence to its distributional history.

There occur in north Asia two genera of salmonids which in some ways suggest counterparts of the lake trout. The lenok, *Brachymystax lenok*, is a large river-dwelling species which never descends to the sea. Its range extends across northern Russia from the Ural Mountains eastward to within 600 miles of the Bering Strait in the Kolyma River basin. However, in its rather small mouth and skull morphology the lenok somewhat resembles the grayling *Thymallus*, and is apparently not very closely related to the lake trout.

The other genus of strictly freshwater Eurasian salmonids is *Hucho*, with four species which range from the Danube to Siberia and south to Japan; of these the taimen, *Hucho taimen*, occurs in the Volga and in Russian Arctic drainages from the Pechora River eastward to within 1,000 miles of Bering Strait in the Indigirka River (*see* second distribution map). It lives either in rivers or in lakes, and never descends to the sea. Like the lake trout, it reaches a large size.

Hucho taimen is without doubt a species perfectly distinct from *Salvelinus namaycush*, but the genera *Hucho* and *Salvelinus* do not differ sharply. Berg characterizes the genus *Hucho* as lacking teeth on the copulae (i.e., lacking basibranchial, or "hyoid," teeth). Norden omits

this character in his summary of generic characters, for he found that although basibranchial teeth were lacking in *H. hucho* they were well developed in *H. perryi*. The lake trout always has several rows of strong basibranchial teeth. The Arctic char, *S. alpinus*, has variable basibranchial teeth, while other species of *Salvelinus* have these teeth weaker and less numerous, or absent. The character most often cited as diagnostic between *Hucho* and *Salvelinus*, the presence or absence of a gap between the palatine and vomerine teeth, is also unreliable. McPhail describes these teeth in *S. malma* as "sometimes continuous, usually not"; in *S. alpinus* Walters illustrates some specimens with continuous tooth rows and some without.

The principal remaining osteological differences between the genera, the proportions of the supraethmoid and the development of the ascending process of the premaxilla are matters of degree only. In several osteological characters *Hucho* shows close relationship to *Salvelinus* (e.g., boat-shaped vomer, two parallel rows of strong teeth on the tongue), often with suggestions of closest relationship to *S. namaycush*.

Arguments based on other types of evidence can also be advanced to indicate that *S. namaycush* is the closest relative, amongst North American chars, to the Eurasian *Hucho*. The lake trout has a remarkably large number of pyloric caeca (94–170, in contrast to less than 75 in other North American chars); so do species of *Hucho*, with 150–250 caeca, many more than in other Eurasian salmonids. Another feature shown graphically by Morton and Miller to characterize the lake trout is the placement of the dorsal fin relatively far back on the body. Measurements of photographs and drawings show that the taimen also displays this backward position in the dorsal fin. Size also has been mentioned; the lake trout is the largest species of *Salvelinus* (over 100 lb., 45 kg.); *Hucho taimen* is even larger, up to 176 lb. (80 kg.).

Salvelinus and *Hucho* differ in coloration, but again the lake trout shows some intermediacy. All *Salvelinus* have light markings on a darker background. All species in the genus other than *S. namaycush* have vivid colored spots, at least at spawning time, and then the sides may become bright orange or red. Lake trout never have vivid colored spots; their nuptial coloration may consist of a yellowish or light orange wash. *Hucho* has no light markings, but small black speckles which may vanish with age.

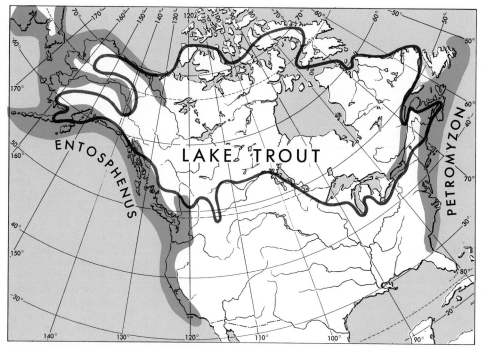

Distribution of *Salvelinus namaycush* (heavy outline) and large lampreys (dark blue)

Like the lake trout, they lack bright-colored spots, but the body may become copper-red during spawning.

All species of *Salvelinus* spawn in autumn, but all species of *Hucho* spawn in spring, evidently in running water.

According to the phyletic tree suggested by Norden, the most primitive genus of salmonine fishes (and the closest to *Thymallus*) is *Brachymystax*, followed progressively by *Hucho*, then *Salvelinus*, then *Salmo*, and finally *Oncorhynchus*. From the evidence given above, the most "*Hucho*-like" (and hence presumably most primitive), species of *Salvelinus* is *S. namaycush*.

The generic distinction between *Hucho* and *Salvelinus* may be questioned. But so may the distinction between *Salvelinus* and *Salmo* (see particularly the autumn-spawning *Salmo trutta* with pale haloes), or the distinction between *Salmo* and *Oncorhynchus* (bridged by the trout-like *Oncorhynchus masou*). In the interests of stability, generic distinctions in this (or any other) family should not be tampered with unless *all* known species are carefully reviewed.

SUMMARY

In summary, the taimen and the lake trout are both largely cold-adapted, almost purely freshwater species, evidently shunning lowland areas, each confined to one continent and approaching but not reaching Bering Strait. The taimen spawns in spring, lives primarily in rivers and has dark speckling; the lake trout spawns in autumn, lives primarily in lakes and has pale markings. The two do not differ strikingly in morphology.

It is suggested that *Hucho* and *S. namaycush* may have had a common ancestor which crossed the Bering gap in early Pleistocene or pre-Pleistocene times. (The ancestor might have resembled *Hucho perryi*, which is char-like in possessing basibranchial teeth, and which evidently tolerates sea water.)

Although they have diverged since, *H. taimen* and *S. namaycush* have apparently been subject to somewhat the same checks to geographic expansion.

LAMPREYS AND LAKE TROUT DISTRIBUTION

A further clue to lake trout distribution may be found by examining the North American distribution of large predatory lampreys. These are, on the Atlantic coast, *Petromyzon marinus*, on the Pacific coast, *Entosphenus tridentatus*, and in the Bering Sea and part of the Arctic Ocean, *Entosphenus japonicus* (probably synonymous with *E. lamottei*). The combined ranges of these, and the range of lake trout, are almost mutually exclusive (*see* third distribution map).

E. tridentatus occupies the lower parts of the Fraser River system, and lake trout the upper part of the system.

E. lamottei runs up the Yukon River to Dawson City, while lake trout occupy only the headwaters above there. In the St. Lawrence River system lampreys were formerly confined to below Niagara Falls; their entry into the upper Great Lakes has caused a catastrophic decline in lake trout there.

Lake trout have not crossed narrow seas to Newfoundland, to Vancouver Island, or the Queen Charlotte Islands; nor have they crossed Bering Strait. All these marine waters contain predatory lampreys. In contrast, lake trout *have* crossed the sea to reach Banks, Victoria, King William, Southampton, and other Arctic islands, all probably beyond the range of marine lampreys. (Exceptionally, lake trout have apparently crossed a narrow stretch of sea to reach Admiralty Island in southeastern Alaska, within the range of *E. tridentatus*.) These phenomena may arise from the higher sea temperatures and salinities existing toward the south, but presumably during ice recession even the more southern sea channels contained relatively cold brackish water.

Lake trout and large lampreys do overlap in a few localities. Lake Ontario contained *Petromyzon* and yet supported a moderate lake trout fishery, but these lampreys evidently did not migrate to sea, and were smaller than the marine form. Cayuga Lake in New York contains both species, but here the lampreys are a somewhat dwarfed landlocked race. In British Columbia a few sea-run *Entosphenus tridentatus* enter Shuswap Lake which also has lake trout. The Naknek River system tributary to Bristol Bay has lake trout and sea-run lampreys. Great Slave Lake contains many lake trout and a few *E. lamottei*, but the latter are non-migratory and much smaller than their Bering Sea counterparts. Several species of lampreys other than those named share lake trout waters in the southeast, but these are either non-parasitic or are smaller than the sea-running species, and presumably do not pose a serious threat.

Experience in the Great Lakes shows that lake trout are peculiarly sensitive to lamprey attack, due perhaps to their behavior or to their life history. There they have been decimated by lampreys, while other salmonid species (including the introduced *Salmo gairdnerii*) have been less affected. It is suggested that the lake trout has evolved in areas of North America not occupied by large predatory lampreys. Long exposure to lampreys in a few areas such as Lake Ontario may have produced by selection local races better able to withstand predation. The recent striking decrease of lake trout formerly protected by Niagara Falls may be due in part to the very long immunity which lake trout stocks had enjoyed in the upper Great Lakes.

The impact of lampreys on lake trout distribution should not be over-stressed, for the subject is highly conjectural. Lampreys are certainly not claimed to be the only, nor even the prime factor in limiting the spread of lake trout. They may, however, be one of the factors which have combined to hold lake trout within their present confines.

CONCLUSIONS

Radforth argued against the lake trout having survived south of the ice sheet, due to the absence of suitable habitats there. However, even now there are natural lake trout populations close to the southern edge of glaciation; at lower temperatures and with melt-water coming from the ice face, suitable environments were almost certainly present. The eastward distribution as far as New England and Nova Scotia suggests one or more southern refugia. The existence of a fossil in Wisconsin shows that the species was certainly present at some time south of the glaciated area; the most recent dating of the adjoining beds indicates that the specimen lived there about the time the last ice sheet was beginning to wane. Absence of lake trout from some suitable lakes along the southern margin of glaciation may be explained by failure to reproduce there during a post-glacial "hypsithermal" period.

Walters argued against the lake trout having survived north of the ice sheet due to its absence from Siberia. However, even now the lake trout is absent from areas close to Bering Strait. Whatever conditions now prevent it from expanding toward the Strait may very well have been operative throughout previous glacial and interglacial periods. Its wide but scattered Alaskan distribution does not suggest that it is a post-glacial immigrant which will shortly expand westward to the Strait.

If indeed it has penetrated from the Mississippi to remote western and northern Alaskan areas in recent times, there seems no reason why it should have failed to reach Alaska and become established there during previous interglacial periods. More likely it, and perhaps its relatives *Hucho* and *Brachymystax*, have survived in the north for a long time, but have failed to reach and cross the Bering area for ecological reasons. These may include the absence of lakes with suitable spawning sites in unglaciated regions circumscribing their present range, the barriers of silt and shallow water in lowland areas (including fresh waters of the land bridge while it was emergent), and blockage of suitable habitats by local ice in the Chukotsk highlands at times when a land bridge existed. Higher sea temperatures and salinities are now a further discouragement to crossing Bering Strait. Another factor which may hold the lake trout in check is the presence of predatory anadromous lampreys in the lower reaches of all but Arctic Ocean drainages.

The lake trout is a distinctive species, which has probably existed in northern North America for a long time. During the last, and perhaps during earlier glaciations, it probably survived in several refugia, some north and some south of the ice sheet. Morphological or physiological differences, such as occur in several other species, may yet be found which will enable us to distinguish between populations originating from the different refugia.
—C.C.L.

(This article is reprinted from the Journal of the Fisheries Research Board of Canada, *Vol. 21, No. 5, 1964, by permission of the author and editor of the* Journal. *Specific references in the text can be found in the reading list at the back of the book.)*

ANGLING VALUE

The lake trout is a popular gamefish, and it may be taken by fly-casting, spinning, or bait-casting when it is found inshore. Streamer flies, spoons, spinners, and plugs are effective lures. However, the most common method of fishing for lake trout is by trolling with large spoons and live bait. This is done principally with wire line (*which see*) at great depths. Lake trout are extremely sensitive to water temperature, and some local knowledge of the area being fished is a great advantage.

FOOD VALUE

An excellent food fish, the lake trout once constituted a large commercial fishery in the Great Lakes. With the advent of pollution and the parasitic sea lamprey (*which see*), the landings of lake trout have fallen from 7,457,000 pounds in 1946 to 385,000 pounds in 1960. Most of the commercial catch today comes from northern Canada.

The lake trout is prepared in a variety of ways such as stuffed and baked, steaked and broiled, and smoked. *See also* Fish Cookery, Smokehouse Cookery

LAKE WHITEFISH *Coregonus clupeaformis* The lake or common whitefish is only distantly related to the familiar mountain whitefish (*which see*) and is more highly regarded for its game qualities. Although most frequently found in lakes, it also enters rivers and provides a considerable sport fishery in the northern part of its range. However, not many anglers specialize in catching lake whitefish, and the methods employed are not widely known.

Lake Whitefish

The general coloration of the lake whitefish is a satiny-white with a faint, olive-green cast along the back. The fins are white or dusky-white, except for the caudal which normally has a dark edge. The body is compressed, and the back in adults is arched in front; the greatest depth is about $1/4$ of the body length. The head is small, being about $1/5$ of the body length. The snout is blunt and the mouth small with the maxillary reaching a point under the pupil of the eye. There are 11 rays in the dorsal and anal fins. The scale count varies around 82–92 along the lateral line, with 11 rows above and 8 below. Lake whitefish are known to attain weights of over 20 pounds, but the average is usually less than 4 pounds.

LIFE HISTORY

Lake whitefish spawn in the fall. Their migrations are made to shoal areas of large lakes, or they ascend tributary streams. There is considerable variation in the size of whitefish at maturity according to the racial stock; whitefish in Lake Huron become mature at 20–21 inches in length (according to John Van Oosten), with a small percentage of the population reaching maturity at 17–18 inches in length. In Great Slave Lake, Northwest Territories, whitefish reach maturity at 18 inches (Kennedy), although 20 per cent of the population is already mature at 12.1 inches. The smallest mature whitefish were reported from Lake Openago in Algonquin Park, Ontario; this dwarf stock matures at a length of 4–5 inches (Kennedy). There is no parental care of the eggs or young after spawning. Although the female whitefish deposits 10,000–12,000 eggs per pound of her body weight, only a very small percentage ever hatches. The adults spawn on gravel where the eggs are preyed upon by yellow perch, the mud puppy, crayfish, and aquatic birds.

Lake whitefish grow slowly, and a considerable time is required for the individual to attain a weight of 1 pound in most waters. The following table for Lake Erie (Van Oosten and Hile) represents the calculated length at the end of each year.

Age	Length (Inches)
I	6.9
II	12.7
III	16.1
IV	18.1
V	19.6
VI	20.7
VII	21.4
VIII	22.1
IX	22.8
X	23.2
XI	23.7
XII	24.2
XIII	24.6
XIV	25.0
XV	25.3
XVI	25.6

Lake whitefish feed principally on small crustaceans and aquatic insects. They also prey on forage fish to some extent, but this vertebrate food usually composes a very small part of their diet.

ANGLING VALUE

Although a natural associate of the lake trout, whitefish are more readily available to surface or near-surface angling methods throughout much of their range. Deepwater populations are most common in thermally stratified lakes along the United States and Canadian border. In their northern range, however, schools of lake whitefish are often found in the company of grayling toward evening as they forage inshore. Despite their abundance, angling is often a hit-or-miss proposition. Unless you are familiar with the area or travel with a competent guide, it's sometimes difficult to locate the grounds. When mayflies are hatching, the activity of a school is unmistakable. On quiet bays their swirling and popping rises are readily visible.

Lake whitefish also enter rivers, particularly in the spring and fall months. A considerable sport fishery exists in streams such as the Kanuchuan River and Gods River in Manitoba as well as the tributaries of Lake La Ronge, Reindeer Lake, and Cree Lake in Saskatchewan. During daylight hours river populations readily strike leadhead jigs and small spinners; toward evening they rise to aquatic-insect hatches and can be taken on dry flies. Whitefish should become an increasingly important gamefish in northern Canada when the techniques for catching them are better understood. Some angling possibilities exist in the northeastern United States also. Maine has many lakes which are not exploited. The common whitefish is abundant in Moosehead, Chamberlain, West Grand, and Sebago lakes where they provide excellent fishing on small dry flies in the spring of the year. Do not confuse the Menominee whitefish with the larger lake species in this region; the Menominee is a round whitefish (*which see*), common to New England, which seldom attains proper angling size.

COMMERCIAL VALUE

Whitefish have a tremendous commercial value the world over. They are largely utilized in smoked form. Due to its market popularity the species has a number of regional names, such as high-back whitefish, or bow-back whitefish, or buffalo-back whitefish, in alluding to the humped-back appearance of the adult. The lake whitefish is also inappropriately called "Otsego bass" at Otsego Lake in New York. In North America whitefish have decreased in number, but as transportation facilities expanded toward the Arctic into remote lakes the market haul has increased. When the northland is frozen and the ice on Great Slave Lake is four feet thick, whitefish are gillnetted by a rather ingenious method of running the mesh between spud holes, then hauled away in heated snowmobiles. Canada produces the largest catch in the world (20 million pounds); however, this reflects a growing exploitation from northern Saskatchewan into the Northwest Territories. Whitefish and lake trout are the dominant species in the Arctic fauna, followed by round whitefish, northern pike, ciscos, and grayling. Brook trout and char have a comparatively limited distribution and are absent over vast areas in these same latitudes.

But the world market for whitefish is immense, and many countries have developed hatchery techniques to increase their production.

FLY-FISHING FOR WHITEFISH

Taking whitefish on the fly requires some study. The fish rise most frequently in the early morning and evening. They seldom forage on the surface in bright daylight. The technique of catching them in lakes requires, first, a calm evening or morning and a good hatch of mayflies or caddisflies. The whitefish cruise a predictable course, rising for the adult insects. Often the fish can be seen very clearly in the water, but you must learn to intercept whitefish without seeing them. Watch for a rise. Within 4–5 seconds it will be followed by another rise in a different location and some yards apart. This is, invariably, the same whitefish. Relating the two rises you now have an indication of its direction. Place the fly in its path, about thirty feet from the last rise, and wait for the whitefish to come take it. It is almost useless to cast directly at a rise, as the fish move continuously and rather fast when feeding.

Whitefish take the fly in two ways. They either roll on it from top, sometimes in a half-jump, to bring the underslung mouth over the fly, or they take it in a body turn from below by sucking it in. Even when mouthing a cut bait they may expel it several times before accepting it. Their rise is wholly unlike that of a trout and very easy to miss if you strike too fast. It's necessary to give the whitefish ample time to inhale the feathers before setting the hook. And you must be very gentle as the fly will tear through their tender mouths. In many Canadian waters they run somewhat heavier than the weights most people are accustomed to dealing with, and it's easy to pull the barb out of an unyielding fish. You can't budge a 5–10 pounder with a 3X leader. An ice-shanty whitefish hooked 40–60 feet down on the lake bottom and hauled up through a spud hole has little chance to display his skill. When taken with a dry fly on top, it makes short but strong porpoising runs and on rare occasions leaps clear of the water.

BAIT-FISHING FOR WHITEFISH

Lake whitefish can be caught on cut bait. However, the most successful methods differ somewhat from normal procedure. In some states where it is legal, some form of chum is employed. The fisherman distributes a chum such as boiled rice, canned sweet corn, chopped minnows, or cooked spaghetti in the area to be fished. The location is marked with an empty capped can which is anchored in 40–65 feet of water. The chum is usually lowered around the marker in a bucket, then spilled on the bottom. The whitefish are then "snatched" as they feed on the ground bait by using a rig consisting of hooks soldered to a lead sinker. A second method consists of using a handline, small dipsey sinker, and two snelled No. 8 hooks baited with cubes of sucker meat. The baits are never left still on the bottom but jigged very gently to attract the attention of a whitefish. Usually, a fish nibbles at the sucker meat two or three times, then takes it with a noticeable pull. It's most important to tighten on the fish rather than strike it with any force. Most whitefish are lost by jerking at the line and ripping the hook out of their soft mouths—or by hauling them too fast from the bottom when they

are hooked. Handlining whitefish is not a very spectacular game, but it does require a gentle touch.   —A.J.McC.

LAMPREY *See* Pacific Lamprey, Sea Lamprey, Silver Lamprey

LANDING NET A baglike net mounted on a wood or metal frame used to lift fish from the water. A landing net is employed after the fish has been exhausted by the rod and is ready to be unhooked. Landing nets are of two principal types. One with a short handle (which seldom exceeds 18 inches in length) is a *stream net* which is designed to be worn on the person by means of an elastic cord or snap; the second type with a long handle is a *boat net* which is designed to be carried by hand or transported aboard the craft.

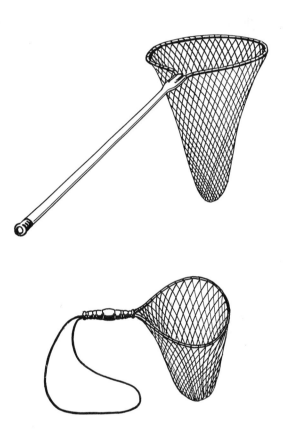

Landing Nets: Boat Net *(top)* and Stream Net

Although usually of fixed construction, either type may be made collapsible or telescopic in part or whole. The net frame can be circular, elliptical, semicircular, or triangular. The depth and strength of the mesh must be consistent with the length and weight of the fish sought.

The stream net is suitable for all small, freshwater gamefish, such as trout and bass. A boat net is required for larger fish, such as northern pike, lake trout, and salmon. The latter type also has broad application to saltwater gamefish such as spotted seatrout, snook, summer flounder, and yellowtail. However, where fish run large and are ordinarily killed rather than released, a gaff is preferable. In the case of gamefish with a stiff caudal peduncle (the "wrist" above the tail), such as Atlantic salmon, a tailer can be used. *See also* Gaff

Landlocked Salmon, 5½-pound Male, Long Lake, Maine

LANDLOCKED SALMON *Salmo salar* A superior freshwater gamefish, highly prized by United States anglers. The anadromous Atlantic salmon (*which see*) is considered by ichthyologists to be structurally the same fish with essentially identical taxonomic characteristics. Nevertheless populations vary in appearance according to environment, and the methods of fishing are dissimilar. A significant landlocked-salmon fishery exists in Maine where the species is considered the state's most important gamefish.

Four different river systems contained the original Maine populations—the St. Croix drainage in Washington County, Union River drainage in Hancock County, Piscataquis River subdrainage of the Penobscot in Penobscot County, and the Presumpscot River drainage in Cumberland County. Sebago Lake is located in the last-named county. The world's record rod-and-reel catch of 22½ pounds was taken from this lake in 1907. That same year, while seining salmon to strip, one of 36 pounds was reportedly netted by some hatchery personnel. Occasional landlocks of 9–10 pounds are caught presently in such Maine waters as the West Branch of the Penobscot, Long Lake in Aroostook County, and East Grand Lake in Washington-Aroostook counties. However, the average in Maine has been closer to 2½ pounds in recent years.

Landlocked salmon have been widely introduced in other lakes in Maine. New Hampshire has limited populations, and New York has established the fish in a few large lakes. The species, introduced in South America, has shown extraordinary adaptability to its new environment in Argentina (*which see*). Growth has been especially good, and some authorities think a new world's record for landlocks may be achieved on that continent. In the Maritime Provinces of Canada the landlocked salmon is called ouananiche (*which see*).

Like the Atlantic sea-run salmon, the landlock once existed over a wider area than it occupied when restocking began (in Maine) in 1875. The original distribution consisted of several waters in the Canadian Maritime Provinces, much of New England, Lake Ontario and a few lakes in New York's Adirondacks. The encroachment of civilization, with deforestation along lake shores and warmer water as a result, fostered the decline of this fish. It survives best in deep, cold lakes that have an abundance of oxygen.

LIFE HISTORY

Fisheries biologists in Maine have been particularly conscientious in their studies of the landlocked salmon. According to Kendall Warner, spawning takes place in the fall, primarily between October 15 and November 30. However, migrations to spawning areas may commence weeks earlier, and salmon may be found gathered near tributary mouths as early as the first week in September. Salmon reproduce successfully in lake inlets and outlets in swift, riffle areas with gravel or rubble bottom. The female constructs the same type of nest as the Atlantic salmon, digging pits by turning on her side and flapping vigorously with the caudal peduncle and caudal fin.

Warner concluded that most of the landlocked salmon taken by sportsmen are 3–6 years old. A new longevity record occurred when an angler recaptured a tagged female (June, 1960) in Long Lake, Aroostook County, Maine. Assuming the original aging to be accurate, the salmon would have been age 13+ in 1960. The landlock was 28 inches long and weighed 7.1 pounds when it was caught. The oldest previously taken was also a female fish of 19.7 pounds. Also from Long Lake, it was aged as 11+ and was caught in 1941. Warner estimates the growth rate of Maine landlocked salmon as follows: age one, 5.9 inches; two, 11.6 inches; three, 15.2 inches; four, 18.1 inches; five, 20.3 inches; six, 22.2 inches; seven, 23.5 inches; eight, 25.2 inches and age nine, 27.9 inches. The legal (minimum) length limit allowed in sports salmon fishing in Maine is 14 inches, with few exceptions; hence, landlocks are 3 years old, at least, when creeled.

DIET: A KEY TO LURES

Landlocked-salmon fry feed on small aquatic insects and other invertebrates, and the young (parr) stay in the river or stream where they are hatched for a year or two before migrating into a lake. Their diet then becomes largely forage fishes (in Maine), such as smelts, young alewives, sticklebacks, yellow perch, and minnows, and occasionally other fishes. Thus, the streamer fly—tied to resemble a smelt—was originated in Maine around the turn of the twentieth century. Herb Welch, of Oquossoc, Maine, was credited with designing the Black Ghost, and Carrie Stevens of Madison, Maine, the popular Grey Ghost. Probably half of the landlocks caught from ice out until late June each season strike streamers and the similar bucktail patterns, trolled a few inches under the surface, and the other half take live smelts which are fished in about the same way. In warm weather, deeper trolling is practiced (about 18–20 feet down), and the lure may be a long, slim wobbler or a live smelt.

Comparatively few sportsmen enjoy the thrilling contest which results when a landlocked salmon takes a small dry fly (in Maine); yet this fish rises gracefully and accepts such insect imitations readily. Patterns on No. 16 and 18 hooks are effective in places like the fastwater slicks below Ripogenus Dam on Maine's West Branch of the Penobscot, on Kennebago Stream in the Rangeleys, and, indeed—particularly in the evening—on nearly all salmon lakes, when the surface is smooth. Spin-casting is practiced increasingly, but landlocked salmon are such spectacular jumpers when hooked that fly-fishermen deplore anything except feathers and tinsel to entice them, or to slow down their action. —R.E.

LANE SNAPPER *Lutjanus synagris* This is one of the smallest and most common of snappers. It is fairly abundant around southern Florida and throughout the tropical American Atlantic. The usual total length is less than twelve inches.

The lane snapper has 10 dorsal spines, 12 dorsal rays, and 8 anal rays. Pectoral rays 15–16, usually 16. Gill-rakers 8–10 on lower limb of first arch, not counting rudiments. Rows of scales around caudal peduncle 25–27, usually 26. Cheek scales normally in six rows. Upper jaw reaching to or beyond vertical from anterior margin of orbit. Pectoral fin not reaching to vertical from origin of anal fin. Anal fin rounded, not angulate posteriorly. General coloration rosy-red with longitudinal yellow stripes; paler below. Black spot on sides of body present. Pectoral and caudal fins reddish. Dorsal fin pale, margined with orange-yellow. Pelvic and anal fins tinged with orange-yellow. Eye scarlet.

This snapper is distinguished from the others by the color pattern and the fewer dorsal rays. The mahogany snapper (*which see*) also has 12 dorsal rays but fewer pectoral rays and cheek scales.

ANGLING VALUE

A bottom-feeding, shallow-water species. The lane snapper takes live or dead bait and, occasionally, artificial lures. Accessible from shore, piers, or bridges.

FOOD VALUE

One of the best-eating snappers. Its small size makes it suitable for panfrying. A common market fish in the Caribbean area and occasionally in Florida. —L.R.

LANYARD A line made fast to anything to secure it
LAPSTRAKE *See* Clinker
LARGEMOUTH BASS *Micropterus salmoides* One of the most important freshwater gamefish in North America. The largemouth bass is regionally known as green bass, green trout, Oswego bass, and black bass. The largemouth can be distinguished from the smallmouth bass (*which see*) on three key points. The mouth of the adult is larger, the upper jaw or maxillary extending behind the eye, while the mouth of the smallmouth doesn't reach beyond it. Secondly, the spiny portion of the largemouth's dorsal is almost separated from the rear soft portion, while in the smallmouth bass both parts are connected in one continuous fin. The smallmouth also has scales overlapping the base of the soft dorsal while they are absent from that part of the largemouth. In color, the smallmouth bass is most often bronze to brownish with prominent vertical markings on its sides, while the largemouth is black to greenish and wears a dark horizontal band from head to tail. These markings may be obscured completely, particularly on older bass.

Largemouth bass are found in almost every state, but originally they were indigenous to southeastern Canada through the Great Lakes, and south in the Mississippi Valley to Mexico and Florida, and up the Atlantic Coast as far north as Maryland. This range gradually extended west of the Rockies about 1887 when bigmouth were introduced to the Columbia River system, then east into New England.

The largemouth thrives best in shallow, weedy lakes or in river backwaters. These bass prefer weedy habitats not

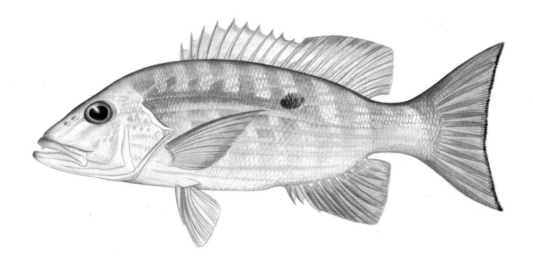

Lane Snapper, 10-inch Male, Deep Water Cay, Bahamas

Largemouth Bass, 6½-pound Female, Lake Seminole, Georgia

only because their food supply is available in these areas, but also because aquatic plants and sunken debris furnish protection. They are usually found in water less than 20 feet deep and rarely go beyond the area where rooted vegetation will grow.

The food of the young largemouth consists of tiny crustaceans, but as they grow larger they add insects, crayfish, frogs, and fish to their diet. Feeding drops off in late fall and winter, but when the water temperatures warm in the spring, heavy feeding again resumes.

LIFE HISTORY

Largemouth bass spawn in the north in the spring when the water temperatures reach 62°–65°F. This can be from early May to late June depending on the latitude. The male bass cleans out a nest about 20 inches in diameter and 6 inches deep in sand or gravel, if it is available. If not, the male will fan out the nest in most any type of bottom including silt and clay. Nesting usually occurs within 7–8 feet off the shore in 12–36 inches of water. The nests are never close together, but are separated by a distance of twenty feet or more. When the nest is completed the male bass entices a female to spawn. Female largemouth usually lay only a few hundred eggs at a time which are fertilized by the male. The eggs are adhesive and

fasten to the bottom of the nest. The female bass departs but may return to spawn with the same male or spawn in the nest of one or more other males. Often several female bass spawn in a single nest. The number of eggs per nest is dependent upon the number of females utilizing it and may vary from a few hundred to several thousand eggs. Female bass usually contain 2,000–7,000 eggs per pound of body weight.

The male largemouth guards the nest during incubation and for a short time after the young emerge from the eggs. The eggs usually hatch within a period of a week to ten days depending upon water temperature. At a temperature of 65°F. hatching takes place in about ten days, whereas at a temperature of 80°F. within only five days. Bass fry remain on the nest until the yolk sac has been absorbed, after which they school, frequenting the shallow water which is rich in microscopic food (plankton). They may remain in schools until over an inch in length, a characteristic which distinguishes them from the smallmouth species, the fry of which scatter when only ½ inch in length. At this stage the largemouth fry are of a yellowish, transparent color with a very pronounced black stripe down the body. They feed on Entomostraca but, as they grow, seek increasingly larger food items, feeding on smaller fish when less than 2 inches long.

Largemouth Bass, 3-pound Male, Black Lake, New York

GROWTH RATE

The growth rate of the largemouth bass is variable depending on environmental circumstances. In the Northern states this bass may grow from 2–4 inches the first year, 5–7 inches in its second year, and 8–11 inches in the third year. By the time Northern largemouths reach 18–19 inches in length they are usually 7–8 years old. A subspecies, the Florida largemouth (*which see*), grows much faster due to a more favorable environment and is known to attain weights of over 20 pounds. Northern bass rarely exceed 10 pounds, and 2–3 pounds is considered a good catch by the angler.

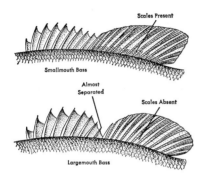

The spiny portion of the largemouth's dorsal fin is almost separated from the softrays, while the dorsal fin of the smallmouth is continuous with a scaled base on the soft portion

GENERAL ANGLING METHODS

The largemouth bass will take almost any type of bait that it considers alive. Worms, frogs, insect larvae, crayfish, and live minnows are all successful natural baits. Flies streamers, plugs, spinners, and spoons all have their ardent followers. In laboratory experiments it has been learned that black bass can distinguish color. Among casting baits the bass preferred red, then white, silver, and black in that order. Among the fly-rod lures, pure yellow, white plus any other color, and brown in a combination of other colors were preferred. *See also* Bait Casting, Bass Bug, Spinning   —K.B.

LATERAL Pertaining to the side; region of the side

LATERAL LINE A connected series of pores or receptors on the side of a fish. These receptors are composed of ciliated cells which are sensitive to the intermediate vibrations or low-frequency water movements. They are used to detect the presence of other fish, obstructions, and changes in the direction or flow of water. In some species the lateral line may represent the chief sensory organ. *See also* Anatomy

LAY The twist of the main strands in a fishing line or rope. The lay of the three main strands in a linen fishing line of conventional construction may be described as *hard laid*, meaning tightly twisted; and *long laid*, implying that is is more loosely twisted with relatively fewer twists per inch of line. Synonymous with long laid is the term *soft laid*. A polished finish to a fishing line strengthens the effect of it being hard laid. *Right-* or *left-hand-lay* indicates the direction of the twist of the main strands of a rope. *See also* Line

LAY TO To come to a stop, as to heave to, except that the stop need not necessarily be made only because of heavy seas, as in the case of stopping and holding to a desired heading to enable someone on another boat to approach and come aboard. When describing her location, a boat may also be said to *lay to* an anchor, mooring, pile, and so forth, at some particular place.

LEADER A variable length of synthetic or metal material connected to the end of a line. Leaders are used in fly-fishing, bait-casting, spinning, and trolling. The choice of a leader varies according to its specific purpose. In fly-fishing, for example, the line generally has a pound-test rating that far exceeds the strength of the leader. The only terminal problem in fly-fishing is to provide a reasonably invisible connection between the line and lure. Therefore the fly leader (*which see*) has a very fine diameter, and is made of a somewhat opaque material. But the prime function of leaders for all other forms of casting is that they provide a safety zone between line and lure to prevent sharp-toothed or rough-scaled fish from breaking free. The leader also protects the line from chafing or breaking against underwater obstacles, such as stumps, weeds, coral heads, and shell beds. When trolling, a leader can reduce or eliminate line twist, abrasion, and stresses against heavy rigs.

FRESHWATER CASTING

When using a monofilament line with spinning or bait-casting tackle there is seldom reason to employ a leader in freshwater fishing. The line itself provides that factor of invisibility. Trout, bass, panfish, and even the needle-toothed chain pickerel are not likely to cut free, and a small-snap swivel at the lure prevents line twist. When using braided line a six-foot length of monofilament spliced to the line with a Blood Knot reduces its visibility to some degree. Such leaders can also be purchased at very nominal cost. They are generally packaged in three-foot and six-foot lengths of ten-pound-test nylon. The nylon is looped at one end, and a snap is tied to the other, which makes lure changing easy. The loop is smooth enough to slip through the rod guides when joined with a Multiple Clinch Knot. With braided casting lines, this basic monofilament leader is an advantage, especially to the plug-caster who fishes civilized ponds.

In North America, the only toothed freshwater fishes which require metal leaders are large pike, walleyes, and muskellunge. However, for inland waters there's no hard-and-fast rule concerning the choice of metal or monofilament leaders, because fishing is frequently a hotchpotch affair. For instance, you may have the opportunity to catch smallmouths and muskies in the same lake—although you have no way of knowing which is going to strike. Primarily, the angler must decide exactly what he wants to catch and choose his terminal tackle accordingly. Fortunately, a very large percentage of the sharp-toothed freshwater species are landed without benefits of a metal leader when using artificial lures. The diameter of the line is a determining factor, and a great many anglers who cast for pike and muskies favor monofilaments of 8-pound-test or stronger. Lines of this size are not easily broken. The use of live bait such as minnows presents another problem, however. A bait is usually swallowed deep, and the line is submitted to a nasty mess of dentures. For all practical purposes, the use of a leader in freshwater resolves itself to whether your casting line is sufficiently strong to withstand abrasion.

SALTWATER CASTING

Generally speaking, some type of metal or synthetic leader is essential to saltwater casting. Almost every ocean-going gamefish is peculiarly equipped by nature, such as the scissorlike mouth of the barracuda, the razor-edged operculum of the snook, or the bony scutes of the jack crevalle—or by habitat such as the coral caves of the grouper or the oyster bars of the spotted weakfish—for cutting a casting line. Inasmuch as refined terminal tackle seems to be comparatively unimportant in saltwater fishing (although there are notable exceptions) the angler has a somewhat wider choice of leader sizes and materials.

Piano Wire Straight piano-wire leaders are popular among saltwater casters. These are made of high-carbon steel, which has been galvanized or tinned, and stainless steel. The advantage of piano wire is that it's relatively cheap, easy to loop for attaching the lure or hardware, and it's strong per diameter. However, wire kinks readily, and the kinks break. Its inherent stiffness also spoils the lure action. These drawbacks are evidently minor considerations as the material is still preferred by many experts when casting for big fish. If you use piano wire for densely packed school fish like the Spanish mackerel, bluefish, or king mackerel, be certain to buy the kind that's colored tobacco brown rather than the bright, tinned finish. When one fish hits the lure, others will slice a reflecting wire with the precision of a switchblade. Of course, plain wire rusts more quickly than tinned, but in saltwater fishing, metal of any kind cannot be trusted for prolonged periods. The same applies to swivels and snaps, which should be black or brown. Piano-wire leaders can be bought ready-made with twisted loops, or swivels attached. Some anglers obtain the raw material in coils and make their leaders on location. Piano wire usually comes in ¼-pound coils and 25-foot coils, and the sizes which are of interest to casters runs as follows:

Size	Diameter (inches)	Carbon Steel (test)	Stainless Steel (test)
2	.011	28	27
3	.012	34	32
4	.013	39	38
5	.014	46	44
6	.016	60	58
7	.018	76	69
8	.020	93	86
9	.022	114	104
10	.024	136	128
11	.026	156	148
12	.028	184	176
13	.030	212	202
14	.032	240	232
15	.034	282	272

Braided Wire Braided- or twisted-wire leaders are more flexible and less liable to kink than straight wire, but they are somewhat heavier in diameter for comparable strengths. They also require a crimping tool and metal sleeves for forming swivel connections if you make your

own. However, none of these disadvantages outweighs the advantage the flexible leader has when you are hooked to an active jumping or rolling fish. Braided wire is also made with a nylon cover, and this kind is most popular in both saltwater and freshwater fishing. The nylon-covered braid has great flexibility, seldom kinks, and the wire strands do not fray. These come ready-made in various sizes, the 6-inch and 9-inch lengths in 20-pound-test for freshwater, and 12-inch and 18-inch lengths in 30-pound-test for saltwater are most popular.

Shock Line The shock line is a leader made of monofilament designed to protect the end of the casting line in many types of heavy saltwater fishing. Unlike the ordinary tapered leader, the shock line is attached to the casting line in reverse; i.e., the heavy or butt end is tied to the lure while the progressively lighter section is tied to the end of the line. A good example of the role of a shock line is its function in tarpon fishing. Although an 8-pound monofilament is perfectly adequate for tarpon up to, say, 90 pounds, that diameter won't hold heavy fish at the terminal end. The silver king is rough on line, not so much from his concrete jaws, but through body contact. Tarpon frequently run directly away from the source of pull, taking the line over their backs and pounding the last 5–6 feet with their powerful tails. Many casters try to avoid using piano wire whenever possible as it's difficult to get maximum action from the lure, and the entire leader has to dangle from the rod tip when casting. Inasmuch as the tarpon doesn't present a dental problem, a heavy monofilament serves the same purpose as wire. A 2-foot length of 18-pound-test nylon joined to a 3-foot length of 36-pound-test makes a suitable a 5-foot leader. The strands are spliced with a Double Nail Knot, but unlike the ordinary tapered leader, the light end becomes the butt section and is knotted to the 8-pound line. Some Gulf Coast regulars prefer even longer shock lines of 10–12 feet in length. This puts the knot on the spool, whereas a 5-foot leader places the knot above the fore-finger when using a standard 7-foot spinning rod. It doesn't really matter exactly where the knots are located because, when correctly tied, they slip through the guides easily. It's important, however, to check them at least once during the day to make certain they are secure. In most waters, a 5-foot shock line will keep you out of trouble around coral heads and mangrove roots. If the tarpon are likely to run over 5 feet long, then obviously a greater length of heavy monofilament is necessary.

TROLLING LEADERS

For two reasons, trolling for any of the larger species, such as lake trout, king salmon, or even rainbow trout, requires a metal leader of some kind when heavy spoons, flashers, cowbells, or dodgers are employed. As far as the multiple attractors are concerned, a wire leader is an integral part of the rig. When hooked in deepwater, these fish will roll and wrap themselves around the line. The other reason is that trolling spoons will twist your line badly, and a properly swiveled leader eliminates that problem. The standard trolling leader for lakers and salmon is a 6-foot piano wire (27–58-pound-test), but a great deal depends on where the fishing is being done. Sinker weights of the slip and crescent type vary from 2–16 ounces, and a man needs heavy terminal gear as conditions demand.

For shallow trolling with small lures, however, the prime purpose of your leader is to prevent line twist. Maybe you just want to comb the rock ledges with a spoon for smallmouths, in which case a 6-inch, nylon-covered wire, or even plain monfilament, would be perfectly adequate. The casual troller can make his own leaders from 3-foot strands of monofilament. At the lure end, knot on a barrel-and-snap (these come in sizes from 1 to 12, the higher numbers being progressively smaller), and at the other end tie on a plain barrel swivel. The line is then joined to the barrel ring with an Improved Clinch Knot. Whenever possible, it's a good idea to use a mono-filament testing a few pounds lighter than your line. If the lure becomes firmly snagged, the leader will break, and there's no yardage lost. The swivels provide the real leader function in this type of angling; so make certain to get a good brand that rotates freely. *See also* Fly Leader

—A.J.McC.

LEADHEAD A colloquial term for various types of small jigs used in fresh- and saltwater casting. *See also* Jig

LEASH A collective name for three fish, e.g., a leash of trout

LEATHER CARP *See* Carp

LEATHERJACKETS *Oligoplites* spp. Also called leather-coats and leathernecks. These interesting fishes are super-ficially more like the scombrids (tunas and mackerels) than the Carangidae.

They are distinguished by the semidetached finlets of the posterior 6–9 rays of the dorsal and anal fins; the flattened, spinelike, embedded scales on the body; the 4–5 short dorsal spines (rarely 3–6), the anterior 2–3 spines inclined forward; and the long, thin jaws (the premaxil-laries are not protractile).

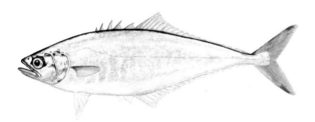

Leatherjacket

There are three Atlantic species (*Oligoplites saurus, Oligoplites saliens,* and *Oligoplites palometa*) and four Pacific species (*Oligoplites altus, Oligoplites inornatus, Oligoplites mundus,* and *Oligoplites refulgens*). One of the Pacific species (*O. inornatus*) is so similar to one of the Atlantic species (*O. saurus*) that it has been classed as a subspecies of the latter. Because these fish are generally similar in appearance and infrequently caught, their common names are less meaningful than their scientific names. The leatherjackets are closely related to the talang or queenfish, genus *Chorinemus* (sometimes *Scomberoides*) of the Indo-Pacific, which usually has seven spines in the first dorsal fin and broad bands of teeth on the pterygoid bones.

LIFE HISTORY

The life histories of the leatherjackets are not known. They appear to have an inshore habitat, mainly in tropi-cal waters. They are found along sandy beaches and in inlets and bays, where they seem to prefer tidal currents, and they have been taken in water of low salinity. Young leatherjackets (*O. saurus*) have been noted drifting twisted and head down at the surface, resembling in shape and color mangrove leaves floating in the vicinity (suggested to be protective mimicry). They also have been observed in this same manner when nothing else was present at the surface. Placed in an aquarium with small herring, they mimicked the herring swimming behavior and changed color from brassy-green to silvery. The two detached anal-fin spines of one species (*O. inornatus*) apparently are connected with toxic glands; in an aquarium this species was seen to thrust the spines into a bat ray, and the bat ray promptly died; but with this in mind, when the anal spines of a freshly caught specimen of another species (*O. mundus*) were forced into an arm, the only result was the mild sensation produced by holes in the skin.

SPECIES

The Atlantic species are separated as follows. *Oligo-plites saliens:* 17–20 gillrakers on the lower limb of the first gill arch (range of Central America and the West Indies to Montevideo, Uruguay). *Oligoplites palometa:* 12–13 gillrakers on the lower limb; teeth on the upper jaw in a band (range of Nicaragua to Rio de Janeiro, Brazil). *Oligoplites saurus:* 11–14 gillrakers on the lower limb; teeth on the upper jaw in 2 distinct rows (range of Woods Hole, Massachusetts, to Montevideo, Uruguay, and in the West Indies).

The Pacific species are distinguished as follows. *Oligoplites refulgens:* 18–22 gillrakers on the lower limb of the first gill arch (range of Cabo Blanco, Peru, to the northern Gulf of California). *Oligoplites inornatus:* 14–17 gillrakers on the lower limb; no series of pores opening onto top of head (range of Santa Elena Bay, Ecuador, throughout the Gulf of California, to southern Cali-fornia, and at the Galápagos Islands). *Oligoplites altus:* about 12–13 gillrakers on the lower limb; a series of small pores opening onto the top of head; the pectoral fin longer than the length of the upper jaw (range of Guaya-quil, Ecuador, to Panamá). *Oligoplites mundus:* 11–13 gillrakers on the lower limb; a series of small pores open-ing onto the top of head; the pectoral fin shorter than the length of the upper jaw (range of Callao, Peru, possibly only southward to the Gulf of Guayaquil, and northward into the southern Gulf of California, and to Santa María Bay on the outer coast of Baja California).

The relatively deep-bodied *Oligoplites mundus* ap-parently attains the largest size of any of the leather-jackets, reaching 15 inches in total length.

ANGLING VALUE

The leatherjackets generally are not listed as gamefish, but one species at least (*O. mundus*) has proven to be an exceptionally strong and stubborn fighter on light tackle. Another (*O. saurus*) reportedly is fished for at times and is favored in certain localities for use as live or cut bait for other fish. They are of little commercial importance; one species (*O. saurus*) has been described as of little value as food with dry and bony flesh; but another (*O. mundus*) is sold and eaten in Mexico. *See also* Carangidae —F.H.B.

LEATHERSIDE CHUB *Gila copei*   A bluish-backed, silvery minnow with a dusky lateral streak. A faint orange smear may be present between the eye and the maxillary. Bright spots of the same color may be present at the bases of the pectoral and ventral fins. Scales small, eighty in lateral line. Origin of the dorsal fin behind origin of the ventral fins. Dorsal rays 8. Anal rays 8. The mouth is small, low, terminal, and oblique; the premaxillary just below the level of the pupil; the maxillary reaching just beyond the

Leatherside Chub

front of the eye. This fish is found only in the Bonneville and Snake River drainages of Nevada, Utah, and Wyoming.

HABITS

The leatherside chub inhabits clear coldwaters where it grows to a length of 6 inches. Spawning is in midsummer.

ECONOMIC VALUE

The leatherside is considered an excellent bait species.
—R.A.J.

LEE   The side opposite to that from which the wind blows; the side sheltered from the weather. If a boat has the wind on her starboard, that will be the "weather" side, and the port will be the "lee" side.

LEECHES *Class Hirudinea*   One of the groups of segmented worms or annelids, commonly called bloodsucker. Leeches range 1–4 inches long. It is an external parasite on fish and other aquatic animals but may also occur in fish stomachs. Leeches also attach themselves to persons swimming or wading by means of a posterior and anterior sucker, making a wound with jaws located inside the mouth. The salivary glands of the leech secrete an anticoagulant, hirudin, while the worm extracts blood. The wound is very minor and will itch more if the leech is removed immediately after biting, than if left in place to suck out the irritating hirudin. Leech bites are not dangerous except in the rare instance of a hemophiliac or "natural bleeder."

Leeches are often an important fish food, particularly to trout. Although no leech imitations have been designed per se, various patterns of the Woolly Worm, especially those with black or dark brown bodies, are frequently effective where these annelids are numerous. For leeches as fish parasites *see* Diseases and Parasites   —A.J.McC.

LEMONFISH   *See* Cobia

LEMON SHARK *Negaprion brevirostris*   A common tropical shark of the family Carcharhinidae, it is readily recognized by its yellowish-brown color, the broadly rounded snout, and the two dorsal fins of about equal size, both of which are placed rather far back on the body. The distinctive teeth, which also help to separate it from other Atlantic sharks, are symmetrical and erect in the central part of the jaw and lack cusps along their margins. The bases of the teeth of the upper jaw have fine, irregular serrations. It reaches a length of about 11 feet but does not grow as heavy as other species at about the same length. Lemon sharks are plentiful in the Caribbean, and are reported regularly elsewhere from Brazil to North Carolina and the Gulf of Mexico, straying north to New Jersey, as well as off the coast of tropical West Africa and Ecuador.

LIFE HISTORY

Although it is predominantly a shallow-water shark, a few have been taken from 50 fathoms. Young lemon sharks are common in very shallow waters while adults occur singly or in loose aggregations, usually in schools predominantly of one sex. Young are produced in late spring and early summer, where they are abundant in shallow water. They feed on fishes, such as mullet, and crustaceans, apparently feeding more at night than during the day.

This species has been implicated in attacks on humans, and its vicious habits in captivity and its common occurrence in shallow water make it a potential danger to bathers.
—D.dS.

LEMON SOLE   *See* English Sole

LENOK *Brachymystax lenok*   An Asian salmonid differing from other genera in having a smaller mouth. The lenok occurs in all Siberian rivers from the Ob to the Kolyma

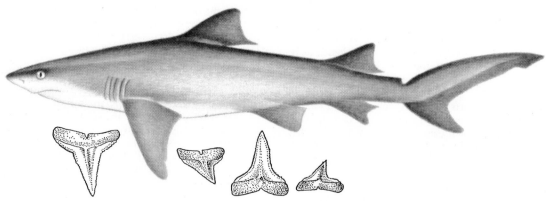

Lemon Shark

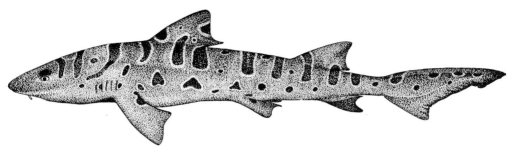

Leopard Shark

and as far south as the Yalu River. The lenok is not anadromous, but lives in rivers where it feeds upon insects, amphipods, and occasionally small fishes. The lenok seldom exceeds 10 pounds in weight, but it has some commercial value to the Soviet fishery. —A.J.McC.

LEOPARD SHARK *Triakis semifasciata* The distinctive color pattern of this shark readily identifies this Pacific Coast species. It has a general resemblance to the brown smoothhound (*which see*). It is only somewhat stout anteriorly, tapering rapidly to a narrow caudal peduncle. The first and second dorsal fins are about the same size. The body is gray with about 12-13 dark crossbands on the back and dark spots on the sides. Males grow to 3 feet long, females to 5, and maturity in about half of the females occurs at approximately 3½ feet long. Found from Oregon to Baja California, it is fairly common in shallow bays of southern California.

ANGLING VALUE

The flesh of the leopard shark is good, and it is commonly taken by sport fishermen.

DANGER TO MAN

This species was involved in an attack on a skin diver in 1955 in California. —D.dS.

LESOTHO *See* South Africa

LESSER AMBERJACK *Seriola fasciata* This is a small and rare species of the western Atlantic.

The dark nuchal band of the lesser amberjack extends obliquely backward from the eye to the nape, ending well in front of the first dorsal fin. The body at all known sizes has eight (rarely seven) split and wavy bars. The body is relatively deep; the greatest body depth goes about 2.6 times into the standard length (standard length is measured from the tip of the snout to the end of the bony plate of the tail—*see* Measurements of Fish).

The first dorsal fin has eight spines. The second dorsal fin has 1 spine and 30-32 softrays. The anal fin has 2 detached spines followed by a spine and 19-20 softrays. The dorsal-fin-lobe length goes about 6.7 times into the standard length. The first gill arch has a total of about 22-28 gillrakers, about 6-8 on the upper limb and 17-20 on the lower limb. The back is olive-brown, the sides and belly silver-gray, and the bars brown.

This species has been reported from Cuba to Massachusetts, in the northeastern and southwestern Gulf of Mexico, in the Bahamas, and from well offshore in the Florida Current and the Gulf Stream. Records of its occurrence in the eastern Atlantic are not substantiated and are doubtful. The largest specimen caught was 10¼ inches in total length.

ANGLING VALUE

The lesser amberjack is seldom caught, and any specimens caught would be useful to future studies, if saved for an ichthyological museum. *See also* Amberjacks, Carangidae —F.H.B.

LESSER ELECTRIC RAY *Narcine brasiliensis* A small ray of the family Torpedinidae, this well-marked species is distinguished from the Atlantic torpedo (*which see*) by its size, its more convex head, the close placement of the spiracles to the eyes, its more rigid snout, and the color pattern. The disk is nearly circular, but the broad pelvic fins appear so nearly confluent with the disk that the disc takes on a triangular appearance. It is dark brown, grading through gray-brown to reddish. The color pattern is highly variable and ranges from a uniform color to a more common pattern of irregular, dark blotches, each of which usually has a light center. Occasionally a band crosses the disk in front of the eyes. It grows to a length of about 15 inches.

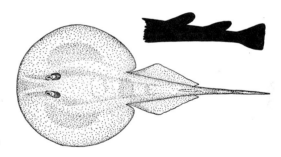

Lesser Electric Ray

LIFE HISTORY

Found in tropical waters, it is commonest from Brazil to Florida and throughout the Caribbean. A few range into the waters of North Carolina and Argentina. This same species also occurs from the Gulf of California to Panama. Shallow waters are its favorite haunt, where it is a bother to fishermen or other persons wading the shallows. The ray's voltage, produced through specialized, batterylike cells on either side of the disk, may reach as high as about 37 volts, and the result is, if not painful, quite surprising. This voltage is sufficient to knock down an adult.

They lie mostly buried in the sand, and occasionally they are taken in water as deep as 20 fathoms. The young are born during the summer, and even then are capable of giving a noticeable shock. Four to fifteen embryos have been taken from females.

FOOD VALUE

This electric ray has no commercial or sport-fishing value, although its flesh is reported to be of fine flavor.

—D.dS.

LESSER WEEVER *See* Weeverfish

LIFE BUOY A ring buoy made of cork and covered with canvas, used for life saving.

LIGHTHOUSE A structure, visible for some distance, placed on or near a dangerous area or on a point of land and equipped with a light which flashes in a set pattern.

LIGHT SHIP A small ship equipped with a distinctive light and anchored near an obstruction to navigation or in shallow water to protect passing marine traffic

LIMBER HOLE A hole cut in the framing of a boat near the keel to allow water to flow back and forth in the bottom so that it may be sponged or pumped out

LIMPETS Primitive gastropods (a large class of mollusks) similar to snails that are found in both ocean and fresh water and have low, cone-shaped shells.

LINE That component of fishing tackle which serves to present the lure or bait at varying distances from the angler when thrown or lowered by hand (handline), or cast from a reel with a rod (casting line), or cast from a rod independent of the reel (fly line) or paid out behind a boat (trolling line). Also used to refer to the ropes or hausers of a ship or vessel.

Lines are made of many natural and synthetic materials, such as linen, silk, nylon, Dacron, terelene, perlon, plastic, copper, and Monel metal. They are classified according to the material, its length, construction, strength, and weight (flyfishing). The characteristics desirable in a line for the different methods of fishing are not uniform; flexibility, resistance to abrasion, diameter, degree of water absorption, and specific gravity are variable factors which have greater or lesser importance according to the purpose. A detailed description of fishing lines can be found under the respective method. *See also* Bait-Casting, Fly-Casting, Spinning, Spin-Casting, Surf-Casting, Trolling. A detailed description of line material and manufacture can be found under the respective subjects. *See also* Dacron, Linen Line, Nylon, Perlon, Silk, Terylene, Wire Line

LINE DRESSING A compound in solid or liquid form which is applied to a fly line to make it float

LINEN LINE A line made of linen which was popular among saltwater anglers until 1955. Linen lines have been replaced by Dacron in the heavy tests, and monofilament in the light tests. Some big-game experts still prefer linen, however, particularly in the 39-thread size because of its negligible stretch and resistance to abrasion. Only a very minor quantity of linen lines is made today.

Linen lines are braided or twisted and rated according to the number of threads in multiples of three, from 6-thread to 72-thread. Thus, a 6-thread line represents 18-pound-test, and the 72-thread represents 216-pound-test. Dry linen is not as strong as wet linen as the absorption of water increases the strength by decreasing fiber slippage.

—A.J.McC.

LING A regional name in the Gulf states for the cobia (*which see*). Also a regional name for the burbot (*which see*).

LINGCOD *Ophiodon elongatus* A Pacific marine species of some value both as a sport and commercial fish. The lingcod is known in many areas as the cultus cod. Lingcod occur in North American waters from California to Alaska. As a rule they run at a wide range of depths from two to more than 70 fathoms.

DESCRIPTION

The lingcod has a large mouth, large pectoral fins, smooth body, and a long, continuous dorsal fin divided by a notch into spiny and soft parts. Young individuals are slender throughout, but older fish are moderately robust with large heads and jaws. Their color is variable, usually mottled against a dark gray or brown body. Fish taken from the same reef are frequently colored alike, and as a result experienced anglers claim they distinguish the locale of capture by their appearance.

Lingcod reach large size. The largest specimen recorded is 70 pounds, but the rather frequent occurrence of 50–60 pounders in commercial catches makes it seem probable that the 70-pound weight is occasionally exceeded. Maximum length runs 4–4½ feet. Males are much smaller than females, and it is doubtful that they exceed 3 feet in length or a weight of 25 pounds. As might be expected from their larger size, female lingcod grow about 2¾ pounds per year, and males 1¾ pounds. The rate of growth is not constant throughout life, so that at 8 years of age a male lingcod will weigh about 9¾ pounds and a female 14¾ pounds.

HABITS

Lingcod spawn in the winter from December to February. The eggs are deposited in porous, pearly masses struck to the rocks, usually, in crevices or beneath overhanging boulders. Egg masses may be 2 feet in length, weigh as much as 30 pounds, and contain more than half a million eggs. A considerable number of egg masses are found in the intertidal zone. Some evidently occur below low-tide mark, but what proportion, or how deep, is not known. The egg masses are tended by the males, who drive away potential predators.

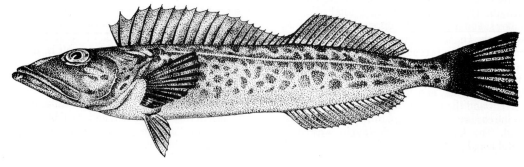

Lingcod

The eggs hatch in 1–2 months to produce larvae about ½ inch long. At this stage they have small yolk sacs on the abdomen with a ten-day supply of food and noticeably blue eyes. The young apparently move around near the surface until they are 3–4 months old, when they are found near the bottom in shallow water. Many of them gradually work down to take up more or less permanent positions in deepwater. In general, the larger lingcod are found on "hard bottom" of rock or gravel.

The data obtained by tagging nearly two thousand lingcod in the Strait of Georgia with strap tags on the gills, or celluloid spirals rolled on the upper jaws, have shown that many of them are very sedentary, as they are recaptured years later in the same place as tagged. Others show considerable movement, and the evidence of the fishery on the west coast of Vancouver Island is that ling-cod appear on fishing grounds as though they were taking part in a mass migration.

FISHING METHODS

The primitive method of fishing for lingcod by Indians was ingenious. A wooden shuttlecocklike lure or hee-hee made of wood and fibers was pushed down toward the reef with a long, three-tined spear. When the spear was sharply withdrawn, the hee-hee spun slowly toward the surface followed by the curious or hungry lingcod. When the fish came close to the surface it was deftly speared and landed. (*Most of the information on this species is from the Information Service of the Department of Fisheries, Ottawa, Canada.*)

LITERATURE OF ANGLING Exceeded in its antiquity only by the literature of hunting, angling literature is now even greater in its extent and diversity, and is today generally acknowledged to be the largest body of literature devoted to any single branch of sport. While a definitive bibliography of angling literature has not been attempted in recent decades, it is obvious that any such masterwork, if attempted today, would have to embrace in excess of five thousand titles in English alone. Even so, it would still be only fractional in relation to the size of a full bibliography on ichthyology, which would exceed fifty thousand entries.

The most written about single fish, considered as a quarry for sportsmen rather than as a subject of commercial or scientific study, is by all odds the trout. And of all the many branches of sport fishing, fly-fishing, with all its attendant studies of entomology, has received by far the greatest amount of literary attention.

Since the kindergarten of angling is still fishing with a pole and a worm, and serious anglers generally agree that the progressive education of an angler culminates in stream fishing with a fly, it is only natural that the highest reaches of the literature should be concerned chiefly with this form of fishing.

The two chief milestones in almost five centuries of angling literature are, and will undoubtedly remain, the works of Dame Juliana Berners, first printed in 1496 although presumably written some fifty years earlier, and Izaak Walton, the latter first printed in 1653, but not issued with its all-important second part by Charles Cotton until 1676. Both of these works are of such cardinal importance that they are given separate entries in this book, and the interested reader will find these two articles under Berners and Walton.

As classics, the Berners and Walton books are in a class by themselves, but there are eight others which, together with these first two, have earned through their longevity and the frequency with which they have been reissued, the distinction of being the Big Ten of angling classics. They are, falling in alphabetical order between Berners and Walton, the works of Thomas Best (1787), "John Bickerdyke" (1889), Richard and Charles Bowlker (1758), Gervase Markham (1631), Alfred Ronalds (1836), Thomas Salter (1814), J(ohn) S(mith) (1696), and W. C. Stewart (1857).

The well-read angler ought also to include, on a par with the rest of the Big Ten, but never heretofore counted among them because it was for centuries a lost classic and only recently rediscovered, *The Arte of Angling* (1577), a bridge between Berners and Walton, which is discussed in the entry on Isaak Walton.

At the risk of seeming to oversimplify the subject, it is possible to blaze a trail through the thousands of titles that together form the almost impenetrable thickets of angling literature by adding to the ten all-time best sellers among the classics, already mentioned, merely another ten authors of vintage works (1828–1935) and another ten authors of modern works (1950–1963). Thus, by reading thirty books, any angler can qualify as being truly well read, without attempting the almost insuperable task of reading everything that has been written about fishing the last five centuries. And while it is unlikely that any of the scholars in the field would agree exactly on the ten moderns, it is equally unlikely that they would disagree seriously on the ten classic or the ten vintage selections.

After running this short course, those whose reading appetites have been whetted to read on would still do well to seek further guidance, in the form of one of the several good "books about books about fishing," before striking out for themselves. For otherwise the unguided angler will have to plough through many for every one that he finds rewarding in any substantial way. Inevitably there has been endless duplication in the literature of angling, and while it is certainly no longer true, if indeed it ever was, that "Walton alone gave it style," as Andrew Lang, eighty years ago contended, still it would not be too severe to say that not more than one in every hundred of its thousands of books has represented a truly original contribution, either from the standpoint of adding to the attraction, through literary distinction, or enhancing the instruction, in the sense of adding to the knowledge of angling.

One short cut across these trackless wastes is, of course, *An Angler's Anthology*, and there are at least two good ones, an English one by A. B. Austin, first issued by Country Life Ltd. in London in 1930, and in the United States by Scribner's, and the other, American, by Eugene Burns, published by Stackpole in 1952. Both browse delightfully among the books on angling, back to the *Treatise*, culling choice blooms from the vast gardens, but their gatherings, like cut flowers, leave the interested angler with nothing that he can plant and cultivate and make his own. Like all samplers, the more he enjoys them, the more they make him want to look for more, and yet by their very nature they can't give him any idea of where to find more of the rare and fragrant blossoms without getting bogged down among the weeds and brambles.

Three books that can give such guidance to angling literature, and are at the same time worth reading in themselves, are *Notable Angling Literature* by James Robb, published by Herbert Jenkins Ltd. (London), 1945; *A History of Fly Fishing for Trout* by John Waller Hills, published by Frederick A. Stokes Co., 1921; and *Walton and Some Earlier Writers on Fish and Fishing* by R. B. Marston, published by Elliott Stock (London), 1903, although first published in 1894. On the last page of the second of these books Hills spoke just as truly for the other two as he did for his own when he said, "There are some who read everything which is written about fishing, for I am of that number . . . there must be others also like myself, whom the history of the sport attracts, who are fascinated by the devices of other days, and who are never weary of going back to the old writers, of reading them again, of getting at their real meaning, and of seeing where they have anticipated us and where we have improved on them."

All three of these writers, Robb, Hills, and Marston, get at the real meaning of the old writers, quote them and characterize them, point out the significance of their contributions, and show both where they are still valid and where later developments have improved upon them. Robb, since he is the most recent, is the most valuable as a guide to further reading.

The thirty books that, together, bridge the five centuries from the *Treatise* to our own times are generally available in metropolitan and university libraries, and the identification of them here given should be sufficient to obtain access to them. For anglers who wish to have copies of their own, the services of a seller of sporting books will undoubtedly be required. Three who among them can be counted on to furnish copies of virtually all of them are Sporting Book Service, Box 181, Rancocas, New Jersey; Angler's & Shooter's Bookshelf, Goshen, Connecticut 06756; and E. Chalmers Hallam, Earlswood, Egmont Drive, Ringwood, Hampshire, England.

The Thirty Books (*indicates attraction—literary value; + indicates instruction—technical value)

Classic: Berners, Dame Juliana, *The Treatise of Fishing with an Angle*, ****+, 1496 (see McDonald *Origins of Angling*, below, which contains two versions of *The Treatise*); Best, Thomas, *A Concise Treatise on the Art of Angling*, **, 1787; "Bickerdyke, John" (Charles Henry Cook), *The Book of the All-round Angler*, **, 1889; Bowlker, Richard and Charles, *The Art of Angling Improved in All Its Parts, Especially Fly-fishing*, **, 1758; Markham, Gervase, *Country Contentments*, ***, 1631; Ronalds, Alfred, *The Fly-fisher's Entomology*, ***+, 1836; Salter, Thomas, *The Angler's Guide*, **, 1814; S(mith), J(ohn), *The True Art of Angling*, **, 1696; Stewart, W. C., *The Practical Angler*, **+, 1857; Walton, Izaak, and Cotton, Charles, *The Compleat Angler*, *****, **+++, 1676.

Vintage: Davy, Sir Humphrey, *Salmonia, or Days of Fly-fishing*, **+, 1828; Francis, Francis, *A Book of Angling*, ***+, 1867; Grey, Sir Edward (Lord Grey of Fallodon), *Fly-fishing*, ***+ 1899; Halford, Frederic M., *Dry-fly Fishing in Theory and Practice*, **+, 1889; Hewitt, Edward Ringwood, *A Trout and Salmon Fisherman for Seventy-five Years*, *++, Scribner's, 1950; LaBranche, George M. L., *The Dry Fly and Fast Water* and *The Salmon and the Dry Fly* (together in one volume), **+, Scribner's, 1951; "Scott, Jock" (Rudd, D. G. H.),

Greased Line Fishing for Salmon, *+++, (compiled from the papers of A. H. E. Wood), Lippincott, 1935; Scrope, William, *Days and Nights of Salmon-fishing in the Tweed*, ***+, 1843; Skues, G. E. M., *The Way of a Trout with a Fly*, **+, 1921 and/or *Minor Tactics of the Chalkstream*, 1910; Taverner, Eric, *Troutfishing from All Angles*, **++, 1929.

Modern: Bergman, Ray, *Trout*, **++, Knopf (revised edition), 1952; Fox, Charles K., *This Wonderful World of Trout*, *+++, Foxcrest 1, Carlisle, Pa., 1963; Grove, Alvin R. Jr., *The Lure and Lore of Trout Fishing*, **++, Stackpole, 1951; Marinaro, Vincent C., *A Modern Dry-fly Code*, *+++, Putnam's 1950; McClane, A. J., *The Practical Fly Fisherman*, **+++, Prentice-Hall, 1953; McDonald, John, *The Origins of Angling*, ****+, (with a new printing of *The Treatise of Fishing with an Angle*), Doubleday, 1963; Ritz, Charles, *A Fly Fisher's Life*, **++, Holt, 1959; Schwiebert, Ernest G. Jr., *Matching the Hatch*, *+++, Macmillan, 1955; Shaw, Helen, *Fly-Tying*, ++++, Ronald Press, 1963; Wulff, Lee, *The Atlantic Salmon*, **+++, Barnes, 1958.

The first dividend to be derived from reading the old angling authors is the realization that there is nothing new under the sun and that every angler practices his pastime under the conviction, voiced by all his elders, that fishing isn't what it used to be.

In 1890, in *Angling Sketches*, ** Andrew Lang summed this up: "Even then, thirty years ago (1860), the old stagers used to tell us that 'the watter was ower sair fished,' and they grumbled . . . ' 'Tis gone, 'tis gone: not in our time will any man . . . need a cart to carry the trout he has slain.' The companions of those times are scattered, and live under strange stars and in converse seasons by troutless waters. But, except for the scarcity of fish, the scene is very little altered, and one is a boy again, in heart, beneath the elms . . . However bad the sport, it keeps you young, or makes you young again, and you need not follow Ponce de Leon to the Western wilderness, when, in any river you knew of yore, you can find the Fountain of Youth."

That passage has as much truth as poetry, for from the time of Walton himself, who lived to be ninety, the great fishers have generally kept young enough to fish to a ripe old age, as witness Scrope who was eighty, Francis, Halford, Grey, and Hills, who all made it past seventy, and those two fabulous old friends of our own time, Hewitt and LaBranche, who both died in their nineties within the past few years.

Further back than Andrew Lang the angling reader will pick up the same old refrain from the querulous voice of the American Charles Hallock complaining, in *The Fishing Tourist*, as long ago as 1873, that it now ran the angler virtually a dollar a pound to find trout and, almost in the same breath, that the ease of modern travel was making them too easy to find.

There is repetition, surely, throughout the literature that is available in such abundance for the angler who would learn as he reads, but in a two-fold sense even the repetitiveness of it constitutes another dividend, for one of the best ways to acquire a solid education as an angler is by having the fundamental lessons drilled in by hearing them taken up again and again by the many voices of the old masters, beginning with Cotton's insistence away back in 1676 upon the most essential necessity of all, that of fishing "fine and far off" in a clear stream for trout. And starting with the *Treatise* itself, the reading angler acquires successive layers of learning, like the successive coats of lacquer on a job of custom coachwork, feeling a growing sense of the traditional as fundamentals are reiterated across the centuries and enjoying successive thrills of enlightenment with the continuing revelations of the various great breakthroughs of angling knowledge and mastery that have been made by the half dozen or so "great originals" across the years down to our own time. These are all certainly included in the thirty volumes that constitute the "short course" above recommended. And while not all of the recommended authors are of anything like the same stature, and not more than half of them are today of full and unimpaired instructional value, of this better half virtually all have made truly original contributions. And it is worth while to read the other half, either for enjoyment just as reading, or as furnishing the forest setting against which to measure the stature of such mighty trees as the most important of them represent.

With the thought of furnishing a further guide to the beginning angling scholar, the thirty authors have been given stars and/or plus signs, as a purely arbitrary way of indicating their relative importance, with the stars attempting to indicate the comparative and approximate degree of their value as purveyors of the attractions of angling and the plus marks indicating a like attempt to estimate their value as instructors to the angler who wants to read more than to be taught than to be entertained.

Walton, for example, wears five stars here, simply because he is and will remain peerless as long as the well of pure English stays even reasonably undefiled by the gathering vulgarities of our assorted gobbledygooks of technical newspeak, but he carries no plus marks at all because he ceased, over a hundred years ago, to possess any actual instructional value to a sophisticated angler. Cotton, on the other hand, here is accorded only two stars, to show how far he fell below his "father" Walton in communicating the pastoral delights of the angling scene in the days of merrie England, but in compensation ekes out his five-star rank with three plus marks, to indicate the simple truth that after 292 years his is still the best school the aspiring clearwater fly-fisher can hope to attend.

James Chetham, however, who wrote within Walton's lifetime, here is accorded only the single star indicating that he is of interest only to the reader who is more "book-worm than angle-worm," delighted as the latter may be to come across, in Chetham's, *The Angler's Vade Mecum* * (1681), such a wonderful complaint as his forthright pronouncement that "this night fishing" was "unwholesome, unpleasant and very ungenteel" and that he would have none of it, since it was "to be used by none but idle pouching fellows."

Since comparisons are at least as odious in this field as in any other, and perhaps even more so, in the light of the reflection that fishing is, at best, one of the world's few truly noncompetitive sports, it may be a matter of passing regret that the stars and plus signs here employed may seem to assign purely arbitrary rankings to writers the way a Michelin guide would assign them to so many restaurants. But the device is used to aid the beginning angling scholar to know what books to look for first, depending on whether he is more interested in entertainment or in instruction, and the stars and plusses merely aim to indicate which books are of the greater interest in each of these two respects, with the possible added service that the angling reader aiming to acquire his own library may want to set about it after the manner of first things first.

Even the briefest outline of history could not possibly attempt to confine the account to events of absolutely equal interest and importance, and however egalitarian and democratic might be the aim to make all good books on fishing equal, there must always be some authors in any field, such as Marlowe and Shakespeare in dramatic literature, and Berners and Walton in angling literature, who will always be "more equal than any others."

In his excellent *History of Fly-fishing* Major J. W. Hills made the fair statement that "there are four names which stand above others in the history of the fly: the author of *The Treatise*, who started it; Cotton, who established it; Stewart, who converted the world to upstream fishing; and Halford, who systemized the dry fly." The good major is, since 1938, beyond reach for consultation, but even he—on record though he is as being of that number who would read everything ever written about fishing— would not argue that all four of those names, though he picked them out from hundreds of others, were therefore, and by that act, all made equal to each other. Their only equality, by even the major's omnivorous interest in the subject, would be in the sense that any book about fishing is better than any book that isn't about fishing.

By the same token, one of the most endearing statements ever made by an angling writer was the one attributed by Hills to Francis Francis: "Some fishing is better than others; but there is no such thing as bad fishing."

Thomas Best, whose *Concise Treatise on the Art of Angling* ran through thirteen editions after its initial appearance in 1787, can be of interest to an American angler of the 1970's chiefly for the purely antiquarian point that his was the first book to mention the multiplying reel, though in its relation to other books that came before and after it, his book was, in Robb's estimation, both practical and sensible.

There is not much more to be said for Thomas Salter, by today's standards, though his book, too, from its first appearance the year before the Battle of Waterloo, as a best seller of wide influence, was a worthy stone in the arch of angling knowledge that has been abuilding from Dame Juliana's day to ours. And one piece of advice he gives is as fresh as ever: "notice that by rubbing gut . . . which has laid in coils, with India rubber, it instantly becomes straight, especially the pieces to which hooks are tied, as these pieces usually are kept coiled up."

"John Bickerdyke" (Charles Henry Cook), though Robb terms him "one of the elect," particularly in the field of coarse fishing and for his pioneering in sea fishing, is a giant of diminished stature today, and though his time (1887) is much closer to our own, *The Book of the All-round Angler* is still chiefly of interest as background and continuity, in relation to others of more lasting originality both before and since.

For that matter, Gervase Markham, though regarded by his peers in 1631 as something of a rascal and an opportunistic jack-of-all-trades, has more to say to those of us who are today still intent upon "matching the hatch," for it was he who first gave us the idea, as follows: "Now for the shapes and proportions of these flyes, it is impossible to describe them without paynting, therefore you shall take of these severall flyes alive, and laying them before you, trie how near your Art can come unto nature by an equall shapes and mixture of colours; and when you have made them, you may keep them in close boxes uncrushed, and they will serve you many yeares."

As for Richard and Charles Bowlker, Hills dated the start of modern fly-dressing from the first appearance of their book in 1747 (begun by the father Richard and continued in subsequent enlarged editions by the son Charles), so many, in fact, as to earn their *Art of Angling* the appellation of "the most successful purely fishing book ever written," and certainly this one of its dicta still stands: "When you see a fish rise at a natural fly, the best way is to throw a yard above him, rather than directly over his head, and let your fly move gently towards him, by which means you will show it to him more naturally."

A half century earlier J(ohn) S(mith), in *The True Art of Angling* (1696), had written another enormously influential book that went through twelve editions and remained a standard work for seventy-five years. It advised fishing upstream in clear water, though with a natural fly, but downstream in thick water with an artificial.

It remained for W. C. Stewart to combine those elements of advice, in *The Practical Angler* **+ (1857), as the first apostle of upstream dry-fly-fishing: "The nearer the motions of the artificial flies resemble those of the natural ones under similar circumstances, the greater will be the prospects of success." As Hills pointed out, this sums up the creed of the dry fly: "He was not the discoverer of upstream fishing any more than Darwin was the discoverer of natural selection, but he was the first for nearly two hundred years to take the trouble to make the case, and the first of any age to do it completely."

Even so, the contribution of Alfred Ronalds was the more lasting, for where Stewart began something that was later pushed to the point of senseless mania, Ronald's *The Fly-fisher's Entomology* ***+, (1836) started not only a whole school of writers but a whole school of thought and gave fishing a new dimension of science. From 1836 to 1921 it was the only book of its class, and is for all time, in Hill's phrase, "the creator of the race of angler-naturalists."

Although Francis Francis, like most of the writers before him, treated of all forms of freshwater fishing in *A Book on Angling* (1867), he showed his estimation of their relative importance by devoting two-thirds of his space of over five hundred pages to trout and salmon. And though Francis standing on Ronalds' shoulders raised "the right fly" to gospel, and Halford right after Francis pushed the mystique of the dry fly to a point of snobbish mania, both are richly rewarding reading even today, and both, in view of the near-fanaticism of their insistence on glorifying the proper fly even at the expense of angling results, are still surprisingly human.

Here is Francis: "And so you walk on, sometimes musing, sometimes marvelling, as each new voice salutes you, 'the voices of the evening,' that you never noticed before, though you may have heard them a hundred times; but it is your mood to hear, and note them, too, tonight, and you do so wonderingly, as though they were all new

things and this some other hemisphere, and so you tramp on homewards under the moonlight. Is your creel light, friend: What then 'Your heart is light too, and there are other things to admire in the world besides fishes,' so take that by way of consolation."

And Halford, too, despite his insistence on the dry fly as the be-all and end-all of fishing, could still be cherished for this one passage alone from *Modern Development of the Dry-fly*: "I have as many disappointing days as any of my readers, perhaps more. I fail continually. I leave flies in the fish's mouth; I am weeded and broken. Some evenings I get home dead beat, tired out, depressed, and ready to declare that I will give up dry-fly fishing altogether. I hope however that I have learned to look at sport from the optimistic point of view, and so the next morning I wake up keener than ever, and once more sally forth to the river resolved to do or die."

That Halford was a man of high resolve, and no egomaniac, is shown in the fact that he quit all business at the age of forty-five to devote the next twenty-five years of his life to fishing and writing about the dry fly, and not only to formulate his own theories but at the same time to play the role of Boswell to Captain Marryat, a great non-writing fisherman. He also served not only as the historian and systematizer of the dry fly but as its transatlantic spark-gap, as it was he whose patterns, sent to the sainted Theodore Gordon, started the development of the dry fly in the United States.

It was the one-two force of Stewart and Halford that raised the dominance of the dry-fly to the almost tyrannical rule that it exerted over fishermen in England over the last third of the nineteenth century, but by the century's last year its exaggerated importance first began to be undermined. In 1899 Sir Edward Grey emerged, in *Fly-fishing*, ***+, as "the first writer of importance on the dry fly who really knew what the wet fly meant . . . and he started that restatement of value that Skues carried so far."

Skues brought the English angling world back to its senses by the revelation that there was no real need to exalt either the dry fly or the wet fly at the expense of the other: "There are days and hours when the wet-fly has not a chance against the dry-fly, and there are days and hours when the dry-fly has not a chance against the wet-fly."

On the salmon side, Scrope in *Days and Nights of Salmon Fishing in the Tweed* ***+, (1843) took up where Sir Humphrey Davy had left off in 1828, and although he too wrote only one book it was—and is—one of the brightest volumes in the whole literature of angling. Scrope is a character, one of the most colorful personalities ever to put pen to paper about angling, and everything he wrote is as individual as a fingerprint.

But if the literature of salmon fishing had to wait several centuries to get started, and poor Sir Humphrey, dictating his *Salmonia* from his bed of pain, had to play the role of its Berners, then Scrope was well worth waiting for, and he can serve as its Walton and Cotton combined. Probably every man who ever fished has sometime had the thought, when taken to task about fishing, that only Scrope ever put into so many words. Has man the moral right to deprive these, his fellow creatures, of their God-given lives? Yes, bellows Scrope, and on these grounds: "Let us see how the case stands. I take a little wool and feather and tying it in a particular manner upon a hook make an imitation of a fly; then I throw it across the river and let it sweep around the stream with a lively motion. This I have an undoubted right to do, for the river belongs to me or my friend, but mark what follows. Up starts a monster fish with his murderous jaws. It makes a dash at my little Andromeda. Thus he is the aggressor, not I; his intention is evidently to commit murder."

Scrope's beguiling logic also conferred dubious immortality upon that warden of Selkirk who "as a water bailiff was sworn to tell of all he saw; and indeed, as he said, it could not be expected that he should tell of what he did not see. When his dinner was served up during close time his wife usually brought to the table a platter of potatoes and a napkin; she then bound the latter over his eyes that nothing might offend his sight. This being done, the illegal salmon was brought in smoking hot, and he fell to, blindfolded as he was, like a conscientious water bailiff—if you know what that is; nor was the napkin taken from his eyes till the fins and bones were removed from the room, and every visible evidence of a salmon having been there had completely vanished . . ."

But Scrope is unquotable without quoting him all intact, for he must be read, as Walton must (though not without Cotton) by every man who would aspire to any status beyond that of the most casual tourist in the rarefied realm of the kingly sport of salmon angling.

Though hundreds fish for trout for every dozen who can afford to fish for salmon, the literature of salmon angling is, in view of that restricting circumstance, surprisingly large. But as far as mastery of the sport's technique is concerned, and forgetting all the purely literary attractions (like Chaytor's *Letters to a Salmon Fisher's Sons*) that beckon down innumerable bypaths, the whole art can be learned from just three books that came after Scrope. They are *Greased Line Fishing for Salmon*, in which the pseudonymous "Jock Scott" (Donald Rudd) played Boswell to the great A. H. E. Wood; LaBranche's *Salmon and the Dry Fly;* and Lee Wulff's *Atlantic Salmon*. These are three of the "great originals," each representing an all-time breakthrough in angling technique. When A. H. E. Wood, of Cairnton on the Aberdeenshire Dee, discovered by accident the greased-line method, he made it possible for the first time to take salmon with any consistency in low water and in warm weather. In this method a sparsely dressed fly (he used only three—Blue Charm, Silver Blue, and March Brown) is cast across the stream and the line consistently mended whenever drag threatens, with the result that the fly barely sinks beneath the surface, the taking fish is seen, and, when it takes, there is no striking, since it hooks itself in the corner of the jaw where a good hold is generally secured. Similarly, when George M. L. La-Branche, teamed with Hewitt, established the possibility of taking salmon on the dry fly, he went on, again almost by accident, to a further discovery that has since been used by many more anglers than the comparative handful who fish for salmon: his great contribution was the further invention of a deadly method for taking almost any fish that refuses to be taken by conventional offerings, the creation of "the artificial hatch" by repeated casts floated over the same spot often enough to convince even the most skeptical of fish that a hatch is on and that he'd better take before it's over. On a par with these two

earlier breakthroughs is the establishment, by Lee Wulff in *Atlantic Salmon*, that the light-tackle angler, though seeming to do things the hard way, actually enjoys an advantage, in playing large or difficult fish, over the angler more conventionally equipped. With this, and the techniques of the skittered or riffled "hitched fly" and the semisubmerged fly, the salmon angler is brought up to the minute in the applied knowledge of his sport.

Mention of Hewitt should probably not be left with the mere indication of his godfatherly role in relation to dry-fly-fishing for salmon with LaBranche, for in the course of his long life he also undoubtedly played the greatest single role in the establishment of nymph fishing in America, and he must also be credited with the invention of one of the most versatile of all lures, the spider as he first fished it in the guise of the Neversink skater. He was taking salmon on a size-14 spider as long ago as the early twenties—a feat that is not even now to be regarded as exactly routine.

To get back to the English, Taverner in *Trout Fishing from All Angles* compiled the book that gives the impression of being comprehensive to the point of being exhaustive, as an exposition of all their methodology and knowledge. Fortunately the last word is never written, or angling would be a science rather than a sport, although this book almost makes the reader forget that it isn't.

Bergman in *Trout* became for Americans what Taverner is to the English, for his is still their best all-around and, to many people their only, book on trout. But Bergman's book, though revised in 1952, was originally written in 1939, and in this sense A. J. McClane's *Practical Fly Fisherman*, first published in 1953, virtually stands on Bergman's shoulders. Until somebody now in knee pants comes along to do it the same disservice, the *Practical Fly Fisherman* must stand as the most comprehensive and useful single volume on all forms of freshwater fly-fishing available to Americans.

Other essential books of the last decade, to enable the angler to feel that he is at least as well educated as books alone can ever make him, are more specialized but, taken with McClane as a prerequisite, like the required reading demanded of freshmen before they are allowed to progress to more diversified studies, will bring the angling scholar up to date.

He who would implement, by today's standards, the most refined application of Cotton's immortal exhortation to fish fine and far off must now sit at the feet of the three Pennsylvania masters of the minutiae, Fox, Grove, and Marinaro, who will certainly some day seem as legendary to us all as Hewitt and LaBranche are already beginning to seem within the decade of their death. And he who would follow, to today's most demanding exigence, the perfectionism upon which Francis and Halford insisted in the natural imitation of artificials, cannot do without Schwiebert. And he who would try today to lead a fly-fisher's life will surely miss a few tricks if he doesn't, somewhere along the way, take time out to study the one now near sundown led by Charles Ritz, one of the most gracious as well as most graceful of its modern practitioners.

No man can call himself a fisher, within the meaning of the masters, unless he ties, or at least tries to tie, his own flies. Some earnest souls, born with ten thumbs, who have often tried but failed, may be heartened by the knowledge that at last they have a woman's help so that now, even for them, this art while still possibly difficult is at least no longer impossible. For with the aid of her photographer husband, Helen Shaw in *Fly-Tying* looks over your shoulders and guides your hands, though performing with her own, to let you see just how you do it, step by single step.

While this is the most elementary last word on the how-to-do-it side, in a brief survey of angling literature to date, scholarly mastery is also not yet lost, for in the same year there was also in John McDonald's *The Origins of Angling* (and a new printing of *The Treatise of Fishing with an Angle*), one of the most intensive and perceptive feats of angling scholarship ever performed over the centuries that fishing has been written about. McDonald who had, although of a later generation, served the memory and preserved the contribution of Theodore Gordon (in *The Complete Fly-fisherman*, Scribner's 1947, collecting and annotating Gordon's letters), just as Halford had done for Marryat and "Jock Scott" had done for Wood, has now done the same service for Dame Juliana herself, thus in one volume serving today's reader as a guide back to the very beginning of the most voluminous literature ever devoted to any one sport and, in that service, attaining the stature of one of its stars—those bright lamps that, in Milton's phrase, nature hung in heaven, to guide the wayworn traveler: in this instance, any man who would know the story of his pastime, his hobby, his addiction, or, in more advanced cases, his mania. —A.G.

LITTLE SKATE *Raja erinacea* A small member of the skate family (Rajidae), it has a distinctively blunt snout and three rows of spines along the midline of the back which are most pronounced in the young. The tail is long and covered with spines, and the dorsal fins are touching one another, with no spines between them.

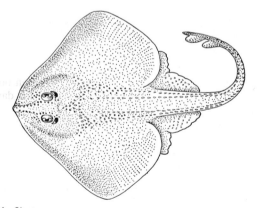

Little Skate

The little skate closely resembles the winter skate (*which see*) but has less than 66 teeth, usually less than 54, in the upper jaw, while the winter skate has at least 72 and usually more than 80. The females are spinier than males. The color is grayish to dark brown with dark mottlings or spots above, and white below with the tail dusky. They grow to nearly 2 feet long, and a specimen 1½ feet long weighs slightly over 1¼ pounds.

LIFE HISTORY

The little skate is a coolwater animal, occurring from Nova Scotia to North Carolina, in the shallow surf zones to as deep as 80 fathoms. In New England, it is the commonest of all skates in that region. Taken predominantly close to shore in the winter, it moves offshore during April and May, reappearing in the shallows in October and November. Mating occurs throughout the year in less than 15 fathoms, with a peak from October to January and another peak in June and July. Tough-shelled eggs are laid which contain miniature skates. These egg cases, about 2 by 2½ inches, have filamentlike extensions at each corner, and are often seen on beaches. Under aquarium conditions the young are hatched out 5–6 months after they are laid, at which time they are about 4 inches long. They evidently grow to 6–8 years of age, and the males grow to a larger size. In the northern part of its range, it feeds primarily on shrimplike amphipods, small crabs, and mud shrimp, and toward the south it eats mostly mud shrimp and clams. Presently there is little commercial value attached to this species, although its flesh yields a good grade of fishmeal. —D.dS.

LITTLE SNOOK *Centropomus parallelus* This is the second largest of the West Indian snooks. It occurs in Florida as far north as Lake Okeechobee and throughout the American Atlantic tropics. The little snook occasionally reaches a total length of about 20 inches, but larger individuals are rare. The largest known specimen measured 28 inches in total length. The robust body is heavier than in the other species at the same length.

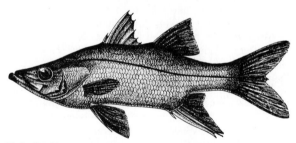

Little Snook

The little snook has 79–92 lateral scales. Gillrakers 10–13, usually 11–12 on lower limb of first arch, not including rudiments. Anal rays 6. Pectoral rays 14–16, usually 15. Second anal spine not reaching beyond vertical from caudal base. Pectoral fin not reaching to vertical from tip of pelvic. Pelvic fin reaching to or beyond anus. Maxillary reaching to or beyond vertical from center of eye.

The greater number of lateral scales and the more robust body distinguish this snook from the others. A closely related species from Brazil, *Centropomus constantinus*, has fewer lateral scales (68–79). Another relative, *C. poeyi*, from the vicinity of Veracruz, Mexico, usually has 9 dorsal rays instead of 10.

ANGLING VALUE

In addition to bays, estuaries, canals, and the lower course of streams, this species occurs along the coast in saltwater. It takes live bait and artificial lures. Although more common than the swordspine and tarpon snook, this species is much less abundant than the snook (*which see*).

A lively fighter on light tackle. Live shrimp and top-minnows are the best natural bait. Good sport on spinning, fly, or plug tackle.

FOOD VALUE

Ideal for baking or broiling whole. Should be skinned.

—L.R.

LITTLE TUNNY *Euthynnus alletteratus* Until 1970 three scombrids and sometimes a fourth of the genus *Euthynnus* were loosely regarded as "little tunas"; *E. alletteratus*, also called false albacore or bonito; *E. affinis*, also called wavyback skipjack or kawakawa (Hawaii); *E. lineatus*, also called black skipjack, and *E. pelamis*, also called skipjack tuna. The common name, little tuna, applies only to *E. alletteratus*.

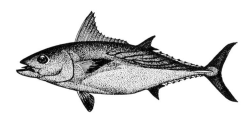

Little Tunny

These are fishes of the mackerel family which have a variable number of black spots on the sides of the body below the pectoral fin and dark markings on the back. A corselet of scales is found on the anterior part of the body, but the posterior part is naked.

The species are difficult to distinguish. *E. alletteratus* is found only in the Atlantic Ocean and Mediterranean Sea. It differs from the other species in lacking teeth on the vomer, a small bone in the roof of the mouth. *E. lineatus* occurs only off the West Coast of America from California to Peru. It typically has 3–5 horizontal black lines on the back, while the other two have wormlike or oblique, wavy lines. *E. affinis* is rare off the American West Coast but is common from Hawaii through the Western Pacific and Indian oceans; it has teeth on the vomer and has wavy lines on the back. All are medium-sized fishes. *E. lineatus* attains a weight of about 10 pounds and a length of about 2 feet; *E. affinis* and *E. alletteratus* both become larger, reaching 15 pounds and more and over 2½ feet. Their food consists of a wide variety of fishes, squids and crustaceans.

The little tunny possibly spawns the year around, possibly with different peaks in different areas. They may shed over a million eggs.

Marlins, sharks, and tunas are known to prey upon the little tunny.

ANGLING VALUE

Because of its abundance in nearshore waters, little tunny and its allied species are often popular sport fishes.

—B.B.C.

—R.H.G.

LITTORAL The coastline, including both the land and nearshore water; particularly that portion between the extreme high and low tides, the intertidal zone.

LIVE BAIT Any natural organism which can be employed to catch fish. Although the bait may not actually be alive at the time of use, the term is broadly applicable nevertheless. A live bait is called *cut bait* or *strip bait* when it has been changed in form to serve some special purpose, e.g., cut mullet or cut menhaden as used in bottom-fishing, or strip mullet or strip mackerel as used when trolling. In general, the most common live baits are minnows and worms; however, insects, crustaceans, and mollusks of various kinds may be preferable for certain species in both fresh- and saltwater.

NIGHTCRAWLERS

These large earthworms are probably the most widely used of all live baits in freshwater. They are relatively easy to obtain and store and are an excellent bait for nearly all species except members of the pike family. Nightcrawlers are especially effective on a trout stream immediately after a rise of water has turned the stream roily, and they will account for above-average fish under these conditions. They are a top bait for smallmouths when the latter are in deepwater. Nightcrawlers are also excellent for early-season walleyes when trolled just off the bottom behind a small spinner.

Nightcrawlers partially emerge from their burrows on nights when the grass is moist because of dew, rain, or recent lawn-watering activities. They can be stalked with a flashlight and picked up easily if care is taken not to frighten them. They are very sensitive to ground vibrations, and it is necessary to tread softly before they become alarmed and retreat under ground. Nightcrawlers are also sensitive to light, and a strong beam is impractical when collecting them. A too-powerful light can be easily modified by taping red or yellow cellophane over the lens.

A supply of nightcrawlers can be kept alive indefinitely by providing a cool place for storage and material in which they will remain healthy. A cellar or basement will usually furnish the required cool spot, but soil (a natural choice) is a rather poor storage material. It is much better to fill an old-fashioned wash tub or a large wooden box with *dry* leaves and sprinkle lightly with water each day. If the sprinkling is done sparingly, the nightcrawlers will thrive, eating the leaves and remaining fresh and lively. Sphagnum moss is another good material if kept damp. Prompt removal of all dead worms is highly important. Mortality rates tend to run high immediately after collection, for a certain amount of injury is unfortunately inevitable. Few will die thereafter, if suitable conditions are provided.

ANGLEWORMS

Angleworms can be collected by spading wherever the soil is rich and damp, and a supply will live a long time in a large can of the same earth if kept cool and moist. These small worms have the same wide fish appeal as do the larger nightcrawlers, and are to be preferred to the latter in some instances. They are better suited to fishing for small stream trout, for instance, and for panfish such as yellow perch and bluegills.

Like all small baits, angleworms should be presented as naturally as possible for best results. The most common mistake is to use sinkers that are too heavy and hooks that are too large. Use small hooks (No. 10 or 12) and wherever possible eliminate the sinker entirely. In ponds and lakes, cast frequently, letting the worm settle slowly under its own weight; in streams, cast upstream and let the current carry the bait back toward you. Freedom from restraint will result in a natural drift in each case which will fool wary fish.

MINNOWS

This term is used loosely to include all kinds of small fishes used for bait. Although various species of the minnow family do comprise the bulk of freshwater bait-fish, other species are also represented in bait buckets, such as suckers, smelt, small perch, and sculpins. Terminology is less important, however, than the fact that since most gamefish are predatory, small fish are their natural forage. It is for this reason that minnows are perhaps the most reliable day-to-day producers of all freshwater live baits, and particularly with respect to trophy-size fish. The larger the gamefish, the more it depends upon small fish for food. Many species reach a size where they tend to ignore other food items and are thus among the minnow fisherman's most likely quarry.

But because minnows are caught, kept alive, and transported with some difficulty, the extent to which they are used probably falls short of their high degree of efficiency as bait. The fisherman who can buy live minnows whenever and wherever he wants them is fortunate and most simply do without whenever, as is often the case, minnows are in short supply. Actually this is seldom necessary because the individual can usually catch his own bait on location with the help of very simple equipment.

Quickest and most efficient is a minnow seine, which, since it need not be longer than 6–8 feet, is easily stored and transported. Such a seine will pay for itself many times over, for there are few fishing waters from which bait cannot be collected after a bit of prospecting. Schools of minnows may be evident in shallow bays and coves, but even though none is seen, a substantial number are likely to be hidden in the weed patches near shore. By starting at a depth of a few feet and hauling straight to shore, sufficient bait for a day's fishing can often be obtained with only a few drags of the net, even in spots where no bait was visible.

Another handy item of equipment is an old-fashioned screen minnow trap. This will usually provide enough minnows for a day's fishing if set overnight in a brook or pond. Crackers or bread may be used for bait, but it is better to moisten dry oatmeal until it can be formed into balls about two inches in diameter. Several of these in the trap will remain much longer than will crackers or bread.

Before collecting bait from freshwaters, be sure to check with the local conservation department regarding state regulations.

Storage of large numbers of live minnows is usually beyond the physical means of most fishermen. Chlorinated water is a common prohibitive factor, as is the lack of space for suitable tank. Fortunately, however, a few dozen minnows will live for a considerable period in a large minnow bucket of the porous, self-cooling type.

The most popular form of minnow fishing is still-fishing. The bait is hooked lightly, preferably just ahead of the dorsal fin, then gently lowered to within a foot or so of the bottom. The minnow's natural swimming action will attract nearby fish, but more ground can be covered by attaching a bobber to the line and paying out slack as wind or current carries the bobber along.

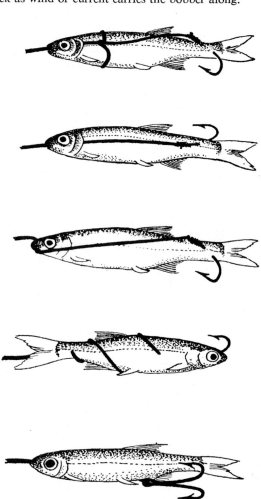

METHODS OF HOOKING MINNOWS FOR CASTING

1. Monofilament is passed through mouth and looped around body with hook inserted near tail
2. Monofilament is passed through mouth and under gill, with hook imbedded near tail
3. Monofilament is passed through both lips, with hook placed in tail
4. Minnow is "sewn" through the mouth and tail and hook snicked through head for reverse presentation
5. Monofilament is inserted internally with needle from mouth to vent. Double hook is tied in place after the leader material is in

Minnows are by no means limited in use to still-fishing, however, nor in the case of still-fishing is it always best to fish live minnows in the conventional manner. When rigged or "sewn" on a hook, minnows are excellent trolling bait for all gamefish. They may be sewn to swim naturally, or curved to spin, and they may be used with, or without, a spinner. Generally overlooked is the fact that a sewn minnow is very deadly when cast and retrieved with either a bait-casting or spinning outfit. It is especially effective on pickerel and northern pike. Also overlooked is the fact that a dead minnow, resting on bottom, holds more appeal for some species than one fished alive and vigorous. Large trout, for example, are quick to pick dead minnows from the bottom, and some fishermen believe that the dead minnow becomes even more effective when partially skinned and the shredded skin left to dangle. Big catfish also have a distinct liking for large, freshly killed minnows.

Minnows intended for trolling, casting, or bottom-fishing can be stored handily by wrapping individually and placing them in the freezer or freezing compartment. Carry your supply for the day in a wide-mouthed thermos, or in an iced cooler if you carry one. By unwrapping only as needed they will stay frozen for hours.

The kinds of baitfish vary from region to region, and favorite species are therefore usually a matter of local opinion and experience. In general, suckers are held in high esteem as bait for pickerel, northern pike, and muskies; smelt are favored by those who fish for lake trout and landlocked salmon. The common shiner is probably the most generally available and most widely used.

The size of the bait used is fully as important as the kind and here the fisherman can exercise a choice. Tiny minnows, usually called "pinheads," are best for panfish, and they are excellent for use on the trout of small streams.

Very small hooks and light leaders are the equipment required to fish small baits most effectively. Medium-size minnows, 3–4 inches long, are the best choice for smallmouths, walleyes, and large trout. Largemouths usually respond best to somewhat larger baits, while foot-long suckers are often used by those who fish for muskies and big northerns.

Restraint should be used in setting the hook when fishing with baitfish of substantial size. The striking fish usually clamps the bait between its jaws, then moves off a short distance before pausing to swallow it. An attempt to set the hook during this initial run is likely to fail, simply because it may be outside the fish's mouth. The common procedure is to pay out line during the first run, then set the hook when the fish moves off again after swallowing the bait.

As a conservation measure, minnow fishermen should resist the impulse to empty minnow buckets into fishing waters at the end of the day. The undetected fingerlings of undesirable species may be released, with serious damage to good fishing waters consequently resulting. Fine trout lakes have been all but ruined by the unintentional introduction of sunfish, yellow perch, and carp through the dumped minnow bucket. Feed surplus minnows to your cat, or bury them near your rose bushes.

FROGS

Frogs are not widely popular as bait, but they are effective at times on both largemouth and smallmouth bass. They can be fished alive by hooking them through the lips or by the skin of a hind leg. Bass will sometimes wallop them when they are allowed to swim at the surface in shallow water, but in greater depths it is necessary to add enough sinker to take them down near bottom. Small frogs are the best choice for this type of fishing.

With the help of a harness a dead frog can be rigged as a casting lure for use with either a bait-casting or spinning rod. A frog "skittered" along the surface will bring strikes from northern pike and pickerel, and from largemouth bass as well.

In a different category, a large, dead frog is one of the best baits for big catfish. It should be fished resting on bottom, and at night when catfish are most active.

CRAYFISH

These small, lobsterlike crustaceans are important items of fish diet wherever they occur and are therefore among the effective freshwater baits. They live in lakes, ponds, and warmwater streams and ditches, hiding under rocks by day and crawling about in search of food by night. The collecting and keeping of a large supply of crayfish is an involved undertaking which most fishermen don't attempt. However, it is important to learn how a small supply can be caught, stored temporarily, and transported alive.

Crayfish are most easily and quickly caught in the riffle sections of a stream. Anchor a seine across a portion of the riffle by weighting the bottom with rocks; then use a hoe or rake to scour the bottom immediately upstream. The current will carry dislodged crayfish into the net, and an ample supply can usually be caught with only a few attempts. Lacking such a spot, stir up the bottom in a pond, slough, or ditch, overturning all rocks, sunken logs, and other natural hiding places. Draw a seine through the stirred-up area, working slowly to keep the lower part of the net close to the bottom. Or you can catch a small supply by hand by using an empty tin can from which the ends have been removed. When a crayfish scuttles from beneath an overturned rock, plunk the hollow cylinder down over it. It is then a simple matter to reach in and grab the crayfish as it sculls around inside.

A small supply of crayfish is best kept alive in a tub containing plenty of damp sphagnum moss, small branches with green leaves left on, grass, or some similar material. Cover the top of the container with wet burlap for an additional cooling effect. Do not try to keep the crayfish in unreplenished water, as they may die from lack of oxygen.

The same rules apply to carrying a supply for a day's fishing. Keep them in a bait bucket packed with the same materials, and guard against high temperatures by draping damp burlap over the bucket. A layer of ice cubes in the bottom of the bucket will help keep the contents cool, but sufficient solid material should be added so that the bait won't become immersed as the ice melts.

Crayfish molt, or shed their hard shells, as they grow, and for a short time after shedding they are soft to the touch—and particularly good bait. Use any softshells you may have in preference to all others. This does not mean that fish are indifferent to the hardshell phase, but the smaller specimens are best when you have only this type to offer.

NIGHTCRAWLER

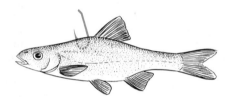

Most of hook
covered (2 worms)

EARTHWORMS

Hook through collar

GRASSHOPPER

Hook through
collar

HELLGRAMMITE

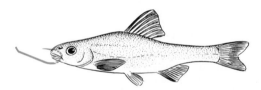

MINNOW HOOKED IN BACK

MINNOW HOOKED THROUGH LIPS

FROG

Hook through leg

MINNOW HOOKED NEAR TAIL

For maximum action, worms should be hooked lightly. A single nightcrawler is suitable for most species of freshwater fish. Two or more earthworms is most effective on panfish, such as perch, sunfish, and bullheads; sliced shank is optional, but helps to hold bait in place. Insect baits are usually hooked through thorax or "collar." Minnows may be hooked in several ways to keep alive in water when still-fishing. Frogs are often hooked through lips, but taken head first by gamefish leg method is better. Whole crayfish is best for bass and trout, particularly in softshell stage, but tail meat is much superior for panfish.

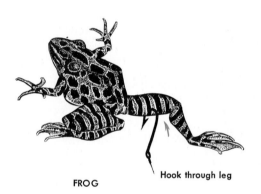

CRAYFISH

Remove shell;
thread on hook

Freshwater Baits

The best method of hooking is to slide the barb of the hook under one or two segments of shell at the top of the tail, drawing the point all the way through until it stands free.

Crayfish are eaten to varying degrees by most game-fish, but they are especially relished by smallmouth and largemouth bass, and are therefore most widely used as bait for these two species. Very small crayfish make excellent trout bait, and are regarded by some fishermen as the perfect answer to difficult early-season conditions in cold- and highwater. The detached tails from large crayfish are standard catfish bait, and these will also account for other bottom-feeding species as well.

HELLGRAMMITES

These are the larvae of the dobsonfly (*which see*). In spite of their vicious appearance hellgrammites are popular as a smallmouth bass bait. They can be used to catch trout, largemouths, walleyes, yellow perch, and other species, but it is for smallmouth that they often seem to hold an almost overpowering appeal.

Hellgrammites live under rocks in the riffles of warm-water streams, eventually growing to a length of 3–4 inches. At this size they are tough, leathery, and armed with formidable pincers which they promptly use with very telling effect when given the chance. They are best handled by grasping the hard shell, just back of the head, between thumb and forefinger, thus preventing them from curling around and drawing blood with the painful nip which they are quite capable of delivering.

Not only does this "collar" afford a safe means of grasping these belligerent larvae, but it provides a handy spot for secure hooking. Slide the hook under the collar and draw the point free; the bait is not only securely hooked, but will remain alive for a long time.

The most difficult problem in gathering hellgrammites is usually that of locating spots where they abound, for they are almost as eagerly sought by fishermen as are the bass for which they will be used as bait. Once located, however, they can be collected by holding a net or screen downstream from large rocks and then flipping these over. Dislodged hellgrammites will be swept into the net, to which they will obligingly cling. A net or screen made for the purpose is best, but an ordinary landing net will suffice when necessary. Although the hellgrammites could pass easily through the mesh, most will cling long enough for capture.

As in the case of crayfish, hellgrammites must be retained alive and transported in moist material such as rotted wood, moss, and leaves. If kept in tubs, a few inches of water can be put in the bottom, then sufficient material added to bring the level well above the water. The contents will remain damp and cool through absorption and evaporation. Guard against overcrowding, for hellgrammites are likely to attack and destroy one another in this event. No more than 2–3 dozen should be stored in each large container.

To carry this bait on fishing trips, use a minnow bucket loosely packed with the same material in which they have been stored. Again, a layer of ice cubes in the bottom will help keep temperatures down, as will damp burlap draped over the bucket.

Fish hellgrammites close to bottom, but not resting upon it, for in this case your bait is almost a sure bet to crawl under a rock where no fish can get at it. Lift the line often to see that this hasn't happened.

Hellgrammites are particularly deadly when used for both stream smallmouths and trout if they are hung from a small bobber and cast with a spinning rig. Adjust the bobber so that the bait will drift close to bottom; then cast upstream to the heads of runs and rips. Let the bobbers carry the bait through the run. This method assures the natural drift of a tempting food item.

GRASSHOPPERS AND CRICKETS

These insects are so common and easily collected that discussion of their capture doesn't seem warranted. They can be carried while fishing in a variety of containers ranging from ketchup bottles to old socks, as well as in cages sold explicitly for the purpose. But the exceptional fish-taking qualities of these two hot-weather baits make them worthy of any effort. During the grasshopper season the trout of most streams are hungrily on the alert to grab any and all grasshoppers unfortunate enough to have tumbled into the water. Fly-fishermen know that an artificial imitation will bring plenty of rises at this time, and it follows that the natural will also be enthusiastically received.

A meadow stream is the perfect location for "dapping" a grasshopper on a small hook and fine leader. The bank should be approached stealthily, the long grass carefully parted so the rod can be poked through, and the insect gently lowered until it floats kicking on the surface. Since the water is seldom visible to the crouching fisherman, he waits for the sudden sound of a splash and the zinging of slack line through the guides to tell him of a hit. It's an exciting form of streamfishing, and one likely to yield good returns when more conventional methods may produce only meager results.

Smallmouths are also likely to become extremely fussy during hot weather, but one way to win them over is to offer them a single cricket on very fine terminal tackle. Clamp a single split shot to a tapered leader, and let the cricket settle slowly; even the most fussy smallmouth is likely to snatch a cricket that has been delicately presented.

Delicacy is the key to fishing both grasshoppers and crickets, in fact, but both are often wonderfully productive when fished in a natural manner.

MISCELLANEOUS FRESHWATER BAITS

The most earnest attempt to enumerate all the natural baits that can be used to catch fish would probably result in only a partial listing. Many regional specialties—catalpa worms for bluegills being one example—would have to be included, plus an enormous list of organisms which are not generally used, but which will take fish—salamanders, tadpoles, freshwater mussels, cockroaches, beetles, etc. No single fisherman can become familiar with the great number of baits known to all fishermen collectively. But perhaps one general observation is warranted. It has to do with the use of very small items such as tiny larvae, nymphs, and grubs, and the generally overlooked high potential which they actually represent.

That these very small tidbits regularly form the bulk of the food eaten by most fish is well-known to all fishermen who have examined the stomach contents of the fish they have caught. Yet very few bait-fishermen use these tiny baits for the simple reason that most fail to provide themselves with the equally tiny hooks and fine leaders which the delicate job requires.

For an example of such a bait, one which can be used with deadly results on a trout stream, it is necessary to look no farther than the common stick caddis larvae which cling to the rocks of most trout streams in great numbers. When drawn from its case the tiny larva looks hopelessly small; yet it can easily be threaded on a No. 14 hook which should be tied to a leader tapered to about 3X. Any fisherman who has taken the pains to try has discovered an unbeatable trout bait. He has, at least if he has fished it properly by casting upstream and allowing the bait to tumble back with the current.

Or for the caddis larva, substitute a stonefly nymph, a corn borer, a maggot, or some equally tiny item. Results are much the same whenever requirements for fishing such small baits have been met. Few bait-fishermen fully explore these briefly implied possibilities, but those who do invariably make some rewarding and surprising discoveries.　　　　　　　　　　　　　　　—H.F.B.

CLAMWORMS AND BLOODWORMS

These annelid worms are sold on the North Atlantic Coast as bait for saltwater fish. Collectors in Maine have a business worth a quarter million dollars a year from these worms. The industry in that state is centered around Wiscasset, but it extends from Long Island, New York, northward. The largest collections usually are taken in April but may continue into August. The worms usually run 6–8 inches in length. They spawn in the spring, at which time the ripe worms are unfit for bait. The spawners are easily identified. When spawners are held up, the insides flow to one end. The fluid from a broken spawner, if mixed with other worms, will kill them.

The clamworms, sometimes called sandworms, are represented by several species along the Atlantic Coast. The most common, *Nereis virens*, is flesh-colored and has a greenish sheen and black jaws. It is found from Long Island to Labrador.

The bloodworms most commonly collected are *Glycera americana* and *Glycera dibranchiata*, which occur from the Carolinas to the Bay of Fundy. The *Glycera*, which have a cylindrical body, elongated snout, four small tentacles, and four teeth, are differentiated from *Nereis*, which have a slightly flattened body, short snout, two small tentacles, and two teeth.

Bloodworms have been reported to three feet in length. Such giants are rare, the usual size is 6–8 inches. There are occasional giant sandworms, too. Specimens up to four feet long have been found. The adult sandworm, however, runs 10–18 inches.

Another name for the bloodworm is the "proboscis worm" because its snout is extended or retracted at will and acts as a burrowing organ. The bloodworm's mouth is armed with four tiny, black, curved "teeth," actually jaws, which may fasten onto a finger, creating the sensation of a bee sting and producing a painful swelling in persons allergic to the bites.

Bloodworms range from pink to red and have short, finlike appendages along the sides, with firm, round, barely visible segments under the smooth skin. They are found in the surface layer of mud. Sandworms will occupy the same flat with bloodworms but burrow much deeper.

Both species are found under stones and among seaweeds, particularly in burrows, but at night they extend their bodies in search of food or leave the burrows entirely. The openings of the burrows are usually covered with sand, but open entrances may be found, and these make excellent places to dig for worms. The sandworms are usually deeper in the mud than the clamworms. The worms may be stalked with a light on the tidal flats during the dark, moonless nights. At the slightest vibration from footsteps or a quick movement of the hand, the worms disappear. Worms are packed in rockweed and may be kept for several days in a refrigerator.

As the *Glycera* may destroy the *Nereis* if the species are placed together, they should be stored separately. Worms are ideally held at temperatures of 38°–40°F. They may be kept for two weeks or more so protected. Heat, particularly sun, quickly kills them.

Even more disastrous to seaworms than heat is freshwater. Bloodworms or sandworms left out in the rain soon turn up their parapods (side feet which are used for swimming). Similarly if worms come in contact with the ice, the icewater spoils them.

The worms refuse to eat in captivity and consequently have not been propagated.

SHRIMP

Shrimp are one of the most widely used natural baits in the Southern United States, and they are used to some extent in the Northeast and on the Pacific Coast. Species which may be caught on shrimp include snook, bonefish, weakfish, Spanish mackerel, king mackerel, spotted seatrout, sand seatrout, jack crevalle, ladyfish, red drum, striped bass, white sea bass, halibut, croakers, bluefish, and snappers. Various sand shrimp (*Crangon*), grass shrimp (*Palaemonetes*), and ghost shrimp (*Callianassa*) as well as the edible shrimp (*Penaeus*) are commonly used as bait. Some dealers sell live shrimp, but the majority stock them in frozen form. The live shrimp is a superior bait for certain species, but the whole or parts of dead shrimp are quite effective nevertheless.

One method of hooking a whole shrimp is to thread the crustacean through the body, starting at the tail so that the hook protrudes among its legs. Fishermen seeking surface-feeding gamefish who want to keep the bait alive usually hook the shrimp head first, inserting the hook in a small V-shaped indentation among the legs close to the head. The hook point is run through the V and emerges at the top of its head. This avoids the vital area which can be seen as a dark spot inside the body. Live shrimp can also be hooked near the tail at the third or fourth segment. Bridge-, drift-, and still-fishermen use the head method because the shrimp appears more natural; the hook underneath the shrimp acts as a keel, allowing the crustacean to swim freely.

Shrimp are a popular chum (*which see*). When chopped in small pieces and scattered on the fishing grounds the chum attracts many different species.

MULLET

The size of the mullet to be used depends upon the size of the gamefish being sought. Seldom, however, is a mullet of more than twelve inches practical for any of the common gamefish. The methods of taking mullet for bait

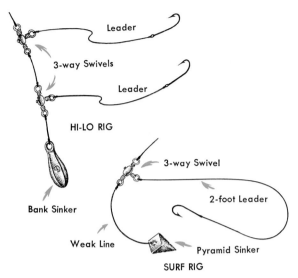

Leader

3-way Swivels

Leader

HI-LO RIG

Bank Sinker

3-way Swivel

2-foot Leader

Weak Line

Pyramid Sinker

SURF RIG

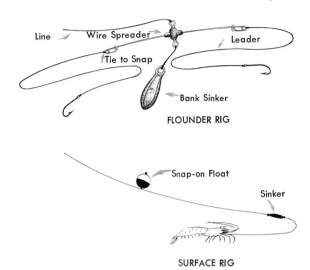

Line → Wire Spreader

Tie to Snap

Leader

Bank Sinker

FLOUNDER RIG

Snap-on Float

Sinker

SURFACE RIG

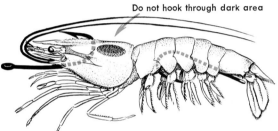

Do not hook through dark area

Shrimp can be hooked through head avoiding penetration of dark spot or through tail. Tail portion may be removed and used as bait for bottom species, and head portion used as chum.

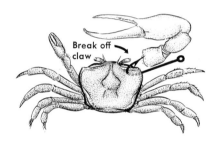

Break off claw

Fiddler crabs are excellent bait for many bottom species. Remove claw to prevent crab fastening under object; use the claw for chum.

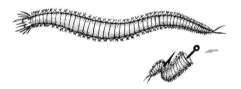

Sandworms or bloodworms are used whole for large gamefish such as striped bass, and hook can be impaled through head into body of worm. For bottom species such as flounders, porgies, and whiting, small pieces of worm are equally effective.

Sandbug, when used behind a lure such as a jig, can be hooked completely through the body under carapace. If used as a live bait, pass hook under carapace in rear portion.

Delicate anchovies are short-lived. For maximum action, hook bait in the flesh behind gill. Scored or partially cut anchovies are effective when casting or trolling.

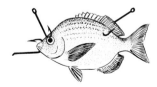

Small baits, such as pinfish, can be hooked through lips in the tough cartilage between eyes or under dorsal near tail.

are with a cast net or treble snatch hook. Mullet are extremely difficult to keep alive in bait cans and tanks, and therefore the vast majority of bait-fishermen catch their own just prior to a fishing trip.

In the shallower, tidal, inshore waters, the usual ways of rigging a mullet include running the hook beneath the dorsal fin, just forward of the tail, or through the fish's side in the rear section of the body. When fishing in inlets or other areas where the current is swift it is advisable to hook a mullet bait in the lips. This not only keeps the bait alive longer but gives the mullet a more natural appearance in the water. Bridge fishermen who fish straight down near the pilings of these spans often hook a mullet just behind the head and keep the bait on the surface to swim against the current.

Snook fishermen usually fish a mullet with the reel in free-spool, or, in the case of spinning tackle, with the bail open. It is necessary to drop back to a gamefish to allow it opportunity to get the bait completely in its mouth.

The spectacular live-bait jamboree on Florida's southeast coast is the annual mullet run each September. At that time of the year huge schools of mullet appear in the surf as they migrate southward. Anglers by the hundreds turn out on the beaches to fish for the tarpon, snook, bluefish, and other gamefish that feed on mullet.

Fishermen seeking tarpon and snook in these mullet schools usually cast out and snag a mullet with a treble hook. They reel in the bait, change to a single hook, and rehook the bait, and cast it back out where the gamefish can be seen feeding. A snap on the end of the line facilitates quick hook changes. Fishing from the beach for tarpon in the 50–100-pound class probably is the most strenuous kind of surf-fishing to be found on any coast, with the exception of shark fishing.

SANDBUGS

The sandbug, erroneously called "sandflea," is popular among pompano fishermen. These little, hardshelled animals, seldom more than 1½ inches long, are dug from ocean beaches at the tideline with a wire-mesh scoop that is pulled through the soft sand. They may also be purchased at bait shops and fishing piers.

In surf-fishing for pompano, sandbugs are fished with bottom rigs. Casters and trollers hook a sandbug onto a feather, jig, or small spoon. The sandbug has feelers at one end of its body that lie flat against its belly. For casting or trolling, the point of the hook should be inserted between the feelers and thence through the sandbug's body dead center. If hooked any other way, the loose feelers cause the bait to spin in the water. —A.J.McC.
—E.C.B.

LOBSTER *See* American Lobster, Fish Cookery, Spiny Lobster

LOBSTERETTES Family Nephropidae Small decapod crustaceans which inhabit the waters of the continental shelves and slopes of the world's oceans. Among the more familiar nephropids are the American lobster (*which see*), the European lobster (*Homarus vulgaris*), and the Norwegian lobster (*Nephrops norvegicus*). The smaller members of the family are called lobsterettes, for in appearance they resemble the lobsters with their large pinchers or chelae and heavily armored head and tail

regions. The abdominal plates or somites are triangular, and terminate in sharp points. The tail fan is broad, with numerous sharp spines along its margins. In deeper-water forms there may be a degeneration of the eyes coupled with a strengthening of the olfactory senses, indicating a dependence on smell rather than sight for locating food and avoiding predators. Often lobsterettes are brilliantly hued in shades of yellow-orange and red, providing them with a rare and unusual beauty not often encountered in the larger, shallow-water lobsters.

In the western Atlantic and Caribbean Sea there are some 6 genera and 10 species of lobsterettes, only three of which are both large enough and numerous enough to be considered as having commercial merit. These are the Caribbean lobsterette (*Nephrops binhami*), the red lobsterette (*Eunephrops bairdii*), and the Florida lobsterette (*Nephropsis aculeata*). The latter is not to be confused with the spiny lobster (*which see*), which belongs to another family of decapod crustaceans. The Caribbean and red lobsterettes are distinguished from the Florida family by their large black eyes and hairless pinchers. The Florida lobsterette has degenerate eyes and highly pubescent or hairy chelae. The Caribbean differs from the red in having a shorter carapace or head region; lighter, more slender, chelae; and alternating red and white coloration, as opposed to the red lobsterette's solid red to red-orange color, elongate carapace, and heavy chelae. Caribbean lobsterettes have been found off the coasts of Central and South America in depths of 125–500 fathoms, and off the coast of Cuba in 400 fathoms. There is evidence that the Caribbean lobsterette may also be distributed in the lesser Antillean region. The red lobsterette has the widest distribution of the three species, occurring from Cape Cod to Brazil throughout the waters of the southwestern Atlantic, Gulf of Mexico, and Caribbean Sea in 100–800 fathoms. Since its introduction to the seafood market it has gained a great deal of popularity as an unusual and delicious seafood.

LIFE HISTORY

Because of the great depths at which lobsterettes occur, very little information has been collected on the biology and ecology of these interesting animals. The eggs are carried on the abdominal appendages of the female for some length of time, and the number is dependent on the size of the individual, with 100–300 eggs per female being the normal complement. The eggs measure 1.5–2.5 mm in diameter in the Florida lobsterette and 2.0–3.0 mm in the Caribbean and red lobsterettes. Egg coloration varies from a deep blue-green during early development to a yellow-orange at the latter stages of maturation. Once the eggs hatch, the larvae become pelagic, remaining so until the postlarval stage is reached. At that time the juvenile becomes benthic or bottom-dwelling. Whether or not the juveniles and adults actually burrow into the substrate has not been documented, though their preference for mud and other soft bottoms would indicate this to be so. Considerable debate has also arisen over the occurrence of eye degeneration as found in several species. This condition is believed to restrict movement about the habitat, thereby creating a burrowing form of behavior. However, the presence or absence of eyes seem to be traits equally distributed among the deep-sea nephropids.

The water temperatures in the depths of the continental slopes inhabited by lobsterettes range from 43°–65°F for the Caribbean and red lobsterettes and 45°–51°F for the Florida lobsterette. The effects of temperature on these creatures is one of the many environmental factors believed to affect the distribution of deep-water animals whose mechanisms are as yet unknown.

FOOD VALUE

Lobsterettes were first introduced to the seafood market in 1962 by shrimp fishermen harvesting deepwater shrimp stocks off St. Augustine on the east coast of Florida. They called these little crustaceans "Danish lobsters" or lobsterettes, reminiscent of the commercially fished nephropids from the eastern Atlantic called Norway lobsters. (These latter crustaceans are imported into the United States as "scampi.") Only the tails are used, since the claws are too small to contain enough meat to merit their cooking and cleaning.

To prepare, boil the tails two minutes. Peel the cooled tails and serve cold with melted butter, or broil or bake in butter until hot. The meat has a texture and bouquet somewhat comparable to, though more delicate than, American lobster. —R.B.R.

LOCH LEVEN TROUT A racial strain of brown trout, *Salmo trutta*, characterized by the absence of red spots, and indigenous to Loch Leven in Scotland (*which see*)

LOCK A compartment in a canal or river for lowering or raising boats to a different level.

LOG A book maintained as the official record of all data and events that take place on a cruise, including, for example, speed, weather observations, and significant happenings. May be submitted as legal evidence in court.

LONGBILL SPEARFISH *Tetrapturus pfluegeri* An Atlantic marine species, of rather small size for this family, occasionally taken off the southeastern and Gulf coasts of the United States. Generally found more or less offshore, in waters of 50 fathoms or deeper.

DESCRIPTION

The longbill spearfish is elongate and slender, with fairly long pectoral fins, a crescent shaped anal fin, and a long, relatively high dorsal fin. The anterior part of the dorsal fin forms a sharp peak, while behind this peak the rest of the fin maintains a fairly even height about equal to or greater than the depth of the body. The vent is located some distance in front of the anal fin. In young individuals the snout is considerably longer than the lower jaw, but in older specimens the snout and lower jaw tend to become more nearly equal although the snout is always the longer. The body is long and slim, the sides flat, the lateral line single and quite prominent. Color is dark metallic blue, or sometimes greenish, above, fading through silver gray to white or silvery on the ventral side. A few hours after death the dorsal colors fade to a dark slatey blue-gray. The fins are all dark and there are no spots or bars on the body.

The longbill spearfish is the smallest member of the group, seldom exceeding 40 or 50 pounds weight.

HABITS

This fish is not at all common, and was only recently recognized by ichthyologists as a distinct species, hence practically nothing is known of its life history. Presumably its food, like that of the shortbill spearfish, includes smaller fishes, squids, and so on. It is primarily a fish of the open waters, occurring most commonly some distance offshore.

Because of its relative scarcity and small size, the longbill spearfish is of but little importance to commercial fishermen. Sportsmen, however, will find it of interest as being a species not commonly met. It is known with certainty only from the western North Atlantic, where it occurs from off southern New Jersey to Venezuela, and from Texas to Puerto Rico.

FISHING METHODS

Longbill spearfish may be taken by trolling with rod and line, by long-lining, or any other means suitable for carnivorous fishes of this size.

LONGEAR SUNFISH *Lepomis megalotis* The longear, a highly colored sunfish, can be distinguished from the other sunfishes by the exceptionally long, flexible gill flap which is narrowly bordered with scarlet. The sides are flecked with blue or yellow, and the cheeks have irregular lines of blue or green. The head profile is sharp, the pectoral fin is short and rounded, and the mouth is moderately large, ending under the eye. The Northern longear grows to a maximum length of about 4½ inches while the central longear reaches 9 inches in length and 10 ounces in weight.

The longear and its subspecies are found from the Dakotas east to the upper St. Lawrence River and south to Florida and Texas. It prefers clear, weedy streams, ponds, and bogs.

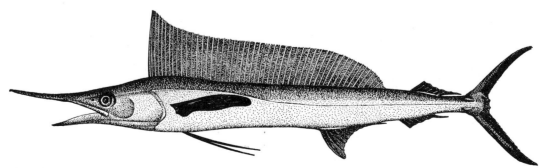

Longbill Spearfish

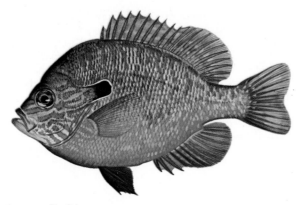

Longear Sunfish

LIFE HISTORY

This sunfish builds a nest like most of the other sunfishes and spawns in the North in late June until early August. They reach sexual maturity in the third summer. It takes five years for the Northern longear to reach 4 inches. The food is principally aquatic insects, crustaceans, and small fishes.

ANGLING VALUE

Although the longear sunfish feeds mostly at the surface and can be taken on artificial flies, it has little value because of its generally small size.   —K.B.

LONGFIN BLUNTNOSE JACK *See* Atlantic Bluntnose Jack

LONGFIN BONEFISH *Dixonina nemoptera* Closely related to the bonefish (*which see*), it is a herringlike fish related to the tarpon and ladyfish. It resembles the bonefish in having an elongate, torpedo-shaped body, with a slender head and a mouth placed beneath the tip of the pointed snout which reaches the middle of the eye. The single dorsal fin is placed about in the middle of the body. It is known in the Atlantic from northern Brazil, Venezuela, Santo Domingo, Jamaica, and, rarely, from the Florida Keys. In the Pacific it ranges from the Gulf of California to Costa Rica. It differs from the bonefish in having a more slender body, a longer maxillary bone, a greater number of lateral-line scales (76–84 versus about 70), a longer and more conical snout, a larger mouth, and an elongate last ray in the dorsal and anal fins, the length of the fin being less pronounced in the young. The body is bright silvery with dark scale lines along the upper half of the body, and dark green about the head. Maximum recorded size is about 16 inches.

LIFE HISTORY

Generally, the longfin bonefish probably has about the same habits as the common bonefish. In Jamaica they are reported to be more numerous near creek mouths than are common bonefish. They are inhabitants of sandy or muddy flats and feed on the bottom on shrimps, crabs, and small fishes. They school with the bonefish in shallow waters. A specimen, which was taken from Costa Rica in January, apparently was almost ready to spawn. The longfin is too rare to be commercially valuable, and, like the bonefish, its flesh is poor and bony. They are periodically abundant about Jamaica, where they are sometimes used as bait for blue marlin.   —D.dS.

LONGFIN SMELT *Spirinchus thaleichthys* This smelt (*which see*) was described in 1934 and first taken in 1921. Sometimes taken in shrimp trawls in 10–70 fathoms. Spawns in freshwater streams at least, and has been taken as far up the Fraser River as Harrison Lake. It is

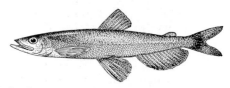

Longfin Smelt

to be found from Central California to southeastern Alaska. Dorsal-fin origin slightly back of pelvic origin; anal rays long; midlateral scales 55–62; pectoral fins long; no striae on opercles; head and body with fine black stippling.

COMMERCIAL VALUE

Although the longfin smelt is of fine flavor, the catch is limited. *See also* Smelt   —J.R.

LONGFIN TUNA *See* Albacore

LONGLINE A method of fishing wherein long lengths of line are buoyed at the surface with floats from which shorter dropper sections are baited. Usually each section comprises 7–10 specially made hooks (with shanks bent inward for automatic hooking) and each of these sections represents a "basket." These baskets may total 50–70 miles in length. The longline is commonly used by Japanese commercials to catch tuna, marlin, and swordfish. It is used to a lesser extent by the Norwegians in the capture of sharks and in the Pacific Northwest commercial fishery to catch halibut. Longlining is of great importance today to American universities and research institutes engaged in studies on large marine gamefish.

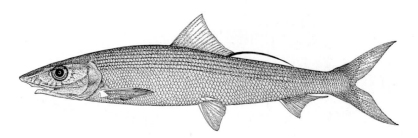

Longfin Bonefish

LONGNOSE BATFISH *Ogcocephalus vespertilio* A member of the batfish family (Ogcocephalidae) which is occasionally caught by angling and is sometimes observed along the bottom in tropical marine habitats. The batfish seldom exceeds a foot in length and is distinguished by its broad body and flattened head, the anterior portion of which is elongated into a snout process with an inferior mouth. The large pectoral fins are inserted horizontally and the skin is covered with bony tubercles. Related species in Atlantic distribution are the spiny batfish (*Halieutichthys aculeatus*), the tricorn batfish (*O. mcgintyi*), shortnose batfish (*O. nasutus*), roughback batfish (*O. parvus*), polka-dot batfish (*O. radiatus*), and in the Pacific Ocean the spotted batfish (*Zalieutes elater*). The batfishes vary in color from black to shades of red. They feed on small fish, crustaceans, and mollusks.

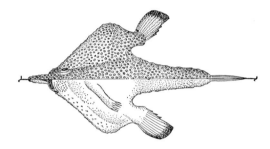

Longnose Batfish, dorsal view, *top*, ventral view, *bottom*

LOCOMOTION

The batfish usually does not swim fishlike but uses its pelvic and pectoral fins in the manner of limbs by trotting, hopping, or jumping forward along the bottom. The modified dorsal spine underneath the forehead is a nasal lure used as a "fishing rod" to attract its prey, similar to the anglerfishes. —A.J.McC.

LONGNOSE DACE *Rhinichthys cataractae* A dark, greenish-olive-backed minnow with a long snout. The snout projects far beyond the nearly horizontal mouth. Fins light olive or transparent. Ventral portions of the body milky-white. The tip of the upper lip is far below the level of the lower edge of the eye. There are many dusky scales scattered over the back giving a mottled appearance. The range of the longnose dace extends over most of the United States except the Southeast coastal region.

HABITS

This species thrives in swiftwaters. A characteristic fish of the small, headwater streams of the mountain-brook type, the longnose is found in association with rushing

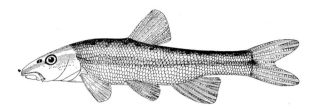

Longnose Dace

torrents and rock pools. The food of the longnose consists of various aquatic insect larvae and some vegetable matter. Its liking for blackfly larvae contributes to its economic value. Little is known of the breeding habits of this species. It apparently spawns in early spring, and the males develop minute tubercles on the head and back. The longnose dace is found up to 4½ inches in length.

ECONOMIC VALUE

Considered of some value in the control of blackflies, this species is also an excellent baitfish. It is easily obtainable and is felt to be unsurpassed as a bait for bass. It undoubtedly provides excellent forage for trout also. —R.A.J.

LONGNOSE GAR *Lepisosteus osseus* This species is the most abundant and widely distributed member of the ancient gar family. Its very long slender beak, whose length is 18–20 times its least width, and a long cylindrical body covered with overlapping diamond-shaped scales distinguish it from all its freshwater relatives. The dorsal fin is inserted far back, almost over the anal fin.

It is found in the Mississippi River system northwest to Montana, through the Great Lakes except Lake Superior, to the St. Lawrence watershed of Quebec, and south to northern Mexico.

LIFE HISTORY

Spawning takes place in the spring, usually May and June, in shallow water. The eggs attach to weeds or other objects and hatch in 6–8 days. Beginning early in life, they spend long periods motionless near the surface, moving only when they break the surface to gulp air into the swim bladder or to capture food. This habit causes gar to be seen more frequently than other species and often gives the appearance of disproportionately high numbers when this is not necessarily the case. After the first few weeks of life man is the only major predator. It grows very rapidly to 19–22 inches the first year. Males mature at 3–4 years and females at 6. An average female has 28,000 eggs. These green eggs are poisonous to higher vertebrates and should not be eaten.

Longnose Gar

It is more tolerant of current than the other species of gar, and is often found swimming and feeding in moderate currents.

Fish compose most of its diet except during the first few days after feeding begins when it takes plankton and insect larvae. Feeding on small minnows begins very early in life.

ANGLING VALUE

It should be utilized as a sport fish to a much greater extent. It can be taken with minnows on a short wire leader or on many other baits including frayed nylon without a hook. The latter is effective because the gar is captured when its teeth become entangled in the nylon.

—C.A.P.

LONGNOSE SKATE *Raja rhina* Characterized by a distinctively long snout which tapers forward rather gradually, this skate's disk has an irregular shape. The anterior margins of the pectoral fins are decidedly concave. It is dark brown above with irregular spots, often with a distinct, large spot, which lacks a white rim, on either wing. The ventral surface is a muddy blue. In size and general characteristics it is somewhat similar to the barndoor skate (*which see*), growing to a length of 4½ feet. It is recorded from southeastern Alaska to southern California. As with other skates, it lays eggs, each egg measuring 3–5 inches long and containing a single individual.

—D.dS.

LONGNOSE SUCKER *Catostomus catostomus* As the name implies, it is a sucker with a bulbous snout projecting far beyond the upper lip. Color dorsally dark olive-slate, sides lighter, ventrally milky-white. Scales sharply outlined with darker color. Lateral-line scales more than 85. The longnose is widely distributed east of the Rocky Mountains from Alaska to Maine.

Longnose Sucker

LIFE HISTORY

A deep, coldwater species, the longnose ascends tributary streams to spawn in April, May, and June. At this time males develop a rosy lateral band. Little is known of the food habits of the longnose sucker except that it apparently feeds primarily on plant material. The average size is 16 inches and 2 pounds.

ANGLING VALUE

The longnose sucker has little angling value. It is caught on worms and is also taken by spearing during the spring migration period. The flesh is edible although very bony. It is of minor importance as a commercial species in the Great Lakes region. —R.A.J.

LOOKDOWNS Genera *Selene* (lookdowns) and *Vomer* (moonfish). These two genera have blunthead profiles, deep and very thin bodies, and minute scales that may be difficult to locate.

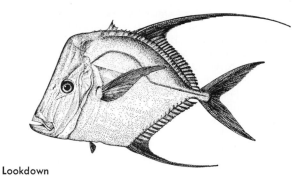

Lookdown

The true lookdowns (*Selene*) have a very high and steep anterior profile, with the head almost 1½ times as deep as long. The dorsal and anal fin lobes are elongated, extending to the ends of the fins when depressed. The Atlantic lookdown, *Selene vomer*, occurs on both sides of the Atlantic; in the western Atlantic it is known to range from a latitude of 35° 31' S. off Uruguay to Massachusetts and at Bermuda. The two eastern Pacific species can be distinguished as follows. The blackfin lookdown, *Selene brevoortii*, has 21 to 22 dorsal softrays and 17–19 anal softrays (range, Peru to Magdalena Bay, Baja California, and Macapule Island, Mexico). The Pacific lookdown, *Selene oerstedii*, very closely related to the Atlantic lookdown, has 16–18 dorsal softrays and 15–16 anal softrays (range, Panama to Mazatlán, Mexico).

The moonfish (*Vomer*) have a head profile that is only moderately high, with the head only slightly deeper than long. The dorsal- and anal-fin lobes are very short (except in specimens smaller than 1 inch in length). The Atlantic moonfish, *Vomer setapinnis*, occurs on both sides of the Atlantic; in the western Atlantic it ranges from Uruguay to Nova Scotia. The Pacific moonfish, *Vomer declivifrons*, ranges from near Chimbote in Peru to Long Beach, California. The two species are very similar.

ANGLING VALUE

Both the lookdowns and the moonfish grow to about 10–12 inches. They are caught by casting artificial lures, such as small (⅛–¼ ounce) jigs and streamer flies in open bays, and also around docks at night in Florida. Their flesh is excellent. Very little is known of their life histories. *See also* Carangidae —F.H.B.

LOUISIANA Angling in Louisiana is considered a year-round recreation by its residents. There are 4,000,000 or more acres of lakes, lagoons, rivers, and marshes which provide perfect habitats for a variety of freshwater game and panfish. There are no real winters, and, with an average annual temperature of 67° F., the fish growing season is long. Saltwater fishing in the bays, outer passes, and the Gulf proper contributes immensely to the sport available and species such as red drum (locally redfish or *poisson rouge*), spotted seatrout, sand seatrout, sheepshead, pompano, Spanish mackerel, and the dolphin exist in abundance. The reputation of New Orleans as a citadel for the gourmet is in a large measure due to the great wealth of its aquatic resources. In recent years, big-game fishing for marlin and sailfish has also become established off the passes of the Mississippi. But exotic or commonplace, from "gigging" flounders by torchlight at night or jumping tarpon with a plug, Louisiana is, above all, diversified.

The freshwater angler will find largemouth bass, warmouth, yellow bass, crappie (locally *sac-à-lait*), and several species of sunfish throughout most of the state. The striped bass is scarce, but it inhabits the areas east of the Mississippi in the Amite, Tchefuncte, Tangipahoa, and Pearl rivers, and adjoining lakes. In the large river basins further inland the yellow bass becomes rare, and the white bass and crappie replace it. However, the largemouth bass and warmouth maintain their abundance throughout the slow-flowing streams of this region. The white bass (*which see*) reaches its greatest concentration in northeast Louisiana, chiefly in the oxbow lakes along the Mississippi and Black rivers and in the Ouachita River itself. Some of the most productive fishing exists in the "backwater" ponds which are located on the flood plains of the Mississippi, Atchafalaya, Red, and Black rivers. These plains are punctured by a large number of shallow lakes which receive backwater from nearby rivers during periods of flooding; some are permanent, some maintain their level during lowwater periods. As a rule the quality of the backwater lake is above average. Two of the most outstanding are Spring Bayou Backwater and the Pearl River Backwater. Largemouth bass, spotted bass, white bass, yellow bass, bluegill, channel catfish, drum, and buffalo are the principal species caught here.

Leaving the larger valleys with their lazy streams and ascending the swifter rivers of the uplands, the fish population is considerably different. The largemouth bass is not as abundant; spotted bass, spotted sunfish (locally redbellied sunfish), and the chain pickerel become more numerous. The fastflowing streams of Louisiana are not comparable in any way to the rapid, clear coldwaters of states in the mountain regions, with their large rocks and boulders.

Geographically, Louisiana offers fishing opportunities almost everywhere because the fish fauna is well-established in hundreds of thousands of acres of water and because the state itself has been protecting its marine assets ever since 1872 by means of a commission initially created for the protection of the oyster industry; this movement grew in scope as the years passed. Presently, almost every pond capable of sustaining fish is surveyed, and if conditions are feasible, it is stocked with fingerlings produced by four state-operated hatcheries. Also an intensive aquatic weed-control program is constantly in operation clearing fishing grounds of water hyacinths and other noxious plants by means of machines and toxins harmless to fish and by managing water levels and pollution control. These methods are not unique but are merely sound conservation put into rigid practice.

The 600-mile Gulf Coast of Louisiana is decidedly discontinuous, being broken up into numerous marshy islands and peninsulas, which, for the most part are inaccessible to an automobile. The most accessible, as well as the most attractive, sand beaches, are at Grand Isle, south of New Orleans, and on the Cameron Coast, south of Lake Charles. There are also beaches along the Chandeleurs, Timbalier, Isle Derniére, and Cheniere au Tigre islands, but the latter may be reached only by boat. All of these beaches are unusually wide and composed of fine sand mixed with broken shell. Southerly winds prevail, and surf-fishing is usually productive.

White and Grand lakes may be entered from Abbeville or Lake Arthur by boat. These are brackish lakes with fresh and saltwater species. From Lake Charles, Calcasieu Lake and Pass can be reached by boat or highway. Croaker and some seatrout work up into Lake Calcasieu, which also has bass and panfish.

As one travels inland by boat from the coast, the water in the bayous and lakes becomes brackish and finally fresh, and the tide slackens, although the watercourses are still practically at sea level. In this region, salt- and freshwater species often mingle. The croaker (*see* Atlantic croaker) ventures farthest inland, to feed on small clams and crustaceans abounding on the lake bottoms. The red drum prefers the mouths of bayous; spotted seatrout are found mainly along the hard-bottomed grassy shores of lakes. The sheepshead prefers shell reefs and barnacle-covered pilings. The largemouth bass can also tolerate minimal salinities and may be found in this section during the summer months along with various panfish.

In the prairie regions streams are usually small and, being near sea level, are sluggish. The Vermilion, Calcasieu, and the Mermentau are the only rivers of notable size which traverse the prairies. Ordinarily, because of this lack of streams, the prairies proper are not considered good for fishing. However, with the introduction of large irrigation systems, the canals themselves, particularly abandoned ones, have become quite heavily populated with crappie, largemouth bass, warmouth, and sunfish.

In the large interior river valleys, or the hardwood valley lands and river basin swamps, and in lakes above Gulf level, the swamps differ from the tide-level swamps chiefly in the density of cypress and tupelo growths and the almost complete absence of open marshy tracts. There are also locations where red maple and ash are quite plentiful. The numerous lakes and bayous of these basins constitute the richest freshwater habitat in the state. Crappie, largemouth bass, warmouth, and several species of sunfish are plentiful and grow to large size. White bass are also common. There is an active commercial fishery for catfish, buffalo, and paddlefish.

In the terraced, longleaf pine hills, composed for the most part of sand and sandy clay, the streams are perhaps the most interesting to the freshwater rod-and-reel fisherman because they closely approach trout streams in appearance. They are fairly swift and, except during heavy rains, are clear since they are fed by springs and ground seepage. The dominant species here is that extremely wary and game fighter, the spotted bass. Where such streams flow out of the flatter country to the southward, both the spotted bass and largemouth bass are to be found. The spotted bass can be taken wherever there is a fair current, while the largemouth is more abundant in water that remains relatively still.

BASS LAKES

Some of the major bass lakes in Louisiana are Toledo Bend Reservoir and Caddo Lake, which are shared with Texas, the Bayou Bodeau lying to the east, Cross Lake near Shreveport, Lake Bistineau near Ringgold, Catahoula and Sabine lakes northwest of Alexandria, and Lake St. John and Lake Bruin to the northeast. All the usual methods are popular, including bait casting, spinning, and fly fishing, as well as live bait. Surface plugs, floating-and-diving plugs, plastic worms, weedless skirted lures, and leadheads are effective, depending on the season and water conditions. The usual run of fish is from 1–3 pounds, but larger bass are caught by skilled anglers. Spring and fall are the most productive seasons for the fisherman; however, in periods of good weather the angling can be fast right through the winter.

GRAND ISLE

The saltwater playground of Louisiana, Grand Isle has much to offer the vacationer who wants to fish for almost every variety of gamefish found in the state. Accommodations are well rounded out on the islands. There are hotels and many tourist courts adjacent to the beach. Although Grand Isle is popular among boating and water-skiing enthusiasts, its greatest appeal lies in the fishing possibilities. There are charter boats for party fishing out in the Gulf; some tie up at the offshore drilling platforms to bottom-fish for blues, red snapper, spadefish, sand seatrout, jewfish, cobia, and pompano. Other boat skippers prefer to troll the openwaters for Spanish and king mackerel, cobia, tarpon, crevalle, and dolphin. Those boats which are equipped for fishing the deepwaters miles offshore seek sailfish, marlin, and bluefin tuna over the deep banks beyond the Passes of the Mississippi's mouth.

When the water is right, the surf-fisherman can fish off the beach where spotted seatrout move in for feeding with the rising tides; or he can cast around the many small islands and shell reefs which dot the inside limits of Barataria and Caminada bays. Favorite locations for schooling fish are Monkey Reefs, Bird Reef, and Middle Bank. Those not familiar with the area can always follow other boats which make the daily run during the fishing season, or they may get directions from the operator of their particular boat landing. Rental and bait services are plentiful on both sides of the Caminada Bridge.

NEW ORLEANS AREA

Beginning just west of Lake Pontchartrain is the only slightly saline Lake Maurepas connected by a seven-mile channel with Pontchartrain, which in turn is connected to Lake Borgne and Mississippi Sound. Maurepas is dominated by croaker. Pontchartrain, however, has both croaker and seatrout along most of the shore, and near Pass Rigolets, tarpon, red drum, sheepshead, and flounder also are caught. Lake Catherine, which opens off Rigolets between Borgne and Pontchartrain, is fished, as is Lake Borgne, for red drum, seatrout, and flounder. So are Grand Pass, Le Petit Pass, Nine-Mile and Three-Mile bayous, Oyster Bay, and Creole Gap, all of which border Mississippi Sound east of Borgne. Deeper waters off nearby Chandeleur and neighboring islands are better known for mackerel, bluefish, ling, and trout. The Black Bay, California Bay, and Breton Island areas of Breton Sound are channel-bass and seatrout waters. There is an October bonanza of spotted seatrout when they move in from the lake with the south winds of fall.

Accommodations for extended fishing trips in the Madisonville, Lacombe, and Slidell areas are adequate the year round. Those fishing camps with lodging and food on the spot may become crowded when fishing is at its peak during the summer and fall runs; even so, U.S. 90, which is a major artery to the Mississippi Gulf Coast, is lined with motels, hotels, and dining places all within reasonable distance of good fishing. Boats are available at all camps which also have good launching facilities for anglers who bring their own rigs. An outboard motor is necessary, and there is no extensive rental service in the area.

Beginning in 1965 big-game anglers began exploring the Loop Current out of New Orleans. The Loop Current, while not as well known as the Gulf Stream, is a similar water mass that flows from the Yucatan Channel northward into the eastern Gulf of Mexico, where it turns in a semicircle and flows parallel to the west coast of Florida in a southerly direction to the Florida Straits. The New Orleans Big Game Fishing Club log indicates a 250-pound average on blue marlin, with the local record at 686; and yellowfin tuna at an average of 40 pounds with the local record at 201½ pounds. White marlin, dolphin, sailfish, and wahoo have been prime targets also, and in the 1971 season six giant bluefin tuna were boated, which included the heaviest fish ever recorded for the Gulf of Mexico— an 859-pounder weighed in at Port Eads. Due to Louisiana's shallow, gradually sloping coastline it requires a long run (35–60 miles) to reach the inside or outside edge of the dropoff. New Orleans skippers look for blue water or weed lines before dropping their outriggers.

LAKE VERRET AREA

Lake Verret, between Grand Lake and Napoleonville, is fished for bass. Grand Bayou is a tributary of Lake Verret. Many fishermen like Lake Boeuf east of Thibodaux and Little Lake des Allemands. Grand Lake (there are two of the same name) is long and sprawling, with numerous bays and feeder bayous. Many parts of this lake yield bass, crappie, sunfish, and channel cat. Bayou Eugene and Big and Little Pigeon bayous are locally popular. Bayou Teche parallels Grand Lake on the southwest.

The settlement of Pierre Part, hub of fishing activity around Lake Verret, has several adequate lodgings for extended fishing trips. There are restaurants featuring seafood cooked in wonderful Creole style. At Bayou Corne accommodations are good. There are small cabins, spacious camping grounds, and outdoor cooking facilities. Accommodations at Belle River are limited as at Shell Beach. There are boats for rent at Bayou Corne, Pierre Part, and Belle River.   —E.T.W.

LOUP   The French common name for the Atlantic wolffish (*which see*)

LOUPE DE MER   *See* Bass

LUCKY BONES   *See* Freshwater Drum

LUMPFISH *Cyclopterus lumpus*   Also called the henfish, lump, and lumpsucker, this unusual-looking fish belongs to the family Cyclopteridae, a group of small, stout-bodied fishes of the northern seas with the pelvic fins modified to form an adhesive disc. The lumpfish is found on both sides of the North Atlantic; on the west side it ranges from Hudson Bay south to Chesapeake Bay; on the east side it is found on both sides of Greenland, Iceland, Faroes, and the White Sea south to Gascoyne Bay, France

Its color is variable, often matching its environment, especially in the young. It ranges from blue, bluish-gray to greenish and brownish; belly often yellowish or whitish; in breeding males the belly becomes red, brightest near the adhesive disc.

Other distinguishing characters of the lumpfish are body stout, thick, greatest depth 2″ in total length about halfway between snout and base or caudal; a partly cartilaginous, partly gelatinous hump on the back engulfing the first dorsal fin in adults; scaleless but covered with hard, wartlike tubercles of various sizes, the larger ones disposed in 7 rows, 1 along the middle of the back plus 3 rows on each side; head 4 in total length; mouth small, terminal, angle in front of eye; small, simple teeth in a single row in jaws. Eye 4 in head.

First dorsal fin has 6–8 spines, but this fin is visible only on small specimens of 1¼ inches or less. Second dorsal fin with 10–11 softrays, located behind hump and ending at caudal peduncle; caudal fin moderate and slightly rounded; anal fin with 9–11 softrays; pectorals large with 20–21 softrays, base extending along lower ⅔ of gill opening, larger in males than in females; pelvics located on ventral side between bases of pectorals, modified to 6 pairs of fleshy knobs surrounded by a circular flap of skin forming an adhesive disc. Lateral line not apparent.

LIFE HISTORY

Adult lumpfish are primarily benthic forms, living on rocky and stony bottoms, but sometimes they are found hiding under floating seaweed. Their food consists of euphausiid shrimp, amphipods, and other small crustaceans; also occasionally jellyfish, comb jellies, and small fishes.

Spawning takes place in spring or summer, and the demersal eggs are deposited in large masses that adhere to rocks among seaweed. The eggs are about ¹/₁₀ of an inch in diameter, pale green to yellowish, becoming darker as development proceeds. Large females will produce about 140,000 eggs. The male guards the eggs during the incubation period which lasts 6 weeks to 2 months.

Lumpfish reach a length of about 4 inches in their third year and about 10 inches by their fifth year. Females may reach a maximum length of about 24 inches and a weight of more than 20 pounds.

FOOD VALUE

In Europe the flesh is used for food and the eggs make a good caviar substitute. —J.C.B.

M

MACABÍ A regional Spanish name for bonefish (*which see*) used in Cuba, Mexico, Central America, and parts of South America.

MACACO A regional Spanish name for bonefish (*which see*) sometimes used in Puerto Rico.

MACHACA The Spanish common name for one or several of the brycons (*which see*) in Nicaragua, Costa Rica, and Panama.

MACKERELS There are at least two species of mackerels in American Atlantic waters, the Atlantic mackerel, *Scomber scombrus*, without spots on the sides below the midline and without a swimbladder, and the chub mackerel or tinker mackerel, *Scomber colias*, with spots or blotches on the sides below the midline, and with a

Atlantic Mackerel

swimbladder. The Pacific mackerel, *Scomber japonicus* (which has been called *Pneumatophorus diego*) is doubtfully distinct, resembling the chub mackerel in possessing a swimbladder, and with spots and blotches on the sides present or absent. Mackerels differ from other fishes in their family by having fleshy, adipose eyelids covering the anterior and posterior parts of the eye, and the two dorsal fins are widely separated from each other as in the frigate mackerels. Adult Atlantic mackerel commonly reach 14–18 inches in length and weigh 1–2 pounds, and occasionally larger ones are found. There is a record of a 7½-pound individual. Chub mackerel are smaller, reaching a length of 8–14 inches. Pacific mackerel seldom exceed 16 inches and 2 pounds; the largest American specimen known was 25 inches long and weighed over 6 pounds.

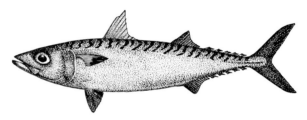

Pacific Mackerel

Atlantic mackerel occur in the Atlantic Ocean and the Mediterranean Sea. In the western Atlantic they are found roughly from the Gulf of St. Lawrence to Cape Hatteras. Chub mackerel have a somewhat similar distribution, but are found farther south, at least to Cuba in the western Atlantic Ocean. Pacific mackerel are known from the Gulf of Alaska to southern Baja California and the Gulf of California. They are also found through much of the Pacific and Indian oceans.

Mackerel feed on a wide variety of foods, including small fishes, crustaceans, squid, worms, and planktonic organisms. They are eaten by a multitude of larger predaceous forms, such as whales, porpoises, sharks, tunas, bluefish, striped bass, cod, and sea birds. In American waters, all species breed in spring and early summer, a single female shedding a total of about half a million eggs in each season.

Mackerels are important commercial fishes on both American coasts, as well as in other parts of the world. Many are caught, if not sought, by anglers, and the flesh is regarded as delicious, though somewhat oily. *See also* Cero, Frigate Mackerel, King Mackerel, Monterey, Sierra, Spanish Mackerel —B.B.C. —R.H.G.

MADTOM *See* Black Madtom, Brindled Madtom, Catfish, Speckled Madtom, Stonecat, Tadpole Madtom

MAHI-MAHI The Hawaiian name for dolphin (*which see*). Dolphin are taken commercially in Hawaii, and are one of the most important food fish in the islands. *See also* Hawaii

MAHOGANY SNAPPER *Lutjanus mahogoni* This rather uncommon snapper is occasionally taken around southern Florida. It occurs throughout the tropical American Atlantic. Not known to reach a large size, most of the specimens taken by anglers or seen in Caribbean markets measure less than 20 inches in total length. The Spanish name, *ojanco*, refers to the large eye.

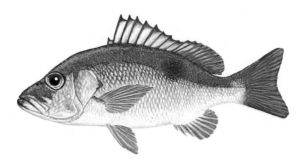

Mahogany Snapper

The mahogany snapper has 10 dorsal spines, 12 dorsal rays, and 8 anal rays. There are normally 15 pectoral rays. Gillrakers 8–10 on lower limb of first arch, not counting rudiments. Rows of scales around caudal peduncle 24–26, usually 25. Cheek scales in 5, rarely 6 rows. Upper jaw reaching beyond vertical from anterior margin of orbit. Pectoral fin not reaching to vertical from origin of anal fin. Anal fin rounded, not angulate posteriorly. General coloration reddish-brown with bronze streaks; silvery below. Black spot on sides of body present. Caudal fin red. Dorsal fin pale, edged with red. Pectoral, pelvic, and anal fins scarlet. Eye scarlet.

The large eye and color pattern distinguish this species from the other snappers.

ANGLING VALUE

This is one of the least known of snappers. Small individuals occur in shallow water, but the larger adults are usually found in moderate depths. A bottom feeder usually taken on live bait. The mahogany snapper is a rewarding catch because of its bright colors and relative scarcity.

FOOD VALUE

Edible. A food fish occasionally seen in the West Indian markets. —L.R.

MAHSEER *Barbus tor* The mahseer, an Asiatic member of the Cyprinidae, is a powerful gamefish and grows to weights of 120 pounds. Mahseer of 15–60 pounds are generally common in Nepal, India, and a portion of Pakistan. A smaller species occurs in Ceylon. Although remotely related to the European carps, the mahseer is omnivorous, and despite its rubbery lips the jaws are extremely strong and its throat contains pharyngeal teeth. The mahseer has very large scales (to the size of a playing card on big fish), and exhibits a great variation in color from gold to almost black according to the habitat. Mahseer scales are often used for luggage labels and even menu cards by devoted anglers. When hooked, the mahseer makes a typical long run of 100 yards or more. Subsequent runs may be shorter and punctuated with occasional jumps, especially from smaller fish, but unquestionably the mahseer is difficult to subdue. Large mahseer (over 100 pounds) have required more than four hours to bring to gaff against heavy tackle.

The main western mahseer rivers in Nepal are the Karnali and Bheri (or Surju) and the Rapti—all of which join to form the Gogra, which in turn flows into the Ganges. In central Nepal the principal streams are the Gandak and its tributaries, notably the Narayani, Seti, Marsyandi, Darondi, and Burhi rivers. Elsewhere and to the east are the Indrawati, Sun Kosi, Dudh Kosi, Arun, and Tamur rivers—all of which eventually merge and flow into India.

The best run of mahseer occurs in March and April, and a fair run takes place in November, depending on how early or how late the monsoon clears. The climate varies with altitude. At low elevations it is subtropical with heavy rainfall, hot and humid in the summer but pleasantly cool during the winter. The uplands have comfortable temperatures during the summer months and a cold winter with heavy snows above 8,000 feet. June, July, and August are the monsoon months.

—A.J.McC.

MAINE One of the most popular states for freshwater fishing. Maine covers an area of 32,562 square miles of which 8 percent is inland water, bog, and swamp. The irregularly indented coastline, cut by tidal river mouths, bays, and inlets, is ten times its straightaway length of 250 miles. There are 5,152 streams in Maine (six rivers 100 miles or more in length, 67 from 20 to 99 miles long, and the remainder are smaller brooks) as well as 2,465 lakes and ponds. Sparsely settled but with more than 16,000,000 acres in woodland, the state still provides some relatively inaccessible brook-trout fishing on such

Canoe trips are popular in Maine and wilderness floats can be made for more than 100 miles

notable streams as the Allagash, Spencer, and Kennebago and for landlocked salmon as well as squaretails on the West Branch of the Penobscot, Moose River, upper Kennebec, and the outlets of Moosehead Lake. Much of the angling is done in lakes and connecting thoroughfares for brook trout, lake trout (locally togue), landlocked salmon, and smallmouth bass. Many warmwater lakes from central Maine to the coast also contain chain pickerel, white perch, and yellow perch. An Atlantic-salmon restoration program initiated in 1949 has been partially successful in establishing runs in five rivers and lesser runs in several others. Sea-run brook trout (salters) are present in a number of coastal streams, and anadromous brown trout ascend from the sea into Alamasook Lake (Hancock County). Inland, the brown has been introduced widely in warmwater lakes. There is an established population of rainbow trout in Maine's Kennebec River in the Bingham area. Saltwater sport fishing in the state is dominated by the striped bass, pollock, and mackerel, but there is some offshore angling for bluefin tuna out of Ogunquit, Small Point, Boothbay, and Bailey Island.

FISH RIVER LAKES

This group of large connecting lakes is in the Fish River drainage located in Aroostook County. Long Lake in the eastern headwaters has an area of 6,000 acres and a maximum depth of 136 feet. Landlocked salmon were introduced into Long Lake at the turn of the century, and an excellent population has been maintained since. This lake is typical of others in the river system such as Mud, Cross, Square, and Eagle. Besides landlocked salmon the principal gamefish is the brook trout. The lake whitefish provides fine dry-fly-fishing at times and is an excellent table fish.

The Fish River drains 890 square miles. It is a tributary to the St. John River. Southwest of Eagle Lake lies 7.7-mile-long St. Froid Lake, and further south is Portage Lake. Fish River Lake is situated to the west of Portage Lake. This last-named lake has landlocked salmon, lake and brook trout. It has been inaccessible except by plane, but a woods road now leads into the area.

DeBOULIE AND ALLAGASH WATERS

West of the Fish River chain of Lakes in Aroostook County lie the famous DeBoulie (Red River) Lakes and the Allagash River drainage. Poushineer Pond supports brook trout and also the rare blueback trout (*which see*). This fish exists in several other nearby lakes. At one time, it was a highly favored table fish in this region, and the unusually heavy brook trout (9–11 pounds) in Rangeley Lake were believed to have attained their size from foraging on small bluebacks. Bluebacks are bottom feeders and difficult to catch. In the early days, they were netted by residents. Gardner Lake is another home presently of both brook and blueback trout.

There are hundreds of trout and togue waters in this section of Aroostook County and on down into Piscataquis County. Long Lake (1,203 acres) lies directly on the Allagash River, for example. South of it is Umsaskis Lake (1,222 acres). Other famous Allagash River waters south of those named are Churchill, Round Pond, Eagle Lake, Big Lake (17.48 square miles).

Chamberlain Lake and its southeasterly arm, Telos Lake, lie close to Baxter State Park—a wilderness sanctuary of more than 200,000 acres. These are but typical of the trout and togue lakes, ponds, and streams in the Allagash Region.

The best smallmouth bass fishing is found in southeastern Maine in waters such as West and East Grand Lake

CHESUNCOOK LAKE

Maine's third largest lake is Chesuncook. It lies northeast of big Moosehead Lake and west of Baxter State Park. Chesuncook has become one of the important landlocked-salmon waters in the state. It also has a good population of brook trout, togue, lake whitefish, and some unusually heavy white perch. Formed by the construction (1916) of Ripogenus Dam, Chesuncook includes Ripogenus Lake, Caribou Lake, Moose Pond, Umbazooksus Stream, Caucomgomoc Stream, and a section of the West Branch of the Penobscot River, in its general system—impounded by the dam. The area is 26,200 acres, and the maximum depth is 150 feet. Chesuncook has good water quality in all basins for coldwater gamefishes. Below Rip Dam, fishing in the West Branch of the Penobscot River is notable. Many fine salmon are taken there.

MOOSEHEAD LAKE

Sprawling Moosehead Lake is Maine's largest inland body of water. Moosehead is an ideal environment for landlocked salmon, brook trout, and togue. Its area is 74,890 acres, and the maximum depth is 246 feet. With a surface temperature of 70°F., the water cools to 43°F. at 210 feet. There are numerous tributaries suitable to trout and salmon spawning. West and east outlets of Moosehead join to form Indian Pond, which flows into the Kennebec River. To the west of Moosehead lie many noteworthy fishing lakes and streams. Up the Moose River from Rockwood is 8,979-acre Brassua Lake. Brassua is shallow (maximum depth 65 feet), but brook trout attain unusual size there. The 65-mile-long Moose River itself is an excellent salmon and trout stream for much of its length. It originates in Somerset and Franklin counties (in the Jackman area), and flows through several ponds and into Moosehead Lake. There are good salmon and trout ponds near the source of Moose River. East of Moosehead Lake are many fine trout waters like Sourdnahunk Lake, sometimes called the "most natural trout factory" in Maine. Sebec Lake is equally famous for landlocked salmon. These are but two of many lakes in the Moosehead-Baxter Park general area.

CHAIN OF PONDS, MEGANTIC WATERS, AND KENNEBAGO LAKES

North of Jackman in Somerset County lie many trout ponds, similar to those in the Allagash region, like Desolation. West of Jackman, in Franklin County, is the (private) Megantic Club. Chain of Ponds (public) and Coburn Gore on the Quebec border are entrance points for club members and their guests. There are seven trout ponds in the club holdings on the Maine side which provide noteworthy fly-fishing for brook trout.

Seven Ponds Stream runs into Little Kennebago Lake, long famous for big brook trout, particularly in the fall. The Kennebago River runs through a series of "logans" into big Kennebago Lake. With an area of 1,700 acres in its 5-mile length, this lake has a maximum depth of 116 feet. It is chiefly recognized as a trout (fly-fishing) lake but has some landlocked salmon. The stream contains several excellent pools, fishable from the shore. At Gravel Bank Pool, trout are sought (above big Kennebago). Downriver, salmon and trout both frequent the stream. Salmon fishing improves in midsummer.

THE RANGELEY LAKES

Generally considered in the chain of Rangeley Lakes are Cupsuptic, Mooselookmeguntic, Rangeley, and Long. Actually, the Richardson Lakes (Upper and Lower) and Umbagog are connecting waters. Umbagog is largely in New Hampshire. North of Richardson, too, are Aziscoos and famous Parmachenee. Like the Kennebagos, all of these lakes have enviable fishing histories and, even in modern times, justifiably so. The Parmachenee Belle (tied to resemble a trout fin), and many other famous fly patterns originated in this region. Records in the old Oquossoc Angling Club indicate that brook trout taken in the early 1900's approached world-record size. No trophies are caught today, but trout ½–3 pounds and occasionally 4 pounds are not uncommon. Most of the heavier ones hit trolled flies and lures in the lakes, where this kind of fishing is allowed (not Parmachenee). The catch of landlocked salmon probably outnumbers that of brook trout.

SEBAGO LAKE

Seventy-five or 80 miles by air from the Rangeleys south lies Sebago Lake. This is one of the original homes of the landlocked salmon and the lake which produced a world's record in this species in 1907. It is 28,771 acres in area, and has a maximum depth of 316 feet. Brook trout and smallmouth bass presently are the other two important species; some notable brown trout have been caught in this lake, but current management suggests precluding further stocking of browns. The water quality is excellent habitat for salmonids. The surface is an average temperature of 78°F., which drops to 41°F. at 300 feet.

Sebago is usually the first lake to shed its icy coat among Northern New England lakes and ordinarily is fishable by April first. During some winters large areas do not freeze over, but it has opened later, at times. Easily reached (only 18–20 miles from Portland) Sebago is under appreciable fishing pressure, but it is one of Maine's largest lakes.

WINTHROP-BELGRADE LAKES

Northwest of Sebago Lake there are a number of bass and/or trout waters; north, in Otisfield, is Moose Pond where largemouth bass have become quite well established. Southwest of Sebago there are stocked trout ponds and, in York County, some promising brooks (for trout). There are several brown-trout and bass waters in Androscoggin County, northeast of Sebago, and on into Kennebec County, are the Winthrop-Belgrade lakes. These are excellent bass waters, largely smallmouth but with some introduced largemouth bass. An attempt to re-establish landlocked salmon has met with considerable success. Although not a dominant species, some of the heaviest brook trout are taken from Messalonskee Lake each spring that are recorded in Maine. Lakes in this section of considerable importance include: Androscoggin, Cobbosseecontee, Maranacook, Echo, Long Pond, Great Pond, North and East ponds, and Messalonskee Lake. Across the Kennebec River from the state capital (Augusta) lie Webber Pond and 3,922-acre China Lake. China Lake has a good brown-trout population, some lake trout, both large and smallmouth bass, and a heavy population of white perch.

HANCOCK COUNTY LAKES

Southeast of Bangor in Hancock County are several lakes of considerable interest. They are part of the Union River drainage (Hancock and Penobscot counties). Total drainage area is 500 square miles; there are nearly 500 linear miles of streams, eighty-one lakes and ponds in the entire Union River system, but consideration here is of only a few waters in the network.

Green Lake is one of the four original homes of landlocked salmon. Others (also landlocked salmon) are: Lower Patten Pond, Branch Lake, Beech Hill Pond, Phillips Lake, Hopkins Pond, Alligator Lake, Upper Lead Mountain Pond, Molasses Pond, Upper Middle Branch Pond, and Floods Pond. Floods Pond is thought to be the last pond in the nation with a pure strain of Sunapee trout (*which see*). Branch Lake holds unusually large brown trout. It also supports togue, brook trout, and smallmouth bass. Phillips Lake has salmon, brook trout, togue, and bass. These waters are similar to others named above; most of them contain trout, bass, and landlocked salmon.

WASHINGTON COUNTY WATERS

Washington County is Maine's easternmost area, and the nation's most easterly point is Sail Rock off Lubec in this county. A great variety of fishing exists in the region. It is bounded on the west by Hancock and Penobscot counties; north by Aroostook; northeast and east by New Brunswick, Canada.

Four of the state's principal Atlantic salmon waters, Narraguagus, Machias, Pleasant, and Dennys, are in this county. The lower third also has lakes containing many

Fly fishing for trout and landlocked salmon is tops in some of the more remote northern lakes. Casting dry flies or trolling with streamer flies are popular methods among canoeists, and both account for large fish

fine smallmouth bass, with white perch the chief competing fish. Bass also are heavily populated in most of the other waters in Washington County. Lake trout are found in East Grand Lake, West Grand Lake (14,340 acres), West Musquash Lake, and Pleasant Lake. While brook trout occur in most waters in the St. Croix River drainage, they are not numerous generally. Major landlocked salmon waters are East and West Grand, and West Musquash. They are incidental to several other waters, where the fishing for bass is primarily important—Big Lake (11,520 acres), Spednic (22.84 square miles), the latter lying partly in Canada, and similar waters.

ATLANTIC-SALMON FISHING

Atlantic salmon once ascended New England streams in such numbers that farmers pitchforked them out to spread on the land as fertilizer. Old records show that it was illegal for employers to feed their hired help salmon more than twice each week in certain townships. However, the fishery was destroyed well before the turn of the century through mismanagement of the forestlands and because of dam building.

Beginning in 1945, Maine has made a dedicated attempt to restore its salmon stocks, and partial success has been achieved on five rivers—the Sheepscot in Lincoln County and Narraguagus, Pleasant, Machias, and Dennys in Washington County. There is considerable interest in two border rivers—Aroostook (a tributary to the St. John River in New Brunswick) and the St. Croix which is a natural boundary between Maine and New Brunswick. Canadians have termed this river as potentially the best for Atlantic salmon on the North American continent. Obstructions and water fluctuation presently limit any appreciable improvement there. Still further work is being done in Maine on a number of other

streams, and progress is slowly being achieved. The annual catch of sea-run salmon by fly-fishermen in Maine (on all rivers) totals 500–600 although many times that number enter the rivers. Atlantic salmon caught by commercial fishermen in Maine waters are taken only incidentally to their pursuit of other species.

Fly patterns favored by veteran sportsmen on Maine rivers are the Cosseboom, the locally originated Bear Hair, a wide variety of English salmon flies, and streamers similar to those used by New Englanders in landlock angling. A few skillful fishermen cast nymphs, and occasional use of dry flies is notable. Maine rivers are more heavily fished in late May and in June than at other times. Fall fishing is particularly light. Almost all angling for sea-run salmon in Maine is done from river banks or by wading. Long stretches that might be fished from a canoe go largely unnoticed.

Experienced anglers drift flies toward salmon lying in pools or riffles by casting across and above the fish. The retrieve is steady, not jerky, and few Atlantics hit when the fly is being brought back in. This is quite the opposite of landlocked-salmon fishing. In casting with streamer flies particularly, the retrieve is a series of sharp pulls on the line and twitching of the rod; in trolling, the fly is given further erratic motion by occasional jerking of the line to incite strikes.

Atlantic salmon spawn in the fall (in Maine, most heavily in late October). Eggs hatch the next spring. Parr remain in streams for 2–3 years. As smolts, 5–9 inches long, they migrate into the ocean, where they usually spend 2 years before returning to freshwater to complete their life cycle by spawning. Adults at this time usually are 29–32 inches long and weigh approximately 10 pounds, although there is variation with many salmon larger and heavier coming in from the sea.　　　　—R.E.

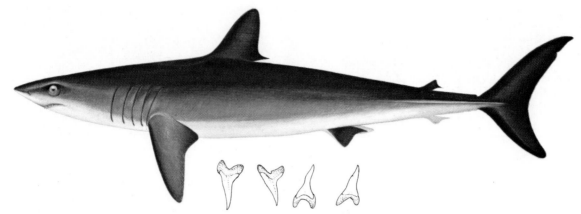

Mako (teeth upper jaw *left,* lower jaw *right*)

MAKO *Isurus oxyrhinchus* Closely related to the white shark (*which see*), this open-ocean shark resembles it in its nearly symmetrical tail, streamlined shape, and pointed snout. The mako's teeth are long and slender and protrude from the mouth. The second dorsal fin is only slightly ahead of the anal fin in the mako but is directly above the anal in the porbeagle (*which see*). The dorsal and pectoral fins have somewhat rounded tips, while those of the white shark are more pointed. The color is a striking cobalt to bluish-gray in fresh specimens, becoming grayish-brown in dead specimens. Fresh specimens also show a sharp line of demarcation between the colored upper parts and the dead white below.

Makos of 12 feet have been measured, and a 10½-foot specimen weighed just over 1,000 pounds. The Atlantic hook-and-line record is 786 pounds, taken off Bimini, Bahamas.

LIFE HISTORY

The mako occurs in the tropical and warmer parts of the temperate Atlantic Ocean, being replaced in the Pacific by the closely related bonito shark (*which see*). Apparently it is entirely an oceanic species of the "blue waters," although a mako has been reported from water about 30 feet deep off Cat Cay, Bahamas. Undoubtedly most reports of "makos" in shallow water are based on the sand shark (*which see*), which has similar teeth and is found inshore. A fast-swimming species, the mako is well-known to anglers for its gameness and leaping characteristics. It is apparently a surface- or near-surface-dwelling fish. Tunas, mackerel, and herringlike fishes are staple foods. It is known as an enemy of the swordfish, which it attacks frequently.

FOOD VALUE

The flesh of the mako and the swordfish are very similar in taste, possibly attesting to the importance of swordfish in the mako's diet. The flesh of the mako is indeed a delicacy, but its importance lies chiefly in its attraction to the angler.   —D.dS.

MALAMALAMA The Hawaiian name for the bluelined wrasse (*see* Wrasse). The bluelined wrasse is a food fish utilized in Hawaii and Johnson Island.

MANATEE A large aquatic plant-eating mammal found in the tropical waters · of the Amazon, West Africa, Caribbean, and portions of the southeastern coast of the United States, primarily Florida. The manatee may reach a length of 12 feet and has paddlelike forelimbs, no hindlimbs, and a rounded powerful tail.

MANDIBLE The bones of the lower jaw

MANEATER SHARK *See* White Shark

MANGROVES When Columbus discovered the New World he noticed a strange kind of tree growing in shallow, saltwater lagoons, its trunk held above the surface by arching, stiltlike roots. In the Gulf of Batabanó, on Cuba's south coast, Columbus wrote in his ship's log that the trees were "so thick a cat couldn't get ashore."

A century later Sir Walter Raleigh, while searching for the land of El Dorado, found the same kind of tree at the mouths of rivers in Trinidad and Guiana and noted that the trees had "oysters upon the branches." The oysters, he said, were "very salt and well tasted" and were found only "upon those boughs and sprays, and not on the ground."

Tourists who visit tidal areas in the tropics where mangrove trees flourish continue to be astonished at the spectacle of oysters "growing on trees." These coon oysters, which attach themselves to the prop roots of the red mangrove, where they are often exposed at low tide, are not generally considered a delicacy today, except, perhaps, to raccoons, but they are quite edible.

The tree described by both Columbus and Raleigh was the red mangrove (*Rhizophora mangle*), which is found throughout the New World tropics. Closely related species grow in Indo-Pacific regions. All trees of the genus *Rhizophora* have the distinctive prop roots that look to some observers like the legs of monstrous spiders wading in shallow water. They are, according to some botanists, the only "true" mangroves. Red mangroves are important land builders, pioneer trees that start new islands and extend old shorelines. They are always found in or near the water. Other mangroves (of which there are only two in the New World—the black mangrove, *Avicennia nitida*, and the white mangrove, *Laguncularia racemosa*) are usually found farther inland.

TREE THAT MIGRATED INTO THE SEA

Botanists are in disagreement over what constitutes a mangrove, since the name "mangrove" itself relates more to habit than form. Generally speaking, mangroves are plants that can live in loose, saturated, salty soils; they have respiratory roots and produce seeds that are more or less vivaparous—that is, the seeds germinate while still attached to the parent tree. Some scholars suggest that mangroves are primitive plants that evolved in shallow seas and never managed to move inland. But as mangroves belong to the highest order of plants, the fruit bearers, the prevailing opinion is that these unique trees developed on land and later began their return to the sea.

In one sense they have completed their return to the sea and might be considered marine plants, for the red mangrove is capable of living, growing, and reproducing without the aid of either "land" or rainfall; it can exist hundreds of miles from the nearest true shoreline (but must, of course, be in quite shallow water for its roots to find a foothold).

But in another sense mangroves cannot be considered strictly marine plants, for they grow best in brackish water—near the mouths of rivers, for example—and can sometimes be found in water that is virtually fresh. Laboratory tests, in fact, show that some mangroves can live and grow for years in water that has no detectable trace of salt.

The way in which the red mangrove propagates itself is quite remarkable. When each fruit matures, the embryo of a new plant begins to grow inside it. A slender, spikelike root emerges and grows to a length of 6–12 inches while still hanging from the tree. When it falls, the seedling, which resembles a green wooden dart whose lower end has been dipped into copper paint, may stick into mud and send out rootlets and soon become anchored to the spot. But most seedlings will float away with the tide before secondary roots develop.

The seedlings may drift for hundreds—or even thousands—of miles, remaining alive for a year or longer and sometimes even producing secondary roots and top growth while afloat. At first they float in a horizontal position, but as they grow older they swing more and more to the vertical. After a month most are floating vertically, the root end downward, ready to take root if it comes into contact with the bottom.

The saltier the water, the longer the seedlings will float. Even those that eventually sink may occasionally survive, since tests show they may live a year or longer while totally submerged. If they sink in water no deeper than 2–3 feet, they may root in the bottom, send a thin shoot to the surface, and then produce leaves.

Ocean currents are undoubtedly responsible for the wide distribution of mangroves. The three American species are found on the west coast of Africa (where they probably originated) and, interestingly, on both coasts of Central America and in the Galápagos Islands. How they got into the Pacific is a perplexing question. Most botanists doubt that the seedlings migrated around Cape Horn, and fossil records indicate that mangroves evolved after the Panama land bridge rose. In recent years the American red mangrove has also been found in Hawaii, where mangroves are not native but where both Old World and New World species grow. It has also been reported from Fiji, Tonga, and even from atolls in the Indian Ocean.

Once the seedling becomes anchored, it grows rapidly, its height increasing as much as two feet the first year.

During the second year it sends out prop roots, which extend outward from the trunk in successively widening circles. After 3–4 years the tree is braced so securely that it can withstand almost any storm. In addition to the main prop roots, aerial roots may drop from branches, forming secondary trunks with their own prop roots.

TREES AND CORAL REEFS

Mangroves are often popularly associated with coral reefs, but while corals and mangroves do in fact exist in close proximity—particularly in Indo-Pacific regions—they thrive best under quite different conditions. Reef-building corals need clear oceanwater which contains little sediment and is in continual motion, while mangroves do best in still, protected, sediment-laden water. Corals require fairly salty water and may be harmed by a drastic change in salinity in either direction. Mangroves prefer brackish water but can tolerate a wide range in salinity from virtually fresh to extremely salty water. Reef corals cannot live long in water that falls below 70°F., while mangroves thrive in much colder water. At the Galápagos, for example, the water temperature is sometimes in the 50's, due to the cold Peru Current; yet all three species of American mangrove are found growing. On the other hand, a drop in air temperature to 25°F. is almost certain to kill mangroves—while, of course, a drop in air temperature per se has little or no effect on corals, unless followed by a drop in water temperature.

Although, obviously, the conditions under which corals and mangroves can exist together are far from the optimum conditions for either, both play important roles in creating tropical real estate—and, in a sense, they often work together. Normally, the corals must first do their work, however, producing conditions where mangroves can grow.

Young mangroves must have protection from waves and currents. On beaches exposed to surf, or on bars and flats where currents are strong, the seedlings cannot

The aerial-rooted mangrove tree is important in the growth of islands and to fish habitats

gain good footholds. They may root in such areas and hang on for months but are almost sure to be killed or swept away by wind, water, or shifting sands before reaching maturity. If, however, a shore or a shoal is protected by a coral reef, the mangrove seedlings can establish themselves.

MANGROVES MAKE NEW LAND

Thus mangroves may become established on the inside of a coral reef, where water that is relatively still is found, sedimentation is rapid, and debris accumulates. These, of course, are conditions that live corals cannot tolerate; so the mangroves take up where the corals leave off. As the reef corals continue to grow outward, toward the sea, the mangroves grow along the rubble-strewn inner edge, trapping in their great spreading roots the seaweed, sponges, shells, chunks of dead coral, and other materials that wash over the reef. By reducing the flow of water, the mangroves aid further in the buildup of sand, marl, and other deposits.

As the mangrove colony increases, broken limbs and roots from the trees decay and form peat; and the land may be further built up by calcareous algae and the shells of mollusks and crustaceans that live among the roots. Birds may roost in the trees and leave deposits of guano. Other species of mangrove may become established in the swamp, as well as other saltmarsh plants. As the land becomes higher, coconuts may float ashore and take root, as well, perhaps, as the seeds of the sea hibiscus, or mallow. In Indo-Pacific areas, screw-pines and casuarinas are frequently found near the mangroves, while in the Americas the seagrape is often present.

In this manner—and over many, many years—an island may be formed on the leeward side of a coral reef.

Similar results may be produced near the mouths of rivers. (Here there are no corals, of course, for corals cannot live in brackish water.) Mangroves become established along the shores of rivers and on shallow bars formed by sand and mud carried downstream by the current and deposited at the mouth of the stream. Hundreds of mangrove keys may be formed near the mouth of a single river. Over a long period of time some of these keys may rise above the reach of high tide, producing conditions for the growth of mahogany, oak, and other hardwoods. A dense hammock may develop which may eventually become a part of the mainland.

1,500 ACRES OF TREE-MADE LAND

The land-building properties of mangroves are substantially in areas such as south Florida, where sedimentation is great. During his study of Florida mangroves, Dr. J. H. Davis found that about 1,500 acres of new land had been formed in Biscayne Bay and Florida Bay over a period of 30–40 years. (For the purposes of this estimate, Dr. Davis considered mangrove swamps to be land.) During this study it was found that the soil of many inland hammocks in the Everglades is composed largely of mangrove peat.

One of the greatest mangrove forests in the Western Hemisphere—and possibly in the entire world—is found in southwest Florida. Extending from the southern tip of the mainland up the Gulf Coast to Marco, the forest includes the area known as the Ten Thousand Islands and the mouths of numerous rivers draining the Everglades. The actual number of mangrove islands is unknown, since the islands constantly merge and new ones are constantly born. Unlike the low, twisting trees of most mangrove swamps, the trees in this forest often grow straight and tall—near the mouth of the Shark River are red mangroves eighty feet high—but occasionally a tremendous tree extends almost horizontally for about one hundred feet, its trunk supported by hundreds of aerial roots. Such trees may have been blown down in storms of many decades ago. Other trees, killed by hurricanes, stand upright, stark and white, like bleached skeletons.

Even the strongest winds rarely uproot the mangroves, but hurricanes may shake the trees so violently that the bark peels off, exposing the soft cambium layers to salt spray and waves, quickly killing the trees. The great storm of 1960, Hurricane Donna, killed thousands of large mangroves in southwest Florida—trees that had withstood dozens of previous hurricanes.

When observed from seaward a mature mangrove forest is like a massive green wall. Up close, twisting waterways are seen among the islands, often virtual tunnels with merging branches forming a canopy. Exploring these islands on foot is a memorable experience—though few visitors leave their boats. The dark interior is a seemingly impenetrable maze of slimy roots growing from the mud and often armed with razor-sharp oysters. The air is humid and still, and the odor of peat and muck is strong. Even in the dry season, at low tide one may sink past his knees in the soft soil.

Sometimes there is dead silence in the swamps; other times there may be the constant whine of insects, the clicking of the shells of bivalves, the rustle of scurrying crabs, and perhaps the haunting cry of a limpkin. Pools of water are often rust-red, caused by tannic acid produced by the red mangroves. This tannic acid is believed to prevent teredoes from infesting the submerged roots.

EVEN BEES LIKE MANGROVES

The larger trees will usually be found away from the shore. And here the black mangroves are often seen. The black mangroves have no prop roots, but the roots often form strong buttresses at the base of the trunk, and then, extending for long distances under the soil, they send up myriad pneumatophores—breathing roots—that project from the soil like pencils. The flowers of the black mangrove are rich in nectar, and beekeepers often place their hives in the swamps to obtain the highly prized mangrove honey. The smaller white mangroves, which also sometimes have pneumatophores, are seen in many Florida swamps, along with twisted, gnarled buttonwoods.

In many parts of the world, the timber of mangroves is economically important. The thick bark of the red mangrove is widely used in tanning leather; and in Jamaica the government has found it necessary to restrict the stripping of bark. A Trinidad botanist has estimated that a single red mangrove with a girth of eight feet (which is a giant of the species) will yield one thousand pounds of bark. The heartwood of all three American mangroves is used in furniture work.

Perhaps the greatest importance of mangroves in Florida is their value in stabilizing and preserving shorelines. Many sections of shore might be washed away in severe storms without the protection of these unique trees. Studies might show that many shorelines now suffering erosion could be stabilized by plantings of mangroves. (Reprinted from *Sea Frontiers*, Vol. 8, No. 4.) *See also* Marine Ecology —W.M.S.

MANGROVE SNAPPER *See* Gray Snapper

MANITOBA This Canadian province has a water area of 39,000 square miles of which approximately 22,000 are fished commercially, making it one of the most valuable freshwater fisheries in the world with an annual harvest of about 30,000,000 pounds. There are seventy-five different species of fish in Manitoba, but the most important to anglers are the lake trout, northern pike, brook trout, walleye, whitefish, and smallmouth bass. Others of commercial importance are the sauger, tullibee, carp, catfish, goldeye, sturgeon, and yellow perch. The geological formation of the province divides it into three definitive regions; Mesozoic shale covers the southwest portion; Paleozoic limestone extends through the north-central portion, and the Pre-Cambrian granite extends fanlike in a northwesterly direction beyond provincial boundaries. The Mesozoic area is typified by small, shallow lakes with only limited fish production. Lakes in the Paleozoic zone are moderately shallow but are large, and heavy producers of commercial fishes such as the sauger, tullibee, and drum. Good examples of the latter type are Lake Winnipeg, which covers an area of 9,398 square miles; Lake Winnipegosis, which covers 2,086 square miles; and Lake Manitoba, which has a 1,817-square-mile surface area. Most of the better angling waters are in the Pre-Cambrian area of the north which is typified by fertile, deep lakes and numerous rivers. Examples of this type are Gods Lake with an area of 400 square miles, Island Lake, which covers 375 square miles, and 100-square-mile Big Sand Lake.

Reed Lake in the Pre-Cambrian shield of Manitoba is a heavy producer of 15-to-25-pound northern pike

WINNIPEG RIVER

Fishing on the Winnipeg River is a family affair with plenty of comfortable accommodations, beautiful scenery, and a variety of gamefish. Ever since fur-trading days, the Winnipeg has been one of the great fishing streams of Manitoba. The river rises in Lake of the Woods and sweeps in a giant arc across the northern limit of the Whiteshell Provincial Park, about 100 miles north of the United States border. At Seven Sisters, 60 miles northeast of Winnipeg city, it broadens to form Lac du Bonnet, then drops through a series of cataracts and bays to join Lake Winnipeg. Cutting the rock-ribbed crust of the Pre-Cambrian Shield for 100 miles, the stream is bordered by coniferous forests and vagrant stands of paper birch and burr oak. The inroads of civilization have been slight. Fishing for northern pike, walleye, smallmouth bass, goldeye, and sturgeon is consistent. Over 30 per cent of Manitoba's *Master Angler Awards* in one season were scored by pike anglers in the Winnipeg and its two small effluents, the Bird and Lee rivers.

Accommodations consist of both lodges and motels. Moose, deer, bear, and waterfowl are plentiful and provide good subjects for the photographer.

The fishing is primarily done by boats, which can be rented from the various camps. The river presents a variety of water types, and, generally speaking, northern pike are caught along the weed beds in quiet bays, the smallmouths around the deep, rocky ledges, and the walleyes on sand- and gravelbars. Goldeyes and sturgeon may appear anywhere. Northerns of about 5 pounds are common, but fish up to 15 pounds can be expected. The walleyes run 2–10 pounds, and the smallmouths average about 2½ pounds. All methods of fishing are practiced, but spinners, spoons, and pork-rind lures are the most popular artificials. The goldeyes ranging 1–2 pounds come readily to wet and dry flies. It's a good idea to have both a fly rod and a casting rod on your Winnipeg trip. Lake trout can be caught also in many of the two hundred lakes of the Whiteshell Park.

American sportsmen motoring into the area from the southwest via Winnipeg travel over Minnesota Highway 75 or North Dakota highway 75, connecting with Manitoba Highway 75 at Emerson. Winnipeg is 60 miles to the north, and here the route to the Winnipeg River lies east for 53 miles over Highway No. 4 to the junction of No. 11 north. The whole route to Seven Sisters Falls and Lac du Bonnet is paved.

The southeastern route from International Falls, Minnesota, is Ontario Highway No. 71 to Kenora, 135 miles north of the International border. West from here, Ontario Highway 17 connects with Manitoba Highway No. 4, thirty-five miles west of Kenora. Twenty-three miles farther west, No. 4 connects with the Brereton Lake road which leads to the lodges along the southern arc of the River, west of Seven Sisters Falls. Another 27 miles west, No. 4 connects with No. 11 north for the lodges which lie west of Lac du Bonnet.

From Seven Sisters Falls, No. 11 highway flanks the west bank of the river for 40 miles, north to Pine Falls. East of Seven Sisters Falls, a good gravel road follows the river through the Whiteshell Forest Reserve. Here the river broadens to form a series of lakes—Natalie, Sylvia, Margaret, Elinore, Dorothy, and Nutimik. There are six fishing lodges and motels along the stretch of the river and several camping grounds.

At Lac du Bonnet, 14 miles north of Seven Sisters Falls, a good gravel road follows the south shore of the lake and extends east along the south shore of the Bird River, which is a tributary of the Winnipeg River. There are eleven motels and fishing lodges along this route. A 27-mile extension of this road leads southeast from Pinawa Lake to Pointe du Bois. East of here the territory is isolated, and the two fishing camps in the area may be reached only by boat from Pointe du Bois or by float plane from Kenora, Ontario, or Lac du Bonnet, Manitoba.

The lodges are connected with the outside by radio telephone. Both operate on the package plan, which includes air or boat transportation, cabin, meals, guides, boats and motors, gas, and packaging of fish. Everything should be planned much the same as a stateside fishing holiday. Summer weather is hot by day and cool by night; so dress accordingly. Tackle and sundries can be bought in Winnipeg, or at several of the camps.

SOUTHERN WHITESHELL

The southern portion of Whiteshell Provincial Park, traversed by the Trans-Canada Highway, contains Falcon Beach resort area, a popular Manitoba vacation spot. Although many of the lakes here are well-developed with cottage sites, good fishing is still available throughout most of the season. This is ideal country in which to combine the family vacation or camping trip with fishing. Angling for smallmouth bass in Falcon Lake is most productive in the early season (June).

There is a wide range of accommodations in the southern Whiteshell, from tenting grounds to deluxe motels. The area can be approached by different routes: from International Falls and Kenora via highways 71, 17, and 1 or 4; from Emerson through Winnipeg via highways 75 and 1 or 75 and 4. The paved Whiteshell Central road connects this area with the Winnipeg River district in the northern part of the park. More adventurous anglers may take the canoe route north down the Whiteshell River to the Winnipeg.

In addition to bass fishing the lakes and rivers contain northern pike, walleye, and some lake trout. Fishing for rainbow trout and brook trout can be found in several small lakes where they have been introduced. Lake trout are native to West Hawk and High lakes.

There are twenty-five fishing lodges, camps, and motels in the Whiteshell between the Trans-Canada Highway at Falcon Beach and the Winnipeg River.

THE INTERLAKE DISTRICT

A large area ranging from farmland in the south to coniferous forest in the north lies between Lake Winnipeg and lakes Manitoba and Winnipegosis. The northernmost two-thirds of this area is sparsely settled and only lightly penetrated by roads, making it a natural reservoir for wildlife. The Interlake also supports fishing spots of more than passing interest. Although these places are widely scattered, all but two can be reached via Highway No. 6 that angles northwest out of Winnipeg and parallels the east shore of Lake Manitoba.

The Narrows of Lake Manitoba, 130 miles from Winnipeg via Eriksdale, produces some of the largest walleyes caught in the province, approaching the 14-pound class. The usual size is 3–5 pounds, and the best time for large fish, according to official records, is May and September into October. Favored lures are spinners and minnows.

Forty miles north of Ashern, Lake St. Martin offers good water for northern pike, but the real hot spot for northerns is 125 miles further north at Cross Lake, part of the Saskatchewan River system. Fish exceeding 30 pounds have been landed from the lake. In the Saskatchewan River west of Grand Rapids walleyes are plentiful, particularly during the spring run.

A cluster of small lakes just west of Lake Winnipeg, known as the St. George Lake area, offers variety fishing for northerns, walleyes, and perch. The lakes are well off the beaten track but are only 140 miles from Winnipeg via Highway No. 7. Accommodations are limited at all the Interlake angling spots, and anglers wishing to explore the fishing potential should make their travel plans well in advance. Boats and motors are available to rent.

EASTERN AREA

North of the Winnipeg-Bird River area, between Lake Winnipeg and the Ontario boundary, lies another vast chunk of Pre-Cambrian lake and river country that stretches to Gods Lake and far beyond. Only the southerly part of this vast land has been touched by civilization with a road serving the Manigotogan-Bissett district. Three fly-in lodges are located north of here, at Aikens Lake and Fishing and Moar lakes, both part of the Berens River system. Northern pike, walleyes, and some lake trout are the species available. The eastern area is the closest "wilderness" country to Winnipeg.

GODS LAKE-GODS RIVER

The angler who seeks both trophy lake trout and brook trout could do no better than travel to the famed Gods Lake-Gods River country of northeastern Manitoba. He would also stand a better-than-average chance of catching a trophy northern pike. Giant lakers, going to 50 pounds and over, are caught every year in the lake, which is one of the largest bodies of water in the north. In the swift whitewater of Gods River 4–8-pound brook trout are not unusual.

At Gods River, in common with all other waters north of the 53rd parallel, the daily creel limit is two brook trout. Only single, barbless hooks may be used in the Gods and Island Lake rivers and at Kanuchuan Rapids. Spoons and wobblers are popular for lake trout. More than half the large brook trout are taken on small spoons and spinners, but flies and jigs are also effective. Fly-fishing is most attractive in July when insects are on the hatch, and large whitefish as well as brook trout are taken in Gods River.

Gods River water is very clear, but skilled canoemen are a necessity to negotiate the violent rapids. The wily brook trout, famous throughout the continent, are brilliantly colored, and the true sportsman usually acknowledges victory after a magnificent battle by releasing his catch. The fish in this river are native, wild stock; no hatchery plantings have ever been made. Although some trout spawn in tributary creeks many miles downriver from Gods Lake, most of them deposit their eggs in early September on gravel beds in slacker water behind islands in the main river itself. Early the following summer the fry inhabit warmer, quiet water along the banks and enjoy the bounty of a plentiful aquatic insect supply. The young fish triple in size during the brief midsummer and soon adopt characteristic hiding places among rocks in deeper and faster water. Trophy fish, over 4 pounds, are about 6 years old, and their diet includes several varieties of forage minnows as well as insects. These brook trout do not retire to deep lakes or go off feed in midsummer but live in the big river the year round.

THE NORTH

North of the 53rd parallel in the western half of Manitoba lies a vast land of blue lakes, spruce-clad forests, and rushing rivers. All but a small portion of this section of the province is in the Pre-Cambrian shield country. The northern area has become increasingly popular with visiting anglers over the past few years. Although this renowned fishing country is several hundred miles north of the international boundary, transportation facilities reaching it are excellent. No. 10 highway, a paved route covering over 500 miles between the North Dakota border and the town of Flin Flon, is the "main street" of the north. Daily (except Sunday) airline flights serve The Pas and Flin Flon, the two main population centers of the area. There is also a daily train and bus service from Winnipeg and other southern points.

Aside from the Red Deer River just south of the 53rd parallel for goldeye and Overflowing River, immediately north of this line for walleye, the first fishing of consequence in the northern area is found at Clearwater Lake. Remarkable for the clarity of its blue-green water, this lake is a consistent producer of large lake trout and is just 20 miles north of The Pas. In The Pas-Clearwater-Rocky Lake area there are seven camps, lodges, and motels which cater to fishermen. Still in the limestone country but not accessible by road is Cormorant Lake, which has large northern pike and fine walleye fishing. There is one lodge on this lake that can be reached by railway or airplane from The Pas.

Sixty miles north of The Pas is Cranberry Portage, a small settlement set in the midst of some of the finest freshwater fishing in North America. The town is located on Lake Athapapuskow which held the world's lake-trout record (63 pounds) for almost thirty years. East of Cranberry Portage lies Grass River Provincial Park. The 100-mile chain of lakes and streams that winds through this Pre-Cambrian country is renowned for its breathtaking beauty as well as its fishing. The chain produces lake trout, walleyes, and, particularly in Reed Lake, an unusually large number of northern pike of 15–25 pounds. There are six camps and lodges and one hotel in the Grass River-Snow Lake section, two of which are not accessible by road.

Flin Flon, largest urban center in the north, is close to a variety of fishing waters including the North Arm of Lake Athapapuskow. In the Cranberry Portage-Flin Flon section there are fourteen camps, lodges, and motels. North of Flin Flon is an immense territory barely touched by civilization where, except for the railway that strikes north to Lynn Lake, airplane is the means of access. However, there are four fishing camps in the area, two at Kississing Lake, one at McGavock Lake, and one at Vandekerckhove Lake. The latter two are reached from Lynn Lake which has connections with the south via scheduled airline. The first two camps are accessible either by charter plane or the Lynn Lake railway line. Kississing is a consistent leader in the large northern-pike division, and walleyes and lake trout are found through the district.

Anglers who fish the northern area invariably make more use of the standard spoon lure for almost all varieties of fish. In the past few years, however, jigs have been successfully used for both lake trout and walleyes.

HUDSON BAY RAILWAY LINE

Only the more adventurous anglers attempt fishing expeditions along this thin line of "steel" that knifes through the wilderness 510 miles from The Pas to the northern port of Churchill. Accommodations, where they exist at all, are scarce throughout this vast frontierland, and, although it is sometimes possible to arrange for guide service with local residents of the small communities along the railway, most anglers travel well equipped.

The principal attraction for fishermen is brook trout and Arctic grayling. The former are native to a number of rivers and streams north of the 56th parallel, including the Limestone and Weir rivers, Sky Pilot Creek, and other streams tributary to the lower Nelson River. Grayling exist in the lower reaches of the Churchill River, some of its tributaries, and the Owl, Deer, and Silcox rivers.

THE SOUTHWEST

There are few large bodies of water in this part of Manitoba. The majority of the small lakes in the southern half of the district are shallow, and, although fertile, natural production sometimes lags behind angling pressure.

Despite this, a judicious stocking program has been successful in maintaining good fishing in most of these lakes. In some cases the introduction of exotic species has resulted in exceptional success. Lake William, right on the North Dakota border and a short distance east of No. 10 highway, and Katherine Lake, in Riding Mountain National Park 165 miles northwest of Winnipeg, produce rainbow trout in the 5–10-pound class.

Many of the lakes in the Manitoba Highland country (Riding Mountain National Park, Duck Mountain Provincial Park, Porcupine Mountain Forest Reserve) are at comparatively high altitudes; their clean waters are ideal for trout.   —C.K.

MANTA *See* Atlantic Manta, Devil Ray, Pacific Manta
MANTIS SHRIMP Family Squillidae This is not a true shrimp (*which see*) but a member of the order Stomatopoda. There are about two hundred species in this family, which fundamentally have the same structure. Mantis shrimp are large, reaching a length of 12 inches, and are distinguished by a pair of raptorial claws with six long teeth. The carapace of the mantis shrimp is of membranous texture and has a longitudinal median ridge with deep grooves. The animal is narrow in the anterior portion but flares outward in the posterior portion. The bright green eyes are mounted on narrow stalks. In some species the body is pale green or yellowish-green tinged with pink, while other species have seven or more bright

Mantis Shrimp

colors. The mantis shrimp bears a certain resemblance to the praying mantis insect, hence the common name.

ANGLING VALUE

Mantis shrimp burrow in mud at or below the low-water mark and there are usually several entrances to each den. They can be caught with a baited wire snare by poking it into the burrow; any small tough piece of fish, mollusk, or crustacean may be used as bait. When boiled or fried, the tail meat is extremely palatable, being similar to that of large shrimp. Due to the difficulty of capture, mantis shrimp are not often utilized as food nor as live bait. —A.J.McC.

MARBLED GROUPER *Dermatolepis inermis* This fairly rare grouper is taken occasionally off southern Florida. It occurs throughout the tropical American Atlantic. The few specimens available in museums or studied in the field measure usually less than 20 inches in total length.

The marbled grouper has 11 dorsal spines, usually 19 dorsal rays, and usually 9 anal rays. Pectoral rays 18–19, usually 19. Posterior nostril 2–3 times larger than the anterior. Insertion of pelvic fin behind lower end of pectoral base. Posterior margin of caudal fin slightly convex,

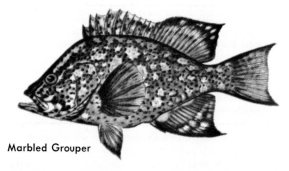

Marbled Grouper

straight, or slightly concave. Head, body, and fins marbled or mottled with irregular light blotches and spots on a dark background.

FOOD VALUE

Edible but not known to be a food fish of commercial importance. —L.R.

MARINA A boat basin developed to serve pleasure craft. Normally offers boats and motors for sale or rent, seasonal and temporary mooring space, bait, fuel, and haul-out and launching facilities. Provisions, ice, and many boating accessories are handled in conjunction with the marina store.

MARINE ECOLOGY As distinct from freshwater ecology (*which see*) and concerned with the oceans of the world. Ecology is the study of the interaction of organisms and their environment. Each organism affects the other; each organism affects its neighbors; and among all these interactions there is a very complex balance. In a scientific experiment it is normal to hold all but one of the variable conditions, and then study the effects of changing this variable. In the same way in ecology it is necessary to simplify the situation by studying one reaction at a time if the complex is to be disentangled. There is, though, a danger in this approach, and it has been too often ignored. We are apt to think in terms of these simplified situations which we can understand and to forget that nature rarely produces such simple test-tube situations.

Any science calls for a system of classification, or the multiplicity of facts will conceal such orderly pattern as underlies them. Once a scheme of classification has been developed, there is a danger of going on indefinitely classifying more material and elaborating the system of classification. It is more difficult to look for reasons for the observed orderliness. Ecology in the past has largely diverged into detailed study of single species or their reactions or into over-all studies of whole communities with little concern with the mechanisms involved. Now a meeting of the two schools of thought is needed.

SEAWATER

Life is believed to have originated in the ocean, and water has certain advantages for a simple life form. The most important of these is that it is wet. The chemical processes of life depend on the presence of water within the tissues, and such water is easily lost by evaporation. To avoid this, special water-conserving mechanisms are required for anything living in a dry environment. So, from this point of view, the water is an advantageous place to live and allows considerable simplification of body structure. The ocean has the advantage of varying relatively little from polar to tropical waters or from the surface to abyssal depths. ·

Salinity The next thing an organism needs, again within its tissues, is salt, mainly sodium chloride, but many others in smaller concentrations. Since the oceans first formed, rain has been leaching soluble materials from the soils, and the rivers have been carrying these into the sea. Evaporation provides the water vapor for the rain, but the dissolved materials remain behind in the sea. Only a small part of these leave the seawater again to be incorporated in the bottom sediments. Today the seas contain about 3.5 per cent of dissolved salts, but the proportion was doubtless less at the time when the first life appeared in them. This earlier concentration is reflected in the roughly 2–3 per cent salt content of the tissues of animals no longer living in the sea. If the salt concentration is different inside and outside a cell, water tends to diffuse through the cell membrane until the concentrations are the same, so that special mechanisms are needed, and work must be done if this is to be prevented. Since serious changes in the salt content of the tissues are fatal to the organisms, the sea again proves an advantageous place to live. However, salinity is a factor which does vary considerably in some parts of the sea.

Evaporation at the sea surface, particularly in the tropics, increases the salinity of the water and at the same time makes it denser. It then sinks and mixes with the less saline deeper waters unless the surface heating is sufficient to counteract the density change and keep it floating at the surface. In this case it will, in time, be carried to an area where such mixing is easier, so that by this means, and by mixing by waves and other agencies, it never attains an extremely high salt content. Only in more landlocked seas, near polar ice, or under coastal conditions does the salinity vary enough to affect most organisms.

Rain falling on the sea surface, or brought to the sea by rivers, is lighter than seawater and tends to float near the surface. Here again mixing agencies are at work, and it is, in general, only locally that salinities drop low enough to have a serious effect on the organisms living in the sea. In estuaries, though, we find all gradations from fresh- to saltwater, and sometimes to very high salt concentrations, and here the organisms must have special protective mechanisms if they are to survive the extreme conditions. Furthermore, the salinity there usually fluctuates rather widely with the state of the tide and seasonally, and, as will be seen, such fluctuations may be even harder to tolerate than steady conditions. In the intertidal zone also, salinity fluctuations are usually extreme.

Other Salts The organism needs to maintain in its tissues not only a certain total concentration of salts, but also a sufficiency of a considerable number of elements which may be present in only minute traces in the surrounding water. This may involve mechanisms capable of achieving a high degree of concentration of the element concerned. For example, phosphorus may comprise 0.13 per cent of the tissues of a copepod, yet only 0.000011 per cent of the seawater in which it is living, a concentration of 12,000 times. It is true that a two-step process is involved here, since the copepod feeds on diatoms which themselves remove the phosphorus from the water. Among the intertidal algae, *Fucus spiralis* can concentrate titanium 10,000 times, and *Ascophyllum nodosum* can concentrate zinc 1,400 times. This ability to concentrate particular substances may be of great importance in the modification of the environment by the organism, as in the case of sulphur-producing or lime-depositing bacteria. On the other hand, in the control of the organism by the environment, it is not the degree of concentration which is important so much as the availability of a sufficient supply of the element concerned. Thus iodine, which may comprise only 0.000005 per cent of seawater, is still present in more than sufficient quantities and is therefore never limiting. In point of fact, salts of phosphorus and nitrogen are the two main limiting factors, with a few others, such as iron, silica, etc., possibly limiting under some circumstances. In this statement we are considering the growth of plants in the sea. Animals in general can obtain their needs from the plants or other animals on which they feed.

Nutrients The various elements in seawater are present in a rather constant proportion, and nitrogen

and phosphorus occur in just about the same ratio in the tissues of the water, plants, and animals. Thus the removal of these salts from the water and their later return on decay of the organisms involve little change in their ratio, and we can get a good over-all picture of the available nutrient in terms of either one of them in most cases. Most of the water in the ocean contains ample nutrients to support a rapid growth of plants.

An empty shell is essential to the environment of a hermit crab, which must always find new shells as it grows. If there is no empty shell, and it cannot dispossess a crab, it will force itself into an occupied one until pushed out

However, most of the water also lies below a depth to which sufficient light can penetrate, and, in fact, nearly all photosynthesis occurs in the top hundred meters, and in most areas even shallower. Only in this zone is solar energy used for the production of organic matter, and these surface waters are therefore the ultimate source of food for all life in the sea. Animals, for example, which live permanently below this depth must find their food in the rain of dead plants and animals which come down from the upper layers or in forms which migrate into these upper zones to feed. Nutrients taken from the water by the plants return and become available for re-use after the death of the plants themselves, of higher forms which have fed on them, or as excretory products. Since most dead organisms sink, there must be a steady removal of nutrients from near the surface and regeneration of them deeper down, and such nutrients need to be brought toward the surface again before they can be used in photosynthesis. The deepwaters are a huge reservoir of nutrient, available in all oceans, and surface productivity reflects largely the efficiency of a mechanism for their upward transport.

It is here that there is a great difference between cold and warm seas. At high latitudes, cooling of the surface waters makes them dense enough to sink, and nutrient-rich deeper waters come to the surface to replace them. In temperate waters this process generally happens in the winter only; so the replenishment of the surface waters is seasonal. Tropical waters, though, never become cool enough at the surface to produce vertical mixing, and as a result their upper layers become and remain impoverished so far as nutrients are concerned. They have to rely on horizontal drift, on turbulence, and perhaps on some transport by vertically migrating animals, and the relative inefficiency of these is reflected in their generally low plankton production. An exception to this pattern is found where the predominant winds carry the surface waters away from the continental shores or where one water mass rides over another. Where either of these happens, as off the coast of Peru, deepwaters rise to take their place, bringing nutrient-rich water and extremely productive surface conditions.

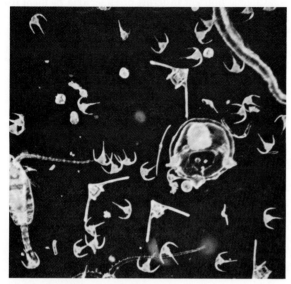

Plankton are drifting minute animals (zooplankton) and plants (phytoplankton) in seas and lakes

Other Chemicals Dissolved organic matter in the sea plays a very important role, but one which is little understood at present. It can be utilized as a food source by many plants, thereby allowing them to grow at depths below those to which adequate light penetrates. Evidence is accumulating which suggests that some animals may be able to use it in the same way. We know that the well-being of many organisms is strongly influenced by the presence of certain metabolites in the water. These may be produced by the same or other species, and may condition the water favorably or unfavorably toward the species affected. We are finding that various species whose larval stages are free-swimming are attracted chemotactically to settle where there are adults of their own species. There are many other similar cases, but in almost none of them do we yet know what organic compounds are involved or how these are distributed, or how they can even be analyzed in the water.

Certain chemical factors whose variations may be very significant in freshwater need be considered in the sea only in extreme circumstances such as are found, for example, in intertidal pools. In the open sea their variations are probably of little biological significance. One of these is the calcium content of the water, and another is the acidity, or pH. Variations in the oxygen content of seawater generally fall well within the tolerance range of most species in the open ocean, although there is a minimum oxygen layer, which in some areas may be seriously depleted. Oxygen depletion may be critical, though, in the deepwater of certain basins such as the Black Sea and the Cariaco Trench. It may also be depleted in areas of heavy pollution, such as in many estuaries, and, finally, this usually occurs below the surface of mud. The low concentration is itself lethal,

but, in addition, absence of oxygen is associated with the presence of hydrogen sulphide which is highly toxic.

Since life ultimately depends on photosynthetic production of organic matter, the distribution of light is a vital ecological consideration. Sunlight is the only significant source so far as photosynthesis is concerned, although at the much lower light levels concerned in vision both moonlight and bioluminescence are important too. Summer illumination at the sea surface is not much less at 60° latitude than it is on the equator, but the greater obliquity of the sun's rays near the poles results in a lower value. The great latitudinal difference is in the degree of seasonal variation, and, as a result, of total annual incident radiation. At two stations on the equator the total annual figure was 11.8 and 16.2 units, whereas at stations at 60° N. and 60° S., respectively, it was 7.2 and 5.7 units. In the polar regions it would have been considerably less.

Light reaching the sea surface loses some energy by reflection, the loss being greater when the sun is low. Once in the water the light suffers further loss by absorption and scattering, and is lost most rapidly at the two extremes of the spectrum so that, in deeper water, the light is progressively restricted to the blue-green region. Of great importance for productivity is the depth at which just sufficient light penetrates for the photosynthesis of the plants, over a twenty-four-hour period, to produce as much oxygen as is used up by their respiration. This is known as the compensation depth, and corresponds roughly to an illumination of ½–1 per cent of the surface light. Above this level active production of plant material takes place; below it, plants may survive but can only grow if another source of energy is available. The depth therefore gives us a limit to the zone of most active plant production, and it varies widely in relation to the transparency of the water. In the very clear waters of the Sargasso Sea it may be as much as two hundred meters, but in the English Channel is only forty-five meters, and in turbid estuaries may be only a meter or less. In such conditions, algae attached to rocks at the low-water mark may, when the tide comes in, be receiving insufficient light. Light at the ends of the visible spectrum is rapidly absorbed, and beyond this, in the infrared and ultraviolet, even more so. This is important in that the further ultraviolet, in the region which produces serious actinic damage, is so rapidly removed that even a thin layer of water provides an efficient filter.

TEMPERATURE

Solar radiation heats the surface waters, and its distribution is responsible for the higher surface temperatures in tropical than in temperate or polar waters. The distribution of temperature is complicated by the drift of surface currents, and water is slow to gain or lose heat. In general each ocean has a circular surface movement which is clockwise in the Northern, and counterclockwise in the Southern Hemisphere. As a result the eastern coast of North America is warmed by the Gulf Stream, and, after this has crossed the Atlantic, a branch also warms the northern European coast. Temperature drops rapidly with increasing depth. While surface temperatures range from about 28° C. at the equator to −1° in polar waters, at 400 meters the maximum temperature is only about 15° C., and at the bottom in water that is

really deep the temperature is always within a few degrees of zero. The seasonal temperature range in the open ocean is low in the tropics, maximal at 30°–40° north and south latitude, and low again in the polar seas. It, too, decreases rapidly with depth, so that at a depth of a few hundred meters it is not of any biological significance. Many animals carry out a diurnal migration, and in doing so are exposed to a considerable temperature change. If they ascend from a depth of 800 meters to the surface, the change may be as much as 24° C. in the tropics, which would be very drastic for an animal which cannot regulate its body temperature. This vertical change also decreases toward higher latitudes.

PRESSURE

A factor which has received surprisingly little consideration is pressure. This increases about one pound per square inch for every two feet of depth, so that pressures of over a thousand atmospheres are found at great depths. Effectively the pressure at a given depth does not vary geographically or seasonally. Tissues are relatively incompressible, so a body is not crushed by high pressures. Only if it contains a gas-filled cavity does this happen. Fishes with swimbladders must be able to regulate the gas content of the bladder when they change depth. Shrimps have no such problem. There are, however, physiological changes in tissues under pressure. Close to shore there is a small pressure change with the tide, and it has been found that this is sufficient to induce a response in various animals.

WATER MOVEMENT

Water movement affects animals in various ways. The permanent ocean currents carry with them such characteristics as temperature, and these change only slowly. They also carry their planktonic and nektonic fauna and flora, and among these the larval stages of many forms which are attached as adults. They thus perform an important distributional function. The same function, on a smaller scale, is performed by tidal currents which are oscillatory in nature, and in general flow parallel to the shore. Tidal currents also cause the flushing of estuaries with resulting interchange of fresh- and saltwaters and their contained organisms. Water movement may be important in bringing food within the reach of attached organisms but may also, if too strong, damage them. It also disturbs bottom sediments, limiting their attached or burrowing organisms. A current of one knot, for example, will shift fine gravel.

Finally, waves, which have little effect on organisms in the open sea, have a tremendous effect on the shore. Besides stirring up the bottom sediments, they hit the shore with very great force. A pressure of 29,700 kilograms per square meter has actually been recorded when storm waves hit the shore. Such wave action is very destructive to the shore itself as well as to the organisms living there. There is a record of a rock weighing 20 metric tons being lifted 3.7 meters vertically and deposited on top of a pier, and another of the windows of a lighthouse 90 meters above sea level being broken by stones thrown up by waves. Waves require a long fetch to build up, so shores facing the open ocean receive the biggest storm waves. Approach to shallow water changes the form of the ocean swell and finally causes it to break, so

the extent and depth of offshore shallows also have an important effect on the wave exposure of a particular coast.

TIDES

The tides, although not directly affecting the shallow-water organisms, do so indirectly through modification of such factors as temperature, desiccation, etc. The intertidal zone is a transitional area grading from aquatic to aerial conditions, and the details of this gradation depend on the type of tides. Tides result from the gravitational attraction of the earth, sun, and moon; the effect of the moon is about twice that of the sun. Depending on the relative positions of the two bodies, the attractions reinforce or partially cancel, so that a lunar month contains two periods of wide-amplitude spring tides and two of narrower-amplitude neap tides. In addition, the spring tides at the two equinoxes tend to be of greater amplitude than those at the solstices. This simple scheme suffers great local modification. The ocean tides are of very small amplitude and only build up into big tidal ranges on the coasts. Depending on the natural period of oscillation of the bodies of water in which the tides operate we find everything from no tide to the fifty-foot tides of the Bay of Fundy. At a particular locality the lunar or the solar component of the tide may predominate, so that there may be two almost equal tides each day, occurring progressively later each day; two very unequal tides each day; or tides which occur at the same time every day. The relation of duration of exposure to tidal level may therefore be a complicated one.

HOW ORGANISMS AFFECT ENVIRONMENT

We have considered so far only the factors in the environment which affect the organism. In the same way, though, the organisms affect the environment and one another. The planktonic plants remove light for photosynthesis and so reduce the level of illumination. The transparency of the water may show a marked decrease during a phytoplankton bloom. The zooplankton also, when abundant, may appreciably reduce the illumination. With active photosynthesis, the oxygen content of the water is increased, often above the saturation level, and in pools in the intertidal zone oxygen can be seen streaming up from the algae on a sunny day. Both plants and animals also respire, and at night there may be a dangerous drop in the oxygen content. Decaying organic matter, as we have seen, also uses up oxygen and may lead to anaerobic conditions. Photosynthesizing plants remove nutrient salts from the water, and decaying plants and animals return it again. Various organisms also can remove dissolved organic matter from the water. Finally, organic matter accumulating in deposits is the source of petroleum deposits.

Another important effect of the organisms on the environment is in the accumulation of particular chemicals and their deposition as minerals. An obvious case is calcium carbonate, and nearly all the world's limestone deposits arise from the calcified skeletons of plants or animals. Silica also is accumulated from skeletons, and may give rise to important deposits such as those of diatomaceous earth. Then again various organisms, particularly bacteria, precipitate sulphur.

FOOD

One of the major ways in which organisms affect one another is in the matter of food. They eat one another; so the predator directly limits the numbers of its prey in proportion to its own numbers and activity. The abundance of the prey modifies that of its predator in a less direct manner. Shortage of food probably rarely kills the predator directly by starvation. If the predator is sufficiently mobile it may move to better feeding grounds when prey becomes scarce. This will result in actual reduction of the pressure on the prey in the original locality and offer it a better chance for recovery. If the predator is unable to move away, shortage of food may result in its slower growth and lower reproduction rate. Similarly, increased food supply may lead both to greater fecundity and to faster growth and earlier sexual maturity. The predator generally grows more slowly than the prey and so adjusts its numbers more slowly to changing conditions. Phytoplankton, for instance, may double its numbers in a day, whereas the copepods which feed on it take a month or more per generation and the fish which eat them a year or more. There is a considerable delay, therefore, before the copepod population can increase its numbers and take advantage of a diatom bloom. Slowed growth of the predator may result in higher mortality if it in turn is being preyed on. Very many bottom-living invertebrates liberate their eggs into the plankton where they develop to the stage when they are ready to settle again on the bottom. During their planktonic existence they are a food source for a host of other animals; prolongation of planktonic life leaves them that much less chance of surviving to settle.

There need not be a predator-prey relation for food to affect the well-being of the organisms. Sediment feeders depend, among other things, on the organic content of the sediment which they eat. Barnacles, which filter suspended food from the water, grow fastest where the food content is greatest, but also show a marked increase in growth rate where water movement brings more food within their reach. Food may be present in abundance, but not in a suitable form for use by a particular species. Planktonic diatoms, in general, can utilize decaying organic matter only when it has been broken down into simple salts. Many dinoflagellates, on the other hand, can use an earlier stage in the breakdown such as amino acids. Brittlestars can eat the newly settled spat of many bivalves before these develop heavy shells but are unable to harm them when they grow slightly older. Filter feeders usually have a lower limit to the size of particle which they can trap and may be unable to utilize anything as small as bacteria, even when these are abundant enough to offer a good food source.

SPACE

Many attached organisms are limited in their spread by direct competition for space, growing to the point where they are in contact with their neighbors, and sometimes overgrowing and killing them. A lesser degree of crowding may still result in competition for light, oxygen, or food. Crowding may result in catastrophic mortality in the organisms concerned. This happens in *Mytilus* beds when the first settled individuals are overgrown by later arrivals and killed. Their attachment to the rock then weakens, and finally whole sheets of *Mytilus* may be peeled off the rock by wave action. When such a clearing of the surface occurs, recolonization may be determined by the species available for resettlement at the time. On the other hand there may be a regular sequence of species each replacing its predecessor.

The aggregation of organisms is not of necessity harmful. It may equally well be beneficial. In marine plants, and in many marine animals, the sexual products are liberated into the water where fertilization takes place. Clearly, the proximity of a number of spawning individuals increases the probability of all the eggs being fertilized. Even in the cases where copulation takes place, aggregation increases the chance of individuals meeting at the possibly brief time when the eggs are mature. This may be a serious problem in the sparse populations of the deepsea. Then again aggregation may provide protection. A fish which will attack a single sea urchin may well avoid a group. Seedlings of the "grass" *Thalassia* are less likely to be washed from the sediment if germinated among the tangled roots of an established colony than in the open, and young fucoids survive better in the damp, shady conditions under older plants than on the open rock. Such benefits may lead to commensal relationships or parasitism. A good example of mutual benefit is found in certain shrimps in tropical coral reefs. Various fishes

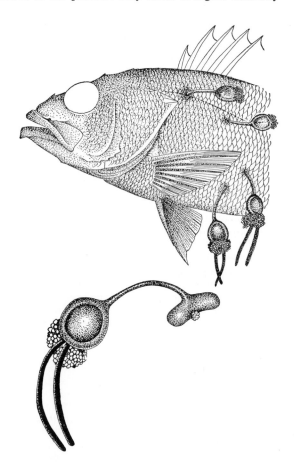

In the ecology of the sea, microscopic copepods serve as food for fish, while a larger parasitic copepod feeds on fish such as ocean perch

come to the hole regularly inhabited by the shrimp, open their mouths and opercula, and allow the shrimp to crawl about removing parasites and eating them.

Metabolites We have already referred to the role of dissolved organic matter in seawater. As well as having a nutritive role, this may have a highly specific effect as in the inducing of spawning in many species by the presence of sperm of their own species in the water. It has been found also that many species of larvae, when ready to settle, are attracted chemotactically by the presence of adults of their own species or even by their dead shells. This is a mechanism of obvious value in ensuring settlement in a habitat where conditions not only are suitable at the time of settlement but also have remained so throughout the lifetime of the adults. Various species condition water in such a way as to make it more favorable for future growth of their own species. This has been shown for aquarium water containing goldfish. Other species condition water so as to render it unfavorable to other species, as in the fish-killing red tide caused by the dinoflagellate *Gymnodinium*. Still other species condition the water unfavorably for future growth of their own species, a mechanism whose value to the species is not apparent. This occurs in the marine diatom *Skeletonema*.

LIFE IN THE SEA

The organisms living in the sea are often so very different from those elsewhere that some discussion of their nature is needed before we can examine the role they play in the various marine habitats. Marine plant life comprises algae almost exclusively, a group ill adapted to terrestrial life, and the higher forms found on land are, in general, represented only along the fringes of the sea. However, algae seem to have left no habitable niches unoccupied. At the single-cell level there are ubiquitous bacteria free in the water, in sediments, and on the surfaces of rocks, plants, and animals. The diatoms with their silica capsules and the dinoflagellates, with or without a shell, comprise most of the phytoplankton, the floating plant life of the water, taking advantage of their small size and relatively uncomplex structure to reproduce rapidly and utilize newly favorable habitats as soon as they appear. Many of them also are adapted to attached or creeping life. The larger, multicellular algae are, with few exceptions, limited to regions where they can attach to rocks or penetrate into soft sediments. Unlike land plants, their weight is supported by the water, so they can grow to great size without a strong skeleton, and the Pacific giant kelp *Macrocystis* has been reported to attain a length of three hundred meters. Species of one of the larger algae, *Sargassum*, have adapted to a permanently floating existence in the open ocean. A few flowering plants occupy the niche of grasses in shallow water, *Zostera* in temperate waters and *Thalassia* and others in warm seas. In the latter, also, mangroves (*which see*) encroach on the water and form their own peculiar habitat.

Among protozoa, flagellates and ciliates play an important role in sediments and in the plankton also. Two other groups of protozoa are important in the plankton, Foraminifera and Radiolaria. The first are amoebae with a calcareous shell, and the rain of these dead shells is the main contributor to extensive deepsea sediments. The Radiolaria, with complicated basketlike skeletons of silica, also rain down from the surface plankton, and they, together with siliceous diatom tests, dominate in sediments so deep that most calcareous shells dissolve.

Sponges, represented in freshwater by only a few forms, range in abundance from intertidal to abyssal waters, and may grow as large as barrels. They are filter feeders whose soft bodies are reinforced with horny material, and calcareous or siliceous spicules, and these spicules also contribute largely to sediments. The coelenterates also are much more strongly represented in the sea than in freshwater. They include attached hydroids whose larvae are liberated into the plankton, larger jellyfish, whose attached generation plays only a minor role, anemones, sea fans, and corals. All the last three are sedentary, and the massive skeletons of the corals so modify their environment that they produce a habitat unlike any other. Their fossil remains testify to their permanent influence. The coelenterates are mostly carnivorous; in the plankton they may be the major predators on such herbivores as copepods, and a coral reef proves to be a surprisingly efficient filter for trapping passing zooplankton.

The echinoderms are a marine phylum, and all but one or two holothurians are bottom-living as adults. They range from the intertidal zone to abyssal depths and include attached, free-living, and burrowing forms. In food habits they include omnivorous, carnivorous, and herbivorous types as well as filter feeders and detritus and deposit feeders.

Of the arthropods, only the Crustacea play an important role in the sea. The insects, so successful on land, are hardly represented in the sea. Small copepods are the most important herbivores in the plankton and comprise a large part of the food of many fishes. Crabs, lobsters, and shrimps are a considerable fraction of the bottom-living fauna.

Of the various groups of worms, the polychaetes are the most important in the sea. Many are mobile forms, carnivorous or deposit-eating, and a few are adapted to a permanently planktonic life. As with other groups, a large proportion of the bottom-living forms release their eggs into the water to develop as plankton. Filter feeding is highly developed among the tube-building forms, and in some the aggregation of tubes may rival coral reefs in massiveness.

Mollusks have diversified into all possible habitats, and range from sedentary tube-building forms, through active bottom-living species with all types of feeding, to specialized permanently planktonic groups, and finally to the very active and intelligent cephalopods. All classes of mollusks inhabit the sea; fewer have invaded freshwater, and fewer still the land.

Other phyla of invertebrates, which it is unnecessary to cover in detail here, play a relatively minor role in the sea. Among the vertebrates, the fishes are by far the most important, and of these the elasmobranchs, including the sharks and rays, are almost restricted to marine conditions. Fishes occur from the greatest ocean depths to the intertidal zone, and a few can tolerate aerial conditions for a while. Many species can tolerate widely varying salinities. The higher vertebrates, because of their air breathing, are generally limited to the upper levels of the sea, and, with the exception of the whales and some sea snakes, must come ashore to breed. Whales and seals are sufficiently abundant to play an important role in the sea, and birds in some areas are extremely abundant. Reptiles play a minor role; amphibia hardly enter sea water.

HABITATS

An orderly arrangement of the various marine habitats might be framed around gradients of depth, temperature, substrate, or other characteristics. Since the ultimate source of food is the zone reached by sunlight, this is perhaps the logical place to start. And, since over 70 percent of the earth's surface is sea, and only 3 percent of this is less than 200 meters deep, that is to say continental shelf, the open ocean is by far the most important part. The photosynthetic production of organic matter takes place only in the upper 100–200 meters, often less, and is carried out mainly by diatoms and what is grouped together as nannoplankton. This comprises the very small organisms which pass through the fine silk nets which we have traditionally used to filter out the diatoms in the water. Many nannoplankton are without a skeleton and are very delicate, so special methods are needed for their collection and study. As a result, although we know that in much of the ocean their bulk is much larger than the diatom population, we know as yet little about them and have to base most of our ideas on the better-known diatoms. It is probable that a very different story will emerge when we know more about the nannoplankton.

The phytoplankton requires solar energy, and, as we have seen, the amount of this energy is rather constant throughout the year in the tropics, but highly seasonal toward the poles. Other things being equal, the same may be said of the basic food supply of everything which depends on the phytoplankton. A good example of this is found in the production of planktonic larvae by bottom-living invertebrates. In the tropics the majority of shallow-water forms produce planktonic larvae, and one species or another span the entire year with their breeding periods. They can count on a food supply for their larvae whenever these are released. In temperate waters the season of phytoplankton bloom is much shorter, and breeding tends to be limited to this period. There is greater competition for the food, and there is need to time the spawning so as to catch the time of best food supply. As a result we find that somewhat fewer species produce planktonic larvae, and more provide their eggs with a yolk supply or guard them in some other way. Finally in the Arctic, where the phytoplankton season is still shorter, almost all species guard their eggs, and only one or two species face the risk involved in catching the phytoplankton bloom, rich as this is while it lasts.

The phytoplankton also requires a supply of nutrients, and these, as well as light, may limit production. As the plants grow they deplete the nutrients. After passing through various steps in the food chain, the cycle of return of these nutrients to the water is completed at a greater depth than that at which their removal occurs. Productivity, then, depends on their return to the surface. In the polar regions sufficient vertical mixing generally occurs through the year to keep an adequate nutrient supply always present, and the seasonal phytoplankton cycle largely parallels the solar energy cycle, with a maximum in summer and a very low minimum in winter. At intermediate latitudes such replenishment tends to occur only in winter when the surface waters are cold enough to sink. In summer the water is stable, and there is little replenishment from below. Vertical mixing in winter carries much of the phytoplankton below the depth at which it can reproduce, and this slowing of reproduction in the population, combined with lower solar energy, more than offsets the good nutrient supply and allows only a small standing crop of diatoms. Stabilization in the spring brings also the ideal conditions of rich nutrient supply and increasing light and temperature, and there is often a dramatic spring outburst of phytoplankton which may increase a thousandfold in a week or two. The nutrients are soon used up, though, and with the grazing of the more slowly increasing copepods, the phytoplankton level drops again for the summer. Frequently it shows a brief, smaller increase in the fall. In the tropics, stability is the rule throughout the year, so there is only slow nutrient renewal. Sunlight and temperature are more constant, and there is but little seasonal change in the amount of plankton.

The species contributing to this general picture, of course, vary geographically and seasonally. There is a general latitudinal trend in the relative proportions of diatoms, dinoflagellates, and blue-green algae. In one series of stations, the percentages were 99.9, 0.1, and 0.0 at latitude 57° S.; 26.7, 53.3, and 20.0 at 38° S.; and 3.0, 22.4, and 74.6 at 3°S. In the same way there is a seasonal species succession at any one place, and even within a particular bloom.

Feeding on the phytoplankton there is a population of herbivores composed largely of copepods, euphausids, and decapods. These are much slower growing than the diatoms and take correspondingly longer to respond to changes in the food supply. The copepods take perhaps a month or more for a generation, and the euphausids and decapods a year or more, although we know less about their life span. The copepods respond to the extra food available in temperate waters in the spring by eating to the point where much of the food passes undigested through their guts. In response to the ample food they lay larger numbers of eggs. A month or so after the spring diatom increases the copepod numbers also rise fast, and their increased feeding accelerates the decrease in the phytoplankton population. In turn those animals which feed on the copepods, such as herrings, fatten on the extra food. Bottom-living animals presumably also benefit, although in water that is very deep the time lag involved in the sinking of dead bodies may eliminate any seasonal effect. On the continental shelf, though, there is sometimes a clear seasonal pattern in the amount of organic matter being deposited in the sediments and so available to their inhabitants. Many of the larger animals take advantage of the seasonal plankton abundance in the polar seas, and the summer assemblages of whales and plankton-feeding birds in these regions may be impressive.

The plankton of inshore waters follows, in general, a similar pattern, although sometimes with more extreme fluctuations. It differs in one marked characteristic though. Larvae in the ocean plankton are almost all those of parents which are themselves swimming or floating there. The bottom is too far away for many of its larvae to rise into the rich surface waters, and the deepwater is too poorly supplied with food to be a good place to rear planktonic larvae. The bottom invertebrates of shallow water, in contrast, can readily utilize the plankton as a food-rich feeding ground for their larvae, and also as a means for their dispersal, and inshore plankton usually contains a very high proportion of larvae. In the English Channel, larvae, of intertidal barnacles provide, for some months of the year, the major food of young herrings.

The illumination in the daytime appears to be too great at the surface for most plants and animals. Maximum photosynthesis is usually somewhat deeper, and the maximum concentration of those animals which are able to swim is deeper still. In the tropics it is possible that high surface temperatures may also be a deterrent. It is typical of the animal plankton and of many of the stronger-swimming nekton also that, both in the open ocean and inshore, there is a diurnal migration from the deeper layers occupied in the daytime toward the surface at night. The significance of this has been argued, but it seems unlikely that the major value of such migration is in avoiding capture by staying always in the dark. The vertical movement involves a considerable change in temperature and other factors. It is quite possible that such climate fluctuation is advantageous since, in some other organisms, it has been shown that fluctuating conditions are more favorable to development than any one fixed condition.

Midwater The food raining down from the euphotic zone, with of course such additions as there may be from the land, is the supply on which all deeper-living organisms depend. Near the coast this means organisms living on the bottom, but in deeper water, before such food reaches the bottom, it passes through a zone of animals whose migrations take them neither down to the bottom nor up to the richer food sources. Although this zone may have a vertical extent of as much as five miles, it is convenient to consider it as a whole.

Its conditions are in striking contrast with those near the surface. Sunlight in any appreciable quantity does not reach it, nor do the seasonal temperature changes associated with the upper waters. There is no wave action and little current. It is relatively cold and as the water deepens, approaches freezing point. At this depth there is less temperature difference between tropical and polar seas than there is at the surface, and with increasing depth this difference steadily disappears. In other words, with increasing depth the temperature conditions become more uniform and unvarying over great areas of the ocean. Until we know more about the distribution of metabolites and other characteristics of particular water masses, we cannot say how regional these are and how much they may affect the distribution of animals. We also know little at present of the physiological effects of hydrostatic pressure and of the difficulties which may be involved in adapting to different pressures. We know that many shallow-living animals are killed by a sudden increase in pressure, and we know that some bacteria from water that is very deep change their character when grown under different pressures. On the other hand we know that some species have a very great depth range. Among these, the brittlestar *Ophiacantha bidentata* ranges from shallow water in the Arctic to 4,450 meters near the Azores. It would appear that the distribution of such a species is governed far more by temperature than by pressure.

The universal factor in this midwater zone is the shortage of food and the resulting sparsity of population. Sinking food is constantly being intercepted en route, and a fraction lost to the sinking process by solution in the water. There is thus a steady decrease downwards in food supply until, at abyssal depths, the rate of accumulation of sediment on the bottom is only a few millimeters in a thousand years. Most groups of marine animals, other than air breathers, have successfully invaded this zone, although the maximum depths to which they have penetrated vary somewhat. Such deepsea animals have rarely been kept alive for observation, but we can reasonably guess the significance of some of their modifications. To begin with, a large dead body not only sinks faster but is likely to reach a greater depth intact. Such a body must be eaten whole if it is not to sink out of reach and therefore be shared with other hungry animals. Furthermore, such a meal is a relatively rare occurrence, and the most must be made of it when it is encountered. To meet this situation we find many deepsea fishes with extremely distensible jaws and stomachs, and have captured specimens which have swallowed other fishes considerably larger than themselves.

Sparsity of population also implies mating problems. There is less chance of a female finding a mate when the eggs are ready for fertilization. Again in the deepsea fishes we find this situation met by some species being hermaphroditic, and by some carrying the males as permanently attached parasites on the outside. We also find in many groups an elaboration of luminous organs. In some, such as deepsea angler fishes, there is a luminous lure dangled in front of the mouth or even inside it. There can be no doubt that these are to attract prey. In many other cases, though, it would appear that the display of lights constitutes a species-recognition system, or even a sex-recognition system, and as such would be valuable in ensuring mating.

In general then, light and temperature, and, for plants, supply of nutrients, are the major controls in the upper waters of the ocean. Geographical differences in these conditions are great, and geographical distribution of species correspondingly restricted. In the deeper waters conditions are far less varied geographically, and species tend to be of wide distribution. Temperature is low and pressure high, but by far the most important environmental condition is the shortage of food.

Deepsea Bottom Some food reaches the bottom in deepwater, and since it accumulates there, this is a richer feeding ground than the waters above it. Dead copepods sink at a rate of about five hundred meters a day, so their chances of reaching the bottom intact are small. At the other end of the scale, whales sink fast, and it is unlikely that anything can eat them whole or even take seriously large bites out of them as they sink. It has been calculated that on the average, one settles each year on each fifty square miles of bottom, and spread out thin it is doubtful whether this would supply a gram of food per square meter per year. So once again the shortage of food is found to be a major factor in this habitat. In point of fact we find that a large proportion of the bottom-living animals at great depths are deposit eaters. Groups which feed on suspended food particles in the water are absent at very great depths, the crinoids, for example. In polar seas, few animals release their eggs to develop as planktonic larvae, since the period of phytoplankton supply is so short. In the same way, the abyssal animals tend to be viviparous, since there would be no food for planktonic larvae, and further there would be little current to disperse them. Mating also is a problem as it is in the waters above, and here too we find such modifications as the complementary males in the mantle cavities of attached female barnacles.

The sediments as they accumulate are compacted and modified to give rise to sedimentary rocks, and the centers provided by animal remains may accumulate various minerals, particularly manganese. The latter may be present in sufficient quantities to offer a rewarding source of minerals if suitable methods of harvesting can be devised. These sediments also provide a valuable record of previous conditions in the sea above them. Deepsea cores are now yielding not only dated records of the ice ages, as indicated by the species of planktonic shells found in them at successive levels, but also data of the actual surface sea temperatures at which these shells lived.

Shallow-Water Bottom In shallower coastal waters the surface and bottom are much closer together, and there is less room for this midwater zone to be distinguished. There are, of course, many organisms living at middepths, but the majority of them have contact with top or bottom, or are strongly influenced by their conditions. Even if the bottom does not lie within the actively producing phytoplankton layer, it is close enough to receive from it a much better rain of organic material. Actually the producing layer is likely to be thinner than in the ocean because of the reduced transparency of inshore waters. An additional source of food is that washed from the land, and large rivers such as the Mississippi spread their load of mineral and organic matter over a very wide area. In one Scottish loch into which only minor streams discharge, the sediments were still accumulating at a rate of 3–6 millimeters a year, which is about a thousand times the rate in some of the abyssal sediments.

Although there are some exposed rock faces in deepwater, the majority of the bottom is an almost flat plain of fine sediment. Coarser-grained sediments become progressively commoner toward land. The heavier particles carried down by rivers or produced along the shore are the first to sink from the water. Where there is sufficient water movement, the finer particles are selectively washed out of the sediments, to be deposited in quieter waters, and only sand or gravel remains. Finally, there are larger areas of exposed rock surface.

The bottom inhabitants fall more or less into two groups, those that live in and those that live on the bottom. Those that live in the sediment face many of the problems found also in deeper water. Even if sufficient light reaches the bottom, it does not penetrate, so plant growth is limited to the surface film, or, in larger attached algae, to the water close to the bottom. The burrowing animals rely for their food on what is contained in the sediment, on what they can remove from the surface film or the immediately overlying water, or, on one another. The sediment is a trap in which detrital material tends to accumulate. This makes it a rich food source for animals which can swallow it whole or selectively pick out the food particles. When the sediment is coarse-grained because water movement keeps the fine material washed away, the organic matter is largely washed away, too,

and much less food remains for deposit eaters. Furthermore, only a large animal can swallow large particles, and the mechanical process of burrowing among large particles is more difficult for small animals. A relation, then, tends to exist between the particle size and the size of the burrowing animals, particularly if these are deposit eaters, although the relationship is readily obscured by other factors.

A second factor in the sediments is the oxygen supply. Organic matter is oxidized in the sediment, reducing the oxygen content of the interstitial water often to vanishing point. At this point poisonous hydrogen sulphide is produced. A fine sediment tends to have a high organic content and is relatively slow in allowing water to circulate through it. A coarse sediment, on the other hand, is generally far more permeable, and this, combined with its lower organic content, allows a better oxygen supply to the inhabitants. The problem of oxygen supply is met in most cases by maintaining a water supply from the surface. This may be done through a burrow, often kept open by a mucous cement on the walls, or by siphons which, being part of the animal, effectively allow it to move around carrying its burrow with it. Other animals are able to go for long periods without oxygen and so can live deeper below the surface without the need of an open connection to it. Nematodes are particularly efficient in this connection. In the muds already referred to in a Scottish loch, oxygen was absent a few millimeters below the surface. Ostracods and copepods, both of which require a good oxygen supply, were much the most abundant in the top centimeter, whereas nematodes were at their maximum below this depth, and extended several centimeters deeper.

The surface of the sediment receives the newly settled debris from the water. In addition, in shallow water, it may support a rich skin of bacteria, diatoms, and other microorganisms. Many of the burrowing lamellibranchs skim this surface film with their siphons. A photograph of the abyssal bottom shows evidence of the same behavior, but with the animal apparently moving on a short distance when each successive area has been exhausted. In intertidal sand it has been shown that *Tellina*, unless too crowded, tend to move apart until the circles traced out by their siphons do not overlap. Other burrowing forms hold their arms or tentacles above the surface to filter the particles from the water as they fall. Still others pump water down into their burrows and filter it there. For all of these feeding types, as well as for the carnivores, there is the need for a suitable sediment texture, suitable food supply, and ability to cope with depleted oxygen below the sediment surface.

On land, ecologists have elaborated a system of classifying recurrent groupings of species into communities, and of relating these to environmental conditions. Some of the earliest communities to be described in the sea were those in and on the sediments of relatively shallow water. These seemed to show a rather clear relationship with the sediment type. There has been much argument as to whether communities are naturally distinct or are a convenient artifact in a system of classification, and in either case whether they should be described in terms of the organisms living in them or of the environmental conditions controlling their nature. Whoever is right, it is certainly convenient to have a system of classification, and

Seaweeds are attached by holdfasts, the equivalent to the roots of higher (vascular) plants

it is equally certainly unfortunate when workers become so wrapped up in classification that they stop trying to understand the reasons underlying the similarities within the communities and the differences between them.

Communities do not seem to intergrade completely, or, if they do, the intergrades are rarer than the typical assemblages. This must mean that either the environment or the organisms vary discontinuously. Organisms certainly do so. The "seagrasses," which are not true grasses, have an extensive rooting system like other flowering plants. Algae have not evolved holdfasts which are as successful in anchoring them in soft sediments. And few other flowering plants have invaded the sea. As a result a grass community, safe from all but extreme wave action, is quite distinct from any other on the soft bottom. The epiphytic algae which grow on the grass, and the many animals which seek shelter and food among the grass, could, unless they are very highly specialized, live as well in other comparable habitats. The grass community is very similar wherever it is found, although the species comprising it vary widely. It is typical of a community that the building blocks from which it is constructed may vary, but the final structure is similar. As a result, the environmental limits within which the community is found over its range may be considerably wider spread than those of the particular species which comprise the community in any one area. The temperature limits of *Zostera* in temperate waters, for example, differ from those of *Thalassia* in tropical waters; yet the two are characteristic of very similar communities.

The chemical characteristics of the soil have less influence on marine plants than they do on land plants. In general it is the physical characteristics that control both the plants and the animals. In many cases, though, it is a biological mechanism which decides which species comprise the community. Predator-prey relations are obviously likely to be involved. In early surveys, some communities were found which contained a lamellibranch and a brittlestar living together. Since the brittlestar feeds voraciously on small lamellibranchs, it was difficult to see how they could survive. The solution to this problem, only recently worked out, is a good example of the way in which important mechanisms may be concealed. It was found that this brittlestar does not have room in its body cavity for large gonads and a functional stomach, so, when the gonads are maturing, the animal ceases to feed. This coincides with the period when the young lamellibranchs are settling on the bottom, and by the time the predator has finished spawning and resumes feeding, enough of the lamellibranchs have grown to a size where they are safe from attack.

Many more subtle relationships are undoubtedly involved in determining which species will live under particular conditions. Conditioning agents, already referred to in the plankton section, play their part, attracting larvae to settle where adults of their own species are already present, and possibly attracting them also to other species with which they are habitually associated. Organics absorbed on sediment particles have been shown to be tested by polychaete larvae which may move on to test other bottoms until they find one which is acceptable, and metamorphose there.

Many of the members of these bottom communities spend only a part of their life on the bottom. The population is usually the maximum allowed by available space, food supply, or some other limiting factor. But conditions are constantly changing, and catastrophic mortalities occur with unusual temperature conditions, heavy wave action, or other causes. The resulting bare areas are then available to such forms as can enter them. Forms which can only expand vegetatively, or walk slowly, are at a disadvantage compared with those which swim. The advantages of protected sedentary life are combined with those of swimming by liberation of eggs or spores into the plankton where they carry out development of varying duration. During this time they are dispersed by the currents, so that any available space is likely to receive some of them when they are ready to settle. Furthermore, small organisms require, relatively, far more food than larger ones, and these larvae pass through their small and hungry stages in a part of the water where they are not competing for food with their parents. There are, of course, disadvantages in this casting adrift of the eggs to fend for themselves. They are vulnerable to predation, mainly in the plankton, but also at the time of settling. Many of them, despite ability to test the bottom and select a suitable settlement area, must be carried into impossible regions. All told the mortality is high, and to meet this the number of eggs liberated must be correspondingly high. Figures for Danish bottom invertebrates with planktonic larvae show an average annual output of about a million per individual, with some species producing over 500,000,000. It will be remembered that on the average only two of the offspring produced by a given female survive to replace it.

We emphasized the changes with latitude in the duration of the period of phytoplankton abundance. In the tropics, production is much the same throughout the year, and there is a steady poleward concentration into a brief period of rich plankton. If the larvae are to take advantage of this food supply, spawning must be carefully timed to coincide. In fact we find that in the Arctic very few species liberate their eggs into the plankton, instead protecting them and providing a supply of yolk for food. Those species which do utilize the plankton, though, are highly successful and abundant. In temperate waters the proportion of species with planktonic larvae is greater, and in the tropics, at least in some groups, these are in the majority. Furthermore most temperate species have a very limited breeding season, and this in the spring or early summer. In the tropics some species breed throughout the year, but many have a more or less limited breeding season. This season varies among the species so that the quantity of larvae present in the plankton probably shows little fluctuation. In northern waters a peak concentration of larvae in a column of water 18 meters deep and under a one-square-meter surface was estimated as 40,000.

There would seem to be advantages in passing as quickly as possible through this dangerous planktonic phase; yet an average of about four weeks seems typical. Furthermore, although development in general tends to be more rapid at higher temperatures, comparison of temperate and tropical larvae yields just about the same average stay in the plankton. It is interesting to speculate what may be the advantages in retaining this particular rate of development. Planktonic larvae are subject to vicissitudes from which protected larvae are free. One result of this is that the protected ones are produced in far smaller numbers, although, since the eggs are usually larger and yolk-filled, the total expense in producing them is probably about the same. Another result is that the settlement of protected larvae is relatively constant from year to year while that of the planktonic larvae is highly variable. The year class resulting from one successful season may dominate a population of a long-lived species for a number of years.

In most groups the number of species in a region increases rapidly toward the tropics. There is about a tenfold increase in marine gastropod species from Newfoundland to Cuba. This increase occurs in the bottom epifauna, but not in the infauna. Although the increase is apparent in comparing the fauna of different regions, the number of species found in comparable square meters of bottom does not increase. This would seem to imply either that the tropical bottom contains more variety of habitats than the temperate, or that its species are more highly specialized. Since the same increase in species occurs in the plankton, where the environment is so constant, the first explanation seems the less probable, but there then remains the problem of lack of speciation in the infauna.

Between surface and bottom in shallow water is a zone whose inhabitants certainly deserve discussion. This is the zone, though, which is the main concern of commercial fisheries, and the studies on the ecology of commercial fishes is so extensive that its coverage cannot be attempted here.

Sub Littoral Although the intertidal zone is clearly distinct from those above and below it, it intergrades into them in many ways. One of its characteristics, where the substrate is hard, is the heavy growth of the larger algae, and these may be even more strikingly developed somewhat below lowwater mark. In the cooler waters of most seas there are submerged beds of kelps whose size far exceeds that of any of the other algae. On European coasts these are mainly species of *Laminaria* which may be in water as much as 10–20 meters deep, but which do not reach the surface from this depth. When the water is shallower, the tops of the fronds float flat at the surface where they form a dense canopy. The plants grow more closely together in shallow water than in deepwater, and in either case are so spaced that about 1 per cent of the surface light reaches through the forest to the sea bottom. This is about the amount of light associated with the compensation point at which photosynthesis just balances the respiration of the plants, and below which they are living at a loss so far as organic production is concerned.

These forests represent a very large standing crop of plant material. The stock in the White Sea alone has been estimated at 1,500,000 metric tons. Individual plants live for 2–3 years and are constantly fragmenting at the tips and replacing this loss by growth lower down, so the annual production is probably greater than the standing crop at any time. Much of the material lost washes up into the intertidal zone where it is an important food source for amphipods and other animals living there. On other coasts, such as those of South Africa and the Pacific Coast of America, much larger algae such as *Macrocystis* and *Nereocystis* comprise the forest. Growth rates as high as twenty-five centimeters per day have been reported, and these algae are regularly harvested in some areas. Despite the impressive density of these forests, though, their annual productivity appears to be less than that of phytoplankton in a comparable situation.

The algae forests, by their density, have a marked effect on the environment. In addition to serving as a food source, they provide shelter for many other algae which grow epiphytically on them and for invertebrates which grow on or among them. They form an effective breakwater for reducing wave action, and many larger animals take advantage of this or of the cover they afford. Among these are many fishes, and, on the Pacific coasts, the sea otter.

Coral Reefs Another special habitat centered slightly below lowwater is that of coral reefs, and, like the algal forests, this is one in which the environmental conditions are largely controlled by the organisms. Reef-building corals are limited to waters with a minimum temperature in the neighborhood of 20° C., and to a depth of less than about a hundred meters. However, there are corals of other types which are found even in water that is very cold and at depths of down to almost six thousand meters. Almost all of the corals which comprise a reef contain symbiotic algal cells, zooxanthéllae, and below the compensation depth there is not enough light for their adequate photosynthesis. It has been shown that reef corals can survive and grow without their zooxanthellae, and their role is not completely understood, but the fact remains that reefs are limited to shallow water, and their lower limit depends on the transparency of the water. Further, the coral growth is greatest just below lowwater mark.

Of the many organisms inhabiting the reefs, others besides corals contribute to the construction. The most important of these are calcareous algae, which comprise a considerable fraction of the structure of some reefs. In fact, some reefs, such as the "boilers" in Bermuda, are composed mainly of algae and trapped sand, with only a minor fraction of coral. Coral reefs build up toward the surface, and rates of 2.5 centimeters a year have been recorded in the Pacific. With any considerable exposure at low tide, corals are killed, and, curiously, the Atlantic reef corals seem to be less tolerant of such exposure than those in the Pacific. Massive corals, in general, grow more slowly than branching ones. On the Great Barrier Reef, the increase in diameter in six months was 10–17 percent in the massive forms, and 33–96 percent in the branched ones. Although there is this steady process of building up of reefs, there is an equally steady process of breakdown due to wave action, particularly on structures weakened by the many boring organisms. On the whole, most reefs have probably achieved more or less of a balance.

Reefs, by their solid nature and highly cut-up surface, provide shelter for a whole range of organisms—fishes, worms, urchins, algae, and many others. They provide food for various fishes which feed on them, and they act as very efficient filter beds for removing the zooplankton from the water which washes them. Corals are specialized carnivores, and most of them expand their polyps only at night, at the time when the zooplankton on which they feed is most abundant in the surface waters.

Reef corals are limited by temperature and light. They cannot begin to grow if the bottom is too far from the surface, but, if the bottom is slowly sinking, may be able to maintain depth by addition to the top of the reef so that the original base may be far below the present surface. It used to be thought that they could not withstand silt in the water, but it has been shown that they have a surprising ability to free themselves from silt which settles on them. It has been observed that there is often a gap in a reef opposite the point at which a river discharges on the coast behind the reef. It seems probable that this gap may result from the low salinity of the discharged water, rather than its silt content, since most corals are intolerant of low salinity.

Intertidal Rocks The intertidal zone is the region which has received the most study because of its accessibility; yet, because of its complexity, it is by no means the best understood. It is the region at which water and air meet, and, even if there were no tides or waves, there would be fringes of organisms on either side of the boundary, graded in proportion to their ability to make the transition from one medium to the other. Considerable migration has taken place across the boundary from water to land, but less from land to water. Tides, with their resulting alternation of aquatic and aerial conditions, have served to spread out these transitional animals and plants, zoning them vertically according to their individual tolerances, and producing many species which are now adapted to the fluctuating intertidal conditions, but no longer able to tolerate either permanent immersion or permanent emersion.

Rocky shores provide a holdfast for attached algae and animals, so that their ecology is in many ways very different from that of soft sediments. Not only do they allow the permanent or temporary attachment of the organisms living on them, but also they are stable, and not easily broken or moved by wave action. As with the sublittoral forests, large algae have evolved in this intertidal zone, although they do not grow as large as the giant kelps. The latter may invade the lower intertidal zone, and penetrate even higher in pools. In addition to possibly greater wave action, the algae in the intertidal zone have to survive desiccation and strong illumination. The latter

The inter-tidal zone is inhabited by burrowing life forms which survive in the absence of water

includes heating infrared and actinically active ultra-violet radiations, neither of which penetrate far through the water. In general, the brown and green algae have been successful in adapting to these conditions, while the red algae are more successful in deeper water. The seriousness of the illumination problems is shown by the general absence of the larger algal grown on intertidal rocks in the tropics. Even in temperate regions growth is sometimes stronger on the shaded than on the sunny side of rocks. Young algae, as with most young organisms, are less resistant than adults, and they may grow much faster if they have settled in the shelter of older plants. Fucoids, which float upward when the tide is high, may form knee-deep beds when left by the tide, and when this happens the upper layers provide protection for those below them. The whole colony also retains moisture so that desiccation is much less than in isolated plants. The adaptation of the intertidal species to their habitat is carried further in the adaptation of individuals to the particular conditions which they have been reared. It has been shown that individuals reared in a dim light thereafter grow best in a dimmer light than individuals reared under bright conditions. They may also adapt similarly to the color of the light in which they have been reared.

Unlike phytoplankton, these attached algae are in no danger of sinking to a depth at which there is insufficient light. However, where the water is turbid, as it is in many estuaries, the light which reaches the low water zone when the tide is high may be less than the compensation value, so that photosynthesis may be limited to the low-tide period. In such estuaries, on buoys which move up and down with the tide, the algae may form quite a narrow zone close to the water surface.

We know little about the needs for nutrients in intertidal algae. We know that the algae must be relatively tolerant of extreme salinity changes, since they are washed with freshwater when it is raining. When exposure to low salinity is more extended, as occurs when there is drainage of freshwater down the shore, fewer species can survive, and the genus *Enteromorpha* is frequently characteristic of such conditions. The algae may suffer severe abrasion by wave action, and the larger fucoids tend to be absent in highly wave-exposed locations. These fucoids also act as abrading agents, and there may be a clear area of rock, with no barnacle settlement, within the radius swept by them under wave action.

Algae become few toward the top of the intertidal zone, and on European shores *Pelvetia* is the highest of the larger species, forming a zone at about highwater of spring tides. At this level, apart from wave action, they are wet by seawater only for a few tides every two weeks. Above this is typically a zone of lichens. A second effect of wave action is to wet the shore above the level which would normally be covered by the tide and so elevate the zonation of the various inhabitants of the zone. The effective shift of the levels may be so great that it is of little value to refer to them in terms of the tide, and the levels of the organisms themselves is the best index of the conditions. On temperate shores, for example, the top of the barnacle zone is usually clearly defined, and in a sheltered locality it coincides with mean highwater of neap tides. On wave-exposed shores it may be considered as the level at which conditions approximate highwater neaps of a sheltered shore.

Where wave action does not complicate the picture, there are various tidal levels at which there is an abrupt change in conditions. The lowest highwater of neap tides is the highest point on the shore which is wet by seawater on every tidal cycle. Anything above this point may go several tides without being wet and therefore suffer a marked increase in the severity of desiccation. Similarly, mean highwater of spring tides will be wet for one or two tides at average springs, but exposed for the rest of the semilunar cycle, and during the two solstitial periods of the year the spring tides will not reach it. A graph of the relation of maximum possible exposure to aerial conditions against tidal level is therefore not smooth but stepped, and these steps have been shown to coincide with the upper or lower limits of distribution of many of the intertidal algae. They can withstand the conditions up to a step, but not the suddenly worsened conditions beyond it.

Although these algae are permanently attached, they effectively perform some migration. Their reproductive products are set free in the water and thus achieve wide distribution. The adult plants spread vegetatively in many species so that their creeping stolons may colonize neighboring areas. Winter storms tear off large quantities of algae and carry them, sometimes for a considerable distance, to accumulate above highwater mark. There they provide a rich food source for a fauna which could not have reached them when alive. Such beds of dead algae are often heavily populated with amphipods and other animals which in turn attract numbers of wading birds which feed on them. Finally, there may be an apparent seasonal movement of algae up and down a shore or estuary resulting from their inability to tolerate conditions at one season, and recolonization of the region when conditions are more favorable.

Certain groups of animals have specialized for intertidal life to the point where they are numerically far more abundant there than deeper down. The sessile barnacles are an example of this. They sometimes cover the rocks so closely that there is little remaining room for other organisms to attach. They may form a wide band along the shore, or, where wave action excludes the larger algae, extend from high- to lowwater mark. It was calculated that the barnacles on a kilometer of one such a shore have a dry tissue weight of about two metric tons. These would yield annually about 1½ tons of tissue and an additional million larvae weighing about ½ ton. Barnacles on temperate shores grow relatively slowly, but in the tropics they may, a month after settlement, be over a centimeter long and be mature and releasing larvae to constitute a new generation.

It is for barnacles that we have the best knowledge of the attraction of the young to settle where there are already adults present. This attraction may even be to the dead shells of adults. The value of such a mechanism to the species is clear, since it reduces the chance of larvae settling in a place where at low tide, or at some later period, conditions will be intolerable. Barnacles filter food particles from the water by beating a cirral net. If the movement of the water is sufficient, though, they use the more economical method of holding the net in the current and letting this bring the food to them. In either case more food reaches them in moving water, and their growth rate is highest in moving water or in water with a high food content. Except for regions where winter ice scrapes the rocks bare, intertidal barnacles are worldwide, with the genera *Balanus*, *Chthamalus*, or *Tetraclita* found on almost all shores.

Some intertidal animals feed directly on the larger algae, but more obtain their food by scraping epiphytes from the surface of the algae or from the rock surface. In the latter category are limpets of various types and coiled snails of the family Littorinidae. These are practically limited to the levels above lowwater, and many have adapted to life above the reach of normal tides at a level where they are reached only by spray or storm waves. There is a tendency, although there are exceptions, for those species which live within the intertidal zone to liberate their eggs into the sea where their larvae are planktonic, but for the higher up ones to brood their young. This obviously useful system has been extended in the case of some land crabs to a return of the normally land-dwelling crabs to the sea at breeding time, with the eggs hatching and developing in seawater. Yet other land crabs have become permanently adapted to the land and may breed in damp burrows there or even in the freshwater in the bromelliads growing on jungle trees. Crabs show a wide range of adaptations to environmental conditions. Below lowwater there are spider crabs so slender they could hardly survive heavy wave action, slow-moving crabs hiding under a mask of sponges or algae, and very active swimming crabs with legs flattened into paddles. Land crabs are generally built with relatively long legs for active movement, and their gills, of less use on land, are reduced. The gill cavities, on the other hand, are enlarged and contain special moisture-retaining tissue. A similar series of modifications exists for protection of the gills from intrusion of sediment. These may range from a sieve of fine hairs to keep out fine silt to a similar sieve of coarse bristles in sandier habitats, and burrowing crabs may bring water down through a bristle-walled tube between the antennae.

The predators of the intertidal zone include both permanent and temporary forms. Gastropods of the genus *Thais* are worldwide, intertidal carnivores, preying largely on barnacles. When the tide is high, various fishes feed in the intertidal zone, and when it is out mammals and birds invade it, playing a more important role than is usually realized. Gulls, for example, may limit the migration of tropical sea urchins above low-water mark, killing every individual they can reach. A number of these predators are most active at night, and in the tropics a considerable proportion of the animals remain in hiding during the sunny hours.

Rocky shores grade to some extent into those composed of soft sediment. Large rocks, not liable to be turned over by waves, have on their upper surface similar algae and animals to solid rock. Underneath, if they are not bedded into the sediment, they carry a special assemblage of animals, often rich in sponges and ascidians. These are adapted to shelter from excessive wave action and light and are killed if the rock is upset. Smaller stones carry progressively fewer organisms, more where they are least liable to disturbance, and probably the most barren type of shore is the pebble beach where the stones are constantly ground together by wave action.

Sand and Mud Sand and mud afford a very different habitat from rock. To begin with, such shores are more nearly flat. The sheltered crevices in and under stones are replaced by the interstices among the particles, or the burrows made and maintained by the organisms themselves. On the other hand the sediments are much more readily penetrated by burrowers, and retreat below a very thin layer of sand or mud affords effective insulation from the surface conditions. Dinoflagellates, which may be abundant on the sand surface, can avoid too bright light by retreat to a depth of one or two sand grains. Heat is transmitted relatively more slowly through a sediment so that burrowing forms undergo much smaller temperature changes than those of the surface. In severe freezes, deep-burrowing animals may survive when those at or near the surface are killed. Water circulates slowly through sand, and still more slowly through mud. Where water of low salinity flows over the surface during part of the tidal cycle, animals below the surface receive considerable protection from the salinity changes. One disadvantage of the habitat is that oxygen also circulates slowly, and a supply must be maintained by open burrows or other means.

Soft sediments are easily shifted by water movements, and few algae have evolved a rooting system which can hold them safely in the sediment. Even if they have, they face the problem of the changing level of the surface, and such changes are frequently extensive. As a result the plant population of soft sediments tends to be restricted to rapidly reproducing microorganisms such as diatoms and dinoflagellates forming a skin on the surface. In sheltered areas a few larger algae may occur, and they are also found attached to such solid objects as surface stones and shells. Some of the burrowing animals obtain their food supply by skimming the rich surface layer with siphons or by other means. These pick up not only the locally produced algal film but also the detritus which settles. Much of this detritus becomes trapped and incorporated in the sediment, where it supports a population

of mollusks, polychaetes, echinoderms, and others. Population densities may be very high in such an environment. The small bivalve *Tellina tenuis* has been recorded up to 7,500 per square meter, polychaetes up to 4,000, and amphipods up to 11,000. Of smaller animals, there are estimates for intertidal sand of 5,000,000 nematodes and about 500,000 each of ostracods and copepods per square meter. On many temperate sandy beaches the night high tides bring an extensive population of crustaceans into the area. For one such population there is an estimate of two hundred myside per cubic meter of water. This night-swimming population spends the day in the sand between tide marks or below low water.

Various species are adapted to particular levels or to particular particle sizes of sediment. It might be expected that filter feeders and detritus feeders, obtaining their food only when covered by the tide, would grow fastest near lowwater. This is the case in the cockle *Cardium edule* but not in *Tellina tenuis* in a similar habitat. Perhaps growth is limited by competition for food in the latter case, and certainly the slowest growth is at the level where the population density is greatest.

Many of the inhabitants of intertidal sediment have planktonic larvae, and the vicissitudes of planktonic life result in much greater year-to-year variation in the successful settlement of young than is typical of animals which protect their young. *Tellina tenuis*, for example, showed a tenfold range of settlement in a period of five years. The Tivelo clam, in California, is recorded as having a settlement density of 871, 44, 199, 0, and 758 in successive years. A successful settlement may therefore dominate the population for a number of years. Many shallow-water animals show a lunar rhythm in their migrations or other behavior, but particularly in their spawning. Some of the most spectacular spawnings occur in sediment-living polychaetes, which leave the bottom and swim to the surface where fertilization occurs. In Bermuda, the fireworm spawns in this way, appearing at the surface three days after full moon and fifty-four minutes after sunset. These, and the equally common diurnal rhythms in behavior, appear to be generally regulated by an internal "clock" mechanism whose timing is kept in phase by such external variables as daylight, tidal changes, and so on.

Since sediments are easily disturbed by water movement, they are an unstable habitat for the inhabitants where there is much wave action. Unlike wave-beaten pebble beaches, sands subject to surf contain a number of animals specially adapted to the conditions. On Florida beaches the small lamellibranch *Donax variabile* occurs in great numbers under conditions under which it is constantly washed out of the sand by waves, only to burrow in again immediately. Some, such as the sandflea, a small crustacean, feed on the detritus which concentrates where the waves run up the sandy beach. They stay with this zone by periodically riding a wave up the beach on the rising tide and down on the ebb. On the whole, though, there is less fauna in wave-exposed sands, possibly because of their lower food content. Light organic matter tends to be carried away from such a habitat, leaving only the heavier mineral particles.

Estuaries The intertidal zone is a graded transition from marine to aerial conditions. Estuaries are a similar transitional zone to freshwater. Typically they have a river entering the head. The freshwater mixes progressively with saltwater as it moves down the estuary, until at the mouth there are more or less fully marine conditions. Typically also, the more brackish water flows out along the surface, and more saline water flows in along the bottom. Tides partially flush the estuary so that on each tide some of estuarine water and its contained plankton are permanently lost to the open sea.

Some estuarine animals, such as fishes, can move up and down the estuary with the tide and so remain at a more or less constant salinity. Sedentary forms, though, are subject to strong salinity fluctuations during the tidal cycle. A large proportion of the animals can protect themselves from adverse external conditions by contracting into their shells, as do mollusks and barnacles, or by retreating into burrows. They need then make contact with the water only at that part of the tidal cycle when conditions are suitable. For filter feeders this has the disadvantage of limiting their feeding period, but most estuaries are so rich in suspended food that the effect appears not to be serious. On the other hand, in some polluted estuaries, oysters have been found to be in very poor condition, apparently because of too short feeding periods.

Life in an estuary calls for either tolerance of fluctuating internal salinity or osmoregulation. Some groups are incapable of adaptation to low salinity conditions. Among these, cephalopods and echinoderms are outstanding. Few of either group penetrate at all into estuaries, and none of them penetrates far. Osmoregulation involves the expenditure of energy, and is favored by high temperature. The eggs of the European shore crab *Carcinus* can tolerate a salinity as low as $20\%_{00}$ at 16.3° C., but only $26\%_{00}$ at 10° C. Just as the growth rate of an organism typically decreases throughout life, so its tolerance increases. The adult *Carcinus* can live at salinities too low for the young to survive. Some estuarine barnacles liberate their larvae into the surface waters where they are carried down toward the mouth of the estuary. There, when the salinity approaches that of the open sea, they sink and ride the bottom current up the estuary again, so avoiding flushing out of the estuary. Once settled they may, at lowwater, encounter water much fresher than that in which they passed their more vulnerable larval life.

Salinity fluctuation is not the only important characteristic of an estuary, but some of its other factors are associated mainly with either the fresh- or the saltwater, and so their distribution parallels that of salinity. Many rivers carry a heavy load of suspended matter. This is often high in organic content and constitutes a rich food source. If water movement slows when the river widens into the estuary, the suspended matter drops out of suspension; so muds are characteristic of much of the bottom. A deep channel and almost flat intertidal zone are also frequently found. Very many estuaries have become polluted with sewage or industrial waste, with resulting changes in their plants and animals. Industrial wastes may be toxic; but if they are not, both they and sewage may be beneficial if not too concentrated; they may be an added food source. However, excess organic matter, oxidized by bacteria, may reduce the oxygen content of the water and the sediment to the point where many animals are excluded.

In temperate estuaries the flow of freshwater is usually greatest in winter, at the time when temperature is lowest. The two combine to produce a seasonal shift in the tolerable limits of various species in the estuary, and a number of species have been shown to change their territory correspondingly. Not all estuaries, though, are of this type. Particularly in the tropics, the rainy season may be in the summer, and quite different seasonal shifts in the population may occur. Other tropical estuaries are cut off from the sea by a sandbar during the dry season, and evaporation lowers the water level and increases the salinity above that of the outside seawater. During the rainy season the bar is cut through and connection with the sea reestablished.

THE SEA

The sea commences at the air-water interface and ends at the water-substrate interface. At both of these there is a much sharper change in conditions than is found within the water itself. Both have an assemblage of plants and animals differing in their mode of life from those in the intermediate zone, and both show some diffusion of conditions and organisms on either side of the actual boundary. Where air, water, and substrate all meet, that is in the intertidal zone, the most complex and variable conditions are found, as well as an assemblage of the most specialized adaptations of the plants and animals. Basically illumination is the most important factor in controlling conditions in the sea. Temperature is affected through illumination, and is probably the most important secondary factor. However, while light distribution is the cause of the major break between plant-producing and plant-deficient waters, temperature rather modifies the species by which a group will be represented. From surface to bottom of the sea there is a gradient of temperature and light, with the temperature gradient steepest near the surface, and the light effectively absent from all but shallow water. Seasonal changes in both light and temperature decrease rapidly with depth and are significant only in the surface waters. In the surface water both light and temperature vary with latitude, and the extent of their seasonal changes varies similarly. In deeper water, latitudinal differences become rapidly less.

—H.B.M.

MARL A grayish-white sediment which comprises the bottom on most bonefish flats. Marl consists primarily of carbonate of lime ($CaCO_3$) precipitated by plants and to a large extent the fragments of shells, mollusks, and corals. When bonefish are "mudding," the milky clouds thus formed are marl in suspension. This sediment is often extremely difficult for the angler to wade on because it is soft, adhesive, and generally deep.

MARLIN *See* Black Marlin, Blue Marlin, Striped Marlin, White Marlin

MARYLAND Although Maryland is only 12,327 square miles in area the state is indented by the 20,000-square-mile Chesapeake Bay. The varied topography ranges from ridges and narrow valleys, which are typical of the Appalachian Mountains in the west, to the rolling plateau which extends to tidewater. The Old Line State, one of the original thirteen colonies, is not only blessed with miles of ocean front but a number of rivers, streams, lakes, and ponds. From the Susquehanna River, which crosses the northeast corner of Maryland, to the Potomac which flows along the southern boundary the visiting angler can find a variety of angling. The moderate climate—42 inches of rainfall and an average temperature of 50°F.—gives Maryland a wide variety of seasonal changes which are very conducive to outdoor living.

INLAND FISHING

Spring gets an early start in Maryland, and by late February brook, brown, and rainbow trout are on their way from the hatcheries to approximately 50 inland streams, totaling 145 miles throughout the western and northern sections of the state. A modest trout fishery is maintained in the Gunpowder River, Hunting Creek, Bear Creek, Beaver Creek, Rock Creek, Principio Creek, and the Savage River. These are, perhaps, the most important Maryland trout streams. The phenomenal runs of yellow and white perch in many tidal streams of Maryland also bring out the early angler. Mid-March witnesses the herring runs up the broad branches of the Bay country. This is closely followed by migrations of alewives, hickory shad, and the American shad. Warm nights find the rivers and streams aglow with Potomac and Susquehanna dippers seeking these sea-run species in the spring season. The Potomac River bank and boat fishermen find the smallmouth bass and channel catfish a real challenge in the big river. Down at the gateholes of the Eastern Shore millponds, many black crappie are taken in the 1–2-pound class. The more than 150,000 acres of lakes and reservoirs in the inland area scattered over Maryland's countryside come alive in early spring with largemouth bass, northern pike, walleye, catfish, and sunfish. Maryland's activity in stocking 3-pound northern pike and walleye along with adult largemouth bass and chain pickerel to control slow-growing perch, crappie, and sunfish in impounded water provides a two-way management technique—better fishing for the anglers and a better balanced population in the lakes and ponds. The response of this program in the multipurpose reservoirs has been very gratifying, particularly in Deep Creek Lake

Deep Creek Lake in Garrett County is one of several multipurpose reservoirs popular among Maryland anglers

in Garrett County, Loch Raven Reservoir in Baltimore County, and Conowingo Reservoir in Harford County.

ESTUARIES

Many broad estuaries headed by tidal streams afford more than 5,000 miles of sport fishing to fresh- and brackish-water anglers. The Susquehanna, which is the "Father of Waters," finds its way southward from New York and Pennsylvania into Maryland where it becomes a broad, drowned valley of the Chesapeake Bay. The North East, Elk, Sassafras, Bohemia, and Chester rivers on the Eastern Shore, along with the Magothy, Patapsco, Back, Middle, Gunpowder, and Bush rivers on the Western Shore, form a vast network of aquatic pasture in the upper Bay region. Striped bass, black bass, yellow perch, northern pike, walleye, and sunfish provide year-around fishing for many anglers.

The midregion tidal-river system includes the Severn, South, West, and Rhodes rivers on the Western Shore, and the Wye, Miles, Tred Avon, and Choptank Rivers on the Eastern Shore. These estuaries are traversed by navigable rivers that produce the spawning runs of the spring season. Excellent summer and fall fishing for striped bass, yellow and white perch, chain pickerel, bluefish, crabs, and clams abounds. The lower estuarine waters become broader, longer, and saltier as you progress southward in Maryland, and the Patuxent, Potomac, Nanticoke, Wicomico, Manokin, and the Pocomoke rivers are all ideal areas for exploration.

CHESAPEAKE BAY

Ninety miles of Maryland's Chesapeake Bay, reaching from the mouth of the Susquehanna to the mouth of the Potomac River, are a sea of fishing boats and pleasure craft from April through November. Due to the many rivers emptying into the bay, the upper part of Chesapeake is fished intensively for species which are normally considered freshwater fishes, while the saltwater species, which require higher salinities, are more common to the lower half of the bay. As a result, striped bass, spotted seatrout, bluefish, croaker or "hardhead," yellow perch, white perch, spot, flounder, and shad may enter the multi-ton annual harvest. Oyster bars, rock jetties, river-channel spoil beds, and other natural and artificial wrecks provide ideal habitat for the various species.

The Chesapeake Bay Bridge, Susquehanna Flats, Turkey Point, Spesutie Island, Battery Light, Betterton, Pooles Island, Worton Point, Tolchester, Tea Kettle Shoals, Hickory Thicket, Bodkin Point, Eastern Neck Island, Love Point, and Sandy Point are all productive spots in the upper bay. Southbound from the Bay Bridge, Dolly's Lumps, Brick House Bar, Gum Thickets, Bloody Point, Eastern Bay, Poplar Island, Holland Point, and Tilghman Island areas are all good locations. Farther south, anglers fish the lower bay near Choptank River, Sharps Island, Winter Gooses, the James Island area, Round Ragged Point, Little Choptank River, Taylor's Island, and Cove Point, and into the Patuxent River. Across the bay, the Honga River with its shallow clearwaters and southward to Tangier Sound and Smiths Island, we arrive at the great seafood capital of Crisfield, Maryland. This area also supports a large blue-crab fishery.

ATLANTIC OCEAN

Thousands of vacationers journey to the Atlantic Ocean front of Maryland. Many modern hotels, motels, and restaurants cater to the fishermen who prefer the limitless, broad, ocean areas of Maryland for their flounder, bluefish, seatrout, croaker or "hardhead," channel bass, and kingfish. Behind the various reefs, there is an abundance of bottom-fishing, and saltwater clams and oysters abound. Starting with the Atlantic runs of codfish from Newfoundland banks in February, the seasons at the Atlantic Ocean areas of Maryland present a continuous change in variety of fishing. White marlin are the champion of the deep and attract many fishermen in the mid-Atlantic area to go for this acrobatic billfish which appears off the coast of Maryland. Ocean City, the most famous big-game fishing port, is a gateway to the favorite offshore grounds such as the Jack Spot, Tide Rips, Fenwick's Ridge, and Winter Quarter. July and August are the best months, not only for marlin but school tuna, dolphin, and various other bluewater species. Surf-casters work the beach of Assateague Island, which extends about 30 miles from Ocean City, principally for channel bass which appear as early as May and linger until fall. —E.M.B.

MASSACHUSETTS The state of Massachusetts covers approximately 8,000 square miles. Of this area, about 3 percent is covered by water. The largest stream is the Connecticut River, and the largest standing body of water is Quabbin Reservoir. The state varies greatly in physical characteristics. In elevation, it ranges from sea level along the 1,800 miles of coastline in the east to 3,491 feet at the summit of Mount Greylock in the Berkshire Hills in the west. The land between the coastal lowlands and the Berkshires consists of low hills, marshlands, and river valleys. A little distance west of the middle of the state, the Connecticut River runs southward through a broad valley that once was a prehistoric lake before the eroding stream cut a notch through a mountain range in the middle of the state. The most important single influence in the soil formation of Massachusetts has been glaciation. Gravel up to several hundred feet deep, deposited by the terminal moraines, underlies much of the land, and small, rolling hills, called drumlins, further attest to the past occurrence of the glaciers in central Massachusetts. Topsoil, formed since the land was free, is seldom over 10–15 inches deep on open, level land, except in river valleys. Massachusetts has been blessed with bountiful groundwater supplies. Good-sized springs are found in the Berkshires, on Cape Cod, and along the sides of the Connecticut Valley. Forest types range from mixtures of hemlock, pine, maple, beech, and birch in the western highlands to brushy hardwoods in the east and scrub oak and pitch pine along the southeast coast. The population of Massachusetts is concentrated in the east, center, and southeast and averages 700 people per square mile, totaling about 5,700,000. Climate is temperate, with both precipitation and sunshine well-distributed throughout the year. Winter temperatures are cold enough to keep the ponds frozen over from the last half of December to the end of March, usually, except within twenty miles or so of the coast where the weather is milder. Almost any part of Massachusetts is accessible by the highway system, and the two most widely separated points in the state are not much over 250 miles apart, so that the distance between them could be traversed in a single day of casual driving.

INLAND FISHING

Inland fishing in freshwater ponds, lakes, and streams attracts about 200,000 licensed fishermen each year, and an unknown number of minors below the age of fifteen who are not required to be licensed. Favorite sport fish are brook, brown, and rainbow trout, largemouth and smallmouth black bass, chain pickerel, white and yellow perch, calico bass, brown bullheads, bluegills and pumpkinseed sunfish. Fishermen polls have shown an inclination toward trout as a preferred gamefish. However, in Massachusetts, most of the larger rivers are polluted by industrial and domestic wastes, and many of the smaller-sized streams dry up in summer. As a result, natural trout habitat is limited to a few small, clear brooks and to some of the deeper lakes. The brook trout, which was the only native salmonid found originally in inland waters of this state, still exists without stocking in the numerous colder, purer, better-shaded streams but does not often attain a size over 12–14 inches. Atlantic salmon were taken by the early settlers in large numbers, but ceased to spawn in coastal streams due to pollution, siltation, and the construction of dams. Brown and rainbow trout are stocked in suitable waters mostly as a put-and-take fishery. In some of the better trout lakes, where large volumes of suitable water last through the critical hot summer weather, stocked browns and rainbows carry over for several years, and specimens of brown trout have attained a weight of almost 20 pounds under such circumstances. Lake trout are caught only in Quabbin Reservoir where they have been successfully introduced. Some anadromous brook and brown trout ascend coastal estuaries in the spring and fall.

Largemouth bass were introduced to Massachusetts about a hundred years ago, and, finding suitable habitat here, have become common almost everywhere. Smallmouth bass also were introduced, and are less common although fairly well distributed throughout the state. Chain pickerel were native to Massachusetts and have been found throughout the state. A former world-record chain pickerel weighing 9 pounds, 5 ounces was captured by a woman fishing through the ice at one of the Berkshire County lakes in 1954. In surveys of fish populations of this state, yellow perch have been the most common fish. Specimens up to 16 inches in length are occasionally captured. White perch were native to coastal estuaries and to any ponds that were accessible from the sea. They have been successfully stocked in many of the waters of the state, and frequently have reproduced to such an extent that they have overpopulated ponds. In such circumstances, they usually never grow large enough to be worth catching and are a hindrance rather than an asset to the fishery. The same thing may be said of bluegills, another exotic, which, in many ponds, grow too slowly and to too small a size to be worth-while quarry. In some of the ponds that are characterized by a high basic fertility, bluegills are large enough to provide good sport and eating. The pumpkinseed is generally regarded as a "bentpin" species fished for by children.

Much sport is afforded each spring by the shad, which run up some of the larger rivers. These gamy fish are eagerly awaited by a large number of enthusiastic anglers, especially in the Connecticut River around Springfield, Chicopee, and Holyoke. The problem of passing them by the dams to spawning grounds upstream has not as yet been adequately solved, but enough adult fish do get through to perpetuate themselves.

Other fishes that provide sport are carp, often of 20 pounds or more, which are taken by bow and arrow and by angling; white suckers, sometimes snagged out of spawning streams; northern pike, which are found only as occasional individuals; and walleye and catfish, which are caught only in a few specialized local fisheries.

BERKSHIRE HILLS REGION

The Berkshire Hills is a popular summer-resort and winter-sport area. The lakes are often hundreds of acres in size, deep and clear. Some of the best-known are Onota Lake, Pontoosac Lake, Stockbridge Bowl, Lake Buel and Lake Garfield. All of these five provide fishing for bass and pickerel, and Lake Onota has given up brown and rainbow trout of trophy size. The Cheshire Reservoir is a good example of the shallow, weedy Berkshire lake where good catches of bass, pickerel, and perch may be made. The largest pond that is open to fishing in the Berkshires is Otis Reservoir, which is over 1,000 acres in size and affords catches of bass, pickerel, and trout. The best-known trout stream in Massachusetts is the Deerfield River, which flows out of Lake Whitingham, just across the border in Vermont and winds southward along the Mohawk Trail 39½ miles to discharge its waters into the Connecticut River. Floods that have occurred during the past twenty-five years have filled in some of the better pools and destroyed stream-bank shade trees and generally disorganized the riffle and pool order of the Deerfield and some of the other large Massachusetts rivers that were formerly famous for trout fishing. However, the Deerfield still receives thousands of hatchery trout each year. Other Berkshire trout streams are the Konkapot, the Farmington, and the Green River. Many of the smaller streams and creeks receive annual allotments of state-reared catchable-size hatchery trout.

CONNECTICUT RIVER

The Connecticut River originates in New Hampshire and flows 68 miles through Massachusetts, occupying over 7,000 acres of water, with its main stream, bays, and backwaters, before it enters the state of Connecticut. This river was more polluted at one time than it is now, but much of the pollutant matter has been rendered harmless by sewage disposal plants and by factory processes that make their manufacturing wastes less dangerous to aquatic life. One of the few walleye fisheries is in the northern part of this river. Channel catfish have been taken in the oxbow near Northampton. Bass, pickerel, and panfish inhabit the backwaters. Several public-access and boat-livery sites are distributed along the length of the river, which is being used more and more constantly for boating, water skiing, and other recreational purposes.

QUABBIN RESERVOIR

In 1937, a dam across the Swift River was completed for the purpose of impounding a drinking-water supply for Boston. Seven years later when the impoundment

Fall fishing on the reservoirs of Massachusetts is a prime season for the skilled bass angler

reached spillway level, it covered almost 40 square miles and was known as Quabbin Reservoir. Bass, pickerel, and white and yellow perch furnished most of the sport until 1957, when anglers began to catch introduced lake trout and stocked brown and rainbow trout. Since that time, the Quabbin has been best-known to fishermen as a trout pond. This reputation is well-deserved, as individual brown trout weighing over 18 pounds have been taken there and many large lake trout and rainbow trout have also been captured. The trout fishery is characterized by a rather low rate of fishing success for all trout fishermen and by a large average size of fish taken. Three state-operated boat liveries and launching ramps provide access to the reservoir. Approximately one-fifth of the impoundment remains closed to prevent contamination of the water where it is drawn off to be used for drinking purposes. Special restrictions include limitation of motors to outboards not over 10 hp and the refusal to permit water skiing, swimming, or any other form of aquatic recreation other than fishing (persons using the reservoir must display a Massachusetts fishing license), and limitation on the number of occupants in a boat. Besides being the state's most famous fishing spot, the Quabbin is also well-known for its scenic appearance and for the opportunities it affords to observe seldom-seen species of birds and animals.

CENTRAL REGION

In central Massachusetts, many of the shallow, weedy waters yield largemouth bass up to 7–8 pounds, although the number of such large fish from any of the better ponds is not often more than six to ten per year. Examples of such ponds are Long Pond, Rutland; Whitehall Reservoir, Hopkinton; the lower end of Lake Quinsigamond, Worcester, lakes Lashaway, Wickaboag, and Quaboag, in the Brookfield vicinity, and the Quaboag River.

For trout fishing in central Massachusetts, the best spots are Comet Pond, Hubbardston; Lake Quinsigamond, Worcester; Lake Mattawa, Orange; Lake Cochituate, Natick; Lake Whalom, Lunenburg; Lake Quacumquasit, Brookfield; Burnshirt and Canesto brooks, Hubbardston; Ware River, Rutland; Quinapoxet River, Holden and the Squannacook River, Townsend. In most of these trout ponds and streams the greater part of the catch is of recently stocked trout averaging about ½ pound or less, but every year fish are taken that have carried over from other seasons and when captured weigh 2–6 pounds.

NORTHEASTERN REGION

In the thickly settled northeastern part of the state, bass and pickerel are found in Lake Quannapowitt, Wakefield; Spy Pond, Arlington; Long Pond, Littleton; and the Concord and Sudbury rivers, as well as many less well-known places. The best trout fishing opportunities would be in Pleasant Pond, Wenham; Sluice Pond, Lynn; Lake Walden, which was memorialized by the naturalist Thoreau; the Shawsheen River, Bedford; the Ipswich River, North Reading and the Nissitissit River, Pepperell. Trout-fishing opportunities in the northeast are comparable to those just described for central Massachusetts.

SOUTHEASTERN REGION

The southeastern part of the state is rather low and has some extensive marshes and many ponds and rivers. The generally agreed best smallmouth-bass pond in the state is Watuppa Pond near Fall River. Sawdy Pond, a few miles away from Watuppa, also harbors many smallmouths. The Norton Reservoir is known as a "porkbarrel pond" for largemouth bass, pickerel, white and yellow perch, crappies, and good-sized bluegills. Largemouths weighing 7–10 pounds are taken here every year. Furnace Pond, Pembroke; Monponsett Pond, Halifax, and many of the other ponds in these and neighboring towns afford fishing for largemouth bass and pickerel. Long Pond, Lakeville, has both kinds of bass, and has produced many large white and yellow perch. This pond, together with Assawompsett Pond, and Great and Little Quitticas ponds and Pocksha Pond constitute the largest natural water unit in the state (ponded), comprising 5,724 surface acres.

Good trout fishing in most of southeastern Massachusetts is uncommon, as most of the ponds are too shallow and the streams are too warm to sustain trout except in the Plymouth-Cape Cod area.

CAPE COD

Cape Cod is a famous summer resort. Throughout most of the year the small towns are relatively inactive, but in the summertime visitors and guests arrive from all parts of the country to enjoy fishing, camping, swimming, boating, and all sorts of outdoor activities. The receding glaciers left blocks of ice in the sand and thereby created kettle-type lakes. The deeper of these lakes now contain some of the best trout-sustaining water in the state. Some of the popular waters are Cliff Pond, Brewster; Peters Pond, Sandwich; Long Pond, Plymouth; Scargo Pond, Dennis; Shubael Pond, Barnstable; and Gull Pond, Wellfleet. Most of these ponds are less than a mile long but contain some large trout nevertheless. A brown trout weighing over 19 pounds was picked up dead of natural causes at Cliff Pond in the year 1954. Live shrimp are one of the most effective baits when fishing for trout in Cape Cod ponds.

Although the emphasis in freshwater fishing is on trout, the possibilities for catching warmwater fish should not be overlooked. Bass, pickerel, and white and yellow perch attain large size in many of these ponds. Among the better warmwater fishing ponds are Lake Chequaquet, Barnstable; Mashpee-Wakeby Pond, Mashpee (also a famous trout pond); Santuit Pond, Mashpee; Pleasant Lake, Harwich; Depot Pond, Eastham; and Lawrence and Mystic and Middle Ponds, Sandwich.

It has been said that there is a pond for every day of the year on Cape Cod. Because of the combination of abundant water resources and low angling patronage resulting from its remoteness from centers of population, the Cape has remained one of the least exploited angling spots of the state, and probably will continue to be so for many years.

Because of the activities of the Massachusetts Division of Fisheries and Game, changes are constantly being made in fishing within the state. By chemical control of undesirable fish populations, technicians have altered or removed all of the fish in some water units and replaced them with species that are more rewarding to the angler and more suitable to the environment. Persons who are contemplating a fishing trip to Massachusetts should investigate to find out what new opportunities the state has to offer by contacting the division for information.

A general idea of the size of gamefish to be expected in Massachusetts may be derived from the length or weight of prize-winning fish registered in the state-sponsored sport-fishing award contest during a two-year period. The following were the largest of each species entered during these two years: lake trout, 13 pounds, 1 ounce; brown trout, 18 pounds, 8 ounces; rainbow trout, 6 pounds, 13 ounces; largemouth bass, 12 pounds, 1 ounce; smallmouth bass, 6 pounds, 10 ounces; chain pickerel, 7 pounds, 11 ounces; northern pike, 13 pounds, 12 ounces; walleye, 8 pounds, 5 ounces.

SALTWATER FISHING

A great variety of saltwater fishing offers itself to the anglers in Massachusetts. The glamour fish of the saltwater fishery is the striped bass. They are taken in great numbers and in large sizes off Massachusetts shores. In August 1960, the women's all-tackle world record was broken twice in one day by two Massachusetts women fishing on Cape Cod. Their two huge stripers weighed 62½ and 64½ pounds. Most fishermen, however, take bass in the 5–15-pound size. The larger bass are always a possibility, and diligent fishermen who pursue the stripers over a period of years usually take bass in the 30–40-pound class sooner or later. Favorite fishing places for stripers are Plum Island, Newburyport; Race Point, Provincetown; Nauset Beach, Orleans; the Cape Cod Canal, Martha's Vineyard; and Cuttyhunk. Most stripers are taken by party-boat fishermen. Large plugs, sandworms, and squids are the usual lures. Since 1960, bass have been present in the greatest numbers ever recorded, probably as a result of favorable spawning conditions and survival circumstances.

Bluefish fishing is a popular sport, but this species is found in much smaller numbers than striped bass. Specimens up to 20 pounds are occasionally caught.

The most popular fish of the saltwater anglers is the winter flounder. More of these fish are caught every year by sport fishermen than any other marine species. In addition, cod, mackerel, haddock, pollock, scup, and tautog are taken in large numbers. Most saltwater fishing is done from small boats, such as rowboats, but shore fishermen make good catches also and congregate in such places as, for example, the Cape Cod Canal, Plum Island, and Race Point. —R.S.McC.

MAXILLARY The bone situated on each side of the upper jaw.

MAYFLIES Ephemeroptera Over 500 species of mayflies are known from the United States and from Canada. Among them they occupy almost every type of freshwater habitat, from the smallest permanent pond to the Great Lakes, and from the tiniest brook to the largest river. One or another may be found on the wing from early spring to late fall and at almost any hour of day or night. Trout-stream species are on the wing in greatest number and variety in afternoon and evening hours between mid-April and mid-July.

Fish feed avidly on nymphs, duns, and spinners, and each stage is a challenge to fly-tier and fly-fisherman alike. There is a great deal of synonymy in common names for the mayfly species; the Green Drake of Europe, for example, includes *Ephemera dancia* and *Ephemera vulgata*, while in the United States it refers to *Ephemera guttulata*, as well as several nonrelated species. Nevertheless, the lore of the mayfly is regionally distinct and the

Mayflies are an important food to trout, which forage on these aquatic insects at all stages in their development from the bottom-dwelling nymph to the emerging dun and the winged adult

angler learns when the important emergences are likely to occur in his area and which artificials best imitate them. The use of the Mayfly Key is suggested for positive identifications.

LIFE HISTORY

Mayfly eggs deposited in water hatch into the nymph which spends the fall and winter months feeding on aquatic plants, diatoms, organic detritus, etc. In spring or early summer the nymphal skin splits, and the first winged stage emerges; about twenty-four hours later the skin is shed again, and the fully mature insect emerges. Mayflies are the only insects which shed their skin after developing functional wings. Mating, egg laying, and death follow in a matter of hours. The winged stages have atrophied digestive tracts and are incapable of feeding.

Mayflies have three (less commonly two) slender tails. Nymphal gills are external, attached at the outer edge of the upper surface of the abdomen. The wings develop in "pads" or pockets on the back of the nymphal thorax and turn dark shortly before emergence, the sign of an imminent hatch.

The subimago or dun, which emerges from the nymph, constitutes the true "hatch" of the angler. Imagoes or spinners often swarm over the water in great numbers to mate and lay eggs. Some anglers refer to this flight as a "brush hatch," since the insects often rest in streamside vegetation while awaiting the final molt.

Mayflies vary in body length (less tails) from ⅛ inch to over 1½ inches. The antennae are short and bristlelike. The wings are almost always four in number, the front pair much larger than the hind pair, which is wanting entirely in a few species. They are supported by a dense network of veins and at rest are folded together vertically over the back like those of a butterfly. In the dun stage the wings are usually cloudy, often appearing pale blue, slate, olive, yellow, or white, sometimes with dark mottling. In the spinner stage the wing membrane is clear, transparent, and with dark mottling in only a few species.

—J.W.L.

DAPPING THE MAYFLY

Although natural mayflies are the prototypes for literally hundreds of artificial flies, the live insect can be used as a bait. This method is almost unknown to United States waters, but the art of "dapping" is brought to perfection in the lakes of Ireland. The large mayfly hatches, notably that of the Green Drake *Ephemera danica* which occurs in the limestone lakes usually between the second week in May and the third week of June, is regarded as an annual holiday for the skillful dapper. The live mayflies are captured around the bushes or rocks near shore. They are placed in a small wooden box which has several large holes that are covered with perforated zinc; the box has two hinged lids for depositing and recapturing the insects.

The dapper uses a long (up to 17 feet), light rod and a plaited silk "blow-line" with a fine leader and small hook. One or usually two mayflies are impaled on the hook through the thorax. While drifting in the boat with the breeze, the angler lets the line blow out so that the mayfly just floats along on top of the water—well in advance of the boat. The mayfly drifts on the surface until seized by the trout. *For details on dapping see* Ireland

THE HENDRICKSON

Ephemerella invaria The natural insect after which this popular artificial fly is patterned is of general occurrence in trout streams throughout the northeastern quarter of the United States and adjacent parts of Canada. It shows a preference for streams with gravel bottoms in which the nymphs find suitable harborage.

It appears on the wing early in the season, when trout are just beginning to shed the lethargy of winter and show interest in surface food. In Michigan, where emergence records have been kept for many years, hatching may start by mid-April when snow is still on the ground, reach a May first peak, and continue in diminishing numbers well into June.

Transformation from nymph to winged state usually takes place between noon and 6 P.M. The nymph releases its grasp on the stream bed and rises to the surface, drifting downstream with the current as it rises. When it is still several inches below the surface the nymphal skin starts to split down the middle of the back, and by the time it actually surfaces, the molt is likely to be complete. For the next 30–60 seconds the mayfly rides its cast nymphal skin downstream like a raft, shaking its wings to open the folds into which they were tightly compressed while still in the nymphal stage. It then rises from the water and, with fairly steady flight, heads for streamside cover. Safely lodged among alder or other vegetation it settles in a protected spot where it can endure the sometimes below-freezing temperatures of night.

In the morning, as the air warms, it undergoes a second molt, thus transforming from the dun (subimago) stage to the spinner (imago or adult) stage. Depending somewhat on weather conditions, it continues to rest in shelter until midafternoon. Then the males take wing and form the typical mating swarm, a loosely formed assemblage of up to hundreds of individuals, each alternately rising and falling through a space from a few inches above the water to about the highest level of streamside vegetation. After the swarm has formed, females start joining it individually. Almost at once, each is seized by a male, and mating takes place on the wing. The act may last from thirty seconds to three minutes. At its conclusion the female leaves the swarm to deposit her eggs, after which she almost immediately dies. The male rejoins the swarm and may mate again. In fact, if the weather is cool the male may survive for a second day and, as death approaches, fly away from the stream and die at some distance from water.

Some of the heaviest feeding by trout on this mayfly is during the transit from stream bed to surface. Stomachs of trout caught at this time contain a heavy percentage of partially transformed insects. Those mayflies that survive to reach the surface continue to be extremely vulnerable during the brief interval when they are floating and testing their wings. The females, of course, come within range of feeding fish during and after egg laying.

Description: Body length, not including tails, ⅜–½ inch. Top of head dark reddish-brown, face somewhat paler. Eyes shiny reddish-brown. Thorax dark, shiny reddish-brown above, sometimes purple just ahead of forewing bases, lightly washed with creamy-yellow on the sides. Legs olive-brown turning to reddish-brown where they join the body. Wing membrane clear, veins amber to medium brown. Abdomen dark reddish-brown, the sides lightly washed with cream color near the tip. Tails smoky-olive with narrow reddish-brown joints.

From a distance the general impression is of a dark, glowing, mahogany-colored insect with olive tails.

Both *E. subvaria* and *E. rotunda* so closely resemble *E. invaria* that all three species of mayflies are represented by the Hendrickson pattern.

THE GRAY FOX; THE DARK CAHILL

Stenonema spp. Three closely allied species of mayflies, *Stenonema vicarium*, *ithaca*, and *fuscum*, serve as models for the Gray Fox while they are still duns or subimagoes, and for the Dark Cahill when they become spinners or full adults. While the species differ from each other in minor details significant to the entomologist, their over-all appearance is very similar, and the difference from the angler's viewpoint is mainly one of size. The body length, less tails, of *S. vicarium* may be as much as ¾ inch; *S. ithaca* may measure a scant ⅜ inch, with *S. fuscum* about midway between. Hence the same basic patterns tied within this size range may cover a wide range of angling opportunity.

Emergence takes place from mid-May to mid-July, *ithaca* generally starting earliest, and closely followed by *fuscum* and *vicarium* in that order.

Nymphs of all three species are strongly flattened, a modification which adapts them to their preferred habitat on the under side of stones or on submerged logs in moderate to rapid current.

Transformation from nymph to dun or subimago usually takes place in late afternoon. The molt from dun to spinner occurs that night or early next morning, and mating flights start to form by midafternoon. Heaviest mating and egg-laying activity takes place at or after dusk, often at 20–50 feet above the stream. The egg mass, yellow to orange in color, may be released from a height of several feet or deposited while the female floats on the water.

Description: Dun (subimago) predominantly brownish- or yellowish-olive in color, wings cloudy-gray with olive reflections, cross-veins heavily mottled with dark olive-brown.

Spinner (adult) predominantly medium to dark reddish-brown, sides of thorax lightly washed with yellow. Wings clear with dark veins. Legs amber with reddish-brown cross-bands. Abdomen reddish-brown, amber to yellow near base, lightly washed with yellow near tip. Tails amber with dark joints.

Each of these species exhibits a preference for medium to large trout streams and appears to thrive not only in coldwaters but in streams warm enough to be considered marginal for trout.

THE OLIVE DUN

Ephemerella lata Both nymphs and adults range from ¼–⅜ inches in length exclusive of tails. Nymphs occur in three distinct color phases. One of these is predominantly medium to light olive brown with little or no detectable color pattern. A second phase is dark greenish brown in color, but with the pronotum or "collar," the middle abdominal segments, and the gill plates light bluish-green, and with cross bands of this color on the legs. In the third color phase the general impression is of a dark greenish-brown insect with a cross band on the "collar," stripes ahead of each wing pad, the middle abdominal segments and the gills bright red.

The dun or subimago is nearly black in color with olive reflections. The legs are pure olive and the wings are very dark, opaque bluish-black.

The imago or spinner is a rather uniform dark brown with olive reflections. The tails are white, contrasting strongly with the dark abdomen.

Nymphs of this species occur rather generally in gravel riffles of trout streams, and the winged stages may appear almost any time in July and early August. The nymphs frequent much the same sites as those of the Beaverkill and the Hendrickson, but the winged stages of the *lata* emerge a month and a half to two months later than either of these species.

Perhaps the greatest interest of *Ephemerella lata* to the trout fishermen centers in its comparatively late season emergence, appearing on the wing, as it does, after most of our abundant mayflies have completed their adult life.

THE BROWN DRAKE

Ephemera simulans Nymphs of this important burrowing species inhabit the beds of both streams and lakes. They generally burrow in a mixture of sand and gravel, unlike nymphs of the larger burrowing species, *Hexagenia limbata*, which prefer silt and mud bars. Nymphs of the Brown Drake, ranging from ⅜–½ inch in length, are hardly large enough to be of significant value as live bait. Both the dun and spinner stages, however, which range from ½–⅝ inch in length exclusive of the tails, are very popular with feeding trout, and artificial lures patterned after them are very effective.

The subimago is dark brown in color with definite olive reflections. The wings are olive, heavily spotted with dark brown. The imago or spinner is characterized by clear but heavily spotted wings and by a body which is predominantly dark brown relieved by yellowish spots above and predominantly yellow underneath. The three tails are light yellowish-brown with dark bandings and are about twice as long as the body.

Subimagoes emerge from the nymphal stage at dusk and are much sought after by feeding trout during the period of transformation. The molt from dun to spinner stage usually takes place later that night or early the next day. The adult mating flight usually forms at about dusk of the day following emergence from the nymph. Swarms ordinarily occur over water at a height of 10–50 feet, but may sometimes form in clearings at a distance from the water. The dun or subimaginal stage is attracted to light, and bodies of dead and dying insects may accumulate in objectionable quantity under street lights.

The Brown Drake is rather generally distributed throughout the north central and northeastern states and adjacent areas of Canada. The extent of dark spotting on the wings will often vary, not only from one part of the range to another but between different bodies of water only a small distance apart.

In parts of its range shared with *Hexagenia limbata*, the Brown Drake, with its earlier emergence date, is thought by many fishermen to help focus attention of large trout on surface feeding and so to prepare the way for the spectacular fishing that attends the hatching and egg-laying of *H. limbata*.

Heptagenia sp., subimago on cascara twig

Rhithrogena sp., female, on cascara leaf

THE GREEN DRAKE

Ephemera guttulata Both nymphal and adult stages of this mayfly are about the same as those of *Ephemera simulans* or the Brown Drake.

The most readily noticed difference between *guttulata* and *simulans* is that in the dun or subimago stage, the abdomen of *guttulata* is pale green devoid of dark markings, and in the spinner or adult stage it becomes creamy white, again without dark markings. The wings of *guttulata* are much more heavily spotted with dark brown than those of *simulans*, and from a distance appear to be almost entirely black.

The Green Drake is widely distributed throughout the northeastern United States and Canada. Its habits resemble those of the Brown Drake, and emergence dates may range from the middle of May to the middle of June, depending upon environmental factors and the part of the range involved.

While Green Drake is the common name widely applied to the dun or subimaginal stage of this species, the spinner or imago stage is known as Gray Drake, Black Drake, or Coffin Fly, depending on the geographic area in which this stage of the species is found.

BURROWING MAYFLY OR "MICHIGAN CADDIS"

Hexagenia limbata This is the largest of our mayflies which is popularly, but erroneously, called the Michigan Caddis. Its nymphs burrow in the muddy bottoms of both streams and lakes where the bottom material is sufficiently compacted for the burrows to remain open. Nymphs range in length from ⅝–1¼ inches and adults attain approximately the same lengths, both growth stages measured exclusive of the tails. The variation in length of mature nymphs and adults depends largely on their sex, the females always being much larger than the males

The nymphs are predominantly amber in color, the thorax and abdomen washed here and there with reddish-brown to purple. The conspicuous feathery gills are essentially purple in color with gray edges.

The dun or subimago is predominantly yellowish-green to olive in color. The wings are opaque olive-gray.

The spinner or imago has clear wings. Body color may vary considerably from essentially yellow with purple markings to dark purplish-brown with olive markings. The outer tails are longer than the body, but the middle tail is very short, providing a convenient means, apart from color and size differences, for distinguishing this species from the species of *Ephemera*.

The nymphs of *H. limbata* enjoy a very real commercial value over much of their range. Known to the winter ice fishermen as "wigglers," they are widely popular with them as a live bait for catching panfish.

The emergence of the winged stages from the nymph, especially over streams, is a most spectacular event. Emergence is usually at its height during the last half of June, although stragglers may appear until frost in the fall. The hatch usually starts about 9 o'clock in the evening and may continue until about midnight.

Duns rest in sheltered places for 24–72 hours after emergence. Then transforming to the spinner stage, they form a mating flight which constitutes one of the most spectacular phenomena of insect behavior in the northeastern United States. Enormous swarms form at or above tree-top height and they follow the course of the stream for miles. The rustle of wings is clearly audible at some distance from the swarm. If one directs the beam of a flashlight into the swarm, he is likely to be covered with the insects in a matter of seconds.

Eggs are produced in a single packet, elongated in shape and creamy yellow in color. Females sometimes drop their eggs into the water while still on the wing, but more frequently they crash land on the surface and squeeze out the eggs with their final death struggle. Each egg packet may contain over 3,000 eggs.

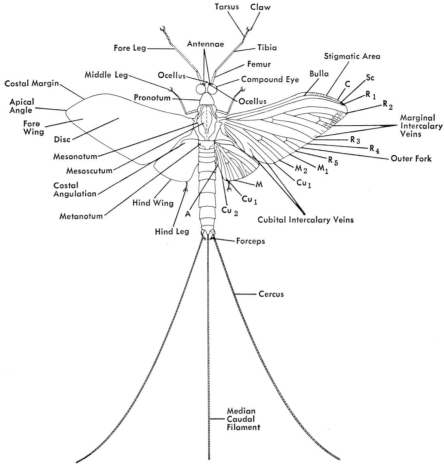

A generalized mayfly

Both during emergence from the nymph and during egg-laying this large species is greatly sought after by feeding trout. During a heavy hatch or flight, trout appear to lose all wariness and may bump against the legs of the wading angler while feeding under his very nose.

—J.W.L.

KEYS TO NORTH AMERICAN MAYFLIES

Structurally, mayflies are similar to stoneflies. Therefore, the description of the stonefly body parts in the stonefly section is also generally applicable to them. There is one difference, however. Adult mayflies are often less well developed. There is a strong tendency for gills to disappear completely and for mouthparts and legs to become vestigial. Wings do not develop well in many genera, some veins disappear, hind wings may be absent, and the venation may be monotonously similar among the genera of certain families. Nymphs are very well developed and in some genera possess better specific characters than adults.

In making the keys, I have relied very heavily on B. D. Burks' excellent monograph, *The Mayflies, or Ephemeroptera, of Illinois,* issued in 1953 by the Illinois Natural History Survey. The various sketches were patterned after illustrations found in this outstanding work. I have followed the systematic arrangement in the 1962 paper by George F. Edmunds, Jr., titled, *The Type Localities of the Ephemeroptera of North America North of Mexico,* published as Number 5 of Volume 12 in the University of Utah Biological Series. A number of other scientific papers and books have been consulted in regard to the classification and distribution of mayflies.

The keys are really easy to use after a little practice. Note that they are made up of couplets, each containing a pair of statements. Here is how to use them. We assume that you have an adult winged mayfly (*see also* Stonefly key) before you. Find its proper family in the key to the families. Read the two statements in the first couplet and decide which fits your specimen. If it has ocelli about half as large as the compound eyes, go, as directed, to the second of the couplets and decide which alternate choice fits your specimen. Repeat this process until your specimen is properly identified as belonging to one of the fifteen families of North American mayflies. (The number in parentheses following the couplet number refers to the earlier couplet where you were directed to go to the present couplet.) Now go to the key to genera for the family represented by your specimen and proceed in a similar fashion until you identify your specimen to genus.

FAMILIES OF NORTH AMERICAN MAYFLIES
ADULTS

(The family Behningiidae, known in North America only in the nymphal stage, is omitted.)

1   Lateral ocellus large, usually about one half as large as compound eye.   2

      Lateral ocellus small, never more than one quarter as large as a compound eye, always much less in males.   3

2 (1) Fore wing with very few crossveins and with median intercalary vein extending to wing base.   *Caenidae*

Fore wing of *Brachycercus*

      Fore wing with relatively numerous crossveins and with median intercalary vein extending only half way to wing base.   *Tricorythidae*

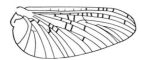

Fore wing of *Tricorythodes*

3 (1) Vein Sc of fore wing absent or united with R_1.   *Oligoneuriidae*

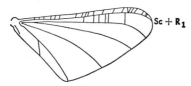

Fore wing of *Oligoneuria*

      Vein Sc of fore wing present as a separate vein.   4

Fore wing of *Baetis*

4 (3) Cubital intercalary veins absent, crossveins in disc of fore wing netlike.   *Baetiscidae*

Fore wing of *Baetisca*

Cubital intercalary veins present, crossveins in disc of fore wing not netlike.   5

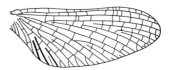

Fore wing of *Heptagenia*

5 (4) Hind tarsus with five segments.   *Heptageniidae*

Hind leg of *Stenonema*

      Hind tarsus with only three or four segments.   6

Hind leg of *Leptophlebia*

6 (5) Vein M_2 of fore wing sharply bent near base running parallel with vein Cu_1 in this area.   7

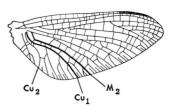

Fore wing of *Neoephemera*

      Vein M_2 of fore wing straight throughout its length or curved no more than in the sketch.   10

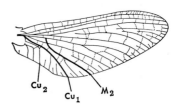

Fore wing of *Ephemerella*

7 (6) Costal crossveins of fore wing in area basad of bulla partly or almost completely atrophied.   *Neoephemeridae*

Fore wing of *Neoephemera*

Costal crossveins of fore wing well developed. 8

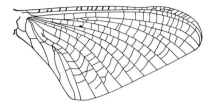

Fore wing of *Tortopus*

8 (7) Marginal veinlets absent from the fore wing, or if present, cubital intercalary veins straight, not attached at bases to Cu₁. *Polymitarcidae*

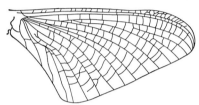

Fore wing of *Tortopus*

Marginal veinlets present in the fore wing and intercubital intercalary veins sinuate, attached at bases to Cu₁. 9

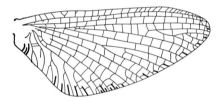

Fore wing of *Potamanthus*

9 (8) First anal vein of fore wing forked near wing margin. *Potamanthidae*

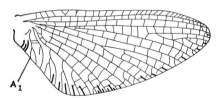

Fore wing of *Potamanthus*

First anal vein of fore wing not forked near wing margin. *Ephemeridae*

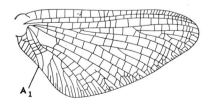

Fore wing of *Ephemera*

10 (6) Fore wing with one or two long intercalary veins between veins M₂ and Cu₁. *Ephemerellidae*

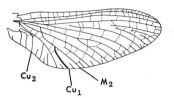

Fore wing of *Ephemerella*

Fore wing without long intercalaries between veins M₂ and Cu₁. 11

11 (10) Vein Cu₂ of fore wing angularly bent toward inner wing margin. *Leptophlebiidae*

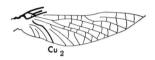

Lower part of fore wing of *Paraleptophlebia*

Vein Cu₂ of fore wing straight or evenly curved. 12

12 (11) Cubital intercalary veins of fore wing consisting of one or two pairs of long, parallel veins; hind wing always present. 13

Cubital intercalary veins of fore wing either a series of short, slightly sinuate veins or one or two basally detached veins with accompanying marginal veinlets; hind wing may be absent. 14

13 (12) Median caudal filament present or absent and first segment of fore tarsus of male slightly longer than second segment. *Ametropidae*

Median caudal filament absent and first segment of fore tarsus of male three fourths as long as second segment. (Genus *Pseudiron* only). *Heptageniidae*

14 (12) Vein M₂ of fore wing detached at base from stem of M. *Baetidae*

Lower part of fore wing of *Baetis*

Vein M₂ of fore wing not detached at base from stem of M. *Siphlonuridae*

Lower part of fore wing of *Isonychia*

FAMILIES OF NORTH AMERICAN MAYFLIES
NYMPHS

1   Gills on abdominal segments 1–6 concealed under a shield-shaped projection of thoracic notum.   *Baetiscidae*

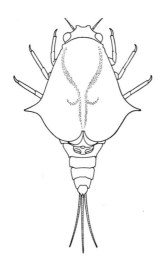

Nymph of *Baetisca*

Gills on abdominal segments 1–6 exposed.   2

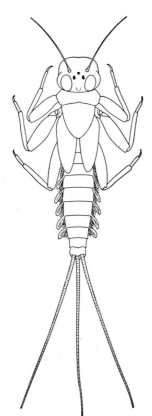

Nymph of *Heptagenia*

2 (1) Second abdominal segment bearing a pair of operculate or lidlike gills which cover gills on segments 3–6.   3

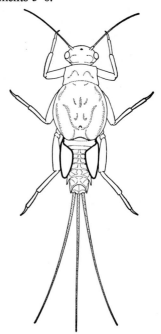

Nymph of *Tricorythodes*

      Second abdominal segment not bearing a pair of lidlike gills.   6

3 (2) Gills ventral.   *Behningiidae*

      Gills dorsal or lateral.   4

4 (3) Operculate gills fused on meson; a hooklike median spine at posterior margin on tergites 6–8.   *Neoephemeridae*

      Operculate gills not fused on meson; no median spine on abdominal tergites 6–8.   5

5 (4) First abdominal segment without gills.   *Tricorythidae*

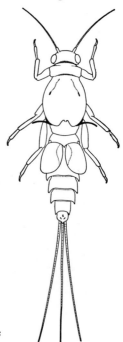

Nymph of *Caenis*

First abdominal segment bearing a pair of single, filamentous gills.   *Caenidae*

6 (2) Gills on first abdominal segment large and situated on the venter.   *Oligoneuriidae*

Gills on first abdominal segment dorsal, or first abdominal segment without gills.   7

7 (6) Gills always absent from second abdominal segment, sometimes from third, also.   *Ephemerellidae*

Gills present on abdominal segments 1–7.   8

8 (7) Tibia of hind leg shorter than hind tarsal claw; or claw at least six times as long as wide.   *Ametropidae*

Hind leg of *Siphloplecton*

Tibia of hind leg at least as long as hind tarsal claw; claws relatively thick.   9

Hing leg of *Leptophlebia*

9 (8) Each mandible with a projecting tusk.   10

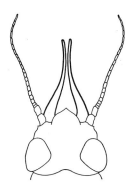

Head of *Hexagenia*

Mandibles without projecting tusks.   13

10 (9) Gills relatively broad with margins ciliate.   11

Gill of *Hexagenia*

Gills slender, filamentous, and bare.   *Leptophlebiidae*

Gill of *Leptophlebia*

11 (10) Gills lateral.   *Potamanthidae*

Gills dorsal.   12

12 (11) Head with a frontal process and mandibular tusks upcurved.   *Ephemeridae*

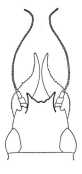

Head of *Pentagenia*

Head without a frontal process, or if with a frontal process, mandibular tusks downcurved.   *Polymitarcidae*

13 (9) Head flattened dorsoventrally; eyes dorsal.   *Heptageniidae*

Head not flattened dorsoventrally; eyes lateral.   14

14 (13) Cerci uniformly clothed with short setae.   *Leptophlebiidae*

Cerci bearing a dense row of setae only on the mesal margin of each.   *Baetidae*

SIPHLONURIDAE

The fishlike nymphs of this family are strong, fast swimmers and live in both lakes and streams. The nymphs of such genera as *Siphlonurus* are so agile that they cannot be picked up with forceps but must be netted. Gills are always platelike and may be single or double. Some of the nymphs in this family, such as those of *Isonychia*, are predacious, but most species are vegetarians like the vast majority of mayfly nymphs.

In adult males each compound eye is composed of an upper portion of large facets and a lower portion of smaller facets. In the fore wing of these mayflies cubital intercalary veins form a series of parallel, often sinuate but normally not branched, veins extending from vein Cu$_1$ to the anal margin of the wing. Many species have wings pigmented wholly or partly with brown, yellow or tan. There is never a developed median caudal filament.

In Michigan the Gray Drake is an artificial patterned after members of the genus *Siphlonurus;* the gray wings of its adult stage are tinted with purple and the body is sometimes russet in color. (The British Grey Drake belongs to a different mayfly genus.)

ADULTS

(Adult of *Acanthametropus* unknown)

1   Gill remnants present at base of rudimentary maxilla and at base of fore coxae. Isonychiinae. Twenty-five described North American species; transcontinental. *Isonychia*
Gill remnants absent. 2
Siphlonurinae

2 (1) Abdominal segments 5–9 with broad, flat, lateral expansions. A single described species; New York. *Siphlonisca*

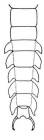

Abdomen of *Siphlonisca*

Abdominal segments without broad, lateral expansions. 3

3 (2) Hind wing with an acute costal angulation, and vein M forked near base. Thirty species recorded from areas across North America. *Ameletus*

M_1
M_2

Hind wing of *Ameletus*

Hind wing with a blunt, or with no, costal angulation, and vein M either not forked or forked well distad of the base. 4

4 (3) Vein M of hind wing simple. Four described species, three from Cordillera, one from Ontario. *Parameletus*

M

Hind wing of *Parameletus*

Vein M of hind wing forked. 5

M_1
M_2

Hind wing of *Siphlonurus*

5 (4) Fore leg of male at least as long as the body. Eighteen described North American species; transcontinental. *Siphlonurus*
Fore leg of male only two thirds as long as the body. A single described species; California. *Edmundsius*

MATURE NYMPHS

1   Each abdominal gill composed of a platelike dorsal element and a ventral fibrillar tuft. Isonychiinae. Twenty-five described North American species; transcontinental. *Isonychia*

Gill of *Isonychia*

Each abdominal gill platelike; usually single, but when double, both elements platelike. 2
Siphlonurinae

Gill of *Ameletus*

2 (1) A stout, median, ventral spine on meso- and metasternum. A single described species; New York. *Siphlonisca*
No median ventral spines on thorax. 3

3 (2) A conspicuous, transverse comb of spines present on margin of each maxilla. Thirty species described from areas across North America. *Ameletus*

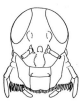

Head of *Ameletus* nymph

No comb of spines present on maxilla. 4

4 (3) Labial palp not forceps-like at apex. 5

Labial palp of *Parameletus*

Labial palp forceps-like at apex, the apical segment and an apposed, thumblike projection of penultimate palp segment forming a forceps. 6

5 (4) Labial palp three-segmented and pointed. Eighteen described North American species; transcontinental. *Siphlonurus*
Labial palp with second and third segments and the third segment is very wide and semitruncate. A single described species; California. *Edmundsius*

6 (4) Gills broad and single. Four described species, three from Cordillera, one from Ontario. *Parameletus*
Gills paired and deeply fissured. Acanthametropodinae. A single described species; Illinois. *Acanthametropus*

BAETIDAE

This is another large family of mayflies, the adults with simplified wing venation. The males have peculiar compound eyes: each is in two distinct parts, the upper stalked. Females have simple, relatively small eyes. Head shape is markedly different in the two sexes and this is true also in the nymphs. Some genera, such as *Cloeon*, lack hind wings.

Nymphs are streamlined, fishlike, the labrum with a square notch on the anterior margin of the meson.

Species are extremely difficult to identify, and in the female sex it is not possible always to place specimens even to genus. Baetids are often abundant at both lakes and streams and are likely important as food for game fish in many places. There appear to be multiple broods of some species as the emergence period extends over a period of many months.

British anglers have given vernacular names to several species of *Baetis*, calling them various kinds of Spinners and Duns.

ADULT MALES

(Adult of *Baetodes* unknown in North America)

1 Fore wing and hind wing with relatively numerous crossveins. Twenty-three described North American species; transcontinental. *Callibaetis*

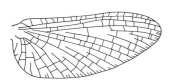

Fore wing of *Callibaetis*

Fore wing with relatively few crossveins. 2

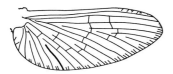

Fore wing of *Baetis*

2 (1) Hind wing present. 3
Hind wing absent. 4

3 (2) Marginal intercalary veins of fore wing single. Twenty-four described North American species; transcontinental. *Centroptilum*
Marginal intercalary veins of fore wing paired. Fifty-nine described North American species; transcontinental. *Baetis*

4 (2) Marginal intercalary veins of fore wing paired. Named genus with nineteen described North American species; transcontinental; two related genera from California with single species.
Pseudocloeon and related genera
Marginal intercalary veins of fore wing single. 5

5 (4) Second segment of male forceps with a prominent, angular projection on mesal margin. A single species described; southern Appalachia. *Neocloeon*

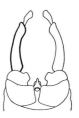

Male genitalia of *Neocloeon*

Second segment of male forceps simple, without a mesal projection. Eleven described species; Appalachia and Alberta. *Cloeon*

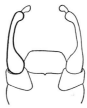

Male genitalia of *Cloeon*

MATURE NYMPHS

1 Gills only on abdominal segments 1–5. Primarily neotropical; one nymph record for Texas. *Baetodes*
Gills on abdominal segments 1–7. 2

2 (1) Gills single, platelike on all abdominal segments. 3

Gill of *Baetis*

Gills double on at least some abdominal segments, or each gill a thin, somewhat irregular sheet with a recurved flap. 8

Gill of *Callibaetis*

3 (2) Hind wing pad absent.   4
         Hind wing pad present.   7

4 (3) Maxillary palps with three segments. One species described; southern Appalachia.
Neocloeon
         Maxillary palps with two segments.   5

5 (4) Median caudal filament usually vestigial. Nineteen described species; transcontinental.
Pseudocloeon
         Median caudal filament usually well-developed.
                                           6

6 (5) Maxillary palp two-jointed. One species; California.
Paracloeodes
         Maxillary palp three-jointed. One species; California.
Apobaetis

7 (3) Median caudal filament well-developed. Twenty-four described North American species; transcontinental.
Centroptilum
         Median caudal filament reduced or vestigial. Fifty-nine described North American species; transcontinental.
Baetis

8 (2) Hind wing pad absent. Eleven described species; Appalachia and Alberta.   *Cloeon*
         Hind wing pad present.   9

9 (8) Maxillary palp with three segments. See above.
Centroptilum
         Maxillary palp with two segments. Twenty-three described North American species; transcontinental.   *Callibaetis*

OLIGONEURIDAE

This is a family of mayflies rarely reported from North American waters. The few specimens taken in Saskatchewan, Utah, Illinois, and Indiana are placed in two genera. Nymphs have the legs positioned in a peculiar manner that is probably an adaptation for securing a relatively firm position in the sandy stream beds where they have been taken: fore legs extended in front of the head, middle legs held straight rearward and hind legs extending laterally and anteriorly.

There is peculiar wing venation in this family. The subcosta has vanished as have all marginal veinlets. Some of the other long veins have disappeared and crossveins are scarce or even absent.

There appear to be no records of mayflies of this family being consumed by gamefish.

ADULTS

Few, if any, crossveins in the costal area; median caudal filament vestigial. Two described North American species; Saskatchewan and Utah.   *Lachlania*
Many crossveins in the costal area; median caudal filament well-developed. One described North American species; Indiana and Illinois.   *Homoeoneuria*

NYMPHS

Coxae of hind legs smaller than femora; size of ventral first gill the same as others.   *Lachlania*

Coxae of hind legs larger than femora; ventral first gill larger than the others.   *Homoeoneuria*

HEPTAGENIIDAE

This is a large family of mayflies of major importance in the diet of trout and other game fish. The adults are characterized by having intercalary veins in the fore wing and having a hind tarsus composed of five distinct segments. Nymphs of many species inhabit rapids and swift currents and are much flattened; all have three tails except *Epeorus* which has two. The nymphs of one genus are evidently predatory, judging from the morphology of the mouthparts. The gills of the nymphs of *Rhithrogena* are modified to form an adhesive disc on the underside of the abdomen for clinging to stones in torrential currents.

The genera *Heptagenia* and *Stenonema* include species of major importance in trout streams throughout North America. As nymphs the two genera are readily separated, but as adults they are difficult to distinguish, and specific differences are even more elusive. Only by painstaking care can the species be identified positively for any given region and then usually only after rearing nymphs to obtain an absolutely positive association with adults.

The Light Cahill fly pattern resembles certain species of *Stenonema* and *Heptagenia*, the Dark Cahill, others. The British March Brown is a species of *Rhithrogena*.

ADULT MALES

1   Hind tarsus with only four clearly differentiated segments. Pseudironinae. Two described species; central and southern United States and Manitoba.   *Pseudiron*
       Hind tarsus with five clearly differentiated segments.   2

2 (1) Fore tarsus not more than three fourths as long as fore tibia. Anepeorinae. Two described species; southeast, central, and western North America.   *Anepeorus*
         Fore tarsus longer than fore tibia.   3

3 (2) Vein R_{4+5} of hind wing unbranched. Arthropleinae. One described species; northeastern North America.   *Arthroplea*

Hind wing of **Arthroplea**

         Vein R_{4+5} of hind wing forked at or near center of wing.   4
                               Heptageniinae

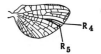

Hind wing of **Epeoris**

4 (3) First segment of fore tarsus as long as or longer than second. Twenty-four described North American species; transcontinental.   *Epeorus*
         First segment of fore tarsus shorter than second.
                                         5

5 (4) Stigmatic crossveins of fore wing anastomosed; penes a pair of relatively undifferentiated,

elongate or stubby lobes. Twenty-one described North American species: transcontinental.

Rhithrogena

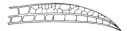

Upper area of fore wing of *Rhithrogena*

Stigmatic crossveins of fore wing not anastomosed, or only partly so, or anastomosed and forming two rows of cellules; penes lobes variously modified, with lateral or apical expansions. 6

Upper area of fore wing of *Cinygma*

6 (5) Penes lobes divided to base or fused on meson at base only. Eleven described North American species; Cordillera and northeastern North America. *Cinygmula*

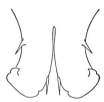

Male genitalia of *Cinygmula*

Penes lobes fused on meson for at least their basal halves. 7

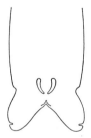

Male genitalia of *Cinygma*

7 (6) Stigmatic area of fore wing with an irregular, longitudinal line dividing the stigmatic crossveins into two rows of cellules. Three described Cordilleran species. *Cinygma*
Stigmatic area of fore wing not divided into two rows of cellules. Twenty-nine of former, thirty-four of latter genus; transcontinental.

Stenonema and *Heptagenia*

MATURE NYMPHS

1 Gills with a small fibrillar tuft near base on ventral side and a narrow whiplike appendage near center of posterior margin. Pseudironinae. Two

described species; central and southern United States and Manitoba. *Pseudiron*

Gill of *Pseudiron*

Gills without both fibrillar tuft and whiplike appendage. 2

2 (1) Second segment of maxillary palp extremely long, recurved over dorsum of thorax. Arthropleinae. One described species; northeastern North America. *Arthroplea*

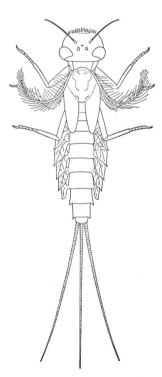

Nymph of *Arthroplea*

Second segment of maxillary palp not recurved over dorsum of thorax. 3

3 (2) Maxillae and mandibles fanglike; gills ventral. Anepeorinae. Two described species; southeast, central and western North America (only a single nymph known, however). ? *Anepeorus*
Maxillae and mandibles not fanglike, each mandible with a broad molar area; gills lateral. 4
Heptageniinae

4 (3) Median caudal filament absent. Twenty-four described North American species; transcontinental. *Epeorus*
Median caudal filament well-developed. 5

5 (4) Gills on seventh abdominal segment slender and semi-filamentous. Twenty-nine described North American species; transcontinental. *Stenonema*
Gills on seventh abdominal segment platelike. 6

6 (5) Front of head incised on meson to expose a portion of labrum when viewed dorsally. Eleven described species; Cordillera and northeastern North America. *Cinygmula*

Front of head not incised on meson, labrum not exposed when viewed dorsally. 7

7 (6) Gills of first and seventh pairs enlarged, converging beneath abdomen to form an adhesive disc. Twenty-one described North American species; transcontinental. *Rhithrogena*

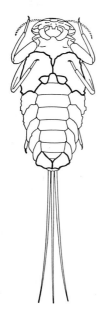

Nymph of *Rhithrogena*, underside

Gills of first and seventh pairs not converging beneath abdomen to form an adhesive disc. 8

8 (7) Each mandible with a heavily chitinized lobe on mesal margin, basad of molar area. Three described Cordilleran species. *Cinygma*

Mandible of *Cinygma*

Mandibles without a chitinized lobe basad of molar area. Thirty-four described North American species; transcontinental. *Heptagenia*

Mandible of *Heptagenia*

AMETROPODIDAE

Mayflies assigned to this family are rarely abundant in the adult stage. The genera appear not to be closely related though all are of the Heptageniid type in wing venation; they also show affinity to the Baetids.

In the adult there are only four distinct tarsal segments, the compound eyes are not divided, and there are two, or often four, cubital intercalaries. In both sexes the abdomen is long and slender.

Nymphs are agile swimmers, the body elongated and fishlike; they are often very common in streams and are no doubt an element in the diet of game fish.

ADULTS

1 Median caudal filament well-developed, almost as long as cerci. Ametropodinae. Two described species; Cordillera. *Ametropus*

Median caudal filament vestigial or represented by only a one- to four-segmented stub. 2
Metretopodinae

2 (1) One pair of cubital intercalary veins in each fore wing. One described species; British Columbia and Alberta, Michigan and New Brunswick. *Metretopus*

Two pairs of intercalary veins in each fore wing. Five described species; Appalachia. *Siphloplectron*

MATURE NYMPHS

1 Eyes directed anteriorly; each fore coxa with a large lobelike, median appendage. Ametropodinae. Two described species; Cordillera. *Ametropus*

Eyes directed laterally or dorsally. Metretopodinae. 2

2 (1) Maxillary palp two segmented. One described species; British Columbia, Alberta, Michigan, and New Brunswick. *Metretopus*

Maxillary palp three-segmented. Five described species; Appalachia. *Siphloplectron*

LEPTOPHLEBIIDAE

This is another sizable family of mayflies abundant in nearly all game fish streams. The compound eye of the adult male is composed of a large upper portion of relatively big facets and a lower portion with smaller facets. The compound eye of the female corresponds in size to the lower portion of the male eye. Adults have paired claws, one hooked and one lobed. Adults of North American species have two pairs of wings; the fore wing has two or four cubital intercalary veins.

Nymphs of this family are typically slender and somewhat flattened. Many live in ponds or lakes; others frequent slow current areas in streams.

Subimagos of *Paraleptophlebia* are called Blue-winged Duns by some American trout anglers. More descriptive terms, like Large Claret Spinner and Turkey Brown, are used by British fishermen for certain species of this family.

ADULTS

1   Hind wing without a costal angulation.   2

Hind wing of *Paraletophlebia*

Hind wing with a well-marked costal angulation.   3

Hind wing of *Habrophlebia*

2 (1) Fore wing with Cu$_1$ and Cu$_2$ closer together than Cu$_1$ and M in subbasal region where these veins are subparallel. Nine described North American species; Appalachia and Cordillera.   *Leptophlebia*

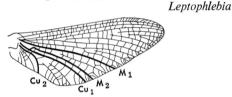

Fore wing of *Leptophlebia*

Fore wing with Cu$_1$ and Cu$_2$ separated in subbasal region by a space equal to that separating Cu$_1$ and M. Thirty-four described North American species; transcontinental.   *Paraleptophlebia*

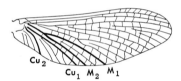

Fore wing of *Paraleptophlebia*

3 (1) Vein M of hind wing forked. Two described species; Texas and Arizona.   *Thraulodes*

Hind wing of *Thraulodes*

Vein M of hind wing simple.   4

4 (3) Vein Sc of hind wing extending nearly or quite to apex of wing. Two described species; Appalachia.   *Habrophlebia*

Hind wing of *Habrophlebia*

Vein Sc of hind wing ending near costal angulation.   5

5 (4) Costal angulation of hind wing small, rounded at apex. Nine described species; transcontinental.   *Choroterpes*

Hind wing of *Choroterpes*

Costal angulation of hind wing prominent, almost or quite acute at apex.   6

Hind wing of *Habrophlebiodes*

6 (5) Small, slender mayflies; male forceps base divided into two triangular lobes. Three described species; Appalachia and Oklahoma.   *Habrophlebiodes*
Medium sized and rather heavy bodied mayflies; male forceps base entire, not divided into two triangular lobes. Two described species; Texas, Utah, Alberta.   *Traverella*

MATURE NYMPHS

1   Gills of first abdominal segment similar in type to gills borne by more posterior segments.   2
Gills of first abdominal segment of a different type from gills borne by more posterior segments.   6

2 (1) Abdominal segments 2–9 with posterolateral spines. Two described species; Texas and Arizona.   *Thraulodes*
Abdominal segments 8 and 9 only bearing posterolateral spines.   3

3 (2) Each abdominal gill lamelliform, the margins of each finely dissected to form numerous, long filaments. Two described species; Texas, Utah, and Alberta.   *Traverella*
Each abdominal gill not lamelliform, the margins not finely dissected.   4

4 (3) Gills on abdominal segments 2–7 each consisting of two clusters of slender filaments borne on a single, narrow stalk. Two described species; Appalachia.   *Habrophlebia*

Gill of *Habrophlebia*

Gills on abdominal segments 2–7 bifid to bases, each part a very slender lamella.   5

Gill of *Paraleptophlebia*

5 (4) Apical margin of labrum only slightly indented on meson. Thirty-four described North American species; transcontinental. *Paraleptophlebia*

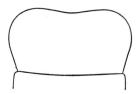

Labrum of *Paraleptophlebia*

Apical margin of labrum deeply indented on meson. Three described species; Appalachia and Oklahoma. *Habrophlebiodes*

Labrum of *Habrophlebiodes*

6 (1) Each gill of pair borne by first abdominal segment a single filament. Nine described species; transcontinental. *Choroterpes*
Each gill of pair borne by first abdominal segment bifid at apex. Nine described North American species; Appalachia and Cordillera.
Leptophlebia

EPHEMERELLIDAE

This family is represented abundantly in the northern and western parts of the United States and Canada probably because of the extensive areas of their preferred habitat, rapid and clear streams. Nymphs are easily collected, are abundant, and possess excellent specific characters; adults are scarce and not well differentiated among the many species. Adults are rather strong flyers and live at most only three or four days. They have big eyes and three tails.

Nymphs are somewhat flattened and are tough; sometimes they are spiny dorsally. Some western species have a ventral abdominal sucker-disc for holding, limpet-like, to rocks in very swift currents.

Members of this genus are very common in trout waters and occur in a variety of stream situations. A few kinds occur in lakes with stony beds. Over eighty North American species of *Ephemerella*, the only genus in the family, have been scientifically named. At emergence in streams, subimagos rise to the surface and then float for a distance before rising. Trout feed heavily on both this stage and on the nymphs.

The subimagos are called Blue-Winged Olive Duns by British and some American trout anglers. Beaverkill fly patterns also imitate certain species in this family.

TRICORYTHIDAE

These are predominantly tiny mayflies closely related to the family Caenidae. The fore wings have numerous crossveins, and the median intercalary vein extends only halfway to the wing base. As in the Caenidae each lateral ocellus is at least half the diameter of a compound eye in the male. The thorax is big, the abdomen small and contracted.

Nymphs inhabit streams and are very hairy with somewhat flattened bodies. The lateral margins of the abdominal segments are platelike.

Adults of *Tricorythodes* conduct the mating flight in early morning, and frequently this occurs late in the season. So many of these hatch at one time that despite their small size, they stimulate trout into feeding on them voraciously.

ADULTS

Fore wing broadest in the anal region. Ten described species; transcontinental. *Tricorythodes*
Fore wing broadest in the center. A single described species; Texas. *Leptohyphes*

MATURE NYMPHS

Operculate gills triangular. Ten described species; transcontinental. *Tricorythodes*
Operculate gills elongate oval. A single described species; Texas. *Leptohyphes*

CAENIDAE

Adults of this family have the median intercalary vein extending to the wing base and crossveins are scarce. Adults sometimes emerge in tremendous numbers. Like *Tricorythodes*, to which they are related, the members of this family of small mayflies emerge and swarm in early morning. Species of *Caenis* occur most commonly in ponds and lakes, but some species occur abundantly in streams.

Swarms of *Caenis* at favored fishing waters evidently inspired the accepted British name Angler's Curse for species in this genus.

ADULTS

Prosternum twice as broad as long. Five described species; Appalachia. *Brachycercus*
Prosternum at least twice as long as broad. Thirteen described North American species; transcontinental.
Caenis

MATURE NYMPHS

Head bearing occipital and frontal tubercles. Five described species; Appalachia. *Brachycercus*
Head without tubercles. Thirteen described North American species; transcontinental. *Caenis*

NEOEPHEMERIDAE

This is a small family of mayflies represented by two species in northeastern North America. The single genus shows affinity in the adult to the family Ephemeridae, in the nymph, to Caenidae. It seems doubtful that they enter into the diet of game fish to any significant degree.

BAETISCIDAE

The single North American genus in this family includes at least ten species which frequent streams at many places across the continent. Both adults and nymphs are very different from other mayflies. The adults have a very stout thorax with a mesonotum highly arched and all tarsi are five-jointed. The nymph has a large dorsal carapace which covers all of the thorax and the first five and a half abdominal segments. It covers the gills.

Gamefish may occasionally consume quantities of members of this family.

POTAMANTHIDAE

Placed by some authorities in the Ephemeridae, the genus *Potamanthus* is given family status by some recent mayfly investigators. The adults are fairly large, delicately pigmented on the body, and the marginal intercalary veins are not netlike. The nymphs are sprawlers with the gills extended laterally. The genus occurs in central and eastern North America, and eight species have been described.

At times *Potamanthus* is probably important in the diet of lake-inhabiting game fish.

BEHNINGIIDAE

This extremely rare family of mayflies was originally described from nymphs collected in the Volga River in Russia. Since then, two adults and more nymphs have been collected from near the mouth of the Amur River in Siberia, and a few nymphs have been taken in Poland and Roumania. Then a few years ago, mayfly specialists were excited to learn that five nymphs of the family had been taken from the Savannah River in South Carolina.

Members of this family are probably so rare in nature as to be of no significance in the diet of fish.

EPHEMERIDAE

These are big mayflies with burrowing nymphs, abundant in lakes and sluggish rivers over much of the continent east of the Rocky Mountains; they are less common westward. Many species are light in color with the wings tinted cream, yellow or brown and the body blotched in straw or yellow. Other species have a browner aspect with spots on the wings. The nymphs have heavy mandibular tusks, and in life the gills are curved up over the tergites.

These abundant, big mayflies are very important as fish food in much of the United States and Canada, in both lakes and streams. They frequently attract attention in some midwestern communities by falling in windrows beneath street lights. The nymphs of *Hexagenia limbata* are sold extensively as bait for winter ice fishing. The June hatch in the North Central States stimulates a feeding orgy by trout, big and small.

ADULTS

(1) Fore wing with crossveins at and posterior to bulla crowded and darkened to form a path extending half-way across wing. Seven described North American species; east of Rocky Mountains.
Ephemera
Fore wing with crossveins in region of bulla not arranged to form a path extending across wing.   2

2 (1) Median caudal filament reduced but relatively well developed, at least one-sixth as long as cercus. Two described species; central and southern United States   *Pentagenia*
Median caudal filament vestigial, reduced to only four to nine small, poorly developed segments. Six described North American species, and several subspecies; transcontinental.   *Hexagenia*

MATURE NYMPHS

1   Head with more or less dome-shaped anterior projection between bases of antennae. Six described North American species, and several subspecies; transcontinental.   *Hexagenia*

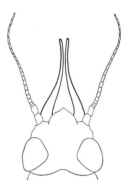

Head of *Hexagenia*

Head with a two-pronged anterior projection between bases of antennae.   2

Head of *Pentagenia*

2 (1) Mandibular tusk with dorsolateral angle smooth, rounded. Seven described North American species; east of Rocky Mountains.   *Ephemera*
Mandibular tusk with dorsolateral angle carinate and toothed. Two described species; central and southern United States.   *Pentagenia*

POLYMITARCIDAE

Species in this family are large, usually snow white, mayflies with many of the legs rudimentary. Like species in the previous two families mayflies in the family Polymitarcidae were earlier included in the one family Ephemeridae. Only seven species of Polymitarcidae, predominantly a neotropical group, occur north of the Mexican border. Nymphs are tusk-bearing burrowers.

These big mayflies are important food for game fish in the lakes and muddy streams where they occur.

ADULTS

1   Veins Sc and R_1 of fore wing curved posteriorly and continued around apical angle of wing, marginal veinlets absent.   2

Campsurinae

Veins Sc and R_1 of fore wing straight at apexes; marginal veinlets present. Polymitarcinae. Two described species; transcontinental in north, south to Maryland and Utah.   *Ephoron*

2 (1)   Middle and hind legs reduced to functionless vestiges, but parts distinguishable. Four described species; central and southern United States.

Tortopus

Middle and hind legs completely aborted beyond the trochanters. One species extending northward to Texas.   *Campsurus*

MATURE NYMPHS

1   Head with a frontal process. Polymitarcidae. Two described species; transcontinental in north, south to Maryland and Utah.   *Ephoron*

Head without a frontal process. Campsurinae.   2

2 (1)   A single prominent tooth on each mandibular tusk. Four described species; central and southern United States.   *Tortopus*

Several teeth on inner margin of each mandibular tusk. One species extending northward to Texas.

Campsurus
—S.G.J.

MAZATLÁN JACK *Caranx vinctus* This species is endemic to the eastern Pacific. It has been called striped jack (in reference to the persistent vertical markings on the body), but this name is not appropriate—because in the most usually accepted terminology, a vertical marking is a *bar* and a horizontal marking is a *stripe* (and oblique marking is termed either of these, or a *band*).

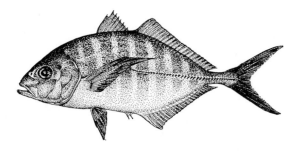

Mazatlán Jack

The Mazatlán jack has 8 dark bars on the body (rarely 7–9) plus one on the nape, which persist to the largest known sizes in live fish and preserved specimens. The second dorsal fin has 1 spine and 22–24 softrays; the anal fin has 2 detached spines followed by 1 spine and 19–21 softrays. Gillrakers on the first gill arch number 10–13 on the upper limb and 27–30 on the lower limb. The vent is about midway between the anal-fin spines and the insertion of the pelvic fins, and the tips of the pelvic fins extend past the position of the vent.

The body is only moderately deep but is thinner, more laterally compressed, than any other eastern Pacific jack crevalle. The dorsal and anal-fin lobes are short and not pronounced. The straight lateral line has about 44–52 pointed scutes, and is about 2–3 times as long as the curved part. The back is darkened, and most of the sides and the belly are light. All fins remain unpigmented. There is a small, elongated opercular spot.

This species has been reported from Manta and La Libertad, Ecuador, to Topolobampo, Mexico, and from Concepción Bay on the east coast of Baja California. The largest known specimen is 13½ inches long.

LIFE HISTORY

This is a relatively rare species and its life history is not known. An 11-inch specimen taken from Costa Rica in June had small eggs in the ovaries. The smallest known specimens, 1–1½ inches long, were taken from under the bell of a jellyfish.

ANGLING VALUE

This fish has little, if any, importance to sport or commercial fishing. Its palatability has not been described It is interesting because of its relative rarity and restricted distribution.

The Mazatlán jack could be superficially confused with a green jack (*Caranx caballus*) that still had the juvenile body bars, but they can be easily distinguished by the more posterior position of the vent in the green jack in which the vent is posterior to the tips of the pelvic fins and close to the anal fin spines. *See also* Carangidae, Jacks.
—F.H.B.

MEASUREMENTS OF FISH For various purposes fish may be measured in different ways. Of primary importance to the angler is the total length in determining the legality of his catch. However, the fishery biologist may use the fork length, while the ichthyologist may use the standard length in his research operations. In the *Field & Stream* Fishing Contest only the fork length is valid. For identification purposes the angler may also want to learn the depth of body, depth of head, and length of body.

Fork Length: Length of the fish from tip of snout with the mouth closed to tip of the shortest ray of the caudal fin. Or to the center of the fin if the tail is not forked.

Standard Length: Length of the body of a fish from the tip of the snout with the mouth closed to the end of the vertebral column (base of caudal fin).

Total Length: The over-all length of a fish, measured from the tip of the jaw with the mouth closed and extending to the tip of caudal fin. The caudal rays are sometimes squeezed together to give the greatest over-all measurement but this is of no scientific value.

Depth of Body: The greatest body depth measured at right angles to the long axis of the body; the number of times that the greatest depth is contained in the standard length.

Depth of Head: The depth of the head measured vertically from the occiput ("neck"); the number of times the depth of the head is contained in the length of the head.

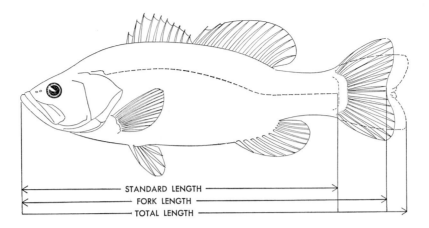

Measurements of the Fish

Length of the Head: Longest length of head measured from the tip of the snout to the end of the operculum; the number of times the length of the head is contained in the standard length. *See also* Anatomy —A.J.McC.

MEDITERRANEAN SPEARFISH *Tetrapturus belone* A marine species of small to moderate size for the family, evidently restricted to the Mediterranean Sea.

The Mediterranean spearfish is elongate and slender, with short pectoral fins, a crescent-shaped anal fin, and a long dorsal fin of medium height. The anterior part of the dorsal fin forms a sharp peak, while behind this the rest of the fin maintains a fairly even height about equal to or somewhat less than the depth of the body. The vent is located some distance in front of the anal fin, in contrast to marlins and sailfish. The snout is moderately longer than the lower jaw, but not as long as that of the longbill spearfish (*which see*) yet longer than the shortbill spearfish of the Pacific. The body is long and slim, the sides flat, the lateral line single and quite prominent. Color is dark metallic-blue, or sometimes greenish, above, fading through silver-gray to white or silvery on the ventral side. A few hours after death, the dorsal color fades to a dark, slaty blue-gray. The fins are all dark, and there are no spots or bars on the fins or body.

The Mediterranean spearfish runs somewhat heavier than the longbill spearfish, reaching a weight of over 100 pounds.

HABITS

This fish is not at all common, so very little is known of its life history. In the Mediterranean it spawns in late spring and summer. Presumably its food, like that of the shortbill spearfish, includes smaller fishes, squids, and so on. It is primarily a fish of the openwaters, occurring most commonly some distance off shore.

The Mediterranean spearfish is of some importance to commercial fishermen, especially around Sicily.

FISHING METHODS

Mediterranean spearfish are taken by trolling with rod and line, but the usual method is with deepdrifted hand-lines. —J.E.M.

MEEK, JONATHAN F. *See under* Bait-Casting (Development of Bait-Casting Reels)

MENHADEN *See* Atlantic Menhaden

MENOMINEE WHITEFISH *See* Round Whitefish

MERMAID'S PURSE A popular name for the horny egg capsule of the skate commonly found washed ashore on beaches throughout the world. Although the living capsule may be of various colors, it is usually turned black by the sun. It is also called "sea purse" and "sailor's purse." The capsules are 3–8 inches in length and contain one or more eggs. *See also* Barndoor Skate, Big Skate, California Skate, Clearnose Skate, Little Skate, Longnose Skate, Roundel Skate, Skates, Winter Skate

MEXICAN GOLDEN TROUT *Salmo chrystogaster* This trout was first described by Needham and Gard in 1959 and named in 1964. The name *chrystogaster* is derived from the Greek meaning "golden belly." A striking characteristic of this species when alive is the bright orange color below the jaw and on the belly. The Mexican golden trout has the smallest number of vertebrae and pyloric caeca found in any North American member of the genus *Salmo*.

The known range of *chrystogaster* comprises an area 35 by 45 miles in the Fuerte, Sinola, and Culiacán river systems in southwestern Chihuahua and northwestern Durango, Mexico.

Descriptive characters of the Needham and Gard holotype are number of vertebrae, 57; scales in lateral line, 108; scales above lateral line, 21; scales two rows above lateral line (lateral series), 147; scales below lateral line, 18; branchiostegal rays, 9 (both sides); gillrakers, 17; pyloric caeca, 19; pectoral rays, 14; dorsal rays, 10; pelvic rays, 9; anal rays, 10; caudal rays, 19. Basibranchials smooth. (Extract from *A New Trout from Central Mexico: Salmo chrystogaster, the Mexican Golden Trout* by Paul R. Needham and Richard Gard.)

MEXICAN SCAD *Decapterus hypodus* This very inadequately known eastern Pacific species has a detached and single-rayed finlet behind the dorsal and the anal fin. There are pointed scutes in the straight lateral line, but no scutes in the curved lateral line. The vertical edge of the shoulder girdle has a moderate-sized papillalike

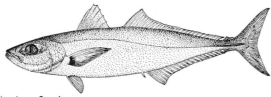

Mexican Scad

projection at its upper and its lower extremities, but no furrow below the lower projection.

The second dorsal fin has 1 spine, about 32–33 softrays, and the detached finlet. The anal fin has 2 detached spines followed by about 26–28 softrays and the detached finlet. The straight lateral line has about 34–41 pointed scutes. The first gill arch has about 38–40 gillrakers on the lower limb.

The Mexican scad is believed to range from the Galápagos Islands to Monterey Bay, California, and to grow to more than a foot in length.

LIFE HISTORY

Apparently there is little fishing intensity or use for this species, and the life history is unknown.

Three other species of the genus *Decapterus* have been reported from the eastern Pacific; but they have not been adequately studied or compared, and the relationships and the correct names that apply are currently uncertain. *See also* Carangidae, Scads   F.H.B.

MEXICO From its 2,000-mile border with the United States, Mexico extends south and east 1,800 miles to its boundary with Guatemala. Although locations such as Acapulco, Guaymas, Mazatlán, and Manzanillo are well-known to tourist fishermen, there are literally hundreds of remote villages along both coasts which are seldom visited by tourist anglers. Two areas, which are becoming of increasing importance, are the Yucatán Peninsula, which separates the Caribbean from the Gulf of Mexico, and the west-coast peninsula of Baja California. Saltwater fishing for striped marlin, Pacific sailfish, tarpon, snook, dolphin, roosterfish, yellowfin tuna, corvina, totuava, and many other game species is most popular. However, a limited amount of freshwater fishing also exists. Three-fourths of Mexico is mountainous, and nearly all of the central plateau lakes and streams have been stocked with rainbow trout or largemouth bass. Rainbow trout are indigenous to the country, but some rivers also contain a unique native species, the Mexican golden trout (*which see*).

Climate in Mexico is determined more or less by altitude rather than distance from the Equator. The *tierra caliente* or hot land is from sea level to about 3,000 feet; the *tierra templada* or temperate land is from 3,000–6,000 feet; the cold land or *tierra fria* is limited to mountain tops and plateaus of 6,000 feet or higher. Though modified to some extent by the nearness of the sea, these differences hold throughout Mexico. The rainy season begins in June and extends to October; however, except for the rare *chubasco* (hurricanelike storm), the rains are not equatorially violent nor continuous. Northerly blows during the winter months sometimes confine ships to port on both coasts, but these storms are normally of short duration.

Mexican charter craft are not usually as modern or well equipped as stateside fleets. Small to medium sportfishermen are the rule (24–32 feet); these are adequate for the normally flat to moderate seas encountered. There are comparatively few days when offshore fishing is scrubbed due to high winds. Although tackle is available on most charter boats, again it is only adequate, and the visitor is strongly advised to bring his own. Twenty-test class for small-game trolling including sailfish and 50- or 80-pound-test class for marlin and swordfish is standard here. Blacks of 500–1,000 pounds, while not abundant are always possible, particularly in southern Baja waters.

Trolling large flying fish baits (imported from California) and sometimes mullet baits is the principal method used for marlin. Blind strikes are obtained, but frequently the majority of the fish, including swordfish, will be sighted finning-out at the surface. The Mexican method is to rush the baits to billfish at full throttle, then let them settle in front of a visible quarry, or work the area in a trolling pattern.

BAJA CALIFORNIA

Baja California is a peninsula contiguous to the state of California but actually a part of Mexico. This peninsula forms the western boundary of the Gulf of California, often referred to as the Sea of Cortez, which supports an immense marine sport fishery. The average width of the sea between the peninsula and the Mexican mainland is a little less than 100 miles and its length approximately 750 miles. Except for the rainy season from July through September along the mainland, and the mountainous inland of the peninsula, the coastal region of the Sea of Cortez is arid. Due to the lack of graded roads on the Pacific Ocean side of Baja California, south of San Quintin Bay (190 miles below the United States border) this region is only sparsely settled. At various points, however, fishing facilities are developed and commonly serviced by air. However, since 1973 the entire length of Baja has become accessible by auto with the completion of the 1035-mile long Benito Juarez Trans-Peninsular Highway.

The sportfishing fleet at Cabo San Lucas. Excellent accommodations nearby make this area a top attraction

The Mulege area, which includes the copper port town of Santa Rosalia and the 25-mile-long Concepción Bay, is inhabited only at about a half-dozen ranches. There are no resorts except at the subtropical and picturesque towns of Mulege and Loreto. The area is noted for large black snook and an abundance of small gamefishes. The snook are taken on live mullet in the river and estuary from October through April; the others by casting from shore or trolling feathers and other lures. Most of the checklist of over one hundred species remain the year around. Included are the roosterfish, yellowtail, pompano, and several other jacks; giant jewfish, groupers, snappers, and sierra. The marlin, amberjack, and dolphin arrive about June 1st, sailfish and yellowfin tuna, a month later.

Loreto, the oldest town on the peninsula, has angling lodges and fleets. It is noted for roosterfish and giant grouper. Migrating big gamefish species and calendar are about the same as Mulege.

Juanaloa, including its 16 islands, is an area of 750 square miles with a population of no more than 30 people. It is unique in having waters that are very calm, an abundance of native and migrating fishes, and esthetic beauty, in comparison to the grotesque landscapes of the Midriff. It has two fine bays, Agua Verde and Escondido. There are no villages or populated places between Loreto and La Paz except at a salt works on San José Island and at some eight or nine ranches.

La Paz is the central port and city for the southern end of Baja California. It has first-rate hotels and large fleets of offshore cruisers. However, little of its native charm has been lost. Surf-casting in the bay for corvina, snook, and sierra exists the year around. Marlin and dolphin may arrive as early as April in warm years; sailfish, black marlin, and skipjack appear 4–6 weeks later. The jacks, including roosterfish, and the groupers, cabrillas, and snappers are always available. They are taken in the outer bay and around islands, as are several other species.

To reach La Paz, gateway to the southern resorts, you can fly from Mexico City or drive down a paved highway along the eastern coast of the Sea of Cortez (mainland Mexico) to Mazatlán and take the ferry across. Resembling a small cruise ship, this modern vessel transports 400 passengers and more than 100 autos, sailing twice a week on a 16-hour crossing. The quick way is by plane.

Between La Paz and Buena Vista, 70 miles south, there are no public resorts at present. However, there is a popular motel-type camp at Buena Vista, which has an airstrip and a good fleet of boats. Continuing south there are hotels at Palmilla, Puerta Chileno, San José del Cabo, and Cabo San Lucas. This latter strip contains Baja's most exotic angling resorts in the form of deluxe hotels in Spanish Colonial style with gardens and fountains to make shorebound hours rewarding. Each hotel has its own boats, and in this area toward "land's end" some of the best black and striped marlin fishing can be found. Swordfish are also numerous and are taken in fair number by deep fishing.

THE NORTH END

This area has a 131-mile paved road from Mexicali to San Felipe, and a passable one extending another 104 miles to San Luis Gonzaga Bay. The north end is fished principally for totuava (which see) and big corvina. A new area for fishermen has been opened by a graded 68-mile road from the border town of San Luis, which is 26 miles south of Yuma, Arizona.

The totuava and corvinas migrate up from the Midriff to spawn in the mouth of the Colorado River when the extreme tidal currents occur on each full and new moon between March 1 and June 15. The totuava is taken a few days after spawning, on foot-long live baits caught on the spot. Corvinas take shrimp, feathers, and other lures.

THE MIDRIFF SECTOR

This narrow waistline of the gulf with a belt of large islands is located astride the 29th parallel. Tides run the full length of the gulf in 5½ hours. Extreme high tides funnel large volumes of water into the narrow channels of the Midriff and surface currents develop a spread of 4 knots. There is some surface "boil" among the islands and off the points of land. Winds of hurricane force can occur in the summer and early fall. The prevailing northwesterlies may kick up a severe chop or dangerous larger waves in the afternoon; "knock-down" winds sometimes sweep into the gulf from the peninsula.

Small-boat enthusiasts are attracted to the Midriff not only by the fishing but for amateur exploring. They fit out at Hermosillo and launch at Kino Bay (reached by paved road from Hermosillo), and cross over to camp on Tiburon Island. The more adventurous go across (65 miles), island hopping, to uninhabited San Francisquito Bay. Still others cruise on down the Baja California coast to subtropical Mulege into Concepción Bay and past the town of Loreto, which contains the oldest church in the western hemisphere, in a wilderness region called "Juanaloa." Another popular trip is to La Paz and to Rancho Buena Vista, visiting the chain of islands along this course.

The best cruising and fishing season is from May through October. Marlin, sails, and tuna arrive about July 1 in this area.

The only resort on the Baja California side at the Midriff is at Los Angeles Bay, reached principally by private planes and a commercial flight from Tijuana. A few visitors arrive via a very rough road, and others by small boats.

On the mainland, there is a rough, camp-out-style lodge at New Kino, five miles above Kino Bay. It is reached by paved road and private planes.

THE MAINLAND COAST

Below Hermosillo, the next accessible sector is the Guaymas area. Included in it: San Carlos Bay, recently developed as an elaborate resort yacht, and small-craft harbor, hotels, cafes, and angling fleets; Miramar Beach with hotels, trailer camps, and a large fleet; the city of Guaymas, motels, and an angling fleet. Fishing for groupers, snappers, and corvinas continues the year around; yellowtail occur May through January 15; marlin, sailfish, dolphin, and numerous other species appear from June 15 through October.

Below Guaymas there are several places where rough roads lead from the main highway to the sea, but there are no shore accommodations short of the booming city of Los Mochis and at nearby Topolobampo—popular as

One of Mexico's famous gamefish is the roosterfish. This 72-pounder taken on light tackle is trophy size

a hunting and fishing area. Roosterfish, yellowtail, snappers, snook, and several jack species are abundant the year around; sailfish and marlin occur in the spring and fall months.

ISLANDS OF THE CORTEZ

The islands south of Guaymas, close up to the mainland, are mostly flat, delta formations detached by estuaries and lagoons which are bordered by thick mangrove bushes. These are good waters for three species of snook, many snappers, and a large number of other edible fishes. However, to most anglers, yachtsmen, and small boaters, it is the islands across the Midriff and down the inner coast of Baja California, as well as its broken shoreline, that are most interesting not only because of the great number of game species and massive schools, but for the adventure and exploration possibilities in this world of seafaring and camping. These islands are dead volcanoes or mountain tops which were isolated from the peninsula through an old geological faulting. Since the Seri Indians moved to the mainland from Tiburon, of the one hundred islands, only San José, Carmen and San Marcos are populated.

MAZATLÁN

The city is a well-known resort with a dozen deluxe hotels and major angling fleets. The angling here is principally for striped marlin and dolphin from October through April; sailfish and black marlin, from May through October. Snook are caught in river estuaries and lagoons south of Mazatlán. Amberjack, crevalle, yellowtail, and other tropical species occur here most of the year.

The general angling methods practiced at Mazatlán are substantially the same as used elsewhere in the Sea of Cortez. Billfish are taken by slow-trolling frozen mullet or California flyingfish or other foot-long baitfish caught on the spot. The black and blue marlins and large sharks show a preference for live surface fish (to 20 inches in length) caught in the same area. For these, an 80-pound-test outfit is recommended. For other billfish, medium tackle, in the 30–40-pound-test class, is suitable.

Other species are caught on light tackle on white feathers, white jigs, or large plugs, in that order. Roosterfish are taken on large, chrome or white spoons, red-and-white plugs, or rubber squid. Several species prefer a fresh skip bait, tobogganed on the surface. The giant basses—grouper, jewfish, and black seabass—prefer fresh-caught fish up to 10 pounds in weight.

ACAPULCO

Equally famous with jet-setters Acapulco is also one of the major sailfishing ports in Mexico during the winter and spring season (peak in April). Nearly all hotels can arrange for charter craft. Although not as numerous as they are on the Baja and Mazatlán grounds, both striped and black marlin occur here also, and rare specimens of the latter exceeding 600 pounds have been taken. Acapulco is located on an oval bay surrounded by mountains, and the scenery is fantastic. Hotels are numerous, ranging from super deluxe to modest. This location is a popular choice among anglers who want to combine fishing with a family vacation.

LAGUNAS DE TERMINOS

Although the Yucatán Peninsula is not developed to any degree for tourist sportsmen, there is a modern camp located directly on the Gulf of Mexico, 2½ miles east of the island of Carmen which is open from early December until late August. The fishing here is done in the Laguna de Terminos, a 35- by 50-mile shallow lagoon, which is fed by three major rivers and innumerable streams flowing from southern Mexico and Guatemala. The many mangrove islands, grass flats, and deep channels make this a remarkable area for the light-tackle angler. The principal gamefish are tarpon, snook, mangrove snapper, dog snapper, king mackerel, spotted seatrout, jewfish, ladyfish, grouper, red snapper, and jack crevalle. Beginning in early June, schools of permit frequent the flats also. Trolling and casting with plugs, spoons, flies, and jigs are generally productive.

The floating equipment of the Carmen camp consists of fifteen-foot skiffs with outboards which are designed for two anglers with guide. Fishing is customarily done from 6:00 A.M. to 6:00 P.M. with time out for a siesta from noon to 3:00 P.M. The lagoon is protected and the water is usually calm with one or two tidal changes per day. The climate is tropical (72–98°F.) with sunny weather the rule and showers of short duration.

COZUMEL

This 25-mile-long island lying off the coast of the Yucatan Peninsula is fast developing as a major east coast resort. The island has a great deal to offer by way of fishing, but the local building program can hardly keep abreast of the in-season tourist traffic. Since the discovery (1968) of giant bluefin tuna in deep water between the mainland and the island during April and

May, which adds a mighty plus to the marlin and sail-fishing available, the number and quality of charter craft and accommodations has increased. Beautiful beaches and crystal clear water can be found all around the island. The weather is hot and humid in the summer months so order air-conditioning in the off-season.

ISLA MUJERES

The "island of women" is reached by the extension of a jungle highway from Valladolid, east of Merida, or by charter plane from Merida. The last half of the bus trip to Puerto Juarez on the coast where you catch the ferry is rough. A low-lying, 4½-miles-long island, Mujeres is a get-away-from-it-all sanctuary (the village, population 1,000, consists of low stone and wooden houses behind unpainted plank fences and a Navy installation on top of the hill) which adventurous anglers might find interesting. There are minimal accommodations on the island. Mujeres is currently the jump-off point for Isla Contoy to the north, undeveloped and offering virgin fishing for tarpon, permit, bonefish, snook, large snappers, and groupers. Sailfish are abundant in the spring, with a peak in April. The only way to make this trip is by charter boat from Mujeres to Contoy, stocking ample provisions and ice.

BOCA PAILA

One of the more unique permit grounds recently made available to angling is at Boca Paila in the Quintana Roo. This east coast Mexican location, long known to a few pioneer anglers who used to make a rough 7-hour boat trip down from Cozumel, then tent on the beach, now features a landing strip and resorts which offer all the amenities of civilization. Although small (2–3 pounds) bonefish are fantastically abundant on these shores, the permit schools are so numerous that you can cast to 40 or 50 fish per morning. Light-tackle action for tarpon, snook, and numerous reef species, including big dog snapper, is top drawer. Boca Paila is best reached from Merida by charter aircraft.   —R.C.
                                                            —A.J.McC.

MICHIGAN Tourist literature and auto license plates proclaim it to be the "Water Wonderland." It is indeed fortunate in the vast amount and wide variety of water it possesses. Michigan is a part of the central lowland area of the United States, and is made up of two peninsulas. The Lower Peninsula is contiguous to Ohio and Indiana and projects between Lake Michigan on the west, and Lakes Erie, St. Clair, and Huron on the east to the Straits of Mackinac. The Upper Peninsula is contiguous to Wisconsin and projects eastward between Lake Superior on the north and Lakes Michigan and Huron on the south to the St. Mary's River on the east. Thus, the state has an extensive shoreline on the Great Lakes of approximately 3,100 miles which affords an enormous recreational angling opportunity.

This vast amount of water also modifies the climate markedly. It results in cooler weather in summer and warmer weather in winter. The effect is profound in a narrow belt near the lakes and diminishes farther inland. The rainfall ranges from 36 inches in the southern part of the state to 26 inches in the northern part, and it is quite evenly distributed through the season. Fortunately,

the soil and terrain are such that a high percentage of the rainfall flows into the ground to supply rivers and lakes with cool clearwater. Well over half the area of the state has forest cover which enhances the ground-water recharge. The major areas of farming land are in the southern half of the Lower Peninsula and on the eastern end of the Upper Peninsula. There are scattered agricultural districts in other sections of the state especially near the Great Lakes shoreline and in river lowlands. However, farmlands are not as porous, with the result that there is less water flowing into the soil and more direct runoff, thus increasing erosion and turbidity of the streams. Another result of the agricultural activity is a greater seasonal fluctuation in stream flow. All these factors influence fish habitat adversely from the angler's viewpoint.

FISHING IN THE GREAT LAKES

For nearly 25 years the quality of the Great Lakes as a fishing resource has declined. These huge bodies of fresh water (⅙th of all the fresh water in the world) became less and less productive and, finally, were virtual water wastelands. The decline began in the early 1930's with the opening of the Welland Canal. While this gave the Great Lakes shipping lanes access to the ocean, it also provided two very undesirable ocean inhabitants with access to the Great Lakes. First came the parasitic sea lamprey. This eel-like predator found a natural host in the lake trout and also ideal conditions for fast reproduction, since there were no natural predators of the lamprey in fresh water. The lamprey thrived, and, combined with overkills from commercial lake trout fishing interests, managed to deal a virtual death blow to a once-great fishery.

Immediately following the decimation of the lake trout came the invasion of another Atlantic migrant, the alewife. This shadlike forage fish proved to be so prolific in the absence of any predators that it multiplied to become 90 percent of all the Great Lakes' fish population by the middle 1950's.

The first faint glimmerings of hope for the Great Lakes fishery began with the development of a selective poison called lampricide. When applied to the spawning streams around the Great Lakes it proved effective in killing lamprey larvae in the early stages.

With the lamprey under some degree of control studies began at the Michigan Department of Conservation Fisheries Division to determine what large predator fish could be introduced into the Great Lakes to make use of the alewife food fish population and also provide good sport fishing. Leading the research group was Dr. Howard Tanner, then Chief of the Fisheries Division, and his assistant Dr. Wayne Tody. They were looking for something that would be "both fast and dramatic," and considered striped bass, steelhead, coho, and chinook salmon. After all factors were evaluated, the coho was selected because of its extremely fast growth pattern, predictable migration pattern, and the fact that it is easily harvested.

Dr. Tanner then obtained 1 million coho eggs from the State of Oregon Fish Commission. 850,000 survived the yearling stage in Michigan's hatcheries and in April of 1966 the first salmon smolts (5–6 inches long) were planted in two lower Michigan streams: Bear Creek and the Platte River. A planting was also made in one upper peninsula stream, the Big Huron River.

The first mature salmon returned to these rivers in the fall of 1967. After spending only 18 months in Lake Michigan, the fish had grown to average nearly 16 pounds; the world's largest fishery-stocking experiment had turned into its greatest success.

In subsequent years other states around the Great Lakes—Wisconsin, Minnesota, Illinois, Indiana, Ohio, Pennsylvania, and New York—all began salmon programs, and in a period of 5 years, the Great Lakes became one of the most productive sport fisheries in North America.

On a longer-term program the coho is not the complete answer, due to its short three-year life span. All Pacific salmon die after spawning, so hatchery and restocking programs must be continued at a high level. To partially overcome this Michigan accelerated its lake trout, steelhead, and chinook salmon-stocking programs. Both the lake trout and the steelhead have an 8–10-year life cycle, the chinook from 4–6. Some spectacular successes were achieved, particularly in the steelhead and lake trout populations.

The economic impact of this resource was considerable. Since it is basically a big-water trolling fishery, it was necessary for fishermen to upgrade their boats, motors, and tackle so that they were similar to light tackle offshore saltwater trolling. New methods and techniques were developed, the most notable being the use of recording fathometers to spot schools of fish and the use of an entirely new piece of equipment to facilitate what came to be called "depth-control fishing." This new technique developed because of the habit of the salmon of stratifying at specific water-temperature levels. Most salmon schools are found "suspended" at the 50°–55° F temperature range, regardless of how deep the water may be. It was therefore necessary to be able to troll at a specific and constant depth. An ingenious new piece of equipment called a downrigger was developed in order to do this. The downrigger is a rather simple mechanical device that utilizes a heavy weight (usually 7–10 pounds), either braided or solid wire line wound on a rather large wheel. The lure and leader are attached to the heavy weight through a breakaway coupling and lowered to the depth required (either by counting the turns of the wheel or by a metering system mounted on the wheel). When a fish hits the bait the breakaway releases and the fish can be landed on a "clean line" without any sinker weight at all. This unique system is also being used in saltwater, and has opened new horizons in ocean trolling.

Trolling has proven to be the most efficient method of taking salmon in this new fishery. Medium- to heavy-duty tackle is needed, particularly as the fish near maturity. Large capacity spinning or revolving spool reels with at least 200 yards of 20–30 pound line are popular. The lures used differ somewhat from those favored on the Pacific Coast in that bright colors predominate. The basic types are: trolling flies and dodgers, wobbling spoons, swimming plugs, spinners, and actionized flies. Lures that have a built-in action are usually trolled behind "cow-bell" type of flashing attractors that simulate a school of bait fish. Productive trolling depths depend on water temperature, and may vary all the way from the surface to water in excess of 100 feet deep, but

normally fall in the 30–70-foot range. The most productive trolling speed is usually 2–4 miles per hour—much slower than the 6–8 miles per hour used by most saltwater salmon trollers.

The season begins in early April when the ice moves out of lower Lake Michigan. As the water warms the schools move up both east and west coasts of the lake. The east (Michigan) side has a much larger group of fish, because Michigan stocks more salmon than all the other states combined. By late April the Chicago, Gary, and Michigan City areas are taking 2–3-pound fish regularly. In May the salmon have moved up to Benton Harbor, then to South Haven. The fish tend to stay between South Haven and Muskegon for about two months. During this time they grow to an average weight of 5–7 pounds. In July the main school moves north to the Pentwater-Ludington area, with individual fish weighing from 8–10 pounds. Mature salmon begin appearing at Manistee in August. By this time they weigh 12–15 pounds and the main school begins to scatter toward their parent streams. Some fish remain off Manistee, others off the ports of Arcadia, Frankfort, Platte Bay, Leland, Northport, Traverse City, Charlevoix, and Harbor Springs.

The season's peak comes in mid-September. Fully grown, the salmon weigh 15 pounds or more. Many fish top 25 pounds, and most experts agree that Lake Michigan will produce a new world-record coho. A 31-pound, 8-ounce coho was taken in Grand Traverse Bay in October of 1971. The chinook stocking program has not challenged the 90-pound world mark, but 4-year-old chinook have been taken that weigh over 40 pounds. October and November still offer some lake fishing, but the salmon start their migration upstream. They cease feeding and begin living off their own body fats about this time, and are not considered prime table fare.

The lake trout forms a more static population, particularly in the northern areas such as Grand Traverse Bay. Fish are taken from April through November, using techniques and equipment similar to the coho fleet, although the trout are usually found in deeper water. They follow a slightly lower temperature range of 48°–51° F, and it's not unusual to troll over 100 feet down to find them.

TROUT FISHING

Trout fishing is the most popular if not the most productive fishing in the state. Brook, brown, rainbow, and lake trout all provide angling in Michigan, with the rainbow trout being the most widely distributed. Many of the streams entering the Great Lakes in the northern half of the Lower Peninsula and the Upper Peninsula have rainbow runs which attract the early-spring and late-fall fisherman. Some rivers tributary to inland lakes in the northern part of the state also have good rainbow fishing. Rainbow trout runs and resident fish may be found in the Muskegon, Père Marquette, Manistee, Platte, Betsie, and Boardman rivers on the west side of the Lower Peninsula. The Au Gres, Au Sable, and Thunder Bay rivers on the east side of the Lower Peninsula are noted for rainbow-trout fishing. In the Upper Peninsula, the Huron, Two-hearted, Chocolay, Black (Mackinac County), and the Sturgeon (Delta County) are well-known rainbow streams. The Sturgeon and Pigeon rivers, tributary to Burt and Mullett lakes, also have good rainbow-trout runs. There are many smaller streams tributary to the Great Lakes which provide rainbow-trout fishing also.

Brown trout are found in nearly all the rivers mentioned for rainbows and inhabit several other streams as well. Outstanding brown-trout streams include the Père Marquette, Manistee, Au Sable, Sturgeon (Cheboygan and Otsego counties), and Pigeon (Cheboygan County). There are numerous smaller streams with good brown-trout fishing, among them, the Little Muskegon, Augusta Creek, and the Pine River (Alcona County).

The headwaters of many of these streams and the colder tributaries are inhabited by brook trout. The Two-hearted and Whitefish rivers of the Upper Peninsula are very good brook-trout rivers as are the Black (Cheboygan County) and Au Sable rivers of the Lower Peninsula.

AU SABLE RIVER

The Au Sable is the most famous trout stream in Michigan, and, like the Beaverkill River in New York, it has contributed a great deal to American angling literature as well as the development of fly-fishing. The Au Sable is located in the northeast section of the Lower Peninsula, rising in the highlands in the central part of the state and flowing generally eastward to Lake Huron.

Steelhead fishing in the lower Au Sable River is very productive in the fall season from Foote Dam downstream

It has in past years achieved an international reputation as a trout stream and has consequently attracted a large number of people. To those who like to fish in isolated places, perhaps this popularity may be deplored, but the Au Sable River, nevertheless, still provides excellent angling. As may be expected in streams which receive a good deal of traffic, the best fishing is almost always early in the morning, before numbers of people arrive on the scene, and late in the evening. During these periods, very fine fishing can be found with both the native brook trout in the headwaters and, in the lower reaches, the brown trout. Several dams have been placed across the Au Sable which modify the angling. The best period begins when the dams are opened late in the evening and the water begins to rise downstream. At this time brown trout come to the surface, and the large fish start feeding. There is also excellent angling to be had during the caddis hatch, which usually occurs in the second or third week of June. Although the insect which brings on this great rise is not a caddisfly, but rather a mayfly (*which see*) *Hexagenia limbata*, the quality of the sport brought on by this hatch is an event which resident and tourist anglers anticipate each year.

For those who are not dry-fly purists, the backwaters of the reservoirs also provide good fishing. This is frequently wet-fly or bait-fishing, but all of the impoundments have appreciable populations of large trout. The angler who plans to fish the Au Sable should familiarize himself with the special regulations in force on this river. There are sections reserved strictly for fly-fishing and sections where only fish of ten inches and longer may be kept.

The lower 12 miles of the Au Sable from Foote Dam to its mouth produces excellent steelhead fishing in the fall season.

WARMWATER FISHERIES

The larger rivers of the southern half of the Lower Peninsula are mostly warmwater streams and sustain some pollution. In the nonpolluted parts of these streams and in many of the reservoirs one may find northern pike and largemouth bass as well as panfish. These areas, being near the centers of population, receive heavy angling pressure. The fish are not as abundant or as numerous as in more northerly areas. At the point where these rivers enter the Great Lakes there is generally excellent fishing for white bass in the spring and early summer, and for yellow perch from early spring until fall. Locally these streams also provide moderately good angling for walleyes, smallmouth bass, and channel catfish. Rivers included in this group are the Lower Muskegon, Grand, St. Joseph, and Kalamazoo flowing into Lake Michigan; the Raisin and Huron tributary to Lake Erie; and the Cass, Shiawassee, and Titabawassee flowing into Saginaw Bay of Lake Huron.

Great Lakes fishing can be spectacular. Anyone aspiring to this kind of angling should establish contacts at the places of interest so they can be notified of the action when it develops. The connecting rivers, St. Mary's, St. Clair, and Detroit, have excellent walleye fishing in the early season. Later they also provide northern pike, smallmouth bass, and musky fishing.

Lake St. Clair is noted as a muskellunge lake, but it offers some walleye, perch, and bass fishing. Saginaw

Fall fishing for rainbow trout in the area north of Alpena on Lake Huron can be extremely productive. The fish feed extensively in the shallows and can be taken on small spinning lures or flies. Similar fishing occurs on the Lake Michigan side of the state

Bay is noted for largemouth bass, smallmouth bass, perch, and cyclically for pike and walleye. Potaganissing Bay and Munuscong Lake in the lower St. Mary's River have excellent walleye and smallmouth-bass fishing. Green Bay and its tributary bays, Big and Little Bay DeNoc, have excellent perch and smallmouth bass fishing and periodically northern pike and walleye are abundant. Grand Traverse Bay has excellent perch and smallmouth bass fishing. Lake Erie provides excellent white bass and yellow perch angling. Smelt are found in abundance near the mouths of tributary streams in lakes Huron, Michigan, and Superior. While the smelt are taken by dipnet rather than by angling, they nevertheless provide excellent sport.

There are times and places where schools of yellow perch of large size appear near shore and attract many people to excellent angling. However, contacts are necessary to inform the angler of the proper time and place. Nearly every year during the duck season of late October and November large schools of yellow perch, locally referred to as lake perch, suddenly appear about Les Cheneaux Islands near Cedarville in the Upper Peninsula. Similarly, big schools of large yellow perch appear in and about St. James Harbor and Beaver Island in May and June. Many of these perch are ¾–2 pounds.

Another fish which behaves much the same way but isn't much sought after is the cisco (*which see*). This fish comes inshore at times of emergence of the burrowing mayflies (May–June) and may be taken on dry flies in the evening. These fish are 10–12 inches and feed at the surface. With their tender mouths, skill is required to land them, but the spirited action warrants a trial.

Michigan is liberally supplied with smaller inland lakes. These lakes are quite generally distributed except in the eastern end of the Upper Peninsula and in the section of the Lower Peninsula lying east of a line from Midland to Flint to Port Huron, usually referred to as the Thumb Region. The great majority of these are warmwater lakes harboring bluegills, largemouth bass, pike, and black crappie. The bluegill is very abundant and readily caught thus supplying excellent angling to a host of anglers. These lakes are most abundant in the southern half of the Lower Peninsula near the centers of population. Consequently, they are heavily fished. While the heavy fishing results in fewer and smaller pike and largemouth bass, it appears to have little effect on the abundance or size of the bluegill, perch, and crappie. The number of bluegill lakes is large, and but a few can be mentioned. Gun Lake, Coldwater Lake, and Chemung Lake in southern Michigan are good bluegill lakes. Houghton Lake in northcentral Michigan is a well-known bluegill lake.

Not all inland lakes are primarily largemouth and bluegill lakes. The walleye provides good angling in Houghton, Hubbard, Burt, Mullett, and Black lakes in the Lower Peninsula; and Manistique, Indian, Michigamme, and Gogebic lakes in the Upper Peninsula. Similarly, several of the deeper lakes provide good lake-trout or rainbow-trout fishing. Among the better-known trout lakes are: Gull Lake near Kalamazoo, Crystal Lake near Frankfort, Higgins Lake near Roscommon, and Burt and Mullett lakes near Cheboygan. Lake Leelanau, Walloon Lake, and numerous smaller lakes also produce good trout fishing.

WINTER FISHING

Most Michigan inland lakes have ice cover for from 3–4 months. This ice cover may be a serious problem in places where it also accumulates snow in excess of 4–5 inches for weeks at a time. The combined ice and snow reflects or absorbs nearly all sunlight, thus resulting in a condition where the oxygen-producing algal cells have no source of energy (sunlight) and begin to use dissolved oxygen instead of producing it. After a few days the water becomes so low in dissolved oxygen that fish begin to suffocate. This is referred to as a winter-kill (*which see*). It may require several years for a lake to return to full production after one occurs.

Ice cover also provides easy access to fishing waters for many anglers, and winter fishing is a popular sport in Michigan. While the majority of anglers seek bluegills or perch, many fish for pike and walleyes with tip-ups. Others try to spear pike or sturgeon from the vantage point of a darkened shanty. Some anglers seek rainbow, brown, or lake trout in one of many lakes with an open winter season on trout. This list of lakes open for winter trout fishing changes from year to year, and each year one must obtain a list from the Michigan Conservation Department, Fish Division.

Such lakes as Gull Lake, Crystal Lake, and Torch Lake provide excellent sport catching smelt on hook and line. This is night fishing with small live bait such as corn borers or small minnows. The smelt are too small to put up a fight, but they make up in numbers what they lack in size and are of course excellent food fish. Catches of 25–75 in a 3-hour period are not uncommon.

Ice fishermen are found angling under a wide variety of comforts. Some have no shelter at all while others may have wind breaks of canvas or wood. Still others have shanties with gas or oil heat. All shanties left on the ice must be marked with the owner's name and address. At such popular fishing places as Houghton Lake or Crystal Lake near Frankfort one may rent a shanty for a nominal fee from nearby bait dealers.   —P.I.T.
—B.McC.

MIDCHANNEL BUOY A buoy placed in the middle of the channel to be passed on either side. In the United States it is painted black and white in vertical stripes.

MIDGES Order Diptera Tiny, mosquitolike aquatic insects of considerable importance as food for fish. These flies are also known as punkies, gnats, no-see-ums, and smuts. Although they do not bite, they tend to swarm around the angler's head and constitute a nuisance. Nevertheless, midges breed abundantly, and they are common to almost every trout water from lowland river to high-altitude lake. Periodically, salmonids consume vast quantities of midges, and the fly-fisher must be prepared to cope with the situation, as trout often show great selectivity at these times. The larvae and pupae are taken more readily than the adult midge.

From an angling standpoint the midge is most important on slowwater streams and in high mountain lakes, particularly in the Rocky Mountain region. Although large insect forms such as the mayfly or stonefly may be scarce or absent at or near timberline, midges are often plentiful and constitute a dominant food for trout. Due to the small size of the natural, the best copies are tied on No. 16–No. 20 hooks which requires a fine leader and line. So fishing the midge is ideally a light-tackle method.

The larvae, when mature, measure less than ¼ to about ⅜ inch in length. They may be green, black, brown, or most commonly red. (The blood worms or their dull-colored relatives burrow in the muck of river and lake beds and subsist largely on dead organic matter.) The pupal stage occurs when the larvae rise to the surface; pupae hang vertically in the water, head up and tail down, with their gills in the surface film. Both the head and the tail of the pupa have distinctive hairy appendages, as well as an enlarged thorax and folded but visible wings. Trout often take the larvae at the surface and always come to the top for drifting pupae; thus feeding signs are evident even in the subaquatic stages. The adult midge looks very similar to a mosquito, except that it holds its front legs in the air. So basically, you need imitations of two or preferably all three stages. The pattern is not often important, but the artificial must be the right size. The standard Grey Midge Pupa, Wetzel's Green Midge Pupa, and Harger's Black Midge pattern prove useful under most conditions.

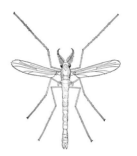

Midge Adult and Pupa

The midge is a significant trout food in both the cold- and hot-weather seasons. Rainbow and brook trout are especially partial to midge larvae. A midge hatch may occur in the dead of winter, particularly on days when the water temperature rises to about 40°F., or under the glare of a steamy August sun. Fished wet, the Black Midge makes an excellent pattern for opening day if the stream is running clear. On the Missouri River, and the Yellowstone of Montana, the midge is known as a "snow fly," and imitations are used for winter fishing. The popular sizes on this river are tied on No. 12, 14, and 16 hooks, but these are 5X Short Shank. The 5X hook takes a dressing comparable to a regular No. 16, 18, and 20—which is similar to the lowwater salmon fly in offering more gap to a sparse pattern.

WHEN TO USE THE MIDGE

The symptoms are easy to distinguish. Trout rise steadily all around you but will not take an ordinary dry fly. Frequently, they will hit the knots in a leader. Usually, the fish's back or tail breaks the surface, and you see its lacquered flank flash in the sun, while others poised on easy fins repeat the roll again and again. Mouths open and close, the water folds back in widening rings, and eventually the game becomes one of snipping off the last pattern and trying a new one. It's difficult to understand why trout, when taking midges, will not readily feed on larger insects which logically furnish more food. The fact remains, however, that selective periods often occur when caddis or mayflies are drifting athwart the current in perfect safety. The angler is invariably deceived by these decoys because the largest of the thousand classified genera of midges is less than ½ inch long.

HOW TO FISH THE ARTIFICIAL

There are two distinct ways of fishing a midge. If a dry pattern is called for, it is oiled and left floating on the surface. Let the fly sit quietly for some time before giving it a twitch. If this doesn't bring a strike, then retrieve the floater slowly with short pauses before picking it from the water. However, if the trout are feeding on the larvae and pupae of the midge you will have to fish below the surface. The idea here is to cast and let the fly sink, then make it behave like the larvae coming up from the bottom. It should be drawn slowly to the surface; then after a sufficient pause to let the midge sink again, you repeat the process. Sometimes trout will strike the instant your fly hits the water, and occasionally they will hit a midge drawn across the surface.

There are times, also, when trout will seek midge larvae along the bottom, and you'll have to fish very deep for them. This takes a nice sense of touch because the strike will be no more than a slight movement of the line. Using a sinking fly line, let the midge go down about 12–15 feet. Sometimes the strike comes when the fly is sinking, but usually it happens on the draw.

THE LEADER

It is seldom effective to present a midge on a leader tapered heavier than .006 inch. A thick point destroys the illusion of a natural and prevents the fly from moving freely with the current. If you have a delicate hand you can work safely with tippets from 5X nylon (.006 inch) to 7X (.004 inch). These sizes are suitable for No. 18 to No. 22 hooks. At first glance, you may think that such terminal tackle cannot hold large trout. This is a mistake because the tiny, fine-wire hooks will slip in the skin of the mouth and bite firmly. As a matter of fact you will often have difficulty removing the barb. There is also a trick to using 7X nylon safely; never make your leader with a short tippet section. Most anglers tend to believe that the less fine material they put in a leader the stronger it will be—whereas the opposite is true. You can feel the difference when unrolling a spool of say, 1-pound-test. If you take a few inches of the nylon between your fingers and pull, it snaps quite easily. Now roll off about 40 inches and pull (from both ends). The monofilament stretches, and it takes considerably more effort to break. You should always add at least 3 feet of tippet, and on a 12-foot leader do not hesitate to use between 40–50 inches of the 1-pound-test for maximum elasticity.

HOW TO STRIKE FISH

The real problem in using a fine leader is in striking the fish, and this requires a little practice. You don't really strike at all. Just tighten on the line, and keep a steady pressure with no wrist jerk. This is difficult, particularly for experienced anglers with whom an instantaneous strike at the taking of the fly is reflexive. The strike in midge fishing must be firm, but it must also be calculated between the fine tippet and the weight of the fish. Fortunately, midge fishing is almost always done in waters that are relatively still, where you can see the trout rise and

play it without the hazard of a wild current. Naturally, you will break off some fish no matter how carefully you work, but if the number of breaks becomes excessive then something is wrong with your tackle.

ADVANTAGE OF LIGHT TACKLE

The tools you use for midge fishing are important. You cannot work with a heavy line or a stiff rod because either one will snap a fine leader on the strike. The rod may be short or long, but it must be flexible. Some builders make extra-light wands specifically for delicate casting; one popular "midge" rod is 6 feet, 3 inches long and weighs 1¾ ounces complete. In a specialist sense these are the ideal dimensions for a very light fly rod. Your regular trout outfit might be perfectly suitable, however, and some idea of its ability can be judged by the line size used. The rod should not require a line heavier than a No. 5. Any larger size will offer too much water resistance for smooth striking with fine leaders. It will also prove a bit splashy for flatwater fishing. Midge fishing may appear as a long step from regular fly work, but it isn't. Casters who have the patience to polish their technique and make the conversion from heavy to light tackle will find greater pleasure in their days astream. You are bound to improve your percentage purely on the numbers of fish struck. If for no other reason than this, you will find the miniature fly worth your while.   —A.J.McC.

MILAM, BENJAMIN C. *See under* Bait-Casting (Development of Bait-Casting Reels)

MILKFISH *Chanos chanos* It is a herringlike fish, belonging to the family Chanidae, which resembles the ladyfish and shad (*which see*) in its streamlined, pointed, and compressed body, single dorsal fin, and deeply forked tail. An adipose (fatty) eyelid is present, and the toothless mouth is small and situated at the end of the head. The gillrakers are long and fine. When alive, it is bright silvery with blue or bluish-olive hues on the back and yellowish-olive on the head. The side of the head reflects pink and gold, and the sides have golden reflections. The dorsal, pelvic, and anal fins are yellow, and the caudal fin is gray to pale with a black margin. Also known as bangos, this is a large herringlike fish, growing to nearly 5 feet long and a weight approaching 50 pounds.

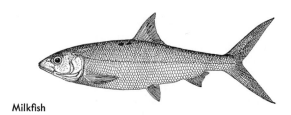

Milkfish

LIFE HISTORY

Milkfish occur from the Red Sea and East Africa along the coastal regions of the northern Indian Ocean eastward to southern Japan, the Philippines and Oceania, northern Australia, and northern New Zealand, to the Hawaiian Islands, central California, and the coast of Mexico. Adults occur most commonly in coastal waters around areas fertilized by estuarine runoff and consequent phytoplankton production. In Indonesian waters, milkfish are thought to spawn inshore in waters of 20–30 fathoms.

Spawning apparently occurs in clearwater, away from influence of estuaries. The eggs float at the surface, and are encountered up to about 20 miles from shore, from March to August in Indian waters. The larvae are elongate, ribbonlike, and transparent, closely resembling typical herringlike larvae. They enter inshore waters, including bays, creeks, and swamps, about ten days after hatching from the eggs offshore, and evidently prefer waters with some stream flow.

Larvae have been taken in coastal waters from Formosa to India and in various parts of the Philippines. Juveniles have been taken from Hawaii, Fiji, Formosa, the Philippines, Sumatra, Borneo, Vietnam, and southern India. The young enter clearwater streams but ascend turbid streams only a short distance. Adults remain in coastal waters at least part of the year. Milkfish are governed in their distribution by temperature, and become sluggish or die at low temperatures.

Sexual maturity occurs at a length of 3 feet in the female. Age estimation has been attempted using otoliths, but results are inconclusive except that pond-raised fish grow more slowly than fish from the open sea.

Larvae feed on plankton, largely diatoms. Adults also feed on bottom diatoms, grazing over the upper surface of the bottom, where they also sift off protozoans, small clams, and snails. Copepods and mysid shrimp are also eaten.

FOOD VALUE

The milkfish is a very important species throughout the Indo-Pacific region, where it is used extensively for food. The adults are taken from coastal waters in seines and in stake traps. The biggest fisheries are those for the fry, which are taken by scoopnets, and the adults which are raised in ponds from young to market size. These are caught with gillnets, seines, and castnets. Extensive pond management has reached a high degree of sophistication throughout the Indo-Pacific. Estuarine waters, including rivers, bayous, ponds, creeks, and tidal sloughs, are diked off to form ponds, and, wherever possible, ponds are built where the water level can be controlled. The fry are captured from coastal waters, selected, and transported to the ponds where they are raised to fingerlings and the fingerlings to adults, all phases of this work re-quiring extreme skill. Algal growth for food of the fish is promoted by periodic freshening of the water. —D.DS.

MILKYMOUTH CREVALLE *Uraspis secunda* The tongue and central portions of the mouth are a milkywhite, surrounded by dark violet on the sides of the mouth. There are more gillrakers on the medial side of the fourth gill arch than on the lateral side of the first gill arch. In specimens up to about 8–10 inches in length, most of the points of the scutes in the straight lateral line are turned outward and forward. There is a scaleless area on the chest and lower sides in front of the pelvic fins (similar to that of the crevalle, *Caranx hippos*, but lacking the small, central patch of scales that distinguishes the crevalle).

The second dorsal fin has one spine and 27–30 softrays. The anal fin has two detached spines (which become covered by skin in medium-sized fish), followed by one spine and 21–22 softrays. The first gill arch has 5–7 gillrakers on the upper limb and 14–16 gillrakers on the lower limb. There are about 32–38 scutes in the straight lateral line. Specimens under about ten inches in length have seven dark bars on the sides; the posterior bars continue onto the dorsal and anal fins.

This is a very unusual and rare species, and is found primarily in offshore waters and around oceanic islands in tropical and subtropical waters around the world. Less than two hundred specimens are known to have been taken. In the western Atlantic it is known from Brazil, Puerto Rico, and Cuba, in the Gulf of Mexico, and from off Florida, North Carolina, New Jersey, and Massachusetts. In the eastern Pacific it has been taken only at Revillagigedo Islands.

The closely related cottonmouth jack, *Uraspis helvola*, has not been taken in the western Atlantic, and is known in the eastern Pacific only from the Revillagigedo Islands.

These white-tongue jacks have been classified under a variety of scientific names. Both have been listed by the generic name *Leucoglossa*, and *Uraspis secunda* has usually been referred to as *Uraspis heidi*.

ANGLING VALUE

Any of these fish that are caught should be deposited in an ichthyological museum. One specimen was kept alive in the aquarium at Woods Hole for several months. *See also* Carangidae, Jacks. —F.H.B.

Milkymouth Crevalle

MINKFISH *See* Whitings

MINNESOTA   Minnesota is a large state, larger than any state east of the Mississippi River. It is a rolling land of varied scenery, and its more than 10,000 lakes of "sky-blue" water have much to offer to fishermen. A small portion of it, the Northwest Angle, is surrounded on three sides by Canada. From a drainage standpoint, it is the roof peak of eastern North America. Minnesota streams flow south to the Gulf of Mexico, east to the Atlantic Ocean, and north to Hudson's Bay. Minnesota lies at a crossroads of vegetation types, hence its varied scenery. The north and especially northeast are covered with coniferous forests of pines, spruce, and fir. Here summers are pleasantly cool. This is deer and partridge country. Central and southeastern Minnesota lie in the hardwood forest belt of maples, oaks, basswood, and elms. The west and southwest, once prairies on which roamed buffalo, elk, and antelope, are now mostly farm-land. This is the corn and pheasant country.

In Minnesota about 1,500,000 people fish; about half of the adult residents purchase a fishing license. In addition about 300,000 out-of-state anglers visit Minnesota each year. There is adequate fishing water for all, nearly two million acres, not counting over a million more which are Minnesota's portion of Lake Superior. At least 2,000 lakes are large, really first-class angling lakes, and thousands of others provide some fish. There are also about 15,000 miles of streams, ranging in size from the wide and scenic Mississippi to the tiny, cold trout streams of the wilderness along the north shore of Lake Superior. From all these waters anglers take each year about 50,000,000 fish, with an aggregate total weight of nearly 25,000,000 pounds.

Fishing is important in Minnesota, and the angler can find comfortable family resorts, with tackle, boats, and guides available at almost any large lake. For campers and trailer travelers there is a fine system of state parks, the best-known of which is Itasca State Park, at the head-waters of the Mississippi in the heart of an excellent fishing area. Both national and state forests, which cover about 25 per cent of the state, have many improved camp grounds. For the fisherman who brings his own boat there are public-access sites on many of the more important lakes and streams.

THE WALLEYE LAKES

The walleye is the most sought-after species of Minnesota fishes. To help satisfy the demand, Minnesota operates a large propagation and stocking program, and about half the acreage of the inland waters is managed primarily for walleye. The best lakes are over 1,000 acres in area and fairly shallow, not more than 40 feet deep. Such habitats are broad expanses of water which the waves keep evenly mixed from top to bottom throughout the summer. Here walleye can feed over the entire lake bottom. There is no thermal stratification (*which see*). Some of the better fisheries are at Mille Lacs in central Minnesota; Leech, Cass, and Winnebigoshish in the Mississippi headwaters region near Walker and Grand Rapids; and Lake of the Woods, Kabetogama, and Rainy along the Canadian border near International Falls. There are also the Red lakes, Upper and Lower, which together constitute the largest body of water within Minnesota. At Washkish, on the tributary Tamerac River, there is spectacular walleye fishing each spring. Other choice spots include Shetek Lake in the southwest, Minnewaska Lake near Glenwood, and some bays of Lake Minnetonka and Spring Lake close to the city of Minneapolis. Perhaps a classic example of these vast, shallow, yet productive fisheries is Lake Traverse located on the Minnesota and South Dakota border. Lake Traverse has a surface area of approximately 11,000 acres. It has a maximum depth of only 16 feet, and the average is close to 10 feet. However, the water has a high mineral content and is very fertile. The principal game-fish are walleye, northern pike, crappies, and bullheads. Lake Traverse supports a considerable winter fishery, and as many as five hundred shanties appear on the ice.

Fishing for walleyes is usually best in the early morning and evening, but some fishing for them is done at night. They are commonly caught on minnows. Since they are sought in big waters, a sturdy boat is essential, and many resorts provide launches for their guests. Walleye may also be found in rivers, especially in the lower Mississippi and in Lake Pepin, which is really a widening of the river. However, in rivers the sauger (*which see*), also called sand pike, is more likely to be caught. The Minnesota record for walleye taken by hook and line is 16½ pounds.

BASS AND PANFISH LAKES

Most of the smaller lakes, especially those of less than 500 acres, and the bays of larger lakes, are bass, panfish, and northern-pike waters. The common panfishes are the black crappie, white crappie, bluegill, and pumpkinseed sunfish. In terms of numbers taken, bluegills rank first in the Minnesota catch and crappies second, but the crappies are usually larger. Black crappies weighing 5 pounds and bluegills of over 2 pounds have been caught, although the average is smaller. The black crappie is dominant in northern Minnesota, while white crappies are common to the south. Bluegills and pumpkinseed are found in the lakes with weedy shores, especially over a muck bottom. These sunfish are the favorite of cane-pole fishermen, but the man with a fly rod and poppers or dry flies will find that bluegill fishing is real sport.

In Minnesota lakes largemouth bass are more common than smallmouth; nearly all lakes with weedy shorelines hold largemouth. Smallmouth fishing is most productive in large streams such as the St. Croix River along the Wisconsin boundary and in the Mississippi between Minneapolis and Brainerd. Certain lakes also supply considerable fishing for smallmouth bass such as Rainy, Brule, Saganaga, Greenwood, and Little Vermilion. One of the best is Basswood Lake near Ely. Casting with fly rod poppers and spinning lures in the month of July provides excellent sport. The bass are not large but abundant and extremely active in this rock-rimmed lake. Farther west, near Alexandria, there are other smallmouth lakes, such as Miltona and Ida.

PIKE AND MUSKELLUNGE LAKES

Nearly every lake in Minnesota, except the laketrout waters of the northeast, contain northern pike. They may weigh up to 40 pounds but will average less than 5 pounds. Pike are taken on spoons and plugs and are often fished by slow-speed motor trolling, which is legal here—or by baitcasting. In terms of total weight of fish taken, the northern pike ranks first in the Minnesota angling catch. Pike occur in most of the lakes and rivers, Ball Club Lake and Winnibigoshish Lake near Bena being especially productive. Numerous walleye lakes also supply about as many northerns as walleyes, and some also yield muskies. The muskellunge, however, has a more limited distribution than the northern pike. The best natural muskellunge waters are those in the Mississippi headwaters area, in lakes such as Cass, Leech, and Winnibigoshish. Leech Lake is the most famous of all, and astonishing catches have been made here during summer flurries. There are smaller muskellunge lakes farther west, in the Park Rapids area, among them Bottle and Bad Axe lakes. Muskies are also taken from the Mississippi in central Minnesota, especially between St. Cloud and Brainerd. Other lakes with muskies are Moose and Spider in the northeast, near Grand Rapids, and Lake of the Woods on the border. The latter also provides fine walleye fishing.

TROUT LAKES

For the trout fisherman who likes lake fishing there are many good locations in the northeastern border country. These lakes are large, cold, and often rock-rimmed. However, deep fishing is necessary during the summer. Most of the trout lakes are best approached from Duluth, Two Harbors, or Grand Marais, all on the north shore of Lake Superior. Some of the better lake-trout waters are Mountain, Clearwater, Seagull, West Pike, Snowbank, and Gunflint. In addition lake trout may be caught in Lake Superior by deep trolling. Those who prefer brook- or rainbow-trout fishing in smaller but often very scenic waters should try the reclaimed lakes of which there are about one hundred in northern Minnesota. Many of these supply excellent fishing, especially in early summer. Grindstone Lake near Pine City in eastern Minnesota is a fine lake with good rainbow-trout fishing. A list of the reclaimed trout lakes, with their locations, is available from the Minnesota Department of Conservation.

TROUT STREAMS

In Minnesota there are about 2,000 miles of coldwater streams which support trout. Perhaps the most scenic are those along the north shore. Here the catch is largely of native rainbow and brook trout. In the spring season there is a run of large steelheads from Lake Superior into the lower portions of these streams. Here, between the high falls and the lake, these fish may be taken during a special early fishing season. Small runs of silver salmon have also appeared in some of these streams in recent years.

In southeastern Minnesota there is considerable trout fishing in the streams that flow through the rugged valleys of the Root and Whitewater rivers. These waters are heavily stocked with rainbow and brown trout, and most of the catch here is of hatchery-reared fish. Other trout streams are scattered through Minnesota. The most famous is near Itasca State Park: Straight River at Park Rapids.

CANOE COUNTRY

The fisherman visiting Minnesota should not overlook the wilderness canoe country of northeastern Minnesota and adjoining Canada. This Quetico-Superior area of primitive forest has hundreds of lakes, connected by streams and canoe portages. There is fishing in all of them. This is primarily walleye lake-trout, and northern-pike country, but other kinds of fish are also taken. There are many camp sites in the area, and complete trips with guide and supplies can be arranged for at outfitters at Ely or Winton. If you want to get away from it all, this is the place.

CANE-POLE WATERS

If you are not inclined toward the adventurous life, there are many relaxing cane-pole waters in Minnesota. Bullhead fishermen, and they are legion, find fishing especially good in southern Minnesota, in the lakes around Waterville, Mankato, and Faribault. Here bullheads are big, fat, and easily caught. For variety there are also crappies and bluegills in many of these same lakes. Those who prefer the north in summer might try catfish fishing in the St. Louis River or on lakes tributary to it on the Mesabi Iron Range. On the Mississippi, the waters below any dam provide good fishing, and the backwaters and bayous between Hastings and the Iowa line are hard to beat for the cane poler. In these waters there are many kinds of fish, and while every bite may not be a prize, it may well be a surprise. And on some of the backwaters it is not hard to imagine that you are way away from everything—except the fish.

WINTER FISHING

It is cold in Minnesota in the winter, but this does not deter fishermen. About a quarter of the total fishing effort is by hardy souls who fish through the ice. Fish houses, usually kept warm with an oil heater, are a common sight on Minnesota lakes in winter. Some, such as Lake Minnewaska at Glenwood, have veritable villages of fish houses, even with street names and a mayor. Fish houses may be rented from many resorts. Most of the winter angling catch is of crappies and bluegills. Crappies are taken with minnows and bluegills with goldenrod grubs or mayfly nymphs. Spearing of northern pike from a dark house in winter is also permitted, but by Minnesota residents only.

SMELT FISHING

Smelting is a popular sport along the north shore of Lake Superior in late April and early May. The smelt are seined or caught in dipnets as they appear in countless numbers to spawn. The water is cold, but the fishermen can always warm themselves around a blazing wood fire on the beach.
　　　　　　　　　　　　　　　　　　　　—J.B.M.

MINNOW PROPAGATION The propagation of baitfish for pleasure or profit. *See* Fish Culture

MINNOWS The word *minnow* has its root in the ancient Anglo-Saxon *myne*, meaning small. While this generally describes the family Cyprinidae, there are notable exceptions. Some species such as the carp, squawfish, and mahseer attain lengths of 3–5 feet, and the latter may reach weights of over 100 pounds. Except in South America, Australia, and New Zealand, cyprinids are endemic to all other continents, with an estimated 2,000 species on a world basis, most of which are found in Asia and South Africa. Approximately 200 are known in North America. But here the collective term "minnows" not only includes the various true genera—such as shiners, dace, and chubs—but even unrelated families—such as the silversides, killifishes, darters, and sculpins.

The role of the minnows in the scheme of aquatic life is manifold. They compete with larger fishes for space and food. Fish-eating birds—such as the ospreys, gulls, herons, and kingfishes—depend largely on minnows for their existence. Minnows feed on unwanted aquatic plants, as well as mosquito larva and other obnoxious pests. Because of their widespread distribution and their occurrence in every conceivable ecological niche, minnows are a tremendously important source of food for gamefish. As a staple item of diet the minnow has no counterpart. However, populations of baitfish can be seriously depleted not only through their vulnerability to capture by all predators, including man, but in fluctuating water levels and other natural phenomena which adversely affect their habitat. Thus, many states prohibit the taking of minnows from waters inhabited by gamefish—and minnow farms have become a big business in the United States. The gross dollar volume for the sale of baitfish exceeds $2 million annually in the larger fishing states. The dealer selects his stock on the basis of how readily it thrives in ponds, its growth rate, and its ability to stand rough handling and transportation. As a result only a few commercially feasible species—such as the golden shiner, fathead minnow (or "Missouri" minnow in the South), and the bluntnose minnow—are familiar to anglers who fish with live bait. To the fly tier, however, the almost infinite variety of wild minnows is a painstaking challenge.

Most minnows are difficult for the angler to identify, as many species are superficially alike. Physical characteristics for distinguishing the various minnows such as the number of fin rays and scale counts may overlap. The type and number of pharyngeal teeth are also used diagnostically; however, the minnow must be killed and dissected to determine these. Even then it may be impossible for anyone but a trained ichthyologist to separate similar-appearing species.

MIRROR CARP *See* Carp

MISSISSIPPI Most of the state of Mississippi is fairly level; actually there is only 800 feet of gradient between the highest point in the northeast of the state and sea level. From the sandy hills and pine woods to the bayous of the south, resident anglers need only travel a few miles from any point to find good fishing. The waters range in size from four large flood-control reservoirs located in northcentral Mississippi and the Pearl River Reservoir, near Jackson, to the old oxbow lakes found in the delta section and in the southeastern part of the state along the Pascagoula River and its tributaries. Then, there is a portion of the TVA chain in the northeast, as well as numerous streams and small artificial lakes scattered throughout the state that afford many hours of fruitful fishing. In sections, principally along the eastern boundary and the southcentral part of the state where fishing waters are limited, the Game and Fish Commission has a lake-building program underway to expand existing facilities.

DELTA LAKES REGION

In the four flood-control reservoirs, located in the northcentral part of the state, there is good bass fishing; however, among local anglers the most popular species is the crappie. Grenada Reservoir attracts more bream fishermen than the other three impoundments. Sardis, Enid, and Arkabutla Reservoir, however, produce excellent bluegill fishing. In the northeastern part of the state, Pickwick Reservoir furnishes varied fishing. Crappie, largemouth bass, smallmouth bass, white bass, sauger, and catfish are found here in abundance. In the northern part of the delta, one finds excellent crappie fishing in lakes such as Tunica Cut-Off and Moon Lake. Bluegill fishermen should not overlook the possibilities in these oxbow lakes, for the willow- and cypress-lined shores produce excellent sport.

In the lower part of the delta fishing is more varied. Here the panfisherman has his favorite lakes, such as Eagle and Mossy. Other lakes also produce excellent bluegill, redear, and crappie. The bass fisherman, whether he uses live or artificial bait, can find largemouths in a receptive mood in most any of the lakes of the Mississippi Delta region.

CENTRAL REGION

In the central part of the state the fishing is somewhat limited to small, man-made lakes, but these produce bass and bluegills in large numbers. In this section, too, there are small streams that furnish excellent fishing for the man who likes to wade and use a fly rod, or for the cane-pole fisherman using worms or minnows. Two of these streams are Strong River and Limestone Creek. There are also some larger streams, such as the Pearl, Bowie, and Chunky rivers, which provide excellent float-fishing (*which see*) at certain times of the year.

SOUTHERN REGION

In the southwest, lakes Rodney, Yucatan, and Mary are the favorites of local anglers. Periodically, Yucatan has some of the best bass fishing found in the state. A man-made lake at Percy Quinn State Park, near McComb, should not be overlooked. Streams such as the Bogue Chitto also provide scenic float trips in this area.

In the southeastern area Mary Walker Bayou, Big Lake, and Graveline are popular locations. Some of the most beautiful streams in the state are in this part of Mississippi. Red Creek, Leaf River, and Chickasawhay are darkwater streams of the coastal plains which provide excellent angling as well as scenic beauty.

ANGLING METHODS

Approximately 75 percent of the fishermen in Mississippi use live bait. The most popular bait for bass and crappie is the minnow. These may be golden shiners, or goldfish raised in artificial ponds, or many different species of baitfish native to Mississippi waters. The most popular bait for the bluegill and redear sunfish, however, is the earthworm, although some panfish specialists prefer crickets, catalpa worms, gall worms, wasp larvae, or grub worms. The avid clan of catfish anglers scattered throughout the state use baits as varied as the locations in which their fishing is done; the most common are commercially prepared "stink-baits" which depend on their odor to attract the bottom-feeding catfish. Carp and buffalo are caught primarily on dough balls.

Nevertheless, the angler who casts artificial lures can catch almost all of the Mississippi game- and panfish. For bass, topwater plugs, spoons, and diving plugs are effective. Bluegills will succumb to popping bugs, flies with spinners, and even small plugs at times. Crappie will hit small spoons and plugs as well as flies with spinners. The redear sunfish or "shellcracker" will also hit flies and plugs, but not as readily as the bluegill. The habits of the white bass are very similar to those of the black bass, but the most productive artificial bait for the white bass is a silver spoon, especially when they are schooling. Naturally, the effectiveness of any method will vary from lake to lake and from season to season. Experience is the best teacher. Generally speaking, bass hide around submerged logs, stumps, or weedbeds. Spits running out from points of land are another favorite hangout. Crappie tend to school in the spring months, and good catches can be made around brush piles or logs, trees, and other underwater objects. The best bluegill and shellcracker fishing is during the spawning season. Beds are usually found where the bottom is hard and the water is 2–3 feet deep. They may be located by moving around and fishing here and there until you get a strike. Some people locate these beds by smell, but this method is for the experienced fisherman only. If you see a group of boats close together, this is usually a good sign of a bream bed, and there is always room for one more boat.

MISSISSIPPI GULF COAST

Although the Mississippi coast is only 90 miles long, it covers more than 200 miles with indented bays and river mouths. This is the most varied fishing area. In many streams which enter the Gulf of Mexico, such as the Wolf, Biloxi, and Pascagoula, the fisherman may hook a black bass on one cast and a spotted seatrout or channel bass on the next cast. Here we find an intermingling of fresh- and saltwater species. The towns of Biloxi and Ocean Springs on opposite shores of Biloxi Bay attract visitors, and boats operate out of both ports for tarpon fishing in the Gulf. There's also fishing throughout Mississippi Sound, which is protected from the offshore winds by a string of islands. The seatrout, flounder, whiting, bluefish, and red drum are the principal gamefish, but many anglers specialize in catching tripletail (which see) in this area.

For the more adventurous anglers, planes may be chartered at Gulfport which fly to the offshore islands for surf-fishing. One of the favorite offshore spots is Chandeleur Island. Others are Ship, Horn, and Cat islands. —B.O.F.

MISSOURI Missouri's fishing opportunities are many and varied: largemouth bass, crappie, and white bass; giant paddlefish; fine-quality rainbow trout; walleye, sunfish, catfish, carp, drum; smallmouth bass and rock bass of the famed float streams. Fishing waters vary from the clear, cool streams of the Ozark highlands to the warm, shallow lakes and bayous of the southeast delta lowlands. The best-known fishing area is the Ozarks region where high-quality float-fishing streams and large impoundments are the major attractions. This region contains many well-developed vacation areas. To the west is the Ozarks border where streams tend to be moderately turbid, but many of them contain excellent populations of black bass, walleye, crappie, sunfishes, and catfish.

In the Missouri and Mississippi prairie regions the large streams are slow-flowing and turbid. Here the channel catfish is the prime game species, and other catfishes, carp, buffalo, sunfishes, and freshwater drum are highly regarded and much sought after. Many of the smaller streams of this area equal those of the Ozarks border and sometimes of the Ozarks itself. Small impoundments from farm ponds to water-supply lakes of several hundred acres abound in this region and furnish much largemouth bass bluegill, and channel-catfish fishing.

Fishing methods vary as widely as waters and species. In addition to the usual well-known methods, gigging, jugging, snagging, grabbing, snaring, bank lines, limb lines, throw lines, longbow, and underwater spearfishing are legal methods during prescribed seasons. Some of these colorful names are for methods unique in the area. They make possible harvest of many species which are seldom taken by the usual methods and provide many hours of unusual sport.

Access to most waters still is not difficult in most places. Where public access is not available, most landowners will grant permission if they are asked. To ensure that streams continue to be accessible the Conservation Commission has begun buying land at strategic locations.

LAKES

Taneycomo is the oldest of the large impoundments in Missouri. Since the impoundment of Table Rock Lake, a flood-control and power-production impoundment immediately upstream from Lake Taneycomo, the water received by this 2,200-acre impoundment has been too cold for the warmwater species formerly abundant. The Missouri Conservation Commission began managing the entire lake for rainbow trout in 1958. This has been a very successful program, and trout fishing is consistently good. While the warmwater fishery is declining, good numbers of bluegills and crappie still are taken plus some bass, walleye, and an assortment of warmwater fishes. In the Taneycomo tailwater, which contains the famous "Pot Hole," fishing remains good with white bass, freshwater drum, channel catfish, and bluegill the most numerous species taken. This area also consistently produces the largest walleyes in the state.

Bull Shoals Lake (9,900 acres in Missouri), immediately downstream from Taneycomo, is famous for large bass. For example, during one unusually successful week in April, 1963, 700 bass weighing 4–10 pounds were recorded as taken from the Theodosia Arm alone. White bass, crappie, and bluegill are abundant. Trout which have moved from Taneycomo also are taken in some portions of Bull Shoals.

Table Rock Lake (43,100 acres), immediately upstream from Taneycomo in the White River system, is the newest lake completed in the drainage. It is now in its peak period of production and is doing moderately well although a premature flooding and draining reduced and delayed the initial high production we have come to expect in new impoundments. Crappie, white bass, largemouth bass, and bluegill are caught most frequently.

The proximity of Table Rock, Taneycomo, and Bull Shoals lakes, with a variety of fishing opportunities and fine scenery, has encouraged the development of a considerable resort area, and tourism is a major industry.

Norfork Lake (1,240 acres in Missouri), which is the downstream impoundment of White River extending into

Missouri, has only one arm in the state. Fishing opportunities are similar to those in Bull Shoals and Table Rock.

In southeastern Missouri, lakes Clearwater and Wappapello are the major impoundments. Clearwater (1,650 acres) is the most productive. Crappie provide over 70 percent of the catch, with channel catfish making up the bulk of the remainder. Good catches of largemouth bass can be made, but few of the fishermen using this area specialize in bass fishing. In the tailwaters of Clearwater there is a heavy catch of crappie, carp, channel catfish, buffalo, and white bass in a relatively few acres of water.

Wappapello (7,200 acres) is shallower and somewhat turbid. Crappie and catfish are the major sport species taken here, also.

The Lake of the Ozarks (65,000 acres), which impounds the Osage River in southcentral Missouri, has another major resort development. It yields large catches of crappie and white bass and some good largemouth bass and channel catfish, particularly early and late in the year. In its extreme headwaters and on up the Osage River the famed paddlefish (spoonbill) fishing takes place each spring. Biologists estimate that over 500 tons of this fish are caught in the Lake of the Ozarks each year.

Pomme de Terre Lake (7,800 acres) in westcentral Missouri was impounded in 1962. Smallmouth bass and white bass are the principal attractions here.

Missouri boasts thousands of farm ponds which are good producers of bass, bluegill, and channel catfish. The bulk of these are on private land where permission is needed for access. Professional construction advice and biological advice in management are constantly upgrading the quality of these waters.

The Missouri Conservation Commission builds fishing lakes in areas where there is a shortage of such waters. The James A. Reed Memorial Wildlife Area near Kansas City and the August A. Busch Memorial Wildlife Area near St. Louis each has a number of small lakes totaling nearly 500 acres which are open to public fishing from May 30 to Labor Day for a small daily fee. Largemouth bass, bluegill, channel catfish, and redear sunfish are present in these waters.

Fishing lakes are built by the Conservation Commission in a co-operative program in which communities provide suitable sites and the Commission builds, stocks, and manages the lake for free public fishing. The lakes already built, their surface acreage, and the counties in which they are located are: Jamesport, 30, Daviess; Ray County, 25, Ray; Vandalia, 44, Audrian; Tri-city, 30, Boone; Miller, 27, Carter; Worth County, 20, Worth; Limpp, 29, Gentry; Tywappity, 37, Scott; Ripley, 20, Ripley; Austin, 22, Texas; Sterling Price, 35, Chariton; Malta Bend, 5, Saline; Little Dixie, 205, Callaway; Deer Ridge, 48, Lewis; Sever, 158, Knox; and the Diggs Area, 30, Montgomery County. Other lakes with similar management but constructed without local financial assistance are Paho, 273 acres, Mercer; Hunnewell, 228, Shelby; Big Oak, 22, Mississippi; and Jo Shelby, 31, Linn. These lakes are all managed for largemouth bass, bluegill, channel catfish, and some have redear sunfish.

Missouri's waterfowl hunting and refuge areas have provided a great bonus of fishing water. The most notable of these is Duck Creek on the Bollinger-Wayne County line in southeast Missouri whose 1,773 acres support very fine bass, crappie, and sunfish. Large bowfin up to 19 pounds have been taken. These armored monsters are extremely fine fighters.

The Schell-Osage waterfowl area near the Osage River in westcentral Missouri has 700 acres of water which was impounded in 1962, but already it is becoming widely known for its bass, crappie, and a host of other species which enter from the Osage River when it floods and reproduce very successfully.

Montrose Lake in Henry County is a 1,500-acre impoundment built by the Kansas City Power and Light Company which has been licensed to the Conservation Commission for management of public hunting and fishing. This lake has a warmwater discharge from the power plant. In the warmer water there is good winter fishing for crappie, channel catfish, and bass. In the summer, fishing is distributed over the lake.

The Trimble Wildlife Area in Clinton County contains 170 acres of water which are productive of crappie, bass, walleye, and channel catfish.

The Swan Lake Federal Refuge in Chariton County also provides an extensive fishing area for channel catfish, carp, and several other species. Many buffalo are taken during a special summer seining season.

Since all the latter group of waters were developed for waterfowl, which prefer shallow water and for which aquatic plants are desirable food, most of them have heavy weed growths by midsummer. Therefore, the early spring fishing is best. However, properly made weedless lures take good catches through the entire open season. Usually no fishing is allowed during the waterfowl season.

OZARKS STREAMS

Missouri has 20,000 miles of streams, almost all of which provide some fishing. However, the widely known Ozarks streams receive the greatest attention. Among these are the Gasconade, Meramec, Bourbeuse, Big, Black, Upper St. Francis, Eleven Point, Current, Jacks Fork, Huzzah, Courtois, Big Piney, Elk, James, and Niangua rivers. The relative proportions of the various species in these streams vary somewhat, but many fishermen think of most of them as smallmouth-bass streams. These are known for float-fishing in which fishermen can travel for days or a week or more by canoe or Johnboat while fishing and enjoying the scenery. Float-fishermen concentrate their efforts on smallmouth bass but get considerable action also from rock bass, several species of sunfish, walleyes, and catfish. The lower reaches of the larger streams such as the Meramec and Gasconade contain a great variety of species, including freshwater drum, crappie, flathead, catfish, carp, and buffalo. Throughout the length of these streams, suckers and sunfishes are the most abundant groups, and are taken by several special means. Gigging accounts for most of these. This is spearfishing, usually from a boat at night, with specially rigged lights of several types, each typical of its area. During their spawning season suckers are taken off their spawning shoals by grabbing (snagging). They also are snared from perches over the water in areas where they are working.

In the southeast lowlands, drainage ditches which were formerly very productive have become less so because of low-water levels and, apparently, the use of agricultural chemicals. Still they produce crappie, sunfishes, bass, carp, and buffalo. Many of the sloughs and bayous in this lowland region are good producers of a variety of species. Fishing success fluctuates considerably in them. This is especially true of the sloughs on the river side of the levee which change with each flood but which are frequently fine fishing waters.

OZARKS BORDER STREAMS

The Ozarks border streams include Spring River, which flows southwest into the Arkansas River system. It remains turbid for longer than normal periods after rains, but it supports good populations of bass, catfish, and sunfish. Several small mill dams on it provide lake-type fishing in which largemouth bass are the major game species. Between them and in the upstream area smallmouth bass and spotted bass predominate. The remaining Ozarks border streams including the Sac and Pomme de Terre rivers, and a number of smaller streams are tributaries of the Osage River. These support a great variety of fishes including basses, sunfishes, crappie, white bass, walleye, and channel catfish. These streams also tend to remain moderately turbid for considerable periods but provide good fishing opportunities. The character of the Sac and Pomme de Terre rivers is being changed by impoundments. An impoundment was constructed on the latter in 1962, and the former will have one in a few years.

MISSOURI PRAIRIE STREAMS

The streams of the Missouri Prairie are characteristically turbid and slow-flowing and have large fluctuations in level after rains. The major streams in this region, all of which drain into the Missouri River, are the Tarkio, Nodaway, Platte, Grand, and Chariton north of the Missouri River; and south of it the Lamine, Moreau, South Grand, and Osage. Channel catfish and carp make up the bulk of the catch in the main streams of the group north of the river. In the headwaters and tributary streams green sunfish and bullheads are important. South of the Missouri river the prairie streams have a wider variety of species in fishable populations. These include channel catfish, carp, green sunfish, bullheads, drum, and bluegill. In the Osage River these species are important through the year. In addition, upstream from the lake of the Ozarks there are spring movements of walleye, white bass, and paddlefish from the lake. Crappie also move in at this time and through the warm months. Although most of the migrating fish move in the Osage, they are not confined to it. Most species also go into the lower portions of the South Grand, Pomme de Terre, and Sac. Below the Lake of the Ozarks the same species are important, but their presence is influenced more by water released for the Lake of the Ozarks than is true above the lake.

One outstanding and almost unique fishing opportunity in the Osage River is paddlefish (spoonbill) snagging. Each spring paddlefish move from the Lake of the Ozarks up the Osage River to spawn over gravelbars. During this movement snagging is permitted from March 15 through April 30 and upwards of one hundred tons are caught. Snagging is done by both trolling and by casting from the bank. Average weight of the paddlefish caught is 38 pounds, with some up to 70 pounds. It was in the Osage that the first fertile eggs and newly hatched paddlefish fry ever reported were found in 1960.

MISSISSIPPI PRAIRIE STREAMS

The Fox, Wyaconda, Fabius, North, Cuivre, and Salt rivers in northeast Missouri tend to be moderately turbid to turbid in their mainstreams. Channel catfish, bullhead, freshwater drum, green sunfish, and carp are the major species here. These streams are the best channel-catfish producers in the state, and this catfish is considered second to no other fish in this region. At times the lower reaches of these streams also receive migrating groups of white bass, crappie, and a few other species.

LARGE RIVERS

The Missouri River provides a relatively small amount of fishing in proportion to the amount of water present. The major fishes taken are carp, channel catfish, crappie, and flathead catfish. This fishery has been affected by channelization for navigation, which has eliminated much good habitat, and by pollution. Fortunately steps have been taken to eliminate the sources of pollution. Conditions should be improved, and fishing should be better when this is accomplished.

The Mississippi River downstream from St. Louis is also seriously affected by pollution, although there is good fishing in the backwaters, sloughs, and bayous out of the mainstream. Crappie, catfish, and carp are important here. In the navigation pools upstream from St. Louis, which are actually river impoundments, fishing is much better, and use is heavy. Crappie, channel catfish, drum, bluegill, carp, and green sunfish are the species taken most frequently, but a host of other species are important. They include white bass, sturgeon, paddlefish, flathead catfish, bullheads, walleyes, and, in the sloughs and backwaters, even largemouth bass.

TROUT STREAMS

The mileage of Missouri's trout water is rather limited, but there is no shortage of trout in the suitable areas. Since there is very little reproduction, rainbow trout are reared in hatcheries and stocked regularly, most at ten inches or larger. In 1962 about 700,000 trout were released. Four of the trout areas are spring-branch streams in parks. These are Bennett Spring, Montauk, Roaring River, and Maramec Park. The first three are state parks; the latter is operated by the James Foundation. In these areas fish are stocked daily, and a daily fee is charged for fishing.

In other waters trout are stocked five times per year, and annual fishing and trout permits are the only requirements. They are Capps Creek, Newton County; Niangua River below Bennett Spring in Dallas County; Dry Creek, Crawford County; Roubidoux Creek, Pulaski County; and the Eleven Point River near Greer Spring, Oregon County. Lake Taneycomo is also stocked five times annually, and the same licenses are required.

SMALL STREAMS

Missouri has many small streams which are barely large enough or too small for boat travel which are excellent fishing streams. These waters receive relatively low fishing pressure, and are to be recommended to the fisherman who is willing either to drag his canoe over frequent gravelbars, or to wade. Bass, sunfishes, channel catfish, bullheads, and green sunfish are taken in most of these, but species vary with the locality. These can be located by local inquiry in almost any part of the state. —C.A.P.

MISSOURI MINNOW A regional name in the Southern United States for the fathead minnow (*which see*).

MISTY GROUPER *Epinephelus mystacinus* Also called the mustache grouper, this rather rare deepwater species may reach a weight of 50 pounds. It is found throughout the tropical American Atlantic, including extreme southern Florida. The name mustache grouper refers to the black, mustachelike band on either side of the snout parallel to the upper jaw. Called *cherna del alto* in Spanish, it is a commercial fish in some of the Antilles but rarely seen in the markets.

It has 11 dorsal spines, usually 15 dorsal rays, 9 anal rays, and 18–19 pectoral rays. Posterior nostril much larger than the anterior. Insertion of pelvic fin under, or in advance of upper end of pectoral base. Posterior margin of caudal fin convex. Dark bars on sides of body. A dark bar around caudal peduncle much darker on top but not forming a well-defined, saddlelike black blotch.

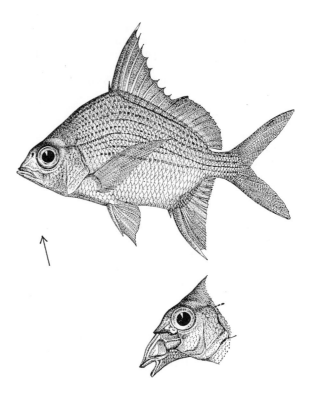

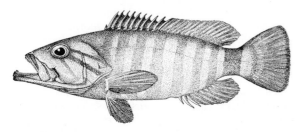

Misty Grouper

The much enlarged posterior nostril distinguishes this grouper from the others, except the snowy grouper (*which see*). The latter, however, has an entirely different color pattern.

ANGLING VALUE

This fish occurs on rocky bottom, usually along the edge of the shelf, in depths of 80–120 fathoms.

Because of its occurrence in deepwater, this grouper has little or no angling value in the usual sense. When taken with a wire line, however, it provides the thrill of an unusual catch by an unorthodox method. It is taken on handlines by West Indian fishermen. —L.R.

MOJARRAS Family Gerridae These small silvery fishes are most abundant from Cape Hatteras south to Brazil, with at least nine species found in Atlantic waters, and one, the spotfin mojarra, *Eucinostomus argenteus*, also occurring in the Pacific. Mojarras have compressed bodies and large, smooth scales. They are noted for an extremely protractile mouth; when pushed out the mouth descends downward in adaptation to bottom feeding. The premaxillary process, which is otherwise hidden, slips into a long groove under the skin on the snout.

Several species of mojarra attain 10–12 inches in length and are sometimes utilized as food. However, the majority are less than 8 inches long and are more commonly used as bait in southern saltwater fishing.

ANGLING VALUE

The Gerridae are actually an important forage to many of the larger inshore species which feed over shallow sand

Striped Mojarra, Showing Protractile Mouth, an Adaptation to Bottom Feeding

or coral shores, such as the barracuda, jacks, and snappers. Commonly called "shad" in the Bahamas, vast schools are often sighted freckling the surface on bonefish flats. —A.J.McC.

MOLLUSK A member of a large phylum of animals that includes some of the most highly developed invertebrates —such as snails, octopuses, squids, mussels, chitons, nautiluses, clams, and oysters. Mollusks have soft, bilaterally symmetrical unsegmented bodies frequently covered with a shell secreted by a fold of the body wall— the mantle. Many have a large muscular "foot." Some mollusks are important as sources of food and such products as pearls and mother-of-pearl.

MONTANA This is one of the most important areas in United States trout fishing. The prime waters are almost entirely in the western portion of the state. A north-south line drawn through Laurel, Montana (west of Billings), separates the trout country from the region suitable mainly for warmwater fishes to the east. Only half of Montana contains good trout habitat, but that segment is about as large as three average Eastern states, and the streams and lakes are very numerous.

Montana fishing has survived as well as can be expected against the onslaught of civilization. Fishing pressure has increased enormously in recent years, but it is still not heavy by United States standards because the state is sparsely populated and removed from large centers of population. In spite of the growing popularity of trout fishing with tourist anglers, nonresidents only account for about 20 percent of the licenses sold.

Irrigation has always been a detriment to Montana fishing. Many small tributary streams have a reduced volume of flow in their lower reaches, and as a result the water level in the big rivers can become seriously low during the summer season. There can be a considerable mortality of trout when they go into irrigation ditches which are later shut off. On some streams it is also the practice to operate bulldozers in the stream beds to create dikes for diverting irrigation water. Much insect life is thereby lost. On the bright side, more efficient utilization of water for irrigation has been recognized and instituted.

Many miles of good trout streams have been impaired by stream straightening in building highways. Unfortunately, in mountainous country the easiest place to run highways is along trout streams. A law against this type of habitat destruction has passed the Montana legislature.

The pollution (*which see*) picture in Montana is promising. Many cities have put in modern sewage disposal plants. Gold-mining operations, which formerly silted some of the best trout streams, have almost all been abandoned. Most industries, of which there are comparatively few in Montana, are in the larger centers like Billings and Great Falls. These are far enough downstream on the main rivers so that their pollution is below the natural trout range.

As fishing pressure grows, access to the best fishing waters will become an increasing problem. Much of Montana is National Forest land where access is free to the public, but the larger trout streams flow through private ranch land. Although the average rancher is friendly and allows fishing with his permission, as the pressure becomes greater, this could become a limiting factor in the future. The state has been buying access areas on numerous streams, but many more are needed. Posting by private clubs is not widespread in Montana, but this will increase as it has in more populated areas. Some resorts and dude ranches have reserved small sections of the best streams for their guests.

The majority of Montana's good trout streams are in the drainage of three large rivers: the Missouri from the mouth of Judith River upstream; the Yellowstone from the mouth of Clarks Fork upstream, and Clark Fork of the Columbia from the Idaho state line upstream. The only good trout streams not in the drainage of these three rivers are the Kootenai and its tributaries in the extreme northwest and a few streams in the eastern part of Glacier Park which are in the Hudson Bay drainage. There is a point in Glacier Park where one could empty a pail of water, and some of it could reach the Pacific, some Hudson Bay, and some the Gulf of Mexico.

The Missouri, sometimes referred to as the "Mighty Mo," is a great trout stream in its own right and has more famous trout tributaries than any other river in Montana. Quality trout fishing on the Missouri does not start until a hundred miles above the mouth of Judith River, which is above Great Falls. The Judith River flows into the Missouri north of Lewistown, and has some good brown and rainbow trout but is most noteworthy for its two tributaries, which are Big Spring Creek at Lewistown, and, of national fame and smaller but equally good, Warm Spring Creek, which flows into the Judith just a few miles downstream from Lewistown.

SPRING CREEK

Spring Creek, referred to as Big Spring Creek, is bigger in reputation as a trout stream than in actual size. It is a true spring creek in that most of its current comes from a single spring at its source and very little from tributaries. It has about 20 miles of good trout water. The town of Lewistown divides Spring Creek into two parts of quite different character. The water upstream from Lewistown to the source is perfectly clear, and rainbows predominate in the catch, although when an exceptional fish is caught, it is usually a brown. This part of the creek is strictly fly water, and dry flies of small size are best. It is a narrow stream, somewhat brushy and difficult to negotiate, but has a strong volume of water. From Lewistown downstream to the Judith the stream flows over some clay banks so that it is not quite so clear. But it makes up for that by being wider and easier to fish. In this downstream section, brown trout predominate, and they run considerably larger on the average than the trout above town.

For information on where to fish Spring Creek and what to use, go to the Sport Center in Lewistown. There you will see what to hope for from Spring Creek, for the owner has a large collection of mounted trout—the largest each year taken from the creek for quite a few years back. All of these are big trout, and the largest is over nineteen pounds.

MARIAS RIVER

Marias River, which flows into the Missouri lower downstream than the other trout tributaries of the river, is not much of a trout stream because it flows through plains country and is heavily silted. The Marias is noteworthy mainly on account of a large rehabilitation program which was carried out and which was not successful. When Tiber Dam was built on the Marias, all of its tributaries and the main river above the dam were poisoned (*see* Rotenone) and later restocked with rainbow trout. Before that time the drainage had been populated mainly by rough fish. Fish are now abundant in the reservoir, but they have not thrived because of a shortage

Montana offers some of the best trout fishing in America. Fish of 4–5 pounds are common in many streams

of food. Nor has there been much improvement in the streams above the lake. There is some good trout fishing for a short distance downstream from the dam where the formerly muddy water has cleared, and there is fair angling in the extreme headwater creeks. The best of these is Cut Bank Creek.

GREAT FALLS

Just downstream from Great Falls on the Missouri is Belt Creek, which is a pretty little mountain stream in its upper reaches with good fishing for rainbows.

Just above Great Falls, Smith River flows into the Missouri. This is a medium-sized stream with about fifty miles of good to excellent trout water. Rainbows and browns predominate in Smith River with some good brook trout in the upper reaches. The upper part of the Smith is a meadow stream, flowing through ranch country. The lower part is through an inaccessible canyon. Fishermen float through this stretch and often take some large trout.

SUN RIVER

The headwaters of the Sun River, which flow into the Missouri, maintain a substantial trout population. There is rainbow fishing in the Sun above Augusta and good fishing which can only be reached by horse in the North Fork Sun and South Fork Sun above Gibson Dam. These are beautiful little wilderness streams which contain some fine trout.

MISSOURI RIVER

The Missouri between Great Falls and Holter Dam near Wolf Creek has good fishing all the way for a distance of about 50 miles. This is big water, and it produces browns and rainbows in the 10-pound class every year. There is no closed season on the Missouri, and fishermen are seen along it on any pleasant day during the winter. During the winter and early spring months, there is usually a hatch of small midges called locally snow flies. Skillful fishermen take many fine trout on tiny flies which imitate these insects.

The Dearborn River flows into the Missouri from the west about ten miles below Wolf Creek. This is a good medium-sized stream, but is posted more heavily than most Montana streams. By cultivating the friendship of the ranchers along the stream one can get permission to fish. The Dearborn also gets too low for the best fishing during the latter part of the season because too much water is diverted from it for irrigation.

Prickly Pear Creek flows into the Missouri at Wolf Creek. This stream is heavily fished by Helena fishermen, but some good trout are taken here. The Montana Fish and Game Department uses Prickly Pear Creek as a test stream because it is easy to electro-fish and make stream population counts there. An interesting finding is that, though it is heavily fished, the stream has a food supply that would allow about 18 percent increase in the wild-trout population. This shows that streams—at least those containing brown trout—do not become fished out. On the other hand, the hatchery rainbows which are stocked in the stream are either caught immediately or do not survive beyond the first season.

The next 50-mile stretch of the Missouri consists mainly of large reservoirs with only small sections of free-flowing river between them. The reservoirs are Holter Lake, Hauser Lake, and Canyon Ferry Lake. All of these have some trout fishing, mostly by trolling. The best fishing, which is principally for rainbows, is in Canyon Ferry Lake.

Reservoirs in Montana have been disappointing as trout producers. Fishing the impoundments is usually good shortly after they are formed, building up to a peak in about five years and then declining to a stable level of relatively poor fishing. Nor is there any improvement in the stream fishing below the reservoirs in Montana's coldwater streams. This is in contrast to southern United States reservoirs where a habitat suitable for trout is often created where it did not exist before. Large dams on the best Montana trout streams always result in a substantial loss in good stream fishing which is replaced by poor lake fishing.

The small stretches of free-flowing river on the Missouri between Wolf Creek and Townsend have good, though somewhat crowded, fishing, particularly during the spawning runs of trout from the reservoirs below. At these locations there is good fishing for large brown trout between September 15 and October 15, and for rainbows in the early spring.

From Townsend at the head of Canyon Ferry Reservoir to the point where the Madison, Gallatin, and Jefferson join to form the Missouri, fishing is good for large trout. The drawback to this section of the Missouri is that it remains discolored during most of the season, with silt coming from the East Gallatin and Jefferson rivers.

A good small tributary of the Missouri is Sixteen Mile Creek which enters the river at Lombard. Some fine rainbow fishing can be found on this stream in a canyon about 10 miles up from the Missouri. One has to hike several miles into this canyon for the best fishing.

GALLATIN RIVER

The eastern fork of the three rivers which form the Missouri is the Gallatin, and this divides again a few miles upstream into the East Gallatin and West Gallatin rivers. The West Gallatin is the larger and the more famous of these branches. Except for its first ten miles where much water is diverted for irrigation, this stream has fine rainbow fishing all the way up to Yellowstone Park. Brown trout are caught in the lower part, and the species is gradually increasing further up the river. A highway parallels the West Gallatin for miles through beautiful Gallatin Canyon. There are excellent National Forest camp sites along the river here. It is very popular because of its beauty and accessibility, and it is heavily fished.

The East Gallatin is a brushy meadow stream which flows through ranch country and is always slightly discolored due to irrigation. Upon first viewing it, it may be regarded as too muddy for flyfishing, but the trout are not affected by the discolored water. They are abundant and average larger here than in the more popular West Gallatin.

MADISON RIVER

The famous Madison is the middle one of the three rivers. It has excellent fishing for browns and rainbows all the way from Three Forks to Yellowstone Park and beyond in the park. Unlike other Montana streams, the

Ennis Lake, in the course of the Madison River, produces trout in the morning and evening to the fly fisherman

Madison has no pools, just a wide rush of water with many large boulders, all of which form good pockets for trout. Headquarters for fishing the Madison is Ennis where there are several good motels.

Just below Meadow Lake on the Madison is a famous canyon called the Bear Trap. This is about 10 miles of water which is inaccessible except by boat or hiking. It is great fishing for enormous trout, but a rough trip by boat or trail, and it also has wild rapids and rattlesnakes.

From the point where the Madison comes out of the Bear Trap down to Three Forks the river flows with a strong but even current. The water in this stretch is always slightly discolored from silt which is picked up where the river leaves Meadow Lake. Though less popular than the water above the lake, the trout in this stretch average larger.

Meadow Lake has good fishing for rainbows and browns, but it is not fished much because the river draws the crowds. Where the river enters the lake, it splits up into a number of channels, some of which are a mile long or more. These channels are particularly pleasant to fish, the current not being as severe as other parts of the river, and each channel is like a medium-sized trout stream.

The popular part of the Madison is from Ennis up to Quake Lake. Formerly it was up to Hebgen Lake, but several miles of the river were lost in the earthquake of 1959, and there is only a short stretch of river now between Hebgen Dam and the new earthquake-formed lake. The best time to hit the Madison is during the hatch of large stoneflies (*which see*) called locally salmon flies. These usually come out on the river in late June and early July. Then every trout in the river is susceptible to any big dry fly which resembles the natural insects.

Just to the west of the upper Madison are Wade Lake, Cliff Lake, Hidden Lake, and Elk Lake. All of these have

produced trout in the twenty-pound class. They are beautiful little volcanic lakes with banks so steep that a boat is essential. Wade Lake produces big ones more consistently than the others, and Hidden Lake has the best fishing, but can only be reached by foot.

Hebgen Lake is about 20 miles long and has good fishing for rainbows and browns. The fishing is less attractive here because it is a controlled lake and large mud flats are often exposed in the late summer.

Good tributaries of the upper Madison, or properly speaking of Hebgen, are South Fork Madison, Grayling Creek, Duck Creek, and Cougar Creek. These are all small streams, but all have big trout which run up from Hebgen. Headquarters for fishing these creeks and the Madison, Firehole, and Gibbon in Yellowstone Park is West Yellowstone, Montana.

The westernmost fork of the Three Forks of the Missouri is Jefferson River, which is a good brown trout stream throughout its length when the water is clear. The river usually clears in the late fall when ranchers quit irrigating.

At Twin Bridges the Jefferson divides and becomes the Big Hole, Beaverhead, and Ruby rivers. All of these are fine trout streams, the Big Hole is the largest and best-known, but its halcyon years are past.

The Ruby is a fine little trout stream with some big browns and rainbows. Being small and brushy, it is somewhat hard to fish. It does not receive much angling pressure because it is so near the more popular Big Hole.

The Beaverhead is a good meadow-type stream, but access to it is somewhat difficult in its lower reaches where it flows through large ranches, and it is a long way from the road.

BIG HOLE RIVER

The Big Hole has declined as a trout producer since the 1960's due to numerous stream diversions for irrigation. Most of the larger fish are taken in the 20 miles of water between Twin Bridges and Divide. Brown trout predominate in this stretch, but there are also many good rainbows.

Above Divide on the Big Hole there are browns, rainbow, brook trout, and grayling. As you proceed farther upstream there are more brook trout and grayling. Here the valley is called Big Hole Basin, which is noted for the thousands of haystacks which can be seen from any point. The irrigated hay meadows breed mosquitoes in abundance, so bring an insect repellent if you fish here. The Big Hole has few tributaries, but the Wise River above Divide is a fine stream with an abundance of small-to medium-sized trout.

YELLOWSTONE RIVER

Montana's other important waters which are east of the Continental Divide are in the Yellowstone drainage. The Yellowstone itself is a tributary of the Missouri, and it could be considered as part of the Missouri drainage. But since it is several hundred miles upstream before there is trout fishing on the main river or the tributaries, it may be regarded as a separate drainage. The first trout fishing worthy of note on the main Yellowstone starts near Laurel, Montana, which is 12 miles west of Billings. Below Laurel the river is polluted by industries and is also heavily silted. There is fishing for browns and rainbows in the river between Laurel and Big Timber, and occasionally very large trout are caught in this section. However, top trout fishing on the Yellowstone starts at Big Timber and extends upstream to the Yellowstone Park boundary and beyond.

The easternmost tributary of the Yellowstone which is worth fishing is Rock Creek, which rises in the mountains back of Red Lodge. This is a fair to excellent rainbow stream with browns in the lower reaches. Above Red Lodge, Rock Creek is a beautiful little stream which has been left in its natural state, but trout are small in this section.

The Stillwater is a good trout stream which enters the Yellowstone at Columbus. Being only 30 miles from Billings, this stream is heavily fished, and much of the water is posted. Permission to fish can usually be obtained from the ranchers or by staying at a resort which has water reserved for its guests.

Good tributaries of the Stillwater are East Rosebud and West Rosebud creeks. The upper part of the Stillwater can be reached only by pack horse, and there is good fishing for rainbow, cutthroat, and brook trout in the river and in many high-mountain lakes.

The Boulder River flows into the Yellowstone at Big Timber. There is good fishing for browns and rainbows from the mouth of the Boulder up to Natural Bridge where a waterfall acts as a barrier to migrating trout. Above Natural Bridge rainbow, cutthroat, and brook trout may be caught. The Natural Bridge also acts as a barrier to Rocky Mountain whitefish, which are plentiful below the falls but are not present beyond it. The Boulder is a pretty trout stream, being of a meadowy character with deep pools in the lower part and a rapid mountain stream in the upper reaches. Much of the river is privately held by guest ranches however, and the best public access is in the headwaters on national forest land. Here the trout are abundant but small.

The mountain whitefish (*which see*) are plentiful in all of the larger streams east of the Continental Divide, and also in many streams west of the divide. The mountain whitefish is classified as a gamefish and rises readily to flies, but most serious trout anglers consider them a nuisance. They are fished for mostly in the winter months with live maggots as bait. Mountain whitefish are excellent when smoked.

Good tributaries of the Boulder are East Boulder River and West Boulder River. Note that in Montana anything big enough that you can't step across is often dignified with the name river. Trout in the East Boulder are mostly small, but West Boulder has some surprisingly large brown trout. Though only rainbows and cutthroat are stocked in this stream, the big ones which are caught are always browns. The West Boulder is a fine stream, but only the expert fly-fishermen take the large browns and the casual fishermen take the smaller, stocked rainbows.

The Yellowstone River has excellent fishing from Big Timber to the Yellowstone Park boundary. Trout in the section between Livingston and Big Timber average larger than those between Livingston and Gardiner, but numerically they are not as abundant. Trout species in the lower river are browns, rainbows, and cutthroat in that order of abundance. The most popular section of the Yellowstone is between Livingston and Gardiner. The same species of trout are found here as in the lower river except that the proportion of cutthroat to rainbows and browns increases as one goes upstream. Cutthroat of over 5 pounds are rare, but several browns and rainbows in the 10-pound class are caught every year, and 4–5 pounders are relatively common.

The National Fresh Water Trout Derby is held every year on a section of the Yellowstone near Livingston. A prize of $1,000 is given for the largest trout caught between the hours of 9:00 A.M. and 1:00 P.M. The best trout is usually around 4–6 pounds. The number of fishermen disturbing the water guarantees that not too many trout are caught at this event, and those which are taken are usually from the deepest pools and are caught with bait.

A popular tributary of the Yellowstone is Mill Creek, 20 miles upstream from Livingston. Mill Creek is a pretty mountain stream, but the fish, which are mainly cutthroat, do not run large. It also has smaller numbers of brown, rainbow, and brook trout.

The only fair-sized lake in the upper Yellowstone drainage is Dailey's Lake where there is good fishing for rainbows up to 4 pounds. Formerly this lake produced many trout in the 10-pound class, but the average size of the trout taken has declined due to overpopulation and the presence of many yellow perch which were stocked in the lake at a time when the water was unsuitable for trout. This lake had become stagnant due to the diversion of its inlet stream for irrigation. Through the efforts of the Livingston Rod & Gun Club, a portion of the original feeder stream was restored, and the lake again became suitable trout habitat.

There are hundreds of small alpine lakes in all of the mountains adjacent to Montana streams, but these are too numerous to list and too variable in the quality of their fishing to recommend. In general the high lakes are unproductive because of a shortage of food, a short growing season, and overpopulation where spawning is possible. In spite of this general rule some high lakes sometimes have fine fishing for anglers who are willing to hike and explore. A few of these lakes contain the rare golden trout.

The waters in the northern part of Glacier Park east of the Continental Divide are in the St. Mary River drainage which flows into the Saskatchewan River and finally into Hudson Bay. St. Mary River has fair to good fishing for rainbow and cutthroat below St. Mary Lake, and there is excellent fishing for large trout in that river above St. Mary Lake which can be reached only by a rough hike.

Duck Lake produced *Field & Stream* prize-winning rainbows in the 1960's, many of them of 10–15 pounds; but the quality of the fishing has declined greatly. The best fishing at Duck Lake is in the early spring just after the ice goes out. There is no inlet in which the trout can breed, and they come in close to shore to seek suitable spawning sites. This fishing is from the shore with large Woolly Worm flies. During the summer most of the trout are caught in the deeper water by trolling. Goose Lake, in the same area, has been stocked with rainbows and may become as good as Duck Lake for large trout in a few years. At present the trout usually run 2–3 pounds. Neither of these lakes has natural spawning, and all trout which are taken are stocked. Many lakes in or adjacent to Glacier Park on the east side have good fishing, and all except the larger ones must be reached by hiking.

Fly rod expert Tom McNally works the swift currents of the Gallatin River. Although not noted for large fish, the stream holds good populations of rainbow, brown, and brook trout. Best section from Gateway upstream

CLARK FORK

Most of Montana's streams which are west of the Continental Divide are in the drainage of Clark Fork of the Columbia, which is usually referred to simply as Clark Fork. This is not to be confused with Clarks Fork of the Yellowstone, which rises northeast of Yellowstone Park and flows into the Yellowstone above Billings.

Clark Fork is a big, beautiful river, but in the past has been badly polluted by industries in Butte, Anaconda, and Missoula. In recent years efforts have been made to control this pollution, and there has therefore been a substantial improvement in the fishing.

There is good fishing in Thompson River for rainbow and cutthroat and fair to good rainbow- and brown-trout fishing in Clark Fork between Thompson Falls and Missoula. As on several other large Montana rivers fishing is open here all year.

FLATHEAD RIVER

The largest and best known tributary of Clark Fork is Flathead River, which flows south from Flathead Lake. Below the lake there is fair fishing for rainbow and brown trout. Above the lake there is good fishing for cutthroat, rainbow, and Dolly Varden in the main Flathead. The river is difficult to fish from shore or by wading, and float-fishing is the most productive method. Jocko River is a good small stream which flows into the main Flathead northwest of Missoula. Jocko has some fine brown trout in its lower reaches.

The South Fork Flathead flows into the main river from the south above Columbia Falls. More than 30 miles of this river has been flooded by Hungry Horse Dam where there is fair fishing. Above Hungry Horse Lake the South Fork is a wilderness stream most of which can only be reached by a long pack trip. In this river and Salmon Lake exists what is probably the best wilderness fishing for cutthroat trout left in the United States. This is a magnificent trip for those with the time to make a pack trip.

North Fork Flathead flows south along the west boundary of Glacier Park. This is one of Montana's most beautiful streams, and the water is crystal clear. Trout here are principally cutthroat. In Glacier Park just off this river are many fine trout lakes, largest of which are Kintla, Bowman, Quartz, Logging, and McDonald.

Middle Fork Flathead flows north and west along the southern boundary of Glacier Park and joins North Fork about 10 miles above the mouth of South Fork. Fishing in this branch is a back-packer's delight. The quality is excellent.

Flathead Lake is a beautiful body of water in a magnificent mountain setting. It has fishing for cutthroat, rainbow, Dolly Varden, and lake trout. There is also some largemouth-bass fishing in the lake and fishing for kokanee.

There are a number of lakes in this section of Montana having good largemouth-bass fishing. Among these, in addition to Flathead Lake, are Lone Pine, Nine Pipe,

Kicking Horse, and Echo lakes. Whitefish Lake at White-fish is noted for its large lake trout which are taken mainly by trolling. Lake Mary Ronan just west of Flathead was formerly one of the best trout producers in Montana. The fishing declined when rough fish became established, but it has been fairly well rehabilitated, and the fishing is now improving.

OTHER CLARK FORK TRIBUTARIES

Just below Missoula the Bitteroot River enters Clark Fork from the south. This is a fine trout river for its entire length. There are large brown trout in the lower part of the river and good rainbow and cutthroat fishing in the upper reaches. Headquarters for fishing the Bitteroot is Hamilton.

Swan River is an excellent tributary of the Flathead which enters Flathead Lake at Big Fork, Montana. It is noted for its fine rainbow fishing and the forested mountains through which it flows. At its headwaters are Holland and Lindberg lakes; both offer good fishing and magnificent scenery.

The Blackfoot River enters Clark Fork just above Missoula. This is one of western Montana's best and most beautiful streams. It has excellent rainbow and cutthroat fishing. A productive tributary of Blackfoot River is North Fork Blackfoot. Another tributary which has good fishing is Clearwater River, adjacent to which there are many fine lakes. Of these, Seeley Lake is the best-known and a popular resort area.

Brown's Lake is a newly created lake on the upper Blackfoot. Trout here have grown very rapidly and some fishermen think it may eventually rival Duck Lake as a big trout producer.

The important fishing tributary of Clark Fork is Rock Creek which flows into the main river 18 miles east of Missoula. It is rated as the best Montana trout stream west of the Continental Divide. It is a good-sized stream larger than many other Montana streams which are dignified by the term river. Rock Creek is mainly a rainbow stream with some large browns in the lower part and some cutthroat in the headwaters.

The upper part of Clark Fork between Missoula and Deer Lodge was formerly so heavily polluted with mining waste that it contained practically no insect life or fish. Recently the pollution has been partially controlled by settling ponds, and the river is now making a strong comeback.

Flint Creek is a good small stream which flows into Clark Fork at Drummond. Pollution of this creek from mines at Phillipsburg is not as bad as it was, but a new highway has been built here, and much of the stream has been spoiled by straightening.

The uppermost good tributary of Clark Fork is Little Blackfoot which flows into the main river at Garrison. This stream is easily accessible because it is paralleled by the highway for its entire length. It is very popular with Helena fishermen, and is heavily fished.

Georgetown Lake is a productive fishery which is about 15 miles west of Anaconda. This lake has good fishing for rainbow, cutthroat, and some brook trout.

EASTERN MONTANA

Eastern Montana fishing is only of local interest among residents who don't have time to get to the good trout waters farther west. This is plains country and the rivers are heavily silted. The fishing is for walleyes, sauger, bullheads, and some channel catfish. There is trout fishing in a few widely scattered lakes and ponds where rainbows have been stocked. Among these are Bear Paw Lake south of Havre, Gartside Lake near Sidney, and Barnum Pond near Miles City. Many other small lakes and farm ponds through this region support largemouth bass.

There is some trout fishing in Fort Peck Reservoir, but these are only taken occasionally by fishermen who are after the more abundant warmwater species. Below Fort Peck to the North Dakota border, fishing is good for walleye and sauger. One unique fish which is taken on the Yellowstone near Glendive is the paddlefish (*which see*). These fish can be taken only by snagging. They run up to 30 pounds in weight and are good eating. —D.B.

MONTEREY SPANISH MACKEREL *Scomberomorus concolor* A fish of the mackerel family related to the other Spanish mackerels. It lacks the golden spots present on the sides of the sierra (*which see*) and has a greater number of gillrakers (20–29 on the first arch).

This species is now found from Panama Bay to the Gulf of California. It was once common in Monterey Bay, California, but in the late 1880's it disappeared from the California coast, and only a few specimens have been taken in that area since then. The flesh was considered a great delicacy and brought a high price on the market.
—B.B.C.
—R.H.G.

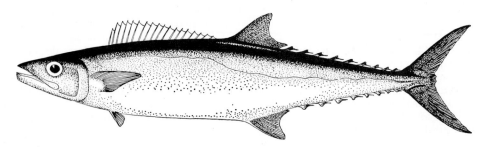

Monterey Spanish Mackerel

MOONEYE *Hiodon tergisus* A freshwater panfish which broadly resembles the gizzard shad and alewives, the mooneye is related to the goldeye (*which see*) and to the southern mooneye (*H. selenops*), which differs mainly in not having a keel on the belly in front of or behind the pelvic fin. These three species of the family Hiodontidae are characterized by having large eyes and mouths edged by small teeth; thus the common name toothed herring is often applied to this family.

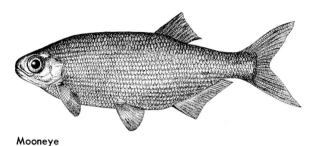

Mooneye

The dorsal surface of the mooneye is olivaceous, with dark blue reflections, and the sides are silvery. The anterior margin of the dorsal fin is inserted in front of the anterior margin of the anal fin (the dorsal fin of the goldeye originates behind the anterior margin of the anal fin). The mooneye generally attains a slightly larger size than the goldeye, and individuals of 2 pounds are not uncommon.

The mooneye is distributed from the Hudson Bay area (in tributary watersheds) to the Lake Champlain drainage system and west through Lake Erie and the Mississippi River to Alabama, Arkansas, Oklahoma, and Kansas.

ANGLING VALUE

Although not commonly taken by anglers, the mooneye will rise readily to small flies when feeding near the surface of large lakes. The fish seldom exceeds 2 pounds, so it is best sought on very light tackle.

FOOD VALUE

The flesh of the mooneye is dry and full of small bones. It is not a very satisfactory fish when eaten fresh but quite palatable when smoked, being similar to the goldeye. —D.dS.

MOONFISH *See* Lookdowns

MORAYS Family Muraenidae Reef fishes found in tropical seas, the members of which commonly reach a length of 6 feet, some may grow to 10 feet. Sometimes, and incorrectly, called moray eels, morays are pugnacious and can be harmful to man if provoked. There are about 120 species, and all have thick, scaleless skins, and large mouths with strong teeth (usually pointed and needle-sharp, but blunt in some species). Morays have small, rounded gill openings and are without pectoral or pelvic fins. In some species the dorsal, anal, and caudal fins are so small and indistinct (or even hidden under the skin) that the morays appear to be as finless as a snake. Many display lavish colors and patterns.

The color of some morays is affected by a skin coating of algae. The common green moray of Atlantic waters is actually blue-gray in color, but its normal covering of yellow algae gives it a chartreuse hue. Sometimes this species is brown instead of green, and this is probably caused by some different kind of algae.

As a rule, morays are rather poor swimmers. Generally they remain on the bottom—in caves, crevices, or tunnels—and only rarely venture into openwater. When well-anchored in rocks or coral they can move the forward part of their bodies with terrifying swiftness—and the movement is much like the strike of a snake.

DANGER TO MAN

Of all the fishes commonly associated with coral reefs, none commands more respect from swimmers and divers than the moray. Slimy, serpentine, and powerful, the moray certainly looks the part of the villain it is reputed to be. The sight of a huge head protruding from a hole in a reef, with tremendous tooth-studded jaws continually opening and closing and the head swelling at every respiration, is awe-inspiring. And when the moray extends 3–4 feet of its length out of its hole and arches its body, it looks as fearsome as a great cobra about to strike.

There is little room for argument over the danger to man from a moray which is injured or threatened, for it will often bite anything it can reach, including its own body. But it appears to be equally true that a moray will attack a man *only* when provoked. Unlike larger animals, such as sharks, morays are utterly incapable of devouring men or even of severing limbs. Most species have pointed teeth that are designed for grasping and holding, not for sawing or chewing; and they eat only prey which is small enough to be swallowed whole.

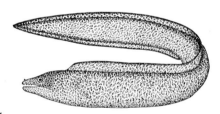

Moray

Obviously, then, a moray is not likely to attack a man out of hunger. In general, it will strike only when disturbed by an invasion of its home territory. Since a moray does not post "Keep Off" signs on the borders of its territory, however, a diver has no way of knowing when he is trespassing. As a result he may interpret certain behavior as offensive or aggressive when actually the fish is only trying to run the man away. In most cases a moray will not leave the safety of its hole to attack or chase a diver; but big specimens do not always follow the general rule.

Morays inhabit reefs and rocky areas throughout tropical and subtropical seas. They are found from the shore to a maximum depth of about 150 feet and are rarely, if ever, found in the open sea. They are common in both Florida and California and in these areas reach a maximum length of about 6 feet. Some of the Indo-Pacific species are much larger—possibly exceeding 10 feet.

In 1948 Vernon Brock, Director of the Division of Fish and Game in Hawaii, was chased and severely bitten by a monstrous brown moray (*Enchelynassa canina*) that he estimated to be about 10 feet long. Brock was spear-fishing on a reef at Johnston Island when he saw the huge moray under a ledge 20 feet below the surface. Diving down, Brock shot a spear through the moray's head, then returned to the surface for air. After 15–20 minutes elapsed, and the moray hadn't moved, Brock decided the fish was dead. Diving to the bottom he grasped his spear, on which the moray was impaled, and dragged the eel upward to the surface. Suddenly the moray lashed at the man with snapping jaws, and Brock dropped the spear and tried to get away, churning his flippered feet on the surface as he swam on his back. The moray overtook him, reared out of the water, and struck downward at his head. Brock raised his elbow to protect his face, and the eel crushed his arm with its immense jaws, then immediately released him. Bleeding profusely, the man swam to his boat, where a friend put a tourniquet on his arm. Ashore, a Navy surgeon spent several hours sewing up the wounds. Brock did not recover fully for three months.

During the war the author spent a year on Johnston Island and, while skin diving on the reefs, saw morays that appeared to be 8–10 feet long. The largest observed (actually measured), however, was a brown moray 7 feet, 10 inches in length, which was caught by Hawaiian fishermen on a handline. On the same island, in 1953, Major Bill Royal speared and landed a 7 foot, 2 inch moray of undetermined species after the moray came out of its hole 40 feet down and swam up at Royal while he floated on the surface.

Throughout Polynesia the natives fear large morays, which they claim are often aggressive. After the raft "Kon Tiki" was wrecked on a Pacific atoll several years ago, the members of the expedition told of being chased from the lagoon by morays.

In 1902 scientists aboard the Royal Indian Marine Survey Ship "Investigator" had an encounter with aggressive morays at Betraper Atoll, in the Indian Ocean. A. Alcock wrote: "As it was low spring tide, we had to leave our boat at the outermost edge of the atoll and to wade across the reef to the island, and during this delicate progress—for growing coral is by no means pleasant stuff to walk upon, even when a man is shod—we were surprised to find ourselves furiously attacked by a swarm of the spotted reef-eel (*Muraena pseudothyrsoidea*), for it was their breeding season, a period when they are always strangely irritable and aggressive."

In 1961 a man was attacked by a huge green moray (*Gymnothorax funebris*) near Key West, Florida. Lieutenant Rudy Enders, an instructor at the Navy Underwater Swimmers School, was spearfishing in thirty feet of water, looking for fish under a ledge. He had not speared anything, and there was no blood in the water. Just as Enders started up for air, a moray lunged out of a nearby hole and grabbed the diver's right wrist, slashing flesh and tendons, then released its grip. Lieutenant Enders shot to the surface and climbed aboard his boat, where a Navy doctor immediately applied a tourniquet. Enders spent several weeks in a hospital.

A few months later, at the same spot, Enders was again charged by a huge moray which he believed was the same one. On this occasion the fish came completely out of its hole and poised to strike at Ender's neck. A companion, Scott Slaughter, shot the moray through the head, whereupon the fish pulled itself off the spear and disappeared into the rocks. Slaughter said that the moray was at least seven feet long.

Attacks such as these are rare. Most injuries from morays occur when divers reach under ledges or into holes while hunting spiny lobsters or shellfish or when trying to retrieve a speared fish that has wedged itself in a crevice. Reaching into a moray's cave is, no doubt, from the moray's standpoint an act of aggression. It is unquestionably a hazardous practice. On two occasions men diving with me have had fingers bitten by small spotted morays (*Gymnothorax moringa*). In California a considerable number of divers have been bitten by *G. mordax* while feeling under rocks and ledges for abalones. According to marine biologists G. E. and Nettie MacGinitie, *G. mordax* feeds largely on octopuses and probably mistakes the movements of a man's fingers for the arms of a small octopus. Some divers say, however, that California morays are very fond of abalone and that men have been bitten when morays tried to take the shellfish away from them. California divers sometimes keep morays at a distance by tapping them on the nose with an iron bar which they carry to pry abalone loose from the rocks.

There are two popular conceptions about morays that seem to be fallacious. One is that the bite of a moray is venomous, and the other is that morays, on grabbing a diver, will hold on tenaciously until the diver has drowned. While it is possible that the bite of some species of moray is toxic, this has never been definitely established, and no venom apparatus has been found in specimens examined. (It should be noted, however, that the flesh of some morays can be highly poisonous to humans when eaten.)

The weight of evidence seems to be against the holding-underwater story, too. A moray can, undeniably, grasp an object with great tenacity; and a diver who panics upon being bitten could easily drown. But virtually all persons injured by morays have reported that the bite was quick and brief and that the fish made no effort to hold them. It is doubtful that a moray could hold a person for long, in any case, since it must open its mouth to pump water through its gills in the process of respiration. Normal respiration for a moray seems to be rather rapid; the animal often seems to pant even at rest. When moving rapidly or attempting to hold a man, it would surely need even more oxygen. The stories of the "bulldog grip" of a moray must, in the absence of concrete evidence, be considered in the same light as the tales of "maneater" clams drowning swimmers—possible, perhaps, but unproven and unlikely.

The wild, frenzied movements of a moray that has been speared or hooked are amazing to behold. This animal's remarkable habit of tying its body into knots is a truly amazing thing to see. It happens so frequently, and with so many different species, that it could hardly be termed accidental; but the possibility that the movements are calculated is also rather incredible. Possibly the behavior is innate, resulting conceivably from eons of close contact with octopuses—for in some areas the octopus and the moray seem to be natural enemies, and the knotting pattern is certainly an efficient method of coping with small octopuses. G. E. and Nettie MacGinitie, who have watched many captive morays eat octopuses, describe the method as follows:

"When the eel grasps the octopus in its mouth, the octopus immediately fastens to the head of the eel with its tentacles. The eel then throws a loop with its tail around its own body and slips its body backward through this loop, thus forcing the tentacles of the octopus loose from its head, and at the same time makes another gobble or two to get the octopus farther down its throat."

Chapman Grant, while collecting specimens for the Key West Aquarium in 1912, saw the same knot-tying routine employed for quite another purpose by a three-foot green moray. The fish, caught in a fish trap, had so stuffed itself with grunts that it could hardly move when Grant dumped it out of the trap onto the deck of a boat. The moray tied itself in a knot, then squeezed itself backward through the loop, forcing the eaten fish out of its mouth, one by one. Continually repeating the process, it divested itself of five grunts and a Bermuda chub. Then the moray slithered over the gunwale and dropped back into the water. Grant reports that he later saw two other green morays regurgitate food by this method.

The same means is often used by green morays caught on hooks to break the line or pull the hook from their mouths. Once at Marathon, Florida, I saw a large green moray that had apparently tried to break a strong wire leader by this method and, unsuccessful in the attempt, had strangled itself.

Almost nothing is known about the breeding habits of morays. There is little or no evidence of migration, and individual morays are believed to sometimes inhabit the same holes for years. When spawning, females release great quantities of eggs into the water; and like other related fishes the young go through a leptocephalus stage in which the larvae are long, ribbonlike and almost transparent, much like the larvae of tarpon, bonefish, and ladyfish.

According to some of the writers of ancient Rome, the people of that day relished the flesh of morays and even raised them in great ponds connected by canals to the Mediterranean. One supplier reportedly furnished six thousand morays for a great feast given by Caesar. Some Romans were said to have trained morays and kept them as pets, though this seems unlikely, as morays in captivity never seem to become really tame (and will in fact climb out of a small aquarium if the tank has no firmly fixed lid). Since the Romans probably used the term *muraena* to apply to both morays and conger eels (and even on occasion to lampreys, which are not eels at all), it is likely that many of the moray legends refer to other fishes.

—W.M.S.

MORPHOLOGY Structure; the study of the gross structure

MOSQUITOFISH *Gambusia affinis* This small member of the livebearer family (Poeciliidae) is of economic importance because it feeds on the larvae and pupae of mosquitoes. It occurs in fresh, brackish, and saltwater. The mosquitofish is common to the southern United States and has been widely introduced to warmwater habitats elsewhere in the world because of its value in mosquito control. Although the female seldom attains 2 inches in length, and the male mosquitofish a length of 1 inch, the species is also an important forage for sunfish, young black bass, and young barracuda.

LIVEBEARER

The female mosquitofish produces live young. Fertilization is internal and a single mating provides sufficient spermatozoa for a series of broods. Its gestation period is from 21–28 days. The number of eyed embryos may vary from about 10–300 depending on the size of the female.

—A.J.McC.

MOSSBUNKER A common name for the Atlantic menhaden (*which see*)

MOTTRAM, JAMES CECIL English (1880–1945) The unsung genius of English angling literature, Mottram published *Fly Fishing: Some New Arts and Mysteries* (1915), an unusually forward-looking book; one of its mysteries is why it has been so consistently overlooked. Major John Waller Hills in his classic *A History of Fly Fishing for Trout* covered English fishing books up to his day with scholarly thoroughness and was conscientious about mentioning even those works, usually American, that lay outside his chosen theme of showing the development and heritage of British fishing. But Hills had a rare talent and eloquence for advocacy of those writers whom he deemed in any way original in the advancement of the sport, and he was unstinting of his space and attention in dealing with otherwise undistinguished authors if he could but point out something in their pages that had some relevancy, however slight, to the subsequent development and refinement of the art. He might logically have been expected, then, to have jumped in joyously as chief drumbeater for Mottram as the most innovative talent of his time. But Hills dismissed Mottram with a sentence, saying in a mention of him among others: "Also there is much new and stimulating matter in Mr. J.C. Mottram's *Fly Fishing*."

Even more mysterious is the faint praise with which Mottram is damned by James Robb in *Notable Angling Literature* (published in 1945 or 1946; it is undated, but interior evidence indicates its approximate date of appearance). Robb lists Mottram's book and, like Hills before him, praises it with minimal mention: "J.C. Mottram's *Fly Fishing* is broad-minded and challenging." He gives equally short shrift to Mottram's next work, *Sea Trout and Other Fishing Studies* (1923), saying simply: "He has much to say about worm fishing, and the use of fly, wet, dry and blow line. It is useful and practical."

Hills published before Hewitt's first book appeared, so he is not mentioned by Hills, although La Branche is; but Robb lists both of Hewitt's first two books (published in 1922 and 1926) and the fact that Robb gives this much indication of being acquainted with Hewitt's work takes on additional interest when it is realized how startlingly Mottram anticipated by from 7–21 years some of Hewitt's most important experiments and conclusions. Comparison of Hewitt's *A Trout and Salmon Fisherman for Seventy-five Years* (1950), which represented all Hewitt's theories and diagrams of the previous 30, from *Telling on the Trout* (1922) through *Manuals on Nymph Fishing and Stream Improvement* (1934), shows that with the sole exception of the reporting of Hewitt's and La Branche's experiences with the Neversink skater there is virtually nothing substantive in Hewitt in 1950 that wasn't anticipated by Mottram in 1915, including the diagram of the study of the stress and strain on a 6-foot rod.

This comparison is not cited to take anything away from Hewitt, whose exploits are remarkable (and are the subject of another entry under his name), but rather to emphasize how extraordinarily prophetic Mottram was with his anticipation, as far back as 1915, of what anglers generally considered news decades later, not only in respect to light tackle and short rods and nymph fishing and stream improvement but even in some of Mottram's anticipations of the use of tiny terrestrials in the case of smutting fish, a phenomenon that also had to wait to appear again in print until the publication of Vincent Marinaro's *A Modern Dry Fly Code* (1950).

Mottram's subsequent books, *Trout Fisheries: Their Care and Preservation* (1928) and *Sea Trout* (1923) previously mentioned, are much less outstanding than his amazing debut in 1915 might have given every reason to expect. In the sweepstakes of angling Mottram showed "early foot" to an astonishing degree, but without the stamina to maintain it over the distance. He did, however, make something of a comeback to his early form with his undated but post-World War II *Thoughts on Angling*, a small but very thought-provoking book. His first book, *Fly Fishing: Some New Arts and Mysteries*, was reissued in 1921, but both editions are extremely hard to acquire and Mottram's turn has not yet come in the current scheduling of reprints of the various angling classics by Crown and Freshet Press. When his day does come, there will be a new star in the fisherman's heavens, and Mottram, after half a century of scandalous neglect, will be recognized for what he is, the most remarkable "sleeper" in at least seven decades of angling annals. When the currency of Mottram's classic is restored, and he receives the same belated justice that is now serving to bolster the reputations of Preston Jennings, Vincent Marinaro, John Atherton, and other innovative figures threatened with being overlooked, he will at last take his place, right next to G.E.M. Skues, in the gallery of great English angling figures. Until then, angling has the paradoxical irony of knowing who its Unknown Soldier is, as well as where the body is buried.   —A.G.

MOUNTAIN SUCKER *Catostomus platyrhynchus* A dark green sucker with fine black specks along the back. Ventral surfaces white. Body slender. Head short. Scales small, 90–100, in the lateral line, crowded anteriorly.

Mountain Sucker

Lips full. Distinct notch between upper and lower lip at the corners of the mouth. The range of this species is from the Columbia River drainage and the headwater of the Missouri to the Bonneville Basin and the Snake River drainage of Utah and Wyoming.

HABITS

The mountain sucker prefers the clear, cold mountain streams where it is found in the rockstrewn riffle areas. This sucker spawns in late spring in the shallow tributaries. At this time the males develop an orange lateral band. The food consists mostly of algae and some aquatic insects. This species reaches a size of 12 inches.

ECONOMIC VALUE

Of little or no importance for food for man, the mountain sucker does provide excellent forage for trout and other sport fish.   —R.A.J.

MOUNTAIN WHITEFISH *Prosopium williamsoni* Also known as the Rocky Mountain whitefish, the mountain whitefish is endemic to lakes and streams on the western slope of the Rocky Mountains from northern California to southern British Columbia. This species has a quasi-game status in that many anglers consider it a nuisance when found in trout streams. It is not as interesting nor as active as the lake whitefish (*which see*). The mountain whitefish is regarded in the same way as the "chub" or fallfish, common to Eastern trout streams. Some fisheries managers also consider the mountain whitefish a detriment in that it competes with trout for both food and space. However, in some heavily fished Western rivers where natural trout reproduction makes an insignificant contribution to the total catch, the whitefish can provide a dividend to the put-and-take type of angling.

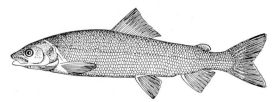

Mountain Whitefish

The mountain whitefish generally resembles the lake whitefish although the body is more cylindrical. The body coloration is brown on the dorsal surface, shading to silver and white on the belly. The snout and lower jaw are short and blunt. The dorsal fin and the anal fin have 12–13 rays. The lateral-line scale count is usually 80–90, although there is some variation, both lower and higher. Although mountain whitefish grow to 5 pounds, the majority caught weigh less than 2 pounds, and a 3-pound fish is considered exceptional.

ANGLING VALUE

Mountain whitefish provide a considerable winter fishery in many parts of the West, and in regions where the steelhead is absent, such as Colorado, Utah, Montana, and Wyoming, they keep the coldfoot clan busy between trout seasons. The fish are also plentiful in Washington and on the eastern slope of the Sierras in California and Idaho. Although shore ice may extend some distance over the water, the main channels of most rivers remain open, and the angler merely drifts his bait along the bottom with a fly or spinning rod. The natural diet of whitefish consists chiefly of caddis larvae, stonefly nymphs, and midge larvae; during the fall months they are heavy consumers of their own eggs. The best baits, therefore, are the natural stonefly nymph and salmon eggs, but maggots and fruitflies are also used.

During warm weather, mountain whitefish rise readily to artificial flies, and may also be taken on spinners.

FOOD VALUE

Mountain whitefish are a palatable food fish, particularly in the winter months. Although they are usually fried or pansautéed, the fish are excellent when poached or smoked. —A.J.McC.

MOZAMBIQUE Mozambique is located on the east coast of Africa and is bordered by Tanzania, Zambia, Rhodesia, Malawi, South Africa, and the Indian Ocean. This Portuguese territory is approximately 297,864 square miles in area and has an estimated population of about 7,200,000. The coast varies from high, rocky cliffs in the north to low-lying mangrove swamps south of the Zambezi River delta. There are more than 50 river systems in Mozambique, and the Zambezi more or less divides the country in half. Portions of the interior are mountainous and the highlands along the Rhodesian border reach about 9,000 feet. There is a great variety of animal life including lion, elephant, black rhinoceros, leopard, buffalo, and various antelopes. There are three game reserves and at least one, Gorongoza National Park (1,150 square miles), is well worth a visit in order to see and photograph African game.

Mozambique has a typical tropical climate, with a hot, rainy season from October to March and a cooler dry season from April to September. Temperatures are moderated by altitude, but the general range is from 75°–80°F in the fishing months, with exceptional coastal highs to a maximum of 107°F. The peak period for marlin fishing is from mid-September to mid-December.

Big black marlin highlight Mozambique's angling. This 900-pounder (left) is weighed in at Bazaruto Island

Mozambique has come into angling prominence because of its superb billfishing and, more specifically, its black marlin. Annually, an increasing number of sportfishing boats are appearing in the angling centers of Mozambique, so the still very critical problem—shortage of boats—is slowly being solved.

In order of frequency black marlin, Pacific sailfish, striped marlin, Pacific blue marlin, and swordfish can be taken from the waters of Mozambique, though there is a feeling among some sportsmen that the broadbill population may be greater than realized and that, undoubtedly, more swordfish would be baited if faster boats were available. Other species include mako and hammerhead sharks, dolphin, yellowfin tuna, barracuda, queenfish, tanguigue, wahoo, cobia, and bonefish. The coastal waters of Mozambique have produced a number of exceptional bonefish (18–20 pounds). These have been caught incidental to the commercial fishery at Pomene, Inhaca, Bazaruto, and Inhambane. Bonefishing has not developed as a sport because this species is not a popular food locally, although some are marketed; and no effort has been made to establish its centers of abundance or season. Indian Ocean bonefish are found in deeper waters than, for example, in the Bahamas and Florida Keys, and generally speaking appear to be more numerous in the rainy season (January through March).

PARADISE ISLANDS

The best place for black marlin is undoubtedly Bazaruto (Paradise) Islands, which are located in the Indian Ocean and can be reached from Vilanculos by boat (scheduled service three times a week) or charter plane or from Beira (about a 40-minute flight). The boat trip is not recommended.

Annually, Paradise Islands produce at least one 1,000-pound black marlin. Of the blacks logged during a 12-month period 24 percent were over 500 pounds, and 12 percent weighed over 800 pounds; thus, this area is one of the most outstanding places in the world for big marlin. The largest black boated to date weighed 1,139 pounds, but much heavier marlin have been hooked. Numerous small black marlin, 20–80 pounds, are usually taken on feathers, while trolling for bait. It appears that the Paradise Islands may be a spawning as well as a feeding area for black marlin.

The best time for marlin fishing is from mid-September to mid-December, but it is also true that blacks have been taken during every month at Paradise Islands. Since most anglers have been fishing this area in the fall season it is logical that the most impressive catches would be made during this period.

The only accommodations available are at Santa Carolina Island (one of the Paradise Islands).

POMENE

In addition to Paradise Islands there is a new fishing center recently established at Pomene (closest town with an airport is Inhambane). This is a very comfortable resort. There are only a few sportfishing boats available, but more have been placed on order. The Mozambique Current is only about 500 yards offshore of Pomene, and some big black marlin have been taken within 2 miles of the hotel. Since this is a new fishing center, little is known at this time about its angling possibilities. A 23-pound bonefish was reportedly taken here by Harry Manners.

INHACA ISLAND

A third possibility for billfishing is at Inhaca Island, which is about 30 miles out of Lourenco Marques. The accommodations, service, and food at the Inhaca Hotel (P.O. Box 1778 Lourenco Marques, Mozambique) are excellent. Dolphin, yellowfin tuna, sailfish, and tanguigue are the important species here, and, while Inhaca is not geared for sportfishing, boats can be procured from Club de Pesca Desportiva (Lourenco Marques, Mozambique) provided sufficient notice is given. Occasionally black marlin are taken from Inhaca, but since most fishermen troll with either feathers or strip bait, the dolphin and sailfish catches predominate.

TACKLE

Bring your own tackle. Although some equipment is for rent at Santa Carolina it is not reliable. The most popular gear is 80-pound test and 130-pound test class for the marlin. The usual bait is a 4–7 pound bonito; however, bonefish of similar size are preferred when available. Trolling is the usual procedure, but good success is had at times by deep drifting a live bonito.   —A.J.McC.

MUD CAT A regional name for the flat bullhead, flathead catfish, green bullhead, and yellow bullhead. (See entries under each of these names)

MUDFISH Regional name for bowfin (which see)

MUD PUPPY A common name for the tiger salamander larva, also called waterdog (which see)

MUD SUNFISH *Acantharchus pomotis* This little-known and secretive sunfish is a small, heavy-set panfish with 5–8 indistinct, dark longitudinal bands along the sides. It has a rounded tail, and the mouth is large, extending beyond the middle of the eye; the body is a dark green color.

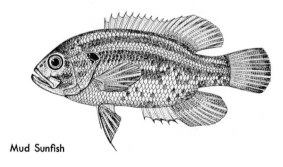

Mud Sunfish

The mud sunfish ranges from southeastern New York to Florida in the lowland streams and sluggish waters of the coastal plain.

ANGLING VALUE

None. The mud sunfish seldom reaches 7 inches in length and is generally much smaller.   K.B.

MULLETS Family Mugilidae Marine and freshwater fishes of worldwide distribution containing over 100 species. Mullet are commonly seen leaping out of the water in bays, lagoons, and estuaries. They jump and then fall back on the surface in a rigid posture making a characteristic fluttering noise with their tails. The reason for this habitual jumping has never been established. Vast schools of mullet are also observed during periods of migration along the coastal shoreline at which time they attract many gamefish. Mullet feed on microscopic animal and plant foods and thus have no apparent angling value. But in a few areas and at certain seasons mullet have been known to strike baits and artificial lures (see Jamaica). Although their capture by hook and line is rare, they do provide sport on fly rod and cane pole. Mullet have great food value and are important as bait for larger saltwater gamefish, such as the tarpon, snook, dolphin, kingfish, and sailfish. The distribution of mullet along North American shores is from central California south and from Maine to Mexico, with the chief center of abundance in the southern Atlantic. Florida provides about three-quarters of the total U.S. mullet landings (35,000,000 pounds per year).

The following is a key to the American mullets of the genus *Mugil*:

A. Soft dorsal and anal fins almost naked; 3 anal rays, 8 softrays (rarely 7); sides with dark longitudinal stripes along the rows of scales; caudal deeply forked; size large.
   B. Scales about 33 in longitudinal series; depth about 4½ in length to base of caudal; teeth very minute, lips rather thin.   *liza*
   BB. Scales about 41 in longitudinal series; depth about 4 in length to base of caudal; teeth close-set and rather small.   *cephalus*

AA. Soft dorsal and anal fins scaled; sides without dark stripes along the rows of scales, caudal less deeply forked; size smaller.
   C. 3 anal rays, 9 softrays; scales 35–45 in a longitudinal series
      D. Pectoral not nearly reaching origin of dorsal; scales 38–39.   *curema*
      DD. Pectoral nearly reaching origin of dorsal; scales 35–36.   *gaimardiana*
   CC. 3 anal rays, 8 softrays; scales very large, about 33 in a longitudinal series; teeth wide-set, larger than in any other species, about as long as the nostril; upper lip thick; pectoral not nearly reaching front of dorsal; size small.   *trichodon*

HOW TO CATCH MULLET

Mullet are easily caught with a cast net. Those captured for use as bait are quite often netted from bridges and on the mud flats of tidal lagoons. For food purposes, mullet caught in the surf or around inlets where the water is clear and the bottom is composed of sand have a superior flavor. Mullet are also snagged by casting a weighted treble hook into the densely packed schools.

FOOD VALUE

Mullet have an iodine content 900 times greater than the best grade of beef. They are also rich in minerals. Fat mullet are utilized in smoked form, and lean mullet are usually marketed fresh either whole or in fillet form. The flesh has a mild, nutty flavor and is best broiled or grilled. The roe and testes of the male (sometimes called white roe) are considered gourmet delicacies. See also Black Mullet, Striped Mullet, White Mullet, as bait see under Live Bait   —A.J.McC.

MUMMICHOG *Fundulus heteroclitus* Also known as the common killifish, this member of the family Cyprinodontidae is recognized by its stout body, deep caudal peduncle, short snout, large scales, and broadly rounded fins. These, in combination with the alternating dark and silvery bars and white or yellow spots on the side, distinguish it from the striped killifish (*which see*). During the breeding season the colors become more intense. Males are dark olive-green with the lateral bars distinct, while the females are much paler and lack distinct bars. The dark-barred pattern of the young disappears with age. Maximum size is 6 inches, but most are less than 4 inches; females are slightly larger.

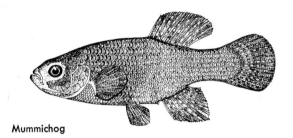

Mummichog

The mummichog ranges in shallow water from Texas to the Gulf of St. Lawrence. Extremely common in coastal waters, it frequents bays, lagoons, estuaries, salt marshes, and ditches, in salt- and freshwaters, but occurs predominantly in brackish water. It is common over mud or muddy-sand bottom, and during the winter it burrows into the mud in a torpid state.

LIFE HISTORY

In spring the mummichog migrates from brackish into fresher waters; it is not known if it returns to deepwater with the onset of cold weather. It is highly resistant to adverse environmental conditions, living in areas nearly devoid of oxygen, and it is moderately resistant to pollution.

Spawning occurs from April to August in only a few inches of water, following extensive courtship. The rather large eggs sink to the bottom. The young grow up in the shallow water and resemble their parents even at a small size. The mummichog is omnivorous, feeding to a large extent on plant material, detritus, worms, crustaceans, small mollusks, and small fishes.

Although of no direct importance, its widespread distribution in shallow waters makes it a ready source of food for many fishes, and even birds.

ANGLING VALUE

It is a very important bait for anglers because of its hardiness and activity on a hook. However, its greatest value perhaps lies in its value as an eradicator of mosquito larvae. —D.dS.

MUSKELLUNGE *Esox masquinongy* The largest members of the pike family, muskellunge are prize freshwater gamefish. They are big (15–30 pounds is not unusual), and are sometimes caught in the 50–60-pound class. Although muskellunge is the accepted common name in the United States, this fish is officially designated in the laws and publications of Canada as "maskinonge." There are more than fifty common names and variations

in spelling which include muskalonge, muskallunge, 'lunge, musky, muskie, pike, blue pike, great pike, jack, spotted muskellunge, barred muskellunge, tiger muskellunge, and great muskellunge. The names have been influenced by local fancy and description and the origin of the fishermen. The latter fact is evidenced by the name "piconeau" given to the muskellunge of the Ohio by the early French settlers. There are many interpretations as to the origin of the common name which has been ascribed to the French, French-Canadian, and Cree dialects. However, Jordan states that it originated from the Ojibway dialect meaning *mas* for ugly and *kinononge* for fish. This, he claimed, has been perverted to muskellunge and wrongly derived from the French *masquallongee*.

The muskellunge is a fish with an elongated body about six times as long as it is deep. The front of the head is shaped like a duck's bill, and the head is scaled. The dorsal and anal fins are set well back on the body. The muskellunge can be distinguished from other pikes by the lack of scales on the lower half of the cheek and gill cover. Also it can be further differentiated from the northern pike by the number of sensory pores on the lower jaw or mandible. The northern pike usually has 5 while the muskellunge has 6–9 mandibular sensory pores on each side. The markings on the sides of the muskellunge may be barred, dark-spotted, or plain, while adult northern pike almost always have light-colored, bean-shaped spots on the sides.

SUBSPECIES

There are three recognized subspecies of muskellunge. Since the descriptions overlap, the subspecies are best separated by geographic distribution. The Great Lakes muskellunge (*Esox masquinongy masquinongy*) is generally considered to inhabit the Great Lakes basin. The Ohio or Chautauqua muskellunge (*Esox m. ohioensis*) is found in Chautauqua Lake, New York, and southward through the Ohio drainage. The tiger or northern muskellunge (*Esox m. immaculatus*) is indigenous to Minnesota, Wisconsin, and the portion of Michigan close to the Wisconsin border. The range of the muskellunge, in general, is north to Lake Abitibi in the James Bay drainage, west to the Lake of the Woods in the Hudson Bay drainage, in Minnesota and Wisconsin in the Upper Mississippi drainage, the Ohio drainage from New York through Pennsylvania to Tennessee, North Carolina, and Georgia in the TVA system, and east in the Great Lakes basin to the St. Lawrence drainage.

EVOLUTION AND DISTRIBUTION

The distribution of the muskellunge can be correlated with the glacial advances and retreats. The teeth of muskies have been found in Pleistocene deposits as far south as northwest Oklahoma. It is believed that they entered the Mississippi drainage from the sea, and were isolated in the Upper Mississippi region during the retreat of the glaciers. Since numerous fossil species are found in the Tertiary of Europe, this would indicate that the origin of this family was in southern Europe, although it is true that most of the living species of the family are in America.

Occasional mention is made of the pikes in the *Jesuits Relations* and other early accounts of the Great Lakes and Canadian fur-trading regions, but none of these re-

Muskellunge (Chautauqua or Barred), 22-pound Male,
Chautauqua Lake, New York

ports gives the impression that the pike was regarded as an important food fish. The Indians regarded the pikes as poor fish for eating and used them only when other fatter fishes were lacking.

Until 1950 the range of the muskellunge was more or less confined to limited sections of the border country from the St. Lawrence through the Great Lakes and northward into Ontario. Muskies were caught in parts of the Ohio drainage system and western New York, the Tennessee River system, Michigan, Minnesota, and Wisconsin. Because of improved methods of artificial propagation that distribution has been extended, and more new muskellunge fisheries are being created each year. A brief review of the top North American muskie waters would include Lake-of-the-Woods and Eagle Lake in Ontario; St. Lawrence River, Black Lake, and Chautauqua Lake in New York; Chippewa Flowage, Lake Court Oreilles, Flambeau Flowage, Mantowish, and Lake Pokegama in Wisconsin. Minnesota offers Big Mantrap, Leech Lake, Lake Winnibigoshish, and Lake Belle Taine. In Michigan the St. Clair River is popular. Ohio has many muskie waters such as the Muskingum River and Rocky Fork Lake. Except in big rivers like the St. Lawrence, streamfishing for muskellunge is not usually productive of heavy fish. The average is apt to be less than 5 pounds, but an occasional 20–25 pounder is taken in Southern rivers like the Obed, Daddys Creek, and Crab Orchard Creek in Tennessee, or the Green River, Tigart Creek, Ohio River, and Barren River in Kentucky. West Virginia offers some muskie holes in the Little Kanawha, Middle Island Creek, Pocataligo River, and the Hughes. Pennsylvania's muskellunge fishing is found principally in Presque Isle Bay on Lake Erie, Lake LeBoeuf, Conneaut Lake, French Creek, the Shenango River, the Allegheny River at Tionesta, and Pymatuning Dam.

SPAWNING

The time of spawning of the muskellunge varies with the locality, seasonal temperatures, and possibly strains. The spawning of the northern muskellunge in Wisconsin may start as early as April 10 and continue through mid-May. The Great Lakes muskellunge may spawn from mid-May to mid-June. Spawning usually occurs at night in shallow bays on muck bottom covered with detritus—preferably in an area with sunken stumps and logs. Eggs are deposited indiscriminately over several hundred yards of shoreline in water 6–12 inches.

Optimum water temperatures for spawning are 48° to 56°F., but muskies will spawn in temperatures as high as 60°F. If the weather turns cold and temperatures of the littoral zone drop below 50°F., the spawning ceases or becomes erratic.

In Tennessee, females were found to become mature when they were 3–4 years old and approximately 25 inches long. Male fish mature at 3 years of age and approximately 22 inches long. Canadian muskellunge mature at 3–5 years and 22½–29½ inches in length. Muskellunge in Wisconsin mature at 4–6 years, and little difference in the age of maturity is found between the sexes.

The first muskies begin to run when the water reaches 42°F. The first run consists almost entirely of males, but when the water reaches 46°F., the females run and very early eggs may be stripped from a few. The spawning of other fish in a lake follows a sequence which leads up to muskellunge spawning. Northern pike spawn when the ice leaves the lake at temperatures of 40°–46°F., followed by the walleye at temperatures of about 45°–50°F. Perch spawn toward the end of the walleye run and usually continue after the walleye are through. The muskellunge are next in spawning order in waters of 48°–56°F., and after they have finished, appropriately enough, other species important as forage begin to spawn.

Muskellunge 25–53 inches in length will produce from 22,000–180,000 eggs. The number of eggs produced is directly correlated to the size of the female. One 40-pounder produced 225,000 eggs. The usual number of eggs from 30–40-pound fish is 220,000–270,000, or 4 or more quarts. When the female deposits her eggs, the male spawns simultaneously at her side. The female does not release all of her eggs at one time but spawns at intervals as she cruises over a suitable bottom. Neither the female nor the male muskellunge builds a nest, nor is there any parental care attempted after the eggs are deposited.

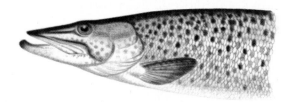

Muskellunge, Spotted Form

Factors limiting reproduction are coldwaters, fluctuating temperatures, fluctuating water levels at spawning time, predation by other fishes and invertebrates on eggs and fry, quantity and size of live zooplankton and fish forage available for musky fry, and hybridization of species.

HABITAT

Muskellunge are found in rivers, lakes, and streams. They prefer the quiet waters normally in an area of submerged weed beds. They are usually associated with clearwaters but an exception to this is in West Virginia where the muskellunge inhabit the muddier streams. This fish usually remains in less than 15 feet of water but is sometimes found in waters to depths of 40–50 feet and in waters that have little vegetation. Muskellunge in Tennessee are found at elevations of 730–1,735 feet in streams with conglomerate or sandstone bedrock. There is little movement of muskies in summer, and the larger specimens will remain in the same pool during this period. If there is any movement in the summer, it will normally be upstream, while in the fall, when more movement occurs, it will be in a downstream direction. Young muskellunge tend to stay in the same locality, hiding in the shade of submerged objects.

Factors which influence migratory behavior of the muskellunge are water temperatures, water-level fluctuations, the food supply, and the movement of food supplies.

AGE AND GROWTH

The muskellunge is considered to be one of the fastest growing of the freshwater fishes. At 6 years they are twice as long as a largemouth bass and almost twice as long as walleye of the same age. The growth of muskellunge varies among and within populations. The differentiation of growth within populations probably has considerable effect on the total population since the faster-growing fish feed on the fish of slower growth, particularly if other forage fish are not available. Five to 7 pounds of forage fish are required to produce one pound of muskellunge.

The greatest growth occurs in early summer and early fall when temperatures are optimum. Growth is more rapid during the first three years, whereas after the second year the growth decreases until about the thirteenth summer when it is hardly more than one inch per year. Females tend to grow faster than males, and at 5 years of age the female will be 3–6 inches longer than the male. However, the females weigh the same as males in proportion to their length. The average Canadian muskellunge reaches the legal length (30 inches) by the fifth summer, but this may vary between 4–7 years. In Tennessee, in the extreme southern range of the muskellunge, few fish are taken over 5 pounds or over 30 inches. The legal limit in this Southern state is 25 inches. Farther to the north, the Wisconsin muskellunge reaches the legal size of 30 inches in the fourth summer.

The usual age of most creeled muskies is 3–6 years. There are several records of 18- and 19-year-old fish, but the oldest fish ever recorded was a specimen of 69.7 pounds, the age of which was determined by scales and vertebrae to be 30 years.

For comparative purposes, the lengths and weights of muskellunge from two different regions are listed in the table on this same page. These two subspecies are from quite widely separated localities.

LENGTH AND WEIGHT RELATIONSHIPS FROM MICHIGAN AND NEW YORK

Lake St. Clair, Michigan		Chautauqua Lake, New York	
Length (inches)	Weight (pounds)	Length (inches)	Weight (pounds)
30.00–30.35	—	30.5–31.5	7.41
30.50–31.25	5.50	31.5–32.5	7.86
31.50–32.25	6.50	32.5–33.5	8.29
32.50–33.25	8.00	33.5–34.5	9.07
33.50–34.25	7.00	34.5–35.5	10.25
34.50–35.25	7.00	35.5–36.5	10.62
35.50–36.25	8.25	36.5–37.5	10.60
36.50–37.25	9.50	37.5–38.5	12.28
37.50–38.25	10.50	38.5–39.5	12.13
38.50–39.25	11.00	39.5–40.5	13.60
39.50–40.25	13.00	40.5–41.5	14.97
40.50–41.25	13.00	41.5–42.5	14.00
41.50–42.25	13.00	42.5–43.5	20.50
42.50–43.25	15.75	43.5–44.5	21.30
43.50–44.25	20.50	44.5–45.5	21.00
44.50–45.25	18.00	45.5–46.5	—
45.50–46.25	21.00	46.5–47.5	28.25
46.50–47.25	22.50	47.5–48.5	17.23
47.50–48.25	23.50	48.5–49.5	—
48.50–49.25	23.00	49.5–50.5	—
49.50–50.25	26.00	50.5–51.5	34.75

For comparative purposes the following age and length relationship for Wisconsin muskellunge may be viewed as typical of their growth.

Age (years)	Length (inches)
I	7.0
II	14.4
III	19.8
IV	24.4
V	28.2
VI	31.2
VII	33.8
VIII	36.4
IX	38.0
X	39.7
XI	41.2
XII	43.1
XIII	44.4
XIV	45.6
XV	47.3
XVI	47.0
XVII	49.5
XVIII	49.7
XIX	51.1

FEEDING HABITS

When muskellunge are feeding, they line up on the prey, look it over, and seemingly try to decide if it is alive. This concentration on a potential prey is sometimes so intent that the young muskellunge can be touched before it takes alarm. This poised position and concentration make the muskies very susceptible to predation. If the musky decides it has a fair prey, it coils into an S-shape and strikes like a snake from above and behind. The lateral body movement of the minnow makes it difficult for the muskie to strike accurately, and the prey often moves before the muskie strikes. A motionless muskellunge is much easier to catch than a moving minnow, and this often results in heavy cannibalism when an abundance of other food is not present. If the prey is caught it is grasped broadside, and with each shake of the head, the minnow is brought close to the mouth and is eventually swallowed headfirst. They become better at catching minnows as they become older, they never become as adept at catching fish as a young largemouth bass.

Little preference is shown by adult muskellunge for food. They take what is most available. In Canada, depending on the region surveyed, their diet consisted of from 55–71 percent yellow perch. It has been stated that they prefer softrayed fishes rather than bass, bluegills, and perch, but this again would probably depend on availability. Other food items found in the stomachs of large muskellunge include snakes, muskrats, ducks, crayfish, walleyes, suckers, minnows, and salamanders. Muskellunge feed best at 68°F., and when the water temperature reaches 90°F., they stop feeding. As temperatures were lowered below 68°F., feeding slowed down.

—K.B.

FISHING FOR MUSKELLUNGE

Muskellunge are generally taken with spinning, baitcasting, or trolling tackle. On rare occasions they are also caught with the fly rod. The key to catching muskellunge is in the retrieve. There is no hard-and-fast rule, but, unlike bass fishing, which counts heavily on slow reeling with long pauses, the veteran muskie man frequently employs a fast retrieve. One would expect that any predator which lies waiting to ambush its food is going to snap at slow-moving baits or even stationary ones; yet it doesn't always work out that way. Nothing excites the muskie more than a lively lure teased along the surface. Topwater plugs are very effective. There's a variety of specials on the market featuring propellers, flaptails, and chugging heads. Darter-type plugs, which run a foot or so under the surface, also have their innings when worked at a fast pace. Next to plugs large casting spinners with a bucktail trailer are preferred by many specialists; these lures have a single or double spinner blade in the No. 3 to No. 5 sizes.

Muskellunge usually remain out of sight in very dense weed beds at depths of 6–15 feet; in some lakes muskellunge go down to 60–70 feet during hot weather. Deep trolling is most popular among muskie specialists in the summer period. Bear in mind, however, that motor trolling or the use of metal lines is illegal in some states. When in rivers, muskellunge are partial to quiet backwaters and the sheltered places where there is some pad cover or thick grass. They also frequent dropoffs and channels at depths of 6–30 feet or more depending on the season.

HOW TO BOAT MUSKELLUNGE

If you want to release your fish, then a large deep, bagged net is necessary. Those made with lightweight aluminum frames are most convenient, provided the handle connection is solid and the mesh is strong. Muskies are rough on nets because they are heavy, razor-toothed, slimy, and active. If the fish are small, you can boat them by using the bowling-ball grip. (Move your hand from behind and grab the muskie across the head with thumb and forefinger in the eye sockets.) When held firmly with fingertips pressed into the eye sockets, the fish can be lifted from the water. This does take practice and is not easy to accomplish on fish of much over 15 pounds.

The other method is the gaff. This is the easiest way to handle giant muskies in the 40-pound-plus class. Presumably, you won't be releasing fish of that size anyway; so for trophy hunters adept at grabbing, the gaff is a good alternate method. Some fishermen prefer a .22 handgun or even a rifle, but this is a dangerous practice and not considered sportsmanlike. Keep an old towel handy to grip the fish and a pair of longnose pliers to facilitate hook removal.

FISHING TECHNIQUE

Most muskie fishermen will agree on the following: by far the greatest majority of muskies caught over 15 pounds are females; the most productive time of day is afternoon fishing; two of the best months are September and October; muskies are solitary fish and will stay in one spot unless driven out by a larger fish or caught; more than one cast in the same place frequently produces a strike or a follow; muskie fishing is hard work; the medium-to-short cast is better than the long cast; the fisherman who works his baits properly, makes the most casts, and stays alert will, in the long run, enjoy the greatest success, and, finally, all muskies are unpredictable.

A muskie may strike the lure at any point along the line of retrieve and has, on occasion, been known to bash its snout on the side of the boat in its belated efforts to grab the lure. Or it may follow the lure to the boat without striking and repeat this procedure several times. The muskie does have a big, toothy mouth, and in most instances it will lunge at the bait in such a way as to have it end up across its jaws. Since it exerts tremendous power downwards, it is almost impossible to move the bait in its mouth. It is only when it realizes that the bait is not what it wants and relaxes the tension of its jaws that the hooks may be driven into its mouth, so it is very important to set the hooks four or five times in rapid succession.

The muskie does not always agree with the fisherman in regard to what constitutes a perfect day for fishing. Weather conditions seem to play a large part in determining whether or not the fish will cooperate. A light to medium chop on the water is generally agreed as being a time more productive than others. A northwest, north, or northeast wind is eagerly anticipated as being far more favorable than winds from other quadrants. Since few fishermen can pick and choose those days which seem most conducive for action, their results do little to stabilize an otherwise already cloudy picture. One of the best times to try is during or after a storm on a rising barometer.

Muskies do not roam all over a lake when feeding. They prefer to lie in wait in weed beds which attract smaller fish, near a point around which other fish must swim, near the mouths of feeder streams or rivers, along dropoffs, and under overhanging tree trunks waiting for the unwary frog, squirrel, or chipmunk. Approximating the natural paths of living creatures on a lake, many times a fisherman will fish from shore out, retrieving his lure toward the shallow water, making it appear that a frog or minnow has ventured beyond its depth and is hurrying back to safety. You will seldom, if ever, see a small creature swimming out toward the middle of the lake, for they instinctively know that danger awaits them there. Every muskie lure was designed to be fished in a certain way—some are fast retrieve, others are slow, and still others must be jerked through the water. The lure must be worked to give it the most natural-looking appearance possible.

If the fisherman sees a muskie following his bait he can do any one of three things. He can stop the lure for a split second and then start reeling as fast as he can, or he can instruct his guide or companion to start rowing at the same speed or faster than he was retrieving the bait, or when the lure has reached the side of the boat, he can swirl it around in the water in a figure eight, hoping to make the muskie mad enough to strike. Generally, the first suggestion is the most successful, although many old muskie fishermen will tell you never to stop a lure in the water.   —D.B.

MUSSELS Family Mytilidae Any of a number of marine bivalve mollusks some of which are used as food. Members of the related freshwater genus (*Anodonta*) are not edible, but the shells are used in the ornamental button industry. Saltwater mussels are found in large colonies on gravel, rocks, seawalls, and literally on any surface that will support them in the intertidal zone of all temperate seas. Along the North American coast the mussel is particularly abundant in New England. The blue-black bivalves are bound to their beds with silken anchor threads. Like the oyster, however, the mussel begins life as a free-swimming "spat" before settling down to community living.

FOOD VALUE

The U.S. Fish and Wildlife Service has long advocated the exploitation of this resource as food. Mussels have been known to be toxic to humans (Pacific) when the bivalve has been feeding on dinoflagellates (*see* Red Tide). However, they are an excellent food in all other localities and are widely cultivated in Europe. The traditional method of mussel farming is on twigs laced between stakes in tide areas of the English Channel. These crude frames are called "bouchot" and are still used by the French commercials today. Vast quantities of mussels are also cultivated in Holland (Zeeland), and that country supplies a large part of the market crop. Maine

provides most of the fresh mussels in the United States, but small amounts are canned in Massachusetts, New York, and New Jersey.

THE EDIBLE MUSSEL

The edible mussel is the one that most commonly colonizes on fishing grounds. It is recognized by its *smooth* shell, which is generally violet-blue in color covered by a bluish-black horny layer. The inside of the shell is pearly and margined by dark blue. When mussel beds are located at medium depths they can be collected with long-handled clam tongs. In shallow water and on rocks below tide level they can be pried loose by hand. In the summer, it is best not to collect mussels from beds which are exposed at low tide. There is always the danger of collecting dead ones among the live mussels. As with clams or oysters, a live mussel will clamp its shell shut when disturbed or irritated. Mussels are usually at their peak for eating during the fall, winter, and early spring. In late spring and early summer they spawn and as a result are lean and watery, though still edible.

THE RIBBED MUSSEL

The ribbed mussel is not edible. Although there are no records of toxicity, the ribbed mussel has a strong and unpleasant flavor. Ribbed mussels are commonly sold at bait stations to be used as chum or flounder bait. These bivalves grow in grassy bogs and along the banks of tidal creeks. They are easy to distinguish because of the heavy fanlike ribs on the shell. *See also* Fish Cookery
—A.J.McC.

MUTTON HAMLET *Alphestes afer* This is a small seabass belonging to the family Serranidae. It is a very distinct species, but has a close relative in the tropical eastern Pacific. The mutton hamlet is confined to the western Atlantic, and extends from Bermuda and southern Florida all the way south to Argentina and the Falkland Islands.

Its color may be described as olive, blotched and mottled with darker olive to brown. There are some dark orange spots on the body. The pectoral fins are dull olive red with bluish spots, the vertical fins olive with darker markings. Some pale spots are present on the ventrum and the anal fin. The lower part of the head is yellowish. Above the maxillary there is a dark reddish brown "mustache." At night this pattern is lost and two dark bands cross the body.

Other distinguishing characters of the mutton hamlet are dorsal fin spines 11, softrays 18 or 19; anal fin spines 3, softrays 9; scales covering head and body; reduced in size at nape and everywhere on head except opercles, where they are larger than on body; scales all cycloid except a distinctly ctenoid patch under or above pectoral; scales above lateral line 12, along lateral line 75–85, below lateral line 32. Gillrakers short, about 15 below angle.

Head length about 2.6 and body depth about 2.7 in standard length; eye 4.6, snout 6, and maxillary 2.4 in head length. Body ovate and compressed, caudal peduncle short; head small and pointed, anterior profile depressed in occipital region; eye large, its diameter greater than length of snout; mouth oblique, maxillary reaching posterior border of orbit or beyond; teeth

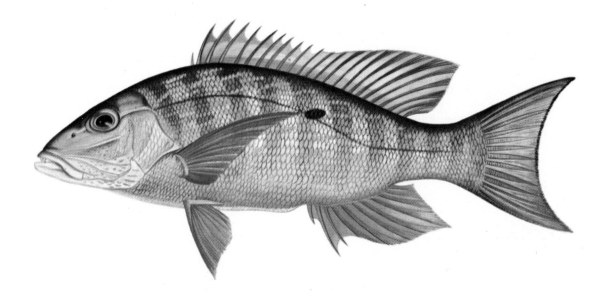

Mutton Snapper, 10½-pound Female, Deep Water Cay, Bahamas

conical and sharp, some of them depressible, in patches on front of jaws; lower jaw slightly projecting; preopercle strongly convex, angle rounded and with a strong, flat spine pointing downward and curved slightly forward; above this are fine serrations along entire upper limb; opercle with three flat spines, middle one strongest, upper and lower nearly concealed by scales.

Attains a length of about 1 foot. Females with well-developed eggs have been taken as small as 7.5 inches. This is an important food fish in the West Indies, but its life history is unknown. —J.C.B.

MUTTON SNAPPER *Lutjanus analis* This is one of the most common of snappers. It occurs along the lower east and west coasts of Florida southward throughout the tropical American Atlantic. A medium-sized snapper, it may reach a weight of 25 pounds or more.

The mutton snapper is a brightly colored fish being olive-green dorsally, reddish on the sides, and paler below. The pectoral, pelvic, anal, and caudal fins are brick-red. A black spot is present on both sides of the body. The iris is red.

When small, the mutton snapper is sometimes confused with the lane snapper (*which see*), while the larger individuals may resemble the red snapper. However, the mutton snapper can be separated from these by the following characteristics: It has 10 dorsal spines, 14 dorsal rays, and 8 rays in the anal fin. The pectoral rays usually number 16. There are 7-9 gillrakers on the lower limb of the first arch, not including rudiments. There are generally 26 rows of scales around the caudal peduncle, and 7 rows of scales on the cheeks. The upper jaw does not reach to a vertical from the anterior margin of the orbit (large adults); it reaches to or somewhat beyond the orbit in the young. The pectoral fins do not reach to a vertical from origin of anal fin. The anal fin is angulate, and not rounded posteriorly.

ANGLING VALUE

The mutton snapper is a strong gamefish and ideally suited to light tackle. Large individuals are often taken by slow trolling near the bottom with bait or artificials. They can also be chummed to the surface and caught with lures such as feathers, jigs, and plugs. However, casting for big mutton snappers over known "holes" is often rewarding even with topwater baits. A recommended lure is a silver-flash plug. It is important to make long casts, as mutton snappers are shy and will generally spook at the sight of a boat.

Although mutton snappers are most frequently caught in blue holes (*see* Blue-Hole Fishing), around coral heads, in channels, and creeks, at depths of 10-30 feet, they sometimes appear on bonefish flats where a variety of spinning and fly-rod lures is successful. At times, they may be seen tailing, and the general procedures used for bonefish can be employed.

The usual mutton snapper is 5-10 pounds, but 15-20-pound fish are not unusual in a good location. Due to their size, sharp gill covers, and teeth, it is advisable to use a short wire leader to prevent line breaks. As a general rule, 12 inches of No. 1 or No. 2 piano wire (tobacco brown color) is adequate and will not interfere with the lure's action.

FOOD VALUE

The mutton snapper is one of the best saltwater fish to eat. The flesh is firm and white, and ideally suited to baking or broiling. Do not neglect the cheek and throat meats, which are considered a gourmet item when taken from the larger fish. The head and bones and skin should be reserved for stock in making soups and chowders.

—L.R.
—A.J.McC.

N

NASSAU GROUPER *Epinephelus striatus* Among fishermen, this is one of the best-known groupers in southern Florida and throughout the tropical American Atlantic. It is also one of the most common of the important commercial groupers. Although it may reach over 3 feet in total length, the usual size is less. The common name probably refers to its being more abundant in the Bahamas than in Florida.

The Nassau grouper has 11 dorsal spines; 16–18 dorsal rays, usually 17; 8 anal rays; and 18, rarely 17 pectoral rays. Its posterior nostril is somewhat larger, up to about twice as large as the anterior. The insertion of pelvic fin is behind the lower end of the pectoral base. The posterior margin of caudal fin is convex. Dark bars occur on the head and body. A saddlelike, black blotch is on top of the caudal peduncle. Scattered black specks are present around eye.

This grouper is distinguished from all the others by the color pattern. It somewhat resembles the red grouper (*which see*), but the latter is much paler and lacks the black blotch on top of the caudal peduncle.

ANGLING VALUE

This grouper prefers rocky bottom in shallow to medium-depth water. Small individuals may occur close to shore whereas large adults are usually found in somewhat deeper water around coral heads and reefs. It takes live bait as well as artificial lures. One of the best-fighting groupers, it is difficult to keep away from holes if hooked on light tackle.

FOOD VALUE

Excellent eating, it is one of the most important commercial fishes in the southern United States and the Caribbean. The skin is tough and strongly flavored. The firm white fillets should be cut in fingers for deep frying or in chunks to make chowders.

—L.R.

NATIVE (TROUT) A regional name for the brook trout in the Eastern United States, which has been in popular usage since the introduction of the brown trout from Europe in 1886. However, the term "native trout" is arbitrarily used, as it is also applied to the cutthroat trout in many parts of the West. The inference in both regions is to distinguish the endemic species from an exotic in waters where other trout species have been planted.

NEBRASKA Many people regard Nebraska as a flat, fertile plain that raises grain, cattle, an occasional dust storm, and little else. But those who travel the state learn quickly that Nebraska is literally laced with streams and dotted with lakes—all of them highly productive and most of them underfished.

Nebraska boasts 11,000 miles of streams and more than 3,300 lakes, and far more fishing than fishermen. The fishing opportunities change as you drive from border to border. Plenty of cool, clear trout water is found in the panhandle and along the northern border. A large variety of fish abounds in the unique Sand Hills, and, farther east, lunker catfish and other river varieties are plentiful. For special attention are the mammoth reservoir chains on the Platte, Republican, and Missouri Rivers. Of the dozens of giant impoundments, three rank above the rest—23-mile-long Lake McConaughy in the west; 13-mile-long Harlan County Reservoir in the south; and 33-mile-long Lewis and Clark Lake in the northeast. All are highly productive fisheries. McConaughy takes top honors, having produced the state's record rainbow, brown, and brook trout, walleye, white bass, smallmouth, and perch.

Trout, white bass, and largemouth bass, northern pike, crappie, sauger, and paddlefish kick off Nebraska's spring fishing show. A little later, smallmouths, walleyes, catfish, drum, bluegills, and bullheads come into their own. Top angling continues through the summer. Fall fishing on most all species is prime, and when the water freezes over, the ice fishermen move in.

To add to Nebraska's variety, nongamefish may be taken with bow and arrow and spear. Snagging, too, is legal in certain waters. Any way you look at it, Nebraska is prime fishing country, with thirty-one different game species available.

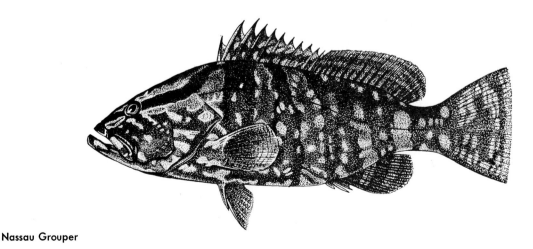

Nassau Grouper

Angling is on a year-round basis, with generous creel limits and no size limits.

SOUTHWESTERN NEBRASKA

Fishing isn't hard to find in the state's southwestern portion. The area has ten major reservoirs, five smaller reservoirs, and five state lakes, totaling 68,847 acres of water open to the public. Two sizable rivers and a vast canal system also add mileage to the area's fishing picture.

Most of the fishing in the southwest is done in the larger impoundments, with the smaller lakes, streams, and canals receiving less pressure. June is the favored month for fishing in the area. However, peak periods of success occur in other months as well.

Lake McConaughy This reservoir has 35,000 surface acres and is the largest water body in the state. It is also one of Nebraska's finest fishing areas. With 105 miles of shoreline, the huge impoundment can handle any number of anglers. Walleyes are probably big Mac's best, but white bass, smallmouth, and channel catfish are also popular species. Rainbow trout are much sought after in summer and fall.

Harlan County Reservoir Another of the state's most productive spots located two miles south of Republican City, this 13,468-acre impoundment supports an excellent population of walleye. Crappie and white bass are also found in the reservoir in abundance.

Medicine Creek Reservoir This reservoir has 1,850 surface acres, and is located 10 miles north of Cambridge. It is a good bet for crappie and channel catfish. Other species which thrive are largemouth, northern pike, smallmouth, white bass, bullhead, and yellow perch.

Maloney Reservoir Maloney covers 1,650 surface acres and features top fishing for crappie and channel cat. Walleyes, yellow perch, white bass, bluegill, and drum are also taken frequently. Other species present are northern pike, smallmouth, and bullhead. Maloney is located 6 miles south of North Platte.

Swanson Reservoir Located 6 miles west of Trenton, this reservoir features black and white crappie, channel catfish, drum, and bluegill.

Enders Reservoir Located 5 miles east of Imperial, Enders is noted for the excellence of its crappie, yellow perch, and channel catfish.

Johnson Reservoir Ten miles south of Lexington, it has good crappie and yellow-perch fishing. White bass are also taken in abundance.

Jeffrey Reservoir Located 7 miles southwest of Brady, its fishing is most productive for crappie, drum, and channel catfish.

Sutherland Reservoir Five miles south of Sutherland, this reservoir has 3,000 surface acres of water. Top-going fish is the channel catfish, with crappie and white bass next in line.

State lakes include Rock Creek, 8 miles north of Parks, excellent for bluegill and largemouth bass; Ravenna Lake, 1 mile east of Ravenna, good for large-mouth, bluegill, and channel catfish; Hayes Center Lake, 9 miles northeast of Hayes Center, fair for bass, bluegill, and channel catfish.

The southwest's streams, creeks, and canals add considerably to the area's fishing potential, but in general these waterways are all but ignored by fishermen.

North Platte River This river provides excellent fishing above McConaughy for largemouth and channel catfish in early spring and summer. Trout can be caught below the Keystone Diversion Dam in the spring. The Republican River offers productive angling for channel cat downstream from Harlan County Reservoir.

Otter Creek On the northwestern side of McConaughy, it provides fishing for brown trout almost year round and some rainbow in late winter.

South Loup River It abounds in channel catfish and also produces largemouth angling in backwater areas. The central Nebraska and Platte Valley Public Power and Irrigation District Canal System also provides full creels. Rainbows are taken regularly from a stretch between Keystone to Paxton. Some rainbows, walleyes, and white bass are caught from Paxton to Sutherland Reservoir. Beyond Sutherland to Maloney, walleyes, white bass, yellow perch, and channel catfish are good to fair. From Maloney to Johnson Lake, fishing for all species is good, with the best results below canal checks and power stations.

NEBRASKA'S PANHANDLE

Western Nebraska, or the Panhandle, is generally known to fishermen as the state's trout country. While Nebraska trout are not confined to this region, it is here that most of the state's strictly coldwater anglers come. At least twenty-nine streams produce rainbow, brown,

The Niobrara River and its tributaries contain some of the best brown trout water in Nebraska

and brook trout in varying numbers. Eight of the Panhandle's eleven counties offer some kind of trout fishing. Trout water in the area can be divided into three general drainages.

North Platte River Trout streams in the North Platte River watershed are concentrated mostly in the Scottsbluff area. Generally the streams are short, and most are small, being comprised primarily of a series of pools and riffles. The brown trout is the most common variety in these streams, and can be found the year around. Rainbows exist in many of the streams in lesser numbers, but most of the larger rainbows migrate downstream to Lake McConaughy in the late spring and summer. Trout waters in this drainage include Lawrence Fork, Blue Creek, Greenwood, Red Willow, Wild Horse, Stucken Hole (Bayard Drain), Nine Mile, Sheep, Spotted Tail, and Winter Creek.

Pine Ridge Here are two drainages—Hat Creek and White River. Hat Creek tributaries supporting trout generally are small. Monroe Creek is typical, with only about four miles of trout water in the upper regions of the drainage. These streams, also, are usually a series of pools and riffles, with trout confined mainly to the pools.

Trout waters in the Pine Ridge area include Monroe Creek, Sowbelly, Hat, Soldier, White River, Chadron Reservoir, Dead Horse Creek, Chadron Creek, Big Bordeaux Creek, Little Bordeaux, Beaver, White Clay, and Larrabee Creek.

Niobrara River Drainage The Niobrara River and its tributaries contain some of the best trout water in Nebraska. In Sioux County, the Niobrara itself is topnotch. Tributaries as far east as Antelope County are suitable for trout. Brown-trout populations are extremely high in some areas.

Streams on the south side of the Niobrara originate in the grass-covered, rolling Sand Hills. Consequently they are often plagued by drifting sand which limits their trout-carrying capacity. Trout waters in this drainage include the Niobrara River, Pine Creek, Deer Creek, and the headwaters of the Snake River.

Warmwater and lake fishing in the Panhandle is not to be ignored. Possibly the number one lake is Smith, twenty miles south of Rushville on Highway 20. This 222-acre, state-owned lake specializes in northern pike, yellow perch, largemouth bass, crappie, bluegill, and some bullheads and channel catfish. Smith Lake is also very popular for ice fishing.

Other top waters include Island Lake, a 711-acre natural Sand Hills lake on the Crescent Lake National Wildlife Refuge, the northern pike center of the Panhandle; Lake Minatare, 10 miles northeast of Scottsbluff and 2,200 acres in size, best for yellow perch with good results also for walleye, crappie, northern pike, and channel catfish; Walgren Lake, 3 miles east and 3 miles south of Hay Springs, a big producer of bullhead and some crappie and bluegill; Box Butte Reservoir, on Niobrara River 30 miles northwest of Alliance, abounds with perch, crappie, and walleye.

Whitney Reservoir An 800-acre impoundment west of Whitney, good for stringers of crappies, catfish, and walleyes; Kimball Irrigation Reservoir, eight miles west of Kimball, best for yellow perch with crappie next; Chadron Water Supply Reservoir, eight miles south of Chadron, big producer of trout.

Adding to the Panhandle's attractiveness for fishermen are twenty-one United States government stock ponds north of Crawford, all stocked with bass and bluegill.

THE SAND HILLS REGION

There is literally fishing at every turn in Nebraska's fabulous Sand Hills. The only problems facing the angler in this vast region is first locating his spot and then getting to it.

The area is dotted with lakes and laced with rivers. Upward of two thousand lakes can be found here, but most are too small, too shallow, or too alkaline to support fish life. More than forty lakes, however, ranging from less than two acres up to more than one thousand, are recognized and managed as fish lakes.

The Niobrara, Calamus, North Loup, Snake, Elkhorn, and Dismal rivers all add considerably to the area's sport fishery. Dozens of tributaries provide trout and warmwater angling in abundance.

For an angler traveling into the Sand Hills for lake fishing, probably the best bet is the Valentine Wildlife Refuge. The area does not necessarily contain the best lakes, but the area is public property. This fact simplifies the access problem considerably for the visiting angler, for many of the other lakes are privately owned and require permission for fishing.

Most of the lakes on the refuge and elsewhere in the Sand Hills are relatively shallow, with the deepest up to 10–12 feet. However, the waters in the best of these lakes are some of the most fertile and productive anywhere in number of fish per acre. Species to be found include northern pike, walleye, largemouth bass, yellow perch, black crappie, bluegill, and bullhead.

Major lakes on the refuge are Watts, Hackberry, Big Alkali, Clear, Willow, Dewey, and Ballards Marsh. Refuge lakes are closed during the waterfowl hunting season.

In quantity, Sand Hills trout fishing perhaps must take a back seat to that in the Panhandle, but in quality it is second to none. Some of the best trout fishing in Nebraska can be found in the tributaries of the Niobrara and Loup Rivers. Long Pine Creek, a Niobrara tributary just west of Long Pine, is the traditional example of Sand Hills trout fishing at its best. Other trout waters in the region include Plum Creek, west of Ainsworth; Coon Creek, north of Bassett; Schlagel Creek, north of the Valentine Refuge; Gracie Creek, northwest of Burwell; the headwaters of the Snake River above Merritt Reservoir; Merritt Reservoir; the North Loup River, northwest of Mullen; Dismal River pits; and Dismal River from Highway 97 south of Mullen to headwaters of the river.

Warmwater fishing abounds in the Sand Hills. The Calamus River, which has its beginning in a Sand Hills lake near Brewster, offers excellent northern-pike angling in spring months. Its pools and oxbows provide topnotch pike habitat and a great deal of cool-weather action. The Elkhorn River, which originates east of Bassett and runs its entire length to the Platte River along one major highway or another, is easily accessible at most points and is particularly good for northern pike.

Major Sand Hills lakes at which permission is not required include in Cherry County—Johnson, 19 miles southeast of Valentine, 96 acres, for bullheads; Rat and

Beaver, 34 miles southwest of Valentine, 450 acres, for crappie and perch; Schoolhouse, 20 miles southwest of Nenzel, 105 acres, for crappie, bullhead, northern pike; Shell, 14 miles northeast of Gordon, 163 acres, for northern, bluegill, perch, crappie, largemouth; Round, 29 miles northwest of Whitman, 245 acres, for largemouth, bluegill, northern pike, sauger.

Alkali, 19 miles northwest of Ashby, 375 acres, for bullheads, yellow perch; Mothers, 18 miles northwest of Ashby, 550 acres, for bullhead, yellow perch; Merritt, on Snake River, 2,700 acres, for trout; Shoup, 23 miles southwest of Nenzel, 47 acres, for largemouth, crappie, bluegill; Flowing Well, 22 miles northwest of Mullen, 64 acres, for yellow perch, bullhead; Meyhew, 24 miles north of Mullen, 38 acres, largemouth, bullheads; Roseberry, 28 miles northwest of Mullen, 82 acres, for largemouth, perch.

In Brown County—Clear, 28 miles southwest of Ainsworth, 194 acres, for smallmouth, largemouth, bluegill; Long, 31 miles southwest of Ainsworth, 155 acres, for bullhead; Enders, 29 miles southwest of Ainsworth, 367 acres, for northern, bullhead, crappie; Hofelt, 13 miles south of Ainsworth, 150 acres, for bullhead.

In Holt County (western half)—Swan, 25 miles south of Atkinson, 240 acres, for northern, largemouth, bluegill, crappie; Brunner, 29 miles southwest of Atkinson, 38 acres, northern, crappie; Overton, 27 miles southwest of Stuart, 137 acres, for bullhead, crappie.

In Rock County—Cameron, 19 miles southeast of Bassett, 96 acres, for perch, bullhead, crappie.

NORTHEASTERN NEBRASKA

Plenty of action exists in Nebraska's northeast portion for the fisherman who knows where to go. Enhancing the fishing picture here are giant Lewis and Clark Lake, four smaller state lakes, three large oxbow lakes with public access, private lakes, over 2,000 miles of Missouri River, six lesser rivers (some of whose tributaries contain trout), and literally hundreds of farm ponds.

Forty-mile-long Lewis and Clark Reservoir with more than 100 miles of shoreline, it is the undisputed fishing capital of the northeastern section. Sauger and walleye are taken in great numbers from the lake itself and also from the tailwaters below the dam. A world-record 8-pound, 5-ounce sauger was caught from the Missouri River just above the reservoir in 1961. Other good-going fish at Lewis and Clark are northern pike, catfish of all kinds, crappie, and drum.

Some of the top-producing lakes in the area are Grove, 2½ miles north of Royal, and perhaps the best of the state-owned lakes, features largemouth, walleye, bluegill, bullhead, channel catfish, northern pike; Pibel Lake, south of Bartlett, noted for excellence of its largemouth-bass fishing; Dead Timber, 2 miles northeast of Scribner, offers unusual scenery along with lots of largemouth, channel catfish, crappie; Goose Lake, 13 miles southeast of Chambers, good for bullhead; Decatur, 550 acres in Burt County, popular for ice fishing and good for walleye, crappie, northern, bluegill the year around; Crystal, 850 acres off Highway 20 just west of South Sioux City, producer for bluegill, bullhead, carp; Omadi Bend, on Missouri River northeast of Homer, a winner for big black crappie in spring; Ericson, just outside Ericson, for bass, bluegill.

Trout fishing in northeast is found in various sections of four different streams, all of which are stocked annually to maintain good populations of browns and rainbows. These include the upper 10 miles of Steel Creek, a tributary of the Niobrara River in Knox County; east branch of Verdigre Creek, 1 mile west, 2 north of Royal; Upper Big Springs Creek, 4 miles northeast of Orchard.

Warmwater stream fishermen score repeatedly for channel catfish and largemouth bass in the Cedar River, 120-mile stream; for flathead catfish, largemouth, bluegill, and sauger in 116-mile-long Beaver Creek; for virtually all warmwater species in the Elkhorn River, which runs much of its length inside the northeast area; for mixed species in 69-mile-long North Fork of Elkhorn; for carp, channel catfish, and bullhead in Logan Creek; for catfish, carp, crappie, and drum in Loup Power Canal; and for walleye, sauger, and flathead catfish in Lake Babcock, 5 miles north of Columbus on Loup Power Canal.

SOUTHEASTERN NEBRASKA

While not as plentiful as in other areas, fishing waters in the southeast are very significant in that they provide sport for thousands of persons each year.

State-maintained lakes are the most significant element in the southeast's angling potential. Included are those at Fremont, Burchard Lake, Verdon Lake, Louisville Lakes, Memphis Lake, Two Rivers Area, Plattsmouth Refuge Lake, Alexandria Lakes, Hord Lake, Mormon Trail Wayside Area, and Crystal Lake.

Lake fishing—the state area at Fremont is probably the most widely used of its type in Nebraska, since it is located within easy driving distance of both Omaha and Lincoln. The area has fourteen manageable sandpit lakes of varying size which are productive for most warmwater species.

Burchard Lake One hundred twenty acres, 3 miles east and 1½ miles north of Burchard, it supports good populations of northern pike, bass, catfish, and bluegill. The lake is complete with a state recreation area.

Verdon Lake It is one-half mile west of Verdon, and offers good action for bass, crappie, and bluegill.

Two Rivers Area Twenty-two miles southwest of Omaha, this region features fine trout angling in a "put-and-take" pay lake. Other lakes there are fair for carp, bullhead, bass, and crappie.

Plattsmouth Refuge Lake Two miles north of Plattsmouth, it is generally excellent for bass fishing but is fairly shallow and subject to winter-kill.

Mormon Trail Area Twelve miles northeast of Central City, it is productive for bass, bluegill, and catfish.

Louisville Lakes Four in all and located near Louisville, it is popular with fishermen for bullheads, carp, bass, crappie, and bluegill.

Hord Lake This lake is two miles southeast of Central City, and is fair for bass and carp.

Memphis Lake Northwest of Ashland, it contains mostly rough fish and bullheads.

Crystal Lake On Little Blue River 3 miles north of Ayr, it also contains mostly rough fish and bullheads.

The southeast has its share of streams. The Missouri River, which borders the area on its eastern side, contributes considerably to its fishing potential. Since the river is considered navigable, its waters are public property, and boaters need have no fear of trespassing while afloat.

Fishing in the Missouri River along its stretch in the southeast is rated from good to fair. Most frequently taken species are channel catfish, other kinds of catfish, and carp. These fish also make up the bulk of the catch on the Big and Little Nemaha rivers, the Platte, Blue, and Republican rivers.

Also available to anglers in the southeast are private or group-owned lakes or ponds. Several cities own their own lakes, and these usually are open to the public. The Hastings City Lake, Schuyler City Lake, and Carter Lake at Omaha fall into this category.

A windfall to southeast fishermen is the Salt-Wahoo Watershed District string of reservoirs near Lincoln.

—D.H.S.

NEEDLEFISHES Family Belonidae The needlefishes are voracious elongate fishes with a superficial resemblance to the freshwater gar; however, they belong to the order which includes the halfbeaks, sauries, and the flyingfishes.

The jaws of needlefishes project into long, thin, and rather fragile beaks, usually with the upper jaw slightly shorter (more so on the young than the adults). A band of long pointed teeth, in addition to a band of shorter ones, arms the jaws.

Six species of needlefishes are known from the western north Atlantic: the Atlantic needlefish, redfin needlefish, timucu, houndfish, agujon, and flat needlefish. The latter four are also found in the tropical Pacific and Indian oceans. Although common in the warm waters

of the West Indian region, the Atlantic needlefish is abundant along the eastern seaboard of the United States as far north as Cape Cod. It often penetrates freshwater. The related California needlefish of the cool water of the eastern Pacific ranges as far north as Point Concepción, California. The classification of the needlefishes is under study. Many of the scientific names are not yet stabilized.

The largest and most heavy-bodied of the needlefishes is the houndfish. It reaches a length of 5 feet. A 52-inch one from the Virgin Islands weighed 10 pounds, 9 ounces.

Needlefishes live at the surface and are protectively colored for this mode of life. They are blue or green on the back, shading to silvery white on the sides and abdomen. They feed heavily on small fishes. When they, in turn, are threatened by predators, they endeavor to escape by skipping rapidly along the surface, often more out of the sea than in it.

LIFE HISTORY

Needlefishes are unique in their possession of large eggs. Those of the 10-pound, 9-ounce houndfish measured 4.1–4.6 millimeters (about $\frac{1}{6}$ of an inch) in diameter. Eggs of most marine fishes, however, tend in general to be less than a quarter of this in size.

Numerous tiny threads can be teased with dissecting needles from the outer, tough covering of the houndfish eggs. These threads probably serve to attach the eggs to floating objects. The eggs have no oil droplets to keep them afloat. A freshly eaten mass of needlefish eggs was found in the stomach of a 5½-pound dog snapper (*Lutjanus jocu*) in the Virgin Islands.

Certain young needlefishes, an inch or so in length, are dark-colored and float motionless and straight at the surface. In this pose they resemble floating twigs. Juveniles about 5 inches long were observed in the Virgin Islands imitating floating pieces of manatee grass (*Cymodocea*). The fish were straw-colored, like many of the grass fragments, and frequently held their bodies in an arc as they floated, seemingly inert, beside curved pieces of the grass.

Needlefishes have at times been observed repeatedly leaping over small floating sticks, as if at play. A single fish may jump back and forth over the same floating object. Usually they seem to rub against the object as they jump over it, suggesting that they may be responding to a skin irritation or trying to dislodge a skin parasite.

DANGER TO MAN

The larger needlefish, and particularly the houndfish, should be regarded as dangerous to man. At night, when startled by a light, they often execute a series of long leaps from the water. Although apparently not specifically attracted by light, they will at times leap in its direction. Anyone in the path of these living javelins can be impaled on the long pointed jaws. A number of cases are known of persons who have been seriously injured, sometimes fatally, by being struck by these fishes. The needlefish hazard has not received the literary attention that it should. By contrast, incidents involving sharks or barracudas are usually widely publicized. A person who is fond of fishing at night with a light from an open boat in tropic seas would be well advised to construct a shield in the boat for his own and others protection from leaping needlefishes.

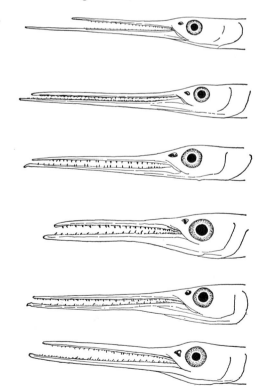

Six Species of Needlefishes (after Berry and Rivas): 1. *Belone argala*, 2. *Ablennes hians*, 3. *Strongylura marina*, 4. *Tylosurus raphidoma*, 5. *Strongylura notta*, 6. *Tylosurus acus*

ANGLING VALUE

Needlefishes are readily caught on flies, plugs, jigs, and live baits. Their habit of "walking" on their tails when hooked makes them rather spectacular fighters.

FOOD VALUE

The needlefishes are edible and, in fact, their flesh has a very good flavor. However, they are not commonly used for food in the United States because of the odd green color of the bones which causes apprehension in persons who may contemplate eating them. In Europe and particularly Scandinavia "hornfisk" is a gourmet item.

—J.E.R.

NEKTON *See* Freshwater Ecology

NEOSHO SMALLMOUTH BASS *Micropterus dolomieui velox* A subspecies of the smallmouth bass which occurs in the Neosho River and adjacent tributaries of the Arkansas River in Oklahoma, Arkansas, and Missouri. Due to the construction of large impoundments on the Neosho River the natural habitat of this subspecies has been greatly reduced to the upper reaches of some of its tributaries, and this distinctive local form of smallmouth has become quite rare.

The Neosho smallmouth is more slender than the northern form and is easily distinguished by its lower jaw, which projects beyond the snout to the extent that its teeth are visible from above. The upper mandible extends to or nearly below the posterior margin of the eye. The coloration is rather uniform, being dark olive above and fading to white below with only faint vertical markings.

ANGLING VALUE

The subspecific name *velox* or "swift" refers to its characteristic as a gamefish. Found in fast-water habitats, the Neosho smallmouth probably made the reputation of many Ozark bass rivers in years past. To what extent the original stock has been modified by interbreeding with the northern form of smallmouth is not known, but the typical Neosho subspecies is prized for its rarity. *See also* Black Bass, Smallmouth Bass   —A.J.McC.

NETHERLANDS ANTILLES The Netherlands Antilles is composed of two widely separated groups of islands, one originating less than 20 miles from the coast of Venezuela—which consists of Aruba, Curaçao, Klein Curaçao, Bonaire, and also Klein Bonaire—and the other group located more than 500 miles to the northeast of Curaçao, or somewhat east of the Virgin Islands which consists of Saba, St. Eustatius, and St. Maarten. Of these, the first or "leeward" group is of angling importance. The islands are volcanic in origin and have sharp dropoffs; the maximum depth between Curaçao and Venezuela is over 500 fathoms. A deep trench, exceeding 800 fathoms, occurs between Curaçao and Aruba; to the north of Aruba the bottom shelves down to 2,850 fathoms. The leeward Dutch islands lie south of the range of hurricanes, but they are exposed to steady trade winds from the eastnortheast and east with a mean velocity of five meters per second. Because of the wind direction and the steep coral coast the best natural harbors are on the calmer west shores.

Due to the extreme drop-offs there are few reefs or extensive shallows around the Leeward Group, and consequently only a very limited amount of inshore fishing exists for small-game species such as bonefish, barracuda, or snappers. The fishing is primarily for blue marlin, sailfish, dolphin, wahoo, occasional white marlin, king mackerel, and blackfin tuna.

Because of the semiarid climate no freshwater fishing exists in the Leeward Islands. In the small basins, where freshwater accumulates during the rainy season (November to March), so-called "tankies" consisting of several species of killifish, gambusia, and mollies occur, as do one or two species of sleepers (Eleotridae).

BIG-GAME FISHING

Ordinarily the big-game fishing period begins at the end of August and extends to April. The force of the Trades abates somewhat at the end of summer, as the Leeward Group lies south of the hurricane zone and frequent low pressure areas to the north cause the prevailing winds to diminish into the fall season. This may not

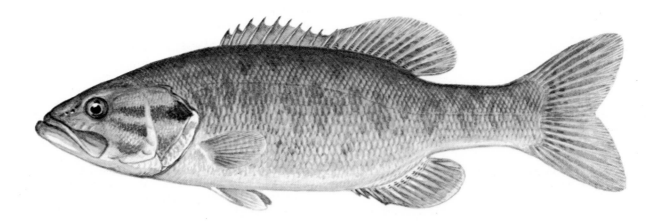

Neosho Smallmouth Bass

provide the best fishing of the year, nor the kind of fishing you seek, but it's the best bet for calmer water. Blue marlin (locally balau blancu) fishing gets under way in the fall and extends through the winter, tapering off toward April. Blues in the 300-400-pound class are fairly common. Sailfish (locally balau bandera) migrate through the Leewards during the same period. White marlin (locally balau cora) display no peak, are seldom numerous, and may occur at any time. Wahoo (locally mula) occur in October and November and again in May. At other times of the year wahoo are scarce or totally absent. The waters around Klein Curaçao are especially productive of wahoo averaging 30–40 pounds. Dolphin (locally dradu) are most abundant from April through the summer months, and average a large size with 30-pounders not uncommon. King mackerel (locally konefes) occur from July to October.

Until recent years the boat situation in the Leeward group was poor, but with the upsurge in tourism, more and more charter craft are becoming available. Most hotels can arrange the details.   —A.J.McC.

NEVADA A desert state, with wide expanses of sagebrush and range land stretching between rough, sometimes isolated, mountain ranges, Nevada nevertheless has some excellent trout fishing in several large lakes and in a few streams. Largemouth bass, too, attract many anglers, due to ease of reaching such premier waters as Lake Mead, with its more than 500 miles of colorful, indented shoreline.

TROUT FISHING

On the state's western boundary, in the towering Sierras, with their rushing snow waters, lies beautiful Lake Tahoe, with 100 miles of forested, attractive shoreline. The lake is very deep, cold, and clear, and once gave up large lake (locally mackinaw) trout, as well as cutthroat and also brown trout. Deep trolling is the usual and best method of taking them. This great fishery declined for various reasons, but the Nevada authorities joined with the California Department of Fish and Game (the two states that share in the Tahoe area) in a very heavy planting program of both broodfish and fingerlings. Satisfactory returns are coming to diligent anglers, and this once-great fishery promises again to lure the faithful to its blue waters. The area has a perfect summer climate—the elevation being just under 7,000 feet.

The beautiful Truckee River, natural outlet of Tahoe, flows down through its wooded canyon, where there are always good trout for the skilled angler, and through the city of Reno. Here, in years past (and still possible), giant brown trout as large as 15 pounds have been caught right in the city.

To the north of Reno, great Pyramid Lake once received all the Truckee flow, and up its current swam the giant cutthroat trout to the spawning beds far above. The world-record 41-pound cutthroat trout came from Pyramid in 1925. Then, as so often in the West, irrigation interests took over the Truckee's flow, and a dam was constructed which effectively prevented ascent of these prize trout to their ancestral spawning grounds. This was a major loss to the state. However, by taking the Lahontan subspecies from a few other waters where they occurred originally, Nevada has rebuilt the cutthroat fishery to a

large extent. In addition, plantings of rainbow and rainbow × cutthroat hybrids have resulted in excellent angling from late October through April. The fishing peaks during the winter months. Pyramid Lake is within the Paiute Indian Reservation and a permit must be obtained from the Indians in addition to a Nevada license.

Not far east and south of Reno is 20-mile-long Walker Lake fed by the East Walker River, flowing down through its canyon from Bridgeport Lake, in California, not far above the state boundary. Here, in the fall, winter, and spring can be found some excellent cutthroat-trout fishing. Mostly winter game at Walker Lake, the big trout are in shallow water at that time. The early spring months can be exceptional as the trout gather at the inflowing river which can, in itself, provide stirring sport for rainbow, brown, and cutthroats. Although most of the Walker trout are taken by trolling, many can be taken by shore-casting from the west side, just below the highway.

Another boundary lake, sharing its waters with California, is Topaz, a short drive down the beautiful Carson Valley below Carson City, the state capital. Here are large brown and rainbow, and some cutthroats, all taking a trolled lure well and responding to live bait. In the shallow bays, just under the highway which follows the west shore, there can be good fly-fishing at times. The Topaz fish ascend the West Walker River up into the meadow waters under the California Sierras.

UNUSUAL RIVER FISHING FOR RAINBOWS

Below giant Hoover Dam, which impounds the Colorado River to form Lake Mead, the river flows clear and cold. This is prime rainbow water. Many years ago fishery authorities of Nevada and Arizona (the river forming the boundary for many miles) joined in planting trout which distributed themselves down the swift current through colorful Black Canyon. A seaworthy boat, with a powerful outboard, makes this spectacular canyon water easily available. A launching area at Willow Beach, on the Arizona side, below Hoover Dam (where there are ample accommodations) will let the angler fish down many miles and into Lake Mojave. Another modern resort at Cottonwood Cove, out of Searchlight, Nevada, or out of Nelson, farther up Lake Mojave, offers access, and a reverse journey—back up the lake and into the Colorado.

The Humboldt River watershed in northcentral Nevada offers excellent fly-fishing in many meadow stretches, and a variety of trout fishing in the many lake impoundments, of which Wild Horse Reservoir, north out of Winnemucca, is outstanding.

LARGEMOUTH BASS

Lake Mead is considered outstanding by visiting anglers. Ever since the first year of its existence in 1935, this Nevada impoundment has been highly productive. It is largely a "boat game," casting plugs and other lures along the steep, rocky shores and under the colorful, overhanging cliffs of innumerable islands. The bait angler does well, too, particularly in the winter months, when the bass are deep, fishing mudsucker minnows or waterdogs.

In spring, when the fish come into shallows to spawn around half-submerged logs and brush, a fly rod or casting popper lure can provide excellent sport. There are also productive crappie holes, where a deep-fished, slow-retrieved fly will fill the creel with these splendid panfish. Boat marinas and launching ramps are on the lakeshore near Boulder City, at other nearby bays, with the great north arm of the lake, out of Overton, some 50 miles east of Las Vegas, providing all necessary accommodations and, perhaps, the best bass fishing in all the great impoundment.

NEW BRUNSWICK The largest of the three Maritime provinces of eastern Canada is best known for its Atlantic-salmon fishing. New Brunswick also offers anadromous brook trout as well as inland trout fishing and smallmouth bass fishing in the southwestern part of the province. New Brunswick attracts many American anglers because of its proximity to the United States border and a comparative abundance of its salmon streams. The province lists 439 miles of public water, which is made available by camps and outfitters at reasonable fees. An additional 676 miles is leased from the Crown by clubs and individuals. Not all the rivers provide good angling, because the salmon either return to them from the sea too late in the season or because the adult salmon are not plentiful. There is excellent angling, however, in many parts of three large river systems, namely the Restigouche, the Miramichi, and the Saint John, as well as in other smaller rivers like the Nepisiguit and Tabusintac.

ATLANTIC SALMON FISHING

More salmon are caught by angling in the Miramichi River than in any other river in eastern Canada. The total Miramichi angling catch usually runs between 20,000-25,000 fish. Of these totals about 25 percent were kelts or "spring" salmon that entered the river the previous year to spawn and which were caught in early spring as they descended to the sea. Such kelt fishing is legal in New Brunswick under special permit. It allows many people to enjoy salmon fishing on stretches of rivers where conditions are unsuitable for regular "bright" salmon fishing. It is not prohibited for biological reasons because so few previously spawned Atlantic salmon survive to be caught or to spawn again—about 5 percent—and it seems best to make maximum use of the adult fish upon their first return to freshwater from the sea. Many of the kelts are in moderately good condition because they entered the rivers in September or October of the previous fall and did not become weaker and thinner through a prolonged sojourn in freshwater to as great an extent as the adults that came in early from May through July. At least half, often a higher proportion, of the fresh-run salmon that are available to anglers during the regular angling season are grilse, weighing 2½–5 pounds, that have spent only one winter in the sea. The rest are mostly 2-sea-year salmon, weighing 8–12 pounds, but some are 3-sea-year fish weighing over 20 pounds. Grilse provide excellent angling on light tackle, and many anglers prefer them to larger salmon for eating.

Since inshore commercial salmon fishing was banned in 1972 the Province is optimistic about the future of its stocks. Despite a downtrend internationally, due to the Danish high-seas fishery, the 1972 season produced an overall total of 21,338 grilse and 13,610 salmon in New Brunswick rivers. These were all bright fish, of which the Miramichi provided 19,101 grilse and 8,933 salmon.

Another popular angling river, the Restigouche, comprising the main river and tributaries like the Kedgwick and Upsalquitch, provides lower total catches but higher average takes per rod-day, and a higher proportion of large 2-sea-year salmon than the Miramichi. Total Restigouche catches have run 3,102–3,620 fish, and the average catch per 10 rod-days was 5.6–6.9 fish.

Angling in the Saint John River has suffered from industrial developments, including hydroelectric development and pollution from pulp mills and forest spraying with insecticides, but total angling catches in the system runs about 2,500 fish per year.

Anglers planning to visit New Brunswick for the first time can obtain advance information on accommodations, guides, and other details by writing to the New Brunswick Travel Bureau, 658 Queen Street, Fredericton. A summary of angling regulations (which are legislated by the federal government) and license fees is issued annually by the New Brunswick Department of Lands and Mines, Fredericton, N. B., and can be obtained by writing to that Department, Fredericton, N. B.

There is individual ownership as well as leasing of riparian and fishing rights in New Brunswick, but some of the waters so held are operated in conjunction with fishing lodges and camps, where accommodations and guides are available at reasonable rates. In recent years the province has made available for inexpensive public fishing some previously leased water in very desirable locations, and application for reservations should be made to the Department of Lands and Mines, Fredericton, New Brunswick, several months in advance of the angling season.

Angling for salmon is restricted to fly-fishing, and no other kind of bait or lure is permitted. The limit is four salmon in any one day, or twenty-one salmon in any week. There is some variation in the salmon angling season throughout the province, but the commonest open season in waters tributary to the Gulf of St. Lawrence is May 15 to September 30. A few rivers where late-run salmon predominate have a slightly later closing date, some waters have an earlier closing date, for example, September 15 for parts of the Miramichi, and August 31 for the whole Restigouche River system. In 1963, Atlantic salmon were given extra protection on parts of the main stems of the Miramichi, Restigouche, and Big Salmon (Saint John County) rivers through special scheduling as salmon angling waters. On these stretches all angling during the open season for salmon is restricted to the use of artificial flies; but other lures can be used for trout on the tributary streams.

On some New Brunswick rivers there is good early-season fishing for fresh-run salmon, from early June through July, if water conditions are favorable. Others have few early-run salmon, and fishing is best starting in early September. Inexperienced anglers might have better success with the September angling, for example, on stretches of the Southwest Miramichi River in the Blackville-Boiestown area. The Miramichi Salmon Association, Inc., is supported by a large membership of salmon anglers in the United States and many New

Brunswick camp owners and outfitters. Information on salmon angling, particularly in the Miramichi area, can be obtained from the Manager, The Miramichi Salmon Association, Inc., Boiestown.

TROUT FISHING

The most common gamefish in New Brunswick, and the Maritime provinces of Canada in general, is the brook trout. The species' wide distribution in brooks, rivers, and lakes assures its availability to trout anglers throughout the province. Obviously abundance varies from place to place depending primarily upon the fertility of waters and their trout-producing capacity, and secondarily upon the intensity of the angling effort and number of fish removed by anglers. Although the brook trout is adaptable to a wide range in water conditions, its numbers can be markedly reduced in those localities where fishing is heavy. The fact, however, that even in these situations New Brunswick anglers continue to enjoy trout angling each year shows that trout can and will persist unless man ruins their habitat by pollution and other adverse actions. Waters are seldom "fished out" permanently, although with increased number of anglers the catch per individual may be less, even with the total number of trout caught remaining relatively constant from one year to the next.

The brook trout is a coldwater species. When waters approach or exceed 70°F. trout will move into cooler waters. Thus by midsummer a trout population that during the spring months ranged over almost the entire area of streams and lakes will tend to congregate where springs and spring seepage moderate the water temperature. It follows that trout angling is most intensive during the spring and early summer and by and large is then most successful. It also follows, however, that when an angler knows his territory he continues to enjoy good trout fishing throughout the summer in the cooler streams and in "spring holes," about whose location he is understandably evasive. Thus the nonresident angler is somewhat handicapped in obtaining midsummer trout fishing without local know-how, but throughout New Brunswick this is not difficult to obtain.

The rainbow trout is not native to the waters of New Brunswick. This species has been introduced into a number of streams and lakes, and in some of these has established breeding populations. Crooked Creek in Albert County is a case in point. Having been introduced some time ago in both streams and lakes, it is spreading gradually to a number of waters, with increasing reports of its capture, in some instances as a steelhead. To what extent these migratory populations may become established is not known.

SMALLMOUTH BASS FISHING

The smallmouth bass is not native to New Brunswick waters. It is now found in a number of rivers and lakes of the southwestern section of the province, in part having migrated from neighboring Maine waters where it has long since been established, and in part by direct introductions. Thus excellent angling for black bass may be had in the St. Croix, Magaguadavic, and St. John River systems, in the rivers themselves and in tributary lakes. The quality of black-bass fishing in these waters has been appreciated only in recent years. Even today resident anglers, perhaps for no other reason than that they have

been brought up as trout anglers, do not seriously fish this species. To the contrary, the nonresident angler, who is well aware of the prowess of the smallmouth black bass as a sport fish, is increasingly becoming aware of the excellent angling that is to be had in the above waters. Through facilities of local guides, hotels, and owners of fishing camps, more and more nonresident anglers are enjoying bass angling, which they acknowledge to be of a quality infrequently encountered in the northeastern area of the continent. Lakes such as Spednik, Magaguadavic, Digdeguash, Utopia, and Wheaton provide uncrowded angling opportunity for black bass under the most pleasing of summer weather.

Information on angling regulations for trout and black bass can be obtained from the Fish and Wildlife Branch, Department of Lands and Mines, Fredericton, New Brunswick. With some exceptions, the trout season is from April 15 to September 15. There is a size limit for trout of six inches, and for smallmouth black bass of ten inches. The daily catch limit for trout is twenty fish or ten pounds. Fly-fishing only is permitted on the main southwest and northwest Miramichi, Restigouche, and Big Salmon rivers, but this regulation does not apply to trout fishing on the tributaries to these rivers. The New Brunswick Travel Bureau, 658 Queen St., Fredericton, provides information on living accommodations, on availability of guides and outfitters, and other pertinent information, in relation to the many fishing waters in New Brunswick. *See also* Atlantic Salmon   —C.J.K.
—M.W.S.

NEWFOUNDLAND This eastern Canadian province offers the most fishing in the Maritimes. It is highly regarded for Atlantic salmon, brook trout, salters, sea trout, landlocked salmon, and bluefin tuna. Newfoundland, which follows the liberal principle of Nova Scotia, has more public salmon waters than any other province, and although the catch is dominated by grilse, the costs are modest and the opportunities abundant. The mainland portion (Labrador) has many fine streams in a comparatively virgin state, but it is difficult of access. There has been a general improvement in the road situation on the island in recent years, and the better salmon streams, notably on the north coast, are more readily available. Generally speaking, accommodations are scarce, and camping out is widely practiced.

WESTERN NEWFOUNDLAND

Western Newfoundland may be reached by plane at Harmon Airport in Stephenville, which is the starting point by road or rail for some excellent fishing. The productive season varies on different rivers; however, good angling can be expected from June 20 until late July. Some of the better streams here are the Little Codroy, Grand Codroy, Crabbs River, Flat Bay Brook, Fishels River, Fox Island River, North Branch River, South Branch River, Harry's River, Highlands River, Southwest Brook, Bottom Brook, Robinson's River, Serpentine, and the Humber. The Humber, both Upper and Lower, holds big salmon which arrive in the first run from about mid June to mid July. After that the take is predominantly grilse. Although a tremendous number of fish are gaffed at spots such as Big Falls and Little Falls, the Humber is heavily fished; being convenient to Corner Brook and Deer Lake, it has no shortage of anglers.

One of the top salmon producers of Newfoundland is the Serpentine River on the island's west coast

However, experts continue to take some exceptional salmon out of the Humber with fair regularity. Deer Lake is a good jumpoff spot for the more remote rivers on the island, and you can also charter aircraft out of here for wilderness fishing in Labrador.

GREAT NORTHERN PENINSULA

The Great Northern Peninsula offers the most to the average fly-fisherman from the point of view of accessibility. The peninsula is open by means of a very good dirt road which crosses virtually every river on the western coast. There is also excellent salter fishing in season in at least two of these rivers (Western Brook and Baker's Brook). Rivers that are most favorably known are Western Brook, Baker's Brook, Portland Creek, River of Ponds, Torrent River, Castor River, and the East River. There are others farther north.

The season is from mid June until mid August; however, July fishing would be considered by far the best. As a matter of interest all these rivers are fairly heavily fished by local rods; however, there is still room for more. Roughly 80 percent of the catch are grilse, although several of the rivers named, e.g., Portland Creek and the Torrent River, have runs of very large fish, up to 35 pounds. But these are very seldom taken.

There is some tourist accommodation along this road, particularly at Portland Creek. However, guides and outfitters are generally available for all rivers.

AVALON PENINSULA

There are four main salmon rivers on the Avalon Peninsula in eastern Newfoundland. These are all located within one hundred miles of St. John's—the Salmonier River, Colinet River, Placentia River, and Trepassey River. Salmon are plentiful, but the fish are usually small. The best fishing period is from July 1 to August 15. Although accommodations are available, guides are difficult to obtain.

Salters enter the streams of the Avalon Peninsula beginning in May and can be taken in the estuaries of the brooks at Seal Cove, Holyrood, Biscay Bay, Colinet, Swift Current, Witless Bay, and many other locations. Large sea trout (*which see*) are also caught in this area at the stream mouths and also in brackish lagoons; two sea trout taken near Witless Bay in 1960 and 1962 exceeded 27 pounds and 28 pounds, respectively. These anadromous browns are caught on bait, flies, and spinning lures.

AVALON PENINSULA TUNA FISHING

Conception Bay offers excellent giant bluefin tuna fishing through August and part of September. However, there is only a limited number of charter craft (Cape Island boats) available, and reservations must be made well in advance.

Conception Bay is a half-hour cab drive from the lovely old city of St. John's, capital of the province. Anglers can headquarter at the Newfoundland Hotel, which offers the best in accommodations and food. After a hearty breakfast (don't miss the cod au gratin), you can be aboard by 8:30 A.M. Newfoundlanders believe in fishing right up until dark. This gives the angler a long day. It's even longer when you realize that there's no time-killing run to make to the grounds. Baits are splashed the moment you clear the slip. Conception Bay is surrounded by hills, and the water is so flat at times that you can spot fish working a mile away. The tuna range 400–800 pounds during the season, with the larger fish generally caught in early September.

CENTRAL NEWFOUNDLAND

The four most important salmon rivers in central Newfoundland are the Gander, Northwest Gander, Southwest Gander, and Exploits River. The latter is Newfoundland's longest stream, but the salmon fishing is confined to the stretch from Grand Falls to the mouth, a distance of about 30 miles. The salmon are usually small, averaging about 4 pounds, with only the very occasional fish in the 12–15-pound class.

Farther east is the 32-mile-long Gander River, a broad, island-dotted sweep of grass-, gravel-, and boulder-studded water which draws such heavy angling traffic during the July and August grilse run that the high-pitched whine of outboards doesn't even scare the moose these days. The river, which is 15 miles from Gander Airport, has become an increasingly popular spa. There are two commercial camps located below Glenwood.

Newfoundland has countless rivers, and naturally the best ones are a bit harder to reach than either the Humber or Gander. The Newfoundland Tourist Development Division puts out a comprehensive seventy-page booklet, *Fishing in Newfoundland*, which can be obtained by writing to that office in the Confederation Building, St. John's, Newfoundland. This is a bible in the back country, and will prove most helpful.

SALMON FLIES FOR NEWFOUNDLAND

Hair-wing flies were developed in North America. In Newfoundland, with a plentiful supply of moose skins, it is easily understood how the fisherman here experimented and developed their own flies with this type of very sturdy hair. Although some patterns originated in Newfoundland, such as Black Silvertip, Black Moose, Black Bear,

Killer Jock, Gander Dilly, and Polar White, virtually all standard salmon flies are now tied by substituting moose hair for the complicated feather wings. Because of its strength and weight moose hair is best suited for wet flies; deer and caribou hair for dry flies. Hair-wing flies can be purchased for half the price of feather flies. They are now so popular with local fishermen and visitors that 80 percent or better of all wet flies used are moose dressings. They can be tied in all sizes and types, such as standard, lowwater, and double hooks.

The visitor to Newfoundland would do well to supply himself with a variety of sizes in standard flies such as a few 4's and 6's for highwater and for early in the year, May and June. Sizes 6, 8, and 10 should be used for July and August, for medium and lowwater. Lowwater flies also have a place—they were developed for salmon fishing when large salmon rise only to small flies. The hook in various sizes is tied using a much longer, fine but strong shank, and the dressing is small and well up the shank toward the eye, giving the appearance of a smaller fly. Dry flies, such as the White and Grey Wulff, Deer Brown, and Grizzly King, are very successful at times. These are used in still pools, slow deepwater, and later in the season.

—A.J.McC.

NEW HAMPSHIRE Primarily a coldwater state, New Hampshire has over 4,000 miles of trout streams and 227 coldwater ponds which contain brook, brown, lake, and rainbow trout, as well as the landlocked salmon. There are approximately 1,200 warmwater lakes in the southern portion of the state in which smallmouth bass and chain pickerel predominate. Many of the small northern waters in the White Mountain area maintain natural populations of native brook trout, but New Hampshire does a great deal of stocking to maintain a put-and-take trout fishery. Most notable among New Hampshire's waters are the Androscoggin River, Ammonoosuc River, Baker River, Swift Diamond River, Connecticut River, Saco River, the Connecticut lakes, Winnipesaukee Lake, Sunapee Lake, Squam Lake, Ossipee Lake, Newfound Lake, Hampton River, Winnisquam Lake, Bearcamp River, and the Smith River. However, there are many lesser streams and ponds which provide fair to excellent fishing at times. The best landlocked salmon fishing occurs in the early spring season, right after "ice out," and some good trout fishing can be had in some parts of the state until late October (check current regulations on dates). New Hampshire also provides some saltwater fishing along its limited seacoast between Newburyport and Portsmouth. The principal species sought is the striped bass.

The saltwater fishery has been expanded somewhat in recent years to include coho salmon. New Hampshire stocked 90,000 yearlings in 1969. Released in Great Bay near Portsmouth and in the Merrimac River at Newburyport, the coho schooled off the mouth of the Piscataqua River (Great Bay's outlet stream) and around Plum Island south of the Merrimac. By late summer of 1970 the coho were averaging 9 pounds in weight, and the odd big fish was caught by fishermen along the Massachusetts and Maine coasts. There are vast shoals of 8–12-inch-long "tinker" mackerel off New England's shores, which the peripatetic coho found as an abundant forage fish. For a short period the coho disappeared, when inshore water temperatures exceeded 60°F, but otherwise it was characteristically a surface fishery with salmon hitting

jigs, plugs, sea worms, and live mackerel intended for striped bass. Comparatively few anglers went out with the idea of fishing for coho. Contacts with the salmon usually paralleled the type of fishing found in the cold Pacific northwest, with schools visibly feeding at the top.

CONNECTICUT LAKES

There are four Connecticut lakes starting with Lake Francis, and, ascending the Connecticut River toward Quebec, they are First, Second, and Third lakes. Although these are all accessible by road and the angling is sustained by stocking, they provide considerable fishing for lake, rainbow, and brook trout as well as landlocked salmon. The fish are generally small, with 4–5-pound lake trout and 2–3-pound salmon making up the usual catch; however, a few larger specimens are caught each year. Some of the better angling in this northern section of the state is found in the smaller ponds, such as Big Brook Bog, Scott's Bog, Munn Pond, Big and Little Diamond Pond, and Stratford Bog. Fishing pressure is heavy, particularly during the summer period, and the best results are usually had right after ice out and late in the season.

CONNECTICUT RIVER

One of the most important trout streams in New Hampshire, the Connecticut River rises in the Connecticut lakes north of Pittsburg and flows south through Massachusetts and the state of Connecticut before entering Long Island Sound. The major sport fishery exists between its source and North Stratford; although trout persist in scattered locations all the way to saltwater, particularly at the mouths of cold tributaries, the best fishing is roughly in the Pittsburg to North Stratford section. This can be a difficult stretch of river. In common with many modern streams, its flow is controlled for hydroelectric power so the normal level can spin a generator—or knock an amateur angler galleywest. Periodically, the torrent is cut to a trickle, but this respite generally occurs toward the end of the fishing season. At summer level the Connecticut hisses well above its rocks and whips through the bank grasses and under spruce roots, which mark its normal margin. It has a subdued sense of force which even the expert will respect. There are only four real pools in the fly-fishing-only stretch between First Lake and Lake Francis. The river is composed almost entirely of pocketwater or long turbulent runs. Unless you understand the habits of trout, it would be easy to believe that the river is far too strong to hold fish. However, this highly oxygenated flow is host to a good population of 8–12-inch brook and rainbow trout. Brown trout are common, and large individual fish are taken from time to time. Small landlocked salmon are numerous. South of the Connecticut lakes region the best trout stretch on the river is in the vicinity of Colebrook and North Stratford. A favorite spot is the Cones Siding Run, which holds some big browns and rainbows in fastwater. In general, the Upper Connecticut is a better-than-average public trout stream.

The Mascoma River is in confluence with the Connecticut at Lebanon. Brown trout is the predominant species in the short stretch of the Mascoma (about 8 miles) between Lebanon and Mascoma Lake. Continuing south on the Connecticut, another stream is seen joining that river at West Claremont. This is Sugar River, which, at Newport (15 miles east of West Claremont), is brook-trout water. The north branch of the Sugar River, in Croydon and Grantham, is stocked with brown trout. Still farther south on the Connecticut, Cold River, a brook-trout stream at Acworth, joins the major river in the village of Cold River. The last important tributary is the Ashuelot River which enters the Connecticut at Hinsdale, 8 miles above the Massachusetts line. In its upper reaches at Marlow and Gilsum, the Ashuelot is a brown-trout stream. Above Ashuelot Pond it becomes a bass stream.

LAKE WINNIPESAUKEE

Island-dotted Winnipesaukee is one of the largest lakes in New England, and is highly developed as a resort region. Although subject to heavy angling pressure it produces good lake-trout and exceptional landlocked salmon fishing in the early season and smallmouth bass during the summer period. In the winter months ice fishermen (*see* Ice Fishing) colonize the lake with their bobhouses to take lake trout and whitefish.

Both Squam Lake, to the northwest, and Winnisquam Lake, to the southwest of Winnipesaukee, have similar fisheries. Newfound Lake, about ten miles to the west, was once widely known as a salmon lake; Newfound still affords some sport for those who like to pursue this species. It is also excellent for lake-trout fishing, both in summer and through the ice.

SUNAPEE LAKE

Sunapee Lake lies within the towns of Sunapee, Newbury, and New London. It is historically associated with the rare Sunapee trout (*which see*), which is probably extinct today. Sunapee does produce brook trout, lake trout, landlocked salmon, and smallmouth bass. Some of the better locations are at Lost Reef, Loon Island Light, Blodgett's Bar, and Great Island. Trolling with live smelt in deepwater is the most popular method of angling in Sunapee.

DIAMOND RIVERS

Rising in the eastcentral part of Coos County, the Dead Diamond and Swift Diamond rivers join with the Magalloway River on the Maine border near Wentworth Location. With the coldwater of Clear Stream coming in at Errol, these rivers build up the big Androscoggin River that flows rapidly south to Berlin and then turns east into Maine at Gorham. In both Diamonds the native brook trout is at its best in New Hampshire. The brookie is successfully fished for in the Androscoggin, too, as far south as Milan. Landlocked salmon are taken occasionally in the Androscoggin. The Androscoggin between Errol and Milan is one of the finest rainbow-trout streams in the state, producing a large number of 5-pound specimens. A good stretch on this stream for the fly-fisherman is between Errol Dam and Pontook Rips.

AMMONOOSUC RIVERS

Fed by the Nash Streams in Stratford and Odell and by Phillips Brook in Odell, both brook-trout waters, the Upper Ammonoosuc River enters the Connecticut River at Groveton. At Kilkenny, the Upper Ammonoosuc is good brook-trout water.

The main Ammonoosuc River flows into the Connecticut River at Woodsville, where Route 302 crosses into Vermont. Upriver from Woodsville to Lisbon on this route (12 miles), the Ammonoosuc is brown-trout water and continues to Littleton and beyond. In the Littleton-Bethlehem area, brook and rainbows are present.

The Wild Ammonoosuc River runs between North Woodstock on Route 3 and Bath (just above Woodsville) on Route 302. It is a brook-trout stream.

SACO RIVER

Rising in the great notches which breach the main range of the White Mountains—Crawford, Pinkham, and Carter—the Saco River provides notable trout fishing of several varieties. High on the side streams, such as the East Branch, brook trout are predominately wild and self-supporting; although not reaching significant size, they are prolific and as beautiful as the clear coldwaters and rocky pools which form their habitat. Many an angler will enjoy losing himself for a few hours here or in the waters of Dry River, Sawyers River, or several others. Near the headwaters of the Saco River are also several remote ponds, such as Sawyers and Mountain ponds, which harbor fine brook trout.

From about the latitude of North Conway, where the East Branch joins it, all the way down to the Maine border, a distance of some 20 miles, the Saco takes on the characteristics of a major trout stream. Here, in the early 1900's, famous fly-fishermen came to stalk the native squaretails, which often reached 3–4 pounds in some of the great slow-moving pools. Nowadays, while a few of them remain resident to taunt the persistent angler, most of their living space has been taken over by brown trout, which often reach still greater size. Although these browns are by no means easy to capture, the very fact that they are in there waiting for the angler is satisfaction enough to lure many a persistent Waltonian to fish the river.

While in the Saco valley, fishermen should not neglect the long and beautiful Swift River, which enters through the Passaconaway Valley as a major tributary from the West and holds good populations of both brook and rainbow trout. Today, the highway to Kancamagus closely parallels this stream for most of its length, making it easy of access. Conway Lake also provides some good sport for the bass fisherman.
    —A.E.N.
    A.J.McC.

NEW JERSEY New Jersey has more people and industry per unit area than any other state in the United States. Yet, nearly 50 percent of the state is still rural, and fully half of this area is forested. Though small in size, New Jersey is a region of contrasting environments; few states can match the variety of fishing opportunities available, which range from bluefin tuna and striped bass in offshore waters to American shad and chain pickerel inland. Inevitably, civilization has put the squeeze on many fisheries, such as the trout angling, but even here, residents enjoy a satisfactory, and often surprising, return to the creel.

New Jersey has an abundant water supply. Two major rivers and the Atlantic Ocean form about three-quarters of the state's boundaries. The state contains over 300 lakes and impoundments, with an average size of 75 acres. It has 75 major watershed units. While some of the lakes are of glacial origin, most are artificial, dating back to colonial times and the need for water power. These old mill ponds provide habitats for a variety of warmwater fishes. In addition, New Jersey farmers have created more than 3,000 acres of farm ponds, many of which produce good fishing.

FRESHWATER FISHING

New Jersey's important freshwater gamefishes include the brook, brown, and rainbow trout, large- and small-mouth bass, chain pickerel, walleye, and channel catfish. The Division of Fish and Game stocks about 500,000 trout annually which run 9–10 inches in length, with a range of 7–18 inches. While the hatchery program supplies the bulk of the trout in New Jersey, many smaller northern streams contain good populations of native brook and brown trout. These highly colored fish, though generally smaller than the average hatchery trout, will provide excellent sport for an ardent group of anglers.

It is somewhat of a paradox that even New Jersey's better waters are crowded only early in the season and even then usually on week ends or days immediately following restocking. Late summer and fall excursions to many trout streams will find the fisherman virtually isolated in delightful natural surroundings.

The Big Flat Brook, in Sussex County, is perhaps New Jersey's most productive trout stream. Its upper tributaries contain native populations of fish, and the lower stretches receive liberal stockings of brook, brown, and rainbow trout from April through June. Many stretches of Big Flat Brook will carry trout the year around, and it is the resident brownie which presents the real challenge to accomplished fly-fishermen. Early autumn also finds an upsurge in rainbow trout activity, probably fish which move up from the Delaware River.

The Musconetcong, Wanaque, Paulinskill, Pequest, and upper Raritan River provide good trout fishing. The best-known stream in southern New Jersey, the Manas-quan, defies the fly angler to take trout from its highly colored waters, but accomplished bait-fishermen are successful throughout the season. Occasionally, a sea-run trout (see Salter, Sea Trout), which has come up from the lower estuary, is caught in the Manasquan. With the liberalized trout-fishing regulations in effect, hunters have found it worth while to bring their tackle along for a few hours of fishing on warm autumn days. Annual breaks in the winter cold snaps also find anglers heading for the major streams to seek those pools where cold-weather trout congregate.

The Delaware River has reached national prominence in recent years as a result of the resurgence of its shad population. Fishing for this species has stirred local Waltonians into a frenzy of action and excitement never before seen in this state. But other kinds of fishing can be found in this delightful river, too. Some trout fishing can be had above Belvedere, especially at the mouths of tributaries. Smallmouth bass and walleyes offer fair to excellent sport from Lambertville north. Here again, nimrods are learning that they can combine their hunting with some late-season walleye fishing along Warren and Sussex County shores. This is usually the best time of year to fish for walleyes. Channel catfish are on the increase in the lower Delaware River. Although they are taken from Lambertville on down, the best fishing is to be had

from Camden south. This lower section of the river also provides good fishing for striped bass, white perch, yellow perch, bullheads, and carp. Major tributary streams, such as the Rancocas, Cohansey, and Salem provide, in addition to the above mentioned species, modest sport for largemouth bass and chain pickerel.

It is the alewife that ushers in the spring for Delaware River fishermen. The best spot to get into the annual run is at Trenton Falls, within the city limits of the capital city. Several other major river systems in the state have alewife runs, and where dams cause them to congregate, fast action is generally assured.

"Gate-hole fishing" in New Jersey should be given a bit more than passing mention. Gate holes, or stilling basins, are the pools below dams where a variety of fish species will congregate. The best gate-hole fishing is in southern New Jersey. Besides alewives, and depending on the season, one can expect to find good to excellent fishing for white and yellow perch, pickerel, largemouth bass, catfish, less frequently shad, striped bass, and "snapper" bluefish.

Lake fishing in New Jersey varies considerably in quality. Most large lakes attract a variety of other recreational activities not conducive to good fishing. In these, fishing is best early or late in the season, or at night. Many lakes are private and not available to the general public. However, the Division of Fish and Game and other state agencies have undertaken a long-range program of acquisition and construction to help alleviate this problem.

Some of the best warmwater fishing opportunities may be listed by species.

Smallmouth bass The Delaware River has already been cited and is without doubt New Jersey's best small-mouth water. Steenykill Lake in Stokes State Forest is under management for smallmouth and has provided fair to good fishing in recent years. New Jersey's larger northern lakes and reservoirs, like Boonton Reservoir, Lakes Hopatcong, Big Swartswood, and Greenwood, provide occasional flurries of good smallmouth fishing in the midautumn, but this is not always so.

Largemouth bass Generally speaking, New Jersey's better-known lakes are not the best for largemouth-bass fishing, except in the off season. However, many of the mill ponds so abundantly scattered throughout the state, especially those off the main arteries, will offer quite adequate rewards to the angler with a car-top boat who likes to explore. The topnotch largemouth waters are on the Tuckahoe Public Hunting and Fishing Grounds in Atlantic and Cape May counties; Union Lake in Cumberland County; the Collier's Mills Public Hunting and Fishing Tract in Ocean County; Imlaystown Lake in Mercer County; the Delaware and Raritan Canal; Shadow Lake and Tinton Manor Reservoir in Monmouth County; Budd Lake, Hopatcong, Big Swartswood Lake, and other north Jersey lakes and reservoirs are good, but the bass here are really "educated" and quite a challenge.

Chain pickerel The pickerel is New Jersey's most widely distributed gamefish, and the only major one in the acid "cedar" waters along the outer coastal plain. In more fertile waters, its growth is rapid, as attested to by the fact that a former world-record pickerel was a specimen from New Jersey. The Tuckahoe, Collier's Mills Tracts, and Union Lake, mentioned above, are also outstanding for pickerel fishing. The Menantico Sand Ponds in Cumberland County, Big Swartswood, and Lake Hopatcong in Sussex County should be investigated. Serious pickerel fishermen should also explore the upper tidal sections of the rivers that drain the outer coastal plain. These areas receive very light pressure, despite biologist reports that "lunker" pickerel lurk in these waters. The stretch around Upper Green Bank on the Mullica River is especially productive.

Panfish Panfishing in New Jersey does not seem to be as popular as in many sections of the country; yet most of the state's freshwaters harbor a variety of species with better-than-average growth rates. Calico bass, yellow perch, brown bullhead, bluegill, and pumpkinseed sunfish are to be found in just about every good bass lake. Some of the larger lakes and reservoirs also contain good populations of white catfish, redbreast sunfish, and white perch. A few impoundments have been managed for channel catfish.

Carp Carp fishing has a few supporters among rod-and-reel fishermen; the devotees are bowmen and cane-pole fishermen. Such river systems as Pompton, Passaic, and the lower Delaware and its tributaries maintain carp populations. Paulinskill Lake in Sussex County, Columbia Lake in Warren County, Carnegie Lake in Mercer County, and the Delaware and Raritan Canal are popular haunts of the bowman.

SALTWATER FISHING

New Jersey is situated in the center of the Middle Atlantic Bight. A wide variety of marinefish habitats are available to the sport fisherman, including tidal rivers and bays, miles of surf with and without jetties, the broad continental shelf studded with natural reefs and wrecks, and the submarine canyons and slope waters which are only beginning to receive the big-game fishermen's attention. Anglers can literally "have their cake and eat it, too," for during the summer months they can catch many of the species generally associated with the south Atlantic area, and during the winter they can catch species generally found in New England waters. Except for an occasional lull in activity, New Jersey offers year-around fishing of high caliber.

Striped bass are probably the most highly rated gamefish in this area. Except for the short closed season during January and February, they can be taken at all seasons by sport fishermen. At the opening of the season on March 1, the bass are still somewhat dormant because of coldwater temperatures, but they can often be enticed with a gob of clam or bloodworms in such popular spots as the surf at Island Beach State Park or the Mullica, Great Egg, or Maurice rivers. The warm spring sun quickly warms the water over the flats of Barnegat and other shallow bays, and by mid March bass can usually be taken by drifting these bays and casting bucktails with light spinning tackle. Surf-fishing, primarily with bait, reaches a peak in April. After this peak, the best fishing is to be had by trolling and surf-fishing in the Sandy Hook area, or bait and bucktail fishing in bays and rivers. During the summer months, some stripers are taken but primarily by the experts. However, excellent fly fishing can be found in both bays and along the surf. The fall run in the surf is best of all; once you've been "in the right place at the right time" you will be "hooked" for life. Metal lures and plugs are the rule at this season.

Far less glamorous, but high in the esteem of a huge army of anglers, is the fluke or summer flounder (*which see*). It is taken by drifting live or cut bait along the bottom of bays, inlets, or inshore ocean waters from May to October. The blackback or winter flounder (*which see*) rounds out the season for the bottom-fisherman. It can be taken during March, April, October, and November in bays and inlets. Bloodworms are the preferred bait, but clams and mussels also take fish.

Sea bass and porgies (*see* Scup) are abundant on the offshore reefs and wrecks during the summer months. Most anglers take advantage of the many well-equipped party boats which take you to the grounds for a day's fishing for a nominal fee. During the winter months cod, whiting, pollock, and hake are taken by the party-boat anglers.

Bluefish certainly deserve a place near the top of any list of gamefish. While some of them are taken as early as June, don't count on them before July. They remain in our waters until late September or early October. Most bluefish are taken by the party-, charter-, and private-boat fleets on such well-known grounds as Shrewsbury Rocks, Barnegat Ridge, and Five Fathom Bank by chumming or trolling. Surf-casting with cut bait or lures is also productive. Not generally known, but far more exciting, is the light-tackle fishing that can be enjoyed in some of our bays, especially early and late in the day or at night.

The angler interested in big-game fish can also be accommodated. School tuna and white marlin are taken regularly by charter boats operating from New Jersey ports during the summer months. The more adventuresome big-game fishermen should be interested in the waters along the edge of the continental shelf. While this area is virtually unexplored, indications are that marlin, several species of tuna, true albacore, dolphin, and mako sharks are there for the catching. However, the 75-to-100-mile haul to the fishing grounds necessitates a weekend operation.

For those interested in more specific information on fishing in New Jersey, information and reprints from the division's magazine *New Jersey Outdoors* may be obtained by writing to the Division of Fish and Game, 230 West State Street, Trenton. —R.F.S.
—P.E.H.

NEW MEXICO When the traveler enters the great state of New Mexico on any of the five main highways, he sees practically no fishing waters. The point at which he crosses the Rio Grande or the Pecos River belies the situation elsewhere. He may even conclude that the state is mostly semidesert and never suspect that it has many clear streams and lakes, extensive mountain ranges, and highly scenic wilderness areas. In a state covering an area of 122,634 square miles there is room to hide many lakes and streams and even vast mountain ranges with peaks reaching 13,000 feet in elevation. New Mexico's size, by way of comparison, is equal to the combined areas of Maine, New Hampshire, Massachusetts, Rhode Island, Connecticut, Delaware, New Jersey, Maryland, and Virginia.

New Mexico is truly a land of surprises and enchantment. Its lowest point is 2,876 feet above sea level, from which it ranges up to over 13,000 feet in several spots. It embraces six of the seven life zones found in the United

States—Lower Sonoran to Arctic. It includes six National Forests with a combined area of nearly 9,000,000 acres, and some 5,000,000 acres of well-timbered areas of private, state, and public-domain lands. It has one National Park, nine National Monuments, and a dozen State Parks.

The climate may be classed as dry and very sunny. Precipitation varies from about 6 inches annually, with practically no snow in the lower areas, to more than 30 inches with 200 or more inches of snow in the high country. Winters tend to be mild enough in the lower and intermediate elevations for year-around fishing, while many of the alpine lakes at elevations above 10,000 feet remain frozen over and isolated from access by snow until well up into June. With this wide range in climatic conditions New Mexico has an unusual variety of fishing resources—brilliantly colored cutthroat trout in the high, cold streams and lakes to sluggish catfish in the warmwaters of the low elevations. In between will be found rainbow, brown and brook trout, smallmouth bass, sunfish, crappie, yellow perch, black bass, white bass, walleye, channel, blue, and flathead catfish, bullheads, Colorado squawfish, buffalo, suckers, and carp. Of all these species the only gamefish indigenous to the state is the Gila trout (which see) found in the Gila River drainage, cutthroat trout in all other mountain streams, catfish, and yellow perch. The rest have been introduced.

New Mexico is really a dry state, and its fishing is relatively limited despite the fact that there is a great variety of fishing waters. Unlike the Northwest states where dams interfere with migrations of anadromous fish and are considered detrimental to fishing resources, here every impoundment adds acreage to the fisheries inventory. The large irrigation reservoirs such as Elephant Butte, Caballo, McMillan, Alamogordo, Conchas, Bluewater, El Vado, and Navajo provide the biggest resources the state has. However, the erratic fluctuation of water levels due to the annual summer drawdown as the water is used for irrigation and the recharging with the spring runoff is not conducive to optimum conditions for fish production.

TROUT WATERS

New Mexico's biggest and best trout stream is the Rio Grande. From the New Mexico-Colorado boundary south for 80 miles this roaring river wends its tortuous way through a 400–900-foot deep gorge of cliffs and boulders. The Rio Grande Box Canyon, as it is known, is truly a fabulous fishing water. The first 50 miles of it is a magnificent wild river, accessible only by foot trails except where one state road crosses it. Rainbow and brown trout abound there and attain great size—regularly 3–5 pounds, frequently to 8 pounds, and occasionally up to 15 pounds or over. They are a wild, fighting trout in turbulent water to tax the angler's skill in an awe-inspiring setting. For the remaining 30 miles to the junction with the Chama River, whose muddy waters put an end to trout fishing, the stream is paralleled by a highway. Here it provides bigwater trout fishing, as well as some smallmouth bass, for the many anglers who like waters accessible by car.

A few miles east of this 80-mile stretch of the Rio Grande the Sangre de Cristo range rises to elevations of up to 13,000 feet. In those mountains there are many small- to medium-size trout streams flowing out on either

side. Costilla Creek near the state line is a good fishing stream. At the head of Latir Creek, one of its tributaries, are the nine famous Latir Lakes nestling against the base of Latir Peaks which tower way above timberline. A jeep road takes one to within hiking distance.

Twenty miles south, Red River comes tumbling down from timberline peaks through the renowned resort town of Red River. A four-mile box near its junction with the Rio Grande is also a wild river. At its head are a number of alpine lakes that afford excellent fishing for those who like it in a primitive setting. Near the town of Questa is Cabresto Lake, which is about 25 acres in extent, and is accessible by car.

The Hondo Creek comes down twelve miles north of Taos, and twenty miles south are the Rio Pueblo and Santa Barbara rivers, which are beautiful trout waters. All of these streams, except the Rio Grande Box, must be stocked heavily throughout the season to meet the intensive fishing pressure. The mountains in which these waters are located are situated mainly in the Carson National Forest.

Eagle Nest Lake, situated in the Merino Valley 40 miles east of Taos on United States Highway 64 at an elevation of 8,400 feet, is an excellent trout water. It is an 1,800-acre irrigation reservoir in private ownership, where special permits must be obtained to fish. It is operated on a commercial basis, but has a reputation for good fishing.

Cimarron Canyon, for 12 miles below the lake, through which the Cimarron Creek flows, is owned by the New Mexico Department of Game and Fish and is very heavily utilized as a public recreation and fishing area. It is in a cool, scenic country. The country northward from the Cimarron Canyon Area is all privately owned, but includes some good trout streams and lakes on the Vermejo Park property. Near Raton is Lake Maloya, a municipal reservoir open to public fishing, which provides considerable sport fishing for the angler after rainbow trout.

In the extreme northeast corner of the state, just north of Clayton, is Clayton Lake, a 170-acre body of water impounded by a dam built by the Department of Game and Fish. It is an excellent rainbow-trout lake and serves well because there is no other fishing water of any real consequence within 100 miles.

West of Raton and north of Cimarron lies the 640,000-acre Vermejo Park Ranch within which are several good trout streams—Vermejo Ricardo, Costilla, and others—containing trout. Also, there are several good lakes on the east slope of the mountains and on the west side there is Costilla Reservoir which is excellent fishing. All this is private property and fishing and hunting is commercialized.

The two Charette lakes with a combined area of 400 acres, located on a high mesa 20 miles northwest of Wagon Mound, also belong to the New Mexico Department of Game and Fish and provide some of the finest rainbow-trout fishing to be found anywhere in the state, especially for those who like to troll.

Near Maxwell, 20 miles south of Raton, are six irrigation reservoirs, 20–1,200 acres, which provide both trout and warmwater fishing.

Northwest and west of Las Vegas the southern extremity of the Sangre de Cristo Range rises to an elevation of 11,000 to 12,000 feet. In front of it huge, double-humped, granite-faced Hermits Peak rises almost as high.

The Peak and El Porvenir Gorge with 1,500-foot perpendicular walls make this one of the grandest scenic attractions in the state. Sightseers can fish, too, for there are several streams, principal of which is the Gallinas River, flowing eastward from the Sangre de Cristo Range.

Three miles north of Las Vegas is privately owned 1,200-acre Storie Reservoir on which the Department of Game and Fish owns the fishing rights. This provides rainbow-trout fishing, but, being an irrigation reservoir with resulting fluctuation of water level, it is not so productive as it otherwise would be. Seven miles east of Las Vegas the State Department of Game and Fish owns McAlister Lake, fed by canal from Storie Lake, which has an area of about 150 acres. This is an amazing trout lake. The fish stocked as fingerlings grow extremely fast and provide some of the best 1–5-pound rainbow-trout fishing in the state.

U. S. Highway 85, twenty-five miles southwest of Las Vegas, crosses the Pecos River at the approximate lower limit of trout fishing. From there on down 80 miles to Alamogordo dam there is nothing much but suckers and chubs. But upstream brown- and rainbow-trout fishing begins and gets better the farther up you go. Twenty miles up is the town of Pecos where the prime trout water begins. Ten miles northwest is Cow Creek with its several tributaries, which also hold trout. The upper Pecos drains a huge horseshoe basin with streams fanning out on either side and heading against the watershed divide made up of two prongs of the Sangre de Cristo Range. Sixteen miles above Pecos the Mora Fork enters. The Mora Fork and its several tributaries are excellent trout streams, accessible only by foot or horseback travel. The river here is partly posted and partly open. Above and below the junction of the Mora the Department of Game and Fish owns 5 miles of the stream and adjacent lands to provide public fishing and camping areas.

Near Cowles the roads end, and just beyond the fabulous Pecos Wilderness Area begins in the Santa Fe National Forest. It embraces 165,000 acres in the upper Pecos River Basin and a fringe lapping over the high, horseshoe divide surrounding it. The wilderness area is characterized by alpine forests, mountain meadows, bunch-grass parks, the finest aspen woods in the world, timberline ridges, and peaks of 12,000–13,150 feet at South Truchas Peak. Besides the main Pecos and the Mora rivers there are many smaller tributaries, all prime trout waters, where cutthroat, rainbow, and brown trout abound and, in some, brook trout also. There are many beaver dams to increase the fishing capacity and enhance the environment.

Best of all, though, are the alpine lakes of 2–20 acres nestling at the base of rugged timberline peaks and ridges. Principal of these are Katherine, Spirit, Stewart, Johnson, Baldy, Truchas, Ruth, Hazel, Alice, Middle Fork, North Fork, Santiago, Encantada, and Lost Bear lakes. Cutthroat and rainbow trout are stocked in these lakes by airplane. Fishing is good in a majestic primitive setting, accessible only by foot and saddle trails.

On the west side of the mountain north from Santa Fe are a few streams, principal of which is the Rio del Medio. Santa Cruz Reservoir, east of Española, is an irrigation project but due to heavy stocking of catchable-size trout each spring it provides excellent fishing in the early part of the season.

The Jemez Mountains in Santa Fe National Forest 60 miles north of Albuquerque has a number of small trout streams—East Fork, San Antonio, Rio de Las Vacas, Cebolla, and others—which are all heavily fished. On Clear Creek is 32-acre San Gregorio Reservoir, and on Rio Cebolla is Fenton Lake of similar size, built by the Department of Game and Fish which, for small lakes, provide a lot of good fishing for cutthroat, rainbows, and browns.

The Chama River enters the Rio Grande a few miles above Española, but upstream for 50 miles it is too muddy for trout. Its first tributary is Vallecitos Creek, which, a bit farther up, is a good trout stream. Near its head is Hopewell Lake built by the Department of Game and Fish in high country accessible by road from Tres Piedras which provides some excellent brook and rainbow fishing. Farther north is Laguna Largo and then the Lagunitas Lakes, several small lakes, and astounding beaver ponds, which are quite popular.

Adjacent to the Colorado line is the Rio Los Pinos, a tributary of the Rio Grande, which, for several miles, is one of New Mexico's best trout waters. A lot of it is posted, but the Department of Game and Fish bought 4 miles of it to provide the public some privileges there.

Back to the Chama, about 60 miles upstream from its junction with the Rio Grande, is El Vado Reservoir, an irrigation project. The lake does provide considerable good trout fishing, but it is drawn too low each year to be anything like prime. The stream below the dam for some 20 miles is pretty good and has the reputation for producing large fish. A 20-pound, 8-ounce brown is the record here.

Near the villages of Nutrias and Canjilon is a series of ponds and small lakes of the same names. Some have been enlarged by the Department of Game and Fish and others by remarkable beaver workings. They are good considering their size.

The Chama River from El Vado Lake to its head in Colorado is prime trout water, as are its several tributaries. The stream is part posted and part open, some of it open with a use charge. Its principal tributary is the Brazos which has a six-mile box between towering cliffs making it a truly wild river, and, for the hardy fisherman, it yields great sport. The Brazos Meadows above the Box are perhaps the most productive waters in the state resulting from natural spawning. Originally there were only cutthroats there, but now other species have invaded the area. It is largely posted.

West of the town of Chama on the Jicarilla Apache Indian Reservation there are a number of excellent natural lakes which yield some fine rainbow trout. There is a nominal fishing fee charged by the Indians.

Another popular spot is the Four Corners Area, so-called because it is the only place in the United States where four states (Colorado, Utah, Arizona, and New Mexico) corner together. The San Juan River, tributary of the great Colorado River, flows through this area for 60 miles above and an equal distance below the city of Farmington. This stream is New Mexico's largest, but formerly it flooded each spring and was so muddy that it did not afford much fishing. Native species were suckers and Colorado squawfish. With the completion of the huge Navajo Dam and reservoir, 30 miles upstream from Farmington, changes occurred, including desilting and stabilization of temperatures and flow, so that the stream below the dam developed into a prime fishing stream for big brown and rainbow trout.

The Animas River, entering the San Juan at Farmington, is a large, good-looking stream, and is regularly stocked with trout, but it is not productive due in large part to the fine silt that it carries from old mining activities in Colorado which impairs its food-production capacity.

A few miles west of Farmington is Jackson Lake, owned by the Department of Game and Fish, which, though very heavily used, is a pretty good rainbow-trout lake. The huge Navajo Dam has impounded 17,800 acres of water with a permanent recreation pool of 2,670 acres. The Navajo reservoir is by far the largest trout water in the state. The permanent pool distinguishes it from most of the irrigation reservoirs. It is fine trout fishing.

When this lake began to impound water it was stocked with rainbow trout, and stocking has kept pace with the volume of water stored.

A hundred miles south of Farmington is the city of Gallup. Near Gallup is McGaffey Lake, a small impoundment made by the Department of Game and Fish, which provides some trout fishing. About 45 miles southeast of Gallup and 8 miles south of U. S. Highway 66 is Bluewater Lake. This is an irrigation reservoir, but to prevent its being ruined by draining every few years, the New Mexico Department of Game and Fish paid the owners $92,000 for water rights sufficient to hold the water level at 20 feet on the dam, thus guaranteeing a permanent 400-acre lake or better. That illustrates the value of water in New Mexico. Then it was cleaned of all rough fish, and is being stocked annually with 300,000 trout fingerlings. The results have been spectacular. During one year, for instance, only 1,800 pounds of catchable-size trout were planted and the creel checks showed over 50,000 pounds of trout up to 2–3 pounds taken out by anglers.

The Gila National Forest north of Silver City, within which is the 516,000-acre Gila Wilderness Area, is in a drier climate, and the mountains are not so high as in the northern part of the state, and fishing waters are more limited. In the Gila River above the town of Gila there are some channel catfish and smallmouth bass. Fair to good trout fishing for browns and rainbows is found in the Middle and West forks of the Gila and tributaries, and in Mogollon Creek. On the west side is Whitewater Creek and Negrito. The best fishing is in the interior of the Wilderness accessible by trail only.

Some years ago the Department of Game and Fish built a dam on Taylor Creek between Silver City and Beaverhead to make a 30-acre trout lake which has proved successful, but it is rapidly silting in. Also the department bought water rights on Bear Canyon Reservoir just off the Mimbres River to guarantee a reasonable recreation pool, and that has improved the fishing there. Just now the department has completed Lake Roberts on Sapillo Creek to make a 70-acre lake only a few miles north of Silver City. That has added greatly to the fishing resources of that area.

In the middle Rio Grande Valley, at and below Albuquerque, and in the lower valley near Las Cruces there are quite a number of drainage canals which contain water suitable for fish, and they are stocked, some with trout and others with warmwater species. Fifteen miles of the Rio Grande between Elephant Butte Dam and Caballo Lake is a good trout stream as water released through the turbines near the bottom of Elephant Butte Lake is quite cold. That affords a lot of rainbow fishing.

The last trout area of the state, the White Mountain country, southeast of Carrizozo, offers a limited amount of fishing. On the west side is Three Rivers, a small, short trout stream, and farther south is Tularosa Creek, most of which is on the Mescalero Apache Indian Reservation. East of Carrizozo is Nogal Lake, an average 30-acre trout lake. Southeast of there is 45-acre Bonito Lake, a municipal water-supply reservoir, where fishing, with a small charge for clean-up maintenance, is pretty good. Above Bonito Creek has a little fishing, and over the ridge Eagle Creek likewise. Rio Ruidoso (Noisy Brook), heading on the Indian reservation and flowing eastward through the City of Ruidoso, provides some trout fishing mainly above the city.

WARMWATER FISHERIES

The warmwater resources of New Mexico are no less important than trout fishing. Of course there are warmwater species found in many ranch and farm ponds and in a few streams, but practically all of this resource is in a dozen or so man-made reservoirs. On the Rio Grande near the city of Truth or Consequences is Elephant Butte Lake with an area, when full, of 42,000 acres. Elephant Butte Lake is stocked with black bass, several kinds of catfish, crappie, yellow perch, bream, and walleye. The latter have not become well-established, however. This lake has a big play the year around. Fishing at times is all that can be desired, but at other times it is slow. High winds in spring often ruin fishing conditions, but its size makes it particularly attractive.

In Caballo Lake, only 15 miles below, with black bass, white bass, walleye, channel catfish, and sunfishes fishing is excellent. White bass are caught in some quantity, and walleye show remarkable growth. If rough fish can be controlled this will be a fine warmwater lake but limited by fluctuating water levels. It covers an area of 11,532 acres when full, but is drawn down quite low each season.

The Pecos River leaves the state at Red Bluff Reservoir. The dam is some distance over the line in Texas, but when the lake fills the water backs up 7 miles into New Mexico. The usual varieties of warmwater fish are found here, but perhaps white bass, at the upper end of the reservoir and on up the river toward Carlsbad, afford the greatest amount of fishing. Along the lower Pecos River are several dams impounding a considerable amount of water—Six Mile, Harroon, and Municipal lakes at Carlsbad and Lakes Avalon and McMillan on above. These, and the river between them, are well stocked by the U. S. Fish and Wildlife Service, but the fishing is disappointing. The water is highly alkaline, not conducive to optimum fish production.

Willow Lake, a privately owned 350-acre reservoir about 15 miles south of Carlsbad, is fed from Black River, and the water is of a better quality for fish production than the lower Pecos. Warmwater fishing there, especially bass, is traditionally good. The state has considered acquiring it.

Near the city of Roswell, about 50 miles above Lake McMillan, are the Bottomless lakes and several other small bodies of water that provide warmwater, and in some cases trout, fishing of fair to good quality. A few miles northeast of the city lies the Bitter Lakes Federal Refuge containing some excellent lakes that provide fishing during limited seasons when it won't interfere with waterfowl use of the area, usually June to October.

It is noteworthy that in past years catchable-size channel catfish have been stocked in considerable numbers in these lower Pecos Valley waters in an effort to improve fishing with some success.

Upstream about 100 miles from Roswell is Alamogordo Dam and Reservoir, a very good fishing water of the irrigation type for the usual warmwater species. It is located about 16 miles northwest of Ft. Sumner, burial place of Billy the Kid. Walleye have been stocked here. The Pecos River, between Bitter Lakes Refuge and Alamogordo Dam, is of little value for fishing of any kind except perhaps at the stilling basin just below the dam and a short way downstream where trout are stocked and provide some good fishing.

On the Canadian River, 31 miles west-northwest from Tucumcari, a truly magnificent lake formed by 155-foot high Conchas Dam, completed by the U. S. Army Engineers in 1940. Its maximum area is 10,000 acres, and the beauty of it is that it cannot be drawn down below the 105-foot elevation of the dam, thus insuring a recreation pool of some 3,500 acres. The warmwater species found there are black bass, crappie, bream, channel catfish, and walleye. It is an excellent fishing lake, and walleye have done very well. The angler familiar with the methods of fishing for them can usually be successful.

The Conchas River arm of the lake is in an open valley for the most part with a spectacular rock-rimmed island in the center. The Narrow Canadian River arm extends about 20 miles up the colorful, cliff-bordered canyon in a magnificent scenic setting. Here the west winds affect fishing less than on the Conchas arm and on other lakes discussed.

At Conchas, as at Elephant Butte, Caballo, Alamogordo, and some others, there are accommodations nearby and boating facilities available.

The Canadian River for 75 miles above the lake wends its exceedingly tortuous course along a rock-walled canyon, most of which is accessible only on foot or on horseback, where is found the best channel-catfish angling in the state. The Mora River, a tributary, has several miles of good catfish water also.

Ute Reservoir, made by a dam on the Canadian River near Logan about 20 miles northeast of Tucumcari, comprises 5,000 acres and the Department of Game and Fish has certain water and fishing rights on it. This has been stocked with warmwater species and undoubtedly will be a warmwater lake, but as an experiment the Department has stocked trout fingerlings in it. This should prove to be an exceptionally good warmwater lake.

The Department of Game and Fish has taken a 25-year lease on 75-acre Lake Van near Artesia in the lower Pecos Valley. This is primarily a warmwater fishing lake. However, the Department is stocking it with catchable-size trout in winter months on a put-and-take basis. This same procedure is being carried on at some spots in the lower Pecos River and in the Municipal Lake adjacent to Carlsbad. This has proven successful and provides the citizens of the general warmwater areas some good trout fishing without their having to travel long distances for it.

—E.B.

NEW YORK The Empire State is endowed with an impressive abundance and variety of freshwater fishing opportunities. It may be a little difficult for a nonresident to visualize good fishing as a permanent feature in a state which is world-renowned for having a towering modern civilization, great economic and industrial wealth, and a rapidly expanding population of 16,000,000 people. But when you consider that over half the population is concentrated at the mouth of the Hudson River in the New York City area and that at least 2,000,000 more people live in five widely separated urban areas across the state, it may be easier to accept the fact that there is still plenty of natural landscape to enjoy. In addition to urban clumping of population there is also the fact that about 9 percent of the state's total land area is classified as either state forest preserve or state park land. The fishing potential here alone is little short of amazing, since this 4,220-square-mile section of natural landscape is roughly half the size of each of the states of Massachusetts, Vermont, New Hampshire, or New Jersey, over three-quarters the size of Connecticut, twice the size of the state of Delaware, and four times that of Rhode Island. In addition there are hundreds of lakes and several thousand miles of trout streams on nonpreserve lands. In all, there are 70,000 miles of flowing water, of which 20,000 miles are considered as suitable year-round trout streams. The lake inventory includes 2,500 lakes of major size (over 6 acres).

The principal warmwater gamefish species are large and smallmouth bass, walleye, northern pike, eastern chain pickerel, and muskellunge. The more widely distributed coldwater fishes include brook, brown, rainbow, and lake trout. Both landlocked salmon and kokanee are comparatively recent additions which are providing excellent fishing in some waters. Both of these new fisheries are

New York's Montauk Point is one of the best surf-fishing locations along the entire East Coast

the result of intensive Conservation Department management programs, which include planting of young salmon for maintenance of future fish stocks.

Panfish varieties represented are yellow perch, pumpkinseed and bluegill sunfish, black and white crappie, rock bass, and bullheads. Coarse fish such as suckers, carp, and fallfish are common, and many attain large size. Probably, due to the abundance of more desirable species, these so-called coarse fish are not very highly regarded either as sport or food in New York State. Anglers in other countries, such as England where coarse fishing has a great following, would be well pleased with the size and abundance of these fish present in some New York waters. Carp commonly attain weights of 5–10 pounds, and 30-pound carp are not unique. The fallfish (locally chub) runs 1–3½ pounds and the white sucker 1–5 pounds.

The possibility of capturing a large fish is better than average in New York. Record northern pike and muskellunge have been taken in the Empire State. The former weighed 46 pounds, 2 ounces and the latter 69 pounds, 15 ounces. Sacandaga Reservoir produced the northern pike in 1940; it currently produces northerns of 15–25 pounds. The big musky was caught in the St. Lawrence River. A brief account of record New York State fish, but not United States records is as follows: brook trout 8 pounds 8 ounces; brown trout 21 pounds 5 ounces; rainbow trout 21 pounds; lake trout 31 pounds; landlocked salmon 16 pounds 14 ounces; smallmouth bass 9 pounds; largemouth bass 10 pounds 6 ounces; and walleye 15 pounds 3 ounces.

THE NIAGARA FRONTIER

This far-western section is best known for its warmwater fishing. The New York shore of Lake Erie is a good area for smallmouth bass, white bass, walleyes, and yellow perch. Smelt have become superabundant in recent years, and these delicious little fish can be taken fishing through the ice toward the east end of the lake, and by dipping in early season.

The Niagara River, connecting between Lakes Erie and Ontario, world famous for the Falls, is less widely known for its fishing, but not because of scarcity of fish. Northern pike, muskellunge, yellow perch, smallmouth bass, and walleye find this deep, dark, powerful river to their liking. This is best classified as a "big-fish" river, but don't expect to hit the jackpot on any given day. The fish have plenty of food and thus are not likely to accept everything that comes their way. There are several hot spots, and in general the river below the Falls may produce a little more variety, although the Grand Island area above the Falls is quite good. In terms of bass, walleye, northern, and musky, a "big" Niagara fish would be the commonly caught sizes of 5, 10, 15, and 25 pounds respectively. As far as average size of fish for a variety of species is concerned, it is doubtful whether any river in the state can equal it. Yellow perch and rock bass are not "panfish" here, as 3-pound fish of either species is a possibility, although not a common one.

Chautauqua Lake has the reputation of being the most stable warmwater fishery in the state. This lake enjoys a dependable production of 30–35 tons of muskellunge annually. To add frosting to the cake, the *average* size is over 10 pounds per fish. If the muskies aren't moving during your visit—and this can often be the case—you still have some excellent largemouth-bass and panfish potential. It almost goes without saying that this is a very fertile lake environment, and fast growth rates of most species are the rule here. For example, black crappies average close to a pound, and 2-pounders are not uncommon. So don't let "musky fever" prevent you from sampling other of Chautauqua's rich gifts.

There are relatively few trout waters to recommend themselves in this region. Among the best bets are the Wiscoy Creek, Ischua Creek, Genesee River above Wellsville, and the Cohocton River. Brown trout predominate in these waters.

THE FINGER LAKES REGION

The six largest, finger-shaped lakes in this region are Skaneateles, Owasco, Cayuga, Seneca, Keuka, and Canandaigua. They run 11–40 miles long. Seneca, at 618 feet, ranks as one of the deepest lakes in the United States.

For large rainbows and lakers, Seneca, Canandaigua, and Keuka have the best potential, although not necessarily in this order. Rainbows and lakers in the 10–20-pound class are usually taken in fair numbers each year from these waters. A state record, a rainbow of 21 pounds, was taken in 1946 from Keuka. Although not a state record, Canandaigua produced a 26-pound laker in 1962. You're liable to run into some good-sized walleyes in Canandaigua also. Trolling is the most consistently successful method in taking these fish. Local tackle shops will be more than willing to suggest the proper artificial and natural lures and also direct you to the more likely spots.

It is possible to take these lakers and rainbows by trolling big bucktails and streamers. A group of anglers working out of Skaneateles village has developed very successful methods and patterns for these species.

Cayuga Lake lake-trout fishing has been very satisfactory in recent years. An extra dividend here is the chance of hooking a landlocked salmon. These fish have appeared more frequently in catches, and their presence is due to an intensive salmon restoration program.

Owasco is somewhat different from the others in that it offers good walleye and cisco fishing. The rainbow- and lake-trout fishing is also fair. A New York State record brown trout of 21 pounds, 5 ounces was taken here in 1954.

Although there is a tendency to think of these six Finger Lakes in terms of salmonids, the warmwater complex should not be discounted since these species are common and attain desirable size. This includes smallmouth black bass, pickerel, yellow perch, and panfish.

In this same area there are also several other good-sized lakes that are well worth mentioning. Lamoka and Waneta are warmwater lakes which have largemouth-bass, pickerel, and panfish potential. Conesus Lake has both large- and smallmouth bass, walleyes, and northern pike. Canadice Lake has smallmouth bass and lake trout. Otisco Lake contains brown trout, smallmouths and walleyes, while Honeoye lists walleye, pickerel, and bass among its game species.

Finger Lakes Rainbow Runs The most famous rainbow run is in Catherine Creek, which enters the south end of Seneca Lake. Each spring, big rainbows ascend from the lake to spawn in this rather small creek, and rainbows to 17 pounds have been taken. The average size is about 5 pounds. The best time is the first two weeks of the season, which opens on April 1. But don't be a bit surprised to find yourself in elbow-to-elbow competition with hundreds of other hopefuls at this time of year. Naples Creek also has a run of these fish. The Skaneateles Lake run occurs in Grout Brook, and these fish do not average as large as the Seneca fish. Two to 4 pounds is the expected during the Grout Brook run.

Fish eggs of any kind are not allowed in Finger Lakes rainbow streams, thus imposing a necessity for finding alternative methods of capture. Necessity in this case turned out to be a very fine mother of invention and resulted in the discovery of many ample substitutes. These include dyed tapioca "eggs," dyed vaseline "eggs," and pieces of red bath sponge. At least one trout has been taken on the proper-colored gum drop.

LAKE ONTARIO AND THE ST. LAWRENCE RIVER

The walleye and smallmouth bass are present along the entire offshore waters from Niagara on the west end to Cape Vincent on the east. The presence of weedy bays along this coast also provides suitable habitat for the largemouth bass and the northern pike. Among these are Braddock's Bay, Irondequoit Bay, Blind Sodus Bay, Sodus Bay, Port Bay, East Bay, and Little Sodus Bay. You'll also find smallmouth, northerns, walleyes, and occasional muskies in this habitat. Chaumont and Henderson bays at the east end of the lake are popular and productive fishing areas.

The St. Lawrence River may be as good fishing today as it has ever been. The smallmouth bass is the principal game species in terms of numbers caught, while the muskie and northern round out the balance. Perhaps the most impressive feature of the St. Lawrence is the abundance of fishy-looking spots to choose from, a feature which is enhanced by the presence of myriad islands and reefs, all of which add up to excellent feeding, shelter, and spawning areas for many fish species. If you're serious about muskies, it would probably be best to get local guide service.

Further downstream, a new fishing area has appeared as a result of dam construction on the St. Lawrence Seaway near Massena. This is Lake St. Lawrence—a 25-mile, man-made lake.

There are numerous inland lakes in the St. Lawrence-Thousand Islands section. The largest of these is Black Lake, a beautiful and very productive piece of water extending for 18 miles. Again, smallmouths, walleyes, northerns, muskies, and panfish are the main fare.

THE ADIRONDACK REGION

This sprawling upland area of emerald-green forest, pristine lakes, and sparkling streams represents a great fishery resource.

The Fulton Chain Lakes have been very fine hosts to thousands of landlocked salmon parr and smolts planted in past years. As a result, a good salmon fishery is being established. Five pounders are quite frequent. Seventh Lake may rate slightly ahead of the others as the best spot. Smallmouths, northerns, and panfish are plentiful.

Schroon Lake on the eastern side of the Adirondacks is a salmon, bass, and northern-pike lake. It has been a good producer of good-sized fish of all three species. You can expect to put in more fishing time for northerns and salmon than you will have to put in for bass.

Lake George also at the southeastern side of the Adirondacks has been a favorite fishing spot for many years. Its clearwaters may yield lakers, salmon, bass, and occasional northerns. A salmon just under 17 pounds was caught here in 1958. The usual size of laker and salmon, however, is more like 2–4 pounds. In addition to the usual lodging facilities, New York State allows permit camping on 48 of their 154 state-owned islands on a first-come-first-served basis. The free Conservation Department pamphlet titled *Lake George* will provide a lake map as well as camping details.

Sacandaga Reservoir at the southern end of the Adirondacks is a fine place for walleyes, bass, northerns, bullheads, and panfish. It is also a favorite ice-fishing spot. A United States record northern of 46 pounds, 2 ounces was caught in Sacandaga in 1940. Today the reservoir annually gives up 15–25-pound fish, thus making it one of the more consistent big pike producers in the state of New York.

Lake Champlain on the northeastern Vermont-New York border is a large aqueous gem of 439 square miles and is about 125 miles long. It is a lake with a variety of fish habitats and a great variety of fish. The lower third of the lake from Whitehall north to Ticonderoga is narrow and riverlike with extensive, shallow weed beds. The middle third is the widest and deepest portion with a considerable amount of water in excess of 200 feet. The upper third is roughly bisected into "separate" lakes by Grand Isle.

A rather amazing variety of sport fishes lives in this lake—large- and smallmouth black bass, northern pike, walleye, chain pickerel, freshwater drum (sheepshead), black crappie, whitefish, cisco, smelt, landlocked salmon, sturgeon, and occasional muskies. The mooneye (*which see*), a rather rare fish, is regarded highly as both food and sport fish. It can reportedly be taken on flies, minnows, grasshoppers, and worms near shore in late summer. The Port Henry area is one of the places where this unique opportunity exists. Fish up to 2 pounds have been recorded. Ice fishing for walleye, smelt, and northern is also an extremely popular pastime here in Champlain.

One of the possible spots for musky is in the Big Chazy River, just below Rouse's Point. Muskellunge have also been caught in the lower river itself.

Indian and Lewey lakes are connected and are excellent bass and northern lakes. You can expect bass to average 2 pounds, and 5-pound northerns are common. Some very sizable northerns are taken annually, including fish above 20 pounds. Whitefish are present, but it takes real know-how to catch up with them.

Raquette Lake has a history of being a consistent lake-trout producer, along with its smallmouth-bass population.

Long Lake, a few miles northeast of Raquette, is particularly well-named. It is about 14 miles long, very narrow, and productive for northern pike and smallmouth black bass. Largemouth black bass have been introduced in recent years.

Lake Eaton and South Pond are both a few minutes' drive from Long Lake. Both contain lake trout and whitefish, with South Pond also producing some brook trout.

The Saranac lakes all have black bass, northerns, and whitefish, and Upper Saranac produces some fine-quality lakers. Saranac and Raquette lake trout are netted each fall and stripped for eggs for fish propagation. About half a million eggs are collected in a good spawning year. Lower Saranac Lake yields some good rainbow trout on occasion.

For every well-known lake and stream there are probably four or five which are just names on a topographic map to most people. This is not for lack of fish in the majority of instances, but for lack of easy accessibility. For anyone who has the time, energy, enthusiasm, and desire to fish these out-of-the-way places this exploration should offer a very rewarding experience, both aesthetically and, usually, poundage-wise. Shoe leather and/or canoe paddle are a necessary part of the transportation system. Don't forget the fly dope if an early-season trip is contemplated because the Adirondack blackfly is as famous as the fishing.

For the sake of example, the St. Regis chain of lakes, in the Saranac Inn–Paul Smith's area, presents interesting possibilities. A cluster of lakes lie in fairly close proximity to each other. These are Nellie, Bessie, Little Long, Lydia, Kit Fox, and St. Regis ponds. All are reclaimed ponds, the largest of which is St. Regis at 1½ miles long. Brookies weighing 1½–2 pounds are present in a couple of these ponds, while others offer sport for fat 10–12-inch fish. The size of the fish in any one pond is mainly due to stocking rate. The lightly stocked ponds have faster-growing and consequently larger fish than the more heavily stocked ones. As usual the larger fish seem to be the hardest to catch, perhaps more by virtue of fewer available fish and their habit of lying in deepwater than actual difference between sizes if we remember that the 10-incher in one pond is exactly the same age as the 2-pounder in another. For coloration, body shape, or fighting qualities these hatchery products are indistinguishable from wild fish. They are stocked in the fall of the year as tiny fingerlings. Ice out through mid May brings best results for pond brookies. After that the fish seek cooler water. This usually means deeper water, but those who know the locations of shallow-water spring holes extend their success through summer.

There are many other possibilities for wilderness fishing. A fishing and camping trip in the Cold River country would qualify as being among the most remote. The country is little changed from the days of the pioneer. This section is available by trail and lies southeast of the village of Tupper Lake and southwest of Lake Placid village.

In general, your best bet for the back-country fishing lies in being well equipped and fishing at the right time. This usually means choosing late April and May for trouting success while September is often a good month for bass and pike. Don't let this prevent you from a summer vacation trip, however, because there will be many "hot" fishing periods during it, but, more often than not, early morning and evening fishing give the best results. No matter what time of year you choose, it is always advisable to get on-the-spot information on the fishing outlook and arrange plans accordingly.

LARGE LAKES AND RESERVOIRS

Oneida Lake, a short distance northeast of Syracuse, is the largest lake located entirely within the borders of the state. Numerous offshore shoals and relative shallowness of the entire lake undoubtedly contribute to the extremely high fish production in this water. Many anglers consider it to be the finest lake of all for bass, walleye, yellow perch, and other warmwater species. Fish of all species usually have high levels of annual abundance with the exception of the walleye. Factors such as the strength of the year-class (abundance of young) several years previous may directly affect adult walleye abundance and, consequently, fishing success for a particular year, according to the findings of fishery research biologists who have conducted extensive studies of the situation. It was also indicated that food supply conditioned fishing success. In years when food was abundant, catches were very low, even though walleye populations themselves might be high. Recent annual estimated catch rates of walleye show that numbers of fish caught fluctuate between 40,000 and 468,000 fish per year. In the peak year 1959, about 650,000 pounds of walleye were caught by Oneida fishermen. This is unique, especially because the state commercial catch for the year was only 230,000 pounds.

Otsego Lake, near Cooperstown, is a deep, extremely clear lake and the largest in the Susquehanna watershed, of which it is the headwater. Lake trout, bass, walleye, and whitefish (see Lake Whitefish) provide the major portion of the angling here. In recent years the walleye fishery appears to be increasing at the expense of the lake-trout fishery. Many lakers are still taken, but veteran anglers indicate that the catch rate has been considerably reduced when compared to the fishing in years past.

Ask locally about whitefish methods, which are quite unusual. At Otsego Lake, baited buoys mark the locations where they are taken by deepwater, snatch-hooking methods. Both baiting and snatch hooking are legal in Otsego. The fish appear on the local menus as Otsego bass, and in food value they rate as an epicure's delight. Whitefish snatching is almost a year-round venture, and many are taken by this method through the ice. The whitefish season opens on the first of the year and continues till fall.

Canadarago Lake, a few miles north of Otsego, is entirely different in physical character. It is a relatively shallow, unclear lake with unpredictable gamefish potential. Bass, walleye, and pickerel, although not abundant, are good-sized. A largemouth bass weighing 11 pounds 6 ounces was reported in 1962. Probably the most productive fishing here is for medium-sized yellow perch. It is possible to boat more than a hundred such fish during a good day.

Located on the eastcentral side of the state, Saratoga Lake has a reputation for sizable largemouth bass and northerns. The walleye fishing is also a good bet. Largemouths of 5–8 pounds have been caught while 10–15-pound northerns (and some over 20 pounds) are caught each year.

CATSKILL RESERVOIRS

Generally speaking there are relatively few Catskill lakes, and many of these are not open to public fishing. Fortunately there are several large water-supply reservoirs which offer fine fishing for smallmouths, pickerel, brown trout, yellow perch, and occasional rainbows. The newest reservoirs invariably produce excellent trout fishing for the first few years of reservoir life, followed by a rather rapid reversion to good warmwater fishing.

The trout are by no means rare, however, and occasional good catches are taken. Some of the largest trout caught in the state are taken annually from these reservoirs. If you're the angler who wants a trophy brown trout, you must expect to put in many hours of fishing, perhaps over a period of days, for the big moment to arrive, but when it comes there is a tendency to forget that the long, dry spell ever occurred. Reservoir trout are not evenly distributed in the lake. To increase their chances of success, many anglers fish the areas where feeder streams enter. The best time of year is "ice out" in April through June and again from late August through September. Not to let the trout overshadow the warmwater species, it is worthy of mention that chain pickerel commonly attain sizes of 3–6 pounds, smallmouths 2–4 pounds, and yellow perch are commonly a pound or better.

There are four major Catskill reservoirs. These are Pepacton at Downsville, Neversink and Rondout northeast of Liberty, and Ashokan north of Kingston. Pepacton Reservoir regularly produces 8–15-pound brown trout in the spring season (April and May) in the area from Cat Hollow near the dam to the Shavertown Bridge. Most fish are caught by slow trolling or drifting with live bait.

TROUT STREAMS

The trout-stream fishery is large, and the streams are of many different types. There are hundreds of miles of rather small, often alder-covered, fountainhead rills, meadow meanders, and feeder brooks which are "unfamous" but far from infamous to those who are familiar with their treasures. Some shelter outsize browns, especially the meadow-meander type, more are host to myriad native brook trout, others contain both species, and here and there the rainbow establishes a foothold. There is a double reason for emphasizing this facet of potential trout fishing. The first is that these small waters have a charm all their own. They are generally lightly fished, which means plenty of elbow room, are consequently quiet and peaceful, and usually offer unrivalled natural scenery. Second—and this surprises many anglers who have been conditioned to put-and-take angling— these trout streams are rarely in need of stocking. It is true that in some waters it is a case of overabundance of wild, naturally spawned trout when determined by the average size they attain. In others, food, space, and spawning success balance out an equation productive of respectable-sized fish. The lower sections of many of these smaller streams—say the first mile or so of the brook above its confluence with a larger river (especially if it is a cool spring feeder)—are often the summer living quarters of big-river fish who have taken up residence to escape the heat. A stream thermometer should provide the means of telling you what to expect. If the temperature of the mainstream is considerably higher than that of the tributary, then proceed with care and caution to fish the confluence and the lower section of the feeder. Although all that glitters is not gold, trout prospecting can very often be extremely rewarding. You won't find these streams on a standard road map, but they are all listed on the geodetic survey 15-minute-series quadrangles. A short cut to success is, again, getting local information, if forthcoming, or to write the local Conservation Department fishery manager who has a running inventory on every stream in his district. These offices are listed in the Conservation Department pamphlet titled *1,001 Top New York Fishing Waters*

The Big Rivers To veteran trout fishermen names like Mettawee, Battenkill, East Branch Delaware, Beaverkill, West Canada, West Branch Ausable, Upper Hudson, Willowemoc, Kinderhook, and Bouquet serve to rekindle memories of many a fine day afield. Some of these rivers are living legends as new chapters are being written yearly to enrich their respective reputations. It is very probable that none of these rivers can offer as many trout as in the "good old days." In all fairness to their present quality, however, it takes a great deal of searching to find a public water categorized as an eastern-brown-trout river anywhere on the Eastern seaboard that *is* the same producer that it was even if we take the "good old days" to mean vintage of 1945. Since then, increased license sales, better highways, shorter working hours, a general renewal of interest in outdoor recreation, an expanding economy, and improvement in fishing tackle have all had a bearing on the problem. Many of our finer rivers have remained virtually unchanged in terms of suitability of the natural environment for trout production, and it is here that it is easiest to weigh the effects of continued high levels of fishing pressure. The most obvious thing is usually the absence of in-between size ranges of trout. Generally there are plenty of 6–9-inch fish, very few 10–16 inchers, and an occasional trophy. A river that naturally produces as many or more 10–16-inch fish than those in the smaller-size group would certainly have to be considered a topnotch stream. There are few such rivers in the state, and the resident trout in them are not easily accessible to angling pressure. This may be one of the main reasons that good-sized fish are available. Accessibility can be limited even if the river is adjacent to a good road for its entire length. Extreme width, depth, heavy flow, confinement of trout to certain sections, late runoff, and hazardous wading are also accessibility factors, and all serve to cut down successful pressure. It takes the average stream trout several years to attain respectable size. For instance, a Beaverkill or Battenkill brown ordinarily must be 4–5 years old or more to qualify as a good-sized fish of 15–18 inches. In poorer streams with less food and space and increased competition from other species, this size may never be obtained due to slow growth. The point is that a catch of five fat 16-inch browns that someone takes today will require at least twenty "growing years" to replace. The chances of numbers of trout surviving an average of 4 years in even the best of our streams in the face of increasing limitations on survival are not as great as they were in former years.

Present methods of attacking this problem of reduction in numbers of fair-sized trout are stream improvement, pollution control, stocking, and restriction of bag limit. Of these, stocking is by far the most popular, but the enlightened utilization of all four methods is generally considered to be the key to better fishing in the future.

What can you expect to catch today on a famous and heavily fished trout river? On the average, a 10-inch fish will be the one that tops off the basket. If you fish shortly after stocking, you will have trouble keeping your lure away from trout. Later, angling success depends on individual skill, stream conditions, weather conditions, and the time of day fished. Rest assured, however, that there is always a fishing potential present in our better rivers. Biologists don't know of any major stream which is really fished out, but it is more a case of relative scarcity of fish of larger sizes. It is a real challenge to take one of these trophies. They seldom feed during the daylight hours, a habit which renders them essentially angler-proof, since only a fraction of anglers are serious night fishermen. The big trout are caught more by accident in daylight and more by design at night. Once the home of a big fish is known, the night fisherman very often keeps with it till it's taken. These fish are commonly residents of the most heavily fished pools on the stream.

The opportunity rarely occurs to get a good look into the lair of big fish. One of these uncommon vantage points is from Buffum's Bridge on the Battenkill, and more often than not, when the water level recedes to allow clear viewing to the pool bottom, you'll see a dark, torpedo-like shape resting along a certain rock fissure, blunt and facing upstream. It has been the history of this location to have another fish of similar proportion move in some time after the original resident is caught. Over the years a single trout of 5–7 pounds or better has called this spot home. How many other natural big fish spots are present on this and the other rivers is anybody's guess, but they are probably more numerous than fishing success would indicate.

Other Trout Rivers The Roeliff Jansen Kill and Kinderhook creeks are primarily brown-trout rivers. These are located in the Rensselaer-Columbia counties section which is southeast of Albany on the Massachusetts side of the Hudson. Neither river is usually a very good opening-day stream, although the feeders may often be. Fishing picks up in late April and May. In the summer, you can get some fair fly-fishing in early morning and toward dusk.

The Mettawee River, northeast of Glens Falls in the Granville area, is a brown and rainbow river and is usually quite a good prospect for early-season angling. This river courses a flatter valley than the Kinderhook and Roeliff Jansen Kill, and, as a consequence, there are numerous wide, deep pools and reaches.

The Battenkill River, east of Saratoga Springs in the Cambridge area, is a small-fish producer with big-fish potential. Fishing pressure, as previously discussed, probably limits the abundance of large-sized fish, especially if past history can be considered reliable. This stream is a "seven-incher or seven-pounder" river, while fish in the in-between-size classes are at present far from numerous, but available in sufficient numbers to show when good hatches occur. The Battenkill is a very fishy-looking river —clear, bank-full flows, rounded cobbles in the bed, well-wooded slopes, and lush green pastureland in the valley areas. A rather extensive stream-improvement program

has served to heighten this impression in recent years. It is considered a fine fly-fishing river, and the current trend has been toward use of smaller flies for consistent success and therefore flies in sizes 18, 20, and 22 should be part of the fisherman's stock in trade. It is an unusual river in that there are fastwater stretches where it is best to wade the center and cast to either shore. Undercut banks provide attractive trout shelter in these spots.

The Saranac River in Clinton County is a boulder-studded river which offers good brown trout fishing. Don't expect to get action every day, every place, every time of year though. Although less heavily fished and basically harder to fish than the Battenkill, trout are still trout and seem to pick their own feeding moments. May and June are good fishing months in this water.

The Salmon River, Chateaugay River, and North Branch Chazy River systems are tucked away in the upper northeast corner of the state in the Franklin-Clinton counties section. Browns and rainbows are available, and many miles of fine trout water are at your disposal. This area deserves more attention from trout fishermen because there is prime water here, and the expectation of big fish is quite high. By downstate standards you would call these waters lightly fished. Once the snow-waters depart fishing is fairly good till season end.

The East and West branches of Fish Creek in Oneida and Lewis counties, northwest of Rome, are quite good, and this applies to many of its feeders. Good-sized browns are taken every year. You have miles of attractive-looking stretches to choose from. Don't pass up the Black River which is also in this area.

The West Branch Ausable located near Lake Placid is considered by many as the best stream in the state. It has natural beauty, plenty of food, living space for trout, and is generally accessible by good road over most of its length. Browns provide the bulk of the fishing although rainbows and brooks often enter the catches. If you are fortunate enough to hit it right when the big fish are on the move you will undoubtedly join the long list of admirers. It may seem somewhat paradoxical to state that anglers have occasionally complained that they caught too many trout! More specifically they were concerned with the experience of taking a couple dozen small fish of 6–8 inches in a short time interval and having yet to see a sizable trout. As fishing goes, many consider this the kind of complaint that should occur more often on more waters.

The Beaverkill-Willowemoc system, located in Sullivan and Delaware counties, is situated a 2½-hour drive from one of the nation's greatest population centers—the greater New York area. It is a tribute to the tenacity for survival of trout populations and the quality of the liquid assets the rivers provide that fairly good trouting exists here in spite of heavy fishing pressure. As is the case in most of our eastern-brown-trout rivers, a 10-incher looks good on most days, and a 14-inch fish is remarkable. Nevertheless, enough big fish are caught each year to provide the fuel for hotstove sessions all winter. The Willowemoc is generally a better early-season prospect than the Beaverkill, which comes into its own about mid May and sometimes as late as the first of June. This is not to say that fish aren't caught in the Beaverkill in early season, but a steadier day-to-day prospect often occurs later on. This aspect is not generally recognized, as witness the appearance of several thousand fishermen in April and early May compared to a few hundreds from June to season-end.

The East Branch Delaware below Downsville (Pepacton Reservoir) dam is a highly productive water which contains numbers of extremely fast-growing brown trout. The cold reservoir bottom waters released to the river thus create many miles of fine trout environment. The water leaves Downsville at 39° F., warms to the mid 40's and low 50's in Shinhopple-Harvard section about 10 miles below, promotes a coldwater environment for the entire extent of the East Branch, and continues to exert its influence on the main Delaware for many dozen miles. The East Branch has large, glassy, deep pools and deep, inviting-looking runs. The trout are extremely wary, and it often takes an angler's best efforts to capture his prize. The river generally gives up its fish reluctantly, even when fish can be observed actively feeding. Some good catches are taken on bait in early season, and mid- and late-season success is generally produced on fly tackle. If you are a dry-fly purist, this river can compare with any for containing extra-selective, good-sized trout, which seem to know the difference between fly patterns, leader sizes, and methods of presenting the fly.

West Canada Creek which enters the Mohawk at Herkimer is a good brown-trout stream from its mouth upstream to Trenton Falls. In this latter area, there are also a few rainbows. This is a tricky river to wade for two reasons: extra-slimy, algae-covered rocks, and fluctuating water levels produced by a regulating dam at Trenton Falls. So watch for quick change in water height when you're wading, and use felt soles, or better yet, hobs. Above Hinckley Reservoir the river contains a few brook trout. Anglers who know the spring holes do fairly well in warm weather. Otherwise, this upper river doesn't offer much.

The Delaware River, which forms the southwest border of the state between Port Jervis and Hancock, is big, extremely productive, largely underfished for a variety of species, and is canoeable for its entire length. It is a good smallmouth-bass river in the lower section, a good walleye river over its entire length, and an excellent rainbow- and brown-trout river wherever fastwater stretches are extensive. Trout are also likely to be found in the main river wherever a good-sized feeder brook enters. Just how good a trout river this is may be indicated by the fact that 10–14 inches is considered a "standard" fish, anything caught below this size is rare indeed, and 14-inch fish are quite common. A combination of factors, such as very large size of river, heavy flow, depth, abundant food supply, and the presence of "hot spots," tends to give the advantage to the trout, and it is not unusual to be completely baffled by these fish. One good day will make up for the difficult ones and then some.

The American shad made a strong comeback in the Delaware River, beginning in 1962. Anglers take thousands of these "poor man's salmon" in May and June. The shad is a remarkable fighter, and its size accentuates this feature. The usual size is 2–3 pounds and 19–21 inches in length. Five and 6 pounders and a few even larger are also taken. The Port Jervis–Pond Eddy–Barryville section is a favorite on the main river, but thousands of fish migrate upstream as far as Hancock and then turn up both the West and East Branches of the Delaware from

this point. A few shad were taken in the lower Beaverkill beginning in 1963. The "shad lure," a bright-colored lead jig, is effective as a spinning lure, and upper-river fishermen have devised several quite effective "shad flies." The popular colors on both jig and flies are red, white (or silver), yellow (or gold), and bright blue. Very often, gold-plated hooks are used. Shad rise to dry flies at dusk, and, although not generally known, they do feed in freshwater. Shad stomachs are sometimes bulging with natural insects. Assuming the factors that are responsible for the return in abundance of this fine native species remain favorably oriented, the major limitation to the future of this fishery in New York State will be centered around the problem of allowing successful upstream passage of adult spawners and downstream migration of young past dams.

KOKANEE FISHING

There are several lakes which have been planted with kokanee (*which see*), but the best fishing is at Lake Luzerne at Hadley. These fish commonly mature at 10–14 inches long, depending on numbers of fish present and available food. Occasionally, when populations are low and food plentiful, 18–20 inchers are produced, but this is rare in most lakes. Kokanee are plankton feeders, but can be induced to hit a hook baited with a tiny piece of worm which is trolled behind a series of spinners. Some call this a "Christmas tree" rig. It is also reported that in the fall they come inshore, a trip perhaps related to the advent of spawning, and can be taken quite readily using regular spinning gear and small spoons and spinners.

SMELT DIPPING

Smelt run the Finger Lakes and Great Lakes feeders in April and provide great sporting variety. It's a nighttime sport, and the fish are caught by dipping the net into the stream in blind fashion. Light scares your quarry, thus making the blind dipping necessary. Hundreds of people of all ages participate in this interesting but zany-appearing pastime. All doubts as to the justification for such darkness deportment vanishes the moment the querulous newcomer puts these creatures to the taste test. Fresh smelt are absolutely delicious.

AIDS IN MAKING YOUR FISHING TRIP MORE SUCCESSFUL

Several brochures published by the New York State Conservation Department are available to aid you in selection of your brand of fishing fun.

Two publications, *Adirondack Campsites*, Recreation Circular No. 3, and *Catskill Trails*, Recreation Circular No. 9, describe the locations, facilities available, and regulations pertaining to over 40 public campsites in these areas. Well over one-third of a million individual campers use these facilities annually, an indication of their popularity. Most of these campsites are located at lake- or streamside, and fishing is one of the major attractions.

In addition to campsite information, the Adirondack pamphlet lists the hundred largest lakes in the region, including particulars such as surface area, length, and altitude. Location of open camps and fireplaces along the mountain trails are also cited.

The Catskill pamphlet contains a 12 x 18-inch map showing marked trails in color, location of public campsites, and major lakes and streams.

Adirondack Canoe Routes, Recreational Circular No. 7, deals primarily with the Fulton Chain Lakes canoeing possibilities. A 14 x 28-detail map is provided, as well as myriad particulars relating to making your trip a success. It is possible to travel up to 86 miles by canoe through the Adirondack wilderness.

The pamphlet titled *1,001 Top New York Fishing Waters* can become an indispensable aid. The top fifty trout streams are listed, as well as a county-by-county rundown of the names of fish-productive lakes and streams. Another section lists three hundred remote Adirondack trout ponds under the very apt title of "Hikers Special." There is also a detailed listing of public fishing rights streams and the mileages involved in each case. The total mileage of public fishing rights is presently 853 miles with more being purchased each year.

The Outdoor Recreation Map, published in 1962 by Division of Conservation Education, features a large-scale map of the state showing over eighty state parks, sixty-six public boat-launching sites, state-stocked streams, etc., and is designed to be used with any standard touring map of New York State.

All of the above are available without charge by writing the New York State Conservation Department, Division of Conservation Education, State Campus Site in Albany.

—W.H.K.

LONG ISLAND

There is very little freshwater fishing available on heavily populated Long Island. Token trout fishing exists in Avon Pond at Amityville, Champlain Creek and Orowoc Creek at Islip, Carmen's River at Brookhaven, Cannan Lake, West Lake, and Swan Lake at Patchogue, Sampawam's River at Babylon, Freeport Reservoir at Freeport, and the Nissequogue River at Smithtown. These waters are stocked annually with brook, brown and rainbow trout. Black bass, chain pickerel, and pan-fish exist in a few warmwater habitats, notably the Peconic River near Riverhead.

Long Island does provide good saltwater fishing, however, and has three ports at Freeport, Hampton Bays, and Montauk where charter boats are available. The fishing is primarily for school tuna, giant tuna, white marlin, and swordfish in the summer season. Striped bass provide an outstanding fishery along many of the south shore beaches where surf-casting is popular.

Sheepshead Bay Sheepshead Bay, located in New York Harbor, is the original sport-fishing center of the East, and it still caters to thousands of anglers annually. And if times are different from the old, most of today's customers arrive in their automobiles rather than on the subway. But the subway is still there and ever popular with important segments of the fishing clan, the youngsters and the oldsters. The Sheepshead Bay fishing fleet, composed largely of big, diesel-powered party boats, heads down the harbor for the fishing grounds lying astride the "crossroads of the world." Ocean liners, tugs, and freighters and even warships are the passing scenery for a New Yorker heading offshore to test his skill against fluke, bluefish, porgies, seabass, blackfish, cod, and a host of other bottom feeders.

New York Harbor's fishing is not limited to the party-boat variety. Charter boats and private boats, basing their operations in Jamaica Bay or in Staten Island's harbors, eagerly respond to the June striper run on Romer Shoals, Ambrose Channel, or at Sandy Hook across the bay. The fish are trolled with big plugs, spoons, and bucktails. Forty and 50 pounders are not uncommon.

In the late summer with the bluefishing at its peak, giant tuna often come into the chum slicks. Each year several dozen tuna of 200–400 pounds and more are caught by fishermen who sometimes bait up with live bluefish.

Freeport Freeport, on Long Island's south shore, built much of its early fishing reputation on the angling for giant tuna in the New York Harbor bight. And a few of the big fish are brought into the port through Jones Inlet each summer. These same tuna grounds are fished by charter and private craft leaving from Point Lookout, Island Park, Atlantic Beach, and various waterfront communities entering on Reynolds Channel, which separates the island of Long Beach from the mainland.

Freeport remains Nassau County's best-known fishing port, although private vessels rather than professionals now dominate the scene. Party boats, docking in Woodcleft Canal, are in operation year round. Most of the charter-boat skippers build their income on the bluefishing, except in August when the school tuna arrive. Trolling for these small bluefins is very popular.

Great South Bay While there is limited inshore fishing in the narrow and channeled waters on the west end of Long Island's south shore, the story is different beginning at Great South Bay and continuing eastward through Moriches Bay and Shinnecock Bay. Miles of shallow waters provide excellent flatfishing. In spring and fall flounders are the quarry. In summer, there are the fluke. Sometimes blowfish, or puffers, arrive in teeming numbers. Outboard fishermen and party-boat fares alike go home with bags of "sea squab," which is the universally accepted name of the plump meat after it has been pulled clear of the sandpaper hide of the fish. Snappers, immature bluefish, are ever popular with skiff- and pier-fishermen during the late summer. Often 2- and 3-pound blues come feeding into the bays. Chum lines are set up for them in the manner of the offshore fishing.

Party boats for Great South Bay may be hired at Babylon and Lindenhurst. The Long Island State Park Commission established a public port at the end of Jones Beach which is called Captree State Park. A score of big party boats depart from here daily, and an equal number of charter boats are available for bluewater fishing. Some of the party boats also fish offshore, particularly in November when the Fire Island cod run develops. Charter boatmen as well as private boatmen troll for blues, school stripers, and school tuna, too. A few marlin are brought in through Fire Island Inlet each season. But the best marlin and swordfishing are products of the east end of the island—Shinnecock and Montauk.

Peconic Bay Skiff-fishermen leaving from the Peconic Bay towns of New Suffolk, Southold, Three Mile Harbor, and Greenport catch big flounders in the early spring only to have the flatfish transcended by schools of sea-run porgies, many of which weigh 3 pounds or more. Peconic Bay once provided spring-run weakfish. These schools of tiderunners no longer exist, however. The cyclic weakfish are now reduced to the point of scarcity.

Party boats and charter boats may be hired at Greenport, the North Fork's largest town, which thrusts its long breakwater into the mouth of Peconic Bay. Spring specialties are the flounders, followed by porgies, blackfish, fluke, and bluefish. The blues are caught in the fast tides of Plum Gut, off Orient Point, and at Fisher's Island. Sometimes school stripers are mixed with the blues, and diamond jigs worked on the bottom from drifting boats will catch both species.

North Shore Trolling School stripers range the rocky, irregular north shore of Long Island from Orient to the threshold of New York Harbor's East River. However, no party-boat or charter facilities are available on the north shore except at Mattituck Inlet where a few craft fish the sound for flounders, blackfish, seabass, and porgies.

North-shore striper trolling, therefore, is entirely in the province of the private boatman. Some of them become so absorbed in the sport, they will fish for nothing else. These school stripers are caught on bucktails or spinners and seaworms. The spring run begins in Little Neck Bay on the New York City border in early April. It spreads with warming weather through Manhasset Bay, Hempstead Harbor, Oyster Bay, Cold Spring Harbor, Northport, Port Jefferson, and beyond. Some shore casting is done on the west side of Little Neck Bay and on the beaches east of Port Jefferson. Private property blocks off most of the north-shore fishing beaches.

Other species popular with north-shore anglers are flounders, blackfish, tomcod, and snappers. Now and then schools of bluefish move in, and are caught by trolled lures. A particularly fruitful sport for blues is at Mount Misery Shoals, just east of Port Jefferson Harbor.

South Shore Casting While the north-shore surf-caster is severely restricted in his sport, the opposite is true along the miles of sandy beaches fronting on the south shore's Atlantic Ocean. At Jones Beach, designated areas are placed at the disposal of the fishermen so there will be no interference from the bathers. On nearly all of the popular bathing beaches, fishing is allowed after bathing hours. After the bathing season, there are few restrictions.

Striped bass and blues are the most popular fish of the surf-caster. Sometimes kingfish are caught on worm bait and even a stray weakfish. Rock jetties and wooden groins stud many beaches and attract both bass and bass fishermen. Favorite beaches on the west end of the Island are Rockaway Beach, Atlantic Beach, Long Beach, Point Lookout, Jones Beach, and Cedar Beach.

Shinnecock Canal Shinnecock Canal, connecting link between Shinnecock and Peconic bays, has its coterie of faithful who, nine months of the year, sit or stand on the bulkheaded banks and fish for flounders, fluke, snapper blues, and occasionally, big bluefish. But it is at Shinnecock Canal where one of the island's busiest offshore fishing fleets is concentrated. Here the first swordfish of the season is invariably landed and invariably the first white marlin. Deepwater sweeps in close to Shinnecock Inlet. Often swordfish are seen finning within the lobster-pot area, a mile from the inlet. Charter boats may be hired at the Canoe Place Dock. School tuna, little tuna, oceanic bonito, and dolphin are also caught by the skippers who tirelessly scan the ocean for signs of swordfish or marlin. Although Shinnecock usually lands the first broadbill and marlin of the season, it is neighboring Montauk that brings in most. When these spectacular gamefish move in from the depths of the Continental Shelf, the charter-boat fleet largely neglects its inshore fishing to seek them. Some skippers still harpoon the swordfish that refuses a bait. But the practice is losing favor.

Montauk Point The village of Montauk, under the shadow of its towering lighthouse, has the largest charter-boat fleet on Long Island as well as a major party-boat fleet. The port at Lake Montauk is also becoming increasing popular with private boatmen, many of whom leave their crafts out there year round. There are also liveries where skiffs and outboards may be hired, although a fisherman must be extremely weather conscious when taking a small boat outside the inlet jetties.

Fishing never stops at Montauk. Party boats sail for cod all winter. In the spring the pollock move up to join the cod. These sporty members of the cod family are caught with trolled jigs in the rips. Fish over 20 pounds are common in May. Spring fishing for cod and pollock may be done under the bluffs at the lighthouse or on Southwest Ledge near Block Island. Close in along the Block Island shore are the "Hooter Grounds" where flounders of snowshoe size are caught in April and May.

Striper fishing begins in early June as the bass move up the coast. At this time casters vie with the trollers. Bluefishing starts in midsummer. By then the codfish boats are heading for distant Cox's Ledge, a deepwater ground said to be washed by a chill eddy of the Labrador Current. Boats that fish local waters catch seabass, porgies, and fluke throughout the summer. Offshore trollers seek the vast schools of tuna which feed in the bluewater south of Montauk and Block Island.

Some Montauk charter boatmen make a specialty of chumming for giant sharks. "Monster Fishing" is the name given the sport. Several records have been made in this fishing. Montauk at one time or another also held records for bluefish and pollock. The largest tuna caught in United States waters, a fish of over 960 pounds, was taken by a Montauk angler. The giant tuna grounds are along the Rhode Island shore, across Block Island Sound from Montauk. Montauk, however, never seethes as it does when the fall striper run begins in early October. Great schools of bass, followed by clouds of gulls, swing in on the rips and reefs. School fish of 3–10 pounds predominate. But sometimes the huge "cows" and "bulls" settle in on Shagwong Reef. Often the fish bite so steadily that the fishermen are worn out in a few hours. The captains make capital of this bass bonanza by arranging, when possible, two trips a day. The first charter begins at daybreak, ends at noon. The second trip begins at 1 P.M. and continues into dark.

The fall bass run is also the signal for the gathering of the Montauk surf-casters. At times the action is along the sand beaches on the south side of the town. Usually, however, the fishermen gather at North Bar, Jones Reef, and on the rocks directly under the lighthouse.   —F.K.

NEW ZEALAND Because New Zealand is small and is bounded on the east by the Pacific Ocean and on the west by the Tasman Sea and because no city or town is more than half a day's travel from the sea, fishing, boating, and other aquatic sports are an integral part of the New Zealander's way of life. New Zealand, with a population of 2,500,000, is a predominantly pastoral country. The capital city is Wellington, situated at the south of the North Island on turbulent Cook Strait, but the largest city is Auckland with a population of about 500,000.

The North Island with an area of 44,281 square miles has many tourist attractions, including thermal activity, skiing, and fishing of all kinds. The South Island with an area of 58,092 square miles is divided down the center by the Southern Alps which rise to a height of 12,349 feet. The main attractions are trout fishing, skiing, mountaineering, and the scenic wonders, such as the Fox and Franz Josef glaciers.

Lake Manapouri on the south island is not only scenic but with its many tributary rivers a prime trout spot

SALTWATER FISHING

From an early age the average New Zealand child learns to use a handline from the nearest wharf or rocks. As he gains experience he improves on his tackle and turns to boat fishing or surf-casting. There are approximately four hundred species of fish in local waters, about 20 per cent of them being peculiar to New Zealand. North Island east-coast waters from Tauranga north are among the finest deepsea fishing grounds in the world. Big-game species caught include black and striped marlin, mako, hammerhead and thresher sharks, swordfish, bluefin and yellowfin tuna, while yellowtail, albacore, and bonito provide wonderful sport on medium gear. Many IGFA (*see* International Game Fish Association) records have been established in these waters. Among light-tackle anglers, boat fishing and surf-casting are equally popular in the North Island, but both are limited in the South Island by rocky coasts and heavy seas, although in the western and northern provinces, some excellent fish are taken from the beach.

Because the continental shelf dips sharply from the coast, commercial fishing has been confined to a fairly narrow area with a resulting decline in the fish population in recent years. The food supply is plentiful, and the angler, to be successful, must learn to present his bait or lure in the most attractive way. An increasing skill in angling techniques has been noticeable since 1945. The use of light tackle has become quite popular, although many still fish from small boats with handlines. In beach-fishing the rod-and-reel angler predominates, using 6–19-pound-test line and casting the bait out into the surf up to 150 yards. Casting as a competitive sport has a large following in New Zealand.

The most important fish in New Zealand waters is the snapper, a fine table fish which is plentiful all round the coast but more so in northern waters. In warmer waters, snapper up to 20 pounds are not unusual. Other common species are John Dory, flounder, mackerel, hapuku, kahawai, tarakihi, and moki. The kahawai (*which see*) averages about 4 pounds, is a terrific fighter, and can provide a real battle on light gear. In the warmer areas are to be found trevally, mao-mao, and porae, while colder waters yield cod, trumpeter, hake, and sea perch. There are many types of eels, rays, and skates which are numerous enough to be a nuisance to anglers. There are also a number of small sharks, such as sevengill, tope, carpet, smoothhound, and dogfish. While none of these is a great fighter, it is good fishing to land a 50-pound specimen on 12-pound line.

Hundreds of amateur fishermen fish from their own small boats off every suitable beach in the country. The larger launches may go 20 miles and more from the coast; the small dinghies will stay within 4–5 miles. The most common equipment for boat fishing with light tackle is a fiberglass rod about 6 feet long, revolving spool reel, and 12–20-pound test line. The light- or medium-tackle angler who is after tuna, yellowtail, bonito, and albacore will also need feather lures, spoons, spinners, jigs, or small plastic fish. The yellowtail can be taken trolling from slower craft, but the other species will not strike at a slow-moving lure.

FRESHWATER FISHING

Fabulous trout fishing has long been one of New Zealand's greatest attractions. In 1883 a shipment of eggs from the United States was hatched in Taupo, New Zealand's largest lake, and the country's entire rainbow-trout population is the result. The brown trout was first introduced in the South Island and still predominates there. Fingerlings from Government and Acclimatisation Society hatcheries maintain stocks in lakes and rivers, many of which are replenished by dropping the fish from low-flying aircraft.

With improvements in transport and access and increased interest in the sport, fishing pressure has grown enormously in recent years, resulting in a smaller average size. Where once Taupo's rainbow averaged 10 pounds, the present average is about 4 pounds, which is still good fishing. Brown trout averaging 6 pounds, with the odd 15-pound catch, are plentiful in the icy rivers and lakes of Southland and Otago, the snow-fed Canterbury rivers, and the inland waters of Nelson, Marlborough, and Westland. Rainbow are found in varying sizes throughout the South Island, but the brown is more common. The brown predominates in the south of the North Island and in westerly flowing rivers, as far north as Taranaki. The east-coast rivers of the island produce rainbow of moderate size, while the Taupo-Rotorua system of lakes and rivers provides some of the best trout fishing to be found anywhere. Within this district there are numerous lakes and streams full of fighting browns and rainbow. Rotorua is one of the few places in the world where an angler can catch his trout in a cold stream and cook it in a nearby boiling pool.

The biggest rainbow in New Zealand are taken from Lake Tarawera in the Rotorua district and average 9 pounds. Over-all, rainbow would average 4 pounds and brown trout 6 pounds, but there are many rivers and lakes where 7-pound rainbows and browns up to 15 pounds are common.

The many snow-fed rivers of the East Coast of the South Island such as the Waitaki, Rangitata, Rakaia, and Waimakariri are popular among New Zealand anglers for chinook salmon (locally Quinnat salmon). The fish begin arriving in February and the season peaks in March and April. These wide, silty, bouldery streams are not too attractive and the quality of the angling by American standards at least is poor. The average weight in New Zealand waters is about 12 pounds with fish over 30 pounds being exceptional. Casting with spoons and heavy tackle is the only method used. These rivers are frequently unfishable because of torrential rains and floods which makes a trip risky for the visitor with limited time and more rewarding choices available.

Sea trout (anadromous brown trout) enter most of the rivers in the South Island between Milford Sound and Haast with the significant runs occurring in the McKerrow-Alabaster and Okuru-Turnbull watersheds. New Zealand sea trout follow the movements of whitebait and smelt into the coastal rivers and lakes between November and January, but because early runs sometimes take place, the angling season for these coastal waters begins on September 1st to coincide with the whitebait season.

American brook trout were introduced to Taupo in 1952 but are not a success there. The only rivers where the species is plentiful are the Hinds in mid-Canterbury and the Whangapoa in the Rotorua district.

The following is a brief summary of the better-known, readily accessible fishing areas, but it must be emphasized that because many excellent fishing waters are so isolated or in such rugged country, they are fished only by those anglers with the time, energy, and physical ability to penetrate these remote districts.

THE NORTH ISLAND

The North Island is smaller than the South Island, and the general character of its fishing is different from the latter. Rainbow trout predominate here, and some of the lakes and rivers, such as Lake Taupo and the Tongariro River, situated in the center of the island are world famous. Generally speaking, the waters of the North Island are at their best early and late in the season, from October 1 to November 15, and again from April 1 to the end of May. Night fishing is very popular in New Zealand, and some large trout are caught during the height of summer (February) on flies after dark in North

Island streams. A great deal of trolling is done in some of the larger lakes, primarily with spoons.

Lake Taupo, with an area of 234 square miles, is the largest lake in New Zealand at a height of about 1,100 feet above sea level. Its main inlet is the rugged Tongariro River, about 70 miles in length, and its outlet is the 270-mile-long Waikato River, with its many man-made lakes resulting from the building of hydroelectric stations. To fish Taupo and the Tongariro strong tackle is recommended. Taupo rainbow are powerful fighters. The banks of the Waikato are not encouraging for anglers, but rainbow and brown trout have been stocked successfully in the hydroelectric lakes and some good fishing is available to the angler on these waters.

Lake Rotorua is not a particularly reliable fishing lake but is popular because of easy access from the city of the same name which is sited on its shores. Brown trout averaging 6 pounds and rainbows 3½ pounds are taken from the lake, but fishing there is often very difficult. Trolling is popular, and boats can be hired.

Lake Tarawera rainbow average 9 pounds, and this fact coupled with good roads encourages hundreds of anglers to travel the 11 miles from Rotorua in search of the big ones. Fish up to 12 pounds are not uncommon. However, it's quality rather than quantity here and the take can be sparse. The best fishing is had in October and again in the fall which peaks in May. This 17-square-mile lake fishes poorly in the summer months.

Lake Rotoiti is a 13-square-mile playground for New Zealand vacationists, and its beautiful shores are well developed for the holiday crowd. Nevertheless, it offers some fine fishing for rainbows averaging 4 pounds and browns in the 7- to 8-pound class. It is a good lake to wade. Fly fishing is best in November and after March, with trolling and spinning most successful in the warm months. The Kaituna River, the outlet stream of Rotoiti, offers a variety of big water for the fly fisherman and while the trout are not large by New Zealand standards, 2- to 3-pounders are not uncommon.

THE SOUTH ISLAND

The South Island is 550 miles long and has an average width of 120 miles. The magnificent alpine range, rising to 12,349 feet at Mt. Cook, runs west of the island's center. Many of the larger rivers rise in the peaks; during the early summer months these snow-fed streams are often highly discolored. However, there are other streams which do not get the melt and run clear. Perhaps the best period on the South Island is from November 15 to January in Canterbury and Nelson provinces, and to the end of March in Otago, Southland, and the Lakes District. Brown trout predominate on the South Island, and the average size varies according to the water fished. Some of the best rainbow fisheries are in Otago Province, and good landlocked salmon fishing is to be found in the lakes.

Buller River, 110 miles long, rises in the Nelson province and flows westward to the Tasman. Brown trout up to 10 pounds can be taken on any tackle provided the angler knows where to fish. The scenery along the Buller is magnificent and worth a visit even if the fish are not cooperative.

Waimakariri, Rakaia, Hurunui, Waitaki, and Waiau rivers are the main fishing waters of Canterbury, and when the quinnat salmon runs are on, they are the scene of great activity. Tackle recommended is a 10–12-foot spinning rod with a revolving spool, and line up to 25-pound breaking strain. Fly-fishing is normally rather unsuccessful, and heavy spoons are most commonly used. Quinnat up to 40 pounds have been recorded, but the usual catch is about 12–15 pounds. Brown trout can also be taken in these waters, but the quinnat runs are the highlights.

Mataura River, 140 miles long, is Southland's—and possibly New Zealand's—most prolific river. The fish are not large, but they are certainly plentiful. Dry and wet fly fishing are profitable in the upper reaches, but dry fly and bait casting are preferable in other areas. Trout up to about 4 pounds can be taken, but larger fish may be caught in the Mataura's tributaries, the Brightwater and the Waimea.

Of all the great southern lakes, Te Anau, the largest, has the greatest variety of scenic and sporting attractions. Te Anau is 98 miles from Invercargill and 89 miles from Gore over excellent sealed roads. The lake is 42 miles long and ranges from 2 to 8 miles wide, with a total area of 132 square miles. Much of its 330-mile shoreline is formed by fiords on the lake's western shore that run into the mountains for 12 to 20 miles. The eastern shore is low lying for the first 24 miles of its length and has little or no vegetation. Snow-capped peaks towering to 6,000 feet are clothed in dense bush from the snowline to the water's edge on the western and northern shores. The rivers of the western fiords are the best in the area and are seldom fished. It's worthwhile to hire a boat or charter an amphibian aircraft, as the waters are truly an angler's paradise. During westerly weather the first 7 miles of the eastern shore give many good fish to threadliners. Brown trout averaging 3½ pounds, rainbow averaging 3 pounds, and salmon averaging 2½ pounds are taken in these waters. Accommodations can be had at Te Anau.

The Upukerora River, rising in the high country east of Lake Te Anau, enters the lake about 3 miles from the Te Anau Hotel. The water courses at a fast pace over a rock bed. It is the only river in New Zealand in which Atlantic salmon has been successfully introduced. Brown and rainbow trout averaging 3 pounds and salmon averaging 2½ pounds may be taken. The river is restricted to fly fishing only. The Clinton River, which runs into Te Anau, is crystal clear, and fishing is therefore not easy. Catches of browns up to 13 pounds are commonplace on wet and dry fly, and rainbow are taken up to 10 pounds in the upper reaches.

Lake Manapouri has a depth of 1,458 feet and is probably the most beautiful lake in the country. Rainbows averaging 2½ pounds, browns 3 pounds, and Atlantic salmon 2 pounds are taken, usually trolling with red minnow, Gold Devon, or Silver Devon respectively; fly-fishing is also productive.

Lake Wanaka provides fishing that is usually successful for fly- and minnow-fishermen on the shoreline, but trolling is undoubtedly the best way to attack the moderate-sized rainbow and browns, which average about 3 pounds. The Clutha River (210 miles) is the outlet of Wanaka but passes through rough country for much of its length. Brown trout of up to 10 pounds can be taken by the fisherman, and they are powerful fighters.

In addition to the rivers and lakes mentioned there are literally thousands of small rivers, streams, and lakes

which provide good fishing. In some remote areas access is being improved, and some wonderful sport will be made available. This is particularly true of the Westland

Wading the river mouths which empty into Lake Taupo produces excellent rainbow fly fishing

and Southern lakes districts where many streams are, at present, practically unfished.

Tackle can be purchased in any of the major cities or fishing centers such as Auckland, Rotorua, Wellington. Christchurch, or Dunedin. Generally speaking, the New Zealander favors somewhat heavy gear for freshwater fishing with powerful 9-foot to 12-foot (double handed salmon type) rods in the majority. To what extent this type of tackle is necessary depends on the experience of the angler. In lake fishing, a 9-foot rod calibered for a No. 8 line is sufficient; the reel should have a capacity for 100 yards of 18-pound-test backing. The same rod would be suitable for fishing on large rivers. There is ample opportunity, however, to employ lighter gear on small waters provided the angler is a skilled caster.

Many rivers and portions of lakes (usually in the vicinity of river mouths) in New Zealand are closed to fly-fishing-only, but the fixed spool reel is used elsewhere both for casting and trolling.

The streamer fly is of more than passing interest in New Zealand trout fishing. The dry and wet fly and nymphs are effective on most rivers, but in the larger lakes where crayfish and forage species such as the native smelts (*Retropinna spp.*), bullies (*Gobiomorphus spp.*), galaxias (*Galaxias spp.*), and the juvenile galaxias or so-called "whitebait" are abundant, the streamer fly is more productive. Many imitative and fanciful local patterns have been devised, but visiting American or Canadian anglers can rely on the White Marabou and Muddler Minnow; the former is an excellent representation of the smelt and whitebait, and the latter suggests the adult galaxias and bullies. Either of these patterns fished slow and deep with a sinking-type fly line are consistent trout catchers in New Zealand. At times when smelt or the transparent juvenile galaxias are shoaling near the surface of a calm lake, numerous rises may be seen that are easily mistaken for insect-feeding trout. Large rainbows and browns take the baitfish at the top in what appears to be a leisurely rise to a mayfly. These "smelting" trout are highly selective and can only be attracted to suitable imitations.

Mayflies are the dominant aquatic insects in New Zealand and the more important species are somewhat large in size (*Ichthybotus hudsoni, I. bicolor*). Caddisflies, stoneflies, dobsonflies, and dragonflies (particularly the red dragonfly) appear in number regionally. Terrestrial insects are in many waters more important than the aquatics; the green manuka beetle, willow beetle, and brown fern beetle will bring on active rises, particularly in the early morning and evening.   —R.T.J.

NEW ZEALAND LONG-FINNED EEL *Anguilla diefennbachi*
The long-finned eel is distinguished from the short-finned eel by its dorsal fin, which extends well forward of the ventral fin; it also has a longer narrow band of vomerine teeth. It is endemic to New Zealand.

The freshwater eels spawn at sea, and the transparent leaflike leptocephali drift in the ocean currents. When they reach the coastal waters they metamorphose into the clear "glass eel," which is about 3 inches long. These glass eels enter the rivers in spring in large numbers and move into the lower mile or so of streams. They soon become darkly pigmented in fresh water, and over the following few years move upstream and penetrate to the headwaters of rivers.

The long-finned eel is the most widespread, the largest, and probably the most abundant of the native fish of New Zealand. Eels have an ecological advantage in that each species comprises a single population recruited from one breeding ground at sea. This enables adult eels to live in a range of habitats without the need to adapt their reproductive cycle to varying conditions.

Experiments have shown that the growth rate of eels is very variable and depends largely on the food supply available. In a typical stream the annual increase in length ranges from 2 inches per year for the smaller eels to 1 inch per year for the larger.

Eels are generally cryptozoic. The juveniles are found buried in loose shingle or in weed beds. As they grow (over 12 inches), these habitats do not provide the required shelter, and so they move to cover provided by undercut banks, fallen logs, and so on. There is a definite correlation between the amount of cover and the quantity of eels found in a stream. Once established in an area eels do not move far. Tagged eels are recaptured close to the point of release; one recaptured after 10 years had not moved more than 100 yards.

Their feeding habits are generalized, and reflect the environment in which the eel is living. All sizes feed on the invertebrate fauna of the streams. The smaller eels feed on mayfly larvae; as they grow they feed on caddis larvae. Eels of 12 inches and over show an increasing tendency to include fish in their diet. However, in most places there are not enough fish to provide a regular diet for the eel population. The larger eels are readily attracted by blood in the water. Liver and rabbit carcasses are used as bait in wire traps to catch eels. It has been thought that eels hibernate during winter, but recent studies on their feeding habits show reduced feeding with no indication of hibernation.

In summer and autumn a proportion of larger eels prepare for the spawning migration to the sea. External physical changes are visible; the eyes become enlarged and the lips thinner. There is a marked streamlining of the head because of a reduction of the jaw muscles. Internally, the gonads become visible to the naked eye, there is an increase in the deposition of fat, and the gut atrophies. The male is considerably smaller than the female at maturity. Typical sizes for the long-finned eel are: males 25.4 inches, 1.4 pounds; females 47 inches, 13.2 pounds (eels of 30 pounds weight are not uncommon).

The downstream migration begins in October and extends to April, the peak being in December; the migration occurs mainly during the dark phase of the moon and is stimulated by rainfall. Each year most of the eels move downstream in two runs, the females running slightly later than the males. The largest run was recorded at a fish

New Zealand Long-finned Eel

New Zealand Short-finned Eel

trap when there was a very heavy rainfall during a new-moon period. The migrant eels congregate in tidal reaches. The movement into the sea has been observed at the outlet of Lake Ellesmere, where migrant eels try to reach the sea during April, May, and June.

Before the discovery of New Zealand by Europeans, fish and birds were the only source of animal protein for the native population. Eels were therefore an important food item for the inhabitants and are still considered a delicacy. The Maoris studied the habits of eels carefully and devised fishing methods which are still used in catching eels. Migrant eels were caught in traps and weirs; Maoris also took into account the season and phase of the moon. Large quantities of eels were caught at migration time and were smoked and dried for future use.

Attempts have been made to utilize eels commercially, particularly in recent years. —A.M.R.

NEW ZEALAND SHORT-FINNED EEL *Anguilla australis schmidti* The short-finned eel differs from the long-finned eel in that the dorsal fin extends only a short distance in front of the ventral fin. The short-finned eel also occurs in parts of Australia and in some islands to the north of New Zealand.

Although the short-finned eel predominates in most samples of glass eels, the adult has a restricted distribution. The juveniles penetrate well inland, but the larger eels are found mainly in the coastal spring-fed streams, in lagoons, and inland lakes. They prefer streams and lakes where the temperature fluctuations are limited. This supports the observation that the rate of feeding of the short-finned eel is affected by low temperatures to a greater extent than that of the long-finned eel.

The growth rate varies from 3 inches per year for the smaller eels to under 1 inch per year for the larger ones. The maximum size reached is considerably less than that of the long-finned eel, and there is a similar difference in the sizes at which the sexes mature. Typical sizes at maturity are: males 18.9 inches, 0.4 pound; females 27.1 inches, 1.2 pounds.

DOWNSTREAM MIGRATION

The downstream migration of maturing eels is mainly in February, some two months later than the main migration of long-finned eels. The migrant livery of the short-finned eel tends toward a gray or silver, with enlargement of the eyes and reduction of the lips. The seaward migration of short-finned eels occurs during March, April, and May, slightly ahead of that of the long-finned migrants. —A.M.R.

NEW ZEALAND SNAPPER *Chrysophrys auratus* This is the southernmost member of a group of closely related species of inshore marine fishes which occur throughout the subtropical and warm temperate Indo-Pacific. Essentially similar, snappers, sea breams, or porgies (family Sparidae) also occur in the Northern Hemisphere. The following account deals only with the New Zealand snapper, though other members of the genus *Chrysophrys* may have similar habits.

Other names for the snapper include bream and brim for smaller sizes of fish, and schnapper, an erroneous spelling of unknown origin perpetuated by the fishing industry. Its Maori name is tamure.

The New Zealand snapper is a typical sparid. Its body is deep, slightly compressed laterally, with an arched dorsal profile and a large bony head. It has strong jaws equipped with several rows of well-developed teeth, conically pointed in front and bluntly rounded at the side of each jaw. The dorsal fin is continuous, with 10 spiny and 12 softrays; the anal fin has 3 spiny and 8 softrays. The pectoral fins are relatively large, with the uppermost rays elongated.

Snapper are reddish-gold in color, slightly darker dorsally, with numerous small blue spots on the dorsal surface above the lateral line. Some color variation occurs; fish from muddy-bottom areas are a pale silvery pink, while those from hard-bottom areas near reefs may be dark reddish-bronze. They are usually most brightly colored during the summer spawning season. Juvenile fish have five darker vertical bands spaced along the body.

DISTRIBUTION AND ABUNDANCE

Snapper occur in the warmer waters of New Zealand south to about Cook Strait (latitude 41–42°S), with a few farther south during summer. The northern limit of the snapper beyond New Zealand and its relationship with Australian and Indo-Pacific forms remain unknown.

In northern New Zealand the snapper is the dominant member of the inshore demersal (bottom-dwelling) fish fauna, occurring in practically all habitats—muddy estuaries and tidal creeks, sandy bays, rocky coastlines and reefs, and over sandy mud bottoms down to at least 100 fathoms. However, it seems to prefer relatively hard sandy sea bottoms near the shore or near reefs, where it is probably able to obtain a plentiful food supply. It is most abundant between 10 and 60 fathoms.

LIFE HISTORY AND SEASONAL MOVEMENTS

Spawning may occur from spring to late summer (October to March), although it usually takes place in December–January. Little is known about spawning, except that it occurs in sheltered inshore areas, probably about the level of a midwater (5–10 fathoms) thermocline, these being the areas and depths where "running ripe" snapper are most frequently caught during the spawning season. The small, spherical eggs are externally fertilized and are pelagic, floating at or near the sea surface. They hatch in 36–48 hours, depending on the water temperature. The larvae and postlarvae are presumably midwater or bottom-dwelling; none have so far been taken in surface plankton hauls. The smallest snapper captured has been 1 inch long, at which size they are fully scaled and in shape and color are miniatures of the adults, even to the tiny blue dorsal spots. These young-of-the-year are first caught in summer in shallow harbors and estuaries, and then in autumn they appear in the more open-water areas adjacent to such embayments. When the coastal waters become cold in winter the small snapper, with most other small fish, move out of the harbors into the open sea, returning to shallow waters the following summer.

These seasonal inshore-offshore movements become more regular as the fish mature at the end of their third or fourth year when they are 8–10 inches long. The summer inshore movement is then reinforced by the spawning migration, and large groups of mature adult "school snapper" assemble in inshore areas before and during spawning; afterward they disperse, first to their inshore summer-autumn feeding grounds and later to their offshore winter grounds.

682 / New Zealand Snapper

A certain proportion of the population, however, particularly those fish inhabiting reefs and rocky shores, are less migratory and may stay in the same area for several years. Tagging experiments on adult snapper have not revealed any long-distance migration patterns; most tagged fish have been recaptured near their original tagging site, and the small distances traveled by the others (5–40 miles) are consistent with inshore summer spawning movements.

FISH SIZES AND GROWTH RATE

Snapper spawned in December–January grow to about 4 inches fork length (nose to V of tail) in their first year. In successive years, on the average, they reach 7, 9, 10½, 12, and 13 inches; from this size they grow about an inch, decreasing to half an inch per year. At first maturity 8–10-inch snapper weigh about ½ pound; adult fish 12–24 inches long weigh 1½–10 pounds; and large snapper may reach 30–35 inches in length and 20–30 pounds in weight. The age of these largest fish is uncertain; on the basis of scale-growth ring counts it may be more than 25 years.

The growth rate varies in different localities, but whether this is caused by variations in water temperature and food supply, by differences in fishing pressure and population density, or by inherent racial characteristics in the snapper stocks themselves is not yet known.

FEEDING

Snapper eat a wide variety of marine animals. The young-of-the-year fish feed mainly on small planktonic or bottom-dwelling crustaceans; the larger juveniles (4–8 inches) feed on larger crustaceans, brittle-stars, various marine worms, gastropod and bivalve shellfish, and small fishes. Adult snapper appear to feed on whatever marine animals are locally most abundant, from the pulpy jellyfishlike salps in the plankton to extremely hard-shelled bivalves, which they crush with their strong molars. Many kinds of small or juvenile fishes are also eaten. Sometimes small groups of snapper feed almost exclusively on one type of organism, for example, chitons scraped off rocks, mud crabs taken in tidal creeks, juvenile flounders from a tidal mudflat, or one particular type of shellfish from a sandy bottom. Most of the food organisms are bottom-dwelling, but during summer, particularly in the spawning season, a greater proportion of small pelagic fishes (herrings, horse mackerel, and so on) are taken, which suggests some midwater feeding at this time of year.

ANGLING VALUE

The snapper is probably the most commonly sought-after marine fish in New Zealand. It can be taken by almost any fishing method; the most common are bottom-fishing or driftline-fishing from small boats with handline or rod-and-reel; surfcasting from sandy shores or rocky headlands; and setlining, either from small boats or by sending the line offshore on a small wind-driven raft (a *kon-tiki*). Some are taken incidentally with beach seines along open beaches during flounder fishing or with bottom gillnets set in harbor channels. Snapper are the main fish taken by charter boats (excluding big-game boats) fishing from northern New Zealand harbors, principally Auckland.

Snapper bite vigorously and fight moderately well, particularly in shallow water, although as a result of pressure changes in their air bladders they tire quickly after being brought to the surface. Their fighting style consists of a series of smooth, powerful runs, which become less frequent and weaker as they near the surface. They take a variety of fish and shellfish baits, being particularly attracted by the carcass and entrails of small fish.

They are very wary fish, and although frequently seen by skindivers, they are difficult to approach underwater, and consequently do not figure prominently in the New Zealand spearfish catches.

COMMERCIAL VALUE

The snapper is also important commercially, and as judged by the frequency of snapper remains in New Zealand archaeological deposits, it has always been a popular food fish. Before the main European settlement of New Zealand in the mid-nineteenth century, the Maori people who lived along the coast caught large quantities of snapper, together with kahawai (*which see*) for local consumption and also for barter with inland tribes and the early European sealers and whalers. These fish were caught in large beach seines or on hooks fashioned from shell and wood.

From the late nineteenth century snapper has always been the main species in the annual New Zealand marine fish landings; in 1966, 203,990 hundredweight of snapper were landed, comprising 31 percent of the total fish landings. Most of the snapper catch is taken in northeastern New Zealand waters by 50–70-foot trawlers working out of several ports. Snapper trawling is generally most successful in the green coastal waters over hard sandy bottoms near the land or offshore reefs; these areas also produce the most desirable type of snapper— medium-sized, brightly-colored, and firm-fleshed. In the deeper, clearer water further from shore trawling is more successful at night, especially during dusk and dawn. Danish seiners and long-line boats from Auckland also contribute to commercial landings, particularly in summer as the snapper move inshore to school and spawn in shallower waters.

The New Zealand snapper, particularly the smaller fish, are sufficiently similar to the Japanese species to be classed in Japan as *tai*, a highly regarded fish cooked and served whole on religious or ceremonial occasions. These snapper command a high price, which has justified the Japanese sending fishing fleets thousands of miles to fish for them in New Zealand's offshore waters.

On local New Zealand markets snapper are seen as a palatable, although rather dry, food fish; their main sale is as whole fish or fillets, but some are smoked.   —L.J.P.

NICARAGUA Excellent fresh and saltwater angling can be found in this Central American country. Although organized facilities are limited, trips can be arranged in the capital city of Managua for tarpon and snook fishing in the larger inland rivers. The San Juan River at San Carlos, an outlet for huge Lake Nicaragua which flows about 120 miles into the Atlantic Ocean, is one of the more popular locations. Both the tarpon and snook run to good size in the San Juan and can be taken by casting or trolling, with the peak season from February to June. Freshwater sharks inhabit Lake Nicaragua and occur also in many of the rivers. Snook and tarpon are numerous at the river mouths along the Atlantic side, and barracuda, king mackerel, various jacks, snappers, and groupers are abundant on the outlying reefs.

NIGHT SMELT *Spirinchus starksi* A Pacific smelt found from southeastern Alaska to Washington, similar to the whitebait smelt but having small teeth, not caninelike, on the vomer. It has short anal rays, 62–65 midlateral scales, and three rectilinear striae on the gill covers.

ECONOMIC VALUE

Of minor sport and commercial significance, it is similar in this respect to whitebait smelt. *See also* Smelt

—J.R.

NILE PERCH *Lates niloticus* A large gamefish not unlike the North American black bass in appearance, it is endemic to Africa. The color is brown or olive above and silvery, sometimes tinged with yellow, below. Young Nile perch have more or less dark brown, irregular vertical bars.

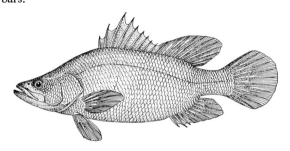

Nile Perch

Various species of the Nile perch are distributed in the big rivers and lakes of tropical Africa with the exception of Lake Victoria. Nile perch of Lake Albert and Lake Rudolf are two subspecies; the Nile perch of Lake Tanganyika is *niloticus*. This fish may weigh up to 300 pounds. Fish of 165 pounds have been caught in the Niger River and 145 pounds in the Benue River, although many of about this weight have been caught at the junction of the Blue and White Niles. A famous place is below the Aswan Dam. Lakes Fayoum and Menzaleh, however, contain very large perch. This fish was well-known to the ancient Egyptians, and pictures depicting men carrying large Nile perch are to be found in many tomb scenes. The mummified body of the fish has also been found.

LIFE HISTORY

The Nile perch follows the floodwaters of the rivers out over the land and channels connecting the river. There is no parental care of the eggs or young after spawning. The fry hatch out and often stay in small pools left by the river until the next year, feeding on the larval forms of various insects. They keep to the shallows for some time to escape predation, but as soon as they are large enough for a fish diet they keep steadily at it, eating all they can devour.

ANGLING VALUE

The best time to catch Nile perch is early morning and evening, both in rivers and lakes. The bait may be any fish of about a pound. The tigerfish (*which see*) of this weight is considered excellent. Tilapia (*which see*) are also good as they are hardy bait. Generally the bigger the bait, the larger the perch. A single hook under the dorsal fin is the best method. The bait is allowed to drift downstream. However, a series of large hooks in proportion to the bait can be used, and this is trolled slowly. Generally there is no hesitation when the Nile perch seizes the bait. There is a long run, followed by two or three more; however, after that the fish is exhausted. The reel should hold at least 300 yards of 36-pound-test, and a powerful rod should be used. In heavy water the fight is a much better one. As a rule a 50–60 pounder will be most active. The smaller Nile perch (20–40 pounds) have some food value, but the flesh of the larger ones is coarse. —A.J.McC.

NINESPINE STICKLEBACK *Pungitius pungitius* The large number of dorsal-fin spines identify this species, there being from 7–11, usually 9–10. A sharp caudal keel, a convex caudal fin, and a rather elongate body also help to distinguish it from other relatives. It lacks the bony plates of the threespine stickleback. Coloration is dull brown above with faint bars or blotches, with a silvery belly. Variations in color and intensity depend on the season, sexual maturity, and habitat. It reaches a length of about 3 inches.

This is a coldwater stickleback, occurring more in circumpolar regions than others of the family Gasterosteidae. It ranges from northern Scandinavia to the Mediterranean and Black seas, from the Arctic Circle to Japan and northern China, and from Newfoundland to New Jersey. It also occurs in the cooler waters of the Great Lakes. Equally at home in fresh- and saltwaters, it prefers quiet waters of creeks, estuaries, and salt marshes. In freshwater lakes it occurs at considerable depths.

LIFE HISTORY

Spawning occurs in April and May, and is accompanied by the nest-building behavior characteristic of other members of the family. *See also* Brook Stickleback, Fourspine Stickleback, Threespine Stickleback —D.dS.

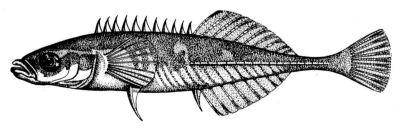

Ninespine Stickleback

NITROGEN NARCOSIS *See in* Skin and Scuba Diving Dangers *under* First Aid

NOMENCLATURE The modern system of naming, or nomenclature, was adopted from the principles of a Swedish naturalist Linnaeus (Carl von Linné) as proposed in his book *Systema Naturae*. His system was first used in 1758. Under this method of naming, each fish or insect, for example, is allotted two names—a generic name and a specific name. The names applied to organisms are from Latin or Greek words, and because these are dead languages, they furnish the advantage of being unchanging and of universal application. Thus, *Salmo salar* can be identified as an Atlantic salmon throughout the world, and *Ephemera guttulata* can be identified as a species of mayfly (the Green Drake). Under the rules adopted in 1901 by an international conference of zoologists, a capital letter is used in the generic name and a small letter in the specific name. The name of the person who discovered or first described and named the species may follow the specific name, thus *Salmo salar* Linnaeus is the complete form. Where a subspecies exists, a third Latin or Greek name is added. —A.J.McC.

NORRIS, THADDEUS American (1811–1877) There is no American counterpart to Walton, for none of our fishing books has ever achieved world stature as literature. For that matter, neither has any other English fishing book; Walton is unique. But as a figure of influence on anglers and those disposed to take up angling, "Uncle Thad" was as meaningful to his countrymen as Old Izaak was to his.

The American Angler's Book (1864), is the cornerstone of American angling literature. It was published in Norris' native Philadelphia and became all that its title staked out for it. It was the book for the fisherman of its time; and it is one of the few early American fishing books that can still be read with pleasure and profit today. Uncle Thad had all of Walton's zestful enthusiasm for the sport, and just as lively an appreciation of the concomitant meat and drink; he was as ready as Izaak himself to talk about things other than fishing in the course of writing a fishing book. Indeed, in this respect Walton is for once outdone. Thaddeus Norris' book, even in its first edition, ran over 600 pages, a lot of it set in type so small that it taxes even today's lighting facilities for readers, and must have constituted a really arduous test of patience and endurance by the coal oil lamps that afforded the best light for most of Norris' contemporaries. Yet within the year he was back with another edition to which he added pages making it run over 700. But if Norris was more than Walton's match for garrulity, he was far from it in piety. In this he was outdone by W.C. Prime, author of *I Go A-Fishing* (1873), although the delightful chapter devoted by Uncle Thad to "The Angler's Sabbath" would more than satisfy even the most devout in our more permissive age.

Norris was far ahead of his time in his perception of the inevitability of conservation measures, and remarkably so in a period when most of America was still wilderness. Theodore Roosevelt's uncle, Robert B. Roosevelt, who wrote under the pseudonym of "Barnwell," showed a more modern attitude than Norris in anticipation of the angler-entomologists of this century, dismissing as old-fashioned the palmered flies that Uncle Thad still swore by, although the Norris book was two years later than "Barnwell's" *Game Fish of the Northern States of America and British Provinces*.

Norris was in fact inclined to scoff at those who were beginning to entertain any notions of exactness in imitation, though he was the first by many years to point out in print the desirability of keeping the fly dry and the line and leader wet. He was impatient with new-fangled ideas, whether expressed in what he considered needless gadgetry or in overtheorized approaches to what was to him essentially a simple sport, and he was openly contemptuous of tendencies to either overintellectualize or over-romanticize fishing. He poked sly fun at "Mr. Barnwell" both for his "fancy in high feather" and for "the Anglomania which has seized him."

In this latter respect he was the very prototype of the purely American breed of dry-fly man in contrast to the Anglophile purists, believing in fishing the water, not the rise, and concentrating on broken water rather than the smooth, feeling that what fly you use matters much less than how you use it.

Typically American in his dry wit, as opposed to the more gentle humor exhibited by English writers, there is a great sense of gusto in everything Norris writes, and particularly in the casual asides he keeps dropping like pebbles along the wayside as he pursues the main theme of his thesis: "My neighbor asked me once if trout fishing was not a very unhealthy amusement—he thought a man must frequently have damp feet. Well, it is, I answered; but if he gets wet up to his middle at the outset, and has reasonable luck, there is no healthier recreation." At another point, speaking of the pipe, and saying that it "must have been instituted expressly for the fisherman," he cannot refrain from interjecting, a few phrases farther on: "What a pity it is that infants are not taught to smoke!"

Though nobody ever paid greater respect to the place of potables in fishing parties, nor surpassed Norris in conveying the sights and sounds and smells and tastes in streamside eating of the quarry, still the fellowship aspect of angling has hardly lacked celebrants from Dame Juliana's day to ours. But Uncle Thad was the first on this side of the water, and among the first anywhere, to emphasize the solo role of the angler, as opposed to all the partying and partnering with which angling's annals have always been replete. In his chapter "Fly Fishing Alone" Norris gave the definitive description of the unique pleasures of solitary fishing in a way that has never been equalled, and if only for this *The American Angler's Book* would be worth going back to for any man who today either professes or aspires to be well read as an angler.

Although the portion of his book devoted to rodmaking was confined to giving the reader pointers on "home-made" rods and repairs, Norris himself went on to become one of the really skilled rod-makers of his day, and the extraordinary quality of Norris rods is extolled by Prime and others in the angling writings of the post-Civil War decade.

Norris died at 66, which is hardly premature against the actuarial averages of a century ago but far short of his own expectations as an angler, as voiced in many different places in his book. With Reverend G.W. Bethune, the first American editor of Walton (1847), and W.C. Prime, Norris stands as one of the three major American angling figures of his century which was, as concerns the recorded history of the sport, virtually the first. And while enthusiasts could make special cases for "Barnwell," George Dawson (*The Pleasures of Angling*, 1876), Genio Scott

(*Fishing in American Waters*, 1869), Charles Hallock (*The Fishing Tourist*, 1873), and James Henshall (*Book of the Black Bass*, 1881) for a place in any such proposed triumvirate [votes for Frank Forester would have to be disallowed on the ground that the author of *Fish and Fishing* (1849) was actually the Englishman William Henry Herbert], still it is inconceivable that Uncle Thad would not be the last to be dislodged, for it is hard to cite any fishing book, Walton's not excepted, that constitutes a more engaging self-portrait of a sportsman. A case could indeed be made that a century hence Thad Norris might well stand alone. —A.G.

NORTH CAROLINA From the 6,000-foot peaks of the Great Smokies to the surf-splashed beaches and beyond, North Carolina is blessed with abundant waters and quality angling. Some of the Atlantic's best red drum fishing exists here, and inland are miles of blackwater-swamp streams as well as the clear, fast-flowing trout rivers of the mountains. The Gulf Stream veers in at Cape Hatteras, reaching a point closer to shore than any place between south Florida and Cape Cod. This north-bound ocean current is the location of exceptional blue-marlin fishing. In species of fish, the Tarheel State offers both variety and quality.

TROUT STREAMS

Starting at the North Carolina-Tennessee border high in the rugged Appalachians, trout fishing ranks first among most anglers. Some two thousand miles of trout water extend as far east as the Upper Dan River north of Winston-Salem. The quality of this water ranges from some of the best in eastern United States to a few miles of marginal waters producing put-and-take fishing at best. These trout streams vary in size from the 100-foot wide, roaring, tumbling Nantahala River to the tiny feeder streams a few feet across. Many of the high headwaters have native brook trout, and are seldom stocked. Stream temperatures rarely exceed 55° F. in these picturesque brooks, but the numbers of trout are decreasing because of logging, farming, and industrial operations.

The brook-trout waters are generally thickly overgrown with mountain laurel and rhododendron. Fly-casting is very tricky here, and a short fly rod is best. Even a 6-foot rod works well in these miniature watercourses since most casts are less than 15 feet. The better streams of this type have interspersed pools and tumbling white water. Dry flies fished upstream on short casts and allowed to float quickly into the pools often get the best results. Most of these small creeks are not rich biologically and do not support heavy fishing pressure. But their secluded nature limits the number of visitors. Brookies of a foot long are considered nice fish, and brightly colored natives of 6–8 inches are satisfying catches. There is no size limit on trout in North Carolina except in waters classified as native trout streams and on National Park Service lands.

As the cold streams rush down the mountains, they become somewhat warmer and acquire other tributaries, thus increasing their volume. The trout waters that reach 60° F. are generally considered rainbow waters, but may contain brook and browns as well. The banks are still lined with lustrous green mountain shrubs and present backcast problems to the fly-fisherman, but this vegetation often means that the stream will remain cool enough during the long summers to permit year-round trout survival.

Many of these streams maintain natural spawning areas, particularly for rainbow and browns. However, many don't produce enough fish to supply the rather heavy demand on the accessible waters. State and federal fish hatcheries annually stock well over 500,000 "eating-size" trout in suitable North Carolina waters. This total tops a million trout when the fingerlings and adult fish are added.

In the late 1950's a few test streams were selected as native trout streams, and a special set of regulations was adopted for them. The standard trout season remained the same, but the creel limit was cut in half, and a size limit of 9 inches was established. No natural baits were allowed, and flies only were permitted in one or two; single-hooked artificials were permitted in the others. These streams have become popular although the desire for additional mileage is not great.

As most fishermen would expect, the larger Tarheel trout streams produce the larger fish, and browns up to 10 pounds are reported each year. Rainbows run a shade smaller, but many over 6 pounds are taken annually. Few brook trout over 2 pounds are caught from North Carolina waters.

TROUT LAKES

Several fine trout lakes give the mountain area a bonus in angling pleasure. Nantahala Reservoir, west of Franklin, is perhaps the best since it has the mighty Nantahala River flowing in for excellent natural rainbow spawning. In 1959, kokanee (*which see*) were added to serve as forage for the rainbows. Within three years, these little salmon had outgrown ordinary forage size and were adding to the sport fishery with hook-jawed adults up to 3 pounds in weight.

Cheoah Reservoir, just below majestic Fontana Dam, is the home of some beautiful rainbows, too. This cold, blue-green "flowing" reservoir is fairly rich and grows trout well. Little natural reproduction takes place apparently, and a heavy stocking of fingerling trout keeps fishing good. As with Nantahala, a boat is almost essential to cover the water thoroughly. Trolling with small spinners is productive, although Cheoah unlike Nantahala is a good fly-fishing lake, too. All North Carolina power impoundments are open to year-round trout fishing. There is no closed season on any warmwater fish in North Carolina.

Two or three of the reservoirs on the Tuckasegee River near Cullowhee in Jackson County have good trout populations, but it is a matter of fishing rather deep (30–60 feet) except in late fall and winter. Actually, the cold season is often the best time for big trout in these impoundments.

Trout are also caught in Fontana and Santeetlah reservoirs, although not regularly. There are many smaller trout lakes (2–25 acres) in the northwestern counties, and these provide fine fishing particularly in the early season.

BASS FISHING

Many of the mountain lakes that have been mentioned are also excellent bass lakes. Smallmouth fishing is very good in Nantahala and Fontana; largemouth fishing is exceptional in Santeetlah and at times in Fontana. Other good reservoirs in western North Carolina include Hiwasee, Chatuge, and Glenville. All have bass and pan-fish; some have walleyes and white bass, too.

Fishing in these lakes is generally done from a boat rowed or paddled a good casting distance from the shore. Standard bass lures are used, with a preference for the noisy surface baits and those imitating salamanders. A plastic black worm fished near the bottom is good. Spinners often take panfish as well as bass. Natural baits such as salamanders, minnows, and earthworms are most productive in the summer. Bluegills and other smaller sunfish hit popping bugs well, particularly in the early morning and evening hours. Night fishing in some reservoirs is spectacular for big bass during the midsummer months.

Smallmouth streams are scarce in North Carolina, but one stands out—the New River in Ashe and Alleghany counties. It is a big river, too deep to wade and too rocky for safe outboard running. Boat drift-fishing is popular, casting into the deep holes as the craft goes along with the rather strong current. Frequent stops are made by pulling up to a rock ledge and fishing the better spots. Large rockbass are common, and an occasional walleye. The medium spinning rod is popular, and spinners work well in the moderately fast water. Nice smallmouth are taken on flies, too, but covering the big water is a problem.

The New River is one of the few Tarheel rivers having a population of flathead catfish. Thirty pounders have been taken although very little real effort is expended to catch them.

The large rivers of the Piedmont are harnessed for hydroelectric power along their entire lengths. Since these streams flow through rolling agricultural lands, turbidity and siltation are real problems both to fish production and fishing. The upper impoundments suffer less than the lower ones, and the problem is decreasing with better land management and soil-erosion control.

CATAWBA RIVER SYSTEM

The Catawba system is headed by Lake James near Morganton. It is the coolest of the several reservoirs of this chain and likely the clearest. The lower mountains form its watershed, and it is most like a high-altitude lake of any of the Piedmont impoundments. It always has produced good bass and panfish angling and now has a thriving population of nice-sized walleyes. Midspring fishing is best, and natural baits produce well. Crappies are often schooled up in drowned timber sections.

Rhodhiss Lake is next in downstream succession and is a good fish producer. Largemouth and crappies are its main claim to fame. Numerous bays and its brushy shoreline sections provide the bass bugger with some fine bass fishing around mid May. Later-season trolling with deep-running plugs is productive.

Lake Hickory, next in order, is one of the most consistent fish producers in the state. The water is often turbid, but bass and panfish still hit. Winter fishing for crappies can be spectacular. Bass up to 11 pounds are caught each year.

All these reservoirs have their share of rough fish, including carp, catfish, suckers, and gizzard shad. The gizzard shad, however, may be an important forage fish rather than a competitor. The difficulty is keeping their numbers in check, and this presents a real fish-management problem. Likely the newly introduced threadfin shad will prove a better choice as a forage fish. Cold winters create a survival problem, however.

Lookout Shoals Reservoir, immediately below Hickory, is quite narrow. The introduced white bass is now a favorite with fishermen in this hydroelectric impoundment.

Large, bay-filled Lake Norman, created by Cowan's Ford Dam, shows promise of being a fine fishing lake. Its population is generally the same as in similar impoundments, but may provide sauger fishing also. Its waters are perhaps too turbid and warm for walleyes.

The farthest downstream Catawba-system reservoir in North Carolina is Lake Wylie (formerly known as Catawba Reservoir). Part of the impoundment is in South Carolina. It is a consistent fish producer, with largemouth and white bass high on the list. Plenty of crappies and bluegills are available for the fly-rod angler. The turbidity and water-level-fluctuation problems restrict top fishing somewhat.

YADKIN RIVER SYSTEM

The Yadkin-Pee Dee system heads from sprawling High Rock Lake near Lexington. This is a fairly shallow impoundment with a turbidity and water-level-fluctuation problem periodically. Although it has had its ups and downs, literally, High Rock manages to come through with some fine largemouth- and white-bass fishing each year. Trolling around the points and steep banks usually does the trick for largemouth. White bass are often found schooling and feeding on the surface during the summer.

FARM PONDS

Some of the best Piedmont North Carolina fishing is in the thousands of farm ponds dotting the landscape in the center one-third of the state. These range from less than ½ acre to a few of more than 10 acres. The average size is around 1½ acres. Those that have been properly constructed and located stay reasonably clear much of the year. Others have turbidity problems. Most are stocked by the U. S. Fish and Wildlife Service with largemouth bass and bluegills. More recently the redear sunfish has been added to this combination.

Under good management of fertilization and harvest, bass reach 10 inches their first year, with bluegills making it to 6 ounces by their second spring. Redear growth at first is slightly behind the bluegill, but this fish soon passes the bluegill and usually reaches a larger maximum size more quickly. Well-cared-for Piedmont farm ponds produce bluegills weighing one pound rather consistently, and bass of over 7 pounds are common. Redear of 2 pounds are frequent. Crappies are discouraged in the small farm ponds because of their great tendency to overpopulate and become stunted. Some of the older ponds, such as the mill ponds of the Coastal Plain, maintain crappies, warmouth, common sunfish, flier, and even yellow perch.

Farm-pond fishing is a year-round affair although it peaks from May to late June. Summer angling is often surprisingly productive at dawn and dusk. Fly-fishing is ideal for the farm pond. Although most of it is done from a small boat, many ponds have even, smooth bottoms which can be waded nicely. In the early spring, wet flies and nymphs are excellent for bluegills. The fly-fisherman concentrating on bream is often jolted by a cruising largemouth that picks up the tiny fly. To be on the safe side, a 4-pound-test leader should be used.

Wet flies in fairly dark patterns (brown, gray, and dark green) in sizes No. 6 to No. 10 work well on bluegills. When this scrapper moves on the spawning bed, fishing can be fast and furious. Deep purple male fish guarding the nests can't resist a nymph or bushy wet fly settling into the spawning area. In good ponds, a productive bed will yield several hundred bluegill up to 24 ounces and even larger. Mid-May in the Piedmont is best for fishing.

Popping bugs also are fish getters, both for bass and panfish. Bluegills prefer the smaller No. 8 and No. 10 bugs, while bass prefer the larger ones, up to size 1/0. Usually these surface lures are most productive beginning in Piedmont, earlier in the Coastal Plain.

COASTAL PLAINS WATERS

It is the dark, swamp-stained rivers that offer the best Coastal Plain angling. Although there are productive mill ponds and a few farm ponds in this section, the slow, meandering rivers are hard to beat. Fish populations tend to be of the more acid-tolerant varieties since the pH of these waters may run as low as 4.6. This means that the bluegills are joined (and often outnumbered) by the "robin" or redbreast sunfish. Bass hold their own, but pickerel are numerous, both eastern chain and redfin. The yellow perch is much more numerous, the fliers mingle with crappies.

Near the mouths of these rivers and creeks, white perch and striped bass move in and out. Even flounders and croakers may occur if lowwater exists. Rough fish—notably gar and carp—are often abundant, and bullheads and white catfish may be numerous. Saltwater migrants, in addition to the already mentioned striped bass, include herring, hickory shad, and the larger American shad.

A normal season in a typical coastal river would begin in early March with the arrival of the hickory shad from the sounds and ocean. Silver schools move up on highwater, and spawning takes place in tributary creeks. Although considerable commercial fishing is done with gillnets, the hickory is a fine sport fish and strikes hard at small spoons and tiny white jigs fished slowly in the current. A 2-pound hickory is considered a good fish, and few go over 3 pounds. By mid or late April, the American or white shad joins the departing hickory. This fish is larger and often weighs 4–5 pounds. The method of fishing and waters fished are about the same as for the smaller hickory.

The shad runs end by early or mid May and are overlapped in the larger streams by spawning migrations of the striped bass. The Roanoke River, plagued by pollution, has been the site of large striped-bass runs. Fish of up to 30 pounds find their way up to the Weldon, North Carolina, area and spawn in the favored fastwater there. Sport fishing is often spectacular although few large female fish are taken on hook and line. The males average about 4 pounds, with some reaching 15. Wobbling spoons and cut herring are favorite baits.

By early summer, the smaller creeks provide fine redbreast sunfish angling, good bluegill fishing, and some fast largemouth and pickerel fishing. The swampwaters stay surprisingly cool, and many of the rivers have no "dog-days slump." Fly-fishing with small popping bugs is one of the most productive methods for bass and panfish. Pickerel prefer a flashing spoon or spinner.

Fall finds better yellow-perch fishing, the stripers returning to winter in the rivers, and the bass feeding well. This blends into cool winters with rarely anything but a little skim of ice to prevent good striped bass and pickerel catches (with nice crappies thrown in) all winter long.

The only reservoir containing landlocked population of striped bass thus far developed in North Carolina is Kerr Reservoir on the Virginia line near Henderson. The early history of this impoundment found spectacular crappies fishing and good largemouth and pickerel angling. The crappies declined, walleyes appeared, bass held their own, but the stripers did well and began spawning runs up two large rivers entering the lake. Fish of 15 pounds were taken by the 1962 season. Black bass growth is slow in the reservoir until they reach 1 pound; from then on, growth is rapid, and 7–8 pounders are common. Much of the fishing is very deep (25–40 feet), using deep-running plugs and live bait.

SOUNDS

Currituck Sound, in extreme northeastern North Carolina, has long been famous for largemouth-bass fishing. This is a shallow (maximum depth about 15 feet), fairly weedy, freshwater sound, whose eastern shore is formed by the narrow strand of sandy beach which is part of the Outer Banks.

Several severe hurricanes and one early March blow almost converted this freshwater into salt. The slight fish-kills resulting apparently did little damage to the over-all bass population.

Although much of the early-season bass fishing is done with minnows, weedless pork-rind spoons and surface lures are productive. Fly-fishing also can be very good. One problem is access to the sound and then knowing where to fish. Fortunately just about any grass bed has its share of bass, but, of course, local hot spots crop up. The fisherman making his first trip to Currituck would do well to look up a guide in the vicinity of Poplar Branch, Grandy, or Waterlily.

Currituck is not noted for panfish, but East Lake (actually a series of bays off Albemarle Sound) is worth a visit. This slightly brackish, shallow bay north of Mann's Harbor is a tricky one to fish and can be frustrating to the newcomer. It is a good fish producer, however.

Mattamuskeet, noted for its fall Canada goose shooting, also must be mentioned in the bass-fishing category. Now rid of the scourge of carp, Mattamuskeet is clear and producing plenty of bass. Large popping bugs on substantial bass fly rods are good. Ten-to-15-pound-test leaders are in order because of numerous stumps and submerged timber.

When these freshwater localities fail (which isn't often) the angler can swing east a few miles and pick up the trail of the red drum, bluefish, spotted seatrout, mackerel, and many other saltwater species. The sounds—Albemarle, Pamlico, Roanoke, Bogue, and others—seasonally contain croakers, flounder, a few bluefish, plenty of stripers, trout, cobia, a few Spanish mackerel, and assorted smaller fish. The surf, from May on, has red drum, spotted seatrout, bluefish, a few mackerel, a few tarpon, whiting, and spot. But no stripers; the beaches are smooth, almost rock free, and apparently don't attract the stripers like the New England surf does. Piers which furnish tackle, bait, and lunch are numerous and can produce fast fishing—at a modest cost. The pier season starts as early as April 15 and hits a peak about May 15, slowing some during July and August and getting the returning migration of fish again in September and October. Surf-fishing is a shade better in the fall, say October, than in the spring.   —D.F.R.

HATTERAS

The Outer Banks, composed of Hatteras and Ocracoke islands, form the eastern perimeter of Pamlico Sound. These two thin strips of sand and scrub trees protect the eastern shore of North Carolina from the cruel buffeting of the Atlantic Ocean. As the mainland falls sharply off toward the southwest, Hatteras Island, separated from Bodie Island by Oregon Inlet, runs almost due south for 45 miles before turning abruptly westsouthwest to meet Ocracoke Island and eventually join up with the mainland again. Hatteras Island, from the Oregon Inlet at the north end to the town of Buxton 40 miles south, at no point exceeds 1,000 yards in width. The largest part of the island is dominated by the famous Cape Hatteras Lighthouse guarding the west end of the Diamond Shoals. This shoal extends 12 miles into the Atlantic, and it constitutes one of the most dangerous sailing areas in the world. The brave little Diamond Lightship rides at anchor 15 miles out in the Atlantic night and day to warn the unwary ship of this treacherous hazard to navigation.

The angler driving to Hatteras cannot help but realize that this is truly one of America's last, great, natural frontiers. For those who know the area and the people of Hatteras, it is hoped that it will remain in this pristine state. Because of the geographical location and its relationship to the ocean currents, Hatteras may be favorably compared to Cabo Blanco on the northwest coast of Peru. There, the Peru Current sweeps up from the south to meet the Equatorial Counter Current from the north before pushing each other out again into the Pacific. Off Hatteras, the Gulf Stream flows up from Florida, and it is here where the Stream most closely approaches the United States after it leaves Florida before heading out into the Atlantic. The other current, which hugs the inner side of the Stream, is an extension of the Labrador Current coming down from Greenland and Nova Scotia. This junction of two major currents creates a condition favorable to fish, but it also creates a rough sea, so the angler must also be a good sailor to test these waters properly.

The striped bass winters off Hatteras, and this area has always been famous for its red drum, or channel bass, run in the late fall. Tarpon migrate north and are seen in June and July rolling in Hatteras Inlet. Cobia are plentiful at Ocracoke Inlet along with pompano, weakfish, flounder, mackerel, and croaker. The bottom-fisherman who does not care for surf-casting or offshore trolling but would rather take a small boat and fish the sound will find excellent fishing for sheepshead, hogfish, weakfish, spots, flounder, and tarpon just north of Bird Island about 3 nautical miles westnorthwest of Buxton in the Cape Channel. There is also good spring and fall fishing for "puppy drum" in this area. Most anglers use a light boat rod or medium spinning gear with not less than 12-pound-test monofilament line. Crabs, shrimp, and pinfish make excellent live bait, but small darting plugs, metal wobblers, feathers, and spoons take their share at

certain times of the year. The area just inside Hatteras Inlet is also a good holding ground for all these species, and in addition, many bluefish stay close to the inlet.

Starting at Oregon Inlet the surf-caster has many spots from which to choose. Just south of the Pea Island Government Bird Sanctuary there is excellent fishing in the gullies along the beach. A good surfer will watch the wave action and can quickly tell where the holes are located and where the fish will most likely be lying. Always keep an eye on the birds, and if they start feeding close to shore, pick up and go where they are. About 5 miles south of Pea Island, the area near the tower at Chicamocomico is very good, and the area between the towns of Rodanthe and Salvo produces very good catches of spotted seatrout, bluefish, pompano, flounder, and channel bass. Bear in mind that the best surf-casting occurs in the early spring or late fall with a very dead period usually existing during the summer. There are several wrecks located along the 60 miles of Hatteras coast, and these generally produce good fishing the year round. One such wreck is located just north of the town of Waves and still another 2 miles south. Running roughly 3 miles between the towns of Avon and Buxton there is a shore condition called the Three Mile Slough. Here, red-and-yellow plugs work very well on spotted seatrout, and in the fall a metal wobbler fished high on the wave attracts bluefish and channel bass. A large white feather is productive on red drum in this area.

Cape Hatteras Point is a very good spot for surf-fishing. In fact, the entire area from this point south until Hatteras Inlet is reached should not be overlooked. At times, the hottest spot on the island is the inlet itself, particularly on the young flood tide. Each of the towns the angler passes on Hatteras has its bait shop and tackle store. By far the best authority on where the fish are biting and on what is the tackle and bait man in that particular area. Your chances of success will be greatly enhanced by taking the time to consult with him before fishing. Beach buggies are available at nominal prices, and they are essential if one wishes to travel on the beach for any great distance.

MARLIN FISHING

Rapidly gaining stature as the number one deep-sea fishing area for blue marlin, the waters in the Gulf Stream near the Diamond Lightship consistently produce big fish. A large blue marlin weighing 810 pounds was taken near the lightship during the summer of 1962 on an artificial bait. The run from Hatteras to the fishing grounds takes a minimum of one hour to perhaps two hours depending on whether the Gulf Stream is running inshore or offshore. It can be as close as 12 miles or as far as 30 depending in large measure on the wind and the strength of the current that is pushing down from the north. The best wind for fishing seems to be a northeaster, but this wind also produces fairly lumpy water since it is going against the Stream. The local boats and crews available at Hatteras are excellent for this particular type of fishing and under the rough conditions which are likely to be encountered. The men are expert seamen, and the boats are safe.

In addition to blue marlin, there are also white marlin, sailfish, king mackerel, wahoo, dolphin, bonito, oceanic bonito, blackfin tuna, and yellowfin tuna. The big bluefin also passes close to Hatteras on the annual migration to the north. A 400-pounder was washed up on the Hatteras beach which seems to bear out this theory; however, they probably go by too deep for fishermen. The numerous wrecks which dot the area around Diamond Shoals provide excellent fishing for amberjack, barracuda, bluefish, sailfish, kingfish, and mackerel. If an angler tires of skipping baits for big fish, he can enjoy a change of pace by using lighter tackle and fishing the dropoffs near the sloughs and shoals. One of the greatest concentration of dolphin exists off Hatteras during the summer and extending into the fall. They range up to 40 pounds, and an angler can enjoy great sport with spinning tackle along the weed lines or logs which float with the stream. However, the angler must be prepared to sit it out on shore if the weather gets nasty. Any boat captain taking a private fishing boat to Hatteras should consult the local guides for inlet conditions and the latest information on the position of the sandbars at the mouth.

The heritage of Hatteras is one of contrasts. Hurricanes have battered but not defeated her; pirates and buccaneers have used her as a base of operations and as a safe refuge from the storms, but the quiet strength and serenity of her people perhaps reflect best of all the tranquility and peace of this remarkable island.   —D.B.

NORTH DAKOTA The state of North Dakota is approximately 400 miles long and 300 miles wide. The state covers an area of 70,665 square miles and has a population of over 632,000. North Dakota is the nation's number one cash grain state. It ranks tenth in proven oil reserves and has the largest deposit of lignite coal in the world just below the surface. Ranching is also big business, with approximately one-third of the state still in native grass. North Dakota is sometimes known as the prairie "pot-hole" state and produces a large percentage of the waterfowl in the United States.

There are numerous lakes of natural origin within the state and several that have been created by the activities of man. Water levels in natural lakes have declined during the past ten years, due to a lack of spring runoff, to the point where the majority of them have been unable to sustain fish life because of winter oxygen depletion. Man-made reservoirs, on the other hand, were constructed with sufficient depth to sustain adequate oxygen levels during the winter to support fishes. These impoundments vary in size from small 60-acre ponds to the huge Garrison Reservoir comprising 300,000 surface acres. A number of new reservoirs have been constructed, and it has been estimated that North Dakota will have one hundred new fishing lakes within the next five years. This type of fishery management has provided, and will undoubtedly continue to provide, the sportsman with quality fishing.

North Dakota winters are quite long and usually severe, with high winds and heavy snowfall. Under these conditions drifting snow accumulates on the lakes to great depths and causes winter-kill in the shallower lakes. The summers are short and hot; consequently, the growing season is of short duration. The natural lakes in the state are quite fertile and produce, during the summer, heavy growths of aquatic vegetation. This situation is not only a nuisance to the fisherman but has also resulted in summer-kills on some of the shallower lakes.

The principal game species in North Dakota are northern pike, walleye, sauger, white bass, largemouth bass, and trout. Of these the northern pike is the most important gamefish. North Dakota is possibly the pike capital of the United States. Fishery workers in this state have been leaders in developing successful hatchery techniques in the culture of this species. Each year millions of northern-pike eggs are collected and supplied to state and federal hatcheries with production figures of 85–95 per cent success not unusual. This species is extremely well adapted to the natural conditions existing in North Dakota, exhibiting rapid growth and being quite tolerant to low oxygen contents during the winter. Although North Dakota experiences a short growing season, northern pike will run 17–18 inches during their first year.

Walleyes are also an important and popular fish in North Dakota. These fish are much slower-growing and require 2–3 years to provide good angling. Numerous lakes and reservoirs have been managed for this species with three lakes—Heart Butte Reservoir, Lake Ashtabula, and Spiritwood Lake—used as sources of walleye eggs during the spawning season.

Sauger are present only in the Missouri River and its tributaries; consequently, fishermen must travel long distances to pursue this species. Sauger are quite abundant in Garrison Reservoir and in the Missouri River below the dam, with good catches being recorded in both areas. The highest level of fisherman harvest on sauger is produced in the tailrace area below the dam. The fish caught in this area are not as large as those caught in the reservoir, but they are more numerous.

Trout, both rainbows and browns, are fast becoming one of the most sought-after fish in the state. Although North Dakota does not have a single mile of natural trout stream, a progressive trout-stocking program has been initiated on newly created reservoirs and rehabilitated lakes. Trout when planted in these areas exhibit excellent growth and provide good angling. As there is no spawning habitat available, they do not overpopulate the area and are easily managed.

Other species, such as largemouth bass, white bass, perch, crappies, and catfish, are not as widely distributed within the state but where present provide good angling.

There are approximately one hundred major fishing areas thoughout the state providing the fisherman with just about any type of fishing he might desire. The state Game and Fish Department annually publishes a small pamphlet, *North Dakota Fishing Guide*, which contains a map of the state, the exact location of the best fishing areas, road directions, the type of fishing available, and the facilities available at each area. This publication is available from the state office in Bismarck.

GARRISON RESERVOIR

Garrison Reservoir offers the most diversified fishing in the state. Over twenty-six species of fish are present in the reservoir, and the fisherman is never quite sure what is on the other end of his line until he lands his catch. The reservoir covers 300,000 surface acres in the western portion of the state, has a shoreline of approximately 1,500 miles, and provides the people of North Dakota with abundant recreation. Although the reservoir is quite turbid near the headwaters, the lower one-half of the reservoir is quite clear and pure. A number of tributaries enter the reservoir, and where each of them enters the nearest town has established boat-docking facilities.

Sightseeing by boat in the tributaries is a favorite pastime of the fisherman. The Little Missouri River, for example, extends approximately 25 miles back off the main reservoir and then meanders on through the North Dakota Badlands, a very scenic trip. Garrison Reservoir is responsible for most of the big fish that are caught each year, and although all species are present throughout the reservoir, some areas consistently produce the best catches. The Little Missouri River and Tobacco Garden Creek are the two areas where most of the northern pike are caught, with catches of 20 pounds or more quite numerous. The rock rip-rap off the face of the dam provides rainbow-trout fishing in the spring of the year, with some of the fish weighing 5–6 pounds. Walleyes are also caught off the face of the dam in the fall as well as in Snake Creek, Van Hook Arm, and the Little Knife River. Sauger are caught throughout the reservoir but tend to concentrate in the lower portion of the reservoir. Crappies and channel catfish are present in Mahato Bay, the Little Missouri River, and Douglas Creek, but the fishermen are usually in pursuit of large northern pike and overlook these two species.

Snake Creek Reservoir is a large reservoir separated by a causeway from Garrison Reservoir. This area will be the water supply of the proposed Garrison Diversion Unit when the project is completed. Water is released into Snake Creek Reservoir through a large conduit from Garrison Reservoir. As there is no feasible method of preventing fish movement through this conduit, all species of fish in Garrison Reservoir have access to Snake Creek Reservoir.

Garrison tailrace is probably the most heavily utilized area in North Dakota. The principal species caught in the tailrace are sauger, northern pike, and walleye. As the banks have been heavily rip-rapped with large rocks, this area is difficult to fish and many lures are lost. Lead-headed jigs and small wobbling spoons are the most popular bait.

Four of the other more important fishing areas in the state are:

Lake Ashtabula A 5,400-acre reservoir formed by impoundment of the Cheyenne River. This is a well-developed area with a number of resorts and camping facilities. The fish population consists of northern pike, walleye, crappie, perch, white bass, and bullhead.

Heart Butte Reservoir A 5,190-acre reservoir constructed on the Heart River. Heart Butte is in the southwest portion of the state and offers walleye, crappie, white bass, and catfish.

Jamestown Reservoir A 1,200-acre reservoir formed by impoundment of the James River and located 2 miles north of Jamestown. Good fishing for northern pike, walleye, bluegill, and bullhead.

Lake Darling 14,000 acres formed by impoundment of the Souris River, about 30 miles northwest of Minot. Some excellent northern pike and walleye fishing, as well as perch, especially for ice fishing in winter.

Also important are North and South Lake Metigoshe, 1,600 acres near the Canadian border, and Spiritwood Lake near Jamestown. —J.W.S.

NORTHERN ANCHOVY *Engraulis mordax* A small marine species of considerable importance as a bait for barracuda, yellowtail, halibut, and other gamefishes in Pacific coastal waters; the commercial catch for the live-bait market runs over 3,000 tons per year in California. The northern anchovy is distributed from Vancouver Island south to Cape San Lucas, Baja California.

Like all members of the anchovy family (Engraulidae), it has a long snout and a large mouth, with the maxillary extending behind the eye almost to the edge of the gill cover. The head length is greater than the depth of body and the anal fin is shorter than the head. The color is blue-green above and silvery on the sides and beneath. The northern anchovy is usually 4–5 inches long with a maximum of about 9 inches. It spawns throughout the year, and the elliptical eggs float near the surface. The fish mature at 2–4 years and live to 7 years.

Four other species of anchovies are of minor importance along the Pacific coast; the deepbody anchovy, *Anchoa compressa;* the slim anchovy, *Anchoviella miarcha;* the anchoveta, *Cetengraulis mysticetus;* and the slough anchovy, *Anchoa delicatissima.*

FOOD VALUE

Anchovies are caught with roundhaul nets. They are not often eaten fresh or whole, but when utilized as pickled and salted fillets they contribute a distinctive rich flavor to a variety of meat and fowl as well as seafoods. Their most frequent use is in a butter sauce on bland fish, such as whitefish and sole, or anchovies can be served with scrambled eggs, salads, and vegetables. The fillets are usually cured in salt and olive oil, or vinegar and parsley. They are a popular chum to attract tuna in commercial fishing operations. Anchovies are also used as whitebait (*which see*). *See also* Live Bait, Striped Anchovy

—A.J.McC.

NORTHERN HOG SUCKER *Hypentelium nigricans* Also known as hog molly or hammerhead, this long-snouted rooter of the riffles has more of the aspects of the darters than of the suckers. Identifying the northern hog sucker is relatively simple. The major features are a large head, with a depression between the eyes and a sucking-type mouth, and four rather broad, dark oblique bars or saddles on the body. The eye is behind the middle of the snout. The whole body appears almost conical, and is covered with large scales. The lower fins are a dull red. Some attain a length of 2 feet, but 10–12 inches is the most usual size seen.

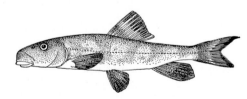

Northern Hog Sucker

The northern hog sucker is found from central Minnesota eastward through the Great Lakes region to New York, down the Mississippi drainage to the Gulf of Mexico. Elsewhere its southern limit extends from northern Alabama to eastern Oklahoma. It is particular as to where it lives and generally is present only in clear streams. Preferred habitats are riffles and adjacent areas of clear, shallow streams with gravel bottoms. It also frequents the shallow areas of lakes near the mouth of a stream.

It has been called the representative species of the Ozarks where it often becomes very numerous. A biological survey crew studying an upstream area of Current River, Missouri, captured 130 hog suckers in a riffle area less than one-half-mile long.

RESEMBLANCE TO DARTERS

The northern hog sucker appears suddenly from among the riffles, darts rapidly away for a short distance, then merges with the bottom. This sort of activity along with a slender body, large pectoral fins, and coloration heightens its resemblance to the darters (*which see*). Like the darters, it has the habit of resting quietly on the bottom, supported by its paired fins. Its coarsely mottled colors help to conceal it among the surrounding stones.

LIFE HISTORY

Spawning occurs in shallow waters or riffles in April to June, as water temperatures reach 60° F. There is some movement from the larger streams to the headwaters at this time. During spawning several males crowd about a female as she takes her position over an area of sand and gravel in shallow water. Two or three usually remain at her sides as eggs are extruded. The eggs are not guarded, and minnows usually rush in to feast upon them as soon as they are laid.

A striking peculiarity of the fish is its feeding habits. The large bony head, streamlined form, and well-developed pectoral fins enable it to seek its food in the more rapid parts of streams. It uses its long snout and large head to turn over rocks while it keeps its position on the riffle with the pectoral fins. Food is obtained by sucking up the ooze and slime which is exposed when the rocks are moved. Many insect larvae and other minute organisms are gathered up in this manner. During these activities the sucker often serves as a provider for other species. As it roots a path through a riffle it is often followed by small fish which feed on the insects that are dislodged. The smallmouth bass is the game species most frequently observed enjoying this free board.

ANGLING VALUE

Bait-fishermen infrequently take hog suckers, but gigging, snaring, and snagging are used quite successfully where legal. Although edible, it is the least sought-after of the suckers due to its soft flesh and the small percentage of usable meat. Though it is not widely used for food by man, it fills an important niche in the stream. Its greatest value is in making much food available for more desired species.   —C.A.P.

NORTHERN KINGFISH *See* Whitings

NORTHERN PIKE *Esox lucius* A freshwater gamefish of circumpolar distribution; in the United States the pike is most common from New York through the Great Lakes regions to Nebraska. However, the species has been widely introduced in many states of the South and West. The northern pike caught by anglers are often large (up to 20 pounds in many areas), and due to their size and activity when hooked, northern pike are a highly desirable gamefish.

The northern pike is a very elongated, somewhat laterally compressed fish. The head is large and has a flat dorsal surface. The duckbill jaws have large, sharp, pointed teeth. The roof of the mouth has short, backward-pointing teeth. The entire cheek is covered with small scales, but only the upper half of the gill cover has larger scales. This scalation pattern is one of the most distinguishing characteristics of the northern pike. Five sensory or mandibular pores are found on each side of the lower jaw. The back is dark green shading to lighter green on the sides and to white on the ventral surface. On the sides are many bean-shaped yellow spots, but the fins are heavily dark-spotted. The young up to 6–7 inches have light vertical bars.

SUBSPECIES

One species of northern pike, *Esox lucius*, is found in North America and Europe, but the pike of the Ob' River in western Siberia and through eastern Siberia are now regarded as a subspecies *Esox lucius baicalensis*. It is possible that this subspecies extends into Alaska and western Canada as do some other Siberian forms, but not enough work has been done to determine subspeciation in this area. In the Amur River, which separates Siberia from Manchuria, the northern pike is replaced by a blackspotted pike, *Esox reicherti*, which is similar to the American muskellunge.

In Minnesota a variant or mutant form of northern pike was found. This is apparently a true-breeding variety called the silver pike. The silver pike was first noticed by local residents in Lake Belletaine near Nevis, Minnesota, about 1930. It was thought to be a variation of the muskellunge and for several years was propagated as such. Superficially they differ from the northern pike only in the markings. The body is usually a dark silver or gray, and each scale is flecked with gold. This mutant form breeds with others of its kind rather than with the muskellunge and typical northern pike. Specimens rarely exceed 10 pounds.

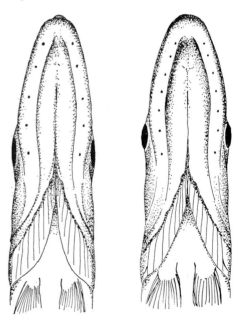

One of the distinguishing features between northern pike and muskellunge is the number of mandibular pores which appear as tiny holes along the ventral margin of the lower jaw. The pike has 5 or less mandibular pores and the muskellunge has 6 or more

Northern Pike, 11-pound Male, St. Lawrence River, New York

Recent studies in Canada have added more information to the knowledge of the characteristics of this mutant form. It was found that the silver pike differ from the normal pike in some morphological characters as well as color. The smaller silver pike are somewhat narrower in body width and appear to have larger eyes than the normal pike. This conclusion, based on measurements of eye diameter, is strengthened by evidence that the interorbital width of silver pike is distinctly less than that of normal pike. There is some evidence that the mandible and maxillary are both shorter in the silver pike. The silver pike has been reported from as far north as Beaverlodge Lake, east of Great Bear Lake, from three lakes in Manitoba, from a lake near Ottawa, and from Minnesota and Sweden.

Crosses between silver pike and muskellunge produced hybrids which were identical with the typical northern pike-muskellunge cross. When silver pike were crossed with normal northern pike, there was a heavy loss of the progeny. The survivors were greatly different from both parents in markings; they were mottled with dark splotches similar to the black crappie, but in all other external characteristics they were identical.

MYTHOLOGY

No species has inspired more fables than the pike. Its malevolent eye and tail-drooping posture once identified it as Luce, the waterwolf. Anglo-Saxons compared it to that ancient weapon the pike, and thus it became *Esox lucius*, the pitiless pike. To account for its presence in unstocked waters, early-day naturalists believed that the fish were bred from weeds and hatched by the sun's heat. Another myth concerns its age. The famous Mannheim pike was supposed to have been 267 years old. Actually, their average life span is closer to 10 years, although the occasional individual will reach 20 years old. As to size, the 350-pound pike from Lake Kaiserwag was, like so many others, a hoax. The mounted specimen consisted of a number of pike sectionally reconstructed to make one huge fish of 19 feet. But pike existed in medieval literature simply to attack swans, men and even mules, and to provide medicines (the heart and gall to cure agues and abate fevers, powdered jawbone to cure pleurisy, and the ashes of burned pike to dress wounds). Pike bones were also worn as talismans against witchcraft. In Bohemia, which is authentically the land where farm-pond management got its start in the eleventh century, the sight of a pike feeding before midday was considered a bad omen. Mystery, of course, has always been an important ingredient in angling, and nothing stirs the soul more than the abrupt arrival of a twenty-pound pike behind the lure. With baleful eyes and underslung jaw, it comes grimly to the feast.

EVOLUTION AND DISTRIBUTION

The northern pike probably evolved in southern Europe in the Cretaceous period, or 60–120 million years ago. Numerous fossil remains are found from the Tertiary period in Europe. One of the earliest and best-known was found from the Miocene epoch, which existed 10–18 million years ago. The progenitors of our present-day pike were a specialized form of the clupeiforms, which originated from the osmeroids (smelts) in this period. Also included in the clupeiforms are the herring, shad, char, trout, tarpon, and anchovy.

The pike were widely distributed throughout North America, Europe, and Asia in preglacial times. Their present distribution resulted from glacial effects and movements. During the Cretaceous period, a broad connection existed at the present Bering Strait, and the pike may have spread through its coastwise marshes. Credence may be added to this theory by the fact that although the pike are considered a freshwater fish and cannot live long in seawater, they are found in brackish water. The pike support an important commercial fishery in the Baltic Sea off of Sweden.

Another theory is that the melting ice in spring may have freshened the waters of the Arctic Ocean. Since the freshwaters float on the saline water of the ocean, the dispersal of this species may have been furthered between the two continents.

Before the arrival of the Europeans, there were no northern pike on Newfoundland Island, Nova Scotia, or in the New England states. In 1838, it is said, the northern pike were introduced into the Connecticut River drainage in a pond connected to the Black River. From this point they spread throughout the Connecticut River system in the New England states. There are still no pike reported in Nova Scotia or Newfoundland.

The range of the northern pike in the United States is New York, western Pennsylvania, through the Great Lakes states and into Missouri, eastern Nebraska, the upper two-thirds of Iowa, and north through the prairie region, but not naturally in Kansas or eastern Colorado.

In Canada the pike range includes Labrador, New Brunswick, and Ontario, except in certain highland regions in Algonquin Park and Haliburton County. They are distributed west through the prairie provinces to British Columbia where they are found only in the Peach River system which drains east into Lake Athabasca. Thus far they have failed to cross the Continental Divide into any major Pacific watershed. The pike are dispersed north into Saskatchewan and the Northwest Territories but are not found in the Northwest Territories east of Bathurst Inlet.

In Alaska, the pike is distributed broadly north of the Alaskan Range and drainages into the Bering Sea and the Arctic Ocean. The northern pike does not occur south of 60° N. latitude, that is, south of the Bering Sea in either North America or Asia.

Esox lucius is found in the northern rivers and streams of Siberia, but does not extend as far south as the Kamchatka Peninsula, nor is it found in most of the drainages of the Sea of Okhotsk in southeastern Siberia. It is found in the northern river systems of Europe but not on the Atlantic coast of Norway. To the south it occurs in the Caspian Sea, but not in the Transcaucasian or Black Sea. It occurs in the Sea of Azov and the basin of the Danube River but not in Greece or the Pyrenean Peninsula. It has never been reported from an Arctic or sub-Arctic island.

Its range has been extended southward through planned introductions in southern Pennsylvania, Maryland, and North Carolina and westward into Colorado and Montana. The ability of the northern pike to live and reproduce in all these new environments has not been definitely established.

SPAWNING

Gesner, the Swiss naturalist, in his *Historia Animalium* (1551–1558), postulated that pickerel weed and other glutinous matter in ponds when helped by the sun developed into pike. However, there was just one condition necessary—the ponds had to be "apted" for pike. Since the days of Gesner and Izaak Walton (who also apparently accepted this theory) much more has been learned about the procreation of northern pike. Why, where and how pike spawn has been investigated both in North America and Europe.

The concept that is advanced by some physiologists is that activity is merely the process of using energy released by metabolism. Whatever controls metabolism must necessarily control other activities. One of the activities of pike is spawning. This activity is not controlled by one stimulus but by a series of stimuli which occur in the early spring. Both internal stimuli, such as increased gonad action and high hormone levels, and external stimuli, such as vegetation, temperature, and increased light, are needed to promote spawning action. However, a high intensity of one stimulus lowers the intensity required of other stimuli.

Pike will concentrate near the spawning site before there is any visible change in water temperature. This assembling action is initiated in response to internal stimuli from increased gonad action and probably the lengthening of the day. After leaving the depths, the spawning desire is further increased by water temperatures and relatively intense light. Therefore, it may be said that spawning activity is influenced by the summation of

internal stimuli, increasing temperatures, the sight of other spawning pike, increasing light intensities, and the presence of vegetation.

Northern pike in the southern portion of their range spawn occasionally at one year of age, but the bulk of their number spawn initially at two years of age. In Minnesota 84 percent of the spawners were 3–5 years old. Only 1 percent were 2 years old, and 15 percent were older than 5 years. It has been observed that the size range and composition of spawning-run catches are indicative of the length composition of fish which anglers will catch later in the season. It has been suggested that an annual study be made of spawning runs to predict the angler's future catch.

Northern pike usually spawn in the early spring as soon as the ice goes out of the spawning areas. The dates vary yearly according to the lateness of the spring. In Iowa they may spawn in the third and fourth week in March; in Minnesota and Pennsylvania they may spawn in the first few weeks of April. In Saskatchewan, they usually do not spawn until May. In Alaska they are reported to spawn in July.

Most spawners run from 6:00 P.M. to 9:00 A.M., with the peak of the run between 9:00 P.M. and midnight. Even though they may run at night there is no spawning until the daylight hours. The height of the spawning usually takes place in the afternoon. The most intense spawning activity has been noticed on sunny days when there was very little wind.

MIGRATIONS

It is during the spawning season that the greatest movement and migration of pike occur. Pike often travel a long distance to reach the spawning grounds. In Michigan two pike, 38 days after tagging, had traveled 25 miles upstream. Michigan pike which were trapped and marked on their way to the spawning ground were later on trapped as they left the spawning areas. It was found that the pike did not start to leave the spawning ground until the run had almost ceased. This would imply that pike do not wander between spawning places or into openwater each day. However, other studies have shown that pike wander within a spawning area. One female may travel 100 yards or 1½ miles. Therefore, catches in nets on the spawning grounds may not reflect the movement or migration of pike but only the intensity of the spawning activity.

Some biologists are of the opinion that the pike are constant wanderers, moving restlessly from place to place in a lake. It is generally agreed, however, that in small lakes with more or less uniform habitat conditions the pike do little wandering. In large lakes, where there may be extensive weed beds scattered over the lake, there is evidence of certain aggregations of pike which move from place to place. In Michigan, river spawners were found to be more restless and far-ranging, while pike which spawned in marshes along the shore were more sedentary in nature. Large pike were also found to move more than the smaller pike. One pike, tagged one year, was caught the following year 49 miles from the point of tagging. Another tagged pike traveled 10 miles in 22 hours at an average speed of about ½ mile per hour.

In summer northern pike are usually found in lakes in or close to weed beds in about four feet of water, but in the fall they may move to precipitous stormy shores. In winter they may return to the summer habitat, but larger pike seem to go to deeper water. Temperature and available food influence the activity, movement, and habitat of northern pike. When temperatures rise above optimum, pike restrict activity and practically stop feeding. The species of fish which pike utilize for food influence their habitat and the depth at which they are found. In Wisconsin where the stomachs of larger pike were found to contain cisco, pike were taken in gillnets in water up to 50 feet. Beyond the 40-foot depth, northern pike weighed 3 pounds or more. Almost without exception the smaller pike were taken in 10–20 feet of water. This lake had a maximum depth of 143 feet, and ciscos were found at 60–110 feet. The northern pike forage in these deeper waters for the ciscos. In Lake Nipigon in Canada, fishermen's nets in late summer often took northern pike in 60–75 feet of water, and occasionally they were taken from depths of over 100 feet.

Most pike, however, are taken from water of less than fifteen feet deep. In New York State, 88 percent of the pike taken were caught in water less than fifteen feet deep. Only 12 percent were taken at 15–45 feet.

FEEDING HABITS

Jordan's classic statement concerning the feeding habits of pike probably is the best description of its voracity. He called them "Mere machines for the assimilation of other organisms." Adult pike are almost wholly piscivorous. Items found in their stomachs include yellow perch, ciscos, suckers, ninespine sticklebacks, brook sticklebacks, brook trout, bluegills, crappies, bass, common whitefish, burbot, walleye, young pike, bridled shiner, and other minnows and fishes when present. A small part of nonfish diet consists of frogs, tadpoles, aquatic birds, muskrats, mice, crayfish, snails, freshwater shrimp, amphipods, leeches, and dragonfly nymphs. Pike feed entirely in the daylight, and yellow perch and suckers seem to be preferred items when present. It is the general rule that food preference is for the most abundant food item.

AGE AND GROWTH

Northern pike are one of the fastest-growing freshwater fish. Under ideal conditions they possess the ability of extremely rapid growth. One pike, under ideal conditions, grew to 17.6 inches from June 25 to October 14, a period of 171 days. In Michigan, yearlings average 14.7 inches. Pike introduced in 1956 into the Youghiogheny Reservoir in Pennsylvania grew to 39.5 inches in five summers. The largest was reported to weigh 15.5 pounds. This was unusual growth, but the circumstances were unique. The water area is south of their range, and because of the small number planted, there was little intraspecific competition from other species. A more normal rate of growth for northern pike is shown in the table.

Growth varies according to latitude. In Great Bear Lake, which is located on the Arctic Circle in Canada, it takes about 7 years for pike to reach 20 inches and 12 years to reach 30 inches. In Pennsylvania, on the extreme southern edge of their range, they reach 20 inches between the second and third year and 30 inches between the fifth and sixth year of life. In Minnesota in the

RATE OF GROWTH FOR NORTHERN PIKE

Age (Years)	Total length (Inches)	Weight (Pounds)
I	8	1/8
II	16	1
III	23	3
IV	28	6
V	32	9
VI	35	12
VII	38	14
VIII	40	16
IX	43	19
X	45	23
XI	46	25
XII	48	28
XIII	49	31
XIV	51	33
XV	52	34
XVI	53	35
XVII	54	36
XVIII	55	37
XIX	56	38
XX	58	39

southern, more fertile lakes, growth is 12–18 inches the first year; in the northern part of the state it is 6–14 inches. Males rarely exceed 24 inches. The largest male reported in Saskatchewan was 30½ inches, weighed 6 pounds, and was 10 years old.

As the fish grow larger the range in weights is more extreme. A 45-inch fish may weigh 15–30 pounds. Also as the fish grow larger, they become proportionately heavier. A 16-inch fish will weigh about 1 pound, while a 32-inch fish will weigh 7–10 pounds.

SHEDDING OF TEETH

Fishermen have long believed that the shedding of teeth in the pike family was responsible for the small catch of these fish in the summer months. This shedding, according to fishermen, reached its peak during "dog days." Research in Michigan proved that this idea was a fallacy and that the number of canine teeth on the lower jaw was constant throughout life, averaging about sixteen per jaw. Although the canines were much subject to loss throughout life, they were constantly replaced by accessory teeth developed in each section of the gum. There was no seasonal change of consequence of the number of teeth in service or being replaced. Further, there was no inflammation of the gums in summer except those caused by the leaders and hooks when the fish were caught. The gums redden chiefly where canine teeth are being replaced because the soft flesh is unprotected and is being supplied by blood vessels which nourish the growing fixed teeth. It was concluded that the failure to catch northern pike in the summer was due to the especial abundance or availability of natural food in summer, or to retirement of these coldwater fish to deepwater at that season, or sluggishness induced by warmwater. Pike often make up a comparatively large percentage of the catch and also the percentage of the weight taken from lakes.

ANGLING FOR PIKE

The northern pike is one of the most reliable gamefish, but there are times when it is more readily caught than others. In the southern part of its range in Nebraska and Iowa and east to Ohio and Pennsylvania the best fishing occurs in cold weather until May and June. For a very brief period after the spawning run, fishing is excellent. Almost all fish returning from spawning runs have empty stomachs, and this has proven to be one of the best times for large catches. Fish taken early in the morning tend to have empty stomachs from the previous night's digestion. This is why morning is considered one of the better fishing periods. Pike are more active during the different times of the day. One study found that they were most active between 8:00 and 11:00 A.M. and 2:00 and 4:00 P.M. There seemed to be a definite rest period between 11:30 A.M. and 1:00 P.M. After 1:00 P.M., activity reached its peak at 3:00 P.M. and then gradually declined for the rest of the evening. These periods of activity probably vary with the seasons and latitude. In the north, where days are longer, the peak of activity may be between 5:00 and 6:00 P.M. The catch of fishermen is influenced by these periods of activity.

After the water reaches 65° F., angling success lessens, and the summer catches diminish. In the north, such as in Great Slave Lake in Saskatchewan, water temperatures rarely exceed 50° F. in the openwater and 60° F. in the shallow water. Consequently, the average catch in June is only slightly higher than in July and August. The most consistent catches of northern pike are made in shallow water by fishing holes in weed beds and patches of lily pads. In the spring, pike concentrate in large numbers in moderate to strong currents on the downstream side of barriers or falls. Fish usually bite readily in these areas, and large catches often result. They visit these areas on and off throughout the summer.

Medium- and shallow-running lures and large, lively live bait are most generally used and are the most productive. A tabulation of artificial baits in Wisconsin indicates that so many kinds were used that there were no significant differences discerned in their ability to catch fish. A breakdown of lures from creel-census returns from different localities probably illustrates the variations more in fishermen than in fish. In Wisconsin, 92 percent were taken on plugs, 7 percent on minnows, and 1 percent on spinners. In contrast, Michigan reports that spinners are best, then plugs, and then minnows. In the Prairie National Parks, plugs caught 0.9 fish per hour, spoons 0.7 fish per hour, and spinners 0.5 fish per hour. Flies were popular and fairly successful. North Dakota suggests bright wobbling spoons, brightly colored plugs, and spinners with live bait. In Manitoba, large flashing baits are supposed to be most successful, but it is noted that northern pike strike at anything. In Alaska, plug and streamer fly are supposed to produce instant action. Added to all baits listed above is the fish worm. Some pike are taken each year with worms when anglers were fishing for other species. —K.B.

NORTHERN PUFFER *Sphaeroides maculatus* Commonly known as blowfish, swellfish, and globefish, the puffer derives its name from its ability to inflate its body with air or water by means of a sac, which is a ventral extension of the stomach. When alarmed or touched, the puffer quickly expands to a large size until it is almost globular; this protects the puffer from its enemies. When left alone, it soon deflates and assumes its moderately slender proportions. The northern puffer occurs from Cape Cod to Florida where a similar species, the southern puffer (*which see*), replaces it.

The northern puffer has a very small mouth, located at the tip of the snout. It does not have true teeth; the bones of the upper and lower jaws form cutting edges, which are divided in the middle giving the appearance of two large incisors both above and below. The skin is scaleless, but the head and body are covered with small, stiff prickles creating a heavy sandpaper texture. The gill openings in front of the pectorals are small and run obliquely backward and downward. The soft dorsal fin has 8 short rays and is twice as high as it is long. The anal fin has 7 rays and originates just behind it when a vertical line is drawn. There are no ventral fins. The northern puffer may reach 14 inches but is usually less than 10 inches.

The northern puffer is dark olive-green dorsally, the sides are greenish-yellow, crossbarred with 6-8 indefinite dark bands or blotches. The belly is white.

LIFE HISTORY

An inshore species, the northern puffer is seldom caught in water more than a few fathoms deep. Puffers are primarily bottom feeders and consume shrimp, crabs, amphipods, isopods, mollusks, worms, sea urchins, and other invertebrates. They spawn from mid May through June according to the location, the eggs sinking and adhering to any object. The larvae are brilliantly pigmented with orange, red, yellow, and black. Puffers of only ½-inch long can inflate themselves to a greater extent than the adult, until the expanded skin completely hides the anal and dorsal fins.

ANGLING VALUE

Puffers are caught incidental to some other bottom species and are often considered a nuisance because of their ability to strip a bait from the hook. Occasionally, they will also strike artificial lures, such as small jigs. However, the northern puffer is highly regarded as a table fish and is sold commercially as "sea squab." It has firm, white flesh similar to that of fowl. The roe should never be utilized. A puffer is a member of the Tetraodontidae. The ovaries, and occasionally the viscera of these fishes may contain a virulent poison, particularly among the tropical species. The fish should be skinned and the whole viscera, including the roe, should be discarded. After several reported cases of food poisoning from eating "blowfish" roe in the year 1945, the material was tested by the Bingham Oceanographic Laboratory of Yale University. Ripe roe was found to be toxic. Despite this, the flesh of this puffer is a popular food and is usually perfectly safe to eat.

HOW TO SKIN A PUFFER

Place the fish belly down on a hard surface, and grasp it over the head, squeezing inward on each side. With a sharp knife, cut down through the backbone just behind the head. Turn the fish on its back without changing your grip, and pin the body of the fish to the table by pressing the butt of your knife blade against the backbone. Simply pull against this with the hand still holding the head. The skin will peel off like a glove. Rinse the two fillets clean. Discard *all* entrails. *See also* Smooth Puffer, Southern Puffer. —A.J.McC.

NORTHERN REDHORSE *Maxostoma macrolepidotum* The northern redhorse is one of the more colorful suckers found in the North and Central states east of the Rockies and throughout central and eastern Canada. The southern extremity of its range is found in Kansas and northern Arkansas, while to the east it ranges through New York, Pennsylvania, and Ohio. It is a cleanwater species found in rivers, moderate-sized streams, and also in lakes. The northern redhorse is especially at home in swift, clear rivers and streams.

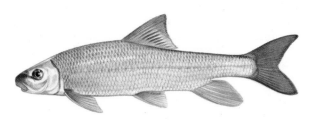

Northern Redhorse

The northern redhorse is bright silvery on the sides, with a somewhat darker back. The fins, including the forked tail, are bright orange or blood-red. The rather short dorsal fin is falcate and has 12–14 rays. The typical sucker-shaped body usually has 42–44 scales along the lateral line. There are no teeth in the mouth or spines on the fins. The head is unusually short, with the suckerlike mouth positioned ventrally.

Other names often applied to the northern redhorse include redfin, redhorse, redfin sucker, and bigscale sucker.

The usual size of the species taken by fishermen runs 2–4 pounds, while maximum weight attained is 10–12 pounds.

LIFE HISTORY

When possible, northern redhorse ascend small, clear streams in April or May to spawn over gravel or rubble. In lakes, they may select clean sand or gravelbars where the water is a foot or two deep. Adult females will spawn 10,000–50,000 eggs, which are scattered among the gravel and rubble. After spawning the parents leave the spawning grounds, and the eggs take about two weeks to hatch. The young feed on minute plankton until they are large enough to begin the adult diet of insect larvae and small mollusks which are sucked from the gravel and rocky bottom. Under average conditions they should attain lengths of 4, 7, 10, 13, 15, and 17 inches at ages 1 through 6, respectively. A 1-pound specimen should measure 14 inches, while a 2-pounder should be 17 inches. An 8–10-pounder will be at least 24 inches. Adulthood is reached at age 3–4, and only a few individuals can be expected to live 8–9 years.

Northern redhorse are particularly vulnerable to muddy or polluted water. They are found only rarely in such waters, and when normally clean waters are occasionally subjected to these conditions, heavy mortality among the redhorse population can be expected. This inability to withstand silt and pollution has greatly decreased the distribution of the species as modern civilization has systematically dirtied most of the major rivers and streams.

ANGLING VALUE

Northern redhorse are viewed with favor by anglers in some localities. They are most readily caught during and just after their spring spawning runs and may be taken on worms, grubs, crickets, etc. They are considered to be one of the best-eating species of the sucker family.

COMMERCIAL VALUE

Commercial fishermen take considerable numbers of northern redhorse, especially during the spring spawning runs. Traps and small seines are the primary methods of capture. Many of these fish are smoked, and demand excellent prices. As fresh fish they bring a lesser but reasonable price. On the commercial market they usually are referred to as suckers. —J.T.S.

NORTHERN SCULPIN *Icelinus borealis* One of the small marine members of the sculpin family. It is dark olive gray or brown above and white to cream below, and has 4 dark saddles across the body. Narrow brown bars are present on the lips, cheeks, and all fins except the pelvic and anal. The male can be distinguished by 2 black spots on the spinous dorsal fin. The spinous dorsal has 9 or 10 rays and is separate from a soft dorsal fin with 15–17 rays. The anal fin has 12–14 rays. The caudal fin is square to slightly rounded.

Compared to other members of the family its head is moderately large. The mouth is also moderately large and is terminal, and the snout is bluntly rounded. It has a short, sharp nasal spine and 3 preopercular spines on the head, the uppermost of which is stout and antlerlike, with 3–6 spinules standing upward from it. It has many slender filamentous projections called cirri along the lateral line and on the head. The gill membranes are united and free from the isthmus. The anus is located ¾ of the distance between the insertion of the pelvic fins and the origin of the anal fin. Rough ctenoid scales are present in two rows on the upper body close to the dorsal fins and on the lateral line. The upper row extends beyond the posterior end of the softrayed dorsal fin to meet the corresponding row from the opposite side of the body.

LIFE HISTORY

This sculpin attains a maximum length of 4 inches. It is found at depths of 10–60 fathoms in the ocean from Puget Sound to northwestern Alaska. *See also* Sculpins —C.A.P.

NORTHERN SENNET *Sphyraena borealis* This close relative of the Pacific barracuda rarely reaches a length of more than 15 inches. It occurs along the coast of New England and intergrades southward with the form called southern sennet (*Sphyraena picudilla*), with which it appears to be conspecific. The southern sennet occurs from Florida southward to Brazil.

The sennet has 5 dorsal spines, 10 dorsal rays, 11 anal rays, and 115–130 scales along the lateral line. The maxillary does not reach beyond a vertical from the posterior nostril. The pectoral fin does not reach to a vertical from the insertion of the pelvic fin. The anterior

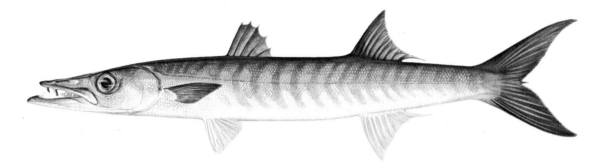

Northern Sennet, 13-inch Male, Lake Worth, Florida

rays of the second dorsal and anal fins do not reach to the tip of the last ray when the fin is depressed. The posterior teeth of the mandible are not slanted backwards. There are no black blotches scattered on the sides of the body.

ANGLING VALUE

Similar in habits to the Pacific barracuda, it is a schooling fish usually occurring not too far from shore. It is usually too small to be considered a gamefish except when taken by anglers on very light tackle with small spoons, plugs, and jigs.

FOOD VALUE

It is excellent eating, and the flesh is never known to be poisonous. Especially in the American tropics, it is a commercial fish of some importance.   —L.R.

NORTHERN SQUAWFISH *Ptychocheilus oregonensis* The squawfishes are the largest of North American minnows. Dusky-green above and silvery below, the northern squawfish has 67–75 scales along its lateral line, 46–56 of which are before the dorsal fin. The dorsal fin contains 9–10 softrays and the anal fin 8 rays. The range of the northern squawfish is limited to the Columbia River drainage and the coastal streams of Washington and Oregon. Three related species, the Colorado squawfish (*P. lucius*), the Umpqua squawfish (*P. umpquae*), and the Sacramento squawfish (*P. grandis*) have a minor western distribution in their respective river systems.

The squawfish are voracious minnows with pikelike habits. The adults feed on other fish including young trout and salmon. These fish are reported up to 80 pounds, but those taken in the Columbia River run 6–10 pounds.

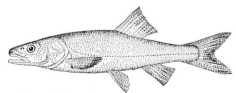

Northern Squawfish

ANGLING VALUE

Condemned by sportsmen for its predaceous habits, the squawfish is easily caught with most lures and natural baits. The young make excellent bait for trout and other gamefish. Though bony, large squawfish have some food value, particularly when smoked.   —R.A.J.

NORTHWEST TERRITORIES The Northwest Territories encompasses an area of approximately 1,352,000 square miles, or about 38 per cent of the total land mass of Canada. It sprawls 2,000 miles across the top of the North American continent from the Yukon on the west to Baffin Island on the east and another 1,700 miles from 60° N. latitude to within 500 miles of the North Pole. This vast land covers part of the sub-Arctic and virtually all of Canada's Arctic. It is populated by some 25,000 people, the majority of Indian and Eskimo descent. In the far northern and northeastern reaches day-to-day life has changed relatively little in the last hundred years, but in the more populated and heavily traveled areas, and more recently in even some of the isolated areas in the Arctic archipelago, new transportation routes, the search for oil and minerals, and nuclear age defense requirements have brought dramatic changes to the territories and its people.

This is a land of infinite variety in topography, climate, and vegetation. At the western extremity lie the 9,000-foot Mackenzie Mountains, home of the snow-white dall sheep, grizzly bear, moose, and mountain goat. The mountains are cut by rivers such as the Nahanni, flowing through the now legendary "Headless Valley" to the mighty Mackenzie River. The miles-wide Mackenzie drains one-fifth of Canada and is one of the world's largest rivers. During the summer months, the Mackenzie is a 1,200-mile water highway from the outlet of Great Slave Lake to the Arctic Ocean. Its valley is relatively flat and well-forested, bounded on one side by the Mackenzie Mountains, and to the east by the Precambrian Shield.

The ancient granite of the Shield provides the basic character for most of the Territories. From the air, the land is a web of thousands of lakes and rivers, with treed valleys and bare-rock hills and ridges. To the north and east, the trees gradually become smaller and more scattered, until the tree line is past and the true Arctic begins —devoid of trees but blossoming in the summer with carpets of flowering shrubs and perennials. Farther north again, the land becomes more rugged, reaching a peak of magnificence in the 2,000-foot sheer cliffs of northeastern Baffin Island and the 10,000-foot mountains and permanent ice caps of Ellesmere.

The North is considered by many people as a land of eternal ice and snow, but this is true only of the few distant ice caps. Winters are long and summers are relatively short and warm. Throughout much of the Northwest Territories, there is little or no spring or autumn, at least not as it is known in southern areas. The arrival of spring is delayed by the large masses of lake and ocean ice. Break-up comes suddenly and then it is summer. Summers range in length from a scant 2 weeks in northern Ellesmere Island to 2–2½ months in the subarctic area around Great Slave Lake. Average summer temperatures range from around 45° F. in southern Baffin Island to 55° F. in the Great Slave Lake area, but temperatures as high as 100° F. have been recorded. The crisp, clear summer climate of the Territories has many advantages for the visitors—up to twenty-four hours of sunshine per day, for this is truly the land of the midnight sun; very light rainfall; relief from the stifling heat of southern latitudes; and beautiful haze-free skies which range through, literally, the complete color spectrum in any twenty-four-hour period.

LAKE TROUT

The lake trout is the most widely distributed gamefish in the Territories and is found throughout the Mackenzie, Coppermine, Back, and Thelon drainage systems. The main angling locations, however, are Great Slave and Great Bear lakes, each more than 10,000 square miles in surface area. Modern fishing camps exist on both lakes. Fish in the 30–40-pound class are common and specimens of over 60 pounds have been recorded in these waters. Of the two, Great Bear Lake is the larger. Lying sixty miles east of the Mackenzie River and largely in the eroded crags of the Precambrian Shield, it presents a barren landscape with steep cliffs and hills along the east and low, timbered shores to the west. The Arctic Circle bisects the northern half of the lake. A number of things make Great Bear fishing unique. It's a remote lake and not fished commercially. The dominant gamefish are lake trout and grayling but there are also scattered populations of whitefish, northern pike, and walleye. Furthermore, the lake trout feed on the surface throughout the summer. Although the ice may break up anytime from mid-June to early July the surface temperatures remain at optimum for lake trout during July and August—with an

No river is too remote for the modern flying sportsman who visits the Northwest Territories

average range of 40°–45°F. The water in a few shallow, isolated bays will reach 50°F. but these are in the minority. The average daily air temperature ranges within 44°–75°F., which is surprisingly comfortable. Because of the cold water and comparatively warm air Great Bear is largely covered by fog early in the morning and late in the evening. But the mysteries of Arctic weather are reducible to the dictum that for good or bad they generally favor the summer angler.

It is not essential to use heavy tackle in Great Bear. The popular methods are casting and trolling at depths of 20–40 feet with all types of metal lures. Many anglers use spinning tackle with 8–10 pound test lines and a spinner or wobbling spoon in nickel, copper, brass, or red-and-white finish. Although lake trout fly fishing is generally done with streamers and bucktails, catching them with dry flies is sometimes possible at Great Bear. Fly hatches are numerous in the gravelly bays and whenever the water is calm it is possible to locate feeding trout.

The angling at Great Slave Lake is similar; however, it is fished commercially. The lake lies 550 miles north of Edmonton. Much of Great Slave is shallow, but in the vicinity of Christie Bay it drops to over 2,000 feet. The shoreline is irregular with many cliffs and with wooded sections. Lake trout are the most common gamefish and are distributed in all parts of Great Slave at depths of 15 feet or more. There are also abundant populations of grayling, northern pike, ciscos, and whitefish. Inconnu or sheefish are scattered throughout the lake and are most commonly caught during their spawning runs in tributary streams such as the Big Buffalo River and the Talston River. Walleyes are present but only in scattered locations.

AMERICAN GRAYLING

The American grayling (*which see*) is particularly common in the Mackenzie, Coppermine, Anderson, Thelon, and Back drainage systems. During the summer months, grayling are found mainly in the cold, swiftly flowing rivers, but they also occur in bays of the larger lakes such as Great Bear. This species generally forages closer to the shoreline at depths to 5 feet, while Great Bear lake trout favor the 20-foot zone for their surface feeding. The grayling in the lake proper are somewhat larger and darker-colored fish than those found in nearby rivers. The lake form averages about 2 pounds and is a thickly built, brownish purple fish wholly unlike the bright, brassy blue tinted grayling in Great Bear River. A tributary to the Mackenzie, the river is an outlet near Fort Franklin on the west shore. In the clear swift currents these river fish often make spectacular jumps when hooked.

ARCTIC CHAR

Arctic char (*which see*) are found in clear waters from the rugged coasts of Baffin Island on the east to within a hundred miles of the Mackenzie River on the west. There are two forms, the landlocked or freshwater char, and the anadromous or sea-run char. Even within these forms, there appears to be an appreciable variation in appearance and behavior between fish in various geographic locations. In general, the char is very streamlined in shape. Its back is dark green in color, shading to silvery sides and belly with pinkish spots on the sides. At spawn-

A big lake trout is pumped to the surface of Great Bear Lake. Fish of over 40 pounds are not uncommon, although the average is considerably smaller. Due to cold temperature fish are taken in shallow water

ing time, the males develop a protruding and hooked lower jaw, and the belly and sides may turn a vivid orange-red.

The Coppermine–Cambridge area in the western Arctic is a popular region for char. While fish of 15 pounds are common in some rivers (they have been recorded to over 27 pounds in the Tree River), the usual run is 5–7 pounds. They can be taken with wet flies but gold, silver, or reddish-colored spinning lures are most commonly used. The char is not a spectacular jumper like the Atlantic salmon, but will frequently take off a hundred yards or more of line with one powerful drive and then jump or thrash on the surface in an effort to shake the lure. Sometimes they can be brought in towards the shore apparently tired and docile, but then suddenly turn and run out to sea for a repeat performance.

INCONNU

The inconnu (*which see*) or sheefish exists in areas which are accessible to anglers and it presents a challenge to the sportfishermen who are looking for something different. The inconnu was appropriately named the "unknown" by Alexander Mackenzie's French-Canadian voyageurs, and it is still largely an unfamiliar fish as far as angling is concerned. Numerous sheefish are caught in the Hay River in May or early June after break-up.

They are also common in the Big Buffalo, Talston, and Anderson Rivers. They are a member of the whitefish family and, with their dark back, silvery sides, and large scales, somewhat resemble a large herring. The inconnu averages 8–20 pounds, but specimens weighing over 70 pounds have been reported by commercial fishermen. They are usually taken on spoons or spinning lures.

NORTHERN PIKE AND WALLEYE

The angling interest in big pike which has been generated in the Precambrian lakes of the provinces and the northern states does not exist in the Territories. The abundance and fighting qualities of the lake trout tend to overshadow the pike. However, there are plenty of pike for the fishermen, particularly in the Great Slave Lake area, and to varying degrees throughout the drainage systems of the Mackenzie and Anderson Rivers. The pike generally run 5–15 pounds, but fish in the 30–40-pound class have been reported.

Walleye have been fished mainly by resident anglers. They are common in many of the smaller lakes around Great Slave, but particularly in the Hay River and Yellowknife areas. They are found to a lesser extent in lakes farther north, including Great Bear. Walleye do not generally run to more than ten pounds.

CLOTHING AND EQUIPMENT

The type of clothing required depends to some extent on the location in the Territories. In the Great Slave Lake area during July and August, the mean daily maximum temperature is 70°F. and the mean daily minimum 50°F. Temperatures occasionally go up to 85°F. and down at night to 35°F. A warm windbreaker is essential and a set of long underwear is recommended. Farther north and east the temperatures gradually decline until at Cambridge Bay and Frobisher Bay on the Arctic Islands the mean daily maximum temperature during July and August is about 55°F. and the mean daily minimum is 40°F. The equivalent of late fall hunting clothes is recommended for these areas.

Long sunny days (up to twenty-four hours) with very light rainfall are the general rule throughout the Territorial summer, but a rain coat or some type of waterproof clothing is recommended particularly in the coastal areas.

At the wrong place and the wrong time, mosquitoes and black flies can be sufficiently numerous to drive men indoors. Generally, anglers will find the insect problem no worse than in forest areas farther south; but take along a good supply of insect repellent, heavy trousers and a head net as insurance. Fly fishermen will find the Arctic grayling are their main target, although lake trout can be taken under the right conditions. Many anglers troll for lake trout, even in shallow water, and in some of the smaller lakes in the southern part of the Territories water does warm up enough in summer to force the lake trout down. In these lakes, trolling gear is essential. Generally speaking, casting or spinning gear is satisfactory all-round equipment for the Territories and will take all species.

Anglers should pack an extra rod and reel and a supply of their favorite lures. All standard supplies can be purchased at any of the towns or larger settlements, but some of the camps and best angling locations are quite remote from any source of repair or replacement.

Other equipment and supplies should include sun glasses and skin lotion for protection during the long hours of sunlight, and cameras to record the catch of a lifetime.

TRAVEL

One relatively small corner of the Northwest Territories is accessible by road. The Mackenzie Highway system, leading north from Grimshaw, Alberta (320 road miles northwest of Edmonton) serves communities in the Great Slave Lake area, including Hay River and Yellowknife. There is some good fishing for motorists who bring their own boats or who are prepared to rent boats in one of the communities. However, the best fishing locations are generally some distance from the settlements and some are accessible by only charter aircraft. A major portion of the Territories is served by scheduled airlines, operating out of Edmonton, Alberta, Winnipeg, Manitoba, and Montreal, Quebec. Connections with these carriers is made through any of the transcontinental or transoceanic airlines. —D.S.O'B.

NORWAY The Fjord Country is an outstanding producer of Atlantic salmon. It also offers exceptional sea-trout fishing and a modest amount of inland trout fishing. However, the salmon has been, historically, the most expensive and desirable sport fish in Norway. The considerable cost of the fishing began with the salmon's scarcity. As man commenced polluting rivers in the nineteenth century, the fish gradually disappeared from many watersheds in America and Europe. This intensified the commercial fishery elsewhere, and soon the cost of a day's sport became exorbitant. For many years one couldn't find the rivers behind a forest of family trees in Norway. But with postwar currency restrictions, the torrent of kroner that once poured down the fjords suddenly became a trickle. To pay between $8,000 and $10,000 for a beat on an Olympian river is not unprecedented, but this is far from the over-all picture today. Norway has more salmon rivers than any other country in the world. Naturally, the quality of its 121 registered streams is highly variable, and many watersheds are not suited to fly-fishing at all. There's no shortage of first-class rivers, however, such as the Namsen, Driva, Alta, Passvik, Tana, Surna, Lakselv, and Laerdal. Some of these 121 registered rivers are quite large and have a constant supply of water. This, for example, is the case with the Numedalslagen and the Drammenselv in southeastern Norway. Other rivers, such as the Tengselv, the Lyngdalselv, the Laerdalselv, the Gaula, and the Driva in the south and west, are also registered but do not have so constant a supply of water. The majority of the larger rivers are situated in northern Norway, in the counties of Nordland and Finmark. The principal rivers here are the Namsen, the Tana, and the Alta.

The supply of water in the rivers depends entirely on the amount of precipitation, especially snowfall in winter. A number of the best salmon rivers originate in glaciers 4,000–5,000 feet above sea level. On warm days during the spring and summer the snow and ice melt, and the rivers swell. The smaller rivers are quite dependent on snow which falls in wintertime. If this is below average, the supply of water is very moderate, and the salmon and sea trout can hardly run up. In this case the fish are outside the river mouth. If there has been a heavy snowfall in winter, the rivers swell up in springtime and early

Fishing platforms are a common fixture on the larger Norwegian salmon rivers like the Laerdal

summer, and the fish have a better chance to enter; consequently the angler has better sport. On the whole it can be said that the salmon run up from the end of May and during the whole month of June. This is the best month for the angler. Salmon continue running up in July and August, but in lesser quantity. The sea trout enters the rivers from the middle of July and for all of August and September. After a winter with a minimum of snowfall, smaller rivers are quite dependent on rainfall. These rivers are called "flood rivers." During a heavy rainfall or continuous downpour the rivers swell up in a day or two. All the fish waiting in the fjord and outside the river mouth will run up.

Probably the easiest way to arrange a maiden trip is through the *Norges Elveigarlag* (an association of the Norwegian salmon river owners) at *C. Sundtsgate 1, Bergen*. This association will assist in providing information and also give advice in regard to leases. The fishing is not necessarily expensive. By careful shopping the angler can often obtain salmon fishing at nominal cost.

ALTA RIVER

The Alta River in Arctic Norway is rated as the finest salmon river in the world. Rising in the plateau barrens above Karasjok in Lapland the Alta flows through a forested valley toward the Altafjord, only a hundred miles south of the North Cape. Regular daily air service connects Oslo with Alta, and the fishing accommodations are along the river. *Mytravel* controls the arrangements for fishing the Alta, and occasional beats are available on a weekly basis. Prices are expensive and vary considerably with the specific beats and seasons, but fishing this almost legendary salmon river is an experience no dedicated salmon angler can afford to miss.

The people of the village of Alta celebrate Midsummer's Eve at midnight on June 23 each year. Everyone participates—men, women and children. Most of them preselect camp spots along the river, for public fishing is permitted and they are free to fish for salmon from the banks until midnight that day. They view this occasion, the day the sun never sets, as being second only to Christmas in importance. At midnight all public fishing ceases, for the 300 land owners along the river have formed "The River Company" which leases the river for the next five weeks, and only the lessee and its clients can fish.

The fishing is exceptional. Skilled salmon anglers often kill as many as ten salmon averaging 27 pounds in a single night. Alta regulars sleep through the day and fish during the eight-hour twilight of the Midnight Sun. The flow in the Alta River is heavy even in July. To get a fly deep and to attract large salmon requires wet patterns such as the Dusty Miller, Red Abbey, Black Dose, Jock Scott, Silver Rat, and Rusty Rat in sizes from 3/0 to 6/0; local preference is for double hooks in 5/0 and 6/0. A heavy sinking line (No. 11) with 220 yards of 30-pound-test backing is standard. Leaders testing 30 to 40 pounds are preferred. Traditional fly rods are two-handed 13-footers but single-handed 9- and 9½-footers are now in fashion. Fishing on the Alta is done from narrow 20- to 22-foot-long boats with substantial freeboard; they are quite stable in rough water and are maneuvered by a man operating a stern outboard motor and a "rower"

who sits in the bow. The fishing is accomplished by slow drifting from the head of the pool to the tail. The angler, sitting amidship, casts quartering down on the fast water side allowing the fly to swing directly ahead of the boat. Thirty- to 40-pound salmon are not uncommon. The record Alta salmon weighed 61 pounds and was killed by the Earl of Dudley in 1951. Such fly-fishing makes the Alta a unique salmon river.

AURLAND RIVER

The Aurland River is situated on the Sognefjord, a short drive from Flaam which is connected with Oslo and Bergen by rail. Aurland can also be reached by car from Oslo or Bergen on the new mountain road from Laerdal to Aurland. There are also excellent fjord steamer connections to the various villages on Sognefjord. The Aurland is probably one of Norway's most beautiful rivers and is famous for its fine run of sea trout. The river also holds a good number of salmon. Sea trout are usually caught on dry flies, and are considered even better sport than salmon by many anglers since light tackle can be used. Sea trout from 12 to 18 pounds are caught every year, and the average is around 6 pounds. Best salmon season is from mid-June to mid-July and top sea trout season from mid-July to the end of August.

Accommodations can be arranged at Flaam, the Frethelm Tourist Hotel, which is situated 20 minutes drive from the river. This is one of Norway's most charming fjord hotels.

DRIVA RIVER

The Driva rises high in the barren Dovrefjell plateau, among the highest mountains in Norway, and flows north through one of the most beautiful valleys in Europe until it reaches the fjord at Sunndalsøra. Its pastoral farmsteads and emerald-green currents are enclosed in a high-walled valley, threaded with countless waterfalls tumbling more than a thousand feet from the snowfields and glaciers to the valley floor. The setting is spectacular.

The Driva lies about two hundred miles north of Oslo, with excellent train service to Oppdal and transfer by chauffeur-driven car the last 40 miles to the Grand Hotel in Sunndalsøra. The beats include several charming fishing huts along the river, and encompass the Hoven and Hol leases which are considered the best stretches. Some boat fishing is done on the larger pools, using small prams designed for such work, but other pools offer excellent wading and bank-casting.

Driva salmon average about 18 pounds and the sea trout about 3 pounds. Fly fishing becomes good after mid-July, and the sea trout begin arriving later. The record salmon for the river is 57 pounds, and its reputation places it among the ten best rivers in Norway.

FLAAM RIVER

A relatively small Norwegian salmon stream, the Flaam has its source in the Storskavlen glaciers, about 200 miles northwest of Oslo in the mountains of the Sognefjord. This tranquil valley has picturesque villages, farms and waterfalls, and its crystalline pools hold salmon in about three miles of water between the fjord at Flaam and the Gilja waterfall upstream. The current is relatively smooth, since the river drops less than 200 feet between the waterfall and its mouth, but it is surprisingly swift.

Flaam is the terminal point of excellent rail service from Oslo, and much of its charm lies in its isolation from outside roads. Charming fjord steamers also serve Flaam from several villages on the Sognefjord. The *Mytravel* lease includes the entire three miles of river, with bankcasting and some wading throughout. There are nine pools in this reach of water, as well as a number of small holding-places at various levels of water.

The salmon run a little smaller than those of most Norwegian rivers, averaging about 14 pounds. There are also numbers of grilse and sea trout arriving after the middle of July.

Salmon of over 30 pounds are possible. A fish weighing 32 pounds was caught on the dry fly in 1968 by John R. Martin of New York using a single-handed 9-foot rod. The visitor cannot expect the same number of salmon on the Flaam as are killed on larger, more costly rivers elsewhere in Norway but it flows among some of the most spectacular mountains in Norway, and its charming Frethelm is one of the most pleasant country hotels in Europe. Fishing its pools is an angling experience of tranquility and comfort, in a high-walled valley almost unspoiled by civilization.

LAERDAL RIVER

One of the best salmon rivers in Norway, the Laerdal is approximately 50 miles long, of which there are about 16 miles of salmon and seatrout water below an impassable falls. The river flows into Sognefjord, Norway's longest fjord, at the village of Laerdal. Nearly all fishing takes place from the banks or from specially constructed platforms built over the water. A few beats can be waded. No boats are used. The main road follows the river, and every pool is accessible by car. Visitors to the Laerdal travel by ferry steamer from Bergen to Laerdal in one day, or from Oslo by rail to Fagernes and then by bus to Laerdal (217 miles). Accommodations are available at Lindstrøm's Hotel in Laerdal.

Laerdal salmon run 20–25 pounds. Fish of over 40 pounds are taken each season. The sea trout (migratory brown trout) range from 8–15 pounds, but individual fish of over 20 pounds are caught.

The Lindstrøm Hotel dominates the village of Laerdal. As pine in functional design has become Early American, the well-built houses and the hotel, which reflect industry and thrift, might be called Early Norwegian. The main street is bisected here and there by forlorn little rivulets that come weeping down from the steep mountainside to seek their parent river. Lindstrøm's has been famous since before the turn of the century. This imperial playpen has been host to all of the crowned heads in Europe bent on catching salmon, the more successful anglers being celebrated by wood carvings and painted outlines of their prize catches which adorn the walls of the inn. Moldebo Lodge is also good for some of its Laerdal fishing.

The salmon fishing commences at the end of May in the lower Laerdal (from the fjord to Vold). The fish usually arrive in the mid-Laerdal about the second week in June (from Vold to Bjorkum). From the beginning of July the salmon are in the upper Laerdal (Bjorkum to Husum Falls). The season closes in the first or second week of September.

Although many fish are caught on spoons by casting from the bank, the Laerdal offers excellent fly-fishing, not only for the salmon but beginning in mid-July for sea trout. Dry-fly-fishing for sea trout is very popular on this stream. The best sea-trout fishing is from the river mouth up to Mo Beat below the Honjum rapids. The best time is after 10 A.M. and preferably when the sun is on the water. In spite of heavy caddis hatches at dusk, there is no evening rise of sea trout.

It is difficult to obtain fishing rights on the Laerdal. Anglers come from all over the world to fish this stream. The beats are usually hired a year in advance, and many are taken under long-term leases. However, many are also sublet for short periods of time and inquiries should be directed to the Lindstrøm Hotel or to the *Norges Elveigarlag*.

MALANGSFOSSEN

This is considered the finest single salmon pool in the world. It is almost 250 miles north of the Arctic Circle in a valley of dense pines and spectacular mountains. Its excellence stems from the size of the river and its thundering waterfall, which churns through 500 yards of broken boulders and mossy ledges until it has dropped almost 75 feet into the pool. The falls block the entire spawning run of a major arctic watershed for almost two months. Sometimes thousands of salmon, darkening after weeks in the river and others still sea-bright and fresh, lie waiting in its tumbling currents until the right water level enables them to ascend the ladder in the falls; this usually occurs in early July.

The Malangsfoss lies only thirty minutes southeast of the airfield at Bardufoss, with daily five-hour connecting flights to Oslo. *Mytravel's* lodge is located in a pleasant meadow surrounded with silver birches, sited on a quiet bend of the Bardufoss river, since the roar of the Malangsfoss waterfall itself makes sleep difficult. The pool itself measures almost 300 yards in diameter, shaped like a gargantuan bottle with the waterfall in its narrow throat. The principal current-tongue churns deep into the maelstrom of whirlpools and white water at the head before sweeping almost 200 yards down the granite ledges across the pool. Strong reverse currents sweep back along the rocky fishing beaches toward the base of the falls, and the river is powerful enough so that salmon are found facing reverse currents and eddies as well as the river itself. The spreading tail shallows divide at a downstream island, widening the river to almost 400 yards in places. Depending on the river level, there is ample fishing room for two to three boats on this tremendous pool.

The fishing at Malangsfossen is unique in terms of a single pool, since about forty salmon averaging 30 to 40 pounds, are killed each summer, and the pool record is 57 pounds. Its depth and turbulence make fly fishing difficult until late July, and most of the fishing is done with an assortment of spoons and Devon minnows. Some bankcasting and wading is possible, but the best fishing is from boats. Some additional bank-casting and wading is available on the beats below the pool. Hip-length waders are recommended, since the fish are landed on the rocky beach after hooking them from the boats.

SULDALSLAGEN RIVER

Also known as the Sand River, this beautiful stream is in Rogaland, about 200 miles southwest of Oslo, and its salmon run upriver about 15 miles between the Suldalsvatn lake and its mouth in the Saudafjord above Stavanger. Its valley varies between narrow gorges, where the river tumbles in white water chutes, to timbered basins where it flows past farms and small villages. Sand is located at its mouth on the fjord, and is a typical coastal settlement that once built sailing ships and now draws its livelihood from fishing and forestry.

British anglers have fished the river since 1884, when its late summer run became known in the United Kingdom and dedicated anglers could travel to Sand when their own fishing slackened in midsummer. Suldalslagen was considered one of the best rivers in the world until about 1925, when its extensive spawning run and the high average weight of the salmon on the river became attractive to commercial fishing interests and the fish were decimated.

Sport fishermen ended this period of exploitation, when all netting and trapping ended and the river was restored. These reforms have brought the river back considerably in the past ten years, until its salmon now average about 25 pounds and the river record of 64 pounds was made in recent years. The salmon run peaks in August and September, making it a late river for Norway. The Sand is reached via daily air service to Stavanger and hydrofoil-boat connections between Stavanger and the village of Sand. There is both boat fishing in the larger pools and bank-casting in other places. Your chances here are excellent for fish above 40 pounds.

TACKLE

Norwegian salmon rivers are swift and their fish average close to 20 pounds, with fish between 30 and 40 pounds in good numbers. Strong tackle is advisable in Norway, although anglers experienced with big salmon on Canadian rivers can use single-handed rods of 8½ and 9½ feet. Longer two-handed rods between 10½ and 13½ feet are more commonly used in Norway, since there is considerable use for flies larger than 3/0. Sinking lines are required through most of the Norwegian season, although floating lines are useful in shallow holding-lies later in the summer. Fly-reels should be sturdy, provide firm drag mechanisms, and have at least 200 yards of 20-pound backing line. Such flies as the Jock Scott, Silver Grey, Blue Charm, Black Doctor, Thunder and Lightning, and Dusty Miller are in widespread use on Norwegian rivers, and an assortment between sizes 4/0 and 5/0 is advisable. Spoon fishermen will find light trolling rods valuable, fitted with heavy-duty casting reels and 30-pound line. Medium to heavy spinning gear is also useful. Spoons and Devon minnows and other lures are available throughout Norway, and the fisherman should perhaps purchase such equipment to meet local conditions. There are well-stocked tackle shops in Oslo, Bergen, and Trondheim.

—A.J.McC.

The Driva River can be fished from the bank or by wading. This is a great stream for the fly fisherman

NOVA SCOTIA The province of Nova Scotia, which includes the island of Cape Breton as well as numerous smaller islands, is about 374 miles long, lying on a southwest to northeast axis, and about 80 miles in width. It is connected to mainland North America by the 15-mile-wide Isthmus of Chignecto. The country is undulating and heavily wooded, except in the wide, fertile valleys. The Annapolis Valley (famous for apples and strawberries) is bounded on the north and south by two ridges 850 feet high. In Cape Breton all the valleys are fertile, the highest peak in the beautiful Highlands rising to 1,747 feet. The climate is never too hot nor too cold. The mean annual range for the entire province is 42.8°F., July and August being the warmest months with a mean annual temperature of 62°F. In most years rainfall is adequate, the average annual for all regions being 46.1 inches.

Historically, more than nine centuries ago, the Norsemen landed on this peninsula and named it Markland. The first attempt at permanent settlement was made by the French in 1605, to be followed by the British in 1621. The abundance of salmon was one of the reasons for the early settlers' locating their town or village sites near the mouths of rivers. The Indians of the province used the salmon but took only a very small portion of this resource as and when required.

Nova Scotia is not troubled with overindustrialization. Apart from coal mines in Cape Breton and pulp and paper mills in western Cape Breton and southwestern Nova Scotia, there is no industrial disturbance of the land. Most damage to the rivers has been done by power dams, which have ruined some of the best fishing streams in the province of Nova Scotia. Unfortunately nothing can now be done to remedy this situation.

The Margaree River of Nova Scotia is one of the top salmon and salter streams in the province

Approximately one-third of Nova Scotia is freshwater. There are over 2,500 lakes and ponds and 550 rivers, brooks, and streams. Not all are fishable. There are, however, 516 trout lakes either adjacent to or within reach of roads, and 314 salmon and trout streams. Though the province always had many trout fishermen, the interest in salmon fishing is of fairly recent date. This explains why records of annual salmon catches have only been kept in recent years. Records have been maintained for seventy-eight streams, and less than half of these yield consistent catches of any number of salmon.

SALMON FISHING

Though only thirty-four rivers are listed as angling streams, almost every river in the province has a run of salmon entering it during the fall when water conditions are suitable. Even among the angling rivers, the fall run is larger than early migrations into the streams. In the late-run rivers the angling season is closed by the time these salmon move into the streams. This anomalous situation stems from the fact that the control over the freshwater fishing rests with the federal authorities. Nova Scotia being a poor province with a small population of 750,000 could not afford to maintain its rivers and streams. So the expense of taking care of the fish life was handed over to the federal government. The problem then arose of the province owning the banks of the streams, and the federal authorities the river, river bed, and fish. Fishing regulations were laid down without too much regard for or knowledge of local conditions. Seasons were decided by area instead of by watersheds and run of fish.

The growing population and increasing pressure of fishermen has had a serious effect on the salmon population. In the 1930's the number of salmon anglers, native and nonresident alike, was very small. Protection regulations were sketchy, and the few protection officers had a large area to travel and control. Though more conservation regulations were introduced and more fishery officers appointed, these measures did not keep apace with the

growing interest in salmon fishing; consequently the salmon stock depleted seriously.

In 1962, a group of public-spirited fly-fishermen formed the Nova Scotia Salmon Anglers Association, the purpose of which was to concentrate on improving the salmon streams in the province. Response from the anglers was more than encouraging, and conservation measures, as suggested to the federal authorities by the association, have been put into practice. The association took as their guideline a document, prepared in 1951 for the parent body, The Atlantic Salmon Angling Association with headquarters in Montreal, by Mr. W. J. H. Menzies. Mr. Menzies toured Newfoundland, Quebec, New Brunswick, and Nova Scotia, dividing his time between the net and rod fishing. The result was a comprehensive report on the position of the Atlantic salmon fisheries of Canada, known as Document 17.

One of the first aims of the Nova Scotia Salmon Anglers Association was to give protection to every possible salmon water. This they did by getting a local team of one chairman, plus a committee of six, formed for each river; each committee advises the parent body what that stream requires in the way of water control, stocking, protection, and antipollution care. Salmon angling depends on two basic things—water and fish. Due to the short rivers and the high runoff, average Nova Scotia salmon rivers can be dry rock piles during July and August. Although western rivers are open in April, due to ice and snow, most rivers are not fishable until May. The best salmon rivers are the Medway and the LaHave, which produce in April and early May. Mid May to mid June, the Medway, LaHave, Musquodoboit, and St. Mary's are good bets, together with the West River Sheet Harbor, Moser, Ecum Secum, Quoddy, Ingram, Gold, and East rivers. Later on in the season, the Margaree, which does not close until October 15, is the best late river producing large fish. Unless the season is wet and rainy, the months of July and August are not to be recommended for salmon fishing. A letter to the Secretary of the Nova Scotia Salmon Anglers Association will give the latest report on the state of the rivers and size of catch.

TROUT FISHING

The Nova Scotia fishing season begins with sea-trout in the spring (about mid April) which appear in literally all the river mouths and reach their peak of abundance in June. The migration becomes progressively later as you travel from west to east, with the latest runs entering at Cape Breton. Inland trout fishing is also productive. Generally speaking the best time is from opening day till mid June and again at the end of the season. During July and August the level of the lakes tends to drop, the water temperature to rise, and the brooks run dry. Trout can be found in all rivers, brooks, and lakes. The waters near the highway are most heavily fished because of easy access. However, if a nonresident angler enters the woods to fish a more remote lake, he must be accompanied by a registered guide. A list of these guides is available at all tourist bureaus.

Five lakes have been stocked with rainbow trout—Giants Lake, Sunken Lake, Rumsey Lake, Lavers Lake, and Clear Water Lake. Giants Lake in Guysboro County, probably holds the largest fish—3-4 pounders. Sunken

Lake in Kings County is overfished. Rumsey Lake in Annapolis County is a spring-fed lake eight hundred feet up on the North Mountain. It is heavily fished in July, but after that produces well from late August through October. The last two weeks of September till the close of the season are most productive. The dry fly produces the largest fish; the wet fly is second best. Late in the season trolling is not generally too productive.

Brown trout were introduced in Nova Scotia successfully in 1933. They flourish in this province, and have been known to reach a weight of 11 pounds in freshwater and to produce even heavier sea-run individuals. Brown trout are more tolerant of high temperature, mild pollution, and a variety of spawning conditions than are brook trout and therefore provide fishing in waters that would otherwise lack trout. They take small dry flies, bait, and spinning lures. Late evening is usually the time when angling for them is at its best. Brown trout may be taken in Milford Haven and Salmon Rivers, Guysboro County; Cornwallis River, Kings County; East River, Sheet Harbour, Halifax County; Mersey River, Queens County; Salmon River, Yarmouth County; and Kilkenny Lake, Cape Breton County.

Landlocked salmon are found in numbers in one place only in Nova Scotia, in Shubenacadie Grand Lake in Halifax County. Locally these fish are erroneously referred to as grayling. Ice out and the end of season are the best times for the larger fish. The season runs from April 15 until September 15. Grand Lake is a very large body of water, and fishing is done mainly by trolling lures, such as large streamer flies or spoons.

Nova Scotia's salmon are seldom large, but even small fish on a small stream like the Ecum Secum are prized

SMALLMOUTH BASS

Smallmouth bass is another fish introduced into Nova Scotia. Several lakes were stocked some years ago and, due to lack of local interest, were not fished, giving the fish a chance to grow. Elliott Lake in Annapolis County has produced smallmouth bass 5–9 pounds. Bucktails and streamer flies are often used. The smaller, deep-going plugs and lures, bass fly spinners, and, in early morning and evening, surface lures are also used. Evening and late evening is the best time. The principal waters in Nova Scotia are Dartmouth Lake, Halifax County; Blair Lake, Cumberland County; Lily Lake, Halifax County; Victoria Lake, Queens County; and Elliott Lake, Annapolis County.

STRIPED BASS

One of the most prolific gamefish during the summer months is the striped bass, which occurs at the river mouths and for some distance upstream. The fishery consists primarily of school bass in the 5–7-pound class, with an occasional 12–15 pounder in the day's bag. At this northern extremity of the squidhound's range, a 25-pound striper is unique. However, most of the angling occurs in rivers where the light-tackle addict can thoroughly enjoy himself with fly and plug.

On the coast of Nova Scotia striped bass are not generally distributed but are inclined to congregate in certain preferred areas. These are of two kind—estuaries entering Bay of Fundy waters and Northumberland Strait, and openwaters beside certain sandy beaches. Good striper fishing is to be found in the lower reaches of the Bear, Annapolis, Gaspereau, Shubenacadie, Stewiacke, Avon, Waugh, Bass, Parrsboro, Shinimicas, Philip, Wallace, and Tidnish rivers. Surf-casting and pier-fishing produce good sport along the shores of Minas Basin and Cobequid Bay and on the Nova Scotia shore of Northumberland Strait. As an exception, boat and shore fishing is most profitable in the freshwater of Shubenacadie Grand Lake, a few miles from Halifax. The gear used and the manner of fishing for stripers vary greatly from place to place. To a large extent these variations reflect local experience with these bass and their habits and preferences. It is a good plan to make contact with a reliable guide. The best time to fish is the last hour to full tide; also about 15 minutes after the turn of the tide.

SALTWATER FISHING

Nova Scotia, being almost surrounded by the Atlantic Ocean and having a coastline of almost 5,000 miles, which is studded with islands on its west, south, and eastern shores, provides fishing grounds that would take a lifetime to explore. Fish of all kinds abound in these waters from giant bluefin and broadbill swordfish to halibut, cod, hake, haddock and pollock. The light-tackle angler will find that pollock are fine gamefish. School pollock run into every bay and harbor, and a few miles offshore they run up to 35 pounds.

Saltwater angling is best from July on, and registered charter boats, fully equipped and captained by qualified masters, under government supervision, are available all around the coast. A letter to the Nova Scotia Tourist Bureau, Halifax, will produce maps, lists of shore stations, and guides, who have fully registered boats available.

For years an international Tuna Cup Match was held annually at Wedgport, Nova Scotia. Angling teams from various nations competed here for the Alton B. Sharp trophy. Due to the increased interest in saltwater fishing, more fishermen have hooked tuna and caught them in other locations. Angling has now developed not only at Wedgport but at such Nova Scotia points as Cape St. Mary, Digby County; Shelburne and Jordan Bay, Shelburne County; Junt's Point and Liverpool, Queens County; East Chester, Lunenburg County; and Ingonish, Victoria County. —W.G.

NOVA SCOTIA SALMON A market name for the Atlantic salmon, usually when sold in smoked form. The product may or may not originate in Nova Scotia.

NUN BUOY A buoy tapered at each end. A red nun buoy indicates the starboard side of the channel when moving upstream and away from the sea.

NURSE SHARK *Ginglymostoma cirratum* This distinctive species is readily recognized by the combination of the two dorsal fins which are about equal in size (*see also* lemon shark), the long barbel at the front of each nostril, and the brown to yellow coloration with dark, evenly spaced spots when young. The caudal fin is relatively long, and the fins, generally, are large and rounded in comparison to other Atlantic sharks. The eye is very small, and the snout is somewhat blunt and rounded. It reaches a length of 14 feet. An 8½-foot fish weighs about 330–370 pounds.

This widespread species occurs in tropical and subtropical waters of the Atlantic. In the eastern Atlantic it is found off Africa, and in the western Atlantic it is known from Brazil to Rhode Island and throughout the Gulf of Mexico and the Caribbean Sea. In the eastern Pacific, it is known from the Gulf of California to Ecuador.

LIFE HISTORY

A shallow-water species, the nurse shark is a reef inhabitant often found resting in caves or under shallow ledges. It may enter mangrove channels as well, occurring either solitarily or in groups. A sluggish species, it is often the target of divers who attempt to ride it or to grasp its tail; yet it can be extremely voracious, and despite its relatively feeble teeth, it has inflicted painful bites on persons molesting it.

It feeds predominantly on squids, shrimps, crabs, lobsters, and sea urchins. Breeding occurs in shallow water, but almost nothing is known on the details of the period of gestation or the time of birth.

ANGLING VALUE

The nurse shark is often caught by anglers, but its comparatively sluggish habits do not make it much sought for even by shark fishermen. Its flesh, particularly the fins, is reported to be excellent. —D.dS.

NYLON A generic term for any long-chain, synthetic polymeric amide which has recurring amide groups as an integral part of the main polymer chain, and which is capable of being formed into a filament in which the structural elements are oriented in the direction of the axis.

The resins are placed in an autoclave at a high temperature. Being forced out under pressure through small holes in a special metal plate, stretched to a predetermined amount, it quickly solidifies in a cooling medium. The approximate tensile strength of nylon is 70,000–100,000 pounds per square inch of cross section, or as strong as mild steel.

Monofilaments may have an elongation before rupture of 15–30 percent dry, and 20–35 percent wet. For practical purposes nylon is waterproof, but actually it is slightly hygroscopic in that it will absorb about 3–12 percent water in weight (depending on the type of nylon), with a slight loss of its tensile strength, usually not over 10 percent. The specific gravity is 1.08–1.15.

—A.J.McC.

NYMPH A subaqueous insect, the larva of the Neuroptera or nerved-winged flies, of which the Ephemeridae are of prime interest to anglers. In a strict sense, the immature ephemerids are called larvae and only become nymphs when their rudimentary wings become visible. Since the difference in appearance between the two stages of the insect's life cycle is slight, anglers find it more convenient to use the term "nymph" to designate all the subaqueous stages of the ephemerids, as well as the larvae of certain other insect species. Thus, nymph in its broadest sense, as applied to angling in the form of an artificial fly, may also encompass the larva of the caddisfly, dragonfly, cranefly, and other aquatic insects. To the angler, nymph fishing implies a specialized method

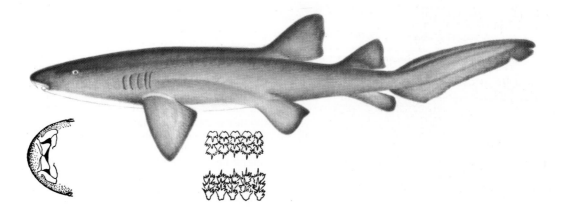

Nurse Shark (teeth of upper jaw, *top*, lower jaw, *bottom*)

rather than an orderly classification. It is most often applied to trout fishing, but may be used for other game-fish.

NYMPH-FISHING

Nymph-fishing is acknowledged to be the most difficult phase of the fly-rod art. Yet, with some degree of casting skill and careful attention to details, it quickly becomes a reliable method of catching trout on artificials. The game originated in England (see Skues, G.E.M.) at a much later date than either the wet or dry fly, and when properly understood, it offers many opportunities which the older methods cannot meet. Natural nymphs are providentially abundant at all seasons of the year, and regardless of weather conditions one can usually take enough fish to make the day successful. Some wet flies are really nymph imitations, and undoubtedly a great percentage of trout caught on sunk patterns are nymphing fish who made their error in the pursuit of subaquatic food. The difference between the wet-fly method and the nymph is arbitrary, but broadly speaking the latter eliminates patterns and techniques that would apply to the imitation of noninsect forms such as fry or shrimp.

Seasonal Picture There is a great deal to be said for the study of entomology, whether it be a formal university course or simply reading a few good books on it at home. It's one of many subjects that can broaden your knowledge of the outdoors. The angler, however, needs no more than working familiarity with trout-hunted insects; he should be able to identify the most important groups and have a capsule idea of their life cycles. He should know which species are most abundant in his area and their expected period of emergence. Four of the groups are wholly aquatic, and it's particularly pertinent to know the size and color of their nymphs and larvae. Although mayflies are the most important insect as far as the dry-fly angler is concerned (with regional variations of course), the underwater larder is more complex. The general picture is seasonal with mayfly nymphs, caddis larvae, stonefly nymphs, and the nymphs of dragon-and damsel-flies dominating at certain periods. However, their very abundance permits the angler a considerable latitude in his choice of artificials. The complete cycle of a mayfly, for example, from the time the nymph hatches from its egg until it emerges from the water as a winged adult, can require two years. Thus, the trout's larder is always full, and proof of that can be found on any stream-bottom rock. Turn it over, and you will discover speckled-brown or amber-colored nymphs clinging to the underside. They have a flattened contour, which, together with their strong clawed legs, enables them to hold their position in a strong current. As the weather warms, you will also find the empty shucks of skins of these same nymphs adhering to sun-dried rocks. When ready to emerge many species complete their metamorphosis by crawling atop the stones to shed. On insect-rich rivers the domes of boulders might literally be encrusted with shucks. All nymphs do not hatch in the same way, and a great many of them live in sand, mud, and silt. Although they are similar in form, nymphs are not always the same color and size. As a matter of fact, there are hundreds of different larvae which are common to American rivers. However, this is something of an advantage because an artfully tied imitation is seldom questioned by a hungry trout. It's not unusual to catch a fish with an artificial mayfly pattern when its stomach contents reveal that it has been gorging on caddis larvae. In brief, there is more to be said for the method than for any preoccupation with what to use. Some patterns are superior to others, but, in general, any of the standards will work. Most important is your ability to present the fly properly and to use suitable tackle.

Methods of Fishing the Nymph Trout feed very little during the winter months, but rising temperatures in the spring whet their dulled appetites for the abundance of nymph life that flourished even while snow banked the hemlocks. In the beginning of the season, when April rivers are still cold and before the hatches have started, an artificial nymph should be handled quite differently from the way it is fished later on. The fly must be presented at the trout's level, which in these early days is near bottom. You can't really fish too slow or too deep. The same condition may hold true of the hottest days in summer, when trout are gathered at the spring holes. By late August, on Eastern rivers, the currents grow quite stale; a few rings of dirty foam float apathetically around the eddies. Downstream fishing is often hopeless. Trout always lie facing the flow, and you can therefore approach them more closely from behind. The nymph also drifts more naturally when fished upstream. The basic attack in August is to work upriver with a long, 5X leader and a small nymph, keeping it as close to the bottom as possible. It's all "fine and far-off" fishing with drag-free drifts and careful wading. The fish strike very gently and one must watch the water and any visible part of line or leader for the slightest movement that indicates a strike. Hooking a trout on the dry fly is easy by comparison. With floaters, the chief difficulty is striking too fast. Nymphs on the other hand are out of sight, and you must acquire an almost automatic reflex to tighten at just the right instant. And there's the additional hazard of breaking off if the strike is made too forcefully. But with experience you will find yourself hooking fish without even thinking about it.

Casting upstream is usually the most effective way to handle a nymph. You must put the artificial in places where trout are likely to feed and let the current carry it along at a natural pace. As with the dry fly, you should raise your rod slightly and strip line by hand to keep the nymph free of drag. Sometimes the best level to work is directly in the surface; there are periods when fish station themselves near the top to grab nymphs which are drifting with the current. On other occasions you'll find most of the trout foraging a few feet down, or, as it so often happens on opening day, they'll be directly on the bottom. If the river is very heavy and you can't face the current, then you can fish downstream by casting a slack line and allowing the nymph to sink deep as it drifts below your position. Don't recast immediately. Give the nymph a few twitches when it swings to a stop. There are runs and pools where you can take trout in both directions and other places where you must face one way to get strikes. But the importance of fishing a nymph at the correct depth cannot be over-emphasized.

Sinking Line versus Floating Line To reach a wide range of depths many nymph specialists carry an extra reel spooled with a sinking-type fly line. Although the more commonly used floating type is adequate to most stream problems, in water that is very deep or very swift it's almost impossible to work a nymph correctly unless the trout are actively feeding near the surface. There are a number of nicely balanced and smoothly finished lines of this type on the market which eliminate the need for split shot to pull a fly under. Depending on the height of the stream, either cast up or down; if the current is normal or at summer level, work up; but if it's high, work down. The trout may hold along submerged ledges 10–12 feet or more in depth. The problem in catching fish here is to get the nymph right on the bottom. To accomplish this, make a slack cast up and across the stream; then by shaking out more footage through the guides, the line sinks quickly as it swings downstream. You shouldn't miss too many trout this way. In deep, heavy water fish take the nymph solidly, and it often happens that they hook themselves against the pull of the line.

In contrast, there are times when the artificial nymph must be fished at the surface. For 1–2 years, a mayfly nymph is subaqueous, but in the last stage of its existence it develops a hump on the part that would correspond to shoulders; this is the growing wings, which fly tiers refer to as the wing pad. When ready to emerge, the nymph rises to the surface, and, while floating downstream, its nymphal shell is split and shucked off. The shriveled-looking insect that appears from the shell is a subimago, which anglers call the dun. Although the dun is at first unable to fly, its wings soon dry and become strong enough to carry the mayfly off to find shelter along the streamside. There it awaits its next metamorphosis to the imago. Two stages in this cycle that are of particular interest to the trout are when the nymph is floating help-lessly in the surface, and of course, when the duns hatch. The latter is a dry-fly problem. The former, however, is a nymphing situation. During the period preceding a hatch, trout take positions in the current where they can expect an abundance of nymphs, and without moving more than a few feet each fish commences to gorge. In quiet runs, trout are often seen balanced on their fins just below the surface, turning left and right, as they sip their food. Under these conditions, a floating-type line is a necessity, and it's often advantageous to grease all but the last few feet of your leader to keep the nymph just under or in the surface film.

Caddis Larvae Although Skues was concerned strictly with the larval mayfly on his lush chalk streams, the game of nymphing has come to encompass a number of insect species on American rivers.

Next to the mayfly nymph, the caddis larvae are very important. As a subaquatic food the caddis probably surpasses the mayfly in many Eastern rivers where the Ephemeridae are seasonally scarce. Although there is no actual nymph stage in the development of a caddisfly (the insect has a complete metamorphosis from egg to larva and pupa to adult), the larva is taken greedily by the trout from the stream bottom even while wrapped in its case. The pupa is eaten just before a hatch. As in the mayfly cycle, some caddis pupae have a vulnerable period when they drift in the surface. So from the angler's point of view he is imitating a caddis "nymph." The presence of these little grubs in any stream is easily established. Caddis are the house builders, whose tiny sand, pebble, and twig cases are visible on the rocks. Some are cemented in place by the larvae, and others are portable; by means of strong hooks in its tail the grub

can drag its home about. But trout often eat the occupant, house and all. This accounts for the sticks and pebbles so often found in fish stomachs. Brook trout are especially inclined to gorge on caddis larvae. There are many good imitations available in white, cream, green, and dirty gray which are the common colors of the naturals.

Stonefly Nymph The stonefly nymph is next in importance. It's generally similar to the mayfly in form and color but somewhat larger in size. Even old cannibal browns are inclined to get careless when stoneflies are abundant, and during a hatch they take the adult voraciously. However, the significant emergences occur on relatively few Midwestern, Western, and Far Northern rivers. In the Eastern United States one does not find anything resembling these cloudlike "salmon" or "willow" fly hatches which create such remarkable angling. But stonefly nymphs are numerous in rocky, fastwater rivers throughout this range and many good patterns are dressed to imitate them, such as Dark Stonefly, Golden Stonefly, Little Yellow Stonefly, Early Brown Stonefly, Large Stonefly, and March Brown. Generally speaking, and especially in the spring season, stonefly nymphs are most effective when fished close to the bottom. It is worthwhile to have at least a few artificials tied with weighted bodies. On turbulent rivers the stonefly nymph is usually fished up-and-across the current so that it sinks deep in the flow and swings downstream without drag. Quite often a nymph will be taken by the trout after it has settled to the bottom and left there for several minutes. This is a good technique to use at the heads of large pools where the current breaks.

The artificial nymphs vary in size from No. 4 down to No. 14 (many of the common Nemourids are quite small although they contribute greatly to the trout's food supply in some streams). As a rule the large No. 4 dressings are most effective in heavy rivers such as the Delaware in the East or the Madison in the West. Most stonefly imitations are brown or tan in color, but these nymphs exist in variety and patterns in green, gray, and black with lighter colored undersides, and bright yellow or orange markings are regionally effective. Although the stonefly nymph is most often associated with brown trout fishing it is the dominant food form of brook trout on Gods River in Manitoba and is thought to contribute greatly to the unique growth rate of this population. Nevertheless, the larval stonefly is a universal trout food and imitations ranging from No. 14 to No. 6 in size are very effective.

Midge Larvae Why trout should forage on this tiny wormlike creature when more substantial insect foods are available is a mystery. Winged adults resemble miniature mosquitoes as they swarm over the water during an emergence. Trout will roll, bulge, sip, and flash at the surfacing pupae, seldom more than ¼ inch long and usually much smaller. As with the caddis, we are not dealing with an actual nymph, but rather a stage in an insect's metamorphosis which requires nymphing technique to emulate. The standard artificial is dressed on a No. 18 hook in black, orange, yellow, red, and white with a simple peacock thorax. The whole trick in fishing these tiny flies is to use a gossamer leader of 5X or 6X and present the midge without movement. *See also* Alderflies, Caddisflies, Craneflies, Dragonflies and Damselflies, Fly Fishing, Mayflies, Midge, Stoneflies

—A.J.McC.

O

OAR A long, narrow implement, usually made of wood, and usually used in pairs for manually propelling or rowing a boat through the water. The end that enters the water is flat and wide and is called the blade. The very end of the blade is the tip. The balance of the wooden shaft is rounded, with the other end or handle turned down to a circumference to fit the hand. The fulcrum of the oar, about two-thirds of the distance up from the blade, is frequently covered with leather or some similar material employed to protect the wood from chafing or splintering where it rests and works in row locks. The top edge of the leather is raised by an additional circle of

Oar

leather, rubber, or rope called a preventer and used to keep the oar from slipping out of the row lock.

The design and shape of the blade may vary according to make and region, but the well-balanced oar is a thing of beauty, sensitive to handle, and springy with power, a highly functional tool. The best oars are made of straight-grained ash. The longer the boat, the longer the oars. Spruce and linden are also used. Hollow aluminum oars are available for small boats. The best wooden oars are varnished clear or left unfinished, enabling the purchaser to note immediately any splits or imperfections. Less expensive but often serviceable oars are painted. They cannot claim the superior grade because defects may be hidden under the paint. Unfinished oars may be kept white and clean by rubbing with sand and canvas. Oars should be stowed flat to avoid warp.   —F.M.P.

OARFISH *Regalecus glesne* A seldom seen inhabitant of the dimly lit depths of the open sea. Its large size, bizarre coloration, and striking appearance engender strange roles for the creature in the minds of almost all who behold it.

Because it is said to accompany or announce the beginning of the herring run, to northern Europeans it is the "king of the herring." Oddly enough, Indians of the Northwest Pacific Coast hold a similar belief with regard to a relative of the oarfish, called "king of the salmon" (*Trachipterus rex-salmonorum*). The "king" appears just before the salmon run, and to kill it, say the Indians, means the salmon run will cease.

BLADES ON FIN TIPS

The name oarfish derives from the unusual pelvic fins. These are long and slender, with a bladelike expansion at their tips, thus resembling a pair of oars. The Japanese, however, call the fish "cock of the palace under the sea," in allusion to the crest of long dorsal-fin rays atop the head. These number up to eighteen in a large individual, and can be raised and lowered like a rooster's comb.

The nickname "sea serpent" comes from the elongate body (a 10-foot fish may be only 5 inches deep), the eel-like method of swimming, the enormous size of some individuals (35–40 feet in a complete fish; a 56-foot "sea serpent" found at Orkney, in 1808, was probably an

oarfish), and the flame-red dorsal fin that looks like a fiery mane. Quite a few reports of sea serpents can doubtless be attributed to sightings of the oarfish.

WASHED ASHORE IN FLORIDA

On May 12, 1958, an oarfish was chased ashore by a shark at Pompano Beach, Florida. Its body had been almost completely cut into three pieces. The pieces were taken to the taxidermy studios of Joseph Reese at Fort Lauderdale and there placed under refrigeration until a biologist could examine them. Thus the first adult oarfish from Atlantic coastal waters of North America became available for scientific study.

The remains turned out to be those of a male, which is of interest since most oarfish that have been examined were females. Had the Pompano Beach fish not been injured earlier in life it would probably have measured 10 feet in length. However, almost all captured oarfishes, other than very young ones, lack up to half their bodies, but show signs of healing and regeneration of their old injuries.

The Pompano Beach specimen, which measured just less than 5 feet in length, for example, shows a nicely healed tail. Apparently the oarfish can survive a loss of about half its body to a predator, although, since the stomach occupies almost half the length of the tail, any greater loss would probably prove fatal.

TOO SLY FOR NETS

Very little is known of the life history and habits of the oarfish. The eggs, which are about the size of air-gun pellets, drift in the open sea for some 3 weeks before the ¼-inch larvae are hatched. It is surmised that, owing to its well-developed eyes, brilliant red fins, silvery body, and blue-black polka dots and slashes, and the great reduction in the amount of bone in the skeleton, the adult lives at depths 300–3,000 feet, where there is still sufficient light for vision.

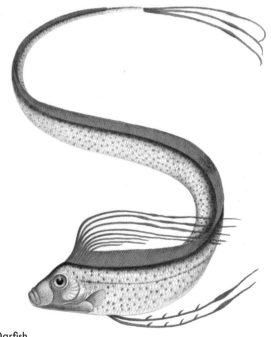

Oarfish

No adult has been taken in an oceanographer's net, presumably because they are too agile to be captured in such a manner. On occasion larvae and juveniles are brought up. The larva feeds on minute crustaceans among the plankton of the sea. The adult favors small, shrimp-like animals, the euphausiids, which occur in enormous numbers in the Deep Scattering Layer. To gather these creatures the oarfish has a large number of long, spiny gillrakers (42–58) which strain the water passing over the gills.

ONLY DEEPSEA FILTER FEEDER

The oarfish is thus an anomaly among deepsea teleosts, or bony fishes, since it is the only one known to be a filter feeder. The others swallow food of large size in comparison with their own bodies and have luminous fishing lures and wicked-looking teeth to obtain their prey.

The oarfish, on the contrary, has a small mouth, lacks teeth, and luminescence has never been observed. It is the longest known teleost fish; marlins and tunas are small when length alone is considered. (Reprinted from *Sea Frontiers*, Vol. 5, No. 2, with permission of the International Oceanographic Foundation.)   —V.W.

OAR LOCKS Old salts and purists will tell you that an oar works in a *row lock*, but that a single oar used as a steering oar or sweep works in an *oar lock*. The distinction seems to be lost in general usage in the United States, where oar lock is frequently used to encompass both meanings. In some types of boats oar locks or row locks are simple, square notches cut in the gunwale or top edge of the transom. One side is sometimes hollowed out to keep the oar from jumping out while being worked. This is called a box oar lock. Another somewhat primitive-type row lock is made of thole pins. These are hard wooden pins set vertically into holes drilled in the gunwales. The oar works between the upright pins, and is held in place by a grommet or endless piece of rope that encircles oar and thole pin to hold the oar in place.

Most row locks are made of brass or galvanized iron shaped in the form of a crutch. The arms of crutch-type row locks are called horns. Metal oar locks swivel in a socket as the rower works, causing less wear and tear on the oar. There are numerous variations in metal locks. Some are permanently screwed to the gunwales with a rigid base, although the open crutch may still swivel with the oar. To avoid loss, nearly all metal row locks have an eye in the base of the pin through which a lanyard should be run and then secured inside the boat. The Davis oar lock, a common-type metal lock, can be

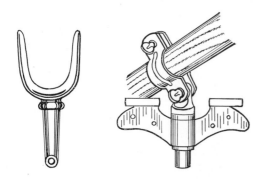

Oar Lock and Canadian Oar Lock

removed by simply lifting it out of its socket and letting it hang down in the boat. It is designed to stay put in an upside down position when not in use, and leaves the gunwale clear for other action. Round-socket or ring oar locks, as the name implies, are simply a circle of iron through which the oar must be passed before the preventers are attached. The design makes it a permanent part of the oar. The oar lock is dropped into the socket when the rower ships the oars ready to work. North River row locks or pin-type locks are also permanently made fast to the oar by means of a metal pin which passes through a hole drilled through the oar. They are frequently used for small boats, dinghies, and the like but are frowned upon as being landlubberly in design. The hole drilled for the pin naturally weakens the oar, and, equally a problem, the oar cannot be rotated or feathered while rowing to account for wind or wave caps that may grab at the flat side of the blade. Row locks are available in angle-plate and side-plate styles that attach inside the gunwales as well as conventional or topside fittings that attach to the surface of the gunwale.

—F.M.P.

OCCIPUT On a fish, the extreme posterior part of the top of its head, or the point at the posterior end of the skull, separating the head from the body. *See also* Anatomy

OCEANIC BONITO *See* Skipjack Tuna
OCEANIC SKIPJACK *See* Skipjack Tuna
OCEANIC WHITETIP SHARK *See* Whitetip Shark
OCEANOGRAPHY The science of the seas. Oceanography consists of the marine aspects of geology, meteorology, chemistry, biology, physics, geophysics, geochemistry, fluid mechanics, and theoretical and applied mathematics. It is an environmental science concerned with all the processes in the ocean and its interrelation with the earth and universe. *See also* Currents, Marine Ecology

OCEAN PERCH *Sebastes marinus* Commonly called rosefish, red perch, and sea perch, the ocean perch is a food rather than game species, taken at great depths by commercial trawlers. In recent years the total landings of ocean perch have surpassed the cod and haddock. The ocean perch is similar to the freshwater perch in general appearance, but the flesh is more strongly flavored. Actually the two are in no way related. Ocean perch are caught at depths of 400–700 feet from the Gulf of Maine to northern Labrador. They are also taken off Iceland and Norway where they are sold as Norway haddock, or red fish. Ocean perch range in color from orange to flame-red and have large, black eyes. Not much is known of their migratory habits, but immense beds of them appear in various parts of the North Atlantic, and in some years as much as 200,000,000 pounds are caught by American trawlers. Ocean perch grow very slowly, maturing at about 10 years of age, but a great many 20-year-olds appear in commercial landings. It has been known to reach 27 years of age. They average about one pound, and a 5-pounder is considered large.

The ocean perch is the only Atlantic member of the rockfish (*which see*) group, although its relatives, the scorpionfishes, are predominantly Atlantic species. The rockfish and scorpionfishes comprise the family Scorpaenidae. The ocean perch is distinguished by 14–15 spines and 13 softrays in the dorsal fin; 3 spines and 7

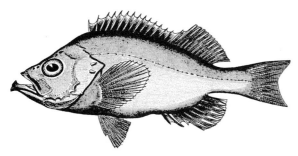

Ocean Perch

softrays in the anal fin; red body color; black eyes; irregular dusky patches on the back; a dusky patch on the gill cover. Length to three feet.

The female ocean perch develops mature eggs (37,000–350,000) by February, when fertilization takes place. Subsequently the sexes separate. The young perch are born with almost all of the yolk sac gone. The first year of life is spent in surface waters. The young feed on invertebrates and fry. Larger ocean perch feed mainly on fish such as herring, capelin, and cod. —A.J.McC.

OCEAN SUNFISH *Mola mola* This huge marine fish is classified in the Mola, or headfish, family (*Molidae*). It is related to the porcupine fishes and puffers.

This large pelagic fish is easily recognized; it has been described as a huge head to which the fins are attached. It lacks a caudal peduncle, and the tail fin is very peculiar, being hardly more than a flap of skin that extends around the rear of the trunk. The ocean sunfish has a small gill opening, and the teeth are fused into a bony beak. The skeleton is not particularly well developed, being tough and cartilaginous. The fish gets protection from a thick layer of cartilage found under the skin along its sides.

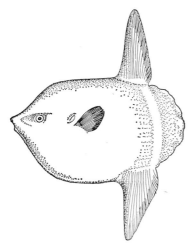

Ocean Sunfish

The high dorsal and anal fins are used to propel the fish by waving from side to side. No pelvic fins are present and the pectoral fins are small. It is dark gray above, and the sides are pale with silver reflections. The belly is dusky-white. It grows to 11 feet, weighing a ton. A 4-foot ocean sunfish weighs about 500 pounds. Most of those seen are from 200–500 pounds.

LIFE HISTORY

The ocean sunfish is a pelagic fish found in tropical and temperate seas. It is known as far north as Nova Scotia on the eastern Atlantic and the Gulf of St. Lawrence. It can normally be seen at sea lying on its side seemingly helpless.

It lays pelagic eggs, and the young are spiny and much different in appearance from the adult fish.

Ocean sunfish feed on jellyfish, various crustaceans, and even at times on floating seaweed.

ANGLING VALUE

This fish is easily harpooned and occasionally taken in pound nets set for tuna. Sometimes it is brought to dock as a curio. The flesh is very oily but edible. —A.J.McC.

OCTOPUS Octopuses are mollusks related to snails, clams, and oysters and, with the squids (*which see*), are part of the class Cephalopoda. They have a flexible, nearly globular body and eight long arms covered with suction cups, united at their base by a weblike membrane. Usually the arms are of equal length. Except for the

Octopus

paper nautilus (*Argonauta*), there is usually no internal shell such as occurs in squids. As in the squids, there is a sharp, parrotlike beak which is supplied by powerful jaw muscles. The octopus lies patiently in wait hidden in caves or crevices for passing prey, which is grasped with its tentacles or crushed with the powerful beak. Food is seized with the arms and introduced to the mouth. Associated salivary glands contain a powerful poison which paralyzes and kills the prey. Crabs are a favorite food, and clams, snails, lobsters, abalones, and scallops are also eaten readily. Other octopuses are eaten, and occasionally, prior to death, an octopus will eat its own arms.

They live in rocky or sheltered areas, feeding primarily at night and hiding during the day. They are found from the shallow tidepools and floating at the surface with their egg case (paper nautilus) to over ½ mile deep, but one species has been taken from a depth of nearly 15,000 feet. The male of the paper nautilus seldom exceeds ½ inch, while the octopus of the North Pacific exceeds 16 feet in spread.

Octopuses are fed upon by predatory reef fishes whenever they can get them, and floating paper nautiluses are regularly eaten by dolphin and sailfish. Morays seem particularly fond of octopuses, and groupers and snappers also eat them. As in squids, octopuses discharge clouds of ink which have a shape of a dummy or "phantom" octopus, this mechanism presumably being used to fool the attacker. Possibly the ink is also used to attract other octopuses or to locate one another.

JET PROPULSION

Like the squids, the octopus uses its funnel to propel itself through the water by jet action, supplementing its ability to crawl and permitting it to dodge its enemies quickly. Occasionally they may even crawl onto land in search of food. They are not as fast as squids but are able to travel 6–8 feet with each jet, while some can shoot a jet of water 10 feet in the air. Young octopuses jet themselves forward or backward with equal ease. In addition, octopuses swim with the membraneous web.

Octopuses have a nervous system as well developed as that of squids and they react quickly to stimuli. Their vision is keen, the structure of the eye being similar to that of a human, and their ability to smell and taste is acute.

REPRODUCTION

Male octopuses have a specialized arm (hectocotylus) for transferring the sperm to the female. Octopus eggs look like rice grains, ranging from about $1/30$ of an inch (paper nautilus) to nearly 2 inches (pearly nautilus), but the eggs of most species are $1/8$–$1/2$ inch long. The eggs are clustered together like a stalk of bananas and are laid over a period of several weeks or more. Eggs are generally laid inshore, attached to rocks, pebbles, or vegetation. The female guards the eggs, usually passing up food altogether. Young octopuses hatch out as miniatures of the adult and swim readily about. Probably the young float about the surface in the plankton for some time before assuming a bottom existence.

FOOD VALUE

Octopuses are considered highly valuable as food in most parts of the world. They are taken in pots, baskets, and traps, and by dynamite, spears, hooks, and a multitude of lures and poisons. They are eaten fresh, baked, fried, boiled, dried, canned, salted, and pickled as well as mixed with other foods. Occasionally they occur in large numbers, where they are a nuisance to fishermen by damaging nets and by eating valuable food fish.

DANGER TO MAN

Documented attacks of octopuses on humans are recorded, but such attacks are uncommon. The beak can inflict a severe bite, sometimes fatal, and conceivably, under the right circumstances, a diver could be held underwater by the powerful arms and suction cups.

—D.dS.

OFFSHORE That area beyond the surf or inshore reefs, therefore in deepwater. *See also* Zones (Sea) under Marine Ecology

OFFSHORE FISHING A term which implies fishing in deepwater some distance from, but not essentially out of sight of land. By inference, fishing for pelagic species, such as the sailfish, marlin, tuna, and dolphin. *See also* Big-Game Fishing

OHIO Squarish in shape, Ohio covers 44,803 square miles. The state is about 225 miles wide in an east-west direction and 210 miles deep. About two-thirds of north-ern Ohio skirts Lake Erie, one of the great producers of freshwater fish in the world. The Ohio River snakes along the southeastern, southern, and southwestern border of the state with its 9,000,000 people. The upper third of the state rests in the St. Lawrence-Great Lakes watershed. The other two-thirds lies in the Ohio-Mississippi watershed. There is a variety of topography from the western portion, which is level or gently rolling, to the eastern part, which is hilly or of a rolling terrain.

To the angler Ohio offers year-around sport. There are no closed seasons, no limits on the fish you can catch or on their size with a few exceptions. Ohio was one of the first states to offer so-called "liberalized" fishing. Because there are so few restrictions on angling, Ohio likes to call itself the "state of relaxed fishing."

Even though winters can produce below zero temperatures, fishermen are out almost every day of the year. In winter, ice fishermen flock to Lake Erie to catch yellow perch. On inland lakes they catch bluegills, crappies, largemouth bass, and walleyes.

Most of Ohio's inland fishing lakes are manmade. Most of the fishing in the state is done in lakes as many streams are polluted or posted against trespass. There are some beautifully clear streams in southern Ohio, but they offer little in the way of angling because of acid mine waste from old abandoned coal mines. Many other streams are polluted by cities and silt from farms.

Ohio's important gamefish are walleye, muskellunge, largemouth and smallmouth bass, white bass, crappies, bluegills, channel catfish, bullheads, suckers, and carp. There are several lakes where chain pickerel and northern pike have been introduced.

The state has little trout fishing, although several private clubs offer superb angling such as the Castalia Trout Club and also the Rockwell Springs Trout Club. Some trout are taken from the Mad River in southwestern Ohio, but generally most Ohioans never see a trout, let alone catch one.

For the angler who likes to go for trophy fish there is excellent fishing for smallmouth and largemouth bass, and muskellunge are rapidly attaining a respected stature.

LAKE ERIE

Lake Erie is, by far, the number one fishing area for Ohioans and visitors, with the angling center being in the Port Clinton-Sandusky area in the northwestern part of the state. An island archipelago, north of those two cities, provides reefs, sandbars and gravel bottoms for fish to spawn. Among the islands are South Bass Island, Middle Bass Island, North Bass Island, Kelleys Island, and various other small clusters of land. These islands are famed for smallmouth bass and yellow perch. At one time many walleye fishermen trolled countless miles around this area and made fabulous catches. In recent years, the walleye population has dropped drastically while yellow perch numbers have exploded. Ohio biologists report that there is some evidence that walleye populations are on the rise. Studies by federal biologists, however, indicate that Lake Erie may be a "dying lake" because of the cumulative effects of pollution by industry, farms, and municipalities. Two fish species that once were plentiful—the cisco and blue pike—are virtually gone from the lake.

Following Michigan's spectacular success with coho salmon stocking, Ohio fisheries personnel first planted

Fishermen crowd the banks of the Chagrin River during the fall run of coho up from Lake Erie

about 25,000 coho smolts in a tributary of the Chagrin River in 1968. After a six-week "imprinting" period the salmon were released to make their way into Lake Erie. That fall a successful run of early-maturing coho (jacks) proved that the species could survive and thrive despite Lake Erie pollution. The fish had attained lengths up to 15 inches. Each year since, Ohio has stocked larger numbers of coho (up to 150,000 in one year) in the Chagrin River, Conneaut Creek, and the Huron River. These streams are located at strategic distances along Ohio's 200 miles of Lake Erie shoreline.

Although Lake Erie contains an unlimited supply of smelt as forage for the coho, the fish here have averaged smaller than Lake Michigan coho, which feed on alewives. Ohio adults run around 7 pounds each. Lake Erie coho are not unerring in returning to their "home" streams. In one survey 60 percent of all fish returning to the Chagrin River were fin-clipped Ohio coho; and 26 percent had been planted by Pennsylvania. The balance were unidentified. In the fall of 1972 stray fish were running up numerous Lake Erie tributaries. Pennsylvania and New York have also stocked coho in streams emptying into Lake Erie.

In the spring of 1971 Ohio augmented its coho project by planting 150,000 chinook fingerlings in the Chagrin River and Conneaut Creek. However, fishing for salmon from boats in Lake Erie has developed very slowly in comparison to the boom in boat fishing that accompanied Michigan's program.

Yellow perch are extremely abundant. During a recent winter, one fisherman at South Bass Island caught nearly one thousand perch in a day through the ice. For the sport fisherman, however, smallmouth bass and white bass provide high excitement around the island area. In May smallmouth may be taken on artificial baits by casting toward rocky shorelines. In the summer they can be taken by fishing in deepwater with softshell crabs (crayfish) being the favorite bait.

White bass also school in the lake, and often the fact that they are around can be noted by the screaming of gulls and terns as they wheel over the school for baitfish. Once in a school of white bass, fishermen can get a fish on virtually every cast. If you miss the first strike, keep reeling as another white bass will hit your bait. Small, pearl-sided spoons are very effective.

Occasional muskellunge, northern pike, and sturgeon also are caught in Lake Erie.

Channel catfish also are taken in Lake Erie on the southern shore in the Sandusky-Port Clinton area and also in Sandusky Bay off Lake Erie. Best time usually is during first three weeks of June. Sandusky Bay alone covers 36,000 acres and teems with boat liveries, fishing piers, and marinas.

On Lake Erie itself, from Toledo on the west to Conneaut on the east, there are numerous boat liveries and piers where thousands of people fish on every pleasant weekend. There are boat ramps all along the lake for people wishing to put in their own craft.

INLAND LAKES

There are 68 major inland lakes in Ohio, and these vary in size from Pymatuning Lake with its 15,000 water acres in northeastern Ohio to much smaller impoundments. In addition, there are some thousands of farm ponds and pay-to-fish impoundments which provide fine fishing for largemouth bass, bluegills, and crappies.

Northeastern Ohio with the most people has the most lakes. Walleyes have been successfully introduced, and are reproducing in lakes in this area, creating a highly desirable fishery. Best lakes for walleyes are Berlin Reservoir (3,650 water acres), Lake Milton (1,685 acres), Mosquito Lake (7,850 acres), and Pymatuning. All these are centered in this section of Ohio, and it would be possible to fish all four with a minimum of driving.

Pymatuning, which lies on the Ohio-Pennsylvania border, also is stocked with muskellunge, and some of these fish top 30 pounds. Walleyes up to 18 pounds also have been taken from Pymatuning. Other species here include largemouth bass, white bass, channel catfish, and usual panfish. Pymatuning is an ideal lake for fishermen as there is no speedboating, because a 10 hsp limit applies on motor boats.

Other principal lakes in northeastern Ohio include the Portage Lakes (1,651 acres) in the Akron area. These provide fishermen with largemouth bass, walleyes, and other popular species. Chain pickerel are caught in Long Lake.

Near Akron is the 900-acre Mogadore Reservoir, which is extremely popular for winter fishing. One of the amazing bits of water in this section is Deer Creek Reservoir, a lake of 303 acres, which has been stocked with muskellunge. In 1962, John M. Charley of Wadsworth caught a 31-pound muskie.

MUSKINGUM CONSERVANCY DISTRICT

A unique system of lakes in eastern and central Ohio is the ten Muskingum Conservancy District reservoirs. These were created for flood control, and the ten lakes together make up 16,000 acres of water. The lakes are Atwood, 1,540 acres; Beach City, 450 acres; Charles Mill, 1,350; Clendening (famous for largemouth bass), 1,800 acres; Leesville, 1,000 acres; Piedmont (well-known for muskellunge), 2,270 acres; Pleasant Hill, 850 acres; Seneca, 3,550 acres; Tappan, 2,350 acres; and Wills Creek, 900 acres. Despite its relatively small size Leesville Lake produced the state record largemouth bass of 9 pounds, 2 ounces and some exceptional muskellunge in years past. Piedmont Lake, however, produces most of the over 20-pound muskies caught in Ohio, including the state record of 55 pounds, 2 ounces (1972); also flathead catfish to 76 pounds (1972). All of the Muskingum Conservancy reservoirs are in scenic, rolling countryside, and all but Beach City offer camping facilities. Motels are nearby. The late Louis Bromfield once called this lake system the "Edge of Paradise," and he lived on a farm near Pleasant Hill Lake.

This lake system has become a fine vacation area, with rental cabins and camping facilities available at many of them. For information, write Muskingum Conservancy District, New Philadelphia, Ohio.

OTHER LAKES

In southern Ohio one of the best bluegill lakes is 664-acre Burr Oak. In central Ohio, Buckeye Lake (3,800 acres) offers fine fishing in spring and fall for bass, crappies, and bluegills. Also in the Columbus area are Delaware and Hoover reservoirs.

In Highland County, Rocky Fork Lake offers muskellunge, bass, bluegills, crappies, and walleyes.

Western and southwestern Ohio have a number of good fishing lakes, such as Great Lake, Cowan Lake, Acton Lake, Clark Lake, Indian Lake, and Kiser Lake.

Loramie and Indian lakes are more than one hundred years old, and were originally built as water-supply reservoirs for canals.

Northwestern Ohio with its pancake-flat land does not have too many lakes. One of the best is Grand Lake St. Marys, covering 11,000 acres. Top species are channel catfish, crappies, and largemouth bass. This lake is shallow but offers superb crappie fishing in April, May and early June. Much of the fishing here is done from shore.

As pointed out previously, Ohio is continually building new lakes. Two of the newest are Dillon Reservoir near Zanesville and LaDue Reservoir located east of Cleveland. Both should offer fine fishing.

STREAMS

Although many streams are polluted there are some that offer hours of sport. In northeastern Ohio there are the Grand River, Chagrin River, Conneaut Creek, Beaver Creek, the Cuyahoga River (in the upper region only), and Rocky River. Much of Rocky River flows through the Cleveland Metropolitan Park System, and fishermen are welcome.

In northwestern Ohio, the Huron and Vermilion rivers provide smallmouth-bass fishing in May. The Huron also produces shovelhead catfish up to 50 pounds. In northwestern Ohio, the Maumee River produces some fair fishing, but this river is becoming more polluted. Also in northwestern Ohio is the Sandusky River, where hundreds of anglers congregate every May for the famous run of white bass into this stream from Lake Erie.

In southern Ohio the Muskingum River produces channel catfish and smallmouth bass. Central Ohio's best streams are the Big Walnut, Big and Little Darby, Paint Creek, Deer Creek, Olentangy, and Kokosing rivers.

Western Ohio has the Big and Little Miami rivers and the Stillwater River, plus tributary streams.

Information on Ohio angling is available from Ohio Wildlife Division, 1500 Dublin Road, Columbus 12. The *Cleveland Press* also publishes an outdoor guide, listing all major fishing areas in the state.   —H.A.

OHIO MUSKELLUNGE *See* Muskellunge

OILFISH *Ruvettus pretiosus* This interesting creature belongs to the family Gempylidae, the snake mackerels, a small group of widely distributed species that inhabit relatively deep pelagic waters. The oilfish has a worldwide distribution in tropical and temperate waters. In the Western Atlantic it extends from Newfoundland and Bermuda to Brazil.

Its color is purplish-brown, darkest above, with blackish patches. The ventrum is a dull white; scales provided with bony, white prickles. Inside of mouth is dusky. It may be distinguished from all other mackerels by the presence of only 2 dorsal and 2 anal finlets. There is no keel on the caudal peduncle and the prickly skin is unique.

Other distinguishing characteristics of the oilfish are first dorsal fin with 13–15 spines, depressible in a furrow; second dorsal with 18 softrays; anal fin with 17 rays under second dorsal and similar in size and outline. Body fusiform, moderately elongate, moderately compressed, greatest depth about 6 in total length; caudal peduncle moderate. Head compressed, 4½ in total length; snout bluntly pointed; mouth large, oblique; lower jaw heavy, projecting slightly.

Pectoral fins situated low on sides behind gill opening, a little more than ½ length of head; pelvics ventral, inserted directly below base of pectorals. Lateral line obscure.

FOOD VALUE

The oilfish grows to a weight of 100 pounds and is utilized for food in some parts of the world (Polynesia). However, extreme care should be used with this species since eating flesh that is not properly prepared, by boiling thoroughly and pouring off the oil, may cause severe poisoning. It is best not to eat it at all. Sports fishermen are not likely to catch this species as they are usually caught on baited hooks at depths of 600 feet or more.
      —J.C.B.

OKEFENOKEE PYGMY SUNFISH *Elassoma okefenokee* This pygmy sunfish was first recognized in 1956 by tropical-fish hobbyists. Specimens were sent to the Academy of Natural Sciences of Philadelphia and, there, were confirmed as a new species. They differ from the Everglades pygmy sunfish by having the top of the head scaleless and the male dorsal fin darker throughout. The color pattern of the female is rather contrasting, consisting of dark brown bars or blotches on a light background.

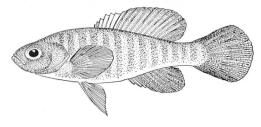

Okefenokee Pygmy Sunfish

The body colors of this sunfish are blue and brown with an iridescent blue crescent on all fins except the pectorals. Its background color is velvet brown. The female lacks blue but has basic brown color. The name of this pygmy sunfish is taken from the locality where it is found, the Okefenokee Swamp of southern Georgia.

This fish is found in very soft, acid waters. It prefers hiding under plants overhanging clean deepwater.

ANGLING VALUE

Because of its small size, it is better adapted to the aquarium than to angling.   —K.B.

OKLAHOMA   There are peak periods in spring and fall months, but fishing in Oklahoma is a year-around sport afforded in a wide variety of settings that have grown at an almost unbelievable rate in the past twenty-five years.

That quarter-century of progress has elevated the state to a point where it now ranks among the foremost in the nation in inland water resources. The state affords wealth of freshwater sport fishing, ranging from the excitement of smallmouth-bass fishing in the mountain streams of eastern Oklahoma to statewide interest in largemouth-bass angling in the many large lakes, as well as small lakes and ponds in each of the state's seventy-seven counties. Crappie, bream, and white bass hold much of the sports-fishing interest. There are seemingly endless opportunities for catfish anglers on streams and lakes. In practically all large reservoirs 24–25 of the larger species are common and there are from 30–40 species of minnows in the tributaries and lakes.

The Oklahoma Wildlife Conservation Department has introduced rainbow-trout fishing for the public on one of its fourteen lakes provided for under its federal aid program, 160-acre Carl Etling in the Black Mesa country of Cimarron County near the Colorado line. Walleye have been introduced in Canton Lake in northwestern Oklahoma and Lake Tenkiller in eastern Oklahoma. Research is being carried out with other species for possible use in fishery management and for sports fishing. The latter includes chain and grass pickerel, trout in the Illinois river and striped bass in Lake Keystone.

Grand, Lake of Cherokees, Eufaula, Tenkiller, Fort Gibson, Wister, the 95,400-acre Texoma lakes are sports fishing centers and rate as prime largemouth-bass lakes. They also provide white-bass and crappie fishing. Spavinaw and Eucha Lakes in northeastern Oklahoma, as well as Lawtonka in southwestern Oklahoma, are among the older lakes that are better-known fishing spots. At the present time the Army Engineer's district office at Tulsa maintains records on fourteen federally owned major lakes in Oklahoma that provide public fishing with something like 320,000 surface acres of water. City lakes and other larger reservoirs account for about 200,000 additional surface acres of good fishing, but the story goes much beyond that point. There are around 200,000 farm ponds and approximately 700 upstream flood-control lakes, the latter averaging about 25 surface acres in size. These are a part of the state's fishery resources.

Oklahoma's Wildlife Conservation Department maintains five hatcheries and a laboratory, the latter in cooperation with the University of Oklahoma. A large hatchery at Tishomingo is maintained by the U.S. Bureau of Sport Fisheries and Wildlife. Better management of the state's expanding sportsfishing resources is a primary aim of the Wildlife Conservation Department, Fishery Division, in plans for the cooperative U.S. Bureau, State Wildlife Department, and university research projects in addition to research work by the University of Oklahoma at its Lake Texoma Fisheries Laboratory and a laboratory near the university city, Norman.

Visitors to most of the state's lakes will find attractive facilities in a system of state-park lodges, as well as private facilities, lodges, and courts. Public-use areas for camping, as well as boat docks and launching ramps, are provided. Concessionaire associations at most lakes provide folders for the benefit of prospective visitors. The Lake Texoma state lodge; Western Hills, on Fort Gibson Lake; Lake Murray State Park; Quartz Mountain State Park at Altus; Lugart Dam; Beavers Bend Park on the Mountain Fork river in the mountains of southeastern Oklahoma; Lake Wister Park; and Tenkiller State Park provide attractive cabins and lodges. Extensive plans have been carried out for facilities at Lake Eufaula.

Year-round fishing is not merely a catch phrase. Oklahoma's climate makes possible fishing through most of the winter months for those who do their angling from boats or along banks. Fishing barges that provide practically all of the comforts of home are popular meccas for those who angle for crappie and other fish. Most of these enclosed barges or docks are heated in winter, as well as being air conditioned for summer fishing. Television is another common convenience many of them afford their patrons. Grand Lake, where this type of fishing first attracted widespread attention, affords about 100 such fishing docks. Boats and motors may be rented at all of the larger lakes, and float trips are available on attractive Illinois and Mountain Fork rivers, two of the popular streams in eastern and southeast Oklahoma. Both rivers are known for their smallmouth-bass population, and visiting sportsmen find the state's fishing license fees reasonable.

Peak fishing months in the spring generally extend from about mid March into June when largemouth-bass, crappie, white-bass, panfish, and catfish spawning periods spur action. During summer months night and early-morning fishing for largemouth bass is more successful. White bass surfacing on Texoma and other large lakes from June into late fall offer an unlimited amount of sport. Oklahoma has no closed season, except that applying to trout on Lake Etling west of Boise City. Six rainbow may be taken daily from April through September 30. Only artificial lures, worms, or other area insects may be used. Any other live bait, such as minnows, is prohibited on Lake Etling.

Walleye seasons were opened at Lake Tenkiller in eastern Oklahoma and on Canton Lake in western Oklahoma in 1964. Walleye have shown exceptional growth in the two lakes during the first 4 years of stocking. If natural reproduction should not be obtained, the Wildlife Department's fishery division plans to maintain permanent walleye fisheries with its hatchery facilities.

All lakes and ponds are provided initial stocking with largemouth bass and channel catfish.

Largemouth bass ranging 6–10 pounds are accounted for in catches at Tenkiller, Texoma, Fort Gibson, Grand, and smaller lakes. Heavyweights of the lakes and streams are the 80–100-pound flatheads. Channel catfish are found in all lakes and rivers, and the big blue catfish range

Once a comparatively arid state, Oklahoma has created tremendous water resources through its growing chain of impoundments. Black bass, channel catfish, various panfish, and even striped bass provide an abundance of angling for resident and tourist alike

in waters of the southern part of Oklahoma, particularly in the Red River and its tributaries. Both white and black crappie abound in lakes as well as in the streams of the state.

Statistics on major impoundments are: Altus, Lugert Dam, southwestern Oklahoma; 6,600 acres, largemouth bass, crappie, channel catfish, white bass predominate. Elevation 1,559 feet.

Canton Reservoir, northwest Oklahoma, 7,700 acres; largemouth bass, crappie, white bass, channel catfish predominate. Elevation 1,614 feet.

Lake Texoma, extreme southern Oklahoma, 95,400 acres; best-known for largemouth bass, crappie, white bass, and catfish species. Elevation 617 feet.

Eufaula Reservoir, eastern Oklahoma, 102,000 acres; largemouth bass, crappie, channel catfish, white bass, and panfishes.

Fort Cobb Reservoir, southwestern Oklahoma, 4,100 acres; opened to fishing in 1961. Crappie, largemouth bass, and catfishing. Elevation 1,342 feet.

Fort Supply Reservoir, northwestern Oklahoma, 1,800 acres; stocked with all common sports-fishing species. Elevation 2,002 feet. Less used than most larger lakes in state.

Foss Reservoir, western Oklahoma, 8,800 acres; general sports species, including largemouth bass, crappie, white bass, and catfishes. Opened to public use in 1962. Elevation 1,652 feet.

Great Salt Plains Reservoir, northwestern Oklahoma, 9,300 acres; salt content of tributaries has effect on fish population. Less widely used but locally popular. Elevation 1,125 feet.

Markham Ferry Reservoir in northern Oklahoma has been producing good runs of spotted bass, as well as several other species, since its completion in 1964.

Heyburn Lake, northeastern Oklahoma, 1,100 acres; most sports-fishing species common to state. Elevation 762 feet.

Hulah Lake, northeastern Oklahoma, 3,600 acres; common sports-fishing species. Elevation 733 feet.

Grand Lake of Cherokees, extreme northeastern Oklahoma, 46,300 acres; all of common sport fishing. Elevation 745 feet.

Tenkiller Lake, eastern Oklahoma, 12,500 acres; deepest of clearwater lakes, all sport-fishing species common to state, as well as introduced walleye. Elevation 630 feet.

Lake Wister, southwestern Oklahoma, 4000 acres; all of common sport fishes. Elevation 472 feet.

While being held below capacity, Oologah reservoir, north of Tulsa, is now providing abundant fishing.

Two Tulsa city lakes, Spavinaw and Eucha, in northeast Oklahoma, Oklahoma City's Atoka Lake in southeastern Oklahoma, Lawton's Lake Lawtonka, and Lake Ellsworth and Lake Murray in the Arbuckle mountain area of southcentral Oklahoma are popular with sportfishing devotees and have good accommodations. The Wichita Mountain Federal Wildlife Refuge has a series of attractive public-use lakes in the Lawton area of southwestern Oklahoma. One of the largest bass, a 10-pound 4-ounce, was taken from Lake Humphreys, a Duncan city lake in northern Stephens County. The new Norman City reservoir, built by the Bureau of Reclamation, was stocked in early 1965. The Bureau is also building Lake Arbuckle near Sulphur and Platt National Park.

Blue River in southcentral Oklahoma, Mountain Fork, Buffalo Creek, and many other southeastern Oklahoma rivers are popular spots. The Illinois River, Spavinaw Creek, Bird Creek, and other streams of northeastern Oklahoma provide equally good fishing and atmosphere.

Further details may be obtained by contacting the State Department of Wildlife Conservation, Capitol, Oklahoma City; the Corps of Army Engineers office in Tulsa; Oklahoma Planning and Resources Board, Capitol offices, Oklahoma City; or various lake associations. —G.H.C.

OLIGOTROPHIC WATERS Waters with a small supply of nutrients; hence they support little organic production. *See also* Types of Lakes *under* Freshwater Ecology

ONO The Hawaiian name for the wahoo (*which see*).

ONTARIO Canada's second largest province has an area of 412,582 square miles. It extends over 1,000 miles from north to south, and approximately the same distance from east to west. Ontario's water area is 68,283 square miles, almost equally divided between its inland waters and the Great Lakes system. The most common fish species in southern Ontario are smallmouth bass, muskellunge, largemouth bass, yellow perch, northern pike, brown trout, whitefish, and walleye. Brook trout can be found in some of the small streams and spring-fed lakes in this same area; however, the native (brook) and the lake trout are more common in larger rivers and lakes of the north. Rainbow trout are found in lakes and streams of the Great Lakes region. Splake (*which see*) have been planted experimentally in various waters, and good angling success for these hybrids has been reported in several Algonquin Park lakes and in the South Bay area of Manitoulin Island. Ouananiche (*which see*) have been successfully introduced to the waters of Trout Lake near the town of North Bay. Arctic grayling (*which see*) have been introduced to several small lakes in the Forest Districts of Geraldton and Port Arthur.

Generally speaking, the quality of Ontario angling ranges from modest near large population centers to exceptional in the more primitive areas.

The climate of southern Ontario is largely influenced by the Great Lakes which modify its winters and add additional moisture in the summers. Northern Ontario summers are cooled by sub-Arctic air which flows over Hudson Bay before settling in valleys and other low areas. The heaviest snowfall in southwestern Ontario occurs from January to early March, while in the settled parts of northern Ontario annual snowfall is 80–100 inches. In general, less than 60 inches fall in the more sparsely settled regions farther north. However, winter is no barrier to Ontario anglers as ice fishing has become a popular winter sport, especially at Lake Simcoe, less than 50 miles north of Toronto. In a recent winter, approximately 200,000 pounds of fish were harvested through the ice, and conservation officers checked more than two thousand anglers with a catch of over 5,000 fish. Two important changes in Ontario regulations have developed this fishery. These were the establishment of a winter season for lake-trout fishing in a number of areas and the extension of the walleye (locally yellow pickerel) season which provided for winter fishing in most southern Ontario waters.

In the Lake Erie District, creel-census studies on five principal ice-fishing areas (upper Niagara River, Long Point Bay, Rondeau Bay, western Lake Erie, and upper Lake St. Clair) demonstrated that approximately 56,000 anglers, including 15,500 nonresidents, caught an estimated 2,500,000 fish in one season. This catch consisted largely of yellow perch and smelt. Elsewhere, there has been a general increase in the numbers of anglers participating, notably in the western part of Lake Erie, the Detroit River, and lower Lake St. Clair.

LAKE TROUT

This species is distributed widely throughout the province and is found in all forest districts with the exception of Lake Erie, Lake Huron, and Kapuskasing. Ontario is noted for quantity rather than large average size of specimens in its lake-trout fishery. Many populations are plankton feeders and average under 20 inches. While a few large specimens can be caught almost anywhere within the normal range of the lake trout, it is an exceptional fishery that provides commonplace trout in the 5–8-pound class. Such lakes are generally those that are underexploited, and are often located in the northern or more remote parts of the province. Lake Simcoe is the exception as it provides excellent fishing for lake trout of good average size.

The sport fishery of Algonquin Provincial Park is predominantly for lake trout and brook trout. This popular park area is frequented by many ardent trout anglers each year. Algonquin Park is situated in the Pembroke Forest District, and is approximately 150 miles north of Toronto. Canoe trips within the park are quite popular, and the best fishing is to be had in some of the more remote lakes.

With the exception of the Kapuskasing Forest District, good lake-trout waters are common in northern Ontario, but here again the better ones are accessible by aircraft, canoe, or bush road only.

BROOK TROUT

The brook trout is native to the waters of fifteen of the twenty-two forest districts. Due to successful introductions by the use of hatchery stock, the range of the brook trout has been extended, and all forest districts, with the exception of Fort Frances, are maintaining a fishery to some degree.

There are many relatively small spring-fed trout streams in the forest districts of Lake Erie, Lake Huron, Lake Simcoe, and Lindsay. While these areas do provide considerable angling for brook trout, the trout so taken are generally of small average size. Also, as these streams lie almost entirely on private land and as there continues to be a definite increase in the amount of posted property and in the establishment of private trout ponds, public fishing has been somewhat curtailed in recent years.

Farther north, in the Crown Land areas of Ontario, there are fewer spring-fed streams but some exceptionally good ones. Many of the tributary streams entering Lake Superior, along the north shore, are in this category, and local populations of brook trout are augmented considerably by substantial movements of coasters, which enter the tributary streams in late August and September. Coasters are brook trout that spend part of their life cycle in Lake Superior and are noted for their rapid growth and large size (usual size: 2–4 pounds).

In the Laurentian Shield area of southern Ontario and extending northward through Algonquin Provincial Park and the forest districts of North Bay, Sudbury, and Sault Ste. Marie, there are numerous streams connecting suitable trout lakes and ponds, and many such streams provide excellent fishing for brook trout during the cool weather of spring and fall.

To the far north, in the Patricia area of Ontario, there are several water courses in the Arctic drainage that contain almost virgin populations of large brook trout augmented periodically by extensive migrations of the sea-run variety which spend a part of their life in the saltwater of Hudson and James bays or in the estuarine areas. While brook-trout fishing is fantastic in portions of the Severn, Winisk, Sutton, Black Duck, and Albany drainage areas, the usual size of fish caught is 2–3 pounds. Although a few larger fish, of 4–5 pounds, are caught, it is very doubtful if record-size brook trout are present in the populations.

Spring-fed lakes and ponds are numerous in southcentral Ontario and throughout most of northern Ontario with the exception of the western region. While there were native populations of brook trout in some of these areas in the past, the extent of lake and pond fishing for this species has increased tremendously during the past decade due to the availability of hatchery fish stocks for new introductions and the use of aircraft in fish-planting activities. In many cases, suitable spawning areas for brook trout are not available in these lakes and ponds, but it is possible to maintain an attractive fishery by restocking periodically with hatchery-reared fish.

Each of the forest districts of Lindsay, Tweed, Parry Sound, Pembroke, North Bay, Swastika, Sudbury, Sault Ste. Marie, White River, Geraldton, and Port Arthur has numerous (50–200) ponds and small lakes under management at the present time. The majority of such fishing areas are not accessible by good roads, but the department is attempting to provide some angling for trout by reclaiming and/or stocking lakes on main access routes and by the development of pond areas.

Among the better areas supporting natural populations of brook trout, the lakes of Algonquin Provincial Park are outstanding, and the wide expanses of Lake Nipigon continue to yield a few trophy fish in the 6–8 pound class each year. Most of the other prize-winning brook trout from Ontario are the result of a successful introduction of the species to very productive waters.

RAINBOW TROUT

Originally an exotic species, the rainbow trout is now found to some extent in fourteen of the twenty-two forest districts. However, some of these occurrences are due to fairly recent introductions to a few inland lakes and ponds in some districts. The main rainbow-trout fishery of Ontario is still to be found in the numerous tributary streams of Lake Ontario, Lake Erie, Lake Huron, Georgian Bay, and Lake Superior. The fish are most vulnerable to anglers during the spring and fall seasons, and this important fishery continues to expand in range, strength, and angler interest.

The new introductions to a few specific inland lakes are experimental in nature. While it has already been demonstrated that some of the rainbows have survived, have exhibited a good growth rate, and have been caught by anglers, it is undoubtedly true that suitable spawning areas are not available in most cases and that the future of such a fishery will depend on plantings of hatchery fish.

BROWN TROUT

This species was introduced to Ontario many years ago, and has been confined to streams in the more southerly forest districts of Lake Erie, Lake Huron, Lake Simcoe, Lindsay, and Tweed. Because the brown trout is a wary species and withstands heavy fishing pressure better than other members of the trout family, its contribution to the sport fishery of Ontario is presently under surveillance. The distribution of brown trout from Ontario hatcheries was drastically curtailed in 1959. An attempt is being made to evaluate the potential of the brown trout in Ontario waters, and a final decision concerning its future will not be made until this study has been completed.

NORTHERN PIKE

The northern pike enjoys the widest distribution of all gamefish in Ontario and is abundant in each forest district with the exception of Lindsay; major portions of the Kawartha lakes area, the Haliburton Highlands, and Algonquin Provincial Park do not contain pike populations either. As a general rule, the largest pike are found in the so-called fly-in lakes which receive little fishing pressure, while those waters close to roads produce pike of smaller average size. Some of the heaviest northerns caught in recent years (30–40 pounds) were taken in Lake Nipigon, Delaney Lake, Lac Seul, Lake of the Woods, Pickerel Arm Lake, Helen Lake, Gibb Lake, and Ninitaki Lake.

WALLEYE

Although the walleye is found in all twenty-two forest districts, it is somewhat more selective in habitat requirements than the pike. Accordingly, it is found in the larger, more fertile water areas and particularly those that provide rock-rubble shoreline or tributary rivers suitable for their spawning. While an angler might catch a large walleye almost anywhere, fish of large average size are taken from relatively broad expanses of fertile water. Such waters are to be found in the Georgian Bay area, the Kawartha lakes area, Lake Nipissing, and numerous large lakes throughout northern Ontario.

SMALLMOUTH BASS

This is a very popular gamefish in Ontario, and is found in twenty of the twenty-two forest districts. The natural distribution of the species is much more limited, however, and many of the occurrences in northern Ontario are the result of new introductions by the use of hatchery stock, and many are very marginal in nature.

Although smallmouth bass are abundant throughout southern Ontario, special attention is given to this species by anglers operating along the north shore of Lake Erie, in Lake Simcoe, the Georgian Bay and North Channel areas, the St. Lawrence River, and numerous waters within the forest districts of Parry Sound, Lindsay, Tweed, North Bay, Sudbury, Pembroke, and Kemptville. In the far westerly part of Ontario, excellent fishing for smallmouth bass is provided in specific waters in the forest districts of Fort Frances and Kenora, and this choice fishery is undoubtedly one of the most under-exploited populations in the province.

LARGEMOUTH BASS

The largemouth bass has specific habitat require-ments, and is therefore limited in distribution to the warmer, more southerly lakes and rivers of southern Ontario. It is an excellent gamefish during the heat of midsummer and is most important in the Rideau Lakes area, the Kawartha lakes region, the Bay of Quinte, Lake Simcoe, and Lake Erie.

MUSKELLUNGE

The muskellunge has a rather spotty distribution throughout Ontario, but it is found in varying degrees of abundance in thirteen of the twenty-two forest districts. While the musky is highly regarded as a trophy fish, few anglers are ever fortunate enough to break into this elite group. In recent years, muskellunge of 45–58 pounds have been caught in some of the larger waters, such as Lake of the Woods, Lake St. Clair, Georgian Bay, Lake Nipissing, St. Lawrence River, and Eagle Lake. However, if the angler simply wants to catch a muskie, good popula-tions in the 8–18-pound range are readily available in the Kawartha lakes area of southern Ontario or the Vermil-ion Lake area near Sioux Lookout in the far northwest.

OTHER WARMWATER SPECIES

Panfish such as yellowperch, sunfish, rock bass, blue-gills, and bullheads are plentiful in most areas and par-ticularly in the more southerly forest districts. Crappies are found in some abundance in Rainy Lake (Fort Frances District), Bay of Quinte, and other sheltered areas of the Great Lakes. White bass contribute to the fishery in Lake Nipissing and the Bay of Quinte.

The carp has penetrated some of the major water-courses in southern Ontario. A limited but active sport fishery exists in the Kawartha lakes area (particularly Lake Scugog) and in some of the marshy bays of Lake Ontario and the St. Lawrence River. There is also con-siderable interest in bow-and-arrow fishing for carp, and this is permitted in certain parts of Lake St. Lawrence and in parts of Lake Erie. —P.O.R.

OPALEYE *Girella nigricans* Also known as the green fish, blue bass, blue-eyed perch, button perch, and Catalina perch, the opaleye is known from Monterey, California, southward to Magdalena Bay, Baja California, but is uncommon in the extremes of its range. The family Girellidae, aptly called the nibblers, includes about a dozen other species, one of which occurs in the Gulf of California; the others are found in the Indo-Pacific region, principally off the coast of eastern Asia.

The opaleye is perchlike in general shape, but is easily distinguished from other fishes of this general appearance that occur within its range by its higher number of dorsal-fin spines, 14. The surfperch family, Embiotocidae, with 19 marine species off California, has 11 dorsal spines. The halfmoon, *Medialuna californiensis* of the family Scorpi-dae might be confused with the opaleye, but it has 11 or fewer dorsal spines. The only other fish that might cause confusion is the blacksmith, *Chromis punctipinnis* of the damselfish family (Pomacentridae), and it has 13 dorsal spines. The body of the opaleye is laterally compressed and moderate in depth. The head profile is evenly convex. The angle of the preopercle is minutely serrate. The dor-sal fin has 14 spines and 12–14 relatively longer softrays, giving the posterior portion of the fin a lobed appear-ance. The anal fin has 3 short, graduated spines and 12 relatively long rays also resulting in a lobate posterior region. The short, broad pectoral fins do not extend to the vent. The pelvic fins are relatively short. The caudal peduncle is deep, and the caudal fin is slightly lunate or subtruncate. The long slender gillrakers number about 15 on the upper limb of the first gill arch and 20 on the lower limb. The scales on the trunk are relatively large, while those on the chest and the back of the head are smaller. The opercles and dorsal aspect of the head generally lack scales. There are about 50 scales along the lateral line. The peritoneum is black, the long intestine is coiled exten-sively, pyloric caecae are numerous, and the swim bladder

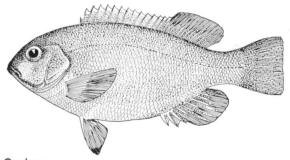

Opaleye

has paired, posteriorly directed horns. The small, subin-ferior mouth has no vomerine or molar teeth but has two unusual bands of small, tricuspid incisors in each jaw. The front rows are loosely imbedded in a shallow depres-sion in each jaw and are thus freely movable. Behind each of these front rows is a broad band of similar teeth, also loosely attached. This type of tooth arrangement allows efficient tooth replacement and is of obvious advantage to grazing fishes such as the opaleye. The juvenile and adult opaleye are light or dark green, depending on the illumi-nation, and are often slightly paler on the ventral surface. The young are easily identified by the pair of whitish or yellowish spots located on the back of each side of the dorsal fin. The eye is a beautiful opalescent blue. The largest fish on record measured 19¾ inches and weighed 6⅛ pounds; however, individuals larger than 15 inches are uncommon.

The closely related *Girella simplicidens* of the Gulf of California has a shorter and deeper body than *G. nigricans*. Also, it differs in color pattern, having a dark background color with darker stripes along the body.

LIFE HISTORY

The adults are thought to spawn from April to June in offshore areas such as kelp beds. The eggs are pelagic, and the larvae remain offshore, feeding indiscriminately on plankton. Late in June the larvae develop into silvery prejuveniles that form schools and move shoreward into the tidepools. Once entering the rocky tidepools the young opaleye undergo a remarkable transformation from omnivorous plankton eaters to algal grazers as they develop into juveniles. A very interesting study showed that these juveniles exhibit homing behavior since they return to the same tidepool after each low tide. They remain in the tidal area for about two years, after which they return to the subtidal area to spend the rest of their life. At this stage they are primarily algal grazers, and are often seen in large schools in or around large offshore beds of kelp (*Macrocystis pyrifera*).

ANGLING VALUE

Despite its moderately small size, the opaleye affords considerable sport to the California fisherman, particularly during the winter months, when certain of the other surf fishes are scarce and the larger opaleye seem to move inshore. Effective baits are redrock shrimp, mussel, razor clams, and moss. Commercially, the opaleye constitutes a minor part of the California fish catch (the average yearly landing was 3,300 pounds during 1956–1961). The food quality of the fish is rated fair to good in California. Closely related species are extensively exploited for food in the Orient. —H.G.M.

OPERCULAR FLAP A fleshy extension of the operculum.

OPERCULUM The posterior bony plate on the side of the head of a fish, or this bone together with its coverings. The gill cover. *See* Anatomy

OPTIC A type of artificial fly in which the head portion is enlarged and painted with eyes. Usually said of an optic streamer fly or an optic steelhead fly. *See also* Fly Tying

ORANGEMOUTH CORVINA *Cynoscion xanthulus* The species is much sought after. It is known as the yellow-finned corvina in Mexico. The orangemouth corvina is the chief gamefish in the Salton Sea, where it was introduced beginning in 1950. From a small introduction of about 275 fish, the population in the sea has increased to an estimate of millions. Here it has reached a maximum recorded weight of 32 pounds. It is a common corvina from the head of the Gulf of California to Mazatlán (*see* Corvinas).

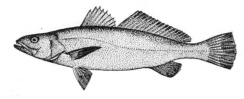

Orangemouth Corvina

The mouth of this species is a bright orange-yellow. The body is long and slim. Its back is tan or blue, and the flanks are silvery. The middle rays of its caudal fin are longer than the top or bottom ones. There are 7–9 anal rays; gill-cover lining black; caudal fin yellow.

LIFE HISTORY

In the Salton Sea the species reaches 2¼ pounds by the second winter, 5¼ pounds in the third, and 11 by the fourth. Plankton is utilized in the sea as food until the fish reaches 30 millimeters. Large fish are piscivorous. The species spawns in April and May. The approximate number of eggs per female in the sea has been estimated as 400,000–1,000,000.

ANGLING VALUE

The orangemouth corvina is a popular gamefish, and will take a variety of lures and live bait. It is readily caught on gold wobbling spoons. The corvina is an excellent food fish. —J.R.

ORANGESPOTTED FILEFISH *Cantherhines pullus* Although there are five synonyms of this species, most recent authors have employed the name *pullus*. Many, however, have used the generic name *Amanses*, but this seems best restricted to the type species *scopas*, an Indo-Pacific form with spines on the side of the body.

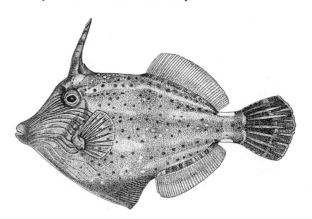

Orangespotted Filefish

The genus *Cantherhines* is distinguished principally from other warmwater filefish genera by the position of the first dorsal spine over or slightly in front of the center of the eye and the presence of a deep, median groove on the back into which this spine folds. Another important character is the immobility of the terminal pelvic element (sometimes called pelvic spine).

Cantherhines has eleven species, two of which occur in the tropical Atlantic. These two, *pullus* and *macrocerus*, have long been confused. The latter is a large fish, attaining a total length of at least 17 inches. *C. pullus*, on the other hand, is not known to exceed 7 inches. Other than the difference in size the two species may be distinguished by the presence on the side of the caudal peduncle of *macrocerus* of two or three pairs of recurved spines (larger in the male) and its usually having 14 pectoral rays. *C. pullus* lacks such spines (but adult males have a large patch of setae on the side of the caudal peduncle); usually there are 13 pectoral rays. In one common color phase *macrocerus* displays large white spots. Except for a prominent white spot at the rear base of the second dorsal fin and another at the rear base of the anal fin, *pullus* has only small indistinct orange spots on the body.

The second dorsal- and anal-fin-ray counts of *pullus* (D 33–36; A 29–32) are not useful in distinguishing the species from *macrocerus* but gillraker counts may be. *C. pullus* has 34–46 gillrakers, and *C. macrocerus* 29–35.

C. pullus has close relatives in *C. pardalis* from the Indo-Pacific and *C. sandwichiensis* from the Hawaiian Islands. All three have the characteristic white spots at the rear base of dorsal and anal fins as mentioned above for *pullus*. There appear to be enough differences, however, to regard them as distinct species. The front part of the second dorsal and anal fins of *sandwichiensis* is markedly elevated compared to the other two species, and the caudal fin is nearly truncate. *C. pardalis* has a deeper body than *pullus* (depth at origin of anal fin 2.1–2.3 times standard length, as compared to 2.3–2.5 in *pullus*), and the spots on the body are larger and more closely spaced.

In addition to the two white spots and the many orange spots, *pullus* may have broad, alternate, longitudinal dark and light bands posteriorly on the body. There is also a resting phase in which there are broad irregular dark bars on the body.

LIFE HISTORY

The species is recorded in the western Atlantic from Massachusetts to Rio de Janeiro, including the Gulf of Mexico. It is also found in Bermuda, and is common in the West Indies. It has been reported once from West Africa. Its occurrence in cooler areas such as New England is probably the result of its transport there in larval form in currents from a warm region. It is doubtful that the species completes its life cycle in a coldwater area.

The postlarvae may occur far from land and are commonly found in the stomachs of large pelagic fishes. The late postlarval (prejuvenile) stage transforms to the juvenile form at a standard length of about fifty millimeters.

As an adult, *C. pullus* is a reef fish. It feeds on bottom growth, largely sponge and algae, but stomachs often contain tunicates, bryozoans, and other sessile invertebrates.

Males attain a slightly larger size than the females. The eggs are green. Ripe females have been found from February to June in Puerto Rico and the Virgin Islands.
—J.E.R.

ORANGESPOTTED SUNFISH *Lepomis humilis* The outstanding feature of this little sunfish is the 20–30 bright red or orange spots scattered irregularly on the sides of the male. The female has the same color pattern but has brown spots. The black gill flap of this species is margined with white, and the sides of the head are often streaked with brown or red. It is called redspotted sunfish, dwarf sunfish, and pygmy sunfish.

This species is widely distributed in the Mississippi Valley from western Pennsylvania to North Dakota and south to Texas, Mississippi, and northern Alabama.

LIFE HISTORY

Like most other sunfishes, the male constructs the nest by making small depressions in the sand or gravel. The orangespotted sunfish usually spawns in colonies in water less than 3 feet deep. Sometimes the water is just deep enough to cover the bodies. The main spawning period is late May or early April, but some may straggle into early August. The females lay 25–300 eggs at a time.

The food consists of insect larvae, crustaceans, and occasionally small fishes.

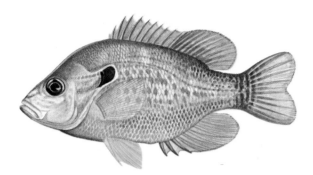

Orangespotted Sunfish

ANGLING VALUE

The orangespotted sunfish has no angling value because it rarely reaches 4 inches. —K.B.

ORBIT The bony socket of the eye

OREGON This is a state of contrasts, from arid rolling lands spotted with sage and juniper to great mountain ranges which rise to 11,253 feet at Mount Hood in the Cascades. This range keeps the western slopes moist and much of the country to the east dry. Yet enough water spills over the east slope to form the mighty Deschutes River. Beyond, to the Wallowa Mountains, the state is crisscrossed with trout rivers. There are more than 15,000 miles of streams and hundreds of lakes. Its fishing is justly famous, and there is some type of outstanding angling opportunity available throughout the year.

In the coastal region a variety of fishing exists unmatched elsewhere in the state. Bay, surf, stream, lake, ocean, and fishing from rocks are to be had. In the streams and bays are salmon, steelhead, striped bass, and cutthroat trout.

In the Columbia, Rogue, and Umpqua rivers, spring chinook salmon are to be taken in April and May on cluster eggs or spinners. Fall chinook and coho or silver salmon are available in August to October. They may be caught with cluster eggs, spinners, and wobblers. Trolling, casting, spin-fishing, or still-fishing are the methods used. Offshore salmon fishing is available from July through September with charter or private boats. At Cape Kiwanda, surf dories (*see* Oregon Surf Dory) are used for exceptional salmon fishing near the mouth of the Nestucca River.

Striped bass are in the lower Coos River, the Umpqua from Reedsport to Winchester, and in the lower Coquille. They may be caught in June to October on plugs, frozen baitfish, and live sculpins. All along the coast, rock and surf-fishing can be enjoyed for surf or sea perch, flounders, lingcod, kelp greenling, many species of rockfish, the cabezon, and others. Though no special equipment is needed in most of the fishing grounds, it is desirable that good spinning or casting tackle be used for surf-fishing.

Shad may be caught in the Coos, Umpqua, Sandy, and Lower Willamette rivers where they are usually present in large numbers in May and June.

Sturgeon are in the Willamette and Columbia rivers. None may be kept that is over 6 feet in length in Washington, Oregon, or Idaho in the Columbia River, a regulation designed to protect the large brood females. The peak of the fishery occurs in March and April.

TROUT FISHING

Trout angling is most productive from late spring to early fall. The coastal lakes are well-stocked with hatchery cutthroat and rainbows. Searun cutthroats enter the river estuaries all summer long and remain in tidewater until the fall rains, providing a peak of angling success in September and October. In the Willamette Valley and on the slopes of the Cascade Mountains large numbers of cutthroat, rainbow, and eastern brook trout are stocked in the lakes and streams. Some of the streams are the Clackamas, Molalla, Santiam, and McKenzie, Rogue, and Umpqua of those flowing out of the Cascades. From the coast range, flowing eastward into the Willamette Valley are the Tualatin, Yamhill, and Luckiamute. The valley is a region of major population density, and the streams are extensively used for power, irrigation, industrial, and domestic purposes, but even so there is much good fishing. In and near the city limits of Portland upwards of 10,000 spring chinook salmon have been caught in March and April of each year.

Brown trout are present in the upper Umpqua and Rogue rivers and in the Deschutes. None is stocked, the species being able to maintain itself reasonably well. The brown is usually much more difficult to catch than the rainbow or brook trout. Actually, all of the lakes and reservoirs of the state, except a very few that are too saline or shallow, are stocked with trout or warmwater gamefish. As a rule, the mountain lakes contain only salmonids. They are inaccessible in the Cascades in winter because of snow. Most of them can be reached by June from the eastern side.

The lakes of the Cascades and eastern Oregon hold a variety of salmon and trout. Kokanee occur in Lost, Suttle, Elk, Davis, Big Cultus, Crescent, Odell, Fourmile, Crane Prairie, and a few other lakes and reservoirs. Lake trout are in Crescent, Odell, Big Cultus, and Wallowa. Fish to 25 pounds have been caught but larger fish have been captured and then released in studies made by conservation agencies. Brook and rainbow trout are scattered throughout the area. The most productive waters include Diamond, Paulina, East, South Twin, Davis, Big Lava, Elk, Sparks, Lake of the Woods, Morgan, and Fish (Steens Mountains) lakes; and Crane Prairie, Wickiup, Ochoco, Ana Springs, Prineville, Detroit, Malheur, Haystack, Thompson Valley, and Beulah reservoirs. Most of the lakes have associated resorts and boating facilities.

In the Wallowa Mountains of northeastern Oregon is a primitive area containing about sixty lakes. Most of them contain brook trout in large numbers. No roads reach the lakes. To encourage anglers to crop the fish population, a special regulation of 30 brook trout per day and 60 in possession has been in effect since 1947. No brook trout have been stocked since that year, and the populations maintain themselves adequately by natural reproduction.

Golden trout occur in lakes on the shoulders of the Three Sisters in the Cascades as well as in several lakes of the Wallowa Mountains.

One of the outstanding streams of the state is the Deschutes, including such tributaries as the Metolius, Williamson, White, and Little Deschutes rivers. The main river can be fished from its banks or in boats above Bend, but below that city no boat fishing is allowed. Rainbows, brooks, and browns are in the upper reaches while below Redmond the catch is mostly of rainbows.

The Metolius is a cold, spring-fed river that has a good rainbow fishery. A portion of the upper river is reserved for fly-fishermen. The White River flows into the Deschutes from the east slope of Mount Hood. Because the stream is discolored at times by water from melting snow, the best season is in July and September.

The Little Deschutes and Crescent Creek are headwater streams providing excellent bank or, in some places, boat angling for browns and rainbows. The fishing here is well-suited to the expert fly-man. Both streams are slick-faced, willow-bordered, and contain many undercut banks. It requires fine leaders and skilled casting to take trout in either the Crescent or Little Deschutes.

The Williamson is a tributary of the Klamath River near Klamath Falls. The largest resident stream trout are to be found here. Brown and rainbow trout are the species. Big rainbows can also be caught in Klamath Lake but the gourmet angler should plan to be there in the winter and spring before algae impart a distasteful flavor to the fish.

The John Day, Umatilla, Walla Walla, Grand Ronde, and Imnaha rivers have a winter and spring fishery for steelhead. In addition, spring chinooks are to be caught in the Imnaha and Grand Ronde in June and July.

In Harney, Lake, and Malheur counties in the southeastern section are great expanses of range and semidesert country, but considerable water is also present. No migratory fishes occur here except for a few salmon in the northeastern corner. The upper waters of the Silvies River near Burns, the Blitzen River near Frenchglen, the upper Chewaucan, near Paisley, Honey and Drift creeks near Lakeview, and the upper Malheur River near Drewsey have rainbow trout in them. A native strain of the inland cutthroat trout is in the Trout Creek mountains in the farthest corner of the southwestern part of the state in such streams as Willow, Whitehorse, and Antelope creeks.

WARMWATER FISHERIES

A few reservoirs of the area are stocked with warmwater gamefish. Possibly the two most important are Gerber in Klamath County and Owyhee in Malheur County. Gerber has had a reputation as a producer of crappie. In Owyhee, largemouth bass and crappie are available in large numbers. The channel catfish was introduced into the Snake River and found conditions that were favorable for good growth. Catches of 17 pounds have been made. The species is to be caught from the vicinity of Ontario all the way down the Snake and Columbia to about 30 miles below Portland. Smallmouth bass inhabit the same rivers down to the vicinity of the Dalles, and are readily taken. The walleye was found in the Columbia near McNary in the late 1950's. Its ultimate population-level potential is not known.

Fishing for warmwater gamefish is done the year around. Bass, perch, crappies, bluegills, and bullheads are also taken in many of the coastal lakes. Sunset and Cullaby lakes are on the north coast in Clatsop County; Devils is in Lincoln County; Sutton, Mercer, Cleawox, Siltcoos, Tahkenitch, and Loon are further south. Tenmile Lakes are further to the southward in Coos County, and Garrison Lake is in Curry County near the southern border of the state.   —J.R.

STEELHEAD FISHING

The giant Columbia River system complex and major coastal streams provide Oregon's noteworthy summer and winter steelhead angling. They are sufficiently diverse in nature and location to offer productive fishing throughout the year.

With just enough exception to prove the rule, tradition confines steelhead fly-fishing in Oregon to summer-run fish. The term "summer run" is unduly confining, however, because these migrations are peaking somewhere in Oregon from spring (March) through fall (November). December, January, and February find peaking winter runs best for baitmen. Few Oregonians emulate anglers in bordering coastal states and fish flies over winter steelhead. As a result, the only significant successes recorded are on Eagle Creek, a small, fast-clearing tributary of the Clackamas River, near Portland, and the more remote coastal streams of short length and quick runoff characteristics. Almost all winter steelhead kills are made on fresh salmon eggs, lures resembling roe clusters, and, in lower water, flatfish and wobblers.

Columbia River steelhead face a gamut of sport fishermen in Oregon from sandbar plunkers near the mouth into the Idaho-Oregon border forming Snake River. En route, the feeder-stream runs in the John Day, Grand Ronde, lower Umatilla, and Imnaha rivers attract bait and lure fishermen. A principal fishing waypoint on the main Columbia is near Boardman, below McNary Dam. Another major tributary, the Willamette River, carries steelhead through Oregon's populous heartland, with winter boat and bank fishermen concentrating at Oregon City Falls.

In contrast to coastal-stream winter runs, peaking December through February, Willamette steelhead run through April, and are not considered as desirable a table fish. The coastal steelheader thinks of winter streams in terms of proximity, north to south, not alphabetically. On that basis, the most productive and popular winter streams are the Nehalem, Wilson, Trask, Big Nestucca, Salmon, Siletz, Alsea, Siuslaw, Umpqua, Smith, South Fork of Coquille, Sixes, Elk, Rogue-Illinois, and Chetko.

The impatient fly-fisherman anxious for an early start should visit either of Oregon's north corners. In the northeast, summer runs that were peaking in October to November continue active—after winter inaccessibility— to mid March in the case of the Grand Ronde, Snake, Wallowa, and Imnaha rivers. A May to July closure provides for their spawning and recovery. For these inland fish, no fly pattern is favored; anglers are divided into "light" or "dark" camps on standard wet patterns. In the northwest, the Santiam River winter run begins in March, peaks in April to May, and continues until July, and the Hood River's summer run, which covers the same period, peaks later, from May to June.

Although the name Deschutes conjures images of large "redsides" or native rainbow for most fly-men, this north-central river maintains a good summer run of steelhead which has a May to October duration with an August to September peak. Much good water exists from the flooded confluence with the Columbia to Warm Springs Bridge, although once popular riffles immediately above the Dalles Dam backwater are not open to public entry. Popular patterns include the Bucktail Coachman, March Brown, and Skykomish Sunrise.

Southwestern Oregon's North Umpqua and Rogue Rivers continue to merit their traditional acclaim as the state's most famous fly streams for steelheads. Veterans consider the rock-ribbed North Umpqua a challenge to wader and caster that, once met, produces bigger summer-run fish up to fifteen pounds. Forty miles upriver from Roseburg at Steamboat Creek lies the favorite water area—Fighting Pool, Glory Hole, the Ledges, and Williams Creek and Honey Creek riffles. The best flies, on No. 4 and No. 6 hooks, are Royal Coachman, North Umpqua Special, Gordon's Favorite, Skunk, and Kalama Special.

Fly-fishermen think of and fish the Rogue in terms of segments—lower, middle, and upper. The famed lower Rogue "half pounders" provide August to October steelheading that peaks in September. Successive runs of increasingly heavier fish can be taken on the fly, weather and water conditions permitting, to the late winter closure. From Gold Beach on the coast to Agness at the Illinois River junction, the lower Rogue's most popular riffles include Gillespie, Lobster Creek, Hawkins, and Coal. In this stretch, double-hook flies in No. 8 and No. 10 should include Red Ant, Silver Ant, Royal Coachman Bucktail, Maverick, Juicy Bug, and Rogue River Special. The middle river is mostly canyon up to Galice, and is fished only by guided boat parties. It includes waters popularized by Zane Grey, who once maintained a fish camp there. Above Galice, the upper river's noteworthy waters include Weatherby Riffle and, above Grant's Pass, the famed Pierce Riffle, just below Savage Rapids Dam, as well as Leaning Tree Riffle. Here, single hooks are more the rule, and, in addition to lower river patterns, the Golden Demon and Weatherwox are popular in No. 6 to No. 10.   —F.C.O.

OREGON SURF DORY This sturdy, safe, and versatile surf dory is used on exposed parts of the Oregon coast more than any other hull type. Hundreds may be seen in good weather and bad in the tide rips at the Columbia River mouth and in the surf at Cape Kiwanda, running when other boats are hove to and always providing a sturdy platform for fishing.

Some hulls are equipped with sail, cat-rigged with about 125 feet of cloth. The reserve stability provided by the large amount of flare makes for a stiff sailer. Commercial fishermen have long used the boat off Pacific City. Guides prefer the boat where any surf work is involved in reaching the fishing grounds. It differs from the banks dory in being completely double-ended, light in weight, and broad on the bottom. There is considerable rocker fore and aft so that she'll answer instantly to the touch of an oar when there is need to prevent broaching in the surf.

Construction is simple. Three sheets of plywood, 22 feet long and 4 feet wide, are needed; the sides are ⅜ inch thick, and the bottom is ½ inch. When the plywood is bent around and firmly fastened, the hull is stressed to remarkable rigidity.

There is no crankiness to the boat. If she has faults they lie in the need for a small rudder to prevent overcontrol when an engine is used, and in the maximal speed under power of about 10 mph. Power required is 5–10 hsp with 7½ hsp ideal. Anything more than 10 hsp simply produces bow and stern waves.

For many years the Oregon Game Commission used the hull for tending nets on large lakes on dangerous leeward shores and in tagging salmon offshore. The commission furnished plans to those who inquired about the boat, and over the years there were hundreds of dories subsequently built. They are in operation from Europe to the South Pacific. Commercial builders now produce the boats in quantity at various places in Oregon.   —J.R.

ORIENTAL BONITO *See* Bonito

OUANANICHE *Salmo salar*   A primitive race of Atlantic salmon which spends its entire life cycle in freshwater, and also in common with the land-locked salmon (*which see*) displays no real taxonomical difference from the sea run form. It was formerly recognized on the subspecific level *Salmo salar ouananiche* as was the landlocked salmon of Maine, *Salmo salar Sebago*. However, there is no evidence to support the distinction between these forms other than their nonmigratory behavior. The ouananiche is highly regarded as a sport fish, and in general appearance may differ in shape and color from an Atlantic salmon. The fins of the ouananiche are larger in relation to total length and girth. It is more elongate and generally

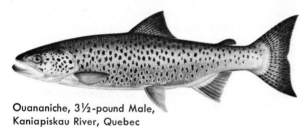

Ouananiche, 3½-pound Male,
Kaniapiskau River, Quebec

darker in color while the body is heavily covered with black or dark brown spots or crosses. Ouananiche are found in Quebec, Labrador, and Newfoundland.

ANGLING VALUE

The ouananiche seldom exceeds 6 pounds in weight with the average 1½–2 pounds. However, this salmon takes the fly readily and is extremely active when hooked. The methods used for trout are successful. —A.J.McC.

OUTBOARD   Outboard boats comprise the biggest group and most varied designs of all classes of recreational craft. The term "outboard" is interchangeably used to describe engine or boat as well as the combination of both. The complete outboard rig also includes a boat trailer. The word "outboard" derives from the location of the engine which is clamped in demountable fashion atop the transome where powerhead, gears, and driveshaft all travel and operate outside of or outboard the stern of the boat.

Many boats are specifically designed for outboard propulsion, but the remarkable adaptability of the portable outboard engine has also led inventive boatmen to convert other designs to outboard power. It's not unusual, for example, to see an outboard motor mounted in a motor-well set deep inside the cockpit of a double-ended dory which was originally designed for rowing. Outboard engines are used to power houseboats, catamarans, canoes, rubber rafts, utilities, skiffs, and runabouts—and this list is by no means inclusive. But all outboard boats fall into two general hull-design classifications—either displacement or planing design.

DISPLACEMENT HULL

The displacement boat sinks into the water until it displaces a volume of water equal in weight to the weight of the boat and everything aboard it. It pushes its way *through* the water rather than on top. A canoe is a displacement craft. So is the houseboat set on a bargelike hull. Displacement outboard craft are not designed for high speed and so require minimum horsepower. In fact it is a waste of money and sometimes dangerous to overpower displacement boats. After a displacement hull achieves its design speed, additional power merely causes it to squat at the stern while the bow climbs skyward. The action creates a heavy wake, erratic steering, and at times a porpoising effect—but does not increase speed.

PLANING HULL

At rest in the water, displacement and planing designs are similar. However, a planing hull operates as a displacement type below its planing speed. As soon as it achieves planing speed, the planing design escapes resistance by dynamically rising above the surface until it is skimming along or planing on a small, wetted-bottom area. The hydroplane is a perfect example of a planing boat. The fast-moving ski boat is another. The planing design makes the most efficient use of outboard power, and it is basic in all modern outboard cruisers, runabouts, and utilities. It provides maximum speed with minimum fuel consumption.

HOW TO SELECT BOAT AND MOTOR

The horsepower capacity of an outboard boat is determined by an involved engineering formula, and manufacturers who comply with industry standards attach a specifications plate to every boat they produce. Often located in a hidden corner of the boat, such as the transom well or beneath the bow deck, the plate will list a serial number and carrying capacity in pounds as well as the minimum and maximum horsepower required for the design. You can determine an outboard boat's carrying capacity with reasonable accuracy if you figure one passenger or 150 pounds for every 12 cubic feet of space in the boat. Here is a simple formula that will provide the answer:

$$\text{Number of persons} = \frac{\text{Length} \times \text{Width} \times \text{Depth (in feet)}}{20}$$

Choosing an outboard boat is easier than it seems; yet, like buying a hunting dog or matching a shotgun to your frame, it involves many personal decisions. You must also be willing to make compromises, for there is no one outboard that is perfect for all needs. Since only you can decide which features are most important, self-analysis and pencil and paper make a good boat-selecting system. Write down all the uses you plan for your boat, how it will be transported, what loads it must carry, and the kind of water you will be traversing most of the time. Check each type of outboard boat that interests you against your listed requirements. The one that fills most of them is the right boat for you.

Here are some thoughts that will help you, and some questions that should be answered. Do you favor speed? Prefer comfort? You really can't have a hull that combines houseboat comfort and skiboat speed. But you can find a good many cruisers and semicruisers that offer live-aboard facilities with reasonable speed. Do you require a family-size day cruiser, or are you shopping for an economic craft that will let you escape on week ends in rough-and-ready style? Such considerations should determine seating capacity, as well as how you will want to use it. There is a vast difference between a rowboat that *seats* four and an outboard cruiser that seats and *sleeps* four. Which do you need? Will you also be wanting to cook on board? There are all kinds of galley systems for outboard boats. Some are portable; others are permanent. Just be sure you choose one that meets all approved marine safety standards. Gasoline camp stoves are out—too dangerous afloat. Bottled-gas, alcohol, and kerosene units are safe. Will bedboards and air mattresses suffice for your sleeping accommodations, or are permanent berths important to you? A good many outboards are equipped with seats that unfold into very comfortable beds for nighttime use. What about a marine head or toilet? Built-in toilets are bulky and heavy. Every pound you put aboard means less speed, greater gasoline consumption. But if you are planning on sharing your boat with children and women, a toilet becomes an essential accessory.

The Auto-Top Boat Perhaps you're not envisioning anything larger than an auto-top outfit. You recognize, of course, that any hull light enough to carry atop your car is normally not big enough to take a family of four and all your fishing gear across big, open bays or coastal waters. But you still need to ask and answer some basic questions, if you would make a sound choice. Will you be lifting the boat on top of a car by yourself, or can you always count on help from your son or a friend? If alone, 80 pounds is a maximum weight, unless you want to invest in some special boat-carrying gear. There are carriers that will let you load a 200-pound boat without help. Seating capacity and motor capacity also affect selection of an auto-top outboard.

The Camper-Top Cabin If you want to combine cruising accommodations with fishing comfort, you need to be realistic about certain decisions. A cabin is a great comfort in raw or wet weather; however even the small cuddy or shelter cabin, characteristic of medium-sized and semicruisers, robs you of cockpit space that makes the difference between a cramped or efficient fisherman. Yet every year naval architects find new ways to meet these problems. The canvas or vinyl camper-top is one example. During the day the convertible camper-top is folded away in self-contained boots. There is no cabin on which to bump your head. There is space in which to maneuver, room for tackle kits, great visibility, and usually better balance with the helmsman's station set farther forward than is possible in a cabin cruiser. By night the camper-top erects into a boat-tent complete with plastic windows and mosquito bars. In some designs the convertible camper makes up into a snug cabin bigger than one a permanent superstructure provides.

Handling Characteristics Where you cruise also affects your choice of boat. Great Lakes country and the coastal waters of the United States dictate a good-sized outboard with superlative sea-handling characteristics— a low freeboard that will avert your being blown about by every crosswind; a bow that will lift to the oncoming rollers; and a transom that will rise with a following sea. Big-water boats carry extra-high transoms of 20 inches. This is 5 inches higher than standard, but motors are available with long shafts to match. Boats in this class should also have a false or second transom forward of the stern. Built in as part of the motor-well, the false transom keeps water from flowing into the cockpit should a wave break over the stern. Scuppers or a self-bailing arrangement in the motor-well lets the water run off harmlessly.

Choice of Construction Material Today's outboard boats come in every conceivable kind of construction material—wood planks, canvas, rubber, fiberglass, planked plywood, molded plywood, sheet plywood, modern plastics, aluminum, steel, and in combinations of these materials. Which should you choose? There is no ready answer, despite the vociferous proclamations of those who favor one over the other. The truth is there are good boats available in each type of material. Your choice again becomes partly a personal preference. Wood has a warmth and a resilience plus the quality of natural flotation that is unequaled by any other material. The modern plywoods are amazingly strong for their light weight. Fiberglass is a minimum maintenance material and gains new adherents every year as well as new application in larger boats. But fiberglass bottoms require antifouling paints as much as any other kind of boat in similar service, and the gel or finish coats do require paint when they begin to fade and lose their luster after a few years. Now you can buy lapstrake hulls made of aluminum planks, and aluminum is rotproof and corrosionproof, light and strong for its weight. It does not require paint except for decorative reasons.

The Balanced Rig If you're buying a complete outboard rig—boat, motor, and trailer—be sure they're matched and will blend into a serviceable and safe combination. You can find horsepower and motor accessories to fit every outboatd boat. If the giant 80–100-hsp outboards don't provide enough power for you, there is a hybrid arrangement called variously an inboard-outboard, a stern drive, and outdrive. It combines inboard power with an external drive that looks and is very similar to the lower unit of a conventional outboard. The flexibility and responsive steering of the outboard engine is thus combined with the nearly unlimited power potential of inboard marine engines. The motor, like the boat, should be chosen to fit your needs. Although most 18-hsp engines will pull a medium-weight water skier, no water-ski buff would be really satisfied with such minimum power. By investing in automated electric controls you can make high horsepower easy fun for every member of the family. Remote steering, throttle controls, electric starting, electric gearshifts—forward, neutral, and reverse —are available on all but the smallest motors. The right motor for your boat relates to many factors. Speed changes with an increase or decrease in propeller revolution, and is affected by different loads, propeller pitch, throttle setting, etc. A motor may be rated 40 hsp at 4,000 rpm; hang it on the stern of a huge houseboat, and it may never be able to turn over faster than 3,500 rpm. Thus you pay for more than you will ever enjoy.

HOW TO SELECT A TRAILER

A boat trailer enables you to keep your boat in your backyard instead of afloat at an expensive mooring; better than this, it makes an amphibious adventurer out of you. With wheels under your boat you can fish or hunt anywhere. Select your trailer after you decide upon boat and motor, and then buy one to fit. The gross weight of your boat and the length of your boat are the two basic figures. Trailer manufacturers list their products according to a rated load and length capacity. A trailer rated for 16-foot boats cannot take an 18-footer without upsetting its basic balance. Be sure that gross weight includes everything you plan on carrying inside the boat as well as the motors. Provisions, camping equipment, and waterski gear all count. Gasoline weighs 6 pounds per gallon; water weighs 8 pounds per gallon. Frame steel, axle strength, size of wheel, ply of tire, and number of axles are all coordinated to accommodate a specified load capacity. Exceed it, and you're asking for bent axles and blown tires. On any four-wheeled trailer, each tire supports one-fourth the load. If you put a 2,000-pound boat on a tandem four-wheeled trailer, its tires will not be the same ply or quality that the same boat demands of a two-wheeled trailer.

Every trailer is designed to take several makes of boats. Review your choice to insure that it can be adjusted to provide maximum support for your hull. Rubber rollers, bumpers, or padded chocks should cradle your craft, hold it in perfect balance, and protect it from road shock. The smaller your boat the less likely that you will need any launching-retrieving mechanism such as a winch or tilt-bed, but they are essential to big boats. A power winch can make loading a 20-footer a pushbutton proposition. In choosing a trailer, keep in mind the fact that the roving trailerboatman often cruises more miles on concrete than he does on water. —F.M.P.

OUTRIGGERS An integral part of equipment for big-game fishing boats. *For details see* Outriggers *under* Sportfisherman

OVARIES The essential female reproductive organs which produce eggs

OYSTERS *Ostrea* and *Crassostrea* spp. Common marine bivalves found in all seas. The United States oyster industry is one of the most valuable fisheries, past harvests yielding 75–90 million pounds of meats annually. In the United States three species are of commercial importance and used as food—the eastern oyster *Ostrea virginica;* the Olympia oyster of the northwest *Ostrea lurida;* and the Japanese oyster *Ostrea gigas*, which has been widely introduced on the Pacific Coast. A fourth species, the European oyster *Ostrea edulis*, was experimentally planted in the Canadian Maritime provinces, New England, and the state of Washington in 1950, and it has also become established in these regions. Traditionally, oysters are identified according to their place of origin, and some culinary distinctions exist in the Blue Point, Cape Cod, Cotuit, Albemarle, Abascon, Tangier, Rockport, and various other regional varieties.

FOOD VALUE

From a dietetic standpoint oysters are better balanced than most foods. Oyster meats contain copper, iron, manganese, iodine, calcium, and phosphorous as well as essential vitamins (A, B, C, D, and G). The protein in oyster meats has an especially high nutritive value. Oysters also contain glycogen, a substance similar to starch, which is readily digested even when uncooked. Because of this high mineral, vitamin, protein, and glycogen content oysters are one of our most nutritive foods.

Oyster

EASTERN OYSTER

The eastern oyster is of primary importance because of its wide distribution and great abundance. It thrives in the inshore waters of our Atlantic and Gulf Coasts from Massachusetts to the southern extremity of Texas, and was at one time found in large quantities on the coasts of Maine and New Hampshire. To the Indians and the Pilgrim colonists these northern oyster beds provided a most valuable food resource, but no industry exists there today. The eastern oyster thrives in seawater of reduced salinity. Under natural conditions oysters are found in brackish waters in depths ranging from halfway between tide-marks to 40–50 feet. Oysters can grow even in deeper water, but no commercially important beds occur below 40 feet. They are well-adapted to withstand considerable fluctuations in temperature and salinity of water, thriving in the bays and estuaries where environmental conditions frequently change. In the Gulf of Mexico and on the flats of the inshore waters in Southern states the temperature at oyster bottoms often reaches or even exceeds 90°F., whereas in the Northern states nearly freezing temperatures occur every winter. Their tolerance to salt content is also very great. Natural oyster beds are usually located near river mouths and in bays where the salt content of the water is greatly reduced.

An eastern oyster will take 2–5 years to grow to marketable size, depending on the locality in which it lives. Oysters which are planted so that they have unrestricted space for growth acquire the most desirable shape, while oysters crowded excessively are thin and poorly flavored as well as ill-shaped. At the present time oysters used for canning chiefly come from the overcrowded natural reefs of the Southern states where they grow in great clusters. If properly cultivated, however, the same beds may produce oysters of better quality equally suitable for canning, shucking, and the half-shell trade.

OLYMPIA OYSTER

The native oyster of the Pacific Coast is smaller than the eastern oyster, seldom exceeding a length of 2¼ inches. It is found from Charlotte Sound in British

Columbia as far south as San Diego Harbor, California, occurring in greatest numbers, however, in the lower part of Puget Sound in the state of Washington, the leading West Coast state in oyster production. For the cultivation of the West Coast oyster an elaborate system of dikes has been arranged whereby large areas of otherwise useless mud flats are converted into a series of pools. The system is so devised that the highest levels will be covered with water at low tide. Because of the great range of tide the enclosed tracts of about one acre each may be arranged at as many as five different levels. Oyster larvae when ready to attach strike near high-tide line. Here they are allowed to remain for a year or two before they are transplanted to a lower level. Growth is slow in this species, 4–5 years being required to reach marketable size.

JAPANESE OYSTER

The imported Pacific oyster differs from our native oysters in appearance by its elongate and rather fragile shell. Imported as seed, it arrives from Japan in February and March. It is then planted rather thickly and left undisturbed until the following spring. It may be transplanted several times, but grows very rapidly, attaining a marketable length in less than two years. Attempts to propagate this species in American waters were successful, but "setting" does not occur every year. It usually fails when summer temperature is low and water remains cold. Because of its rapid growth and high glycogen content the Japanese oyster is considered well-suited for canning. As to flavor and appearance it is decidedly inferior to our eastern oyster and cannot take its place in half-shell trade. Its very rapid growth may also contribute a serious handicap for the oyster often overgrows a marketable size and is not acceptable by trade. Failure to spawn presents another serious difficulty because the presence of large amounts of spawn in the oysters impairs their flavor and renders them unpalatable.

EUROPEAN OYSTER

The European oyster thrives in coldwater from Spain to Sweden. As an exotic to United States waters it thrives in regions where our native eastern oyster will not propagate. Unlike the American species, the European oyster fertilizes its eggs within its shell. The larvae are held within the gills of the parent where they feed on microorganisms siphoned by the adult.

OYSTER FARMING

The cultivation of oysters began more than 2,000 years ago in ancient China. Oysters do not grow on the ocean bottom but in bays and river mouths where the salinity of the water has been diluted to some extent by tributary streams or rivers. Natural oyster beds are usually in 3–4 feet of water, but they grow through the intertidal zone, and in semitropical areas they even grow on the aerial roots of mangrove trees and marsh grass where they are only covered by water at high tide. This proximity of freshwater determines the flavor of the oyster to a large extent, because the bivalve is a vegetarian, eating minute, one-celled plants known as diatoms. The diatoms, like other marine plants, are nourished by various minerals in the water, such as copper, iron, and iodine, which are reflected in the oyster's food value, flavor, and color.

Occasionally, abnormally colored oysters—green, brown, and almost black—are found in certain localities. Greening may be due to a certain variety of diatoms in the diet, in which case the color is usually limited to the gills. Green-gilled oysters are of fine quality, and, while not generally acceptable to the American public, are regarded in France as a superior product, and special methods are used to grow them. Greening caused by an excess of copper in the tissues colors the entire body. It does not render the oysters inedible but gives them a coppery taste.

The task of an oyster farmer is first to prepare his ground by dredging and clearing away old shells and natural enemies of the oyster. He then plants clutch or material on which to catch the set. For this purpose material such as gravel and the shells of oysters, clams, and scallops is being used in different parts of the coast. To increase the area available for setting, various spat (young oysters) collectors can be used. Cement-coated tubes and poles have proved satisfactory for gathering seed in certain localities. Wire bags filled with shell are commonly used. A particularly efficient collector has been developed from the ordinary egg crate partition which, when coated with a mixture of lime and cement and placed in the water, affords a maximum area for "setting." In some places brush stacked in rows on mud flats can be used with great advantage. Set obtained on shell collectors may be left until the following fall or spring, but more often it is transplanted to growing grounds. *See also* Fish Cookery —A.J.McC.

OYSTER TOADFISH *Opsanus tau* This species is a member of the family Batrachoididae, a small family of shallow-water marine fishes with a worldwide distribution in tropical and temperate waters. Two related species belonging to the same genus occur in Florida waters and in the Gulf of Mexico, and a third was recently described from the Bahama Islands. The oyster toadfish is found from the Gulf of Maine south to Miami, Florida.

Its color on back, sides, and head is predominantly dull greenish or brownish with dark vermiform markings. There are no white spots or "H"-shaped markings. The soft dorsal and anal fins have 5–9 oblique, irregular black bands; caudal, pectoral, and pelvic fins with 5–7 sharply defined cross bands. Belly and underside of head yellowish and sometimes dark spotted.

Other distinguishing characteristics of oyster toadfish are body stout, scaleless, with loose wrinkled skin and obscure lateral line; numerous flaps or cirri on head; mouth very wide, with fleshy lips and with a single row of blunt teeth on jaws, vomer, and palatines; opercle with 2 concealed spines; dorsal spines 3; a large foramen in axil of pectorals.

Body depth greater than .2 in standard length; head broad, about .37 in length. Dorsal rays 24–27, usually 25–26; anal rays 20–22; pectoral rays 18–21, usually 19 or 20.

LIFE HISTORY

In the northern part of its range the oyster toadfish spawns in June and July. The eggs are large, about 5 mm in diameter, and adhesive. They are deposited in a single layer within a shell or some other nesting cavity. Each egg is attached to the substrate by means of a peculiar adhesive disc. Even after hatching, the larvae remain attached to the disc until the egg yolk is well absorbed. Separation occurs when the larvae are about 15 mm long.

The nest is guarded by the male who expends considerable energy in keeping the eggs clean. He will remain with the nest even though it may become exposed at low tide. Incubation takes 2–3 weeks.

This species attains a maximum length of about 18 inches and a weight of a little over 1 pound. The males become larger and live longer (to 12 years compared to 7 for the females). Food consists mainly of bottom-dwelling crustaceans and mollusks but sometimes small fishes and fish eggs are eaten.

ANGLING VALUE

Due to its small size the oyster toadfish has no angling value. It is caught by bottom-fishing with natural baits, usually incidental to some other quarry, such as flounder or porgy.

The flesh of the oyster toadfish is edible, but individuals need to be handled with care since both the dorsal and opercular spines are poisonous. —J.C.B.

P

PACIFIC AMBERJACK Seriola colburni This species is endemic to the eastern Pacific.

The Pacific amberjack has a dark nuchal band extending diagonally from the front of the first dorsal fin through the eye. The dorsal- and anal-fin lobes become more elongated with growth; the dorsal lobe is greater than ¼ to less than 1/7 as long as the head and body (without the tail) in specimens 12 inches and longer. First dorsal fin

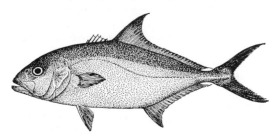

Pacific Amberjack

with about 7 spines; second dorsal fin with one spine and about 28–31 softrays; anal fin with 2 detached spines followed by one spine and about 21 softrays. First gill arch with about 14–19 gillrakers on the lower limb, the rakers becoming shorter and rudimentary with growth.

The body is elongate, moderately compressed, and fairly deep for an amberjack. The head profile is not as pointed as in the California yellowtail, and the body and fins are darker than in that species.

The range extends from the Gulf of Guayaquil, Ecuador, through the Gulf of California, to Oceanside, California, and at the Galápagos and Tres Marías islands.

The first specimen identified as this species was 49 inches long. A specimen from Cape San Lucas was reported to weigh about 112 pounds.

LIFE HISTORY

The life history is unknown. Stomachs were reported to contain fishes, crabs, shrimps, other crustaceans, and bottom-living mollusks, the last suggesting bottom-feeding habits as well as pelagic.

ANGLING VALUE

The Pacific amberjack is a very fine gamefish. It is taken trolling and still-fishing with cut bait. Its palatability is only fair. *See also* Amberjacks, Carangidae
—F.H.B.

PACIFIC ANGEL SHARK Squatina californica Closely related to the Atlantic angel shark (*which see*), it differs from it primarily in the shape of the inner barbel of the nostril, that of the California species being expanded into a spoonlike structure, while the Atlantic species is narrow and tapering. It is reddish-brown, grading through brown to black above, spotted with dark or olive markings. The underparts are white, and the fins are gray on their posterior edges. It usually grows to about 3 feet, although 5-foot, 60-pound specimens have been reported.

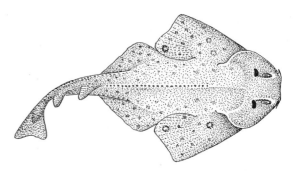

Pacific Angel Shark

It is found only along the Pacific Coast of North America, from lower California to southern Alaska. More common along the southern California coast, it occurs on the bottom in shallow, inshore areas. As in the Atlantic species, it bears live young which hatch from the egg within the mother. —D.dS.

PACIFIC BARRACUDAS Sphyraena spp. There are four described species of barracudas occurring in the eastern Pacific. Of these, the Pacific barracuda, *Sphyraena argentea*, is the best known. Also called California barracuda, barrie, snake, scoots, and scooter, this species occurs along the Pacific coast of North America from Alaska southward to Magdalena Bay, Baja California. Its common range, however, is between Point Conception, California, and Magdalena Bay. This species reaches a length of 44 inches and weight of about 12 pounds but most of the individuals captured by anglers are much smaller. Weights of 14 to 18 pounds have been reported but are unverified.

The Pacific barracuda is brownish with a blue tinge, metallic black or gray on the back, shading to silvery white on the sides and ventral surface, with the tail yellowish. It lacks black blotches scattered on the sides of the body as does the great barracuda (*which see*). It has 5 dorsal spines, 10 dorsal rays, and the anal elements consist of 2 spines followed typically by 9 rays. There are more than 150 scales along the lateral line. Its maxillary

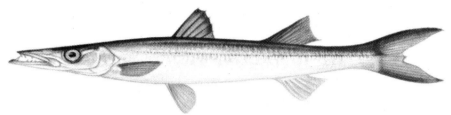

Pacific Barracuda

does not reach beyond a vertical from posterior nostril, and the pectoral fin does not reach to a vertical from the insertion of the pelvic fin. The anterior rays of the second dorsal and anal fins do not reach the tip of the last ray when the fin is depressed. Its posterior teeth of the mandible are not slanted backward.

In southern California, it reaches a peak of abundance during the spring and summer, with only a few being taken during the winter. It is, however, taken in Mexican waters throughout the year, reflecting a northerly spring migration and a southerly fall migration. Spawning occurs offshore in the open ocean, from April to September, with a peak in June. The spawning location probably is somewhere off outer Baja California and perhaps off southern California. The eggs are pelagic, and young barracuda resemble the adults in having well-developed teeth. The young drift inshore and live in the shallow, quiet bays and coastal waters. Those spawned in early spring grow to about 4 inches by July, and average about 16 inches by the following July. They grow to at least 11 years old, and the females grow larger than the males. Most fish weighing over 8 pounds and all fish weighing over 11 pounds are females. Growth rate is about the same in both sexes up to the fourth year of life, after which the females grow slightly faster. Most females spawn in their second year and all by their third year, while a few males spawn in their first year, and all by their second year. It eats small herring, smelt, squids, and other small, schooling forms.

Commercially it is taken with gillnets and trolling lines in California, while in Mexico it is caught in purse seines. The market is almost exclusively for fresh fish, although a few are smoked or canned. Historically, it has always been one of the most valuable of California's resources, both commercially and to sportsmen.

There are at least three other species of barracuda in the eastern Pacific: *S. lucasana*, commonly called the Gulf barracuda, is distributed from Cedros Island to Cape San Lucas and throughout the Gulf of California (usually not north of San Juanico Bay on the outer coast). The exact northern and southern range of two other species, *S. ensis* and *S. idiastes*, is not known, but the former may be given as Mazatlán (one record) to Panama; and *S. idiastes* from Panama to Peru and the Galápagos Islands. These three Pacific barracudas are not as large as *S. argentea*; none has ever been measured at over 30 inches or a weight in excess of 4 pounds.

ANGLING VALUE

During the fishing season (summer), the Pacific barracuda is found along the coast from close to shore to about 7–8 miles out. This is one of the most popular of the small game fishes in southern California. It may be caught by trolling or casting with ¼-ounce to 1-ounce feathers, stripbait, or a live bait such as sardine, queenfish, or anchovy. When using artificials a fast retrieve is usually most effective.

FOOD VALUE

It is an excellent food fish. Several million pounds are sold in West Coast markets each year. The roe of this species is highly esteemed. —D.dS.
—A.J.McC.

PACIFIC BLUNTNOSE JACK *See* Atlantic Bluntnose Jack
PACIFIC BONITO *See* Bonito
PACIFIC BUMPER *See* Atlantic Bumper
PACIFIC COD *Gadus macrocephalus* A close relative of the Atlantic cod (*which see*), this Pacific species varies from its Atlantic kin only in minor details, mainly in the pointedness of the fins of the Pacific cod. The heavy body is elongated, bearing 3 dorsal fins and 2 anal fins. A well-developed barbel on the chin and a large mouth help to typify this species. The position of the anal opening, placed below the anterior part of the second dorsal fin, and the large barbel, which is about equal to the eye diameter, distinguish it from the Pacific tomcod (*which see*). The body is brown to gray on the back, becoming lighter on the belly, with scattered brown spots on the upper parts. The fins are all dusky, and are edged with white on their outer margins. Specimens have been taken in excess of 3 feet, but the species does not attain the size of its Atlantic relative.

It generally occurs from Oregon to the Bering Sea; it has been recorded from northern and central California, but is more common to the north. Specimens have been taken from shallow water to nearly 800 feet.

Spawning occurs in winter and early spring, and the eggs are believed to be pelagic. Food consists of fishes, such as herrings and sand lances, as well as crustaceans. Its habits are similar to those of the Atlantic cod.

ANGLING VALUE

Formerly an important commercial species, its full potentiality has never been realized, particularly off the western and northern Alaskan coasts, which appear most promising. It is taken in trawls and on longlines set for halibut, and sold fresh, smoked, and salted. Some are taken by anglers using fish or cut bait. —D.dS.
PACIFIC CUTLASSFISH *See* Atlantic Cutlassfish
PACIFIC ELECTRIC RAY *Torpedo californica* A Pacific species of the family Torpedinidae, it is similar to the Atlantic torpedo (*which see*) in the shape of the subcircular disk, the short tail, and the smooth skin. It is blue-black to lead-gray, with small spots on the dark background of the upper sides of the disk. It grows to at least

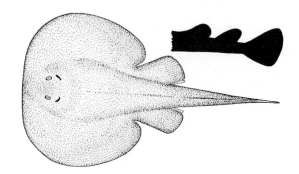

Pacific Electric Ray

50 pounds and 3 feet. Known from British Columbia to southern California in waters that are moderately deep, this ray possesses the ability of other members of the family to generate a powerful electric shock which originates from modified muscles located on either side of the head. —D.dS.

PACIFIC HAKE *Merluccius productus* Sometimes placed in a separate family, Merlucciidae, this cod is distinguished from its other Pacific relatives by the two dorsal fins and the single anal fin; the second dorsal and anal fins are deeply notched, giving the appearance that the fin is divided. As in other cods, the head is large, but this species has a very large mouth, with strong, sharp teeth. The lower jaw projects and lacks a barbel. The body is elongated and tapered, ending in a square-shaped caudal fin. The thin scales fall off readily. It is a dull silvery-gray to metallic-black above, grading to silvery-white on the lower parts. The head and body are usually covered with irregular black dots. The lining of the mouth and gill covers is black. It is larger than the Atlantic hakes, reaching about 3 feet.

Found from the Gulf of California to Alaska, it is most common from central California to Washington in moderate depths.

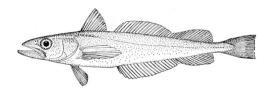

Pacific Hake

LIFE HISTORY

Spawning occurs largely from February through April, and the larvae are extremely abundant from Baja California to San Francisco, up to 300 miles offshore. To the north, the young are taken in shrimp trawls in 300 feet or more of water, but adults have been taken off California, as deep as 3,000 feet. Small fishes and squids are eaten.

ANGLING VALUE

Because of its abundance, this hake is common in commercial and sport catches, but its flesh is not desired and has poor keeping qualities, although some hake is sold fresh. —D.dS.

PACIFIC HALIBUT *Hippoglossus stenolepis* The largest flatfish of the Pacific Coast, and a member of the righteye flounder family, it has a high arch of the lateral line over the pectoral fin, with no accessory dorsal branch. A lunate caudal fin and the middle rays of the dorsal and anal fins, which form a peak, help to identify the species. The scales are smooth, and the small mouth, which does not extend past the middle of the lower eye, contains well-developed teeth on both sides of the jaws. It is dark brown with irregular blotches and is uniformly white on the pale side. Reaching nearly 500 pounds and 9 feet, it is found from central California to the Bering Sea and northern Japan in depths of 60–3,600 feet.

LIFE HISTORY

It spawns in the winter, in deepwater, and a 140-pound female may contain about 2,700,000 eggs. The young fish settle to the bottom of the inshore waters by spring, where they live in sandy bays and inshore banks, eventually

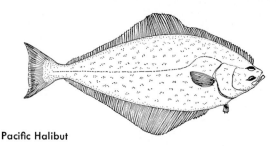

Pacific Halibut

returning to deeper waters with age. Females grow faster and reach a larger size, attaining an age of at least 35 years. Immature fish do not migrate extensively, but the mature adults may migrate at least 2,000 miles. They eat fishes, crabs, clams, worms, and squid.

FOOD VALUE

This is an excellent table fish. The commercial fishery uses only longlines, usually in depths of 60–900 feet, and in 1960, for example, over 50,000,000 pounds were taken commercially in the United States. The liver and viscera are used in the production of vitamin A. —D.dS.

PACIFIC HERRING *Clupea harengus pallasi* This species is closely related to the Atlantic herring, from which it is separable only on a subspecific level. It is found from northwestern Alaska to San Diego. Its greatest abundance is around Kodiak Island and Sitka, as well as in British Columbia. The Pacific species also ranges from the eastern Soviet Union south to Japan and the Yellow Sea.

Like the Atlantic herring, the Pacific herring reaches a length of about 18 inches. Throughout its range, the Pacific herring seems to be broken up into a number of localized populations which have an annual migration between the inshore spawning area and the open-ocean feeding ground.

The fishing season is from December into the late summer where herring are taken with beach seines, gillnets and haulnets. Sportsmen in various areas take them with dipnets. During the winter and spring, Pacific herring enter the bays and shallows to spawn, and the eggs are deposited on weeds and rocks in shallow water. They reach an age of at least 8 years, with occasional individuals living to be 20 years old.

ECONOMIC VALUE

These herring travel in vast schools, feeding on small plants and plankton with their comblike gillrakers. As

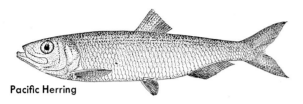

Pacific Herring

with the Atlantic herring, this species is eaten by a great number of predatory fishes, such as sharks and salmon, as well as by waterfowl, seals, and probably sea lions. The commercial catch is sold canned, smoked, or fresh, while other Pacific herrings are used for bait or for reduction to oil and meal. —D.dS.

PACIFIC HORSE-EYE JACK *Caranx marginatus* Also called big-eye jack, this eastern Pacific species is closely related to *Caranx latus*, the Atlantic horse-eye jack (*which see*) and to the Indo-Pacific *Caranx sexfasciatus*.

The chest in front of the pelvic fins of the Pacific horse-eye jack is completely scaled. The second dorsal fin has one spine and 19–21 softrays; the anal fin has two detached spines followed by one spine and 15–17 softrays. The first gill arch has 6–8 gillrakers on the upper limb and 16–18 gillrakers on the lower limb. The body and fins are never black or dark brown. The body is moderately deep, the head profile is convex, and the prominently large eyes are placed well forward in the profile. The dorsal- and anal-fin lobes are moderately elongated. There are about 29–35 scutes in the straight lateral line. Some of the gillrakers on the anterior parts of the upper and lower limbs may become very short with growth. The bluish-green back grades into silvery or white sides and belly. The dorsal-fin lobe is black-tipped in the young, and both the dorsal and anal fins become dark in large specimens. A small spot usually occurs at the upper margin of the operculum. The young, up to about 8–10 inches in length, usually have five broad bars on the body and one on the nape.

The Pacific horse-eye jack has been taken from La Plata Island, Ecuador, into the southern Gulf of California at Topolobampo and at Cape San Lucas, Baja California, and at the Galápagos, Cocos, Clipperton, Tres Marías, and Revillagigedo islands.

A photograph has been published of a specimen 36 inches long, and this is the largest recorded specimen.

This species may have been confused sometimes with the crevalle, *Caranx hippos* (*see under* Atlantic horse-eye jack). It is very different from the spotted jack, *Caranx melampygus*, which tends to have more dorsal and anal rays, gillrakers, and scutes, but the ranges of these numbers overlap slightly in the two species. The spotted jack has a deeper body, less rounded head profile, smaller eyes, and longer dorsal- and anal-fin lobes, and specimens more than about 10 inches long have small spots on the head and body.

The life history remains to be studied and documented.

ANGLING VALUE

This has been described as a fair gamefish. Its flavor is not well-known in the eastern Pacific. The closely related

Caranx sexfasciatus is considered an excellent food fish in Hawaii and other parts of the central and western Pacific, where a few specimens have reported to be toxic, with the toxicity increasing with age. *See also* Carangidae, Jacks —F.H.B.

PACIFIC JACK MACKEREL *Trachurus symmetricus* It is also known as California horse mackerel. Large adults were described under a different name, *Decapterus polyaspis*.

The Pacific jack mackerel has enlarged scutes along the entire portion of both the curved and the straight lateral lines. There are no detached finlets behind the dorsal and anal fins, although the last ray of each fin is slightly more separated than the other rays; and there are no papillae or furrow on the shoulder girdle.

The second dorsal fin has one spine and 30–35 softrays. The anal fin has two detached spines followed by one spine and 28–31 softrays. The first gill arch has about 13–16 gillrakers on the upper limb and about 39–42 gillrakers on the lower limb. The curved lateral line has about 48–51 scutes, and the straight lateral line has about 43–48 scutes. There is an iridescent green color above, sometimes with a bluish luster, often mottled with lighter and darker shades, and the sides and belly are silvery.

The Pacific jack mackerel ranges from Cape San Lucas, Baja California, to southern Alaska. It occurs from inshore waters up to 600 miles offshore. The largest recorded specimen was 32 inches long and weighed 5 pounds.

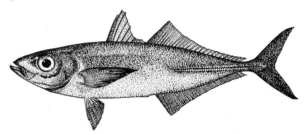

Pacific Jack Mackerel

LIFE HISTORY

Because of its abundance and importance off California, the life history has been fairly adequately studied. Based on studies of otoliths, some large adults are thought to live 30 years or more. Spawning is known to occur from Magdalena Bay, Baja California, to Washington, and is concentrated in offshore waters. The spawning season extends from February through September with peak spawning around May. The early development, from the egg through the larval stage and into the juvenile stage has been well-documented. The early larval growth rate and survival have been studied. The jack mackerel is a schooling fish, and is frequently taken with schools of sardines (*Sardinops*) and Pacific mackerel (*Scomber*). The principal food is pelagic crustaceans and mollusks, although at times they feed heavily on anchovies, lanternfish, and small squid. Schools of jack mackerel are preyed upon by several kinds of larger fish and marine mammals.

The relationships of the genus *Trachurus* have not been adequately studied. In the eastern Pacific Ocean there may be 3–4 species. *Trachurus murphyi* is usually applied to the species from Chile to Peru and the Galápagos Islands.

ANGLING VALUE

This is an important light-tackle gamefish in California where they occur in local abundance and where they are usually caught using live anchovies for bait. In California and Baja California it is of increasing commercial importance, is usually taken by purse seines and lampara nets, and canned. It is very good smoked. *See also* Carangidae, Scads —F.H.B.

PACIFIC LAMPREY *Entosphenus tridentatus* This eel-shaped member of the family Petromyzontidae is recognized by its peculiar sucking mouth, the lack of paired fins, and the long dorsal fin which is confluent with the tail fin. It differs from the sea lamprey (*which see*) in having only a single dorsal fin, rather than having it divided in two by a deep notch, and lacks the well-developed arrangement of rasping teeth on the sucking disk, there being only 5–6 cusps. It is dark bluish to brownish gray, and is seldom mottled. A length of over 2 feet is attained. It occurs from southern California to northwestern Alaska.

LIFE HISTORY

Adults live in the sea, ascending estuaries during the spring to spawn. After lengthy journeys, they build nests in the upper headwaters of streams. As in the sea lamprey, death follows spawning. After the eggs, which are buried in gravel, hatch, the young ammocoetes burrow into mud for about two years, toward the end of which transformation into the adult stage begins. Adults drop downstream into the sea, where they take up a parasitic life on such forms as salmon and trout. With its rasping teeth it bores a hole through its host's skin and lives on blood and body fluids.

FOOD VALUE

The flesh of most lampreys is edible, even delicious, but it is seldom utilized in the United States. —D.dS.

PACIFIC LOOKDOWNS *See* Lookdowns
PACIFIC MACKEREL *See* Mackerels
PACIFIC MANTA *Manta hamiltoni* Its disk somewhat resembles that of another Pacific ray, the bat stingray (*which see*), but the hornlike projections on the head readily separate it from the bat ray. The tips of the pectoral fins are pointed, the pelvic fins are short and confluent with the posterior margin of the disk, and there is a short dorsal fin. Its short tail and the terminal position of the mouth separate it from a southern, closely related species, *Mobula lucasana*, which has a tail nearly as long as the disk, and the mouth is located beneath the tip of the

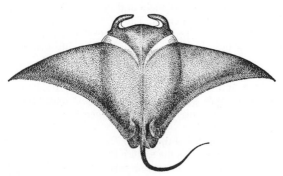

Pacific Manta

snout. It is black above and white to bluish beneath. All mantas reach a large size, this species growing to 18 feet and over 2,300 pounds.

LIFE HISTORY

An inhabitant of warmwaters of the eastern Pacific, it is known as far north as Redondo Beach, California. An 18-foot specimen contained a 28-pound embryo, but little else is known about these fish except that young have been seen being born during the frequent somersaulting and leaping displays which characterize mantas. —D.dS.

PACIFIC MOONFISH *See* Lookdowns
PACIFIC OCEAN PERCH *Sebastodes alutus* This rockfish (*which see*) has been exploited commercially on an extensive basis relatively recently. It is taken all along the coast and occurs in waters of 200–2,000 feet in depth from southern California to the Bering Sea. The interorbital space is slightly convex or flat; lower jaw very long but not extending beyond the upper head profile; knob on lower side of lower jaw tip large; frontal spines medial; no spines under eye; peritoneum dusky to black. It is carmine-red with black markings, and grows to 18 inches.

IMPORTANCE

The fish forms a significant part of the food of albacore and halibut. In 1958, 2,000,000 pounds were landed in Queen Charlotte Sound. —J.R.

PACIFIC PERMIT *Trachinotus kennedyi* This eastern Pacific species has also been called the palometa, and is the same species as *Trachinotus culveri*, Culver's pompano, under which name it has sometimes been described. It is very similar to the Atlantic permit (*which see*).

The first dorsal fin of the Pacific permit has 6 short spines. The second dorsal fin has one spine and 17–18

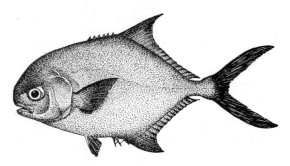

Pacific Permit

softrays. The anal fin has two detached spines (3 reported once, but aberrant, if correct), followed by one spine and 16–17 softrays. The body is moderately to very deep, but variable, and the body depth decreases with growth of the fish. The dorsal- and anal-fin lobes are relatively short; the length of the lobes is shorter than the length of the head. There are no dark bars on the body.

The Pacific permit ranges from San Pablo, Ecuador, into the Gulf of California, and north on the western coast of Baja California at least to Abreojos Point. It possibly extends to southern California. It has been reported to attain a length of 2–3 feet, but there are no apparent recognized records of fish of this large a size.

There are two other sympatric species of permit found in the Indo-West-Central-Pacific. They are readily separable by the greater depth and longer dorsal fin lobe in Trachinotus blochii. Also at sizes larger than about 12 inches total length, the osteology is appreciably different; *T. blochii* has hyperostosis of the "Tilly-bone" and has no osseous enlargement of the ribs. In *T. mookalee* there is no hyperostosis of the "Tilly-bone" (just in advance of the three free supraneurals in advance of the dorsal spines); there is hyperossification of the nasal bones and an extreme enlargement of the second plural rib on each side.

LIFE HISTORY

The life history of the Pacific permit has not been studied. Young, deep-bodied specimens have been observed drifting on their sides at night in bays, and have been speared just beyond the surf.

ANGLING VALUE

This is an excellent game- and foodfish. It has small commercial importance, but both its sport and commercial potential are great. *See also* Atlantic Permit, Carangidae   F.H.B.

PACIFIC SAILFISH *Istiophorus platyperus* This species is the Pacific representative of the sailfishes along the American coasts. Whether or not it is really a different species from the Atlantic sailfish is uncertain. The chief difference between the two seems to be that the Pacific sailfish gets much bigger than the Atlantic one. The Pacific sail grows to 275 pounds, more than twice the weight of the Atlantic record.

As far as we know, everything that has been said about the Atlantic sailfish will apply also, with appropriate modifications, to the Pacific form. In appearance, they are very much the same, with a long, high dorsal fin, long pelvic fins with a membrane, similar coloring, and so on.

Nothing is known definitely of the spawning and migratory habits of the Pacific sailfish, but presumably they are similar to those of the Atlantic form.

The Pacific sailfish is found all the way from southern California to Ecuador. In times of El Niño, an occasional warm, southerly extension of the Equatorial Counter Current, it follows the warmwater even further south, to the northern coast of Peru. But in ordinary years it probably does not range much south of the Gulf of Guayaquil. Sailfish, whether of the same or another species, are also to be found around the Hawaiian Islands, the Line Islands, and throughout the South Pacific generally. They are quite common along the Asiatic coast, from Korea southwards, and have been recorded occasionally from New Zealand and Australia.

FISHING METHODS

Angling for Pacific sailfish is done in the same manner as for Atlantic sails. In the Pacific, however, fairly large numbers are taken by commercial fisheries, either by longline or harpoon. However, like the Atlantic fish, the flesh tends to be tough, and is regarded as much less desirable than, for example, that of the striped marlin. It is excellent when smoked.   —J.E.M.

PACIFIC SALMON *Oncorhynchus* **spp.** There are six species of Pacific salmon, five of which occur in North America—the chinook (*O. tshawytscha*), coho (*O. kisutch*), sockeye (*O. nerka*), pink (*O. gorbuscha*), and the chum salmon (*O. keta*). The sixth species is the cherry salmon (*O. masou*), which occurs only in Asia. The genus has a range from Formosa to San Diego, California. In general, only two species, the chinook and coho, are important sport fish, but the chum, pink, and sockeye are also taken in some waters. The pink salmon holds first place quantitatively in commercial catches with the sockeye next but the positions are reversed in value of catch. The chum and chinook differ little from each other in quantity caught commercially. However, salmon stocks on the Pacific coast have diminished, especially in the southern part of their range, as a result of overfishing, habitat destruction, barrier emplacement, and pollution. At high dams there is no known satisfactory way of passing the young fish downstream unharmed.

The American species have 12–19 rays in the anal fin; they have abdominal pelvics, a soft-rayed dorsal, and an adipose fin. As the fish mature and reach spawning time, their silvery appearance with blue backs and some spotting changes to shades of red, yellow or black, dependent on the species and sex and the males develop a hook (kype) on the tip of the lower or both jaws.

Unlike the Atlantic salmon, after the long and arduous journey upstream to spawn, all Pacific species die

LIFE HISTORY

All the species spawn in freshwater in gravel from June (chinooks in Siberia) to February (coho in Oregon) and die shortly thereafter. The young (alevins) remain in the gravel until the large yolksac is wholly or almost used up and then emerge to go to the ocean immediately as with the chum and pink or remain in freshwater for 3–4 months, as does the fall chinook, or for a year or more, as with coho, spring chinook, and sockeye. The kokanee or resident sockeye usually spends its entire life in freshwater. The ocean life is varied, from 2 years with pinks and cohos to 7–8 with some sockeyes. Most of the species and races probably feed in the north Pacific and the Gulf of Alaska.

There is considerable intermingling between populations of widely different origins while at sea. Chum salmon for example, tagged within a relatively small area of the Gulf of Alaska, provided returns from Japan, the USSR, and as far south as the state of Washington which is practically the entire geographical range of the species.

Comparatively little is known of the vertical distribution of Pacific salmon while in the ocean. On the basis of echo sounding experiments by Japanese researchers in the Aleutian region, it was observed that salmon were closest to the surface after sunset and descended after daylight. The concentrations of fish shifted in relation to the depth of the thermocline. Canadian researchers found that sockeye and chum salmon exhibit differences in behavior toward the thermocline; this cold layer of water appears to act as a barrier through which the sockeye will not pass either during the night or day, whereas the chum salmon found the thermocline a barrier only during hours of darkness in the late season.

PACIFIC SALMON MIGRATIONS

The chinook, sockeye, and chum salmon from North America travel great distances to reach their ocean feeding areas. Chinooks from the Columbia River have been known to travel 2,500 miles to the Aleutians. Sockeyes swim over halfway to Asia from British Columbia. Chums from southeastern Alaska journey to the Aleutians. Pink salmon from southeastern Alaska cross the Gulf of Alaska, at least, in their peregrinations. The coho from Oregon and Washington is not given to extensive migration. They are caught in the ocean by commercial fishing fleets from Northern California into British Columbia. Some of the northern stocks of the species travel into the Gulf of Alaska, at least.

Salmon which survive to maturity in the open ocean return with a high degree of constancy to the freshwater rivers of their origin. This phenomenon has been the subject of extensive research to isolate the homing mechanism. The well-ordered direction and timing of the shoreward migrations from the high-sea are relatively rapid journeys which do not appear to be oriented by currents, temperatures, or salinities. It has been suggested that the detection of odors of certain rivers near coastal localities is the homing mechanism but this does not explain orientation in migration and would require strict adherence to a shoreline after making a blind landfall. It is known that salmon can maintain widely divergent courses while hundreds of miles at sea and arrive at a coastal locality, converging with a high degree of precision at their place of origin. Salmon also show a keen awareness of changes in light intensity and length of day which suggests that ocean life is an integrated whole involving the seaward migration of young, seasonal movements, and exploitation of the environment during the ocean years before returning to the river.

See also Chinook Salmon, Chum Salmon, Coho Salmon, Kokanee, Pink Salmon, Sockeye Salmon   —J.R.
—A.J.McC.

PACIFIC SANDDAB *Citharichthys sordidus* A left-handed flatfish, this dab has a straight lateral line, with no arch as in many flounders. The pelvic fins are dissimilar in shape, that on the eyed side being attached to the belly ridge. The eyes are large, and the left pectoral fin is shorter than the head length, distinguishing it from the related longfin sanddab, *C. xanthostigma*. The thin scales fall off more easily than in other flatfishes. The color is tan to brown, variously mottled with dull orange to black. It reaches 2 pounds and 16 inches.

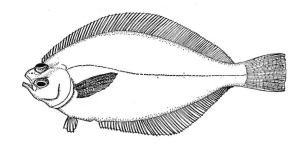

Pacific Sanddab

The Pacific sanddab is found from southern California to northwestern Alaska in water of 10–100 fathoms, being commonest at depths of 20–50 fathoms. Like other flatfishes, they spend most of their time on the bottom but are capable of swift movement in the capture of small fish, squid and octopods, shrimps, crabs, sea squirts, and worms. A number of predatory species feed upon the Pacific sanddab.

LIFE HISTORY

Sexual maturity occurs at about 7 inches. Spawning occurs from July to September, the ripe eggs being ½–¾ millimeter. The smallest stages of the pelagic young have an eye on either side of the head, but, as in other flatfishes, one eye migrates around to the colored side prior to the young fish settling to a bottom existence. They attain an age of at least 10 years, and an 11½-inch female is 9 years old, the females growing faster and larger than the males.

FOOD VALUE

This species, as well as its relatives, is excellent eating, being sold fresh, although split and dried dabs are prepared in some areas. It is taken primarily in trawls and by hook and line.   D.dS.

PACIFIC SARDINE *Sardinops sagax* The Pacific sardine is a member of the herring family and is one of the true sardines, being separated from the Pacific herring by the presence of low, oblique ridges on the gill cover. The belly does not have a sharp, sawtoothed edge as in the shad, being less prominent than in the Pacific herring.

Pacific Sardine

The body is elongate and round in cross section, with a compressed head and a small mouth, which contains no teeth. The color is dark blue on the back, becoming silvery on the ventral surface, with round, black spots forming one or more rows on each side of the body, as well as a row of black dots along the back. The sides are iridescent, reflecting shades of purple and violet.

The range of the species is from southeastern Alaska into the Gulf of California. Close relatives are found in Japan, western South America, Australia, New Zealand, and South Africa. This open-ocean fish travels in large schools of varying size of from a few tons to hundreds of tons.

LIFE HISTORY

Spawning occurs in the open sea up to 300 miles offshore, mostly in the southern part of California. The young migrate toward shore at a length of 3–5 inches. When they reach about 7 inches, they will move back offshore to resume an open-ocean life, where they become subject to the commercial fishery. An age of at least 13 years is attained, although the average life span is only about 10 years. Regular migrations occur between California and British Columbia, with indications of a northward feeding migration during spring and summer, followed by a southerly movement during the fall and winter.

ECONOMIC VALUE

Due to fluctuations in the environment, this species has undergone marked changes in abundance during the past years. Water temperatures and food supply seem to be responsible for these fluctuations, and on several occasions the commercial fishery has virtually failed. The species is used principally for canning and for production of fishmeal and oil, although a small percentage of them is used for bait and chum. Young sardines are used as live bait, principally for tuna and mackerel.   —D.dS.

PACIFIC STAGHORN SCULPIN *Leptocottus armatus*   This abundant Pacific coastal sculpin is important as a baitfish. Some striped-bass anglers use it exclusively. It is often a nuisance, taking bait intended for more desirable

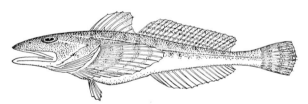

Pacific Staghorn Sculpin

fishes. Its sharp preopercular spines are a formidable weapon which are thrust upward as the fish flattens its head when disturbed. It is found in bays and inshore, also in and near freshwater at the mouth of streams, from northern Baja California to northwest Alaska. It grows to twelve inches.

The Pacific staghorn sculpin has a scaleless body; an antlerlike preopercular spine; coloration green to gray-olive with yellow and black markings; a conspicuous, large black spot on the posterior portion of the spinous dorsal fin. *See also* Sculpins   —J.R.

PACIFIC THREADFIN *Alectis ciliaris*   Also called goggle-eye jack and previously designated as *Hynnis hopkinsi*, this Pacific species is very similar to the African pompano (*which see*), but is even less well-known than that species. The very large, bluntheaded carangid from Hawaii that has been called white ulua, *Carangoides ajax*, is the Pacific threadfin.

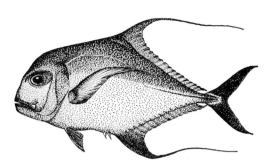

Pacific Threadfin

The Pacific threadfin occurs in the Indo-Pacific from the east coast of Africa to the Hawaiian Islands and Tahiti. In the eastern Pacific, it is known from off Chimbote, Peru, to south of Ballenas Bay, Baja California, Mexico, and at the Galápagos Islands and the Tres Marías islands. It apparently occurs throughout the tropical Indo-Pacific waters. It attains a length of at least 3 feet.

LIFE HISTORY

The smallest known specimen, ½ inch long, from the eastern Pacific was taken in June off Mexico, and other small specimens, taken from May to October off Mexico and Guatemala, suggest a spawning season of about March to September. Newly hatched larvae that may have been this species were once described from the Java Sea.

ANGLING VALUE

It is caught trolling or bottom-fishing, and gives a good fight on light tackle. *See also* Carangidae, Threadfins
            —F.H.B.

PACIFIC TOMCOD *Microgadus proximus*   A small, Pacific member of the cod family, it resembles the Atlantic cod and Pacific cod (*which see*). It differs from the latter in having the anus positioned beneath the first dorsal fin, and by its small barbel which is equal to about half of the eye diameter. Codlike in appearance, it has a large mouth with fine teeth, a large head, and 3 dorsal fins and 2 anal fins. The body is covered with small, thin scales. It is olive-green to brown on the back and white to silvery on the lower sides and belly, with dusky edges to the light-colored fins. It reaches a length of about 1 foot.

ANGLING VALUE

It is known from central California to Alaska, in 60–300 feet, occasionally entering shallow water. It occurs in otter trawls sporadically and is of only minor commercial importance, although the flesh is good. In central California it has some value as a sport fish.   —D.dS.

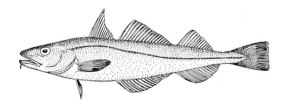

Pacific Tomcod

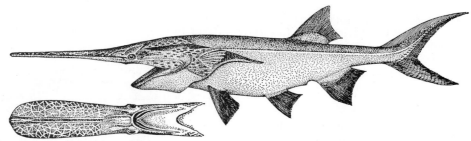

Paddlefish, with under view

PADDLEFISH *Polyodon spathula* Also known as spoon-bill, spoonbill cat, shovelnose cat, and boneless cat, the paddlefish is a living representative of an old group of fossil fishes. Its only near relative is a native of the Yangtze River in China. This species can be recognized by the long, flattened snout in front of a large head and mouth; the sharklike tail whose upper lobe is upturned and is longer than the lower; and the skin, which is scaleless except for a very few scales that are inconspicuous. The eye is very small, and the gill cover has a long, pointed flap. Color is gray to bluish-gray in turbid water and grades to nearly black in clearwater. The skeleton is chiefly cartilage. One 200-pound specimen was recorded, but about 90 pounds is the normal maximum. Average weight of paddlefish caught by anglers in the Osage River, Missouri, in 1961 was 38 pounds.

Paddlefish are found in the large rivers and lakes of the Mississippi River system, including the Missouri River into Montana, the Ohio River, and their major tributaries. They have thrived in large impoundments where extensive areas of gravelbars remain in large tributary streams to provide spawning areas and have declined in places such as the upper Mississippi River where the slowed waters of a continuous series of dams has caused siltation of these spawning areas.

LIFE HISTORY

Spawning occurs in April and May. The fish in lakes often make extensive movements to find the gravelbars in streams needed for spawning. This movement and spawning occur when significant rises in the river level occur which allow the large fish to move over normally shallow riffles and provide current which they appear to need for spawning. At this time they move in groups, often near the surface, where they frequently are hit by boat propellers. The eggs are scattered over the gravelbar and fertilized by accompanying males. Immediately upon fertilization the egg forms an adhesive coating which causes it to sink and to adhere to the first object it touches. Most adhere to the gravel where they hatch in 5–10 days, depending on the water temperature. Upon hatching they depend on the attachment to the rock to hold the capsule as they wriggle free. When hatched the young paddlefish has no indication of the snout that will begin to be apparent in 2–3 weeks, but it grows rapidly after that and soon is the most conspicuous part of the fish. It is proportionately longer on young fish than on those that are nearing maturity. The newly hatched larva begins to swim soon after hatching and does so continuously thereafter; thus it is removed from the gravel to the stream and, in many areas, to the lake very early in life. Growth varies greatly with the abundance of food, but they usually grow 10–14 inches the first year and to about 21 inches

the second. They are long-lived, up to 30 years in the Lake of the Ozarks, Missouri.

The paddlefish feeds by moving through the water with its huge mouth agape. If attracted by a swarm of plankton it begins to circle and feeds actively through it. Food is retained on large, comblike gillrakers, and periodically the mouth is closed and the fish gulps to swallow it. This consists primarily of plankton and insect larvae. Small fish have been reported taken infrequently. They appear to be ingested accidentally by adults but have been noted more frequently among young fish during the only period of life when teeth are present.

ANGLING VALUE

Paddlefish are usually caught by anglers using heavy snagging tackle including ½-pound sinkers and large treble hooks. These are cast from the bank or trolled from a boat. It is not a strong fighter, but its large size and the strong currents usually found where they are taken combine to provide real sport. There are few bones in the body, which is a good food fish, particularly smoked.

—C.A.P.

PAINTER A rope secured to bow of small boat to make it fast.

PALLID STURGEON *See* Sturgeon

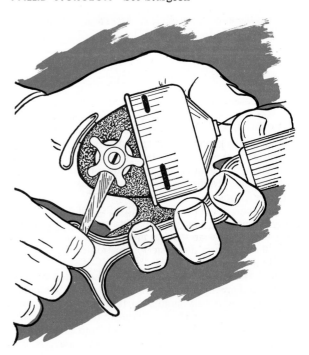

Palming a reel

PALM A term used in bait-casting to describe a manner of holding the reel when retrieving a lure. The angler palms a reel by grasping it comfortably across the side plate, and, when using a reel without a level-winding device (tournament type), he may take the line between his thumb and forefinger to lay it evenly on the spool. *See also* How to Bait-Cast *under* Bait-Casting, Spin-Casting

PALOMA POMPANO *Trachinotus paitensis* This eastern Pacific species was previously sometimes listed by the scientific name of *Trachinotus paloma*. It is very closely related to the pompano, *Trachinotus carolinus*, of the western Atlantic.

The first dorsal fin of the paloma pompano has 6 short spines. The second dorsal fin has one spine and 24–27 softrays (usually 25–26). Its anal fin has 2 spines (which become detached in large fish) followed by one spine and 20–25 softrays (usually 22–24). The dorsal- and anal-fin lobes are moderately short, and there are no black bars on the body.

The range is from Independencia Bay, Peru, to the northern Gulf of California, and northward to Redondo Beach, California. An unsubstantiated report lists it from as far south as Valparaiso, Chile. A specimen from Peru of about 15 inches in total length may be near the maximum size attained. The life history is not known.

ANGLING VALUE

Presumably, this would be a good light-tackle game-fish and equal in palatability to the common pompano of the Atlantic. It has been reported to be one of the best food fishes of Peru, entering the commercial catches in fair quantities; it is usually found there on fairly rough sand beaches and is caught in seines, gillnets, and trammelnets. It is also sold in markets in Panama and Mexico. *See also* Carangidae, Pompanos —F.H.B.

PALOMETA *Trachinotus goodei* Also called the gafftopsail pompano and the longfin pompano, this species is endemic to the western Atlantic, and is very closely related to the gafftopsail pompano, *Trachinotus rhodopus*, in the eastern Pacific.

The palometa has a first dorsal fin with 6 short spines. The second dorsal fin has 1 spine and 19–20 softrays. Its anal fin has 2 anterior spines (which become detached in larger fish), followed by 1 spine and 16–18 softrays. The body has four narrow bars high on the sides with a trace of a fifth bar in back of the fourth. The dorsal- and anal-fin lobes are greatly elongated (especially in specimens of 6 inches and longer); the dorsal-fin lobe may extend beyond the fork of the tail when the lobe is depressed.

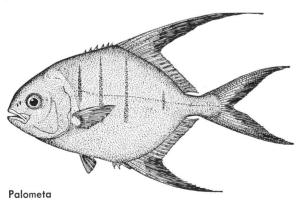

Palometa

The body is moderately deep. The coloration of the palometa is dark silvery above with silvery or golden sides, a yellowish belly, and a bright orange breast. The lobes of the dorsal and anal fins are almost black, the remainder of these fins dusky or pale with bluish edges; the caudal fin is dusky or bluish, the pectoral fins golden and bluish, and the pelvic fins whitish. The narrow, dark body bars and the dark, falcate lobes of the dorsal, anal, and caudal fins make this a beautiful and striking fish.

The species has been assigned three different scientific names—*Trachinotus glaucus* by Bloch in 1787, *Trachinotus goodei* by Jordan and Evermann in 1896, and *Trachinotus palometa* proposed by Regan in 1903 (who technically invalidated the name established by Bloch). According to the rules of zoological nomenclature, the correct name for this species is now *Trachinotus goodei*.

We know now that the very large pompano from Florida, called permit, is the same species as the smaller-sized, deep-bodied pompano there, called round pompano. Some years ago fishermen and scientists alike considered these to be two distinct species. It was definitely known that the scientific name *Trachinotus falcatus* applied to the form called round pompano. The large permit-form was first thought (1879) to be the same as another species that had been described from Africa as *Trachinotus goreensis*. When it was determined (1896) that the African species and the Florida permit were not the same, a new name was proposed for the permit from Florida to clarify the distinction. Unfortunately, although this was the intent, it was not the result, because the name proposed, *Trachinotus goodei*, was officially connected with only two small (1½ inch) specimens that are the young of the palometa. Although it has been used as such for many years, *Trachinotus goodei* is not the scientific name of the permit; and it must be the name used for the palometa. *See also* Carangidae, Pompano

—F.H.B.

Piñas Bay anglers enjoy a very high ratio of success when they fish for marlin

PANAMA The word *panama* means "abundance of fish," and, in fact, this part of Central America rates as one of the top angling regions in the world. Bordered by the Caribbean Sea on the north and the Pacific Ocean on the south, Panama offers a variety of saltwater fishing as well as considerable fishing in its inland rivers. Panama is tropical and has a dry season from December through

April and a rainy season from May through November. The rainy season is typified by brief but heavy showers during some part of the day.

GULF OF CHIRIQUI

Beginning in 1972, when a camp was established on the island of Coiba, anglers began exploring the Gulf of Chiriqui which lies west of the Gulf of Panama near the border of Costa Rica. The fishing here has proved to be exceptional for various snappers, groupers, jacks, roosterfish, wahoo, dolphin, sailfish, and black marlin.

The cove at Tropic Star Lodge is a well-protected anchorage for charters. These seas can sometimes be quite rough

GULF OF PANAMA

Until the 1960's the prime fishing grounds in the Gulf of Panama at Piñas Bay were difficult of access. Adventurous anglers cruised from the Canal Zone with an overnight stop at Cocos Point to fish the Piñas Bay area for black and striped marlin, yellowfin tuna, Pacific sailfish, dolphin, amberjack, mako, and a great variety of reef species, including the corvina. Today, it can be conveniently reached by plane service from Tocumen Airport, and excellent accommodations as well as boats and guides exist on location. This is one of few areas where black marlin (*which see*) can be caught in quantity. The system of fishing for black marlin at Piñas Bay differs from that used at say, Cabo Blanco. For one thing outriggers aren't necessary at Cabo. Here, the best results are usually obtained by trolling in the boat's wake. Too, at Cabo it's primarily sightfishing. You can see those Peruvian giants finning at the surface, although blind strikes occur from time to time; the opposite condition is true in Panama.

Black marlin have been caught in Piñas Bay during all months of the year. However, they are more abundant during January, February, and March. The boats often average fifteen marlin strikes per day during this period. Some large black marlin (600–700 pounds) have been caught in the summer months, and it would appear that the heaviest fish occur here from July until early fall.

Pacific sailfish are boated the year round, but because the conventional method of fishing for marlin is to use a whole bonito from the outriggers, many sailfish are not hooked on these 5–6-pound skip baits. A similarly large bonito is employed when live baiting on the flat lines. However, sailfish are readily caught on smaller whole baits as well as strip baits. Wahoo, dolphin, roosterfish, and amberjack also come to these smaller baits.

—A.J.McC.

PANFISH Used in a collective sense to indicate a group of freshwater (usually) fishes which are ordinarily too small to be considered gamefish. The most common panfish are yellow perch, bluegill, crappie, bullhead, and rock bass. Panfish are sought largely as food. They provide the greatest percentage of United States fishing and are found in all kinds of waters from city parks to more than 1,000,000 farm ponds. Although no panfish is capable of a prolonged struggle against ordinary fishing tackle, they do offer some sport when caught with very light equipment. Panfish also represent a large winter fishery, particularly in our Midwestern states where they are taken through the ice. On the debit side, panfish are not harvested sufficiently in many areas where they exist as stunted populations; in some instances they have caused the decline of more desirable gamefish.

THE BASIC ART

If one item were to be singled out as the pivotal invention in panfishing equipment, it would be the flat Prince Albert tobacco tin which first put the worm in small boys' Sunday pockets. Like a magic lantern, it materialized the redwings cackling in the cattails and squirrels racing along oak limbs and bonnets vibrating like drumheads from the sound of crappie chomping on fry. Next to the height of August corn, the most amazing sight was a string of perch ringed in yellow and black with transparent vermilion fins—and the way a granddaddy bream could stare at you through its purple mask. There was then, and always will be, many things to learn with a cane pole which escape modern philosophers.

All panfish can be caught on worms, minnows, grasshoppers, and other insect baits. If we were to take a vote, probably the manure worm, cricket, and roach would win in that order. Ever since the Alleghenies began leaking into farm ponds, the rearing of crickets and roach trapping have become a considerable business in our Southern states. Such specialist items as catalpa worms, bonnet worms, and the meal worms or golden grubs which gave winter bluegill fishing a jolt in the Midwest are also locally important. But live-bait fishing for panfish is a simple mechanical process. As a rule, the line is run through an adjustable float, and two small split shot are added just above the hook. The angler estimates where the fish are located, then starts to work. If nothing nibbles within a few minutes, he may vary the depth of the bait or move on to a new location, This pursuit of a large school is enough to satisfy any angling appetite, and it requires a devotion hardly less concentrated than that of a hairline caster working with artificial lures. Yet the real art rests on how much the angler has absorbed about the habits of his quarry.

Panfish generally inhabit the marginal areas of a lake, but the larger specimens are apt to be found on shoals which rise from deepwater, or over submerged weed beds. Much depends on the season, character of the pond, and the available food. In lakes where thermal stratification occurs, large yellow perch are usually most abundant just above the thermocline (about 20–30 feet down), but in some waters they frequent the stagnant area *below* the thermocline where there is little or no dissolved oxygen. By comparison, bluegills are unable to venture into deepwater where oxygen values are too low. The sunfish isn't as tolerant as the perch, thus, fortunately, keeping their schools within easy reach. White perch, on the other hand, generally move according to the light, seeking deepwater during the bright hours and schooling in the shallows toward dark. For this reason, the best fishing is usually at early morning and again in the evening. But the feeding places of panfish also depend to a large extent on the abundance and type of food. Our casual panfisher might assume that all small fish can be taken on any small lure; however, it's not that simple. The individual species adheres to a well-defined pattern in each locality.

For example, in a study on the food habits of black crappies in Orange Lake, Florida, it was observed that the consumption of minnows is seasonal; stomach contents revealed that the amount varied from 90 percent in the fall and early winter to a low of 65 percent during the summer months. Furthermore, during the spring breeding season, male crappies consumed 33 percent less minnows and 33 percent more crustaceans than females. Food preferences of the sexes is revealing because it's not limited to the crappie—nor the spawning season. Based on a study in Michigan, it was concluded that the yellow perch of Ford Lake were distributed according to their preferred diet. Females dominated the shallows where minnows were most abundant while the males congregated in deepwater where midge larvae were almost the sole item consumed. A similar phenomenon was observed on Saginaw Bay. The catch made by bottom trawling was composed primarily of males which had been feeding on larval insects, whereas the females foraged on small fish in open water. The picture that emerges, then, is that the selectivity of panfish schools is definitive and local knowledge of fishing conditions really pays off.

PANFISH TACKLE

Of the three different types of modern panfish tackle, most specialists will want to own at least two of them—a panfish fly rod, and a spinning or spin bait-casting rod. At the extreme, one popular fly rod outfit consists of a 4-foot 4-inch fiberglass rod which weighs exactly 1 ounce. The matching reel is a single-action aluminum with silent click that weighs 2⅜ ounces. A custom-tapered fly line fits the rod, and, depending on your skill, casts up to 40 feet or more can be made. The assembled outfit feels featherlight, and it provides plenty of thrills against the pull of a fat bluegill or crappie. However, any fly rod up to 4 ounces in weight is suitable for panfish; so the second outfit should be calibered to toss baby jigs, spoons, spinners, and live bait.

Spin bait-casting designed to handle 4-pound-test line is most practical, and should appeal to the great majority of panfishers. The thumb-controlled top-mounted spool is ideal for beginners. A popular 5-foot-long fiberglass rod-and-reel combination weighs just 7½ ounces complete. A husky perch can make the drag buzz merrily. Experts who want to go down to very fine lines of 1–2-pound-test will probably choose one of the many rods and reels in the orthodox ultralight range. One popular outfit consists of a 4½-foot fiberglass rod which weighs 1¾ ounces, matched with a precision-built 6-ounce reel. The reel is designed for lines testing up to 4 pounds, which should satisfy everybody. Even with large panfish available, it's rarely necessary to use anything heavier than 4-pound-test, and smaller diameters are preferable for casting the tiniest lures. But between these two types of spinning outfits, you should have one to supplement the fly rod.

Of all the panfish—white and yellow perch, rock bass, the sunfish, white and black crappie, and the white and yellow bass—some kind of sunfish is the most likely catch of the majority of anglers, and broadly speaking, "bream" are the prototypes for our panfish techniques. There are numerous hybrid sunfish in addition to the eight species, of which the bluegill is the largest and most highly esteemed among panfish specialists. Distinguished by long pointed pectoral fins (equal to almost one-third of its body length) and black ear flaps, the bluegill is usually a dark greenish-blue on the back and yellowish to orange on the belly parts. It also has 6–8 dusky vertical bars on its flanks. Actually, the coloration of bluegills is more variable than in other sunfish, and only the fins are a reliable gauge. The redear sunfish also has elongated pectorals, but the red margin of its opercular flap is distinctive and is not to be confused with the black "ears" of a bluegill. Although widely distributed throughout the United States, the bluegill is of prime importance in the Midwest and South. However, the redear, better known as the "shell-cracker" because of its ability to crush and grind mollusks, often weighs ½–3 pounds in the Swamp Belt and is seasonally popular during the spring bedding period. Taken in its native waters, either sunfish is no slouch on light tackle, and both can be extremely fastidious about your choice of lures.

PANFISH TECHNIQUE

Just as the over-all rule for panfish tackle is light, the best method of fishing is slow. It doesn't matter whether you use a spinner or fly; all panfish are more readily caught at minimum retrieving speed. The exceptions are rare. Panfish are comparatively slow swimmers when measured against a trout or bass, and it's apparent that quick motions frighten them. Sunfish, for example, usually study a surface lure for some time, finning toward it, and backing off as though waiting for it to explode. Occasionally one will strike immediately if the school is actively feeding, but their normal approach to a bait is cautious. There are times when big bluegills will flee at the faint sound of a popping bug. Yet, they might hit the same lure provided it is left on the water for a considerable period without being popped. All things considered, poppers are not ordinarily as effective for bluegills or other panfish as quiet, swimming bugs of the old-fashioned moth design or the sponge-rubber crickets and spiders. The ideal lure seems to be one that looks completely helpless and just barely disturbs the surface, and it must be small. You can hardly poke your finger between the rubber-tire lips of a big bluegill, and for this reason its lures must be dressed on the correct hooks. Although an occasional sunfish will become fastened to a bass bug, this is the exception rather than the rule. Stay within the limits of a No. 8 to No. 12 hook size, and you won't miss many bream.

Another popular sunfish is the pumpkinseed. This gaily colored species sometimes reaches a weight of over 1 pound. There's no mistaking the pumpkinseed because its dark blue ear flaps end in a red border, and its body which shades from a coppery-brown on the back to a yellow or orange breast is brilliantly marked with a thatching of powder-blue stripes and orange spots. This sunfish is easier to catch than either the bluegill or shellcracker, and it'll hit any small wet fly, nymph, dry fly, or panfish bug. However, the rule of fishing slow still applies; in fact, the only thing that will discourage a pumpkinseed is fast or erratic retrieving. The spinning-rod fisherman suffers most on this count because many lures are not designed for really slow work. If a spinner blade is too thick or the lure body too heavy, the angler must reel quickly to activate the lure or keep it from snagging bottom.

An ideal spinning lure for most panfish is an ordinary weighted spinner. There are countless hundreds on the market, but the size is important. It should have a blade about one inch long. It must be free swinging, slender rather than oval in design, and thin enough to spin at the slightest pull. It shouldn't weigh more than ⅛ ounce, and preferably about $1/10$ ounce. Although the bare spinner is usually effective, it sometimes helps to add a tiny sliver of pork rind. You can buy the rind in paper-thin two-inch strips which is labeled as a fly-rod size, but it's ideal for decorating ultralight lures. It wiggles enticingly at slow speeds. The spinner should be cast out and left to sink near a school. Being light, it seldom snags in weeds; so when it gets near the bottom, retrieve *very* slowly with just the faintest hopping motion.

The second most popular panfish in United States waters is the crappie. One or both species of the crappie is found nearly everywhere today. The white and black crappie are very similar in appearance. Their general color is a silvery-green or olive-drab on the back fading to a silvery-white or pale yellow on the belly. The dorsal and caudal fins are spotted with darker green, and the flanks of the white crappie are marked with dark vertical bands; the black crappie wears irregular dark blotches. Generically, the black crappie is a member of the sunfish family, but it's temperamentally different from the bluegill. A school doesn't often roam in the open—they have a passion for getting under things such as fallen trees, pad beds, or sunken brush piles.

One of the best methods of catching crappies on big Southern creeks is to troll close to the bank. This is done by throttling the outboard down until it purrs and trolling a live minnow along the deep banks, pushing through overhanging limbs where necessary. This live-bait trolling method vividly explains why crappie addicts go to extreme pains to find sunken brush piles. A dedicated black crappie fisherman will build one if he can't find one. Willow mats are anchored in many Midwestern lakes for that reason. Nearly all Western and Southern impoundments have natural brush heaps, however, created when the land was inundated. The secret of fishing is to find these areas where the fish school, and once you have a hot spot, the rest is easy. A popular lure is a miniature yellow jig for the spinning rod, but many small spinners and spoons worked slowly and deeply will pay off also. Crappies are not consistent surface feeders, but, in common with the voracious white bass, they school periodically to feed on clouds of forage fish, notably the threadfin shad. At such times, fly-rod lures of the feather-minnow type, bucktails, and even top-water bugs will take fish. *See also* Black Bullhead, Black Crappie, Bluegill, Brown Bullhead, Green Sunfish, Ice Fishing, Pumpkinseed, Redbreast Sunfish, Redear Sunfish, Rock Bass, Ultralight Spinning, White Crappie, White Perch, Yellow Bullhead, Yellow Perch

PARABOLIC ACTION   A type of rod which is slower than the tip-action (*which see*) due to the flexion being distributed throughout its total length. The butt of a parabolic rod has a low taper; the tip has two compound tapers. In casting, the butt section will flex as far down as the angler's hand. Such a rod may be extremely powerful and better suited to some purposes than the tip- or progressive-action (*which see*) rod. *See also* The Theory of Rod Function in Casting *under* Rod Building

PARAGUAY   This country in central South America has much to offer the sportsman, but the dorado fishing is clearly its best angling. Paraguay is the least populated country in South America (estimated less than 2 million) and many of its numerous rivers receive very little rod pressure. The land is not for the tourist who expects to find everything comparable to home; there is a great deal of primitive jungle and roads are nonexistent in many areas. The river port capital, Asunción, is the only concession to civilization, and here ox carts and donkeys plod among the taxis and imported cars. The best and easiest way to arrange a dorado trip here is through Tiger Hill Safaris in Asunción, which maintains camps on a number of Paraguayan rivers. The accommodations may consist of hotels, ranch houses, or tents, depending on the river being fished. All supporting equipment including small aircraft and car, service personnel, and a bilingual guide are included in these package trips.

Dorado fishing in Paraguay starts and ends later than the same angling in Argentina. The best period here is from October through March. This is the summer season and temperatures ordinarily run from 80°–90°F, accompanied by moderate rainfall in the form of thundershowers.
                                                                —A.J.McC.

PARGO   The Spanish name for any one of a number of snappers (*which see*).

PARROTFISH   *See* Queen Parrotfish

PAYARA Family Cynodontidae   South American freshwater fishes of at least 4 genera and 10 or more species, all cynodons are formidable predators, closely related to the tigerfish of Africa. The payara is known in Brazil as *peixe-cachorro* or dogfish because of its pair of long canine teeth in the lower jaw which project upward

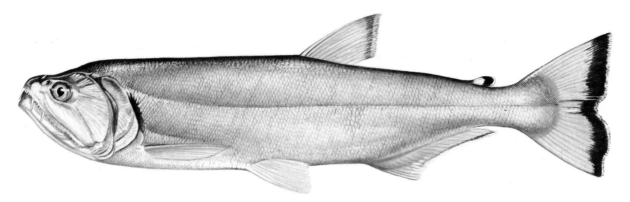

Payara, 16-pound Male, Cinaruco River, Venezuela

through the snout. Payara are distributed from Colombia to southernmost Brazil. All species have elongate, compressed bodies; dorsal fin origin about the middle of the body; a complete lateral line, slightly downcurved; adipose fin present. Payara are generally dark blue to olivaceous dorsally, blending to silver along the sides and belly. The most common species (*Hydrolicus scomberoides*) in the northern part of its range has strong black margins on both adipose and caudal fins and less intense black margins on its dorsal and anal fins.

Payara occur in both standing and running waters. They are a schooling fish. Little is known of their life histories and the taxonomic position of the various species is under revision.

ANGLING VALUE

Payara are among the gamest of South American freshwater fishes. Because of their sharp teeth, wire leaders are essential. Almost any artificial lure, particularly topwater plugs seem irresistible to these fish. Their multitoothed mouths make them difficult to hook, and after touching a lure they instantly leap in the air. Large payara make very strong, fast runs. At least one species attains lengths of 40 inches or more and has been reported to 30 pounds. *See also* Brazil, Colombia, Venezuela
—A.J.McC.

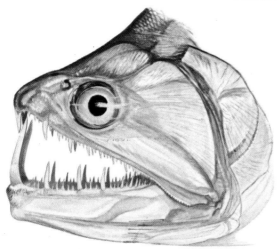

Dentation of payara

PEACOCK FLOUNDER *Bothus lunatus* This species belongs to the Bothidae, the largest family of flatfishes, which contains about 40 genera and about 200 species. It is restricted to the Western Atlantic, where it has four close relatives, and ranges from Bermuda and Florida south to Fernando de Noronha, Brazil. It is common in the Bahamas and the West Indies.

The peacock flounder is one of the most colorful of all the flounders. It has bright blue rings and spots on a brownish or grayish background. Large individuals generally have dark dorsal, anal, and caudal fins with blue spots on the bases and white dots on the margins. There are two or three large diffuse blotches on the straight portion of the lateral line and the pectoral fin has three narrow, dark crossbars.

Other distinguishing characteristics of the peacock flounder are dorsal fin rays 91–99; anal fin rays 71–76; pectoral fin rays on ocular side 10–12; gillrakers on lower limb short, 8–10; scales in lateral line 83–92; vertebrae 10–30. Body depth 54–59 percent of standard length; head length 26–31 percent of SL; eye diameter 16–22 percent of head length; upper jaw length 30–35 percent of HL, extending posteriorly to a vertical through anterior edge of eye or slightly beyond.

Anterior profile of head notched in front of lower eye. Anterior margin of upper eye over posterior margin of lower eye on specimens larger than about 100 mm; over middle of lower eye on specimens about 50 mm in standard length. Tentacles on eyes short, not present on specimens less than about 100 mm. Interorbital space in both sexes as wide as or wider than eye diameter. Interorbital spines reduced in size, not prominent when present. Anterior pectoral fin-rays of the adult males greatly produced.

This species and other bothids produce large numbers of pelagic eggs. The young larvae are bilaterally symmetrical, having one eye on each side of the head. At metamorphosis one eye migrates through a slit in the head below the anterior dorsal fin base and comes to rest adjacent to its counterpart on the other side. At this time the fish takes up a bottom existence with its eyed and pigmented side uppermost.

It prefers a sandy bottom in shallow water (usually less than 20 feet) around patch reefs and rocky shore lines. It is edible and is said to reach a length of about 18 inches.
—J.C.B.

Peacock Pavón, 17-pound Male, Paguey River, Venezuela

PEACOCK PAVÓN *Cichla orinocensis* One of the most widely distributed cichlids found in the freshwaters of tropical South America. Lack of research has caused numerous authors to lump a number of species together under the name *Cichla ocellaris*. The *Cichla* genus is presently being revised and as many as a dozen species may emerge. Also called the pavon cinchado (Spanish) and tucunaré comum (Indian). This fish is generally basslike in appearance with a prominent hump developing on the posterior region of the head in breeding males. The adult body coloration is a gray-green or purplish-green on the dorsal surface, shading to golden yellow or bronze on the sides. The belly coloration varies from snow white to dusky yellow and is often bordered by bright orange. The peacock pavón has three black to dusky bars on its sides. All pavón possess a prominent ocellated black spot on the base of their caudal fins; which suggest the vivid eye of a peacock tail plume; hence the popular American name, peacock bass. The pelvic, anal, and lower half of the caudal fins are yellowish-green to brick red in color. The dorsal fin and upper half of the caudal fin is a translucent blue-green sometimes with white spots. Some are characterized by an interrupted lateral line canal, while others have a continuous lateral line. The caudal fin is slightly rounded and completely scaled; the anal and pelvic fins are partially scaled. The peacock pavón attains weights up to 28 pounds or more, with the average in some Venezuelan streams running 5–6 pounds.

ANGLING VALUE

An excellent gamefish, the peacock pavón can be caught on bait-casting, spinning, or fly tackle. It will strike plugs, spoons, spinners, streamer flies, and popping bugs. The play is typical of a largemouth bass with strong runs and occasional jumps. However, the strike of a peacock pavón is swift, and anglers usually experience some difficulty in hooking the fish at first. Peacock pavón also tend to feed in schools, and once located it's often possible to catch several or more than several fish.

An excellent food. The flesh of the peacock pavón is firm in texture and varies from white to a creamy white in color. It can be prepared by frying, baking, broiling, or being made into a chowder. *See also* Butterfly Pavón, Colombia, Venezuela —A.J.McC.

PECTORAL FINS The anterior paired fins

PELAGIC A fish which spends its life close to the surface waters of the sea, such as the tuna. Fish of pelagic habits are opposed to demersal species, which live close to the bottom.

PELICAN HOOK A hinged hook held together by a ring. When the ring is freed, the hook swings open.

PELVIC FINS The posterior paired fins

PENNSYLVANIA The commonwealth's 45,126 square miles sit astride the Appalachian and Allegheny mountains, dividing the coastal plains and metropolitan areas of the east from the farm lands and the industrial complex of the Ohio River drainage. It could be called a transition state as diverse in its fishing opportunities as in its topography. The mountainous areas, running from the northeast to the southcentral portion, provide the principal trout-fishing areas. The two major lake regions are in opposite corners of the commonwealth, in the northeast and northwest. However, man has affected the natural distribution of lakes by building impoundments in many areas previously devoid of standing waters. The distribution of fishes also has been affected by the stocking program of the Pennsylvania Fish Commission. Over 4,500 miles of stream and 69 lakes are annually planted with more than 2,000,000 legal trout. Warmwater species, such as muskellunge and northern pike, have been introduced successfully into new drainages. On the debit side of this picture is the 3,000 miles of running water adversely affected by pollution.

THE POCONO REGION

The Pocono region, in the northeastern section of the commonwealth, is one of the great resort areas of Eastern United States. Into this locality, because of its many lakes, streams, and mountain beauty, come many tourists from large Eastern cities. The largest lake in the Poconos is 5,670-acre Lake Wallenpaupack at Hawley. It is an artificial impoundment located on the Pike-Wayne County border. This lake is generally known for its bass and walleye fishing, but many panfish and some trout are taken in the spring and early summer. Located nearby are many glacial or artificial lakes which also provide fishing for chain pickerel, bass, and panfish. Pecks Pond, Promised Land Lake, Lower Promised Land, and Fairview Lake are a few of the better lakes open to the public in Pike County. In Monroe County, Tobyhanna Lake and Bradys Lake are open to public fishing for the usual warmwater species of this locality. Wayne County provides bass, pickerel, and panfish angling in 250-acre Gouldsboro Lake, Elk Lake, Duck Harbor Pond, Lake Quinsigamond, Lower Woods Lake, Belmont Lake, Miller Pond, and 357-acre White Oak Pond at Aldenville.

The angler who likes to fish for smallmouth bass can have some of the best fishing in the east on the Delaware River between Stroudsburg and Hancock, New York. The beauty of this 139-mile stretch is that the bass fishing is at its best in the dry summer months when lakes rarely produce. The live-bait fishermen usually do well with hellgrammites, while those who cast artificials should try popping bugs in the morning and evening.

The trout fisherman can find angling for his favorite species in the picturesque streams which cascade off the Pocono plateau. Coursing through this area are the Lackawaxen River, Shohola Creek, Equinunk Creek, Big Bushkill Creek, Brodheads Creek, Pocono Creek, Pohopco Creek, Tobyhanna Creek and the upper Delaware River. These streams because of their size and nature are particularly adapted for fly-fishing. Brook trout, rainbow trout, and brown trout are stocked in most of these waters.

Upper Woods Lake at Cold Springs is one of the most beautiful mountain lakes in the state. This contains not only rainbow trout but is the only lake in the commonwealth where one can catch kokanee.

Although only the major lakes and streams were listed, some of the best fishing for trout can be found in the unheralded headwater streams.

THE ANTHRACITE REGION AND VICINITY

The anthracite region lies west of the Pocono region and centers around the cities of Scranton and Wilkes-Barre. In this region there are two unique waters which are the only lakes in Pennsylvania where an angler can catch not only warmwater species, but also rainbow trout and lake trout. These lakes are 658-acre Harvey's Lake in Luzerne County and 190-acre Crystal Lake in Lackawanna County. Harvey's Lake is the second largest natural lake in the state and one of the deepest, with depths up to 100 feet. Bass, walleye, pickerel, and assorted panfish are also available. In the winter time, smelt are a prime species for the ice fisherman. The same species are present in Crystal Lake. Nearby, Lake Winola is another "two-story" lake, with rainbow trout and warmwater species awaiting the fisherman.

Other lakes in this immediate area with population of bass and pickerel are Spring Lake in Bradford County, 110-acre Lake Harmony in Carbon County; 254-acre Lake Jean, Lily Lake at Pond Hill, and 32-acre Mountain Springs Lake all in Luzerne County. In Sullivan County is Hunters Lake at Muncy Valley. In Susquehanna County, the countryside is dotted with small glacial lakes. The largest of these is 127-acre Quaker Lake near Montrose. One of the better-known lakes in Wyoming County with bass, pickerel, and walleye is 250-acre Lake Carey located near Tunkhannock.

Through this region flows the North Branch of the Susquehanna River which is noted for its exceptional smallmouth-bass fishing. The stretch of river from Tunkhannock to the New York line is considered one of the better areas. Public-access areas on the Susquehanna River are on State Game Lane No. 35, one mile east of Hallstead; and the Oakland access areas, two miles north of Oakland in Susquehanna County. Three access areas are available in Bradford County, the Sayre access, 2 miles northeast of Sayre; at Terrytown; and the Wysox access which is 2 miles south of Towanda. In Wyoming County there is an access at Laceyville on Route 6 and one located a mile south of Tunkhannock. These access areas make it possible to fish the most productive waters of the North Branch of the Susquehanna River.

An outstanding trout stream in this area is the headwaters of the Lehigh River flowing from the Pocono plateau through Carbon and Luzerne counties. Six miles are accessible at Stoddartsville and 15 miles at White Haven on Route 940. Fourteen miles of Fishing Creek near Benton in Columbia County are considered among the best trout waters in that region. For the fisherman who prefers mountain streams, 15 miles of Bowmans Creek and 16 miles of Mehoopany Creek in Wyoming County give fair trout fishing.

NORTH CENTRAL REGION

The north central region embraces the more remote and mountainous areas from Bradford County to McKean County along the New York State line. In this wooded and comparatively little-inhabited area extending south to Union County in the east and Clearfield County in the west are some of the better trout streams in the commonwealth. Since there are few lakes, trout fishing and deer hunting are the major forms of recreation.

A prime brown-trout water is the headwaters of the Allegheny River from Coudersport in Potter County along Route 6 to Port Allegany in McKean County. During the warmer months some good smallmouth fishing is evident particularly around Smethport farther downstream.

The "Grand Canyon" of Pennsylvania is on Big Pine Creek in Tioga County. Some excellent trout fishing exists above the canyon, but in the canyon proper trout fishing is good, and float trips are offered for the fishermen. Route 6 west of Wellsboro leads to a popular area on this stream. Fishing remains above average as it traverses Lycoming County, but smallmouth bass become dominant in the lower reaches.

Kettle Creek in Potter County is another famous north-central trout stream. Over 9 miles of the better trout fishing is above Cross Fork on a tributary, Cross Fork Creek, of which 3½ miles are reserved strictly for fly-fishing. Another good tributary is Hammersley Fork Creek.

Sinnemahoning Creek, both the First Fork and the Driftwood Branch, are heavily stocked with trout. To increase the interest in these two streams, summer vacationists get the added bonus of smallmouth bass.

Loyalsock Creek in Lycoming County near Montoursville and in Sullivan County near Forksville is a picturesque stream flowing through a steep-sided mountain valley. This stream along with one of its major tributaries, Little Loyalsock, is trout fly-fishing water of renown. Since practically all the streams of this region are suited to trout, the fisherman can put in successful days on such waters as Medix Run, Mosquito Creek near Karthaus, and Trout Run at Shawville in Clearfield County. All of these could be considered wilderness streams with few access areas.

Slate Run and Grays Run are two of the lesser known streams in Lycoming County that a trout fisherman would enjoy.

Potter County seems to be the heart of the trout fishing in this area. Almost all the smaller streams afford natural reproduction of both brown and brook trout. Coudersport on Route 6 is the center of activity for this region, and a fisherman can spend many fruitful days fishing here.

Tioga County is also blessed with numerous trout streams. Asaph Run offers 15 miles of water, Black Creek 10 miles, and Cedar Run 28 miles of riffles and pools.

In Union County, White Deer Creek, flowing out of the mountains to the Susquehanna River, is considered a good trout stream.

For those who like to fish the limestone streams, 18 miles of Big Fishing Creek near Lamar is beautiful water featuring good brook- and brown-trout fishing. The stretch called the "Gorge" above Lamar has an exceptional population of native brook and brown trout. Elk Creek in Centre County is spring-fed with the best fishing time for big brown trout around Memorial Day when the large mayfly hatch comes off. Nearby Penns Creek has the same fly hatches, and skilled anglers can have a field day, during this same period when the large mayflies emerge. Fisherman's Paradise, near Bellefonte, is no longer in operation but has been converted to a "Fish for Fun" stream where one can catch as many fish as is possible at any time of year, but none can be kept.

If one wants some good fishing for native brook trout, angling in late May and early June in the headwaters of most of these streams is exceptional, especially in northern Centre, Clearfield, Elk, Cameron, McKean, and Potter counties. However, this is also the season when rattlesnakes come out of hibernation. For the rare angler who has no fear of snakes the fishing may be excellent.

Warmwater anglers can try 46 miles of the North Branch of the Susquehanna in Bradford County near Towanda for smallmouth bass and walleye. For pristine beauty and bass, 90-acre Hunters Lake at Muncy Valley is a spot that shouldn't be missed.

Black Moshannon Lake near Phillipsburg in Centre County offers chain pickerel, muskellunge, and yellow perch in a mountain setting. In Tioga County, the same species are available in 130-acre Hills Creek Dam near Mansfield.

This entire region is picturesque, and the "Keystone Shortway," a four-lane highway across Pennsylvania, makes this section of the state accessible to fishermen from all parts of the metropolitan east.

NORTHWEST REGION

Some of the better and most expansive water areas in the state lie in the northwest region. Pymatuning Lake is situated in Crawford County on the Ohio-Pennsylvania border. This 16,000-acre impoundment is a shallow, rich body of water stretching 16 miles and averaging over 1½ miles in width. Some 8,000 acres of land surrounding the lake are in public ownership. Fishing starts in the early spring around Memorial Day when crappies and

A brown trout from the limestone water of Big Fishing Creek

walleyes are caught in large numbers. Largemouth bass and muskellunge help to fill the fisherman's quota. On the shore of the lake, near Linesville, the Pennsylvania Fish Commission maintains a large hatchery for the warmwater species. This is open to the public. Nearby the Game Commission has a waterfowl museum featuring most of the birds found in the Commonwealth.

The portion of Lake Erie touching Pennsylvania has outstanding fishing most of the year. Following Michigan's success in establishing salmon in the Great Lakes, Pennsylvania began stocking coho in 1968 and chinook salmon in 1971. Although the coho do not attain the size in Lake Erie which typifies Lake Michigan, the fish provide an abundance of sport for thousands of people. The chief angling center is the city of Erie and neighboring communities to the east and west. There are numerous public access areas and launching facilities. Bordering the city of Erie is Presque Isle Bay. During the winter months, the ice is covered with fishermen angling for smelt and yellow perch which are taken in large numbers. In the spring, after the water temperatures climb into the 60's, the panfish, including yellow perch, bullheads, and sunfish, begin to move into the lagoons on the peninsula. A good population of northern pike supplements the large catches of panfish. Trolling in the bay proper is the chief pastime of muskellunge fishermen. The evenings of the summer months are spent by many anglers seeking the largemouth bass which are present in the weeded areas. The peninsula is a state park and provides access for boat launching.

For the fisherman who likes variety, 928-acre Conneaut Lake in Crawford County furnishes the largest variety of gamefish of any lake in Pennsylvania. Muskellunge, northern pike, largemouth bass, smallmouth bass, walleye, and exceptionally large bluegills, crappies, and bullheads are found in this natural habitat.

There are other fine muskellunge lakes in this area including 169-acre Canadohta Lake near Union City in Crawford County; Edinboro Lake; and Lake LeBoeuf at Waterford, in Erie County. In recent years, the hottest muskellunge fishing has been in the 480-acre Tionesta Flood Control Reservoir. Tionesta Creek, below the dam, is also known for its muskellunge and smallmouth.

Flowing from the northeast out of New York State to the southwest toward Pittsburgh is the Allegheny River, which some anglers consider the top smallmouth river in the East. In addition, this river can supply a mixed creel, including muskellunge, northern pike, and walleye. Public-access sites are at Starbrick on the River Road, 2 miles south of Tidioute on Route 62; and ½ mile south of Hunter Bridge on Route 537 in Warren County. Venango County has four access sites, one at Kennerdell, another at Elk Street in Franklin, the third ½ mile southwest of Oil City on Route 62, and the fourth ½ mile south of Hunter Bridge on Route 537. In Forest County there is an access area in the borough of Tionesta.

For those who wish to pursue the musky fishing a little further, the smaller rivers often produce some big surprises. Twenty-eight miles of Conneaut Creek near Conneautville, Cussewago Creek at Meadville, and 41 miles of French Creek near Meadville yield more than their share of muskellunge each year from Crawford County. In this region emphasis is placed on warmwater

fishing, but good trout fishing is available in the Allegheny National Forest. Many heavily stocked streams can be reached on roads leading from Route 6 between Warren and Kane. Route 62 from Tionesta is a main traffic artery skirting the western edge of the forest.

SOUTHEASTERN REGION

The southeast region located between the Delaware River on the east and the Susquehanna River on the west is one of the heaviest populated areas of the state. This is also Pennsylvania Dutch country and includes the fertile Lancaster and York valleys. Because of the large industrial complex and intensive farming much of this area does not contain top-notch trout streams. However, heavy stocking is utilized to provide these fish in suitable waters. The outstanding fishing features of this area are the three large power dams on the Susquehanna River below Harrisburg. The 6,000-acre Conowingo Dam at Drumore, the 2,400-acre Holtwood Dam at Pequea, and the 5,000-acre Safe Harbor Dam near Columbia provide excellent tailrace fisheries in the spring. The tailrace of Holtwood is rated the best of the three dams for smallmouth bass and walleye.

Two water-supply reservoirs, 1,080-acre Ontelaunee Reservoir at Leesport, in Berks County, and the Chester-Octorara Lake near Mt. Vernon in Chester County have good warmwater fishing. However, only shore fishing is allowed. Green Lane Reservoir is another dam built for water supply which provides 814 acres of angling. Largemouth, smallmouth bass, and muskellunge are three important game species present. On this area, anglers must pay a fee for the use of the facilities.

Two state-park lakes, Hopewell Lake at Birdsboro in Berks County and 340-acre Pinchot Lake at Rossville in York County, have better than average fishing for the usual warmwater species. Sweet Arrow Lake at Pine Grove has good fishing in the spring for crappie and walleye and in the early fall for largemouth bass.

The Susquehanna River, north of Harrisburg, is known for its smallmouth fishing. The same can be said of the Delaware River north of Easton. The area between Belvedere, New Jersey, and the Delaware Water Gap is particularly productive.

The trout fishing in this region generally is a put-and-take fishery. A breakdown of some of the better streams would include Tulpehocken Creek at Reading, Cooks Creek at Springtown, French Creek at Pughtown, Phoenixville and Stoney Creek at Dauphin, also Clarks Creek at Dauphin, Fishing Creek at Chestnut Level, Little Lehigh Creek at Allentown, Bushkill Creek at Easton, Deep Creek at Valley View, and Muddy Creek at Woodbine.

SOUTHCENTRAL REGION

The southcentral region is best-known for its large limestone springs and fertile streams which form below them. Because of the warmer temperatures in winter and more constant flows in the late summer, many streams in this area have natural reproduction of brook, brown, or rainbow trout and the carryover from year to year is good. Heavy plantings of hatchery trout help to increase the catch.

There are not many lakes in this region, but two larger reservoirs, 275-acre Gordon Lake and 268-acre Koon

Lake, both near Centerville, in Bedford County, yield some of the best angling in the state. Gordon Lake has been stocked with muskellunge but also has some exceptional largemouth-bass fishing. Good walleye, bullhead, and bluegill angling are also available. Koon Lake is noted for its big rainbow trout, many resulting from natural reproduction in its headwaters. Largemouth bass and panfish angling are better than average in this lake. The 426-acre Shawnee State Park Lake near Schellsburg has been stocked with largemouth bass, smallmouth bass, muskellunge, walleye, and panfish.

In Bedford County, eighteen miles of Yellow Creek near Loysburg, is one of the better limestone streams with a good brown-trout population. Brook-trout fishing is better than average in tributary streams, such as Potter Creek and Three Springs and the headwater springs. Bobs Creek, near Pavia, and Cove Creek are also heavily stocked areas.

Huntingdon County has warmwater fishing in the 576-acre Raystown Dam for muskellunge and bass. Early-spring fishing for crappies can be excellent. For those who like to fish for brook trout in mountain streams, Laurel Run near McAlevy's Fort (above Whipples Dam) is recommended. Standing Stone Creek near McAlevy's Fort, has 31½ miles of fishing with trout in its headwaters and smallmouth bass fishing near its mouth.

One of the better streams in Mifflin County is Honey Creek near Reedsville. The headwaters of this stream flowing from the mountains is known for its brook-trout and brown-trout fishing. Biological surveys have shown a good population of large brown trout in its lower reaches.

East Licking Creek near Mifflintown, in Juniata County, is a mountain stream flowing through forested land which produces its share of brown trout. A sleeper in this same county is Willow Run near Honey Grove. This stream is comparatively small and lightly fished. It maintains natural populations of brook and brown trout.

Perry County contributes Laurel Run and Landisburg and Shaffer Run near Blair to the trout angler. Shaffer Run is a better-than-average mountain stream because it holds its flow better than most creeks of this area.

Cumberland County has big limestone springs. The largest spring in the state, Big Spring at Newville, is the source of Big Spring Creek. This watercress-laden stream holds a good population of trout up to 16 inches in the area near its source. Thirty-eight-mile-long Yellow Breeches Creek near Carlisle is another favorite limestone stream of this region. Because of good water quality it is heavily stocked. Mountain Creek near Mt. Holly Springs is, as the name implies, a mountain stream flowing through the laurel and hemlock. The best fishing for brook and brown trout is above Laurel Lake.

Recommended for trout fishing in Franklin County is the East Branch of the Antietam Creek near Waynesboro which starts in the mountains. The West Branch of the Antietam also at Waynesboro is more typically a meadow stream. The East Branch of Conococheague provides 42 miles of the best brown-trout fishing above Chambersburg. The West Branch of the Conococheague is most productive for trout anglers above Fort Loudon. Falling Spring Creek near Chambersburg has natural rainbow-trout reproduction and good fishing for this species in some sections. Brown trout are also present.

Another heavily stocked stream in Fulton County is Cove Creek near McConnellsburg. This stream also has a population of smallmouth bass.

Flowing west to east through this region is the Juniata River, a better-than-average smallmouth and walleye river. From Mt. Union to Amity Hall it is paralleled for 65 miles by Route 22. The Pennsylvania Fish Commission has access sites for fishermen to launch boats near Mifflintown, Mexico, Thompsontown, and Newport.

Many of the streams in Blair County arise from limestone springs and sustain good trout populations. Clover Creek, near Williamsburg and Martinsburg, is one of the top streams in this area whose source is made up of many of these springs. Piney Creek also at Williamsburg flows through a comparatively narrow valley and, because of its spring source and minimum farming in the valley, seldom becomes turbid or flooded. The Frankstown Branch of the Juniata River near East Freedom is a good stretch of trout stream with probably some of the best fishing in the vicinity of Claysburg.

SOUTHWEST REGION

The southwest region is in general a coal-mining area and contains a large industrial complex. However, some warmwater fishing can be obtained in the Allegheny River from Freeport north through Armstrong County. Crooked Creek Flood Control Reservoir near Ford City, and Mahoning Flood Control Reservoir at Dayton, both in Armstrong County, have bass and northern pike as the principal game species. The 2,172-acre Youghiogheny Flood Control Reservoir is one of the better fishing spots in this area. Largemouth bass and northern pike reach trophy size. In Washington County, the Fish Commission owns Dutch Fork Lake near Claysville, which has been heavily stocked with largemouth bass, smallmouth bass, muskellunge, and panfish. Very close to the town of Somerset, within view of the Pennsylvania Turnpike, is another Fish Commission area, 253-acre Somerset Lake. This, too, has been heavily stocked with largemouth bass, northern pike, walleye, and panfish.

The southwest region is not generally known for its trout fishing although the mountainous section around Somerset has a few good streams. Of these, Laurel Hill Creek at Bagersville is considered one of the best. Wills Creek near Berlin, Whites Creek at Listonburg, Brush Creek, and Clear Shade Creek are also heavily stocked.

For those who like put-and-take fish, there are five lakes which are planted with trout every Friday for 7–8 weeks. These lakes are North Park Lake near Pittsburgh in Allegheny County; Virgin Run Lake at Perryopolis, in Fayette County; Canonsburg Lake near Donaldson Cross Road and the previously mentioned Dutch Fork Lake in Washington County. In Westmoreland County, Keystone Lake at New Alexandria receives the weekly stocking.

The Pennsylvania Fish Commission, Harrisburg, will supply upon request a detailed booklet *Fishing and Boating in Pennsylvania*. This publication has a comprehensive compilation of all fishing waters in Pennsylvania with a list of the species present and the closest access points, including public-access sites on large rivers and lakes. "Fly Fishing Only" and "Fish for Fun" areas and waters stocked with muskellunge are also listed. Illustrations aid the fishermen in identifying the important fish species

—K.B.

PERCH *See* Black Perch, European Perch, Kelp Perch, Nile Perch, Ocean Perch, Pacific Ocean Perch, Pile Perch, Pirateperch, Rio Grande Perch, Sacramento Perch, Surf Perch, Troutperch, Tule Perch, White Perch, Yellow Perch

PERIWINKLES Periwinkles are snail-like mollusks which are generally small. There are nearly 200 species, which freely move between saltwater and whatever substrate they can cling to, such as rocks, pilings, trees, or wharves. Their shells usually have a pointed apex, and most have intricately sculptured shells, often marked with beautiful, delicate colors. They move about slowly, grazing the microscopic algae from the substrate with the radula or tongue. This organ is worked continually to scrape off the thin film, which they love, of diatoms and other algae covering the intertidal area. Some species also eat small mollusks and crustaceans. Related to river snails, periwinkles have gills, which are modified so that they can breathe atmospheric air, as long as the gills are moist, when they are foraging about out of water. Periwinkles are delicious to eat and form the ingredients for many excellent seafood sauces and broths. —D.dS.

PERLON A caprolactam-based material used in the manufacture of fishing lines. Perlon is most often seen in the form of monofilament. Perlon is the registered trademark of Perlon-Warenzeichenvervand e. V., Frankfurt-am-Main, Germany. *See also* Monofilament, Spinning

PERMIT *See* Atlantic Permit, Pacific Permit, Saltwater Fly-Fishing

PERU This west-coast South American country offers limited but rather spectacular fresh- and saltwater fishing. The two important centers are located at Lake Titicaca, where rainbow trout of exceptional size have been caught in years past, and at Cabo Blanco, where big-game anglers score heavily on black marlin, striped marlin, broadbill swordfish, yellowfin tuna, and big-eye tuna. Cabo Blanco also provides interesting light-tackle surf-fishing for snook, corvina, and mackerel. The year-round temperature in Peru is about 70°F. Spring begins in September, and summer starts in December. It seldom rains, but in winter there are heavy fogs. Generally speaking, Peru offers some excellent saltwater fishing through all months of the year.

LAKE TITICACA

Located between Peru and Bolivia, Lake Titicaca supports the highest trout fishery in the world (14,000 feet altitude) and is famous for its large rainbows. From 1940 to 1960 Lake Titicaca produced rainbow trout of 12–15 pounds with monotonous frequency. The record ran to 34 pounds. A 20–25-pounder was not at all unusual, and if one enjoyed trolling or casting with spoons, the delirium of catching nothing but trophies spoiled a man for the rest of his angling life. The secret of the lake's trout production is the pejerrey, which the Aymara Indians call *bocarón*. This rather large and prolific forage fish puts weight on rainbows very rapidly. But it also instills them with a catholic appetite, and the fly-fisher rarely finds any sport on the lake proper. Today fishing in Titicaca is fast becoming a thing of the past. Netting and dynamiting have taken a heavy toll of the larger trout, and the once common 12-pounder will soon be as ancient as Machu Picchu. In spite of the decline, Titicaca is one of those alien aqueous places that hypnotizes the angler, and realization does not seem to lessen its in-

fluence. There are some huge rainbows still to be caught, and the lake will remain important for that reason.

To reach this world's highest trout lake, you can come from the Peruvian side in Lima or the Bolivian side in La Paz. Lima is the better of the two. This Pizarro *cum* Dior city has everything from noisy jazz cellars to plush hotels and restaurants. But here all animal comforts end. As in Caracas, the city reflects the country beyond with no more accuracy than does the upsidedown face of Titicaca where, on a hazy morning at 14,000 feet, a giant rainbow trout rolls out of the crystal water and shatters the mirrored surface into a hundred images of itself. To make the ascent from Lima you have the choice of Puno or Juliaca, two towns which provide minimum-comfort hotels. They can be reached via Cuzco or Arequipa by a railroad which supplies oxygen for needy passengers as it crosses a nearly 3-mile height. There is also limited air service into Juliaca from Arequipa, but don't regard the schedule too seriously.

Titicaca Lake Indians spear boga, a tasty little fish, from native craft made of dried grass

At Puno you can fish the Llave River, and at Juliaca the Cabanillas River or the Ramis River. These three streams are Titicaca tributaries which provide an occasional 8–10-pound fish. Perhaps the best bet in the entire area is Lake Arapa which is just beyond the Ramis. However, you would have to camp out at Arapa, and between the altitude and chill winds it's hardly ideal for the casual tourist. Bear in mind that the weather is cold from June through August, with freezing temperatures occurring whenever the sun drops below the Cordillera. The season for Titicaca fishing differs from all other regions in South America. During the rains from November until March even trolling is almost impossible on the lake. It usually gets better around the first of April, and until May the rivers run high and roily, which is the period when the largest trout are caught. By June the waters become clear, but they still can't be fished properly with flies until the level has gone down. The time for fly-fishing here is in August and September. However, big, silver-bodied streamer flies that resemble the slender pejerrey are necessary because aquatic insect life is scarce and unimportant at 14,000 feet. The dry-fly man would be disappointed. —A.J.McC.

PETRALE SOLE *Eopsetta jordani* Also known as brill, this rough-scaled, righteye sole has a pointed tail and a rather broadly rounded snout. The unbranched lateral line curves gradually upward anteriorly. The eyes and mouth are of moderate size, with well-developed teeth on both sides of the jaws, the teeth in the upper jaw occurring in two rows on each side. It is a uniform olive-brown on the eyed side, with indistinct pale blotches on the body and fins. It grows to 24 inches and 6–8 pounds.

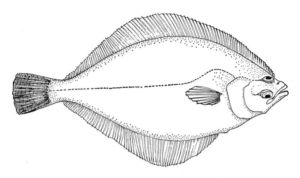

Petrale Sole

Found from the Mexican border to northwestern Alaska, it occurs in depths of from 60–1,300 feet. It reportedly eats crustaceans and small fishes, such as anchovies.

An extremely desirable and important commercial fish, it is taken chiefly by otter trawl, and a small part of the catch is taken by anglers. —D.dS.

pH A measure of acidity and alkalinity (hydrogen ion concentration) based on a 0–14 scale. The pH of pure water is 7; it represents neutrality. Below 7 acidity increases as hydrogen ions increase; above 7 alkalinity increases as ions decrease.

PHARYNGEAL TEETH Teeth located in the throat

PHYTOPLANKTON Plant microorganisms, such as certain algae, living unattached in the water.

PHILLIPPE, SAMUEL American Credited with building the first split-bamboo fly rod in America and possibly in the world. Phillippe's work is commemorated in a historical marker in Easton, Pennsylvania, at the site of his shop. The marker reads: "Samual Phillippe recognized as the inventor of the split-bamboo fishing rod in the United States. His first rent and glued-up cane rod was made about 1846 in his gunsmith shop that stood on this site." Samuel Phillippe's son Solon was also a rod builder, and an example of his work made in 1862 is now in the Pennsylvania State Museum.

PIABANHA. A regional Portuguese name for the brycon (*which see*) in Brazil.

PICKEREL A regional and erroneous name used for the walleye (*which see*) in central and eastern Canada. In correct usage a member of the pike family. *See also* Chain Pickerel

PICUA The Spanish name for barracuda (*see* Great Barracuda) and also a number of barracudalike freshwater fishes of the genus *Hydrocinus* found in South America.

PIKEPERCH (1) A regional name in the United States and Canada for *Stizostedion vitreum* the walleye (*which see*), and *Stizostedion canadense* the sauger (*which see*).

(2) The accepted common name in Europe for *Stizostedion volgense* the eastern pikeperch. All are members of the family Percidae and not related to the true pikes. In Europe it is also known as sandre (France), zander (Germany), Gjørs (Norway), smud (Yugoslavia), sandart (Denmark), zander (Holland).

PIKES Family Esocidae Elongate freshwater fishes characterized by their highly carnivorous feeding habits. The family consists of 6 species of which 5 are found in North America. The Amur or black spotted pike (*Esox reicherti*) is strictly an Asian species, but was introduced on an experimental basis in the United States (Pennsylvania, 1968) with limited success. Except for size, pikes are remarkably alike in appearance. The anal and dorsal fins are located near the posterior end of the body and the ventral fins are abdominal in position. The front of the head is like a duck's bill and the mouth is large and supplied with formidable canine teeth. The fins are softrayed.

Three species considered as gamefish are the chain pickerel (*Esox niger*), northern pike (*Esox lucius*), and muskellunge (*Esox masquinongy*). Of these the chain pickerel commonly reaches a weight of 2–3 pounds, the pike 5–10 pounds, and the muskellunge 10–30 pounds. The other two American species are small and rarely exceed 12 inches in length. They are the redfin pickerel (*Esox americanus*), which is found in the Atlantic coast drainage, and the grass pickerel (*Esox vermiculatus*), which is found in the Mississippi drainage.

The latter two species may be separated from the others by their short snouts and by the nearly vertical dark bars on their sides. The three game species are separated on the basis of their scale pattern on cheek and opercle and by color pattern.

In the chain pickerel both the cheek and operculum are completely scaled, and the color pattern consists of black, chainlike markings on a yellow background. The northern pike has scales on the cheek, but the lower half of the operculum is scaleless. The coloration consists of distended light ovals on a dark background. The muskellunge has no scales on the lower half of both cheek and operculum, with dark vertical bands or dark spots on a light background.

Hybrids of pike and pickerel or pike and muskellunge are common in some areas. *See also* Chain Pickerel, Muskellunge, Northern Pike, Redfin Pickerel

—A.J.McC.

PILCHARD A common name in the western Atlantic for the false pilchard, *Harengula clupeola*, as well as other herrings of this genus. Also a common name for the Pacific sardine (*which see*). More correctly, it represents the European sardine, *Sardina pilchardus*. *See also* False Pilchard, Sardines.

PILE PERCH *Rhacochilus vacca* A common shore-dwelling surfperch (*which see*), it affords much sport to the angler.

It is dusky brown or blackish on the back; silver ventrally; it may have 3–4 darker blotches on upper body; a black spot on preopercle just behind posterior tip of maxillary; fins dusky except for clear pectorals; pelvics may be pale yellow or orange tipped with black; a broad frenum interrupts posterior groove of lower lip; tail deeply forked; first softrays of dorsal sharply elevated above spiny portion. Length to sixteen inches. Its range is from Baja California to Alaska.

The life history, food, and angling value is the same as for surfperch in general.

COMMERCIAL VALUE

It is of considerable importance in northern California.
—J.R.

PILOTFISH *Naucrates ductor* This popularized species is one that appears to have more different scientific names than common names. It is worldwide in tropical and subtropical waters, and has been known for several centuries to naturalists and ichthyologists. The pilotfish is superficially very similar to the amberjack genus *Seriola;* the most obvious difference is in the low, unconnected spines of the first dorsal fin of the pilotfish.

The first dorsal fin of the pilotfish usually has only 5 spines (rarely 3, 4, or 6), and these are short and unconnected in specimens longer than about 3 inches. The body has 5-6 broad, dark bars at all sizes.

The body is relatively slender and rounded, the head profile is pointed, and the mouth small. The second dorsal fin contains 1 spine and 26–28 softrays. The anal fin has 2 short, detached spines, followed closely by 1 spine and 15–17 softrays. Gillrakers on the first gill arch number about 6 on the upper limb and 15–18 on the lower limb. The body is brown above and pale below, with the body bars and nuchal band darker brown or black.

The tropical to temperate, and usually oceanic, worldwide distribution is well-known. In the western Atlantic it has been recorded from a latitude of 35° 30′ S. off Argentina to Nova Scotia, at Bermuda, and in the West Indies. In the eastern Pacific it has been reported from west of northern Chile to off California. The pilotfish has been reported to reach a maximum size of about 24–27 inches.

LIFE HISTORY

Despite the many observations that have been made of this fish, its life history is not well-known. It is most frequently observed in its commensal relation to sharks, with one or more pilotfish closely following a shark and feeding upon scraps left by the shark, or symbiotically feeding on parasites of the shark and remaining unmolested by the shark. It has been speculated, somewhat expansively, that the pilotfish leads the shark to its food and that the shark does not eat the pilotfish because the flesh of the pilotfish may be unwholesome to the shark. Other accounts suggest that the principal food of the pilotfish is the shark's excrement. Pilotfish have also been reported in association with large rays and are said to follow sailing vessels frequently. The larval and early juvenile stages are well-known, but not spawning places or seasons. Small specimens frequently stay under jellyfish.

ANGLING VALUE

There is no sport or commercial fishery for this species in the Americas. *See also* Amberjacks, Carangidae
—F.H.B.

PINFISH *Lagodon rhomboides* There is but one species in this genus, ranging with little variation from the south side of Cape Cod south to the Yucatán Peninsula in Mexico. It also is found at Bermuda, but other island records, such as Cuba, Jamaica, and the Bahamas, apparently are erroneous. The pinfish probably is one of the most abundant of inshore fishes, especially in the more southern parts of its range.

Pinfish

In life, the ground color of the pinfish is bluish-silver, darker above than below. There are 4–6 dark crossbars (varying in intensity) on the sides and numerous longitudinal golden stripes on the length of the fish. There is a dark shoulder spot. The fins are yellowish, with tinges of blue.

Like many American sparid fishes, the pinfish has a series of humanlike incisor teeth in the front of the jaws. However, it can be distinguished from members of the other genera by the conspicuous notching of these teeth. Using these teeth, the pinfish is a grazer, and its food is quite varied, the bulk apparently consists of small animals, particularly crustaceans, and perhaps plant material to some degree.

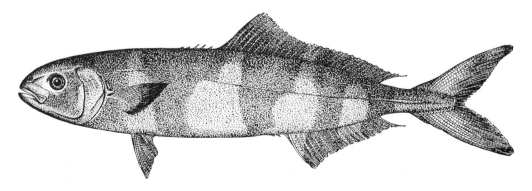

Pilotfish

LIFE HISTORY

Spawning apparently takes place offshore, for gravid adults are found only in a few areas, despite the wide distribution of the species, and postlarvae smaller than about 11 millimeters rarely are seen, but are common larger than this after they have migrated or been swept inshore. Spawning usually occurs in the late fall and early winter.

Inshore, pinfish occur most commonly on shallow, fully marine grassy flats, but they also come up rivers into water that is essentially fresh, and the larger adults occur at or near the bottom far beyond the zone of vegetation. Pinfish apparently are quite tolerant to changes in their environment, and this may account in part for their great abundance.

ANGLING VALUE

Members of this species form a major portion of the diet of a number of gamefish, and consequently often are used for bait. Larger specimens, usually up to about 8 inches but sometimes reaching nearly 14 inches, are used for human food and themselves often are sought as a bottom-dwelling gamefish. *See also* Spottail Pinfish

—D.K.C.

PINK SALMON *Oncorhynchus gorbuscha* This species is the smallest of the Pacific salmon (*which see*), usually 3–5 pounds at maturity, reaching 10 at maximum. The size varies with the abundance of year-classes. It is recognized by the large, oval, black blotches on the caudal fin, the small scales (170–229 in the row above the lateral line), and the 24–35 rakers in the first gill arch. The young have no parr marks.

LIFE HISTORY

The fish reaches maturity in two years. At that time males develop a large hump on the back in addition to a hooked snout. Spawning takes place in September and November in freshwater, usually near the sea, but a few races migrate several hundred miles. They enter the river as early as July. The timing of runs varies widely from odd to even years to disproportionate numbers between years or to more or less even numbers between years.

Food consists largely of crustaceans but sometimes includes fish and squid.

The ocean and Puget Sound sport fisheries take many pinks, but it is the commercial effort that accounts for the greatest take—$17,227,477 in 1960, the second highest value for Pacific salmon, exceeded at that time only by the sockeye, but more pinks than sockeyes are caught. Those caught by sportsmen in the ocean are usually called "young chinooks." It ranges from California to Korea and Japan.

ANGLING VALUE

Although the pink salmon does not provide consistent angling over most of its range, this species is occasionally caught on flies, wobbling spoons, and spinners in certain rivers, particularly in British Columbia. Planted in the Dennys River, Maine, in 1926 this species was established there for several generations, but despite an intensive Atlantic salmon fishery at that time no pinks were caught by angling. Along with the chum salmon the pink is taken in waters around the Queen Charlotte Islands and in northern Norway. *See also* Pacific Salmon —J.R.

PINK SEAPERCH *Zalembius rosaceus* The species is found in deeper water than other surfperch (*which see*), usually at from 15–50 fathoms. Its color is a silvery-white suffused with rose; there is a chocolate spot just under the junction of the spinous and soft dorsal and another on the body at the end of the dorsal fin. A frenum (a connecting membrane) interrupts the posterior groove of the lower lip. Soft dorsal rays lower than longest dorsal spine; caudal and anal upper rays often elongated, filamentous in male; 16–19 soft-dorsal rays; 18–22 soft-anal rays. Its length goes to about 8 inches. Its range is from central California to northern Baja California.

It is rarely caught by sportsmen but is to be found in purse-seine catches. —J.R.

PINTADA *See* Cero

PINTLE (1) In big-game fishing equipment the short metal shaft or pipe fitted to the underside of the seat of a swivel fishing chair so that the chair can pivot. The pintle is seated into a pipe of larger diameter supporting the chair. The pintle on a fishing chair generally is between 6 inches and 1 foot in length, especially when sliding into an oversize pipe extending above the deck, but may be as much as 2 or 3 feet long if the pintle itself extends through a round plate on the deck and is seated into a fitting located in the bilge.

Pink Salmon

(2) In boating terminology, a pin in a rudder which slips into the gudgeon on the transom is also a pintle.

PIRANHAS Also known as *caribe* (Spanish) These freshwater fishes of the family Characidae inhabit South America and are the counterpart of the North American minnows. Fortunately for North America, minnows don't have the teeth that characterize some species of piranha (pronounced per-on-yeh). Unlike minnows and carps, they are generally flattened from side to side, have a high body, and all have a fleshy adipose fin on the back between the dorsal and caudal fins. The head is blunt, with short, powerful jaws containing many sharp cutting teeth. Of the many characins in South America, only a few are piranhas, and of approximately twenty-five piranhas only about four species are dangerous to man. One species grows to 2 feet, but the others are smaller. Piranhas have a wide distribution throughout the rivers of Colombia, Venezuela, the Guianas, Brazil, Paraguay, and south to central Argentina. They occur in swarms, at which time they pose the greatest danger, especially in muddy waters; but are reportedly less dangerous in clear waters. Small fishes are their usual diet, but injured or dead animals are readily and eagerly devoured. Their ability to detect blood in the water is legendary, but more likely they are able to perceive the vibrations of the injured or struggling animal as sharks do.

Red Piranha, (2-inch Juvenile)

There is great hearsay about the danger of the piranha, but some authorities feel that, while the piranha is indeed a potential danger and undoubtedly has taken its toll of humans and others, many of the more spectacular stories may be traceable to a relatively few yet spectacular instances, which have been repeated and embellished over the centuries, making it appear that they do nothing but actively seek out human blood and devour hapless beings. Nevertheless, these tales are remarkable, and one authenticated report tells of a 100-pound capybara (a large rodent) from which the flesh was stripped in less than a minute; while another, no less authentic, documents a man and his horse falling into the water both being picked clean except for the man's clothes, which were undamaged. Thus, because of its sharp teeth, its speed, the large numbers in which it travels, and reports of its at least alleged danger, the piranha should certainly be treated with caution.

In past years piranhas were brought in alive to the United States as special "pets" for aquarists, and there were some reports that these were accidentally or

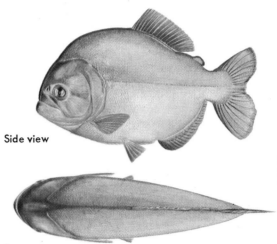

Side view

Top view

Red Piranha, 14-inch Female, Orinoco River, Venezuela

deliberately being released into local waters. Because there is always the possibility that these might successfully reproduce and become established in warm waters, Federal injunctions have been levied against importing piranhas for sale.

Piranhas are of limited angling value. They can be caught on any strip or cut bait and occasionally are taken on artificial lures. A wire leader is essential. The smaller, less aggressive species are often timid quarry. Piranhas have some food value and are consumed by Indians of the Orinoco and Amazon. The teeth are sometimes used to fashion arrowheads for small game and birds. —D.dS.

—A.J.McC.

PIRARUCÚ *Arapaima gigas* This is a native freshwater species of tropical South America. Although originally assigned to the family Osteoglossidae, its scaled pelvic fins, different dentation, and lack of barbels are the basis for a more recent family classification (Arapaimidae). This is one of the largest strictly freshwater fishes, reaching 15 feet and 400 pounds. The pirarucú is common in the Amazon River, its major tributaries and associated lakes, and in the larger rivers of the Guianas. It is a valuable food fish in Brazil; however its numbers have declined greatly. The flesh is very firm, white, and of fine flavor. The pirarucú is also known as paiche, payshi, pirarocou, anatto, lou-lou, warapaima, and arapaima in various Indian languages; pirarucú is given precedence due to its wider usage.

ANGLING VALUE

The pirarucú is not noted as a gamefish; however, pirarucú can be caught on artificial lures, including spoons, plugs, and streamer flies. The fish are usually spotted drifting or rolling at the surface. Indian fishermen use harpoons, arrows, and trotlines. —A.J.McC.

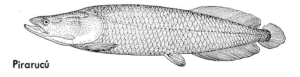

Pirarucú

PIRATEPERCH *Aphredoderus sayanus* This is the only living species of the *Aphredoderidae* family, although it is related to the troutperch. It is not a true perch.

It is a small fish with spiny rays and rough ctenoid or comblike scales. The vent or anus is located in the throat region rather than in the more normal position in front of the anal fin. It is a dark olivaceous fish with heavy specklings of dark over the entire body, except the belly. Breeding specimens show much iridescent purple. Most adults are between 3 and 4 inches in length, but may reach a size of 5–6 inches under good conditions.

It is found from Minnesota eastward to Ontario and southward to Florida and Texas. It is rather widely distributed in the north in sluggish weedy creeks. It is very common along the Atlantic coastal plain in swamps and backwater creeks.

LIFE HISTORY

The pirateperch spawns in the spring and both parents build a nest. They guard it and the young until the latter are ⅓-inch long. It is a predaceous fish which attacks insects, crustaceans, and other small animals.

Peculiar to its life history is the location of the anus; the anus migrates forward as the pirateperch grows and eventually locates under the throat of adult fish.

ECONOMIC VALUE

The pirateperch is an interesting aquarium species, but its pugnacious character makes it difficult to keep with other fish. It has limited use as a bait minnow.
—A.J.McC.

PISCIVOROUS Fish-eating

PITCH A measuring factor applied to a propeller, it is the distance the propeller would advance in one turn or revolution provided there was no slippage. A propeller marked 10⅜ inches by 12½ inches indicates that the diameter of the blades is 10⅜ inches and the pitch is 12½ inches. The greater the pitch the farther the boat travels for each revolution. Pitch and diameter are only two of the factors that affect efficient design in a propeller. Blade area is also considered. If blade area is too limited, it may not work hard enough; and if too large, it may create a limiting disturbance.

PLACOID *See* Scales (Fish)

PLAICE *Pleuronectes platessa* A well-known and much-appreciated European marine flatfish, unlike most common food fishes, it has only one English name by which it is generally known. Its appearance is very characteristic. It lies on its white *left* side, the right or upper side being deep brown with ¼-inch red spots. These spots do not fade after death, so the plaice can be readily identified. The lateral line is nearly straight from head to tail, curving only slightly near the pectoral fin. Along the back the scales are very small, and the skin mucous thick and slimy. There is a sharp spine at the forward or anterior edge of the anal fin; and the anterior edge of the dorsal fin is level with the eyes. The whole head has a very characteristic "twisted" appearance, with a mouth full of broad and blunt crushing teeth.

Plaice are generally distributed in European Atlantic waters from Biscay to the Baltic, penetrating rarely into the Mediterranean. Its numbers and position are subject to fluctuation; in summer it is in shallow waters, in winter in the deeper areas up to 600 feet. Feeding is equally seasonal; it feeds mainly in summer on bivalve mollusks which it crushes with its blunt teeth. In winter only 10 percent of commercially landed fish have anything in the gut, the usual diet item being sea worms.

The maximum length most plaice reach is 30 inches; maximum weights of 12–15 pounds have been reported.

LIFE HISTORY

Because of their commercial importance and fluctuating numbers plaice have been the subject of much investigation by fishery scientists in most European countries with an Atlantic seaboard.

Spawning occurs around February in the English Channel, but farther north it may be delayed until as late as May. It always occurs well offshore in large gatherings in well-known areas of the European seas. The largest single area is the so-called "Flemish Bight," the area of sea between southeastern England and the coast of Holland. Other, though smaller, centers are off the English Yorkshire coast, in the Irish Sea, and off Heligoland in Germany.

Mating occurs in midwater, male and female plaice lying one on top of the other. The female lays around 100,000 eggs per pound of body weight; figures of 300,000–500,000 eggs per female have been quoted as averages. The egg itself is one of the largest of flatfish eggs, 1½–2½ mm in diameter. It has a wrinkled outer coat and no oil droplets, but despite this it still floats. It was once feared that plaice eggs were not pelagic but were laid on the bottom and could be destroyed by trawling. Fears of depletion of stocks for this reason prompted some of the early European fishery work.

The greatest concentrations of floating plaice eggs occur in the "Flemish Bight" area; large numbers are eaten by the plankton-feeding herring, *Clupeus harengus*. But the majority survive and float in the plankton for 10–12 days before hatching.

The larvae which emerge are ⅕-inch long, with black and yellow spots. The yolk sac is absorbed about a week later, leaving a normally-shaped young fry feeding actively first on diatoms and then small planktonic crustaceans.

As it is therefore entirely planktonic at first, much of its subsequent fate will depend on North Sea currents. Eggs and fry spawned in the "Flemish Bight" area are carried from the southwest by the general drift of the English Channel currents at a rate of between 1½–3 miles per day. This speed means that the plaice have begun to change to a more normal flatfish shape (metamorphosis) by the fourth week, and should be over the coastal "nursery" grounds of Britain and Holland.

If, however, strong northeasterly gales in March slow down the normal southwest surface drift, then the young plaice will not reach the "nursery" grounds until too late. This will result in "bad years" of plaice catches to come.

Metamorphosis is slow, taking 2½–3 weeks, but generally it is complete by the seventh week after spawning. By then the eyes have finally moved over to the right side. The young plaice tend to stay in the coastal "nurseries" for two years or more. They attain a length of about 5½ inches by this second year. They then will move out from the coastal "nurseries" toward the deeper waters of the North Sea.

Plaice

Sexual maturity is gained at about the fourth or fifth year of life. This means an average in female plaice of 12–16 inches, and in males of 8–11 inches. Irish Sea plaice show a slightly faster growth rate, 7¾ inches at two years to over 13 inches at four years. There is evidence in fact to suggest that maturity in plaice is a function of size rather than age, as exceptional fish may be only two years old at the 8–16-inch size range, and yet will mate.

COMMERCIAL VALUE

Plaice are certainly among the most generally appreciated of European food flatfish, and the easiest for a housewife to identify on the slab. Hence it is very difficult for unscrupulous traders to substitute an inferior flatfish.

Most of the large European catches of plaice are taken in trawls in the central North Sea area. Parts under 100 feet deep, like the Dogger Bank, are much fished, though plaice will range into waters over 500 feet.

The size of trawl nets is most carefully regulated, especially for inshore work, in order not to catch immature fish. Films have been taken by fish biologists in Scuba gear to show the selective effect of such trawl mesh sizes.

As the ultimate growth, maturity, and abundance of plaice in the North Sea as a whole is dependent on the conditions in the "nursery" waters, attempts have been made to "farm" plaice by keeping young plaice in land-locked arms of the sea and fertilizing the water. But these experiments are still very much in the pioneer stage.

The Baltic Sea has a plaice fishery of its own; it is unique in that only the larger and mature plaice are ever caught. The smaller two- and three-inch plaice are conspicuous by their absence, though the Baltic does not lack "nursery" type of shallows. This is believed to be due to the low salinity of the Baltic, where freshwater and marine life may grow side by side. The lowering of buoyancy by this brackish Baltic water causes entering plaice eggs to sink and die. Hence any plaice which enter the Baltic must do so under their own efforts as adults.

ANGLING VALUE

Plaice are one of the several inshore commercially-sought fish which have caused rancor between anglers and netsmen, the latter trawling good plaice grounds and removing fish. Plaice-angling grounds are often, therefore, on bottoms the netsmen would rather not risk gear on, the governing factor being the presence of mussel and other shellfish beds.

They are taken like other flatfish: by accident on baits trailing the bottom from multihook rigs and by design on light gear and a leger rig with running sinker. Taken this way they put up a respectable fight. The normal baits are shellfish and various marine worms. Like most flatfish the first gentle indication of a bite should not be struck. The fish should be given slack line and struck firmly on the harder tug which indicates it has the bait in its mouth. (*See also* American Plaice)   —D.M.

PLAINS CARPSUCKER   *See* Quillback

PLANKTON   Animals that float and drift passively in the water of the seas, lakes, and rivers as distinct from animals which are attached to, or crawling on the bottom. Plankton are mostly of microscopic size and have a large surface area in relation to their weight. Many crustaceans, some mollusks, a few worms, a variety of small larvae, and minute plants (phytoplankton) compose a plankton population. The abundance of different organisms varies according to the season. *See also* Freshwater Ecology, Marine Ecology

PLASTIC LURE   A type of lure made of flexible vinyl plastic. Plastic lures first became popular in the United States in 1957, and are marketed today in a variety of forms and sizes suitable for the fly rod, spinning rod, bait-casting rod, and for trolling in saltwater. Although the first "soft" lure was patented in 1860's (a rubber worm), it wasn't until 1935 when the B. F. Goodrich Company produced a vinyl under the trade name Koroseal that any significant progress occurred. This plastic material is ideal for molding, and it doesn't become brittle with age or variations in temperature. Lures designed to imitate worms, grasshoppers, crickets, hellgrammites, minnows, eels, maggots, shrimp, bloodworms, sandworms, mackerel, mullet, and a variety of other fish foods are now widely used. The effectiveness of plastic baits varies according to the season and the fish sought, although their strongest appeal is in Midwestern and Southern lakes where the plastic worm-and-spoon, worm-and-spinner, and worm-and-jig combinations are virtually standard lures when "bottom scratching" in deepwater for bass, walleye, and panfish. Nearly all impounded waters cover large areas of submerged trees, and active plastic baits can be jigged among the branches and stumps without hanging up too often. A weighted weedless worm (or gollywhomper) is used with great success in dense weed beds for Florida bass. Being flexible, the lure glides snakelike over any vegetation. Large trout have also been caught on plastic worms, notably in the tailwater fisheries of Tennessee and Arkansas. Attempts to create appropriate plastic lures for many other types of fishing, however, have not been wholly productive.

HOW TO RIG THE PLASTIC WORM

The most popular method of rigging a plastic worm is the self-weedless sliding-sinker style. This requires a bullet-shaped sinker with a hole through the center which is threaded on the line in front of a single large hook (usually 3/0–6/0). The hook point is pressed into the nose and back out the side of the worm, turned 180°; the eye of the hook is then imbedded in the nose and the hook point pushed back into the worm so that it forms its own weedguard.

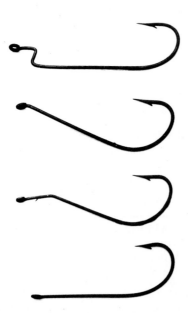

Specialized hooks, varying from 3/0–7/0, are made for plastic-worm fishing. Bends or shank barbs help hold the worm in place

Thread the monofilament through the bullet type of slide sinker and tie on the hook

To thread the worm, start the hook in the center of the worm's head at about a 30° angle, allowing some slack in the worm body so it will be straight when it is imbedded. Then force the point outside the worm

Turn the hook 180° in the worm

Impale the hook in the worm. The rig is now completed

Bass fishermen have developed a method of fishing this self-weedless worm that is as unique as the rigging. It employs a very slow retrieve, moving the lure only a foot or two at a time. The reel is used only to take up slack line, while the rod moves the worm in short hops along the bottom. The sequence is to cast, let the lure sink with line taut (watch the line—if it moves, strike), then retrieve with the rod moving from near horizontal to vertical before dropping the tip to reel in slack. The fisherman has to "feel" his way along the bottom. Bass seldom strike a worm hard. A typical strike is felt as if a small child were tugging at your sleeve, just a light "tap-tap." Experienced bass fishermen *always* strike as if they were going to break the rod. A forceful strike is necessary for two reasons. The large hook has to be driven through the worm and into the fish's jaw; secondly, the bass is usually in or close to heavy cover on the bottom where any hesitation can mean a lost fish.　　　　—A.J.McC.

PLATYL A material used in the manufacture of fishing lines. Platyl is most often seen in the form of monofilament. The physical properties of platyl are similar to those of other caprolactam-based nylons. The name platyl is the registered trademark of Dr. Plate, Chemische Fabrik, Dransdorfer Weg 21, in Bonn, Germany. *See also* Monofilament, Spinning

PLUG A casting lure usually designed in the shape of a small fish. However, these are often fanciful in both form and color. Plugs are also made to suggest frogs, mice, ducklings, and other forms of life utilized by gamefish as food. There are literally thousands of different plugs on the market, but these can be separated or selected on the basis of their individual function.

SIZE STANDARD

The first consideration in selecting a plug is its size. Back at the turn of the century, the standard bass lure weighed just a shade under one ounce. The weight had nothing to do with performance in the water—it was the amount necessary to put a casting bend in the stiff rods of 1900. Today's equipment is greatly refined. With ultralight spinning tackle the angler can cast $\frac{1}{16}$-ounce plugs which are no bigger than a natural minnow. But for the man who uses regular spinning, spin bait-casting, or bait-casting tackle, the standards are $\frac{1}{4}$-ounce, $\frac{3}{8}$-ounce, $\frac{1}{2}$-ounce, and $\frac{5}{8}$-ounce plugs. Broadly speaking, the $\frac{1}{4}$-ounce to $\frac{3}{8}$-ounce sizes are for refined fishing in clear-water with light tackle, while the $\frac{1}{2}$- to $\frac{5}{8}$-ounce plugs are the ncrm for nearly all other freshwater work. For beginners using regular bait-casting gear, an assortment of lures in the $\frac{3}{8}$-ounce and $\frac{5}{8}$-ounce weights are most practical. At the extremes, these are the easiest sizes to cast with a revolving-spool reel. It takes some thumbing skill to handle the lighter $\frac{1}{4}$-ounce plugs. But if you are using any kind of fixed-spool reel, don't hesitate to try these midgets on civilized ponds.

PLUG COLOR

The color of a plug is sometimes a determining factor in getting strikes. There is no one universal rule, not even for one species of fish. Local preferences can be learned at any tackle shop or boat livery. Just as a general guide for the beginner who is far from his fishing grounds, the following are basic: a red-and-white finish, frog finish, black-scale, silver-flash, and yellow-polka-dot. These five color patterns are old reliables throughout the country. If you are going to plug-cast in saltwater, then the silver-flash, blue-mullet, gold-flash, yellow-polka-dot, and a green-scale finish are good colors to start with. As a rule of the thumb, small, dark, natural-looking plugs work best in transparent lakes, the kind of water where you'd fish for smallmouth bass; the bright colors and larger plugs are more suited to turbid water or periods when the light is dim. Needless to say, there are plenty of exceptions, but you can't go too far wrong by using imitative patterns, such as the perch, shad, frog, or mullet. The important thing is to select plugs that function at the correct level or otherwise act in a way that will attract the fish.

POPPING PLUGS

Poppers float on the surface, and when jerked with the rod tip they bury their hollow faces under the surface to create sounds and bubbles. Popping plugs come in all sizes from the $\frac{1}{4}$-ounce spinning model to $4\frac{1}{2}$-inch-long musky baits. Some saltwater popping plugs weigh as much as $2\frac{1}{2}$ ounces. They are also made in jointed models and skirted models which add a bit of wiggle in addition to the noise, and when the face is elongated they make a chugging sound instead of the usual *blup*. Poppers get their biggest play in shallow-water casting. It's customary to let them lie still until the splash made from falling on the surface has subsided. Then they are retrieved in a series of well-spaced jerks. Those plugs which have a pronounced action (some pop more loudly than others) will bring fish from greater depths than those that make a mere bubble. When bass are bottom feeding or even hiding among weeds in ten feet of water, they will sometimes come up for a noisy bait. However, and this is significant, popping plugs do not always get strikes. Although a noisy surface plug might be blasted to splinters on occasion, there are times when that which attracts merely repels. Under these conditions a surface-disturbing lure such as an injured-minnow or a nodding plug should provide just the right amount of action to bring the strike.

There are two fishing situations in which the popping plug is ideal. The first is when gamefish are chasing large schools of forage, such as the shad or the mullet. This occurs most often in Southern impoundments and tidal creeks, but it also happens periodically in large Northern lakes when alewives and smelt are schooling. With clouds of baitfish in the water, the predators have plenty of targets, and the easiest way to get their attention is to put a popping plug in the area. For one thing, the lure looks like the helpless result of their feeding spree, and the sound will invariably command at least one fish to strike.

The second situation is more common. During periods of highwater, when the lake or river level is well up in the bank brush, a deftly placed popper sitting at the edge of the branches will attract fish from under their cover. Other types of baits would have to be in motion to get strikes, and this is one time when the sitting-and-talking plug has a tremendous advantage. The great majority of lunker bass caught on popping plugs are hooked in this fashion by casters who have the patience to work slowly. You must give the fish a chance to hear the lure, then allow enough time for the fish to find it.

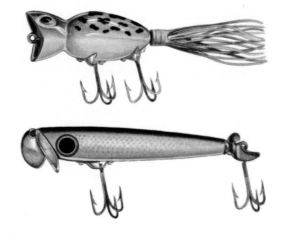

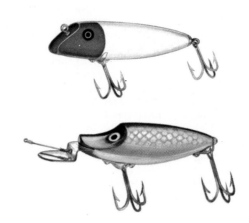

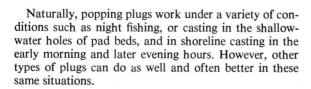

(*Left to right top*) Popping Plug, Floating and Diving Plug, (*bottom*) Surface Disturber, Deep Diving Plug

Naturally, popping plugs work under a variety of conditions such as night fishing, or casting in the shallow-water holes of pad beds, and in shoreline casting in the early morning and later evening hours. However, other types of plugs can do as well and often better in these same situations.

SURFACE DISTURBERS

Plugs of this type are more versatile than poppers and will often work when the bubble makers are ignored. The surface disturbers also float on top of the water, but unlike the popper which must be fished slowly, with pauses and jerks, these baits can be fished at varying speeds. Some surface disturbers can be "nodded" or twitched in one spot, others can be worked from very slow to very fast and even skipped over the water, and still others have a regular swimming action at slow to moderate speeds. Surface disturbers are made in a variety of designs incorporating metal arms, propellers, swinging legs, and even metal tails which flap on the water.

On calm days and even in bright sunlight, the nodding plug is often a killer on big bass. Nodding is pure fish psychology. It differs from popping in that you must assume that an old mossback is nearby and studying the plug. There is no need to attract his attention with noise. If the bass comes up for a look and swims away—fine. Just leave the plug there, and after awhile the fish will come back. Then nod your plug just a bit. The lure sits with its tail slanted down and its nose out of water, so when you move it slightly it tips forward like a paralyzed minnow. If the bass still isn't convinced, wait a bit longer and nod again. Do this often enough and the bass will work up some real enthusiasm. You can also reel the plug along for 1–2 feet, and the rear propeller will make a wet purring sound. Then stop and nod. This plug should never be fished fast. It does its best work with a minimum of movement and motion.

By contrast, the fore-and-aft propeller lure works at all speeds. Its basic action is that of an injured-minnow when retrieved very slowly with long pauses and repeatedly directed with the rod tip from left to right. This is usually a good technique for evening bass fishing along rocky shores and lily beds. On days when the bass act like they all went asleep you might try reeling this type of plug just as fast as you can crank. Skip it over the surface by jerking the rod tip. You will get the best action if you are using a long casting rod and standing on your feet. You have to keep a maximum length of line elevated from the water to make the plug act frantic. The idea is to convince the fish that something edible is hightailing for cover. This retrieve brings explosive strikes from logy summer gamefish. There are similar plugs made without the propellers and having a longer and more slender shape which are equally effective.

Many surface-disturbing lures have been created to resemble mice, frogs, and even ducklings. These all have to be fished slowly or at moderate speeds with short pauses. Such plugs are wholly imitative and give best results when a normal swimming action is duplicated. The proper way to fish a frog plug, for example, is to impart gentle kicking strokes with brief pauses. Allow the lure to stop occasionally, and, if possible, direct it toward a stump or lily pads. Live frogs are invariably heading for cover when they pass within reach of a gamefish.

DARTERS

The name "Darter" is trademarked by the bait company which made the original plug of this type. However, most anglers have come to identify the action as "darting," and thus we use the term here in its broadest sense. The darter-type plug floats when at rest. Most darters float horizontally, but some float vertically with the tail of the plug pointing straight down. When in motion the plug submerges from a few inches to a maximum of 3 feet under the surface, and its action during the retrieve is a slow, tantalizing wobble. The wobble is caused by the grooved head design which gives all darters an open-mouthed appearance. Although the basic shape is snub-nosed and slim, some darters have a curved back; this type can be repeatedly jerked underwater with little forward momentum and the plug will resurface in almost the same spot. Spinning-size darters are favorite lures in Northern lakes and rivers for both largemouth and smallmouth bass. The standard ⅝-ounce darter in frog finish is one of the most popular plugs for shallow-water casting in the South.

The darter has some of the virtues of a surface disturber and also the next group of baits, the floating and diving plugs. The darter doesn't do both their jobs; in fact, its chief appeal is the weaving action which not only hypnotizes bass but excites big tarpon, snook, northern pike, and striped bass. The beginner will not get as much action out of a darter as an experienced angler who knows how to handle a rod. It can be reeled at all speeds and "rolled" over the surface with pauses, stops, and suddenly accelerated. There is no metal lip to interfere with the change of pace. The ideal situation for a darter is in shore-line casting, or on shallow bays of uniform depth. It isn't much good over deepwater because unlike the next group of lures which can be pulled down to more effective levels, the darter is buoyant.

FLOATING AND DIVING

Plugs of this type float at rest and dive when retrieved. They differ from the darters in having a more erratic side-to-side action which is induced by a metal lip, grooved head, or flat front profile. Floating and diving plugs also work somewhat deeper, planing 3–7 feet down, depending on the length of your cast and the speed of your retrieve.

There are two ideal situations for floating and diving plugs. The first is when you are casting toward a bank with a sloping shoreline; the plug can be reeled slowly in the shallow area and fished almost like a surface disturber, then speeded along to dive deeper as it passes over the dropoff. Naturally, this works in reverse for the bank caster or wading angler. The plug can be tossed far from shore, worked back deep, then by slowing the retrieve it can be steered over the inshore weed beds. Reflected light or water color will give some indication of the depth at various points, and the reeling speed should be adjusted accordingly.

The second spot is over a submerged weed bed in deepwater. Often you will find weed beds which come within 4–5 feet of the surface way out in the middle of the lake. Big bass, northerns, and muskies hide in the plant fronds and watch for food in the open area above. The floating-and-diving plug can be passed just over the weed tops when retrieved at the correct speed. Reel very slowly where the weeds are nearest the surface and faster as the plug approaches a deep hole. Rapid reeling causes the plug to dive deeper, but you can stop reeling in a fishy-looking pocket and twitch the plug with short pulls as it slowly rises toward the surface.

Floating and diving plugs are also very useful in early-morning and late-evening trolling when the fish are feeding in water of moderate depth. Unlike straight sinking plugs, lures of this type are buoyant and will come to the surface when you slow the boat's speed or execute short turns. This prevents getting snagged and is ideal for the solo angler who is paddling or rowing his own skiff.

SINKING PLUGS

Plugs of this type sink immediately upon contact with the water. Some sink slowly and can be worked at various depths according to how long you wait before beginning the retrieve. Inasmuch as the rate of descent is consistent with any one plug, it's a good idea to count how many seconds it requires for the lure to drop to a fish-taking level. Although most sinking plugs have a slim profile and must be worked with the rod, others are fish-shaped and have some incorporated action in the form of propellers. Fast-sinking plugs are designed for special conditions. One popular bait used in saltwater is exceptionally heavy for its over-all size; the plug is 3¼ inches long; yet it weighs 1 ounce. Due to its nose design and location of the eye ring the plug has a violent wiggling action.

The thing that makes a sinking plug valuable is that it can be handled in several ways. When casting on strange water, use different retrieves, starting with slow, steady reeling at various depths. After the plug has been worked from a few feet below the surface to near bottom without a strike, let the lure go down and bump gravel. If this doesn't produce, repeat the original casts in depth, but this time using a somewhat faster retrieve with short pauses every few feet. This causes the plug to dart ahead, then settle down. The sinking plug can also be pumped in short and long strokes at fast speed, which give it a very enticing action. The latter technique is more effective in saltwater, however, than in freshwater. Actually, the practical distinction between a sinking plug and a deep diver is seen right here; the former can be varied to a greater degree in speed and action. The strike-provoking side-to-side wiggle of a disc-lipped deep diver which must swim at a more or less constant speed is not nearly as effective for species such as the spotted sea trout, bluefish, snook, and ladyfish as the "straight" sinker which has little if any lateral motion.

Midget sinkers are first-rate lures for river small-mouths. This plug can be fished in fairly rapid water, whereas baits which have metal lips, hollow faces, or widely curved surfaces will not function properly. Water resistance would force them to the top or destroy their built-in action completely. The sinker with a propeller fore-and-aft has enough flash and motion to attract gamefish, and yet its streamlined shape keeps the plug deep. Naturally, midget sinking plugs can be used in lakes and for species other than the smallmouth. Remember that a sinking plug doesn't necessarily have to be used in water that is very deep.

DEEP DIVERS

These are the important walleye and smallmouth-bass plugs. They are also periodically effective for large-mouths, northerns, and muskellunge. Most deep-diving plugs sink immediately upon contact with the water. However, some are designed to float before diving down to 30 feet or more. Unlike regular sinking plugs, whose depth is regulated by their specific gravity and by your retrieving speed, the deep divers have broad metal lips which cause the lure to plane downward as you reel. Therefore, the longer the cast or the more line extended when trolling the deeper the plug will swim.

The ideal situation for deep-diving plugs is in a lake or stream where the fish are holding below the 15-foot level. This generally occurs in July and in August and on bright days when adult gamefish retreat to deeper water. Finding the right spot depends to a great extent on the type of lake you are fishing. A rock-rimmed pond, for instance, with little or no weed area inshore is usually more productive out where there are submerged beds of rooted vegetation or gravel shoals. You will often see yearling bass chasing schools of minnows along the pond margin, and consequently the natural impulse is to favor shoreline casting with topwater baits. But heavy bronzebacks feed beyond the drop-off in warm weather, and they can be reached with deep-running plugs. As a rule of thumb, topwater baits work best after the sun has touched the horizon and again from dawn until 9 A.M. Sinking plugs and deep divers fished over the dropoff adjacent to gravel point, shale banks, shoals, and submerged weed beds at the 15–30-foot level are productive midday lures. Black bass are often caught at the 40–60-foot level in Southern impoundments during hot weather. Most deep-diving plugs will not reach these extreme levels; spoons, black eels, jigs, plastic worms, spinners, and various combinations of each are better suited to bottom fishing. —A.J.McC.

PLUG-CASTING A colloquial term for bait-casting (*which see*). *See also* Plug

POACHERS *See* Sea Poachers

POD A collective name for a number of whiting—"a pod of whiting." In modern American usage pod encompasses other species, e.g., a pod of sailfish, and may also include a number of similar species, e.g., a pod of billfish, whales, or seals.

POINT In fly-fishing, another name for the tippet or last section of a tapered leader. When more than one fly is mounted on the leader, the fly tied to the tippet is called the point-fly; in such cases, a second fly is tied to an additional strand of leader material or dropper and is called a dropper-fly.

POLE FLOUNDER A common name for the witch flounder (*which see*).

POLLOCK *Pollachius virens* This sportier member of the cod family Gadidae is popular with anglers. It resembles the Atlantic cod (*which see*) in general body form, but can be easily distinguished from the cod, haddock, and tomcod by the projection of the lower jaw beyond the upper and the deep, plump body ending in a pointed snout. The presence of the long, lower jaw, the forked tail, and the light lateral line readily separate it from its relatives.

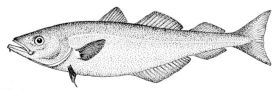

Pollock

The freshly caught pollock is a striking olive-green, varying from rich olive-green or brownish-green above to yellowish or gray on the lower sides, becoming silvery-gray on the belly. This species attains a maximum weight of about 35 pounds corresponding to a length of about 3½ feet, but most caught are around 4–15 pounds.

Found on both sides of the Atlantic, in the western Atlantic it occurs from the Gulf of St. Lawrence south to Chesapeake Bay, being occasionally taken off North Carolina. In the eastern Atlantic, it is taken from the Bay of Biscay, north to Iceland and the North Sea. This active species is taken in large numbers and is found in shallower waters than the cod and haddock, although a few are taken in deeper water between the surface and the bottom.

LIFE HISTORY

Spawning occurs in the late autumn and early winter, the eggs drifting about on the surface. Larval stages occur in the upper water layers for the first three months or so. The pollock grows relatively slowly and reaches about 30 inches when it is about 9 years old. Large schools actively feed upon small fish and on pelagic shrimps as well as small herring, small cods, and their relatives.

ANGLING VALUE

This is an important species for the hook-and-line fishermen who take it by trolling and casting, using spoons and artificial flies. Commercially, it is taken by trawls and gillnets, as well as by handlines, seines, weirs, and traps. Most of this species is sold as frozen fillets or fresh, although some is sold smoked. —D.dS.

POLLUTION The population of the United States has expanded, and industrial and agricultural production has increased tremendously since the turn of the century, but streams, lakes, and estuarine waters have remained static in number. Thus, waste-water disposal problems and their reasonable solution are today a major concern of all. In 1900, there were 76,000,000 people in the United States. In 1950 our population was 150,000,000; in 1960, 180,000,000; in 1980, about 260,000,000. Obviously, the more people there are, the more water will be used.

We have become a nation of concentrated communities, with nearly half our population crowded on 1.5 percent of our land surface. Municipal demands for water are eight times the 1900 level, reflecting in part the larger urban population and in part our higher standard of living and our growing industry.

Agricultural irrigation uses 141 billion gallons of water each day, compared to only 22.2 billion gallons in 1900. No more than 12 percent of the water used in cities is evaporated or transpired to the atmosphere; however, about 60 percent of the water used in irrigation is depleted and thus not recoverable for reuse. That portion returned to the watercourse often is laden with salts, other minerals, and chemicals, including pesticides.

City and agricultural needs for water are minor in comparison with the staggering increase in water use by industry. Since 1900 this country's industry has increased more than nine times, and its estimated use of water is eleven times greater. In 1960, industry used 160 billion gallons of water per day; by 1980, this will jump to 394 billion. Water has many different uses in industrial production, including serving as a source of power, a coolant, a transporting device, an ingredient, and a washing agent. And our factories use water in amounts per unit of final product produced that are astonishing to the average person. For instance, it takes approximately 1,400 gallons of water to manufacture a dollar's worth of paper; the manufacture of 1 yard of woolen cloth requires about 500 gallons of water; a ton of aluminum takes 320,000 gallons.

All water users should be interested in alleviating pollution. With abatement of pollution, danger from disease is lessened; a better potable water is produced; new industries can be attracted to communities; property values increase; and recreation in the form of fishing, hunting, boating, swimming, and other water sports can be available locally.

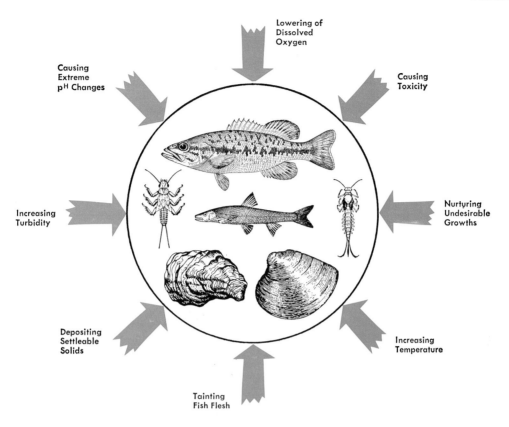

Ways in which industrial wastes may affect aquatic life

History illustrates that in many sections of the United States we defiled our land by overtimbering, overgrazing, and by unwise use of the plow. For many years, we were able to move away from such destroyed, "polluted" land and still subsist. When there was no more new land, we became land conservationists, realizing that in the land lay our survival. The history of land depredation could be repeated in our depredation of water. The number of streams and lakes is static, and there is a minimal number of impoundment sites; there is no moving over a ridge to discover a new waterway. Today, we must become water conservationists, realizing that water is limited and that in water lies a great part of this nation's strength. The available bodies of water must be protected for the multiple uses described, which include the maintenance of a healthy aquatic biota. Ours is the choice of having polluted, barren streams or those with clean water supporting a bountiful healthy life including fish, waterfowl, and other wildlife. The basic aim in conserving our waters should be a multiple use for the many rather than a single use for the few. Thus, with pollution prevention and abatement, we can assure ourselves and our posterity that water will be maintained satisfactorily for a number of interests over a long period of time.

Because of the concern regarding fish destruction by pollution, the Surgeon General of the Public Health Service in early 1960 asked state conservation and fish and game agencies to assist him by reporting instances of fish kills that were attributable to pollutants entering the waterways of the nation. A form for this purpose was devised in cooperation with the U. S. Fish and Wildlife Service and various independent conservation organizations.

Recent controversies associated with the programs for the control of the fire ant, the spruce bud worm, the gypsy moth, and other forest insects, and extensive pesticidal application on food crops have focused attention on the problems of those interested in the preservation of the aquatic habitat. Most pesticides are toxic to aquatic life. Some are highly toxic (e.g., 0.6 pound of Endrin in 120,000,000 gallons of water will kill bluegill sunfish); some are accumulative in the fat and flesh of organisms and in bottom muds. Their use has resulted in the killing of fish and waterfowl, as well as invertebrates such as crabs, crayfish, and aquatic insects that are important in food chains.

Use of pesticides by the aquatic biologist at times has been an important aspect of lake and stream management; such use has been directed toward the control of nuisance midge, mayfly, and mosquito populations, undesirable algae and aquatic weed growths, the sea lampreys, and stunted or undesirable fish populations. Pesticides exhibit tremendous variation in their impact upon the aquatic community; great variation is also shown in the susceptibility of the many kinds of aquatic invertebrates important in fish and waterfowl food chains within that community. Various additives such as solvents, wetting agents, and diluents tend to decrease the hazards to birds and animals and increase the toxicity to aquatic organisms. The kinds of animals associated with the pesticide-treated habitat, and their activities within the treated area are important factors in governing the hazards of the application. The season of the year greatly influences the effect of the pesticide because of the migration, hibernation, and life cycle of the aquatic organism, waterfowl, and other wildlife. The recovery of an affected area depends upon many factors, among which are the proximity of similar habitats, the migratory tendency and range of the animals, and the number of generations per year.

Pesticides must be considered individually rather than collectively, and toxicity problems must be balanced between the beneficial and harmful effects of a particular compound. It is necessary to assay the total effect of a proposed application upon the aquatic environment; to do this necessitates a knowledge of the toxicity and associated hazards of the control agent. Usage must be governed by rigid controls, and adequate safeguards must be installed against "careless use," which has so often been the chief cause of unwarranted aquatic mortalities.

The following environmental changes brought about by industrial waste effluents can be detrimental to aquatic life to varying degrees: decreases in dissolved oxygen to harmful levels; increases in turbidity; formation of sludge deposits by settleable solids; increases in chemicals to toxic levels; changes in pH toward extremes in acidity or alkalinity; increases in temperature; tainting of fish flesh; and production of nutrients resulting in undesirable aquatic growths.

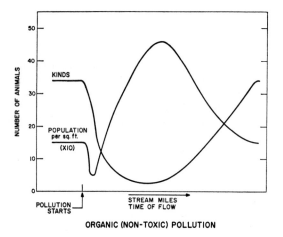

ORGANIC (NON-TOXIC) POLLUTION

The pollutional effect of temperature increases on aquatic life in natural waters has long been overlooked or ignored. A subtle effect is illustrated by the decrease in solubility of oxygen with temperature increases. For example, the solubility of oxygen in freshwater under a pressure of 760 millimeters of mercury at sea level at 32°F. is 14.62 parts per million, at 68°F. it is 9.17 parts per million, and at 86°F. it is 7.63 parts per million. Thus, heat alone can deny aquatic life the necessary oxygen reserves. Where putrescible waste pollution creates a high biochemical oxygen demand and takes additional oxygen from the stream, increased temperatures are dangerous as they may be related to depletion of dissolved oxygen to suffocating levels for aquatic life.

Another subtle effect of temperature increase is reflected, on occasion, in the increased toxicity of certain

chemicals to aquatic forms; for example, high temperatures increase the toxicity of rotenone (a poison used to kill fish) to fish. Brown trout die much more rapidly at 70°F. than they do at 55°F., the time being about 15 and 70 minutes, respectively, with a 0.40 parts per million dosage; with dosages of 0.20 parts per million they die in about 22 minutes at 70°F., and in 100 minutes at 55°F. To the contrary, certain temperature extremes may not be related significantly to toxicity and time of death. Temperatures at 50° and 77°F. have not affected toxicities of ammonia to chubs. Further, toxicities of potassium dichromate and naphthenic acid were very similar at 65° and 86°F.

For extensive data on the effects of temperature increases on fish, one must turn to laboratory research studies where a wealth of data exists, all of which cannot, of course, be summarized or even listed in a summary of this nature. In field investigations involving industrial wastes on large streams, it may be difficult to relate detrimental effects of temperature—heat pollution—to specific aquatic organisms. High temperatures may adversely affect the over-all biota by eliminating many organisms but, in doing so, allow a few, such as certain heat-resistant blue-green, scum-forming nuisance algae, to become dominant.

Gross limits of temperature to which most warmwater fish are subjected in natural bodies of water are somewhere within the range 32°–95°F. If waters of 86°F. are available, warmwater fish may seek them, leaving 90°F. water. Examples of warmwater fish include sunfish, catfish, carp, and many minnows. Coldwater fish, such as salmon and trout, normally live in natural waters somewhere in the range of 32° and near 65°F (summer temperature) and usually do not tolerate temperatures above 81°F. Certain trout have been reported as surviving temperatures of 82°–83°F. for very short periods in natural waters. The Aquatic Life Advisory Committee of the Ohio River Valley Water Sanitation Commission, in reference to waste discharges, recommended that temperatures should not be raised above 93°F. ". . . at any place at any time," and that temperatures during December through April should not exceed 73°F. ". . . at any place or at any time." In streams suitable for trout propagation, temperatures should remain unchanged from those of the natural water. Current knowledge does not permit a precise statement regarding the effects of varying temperature levels on the over-all biota of a stream. In general, in most temperate-zone streams of low gradient, large reaches should not exceed 86°F. for prolonged periods; headwater streams will probably have an upper limit of 72°–77°F. for extended periods of time. Additional research is likely to lower than raise these limits.

Turbidity, which is an expression of the optical property of water that causes light rays to be scattered and absorbed rather than transmitted in straight lines, is caused by a variety of particulate suspended matter. Such matter may be living or dead phytoplankton or zooplankton cells, as algae, protozoans, bacteria, and small crustaceans, or silt or other finely divided inorganic as well as organic waste materials.

Many industrial operations affect turbidity by contributing settleable solids to the water, with resulting bottom deposits that affect aquatic life in varying severities. These include metal, coal, and other mineral mining, including coal washery, gravel washery, glass sand, lumber, aluminum, steel, pulp and paper, slaughterhouse, canning, tannery, milk and cheese, and oil. Only the physical effects of particulate matter in the water are considered here.

Fine particulate inorganic and organic waste materials that remain in suspension can limit the penetration of sunlight, thus restricting the growth of attached bottom plants as well as floating or weakly swimming algal forms, which, because they are photosynthetic organisms, are dependent on light for their existence. Also, solids flocculate planktonic algae and animals out of water and carry them to the bottom to die. Thus, by limiting growths of aquatic-plant meadows, food chains are interrupted, which results in a sparsity of animal life.

As particulate matter settles to the bottom, it can blanket the substrate, forming undesirable physical environments for organisms that would normally occupy such a stream habitat if it were not subjected to these continual deposits. Erosion silt alters aquatic environments chiefly by screening out light, by changing heat radiation, by blanketing the stream bottom, and by retaining organic material and other substances that create unfavorable conditions at the bottom. Developing eggs of fish as well as fish-food organisms may be smothered by deposits of silt; fish feeding may be interfered with. Direct injury to fully developed fish, however, by nontoxic suspended matter occurs only when concentrations are higher than those commonly found in both natural and polluted water.

Bottom-blanketing deposits of dominantly organic solids (as from human sewage) can have quite different physical effects on stream life than those of dominantly inorganic solids (as from coal washeries). In the former instance, if marked toxicity does not exist and dissolved oxygen is satisfactory, stream life that is not adapted specifically to a bottom made up of soft, organic, decaying sludges will be replaced by organisms that are adapted for life in such deposits. In the latter case, inert solids, as those from glass-sand operations, coal washeries, and mineral mining operations, typically destroy bottom life, there being a paucity of organisms that can live among compacted, heavy abrasives. These wastes may form actual "ball-mills" on a stream bottom, grinding and crushing life that is contacted as materials may be resuspended and moved further downstream at high stream-discharge periods.

The physical and nutritional changes effected by organic sludges of certain industrial or sewage origin may result in the formation of zones in a stream characterized by different organisms associations. Above pollution in the clean-water zone the bottom may be composed of small and large stones. Here are to be found many different kinds of the bottom-fish-food organisms, plankton, and fish. Fish-nesting areas are numerous. The typical association of clean-water-dwelling animal species are immature caddisflies, stoneflies, and mayflies; hellgrammites; gill-breathing snails; and pearl-button clams. Smallmouth black bass, sunfish, and various minnows abound. Numerous kinds of plankton are present. Thus in the unpolluted zone there is a great variety of animals and plants, but because of predation and competition for food and living space these are represented by few individuals.

In the zone of recent pollution, floating solids that become settleable blanket out light penetration and, on moving into the zone of active decomposition, settle to form sludge deposits over the entire bottom. Turbidities here are high. Only a few kinds of animals and plants can survive on the soft, shifting blanket of sludge. Such organisms, isolated from many predators, form huge populations of individuals. Solids, in settling, flocculate floating small animals and plants out of water; thus these are scarce. The few animal forms that are adjusted to living in a sludge substrate are sludgeworms, some kinds of bloodworms, water sow-bugs, certain snails, and various leeches. Fish are absent or are scarce and prefer to form their nests elsewhere. Flowering water plants are absent, not being able to root in sludge deposits. Most algae are extremely scarce, being represented by dominating blue-greens that form gelatinous, slimy coverings over the sludge in shallow, marginal water. At some point downstream, turbidities gradually decrease, sludge deposits are reduced, and the stream becomes healthy again, teeming with many different kinds of animals and plants. Because the available food supply is reduced, there is a reduction in the total population. As more different organisms become established in the environment, after many miles stream conditions become similar to those that exist in the clean-water zone.

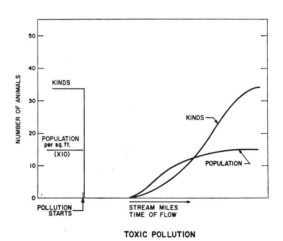

TOXIC POLLUTION

The physical effects of inert, inorganic solids, as from glass-sand operations, can be more severe in reducing populations than those of settleable organic solids. Data collected in a stream survey vividly relate the physical effect on aquatic life of particulate mineral matter wasted from a glass-sand operation to a small creek that flowed into the Potomac River. Below this creek the true "Sahara Desert" of waters was found, with oases being extremely sparse. Above the point of confluence, the sparkling clearwater of the Potomac was bedded by rocky ledges, rocks, coarse gravel, and some naturally occurring clean sand. Beds of higher rooted aquatic plants lushly abounded. Gill-breathing snails and immature mayflies dominated the invertebrate fauna, and were found everywhere on the substrate. Large pearl-button clams were common marginally. Minnows were observed in abundance, and filamentous algae covered much of the rocky area. Eleven kinds of floating and attached filamentous algae and eight kinds of animals were represented in collections before pollution entered the stream.

At a station six hundred yards below the confluence of the Potomac with the small creek that received the glass-sand wastes the bottom of the river was devoid of life. Blue-green algae grew marginally on the wave-washed area of the bank. This paucity of organisms existed to midstream where three kinds of snails and ten kinds of floating algae were collected. From the right bank to midstream, rock ledges, rocks, gravel, and sand of the original Potomac River bottom were completely covered by a blanket up to two feet of wasted glass-sand fines. During the period in which samples were collected the water was clear and the sand-fines desert was spectacularly visible. Turbidities attributable to this operation varied tremendously with varying waste discharges, as from 130 units to 50,000 units. The effects of such deposits suppressed the abundance of bottom organisms as far as ten miles downstream.

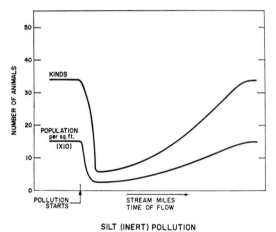

SILT (INERT) POLLUTION

In the years 1910–1950, 10,000,000 tons of sandy silt attributable chiefly to improper agricultural practices was deposited in the Bear River from Preston, Idaho, to Cutler Reservoir, covering the natural substrate to a depth of 5–6 feet. Above the source of silt pollution, a recent survey indicated over four hundred bottom-dwelling organisms per square foot. Below the source, for a distance of forty-three miles, organisms were present only on the rocks that had not been covered by silt near bridge abutments. On masonite panels placed in the stream for 5 weeks, 250 organisms per square foot were found during periods of low siltation, indicating that the major limiting factor was the availability of living spaces for benthic forms.

Pollution by oil wastes is also a matter of concern. Many thousands of waterfowl have been destroyed by the effects of oil pollution. This wasteful loss has deprived many thousands of nature lovers, waterfowl hunters, and bird watchers of immeasurable enjoyment. The destruction of many duck species, such as the canvasback, redhead, and scaups, comes at a critical period for these species that are fighting for survival against the forces of nature. In future years additional waterfowl will be destroyed if oil dumping is continued, especially in late winter. In this modern age of technical development, the discharge of oil into a river system indicates man's lack of responsibility for the preservation of our natural resources.

Oil causes matting of the duck feathers so that ducks become waterlogged, lose their ability to fly, and drown if they cannot get out of the water soon enough. It breaks down the insulating power of the feathers; body heat and stored reserves of energy are rapidly lost. Diving ducks may starve, and, following the preening of oil from contaminated feathers, bleeding ulcers may be produced in the digestive tract causing mortality.

Wastes with substrates of nitrogen and phosphorus (fertilizers) pollute our waters and increase certain organism populations to such magnitudes that water uses are interfered with and nuisances are created. Organisms that respond to such nutrients are certain floating and attached algae and rooted aquatic plants. If streams, lakes, and man-made impoundments continue to become enriched with wastes of industrial, municipal, and agricultural origin, biological nuisance problems that exist today will become intensified in many areas; other areas that do not have them now can certainly expect them.

Inorganic and organic nutrients containing nitrogen and phosphorus are among the major factors that contribute to plant abundance, including nuisance algal blooms. In modern waste-treatment practices, dissolved inorganic or mineral constituents of municipal sewage and industrial wastes are removed only incidentally by sedimentation and oxidation; also, certain organic materials are broken down with treatment to liberate inorganic nitrogen and phosphorus, thus making them more available as fertilizers for plant growth. Treatment-plant effluents may actually contain more readily available nutritional (fertilizer) substrates than are found in raw sewage effluents. Thus, to prevent acceleration of the fertilizing effect of sewage and certain nontoxic industrial wastes and attendant nuisance problems, all such wastes ideally should be excluded from natural lakes and impoundments. Even if nutrient-bearing wastes are excluded, agricultural drainage carrying nitrogenous and phosphorus compounds may still provide nutrients that encourage nuisances in certain regions.

A two-year study of seventeen lakes in southeastern Wisconsin indicated that if assets of inorganic nitrogen and phosphorus exceeded 0.30 and 0.01 parts per million, respectively, at the start of the active growing season (the time of spring turnover in Northern climates), a season with nuisance blooms could follow. This undoubtedly does not apply in strict manner to all lakes, but the finding should stimulate further investigations along these lines.

The facts today indicate that algal nuisances have only just begun to disclose what monsters they can become in future years if nutrient enrichment of waters with certain industrial wastes, sewage, and agricultural fertilizers through runoff is continued. The secondary treatment effluent of the combined sewage and industrial wastes of Madison, Wisconsin, has an annual per capita contribution of 8.5 pounds of inorganic nitrogen and 2.8–3.7 pounds of soluble phosphorus. By diverting this effluent around Lakes Waubesa and Kegonsa, this city reduced the inflow of nutrients into those waters by 3,143 pounds per day of inorganic nitrogen and 1,342 pounds per day of soluble phosphorus. If the suggested nutrient concentrations for bloom production are used (namely 0.30

parts per million inorganic nitrogen and 0.01 parts per million inorganic phosphorus), the annual per capita contribution of treated sewage effluent would supply sufficient inorganic nitrogen to fertilize one acre of lake water to a depth of five feet and sufficient inorganic phosphorus to fertilize seven acres of lake water to a depth of five feet, which would probably cause nuisance algal blooms to occur during summer months.

Land runoff from the drainage basin may be the principal nutrient contributor to the tributary stream. The annual loss per acre in Wisconsin from a planting of corn on a 20-percent slope of Miami silt loam was found to be 630 pounds of organic matter, 38 pounds of nitrogen, and 1.8 pounds of phosphorus. The annual contribution per square mile of drainage area may be as high as 4,100 pounds of inorganic nitrogen. Research in Washington indicated that water samples collected from the gutters on Seattle streets carried 0.53 parts per million of nitrate nitrogen and 0.076 parts per million soluble phosphorus following rainstorms; water from irrigation return flows carried as much as 2.5–24 pounds of total nitrogen per acre of drainage per year and 0.9–3.9 pounds of total phosphorus per acre per year.

The effects of algal nuisances have long been known to the waterworks field. Algal blooms cause tastes and odors in water, clog rapid sand filters in water-treatment plants, and form unsightly scums on various basins in such installations. The writers wish to re-emphasize the problems that can in future years greatly plague those charged with management of water projects, such as the many multiple-purpose reservoirs that are being constructed in this country. At the heart of biological nuisance problems there will be algal blooms, which are nurtured by nutrients from various sources.

There is considerable literature on the enrichment of water, which is called eutrophication. Little has been published, however, on lake fertilization to show systematically the effects of nutrients on the entire ecology of a lake and on man's ultimate uses of lake water.

The effects of algal blooms on lakeside dwellers have been well-documented for certain lakes in the Madison, Wisconsin, area. Especially during hot summer periods algal blooms have accumulated to give lakes a thick, green, pea-soup appearance and consistency. At times of blooms, lakes are no longer inviting to bathers, fishing is impaired, boating becomes a sport out of season, and vile odors produced by decomposition permeate the area. The odors make life in the area hardly bearable, sometimes forcing the residents to move.

Algal blooms have been related specifically to fish kills through removal of dissolved oxygen from water during respiration. In daylight hours algae and submerged aquatic plants give off oxygen by photosynthesis, commonly raising the dissolved oxygen resources to supersaturation levels. Photosynthesis does not occur during hours of total darkness. Respiration, of course, continues over twenty-four hours with algae and other aquatic plants as it does with animals. In streams with huge algal blooms, dissolved oxygen resources can be reduced to suffocating levels by the respiration of the organism mass, resulting in fish kills.

For example, in Lytle Creek, Wilmington, Ohio, dissolved oxygen was observed to fluctuate over 24 hours from 19.4 parts per million in the afternoon to 0.7 parts per million before dawn. A fish kill occurred in this creek that was attributed to low dissolved-oxygen levels resulting from organism respiration. Fish kills related to oxygen depletion have also been reported for East Okobeju Lake and Storm Lake, Iowa, as well as the lakes at Madison, Wisconsin. Field surveys of streams in the Ohio River Basin disclosed disastrous reductions of dissolved-oxygen resources for aquatic life during early-morning hours. Reduction of dissolved oxygen to levels endangering aquatic life during nighttime hours and during a consecutive series of cloudy days when oxygen production was curtailed was also reported. *See also* Freshwater Ecology and Marine Ecology   —W.M.I.
—K.M.M.

POMPANO *Trachinotus carolinus* This eastern Atlantic species has also been called pompano, or sunfish. The slender-bodied form that previously was named *Trachinotus argenteus* is merely a growth stage and the same species as this. Very large specimens may have been confused with the permit, *Trachinotus falcatus*.

The first dorsal fin of the common pompano has 5–6 short spines. The second dorsal fin has one spine and 22–27 softrays (usually 23–26). The anal fin has 2 spines (that become detached with growth) followed by 1 spine and 20–23 softrays (usually 21–22). There are no dark bars on the sides.

The body is relatively shallow, and the body depth decreases proportionally with growth. The dorsal- and anal-fin lobes are relatively short at all body sizes, but the proportional length changes with the growth of the fish; in fish about 12 inches long and larger, the length of the dorsal-fin lobe is about equal to or less than the length of the head. The back and upper sides are grayish-silvery-blue or bluish-green, the sides silvery, and the ventral surfaces flecked with yellow. The dorsal fin is dusky or bluish, the anal fin yellowish or light orange, and the caudal fin dusky or yellowish.

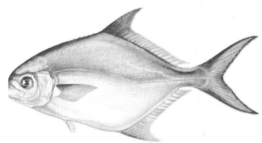

Pompano

The common pompano ranges from Santos, Brazil, to Massachusetts, in the West Indies, and at Bermuda. The largest known specimen is 25 inches in total length (obtained from the New York market, the location of capture unknown). A maximum weight of 8 pounds has been mentioned, and some fish of about 30 pounds were thought to be this species by commercial fishermen.

LIFE HISTORY

The life history is imperfectly known, although this is the most abundant and the most important pompano of the United States and probably of the American continents. There have been a number of speculations about the place of spawning of the common pompano, and these have been accepted over the years to imply that the pompano comes inshore to spawn. Spawning probably occurs in offshore waters. The two smallest known specimens of this species, ⅜ and ½ inch long, were taken 60 and 30 miles off the coast of South Carolina in August and September. Spawning off the Southeastern United States probably extends at least from March into September. The developing young move inshore and northward along the Eastern states from about May to December and then move out. Young and adults appear to be influenced greatly by water temperature changes. They run in schools, are abundant around inlets and along sandy beaches, and at times move in and out with the tide. Young fish eat a variety of pelagic and benthic invertebrates and sometimes smaller fish. Larger pompano are thought to prefer bivalve mollusks and small crustaceans, and have been described as rooting in the sand and mud for these.

ANGLING VALUE

Epicures have proclaimed this to be a food fish without peer from either fresh- or saltwater. The flesh is firm and rich. Pompano cookery is an art in Florida and Louisiana; the classic dish is pompano papillote (in a paper bag). This is an excellent gamefish on light tackle. It strikes fast and runs fast. Fishing success is definitely improved with skill and know-how. Beach-casting with live sandbugs is a popular method.   —F.H.B.

ANGLING METHODS

Because of its high commercial value, the common pompano is sought principally by fulltime and parttime market fishermen. Due to its esteemed position on the menus of seafood restaurants and its high monetary return to commercial fishermen as compared to other species, the pompano is often overlooked as a gamefish. On light spinning tackle, this fish, which averages about 2 pounds, is a spirited fighter.

The flat-sided pompano uses its body surface to execute sudden reversals of its forward motion. The pompano is unpredictable with respect to its fighting tactics. It is a "nervous" fish. This is noticeable during the spring season in particular. Occasionally a pompano will dash across the water in a semicircular course around a boat and may even skip along the surface like a flat rock. Approached by a boat in the shallows it will often streak through the air like a projectile. Panicky pompano have even been known to leap into a boat, and some fishermen have been struck by them. The high-strung nature of the pompano becomes plainly evident as it is reeled close to the angler. The fish may do just about anything in its frantic attempt to escape; it may bolt beneath the boat to the other side or take a hitch around an anchor line.

Pompano are present in Florida waters of the Atlantic and Gulf coasts the year around. However, they are most plentiful in the fall, winter, and spring seasons. Migratory fishes for the most part, they head southward down the east coast of Florida before the fall storms to spend the winter in warmer waters. In spring, the pompano move back north.

The pompano is second only to the bluefish in Florida in importance as a surf gamefish. The species is also taken from ocean piers and jetties, and by skiff and bridge fishermen in tidal bays and estuaries.

Probably the sportiest way of catching pompano is by spinfishing from a drifting or anchored skiff. Because the pompano has a soft mouth, some anglers use no leader material, tying a jig or feather lure directly to a 6–10-pound test monofilament line. There is always a very good chance of hooking other species while fishing for pompano, however; so it is good practice to tie on a two-foot length of monofilament leader material of 20-pound-test.

Pompano may be taken on artificial lures, and nylon jigs in particular. This is true especially when a new school of hungry, migrating fish first put in an appearance. But the great majority of pompano fishermen use natural bait. The pompano prefers crustaceans to baitfish, and the sand bug (*which see*) or "sand flea" is without a doubt the most widely used bait for this species both in surf and bay fishing. Fishermen who cast from skiffs in inshore tidal waters usually bait a nylon jig with a sand bug. If this lure-bait combination is used, it is desirable to keep the amount of nylon skirt on the lure to a minimum. This can be accomplished simply by cutting off the nylon material even with the bight of the hook.

Since the pompano is a bottom feeder, the trick is to keep the lure bouncing on the sand. After the cast, the lure should be allowed to sink all the way to the bottom. A popular technique is alternately to raise the rod tip somewhat briskly and then lower it as the reel crank is turned to pick up the slack.

This retrieve, a slow, less vigorous version of the whip retrieve (*see* Bait-Casting), allows the lure to bounce along the bottom. Pompano usually hit when the rod tip is lowered and the lure drops downward. The selection of a jig depends upon the depth of the water and speed of the current. In a strong tidal flow where the water is relatively deep, an angler will have to use heavier jigs.

Pompano can also be taken trolling in inshore tidal waters. This method is generally employed by small-boat commercial fishermen. A jig baited with a sand bug should be trolled slowly while jigging the rod tip to give the lure the same bottom-bouncing action as already described. A more effortless trolling method can be obtained with a small spoon and a weighted terminal rig. The spoon, baited with a sand bug, is tied to the end of a 6–7-foot length of 20-pound-test leader material. A small swivel is used to join leader and line. To this swivel—or the line just above it—a trolling sinker or teardrop-shaped lead is attached. The weight should be just heavy enough to keep the lure and bug very near the bottom. With this method, no jigging of the rod tip is necessary as the wobbling spoon provides sufficient action.

Pompano fishermen also still-fish from anchored skiffs in bays and estuaries. Sand bugs are a common bottom-fishing bait, but in some areas other natural baits such as clams are used. Terminal rigs for this type of pompano fishing vary from a singlehook fishfinder rig to more complicated rigs with multiple hooks. The common surf rig has two or three hooks, and is made up of monofilament leader material. The hooks are usually placed above a pyramid sinker. Weight of the lead depends upon the surge of the sea, the current, and the distance required to reach the fish.

On the southeast coast of Florida, long casts are usually necessary as the pompano are often located along or beyond the first sandbar from shore. Both spinning tackle and revolving-spool reels are used, the latter being the most popular. Monofilament lines are in wide use with both types.

On the Florida east coast, which is prime pompano territory, hollow fiberglass surf rods used for pompano range 11½–13 feet in length. The surf stick must be sturdy enough to handle 3–5-ounce sinkers, yet have a tip limber enough to prevent a bait from snapping off the hook on long-distance casts. A great many of these surf rods are custom made in Florida.

Although the pompano averages about 2 pounds, there are times during each season when fish ranging from 3 to more than 4 pounds put in an appearance. Infrequently, a true pompano weighing as much as 7–7½ pounds is taken. Anything much larger is generally the close relative of the pompano—the Atlantic permit (*which see*)—which may achieve a weight of more than 30 pounds. *See also* Carangidae   —E.C.B.

POMPANO DOLPHIN *Coryphaena equiselis* This smaller relative of the dolphin is probably more common than records indicate, but it is easily confused with females and smaller males of that species which lack the high vertical forehead of larger males. Pompano dolphin are most easily distinguished from dolphin by their greater body depth; the greatest body depth goes into the length from tip of snout to fork of tail fewer than four times, and this greatest depth occurs near the middle of the body, rather than just behind the head, as in the dolphin. There are usually fewer than 200 lateral-line scales and fewer than 56 dorsal rays. The few recorded observations indicate that the color of the pompano dolphin is similar to that of the dolphin. Pompano dolphin may reach a length of 2 feet and a weight of 5 pounds.

Because of the difficulty in distinguishing between the two species of dolphins, the published information does not accurately depict the range of the pompano dolphin. It is probably found around the world in warm seas, but the pompano dolphin generally appears to be a more oceanic species than the dolphin.

Little is known of the life history of the pompano dolphin. Females mature at a length of 10–12 inches. Spawning is believed to occur throughout spring and summer in the Gulf of Mexico, and perhaps over a longer period in the Caribbean. Although adults are not commonly reported, juveniles of this species are abundant offshore where they have been taken along with dolphin by the use of lights at night with dipnets. *See also* Dolphin
                    —B.B.C.
                    —R.H.G.

POMPANOS In American waters there are ten species of three genera of pompanos (*Trachinotus, Parona,* and *Zalocys*).

They are collectively distinguished by their generally deep and compressed bodies; six spines in the first dorsal fin; the anal fin only slightly shorter than the dorsal fin; no scutes in the lateral line; and small, rounded, cycloid scales on the body. *See also* Carangidae, Gafftopsail Pompano, Paloma Pompano, Palometa, Pompano
                    —F.H.B.

POND SMELT *Hypomesus olidus* Though found in the North Pacific and eastern part of the Arctic Ocean from the Copper River, Alaska to Hokkaido, Japan, as well as in the McKenzie River, Northwest Territories, Canada, it is of interest to us because it was introduced from Japan experimentally into a freshwater lagoon in northern California as a possible foragefish. It is almost a completely freshwater species, venturing rarely into brackish water. It spawns in the spring and its eggs are the same type as *Osmerus* (*see* Smelt). It is distinguished by having 0–3 pyloric caecae, an extended longest anal fin ray, and the attachment of the pneumatic duct behind the anterior end of the air bladder.   —J.R.

PORBEAGLE *Lamna nasus* A member of the swift-swimming mackerel shark family, the porbeagle, sometimes called mackerel shark, is a heavily-bodied, open-ocean fish closely resembling the mako, bonito shark, white shark, and salmon shark (*which see*), being most closely related to the latter. From its Atlantic relatives, it is separated from the white shark by its pointed, slender teeth, each of which has a sharp cusp at the base. The base of the porbeagle's caudal peduncle has a secondary,

Pompano Dolphin, 3-pound Male, Miami, Florida

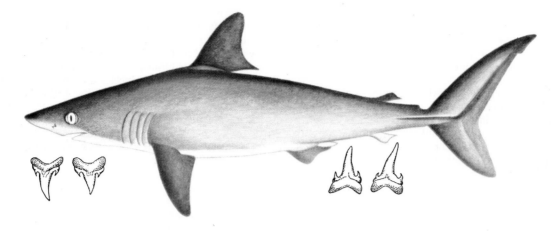

Porbeagle (teeth of upper jaw, *left*, of lower jaw, *right*)

smaller keel, which is lacking in its relatives. Its dorsal fin is directly over the pectoral fin, whereas it is behind the pectoral in the mako; it is only somewhat behind in the white shark. But the second dorsal is located directly above the anal fin in the porbeagle, which separates it from both the mako and the white shark. The porbeagle's caudal fin is less symmetrical as well, the upper lobe being decidedly longer, yet not as long as in the sand shark (*which see*). It is blue-gray to blackish above to white on the belly, with a white or dusky anal fin. It is not a large shark for this family, the largest recorded being 10 feet, although fish of 12 feet have been reported. A 400-pound specimen was 9 feet long.

LIFE HISTORY

Found in the nearshore waters of the Atlantic Ocean, it has been reported from both sides of the Atlantic from the Murman coast south to Africa and the Mediterranean. In the western Atlantic, it has been taken from the Gulf of St. Lawrence to South Carolina. It is a shark of the temperate zone which occasionally enters water that is rather cool. But they apparently move into deeper strata during the winter to avoid water temperatures that are very low. It is less vigorous a swimmer than its Atlantic relatives, and is also found in deeper strata, being reported from depths of 80 fathoms.

Porbeagles feed on schooling fishes, such as mackerel, pilchards, and herring, and on bottom-dwelling species such as cod, hake, and flounders. In the mackerel-shark family, the eggs are hatched within the female, and the young then remain inside for some time afterwards. Although embryos have been found in the mother during the winter, evidence suggests that birth occurs during the summer.

FOOD VALUE

The porbeagle is not considered a sport fish, but formerly its liver was in commercial demand because of the large amount of oil it yielded. Some porbeagle is still sold because of its resemblance in taste to swordfish meat, but the market is not large. Most are taken in gillnets, and the rest are captured on hook and line and in various types of seines and traps. —D.dS.

PORCUPINEFISH *Diodon hystrix* This well-known fish, aptly named for the quill-like spines over the head and body (except snout, chin, and caudal peduncle), was given its scientific appellation by Linnaeus (1758). It is said to occur in all warm seas (in the western Atlantic straying north to Massachusetts) and to reach a length of over 2 feet. It has small black spots over the upper part of the head and body. A related species, *Diodon holacanthus*, is reported to differ principally in having longer head spines relative to those on the side of the body. The spines on the forehead of *hystrix* are equal to or shorter than those behind the pectoral fin, whereas those of *holacanthus* are longer than the postpectoral spines. Both *hystrix* and *holacanthus* are readily distinguished from the burrfishes (*Chilomycterus* spp.), which are also placed in the porcupinefish family (Diodontidae), by having movable spines; the spines over the head and body of the burrfishes are short and immobile.

A JAPANESE LANTERN

When a porcupinefish is harassed, it inflates itself to nearly spherical form, and the spines, which are usually laid nearly flat against the body, are forced outward at approximately right angles to the body, thus presenting a rather uninviting appearance to a predator. In the sea, the porcupinefish enlarges itself with water, but if held out of the water it gulps air to inflate. When dried in the inflated position it makes an interesting curio, sometimes termed a "Japanese lantern."

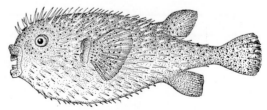

Porcupinefish

The beaklike jaws of *Diodon* are not divided at the front by a suture like the related puffers. The jaws are powerful and used to crush hardshelled invertebrates, such as mollusks and echinoids, which form the principal items of the diet.

The porcupinefish possesses an even better protection than the formidable spines alone would indicate. Each spine has a long lateral root on each side and a short anterior root (except frontal spines on which the anterior root is reduced or absent). These roots are nearly in contact with one another and form a kind of inner armor.

Although the porcupinefish is difficult to prepare for eating, it is generally regarded as a good food fish. The internal organs, however, have at times been reported as poisonous. —J.E.R.

PORGY *See* Jolthead Porgy, Red Porgy, Scup, Whitebone Porgy

PORKFISH *Anisotremus virginicus* The porkfish is a member of the grunt family (Pomadasyidae). Its genus, *Anisotremus*, is distinctive from other American grunts mainly in the deeper body, blunt snout, and thick lips. *Anisotremus* is well-represented in eastern Pacific waters, but there are only three species in the western Atlantic, of which only the porkfish and the black margate (*A. surinamensis*) occur in the West Indies and Florida.

The porkfish is easily distinguished from the drab black margate by its striking color. The head is yellowish and silvery with a black bar running from the forehead through the eye to the corner of the mouth. Anteriorly on the body is another black bar running vertically from the origin of the dorsal fin to the axil of the pectoral fin. The body is longitudinally striped with light blue and yellow, and the fins are yellow. The young are very differently colored. They have a yellow head and a thin horizontal black stripe running posteriorly from the eye to the caudal peduncle, followed by a large, round black spot at the base of the tail; there is a second black stripe on the upper part of the body.

Porkfish

LIFE HISTORY

In spite of its scientific name *virginicus*, bestowed by Linnaeus in 1758, the porkfish does not appear to range north of Florida (it has been introduced into Bermuda), but occurs southward to Brazil. It is not a common species in the West Indies, but is often encountered in large schools in Florida.

Adults feed on a great variety of small invertebrate animals, such as crabs, shrimps, mantis shrimps, mollusks (gastropods, pelecypods, and chitons), isopods, amphipods, and brittlestars. The young feed at least in part on the ectoparasites of other fishes.

FOOD VALUE

Although not a large species (it attains about 14 inches), the porkfish is a good eating fish. —J.E.R.

PORK RIND A type of lure made from hog skin which is cut in strips or a variety of shapes and chemically preserved. Pork rind is used chiefly in freshwater fishing for bass, pike, and muskellunge. It has a wide application to saltwater angling when used in tandem with jigs, feathers, spoons, and spinners.

Crude pork-rind lures can be made at home, but the commercial product is relatively inexpensive and more durable. Just the choice skin (6–8 inches wide) is taken from the back of a hog on either side of the spine; this is the only usable skin on the entire animal, as the remainder is too soft or too fragile. The skin is cured immediately to prevent spoilage. After curing, it is processed by machine to split away the fat side, and again to split off the dirty outside layer so that both sides are uniformly white and without imperfections. The skin is then split a third time to obtain the required thinness. Next, it is die-cut to various shapes and sizes. However, because of the great variation in skins, considerable handwork is still required for uniformity. When cut, the baits are put into a finishing cure to prevent spoilage and to maintain their flexibility. —A.J.McC.

PORPOISES This group constitutes a family (Delphinidae) belonging to the mammalian order of whales (*which see*), the Cetacea. They are popularly known as porpoises and dolphins, but the name dolphin is sometimes confused with that of a fish (*see* Dolphin). Porpoise usually refers to members of this family which are small, lack a definite beak, have a triangular dorsal fin, and possess spadelike teeth, while the rest of the family members are referred to as dolphin, save for the killer whale. Generally, porpoises are small and usually have teeth in both jaws and a dorsal fin. They seldom exceed 14 feet, but the killer whale reaches at least 30 feet. The characteristics of this family, including a single blowhole, the lack of whalebone, and the presence of crests on the skull, separate them from other whales, while a closely related family, the river dolphins (family Platanistidae), differs in the number of specialized ribs.

The family contains the subfamily Delphinapterinae, which includes the unique narwhal, which may reach 9 feet and which has a spirally twisted tooth in the male. It occurs in the Arctic, where it is hunted for its oil and the tusk, which yields an excellent grade of ivory. The white whale, or beluga, is closely related to the narwhal, which it resembles, but lacks the long spike and has teeth in both jaws. Adults are pure white, while young are gray to mottled. They reach 14 feet, and have been reported as growing to 18 feet. They are found in the Arctic areas, sometimes ranging southward to the Baltic and the Gulf of the St. Lawrence.

The rest of the family is included in the subfamily Delphininae, divided into those with a more or less well-defined beak and those without. The killer whale belongs to this group, and is known for its speed and ferocity. Its streamlined body is distinctive, and it gives the impression of great strength. The male has a high, triangular dorsal fin, and that of the female is relatively smaller. The black body is variously marked with white patches on the side of the head and along the belly. Males grow to at least 30 feet, females about half that. Killer whales occur in all waters and are especially abundant in polar waters where food is plentiful. They are voracious, feeding on whales, porpoises, fishes, aquatic birds, and seals. They hunt in packs, attacking dead whales which have been harpooned, as well as live ones. Their fearlessness is legendary, but despite their aggressive behavior there is no authentic record of a killer having attacked man. Other members of this group include the false killer whale, identified by a smaller dorsal fin and the absence of white markings, and the pilot whale, or blackfish. The blackfish has a large, rounded head, a low dorsal fin, and a black body, usually with a white chin area. They occur in temperate waters, and have been reported from Europe, the Atlantic Coast of the United States, South Africa, and New Zealand. Reaching nearly 30 feet long, they travel in large numbers, sometimes becoming stranded on the beaches in great schools. Various explanations have been given for this behavior, but it is believed that their radar system, used by whales to locate obstacles, may become inoperative in shallow water under certain conditions.

Another porpoise in this group includes the common porpoise of European seas, marked with a black back and white belly, and found in temperate areas of the Atlantic and the eastern Pacific. It eats fishes, squids, and crustaceans.

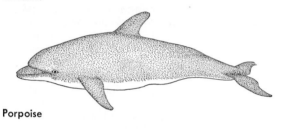

Porpoise

DOLPHINS

Of the so-called dolphins found in the many waters of the world, perhaps the bottlenosed dolphin (*Tursiops truncatus*) is best-known to American readers. This is the acrobat commonly used in public aquaria. It has a well-defined snout about 3 inches long, a triangular dorsal fin which is concave on its posterior edge, and a gray-brown body with a white belly. It grows to about 12 feet. Found from Maine to Florida and throughout the Gulf of Caribbean, it occurs as well from Spain to England, and in the Mediterranean Sea and New Zealand. It travels in large schools, usually in coastal waters, often entering water only a few feet deep. Little is known about its habits in the sea, although the ease with which they are maintained in captivity has made them the intensive subject of numerous behavior studies. Their ability to learn indicates that they have a high degree of intelligence, and their methods of communication with one another are being studied. A high degree of echo sounding is developed, so that they are able to locate prey and submerged objects, a feature common to other whales.

The common dolphin of Europe (*Delphinus*) is the creature whose grace and habits pervade the rich mythological literature. It was known to the ancients for its human characteristics, and many sea tales are associated with dolphin legends. Huge schools of this playful animal cavort wherever the sailor ventures. The narrow, slender beak, the dark brown to black back, the white belly, and the wavy bands on the side easily separate this species

from the bottlenose dolphin. They are reported to eat vast quantities of herrings, and have been observed, like the bottlenose, to leap clear of the water at high speeds as they follow vessels at speeds of up to 30 knots.

FOOD VALUE

The meat of the dolphins and porpoises is said to be excellent, but lovers of the sea religiously attach bad luck to eating this flesh, even though men have eaten the meat when rations were low, fortunately without punitive effects. —D.dS.

PORPOISING Said of a fast, planing boat which bounces along the surface with the bow alternately rising and slapping the water, although the stern may not necessarily come clear of the surface.

A fish, such as a trout, is said to porpoise when feeding in slow, surface rolls. This usually occurs when certain types of subaquatic insect forms are abundant.

PORT Left side of the boat looking forward. A harbor.

PORTUGUESE MAN-OF-WAR *Physalia physalis* A beautiful member of the phylum Coelenterata, it is related to corals, sea fans, and jellyfish. The group to which it belongs (order Siphonophora) contains largely drifting animals, unlike the bottom-living corals and sea fans. Siphonophores form colonies of many animals of the same species, and may float or actively swim. *Physalia* has a large crested float, colored blue-green to violet with many iridescent tints from ruby-red to lilac, which may reach 14 inches long. Long, brilliant blue tentacles hang beneath the gas-filled float, interspersed with shorter, pinkish tentacles. Specimens found on the beach usually have only short tentacles remaining, but in the sea they may exceed 50 feet long. The tentacles are muscular and contract when touched by an organism, the prey being raised into the mouths of the colony. Organisms thus caught are leisurely digested by the powerful enzymes.

Physalia occurs throughout the tropics, drifting poleward during warm months. It usually occurs in bluewater far offshore, but onshore winds may bring it onto the beaches in large numbers. They are often accompanied by the man-of-war fish (*Nomeus*), a jacklike fish with a beautiful blue and silver coloration. It artfully dodges the tentacles, and is believed to act as a lure, bringing predatory fishes within range of the tentacles.

DANGER TO MAN

The tentacles contain stinging cells (nematocysts), tiny spherical cells containing a hollow, coiled tube. Each tube is tipped with barbs. Pressure on the stinging cells causes them to be released, and the barbed tubes, or arrows, still attached to the tentacle, stick to the captured organism harpoon-fashion. Simultaneously, a toxin is injected into the prey, be it fish or human, the poison being a neurotoxin similar to cobra venom and affecting the nervous system. Fishes and invertebrates lose their equilibrium, suffer paralysis, and die within a very short time. Experimental mice, when injected with the toxin, suffer respiratory paralysis and die quickly.

Treatment for *Physalia* stings is first to remove the tentacles, then to neutralize the toxin with alcohol, gasoline, kerosene, or any other organic liquid. Ammonia or calamine lotion is sometimes helpful. Since shock and respiratory paralysis may occur in severe cases, a physician should be consulted.

Portuguese Man-of-War

SIMILAR SIPHONOPHORES

Two other blue siphonophores are commonly mistaken for the Portuguese man-of-war. These are the by-the-wind sailor, *Velella*, which has a flat, oval, gelatinous plate containing air spaces, below which its tentacles hang, while the upper surface bears a transparent, triangular sail. The second is a circular float, rarely larger than a half-dollar, which is known as *Porpita*. The tentacles of either species are seldom more than 3 inches long, and while capable of stinging (a burning sensation) their nematocysts are not capable of penetrating the human skin. *See also* Dangerous, Poisonous, and Injurious Aquatic Life *under* First Aid —D.dS.

POSTERIOR Rear or rearward; region of the rear or pertaining to the rear

PRAWN A crustacean of the order Decapoda. Prawns are often mistaken for shrimp, but their abdomens are more slender.

PREOPERCLE One of the bones on the side of the head of a fish, just ahead of the opercle and just behind the cheek. *See also* Anatomy

PRESENTATION A term used in fly-fishing to denote the end product of a cast. Specifically, it is that phase of the final forward cast from the moment your line straightens in the air until the fly has dropped to the water and is accepted or rejected by the trout. An angler may cast well but present the fly badly, and, conversely, he may be a mediocre caster, yet have enough facility to present a neat fly. The latter case is rare, because as a rule the awkward hand is too concerned with rod strokes to consider the end result. Fortunately, there are always fish which can be caught no matter how the fly is presented, and thus many casters go along with the law of averages part of the time. However, there are basic elements in consistently good presentation which are worth learning. *See* Fly-Fishing

PRICKLEBACK Family Stichaeidae The members of which are bottom dwellers inhabiting and feeding on algae in the colder portions of northern oceans, especially the Pacific. None of them is of importance in the commercial or sport catch. They are oddities and usually rare, many of them inhabiting water to a depth of at least 200 fathoms, though a few are taken in the intertidal area.

The membranes of the prickleback's gills are united; body long, slender; dorsal and anal fins long and usually of nearly uniform height or depth for most of their length; dorsal supported by spines only; pelvic fins, when present, thoracic with one spine and 3–4 rays; lateral lines four or one or absent.

Prickleback

They occur from San Diego to Bering Sea and from Cape Cod to the Arctic.

Many are small, not exceeding 12 inches, but there is one large deepwater species, the giant wrymouth (*Delolepis gigantea*), occurring from northern California to the Bering Sea, which reaches a length of 46 inches. There is one of the species whose blood shows through its transparent skin giving it a red color. The largest of the shore species is the rock blenny, reaching a length of 20 inches. The heads of some species are decorated with a fleshy crest or plumed or blunt tufts giving rise to such names as decorated blenny, mosshead prickleback, or cockscomb.

The rock blenny is the only species which seems to enter the sport catch, and then in only a minor way in central and northern California. It is caught among rocks with a specially made stick with a hook on the end. —J.R.

PRIME, WILLIAM COWPER American (1825–1905) An acknowledged angling classic, *I Go A-Fishing*, was first published both here and in England, in 1873, with additional editions in 1901 and 1905. Few American fishing books have been more affectionately referred to in subsequent angling literature, both here and abroad, and Prime's is one of the frequently quoted voices out of America's sporting past.

But *I Go A-Fishing* qualifies increasingly as a classic that everybody talks about and hardly anybody reads. So much more of it is not about fishing than is, that trying to get to the fishing in Prime is like the proverbial attempt to pick fly specks out of pepper with boxing gloves on.

While a few of the plethora of nonfishing stories in Prime are exotic or amusing enough to be rewarding, most of the nonpertinent matter is, in his own phrase, "garnished with abundance of rhetorical figure, loaded with imagery and sonorous with words." And since the wordy part of Prime is so largely religious, the average reading angler will find wading through it as tedious as sitting in prayer meeting during the one time he could be out fishing.

Prime's incessant Godhopping could perhaps be indulged, since anglers are noted for patience, if only the fishing parts were more pertinent than they now seem. Walton himself was pious, and discursiveness has always been pardoned in angling literature from his day to ours. But by today's standards of decency, as concerns conservation, Prime's unabashed accounts of the weight of his baskets now verges on the pornographic. His constant tallying of the size and number of trout that he and Dupont, his constant fishing partner, and "P————" and even "————" and other guests took from this pool of that river soon begin to pile up in an accumulation of angling guilt and shame that would make a Casanova's account of his conquests sound demure. Thad Norris, by contrast, and for all his enjoyment of trout roasts by the riverside, always seems much more aware than Prime of the necessity of leaving some fishing in the stream for the rest of us to enjoy a hundred years later.

Between his loquacity as a moralizer and his rapacity as a fisherman, Prime would seem on reappraisal to be one of the shakier titans in our gallery of great angling figures of the past, and like some of our statesmen, better to be admired from a distance than examined too closely. Like Audubon's hunting, Prime's fishing tends to give the lie to some of the veneration that over the years has enhanced his name. That he enjoyed angling and possessed the capacity for communicating that enjoyment cannot be questioned, nor can either of those certainties be taken away from him. But between his prim mentions of dressing for dinner after the day's fishing and his noting that the room in the baskets taken by the wine bottles would soon be needed for trout, it is like opening the windows and letting a gust of good fresh air in to turn to Uncle Thad Norris and his rollicking expatiations, when counting up the angling parties' supplies, on the importance of gin.

Prime suffers from some of the snobbery that keeps Robert Barnwell Roosevelt from being as endearing a figure to us, the readers of today, as his importance in the evolution of American angling would warrant. And as for the piety, Henry Van Dyke was a minister but it never kept him from imparting in *Little Rivers* and *Fisherman's Luck* as keen a sense of the uniqueness of the angler's mania as ever was put on paper. He, too, was essentially a man of the nineteenth century (1852–1933), but to an angler Reverend Van Dyke can never seem dated, as Prime is beginning to. —A.G.

PRINCE EDWARD ISLAND Trout fishing was the only real sport fishing on Prince Edward Island until 1970 when a 1,040-pound bluefin tuna was caught out of North Lake by Mel Immergut—the first over-1,000-pound tuna taken on rod-and-reel. Since then, the record has been broken and the province is an established big-game fishing area.

FRESHWATER FISHING

Many indented bays and tidal rivers, some of them fed from inland, freshwater springs, make Prince Edward Island a first-class trout-fishing province. All fresh- and saltwater rivers, all mill ponds, and the few lakes in the province are well-populated with brook and rainbow trout.

The season on brook trout—the most popular and numerous fish on the island—generally opens in mid April and closes at the end of September. The season on rainbow trout is from the beginning of July to the end of October. Surveys made in recent years have shown that island streams are among the most prolific trout-breeding grounds to be found anywhere on the Atlantic Coast. But it must be remembered that trout have been fished in the province for more than a century and that the island has no virgin fishing streams or lakes such as exist in northern Quebec or Labrador. But, for the skilled angler, there are plenty of salters (*which see*) to be had and, in some parts of the province, the sporty rainbow trout.

Although the province does not offer the fisherman the variety or quantity of fish to be obtained in the more remote parts of Canada, it is not necessary to make an expensive expedition into wild country to have a day's sport. It takes little more preparation to have a day's fishing in Prince Edward Island than it does to have a game of golf or a swim on one of the excellent island beaches.

The fisherman must acquaint himself with the best lures and flies or bait to be used on the island to achieve the best results. The accumulated experience of many anglers down through the years is, of course, available to all visiting fishermen. It is generally acknowledged that bait-fishing, for instance, is at its best in the spring and early-summer months. The angleworm is still as popular as ever, but many fishermen use live shrimp, capelin, or other small, live species. The more skilled anglers seldom resort to bait-fishing after the first of July; they depend on the fly exclusively.

By far the most popular flies in island waters are the Parmachene Belle and the Dark Montreal. Scarcely less popular are the Orange Shrimp and the Ibis. Until most recently, these old standbys, in sizes 8–12, were the top-heavy favorites. However, since the advent of the streamer fly, these same patterns have appeared in streamer design and also as bucktails. Although the Belle, Montreal, and Shrimp are essential to any fishing trip, they do not have any monopoly in trout fishing. The Silver Doctor, White Miller, Jock Scott, Cow Dung, Stone Fly, Dusty Miller, and Mosquito have found an important niche in the local fisherman's fly book.

The most popular time of the day to fish is in the evening, but there are those anglers who fish in the early hours of daylight, preferably on a dark day when there is a ripple on the water. It must also be kept in mind that many experienced fishermen prefer to fish in saltwater when the spring tides are running. These high tides occur

3 days before the full or new moon and last until 3 days after these moon phases.

Still another point about salter fishing to be remembered is the height of the tide. Trout follow the river channels and feed on shrimp and other food which is washed off the shore. For this reason, it is advisable to fish just at the edge of the channel, and this can best be done at low tide. Therefore, most fishermen work the first 2–3 hours of the rising tide or the last 2 hours of the dropping tide.

For some reason, the trout select their own particular month for entering certain streams. They make the change from saltwater to freshwater mostly in June, but they do not begin the ascent of some rivers until July or even August. They do, however, keep practically the same timetable on each stream. Year after year, they can be found in certain streams early in June, and the experienced fisherman knows just about when to find them.

Atlantic salmon are native to Prince Edward Island rivers but are not present in any quantity until the autumn months. They do not rise readily to the fly, perhaps because there are no very deep streams and very little fastwater.

Rainbow trout are not native to the province; they were placed in several lakes and ponds on the island some years ago. They have thrived well in Scales' Pond at Freetown and at Glenfinnan Lake, about 15 miles from Charlottetown. They have also been placed in Keefe's Lake, about 16 miles from Charlottetown. The rainbows grow much bigger than brook trout, quite often reaching a weight of 6–7 pounds. Within the past few years, rainbow trout have been caught in some of the tidal rivers, notably in the Cardigan, Seal, and Mitchell rivers. The Mitchell and Seal rivers are tributaries of the Cardigan River. It is altogether likely that rainbow trout now appearing in these rivers have escaped as fingerlings from the Dominion Government rearing pond at the head of the Cardigan River. This probably represents one of the few token steelhead populations in the Atlantic.

—G.V.F.

PROGRESSIVE ACTION The purpose of progressive tapering in a rod, whether applied to glass or bamboo, is to allow the caster a maximum range of casting weights. Most rods are designed to assume one load with a comparatively small margin or more or less weight. The load factor is critical. The progressive action on the other hand implies that a light weight will bend the rod almost at its tip and very little elsewhere; as the weight (i.e., force) is increased, the point of curvature goes farther and farther down the rod. At the final and most extreme loading and application of force, the bend then, and only then, becomes almost circular. See also The Theory of Rod Function in Casting under Rod Building

PROPELLER A two- or three-bladed device on a shaft under the stern which when revolved by the engine provides thrust against the water to propel the boat forward. The primary parts of a propeller are the blades and the hub, which is drilled out in a proper taper to fit the taper at the end of the propeller shaft extending from the engine. In sea-going terminology a propeller usually is called a wheel and sometimes it is referred to as a prop.

Most boats having but one engine are driven by propellers turning right-handed, or clockwise, when viewed from aft of the stern. Twin-screw boats, those having two engines, generally have propellers revolving outward at the top, when viewed from astern, to propel the boat forward. A left-hand wheel revolves counterclockwise when viewed from astern. Very few craft in this field are triple-screw, having three engines and three propellers.

To put it briefly, a propeller may be called a screw because a complete revolution of a propeller pushes a boat forward exactly as a full turn of a screw, or a bolt in a nut, carries the head of the screw forward. In other words, the blades of a propeller may be visualized as cutdown wings out of the head of a screw, with the pitch corresponding to the thread of the screw or at least having the same effect.

A feathering propeller is one in which the blades are mechanically adjustable on the hub so that they may be faced fore and aft in such a way as to prevent excessive drag to the boat when the propeller is stationary, as is often employed in sailing.

A variable-pitch propeller is one in which the pitch of the blades may be altered so as to minimize slippage at various engine speeds.

A propeller, especially on an outboard motor, which is designed to prevent entanglement with weeds and long grass through which the boat may travel, is described as weedless.

PRUSSIAN CARP See Crucian Carp

PUERTO RICO The island of Puerto Rico is located 1,063 miles southeast of Miami and 425 miles north of La Guaira, Venezuela. It is bordered on the north by the Atlantic Ocean and on the south by the Caribbean Sea. Puerto Rico rises as a peak from the ocean floor. Nearby is the deepest spot in the Atlantic (30,246 feet) known as the Milwaukee Deep. The 100-fathom line is within 3 miles of Arecibo and San Juan. Puerto Rico is also very close to shore west of Aguadilla and Rincón, and about 15 miles offshore of Mayagüez. This marine habitat is host to more than four hundred species of fish, of which at least seventy are of angling interest. Big-game fishing, however, is the principal attraction in Puerto Rico.

Because Puerto Rico is in the trade winds zone, fresh easterly or northeasterly winds are the rule. In the spring (March through May), there are strong winds averaging around 18 mph and ranging up to 25 mph, with gusts to 30 mph. In summer (August through October) there is some fairly calm weather. Winds in June and July are stronger, and while waters tend to be rough on the north of Puerto Rico, the wind usually drops after midday, and invariably you will find smooth fishing conditions.

NORTH COAST

Blue marlin, white marlin, sailfish, yellowfin tuna, and dolphin are abundant along the north coast of Puerto Rico. Of the billfish, blue marlin are apparently the most numerous. Although marlin are caught during all months of the year, relatively small blues are boated between February and June. In June, they begin to appear in numbers, and from July to October there is unusually good fishing. The blue marlin in June, July, and until the middle of August are larger than those caught in September and October. Usually, blue marlin vary around 225–450 pounds during the summer period. However, a world's all-tackle record was held twice in Puerto Rico. The heavier fish weighed 871 pounds. Several blue marlin have also been sighted or hooked which were estimated to be over 1,000 pounds. Paradoxically, there are few charter boats available in San Juan, and only week-end fishing is popular among local anglers. Despite the small fishing effort, more than 200 marlin are caught at San Juan each year.

White marlin have been caught in every month of the year but they seem to be more plentiful in April, May, and June. One of the heaviest white marlin boated off Puerto Rico weighed 91 pounds. Whites usually range within 45–65 pounds.

Sailfish enter the north coast late in October, and they are fished in abundance in November and up to the middle of December when they disappear.

Yellowfin tuna are plentiful along the north coast, and May through July seems to be the best period for this species. There are times during the early summer months when very large schools may be seen feeding in the company of two or three whale sharks. The usual size of the yellowfin tuna north of San Juan is large, running 60–150 pounds. The really big ones caught in Puerto Rico approach 190 pounds.

The north coast is also prolific in dolphin schools. Although dolphin are abundant in the summer time, the best month for fishing is February. The usual weight of these fish is 10–15 pounds; however, sizes of 30–50 pounds are not uncommon. In general, dolphin run quite large off Puerto Rico. This, of course, is a choice food fish and is eagerly sought during peak periods.

Wahoo fishing is very good off San Juan, close to shore in January and in great abundance in late December.

There is fair reef-fishing off the north coast of Puerto Rico, a great deal better in Arecibo than in San Juan. The reefs on the east coast of Puerto Rico, in the Fajardo, Culebra, and Vieques perimeter, provide the best reef-fishing on the island. South of Vieques there is an extremely sharp dropoff, reaching a depth of over 1,000 fathoms, very close to shore. Not very much sport fishing has been done south of Vieques, but marlin and sailfish have been raised there.

EAST COAST

On the east coast closer to the southeast of the island, deepsea fishing is also excellent. A few miles off Guaynabo are the Grappers Banks where blue marlin have been caught, but the banks are considered a wahoo paradise.

SOUTH COAST

In the south, reef-fishing is good between Ponce and Santa Isabel, but very few billfish have been caught in that area. Billfish, tuna, and dolphin are plentiful in the south coast from south of Guanica up to Cabo Rojo, consistently more abundant south of Guanica and La Parguera. The fish in the south of Puerto Rico seem also to be migratory, but the fish seem to come and go more with these currents than those flowing on the north of the island. Billfishing and tuna fishing off the south coast of Puerto Rico begin in March, and it is consistently good until May. April and May are the best two months for billfishing in the south coast of Puerto Rico. Reef-fishing, including snappers, groupers, cero, king mackerel, and barracuda, is unusually good at La Parguera close to the shore.

WEST COAST

In the west of Puerto Rico off Mayagüez, Rincón, and Aguadilla, there is excellent blue-marlin fishing. There seems to be two runs off Mayagüez—one in the summer, which may have its origin in the run of fish off San Juan, and the other one in April and May, which may be accounted for by the migration of fish through the Mona Passage coming from the south of Puerto Rico. There is also excellent reef-fishing well off Mayagüez, and unusually good wahoo fishing around the Sponges Bank.

BAITS AND TACKLE

The most popular bait used in Puerto Rican fishing waters is the mullet, which is used chiefly for white marlin, sailfish, dolphin, and wahoo. For blue-marlin fishing the most popular bait is the mullet. However, small barracuda, ladyfish, and even small tarpon (4–6 pounds) have been employed with great success for blues. The blue marlin in Puerto Rico display a varied diet with tunas, especially frigate mackerel, needlefish, pompano dolphin, baby swordfish, snake mackerel, and round robins being important items of their food. The white marlin eat a great quantity of squids as well as small fishes, such as the blue runner, surgeonfish, filefish, and little tuna. Sailfish feed on substantially the same forage and in addition the flyingfish. Flyingfish are the chief item of food to dolphin in Puerto Rico. As in most big-game areas, the baits used do not necessarily reflect the actual diet of the fish sought.

Artificial lures, such as feathers, are used primarily for bonito fishing. There are very large schools of bonito present in the summer months. The bonito run large; seven world's records have been established in these waters.

Anglers trolling off Puerto Rico generally fish on the surface. Little success has been obtained by deep trolling. Hovering flocks of birds generally indicate the presence of bait- or gamefish, and drifting Portuguese man-of-war will usually reveal marlin or dolphin feeding at the surface.

The majority of Puerto Rican anglers favor light tackle. On most boats, 50-pound-test is the heaviest gear used.

FRESHWATER FISHING

There is interesting freshwater fishing in the artificial lakes developed for hydroelectric power. The best spots are Lake Guajataca in the northwest, Dos Bocas and Caonillas in Utuado, Carite in Guayama, Villalba Dam, and the impoundments at Aguas Buenas and Cidra. These lakes provide excellent largemouth-bass fishing.

—E.A.B.

PUFFER *See* Northern Puffer, Smooth Puffer, Southern Puffer

PULMAN, GEORGE British Author of *The Vade Mecum of Fly Fishing for Trout*, which was published in 1841. A second edition was published in 1846, and a revised third edition in 1851. In his revised work Pulman described the technique of dry-fly-fishing. Although the principle had been alluded to by earlier authors (*The Fly Fisher's Legacy* by George Scotcher, 1800) Pulman was the first to detail the method of floating a fly over the trout by false casting and placing the fly lightly just upstream of a rising fish.

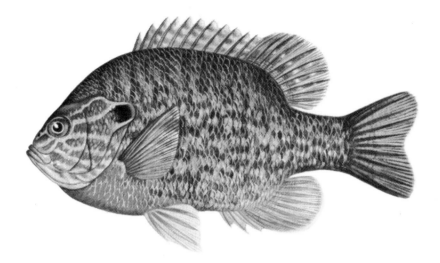

Pumpkinseed, 6-inch Male, Housatonic River, Connecticut

PUMPKINSEED *Lepomis gibbosus* The pumpkinseed, or common sunfish, is a popular freshwater quarry among children. Undoubtedly more fishermen in the Northern United States have started their angling career on this species than any of the other panfishes. It is easily caught, stays within angling reach of shore, and it is a colorful and scrappy individual. It is easily identified by the rigid black gill cover with a bright red or orange spot on the tip. The body is light olive with a sprinkling of various colored spots on the sides. Emerald-blue lines radiate backward from the snout and eye region. The mouth is small and does not extend beyond the front of the eye. The pectoral fins are long and pointed. The young of the pumpkinseed have a yellow belly which aids in distinguishing them from young bluegills. Maximum length is about 9 inches.

The pumpkinseed is distributed from the Dakotas east to the Maritime provinces of Canada, south along the Atlantic Coast to northern Georgia, and in the Mississippi River system from western Pennsylvania to Iowa.

Pumpkinseed inhabit standing waters with soft bottoms covered with sunken plant material. It prefers weed patches, docks, and logs for cover, and is most often found in these localities. The larger fish are not so apt to be found in the openwater as is the bluegill.

They feed on small mollusks, insects, and fishes. Some biologists feel that the diet consists more of small fishes than does that of the bluegill. Therefore they are less likely to become stunted since they help to decrease the number of their own young.

LIFE HISTORY

The pumpkinseed spawns in the same manner as the bluegill and at the same time. Saucer-shaped nests are excavated in colonies sometime between late May and early July. The height of the nesting usually occurs in June. Each nest usually contains several thousand eggs deposited by one or more females depending on how enticing the guardian male was. The eggs incubate for 5–10 days depending on the temperature. The young grow ½–3 inches the first year. In many waters it takes three years to reach 4 inches and six years before growth exceeds 6 inches. Maturity is usually reached at 2 years, and in stunted populations the spawning fish may be no longer than 2½ inches.

ANGLING VALUE

What makes the pumpkinseed such an interesting panfish is the wide variety of baits which it greedily takes. The ordinary garden worm is about as productive as any, but in the springtime, wet-fly-fishing can be fun for all. In some areas in late May or early June they are very partial to yellow flies regardless of the pattern. In summer they are often more easily caught on a grub or the larvae of wasps. In winter they can be taken through the ice on worms.

—K.B.

PUPA An intermediate, usually quiescent form assumed by insects after the larval stage, and maintained until the beginning of the adult stage.

PURSE SEINE A net used in commercial fishing which is particularly suitable to the capture of schooling fish such as menhaden, mackerel, and salmon. The net may be 1,200 feet long and 70 feet deep. When placed in position around a school of fish, it stands like a fence in the water. It is supported at the surface by floats of metal, cork, or glass and held down by weights along the bottom. The pursing rope is strung through large metal rings spaced every 12 feet along the bottom of the net. When the rope is tightened, the bottom is drawn together forming a huge purse or bag.

PYGMY SPERM WHALE *See* Whales

PYGMY SUNFISH *See* Everglades Pygmy Sunfish, Okefenokee Pygmy Sunfish

Q

QUEBEC The largest of the ten Canadian provinces, Quebec covers 600,000 square miles from Ungava Bay on the north to the St. Lawrence in the south. It contains more than one million lakes, thousands of miles of rivers, and an extensive seacoast. The diversified topography provides habitat for a large variety of gamefish, including brook trout, lake trout, Arctic char, Atlantic salmon, smallmouth bass, walleye, northern pike, landlocked salmon, and whitefish. About 900 licensed outfitters operate in the province. There are excellent bush camps, hotels, motels, comfortable inns, and fine restaurants. A critical inspection of these establishments is maintained by the Hostelry Branch of the Department of Tourism, Fish and Game.

Practically all the accessible salmon waters in Quebec are leased and with comparatively few exceptions the angler must be a lessee or the guest of a lessee. The provincial government has opened some rivers to the public, including the Mantane, Romaine, Little Cascapedia, and Port Daniel where camps and fishing privileges are available at reasonable cost. However, the famous and more productive streams along the north shore of the Gulf of St. Lawrence, on the Gaspé Peninsula, and Anticosti Island are operated and maintained by private clubs or individuals. Historically, the Moise, Natashquan, Grand Cascapedia, Bonaventure, Matapedia, Restigouche, and York rivers are Quebec's standard bearers. In contrast to these, some angling can be obtained in the isolated northeastern portion around Ungava Bay.

UNGAVA BAY REGION

The Ungava Bay watershed is vast and partially unexplored. The terrain is part of the Canadian Shield, with a general low-lying topography to the south and west and the mountains of Labrador to the east. Five major rivers drain into Ungava Bay—the Koksoak, George, Leaf, Whale, and Payne in that order of size—and several lesser rivers, the most important of which are the Mukalik, Tuktuk, Tunulik, and Korok. The treeline weaves across the watershed dominated by tamarack and black spruce. Frozen conditions on the lakes in the Ungava area may begin in October and extend to July. The duration of snow cover varies; many of the hills and steeper slopes may be bare by June, while it persists in protected places until well into July. The small Eskimo population of Ungava Bay is scattered along the shores, and their activity in fishing is directed principally at Arctic char and to a lesser degree the Atlantic salmon. The Indians inland from the bay are also few in number. There are several fishing resorts in this region on the George River. A few outfitters also specialize in flying trips and put their parties under canvas at suitable locations.

The Atlantic salmon ascends the larger rivers of the eastern half of Ungava Bay between the George and the Koksoak. Although the Eskimo report that salmon are occasionally caught in the Leaf River, farther west, for all practical purposes the Koksoak is the extreme western limit of the salmon's range. When the angler comes early in the season, he will usually find a full stream in great angry volume. These rivers mutter and hiss with the sound of frightful forces. The spawning areas of Ungava salmon lie well within the treeline, but they seldom begin their upstream movement before the end of July. The season on the George really starts about August 1st and continues through September. The tides at the mouth of the George rise from 40 to more than 50 feet, and their influence can be seen as far upriver as Helen Falls, which is some 50 miles inland. The rise and fall of water send the salmon on their journey—the runs pulsing into the camp area still fresh with sea lice. As far as has been determined, Helen Falls is their first real stop in the migration. Unlike many Labrador and Newfoundland Island streams where grilse dominate the catch or where one finds an abundance of small salmon but no large fish, the George provides many specimens in the 15–20-pound class.

The raw beauty of the George River is irresistible to a dedicated salmon angler. Ever since the year 1956, when a tent camp was established in the wilderness borders of Ungava Bay, adventuring tourists have been trekking up the northeasternmost spur of land on the North American continent. Geographically, the western half is known as New Quebec, while the more precipitous eastern portion is Labrador. Labrador, which in its entirety is the mainland of the province of Newfoundland, covers an area of 110,000 square miles and has a coastline of 4,560 miles. The George River drains a 400-mile-long watershed, rising in western Labrador and entering Ungava Bay in New Quebec. This is a region not only rich in salmonids but most of its waters are yet to be fished. There are nine solid months of winter in what is actually the sub-Arctic, a month of spring and two months of restless summer. Roads are nonexistent.

Salmon fishing on the George is not what one might describe as within walking distance of the camp. The

With a knowledge based on necessity, Eskimos in northern Quebec make skilled guides

routine is to board an Eskimo freight canoe powered by 3 horses and run about 4 miles upriver to the rapids; from there to the topmost beat the angler has a 1½–2-mile walk over the boulders and along a portage trail creased in caribou moss. This is important to undersand because you must wear good, hightop hunting shoes for the hike. Your Eskimo guide will carry the necessary felt-sole waders or hip boots for you, but you should bring along a warm jacket as well as rain gear, as the weather and temperature fluctuate widely during the day. A snow squall can appear in late August, and the thermometer may run 25–75° F. during the peak weeks of the salmon season. When the sun shines, the glare requires Polaroid sun glasses, as seeing the salmon is at least half the battle in catching them. Bugs are present right up to the first heavy frost in September, so a repellent is absolutely essential.

The raw beauty of the George River attracts salmon anglers from all over the continent in the summer season

It's also wise to inventory a fair stock of artificial flies. Their loss among these boulder-studded pools is heavy. Most casting is done from the bank, and even where wading is possible, the shores rise steeply behind the angler. One can easily find a whole trail of salmon flies with broken hooks along the George at summer's end. There are a few pools which in the tradition of Norway's torrents can be attacked from a platform between the shore and a convenient boulder, but otherwise it helps to have the agility of a chamois and a wrist like the village blacksmith. Actually, George River anglers merely nibble at the edges of the stream, so to speak, because there are a thousand more visible lies beyond casting range where any boat would be smashed to splinters. Nevertheless, fishing the George is a leisurely affair. There are eight main pools on the west bank, three main pools on the east bank, and dozens of inconspicuous lies between these stations which generally hold fish.

The ideal tackle for Quebec or in point, George River salmon fishing, is an outfit that you can swing comfortably in a high wind and rough water. It should have enough backbone to extend any length of cast even under the wicked, veering wind that sometimes engulfs the valley.

Big flies are seldom effective on the stream; in fact most of the fish are caught on No. 1 to No. 8 dressings, so you don't need a heavier line to kick the feathers out. The most effective patterns are usually dull in color such as the March Brown, Blue Charm, Lady Caroline, Black Cosseboom, and Black Rat. The fly which accounts for the majority of George River salmon is the Black Bear Hair. This consists of nothing more than a black hair-wing and a black chenille or peacock herl body. As to floating patterns, some anglers prefer the skater-type flies rather than the hair-wings. But wet or dry, sparsely tied flies are most productive in these rivers. Bushy or full dressings don't swim as well in these turbulent, bell-clear waters. Of course, these are ephemeral details which can very well change from day to day for inexplicable reasons.

LAKE ST. JOHN REGION

The Lake St. John region offers brook-trout, lake-trout, and landlocked-salmon fishing. The lake has over 100 miles of shoreline and numerous tributary rivers, such as the Peribonca, Ashuapumuchuan, and Mistassini. There are also the smaller streams such as the Manouan, which is quite famous for its salmon; and one larger river, the Grande Décharge, which is a maelstrom of white water; the Grande Décharge, which has been harnessed for hydroelectric power, is also a salmon fishery. The landlocked salmon or ouananiche (*which see*) in this region are not large (seldom exceeding 5 pounds), and their numbers have declined in recent years. *See also* "Canadian Salmon Fishing" *under* Atlantic Salmon

—P.H.
—A.J.McC.

QUEEN ANGELFISH *Holacanthus ciliaris* The angelfishes are moderately large, deep-bodied, compressed, and frequently beautifully colored. They differ principally from their near relatives, the butterflyfishes, in possessing a stout spine at the angle of the preopercle. The genus *Holacanthus* is distinctive in having, in addition, smaller spines on the rest of the preopercular margin, 50 or fewer scales in longitudinal series on the body, and a truncate caudal fin. There are three species of *Holacanthus* in the tropical western Atlantic—the queen angelfish (*H. ciliaris*), the blue angelfish (*H. bermudensis*), and the yellow-and-black rock beauty (*H. tricolor*). The queen angelfish is primarily yellow but has bright blue margins on the dorsal and anal fins, blue markings on the head, and a black spot with broad blue border on the forehead; the caudal and paired fins are yellow. The caudal fin of the blue angelfish is yellow only on the hind border, and this fish lacks the ocellus on the forehead. The young queen angelfish has three vertical, light blue bars on the body and two on the head which border a dark bar passing through the eye.

The queen angelfish is found on coral reefs in the West Indies and Florida. Although reported to reach a length of nearly 2 feet, it probably does not exceed 18 inches. The blue angelfish, which attains about the same size, occurs in Florida, the western Bahamas, and Bermuda.

The adults feed primarily on sponges, including those with siliceous spicules, but also ingest algae, tunicates, hydroids, bryozoans, etc. The young feed partly on the crustacean ectoparasites of other fishes.

Queen Angelfish

ANGLING VALUE

Although not specifically sought by anglers, the queen angelfish sometimes enters the catch of bottom fishermen when using live or dead bait for snappers, groupers, and other reef species. Like other angelfishes, it has some food value and is usually prepared by pan frying or sautéeing. —J.E.R.

QUEENFISH *See* Drums

QUEEN PARROTFISH *Scarus vetula* Parrotfishes are well-named for their beaklike jaws and gaudy colors. The queen parrotfish is one of the most common of the thirteen species known from the western Atlantic, most of which fall into the genera *Scarus* and *Sparisoma*. The two genera are readily distinguished from one another by the position of the upper jaw relative to the lower. In *Scarus* the beak of the lower jaw fits inside the upper when the mouth is closed; in *Sparisoma* the upper fits inside the lower. *Scarus vetula* differs from all other Atlantic species by having 4 not 3 rows of scales on the cheek.

Like most parrotfishes, the queen parrotfish displays one color pattern for the female and small male form and a more colorful phase for the large male. So different are these two color patterns that both were given different scientific names. The female-small-male phase is reddish-brown with a broad, lengthwise white band just below the midline of the body. The large adult male is blue-green with rose-orange edges on the scales; there are alternate blue and orange stripes on the upper lip and chin, the blue stripe on the lower lip running under the eye; the fins are orange and turquoise-blue.

FEEDING HABITS

Like other Atlantic parrotfishes, it feeds mainly by scraping algae from the bottom. If the bottom is not too hard, the beak scrapes up some of the substratum as well, and this is finely ground, along with the plant material, in the unique pharyngeal mill (a convex-concave set of plates studded with closely spaced nodular teeth above and below the alimentary tract in the gill region). This grinding tears down the cellulose plant-cell walls which are resistant to digestion.

Queen Parrotfish

FOOD VALUE

The queen parrotfish is known throughout the Caribbean area, Florida, and Bermuda. It reaches a length of about 18 inches. Although widely eaten, this and other parrotfishes are not highly esteemed as food.   —J.E.R.

QUEEN TRIGGERFISH *Balistes vetula* The triggerfishes are a distinctive group of fishes named for the interlocking arrangement of the bases of the first three dorsal spines such that the enlarged first spine can be fixed in the erect position. If the second spine is depressed with the finger, the first spine is no longer locked in the vertical position. The fishes are already deep-bodied, so the elevation of the dorsal spine plus the additional depth from depression of the ventral flap ostensibly makes them less desirable to a predator. Also, these fishes use their extended first dorsal spine and ventral flap to wedge themselves into small holes in reefs in which they seek refuge.

Other characteristics of the family and the related filefishes are a tough skin with platelike scales that often bear spinules or tubercles; a single short but stout spine in place of pelvic fins; a short gill opening; a mouth which is small but bears powerful jaws with close-set, projecting incisiform teeth.

Queen Triggerfish

The queen triggerfish is easily separated from other Atlantic species by the long filaments from the tail and front of the soft dorsal fin and by its color. It is olive with two broad, curved blue bands from the snout to the pectoral base. Chin and lower cheek are yellow-orange; yellow-edged dark lines radiate from the eye. There are blue submarginal bands in the dorsal, anal, and caudal fins.

The queen triggerfish is broadly distributed in the Atlantic from Brazil to Florida, straying north to Massachusetts. It is common in the West Indies and is recorded from Bermuda, the Azores, and Ascension Island. A record from South Africa should be confirmed. The largest of eighty-six adults collected in Puerto Rico and the Virgin Islands measured 22 inches in fork length (which is the length to the end of the middle caudal rays; i.e., without the long upper and lower caudal filaments).

The stomach contents of fifty-three of the aforementioned adults consisted mostly or entirely of sea-urchin remains, particularly the long-spined *Diadema*. The other fish had eaten primarily other echinoderms, mollusks, and crustaceans.

ANGLING VALUE

Where abundant or when chummed, the queen triggerfish will strike almost any small artificial lure, including jigs and plugs. An effective bait is a piece of conch on a No. 1/0 or 2/0 hook. Softer baits such as a whole or cut fish are easily stripped from the hook by the triggerfish's nibbling. A strong gamefish, it makes determined runs to the bottom using its broad body to advantage. Despite its coarse skin and odd appearance it is a fine food fish. The flesh is firm and white and is often likened to frogs legs in texture. But the tough skin must be removed.   —J.E.R.

QUILLBACK *Carpiodes cyprinus* The quillback is one of four species of carpsuckers (*Carpiodes* spp.), all of which have very similar characteristics. In fact, they are so difficult to distinguish that ichthyologists have been confused over the natural range of each species due to obvious misidentifications reported in the literature. The other three species are the river carpsucker, *C. carpio*; plains carpsucker, *C. forbesi*; and the highfin carpsucker, *C. velifer*.

The four species of the genus *Carpiodes* are silvery, deep-bodied fish, with the anterior rays of the dorsal fin much longer than the rest of the fin rays, especially in the quillback. Its color is light olive above with silvery sides and white belly. The scales give off silvery, greenish, and bluish reflections. The mouth is toothless, small, and subterminal, with rather thin lips which are flesh or white in color. The number of lateral-line scales runs 33–41 in the four species. The tails are deeply forked, and there are no spines on the fins. The flesh is exceedingly bony.

The primary range of the carpsuckers includes the Missouri, Mississippi, and Ohio River drainages and eastward to the Atlantic drainage with the exception of the northern New England and southeastern coastal states. They are primarily large-river fishes, though the quillback may be found in most of the Great Lakes.

Carpsuckers often are referred to as white carp, silver carp, highfin, white sucker, quillback, or river sucker.

Maximum weights for the four species varies from about 3 pounds for the highfin carpsucker to 10–12 pounds for the river carpsucker.

LIFE HISTORY

Spawning of carpsuckers takes place in April or May when water temperature is about 60°F. The tiny eggs are scattered randomly in shallow water, and no parental care is given before or after they hatch. The number of eggs per female may approach several hundred thousand. Incubation takes place in 8 to 12 days. The tiny fry feed on minute plankton and reach a length of 2–4 inches by the end of the year. Averaging 3 inches in growth the first year, they will measure about 6, 9, 11, 13, and 15 inches at ages 2–6, respectively. Weight will be about 1 pound at 13 inches, 2 pounds at 16 inches, and 3 pounds at 19 inches. Adulthood is attained at 3–4 years of age. Few live longer than 8 years.

As adults, carpsuckers have a tendency to travel in schools. They usually remain close to the bottom where they apparently browse on minute plant and animal organisms (periphyton) associated with rocks and debris. Until very recently they were described as filthy mud or bottom feeders which ate any animal or plant matter they could find in the bottom ooze. This misconception resulted from investigators' inability to identify the mudlike contents of their stomachs. Recent studies, however, have corrected these misconceptions and shown carp-suckers to be rather selective in gathering their fare of periphyton. These feeding habits are in accord with the carpsucker's preference for the least turbid waters and for rocky bottoms.

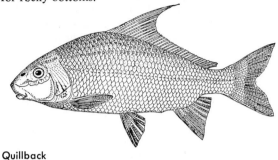

Quillback

Annual mortality is high, especially when the carp-suckers are 6 inches or shorter and ideal forage for pre-daceous fish. Even as adults, mortality probably runs 60–70 per cent annually.

ANGLING VALUE

The carpsuckers are not of particular importance to anglers. Though occasionally taken on worms, dough-balls, bread, or snag hooks, they usually are caught by fishermen in quest of other species.

COMMERCIAL VALUE

There is not a great demand for carpsuckers on the commercial market due to the small usual size (2–4 pounds) of the commercial catches and the bony struc-ture of the species. Where commercial fishermen do harvest them (usually in conjunction with other species), they generally are marketed as carp and bring a few cents per pound. —J.T.S.

QUILLBACK ROCKFISH *Sebastodes maliger* Although this rockfish (*which see*) is found from southern Cali-fornia to the Gulf of Alaska, it is best-known for the commercial and sport catch in the middle of its range. It readily takes a jig or herring, and is sought after at depths of 180–900 feet. It is a fine sport fish because of its fighting ability.

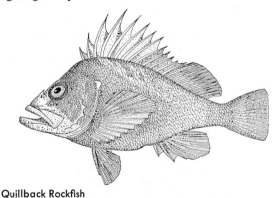

Quillback Rockfish

It is distinguished by a high dorsal fin which is deeply incised, and the yellow-to-brown coloration with orange or brown spotting. It reaches a length of 24 inches. —J.R.

QUINNANT SALMON A regional name (New Zealand) for the chinook salmon (*which see*)

R

RABBITFISH *See* Smooth Puffer

RACE A confused flow of water caused by conflicting tides and currents; the momentary speedup of a propeller created by the lack of bite when a boat's propeller operates above the surface of the water

RADIO DIRECTION FINDER (RDF) An instrument for taking bearings of the source of radio transmission

RAINBOW RUNNER *Elagatis bipinnulatus* Also called rainbow yellowtail, runner, skipjack, and shoemaker. This species, of worldwide occurrence in tropical marine waters, is structurally similar to the amberjack genus *Seriola*.

The rainbow runner has a detached finlet behind the dorsal and the anal fin, composed of the last two, closely spaced rays of each of these fins. The color pattern is unique (*see below*).

Rainbow Runner

The body is slender and spindle-shaped, with a rela-tively sharp-pointed head profile. The first dorsal fin has 6 spines. The second dorsal fin has one spine and 25–27 connected softrays followed by the 2-rayed finlet. The single detached spine at the origin of the anal fin is covered by skin in most specimens more than 1 foot long; the remainder of the fin consists of one spine and 16–18 connected softrays followed by a 2-rayed finlet. The dorsal- and anal-fin lobes are relatively very short. There are 10–11 gillrakers on the upper limb and 25–28 gill-rakers on the lower limb of the first arch.

The back is greenish-blue; high on the sides is a broad, dark blue stripe, followed in succession down the sides by a narrow, light blue stripe, a broader cadmium-yellow stripe, frequently another narrow, light blue stripe, and the remaining third of the sides and the belly are white or yellowish-silver. The fins are greenish-yellow.

The rainbow runner occurs in tropical waters around the world. In the western Atlantic it has been reported from Colombia to Massachusetts and in the West Indies. In the eastern Pacific it has been recorded from northern Peru and the Galápagos Islands and Cocos Island to Cape San Lucas, Baja California.

The largest known specimen was 3½ feet long and weighed 23 pounds, from Hawaii. Statements have been made that it reaches a length of 4 feet.

LIFE HISTORY

The life history is unknown, and habits that were attributed to this species from Pensacola, Florida, in the 1880's, and have persisted in the literature ever since, were most probably those of another species. There is one report of a "female more than one meter in length" taken in October from the central Atlantic, almost midway between Liberia and Brazil. This is a widespread species but apparently is nowhere abundant. Some of the smallest known juveniles, down to ½ inch in length, were taken from July into September in the Florida Current. Young fish have been seen accompanying a large shark with several pilotfish.

ANGLING VALUE

This is an excellent gamefish for light tackle, and its striking color pattern when landed adds an extra touch to the pleasure of the catch. It has been recommended as a fine table fish, and in Japan it is considered a delicate food fish, cooked with a special sauce, or sometimes eaten raw. *See also* Amberjacks, Carangidae   —F.H.B.

RAINBOW SEAPERCH *Hypsurus caryi* Striking and beautiful colors make the species an outstanding surfperch (*which see*). The body is marked by horizontal stripes, of red, orange, and blue; streaks of sky-blue and orange on head; orange on fins; a black blotch anteriorly

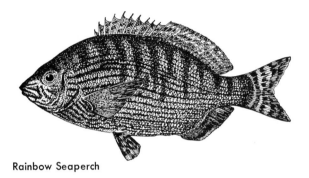

Rainbow Seaperch

on the dorsal. The lower body margin is long and straight; the vent is behind origin of soft dorsal; a frenum interrupts posterior groove of lower lip; 21–24 dorsal softrays; 21–23 anal softrays. Length to 12 inches. Its range is from northern California to northern Baja California.
   —J.R.

RAINBOW SMELT *Osmerus mordax* This species of smelt (*which see*) inhabits the western Atlantic, Pacific, and Arctic West to the White Sea, and their drainages. It occurs as an anadromous form or is landlocked as in the Great Lakes and many other smaller lakes in southeast Canada and Northeast United States. The slender body of the smelt is only about one-fifth as deep as it is long (exclusive of caudal fin), and is somewhat flattened in

Rainbow Smelt

shape. The body color is greenish on the dorsal surface while the sides are of a paler shade with a broad longitudinal silver band. The ventral surface is silvery, and the fins are flecked with tiny, dusky dots. Rainbow smelt have one large canine tooth on either side of the vomer, sometimes accompanied by smaller ones; 8–10 rays in the dorsal fin; 13 rays in the anal fin; 14–28 (rarely 13–30)

pored scales in the lateral line. Smelt grow to a maximum size of about 14 inches; however, the adults usually run 7–9 inches.

In saltwater the rainbow smelt is confined to the coastal area and is seldom found more than one mile from shore or at depths greater than twenty feet. The schools feed on crustaceans (chiefly shrimp), annelid worms, and other small fishes such as silversides, mummichogs, sand launce, and sticklebacks.

ANGLING VALUE

This smelt is taken in large quantities for both sport and commercial purposes. It is caught in harbors and estuaries in New England, as well as in tidal rivers. Sea worms (*Nereis*), shrimp, and small minnows are used as bait. The rainbow smelt is also the sole quarry of an extensive ice-fishing effort on many inland waters.

Smelt are an excellent food fish. They are usually pan fried or broiled whole, and can also be smoked. Due to the oil content of the flesh, smelt must be kept absolutely fresh to maintain their flavor. Store smelt in an ice chest and do not expose to the sun after capture.   —J.R.

RAINBOW TROUT *Salmo gairdneri* This native American trout is high on the list of gamefishes of the world. Its natural range is from the mountains of northern Mexico to the Aleutian Islands and perhaps into the eastern U.S.S.R. as the Kamchatka trout.

The rainbow trout is presently considered synonomous with the Kamchatka trout (*S. mykiss*); the only apparent distinction between *mykiss* and *gairdneri* is in the number of vertebrae. Early-day taxonomists considered the Kamchatka trout conspecific with the North American cutthroat series; however *mykiss* lacks basibranchial teeth (present in the cutthroat) and has 10 pelvic rays, which is typical of *gairdneri* (all other species of *Salmo* have 9 pelvic fin-rays). The Kamchatka trout is redbanded, black-spotted, and except for a lower vertebrae count the fish is meristically similar to the rainbow. It occurs as resident and anadromous populations, and is reported as far south as the Amur River mouth.

Nonmigratory rainbows show extreme variation in outward appearance. Those in clear lakes lack spots, are blue or green on the back, silver on sides grading to whitish on the belly when immature. Stream dwellers tend to be heavily spotted on the body, upper fins, and tail. Mature fish become darker and have a red lateral band. The rainbow has no hyoid teeth; this absence of teeth on the back of its tongue is the most reliable character distinguishing the rainbow from the cutthroat trout. The anal fin has no more than 12 rays, which distinguish it from the Pacific salmons (13 or more). The maximum weight for rainbow trout exceeds 50 pounds; a 52½-pound fish was netted in Jewel Lake, British Columbia, during spawn-taking operations. However, average weights vary greatly according to locale.

The temperature tolerance of rainbow trout is from below 32°F to over 80°F, with the preferred level below 70°F. Survival at lethal temperatures in the mid-80's depends on the size of the fish, the rate of change, and how well the trout are acclimatized. In lakes rainbows may be found near the surface if the temperature is below 70°F, but as the upper layer warms they tend to seek a level between 56.5°F and 60°F. They will also tolerate a considerable pH range from 5.8–9.5 ppm, or from acid to highly alkaline water.

Rainbow Trout, 2-pound Male,
Green River, Wyoming

LIFE HISTORY

Inland populations of rainbow trout spawn from January to June in North America and even later (early August) in some cold-water lakes at high elevation. By selective reproduction in hatcheries strains have been isolated which can breed at all months of the year. Generally speaking, wild fish are early spring spawners on all continents in which they occur. They spawn in streams; the females dig their redds in riffles or near the lower end of a pool, or in inlet or outlet streams when found in lake environments. Reproduction in lakes without tributaries is extremely rare if it occurs at all. Lacking a suitable spawning area the females gradually reabsorb their eggs. During the spawning act, which lasts a few seconds, male and female settle on the redd with their vents in close proximity, then arch their bodies and deposit eggs and milt simultaneously. A second male may also take part. The female immediately covers the eggs with loose gravel. This process is repeated by digging new redds upstream from the first pit until the female is spent, which may take from a half-day to a week. There is no parental care of the young. The female trout move downstream soon after spawning; the spent fish lose considerable weight, with losses as high as one-third in females and one-half in males.

The life span of the rainbow is from 7–11 years depending on the race and locality. Among interior stocks the rainbows of Eagle Lake, California, a recognized subspecies (*Salmo gairdneri aquilarum*), are the longest-lived attaining at least 11 years. Although 7 years is considered maximum for the anadromous form, 8–9-year olds have been recorded. A 9-year-old female steelhead with newly developing eggs was gillnetted in the eastern North Pacific (1969); it probably would have survived to its 10th year; scale studies indicated that it had a freshwater age of 3 years and an ocean age of 2 years before the first of four successive spawnings, plus additional summer growth at the time of capture.

SUBSPECIES, RACES, AND HYBRIDS

At the turn of the century when Jordan and Evermann were cataloguing the western trouts (*American Food and Game Fishes*) it was believed that a number of rainbow trout species existed. The major differences described other than color were in the scale counts. This is a standard and reliable meristic procedure with all kinds of fish. However, some 30 years later Dr. Charles M. Mottley discovered that scale counts in the rainbow complex are a reflection of existing environmental conditions during the early development of the fish. The progeny of rainbows in Kootenay Lake, British Columbia, were found to have a scale count which varied with the time at which egg deposition took place, and the difference was found to be related to temperature. Fish resulting from spawning which occurred late in the run and at a higher temperature varied significantly in scale count from their parents and from the population as a whole. A further change was induced by rearing fish at a still higher temperature in a hatchery. The number of scale rows decreased as temperature increased. (Coastal rainbows, both anadromous and nonanadromous have 120–140 scales in the lateral line series. Several races or subspecies are more finely scaled, with counts up to 180, such as the Kamloops, Shasta, and Kern River rainbows.)

In a textbook sense the western rainbow seems to be in the process of evolving into isolated races and perhaps into other species, but physical change has only begun in that direction. It is much less advanced than in the brown complex. Experimental work has been done which indicates that the characters on which early-day descriptions of supposed species have been based may revert to the original type in a single generation. In view of such phenomena it has generally been accepted that the rainbow trout may be considered to belong to one species—of many strains or races.

Races of nonmigratory rainbows are legion; they bear such names as Kamloops, Nelson trout, red-band, Eagle Lake, Kern River, Shasta, San Gorgonio, and Royal Silver. Nevertheless, various strains of trout, whether wild or domesticated, have potential management implications in terms of catchability, life span, and adaptability to specialized environments. From a fish culturist's standpoint the Kamloops, for example, is not an ideal hatchery product; this strain is slow-growing and requires greater care, which makes production more expensive. In determining a price per pound in the creel California estimates that Kamloops rainbow cost three times more than domestic stocks such as the Shasta, Whitney, or Wisconsin strains. Another consideration is whether the trout are to become established in a stream to provide year-round fishing as opposed to a race that will migrate. Presumably, a certain percentage of any rainbow strain will head for saltwater, but the number varies from exceedingly low to totally high. Both the original McKenzie River and McCloud River races are genetically "resident" stocks which do not migrate to the

Rainbow Trout, 6½-pound Female,
Lake Taupo, New Zealand

sea as do the steelhead strains. Eyed eggs of the McCloud River rainbow were shipped not only to eastern United States hatcheries but to Japan, New Zealand, and various parts of Europe in 1877, and in subsequent years to South America. It is probable that the McCloud race exists in its pure form in remote areas where the breeding and mixing of other wild and domestic strains has not occurred. Anadromous rainbows are rare—for example in Chile, Argentina, and New Zealand—despite the many trout rivers with access to the sea.

Rainbow trout readily hybridize with both the golden and cutthroat trouts. The rainbow × golden is perhaps more common in Wyoming, where the golden was introduced in high-altitude lakes which already held rainbow, than in the isolated alpine waters of California, where the golden existed without other trout species. However, hybrids occur in both states. These resemble highly colored rainbows with a brilliant orange lateral blotch and a similar bright color along the ventral surface. The largest golden cross reported is a 9-pound fish from Washakie Lake, Wyoming. The so-called "golden" trout originally stocked by West Virginia, which has gained some distribution in the eastern United States, is neither a true golden trout nor a hybrid; despite its coloration it's simply a mutation of the rainbow isolated by selective breeding. A similar mutation is found in brook trout which occasionally produce albino progeny; among salmonids albinism is a novel genetic situation in which the eyes may be pink or black and the fish a yellow-gold color rather than white. The rainbow × cutthroat is much more common and, in fact, this cross has been a major factor in the decline of cutthroat stocks in many Rocky Mountain watersheds. Again the rainbow characteristics

remain dominant, including the red lateral band, but with the bright orange or red "cut" marks under the dentary bone of the lower jaw. This cross is common in Yellowstone Park waters, north into Montana, and south through Wyoming in east-slope rivers where cutthroat trout were originally the only salmonid present. In common with all hybrids the rainbow × cutthroat is a vigorous fish and, where established, often run to good size. They are particularly common in Henrys Lake, Idaho, and have been widely introduced in the high mountain lakes of Ecuador.

STEELHEAD

The migratory rainbow, whether anadromous or lake type, is known as a steelhead. The sea-run fish resembles the lake-dwelling form in color as it comes from the sea, but as it proceeds up the rivers and nears spawning time it becomes dark and spotted; the red band appears; and it resembles the mature nonmigratory form, though its body is generally slimmer. The largest steelhead on record weighed 42 pounds and was taken at Bell Island, Alaska. Owing to the wide range of habitat over a large area in Pacific coastal streams, it is probable that steelhead evolved from early geological times into season-differentiated spawning populations in order to occupy viable breeding areas as they became available after each succeeding glaciation or volcanic action.

Steelhead do feed to some extent when in freshwater and lose considerable weight during spawning, but their capacity for survival is exceptional. The anadromous form has been held for egg-taking in a hatchery for a year after migrating into a river from the ocean, and during that time the fish were not fed. One such steel-

Rainbow Trout,
Beaverkill River (headwaters), New York

head, tagged and released, returned to spawn the following year in excellent body condition.

There are steelhead returning from the ocean at any month in the year on the Pacific coast. Those which enter the river as immatures to mature in freshwater six months to a year later are known as spring or summer fish. Those which enter in the fall or winter to spawn shortly from December to May are called winter fish. The winter fish is the most widespread in distribution; the summer form being found in relatively few streams. All of the fish passing above Bonneville Dam on the Columbia River are spring or summer fish.

The ocean migrations and habits of the steelhead are becoming better known because of the attention focused on the Japanese fisheries in the North Pacific Ocean. Marked steelhead have been released from Oregon, tagged in the Gulf of Alaska, and again taken in Oregon at the place of original release. There have been recoveries of tagged or marked steelhead to indicate that the limit of western migration in the ocean for the majority of fish may be somewhat west of 175°W. A steelhead tagged by a Japanese research vessel at 177°W south of Kiska Island in the Aleutians in September 1970 was recaptured by an angler in the Wynoochee River of Washington in March 1971. The fish had returned 2,200 nautical miles to its parent stream. However, Japanese fishery workers report steelhead as far west as 168°E. The Japanese have not been fishing for salmonids in the Pacific Ocean east of 175°W longitude by international agreement (1953), and continue to catch some steelhead. No trout have been taken below latitude 48°N.

ANGLING TECHNIQUES

There are as many ways to catch rainbow trout as we have fishing methods. Broadly speaking, rainbows are taken on all kinds of lures and baits from trolling spoons to frozen lumps of vaseline. However, many methods are only of local importance, and the majority of anglers seeking the rainbow use either fly-casting or spinning equipment. The exceptions may be distinguished by the habitat and food of the trout. Fly-fishing in lakes, for example, is usually more productive in habitats where insects and shrimp are dominant food items, as compared to waters where large forage fish such as the kokanee and cisco are major components of their diet. The trolling and spinning methods excel in lakes of the latter type. Although both the Pacific Coast purist and the steelhead angler of the Great Lakes region are casting for what amounts to the same migratory form of rainbow, regulars of the Pére Marquette and Manistee are essentially limited to plugs and spoons. Eastern anglers face a similar choice in having on one hand lakes where alewife and cisco are the principal forage, but precious few waters where mayflies and other winged delectables create the magic of an evening rise. Consequently, the highly adaptable rainbow becomes a number of fish in the eyes of an angler instead of just one species.

Fly-Fishing for Rainbow Trout Perhaps the chief difference between the rainbow trout and the other common species is because it is pre-eminently a fastwater fish. Rainbows favor the swift runs and riffles of large streams, and a practiced technique is required to take them consistently (*see* Fly Fishing).

The epitome of rainbow-trout fishing is with the dry fly on rivers like the Henry's Fork of the Snake River in Idaho, or the Dean River in British Columbia, where reasonably an angler can expect a 2 or 3 pounder to come up for a floating pattern. Here, in the very best weather, rainbow trout can be found feeding wherever the current will bring them nymphs and duns. As evening approaches, the fish move around more freely, and one can take rainbows ranging 10–18 inches long without covering too much water. The trout jump and hang in the current shaking your wrist, and now and again you meet an old bruiser who demands a bit more skill in placing the fly right.

Another type of rainbow-trout fly-fishing is found in the mountain lakes of the Kamloops region in British Columbia. Again, this is a distinctly different kind of angling, with fish running from 1½ to a possible 7–8 pounds, but it exists primarily in lakes which are rich in insect life. There are many waters of this kind where you may see hundreds of rainbows boiling the surface during an evening caddisfly hatch, such as Babine Lake, Mile-High Lake, and Hylas Lake. You don't explore such waters expecting the 20 pounders trolled in Kootenay, but there is the pleasure of casting small floaters on fine leaders to cruising fish, which can be plenty exciting when your trout are even modestly sized. The Kamloops rainbow in its prime is reminiscent of a landlocked salmon because it wages a spectacular aerial offensive.

Alaska, New Zealand, Chile, and Argentina also afford unique rainbow-trout fishing; however, the emphasis here is on the wet fly in both rivers and lakes. With the exception of Argentina, the migratory form of rainbow or steelhead provides some sport for the tourist angler in these same areas. Nevertheless, steelhead fishing is one of the most productive games in the United States, where it had its origin.

Fly-Fishing for Steelhead On the western coast of the North American continent there are many rivers and streams with annual runs of steelhead. Some occur only in the fall and winter; others, unfortunately not as many, attract summer runs. These runs usually present ideal conditions for the fly-fisherman. Water that is extremely clear may require fine terminal tackle calling for exceptional skill to handle the bruising fighter. Fall will bring occasional storms which may raise and discolor the river for a short time, but one can usually depend on weeks of excellent water and good fishing. Winter presents a real problem to the dedicated fly man as rivers are high and roily with only short periods of clearing or lowering water. Close contact by telephone with local tackle firms or anglers is essential. When favorable, get there immediately, as the river can change in just a few hours.

The southern boundary of fly streams for steelhead is the Russian River north of San Francisco (*see* California). A few streams south of the bay have minor runs but are only of local importance. The Eel River in the northern part of the state was once a fabulous fly stream, but it now has limited productive periods due to extensive lumbering operations which silt the water after each rain. However, the fish are large and worth trying for. The Klamath and Trinity rivers have good fall runs, and occasionally winter fishing occurs. The Smith River next to the Oregon border is noted for the size of its steelhead, which begin to arrive in December.

Oregon (*which see*) has many excellent small streams such as the Rogue River in the south. Its water is normally crystal clear, requiring long leaders and some skill to work effectively. In the winter extremely large steelhead enter the stream, and on those rare days when the water is not roiled from rains, some good fly-fishing can be had. Boat fishing is very popular on the Rogue. The Umpqua River in the central section of Oregon has a run of steelhead almost year round; summer fishing is exceptional and continues until the winter rains make conditions impossible. The North Fork of the Umpqua at Steamboat Inn offers 36 miles of prime water which is closed to fly-fishing only. Oregon rivers entering the Columbia have limited stretches suitable for steelhead fly-fishing. However, the fish are unusually large. The Deschutes, Grande Ronde, and John Day offer a few miles each. Near the Portland area the Kalama, Lewis, Willamette, and Cowlitz are also popular.

Washington (which see) is laced with steelhead rivers from border to border. The Kalama, Klickitat, Skagit, Skyomish, Stillaguamish, Wind, and Sol Duc are some of the more famous ones. Others are becoming popular ever since the development of the lead-core shooting heads which can put a fly in front of a steelhead at depths not attainable with ordinary lines in years past. These are big, turbulent waters which are otherwise difficult to work with flies.

British Columbia (which see) offers many fine streams, some of which are excellent for fly-fishing but many of these can only be covered with baits and lures. The Kispiox River near Hazelton, for example, produced a 33-pound steelhead to the fly; larger specimens have been caught on salmon eggs and spoons and taken in nets. Other good streams in the province are the Morice, Thompson, and Bulkley rivers. On Vancouver Island, the Ash, Campbell, Capilano, Sproat, Cowichan, and Stamp are also excellent steelhead rivers with both winter and summer runs.

Steelhead Tackle Steelhead fly tackle is heavier than ordinary trout gear. Rods of 8½–9½ feet in length are standard. In bamboo, some of the favorites are made in fluted hollow construction; these are extremely powerful for their weight and were responsible for many tournament distance records when they first appeared on the market. Rods of five-strip construction (see Rod Building) have a loyal following, as do impregnated bamboo rods. Fiberglass rods have, of course, captured a large audience, and one development in that construction is a method of joining the sections by using hollow glass as a ferrule to keep the total rod weight down and to produce an action very similar to one-piece blanks. Regardless of the construction, the emphasis is on power; the tip must not be soft, and the action must extend well down into the butt. The guides should be correctly spaced, and of large size to permit smooth shooting of the line. A screw-locking-type reel seat is essential.

The reel must be large enough to accommodate at least 100 yards at 15–18-pound-test backing as well as the fly line. If the angler plans to fish some of the Canadian waters where steelhead in excess of 25 pounds may be encountered, it is advisable to use a reel that will hold at least 150 yards of backing. A single action reel with an adjustable brake is most popular, although some casters use automatic fly reels. In most models the 3⅝-inch and 3⅞-inch sizes (spool diameter) are suitable for steelhead fishing. Although brakes are usually of the friction type, at least one reel has a floating disc brake which eliminates brake failure and heat distortion.

The majority of fly lines used for steelhead are of the sinking type. An occasional river will offer dry-fly-fishing, but such conditions are rare. The rod, of course, will determine the correct line weight to use.

Shooting-Head Lines In 1949, the shooting head was introduced on the Eel and Klamath rivers. A development of the Golden Gate Casting Club, it led the way to new distance records in tournament competition. A shooting head is a short, 28–32-foot-long, single-tapered line of suitable weight for your rod. A loop is spliced at both ends, one for the leader and the other for the monofilament line. Ordinarily, a .021-inch monofilament is used, and this is attached to the loop with a Five-Turn Jam Knot. Some anglers attach the head directly to the monofilament with a Nail Knot (see under Knots) and dispense with the loop. About 75 feet of monofilament is sufficient unless you are an above average caster. A backing line is then attached to the monofilament with the Nail Knot or Five-Turn Jam Knot. These heads are usually custom-made and may be obtained from at least four West Coast shops which specialize in steelhead tackle. If you wish to make your own shooting heads, these same firms offer tapers of various weights and can advise you.

The virtue of a shooting head is that distance with less effort is easily accomplished. A single false cast is all that is necessary to shoot the fly to fishable distances. A regular forward-taper line will handle much more satisfactorily in strong winds and is preferable under this condition. Also, beginners who are not skilled at casting will find a forward-taper line easier to use. It is essential to master the double haul (see under Fly-Casting). The double haul requires considerable practice before the steps become reflexive. There is a slight difference in trajectory with shooting heads, and the general procedure is as follows: Grasp the line near the butt guide with the left hand (reverse the procedure if you are left-handed). As you lift the rod to throw the line up and to the rear, bring your left hand down smoothly. It must be timed perfectly with the lift of the rod. The movement of the left hand will vary in force depending on the distance required. A long cast may require bringing the hand beyond your hip. The next step is simplified when using a shooting head due to the fine diameter of the monofilament. As the line flows to the rear you will feel the pull of its weight as it begins to straighten out. Allow your left hand to follow the line up to the butt guide. Before the line loses its momentum, start the forward cast by bringing the left hand down sharply (as before) and timed exactly with the forward movement of the rod. Aim this forward cast higher than you would with an ordinary fly line. The shooting head differs from the regular forward-taper line in that perfect timing results in a long cast with no need for great power. Don't force the cast, or it will collapse and fall short of the distance required.

The loose monofilament line can be held in various ways. Carefully formed loops draped around your hand or fingers can be released smoothly as the cast shoots away. Or the loops can be held between the teeth or lips, or draped over clothespins on your wader top, or in a specially designed "shooting basket" suspended from the shoulders. The preference is an individual one, but the point, of course, is to become adept enough in handling the loose monofilament to prevent tangling.

How to Make a Shooting Head To make your own shooting-head line the following steps are recommended:

Use acetone or a similar solvent; soak about 1½–2 inches of both ends of the line in it. Scrape off the finish with a dull knife. It may take several applications before the finish is soft enough to come free. Fray about ¼–½ inch of the tips with a needle. On the heavy end of the line it helps to taper the plastic finish with a razor blade. Turn the line back on itself forming a loop. Part of the frayed line should touch the cleaned line with the remainder extending over the plastic surface. Bind this down tightly with silk or nylon thread, and finish with a whip loop. A rod winder may be used by letting the coils of line dangle and slowly turn as you wrap the thread. A fly-tying bobbin is also helpful, and when properly adjusted you can whirl it around the loop forming a rapid and neat tie-off. Cut the end off closely with a razor blade, and apply three coats of varnish or lacquer.

The weight of shooting heads will vary, but 275 grains balances well with rods of medium power; 290–310 grains is for fairly stout-action rods; and 320–340 grains is for heavy, powerful steelhead rods. Not many rods require extremely heavy heads, and these demand a skilled caster to make them work properly.

It is also possible to make a lead-core shooting head for deep rivers by using a plastic-coated lead trolling line. A 30-foot section of this material weighs 385 grains. You can custom the head to fit your rod by cutting off the length of line required. The diameter of such a line is small, and it will sink like a stone. This results in a very deep-running fly, and, while not always practical, the lead-core head is ideal for winter fishing. Lines of this type usually come in 100-yard coils, but sections can be obtained from specialist West Coast tackle shops. The ideal method for attaching both leader and backing is with the Nail Knot; a short piece of nylon is attached at both ends, then barrel knotted to the leader and shooting monofilament.

Leaders Leaders of 9–12 feet are used for steelhead fishing. On clear rivers, such as the Rogue in Oregon, leaders up to 14–15 feet have proven very successful in outwitting the extremely wary trout on that stream. For general purposes the tippet should be 6–8-pound-test.

Steelhead Flies A good steelhead fly should be sparsely dressed so that it will sink readily. It must be tied to withstand hard use. Patterns are varied and range from gaudy to conservative hues, and those illustrated in the color plates represent a working assortment for most Western streams. Minor changes are made in the dressings occasionally; the Skyomish Sunrise, for example, started as a red chenille body fly, and is now being used with red fluorescent chenille as well as yellow fluorescent chenille. However, the original pattern is often the best. Other steelhead dressings, such as the Boss, a Russian River favorite, differ from the standard steelhead patterns in having a very long tail of black hair. It seems out of proportion, but the Boss is highly successful, nevertheless. The somber Silver Hilton and the dull, crude-looking Burlap pattern rarely attract neophyte anglers; yet both flies are far above average and should never be neglected. You must also remember that a particular river may be influenced by a local fly-tier who is an excellent angler. His selections will be used by more casters, and hence they will take a greater percentage of steelhead. It is wise to have a few of the local favorites, but do not neglect the standard patterns.

On any fly a quality hook is essential. It must be top-grade steel, and the points must be sharp. This is important. Many hooks used for this fishing are 4X- and 5X-weight wire, and usually Limerick bends. This type will tolerate considerable punishment against rocks on low back casts; however, the hook should be honed occasionally with a fine file. The forged 7957BX Round-bend Mustad hook is exceptionally sharp and is also popular. Flies tied on the latter hook should be weighted slightly. Another favorite is the Allcock W209 in sizes No. 2–8. This is a round-wire hook, sproat bend, 2X Stout, and also has an extremely sharp point. A round wire does not cut through the flesh as rapidly as a forged hook, which may result in more fish landed. However, this is a theoretical consideration. Double hooks are still favored on the lower Rogue River in No. 6–10. The local anglers believe that the fly rides better when tied on a double hook.

Angling Technique for Steelhead One must realize a basic fact in steelheading—the fish are only in the stream at certain periods of the year, and for many months the water may be barren or simply hold small trout. Steelhead move into the rivers in groups, and a stretch of stream that was productive last week may be empty until a new group arrives. Often, a riffle that produced a steelhead in the morning may have another fish in the same spot by late afternoon. The angler's ability to locate or anticipate good holding water is no small part of the charm of this kind of fishing.

As the fish travel up-river, they will follow identical routes through each riffle and pool, as they have for countless generations before. They will rest in the same spots, bunch up in certain pools, or stay in a favored 5–10-foot area in a riffle that may be 100 yards long. This will be repeated year after year unless a flood scours and alters the stream bed. Oldtimers learn these spots through constant fishing, and by trial and error. Many experts can look at a strange river and instantly pick out the best riffles. Submerged ledges, changes in the bottom revealed by a slight variation in the surface flow, and the location of rocks—all of these have their special meaning. You can save a lot of time by avoiding the kinds of water that steelhead will not hold in and the places that cannot be fished properly even if the trout are present. For example, water that is extremely fast is not likely to contain steelhead. They prefer moving water, of course, but as a rule of thumb, if it is flowing too fast to wade comfortably it is too fast to fish. Dead water is a poor producer on most rivers, although there are a few exceptions. The reliable places are the slicks above a rapid, which are usually created below big pools where the stream spreads out. Another kind of water that is consistently good is a long, uniform flow of moderate speed. Steelhead habitually lie in the channel of a run of the latter type, and it pays to study the deeper sections carefully.

There is a riffle above Lobster Creek in the Rogue River. The mail boats enter this each year and create a narrow channel through the shallower sections of stream. To achieve this, they tie a cable to a tree or ledge at the head of the riffle and winch the boat upstream. A rotary device scours the bottom, pushing the rocks up on each side and leaving a deeper channel in the center. It is never too wide, just a few feet more than required by the boats. This particular riffle is so long that a cable can't reach the length of it, so two changes are necessary and the boat must make a sharp turn near the top. The boat turns at almost a right angle to the current, thus creating a big pocket in the otherwise swift current. The productive way to fish this water is to wade out and make 75–85-foot casts so the fly covers the pocket. The steelhead always hold in the slower, bottom currents behind the rock "wall." This is just one of many situations with which experienced anglers become familiar, not only on the Rogue but all Western rivers.

The basic technique of steelhead fly-fishing is to wade in at the head of a run and cover the water with cross-stream casts until every portion of the riffle is reached. The fly will swing around in arcs, and you are most likely to get a strike between the time the line tightens as it quarters downstream and when it completes the swing directly below you. Keep your rod low and pointed toward the fly. You can let the fly drift dead or jiggle it a bit either by twitching the rod or pulling the line. Try both methods. Make three short casts in all; then, having covered the close water, extend the line 10 or 15 feet. Make three more casts, and then extend the line again to reach the maximum distance so the entire run has been covered from one side to the other. Now wade eight or ten steps downstream and repeat the procedure until the length of the riffle has been fished. This is the standard method. You can vary it, of course, by changing the direction of your casts, working the fly deeper by casting upstream, and running it near the surface by casting more directly downstream.

Catching steelhead is not difficult. The technique is quite simple compared to some other types of trout fishing. The ability to "read" the water and to cast a long line is most important. Wading ability also goes a long way in successful steelhead fishing because of the volume of flow typical of most coastal rivers. —W.B.
—J.R.
—A.J.McC.

RATFISH *Hydrolagus colliei* This relative of the sharks has only a single gill opening on either side, rather than the 5–7 which occur in sharks. A fleshy gill cover superficially resembles that of bony fishes. The body is stout anteriorly, tapering into a slim tail. Its head is relatively large, with a pointed snout, and a clublike projection is located between the eyes of the male. Each of the two dorsal fins is preceded by a heavy spine. The body is silvery, with hues of green, golden, blue, or pale metallic-brown; many white spots cover the body in some specimens. The skin is smooth, and the teeth are fused into bony plates which are incisor-like on the upper jaw.

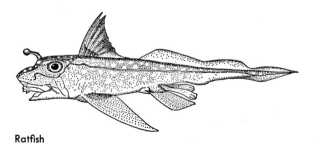

Ratfish

LIFE HISTORY

This peculiar species belongs to a group which contains about twenty-eight species found all over the world, usually in moderately deep coldwater. The ratfish occurs

from northwestern Alaska to Ensenada, Baja California. In the southern part of its range it is found in water that is relatively deep, but is taken in relatively shallower water in its northern habitat, usually at depths greater than 40 fathoms. They occur in large numbers during the fall. They are sluggish swimmers, moving by feeble undulations of the tail and second dorsal fin.

Fertilization is internal, the male introducing sperm via the sharklike claspers. Its eggs are tough-skinned capsules which are deposited vertically in the mud. The young, which resemble the adults upon hatching, have been taken in British Columbia during October.

It eats mostly fishes, but mussels and other invertebrates are also taken. There is no commercial value to this species, but its liver produces a fine cleaning oil and gun lubricant. —D.dS.

RATON A regional Spanish name for the bonefish (*which see*) used on the northeast coast of South America. The connotation of *raton*, meaning "rat," is due to the characteristic feeding posture of the fish in nibbling at a bait. *See also* Ratfish

RAY (FIN-RAY) A bony rod, usually connected to other rays by a membrane (interradial membrane) to form one of the fins of a fish. Rays are generally of two kinds, spines and softrays. Softrayed fishes are exemplified by the trouts, minnows, and suckers, which have only softrays in their fins. Spinyrayed fishes such as the snappers, sunfishes, and perches have one or more spines in their dorsal, anal, and pelvic fins, with the remainder of these fins usually made up of softrays (some fish have one spine in each pectoral fin; spines do not occur in the caudal fin).

Spines and softrays take different forms in various kinds of fishes, and a strict definition of either kind of ray is not possible. In some species, such as the mullets, one of the softrays in young juveniles regularly transforms into a spine. In the usual case a spine is rigid, pointed at the tip, and nonsegmented and nonbranched. Softrays are usually flexible, not pointed at the tip (fimbriated), and segmented, and often they are branched.

The kind and number of rays are characteristic of a species and may be described in scientific text by a fin formula with the following abbreviations:

D Dorsal fin (D_1 and D_2, the first and second dorsal fins when the fin is divided into two units)

A Anal fin

P_1 Pectoral fin

P_2 Pelvic fin (sometimes given as V when the fin is called a ventral fin, in which case the pectoral fin is designated only as P)

C Caudal fin

When the fin formula is given, upper case Roman numerals are used to designate spines and Arabic numerals for softrays (at times lower case Roman numerals are used to designate unbranched or unsegmented softrays). The fin formula is not universally standardized, but the following conventions are recommended: In a single fin containing both spines and softrays, the two kinds of rays are separated by a comma if all the rays are connected by a membrane (D VI, 12 represents a dorsal fin with 6 anterior spines connected to 12 softrays), and by a hyphen if the membrane is discontinuous somewhere in the fin (A II-I, 16 represents an anal fin with two anterior spines separated from the remainder of the fin which consists of one spine and 16 softrays). When finlets occur in the posterior portion of the dorsal or anal fins, they are separated from the remainder of the fin by a plus sign (for the bluefin tuna: D_1 XIII; D_2 I, 14 + 8 represents a first dorsal fin with 13 spines and a second dorsal fin with 1 spine connected to 14 softrays and followed by 8 finlets).

The softrays of the caudal fin are usually given as the unbranched rays in the dorsal part of the fin plus the branched rays plus the unbranched rays in the ventral part of the fin (as C 8 + 15 + 7).

The numbers of rays in some fins may be constant in a species; in others they may vary (D_1 XII to XIII; D_2 I, 14 + 8 or 9 indicates that in the first dorsal fin the spines vary from 12 to 13 and in the second dorsal fin there are constantly 1 spine and 14 softrays and the finlets vary from 8 to 9).

The fin formula is not used in this volume, designed primarily for the angler, because it exceeds the needs of our generalized descriptions of the species. *See also* Anatomy.   —F.H.B.

RAYS Order Squaliformes Rays are fishlike vertebrates closely related to sharks in that they have five pairs of gill clefts, each opening separately to the outside, and a cartilaginous skeleton lacking true bone cells. But the teeth of skates and rays are pavementlike in contrast to the well-developed, pointed teeth characteristic of most sharks. They resemble skates in having gill openings, which open to the ventral surface, and pectoral fins joined to the head. Their skin is generally smooth, they have a slender tail which lacks a caudal and anal fin, and they usually have one or more well-developed serrated barbs, or spines, at or near the tail base. Rays typically have the embryos developing within the oviduct up to the time of hatching, and thus differ further from the egg-laying skates.

While predominantly a saltwater group, some species live exclusively in freshwater, and individuals of other related families freely enter freshwater. They are far more active than skates and spend much of their time browsing actively over the shallow sandflats, rolling and jumping during their forays. They use the pectoral "wings" to stir up the bottom and unearth burrowing forms, such as worms, clams, crabs, shrimps, snails, and small fishes. Pelagic species, such as mantas, also feed on plankton, using the peculiar head fins to funnel the food into their mouth.

Rays are eaten all over the world, but only to a small extent in the United States. The "wings" are sometimes used as a substitute for scallops, and at times large rays are used variously for fishmeal, fertilizer, and as crab-pot bait. Some species take heavy tolls on oyster and clam beds during their incessant foraging, but the chief relation of rays to man is in their sharp, sometimes poisonous barb or barbs on the tail. A wound from these is usually painful and may cause death. The spine injury of stingrays is often accompanied by poisoning from accessory poison glands. In either event, first aid and medical attention are desirable, and, although not always effective, in the majority of cases washing of the wound, followed by application of a mild antiseptic, and a trip to the doctor alleviate the pain and possible complications. *See also* Atlantic Guitarfish, Atlantic Manta, Atlantic Stingray, Atlantic Torpedo, Bat Stingray, Bluntnose Stingray, Bullnose Ray, Cownose Ray, Diamond Sting-

ray, First Aid, Lesser Electric Ray, Pacific Electric Ray, Pacific Manta, Roughtail Stingray, Round Stingray, Shovelnose Guitarfish, Skates, Smalltooth Sawfish, Smooth Butterfly Ray, Southern Stingray, Spiny Butterfly Ray, Spotted Eagle Ray, Thornback Ray, Yellow Stingray   —D.dS.

REDBELLY DACE *See* Southern Redbelly Dace

REDBREAST SUNFISH *Lepomis auritus* Regionally known as the yellowbelly sunfish, longear sunfish, sun perch, redbreast bream, it is one of the brightest colored and gamiest of the medium-size sunfish. It is usually yellow on the sides and crimson on the ventral surface, particularly in the breeding season. The distinguishing character of this sunfish is the long, black gill flap, which is narrower than the eye and has no yellow or red trim. The mouth is small and does not extend beyond the eye. The pectoral fins are short and round. The maximum length is about 11–12 inches and a weight of 1 pound.

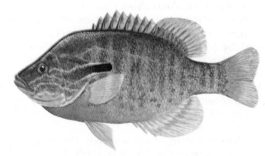

Redbreast Sunfish

Although this fish is sometimes found in lakes and ponds, it reaches its greatest abundance in the rivers of the Atlantic drainage in association with smallmouth bass and rock bass. The redbreast sunfish ranges from New Brunswick east of the Alleghenies to Florida.

The food consists of crustaceans, insects, and small fishes. On this varied fare it grows to 1–2 inches the first year, 2–3.5 inches the second year, and by the fourth year it may reach 6 inches.

LIFE HISTORY

The spawning habits of the redbreast are very similar to the bluegill. When the water temperature reaches 68° F., a shallow nest of about 12 inches in diameter is fanned out in the gravel by the male. It guards the nest and protects the young for a short period after hatching.

FISHING

This is a very sporting fish, taking most any type of small bait and particularly surface lures. It differs from many sunfishes in that it can be caught at night. Small spinners, spoons, plugs, flies, and popping bugs are all effective baits on this hard-fighting panfish.   —K.B.

REDD A type of spawning bed or nest scooped in the gravel of a river bottom for the purpose of protecting the fertilized eggs. The construction of a redd is typical of most salmonids. *See also* Atlantic Salmon

RED DRUM *Sciaenops ocellata* This species is better known along the South Atlantic and Gulf coasts as "redfish," and as "channel bass" in some other localities along the Eastern seaboard of the United States. Red drum occur along the Atlantic Coast of the United States from Massachusetts to Texas. Specimens weighing more than 50 pounds are rare, but many of the individuals taken weigh up to 40 pounds, usually much less. The largest specimen on record weighed 83 pounds and measured 4 feet 4 inches.

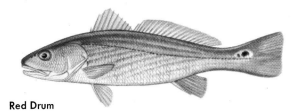

Red Drum

The red drum can be distinguished from the black drum (*which see*) by the absence of chin barbels and the presence of a black spot on the base of the tail. The body coloration is copper- or bronze-colored rather than silvery or gray. Otherwise the fish are generally similar in appearance. The red drum has 11 dorsal spines; 23–25 dorsal rays; 2 anal spines; 8 anal rays; and 40–45 scales along the lateral line. There are 8–9 gillrakers on the lower limb of the first arch. The upper jaw projects beyond the lower. The maxillary reaches to, or beyond, a vertical from the posterior margin of the orbit.

LIFE HISTORY

Comparatively little is known of the life history of this gamefish. Studies have shown that red drum in the Gulf of Mexico do not undertake extensive coastal migrations; in fact there is little movement between bays. Great fluctuations in abundance have been caused in the Gulf area by mass mortalities due to freezing weather, plankton blooms, and excessive salinity. Along the northerly part of its range in the Atlantic, the red drum is apparently migratory and seasonal in abundance.

ANGLING VALUE

A bottom fish, it feeds mostly on crustaceans and mollusks, although it consumes other fish (notably mullet) at times. The red drum is a favorite of surfcasters along the Southeast coast of the United States. Popular live baits include crabs, clams, bloodworms, sandbugs, mossbunker, and cut mullet. Red drum also hit spoons, plugs, metal squids, and leadhead bucktails. The larger drum are usually caught in the northern part of their range along the Carolina coast to New Jersey. Young "redfish" or "puppy drum," generally weighing less than 10 pounds, are also taken in southern Florida and along the Gulf Coast on fly, plug, and spinning tackle. When fishing artificials, the retrieve should be slow. The red drum does not jump when hooked but puts up a steady, hard fight and often makes strong runs.

The larger red drum have coarse flesh and are only fair as food. Small drum (up to 15 pounds) are excellent eating, however, particularly when deepfried in "fingers" or baked. *See also* Saltwater Fly-Fishing, Surf-Casting
—L.R.
—A.J.McC.

REDEAR SUNFISH *Lepomis microlophus* A popular panfish in the Southern United States, it is regionally known there as the shellcracker, stumpknocker, and yellow bream. The redear can be distinguished from the pumpkinseed, which it most closely resembles, by the lack of spots on the dorsal fin and the missing bluish bands on the side of the head. The gill flap of the redear is semiflexible, bending to right angles, while that of the pumpkinseed is rigid.

Redear Sunfish

The body color is variable, from bronze to blue-green with darker spots. There are 5–10 dusky vertical bars on the sides. The gill flap has a whitish border, with the tip accented with a bright red spot on the males and orange on the females. The mouth is small, but not extending beyond the front of the eye, and the pectoral fins are long and pointed. Redear sunfish of over 4 pounds have been caught in Florida, North Carolina, and Virginia. The record is 4½ pounds (1970).

The original range of the redear was south of the range of the pumpkinseed from southern Illinois south to Florida and Texas. In recent years it has been stocked in many states just north of its natural area, and in some Western states, notably New Mexico. The redear has a definite preference for large, quiet waters and has a tendency to congregate around stumps, roots, and logs. It will frequent openwaters, and seems to require less vegetation than the pumpkinseed.

LIFE HISTORY

The redear has been widely introduced into farm ponds because it is believed to be less prolific than the bluegill and therefore less likely to cause an overpopulation of stunted fish as rapidly. It depends largely on mollusks for food and does not compete severely with insect-eating fish. The redear has highly developed grinding teeth or "shellcrackers" located in its throat which are capable of crushing snails—its favorite item of diet.

The redear sunfish has the same breeding habits as the pumpkinseed. It has been known to hybridize with bluegill and green sunfishes.

ANGLING VALUE

Like the bluegill it is an excellent panfish and highly palatable. It can be kept for food at a smaller size because of the plumpness of the body.

Redear sunfish are ordinarily widely distributed throughout the lake or river system in which they occur. As a result they do not enter the angler's catch in appreciable numbers until the spring spawning season. Fishing the "beds" is most productive and eagerly anticipated from April to June in various parts of the South. The

Redeye Bass,
Apalachicola River Form

redear is less susceptible to artificial lures than most sun-fishes, and, consequently, grubs, catalpa worms, earth-worms, and shrimp are preferred baits. The great majority are caught on cane poles with worms, using No. 6 or No. 8 hooks; the bait is simply lowered in the vicinity of a visible bed. On rare occasions, the redear will take a wet or dry fly or small panfish bug.   —K.B.

REDEYE BASS *Micropterus coosae* A black bass which greatly resembles the smallmouth, it is sometimes called shoal bass or Chipola bass. When young, the distinctive color pattern of the redeye consists of dark vertical bars (which become obscure with age) and brick-red dorsal, caudal, and anal fins. The red color of eyes and fins easily separates this species from other bass.

The redeye bass was first identified from the upland tributaries of the Alabama and Chattahoochee River systems in Alabama, and the Savannah River drainage in Georgia. In more recent years it has been found in the Conasauga drainage in southeastern Tennessee and the Chipola River system in Florida. They usually inhabit the upland drainage areas, being present in small streams and ponds built upon these watersheds.

LIFE HISTORY

The spawning habits of the redeye bass are similar to the smallmouth bass except that the redeye will not spawn in ponds or lakes. In the northern part of their range they spawn in late May, June, or early July. Three-year-old fish as small as 4.7 inches have been found to be mature. One 5.7-inch female contained 2,084 eggs.

In Tennessee the growth rate of the redeye bass is slow when compared to other warmwater fishes. Growth is fast the first year but decreases as the fish becomes older. On the average a 10-year-old fish grows about 1 inch a year. In Alabama the average size is about 12 ounces, but fish of over 6 pounds have been caught.

The redeye bass occurs in two forms or racial stocks; the Apalachicola form, which has prominent basicaudal and opercular spots but superficially resembles a small-mouth bass (erroneously called the "Flint River small-mouth"), and the Alabama form, which is usually much brighter in color but the basicaudal spot is faint or absent.

ANGLING VALUE

These bass are prized by many anglers because they are scrappy, colorful, and highly palatable. Since a large portion of their food is insects taken from the surface of the water, the redeye have the characteristics of a good gamefish. Redeyes can be caught on artificial lures or live bait, especially hellgrammites. Typically, these fish are found in deep pockets in riffles and in pools with

Redeye Bass,
Alabama River Form

Grass Pickerel

Redfin Pickerel

some current. In rivers, such as the Flint in Georgia and Hallawakee Creek in Alabama, where redeye bass are numerous, they are often difficult to catch unless fine terminal tackle is used. *See also* Black Bass —K.B.

REDEYE MULLET *See under* Silver Mullet

REDFIN PICKEREL *Esox americanus americanus* The redfin pickerel and the grass pickerel, *Esox americanus vermiculatus*, are the smallest members of the pike family, seldom exceeding 14–15 inches in length. Collectively, they are known as "little pickerel." They can be distinguished from the young of muskellunge, *Esox masquinongy*, and the northern pike, *Esox lucius*, by the scales on the cheeks and opercles. Like the chain pickerel, *Esox niger*, both the cheeks and opercles are fully scaled. They differ from the chain pickerel in branchiostegal count. The little pickerels have 11–13 branchiostegals (throat bones beneath the gill covers), and the chain pickerel have 14–16 branchiostegals. The adult chain pickerel has chainlike vermiculated markings on the sides, while the adult redfin or grass pickerel has vertical bars on the sides. Also the little pickerels have a short, broad snout. The distance from the tip of the snout to the front of the eye is shorter than the distance from the back of the eye to the posterior margin of the opercle. The chain pickerel has a slimmer snout, with the length of the snout being longer than the distance from the back edge of the eye to the edge of the opercle.

Many taxonomists claim that there is no constant characteristic to distinguish the two subspecies of *E. americanus* with the exception that the grass pickerel is seldom as distinctly barred and lacks the red fins of *E. a. americanus*. However, Legendre (1954) separates the two subspecies in this manner:

Redfin pickerel (*E. a. americanus*)	Grass pickerel (*E. a. vermiculatus*)
1. Length of snout contained more than 4½ times in length of body.	1. Length of snout contained less than 4½ times in length of body.
(Measurement from nape, where scales begin at back of head, to origin of dorsal fin)	
2. Head seen in profile, top outline of snout often appears convex from orbit to tip of snout.	2. Head seen in profile, top outline of snout often appears concave from orbit to tip of snout.
3. Between pelvic fins, abdomen with more than 5 cardioid (heart-shaped) scales.	3. Between pelvic fins, abdomen with less than the 5 cardioid scales.

Except for transition zones in the northern and southern extremities of the range of the two species, the redfin pickerel is found in the Atlantic drainage, and the grass pickerel is found in the Great Lakes and Mississippi drainage system. It is thought that the northern dispersal of *E. americanus* was facilitated by the blocking of the St. Lawrence River by ice dams. The water from the St. Lawrence River and the Great Lakes was then discharged south through Lake Champlain and the Hudson River, giving the redfin an access to its most northern limits.

The redfin is confined to the Atlantic drainage and extends south through the coastal plains from Maryland to Georgia. It is widely distributed in Florida but diminishes in numbers south of Lake Okeechobee. It

extends west in the Gulf states through Georgia and Alabama. In Alabama it is reported to intergrade with the grass pickerel.

The grass pickerel is considered the Western subspecies of *americanus*. The eastern border of its range extends from the St. Lawrence River near Montreal southwest in the tributaries of Lake Ontario and Lake Erie to the western slope of the Appalachian drainage in Pennsylvania, eastern Kentucky, Tennessee, and into Alabama where it intergrades with the redfin pickerel. Its northern range in Canada is limited to the drainage of the St. Lawrence, Lake Ontario, and Lake Erie. In the United States, its range extends from western Pennsylvania through Ohio, Indiana, Michigan, and Illinois. In Illinois it is the only representative of the pike family. It is also found in southern portions of the Lake Michigan drainage through southern Wisconsin to the tributaries of the Mississippi in southeastern Iowa. It has not been reported in Minnesota for the past fifty years. It is reported in abundance in the sandhill-lake region of Nebraska and widely distributed in Missouri, Arkansas, and Louisiana. It is also found in southeastern Oklahoma, eastern Texas, and east to Alabama along the Gulf Coast. There was an unrecorded introduction of the grass pickerel at some unknown time into the northeast portion of the state of Washington. Colorado also reports an introduction of grass pickerel in the early 1900's in the vicinity of Colorado Springs. Since that time they have been distributed into lakes and ponds in the immediate area.

SPAWNING

The little pickerels spawn early in the spring soon after the ice goes out. Grass pickerel spawn in Michigan and Illinois in March and during April in Pennsylvania. In North Carolina, the redfin spawns as early as February. Ripe grass pickerel are often taken during the northern-pike spawning runs. Since the pike family is the first to spawn in the early spring and the resulting fry are the first fish species available to predators such as perch, it is possible that the young of grass pickerel hatched at the same time may act as a buffer species or may be a competitor to the young of northern pike. There is no evidence concerning this relationship.

There are indications that grass pickerel spawn both in the spring and in the fall. If these fish do spawn successfully in the fall, survival must be difficult because zooplankton populations are declining and the very small fry of other species are nonexistent. Therefore, no food, or very little food, would be available for the normally fast-growing fry.

FOOD

The food of the redfin and grass pickerel is apparently about the same as that of the larger members of the pike family—the young eat midges, mayflies, other small aquatic insects, and crustaceans. When they grow larger or later, their diet consists of tadpoles, larger aquatic insects, and fish. In a study made in Connecticut it was found that pickerel—both chain and redfin—under 6 inches fed more on crustaceans than any other kind of organism. Algae and insects ranged next in importance. Remains of higher plants, fish, and annelid worms each represented approximately 10 percent of the diet. Fish made up 62.4 percent of the food of pickerel over 6 inches. Minnows made up the largest percentage of fish remains, with perch, sunfish, darters, and bullheads following in that order of abundance.

HABITAT

The habitat of the little pickerels resembles that of the other pikes, although they are more likely to remain in swamps and creeks in dense vegetation. They seem to spurn larger openwaters. Along the St. Lawrence River and Lake Ontario they were found in creek mouths, but none is taken in the larger bodies of water.

They are most abundant in shallow, weedy environments of lakes and streams. Usually the type of habitat the little pickerels prefer has a slow current, if any, and a soft bottom, which are conducive to heavy growths of vegetation. Overflow ponds or small river lakes are optimum habitats, but often these fish are trapped and die when these environments dry up. On the eastern shore of Maryland they are found in millponds on muddy and sandy shores. In North Carolina, the redfin is considered primarily a stream fish, preferring habitat offered by the black acid waters in swampy lowlands. They prefer water that is clean and free of excessive silt and municipal and industrial pollution. In Florida, they are found in the shallow, weedy margins of sandhill lakes.

In Ohio, populations have decreased or disappeared in some areas since 1900 due to ditching or increased turbidity which destroyed the aquatic vegetation in formerly clean vegetated waters. In this state, the grass pickerel is found in ponds and low-gradient streams with clear water and heavy aquatic vegetation. The grass pickerel seemed to suffer from interspecific competition because it was rare or absent where other pike were present.

ANGLING VALUE

Some anglers in Southeastern United States prefer fishing for the redfin pickerel because of its scrappiness. Cane-pole fishermen in southeastern North Carolina go after the redfin in the more remote backwaters. The conservation commission of this state feels the modern sport fisherman is missing a chance for excitement by not pursuing these belligerent little pike with ultralight spinning tackle. Lures should include tiny spinners, inch-long spoons, or miniature plugs. Slamming strikes are often produced by casting around vegetation, an old log,

or other hiding places and reeling the tiny lure at a fairly rapid rate. The length of the average fish taken is about 10 inches; a 15 incher is exceptional.   —K.B.

REDFIN SHINER *See* Common Shiner
REDFIN SUCKER *See* Northern Redhorse
REDFISH *See* Red Drum
RED GROUPER *Epinephelus morio* This is one of the most common groupers in southern Florida and the tropical American Atlantic. It reaches a size of usually less than 4 feet in total length. The common name refers to the reddish general coloration.

The red grouper has 11 dorsal spines; 16–17 dorsal rays; 9, rarely 10 anal rays; and 16–18, usually 17 pectoral rays. Posterior nostril about equal to, or somewhat larger than the anterior. Insertion of pelvic fin behind lower end of pectoral base. Posterior margin of caudal fin straight or concave. Dark bars on head and body and sometimes also scattered white spots. Black specks scattered around eye.

The lack of a notch in the membranes between the dorsal spines distinguishes this grouper from the other tropical Atlantic species of the same genus.

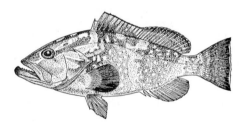

Red Grouper

ANGLING VALUE

It occurs on rocky bottom in waters of medium depth. Smaller individuals may be found in the shallows close to shore. It takes live or dead bait.

An abundant grouper, it is accessible to smallboat anglers operating not far from shore. Large adults fight well on light tackle.

Because it is excellent eating, it is one of the most important commercial groupers in the United States.
          —L.R.

RED HIND *Epinephelus guttatus* This is one of the smallest of groupers. The usual size is less than 20 inches in total length. It occurs in southern Florida, but it is more abundant in the Bahamas and the West Indies.

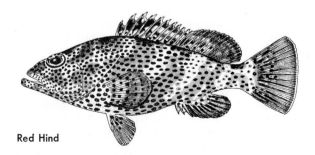

Red Hind

The red hind has 11 dorsal spines; 15–16, usually 16 dorsal rays; 8 anal rays; and 17, rarely 16 pectoral rays. Posterior nostril somewhat larger than the anterior, to about twice as large. Insertion of pelvic fin under, or slightly behind, lower end of pectoral base. Posterior margin of caudal fin convex. Head and body with red spots.

This species is superficially similar to the rock hind (*which see*), but it lacks the dark blotches along the dorsal-fin base and the black blotch on top of the caudal peduncle. There is no other western Atlantic species which it resembles.

ANGLING VALUE

Usually found on coral bottom in relatively shallow water, it takes live or dead bait.

Small enough to be treated as a panfish, its excellent flavor makes up for its poor angling value. This grouper is a highly valued food fish in the West Indies, and is considered a delicacy in some of the Greater Antilles.
—L.R.

REDHORSE *See* Northern Redhorse

REDLIP SHINER *Notropis chiliticus* A small minnow seldom exceeding 2 inches in total length, the redlip shiner is found in the Pee Dee River system of North Carolina. The body of this small minnow is elongate; the depth contained 5.5 times in its total length. The head of the minnow is broad; its length 0.25 its total length. The eye is large, contained 0.35 in the length of the head. The pharyngeal teeth are in two rows 2, 4-4, 2. The lateral line is strongly decurved, complete, and has 34–37 scales in the lateral series. The anal and dorsal fin-rays number 8 each. The interior of the mouth has no black pigment, nor is there any around the area of the vent, anal fin, and caudal peduncle. The body color of breeding males is crimson and there is a pale emerald stripe. The top of the head is greenish, snout red, and the fins are yellow. The dorsal and anal fins are splashed with red or orange. The lips of the redlip shiner are red. This species is similar to the saffron shiner (*Notropis rubricroceus*), greenhead shiner (*Notropis chlorocephalus*), and the yellowfin shiner (*Notropis lutipinnis*).

Redlip Shiner

LIFE HISTORY

Very little is known about the life history of this minnow. The redlip shiner is found in small streams, both turbid and clear. It inhabits streams having sand and gravel bottoms and prefers a pH range of 6.9–7.4.

The redlip shiner serves as forage for the redbreast sunfish, largemouth bass, and other predator stream fishes. It is also used as bait by local fishermen, who seine them from nearby streams.
—D.E.L.

RED PIRANHA *See* Piranhas

RED PORGY *Pagrus sedecim* Although a closely related species occurs in European waters, only this one species is found in the western Atlantic, from New York to Argentina and in the Gulf of Mexico.

Representatives of *P. sedecim* have conical teeth and a rounded posterior nostril (instead of slitlike, as in the members of the genus *Calamus*).

In life, the color basically is reddish-silver, with numerous, minute blue spots.

No data are available on food and spawning habits, but it likely is carnivorous and an offshore winter spawner.

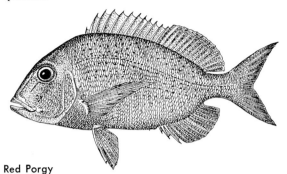

Red Porgy

ANGLING VALUE

The red porgy occurs in water that is rather deep, more so on the average than do other American sparids, but it often forms part of the catch in sport bottom-fishing, where it may reach a length of 3 feet. Good numbers often are taken in bottom trawls fished off the coast of the Southeastern United States, and in this way enter the commercial fishery.
—D.K.C.

RED SHINER *Notropis lutrensis* This minnow is a brilliant, steel-blue-backed, silvery shiner. Males have an orange-red belly, a violet-colored crescent behind the shoulders, followed by a crimson crescent. The fins are reddish, the anal and caudal blood-red. Female plain greenish. Mouth large and quite oblique. Body compressed, back arched. Lateral line strongly decurved. Scales large, 13 in front of dorsal. The range of the red shiner is from Wyoming to southern Minnesota and Illinois southward to Mexico.

The usual habitat of this fish is small ponds and quiet streams. Omnivorous in its food habits, this little minnow subsists on small bits of aquatic vegetation, one-celled animals, small insects, and crustaceans. Spawning in early summer, the red shiner deposits its eggs on submerged water plants. At this time males become even more brilliantly colored and develop small tubercles on the head and body. A small species, the red shiner seldom exceeds 3 inches.

Red Shiner

ECONOMIC VALUE

Although small, the red shiner is a hardy and attractive bait species.
—R..J.

REDSIDE SHINER *Richardsonius balteatus* A silvery shiner with a bluish back and blackish lateral band, it has a slender and moderately compressed body. Head short. Eye large. Mouth small and oblique. Scales large. Dorsal rays nine. Anal rays 10–13. The range of the redside shiner is in the Columbia River basin and the Salt Lake basin.

Redside Shiner

Inhabiting lakes and streams alike, the redside shiner in streams is most abundant in slow-moving pools. This species is carnivorous, and although its main diet is small aquatic insect larvae and crustaceans, it has been observed feeding on fry. Spawning time is in early summer when males develop a red stripe below the dorsal band and fine tubercles on the head, body, and upper sides of pectoral fins. At this time a light red stripe appears on the females. The redside attains a length of little more than 5 inches.

ECONOMIC VALUE

In some areas of its range, the redside shiner is considered the finest live bait available.   —R.A.J.

RED SNAPPER *Lutjanus blackfordi* (The correct scientific name for this species is still controversial. There is evidence that two species of red snapper may exist; *L. aya* and *L. campechanus* have also been given.) The species occurs along the Middle Atlantic and Gulf coasts of the United States southward throughout the tropical American Atlantic. A medium-sized snapper, it may reach 35 pounds and over 30 inches in total length.

The red snapper has 10 dorsal spines, 14 dorsal rays, and 9 anal rays. Normally 17 pectoral rays. 8–10 gill-rakers on lower limb of first arch, not counting rudiments. Rows of scales round caudal peduncle 25–27, usually 26. Cheek scales in 6, rarely 5 rows. Upper jaw reaching to or beyond vertical from anterior margin of orbit. Pectoral fin reaching to or beyond vertical from origin of anal fin, except in large specimens. Anal fin angulate, not rounded posteriorly. General coloration rose-red, paler below. Fins red, the dorsal margined with orange. Black spot on sides of body present; faint to obsolete in large individuals. Eye red.

This snapper is distinguished from the others by the color pattern, the longer pectoral fin, and the more numerous anal rays.

ANGLING VALUE

The red snapper usually occurs in schools, a few feet above hard bottom. This fish may frequent depths of about 100 fathoms, but it is usually found at 20–60 fathoms. Smaller individuals also occur in shallow water. It is usually taken on dead bait. A good fighter frequently caught by anglers on rod and reel, it is seldom caught on artificial lures.

This excellent eating fish is the most important commercial snapper in the United States and many tropical American countries.   —L.R.

THE COMMERCIAL FISHERY

The red-snapper industry began in 1870 at Pensacola, Florida, where the first fish house was built by an enterprising New Englander, one S. C. Cobb, Mr. Cobb sent his live-well smacks out into the Gulf, and those snappers caught at less than 20 fathoms could be kept alive in the wells until the ships' return. In time, artificially made ice made it possible to send larger, long-range schooners to the Gulf banks, some of them going 600–700 miles to the Campeche Banks west of Cuba. If a vessel finds a good fishing spot, a crew of nine men is said to be able to catch 1,000–4,000 pounds in an hour with handlines or 7,000–10,000 pounds in a day, depending on depth of water, tide, and wind. Even larger daily catches have been reported, one fishing captain stating that his crew once caught 1,800 red snappers.

A number of species of at least three distinct families of fish have been sold as red snapper by distributors, such as the mangrove or gray snapper, which when dead has a reddish color, the "hambone" or blackfin snapper, the silk snapper, red grouper, yellowfin grouper, speckled hind, black grouper, gag, scamp, and even the snook have at times been marketed as red snapper. Grouper steaks or fillets are skinned, but real red snappers are marketed in the round (whole). The skin has a bright reddish color, and the purchaser is insured against substitution. If the whole fish is bought, then save both the head and the throat. Small pieces of flesh, roughly triangular in shape, can be taken from the ventral side of the head, reaching down to the border of the gill flaps. This flesh is the richest and most delicately flavored part of the fish, and is

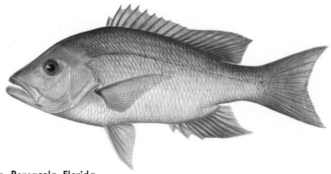

Red Snapper, 8-pound Male, Pensacola, Florida

usually thrown away with the head. In some areas, it is cut out and sold, a considerable demand having been built up for "throats" in some markets. The head makes a fine stock for fish chowder or bouillabaisse. —A.J.McC.

REDSTRIPE ROCKFISH *Sebastodes proriger* The species ranges from southern California to the Bering Sea. It is distinguished from other rockfishes (*which see*) by the shallow notch in the dorsal fin, the distinct red stripe along the lateral line, the knob on the underside of the tip of the lower jaw, the convex interorbital space, and the black peritoneum. Its color is red, mottled with dusky olive-green in the back; the lips are blackened. It has been taken to depths of 600 feet.   —J.R.

REDTAIL SURFPERCH *Amphistichus rhodoterus* Much like the barred surfperch (*which see*), but a frenum does not interrupt the posterior groove of the lower lip; the lower jaw projects slightly; the dorsal spines are higher than the contour of the softrays; there are 20–22 scales between the lateral line and the anterior end of the vent; softrays of the dorsal 25–28; anal softrays 28–31. There are 9–11 vertical, reddish-brown or brassy bars on the sides; the pelvic and caudal fins usually reddish. Called "porgy" north of California. Common in surf along sandy beaches. Found from Washington to central California.

COMMERCIAL VALUE

It is an important commercial species in the Eureka region.   —J.R.

RED TIDES The term "red tides" is given to a number of phenomena, some widely different in origin, which cause a discoloration of the water and, at times, may kill fishes and other aquatic organisms. Most red tides are caused by plankton organisms which grow rapidly to epidemic proportions to cause a "bloom." The large number of organisms in the water, which may be ordinarily transparent or only slightly colored, thus tint the water. But the term "red tide" is not always accurate, for water blooms may be red, yellow, pink, green, blue, black, purple, or brown, and even a bloom from a single organism may range from green to pink to red to rust to purple depending on the stage of the bloom.

CAUSE OF RED TIDES

Most red tides are caused by dinoflagellates, one-celled plants capable of swimming, some of which are so small that 25,000 of them are required to make an inch. One of the most notorious dinoflagellates is the suspected red-tide producer off Florida's west coast, *Gymnodinium breve*, and although many species cause red tides, fortunately only a few species cause death of aquatic organisms. Some water blooms, particularly those in freshwater which are caused by filamentous blue-green algae, can cause fishy tastes in drinking water, and, during certain stages of their decomposition, have killed livestock which drank heavily contaminated water.

Mortality of marine organisms by red tides is usually caused by powerful neurotoxins released from the body cells of the dinoflagellates. Poison from the blue-green algae is an alkaloid toxin. Low-oxygen conditions which occur during red tides may also contribute to mortality of organisms, and it is likely that man-made pollution as

well as pollution caused by the organisms killed by water bloom may be factors. Hydrogen sulfide might be the factor in such cases as well, resulting from the decomposition of dead organisms.

A red tide "gas" sometimes associated with water blooms is the result of mechanical breakdown of dinoflagellates, the toxin being carried about by wind and waves in a finely suspended mist.

Red tides usually occur in tropical areas or during warm seasons where the plantlike dinoflagellates are "fertilized" by certain naturally occurring chemicals in water. Warm weather, low salinities, and calm sea conditions may hasten red-tide growth, although the exact combination of factors which must exist before a red tide will occur are unknown. Among the factors believed responsible for red-tide growth are nitrates, phosphates, silicates, vitamins, minerals, organic acids, and certain microorganisms, including yeasts and bacteria. Metabolic by-products of previous innocuous plankton blooms may also be a contributing factor.

Runoff of nutrient-rich rivers, streams, or lagoons may mix with coastal waters containing dinoflagellates, resulting in rapid growth and division of cells, such as occur off Florida's west coast. The mixing of cold currents containing nutrients with warm currents containing dinoflagellates may cause red water. An example of this type occurs off Peru and Chile where it is known as *aguaje*. Upwelling of cold, nutrient-rich water, resulting from winds blowing waters offshore, brings chemicals into the sunlit area where red-tide organisms multiply.

CONTROL

Charcoal and copper sulfate have been used experimentally to try to prevent the spread of red tide, but insufficient research has been carried out to prove the efficiency of this method. Networks of volunteer observers in some areas are instrumental in spotting early outbreaks so that, if necessary, copper sulfate can be dusted on the water bloom.   —D.dS.

REEF SHARK *See* Springer's Reef Shark

REEL A device consisting of a spool set in a frame which is mounted on the rod butt for the purpose of controlling the movement of the line. The spoon may rotate (revolving-spool reel), or it may be stationary (fixed-spool reel). There are two broad categories of reels: those used in freshwater and those used in saltwater. However, some types of reels are common to both forms of angling, such as the bait-casting reel, spinning reel, and fly reel. In a strict sense only big-game trolling reels and surf-casting reels are limited to marine angling.

First mention of a fishing reel appears in *The Art of Angling* written by Thomas Barker and published in England in 1651, two years before the appearance of the first edition of Izaak Walton's *The Compleat Angler*. Barker, who "served at the Lord Protector's charge in the kitchen of foreign ambassadors," according to author Eric Taverner, refers to the reel as: "Within two foot of the bottom of the rod there was a hole made for to put in a wind to turn with a barrel to gather up his line, and loose at his pleasure."

In 1967 Dr. John T. Bonner, Chairman of Princeton's Department of Biology, presented evidence in a painting

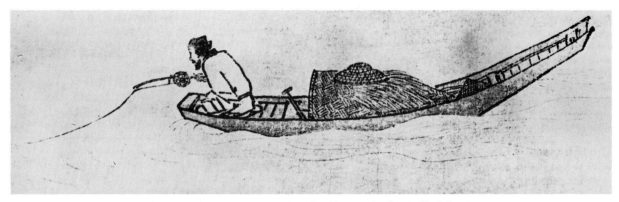

Patient fishermen with rod and reel in a painting attributed to Ma Yuan in the first half of the thirteenth century

by the celebrated Chinese artist Ma Yuan, who is known to have been active in the period 1190–1230 A.D., that the reel is many centuries old. The painting, which hangs in the National Museum of Tokyo, has been reproduced many times in art publications, but never in fishing literature prior to Dr. Bonner's exposition in *The Atlantic Salmon Journal*.

Dr. Bonner found additional evidence of the reel's early use in an encyclopedic series, *Science and Civilization in China*, by Dr. Joseph Needham. One volume ("Mechanical Engineering") clearly shows that the first fishing reel was well known at least by mid-13th century A.D. and possibly as early as the 3rd and 4th century A.D. Dr. Needham suggests that the Chinese reel was patterned after the early use of the bobbin in the silk industry.

Although Dr. Needham gives the exact date of the Ma Yuan painting as 1195 A.D., there is apparently some uncertainty, according to Dr. Bonner. In the lower right-hand corner of the painting there is a collector's seal bearing a cyclical date corresponding to either 1195 or 1255 A.D., "the latter being more likely." Dr. Bonner's authority is Dr. Roderick Whitfield of Princeton's Department of Art and Archaeology. *See also* Bait-Casting, Fly-Casting, Spin-Casting, Spinning, Surf-Fishing, Trolling.

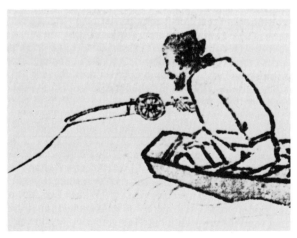

Detail of the painting at the top of the page shows the reel mounted below the rod, which has two guides
(Photos courtesy of Dr. J. T. Bonner, Princeton University)

REMORAS Family Echeneidae Elongate marine fishes which are most often seen attached to sharks by means of a laminated disk located on top of the remora's head. Remoras are not parasitic but secure themselves to large predators to share scraps of food. Although some remoras can be swift swimmers, it is believed that they cannot travel long distances. They also select turtles, rays, barracudas, and billfishes as hosts.

THE LIVING FISH HOOK

Among the many weird and wonderful tales carried back to Europe from the New World was the story of how the Arawak Indians of southern Cuba used suckerfish as "living fish hooks." Peter Martyr wrote the first published account of this incredible method of catching large sea turtles, manatees, and sharks, and Martyr is believed to have received his information directly from Columbus. According to Martyr, the Arawaks kept a supply of live suckerfish, which they called *guaicanum*, in shallow-water pens. Upon seeing turtles near shore, they would release a suckerfish with a line tied to its tail. The fish would clamp itself to a turtle so tightly that the fishermen, by pulling the line, were able to draw the turtle to shore or to a boat.

Martyr's first mention of the suckerfish (which he called "Reversus" or upsidedown fish) was published in 1504. Some years later, when he wrote further about the "hunting fishes," he complained that he had been strongly ridiculed in Rome for insisting that the story was true. The people of sixteenth-century Europe, it seems, were willing to accept the reports about the land of the Amazonian women and the races of one-eyed people, but the tale of the suckerfish was just too much to swallow. Admittedly, Martyr's full account of the Reversus did indeed have overtones of fable, and as a result most naturalists for hundreds of years considered it highly improbable.

REMORAS IN HISTORY

Scientists and other educated people of the Mediterranean had long known of the existence of the remoras, or suckerfishes, but most of the literature on the subject was even more farfetched than Martyr's account. The ancient Greeks and Romans had written widely about remoras and had ascribed to them all kinds of magical powers. One belief was that handling a remora in a certain way could cause an abortion. (Even today in Madagascar shamans are said to attach portions of remoras' suction disks to the necks of wives to assure faithfulness in their husbands' absence.)

The ancient Romans were greatly impressed by the power of the remora's suction disk and attributed the death of the Emperor Caligula to remoras, which were believed to have fastened onto his ship and held it back, allowing enemy ships to overtake it. Mark Antony's defeat at Actium was also reportedly caused by suckerfish holding back his galley. The Greek name for the suckerfish, *Echeneis*, came from two words meaning "to hold back" and "ship," and the Latin name *Remora* means "holding back."

In the Eighteenth and Nineteenth centuries quite a number of reputable observers brought back stories of natives in many remote areas using suckerfishes in the same way that Martyr described. Reports came from Zanzibar, India, Malaya, Japan, the South Pacific, South America, and other places. (The fact that the method was apparently so well-known in widely separated primitive cultures is almost as incredible as the fact that the method works.)

WIDESPREAD FISHING METHOD

Dr. E. W. Gudger, in a comprehensive paper published in 1919 on the use of remoras in fishing, wrote that a Lady Annie Brassey saw Indians fish with remoras off Venezuela as late as 1885. And in 1898 Professor A.C. Haddon, leader of a Cambridge University expedition to the Torres Straits, saw Australian aborigines catch turtles with remoras, and he later wrote a lengthy report on it. In a book published in 1904, Frank T. Bullen told of seeing the same thing off China.

Presumably Australian aborigines still employ the method. Using the large sharksucker *Echeneis naucrates*, they pierce the base of the tail and run a cord through the hole. (In some other areas a ring is fastened around the base of the tail, and a line is tied to the ring.) When setting out to catch a turtle, they pass a second line through the fish's gills and mouth, then sling the fish over the side of their boat. This line keeps the fish's head into the current, allowing normal respiration, and also keeps it from fastening its disk to the bottom of the boat. (In some areas fishermen permit the remoras to cling to the hull, and a bamboo pole is used to dislodge them when their services are required.)

When a turtle is sighted, the fishermen pull the line from the fish's mouth and heave the fish in the direction of the turtle. When the suckerfish takes hold, the men keep a tight line and "play" the turtle carefully until it has been drawn to the boat or has settled down on the bottom. In the latter case a diver follows the line down and ties a heavier line to a flipper.

Just as it is considered best practice in rod-and-reel angling, no attempt is made to lift the catch aboard by the fishing line itself. In the struggle at boatside, the remora might dislodge itself; and even if it held fast, the turtle's dead weight might pull the fish apart. So heavy ropes or gaffs are used to boat the turtle.

THE SECRET OF ITS TENACITY

The holding disk of suckerfishes is located atop the head and is composed of numerous transverse ridges or flanges which, when raised slightly, create a partial vacuum. The fish can raise or lower the flanges at will. A backward pull on the fish's tail increases the suction by further raising the ridges—the harder the pull, the greater the adhesive force. A number of tiny spines project tailward from the ridges, giving additional insurance against the disk's sliding backwards. Presumably, once it has attached itself to an animal, the suckerfish can relax its muscles completely, and, no matter how fast its host swims, it will not be thrown off. The pressure of water flowing over its body constitutes a backward pull that increases the suction as the speed is increased. (This is definitely indicated by the fact that a dead remora is as hard to remove from a smooth object as a live remora, as long as the pull is from the rear.)

Apparently, then, if a tethered remora latches onto an animal and a tight line is maintained, the suckerfish cannot release its grip even if it tries. In theory, the maximum size of a prey that can be landed is limited only by the skill of the fisherman, the breaking strength of the line, and the breaking strength of the remora's body.

In tests made at the New York Aquarium a bucket of water weighing 24½ pounds was lifted into the air by a line attached to the tail of a 26½-inch sharksucker (*Echeneis naucrates*), which had attached itself to the bucket. A 40-pound sailfish can be lifted almost off the deck of a boat with a 4-inch specimen of *Remora osteochir* and might lift it all the way if the suction disk doesn't tear loose from the remora. A similar experiment, with identical results, can be performed with a dead remora of the same size.

Suckerfish can be easily dislodged from any surface by pushing the head forward (which lowers the flanges of the disk) or pinching the disk, which permits air or water to enter and equalize the pressure.

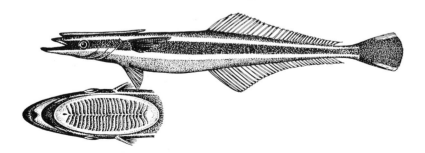

Remoras (showing shark sucker on top of head)

ECHENEIS IS NOT CHOOSY

There are several genera and about a dozen species of remoras. The most common seems to be *Echeneis naucrates*, the sharksucker, which grows to be 3–4 feet long. *E. naucrates* is not choosy about whom or what it takes up with and can be found attached to sharks, whales, jewfish, rays, boats, floating timbers, or other objects. A large shark may carry a half-dozen or more individuals of *Echeneis*. These sharksuckers are occasionally seen swimming free, and nothing gives a skin diver such a start as to see a large *Echeneis* appear from the opaque depths and circle the diver's body, seemingly sizing him up. It's not the *presence* of the fish that's so disturbing—it's the inevitable worry about where it just came from.

Echeneis has a rounded tail and is not a rapid swimmer. Its body is usually grayish-brown or greenish-blue, and it has a black band edged with white stripes down the side. Its belly is white. *Echeneis* has the ability to reverse its coloration when it flops onto its back, as when fastening onto the upper surface of a shark or turtle, and in that position it strongly resembles a right-side-up fish with its suction disk located beneath its chin. Its ability to reverse its coloration is probably responsible for the name "Reversus."

THEY HAVE THEIR PREFERENCES

Suckerfishes of the genus *Remora* are rather uniformly brown or gray. These fishes seldom exceed 15–18 inches in length and are generally much smaller. They have forked tails, are faster swimmers than *Echeneis*, and are often found on speedy oceanic fishes. Some suckerfishes —*Remora osteochir*, for example—are generally found in pairs. Dr. C. Richard Robins of the Institute of Marine Science, University of Miami, has noted that specimens found by him on blue marlin are usually larger than those found on white marlin, and these in turn are larger than those found on sailfish. The reason for this apparent disparity in size is unknown.

Some suckerfishes appear to be always found on the same kinds of fish. *Remora osteochir* commonly enters billfish gill chambers, but Gudger reports that it has also been found in the gill chambers of sharks, ocean sunfish, and barracuda. One fairly rare species, *Phtheirichthys lineatus*, is said to be found only on barracudas.

It is interesting to speculate on how the suction disk of the suckerfishes developed. The disk is a modification of the dorsal fin. During untold millions of generations the spines of the fin divided and flattened out and became an oval plate with movable parts that operate like the slats of Venetian blinds. During its period of development the plate moved forward on the body until it became located on the top surface of the head.

As evidence of how long the disk may have taken to evolve, a fossil suckerfish from the Tertiary period (about 60,000,000 years ago) had a suction disk almost exactly like that of *Echeneis* of today. Another fossil fish, however, had a narrower, imperfectly formed disk located farther back on the body. This fish had larger gill plates and a forked tail and in some ways resembled the pilotfish (*Naucrates ductor*), the striped jack that swims with sharks and is often confused with the suckerfishes. The suggestion has been made that the ancestors of suckerfishes were similar in habit to the pilotfish before they developed their hitchhiking technique. (Interestingly, the pilotfish also seems to have developed a different hitchhiking technique—riding the pressure waves pushed forward by sharks' movements through the water.)

Strictly speaking, suckerfishes are not parasites, but commensals. They do not harm their "hosts." They're just along for the ride. (It has been suggested, in fact, that remoras occasionally pick parasites from their hosts.) When their hosts feed, they dart about and gather up the scraps. Occasionally they swim away to catch small fish on their own.

It is widely believed that sharks tolerate their clinging companions and never harm them. According to Norman and Fraser, no remoras have been found in the stomachs of sharks. But whether the sharks actually tolerate them or just can't catch them hasn't been definitely established. Generally, suckerfish stay in spots where the sharks can't reach them. But even these spots don't always seem very "safe." The late Captain W. E. Young, who caught sharks commercially for a half-century, stated that he had often found small remoras inside sharks' mouths, clinging to the roof. Presumably they got there by going through the gill slits.

Practically nothing is known about the breeding habits or larval development of suckerfishes. Specimens as small as an inch in length have been noted to resemble adults in all characteristics except size. The late Dr. Å. Vedel Tåning of Denmark examined several smaller specimens that showed postlarval development, but just how and where spawning takes place is unknown.

Suckerfishes are not generally held in high esteem as food, although the Australian aborigines are said to eat their remoras after using them on fishing trips. Which only goes to show that the Australians are more practical than were the aborigines of the West Indies, who, according to Martyr, never ate their "hunting fishes" but sang songs of praise and reverence to them.   —W.M.S.

REX SOLE *Glyptocephalus zachirus* A member of the righteye flounders, Pleuronectidae, this has a close relative on the Atlantic Coast. The long pectoral fin on the eyed side and the thin, slender, and tapering body help to distinguish it from its relatives. The mouth is small, the eyes are relatively large, and the straight lateral line lacks a dorsal branch. The color is uniformly light brown on the eyed side, and is white to dusky on the blind side.

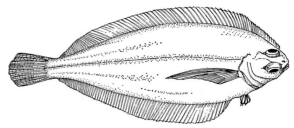

Rex Sole

Reaching a length of 20 inches, it occurs from southern California to the Bering Sea. Although a few are taken in relatively shallow water, they generally are taken in trawls at 60–800 feet, the greatest depth (in Alaska) being about 2,100 feet.

FOOD VALUE

Although comprising only a small percentage of the commercial catch, the flesh of this superior table fish is exceedingly delicate.   —D.dS.

RHEAD, LOUIS American (1857–1926) This great contemporary of Theodore Gordon was a successful commercial artist who turned tackle dealer in order to devote his talent full time to what had originally been his avocation, the design of lures in imitation of natural-bait fish. In the process he only very narrowly missed, by one basic error of judgment, the hagiographic stature of being enshrined today as the American Ronalds and the father of our angling entomology. Alfred Ronalds gave angling a new scientific dimension when he published *The Fly-Fisher's Entomology* (1836). Rhead's aim, at the outset, was unerring, and it has been best appreciated to date by the Boston fly-tier and angling historian Austin Hogan: "By going directly to the minnow Rhead took the old non-imitative streamers and reshaped them to what he looked upon as imitative smelts and shiners. His bugs were copied from the crawling things on the bottom, and his terrestrials actually looked like crickets, grasshoppers and beetles."

But the artist's eye and perception that led Rhead to this impressionistic approach was also linked with the artistic temperament that made him impatient with the tedium of scientific discipline involved in conforming to the accepted and established Latin terminological pattern of entomology. His approach to the nomenclature of his insect patterns was also impressionistic, Rhead contenting himself either with following the colloquial folk designations, or bestowing fanciful names such as Brown buzz, Longhorn, and Pinktail, instead of the more exact and readily identifiable traditional and scientific names of flies.

The result is that Rhead's remarkably original work, perceptive almost to the point of divination and augury, was too generally shrugged off as the amateurish fancy of a dilettante or dismissed as a sales gimmick for specific flies of his own creation; and from 1916, when he brought out the first American book on insects of the stream, *American Trout Stream Insects, A Guide to Angling Flies and Other Aquatic Insects Alluring to Trout*, until his death a decade later Rhead's pioneering work received insufficient recognition.

It had to wait until 1935, with the publication of *A Book of Trout Flies* by Preston Jennings, before American fly fishermen felt that a step had at last been taken on that proper track that had been laid out for the English a century before by Ronalds.

The irony is that while Preston Jennings has been accorded the honor he deserved, even though posthumously, with revival of his influence through reprinting of his book after more than three decades, Rhead still awaits his due.

As Hogan points out: "In retrospect it seems strange to find that the finger pointed by Louis Rhead, the off-beat designer of curious imitations, was the finger of a prophet. Nymph, streamer and bucktail have kicked the old-fashioned wet fly into the curio cabinet. And the dry fly, so ably presented by the gentle Theodore Gordon, and so full of promise, has become just a status symbol."

Rhead's other work, both as editor and author, is representative of its time, but of no extraordinary pertinence today. It is his one blinding flash of revelation, *American Trout Stream Insects* (1916), that has so unfortunately become the light that failed and that should ultimately illumine his name far into the future. —A.G.

RHODE ISLAND Although Rhode Island is the smallest (1,497 square miles) and most densely populated state in the United States, it offers some excellent fishing opportunities. With 400 miles of the state's shoreline twisting around into bays and estuaries, the angler has access to a wide variety of salt- and brackish-water species. Numerous harbors provide jumpoff points for unexcelled surf-, big-game, and bottom-fishing. Several freshwater lakes and ponds provide better than average largemouth and smallmouth bass angling, and most waters abound in panfish, including white and yellow perch, sunfish, bluegills, and bullheads. Only a few streams maintain a year-round and carryover trout population; however, more than sixty streams and ponds receive an annual stocking of brown, brook, and rainbow trout on a put-and-take basis to provide anglers some opportunity.

STRIPED-BASS FISHING

The striped bass, the glamor fish of the surfcaster, appears in great schools around the first of May, although a few winter over in inland salt ponds and estuaries. School fish range in size from below the 16-inch legal size to 5–7 pounders. Once the migration is underway, bass can be taken just about anywhere in Rhode Island and on a variety of artificial lures, baits, and tackle. Some of the favorite hot spots include Weekapaug Breachway, Quononchontaug Breachway, Charlestown Breachway, Matunuck Bar, Warwick Light, Sapowet Point, Sakonnet Point, and the entire Ocean Drive at Newport. After the school fish pass through or settle in the bays and estuaries, the larger stripers appear, ranging up to 50–60 pounds. These are not so easily taken, and require a great deal of fishing skill. In general, the trophy stripers are caught at night with eels and plugs from shore, but in recent years small boats working just outside the breaking surf have been more successful. Late summer is the slowest period for the striper fisherman, but commencing in September, schools begin to form and the fish go on a feeding orgy. Once again, the surf angler is in his glory, especially if he happens to be in the right spot when a school of stripers attacks a pod of baitfish. The striper schools continue to move until late November under favorable weather conditions.

BLUEFISH

Although considerably smaller, the bluefish rivals the striper as the favorite of many anglers. Migrations of bluefish to Rhode Island are not as dependable as the bass runs, but substantial numbers are usually present. Bluefish follow closely behind the stripers and visit most of the same areas previously listed. Greenwich Bay, an arm of Narragansett Bay, year in and year out is the most dependable area to troll for bluefish. These fish are savage feeders, and by the time they leave in November they have increased so much in size that it is hard to believe they are the same fish. As would be expected there is a wide choice of lures taken by this species, although feathered jigs are perennial favorites, with whole eels, eel skins, and plugs equally effective at times. Snapper blues, or the pint-sized juveniles, have the same characteristics as the adults, although not arriving until midsummer and rarely exceeding 6–8 inches in size. Fishing for them is popular from bridges and along banks wherever the tide runs swiftly. These little fish are so voracious that by migration time, in November, they will have doubled in size. It is easy to see how spectacular fishing on light tackle can be in a school of snappers.

BOTTOM-FISHING

Geographically, there is little variety in this state's fishing; yet, as would be expected among saltwater species, there is a great seasonal variation. Commencing in early March, the winter flounder can be taken by those hardy enough to stand the prevailing raw weather. Early fishing is generally from bridges and along the banks of deepwater channels; later, boat fishing in the bays and salt ponds is popular. Such places as Pettaquamscutt River and Salt Pond in Narragansett, Charlestown Pond, Brightman's Pond, and Quononchontaug Pond along the south shore provide opportunities for bridge, bank, and boat fishing. Upper Narragansett Bay does not offer the bridge and bank access, but good fishing is within rowing distance of numerous boat liveries. The winter flounder is a year-round fish with two peaks—the spring and the fall. The spring run continues through June, presumably after the fish leave their shallow-water spawning beds and head for deepwater, while the fall run commences in September and continues through November or until it's too cold to fish.

Although not as numerous nor as popular as the flounder, the white perch follows about the same pattern and seasonal migration, usually penetrating brackish water to a greater degree of freshness.

A little later in the spring, another native bottom feeder, the tautog or "blackfish," comes into the shallow water of upper Narragansett Bay to spawn. This fish, with its very powerful jaws, ranges up to 20 pounds, but averages about 3 pounds. It was formerly sought with heavy tackle, strong line, big hook and sinkers. In recent years the trend has been toward light tackle and monofilament line, with the resulting sport elevating the popularity of the tautog to a higher plane than ever enjoyed before. As the water warms and summer approaches, the tautog returns to the ocean shore where it is found along rocky outcroppings and pilings. It takes a variety of baits, including green crabs, clams, mussels, and worms. Most of the fishing in upper Narragansett Bay is from boats, but along the ocean front at Little Compton, Newport, Narragansett, and Weekapaug, giant rocks provide the ideal habitat for tautog, and a short cast reaching deepwater is generally productive.

Few fish have more followers than the summer flounder. Although a bottom feeder, it drives bait, hits hard, and fights enough to satisfy the most critical. Fancy tackle is not required, but the lighter the rod and line, the greater the thrill bringing one to gaff. "Doormats" of 8–10 pounds are not uncommon, but the usual run of inshore fishing runs 1–5 pounds. Almost any ocean-front area produces throughout the summer months, with the productive spots found where the tide runs strong. Small minnows are very effective, but cut baits also take fish.

Another bottom feeder without the glamor of the more publicized species is the scup. Arriving in May, it spends the summer along the ocean shore and in deeper inshore waters, such as Narragansett Bay and Sakonnet River. Ranging ½–3 pounds, it is not a critical feeder and will take worms, clams, shrimp, squid, and any other live bait. The angler can usually depend on this species when luck fails on all the others.

Coming into the picture when other fish are leaving, cod and pollock provide the cold-weather angler with plenty of sport during the winter months. Neither species penetrates the bays or breachways, but is found along the entire outer shore, favoring rocky ledges, wrecks, and shoals. Both species move inshore as the water cools, yet can be taken year round at offshore hot spots. The pollock, although generally a bottom feeder, will come to the surface for feathers, jigs, and other artificials during the inshore migration periods. The cod, however, is exclusively a bottom feeder, and a favorite of the party boats. It weighs up to 50 pounds, although 3–20-pound fish are taken most frequently. Hot spots reached from Watch Hill, Point Judith, Newport, or Block Island are Shark Ledge, Brown Ledge, and Coxes' Ledge all within reasonable cruising distance. Block Island, a fairly small island 12 miles off the southern coast, for years has been acclaimed the cod capital of the state, and as a matter of fact could lay similar claim to about any other species one cared to mention. Several light-tackle records have been made for striped bass in its adjoining waters.

Other inshore bottom species of lesser importance in Rhode Island include the mackerel, a universal favorite with light-tackle addicts; the northern kingfish, which puts in a regular summer appearance; the tomcod, a year-round resident, though seldom taken except in cold weather; and the sea bass, a bottom fish believed by many to be the best eating fish of the sea.

BIG-GAME FISHING

The selection of Galilee at Point Judith as the site of the annual United States Atlantic Tuna Tournament and the presence of more than one hundred sport-fishing boats fishing for big-game fish are the best testimonial to the abundance of giant bluefin tuna in the waters of Rhode Island. This state has produced among the largest tuna taken on rod and reel, including a 962 pounder boated within 2 miles of the Matunuck shore, and during one tournament 34 giant tuna were caught in 3 days of fishing, totalling 17,854 pounds. Twenty of these fish exceeded 500 pounds, and one reached 758 pounds. These giants, of course, require special equipment; however, a number of charter boats are equipped and specialize in this type of big-game fishing. School tuna arrive in early summer, a month or so prior to the giants, and remain until late fall, usually November. They range 20–100 pounds, and are usually taken by trolling offshore in the vicinity of Block Island.

The same waters that produce the tuna are also productive of marlin, swordfish, and bonito. The white marlin has become a very popular trophy fish. In these waters it ranges up to 100 pounds, although most catches are around 70 pounds. The blue marlin is quite rare, but swordfish are very plentiful, and there is a considerable number landed in several ports for the commercial trade; these fish are harpooned. To hook and boat one of these giants on rod and reel is no small chore; yet several are caught each year by this method. The same rig used for giant tuna is also employed for the swordfish, and several charter-boat skippers specialize in fishing for both species.

FRESHWATER FISHING

With such a wealth of saltwater species, it would seem that the freshwater angler would be out of the picture. This is not the case, for there are many who prefer the peace and quiet of a cool-running stream or calm lake to the spray of the surf or chopping and bouncing in a boat. The Wood River is one of the few streams that carries over trout from year to year. Several streams make up the watershed, including Falls River, Breakheart Brook, Flat River, Paris Brook, and Roaring Brook most of which flow through Arcadia State Reservation, therefore, presenting no trespass problems, and as a matter of fact, access and parking sites have been provided as part of the state's management plan. Although three species of trout can be found, Wood River is noted for its oversize browns, some going up to 5 pounds. Trout fishing in Rhode Island runs from mid April until the last day in October.

Two large border ponds, Beach Pond, half in Connecticut, and Wallum Lake, half in Massachusetts, have been reclaimed for trout, and in Stafford's Pond, Tiverton, a good trout population has successfully been superimposed on an excellent smallmouth population. All three ponds exceed three hundred acres in area and afford boat as well as bank fishing.

The largemouth bass can be taken from mid April until late February. Along with the pickerel it is a favorite through the ice. Worden Pond, which is about 1,000 acres, is generally considered the best bass pond in the state; however, this is disputed by many. Other large waters rivaling Worden in popularity as well as production are Watchaug, Bowdish, and Johnson's. Warwick Pond and Brickyard Pond are smaller, yet have produced a good many 8-pound largemouths over the years.

Only a few waters of a hundred acres or more have retained good smallmouth-bass populations. The most outstanding is the aforementioned Stafford Pond, with Indian Lake or Herring Pond running a poor second. Unfortunately, many smallmouth-bass waters were ruined when the largemouth was introduced. —T.J.W.

RHODESIA *See* South Africa

RIBBONFISH *See* Drums

RIFFLE A shallow extending across the bed of a river; a small rapid.

RIVER CARPSUCKER *See* Quillback

ROACH *Rutilus rutilus* The roach is sought by more European anglers than any other fish. This is not due to its intrinsic sporting value, but because it is extremely common and its capture requires some skill. Wherever they occur, roach exist in numbers, and they invade almost every type of water successfully. In rivers, they are found from the source right down to brackish water. Canals hold very large stocks, and roach are equally at home in lakes or ponds. They are even known to establish populations in small, industrial water-storage tanks. The only criterion appears to be that the water should be permanent and not liable to dry up completely.

Roach are abundant throughout Europe north of the Alps and Pyrenees. They are not recorded from north Scotland, but may in fact be present. Ireland was roachless until fairly recently, but a population is now established in the River Blackwater, County Cork. Their spread is feared by the Irish Fisheries Trust, who believes they would reach vermin proportions in nearby trout waters.

The roach is a typical cyprinid five times as long as it is broad; in old fish this ratio is somewhat lessened by lateral compression and the development of a humped back. The flanks and belly are bright silver-white, the back blue-green or gray. The pelvic and anal fins are bright red or orange, the others gray, though often with pinkish tints. The iris of the eye is red, the tail deeply forked. The mouth is terminal or subinferior.

Roach

Roach are often confused with the rudd, *Scardinius erythrophthalmus* which is indeed very similar. The following distinguishing characters should be noted:

1. Mouth of rudd *always* terminal.

2. Iris of rudd eye yellow rather than red.

3. All rudd fins are bright red-orange, not just the pelvic and anal as is typical in roach.

4. Brassy tinge frequent in the back and flank scales of rudd; this is rarely seen in roach, except those which live in lakes or which are of advanced age.

5. Rudd are rarely found in fast-flowing water, whereas roach are.

6. Rudd are normally surface or midwater feeders; roach more typically stay nearer the bottom.

7. The leading edge of the roach's dorsal fin is vertically over the base of the pelvic fins; the rudd dorsal fin is 3–5 scale rows behind (posterior to) this position.

8. The scales between the pelvic and anal fins in the rudd are sharply keeled; in the roach the keel is barely discernible or, more usually, absent.

Confusion with rudd is likely in fish caught from lakes; from running water, roach have been confused with dace or chub. The differences here are more obvious—the chub has prominent white lips; the dace lacks any trace of red in any of its fins.

Roach present another problem in identification by hybridizing readily with other species, especially the rudd and bream. These hybrids are sterile F_1 (first) generation "mules," displaying characters intermediate between their two parents. Hybrids grow larger than true roach for three reasons—they inherit the other parent's superior size; there is probably some hybrid vigor; and they do not have to waste protein laying down spawn. Fertile hybrids are known, but they are so rare they can be discounted. Much importance is attached to verifying that specimens for competitions are indeed true roach, as the larger size of hybrids otherwise gives them an advantage. Where examination of the fish is not enough, the absence of spawning marks on the scales of hybrids is normally used.

Roach grow to 4 pounds in England and 5 pounds or more in Holland. Anything over 2 pounds is an excellent fish, usually only caught consistently by real experts. The general run of fish taken by anglers is perhaps ½–1 pound and generally smaller.

LIFE HISTORY

Roach spawn from April to July in dense weed beds. The males assume a breeding dress of spotty white tubercles on the anterior part of the body. The spawning act is easy to observe, as it is gregarious and splashy. Females produce 110,000 or more minute eggs per pound body weight; the eggs are sticky and adhere in masses to plant stems. Such small eggs contain little yolk; so the fry hatch quickly and adhere to water plants for several days.

The summer following the hatch, the young congregate in shoals in the shallows near where they were spawned, feeding upon zooplankton and algae. When winter comes, they emulate the older fish and retire to deeper water.

Throughout life roach tend to feed on foods similar to those of the first year. A typical analysis of a roach's stomach contents reveals 78 percent by volume of algae (especially diatoms), 10 percent vegetable matter, and 12 percent mollusks, insects, and small crustaceans. In some waters the proportion of animal food has been 20 percent; this is especially true in summer, when small animals are more abundant, and for fish over 10 inches long.

Observations by the University of Reading (England) on roach in the River Thames show changes in animal diet with size; larger roach take more mollusks, smaller roach more crustaceans. They also calculate an average density in some parts of the Thames of one roach per square meter—only counting the larger fish.

Roach attain their maximum growth rate in reservoirs and lakes (where the large ones rarely come close inshore) or in moderately fast, clear rivers such as the Scottish Tweed. Gravel bottoms and beds of light green weed are preferred in either of these optimum environments. In more turbid waters the growth rate is slower, the average size less, but their numbers are much greater. Trophy roach have been taken from ponds, canals, and very shallow lakes.

Clearly the growth rate varies widely from place to place. From an optimum water, a 2-pound roach would be 10–15 years old, whereas in turbid reaches of the Thames, 10-year-old fish are only 8 inches long. These represent extremes between which the expected growth rate will vary from one population and ecosystem to another. The life expectancy is over 20 years.

The cause of such wide variations in growth rates is still a matter of suggestion and dispute, especially as the ecology of larger roach has not been properly investigated, whereas that of stunted ones has. If one can argue from negative evidence, the optimal conditions appear to be where the bottom is clean and higher plants can photosynthesize. These in turn hide crustaceans; and it is noteworthy that crustaceans and other animal foods are the preferred diet of large fish. Under optimum conditions, the growth of attached and epiphytic algae (as distinct from planktonic ones) is also enhanced. Both these foods in abundance provide good growth among roach.

Roach are a major forage fish in most waters. They are a natural intermediary in food webs at all stages—roach fry are eaten by many predacious insects (dragonfly nymphs and larvae of the *Dytiscus* beetle). Adult roach provide forage for northern pike. Against such perpetual pressure, the individual roach's chances of survival are slight, but this is more than compensated for by overbreeding. So prolific are most roach that the numbers of individuals are not greatly affected by quite intense predation. Most attempts to improve the average size of roach by introducing pike into the ecosystem have not had the desired effect at all. Netting and wholesale removal have been much more effective, for short periods at least.

Roach are shoal fish throughout their lives, forming typical compact and orderly schools—the members all of similar size. There appears little segregation or order, except that the smaller fish tend to be to the front and above the main body of larger fish. They intercept particles falling from the surface or drifting down with the current, "filtering" them out, while the main body of the shoal takes its food from the bottom. The whole shoal patrols a territory and shows distinct homing patterns.

Feeding occurs at any temperature between 32°F. and 70°F., but they are often shy of strong light. Most notable roach catches have been on dull days, at dusk, or at night.

ANGLING VALUE

Roach are the main quarry of most European working anglers, particularly in England. Very often roach are the only worth-while fish in canals in the center of industrial cities. As roach occur practically everywhere, it is not surprising that anglers practice traditional regional styles of fishing for them, based on meeting local conditions. Common to them all is light tackle, usually with a float, for the roach is a delicate biter. Baits are usually bread or maggots, less frequently worms.

The major differences in local styles are revealed in the rod. The general English style uses a long rod (up to 16 feet), very light, with most of the action in the top three feet. This is to strike delicate bites; such a rod is poor at playing fish. Roach fishing in faster rivers, such as the English Trent, has evolved a stouter and shorter rod, with more action in the midsection. More common in Continental Europe, and still a traditional and very skillful method in the London area, is the roach pole. This is a very long rod, up to 25 feet, of light cane without rings or a running line; this is attached to the tip only.

In recent years experiment has led to some merging of these styles, but no one method is universal. Apart from the traditional methods, roach are caught on wet flies and nymphs, and in Holland very light spinning lures have been used with success. Presumably the largest roach include small fish in their diet—whatever the explanation, roach up to five pounds have been taken from large inland waters such as the Dutch Ijsselmeer.

Roach are the main quarry in large, organized fishing contests, where a premium is put on "snatching" large numbers of fish from allocated swims. Most traditional roach tackles are admirably suited for this, which tends to keep them in use.

Roach fishing is static, the shoals being attracted into a swim by means of meal-based "cloud" groundbaits. In less conventional methods, and in waters where conditions are optimal, roving in search of fish seems more profitable.

Besides being sporty in their own right, roach are extensively used as baitfish in fishing for pike. They are mounted on spinning flights or else used live on liphooks and snap tackles.

ECONOMIC VALUE

More money is spent in England on conserving or shifting roach stocks than on any other species except trout and salmon. Certainly more is spent on licenses and tackle to fish for roach than even on the gamefish. Small roach bite freely and more boldly, so there is incentive for whole families to become roach fishers; volume sales are a feature of roach-tackle selling. Bait companies do considerable business in roach baits, especially maggots.

Conservation for sport is widely practiced, and minimum size limits are laid down universally. Unfortunately, conservation may be widespread but not always intelligent or informed. Many introductions are mere shiftings, often of unsuitable and stunted stock. In consequence many roach populations are uniformly composed of small fish, protected not infrequently by unrealistic legal minimum size limits. The University of Reading's example may be referred to again; roach from the river Thames of the legal minimum size limit (8 inches) proved to be 10 years old. Although other reaches and other waters show better rates of growth, the cumulative effects of such policies have not improved the fishery.

Fortunately more enlightened conservation and stocking methods are coming into favor now.

As a food fish it is little sought because the flesh is bland and bony. In northern Germany it is taken in traps and seines to be eaten, but in southern Germany it is little regarded. It is not normally commercially bred in hatcheries. —D.M.

ROANOKE BASS *Ambloplites cavifrons* A freshwater panfish which closely resembles the rock bass. It differs in having a concave cranium profile, whereas the profile of the rock bass is straight or slightly convex in older fish. The cheeks of the Roanoke bass are scaleless or have only a few deeply imbedded scales, as compared to the completely scaled cheeks of the rock bass. There are 3 spines in the anal fin, whereas the rock bass has 6.

First described from the Roanoke River in Virginia and presumed to be confined to that drainage, it remained unrecognized in the Tar and Neuse River watersheds of North Carolina until 1963. It is a fish of moderately large streams with a hard substrate, usually rock or gravel. It feeds principally on fish and crayfish. The Roanoke bass attains a larger size than the rock bass, with 1-pound fish not uncommon, and has reportedly been taken in excess of 4 pounds. —A.J.McC.

ROBALO The Spanish name for snook (*which see*)

ROBIN A regional name in the southern United States for the redbreast sunfish (*which see*).

ROCK BASS *Ambloplites rupestris* This robust sunfish is aptly named. The more stone rubble and large stones in an area, the more likely one will find a good concentration of these fish. The Latin species name literally means "of the rocks." Regionally, it is sometimes called black perch, goggle-eye, red-eye, and rock sunfish. There is at least one subspecies in the southern United States.

The rock bass is a rugged-appearing sunfish of dark olive coloration. The sides are mottled with brownish and brassy blotches. The scales have a basal spot forming in-

terrupted lateral streaks. The eye is red, the mouth extends beyond the eye, and the dark blotch on the gill flap is typically margined with white or gold. There are 6 spines in the anal fin and 11–12 in the dorsal fin.

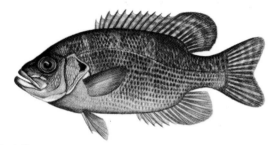

Rock Bass

The rock bass is distributed from Vermont to lower Lake Winnipeg in Manitoba and south to the Gulf states. It has been widely introduced into other states.

LIFE HISTORY

The spawning habits are similar to other sunfishes which nest in shallow excavations on gravelly or sandy bottoms. Spawning starts when water temperatures reach 60°–70°F. The females will lay an average of 5,000 eggs, but as many as 9,000 have been counted. The nest is vigorously guarded by the male. The young grow to 1½–2 inches the first summer. It usually takes 5–7 years to reach 8–9 inches.

The adults move about in schools, and are commonly found in association with smallmouth bass. In the East they are one of the most common fish in the large bass rivers and often occur in Southern trout streams.

ANGLING VALUE

The rock bass will take a variety of artificial and natural baits. On summer evenings, a small popping bug will be greedily grabbed from the surface with a characteristic sucking sound. It is vigorous when first hooked but quickly tires and can be easily reeled in. Although it occasionally reaches 10 to 12 inches and weighs 1 pound, the usual catch is 6–9 inches weighing ½ pound. —K.B.

ROCKCOD *See* Rockfish
ROCKET TAPER LINE *See* Weight Forward Line
ROCKFISH Scorpaenidae A large family of marine fishes of wide distribution in tropical, temperate, and boreal waters, it contains about 250 species, many of great sport and food value. They have firm, white, tasty flesh. Most of the North American commercial catch is filleted for the fresh-fish trade. They are usually abundant where found, and are easily taken by means of cut or whole bait, or jigs. The Pacific species are often called "rockcods," but have no close relationship with the true cod.

The Eastern Pacific members of the family Scorpaenidae are described in *Fishes of the Pacific Coast of Canada* by W. A. Clemens and G. V. Wilby.

The body is stout anteriorly, perchlike; head large, often with spines and ridges; scales ctenoid, large; a single dorsal fin with 13–15 spines and 9–16 rays; anal with 3 spines and 5–9 rays; thoracic pelvics with 1 spine and 5 rays. Many are so much alike that the species are extremely difficult to determine.

HABITS

They are carnivorous. Most are viviparous (all species of *Sebastodes* have internal fertilization of the eggs), and the young are born at about 2 millimeters. Often strongly delimited in ecologic niche, they are nonmigratory, and are found usually over rocky bottom or among algae in shallow water, to depths of 5,000 feet.

In 1960 the Pacific Coast landings in the United States including Alaska were 27,286,000 pounds.

See also Black-and-Yellow Rockfish, Black Rockfish, Blue Rockfish, Bocaccio, Canary Rockfish, Chilipepper, China Rockfish, Copper Rockfish, Flag Rockfish, Greenstriped Rockfish, Quillback Rockfish, Rasphead Rockfish, Rosy Rockfish, Shortspine Channel Rockfish, Tiger Rockfish, Vermillion Rockfish, Yellowtail Rockfish

ROCKHIND *Epinephelus adscensionis* Although frequently taken in southern Florida, this species is more abundant in the Bahamas and throughout the Caribbean area. It is a relatively small grouper, reaching a length of usually less than 30 inches.

The rock hind has 11 dorsal spines; 16–17, usually 17 dorsal rays; 8 anal rays, and usually 19 pectoral rays. Posterior nostril about equal to the anterior. Insertion of pelvic fin behind lower end of pectoral base. Posterior margin of caudal fin convex. Head, body, and fins with dark red spots which are larger on ventral area. Three dark blotches along base of dorsal fin. A saddlelike black blotch on top of caudal peduncle.

ANGLING VALUE

This species is found on rocky bottom in relatively shallow water. It is frequently taken around coral heads in water only a few feet deep, although it may occur in much deeper water. The rock hind takes live or dead bait and artificial lures. It is good eating and a grouper of commercial importance throughout the tropical American Atlantic. —L.R.

ROCK LOBSTER A market name for one of the species of spiny lobster (*which see*) of South Africa and Australia, *Jasus lalandi* Only the tail portion of the spiny lobster is utilized, as this contains most of the edible meat. Spiny lobsters do not have claws.

ROCK SOLE *Lepidopsetta bilineata* Belonging to the flounders with a short, accessory branch to the lateral line, this righteyed flounder is readily identified by the added presence of a high arch over the pectoral fin. The

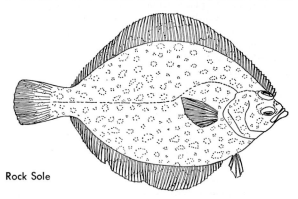

Rock Sole

deeply oval body is dark brown, mottled with dark markings, sometimes with red spots or pale blotches. The fins are marked with dark, broken lines. It grows to 20 inches and 5 pounds. Found from southern California to the Bering Sea, it is also taken south to Japan. Along the American Pacific Coast, it is most abundant in the central California region. A fairly common species in the cooler waters, it occurs from depths of about 400 feet to shallow waters of a few feet deep over sand and gravel bottom. Spawning occurs from late winter to early spring. Crabs, worms, clams, and shrimps are eaten.

ANGLING VALUE

Although the flesh is good, the species is of minor angling importance. Rock sole are only occasionally taken by hook and line. —D.dS.

ROCKY MOUNTAIN WHITEFISH *See* Mountain Whitefish

Rock Hind, 3-pound Male, Reef Near Whale Bay, Bermuda

ROD A tube or shaft, mounted with guides, hand grasp, reel seat, and ferrules, which is used to cast, troll, or otherwise present a bait or lure to the fish. A rod may consist of one or more connecting sections although the number seldom exceeds three; its total length depends on a variety of special conditions, but the general range is 4–12 feet. Although a rod is progressively tapered from the butt end to the tip end its cross section is usually round or hexagonal (six-strip). However, a limited number of rods are made in square, pentagonal, and octagonal forms also. *See* Rod Building, Rod Repairs, Bait-Casting, Fly-Casting, Fly-Fishing, Fly Rod, Spinning, Spin-Casting, Surf-Fishing, Ultralight Spinning

ROD BELT Used only in salt-water fishing, this is a sturdy leather belt that fastens around the angler's waist and has a cup to hold the butt of the rod. By offering a resting place for the rod butt it takes some of the strain from the angler's arms and also helps to keep him from bruising himself with a flailing rod butt. Unlike the various harnesses used in big-game fishing, however, the rod belt is not fastened to the reel. The rod belt is used by surf casters because of the size of rod involved and the size of fish sometimes caught. The preferred type of rod belt has a wide triangular leather backing that tapers to a cup. *See also* Big-Game Fishing, Surf Casting

ROD BUILDING The art of constructing fishing rods. Since 1948 rod building has undergone a complete change, with impregnated glass fibers largely replacing the use of bamboo as the basic material—just as bamboo once replaced various hardwoods such as hickory, bethabara, and lancewood. These woods were tough, strong, and resilient. But they were also heavy and would take a "set" in use. With the discovery of bamboo for rod building, British craftsmen imported canes from India (so-called Calcutta cane) as early as 1850. At first, the bamboo was split and used only as rod tips of three-strip and four-strip construction. However, the rod butts were still made from hardwoods. The six-strip rod as we know it today appeared at a later date. Our modern precision-fitted nickel ferrule was unknown, and the British angler of a century ago laboriously had to splice together the tapered ends of his rod sections with strong twine—often while a hatch of mayflies was bringing brown trout to the surface.

The ascendancy of fiberglass rods is due to the material's resiliency, freedom from "set" even under hardest use, and, perhaps above all, its adaptability to mass-production methods. Glass fibers are woven into cloth, cut to patterns, wrapped around finely calibrated steel templates to provide a desired taper and size, and are then treated with heat and pressure. A second method is to apply a floss of parallel glass fibers about a light-weight core such as balsa wood, subsequently impregnated with liquid resin, wrapped with a thin film of cellophane, and cured with heat. This is a process which cannot be duplicated by the amateur rod builder. Of course, fiberglass "banks" may be purchased and finished by mounting the appropriate hardware and reel seat, but rod building per se begins with the raw materials.

SPLIT-CANE-ROD CONSTRUCTION

Fine rods are still being made from bamboo by both amateurs and a comparatively few skilled professionals.

The cane rod is classical, traditional, and, from the standpoint of casting perfection, the experts' ideal. Bamboo is a giant species of grass which is imported in the form of canes of 6–8 feet in length and 1¼–2 inches in diameter. The best canes are straight, hard, and thick-walled. Bamboo is actually composed of multitudes of long, cellulose fibers, thinner than any hair, lying parallel beneath a dead, outer, enamel layer and bound tightly together by a substance called lignin. Progressing inwardly these fibers become coarser, and are separated by layers of pith which have no strength. Thus the sections which are to be shaped into rod splines are composed of the hard outer portion. The cane walls must be of sufficient thickness so that all of the pithy interior is removed during the shaping operation. It naturally follows then that a heavy rod, such as for saltwater use, must be started with the thickest walls available. Examination of the sawed end of a good culm will reveal the outer portion very dark, the fiber ends appearing as a homogeneous mass even under a lens of low magnification. But in large-caliber rods even the best bamboo will not provide a dense fiber to the core. This is compensated for by use of double-building or triple-building for added strength through the laminated construction. This is perhaps the most demanding of the rod builder's skills.

Raw culms are first split down the center with a heavy knife or motor-driven tool. Either method serves well, as the grain runs so straight that there will be little deviation from end to end to cause weakness. After halving, the inside, thin, solid partitions (where the leaf nodes occur) must be removed, either with a half-round chisel, or by other mechanical means. The finest canes will have nodes which are spaced 15–18 inches apart—and the exterior ridge of each should not rise much above the cane surface. While the leaf-node area may be the strongest part of the cane in its natural state it must be leveled down for rod building, and thus becomes the weakest portion because of the random local grain structure. To preserve the maximum strength of the glued-up rod section, these node areas must be staggered so that not more than one is found at any single point along the length of the rod. It follows that some trimming of length will be required. Usually an extra foot is allowed over the length of the finished rod. This is done while the strips are in the "as sawn" or "as split" condition.

Heat treatment is given the bamboo by many rod builders to stiffen the fibers. This may be done in the halved state, or preferably after splitting. The effect then is somewhat like that used by aborigines to harden arrow points by thrusting them into the hot coals of a fire for a few minutes. There is widely divergent opinion among expert craftsmen as to the degree of heat treatment to be used. The heat will stiffen it, but too much can also make the bamboo brittle. Commercial rod builders use various methods of heat tempering the bamboo; some use ovens for quantity production, others simply a blow-torch flame passed rapidly up and down a complete cane. Still others treat the roughed-out splines. A handy and sure method for the amateur builder will be described later.

In addition to heat tempering, some makers use an impregnating process to soak or force a liquid plastic resin into the bamboo. The function is to waterproof the rod, making it safe from mildew and to enhance its compressive strength. The Orvis Company of Manchester,

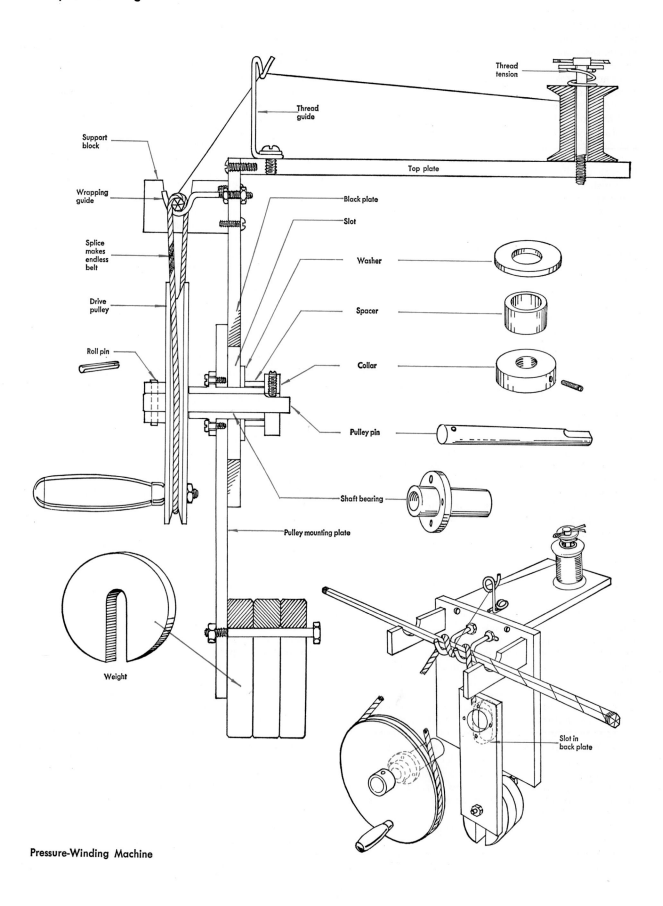

Thread tension

Thread guide

Top plate

Support block

Wrapping guide

Black plate

Slot

Splice makes endless belt

Washer

Spacer

Drive pulley

Collar

Roll pin

Pulley pin

Shaft bearing

Pulley mounting plate

Weight

Slot in back plate

Pressure-Winding Machine

Vermont, employs this system, and any angler who has used one of their fine tools will attest to their power and fine action. The impregnating process seems to render a fly rod almost impervious to setting. Neither heat treatment nor impregnation can make poor bamboo good, but either process will improve quality bamboo.

Every manufacturer has his own method of charting, or planning, his machine setup for a given rod. But he works to a tolerance of .001–.002 inch in taking micrometer calibrations at any point along the stick. Each, also, uses one of the modern resin adhesives for the most important item in rod manufacture—a solidly glued stick, showing no "glue line" at any seam and one which will withstand both heat and moisture.

The oldtime bamboo devotee will recall that nasty set in his favorite rod after a hot, humid day. Or that rod that actually came apart after having been left in a damp case or rod tube. Those were the days of hot animal glue and then, later, casein, neither of which could stand heat and dampness. Modern resins are a boon to the rod builder, easy to apply, and permanent.

Many firms have designed their own pressure-gluing machines. All employ the same principle of applying heavy pressure to the freshly glued sticks, at the same time winding a strong thread spirally to maintain pressure on the glue line until the adhesive has cured. Such a device will be described later for use of the amateur rod builder.

After curing of the glued stick, the wrapping string is removed and the surfaces scraped or lightly sanded to remove adhering glue and the thin outer enamel of the cane, only enough to expose the beautiful fine and straight grain of the bamboo.

Ferruling is usually done with the rod held in a lathe, only the necessary length for the ferrule projecting from the chuck. It is by this method alone that the true cylindrical surface required for a good fit can be achieved. Fitting ferrules, building and shaping of cork grip, addition of reel seat, and final wrapping of guides may be done with machine help, but the willing amateur can secure the same result by hand.

Making ready will require some time and planning. First will be needed a special appliance, a steel or hardwood planing form with properly sized and tapered grooves, in which the rough bamboo strips are reduced to triangular shape with a sharp plane. Secondly, we will need the little pressure-winding machine mentioned above. Both can be built by a machine shop, total cost is not great, and fully justified if the amateur is serious in wishing to follow this absorbing hobby through with many rods of his own design.

The pressure-winding machine illustrated was designed by Robert Crompton, a craftsman of the old school, who delighted in helping amateur rod builders throughout the country some years ago. Drawings and advice were freely given; the machine was purposely not patented to permit its use by anyone.

The base is ¼ inch thick, cold-rolled steel 16 inches in length, bent at right angles to permit the bed, 4 inches wide, to be bolted to the edge of the work bench through two holes taking ¼-inch bolts. The vertical portion, 12 inches long, takes the slide ¼ x 4 x 10 inches, carrying two guiding bolts (set loosely) to slide in the channel milled in the standing section. A small pulley is grooved deeply, to

drive an endless belt made of cotton "chalk line," the ends of which are spliced together or simply overlapped and bound with thread.

Note that at each side of the bed there is an attached block with half-round "U" about ⅞ inch across to support the rod stock as it passes through the two narrow "wrapping fingers" in the center. These are usually spaced to give a spiral wrap of about ⅜–½ inch. The endless belt is wrapped twice about the stick and propels it as the handle is turned. The principle of this machine is that a weight suspended from the slide applies compound force through the belt to provide a uniform and proper glue-line clamping pressure, maintaining this through tension of the wound thread. Tension from the spool is regulated by a sewing-machine tension plate, which can be purchased at any store which generally supplies parts for sewing machines.

Before ordering or making a planing form, one decision must be made. Is the type of rod construction to be the conventional six-strip (hexagonal cross section) in which each strip is planed to an exact 60-degree angle, or of the five-strip (pentagonal shape) developed by Crompton. Many competent builders believe this design has definite advantages.

Briefly compared, the six-strip rod, having six sides, with the guides placed on a flat side, has opposite another flat side, a continuous glue line midway between them. In five-strip design, the glue line does not "divide" the stick as in the six, as each glue line extends only to the center. If we accept the fact that strain on glue line is important, pentagonal construction is to be favored. However, this is a matter of personal preference and experience. The six-strip method is employed by the majority of modern rod builders.

In the six-strip planing form your machinist will start with a slab of mild steel, 48 inches long and 4 inches wide, about ¾ inch thick, and space four 60° (included angle) grooves along its length.

Five-Strip Planing Form With the five-strip planing form, four pairs of grooves are required in the same type of mild steel, 42 inches long. Each pair of grooves consists of an identical right- and left-hand groove, their angles and depths.

In planing strips for the five-strip rod, the spline is alternately placed in each groove every two or three strokes of the plane which develops the correct apex angles as the work progresses. If the builder wishes to try rod building "for size," so to speak, he can make an inexpensive wooden rod-planing form which will serve for two or three rods before it loses its accuracy. This can be done in any home workshop equipped with a circular saw. Birch or maple stand up very well, and the narrow mold is a better tool when draw-filing to final dimensions.

A very important item is a vise mounted on a workbench not higher than 32 inches from floor. The workbench should be made of heavy planking and be well-braced.

Good rod-building canes may be secured from the Charles H. Demarest, Inc., P.O. Box 238, Bloomingdale, N.J. 07403.

First split the canes in half, to prevent possible splitting later through drying out. Remove the inside dams; then prepare your chart for that first rod.

TOOLS REQUIRED

1. A pair of leather-faced gloves
2. 60-degree center gauge
3. Vise, heavy, 3–4-inch smooth jaws
4. 8-inch carpenter's plane for rough shaping
5. 6-inch "low-angle" plane for finishing cuts
6. Heavy (hunting) knife and mallet for cane splitting
7. Half-round gouge chisel for removing "dams" at nodes
8. Small hacksaw, fine-tooth (48/in) blades
9. 1-inch micrometer
10. 8–10-inch mill bastard file for leveling exterior nodes
11. Two 8-inch warding bastard files
12. Outside caliper for shaping cork grips
13. 8-inch fine-grain oil stone for sharpening plane blades
14. Fine grades sandpaper—
     220 (6/0) garnet paper
     280 (A) carborundum paper
15. Small carpenter's scraper
16. No. 00 steel wool for final polishing of sticks

The Six-Strip Rod This rod has been almost the universal construction since the first was placed on the American market by H. L. Leonard of Bangor, Maine, in 1870. Their workmanship was superb, as anyone fortunate enough to own one still as a museum piece will testify. Also, the early makers, particularly in building fly rods, adhered to the early British idea of a "whippy" rod; but its casting ability is limited, and the modern fly rod possesses far more power for a given weight. Much of this improvement is in proportion to and placement of tapers.

We can give credit for improved rod design to members of many tournament-casting clubs, and, of course, to discriminating anglers who have applied scientific theory to their art. Old tournament records will show a champion distance fly-caster achieved 80–90 feet. Today that is "fishing distance," and the tournament man can cast a fly 200 feet.

Many innovations have been worked out by rod builders in an effort to secure more power. While actual weight, as such, is not too important in heavy-duty saltwater service, the lightest possible rod for the intended job is appreciated by the experienced angler. The hollow-built principle has been applied, in which the inner apexes of the shaped strips, which are of coarser fiber than the exterior, are cut away, leaving a hollow interior. We then have a "tube" which, for its weight, is stronger than a solid stick. But a thin-walled tube is easily collapsed; so when the hollow is considerable some sort of internal support is needed. Thus, hollow-built fly rods, such as those of E. C. Powell, of Marysville, California, include internal bulkheads of softwood, glued in place at intervals. The result is a beautifully light, but powerful stick. A fly rod of 9 feet weighs less than 5 ounces, but is capable of handling a moderately heavy tapered line. Improved methods of rod-building, smooth-flowing line through the guides—such as monofilament—and ability to shoot it strongly, all have contributed to these phenomenal distance casts. But in the final analysis, it is the rod which propels the cast

In saltwater work, we are continually amazed at the mighty fish weighing hundreds of pounds, taken on 20-pound-test line, the rod a mere wisp of bamboo or glass. Similar records are going to light spinning tackle.

Perhaps best, for six-strip design, is to copy a favorite rod after first becoming acquainted with the micrometer, which should be used for all future calibrating. A little practice will indicate how the instrument is read. Care must be exercised that the spindle is not screwed too tightly against the 60° (or 72°) apex causing it to be crushed and resulting in a grossly erroneous reading.

Lay the rod you are measuring beside a scale and take the over-all calibrations at 6-inch points along its length. Then note ferrule size, and make a chart as on page 809. This is a chart of "diameters" for a fine commercial 8-foot-rod.

With an 8-foot cane split in half, dams removed, and outer nodes leveled with the 8-inch warding bastard file, the butt portion of one-half may be split into six or eight sections, for the butt joint of the rod, doing this by splitting the halved cane along the middle successively until the desired rough width is attained. Normally after the knife starts the split the two portions may be grasped and quickly separated. A good rule in sawing or splitting butt segments is to have the rough segments or sections at least ⅛ inch wider than anticipated finished dimension. Allowance should be 3/32 inch wider than large end of finished tip segment.

Lay the strips side by side on the bench, slide each until the nodes are separated by at least 4 inches, and cut off the projecting ends, leaving the strips 50–52 inches long. Note that the butt portion of the cane will have thicker walls—necessary for the rod butt—than will the end. If the cane is without flaws, use the upper, or thinner part for rod tips. Next flex each spline, feeling for "soft" or lifeless areas which may indicate injury or inherent weakness of the cane, which should be rejected.

After splitting, each strip will be somewhat crooked. This is easily corrected by wearing gloves, passing the strip over a gas flame until quite warm, then straightening. Upon cooling it will remain straight. At this stage these rough strips are to be heat treated to remove excess moisture. If done later, work might be spoiled through uneven heating at the thin-planed edges of the splines.

Heat Tempering There are several methods, and a good one is the use of a length of 1½-inch iron pipe, several inches longer than the rod sections, hung on a pair of looped wires. Each end is fitted with a wood plug through which an ⅛-inch hole has been drilled.

Place the strips in the pipe, and with a blow torch apply the flame back and forth along its length, turning the pipe frequently with gloved hands. In ten minutes or so steam will issue from the vent holes in the plugs—showing that water is being driven out of the bamboo. Continue to heat and turn another 10–15 minutes; note now the vapor has lessened, has a slight "wood" odor. Remove a plug for inspection, and if the strips show a light brown or dark tan color, the tempering is completed.

It is best to plane down the butt strips first, starting each in the largest groove, taking several cuts from each upturned edge—with the enamel side always against the groove side, since the enamel side is not to be touched. As the strip is reduced, in planing the upturned corners, it

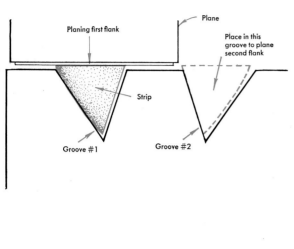

Planing first flank

Plane

Place in this groove to plane second flank

Strip

Groove #1

Groove #2

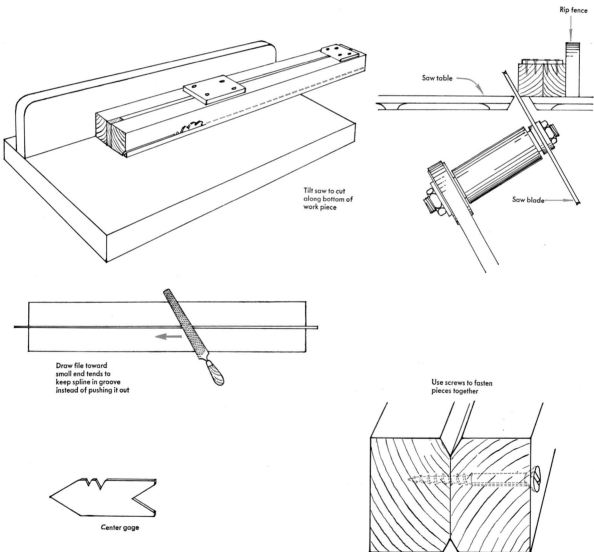

Rip fence

Saw table

Tilt saw to cut along bottom of work piece

Saw blade

Draw file toward small end tends to keep spline in groove instead of pushing it out

Use screws to fasten pieces together

Center gage

Planing a 5-Strip Rod; Making a Wooden Form

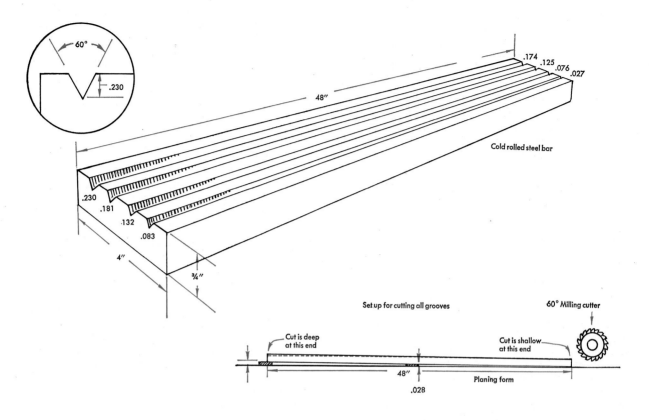

60°

.230

.174
.125
.076
.027

48"

Cold rolled steel bar

.230
.181
.132
.083

4"

¾"

Set up for cutting all grooves

60° Milling cutter

Cut is deep
at this end

Cut is shallow
at this end

48"

Planing form

.028

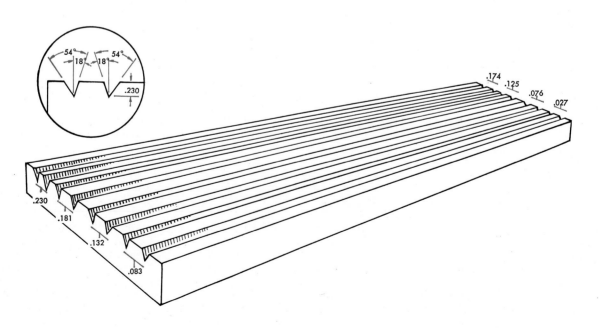

54°   54°
18° 18°

.230

.174
.125
.076
.027

.230
.181
.132
.083

5-Strip Planing and 6-Strip Planing Form

8-Foot, 2-Piece Fly Rod

			6 in.	12 in.	18 in.	24 in.	30 in.	36 in.	42 in.	48 in.
Diameters	Butt	.350	.350	.320	.290	.280	.270	.255	.240	.220
	Tip	.220	.210	.200	.185	.165	.140	.115	.085	.062

For comparing calibration of the five-strip with six-strip construction, following is a chart for a rather powerful five-strip eight footer. It might serve for the amateur deciding upon the pentagon rod and having none for copying.

			6 in.	12 in.	18 in.	24 in.	30 in.	36 in.	42 in.	48 in.
Diameters	Butt	.360	.360	.360	.340	.320	.295	.275	.250	.235
	Tip	.235	.220	.200	.180	.160	.140	.120	.095	.075

will of course become roughly triangular, and, as work progresses, sharpen the plane blade, and take lighter cuts first on one flank then the other.

The slots in the mold position the segment while planing and draw filing and also give one a rough check on size and taper as the segment or spline is being worked.

Frequent use must be made of the center gauge and micrometer when segment is planed to approximately $\frac{1}{32}$ of the anticipated finished diameter. The segments must be equal on both angles, and if any light is to show when checking with center gauge it should be very slight at apex.

A No. 0 Stanley scraper mounted in vise can help to cut down and hold segments to proper 60°. There is a limit to the accuracy of planing, and the time will be well spent with the use of scraper and draw filing with a 10-inch mill bastard file. An 8-inch warding bastard file will cut the nodes better than a mill file. Thus, an accurate triangle will result, the groove helping bring this about— *if* the plane is always kept level with the work.

Previously, the form should have been lightly marked with a narrow file across its face at 6-inch intervals. Thus, as each strip is reduced an approximate idea of the dimension is constantly at hand. This should be frequently verified by use of the micrometer. Six-strip splines should measure just half the diameter of the finished rod, and the necessary spline diameters can be noted below over-all dimensions on your chart.

Five-Strip Calibration   Here, the "one-half" reading will not do. A rod measuring .290 over-all would have a strip diameter of only .130, rather than .145, as for the six-strip. The factor for converting strip diameter is 2.236. Thus, for a five-strip butt of .290, we divide .290 by 2.236 and come out with .130 inch. Using this method, any six-strip rod may be used as a pattern for the five-strip. But, noting the comparison in calibrations of the six- and five-strip 8 footers, over-all dimensions of the five-strip design are greater, particularly in the lower portions.

Before the strips have reached finished size, change to the little low-angle plane, with the blade kept very sharp and set for the lightest possible cut to prevent possible tearing of the bamboo at the cross-grained nodes. If this

becomes apparent, use a small, flat mill file or sandpaper block to smooth.

With all strips reduced to exact size (try to achieve a variation of not more than .002 inch at each 6-inch station) wrap them together in proper position with strong cotton string, wound spirally. Examine for close fitting, and measure the over-all dimensions for comparison with the chart. Any slight sign of poor fitting can be marked, the strips laid out again, and the "bad" spot corrected with plane or file.

Gluing   Several fine glues of the "resin" type are available for the amateur, simply to be brushed on the splines. One of the most satisfactory is Borden's "Elmer's Glue" which can be obtained in almost any hardware store in small cans. The liquid in one is a deep wine color, to which is added the powdered catalyst as directed on the can. With the splines for a rod section properly placed, roll them together with short strips of Scotch tape around them at about 18-inch intervals. Now open them up and place them back down on the bench. Apply the glue to the upturned flanks, brushing to coat all surface area thoroughly. Roll the splines together, and start, butt first through the pressure-winding machine, the endless belt passed twice around the stick as described, the wrapping cord under the belt. A weight of 5 pounds on the sliding member should be sufficient for fly-butt joints, particularly if Epoxy resin is used. Recently Epoxy adhesives have been developed. They are suitable for rod building as they are water- and heatproof. More importantly, they do not set by drying, losing moisture. Therefore there is no shrinkage. Any gap or void is filled. A weight of 2–3 pounds will be ample for tips.

Tie off the cord with a few half hitches when this first wind is completed; then rewind the belt—in opposite direction—for the second wrapping, the cord thus going on "crisscross," and removing all, or most, of the twist resulting from the first winding. Sight down the wrapped stick, and straighten any slight deviations; also correct any twist which may remain while the glue is still soft. (If, after drying, the sticks show twist or a slight bend, these may be corrected by passing finished rod section over gas burner until hot to touch. Reverse twist, and hold until rod joint cools.)

It may be found that for most sticks, a greater weight may be necessary for the second winding to correct the twist resulting from the stick's first passage through.

Glue should set in 24–36 hours, with the sticks suspended in a warm spot; then the wrapping cord may be removed and the exterior faces gently scraped down to remove adhering glue and *only* enough of the enamel to show the fibers beneath. A final light sanding with 280 (A) carborundum paper wrapped about a wood block, followed by burnishing with fine steel wool, and the rod is ready for finishing.

Ferruling and Finishing Only high-grade, nickel-silver ferrules should be used, these with tapered, split (or serrated) ends. Ferrule sizes are indicated by the inside diameter of each, in sixty-fourths of an inch, this being .0156. Thus, to determine proper size for a given rod, measure the six-strip across the flats at the end, and order a ferrule size to match this, which will just permit a true circular seat without cutting into the outer fibers. The 8-foot, six-strip rod charted above, then, is .220 at the ferrule end of the butt stick, and a ¹⁴⁄₆₄ ferrule (.218) will be required.

The five-strip, because of its shape, will have more taken off for a ferrule seat, the corners more prominent; so note, in the five-strip rod charted, the diameter of the stick's end is .235, to take the same ¹⁴⁄₆₄ ferrule.

A bench lathe is ideal for fitting ferrules (note illustration) and for holding the section in the lathe chuck while the ferrule is forced home with the tail stock. Acceptable work can be done, however, holding the section in a padded vise, shaping with a strip of sandpaper wrapped around it. Take care to prevent crushing the section by too much force. The micrometer should be used often to prevent a loose fit. Rather than the hot stick cement, a better preparation is a rubber-type cement, such as Goodyear's Pliobond, and with it a barely snug fit (in which you can force the ferrule into place with the fingers alone) is sufficient. Then, with a thin application of the cement the ferrule is easily forced home in the lathe, or alternatively by pressing it firmly in place by hand.

With ferrules fitted, assemble the rod, and sight down its length, and any deviation at the ferrules can be overcome by turning one section, a "flat" at a time, until the whole matches up.

Reel Seat and Cork Grip These can usually be found in sporting goods stores, the latter with rings ready glued together and shaped, with a hole to fit the rod butt. Lacking the finished grip, cork rings may be had, which you force onto the butt section, glue together, with pressure (the lathe here excellent) applied. After the glue is set, the grip then may be shaped with sandpaper strips to suit the fancy of the user.

Applying Guides and Finishing The best hardened steel guides should be used, those of "snake" type for fly rod; ring guides, chrome-plated, for fly-rod butts and for spinning rods, the latter of light-weight, large size. Spacing will depend upon rod taper; but ten, for example, will serve nicely on an 8-foot fly rod.

The guide positions may be positioned by trial and error, keeping in mind the need to reduce the spacing

In freshwater fishing the strength of a fly rod is less important than its design, with respect to casting conditions

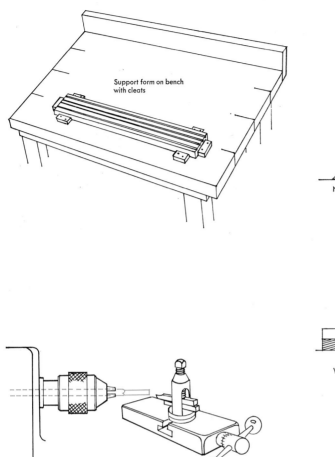

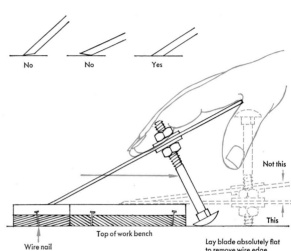

Workbench—Turning Ferrule Diameter

toward the tip. Generally the distance between last guide and tip should be not more than 4–5 inches. No. "0" wrapping thread in nylon or silk, color as desired, is best for light rods, size "A" or heavier for larger rods.

No wrapping jig is needed for home work, and the spool mounted on a nail driven into a heavy block will feed the thread, one hand holding tension, while the other revolves the stick held under the arm. Starting a few turns from the end of the guide foot, take five turns over the thread end, trim it with a razor blade, and proceed to the end of the foot, always crowding the thread closely. When a few turns from the finish, lay a loop of thread along the flat, wrap over it; then cut the wrapping thread, insert the end in the loop, pull under, and trim flush.

Ferrule wrapping should start a few turns from the serrated end and finish snug under the tiny shoulder turned on the barrel. And a second wrapping may be advisable to prevent cement showing through at the serrated end after varnishing.

Thread should be given three coats of thinned clear lacquer using a small brush. This preserves the color of windings which, if varnished directly, would become transparent. Ten minutes between coats will be ample.

Any good, light spar or rod varnish will serve, applied in long strokes with a ⅜-inch wide brush, kept well-filled, and the varnish actually "flowed" on. But this only after the sticks have been carefully wiped with a cloth to remove finger marks, then brushed clean to remove adhering lint.

Two coats of varnish are sufficient for a long-wearing, glossy coat; too much can slow and "deaden" the action of a light rod. An additional coat may be given the wrapping, if necessary, for protection.   —C.M.K.
—L.B.F.

FIBERGLASS ROD CONSTRUCTION

Fiberglass Processes The basic component of a fiberglass fishing rod is the blank (the shaft to which the handle and guides are attached). The size and shape of the blank depends on the method of fishing for which it is intended, the species of fish being sought, the size of the water being fished, and other considerations such as the personal preferences of the angler. All blanks must have adequate strength when flexed. They should also be light-weight, durable, and capable of a rapid recoil. Modern technology allows the arrangement of fibers in the optimum position to obtain the qualities desired. High

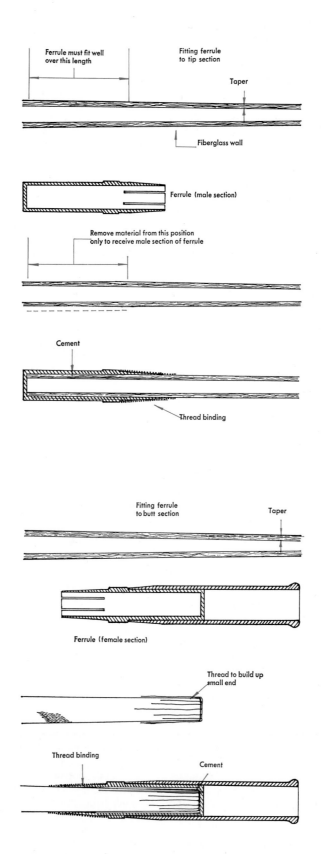

Ferrule must fit well over this length

Fitting ferrule to tip section

Taper

Fiberglass wall

Ferrule (male section)

Remove material from this position only to receive male section of ferrule

Cement

Thread binding

Fitting ferrule to butt section

Taper

Ferrule (female section)

Thread to build up small end

Thread binding

Cement

Fitting Ferrules

flexural strength is achieved by positioning the fibers so they are straight and parallel to the axis of the shaft. Rapid recoil is obtained by the use of a high modulus (stiff) material with maximum resistance to stretching.

There are three primary methods of manufacturing fiberglass rod blanks:

Solid Fiberglass Blanks are made generally by a pulltrusion method of drawing fiberglass through a liquid resin bath and then through a forming die and curing tube. The blanks then are cut to length and ground to the required taper. Since all the fibers run parallel to one another, fair stiffness and durability (excellent crush strength) is achieved. However, the fibers nearest the axis of the blank contribute very little to the stiffness and the recovery properties from flexing. The process is rather simple and the raw materials are inexpensive, so that it is possible to turn out low-priced blanks. The action, however, is generally heavy, and rods made by this process usually are used for heavy-duty boat fishing or as children's rods.

Howell Process This is a patented process in which machines are used to saturate fiberglass yarn with polyester resin. The saturated yarn then is placed over a removable mandrel and an outside mold is formed by a spiral wrap of cellophane tape. The tape is removed after

curing (hardening of the resin). This process uses a type of polyester resin especially suited for rods. Color is mixed into the resin. The outside fibers run longitudinally and the inside fibers are circumferentially spiraled. The latter is necessary to keep the tube from collapsing during flexing. Fine tip sections are made solid because the inside circumference is too small to wrap with fiberglass yarn. Rods of this type have excellent durability and achieve adequate performance under most casting and fishing conditions. They are lighter than solid fiberglass rods, but still are somewhat heavier than rods made by the conventional tubular process. Economies are possible in the production of these shafts because basic resins and fiberglass are used and the blanks are machine-made, requiring relatively little hand work.

Conventional Tubular Fiberglass The great majority of fiberglass rods now are made by this process. The raw materials are designed especially to obtain the optimum qualities desired in fishing rod blanks. Two pre-impregnated fiberglass fabrics are used in the manufacture of nearly all tubular glass rod blanks. Both fabrics are semiunidirectional with a crowfoot satin weave. This means a large proportion of the fibers run in one direction and are woven in such a manner that the fibers are held straight over a relatively long distance. The straighter the

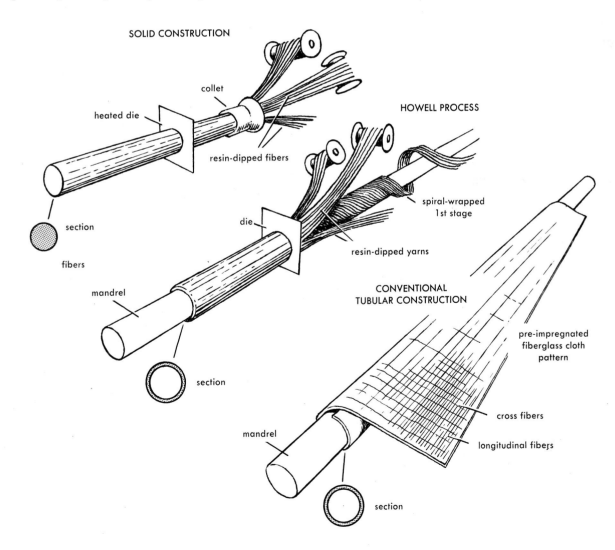

fibers, the better the strength and recoil characteristics of the rod blank. The yarns are bound periodically by the cross weave to keep each straight fiber in its exact place for uniformity and consistency.

The heavier of the two fabrics has 10 longitudinal fibers for every cross fiber. The lighter fabric has a 6–1 ratio. When the fabric is cut for a tubular glass rod blank the pattern is laid out so that the larger number of fibers lies along the length of the rod. The cross fibers then will run circumferentially around the blank to give it the proper crush strength and maintain a circular cross section which is vital to the strength and action of the rod.

Several thermosetting resin systems have been developed for the manufacture of rod blanks. Early rods generally were made of nylon-plasticized phenolic. This is an excellent resin for the purpose, except for color. Phenolics tend to darken with age, and later developments in the fields of epoxy and polyester resins have replaced the phenolics, except in processes where the blank is painted. Most rods now are made with the pigment of the finished rod mixed in with the resin. Epoxy and polyester resins are very durable, and the colors usually are stable even under severe weathering conditions.

An unlimited number of different rod designs is possible with the tubular glass method of construction. The cost varies according to the design.   —A.M.

Rod Actions The action of a rod is best described as the curvature it assumes when stressed. If all of the curvature takes place in the upper quarter of the blank it has an extra-fast action. If the curvature is confined to the upper third of the blank it is described as having a fast action.

If the curvature is in the upper half of the rod blank the action is described as moderate. A slow-action rod assumes a progressive curvature all the way from the butt

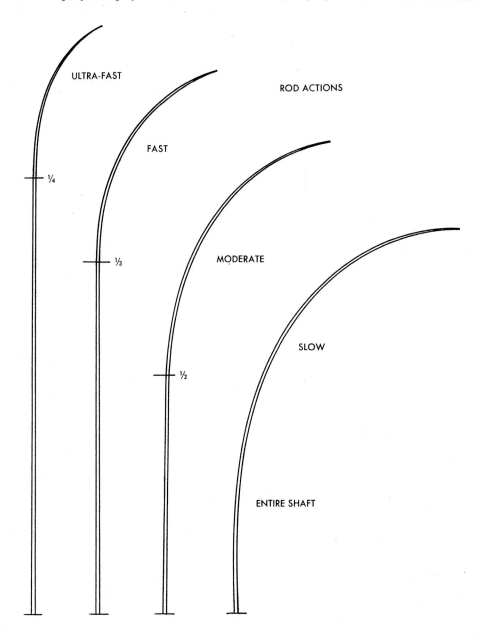

ULTRA-FAST

FAST

ROD ACTIONS

MODERATE

SLOW

¼

⅓

½

ENTIRE SHAFT

of the blank to its tip. It is possible to design any type of rod—whether for fly-fishing, spinning, trolling, or bait-casting—to have any of the actions outlined above. However, in actual practice it is accepted that certain types of actions are more or less suited for certain types of rods.

Ultralight spinning rods used for trout and panfish usually are made with an extra-fast action. This action makes it possible to cast the lightweight lures used in this type of fishing and obtain the distance necessary.

Spinning rods of 6½–7½ feet are made with both extra-fast and fast actions. Lighter lures may be cast with the fast-action rod, which is excellent for black bass where it is necessary to feel the fish take a live bait and still have enough power in the rod tip to set the hook quickly.

Casting rods of 5–6-feet long are manufactured in the full range of rod actions. However, in tournament casting, where pinpoint accuracy is required, the slow or moderate action is preferred. A fast-action rod is better suited to actual fishing, where a rod with a light, sensitive tip is necessary for the angler to detect a fish taking the lure. This is especially true in the new and popular method of artificial worm fishing.

Longer spinning and casting rods (8–9 feet) used for steelhead or salmon again usually are made with a fast action. The sensitive tip is necessary to feel the very light take of a winter steelhead, especially when bait is being used. The rod still has power enough to handle a strong, heavy fish.

Saltwater angling off the southern California coast calls for a rod with an extra-fast tip combined with an especially strong butt. A live anchovy is used for bait and the light tip is needed to cast the light, fragile bait. At the same time the rod must have strength enough to handle the strong, fast saltwater fish that may run as heavy as 35 pounds. This provides an excellent example of how the characteristics of the fish have a direct bearing on the design of the rod, and proves the flexibility of designs possible with tubular fiberglass.

Fly-rod design is influenced primarily by casting conditions. Only in certain types of saltwater angling does the strength of the fish become a more important consideration than the requirements for casting. Quality fly rods are manufactured either with slow or moderate actions. The choice really depends on the preference of the angler. His individual casting stroke may be more suited to the moderate action than the slow rod or vice-versa. On the other hand, fly rods with a fast action are very difficult to cast and very tiring to the caster. If only the tip of the rod is working it becomes difficult to roll the fly line through the air. But if the rod flexes throughout it is possible to apply smooth, consistent power to the line.

All these factors are taken into consideration in the design of rods.

Rod Design Weighing the factors outlined above, the manufacturer determines the required length and action he wishes to achieve and then proceeds to the design of a rod that will meet the objectives he has in mind.

The amount of glass fiber at a given point in the rod blank determines the power and action of the rod. The amount of fiber is determined by varying the pattern which is cut from a roll of glass cloth at the beginning of the manufacturing process.

The pattern itself is tapered. The butt portion is of greater width than the tip. Different rod actions are achieved by increasing or decreasing the width of the taper over any portion of its length.

Increasing the number of glass fibers at any point will stiffen the action of the blank at that point. Conversely, fewer fibers result in greater flexibility. A multitude of different actions may thus be achieved by making small alterations to the pattern at any point along the length of the blank.

A hollow blank is made by rolling the tapered cloth pattern onto a tapered mandrel. The type of mandrel used is very important. If a small-diameter mandrel is used, a thick-walled blank is the result. But if the manufacturer has the necessary sophisticated machinery and know-how he may apply the same pattern to a large-diameter mandrel and produce a thin-walled blank. Because identical patterns were used, both blanks would weigh the same, but the thin-walled blank would have far greater power due to its larger diameter. The right combination of pattern design and mandrel size must be blended to produce a blank with the optimum qualities of power, action, and weight. Thin-walled blanks, while far more desirable than their thick-walled counterparts, are much more difficult and expensive to manufacture.

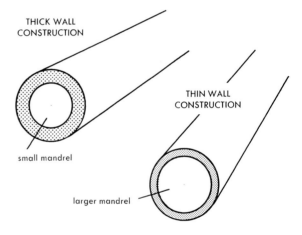

THICK WALL CONSTRUCTION

small mandrel

THIN WALL CONSTRUCTION

larger mandrel

In the actual design of a new rod a test pattern and mandrel are selected and the resulting blank is made into a finished rod, which is field-tested. If the rod lacks the characteristics necessary for its intended purpose the designer alters the pattern-mandrel relationship until the desired results are obtained. Then the rod is put into the hands of expert fishermen who test it under the varied conditions of actual fishing. If the anglers report deficiencies in the design the designer again makes alterations to correct them. The process of design, test, and alteration takes a great deal of time, but it must be carried out before the manufacturer is ready to begin full-scale production of a new model rod.   —J.Gr.

The Manufacturing Process Once a new design has been tested satisfactorily the manufacturer prepares for

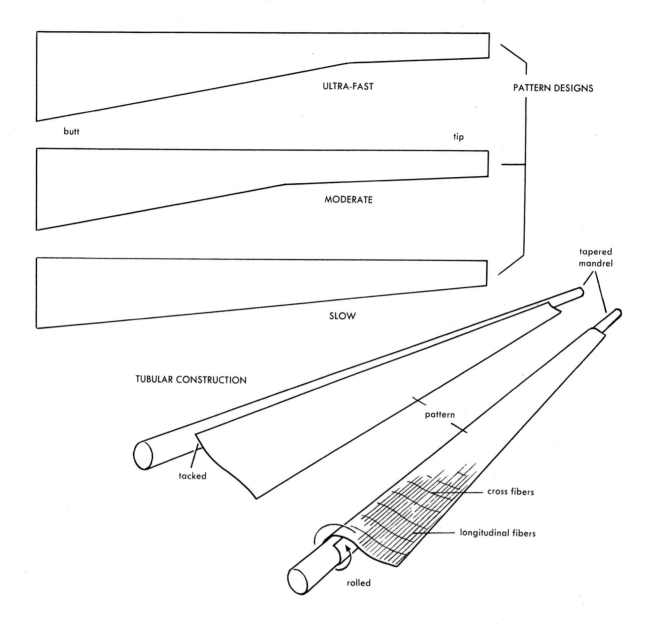

ULTRA-FAST

butt

tip

PATTERN DESIGNS

MODERATE

SLOW

TUBULAR CONSTRUCTION

tapered mandrel

pattern

tacked

cross fibers

longitudinal fibers

rolled

production of the new rod. Preimpregnated fiberglass cloth is used. The preimpregnated process involves taking woven fiberglass cloth, dipping it in resin, and running it through squeeze rolls to control the amount of resin that remains in the cloth. The cloth is then heated in an oven to drive off excess solvent and to dry the resin until it becomes tacky. The cloth is cooled and then rerolled with a polyethylene separator sheet.

In the conventional tubular-manufacturing method used by most manufacturers a roll of the preimpregnated cloth about a yard wide is cut and pulled in layers onto a pattern-cutting table with the longitudinal fibers running lengthwise, the length depending on the length of the blank to be produced.

The cloth sheets are stacked up to achieve the quantity necessary for a production run. Then a metal template is laid on top of the stacked sheets and the desired pattern is cut from each sheet of cloth. Metal templates are used to assure that the exact pattern dimensions are duplicated in each production run.

Heat is used to attach one edge of the fiberglass-cloth pattern to the tapered-steel mandrel. The pattern now is ready to be formed into a tapered tube. This may be accomplished by several methods, but the most common is to roll the mandrel between two heated platens under pressure.

This operation is critical to the production of a high-quality laminate. Precision equipment must be used to

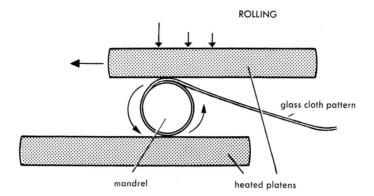

ROLLING

glass cloth pattern

mandrel   heated platens

maintain uniform pressure along the entire length of the blank while the pattern is being rolled onto the mandrel.

The density of the laminate is the major difference between a blank of high quality and one of low quality. A dense laminate (porosity free) such as is found in high-quality blanks is essential to obtain maximum strength and durability. It also allows the manufacturer to produce a rod of optimum strength and light weight.

To make a dense laminate it is necessary to have both an inside and outside mold. The mandrel is the inside mold and the wrapped layers of fiberglass cloth form the laminate. The outside mold may be made of various materials. Cellophane film is used most often, but polyester film or FEP fluoroplastic films also may be used. Another method is to use silicone rubber tubing molded to the shape of the wrapped fiberglass. In the cellophane film method a narrow width (½–1 inch) is spiral-wrapped under tension starting from one end of the blank. This may be done by hand, but it is more desirable to apply the film in a controlled, uniform tension using special equipment. Again, the quality of the laminate depends on the uniformity of the tension applied to the film during the wrapping operation.

The cellophane film does two things: It applies pressure to the laminate during the spiral-wrapping process and, later, it applies further pressure by shrinking during the baking or curing cycle. It also forms a smooth surface against which the resin will flow.

Once the laminate has been wrapped in cellophane, it is ready for final curing of the resin. This is done by placing the wrapped mandrel in a vertical position in an oven and heating to 300° or 350° F (depending on the resin used) for 30–60 minutes. As the resin is heated, it goes through a lower-viscosity flow stage. At this time the cellophane film begins to shrink and applies pressure to the wrapped layers of fiberglass cloth and resin. After a certain amount of time at the proper temperature the resin will harden into gelatin and finally into full cure.

When the curing cycle is complete the mandrel must be extracted from the now-hardened blank. This usually is done by using a power ram to pull the laminate against a metal die, extracting the mandrel through a hole in the die. The mandrel then is cleaned and made ready for another pattern.

At this point the tubular blank has its full properties and is ready to be prepared for finishing. The first step is to remove the cellophane film, which may be done by using a wire brush, tumbler, by high-pressure steam, or by splitting or stripping.

With the cellophane removed, the blank still bears the marks left by the film when the resin flowed against the spiral wrap during the curing stage. These small resin ridges may be left on the surface of the blank, but they add nothing to its strength. A high-quality blank will be lightly sanded to a smooth finish. This adds to the good appearance of the blank when a final protective coating is applied.

The final protective coating adds to the durability and appearance of the rod and is designed to give maximum protection from scratches, mars, moisture, gasoline, solvent, and ultraviolet rays from the sun. It also is designed to hold up under extremes of hot and cold temperature.

Various materials are used for this exterior coating. The primary concern is to avoid applying too thick a coat, as excessive thickness may drastically change the rod action and make it feel sluggish. The same may occur if the coating remains soft and does not dry into a hard finish.

The finish is applied in several coats with buffing operations between coats to achieve a level, "smooth as glass" finish that does not affect the rod's action.

The blank now is complete and ready for final inspection and rod assembly.   —D.Gr.

ROD ASSEMBLY

There are several steps involved in assembling a completed fishing rod which must be followed whether the job is being done by a custom rod builder or by a major manufacturer. The steps are ferrule assembly and mounting; assembly and gluing of the grip and reel seat; wrapping of guides, and finishing of the guide wraps.

A description of the components involved is in order before proceeding to an outline of the assembly process.

Ferrules Nearly all fishing rods are built in two or more sections. This is done so that the rods may be disassembled for ease in transportation. In the long history of rod development, a number of methods have been devised to join and separate the different sections of a rod.

The most common method now used is the metal ferrule, which consists of two parts. On a two-piece rod a female section is mounted on the butt section of the rod and a male section is mounted on the tip. The rod may

FERRULES

METAL FERRULE

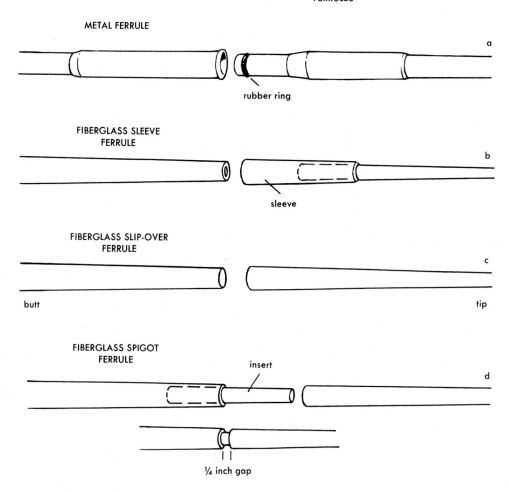

rubber ring

FIBERGLASS SLEEVE
FERRULE

sleeve

FIBERGLASS SLIP-OVER
FERRULE

butt   tip

FIBERGLASS SPIGOT
FERRULE

insert

¼ inch gap

then be joined easily by fitting the tip section into the butt, and separated by pulling the two sections apart.

Chrome-plated brass is used in the manufacture of some metal ferrules. The advantage of this material is that it is easily shaped; the disadvantage is that it is heavy and has a tendency to wear easily.

Nickel silver also is commonly used. It lends itself to deep drawing and the types of forming necessary to produce a ferrule of high quality, but its high cost precludes widespread use.

Another common metal used for ferrules is aluminum. It is light, strong enough to do the job, and well suited to drawing and shaping by machine.

For the most part metal ferrules rely on the friction generated between the inside of the female ferrule section and the exterior of the male section to hold the rod together. The fitting of these ferrules is critical, and it is of utmost importance to keep to the proper clearance in the manufacturing process. A small amount of wear may cause this type of ferrule to loosen; the angler soon will experience problems if this occurs.

A development of major importance in recent years was the perfection of a fiberglass ferrule. Nearly all the manufacturers of fiberglass rods now use some form of fiberglass ferrule.

The slipover style of fiberglass ferrule (in which the tip section of the rod slides down over the butt section) was pioneered by the Fenwick Rod Company with its Feralite Ferrule in 1962. This ferrule is protected by patent, but there is a variety of alternatives available. Slipping the tip section into the hollow butt has proven practical and is utilized by some manufacturers. Others use a sleeve type of ferrule. Probably the most common fiberglass ferrule is the spigot type, and while this adds stiffness at the ferruling point it still provides a measure of flexibility and has proven satisfactory in most instances.

Fiberglass ferrules rely upon a taper fit. Because of this, wear is not a problem as it is with metal ferrules. Fiberglass ferrules also do not have a tendency to stick, as friction-type ferrules do, because once the taper fit of the fiberglass ferrule is broken the lock is released over the entire length of the ferrule and the two sections may be separated easily.

Grips   Nearly all fishing-rod grips are made of cork, though other materials are used occasionally. Cork is used primarily because it is light in weight, easily shaped, and has a composition that keeps it from becoming slippery when wet or covered with fish slime.

Two types of cork are used in rod construction—specie cork and mustard cork. Specie cork rings are cut from cork-tree bark on an axis perpendicular to the core of the tree. This gives the rings an appearance of consisting of multiple layers, but in fact these layers are merely the growth rings of the bark. Mustard cork is cut in rings on an axis parallel to the core of the tree, and the layers are not seen in the finished product. Mustard cork is less durable than specie cork and thus is considered less desirable for rod grips.

An adequate substitute for cork in fishing-rod grips has not been found. However, the most recently developed synthetic foam-rubber materials are receiving some use, even though their weight is considerably greater than that of cork. These materials are extremely durable, and in the construction of heavier rods their use seems to be supplementing or even replacing the increasingly costly cork.

These foamed plastic materials are mostly urethane or neoprene compounds. They are now being used on the majority of the higher-priced production saltwater rods. More experimentation in the development of lightweight synthetics is necessary before their use will become widespread in the construction of spinning and fly rods.

Wood and cloth also are used in the construction of rod grips, again primarily for saltwater rods. The majority of trolling-rod detachable butts are made of wood, fitted to the rod through a ferruling method. Wooden foregrips also are used sometimes, particularly when there is a metal rod holder. (Cork or foam plastic foregrips wear very quickly when used with a metal rod holder.)

Cloth grips appear very rarely in the construction of modern rods. Their use dates from the early days of tournament saltwater angling when layers of felt or other material were used to build a handhold on the rod shaft when fighting large fish.

Different types of rods require grips of varying design and placement. In fly-rod construction the reel seat is placed at the extreme butt of the rod so that the reel may be kept out of the way while the angler handles the rod and line to make a cast. The grip is placed just forward of the reel seat and may be shaped in any one of a number of traditional patterns.

Single-handed spinning rods usually have two grip sections—a short foregrip and a somewhat longer rear grip—with the reel seat mounted in the middle between the two. Heavier rods, known as two-handed spinning rods, traditionally have a longer rear grip so that the angler may free both hands on the rear grip when casting. Using both hands allows the angler to impart greater speed to the rod and thus achieve greater distance in the cast.

In surf casting the distance of the cast is of major importance and the rod is designed so that there is considerable distance between the butt and the reel. This distance is a matter of the angler's choice, but usually it is 22–24 inches. Because of the distance involved, a full rear-grip section is not considered practical and the usual design calls for two grip sections on the rod butt.

In saltwater rods the foregrip is more important because the angler is likely to encounter large fish, and a handhold high on the rod is necessary. The rear grip on these rods is usually between 14 and 18 inches long, this being the length necessary to control a heavy rod properly while fighting a large fish.

A detachable handle is used in tournament or offshore game-fish trolling. The most common design is a straight handle, 16–18 inches long, made of straight-grain hickory.

The strength of the handle is important because, in most cases, the rod is trolled from a rod holder and the force of the strike must be absorbed by the handle. In recent years detachable aluminum and fiberglass handles have been developed for this purpose. These materials cost more and weigh more than the wooden handle, but they are very strong and will not fail under stress.

The trolling-rod butt also is used in fighting a fish and is equipped with a gimball on the butt which fits into a socket on a rod belt or fighting chair. The additional leverage provided by a fighting chair is necessary when fighting fish over 100 pounds with 80–130-pound-test line. For fighting fish of extreme size a curved aluminum detachable butt has been developed which allows the angler to apply even greater pressure.

Reel Seats Reel seats are made from a variety of materials. Aluminum tubing probably is most commonly used. It is strong, light in weight, and inexpensive. Its disadvantage is that when it is exposed to sea water or other corrosive solutions it has a tendency to deteriorate rapidly, even if it has been anodized. For this reason a reel seat of chrome-plated brass is used extensively on saltwater rods, particularly where weight is not a factor.

Reel seats of reinforced plastic also have been developed, and while these have been maligned as being "cheap," they are superior to either aluminum or chrome-plated brass on lightweight saltwater spinning and fly rods.

There has been quite a diversity of opinion over the best design for a reel seat. The straight reel seat with fixed and movable hoods has been adopted by most manufacturers. In this type of reel seat one end of the reel's foot is inserted into the fixed hood and the movable hood then is screwed into position over the other end of the foot by means of screw threads in the reel seat shaft. Some manufacturers place the movable hood and screw threads at the butt end of the reel seat; others place them at the tip end; and there are various arguments in support of both designs. Regardless of which design is used, this type of reel seat is mounted at the extreme butt end of a fly rod or between the foregrip and rear grip of a spinning rod.

A straight reel seat with a trigger grip sometimes is used with casting reels. The main purpose of the trigger is to assist the angler in imparting motion or popping action to the lure without running the risk of having the rod pulled from his hand by a forceful strike.

Some rods are made with a pair of rings to secure the reel to the rod handle. With sufficient pressure these rings will lock the foot of the reel to the cork handle through a wedging action. This type of mechanism is particularly useful in very light rods where weight is a factor or where the angler may desire to change the location of the reel from time to time.

An offset reel seat is sometimes seen, particularly with spin-casting or bait-casting outfits. The advantage of the offset reel seat is that it offers better reel control and makes casting easier.

Reel seats for tournament big-game rods traditionally are made of chrome-plated brass and are manufactured in a variety of sizes. Nearly all of them incorporate

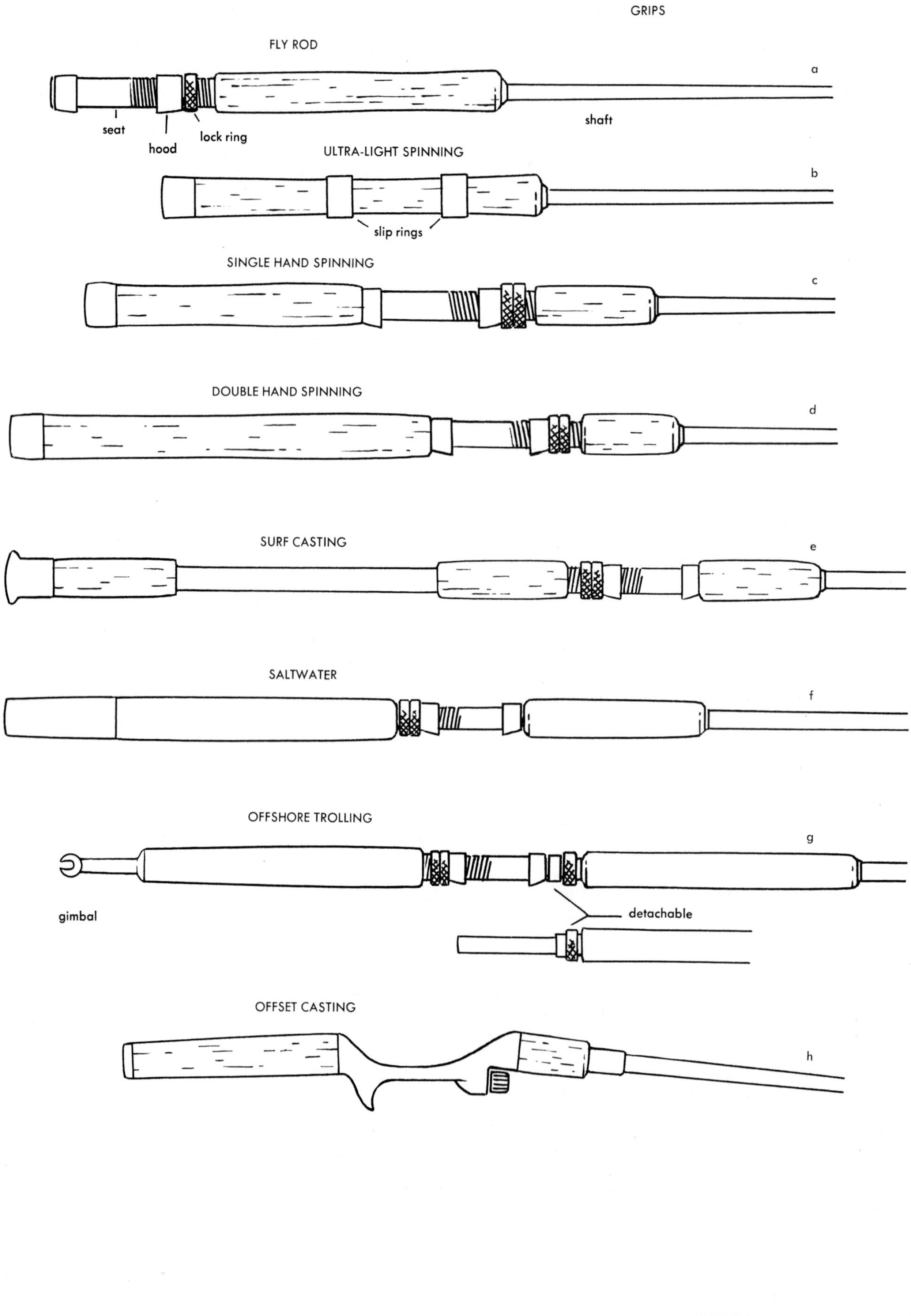

GRIPS

FLY ROD

a

seat

shaft

hood

lock ring

ULTRA-LIGHT SPINNING

b

slip rings

SINGLE HAND SPINNING

c

DOUBLE HAND SPINNING

d

SURF CASTING

e

SALTWATER

f

OFFSHORE TROLLING

g

gimbal

detachable

OFFSET CASTING

h

heavy-duty hoods and an extra lock nut. These features are necessary due to the tremendous strain on the reel seat when lines testing 30, 50, 80, or 130 pounds are used and heavy fish are being played. These reel seats also traditionally are of the ferruled variety, and in most cases the tip section of the rod is removable from the handle assembly at the upper end of the reel seat. A high-grade trolling rod reel seat will have an alignment pin, preferably centered in a V slot on the male portion of the ferrule so that a secure-locking fit is achieved.

Guides Guides are used to control the line in casting and to distribute the stress on the rod evenly when it is flexed by pressure on the line. Guides are made from many different types of material and in many designs.

Stainless steel or brass wire is most often used. Stainless steel has several advantages. It is a fairly hard material, is shaped easily, and does not rust readily. However, it has the disadvantage of being difficult to weld, and by itself it is not nearly so resistant to wear as it is after having been chrome-plated.

Brass probably is used in the majority of guides because it is easily shaped and welded. It must be chrome-plated because its wear resistance in the unplated state is extremely low.

Years ago agate guides were used commonly because of their resistance to wear. They could not be welded or otherwise attached to a wire frame, so it was necessary to build a wire framework around them and attach it to the rod. This made agate guides both heavy and expensive. More recently ceramic guides have been developed which feature the same qualities but are considerably less expensive.

The most popular high-quality guide now on the market has a ring of tungsten carbide and a frame of nickel silver. This is a nearly indestructible combination which offers the fisherman a long lifetime of usage.

Of the many different styles of guide, perhaps the most common is the bridge type. This features a ring and a separate framework which is mounted on the rod shaft. Two styles of framework are used, one U-shaped, the other V-shaped. There is very little difference between the two, and the choice really depends on which the angler finds more esthetically pleasing.

Large-diameter, lightweight bridge guides are known as spinning guides and are used primarily on rods designed for use with open-face spinning reels. The large diameter allows the guides to handle line paying off a spinning reel with a large diameter spool, and their light weight does not affect the action of the rod. When the guides are extremely large a brace often is added to the framework to keep the ring from becoming twisted or knocked loose during use.

The second type of bridge guide is known as a trolling or casting guide. It is built on a heavier framework and has a much heavier ring. It is a more durable guide, but because of its weight it cannot be used in the large diameter sizes required on spinning rods.

Another style is called the wire guide. This consists of a single piece of wire bent into any one of a variety of loop shapes. The ends of the loop are attached directly to the rod and there is no separate framework. The advantages of this design include lightweight, relatively low cost, and the important fact that it does not at all hinder the action of the rod. However, this design also has the disadvantage

of being less durable and resistant to line wear, plus the fact that the guide may easily be twisted or deformed. Wear resistance may sometimes be increased by chrome-plating.

Several styles of wire guide are used. They include the popular "foul-proof" style, the double-footed style, and the snake guide that is used on fly rods.

Last among the various designs of rod guides is the roller guide, which was developed almost exclusively for use with heavy tournament and offshore trolling rods where heavy lines and wire leaders must be used. Many types of rolling guides have been developed, all of them working basically on the same principle and having essentially the same method of construction. In the early 1960's J.C. Axelson of the AFTCO Company made a series of tests to determine the usefulness of the roller guide in preventing line wear.

These tests confirmed the popular supposition that the most important place for a roller guide is at the tip top of the rod. But they also led to the finding that the second most important place for a roller guide is in the position immediately adjacent to the tip top, and that a roller guide becomes less important the farther away it is mounted from the tip. These findings contradicted the widely-held theory that it is important to have a roller guide at the point nearest the reel.

Due to their weight and method of construction roller guides are not practical for use on spinning or casting rods. Several styles of lightweight plastic roller guides were developed for use with these types of rods, but the experiments ended in failure. The problem seemed to be that the plastic guides had a tendency to freeze up; and once they stopped turning freely they generated enough friction to burn the line.

Aside from the roller guides used on the tips of heavy tournament or big-game rods there are a number of other tip-top guide designs for use with other types of rods. By far the most popular are the bridge and ring-and-tube designs. These are made of the same materials used in the manufacture of other styles of guides. The twisted wire tip-top is not so common, but it is very well suited in rods where weight and light action is a critical factor.

Miscellaneous Components There are several other components of lesser importance used in the final assembly of rods. These include housels and/or winding checks placed on the rod shaft in front of the cork handle in order to prevent damage to the handle. Small wire hook-keepers are used on fly and light spinning rods; the angler hooks his fly or lure into these when he intends to transport his rod without taking it down. Butt caps come in a variety of sizes and shapes and usually are made from rubber or plastic. They are used to protect the angler from the sharp corners at the end of the rod butt or, in the case of a fly rod, from the reel seat.

Ferrule Fitting and Final Assembly Final assembly of a new rod begins with the fitting of the ferrule. In production work the rod blanks are made with an extra tab of fiberglass at the point where the ferrule will be inserted. The blank is cut at this point and a centerless grinder is used to size the ends of the rod section to an accurate fit. A hot-melt cement is heated and placed in the ferrule and the male and female sections are then fitted to the blank; without further adjustment a perfectly straight and true connection is made.

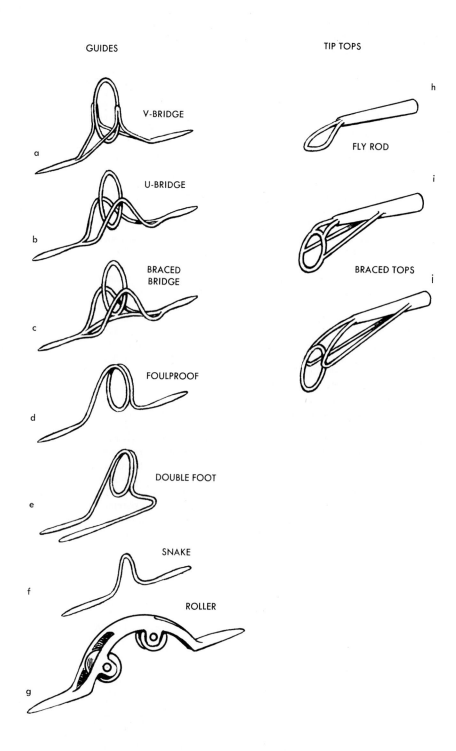

GUIDES

a — V-BRIDGE

b — U-BRIDGE

c — BRACED BRIDGE

d — FOULPROOF

e — DOUBLE FOOT

f — SNAKE

g — ROLLER

TIP TOPS

h — FLY ROD

i — BRACED TOPS

j

The custom rod builder must go about it in a somewhat different way because he does not have the same facilities and he does not have blanks which are pretabbed for cutting. The most common method is to take the female section of the ferrule and slide it down the blank to the point where it will go no farther. This is the point where the blank must be cut and the ferrule fitted into place.

Usually it is necessary for the custom builder to cut a small section out of the blank in order to achieve the proper fit of male and female sections. The male portion is fitted to the tip section and the female portion to the butt section. Often the butt end of the tip section must be sanded to achieve a proper fit. Also, due to the taper of the rod blank, it sometimes becomes necessary to apply a few turns of thread near the butt end of the tip section so that the male ferrule section will be centered in proper alignment. A hot-melt glue or rubber cement should be used so that the ferrule alignment may be adjusted after the original gluing.

After ferruling, the next step is to glue the various components in place. In lower quality mass-produced rods the entire handle assembly is built onto an aluminum tube and this tube is glued onto the blank. In more expensive production rods the handles are preshaped, bored to fit the blank, and then pressed down into position. The reel seat is filled with a bushing of cork, wood, or (where the fit is close) masking tape to achieve a proper fit. Most manufacturers use an epoxy glue to hold these components in place. Once the grips have been mounted, the reel seat is turned to align the hoods with the blank.

In custom building it is necessary to buy individual cork rings and slip them over the tip of the blank and glue them in position one by one, thus gradually building up the cork grip.

Once the rings are in place the builder will use a lathe to shape the handle he wants. In many instances a custom builder also will size down the cork rings to provide a bushing for the reel seat, which is then placed over the cork and glued into place.

When the rod has been assembled to this point it is necessary to determine the number and spacing of the guides to be mounted. A number of methods have been developed to determine proper guide spacing. Probably the most common is the "vibration method" wherein the rod is allowed to vibrate and seek its own natural period of oscillation. There will be one or two nodes in this oscillation, and the theory indicates a guide must be placed at each node. The remaining guides should be spaced evenly up and down the shaft from these points.

An alternative method is to mount a reel on the rod and draw a line along the rod shaft to obtain proper alignment. Then the builder follows a rough rule of thumb which indicates there should be approximately one guide per foot of overall length of the completed rod. It is im-

portant to remember that each guide increases friction on the line, thus shortening the cast; but, conversely, too few guides will cause the line to sag and again create friction which cuts down casting distance. So the number of guides becomes partly a matter of the angler's own choice and partly a matter of what he wants the rod to do.

Once the number of guides has been determined, the guides are mounted temporarily with tape. A line is threaded through the guides and pulled taut so the builder can observe how the stress is distributed over the rod length and whether the line lays against the shaft. The guides should be moved up and down the shaft and positioned so that there is the least possible contact between rod and line when the rod is in a flexed position. Once the builder is satisfied with the guide placement the guides are taped firmly into place prior to wrapping.

The thread used to bind the guides to the shaft usually is made of nylon. In custom work and in higher-priced production rods size A thread is used. Where speed of production is important, a larger size—usually size D—is used. Nylon is practically a universal choice because it is extremely durable, relatively inexpensive, and comes in a wide variety of colors.

Whether the rod is part of a mass production run or is being assembled by a custom builder the wrapping operation is accomplished in much the same way. The method most often used by manufacturers is to turn the rod by a small electric motor controlled through a foot-operated rheostat. The rheostat allows the operator to govern the speed at which the rod is turned. The rod is supported by V blocks and the wrapper applies the thread to the turning shaft. Custom builders usually turn the rod in the palms of their hands, keeping the thread under tension and supporting the rod with two blocks.

The two methods are essentially of the same speed and the choice is pretty much up to the individual where he has access to the equipment necessary for both.

To provide a smooth, continuous wrap it is sometimes necessary to reshape the foot portions of the guides with a grinding stone so that there is no interruption at the

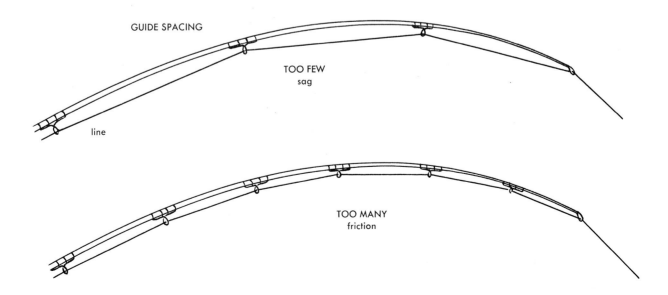

GUIDE SPACING

TOO FEW
sag

line

TOO MANY
friction

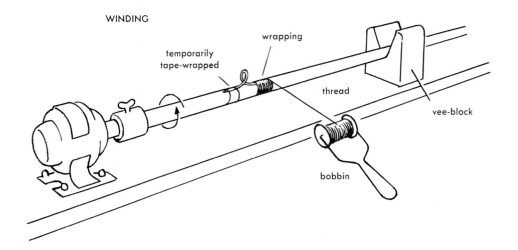

WINDING

wrapping

temporarily
tape-wrapped

thread

vee-block

bobbin

point where the winding leaves the rod shaft and goes onto the guide foot.

The tension applied to the thread during the winding process is of utmost importance. Nylon thread tends to stretch, and if the tension is too tight tremendous force on the guide foot results; it is quite possible to force the guide foot through a wall of the blank. A number of tension-controlled devices have been developed, but the human hand still offers the most reliable gauge.

Many custom builders and some manufacturers produce rods with an underwrap. The underwrap is applied to the blank before the guides are placed in position. Thus, when the guide is placed and wrapped, a double layer of thread results. This method offers a stronger guide attachment and locks the guide firmly in place.

Trim wraps sometimes are placed on either end or in the middle of a standard guide wrap. These usually consist of a smaller-size thread in a color different from that used for the main winding. Trim wraps are for decoration only. It also is customary to wind those portions of the rod adjacent to the grip, the ends of the ferrules, and the base of the tip-top guide.

Once the windings are complete and excess thread is trimmed away the rod is finished except for the application of a coat of lacquer, varnish, or other material designed to protect the windings. The most common material used for this purpose is lacquer. Lacquers tend to dry rapidly and provide a high luster and at least some protection. However, for the custom builder an application of several coats of lacquer is not enough. Usually he also will want to apply one or two coats of spar varnish to the lacquer base which has been built up over the guide wraps.

Today's rod maker also has at his disposal epoxies, urethanes, and acrylics which offer far greater durability and weather resistance than lacquers and spar varnish. The urethanes are most readily obtainable, and though they offer a high degree of durability they are difficult to handle and take a long time to dry.

The two-part epoxies now on the market are extremely durable if properly formulated with ultraviolet absorbents. The acrylics are noted for their use on automobile exteriors; they are not commonly available in clear solutions suitable for rod finishing.

A dip method of finishing is used on cheaper-grade production rods. In this method the entire rod is dipped in a thin mixture of finish. It is then withdrawn slowly while the guides are blown out with air. Many manufacturers also spray a finishing coat on the wraps, and while this method is fast and easy overspraying is a problem. The equipment necessary is expensive and not usually available to the custom builder.

For the custom builder and producer of high-quality rods the time-proven method of using a brush to apply the finish coat is most satisfactory.

All the types of finishes described may be applied by brush; a brush finish results in the best appearance on the completed rod.   —P.T.C.

THE THEORY OF ROD FUNCTION IN CASTING

The purpose of any casting rod is to take a muscular impulse and use it to propel a weight. Obviously, if that impulse were applied directly to the weight without a rod, it wouldn't be nearly as efficient. A fisherman has cast a 4-ounce sinker more than 900 feet. He has also cast a fly line over 200 feet. This cannot be done by the hand alone. Thus we may assume that the flexing of a rod allows a much longer power stroke, and the sum-total energy that goes into the cast is increased as a result. So the prime function of any rod is to bend, and the ability to send a weight through the air is called recoil power.

It is not a hypothetical spring. If a rod were a weightless and inertialess spring, it would have maximum deflection at maximum acceleration and would have theoretically no deflection at maximum velocity; the original stretch of the spring would be given back to the projectile. But a rod has both mass and inertia as well as spring. As a result it has a typical way of vibrating at a specific rate. Maximum recoil power depends on two factors that are built into the rod—its stiffness, or "moment of inertia," and its distributed weight. If our rod builder somehow adds stiffness to a rod without adding weight, the result is a faster rate of recoil—which is the reason for hollow-built bamboo rods, tubular glass rods, and heat-treated bamboo rods. These are a few of the methods used to stiffen a rod without adding weight. In the old days, steel-cored bamboo rods were made in an attempt to get a faster recoil vibration rate, but conversely, adding weight without increasing the stiffness resulted in a less powerful rod. What pioneer bamboo builders failed to see was that the stiffness of a rod at any point in its length is a function of the cross section at that point, and of the material's characteristics. Eventually, arguments were advanced for the six-strip, five-strip, four-strip, ad infinitum. Rods have been made in every form from a solid to one of twelve strips. Many fine rods are built in the United States today in all cross sections from hollow to solid, including those from two-strip to six-strip.

ROD ACTION

Fly rod action may be even less comprehensible to most fishermen than an explanation of how the modern computer or rocket missile works. But, being a functional tool, like the refrigerator, or a vacuum cleaner, the angler will soon learn whether or not the fly rod is producing.

Fly rods are usually identified as being wet-fly action, dry-fly or trout action, bass-steelhead action, and salmon action. These terms are descriptive enough for the novice, but more precise information is desirable for the experienced angler because these terms are interchangeable. A dry-fly "action" is quite suitable for sunken fly fishing, and a quality wet-fly action often makes a perfect rod for floaters. For salmon, never use anything heavier than a bass-steelhead action; perhaps best for salmon, though, is a light dry-fly action. The wet-fly rod is a lighter rod at any given length than a comparable dry-fly rod. Rods for the wet fly are soft, as there is little false casting to be

done. A stiffer rod would dry the fly while false casting and is therefore less desirable. So the dry-fly rod is comparatively stiff and has a more pronounced tip movement, quality that is built into the rod rather than added to it by increase in weight.

Bass-steelhead rods are heavier and stiffer because the flies and rods used for these fish are heavier and more wind resistant. Essentially they are slow but powerful. Salmon-action rods are the heaviest and stiffest by far because of the weight of line and the size of the flies these rods must throw. But if the fisherman chooses to ignore the traditional large double-hook salmon flies and has the skill to lay out a long line with a light rod—any of the other rods can be used.

These terms, then, are simply a guide for the beginning angler.

A rod is really a simple beam with cantilevers at both the ends. It is a subject of dynamics rather than static mechanics. When put in motion it acquires properties of acceleration, impact, rotation, and momentum. There are two supports: the hand which is supporting the butt section and the nodal point in the tip. The nodal point is the area of transition where the force applied to the butt of the rod is being translated into motion. This can be simply demonstrated by holding a fly rod a few inches over and parallel to a table. When the rod is raised sharply to flip the tip upward, as in a cast, the butt portion of the rod comes up with the hand, but the tip moves in the *opposite* direction, striking the table top before rebounding and following the direction taken by the hand. This can also be seen by holding a fly rod horizontally in the air and setting up a side to side vibration, observing how the tip portion fans out.

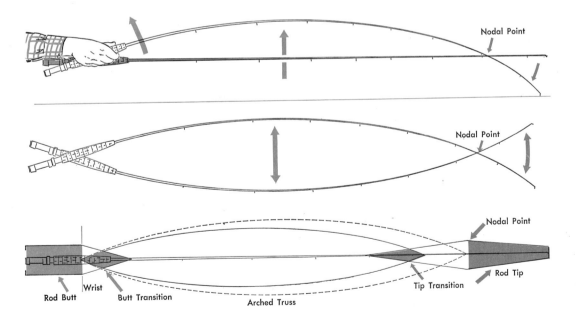

A simple test will demonstrate that rod action is controlled by the stiffness of the middle portion. Hold a rod parallel to a table top, as in the top drawing. Raise the butt sharply as if to flip tip upward, as in a cast. The butt part will come up with your hand, but the tip will move in the opposite direction, striking the table top before rebounding and following the direction taken by your hand. In the second test, hold the rod horizontally, and set up a side-to-side vibration with your wrist, as shown in the middle drawing, and observe how the tip fans out. Note the nodal point and the shape of the vibrating middle. The diagram on the bottom shows theoretical dynamic "linkage" between the three rod portions. Stiffness of the mid-portion governs rod action.

A rod, therefore, can be divided into three convenient and easily recognized sections: the tip, mid-section, and butt. In actual casting the hand drives the butt, the butt drives the mid-section, the mid-section drives the tip, and the tip drives the line or lure. The tightness or looseness of this linkage is the action of the rod. Thus, rod action is controlled largely by the stiffness of the mid-section. The butt is the driver; the tip its translator; and the mid-section is an arched truss between the two.

The Stiffness Factor   The stiffness of a rod at any point of its length is a function of the cross section at that point and of the characteristics of the material from which it is made. This became apparent during the years when steel was a popular rod-building material (1920–1947). Steel rods were strong, but they lacked casting "power." The decline of steel, however, was largely due to metal fatigue. With the advent of fiberglass the limited-life steel rods gave way to the new material. But steel did illustrate that there is a vast difference between a material's tensile strength and its stiffness factor; where the former resists breaking, the latter resists bending. Weightwise, solid steel was the least efficient rod material. If you bend a rod downward, all the surface on top is under compression; inside the rod there exists a point where there is neither tension or compression. This center is called the neutral axis. It exists as a solid or empty space. Under dynamic conditions (i.e., casting) it is also the location of maximum horizontal shear, which is the tendency of fibers to slip past neighboring fibers. Actually, it may be viewed as induced stresses working down and up the length of the rod. Some idea of the force can be realized when a rod "mysteriously" snaps in two at the peak of a cast. The impulse that bends a rod butt in casting is the momentum of the moving tip and the lure; when the cast is checked, this momentum travels down the rod to the butt by way of the ferrule. The bamboo or fiberglass that is under the ferrule takes a terrific pounding because the force is exerted across its diameter, and to compound the stress, the ferrule must bend the butt section. In a bamboo rod, this longitudinal shear sometimes pulverizes the wood under the ferrule. With hollow-glass rods, the force just breaks the joint square off. Solid steel didn't break very often, but it had one major failing in that the extreme or outer working fibers were in close proximity to the neutral axis. The stiff, thin, steel shaft fought a vibrational war within itself.

In order to eliminate the literal core of the problem, one manufacturer originated a system of making tubular rods by stepping down a steel tube in repeated drawing operations. Each die thus successively reduced both the outside diameter and the wall thickness. Solid steel continued to have a large market among trollers and sinker bouncers, but casting men found that in tubular form, steel had some of the "life" of bamboo. Tubular steel rods competed strongly with the cane market. But after World War II, fiberglass appeared, and steel vanished; glass is stronger for its weight and is not subject to rust or wall collapse. Furthermore, both the stiffness and the strength of a fiberglass rod could be controlled by its bonding agent, or the thermoplastic substance that holds the glass fibers together. But the problem that has perplexed rod builders through the ages is that using the structure and material that you would expect to produce maximum recoil is not the answer to a perfect rod. If so,

all rods would be made of tubular glass and have a profile that looks something like the Eiffel Tower. It would be the stiffest and lightest rod ever made, yet not be efficient for casting. The Eiffel Tower profile is for a static cantilever beam—not a vibrating casting rod.

Luxor Method   In 1936, the French tackle firm of Pezon & Michel adopted a spinning-rod classification system known as the Luxor method. This is predicated on the strength of a rod. Under the Luxor system, it is assumed that the optimum lure weight should be $\frac{1}{50}$ of the static resistance of the rod. This is expressed in grams; thus a spinning rod of "400 grams strength" is calibered to cast a lure of 8 grams (eight times the unit of 50 equals 400). Obviously, the 400-gram rod can cast lighter and heavier lures, but 8 grams is optimum for perfect casting. Factory checking is done on a graph board with the rod clamped in a horizontal position; a cord is run from the rod handle through the guides, and weights are attached to the cord until it forms a tangent to the rod tip. The total weight that creates the tangent is the grams-strength measurement, which may be 200, 300, 400, and so on. This is some index of net recoil power.

The argument against graph-board data is that while it may be the best way of determining a rod's strength it does not reveal the moving curve of the rod. The graph board provides a purely static measurement, which isn't enough to explain how the rod will act. The location of the ferrules, for instance, greatly affects rod action, and their influence doesn't show up on the graph board at all. At best, the board can only indicate which rods are downright poor. It cannot take into account the response of a rod in suddenly applied rapid motion. We learn nothing of the rod's action. Is it fast or slow? Three men who tried to carry the graph board to a logical conclusion were the Englishman Hawksley and two Frenchmen, Robin and Biscarbelcha. They recognized that the rod is not a static beam, nor the commonly conceived spring, but a vibrating cantilever beam. Accordingly, they further measured their rods in wave lengths. The conclusion drawn by wave-length researchers was that a good casting rod vibrates in quarter wave lengths.

The Ideal Rod in Theory   Velocity is the end product of casting, which you achieve through muscular impulse (acceleration) multiplied by the time of the cast. The action of the rod to a large extent determines the time factor (fast or slow). Action is controlled by the rod's taper. Thus, the ideal rod is one that is harmonically sound and whose effective bending length is *longest* for the weight being propelled—be it frog, plug, spinner, sinker, or fly. This doesn't mean that long rods are better than short rods, or light ones are better than heavy ones. It means the slowest rod to reach any hypothetical maximum of recoil power is close to, if not actually, perfection.

An example of how rod design relates to performance can be realized in a short ultralight tip-action spinning rod. Casting very light spinning lures with a tip-action rod is awkward and inaccurate because the effective bending length of the rod is short, and therefore the time factor defeats our purpose. With baits weighing around $\frac{1}{20}$ of an ounce, all the initial bend put into the rod is from air resistance alone. We are dealing with weights so light that you can neither feel the lure nor direct its flight until the last instant. Consequently, if we can slow the casting swing so that it's in phase with and aids the casting operation, we have much better control of the lure. Ideally, the rod for ultralight casting must be slow, which on a 5-foot rod means flexing right down into the corks. To shorten the bending length is to decrease the time factor. It's almost axiomatic that the lighter the weights to be cast, the greater the bending length required. Merely using a *longer* rod is no solution. When a builder increases the length of a rod of any given power, to keep that power equal in the longer rod he has to add increments of weight that are out of proportion to the added length; the tip section must remain proportionate to the range of weights being cast. You can't cast heavy weights with a fine tip, nor light weights with a heavy tip. So any extra length must be added to the butt section, which makes the rod heavier, and, failing to provide more bending length, the time factor remains the same. Nor does the answer lie wholly in our first premise; i.e., recoil power is a result of the moment of inertia and distributed weight. The rod's action is ultimately responsible for utilizing the weight to be cast.   —A.J.McC.

ROD REPAIRS There are a number of simple procedures which can be accomplished at home or in camp for minor rod-repair work. Aside from actually breaking a rod the most common damages are to the guides and ferrules. In most cases the angler will need no more than a few basic items, such as thread, lacquer, transparent tape, and scissors to effect these repairs.

CHANNELED GUIDES

Channeling is a result of the line cutting grooves in the metal guides. This usually appears first in the top guide of a bait-casting or spinning rod, or on the butt guide of a fly rod. Although modern chrome carbide, tungsten carbide, and tungsten steel guides are far more sturdy than the soft metals popular in years past, our present-day synthetic lines are also rugged, and this is especially true of the monofilaments. Too, many low-priced rods still come equipped with expendable hardware. The first symptoms of channeling are apt to be costly in losing fish and lures. The bait-casting or spinning line snaps for no particular reason that you can see, but a careful check will usually reveal a sharp spot on one of the rings. A channeled fly-rod guide is less noticeable because the line finish chips off gradually. But if you check your guides periodically under strong light, trouble can be prevented.

HOW TO REPLACE A GUIDE

Both silk and nylon thread may be used for winding guides and binding ferrules. In general, silk sizes No. 0 and No. 00, or nylon size A make the neatest work on fly rods and light spinning rods. But for heavy rods whose guides will be abused and subject to line wear, a size E nylon is most durable. Use size E on any fly rod that casts a heavy three-diameter line and for spinning rods meant to handle monofilaments of 8-pound-test or more. Turning out a neat winding takes experience, but you can make immediate practical repairs if you follow the accompanying diagram carefully. You can practice by wrapping thread around a pencil. With transparent tape, position your guide on one leg. Cut off a 4–5-inch piece of thread for your pull-under loop and keep it handy. Begin the winding about $1/16$ inch ahead of the untaped

leg. Secure the thread by starting the first turn around the free end, and after 2–3 turns slide your hand down the thread so that you are holding it about 10 inches from the rod. The thread must be held at a slight angle to force it against each previous turn. After you have made 5–6 turns, snip off the free end. Continue winding until you are about 5–6 turns from the point where you will stop, which on a guide is where the foot starts to rise away from the rod, and secure the pull-under loop. Wrap around the loop, and then, holding the winding with your thumb, cut the thread, leaving a 3-inch end, and poke this end through the loop. This is probably the most critical step in neat work because the free end must dangle loosely and not be drawn down under tension. If there is no slack, either thread will break or fuzz out when pulled through.

To finish your windings they must be lacquered, then varnished. Use five coats of clear lacquer which is thinned so that it runs like water. Lacquer dries fast enough, so that the five coats can be applied all in one day, and the first coat of varnish may be applied that night. The windings also get five coats of varnish, and preferably a slow-drying one like clear-gloss Super Valspar. Although many factory rod windings are not varnished, it's a good idea to do so because plain lacquer flakes off in a short time. You have probably seen dry, colorless threads appear around your guides after the rod is used for a few weeks—this is due to the lack of varnish. It's a common problem with low-cost glass sticks but easy to remedy.

INCORRECT SPACING OF GUIDES

In mass-produced rods, and this is particularly true of fly rods, the most costly item to the manufacturer is labor and secondly the hardware. Very often, the only difference between a cheap rod and a first-class stick of the same make is the guides and windings. The rods themselves may be identical. Sometimes the original mountings are not spaced correctly, or there are too few guides for uniform stress distribution. Points of stress are greatest between any two adjacent guides, and, logically, the farther they are apart the greater the pressure at these points. When the number of guides is increased, the points of stress are decreased. There is a limit, however, because too many guides add too much weight and create additional friction against the outgoing line. Generally, spinning and bait-casting rods are mounted with 5–6 guides, not including the tip-top, and fly rods get 7–12, depending on their length, quality, and performance.

How to Correct Guide Spacing As a general rule for guide placement on fly rods, a three-piece 9-foot rod will have twelve guides, six on the tip section, exclusive of the tip-top, five guides on the middle section, and just the stripping guide on the butt section. To rough out their spacing, place the No. 11 guide (they are usually numbered, counting from the first below the tip-top down the rod) 9 inches above the stripping guide; then reduce the spacing by $1/2$ inch for the next four on the mid-section. For the tip section, bridge the ferrule $6\frac{1}{2}$ inches from your No. 7 guide and reduce the spacing $3/4$ inch on each of the six guides, bringing the last one to within 4 inches of the tip-top. A two-piece 9-foot fly rod, having one less ferrule, can take two snake guides on the butt as well as the shooting guide with the eight or more guides on the tip. Fly rods of 8–8½ feet in length usually require 8–9 guides exclusive of the tip-top, while shorter lengths down to 6 feet require 7–9, depending on whether they are two- or three-piece rods. The thing to keep in mind is that the butt or shooting guide on a fly rod should be far enough from the grip so that your angle of pull isn't too short. Some makers get generous with the hardware and the big ring is so close to your hand that there's no slack to work with—and then it has to be pulled around corners. Depending on the length of the rod, it should be from 28–34 inches up from the base of the butt.

The function of spinning-rod guides is to "choke down" the line as it comes off the spool. Unlike the situation in fly rods, keeping the line close to the spinning rod is secondary. To cast smoothly, the rings must be large, lightweight, and positioned at minimum points of friction. In spacing spinning rods for trial, the very general rule to use on a 7-foot blank, two-piece, with 10-inch grip is as follows: butt (No. 5) guide, 33 inches from base end of rod shaft, No. 4 guide 13 inches from butt guide, No. 3 guide 11 inches from No. 4, No. 2 guide 10 inches from No. 3, No. 1 guide 9 inches from No. 2, making No. 1 guide 8 inches from the tip-top. For a 6-foot blank, two-piece with 10-inch grip as follows: butt (No. 5) guide 26 inches from base end of rod shaft, No. 4 guide 12 inches from butt guide, No. 3 guide 12 inches from No. 4, No. 2 guide 9 inches from No. 3, No. 1 guide 8 inches from No. 2 making No. 1 guide 6 inches from tip-top. For a 5½-foot rod, use four guides instead of five, as follows: butt (No. 4) guide 24 inches from base of rod shaft, No. 3 guide 12 inches from butt guide, No. 2 guide 12 inches from No. 3, No. 1 guide 10 inches from No. 2, making No. 1 guide 8 inches from tip-top. After mounting the guides with transparent tape, assemble the rod and pass the line through the guides. Hold the rod in a workable arc by tying the line to some object against which you can pull, and note if there are any flat spots. You may have to shift two or three of the guides less than an inch according to the taper of the rod. To make certain you have the spacing correct, take the rod out and cast with it for about 15 minutes. Note particularly whether the line cuts the transparent tape holding your butt guide (if so it should be moved up the rod ½-inch per trial). Also, the line shouldn't wrap around any section of the rod between guides.

LUBRICATE FERRULES

Most ferrule problems begin with the angler taking his rod apart. Get careless and forget to lubricate the male plug, or leave jointed rods standing in the rack for long periods and the ferrules become stuck. But unjointing a rod must be done properly, which means no twisting or yanking. The correct way to unjoint a rod is to grasp it on both sides of the joint with your hands close together and thumbs opposed. Then push your thumbs one against the other, which forces your hands and the ferrule apart. This prevents bending or twisting the ferrule. On a cold day, the fit might be tighter than usual; hold the ferrule between both palms and rotate the rod rapidly. The metal will get warm and expand in a few seconds. If the ferrule won't budge, then bend over at the waist and get in a semisquat position with your knees together and hold the rod behind them parallel to the ground. Grasp the rod on

each side of the ferrule and pull steadily. If you are with a companion, you can work together, but each of you should have one hand on opposite sides of the ferrule. Don't grab it like a mule's tail because you'll both angle off the horizontal. If this doesn't work, then your last course short of removing the ferrule completely is to warm the metal with a match. Hold the flame about ½ inch from the end of the outer ferrule while you rotate the rod with your other hand. A few seconds of heat should expand the metal sufficiently before the inner portion gets warm.

REPAIRING LOOSE FERRULES

When exposed to cold weather, the metal of a ferrule contracts, making its internal diameter slightly smaller than normal. On a bamboo rod the wood is compressed. In hot weather the metal expands, leaving a space between ferrule and wood. This expansion and contraction plus the routine stresses of casting eventually work the metal free. Loose ferrules should be recemented as soon as they are noticed. If you continue using the rod, the rocking joint will snap. If you have to replace a ferrule, buy the best quality obtainable. Nickel-silver is still the most widely used metal; an alloy consisting of 18 percent nickel, 12–18 percent zinc, and the balance copper, it has high tensile strength for comparatively light weight, and it doesn't fatigue readily. Don't confuse it with cheap nickel-plated brass ferrules as their life span and strength are both limited.

For quick, streamside repairs there are many brands of ferrule cement available which are composed chiefly of resin, linseed oil, and beeswax. All you have to do with stick cement is hold it over a flame for a few seconds, then daub the softened mixture on the rod end. Spread the cement evenly with a knife blade, reheat, and push the ferrule (which you should also warm) into place. The brittle character of quick-drying cements, however, makes them undesirable for permanent repairs. Eventually, they cease to bind. If you are in camp and have a few hours to spare, you can get more mileage out of a ferrule that is being hot-cemented by wrapping the rod end with one or two layers of thread. The cement will saturate the wrapping, which acts much like a breaker in a rubber tire. Strands of linen line can be laid ¹⁄₁₆ inch apart parallel to and around the neck where the ferrule will be seated. But for home or permanent repairs, the solution is an adhesive with elastic qualities—and none of these is quick-drying. Many professionals use a cold cement like Goodyear's Pliobond. Although it takes forty hours to dry, the cement remains pliable even years afterward.

—A.J.McC.

ROE The eggs of a female fish usually when still enclosed in the ovarian membrane. Also the eggs or ovaries of certain crustaceans, such as the "coral" of the lobster. The most common roe marketed are from the shad, salmon, and sturgeon. However, many other roes are desirable such as the dolphin, flounder, mullet, Spanish mackerel, and bluefish. To be edible, roe must be obtained at the right period of development. Once the eggs develop to match-head size, the roe becomes too oily for cooking. The roes of some fish, such as the puffers and the gars, are known to be toxic and should not be eaten. *See also* Anatomy, Caviar, Fish Cookery

ROOSEVELT, ROBERT BARNWELL, American (1829–1906). The uncle of President Theodore Roosevelt, he wrote under the abbreviated by-line "Barnwell," and was a key figure in the early development of both the entomological approach to fly tying and the modernization of tackle. He was also a pioneer of North American fly fishing for Atlantic salmon. His first book, *Game Fish of the Northern States of America and British Provinces* (1862), was a landmark in that it was this country's first introduction to angling entomology. Heavily derivative from Ronalds, his approach was dilettantish and slight, but it was a significant start. It was also the first American book to treat of salmon fishing, although anticipated by *Salmon Fishing in Canada* (1860) by a Resident (Reverend W.A. Adamson), which was published in London. A perfectionist, rather pompously opinionated, insistent on the newest and best, and remarkably gadget-minded for his time, "Barnwell" drew the sallies of Uncle Thad Norris for his fuss-and-feathers attitude, including dressing for dinner (Prime would have caught the same jibes, except that he wrote after Uncle Thad). As his subsequent books showed, he was not entirely untrammeled by traces of vainglory. His other books were *Superior Fishing, or, the Striped Bass, Trout and Black Bass of the Northern States* (1865); *Fish Culture Compared in Importance with Agriculture* (1872), the pamphlet of a speech he made in Congress as a Representative of New York; *Fish Hatching and Fish Catching*, with Seth Green (1879); and *Love and Luck* (1886).   —A.G.

ROOSTERFISH *Nematistius pectoralis* Also called *papagallo*, *gallo*, and *pez de gallo*, this unique species lives only along the western coast of the Americas in the eastern Pacific. This fish is classed in a distinct family, Nematistiidae, but is very closely related to the Carangidae.

The roosterfish has 7 elongated rays in the first dorsal fin, the longest about half as long as the total length of the fish.

The body shape tapers like that of an amberjack. There are 8 spines in the first dorsal fin, the last 7 greatly elongated; the second dorsal fin has 1 spine and about 25 softrays; the anal fin has 3 spines and about 15 softrays; the anal fin is much shorter than the second dorsal fin, the lobes of both fins are short; and the pectoral fin is elongated. Color is green to black on the back and white or golden below; there are two black stripes curving downward and backward from under the first dorsal fin, a black nuchal band, and a black spot on pectoral fin base; the dorsal spines are striped with alternate blue-black and white.

The roosterfish is known from Cabo Blanco, Peru, into the Gulf of California and up the outer coast of Baja California to Turtle Bay, and at the Galápagos Islands; there is a sight record for this species from San Clemente Island off southern California. It is most common over sandy beaches from the surf zone to moderate depths, and has been said to be most abundant off Ecuador. The maximum recorded size and total length are 111 pounds and 5 feet 2 inches.

LIFE HISTORY

Essentially nothing is known of its life history. Ripe specimens have not been reported, and some specimens examined in December to June were reported to be sexually immature. The smallest specimen known, ⅜ inch in total length, was taken in July off Costa Rica. Specimens under a foot long may travel in close schools, while larger fish seem to move in looser groups. They are known to feed on small fishes in the surf.

ANGLING VALUE

Roosterfish are excellent and exciting gamefish. When chasing prey they may leap 3–6 times in dolphin fashion. When swimming at the surface they often "flash the comb" by erecting the long spines of the first dorsal fin out of the water. Very palatable. Commercial use seems to be mainly limited to fresh-fish markets in Central American ports, but in Mexico it is frequently transported to interior cities for sale.   —F.H.B.

RORQUAL WHALE *See* Whales

Roosterfish

ROSYFACE SHINER *Notropis rubellus* A small, silver-blue minnow with a lavender lateral band, its sides are silvery with a lavender sheen. Snout sharply pointed. Body rounded. The origin of the dorsal fin is distinctly behind the origin of the ventral fins. Anal rays 10–13. This species is found from North Dakota to the St. Lawrence and Hudson River and south to Virginia and part of the Ohio River drainage.

Rosyface Shiner

HABITS

The rosyface shiner inhabits moderate-sized streams with clearwater, relatively high gradients, and clean bottoms. It apparently winters in deeper riffles and pools. It is intolerant of turbid water and silt bottoms. The food of the rosyface consists of insects and vegetable matter, including midge larvae, blackfly larvae, caddis worms, and green algae. This species spawns over sandy gravel, gravel, or bedrock in spring or early summer. The males become more intensely colored and develop tiny tubercles over most of the body. Another one of the small minnows, the rosyface seldom exceeds 3 inches.

ECONOMIC VALUE

The rosyface shiner is considered excellent bait for bass, perch, and other panfish. —R.A.J.

ROSY ROCKFISH *Sebastodes rosaceus* This rockfish (*which see*) is a minor commercial species found from northern Baja California to central British Columbia. It

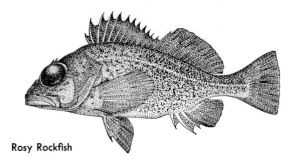

Rosy Rockfish

is distinguished by having strong spines on top of its head; naked under side of lower jaw; a second spine of the anal fin longer than the third; a concave interorbital space. Basic color is yellow in the young; orange-red in adults, with dark red or purple bordering 3–5 white blotches. Length to twelve inches. —J.R.

ROSYSIDE DACE *Clinostomus funduloides* A brilliant-colored, medium-sized, minnow seldom exceeding 5 inches in total length and being found in the upland streams from the Chesapeake Bay southward to Georgia. The snout of this minnow is short; and the lower limb of the pharyngeal arch is short and stout. Its distinguishing characteristics are 7–9, usually 8, dorsal rays, and 7–10, usually 9, anal rays; a sharply forked caudal fin; sides of the body being pale to dark with scattered spots or

mottling; a dark prominent lateral band, being more pronounced on the caudal peduncle; a complete lateral band curving downward from the upper edge of the gill opening, reaching its lowest point about 7 or 8 scale rows from the head; a lateral line scale count of usually 50; dorsal fin originating about 2–3 scale rows posterior to the base of the pelvic fins; outer margin of the dorsal fins nearly straight; pharyngeal teeth in two rows, the teeth being slender and well hooked, with the teeth in the outer row numbering 5-5 and on the inner row usually 2-2; a short intestine with but one anterior loop; no barbels, with the lower lip being normally formed; and the belly between the pelvic fins and the anus being rounded. Another significant characteristic is that the first ray of the dorsal fin is slender and closely jointed to the second ray, there being no membrane between them.

Rosyside Dace

LIFE HISTORY

The rosyside dace is generally associated with small to medium-sized, relatively shallow, clearwater streams. It is found most numerous in streams having gravel and sand bottoms. During June and July the rosyside dace reaches its highest coloration, which is rosy pink. It spawns in early spring laying from 409–1,526 eggs. The rosyside dace reaches reproductive size at 3 inches. The average length of an adult is 3½ inches, and the maximum length is 6 inches.

It serves as forage for the smallmouth bass and the redbreast sunfish. It is used locally, on occasions, for bait. —D.E.L.

ROTENONE The original of various fish toxicants now in use as a fisheries management tool in poisoning lakes to remove undesirable species. Rotenone is an organic compound, $C_{23}H_{22}O_6$, found in the roots of various Leguminosae marketed under the name Derris or Cubé Root, and was originally used by South American Indian tribes for catching fish. Rotenone was first applied to the rehabilitation of two Michigan lakes in 1934, and since that time thousands of waters have been treated with it in the United States and Canada. There are many factors to consider in applying Rotenone successfully, and it requires experienced professional biologists to obtain the desired results. Rotenone has little if any effect on other aquatic organisms when used in a weak concentration, which is strong enough to kill fish. With Rotenone, detoxification can be very rapid, especially in alkaline, turbid, and warm water; in clear, acid water in cold lakes, detoxification may require many months. —A.J.McC.

ROUGH SCAD *Trachurus lathami* Also known as saurel, this species of the western North Atlantic has also been listed as *Trachurus trachurus*, *Trachurus pictaturus*, and *Trachurus binghami* (*see below*).

Enlarged scutes cover the entire portion of both the curved and the straight lateral line. There is no detached

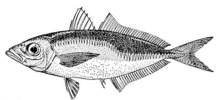

Rough Scad

finlet behind the dorsal or anal fin, and there are no papillae and no furrow on the shoulder girdle.

The second dorsal fin has one spine and 28–33 softrays. The anal fin has two detached spines, followed by one spine and 26–30 softrays. The first gill arch has 12–14 gillrakers on the upper limb and 34–37 gillrakers on the lower limb. The curved lateral line has 30–37 scutes, and the straight lateral line has 31–41 pointed scutes. Color is bluish-green above and silvery below, with a small, sometimes indistinct, opercular spot.

This species is known from Maine to Florida and throughout the Gulf of Mexico. It grows to about 8–10 inches, possibly larger.

LIFE HISTORY

The life history has not been studied. It is a schooling fish. Young juveniles are sometimes taken far offshore, and the young have been noted in association with jellyfish.

ANGLING VALUE

This species does not appear to be common enough to provide a concentrated sport or commercial fishery. It has been used as bait for other fishes.

As with the Pacific species of this genus, the different isolated populations of *Trachurus* in the Atlantic have not been adequately studied. There appears to be only one species off the Atlantic and Gulf coasts of the United States, and the name *Trachurus lathami* should apply to this. The species off the coast of Brazil is frequently designated as *Trachurus trachurus*, the name of the species in the Mediterranean. *See also* Carangidae, Scads   —F.H.B.

ROUGHTAIL STINGRAY *Dasyatis centroura* It resembles the southern stingray (*which see*) in general body shape and in having the outer corners of the disk only narrowly rounded. Its long tail is quite thorny, and there are one or more long, barbed spines near the tail base. The body is rhomboid, with the anterior edges of the wings approximately straight-edged, the posterior margins being slightly convex. Along the midline of the back is a series of irregularly spaced low thorns, bordered on either wing by additional, widely scattered thorns of a slightly larger size. There is no fold along the dorsal midline of the tail, but it possesses a skinfold along the lower surface of the tail. This ray is dark brown to black above with a black tail, and the lower parts are whitish or gray-white, occasionally with dusky to black blotches. It is one of the largest of the stingrays, growing to a recorded length of 10 feet and an estimated length of 13–14 feet and several hundred pounds.

LIFE HISTORY

This species occurs in cooler waters than the closely related southern stingray. It is known with certainty from Georges Bank, off New England, to North Carolina, and is believed to occur in Florida. Closely related species occur in the eastern Atlantic, and in Uruguay. Its center of abundance is from Delaware Bay to southern New England. Warm temperatures bring them into the Middle Atlantic area from June to October, and thereafter they move offshore into deeper water. Found in bays, sounds, and other relatively quiet bodies of water, it tolerates estuarine waters to some degree. Although it enters shallow water, it is usually taken in at least 5 fathoms, occurring regularly in water of 10–20 fathoms. But it is encountered less often in shallow water than the southern stingray. Sexual maturity occurs at a width of at least 4 feet, and the young, resembling the mother, are born alive. It eats shrimp, crabs, clams, snails, squid, worms, and small fishes.

FOOD VALUE

Its flesh is good, and though not widely eaten it resembles scallops in flavor. Because of its large size and the formidable spine of large specimens, it is highly respected by fishermen.   —D.dS.

ROUNDEL SKATE *Raja texana* The body is diamond-shaped, with the corners meeting nearly at right angles. The skin is fairly smooth except for a row of thorns along the tail. On each pectoral fin is a distinct ocellus, or a dark spot surrounded by a light area. These ocelli distinguish it from other common skates, except for the closely related ocellate skate, *Raja ackleyi*, which has elliptical ocelli and broadly rounded corners on the disk. The roundel skate is chocolate- to coffee-colored with a translucent area on the snout as in the clearnose skate (*which see*). Small specimens are sprinkled with pale spots and blotches. It grows to about 21 inches long. Compared to other skates, this is an uncommon species. It is known only from central Florida to Aransas Pass, Texas.

LIFE HISTORY

Its life history is unknown, except that it is apparently a shallow-water species.   —D.dS.

ROUND SCAD *Decapterus punctatus* This is the more common of the two species of this genus occurring in the western Atlantic.

The round scad has a detached, single-rayed finlet behind the dorsal and the anal fin, pointed scutes in the straight lateral line, and no scutes in the curved lateral line. The vertical edge of the shoulder girdle has a moderate-sized papillalike projection at its upper and its lower extremities, but no groove below the lower projection.

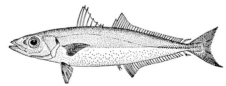

Round Scad

The second dorsal fin has one spine and 28–32 softrays and the detached finlet. The anal fin has two detached spines, followed by one spine and 25–27 softrays and the detached finlet. The first gill arch has 12–15 gillrakers on the upper limb and 34–40 gillrakers on the lower limb.

There are 36–44 pointed scutes in the straight lateral line. There are usually 20 rays in each pectoral fin (range of 19–21). The color is dark above and silvery below with a golden tinge. A row of small dark spots occurs along the anterior part of the lateral line, and there is usually a small opercular spot.

This species ranges in the western Atlantic from Rio de Janeiro, Brazil, to Nova Scotia, and at Bermuda. A very similar form from the eastern Atlantic has been reported under this name. The maximum size is not known; it may be less than 12 inches.

The mackerel scad, *Decapterus macarellus*, ranges from Fernando de Noronha, Brazil, to Nova Scotia, and at Bermuda. It has more scales in the straight lateral line (59–65) than the round scad, but fewer pointed scutes (28–37) than that species. The mackerel scad also has more rays in each pectoral fin (22–24). The round scad was reported to have a blue color and a slimmer body, and the more abundant mackerel scad to have a pronounced yellow stripe on the body.

LIFE HISTORY

The life history is not adequately known. A series of larvae and developing juveniles from North Carolina were described and attributed to the round scad. These young were taken from May to December, and most were taken in July through September. The majority were captured offshore, eastward to the Gulf Stream.

ANGLING VALUE

These two relatively small species are not often taken in sport fishing. They are used primarily for bait, usually salted or frozen. A small commercial fishery exists on the west coast of Florida, where they are caught primarily with haulseines. The taste is reported to be good, and they are occasionally sold in fresh-fish markets. *See also* Carangidae, Scads —F.H.B.

ROUND STINGRAY *Urolophus halleri* The nearly circular shape of the disk identifies this stingray from others along the western coast of North America. The skin is smooth, and the tail is short and lacks a dorsal fin. A well-developed spine is located near the tip of the tail.

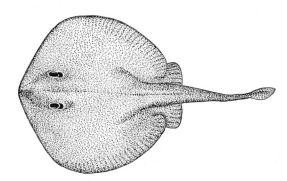

Round Stingray

It is light brown above with wavy, wormlike markings covering the entire surface, these occasionally showing up as round spots. It is yellow or yellowish below. The largest recorded specimen is a 22-inch female.

LIFE HISTORY

It occurs from Monterey Bay in central California to Panama Bay where it is common in quiet waters and along sandy or muddy beaches. Most common in 2–3 fathoms, they have been taken from a few inches of water down to about 100 feet. Indications are that there is some inshore movement with warming temperatures and a converse, offshore drift in the winter. Reproductive activities occur in spring, and young are born from June to November, the mother producing an average of three young with up to eight being known. The young are about 4 inches wide and possess a functional sting. Worms, crabs, shrimps, and small fishes are obtained by the stingray scooping out depressions by beating the "wings." In turn, they are eaten by sharks and large groupers.

DANGER TO MAN

Their sting, depending on the size of the ray, can inflict a painful or even fatal injury. Recommended treatment for stingray wounds is to clean the wound as completely as possible and then immerse the wound in water as hot as possible. Medical attention, including a tetanus shot and further cleaning of the wound, is prescribed. *See also* First Aid

FOOD VALUE

There is no commercial use for this stingray. Although its flesh is reportedly edible, the species is generally too small to make any kind of commercial venture profitable. —D.dS.

ROUND WHITEFISH *Prosopium cylindraceum* A widely distributed member of the whitefish family, also called Menominee whitefish and grayback, it differs from other North American members of the whitefish family (which include the ciscoes) in having only a single flap between the opening of the nostril, rather than two. Unlike the lake whitefish, which is laterally compressed, its body is cylindrical in shape except at the head and tail, and rather uniformly tapered.

The round whitefish is silvery in color, with the dorsal surface including the head a bronze tinged with green. The sides are brownish and the belly light. Sexually mature individuals are more highly colored, with some red or orange on the belly; ripe fish of both sexes develop pearl organs which are more prominent on the males. It is a small species seldom exceeding 15 inches in length and a weight of 2 pounds, although fish to 4 pounds have been recorded in the Great Lakes.

The round whitefish is distributed from New Brunswick northward to Ungava Bay and westward through the Great Lakes and Canada to Alaska and the Arctic Ocean. A subspecies is found in Siberia.

LIFE HISTORY

This fish spawns in early winter (late November and December) in lakes on gravelly shoals at 3–20 feet in depth. The spawning whitefish do not congregate in large schools, but pair off over gravel-rubble bottom. The number of eggs per female varies between 2500–10,000. The eggs usually hatch out in the following spring (April). The fry are heavily preyed upon by yellow perch,

Round Whitefish

as well as larger gamefish such as lake trout, landlocked salmon, and chain pickerel. Round whitefish feed on insect larvae and crustaceans.

The growth rate of round whitefish is variable, with populations in the southern limits of its distribution reaching larger sizes more rapidly and maturing earlier than populations in its northern range. Round whitefish in Lake Michigan reach a weight of 1 pound in 5 years; Lake Superior fish in 8 years; while those in the Ungava Bay area require 10 years before attaining this weight. Its life span is about 12 years.

ANGLING VALUE

Due to its small size the round whitefish has limited angling value. However, it is an important forage species in most areas.

FOOD VALUE

Commercially it is considered a better fish than the ciscos, but it is not rated in the same class as the lake whitefish. Its flesh spoils readily and it contains little oil, so that it is not particularly good for smoking. This species is utilized either fresh or salted.   —A.J.McC.

ROWBOAT A displacement hull designed to be propelled by oars in row locks (*see* Oar Locks). Rowboats are generally 10–14 feet long and usually have a pointed bow and a square stern. *See also* Inboard-Outboard, Outboard

ROYE The Norwegian name for Arctic char (*which see*)

RUBBERLIP SEAPERCH *Rhacochilus toxotes* Considered to be the best food fish of the many surfperch (*which see*). It has very thick lips; a frenum does not interrupt the

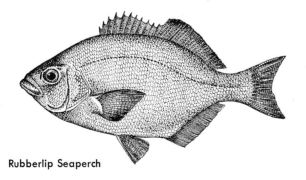

Rubberlip Seaperch

posterior groove of the lower lip; the soft portion of the dorsal fin is higher than the spinous part; 22–24 soft dorsal rays; 27–30 soft anal rays. Color usually whitish with brassy or bluish-black tinge; overlaid with blackish on belly and sides; yellowish pectorals; black or dusky tips on anal, dorsal, and pelvic fins; white or pink lips; one or two dusky vertical bars on juveniles only. Central to southern California. Length to 18 inches.

COMMERCIAL VALUE

One of the two leading commercial species in the Monterey area, of lesser importance near San Francisco and southern California.   —J.R.

RUDDERFISH *See* Banded Rudderfish, Bermuda Chub

RUFF *See* Kahawai

RULES OF THE ROAD Regulations enacted to prevent collisions of all craft underway. Rules specify legal lights for vessels, signals that must be rendered in approaching bridges, locks, and other boats. The rules define the position as well as the procedure for all boats meeting on the water in relationship to each other.

RUNABOUT A small inboard or outboard boat where the forward part of the cockpit is enclosed by a small bow deck.

RUNNING LIGHTS A nautical term for the side lights on a boat. These consist of a green light on the starboard side and a red light on the port side. Each light is visible through an arc directly ahead to two compass points abaft the beam on its own side of the boat. Thus, a red port light cannot be seen from a position forward off the starboard bow, but it can be seen from a position dead-ahead and throughout the arc around to the port to a position two points abaft the light. Each light is screened so as not to show across the bow or further aft than described.

RUSTY DAB *See* Yellowtail Flounder

S

SÁBALO The Spanish word for tarpon (*which see*). Although tarpon are caught chiefly for their angling value in North American coastal waters, they are utilized as food fish in Mexico, Central, and South America.

SABLEFISH *Anoplopoma fimbria* Also called the coalfish and blackcod, the sablefish belongs to the family Anoplopomatidae, a small group confined to the North Pacific Ocean. It extends along the west coast from the Bering Sea to southern California.

Its color is slaty-black or greenish-gray on dorsal surface, somewhat reticulated; light gray on ventral surface; pale on outer margins of all fins except spinous dorsal; narrow, black margin on spinous dorsal fin; black on lining of operculum. In young, colors are brighter and more contrasting, often light green with dusky bars on the dorsal surface.

Other distinguishing characters of the sablefish are body elongate, slightly compressed, tapering to a rather long, slender caudal peduncle. Head conical, elongate; mouth terminal, moderate; lower jaw included; maxillary very narrow, reaching to a point below front of pupil;

teeth small, cardiform, on jaws, vomer, and palatines; nostril double; gill membranes united, joined to isthmus.

First dorsal fin with 17–21 spines, second dorsal with 1 spine and 16–19 softrays, interspace between two dorsals about twice diameter of eye or more; anal fin with 3 spines and 15–19 softrays, spines usually embedded in adults, origin below that of soft dorsal; pelvic fins with 1 spine and 5 softrays, thoracic in position; caudal deeply emarginate. Lateral line moderately high following dorsal contour. Scales weakly ctenoid, small, elongate, covering body and head; about 190 in oblique rows above lateral line.

ANGLING VALUE

The sablefish has considerable commercial value being one of the best of the smoked fishes. Its flesh has a high oil content. Capture is generally from deep water by set line or trawl. Spawning apparently takes place in early spring since postlarvae about an inch in length have been taken off the Oregon coast in the latter part of May. The males do not attain as large a size as the females and reach maturity at an earlier age. Large individuals 3 feet in length and about 40 pounds in weight have been taken on halibut banks at depths to 170 fathoms. It has been estimated that a 40-inch fish is about 20 years of age. Its food consists of crustaceans, worms, and small fishes. Maximum size is about 3 feet 4 inches. —J.C.B.

SAC-A-LAIT A regional (Louisiana) name for the white crappie or black crappie

SACRAMENTO PERCH *Archoplites interruptus* This is the only member of the sunfish family native west of the Rockies. It is blackish over the back, with mottled black-brown and white sides, and usually marked with seven vertical black bars. The anal fin has 6–7 anterior spines, and there are 12–13 dorsal spines. The dorsal-fin base is much longer than the base of the anal fin.

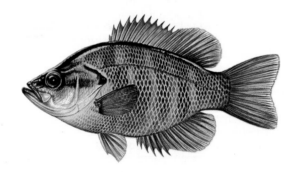

Sacramento Perch

The Sacramento perch was indigenous to the Sacramento-San Joaquin drainage and the smaller Pajaro River systems. It since has been introduced into Nevada and western Utah. This is one of the largest sunfishes, reaching 20–24 inches in length and a weight of nearly 10 pounds.

LIFE HISTORY

Spawning takes place in May or June in waters 1–2 feet deep. The females produce a large number of eggs; one female of 10½ inches contained 84,000 ova. Spawning takes place over boulders with heavy algae cover. No nest building is evident, but rather the adhesive eggs are attached directly to heavy growths of algae on rocks or to plants in an area 18 inches in diameter. This "perch," which is actually a sunfish, differs from the other members of its family because it does not make a nest in a sandy or gravel depression; the eggs do not need constant care, and the eggs and young are left unguarded. This trait of abandoning the nest was not originally detrimental to the survival of the Sacramento perch, but the introduction, by man, of competing species has had an adverse effect on its numbers.

FEEDING HABITS

The food of the Sacramento perch is similar to that of many other sunfishes. It consists of insects when young and forage fish in later life. The young leave the shallows at about 2 inches in length. The growth is generally 6–7 inches in the first year, 8–9 inches in the second year, 8–10 inches in the third year, and 9–11 inches by the fourth year.

ANGLING VALUE

The importance of the Sacramento perch as a sport fish has decreased in California. However, it does supplement the Nevada fisheries. In California, the adults are taken on spinners and live minnows but are rarely captured on worms. In Nevada it is taken by almost any lure dragged slowly through the spawning area. The bait is apparently accepted only to remove it rather than as food. Consequently the fishing season lasts 6–8 weeks while the fish are spawning. Very few are caught during the remainder of the year. —K.B.

SACRAMENTO SQUAWFISH *See* Northern Squawfish

SAILFIN MOLLY *Mollienisia latipinna* This livebearer is found in the wild along the coast from South Carolina into Mexico. It is also bred as an aquarium fish and is the species most usually called the "Mollie." Wild specimens have a body which is light olive green above and lighter below. It has 6–8 rows of dots forming horizontal lines. The dorsal fin has rows of spots and is very long and high. It is almost as long as the back and is especially high in some males. Maximum length is 3–4 inches.

When bred for aquarium use many variations are possible, including the black sailfin molly. Since it sometimes lives in salt or brackish water naturally the addition of a tablespoon of salt per gallon of water is required for its maintenance. It requires a higher temperature than many aquarium species—78°–80° F. It eats both plant and animal food, but prefers algae and other plant material along with insect larva and other small animals. In the aquarium it requires special diets which are high in cereals and other vegetable material.

The eggs are fertilized internally by the male, and the milt may be stored so that one fertilization is sufficient for 4–5 broods. The eggs hatch internally, growing to the same maturity as the young of fishes which are normally hatched from eggs do when they have absorbed their yolk sac; after this they are expelled ready to swim. They mature in 3–4 months. —C.A.P.

SAILFISH *See* Atlantic Sailfish, Pacific Sailfish

SAITHE A common name (Great Britain) for the Pollock (*which see*).

SAILORS CHOICE *Haemulon parrai* This grunt is less common than others and occurs in southern Florida,

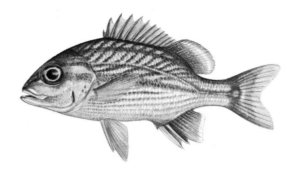

Sailors Choice

Bahamas, West Indies, and along the coast of Central and South America to Brazil. The average total length of mature individuals is about 10 inches. Larger specimens are sometimes taken. This grunt is distinguished from all the others by the color pattern and the scaled pectoral fins. The sides of the body have dark stripes running along the scale rows. The inside of the mouth is red. The sailors choice has 12 dorsal spines; 16–18 dorsal rays usually 17–18; 8 anal rays; and 17 pectoral rays. There are 51–52 pored lateral-line scales, but usually 52. Gillrakers number 21–24, usually 22–23. The pectoral fins are scaled.

ANGLING VALUE

This species occurs on or near the bottom in shallow water close to shore and about reefs in deeper water. It is readily taken on dead shrimp, cut mullet, or cut pilchard. It is good sport on light tackle when taken in deeper water. The sailors choice is good eating and is frequently seen in West Indian markets. —L.R.

SALMON See Atlantic Salmon, Chinook Salmon, Chum Salmon, Coho Salmon, Kokanee, Landlocked Salmon, Ouananiche, Pacific Salmon, Pink Salmon, Sockeye Salmon

SALMON SHARK *Lamna ditropis* This Pacific member of the mackerel-shark family is similar in most respects to the porbeagle (*which see*) but differs in having black blotches on a white background on the lower parts of the body of the adult. The color is bluish-black above. Its snout is broader and shorter than that of the porbeagle. It is reported to reach 12 feet, although 8½ feet is the record measurement.

It is found from San Diego to Alaska and Japan, essentially in deeper waters to the south and shallower depths to the north. Warmwaters are avoided, and its distribution, like the porbeagle, parallels cooler temperatures. It bears living young, and a 6½-foot female from southern California had four young, each of which was 2½ feet long and weighed 18 pounds. Adults are fast swimmers of the open sea and coastal waters, and they are reported to feed voraciously on salmon and to damage fishermen's nets.

ANGLING VALUE

This shark is caught by anglers using salmon for bait. —D.dS.

SALTER A sea-run or anadromous brook trout, *Salvelinus fontinalis*. A salter cannot be identified in freshwater with any accuracy unless the fish has recently migrated from its marine environment (within two weeks), at which time the dorsal surface is a dark greenish-blue and the sides are very silvery. There does not appear to be any genetic difference between freshwater and anadromous brook trout. Presumably a certain percentage of any population will migrate to saltwater in coastal streams. Salters are found in increasing numbers from New Jersey northwest to the Maritime Provinces of Canada and from Labrador to Hudson Bay. They are often incorrectly called "sea trout," a term applicable only to the anadromous brown trout. *See also* Brook Trout, Sea Trout

SALTWATER FLY-FISHING As distinguished from fly-fishing in freshwater. This sport has developed slowly. Even though a number of anglers in various parts of the United States have been catching saltwater species on the fly since the 1930's, it is still considered a highly specialized method. At first, the pioneer anglers caught tarpon, snook, ladyfish, and red drum. Later they added the bonefish, jack crevalle, spotted seatrout, the permit, and barracuda, all of which showed a willingness to take a fly and proved strong fighters. The "tailing" species, however, had a lot to do with the increased interest in saltwater fly-casting. Bonefish, permit, and red drum (redfish) all tend to cruise the flats and grassy shallows, digging in the bottom for food, and when the water is low enough, their tails protrude above the surface, presenting a fine target. The excitement is augmented by the fact that the slightest noise will send these shallow-water foragers scooting for the deep. Saltwater fly-fishing for tailers is a nerve-tensing combination of stalking and casting that can tie the most experienced angler's nerves in knots.

BONEFISH

Bonefish are easily frightened. The crack of a pushpole on the side of the skiff or the sound it makes as it grates on coral on the bottom will send them heading for the deep like a comet shooting across the sky. Bonefish present a constantly moving target. They seldom stop for more than a couple of seconds to explore a hole under a sponge or coral rock or in the grassy flats. As they move along, investigating one likely spot after the other, up comes that tail, to waggle and wave in the sunlight. Then down it goes, only to reappear a second later a few feet further along. The moment the angler first spots such a feeding bonefish is one of the great thrills of his career as a fisherman, which, even after many years of fishing can still panic even the most experienced veteran.

When they feed over a soft bottom, in water too deep for their tail to show above the surface, bonefish put up muds which progress in this same way, indicating the direction in which they are traveling. The angler may also see the fish swimming along at times when they are not feeding. Polaroid glasses are a must for locating bonefish. They allow you to look through the inevitable glare. And you must always remember to look *through* the water down to the bottom, not stopping to gaze at the surface. In this way it is possible to sight a movement quickly.

Most anglers go in a skiff, with a guide poling them slowly along, usually with sun and wind behind them. Bonefish generally feed into the tide, or into the wind if it is strong enough to move the shallow water. Bonefish have a keen olfactory sense, and if a good tide is running they can detect a shrimp bait one hundred feet away. Without a guide, a pair of anglers can work in a rented skiff, taking turns at the pole. It does not pay for both to cast at once. If a bonefish is chasing the offering of one angler the cast of the other may frighten it off. It is also fun to wade for bonefish where the bottom is hard enough, the angler moving along in knee-to-ankle-depth water, watching for oncoming fish or a flashing tail.

The best retrieve is a slow, foot-long jerk of the fly. If the bonefish rushes it and then slows and follows along in back of it, a quick jerk will usually stir it to action, as the bonefish thinks it may be some item of food that is about to escape it and hits the fly fast.

The best flies are hair-wing wet patterns tied in modified streamer style. Bucktail and polar bear hair are popular wing materials. Small marabou streamers are also effective. Hook sizes range from No. 6 to 1/0. The fly should sink readily, particularly when fishing in deep water (3–4 feet). The thing to remember is that bonefish swim along the bottom. You seldom see them in midwater or just under the surface.

PERMIT

Permit are sometimes difficult to distinguish from bonefish. Their coloring is much the same, but the deeper body can usually be identified, and when a permit tails, its caudal fin looks black while that of the bonefish is silvery.

The greatest known concentration of permit is in the area of the Content Keys in Florida Bay, westward from U.S. 1 along the Florida Keys. The permit is extremely tough to take on a fly, and as far as is known only a few have been caught in this way. But they will hit, and to a fly man they present probably the greatest challenge of the sport. They like a small bucktail or a pink-shrimp fly, and also marabou streamers. Hook sizes for permit are usually No. 4, 2, or 1/0. Permit are bigger and longer than bonefish and feed in deeper water, and the larger fly is needed to get down to them.

BARRACUDA

Barracuda often fool anglers into thinking they are bonefish. They will lie just under the surface, motionless, or you may see them swimming slowly along just under the surface. If the fish is lying still, you can almost bet it's a barracuda, because bonefish hardly ever lie still. And if it is swimming, you can usually spot it for a barracuda by the black tail. (You can distinguish a shark, which also appears on the flats, by its wagging tail, different from the tailing action of the bonefish.)

Barracuda are great fish on a fly, but they have built-in choppers that can bite through a nylon leader instantly. Most saltwater fly-fishermen use a 12-inch length of wire attached to the end of their leader tippet when they are going just for barracuda.

You can make a barracuda mad by using a fly-rod popping bug, throwing it a few feet away from a visible fish and popping it time and again. If the cuda turns from the noise and starts away, do not pick the bug up; keep popping, and often it will circle, move in, then charge at the lure. Barracuda will also hit a streamer fly or bucktail, and the faster you make the retrieve the better. Cudas have sharp eyes, and once they get in close and see you, they lose interest.

A hooked cuda of 12–20 pounds will run like a streak just under the surface then come out in amazing, long-distance leaps, sometimes for 25 feet. They like bugs and flies in red-and-white, red-and-yellow, and they will also hit an all-white or all-yellow fly or bug. The best hook sizes to use are 1/0 and 3/0.

RED DRUM

Red drum or channel bass are not so scary as bonefish and permit and feed in some of the same places in the shallows of Florida Bay and along the Keys. They have a habit of sticking their big heads down in the grasses to probe for shrimp, crabs, and small fishes, and sometimes they will stay that way while you cast and cast and don't connect. They just don't see your offerings. Veteran redfishermen slap their flies down hard to attract their attention, and any man who has been out after redfish a couple of times soon learns that it pays to put the fly only a foot or so in front of them because their eyesight is so poor.

Redfish can also be seen as they swim along in the shallows, and like bonefish they sometimes create a mud in deeper water as they feed. At times you can see a school approaching in the distance, as they push up a wave in front of them as they travel. A fly dropped ahead of them then, and retrieved fast so they can see it move, may get a strike where a slow retrieve would not, because they might easily mistake the slow-moving fly for a piece of floating vegetation.

Redfish will hit a popping bug, and they are a push-over for a big feather-type streamer fly tied on 1/0 and 3/0 hooks. Bright colors help the fish to see your fly. Those streamers tied with red hackle and yellow wings are good, as are the red hackle and orange wings.

CREVALLE

Crevalle and the Atlantic horse-eye jack are also found in the southern shallows and both are avid for flies and poppers. Both are as strong as they come. Jacks work the channels and the deeper flats. You see schools of them hitting into baitfish along the dropoffs out from the bonefish flats. They are great travelers and always seem to be hungry. Once you find them you are almost sure of plenty of fast action, as they chase down and slap into your feathery fooler. Almost any kind of retrieve will do the job, but the slow bring-back at first, speeded up as it goes, does the most consistent job of teasing them into striking. Jacks are stronger than almost any other fish. This is one case where the "pound for pound" story holds true.

Color doesn't seem to make any difference to the jack, and the best hook sizes for them are 1/0 and 3/0.

LADYFISH

Ladyfish are aerial artists. One lady going in and out of the water moves so fast that you'd think several fish were hooked simultaneously. They are great night-time feeders, and that is a good time to go for them. Work the channels on the outgoing tide at night, and you can score with popping bugs floated on the surface. The cast should be made uptide so the floater resembles the shrimp which are riding out with the current.

Ladyfish will also hit during the day. There are large concentrations scattered through the Everglades National Park waters and around the Florida Keys, and you can get results even in bright sunlight. The average weight will go about 1½ pounds, with many in the 2–2½-pound class. With both poppers and flies the 1/0 hook is the best size.

SPOTTED SEATROUT

Spotted seatrout will strike a fly. They are found on the Gulf side of the Florida Keys and along the west coast of Florida, and also extend far northward on Florida's east coast with the largest being taken in the Melbourne, Cocoa, and Vero Beach sections. There are consistent catches of spotted seatrout in these waters going 6 pounds and better, with 10-pounders not unusual.

This is one saltwater fish that likes the fly slow at first; then when the retrieve is speeded up they often dash for it at the last minute and sometimes hit within ten feet of the skiff. They like the red-and-yellow and red-and-white combinations in streamer fly and bucktails, and the same colors in popping bugs. They readily strike a popper, also played very slowly. The spotted seatrout is not the hardest-fighting fish in the ocean, but it is fun to take on a fly. Remember to play them slowly and easily, and don't try to horse them as they have very soft mouths and the hook may pull out.

SNOOK

Snook are as crafty as any fish you'll find in the salty shallows. A snook carries an unsheathed knife on his cheek covers, the better to slice through your leader. Most saltwater anglers who are going for snook add 12 inches of 30-pound-test nylon leader material on the end of their regular leaders, which are usually tapered down to a 12-pound-test tippet. Others add 12 inches of No. 3 wire. With both of these methods they manage to bring in some substantial snook.

Snook grow big, 30–35 pounds or more, with record fish in the over 50-pound class. Big or little, they're rambunctious, hard hitters, a pleasure to catch. They will hit a popping bug well, especially along the edges of bars, and channels, and over grassy flats or along the mangrove bushes where the branches dip down to the water. Pop the bug slowly, let it sit still, pop it again, and when a snook explodes on it, you are in for a surprise. They make long runs, jump several times, have a habit of boring into the mangroves, threading their way among the roots and drawing your leader after them so as to cut it or break it off on a snag.

Snook also like to lie in sandy holes among the grassy flats. Drifting across with a slight wind, or with a guide to pole you along, you can spot these fish in plenty of time to cast to them, and it pays to go slowly because a little bit of water can shelter a really big snook, in the 15–20-pound class.

Fishing sandy beaches along the Florida west coast is fun because you see the snook so close to the shore that sometimes their backs are out of water. Other times you see a big female fish, perhaps 35 pounds, moving slowly along, 60 feet out from the beach, surrounded by a drove of 2–3-pound males. Any of them will hit, and if you tie into the big one you will be busy for a good long time.

They like brightly colored flies and poppers, the same old standard patterns of red-and-yellow, red-and-white, blue-and-white. Best hook sizes are 1/0 and 3/0.

TARPON

Tarpon from less than a pound to 20 pounds are called baby tarpon. A 5-incher is a miniature copy of its parents down to the last detail, and it'll take a fly with the same forthrightness. Many anglers use trout flies for the very small ones. But when a 10-pounder is around, you want something a bit larger, and when one of those babies hits, you'll wonder why anyone ever tagged them with the infantile name. They are acrobatic, strong, and have a single idea—to get rid of the hook.

Tarpon are found year round in most parts of their habitat from Florida to the Bahamas, and down through Mexico and British Honduras to Panama. They are found elsewhere in the Atlantic, but these are the best locales for fly-fishing as here you find them in fairly shallow water. The usual time to go for them is from April 15 to the middle of July, with May probably the top month. All tarpon do not migrate but instead move out to the deep when there is a cold spell, and back to the shallows when the weather warms up. Some big tarpon are caught on the Florida Keys in January and February, as long as the weather is normal.

Along the Keys fly-fishing for tarpon has been developed into a highly specialized sport. Here you see tarpon in the lakes which lie between the mangrove flats, as they roll and strike. Then you stake out the skiff and wait for the fish to come to you, or the guide will pole quietly along until you are within casting range. Sometimes they lie just under the surface and suddenly come up and breathe air, then settle back again in the same spot. This maneuver is deceptive because you expect them to be moving when they roll.

When you are after fish of 3–15 pounds, a 1/0 hook is used on flies. For fish 15–40 pounds, a 3/0; and for fish heavier still, a 5/0 does the job. Because tarpon have very rough jaws and scales, it pays to add 12 inches of 100-pound-test nylon leader to the end of your 12-pound-test tippet. Purists stay with the minimum terminal tackle, but it's almost impossible to take a 100-pound tarpon on such a tippet because it takes a long time to land such a tarpon and almost always it will have time to fray and cut the thin leader. With the heavy shock tippet of 80–100-pound-test material, many tarpon over 100 pounds have been caught on flies.

Tarpon of all sizes like the same colors—red-and-yellow, red-and-white, blue-and-white. The 3/0 and 5/0 Honey-Blonde and Platinum-Blonde streamers in the same sizes get plenty of hits.

As with all saltwater fish, the cast should not be allowed to fall behind the fish. Figure the direction and the speed at which it is traveling, then drop the fly quietly in front of it, let it sit still for a moment, then bring it back in slow, foot-long jerks. The fish will often follow right in back of the fly, then zoom forward and strike. It pays to hit hard when setting the hook before the fly is deep in the throat of the fish. When this happens it is almost a foregone conclusion that the tarpon will fray the leader with its rough mouth, even with an 80-pound-test tippet.

It is also a good idea to drop the rod tip when a tarpon jumps, to prevent the leader from brushing across its scales and to avoid having it fall on a tight leader and break it. Experienced tarpon fly-fishermen have also learned to put on all the pressure possible when playing a tarpon. It is almost impossible to break a 12-pound-test nylon leader, and it is hard to break a fly rod unless the angler is a beginner and doesn't know his stick, leader strength, or drag; so set the drag near maximum, and lay back on the fish for all your tackle will take. Each minute added to the lengthy fight favors the tarpon. They are so strong they tow skiffs and cause reels to freeze.

DOLPHIN

Offshore fish also offer some exciting targets for fly-fishermen. Anglers trolling for dolphin have found that if you hook one from a school and keep the hooked fish in the water, the others will stay with it. Then, when it is close behind the boat, the fly man has his chance. Sometimes the hooked dolphin will come in with just one other beside it, and often these are big fish, 20, or even 30–40 pounds. A 40-pound dolphin, while certainly a spectacular catch on a fly, can be landed, and when this happens, the angler will have a lifetime memory. It may seem a little difficult to cast around outriggers, or even from a boat without outriggers, but if you watch your back cast and keep the line low, you can get to them. The dolphin will often be only fifty feet out, and sometimes much closer. When they see the fly and bolt for it, their pectoral fins turn bright blue and their bodies turn glistening green and gold; it's a wonderful sight. Impart 2–3-inch quick jerks to the fly. Dolphin do not fray or bite through a leader, so conventional 12-pound-test tippets are generally used. White or yellow bucktails, on 1/0 and 3/0 hooks are the most successful, and in streamers you want the same sizes in red-and-yellow, red-and-orange, and red-and-white. Use the 1/0 for smaller fish, the larger for bigger ones. Over-all, the 3/0 is the best size.

The best season to find dolphin is from the last part of May through June, July, and into early August.

CHUMMING

Chumming deeper-water swimmers within reach of flies is very successful in Bermuda. A chum line containing inch-long silvery minnows, called hogmouth fry, and pilchards, is used to tempt snappers and yellowtails topside. The mangrove snapper is as wary a fish as you'll encounter anywhere, and it is better to wait until it has forgotten all discretion in its hearty feeding on the chum, before you offer it anything artificial. As a snapper becomes more excited, the "feeding line," which goes back from the eyes and meets at the top of the head, grows blacker and blacker. This means caution has been forgotten. Then cast a "fry fly," a small white bucktail on a 1/0 hook, tied to represent the chum. The yellowtail, a close cousin of the snapper, will take a fly, too, and puts up the same hard fight.

Over 45 fathoms of water, along the drop-offs of the Challenger Banks and the banks off St. Georges, the chum line produces all manner of fish—the blackfin tuna, Bermuda amberjack, called bonito, the little tuna, and many others. Little tuna to 12 pounds have been caught on flies, and yellowfin tuna to 14, and it is only a matter of time till heavier ones will be taken. One-hundred-pound tuna have hit the little fry flies, although none that large has been landed.

STRIPED BASS

The striped bass are at their best as far as the fly man is concerned from North Carolina northward to Cape Cod; and on the Pacific Coast from San Francisco Bay northward to about Coos Bay, Oregon.

The striped bass is one of the hardest hitters of any fish. The striper's sock at a fly-rod popping bug is something to be in on, and once you hook a big one you are in for a good battle, especially if the fish is hooked in the shallows. Sometimes they run four hundred feet at top speed on their way to deeper water.

Stripers are taken by fly rodders who wade the shallow bays, walk the banks of saltwater marshy guts, or use a skiff to fish the grassy flats, drifting along and casting ahead or to either side. Points are great places to work a fly, as are inlets and the undercut saltwater banks of the mainland or islands. If you are walking along the banks and see a point jutting out, undercut, and with tide swirling along, be sure to cast from 10–15 feet back before moving in to the edge of the bank. Otherwise you will run off any stripers that may be in there feeding. At all times it pays to be as quiet as possible, because stripers scare easily in the shallows.

When stripers school, and are chasing baitfish out in the bays, you can spot them by the gulls wheeling and diving on them. Stay off from the school and cast in to them. In this way you can take fish after fish, whereas if you run right into the middle of the school with your boat you will down them fast. When they go down, most boats wait until they come up again, then race for the breaking fish and, keeping off to the side, cast ahead of them.

A fly-rod popping bug should be played for stripers in the same manner as for largemouth bass. Pop it once, let it sit for a good long time, pop it again, let it sit again, then bring it back in a series of pops. A striper may explode on the bug at any time in this retrieve. Bucktails and streamers are retrieved in a slow pull-back, usually 1–2-foot-long jerks.

Best color in lures for the striper are all white, red and white, red and yellow, blue and white. Popping bugs should be on 3/0 hooks and the large, 4-inch-long winged streamers and bucktails on both 3/0 and 5/0.

BLUEFISH

The bluefish is a species you don't get many chances at with a fly, and when you do, usually it is to a school breaking on top. They are strong fighters and will often chop through a leader, so a great many anglers use a length of wire on their leader tippet. The bluefish is not particular about color. They'll hit all white flies, all yellow, and various combinations of colors. All the fly man has to do is throw the fly out where they are, start it back, and he has a hit. If there ever was an all-out feeder, it is the bluefish. Best hook sizes are 1/0 and 3/0.

SHARKS

Sharks which swim the shallows are often encountered by the fly-rod fisherman. The small sharks which come onto the flats include the shovelnose, blacktip, sand shark, and, in places, the lemon shark. All of them will take a fly, and a 10-pounder will run for about 100 yards. They put up a good fight, but their skin is very rough, and unless you use about 12 inches of wire on the end of your tippet you'll lose a lot of flies. With such gear, sharks in excess of 100 pounds have been caught.

In casting to sharks, remember that they are very nearsighted, and the fly must be dropped an inch in front of their noses and retrieved slowly just ahead of them, maintaining that distance. If your particular shark decides to take, it'll snatch that feathery fooler in a hurry.

Standard tarpon streamers can be used for sharks, but as a rule, a white polar bear hair streamer on a No. 5/0 or 6/0 hook is most effective. —J.W.B.

SANDBAR SHARK *Carcharhinus milberti* Also known as the brown shark, this very common shark of the family Carcharhinidae belongs to the ridgeback group. It can be identified by the high dorsal fin, which is placed far forward, originating over the inner corner of the pectoral fin; the pointed snout which is not broadly rounded in dorsal outline; and the short second dorsal fin, whose free rear corner is only about the length of the base. It resembles the bull shark (*which see*) in general appearance, but the bull shark lacks a dorsal ridge between the dorsal fins. The sandbar's color varies from gray to brown above to white below, and the fins lack markings. It grows to nearly 8 feet and about 200 pounds.

LIFE HISTORY

This abundant shark is divided into several populations throughout the warmer parts of the Atlantic Ocean. In the eastern Atlantic, it occurs in the Mediterranean, off Spain, and off West Africa. It is known in the western Atlantic with certainty from New England to southern Brazil and the Gulf of Mexico. A shallow-water species, it is found on or near the bottom of depths of 100 fathoms, occasionally moving out in midwater to oceanic habitats. But its commonest haunts lie in 10–30 fathoms. It occasionally enters river mouths and brackish water, where the young are presumably brought forth. In northern Florida, the young are born in late spring and early summer. An average of 9 is born after 8–12 months gestation, and the newborn sharks are about 2 feet long. Adults eat small, bottom-living fishes, such as goatfishes, flounders, searobins, snake eels, and cusk eels. Crabs and octopus are also taken. It is an important commercial shark, and its skin and liver yield valuable products.

DANGER TO MAN

Apparently it has never been involved in any attacks on man. —D.dS.

SAND BASS *Paralabrax nebulifer* A small Pacific marine species of minor angling importance. The sand bass belongs to the sea-bass family Serranidae. Anglers take sand bass from boats, piers, and barges usually in the vicinity of kelp beds. The sand bass attains a length of about 18 inches. It is often lumped with a very similar species, the kelp bass, *Paralabrax clathratus*, as a "rock bass" in commercial and sport catches.

SAND BASS A regional name for the white bass (*which see*)

SANDBUG *Hippa talpoida* Sometimes called sandflea or mole crab. Sandbugs are found along the saltwater beaches of both the Atlantic and the Pacific. They occur in large colonies. These crustaceans burrow in fine sand at the edge of the water and move in and out with the tide. They are distinguished by a heavy, curved carapace and plume-like antennae. The antennae are used for catching organic matter upon which the sandbug feeds.

ANGLING VALUE

Sandbugs are an important bait for many saltwater fish in the Southern United States. In Florida, where they are known as sandfleas, these crustaceans are of great importance in catching pompano. The sandbug is used alive and whole, or attached to a small leadhead jig.

FOOD VALUE

The sandbug is sometimes used for making a broth or soup in the South. Although the usual sandbug is small (1–1½ inches in length) and contains very little meat, they are cooked in boiling, salted water to which a julienne of vegetables has been added. —A.J.McC.

SANDDAB *See* Pacific Sanddab

SAND EEL *See* American Sand Lance

SANDHOPPER Any one of a number of amphipods which, like the sandbug, are sometimes called sandfleas. In contrast to the sandbug, the sandhopper seldom exceeds 1 inch long and is laterally compressed, more nearly resembling a shrimp. Unlike the sandbug, which moves in

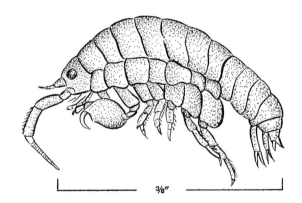

Sandhopper

and out with the tide level, some species of sandhoppers live in dry sand and decaying seaweed, while others live in the intertidal zone and still others are free-swimming in both fresh and saltwater. The freshwater amphipods are called scuds (*which see*). When masses of seaweed on the beach are disturbed, the diminutive beach dwellers, such as *Orchestia agilis*, hop flea-like to escape, thus providing their common name. Due to their small size, sandhoppers have little value as bait, although amphipods are an important source of food for many fish. Though edible, sandhoppers are seldom utilized by man. —A.J.McC.

SAND LANCE *See* American Sand Lance

SAND PERCH A regional name for the barred surfperch (*which see*), a Pacific marine species.

SAND PERCH *Diplectrum formosum* An Atlantic marine species of little angling value. The sand perch or sandfish is one of the small sea basses distributed from North Carolina to Texas. Sand perch seldom attain a length of 12 inches.

SAND SEATROUT *Cynoscion arenarius* Also called the white trout, it is apparently closely related to the weakfish (*Cynoscion regalis*), a species found on the Atlantic Coast from Nova Scotia to northeastern Florida. The sand sea-trout occurs from the west coast of Florida to Texas and Mexico as far south as the Gulf of Campeche. Its body coloration is pale, without well-defined spots, yellowish above, silvery below, the center of the scales above level of gill opening sometimes forming faint, oblique rows of cloudy areas. The back of young sand seatrout is cloudy, the cloudy areas tending to form indefinite crossbands.

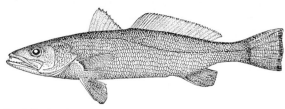

Sand Seatrout

Other distinguishing characteristics of the sand seatrout are the 11 soft anal rays (sometimes 10–12); total number of gillrakers usually 13–14, frequently 15. The most usual number of gillrakers on the two limbs of the first arch is 4 + 10 or 3 + 10. Caudal fin not emarginate in individuals over 300 millimeters, the middle rays being somewhat longer. Least depth of caudal peduncle usually shorter than snout; 1.57–1.82 times in maxillary. The dorsal softrays have a modal number of 26, quite commonly 25–27.

LIFE HISTORY

The life history is not well-known. The young are found in the shallow bays of the Gulf Coast and seem to be particularly abundant where the salinity is reduced. There is a general migratory movement from the bays into the Gulf with the onset of cool weather in the fall. Also, in the spring and summer there is a spawning migration of adults into the Gulf. The young move into the bays from April to September, indicating that this species has a prolonged breeding season.

ANGLING VALUE

This is a small species, the adults usually ranging from 12–15 inches in length. The food seems to be mainly small fishes and shrimp. It supports a minor commercial and sport fishery.   —J.C.B.

SAND SHARK *Carcharias taurus* Also known as ground shark, this common species is identified by its two large dorsal fins of equal size, the large anal fin, which is about the size of the pelvics, and the slender, pointed teeth which overhang noticeably. The gill openings are all placed in front of the pectoral fins, and the first dorsal is well behind the pectoral-fin tips. Its distinctive teeth have a small cusp on either side of the main ones. It is pale gray-brown on its upper parts, becoming grayish-white below. Numerous small, yellowish spots cover the mid-parts and posterior parts of the body and fins, giving it a mottled coloration. Some specimens have the rear of the fins with black edges.

LIFE HISTORY

The sand shark grows to slightly over 10 feet, and a specimen nearly 9 feet long weighed 250 pounds. Most taken are less than 6 feet long. It occurs in the western Atlantic from Maine to Florida and to Brazil, and in the Mediterranean Sea, the Canary Islands, and the Cape Verde Islands. A relatively common species in the Middle Atlantic and New England area, it is a rather sluggish species which is essentially a bottom dweller of shallow waters. They occasionally enter estuaries and penetrate upstream to where the water is quite fresh. Sand sharks are taken inshore during the warmer months, and it is thought that during the winter they move into deeper water. Its spawning habits are not known, but it is believed to reproduce in southerly waters. The eggs are hatched within the mother, the young eating unfertilized eggs until the time they leave the oviduct.

Small fish are their chief diet, including mackerel, menhaden, flounders, skates, sea trout, and porgies, and crabs and squid are eaten as well by the sand shark.

DANGER TO MAN

Although sluggish in its habits, it is well-equipped with a formidable set of teeth. It has been only recently implicated in an attack on man, but an African relative has been suspected of several fatal attacks. The size of the sand shark and the muddy, coastal waters of the subtropical and temperate zone which it inhabits make this species a potential danger.   —D.dS.

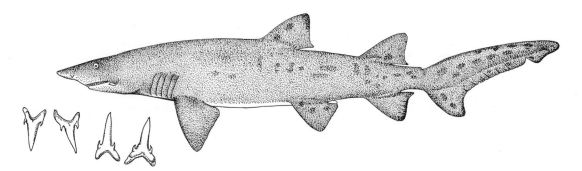

Sand Shark (teeth upper jaw *left*, lower jaw *right*)

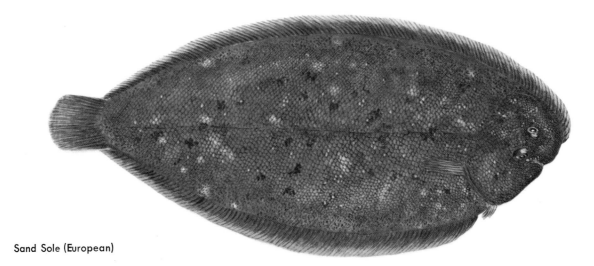

Sand Sole (European)

SAND SHINER *Notropis stramineus* The sand shiner has a moderately stout body and large eyes. Its coloration is light olive or straw yellow with a silvery cast above. Sides are silvery and scales are faintly dark-edged. The abdomen is silvery and milk-white. Fins are transparent or tinged with white. It usually has 7 anal rays, but occasionally has 8. The front of the dorsal fin is about halfway between the base of the tail and the tip of the snout. An irregular and sometimes indistinct stripe, which expands just in front of the dorsal fin and does not surround the base of the dorsal, also distinguishes it from close relatives. The breeding male develops small tubercles on the head. Most adults are 1.5–2.5 inches, with the largest about 3 inches.

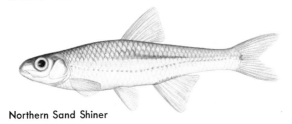

Northern Sand Shiner

LIFE HISTORY

Spawning occurs in July and August in Iowa, but has been reported in late April through July in Missouri. It is longer-lived than some minnows; some live three years but most spawn at one year. One-year-old fish produce 250 eggs, 2-year-olds 1,100, 3-year-olds 1,800 eggs.

The sand shiner is found in the Mississippi, Missouri, and Ohio river drainages, southward into Texas and northeastward to the St. Lawrence River. In streams it prefers sand- and gravel-bottomed riffles and pools having considerable current, and in lakes exposed sand- and gravel-bottomed shores. The sand shiner is seldom found among vegetation or over silt bottoms. It does not withstand low oxygen or crowded conditions; therefore its use for bait is limited.   —C.A.P.

SAND SOLE (1) *Psettichthys melanosticus* In North America a fringe sole, this flatfish of the flounder family is found from southern California to southeastern Alaska.

The sand sole has a lateral line curving only slightly over the pectoral fin and a dorsal branch. The first 8 or more rays of the dorsal fin are elongated and not connected by membrane for about half their length. The teeth and jaws developed about equally on each side. Its maxillary extends to a point below the pupil of the eye. The eyes are small and are on the right side, widely spaced. It has a rounded caudal and a pectoral shorter than the head. The color is light green or brown obscurely mottled with dark spots, and a light brown tinge finely speckled with black or brown.

It feeds on crustaceans, worms, small mollusks, and small fishes such as anchovies.

(2) *Solea lascaris* The true sand sole of Europe found from the Mediterranean to southwest Britain, occasionally occurring in the North and Irish Seas. It can be separated from the common sole (*see* Sole) by its nostril on the blind side being nearly circular and surrounded by short branched filaments. Its body is also covered with numerous small black dots which are absent in the common sole.

SANDWORM *See* Clamworms and Bloodworms *under* Live Bait

SARDINATA A regional Spanish name for the brycon (*which see*) in northern South America.

SARDINES A term as used in western Atlantic waters which refers to the young of herrings. Sardines canned in the eastern United States are one of the herrings rather than true sardines. The Pacific sardine (*which see*) is authentic, and more closely related to the Spanish sardine of the eastern Atlantic, *Sardinella anchovia* and the European sardine, *Sardina pilchardus*.

SARGASSUMFISH *Histrio histrio* One of the more interesting and colorful small fishes of the tropical waters of America is the sargassumfish or fishing frog. It is a member of the family Antennariidae, the frogfishes, a highly specialized group that is closely related to the batfishes, Ogcocephalidae, the goosefishes, Lophiidae, and the deepsea anglers, suborder Ceratioidea, all belonging to the Order Pediculati.

The frogfishes are characterized by their globular bodies; more or less rough skin, depending on the presence or absence of denticles; pectoral fins limblike; gill openings restricted to a pore near or behind the axilla of the pectoral fins; first dorsal spine, if free, with a "lure" at its terminus; second and third spines separate, a fourth, free spine completely embedded, followed by the soft dorsal fin; caudal rays usually all divided and 9 in number; mouth almost vertical; and small conical teeth in rows on jaws, vomer, palatines, and tongue. Frogfishes generally are carnivorous, very voracious, solitary, and sedentary in nature. Of the approximately fifty-four species, twenty are to be found in American waters.

Sargassumfish

Histrio histrio can be distinguished from its relatives by the following characters: dorsal fin with 12–14 rays, first spine small, somewhat bulbous at tip, with two or more filaments; anal fin with 7–8 rays; dorsal part of first gill arch without filaments; 2 dermal cirri on middorsal line of snout in front of first dorsal spine; body smooth, skin minutely granular; head, body, and most of fins with long, fleshy flaps; caudal fin rounded; pectoral with rather long or slender "wrist." Color is very variable, usually pale yellowish, marbled variously with deep brown areas and three brown bands radiating from the eye; belly and sides with whitish spots; fins all marked with broad, irregular, wavy crossbars. Habitat: tropical seas, inhabiting attached and floating *Sargassum* seaweeds. Size to about eight inches.

LIFE HISTORY

The sargassumfish is one of nature's best camouflage artists. Its coloring matches that of the weeds in which it lives, having irregular dark markings like that of the branching fronds, golden rings on its sides exactly resembling the air bladders of the sargassum. White dots even simulate with remarkable fidelity the white encrustations of tiny marine animals living on the sargassum plants. It even has the trick of changing its skin coloring to match the background of its changing environment. In the drifting world of weeds, *Histrio* is hidden from view, but it sees everything; when a smaller fish, shrimp, or worm passes by, the sargassumfish approaches each, not in the form of the ferocious predator it is, but in the guise of an innocuous vegetable.

Other adaptations for its way of life include flexible fins which can be used much the same as arms, wrist, and fingers, enabling the animated weed to clamber about its home. In getting about in the water, *Histrio* frequently moves by a series of thrusts of jets of water from its small, round gill openings, one under each "arm." This allows it in many cases to approach its prey without being

detected. It can draw near with closed mouth, and, suddenly opening its mouth, take in the unsuspecting prey in an instantaneous gulp. A *Histrio* gulp is no ordinary gulp, for when this fish opens its mouth to catch a victim, its jaws open so suddenly and widely that a powerful suction is created; the unfortunate prey is sucked down a capacious throat. It can also use this technique in self-defense. If attacked, *Histrio* can throw open its jaws, swallow water, and pump itself up to a size too large to swallow.

Histrio has a voracious appetite, and it is very cannibalistic. This glutton will take anything offered it, even prey nearly its own size. And, strangely enough, when given a choice, *Histrio* selects its own relatives in preference to different species. Dr. William Beebe told a story of *Histrio* cannibalism on the Sargasso Sea. In a jar in his laboratory he placed three sargassumfish sized like the three bears. In half an hour an inverted magician's trick had been performed—now there was but one, very fat and gulping uneasily. It was not known whether it was a case of the Japanese boxes, one within the other, or whether the big cannibal had engulfed in turn his spiny and much tentacled brethren.

Sargassumfish are helpless victims of oceanic disturbances which dislodge their host seaweed or send their already floating home on a journey far from its normal range. On occasions such as these, sargassum can be collected when it washes near the shore, and searched for its passengers. In an aquarium, the fish soon become acclimatized and act in accordance with their stomachs. For this reason, it is advisable that they be kept out of reach of more valuable tropical aquarium animals and of their own species, which they will eat, or fight viciously if they are the same size.   —F.W.B.

SASKATCHEWAN The borders of this Canadian province encompass 251,700 square miles, of which roughly one-eighth is composed of water ranging from tiny pothole lakes in the Great Sand Hills of the southwest to the vast lakes of the Precambrian Shield, and from tiny trout streams of the Missouri watershed to the mighty, clear, cold rivers of the north, such as the Churchill and Fond du Lac. These gigantic watersheds and the tens of thousands of lakes and ponds that drain into them comprise one of Canada's major inland fisheries. This resource played a vital role in the development of the province by providing a readily available supply of food for the explorers and the fur traders, and later for the settlers.

In the 1960's, Saskatchewan was the top Canadian producer of whitefish (7,500,000 pounds) and lake trout (2,200,000 pounds) in the commercial fishing industry. In addition, the industry harvests approximately 5,300,000 pounds of other species such as walleye, pike, and ciscos, making the total harvest about 15,000,000 pounds annually. Roughly 75 percent of this total is exported to the United States. The mink-ranch industry, utilizing rough species, accounts for an additional 5,000,000 pounds, and another 2,000,000 pounds are taken by domestic and free permit Indian fishermen. But in recent years, Saskatchewan has enjoyed a period of relative prosperity with increasing leisure time for its populace, and this has sparked a tremendous interest in angling.

Sport-fishing enthusiasts, pursuing one of the main attractions of outdoor recreation, summer and winter, purchase approximately 100,000 angling licenses annually. Thus, about one in every nine of the population is an angler, in addition to the thousands of Americans who visit Saskatchewan each year. During the fishing season, from the first Saturday in May to April 15 of the following year, anglers will harvest an estimated 6,000,000 pounds of gamefish—the second largest take of the total provincial fishery.

Since its inception in 1949, the Anglers' Derby, sponsored by the Saskatchewan Fish and Game League, a sportsman's organization, and the provincial government, has maintained a record of some of the trophy fish taken from Saskatchewan waters. In 1958 Kingsmere Lake yielded a 51-pound 10-ounce lake trout. Other record species taken by rod and reel have included a 42-pound 12-ounce pike caught near Stony Rapids; a 13-pound 9-ounce walleye from the South Saskatchewan River; a 4-pound Arctic grayling from the Clearwater River; a 3-pound 1-ounce goldeye from the South Saskatchewan River; a 2-pound 7-ounce yellow perch from Fishing Lake; a 13-pound 3-ounce rainbow trout from Piprell Lake; a 15-pound 8-ounce brown trout from Reid Lake; and a 4-pound 7-ounce brook trout from Cypress Lake.

FISHERIES MANAGEMENT IN SASKATCHEWAN

The successful management of the fish population of any lake is dependent on an adequate research program. In conjunction with research, a clear understanding by commercial and sport fishermen of the need for research and management is required.

On the recommendation of the Royal Commission on Fisheries of the Province of Saskatchewan in 1947, a fisheries research program was inaugurated to secure scientific information on the fisheries resources in provincial waters. The program was initiated under the direction of the late Dr. D. S. Rawson, Head, Biology Department, University of Saskatchewan. The first major biological and fisheries investigation was undertaken on Lac la Ronge. Since the initiation of fisheries research in Saskatchewan, twenty-five biological and fisheries surveys have been carried out on major water areas to date. In addition, many other small lakes and reservoirs have been examined.

Investigations have been completed on the major water areas of the Qu'Appelle drainage system; the Saskatchewan River has been examined, as well as a number of larger lakes in the Park Belt region; larger lakes in the Precambrian Shield have been investigated; also Lac la Ronge has been considered as a pilot area where ecological projects (life history studies of walleye and lake trout) have been carried out. The findings and recommendations resulting from these investigations have been published in a series of fisheries reports.

Whereas the basic objective of fisheries research is to provide information for the development of fisheries management programs, study projects are conducted on Saskatchewan waters to determine productivity of water bodies; secure information on relationship of fish species; investigate ecology and assess factors which may affect environment of fish; and develop techniques to achieve maximum harvest of fish populations without prejudice to continued production.

To date, the agricultural, commercial, and industrial development of Saskatchewan has not had an adverse effect on the province's fishery resource. The fishery is, in some respects, in better condition today than before the coming of the white man. This improvement has been achieved through the introduction of species such as the eastern brook, brown, and rainbow trout which have added variety to the species available for angling, and through the introduction of exotic and native species to new water impoundments. Further improvements will be possible through proper management techniques, including the control of pollution and siltation.

The building of access roads into northern Saskatchewan will bring about a changing pattern of use. There is room for further development of the mink-ranching industry, which utilizes fish not suited to sport or commercial fishermen. The commercial fishing industry will be on a firmer and more profitable basis.

This road-construction program will make lakes previously inaccessible now available to anglers. Thus, the average Saskatchewan angler and the family vacationers from other provinces and the United States will have "new" areas to explore. Saskatchewan's fisheries resources will continue to play an even greater role in the development of the outdoor recreation industry.

NORTHERN PIKE

The northern pike is one of Saskatchewan's most widely distributed fish species, occurring in almost every stream and lake in the province which is capable of supporting fish life. Due to their availability, more pike are taken by anglers than all other species combined. The big ones of the northern lakes, which can put up a good fight, are prized by fishermen who fly into the Precambrian country. Some of the better-known pike waters of northern Saskatchewan are Athabaska Lake, Beaverlodge Lake, Black Lake, Crean Lake, Deception Lake, Fond du Lac River, Foster lakes, Frobisher Lake, Grease River, Hatchet Lake, Hickson Lake, Jewett Lake, Reindeer Lake, Riou Lake, Tazin Lake, Unknown Lake, Wapata Lake, Waterbury Lake, and Wollaston Lake. Camps exist throughout the area, and are usually reached by float-plane service from Lac la Ronge, Meadow Lake, Buffalo Narrows, Carrot River, and Flin Flon.

In the more southerly and accessible portion of the province the following lakes are popular for pike fishing: Besnard Lake, Bear Island Lake, Churchill River, Drinking Lake, Emmeline Lake, Lac la Ronge, Little Deer Lake, MacKay Lake, McIntosh Lake, Nemeiben Lake, Nipew Lake, Histowiak Lake, Otter Lake, and Wapawekka Lake. Heading east into the provincial-park area, anglers catch pike in Buffalo Pound Lake, Crooked Lake, Crystal Lake, Echo Lake, Fishing Lake, Good Spirit Lake, Greenwater Lake, Katepwa Lake, Kenosee Lake, Last Mountain Lake, Madge Lake, McBride Lake, Mission Lake, Moosomin Reservoir, Pasqua Lake, Qu'Appelle River, Round Lake, Souris River, and York Lake.

WALLEYE

Of the sixty-one species in Saskatchewan the undoubted favorite is the walleye. The walleye is not a spectacular antagonist, but as a table fish it is considered unsurpassed by any other species, particularly when cooked by the waterside on a wilderness lake. Although one may seek larger or more active gamefish, veteran anglers consider it almost essential to catch a few walleyes for a shore lunch.

The walleye ranges throughout a lake in its search for food and is far more destructive of young whitefish, ciscos, and suckers than the pike. It has been estimated that a mature walleye accounts for 2,000–3,000 small fish annually, in addition to a substantial number of crayfish, smaller crustaceans, and insect larvae. In spite of its tremendous appetite, this active predator grows very slowly, adding only 6–8 ounces to its weight each year, and does not begin spawning until the age of 6. A spring spawner, the walleye moves upstream in April, in some areas traveling up to 35 miles or more to find ooze bottoms suitable for spawning. The eggs are extremely small, and a large female of 6 pounds will deposit about 200,000 eggs in a season. The average size of walleye caught in Saskatchewan is about 3 pounds, although 13 pounders have been taken.

Among the better-known walleye lakes of southern Saskatchewan are Buffalo Pound Lake, Cannington Lake, Crystal Lake, Echo Lake, Fishing Lake, Good Spirit Lake, Greenwater Lake, Katepwa Lake, Kenosee Lake, Last Mountain Lake, Lenore Lake, Little Quill Lake, Madge Lake, Mission Lake, Moosomin Reservoir, Pasqua Lake, Qu'Appelle River, Round Lake, and Souris River.

In the northwest portion of the province, walleyes are caught at Beaver River, Brightsand Lake, Canoe Lake, Chitek Lake, Clarke Lake, Cold Lake, Delaronde Lake, Dore Lake, Flotten Lake, Green Lake, Greig Lake, Jackfish Lake, Keeley Lake, Lac des Isles, Lac Ile à la Crosse, Makwa (Loon) Lake, Meeting Lake, Murray Lake, North Saskatchewan River, Perch Lake, Pierce Lake, Smoothstone Lake, Turtle Lake, and Waterhen Lake.

Elsewhere in the north walleyes occur in nearly all of the major lake-trout and pike waters.

LAKE TROUT

The lake trout is a coldwater species, abundant in the deep lakes of the Precambrian Shield. Except for a few lakes in the central forest areas, its distribution in Saskatchewan is limited to the Shield. Its spawning season takes place in Saskatchewan during September and October as the water cools. The eggs are laid on the shallow, rocky, rubble bottoms of bays and inlets of the lakes. These lie dormant during the winter, hatching when the water warms again in the spring. During the spring and fall seasons, the adult laker is at its best as a sport fish, responding to spoons and plugs and putting up a good fight when hooked. In midsummer, as the surface waters warm up, the trout go deep and can only be taken by trolling with heavy tackle.

Perhaps the most southerly of the outstanding lake-trout waters in Saskatchewan is Lac la Ronge. This fabulous sport-fishing lake where anglers take annually approximately 200,000 pounds of lake trout, pike, and walleye is accessible by road, has an area of 450 square miles, and has more than a thousand islands. The shoreline of the lake and its islands consist mainly of gray Pre-Cambrian granite, dropping off into water up to 140 feet deep. The water is cold enough to produce vigorous

fish of the highest quality and is more fertile than the lakes farther north. Fishing usually commences between May 20 and June 1. In the first month, lake trout may be taken by casting before they migrate to the deeper waters where trolling equipment is then required to catch them. They again migrate to the shallower waters during the latter part of August, and angling usually lasts until the latter part of September.

Fishermen may use Lac la Ronge as a jumpoff spot to fly into the other northern major lakes—Athabaska, Wollaston, Cree, and Reindeer. The same species of fish exist in these waters. Northward from Lac la Ronge, there are many smaller lakes which are rarely if ever fished. One of the largest lake trout ever recorded, weighed 102 pounds, and was taken in a commercial fisherman's net in Lake Athabaska.

Athabaska Lake covers 3,050 square miles of which approximately two-thirds is in Saskatchewan and the remainder in Alberta. The lake has an irregular shore, and is surrounded by granite ridges and stands of spruce or poplar except at the south end where sand beaches and dunes predominate. The maximum depth of Athabaska is 405 feet near its geographic center, but there are considerable shallow areas as well as deep ones. The dominant gamefish is the lake trout which attains very large size. There are also grayling which can be taken by fly-fishing along the rocky cliffs of the north and east shores; most of the grayling run 12–16 inches (1½ pounds). Goldeyes are numerous in the river channels at the west end of Athabaska, and are frequently caught on dry flies in weights up to 2 pounds. Walleyes and northern pike are taken by casting or trolling. Whitefish and ciscos are present.

ARCTIC GRAYLING

The Arctic grayling (*which see*) is one of the most beautiful freshwater fish on the North American continent. It has been often called the sailfish of the north. It is easily distinguished by its magnificent dorsal fin which is a deep blue color, with white spots and a gold and purple band along the outer edge. As an angler's fish, the Arctic grayling has few equals in North America. It is found in the purest, clearest water in Saskatchewan's far north. Weighing up to 4 pounds (occasionally more), the grayling is found in large schools in the rapid portions of the rivers and streams. In August or September, or on most summer evenings or cloudy days, it responds to almost any lure, including dry and wet flies. Taken on light tackle, this fish provides a fight that tests the angler's skill. As a table fish, the Arctic grayling is perhaps equal to the brook trout and is superior to most others.

Arctic grayling spawn in the rapids of the northern streams, usually around the latter part of May and early June. About 2,000–2,500 eggs are deposited in a spawning season by each female. The grayling is mainly insectivorous, and in the evening may be seen rising from the fastwater to feed on low-flying caddisflies, mayflies, and midges. Insect larvae probably make up a large proportion of its diet, but in the winter months smaller fish may be important as food.

Generally speaking, grayling anglers seek their fishing in the same waters where lake trout are abundant. The fish occur both in the lakes and tributary rivers. Among the better-known spots are the aforementioned Athabaska Lake, Black Lake, Crean Lake, Cree River, Fond du Lac River, Geikie River, Hatchet Lake, Reindeer Lake, Tazin Lake, Wapata Lake, Waterbury Lake, and Wollaston Lake.

WHITEFISH

The whitefish (*see* Lake Whitefish) is important in Saskatchewan almost solely as a commercial species, although in recent years they have been caught by anglers at certain times of the year when they feed on the surface.

The reason for the abundance and quality of Saskatchewan's whitefish is in the multitude of deep, clear, cold lakes of the northern part of the province, with their bountiful supply of the kind of food utilized by these fish. The whitefish is a bottom feeder, its mouth being well-adapted to scouring the bottom ooze of the lakes for freshwater shrimps, mollusks (mainly small clams), and the larvae of the fishflies which teem in the waters of such lakes as La Ronge, Ile à la Crosse, Peter Pond, and dozens of others in the forest area and the southern part of the Pre-Cambrian Shield.

Whitefish are mature and ready for spawning at 4½ years. They are fall spawners and in October and November migrate in large schools to the shallow reefs. Here, at sunset for several days, each female deposits small batches of eggs—35,000–150,000, depending on the size of the female.

BROOK TROUT

Brook trout were first introduced to Saskatchewan as fry planted in the streams of the Cypress Hills in the late 1920's. The species was established but did not thrive in that environment. In 1931 and 1937, they were introduced at Hudson Bay. They are thriving well in the Fir River and other tributaries of the Red Deer River. Further stocking has resulted in their establishment in some other streams of the Pasquia Hills area and in the Nipawin Provincial Park. In addition, they have been stocked in a rehabilitated lake (184 acres in size) and are providing excellent angling.   —G.E.C.

SAUGER *Stizostedion canadense* The sauger is closely related to the walleye and is similar to the walleye in nearly all respects. Everything that can be said about the walleye can be said about the sauger with either more or less emphasis. For example, the walleye is known to inhabit only large bodies of water, but the sauger inhabits only the *largest* bodies of water. Sauger are found primarily in the Great Lakes, the very large lakes in the Northern States and Canada, and in the Mississippi, Missouri, Ohio, and Tennessee rivers and some of their major tributaries. Persistent artificial stocking of adult sauger in smaller lakes has always ended in failure. Why the sauger will not thrive in smaller lakes or rivers remains a biological mystery. The species is known to travel great distances, but there is no explanation as to why movement is vital to its existence.

Only in recent years has the sauger attained a position of prominence among anglers in the United States. This increasing recognition is due to the huge dams constructed across the major rivers of the nation, especially the Tennessee River and its tributaries, and the Missouri River. The huge reservoirs formed by these dams make an ideal home for the sauger. And perhaps of equal importance, these dams block the upstream migra-

tions of the sauger and provide concentration points and excellent angling in the tailwaters immediately below the dams.

The sauger, like the walleye, has a round and elongate body, forked tail, spines on the first dorsal fin and the anal fin, sharp canine teeth on the jaws and palatine (roof of the mouth), and large, glassy-colored eyes. The white belly blends into an olive-gray on the sides and back, sometimes with a brassy tinge. The back is crossed with 3–4 dark saddles which extend down the sides. The dorsal fins are marked with small dark spots, which are arranged in the form of definite longitudinal rows. The white color of the belly extends to the tip of the tail, but this coloration does not spread out at the end of the tail and form a definite white tip as it does in the walleye.

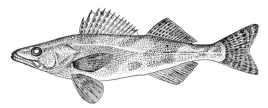

Sauger

Internally, the sauger has 3–9 (usually 5) pyloric caecae (dead-end appendixlike projections attached to the intestinal tract just ahead of the stomach), each of which is much shorter than the stomach. The second dorsal fin of the sauger has 18–22 rays, usually 19–20; anal fin with 2 spiny and 11–12 softrays; 85–91 scales along the lateral line; and cheeks usually, but not always, well-scaled.

The name sauger is becoming more widely used and accepted as the species gains prominence with anglers. However, the name sand pike continues to be used in many localities. Other commonly used names include river pike, spotfin pike, jackfish, and jack salmon.

The sauger attains a maximum weight of about 8 pounds in the Missouri River, but only 3–5 pounds elsewhere. The reason for this size discrepancy is not definitely known, but probably reflects a racial or perhaps even a subspecific difference. Sauger weighing 4–6 pounds are rather common in the catches of anglers fishing in the reservoirs and tailwaters of the huge Missouri River dams. Usual catches by these anglers weigh from 1–3 pounds. Elsewhere, sauger catches run from ¾–1½ pounds, with a 3–4 pounder a rarity.

LIFE HISTORY

As far as is known at present, the life history of the sauger is similar in all respects to the walleye. It is generally believed that the sauger spawns a few days later than the walleye, but otherwise their spawning habits and requirements are believed to be very similar.

Food habits and habitat requirements are also similar to the walleye, with the noted exception that sauger require vast areas in which to roam.

Maximum age attained by sauger in the Missouri River and the Southern states is 5–7 years, while individuals in the Northern states and in Canada may live 10–14 years. Growth of the Missouri River sauger averages 6 inches during each of the first 2 years of life, and 3 inches each year thereafter. Sauger from the southern states grow 6–8 inches during each of their first two years of life, but only 1½ inches each year thereafter. In waters from the far north, sauger grow about 4 inches the first year, 3 inches the second, 2 inches the third, and about 1 inch each year thereafter. Sauger from the Missouri River and the Southern states generally attain adulthood in their third year of life, while those from Northern waters may be 5–6 years old before reaching maturity.

Sauger will weigh a pound at a length of about 14–15 inches, 2 pounds at 18 inches, 3 pounds at 20 inches, and will add an additional pound for each 1½ inches in length thereafter.

ANGLING VALUE

The sauger has always contributed to the catches of fishermen in the Central states and to anglers in the largest lakes of the North. However, the advent of the large dams on the rivers of the Central states has elevated the sauger to the role of a major angling species. Its seasonal runs, especially during the late fall and early winter, attract thousands of anglers to the tailwaters below large dams where the sauger concentrate. Generally speaking, sauger strike a lure or bait lightly and fight less vigorously than walleyes. Other than this, little can be said to distinguish between angling for sauger and walleyes. A successful walleye fisherman usually is a successful sauger fisherman.

COMMERCIAL VALUE

Commercial sauger fisheries exist in the large waters of the North (such as Lake of the Woods in Minnesota) in conjunction with walleye fisheries. The smaller size of the sauger does, however, make it a less valuable species than the walleye. The flesh of the sauger is identical to the walleye. Gillnets are the primary method used in the commercial harvest of the species. —J.T.S.

SAURY *See* Atlantic Saury

SAWFISH *See* Smalltooth Sawfish

SCADS There are three genera and possibly ten species of scads in American waters.

The scads are distinguished by having 8 spines in the first dorsal fin, pointed scutes in the straight lateral line, the anal fin only slightly shorter than the dorsal fin, and none of the rays of the dorsal and anal fins produced into long filaments. They are very similar to the jacks but generally have less deep and more rounded body shapes. The scad genera can be distinguished individually from the jacks; *Trachurus* has enlarged scutes in the curved lateral line as well as in the straight part. *Selar* has two papillae on the shoulder girdle, with a furrow or groove ahead of the lower one. *Decapterus* has a detached finlet, composed of a single ray, behind both the dorsal and anal fins. *See also* Bigeye Scad, Carangidae, Jack Mackerel, Mexican Scad, Rough Scad, Round Scad —F.H.B.

SCALES (FISH) In general terms there are four types of scales in fishes: *placoid* scales or dermal denticles, resembling a tooth in structure, form the roughened skin covering the entire body of most sharks, and occur in various patterns and areas on most skates and rays (but are entirely lacking in some). They also occur in very localized areas of chimaeras. *Cosmoid* scales occurred in many of the fossil fishes and derivatives of this scale type exist now in the coelacanth and in the lungfishes, although these two fish groups have scales that superficially resemble cycloid and ctenoid scales, respectively. *Ganoid* scales occur in some of the more primitive bony fishes, the reedfishes, and the gars, and on the upturned lobe of the tail in sturgeons and paddlefishes. *Bony-ridge* scales, occurring in most species of fishes living today, are characterized by concentric bony-ridges (*circuli*) alternating with concentric depressions on the external surface of the scale. In most fishes these alternating ridges and depressions surround the first portion of the scale to develop (the *focus*). Bony-ridge scales are classed as two kinds, *cycloid* and *ctenoid*. The major difference between these two kinds is that ctenoid scales have pointed projections (*teeth* or *ctenii*) arising from the exposed portion and/or posterior margin of the scale. In some species the ctenii are microscopic; in others they are so pronounced as to make the surface of the fish feel rough to the touch. Most species have either cycloid scales or ctenoid scales; some species have both kinds.

Scalation or squamation is quite various. A relatively few species of fish lack scales entirely (common in most of the catfish and some of the deep-sea families); others have small scales completely buried under the skin (as some eels and the ling); in some fish the scales are reduced to bony plates (sticklebacks) or lateral-line pores; in most fish scales generally cover the entire body. Scales on a fish usually overlap the scales posterior to them (*imbricated*), but they may have separated or only touching bases. *See also* Body Covering *under* Anatomy

SCALLOPED HAMMERHEAD *Sphyrna lewini* A member of the hammerhead family, it is recognized by the broadly expanded head which forms a flat, shovel-like structure. It differs from the bonnethead (*which see*) in having a less rounded anterior margin of the head. The dorsal fin is high, as in all hammerheads, and the head is tapered in lateral view. It differs from the smooth hammerhead (*which see*) in having a distinct indentation at the midline of the anterior portion of the head, a character which it shares with the great hammerhead (*which see*), but differs from the latter in having smooth teeth which have cusps only on their bases, if at all. It also differs from the great hammerhead in having the free rear tip of the second dorsal much longer than the anterior margin. A closely related species (*Sphyrna tudes*), known from the northern Gulf of Mexico, Brazil, and Uruguay, differs from the scalloped hammerhead in having the posterior margin of the anal fin only slightly concave and the eye relatively far forward of the front of the mouth. The scalloped hammerhead is light gray above and white below, with black on the ventral surfaces of the pectoral fins.

LIFE HISTORY

Specimens of 10 feet are reported, although the maximum size is not known. It occurs in the warmer parts of the Atlantic, as well as the Mediterranean, the eastern and western Pacific, Hawaii, and Australia. It is known

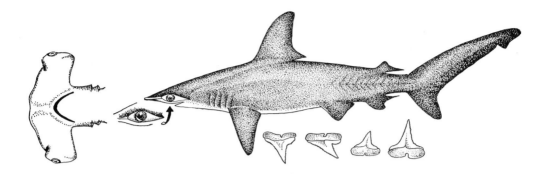

Scalloped Hammerhead (teeth upper jaw *left*, lower jaw *right*)

with certainty in the western Atlantic from New Jersey to Rio de Janeiro, but confusion with other species precludes definite identification of this species from other areas. Males mature at 6 feet, and gravid females occur in south Florida waters, but little else is known about their habits. —D.dS.

SCALLOPS Family Pectinidae Marine bivalve mollusks distinguished by their colorful, orb-shaped shells bearing radiating ribs. Scallops occur in both the Atlantic and Pacific oceans. These mollusks may be either free or attached like an oyster. The adults, however, are free in most species and can move in rapid zigzag flights by forcefully opening and closing their valves and expelling a jet of water which drives the scallop in yard-long jumps to avoid capture. This movement of the shell is achieved by a single, large adductor muscle which is opposed by an elastic ligament. Eyes are located on the mantle margin (30–40), each having a lens, as well as a retina, and an optic nerve which connects with the pallial nerve.

FOOD VALUE

Only the large, tender adductor muscle is eaten in North America. As a seafood the scallop is unique and commands a high price in most markets. Of prime importance to the gourmet is the shallow-water species, *Pecten irradians,* commonly known as the bay scallop. This mollusk is abundant from Cape Cod to Cape Hatteras but has a Southern counterpart, *Pecten dislocatus,* found south to Florida. The shell is usually about 2 inches across and varies from gray to almost black in color, and is found on mudflats or sandflats where eelgrass is common. It reproduces at the end of one year, and it doesn't live through the second year. A scallop must show an annual growth ring to be of legal size.

Small illegal scallops are called "bugs." Because of their short life span and intensive harvesting, scallops are seldom found in great abundance in one area.

The commercial market today depends on the sea scallop, which is not only larger, but more abundant. The sea scallop, *Pecten grandis,* is usually about 5 inches across the shell and its color is reddish or brown. This species is dredged in deepwater, as deep as 900 feet, and it ranges from the mouth of the St. Lawrence River down to the east coast of Florida.

The amateur can obtain scallops of better quality than those commonly marketed. Because they are somewhat difficult to procure in quantity, commercial distributors often put scallops through a process of "soaking" which depletes the delicate flavor of a fresh bivalve. The small cream-colored eye, or adductor muscle, which is the part that goes to market, is placed in freshwater for several hours until the meat has absorbed enough water to increase the bulk by about one-third. Actually, this improves the appearance of the scallop in that it becomes very white, but, from an epicurean standpoint, the flavor is inferior.

HOW TO COLLECT SCALLOPS

Scallops have regionally become more abundant in recent years because of improved coastal conditions. The recurrence of eelgrass (which is the shelter of scallop larvae) in many Atlantic bays and accelerated "seeding" have produced large crops of these tasty bivalves. Scallops may be taken by hand rakes, but because they can move around fast, they are more easily netted. Shellfish permits are required to take scallops, and licenses are issued by the various conservation departments. Residents of a coastal township may purchase a town permit to catch enough scallops for home consumption. *See also* Fish Cookery —A.J.McC.

Scallop

SCAMP *Mycteroperca phenax* This grouper, apparently very rare in the West Indies, is fairly common along the South Atlantic and Gulf Coasts of the United States. The usual size is less than thirty inches in total length.

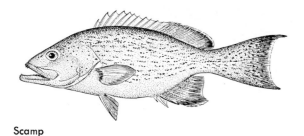
Scamp

The scamp has 11 dorsal spines, usually 18 dorsal rays, and usually 11 anal rays. Posterior nostril much larger than the anterior. Insertion of pelvic fin under lower end of pectoral base. Posterior margin of caudal fin concave. Coloration light brown with small dark spots arranged in round or elongate clusters.

This grouper is distinguished from the others by the color pattern.

ANGLING VALUE

Occurs in shallow water to water that is moderately deep. A good fighter, especially when taken by trolling with natural bait, plugs, spinners, or spoons.

A food fish of some importance in the Southern United States. —L.R.

SCAMPI A seafood dish which in the United States usually consists of large Gulf shrimp which are split and broiled and served with a garlic butter sauce. In European countries the authentic scampi is the tail portion of one of the lobsterettes (*which see*). These latter crustaceans are imported to the United States in small quantities and are also caught off the coast of Florida and in the Caribbean. *See also* Fish Cookery

SCARF A joint, sometimes made in ribs or in the keel of a boat. Made by carefully fitting and overlapping two pieces of wood together by notching.

SCHOOLMASTER *Lutjanus apodus* This is one of the smallest of snappers. It is fairly common around southern Florida and throughout the tropical American Atlantic. Seldom reaches a weight of 5 pounds, and most of the individuals seen weigh less than a pound.

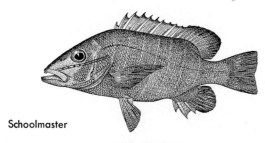
Schoolmaster

LIFE HISTORY

The schoolmaster snapper has 10 dorsal spines, 14 dorsal rays, and 8 anal rays. Pectoral rays 16–17, usually 17. Gillrakers 7–9 on lower limb of first arch, not counting rudiments. Rows of scales around caudal peduncle

21–22. Cheek scales in 7, rarely 6 rows. Upper jaw reaching to or somewhat beyond vertical from anterior margin of orbit. Pectoral fin not reaching to vertical from origin of anal fin. Anal fin rounded, not angulate posteriorly. General coloration brassy-yellow, paler below; sides of body usually with vertical bars. Fins yellow or orange-yellow. No black spot on sides of body. Eye red.

This species differs conspicuously from the other snappers in the color pattern. The schoolmaster occurs in shallow water along the shore. It is most frequently found among rocks. Takes live or dead bait and artificial lures.

ANGLING VALUE

Usually too small to be classified as a gamefish. Larger individuals, however, fight well on very light tackle. A pan-sized snapper of excellent flavor. Seldom seen in markets because of its small size. —L.R.

SCHOOL TUNA A young bluefin tuna which has an arbitrary weight range of 8–100 pounds. Usually, they are caught by sport fishermen in the 10–35-pound class, and the designation of "school" fish merely separates them from the adult bluefin which commonly weighs over 300 pounds. May also refer to small yellowfin tuna in the 10–20-pound size class, as well as any of the tunas found in large schools rather than found singly. *See also* Bluefin Tuna

SCORPIONFISH *Scorpaena* spp. When large enough to eat, these rockfish (*which see*) are an excellent food fish. The California species is highly prized. There are about six species on the East Coast, one in the West. Poison glands are to be found at the base of the dorsal-fin spines; thus, a wound is extremely painful. The fish periodically sheds its skin, which is replaced. One species sheds about once every 28 days, the time varying with the food intake.

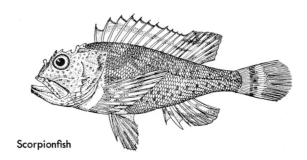
Scorpionfish

Scorpionfish are characterized by 12 spines and 13 softrays in the dorsal fin; 3 spines, 5 rays in the anal; 2 spines on top of head; body scales ctenoid or with dermal flaps; the head-scales are cycloid or absent.

All scorpionfish feed on crustaceans and fish, the prey often being one-half as large as the predator. Spawning occurs in the spring. In some species the egg masses form twin, hollow balloons which float to the surface to become pelagic. As the eggs hatch the balloon sinks. Some species reach a length of 17 inches. —J.R.

SCOTLAND Mountains mirrored by lochs, jagged headlands, coasts eroded by a pounding surf, and intensely green slopes make an idyllic background for salmon and trout fishing. Scotland is the perpetual fountain of whisky, a misty land with a tartan complex, home of the Loch

Ness monster, bagpipes, haggis, and Bobby Burns. Roads wander whimsically through Lowlands and Highlands and driving is much the best way for an angler to see it. Though small as countries are measured (29,795 square miles including its 186 inhabited islands), Scotland is surprisingly "wild" outside of its major cities. Good salmon fishing in Scotland is not cheap, but by world standards it is not expensive either; the only problem is the universal one of getting a beat on a top stream at the right time of the year and hoping the fish arrive. Although four Scottish rivers have become synonymous with the art of salmon fishing—the Tay, Dee, Spey, and the Tweed—there are fifty others such as the Nith, Awe, Oykel, Thurso, Glass, and the Beauly, which give satisfactory sport and may at times outproduce the more celebrated waters. Quality sea-trout fishing is common to Scotland, and brown trout are found in almost every loch, burn, and river.

The Sligachan Hotel on the Isle of Skye in the Hebrides is typical of the fishing resorts in Scotland

The salmon season in Scotland varies from river to river. The only month of the year when there is no fishing available is December; some rivers open as early as mid-January and all waters are open April 15th. Closing dates are also variable, but the season is finished on December 1st. The closed season for trout runs from early October to mid-March. No fishing is permitted in Scotland on Sundays.

Scotland has a cool climate. The western coast of the mainland and the Hebrides have mild but wet and windy winters with temperatures in the 40°–45°F range during January, while the east coast may be slightly colder and have less rainfall. Spring and early summer are often relatively dry, though remaining cool (April means at 43°–45°F); midsummer to late summer conditions are often fairly cool, with temperatures in the mid-50's in the extreme north and the low 60's in the center and south. However, the weather can become briefly hot (in the high 80's) and drought conditions may occur, particularly in the east coastal areas. Because of the latitude daylight lasts long in summer—until about 11:00 P.M.—and those additional hours are a bonus for anglers.

There is no national license required for fishing in Scotland. The waters are held by angling clubs, hotels, or the Crown, and a fee is charged on a daily (day ticket), weekly, or seasonal basis. The costs vary according to

the quality of the fishing, ranging from less than $5 per day up to $100 per day for a rod on a top salmon beat. To plan a trip to Scotland write to the Scottish Tourist Board (2 Rutland Place, West End, Edinburgh 1) for a copy of *Scotland for Fishing.* This comprehensive guide lists fishing fees as well as the rates for accommodations on every river and lake in Scotland. The following is a sampler of some of the better trout and salmon waters.

TWEED RIVER

Among Scotland's southeast rivers the Tweed is a classic. It is probably the most productive water in Great Britain today, and rod privileges are at a premium. The river is approximately 100 miles long, flowing into the North Sea at Berwick-on-Tweed, and forms a considerable portion of the boundary between England and Scotland. It is an early river and yet it also has a very late run of fish in October and November. The Tweed is the only river in the British Isles which can be fished for ten months of the year—from February 1st to November 30th. February to May is considered the peak period, but November can be extremely good if the weather is normal. Salmon are plentiful in the Tweed, but they average on the small side, between 7 and 9 pounds; large salmon of 30 pounds or more are taken in the late fall. Most of the fishing is done from boats, although there are places where bank casting is possible. During the first two weeks of the season only fly-fishing is permitted to minimize rod pressure and allow a maximum stock of salmon to enter the stream. Beginning on February 15th spinning is allowed. Good fly-fishing usually starts about the end of March. Advance bookings are essential for the lower beats below Kelso, where spring and fall fishing is in great demand.

The Tweed is also a first-class trout river, and in April and May the fisning is particularly good. Any visitor staying in the district can find plenty of trout angling, as there are at least twenty tributaries to the Tweed which provide browns in good number, such as the Gala, Blackadder, Teviot, Yarrow, and Rule rivers.

SPEY RIVER

The Spey is one of Scotland's great salmon rivers. It is big water, requiring deep wading but is well suited to fly-fishing. The Spey produces fish from the beginning of February in the lower reaches right through to August in the upper reaches. Several waters can be rented by the fortnight or month. The best of the season would be from the beginning of April to about the middle of June. The fish average good size (about 12 pounds) and are strong fighters for their weight. There are hotels at Fochabers for the lower beats; Craigellachie, Archiestown, Aberlour for the middle river; and Grantown-on-Spey for the upper reaches. The old Palace Hotel at Grantown is a popular headquarters. The Spey also fishes well late in the season. It produces excellent brown and sea trout in the summer months.

TAY RIVER

For the fisherman who does not like wading, and for the one who likes to catch big fish, there are few Scottish rivers that can compare with the Tay. The season opens there on January 15th, and fish are caught on the opening day if the river is normal. The best fishing falls within a

Famous American angler Jack Samson works the Seafield beat on the Spey. This is one of the great salmon rivers

comparatively short season—January to the end of April—with a peak period in the last week of March and the first week in April. The seasons, however, vary, and the fish run earlier in some years than in others, but you would not go very far wrong in the periods mentioned.

Fishing in the Tay, which is a very wide and fast-running river, is practically all spinning or harling from a boat. The fish run large, averaging around 18–20 pounds, and big fish up to 40 or more pounds are killed there every year. Popular locations for Tay fishing are at Perth and Dunkeld.

DEE RIVER

The Dee is the site of Balmoral Castle and is fished by Queen Elizabeth when in residence. The river rises in the Wells of Dee, a spring on the mountain slope of Ben Braeriach in the Cairngorms. It is little more than a brook as it runs through Mar Forest to Braemar; below Braemar it becomes a turbulent woodland stream gaining water from the rivers and burns that spill into it from the high hills along both banks. From Aboyne to Aberdeen the Dee becomes a large river meandering through broad fields rather than woods; the banks are carefully maintained with stone and concrete retaining walls at points where erosion would be a problem. There are numerous hotels with Dee fishing rights. The open season for salmon on the Dee is February 1st to September 30th; the best months are March through May, although fresh salmon

continue running in June provided rainfall has been sufficient to keep the water level up.

THURSO RIVER

Among the northernmost mainland waters beyond Inverness the Thurso rises in the moors near Knockfin Heights as two branch streams which form the river at Dalganachan. The Thurso is one of the largest rivers here, and while not in the same class as the Spey or Tweed, it is an easy stream to fish from the bank. The Thurso is productive beginning in March and peaks from July through September. Since it is popular during the summer months most anglers book their fishing a year in advance, although it's sometimes possible to get a day on the river at short notice due to cancellations.

OYKEL RIVER

The Oykel north of Inverness and flowing into the Bornoch Firth is another good spot for both salmon and sea trout. The river is popular, but a limited number of openings are available each season. The Oykel is a good wading stream and can be fished in part from the bank. Salmon average about 9½ pounds, with occasional large fish; beats are taken in daily rotation; fly-fishing-only is the rule. The lower 7 miles of river averages 730 salmon per year. The peak period is from the end of March to June 1st.

LOCH MAREE

Twelve-mile-long Loch Maree is one of the most productive waters in the Western Highlands. It flows into the sea through the 2-mile-long Ewe River. The average width of Loch Maree is about one mile, but sea trout and Atlantic salmon are found along the shallow shores near rocky headlands and islands in water 8–12 feet deep. The salmon season starts in April and peaks in May. Salmon are caught by spinning and trolling as well as on the fly. However, after the sea trout appear in Loeh Maree the rule is fly-fishing only. Sea trout begin running in July with the first summer flood tide; successive runs occur until mid-September, but the fishing continues until the season ends on October 15th. The record sea trout for Great Britain (21 pounds) was caught on a fly in Loch Maree in 1948. Although the average weight for sea trout is slightly over 2 pounds, many 3–10-pound fish are taken each year. Brown trout up to 6 pounds produce good sport throughout the season. A popular technique in Maree fishing is dapping with the dry fly. The percentage of missed strikes is high, but it does attract the fish. Dapping equipment (13–15-foot rods with blow-lines) is available for sale or rental locally.

Due to its popularity Loch Maree fishing must be booked well in advance; most reservations are made by January for the next season.

LOCH LEVEN

North of Edinburgh across the Firth of Forth (via the new Road Bridge) is world-famous Loch Leven. Although Scotland has an abundance of brown trout waters, this lake is identified with a racial strain, the Loch Leven trout which is widely spread through the country. Brown trout from Loch Leven were introduced in the United States, and that name still persists in some Western states where heavily black-spotted trout are common. Loch Leven was acquired by the Kinross Estates in 1922, but visiting anglers can fish the loch for a nominal fee. Accommodations can be obtained at Kinross. The trout population is entirely natural, as the mature fish spawn in tributary streams; the lake had a high level of production in years past, with a rod catch as high as 86,000 fish in one season. Angling is restricted to fly-fishing in Loch Leven, and catches of 1½–3-pound trout have not been unusual. However, it has not produced great quantities of fish in recent years.

SCOTLAND'S ISLANDS

Sea trout are common to Scotland, but they provide the most fishing on the islands off the west and north coasts. Brown trout are abundant and some salmon fishing is available also. The Inner and Outer Hebrides encompassing islands such as Skye, Lewis, Harris, and North and South Uist attract good runs of sea trout beginning in June. There is a hotel on South Uist, which is well known for its excellent fishing and is worth a special visit from July to September. Hotels at Tarbert on Harris Island and at Lochmaddy on North Uist are also popular. The Isle of Skye provides sea trout, brown trout, and salmon through an old Highland inn which has exclusive rights on a number of lochs and rivers. Another popular spot is at Sligachan.

To the northeast lie the wind-swept Orkney Islands, which can be reached by air from Inverness or by car ferry from Thurso. Large sea trout and brown trout are caught here. There are about 28 inhabited islands in the Orkney group, and Kirkwall and Stromness are the two main centers. It is wild, hilly country with a definite fascination for visitors. The principal lochs here are Harray, Boardhouse, Hundland, Stenness, and Swannay. Sea trout peak in the spring and fall and can be caught in bays and inlets around the islands' shores.

The Shetlands are the most northerly group of islands and can be reached by air service from Inverness or Aberdeen. Among the low hills and fjords there are a number of lochs and small rivers which hold brown and sea trout. There is a hotel at Lerwick which has fishing for its guests. July to the end of September is the best season. —A.J.McC.

SCRIPPS INSTITUTION OF OCEANOGRAPHY The branch of the University of California concerned with investigations in all areas of the marine sciences. Located at La Jolla, in the northern part of the city of San Diego, the Institution is an administrative unit of the University of California, San Diego campus. Founded in 1903 as the Marine Biological Society of San Diego, the Institution became a part of the university system in 1912 as the Scripps Institution for Biological Research. The name was changed to the Scripps Institution of Oceanography in 1925, to reflect an expanded scope of research.

Scripps has long been a center for education in the marine sciences. Instruction is on the graduate level only, and most of the students are Ph.D. candidates. The teaching departments are the Department of Marine Biology and Department of Oceanography. The Department of Oceanography offers training in biological oceanography and marine geology, as well as in physical and chemical oceanography. The Academic Staff of the Institution consists of over two dozen faculty members and three times that many research scientists, many of whom have a regularly scheduled part in the instructional program.

The scope of research conducted at Scripps is broad, embracing physical, chemical, geological, geophysical, and biological investigations of the sea. Continuing programs are concerned with the relationships of marine organisms, and to the effects of the environment upon them, the topography, composition and history of the sea floor, waves and currents, and the exchange of heat and material between the ocean, the atmosphere above, and the sea floor below.

In addition to the teaching departments, research is carried out by the staff of the Oceanic Research Division, the Marine Physical Laboratory, the Visibility Laboratory, the Physiological Research Laboratory, the Marine Life Research Group, and the Applied Oceanography Group. Studies range from the propagation of sound in the sea to the nature of the process by which sunlight and simple ions are converted through the food chain into tuna and sardine flesh.

Also associated with Scripps are the Institute for Geophysics and Planetary Physics and the Institute of Marine Resources.

At the north end of the campus is the Department of the Interior Fisheries-Oceanography Center, which houses the California Current Resources Laboratory and the Tuna Resources Laboratory of the Bureau of Commercial Fisheries, the Inter-American Tropical Tuna Commission, and the offices of the California Cooperative Oceanic Fisheries Investigations.

The Scripps campus consists of over 150 acres. There are a dozen buildings. Docking facilities for the ships of the Institution are located at Point Loma.

In a real sense, the sea is Scripps' laboratory, and the Institution operates a fleet of ocean-going vessels, and many small craft. In addition, the Institution operates the unique vessel, FLIP (Floating Instrument Platform), which is towed horizontally to station and then "flipped" into a vertical position by flooding ballast tanks, so that 300 feet of her 355 foot length is underwater. In this position FLIP is remarkably insensitive to motions caused by wind and waves, and provides a stable platform from which delicate measurements may be made.

Since 1950, the Scripps vessels have made many major expeditions, mostly in the Pacific and Indian oceans, and two ships of the Institution have circumnavigated the globe.

The Institution operates the T. Wayland Vaughan Aquarium-Museum which is open to the public. The museum displays cover oceanography and allied topics. The aquarium houses Southern California marine animals in tanks ranging in capacity from 80 to 2,500 gallons.

—R.R.

SCROD The market name for a fillet of young Atlantic cod (1½–3 pounds), but may also include haddock of similar size.

SCUBA DIVING The art of diving with a self-contained underwater breathing apparatus. Scuba diving permits descents to greater depths and for longer periods of time than can be achieved by skin diving without respiratory equipment. No one should participate in skin or Scuba diving without a complete physical examination and periodic checkups. Qualified instruction in the use of Scuba-diving equipment is also essential. Preferably, the beginner should be young (18–35 years), a good swimmer and not be overweight. The minimum requirements for good swimming ability are as follows:

1. Tread water, with feet only and without fins, for 30 seconds

2. Swim 300 yards without fins

3. Tow an inert swimmer 40 yards without the fins

4. Stay afloat 15 minutes without fins or other accessories

5. Swim underwater 15 yards without fins and without a pushoff

If you can do these things and you don't panic when you get water in your eyes or nose, you're ready to start using mask, snorkel, and flippers—*but not before*. A novice who uses these aids develops a false sense of security and grows to depend on them so much that he tends to be lost without them.

HISTORY OF THE SCUBA

Men have gone underwater to obtain seafood and pearls since the earliest times of which we have record. And for many centuries divers have contrived various means of taking air with them. More than two thousand years ago, Alexander the Great is believed to have used a diving bell (basically an inverted tub forced underwater) during the siege of Tyre; and the use of diving bells for salvaging sunken ships in the sixteenth century is well-documented.

In 1837 the Siebe helmet and closed dress went into use. Essentially the same unit employed today by "hard-hat" salvage divers, the Siebe equipment relied on air pumped through a hose from the surface to the diver, who walked on the bottom. With this gear divers have worked in all seas to depths of more than 200 feet, gathering sponges and precious coral, salvaging wrecks, and building or repairing bridges, docks, and other underwater installations.

Until recent years divers went underwater strictly for profit, not pleasure. Few early divers were impressed by the beauty and uniqueness of the underwater world. They had no time to appreciate it. Whether they held their breath while submerged or were tethered to their boat by an air hose, their time below was extremely limited; and dreadful, little-understood things happened to those who overstayed their time on the bottom. Consequently, they paid little attention to the behavior of fishes or other marine animals—except for those species that represented, they felt, a threat to their work or their lives. And in regard to these animals (sharks, barracudas, eels, octopuses, sea snakes, giant clams), the divers, confident their accounts could not be disputed by the lay public, often embellished—or completely fabricated—their tales of personal encounters.

Almost no reliable observations of marine life were made by divers until the 1920's when a few naturalists donned diving helmets and walked about on the bottom of shallow tropic seas. Notable among these were Dr. William Beebe and Dr. William H. Longley. In many of his popular books and articles, Beebe described his underwater experiences and observations in Bermuda and the Caribbean, while Longley made a systematic study of the fishes of Dry Tortugas, taking many excellent underwater photographs and writing numerous scientific papers on the behavior, color patterns, and mating habits of coral-reef fishes.

Nowadays most oceanographic institutions accept diving as routine, and literally hundreds of scientists go underwater as a regular part of their jobs. In addition, thousands of amateur naturalists, photographers, and "fish watchers" investigate, observe, or record the marine life of all seas, from polar regions to the Equator.

Anglers, too, are taking up diving. Watching how fishes behave under natural conditions is always fascinating and is often rewarding, as well. Through observing different species in their own habitats, a sharp-eyed person can learn things about their feeding habits and food preferences and what attracts or frightens them that he might never learn while casting from a boat.

Fish watching can be enjoyed by anyone who has access to a body of water with underwater visibility of more than a few feet. Floating down a clear mountain stream can be almost as exciting as drifting over a grassy tidal flat. The major difference is the greater variety of species in the marine environment.

The basic piece of equipment is a simple diving mask—the indispensable window to the underwater regions. Also extremely helpful are a snorkel tube (for breathing while the face is submerged) and a pair of foot-fins, or flippers. For deeper diving without the tiring necessity of con-

Free Diver

tinually rising for air, a Scuba (Self-Contained Under-water Breathing Apparatus) is required.

Although the term "Scuba" is newer than the atomic bomb, a workable, self-contained breathing unit was invented in 1865 by two Frenchmen, Benoit Rouquayrol and Auguste Denayrouze. Like the Scubas of today, it employed an automatic regulator that gave the diver air on demand (when he inhaled) at the same pressure as the pressure of the surrounding water. Compressed air was stored in a metal cylinder secured to the diver's back. This remarkable apparatus failed to achieve widespread use for two reasons. First, its tank was capable of holding air compressed to only about 30 atmospheres; consequently it could be used as a self-contained unit for only a few minutes on a working dive to 50–60 feet. Secondly, the divers of that day failed to realize that they could operate most efficiently by wearing only enough lead weights to overcome their natural buoyancy. Instead, they went down heavily weighted and walked about clumsily on the bottom. This eliminated any advantage they would otherwise have had over helmet divers.

So this first "Scuba" never became widely known or extensively used. It did, however, serve as the model for the diving apparatus worn by Captain Nemo and his crew in Jules Verne's famous novel *Twenty Thousand Leagues under the Sea*, which was published four years after the introduction of the Rouquayrol-Denayrouze units.

In 1934 Yves Le Prieur designed the first self-contained unit that permitted a man to swim like a fish instead of crawling like a crab. Wearing flippers on his feet, the diver breathed through his nose from a full face mask and regulated his air manually from a cylinder holding 38 cubic feet of air compressed to 120 atmospheres—sufficient for a 30-minute dive in shallow water.

Then in 1943 the famous Aqua-Lung was invented by J. Y. Cousteau and Emil Gagnan. This unit combined a stronger and larger air cylinder with an improved version of the Rouquayrol-Denayrouze automatic regulator. With this apparatus the "man-fish" was born.

THE SCUBA

All compressed-air, mouthpiece-type Scubas in use today are essentially the same as the Cousteau-Gagnan "lung." There are single-hose and twin-hose regulators,

Scuba Diver

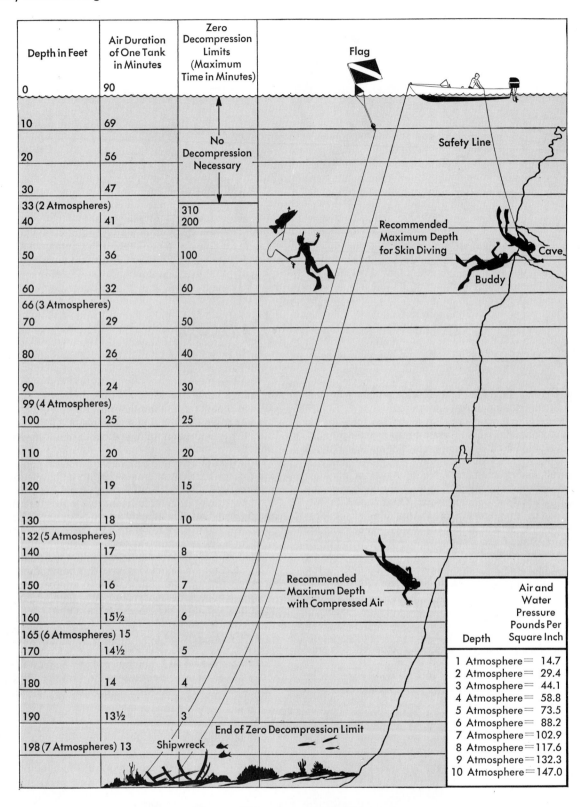

Depth in Feet	Air Duration of One Tank in Minutes	Zero Decompression Limits (Maximum Time in Minutes)
0	90	
10	69	
20	56	No Decompression Necessary
30	47	
33 (2 Atmospheres)		310
40	41	200
50	36	100
60	32	60
66 (3 Atmospheres)		
70	29	50
80	26	40
90	24	30
99 (4 Atmospheres)		
100	25	25
110	20	20
120	19	15
130	18	10
132 (5 Atmospheres)		
140	17	8
150	16	7
160	15½	6
165 (6 Atmospheres)	15	
170	14½	5
180	14	4
190	13½	3
198 (7 Atmospheres)	13	

Flag

Safety Line

Recommended Maximum Depth for Skin Diving

Cave

Buddy

Recommended Maximum Depth with Compressed Air

End of Zero Decompression Limit

Shipwreck

Depth	Air and Water Pressure Pounds Per Square Inch
1 Atmosphere =	14.7
2 Atmosphere =	29.4
3 Atmosphere =	44.1
4 Atmosphere =	58.8
5 Atmosphere =	73.5
6 Atmosphere =	88.2
7 Atmosphere =	102.9
8 Atmosphere =	117.6
9 Atmosphere =	132.3
10 Atmosphere =	147.0

one-stage and two-stage regulators; but all utilize the same principles, and probably all are basically sound in design. The more expensive units are, as a rule, better engineered and more sensitive to slight changes in pres-sure, hence somewhat safer—particularly when a diver has to work in deepwater.

The basic Scuba consists of a cylinder, or "bottle," holding compressed air, plus a regulator that automatically delivers air at the same pressure as the surrounding water. Exhaled air escapes through an exhaust valve. The diver's lungs always contain air at the same pressure as the water at that depth; therefore, no pressure is felt. Closed-circuit units, containing pure oxygen, and semi-closed-circuit units, employing a mixture of gases, are inherently dangerous and intended only for highly specialized or military use. These are not discussed here.

A standard Scuba tank holds the equivalent of 72 cubic feet of atmospheric air. The possible duration of a dive with this amount of air will vary in accordance with the depth of descent and, of course, the amount of exertion involved beyond the norm (such as working with tools). As a general estimate for normal dives Boyle's Law has a practical application to the Scuba; the volume of a gas varies inversely as the pressure, if temperature is constant. Since temperature change is usually negligible the formula works as follows:

$$P_1 V_1 = P_2 V_2 \qquad\qquad V_2 = \frac{P_1 V_1}{P_2}$$

P_1 = 1 atmosphere pressure at surface
V_1 = volume of compressed air, in cubic feet
P_2 = pressure at a given depth
V_2 = volume of air needed at a given depth
Problem: Air duration at 66 feet (3 atmospheres pressure).
Answer: One 72-cubic-foot tankful = 90 minutes at surface

$$V_2 = \frac{1 \times 72}{3} = 24 \text{ cubic feet } \frac{24}{72}$$

$$\times\ 90 = 30 \text{ minutes}$$

At 66 feet, one 72-cubic-foot tankful supplies air for 30 minutes.

The pressure inside the cylinder is about 2,500 pounds per square inch. Obviously, it takes a strong container to hold it—a good reason for using top-quality equipment. A tank that's several years old is likely to be rusty inside (the result of condensation of moisture in the enclosed air; only in the past few years have manufacturers effectively coated the interior of the cylinders to prevent oxidation). Filling a rust-weakened tank to capacity and letting it roll about the hot, unshaded deck of a bouncing boat is about as safe as playing catch with a live hand grenade. Even if such a tank doesn't explode, the fine bits of iron oxide passing from the tank into the regulator may clog up the works, or, worse yet, pass on through the mouthpiece into the diver's lungs.

It is important to have a checkout before making one's first Scuba dive. Scuba diving is remarkably simple; but so is flying; yet few persons would try to solo without hours of dual instruction. With Scuba, a few hours of pool instruction is highly recommended. No matter how fine the equipment, the factors of human error and bad weather can create sudden emergencies. If an untrained diver strays too far from his boat, runs out of air and comes up to find a strong current running against him, he may panic and drown. The steel tank he wears (which is weightless under water and weighs about 35 pounds in air) is like an anchor rope around his neck as he tries to hold his head up to breathe.

The solution is simple if it has been practiced in calm water. The diver can roll over onto his back, using the buoyancy of the empty tank for support, or he can dog-paddle back to the boat while breathing through his snorkel with his head submerged. In extreme cases he can drop his weight belt and, if necessary, remove his tank and push it ahead of him like a log.

The checkout course includes the technique of "buddy breathing" (sharing a mouthpiece with another diver—a lifesaver if one runs out of air in a cave or in water that is very deep, where it may be impossible to reach the surface on the residual air in the tank); also the methods of donning and removing equipment on the bottom; and how to clear the mask if it should become dislodged and filled with water.

PRESSURE HAZARDS

As the diver descends, the pressure on his body increases at the rate of 0.445 psi (pounds per square inch) per foot of depth in seawater, or 1 atmosphere for every 33 feet of descent. The human body can tolerate a great deal of pressure provided it is uniformly distributed (600-foot descents have been completed with no serious effects from compression). During a diver's ascent air contained in his lungs expands. Normally, the air vents freely, and no physical difficulties arise. If the diver holds his breath, however, or if he has a localized airway obstruction, the expanding air may cause overinflation of the lungs. While ascending from only 33 feet of depth without exhaling, the air in the lungs would expand to double its original volume, possibly resulting in gross rupture of the lungs or, more likely, an air leakage into the system known as air embolism—usually fatal or crippling. Naturally, a person with a ruptured ear drum should not dive. The use of ear plugs is not compensatory because the water pressure will force them deeply into the ear. Water entering the middle ear can create a fatal situation.

The other grave danger from pressure—the bends—can be avoided by conforming to recommended depth-time limitations.

Limits of Dives Without Decompression Stops According to the latest Navy tables, divers using compressed air can safely stay at the indicated depths for the periods shown without need to make stops for decompression while surfacing. The times given include descent time. In no case should you rise faster than one foot per second. If you make a second dive without waiting at least twelve hours, you may still have excess nitrogen in your body and you cannot count on being safe under these no-decompression tables.

Depth in feet	Time in minutes
33– 35	310
36– 40	200
41– 50	100
51– 60	60
61– 70	50
71– 80	40
81– 90	30
91–100	25
101–110	20
111–120	15
121–140	10
141 to 190	5

IMPORTANCE OF SAFETY PRINCIPLES

There are numerous physiological dangers in diving. Anyone planning to dive should familiarize himself with these hazards (*see table* Skin and Scuba Diving Dangers). Fatalities among recreational divers are high when compared to the more hazardous professional diving done by the U.S. Navy. During a 32-month study period, 37 deaths were reported in Florida alone; the U.S. Navy had only 7 fatalities in a 15-year period of extensive operational diving. Analysis of the Florida reports (Taylor et al. "Skin and Scuba Diving Fatalities." *The Journal of the Florida Medical Association* April, 1963.) indicated that about two-thirds (24) of the fatalities occurred in springs associated with cave diving when the individuals failed to observe basic rules, such as not using a safety line, going beyond the end of the safety line while in a cave, and failure to wear a depth gauge or diving watch (in fourteen cases exhausted air supply was a major factor in the death). Of the eleven ocean fatalities only one was from shark attack; the remainder were drownings occurring from exhausted air supply; none of the victims wore a depth gauge or diving watch. Although recreational skin and Scuba diving can be perfectly safe, the neophyte cannot afford to ignore the rigid safety principles which have been evolved for his protection.

DIVING SUITS

Except for short dives (thirty minutes or less) in warm, shallow waters, Scuba-divers need protective clothing. The body loses heat rapidly when totally submerged—even in the tropics—and the water temperature only 50 feet down may be ten degrees colder than on the surface. Unlike a swimmer, a Scuba diver does not—must not—exercise strenuously. Maintaining body heat by this method burns oxygen rapidly and increases carbon dioxide build-up.

The choice of a diving suit depends roughly on the following water temperature ranges:

Below 45°F.   A dry suit worn over a wet suit or over long woolen underwear
45°F.–65°F.   Either wet or dry suit
65°F.–75°F.   Woolen underwear, sweat shirt or wet-suit jacket
Above 75°F.   No suit required except for deep dives or long periods of immersion

The wet suit (foam neoprene) is the best and safest for most purposes. A dry suit can have a deleterious effect on the diver (suit squeeze) if air is not released into the suit during deep descent. In a hooded suit ear squeeze can also result.

FISH WATCHING

A Scuba diver is like a part of the underseascape, and the fishes show no fear unless he makes a sudden or aggressive move. Some fishes, in fact, may exhibit great curiosity, rolling their eyes ludicrously as they circle and examine the intruder. In tropical areas a tiny wrasse or a neon goby may nuzzle against the diver's bare skin, insultingly friendly as it searches for parasites. A two-inch damselfish or another territorial species (that is, one that sets up a "home base" and keeps trespassers away) may dart at a diver in an attempt to run him off and then retreat to its hole to peer out with keen interest.

By drifting quietly along the bottom in clearwater areas one can see where fishes stay in the heat of the day; what they do when the tide is running or is slack; which species face into the current, which ones swim with it, and which ones seek cover; how they behave toward one another; how and when they feed; or how they respond to different sounds.

Interestingly it seems that certain sounds attract fishes as strongly as others repel them. A loud, sharp noise, such as the banging of oars, usually frightens them, while scraping or grinding sounds—like the rubbing together of seashells or the scuffing of feet on the deck of a boat—often attract them. The sound of an outboard motor will frequently bring saltwater fishes out of their holes. On many occasions barracuda have been observed to appear suddenly and head for the surface to follow a passing boat.

One of the more striking things that divers notice is that most fishes are attracted by others that are wounded, sick, or in trouble. A nervous or injured fish swims erratically and beats its fins in a frantic, irregular manner. Sometimes it moves vertically or upside down; it may spin, circle, or swim in sudden spurts. A wounded bottom dweller will often go to the surface, while a surface dweller may sink. These abnormal movements excite nearby healthy fishes. They'll gather about the creature in distress. Tiny ones will nip at it, while larger ones may slash it or swallow it. (This phenomenon may explain why actively feeding predators, such as snook, bluefish, tarpon, or channel bass, will almost invariably strike a hooked fish cast into the midst of a school of baitfish. With thousands of milling fish to choose from, the feeding fish will grab the one whose movements are unnatural.)

Obviously, personal observations of this type can benefit any serious angler. And they may explain why some of the time-honored saltwater lures which resemble nothing that swims are effective. The weighted clothespin-plug, for example, when worked properly, darts and dips like a scared or wounded fish. It doesn't look like any particular species. It's "out of phase," and predators may instinctively strike it—even when not actively feeding.

It's quite instructive to study the movements of lures in the water and the ways that fishes react to them. Hovering quietly on the bottom in a fish-filled pocket while a companion in a boat works various artificials through the water is a fascinating pastime. For every strike elicited by a lure, the attention of a dozen or more fish may be attracted. Certain fishes will often snap around and appear to study passing lures intently; they'll jerk forward and follow for a short distance; they'll execute half-hearted passes without making contact; and they'll often flick their tails and turn away in apparent disgust. Sometimes, though, without hesitation, a fish may grab the same lure it ignored on the previous cast. The Scuba-equipped observer can often detect small differences in the angler's presentation which may account for these changes in attitude on the fish's part.   —W.M.S.

UNDERWATER PHOTOGRAPHY

Louis Boutan made the first underwater photographs in the 1890's, and W. H. Longley went diving with color film in the 1920's; yet the scientific use of underwater photographs is still in its infancy. While aerial cameras and techniques have progressed to the point where a single photograph can show hundreds of square miles of the earth's surface in remarkable detail, no more than an infinitesimal portion of the ocean floor has been photographed; and only recently have we been able to depict accurately in a single photograph a bottom area of more than 100 square feet.

To understand why underwater photography has not developed more rapidly, it is necessary to consider some of the limiting factors. Besides the obvious difficulties of working in a foreign and inhospitable medium, there are optical and photometric problems of considerable magnitude.

The Underlying Problems When a ray of light passes from air into water, or from water into air, certain changes take place in the light. The most obvious change is an immediate and pronounced bending, or refraction, of the light ray itself. This is what causes "double vision" when a swimmer wears goggles, the lenses of which are in different planes. This is also what makes submerged objects appear one-fourth larger than they actually are.

Other changes in the light, caused by reflection, absorption, and diffusion, are less apparent to the casual observer but even more important to the photographer. To begin with, a part of the light from the sky is reflected by the ocean's surface and never enters the water. This loss is usually insignificant for photographic purposes, amounting to as little as 3 percent when the sun is high and the surface calm and increasing to about 25 percent when the sun is as low as ten degrees above the horizon; but the loss may be much greater when the sea's surface is disturbed by choppy waves.

The effects of absorption and diffusion are the big problems of the underwater photographer, and these effects are highly variable, depending upon the amount and kind of suspended particles in the water. Generally speaking, dark particles absorb light, while other particles reflect or diffuse the light.

Under the best of conditions (in clear Gulf Stream or Bahama waters, for example), loss from absorption is so great that a light meter held just below the surface will generally indicate less than half as much available light as is found just above the surface; and at a depth of about twenty feet the meter will rarely show more than one-fourth as much light as is indicated on the surface. (In many coastal areas, of course, all light is extinguished, as far as photographic use is concerned, at a very shallow depth.)

The Light Dims, But Unevenly Along with the general absorption of light, there is selective absorption, or "filtering," that has nothing to do with suspended particles and occurs in all water, even distilled water. This filtering is particularly destructive to the red end of the color spectrum. Tests in the Mediterranean showed that only about 10 percent of the red light penetrated to a depth of 5 meters (16 feet 4 inches), while 50 percent of the yellow was still present at that depth and about 80 percent of the blue. (While this rapid disappearance of the red light takes place in all bodies of water, the loss of the other colors is not constant. In clear ocean waters, blue seems to penetrate better than other colors, but in some inshore areas blue light is absorbed as fast as red, and this water is said to have a "yellow cast.")

Because of the strong absorption of the red light—which for photographic purposes is totally absent below 40 feet—color photography in all but extremely shallow water (where corrective filters can improve the color balance) is practical only with the aid of artificial light.

Diffusion, or scattering of light, is the most serious obstacle to long-range underwater pictures. Diffusion causes "distant" objects seen underwater to appear ghostly and indistinct, as though enshrouded by fog. In the clearest seawater, where underwater visibility may occasionally exceed 150 feet, diffusion is still sufficiently bothersome to limit the effective range for pictures to about 30 feet. Diffusion has the effect of redistributing rays of light so that light appears to come not only from the surface but from all directions. This effect is more noticeable at greater depths, where shadows tend to disappear.

Problem of Fog To overcome the "fog" created by diffusion, photographers often use wide-angle lenses, thereby increasing the angle of view and allowing the camera to operate closer to the subject. Wide-angle lenses, in fact, are almost vital for all but closeup work, since the magnification of water has the effect of increasing the focal length of any lens by about 25 per cent, turning the normal lens into a mildly telescopic lens with a consequent decrease in the area covered by the lens. (If the photographer tries to solve the magnification problem by "backing off," he loses sharpness, due to the scattering effect.)

Pillow Distortion The use of a wide-angle lens creates a new problem, however—distortion at the edges of the picture, caused by the sharp bending of the light rays that come from the sides. While this distortion is not sufficiently severe to bother the average underwater photographer and, in fact, is often not noticeable, it presents serious difficulties for the photographer who is striving for scientific accuracy.

Many attempts have been made to overcome this "pillow" distortion (which causes objects near the sides of a picture to be magnified more than objects in the center) by the use of concave outer surfaces on the windows of the camera housings, but results have been unsatisfactory. Under the sponsorship of Woods Hole Oceanographic Institution, Professor Robert Hopkins of the University of Rochester has developed a special lens designed to eliminate pillow distortion. This lens is intended for underwater use only, and cannot be used out of water without causing "barrel" distortion. When mounted on deepsea remote-operated cameras built by Edgerton, Germeshausen & Grier, Inc., this 35-mm lens is said to be capable of producing distortion-free photographs of the ocean floor at a lens-to-subject range of 30 feet, thereby including an area of over 500 square feet of the sea bottom. (Until now, most deepsea photographs have been made at a lens-to-subject distance of about 10 feet, covering a segment of sea floor of only about 50 square feet in area.) Lowered from the Woods Hole research vessel "Chain," the new lens has been used at a depth of about 20,000 feet in the Puerto Rican Trench.

Equipment Need Not Be Complex Most underwater photographs are, of course, made with standard cameras and lenses, which are encased in waterproof housings of metal, wood, or plastic. In water that is reasonably clear and not over 50–60 feet deep, good black-

and-white photographs can be obtained with simple, inexpensive equipment. Acceptable results, in extremely shallow water (about 10 feet or less), can be obtained by inserting a small camera in a makeshift housing made from an ordinary diving mask and a plastic bag, and manipulating the camera controls from the outside of the bag.

Stock housings are available for many 35-mm cameras and for some larger cameras, and certain firms specialize in building custom housing of Plexiglas for any and all cameras. Underwater Sports, Inc., of Miami, produces an inexpensive underwater camera, the *Mako Shark*, that needs no housing, while the Cousteau-designed *Calypso* and *Nikonos* cameras are compact 35-mm cameras with full aperture, speed, and range controls that need no housing and have been tested to a depth of 200 feet.

As mentioned above, the use of color films underwater is hardly practical without artificial lighting. Flash units can be coupled to most cameras, the batteries and capacitors being encased within the waterproof camera housing. The bulb socket on the flash gun need not be protected from the water. Most divers use clear flash bulbs (instead of the blue bulbs normally recommended for color photography), since the strongly red light emitted from clear bulbs tends to compensate for the loss of the natural red light by selective absorption. The flash reflector should be mounted at least 18 inches from the lens to minimize the effect of bounce-back from suspended particles between the camera and the subject (which show up as white or pink spots on the picture). Spare bulbs can be carried in a net, and gloves should be worn, as bulbs sometimes explode while being removed from the socket.

For closeup work, electronic flash is highly recommended, as the color balance of its light approximates that of sunlight. A light meter, invaluable for critical color work, can be encased in a special housing or carried down in a glass jar.

A Sharper Eye for Science With the improvement and increased availability of Aqua Lungs and other self-contained diving units, the uses of underwater photography for scientific work have increased greatly. By taking time-lapse photographs, zoologists can now study the growth and budding of live corals, the manner in which artificial reefs become populated by fishes, the riddling of timbers by shipworms; geologists can learn how sediments build up, how ripples are formed on the ocean floor, how turbidity currents operate; botanists can study the growth of algae and the flowering of marine grasses. Archaeologists can photograph an entire ancient shipwreck by making a series of pictures and pasting them together in a montage, whereby they can study at leisure a picture of the whole wreck—a sight that no diver can see while submerged.

Some day, perhaps, the floor of entire seas may be accurately mapped through the use of montages of stereoscopic photographs in full color. Only by such ambitious undertakings can the vast world of the undersea be brought into sharp focus. (Reprinted from *Sea Frontiers* Vol. 8, No. 5, with permission of the International Oceanographic Foundation.) —W.M.S.

SCUDS Order Amphipoda Erroneously called freshwater shrimp. The order of amphipods includes marine forms as well as most terrestrial species which live near the high water mark, such as the sand bug (*which see*).

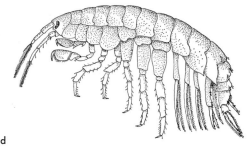

Scud

Amphipods are elongate and more or less compressed. There is no carapace, and the abdomen is usually composed of six segments exclusive of the terminal segment, which forms the telson. The breathing organs or gills are attached to the first joints of the thoracic legs on the ventral surface of the body.

There are about 50 species of scuds in North American freshwaters. They are shrimplike in appearance, the body arched and flattened laterally. The body is smooth and pale, often greenish in color. Scuds have seven pairs of thoracic legs, and two pairs of antennae. They vary from 5–20 mm in length (⅕ to ⅘ of an inch). Scuds are omnivorous scavengers and are most common among aquatic vegetation; they swim rapidly and dart about when disturbed. Freshwater scuds are an important source of food for trout, especially in the western United States, and for largemouth bass in the south. Artificial flies tied to imitate the scud are usually very effective in waters where this forage is abundant. See also Freshwater Ecology —A.J.McC.

SCULL A boat oar. To scull is to propel a boat with one oar by working the oar from side to side over the stern.

SCULPINS Family Cottidae This large fresh- and saltwater species is made up for the most part of small fishes. They vary in length between species of from 2–30 inches. A few are large enough to be used as food, and some are taken for use as bait, but only a half dozen or so are of any commercial or sport importance. They are found from very shallow waters to great depths. Some remain on shore between tides.

Sculpins are distinguished by a bony support extending under the skin from the cheek to the eye; anal spines absent; pelvic fins thoracic when present and each with 1 spine and 2–5 softrays; fewer than 20 dorsal spines; preopercle with one or more spines, variously developed, the upper sometimes antlerlike; scales may be platelike along the lateral line, ctenoid or modified ctenoid, and not covering the body below the lateral line, or absent; pectoral fins large; a greatly developed anal papilla in males of some species; the head usually large and depressed; the eyes high and closely set; gill membranes connected, often joined to isthmus. The environment has a marked effect on coloration, as does the sex in some species.

The family is most numerous in the North Pacific. There are 84 known species in the United States and Canada, exclusive of about 45 which occur only in Alaskan waters. Many of the Pacific coastal species are to be found in the volume *Fishes of the Pacific Coast of Canada* (Clemens, W. A., and G. B. Wilby, Bulletin of the Fisheries Research Board of Canada, No. 68, 368 pp., 1949 [revised edition 1963]).

Egg masses are usually deposited under or on tops of rocks or in crevices. They are orange, brown, pink, cherry-red, green, or blue. The male of some species guards the eggs for as much as 5 weeks, which is the incubation period of at least one species. Egg numbers are known for only a few species and vary from 600 to 3,000. *See also* Bigmouth Sculpin, Cabezone, Great Sculpin, Pacific Staghorn Sculpin, Shorthorn Sculpin

—J.R.

SCUP *Stenotomus chrysops* Commonly known as "porgy" along the Northeastern United States coast. Apparently there are only two species in this genus, this and the common species of the Gulf of Mexico, the longspine porgy, *S. caprinus*. *S. chrysops* ranges from Nova Scotia south to the Atlantic coast of Florida, but has not been shown to occur in the Gulf of Mexico as some writers have supposed. *S. caprinus*, on the other hand, does occur off the Carolina and Georgia coasts along with *S. chrysops*. *S. aculeatus*, the so-called southern porgy or scup of the Atlantic Coast, apparently is a synonym of *S. chrysops*.

The scup has lanceolate incisor teeth, which distinguish the members of this genus from other American sparids.

Scup

In life, the ground color is silvery to brownish, without distinct markings except sometimes for traces of darkish vertical bars on the side, the bar midway the length of the body being usually more distinct than the several others. It sometimes reaches about 18 inches and 3–4 pounds.

LIFE HISTORY

The food consists primarily of small crustaceans, mollusks, worms, and some vegetable matter.

The scup live on or near the bottom in the mid depths of the Continental Shelf. Spawning takes place offshore in the spring.

ANGLING VALUE

The scup often enters importantly both the commercial and sport catches, especially in the more northern parts of its range. Although it readily takes bottom-fished baits, the scup is often regarded as a nuisance by anglers seeking larger species. It is a good table fish. *See also* Jolthead Porgy, Red Porgy, Whitebone Porgy —D.K.C.

SCUPPERS Openings in the side or stern of a boat to carry off water. The outboard transoms often have scuppers fitted into them to serve as a self-bailing arrangement.

SEA ANCHOR A cone-shaped device made of canvas to keep a boat's head into the wind when drifting. Works in water the way a kite works in the wind.

SEA BASS *See* Black Sea Bass

SEA BREAM *Archosargus rhomboidalis* Until recently, the most often used scientific name for this species was *A. unimaculatus*. The species is primarily tropical and ranges certainly from south Florida to Rio de Janeiro.

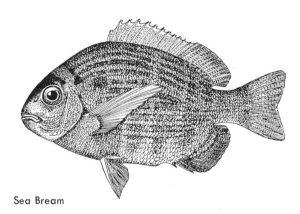

Sea Bream

It questionably has been recorded from as far north as New Jersey. Although common in the proper habitat in the West Indies, it has not been recorded from the Bahamas. This species probably replaces the pinfish *Lagodon* (*which see*) in the tropics, for the two forms have similar ecological and food habits.

A close relative, *A. pourtalesi*, occurs only in the Galápagos Islands of the eastern Pacific.

In life, the color is much like that of the pinfish, being basically bluish-silver with several indistinct dark crossbars, which vary in intensity, on the sides; numerous longitudinal golden stripes on the sides (somewhat wider, more distinct, and less regular than in the pinfish); and a dark shoulder spot. The fins are yellowish, with tinges of blue. In size, the sea bream may reach about a foot.

LIFE HISTORY

The sea bream lives on grassy flats and feeds on small animals and on plant materials, using its lunately edged incisor teeth in a typical grazing type of feeding behavior. Records of *Lagodon* from the West Indies actually are the sea bream, and where the two occur together, as in the Florida Keys, they usually are not distinguished by local fishermen despite the deeper body and different tooth form of the sea bream. Spawning apparently takes place not far offshore in winter.   —D.K.C.

SEA CATFISH *Arius felis* Also called the hardhead, this species is confined to the western Atlantic and is mainly found in warm, temperate waters. It ranges from Cape Cod to the West Indies and throughout the Gulf of Mexico. It has several relatives that occur along the tropical parts of the Pacific Coast.

The body of the sea catfish is rather elongate and rounded, tapering to the slender tail; profile from tip to snout to origin of dorsal is slightly convex; body depth about 5.0 in standard length; head subconical, depressed, 3.8 in standard length; dorsal rays I, 7; anal rays 16; pectoral rays I, 6; eyes located much closer to end of snout than to opercular margin; teeth on vomer in two small, separate groups that may or may not be continuous with the much larger, rounded patches of palatine teeth; all teeth are villiform; gill membranes broadly united forming a narrow, free fold across the isthmus; occipital process with a median keel about one-third length of head, its tip convex; fontanelle forming a narrow groove; top of head comparatively smooth; humeral process nearly one-half the length of pectoral spine; maxillary barbels extend to or nearly to end of operculum; outer mandibular barbels about half the length of head; basal bone of dorsal spine small; dorsal spine rather strong, about three-fifths of head length, granulated in front and serrated behind; adipose fin shorter than dorsal; pectoral spine serrated interiorly and also exteriorly toward the top; caudal fin deeply forked, the upper lobe longer; dorsal and pectoral fins without filaments.

Sea Catfish

Color of the back varies from steel-blue to grayish or gray-green. The sides and ventrum are white to yellowish.

LIFE HISTORY

In contrast to the gafftopsail, the sea catfish seems to prefer high salinities, most individuals being caught where the salt content is 30.0 or more parts per thousand. However, a wide salinity range can be endured, and the very young fish tend to occur in the more brackish waters. In November, a migration takes place from the bays and estuaries to the shallow parts of the open ocean. A return migration takes place in February, and from that time through the summer and early fall, this species is one of most numerous, shallow-water marine fishes.

Most of the breeding takes place in June and July. Like the gafftopsail, the male broods the fertilized eggs in his mouth. The mouth and pharyngeal region of the male become enlarged apparently just before the breeding season. At that time, the female develops an enlarged, spatulalike protuberance on the pelvic fins. The function of this structure is unknown. It has been estimated that it takes 60–80 days for the young to develop to the point where the yolk sac has been absorbed. At this time, they are ready to leave the mouth of the male. The eggs are large, more than ½ inch in diameter, and each female produces 40–60.

ANGLING VALUE

The maximum length is about 1½ feet, and such a fish would weigh about 3 pounds. This species is easily caught with hook and line by bottom-fishing with bait. Although not generally regarded as a food fish, the flesh of the sea catfish is edible.

DANGER TO MAN

Both the sea catfish and the gafftopsail possess a single, sharp spine at the anterior end of the dorsal and pectoral fins. These spines are enveloped by a thin layer of skin called the integumentary sheath. Within the epidermal layer of the sheath is located a series of glandular poison cells. These will rupture and release their contents when the spine penetrates the body of a victim. The result can be a painful wound although it is usually not severe. If extensive, the wound should be thoroughly washed in seawater and then soaked in hot water. After this, it should be treated with an antiseptic and a sterile dressing.

—J.C.B.

SEA CUCUMBER A member of the echinoderm class Holothurioidea. Sea cucumbers can be distinguished from other echinoderms by their long soft bodies. When gutted, boiled, and dried, the sea cucumber is an edible product marketed in Japan as *iriko* and in the Philippines as *trepang*.

SEAHORSES *Hippocampus* spp. The seahorses belong to the family Syngathidae which includes the pipefishes. The seahorses are of no angling value, but they are a popular subject in saltwater aquaria. Seahorses are world wide in distribution occurring chiefly in warm seas, although some species are regularly found as far north as Cape Cod and beyond the Gulf of Maine as strays. The name is derived from the curiously horselike head which joins the axis of the body at an angle. The snout is tubular and terminates in a small oblique mouth. The neck, body, and long tail are circumscribed with rings of bony plates, the number of which varies according to the species. Three species common to Atlantic shores of the United States are the spotted seahorse, *Hippocampus erectus*, dwarf seahorse, *H. zosterae*, and the offshore seahorse, *H. obtusus*. The Pacific seahorse, *H. ingens*, is common to western shores. Seahorses range from 2–6 inches in length, but have been recorded to over 12 inches in Asiatic waters.

They move by rapidly vibrating the dorsal and smaller pectoral fins. Slow of movement, they can hide in weeds and coral.

—A.J.McC.

SEA LAMPREY *Petromyzon marinus* The lampreys are primitive, eel-shaped creatures lacking true jaws and paired fins and having soft cartilaginous skeletons. The sea lamprey is one of the best-known species. It has the dorsal fin separated into two parts by a deep notch, the second part confluent with the caudal fin. The mouth is merely a sucking disk lined with horny cusps, which are also present on the tongue. The closely spaced teeth are arranged in curved, radiating rows. Adults are dark tan to olive or red-brown, with chocolate blotches; spawning adults are purple or blue-black. The young ammocoetes are tan above and lighter below, occasionally with darker mottlings. It grows to 3 feet and nearly 3 pounds.

Sea Lamprey

LIFE HISTORY

The sea lamprey occurs in saltwater from Greenland to Florida, and from northern Norway to the Mediterranean Sea, ascending freshwater to breed. Some occur land-locked in freshwater lakes. Following spawning, the young spend 5–10 years or more (individuals have been recorded to 13 years) buried in the mud, after which they transform and move downstream into the ocean or a lake. Adults spend about two years parasitizing various fishes, then return to freshwater. Nests are built in the stream bed, large depressions being made by the adult moving large stones with its mouth. Adults die following spawning.

The sucking disk is used by the lamprey to attach itself to its prey and to bore a hole through the skin with the rasp tongue, after which it sucks blood from the host. Lamprey scars are visible on many different kinds of fishes.

ECONOMIC VALUE

During spring runs, large numbers were formerly taken and used for food, their flesh being considered a delicacy. Adults are important to biological classes, and are sought by biological supply houses. Because the adults destroy valuable commercial species, particularly in freshwater, attempts have been made to control their numbers. Selective chemical poisoning was effective in certain areas.

ANGLING VALUE

Young "lampers" are used as bait by anglers, and are particularly effective for smallmouth bass and walleye. *See also* Pacific Lamprey   —D.dS.

SEAPERCH *See* Island Seaperch, Pink Seaperch, Rainbow Seaperch, Rubberlip Seaperch, Striped Seaperch, Surf Seaperch, White Seaperch

SEA POACHERS Family Agonidae This family, which includes the alligatorfishes, have a body covering of bony armor made up of rows of shields which do not overlap and do not have free margins. They are small fish, found on rocky or muddy bottoms. They are most abundant in the North Pacific into Arctic seas, but are also found in the North Atlantic and the east and west coasts of South America. Rarely are they found deeper than 3,000 feet and can occur in shallow water in tide pools. Though abundant, they are of no commercial value.

Atlantic Poacher

Alligatorfish

Long, slim, and angulated for the most part, the bony shields of the agonids give an eight-angled appearance to the body; pelvic fins thoracic, each with one spine and two rays. Poachers are separated from alligatorfishes in having a single dorsal fin, whereas the latter have two dorsals.

LIFE HISTORY

Little is known of the habits of the family. A European species spawns in late winter and spring. The large eggs, 1.76–2.23 millimeters, are laid in yellow masses on the bottom, and the incubation period may be as long as a

year. The young are pelagic but settle to the bottom upon reaching 20 millimeters. Food of the pelagic young is zooplankton, of the adult it is crustaceans, worms, and other bottom invertebrates.

They reach a length of 12 inches, but most specimens are much shorter.   —J.R.

SEA RAVEN *Hemitripterus americanus* This sculpin (*which see*) is common north of Cape Cod but occurs to Chesapeake Bay. It has the ability to inflate the belly when disturbed. Its colors vary from purple to reddish-brown or yellow. The eggs are yellow and about 4.0 millimeters

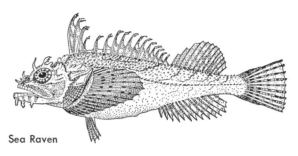

Sea Raven

in diameter. It grows to a length of 25 inches and a weight of 5 pounds. It is distinguished by the spinous dorsal being larger than the softrayed portion. There are 4 spines in the first part of the dorsal fin, 12 in the second, and 1 spine and 12 rays in the last   —J.R.

SEAROBINS *Prionotus* **spp.** Several searobins (genus *Prionotus*, family Triglidae) are common along the Atlantic Coast and from time to time are common in anglers' catches, depending on season and locality. One of the most common, the northern searobin, *P. carolinus*, occurs from the Bay of Fundy to South Carolina. Like its relatives, its large head is covered with bony plates and spines. The large pectoral fins are fan-shaped, each with two dusky blotches. There are a spiny and a soft dorsal fin, and the ventral fins are located beneath the pectorals. The first three rays of the pectoral fins are free and unconnected to the remaining rays by a membrane. The body is reddish to red-brown or gray, with fine black markings and saddlelike blotches. It grows to about 16 inches and 1¾ pounds. Most specimens are less than a foot long. A closely related species, the striped searobin, *P. evolans*, has a distinct stripe on each side of the body, and the pectoral fin has only a single broad blotch. It grows to 18 inches and has about the same distribution as the common searobin.

LIFE HISTORY

Searobins are bottom dwellers, but they can be taken close to the surface, and apparently they can swim rapidly in short bursts. The modified pectoral rays are

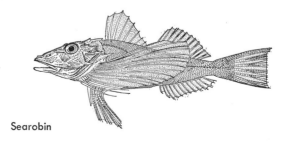

Searobin

used in walking along the bottom and in searching for or stirring up food. They may be on the bottom with the pectoral fins spread, but if disturbed they burrow into the sand, exposing only the top of the head and the eyes. Common searobins occur over a depth range from the tidal zone commonly to at least 40 fathoms, to a maximum of 93 fathoms, but the striped searobin is found in shoaler water. They appear in shallower waters during the summer and move offshore during the cold months.

They are omnivorous and voracious and eat fish, shrimp, crabs, amphipods, squids, clams, and worms. Spawning occurs from at least June to September. The eggs float at the surface, and the young grow rapidly, reaching 7 inches at the end of the first year.

FOOD VALUE

Although the meat is good, few searobins are eaten, even though large numbers are taken in trawls and would provide inexpensive and tasty fare. —D.dS.

SEA SERPENT *See* Basking Shark, Oarfish

SEA SNAKES Family Hydrophidae Sea snakes are reptiles and are specially adapted to their mode of life. The nostrils are provided with valves, the scales are reduced or absent to reduce friction while swimming, and the specialized, flattened tail permits efficient swimming. Most are less than 4 feet long, but a few approach 9 feet. They are usually variously banded, but the yellow-bellied sea snake (*Pelamis platurus*) is black above and sharply separated from the yellow underparts, with incomplete rings around the tail. Sometimes snake eels (*which see*) of the family Ophichthidae are mistaken for sea snakes, but these are distinct classes.

LIFE HISTORY

With the exception of a single species from Lake Taal, Luzon, all sea snakes are found in the tropical Pacific and Indian oceans. The rest of the 50 or so species occur from the Persian Gulf to the Yellow Sea and Japan, southward to Tasmania, northern New Zealand, and western Oceania, being found throughout the Netherlands Indies. These are all essentially coastal species inhabiting shallow water and even river mouths, but the yellow-bellied sea snake is pelagic, swimming hundreds of miles from land. It occurs from East Africa, throughout the Indo-Pacific, to the Gulf of California southward to Ecuador. Sea snakes are seen in large schools, strongly swimming, or perhaps even migrating, in the open sea. Swimming is typically eel-like, with lateral wavy movements of the body, and they can float at the surface or swim backwards or forwards with dexterity, but on land they are helpless.

The reproductive habits are unknown, except that some lay eggs, at least some species coming ashore do so, while others produce living young. Some species are diurnal, while others are nocturnal. Yellow-bellied sea snakes, among others, can be attracted to a light at night, but they have not been observed to feed on the small fishes thus attracted. Sea snakes are fish eaters, and their stomachs have revealed anchovies, small herrings, eels, and mullet. They are reportedly docile but can become aggressive when annoyed.

DANGER TO MAN

This family is a highly poisonous one, the toxin of some species being more lethal than that of the cobra. The fangs are reduced in size but are still effective similar to those of a cobra. Venom injected into a victim usually acts within 20 minutes to a few hours and the mortality from such bites is about 25 percent. *See also* Dangerous, Poisonous, and Injurious Aquatic Life *under* First Aid. —D.dS.

SEA TROUT (1) A sea-run or anadromous brown trout *Salmo trutta*. Sea trout are found in some eastern United States and Canadian rivers. They have a minor distribution in Chile, Argentina, and New Zealand. This migratory form is most common in Iceland and northern Europe. The sea trout has many local names. It is known as a peal in the west of England; in Wales it is called sewin; in Ireland, white trout; and in Scotland, bull trout. Most sea trout migrate to sea at 3 years old; some return to the rivers after only 2–5 months in saltwater, and from then till the following spring they have another set of names—finnock on the east coast of Scotland, whitling on the west, herling in the Solway. All these names, however, apply to the same fish which run up many rivers in Scotland, Wales, and the west of England. They are much smaller than salmon; 3–10 pounds is about the usual size. Very large sea trout of 10–30 pounds are caught in the rivers of Norway, Sweden and Argentina.

AMERICAN DISTRIBUTION

The Connecticut Board of Fisheries and Game made the first imports and introductions of true sea trout to North America in 1958. Before this initial effort the brown trout provided what might be considered token populations in the lower reaches of streams and estuaries of some of the Atlantic coastal states and Canadian Maritime Provinces. Specifically, these included several small streams on the north shore of Long Island, New York, a half dozen streams in Connecticut, a few rivers in Maine, some streams in the northeastern tip of Nova Scotia, as well as on the island of Newfoundland. It is apparent that these large fish are simply stream-resident brown trout which have strayed or wandered to the estuary. As with most salmonids they are able to make the physiological adjustment to saline waters. They find ideal foraging conditions, grow rapidly, and acquire a silvery coloration similar to the Atlantic salmon when living in the sea. Although the brown trout has become well-established in North America, and particularly in the North Atlantic coastal region, they do not display the definite sea-run habit as do other members of the species in Europe and the British Isles.

There are apparently two schools of thought on the basic problem of developing the sea-run characteristic. Some theorists believe that if the population is dense enough in the stream and the environment is favorable, the fish will migrate to saltwater and behave as a sea-run population. Others feel that genetic or hereditary factors are significantly involved and that the offspring of sea-run parent stock are more apt to behave in this fashion. In all probability, both factors are operating; the environment has to be suitable and the hereditary factor is probably a strong one and cannot be discounted.

Sea Trout or Anadromous Brown Trout, 22-pound Male,
Morrum River, Sweden

Results from the introductions in Connecticut indicate that there is validity to the heredity theory. A relatively small plant of about 6,000 2-year-old European sea trout (7–8 inches), in an experimental stream in February 1960, resulted in the return of forty-eight fish that had been to saltwater (twenty-nine adults and nineteen immature) in the fall of 1961, and over 50 adults in the 3½–9-pound-size class in the fall of 1962. This was a more positive indication of a run than ever before. Previously, only occasional fish would appear in the estuary or the stream at various times of the year.

MIGRATIONS

As for the distance of their migrations or whereabouts while in the saltwater, here again there is little information due to a lack of well-planned studies. European biologists are of the opinion that the fish may be confined to the long, meandering estuaries, fjords, or the immediate influence of the particular river system. Yet, others seem to feel that the sea trout leave the river system and range along the coastline for distances not exceeding 100 miles. In Connecticut there has been a known movement of approximately 4 miles to the eastward of the mouth of the stream in which these fish were stocked. Catches by sport fishermen of at least six marked or tagged individuals in this one area indicate the migration pattern and establish the fact that the fish do leave the estuary.

The migrations of sea trout are comparable to the rainbow-trout populations on the West Coast of the United States and Alaska. Here biologists and anglers alike recognize the steelhead as a strain or variety of rainbow trout that runs to the sea. Anatomically, they are the same species, but superficially (coloration, growth rate, behavior) they are dissimilar because of the difference in their environment. It would appear that the sea trout is to the brown trout as the steelhead is to the rainbow.

GROWTH RATE

Despite this lack of information on growth rate, it is fair to state that in areas such as southern New England and the Maritime Provinces sea trout attain an exceptional size. The small amount of data collected in Connecticut suggest the following general growth pattern. It appears as though most of the young trout spend about two years in the stream or freshwater environment. This would be the fingerling or parr stage. They reach the smolt stage and migrate seaward at 2+ years of age and are about 6–8 inches long at this time. This smolt migration usually takes place in February or March with the early spring freshets as it does with the Atlantic salmon. Approximately a year and a half later, or after a full summer and part of the second, fish return to the estuary, many as immature individuals. These immature fish were called "whitling" by the early British naturalists, and are comparable to the grilse of our Atlantic salmon. They run 15–19 inches in size and weigh 1½–3 pounds. The mature individuals returning at this same time in spawning condition may be slightly larger than their immature brethren, run 17–22 inches in size and have a usual weight of 3½–4½ pounds. It is believed that the main run of fish and most mature individuals will return to the parent stream to spawn after the third summer of marine life. Information on some 50 specimens in the 4+ age group indicates that they run 22–23 inches and 4–9 pounds. These are trophy-size specimens considering the high demand on trout fishing in this densely populated and highly industrialized region. However, sea trout provide only a "token" fishery in the eastern United States.

ANGLING VALUE

The sea trout is unquestionably one of the finest gamefish when taken in freshwater rivers. They are caught by a variety of methods and baits but sea trout are preeminently a quarry of the fly-rod angler. Many references to the quality of sea trout appear in angling literature.

"The fight of a sea trout is thus stronger than that of a brown trout and, if possible, even more active and full of quick turns. There is no fish with which one has to be so much on one's guard against being surprised, whether by sudden rushes or by jumps in the air, and as far as the actual playing of the fish is concerned, for sheer enjoyment and rapidity of sensation, I prefer a good fresh run sea trout of three or four pounds in a river on a single-handed rod and fine tackle to anything else." (Grey, 1919)

"Even a little fellow of half a pound is a source of amazement, a fighter from start to finish, that kills himself by his own exertions, while one of three pounds or more is a conquest of which anyone has every reason to be proud. Fierce is its fight, impossible to anticipate or even follow are its wild rushes, violent changes of direction executed with lightning suddenness and rapidity; and, not until the net has securely enclosed it can the struggle be considered at an end or victory won." (Bridgett, 1929)

"If he has caught his quota of perhaps a dozen nice trout on some loch and then suddenly finds himself attached to a jumping rushing silver torpedo which is a 4 lb. sea trout he will there and then become convinced that here is the finest sporting fish of them all. I think this is no exaggeration. The sea trout is definitely the most elusive, the wildest, and the most fascinating game fish which we possess in Great Britain." (Brennand, 1951)

Bridgett's description of the behavior of this fish when hooked seems to summarize well the experience of many anglers. As an angler's fish, the smaller sea trout are more readily caught than the larger ones, and in rivers they are difficult to catch except after dark. A river system containing lakes provides good sport since the sea trout may remain in the lake for a considerable period during the summer. *See also* Argentina, England, Iceland, Ireland, Norway, Scotland, Sweden, Wales

—J.G.

SEATROUT (2) As distinguished from "sea trout" and when used as one word it is the common name for three inshore saltwater gamefish—the spotted seatrout (*which see*), the sand seatrout (*which see*), and the silver seatrout (*which see*). These fish are not trout (family Salmonidae) but members of the drums (family Sciaenidae) and closely related to the weakfish and croaker.

SEA URCHIN A member of the echinoderms or marine animals having limy plates which may or may not be connected, or may be continuous such as the starfish and sea cucumber. The sea urchin has a continuous shell and looks like a pin cushion 1½–10 inches in diameter. The spines of the sea urchin can cause a painful injury to wading fishermen (they are common on bonefish flats), and some tropical species can extrude a poison.

FOOD VALUE

This spiny delicacy is virtually unknown to the average American. Although the short-spined edible varieties can be picked up by hand if held gently, it is advisable to wear gardening gloves when collecting urchins. The demand for the cream-to-orange-colored urchin roes always exceeds the supply. In the French Mediterranean, urchins are called *oursins*, while along the Pacific coast of South America, more particularly Chile, they are known as *herizos*; many natives of the West Indies eat them under the name of "sea eggs." In fact, they were so abundantly sold in the streets of Barbados that laws have been enacted to prevent their extinction.

There are some 500 species of these echinoderms in world distribution and all contain edible gonads when mature (both male and female are utilized). In some areas they can be collected in huge quantities in tide pools, along shallow rocky shores, on reefs, and in creeks. Gathering roe-bearing urchins is highly seasonal and dependent on water temperatures. In Florida, for example, the large Black Urchin (the one with white spines and a black "shell" or test) may commence bearing roe as early as February or as late as July. It requires local knowledge and considerable patience to savour this delicacy. Generally speaking, urchins are ripe on the east and west coasts of North America from late summer to spring (August to April). Due to their perishability, urchins are largely a cold weather item at Fulton Market, New York, and reach their peak abundance around Christmas. The primary source is the state of Maine.

The most widely distributed species is the Green Urchin, which occurs in both the Atlantic and Pacific oceans. There is also a Brown Urchin and a Purple Urchin found along the east coast of the United States, but these common names are misleading as the colors are quite variable. The Purple Urchin, which is found from Alaska to northern Mexico, is marketed in California, particularly at Fisherman's Wharf in San Francisco, where the local Italian population quickly absorbs the daily landings. The supply is limited, however, and orders are placed in advance.

Eating an urchin is simple. You merely cut around the bottom or "mouth" side of the shell with a scissors, or break a circular section loose with a knife and shake out the viscera. Firmly attached to the top side of the shell you will find the five-branched roe, which can be scooped out with a spoon. Depending on the species and maturity, it may require 6–12 urchins to gather enough roe for one portion. The female ovaries are naturally more egg-like, whereas the male gonad has a finer texture. Heaped on crusty French bread and squirted with lemon, the only other accompaniment might be a cold glass of white wine.

Japan is an important consumer of sea urchin roes both as a fresh product and in the making of *Uni-Shiokara*, a fermented urchin paste. As a result, a profitable fishery has developed in British Columbia, Canada. The urchins are collected in waters 20–40 feet deep by specialist scuba divers. They rake the spiny animals into special cages that hold up to 5,000 urchins. Then the live urchins are delivered to a processing plant at Tofine, where they are sliced open and the roe is carefully separated, packed in boxes, and trucked to Vancouver. The product is then airfreighted to Tokyo, arriving in less than forty hours after being taken from the live urchin in Canada. Also known as *Riccio di mare* (Italy), *Morski jez* (Yugoslavia), *Achinos* (Greece), *Sopindsvin* (Denmark), *Sjoborrar* (Sweden), *Krakeboller* (Norway), *Igulker* (Iceland), *Seeigel* (Germany), *Oirico-do-mar* (Portugal), *Erizos de mar* (Spain), *Uni* (Japan).

—A.J.McC.

SEAWEEDS A collective term given to a number of marine plants, it usually refers to marine algae. Most seaweeds fall into three major groups: green algae, brown algae, and red algae. These are generally large, but most of the planktonic algae—such as the diatoms, flagellates, dinoflagellates, and blue-green algae—are microscopic. When occurring in large concentrations, however, they appear as scum or slicks resembling green patches.

The larger seaweeds are usually attached, while the smaller forms are drifting. They are attached by holdfasts, which are equivalent to the roots of higher (vascular) plants. These structures fasten the plant to the substrate and prevent it from being swept away by current, surf, or tidal action. Some seaweeds grow on flat rocks, in crevices, on tree roots, or among boulders; and nearly all require some type of place for attachment.

Among the green algae, the most conspicuous of the plants of the eastern United States is sea lettuce, *Ulva lactuca*. This delicate, flat, green leaf is common along the northeast coast, and although it is initially attached, most sea lettuce is seen drifted in along the beaches. Its bright green coloration is aptly mimicked by the young of the tautog (*which see*).

Red algae include a number of species having commercial importance. Because of a number of pigments in the cells, the plants may not always appear red, and may be brown, purple, green, or blackish. Generally, red algae have slender tubular branches which often are slimy to the touch. One of the commonest, *Gelidium*, is used for making agar, an important medium for bacterial culture; and others are used also in the manufacture of drugs, cosmetics, and other products. Tropical red algae have limestone branches, and the bodies of dead plants sometimes comprise the better part of tropical reefs.

Brown algae are widespread in tropical seas, but rockweed (*Fucus* spp.) is one of the dominant weeds in the northeastern United States and the European coast. Its bifurcate leaves have a small gas-filled bladder which enables the fronds to float at the surface. The Pacific coast of the United States has several species of large brown algae, such as kelp, which are used in the manufacture of algin, which is important in the manufacture of ice cream, drugs, paints, and cosmetics. In tropical waters several species of sargassumweed or gulfweed (*Sargassum* spp.) float at sea in large clumps, harboring myriads of tiny fishes and invertebrates. Dolphins and other fishes are attracted to these weeds, often ingesting mouthfuls of weed along with its inhabitants. In shallow areas it is attached, but after breaking off from its "roots," it drifts in the tropical currents. In such still vortices, where currents are weak, such as the Sargasso Sea, huge patches of sargassumweed accumulate. During sailing days, legends of ships becoming slowed and even sucked under by the sargassumweed and its inhabitants were legion, and were undoubtedly spurred by the lack of favorable sailing winds in such quiet areas.

The term "seaweed" is often applied to the few yet important flowering plants. Eelgrass (*Zostera marina*), a broad-leafed, rooted plant, was one of the common marine plants of cooler coastal waters of the United States prior to a fungal infection which decimated its ranks. This species was well-known to anglers, for many species of marine fishes fed on the fishes which inhabited it in search of food. The young of many marine fishes inhabited these beds, as did numerous invertebrates that were fed on by fishes. Ducks, geese, and other wild fowl formerly fed heavily on eel grass, and with the gradual but slow reappearance of eel grass, waterbirds are now slowly returning to eel grass areas to feed.

Similar in shape and color is turtle grass (*Thalassia testudinum*), the counterpart of eel grass in the southeastern part of the United States. It is found over the flats of quiet, shallow tropical areas to depths of 5 or 6 fathoms or more, and is inhabited by myriads of the young of many food, game, and forage fishes, as well as by numerous invertebrates. It is eaten by grazing invertebrates and is extremely important in the economy of the shallow parts of tropical seas.

Also present in the waters of the southeastern United States are the manatee grass and the diplanthera, which are slender, filamentous plants that are often found with turtle grass. They form an important substrate in shallow, quiet waters for small fishes and their food.

One of the pressing problems of conservation is the destruction of the seaweed habitat, also called grass beds, through uncontrolled and unplanned dredging, filling, and bulkheading for housing developments, ship channels, and through pollution and other by-products of civilization. Man is usually contemptuous of such piles of seaweed, but they form an important habitat for invertebrates and small fishes on which the adults of many sport and commercial fishes, as well as numerous waterfowl, feed, and as a nursery ground for the young stages of sport and commercial species. The blades of these plants offer a substrate on which great quantities of tiny plants and animals find a home and are in turn eaten by other organisms. Seaweeds are also very important in the ecology of coastal waters, because the nutrients they produce when they die are returned to the sea and thus become available for the use of plankton and bottom living microscopic plants.

In addition to its direct importance to fish and wildlife resources, seaweeds are important to man commercially. As already mentioned, several seaweeds are used for the manufacture of agar and algin. Some seaweeds are used as fertilizer because they yield a ready and quick supply of the basic chemicals required by plants, especially the all-important trace elements and organic matter. Seaweeds are also used as a dietary supplement for cattle and poultry.

Although seaweeds have, in addition, excellent nutritional value for humans, popular acceptance has only occurred in the Orient and parts of Europe. The Japanese, Koreans, and Chinese eat various types of seaweeds as a side dish, and the Japanese people have successfully marketed seaweed cakes, cookies, candy and bread. *See also* Algae, Marine Ecology, Red Tide

SECCHI DISK A circular metal plate, 20 cm in diameter, the upper surface of which is divided into four equal quadrants and so painted that two quadrants directly opposite each other are black and the intervening ones white. The Secchi disk is used to measure the turbidity of water.

SEI WHALE *See* Whales

SENNET *See* Northern Sennet

SEÑORITA *Oxyjulis californica* A small member of the wrasse family Labridae, this common species is one of the few representatives of the family taken off the California coast. It is a slender, elongate fish with a long, low, dorsal and anal fin and a convex tail. The snout is somewhat pointed, and the mouth has small, sharp teeth which project forward. It is brown above and cream-colored below, the center of the scales with orange-brown markings. Along the sides of the head are brown and blue streaks, and a large black spot occurs at the caudal-fin

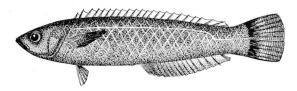

Señorita

base. A closely related species, the rock wrasse, is similar to the señorita but lacks the black spot on the caudal base. The señorita differs from the California sheephead (*which see*) in its more slender body and the smaller number of dorsal spines (9–10). The California sheephead has 11–12 and is deep-bodied.

ANGLING VALUE

It reaches a length of about 10 inches, and is found from central California to Baja California. Common around kelp beds and in inshore waters, it has no sport or commercial value. It is seldom taken by anglers since, like other small wrasses, it is a superb bait stealer.

—D.dS.

SERRATE Rough or sawlike

SET The direction *toward* which a current is flowing. When the wind blows *from* the south it is called a *south* wind. When the flow of the current is *from* the south it is referred to as a *north* set. To *set a course* is to designate to the man at the wheel the course to be steered.

SEVENGILL SHARK *Heptranchias perlo* Somewhat resembling the sixgill shark (*which see*), it has seven pair of long gill openings. The body is thin and elongated, the head narrow, and the snout pointed. The large, oval eye is similar to that of the sixgill shark. Its teeth are very similar to those of the sixgill in that the upper and lower ones are unlike, the upper ones being relatively simple, while the lower ones are flattened and have 6–10 cusps. The single dorsal fin is placed relatively far back, and is slightly larger than the anal fin. The pelvic fins are large, with their bases well in advance of the dorsal fin. The color is gray with brownish shades, becoming paler below. The caudal and pectoral fins have white edges, and the pelvic and anal fins are pale. There are two white spots on the dorsal, and the dorsal and caudal fins each have a black tip. It is a rather small shark, growing only to about 7 feet.

LIFE HISTORY

It occurs on both sides of the Atlantic and in the Mediterranean, being most common in the latter area, and is known from South Africa, Japan, and the North Pacific. A related, if not identical, species occurs in Australia. It resembles the sixgill shark in habits, generally being found in deepwater, but it may enter shallow lagoons in West Africa. Although nowhere numerous, it occasionally becomes sufficiently abundant in Spanish waters, where it is a predator on commercially important hake.

The breeding habits of this shark are unknown, except that the young are hatched in the mother where development is completed. The embryos resemble the adult and are about 10 inches at birth. Males mature at 2–2½ feet, while females mature at about 3 feet or less.—D.dS.

SHAD Family Clupeidae A group of fishes in the herrings of which the American shad (*which see*) is the most sought gamefish. *See also* Hickory Shad

SHARKS The order is composed of about 250 species, representing a wide diversification of habits. Their size varies from less than 2 feet (cat shark) to at least 60 feet (whale shark).

The sharks and their close relatives, the chimaeras (*see* Ratfish), comprise a class (Chondrichthyes) of the phylum Vertebrata, which also includes birds, mammals, reptiles, and amphibians. The Chondrichthyes are fishlike vertebrates having well-developed lower jaws, bony teeth, and paired fins with pelvic and pectoral girdles, in contrast to the circular mouth and the lack of jaws and paired fins characteristic of the lampreys. Hence, sharks are considered to be true fishes.

Within the Chondrichthyes are the Elasmobranchii, containing the sharks, skates, and rays which differ from the chimaeras in the presence of 5–7 pairs of gills and an equal number of gill clefts, each of which opens separately to the outside. Sharks differ from skates and rays in having the gill openings placed on the side, and the edges of the pectoral fins are free from the sides of the head.

The sharks, which represent a very old group of fishes, lack true bone cells, and the skeleton support is received from cartilage. The skin is generally rough and is composed of tiny, specialized scales (placoid scales), which are similar in origin to the teeth. The teeth are variable in shape and number, depending on the species and its feeding habits. Throughout the life of the shark, a con-

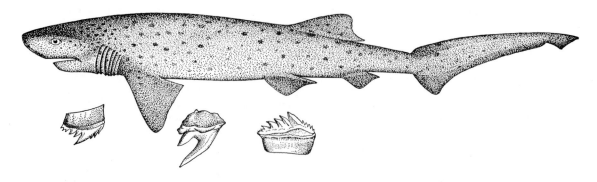

Sevengill Shark (teeth upper jaw *left*, middle and lower jaw *right*)

tinual replacement of teeth supplies the owner with fresh, sharp ones.

Fertilization, which occurs internally, is accomplished through claspers which introduce the sperm into the female. Some sharks lay eggs (oviparity), the egg case usually bearing filamentous tendrils which attach to grass, algae, or debris. In most sharks, eggs are produced which hatch within the mother and the young are subsequently born alive (ovoviviparity), while in other species, the young are born alive following contact with the yolk-sac placenta (viviparity).

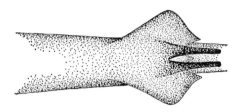

Reproductive Organ (Claspers) of the Shark

FEEDING HABITS

Sharks generally feed through detection of low-frequency sound and by their well-developed sense of smell, but the offshore, pelagic sharks also use sight to capture their prey. Some are aggressive predators, while others are sluggish, harmless species. Some feed actively on anything that moves; yet other sharks feed on floating microscopic plants and animals. Most predator species eat fishes, crustaceans, turtles, seals, and squids, as well as any kind of rubbish and garbage. Some sharks are cannibalistic or will eat other species of sharks. Large sharks should always be considered potentially dangerous, as there are many documented records of their danger to man. In general, sharks do not attack man, but certain species, such as the lemon shark, bull shark, tiger shark, white shark, and the hammerhead shark, should be especially viewed with caution. But sharks are unpredictable, and any shark over 3–4 feet long should be treated with respect. Certain areas, such as Australia, South Africa, California, and the west coast of Florida seem to be more prone to shark attacks, although the reasons are not clear.

FOOD VALUE

Although the flesh of some sharks is known to have a strong purgative effect on man (the cow sharks) and in some instances may be toxic, as in the case of the Greenland shark (which is perfectly edible when dried or allowed to decay in making the Eskimo *tipnuk*), other species are an excellent food. In years past, shark flesh has been sold in the United States, notably on the West Coast where bonito shark, thresher, leopard shark, smooth dogfish, spiny dogfish, and soupfin shark found traditional markets. From 1937 to 1941, when an intensive commercial fishery was conducted for high-potency Vitamin A shark livers the flesh was purveyed under the name "grayfish" or "whitefish." The major source of vitamin oils was from the soupfin shark—an ancient and esteemed item of Oriental cuisine. The Chinese dehydrate both the dorsal and pectoral fins to make a delicate soup stock. As much as 9,000,000

pounds of shark was landed in one year in California alone, and after being processed for the liver the edible parts were sold. This was the peak period of shark consumption in the United States.

On the East Coast both mako and blue shark are highly prized, the mako being an important source of "swordfish" steaks. Swordfish are comparatively rare within their range and command top prices. Makos are similar in flavor and texture and being readily available are sometimes substituted for swordfish. The blue shark differs from the mako in that it is snow-white in color and is somewhat dry. Although sharks are eaten the world over, especially in Mexico and Japan, they are not popular in America for esthetic reasons. —A.J.McC. —D.dS.

SHARK FISHING

Saltwater anglers are inclined to be pedantic when discussing subjects like the characteristics of sharks as fit quarry for gamefishing. To put it mildly, there's a diversity of opinion. It depends on the species sought and the method of capture.

Marlin and swordfish addicts, trolling the bluewater with substantial tackle and using such accessories as fighting chairs and kidney harnesses, generally downgrade shark fishing—and they're right. Sharks are overgunned on heavy gear. On the other hand, mako fishermen off Montauk, New York, who chum deliberately for their sharks, taking the fish on 20–30-pound-test outfits, with rod butts jammed in a belt cup gimbal and the anglers on their feet in an open-boat cockpit, are lyric about the mako's fighting ability. Individual experience, as well as the kind of shark sought, has much to do with the quality of the sport. It is a highly specialized game.

When you troll for tuna, dolphin, yellowtail, and sailfish, the species is immediately identifiable by name. A tuna is a sporting fish whether it's a bluefin or a yellowfin. Atlantic and Pacific sailfish put up a similar, thrilling battle. But a shark is not just a shark. There is as much difference between a blacktip and a dusky as you'll experience playing a rainbow trout versus a sunfish. There are about 250 species of shark—some of them fighters on rod-and-reel, others simply dead weight.

The International Game Fish Association lists records on mako, maneater (white), porbeagle, thresher, tiger and blue sharks. Anglers who have hooked the spinner or large blacktip, *Carcharhinus maculipinnis;* the small blacktip, *Carcharhinus limbatus;* the mako, *Isurus oxyrinchus;* or the bonito shark, *Isurus glaucus,* on reasonably light tackle will rave about their acrobatics on the end of a line. These species will shoot into the air nearly vertically, pancaking with a tremendous splash as they land. The mako is liable to leap four or five times in rapid succession, barely touching the water at the conclusion of one somersault before the fish is off on the next. The spinner revolves on its axis as it jumps, whirling like a ballerina, tangling terminal gear and leaders with devastating effect.

Chumming for Sharks Chumming, quite simply, consists of distributing a batch of fish bait around your angling area so the game is attracted. You may dice up chunks of squid and scatter them near a rowboat to attract scup, trail live grass shrimp in a tideway to entice weakfish, or ladle a watery mixture of ground menhaden over the side of a cruiser for sharks. Chumming produces

The voraciousness of sharks is legendary. Few fish are as aggressive or as potentially dangerous to man

fish because it appeals to their most basic instinct—feeding.

Off Montauk, at the eastern tip of New York's Long Island, menhaden or bunker chum for sharks is favored. Ground-up menhaden are available in five-gallon tins of frozen mash. By mixing small quantities of this brew with seawater in an ash can, one can formulate an odorous pulp that can be ladled over the side of a boat. Since the oil content of the trash fish used is extremely high, the mixture causes a slick on the sea's surface, easily visible for miles. Gulls swoop over the slick, calling raucously, forever diving for tidbits large enough for them to swallow. Quite frequently, large schools of mackerel gather to feed on the bunker, unwittingly adding to the attractiveness of the slick for sharks.

Chumming is a dirty, dull business when you're drifting across the open Atlantic, and the action is slow. It is a sickening method when there is any "wind sea," for your cruiser wallows in the swell, the stench of the rotting bunker permeating everything on the boat. But when cut-water fins are spotted swimming toward the fishing craft, when sharks are grouped within hand's reach of the rail, cruising lazily up and down the hull as they search for the source of the chum, then it becomes thrilling beyond belief.

Since the ocean is vast and the movements of sharks little understood, drifting and chumming is probably the best way to cover a maximum distance with a minimum expenditure of bait. According to the theory, the sharks

will cross your slick sooner or later, coming to you. It is best to rig some sort of flag buoy on a stick with a short length of twine and a heavy lead sinker, heaving this contraption overboard to mark your slick once you strike a shark. If the fight is extended and you never recover the buoy, little is lost. If your shark turns out to be one of the less desirable or smaller species and you want to resume the chumming operation, the buoy marks the spot accurately.

Any trash fish, meal, meat, quantity of blood, refuse, or edible oil may be used as a shark chum. Use whatever is readily available in your area before going to the unnecessary expense of importing bunker. Perhaps there is a local commercial dock where you can arrange for bushel baskets of the trash species or entrails left from trawling operations. Anyone running pound or gillnets has leftovers that can be used. A slaughterhouse may provide exactly what the sharks want.

Locating Sharks Where do you start chumming? If there are schools of small tuna, bonito, or mackerel in your area, look for sharks in the vicinity of these food fish. Makos will follow school bluefins, picking off the weaker or wounded members. So, if you know where there are large quantities of potential shark feed, cut your engines there and start chumming. If you're cruising out over a completely dead ocean, try utilizing your hydrographic charts and pick a bottom where ling, cod, pollock, snappers, grouper—any concentration of local bottom feeders—may occur. The sharks often linger where food is easy to find. At all events, get as much information as possible from chartermen and commercials who spend time afloat in the area. Most of them have little use for sharks and will gladly give you any information they possess.

If you see sharks finning offshore, it pays to attempt a strip bait or whole fish trolled slowly either directly behind the transom or off an outrigger. When they won't take such an offering, deep drifting sometimes turns the trick. New Zealand Islanders, who take tremendous thresher sharks off areas like the Bay of Plenty and Mayor Island, use a baitfish called the *kahawai*, hooked completely through the lips so that the barb is twisted backwards and imbedded in the bait's back. New Englanders, angling for sharks along the Northeastern seacoast, usually use a whole menhaden, bluefish, squid, or mackerel.

Ladle just enough chum overboard to cause an unbroken slick to extend from your boat. Don't overchum since your object is to attract hungry fish to the baited hook, not permit them to lay back and feed as the current brings food toward them.

Rigging the Bait Obviously, your whole baitfish attached to a hook and leader will sink far below the chum unless it is artificially buoyed. Cut a rectangular piece of cork about a foot long, placing a shallow slice in it lengthwise with your knife blade. Press the line into this cut about five feet above the swiveled end of the leader. You'll be able to see your cork floating on the surface, marking the bait. When a shark hits and swims away, the buoyancy of the cork will pop it free of the line without undue pressure on the fish.

Using light tackle and hooks ranging from Nos. 9/0 to 12/0 on approximately 15 feet of leader, you want to "still-fish" for sharks in a chum slick exactly the way you'd dunk a live shiner for a largemouth bass in a river or moss-covered lake. Do not hit the fish as soon as you feel the strike. Let it go with the bait as long as the shark doesn't jump or make a prolonged, rapid run. In the latter event, the fish has sensed something wrong, and you'll have to take your chances, striking immediately.

The normal shark may play with the bait, swimming in fairly tight circles, remaining near the boat. Many of· the big fish will pick it up and continue up the chum streak, never noticing the line and leader trailing behind them. If you're fishing two rods, sharks will often pick up both baits.

Fishing Technique The object of the delay period is to permit your mako—or other shark species—to swallow the baitfish. Once the hook is imbedded deep in a shark's stomach after a delayed strike, even slack line is unlikely to cause a break-off. Your only problem is that a swipe of the tail or a chance contact between the abrasive shark's skin and your line will snap leader or line.

Since chumming is often a slow, tedious operation until the action begins, Montauk skippers stand their shark rigs in a rod holder, leaving the reels on free spool with the drag-click on. You can hear a fish striking if you don't see the cork go under—and there's plenty of time to release the click, permitting the shark to swim freely for anywhere from 30 seconds to 2–3 minutes before bringing the line taut and striking.

You don't have to strike more than once, or twice, at most. When the barb bites into a shark's stomach wall, the fish is either hooked or will shortly break free. Once the rod bows, the technique is to keep the line as tight as possible, fighting the fish hard and consistently. Remember, any time you lay back on the rod, not pumping and striving to gain line, the shark is resting. On a 100–200-pound mako solidly hooked with a 15-thread outfit by an experienced angler, figure a 30–45-minute fight and 2–4 spectacular leaps. Be extremely careful when the swivel shows on top of the water and the leader comes within reach, since makos have a nasty habit of becoming sufficiently irritated to swim alongside a boat, attempting to take a bite out of the planking while they're still green. You don't want to stick a flying gaff into a live and active mako for fear of the shark leaping into the boat. You can tell when a mako is nearly finished for the shark will be rolling, the cobalt blue-black of its back and the white underside showing alternately on top of the sea.

How to Boat Sharks If the fish has enough strength to stay deep, let it run again rather than attempting a maneuver with the gaff that could end in disaster. Use a flying gaff, the rope snubbed to a solid bit on your boat. Don't attempt to hold the rope by hand against the shark's first furious flurry. Do wear a pair of canvas gloves to protect your hands from rope burns. Once you have a shark alongside, the flying-gaff barb sunk deeply into its flesh, use a straight gaff to raise the tail section and drop a loop of heavy rope over the caudal fin. Drawing this tight, drag the shark backwards aft of the boat, letting the water pour through its gill slits. That process calms sharks quicker than blasting the fish with a rifle, pounding them over the head with a persuader, slitting their stomach walls, or any of the other methods often attempted.

Nearly all species of sharks will strike flies and plugs in shallow water. The trick is to cast directly in front of the shark, virtually on its nose—as they are somewhat nearsighted. This blacktip fell to a well-placed streamer

Sharks die slowly. They can be hung by the tail from a block and tackle for hours; then suddenly they tense, striking out at anything within range of their deadly teeth. Obviously, they are not to be trusted in the cockpit of a boat. If you string them up on a gin pole, supplement the tail loop by lines strung fore and aft, attached tightly just behind the shark's ventral fins. If they can't get started in any direction, they certainly can't break free or flip backwards and strike at someone aboard.

For neophytes about to try chumming or deep drifting for sharks on an initial voyage, it's wise to have someone aboard with prior experience. Remember that you're dealing with one of the most primitive of fish, a biological engine behind teeth that is insensitive to pain and capable of an enormous amount of destruction. Handled correctly, there's no more danger connected with the fishery than dunking your toe in your bathtub. Handled carelessly, sharks can cause a catastrophe quite easily. *See also* Atlantic Sharpnose Shark, Bigeye Thresher, Blacknose Shark, Blacktip Shark, Blue Shark, Bonito Shark, Bonnethead, Brown Smoothhound, Bull Shark, Dusky Shark, Gray Smoothhound, Great Hammerhead, Leopard Shark, Lemon Shark, Mako, Nurse Shark, Saltwater Fly-Fishing, Sandbar Shark, Sand Shark, Scalloped Hammerhead, Sevengill Shark, Sickle Shark, Sixgill Shark, Smooth Dogfish, Smooth Hammerhead, Soupfin Shark, Spinner Shark, Spiny Dogfish, Springer's Reef Shark, Thresher Shark, Tope, Whale Shark, White Shark, Whitetip Shark   —C.R.M.

SHARPNOSE SHARK *See* Atlantic Sharpnose Shark

SHEEFISH The common name for the inconnu (*which see*) thought to originate from the Eskimo "chi." The Eskimo *i* is pronounced with a long *e* hence the similarity. *See also* Alaska.

SHEEPSHEAD *Archosargus probatocephalus* There are three named species in the genus *Archosargus* which apparently, at best, are only of subspecific rank within the species *probatocephalus*. One of these subspecies, *probatocephalus*, occurs from Nova Scotia south to the northeastern Gulf of Mexico. The second subspecies, *oviceps*, ranges from the northeastern Gulf of Mexico to the Yucatán Peninsula in Mexico. The third subspecies, *aries*, is known from British Honduras to Brazil. There are no records of *A. probatocephalus* from any of the West Indian islands or from Bermuda, and apparently it is restricted to mainland coasts where it is often quite common.

In life the ground color is silvery, darker above than below, and there are usually 5–6 distinct, dark vertical bars on the side which give this species the sometimes used common name of "convict fish." There is some variation in this color pattern, and the bars *may* be higher in number, lower, or different on different sides of the fish, or odd in shape so that they cannot really be counted at all.

LIFE HISTORY

Like the pinfish, the sheepshead has strong incisor teeth, unnotched, which are used by the adults to pick mollusks and crabs and to scrape barnacles off pilings and rocks. Underwater divers have reported that the sheepshead is quite noisy when heard while it was so feeding. Young sheepsheads live on grassy flats and feed on softer animal and plant foods.

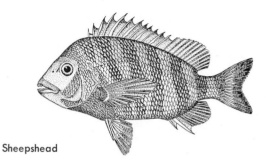

Sheepshead

Although data are scarce, spawning apparently takes place offshore in the spring.

ANGLING VALUE

This is a popular game- and food fish in some areas, particularly in Florida, and some sport fishermen specialize in them because they often are such a challenge to catch. They may reach a size of 2 feet commonly, although individuals over 3 feet in length have been reported.

The sheepshead is a very suspicious quarry, and when located the experienced angler frequently chums the area with crushed fiddler crabs to stir them into feeding. Fiddler crabs, hermit crabs, shrimp, and sandbugs are popular baits. Sheepshead rarely strike an artificial lure, although they may display interest in small flies and jigs. It is an excellent table fish.   —D.K.C.

SHEEPSHEAD MINNOW *Cyprinodon variegatus* A small member of the killifish family Cyprinodontidae, this common species is characterized by its short, stubby body, with a rather high-arched back and a high, short dorsal fin. The small mouth is studded with a row of well-developed incisor teeth. The tail is broad and square-edged. Unlike other killifish, its dorsal fin is well forward of the anal fin. The head and body are covered with large scales. The color of this species is particularly captivating during the mating season, being steely-blue with green hues on the upper part of the male and orange-red to salmon color on the belly. At other times, the sexes are brassy-olive above, grading to buff or white below. The young and the female have black bands, but those of the male become pale.

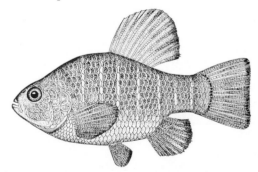

Sheepshead Minnow

It grows to about 3 inches. A coastal, inland form, it is found from Cape Cod to Mexico in shallow, brackish, and hypersaline bays and marshes. It is extremely abundant in such areas, occurring over a wide range of temperature and salinity.

LIFE HISTORY

Spawning occurs from April to September, in shallow water. The spawning act is accompanied by extensive prespawning behavior, including vigorous fighting among the males. The eggs stick to one another and sink to the bottom. It occurs in the company of the mummichog and striped killifish (*which see*). An aggressive species, it attacks larger fishes with its sharp teeth. It feeds on both plant and animal matter. Because of its abundance, it is important as a forage fish for the larger predatory fishes.

ANGLING VALUE

It is used for bait by anglers because of its hardiness.
—D.dS.

SHEER The longitudinal upward curvature of the lines of a boat.

SHELLCRACKER A common name for the redear sunfish (*which see*). The redear feeds on various mollusks, the shells of which are crushed by a pair of rough surfaced bones or "shellcrackers" located in the back of the mouth.

SHELLFISH (1) In broad generic use any aquatic invertebrate animal having a shell, such as a mollusk or crustacean.

(2) *Lactophrys bicaudalis* Better known as the spotted trunkfish, this member of the trunkfish family is found throughout the West Indies north to Florida. The name refers to the rigid, bony, scaled body, which has a triangular cross section; swimming is accomplished by rapid sculling motions of the dorsal and anal fins. Although a rather odd-looking reef-dweller, the shellfish is highly esteemed as food, particularly by people in the Caribbean Islands. The flesh is firm, milk-white, and very similar to spiny lobster in texture and flavor. *See also* Cowfish, Trunkfish

SHINER Any of a number of minnow species (Cyprinidae) which serve as forage for freshwater gamefish. Some shiners are popular as live baits and a few of the larger ones are utilized by man as food. *See also* Bigmouth Shiner, Blackchin Shiner, Blacknose Shiner, Bridle Shiner, Common Shiner, Emerald Shiner, Golden Shiner, Live Bait, Propagation of Baitfish as a Business *under* Fish Culture, Red Shiner, Redside Shiner, Rosyface Shiner, Spottail Shiner, Steelcolor Shiner.

SHINER PERCH *Cymatogaster aggregata* An abundant surfperch (*which see*) found in shallow and deepwater (to 240 feet) from northern Baja California to northwestern Alaska. It is silvery; greenish upper body; about 8 longitudinal, partially interrupted horizontal lines on body; 3 vertical yellow bars on body; males nearly black in winter and spring. Length to 8 inches. The posterior groove of lower lip is not interrupted by a frenum; scales large, caudal peduncle short and slender, 18–23 rays in dorsal fin.

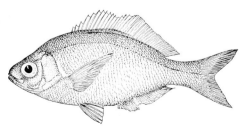

Shiner Perch

Life history, food, and angling similar to all surfperch in general.

COMMERCIAL VALUE

Most important in the British Columbia part of its range.
—J.R.

SHIPWORM The common name for a marine wood-borer or teredo (*which see*)

SHOEMAKER *See Rainbow Runner*

SHOOTING HEAD *See* Rainbow Trout

SHOOTING LINE The level portion of a weight-forward fly line which follows the back taper. The term is not applicable to level or double-taper lines which have a dissimilar profile. *See also* Fly Line

SHOOTING THE LINE A fly-casting term that means releasing the slack, previously stripped from the reel, at the point when the forward cast begins to pull. Although the forward velocity of the cast has ceased, the momentum of the outgoing length is sufficient to pull extra yardage through the guides. This is done to lengthen the cast. *See also* Fly-Casting

SHORT BIGEYE *Pseudopriacanthus altus* This single representative of this genus in the western Atlantic ranges from just north of Cape Cod south to the islands and mainland of the Caribbean and West Indies, including the Gulf of Mexico and Bermuda.

The short bigeye can be distinguished from other western Atlantic priacanthids by its low lateral-line scale count (31–39) and the low number of dorsal (10–12) and anal (9–11) soft fin rays.

In life, the color of the adult is bright red, the vertical fins having black borders.

Short Bigeye

The sometimes used generic name *Pristigenys* apparently should apply only to a fossil form from Europe.

LIFE HISTORY

Spawning apparently takes place offshore, from mid-July to mid-September. The larvae are pelagic, and are widely distributed by currents. The carnivorous adults are secretive and live on the bottom around rocks in depths of about 60–110 fathoms.

ANGLING VALUE

Short bigeyes have no commercial or sport value as a food fish, but they often are taken with hook and line in deep-bottom sport fishing and make a colorful addition to the catch.
—D.K.C.

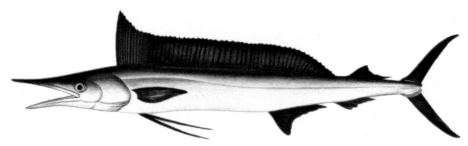

Shortbill Spearfish

SHORTBILL SPEARFISH *Tetrapturus angustirostris* This is a marine fish of the Pacific Ocean, known from Hawaii and, very rarely, from off southern California in the United States and off the western coast of South America. It occurs more frequently in the Central Pacific and in Oriental waters, where it is of fairly common occurrence in the longline fisheries. It is of relatively small size, and is generally found well off shore.

The shortbill spearfish is elongate and slender, the sides of the body flat, with a single, rather prominent lateral line. The pectoral fins are short, the anal fin crescent-shaped, and the dorsal fin is long and relatively high. The anterior part of the dorsal fin forms a sharp peak, behind which the fin maintains a fairly even height about equal to the greatest depth of the body. The vent is located anterior to the anal fin by a distance nearly equal to the length of the anal-fin base. The shortbill spearfish is metallic-blue or greenish above, fading rather abruptly to silvery or white on the lower sides and belly. The fins are all dark, and there are no spots or bars on the body. The snout, at least in adults, is scarcely longer than the lower jaw.

The shortbill spearfish reaches a maximum weight of over 100 pounds. The largest recorded in the literature is one of 114 pounds, but the average weight of those taken by commercial longlines seems to be somewhat under 40 pounds.

HABITS

Almost nothing is known of the habits of the shortbill spearfish. It is primarily piscivorous, feeding on any smaller fish of suitable size. It is also known to feed on squid.

Although rare in North American waters, it is known to occur in concentrations off Taiwan, where it is reported to spawn in the fall of the year. This statement appears to be based on the record of one fish taken on November 22, 1936, by the Japanese fishing vessel, "Shonan Maru," at 21° 46′ 30″ N., 124° 22′ 30″ E., which, when brought on board, "released eggs all over the deck." It is a pelagic species and apparently does not often enter coastal waters or enclosed seas. Although rare, it is widespread in the Pacific, and has been recorded from California, Hawaii, the Line Islands, Japan, Taiwan, and the Celebes-Philippine area. It probably occurs in the Indian Ocean also.

Shortbill spearfish are taken almost exclusively by long-line. Some few may be harpooned or taken by angling, but these most certainly appear incidentally to other operations. —J.E.M.

SHORTFIN CORVINA *Cynoscion parvipinnis* Rarely is the species found north of Mexico where it is known as the blue corvina. Its normal range is from central Baja California into the Gulf of California and as far south as Mazatlán. It was introduced into the Salton Sea, but evidence of reproduction is lacking.

The shortfin corvina is distinguished by a pair of enlarged caninelike teeth in upper jaw; no scales in soft portion of anal and dorsal fins; posterior margin of caudal fin S-shaped or slightly concave; 10–11 anal rays. Pale blue on back, becoming silvery on sides and white on belly; anal and pelvic fins yellowish. Reaches a length of 18 inches or more.

ANGLING VALUE

As with other corvina (*which see*) the flesh is of high quality. It is prized by anglers and commercial fishermen alike. —J.R.

SHORTHEAD REDHORSE *Moxostoma breviceps* A red- or pink-tailed sucker with dark spots at the base of each scale, the shorthead resembles the common redhorse except that its head is smaller and more pointed. Its dorsal fin is falcate; that is, its anterior rays do not extend to the end of the last rays when depressed. The range of the shorthead redhorse is the Ohio River drainage in Ohio, Pennsylvania, and Kentucky.

This sucker is found in small and large streams and also in lakes. It avoids clearwater and appears to prefer warmer temperatures. The food of this redhorse consists mostly of animal matter including mollusks and insect larvae.

ECONOMIC VALUE

The shorthead redhorse apparently enjoys some popularity with anglers as it is often seen on anglers' strings along with the common redhorse. Where it is abundant it is taken commercially in poundnets. —R.A.J.

SHORTHORN SCULPIN *Myoxocephalus scorpius* A sculpin (*which see*) found on the northern Atlantic Coast at least as far south as New England. It reaches a length of 25 inches. It is distinguished by the presence of a small slit or pore behind the last gill arch; the dorsal fin has 9 spines and 15 rays; the anal fin has 14 rays. It lives primarily inshore in the summer, migrating to greater depths in winter. It spawns in the fall and winter. It feeds on crustaceans and small fish. —J.R.

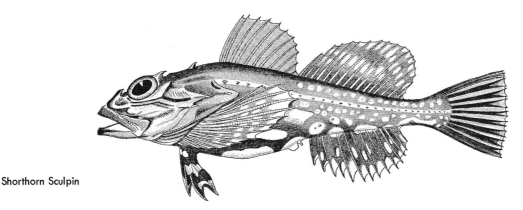

Shorthorn Sculpin

SHORTNOSE BATFISH *See* Longnose Batfish
SHORTNOSE GAR *Lepisosteus platostomus*   A member of
an ancient group of predaceous fishes, the gar can be
recognized by a long, cylindrical body covered with
heavy, diamond-shaped (ganoid) scales behind long,
snoutlike jaws containing many sharp teeth. The dorsal
fin is far back and is nearly opposite the anal fin. The
shortnose gar has a comparatively short beak whose length
is about 5½ times its least width. It has no spots on the
head, but there are small, round black spots on the fins.
It has 60–64 scales in the lateral line. The very young fish
have short jaws and a wide black stripe on the sides.

It is found in the Mississippi River drainage as far
north as South Dakota and Minnesota to the north and
west, in the Ohio River drainage, and southwestward to
eastern Texas. It is more abundant in the southern part
of this range. It prefers slow-flowing streams, lakes, and
backwaters and avoids strong currents. Although it feeds
by sight and thus prefers clearwaters, it is tolerant of
muddy waters, and is found in such waters more frequently than some other species of gar.

LIFE HISTORY

Spawning occurs in the spring in shallow bays and
sloughs. Its dark green eggs are adhesive and attach to
weeds or other objects. The young are solitary, and beginning early in life they lie motionless close to the surface;
its shape and color resembling a floating stick. Both
young and old occasionally break the surface to expel
gases and gulp air into the swim-bladder. This allows it to
live in waters long after they are unfit for many other
species.

Fish compose most of its diet. It is not particular and
takes whatever is most abundant. Since many of the
waters it inhabits contain large populations of coarse and
panfishes which need to be controlled, in many places
they perform a useful function. In others they become
very abundant and are considered a serious problem.

ANGLING VALUE

Gar flesh is not sought by a great many fishermen, and
its roe is toxic. Yet they are a very good sport fish and
should be enjoyed as such. Frayed nylon lures with or
without hooks cast at the surfacing gar are effective. The
hookless lure holds the fish when the teeth are entangled
in the nylon. Dead minnows also are favored baits. Wire
leaders often are used to prevent cutting the line by its
many sharp teeth.   —C.A.P.

SHORTSPINE CHANNEL. ROCKFISH *Sebastolobus alascanus*
This rockfish (*which see*) is considered by fishermen to be
one of the choicest of the family. The short-spine channel
rockfish has a knifelike ridge under the eye; lower rays of
pectoral fin thrust out to form a lobe; 15–18 spines and
9–10 softrays in dorsal fin. Color black on fins, body
bright red.   —J.R.

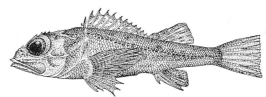

Shortspine Channel Rockfish

SHOVELHEAD CATFISH *See* Flathead Catfish
SHOVELNOSE GUITARFISH *Rhinobatos productus*   This
Pacific ray is very similar in shape to the Atlantic guitarfish (*which see*), and is limited to between central California to the Gulf of California. Like that of its Atlantic

Shortnose Gar

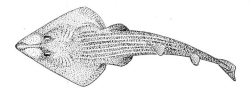

Shovelnose Guitarfish

relative, the snout is sharply pointed and wedge-shaped, tapering into a thick tail bearing two dorsal fins. The area in the front of the snout is translucent. The back is brownish-gray and white below, with a black blotch beneath the snout. The young are born alive after being kept, following hatching from the eggs in the mother, for a period of time within the mother. It grows to about 4 feet, feeding on worms, crabs, and clams. There is no commercial value for it, and it is a nuisance to gillnet fishermen and to anglers. —D.dS.

SHOVELNOSE STURGEON *See* Sturgeon

SHRIMP Order Decapoda There are numerous species of shrimp found in both fresh- and saltwater throughout the world. The freshwater species range from very small to over 12 inches in length (*Macrobrachium* spp.) in the southern United States, the Caribbean, and South America. The latter is common to the Gulf Coast region and may locally be known as "crawfish" as is the true crayfish and spiny lobster. Freshwater species are often confused by anglers with scuds (*which see*). Saltwater species also display a wide range in size with at least one Pacific species attaining a length over 12 inches (*Penaeus monodon*). The large species of shrimp that are utilized for food and fish bait are most abundant along the South Atlantic and Gulf Coast of the United States. The commercial shrimp fishery is concentrated almost entirely in these areas. The six most common species are all members of one family, the Penaeidae, which is characterized by having the first three pairs of walking legs (there are five pairs in all) ending with small pincers or chelae.

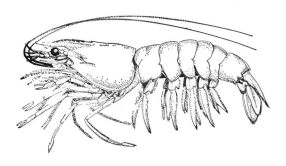

Shrimp

A shrimp can be divided into two principal sections: (1) the head or cephalothorax which bears the rostrum or head spine, eyes, antennae, mouthparts, and the 5 pairs of walking legs; (2) the abdomen or tail which has 7 segments. There are swimming legs beneath the first 5 abdominal segments, and the telson or tail spine is on the last.

The six species may be identified as follows (adopted from a key published by William W. Anderson, 1958):

I. Spines on underside of rostrum (if this area is smooth go to II).
  A. A pair of deep grooves on top of head reaching from behind eyes to almost end of cephalothorax.
    1. A pair of wide grooves on top of next to last tail segment that will permit fingernail to be inserted. No brown spot on side . . . brown shrimp (*Penaeus aztecus*)
    2. A pair of narrow grooves on top of next to last tail segment that will not permit fingernail to be inserted. A brown spot on side . . . pink shrimp (*Penaeus duorarum*)
  B. No such grooves on top of head . . . white shrimp (*Penaeus setiferus*)
II. Underside of rostrum smooth except for small hairs or bristles.
  A. Rostrum long, slender, and arched upward. Last pair of walking legs very long and slender . . . sea bob (*Xiphopeneus kroyeri*)
  B. Rostrum normal and last pair of walking legs normal.
    1. Shell heavy and sculptured. No postorbital spine on side of head . . . rock shrimp (*Sicyonia brevirostris*)
    2. Shell normal. Postorbital spine on side of head . . . royal red shrimp (*Hymenopenaeus robustus*)

The color of the shrimp species is apt to vary widely and so cannot be depended on for identification purposes, but it is sometimes used along with the key characters given above. Brown shrimp are usually a reddish-brown color, with tinges of blue or purple on the tail and on some of the legs. Pink shrimp seem to vary according to geographic locality; along the Atlantic Coast they are usually light brown, in the Tortugas fishery they are pink, and along the northern Gulf Coast they are often lemon-yellow.

White shrimp are generally a grayish-white, and are variously tinged about the tail and legs with green, red, and blue; occasionally a diseased condition will turn this species blue-black. The sea bob is usually red or pinkish-red when alive but will turn black when cooked or frozen. Rock shrimp tend to be brownish on the dorsal surface and pale on the sides; the underside and appendages are variously colored with red or purple. Royal red shrimp are usually deep red all over but sometimes are only a gray-pink.

LIFE HISTORY

In the Gulf of Mexico, white shrimp spawn offshore in about 10–15 fathoms of water, although there are reports of spawning near the passes that lead to the bays. The female, which is larger than the male at maturity, lays about 500,000 eggs. The spawning season begins in March and continues through September, with two distinct peaks, one in May or June and the other in August or September.

During mating, the male attaches a saclike spermatophore to the female so that the eggs may be fertilized as they are laid. The eggs sink to the bottom and then hatch into the first of a series of larval stages; there are at least five naupliar stages, followed by three protozoal stages, two mysis stages, and several postlarval stages. For the first 2–3 weeks, the young are capable of very little movement and are carried mostly by the currents.

The juvenile white shrimp, about ¼ inch long, will migrate along the bottom toward the nursery grounds. They move close to the shore and seem to prefer shallow bays with mud bottoms and relatively low salinity. Here they will grow rapidly, sometimes as much as 1¼ inches per month. As the shrimp grow larger, reaching an average of about 3½ inches, they tend to migrate from the nursery grounds into the deeper bays that are located closer to the ocean. After this, when they reach 4½–6 inches, they become mature and move to the spawning grounds in the open ocean.

The life history of the brown shrimp is similar to that of the white, but the adults appear to spawn in deeper water. These two species are by far the most common in the shallow waters and the bays. The pink shrimp is most abundant in the warmer waters around the Tortugas Islands and the southwestern Gulf of Mexico. Research by the University of Miami Marine Laboratory indicates that the Tortugas fishery is dependent on the brackish water nursery afforded by the Everglades region of southwest Florida, with the intermediate growth stages taking place during the shrimps' migration from the deepwater breeding grounds back to the coast. The young shrimp live in the mangrove creeks, canals, and bays until half grown (3–4 inches long), then return to the Tortugas breeding grounds. Very little is known about the life history of the sea bob or the rock shrimp. The royal red shrimp occurs mainly in deepwater (from 175–300 fathoms) off the edge of the Continental Shelf in the area where it occurs.

ANGLING VALUE

Shrimp are of great indirect value to anglers in being an important food source for many gamefish. They are also readily obtainable bait. Shrimp provide a large commercial fishery in many parts of the world, and in dollar yield may exceed the sum total of all other sea foods in certain countries. The Japanese have been successful in raising edible shrimp through intricate hatchery technique; however, the bulk of all landings are captured with otter-trawls. *See also* Fish Cookery, Shrimp *under* Live Bait

—J.C.B

SIDE LIGHTS The red and green running lights carried on the port and starboard sides, respectively.

SIERRA *Scomberomorus sierra* A fish of the mackerel family that is closely related to the Spanish mackerel relative, the differs from its only close Pacific Coast relative, the Monterey Spanish mackerel, in having several rows of prominent golden spots along the sides of the body and

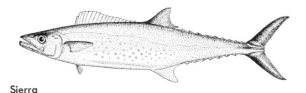

Sierra

fewer gillrakers (14–16) on the first arch. It attains a weight of about 12 pounds.

Sierra are found along the Pacific coast of America from San Diego to Peru. They are one of the most abundant sport fishes along the coasts of Mexico and Central America, occurring in large schools, and are often taken by trolling. Little is known about the food or breeding habits. —B.B.C.
—R.H.G.

SILK SNAPPER *Lutjanus vivanus* This snapper occurs around southern Florida and throughout the tropical American Atlantic. It does not reach a large size, and most of the specimens captured weigh less than 10 pounds.

The silk snapper has 10 dorsal spines, 14 dorsal rays, and 8 anal rays. Pectoral rays normally 17. Gillrakers 11–12 on lower limb of first arch, not counting rudiments. Rows of scales around caudal peduncle 27–29. Cheek scales in 7, rarely 6 rows. Upper jaw reaching to or beyond vertical from anterior margin of orbit. Pectoral fin not reaching to vertical from origin of anal fin. Anal fin angulate, not rounded posteriorly. General coloration rose-red, paper below. Dorsal, pelvic, and anal fins pale rose; dorsal fin edged with yellow. Black spot on sides of body present, faint to obsolete in large individuals. Eye bright yellow.

The color pattern, especially the bright yellow eye and the black-margined caudal fin, distinguishes this snapper from the others.

Silk Snapper

HABITS

A deepwater species, it occurs on the bottom and is most abundant at depths of 60–120 fathoms. Small individuals of the species may occur in shallower water (20–60 fathoms). It is usually taken on live bait.

ANGLING VALUE

The occasional individuals taken on rod-and-reel in shallow water are usually small. The larger specimens occurring in deepwater can be taken with electric reels and wire lines.

FOOD VALUE

Excellent eating, the silk snapper is a commercial fish of importance frequently marketed as "red snapper."
—L.R.

SILKY SHARK *Carcharhinus falciformis* One of the most common of the offshore sharks, the silky is so called because of its very smooth skin. It superficially resembles the dusky and sandbar sharks (*which see*), but differs from them in having a slender second dorsal and anal fin which are more than twice as long as they are high. From the bull shark, blacktip shark, spinner shark, and blacknose shark (*which see*), it differs in having a dermal ridge between the dorsal fins. Its body is elongate and the snout long, with the first dorsal set back about midway between the pectoral and pelvic fins. Adults have pectoral fins which are relatively longer than other species of *Carcharhinus*, and are almost as long as the pectoral fins of the blue shark (*which see*). But pectoral fins of small specimens are relatively much shorter. The inner and outer edges of the pectoral fins are broadly curved, particularly in small specimens. Its color is dark gray to gray-brown, grading to lighter below. The pectoral-fin tips are dusky to black, especially in small individuals, but this coloration in the silky shark disappears with age. It reaches a length of 10 feet.

LIFE HISTORY

Silky sharks are known from the warmer parts of the Atlantic including West Africa and the Caribbean, from Trinidad to Florida, with a few being reported from North Carolina and off Delaware Bay in late summer and autumn. It also occurs in the tropical eastern Pacific Ocean. Although it is occasionally taken in water as shallow as 60 feet, it is essentially an offshore species of the outer reefs and bluewaters. In the Pacific, squid, crabs, and puffers have been found in their stomachs. Silky sharks from the Pacific have been found carrying an average of six young throughout the year, which probably are upwards of 2 feet long at birth. As with some other pelagic sharks, this species tends to run in schools of one sex only at certain times of the year. In Florida, this species has been caught commercially for its hide. —D.dS.

SILVER BREAM *See* Bronze Bream

SILVER HAKE *Merluccius bilinearis* This member of the cod family is distinguished from the cod, pollock, tomcod, and haddock by the presence of only two dorsal fins, the second of which is long and low, somewhat similar in shape to the anal fin. The first is a short and relatively high fin. The body is long and slender, with a large mouth well-armed with sharp teeth. It lacks the chin barbel typical of the cod and haddock and most other relatives of the cod family. The general body shape is slender, with a flat-topped head. Dark gray above with brown and purplish reflections, the sides and belly are silvery with gold and purple hues, with the belly and lower parts silvery as well.

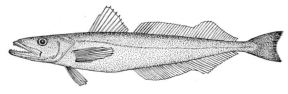

Silver Hake

Although it reaches the maximum length of about 2½ feet and a weight of about 8 pounds, the average length is less than 14 inches.

This Continental Shelf species is found from the Newfoundland banks southward to off South Carolina, being taken in large numbers between Cape Sable and New York. Closely related forms are taken in the southern parts of the United States and in the Gulf of Mexico. It occurs in shallow waters to depths of about 1,800 feet, although, generally speaking, many of the adults are found in deeper waters. They are found in comparatively deeper water than their relatives, but they travel in pursuit of prey into very shallow water. These voracious swift swimmers travel in large schools, and thus they will occasionally strand themselves while in aggressive pursuit of schools of their prey.

LIFE HISTORY

A summer spawner, the silver hake scatters its eggs over the surface, generally in water shallower than 50 fathoms. The young are found successively further inshore, and as they grow, the juveniles are found in the lower parts of the estuaries and in shallow parts along the coastal regions. The adults feed on herring, silversides, menhaden, young mackerel, and on squid and other invertebrates.

ANGLING VALUE

This is a relatively important species, although difficult to handle because of the soft flesh. Most of the catch is frozen and sold in packaged form. A few are taken by hook and line by anglers, and the voracious feeding habits of the silver hake make it a ready sport fish, although somewhat sluggish in character. —D.dS.

SILVER LAMPREY *Ichthyomyzon unicuspis* This member of the family Petromyzontidae is characterized by its eelshaped form, the sucking disk for a mouth, and the lack of paired fins. There is a single dorsal fin, which distinguishes it readily from the sea lamprey (*which see*). It resembles other lampreys in general shape, but its cusps have only one point, in contrast to many other freshwater lampreys. Like the sea lamprey, its cusps are arranged in radiating series but are more widely spaced than in the sea lamprey, and lack the arrangement of larger cusps around the tongue cavity. Its color is light

Silver Lamprey

tan to silvery-tan becoming darker during the spawning season, when they are a bluish-black. It grows to a length of 14 inches, the young ammocoetes reaching a maximum of 7 inches.

LIFE HISTORY

It is found exclusively in freshwater, throughout the Mississippi drainage and the Great Lakes to Hudson Bay and the St. Lawrence River. It is a parasitic lamprey, undergoing an extensive spring migration and nest-building activities. Adults spawn over sand and gravel bottom. After the young emerge from being buried in the gravel, they burrow into soft mud, where they remain for long periods.

In spring, at a length of about 4–6 inches, the ammocoetes larvae drift downstream to take up a parasitic life on fishes in large bodies of water. They remain in these areas in late spring and early summer, where they stay until late in the following spring. In recent years, siltation, pollution, and other man-made alterations in the environment have drastically reduced the numbers of silver lamprey. In former years, large quantities were sold to biological supply houses for use in teaching.   —D.dS

SILVER MULLET *See* White Mullet

SILVER PERCH *See* Drums

SILVER PIKE A mutant form of the northern pike (*which see*)

SILVER REDHORSE *Moxostoma anisurum* A silvery sucker with the rear edge of the dorsal convex. The length of the largest dorsal ray is usually as long as the distance from the space between the eyes to the origin of the dorsal fin. The lower lips of this sucker are very full. The body is silvery and white with dark-edged scales without dark spotting at their bases. The tail is light slate-colored. The range is from Manitoba to the St. Lawrence drainage and south to northern Alabama and Missouri.

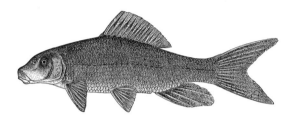

Silver Redhorse

The silver redhorse is an inhabitant of large streams where it prefers long, deep pools with slow currents. It is especially intolerant to turbidity and siltation. The food of this redhorse is primarily immature, aquatic insects. Spawning takes place over gravelbars. The usual size of this sucker is 11–22 inches, and they have been reported to 8 pounds.

ANGLING VALUE

With virtually no sport value and only slight commercial value, the silver redhorse ranks with other suckers in palatability.   —R.A.J.

SILVER SALMON A regional name for the coho salmon (*which see*)

SILVER SEATROUT *Cynoscion nothus* Also called the silver trout, it is related, but not closely, to the other members of its genus. Occurs from Chesapeake Bay to Florida and throughout the Gulf of Mexico. Color pale, without conspicuous pigmentation, the upper part usually straw or walnut, the lower part lighter silvery; sometimes an indication of irregular rows of faint spots. Small individuals, up to about 3½ inches standard length, have the upper part more or less faintly clouded, the cloudy areas tending to form transverse bands.

Other distinguishing characteristics of the silver seatrout are the 9 anal softrays, sometimes 8 and infrequently 10 in specimens from the Atlantic Coast. Total number of gillrakers on the first arch in individuals of 1–6 inches is a mode of 13, frequently 12–14, rarely 15. Most common number of gillrakers on first arch 3 + 10 (3 on upper, 10 on lower limb).

Snout rather short, shorter than the least depth of caudal peduncle. Caudal peduncle short, the length of the rather short maxillary greater than the distance from posterior end of insertion of dorsal to base of caudal on midline. Eye conspicuously larger than in the other species. Dorsal rather long, the usual number of softrays 28–29, frequently 27, less frequently 30, the number of rays increasing in more northern latitudes, and the mode being 28 in Gulf specimens.

LIFE HISTORY

Very little is known about the life history. In contrast to the sand seatrout, this species is more common in the ocean rather than in the bays. In fact, it seems to enter the bays only during the cooler months of the year. It spawns offshore, probably in deepwater, in the early fall. Young have been reported (Gulf Coast) only in October and November. This is the smallest seatrout, the adults seldom growing to more than 10 inches. No food studies have been reported.

ANGLING VALUE

As in the case of the sand seatrout, it supports a minor commercial and sport fishery.   —J.C.B.

SILVERSIDE *See* Atlantic Silverside

SILVER SURFPERCH *Hyperprosopon ellipticum* It does not have the black-tipped pelvics of the walleye surfperch (*which see*); otherwise it is similar. It has no commercial value, but is taken in the surf by sportsmen. Found from Washington to southern California.   —J.R.

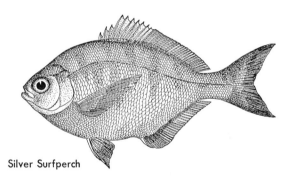

Silver Surfperch

SILVERY MINNOW *Hybognathus nuchalis* An olivaceous, silvery minnow with a broad, slatey middorsal stripe. Sides whitish-silvery. Ventrally milk-white. To separate it from the genus *Notropis* a small knob can be found on the tip of the lower jaw inside the mouth. Dorsal fin well forward. Snout slightly overhangs the horizontal mouth. Scales 35–38 in the lateral line. The range of the silvery minnow is from the Missouri drainage of Montana to Lake Champlain and south to the Gulf.

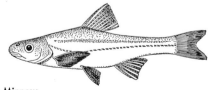

Silvery Minnow

HABITS

The silvery minnow prefers shallow, weedy waters with little or no current. They are found over bottoms of sand or muck but where siltation is absent. Little is known of the food habits of this species except that it prefers waters rich in phytoplankton and probably subsists primarily on microscopic plant and animal life. The silvery minnow spawns over organic debris or vegetation in early spring. A medium-sized minnow, this species averages 6 inches.

ECONOMIC VALUE

Not considered a satisfactory bait species due to its lack of hardiness, the silvery minnow does have some food value, and it takes a hook freely during the spawning season. —R.A.J.

SINKER A metal weight, usually lead, molded in various shapes and sizes, each according to its purpose. Sinkers are used to lower, anchor, drift, or troll baits at a desired depth. They also are used in conjunction with artificial lures in fresh- and saltwater fishing.

Ever since stone-age man turned to the waters for food, the sinker has been an important item of angling equipment. Archaeologists have discovered stone sinkers among the artifacts of ancient Inca and pre-Inca civilizations in South America. Many of these are remarkably similar to the modern dipsey and bank types used by sport fishermen.

While in many parts of the world stones are still used as weights to lower a baited hook to the bottom, and while such assorted articles as metal nuts, bolts, and scraps of iron will suffice in an emergency, modern anglers have developed a family of sinkers, each designed for a specific task.

Among these are sinkers for bottom-fishing, for drifting, live-lining, and trolling. Such weights are employed by freshwater and saltwater anglers, although the latter require a greater diversity of types.

BOTTOM-FISHING SINKERS

Weights designed to take a fresh bait to the bottom and to hold it without fouling are of two basic types. These are the angular, sharp-edged sinkers designed to dig into a soft bottom, best represented by the pyramid; and those which are rounded, and so less likely to foul on rocky or coral-encrusted bottoms, represented by the dipsey.

Where tidal currents and wave action are not excessive, the egg sinker is a popular shoal water type. Tropical anglers use this one on the flats, as it is ideally suited as an anchor for a bonefish or permit bait.

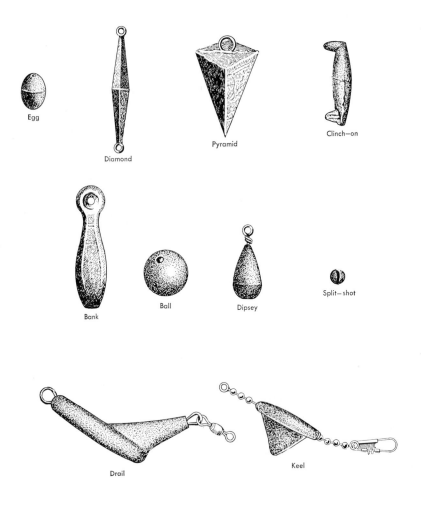

Egg

Diamond

Pyramid

Clinch—on

Bank

Ball

Dipsey

Split—shot

Drail

Keel

Types of Sinkers

At the opposite extreme, for angling in water that is exceptionally deep, and when seeking such bottom feeders, as cod and haddock, the heavy, swiveled drail is a favorite.

Double and triple pyramids are designed to insure greater holding action through the presentation of more edges and flat surfaces. Similarly, multiple-cone sinkers are used to defeat the action of currents and waves, the theory being that one sinker counteracts the movement of another.

Freshwater anglers generally favor the dipsey types for bottom-baiting and find that egg-shaped or round weights are ideally suited to many purposes. Split-shot, ranging from BB size up to 00 Buck, are effective in light-tackle baitfishing. Wrap-on and clinch-on sinkers often are practical.

Since bottom-fishing must take into consideration the ground that will be baited, the depth of water, strength of currents, and effect of wave action, sinker types, shapes, weights, and terminal rigs are important.

In surf-casting, the angler is often handicapped by a current running parallel to the shore and by sweeping combers. Winds may prove equally troublesome. Finally, many game species will drop a bait if they sense the weight of the anchoring sinker.

The required sinker weight depends upon angling technique and the tackle employed. Where trophy striped bass and channel bass are sought in the surf, pyramid and dipsey sinkers weighing 3–6 ounces are most practical, and 4 ounces is probably an average weight.

On the offshore grounds, particularly where it is necessary to lower a baited hook to the 100-foot level, 8–16-ounce weights are necessary. Here the dipsey or bank and the drail are most practical.

The standard terminal rig for wary gamefish found in the surf or in shallow water is the fish finder (*which see*). This is, simply, a sliding-line arrangement. When the fish takes the bait, it is able to move off without disturbing the sinker itself. Fishfinders are available at sporting-goods shops but can be made on the spot. Use one barrel swivel, one snap swivel—and a practical sinker. The snap swivel, to which the sinker is attached, is threaded over the running line. Tie the barrel swivel to the end of the line—and then attach a leader and hook to the opposite eye of the barrel swivel. Leather thongs, often specified, are not essential.

Obviously, the egg sinker with a hole drilled lengthwise, is in itself a fishfinder type, best employed in shoalwater or where scouring currents and pounding waves are no problem.

Many gamefish seem insensible to the drag of a sinker; where these are sought, leaders may be attached to the weight itself. Numerous rigs are employed, among them the "high-low" combination, in which the sinker is attached to the terminal end of the leader, and hooks—on dropper loops—are secured above at intervals so that the baits will tempt bottom feeders as well as those cruising somewhat above the bottom.

A rig often used for channel bass consists of a three way swivel to which is attached a heavy monofilament or wire leader and hook, with a sinker suspended below.

The swiveled drail, shaped something like a distorted banana, often features two hooks, each attached to droppers. The rocking action of the drail makes it possible to feel the slightest strike. Drails, originally, were designed for bait-casting from shore, as well as for bottom-fishing from boats.

TROLLING SINKERS

Modern anglers have developed several sinkers which are primarily suited to trolling with natural or artificial baits. These include the torpedo or cigar-shaped sinkers, keeled sinkers, diving sinkers, and ball sinkers; the latter are often used in conjunction with release devices.

Most popular are the torpedo types. These are produced in a variety of weights and are attached at the junction of running line and leader. Swivels are optional.

Keeled sinkers also serve anglers employing a wide range of tackle combinations. Most of these are swiveled, for one of their purposes is the elimination of line twist.

Diving sinkers of several types are available, some with diagonal, inclined planes forward; others are fitted with line-connecting eyes at the balance, so that they normally tend to drop into the depths.

In some areas, particularly on the Pacific Coast, cannonball sinkers are popular. These often range up to 3 or more pounds and are molded of cast iron. The ball sinker is considered expendable and is dropped, by means of a quick-release swivel, when a fish strikes.

With the exception of the cannonball sinker, most trolling weights are carefully streamlined. The object is a minimum of resistance to the flow of water and prevention of air bubbles which might detract from the appeal of the following bait.

A "hidden sinker" rig, first developed on the Pacific Coast and currently used in many areas, is worth noting. Here, the sinker, a ball or dipsey type, is encased in the sewed-up body cavity of a baitfish which will be trolled. The same general principle is employed in the eel bob, a natural eel with a lead weight attached to the head.

In freshwater trolling, the keeled sinker is most often used. The clinch-on can be substituted when it is necessary to take a lure or bait a short distance below the surface, and split shot may serve the same purpose.

DRIFTING AND LIVE-LINING

Ball, clinch-on, wrap-around, and dipsey sinkers all are used by anglers who drift or liveline natural bait. In most cases the weight is used to achieve a natural buoyancy or to keep the bait suspended below a float at the desired depth. The weight selected depends on the force of currents and, of course, on depth. Shape is dependent upon the angling technique employed.

Where it is deemed advisable to roll a bait along in a marine current or inland stream, egg, splitshot, and wrap-around weights prove most useful. The wrap-around tends to foul in woods or on bottom; so it is effective when used in a strong flow where the bait will be presented just below the surface.

Sinker designers have produced hundreds of shapes which are particularly well-suited to specific employment. However, most of these evolved from the basic sharp-edged (pyramid) or the rounded (dipsey) prototypes. Thus, variations of the pyramid include the triangular bank, diamond, arrowhead, and similar shapes. Dipsey

Sixgill Shark (tooth upper jaw *left*, lower jaw *right*)

variations include the bank, tournament-casting, cone, egg, ball, and disk.

Multiple sinkers often are employed, both in an attempt to increase weight and to aid holding action. Multiple pyramid and cone weights offer the best example, together with strings of egg and split-shot weights.

The drail is specialized, primarily used on the cod banks of the Northeast. Keel, torpedo, and other trolling sinkers have been developed for specific use.

In most cases, sinkers should not be painted or chromed. The dull finish of lead is particularly desirable because it does not detract from the bait itself. There are exceptions; flounder fishermen sometimes find that a bright red sinker will serve as an attractor and may increase the effectiveness of the primary bait.

Basically, sinkers should be chosen on the strength of their efficiency in taking a bait or lure to the desired depth and/or on their ability to hold bottom without excessive fouling.   —F.W.

SINUS SQUEEZE *See* Aerosinusitis *in* Skin and Scuba Diving Dangers *under* First Aid

SISCOWET *See* Lake Trout

SIXGILL SHARK *Hexanchus griseus* This peculiar species is recognized by the 6 pairs of gill openings rather than the usual 5 of most sharks. The single dorsal fin is set far back on the body, almost directly above the anal fin, which is about the same size. The caudal fin is long, and about half the length of the body without the tail. The gill openings are rather long, reaching from the ventral midline well up on the sides. Its eyes are elliptical, long, and relatively large, particularly in young specimens. The teeth are unusual in that the upper ones are relatively simple. The middle upper teeth have single cusps, with the outer teeth having 2 cusps, the number of cusps increasing to 3 auxiliary smaller cusps at the corners of the mouth. The lower teeth, however, are multicusp, and all are approximately the same shape, save for the 10 very small unicusp teeth at the angles of the mouth, and the single median tooth on the lower jaw which is symmetrical. The large teeth are trapezoid in form, with 7 or 8 pointed cusps regularly decreasing in height. The color is gray-brown to dark gray above, becoming paler below. The eyes are bright emerald-green. Some specimens have a pale area along the well-marked lateral line. Young specimens are slate-gray. The sixgill shark grows to over 26 feet, and individuals of 15 feet are not rare.

LIFE HISTORY

This deepwater species occurs on both sides of the Atlantic and the Mediterranean Sea. In the Pacific it is found from British Columbia to southern California and Chile, and off Japan, Australia, and the southern parts of the Indian Ocean and South Africa. It is debatable if the species found in the western Atlantic is the same as that found in other areas.

A sluggish species, it is caught in deeper water toward tropical latitudes and shoaler water toward colder latitudes. Specimens have been taken off Portugal at depths of over a mile, while specimens in the North Sea are taken as shoal as 90 feet. In the Caribbean, most specimens are taken at depths in excess of 600 feet. The spawning season is not known definitely, but it is reported to be in spring and autumn. Eggs are hatched within the mother, where the young complete their development. Young are born at lengths from 16–26 inches, and sexual maturity probably occurs at 6–6½ feet long.

ANGLING VALUE

Adults eat fishes, including hake, dolphins, small marlins, and swordfish, and crabs and shrimp. They evidently feed more actively at night, when they reportedly come to the surface. In Cuba, they are caught by the deep-line fishing method, and their flesh is used for oil; in Germany the flesh is reportedly marketed for its purgative action. Specimens are occasionally taken off southern Florida and in the Bahamas in deepwater, and it has been theorized by some anglers that "sea monsters" which take deep-drifted baits, only to snap wire cable, are perhaps giant sixgill sharks.   —D.dS.

SKATES Skates are fishlike vertebrates possessing 5 pairs of gill clefts, a cartilaginous skeleton, and generally a flattened body. They differ from the sharks in having the gill openings located on the ventral surface, rather than on the sides, as in sharks. And the anterior edges of the pectoral fins are joined to the sides of the head, past the gill openings, usually resulting in a flattened appearance. Unlike sharks, the upper edges of the eye orbits are not free from the eyeballs. Further, skates lack anal fins, as do rays. Their bodies are strongly compressed, and the tail is well marked off from the body, and there are usually two dorsal fins and a small but distinctive caudal fin. The skin of most skates usually has numerous thorns, but a few species have completely smooth skin. Skates do not have the poisonous barb at or near the base of the tail which is characteristic of most rays.

Most skates spend their lives lying on the bottom, cruising sluggishly in search of clams, snails, shrimp, and other bottom-dwelling forms. They are generally less active than rays and school to a lesser extent. Skates range from only a few inches to perhaps 5–6 feet, but most are under 2 feet.

All skates lay eggs, the young subsequently being hatched from a horny capsule. Found exclusively in saltwater, they are largely inhabitants of cooler waters, being most abundant in temperate and subpolar waters. Although they occur in tropical latitudes, such specimens are generally taken from deepwater. Some species of skates have been captured from depths as great as 1,500 fathoms, and they are often abundant in areas of 20–100 fathoms.

FOOD VALUE

While not widely eaten in the United States, the European countries and some Oriental countries highly regard the skates as food. Skate flesh is excellent, and this valuable resource is not being utilized to the fullest. Occasionally, skates are ground for use as fishmeal and fertilizer, and the pectoral fins of some species are regularly used in the United States to make "scallops," which are cut out with a pipe or cookie cutter. *See also* Barndoor Skate, Big Skate, California Skate, Clearnose Skate, Little Skate, Longnose Skate, Roundel Skate, Winter Skate   —D.dS.

SKEG A metal or wood extension to the keel of a boat to protect the propeller from underwater obstruction.

SKIFF An arbitrary classification which encompasses any small utility boat, usually under 16 feet in length, propelled either by oars or power. *See also* Inboard-Outboard, Outboard

SKIN AND SCUBA DIVING DANGERS *See under* First Aid

SKIPJACK *See* Little Tunas, Skipjack Tuna

SKIPJACK HERRING *Alosa chrysochloris* A member of the herring family Clupeidae, this species has a strongly compressed body, thin scales, and a curved belly edged with a row of scutes (sharp-edged scales). The upper jaw is notched, and the lower jaw projects far beyond the upper. The young and, usually, the adults have weak teeth in the lower jaw. The back is green with bluish reflections, and the sides are silvery. Usually there are no dark spots behind the gill covers as in the closely related hickory shad (*which see*). It reaches 21 inches and 3½ pounds, usually 12–16 inches.

This species is found from the marine waters of the Gulf Coast from Texas to Florida, up the Mississippi River and its larger tributaries, north to Minnesota and Pennsylvania. This large-river fish spawns in late April during upstream migrations, probably drifting downstream during the fall.

ANGLING VALUE

On light tackle, the skipjack herring is an excellent fighter, and is taken on flies, small spinners or spoons, or on live minnows. It eats insects and crustaceans, as well as small fishes. It is not valued for food, largely because of its bony flesh.   —D.dS.

SKIPJACK TUNA *Katsuwonus pelamis* Also called oceanic skipjack, striped tuna, and many other names, it is a fish of the mackerel family with prominent, dark longitudinal stripes on the lower half of the body. It has more gill-rakers (53–63) than any other mackerel-like fish in the Americas. The largest fish caught by hook and line, taken in the Bahamas, was 3 feet 3 inches long and weighed 39 pounds 15 ounces.

This species is found around the world in tropical and subtropical seas. It forms schools that at times may include 50,000 fish. The food consists mainly of fishes, squids, and crustaceans. Spawning probably occurs throughout the year in equatorial waters but tends to be restricted to the summer months as distance from the equator increases.

This is one of the most important commercial fishes, particularly in the Pacific, where many are taken near Japan, Hawaii, and the Central American coast. *See also* Little Tuna   —B.B.C.
                                                     —R.H.G.

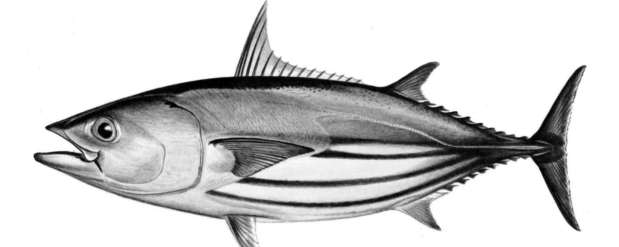

Skipjack Tuna

SKIPPING BLENNY *See* Skipping Goby

SKIPPING GOBY Family Periophthalmidae The skipping gobies or tree-walking fish have a scattered distribution on the shores of tropical seas. These curious fishes are semi-terrestrial in habit and occur among mangrove roots on mud beaches usually near the mouths of rivers. Unlike the skipping blennies (Blenniidae), which swiftly skip from one tide pool to another among rocks where they feed on algae, the gobies climb trees in search of insects. The gobies' land existence is made possible by respiratory organs modified for breathing air, and fins which are especially adapted for walking. Actually, the skipping gobies can travel very rapidly, even over mud, and are most difficult for a man to catch by hand. These gobies live in waterfilled burrows which interconnect, and often have a "main" entrance used by any number of gobies within the community. Skipping gobies are small, seldom more than 8 inches in length, and have keen aerial vision in that one eye can work independently of the other. Their skin is thick to conserve body moisture while on land.

Skipping gobies can be caught on artificial flies by casting near individual fish on the mud flats or by dangling the fly near a goby feeding in the mangroves. There is no sport in this connection, but the larger fish are good to eat; on the *Ile des Poissons Qui Marche*, where they appear by the thousands in the mouth of the Congo River, native people net great quantities of gobies which are both smoked and dry salted for local consumption. Their flesh is very delicate and is sometimes sold in west African cities. —A.J.McC.

SKISH *See under* American Casting Association

SLEEPERS Family Eleotridae Of world-wide tropical and subtropical distribution, the sleepers are of little angling interest, but at least seven species occur in Southern United States freshwater and tidewater streams and canals, ranging from South Carolina through Central America and to Brazil. In contrast to the marine gobies (Gobiidae), in which the ventral fins are united to form a suckerlike disc, the ventral fins of the sleepers are completely separated. The body is elongate, usually cylindrical anteriorly and compressed posteriorly. Sleepers have two separated dorsal fins; the first is composed of short, flexible spines and the second contains soft rays, which may be preceded by a single spine. The caudal fin is rounded.

Many species of the Eleotridae are voracious and predatory, concealing themselves in weeds, rock crevices, or soft mud bottoms, where they move with great speed in capturing other fishes. However, sleepers are of small size and the larger bigmouth sleeper, *Gobiomorus dormitor*, which is caught in Southern states, seldom exceeds 20 inches in length. Sleepers take live baits and occasionally strike spinners, flies, and small plugs. They are fairly common in the Florida freshwater catch, but seldom correctly identified. Large individuals have some food value. —A.J.McC.

SLIME EEL *See* Atlantic Hagfish

SLIP CLUTCH A clutch in the gear housing of an outboard which disengages when the motor strikes an underwater obstruction.

SLIPPERY DICK *Halichoeres bivittatus* This brightly colored member of the wrasse family Labridae is recognized by its elongate body, long dorsal fin, small mouth, and protruding canine teeth. Two black, lateral bands characterize the species, and these bands occasionally are broken up into squarish blotches. The fins and body are brightly colored, the fins with narrow bands of blue, pink, and yellow, with a row of yellowish spots. The body is olive-buff to pale yellow. It reaches a length of about 8 inches.

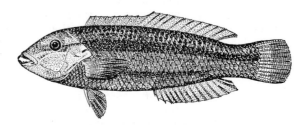

Slippery Dick

Found throughout the West Indies, it ranges from Brazil to North Carolina and Bermuda. It occurs from a few feet deep to at least 100 feet. An extremely common species of the coral-reef environment, it also occurs around wharves, pilings, and debris, and over sand, grass, or silt bottom. However, the larger schools are usually associated with coral reefs.

LIFE HISTORY

It feeds on small fishes and crustaceans, continually foraging about reefs in search of food. Loose aggregations of young and adults occur about coral branches during the daytime, and the species burrows into the sand at night. Ripe specimens are taken during July, but, like other tropical wrasses, it may spawn year round.

Bigmouth Sleeper

ANGLING VALUE

A well-known bait stealer, it is often taken by anglers, but its flesh is poor. —D.dS.

SLOUGH A narrow and not especially deep channel, particularly one that runs through a shallow area in a bay situated near marshlands.

SLUE A small channel or cut through a sandbar.

SMALLMOUTH BASS *Micropterus dolomieui* One of the most important freshwater gamefish found in North America. The robust body of this member of the black basses has a brownish or bronze cast with vertical, dark, olivaceous bars. In contrast to the largemouth bass, the upper jaw does not extend beyond the eye, and the dorsal fin has a very shallow notch. The young can be distinguished by the tricolored tail which has the outermost portion edged in white, the middle portion with a black band, and closest to the body an orange color. The maximum size is about 12 pounds.

The range of the smallmouth is from Minnesota to Quebec and south to northern Alabama, then west to eastern Kansas and Oklahoma. It has been introduced in many other states from coast to coast.

The geography of the smallmouth bass can be traced by the growth of American railroads. Until the year 1869, its range was largely confined to the Lake Ontario and Ohio River drainage systems, but as the wood-burning diamond stackers rolled south and west, the bass became a commuter. The original brood of the Potomac basin, for example, came from the Ohio River by riding over the Alleghenies on the Baltimore and Ohio in a bucket hanging in the water tender. This resulted in some widely scattered plantings, and eventually the smallmouth arrived in California from Lake Ontario via New York.

The smallmouth is usually found in rocky locations in lakes and streams. They prefer clear, rocky lakes with a minimum depth of 25–30 feet and with temperatures in the summer no less than 60°F., and no more than 80°F. In streams, this bass prefers a good percentage of riffles flowing over gravel, boulders, or bedrock.

The first food of this species consists of minute crustaceans, and later it graduates into insect larvae, crayfish, and fish.

LIFE HISTORY

The smallmouth bass matures at different ages depending on its growth and the latitude of its environment. In the north it was found that the males mature at 3 years of age and about 9 inches in length. In more southerly locations, both sexes were found to be mature at 2 years. Smallmouth often move into small and large tributaries to spawn. Spawning normally takes place when the water temperature reaches 60°–70°F. This may occur from late April to early June, depending on the season and location. The nest is built by the male by fanning out the gravel, coarse sand, or stones with his tail. The nest is built in 3–22 feet of water depending on its clarity. The nests, which are 14–30 inches in diameter, will be deeper in clearwater than those found in turbid water. After the nest is completed, the male selects a ripe female and drives her to the nest. After she has spawned, she is driven from the nest and another ripe female selected. Often as many as three females lay their eggs in one nest. Although a

female will produce 2,000–7,000 eggs per pound of her body weight, all the eggs do not ripen simultaneously. A nest may contain from 200 to several thousand eggs with the average being about 2,000. The eggs incubate in 2–9 days depending on the temperature. After hatching, the fry leave the nest a few hours after swimming up. There is little or no parental care. Except for the gold iris of the eye, young smallmouth are pitch black.

GROWTH RATE

The growth of smallmouth depends on the amount and kind of feed, the temperature of the water, and the length of the growing season. In some infertile streams, it takes four years for the bass to reach 9 inches. In the larger fertile rivers, 9 inches will be reached during the second summer; it requires 7–10 years in these rivers to attain 18–20 inches. —K.B.

PARASITES

The smallmouth bass has a common parasitic enemy, *Proteocephalus ambloplites*, or bass tapeworm. This internal parasite doesn't kill the fish, but it shrinks the capacity for reproduction to the point that smallmouths have been virtually eliminated from some Eastern lakes. The tapeworm infests largemouth bass also, but not with the same serious result. Anglers seldom see the parasite, nor eat it accidentally, as it penetrates the intestine and gonads which are removed when the fish is cleaned for cooking. The tapeworm is not related to the "grubby" fish which every angler catches once in awhile. These larval worms (*Clinostomum marginatum*), easily distinguished by their large size and yellow color, occur in the muscle tissue and gill covers. Through a rather complicated process of development, the adult yellow grub passes from the great blue heron to the bass with a freshwater snail as the intermediate host. When an infected fish is eaten by another heron, the worm fastens itself to the mouth, throat, or esophagus of the bird and thus completes the cycle. The yellow grub infestation is harmless to man and not lethal to the smallmouth bass. All parasites occur more abundantly in some localities than in others, and the endemic areas of infection probably shift from year to year. However, the possibility of introducing the tapeworm by unsupervised stocking is an ever present threat to conservation.

ANGLING VALUE

The smallmouth bass is widely acclaimed as the top trophy of the bass family. The fish is extremely active and usually jumps when hooked. The average smallmouth is not nearly as large as many freshwater fish, but the capture of a 4–5 pounder requires more skill and more patience than the taking of many species of comparable size.

Baits used for smallmouth fishing vary with the locality and the season. The natural baits generally accepted in Eastern rivers are hellgrammites, softshell crayfish, stonecats, night crawlers, and minnows. A survey in Iowa revealed that the best bait-fishing is in the early fall of the year. In June the spinner-and-wet fly were most effective; the hair floater was the most productive in July; and in August the plug and hair floater caught the most fish per

Smallmouth Bass, 3-pound Female, Big Lake, Maine

hour. The main thing to remember is that they usually feed actively in the morning and evening and will often hit during the night particularly on surface baits. For the ultimate in sport the fly rod with surface lures is best, but spinning, casting, and bait-fishing are also productive. Smallmouth-bass fishing is best in rivers in late summer when the lake fish refuse to hit. The lower and clearer the river, the better the fishing.

Perhaps the most outstanding area from the standpoint of record or near-record fish is in southern TVA impoundments, such as Dale Hollow Reservoir bordering Kentucky and Tennessee, or Wheeler Dam in Alabama. These lakes produce smallmouths in the 8-pound class every season. By contrast, the dedicated light-tackle man seeks his fishing in rivers like the Delaware in New York and New Jersey, the North Branch of the Susquehanna in Pennsylvania, the Rappahannock and James in Virginia, Ohio's Whetstone, the Elkhorn, Kinninick, and Green of Kentucky, or the St. Croix in Wisconsin. There is little chance of hooking heavy smallmouths in these running waters. A 4-pounder would be exceptional. But the thrill of drifting a bug over strong and oftentimes selective fish epitomizes the fly-rod game. The smallmouth is a fish of large lakes, and it prefers water that is clear and rocky such as that found in southeastern Maine, which is noted for its May to June bass fishing. A good spot to locate bronzebacks is over gravelbars between submerged weed beds in 10–20-foot depths. You will also find bass at the dropoff near shale banks and on the gravel points which run out from shore. Another hot spot is the reefs which often occur far out in a large lake. You may find mounds of rock rising near the surface many miles from shore. Smallmouths regularly hunt crayfish on these shoals, particularly in the Great Lakes region. If you work these places with a deep-running plug or spoon and keep your lure down on the gravel, you should be covering big bass. On the reefs you may be able to take them with surface plugs and darters as the water is likely to be shallow here. But the best surface fishing is usually had in the early morning and evening, when the smallmouths invade the shoreline looking for minnows and frogs.

FLY-FISHING FOR SMALLMOUTHS

Fly-fishing for bass in rivers is not difficult to learn. Most of the pools and runs you will fish are fairly shallow,

and the bass will come readily to a surface lure. The fish generally locate themselves in the feeding lanes which are marked by a line of froth or bubbles at the head of a pool, either in its center or to one side. Smallmouths do not hold in water that is very swift like the rainbow trout, for example, but you will find them in pockets having a moderate current and around all the obvious covers such as boulders, logs, ledges, and grass banks. They sometimes wander into backwaters from the mainstream, particularly if there's a good depth and some vegetation which hides food.

TECHNIQUE FOR RIVER SMALLMOUTHS

The most important thing you can learn about bass fishing in a particular river is the seasonal "pattern" in fish behavior. Different types of habitat will attract and hold smallmouths at certain times of the year. To be sure, you will find young bass scattered over various parts of any good river, but their presence can be misleading as the catchables of 12 inches or more (or from 1 pound up) are more selective in a territorial sense. Although river smallmouths do not undertake extensive migrations, they do move short distances—from shallow to deep riffles or from pools to pocket water and even into backwaters and sloughs according to the season. There is a variety of reasons for this phenomenon, such as the abundance or scarcity of specific foods, the loss of cover during lowering water levels, or the availability of new forage during rising water and correlated temperature changes (smallmouths begin active feeding at about 60°F with the preferred range at 70°–80°F, but feeding ceases at about 50°F). The skilled angler recognizes the productive spots; it may be shallow rock-bottomed pools with only a moderate current in the spring season, the main channel edges during summer, or the slack water of deep pools where there is no apparent current in the cooler temperatures of autumn. There is no universal rule; and it's difficult for the angler on a strange river to get an immediate "reading." The substrate or type of bottom is a useful clue to begin working with in most cases.

The least productive are bedrock and sand. These substrates are low in productivity, the bedrock being constantly scrubbed by the current and the sand shifting with every change in velocity. Aquatic organisms will not thrive here. Coarse gravel and slab rock (as opposed to rounded stones or boulders) are usually most productive of bass foods, but ledges and long grassy banks often attract smallmouths for brief periods regardless of the bottom composition. Remember that river bass, like their lake counterparts, are cover conscious and most commonly hide in rock crevices when not actively feeding. Normally, this is where the smallmouth remains during the winter months when water temperatures hit the low 40's. Once the possible lair is established, it must be fished slowly and carefully, with a minimum of casts. Throwing a lure out and bringing it back again and again is a habit that the trophy hunter cannot afford. The first cast should swing into the holding water at the proper depth and then be worked with all the art you can muster. Never be in a hurry. Sometimes a smallmouth will take a bait the instant it hits the water, but more often the area has to be covered carefully and the fish may not make a pass until the fifth or sixth swim. If you are lucky and take a good bass, continue working the same area, as smallmouths are seldom alone and frequently there will be a fair number of comparable-sized fish within a few feet of where the first one was hooked. Rest the area or change lures, but don't move too quickly to a new location. The active feeding area on that particular day may be a short stretch of no more than a hundred yards in a half-mile long riffle, which is often the case on big bass streams. For this reason the wading angler often has an advantage over the floatboat caster. When float-fishing it is profitable to anchor, or at least beach the boat after hooking a fat smallmouth, and comb the surrounding water. A float trip should consist of at least 50 percent wading, whether the quarry is bass or trout. A boat is a great advantage in that you can cover many more hotspots than the angler traveling by foot.

When you begin to catch bass make a mental note of the depth, type of bottom, and current velocity. If it's a gravel-bottomed shoal of 2–4 feet in depth with a moderate flow, look for identical situations along the river. Try other types of water if you must, but the chances of success are greatly enhanced at every similar location. This may go on for a week or even a month, then abruptly the pattern will change; the shoals are literally barren and the bass congregate in stillwater along deep shores at dropoffs, or they may move into the deepest portions of the main channel and remain at depths of 12–15 feet.

The successful angling for stream smallmouths requires not only attention to details but a flexible method of casting. You must be able to work from top to bottom at various speeds and with light lures. Fly-fishing is dependent on the bass being in shallow water or at least rising to insects of some kind, and based on the results of many seasons; it more or less boils down to those glorious periods in June and September—with exceptions of course. Bait-casting with a multiplying reel is somewhat more effective through the angling year, but some of the best smallmouth lures weigh less than the ¼-ounce weight which is the practical minimum for revolving spool outfits. The ideal tackle is a 6- or 6½-foot spin stick with a total weight of about 3 ounces, mounted with a light spinning reel spooled in 4-pound-test monofilament. This is plenty strong for river bassing (where 4-pound fish are exceptional), and permits long delicate casts with ⅛–⅜-ounce baits.

The chief difference between fly-fishing for largemouth bass and smallmouth bass is that the latter requires techniques and terminal tackle which are more nearly comparable to those used for trout. Generally speaking, the heavy leaders and big bugs used for largemouths are much less effective for the bronzeback and parenthetically, the 6X points and tiny flies which can be necessary for brown trout are not practical. The skilled smallmouth angler will favor 2X to 3X tippets with flies and bugs on No. 4 and No. 6 hooks; occasionally a very large streamer fly on a No. 2/0 hook can stir reluctant fish into striking, but under normal conditions the bronzeback wants something "alive" without too much bulk. The Muddler Minnow, Woolly Worm, and Marabou streamer are classic examples of reliable bass flies. However, there is a variety of bugs made of various materials which are frequently more productive than the standard bass flies.

Smallmouth bass will take dry flies at times, but as a general rule they are not partial to the ephemeral patterns employed for trout. Clipped deer hair bugs or very "bushy" dry flies are favored. These seem to provide a bit more bulk, which is important, of course, in getting a smallmouth to come topside. All the deer-hair floaters evolved one from the other; Devil Bug, Cooper Bug, Delaware Bug, and even the Horner Deer Hair are part of the development. Patterns that feature fat, buggy bodies are ideal for smallmouths when they're inclined to rise.

Soft plastic bugs which imitate crickets, spiders, or grasshoppers are also excellent smallmouth lures. These are made in both floating and sinking models, and although starkly simple in appearance, the flexible legs provide just the right touch of action to attract fish. The patterns may vary from one maker to the next, but an all-black bug on a No. 6 hook is usually very productive, not only on smallmouths but panfish as well.

Another popular daytime bug is a quiet-swimming frog pattern on a No. 6 hook, which in overall size is no bigger than a half-dollar. If the water is real low and clear, wade the quiet pools of big-bass streams, and with a long 3X leader, lay it over the channels, or close to undercut banks. If the fish are holding deep, as they might be in a heavy river or lake, use the frog with a sinking-type fly line. Although the bug is a floater, the line will pull it under, and because of its buoyancy, it will "swim" just like a live frog.

The difference between a natural-looking bug and a fanciful popper should not be underestimated when it comes to catching smallmouths. Poppers are fun to use because they float high, and the *gerblub* sound of the bug walking across the surface certainly suggests some form of life. Loud popping is often deadly on bigmouth bass, particularly in turbid or weedy water, and at night. However it can be more attractive to the angler who gets hypnotized by the game, than to the smallmouth. To get strikes from cagey bronzebacks, go easy on the bug action. Just a gentle pop or gurgle will do the trick. One reason why soft plastic bugs will outfish poppers at times is because they don't make any noise. Quiet swimming plus the leg action of the bug is all that's needed.

There is no answer to the question in so far as which type of bug is better. Chiefly, the idea is to stock a variety of bugs and be prepared to fish them below the surface as well as on top. In trout fishing we can generally offer pretty good reasons for the success of a nymph as opposed to a dry fly, for example but bass fishing is less definitive. There are days when not a single bass can be seen rising; yet they will splinter a popper from dawn to dusk. And if you should dress one out, the chances are its belly will be full of crayfish or minnows which only makes the experience more puzzling. Smallmouth bass do eat a lot of insects. More so perhaps than the bigmouth as a rule. Even in streams or lakes where minnows are abundant a bronzeback loves to forage on beetles, caterpillars, grasshoppers, grubs, ants, bees, dragonflies—and anything that crawls, flies, or falls into the water.

For details on the techniques of catching smallmouth bass see also Bait-Casting, Bass Bug, Spinning, Streamer Fly

For details on the propagation of smallmouth bass see Fish Culture —A.J.McC.

SMALLMOUTH BUFFALO *Ictiobus bubalus* The smallmouth buffalo is second only to the bigmouth buffalo in size attained by species of the sucker family and in economic importance. Though seldom caught by anglers, it contributes significantly to the commercial harvest of fish in the Central states. Its range is similar to that of the bigmouth buffalo, being found from North Dakota east to Pennsylvania and south to the Gulf. Found principally in large rivers and warm lakes of the Plains states, it requires somewhat cleaner and deeper waters than its close relative the bigmouth. This requirement has caused a general decrease in abundance and restriction of range as civilization in the Central states has gradually dirtied and polluted the major rivers and lakes.

The body of the smallmouth buffalo is more compressed and the back more elevated (humpbacked) than either the bigmouth or black buffalo. The mouth is small, subterminal, almost horizontal, and protracts downward. Lateral-line scales number 37–39. The color generally is lighter than that of the other buffaloes, being a slatey-bronze or olive above and fading into white or yellowish on the belly. Other characteristics are similar to those described for the bigmouth buffalo.

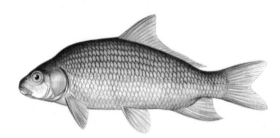

Smallmouth Buffalo

Other names often given the smallmouth buffalo are razorback buffalo, roachback, and thicklipped buffalo.

Average size of the species runs smaller than the bigmouth buffalo. Commercially harvested specimens run 2–10 pounds, but occasional fish will get up to 15–20 pounds. One smallmouth buffalo taken in Tennessee weighed 28½ pounds, while 40 pounds is listed as maximum weight.

LIFE HISTORY

Most aspects of the smallmouth buffalo's life history are similar to or the same as the bigmouth buffalo. Primary differences are that the smallmouth relies more on insects and bottom organisms for food, requires cleaner

waters, and grows slower. Average length will approximate 5, 9, 12, 15, 17, and 19 inches at ages 1 through 6, respectively. Weight will average 2 pounds at 15 inches. 5 pounds at 20 inches, and 10 pounds at 26 inches. A 30-inch specimen weighs about 17½ pounds.

ANGLING VALUE

The smallmouth buffalo is not considered to be of value to the angler since only an occasional, accidental catch is made by sport fishermen.

COMMERCIAL VALUE

The flesh of the smallmouth is said to be of higher quality than the bigmouth, but the species is not as abundant. Of 5,000,000 pounds of buffalo marketed through Chicago in 1961, it is estimated that less than 1,000,000 pounds were smallmouth buffalo. It is slightly more difficult to harvest since it prefers deeper waters. Decreasing abundance of the smallmouth buffalo can be expected to continue due to gradual depletion of the clearwaters it requires to thrive in abundance. —J.T.S.

SMALLMOUTH GRUNT *Haemulon chrysargyreum* This small grunt occurs in extreme southern Florida including the Keys, southward through the West Indies to Brazil.

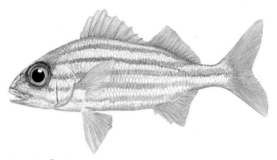

Smallmouth Grunt

Mature adults run 7–8.5 inches in total length. This grunt is distinguished from the others by the color pattern combined with the number of gillrakers. The sides of the body have yellow and bluish-gray stripes. The inside of the mouth is red. The smallmouth grunt has 12 dorsal spines; 13 dorsal rays; 9–10 anal rays, usually 9; and 15–17 pectoral rays, usually 16. Pored lateral-line scales 49–51, usually 50. Gillrakers 30–33. The pectoral fins are not scaled.

ANGLING VALUE

This species forms large schools about the reefs off Florida. It is also found in shallow water along the shore. It feeds on or near the bottom. It is too small to be considered a gamefish but is easy to catch with cut bait. The smallmouth grunt is good eating, but it is often too small to be worthwhile cleaning and cooking. —L.R.

SMALL SPORTFISHERMAN An inshore-offshore fishing boat of 16–25 feet in length. *For details see* Small Sportfisherman *under* Sportfisherman

SMALLTOOTH SAWFISH *Pristis pectinata* Also called the common sawfish, this ray is found on both sides of the Atlantic. In the western Atlantic, it ranges from New

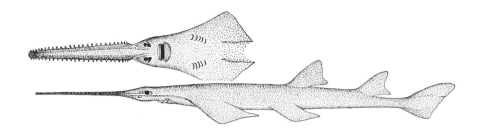

Smalltooth Sawfish

York and Bermuda to middle Brazil and the northern part of the Gulf of Mexico. It is a year-round resident in Florida, but northward it is only known as a summer visitor. There are nine recognized species in the genus *Pristis*. They are found along tropical and warm-temperate coastlines in all parts of the world.

The smalltooth sawfish may be separated from the only other sawfish (the largetooth sawfish, *Pristis perotteti*) known from the western Atlantic as follows: Its first dorsal fin originates about over the origin of its pelvics (rather than considerably in front as in *P. perotteti*); its caudal fin is much shorter with lower lobe only faintly indicated; its rostral teeth are more numerous; there are 24 or more on each side; its saw is relatively shorter; its second dorsal has a posterior margin much less deeply concave; and its pectorals are much smaller. It agrees with *P. pristis* of the eastern Atlantic in the shape of its caudal and in the position of the first dorsal fin relative to the pelvics, but it is separable from *P. pristis* by its numerous rostral teeth.

Color nearly uniform dark gray to blackish-brown above, paler along margins of fins. White to grayish-white or pale yellow below.

LIFE HISTORY

This species, like other sawfishes, is almost exclusively restricted to the immediate vicinity of land in water only a few feet deep. It is most often encountered in partially enclosed waters, lying in the deeper holes on bottoms of mud or muddy sand. It runs up large freshwater rivers regularly and perhaps may live permanently in such places. It has been taken from the lower reaches of the Amazon, the Essequibo, the Atrato and San Juan rivers of Colombia, the lower Mississippi, and in the St. Johns River, Florida.

The smalltooth sawfish obtains for its prey various kinds of small animals chiefly by stirring the mud with its saw. This activity has often been seen, and the motion of the saw has been described as principally backward and forward. It has also been seen attacking schools of small fish by slashing sideways with the saw, then eating the individuals that are wounded. It will take a hook readily if it is baited with freshly cut fish.

Gravid females, with the young well-advanced in development, have been taken in southern Florida waters in April and in July. Small, free-living specimens have been caught there in January, suggesting that the young are born in that region from late spring through the summer. Also, young specimens have been seen in abundance off southern Texas in May and June. Further south, where the seasonal range in temperature is narrower and where winter temperatures are higher, it is likely that young are produced throughout the year.

The smalltooth sawfish is of no commercial value anywhere in the western Atlantic, although the small ones have been described as being good panfish and the larger ones as yielding good steaks. They are of considerable concern to fishermen because of the damage they do to driftnets, seines, and shrimp trawls.

This species of sawfish is about 2 feet long at birth and will grow to a length of 18 feet, or perhaps more. Most of the individuals that wander northward along the Atlantic Coast to North Carolina and beyond are large. Specimens 16 feet long have been taken from both North Carolina and New Jersey. An individual of this length would weigh about 700 pounds.

Sawfish can utilize their saws by striking sideways with great power. Consequently, even small ones should be handled or approached with caution. Although people have suffered severe injury through handling or disturbing sawfishes, there is no evidence of unprovoked attacks.

—J.C.B.

SMELT Family Osmeridae It is characterized by a complete lateral line; the stomach in the form of a blind sac; the short dorsal fin; the slender body; small size; the adipose fin; and the lack of a fleshy appendage at the pelvic-fin bases. Colors range from brown to blue above to silver on the belly.

Smelt are marine, anadromous, or freshwater fish in the Arctic, northern Pacific, and Atlantic oceans and rivers that empty into them. The females are larger; the males may develop tubercles on the fins, scales, and head, and have enlarged lateral-line scales and longer paired fins at maturity. Spawning takes place on sandy beaches. The smelts occur in large schools, are rich in oil, and are excellent food fishes. *See* Capelin, Eulachon, Ice Fishing, Longfin Smelt, Night Smelt, Pond Smelt, Rainbow Smelt, Southern Smelt, Surf Smelt, Whitebait Smelt   —J.R.

SMOKEHOUSE COOKERY (FISH) The average sportsman can easily learn the art of smokehouse cookery. Such expensive delicacies as smoked trout, salmon, and eel may be produced with minimum equipment by anybody capable of lighting a fire. It does require a little experimenting to learn the correct application of brine and heat due to local differences in climate, fuel, and the smokehouse itself, but these details are not complicated. There are two general methods of smoking foods—hot smoking and cold smoking. In hot smoking, the fish is completely

A large smokehouse to handle greater volume. Metal box with holes spreads the smoke

Wooden or metal barrel smokehouse. Burlap over the top controls the flow of smoke

cooked and flavored at 160–180° F. Although a hot-smoked product will not keep for more than a few days unless refrigerated, frozen, or canned, it is the most popular for home consumption. It is the shorter method. Cold smoking is primarily a commercial process for treating large quantities of food to be preserved for several weeks or more. In cold smoking, the fish is *not* cooked but cured through drying at a temperature of approximately 90° F. for a prolonged period. Preservation depends on the length of time the product is smoked and the amount of salt used. In general, the longer the salt cure and the slower the heat is applied, the longer food will keep.

BRINE AND SMOKE

The strong salt brine in which the fish are first immersed is a preservative. Salt solution has an inhibiting effect on spoilage bacteria. Most bacteria with few exceptions are retarded by 5 percent of salt and higher. The removal of body fluids from the fish by salt deprives the bacteria of water without which they cannot survive. The fluid which is extracted from the fish is partly replaced by the salt itself. The addition of smoke to the fish not only adds flavor but increases the tensile strength of the connective tissues. If the smokehouse gets too warm, for example, the fish will drop from the S-hooks or fall apart. This is because the connective tissue has become weakened by *moist* heat before the smoke was able to exert its curing action. Smoke, therefore, makes the fish firmer and with heat dehydrates the food product. Try to find a good balance between the strength of the brine solution and the correct application of smoke. Don't use too much salt or leave the food in brine any longer than necessary; also, vary the smokehouse temperatures to prevent sudden cooking.

THE DRYING RACK

Atmospheric moisture can be detrimental to good results in the smokehouse. Cool, clear days are the best for smoking and drying. Avoid starting your fires during damp or rainy weather. Also dry the fish *completely* before placing it in the smokehouse. Do not expose it to direct sunlight—but dry it in a shaded breezy place. Use an electric fan if necessary. For semipermanent and permanent units, build a separate drying rack. The rack is simple to make. Use two boards, 2″ × 4″ × 8′. Lay them on ground 15 inches apart (inside dimension), and nail on two cross pieces, one at each end. This will look like a ladder without steps. At 9-inch intervals drive nails along each inside edge of the legs. The nails should be long enough to hold S-hooks which fish can be suspended from. S-hooks can be made from bailing wire. The rack should be leaned against a building or tree when the thin glossy skin or pellicle is formed. This may take about 2–3 hours depending on the amount of breeze and also upon the moisture content of the atmosphere.

THE SMOKEHOUSE

The smokehouse need not be elaborate. Excellent results can be obtained with a wooden barrel, an old oil drum, or even a converted icebox. Amateurs can buy portable outdoor smokers, small electric hotplate units,

or even convert the patio fireplace into a suitable smoking unit. Of course, a permanent cabinet-type smokehouse is preferable. Regardless of the structure, the unit must have vents to insure the proper circulation of smoke and fresh air. It must also have racks, trays, or hooks for holding the food in such a way that the smoke and heat will contact all surfaces evenly. Ventilation must be controlled carefully so the wood smoulders and smokes but does not flame. Excessive or sudden heat must be avoided. A thermometer inserted in a cork and suspended at the top of the smoking unit is necessary for the beginner. With experience you will be able to judge the correct temperatures. If the smoker has a hotplate, it should be grounded. This can be done by running a wire from the plate to a rod driven in the ground. All smokehouses "cook" differently due to their shape, material structure, and location of the fire. Therefore you may find it necessary to vary suggested heating cycles according to the results obtained. In general, the food to be smoked should be at least four feet away from a wood fire and at least two feet away from a sawdust or chip fire.

FUEL

The fire should be started at least an hour before the fish are put in the smokehouse. Two hours is better. Any nonresinous wood may be used as fuel in smoking. Oak, hickory, maple, and beech are preferred in the North, but on the seacoast old driftwood is commonly used. Alder, vine maple, and manzanita roots are favorite fuels in the West. In the Southern states, scrub oak, live oak, hickory, sweet bay, river mangrove, and palmetto roots are popular. Dry corn cobs make a good fuel, but the fire must be watched carefully or it will flare up and become too hot. This also applies to coconut husks in tropical and subtropical areas. All dry fruit woods, such as apple and cherry, make excellent fuel and give an especially fine flavor to fish. Hardwood sawdust and chips are easier to handle because they make a rich smoke and smoulder slower. However, there are two tricks worth knowing. You can maintain an even fire with a good smoking wood, such as maple, by adding a few charcoal briquets from time to time. Briquets burn for hours and require little attention. Or, you can combine two woods such as oak and hickory, or oak and maple. Oak produces excellent coals but a comparatively poor smoke. The addition of hickory or maple, which are both rich in smoke, results in an excellent fuel. Always remember to remove all bark and moss from old wood as these impart a bitter flavor to the food.

PREPARATION

It is important to clean and prepare fish properly before brining. The best results are obtained with fresh fish, although fish which have been frozen can be thawed and smoked provided all air has been excluded from the product during storage. Fish can be smoked whole, in chunks, or fillets. Small fish, such as brook trout or alewives, should be left whole, while larger species, such as salmon or king mackerel, should be smoked as fillets. If the fish are very large, then cut the fillets crosswise in large chunks. Fish which have a strongly aromatic skin, such as northern pike and barracuda, should be filleted and skinned. Both are superior smoked foods. In some cases with very small fish, such as herring and butterfish, it may be desirable to smoke them in the round without cutting. These fish can be gibbed. Gibbing consists of making a small cut just below the gills and pulling out the viscera (including the gills) with the thumb and forefinger. This leaves the belly portion uncut. Whether to leave the head on the fish or not depends on how you rack them in the smokehouse. Most small fish are easier to handle with the heads on even if spread on trays. They can also be hung on S-shaped iron hooks, which are in turn hung over sticks running from one side of the smokehouse to the other. If whole, they may also be hung on round wooden sticks, inserted under the gill flap and out of the mouth. When these sticks have been filled with fish, they are suspended from one side of the smokehouse to the other. If the fish are split, the smokehouse sticks may be two inches square with a line of nails driven through two sides at a 45-degree angle. The sides of the fish are hung on the nail points just below the bony neck plate, holding the fish open so that all the flesh surface will be smoked. Another method is to run ¼-inch iron rods through the fish just under the hard bony plate of the pectoral fin, one rod on each side. Thus each fish hangs from two rods. Twelve or more fish may be hung on a set of two rods 4 feet long. Fillets may be hung over three-sided sticks of wood, which rest on supports at each side of the smokehouse. Always remember when using trays to place the fish skin side down.

HOT SMOKING

This process may be used with any fish, but it is intended for foods that are to be eaten within a few days. The cold-smoking process is recommended for extended preservation. To hot smoke fish, split them along the back just above the backbone, leaving the belly solid, so that it will open in one piece. Scrape away all viscera, blood, and membranes. Wash thoroughly and soak in a brine solution made of one cup of salt to one gallon of water for thirty minutes to leach blood out of the flesh. Then prepare a brine in the following proportion of ingredients: 4 cups of salt, 2 cups of brown sugar, 2 tablespoons of crushed black pepper, and 2 tablespoons of crushed bay leaves to each gallon of water. The brine in which you now submerge the fish will inhibit the spoilage action of bacteria. It will also continue to remove blood and body fluids from the tissue and replace them with salt, which is a preservative. The fish are soaked in this brine for 2–4 hours, depending on their size and thickness, amount of fat, and the degree of cure wanted. After brining, rinse the fish in freshwater and hang in a cool, shady, breezy place for about three hours, or until a thin shiny skin or pellicle has formed on the surface. Then place them in the smokehouse. During the first four hours that the fish are in the smokehouse, the temperature should be kept low (about 110–120°). A dense smoke should then be built up. The temperature can then be leveled at 160–180° for the next four hours, at which point the fish should be finished. They have been completely cooked and flavored with smoke.

A discarded box smokehouse. Note vents for proper circulation of smoke and fresh air, hooks for holding food for smoking all surfaces evenly

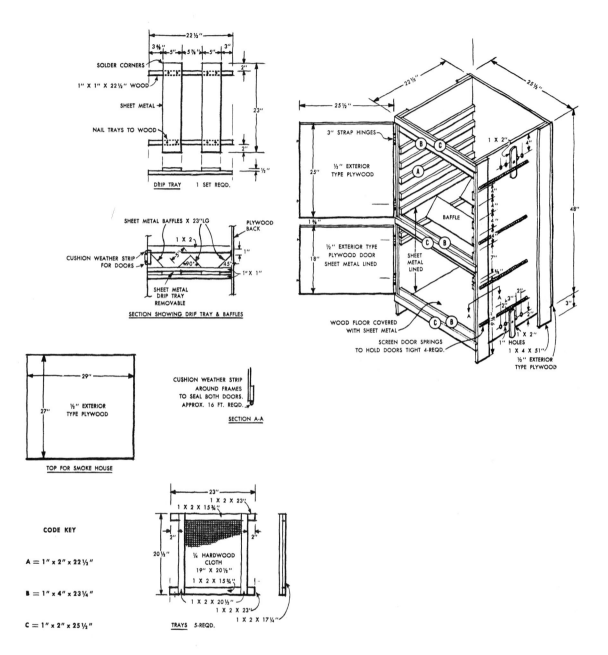

Plans for an Electric Smokehouse

HOT SMOKING—SHORT METHOD

This process is essentially the dry-salting method of smokery. In the opinion of many professionals it produces a better product than the leaching and brining method. It is used primarily for large saltwater fish such as king mackerel, barracuda, striped bass, and marlin. Split or fillet, and chunk the fish; then wash thoroughly to remove all blood and viscera. While the fish is still *wet*, sprinkle the flesh side with salt. The amount of salt used depends on the thickness of the fish. A chunk of

marlin 2–3 inches thick obviously requires more salt than a mackerel fillet. Get an even layer of salt of about ¹⁄₁₆-inch deep on the fish, and when it is completely absorbed (about one hour) the fish is ready for smoking. The dry-salted product requires 8–9 hours in a rich, dense smoke with the temperature leveled at 160–180°F.

Always set aside one fish to test in the smokehouse when processing a large number. It helps to keep a good smoke by stirring the fire with a stick once in awhile, and on these occasions you can sample the fish to see how it's coming along. Testing is important. You can judge whether your fire is going too fast and if the smoke is dense enough. Keep a small fish on hand for this purpose.

COLD SMOKING—DRY-SALT METHOD

To cold smoke fish, clean them thoroughly and place them in a brine of one cup of salt to one gallon of water, and leach for thirty minutes. Remove fish from the brine and rinse in freshwater. Drain off all surplus moisture. Next place each fish in a shallow wooden box or tub of fine salt (Morton's Iodized table salt is the best for fish smokery) and dredge. Pick up the fish with as much salt as will cling to them and place in even layers in a second box. Scatter a small amount of salt between each layer. Leave the fish in salt for 6–12 hours—6 hours if split and therefore having a more absorptive surface, or 12 hours if whole or in the round. After the fish are taken from the salt, rinse them in freshwater and leave to dry in a shady place until the pellicle is formed. This should take about three hours under average conditions. If fish are placed in the smokehouse while still moist, the time required is longer. The color will not be as good as the fish will steam and soften in the smoke.

The principle of cold smoking is to dry out the product with warm smoke at temperatures not exceeding 90°F. This may take 1–5 days. The fire must not produce too much smoke during the first 12 hours if the total curing period is to be 24 hours, or for the first 24 hours if the curing period is longer. Check the thermometer occasionally. If you do not have a thermometer, a rule-of-thumb test is to insert your hand in the smokehouse, and if the air feels distinctly warm, the temperature is too high. When the first curing phase of the process is completed, a dense smoke should be maintained. If the fish are to be kept for two weeks, they should be smoked for twenty-four hours; if for a longer time, smoking may require five days. Smoking need not be a continuous day-and-night process, but it should be completed as rapidly as possible.

COLD SMOKING—BRINE METHOD

This differs from the dry-salt process only in so far as the fish are placed in a brine solution of 1 pound of salt, ½ pound of brown sugar, and ½ ounce of saltpeter for 12 hours. Do not wash, but drain and dry thoroughly before placing in smokehouse. Follow the same heat cycle as described for the cold-smoking, dry-salt method.

EMERGENCY METHOD OF SMOKING FISH

You can usually find enough cast-off materials around campsites to build a crude smoker—barrels or pieces of galvanized sheeting to form the house and screening or wire mesh to make trays. With a little ingenuity some very workable units may be manufactured. However, for anglers in out-camps who have absolutely nothing to start with, the following method is practical:

Split the fish along the backbone so they can be spread open like a kite. Score the skin side longitudinally with ¼-inch-deep cuts and 1 inch apart. After washing thoroughly and wiping dry, rub the fish with a mixture of 1 pound of salt to 1 ounce of pepper. Store the fish in a cool place overnight, and rinse them thoroughly the next

morning. If you can't find any material to build a tray or S-hooks, weave a rack with green sticks across the back of each fish to hold them open (these can be pointed and passed through the skin). Leave the fish in a breezy, shady place until surface moisture has dried and the pellicle is formed. In the meantime, dig a shallow fire pit of about three feet in diameter, and start the fire while the fish are still drying so a good bed of coals is created. Fasten each racked fish to a pointed pole 3–4 feet long. The pointed end should be thrust into the ground so that the stick hangs over the fire pit at an angle. Next make a tripod of poles over the pit which are higher than the smoke sticks. Around the tripod you can place a tarpaulin (which can be kept wet to prevent burning), or a thick thatching of green boughs or any other material you can find which will serve to hold the smoke down. Process the fish for 6–18 hours depending on their size and the efficiency of the "smokehouse." After cooling, the fish should be stored in a dry place. They will remain in good condition for about a week or more in Northern climates.

YOUR OWN RECIPES

There is a variety of flavorings which can be added to smoked foods, such as onion, garlic, Tabasco, or pepper according to the tastes of the family. However, some of the foods that you try which are not generally considered by the amateur are razor clams, oysters, and shrimp. Peel the shrimp while raw, sprinkle generously with salt, and smoke for about 90 minutes. Be sure to make plenty of them because they go fast. You can also smoke needle-fish, bar jack, mullet, and other small nongamefish. One of the best smoked fish on the market is smoked carp. And don't overlook catfish or smoked eels. The following are some basic recipes for smoked fish, which can be elaborated on as you see fit:

Smoked Fish in Milk

3 pounds *smoked fish*
1 cup whole *milk* or *cream*
3 tablespoons *butter* or good cooking *oil*
pepper and *salt* if needed

If the fish have been heavily salted before smoking, freshen one hour or more before cooking. Drain, dry, and place skin side down on a greased baking pan or skillet. Pour over the milk, adding butter and pepper and cook slowly in oven, or over slow fire for 8–12 minutes. Remove to platter, and pour the liquid about the fish. Garnish with parsley.

Smoked Fish Soufflé

2 *eggs*, yolks and whites beaten separately
2 cups cooked *rice*
1½ cups *milk*
1 cup cold, cooked, *smoked-fish flakes*
2 tablespoons *fat*
salt, pepper, paprika

Beat egg yolks until thick and lemon-colored. Add fish flakes, milk, rice, butter, and seasonings. Blend. Fold in carefully the stiff-beaten egg whites. Pour into a greased baking dish, set dish in a pan of hot water, and bake three-quarters of an hour at 350°F. Serve with or without a tasty fish sauce.

Smoked Fish Croquettes

2 cups of *fish flakes*
1 cup of mashed *potatoes*, either hot or cold
1½ teaspoon *salt*
⅛ teaspoon *pepper*
2 *eggs* (Use one in croquette mixture and one in which to dip croquette when crumbing)
1 clove *garlic* mashed and rubbed over the mixing bowl if desired
Bread crumbs

Combine potatoes, salt, pepper, fish flakes and eggs, well beaten. Mix thoroughly, and form into croquettes. Roll in fine bread crumbs, then in beaten egg to which water has been added, or thinned canned milk; drain and roll in bread crumbs again. Fry in deep, hot cooking oil or fat at 390°F, until browned. Drain and serve hot.

SALMON AND LARGE TROUT

Atlantic, chinook, and silver salmon as well as steelhead and lake trout can be smoked by the following method which is shorter than cold smoking but a bit longer than hot smoking. This method also produces an appetizing product from king mackerel, small sailfish, and dolphin.

The fish must be split in two, removing the backbone. To do this the shoulder of the salmon is forced down on a sharp-pointed nail protruding from the cleaning board to prevent slipping. Short incisions are made under the anal fin and just above and below the backbone. With the upper lug or shoulder of the fish held by the left hand, enter the knife at the shoulder above the backbone, holding the blade steady with the edge at a slight downward angle touching the bone, and take the whole side off with one sweep of the knife. To remove the second side, a cut is made at the shoulder just under the backbone. With the edge of the knife blade resting against the backbone at a slight upward angle, one sweep of the knife down to the base of the tail separates the backbone from the flesh without removing the fish from the nail.

Both pieces are then washed thoroughly, trimmed of any ragged edges and any blood clots. Blood remaining along the belly cavity is removed by pressing it toward the back either with the fingers or the blade of a knife. If the blood is not removed, it will harden and discolor the flesh. The sides are then placed in a tub of 90% salinometer brine (a saturated salt solution), chilled with ice. This removes diffused blood, makes the sides a little firmer, and stops oil from oozing out of the flesh. The fish should remain in the brine for 60–90 minutes.

The slabs are then drained for 15–20 minutes. A shallow box is filled with a salting mixture made in the following proportions: 2 pounds salt, 1 pound brown sugar, 1 ounce saltpeter, 1 ounce white pepper, 1 ounce crushed bay leaves, 1 ounce crushed allspice, 1 ounce crushed cloves, and 1 ounce crushed mace. This amount should be enough for about twenty pounds of fish. The salmon is placed in the box, one side at a time, and dredged in the mixture which is also rubbed lightly into the flesh. The sides are then packed in a tub or other suitable container, with as much of the curing mixture as will cling to the flesh. A loose-fitting cover is placed on top and weighted down.

The fish are left here for 8–12 hours, then rinsed and scrubbed to remove all traces of the mixture. The sides are fixed on hangers and dried in the air for about 6 hours. If air-drying conditions are unfavorable, fans may be used. Hang the fish in the smokehouse, and smoke in a gentle heat (not more than 100°F) for 8 hours. Build up a dense smoke, and continue the cure for 16–24 hours at temperatures not higher than 70°F. To obtain a product with the maximum of preservation, the second part of the smoking period should be 48 hours. The fish should be allowed to cool for several hours before handling, then brushed with vegetable oil and stored in a cool, dry place.

Dry-Salt Scotch Method Scotch-smoked salmon is uniquely different, and this method may be applied to other kinds of fish, such as lake trout, inconnu, and large lake whitefish. The salmon is first split (halved) from head to tail and the backbone removed. The two slabs should then be laid skin side down in large pans or on boards. They are then completely covered with a salt preparation composed of 7 parts salt, 1 part saltpeter, and 1 part brown sugar. No flesh should show through the salt. Let the salmon stand in a cool place for 24 hours to marinate. Rinse the slabs gently in cold water for 10 minutes; then hang them on hooks to dry for 6 hours, or until the pellicle forms. Smoke heavily in applewood chips or other suitable woods, such as maple or birch, for 6–8 hours. Remove from smokehouse and let firm for 48 hours.   —A.J.McC.

SMOOTH BUTTERFLY RAY *Gymnura micrura* This distinctive ray is recognized by its very broad disk which is much wider than long, forming a diamond shape. At all stages the tail is very short, and this species has a keel on the upper surface and there is no tail spine, the latter characteristic distinguishing it from the spiny butterfly ray (*which see*). It is usually classified with the stingray family, although some ichthyologists prefer to retain it in a separate family. Color varies from gray, brown, or light green above with small spots and wormlike markings of a lighter and darker color than the background. The tail is pale with 3–4 dark crossbars, and the ventral color of the disc is white with grayish, yellowish, or rosy hues. Characteristic of this species is its ability to vary its color depending on its background. About 4 feet is the maximum width.

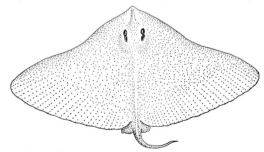

Smooth Butterfly Ray

LIFE HISTORY

It ranges regularly from Brazil to Chesapeake Bay, drifting northward as far as southern New England. Sand bottoms of shallow, coastal waters are its favorite haunt, from a few feet to as deep as about 150 feet. It occurs in warm, shallow waters during the late spring and summer,

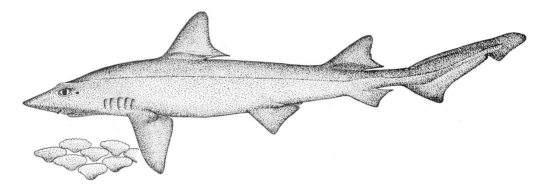

Smooth Dogfish, Showing Tooth Structure

moving offshore into deepwater with the advent of winter temperatures. At home in brackish waters or in full-strength seawater, it forages the flats for fish, crabs, shrimps, and clams.

Young are born from late May to August in the northern parts of its range and throughout the year in tropical waters. Maturity occurs at about 2 feet wide, and the young, resembling the parents in shape, are 6–9 inches. Its flesh is good, and is eaten in French Guiana, while the wings are used as bait in crab pots in the Chesapeake area. —D.dS.

SMOOTH DOGFISH *Mustelus canis* One of the most common sharks in the United States, this small species is well-known to anglers who catch large numbers during the summer months. It has a slender body, the pectoral fins are long, and the first and second dorsal fins are large and are about equal in size. The teeth are flat and low, without sharp points. It is gray or brown above, depending on the type of bottom, with pale coloration beneath. This widespread species is taken from Cape Cod, Massachusetts, to Texas, Bermuda, the Caribbean, and Uruguay. Several closely related species occur in the Caribbean and the western South Atlantic. Five feet is the maximum size, but most taken by anglers are about 2 feet long.

LIFE HISTORY

It is a bottom dweller, commonly found in depths less than 60 feet, but they are taken at times as deep as 80–90 fathoms. It enters mouths of bays and estuaries, occasionally entering freshwater. There seem to be several relatively isolated populations of dogfish along the Atlantic Coast. A northerly migration occurs in the spring, a southerly drift in fall, and the winter is spent in deepwater off the Carolinas.

The reproductive period is in early July, and gestation takes about ten months. The young are about a foot long at birth. Sexual maturity occurs at about 3 feet. Crabs and lobsters are eaten, as are squid and fish, predominantly menhaden and tautog. Collectively, the large schools of dogfish account for vast amounts of the valuable food supply of the sea. Historically, because of their abundance, this species and the spiny dogfish (*which see*) have been staple animals for biological supply houses. —D.dS.

SMOOTH HAMMERHEAD *Sphyrna zygaena* It is easily recognized from its relatives by the combination of a slightly convex anterior margin of the head, which is not indentured; the high, erect dorsal fin; and the smooth edges to the teeth, which are serrated only weakly and irregularly. The color is dark olive to brownish-gray

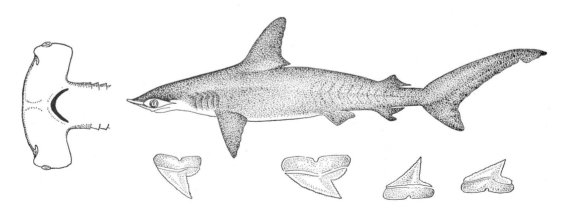

Smooth Hammerhead (ventral view of head and upper teeth *left*, lower teeth *right*)

above and gray-white beneath. The fin tips are dusky, and the pectorals are often black-tipped. It grows to 13 feet and to a weight of at least 900 pounds. As with other hammerheads, because of uncertainties of field identification, several species may be confused with information on the smooth hammerhead. It has been recorded from the tropical parts of the Atlantic, and this species is believed to occur in the eastern Pacific and throughout the Indo-Pacific. It is widespread in the tropical western Atlantic, and has been reported at various localities from Cape Cod to northern Argentina and the northern Gulf of Mexico. A spectacular northward migration is undertaken each summer, and they occur in large numbers at various coastal points during this migration. Most of these migrants are less than 6 feet, but some of 12 feet have been recorded during this coastal movement.

Eggs are apparently hatched within the mother, and the young are born alive. As with other hammerheads, this species is very prolific, producing upwards of forty embryos at a time. Adults occur in shallow water or far out to sea, although it is more of a coastal species than the mako and its relatives. Specimens commonly enter bays and there is a report of a hammerhead from tidal freshwater in Maryland. They eat fish, including stingrays, mackerel, porgies, and other sharks, as well as squids, and shrimp, crabs, and other crustaceans.

DANGER TO MAN

This is a strong-swimming shark which has been known to attack boats and man. Their skin makes a good leather and the flesh has been used for meal and oil.   —D.dS.

SMOOTH PUFFER *Lagocephalus laevigatus* Also known as rabbitfish, the smooth puffer is distributed on both sides of the Atlantic. In the western Atlantic it ranges from Massachusetts south to Argentina, including the Gulf of Mexico. This puffer is distinguished from other Tetraodontidae in its geographical range by its smooth skin (only the belly has short prickles), large dorsal and anal fins, and the concave caudal fin. The smooth puffer is not able to expand its body as greatly as the northern or southern puffers, possibly because of its larger size. It may grow to 2 feet and 7 pounds.

The color is greenish-gray above, silvery on the sides, and white on the belly. The fins are dusky.

FOOD VALUE

Although this puffer attains a fair size, it has no angling value. It is most often caught in shallow channels while bottom-fishing. The "rabbitfish" is considered a table delicacy, however, and is usually cut in half across the body. The rear or tail section contains firm white meat which can be rolled in corn meal and panfried or deep-fried. As with all puffers, care should be used in cleaning the fish, and no part of the fish other than the tail section should be eaten.   —D.K.C.

SNAIL An organism that typically possesses a coiled shell and crawls on a single muscular foot. Air-breathing snails, called pulmonates, do not have gills but typically obtain oxygen through a "lung" or pulmonary cavity. At variable intervals most pulmonate snails come to the surface of the water for a fresh supply of air. Gill-breathing snails possess an internal gill through which dissolved oxygen is removed from the surrounding water.

SNAIL CAT A regional name for the green bullhead (*which see*) and the spotted bullhead (*which see*).

SNAILS as Fish Parasites *See* Diseases and Parasites

SNAKE EELS Family Ophichthidae These snake eels are related to the morays (*which see*), but from which they differ in lacking rays at the tip of the tail, which ends in a horny point. The tail projects beyond the dorsal and anal fins, and the posterior nostril is placed on the edge of the upper lip, while the anterior nostril is usually a small tube placed near the snout tip. The tongue is attached to the floor of the mouth. The body is elongate and sinuous, and the skin lacks scales.

There are about forty species in the family in the Western Hemisphere. One of the common species, the sharptail eel, *Myrichthys acuminatus*, has a pointed tail, blunt teeth, and a series of round, yellowish-orange blotches covering the olive to greenish body. They are commonly seen about coral reefs, or, in particular, over grass beds or detritus where suitable burrows can be made. Secretive in habits, they are commonly mistaken for sea snakes (*which see*), from which they can be distinguished at a glance in their pointed tail. Sea snakes have the tail flattened, and are generally banded, besides differing in many anatomical details. The sharptail eel is found from southern Florida to the Lesser Antilles, along shallow reefs, turtlegrass beds, and occasionally in deeper water. It grows to about 2½ feet.

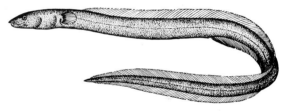

Snake Eel

ECONOMIC VALUE

Snake eels have been found in stomachs of tuna, barracuda, and groupers. Those eaten by groupers often bore through the stomach into the body cavity, where they dry up and resemble mummies.   —D.dS.

SNAPPER *See* Blackfin Snapper, Black Snapper, Cubera Snapper, Dog Snapper, Glasseye Snapper, Gray Snapper, Hogfish, Lane Snapper, Mahogany Snapper, Mutton Snapper, Red Snapper, Schoolmaster, Silk Snapper, Yellowtail Snapper. Also a regional name in the northeastern United States for the young bluefish (*which see*)

SNOOK *Centropomus undecimalis* An important marine gamefish. In the United States, this species occurs in most of Florida and also in southwestern Texas. As a stray, it has been reported from as far north as Delaware. The snook is found throughout the American tropics on the Atlantic and Pacific sides. This is, by far, the largest and most common species of snook. One of the heaviest specimens on record measured 4 feet 7 inches in total length and weighed 50 pounds and 8 ounces. A related species, the black snook (*which see*) occurs on the Pacific side of tropical America.

The snook is long-bodied but thick through the middle, with the upper snout depressed and a protruding lower

Snook, 6-pound Male, Florida Bay, Florida

jaw. The color is variable according to habitat, but is usually a brownish or brown-gold on the back shading to a lighter color on the belly; it has a pronounced black lateral stripe along the sides which extends to the tail. Lateral scales 67–78. Gillrakers 7–10, usually 8–9 on lower limb of first arch, not including rudiments. Anal rays 6. Pectoral rays 14–16, usually 15. Second anal spine not reaching to vertical from caudal base. Pectoral fin not reaching to vertical from tip of pelvic. Pelvic fin not reaching to anus. Maxillary reaching to or beyond vertical from center of eye.

This species is distinguished from the other Atlantic snooks by the fewer gillrakers, the shorter second anal spine, and the pelvic fins not reaching to the anus.

HABITS

This snook occurs along the coast in saltwater, in addition to bays, estuaries, canals, and the lower course of streams. Small, immature individuals, less than a year old, usually occur in the marginal areas of coastal lagoons and estuaries. Adults may occur well inland, in waters generally regarded as fresh, or in saltwater relatively far from estuaries.

The common snook feeds primarily on fishes, but crustaceans are also an important food item. The spawning season extends from June to November. This species may reach the age of at least 7 years, and nearly all specimens are mature by their third year of life. The common snook, and probably the other species of snook also, is very sensitive to cold. The minimum temperature tolerance is about 60°F.　　　　　　　　　　—L.R.

TACKLE FOR SNOOK

Snook are caught on nylon, feather, and bucktail jigs, especially in chilly weather when the fish stay in deep holes. They will also take spinners and spoons at times, although metal baits are not very popular in Florida. Virtually all of the *Field & Stream* prizewinners are hooked on a plug or live mullet. Whether you prefer bait-casting or the spinning rod, there are a number of things both methods have in common, beginning with the rod itself. It must have a stiff tip. A limber rod just won't handle the plug correctly, nor will it have enough rigidity to set the hook. You can't make the lure get up and dance with a willowy stick, and when a snook wolfs the plug, you must hit the fish hard. All synthetic lines are elastic, and if the tip doesn't have considerable backbone, the barbs won't penetrate. The ideal bait-casting or spinning rod is somewhat heavier than you would use for freshwater bass. And it should be a bit longer for better lure control; a great deal of snook fishing occurs at a time when strong breezes are blowing, and it's difficult to keep slack out of the line in a cross-wind unless you can get elevation. A 6½-foot casting rod, or a 7–7½-foot spinning rod is about right for openwater and big surface plugs. Back in narrow mangrove creeks where short, accurate casts are the rule, you can switch to ordinary bass tackle. The reel should be a heavy-duty spinning mill or one of the service bait-casting reels designed for line in the 18-pound-test class. In either case, it must have a smooth drag and an ample cranking radius so you can wind at top speed without dislocating your wrist. Small freshwater reels will do the job but not comfortably.

When casting in shallow water on open flats or along the mangrove banks, most anglers favor surface-disturbing plugs. These are mainly cigar-shaped lures with or without a propeller aft, which have no inherent action of their own. Darter-type plugs are probably second in popularity, then various kinds of poppers all of which are worked a bit faster and more erratically than you would handle them on bass. For deepwater casting around bridges, channels, and inlets a plug with a metal lip to make it dive and wobble is very effective, as are straight, flashing plugs retrieved with snappy jerks of the rod tip. These lures are usually silver in color, with some red, blue, or green trim generally suggesting a mullet or other baitfish.

RETRIEVING THE PLUG

Speed of retrieve is most important in snook fishing. The basic technique in surface plugging is called the "whip." After the cast is made, the angler works his lure back with violent sweeps of the rod, causing it to dart erratically over the water. You can sometimes catch snook by reeling slowly with a darting plug or popping a hollow-nosed bait at a medium speed, but day after day the whip retrieve accounts for more fish than any other technique. A skilled snook caster gets his cigar-shaped bait swimming rapidly with a rolling side-to-side motion so that it barely pauses with each jerk of the tip. This is hard work. When done right, your hands will be cramped after 2–3 hours of fishing. Underwater plugs can be retrieved somewhat slower, but they should achieve that same dart-pause-dart posture. Lure manipulation is the key to the whole game, and the best way to learn it is to watch a veteran snook angler on location.

Casting from bridges at night is quite different because of the tide flow and depth. The trick in fishing a plug in the dark from a bridge is to know where the pilings are, and then to cast "upstream" or against the tide. Always fish from that side of a bridge that faces the flow. The cast should be made at an angle that allows the plug to swim downcurrent and swing under the span somewhere near the pilings. Actually, the tide gives the plug its motion and speed. You only have to retrieve fast enough to keep slack out of the line and lead the lure to the snook. Bridge-casting requires heavy tackle (30-pound-test) because the fish have to be walked off the span and beached.

THE CORRECT LEADER

An important factor in plug manipulation is the leader size. It would be ideal to eliminate wire entirely; however, a length of stainless steel or carbon steel is necessary to hold big fish. A snook's teeth are no more apparent than those of a bass, but the edges of its gill covers are so sharp that they'll cut a line instantly. Too, the snook lives and feeds around oyster bars and shell-encrusted roots where 18-pound-test casting line pops like thread. Even with a wire leader you'll still lose fish because some of them will burrow way back in the mangroves.

The choice of a wire depends on where you'll be fishing. Florida east-coast anglers prefer a No. 6 stainless steel (58-pound-test) in a 24-inch length. This is for the *big* snook in the 25–35-pound class. Specialists use this 24-inch leader on underwater plugs only; for surface baits they will cut back to 6–8 inches. The longer length makes a topwater plug nose heavy, and you can't make it get up and shake. Twist the wire directly to the eye of the plug and eliminate snap swivels. Also use braided line in preference to monofilament because at 18-pound-test the latter sinks too quickly and spoils the lure action. In regions where snook do not often run over 15 pounds use a No. 3 stainless steel (32-pound-test) wire of 12 inches in length on both topwater and sinking plugs.

IMPORTANCE OF TIDE

The ideal in snook fishing is to have visible targets. Sometimes you'll see them cruising on the flats or in canals making humps in the surface as they push water. Or you'll see them smash into schools of baitfish. But most of the time one must fish blind—casting at the mouths of creeks, back up in mangroove pockets, into the holes on the downtide side of sandbars and oyster bars, and the deep spots at the edge of a current. The shelving points of islands are also productive. However, much depends on the stage of the tide in relation to the area you are fishing. As a rule a high, falling tide is considered best for both snook and tarpon around river mouths and along coastal shores, and a flooding or rising tide at the creek heads. Plan to arrive at the fishing grounds one hour before high, and look for the best fishing during the first two hours of the ebb. Falling water pulls baitfish out of the roots and into holes where big snook can get at them. A dead low tide might be productive for the same reason in areas where there are channels and cuts deep enough to hold gamefish. Creek heads, on the other hand, are usually quite shallow, and the fish will move in on the rising water for a feast of crabs or mullet, then drop back. It all seems to boil down to the availability of cover and food; in shoreline casting a high falling tide provides optimum conditions. For this reason a competent guide will keep his client on the move, fishing the "holes" in a pattern corresponding to the tidal flow. It's not unusual to cover twenty miles in the course of a day—and enjoy fast fishing at each stop. *See also* Black Snook, Florida, Little Snook, Saltwater Fly Fishing, Swordspine Snook, Tarpon Snook

—A.J.McC

SNOWY GROUPER *Epinephelus niveatus* A deepwater grouper occurring in southern Florida and throughout the tropical American Atlantic. The common name refers to the snow-white, round body spots of the young. Large adults are called "golden grouper" and may reach a total length of 4 feet.

The snowy grouper has 11 dorsal spines; 13–14 dorsal rays, usually 14; 9 anal rays; and 18 pectoral rays, rarely

Snowy Grouper

19. Posterior nostril much larger than the anterior. Insertion of pelvic fin under, or in advance of, upper end of pectoral base. Posterior margin of caudal fin convex (young), straight or slightly concave (adult). Body with white spots in longitudinal and vertical rows. Top of caudal peduncle with a black, saddlelike blotch. These color marks gradually disappear with age and are absent in specimens over 15 inches in total length.

The enlarged posterior nostril distinguishes this grouper from the others, except the misty grouper (*which see*). The latter, however, has an entirely different color pattern.

HABITS

Adults are taken on rocky bottom along the edge of the Continental Shelf, at depths usually around 80–120 fathoms. Large adults have been taken in 250 fathoms, probably a depth record for grouper. Juveniles and young occur in water as shallow as 50 feet.

ANGLING VALUE

Since it occurs mostly in water that is very deep, this grouper has little angling value. It provides, however, an unforgettable experience when taken on a wire line. It is taken on handlines by West Indian fishermen.

A food fish in some of the Greater Antilles but rarely seen in the markets. —L.R.

SNYDER, GEORGE *See under* Bait-Casting (Development of Bait-Casting Reels)

SOCKEYE SALMON *Oncorhynchus nerka* The species is the most commercially valuable of the Pacific salmon (*which see*), but it is second to the pink salmon in landings at United States ports. It is highly prized for its high oil content, excellent flavor, color of flesh, and rather uniform size.

Its distinguishing characteristics include a small number of gillrakers and minute spots on the back. Mature males often become bright red on the body, females dirty olive to light red, darker on sides than in the male. Young with parr marks extending to near the lateral line.

Sockeye Salmon

LIFE HISTORY

It is found from Japan to California, but enters rivers south of the Columbia River only as a stray. It enters rivers, usually those that are fed by lakes, in March to July with some variation in time. A few spawn in streams without lakes. Spawning takes place in lakes or immediately adjacent in inlet or outlet streams from August to December. Most of the adults are 4–6 years old, but some reach 8 years of age. The young spend 1–3 years in lakes, migrating to the ocean in March to May. Some fish enter the sea as fry. Some sockeye races are nonmigratory and

are known as kokanee (*which see*), which are widely popular among sportsmen because they are often abundant, easy to catch, and delicious to eat. Some sockeyes of sea-run stock have been known to live their whole lives in freshwater. Vast numbers of fish utilize a relatively small area in spawning. For example, the optimal number of fish utilizing the outlet of Chilko Lake in British Columbia is 500,000 over a 3¾-mile reach of the stream, covering 269 acres or roughly 2 square yards per fish.

Food of the sockeye in the ocean consists of euphausiids and other small crustaceans. As kokanee the species subsists largely on water fleas and copepods.

Weight at maturity is 5–7 pounds, maximal weight recorded is 15½ pounds. The kokanee has a wide range in length at maturity, dependent upon freshwater food supplies, varying from 4–24 inches. —J.R.

SOCORRO JACK *Carangoides orthogrammus* This eastern Pacific species is very similar to *Carangoides ferdau* reported from the Hawaiian Islands, and further study may show them to be identical.

There is a scaleless area on the chest, just in front of the pelvic fins of the socorro jack (similar to that of the crevalle, *Caranx hippos*, but lacking the small, central patch of scales that distinguishes the crevalle). The dorsal- and anal-fin lobes are relatively long but decrease in proportional length with growth of the fish (the dorsal-fin lobe is longer than the head in specimens less than about 14 inches in length).

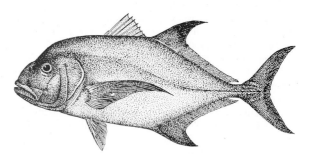

Socorro Jack

The second dorsal fin has one spine and 29–31 softrays. The anal fin has two detached spines (which are overgrown by skin in larger specimens), followed by one spine and 23–26 softrays. The first gill arch has 8–10 gillrakers on the upper limb and 20–23 gillrakers on the lower limb. There are about 22–33 pointed scutes in the straight lateral line. The color is basically silvery and dusky, and darker above, usually with dark fins. Live fish have about 3–13 brightly contrasting yellow spots on each side.

The socorro jack is known from the Revillagigedo Islands (Socorro and Clarion), the Tres Marías Islands, and at Cape San Lucas, Baja California. The largest specimen recorded is 25 inches in total length.

The life history is not known. The smallest specimen preserved is 10½ inches long.

ANGLING VALUE

These fish are not commonly caught, but they are very strong fighters. Several were caught fishing with cut squid on the bottom in about 100 feet of water at the Tres Marías Islands. —F.H.B.

SOFTRAY *See* Ray (Fin Ray)

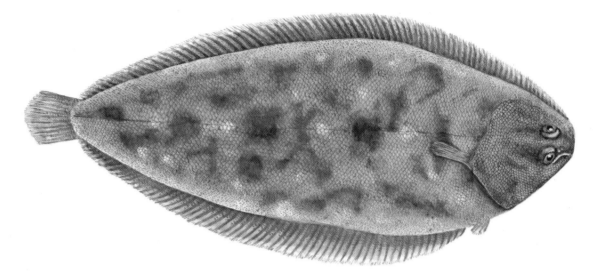

Common Sole

SOLE (1) Any of a number of flatfish in the Bothidae, Pleuronectidae, and Soleidae. Due to the popularity of sole as a food fish and its long history as a gourmet item in Europe the word has been rather widely applied, to the extent that Dover sole and English sole are accepted common names for two Pacific flounders which bear no resemblance to the British original. Other species, such as the summer flounder and yellowtail flounder, are sometimes marketed as "sole" at the retail level. Of the four true soles (Soleidae) found in western Atlantic waters—the hogchoker, lined, naked, and scrawled soles—none attain a size of commercial value. *See also* Butter Sole, Curlfin Sole, Dover Sole, English Sole, Hogchoker, Petrale Sole, Rex Sole, Rock Sole, Sand Sole, Yellowfin Sole

(2) Solea vulgaris A common European marine flatfish, lying on its left side. The true or common sole is of a characteristic oval shape, with both nostrils on the blind left side. The upper or right side is yellowish-brown overall, with darker brown blotches. The mouth curves downward, a noticeable characteristic. The pectoral fins are equally well developed on both blind and upper sides. Diagnostic scale and fin-ray counts are as follows: dorsal-fin rays: 73–90; anal-fin rays: 61–74; lateral line scales: 130–160.

The caudal fin is small, only $\frac{1}{8}$–$\frac{1}{11}$ the total body length. Both dorsal and anal fins have a thin white border.

Confusingly, several other European flatfish are commonly called "soles," or may be mistaken for the true sole. The variety of names and misnomers undoubtedly reflects the value placed on soles and related fishes as food. However, some characteristics may readily distinguish common and other "soles."

The French sole (*Pegusa lascaris*) has large pectoral fins like the true sole, but only one nostril on the blind left side. Fin-ray counts are: dorsal 78–79, anal 67–81. Another sole, the thickback sole (*Microchirus variegatus*), has small pectoral fins and a banded, rather than a blotched upper side. Fin-ray counts of the thickback sole are: dorsal 65–74, anal 55–58.

A diminutive "sole," the solenette, may be mistaken for a young *S. solea.* The solenette is variously known scientifically as *Solea lutea* or *Buglossidium luteum.* It rarely exceeds 5 inches long, has small pectoral fins, a dappled upper surface, and every fifth ray of its fins is dark-tinged. The counts of those fins are: dorsal 65–72, anal 50–56. The lateral line scale count is 72. (*See also* Common Sole)

Commercial fish dealers have invented various "sole" names to sell other species under the same or similar names. The name "Lemon Sole" is commonly used for the lemon dab (*Microstomus kitt*) or for the French sole. In Irish fish-trading circles the witch flounder (*Glyptocephalus cynoglossus*) is sometimes known as the "white sole." The name "Dover Sole" is also used for the common sole in British fish stores. This name has an historical background: It arose when enterprising fish dealers in the days of horse transport arranged fast carriage for fish from the south coast of England to the main Billingsgate Fish Market in London. Naturally these soles were extra-fresh in comparison with sea fish carried by slower means in those days; and, as many were landed at the port of Dover, the name "Dover Sole" became synonymous at Billingsgate with prime fresh south-coast soles. Equally naturally, all dealers jumped on the bandwagon, and soon any fresh sole, regardless of origin, was called a "Dover" sole.

The soles as a group are among the most specialized of flatfish, and are mostly a tropical or warmwater group. In Europe the common sole ranges from the Mediterranean up to the latitude of Denmark on the eastern Atlantic.

Soles normally live in water between 30 and 200 feet deep, preferring the deeper water in winter and the shallower inshore waters in summer. The bottom soles prefer sand or coarse mud broken with rocky ground.

Its habits are moderately inactive, as it mostly feeds by night and rests by day, relying on color camouflage for protection. The hunting habit is unusual; it skims slowly over the bottom on the tips of its anal and dorsal fins, with its head slightly raised. Beneath its head trail many sensitive villi or barbules with which it explores the bottom as it moves. When it finds food it drops its head and grabs it with the peculiar down-curving mouth, which is obviously specialized to perform this act. It is not surprising, therefore, that the food of soles is almost entirely composed of worms, starfish, and occasional bottom-living fishes, such as gobies.

The usual length of soles taken to market is 12–20 inches, reaching a weight of up to 5 pounds.

LIFE HISTORY

Soles spawn in spring and late summer in water over 30 feet deep. Like those of other flatfish, sole eggs float for dispersal. They are 1–1½ mm in diameter, and can be distinguished when found in plankton hauls by the divided yolk and multiple oil droplets. The female sole lays about 130,000 eggs per pound of body weight.

The eggs hatch in 10 days or so into a black and yellow normal-shaped fish of 3½ mm long. At a length of about ½ inch (around 12 mm) the young soles move into shallower water, turn onto their left sides; their eyes migrate over to the right; and they metamorphose into typical baby flatfish. From this point they grow into mature adults at about 8–9 inches long for males, and 9–10 inches long for females.

ANGLING VALUE

Soles are most commonly taken inshore in summer in June and July. Movements of the fish during this their spawning period make soles "in" or "out" in any given area. It is fished for with light tackle on the sandy bottoms it prefers, using a running lead stopped by a swivel 2–3 feet above the fine-wire, long-shank No. 4 or 6 hook, the "leger" rig so effective with many species of flatfish. The line need not be in excess of 10-pounds test, even from a pier.

They are said to be nocturnal feeders, but in fact good bags can be had on dull or hazy summer days with a "soft" light. The bait is invariably a marine worm presented on the bottom, threaded carefully up the shank of the hook to cover it. As soles rear up and "pounce" on their food the first indication should not be struck. Slack line should be given, and a firmer tug is the signal. They are extremely slippery in the hand and perform contortions while being unhooked.

Taken on suitable light tackle, a day's sport when the fish are "in" is a most restful form of angling. Normally soles are not sought deliberately, but are taken on the bottom hooks of the multihook "paternoster" rigs sold to holiday anglers in seaside towns.　　　—D.M.

SOLENOID An electrical switch which can be operated by remote control.

SOUPFIN SHARK *Galeorhinus zyopterus* This famous commercial shark is characterized by a pointed snout, a slightly concave head, a large first dorsal fin, and teeth which are notched on the outer edge below the point. The body is deepest at about the middle of the body, tapering sharply to the snout and tail. The second dorsal fin is directly above the anal fin and about the same size, in contrast to the small anal fin of the brown smoothhound (*which see*). The color is dark or dusky-gray to blue above, shading to pale on the lower parts, with black edges on the anterior parts of the dorsal, pectoral, and caudal fins. It grows to about 6½ feet and 100 pounds, the females growing slightly larger than the males.

LIFE HISTORY

Found from British Columbia to southern California, it is thought to be identical with a species taken in the eastern Atlantic and Mediterranean, both coasts of South America, and the central, western, and South Pacific. They are taken down to depths of 225 fathoms. Males are more common in northern California, females being more common, in shallow water, in the southern part of the state. Males mature at about 5 feet, and females mature at a somewhat larger size. The eggs are hatched within the female, the total gestation period being about a year, and an average of about thirty-five young is produced in each litter. The soupfin eats predominantly fish, including flounders, salmon, rockfish, sardines, mackerel, barracuda, and squid. An extensive commercial fishery was formerly conducted for the liver of this species in California, but this is not as intensive as formerly as a result of the synthesis of vitamin A.

—D. dS.

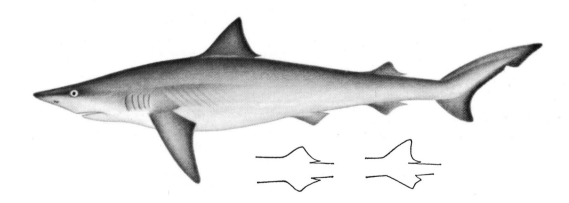

Soupfin Shark (comparing second dorsal and anal fin to brown smoothhound)

SOUTH AFRICA A land of contrast, from lush tropical beaches to rugged cold mountains and endless stretches of veld, South Africa offers considerable freshwater angling and excellent saltwater fishing to the tourist. Although the only trout endemic to the African continent is the Mediterranean subspecies of brown trout (*Salmo trutta macrostigma*) extensive plantings of both brown and rainbow trout from Europe since the turn of the century have become established in many watersheds, notably in the mountains of southwestern Cape Province, along the eastern escarpment of South Africa, and in the Maluti and Drakensberg massif of Lesotho. In general, African trout attain only a moderate size, as their life span tends to be shorter in a warm climate outside of their native range. They thrive near sea level in streams of the wet-winter area within about 100 miles of Cape Town; but as one goes north into the summer rainfall areas the heat increases in the low country and trout exist only by virtue of altitude in waters above 4,000 feet. There are no natural high-altitude lakes, but a number of artificial impoundments carry trout. In the majority of the trout areas rainbows predominate, but there are brown trout strongholds in the southwestern Cape and in Natal from the original plantings of the 1890's.

The introduction of North American centrarchid fishes to South Africa brought about a complete change for the prospects of very numerous waters unsuitable for trout. This coincided with the great increase in the number of artificial impoundments all over the country, and thousands of farm ponds for which only inferior fish were available. Such impoundments soon become populated with frogs, freshwater crabs (which take the place of crayfish of other countries), and small indigenous fish to provide forage for the predatory bass.

The importation of largemouth bass was a private enterprise of the Rand Piscatorial Association of Johannesburg; the fingerlings were obtained from Holland and sent to a trout farm in England before shipment to South Africa. Two members of the Association brought the cans of bass on mail steamers from Southampton on their return voyages from England; one batch was taken to the Jonkershoek Hatchery and the other to the Pirie Hatchery; the former was the most successful.

A tiny nucleus produced a prodigious population explosion in a few years. Forty-five largemouth fingerlings were received at Jonkershoek in February 1928 and some spawned there in October 1929. It was not a large production; only a few hundred fingerlings were available for distribution from June 1930 onward; but the results in many waters seemed almost miraculous. In three large reservoirs batches of only 21, 30, and 50 fingerlings were planted, but enough matured to provide breeders in the spring of 1931; and a wild population of bass up to 2 pounds was available by the summer of 1933. In another instance only 15 largemouth fingerlings taken on a two-day road journey provided the complete stocking of a natural lake, which became the most famous bass fishery in the Cape. So it went, and in a few years largemouth in their myriads existed in thousands of waters, large and small, all over southern Africa. The general size of largemouth bass has been satisfactory, fish from 5–7 pounds being common, but no records over 9 pounds have been substantiated. The last of the largemouth bass imported in 1928 died at the Jonkershoek Hatchery at the age of 14 years. The bass weighed only 5½ pounds, and its scales showed the European winter check of 1927–1928 followed by thirteen checks of the Cape winters.

The remarkable success of the largemouth bass inspired interest in the possibilities of other North American species, particularly the smallmouth bass. It was before the days of government interest in such matters, and the field was open for private enterprise. There was no air service, but vessels ran from New York to Cape Town in about 28 days. No smallmouth were available in Europe, so the Cape Piscatorial Society undertook the organization of an importation program from the United States. With the cooperation of the inland fisheries interests in Natal and diplomatic services in Cape Town and Washington, D.C., the proper contacts were made. Nothing could have been done without the dedicated interest of A.M. Powell, Superintendent of Hatcheries, Lewistown, Maryland (who supplied the fish, tanks, and equipment and internal transport), the owners of the *City of New York* (sunk in the war), and the ship's chief radio operator, A.M. Vida, who nursed the fish during the voyages as deck cargo. South Africa owes much to these Americans.

Large trout are uncommon in South Africa as climactic conditions result in their relatively short life span

After several unsuccessful attempts, due to the hazards of the sea, swamp cypress shipping tanks and electric aerators under the care of Vida kept 29 smallmouth bass fingerlings alive to arrive at Cape Town in October 1937. Some of these immigrants matured and bred at the Jonkershoek Hatchery when 17 months old, in September 1938, and numbers of their progeny were distributed in the Cape and Natal. The offspring of the few stock fish established thriving wild populations in a few years, particularly in rivers where they were most wanted. In a test section of the Berg River in the Paarl district small-mouth fingerlings from the 1938 breeding were planted and some had grown to 12 inches in a year. Although great winter floods in 1940 had removed a population of largemouth bass, the smallmouth remained and bred in the spring of that year (October–November 1940), and by summer the river was swarming with banner-tails. After that this picture was repeated in other river systems and impoundments, and hard-fighting smallmouth from 4½–6 pounds are a feature of southern Africa.

Another development under the cooperative plan was the importation of spotted bass (*Micropterus punctulatus*) from Ohio. These spotted bass were larger than the small-mouth received in 1937 and had survived contamination by sea water in a stormy voyage when two tanks were overturned and their contents lost. Those at the Jonkershoek Hatchery proved to be the easiest bass to handle. They bred 12 months after landing. They were widely distributed but, except when identified by the initiated, it is difficult to get reliable reports of them as most people cannot distinguish them from largemouth bass. However, the spotted bass have lived up to their Ohio reputation of suitability for certain types of rivers not favored by other species, and have done very well in a large conservation reservoir in Natal.

Bluegill sunfish (*Lepomis macrochirus*) were sent out under the importation plan in October 1938, 40 for the Jonkershoek Hatchery and 40 for Natal. Although very small when landed, they were 4 inches long by January 1939, when they nested and fingerlings were soon ready for distribution. Bluegills have reached a weight of 2 pounds in some waters, but on the whole the importation has come under criticism due to their high productivity in a warm climate, and tendency to overstock waters with stunted fish. However, in numerous places bluegills are valued as food for the populace and for light-tackle angling.

The only other significant introduction to South African waters was the carp (*Cyprinus carpio*). The earliest record of the importation of carp to Cape Town was in 1859. Carp were bred at the Jonkershoek Hatchery until 1921, when the stock was destroyed and the spread of carp forbidden by law in the Cape, because of the damage by carp to farm ponds and potential rainbow trout waters. This step came too late to save many waters suitable for bass. Carp are more appreciated in the extensive dry areas of the Cape Province, Orange Free State, and the Transvaal. In the Orange/Vaal river system, large carp are the target of thousands of anglers. Most of the carp are of the mirror variety, with reversions to the fully-scaled type. The Aeschgrund variety of carp is bred in the Transvaal for food. The record carp in the Transvaal weighed 83 pounds.

NATIVE GAMEFISH

There are few species of large indigenous fish in the rivers of the Southern Cape, but their numbers increase northward into the tropics. Members of the family Cyprinidae occur in most parts of southern Africa where there are permanent natural waters. The yellowfishes of the genus *Barbus* are popular angling fish, but like all carps are rather too bony for table purposes. This genus also includes many minnow-sized species found throughout the region. The southwestern Cape Province has a

fine endemic species in the Clanwilliam Olifants River, *B. capensis*, taken up to 30 pounds, popular because it takes artificial lures fished for smallmouth bass as well as bait. The Berg and Breede rivers have another species, *B. andrewi*, that rarely exceeds 8 pounds and is taken on bait. There is then a complete gap in the occurrence of the yellowfish group until the Natal border is reached, where the "scaly" *B. natalensis*, up to 10 pounds, is popular with anglers in that province. The Orange/Vaal river system contains two large species—the smallmouth yellowfish (*B. holubi*) up to 30 pounds, and the largemouth yellowfish (*B. kimberleyensis*) up to 40 pounds—which are fished for by hordes of anglers from the industrial areas of the Witwatersrand. There are 5 other yellowfish species, including *B. polylepis* and *B. marequensis*, which do not grow so large, and occur northward from Zululand to the eastern-flowing rivers of the Transvaal and Rhodesia to the Zambezi.

The most renowned native gamefish in southern Africa is a characin, the tigerfish (*Hydrocynus vittatus*), of tropical rivers and lakes, occurring from northern Natal through the eastern Transvaal to the Zambezi system. In the great Kariba lake on the Zambezi exceptionally large tigerfish up to nearly 40 pounds are taken, and many angling clubs join each year in international competitions.

The tilapia (known as "bream" in Africa) is a mouth-breeder, which has been widely spread to other countries for pond-fish culture. It is native to the Indian Ocean rivers of southern Africa and has a high tolerance for salt water, being found in tidal waters as well as far inland. The southern limit of its natural range is to the north of Algoa Bay (Port Elizabeth), but its distribution has been extended to many waters near sea level for economic purposes. In the Transvaal the Mozambique bream is known as the "kurper" and is much sought after by anglers. It ranges from 2–4 pounds, but large males reach 6½ pounds. The red-breasted bream (*Tilapia melanopleura*) is native to Zululand, grows to 2½ pounds, and is much used in Natal for pond-fish culture. It has a wide tropical range, including the eastern Transvaal and Rhodesia. There are several other species of the Cichlidae in Rhodesia valuable for angling and table purposes. The so-called "largemouth bream" are predatory cichlids, for example, as the olive bream of the Zambezi (*Serranochromis robustus*) with a record weight of 13 pounds taken on the bass plug.

The clariid catfishes (commonly known as "barbel" in South Africa) are a group with supplementary respiratory organs behind the regular gills, enabling estivation in drying waters and overland night journeys for short distances. They do not occur south of the Orange/Vaal system and Natal, but are plentiful northward into the tropics. The species, which was originally described in 1822, *Clarias gariepinus* (from the Hottentot name of the Orange River, *gariep*), can attain a great size; the largest on record being 7 feet long and weighing 130 pounds when caught in the Vaal River in 1898. There are several other species of *Clarius*. In the Zambezi system there is a large and powerful catfish (*Heterobranchus longifilis*), "the vundu," attaining 100 pounds, and commonly caught from 60–70 pounds, a scavenger taken on any bait and sometimes on spinners. The tropical region of southern Africa has many other catfishes, from tiny catlets to great bagrids up to 100 pounds. Many of these have poisonous spines. There is also the electric catfish of the Zambezi. Much valued for their excellent eating quality are the medium-sized "butterbarbel," *Eutropius*.

There are four species of freshwater eels, Anguillidae, bred in the Indian Ocean beyond Madagascar. Their larvae drift westward to the South African coast, transforming to elvers. Those of the commonest species, *Anguilla mosambica*, a long-fin eel, grow as they come southward, being small when they enter Natal rivers and larger when they reach rivers such as the Buffalo, East London, but still agile enough to climb the rocky crevices of waterfalls. Post-elvers enter False Bay, but are not known to round the Cape of Good Hope into the Atlantic. This species ranges from False Bay around southern Africa to East Africa and Madagascar, and attains about 4 feet and 16 pounds. Much heavier eels were reported from the rivers of the Transkei; preserved specimens in the South African Museum were up to 45 pounds. But after 1961, when the research work of R.A. Jubb was published, they were identified as the long-fin mottled eel (*Anguilla marmorata*) attaining 6 feet and 50 pounds, which occurs as far south as Knysna in the Cape Province and has a range along the east coast of Africa and across the Indian Ocean to the South Pacific. Similar in color and markings is another long-fin mottled species (*Anguilla nebulosa labiata*) which is more slender in body, and

ranges from Natal northward. It is plentiful in the cold headwater streams of eastern Rhodesia. In Rhodesia both mottled eels have been recorded up to 6 feet and 40 pounds; *A. mosambica* is more common south of the Zambezi. The fourth species is the short-fin eel (*A. bicolor bicolor*) appearing only occasionally in rivers and swamps near the coast and with a wide distribution in the Indian Ocean to northwest Australia. The freshwater eels are much favored as food, but are usually taken on strong handlines and setlines.

Other kinds of freshwater fish are very numerous in the northern parts of southern Africa. These include the Mormyrids; the smaller species of the Characidae (apart from the tigerfish); and the Citharinids, such as *Distichodus*; the "nkupi" up to 6 pounds; and the "chessa" up to 4 pounds, which provide good angling in the middle Zambezi River. In some rivers above tidal waters the Indian Ocean tarpon (*Megalops cyprinoides*) can give amazingly active performance on bass-spinning and fly-rod tackles.

CAPE PROVINCE

The trout streams in the vicinity of Cape Town are all within a day's drive on good paved roads. The open season in Cape Province is from September 1st to June 1st. The nearest stream is the Eerste River, which holds a

There are 1,000 miles of trout streams in Natal and this province offers the most convenient waters to visiting anglers. The best fishing is in spring (September and October), and again in the fall (April and May). Summer often brings flood conditions

good population of rainbows; some "steelhead" or anadromous rainbows, which range from 1½–5 pounds in size, occur here also. Unlike the steelhead of western North America, which undertake extensive migrations and achieve heavy weights through sea feeding, these South African fish apparently do not wander far from the Eerste estuary. For topographical reasons most rivers in South Africa provide no trout habitat in their lower reaches; the Eerste is a notable exception.

Other trout streams within easy reach of Cape Town are the headwaters of the Berg River, flowing to the Atlantic, and of the Breede River, flowing to the Indian Ocean. In addition to numerous rainbows these river systems have produced brown trout up to 8½ pounds. The Breede also produces good smallmouth bass fishing near Swellendam.

The Olifants River is one of the most interesting waters in the Western Cape Province both because of its size and its indigenous fish species. It is the largest river system, draining into the Atlantic Ocean south of the Orange River. One unusual gamefish found here is the Clanwilliam yellowfish (*Barbus capensis*). Native only to the Olifants, this species is distinct from the Orange River yellowfish (*Barbus holubi*). Members of the genus Barbus in Africa are related to the mahseers of Asia. Yellowfish are most commonly caught by bottom-fishing with live baits, but they are readily taken on artificial lures. In clear tributaries or the riffles of the main river the Clanwilliam yellowfish provides good sport on the fly rod, and large specimens are frequently taken on spinning tackle in deep pools. This yellowfish is reported to weights of over 20 pounds, although 7–15 pounds is the usual range in the Olifants River.

Another Olifants River species is the sawfin (*Barbus serra*), locally known as the "freshwater snoek" or "witvis," although its mouth is toothless and it is distinct from the witvis of the Berg and Breede river systems. It does not grow as large as the yellowfish and lacks the golden coloration. It has a long head and dark patches on the body, and the back fin has a serrated spine like a carp. The sawfin provides fair sport on light tackle.

The Olifants River is also one of the best smallmouth bass waters in South Africa, and many fish up to about 4 pounds are caught. Fishing spots have to be selected, as long stretches of the riverbed are covered with white sand where bass are scarce. Largemouth bass are also present, particularly around large irrigation dams on the river at Clanwilliam and Bulshoek, the record for the former standing at 7 pounds, 11 ounces. The most accessible fishing places for smallmouth bass and yellowfish are the runs below the Clanwilliam rapids and other rocky sections downstream, the running water at the top of the Bulshoek dam, and the large pools below the Bulshoek rapids. A rocky section known as the "Cascades" is a good place. All kinds of spoons, plugs, and spinners are effective.

There are good hotels at Citrusdal and Clanwilliam, and visitors will be able to obtain information about local fishing spots there. As this district is usually very hot in the summer the most popular times for this river are in spring, autumn, and winter.

Passing eastward around the southern tip of Africa, there is a troutless gap for about 600 miles as the streams are too heavily peat-stained and acid for trout. There-

after the real beginning of the eastern trout region of South Africa starts and extends along the eastern escarpments of the Cape, Natal, Transvaal, and Rhodesia. In contrast to the rocky bush-clad mountain streams of the southwestern Cape in the wet-winter area, the summer-rainfall trout streams of the eastern escarpment flow from high mountains through a very different type of country where they meander through grasslands in the rolling uplands.

A number of streams from the Amatole Mountains, which were stocked in the early days from the Pirie Trout Hatchery, continue to yield trout of up to 7 pounds. Across the divide on the headwaters of the western-flowing Orange River, the Barkly East district at an altitude of 6,000 feet has more than 20 streams, and is one of the richest districts for rainbows up to 7 pounds. It also has a number of stream-fed farm ponds which have produced rainbows from 7–10 pounds.

Across the Kei River, the boundary between the Cape Province and the Transkei region, the High Drakensberg range begins, and upper tributaries of the Kei, Bashee, and Umtata rivers hold rainbows. The Umzimbuvu River system, the largest on the eastern side of the Drakensberg escarpment, includes in its large branches the Tsitsa, Tina, Kenegha and Umzimkulu, and reaches the sea at Port St. Johns. In the complete absence of all indigenous river fish, except eels and minnows, these streams were virgin waters for the exotic rainbow trout which were prodigiously successful in the early days, but later showed a tendency to overbreed—although good fishing is maintained in a number of well-known streams reached from various centers.

NATAL

The province of Natal offers the most convenient trout fishing for visiting anglers, for its best streams, amidst wild and grand scenery, are in a compact and accessible area under the supervision of the Natal Parks, Game and Fish Preservation Board of Pietermaritzburg. All the most important streams are in the foothills of the Drakensberg at altitudes between 4,000 and 6,000 feet, and many contain brown trout from the original plantings. The Umzimkulu River system in the Himeville/Lindenberg district in the southwestern corner of Natal is famous for its rainbow trout. Facilities are well organized, as the Parks Board and the local angling association control long stretches of the rivers with offices for the allocation of angling beats, and there are hotels and guest farms catering to anglers. The Parks Board has a hatchery at Underberg. The district has such famous rainbow waters as the Indowana, Ingangwana, Umzimouti, Umzimkulu, Umzimkulwana, and Polela rivers, open from September 1st–May 15th. There are also some 25 ponds and small lakes formed by dams across streams, stocked from the hatchery, and producing trout up to 7 pounds from boat or bank.

Within easy reach of this center are the headwaters of the Umkomaas River system, containing brown trout of good size. The Tugela River system, the largest in Natal, has a number of famous brown trout streams from the High Drakensberg range, flowing from several nature and game reserves which are a feature of this province. The best known are the Mooi and Bushmans rivers. The

Umgeni River system has a large catch area and tributaries nearer to populated centers. Its population of brown trout is descended from those first available in southern Africa in 1890.

The best months for trout fishing in Natal are September and October in spring and April and May in fall, as the rivers are liable to be flooded with the summer rains.

BASUTOLAND

Some of the headwaters of the Orange River in the high Maluti and Drakensberg ranges in Basutoland (Lesotho) have proved very suitable for trout. In spite of its location in southern Africa, Lesotho can be intensely cold on account of its high altitude, and frosts and snow can occur even in summer. It is also in a summer rainfall area, but serious droughts occur at times.

Repeated attempts were made without success from 1904 onward to introduce trout from Cape eggs. It was not until 1935 that members of the Basutoland Mounted Police succeeded in transporting a few adult brown trout from the Bushmans River, Natal, over the Giant's Castle massif of the Drakensberg to the nearest river in Lesotho. Only seven brown trout survived the grueling journey in five-gallon cans on mules, but they bred in the virgin water so successfully that in a few years it was overpopulated. In 1943 rainbow ova from the Pirie Hatchery were taken from the Cape province by the rough Ramatseliso Pass to a trading post at Sehlabathebe in Lesotho, where the trader hatched them in a stream and stocked some high tributaries which were later to produce record fish.

In 1952 local enthusiasts started a makeshift plant for hatching 20,000 Cape ova each year; and fry were transported by car, jeep, aircraft, horse, mule, and man to most of the suitable rivers, so that in time Lesotho became a recognized trout-fishing country. It is, however, a borderline country for trout, suffering from overpopulation by rainbows on the one hand and kills from severe droughts, hailstorms, and floods on the other.

Apart from entry by difficult mountain tracks, Lesotho has a main road and short railway from the Orange Free State to its capital, Maseru, which is a good center for accommodation, the hiring of light aircraft to a number of landing fields, and organized safaris on ponies. From Maseru an all-weather mountain road runs for over 70 miles in the heart of the mountains to several trout rivers.

In addition to rainbow trout in some clear waters the indigenous yellowfish (*Barbus holubi*) up to about 6 pounds will take a fly and make strong runs before being landed. Semonkong in the Maseru district has a productive stretch of the Maletsunyane River above a sheer waterfall of 637 feet, and is reached by a short flight to a landing field or by a longer approach on horseback. The first stocking of trout in this river in the 1950's produced some rapid growth of rainbows; 2-inch fingerlings grew to 13 inches during the four summer months, and two years after the introduction a female heavy in roe was 28 inches long when caught and released. Both brown and rainbow trout up to 6 pounds were taken. A number of other productive streams in the district have to be reached on horseback.

Entering Lesotho further north from the Orange Free State, via Butha Buthe, the Oxbow area, now reached by four-wheel-drive vehicles up the very tortuous Moleng Pass, may well become one of the most famous trout areas when the proposed Oxbow Dam is constructed for power and water supply. Oxbow Dam rivers have already achieved fame, for many rainbows up to 6 pounds have been taken as well as hosts of smaller fish. There is a vehicle and visitors' camp service at Oxbow running regular tours.

Entering from the Cape province, the upper Orange River tributaries can be approached by road through the permanent Qacha's Nek Pass; but the famous rainbow trout streams at Sehlabathebe have to be reached by a very rough cutting up the Drakensberg. The Tsoelikana River in that area has yielded some of the best rainbows in southern Africa, including the present record of 9 pounds 5 ounces, taken on a Jock Scott fly, and numbers from 5–7½ pounds.

A much more popular route into Lesotho for anglers is from Himeville, Natal, the base for the Sani Pass four-wheel-drive service across the Drakensberg to Mokhotlong, where there is good hotel accommodation and the choice of several trout streams yielding brown and rainbow trout.

TRANSVAAL

Trout are established in streams and ponds in the foothills of the Transvaal Drakensberg range, which forms part of the Great Escarpment in the eastern side of the province. These trout waters are in two main river systems flowing into Mozambique territory. The introduction of trout to the Transvaal occurred later than in the Cape and Natal. It was done by private effort and the earliest attempts in 1903 did not have much success.

In the same year a society was formed and a hatchery started on the Mooi River at Potchefstroom with the services of an experienced operator. This again had only moderate success, and it was far away from the prospective trout waters involving slow train journeys and slower hauls by ox-wagon over mountainous tracks. As was more appropriate a private hatchery was started in 1910 at Lydenburg near the Eastern Escarpment, which later became the site of the Provincial Fisheries Institute. Local enthusiasts cooperated to hatch Cape ova in streams of mountain water, and fry were widely distributed in the district by primitive but successful methods of transport. Before the Transvaal Provincial Administration took over in 1947, some 600,000 ova had been bought from private funds and hatched successfully, the fry being spread to many streams of the eastern Transvaal. As in the case of so many preliminary plantings of rainbows in virgin waters, there were many instances of rapid growth before the fish bred too abundantly. However, in this region, like Natal and Lesotho, the trouble of overstocking and reduction of size is liable to be checked by climatic disasters—the ravages of drought and the destruction by sudden hailstorms which drop the water temperature too suddenly for the survival of fish. Thus there is a need for the continuation of hatchery work.

The Transvaal trout rivers, lakes, and farm ponds are 200 miles or more eastward of Pretoria; the best known are in the Belfast, Dullstroom, Machadadorp, and Waterval Boven districts; in the vicinity of the surface gold-mining camps of the early days at Sabie, Pilgrim's

Rest, and Graskop; and further north at Haenertsburg and Magoebaskloof. There are considerable restrictions due to private ownership and the leasing of waters by syndicates.

SALTWATER FISHING

South African saltwater fishing runs the gamut from kite-fishing for big sharks from shore to bay, party boat, and big-game trolling. Black marlin (local record 1,002 pounds), striped marlin, sailfish, dolphin, bluefin tuna, yellowfin tuna, bigeye tuna, mako, and numerous in-digenous game species occur along the 2,000-mile coast. Influenced by the Antarctic Drift, whose cold waters cir-culate in the south and flow eastward, and the warm Mozambique Current, flowing south to become the Agulhas Current at the tip of the continent, South Africa has a diverse fish fauna of more than 1,300 species, most of which originate in the Indo-Pacific region. Seasonal migrations of large gamefish moving down with the Mozambique Current provide unusual angling out of Cape Town, Hout Bay, Simonstown, Kalk Bay, Gordon's Bay, Hermanus, Gansbaai, Mossel Bay, Plettenberg Bay, Port Elizabeth, East London, and Durban.   —A.C.H.

SOUTH CAROLINA South Carolina offers a modest range of fishing—from trout in the mountain streams of the northwest corner to excellent red drum fishing along the coast.

For fishing purposes the freshwaters of the state might be divided into three parts—mountains; the Piedmont, which contains all the reservoirs except Santee-Cooper; and the coastal plain, a land of blackwater rivers and swamp ponds and streams. There are over 25,000 farm ponds scattered throughout South Carolina, but since access is generally restricted to the owner and his family or friends, these do not enter the public-fishing picture.

The trout waters consist of approximately 200 miles of streams in Greenville, Oconee, and Pickens counties. All stocked trout are 8 inches or perhaps longer and consist mainly of rainbows, with some browns and a few brooks. As in all states which depend upon hatcheries to maintain the fishing, a few trout survive the comparatively heavy fishing pressure, an example being a 13¼-pound brown caught in the Chauga River.

However, an angler unfamiliar with the area might best start on the east fork of the Chatooga below the federal hatchery near Walhalla and work downstream. Other good streams are the Chauga and the Middle Saluda. The lower reaches of these trout streams have been stocked with smallmouth bass in recent years, but the bronzebacks have not become well-established and re-main an unimportant species locally.

The rivers flowing through the Piedmont (the upper part of the state below the mountains) are generally muddy and provide little fishing except for catfish. Up-state or in the "Up Country" of South Carolina, the stream gradients are steep in the hilly regions, and they gather silt from every slope. In the Low Country they hit the plain and slow down, depositing much of their earthen burden and clearing as they go. But as they drop the silt, they pick up tannic acid from lush vegetation and long before they reach the sea they nearly all become stained a dark brown, which, nevertheless, has caused them to be called blackwaters. But the upstate reservoirs provide good fishing for black bass, crappie, white bass, and bream. The fishing in these reservoirs is generally similar and should be considered separately from that in the fish-famous Santee-Cooper, which is near the coast.

RESERVOIR FISHING

There are two reservoirs on the Savannah River, the border between South Carolina and Georgia. The first, 78,500-acre Clark Hill, has fairly good populations of all warmwater gamefish in the state. Commercial landings are limited, but several camp sites and launching ramps have been constructed by the Corps of Engineers. Camps include Fishing Village near Plum Branch and one at Little River.

Hartwell Reservoir is located about 20 miles above the headwaters of Clark Hill and contains 60,000 acres. Hart-well, whose headwaters extend back into the foothills, is colder than the other reservoirs and possibly suitable for walleyes, which have been stocked there as well as in Clark Hill.

The other two reservoirs of the westcentral part of the state are Lake Greenwood, 11,800 acres, and Lake Murray, 50,800 acres, the two lakes very similar as re-gards species of fish, seasonal activity, and methods of angling. The five major species of gamefish are large-mouth bass, black and white crappie, white bass, and bream, the last chiefly bluegill but including redbreast, shellcracker, warmouth, and miscellaneous species of sunfish. Also found in lesser numbers are chain pickerel and yellow perch.

The fishing in these two lakes is fair throughout most of the year and sensational in early spring, particularly for bass and crappie as they move into shallow water. The bream fishing is not as good as in the lower part of the state, and the fish run rather small, due to overcrowding and competition from gizzard shad. White-bass fishing is seasonally good but unpredictable. Crappie fishing is only fair. However, these lakes, and particularly Murray, are excellent bass lakes for those who know something of fish-ing and realize that at different times of the year the fish are at different depths and prefer different lures.

A feature of Lake Murray is the 12-mile stretch of the Saluda River below the dam, where the cold, drawoff water from the bottom of the lake keeps temperatures low and where rainbow and brown trout are stocked. All stocking is with 8-inch fish, and the growth has been phe-nomenal, browns up to 19 inches being caught the first spring after stocking. One hazard is the number of big striped bass that come up the Congaree River from San-tee-Cooper, where they are landlocked. A 28-pounder caught shortly after a stocking had three just-released trout in its stomach.

The Catawba and Wateree reservoirs are on the same river, which changes its name from the Catawba to the Wateree some distance after it has flowed into the state from North Carolina.

The Wateree reservoir lies between Camden and Great Falls, and its 13,710 acres support large populations of crappie, white bass, and white catfish, with comparatively small populations of black bass and bream. The crappie is the favorite fish, and many are taken both night and day with minnows. Night fishing is carried on mostly from bridges, using one or more kerosene lanterns which are lowered to the surface of the water. White-bass fishing is done by trolling, or by casting when a school is located feeding on gizzard shad.

Catawba has fair populations of crappie, white bass, largemouth bass, and catfish, but few bream. For some reason the crappie are neither as numerous or as large as those of Wateree, but to balance this the largemouth fishing is considerably better.

SANTEE-COOPER

Santee-Cooper actually consists of two lakes (100,000-acre Marion and 60,000-acre Moultrie) joined by a 7-mile diversion canal. The project, completed in 1941, is an outgrowth of the old Santee canal, completed in 1800 and abandoned in 1850. It involved damming the brawling Santee River, diverting most of its flow into the Lake Moultrie basin through the hydroelectric dam and down the Cooper River to the ocean. The prize of Santee-Cooper is the landlocked striped bass (locally rockfish). There is some question as to whether these fish were "functionally landlocked" even before the dam was built or whether the nonmigratory characteristics were developed by the fish trapped in the lakes when the dams were built. However, a 55-pound striper was caught in Lake Moultrie in 1963.

The striper catch has fallen off somewhat in recent years from the high point reached in 1957 when an estimated 300,000 stripers averaging 5 pounds were caught, and the average catch per angler was three stripers. But it is still high. It is difficult to make predictions as to when, where, and what the stripers will be hitting, particularly since they seem to change their habits from year to year. Generally speaking the best fishing is in the early spring and late fall, although the catch is remarkably consistent throughout the year. During the spring run the hot spots are the diversion canal and the old Santee River bed from around Eutawville on up to the junction of the Congaree and Wateree. During the remainder of the year the striper fishing is generally better in Lake Moultrie. The three most productive methods are trolling, fishing cut or live bait near the bottom in deepwater, and casting lead-head bucktails into schools feeding on shad.

Black bass, although overshadowed by the stripers, are plentiful, with the best fishing in the early spring or in warm spells during the late winter. The last creel census showed an average catch of 2.3 bass per angler and an average weight of 2.3 pounds. Black bass up to 14 pounds have been reported. They are generally caught in fairly shallow water where there is not so much competition for food with the striped bass, which is almost entirely a fish of the deeper water.

May, June, and July are the top crappie months, although some fish are caught every month in the year. Both white and black crappie are plentiful in the two lakes, with the average catch through the year slightly over ten fish.

Lake Moultrie is noted for the number and size of its channel catfish, a world record of 57 pounds having been set by Blease Dennis of Moncks Corner in March, 1960. The big cats congregate in great numbers in front of the powerhouse. where they are caught on cut shad or needlefish fished deep. In Lake Marion smaller white catfish take the place of the channel cats.

Santee-Cooper is also the home of white bass, chain pickerel (locally jackfish), various species of sunfish, carp, yellow perch, and warmouth.

There is good fishing in the lower reaches of the rivers that make up inland—the Edisto, Black, Pee Dee, and Salkehatchie-Combahee—as well as in the comparatively short coastal rivers of the Low Country. These include the Ashepoo, Cooper, and Waccamaw.

These rivers of the Low Country furnish some top-notch fishing for black bass, bream, and the fish that many consider the best of all—the redbreast. Striped bass come up most of the coastal rivers, and in the early spring there are good runs of white shad up those making up far inland. The rivers of the Low Country are mainly blackwater and the choice of those who like scenic beauty as well as fish on their fishing trips.

SALTWATER FISHING

Although saltwater fishing is pursued the year around in South Carolina the best seasons are in the spring and fall. The most popular inshore species are the red drum, spotted seatrout, spot, croaker, flounder, and whiting. Farther offshore, mackerel, bluefish, amberjack, cobia, barracuda, grouper, and snapper may be taken at times. Sailfish and marlin are occasionally caught in bluewater; however, the Gulf Stream lies some 40 miles from the coast so billfish are not readily available to the angler. Tarpon occur off the beaches and near river mouths. Charter boats are available at Little River, Murrell's Inlet, Georgetown, and Charleston. Piers exist along the coast from Edisto Beach up to the North Carolina border. Most of these are found in the Myrtle Beach area.

—E.F.

SOUTH DAKOTA This state has long enjoyed a reputation as "The Pheasant Capital of the World." Few people, however, are aware of the fact that it ranks first or second in per capita ownership of outboard motors or provides its citizens and visitors some of the finest fishing in the United States. Indeed, South Dakota's state slogan, "Land of Infinite Variety," could very well apply to its fishing opportunities. Generally speaking, the fishing is liberal, as creel limits are generous and a minimum of restrictions are placed on the sport fisherman. For example, the daily limit on panfish is generally 50 or more; bait restrictions apply only to the use of minnows in a few lakes (particularly the Black Hills trout waters); there are no size limits on any species, and the use of artificial light as an aid in angling is permitted. Perhaps even more important is the fact that fishing is not crowded. The extent of the fishery resource, coupled with a relatively sparse human population, makes for plenty of "elbow room."

From the standpoint of sport fishing, South Dakota can be divided into five rather well-defined geographic areas: (1) the Black Hills, (2) the "west river" prairie, (3) the Missouri River impoundments, (4) the southeastern area, and (5) the northeast "lakes region." Each of these areas has its own characteristic waters and particular fishery.

THE BLACK HILLS

The Black Hills sport fishery is characterized by lakes and streams which support trout. All of the trout lakes are artificial impoundments. These range from small 10-

acre roadside ponds to 4,000-acre reservoirs. All impounded waters are intensively managed to provide a sustained fishery through the peak angling months of the year—May through September. This has been accomplished by a program of lake rehabilitation and systematic stocking with both fingerling and catchable-sized fish. The fisheries program, which is carried out co-operatively between state and federal agencies, emphasizes rainbow trout, although brown trout and eastern brook trout also are stocked in limited numbers. Some of the more important trout lakes are:

Pactola Reservoir, Pennington County. Located about 25 miles west of Rapid City, Pactola is a large water-storage reservoir which provides an excellent rainbow and brown trout fishery. The state record brown (20 pounds, 2 ounces) was caught here in 1972. Pactola Dam impounds Rapid Creek, one of the major trout streams in this area. An excellent stream fishery is therefore available immediately above and below the reservoir.

Sheridan Lake, Pennington County. This impoundment is located about 6 miles northeast of Hill City and has the distinction of providing a fishery for both trout and warmwater species. The scenic surroundings and excellent recreational facilities make this one of the most popular lakes in the Black Hills. In addition to trout, anglers take largemouth bass and crappies.

Sylvan Lake, Custer State Park, is situated 7 miles north of Custer. The lake is relatively small, but the spectacular setting and fine trout fishing are a prime attraction to both visitors and residents.

Center Lake, Custer State Park, about 14 miles northwest of Custer, is readily accessible, but the "out-of-the-way" location provides a tranquil and scenic setting where the angler-camper will enjoy his sport and the basic accommodations provided for camping.

Deerfield Reservoir, Pennington County, is another somewhat remote lake that provides a first-class trout fishery. Accommodations at the lake proper are nonexistent and the visitor should be prepared to provide for his own angling necessities. Nearby campgrounds and a store, however, can be utilized for provisions and a place to stay. This is another favorite of the camping angler.

These are only a few of the trout lakes to be found in the Black Hills. There are others that will often provide top-notch fishing. The visitor should inquire locally regarding fishing opportunities as some of the lesser known areas will at times be worth investigating. All of the lakes are readily accessible by car and, generally speaking, a boat is not required. Camping facilities, provisional stores, cafes, and overnight accommodations are always available either at the lakes or very nearby.

Stream Fishing For those who prefer stream fishing, Rapid Creek and Spearfish Creek are the most noteworthy in the Black Hills. Rapid Creek heads in the Rochford area of Pennington County, courses through Pactola Reservoir and thence easterly to Rapid City. Some brook trout are found in the upper reaches of Rapid Creek, and a few brown trout may be taken in the major portion of the stream, but the bulk of the sport fishery is supplied by rainbows. Access to the stream is not difficult, although there are some remote stretches.

Spearfish Creek, in Lawrence County, heads south of Cheyenne Crossing and courses north through Spearfish Canyon. This stream is a favored area, not only because of the trout fishing that is available, but also because of its accessibility and scenic setting. Here again, rainbow trout provide the basic fishery, although browns and brook trout are also present.

THE WEST RIVER PRAIRIE

This region would scarcely be considered a vacation area. The rolling, treeless, wind-swept plains appear inhospitable and forlorn to the casual traveler accustomed to tall corn, hills, and trees. To the serious fisherman, however, the several thousand ranch ponds located in this area present a unique opportunity. Although these ponds are private property, local inquiry and proper contact may provide some of the most productive fishing available anywhere. Here the largemouth bass is king, and specimens up to 8 pounds are taken every year. Bass in the 3–5-pound class are common. Bluegills and/or crappies also are generally available in these ponds.

In addition to the private ponds there are several state-owned artificial impoundments that offer fishing for bass, panfish, catfish, and occasionally walleyes or northern pike. Also, the Rosebud and Pine Ridge Indian reservations in the southcentral part of the state contain some artificial impoundments that on occasion provide excellent fishing. Seeking local advice and guidance is of paramount importance here as tourist facilities are generally remote and fishing opportunities receive scant publicity.

MISSOURI RIVER IMPOUNDMENTS

These impoundments afford the angler an opportunity to sample some of the best and most unique fishing in the United States. Four gigantic dams have been thrown across the once rampant "Big Muddy" to form the Great Lakes of South Dakota, a series of bluewater lakes stretching for nearly 400 miles across the heart of South Dakota. From south to north these lakes are:

Lewis and Clark Lake, Yankton to Springfield. A 33,000-acre body of water that furnishes fishing for channel catfish, sauger, and crappie. This reservoir is the most highly developed of those on the Missouri River. Tourist and recreation facilities are available. The tailwaters area below the dam provides a good fishery for sauger, catfish, and walleye.

Fort Randall Reservoir, Pickstown to Chamberlain. Although not highly developed to accommodate fishermen, this 80,000-acre reservoir provides a superior sport fishery. Sauger, walleye, northern pike, catfish, and crappies are the mainstay of the fishery. The bass specialist, however, should find the fishing for this species excellent, especially in the spring and early summer. The tailwaters below Fort Randall Dam have been noteworthy from the aspect of providing anglers with tremendous numbers of sauger (locally sand pike) and paddlefish during certain seasons.

Oahe Reservoir, Pierre to Mobridge. This body of water extends 250 miles from Pierre, the capital of South Dakota, to Bismarck, the capital of North Dakota. The reservoir inundates approximately 376,000 surface acres. Since its impoundment, there has been an explosive development of the northern pike and perch populations. These species, particularly the northern pike, have furnished an exceptional fishery. In the tailwaters of Oahe

Dam, northern pike, sauger, and crappie, walleye, catfish, and paddlefish have made up the bulk of the angling take. Not only have the numbers of fish taken been spectacular, but the quality of the fish also has been outstanding. Northern pike up to 20 pounds, walleye to 8 pounds, sauger to 6 pounds, catfish to 30 pounds, and paddlefish up to 60 pounds regularly enter the catch, especially during seasonal runs from downstream.

Big paddlefish or "spoonbill" are caught below Oahe Dam. Good eating, the roe also makes a caviar substitute

In total, the Missouri River impoundments support more than thirty species of fish. Several species not mentioned in the foregoing account are available to a limited extent or to the angling specialist. Noteworthy among these fish are the flathead catfish and sturgeon. Angler facilities and accommodations are rudimentary, especially on the northernmost reservoirs. Boat rentals, however, can usually be arranged, and angling equipment can be purchased in adjacent towns. As usual, local advice on where and when to fish and an investigation of methods (especially in the tailwater areas) will be of much help to the visiting angler.

SOUTHEASTERN AREA

This region is characterized by relatively small artificial impoundments that provide a panfish type of fishery. Visitors are usually seeking bullheads, crappies, perch, or bluegills. Some of the more important artificial lakes include East Vermillion Lake at Canistota, Lake Alvin near Canton, Lake Mitchell at Mitchell, as well as Lake Hanson near Alexandria.

Natural lakes in this area include Lake Herman, Lake Madison, and Brant Lake in Lake County. This chain of lakes provides, besides panfish, a good fishery for walleye and northern pike.

NORTHEASTERN AREA

The northeast is dotted with natural lakes which for the most part have rocky, wooded shorelines. Some of South Dakota's most beautiful and productive lakes are located here. Generally speaking, facilities for the angler are adequate, although a few of the lakes have not been developed, and boat rentals, for example, are not possible on these underdeveloped lakes. A few of the lakes that a visitor to this area should consider include:

Big Stone Lake, Grant and Roberts Counties, is shared by South Dakota and Minnesota as part of their common boundary. The lake covers about 20,000 surface acres and is a ribbonlike lake 30 miles in length. Gamefish taken by anglers include crappies, walleye, perch, northern pike, largemouth bass, and bluegills. This lake is a consistent producer of gamefish and seldom fails to reward the angler with a handsome catch of at least one of the species mentioned. In spring and early summer, the experienced bass fisherman especially will find this lake well-suited to his talents. This, incidentally, applies to several lakes in the general area. Although excellent largemouth-bass populations exist in these lakes, the bass fisherman will find little competition for the species. During the early summer period and again in the fall most of the walleyes and northern pike are taken. The midsummer fishery is sustained primarily by crappies and bluegills.

Lake Traverse, Roberts County, covers about 12,000 acres and is a highly productive body of water. Here perch, crappies, northern pike, walleyes, and bullheads furnish the bulk of the sport fishery. The summer crappie fishing and the winter perch fishery at this lake are particularly outstanding. Facilities at both Big Stone Lake and Lake Traverse are excellent. This lake also forms part of the South Dakota-Minnesota boundary.

Lake Poinsett, Hamlin County, is South Dakota's largest inland natural lake, covering 8,800 acres. The fishing here tends to be somewhat erratic in that the sport fishery may vary from poor to exceptionally good from one season to another, and even from one week to the next. Nevertheless, the lake bears investigation as it often provides an unsurpassed walleye fishery. Crappies, bullheads, and perch also are at times readily taken. Angler facilities are excellent.

Clear Lake, Marshall County, is one of the better walleye lakes in the northeast area. Perch and northern pike also contribute to the fishery, especially during the winter ice-fishing period. This lake should not be overlooked by the walleye fisherman, and facilities for the tourist are available.

Roy Lake, Marshall County, is noted for its large walleyes, as 8-12 pounders are quite common. Generally speaking, fishing for walleyes is not "fast," although it would be a mistake to term the fishing as poor. Lunker walleyes are usually taken during the spring and fall months, and most often during the late evening or nighttime hours. Bluegills, perch, and northern pike are other species taken by sport fishermen. Facilities for the angler are very good.

Cottonwood Lake, Marshall County, is a relatively small walleye lake but is one of the favorites with local anglers. As at Roy Lake, much of the walleye fishing is done after dark, and often provides excellent results. Other species sought include perch and northern pikes. Facilities required by the angler are adequate.

Pickerel Lake, Day County, is a recreational center and one of the state's most beautiful lakes. Walleye and northern pike are the sport fish most commonly sought at this lake during the summer months. Panfish (perch and rock bass, for example) are not heavily fished, although perch do become an important species during the winter ice-fishing season. Recreational facilities at Pickerel Lake are excellent.

Enemy Swim, Day County, is best known for its walleyes, perch, and bluegills. Relatively shallow and highly productive, this lake is of major importance to the northeastern lakes region. When the fish are biting at Enemy Swim Lake, few lakes can boast of providing more or better sport. Fisherman accommodations are excellent.

Although redundant to the experienced fisherman, a word of caution: Do not expect even the best waters to produce a superlative fishery every day or every year. Most of the specific sport-fishing opportunities noted herein are at least partially seasonal and of course may vary in quality from year to year.

Additional information in respect to fishing, hunting, and recreational opportunities may be secured by writing the Publicity Division, Department of Highways, Pierre, or the Department of Game, Fish and Parks, Pierre.

—M.B.

SOUTHERN FLOUNDER *Paralichthys lethostigma* In contrast to its relative the summer flounder, this species has a white underside and an olive color on the dorsal area. Although it resembles the summer flounder, the gillraker count on the lower limb of the first arch is 10–13 (usually 11–12) in the southern flounder, whereas in the summer flounder it is usually 13–18, generally greater than 15. Where it occurs together with the summer flounder, it can be told by the lack of distinct spots. It is also similar to the Gulf flounder, but can be distinguished by its distinctive color; all of the spots on the southern flounder are diffused, with no distinct ocelli (spots ringed with lighter distinct areas). The usual size of this species is 12–20 inches, and one of 26 inches was reported from North Carolina.

The southern flounder is found in comparatively shallow water over mud bottoms in bays, sounds, and lagoons. Occasionally it occurs in large numbers in freshwater throughout its range, which is from North Carolina to Texas. In the Gulf of Mexico, it is taken during all seasons and in bays over a wide salinity range, from brackish water to full-strength seawater, although the greatest numbers occur where freshwater mixes somewhat with the salt.

LIFE HISTORY

Spawning apparently takes place during the winter, as ripening fish have been caught in October, and young fish of 1–2 inches are taken off the Texas coast from December to April. They feed primarily on mullet, anchovies, and other small fishes, as well as on shrimp.

ANGLING VALUE

This species is taken during all seasons in the inshore waters of the Gulf. A considerable volume is harvested by shrimp trawlers offshore during the spring. Another important method is by gigging using a torch or flashlight, the flounders being speared as they come into shallow water at night. —D.dS.

SOUTHERN HAKE *Urophycis floridanus* Also known as Gulf hake, it belongs to the cod family (Gadidae). This hake is characterized by having the dorsal fin rays not elongate and the scales small, there being about 120 in transverse series. Its color is reddish-brown above and lighter below, with a small dark spot above the eye, a vertical series of 3 or 4 spots behind the eye, and 2 spots on the opercle. The lateral line is black and is interrupted at intervals by white spots. Its maximum length is about 12 inches.

LIFE HISTORY

The southern hake is found in the Gulf of Mexico where it comes inshore during the winter, usually from February to May. In the summer it is found in deep offshore waters. It feeds mostly on invertebrates and fish taken near the bottom.

ANGLING VALUE

The southern hake is caught on hook and line during the winter when it frequents the shallows. It is occasionally taken on small jigs with light spinning tackle.

—A.J.McC.

SOUTHERN KINGFISH *See* Whitings

SOUTHERN PUFFER *Sphaeroides nephelus* Known from southeastern Florida and from throughout the Gulf of Mexico, southern puffers occur in a variety of habitats, including both grassy and smooth, unvegetated bottoms. They often are found near pilings and rocks as well.

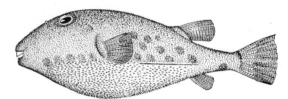

Southern Puffer

In life they are brownish above, with small black and green spots; white below. There are 7–8 irregular black bars on the sides posterior to the pectoral fins and a black spot in front of the pectorals. A dark brownish area at the base of the dorsal fin and between that fin and the caudal. Dorsal and anal fins plain; pectoral pale brownish-yellow; caudal yellowish-brown. Said to reach a length of 14 inches, but seldom exceeds 10 inches.

LIFE HISTORY

Members of this species are carnivorous, feeding on crustaceans and mollusks and on small amounts of plant material.

Spawning occurs in late spring and summer, probably a short distance offshore.

ANGLING VALUE

Of no commercial or sport value in themselves, southern puffers often are considered a nuisance inasmuch as they steal bait by nibbling it with their beaklike dental structures, and themselves often are caught instead of desired species. The flesh of the southern puffer is frequently toxic and should not be utilized as food. *See also* Northern Puffer, Smooth Puffer —D.K.C.

SOUTHERN REDBELLY DACE *Phoxinus erythrogaster* A small, fine-scaled minnow with two dusky longitudinal bands. Deep greenish-olive with a series of dark blotches along the dorsal ridge. A reddish or yellowish streak between longitudinal bands. Lower sides and belly silvery, white, or flushed with yellow, red, or crimson. Body scales are very small, 70–95 in the lateral series. Mouth small and slightly oblique. Jaws equal. No barbel. The range of this species extends from southern Minnesota to Pennsylvania and south to northern Alabama.

Southern Redbelly Dace

HABITS

The southern redbelly dace inhabits permanent brooks with clearwater which are not subject to frequent flooding. It appears to require sufficient water throughout the year as it does not migrate downstream in summer. The largest populations are found where there are undercut banks for escape cover. Primarily a vegetarian, this dace subsists on mud-inhabiting algae. During the spawning period, this fish becomes exceedingly brilliant. Colors indicated above become more distinct, and the ventral surfaces of the head and body become a deep carmine. The fins are flushed with yellow, and a carmine spot appears on the base of the dorsal fin. Although colorful, the females are less so than the males. This species reaches a maximum length of 3 inches.

ECONOMIC VALUE

Although small and for this reason not a popular bait in some areas, the redbelly is easily captured by seining due to its habit of schooling in open-water when frightened, especially where undercut banks are lacking. This species is considered a good aquarium species. —R.A.J.

SOUTHERN SMELTS Family Retropinnidae Southern smelts are small shoaling fishes related to the southern graylings (family Aplochitonidae). They can be considered the southern hemisphere counterparts of the northern Osmeroid smelts. The most noticeable distinguishing feature, in addition to the small salmonoid adipose dorsal fin, is the rearward position of the softrayed dorsal fin, as is suggested by the family name. All species are from 2–6 inches in length, silvery, with a little dark pigment dorsally; and they have a reflecting layer in the midlateral scales which may appear blue or purple. The smell of cucumber is typical of all species when freshly caught.

It has been assumed until recently that the southern smelts represented an ancient line of freshwater fish. But now that a very close relationship is seen between all lake populations and estuarine *R. retropinna* it is clear that estuarine fish are colonizing the freshwater environment. However, evolution does not appear to have advanced far in this direction. The only species which can be identified on appearance and without reference to locality are the three coastal forms in New Zealand.

The freshwater populations present an intriguing problem in investigating the nature of speciation.

DISTRIBUTION AND TAXONOMY

Of the 10 species recognized, 3 live in marine conditions and enter rivers in New Zealand. These are *Retropinna retropinna*, which is common throughout New Zealand; the largest species of the family *R. osmeroides*, which has a similar range but is uncommon at least in freshwater; and *Stokellia anisodon*, which is abundant seasonally in river mouths in southern and southeastern New Zealand. The latter is the only species of fish with a restricted geographic range in New Zealand of those which regularly enter freshwater from the sea. *R. semoni* and *R. tasmanica*, both of which closely resemble *R. retropinna*, similarly enter rivers in southeastern Australia (South Australia, Victoria, New South Wales, and southern Queensland) and in Tasmania respectively. *R. victoriae*, described from a sample from Victoria, Australia, has not been collected again.

R. semoni, in addition to living in the sea and coastal streams, also lives and breeds in inland rivers, lakes, and ponds in Australia. Recent work suggests a similar situation in New Zealand, where numerous lake populations are probably of the same species as the common estuarine smelt, *R. retropinna*, although separate species have been described from lakes in three regions of New Zealand. A related form in lakes on Chatham Island, which lies 500 miles east of New Zealand, is part of the same species complex; the estuarine form of *R. retropinna* occurs in lagoons and coastal areas of this island.

The numbers of rays in the dorsal and anal fins, the numbers of scale rows, numbers of teeth, size, and relative size of the head of estuarine *R. retropinna* and of lake populations in New Zealand vary with environmental conditions. Within each sample there is considerable variation in all these characters, but the typical (average) values vary between populations in a more or less predictable way. Coastal fish tend to have relatively shorter heads (and thus a more elongate form) and more fin-rays, teeth, and scales than lake fish at the same latitude, with fish from brackish lagoons at intermediate values. Fish from the south of New Zealand tend to have short heads and a maximum number of fin-rays, and so forth, and these characteristics give way northward (towards warmer conditions) to opposite values within lake and estuarine populations when these are considered separately. *R. semoni* shows similar trends in Australia. That temperature is not the main or sole factor in producing these changes is apparent from the observation that the number of dorsal rays and scales also decrease with increase in altitude; that is, towards cooler conditions. Several parallels can be drawn between these results and similar data for other types of fishes elsewhere, but as yet no satisfactory explanation is known which accounts for the phenomena.

LIFE HISTORY

As far as is known, all southern smelts breed in a similar manner during the warmer months. Shoals containing both sexes congregate over a suitable sandy or muddy area in a rivermouth or on a lake shore, and large numbers of small sticky eggs are spawned in midwater and are fertilized immediately. The males have longer fins than the females and also a rougher touch, due to tubercles which develop on their fins and scales at breeding time. Their rapid swimming is probably responsible for clouding the water during spawning by stirring up fine sediment. This adheres to the eggs and causes them to become heavy and to sink to the bottom, where they lie hidden from predators. Hatching takes place in about 1–2 weeks. The larvae become planktonic at once and move to the sea or to open lake water.

The size of mature fish varies considerably from one locality to another, with fish from lake populations usually smaller than those from coastal localities. Information has been collected only for fish from a few lake populations. These usually mature within their second year, and it is suspected that they may occasionally live long enough to breed more than once.

Food consists mainly of planktonic crustacea and small bottom-living insects, but other animals of suitable size are also taken by the larger fish.

ECONOMIC VALUE

Small commercial catches are made in a few localities as the adult fish migrate into rivers in late spring, notably in the Wanganui River, North Island, New Zealand; and larvae are caught similarly for local consumption on Chatham Island. These catches are called "whitebait," but this term is better restricted to a species of migratory *Galaxias* in New Zealand which is more abundant and of greater economic importance. Smelts are considered inferior eating to *Galaxias* "whitebait" and mixtures of the two are considered undesirable. Smelts do not occur in commercial numbers in Australia.

Southern smelts have occasionally been used as bait for larger fish, but are principally favored as food fish for lake populations of introduced trout. Several lakes have been stocked with smelts in New Zealand for this purpose, but their value remains to be determined. In many areas their natural distribution probably has not been disturbed by man. The opportunity remains for studying the differences between populations so as to gain an understanding of such processes as their evolution. —C.S.W.

SOUTHERN STINGRAY *Dasyatis americana* Its disk is roughly rhomboid in shape, with the anterior edges shorter than the posterior. The tail is long and whiplike, with a barbed spine near the tail base. It resembles the roughtail stingray (*which see*) in having the outer corners of the disk narrowly rounded, both differing in this respect from the Atlantic stingray and the bluntnose stingray (*which see*) which have broadly and evenly

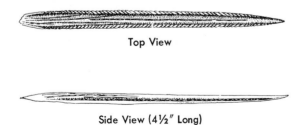

Top View

Side View (4½″ Long)

The barbed spine found at the base of the tail of the southern stingray can give unwary waders a painful wound. The spine has a venom apparatus

rounded outer corners of the disk. It differs from the roughtail stingray in having a long, wide skin fold along the lower part of the tail and in lacking well-developed stubby thorns on either side of the tail. The skin is smooth save for a single row of spines along the midline and a small row of secondary, small thorns on either side of the midline. It is gray to dark brown to green above, and with a light blotch in the middle of its forehead. The ventral surface is gray-white with dark edgings. This species reaches a width of 5 feet and a length of over 7 feet.

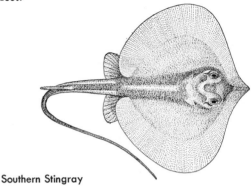

Southern Stingray

LIFE HISTORY

Its range is in the western Atlantic, from New Jersey to Rio de Janeiro, and throughout the Gulf and Caribbean areas, its center of abundance being from the southern Caribbean to North Carolina. An inshore species, it frequents shallow, open areas of sand and mud bottoms in search of clams, crabs, shrimp, worms, and small fishes. Occasionally it is abundant and occurs in small schools. Young are born alive, and they closely resemble their parents in body shape. The southern stingray has excellent food value if properly prepared. *See* Ray and Skate Cookery under Fish Cookery   —D.dS.

SPADEFISH *See* Atlantic Spadefish

SPADE POINT A very strong fishhook point used mainly for big-game fish. The surface of the barb is flat and wider than normal, thus making it difficult for a big fish to throw the hook. *See also* Types of Points *under* Hooks

SPAIN Spain has an intensive fishery management program concerned primarily with its native Atlantic salmon, searun brown trout, and the nonmigratory brown trout. Rainbow trout have been introduced from California. The building of access roads and new hatcheries has kept pace with the increase among resident anglers presently estimated at about 250,000. Sport fishing has become extremely popular during recent years, and the availability of good salmon beats is limited. Quality trout fishing is, however, readily obtained.

Angling facilities are well developed. Government hotels or *paradors* operated by the Tourist Bureau are located near all the major rivers. Spain makes a distinction between its *paradors* and *albergues de carretera* in the sense that the latter are strategically located along main highways and are considered "wayside inns." In either case the facilities are mainly first class and include a variety of lodgings—even old castles and palaces which have been restored and fitted with modern conveniences. The *paradors* are (each room with its own bath) very inexpensive. Fishing huts or *refugios* are also built on Spain's rivers; these 2–4-room masonry houses with a fireplace offer shelter in wet and cold weather. The beautifully landscaped buildings are maintained by the local *guardas pesca* or fish wardens, who are competent professionals. In addition to patrolling the rivers (often on motor scooters) the uniformed *guardas* cooperate in all phases of river management from spawn-taking to building dams and fishing piers. Stone piers similar to those in Norway are placed at strategic intervals on the larger streams to facilitate casting.

ATLANTIC SALMON FISHING

Salmon fishing in Spain starts on the first Sunday in March and closes on the 18th of July. The best months for salmon are March, May, and June in that order. Peak months for trout are April, June, and July. The trout-fishing season normally lasts from the first Sunday of March until August 15th. But in the case of trout in the rivers of high mountain zones the fishing season begins on May 16th and ends on September 30th. (It should be remembered the term "high mountain zone" only includes streams which are above an altitude of 1,500 meters.)

There are 15 recognized salmon rivers in Spain, of which 9 are above average. About 80 percent of the total annual rod catch (between 7,000 and 8,000 salmon) is taken from the Ason, Bidasoa, Deva-Cares, Eo, Lerez, Narcea, Navia, Pas, Sella, and Ulla rivers. All the salmon rivers of Spain flow in a northerly direction into the Bay of Biscay. The north coast runs east and west on approximately the 43rd parallel, which is about the same latitude as Portland, Maine. It is reached by a road that runs east for some 500 miles from Biarritz, France, to La-Corruna, Spain, through the Basque, Asturian, and Galician provinces.

The Cantabrian Mountains, where the salmon rivers rise, are close to the sea, and as a result these boulder- and gravel-bottomed watercourses contain numerous rapids interspaced by pools. There are at least 10 peaks in this range that are snow-covered well into summer (all at over 8,000 feet altitude).

Miño River The Miño is the largest river in Galicia, and in part forms the boundary between Spain and Portugal. All the fishing is in the lower 90 miles from its mouth, as the upper river is blocked by dams.

Ulla River The Ulla is one of the best streams in Galicia. It offers about 60 miles of good fishing water and produces about 1,400 salmon to anglers each season.

Deva-Cares The Deva-Cares is a late stream with its peak fishing in June. This river ranks as one of the better fly-fishing waters in Spain and produces over 1,800 salmon each season.

Eo River The Eo River flows from the mountains into a broad tidal estuary at the town of Vegadeo. Normally the salmon run peaks in the month of May, with fish of 9–12 pounds as the average. It is a deep stream and more successfully fished with a spoon than the fly.

Narcea River Like all rivers in northern Spain the Narcea has its source in the Cordillera and flows into the Bay of Biscay. It is broader and shallower than the Eo and is one of the best fly-fishing streams in the country. There are 9 reserve beats which start high up in a canyon about 14 miles from the town of Cornellana. Much of the water is torrential, with rapids and pools running at least 50 feet below the road. Steps have been carved out of the rocky banks to allow a safe descent to the river. The Narcea produces about 1,400 salmon each season.

TROUT FISHING

There are 150 trout rivers in Spain offering over 1,000 miles of water. These are principally in the northern tier of provinces extending along the French border and the central mountain region. A few isolated trout streams exist in southern Spain. Among the better rivers are the Tormes, Segre, Mero, Mandeo, and Jallas.

Spanish trout streams are very productive to the light-tackle fan. These beautiful and crystalline waters require fine tippets and small flies for consistent results; sparsely tied No. 14's and 16's are more or less standard, and the local preference is for patterns with green, maroon, and white bodies. The fish, mainly brown trout, average 12–18 inches in length, and during a good hatch a skilled caster can expect plenty of action.

LICENSES

In order to fish in Spain the angler has to obtain a National Fishing License. This is valid for a full year from date of issue. To fish the managed or preserved sections of river known here as *cotos* an additional permit is also necessary. Permits valid for any of the 400 *cotos* can be obtained at the regional headquarters of the Inland Fishing, Hunting and National Parks Department (Servicio de Pesca Continental, Caza y Parques Nacionales), if the water is under its jurisdiction.

If the *coto* which interests the angler is administered by the Ministry of Information and Tourism, then the fishing permit may be applied for at the Ministry's regional offices.

REGIONAL HEADQUARTERS OF THE S.P.C.C.P.N.

Guipuzcoa	1st Inland Fishing and Hunting Region. Alfonso VIII, 7 Tel. 17750 San Sebastian.
Pontevedra	2nd Inland Fishing and Hunting Region. Michelena, 1. Tel. 51754.
Burgos	3rd Inland Fishing and Hunting Region. Lain Calvo, 17. Tel. 6338. P.O. Box 203.
Madrid	4th Inland Fishing and Hunting Region. Luchana, 17. Tels. 257 57 29 and 224 82 89.
Seville	5th Inland Fishing and Hunting Region. Virgen del Valle 46. Tel. 27 38 02 and 27 33 22.
Valencia	6th Inland Fishing and Hunting Region. Gran Via Fernando el Catolico 10. Tel. 21 84 03.
Barcelona	7th Inland Fishing and Hunting Re_ion. Plaza Doctor Letamendi, 5. Tel. 254 02 40.
Oviedo	8th Inland Fishing and Hunting Region. Calle 19 de Julio, 10. (3rd). Tel. 18836.
Santander	9th Inland Fishing and Hunting Region. Forestry District, Pasaje de Arcillero, 2. Tel. 20683.
Leon	10th Inland Fishing and Hunting Region. Avenida de Roma, 3. Tel. 5661.

—A.J.McC.

SPANISH GRUNT *Haemulon macrostomum* This medium-sized grunt occurs in the Florida Keys and southward throughout the West Indies to Brazil. Mature adults average about a foot in total length, and larger individuals are frequently taken. The Spanish grunt is distinguished by the upper sides of the body having longitudinal black stripes converging with a median straight black stripe which extends from eye to tail. The inside of its mouth is red. This species resembles the Caesar grunt (*which see*) from which it is distinguished by the number of pectoral rays, anal rays, lateral-line scales, and gillrakers. The Spanish grunt has 12 dorsal spines. It has 15–17 dorsal rays (usually 16), and 9 anal rays. It has 18 pectoral rays, rarely 17. Pored lateral-line scales 50–52, usually 51. Gillrakers 26–28. The pectoral fins are unscaled.

Spanish Grunt

ANGLING VALUE

The Spanish grunt is a bottom feeder and prefers clearwater about coral reefs. It is caught on cut bait, such as mullet, pilchard, or dead shrimp. Fights well on very light tackle. It has good table value, and is frequently seen in West Indian markets. —L.R.

SPANISH HOGFISH *Bodianus rufus* This colorful member of the wrasse family Labridae has the general body shape of the hogfish (*which see*). The thick lips reveal the well-developed, protruding teeth. The dorsal, anal, and caudal fins do not possess well-developed rays as in the hogfish, and there are only 11–12 dorsal spines. The coloration of this beautiful reef fish, as in most other members of the family, is striking. The upper, forward part is violet to violet-red or purple above from about the eye to the last dorsal spine, grading abruptly to bright yellow to orange beneath, with the anal and soft dorsal fins orange. It reaches a length of about 2 feet and about 3 pounds.

Found throughout the West Indies and Bermuda northward to Florida, it is a coral-reef dweller which is generally seen in the shallows. It is not a schooling fish, being generally solitary or occurring in small groups. The young are found in somewhat deeper water than the adults.

ANGLING VALUE

The hogfish is occasionally taken from coral areas by anglers using small bits of shrimp or squid as bait. Its firm, white flesh makes this species an exceptional foodfish. —D.dS.

SPANISH MACKEREL *Scomberomorus maculatus* A fish of the mackerel family that differs from the king mackerel and cero in having spots on the sides and no stripes and in lacking scales on the pectoral fins. There are 17–18 spines in the first dorsal fin as in the cero, and 13–15 gillrakers on the first gill arch. Spanish mackerel reach a maximum weight of about 20 pounds, but 9–10 pounds and a length of about 3 feet are generally considered large.

Spanish mackerel are found south to Brazil and north commonly to the Chesapeake Bay, occasionally to Cape Cod.

SPINNING FOR SPANISH MACKEREL

School mackerel on the move will tear into almost any small lure or bait, but when they take up residence in an area they tend to become more particular about their diet with each successive week. At such times it requires refined equipment to catch them. Light spinning tackle, and even ultralight gear, are ideal for Spanish mackerel, which generally run 1½–3 pounds. Occasionally they run larger, with a 10–11 pounder being an exceptional catch. Nylon jigs, feather lures, and spoons, in that order, are the most popular lures for Spanish mackerel. Casting is preferred by most anglers seeking this gamefish, but they may be taken trolling also. The species definitely prefers a darting lure. Casters usually use a rather rapid retrieve, with regular snaps of the rod tip to cause the lure to jump or dart ahead as it moves through the water. This retrieve is sometimes referred to as the "Florida whip." The same rod-tip snap is used in trolling and is commonly known as "jigging." When using a spoon, a steady retrieve with no snap often will suffice.

Although the three types of lures mentioned are the most widely used, they will not always take mackerel. The Spanish mackerel is notorious for its persnickety fits that sometimes cause an angler to go completely through his inventory of lures without finding one that will attract a strike. When the mackerel are in one of these moods, fishermen often resort to placing a small strip of cut bait or a tiny piece of shrimp on the hook of the lure. Sometimes even that fails. During these frustrating periods, the mackerel occasionally will strike strange lures that ordinarily they would not touch. These lures may be spinners, odd little plugs, and lightweight, thin spoons that can be made to flutter across the surface of the water. They will even strike popping bugs of the type used for freshwater bass.

In Florida waters, it has been noted that the mackerel are often difficult to catch when they are feeding on tiny "glass minnows" no larger than the shank of a No. 1/0 hook. Under these conditions, it is advisable to use a very small jig or spoon and the lightest leader possible. A favorite mackerel lure in southeast Florida waters is a tiny jig of the type used for freshwater panfish. For all occasions, other than wild feeding periods, fine terminal tackle is recommended for mackerel. Leader wire preferably should be No. 1 or No. 2, with certainly nothing heavier than No. 3. When the mackerel are being particularly difficult, anglers sometimes use 30–50-pound-test monofilament as leader material. Because mackerel have small, razorlike teeth, nothing lighter is recommended in monofilament. Black swivels should be used, as the mackerel will strike a brass one, cutting the line. Of great importance—especially when trolling—is a straight leader, free of bends or kinks. A bend in a wire leader can change the action of a small lure. Mackerel

Spanish Mackerel, 5-pound Male, Palm Beach, Florida

are highly sensitive to motion. No mackerel fisherman should be without a simple wire-straightening device.

BAIT-FISHING FOR SPANISH MACKEREL

Live shrimp and dead fresh minnows are the two important baits for taking Spanish mackerel. Live shrimp, on a No. 1/0 hook, may be fished with or without a plastic float. When the mackerel are located near the bottom, the float may be discarded and one or two shot weights added.

Small minnows are usually fished in the same manner, but the size of the hook should be in proportion to the size of the bait used. *See also* Cero, Florida, Monterey Spanish Mackerel   —E.C.B.
—B.B.C.

SPEARFISH *See* Billfish, Longbill Spearfish, Mediterranean Spearfish, Shortbill Spearfish

SPEARING *See* Atlantic Silverside

SPECIES (both singular and plural) An organism or organisms forming a natural population or group of populations that transmit specific characteristics from parent to offspring. They are reproductively isolated from other populations with which they might breed. Populations usually exhibit a loss of fertility when hybridizing.

SPECKLED DACE *Rhinichthys osculus* A grayish, speckled minnow with a faint lateral band. All fins tinged with color. Body slender. Head short. Eye large. Scales 60–64 in lateral line. Small barbel usually present in a depression at junction of jaws. Premaxillaries protractile. The speckled dace and its many subspecies range west of the Rocky Mountains in coastwise streams of Washington and Oregon, and in the Columbia River basin south to southern California and the Colorado River drainage.

This dace is found in clear lakes and streams and also is abundant in warm springs and spring flows. It seems to prefer rubble-strewn riffle areas. One subspecies is known

to inhabit spring flows with temperatures of 84°F. An omnivorous feeder, the speckled dace subsists on algae and other plant material, small crustaceans, insect larvae, and small snails. Depending on water temperatures, this dace may spawn between midspring and midsummer.

ECONOMIC VALUE

The speckled dace is a favorite bait species within its range.   —R.A.J.

SPECKLED HIND *Epinephelus drummondhayi* This rather rare species occurs off southern Florida and throughout the tropical American Atlantic. It is one of the smaller groupers, rarely reaching over 20 inches in total length. Also called "calico grouper" in reference to its color pattern.

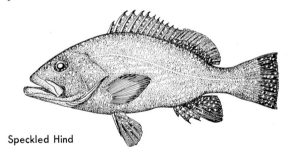

Speckled Hind

The speckled hind has 11 dorsal spines; 15–16 dorsal rays, usually 16; and 9 anal rays. Pectoral rays usually 18. Posterior nostril about equal to, or somewhat larger than, the anterior. Insertion of pelvic fin under lower end of pectoral base. Posterior margin of caudal fin straight or slightly concave. Head, body, and fins profusely speckled with white spots on a dark background.

This species is distinguished from the others by the unique, striking color pattern.

ANGLING VALUE

One of the least known of the groupers. The speckled hind occurs in water that is moderately deep. It is not usually taken on conventional angling gear. A rewarding catch due to its scarcity and beautiful color pattern.

FOOD VALUE

Not known to be a commercial fish anywhere but edible like all other groupers.   —L.R.

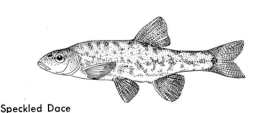

Speckled Dace

SPECKLED MADTOM *Noturus leptacanthus* It is found from eastern Louisiana to Florida and north to South Carolina. Anal fin with 18 rays or less. Occurs in sandy and rocky streams. An inhabitant of small- to moderate-sized creeks with a coarse sand or gravel bottom and

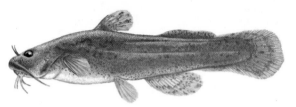

Speckled Madtom

moderately swift currents, it reaches a maximum length of about 3 inches. Seldom used as bait, but it has some value as a forage fish for bass.

SPECKLED PERCH A common regional (Southern United States) but erroneous name for either the black or white crappie. *See also* Black Crappie, White Crappie

SPECKLED TROUT A regional name for the brook trout in central and eastern Canada. Also a regional name for the spotted seatrout along the Gulf Coast of the United States. *See also* Brook Trout, Spotted Seatrout

SPENT-WING A type of dry fly in which the wings are made of the points of hackle feathers tied horizontally and at right angles to the hook shank. The extended wings are designed to suggest a dead or "spent" mayfly. One of the most popular spent-wings is the Adams; however many other patterns can be dressed in spent-wing style. *See also* Fly Fishing, Fly Tying

SPERM WHALE *See* Whales

SPIDER A type of artificial fly, which may be wet or dry, that features overlong hackles in comparison to its hook size. Although wet spider patterns are used to a limited extent, it is chiefly the dry version which United States anglers favor. Because of its air resistance (due to the large diameter of the extended hackles), it is almost impossible to bring a spider down heavily on the surface of the water. It is a great boon to the mediocre caster, and ideal for difficult trout. The fly does not imitate a natural spider, although it may suggest one, but it does have some of the ethereal qualities of many aquatic insects because it is delicate and rides high on the water. The key in its design is the lightness of the hook. A light-wire hook permits the use of minimum hackle, and when that hackle is long the hook will stand away from the surface, provided it is supported by an equally long tail. Furthermore, it falls easily to the water and has less tendency to drag on complex currents; it literally bounces over them. This ability to move almost independently is no small part of the attraction of spider design.

The spider-type fly is most effective on water that is glassy or reasonably flat. In very fast runs the bulkier bivisibles and clipped hair-bodied flies float better, and their larger impression against the surface is undoubtedly more useful in tempting trout to the top. However, on most rivers the problem fish are in the still places where artificials are easily distinguished from the real thing. The stiff, long, sparsely dressed spider is a brilliant suggestion of insect life under these conditions.

It is usually difficult for the amateur fly tier to find quality spade and saddle hackles which are necessary in dressing a' spider; a rooster doesn't grow more than a half-dozen of the former, and commercial skinners are inclined to trim off the saddle hackles. For this reason, many of the popular spider patterns consist of two different mixed spades, such as ginger and grizzly, or mahogany and grizzly. To get maximum flotation do not make a body on the fly, but wind the hackles around two-thirds of the shank length of the hook.

Fly types which are similar to the spider are the variant, a long, hackled fly of conventional design featuring wings and body, and the skater, a spider without tail.

—A.J.McC.

SPIKE A common name for a small Atlantic mackerel about 6–7 inches long. The term is used by commercial fishermen, and comes from the fact that these fish are not any bigger than a big nail or spike.

SPIN-CASTING Distinguished from spinning (*which see*).

The closed-face reel works on the fixed-spool principle. The stationary drum is mounted so that the line "peels" off the end. Its most popular application is to bait-casting-type rods, although it can be used on spinning rods when necessary. But unlike the orthodox open-face reel, the entire mechanism is enclosed in a cone-shaped hood. The casting action is controlled by the thumb resting on a push-button or lever rather than on the spool itself, as in the case of a multiplier. Although the line spirals off the end of the spool, this motion is contained within the hood, and it passes out through a hole in the front. This is the only limitation to closed-spool reels, by that is meant the friction created by the spiraling line as it escapes from the inside of the hood. Friction cuts down the distance, and the purist caster will go to great extremes to eliminate it, but from a practical point of view a well-made closed-spool reel does a quite effective job at average casting ranges. As far as most plugging situations are concerned the loss in efficiency isn't even noticeable. The optimum lure weights are $3/8$–$5/8$ ounce. Casting distance falls off sharply with very light lures not only because of friction but because the fine lines they require have a tendency to foul in the housing.

GENERAL

There are two general types of closed-spool reels. One type is mounted below the rod, the same as the regular spinning reel. Some models require grasping the line to control casts. Other models have release mechanisms for line control, including a reel built as an integral part of the rod with the push-button located in the rod-butt section. This is a most comfortable unit, providing for rod options in that the reel can be unscrewed and removed if you need to use a lighter or heavier stick.

The other type, the top-mounted spin-casting reel, is designed for any bait-casting rod having an offset reel seat. Although it can be slipped on a straight-grip rod, this combination is not too comfortable. You will have to reach up with your thumb which is both awkward and fatiguing. It's a good idea to buy both the rod and reel at the same time to make certain that one fits the other.

Many manufacturers prewind the reel spool with line, but if this is not the case make certain to use the recommended size. The general range for closed-spool reels is from 6-pound-test to 15-pound-test in monofilament. Don't use braided line because it will pile up inside the housing. Occasionally, a monofilament line will be missed by the pickup pin (then simply pull on the line with your left hand or raise the rod tip to eliminate the slack and it will engage), but otherwise you'll experience a lot less trouble with slack under the hood, than you would with an orthodox spinning reel. In practice, the closed-face mill is so trouble free that it's by far the easier reel to use for night fishing because it doesn't require any manual dexterity to keep the line on the spool. It's ideal for the man who tosses surface baits on moonlit bass ponds, as you don't have to worry about loose loops of slack.

HOW TO CAST

Body position is important in all casting, and while actual fishing conditions may require some modifications you should practice in what might be termed the "natural" stance. Face your target; then make a quarter turn to the left so your right shoulder is pointed directly toward the target and your left foot is to the rear of your right foot. Spread your feet slightly, get comfortable, and stay relaxed. Line up the target with your eye and the rod. Hold the rod so the tip end is slightly above your head with the rod handle above your belt but extended

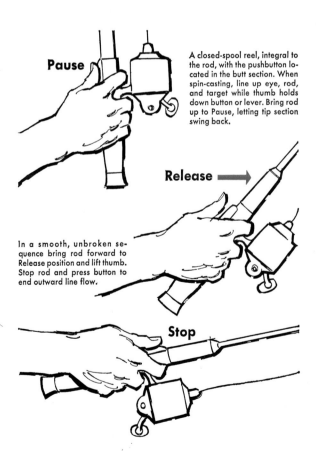

Pause

A closed-spool reel, integral to the rod, with the pushbutton located in the butt section. When spin-casting, line up eye, rod, and target while thumb holds down button or lever. Bring rod up to Pause, letting tip section swing back.

Release ➡️

In a smooth, unbroken sequence bring rod forward to Release position and lift thumb. Stop rod and press button to end outward line flow.

Stop

Hand positions of casting sequence

forward with your forearm paralleling the angle of the rod. Don't stiffen your wrist. Try to keep it relaxed. Cocking the wrist doesn't help in gaining accuracy. Both the back stroke and the forward stroke consist of a forearm movement with just the slightest wrist bend on the forward stroke for emphasis. Start your cast by lifting elbow and shoulder in line with the target until your hand comes up to eye level. The rod must stop in a vertical position and should never be allowed to drift back over your shoulder. Without hesitating, begin the forward stroke in exactly the same path the rod made before. The movements should blend together with the forward stroke made in a crisp, chopping motion. When the rod reaches a position halfway between vertical and your starting point, release your thumb pressure from the button to permit the lure to start its flight. A properly designed rod virtually does all the casting; so don't try to force the rod, as too much arm movement will merely break up the rhythm of the bending and straightening shaft. Try to shoot the plug in a low arc. If you cast too high the monofilament will drift even in a slight wind and reduce your accuracy.

One thing the veteran bait-caster misses in the closed-face mill is the lack of "feel." Stopping the flight of a lure can be done through the push-button. However, you can't actually thumb it, and consequently feathering the plug to its target is not a precise maneuver. Some reels have a feathering device (a spring-controlled pin which the line spirals against), and some anglers develop a sensitivity even for the nonfeathering buttons and can more or less "bump" the line into a corrected speed. The purpose of a closed-face reel is to keep fingers off the spool in any case. Through practice you can establish an exact release point for various distances. The plug can be stopped at any point, of course, by depressing the button.

Retrieving with a closed-face reel is simply a matter of turning the handle. The line will be caught by a pickup pin and wound back on the spool. The spool of an orthodox spinning reel oscillates or rides in and out to crosswind the line, so that one coil doesn't snag another coil. On closed-face reels, the spool may or may not oscillate depending on its design. Obviously an oscillating spool can be made wider and have a larger capacity than a nonoscillating one, but both kinds are popular. The closed-face spool lies inside a spinner head or winding cup that works on the same principle as the rotating head of an open-face reel. Instead of a bail, however, to engage the line, the closed-face reel has a pin to do the same job. Although many models have just one pin, some reels have two pins, and still others are notched completely around the winding cup. Multiple pins or notches not only help to distribute wear but allow a much faster pickup of the line. When the reel is in the casting position with the button depressed the pickup pin is retracted flush with the winding cup. When the handle is turned the pin extends and catches the line. To keep the line from spiraling off the spool when you push the button and retract the pin, the winding cup moves forward and presses against the nose of the hood. The line is held in place against a smooth nylon or rubber ring so that it can't be damaged.

When retrieving and working the plug, many anglers like to palm their reels and this is probably the most

Spin-Casting Reels: (*top row*) Martin 80-XL, Bronson Regent 990, the Pflueger Jupiter 99; (*second row*) Shakespeare 1795 Dual Drag, Heddon Scandia Mark IV 90, the True Temper 420; (*third row*) Heddon 100, the Wright & McGill 88SS; (*bottom*) Johnson 710A, Zebco 33, and the Garcia Abu-Matic 140. Reels courtesy of Abercrombie & Fitch, Bronson Reel Co., Pflueger Corp., Shakespeare Co., Heddon & Sons, Wright & McGill Co., Johnson Reels, Inc., and Zebco Corp.

comfortable way of holding the outfit because the reel usually fits naturally in the hand. By laying one side of the reel in your palm you can also let the line pass between your thumb and index finger when there's too much slack on the water to maintain an even tension. The reel should have a substantial handle to provide a good cranking radius so the line comes back at a reasonable speed without tiring the other hand. And, of course.

the drag must be conveniently located and easy to operate. The adjustable drag mechanism of a spin-casting reel may be located on the front, top, or side of the spool. In any case it should be smooth and display no jerkiness or build-up in operation. The drag isn't too important for most freshwater fishing, but heavy gamefish are definitely going to put it to the test. —R.C.W.
—A.J.McC.

SPINE Unbranched and unjointed fin rays, either stiff or flexible

SPINNER (1) A fly-fishing term used to identify the imago stage of the mayfly. This is the mature insect at the time of mating. Spinners are often seen in great numbers as they gather in clouds and dance over the surface of the water.

(2) A lure in which the principal part is an oval metal blade designed to spin when drawn through the water. The blade generally revolves around a shaft; however, there are some variations in construction. Although spinners are often mounted in tandem with other lures the blade in itself is sufficient to attract game- and panfish. A spinner creates the illusion of a minnow, or at least something edible, in three ways. It has vibration, flash, and motion. Water is a more positive conductor of sound waves than air. External noises, such as a man shouting, bounce off the surface, and fish pay no attention to them. But let the same person step too hard on a hollow bank and the vibrations pass through the earth into the water and into the lateral line of his quarry. Although the "ears" of a fish do not function in the same fashion as the angler's, the fact remains that fish can hear underwater sounds and in themselves emit vibrations which are audible to other fish (*see* Anatomy). Considering the fact that spinners are often effective in muddy water and after dark, this vibration factor is of great significance. Both the size and the speed at which the blade rotates probably has more to do with earning strikes than its actual appearance in the water. Spinners used for casting are ordinarily from 1–3 inches long, but those made for trolling are often 5 inches and as many as seven blades may be mounted on the same shaft. A popular lake-trout trolling rig is composed of three Willowleaf and five Bear Valley spinners mounted on a 48-inch length of wire. This armament either gives the illusion of a whole school of baitfish, or else it has the same effect as a "silent" whistle on a dog. When a lure such as a fly, or pork rind, or worm won't attract fish, it often happens that the addition of a small spinner with its glittering movement is successful.

CONSTRUCTION OF SPINNERS

A spinner consists of a shaft and clevis upon which the blade is mounted. The shaft is generally made of tinned piano wire, brass, or nickel silver. At one end of the shaft is a lure-locking device of either the cross-snap or coil-spring type. The cross-snap is sturdy and reliable on large spinners, but it may have a tendency to pop open on small sizes because of the fine diameter shaft. The coil-spring is, conversely, the better one for small spinners, but the old-fashioned kind tends to creep up the shaft in the large sizes. The clevis is the revolving arm or ring which holds the blade to the shaft. It is important to remember that the clevis can be bent in the mouth of a heavy fish or damaged against rocks. Then the spinner won't rotate

properly. The clevis is usually separated from the eye and the lock by two or three metal or plastic beads. These beads keep the clevis from jamming against either end of the shaft; they also, in the case of the Bear Valley, for example, which has bright red beads, provide some decoration. The Bear Valley is a Colorado blade with a bit of decorative flash. Other spinners, such as the June-bug, do not have a clevis, but are attached blade to shaft, being braced at an angle by an underextension of the blade, which can be cocked or bent to vary the amount of spin. The only other basic component is the hook which may be single, double, or treble, and it can be feathered, covered with bucktail, or mounted with a weed guard. Many anglers dislike treble hooks and avoid using them on any lure that doesn't require it. Certainly, all fly-rod spinners and many weighted blades used with orthodox spinning tackle can be mounted ice-tong style with two single hooks face to face. These are less apt to snag bottom and won't cause any injury to small fish.

Blade Finishes Spinner blades are finished in brass, nickel silver, copper, and gold. They are also enameled in various colors such as black, white, and yellow. By far the most popular in both fresh- and saltwater, however, is a highly polished nickel-silver blade. Yet, under clear-water conditions gamefish often shy away from bright blades and the duller brass, copper, and even black spinners can be more effective. Nevertheless, the size and shape of a blade are equally important from the standpoint of providing constant movement and the right amount of vibration. There seems to be a time for small, slow spinners as well as a time for the large, fast ones.

Blade Design Unlike a spoon, which is a curved blade that breaks rotation because of its shape and thus wobbles, a spinner embodies the principle of a blade mounted on a shaft so that it revolves completely when drawn through the water. Therefore the basic distinction made among spinners is the shape of their blades. The shape is important because it determines how fast or how slow the blade turns, and also the angle at which it rotates with relation to its axis. A near-round blade, such as the Colorado, swings wide and rather slowly while the narrow Willowleaf design spins fast and close to the shaft. This suggests two things: (1) The Colorado has more resistance in the water, and is best adapted to slow currents and ponds; and (2) the Willowleaf has a minimum resistance, and can be used in fastwater without twisting the leader. Between the Colorado and the Willowleaf are a number of designs which are oval in shape, such as the Indiana, Idaho, and Bear Valley patterns, which rotate at an angle close to 45 degrees from their shafts. But both the thickness and size of the blade have a cumulative effect.

FLY-ROD SPINNER FISHING

Casting a spinner with the fly rod is no more difficult than casting a small bass bug. The metal bait has more air resistance than an ordinary fly; consequently, the cast must be slowed down a bit. Once the angler masters the timing necessary in false casting, he can toss the lure 50–60 feet with no effort. The only thing that might cause a problem is the pickup. The harder a spinner is pulled through the water, the faster it spins and the more resistance it creates. Therefore it is essential that the blade be on the surface before the line is picked up for a cast.

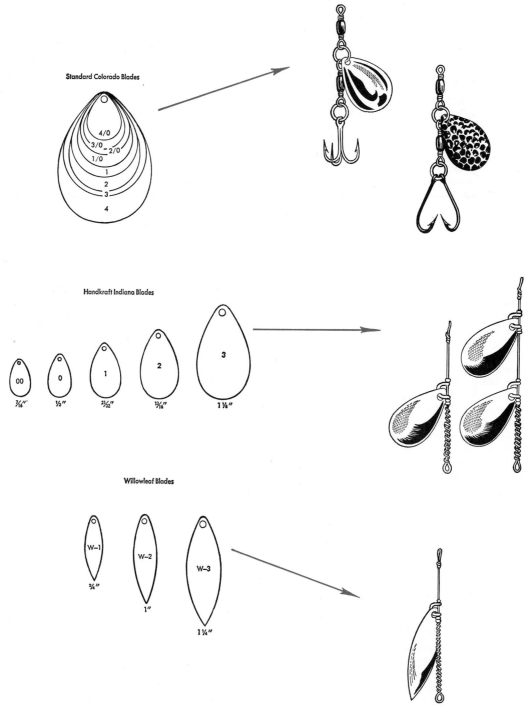

Standard Colorado Blades

Handkraft Indiana Blades

Willowleaf Blades

Spinner Sizes and Types

When you have finished the retrieve, lift the rod until the spinner is on top, skipping over the water, and make a high back cast. Naturally, the bigger or broader the blade used, the more tricky it will be to handle. But this can be simplified at the very outset.

Select the Right Blade   The two important spinners for the fly-rod angler are the Colorado and the Indiana. Each has a specific use—the Colorado is designed to be fished by itself with no other adornment except its hook, while the Indiana pattern is designed to be used in combination with another lure, such as a fly, worm, or pork rind. The Colorado type is mounted on a clevis between two swivels, and thus the action of the blade is nullified by any added weight. Whichever is used the same general rules apply to leader and blade size.

METHODS OF SPINNER FISHING

The most effective way to work a spinner with the fly rod is on a 9-foot leader tapered to 2X. A longer length is difficult to turn over properly, and one tapered to a finer point will twist or snap quite easily. The conventional way to handle the lure is slightly up and across stream, letting the current push against the floating line so there's always enough resistance to keep the blade rotating. If the water is deep, the spinner should be allowed to sink on an almost slack line until it reaches the desired depth or location, then retrieved. It has been theorized that cross-stream fishing is most effective because of the relative position of the blade to the fish. Assuming that most fish lie facing the current, a cross-stream cast will carry the lure at right angles over the lie—in effect giving the fish full view of the spinner and not a rear or head-on glance. This may or may not be so. More important, it's about the easiest way to handle the lure—and even a clumsy caster can provoke strikes all day long just by letting it swim across and down current.

To get results from a spinner in swiftwater, cast quartering upstream; then raise your rod, and start to retrieve. The blade will be almost opposite your position by the time you have actually pulled the slack out of line and leader. When the line bellies with the current as the spinner passes downstream, don't fight it, but let the dragging line carry the spinner around to the point where it hangs in the flow. Then it can be fished out to the quiet places with a slow retrieve. The spinner should always be allowed to weave in the current for a few seconds before you begin to strip back.

A spinner is most effective when fished slowly, and this eliminates all narrow-blade patterns. To be practical on a fly rod, the spinner must be small, but a narrow, small blade has to be pulled *faster* than a broad, small blade to maintain rotation. The best size in clear streams is the 4/0 Colorado (or No. 1 Indiana) if the tandem fly and spinner are used. Narrow blades don't offer much face to the current, and the very tiny ones of a ½-inch or less just hang limply from the shaft unless they're jerked through the water. The standard Colorado blades are the 1/0, 2/0, 3/0, and 4/0. This is a length range from ¾ inch down to ½ inch; although the difference appears minor on paper, it's very considerable in the stream. If the water is silted or cloudy, a bit more flash may be desirable, and then a No. 3/0 would be right. If you are fishing in ponds where there is no current to help animate the blade a 3/0 might be in order for clearwater (because the larger size rotates more readily) and a 2/0 for murky water. As long as there's no current to pull against, you can go up to No. 1/0 if necessary. Any size larger than 1/0 is no good for fly-casting because it will hit the water with a splash, twist the leader, and create a heavy tension against the rod.

THE SPINNER-AND-FLY COMBINATION

There's no denying that balanced spinning tackle is ideal for casting spinners. However, if the angler is

basically a wading fly-fisherman he's not going to carry two rods or go trotting back to camp to switch gear. A plastic tube of spinners in his fishing vest is the only equipment needed to spin with the fly rod. Considering the fact that the majority of anglers use glass rods, the transition is no problem at all. Tactically speaking, he may even have something of an advantage over the spincaster because tandem fly-and-spinner combinations are too light to be cast with fixed-spool reels. A chain of split shot can be added at the terminal end of a monofilament, or one of those plastic bubbles, but the same results are seldom obtained. At best the line would have to be extremely light, the rod soft, and the angler an expert to get any distance with his rig. Even then the effect isn't the same. An unweighted blade swims delicately—it sputters across the current without a hint of artifice. The inertia of any weight suspended in front of a spinner destroys the undulating motion of that portion of leader or line in front of the blade. If the spinner is very small, say ½ inch long, and combined with a fluttery, hackled fly, it can provoke strikes from large fish. Properly handled, the little blade can be cast with the ease and accuracy of a dry fly and made to flash through tricky places where weighted lures would snag.

Fishing with the spinner-and-fly combination is no different from casting a plain spinner in so far as technique is concerned. It's only a question of which might be the more effective lure under specific conditions. Any bucktail, wet pattern, or streamer fly can be added behind a spinner. Bear in mind that ringed-eye hooks (with the eye flush to the shank) are better than the turned-up or turned-down eye hooks which have a tendency to cock at angles or become ensnared on the spinner shaft. The flies should also be rather small and sparsely dressed. A thickly winged bucktail, for example, would buoy a 4/0 spinner at the surface. Simple hackle patterns like the Brown Hackle, Grey Hackle, Black Hackle and for that matter any of the wet spider patterns and Woolly Worms are ideal for trout, bass, and panfish. *See also* Spinning, Ultra-light Spinning   —A.J.McC.

SPINNER SHARK *Carcharhinus maculipinnis* Also known as the large blacktip shark, this is a long-snouted member of the requiem-shark family which is recognized by its long gill slits, well-marked black tips to the fins, lack of a dorsal ridge, small eyes, and smooth edges of the lower teeth (*see* the blacktip shark for comparison). It is gray above and white below, with a faint dark band on the sides up to the pelvic fins. Individuals of 8 feet are known. Known from southern Florida, Cuba, and Puerto Rico, it occurs in schools, and, like the blacktip, is commonly observed leaping from the water and twisting. It is a strong swimmer, occasionally provides sport for anglers, and is also taken in the commercial shark fishery for its hide.

ANGLING VALUE

The spinner shark, like several other species which seasonally and geographically occur in shallow water, notably the blacktip, hammerhead, and lemon shark, provides excellent light tackle angling with artificial lures. Spinning or bait casting equipment with suitable topwater plugs and the fly rod using large streamer flies (No. 4/0–6/0) will take sharks. There are large concentrations of both spinners and blacktips on the flats around Flamingo, Florida, and as far north as Marco, where conditions for this type of fishing are ideal. Flamingo is considered one of the best shark fly fishing areas in the state.

When casting artificials, it is very important to place the lure directly in front of, or slightly to one side of the shark's head for consistent strikes. Sharks will bolt at a nearby lure, but display some visual difficulty in finding a moving bait which is off-target. Accurate casting pays off. Equally important, the retrieve must be slow and erratic. Shark-proofing terminal gear is impossible, but a short wire leader in front of the fly or plug allows a fair percentage of boated fish.

DANGER TO MAN

A spinner shark is known to be responsible for an attack on man in Florida in 1944.   —D.dS.

SPINNING A method of casting and fishing which is distinguished by the use of a fixed-spool reel. The equipment was introduced to America in 1935 from Europe; however, it did not become popular until more than a decade later when United States manufacturers recognized the virtues of spinning equipment and contributed in part to its further development. Although the modern fixed-spool reel was not "invented" by a single individual, but rather evolved from the work of several men, Alfred Holden Illingworth, scion of the Bradford Worsted trade in England, obtained the first patent on a reel which resembles present-day spinning reels. Peter Malloch of Perth, Scotland, had made a fixed-spool reel in 1884. However, the Malloch spool was mounted on a turntable, and in casting the angler moved the spool so that its axis was at right angles to the line and the spool could be rotated. In total effect, it was a combination fixed spool and multiplying reel. Illingworth recognized the advantages in the stationary part of the Malloch reel and saw the similarity in principle to the spinning spindles used in wool manufacture. His first reel consisted of a fixed wooden spindle for the spool, around which he built an aluminum framework of two circular plates to house the working parts. The flier, or pickup mechanism, rotated around the spool, laying down the line and simultaneously reversing the twists made by casting.

After Illingworth made his reel, European manufacturers, chiefly Hardy Brothers in England and Pezon-Michel in France, redesigned and improved it. As agent for Pezon-Michel, Bache Brown introduced the Luxor reel to the United States in 1935; the reel was advertised in *Field & Stream*. By the time a market was developed in 1939, his source of supply was cut off because of the war. Thus, it remained until 1947 before spinning tackle received broad public acceptance in the United States.

ADVANTAGES OF THE SPINNING REEL

The spool of a spinning reel remains stationary when casting and retrieving. The pull of the lure uncoils the line from the spool as it travels through the air. Unlike the conventional revolving-spool reel upon which inertia must be overcome by the momentum of the lure being cast, a fixed-spool offers no initial resistance thereby eliminating the chief cause of backlashes. Because there

is no inertia to overcome at the start of a cast, the spinning reel also permits the use of extremely light lures which do not have the weight to set a revolving spool in motion. So the advantage to a beginner is that he can learn to cast in a fraction of the time required to master orthodox tackle. To the expert, spinning is a method which is ideally suited to casting lures that are too light for practical bait-casting equipment (less than ¼ ounce); this has broad application, ranging from fishing the flats for bonefish to casting on small brooks for trout. There are other advantages, such as ease of casting in headwinds, a greater versatility in the effective lure weights which can be used, and cost; a more efficient spinning reel can be manufactured at a lower cost than a comparable bait-casting reel in which parts and tolerances must be more critical.

REEL SIZES

Spinning reels are designed for all types of freshwater and saltwater fishing. Excluding reels used for ultralight spinning (*which see*), their general weight range is 10–25 ounces, with spool capacities of 200–400 yards. Although reel weight is not the sole feature to evaluate, the lighter models of 10–12 ounces are ordinarily designed for lines up to 8-pound-test. Spinning reels which weigh 12–18 ounces encompass the 8–15-pound-test line class, and those exceeding 18 ounces are spooled for 15–30-pound-test lines. This classification represents light, medium,

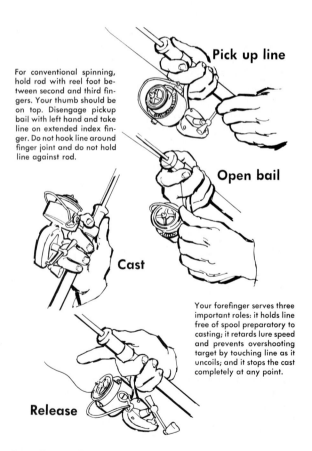

For conventional spinning, hold rod with reel foot between second and third fingers. Your thumb should be on top. Disengage pickup bail with left hand and take line on extended index finger. Do not hook line around finger joint and do not hold line against rod.

Pick up line

Open bail

Cast

Release

Your forefinger serves three important roles: it holds line free of spool preparatory to casting; it retards lure speed and prevents overshooting target by touching line as it uncoils; and it stops the cast completely at any point.

Open-face Reel

Spinning Reels: (*top row*) Alcedo 2C/S, the Garcia-Mitchell 300, Roddy Gyro 22S; (*second row*) Quick Finessa 280, H-I Record 400, Orvis 100; (*bottom*) Ocean City 300, Luxor 1-S, Abercrombie & Fitch 150-Three, Zebco 822   Reels courtesy Continental Arms Corp., Abercrombie & Fitch, Roddy Manufacturing Co., Bradlow, Inc., True Temper Corp., LeTrappeur, Inc., Zebco Corp.

and heavy categories which the manufacturer may further delineate on the basis of purpose such as *general fresh-water*, *light saltwater*, *heavy-duty*, *surf-spinning*, or by whatever descriptive method is suitable to his inventory. Trained tackle salesmen determine the correct reel for a rod on the basis of the various sizes of line to be used and the maximum capacity required. For general fresh-water purposes, it is not necessary to spool more than 200 yards of 8-pound-test; thus the model selected will be light (less than 12 ounces). If the reel is to be used in surf-casting for large gamefish where a minimum of 250 yards of 15-pound-test is essential, then the choice would rather tend to be in the medium category. Therefore, the signifi-cance of spinning-reel weight is a relative factor which should be as light as possible for comfort within the limits of durability and design.

THE SPOOL

For stability in casting, and to keep the line from slapping against the rod, a spinning reel is mounted underneath the grip. The spool is inclined slightly upward (3–5 degrees) from horizontal by the curvature of the reel leg, so that its axis centers or passes slightly below the butt guide. Due to centrifugal force, the line "spins" in a larger arc than the circumference of the spool would indicate until it is choked through the first ring. By mounting the reel below and some distance away from the butt guide, gravity causes the uncoiling line to fall away from, rather than upon the rod. For this reason there is an optimum size to the spool diameter for any given rod.

The diameter of spinning-reel spools may vary from 1⅝ to 3⅛ inches. Generally speaking, a larger spool has the advantage of permitting longer casts and a faster rate of retrieve. When the line uncoils from the spool, its level sinks deeper and deeper. The friction of the uncoiling line against the spool flange increases as the length of the cast is extended. Obviously, a large-diameter spool, with its greater circumference, is less subject to friction (within the limits of any comparable cast) because the line level does not dwindle as rapidly. The width of the spool bears a similar relationship; i.e., the uncoiling line does not sink as fast on a wide spool as a narrow one. However, there

are mechanical limits in both dimensions which must be considered in the reel's design. The greater the circumference, the more the line tends to "slap" the rod because of the larger coils formed; the greater the width, the more friction is created by adjacent coils of line (this is reduced to a large degree by cross-winding). But on all reels it's important to keep sufficient line on the spool. At no time should the spool be filled to less than 1/16 inch below the outside diameter of the rim.

PICKUP MECHANISMS

The pickup is that part of a spinning reel which engages and winds the retrieved line back on the spool. There are three types of pickup mechanisms: the *bail pickup, manual pickup,* and *automatic pickup arm.* Each type has a *roller* over which the line passes. The roller may be fixed, or it may actually roll under the movement of the line. Since the rotating kind cannot be wholly efficient (the slightest dirt or corrosion will freeze it), the fixed roller is commonly employed. All rollers are subject to wear and should be checked periodically for possible replacement.

Bail Pickup The bail is the most popular pickup for conventional spinning reels. The bail consists of a metal hoop which forms an arc across the face of the spool, one end being set in a socket on the revolving cup and the other end attached to the pickup bracket. To open the bail you merely pull it out and down with your free hand —although it can also be opened by holding the forefinger of your casting hand against the spool and rotating the crank handle. The bail closes when you operate the reel again, moving over and around the spool. As the bail starts rotating the line automatically slips along the bail until it comes to rest against the roller.

Manual Pickup The manual pickup simply consists of a roller mounted on the revolving cup instead of a bail or pickup arm, and the angler's forefinger flips the line over the roller before a retrieve is made. Many experienced casters feel that this is the simplest and most foolproof design for a spinning reel as there are no working parts to get out of order. A manual pickup becomes so easy to operate after a little experience that your finger motions become automatic.

Automatic Pickup Arm The automatic pickup arm was most popular in the years 1940–1950. It is still preferred by many anglers and is featured on several standard reels. The pickup device consists of a spirally curved metal arm which engages the line automatically. The whole assembly rotates through an angle of about 45 degrees from open to closed position. When casting, the line is held on the angler's forefinger, and the pickup is rotated backward and out of the way before being disengaged. After the cast is made the crank handle is turned, and the pickup automatically closes when contacting a cam or stud. The objection to this type of pickup is that the line sometimes catches the metal arm when casting in strong winds. However, this slight disadvantage is offset by its strong construction.

A modification of the automatic pickup consists of an abbreviated arm which spans the spool width in rotating around a bevelled edge of its innerface. The arm may be (1) disengaged for casting or (2) the fixed type, which requires rotating the handle backward to free the line. While

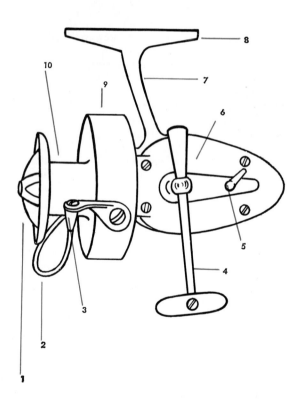

1 Brake Screw or Drag
2 Bail or Pickup Arm
3 Line Guide or Roller
4 Handle
5 Anti-reverse Lock
6 Gear Housing Cover Plate
7 Leg
8 Foot
9 Cup or Flyer
10 Reel Spool

Spinning Reel Nomenclature

reels of this type are simplified versions of the automatic pickup arm, more friction is created in the cast because of the essential lower line level of a bevelled spool.

BRAKE OR DRAG

The drag in a spinning reel is an adjustable arrangement whereby a hooked fish can take the line out without breaking it, while the reel handle is stationary, held either by the angler's hand or by the anti-reverse lock. Its function is identical to the star-drag on conventional saltwater reels. While the principle of operation is the same in all spinning reels, the mechanical details differ with the make. In general, the reel-spool seat is mounted in an exact position on the spindle. It has a round flat side facing forward. The flat rear side of the line-spool rests against the spool seat with a brass, asbestos, or composition friction washer in between. The spindle protrudes through the spool, and this portion of it is threaded to receive the adjustable wing-nut washer creating increased friction or drag which resists spool rotation. Loosening it reduces the drag. Perhaps the most important quality of a good spinning reel is an absolutely smooth drag which operates without jerkiness or "freezing."

ANTI-REVERSE LOCK

This anti-reverse lock is a ratchet and dog combination which may work against the revolving cup itself, against the main gear, or the main gear shaft. When a large fish is hooked and begins taking out line, putting the lock in the "on" position immobilizes the crank handle except when you want to take line back, and the lock should remain on right up until the time you net your fish. This leaves one hand free to use the net, and if the fish decides to make a last-minute flurry it is held in check by the friction of the dragbrake. The lock is also used in trolling. After you let your bait or lure drop back to trolling distance, snap the lock on before putting your rod in the holder. In this way, the bait is held against the dragbrake which you've presumably set lower than the breaking strain of the line. When a fish strikes, the pull will overcome the resistance of the drag, and there will be an audible click as it takes line, but the brake tension is sufficient to set the hook. The anti-reverse lock is also used when traveling from one spot to another; reel your line up tight with the lure hooked in the keeper-ring or over the butt guide and snap the lock on. In this way the bait won't dangle or get snagged in bushes or clothing.

THE SPINNING ROD

Spinning rods run 4–12 feet in length and may weigh 2–30 ounces, depending on the function of the individual rod. The great majority are made of fiberglass, although some excellent bamboo models are handcrafted by a number of builders. Generally speaking, spinning rods can be divided into five classes: *ultralight, light, medium, heavy-duty,* and *extra-heavy.* These classifications are determined by the optimum lure weight range of each rod (*see* table for Balanced Spinning Tackle). For single-handed casting we are concerned with weights up to ⅝ ounce. Spinning rods are of one-, two-, or three-piece construction and are distinguished by a comparatively long handle and a set of graduated ring guides which, if properly spaced, appear in a conelike series when viewed from the rear. The guides are responsible for reducing the spiraling motion of the line so that it passes from the reel without slapping against the rod shaft and with a minimum of friction. The size and spacing of guides is a critical factor in designing a good spinning rod.

The action, or stiffness factor, of any rod depends upon the material, construction, and taper of the shaft. The original spinning rods made in Europe during the 1930's had a slow casting cycle; the shaft was fully utilized under load. A series of these rods sold in France under the trade name *Parabolique* has been identified with that type of action ever since. The rod does not assume the shape of a parabola, but is more nearly a uniform curve when flexed; it bends "into the corks" in angling parlance. This slow time phase is compatible with casting very light lures, which in themselves have little weight and therefore contribute nothing to develop the rod's maximum resistance to bend or recoil power (*see* The Theory of Rod Function in Casting *under* Rod Building). Faster tip-action rods which only utilize the upper portion of the shaft are popular in the United States for casting heavier lures.

ROD HANDLES

Spinning reels may be secured to the handle in one of several ways—by a pair of sliding rings, a fixed-reel seat, or a sliding-reel seat. Sliding rings are the most comfortable to grasp, but because the reel foot is squeezed directly against soft cork, the arrangement has never proven to be perfectly secure. However, with modern *tapered* sliding rings, the problem is negligible. The fixed-reel seat is the metal, screw-locking type and provides maximum security of reel foot to handle, which is advantageous on saltwater

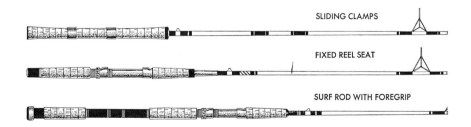

SLIDING CLAMPS

FIXED REEL SEAT

SURF ROD WITH FOREGRIP

Types of Spinning Rod Handles

Small guides or improperly spaced guides cause line to slap against rod (top).
Large conelike series reduces spiral quickly and thereby minimizes friction (below)

rods used for big fish. But the fixed-reel seat sacrifices some comfort and may cramp the hand after long periods of casting. The sliding-reel seat is something of a compromise, consisting of sliding rings over a metal sleeve. This is not always a satisfactory seat, as metal is uncomfortable, and it still has some tendency to slip around the cork. On rods with sliding rings it's often practical to secure the reel in place with transparent tape and remove the rings, or tape them to both ends of the handle. Modern plastic tapes are extremely strong and pliable. The angler can custom tailor his rod handle by binding the reel foot to the cork, thereby eliminating metal corners entirely.

THE OVERHEAD CAST

In spinning as in all other types of casting, the overhead cast is basic and can be used at all times unless branches or other obstructions require an underhand cast. Actual fishing may suggest modifications, but the comfortable stance for a right-handed caster is to face the target, then take a quarter turn to the left, so that your right shoulder is pointed toward the target with your left foot to the rear of your right foot. When casting your body weight should be shifted to the right foot. The procedure should be reversed by a left-handed caster.

Next, lift the line free of the pickup by holding it on the ball of your index finger and backing the pickup mechanism off a quarter turn to disengage the ball or arm. Some casters prefer to hold the line by placing the index finger against the spool rim; however, this will prove to be uncomfortable, unless you have long fingers, and impractical when using the larger saltwater reels and heavy lures. It is easier and in perfectly good form to hold the line with a relaxed forefinger. Just remember not to hook your finger around the line and not to hold it against the rod handle.

To make the overhead cast, hold the rod so that the tip is slightly above the level of your head with the shaft centered on the target. Your forearm and rod should form a straight line with the elbow at a right-angle position and the upper close to but not pressing against your body. Begin the cast by raising the hand to eye level, pivoting on your elbow so that the forearm and rod come to vertical and stop. At this point the weight of the lure is flexing the rod in a rearward direction. Without pausing bring the rod forward with a smooth, crisp chopping motion of the forearm. Some wrist emphasis is proper, but if the arm

action is correct, the extra punch will come naturally. Casting is not a "wrist flick." The rod itself is being loaded during the backward and forward strikes, and in that fraction of a second when the energy is transmitted into the tip it's perfectly capable of tossing the plug across the pond. The cast is not executed by the actual forward motion of your arm except in so far as it provides energy and direction to the rod. As the rod approaches its starting point, release your finger hold on the line, and the lure should be in the right trajectory for an accurate and long cast. The correct release point does take some "feel" or at least previous experience at casting, so you

CLOSED-FACE (Overhead Cast)

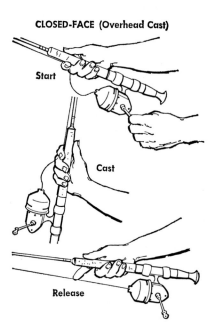

American closed-face reels differ from European open-face reels in that the entire working mechanism is enclosed in a cone-shaped hood. Instead of the line spiraling off an exposed spool, it comes out on the point of the cone. Line is disengaged from pick-up mechanism by backing handle one-half turn. Some enclosed-spool reels have a circular finger guard instead of a foot, and the line is disengaged for casting by pressing a lever don't release too early and send the plug straight overhead or release too late and bounce it at your feet. Through practice, however, you will quickly learn when to let go.

After the lure is in flight you can retard its speed to prevent overshooting the target by bringing your forefinger back toward the spool to create friction against the uncoiling line. This is called "feathering" and serves the same purpose as thumbing the spool when bait-casting. To stop the lure completely, simply touch the spool rim with your forefinger. Even if your cast was absolutely on the button, the forefinger should come down to the spool automatically to prevent winding up slack. Slack coils of line will tangle on a spinning reel. To minimize the problem, always finish each cast by touching the spool rim. Immediately catch the line with your forefinger and lift the rod tip, taking all the slack out of the line before you begin to retrieve. Once you get the timing of this movement the line will lay tight after every cast.

THE UNDERHAND CAST

When casting from the bank of a pond or stream, you will often get into a position where obstructions prevent the use of an overhead cast. In such places the underhand cast is most practical. Because the underhand cast is essentially a "toss" and the lures used are often very light, there is an inclination to help the rod in this particular cast by emphasizing the hand motion. The trick is to rely on the rod which has enough recoil power to do the job with very little help from you. The rod is loaded with a quick upward lift, which is instantly reversed by a sharp downward push to develop the maximum resistance to bend. When practicing, assume your stance by facing toward the target. Then take a quarter turn to the right (which is opposite to the overhead position) so the left shoulder is pointed toward the target and the heel of your right foot is opposite the ball of your left foot. The feet incidentally, should be spread comfortably apart with your weight shifted largely to your left foot. Of course, the stance is reversed by left-handed casters. Extend the rod parallel to the water at waist level so that it points directly at the target. Free the line from the pickup mechanism, and hold it across the tip of your forefinger.

Start the cast from the horizontal rod position with an upward motion by bending your elbow but not the wrist until the rod tip is at about eye level. Without hesitating, bring the rod back down to the starting position, using a positive thumb push on the handle as you do so. When the starting position has been reached, stop abruptly. The combined upward and downward movements provide the necessary casting energy to your rod tip, and when the down thrust is stopped, the lure will flex the rod in toward your feet. As the rod tip begins to reach the horizontal position again, release the line from your finger, and the lure will sail out in a low arc. Remember, let the rod do the work. Do not attempt to help things along by adding a tossing motion with your hand.

SPINNING-REEL MAINTENANCE

The spinning reel used in freshwater fishing won't require too much maintenance. About twice a year the side plate should be removed and the gears cleaned and greased. The mechanism can be washed in gasoline using an old toothbrush to scrub all the working parts. When dry, the gears should be repacked with grease, and all moving parts should be lubricated with a light machine oil. Otherwise, in most inland regions an occasional oiling according to the manufactuer's instructions is sufficient. However, if used in saltwater fishing the reel must be washed each time it is used.

No reel regardless of how well it is made will remain functional if it's allowed to corrode. Once corrosion begins it is only a matter of days before all moving parts become inoperable. To prevent corrosion, you must conscientiously clean the reel in tap water immediately after fishing. Don't wait until the next day. That's too late. The best method of cleaning is to remove the spool, then hold the reel under the warmwater faucet, turning it in all positions to make certain it is washed thoroughly. To clean the spool, use a bit more force to get as much of the salt off as possible. An unwashed line has a tendency to cake, and the residual salt will cause the spool to corrode inside the flanges. When the reel is clean, it should be dried carefully. All moving parts can then be given a coat of reel oil, making certain the areas around the pickup, the crank, and crank knob are well saturated.

HOW TO SELECT A SPINNING LINE

The two types of line used for spinning are *braided* and *monofilament*. Which to use depends in equal parts on your casting ability and the qualities you consider most important in a line. Generally speaking, braided line is easier for the beginner to use on a spinning reel. It is less elastic than monofilament, and it spools evenly. Braided line is completely limp, a quality which tolerates many casting errors without producing a snarl. Monofilament will "lay" loose unless the retrieved lure is kept under constant tension; it's a poor line for fishing with surface plugs for this reason. However, monofilament is more durable than braided line. It has a greater resistance to abrasion. It casts easier in the lighter diameters, absorbs less water, and is less visible. Monofilament also has a smoother surface which minimizes friction against the housing or lip of a spinning-reel spool, thereby permitting longer casts. But because of its inherent stiffness there is a limit to how large a diameter of monofilament you can put on any reel. No matter what the maximum practical size might be in monofilament, you can always spool a heavier (i.e., stronger) braided line on the same reel.

Whichever type of line you choose, the spinning-reel spool should be filled with line to its maximum which is $1/16$–$3/16$ inch below the flange. If a spinning reel is overfilled it will not lay evenly, and it will tangle after the first cast. If a spool is underfilled, friction will retard the cast; on a spinning reel, friction increases over the lip of the spool as the level of the line diminishes. It is important therefore to keep a spinning line at the correct level. As the line is used, the end portion wears and must be removed, foot by foot, to be replaced when the level drops appreciably below the spool lip.

For nearly all freshwater spinning you do not need a leader on monofilament line. It's durable enough even in light tests to resist normal abrasion. Also, one of the advantages of monofilament in clearwater is that it's almost invisible. With braided line a leader is often advisable, particularly on shy fish like brown trout. The

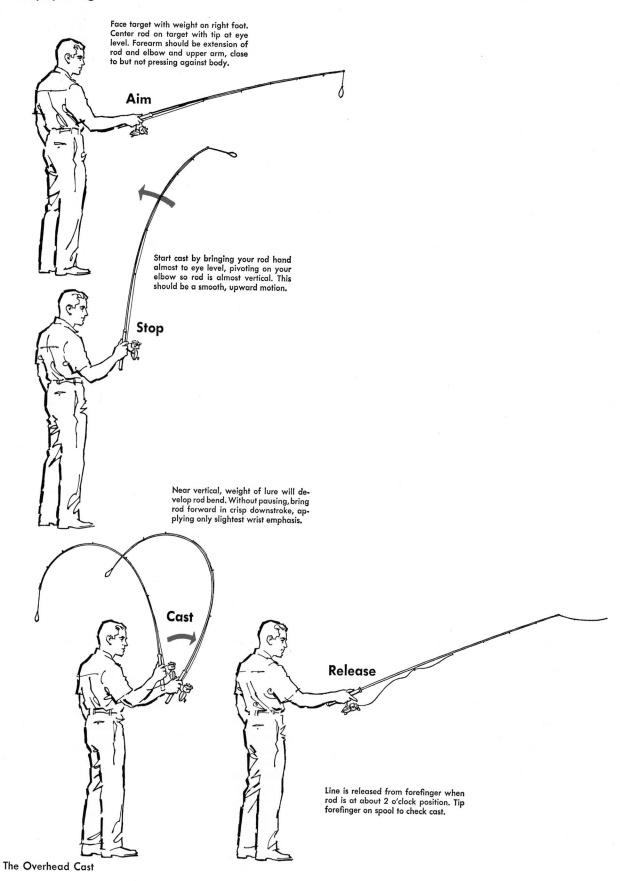

Face target with weight on right foot. Center rod on target with tip at eye level. Forearm should be extension of rod and elbow and upper arm, close to but not pressing against body.

Aim

Start cast by bringing your rod hand almost to eye level, pivoting on your elbow so rod is almost vertical. This should be a smooth, upward motion.

Stop

Near vertical, weight of lure will develop rod bend. Without pausing, bring rod forward in crisp downstroke, applying only slightest wrist emphasis.

Cast

Release

Line is released from forefinger when rod is at about 2 o'clock position. Tip forefinger on spool to check cast.

The Overhead Cast

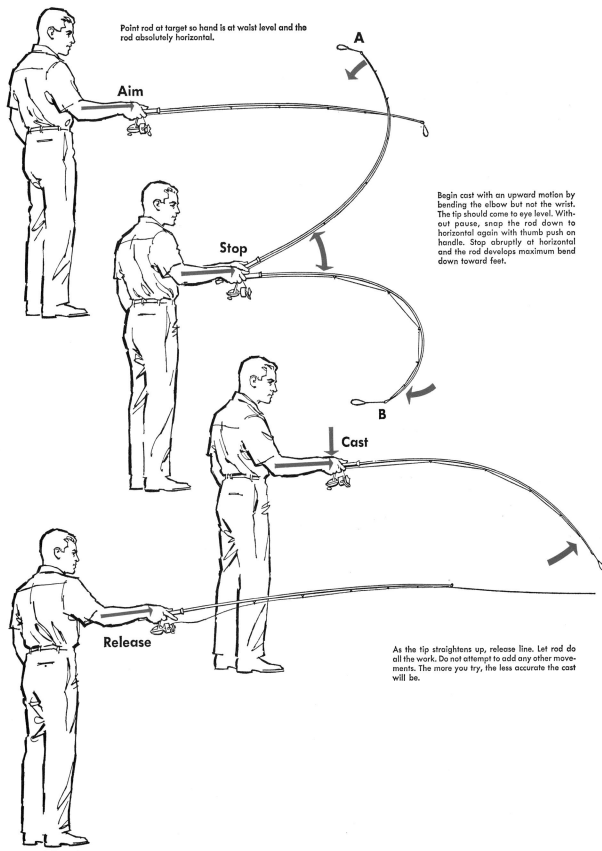

Point rod at target so hand is at waist level and the rod absolutely horizontal.

A

Aim

Begin cast with an upward motion by bending the elbow but not the wrist. The tip should come to eye level. Without pause, snap the rod down to horizontal again with thumb push on handle. Stop abruptly at horizontal and the rod develops maximum bend down toward feet.

Stop

B

Cast

As the tip straightens up, release line. Let rod do all the work. Do not attempt to add any other movements. The more you try, the less accurate the cast will be.

Release

The Underhand Cast

simplest rigging is to use 4–5 feet of monofilament which can be joined to the casting line by means of a Nail Knot (*see* Knots). Although leaders are used primarily to disguise or reduce the visible attachment of line to lure, they are a safety measure in saltwater fishing. The addition of 12–18 inches of piano wire, braided wire, or any of the vinyl-coated wires will save a lot of baits. Ocean-bred gamefish are rough-scaled and sharp-toothed. The short leader in this case keeps your line away from abrasive danger zones.

Test and Elasticity A light lure will not function with a heavy line, nor a light line with a heavy lure. Light lures can't create enough velocity to pull a heavy line any distance, and the heavy lure is going to snap a light line when you whip the rod into a casting bend. A relationship exists therefore between the strength (or diameter) of a line and the weight of a lure. The line must be strong enough to take up the shock of casting when the rod produces backward momentum, and light enough to follow the lure off the spool with a minimum resistance to the lure's velocity.

There is also an obvious correlation between the stiffness factor of a rod and the line test. In effect, the line should not be stronger than the rod's capacity to absorb any given weight. A heavy line belongs on a stiff or heavy rod. Although a fine line can be cast with a very stiff rod, the chances of holding a fish on this mismatched combination are slight. If it requires a pull greater than the line's strength to make full use of the rod's flexibility, the line will snap. In other words it wouldn't be practical to use a 6-pound-test on a heavy-duty or extra-heavy rod. At close range a strong gamefish could pop the line with one quick jerk. The rod must be sensitive enough to work as an elastic unit with the line at all distances.

When a running fish like the bonefish, permit, or steelhead heads for the horizon the natural tendency of the angler is to tighten his drag. This is the precise moment when drag should be minimized. The strain on a line is multiplied by water resistance as the length taken from the spool increases. Furthermore, an additional strain is created as the diameter of the line on the spool decreases because the pull against the reel must overcome increasing friction. Mechanically, the strain on the line may be six times greater as the spool nears empty without the angler even touching his drag. The principal burden of the rod now is to "fight" the line rather than the fish. Paradoxically, and this is where experience counts, the more line a fish peels off (within reasonable limits) the easier you can handle him. By holding the rod tip high to decrease water resistance along the surface, and taking advantage of the full bend of your rod you can finger the spool and use the stretch of the line to subdue a heavyweight into submission. The most critical moments are when the fish has literally emptied the spool and when you play a "green" fish just a few yards away.

All lines do not have an equal amount of elasticity. The safety factor required in a line depends on the type of fishing you will be doing. If you are going to troll, for example, the chances are that you will use Dacron. Dacron is superior to nylon for this purpose. Nylon stretches 17–30 percent as compared to a maximum of 10 percent for Dacron, and most of this occurs in the heavy-stretch phase with the latter material. Dacron also

has a higher degree of resistance to the deteriorating influences of sun and saltwater. Nylon doesn't survive as well. Dacron is also heavy for its diameter. It's inherently a sinking line while nylon tends to float. But for all these good qualities, Dacron is not perfect. Dacron does not hold a knot well. The knots don't slip as they do in monofilament but cut off under pressure. This problem can be solved by the use of the "twist" or overhand whip knot and better yet by eliminating knots altogether and splicing the line instead. So the picture that emerges is that Dacron makes a better trolling line. Because of its weight per diameter and its inelastic quality, the lure runs deeper and is in constant contact with the rod tip.

BALANCED SPINNING TACKLE

Line diameter (inches)	Approximate test (pounds)	Lure weight (ounces)	Rod class
.005–.006	1.75	$\frac{1}{16}$–$\frac{3}{16}$	Ultralight
.006–.007	2.25	$\frac{1}{16}$–$\frac{1}{4}$	Ultralight
.007–.008	3.00	$\frac{1}{16}$–$\frac{5}{16}$	Ultralight
.008–.009	4.00	$\frac{1}{4}$–$\frac{3}{8}$	Light
.009–.010	5.00	$\frac{1}{4}$–$\frac{3}{8}$	Light
.010–.011	6.00	$\frac{3}{8}$–$\frac{5}{8}$	Medium
.011–.012	7.00	$\frac{3}{8}$–$\frac{5}{8}$	Medium
.012–.013	8.00	$\frac{1}{2}$–1	Heavy-duty
.013–.014	9.50	$\frac{1}{2}$–1	Heavy-duty
.015–.018	14.00	1–2	Extra-heavy
.018–.020	17.00	1–3	Extra-heavy
.021–.024	22.00	2–4	Extra-heavy

THE TWO-HANDED SPINNING ROD

The two-handed spinning rod is a heavy-duty freshwater or saltwater model. Most rods in this class are 7–8 feet long, with a glass blank weight of 4–6 ounces. They may be termed as intermediate between standard spinning rods and surf-spinning rods. The chief targets are tarpon, snook, winter steelhead, and salmon. Both hands are used in this style of casting because the weight of the lures involved are too heavy for continuous single-handed work. Such baits weigh $\frac{7}{8}$ ounce or more, and require active rod manipulation for popping and rapid retrieving. To some extent the two-handed spin stick is a counterpart of the more specialized popping rod. Logically, big lures require powerful rods and heavy reels, so the shift to a two-hand style is a compromise to the tackle.

The basic difference between the two-handed cast and other styles is that no actual back cast is required with the two-handed rod. The caster may swing his rod back to get body rhythm as much of the casting power comes from the hips and legs, or he may start from a stationary position with the rod already extended to the rear. Essentially, however, it's the rod's taper and speed plus the right application of force behind it which make the cast. With the standard light spinning rods which have a shorter bending length, the angler must develop recoil power by first making a back cast. In brief, the angler's body becomes a dominant factor in all forms of two-handed casting, and personal styles vary greatly as the rods get longer and heavier.

There are two fundamental casts with the two-handed rod—the overhead cast, which is used in normal winds,

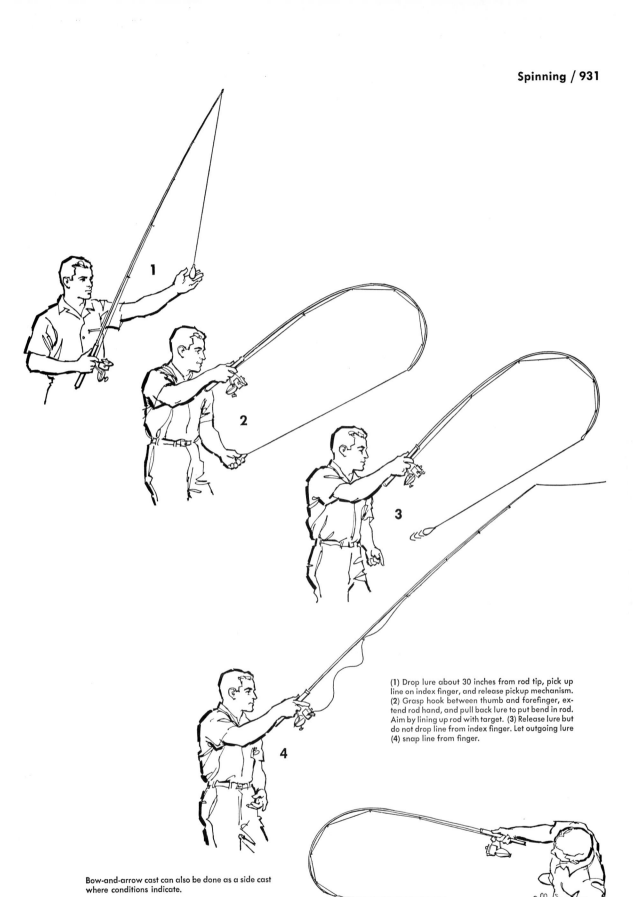

(1) Drop lure about 30 inches from rod tip, pick up line on index finger, and release pickup mechanism. (2) Grasp hook between thumb and forefinger, extend rod hand, and pull back lure to put bend in rod. Aim by lining up rod with target. (3) Release lure but do not drop line from index finger. Let outgoing lure (4) snap line from finger.

Bow-and-arrow cast can also be done as a side cast where conditions indicate.

The Bow-and-Arrow Cast

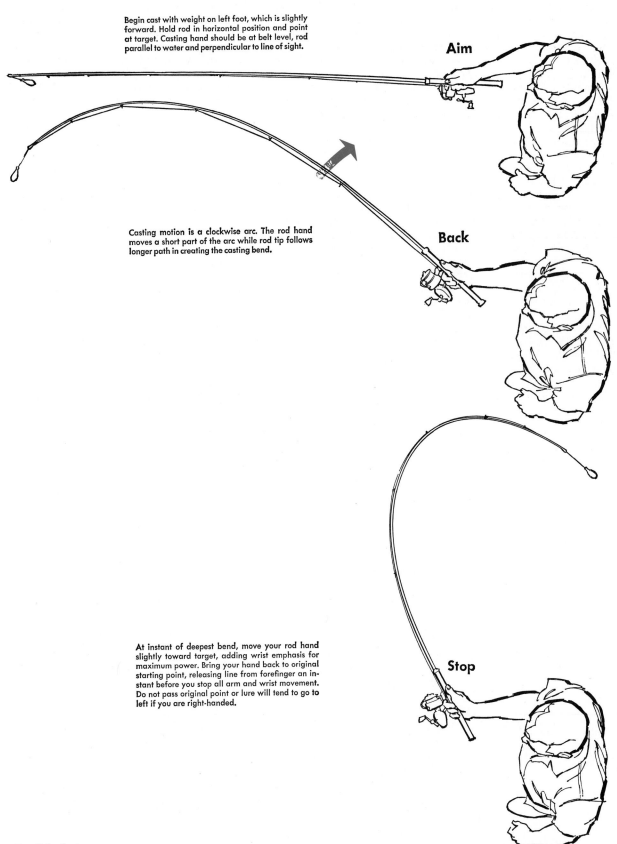

Begin cast with weight on left foot, which is slightly forward. Hold rod in horizontal position and point at target. Casting hand should be at belt level, rod parallel to water and perpendicular to line of sight.

Aim

Casting motion is a clockwise arc. The rod hand moves a short part of the arc while rod tip follows longer path in creating the casting bend.

Back

At instant of deepest bend, move your rod hand slightly toward target, adding wrist emphasis for maximum power. Bring your hand back to original starting point, releasing line from forefinger an instant before you stop all arm and wrist movement. Do not pass original point or lure will tend to go to left if you are right-handed.

Stop

The Side Cast

and the side cast, which can be delivered with a flatter trajectory and is therefore more suitable for casting against the wind.

To make the overhead cast stand with your left foot slightly in front of your right foot and facing your target. With the line free of the pickup mechanism and resting across your forefinger, point the rod to the rear so that the tip is below horizontal. Your weight should be on your right foot with your body leaning slightly backward and to the right from the hips. Your right arm should be not quite completely extended. The casting motion is in a complete overhead arc, during which power is applied progressively. Start slowly, and increase the tip speed by swinging the rod up and forward with your right hand and turning both shoulders into the cast in much the same way as you would if chopping with a two-handed axe. Your body weight will shift from the right foot to the left at the moment you reach the release point about 45 degrees above the target. The left hand merely follows through, acting as a fulcrum on the rod butt.

There is a great similarity between making the side cast and hitting a baseball. The rod is literally swung from the rear to the forward position across a horizontal plane with increasing power to the point of release. The stance for the side cast differs from the overhead in that the left foot and shoulder point at the target with your feet spread well apart. Hold the rod horizontally with the line free of the pickup mechanism and resting across your forefinger. To get a full body swing, point the rod at a right angle to your target, and slowly sweep the rod back slightly below horizontal so the tip is pointing in a line with, but directly opposite to the target. This movement shifts your body weight from the left to the right foot, and your hips turn with your shoulders. When done smoothly the rod will bend slightly, although the idea is not to make a back cast in the single-hand rod sense. As the rod swings back to casting position, sweep it forward with accelerating force, "hitting" your release point just before the tip comes over your target.

SURF-SPINNING

Surf-spinning rods are 8–11 feet long and can cast lines from 8-to-45-pound-test. These specifications also encompass the range of the standard high surf rod, but the real virtue of spinning from the beach is in the use of light tackle; i.e., with rods 8–9 feet long, handling 8–18-pound-test lines and lures of ¾–2 ounces. This gear is particularly suited to working in a calm to moderate surf when small artificials are in demand. Heavier surf-spinning tackle reduces the backlash problem but doesn't match the distance of the standard surf rod. Large spinning reels are made especially for surf-fishing with either a bail or manual pickup.

There are two basic casts to be made with the surf-spinning rod—the overhead and the side cast. As with the lighter two-handed spinning rod no actual back cast is required. The angler may swing his rod back to get body rhythm, generating the power from legs, hips, and shoulders, or he may start from a stationary position with

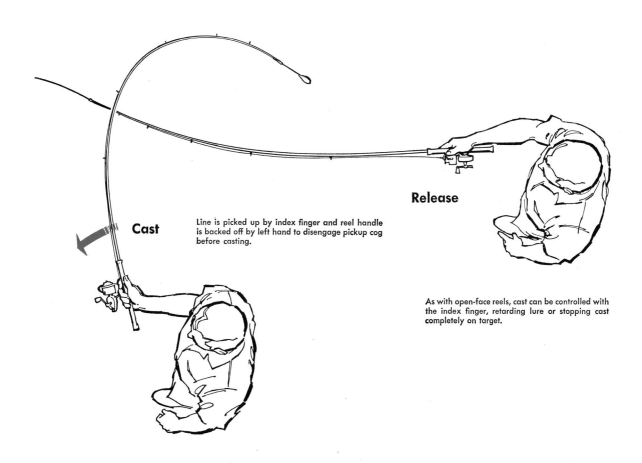

Cast

Line is picked up by index finger and reel handle is backed off by left hand to disengage pickup cog before casting.

Release

As with open-face reels, cast can be controlled with the index finger, retarding lure or stopping cast completely on target.

the rod already extended to the rear. When fishing with bait rigs, many casters simply drop the sinker on the sand behind them and cast from that position.

To make the overhead cast stand with your left foot slightly in front of your right foot and facing your target. Free the line from the pickup mechanism, and rest it across your forefinger. Now, twisting your body at the hips and bending the right knee slightly, lean as far back as possible without losing your balance. Your body weight should be almost entirely on your right foot. With the rod fully extended to the rear, make your cast by pivoting hips and shoulders as you swing the rod up and forward with increasing speed. Your body weight will shift from right to left foot.

To make the side cast, stand with your left foot placed well ahead of your right foot. Both feet should be quartering away from the direction of your target. Release the line from the pickup mechanism, and rest it across your forefinger. Grasp the butt near the end with your left hand, and swing the rod to the rear with the reel down. Both arms should be bent at the elbows. With your body weight on your right foot, twist at the hips bending slightly on the right knee. The cast starts with a body pivot from the right heel, and your weight will shift from right to left as the cast progresses. Swing the rod up in a 45-degree plane with your right hand pushing upward while the left hand pulls backward. As the rod nears the forward position, release line from your finger, and follow with the rod pointing toward the outgoing line.

THE SELECTION OF LURES

The basic lures used in spinning are spoons, spinners, jigs, and plugs. A variety of other baits may be employed; however, these four types receive the widest application to fresh- and saltwater fishing. The plug (*which see*) is, of course, equally popular in the bait-casting method, and its use differs little with spinning tackle and need not be considered here. The selection of a spinning lure depends in part on the species of fish sought, the casting conditions, and the water conditions.

Spoons Selecting the right spoon is not difficult. The only thing to keep in mind is that between two spoons of equal weight but of different size, the one with the smallest blade area will sink faster, work deeper, and cast easier against strong winds. The spoon with the greater surface area (which may be better for your purposes when casting in lakes) will sink slowly and swim higher in the water. This latter characteristic is ideal when fishing for rainbows, squaretails, lake trout, or landlocks right after ice out.

A good choice for river fishing is a compact wobbler 1½–2 inches in length, weighing ¼ ounce. Such a blade will sink deep in high fastwater. Aim the lure quartering upstream, and work it back at the same pace as the current as close to the bottom as possible. The best spot for presenting a wobbler is in pools and at the foot of heavy riffles. You'll have to judge the depth of the water as you move along and correct the angle of your casts so that the spoon is wobbling at fish level. In the average big stream the effective swim of a lure is 6–8 feet down, and generally the speed of the current is such that you have to cast well above the fish's lie. If you cast directly at or even a short distance above its position, the wobbler will be at the very end of its swing before it starts dropping to the gravel. The trick is to angle the blade well upstream and let it sink before retrieving; make a few slow turns of the reel, twitch the rod, and then let the wobbler flutter in the current until it is over the hotspot.

Spinners There are times when a spinner will catch fish and a spoon will not or vice versa. In some respects a spinner is more versatile than a spoon because it can be fished slowly (the blade offers more resistance in the water) and handled without snagging in knee-deep creeks. The trick in using a spinner is to estimate where the fish are hiding and then to bring the lure near the lie. In shallow brooks where most of the casting is done in pockets 1–3 feet in depth, working downstream will probably be more effective. You will have absolute control over the lure, and it can be fished at any speed, or even held stationary against the pull of the current. If the water is a bit deeper, with riffles running 3–5 feet deep, you might try working directly upstream. At these depths you can swim a spinner without snagging, and you're less apt to alarm the fish. In other words, make it a rule to cast against the current wherever the conditions are suitable. The ideal lure weights under these conditions are $\frac{1}{16}$–$\frac{1}{5}$ ounce. This requires light spinning tackle with a 3–4-pound-test line.

In a big river your problem is to get maximum water coverage, and this is easy to accomplish by casting across and slightly upstream, swimming the lure in long swings or drops. Here you might run into difficulty by fishing too "high" in the stream; so the lure weight can comfortably run ⅛–¼ ounce. The ¼-ounce size will probably be your best bet. To cover a pool thoroughly, quarter your first cast about 40 feet upriver; the current will carry the spinner down with a semicircular sweep until it swings around below your position, where it will hang spinning in the current near bottom. Don't hurry the lure back. The second cast shouldn't be as far *up* the river but quartered more toward the opposite bank to a distance of about 50 feet this time. Let it swim downstream again to the lowest point of its arc. By casting in a pattern of widening half circles you can cover every inch of a pool or deep riffle, then move on to the next spot. This sounds like a mechanical procedure, but it takes some skill to keep in contact with the spinner and adjust its speed according to the current to keep it working deep.

Jigs Miniature jigs of $\frac{1}{16}$–⅛ ounce and 1–1½ inches in length can be deadly on trout, smallmouth bass, and panfish, while the larger sizes are more effective on the walleye, largemouth bass, pike and nearly all inshore saltwater species as well. When cast slightly up- and across stream, the lure can be teased very slowly along the bottom and even left motionless when necessary. This slow, bottom knock can't be duplicated with a spoon or spinner. In lakes, the technique differs little, except that no compromises need be made for a current.

The important feature of a jig is the hook. On a lure of this type, a dull point won't penetrate. Because of its hopping and diving action a jig is often struck by the fish when the hook is a tangent to the direction of the rod. When jigging in a deep pool, for example, the hook bend instead of the point may be facing the fish as the leadhead falls free to the bottom. There is no reeling motion to start penetration such as you have when retrieving a spoon through the water—a great percentage of the time.

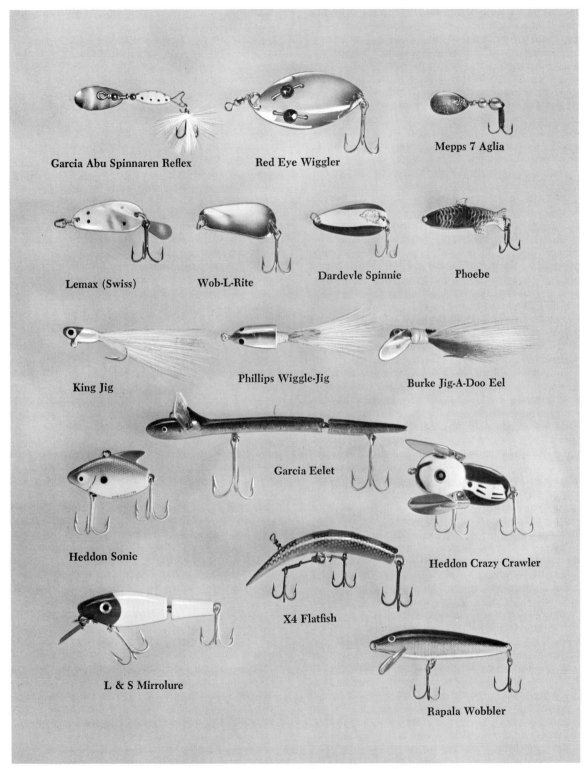

A selection of freshwater spinning lures *All lures courtesy of Abercrombie & Fitch*

Furthermore, the jig is often grabbed by the fish when it is sitting perfectly still. Consequently, the point must be needle sharp. Until quite recently, most jigs were made on heavy spearpoint hooks, as they were used chiefly for clam busters like the striped bass. This didn't make much difference because heavy ocean gear can drive a blunt nail home. But with refined spinning tackle, the hook must be needle sharp.

The value of a jig is that you can worry a fish into striking. This lure is ideal for the trout which swims behind a spinner without hitting. Such fish usually make a few excited passes; then they cruise behind it until the blade is handing on your tip-top. If you locate a lure inspector, try the jig. Hop the lure near its position and if it comes out to examine it, let the jig rest on the bottom. Wait until it backs off or starts swimming away, then hop it again. If it looks excited start retrieving in a series of short hops. By this time it should strike, but if it's still uncertain—drop the jig on the bottom again. Remember, with a leadhead you don't have to keep reeling to catch fish. They're just as likely to scoop the lure off the bottom as in motion.

SPINNING WITH LIVE BAIT

Spinning tackle is extremely effective in casting live baits, such as worms, minnows, hellgrammites, and crayfish. It has virtually replaced all other methods of bait-fishing practiced prior to the introduction of the fixed-spool reel, and can be applied to any lake or stream situation. Aside from the obvious limitations of a cane pole, bait-casting demand sinkers to make the reel turn, and the fly rod requires heavy lines; either condition is a compromise at best, because bait-fishing must be independent of weights before it can become an art. Although you may need one or two split shot when spinning, ordinarily the bait alone has sufficient weight for good casts. This doesn't mean that you can use any kind of rod or line, because spinning with live baits is precise in its requirements; the rod must have a soft or light action. A rod designed for casting plugs and spoons will generally be too stiff to toss a nightcrawler or minnow. In perusing the catalogues of various manufacturers, you'll find the right rod designated as one designed for lures in the $\frac{1}{16}$–$\frac{1}{4}$-ounce class. Such a rod will ordinarily be 6–7 feet long and range within $2\frac{5}{8}$–$3\frac{1}{2}$ ounces. Your monofilament line should run from .006–.009 inch in diameter which will test 3–6 pounds. Monofilament line is a vast improvement over the other types of lines once used in worming. To begin with you don't need a leader. It is nearly invisible in the water, and because of the fine diameters that are practical in most fishing, drag is no problem. You can even hold the line off the surface when fishing short casts, which eliminates any unnatural pull from the current.

One reason why the fly rod never achieved great popularity in casting a worm or minnow is because it frequently popped the bait off when casting. It was easy to lob a bait 20–30 feet, but whenever the water demanded a 40–50-foot toss the angler was never certain whether he would show the trout a bait or a bare hook. That problem is neatly solved with the spinning rod—but your casting must be more gentle than with artificial lures. A fast snap will still shed the bait. Depending on the length and bending capacity of your rod, the bait should dangle 6–10 inches below the guide when you are ready to cast. The rule to be followed is the lighter the bait, the more distance needed between it and the tip-top. Although the side cast is generally less accurate than the overhead, it is by far the better for economizing on your bait stock. Hold the rod nearly parallel to the surface and pointed just above your target; swing the rod back gently to get just the slightest bend in the tip, then bring your hand forward with a minimum of wrist emphasis, releasing the monofil at about 45° from your line of sight. After a little practice the correct release point will become instinctive, and you can zero on targets up to 50 feet away.

No matter which direction you cast, the worm or minnow should always be dropped some distance from where you expect to catch the fish. When fishing across or downstream, your cast should be aimed far enough above the spot to allow the bait to sink, so that it comes to the fish wiggling just over the bottom. After casting you can pay out slack to adjust for the proper depth. Leave the pickup open, and control the drift of the line by touching the spool with your forefinger. There's no need to close the pickup until you are ready to strike. If the current is particularly fast, one or two split shot pinched on the monofilament will keep your bait deep. The important technique in downstream fishing is control; with each accelerated motion, as the worm or minnow passes through an eddy, so much additional slack must be paid out. Since a worm is a natural food with no actual means of locomotion in the water, it should be presented rolling freely. Your results depend on interpreting the point where a trout will hold and how the bait might normally be carried into its feeding area. In the length of a single drift it may be necessary to make a dozen adjustments with your line.

When casting upstream, the basic rule still applies—drop your bait well above the fish, and whenever possible quarter the cast so your line doesn't come directly over its position. The bait will drift at the same pace as the current, and do not hurry it along. Simply keep your rod tip low, and reel in the slack. When a fish takes the bait your line will stop moving. Raise the rod, but do not let the fish feel any tension. If after 3–4 seconds the fish hasn't moved, this means it has the bait in its mouth and you can set the hook. Should the fish take the worm or minnow lightly and immediately swim off to a new position, keep your rod down and feed slack to his run. This often happens in fastwater, where a fish will dash out and seize the end of a worm and scurry back to some quiet place before actually taking the hook in its mouth. Don't let it feel any resistance from your rod until you are certain it has mouthed the bait. There is no hard and fast rule to cover the way fish strike, but a little common sense will tell you what's going on just by the way your line acts.

When to use split shot also requires some judgment on your part. You must gauge the bait drift in each new situation. For instance, fishing directly downstream in moving water causes a worm to ride near the surface. Some fish can be caught that way, but the bait will quickly drag, and you'll lose many opportunities at large fish. This can be overcome in whole or part by quartering your casts across stream and paying out slack; if you can't mend the drift, then add shot. By contrast, if the current is slow and the worm sinks readily to the bottom, there's no need for shot. Most anglers prefer to work quartering down and do so whenever possible. However, in small streams and during periods of lowwater, an upstream approach is most deadly for the same reason that it has become standard fly-fishing procedure—the fish can't see you as easily.

You can nearly always cast a worm or minnow upstream without using split shot. If water conditions require additional weight on the line, then pinch a shot or two in place. Remember, however, the rig shouldn't be too heavy. A weight that moves slowly with the current is better than one which wedges in the bottom or stays in one spot. A rolling bait is going to find fish because it is more lifelike, and furthermore, fish that bite cautiously can feel the resistance of heavy shot. Start by pinching the first shot about one foot above the bait, and if this doesn't slow your drift, then add the second shot a foot above that; although you'll have to modify your casting somewhat, the widely spaced weights will prevent the bait from tangling on the line when casting or drifting. Soft lead wire and lead ribbon are also convenient to handle when wading, and you can buy strips at most tackle shops. As with the shot, the amount to use depends entirely on the current. *See also* Live Bait, Spinner, Surf Fishing, Ultralight Spinning   —A.J.McC.

SPINNING REEL *See* Spinning

SPINY BUTTERFLY RAY *Gymnura altavela* The presence of a well-developed tail spine separates this butterfly ray from the smooth butterfly ray (*which see*). Its disk, like that of its relative, is diamond-shaped and very much wider than long, but the leading edge of the disk is slight convex instead of being concave. Small tentacles behind the spiracles separate it from the smooth butterfly ray. The skin is smooth except in large adults. Its disk color is dark brown with a red to gray cast, with small spots or blotches. The tail is the same color as the disk in adults, but small specimens have light and dark bands. The lower parts are whitish, grading to pale brown or rosy, with the disk edged in dusky markings. A western Atlantic specimen of nearly 7 feet wide has been reported, but the species has reached as much as 13 feet in the waters off West Africa.

LIFE HISTORY

This ray is found on both sides of the Atlantic, being known from Portugal and the Mediterranean to West Africa and from southern Massachusetts to Argentina, but it is less common in the western Atlantic than in the eastern Atlantic. It occurs in deeper water than its relative, although most specimens have been seen in shoal water.

Young rays are born at a size of about 15–18 inches, and at birth are larger than the young of the smooth butterfly ray.   —D.dS.

SPINY DOGFISH *Squalus acanthias* This is a very common shark which is characterized by the sharp spine in front of each dorsal fin. The head is flat, and the tapering snout ends in a blunt tip. Both dorsal fins are nearly identical, the second being about two-thirds the size of the first. The lack of an anal fin also helps to distinguish this species. The small, reduced teeth are directed toward the corners of the mouth. It is usually slate or brown above, grading to pale gray or white beneath. A row of small white spots along the sides occurs in smaller fish, but those disappear in large adults. Most dogfish are 2–3 feet long, and maximum size is about 4 feet. Weights of 20 pounds have been reported.

LIFE HISTORY

It occurs in the northern parts of the North Atlantic and North Pacific oceans. On the United States Atlantic Coast it occurs from Nova Scotia to North Carolina, and is replaced in Caribbean waters, apparently, by a closely related species (*S. cubensis*). Essentially a coolwater shark, it migrates inshore with the advent of colder temperatures, moving offshore or northward as temperatures increase inshore. They swim in swarms of many thousands, roaming over depths from the surf zone to as deep as 100 fathoms. Although they are found in brackish water, they apparently never are found in freshwater. One to four eggs can be found in the female oviduct, where they remain until hatching, at which time the young are about a foot long. Gestation takes 18–22 months.

Spiny dogfish are voracious and feed on any type of fish or invertebrate. Their aggressiveness includes driving off schools of mackerel, herring, cod, and haddock, and eating fish taken in gillnets and traps. They cause great loss to commercial fishermen through the fish they destroy, in the gear they damage, and in the loss of time to fishermen in extracting the dogfish from nets. Many spiny dogfish are caught by anglers, but this species offers little sport.

FOOD VALUE

Although its flesh is good, there has been no demand for it in the United States, even though it is widely eaten in Europe. In the United States it has been used to some extent for making fishmeal and fertilizer.   —D.dS.

SPINY LOBSTER *Panulirus argus* The spiny lobster is a crustacean related to crabs, shrimps, and crayfish. Its shell and legs are jointed, and it has five pair of legs, like other crustaceans in this order. The spiny lobster, also called crawfish or crayfish, and other members of this family (Palinuridae) lack claws, unlike the true or American lobster (*which see*), Nephropsidae. In the western Atlantic there are six species of spiny lobsters, of which the most important is *P. argus*. Numerous spines

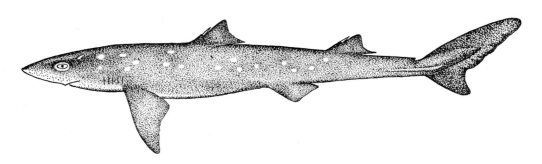

Spiny Dogfish

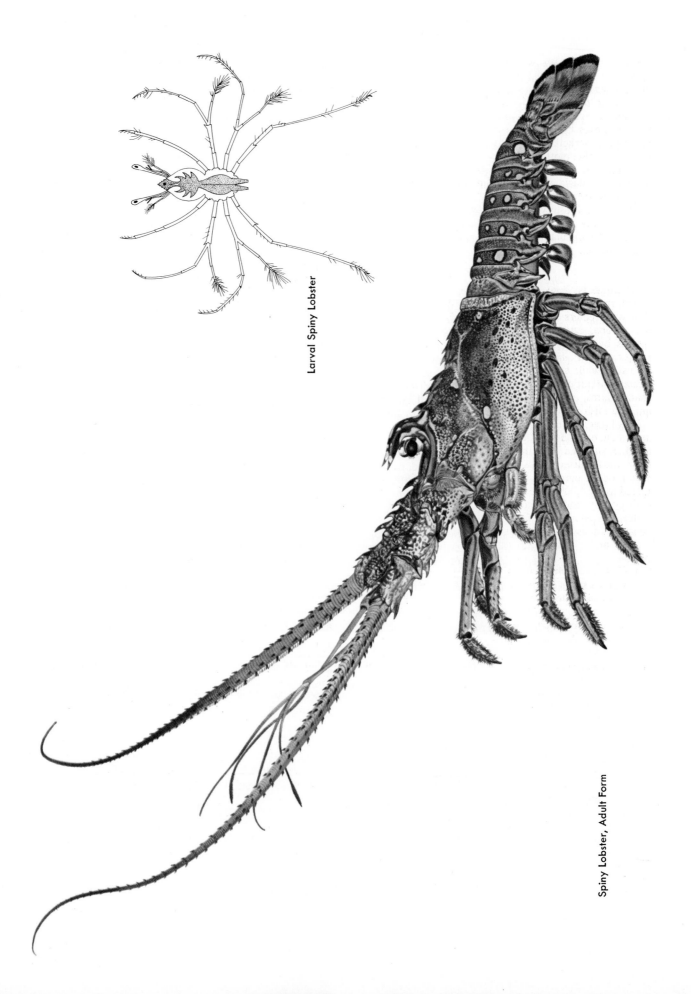

Larval Spiny Lobster

Spiny Lobster, Adult Form

cover the body, with two large hooked horns over the eyes. The antennae, or whips, are long and jointed, like the legs. The tail is segmented, and can be curled up beneath the lobster, the curling being used to propel the animal rapidly backward, although the lobster usually moves by walking forward or sideways. It is a beautifully marked species with browns, yellows, orange, green, and blue mottled over the upper parts and underside of the tail. Over dark bottom or in deep water, spiny lobsters are dark, while over light bottom or shallow water they are lighter. They may grow to as much as 17 pounds, but lobsters over 5 pounds are uncommon. Commercially important relatives of the spiny lobster occur in California, the Mediterranean, South Africa, and Australia.

LIFE HISTORY

Its range is from North Carolina and Bermuda to Brazil, the southern Gulf of Mexico, and the Caribbean Sea, with centers of abundance in south Florida, Bahamas, Cuba, and British Honduras. It is a secretive species by day, emerging from ledges and crevices at night to feed. *P. argus* is usually taken in less than 30 feet of water, while some other species of the family in the western Atlantic may occur only in deeper water. It eats snails, clams, and young of its own, as well as seaweed and dead fish of any type.

The breeding season is between February and April and in June and July. The male fertilizes the eggs which are then attached beneath the female's abdomen. Shortly after, the fertilized eggs are released to float at the mercy of the ocean currents. A 15-inch female has been estimated to lay 4,000,000 eggs in a season. Breeding usually ends by July, and following releasing of the eggs in deepwater, the females return to shoalwater. Sexual maturity generally does not occur before a body length of 8–9 inches, and possibly the females may breed twice a season.

Following hatching from the egg, the young lobster undergoes a series of transformations as it floats near the surface of the water. One of the early stages is termed the phyllosoma or "leaf body." In this, the flat body is rimmed with long, fringed legs and large, stalked eyes. The prolongations of the legs and eyes and the flattened body help to keep the animal from sinking. Usually, however, they are near the surface at night and sink deeper during the day, following the classical pattern of plankton migrations. The young are carried inshore by currents and tides where they complete their development among the sheltered grassy flats and rocky habitats.

Adult spiny lobsters may migrate up to 100 miles, at a speed of at least a mile per day. Most migrations are between shallow and deepwater, but may be longshore as well. At times, mostly during the spring, spectacular migrations of lobsters are sometimes seen by divers, in which hundreds of lobsters migrate single file, or at times in columns, from shallow to deepwater, possibly in a prespawning migration. Lobsters move offshore into deeper water during cold weather and migrate inshore during the warm season. As with all crustaceans, the shell is shed and a new one is grown, between which stages growth can occur. Shedding of the shell, or moulting, usually occurs after food has been plentiful.

FOOD VALUE

All spiny lobsters are delicious to eat, and there is a heavy demand for them. Large quantities of South African and Australian rock lobsters (*Jasus*), belonging to the same family, are imported into the United States annually, and the demand seems always to exceed the supply.

The various methods used for fishing for spiny lobster include the use of wooden slat traps, wire traps, hoopnets, spears, bully nets, drums, rafts, trammelnets, and also skin diving. The fishery is highly valuable to the economy, and the product is excellent. Spiny lobster heads, following shucking of the tail, are also used as chum and bait for fishes, although the spiny lobster gourmet prefers the head parts to the tail. *See also* Fish Cookery

SPINYRAY *See* Ray (Fin-Ray)

SPLAKE A trout hybrid produced by the lake trout X brook trout cross. Suggested by biologists of the Ontario Department of Land and Forests, the name is derived from "speckled" (brook) trout and lake trout—hence splake. *See also* Hybrid Trout *under* Fish Culture

SPLASH POLE *See* Spotted Seatrout

SPLAYED WING A type of streamer or bucktail fly. Splayed wings are made by tying the two or more feathers on each side of the wing back to back, so they will curve outward in the form of a V. For splayed-wing bucktails, the wing is separated into two equal parts by crisscrossing thread between; this gives the same appearance. The current, or manipulation by the angler, opens and closes the wing slightly and gives added action to the fly.

SPOON A metal lure used in fresh and saltwater fishing, spoons are made in a variety of sizes from little 1-inch long, $\frac{1}{16}$ ounce blades suitable for panfish and trout to 10-inch long, 7 ounce trolling spoons designed for wahoo and giant barracuda. They can be cast with all kinds of tackle and fished at all depths from surface to bottom. Despite the fact that the first patent for a metal spoon was issued in 1834 to Julio Buel (his lure was actually a large trolling spinner) of Whitehall, New York, primitive people used pieces of polished shell and bone for the same purpose as early as 3,000 B. C. Presumably the spoon simulates a fish swimming through the water because of its erratic motion and flash, which attracts any larger predatory species. Yet, like any other fishing lure, it has limitations as well as virtues.

The basic wobbling spoon resembles an oval-shaped metal blade, not unlike the familiar teaspoon. The blade may vary somewhat in being broader to reduce its swimming speed or more elongated to increase its speed, but all spoons are meant to "wobble" rather than spin. Regardless of the actual blade shape the distinction is that it does not perform like a spinner. A correctly designed spoon has a calculated balance instability which causes it to break rotation from one side to the other. The chief difference between spoon patterns is the relationship of weight to mass in hundreds of possible curvatures. The theoretical ideal is to design a spoon that swims with a maximum motion through any speed range. The perfect spoon, like the perfect shape for a fish, has never been created; each variation suits a particular environment and circumstance.

Both castability and the spoon's sinking coefficient are interrelated; a blade heavy and streamlined enough to sail across the pond will also drop to the bottom rather quickly. A wide, shoehorn-shaped spoon may achieve only half the distance yet be more "fishable" in sinking and swimming slowly. Obviously the larger the surface area of a lure for a given weight, the greater its wind and water resistance. At times the most effective lures are the most difficult to cast and vice-versa. As a rule of thumb lure weights and blade lengths can be categorized according to the tackle employed as follows:

	Ultra-light	*Spinning*	*Bait-casting*
Line Test (pounds)	1½–3	4–8	8–12
Lure Weight (ounces)	1/16–¼	¼–⅝	⅜–⅞
Blade Length (inches)	1–1¾	2–3	3–4

Trolling spoons are not cast, and while the angler may troll a small wobbler on occasion with spinning and bait-casting gear, in a strict sense the line tests used by specialists ordinarily range from 12–50 pounds with spoon weights varying from ⅝–7 ounces and blade lengths of 3–10 inches. The selection of a lure for this equipment is dependent on how deep the spoon runs and how fast it works. On the other hand, the angler who casts a spoon can be defeated by fractions of an ounce or the slightest variation in blade shape, because wind conditions do not always complement fishing conditions. *See also* the Selection of Lures *under* Spinning

SPORE A reproductive cell of a protozoan, fungus, or alga. In bacteria, spores are specialized resting cells.

SPORT FISHERMAN One who fishes for sport. The term is interchangeable with angler. Although sport fisherman and sport fishing have gained popularity in our spoken language, *angler* (noun) and *angling* (verb) are the classic forms in contemporary American usage.

SPORTFISHERMAN (BOAT) Any inboard power boat, the majority of which are 36–42 feet in length, but which may be shorter or longer, designed specifically for offshore fishing. Fundamentally, the craft is a mobile platform capable of transporting the angler with crew and essential gear to the fishing grounds, maintaining him there as long as necessary, and having adequate range to return to home port. These requirements allow considerable latitude for variations in hull design, building materials, power, accommodations, and equipment.

The basic factor in the selection of a boat is, of course, the type of fishing its owner seeks. The area in which the boat is to be used is also a considerable factor because the fishing could be close inshore and within the range of a rather simple craft—or it could be far offshore, which requires a larger boat with more emphasis placed on range and stability. An offshore boat must have a hull design that can tolerate at least moderately bad weather at a good cruising speed.

DEVELOPMENT

The development of the modern high-performance sportfisherman whose design makes it possible to drive a boat in quite heavy seas with a minimum of punishment to its occupants has completely changed the marine engineer's concept of almost all hull designs. The entire industry is indebted to anglers who had the first sport-fishing boats built.

Paradoxically, one of the greatest incentives in the development of the high-performance sport-fishing boat has been a persistent but surmountable shortage of the anglers' favorite gamefish. This, along with the impetus provided by competitive fishing tournaments, has produced a hull design, as well as several items of specialized equipment, which practically every successful big-game angler is using today.

Perhaps the best illustration of the need for an incentive would be the extremes in boats used on the east and west coasts of Florida. The Boca Grande guide boat has changed little since the installation of the first dependable inboard engines. This is a small V-bottom hull with minimum accommodations and a limited cruising range because the tarpon—which is the gamefish of that area—appears in quantity each year in the Boca Grande Pass or the adjacent flats. There is no need to range very far in search of fish.

On the other hand, along the lower Florida east coast and the nearby Bahama Islands the modern sportfisherman was created simply because there was the need for a boat which had the range and maneuverability to reach the giant bluefin tuna which appear along the eastern edge of the Florida Straits. These are fish which must be located by sight before they can be baited successfully, and a boat must cover literally hundreds of miles in a few days to keep the angler in fish. Here, the pressure of tournament fishing is responsible for the fast hull design, along with equipment which once was considered unique, such as flying bridges and the more recent tuna towers, heavy-duty fighting chairs with integral footrests, gin poles, and now the more efficient transom door to get the fish aboard. Today, these are virtually standard, and have done much to improve fishing in other areas also. Certainly no one feature has done more to increase the taking of swordfish on rod and reel than the tuna tower. This elevates the guide to a position comparable to the harpooner and his mast in spotting and baiting these gamefish in the waters from Long Island north.

STANDARD SPORTFISHERMAN

The standard sportfisherman is a day boat which would be a hull of under 40 feet in length designed primarily as a high-speed fishing machine. It is surprisingly seaworthy. Of course, the inboard equipment will vary depending on the area. But to be complete for the Atlantic Coast of the United States it should include a tuna tower complete with steering and engine controls, flying bridge, and a third control station in the cockpit, so the guide is always near a control station even though he may be assisting the mate in boating a fish. It should also have aluminum outriggers strong enough to troll a heavy bait for marlin, a fighting chair with integral footrest, perhaps two smaller chairs for lighter fishing, and some facility for getting large fish on board—either a gin pole or the more efficient transom door. It must also have a large live-well to carry live bait, a refrigerated bait box (either ice or mechanical for transporting the fresh bait which might be needed during the day), and a fish box to hold the smaller catches. Electronic equipment should

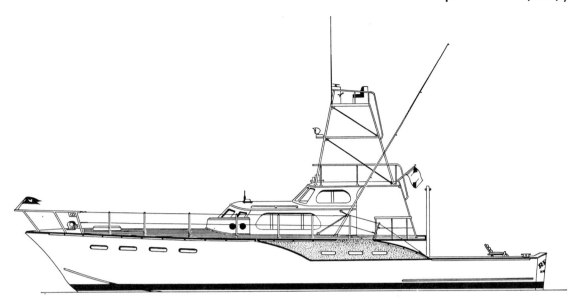

A cruising Sportfisherman (over 40 feet) offers greater range and
more accommodation than the Standard Sportfisherman and is most
practical in regions where the angler has to work a long distance from port

include a marine radio telephone, a good depth recorder, and Loran if the boat is used in an area where the fishing is well offshore. If fog is prevalent radar is almost essential for safety.

While it may be possible to install small diesels in a boat of under 40 feet, to obtain maximum performance, gasoline engines (twin-screw) are generally used, since this is a craft which will return to its home port each day. Speed is more important to give the angler the daily range required to take fish consistently. If anything, a boat of this type could be considered as overpowered. It's much better to have the extra power available, since the engines can always be throttled back, but there is no way to get the extra power out of a smaller engine. The fuel capacity will depend on range, of course, but for this boat a 10–12-hour capacity is sufficient.

For the angler overnight accommodations would be rudimentary, although the crew may live aboard when away from home port. There should be ample lounge space provided in the deckhouse so he can be comfortable and dry on the way out and back as well as between strikes. There must also be adequate locker space both for fishing-tackle storage and other gear. A large head with shower, located amidships so it can be used while underway rather than in the extreme bow, can be a blessing. Cooking facilities are of no importance. A space to make up lunches and store cold drinks, plus a small freshwater supply and sink, is more than ample in this department.

Hull design is dependent on many things. The high performance hull is a hard-chine, deep V-bottom, raised deck hull for fast, dry running in a rough sea. It also has the stability to cruise at slow speeds in a beam sea without excessive rolling. This boat should prove itself superior to most of the basic local designs which will be found throughout the world. These may have features and refinements that have been built into these boats as a result of literally hundreds of years of experience with their particular sea conditions and fishing requirements, but as a rule such hulls can only be driven at low or moderate speeds and lack the versatility of the newer V-bottom hulls.

Since this is to be a fishing boat primarily, particular attention must be given to the design of the working area and control position. Naturally, the cockpit must be ample, and including the area under the deckhouse it represents more than half the over-all length of the boat. The exposed area from the aft end of the deckhouse to transom, which is the cockpit, will require certain definite considerations. It must be spacious enough to take either chairs or a fighting chair, and be deep enough to be safe yet also make it possible to reach the fish. A point to remember here is that the height of the cockpit floor above the waterline is the determining factor in reaching the water. The lower the cockpit floor the easier it will be to bill a fish, but since it is essential that the cockpit be self-bailing it must be 6–8 inches above the waterline. The cockpit depth to floor should not be less than 24 inches, with a depth of 30 inches or deeper preferable. There cannot be projections either in the covering boards or on the coaming on which a line or leader might foul or the crew be injured while trying to boat a large fish. The cockpit floor should be of some nonslip material. So far nothing has replaced teak for decking; it may be a little difficult to keep clean, but it still affords the most permanent type of nonskid surface available.

Cockpit visibility for the guide is of course most important, so he can see what the angler is doing at all times. This again presents no problem from the lower station and the tuna tower but quite often the flying-bridge station is located so far forward on the deckhouse that the chair will be hidden from the helmsman. The correct location gives a view of the fighting chair from the bridge position.

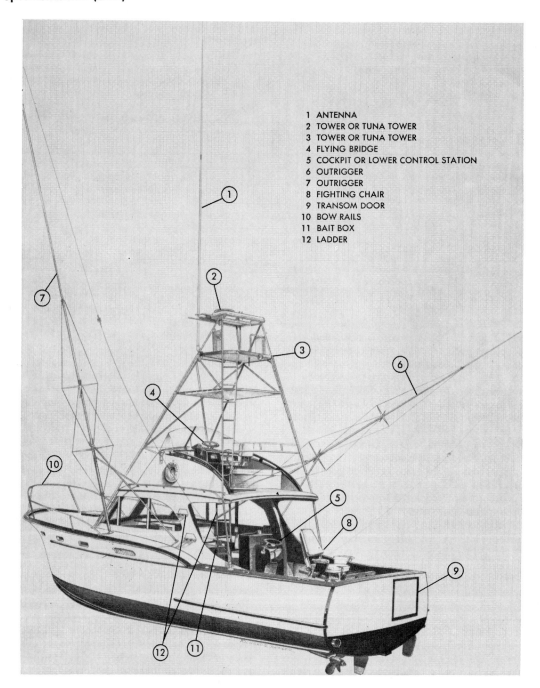

1 ANTENNA
2 TOWER OR TUNA TOWER
3 TOWER OR TUNA TOWER
4 FLYING BRIDGE
5 COCKPIT OR LOWER CONTROL STATION
6 OUTRIGGER
7 OUTRIGGER
8 FIGHTING CHAIR
9 TRANSOM DOOR
10 BOW RAILS
11 BAIT BOX
12 LADDER

Antenna (mainly for radio telephone use, but also for some electronic navigating aids)

Tower or Tuna Tower (welded tubular aluminum structure installed to give fish guide maximum height of locating fish and also provides third control station)

Flying Bridge (the principal operating station for the boat, with all the necessary controls and electronic gears centered here; also makes an ideal observation point for the boat owner)

Cockpit or Lower Control Station (auxiliary station located near angler so guide can assist in boating fish without leaving controls)

Outriggers (anodized aluminum tubes which are rigidly based for the purpose of towing along heavy baits)

Fighting Chair (with integrally mounted footrest), gimbal and rod holders allow angler to fish with heavy tackle from any quarter as chair can be turned to line up with fish)

Transom Door (for taking larger gamefish aboard without need for lifting over rails)

Bow Rails (installed to allow safe handling of anchor or dock lines on forward deck)

Bait Box (refrigerated storage for fresh or frozen bait)

Ladder (for access to bridge from cockpit with steps for quick access from deck)

CRUISING SPORTFISHERMAN

This larger boat is for the angler who believes that the best way to be certain of having good accommodations in a remote port will be to take them along. Living aboard this larger boat can be most enjoyable without sacrificing any of the important features of the standard sportfisherman except speed and perhaps a little maneuverability—two features most important to the angler addicted to the use of very light lines for large fish or to the inveterate tournament participant.

The cruising sportfisherman is a boat of 40 feet or more in length. The larger the boat the more extensive will be the accommodations. Basic fishing equipment is the same as on the smaller boats but can be more complete, particularly in electronic aids, since space and weight are no longer a major concern.

Power could be the larger gasoline engines, but is usually diesel which with its fuel economy can double the cruising range per gallon of fuel carried. Power for operating the necessary ship's services, refrigeration, air conditioning, heating, blowers, pump, and much of the electronic gear can best be supplied by 110-volt generating plants, and for maximum dependability two smaller plants are preferred to one large unit; i.e. two 5,000-watt units would be better than one 10,000-watt unit. Heavy-duty batteries provide starting, and can be made large enough to take care of the refrigeration along with pumps and sanitary system. This is an advantage if there is any objection to the noise of a generating set, which, if the boat is run on alternating current, must run continuously when away from the dock. Fuel and water tankage must be predicated upon the availability of these two most essential needs in the boat's normal operating area. If fuel will be readily available, then capacity for a couple of days cruising would be ample. On the other hand, if it's going to be a ten-day trip with no fuel stops, then considerable thought must be given to providing tankage for that period. In a wooden hull this can be a problem; in metal hulls it's relatively easy to convert the double-bottom areas to either fuel or water tanks. The water problem to a certain extent has been considerably eased recently by the marketing of small evaporators. These can produce excellent water from seawater, taking up very little room. The only requirement is a source of heat which can be had either from the main engine or preferably from the generator, since on a sportfisherman the main engines are used for long periods at such low-power output that little heat is available to operate the evaporator.

Construction materials will parallel those used in the smaller sportfisherman except that as the length increases there will be more wooden hulls and less fiberglass, and for the larger boats the metal hull will become practical again.

SMALL SPORTFISHERMAN

In areas adjacent to inlets or other openings to the sea and where the ocean fishing is relatively near the shore and the weather and sea conditions allow their use, the small sportfisherman is the most predominant boat in use numerically. These are 16–25-foot rigs. Improvements in hull design along with reliable motors have proven these boats to be real fish catchers. Their hulls are now almost universally fiberglass, with metal (aluminum) and wood being second and third choices. This offshore use of a small boat is not completely new since dories have been used for centuries on the Banks, but these were man-powered hulls so the main requirement of seaworthiness was at anchor or under oars. The boat built for today's needs of a fast access to the fishing grounds plus stability for trolling at low speeds is a much more complex design, and a visit to any boat show will reveal that there are many types of hull designs available. For offshore fishing this boat, in addition to having a proper hull design, must have ample freeboard below the waterline with a deck or cabin forward to help keep things dry. In an outboard, it must have the double-transom arrangement to prevent swamping and of course fuel capacity must be ample to give a safe daily range.

Power will be outboard in the smaller boats, but the inboard-outboard drives which utilize the conventional four-cycle marine engine driving through an outboard lower unit are very popular. For the fisherman the economy of operation, dependability, ease of servicing the engine when needed, higher transom, plus availability of larger engines make this a preferred power unit, particularly where range and seaworthiness are of some importance. The boat-trailer combination gives the smaller boat a range and versatility not available to the larger boats which are confined to the waterways to reach other areas. Sometimes two fishing areas can be separated by only a few miles of land, yet be several hundred miles apart by a water route. So the small boat owner often has a greater choice of daily fishing locations.

Fishing equipment need not be too extensive. These small boats, making little disturbance in the water, seem to attract fish. Simple, short demountable outriggers, a lightweight fishing chair with gimbal, fish box, and, for some types of fishing, a tank for live bait are desirable; for safety, particularly for offshore fishing, a radio-telephone, and, if space is available, a depth finder can be most helpful.

FISHING CHAIR

Originally, fishing chairs were office chairs which were bolted to the cockpit floor and served more as a secure place to sit than as an aid to fishing. Leather cups were later attached to the front of the chair to help hold the butt of the rod. The fishing chair as we now know it was originated by Harlan Major in the early 1930's. His chair had a gimbaled rod socket, removable back, and a locking chair base; all fittings were bronze, and chairs were heavily built of teak or mahogany to give years of service.

Fishing chairs today could be grouped into several general classes. The most common is a portable, lightweight chair, usually made of tubular aluminum with a gimbal secured to the front chair frame. This chair is not of the swiveling type; so it can only be used for very light fishing.

The type of chair originated by Major is now used with medium-weight tackle, and while it has been improved it's still a chair with a simple locking base so the angler can turn to face the fish. This chair is installed in the boat at a standard chair height, since the angler will have his feet on the deck. It may have a simple rod holder attached to allow the angler to rest the rod between strikes, and occasionally a holder is furnished to keep a glass or bottle near at hand.

The third type of chair and which is a must for the angler using medium and heavy tackle is the fighting chair. This is a very heavily built chair with attached footrest, which can be adjusted to suit the angler, and an oversized stanchion and mounting plate. This chair is mounted quite high. It should be approximately level with the cockpit coamings so the angler can get full use of his rod, particularly to raise a fish which has gone deep. The chair must have a spindle, which is carried on anti-friction bearings so the chair can be kept in line with the fish even when all of the angler's weight is on the footrest. A hand brake must also be provided to hold the chair securely when not in use. It should have a gimbal which can be adjusted to several positions up and down to allow for different-length rod butts. It must have integral rod holders so the rods are always on the chair in case of a sudden strike. The back must be either hinged or movable to several positions, ranging from almost upright for comfortable sitting during the long periods between strikes to an almost horizontal position to allow the angler to pump a heavy fish in using his whole body and not just his arms. While this chair might appear massive, long years of experience have proven that there is no alternative to size because it must accommodate a person with a harness and be strong enough to withstand a downthrust of as much as four hundred pounds on the extended footrest.

FISH BOX

In the initial conversion of cruiser to sportfisherman, the aft deck was cut out and a recessed fish box built into the area between the transom and cockpit, with flush hatches to make the change as inconspicuous as possible. The fish box was metal lined and had a drain provided which ran overboard. While this location was almost ideal, it did make the boating of a fish rather awkward, since it was almost impossible to reach over the transom. Furthermore, with the increasing interest in large game-fish, such as marlin, tuna, and swordfish, and the installation of fighting chairs near enough to the transom so the rod would clear properly across the stern, most boat owners have favored the portable fish box.

The fish box should of course be large enough to accommodate the average daily catch of fish which the angler wishes to take home. Its size will in the end be determined by the width of the stern; if possible, enough room should be left at each end so the mate can still get to the transom. It should be well constructed of materials which are compatible with the other materials in the cockpit. It must be lined with a material that is easily cleaned, either metal or fiberglass; and if large enough, a small section at one end can be separated and insulated for carrying the rigged bait. The fish box should be held in place with removable chocks and blocked up slightly off the cockpit floor to allow washing. A piece of canvas should be carried to wrap fish which are too long for the box. A canvas helps keep these larger fish from spoiling or drying out as well as keeping the cockpit clean.

Some of the newer boats have dispensed with fish boxes entirely and use wells built under the cockpit floor. These serve a dual purpose since they can be used to carry live bait when this is needed as well as to carry the catch. If possible it's best to have two so one can be used for each purpose.

OUTRIGGERS

In their simplest form, outriggers may consist of short sections of almost any rod or tube that projects outward from each side of the boat. Outriggers used by commercial trollers are often only 5–10 feet in length; however, these have no value to the angler. In sportfishing, the outriggers are used to accomplish one or all of the following purposes:

1. to spread the baits far apart
2. to make it possible to fish more than one line
3. to present another kind of bait; i.e., skipping as well as swimming
4. to fish the baits at a long distance behind the boat out of its wake, without strain on rod or angler
5. to allow the angler to troll heavy baits for large fish

Ordinarily, the offshore boat will troll two stern or "flat" lines. These baits skip or swim astern in the wake of the boat. With the addition of outriggers, four lines can be fished, which make a different presentation in that the baits ride clear of the wake. There is also the "automatic" dropback feature provided by the slack line needed to go from tip of rod to tip of outrigger. This is a distinct advantage in billfishing since it gives the angler a little time to reach his tackle at the strike. Furthermore, the fish could, and often does, hook itself.

The outrigger for most fishing need not be over 30 feet in length. The outrigger pole itself can be bamboo, wood, metal, or, more recently, fiberglass. There are numerous methods of supporting the outrigger, but some arrangement has to be made to keep the outrigger inboard for laying alongside a dock or another boat as well as strong enough to support it in its fishing position, which is generally at a 45-degree angle. The outrigger pole must have guides secured to it so the halyard can work freely and the outrigger pin to which the fishing line is attached can be hoisted to the tip of the outrigger.

Trolling heavy baits requires an outrigger which is solidly braced. The most successful have been made of anodized aluminum with aluminum spreaders and stainless-steel guying wires. This is the workhorse and can troll almost any bait, from mullet or ballyhoo used for sailfish up to baits weighing 8–10 pounds for large marlin. Depending on the size of the boat, and again the requirements of the angler, these outriggers will range in size from 30 feet in length with one spreader, up to 45 feet with four sets of spreaders. Whereas the smaller outrigger can be base mounted only, these larger outriggers require well-engineered attachment fittings to spread the loads properly both to the boat and the outrigger. The strain on a long outrigger in a rough sea is almost unbelievable, even without towing a bait.

Most of the outrigger development has been brought about by the angler who needed equipment strong enough to troll large baits. Zane Grey in an account of his pursuit of the large Pacific marlin tells of sitting in a chair all day with a harness to his heavy rod dragging a 5-pound bait directly astern. This must have been extremely tiring, particularly when, at its best, fishing for large fish is slow. Before the buildup of the Florida fishing fleet, the California anglers had used rudimentary outriggers and then turned to kite fishing (*which see*) to troll a surface bait. While one of the most fascinating ways to fish, and one which requires considerable skill, a kite is limited on its use—it cannot keep anything other than small baits skipping. There has to be wind enough to keep the kite flying, and the direction of the boat is limited since at its best the kite can only stay up in a beam wind or going to windward—unless it is blowing a gale. In the past few years there has been renewed interest in kite fishing, and they are again available. The bait is towed by the kite, and it is fished in much the same fashion as an outrigger. It does lie much steadier on the water since the motion of the boat is never imparted to the bait as is the case with outriggers, except that sometimes a gust of wind can hit the kite at about the same time a fish is about to take the bait.

Since the early-day kites were expensive and somewhat erratic the fisherman had to turn to something better. First, the long bamboo poles, which were worked from light masts and rigged in much the same way as a boom on a sailboat, gave way to the covering-board-based outrigger with main support back to the cabin top. As the length increased, it became necessary to add braces in the form of spreaders. The first pair of metal outriggers was built by Tommy Gifford in 1934. These were of duraluminum and were about 45 feet in length, and, considering the small size of his craft, it was suggested that his boat resembled an overgrown insect.

FLYING BRIDGE

The flying bridge was formerly known as the topside controls. Here again necessity forced the addition of this piece of superstructure, which at the outset was unsightly since the early ones were crude pipe enclosures with the simplest of control extensions to reach from the lower station up through the cabin top. In later years, flying-bridge design has made it an integral part of the boat which, along with simplified engine controls, seems to improve the appearance of most boats, and a sportfisherman just isn't one until this control station is added.

By 1935 all of the better charter fishermen had equipped their boats with topside controls, and the private boats were beginning to add flying bridges as well. There are basic requirements covering the installation of a flying bridge. The boat must of course be large enough to support the extra weight without becoming topheavy. The cabin top must be strong enough to stand the wracking the extra weight will impose. Bridge enclosure should be of sufficient height to contain the crew safely. The helmsman position should be far enough back on the cabin top so he will have good visibility into the cockpit and particularly of the fighting chair. A ladder or steps must be provided to allow safe access to and from the bridge. Control grouping should be such that the guide can operate the boat standing up. It's impossible to give the angler the attention he will need from a position requiring the guide to face forward and reach so low as to be uncomfortable. Some type of windshield should be provided as well as shelter from the sun and rain. Finally, it's best if the electronic equipment, if not located on the flying bridge, be extended to it, since this will be the main point for the boat's operation both in fair weather and more important in foul weather.

For locating and baiting fish which are on or near the surface a fly bridge is a necessity. The tuna tower will do much to extend the range of vision and should prove of considerable help in areas where it has not yet been tried.

GIN POLE

Until the angler has tried to get a 500-pound tuna aboard without the help of ship's gear he can't appreciate how important this can be; for the lack of a proper method many a fine fish has been lost either to sharks or simply broken off in attempting to get it aboard by makeshift methods. Until recently, practically the only method used was the gin pole. This is a wooden spar set inside the coaming and secured to the cockpit floor and cabin top, having at its top a cap with an eye to tape the hook of the upper block of the falls. For heavy fish it's best to use at least two 3-part blocks with ½ inch or larger line. Enough line must be rove through the blocks to reach the water. In use, the fish are hoisted out of the water and swung into the cockpit and eased onto the cockpit floor. The length of the fish the angler intends to catch will determine the length of the gin pole. Usually these are 12–14 feet above the cockpit floor and are 5 inches × 5 inches or larger spruce or fir timber. A piece of aluminum pipe of 4-inch diameter also makes an excellent gin pole. Using pipe also offers the possibility of making a telescoping gin pole by using the next size smaller which will slide inside the 4 inches. When not in use this gin pole need not extend but slightly above the cabin.

TRANSOM DOOR

Although the transom door does involve some structural alterations to the transom, it is by far the most efficient way to get a large fish aboard both from the standpoint of time as well as effort. There is less chance of losing a fish with it than by lifting on the gin pole. However, the all-time hard-luck story happened during a Cat Cay Tuna Tournament. Dale Shaffer had the winning tuna in his boat and the transom door closed when the tuna kicked the latch open with its tail at the same time the boat was speeded up. The fish, of course, slid back into the sea. Transom doors are of two types, a sliding gate which when lifted out gives a clear opening generally to the cockpit floor. The second and more practical method is to cut out a section at one side of the transom from the under side of the upper transom frame or covering board to the cockpit floor. This has the advantage of providing a transom frame with sufficient strength to retain its shape plus bringing the fish into the cockpit at one side so the chair isn't in the way. There is also some protection for the crew since the covering board and coaming would also prevent someone being pulled or knocked overboard while boating a fish.

TUNA TOWER

The last of the major pieces of fishing equipment is the tuna tower—so called since the initial installation was on one of the boats in competition at the Cat Cay Tuna Tournament of 1952. In comparison to the towers being installed today this original effort was almost primitive, but the basic thinking behind the first tower still holds true—to put a man high above the water on a platform which is easily and safely accessible from the lower deck. Within two years every boat in competition at Cat Cay was equipped with a tower, but these were no longer simple lookout platforms; now they are complete control stations so the guide can first locate the school of tuna and then place the bait exactly where he wants it to assure his angler of a strike. Guides today insist the bait can't just be put near a school but must be presented to an individual fish, and since this is being done at distances of 200–300 feet it is most important that the guide be able to see as well as handle the boat properly. The tower has also contributed considerably to the increased take of swordfish on rod and reel in recent years. Here again is a fish which must first be found and when located the bait must be presented with absolute precision. The more successful guides take the line from the rod up to the tower so they can place it precisely where it is most likely to appeal to the swordfish. The swordfish probably has the hardest strike of any of the gamefish, and the guide is able to drop the line at exactly the instant the fish strikes the bait. Another advantage of the height gained by being in the tower is that fish can be seen at a considerable depth so a bait can be placed over a fish even though it isn't visible on the surface.

A fast and highly maneuverable boat is essential to big-game fishing, particularly when a greyhounding marlin heads for the transom

A tower is constructed of welded aluminum tubing or pipe braced to take the strain it's certain to receive on rough days with two or sometimes three men on the platform. Points of attachment to the cabin or decks must be chosen carefully since these must be where there is sufficient strength to support the tower loads. It's always best to locate at least two of the main tower legs at or near a bulkhead or some main-strength member. It's almost impossible to design and build a tower sufficiently sturdy to be able to support itself from the base only, so consideration must be given to the secondary bracing which ties the tower to the upper house and flying bridge. Access to the tower platform is by ladder, either one down the center to the deckhouse aft of the flying bridge, or better still, integral ladders worked into the two aft tower legs which allow access from cockpit to tower. Platform and enclosure should accommodate two persons with a padded coaming to prevent bruising; a 24-inch × 48-inch size has proven ideal, with the railing about 36 inches above standing platform. Tower height will be determined by the size and stability of the boat onto which it's to be placed. Generally, the height to standing platform should not be more than one-half the boat's length; a 30-foot boat could have a 15-foot tower, a 40-foot boat could take 20 feet of tower height; this is figured to the waterline. If clearance under a fixed bridge is important, 4 feet should be added to the platform height which will be the 36 inches plus the controls. Steering and controls will be whatever adapts best to the boat's existing controls; if hydraulic, the problem is simple since additional hydraulic units can be added with a hook-up requiring only tubing; otherwise, steering can best be accomplished using cable and sheaves. A throttle hookup can most generally be made with the push-pull cables although cable and sheaves might be used here as well.

ELECTRONIC EQUIPMENT

Presently some of the most useful fishing equipment is electronic, either indirectly by means of direction finders or Loran, or directly by means of depth recorder or one of the cathode-tube fishfinders. For that matter the boat's radiotelephone can give the angler quick and up-to-the-minute information on where the fish are and how they are biting and save hours of searching.

The recording depth sounder is the best device for locating wrecks, ledges, shoals, and dropoffs as well as determining the type of bottom. A good machine will also indicate fish above the bottom by shadows or blips on the paper. In some areas where bottom contours are chartered, it can also be an excellent navigational aid, and many a skipper has been guided to a safe berth by his depth sounder.

The cathode-tube machine works in much the same way as the depth recorder by bouncing a signal off the bottom or any object between the surface and bottom. These are tunable to depth so that the operator can examine any 10-fathom stratum he wishes instead of reading the total depth. A trained operator can identify fish as to species and size and can almost direct the bait to the larger fish if he wants to do so.

Direction finders locate the boat's position by triangulation; so when used with a chart they can put the operator exactly where the chart indicates conditions are best for fishing. Direction finders also can home in on any radio signal so it's also possible to pinpoint the location of another boat which is in the fish—so long as the other captain is willing to say so over the air.

Loran is the most accurate of electronic navigational aids and can locate the boat's position within yards. A good operator can return to his fishing buoy without groping or running any extra time. When the Loran indicates that this is the spot—it definitely is.

CONSTRUCTION MATERIALS FOR SPORTFISHERMAN

The angler is going to be subject to the materials available to his builder as well as that craftsman's ability to handle the material. While most small boats are built of wood, there are areas which have gone over to metal, either steel or aluminum, both of which have proven satisfactory. The so-called plastic hull of fiberglass while not particularly well-adapted to the custom-built boat is better adapted to mass production than any other material. This is particularly true in areas where maintenance is difficult. A combination of a basic wood hull with the protection of fiberglass is perhaps the ideal solution, since it affords the flexibility of design and building the angler might need plus the durability of fiberglass surfacing.

Wooden hulls, no matter what design, were traditionally built of cedar and oak with mahogany or teak for trim and joiner work. The combination is as good today as it was fifty years ago. Oak remains an excellent choice for frames, stem, keels, and most of the basic structurals. It holds fastenings well, works easily, can be steam-bent nicely, and is reasonably plentiful. In parts of the world where oak may not be available, almost any dense-grained wood which does not check or split easily could be used. Fortunately almost every country that has water also has some type of boat building, and the local craftsmen know what is best.

Planking for the smaller boat should be a wood which can be easily worked, resists rot, is dimensionally stable so it doesn't swell or shrink, won't soak up water excessively, and does not contain oil or sap which could make painting difficult. Cedar and mahogany are first choice. Plywood, either in full widths if the hull design will accept large sheets or cut into planking, is most satisfactory.

Engine stringers, ribbands, risers, clamps, and rails will require extra-long length; so careful selection must be made to obtain the best wood available—fir, pine, spruce, oak, even mahogany can be relied on for this purpose. Bulkheads, decking, and interior partitions can be best made of marine-grade plywood.

Cabin sides and joiner work are almost universally made of mahogany, although plywood again lends itself very well to cabin construction but will require more trim than solid wood. If the owner wishes to have this portion varnished he must be careful in his selection of woods, either solid or ply.

FASTENINGS

If the boat is lightly built, planking should be secured to frames and bottoms with screws or rivets; but if frames are sufficiently heavy, nails can be used. Presently the favorite nail has annular rings which make it resistant to pulling, but the time-proven square-pointed boat nail still can be counted on for years of service. Screws for holding planking to frames should be at least twice the planking thickness in length—¾-inch plank, 1½-inch screws—but nails should be three times the planking thickness in length. Fastening material will determine how long the hull will last. For maximum life where cost is not too important, Monel is the first choice, then bronze or other copper-based alloys, then galvanized iron, and finally iron. It might be observed that while Monel may cost three times as much as bronze or possibly ten times as much as galvanized, the total cost of fastenings required to build a boat is only a small portion of the over-all cost. Therefore extra money spent here can add many years to the life of a boat as well as increase its strength. Bolts and other heavy fastenings can be either bronze or galvanized. Bronze should be used wherever the bolt might come in contact with saltwater, but galvanized fastenings are perfectly fine for all interior bolting.

PROTECTIVE FINISHING

Protective finishes will be needed for all wooden surfaces except teak. Good-quality marine paints and finishes will insure beauty as well as protection for topsides and houses; bottoms must be protected with an antifouling paint, and here the best is none too good. Only a small portion of our waters is free of marine growth, and, even worse, marine borers (their incidence increasing wth the temperature of the water) are a constant problem. While one paint may be ample for use in 60° F. water it will be of little use in 80° F. water. With respect to marine borers (*see* Teredo) there is another reason why they give less trouble in the colder areas, and this is because the boat is rarely in the water a half year so these mollusks have little chance to get started from launching to haul out. But in tropical waters a boat is usually afloat the year around which means the borers have plenty of time literally to eat a boat up. Fiberglassing is the ideal solution to the marine-borer problem, but it must still be painted to prevent fouling. *See also* Inboard-Outboard, Outboard

—J.Ry.

CAUTION

Necessity for using a larger boat will increase with (a) uncertainty of weather, (b) distance to fishing grounds, (c) length of stay aboard, and, finally, (d) amount of equipment required for the area. Conversely, need for smaller equipment will be more pronounced as the angler moves inshore and into shallow bays and flats. Here the small inboard with outdrive and outboard is still the best type available.

SPORT FISHERY RESEARCH FOUNDATION The Sport Fishery Research Foundation was organized in 1962 under the laws of the District of Columbia as a nonprofit corporation, and is now operating as a tax-exempt organization under the Internal Revenue Code. Its formation coincides with the development of a national system of Cooperative Fishery Units being established at selected universities, nationwide, to augment the supply of needed new sport-fishery workers. It is an immediate purpose of the foundation to seek contributions to finance a series of graduate fishery fellowships at the new Cooperative Fishery Units.

Thus, the foundation seeks help to implement one of the findings of the Outdoor Recreation Resources Review Commission, with respect to future development of the important sport fisheries, by providing an opportunity for private interests to participate in the training of fishery biologists. That is to help accelerate vital research efforts needed to generate new and improved methods of fish management required to meet the challenge of greatly increased (threefold) fishing pressures expected to develop in future decades. The foundation does not operate as an action organization, take positions on issues of any kind, or employ any salaried personnel. Its sole objective is to help finance the training of professional workers and to support research in the sport-fishery field. —R.H.S.

SPORT FISHING INSTITUTE Created in 1949 by a group of fishing-tackle manufacturers who recognized an industry responsibility to reinvest part of their earnings in conserving the resource upon which recreational angling depends. SFI began active operation in 1950. The institute was set up as a professionally staffed, nonprofit conservation organization to assist the public in the improvement of angling through progressive research and management programs. The institute is now principally supported by two hundred manufacturers of fishing tackle and accessories, outboard motors, boats, trailers, sporting goods, petroleum and other products used by anglers out fishing. In addition, many interested individuals contribute funds.

The immense progress made in other fields, such as agriculture, has resulted mainly from fact finding, education, and professional services. Future progress in fish conservation seems equally to depend on these same factors. For this reason the SFI program is organized around three major functions.

1. *Research* in fishery biology
2. Fish-conservation *education*
3. Professional *service* to official agencies, key citizen groups, and industry.

The specific objectives of the institute are laid out in its charter (which its three-point program is designed to implement), as follows:

1. To promote and assist in conservation, development, and wise utilization of our national recreational fisheries resources
2. To advance and encourage the development and application of all branches of fishery research and management
3. To collect, evaluate, and publish all information of value to advance fishery science and the sport of fishing
4. To assist existing educational institutions in the training of personnel in fisheries science and management
5. To encourage a wider participation in sport fishing through the distribution of information pertaining to its health and recreational values
6. To assist and encourage co-operative effort between all existing conservation organizations

RESEARCH

The founders of SFI recognized that maintenance and improvement of sport fishing depend on a strong foundation of research-established facts and that these facts must be published widely to establish public confidence in proper management. As a result, fishery research and its interpretation is a major part of the SFI program. SFI's research program is necessarily small in comparison with the total national effort. But it is clear that the public agencies need the understanding and support of informed organizations like SFI. The pump-priming efforts of the institute are vital to demonstrate industry support for basic fishery research and to supply inspired direction and emphasis.

The total research effort of the institute has risen sharply in recent years coincident with strengthened financing, and now accounts for about 25 percent of annual budgets. A large sum is utilized in a selective grant program to stimulate new sport-fish research. Ninety-five grants for basic research have been given to forty-four universities and agencies. Co-operating research initiated as a result of SFI-sponsored studies accounts for an additional fund which has been pumped into these problem areas. Considerable research is done directly by the institute staff. Recent examples include periodic nationwide reviews of fishery programs, publication of a bibliography of unpublished fishery research theses, and compilation of information on future needs of fishing for the Outdoor Recreation Resources Review Commission.

The research funds were awarded to these institutions, agencies, and organizations: University of Alaska, American Fisheries Society, University of Arkansas, Auburn University, Boy Scouts of America, Cornell University, University of Delaware, Illinois Natural History Survey, University of Indiana, Iowa State University, Izaak Walton League of America, Long Beach State College (California), University of Louisville, University of Maine, Maryland Department of Research and Education, University of Massachusetts, University of Miami, University of Michigan, Michigan State University, University of Minnesota, University of Missouri, Montana State College, Murray State College (Kentucky), National Academy of Sciences, Nebraska Game, Fish and Parks Department, North Carolina State College, Northeast Missouri State College, University of Oklahoma, Oklahoma Game and Fish Department, Pennsylvania State University, University of Rhode Island, St. Mary's College (Minnesota), South Dakota Department of Game, Fish and Parks, University of South Florida, Southern Illinois University, Texas Agricultural and Mechanical College, Tulane University, Utah State Agricultural College, Virginia Institute of Marine Science, Woods Hole Oceanographic Institution, and Yale University.

EDUCATION

Good fishing must be created by well-trained and long-experienced professional fishery biologists. Modern fish-conservation methods improve fishing, but lack of knowledge of new fish-management concepts by many key laymen and some career conservation workers alike retards the acceptance of modern programs. The educational phase of the SFI program is designed to help meet the needs for communication of the latest developments and their informed interpretation. This is accomplished by publishing the monthly *SFI Bulletin*, reviewing and commenting upon national fish conservation progress and problems, and special publications to fill specific needs. About half the institute's annual budget is devoted to these activities.

The *SFI Bulletin* permits direct, continuing contact with some 20,000 or more key people who develop and/or influence policies affecting sport-fishery programs. These include administrators, commissioners, fish and game workers, conservation officers, outdoor writers, legislative groups, and officials of sportsmen organizations. Items from the *SFI Bulletin* are widely reprinted and used as source material for original articles in both outdoor and general magazines, sportsmen publications, and a variety of other news media.

A portion of SFI's educational effort is directed toward future citizen leaders. School materials, such as *SFI's Conservation Chart* depicting proper land and water management, have been widely used. SFI actively assists the Boy Scouts of America by helping formulate conservation scouting programs, the Fishing Merit Badge, and the Outdoor Code. The institute's illustrated series of essays entitled *Land, Water and Fishing* has enjoyed outstanding success as supplementary instructional materials. The cartoon-illustrated *Fish Conservation Fundamentals*, a unique digest of fishery principles, enjoys world-wide recognition. Such special publications are made available at the approximate cost of the printing, handling, and mailing to the institute.

SERVICE

Since 1950, SFI has constantly expanded its program to provide a variety of professional conservation services. These have developed in response to specific demand for them on the part of conservation interests and now require the remaining fourth of annual budgetary expenditures. SFI acts as a technical consultant to conservation agencies and serves on advisory committees to help direct natural-resource programs. SFI publishes *Fish Conservation Highlights*, periodic national progress reports, and reports of the Federal Aid in Fish Restoration (Dingell-Johnson) program. These reports are an effective guide to the expenditure of excise-tax and fishing-license funds.

The institute encourages higher professional standards and salaries for fishery workers. A monthly newsletter, *Items for Fishery Scientists*, is an important means of communication among professional fishery biologists. SFI also operates a limited employment service for fishery workers.

The institute serves as a technical advisor to lay groups and legislative bodies on matters affecting sport fishing. SFI is invited to testify and gives its own views on fish-conservation legislation. Major programs of concern since 1950 have included such matters as the Dingell-Johnson Act, earmarking excise taxes for sport-fish restoration; the start of the saltwater sport-fish research program; initiation of a reservoir fishery research program; establishment of Cooperative Fishery Units program at universities; program of speeded up public access on federal reservoirs; and strengthening water pollution control programs.

SFI acts as a national clearing house for fishery information continuously sought by private conservation groups. Simply answering the inquiries for authoritative information on sport-fishery matters has become a major task. Mimeographed summaries of staff activities are sent regularly to SFI members, along with statistical information on fishing. Considerable emphasis is placed on dissemination of information on water-pollution problems.

The institute also collaborates closely in the conservation and jamboree programs of the Boy Scouts of America. Special-events fish-conservation materials are furnished. Publications like the merit badge book, *Fishing*, an *Outdoor Code*, and a feature *Conservation Kit* have been prepared and widely used. SFI cooperates in the annual summer program to train scout leaders in conservation principles. Current emphasis is on cooperative development of an instructional handbook of conservation activities for use in summer camps by scout counselors and development of active fish-conservation programs on scout properties. In all, about 3,000,000 scouts, who constitute a reservoir of potential future leaders, are influenced annually.

FISHING IMPROVEMENT

The three-point program effort by Sport Fishing Institute is aimed at providing more and better fishing. Significant progress has been made by the states since 1950 in developing their fishery resources, with fishing opportunities about doubling over the decade as a direct result. Some of the significant state action programs serving to accomplish this have included the creation of many thousands of acres of new water, through construction of strategically located public fishing lakes; restoration to good fishing of several hundred thousand acres of unbalanced waters, through chemical treatment and restocking; establishment of year-round fishing for bass and other warmwater game- and panfish in the majority of states, affecting some 45,000,000 acres of fishing waters; opening to public recreational fishing of extensive acreage of previously closed municipal water supplies, on a properly controlled basis; permanent acquisition of access to many hundred thousands of acres of previously inaccessible lakes and 6,400 miles of rivers and streams; and improvement of fisherman access to several million acres of federally built reservoirs.

SFI has been widely acknowledged as one of the important external stimulants motivating a large portion of these developments. It has provided a significant element of national leadership and coordination. *SFI Bulletin* articles, staff consultation, nationwide surveys, and talks to recreation leaders have helped to initiate the needed public action and provided vital support to permit informed and dedicated conservation officials to do the things they know need doing.

The expanding population, the trend toward more leisure time, more urbanization, more travel, more need for relaxing outdoor recreation—all these present opportunities and problems for the sport-fishing interests. The following key programs are therefore of special interest to SFI:

1. Develop widespread public recognition of the need to protect and develop fishing as an integral part of water-resource development
2. Create new fishing waters for urban populations
3. Clean up water pollution nationwide, most pressing in urban areas
4. Assuring public access to our 100,000,000 acres of fresh- and saltwater

5. Accelerate substantially lagging basic research on fishes and their environment to provide needed new knowledge, prerequisite to attainment of increased sustained yields on existing and new waters through improved fishery management practices

No industry concerned with its future could long tolerate the situation now existing in sport fishing where the basic facts for management of many important species are almost unknown. The few fortunate exceptions—some managed fishing lakes already provide 10–20 times better fishing than unmanaged waters—serve to emphasize the potential rewards from intensified research efforts.

—R.H.S.

SPOT *Leiostomus xanthurus* A small well-known member of the croaker family, the spot is distributed along the Atlantic coast from Cape Cod into the Gulf of Mexico as far as Campeche, Mexico. Its most common occurrence is south of New Jersey.

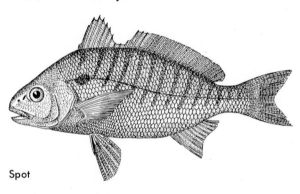

Spot

The spot can be separated from the Atlantic croaker (*which see*) in that the body is comparatively short and deep and there are no barbels on its lower jaw. The mouth is small and horizontal; teeth are present on the lower jaw of the young but are lacking in adults. The body coloration is usually bluish-gray with gold or bronze reflections above and a silvery cast below. There are 12 to 15 oblique, yellowish bars on the sides, which become indistinct with age. The maximum size is about 14 inches, weighing less than 2 pounds, but the average is generally smaller than 10 inches, particularly in the southwestern portion of its range.

LIFE HISTORY

Spot range from freshwater to salinities which are nearly twice that of oceanwater, and can also tolerate a wide range of temperatures. Sometimes they occur in large schools, from the shallows of coastal marshes to at least 112 fathoms, and occasionally they are extremely abundant in deepwater. They appear to be more common in deepwater during fall and winter. Spot occur over mud and sand bottom, as well as about oyster and shell reefs.

Spawning evidently occurs offshore in deepwater. Spot leave inshore waters in the fall, and ripe specimens occur during the winter. The smallest young (about ⅛ inch) occur in November and December and move inshore during late winter and early spring and summer, where they spend their first and second summers in the quiet nursery grounds of tidal creeks and sloughs. At the end of the second summer most fish are sexually mature and move off to spawn in deeper waters. Movements of both young and adults are largely governed by temperature. They grow to about 6 inches by the end of their first year and about 8 inches by the time they are two.

They eat a variety of animals and plants, principally small planktonic and bottom-dwelling crustaceans, although worms are also of importance. Young spot feed more heavily on plankton, with older fish eating worms and small fish. In turn, spot are fed on by striped bass. Like other croakers, the male spot makes a drumming sound using the swimbladder.

ANGLING VALUE

During peak runs, spot are readily caught on hook and line and cut bait, such as clams or worms. The flesh is soft and sometimes wormy, but the flavor is good.

—A.J.McC.
—D.dS.

SPOTFIN CROAKER *Roncador stearnsi* A distinctive species with no close relatives. Its range is confined to the warm-temperate Pacific coast from Point Concepción to San Juanico Bay, Baja California. Distinguishing characteristics: lower jaw included; dorsal spines 10 in the first dorsal fin, 1 in second, 21–24 dorsal softrays, anal fin with 2 spines and 8 or 9 softrays; chin without barbels; a large black spot at base of pectorals.

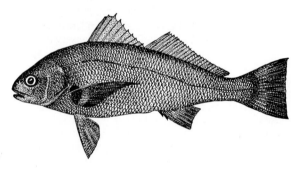

Spotfin Croaker

A shallowwater species that prefers beaches and sloughs, it often congregates in bottom depressions just outside the breaker zone. Its food is mainly small mollusks and crustaceans. Best fishing in late summer with sand crab, clam, mussel, or pileworm bait. Maximum weight about 9 pounds; greatest length about 26 inches.

—J.C.B.

SPOTFIN SURFPERCH *Hyperprosopon anale* Similar to walleye surfperch but without black-tipped pelvics; a black spot on spinous dorsal and usually a small black

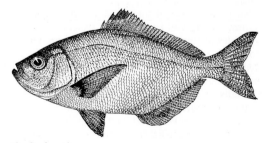

Spotfin Surfperch

area on anal. Found from lower California to San Francisco. It has no commercial value, but is taken by sportsmen. *See also* Surfperch   —J.R.

SPOTTAIL PINFISH *Diplodus holbrooki* Four members of the genus *Diplodus* occur in western Atlantic waters, but except for the Atlantic waters of central and southern Florida, the species usually encountered in the continental waters of the United States is *D. holbrooki*. It ranges from about Chesapeake Bay south to about New Smyrna Beach, Florida, and from the Florida Keys to the northwestern Gulf of Mexico. The West Indies Islands species, *D. caudimacula*, appears to replace *D. holbrooki* from about New Smyrna Beach to the Florida Keys. The other two American species are confined one to Bermuda and one to the mainland coast of South America.

In life, the body of the spottail pinfish is plain silvery, sometimes with several faint, narrow crossbars on the sides. However, it has a distinct dark blotch or saddle on the caudal peduncle which distinguishes it and other American members of the genus *Diplodus* from the other American sparids.

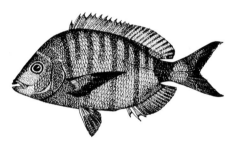

Spottail Pinfish

Species of *Diplodus* have strong, unnotched, anterior incisor teeth. *D. holbrooki* is not as deep-bodied (depth about 2.0–2.2 in standard length versus about 1.9), has a smaller eye, has fewer lateral-line scales on the average (50–61 versus 57–63), and has a less extensive caudal blotch or saddle than *D. caudimacula* The dorsal profile of *D. holbrooki* is regular in general outline, while that of *D. caudimacula* is steep, almost S-shaped.

LIFE HISTORY

Spottail pinfish, like pinfish, occur on grassy inshore flats, but they also are found frequently over sandy bottoms. Spawning takes place in winter, offshore.

Food of the spottail pinfish consists primarily of small animal life, but some plant material also is ingested.

Some small individuals (up to about 6–8 inches) of this species are taken with hook and line in bottom-fishing, and are popular as a bait. The larger specimens, which may reach lengths of some 18 inches, occur too far offshore to enter the sport fishery more than only occasionally.   —D.K.C.

SPOTTAIL SHINER *Notropis hudsonius* A very silvery shiner with a usually distinct caudal spot. In some large adults from turbid waters this spot is faint or absent. Usually the lower edge of the caudal fin is milk-white. The eyes are large, greater in diameter than the length of the upper jaw. The lateral line contains 36–40 scales. The range of the spottail shiner extends from North Dakota and adjacent Manitoba to the Hudson River and south to Virginia, Illinois, and Iowa. Extensions of this range into New England have undoubtedly been effected by bait-fishermen.

LIFE HISTORY

The spottail is a minnow of large, clear rivers and lakes. It is usually found in large schools over sand or gravel bottoms where vegetation is scant or lacking.

Spottail Shiner

Apparently spawning takes place in mid-spring in shoal areas or creek mouths. During spawning the fish attain tiny tubercles on the upper half of the head and at the base of the pectoral fins. The food of the spottail shiner consists of insects, crustaceans, and vegetation. A small minnow, the spottail seldom exceeds 5 inches.

ANGLING VALUE

The spottail shiner is one of the more popular bait species. It also is of considerable importance as forage for gamefish.   —R.A.J.

SPOTTED BASS *Micropterus punctulatus* A popular freshwater gamefish, sometimes called the Kentucky bass, or Kentucky spotted bass, the spotted bass was not properly identified by fishery taxonomists until 1927, although a naturalist, Rafinesque, and fishermen on the Ohio River recognized it as a separate species long before this time. A cursory examination of this species would indicate that it is a hybrid between the largemouth and smallmouth basses because it has some characteristics which are similar to one species or the other or are intermediate between the two. The spotted bass is olive-green on the back with many dark blotches which are usually diamond shape. The lateral band is a series of short blotches. Below the lateral line the scales have dark bases that give rise to the lengthwise rows of small spots which are responsible for the common name. Often confused with the largemouth, the spotted bass differs in having a mouth which does not extend beyond the eye and spotting below the lateral line. It differs from the smallmouth in having spotting below the lateral line and no vertical bars on the sides.

Young spotted bass resemble the young largemouth, but the juvenile spotted bass have spots along the belly and a prominent black spot at the base of the tail. The tricolored tail is marked like a smallmouth in orange, black, and white.

It does not grow as large as either the largemouth or smallmouth. The maximum size attained is about 4–5 pounds. This black bass occurs in the Ohio-Mississippi drainage from Ohio south to the Gulf states and west to Texas, Oklahoma, and Kansas. In the east its range extends to western Florida.

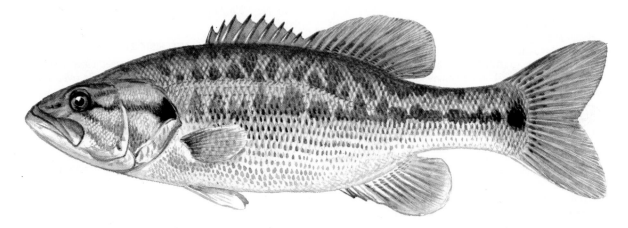

Alabama Spotted Bass

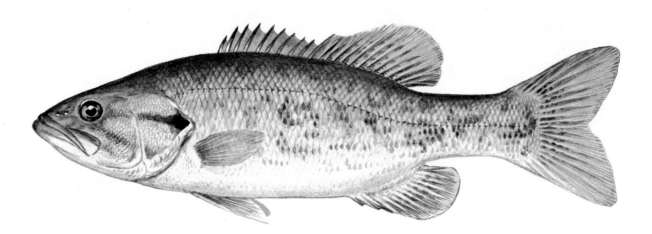

Wichita Spotted Bass

There are two subspecies which occur in limited areas, the Alabama spotted bass and the Wichita spotted bass. The Alabama form has been authenticated to 8 pounds in weight and 24 inches in length (Smith Lake, Ala., 1966).

In the North, the habitat of the spotted bass in streams might be called intermediate between the largemouth and smallmouth bass. In streams the smallmouth inhabit the riffle area, the largemouth the weeded coves, but the spotted bass prefer long, deep, silted pools in sluggish waters. In the South the habitat of the spotted bass is entirely different for it occurs primarily in cool, gravel-bottom streams and clear, spring-fed lakes. In a lake in the TVA system in Tennessee, spotted bass were taken at a depth of 100 feet while the smallmouth were caught no deeper than 60 feet and the largemouth were found close to the surface.

LIFE HISTORY

The food of the young spotted bass is small crustaceans and midge larvae, but as they grow larger they eat larger insects, fish, crayfish, frogs, worms, and grubs. Breeding follows migration upstream into shallow waters where nests much like the other two species of black bass are constructed. The spawning habits are similar to the largemouth, but the nests are small, not over 15 inches in diameter. The young grow to 1½–4 inches the first summer. Maturity is reached at about 7 inches.

ANGLING VALUE

The spotted bass is an important gamefish in areas where it is abundant. It takes the same type of artificial lures and natural baits as does the smallmouth. *See also* Black Bass   —K.B.

Northern Spotted Bass

SPOTTED BATFISH *See* Longnose Batfish
SPOTTED BULLHEAD *Ictalurus serracanthus* Found from northern Florida to southern Georgia and westward to southeastern Alabama, the spotted bullhead has a very limited range. This species has 20–23 anal rays, a flattened head, and is readily distinguished by its spotted body and the strong serrations on its pectoral fins. This bullhead occurs in large streams and rivers with moderate currents and in impounded lakes within its range. Little is known of its life history. Ripe fish are found from December to July. Relatively abundant in limited areas, it may outnumber the white and channel catfish in certain locations. A mollusk feeder, it is often called "snailcat."

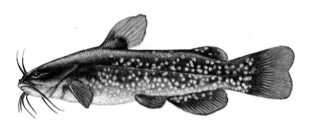

Spotted Bullhead

It is rarely taken with nets, but commonly in commercial slat traps and on hook-and-line. Edible but small, its maximum weight is probably about 1 pound, with the average in Suwanee, Ochlockonee, and Apalachicola rivers running ¼ pound. —A.J.McC.
SPOTTED CUSK-EEL *Otophidium taylori* Cusk-eels belong to the family Ophidiidae. They resemble a true eel in appearance, but they differ in having ventral fins in the form of forked threadlike throat filaments, which probably have some function in finding food. There are thirty known species of cusk-eels, which range from less than a foot long when full grown to over 5 feet in length. The spotted cusk-eel is common to the Pacific coastal areas of the United States, and although occasionally found in shallow water it is more frequently caught in depths of

over 100 feet. In captivity the spotted cusk-eel has been observed to stand on its tail when at rest; it also enters crevices or holes on the bottom tail first, with only a portion of its head visible.

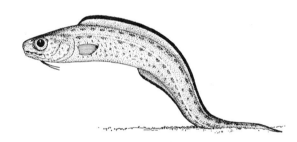

Spotted Cusk-Eel in "Alert" Position

SPOTTED EAGLE RAY *Aetobatus narinari* This beautifully marked member of the family Myliobatidae has regularly arranged spots which vary from white to greenish to yellow on the upper part of the disk. The lower parts are white, and the tail is black. One or more sharp barbs are placed at the base of the long tail, which may be twice as long as the disk. Its body is roughly diamond-shaped, with the anterior edges of the disk convex and the posterior edges concave. A shovel-shaped snout with a peculiar duck-shaped bill further characterizes this species. It has only a single series of broad, flat teeth in each jaw, a character which readily separates it from the closely related cownose ray and bullnose ray (*which see*). Individuals 7½ feet wide and up to 500 pounds are known; their bodies are relatively thicker at the same size than other rays.

LIFE HISTORY

The eagle ray occurs from Angola to Cape Verde in the eastern Atlantic, and in the western Atlantic from Brazil to Chesapeake Bay and throughout the Caribbean Sea. It is also known from the Red Sea and the tropical parts of the Pacific.

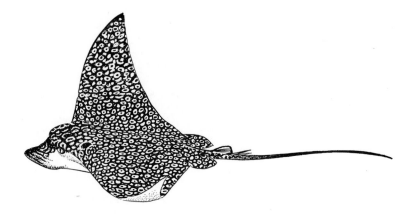

Spotted Eagle Ray

Like other large rays, they are seen swimming singly or in pairs, or in large schools, depending on the time of year. They also share with the other large rays the habit of leaping from the water, during which time they may emit loud, croaking sounds. Their duck-billed mouths are used as plows to dig up clams, oysters, and other hard-bodied burrowing organisms which they crush with their pavementlike teeth. Worms, shrimps, and fish are also eaten.

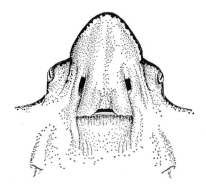

Spotted Eagle Ray, Bottom View

Although it journeys across open stretches of the sea, its relative abundance in protected situations indicates that it is predominantly a coastal species, at least during part of its life. They do enter river mouths but are more at home in salty lagoons, over coral reefs, or sand beaches with little surf action. Small eagle rays, measuring less than 8 inches across, have been taken, but individuals about 14 inches wide have been collected from a mother eagle ray.

DANGER TO MAN

There is no wide commercial use for this species as food, although its flesh is edible. But its chief relation to man is the pain it causes through its large tail spines, and acute poisonings and even deaths have resulted. It causes severe damage to commercial beds of clams and oysters through its feeding forages.   —D.dS.

SPOTTED FLOUNDER   A common name for the windowpane (*which see*).

SPOTTED GAR *Lepisosteus oculatus*   The spotted gar can easily be mistaken for the shortnose and Florida gars. It can be distinguished from the shortnose gar by large, round spots on its head and by the 54–58 scales in its lateral line and from the Florida gar by the distance from the front of the eye to back of the opercle. The snout is much broader than that of the longnose gar. Its body appears heavier than the longnose or shortnose gar. It is deep olive-green, with darker spots on the back. Its sides are lighter and the fins are heavily blotched and spotted.

The spotted gar is found from Minnesota to Ohio in the north, and southward to Texas and northwest Florida.

LIFE HISTORY

It prefers shallow, weedy lakes and bayous and is seldom abundant elsewhere; otherwise its habits are similar to the other gars. It spawns in the spring in grass-grown sloughs, and the young grow very rapidly the first year. Basking on the surface on warm days, it floats like a small log, occasionally gulping air into the swim bladder. It attains a maximum of 3 feet and can be caught by a variety of lures. Dead minnows on a line fished just below the surface are quite effective. Wire leaders prevent the sharp teeth from cutting the line.   —C.A.P.

Spotted Gar

SPOTTED GOATFISH *See* Yellow Goatfish
SPOTTED JACK *Caranx melampygus* Also has been called blue jack and blue crevalle. This species ranges into the Indo-Pacific. In the eastern Pacific it has also been erroneously designated as *Caranx stellatus* and *Caranx medusicola.*

The chest in front of the pelvic fins of the spotted jack is completely scaled. The second dorsal fin has 1 spine and 20–23 softrays. The anal fin has 2 detached spines, followed by 1 spine and 17–20 softrays. The first gill arch has 7–9 gillrakers on the upper limb and 17–21 on the lower limb. The body is never entirely black or dark brown.

The body is fairly deep, and the convex head profile in 8–10-inch fish becomes more angular in larger specimens. The dorsal- and anal-fin lobes are moderately elongated.

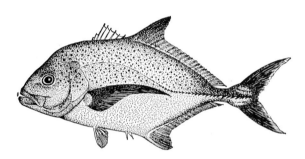

Spotted Jack

The scutes in the straight lateral line number about 30–42. Specimens up to about 4 inches long have 5–6 bars on the body and one on the nape, and specimens of this size and slightly larger have dark dorsal- and anal-fin lobes. When about 9 inches long, small spots begin to form on the body and head, and the number of these spots increases rapidly with growth. The dorsal and anal fins become very dark, frequently with dark blue at their bases. The back of larger specimens is dark blue or bluish-green that fades into lighter sides and belly.

The spotted jack occurs in most areas of the tropical Indo-Pacific westward to South Africa. In the eastern Pacific it is known from Mazatlán, Chacala, and Cape San Lucas, Mexico, and at the Revillagigedo, Tres Marías, Clipperton, and Cocos islands. It has been reported from Panama and the Galápagos Islands. A specimen 28 inches long has been preserved, and the photograph of a 30-inch specimen has been published from the eastern Pacific. A specimen 33 inches long is recorded from East Africa, and an unconfirmed report claims that the species attains 48 inches. Another account, unsubstantiated although feasible, stated that this is the largest member of the jack family and reportedly grows to about 150 pounds.

LIFE HISTORY

Life history information is wanting. It is known to eat small fish. Specimens were reported as having ripening ovaries in March. Nearly ripe males and females were taken at the Tres Marías Islands in August—the males were noticeably darker than the females. The smallest known specimen is about three inches long. While this species has been taken inshore, in the eastern Pacific it is more common around rocky, offshore islands.

ANGLING VALUE

This is a fair gamefish, the larger ones strong and obstinate when hooked. One report stated that it was commonly marketed as a food fish. *See also* Carangidae, Jacks   —F.H.B.
SPOTTED SEATROUT *Cynoscion nebulosus* One of the most popular inshore saltwater gamefish in the Southern United States, it occurs from New York to Florida and throughout the Gulf of Mexico. The spotted seatrout is not closely related to other members of its genus. Also called "speckled trout" or simply "trout," the fish is widely caught on artificial lures as well as live bait.

The body coloration of the spotted seatrout is dark gray above, with sky-blue reflections, shading to a silvery below. The upper parts of its sides are marked with numerous round, black spots, the spots extending on dorsal and caudal fins. Very young with a broad, dark, lateral band; blotches of the same color on the back; base of caudal black. Fins pale to yellowish-green; the dorsal and caudal fins spotted with black in the adult.

Spotted Seatrout, 6-pound Male, Florida Bay, Florida

The spotted seatrout has 10 spines (rarely 11) in the first dorsal fin, 1 spine and 24–26 softrays in the second dorsal fin. The anal fin has 2 spines followed by 10–11 softrays. There are 90–102 scales in the lateral line. The body is elongate and somewhat compressed; the back is a little elevated, while the head is long and low; snout pointed, 3.75–4.2 in head; eye 4.45–5.35; interorbital 4.5–5.9; mouth large, oblique; lower jaw projecting; maxillary reaching nearly or quite opposite posterior margin of eye, 2.2–2.3 in head; teeth as in *C. regalis;* gillrakers rather short, 8 on lower limb of first arch; scales, small, thin ctenoid, extending forward on head, cheeks, and opercles, not present on fins, 11–12 between origin of anal and lateral line; dorsal fins contiguous or separate, spines of the first weak, flexible, the longest spines scarcely longer than the longest softrays; caudal fin pointed in very young, becoming straight to somewhat emarginate in adults; anal fin small, the spines very weak, base of fin ending about an eye's diameter in advance of the end of base of dorsal; ventral fins rather small, inserted a little behind base of pectorals, 1.85–2.25 in head.

LIFE HISTORY

The life history of the spotted seatrout is quite well-known. Spawning takes place from March through November, primarily within the coastal bays and lagoons. The larval and juvenile development is in the protected beds of vegetation found in many parts of the inland waters. The egg and larval stages have not been described, but are apparently similar to those of the weakfish (*Cynoscion regalis*).

The majority of the young fish are found within fifty yards of a shoreline usually in the marine vegetation. The vegetation affords the small fish protection and contains many small crustaceans and fish upon which the juvenile trout feed. The young fish remain in the shallow, grassy areas until winter approaches, when they move into deeper waters.

Although part of the population moves out into the ocean during the winter, becoming distributed up and down the beaches, the majority remains within the bays. Here they are subject to being killed by the millions during cold weather. Such kills occurred along the Texas coast in 1962 and 1963, and earlier instances have been reported in the literature.

Shrimp are the preferred food, and when they are in abundance the spotted seatrout feed on them almost exclusively. When shrimp are scarce, they turn to fish and seem to prefer mullet (*Mugil cephalus*) although they have been taken with menhaden (*Brevoortia* sp.) or silversides (*Menidia* sp.) in their stomachs.

ANGLING VALUE

As far as the Gulf states are concerned, the spotted seatrout is the fourth most valuable commercial fish, ranking behind the menhaden, mullet, and red snapper. It is the most popular of the bay fishes for the sport fisherman. Live shrimp is the most widely used bait, but good catches are often made on small live fishes, cut mullet, or small crabs. Plugs, both topwater and sinking types, as well as jigs, spoons, streamer flies, and popping bugs are all successful lures of regional importance. As a rule, plugs with silver flash finishes and those which imitate mullet and needlefish are very popular.

One of the basic methods of catching seatrout is with the "splash pole." This is a popular technique among commercial fishermen and essentially effective. The splash pole is really a long cane pole rigged with a big float or bobber and a single hook to which is attached a shrimp, pinfish, mullet, needlefish, or similar live bait. The object is to drift slowly over the grass beds with the pole extended and let the seatrout find the bait. To expedite contact, the float is splashed on the surface to attract the fish. The operator often slaps the tip of the pole on the water also, thus the name of the technique. Of course, a properly handled surface plug may accomplish the same effect.

Spotted trout are caught the year round, but the best fishing seems to be in the spring and fall. They take the bait most readily during the early morning hours when the water is calm and clear.

A mature fish averages around 4 pounds, but many run as high as 7–8 pounds, and a rare few go as high as 12 pounds. A world's record seatrout was taken in Florida waters and tipped the scale at 15 pounds 3 ounces.

FOOD VALUE

The spotted seatrout ranks high as a table fish. The flesh is fine and delicately flavored. However, it spoils rather quickly, and it should be cleaned or stored on ice as soon as possible after capture. It usually appears on the menus of Southern restaurants as "trout." *For recipes see* Fish Cookery.

See also Saltwater Fly-Fishing, Sand Seatrout, Silver Seatrout, Weakfish   —J.C.B.

SPOTTED SUCKER *Minytrema melanops* The presence of dark spots on the base of each scale distinguishes this

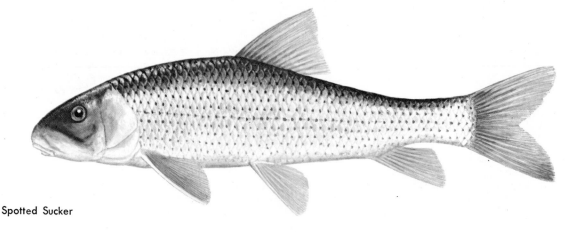

Spotted Sucker

species from others of the sucker family. Color silvery with a dark olive back. Spots on the scales forming prominent longitudinal stripes. Lateral line indistinct or wanting. Outer margin of dorsal fin concave. Scales in lateral series 43–45. Lips thin and striated. The range of this species is from southern Minnesota to Pennsylvania and south to Texas and Florida.

HABITS

An inhabitant of larger streams and lakes with sand, gravel, or hard-clay bottoms, the spotted sucker is intolerant to turbid waters and industrial pollutants. Little is known of the breeding habits of this species. It apparently spawns in early spring when males develop three lateral bands; the lower is chocolate-gray, the middle grayish-pink, and the upper dark lavender. The food of this sucker consists of mollusks and insect larvae. It reaches 18 inches long.

ECONOMIC VALUE

Due to its smaller size and relative scarcity, the spotted sucker is thought to have slight commercial value.

—R.A.J.

SPOTTED SUNFISH *Lepomis punctatus* The spotted sunfish is one of the least known of the small-size sunfishes. Like the warmouth (*which see*), it is regionally known as a "stumpknocker." The olivaceous body of this fish is heavily spotted with black or brown. It has a plain spot on the gill flap and no blotch on the dorsal fin. Each scale is pigmented at the base, and the pectoral fins are rounded. The form which occurs from southern Illinois to Texas is prominently lined with horizontal rows of red spots with a few diffuse, dusky spots on the head. The maximum length is about 6 inches.

Spotted Sunfish

Its range is from South Carolina to Florida and from southern Illinois to Mississippi and west to Texas.

ANGLING VALUE

Because of its small size the spotted sunfish has limited value to the angler, but it is an active and tasty panfish.

—K.B.

SPOTTED WOLFFISH *Anarhichas minor* This species is related to the Atlantic wolffish and the northern wolffish as well as the Bering wolffish of the North Pacific. It possesses the same family characteristics that were given for the Atlantic wolffish (*which see*). The spotted wolffish is also called the leopard fish or spotted catfish. It is found on both sides of the North Atlantic; in the west it occurs from Nova Scotia to Cape Ann, Massachusetts; in the east it has been taken at eastern Greenland, Iceland, the Faroes, Spitzbergen, and from the White Sea to Scotland.

Its color varies from pale olive to chocolate, but the upper parts, including the dorsal and caudal fins, are well marked with blackish-brown spots, irregular in size and shape. Similar spots are on the upper part of head behind the eye.

Other distinguishing characters of the spotted wolffish are body stout, elongate, moderately compressed, greatest depth 6½ in total length, occurring at about middle of pectoral fin, body then tapering to a small caudal peduncle. Head 5¾ in total length, heavy, blunt, profile rounded, mouth terminal, oblique, angle under posterior edge of eye, large canine teeth in front of both jaws; the central patch of vomerine teeth not extending farther back than the flanking rows of palatine teeth on the sides, eyes small, 6½ in head.

Dorsal fin with about 78 spines, fairly uniform except the last 3–6 spines are abruptly shorter making an indentation; the fin originates over the posterior part of the head and extends to the base of the caudal; caudal small, slightly rounded; anal fin with about 46 softrays, fin a little more than half the length of the dorsal ending at the caudal base; pectorals longer than broad, rounded, longest rays almost equaling head length, base low on sides of body and a short distance behind gill opening, pelvics absent. Lateral line absent. Head scaleless; body with poorly developed scales.

This species lives in deeper water than the Atlantic wolffish and has been taken as deep as 250 fathoms. Its diet is apparently similar to that of the latter species.

FOOD VALUE

In Greenland the spotted wolffish is used for food and the skin is tanned for leather. On North American shores it is quite rare and has no commercial value. It is reported to grow to a length of about 6 feet.

—J.C.B.

SPRINGER'S REEF SHARK *Carcharhinus springeri* Although not common in the United States, this is apparently one of the most widespread sharks in the Caribbean. A member of the ridgeback group, it closely resembles the dusky shark (*which see*) but has a larger eye, a lobed nostril, and a larger first dorsal fin with a shorter rear free tip. The distance from the pelvic tips to the anal base is short (about 0.7 of the anal base in *springeri* and about 1.3 times in the dusky), and the second dorsal is inserted slightly more in front of the anal fin. It is grayish-olive to olive-brown above and yellowish-white to white below. Specimens up to 9 feet have been caught. In the Caribbean it occurs around deep reefs, occasionally in some numbers. It apparently replaces the dusky shark as a reef shark in these areas. —D.dS.

SPRING LINES Additional dock lines used to prevent a boat from moving forward or backward. Spring lines are secured at an angle of about 45 degrees to the center axis of the boat.

SQUAWFISH *See* Northern Squawfish

SQUIDS Squids belong to the phylum Mollusca, which includes limpets, clams, snails, and tooth shells. The particular class to which squids belong (Cephalopoda) includes (1) the chambered nautilus and its relatives, (2) fossil ammonites having highly coiled shells, and (3) squids and octopuses. Cephalopoda are characterized by a large head and eyes, with a tubular funnel beneath; horny, beaklike jaws; and 8–10 arms. Squids have 10 arms and usually have a long, cigar-shape body with fins at the end, while octopuses (*which see*) have 8 arms and more of a stubby body. A mantle or envelope covers the entire body and is open at the anterior end only. There is no "backbone" as in fishes, but a shell or pen is beneath the mantle of the body.

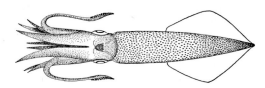

Squid

The arms are covered with suction cups and sometimes with horny, toothed disks or hooks for holding prey. Of the 10 arms, 2 (the tentacles) are long and retractile, and are used in seizing food, which is then held by the remaining arms and moved to the parrotlike beak.

Squids have a marked degree of intelligence and a highly developed nervous system. The color cells in the skin are able to change quickly, causing considerable and rapid changes in color and pattern. They may be red, pink, brown, blue, or yellow, with many iridescent reflections. Some squids contain highly specialized light organs, or photophores. Squids swim backward or forward with amazing rapidity, using the funnel, or siphon, to propel them backward or forward, jet-fashion, the fins assisting in steering. A sac contains ink which may be emptied at the time of sudden propulsion, with the result that a dark cloud of ink appears as a "phantom" squid to a predator while the real squid evades capture. Some squids regularly "fly" or glide over the surface of the water.

They are voracious predators, feeding on small and large fishes of all types as well as on other squids. Squids as small as an inch travel in large schools, while giant squid, which may exceed 6 feet, evidently are more solitary. They live near the surface to depths of a mile, those living in the upper layers often coming near the sea surface at night to feed on fishes following the migrating plankton. Some squids also approach the shore at night, following schools of foraging fishes.

REPRODUCTION

Male squids have a specialized tip on one of the arms called a hectocotylus which is used to transfer the sperm to the female. Following mating, the eggs are laid in long, gelatinous capsules, and the young hatch as miniature adults. Sometimes they swim about the capsule before hatching. Some species die following mating.

ECONOMIC VALUE

Squids are extremely important in the economy of the sea both as predators on all organisms and as food for nearly all predatory fishes. Squids sometimes form the bulk of the food of some species like tunas, some marlins, swordfish, and certain whales, while sea birds feed heavily on surface-dwelling squids. They are widely used as bait, both as trolled squid for pelagic gamefish and as cut bait for flounder, sea bass, and striped bass. Throughout all parts of the world they are utilized as food, either fresh, salted, dried, candied, smoked, canned, or frozen. Seines, trawls, traps, gigs, and lights are used to catch them. In certain areas and at certain times, squids appear in such numbers that they destroy large quantities of food fish, then they become a nuisance to the fisherman.

FISHING FOR GIANT SQUID

For the angler who feels he has tried everything the legendary giant squid of Chile (*which see*) is a hard-to-resist challenge. The *jibia* (*Dosidicus gigas*) grows to 6 feet; it is fast, strong, and wary. Schools of these giants patrol the coastline like herds of wolves waiting for passing prey. The best gear seems to be a tandem of two treble hooks, about 6/0, rigged one on top of the other and weighted with several ounces of lead. Pieces of *bonito* or *barrilete* are cut up and securely tied to the hook. The rig can be jigged by hand or secured to a heavy boat rod and lowered to about 25–50 feet at night, somewhat deeper during the day, although variations in fishing depth should be attempted. These animals grow up to 100 pounds or so, and your line should be strong. You need a wire leader lest their sharp, parrotlike beak or the serrated suction cups on the arms and tentacles cut your lines. They are hard to hook, and their bite is gentle. Patience is required, and it's almost a case of the squid's IQ against the angler's. They are strong swimmers and they pull hard.

If you want to bring one of these aboard, a sharp gaff must be used to pierce the body, *not* the "fins," otherwise the soft flesh will tear. Beware the suction cups, sharp beak, and ample blast of ink they carry with them. In reality, the odds are with the squid, and this is real challenge fishing. Because of their large size, the flesh is tough, though edible, but the mantle (outside covering), arms, or tentacles make good strip bait for fishes.

—D.dS.

SQUIRRELFISH *Holocentrus ascensionis* This species belongs to the family Holocentridae, a group of tropical reef fishes with big eyes and very spiny scales and heads. The family is a primitive group of spiny-rayed fishes consisting of about 6 genera and 25 species. The squirrelfish has been recorded from both sides of the Atlantic; in the Western Atlantic it extends from Bermuda and Florida to southeastern Brazil including the West Indies and the Gulf of Mexico. In the Eastern Atlantic it ranges from Gabon to the Cape Verde, Principe, Sao Thome, and the Annobon Islands; also at Ascension, St. Helena, and St. Paul's Rock in the mid-Atlantic.

The coloration consists of alternating red and white stripes on the body. The leading edges of the pelvic, anal, and second dorsal fins and the outer margins of the caudal fin are white. There is a slightly diagonal white bar on the head below the eye. The membrane between any two dorsal spines is orange anteriorly and greenish posteriorly.

Other distinguishing characters of the squirrelfish are dorsal fin with 11 spines and 15 (rarely 14 or 16) softrays; anal fin with 4 spines and 10 softrays; pectoral rays 13–15; pelvic fin with 1 spine and 7 softrays; tube-bearing scales in lateral line 46–51; 3½ scales from lateral line to origin of dorsal and 8 scales between lateral line and vent. Gillrakers on first arch, 8 on upper limb, 1 at angle, 14 or 15 on lower limb; total 23 or 24.

Depth of body 2.69–3.13, length of head 2.80–3.17, length of snout 11.8–15.3, diameter of eye 6.35–9.45, width of interorbital 14.0–19.2, length of upper jaw 6.62–7.37, length of preopercular spine 16.0–18.7, depth of caudal peduncle 11.5–13.9, length of pelvic fin 3.01–3.60—all in standard length. Mouth large, upper jaw reaching posteriorly to below center of pupil or beyond; lower jaw generally not extending anterior to upper in small specimens, in large specimens even with or slightly protruding; anterior softrays of dorsal and anal greatly elongate; upper caudal lobe considerable longer than lower.

This species prefers shallow water (to a depth of 50 feet) with a rocky or coral bottom. Its life history is unknown.   —J.C.B.

SQUIRREL HAKE *Urophycis chuss* It is a member of the cod family (Gadidae) and closely resembles the mud hake. The scales number from 100–110 rows in the squirrel hake, while the mud hake has scales in about 140 rows. In addition, the filamentous part of the first dorsal fin is much longer in the squirrel hake and the nose is somewhat blunter.

The squirrel hake is brownish-gray or reddish on the upper sides of the back, with more or less dark mottlings, and is usually yellowish on the underside with some dusky spots. The lateral line is pale. Its maximum size is about 30 inches, and its weight about 8 pounds. Most of the commercial catch runs between 2 and 5 pounds.

It is distributed from the banks of Newfoundland and the Gulf of St. Lawrence as far south as Chesapeake Bay. It is normally found over soft bottoms; few are taken over rocks. It is found from the tide mark down to about 1,800 feet.

LIFE HISTORY

The squirrel hake spawns in June and July in the Massachusetts Bay region. The eggs float at the surface and young hake from an inch to 4 inches long are often found under floating eel grass or other vegetation. When slightly larger it takes to a bottom existence.

It feeds on prawns, shrimps, amphipods, squids, and fish.

FISHING TECHNIQUE

It takes a hook readily when baited with herring or clams. It apparently forages mostly at night, as the largest catches are taken at that time. Commercially it is taken with line trawls, and is a fine table fish.   —J.C.B.

STAGHORN SCULPIN *See* Pacific Staghorn Sculpin
STANDARD SPORTFISHERMAN An offshore fishing boat of under 40 feet long. *For details see* Standard Sportfisherman *under* Sportfisherman
STARGAZERS *Astroscopus* **spp.** This genus is characterized by its robust body and a large bony head, with small eyes placed on top of the head directed upwards. The mouth is large and obliquely upturned nearly vertically, and is fringed with fleshy filaments. The body is relatively small and tapers abruptly backwards to a small

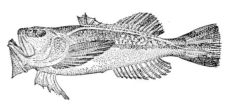

Stargazer

tail. The pectoral fins are broad and large. The first dorsal is composed of short, sharp spines, while the second dorsal is long and much higher. The body is dark with numerous small, white spots.

LIFE HISTORY

Two species, the Northern stargazer, *Astroscopus guttatus*, found from North Carolina to New York, and the southern stargazer, *A. y-graecum*, found from North Carolina to Brazil, occur on the Atlantic Coast, and are separated by the relative positions of the nostrils to the eye and the shape of the top of the head. The Northern species has small, closely spaced white spots on top of the head and body, and the Southern species has large, widely spaced white spots. Most Northern stargazers are less than a foot, while the Southern species grows to about 15 inches. Both species have a specialized area just behind the eyes which contains modified muscles capable of giving an electric shock. The mechanism is used in capturing food and possibly also for protection against enemies. Small fishes and crustaceans are eaten. It habitually lies partially buried in the sand, with only the eyes and lips exposed, and its tendency to live thus buried is also seen in its ability to live out of water for many hours. Young stages of the Northern stargazer have been found offshore, at a length of about ½–¾ of an inch. They too have a large head, which is provided with long spines similar to those of the flying gurnard (*which see*). Spawning possibly occurs in spring and early summer in deepwater, the young subsequently drifting inshore and settling to the bottom.

FOOD VALUE

Stargazers are occasionally caught in nets and traps, and the flesh is edible.   —D.dS.

STARRY FLOUNDER *Platichthys stellatus* Easily recognized by the alternating pattern of orange-white and dark bars on the fins, the species has a small mouth and a nearly straight lateral line. Although usually a lefteyed form, it may have the eyes on the right side. The body is rough, being covered with scattered, spinous plates on

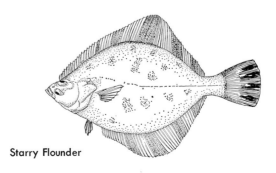

Starry Flounder

the eyed side. It is dark brown to black, with mottlings on the eyed side. Reaching a weight of 20 pounds and 3 feet long, it occurs from central California to Alaska, and south from the Bering Sea to Japan and Korea. It is most abundant in shallow water but also occurs to depths of at least 900 feet, generally over sandy bottoms.

LIFE HISTORY

The species, particularly the young, sometimes enters brackish water and the mouths of rivers. Males mature sexually in their second year (about 1 foot long), while the females mature during their third year (about 14 inches). Spawning occurs in late winter and early spring, taking place in California waters in depths of less than 25 fathoms. It eats crabs, shrimps, worms, clams, and their relatives, and small fishes.

ANGLING VALUE

Most starry flounder are taken by still-fishing throughout the year, chiefly on clams, shrimp, and small, live fish. Although it occurs in the commercial trawl catch, it is important chiefly as a sport fish. —D.dS.

STEELCOLOR SHINER *Notropis whipplei* A bluish-silvery shiner of moderate size, it has pronounced cross-hatching on the scales of back and sides. The lateral band is steel-blue, and a dusky blotch is found on the webbing among the last three dorsal rays. Anal rays 9. The snout is pointed and the head triangular in lateral outline. Eye small. The body of the adult averages deeper than that of the very similar spotfin shiner. The steelcolor shiner is found from Illinois through Ohio.

HABITS

This shiner is found most commonly in rapidly flowing streams of clearwater. Its food consists of insect larvae, both aquatic and terrestrial, and small crustaceans. The steelcolor shiner spawns in late spring and early summer over gravelly riffles. This species averages 4½ inches in length.

ECONOMIC VALUE

Although often confused with other species, the steelcolor shiner is considered a good bait species for bass, as it is attractive and hardy. —R.A.J.

STEELHEAD TROUT The anadromous form of the rainbow trout (*which see*)

STEEL ROD *See* The Stiffness Factor *under* Rod-Building

STEM The timber which forms the bow of the boat and to which the two sides of the boat are secured.

STERNSHEETS That part of a small boat which is farthest aft.

STICKLEBACK *See* Brook Stickleback, Fourspine Stickleback, Ninespine Stickleback, Threespine Stickleback

STINGRAY *See* Atlantic Stingray, Bat Stingray, Bluntnose Stingray, Diamond Stingray, Freshwater Stingray, Rays, Roughtail Stingray, Round Stingray, Southern Stingray, Yellow Stingray

STINK BAIT Stink bait is used extensively in some parts of the country for catching channel and flat-head catfish. Almost everyone who does very much of this type of fishing has his own formula for making the bait. The most common procedure, however, is to take a quantity (usually the content of a 5-gallon oil can) of minnows or small gizzard shad and allow them to decompose until there is nothing but a thick oily substance in the can. Other ingredients such as sliced bananas and oil of anise are added. Ordinarily a piece of sponge is dipped into this liquid and then placed on the hook for bait. Another method of preparation is to make a stiff dough, saturate it with the aromatic solution just described, and mold it around the shank of a treble hook.

STONECAT *Noturus flavus* A yellowish catfish with rounded or square tail and an inconspicuous adipose fin, it is yellow-olive to blue-black above, with lighter sides, and yellowish or milk-white underparts. Caudal fin with a light border. Adipose fin bound to the body over its entire length. Upper jaw much longer than lower jaw. No teeth or serrations on the rear edge of the pectoral spine but with poison gland at its base. Body slender. The range of the stonecat is from Montana to the Great Lakes and south to Texas.

HABITS

Primarily a riffle species, the stonecat, as its name implies, is found in rocky streams and rocky, windblown lake shallows. Spawning in early summer in much the same manner as other catfish, the stonecat deposits its eggs on rocks and logs, and the adults guard the eggs

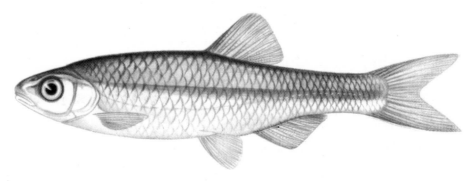

Steelcolor Shiner

Stonecat

and young for some time. An omnivorous feeder, the stonecat consumes a variety of aquatic animals and plant material. The stonecat is a small species seldom reaching 12 inches in length.

ECONOMIC VALUE

Often mistaken for the black bullhead, the stonecat is a fair food fish and is taken in number by youthful fishermen who consider the sting of its poisonous spine inconsequential. In some areas the stonecat is said to be of extreme importance as food for the smallmouth bass.
—R.A.J.

STONE CRAB *Menippe mercenaria* A very popular commercial crab, it is a member of the mud-crab family (Xanthidae), characterized by a somewhat flattened shell which is oval in shape. The large claws have black tips, and the body grades from purplish to dark brown or reddish-brown, with brownish mottlings. The legs, which are fringed with hair, have red and yellow bands and sharp points, and are not adapted for swimming as in the blue crab (*which see*).

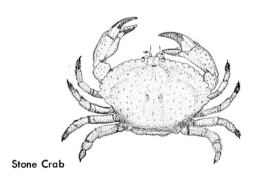

Stone Crab

LIFE HISTORY

The stone crab grows to about 5 inches between tips of the shell, and about 2 inches deep, giving it a more bulky appearance than most crabs. Its shell is very hard and heavy. Found from North Carolina to Texas, it reaches its peak of abundance and size in southern Florida, although nowhere is it as abundant as the blue crab. It is a burrower, living in deep holes of mud and sandy mud, near creeks and estuaries, as well as under rocks and among mangrove roots.

COMMERCIAL VALUE

Although sluggish in habit, the stone crab can inflict a severe bite with its powerful claws, and it is difficult to capture by hand. Iron hooks, hook and line, and crab

pots are used, but the fishery is limited in size. The most important fishing areas are Beaufort, North Carolina; Charleston, South Carolina; Miami, Naples, and Key West, Florida. Its flesh is rich, sweet, and delicate, somewhat like that of the claws of northern lobster, and perhaps is the most prized of all crabs. —D.dS.

STONEFISH *See* Scorpionfish

STONEFLIES Plecoptera Nearly 400 species of stoneflies occur in both the United States and Canada. Stoneflies constitute a major food item for several kinds of gamefish. Almost all of the species pass their early life history in cool, well-oxygenated, flowing streams and are thus particularly important in the diet of trout. Substantial flights of small, blackish species often occur during the winter, and are eagerly sought by trout and other fish. In Western streams countless thousands of very large stoneflies fairly swarm in May or June and are voraciously eaten by large browns and rainbows. Dainty little yellow stoneflies emerge in sizable hatches in spring and early summer, and these too tempt trout and other gamefishes. The adult insects are frequently used as bait and are usually floated like a dry artificial fly. Numerous fly patterns simulate stoneflies—the Golden Stone, Little Yellow Stone, Early Brown Stone, Bird's Stonefly, Sofa Pillow, and California Salmon Fly are popular examples.

In addition to being of value as a food source for fish, stonefly nymphs are important in pollution studies since this group of insects can live only in waters which are clean.

LIFE HISTORY

Stoneflies lay their eggs in flowing streams or occasionally along gravel-strewn lake shorelines in northern areas. Winged adult females normally deposit the egg mass by dipping the tip of the abdomen beneath the water surface in flight. Some small, short-winged females actually crawl under the water surface to deposit their eggs. After hatching from the egg, the tiny nymphs may remain dormant for some months during late spring and summer after which they pass through several molts before attaining full maturity. Most small species require only a year before transforming to adults, but some of the larger forms require at least two full seasons. Stonefly nymphs vary in their feeding habits, some being herbivores and others carnivores. Many species of adults do not feed, but others feed on algae or, rarely, the tender buds of higher plants.

North American stonefly nymphs always have two tails, and there are always two claws on each foot. Similar-appearing mayfly nymphs have a single claw. External gills are characteristic of many stoneflies, and these may be on the underside of the head, laterally on the thoracic or abdominal segments, or extruding from the anus. Many other species apparently absorb dissolved oxygen through the body covering.

At full maturity, nymphs crawl from the water and rest on an exposed rock, tree trunk, or other resting place. After emerging from the nymphal skin, adults rest for some time while the soft wings and other body parts harden. Emergence may occur during the night, early-morning hours, or occasionally during the day.

Stonefly Adult

The small, winter-emerging species must eat algae before mating, but other species require no food in the adult stage. Mating may take place at any hour and occurs when the adults are not in flight. The males of some of the small, winter forms have the odd habit of "drumming," thumping the abdomen to create sound to attract the female.

The majority of stoneflies are fully winged. The four wings are held folded over the abdomen when the stonefly is at rest. Some species have flightless, short wings, and a few are entirely wingless. A most peculiar species has recently been discovered that is wingless and apparently passes its entire life history deeply submerged in Lake Tahoe. Stoneflies have fairly long antennae. Most summer-emerging forms have long tails; some of the small, winter-emerging species are almost tailless.

Stoneflies vary greatly in size. Some small, wingless forms are only about ⅛ inch in length while some giants have a body length of at least 2 inches and a wing expanse of 4 inches. Most North American species are gray or brown; several forms are bright yellow, and a few are green. In New Zealand and Australia some large, showy species have purple or reddish patches on the wings.

Stonefly Nymph

Some adults are nocturnal and may be attracted to artificial lights like mayflies. Most species are diurnal. All are weak flyers and spend most of their time close to their natal stream. There is a succession of species throughout the year in North America, with the greatest number of species and the greatest variety of forms occurring during the spring season.

IMPORTANT SPECIES

From the standpoint of the angler, stoneflies are of much importance both as a source of bait or as models from which to fashion artificial lures. The nymphs and adults of the larger forms may be used as bait for smallmouth bass or trout. Artificial stonefly nymphs are fished deeply submerged, and artificial flies patterned after the adult stonefly are often effective lures, particularly for large rainbows and browns on such Western streams as the Madison and the Deschutes.

The small, blackish species belonging to such genera as *Allocapnia*, *Capnia*, and *Taeniopteryx* often emerge in abundant hatches during the late winter and are eaten in huge numbers by gamefish. As the spring season advances, stoneflies occur in increasing variety on most trout streams. In late spring—May or June—hordes of large stoneflies emerge on many of the large Western streams, and trout gorge on them. Most abundant is the large *Pteronarcys californica*, but other large stoneflies of the genus *Acroneuria* also occur abundantly, not only on Western streams but also those of Eastern North America. On the Pacific Coast these large species are known collectively by trout anglers as salmon flies. Delicate little bright yellow or green stoneflies of the genus *Alloperla* occur abundantly during warm periods just before dusk along many Eastern and Western trout streams. All of these, and many other varieties, contribute importantly to the diet of trout, grayling, smallmouth bass, and other gamefish.

YELLOW SALLY

Alloperla spp. The name Yellow Sally was originally given to an English stonefly in a different genus, but the name seems so appropriate for our species of *Alloperla* that the name is used here.

Members of the genus *Alloperla* are very similar in general appearance, nearly all having yellow bodies and being approximately ¼–½ inch in body length. A few species have green bodies. Many species in another genus, *Isoperla*, are similar in general aspect to species of *Alloperla*.

Most species of *Alloperla* emerge in late spring or early summer and occur abundantly in nearly all gravel-bottom, unpolluted streams in temperate North America. They are much less common in the Southern United States and in the prairie states.

Frequently a hatch of *Alloperla* affords an abundant food supply for trout in the late evening when the insects become very active and swarm over the surface of a trout stream. At such times an angler's skill is tested in matching an artificial to the size and performance of the natural insect.

The body of *Alloperla* is usually yellow, sometimes with a black, longitudinal dorsal band, and in the larger species is about ½ inch in length. The wings are clear, tinted with yellow. The various species are fairly strong fliers and are most active in late afternoon. During most of the daytime they will rest on green foliage bordering streams, with their wings held horizontally over the abdomen.

WILLOW

Leuctra spp. Again, this name is applied to an English stonefly but in the same genus. Since the species of *Leuctra* are very similar in general appearance, the name Willow is equally applicable to all of the species.

Most species of *Leuctra* emerge during early spring and are among the small gray and brown stoneflies that furnish early-season meals to trout. Some species make their advent into the terrestrial world in late winter before the last snow banks melt. Together with early-season species of *Nemoura*, the Early Brown of British trout anglers, these hardy little aquatics may fly in some numbers during sunny periods.

The adult Willow and its allies differ from other stoneflies in that they require a meal, usually of minute blue-green algae, before they can successfully reproduce. The eggs are laid at water's edge.

The adult has a body length of ¼–½ inch in length. Differing from most other kinds of stoneflies, the wings of the Willow do not rest flat along the top of the abdomen but curl over the sides.

The slender nymphs, herbivores, are most commonly found among decaying vegetation lodged among rocks on stream beds. When they have attained full maturity they crawl a short distance from the water, rest upon some solid object, and shed their last nymphal coat. The soft and pale gray insect at first holds the wings erect, but as the wings and body covering harden and darken, the wings lie wrapped around the upper half of the abdomen.

WESTERN SALMON FLY

Pteronarcys californica This is a very large gray or blackish stonefly that occurs abundantly in many Western rivers during late spring. During the hatch, which may last a week or even longer, large trout gorge themselves on both the mature nymphs and on the adults. Enormous numbers of the large, awkward, flying adults sometimes create traffic hazards on highways skirting rivers.

The species ranges along the Pacific Coast from British Columbia into California and eastward to New Mexico. Related species of the same genus occur across Canada and down the Eastern seaboard into the Appalachians and down the Rockies into Wyoming. Only in the West, however, do vast hordes of *Pteronarcys* emerge each season in large rivers such as the Madison, Rogue, and Deschutes.

The adult has a body length of about 2 inches. The slender antennae are nearly an inch in length, the tails somewhat less than ½ inch long. The body and wings are usually gray, though sometimes the wings are blackish. The soft parts between head and thoracic segments are often orange in color. Unlike most other stoneflies both the fore and hind wings have an extensive network of cross-veins something like those that are found in dragonflies. The entire wing span may exceed four inches.

The dark brown nymphs are often extremely abundant among the gravel and detritus of stream beds. They are herbivorous and crawl about slowly. When disturbed they curl and do not attempt to escape. Usually there are at least two sizes of nymphs, and it is believed that the nymphal stage lasts a full two years.

The California Salmon Fly is a name best applied to another large stonefly, *Acroneuria californica*, that is yellowish-brown in color and with a body and wing length of up to ½ inch. Generally it is on the wing somewhat later than the larger and grayer Western Salmon Fly. —S.G.J.

THE SALMON-FLY OR WILLOW-FLY HATCH

The so-called salmon-fly hatch or willow-fly hatch is a celebrated occasion on many Western United States rivers. Very large trout (up to 15 pounds according to the records of the *Field & Stream* Fishing Contest) are caught on floating imitations during the comparatively brief period when the stonefly emergences are at a peak. Either because of their size or food value, the Plecoptera have the capacity to bring heavy trout to the surface. However, as with the leaf roller or inchworm (*which see*), and also beetles, and ants, the stonefly is a unique insect form which must be matched in size and in color for the best of angling results.

There is a considerable variation in emergence dates for nearly all aquatic insects. Many mayflies have successive broods throughout the season, and the bulk of the single-brooded species hatches during a relatively short period in late spring and early summer. The caddisflies also appear erratically. But stoneflies are an exception in having a well-defined succession of species emerging through most of the year. The approximate dates, of course, are of local value, and your favorite fly tier can probably make a qualified guess on when to expect the important hatches. There are more than forty species of stoneflies in western Oregon alone; so learning about even a few of the more important ones is a big advantage in stream craft.

The life cycle of a stonefly parallels that of the mayfly with a few exceptions. The nymphal stage of both insects ordinarily lasts about one year, and in some species two years. But unlike mayflies, which thrive in a great variety of aquatic habitats, the stonefly nymph is largely restricted to fastwater, and reaches its peak abundance in swift, well-oxygenated streams. This obviously accounts for their greater importance in turbulent Western rivers. Also, unlike most mayflies, the stonefly nymph crawls out on the shore or on the side of a rock when emerging into a winged adult; hatching mayflies on the other hand struggle to the surface and drift with the current until the winged adult pops from its shuck. This, plus the fact that stoneflies do not often return to the water in blizzardlike swarms to mate and deposit their eggs (mayflies often do), normally makes them targets of opportunity to the fish. The winged female of most species releases her egg mass by dipping the tip of her abdomen below the surface while in flight—which triggers some eruptive rises from alert trout—but except for the great hatches on Western rivers there are seldom enough stoneflies in the air to bring on a general feeding period. It may be said, therefore, that the nymph is more important than the winged insect. However, at certain times of the year, beginning as early as April and running through August, major emergences do occur, and if you're fortunate enough to be on the water, the fishing can be phenomenal.

STONEFLY IMITATIONS

It's apparent that the so-called Bucktail Caddis series of flies, which are so popular in the West, are basically stonefly representations. These palmered, bucktail-wing dry flies are of a size and configuration that suggest the insect. It's also likely that some of the Woolly Worm patterns are accepted as stonefly nymphs by the trout. However, during the significant hatches a "close approximation" of the natural is far more rewarding for obvious reasons. The strikingly colored Golden Stonefly Nymph, for example, is hard to imitate with anything other than a correctly tied counterpart. As a general rule, a good presentation of the nymph requires that it be fished slowly and deeply along grass- or shrub-covered banks in the early morning when nymphs are crawling from the water prior to transformation to the adult stage. In streams where large boulders project from fastwater, you should find trout feeding nearby as nymphs will be climbing out on the rocks. Empty and split shucks of larval stoneflies still clinging to boulders just above water level are a good indication of where you can expect results.

The clarity of the water and the shyness of the fish dictate in a large part what size leader you will need to fish the stonefly imitation. It's wise to keep in mind that trout which are bigger than ordinary are likely to be on the move so 2X or 3X points are the safe rule. On streams like the Yellowstone, Madison, Green, and Deschutes, which are so opulently filled with splendid browns and rainbows, the fish slash furiously at stoneflies, and leader breaks are common. Eastern anglers who fish at night, in states where it is legal, enjoy the same heavy-mouthed strikes, but under the cover of darkness a No. 4 fly can be worked with IX or even OX tippets without putting the trout down. The ferocious lunge, so unlike the dainty sipping at a mayfly, does require some restraint in setting the hook even with the heavier points. You may observe also that when trout are feeding on stonefly nymphs the strike is more forceful, probably because the natural moves rapidly when disturbed. For this reason, you should try varying the action of the artificial; fish the drift slowly and deeply without any rod movement, but when the line swings around and tightens in the current, bring the nymph to the surface in short, snappy jerks before picking up for the next cast. This is especially productive if you can finish each drift close to the boulders or along streamside brush.

For Western anglers there are three bountiful hatches worth anticipating. These are matched with the Dark Stonefly, Golden Stonefly, and Little Yellow Stonefly patterns. The first is an imitation of one of the *Pteronarcys*, which are the largest North American stoneflies. The dark gray or blackish adults have a body length of about 2 inches, and the wing span may exceed 4 inches. Although various species occur in trout streams all across the country, it is only in the West, where they emerge in great numbers, that *Pteronarcys* has angling significance. The clumsy flying adults not only bring big trout to the surface but often create a traffic hazard on nearby roads. One species, *P. californica* (the Western Salmon Fly), is represented by the Dark Stonefly patterns. The nymph is dressed on a No. 4 (3XL) hook as is the wet version, while the dry pattern is usually tied on a No. 8 (3XL). Actually, a No. 8 is somewhat smaller than the natural, but most anglers prefer it because it floats better. When tied full, the No. 8 is suitably close.

Dark Stonefly (Wet)

Tail	¼-in. barred or spotted dark brown turkey
Body	Tangerine-colored wool ribbed with nickel-gray silk in buttonhole twist. Body is started in front and wound to curve of hook then wound forward and tied off. Clear cement is applied between the two layers. Flatten with smooth-jawed pliers both before and after applying the rib.
Hackle	Dark furnace, long and soft
Wing	Dark Eastern deertail dyed with coffee-brown hair dye
Head	Long and flattened. Black with fluorescent orange band across top in front of wing

Dark Stonefly (Dry)

The dry version requires the same materials as the wet Dark Stonefly. The only difference is that a narrow, dark furnace hackle of dry-fly quality is tied in at the rear of the fly and palmered. A second, stiff, dark furnace hackle is tied in at the front of the fly to form a collar.

Dark Stonefly (Nymph)

Tail	¼-in. barred or spotted dark brown turkey
Body	Spun dirty (offwhite) badger-fur dubbing. Top with dark brown turkey tail. Rib this down with tan silk in buttonhole twist. Color turkey top with black head cement on each rib
Legs	½-in. barred or spotted dark brown turkey
Wingcase	Dark brown turkey ⅓ as long as body, flared and V-notched in middle
Head	Piece of wool yarn, same color as underbody, stained dark brown on top. Thick enamel good for this

Another genus of large stoneflies is *Acroneuria*, which emerges a bit later than the Dark Stonefly. The most important one, *A. californica*, called the Golden Stone or California Salmon Fly, is yellowish-brown, almost gold in color, and is generally dressed on the same hook sizes as the Dark Stonefly. The huge mating flights of this stonefly occur in the Rocky Mountain region beginning in late spring (early June). However, it is definitely of greater importance on west-slope streams in Washington, Oregon, and California. The Dark Stonefly on the other hand is regionally more valuable on the east slope. Other species of *Acroneuria* appear all the way into the Eastern United States, but these are not comparable in importance to the large, brightly colored Golden Stonefly.

Golden Stonefly (Wet)

Tail	¼-in. spotted teal, dyed gold
Body	Spun mohair yarn (antique gold), ribbed with No. 3715 Belding (same color) silk thread in buttonhole twist. Use same procedure as in Dark Stone, flattening body into the clear cement
Hackle	Dyed gold, long and soft. Small bunch of dyed teal in front under head same length as hackle
Wing	Dye pale-backed whitetail deer hair gold. Wing should be two shades darker than body
Head	Gold Belding thread flattened in clear cement

Golden Stonefly (Dry)

The dry version requires the same materials as the wet Golden Stone. The only difference is that a narrow, dyed gold hackle of dry-fly quality is tied in at the rear of the fly and palmered. A second, stiff gold hackle is tied in at the front of the fly to form a collar.

Golden Stonefly (Nymph)

Tail	¼-inch spotted teal, dyed gold
Body	Spun mohair yarn made in the same manner as the wet version. This stonefly displays little if any change in color between the nymph and adult stage. The back is tied in above tail; a long bunch of gold-dyed spotted teal, ribbed down with a button-hole twist. Lacquer with clear varnish
Legs	½-inch of gold-dyed spotted teal
Wingcase	Gold-dyed spotted teal ⅓ as long as body, flared and V-notched in middle
Head	Piece of gold yarn wound into head cement and flattened over Belding tying silk

The traditional Yellow Sally fly pattern was a crude attempt at representing a species of *Isoperla*, a stonefly genus which is distinguished by its yellow color. The Little Yellow Stonefly of the genus *Alloperla* is a better representation, particularly as a dry fly. Most of the species of *Alloperla* have small bodies ¼-½ inch in length, which makes them somewhat easier to imitate than the big species. They emerge in the late-spring or summer months and bring on such a good rise in willow-bordered Western rivers that you can hardly afford to be without an artificial. Most of the species are bright yellow; a few are chartreuse or actually green. The nymph should be dressed on a No. 8 hook, and the wet and dry patterns on a No. 10, all in regular weight and shank length. Both the wet and dry versions are tied with a crimson egg sac to represent the female. E. H. Rosborough of Chiloquin, Oregon, asserts that the Little Yellow Stone female will outfish its eggless mate by a wide ratio; so there's hardly any point in using a male copy. Rosborough made it with fore-and-aft hackles for maximum floatability because this fly must ride high on the water to take fish.

Little Yellow Stonefly Female (Wet)

Tail	Short, pale yellow grizzly fibers
Egg Sac	Short, heavy, bunch, crimson hackle fibers clipped to ¹⁄₁₆ inch in length. This is better than floss because it provides truer color
Body	Chartreuse or yellow wool or nylon. Rib with chartreuse or yellow silk (which can be used as tying thread) very closely as the natural has a narrowly segmented body
Hackle	Pale yellow grizzly
Wing	Clear-veined plastic wings tied flat over body, or pale yellow, grizzly hackle points
Head	Chartreuse or yellow tying silk, flattened

Little Yellow Stonefly Female (Dry)

The same materials are used in the dry version except that it is wingless and tied with fore-and-aft hackles. The hackles are a very pale yellowish grizzly; the rear one should be the size used on a No. 12 hook, and the front hackle the correct size for a No. 10 hook. Both should be of good quality.

Little Yellow Stonefly (Nymph)

Tail	Speckled mallard fibers, dyed chartreuse or yellow
Body	Soft polar-bear dubbing, dyed chartreuse or yellow and spun on a tying loop. The back is tied in above tail; a bunch of chartreuse or yellow-dyed, speckled mallard fibers, ribbed down with a buttonhole twist. Lacquer with clear varnish
Legs	Speckled mallard fibers
Wingcase	Chartreuse- or yellow-dyed, speckled mallard fibers ⅓ as long as body, flared and V-notched in middle
Head	Chartreuse or yellow tying silk

Eastern anglers experience few important stonefly hatches during the season, even though each riffle in every rocky trout stream contains the strikingly marked black-and-amber nymphs. Besides *Alloperla* there are species of *Isoperla*, *Leuctra* and *Nemoura* as well as the big *Pteronarcys*. Most of the Eastern stoneflies are nocturnal insofar as the adults being on the water is concerned, which probably accounts for the success of large flies for brown trout after dark. Unfortunately, the magic *Pteronarcys*, which bust Western streams wide open, is not only nocturnal in the East but limited chiefly to small, cold headwater streams. The prospect of catching an 8-inch trout on a No. 4 fly after dark is of inverse significance. In years past, before the ecology of the river changed, the East Branch of the Delaware had some lush flights of big *Pteronarcys*. Two naturals are effective in the East, however. One appears to be a species of *Acroneuria*, which is simply called Large Stone Fly by most fly dressers and anglers, and the Early Brown Stone, or *Taeniopteryx fasciata*, which emerges in profusion beginning in April. Harry Darbee of Roscoe, New York, has always tied four patterns which serve admirably during these hatches. The first, a wet version of the Early Brown Stone, should be tied on a No. 14 hook of regular length and weight. The dry pattern, a Dun Variant, should be tied on a No. 14 IXS hook. The adult Early Brown Stonefly floats high on the water with its wings held more nearly upright than in the typical down stonefly position. For this reason it is often mistaken for a large, dun mayfly at a distance. A reliable nymph pattern for the Early Brown Stonefly has not been worked out, but the wet version is reliable when fish are not surface feeding.

Early Brown Stonefly (Wet)

Tail	Rusty-dun hackle fibers
Body	Quill stripped from dark brown hackle
Hackle	Rusty-dun
Wing	Two small, dun hackles tied flat over body

Dun Variant (Dry)

Tail	Dun hackle fibers
Body	Brown quill stripped from dark brown hackle feather
Hackle	Dun. The hackle should be large and dressed moderately full

For the Large Stonefly, there are two Darbee nymph patterns as well as a dry pattern. For best results, the nymph should be fished early in the morning and the floater at evening. These are all tied on No. 10, 3XL hooks, but both larger (up to No. 4) and smaller (down to No. 14) sizes are productive as general stonefly imita-

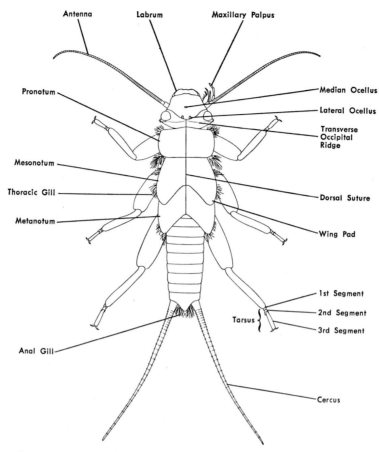

A constructed stonefly nymph

tions for Eastern fishing. Although the thorax of a natural stonefly nymph is divided into three segments (the pro-thorax, metathorax, and mesothorax) fly dressers usually refer to these as "joints" for the sake of simplicity. Two segments bear wingcases in the realistic Darbee manner. The third segment is for all practical purposes indistinguishable from the artificial's head.

Large Stonefly #1 (Nymph)

Wing	Two strands ringneck-cock-pheasant tail center
Wingcases	Pair of junglecock eye, split over two joints
Body	Fox fur dubbing mixed with dyed yellow seal. Body is tied from rear. Tie abdomen first, and rib it with dyed brown monofilament. Tie off. Tie in dubbing for first joint, and add wingcases. Tie second joint and add wingcases. Tie in bunch of dubbing to form head, and collar it with partridge hackle to form legs. Finish head with orange-brown lacquer

Large Stonefly #2 (Nymph)

Tail	Two strands ringneck-cock-pheasant tail center
Wingcases	Clipped pheasant feather, brown and buff, well-marked. Feather should be notched, bent over thumbnail, and tied down.
Body	Fox fur dubbing mixed with dyed yellow seal. Body is tied from rear. Tie abdomen first, and rib it with quill stripped from a large brown hackle. Tie off. Tie in two leg strands from a brown peacock primary-wing quill. Tie in dubbing for first joint, add wingcase and legs as before. Tie in second joint; add wingcase and legs again. Tie in a small amount of dubbing to form head, and finish off with brown embroidery cotton. Cement with orange-tinted ambroid

Large Stonefly (Dry)

Tail	Small bunch of brown deer hair
Body	Gray caribou hair, dyed yellow and trimmed rather flat
Wings	Two rusty-dun hackles, slightly longer than body and laid down flat
Hackle	A small bunch of brown deer hair to form collar as in Muddler Minnow

—A.J.McC.

KEYS TO NORTH AMERICAN STONEFLIES

Before starting to identify stoneflies, you will need a good hand lens, or even better, a binocular microscope with a magnification of 10 to 30 times natural size. Without a microscope, it is best not to attempt to identify stonefly nymphs with a body length of less than a quarter

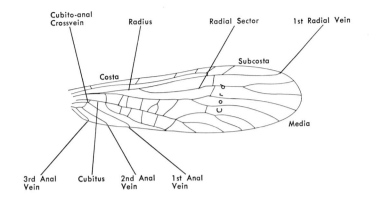

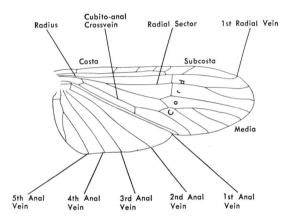

Wings of *Isoperla bilineata*

of an inch. A hand lens, however, will suffice for larger nymphs and for all adults.

If you are not already familiar with insect structure, read the paragraphs below carefully, making frequent reference to the accompanying drawings. Then, with actual specimens for study, refer to the keys.

The stonefly body includes the general areas of head, thorax of three segments, and abdomen of ten segments. Anteriorly, the head bears a pair of slender antennae or feelers, and a pair of large compound eyes, one on each side. Most genera have three ocelli, which are small, simple eyes, arranged in a triangle on the top of the head between the compound eyes. The anterior ocellus is missing in a few genera. The underside of the head may bear gills, either in tufts, or as slender fingers. These are most commonly located at the outer rear angles.

Mouthparts are rather complex. From above, the labrum corresponds to our upper lip. At either side is a sort of upper jaw, a maxilla, adjacent to which is a maxillary palpus, or palp, of five segments or joints, a structure something like a stubby antenna. Below is a structure of major importance in classifying stoneflies, the flaplike labium, or the insect's lower lip. It is made up principally of two pairs of jointed plates, the glossae and paraglossae. In the suborder Filipalpia these structures are all of about equal length; in the Setipalpia the upper pair, the paraglossae, are larger and longer than the lower, innermost pair, the glossae. The accompanying figure in the first key shows the type in each of the suborders. The labium has a short, three-segmented palpus on either side. The heavy, massive mandibles are the stonefly's lower jaws. These are structurally variable and are therefore useful in classifying stoneflies, especially to subgeneric levels which are not considered in this article. The large, platelike submentum at the base of the labium actually covers most of the underside of the insect's head.

The thorax is the strongest part of the insect body. It supports legs and wings (wing pads in nymphs) and frequently has external gills on its sides or on its under surface. The dorsal plates of each of the three segments are termed nota, the ventral ones, the sterna. The anterior segment, the prothorax, bears a pronotum dorsally, a prosternum ventrally. On the middle segment, or mesothorax, there is a mesonotum above, a mesosternum below. Similarly, the third segment is called the metathorax, the dorsal plate is the metanotum, and the ventral plate is the metasternum.

Each of the three thoracic segments bears a pair of jointed legs. The small roundish basal joint is termed the coxa, and next to it is another, rather short segment, the trochanter. Femur and tibia follow; these are comparable to our fore and upper arms and legs. The three-segmented foot terminates in a pair of claws on the last segment. Tufts of gills may be present at the bases of the legs, or there may be slender gills on any of the segments at the leg bases or on the sides between coxae.

The wing veins of insects have special names and are important in identification. See these on the labeled wing and also note in the keys the small wing sketches which pinpoint identification features.

In nymphs, the abdomen bears a pair of long cerci or tails at its posterior end. Adults may have long or very short cerci. There may also be a tuft of branched gills extruded from the anus in either nymph or adult, or a pair of them may be on the underside of the first two or three segments. In one rare species, recorded only from the Sierra Nevada, paired slender lateral gills extend from the first seven segments. The male sex organs are borne behind the tenth segment, those of the female on the underside of the seventh or eighth sternum. However, in both sexes additional segments may be involved in the secondary sexual modifications.

The stonefly keys have been modified from those in several scientific papers and have followed the pattern of presentation found in the chapter on stoneflies in *Aquatic Insects of California*, edited by Robert L. Usinger and published by the University of California. The labeled drawing of the hypothetical stonefly nymph has been modified from the original drawing in the late T. H. Frison's *Stoneflies, or Plecoptera, of Illinois*, issued by the Illinois Natural History Survey. The wing of *Isoperla bilineata*, with the veins named, has been relabeled from a figure in Needham and Claassen's classic work on stoneflies, *Plecoptera or Stoneflies of America North of Mexico*, published by the Thomas Say Foundation. The various sketches were suggested by many drawings found in scientific articles on stoneflies.

The keys are really easy to use after a little practice. Note that they are made up of couplets, each containing a pair of statements. Here is how to use them. Assume that you have an adult winged stonefly before you. First find its proper family in the key to the families. Read the two statements in the first couplet and decide which fits your specimen. Are the paraglossae (mouthpart structures described in the beginning of the key) the same length as the glossae? If so, your specimen belongs to the suborder Filipalpia. Now go, as directed, to the second couplet to make another choice. Repeat this process until your specimen is properly identified as belonging to one of the six families of North American stoneflies. (The number in parentheses following the couplet number refers to the earlier couplet from where you were directed to go to the present couplet.) Now go to the key to genera for the family represented by your particular specimen and proceed in a similar fashion until you are able to identify your specimen as to its genus.

FAMILIES OF NORTH AMERICAN STONEFLIES
ADULTS

1 Paraglossae and glossae of about equal length. 2
Suborder **Filipalpia**

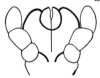

Paraglossae and glossae of *Taeniopteryx*

Paraglossae much longer than the glossae. 4
Suborder **Setipalpia**

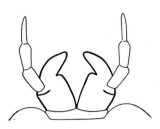

Paraglossae and glossae of *Isoperla*

2 (1) Anal area of fore wing with two or more rows of crossveins; 1–3 inches in length. **Pteronarcidae**

Fore wing of *Pteronarcys*

Anal area of fore wing without rows of crossveins; an inch or less in length. 3

Fore wing of *Nemoura*

3 (2) Ocelli two; straw or gray in color; ½–1 inch in length. **Peltoperlidae**

Head of *Peltoperla*

Ocelli three; brown or gray in color; ¼ to nearly an inch in length. **Nemouridae**

Head of *Nemoura*

4 (1) Branched gill remnants at the lower angles of the thoracic segments. **Perlidae**
Branched gill remnants absent from thoracic segments. 5

5 (4) Fork of second anal vein of fore wing included in the anal cell, branches leaving separately; gills absent or simple gills present on the submentum, the thorax, or the abdomen. **Perlodidae**

Fore wing of *Isogenus*

Second anal vein of fore wing not forked or forked beyond the anal cell except in *Kathroperla* which has the fork at the margin of the cell or included in it. **Chloroperlidae**

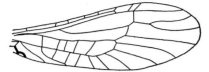

Fore wing of *Alloperla*

NYMPHS

1 Paraglossae and glossae of about equal length. 2
Suborder **Filipalpia**

Paraglossae and glossae of *Taeniopteryx*

Paraglossae much longer than the glossae. 4
Suborder **Setipalpia**

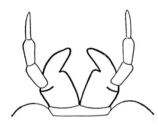

Paraglossae and glossae of *Isoperla*

2 (1) Abdomen without branched gills on the ventral side. 3
Abdomen with branched gills on the ventral side of the first 2–3 segments. **Pteronarcidae**
3 (2) Form roach-like; ocelli two; thoracic sterna produced posteriorly into thin plates overlapping the segment behind. **Peltoperlidae**

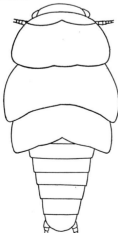

Nymph of *Peltoperla*

Body shape normal; ocelli three; thoracic sterna not produced posteriorly to overlap the segment behind. **Nemouridae**

Nymph of *Nemoura*

4 (1) Branched gills at the lower angles of the thoracic segments. **Perlidae**
Branched gills absent from the thoracic segments. 5
5 (4) Body usually pigmented in a distinct pattern; cerci usually at least as long as the abdomen; gills absent or simple gills present on submentum, thoracic segments, or abdomen. **Perlodidae**

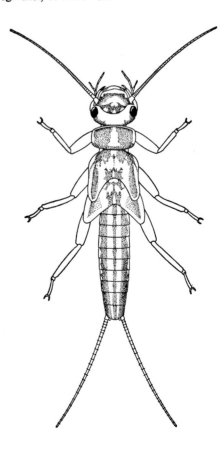

Nymph of *Isoperla*

Body almost concolorous, without a pattern; cerci not more than three-quarters as long as the abdomen; external gills always lacking. **Chloroperlidae**

Nymph of *Alloperla*

NEMOURIDAE

This family includes three subfamilies, separable in both adult and nymph stages by the keys below. The Nemourinae and the Taeniopteryginae emerge mostly in early spring and include the insects after which artificial flies such as the March Brown are patterned. The Capniinae include a number of winter emerging species in *Capnia* and related genera. Most of the species of the genus *Isocapnia* are larger than the species in other genera of the subfamily and emerge in early spring, in contrast to species of *Capnia* which are typical winter stoneflies. The Leuctrinae contain many species of the genus *Leuctra*, which are also abundant in the British Isles and elsewhere in Europe, where trout anglers refer to them collectively as Needles in allusion to their slender form. Some larger species in related genera occur in western North America.

The Nemourids, as a group, while generally rather small and inconspicuous, contain a host of species that no doubt contribute greatly to the food supply of trout and other fish throughout the entire year.

ADULTS OF THE SUBFAMILIES AND GENERA OF NEMOURIDAE

1   Second tarsal segment much shorter than the first.   2

Leg of *Leuctra*

Second tarsal segment at least as long as the first.   11
                       Taeniopteryginae

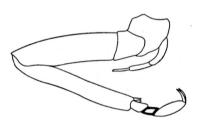

Leg of *Taeniopteryx*

2 (1) Wings lying nearly flat when at rest; second anal vein of fore wing forked; cerci one-segmented.
                       Nemourinae

Fore wing of *Nemoura*

About fifty described North American species; distributed generally; abundant.   **Nemoura**
Wings either rolled around the body at rest, or wings flat when at rest and with second anal vein of the fore wing simple; cerci either one-segmented or with more than four segments.   3

Fore wing of *Eucapnopsis*

3 (2) Wings rolled around the body; cerci one-segmented. 4
Leuctrinae
Wings flat; cerci with more than four segments. 6
Capniinae

4 (3) Anal area of hind wing with six long veins. One Appalachian species, three species in Pacific Northwest; rare. *Megaleuctra*

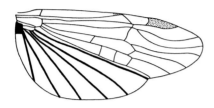

Hind wing of *Megaleuctra*

Anal area of hind wing with three long veins. 5

Hind wing of *Leuctra*

5 (4) Fore wing with veins R$_s$ and M with a common origin on vein R. Two species, western North America; common. *Perlomyia*

Fore wing of *Perlomyia*

Fore wing with vein R$_s$ originating well beyond origin of vein R. About twenty-five described North American species; distributed generally; abundant. *Leuctra*

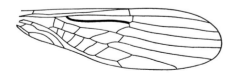

Fore wing of *Leuctra*

6 (3) Cerci with fewer than eleven segments. Two species in western North America, one abundant. *Eucapnopsis*
Cerci with more than eleven segments. 7

7 (6) Two or more crossveins beyond the cord in the fore wing. Ten described North American species, mostly western; one species common, others scarce. *Isocapnia*

Fore wing of *Isocapnia*

No cross vein beyond the cord in the fore wing. 8

8 (7) Vein R$_1$ of fore wing bent abruptly upward at its origin; vein A$_1$ of fore wing bent abruptly caudad at its junction with cu-a and then curved outward again. About twenty-five described North American species, mostly western; often abundant. *Capnia*

Fore wing of *Capnia*

Vein R$_1$ of fore wing not bent abruptly at its origin; A$_1$ of fore wing without an abrupt bend at its junction with cu-a. 9

9 (8) Vein Sc of fore wing ending much before the cord. Nineteen described North American species; east of Rocky Mountains; often abundant. *Allocapnia*

Fore wing of *Allocapnia*

Vein Sc of fore wing ending at or beyond the cord. 10

10 (9) First anal vein of fore wing slightly bent beyond cu-a. One species; eastern North America; common. *Nemocapnia*

Fore wing of *Nemocapnia*

First anal vein of fore wing without a bend beyond cu-a. Two species; eastern North America; common. *Paracapnia*

Fore wing of *Paracapnia*

11 (1) Male cerci with at least three segments; female ninth sternum with a long projection. Fifteen described North American species; transcontinental; common.   *Brachyptera*
Male cerci with one segment; female ninth sternum without a long projection. Three North American species; eastern North America, one species occuring also in Oregon; common.   *Taeniopteryx*

NYMPHS OF THE SUBFAMILIES AND GENERA OF NEMOURIDAE

1   Second tarsal segment much shorter than the first.   2

Leg of *Leuctra*

Second tarsal segment at least as long as the first   7
Taeniopteryginae

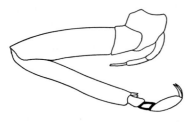

Leg of *Taeniopteryx*

2 (1) Stout nymphs; hind wing pads strongly diverging from the axis of the body. About fifty described North American species; distributed generally; abundant. Nemourinae.   *Nemoura*

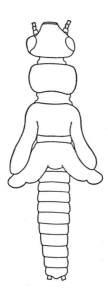

Nymph of *Nemoura*

Cylindrical, elongate nymphs; hind wing pads nearly parallel with the axis of the body.   3

Nymph of *Leuctra*

3 (2) Abdominal segments 1–9 divided by a membranous fold laterally.   4
Capniinae

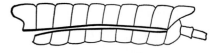

Abdomen of *Capnia*

At most only the first seven abdominal segments divided by a membranous fold.   5
Leuctrinae

Abdomen of *Leuctra*

4 (3) Cerci with lateral fringes of long silky hairs, several to a segment. Ten described North American species, mostly western; one species common, others scarce.   *Isocapnia*
Cerci without silky fringes. About fifty described North American species; generally distributed; often abundant.   *Capnia* and related genera
5 (3) Segments 1–7 of the abdomen divided laterally by a membranous fold.   6
Only the first 5–6 abdominal segments divided laterally. About twenty-five described North American species; distributed generally; abundant.   *Leuctra*

6 (5) Body covered by rather coarse, appressed pile, the individual hairs of which are about a fifth as long as a middle abdominal segment. One Appalachian species, three species in Pacific Northwest; rare.

Megaleuctra

Body with extremely fine pile, appearing naked. Two species, western North America; common.

Perlomyia

7 (1) A single gill on each coxa. Three North American species; eastern North America, one species also occurring in Oregon; common. *Taeniopteryx*

Leg of *Taeniopteryx* nymph

No coxal gills. Fifteen described North American species; transcontinental; common. *Brachyptera*

PTERONARCIDAE

This family of large stoneflies contains only two genera, *Pteronarcys* and *Pteronarcella*. Species of *Pteronarcys* are larger than those of *Pteronarcella* and have gills on nymphs or gill remnants on adults on the underside of only the first two abdominal segments, while in *Pteronarcella* there is also a pair on the third abdominal segment. The two species of *Pteronarcella* are found only in the West, one in the Rocky Mountain region, one in the Sierra-Cascade system. *Pteronarcys*, with eight American species, is not an important game fish food in most eastern States but is a major trout food in western streams where it is justly famous among anglers. The Western Salmon Fly, *Pteronarcys californica*, emerges in spectacular hatches on large western rivers and trout gorge on them.

PELTOPERLIDAE

These peculiar stoneflies with nymphs resembling a cockroach are typically found in small, cold mountain streams. Two species found along the Pacific Coast occur in some abundance in headwater trout areas. There are twelve species described from North America. Appalachia and the Cordillera have several species each, and all belong to the genus *Peltoperla*.

PERLIDAE

This is a very large family of stoneflies abundant on all of the continents except Australia. They have attracted much attention from anglers. A major characteristic of the family is the invariable presence of profusely branched gills at the lower angles of the thorax, often shrivelled in the adults but nevertheless always discernible. The family contains many genera and a host of species. Many are of large size. Most are light in color, often straw or light brown, frequently yellowish or strikingly patterned in black and yellow.

Males are needed to make the most satisfactory identifications of genera in this big family. Included in the following comments are points that may help in differentiating the females of the various genera.

Paragnetina and *Acroneuria* are large brown, straw, or dull yellowish stoneflies, readily separable in the male because of very distinctive sex organ characteristics, not so easily in the female. The *Paragnetina* female has a median square notch in the subgenital plate; the female *Acroneuria* has plates of various shapes, usually not a square notch. *Paragnetina* occurs only east of the Rocky Mountains. *Acroneuria* is widespread in North America, often emerging in enormous numbers. In the West, large flights often follow a hatch of the truly huge Western Salmon Fly, *Pteronarcys californica*. Artificials patterned after *Acroneuria* species are well-named the Golden Stonefly.

Three genera lack an anterior ocellus and can be separated easily in the male sex. *Anacroneuria*, recorded once from Texas, has a small disc or hammer on the ninth sternum as in *Atoperla*, but there are several crossveins in the costal area of the fore wing before the end of the subcosta. *Atoperla* can be distinguished from *Neoperla* by the lack of crossveins between the costa and subcosta before the cord and in not having a cleft tenth tergum. Both of these genera occur east of the Rocky Mountains.

Phasganophora is of good size, about an inch in length, and is strikingly colored in contrasting black and yellow on the head, thorax, and legs. *Claassenia* is another distinctive stonefly. It is a big species occurring in the Cordillera and in northern Manitoba. Females have fully developed wings but males are always short-winged. This species likes to hide among coarse gravel and stones adjacent to riffle areas; adults are crepuscular or nocturnal.

Perlinella and *Perlesta* are of moderate size, under an inch in length, and occur east of the Rocky Mountains. *Perlesta* is nondescript, straw colored, and very abundant in the Great Plains and in southeastern United States. In both sexes, *Perlinella* is distinguished from it by having a well-defined black area surrounding and filling the ocellar triangle on the head. There is also a distinct brown stripe on the pronotum.

SUBFAMILIES AND GENERA OF PERLIDAE
ADULT MALES

1 Males with subanal lobes produced inward and upward, sharply pointed or hooked and tenth tergum of male not cleft; male with a disc or knob on ninth sternum. 2

Acroneurinae

Male terminalia of *Acroneuria*

Male subanal lobes not modified as above; hind margin of tenth tergum deeply cleft; no knob on ninth sternum. 7

Perlinae

Male terminalia of *Paragnetina*

1 (1) With two ocelli.   **3**

      With three ocelli.   **4**

3 (2) Several costal crossveins in the fore wing before the end of the subcosta. Recorded once for the United States; common in Mexico and southward.

Anacroneuria

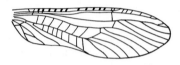

Fore wing of *Anacroneuria*

Usually no costal crossveins in the fore wing before the end of subcosta. One species; eastern North America; common.   *Atoperla*

Fore wing of *Atoperla*

4 (2) Anal area of fore wing with a single row of crossveins. One species; eastern North America; common.   *Perlinella*

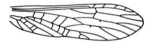

Fore wing of *Perlinella*

Anal area of fore wing without a row of crossveins.   **5**

5 (4) Ninth ventral abdominal segment of male with a knob or disc in middle of posterior part.   **6**

Ninth sternum of *Acroneuria*

Ninth ventral abdominal segment of male without a knob or disc in the middle of the posterior part. One species; east of Rocky Mountains; abundant.

Perlesta

6 (5) Tenth tergum of male with prolongations arising from lateral angles. One species; Cordillera and northern Manitoba; common in Cordillera.

Claassenia

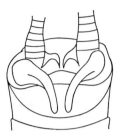

Terminalia of *Claassenia*

Tenth tergum of male without prolongations. Nineteen described North American species; transcontinental; common to abundant.   *Acroneuria*

Terminalia of *Acroneuria*

7 (1) With two ocelli. Two species; each of Rocky Mountains; common.   *Neoperla*

      With three ocelli.   **8**

8 (7) Male genital hooks extending to anterior border of eighth tergum. One species; east of Rocky Mountains; common.   *Phasganophora*

      Male genital hooks extending at most to posterior margin of ninth tergum. Five species east of Rocky Mountains; common.   *Paragnetina*

SUBFAMILIES AND GENERA OF PERLIDAE NYMPHS

1   Eyes situated much anterior to the hind margin of the head.   **2**

Head of *Atoperla*

Eyes situated close to the hind margin of the head. 3

Head of *Neoperla*

2 (1) Two ocelli; body uniformly colored. One species; eastern North America; common.   *Atoperla*
     Three ocelli but anterior ocellus inconspicuous in very young nymphs. One species; eastern North America; common.   *Perlinella*
3 (1) A closely set row of spinules across back of the head, which is usually set on a low ridge.   4

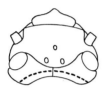

Head of *Perlesta*

No continuous row of spinules across back of the head, no ridge.   9

Head of *Acroneuria*

4 (3) Three ocelli.   5
     Two ocelli, set close together. Two species; east of Rocky Mountains; common.   *Neoperla*
5 (4) Abdomen freckled. One species; east of Rocky Mountains; abundant.   *Perlesta*
     Abdomen without freckles.   6
6 (5) Dorsal surface patterned.   7
     Dorsal surface almost uniformly brown. Eastern North America.   *Acroneuria ruralis*
7 (6) Anal gills present.   8
     Anal gills absent. Five North American species; east of Rocky Mountains; common.   *Paragnetina*
8 (7) Abdominal segments yellow, broadly bordered with black. One North American species; east of Rocky Mountains; common.   *Phasganophora*
     Abdominal segments almost wholly brown. One species; Cordillera and northern Manitoba; common in Cordillera.   *Claassenia*
9 (3) Two ocelli. Recorded once for the United States; common in Mexico southward.   *Anacroneuria*

Three ocelli. Nineteen described North American species; transcontinental; common to abundant.
    Acroneuria

PERLODIDAE

Many of the species in this family are attractively colored in contrasting black and yellow or orange patterns on head and thorax. Many are of moderate size, one or two inches in length. The genus *Isoperla* emerges in swarms at times. Many a placid brown trout stream is dimpled at dusk during June and July when a hatch of these is emerging.

This family contains three subfamilies not easily separable, except in males, because of the wide variation in structure among members of the family. Female specimens are difficult to identify unless they have a network of crossveins in the outer half of the fore wing in which case they are in the genus *Arcynopteryx*. Some of the small yellowish species of *Isoperla* can be easily confused with *Alloperla*, a genus in the family Chloroperlidae. There is great variety in size and color pattern among species of *Isogenus*, a group that is difficult to identify without male specimens. The male genitalia of *Diura*, the only genus in the subfamily Perlodinae, is quite unique and readily identifies it (*see* sketch in key).

Nymphs of most kinds of *Isoperla* are readily recognizable because of the longitudinal striped patterns on the abdomen. Many of the species of *Arcynopteryx* have paired, finger-like gills on the thorax, and all have a lateral pair extending from the submentum, one from either side. *Isogenus* also has submental gills in most species, but some lack them and resemble certain kinds of unstriped *Isoperla*. Since there are no structural characters of nymphs that always separate members of the six genera in this family, no key is presented for them.

SUBFAMILIES AND GENERA OF PERLODIDAE
ADULT MALES

1   Male tenth tergum completely cleft.   2
    Isogeninae

Terminalia of *Isogenus*

Male tenth tergum entire, or at most, slightly notched.   3

Terminalia of *Isoperla*

2 (1) Wings with four to many crossveins beyond the cord, and these usually arranged in an irregular network. Thirteen North American species; transcontinental in boreal areas; a few common species.
Arcynopteryx

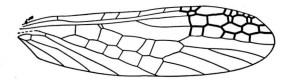

Fore wing of *Arcynopteryx*

Wings normally with no more than two crossveins beyond the cord. Thirty described North American species; transcontinental; a few common species.
Isogenus

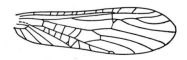

Fore wing of *Isogenus*

3 (1) Male subanal lobes produced inward and backward, meeting along their inner face. **Perlodinae**

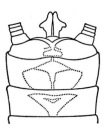

Terminalia of *Diura*

Three species in North America; one species in far north, one in White Mountains of New Hampshire, one in Cordillera; uncommon. *Diura*
Male subanal lobes not as above, either little modified or produced into erect or recurved hooks; usually a lobe at the hind margin of the male eighth sternum. 4
Isoperlinae

Terminalia of *Isoperla*

4 (3) Subanal lobes not formed into hooks; male tenth tergum slightly notched dorsally. One species; coastal Oregon and northern California; scarce.
Calliperla
Subanal lobes of male produced into erect or recurved hooks. 5
5 (4) With a lobe, sometimes obsolescent, on hind margin of eighth sternum. Nearly fifty described North American species; transcontinental; many common species. *Isoperla*

Ninth sternum of *Isoperla*

Without a lobe on the eighth sternum but one on seventh sternum. One species; Cascade-Sierras in California and Oregon. *Rickera*

CHLOROPERLIDAE

This is the family that contains the abundant little bright yellow, chartreuse, or green stoneflies that abound at trout streams in spring and early summer. Other, mostly larger and less common, stoneflies of this family are principally western in distribution.

The mature mymphs of *Paraperla* and *Kathroperla* are easy to distinguish because of their large size and the position of the compound eyes. The head of *Kathroperla* identifies it at once. The nymph of always-rare *Utaperla* has not been discovered. The mature nymphs of *Hastaperla* and *Chloroperla* measure about ¼ inch in length; larger mature nymphs are surely those of *Alloperla*. However, there are several small species of *Alloperla* so it is not possible always to identify specimens with certainty.

SUBFAMILIES AND GENERA OF CHLOROPERLIDAE ADULTS

1 Eyes set far forward; body narrow and elongate; adults usually an inch or more in length. 2
Paraperlinae

Head of *Paraperla*

Eyes normally situated; body less elongate; usually about ½ inch or less in length. 3
Chloroperlinae (and genus *Utaperla* in the **Paraperlinae**).

·Head of *Alloperla*

2 (1) Head longer than wide. One described North American species; Pacific Coast; common.
Kathroperla

Head of *Kathroperla*

Head about as wide as long. *Paraperla*
3 (1) Anal area of hind wing absent. Three North American species; transcontinental; sometimes common. *Hastaperla*

Fore wing of *Hastaperla*

Anal area of hind wing present. 4
4 (3) Third anal vein of fore wing absent, or if present, not fused with the second. One described North American species; southern Appalachia; rare.
Chloroperla

Fore wing of *Chloroperla*

Third anal vein of fore wing with basal part fused with second anal vein so that second anal vein appears branched. 5

Fore wing of *Alloperla*

5 (4) General color dark brown; male supra-anal process suspended at anterior edge of tenth tergum; female subgenital plate large, greatly expanded beyond a basal, broad stalk. One described species from Cordillera; rare. (In subfamily Paraperlinae).
Utaperla
General color yellow; male supra-anal process never suspended from anterior edge of tenth tergum, may be suspended from sides; female subgenital plate never greatly expanded beyond a stalked base. Nearly fifty described North American species; transcontinental; often abundant.
Alloperla
—S.G.J.

STONEROLLER *Campostoma anomalum* Also known as hornyhead and knottyhead, it is a brownish-olive minnow with a brassy luster and has many dark scales scattered, usually singly or in pairs, over back and sides. Ventrally whitish or yellowish. Snout overhangs mouth. Mouth with a prominent, gristly biting edge. Mouth subterminal and almost horizontal. The stoneroller has 8 dorsal rays and 7 anal rays. This minnow and its various subspecies are found from Minnesota to Texas and eastward.

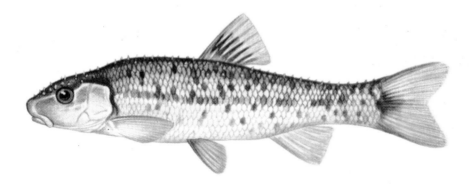

Stoneroller

HABITS

A fish essentially of riffles, the stoneroller is found in small streams of moderate gradient and sandy-gravel bottoms in the spring. In summer and winter it is found in larger waters but is virtually restricted to riffle areas. A bottom feeder, the stoneroller subsists on diatomaceous scum, mud with its insect larvae, and small mollusks and filamentous algae. The stoneroller ascends the smaller streams in spring to spawn. At this time the anal and dorsal fins of the male become brilliant orange and black, and almost the entire upper half of the body is covered with sharp tubercles. The male builds a nest by making a shallow depression in the gravel, a foot or more in diameter. A number of males may work on the same nest. The stoneroller grows to a length of 11 inches in some localities.

ANGLING VALUE

The stoneroller is exceptionally hardy and active on the hook, making it an attractive bait species. In Tennessee, this minnow is highly regarded as a food fish. Stonerollers can be caught with bits of worm or small wet flies. —R.A.J.

STOPNETTING A commercial fishing term which covers a wide variety of methods. These all have in common the principle of enclosing a segment of shoreline at high tide and capturing the fish which accumulate against the net as the tide falls. The variety comes in the methods of concentrating and catching the fish that accumulate against the net. In the simplest form the fish are picked out of mud or very shallow pools where they are stranded by the receding tide. In the more complex techniques the nets are dragged by small engines to decrease the area enclosed by them and driving the fish into a small special "bank net" where they are finally captured. —A.J.McC.

STRAKE Pronounced streak, and meaning one continuous line of planks or metal plates from bow to stern in the hull side of a boat. Each line of lengthwise planking is a strake. *Bilge strakes* refer to heavier planks which may be fastened in place at the turn of the bilge. A *binding strake* is a thick plank fitted immediately below the *sheer strake*. A *rubbing strake* is a heavy strake not far below the gunnel. A *sheer strake* is the topmost continuous line of planking from bow to stern, and thus may considerably influence the general appearance of the boat. *Garboard strakes* or *garboards* are those next to the keel. *See also* Clinker

STREAMER FLY An artificial fly made with a long feather or hair wing and designed to imitate a minnow or other forage fish. Streamer flies are used in both fresh- and saltwater fishing.

Angling success with streamer flies is dependent on the pattern and how it is fished. One factor may be more important than another under some conditions, but it is generally agreed that gamefish can be highly selective with respect to color and size and the speed and depth at which the streamer is retrieved. Despite the implausibility of some garish patterns, which seemingly have no counterpart in nature, the fact is that many forage fish are brightly colored and this is particularly true of the males during the spring spawning period. However, due to the secretive habits of most minnows in the wild and the difficulty in identifying many species which are superficially alike, the lore of the streamer fly is largely based on tradition or whimsy and even the names of the great majority of established patterns—such as the Edson Tiger, Gray Ghost, Wizard, Golden Witch, or Colonel Fuller—provide no clue as to their designer's intentions. This is in sharp contrast to insect imitations, which to a large extent provide a practical reference in the names Blue Dun, Yellow May, Green Drake, Early Stonefly, and a swarm of other recognizable winged trout foods.

One of the most outstanding streamer patterns is the Muddler Minnow. Designed by Don Gapen and first presented in *Field & Stream*, the dressing and all its subsequent variations is a good example of an observant fly-tier's art. The natural muddler, more commonly known as the mottled sculpin and regionally known as a "bullhead" in Western streams, is a choice item of trout food, particularly large trout. Sculpins also occur in lakes in the northern part of their range, but in either habitat they find protection by lying quietly between stones and rock crevices. They obtain insect food by prying their flattened heads under the stones; because of their protective coloration sculpins are easily overlooked by the angler. What Gapen achieved with his simple choice of materials was the large head (natural deer hair spun around the hook, flattened, and trimmed to shape) and slim body form of the living sculpin. Fished slow and deep over stream-bottom rocks, the Muddler Minnow began scoring heavy prize winners from the Nipigon in the late 1940's, and has since become a favorite in trout country everywhere. A versatile pattern, it can even be fished as a dry fly, but Gapen's brainchild did a great deal to expand streamer-fly technique, for it demonstrated the potential of a color and form that looked natural swimming over gravel.

There have been comparatively few attempts to create a series of regional imitative streamer-fly patterns. Lew Oatman of Shushan, New York, was one of the first tiers to single out some of the important minnows in the eastern United States and devise feather-winged counterparts for each species. At least two of these, the Silver Darter and Golden Darter, are still popular. The small, mostly brightly-colored darters encompass 95 species in the United States and southern Canada, and like the sculpins (which belong to the family Cottidae) they are not true minnows but members of the Percidae or perch family. The distinction is important because unlike minnows, which swim in the usual sense of the word, darters lie quietly among the rocks (braced in position by their paired fins) then literally dart from place to place when disturbed. This erratic "flight" of a few feet and seldom more than a few yards before resting on the bottom is not easy to emulate with a fly rod, but once learned it can be a deadly game.

WHEN TO USE STREAMER FLIES

Streamer flies (including bucktails) have a high ratio of success in hooking big fish. However, if an angler devoted all of his time to casting minnowlike flies he would not catch fish all of the time, nor necessarily very large ones. This apparent inconsistency is because streamers, like other types of flies, have a specific role in the seasonal picture of angling. Ideal situations for the streamer are in waters where gamefish are conditioned to feeding on a periodic abundance of forage, such as the sockeye-fry migration in British Columbia, or the smelt runs of New England, or the candlefish and herring runs in the Pacific Northwest. But there are also important periods in suburban trout country—late in the evening or after dark and immediately after a summer rain. Big browns are especially cautious about chasing minnows in bright sunlight. On rare occasions they will go on a daytime rampage, but in the protective cloak of night or discolored water they cruise the shallows looking for baitfish. There are no great clouds of fry to stimulate reckless attacks on hair and tinsel. More so than in other methods of fly-fishing, the streamer-fly angler is dealing with an art that may provoke strikes because of hunger, curiosity, excitement, or just plain pugnacity. The Mickey Finn pattern, for instance, is accredited with the power of exciting fish into striking. The White Marabou (often used as locator fly) apparently arouses their curiosity, as otherwise cautious gamefish will follow the fluttering wing again and again. Nevertheless knowing when and how to use streamer flies requires some knowledge of regional conditions.

STREAMER FLY FISHING IN RIVERS

Under normal river levels, the streamer or bucktail is cast across and downstream, and as the lure drifts with the current a regular movement of the rod keeps the fly alive and the slack out of your line. The darting motion should be very short but spaced at regular intervals to simulate a minnow struggling in the current. Don't lift for a new cast too often. A deep-sunk fly left to be shouldered by the current and seldom fully retrieved can be tantalizing to big trout. In any kind of downstream casting, where the lure swings around and is retrieved directly upcurrent, the angler always runs the risk of spooking his fish. After stalking the lure for some distance, the trout may decide to strike at the very moment his angler comes into view, and the result is an involuntary pass at the fly. This can happen with streamers as readily as any other lure, but the minnowlike fly can run through periods of refusal rises even when you are well out of sight. The fish will boil short or even roll so close that you might foul hook several of them in a very short time. Such fish can sometimes be caught on a smaller-size or a darker-color streamer.

When fishing streamers it is important to vary the retrieve from time to time. Ordinarily, a slow, jerky movement will attract and catch trout, but there are situations where a rapid pull will provoke more strikes. In general, the slow, bottom-scratching retrieve is effective in cold-water periods, and the faster, near-surface swim is better in summer weather.

MARABOU STREAMERS

One streamer which should be stocked in both the weighted and unweighted types is the marabou. Basically, a marabou is an attractor-type fly that depends on its quivering wing action to tempt strikes. It will often hypnotize cautious gamefish into rushing out of their dens for a close look, if nothing else. Even that can be helpful in locating big trout or smallmouth bass. But in high, discolored water, a White Marabou dressed on a weighted body can be cast across stream with telling effect. On deep pools make a slack-line cast up- and across stream to let the streamer sink near bottom before tightening to retrieve. Then work the fly in short, rapid pulls so that it flutters over the gravel. This method will often get a few fish when nothing else seems to click. The marabou is particularly effective on rainy or overcast days, when the river level has come up a few inches. On miniature streams or in shallow water the ordinary unweighted White Marabou is preferable; it is most effective when cast directly upstream. A fluffy, stork-feather wing is difficult to sink. However, that's an advantage when you are casting in knee-deep runs. The fly will hang just a few inches under the surface and come puffing back with the current.

Of course, marabous also attract lake-dwelling gamefish and can be applied here in much the same way. You might try the weighted fly in deep-water and use the unweighted kind in situations where you find cruising fish in the shallows and are in a position to drop the marabou 20–30 feet ahead of visibly moving fish. Dressed on a small, light-wire hook, the fly simply clings to the surface film until you begin twitching it at the approach of a trout. Cruising fish of any kind are usually spooked by a direct cast. This is also a favorite method of casting to bonefish on the grass flats. It solves the problem of frequent bottom snagging with orthodox types of salt-water streamers—many of which are too big and too heavy for proper fishing in shallow water.

SEMIDRY STREAMERS

The semidry streamer is epitomized by the Muddler Minnow pattern. The Muddler has another kind of versatility from the marabou. You can float it, sink it, skim it across the surface, or dive-and-bob it, depending on what you are trying to imitate. The Muddler has scored a respectable number of *Field & Stream* prize-winners as it contains the basic elements of both insect and minnow imitation. It can look like a stonefly, grasshopper, dragonfly, sculpin, stickleback, or a dozen other tidbits when operated by a skilled caster. The Muddler is most effective in lakes where gamefish are conditioned to feeding on large surface foods. You can begin by fishing the pattern dry. Grease the hairs lightly, and pitch the fly under overhanging limbs and along the edges of grass beds. If nothing responds after floating it quietly for a minute or so, bring the fly back in short twitches, long hops, or whatever seems appropriate. Naturally, there's more fun in getting topwater strikes, but if the fish are holding deep, then it's a simple matter to tie on an ungreased Muddler and work at their level.

The easiest way to get a streamer fly down near bottom is with a sinking-type fly line. If you don't carry a line of this kind, then the next best thing is to have some of your flies dressed with slightly weighted bodies. Too much weight will spoil the action of the fly and make it difficult to cast; so get your patterns tied by a professional who knows how much lead the various hook sizes require. As a last resort, you can always pinch a split shot at the head of the fly. Never place the shot up the leader because it will tangle in casting and snag bottom. When pinched directly at the hook eye, the nose-heavy fly will have a diving action which you can work to advantage by jiggling the rod tip as you retrieve.

MINIATURE STREAMERS

Another useful streamer fly is the miniature. A good example of small, imitative patterns is the Blacknose Dace dressed on a 3X Long, No. 10 hook. The brown-and-white wing with a black stripe running through its center suggests various kinds of minnows. Many experts fish the bucktail on a 9–12-foot leader tapered to 4X. The fine tippet permits maximum animation even in quiet water. Miniature bucktails are overlooked by many anglers; yet the approximately 1½-inch wing that fits a No. 10 hook is comparable in size to most common minnows. During the hot summer months, when the water is low, try the Dace pattern dressed on a No. 12 hook. The spot to look for big trout at that time of the year is at the head of a deep pool where the whitewater begins to flatten. Cast the Dace across stream with sufficient slack to let it swing around below; then feed more line out so the fly drops back slowly into deeper water. The idea is to keep the bucktail swimming as long as possible without picking up for a new cast. Let the fly sink, then dart forward a few inches before changing its position by mending the line.

Tactically speaking, the miniature streamer should be suggestive of a tiny minnow and therefore dressed sparsely so the fish doesn't have much to examine. This more or less limits the number of useful patterns to a few basic color combinations such as the black-and-white, brown-and-white, red-and-white, or whatever is most effective in your region. You might get a better imitation locally with a striped badger or barred, grizzly, feather wing. However, the choice of materials is nearly as important as the size and translucent appearance of the fly. Needless to say, any collection of miniatures doesn't stop at the Dace pattern.

Bucktails tied on hook sizes larger than No. 6 are preferable for highwater fishing, night fishing, and in those situations where gamefish find an abundance of smelt, herring, golden shiners, or other large forage species.

BREATHER-TYPE STREAMERS

The splayed-wing or "breather"-type fly is generally made in two styles—the normal dressing with hook down, which is best-known to Western anglers in the Spruce pattern, and a weedless dressing with the hook inverted. The upsidedown hook on a breather is especially useful for largemouth-bass, pickerel, and northern-pike fishing. The breather has wings made of hackle feathers tied back to back so that they curve outward. When pulled in short hops through the water, the opposing feathers close and open. The rhythmic movement of the wing doesn't imitate anything specific, but it suggests life of some kind, and that's ample reason to provoke a smashing strike from predatory fish. The inverted style can be cast ahead of cruising tarpon or permit and left to sink. When the fish approach, a few pulls will raise the streamer from the bottom with its wings kicking, whereas an orthodox hookdown fly is invariably snagged in a crab hole. What makes the breather particularly effective, however, is the fact that it can be animated in a confined space. Just a few short twitches are enough to get the fly working in a small area between lily pads, for example, and the up-turned hook can be slid across surface vegetation.

SALTWATER STREAMERS

The streamer flies used in saltwater fly-fishing (*which see*) are usually very much larger than those used in freshwater. In casting for coho salmon, striped bass, snook, or tarpon, the fly size often ranges from 1/0 to 6/0 with the streamer-fly wing to lengths of 5–6 inches. This poses certain limitations. Often, when projecting a standard pattern into the 0 sizes, it becomes overdressed and lacks action. It's usually best to avoid fancy patterns and select those with simple, durable materials. Streamers such as the Coronation Bucktail and Strawberry Blonde are typical saltwater patterns, consisting only of a colorful hair wing and tinsel body. —A.J.McC.

STRIKE A term used in angling which may imply the strike (attack or bite) of a fish at a bait or lure, or the strike of an angler as he raises the rod sharply to set the hook upon feeling the fish. The manner in which different species of fish strike is highly variable; a live bait may be swallowed directly, as in the case of bluefish, or it may be "nibbled" and even dropped several times, as in the case of a flounder. A rainbow trout may strike a fly swiftly and with obvious force, whereas a bonefish often strikes so slowly and gently that it goes unnoticed by the angler. A knowledge of the feeding posture of the species sought is important.

The technique of the angler in striking the fish is also variable, depending on the kind of bait or lure used, the tackle, and the mouth structure of his quarry. Live bait (*which see*) is a natural food, and speed in striking when using a worm or minnow is seldom necessary or even desirable. By contrast, an artificial fly or plastic plug is instantly recognized by the fish upon acceptance, and the angler must strike before the lure is expelled. The force to be applied ranges from a mere tightening of the line, as in the case of a trout taking a fly on a very fragile leader, to a sharp arms-and-shoulders pull when hooking big gamefish, such as the bluefin tuna. Species with soft mouths, such as the weakfish and spotted seatrout, are frequently lost at the strike because of excessive force while hard-mouthed fish like the tarpon and permit are not hooked because of the lack of it; some experience is required before the angler learns to strike reflexively. —A.J.McC.

STRIPED ANCHOVY *Anchoa hepsetus* A small marine species of considerable importance as a forage fish for gamefish such as the bluefish, mackerel, striped bass, and tunas. The striped anchovy is one of the most widely distributed members of the family Engraulidae in Atlantic coastal waters of the United States. It is abundant from Delaware Bay through the West Indies and south to Brazil; it occurs north of Delaware Bay to Maine and the coast of Nova Scotia as a stray.

The striped anchovy is a larger (4–5 inches long, rarely to 6 inches) species than the eight other anchovies identified in the western Atlantic. The striped anchovy has a

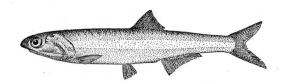

Striped Anchovy

very bright silver lateral band; it is iridescent pale gray above with faint dusky dots and grayish-white below. Anchovies are omnivorous feeders, usually on plankton, of both inshore and offshore regions, and are occasionally found in brackish water at the mouths of streams. They travel in densely packed schools, frequently mingling with other baitfish such as the silversides (*which see*) and the so-called green fry of young herring.

ANGLING VALUE

The striped anchovy is sometimes utilized as a baitfish on the Atlantic coast, but due to its small average size and fragility on the hook, it is not as popular in the East as larger and more durable species, such as the herrings and mullets common to the same range. Like the northern anchovy (*which see*) of the Pacific, it has some food value to man in pickled and salted forms. *See also* Live Bait
—A.J.McC.

STRIPED BASS *Morone saxatilis* An important marine gamefish which belongs to the family Percichthyidae. Regionally known as the rockfish (south of New Jersey) and infrequently called squidhound or greenhead, the striper is easily identified.

The trunk of the striped bass is 3½–4 times as long (to the base of the caudal fin) as it is deep. It has a long head, a moderately pointed snout, and a projecting lower jaw. The two dorsal fins are about of equal length, and both are triangular in outline; these fins are separated. Although the color may vary, as a rule the striped bass is dark olive-green (hence the name greenhead) to steel-blue or almost black above, becoming silvery on the sides and white on the belly. The sides have 7–8 longitudinal dark stripes which follow the scale rows; 3–4 stripes are above the lateral line, one on it, and three below it. The upper stripes are the longest and may reach to the caudal fin. The stripes are often interrupted or broken and are usually absent on young fish of less than 6 inches. There is little chance of confusing striped bass of over 10 inches with any other species of fish along the Atlantic or Pacific coasts. The prominent stripes, separated dorsal fins, and the general outline are unique. In young specimens of less than 7 inches it may be difficult to distinguish the striped bass from the related white perch. However, the dorsal fins of the white perch are connected.

The striped bass on the Atlantic Coast has an extreme range from the Gulf of St. Lawrence to the St. Johns River in northern Florida and in the Gulf of Mexico from western Florida to Louisiana. The center of abundance appears to be from South Carolina to Massachusetts. On the Pacific Coast, where it was introduced in 1886, the extreme range is from the Columbia River in Washington, to Los Angeles, California. The present center of abundance on the Pacific Coast is in the San Francisco Bay region. The fish are coastwise in distribution, and are rarely taken more than a few miles offshore. The striped bass is anadromous and is found in fresh- and brackish water, with preference shown for bays, deltas, and estuarine areas. It exists as a landlocked form also, notably in the Southeast Atlantic states.

LIFE HISTORY

Striped bass females reach sexual maturity beginning at the fourth year at a length of 18–24 inches and 4–6 pounds. By the sixth year all females are mature. Males begin to mature at 2 years, and nearly all are ready for spawning at 3 years. Stripers in the Chesapeake region continue to breed to the age of 14 years. Elsewhere spawning is somewhat curtailed, however, after the fish reach 10 years. Four-year-old females produce about 65,000 eggs while those about 13 years old produce nearly 5,000,000 eggs.

During the spawning period striped bass ascend rivers from brackish or saltwater. The season usually begins in April in Southern waters and will extend into July in the St. Lawrence River area. Water temperature is an important factor, and actual spawning may vary as much as a month from one year to the next. Spawning begins at 55°–65°F. with a peak of 60°–67°F. Probably the most

Striped Bass, 22-pound Female, Montauk Point, New York

famous breeding grounds are to be found on the Roanoke River at Weldon, North Carolina, about 100 miles above tidewater. Here, spawning takes place in the rapids in an area of boulders and rocks. New York investigators found eggs and young striped bass in the Hudson River at locations with a pronounced current and sand or gravel bottom. In California the delta areas of the Sacramento and San Joaquin rivers are the principal spawning grounds. In the Chesapeake region spawning occurs in relatively quiet, upper tidal areas in fresh- or brackish-water streams.

During the spawning act a single, large, female bass is surrounded by a number of smaller males. These so-called "rock fights" are frequently observed but are really courtship and spawning antics. The greenish-colored eggs are 1.1–1.35 millimeters in diameter. One hour after extrusion, the egg absorbs water creating a protective perivitelline space, and its size increases to an average of 3.63 millimeters. There is no parental care, and the semi-buoyant eggs drift downstream for some distance. Hatching takes place in three days at 58°–60°F. or less than 48 hours at 71°–72°F. The yolk sac is absorbed in about 6½ days. Due to the fact that freely spawned striped bass eggs must remain suspended in a current until hatching, most landlocked environments, such as reservoirs, are physically deficient for natural reproduction. Freshwater populations have been maintained by stocking young striped bass, and, despite initial difficulties in hatchery procedures for obtaining females with freely flowing eggs, a modern technique of inducing ovulation with the use of a hormone (chorionic gonadotropin) has been proven to be very successful.

AGE AND GROWTH

The striped bass grows to moderately large size. The heaviest recorded weighed 125 pounds (Edenton, North Carolina, 1891). This fish was probably at least 6 feet long. A 73-pound striper was caught by C. B. Church in Vineyard Sound, Massachusetts, in 1913.

Striped bass weigh about ¾ of a pound when 12–13 inches long or two years old; 2¾–3 pounds at 18–20 inches; 5 pounds at 24 inches; 10–15 pounds at 30–32 inches; and 18–20 pounds at 33–36 inches. A 20-pound bass averages 36 inches and 7 years old, a 30-pound bass is about 38 inches and 10–11 years old, and a 40-pound bass about 40–42 inches and 14 years old. Fifty-pound striped bass run about 50 inches and are probably 17–18 years old. A 23-year-old striped bass has been recorded. This length-weight relationship is about the same on both the Atlantic and Pacific coasts. The striped-bass females grow larger than males, and will weigh more than the male at any given length. The biggest striped bass are "cows," which appear in the summer and fall along the Northeast Atlantic seaboard.

FOOD

The striped bass is a voracious feeder and consumes any kind of small fish and a variety of invertebrates. The food selected varies from one locality to another but may include herring, menhaden, flounders, mullet, eels, shad, anchovies, silver hake, lance, lobsters, crabs, shrimp, squid, sea worms, soft clams, and mussels. However,

striped bass feed more actively at night than when the sun is high. When bass are gorging on a particular food item, it is also apparent that they will ignore food of other kinds during that period.

RACES OF STRIPED BASS

Studies have been made to determine the racial structure of Atlantic Coast striped-bass populations. These investigations together with tagging experiments proved that definite races do exist. Among the distinguishing features are fin-ray and lateral-line scale counts. The term "race" is used in the sense that it implies a lower level of differentiation other than that of a subspecies. Evidence shows that races exist in the Nova Scotia-New Brunswick area, the Hudson River area, the Chesapeake area, Albermarle Sound area in North Carolina, the Santee-Cooper area in South Carolina and in the St. Johns River area of Florida. The Hudson River race showed 70–80-percent separation from Chesapeake stocks. In addition, differences were noted in upriver and downriver fish from the Hudson. Subraces were also noted in the Chesapeake area, and the landlocked fresh-water population appears to be different from a down-river brackish-water population in the Santee-Cooper area.

MIGRATIONS

Striped bass make two types of migrations. One is for the purpose of spawning. The other type occurs in fish of 2 years of age or older and is far more spectacular. A small percentage of the bass move out of their wintering areas, such as the Chesapeake and Delaware bays, and travel northward along the coast to New England and southern Canada. After mingling with northern populations during the summer, most of the bass return again to their southerly wintering areas. During these lengthy coastal migrations the striped bass is subject to an extensive sport fishery along the New Jersey, New York, and New England shores.

Local populations also migrate for relatively short distances. For example, among striped bass tagged in the western quarter of Long Island Sound, 70 percent of the recaptures were made in the Hudson River.

On the Pacific Coast, stripers migrate in the fall season into the freshwater of the Sacramento-San Joaquin Delta, where they remain during the winter. In the spring they disperse over the delta and tributary rivers to spawn, after which they return to the San Francisco Bay and adjacent salt- or brackish waters for the summer. Similar migrations take place in the Coos Bay region of Oregon. However, there is no mass movement at any place on the Pacific Coast such as occurs in Atlantic waters.

SPORT AND COMMERCIAL FISHERIES

Commercial fishing for striped bass is presently limited to the Atlantic Coast. The gear used includes haul seines, pound nets, stake gillnets, drift gillnets, anchor gillnets, and occasionally otter trawls and fyke nets. In the Chesapeake area the winter driftnet fishery is the only effort made exclusively for striped bass. The value of the commercial haul has been increasing each year. The sport fishery for striped bass is most important from the Carolinas to New England and, due to the various migratory patterns, is quite seasonal. In the Chesapeake region this fish can be taken in varying sizes during all seasons of the year. Fishing methods include surf-casting with baits or artificial lures, and trolling and plug-casting from a boat offshore. Baits used include squid, bloodworms, clams, shedder crabs, mullet, and sand eels. Striped bass were formerly known to reach a weight of 125 pounds, but at the present time the largest fish taken along the Atlantic Coast are less than 70 pounds.

HISTORICAL NOTES

Many references to the striped bass appear in early American literature. In 1623 the Plymouth colonists with only one boat available were able to operate a net and catch enough bass to support themselves all during that summer. Captain John Smith wrote about their excellent eating qualities. William Wood wrote in 1635, describing a method of catching striped bass with a handline using a piece of lobster as bait. He also described methods of taking them with nets by trapping fish at high tide.

Although the striped bass existed in great abundance during these early days, the value and inevitable limited supply were realized by the colonists shortly after landing at Plymouth. This was demonstrated in an act passed by the General Court of Massachusetts Bay Colony in 1639 which ordered that neither cod nor bass should be used as fertilizer for farm crops. A subsequent act of the Plymouth Colony in 1670 provided that all income incurred annually from the fisheries at Cape Cod for bass, mackerel, or herring be used to establish a free school in some town of the area. As a result of this legislation the first public school in the New World was made possible through funds obtained largely from the sale of striped bass.

LANDLOCKED STRIPED BASS FISHING

Most striped bass fishing in freshwater lakes is done by trolling deep running baits such as plugs, spoons, leadheads, and a spinner with plastic worm rig. Trolling accounts for the most fish when they are on the bottom, but many anglers prefer to still-fish or drift with live bait such as gizzard shad. The fact that 20–30-pound bass are fairly common indicates that heavy spinning and bait casting gear is the rule. A 20–40-pound test monofilament line with hook sizes from 3/0 to 8/0 for both live bait and lures is standard on impoundments such as Santee Cooper (*see* South Carolina) and Kerr Reservoir (*see* North Carolina). However, stripers frequently come to the surface, especially in the spring and the late summer to early winter periods when they are feeding on shad schools. Popping plugs can be used very successfully in topwater work with much lighter gear in the 8–10-pound test class.

The technique in jump fishing is to watch for signs of feeding bass. They can often be located at long range by gulls or terns circling the shad schools. The angler must get to the fish fast. The stripers (and the same is true of white bass and black bass when jump fishing) may surface only briefly and the action lasts from a few minutes to a half-hour before the fish sound. Veterans at the game usually rig one rod with a popping plug and a second rod with a silver spoon. If the plug doesn't get an immediate strike the spoon is whipped into the melee of feeding bass

for another try. There are occasions when shad-gorging stripers seem to be very temperamental about the kind of lure that will attract them and the jump fisherman is working against time.

Despite the lake environment, in fertile waters landlocked striped bass in excess of 50 pounds have been caught. *See also* Saltwater Fly Fishing, Surf Fishing.

—A.D.B.
—A.J.McC.

STRIPED CORVINA *Cynoscion reticulatus* A large corvina (*which see*) reaching about 3 feet in length. It is found from the Pacific coast of Baja California to Panama.

Caninelike teeth are present in the striped corvina. The fins are scaleless. The caudal fin is slightly pointed in the middle. Its mouth lining is orange. The body coloration is blue-gray or brown on the back, and silvery on the belly. There are dark brown or blackish stripes on the back and sides.

ANGLING VALUE

The striped corvina is a good gamefish on light tackle. It is also an excellent food fish and is often imported into the United States.

—J.R.

STRIPED JUMPROCK *Moxostoma rupiscartes* The striped jumprock is a small sucker rarely exceeding 10 inches in total length. Its geographical distribution is the Piedmont and Mountain portions of the Santee, Savannah, Altamaha, and Chattahoochee river systems of North Carolina, South Carolina, and Georgia. The distinguishing characteristics of this species, which separate it from other *Moxostoma*, are: Its head is wider than deep and the lips are semipapillose; the lower-most caudal ray is dusky in color; it has 10, but occasionally 11, dorsal rays; a head depth, at occiput, entering the predorsal distance 3 or more times; its midscales on the lateral line are smaller than the eye; a lateral line scale count of usually 44; a dusky-colored edging appearing on the dorsal fin; the anterior edge of the eye lies decidedly behind the lower lip; the occipited line is curved forward; the last dorsal ray is shorter, more than 1½ times in the dorsal base; there are 12 or less, rarely 13, dorsal rays; the margin of the dorsal fin is falcate; and the scales around the caudal peduncle number 16.

Striped Jumprock

LIFE HISTORY

This sucker is essentially a small-stream fish found in the Piedmont and the Mountains. In most cases it can be associated with fairly fast water or riffles and it prefers a sand, gravel, or rubble bottom. The striped jumprock spawns when the water temperature approaches 56°F. At this time the male has minute white tubercles scattered over the head, snout, anterior scales, and on the anal and caudal fins. This pattern is also noticeable in females, but the number of tubercles are fewer and they are much smaller. This fish received its name "jumprock" because of its peculiar habit of leaping from the water.

The striped jumprock has little commercial or sport value. It serves as forage, when small, for the redbreast sunfish and the smallmouth bass. It is occasionally taken by anglers.　　　　　　　　　　　　　　—D.E.L.

STRIPED KILLIFISH *Fundulus majalis* This small member of the family Cyprinodontidae is characterized by the vertical bars of the female and the distinctive stripes of the male. It resembles the mummichog (*which see*) in body shape. The striped killifish has a pointed snout, its length being much greater than the eye diameter. The body is less stout and the caudal peduncle less deep than in the mummichog, and the pointed shape of the fins is distinctive. The species is olive-drab to brassy olive-green above and has a pale olive belly, and the male has black, longitudinal stripes. During the breeding season, the colors of the male are intensified. It is one of the largest of the family, reaching a length of 8 inches.

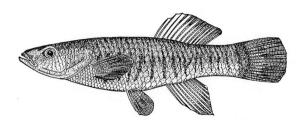

Striped Killifish

It is a shallow-water coastal species occurring all year from Massachusetts to Florida. Bays, lagoons, and estuaries are its common haunt, but it prefers saltier water than the mummichog. Sand or sandy-mud bottom and salt marshes are a favorite haunt, and large, loose schools can be seen in such areas, occasionally in the company of the mummichog.

LIFE HISTORY

Spawning occurs from April to September in shallow-water habitats. The eggs are large, and only a relatively small number is produced. The eggs are laid on sand, and the young are relatively well-formed upon hatching.

Sexual maturity is reached at a length of about 3 inches, and the females reach a larger size. They are predominantly carnivores, eating worms, crustaceans, horseshoecrab eggs, insects, small clams, and fishes.

ANGLING VALUE

Although of no commercial importance, it serves as forage for large predatory fishes, and is used as bait by anglers.　　　　　　　　　　　　　　—D.dS.

STRIPED MARLIN *Tetrapturus audax* An extremely valuable sport and commercial fish from the Pacific and Indian oceans, the striped marlin occurs in eastern Pacific waters from southern California to Chile. They are ordinarily caught fairly close inshore by sport fishermen, but commercial fisheries take them all the way across the Pacific.

The striped marlin is most easily distinguished by its high, pointed dorsal fin. The sickle-shaped anterior part of this fin is higher than the greatest depth of the body, while the posterior portion is long and low. Rarely, a large individual may have the dorsal height less than the body depth, leading to possible confusion with the blue marlin; and in young specimens, up to about 40–50 pounds, the posterior part of the fin is relatively high. This has sometimes led to confusion with the shortbill spearfish. However, the large striped marlin have flatter sides and a more uniform taper to the body than does the blue, as well as generally more prominent stripes, while the young striped marlin are short and chunky and the spearfish of the same weight is long and slender.

In fish of average size, the body is slightly slab-sided, and the depth decreases gradually from the shoulder hump to the anal fin. The anus is close in front of the anal fin. The spear is long, as are the pectoral fins.

The color of the striped marlin is typically dark steely-blue above and on the snout, fading to white on the ventral side. The sides of the body are marked with a varying number of prominent, pale bluish, lavender, or whitish vertical stripes. The fins are dark, except for the first dorsal and first anal, which are, in life, brilliant cobalt-blue with dark tips. The intensity of the colors, particularly of the stripes on the sides, varies widely in different individuals and in fish from different regions. In some, the stripes are prominent and brilliant; in others they may be scarcely visible. In all, the stripes tend to fade out after death, and the whole fish slowly assumes a dull, dark blue-gray color.

Striped Marlin

The usual weight of fish caught by angling will be something in the neighborhood of 200–250 pounds. The present record for rod and reel is 483 pounds, and a fish over 300 pounds is something to brag about. The maximum size seems to vary from one area to another. The 483-pounder was from Chile. At La Jolla, California, a fish of 406½ pounds was taken in 1955. In the Honolulu fish market, the maximum seems to be a little over 300 pounds, but in New Zealand waters they approach 400 pounds. These weights may reflect real differences in the maximum size reached by fish in the several areas, but they may equally well express angling intensity.

HABITS

The habits of the striped marlin have probably been studied almost as much as those of any other member of the family; yet surprisingly little is really known on this subject. Spawning seems to occur chiefly in the spring and summer, roughly June through September, but local populations show considerable variation in this respect, Thus, fish brought in to Kaohsiung, Taiwan, frequently have running eggs and milt in July, and the commercial fishermen in that port claim the major spawning season is in April and May. In the South Pacific, the major breeding season seems to be in the fall—October and November. This, of course, is the southern spring, corresponding to the April-May period of the Northern Hemisphere.

The various local populations of striped marlin in different parts of the world undertake north-south coastwise migrations according to the seasons, moving polewards in the warmer months and toward the equator in the winter season. This has been observed in various localities, notably the Gulf of California, off Taiwan and Japan, and in the South Pacific. There is no evidence to support the old theory that marlins "ride" the ocean currents in a great circle around the southern Pacific. The local populations are too well-marked and discrete to allow for any possibility of such mixing.

The striped marlin, like other members of this family, is a feeder of opportunity, eating virtually anything it can capture. The main articles of food vary from place to place and from time to time, apparently according to what is most readily available. Off San Diego, California, sauries and anchovies seem to be preferred. At the Bay of Islands, New Zealand, sauries and the "New Zealand salmon" or kahawai form the main items in the diet. Along the coasts of Peru and Chile, squid are most often taken, and the list of food items from other studies includes a number of deepsea fishes, squids, octopus, crustaceans, and so on. In the central Pacific, tunalike fishes are often present, notably the oceanic bonito and frigate mackerel, and even broadbill swordfish have been found in the stomachs of striped marlin.

In its geographical distribution, the striped marlin is almost worldwide in warm and temperate seas. It is found in the Pacific and Indian Oceans all the way from southern California to the east coast of Africa, while its north-south range extends from northern Japan to Chile, New Zealand, and Australia. Recently, exploratory fishing has shown that the striped marlin enters the Atlantic along the west coast of South Africa in the water of the Agulhas Current. This, of course, is really Indian Ocean water that flows around the Cape of Good Hope into the Atlantic, and it is not yet known if the striped marlin ever escapes into the waters of the Atlantic proper.

FISHING METHODS

Most striped marlin are taken on commercial longlines, for the species is highly esteemed in the Oriental fisheries. The flesh is of high quality as human food, and millions of pounds are taken annually in the Indo-Pacific region. Some harpooning of striped marlin is also carried on, made possible by the fishes' habit of cruising slowly at the surface, sometimes with the dorsal fin and part of the back out of water. Anglers customarily take striped marlin by trolling, using a whole fish or a strip bait so rigged that it rides the surface of the water. In a few areas, still-fishing, with or without the aid of floats and balloons, is also a popular method.   —J.E.M.

STRIPED MULLET *Mugil cephalus* The striped or black mullet is one of the most abundant and important food fishes of the Southern United States. The Florida mullet fishery alone represents about 30,000,000 pounds annually; mullet fisheries of considerable value exist in other states, notably North and South Carolina, Alabama, and Mississippi. Mullet are caught by means of gillnets, trammelnets (entangling nets of three walls of mesh), haul seines, stopnets, castnets, and occasionally by hook and line. The flesh is firm and of excellent flavor. The roe and testes of the male (white roe) are considered gourmet delicacies.

The striped mullet has a spiny first dorsal with 4 spines, and soft dorsal fin with one spine and 8 softrays, the two well-separated. The ventral fins are on the abdomen behind the point of insertion of the pectorals; the anal fin usually consists of 3 spines and 8 softrays, with only 2 spines in very small fish; the caudal fin is forked moderately deep. The soft dorsal and anal fins are almost naked (scaled in most other American mullets), but the body and head are clothed with large, rounded scales. Adults are bluish-gray or greenish above, silvery on the lower part of the sides and below; the scales on the sides have dark centers which form longitudinal lines. The lining of the body cavity is black. The striped mullet grows to 30 inches or more and over 15 pounds in warmer waters.

Mullet feed chiefly on vegetable matter, but they feed also on eggs and small marine animals such as snails. They nibble at marine plants or scoop up mud and, after sucking out the edible portion and straining it through long gillrakers, reject the residue. Most of the one hundred or so species have a muscular, gizzardlike stomach which enables them to grind their food before it starts through an exceptionally long digestive tract. A 13-inch mullet with a digestive tract 7 feet long is not unusual. Because of the presence of a "gizzard," the striped mullet was once ruled in a Florida court to be a bird, for, said a biologist testifying for the defense, only birds have gizzards. This decision freed a commercial fisherman from a charge of fishing out of season.

LIFE HISTORY

The striped mullet has a very wide distribution, being found on both sides of the Atlantic and Pacific oceans and in the Indian Ocean. In the New World it is found from Brazil to Cape Cod, and as a stray to outer Nova Scotia; it also occurs along the West Coast from Monterey to Chile. This timid and inoffensive fish is structurally related to some of the most ferocious of fishes, the barracudas. It also closely resembles the silversides, Atherinidae, differing in having shorter, broader heads, small eyes, relatively deeper and thicker bodies, lack of a silver stripe, and 24–25 vertebrae (35 or more in the silversides).

The family of mullets, Mugilidae, is worldwide in tropic and temperate seas and is of considerable economic importance wherever found in abundance. Most of the species are marine, although many invade brackish and freshwater in the United States, particularly the freshwater mullet, *Agonostomus monticola*, which differs from the striped mullet in having no gizzard. The striped mullet also is a frequent invader of freshwater; here they may be seen making high, very ungraceful leaps, often several in succession. They do not dive back in the water headfirst; instead they rigidly maintain the position in which they began the leap and land with a splash. Various theories have been proposed for this leaping behavior; among them are leaping for the sheer joy of it and attempting to shake off parasites. Their schooling behavior in saltwater is different, however; here they usually jump more when pursued by predators or when jumping over a fisherman's net when the school realizes it is surrounded.

The striped mullet is not commonly taken on hook and line, but many are taken on small worms in brackish and freshwaters. They fight with great strength, speed, and agility. Smaller "finger" mullets are favored live bait for such gamefish as jacks, snook, and tarpon, while larger mullet are often used as cut bait for bottom fish or fished whole for trolling. *See also* Fish Cookery, Mullets, White Mullet —F.W.B.

STRIPED SEAPERCH *Embiotoca lateralis* The species is one of the most beautiful marine fishes of the Pacific Coast. A surfperch (*which see*), it is striped horizontally with subdued orange and bright blue along the scale rows; bluish-black on anal and dorsal fins, pectorals clear, pelvics black, caudal dusky; some variation in fin color; over-all body color dull red to brown; a frenum interrupts the posterior groove of lower lip; rayed portion of dorsal high anteriorly; dorsal softrays 23–25; anal softrays 29–33; head with several series of blue spots or streaks. Length to 15 inches. It is to be found from northern lower California to northwestern Alaska.

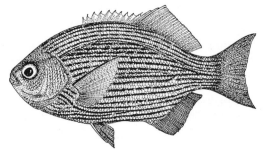

Striped Seaperch

Life history, food, and angling as with all surfperch (*which see*) in general.

The striped seaperch represents only a small portion of the catch in California. —J.R.

STRIPED TUNA *See* Skipjack Tuna

STRIPPING A term in fly-casting which describes pulling line from the reel preparatory to making a cast. The amount of slack line stripped out by the angler determines the length of his cast. To strip line may also imply the act of retrieving slack after the cast has been made; the line is again returned to the angler's hand in loose coils, preparatory to the next cast. *See also* Fly-Casting

STUFFING BOX A metal cylinder enclosing the motor shaft of an inboard. It contains packing to prevent leakage of water into the boat.

STUMPKNOCKER A regional name in the Southern United States for the spotted sunfish (*which see*), and for the warmouth (*which see*)

STURGEON *Acipenseridae* A family of large fish found throughout the Northern Hemisphere which occur in the oceans and freshwater rivers. A total of sixteen species are known, seven of which occur in the United States; the white sturgeon (*which see*) of the Pacific Northwest, the Atlantic sturgeon (*Acipenser oxyrhynchus*), which ranges from Maine into the Gulf of Mexico, the lake sturgeon (*which see*) of the Great Lakes region, the shovelnose sturgeon (*Scaphirhynchus platorynchus*) of the Mississippi Valley region, the green sturgeon (*which see*) of the Pacific coast, the pallid sturgeon (*Scaphirhynchus albus*) a freshwater species, and the shortnose sturgeon (*Acipenser brevirostrum*).

The sturgeons are primitive fishes and were widely distributed in early geological history. They are characterized by a head covered with bony plates and the presence of five rows of bony scutes on the body. There are four small barbels anterior to the mouth; the mouth is protrusible in adaption to bottom feeding. This family consists of four genera of which the beluga (*Huso huso*) ranging in the Caspian Sea, Black Sea, Sea of Azov, and the eastern Mediterranean to the Danube is the largest, attaining a weight of 2,500 pounds. The beluga is synonymous with the Russian commercial fishery because of the exporting of caviar (*which see*), but it is not as important in the annual landings as the sum total of several other species.

All sturgeons are slow-growing fish, seldom maturing before age 12 (according to species and sex), but they are long lived, with individuals attaining 75 years or more.

Although sturgeon are taken primarily in the commercial fishery of the United States and Europe, they are excellent gamefish when caught on rod-and-reel. Methods vary according to species and location. Ordinarily, very heavy spinning or surf tackle is employed. Baits include night-crawlers, lampreys, scraps of meat, and cut bait made from suckers or other fish in rivers such as the Snake of Idaho, and the Columbia in Oregon—or dried river moss (algae) used by specialists in the Apalachicola River of Florida. Sturgeon also provide a winter spear fishery in some midwestern states. Due to the widespread decline of sturgeon populations, many local laws with respect to season and size limit have been established, and some waters have been periodically closed to this type of angling.

With few exceptions (the green sturgeon in the United States) sturgeon have excellent food value and are a significant source of protein. Smoked sturgeon is a gourmet delicacy. The most desirable species in the commercial market is the lake sturgeon, which has been imitated on American markets with the substitution of the more available paddlefish (*which see*). However, all female sturgeon provide caviar. *See also* Fish Cookery
—A.J.McC.

STURGEON CHUB *Hybopsis gelida* A slender-bodied, silvery chub with small dark specks. Caudal fins with narrow white border along lower edge. Snout long, overhanging large mouth. Barbel at junction of jaws. Caudal fin long and deeply forked. Scales each with a small longitudinal keel. The range of this chub is in the Missouri River basin from Iowa to Wyoming and Montana.

HABITS

Little is known of the habits of the sturgeon chub. It is typically a river fish, and is found in stream riffles. Its average length is 2 inches, and it reaches a maximum size of 4 inches.

ECONOMIC VALUE

Undoubtedly this species is of some value for forage for stream-dwelling predators. —R.A.J.

SUBSTRATE The layer or base on which an animal or plant lives.

SUCKER Family Catostomidae Softrayed fishes with a toothless and more or less protractile mouth and thick lips. *See* Bigmouth Buffalo, Humpback Sucker, Lahontan Sucker, Lake Chubsucker, Longnose Sucker, Northern Redhorse, Silver Redhorse, Smallmouth Buffalo, Spotted Sucker, Striped Jumprock, White Sucker

SUCKERMOUTH MINNOW *Phenacobius mirabilis* As the name implies, it is a suckermouthed minnow, and is yellowish or slaty-olive above and silvery below. Distinguished from the sucker family in that the suckers have more than 8 dorsal rays; the suckermouth minnow has 7. A narrow, dark stripe extends along dorsal ridge.

Suckermouth Minnow

Dusky lateral band encircles snout and ends in deep-black, oblong caudal spot. Tip of upper jaw separated from remainder of snout by a deep groove. Lips large and fleshy, the upper curved around the angle of the mouth. The suckermouth minnow has a range from Colorado and South Dakota to western Ohio, Louisiana, and Texas.

HABITS

The suckermouth minnow prefers shallow, rapid streams rich in organic matter. When found in turbid waters, the current must be sufficient to prevent siltation. The suckermouth feeds on small insect larvae and snails from the stream bottom. A late-spring and early-summer spawner, the suckermouth male develops tiny tubercles on the upper part of the head, predorsal region of the body, and on the pectoral and ventral fins. This species reaches a length of 4 inches.

ECONOMIC VALUE

Although used as bait, the suckermouth minnow apparently is not too popular. Undoubtedly it enters the diet of stream-resident predator fish. —R.A.J.

SUMMER FLOUNDER *Paralichthys dentatus* The summer flounder, or fluke, is a member of the flatfish family Bothidae. This is a "left-handed" flounder, its eyes being on the left side as the fish lies on the bottom, the left side also being the dark side. Like other flatfishes, it has a wide body, rimmed by long dorsal and anal fins, and both eyes are together on the same (upper) side of the head. Its mouth is rather large and well-equipped with teeth.

The background color of the summer flounder normally appears gray, brown, or olivaceous with tints of orange, pink, and brown nearly to black. Pale to dark mottlings with regularly placed small spots are distinct or pale, depending upon the bottom on which the fish is lying. Although the species is reported to reach 25–30 pounds, 15 pounds and a length of 3 feet are unusual, and the most common size of the fish is 2–5 pounds.

It is distributed in the continental waters of the Eastern United States, from Maine to South Carolina, to the south of which it is replaced by the southern flounder (*which see*). The summer flounder is found from the shallows to water that is relatively deep, where it spends its life either on the bottom or close to it, as in the case of most flatfishes. It prefers sandy to sandy-mud bottom in bays and harbors as well as the mouths of estuaries. During the summer, it frequents shallow water, while during the winter the medium and larger specimens are found at 25–50 fathoms offshore.

It is believed to spawn in late fall, winter, and early spring, depending on the latitude, young fish drifting in during the spring and growing up in the shallow, inshore nursery grounds. Although the species lies buried in the sand or mud most of the time, it is a rapid swimmer, being able to pursue successfully small fish, squid, crabs, and shrimps, as well as shellfish and worms burrowed in the sand.

ANGLING VALUE

This valuable fish is a mainstay of the sport fishery along the Middle Atlantic Coast, accounting for a proportionately large catch from bridges and jetties, and by small-boat fishermen. The use of live bait consisting of small fishes (killifish) is successful, and summer flounder are also taken on squid, small spoons, and spinners. Although not as strong a fighter per pound as some other sportfishes, the fluke provides lively action, especially on light tackle. This species is important commercially, being one of our most important and valuable flatfishes in the mid Atlantic states. —D.dS.

RATE OF EXPLOITATION

A paper by New York fishery biologist John C. Poole, in the *New York Fish and Game Journal* for July, 1962, describes a D-J (Dingell-Johnson—federal aid in fish restoration) study of the fluke population of Great South Bay (Long Island) in relation to the sport fishery. The purpose of the D-J project was to investigate the causes for a decline in recent years in late-season fishing success for fluke in Great South Bay. In the principal approach to the problem, 5,845 fluke were tagged from 1956 to 1959. Tagging was done in Great South Bay and in oceanwaters of Shinnecock Inlet and Fire Island Inlet.

Biologist Poole found from tag returns that little movement of fluke occurred out of the bay during summer, but that heavy, early-season fishing appeared to be an important factor in the decline. In 1956 and 1959, when 25–30 percent of the calculated population was taken by sport fishing during June and July, the catch declined sharply during August and September. In 1958, on the other hand, the early catch was only 14 percent and that in August and September increased markedly.

The study showed that rates of exploitation of the fluke population by the sport fishery in Great South Bay each summer averaged about 20 percent. Since the bay is the primary summer nursery ground for young fluke, Poole considers that such rates permit a low degree of escapement of young fish. At present, the sport fishery is to a large extent dependent upon the abundance of fluke about a foot or less in length.

Recoveries of tagged fish in years subsequent to the one in which fluke were tagged in Greath South Bay indicated a strong tendency for the population to return to the bay itself after wintering elsewhere. From 25 to 53 percent of recovered tagged fluke during the second and third summers were taken in Great South Bay, and 50–80 percent in all the South Shore bays of Long Island.

Estimates of survival from year to year indicate that the sport fishery, the winter trawl fishery, and the summer commercial fishery are overexploiting the fluke population at the present time. Poole concluded that management to stabilize the catch in Great South Bay throughout the summer seems feasible by limiting in some manner the early fishing pressure. There also appears to be a need for size or catch limits to permit greater escapement of small fluke.

FISHING METHODS

Various methods are employed to catch fluke. These include drifting, fishing at anchor and using chum, trolling, casting from shore, and angling from piers and banks.

Drifting is one of the more popular and effective techniques. The procedure is to let the boat drift with the wind or tidal current. In confined waterways the craft drifts as far as is practicable and safe, then returns to a point near where the drop was begun and repeats the process. Drifting can be particularly effective diagonally across channels, where fluke move along "lanes" in search of current-borne food.

Drifting increases the fisherman's chances by covering more bottom where fluke are apt to be lurking or on the prowl for food. It also keeps the bait or lure in motion. Because of their aggressive nature, fluke find a moving bait attractive. But drifting does have certain limitations. It can be dangerous in rocky areas. A boat's skipper also must keep an alert watch for sandbars in shallow waters. Furthermore, the current and wind must not be too strong. Caution must be exercised in areas where there is appreciable boat traffic. This is especially true in channels, which are often busy thoroughfares.

Chumming, or fishing at anchor and using chum, is a popular method for both fluke and winter flounders. It also can be done while drifting, provided the drift speed is not too fast; and it is effective when the fish are scattered. Chumming for fluke is accomplished in either of two ways.

1. A chum pot, fashioned from a square of netting or other material, such as a meshed sack in which oranges or onions are sold, is filled with cracked mussels. Or, if the mesh is not too large, it can be filled with ground menhaden (mossbunker) pulp. As a substitute for ground menhaden some anglers use the canned fish food sold for cats. The chum pot is attached to a length of twine, by means of which it can be bounced on the bottom at intervals to release the tiny bits of meat and juices which draw fish to the angler's vicinity.

2. Chumming also can be done by dropping a few mussels, their shells cracked to liberate meat and juices

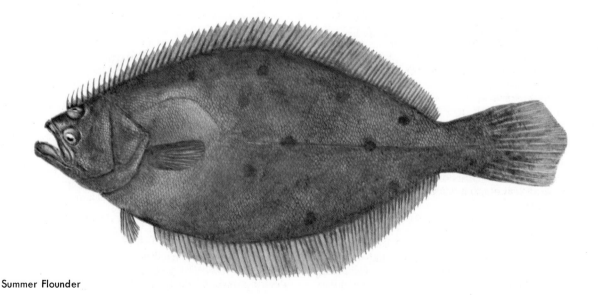

Summer Flounder

into the surrounding water periodically. This method can be carried on in conjunction with the use of a menhaden chum pot, but usually is employed when the boat is anchored.

When conditions are unfavorable for drifting, and you have no chum aboard, anchor in a likely looking spot, then cast out from the boat, retrieving line to keep the bait in motion. Repeat this procedure. If you're anchored in a channel where the tide is moving at a fair clip, you can let it carry the bait away from the boat (use a round or oval sinker for this), then reel it in along the bottom. You won't cover as much territory with these methods, but they approximate drifting because the bait is moving.

Although not practiced as frequently as drifting, trolling has an advantage in that it also covers more ground than fishing at anchor. It introduces an element of suspense, too, for it not only accounts for the larger "doormats" (large fluke) but also for bluefish, striped bass, and weakfish. A fluke taking a trolled offering tends to strike with greater impact because the fish is capturing its prey while in motion. Fluke-trolling speed is a matter of opinion, but best results are obtained when the boat's motor is kept on low throttle to yield a headway of about 1½–2 miles an hour.

Pier, shore, and bank angling can produce fluke in channels and deep creeks, at inlets, and in close-inshore ocean zones. In such locations anglers are limited in their movements, but they can also improve their chances by keeping their bait in motion. Channels and inlets can be particularly productive of fluke. A former world record of 20 pounds was made by an angler fishing in the tidal flow of Fire Island Inlet, New York. Occasionally fluke will come very close to shore, and at such times surf and jetty anglers hook them while bottom-fishing with natural baits. If a surf-caster purposely tries for fluke, it will pay him to use the cast-and-slow-retrieve technique.

TACKLE FOR FLUKE

As in fishing for winter flounder (*which see*), fluke tackle can be as plain or as fancy as the fisherman's tastes and wallet permit. One general rule applies: the lighter the equipment, the greater the sport. A newcomer, however, should bear in mind that summer flounders can attain weights of 10–12 pounds and more, and they offer spirited resistance. A choice lies between conventional tackle and spinning equipment, with selection influenced by such factors as the angler's experience, method involved, general size of fish running, and the hook rig and weight of the sinker for keeping it on bottom.

Almost any light- or medium-weight conventional fiberglass bay rod will do. One with a 5-foot tip section is ideal for fishing from boats, piers, and banks. (In pier-angling, where fish have to be lifted some distance over the water, the rod should have considerable backbone.) This is mounted with a standard saltwater reel with or without a drag. The reel should spool 150 yards of 20–30-pound-test line.

Along an oceanfront or anyplace where some casting distance is required, the fluke angler can use a light conventional surf rod matched with a surf reel of suitable size. A light surf rod may be 8–9 feet in length, and will handle lures of about 2 ounces and sinkers up to perhaps 4 ounces. Its complementing reel will have a star-drag, a

wide or narrow spool (according to preference), and a gear ratio of 3 or 3½ : 1 for fast retrieves. Level-wind and antibacklash devices are optional but convenient. This reel should also hold about 150 yards of line of 20–30-pound-test.

When heavier lures or sinkers are used and when greater casting distance is needed, use a medium conventional surf outfit. The rod will be about 8–10 feet long over-all and versatile enough to handle sinkers up to 5–6 ounces in bottom-fishing and cast lures ranging up to about 4 ounces. The reel for this rod will incorporate the same features as the light surf reel but have a capacity of at least 200 yards of 36-pound-test line. A medium surf-angling outfit will handle not only fluke but also most of the surf-run fishes.

Spinning tackle has certain limitations with respect to the weights of lures, rigs, and sinkers it can handle satisfactorily. These items, in turn, are influenced by such factors as the method used, the size potential of the fish available, casting distances required, depths, current strengths, and other local conditions. Such details determine whether or not light spinning gear is suitable for fluke fishing. It also should be kept in mind that longer playing time usually is required for fish hooked on light tackle. On a crowded, public fishing boat this can cause problems, not the least of which are a tangling of lines and the consequent annoyance of fellow passengers.

A light or medium spinning outfit may be employed in fish from skiffs, piers, and banks. Light gear consists of a rod 6–7 feet long, mounted with a small, saltwater spinning reel with a capacity of 150–300 yards of 10-to-12-pound-test. This outfit will handle lures to 1–1½ ounces and sinkers up to about 3 ounces.

A similar general rule applies in surf-spinning for fluke. Light tackle can be used as long as the water is fairly calm (so that a heavy sinker is not demanded) and considerable casting distance is not required. If local water or wind conditions necessitate a heavier sinker or lure, and maximum casting distance is a factor, medium-weight surf-spinning equipment is preferable. A light outfit's components are a rod 7½–9½ feet long and a saltwater spinning reel which can spool 250–300 yards of line to 20-pound-test. This combination will handle lures to about 2 ounces and sinkers to about 3 ounces. The medium-weight combination consists of a rod measuring 8–10 feet in length and a saltwater spinning reel of about the same size used on the light rod. Such an outfit will operate lures up to 3 ounces and sinkers up to about 4 ounces.

Lines used in fluke fishing are light, with the choice of material being a matter of angler's preference. Some fishermen using conventional-type tackle stay with linen. Many others favor synthetics such as nylon and Dacron. In several kinds of angling, notably bottom-fishing, the trend is toward a replacement of linen lines by monofilament.

THE BASIC FLUKE RIG

Several types of fluke rigs have been used successfully. Again, as in other kinds of fishing, these terminal-tackle arrangements usually are variations of certain basic plans. Also as in other kinds of angling, the terminal tackle for fluke is designed primarily to conform with the quarry's feeding habits. In this case the hooks are rigged for the bottom. That requirement met, variations come about as anglers experiment and find certain modifications and refinements which prove effective.

The basic rig starts with a three-way swivel tied to the line. To the middle of the swivel's remaining two loops attach a hook on 2–3 feet of monofilament or gut leader (about the same strength as the line). To the lowest loop tie a sinker.

A refinement can be added to this rig by attaching one or two shiny spinner blades to the leader not far above the hook. Their motion and glitter provide an extra eye-catching attraction.

A more complicated variation of the basic rig requires these components: a three-way swivel; a 3-foot leader of monofilament or other material; a No. 2 or No. 4 June Bug spinner with a two-way swivel attached; 5–6 inches of No. 7 steel wire; a double hook (this has separate shanks in the form of a narrow, elongated "U"); and a sinker. There are four steps in making the rig:

1. Make a small loop at each end of the piece of wire. Wire loops should not be more than about 2 inches long.
2. Attach one of the wire's loops to the lower end of the spinner (this device has an eye kept closed by a sliding collar; slide the collar up, put the wire on, then slide the collar back).
3. Feed the double hook onto the piece of wire's remaining loop.
4. Attach the leader between the spinner's two-way barrel swivel and the remaining loop of the line. To facilitate changing of rigs, a snap-clip type of connector can be added between the line's three-way swivel and leader.

TWO-HOOK RIG

This is essentially the same as the basic rig except that a second hook is added. The first hook is rigged as before. The second hook (on a snell only, no leader) is tied into the first hook's leader at about the midpoint or slightly lower. With this rig two kinds of bait can be used simultaneously. Whichever bait takes the first fluke will indicate how both hooks should be baited.

TROLLING RIG

The rig must travel deep, near the bottom. To accomplish this a trolling sinker is attached to the line. Following the sinker is a 2–3-foot monofilament leader. Completing the rig is a small artificial, such as a spoon or feather lure, secured to the leader. Some anglers use swivels between the line and trolling sinker, between sinker and leader, and between leader and lure to minimize twisting of the line during trolling. A keel attached above the leader will help; there are keeled trolling sinkers designed for the same purpose.

SURF RIG

Either a standard surf bottom-fishing rig or a fishfinder arrangement can be used. The former calls for a three-loop swivel attached to the line. On one remaining loop of the swivel is tied a pyramid sinker of sufficient weight to hold bottom. To the last loop are 2–3 feet of leader carrying the hook.

The fishfinder (*which see*) surf rig is substantially the same, except that the sinker is equipped with a linkage which permits it to slide freely up and down the line. This linkage goes on the line above a two-loop barrel swivel connecting line and 2–3-foot leader. The idea is that the sinker will go as far down on the line as it can (stopped by the swivel) during casting to add momentum to the rig; yet, because of its freedom on the line, it will not hamper a fish's fight.

In both of the aforementioned rigs a small cork float can be added to the leader to keep the bait up out of the reach of crabs.

SINKERS

Except in trolling and surf-fishing, a bank-type or a round sinker (some have a built-in swivel) can be used. The latter is preferable because it gives more movement to the rig and is a bit less apt to get caught on obstructions when drifting. In trolling, as already noted, a trolling sinker or drail is employed. In surf fishing a pyramid sinker is used. This type is designed to hold bottom in sand. Sinker weights are determined primarily by currents and depths in the areas fished. This is true in both bottom-fishing and surf-angling. In shallow water and when currents are weak, 3–4 ounces are standard. In deeper water and stronger currents it may be necessary to use 5 ounces or more. The important thing is that the sinker be only heavy enough to keep the rig on bottom. Any extra weight tires the fish and detracts from its fight. Similarly, a trolling sinker should be only heavy enough to carry the rig deep. Four ounces or more may be the weight required.

HOOKS AND BAITS

There are numerous suitable patterns. The choice is a matter of preference. The Carlisle is one pattern in use. Another is the Sproat. Still others are the O'Shaughnessy, Eagle Claw, and the long-shank Kirby bass design. There is a certain amount of flexibility with respect to size, because the fluke has a well-developed mouth. A 1/0 will handle the small fluke; a 2/0 will take care of medium-size fluke; and a 5/0 or 6/0 will handle the heavier fish in the "doormat" class.

Fluke are voracious, rather omnivorous feeders, and various baits can be used to catch them. The list includes a strip of fresh or frozen squid, live killy (mummichog), a piece of blue crab, or strips cut from the undersides of menhaden, herring, scup (porgy), young bluefish, and searobin. The most popular fluke baits are a strip of squid, live killy, and a spearing, used separately or in combination. The most effective is often a combination of a live killy and a spearing on the same hook. The killy's movements add to the bait's attraction because it is practically impossible to keep spearing alive. The killy is much hardier.

Squid is sold, frozen, in packages for bait. Used alone or in combination with another bait, the squid is cut into strips. These are taken from the squid's mantle (skirtlike portion), cut 3–4 inches long, and ½ inch or so wide. The outer layer of skin can be peeled away to expose the white flesh underneath for greater visibility in the water. Each strip should be cut up the middle of one end to create two little "tails" which flutter in the water and add to its lure. The hook point is then run through the other end of the squid strip. The strip can be turned up on the hook's bend; then the point is thrust through the strip again in such a way that the two tails are left to dangle.

When a killy or spearing is added to a squid strip, the little fish is hooked carefully through the lips so as to present it in the most lifelike fashion possible. Hooking through the tail or flesh of the back will secure the baitfish, too, but in an unnatural fashion. If impaled on a hook properly, a killy will stay alive for a long time. Killies and spearing also can be placed on a hook by carefully passing the hook's point in through the mouth and out under one gill cover. But the lips method is preferable, especially in the case of a killy.

A strip of white squid and a live killy about 2–3 inches long comprise a bait that is practically irresistible to fluke. The squid's white color is an eyecatcher. So are the killy's movements. And both are attractive to fluke.

FISHING TECHNIQUE

Although fluke are aggressive predators, in shoalwater they sometimes act shy of boats. This can be overcome by letting the rig be current-borne away from the craft. Depending upon the depth, 50–100 feet of line paid out is generally enough. Ordinarily, the fluke's approach to a bait is a hard strike, so enthusiastic that the fish practically hooks itself. If an "automatic hooking" does not occur at the strike, a short upward lift of the rod tip usually plants the barb.

Occasionally the approach is more of a delayed-action type. The fluke seizes the bait to prevent its escape, but has not yet mouthed it for swallowing. This is translated at the angler's end as a light tap. Any attempt to set the hook at that particular moment can tear the bait out of the fish's jaws. The fisherman should pause alertly, just long enough to give his quarry time to mouth and swallow the bait, feeling for a firmer tug which tells the fisherman that the fluke definitely has accepted it. Then a short, smart lift of the rod's tip section will set the hook.

At times a fluke will toy with the bait. This is apt to be the case when a dead bait is used. Toying with the bait is recognized as a series of sharp twitches on the line as the fluke either takes a bite out of the offering or seizes it and backs away with it. When this occurs the angler must give his fish a little line, then retrieve slowly, constantly feeling for the fluke's weight. It may be necessary to repeat the procedure a few times. Finally, if there is no further response the rig should be checked to see if it has been stripped of bait.

Almost any sport fish will seize a live bait or moving lure harder than it will a dead bait or one that is not in motion, the reason being that the former has to be pursued and captured. But not infrequently fluke will come up behind a live killy and bite it off at the midsection, thus escaping the hook. The fluke may return to the bait to finish the job and become hooked. Or, with the killy now dead, the fluke may lose interest; the mutilated bait should be replaced.

An important accessory in this angling is a landing net. Fluke are likely to wiggle violently as they are being lifted from the water, and if the hook is not set securely they can flip themselves free. Many a catch has been lost in this way. What also can happen when they are reeled in close alongside a boat is that they slap against the hull, and they can knock themselves off a hook. A landing net

should be held in readiness as the fish nears the surface, to be slipped under the fluke just before it clears the water.

PLACES AND SEASONS

Fluke frequent ocean and bay areas. Public fishing boats and private craft find them in inshore ocean zones and bays. When the fish are not far off the beach, surf-casters, jetty anglers, and pier fishermen catch them too. Inlets between ocean and bays are also productive as fluke move in and out in search of food or when looking for more satisfactory water temperatures. Inlets have been known to produce doormats of 10–15 pounds for boat and pier fishermen, and even for anglers fishing from shore.

These flatfish range freely over sand and mud bottoms, and they exhibit a preference for the former. Fluke often bury themselves in the bottom, an act which they can perform with amazing speed, and leave only their eyes exposed to watch for passing prey. They also lurk near patches of marine vegetation such as eelgrass, and around pilings and in rocky places which harbor food. Freely moving, fairly deep channels are grounds with potential. Angling can be done there from banks, docks, and drifting boats. Junctions of inlets and channels, where tidal currents swirl food, also can be productive. So can deep creeks with steep banks. Still other likely locations include the junction of a channel and a saltwater creek, and the end of a sandbar, or at a point of land where currents bring food. In channels the flatfish often travel along "lanes," knowing instinctively that currents carry food to them. Generally speaking, they are more likely to bite on a running tide than at slackwater in channel and bay fishing.

In winter, fluke live offshore in the ocean, probably to escape the chilling shallow water. In the spring they move inshore, invading inlets, bays, harbors, and sounds. They spend the late spring, summer, and early autumn in such areas. When cooler weather arrives they again move outside and offshore for the winter.

The start of the fluke season depends on how quickly inshore waters warm to their liking. Their first spring appearance can occur in late April or early May. The numbers of fish increase with springtime warmth, and their run begins to peak in June and July and continues through the summer. Their over-all size increases as the season progresses. The earliest fish caught are seldom larger than winter flounders, going perhaps 1½–2 or 2½ pounds. Later their weight range advances to 4, 5, and 6 pounds. Toward the end of the season "doormats" occur up to 12–13 pounds and heavier.

EDIBILITY

Fluke are superb table fish. Their meat is white, firm, and delicately flavored. Like winter flounders and other flatfishes, fluke have many bones; but considering the quality of their meat this is not a substantial objection. After gutting and dressing, the smaller fish can be cooked whole, by frying or other methods. *See* Fish Cookery

—B.W.

SUNAPEE TROUT *Salvelinus aureolus* The Sunapee trout is very similar to the blueback trout and Marston trout, and the three are presently considered a landlocked population of Arctic char (*which see*) by some taxonomists. However, at least one scientist (Dr. V. D. Vladykov, of the Fisheries Research Board of Canada) who has made an extensive investigation of the char group showed evidence that the Sunapee trout is a distinct species. Thus, its taxonomic position is not clear.

Originally described from Sunapee Lake, New Hampshire, it is also known to have occurred in Big Dan Hole Pond, New Hampshire; Averill Lake, Vermont; and Floods Pond, Maine. It has been unsuccessfully introduced into several other New Hampshire waters. A population of this species was once established in the Third Connecticut Lake, but a few years later they disappeared when lake trout were introduced. There is an occasional Sunapee trout caught in Cornor Pond, Ossipee, where it exists in competition with brook trout. It is not known whether or not the Sunapee trout ever reproduced naturally in either of these ponds. One reclaimed pond, Tewksbury Pond, shows some promise of sustaining the sunapee-trout population.

During the summer months in Sunapee Lake, this species resides in depths of from 60–100 feet; where the temperature is in the neighborhood of 50°F. or less. In the spring it occurs in shallow water along the shores. About mid October it may be found on a reef near the entrance to Sunapee Harbor where it spawns.

BEHAVIOR

The only known information concerning the behavior of this species is the fact that it moves into shallow water on one reef (in Sunapee Lake) to spawn between October 20 and November 20. In the spring it may be found in the shallow water presumably feeding on the smelt, and during the warmer months it is found in the deepest parts of the lake down to 90–100 feet. Little is known of the winter habitat except that an occasional specimen has been caught by pickerel fishermen indicating that they are to be found in shallow water at that time of year.

MANAGEMENT

For years the major conservation procedure has been to capture the trout at spawning time, strip them, and raise the offspring to fingerling or yearling size in a hatchery before returning them to Sunapee Lake. This procedure was believed to be more satisfactory than allowing the fish to reproduce naturally. They have also been protected with a twelve-inch length limit and a two fish per day bag limit. In spite of these measures the Sunapee trout has virtually disappeared.

HYBRIDIZATION

It is known that this species can be artificially hybridized with both the brook trout and lake trout. In Sunapee Lake, hybridization with the brook trout is not believed to be of any consequence as the two species spawn in widely separated locations. The lake trout, however, spawn on the same reef as do the Sunapee trout and at approximately the same time. (Hybridization with

Sunapee Trout, 12-inch Female

Sunapee Trout, 12-inch Male, Flood's Pond, Maine

the latter species is believed by some to be quite common.) Reports indicate that in time past a shortage of mature males was common. It is reported that at such times male brook trout and lake trout were occasionally used to fertilize the Sunapee trout eggs. On one occasion male Sunapee trout were used to fertilize landlocked salmon eggs. No further information concerning the fate of these hybrids is available. At present, the only pure strain population of Sunapee trout exists in Floods Pond, Maine.

ANGLING VALUE

The yield to angling is practically nil. There are only two methods of fishing which are sometimes successful. One consists of deepwater trolling similar to the technique used for lake trout; the other consists of handlining with cut bait in deepwater. Frequently, the angler will have a second line with a live-smelt bait. Usually still-fishing sites are marked with a buoy and periodically chummed with cut bait.   —A.E.N.

SUNFISH Family Centarchidae The sunfish family consists of 30 recognized freshwater species native only to North America and ranging in size from the inch-long Pygmy sunfishes to the over 20-pound largemouth bass. Dated fossils indicate that their probable origin was about 60 million years ago during the Cenozoic epoch, or after the disappearance of the dinosaur. With the sole exception of the Sacramento perch all sunfishes were originally distributed east of the Rocky Mountains. The structure of the dorsal fin is a characteristic of this family; it consists of two parts, a spinous portion and a softrayed portion, united in a single structure instead of being divided into separate fins. All sunfishes (with the exception of the Sacramento perch) are nest builders, and all breed in the spring to late summer period when water temperatures range from 60°–70°F. The pygmy sunfishes prepare their nests from plant material, but all other males construct a shallow saucerlike depression at a depth correlated with water clarity and light intensity, and aggressively protect the eggs and fry until they become free swimming. Thus, centrarchids achieve a high degree of survival which sometimes results in overpopulation and ultimately stunting.

Due to the similarity in spawning behavior natural hybridization is not uncommon among sunfishes, although crosses are mainly confined within "tribes" or congeneric species, such as a bluegill with a pumpkinseed (*Lepomis*) or a white crappie (*Pomoxis*). More than 20 different crosses have been identified among wild hybrids, and in some waters these have represented a substantial portion of the sunfish population. The chief factor in the occurrence of sunfish hybrids is the competition for nest sites, which among the smaller species may exist in dense colonies (25 nests within 50 square feet); the black basses on the other hand exercise more territorial rights, and their nests are ordinarily 20–30 feet apart. However, the resulting sunfish hybrids are predominantly males and are either sterile or have low fertility rates despite growing larger than the parent species. This has been of interest to modern fish culturists in the artificial production of hybrids both from the standpoint of developing larger sunfish and as a management tool in controlling those species which tend to overpopulate, such as the bluegill and green sunfish.

By contrast, the Sacramento perch, the only endemic western centrarchid, has steadily declined in size and numbers. When spawning, this sunfish emits long gelatinous egg masses which adhere to stones and plants. The parents quickly abandon the eggs which are eaten by other fishes, and the young are left unprotected. In centuries past when the Sacramento perch existed in noncompetitive environments this trait was no handicap, but the introduction of exotic species to its native waters soon limited its survival rate. Formerly one of the larger sunfishes—recorded to a length of 24 inches and a weight of almost 10 pounds—it now seldom exceeds 16 inches or 3 pounds.

A fossil sunfish from the Cenozoic epoch

Purely in terms of number of freshwater fish caught in the United States today the sunfishes outrank all others. While sunfishes encompass 11 genera, from an angling standpoint the only important distinction is size. Widely known as bream or "brim" (a name adapted by early-day Southern colonists who saw a slight resemblance between our sunfishes and the nonrelated European bream, *Abramis* spp.) they are either the panfish that glorified the barefoot boy or gamefish in a group collectively known as the black bass. Some methods of fishing are common to both, but each has its lore and an infinite variety of regional techniques. *See also* Banded Pygmy Sunfish, Banded Sunfish, Bantam Sunfish, Blackbanded Sunfish, Black Bass, Black Crappie, Bluegill, Bluespotted, Sunfish, Dollar Sunfish, Everglades Pygmy Sunfish, Flier, Green Sunfish, Longear Sunfish, Mud Sunfish, Okefenokee Pygmy Sunfish, Orangespotted Sunfish, Panfish, Pumpkinseed, Redbreast Sunfish, Redear Sunfish, Roanoke Bass, Rock Bass, Sacramento Perch, Spotted Sunfish, Warmouth, White Crappie—A.J.McC.

SUPRALITTORAL That area of the shoreline which is ordinarily not covered by water, above the high tide line.

SURF-FISHING The art of surf-casting applied to the capture of marine gamefish which frequent inshore waters. Using various tackle combinations, some of them highly specialized, the angler casts an artificial lure or natural bait from the shore, from a jetty, or from a small boat, hooks his fish, and plays it through the surf to breach, net, or gaff.

SURF TACKLE

Surf-fishing usually conjures up the vision of a lonely figure chest-deep in pounding waves, armed with a long, two-handed casting rod. This is, indeed, a reasonably accurate picture of the classic surf-caster or squidder. But recent years have seen almost every tackle combination successfully put to use in surf-fishing. Depending on water conditions, the size of the fish present, and their availability to the angler, the surfman may use anything from a saltwater fly-casting outfit to the heaviest of surf rods.

Choice of the most practical rod, reel, and line for any specific task is made difficult by a present lack of standardization. Since the advent of fiberglass, it is no longer feasible to rate the action and performance figures of a rod by its length and weight. The most accurate description must be provided by the weight range of lures for which the rod is calibrated.

With few exceptions, tubular fiberglass has been accepted as the most practical material with which to make saltwater bait-casting, spinning, and surf-casting rods. Glass fly rods are gaining in popularity, although many fly-casting enthusiasts still demand the "feel" and action of fine split bamboo. While the Calcutta or natural cane rod (see Tonkin Cane) remains in favor in some areas, split-bamboo surf rods are swiftly disappearing from the sea beaches.

Two surf-casting outfits, each boasting a number of variations, are favored by American anglers. They are the so-called "conventional" or revolving-spoon reel–squidding combination and the big surf-spinning rig.

The conventional surf rod is a casting instrument, and not a particularly effective fish-fighting tool. Its primary task is to hurl an artificial lure or natural bait to maximum distance. Obviously, manufacturers of surf rods find it necessary to strike a delicate balance between power and flexibility, so that an angler can make the long cast, then set the hooks, and play a strong fish without breaking the line. With such a rod, all surf-fishing authorities recommend and use the wide-spooled squidding reel fitted with free-spool and star-drag features. Reel size and line test will depend on the rod's action and the type of surf-casting contemplated. The reel should always have a 150–250-yard capacity.

A one-piece rod is always preferable to the two-piece model, and such rods are manufactured with ferruled spring butts for those who anticipate difficulty in transporting the longer stick from home to fishing grounds. Standard spring butts usually measure 30 inches from butt cap to reel seat. This is correct for a man of average height, but may not fit the shorter individual or the caster with exceptionally long arms. A one-piece rod with a generous portion of the butt section cork-taped permits an angler to clamp his reel at the proper location.

Today's guide arrangement is a complete reversal of the old system wherein a surf rod was fitted with a reversible tip-top and two facing guides—theory being that you could reverse the rod when it began to "take a set." Unfortunately, doing so usually caused the rod to break at the point where fibers had stretched, crystalized, and created the original set. Modern guides, three to four of them, are usually rifled to the tip-top. Guides should be the best obtainable, with strong bridges and quality rings. Agate rings offer the least friction; carbaloy is hard, but the friction factor is somewhat increased. Cheap, plated rings are to be avoided; they crack and subsequently fray the line.

Most popular of the conventional surf rods is a medium-action stick which measures 9½–10 feet from butt to tip-top and is calibrated to handle lures in the 2–4 ounce weight bracket. Lighter—and heavier—lures may be cast, but performance falls off on either side of the optimum.

Among major variations are: "The Tidewater Anglers Club of Virginia" tournament rod, a 10½-foot, heavy-duty stick which is designed to cast lures in the 4–6-ounce weight range to maximum distance. This rod currently holds all major East Coast tournament records; yet it is a practical fishing stick in areas where heavy lures or a heavy bait-sinker combination must be cast to extreme range. It is, understandably, a fatiguing rod for the fisherman to use.

Cape Cod's "Production Rod," so-called because many of the rod-and-line commercial striper fishermen of that area use it to take big bass in the surf, also measures 10½ feet, and is calibrated to cast lures and baits weighing 3–5 ounces. The rod is popular only in New England and along the Outer Banks of North Carolina.

New Jersey's "Jetty Rod" is a cut-down version of the standard surf-casting stick. Over-all, it measures 8–9 feet, and butt length is shortened (to 20–24 inches) to facilitate snap casts when the angler is precariously balanced on a barnacle-covered rock. This rod is also used by many boat fishermen who steer their craft just outside a breaking surf and cast in to the shore. Its lure-weight bracket is similar to that of the standard medium.

Popping rods are still popular on all coasts. These are simply short, light, squidding sticks, the link between a saltwater bait-casting rod and a surf rod. Calibrations would fall at 1–2½ ounces of lure weight. The rod is ideally chosen for light plugging and for short-range surf-casting for such species as the northern weakfish and small channel bass. It is also effective on school stripers.

Spinning, now fully as important as squidding in the sport of surf-casting, is essentially a light-tackle technique. Hence it does not supersede squidding but adds a new and efficient weapons system to the angler's arsenal.

With certain exceptions, the heavy surf-spinning rod is similar to the two-handed conventional surf rod. Its guides are much larger, rifling from a relatively huge gathering guide down to a standard tip-top. Lengths run 8–9 feet over-all, and rods usually boast "fast," i.e., whippier, tips. These big fixed-spool outfits are calibrated to cast lures in the 2–4-ounce weight range. The heavy surf-spinning reel, usually an open-face type with smooth, adjustable drag, should hold 200 yards of 15–18-pound-test monofilament line. Heavier tests are impractical. The combination is specialized, popular in some areas of Massachusetts and Rhode Island, along the Outer Banks of North Carolina, and on some sections of the Pacific Coast.

A more popular outfit is the medium-weight rod, which is favored by a great many surfmen on all coasts. This two-handed stick measures 8–9 feet, and is calibrated to cast lures or baits in the 1½–3-ounce weight bracket. Again, the reel should hold at least 200 yards of line, with tests running 12–15 pounds.

Although not considered surf-casting tackle, any of the various light spinning, bait-casting, and fly-casting outfits can be used to take fish frequenting inshore waters. These are at their best when it is necessary to present light lures on fine lines and when the fisherman does not have to cast his lure or bait an appreciable distance.

THE PROPER LINE

To insure optimum results, a surf-fisherman must choose the proper line for his tackle combination and method. In spinning, the problem is simply that of choosing a round monofilament of the correct pound-test to match rod action. (Flattened or ribbon monofilaments should never be used on a spinning reel, and the various braids are best suited to use on revolving-spool reels.)

Linen or Cuttyhunk, once considered the classic line for surf-fishing, no longer sets the pace—having been superseded by nylon braid, Dacron braid, and nylon monofilament. Each of these synthetics offers advantages and disadvantages.

Nylon braid is the most effective in the casting of heavy artificial lures. The line is smooth, it picks up enough water to provide some measure of "coolant," for the caster's thumb, has a good knot factor, and is not excessively elastic. Squidders consider 36-pound-test the classic weight but often use lighter lines—and heavier. Where big channel bass or stripers are sought, 45-pound-test may be a good choice.

Dacron braid is finer in diameter per rated pound-test than is nylon and has far less stretch. This increases the angler's chances of hooking fish but contributes to a slightly inferior knot factor. For casters with tender thumbs, Dacron is a "hot" line. On the credit side, again, Dacron's fine diameter and lack of buoyancy make it an exceptionally good choice for the angler who plans to fish with bait on the bottom.

Nylon monofilament is well-chosen for certain phases of surf-fishing. Round mono in the lighter tests, say up to 30 pounds, vies with Dacron in bottom-fishing where wave action, current, and wind tend to handicap the angler. Flattened or ribbon monofilaments in tests up to 30 pounds are effective in the casting of artificial lures. Heavier monos become unmanageable—and all of the single-strand lines are excessively elastic by comparison with the braids.

LEADERS

While rod, reel, and line comprise the heart of a surf-fishing outfit, leaders are sometimes necessary. These may be made of heavy monofilament for the taking of gamefish which lack sharp cutting teeth, or wire or nylon-covered wire if the quarry is sharp-toothed. When using artificial lures, the leader should be encumbered with a minimum of hardware. One terminal snap is sufficient, and this only to facilitate the rapid changing of lures. Swivels of various kinds, together with sinkers, are necessary only when bottom-fishing is the method used.

ACCESSORY EQUIPMENT

The surf-caster who fishes cold northern waters will require hip boots and complete foul-weather clothing. Better still, use full-length waders and a foul-weather top. Ice creepers should be worn when fishing rocky areas, but are unnecessary on a sand beach. Tropical surfmen dispense with boots and waders but wear tennis shoes to avoid injury from sea urchins and sharp coral.

Two types of gaff are useful. The folding gaff which may be clipped to the angler's belt is ideally chosen when it is necessary to wade far out on a bar where a fish cannot be beached. A long-handled gaff is best for jetty- or small-boat fishing. Paint it white so that it can be seen after dark. Gaffs are of questionable value when it is possible to beach a gamefish. A weighted billy club is more effective to quiet the thrashing of a large fish so that hooks may safely be removed.

The well-equipped surf-fisherman will also need a compartmented bag, with shoulder straps or belt loops, to carry a selection of lures, leaders, and basic tools; a stringer to secure his fish when wading; a flashlight, if he fishes after dark. The miner's headlamp is favored in many areas, but a penlight may be sufficient in a few of the night-fishing hot spots; the indiscriminate flashing of lights is frowned upon.

ARTIFICIAL LURES

Artificial lures will tempt any of the gamefish coveted by surf-fishermen on the Atlantic, the Gulf, or the Pacific coasts. Even cod and flounder find it impossible to resist a properly fished lure. Success for the angler lies in presenting the right tempter at the right time—and in the strike zone.

Five major types of artificial baits (one actually a natural bait rigged for casting) are used by the surf-caster. These are metal squids; weighted bucktails or feather lures; plugs; rigged eels and eelskin rigs, and a variety of soft plastic lures.

Metal Squids A bewildering assortment of metal squids are available to the surfman. Originally cast of block tin—which has a soft, almost translucent glow—many of the modern squids are made of stainless steel or baser metals that have been chrome-plated. In type they range from the old, bent sand eel through keeled and diamond jigs to spoon-shaped creations. All are intended to simulate the flash and frantic swimming action of small baitfishes, and all are at their best in the froth of a breaking surf.

Metal squids are produced with single and treble hooks, with and without bucktail or feather dressing. Often they are improved by attaching strips of pork rind to their hooks. These lures are offered in all weight ranges, from ultralight spin sizes, on up to 4–5-ounce models. Metal squids are most effective during daylight hours but sometimes tempt fish at night.

The weighted bucktail (called bugeye, doodlebug, and weighted streamer on some sections of the coast) is a leadheaded jig, usually dressed with natural bucktail or synthetic fibers, feathers, plastic, or rubber strips. It is manufactured in a variety of weights and sizes. This lure is most effective when cast up and across a strong current, then retrieved in a series of hops. The bucktail is an excellent nighttime bait and often produces as well in daylight hours. Like the metal squid, its fish-taking potential may sometimes be increased by the impaling of a pork-rind strip on its single hook.

Plugs Squidding at one time reigned supreme as the province of the surf-casting purist. Today, the plug-caster often scorns any other method and maintains that his lure and technique are most sporting, most spectacular, and most effective.

These claims are open to debate but the treble-hooked plug certainly catches tons of surf-running gamefish. Sporting-goods shops offer a wide assortment of these lures, and the selection ranges from large surface swimmers and subsurface wigglers, through poppers, darters,

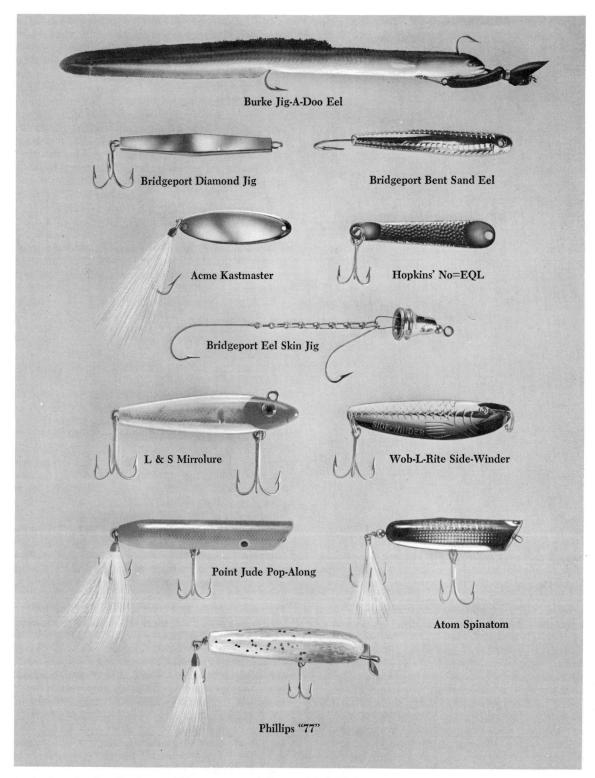

Burke Jig-A-Doo Eel

Bridgeport Diamond Jig

Bridgeport Bent Sand Eel

Acme Kastmaster

Hopkins' No=EQL

Bridgeport Eel Skin Jig

L & S Mirrolure

Wob-L-Rite Side-Winder

Point Jude Pop-Along

Atom Spinatom

Phillips "77"

A selection of surf-casting lures *All lures courtesy of Abercrombie & Fitch*

and torpedo-shaped types with no action other than that imparted by the angler's rod. The lures are manufactured of plastic and wood, and for heavy saltwater use the treble hooks are strung on end-to-end rigging. Plugs are effective on day or night tides.

Rigged Eels Rigged eels and eelskin rigs are most familiar to the striped-bass and bluefishing enthusiast of the North Atlantic Coast. The whole eel, a 10–14-inch specimen preferred, is strung with heavy nylon or linen when striped bass are the quarry. If bluefish are present, chain is used to keep these sharp-toothed marauders from chopping the bait into small pieces. Two or three single hooks are sewed in at the appropriate locations.

To differentiate between weighted and unweighted eel rigs, that with a leadhead is called an eel bob; the unweighted version is usually referred to as a whole eel. These baits are most effective at night when they are cast and retrieved slowly with a periodic pulsing of the rod tip.

Eelskin Rigs The eelskin rig is a far different lure, and two basic types concern the surf-caster. One, used in canals and estuaries where the current is strong and the lure is fished close to a hard bottom, is simply the skin of an eel fitted over a double-hooked, hollow-headed lead jig. Water, passing through the jig's hollow head, inflates the skin and gives it action.

On sand beaches the eelskin is often used in conjunction with a keeled squid. Here, a ring is soldered to the jig so that the skin can be attached. This lure rides higher than the hollow-headed type and works above the sandy bottom. Both lures are most effective during the hours of darkness, although they often take fish in broad daylight. While famous for execution on striped bass and bluefish, eel rigs will take other inshore gamefish.

Soft plastic baits are relatively new on the surf-fishing scene; yet they have succeeded in catching fish and may soon become as important as the old favorites. Plastic eels and seaworms, some of them fitted with wobble plates to insure swimming action, have earned the admiration of saltwater anglers.

All of the artificial lures favored by surf-casters are manufactured in a wide range of weights and sizes. Many simulate specific bait species, and others (among them some of the most effective) rely on action alone.

RIGS AND BAITS

The striped bass, that unpredictable surf-fish with a host of admirers on America's Atlantic and Pacific coasts, will eat just about any marine tidbit that happens along. The striper's bill of fare includes herring, menhaden, anchovies, mackerel, bullheads, sand launces, and any other small fish—including baby stripers. In addition, no crab, clam, shrimp, squid, worm, eel, sandbug, or chicken lobster is safe if a bass is hungry.

Channel bass are nearly as catholic in their tastes, although—as they grow to trophy size—the big reds are primarily bottom feeders. Bluefish have been likened to animated chopping machines; they seem to kill for the sheer love of killing and will attack a wide variety of marine bait species.

Obviously, the fish that frequent inshore waters may be baited with many natural offerings. It is the angler's task to determine which of the tempters is most in demand at the moment. All of the various gamefish tend to be selective.

Among common and useful bottom rigs for bait-fishing, first on the list is the fishfinder rig (*which see*). This is a simple, sliding sinker arrangement which permits the biting gamester to move off with the hook and line while the sinker remains anchored. The rig is most effective on bottoms that are not swept by heavy currents; there the pressure of water on the line creates considerable drag and cancels out the benefit of the fishfinder.

Anglers seeking red drum or black drum, neither of which species is particularly adverse to dragging a sinker attached to a bait, use a three-way swivel with the hook attached to a short leader and the sinker to another and even shorter trace.

Choice of sinker shape and weight is of major importance in surf-fishing. On sand or mud bottom the pyramid type with its sharp, angled edges is most likely to hold. Where rocky outcrops or coral are obvious, use the dipsey or bank sinker, which is rounded and so less likely to foul. Sinker weights will range from about 1 ounce, on up to 4–6 ounces, with the heavier rigs necessary wherever pounding surf and strong currents predominate.

Baits can be lifted off the bottom—out of the range of bottom-feeding trash fish, or to lure gamesters feeding several feet over the bottom—by attaching a small float just ahead of the hook. Sometimes the cork or balsawood float can aid in luring a hungry fish, and for that reason it is often painted bright red or yellow.

A technique that often produces strikes is the presentation of a live baitfish on a fishfinder rig. Hook the baitfish through the tough skin just ahead of the pelvic fins, so that it will be able to maintain balance in the water, even though held in one place by the restraining line and sinker.

Proper choice of hook patterns and sizes is important in bait-fishing, with size often most critical. The angler who is seeking school stripers, for example, will be most successful if he uses a hook in the 1/0–3/0 size range. If large bass are expected, choose hooks ranging 6/0–8/0— depending also on the type of bait employed.

Natural presentation is of major importance. Seaworms bunched on a hook may take a hungry fish, but the wary and selective gamester is more likely to accept a worm that has been threaded well up on the hook shank so that it streams naturally in the current. Always use fresh bait. Remember that a stale, bleached-out offering discharges little of its fresh, basic scent into the surrounding water. Most gamefish rely on their sense of smell as well as their eyes to locate food.

SURF-FISHING TECHNIQUE

The surf-caster must be both hunter and fisherman. Whatever his quarry, it will be necessary for the angler to search for the most promising locations and then take due notice of signs which indicate the presence of feeding gamesters. Tide, wind, weather, and water conditions must be taken into account.

Upon visiting an unfamiliar beach, the experienced surf-fisherman launches a quiet reconnaissance. If possible, he surveys the area during a period of low tide when the location of inshore holes, gullies, and sloughs are easily determined. These will serve later on as the aquatic highways of gamefish when the tide begins to flood back in. The points and bars which produce clashing rips at specific stages of the tide are worth particular attention, for here the bait-fish and other sea creatures will be tumbled and predators will lie in wait. Inlets or openings that pour water into the sea are potential hot spots, since they discharge hordes of bait as the tide ebbs. In such a spot the falling tide may be more productive for the fisherman than the flow.

Evidence of feeding fish is often graphic. You may see the gamesters rushing bait on the surface—or perhaps they will be betrayed by sudden, swift flurries of harried

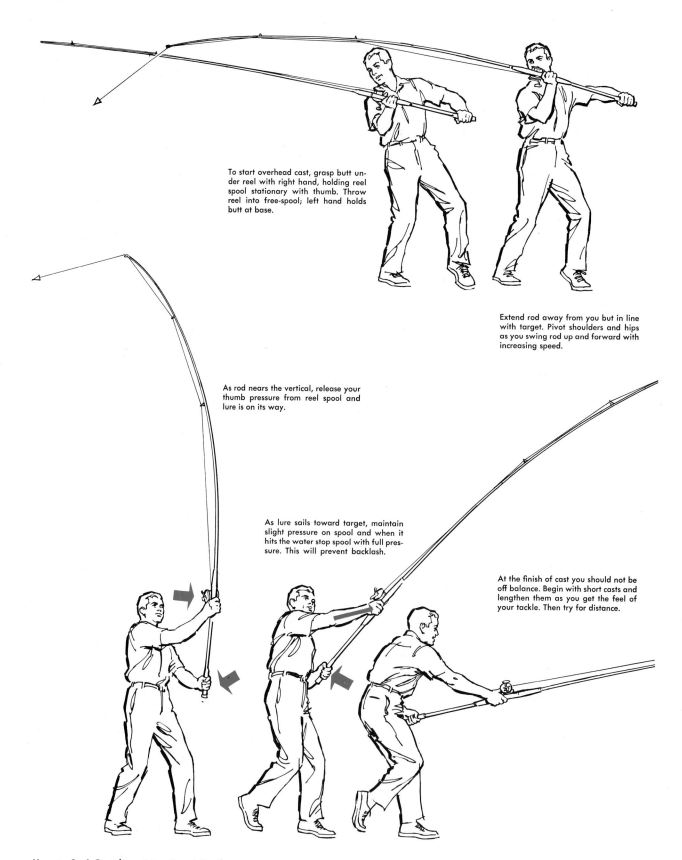

To start overhead cast, grasp butt under reel with right hand, holding reel spool stationary with thumb. Throw reel into free-spool; left hand holds butt at base.

Extend rod away from you but in line with target. Pivot shoulders and hips as you swing rod up and forward with increasing speed.

As rod nears the vertical, release your thumb pressure from reel spool and lure is on its way.

As lure sails toward target, maintain slight pressure on spool and when it hits the water stop spool with full pressure. This will prevent backlash.

At the finish of cast you should not be off balance. Begin with short casts and lengthen them as you get the feel of your tackle. Then try for distance.

How to Surf Cast (Revolving Spool Reel)

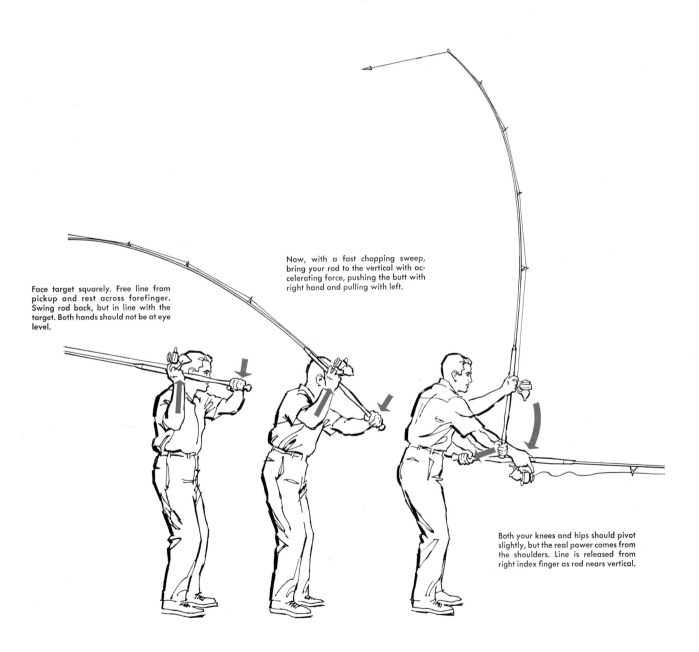

Face target squarely. Free line from pickup and rest across forefinger. Swing rod back, but in line with the target. Both hands should not be at eye level.

Now, with a fast chopping sweep, bring your rod to the vertical with accelerating force, pushing the butt with right hand and pulling with left.

Both your knees and hips should pivot slightly, but the real power comes from the shoulders. Line is released from right index finger as rod nears vertical.

Start side cast with body pivot from right heel. Shift weight to right.

Swing rod up in 45-degree plane with right hand pushing, left hand pulling.

As rod nears forward position, release line; follow through in line direction.

How to Surf Cast (Spinning Reel)

bait. Terns, herring gulls, and other sea birds gather in frantic gaggles over feeding fish. Indeed a single tern may pinpoint the quarry by pausing in its straightaway flight to dip down and then to swing around in a tight, exploratory circle.

Even at night, the surf-caster looks for "sign." A half-dozen flipping baitfishes on the beach may mean that predators are feeding close to shore. The slap of a gamester's tail can be distinguished through the hiss and crash of breakers. Some of the popular gamefish betray themselves to the angler who has a sensitive nose. Striped bass smell like thyme, bluefish throw off the aroma of fresh-cut melons, and channel bass exude an acrid, chemical scent.

Surf-fish often run close to the beach, searching for food right in the wash of the breakers. For that reason it pays to work a lure or bait all the way to the rod. The speed of retrieve may be varied until the ideal pace is rewarded by a strike. Note that retrieves are slowed to a minimum after dark.

In squidding, particularly where the lure is fished through the whitewater of breaking waves, the cast should be timed so that the artificial drops right behind an onrushing breaker. Begin the retrieve immediately, and keep the squid swimming in the water behind the tumbling wave which is relatively clear. Gamefish have a chance to see it there.

Most gamefish prefer to feed in "live water"; that is, where there is some current to stir bait. For that reason, look for action when the tide is rising or falling. The old rule is to fish "two hours before and two hours after the top of the tide." Don't leave it at that, though. A flurry of bait can produce sport at any time, and natural conditions may create ideal fishing conditions at any stage of the tide. Every successful beach fisherman is an opportunist.

Wind is no foe of the surf-caster. In fact the angler's chances are always brighter when the surface is disturbed. Some species will feed in tremendously rough water. It rarely gets too turbulent for striped bass, but it can be too calm and bright.

Since gamefish are selective, a change of artificials—or of bait—may trigger fast action. Sometimes a plug of one color will be scorned, while the same lure which is painted a different hue will draw immediate strikes. Fish feeding on the bottom are likely to ignore a surface-swimming lure, but may pounce on a jig bounced along on the sea floor. Sometimes a combination of lures hits the jackpot.

One of these, popular in many striped-bass fishing areas, and just as effective on weakfish, is the plug and dropper-fly combination. Use a swimming plug and a small fly or a single hook and strip of pork rind. Attach the fly or pork-rind-tipped hook to a short dropper tied to the loop of a longer leader snapped to a swimming plug. In theory a gamefish sees a small bait pursued by a larger bait—and can't resist beating the follower to the punch!

Where fish are concentrated in a specific area, say at the edge of a rip or in the turbulent water piling upon a bar, it may be unnecessary to impart motion to fresh bait. Usually, though, it pays to cast the bait well out and then bring it back toward the beach to cover a greater area.

This should be done slowly, with appropriate pauses, so that a striped bass, channel bass, surf perch, or any other inshore gamefish will have an opportunity to examine the offering.

Surf-casting from a small boat is profitable in many areas. While this should not be attempted unless the angler is familiar with sea conditions on the fishing grounds, or is casting from a boat skippered by a competent local guide, it is a highly effective method. Often lures or bait cast in toward the beach and retrieved through the onrushing waves generate a greater percentage of strikes than the same tempters cast from shore.

In some areas surfmen locate gamefish by aerial spotting, beach buggy (*which see*), or small-boat reconnaissance before they fish. When waters are reasonably clear, the larger gamesters can be seen from a low-flying light plane. They can also be spotted from the forward deck of a small boat proceeding at cruising speed. Beach buggies, of course, permit the angler to cover a great deal of territory and look for the obvious signs of feeding fish.

Surf-casting often is a "hurry up and wait" game. It always pays to question local anglers about the recent feeding habits of gamefish. If all hands have scored on the previous day's flood tide, by all means wait for a repeat of conditions. Sometimes the bass, blues—or whatever the quarry—will return exactly on time. Dawn and dusk are magic hours for surfmen, regardless of tide, but these periods are even more promising if they coincide with the flood.

STRIPED BASS

Four great gamefish are responsible for the tremendous interest in American surf-fishing—the striped bass, red drum, bluefish, and common weakfish.

The striped bass is most plentiful from the Chesapeake Bay region north to the Maritime Provinces on the Atlantic Coast, and from central California to Oregon on the Pacific seaboard. Large bass are haul-seined on the Outer Banks of North Carolina during the winter months, but these trophy fish are rarely hooked by local surfmen.

The surf-caster who seeks striped bass is a dedicated and highly enthusiastic angler who delights in the unpredictable nature of his chosen quarry. Bass are extremely selective; although they feed on a vast number of marine creatures, the species often harries one type of bait for a considerable period of time. Then, on a single tide, another bait may become the primary target.

Stripers are not regular feeders. They appear to gorge at an appointed time, all members of a school slashing into available bait, and then fast for hours or days. No pattern of feeding periods has been established, and individual fish take baits and lures at all hours of the day and night.

During the summer months, when water temperatures are high and the sun is brilliant, stripers may become more than normally nocturnal. In July, August, and early September, Atlantic Coast anglers often prefer to fish between dusk and dawn. The practice is forbidden by law in California.

Striped bass will strike surface, subsurface, or deep-going lures. When a large bass hits a surface lure it often cartwheels on top, slapping a broad and powerful tail.

Smaller bass occasionally come clear in a salmonlike leap, but this is not characteristic. The first run is powerful and determined, usually parallel to the shore rather than straight out to sea, and may peel 50–100 yards of line from the reel. Succeeding runs are shorter, and trophy bass often stubbornly position themselves broadside to the direction of line tension as they weaken.

Surf-casters lose stripers because they insist on fighting the fish from a tight reel drag. A bass of 30 pounds can part a 45-pound-test line if the angler attempts to hold the frantic battler. The drag should be set up only to that point where the hooks can be set, and the star should not be touched thereafter.

In beaching a large striper, the surfman uses wave action to accomplish his purpose. The fish should be kept coming while a breaker is carrying it shoreward, but allowed to drop back when the wave has tumbled and is receding. Proper timing and tension will cause the fish to ride ashore on a comber and to be deposited high and dry as the wave breaks. Don't wait for another comber to rescue the fish; get down there, fast! Tap your prize with a billy club, and drag it up above the high-tide markers.

RED DRUM

On a par with the striped bass as a truly great surf-fish is the red drum or channel bass of the Southern United States and the Gulf of Mexico. The redfish ranges from Maryland southward but is largest along the eastern shore of Virginia and the Outer Banks of North Carolina. Large drum are taken from the shores of South Carolina, Georgia, and northern Florida, but rarely approach the eye-popping weights of Virginia and North Carolina fish. Gulf of Mexico fish are smaller still, seldom exceeding weights of 30 pounds and averaging less than 10 pounds.

Most of the heavyweights are taken on natural baits, rather than on artificial lures, but the red drum will hit a plug, a metal squid, or a bucktail jig. Because the species has an inferior mouth it does not readily strike a surface lure.

Among the better natural baits used to tempt big channel bass are cut mullet and menhaden and whole or quartered crabs. These offerings are fished in sloughs along the beaches and are likely to produce on either the ebb or flow. Like so many inshore gamefish, the red drum prefers "live" water with enough depth to pursue its prey. During the fine spring and fall runs along the Virginia and North Carolina coast, these popular gamefish are taken on day and night tides.

When a channel bass takes a bait it often scoops it up without temperamental picking—and moves along in search of another tidbit. When hooked, the big redfish uncorks a powerful run, often straight out to sea. Pound for pound, the red drum is more powerful than the striped bass but lacks the speed and surface antics of the latter. The channel bass's fight is characterized by brute power and a tendency to bulldog toward bottom; they resist to the last any effort to ride them ashore on a wave.

BLUEFISH

If the bluefish grew to weights comparable to those attained by trophy stripers and red drum it would be the champion of all surf-running gamefish—including, perhaps, the famed roosterfish of the South American coast. The chopper is clean-lined, fast, vicious, and powerful. For a great many saltwater anglers, this fish is unsurpassed on a light surf rod.

Bluefish are virtually worldwide in distribution, but they do not appear along the United States Pacific Coast. On the Atlantic seaboard they are plentiful during the peak of their cycle, from the Gulf of Mexico to southern Massachusetts. Wherever blues swarm into the surf, there you will find bluefishing addicts.

This swift welterweight ordinarily travels in huge schools and ravages all bait in its path. Therefore, when a bluefish invasion is reported, anglers rush to the beaches and hurl tin squids at the slashing battlers. When choppers are frenzied, almost any lure tossed in front of them will draw an immediate strike. They can be selective, though, and a surf-caster is then forced to try various artificials at different depths, perhaps even go to cut or whole bait on the bottom.

The strike of a bluefish is sharp, vibrant, and decisive. Sometimes the chopper jumps like a salmon immediately after the barb goes home. More powerful and far swifter than either the striper or channel bass, blues are the mighty midgets of the surf. They grow to approximately 20 pounds on the Atlantic Coast and have been reported to reach 45 pounds in the Mediterranean.

This surf-running marauder will take plugs, but often manages to shake free of treble hooks. The most effective weapon in a caster's arsenal is the block tin squid with a single hook. Use a short wire leader, and beware of those forever chopping jaws when you bring a blue to beach.

WEAKFISH

When weakfish are at the peak of their periodic cycle of scarcity and abundance, they provide grand sport for surf-fishermen along the Atlantic Coast from Chesapeake Bay to southern Massachusetts. In off years the fish is caught incidentally by anglers seeking striped bass or other surf-running species.

The southern counterpart of the weakfish, or spotted seatrout, is plentiful south of Chesapeake Bay. They are taken in the surf of Virginia, North Carolina, South Carolina, Georgia. Further south, and through the Gulf of Mexico, spotted seatrout are the most popular of saltwater gamefish.

Although the weakfish occasionally grows to 17–18 pounds, it is a light-tackle fish—made to order for the light-to-medium spinning or popping rod. Metal squids, bucktails, and small plugs are the favored artificials, with shrimp, seaworms, mummichogs, and other minnows most often used as natural bait.

The weakfish has a soft mouth—hence its name, and one of the reasons why light tackle is recommended. A weakie hits lure or bait with a solid smash and then launches a short, fast run. At the end of this initial dash, the fish often swirls on the surface and, gradually, yields to rod pressure. To be successful, though, the angler must play his quarry with extreme care—or chance tearing the hook out of its fragile mouth.

Catch a striped bass, a red drum, bluefish, or weakfish and you will have bested one of the Big Four among surf-

Surf-Casting and Surf-Spinning Reels: (*top row*) the Shakespeare 2091, Quick Super 270, Shakespeare 2080, (*second row*) Penn 700, Zebco 870, Mitchell 402, (*third row*) the Garcia-Mitchell 600, the Penn 200, the Ocean City 903, the Penn 140M, (*bottom*) the Pflueger Sea King 2288, the Ocean City 905. Reels courtesy of Shakespeare Co., Bradlow, Inc., Penn Fishing Tackle Co., Zebco Corp., Abercrombie & Fitch, True Temper Corp., Pflueger Corp.

fish. These are the classic species, perhaps because they were first to thrill a multitude of anglers who delight in solitude, the sea beach, and the tumbling breakers. There are others, a few of which may some day rightfully be ranked among the greats. South America's astonishingly fast and powerful roosterfish has already earned the respect of surfmen who have challenged it from the beach.

—F.W.

SURFPERCH Family Embiotocidae Discussed in California Fish Bulletins 88, *A Revision of the Family Embiotocidae (the Surfperches)* by F. H. Tarp; 91, *Common Ocean Fishes of the California Coast* by P. H. Roedel; and 109, *The Barred Surfperch (Amphistichus argenteus Agassiz) in Southern California* by J. G. Carlisle, Jr., J. W. Schott, and N. J. Abramson. There are 23 species, many of which are important to the sport and commercial fisherman. Their range is from Baja California to Japan, with no species found throughout the range although two species range from Baja California to southern Alaska. All bear live young. There are two Japanese species. They are 5–18 inches long and live in shallow waters or in the surf in the ocean proper, in tidepools or in bays, except for one to be found in freshwater streams of northern California and one in deepwater. The color usually varies with the species although most are silvery.

The anal fin of the male has a large, prominent, glandlike oval structure opening to the front or a ray, usually the twelfth, enlarged and bony, resembling a strong, triangular plate with serrated edge and the next following ray somewhat modified or a large oval depression, with a well-defined rim, in front of the anal fin on the body and an oval glandlike body with an anterior horn developed on each side of the fin. The female has some modification of the anal-fin rays.

The common names indicate various habitats; those in the ocean but not primarily in the surf are "seaperch"; those in the surf are "surfperch"; those varying in habitat are "perch."

LIFE HISTORY

Mating takes place in the spring or summer near the time a brood is spawned. The sperm is carried by the female until late fall or winter when the eggs are fertilized. The 8–113 young develop in membranous sacs and receive nourishment from the ambient ovarian fluid. The young are about 1–2 inches long and look like adults except that there are vascular, diaphanous dermal folds or extensions among the ends of the rays of the vertical fins. Mating fish take on new or accented coloration. Copulation has been observed as, facing in the same direction, the male and female swim on their sides, vent to vent, over a sandy bottom in shallow water.

Surfperch feed on sandbugs, clams, eggs of fishes, crabs, polychaetes, amphipods, isopods, and fish.

ANGLING VALUE

Surfperch can be caught still-fishing or by drifting bait along bottom in surf or tidal currents over rocky or sandy bottom. The ghost shrimp (*Callianassa*) is excellent bait, but clam necks, mussels, pileworms, prawn chunks, or cut fish are effective. One surfperch, *Micrometrus*, is herbivorous. An important sport fish, different species predominate in different coastal districts. The family contains the most important surf-fish in California. Various species are fished for throughout the Pacific Coast.

See also Barred Surfperch, Black Perch, Calico Surfperch, Guadalupe Perch, Island Seaperch, Kelp Perch, Pile Perch, Pink Seaperch, Rainbow Seaperch, Redtail Surfperch, Rubberlip Seaperch, Shiner Perch, Silver Surfperch, Spotfin Surfperch, Striped Seaperch, Tule Perch, Walleye Surfperch, White Seaperch   —J.R.

SURF SMELT *Hypomesus pretiosus* This smelt (*which see*) spawns in fresh- as well as saltwater. Found from Prince William Sound, Alaska, to Monterey Bay, California. The

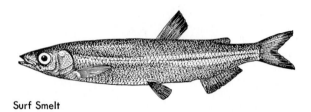

Surf Smelt

male is smaller than the female. Distinguished by the silvery or dusky band along the side of the body and the dorsal-fin origin in front of that of the pelvic; a high midlateral scale count. Greenish on back with silvery sides. Females produce about 1,800–37,000 eggs. Length to 10 inches. Used as bait, in commercial and sport fishing.

ECONOMIC VALUE

Caught throughout the year. Taken by sportsmen with small nets in the surf. *See also* Smelt   —J.R.

SURGEONFISH *See* Blue Tang

SUWANNEE BASS *Micropterus notius* This species was first distinguished by biologists from the University of Florida in 1941 at Ichtucknee Springs in Columbia

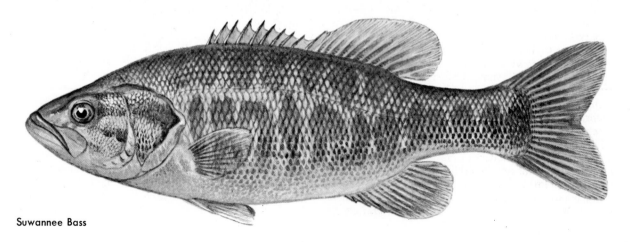

Suwannee Bass

County, Florida. Since that time it has been located by other workers in Florida in the Santa Fe River, the Withlacoochee River (in Madison County), and the main body of the Suwannee River to its mouth. Essentially a stream bass, the species is unique in tolerating the highly acid and low-fertility habitat of the Suwannee River.

It has markings similar to the redeye and spotted bass and other characteristics more like the smallmouth bass. The sublateral dark streaks of the redeye-spotted basses are imperfectly developed and only regularly aligned in the region of the tail. The shallow, notched dorsal fin, the deep body, and the vertical elongation of the lateral blotches are similar to the redeye-smallmouth complex. The spot at the base of the tail fin and the broadened lateral blotches can be likened to the markings of the spotted bass. The one unique marking of this species is the bright blue on the lower anterior parts.

ANGLING VALUE

It is of little value to fishermen. The Suwannee bass seldom attains a length of 10 inches or a weight of 12 ounces, however, individuals up to 2½ pounds have been taken. Unlike other bass species, which tend to lie and feed along the deeper edges of a river around brush and undercuts, the Suwannee bass always remains in midstream. Subject to extreme fluctuation, often 20–30 feet below its banks in dry periods, the Suwannee provides its best fishing when the water is low and the fish are concentrated. *See also* Black Bass —K.B.

SWARM A collective name for a number of eels; i.e., "a swarm of eels"

SWEDEN Sweden is a nation of ardent anglers and some of the precision-built tackle manufactured in this country by ABU is world famous. Sweden covers an area of 175,000 square miles, of which 8 percent is rivers and lakes, not including its extensive Baltic shores. This is not a country that many tourists visit specifically for the purpose of fishing, yet various other attractions make it a popular vacation spot. Perhaps the most popular sport here in terms of total rod catch is fishing for northern pike and perch. There is also a limited mileage of sea trout and Atlantic salmon water along the east coast, and a few quality streams in Lapland for grayling, brown trout, and char. Smallmouth bass have been introduced from North America on an experimental basis in two lakes.

The Atlantic salmon which once occurred in about 50 river systems has been seriously affected by hydroelectric development in Sweden; less than half of these streams carry more than a token population today. The salmon are confined to the Baltic and the main feeding areas are in the sea proper, where the species has been heavily exploited by the nets of commercials from several countries. Pollution is also a factor in its decline. An intensive program of hatchery-reared smolts (2-year-olds), which comprises about 2 million fish annually, has artificially maintained Sweden's salmon production.

The European grayling (*Thymallus thymallus*) is found in rivers from the Dalalven in the south to the Finnish border in the north. South of this area there is grayling in the Lake Vattern and Klaralven watersheds. Although the species inhabits both rivers and lakes in the northern part of its range, in the south it appears only in rivers. Grayling also occur in brackish water along the coast of

Sweden from just south of Sundsvall Bay north around the Gulf of Bothnia and down the Finnish coast. In some areas these Baltic populations were once so abundant that they provided a considerable commercial fishery. The Swedish record for grayling is 7 pounds, 7 ounces taken in Rastojaure (1970), which is about 300 miles north of the Arctic Circle.

Brown trout and char commonly inhabit the same waters in northern Sweden. In the deep and cold water of Lake Vattern a stock of char (*Salvelinus alpinus*) has survived since the period after the Ice Age. The char is the most important fish in the lake, an average yield being some 90,000 pounds a year. Char weighing 8 and 10 pounds have been caught, but the average is less than a pound. Vattern has also been stocked with rainbow trout.

The Morrum River is Sweden's most productive salmon and sea trout water. Fish are large but not numerous

In northernmost Sweden (Norrland)—in the districts of Jamtland, Vasterbotten, Norrbotten, and Lapland—the best time for angling is ordinarily July and August. The rivers in this area are affected by snow runoff, which may hold water levels high until mid-July. In southern Norrland and the middle districts of Sweden fishing begins in June; south of here (Morrum) the fishing begins with the first sea-trout run in May. It is usually snowy and cold at that time.

Morrum River The Morrum River is Sweden's most outstanding salmon and sea-trout fishery. Many foreign visitors as well as local anglers fish the Morrum. The total rod catch runs a modest 700–800 salmon and sea trout each year. However, average sizes are high. Angling begins on April 1st and continues through September. The best fishing occurs in April when the bulk of the catch consists of sea trout, some going 24 or 25 pounds in weight (33 pounds is the local record). A small run of salmon also begins in May, and fish of over 30 pounds are not uncommon. An autumn run of sea trout commences again in September, which though numerically smaller than the spring migration often provides exceptionally large fish.

Both spinning and fly-fishing are permissible and the majority of fish are caught on spoons and other metal lures. Fishing is done from the banks, platforms, and in some places by wading. During peak periods the Morrum gets considerable rod pressure. Permits to fish the Morrum can be obtained from the Fishing Office in Morrum village.

Dalalven River The Dalalven is fairly wide and swift in comparison to the Morrum. The only fishable stretch is the last two miles near its mouth at Alvkarleby. This water is subject to fluctuation by a hydroelectric dam. Salmon, sea trout, grayling, and pike inhabit the Dalalven. Salmon up to 50 pounds have been caught, but the number and size of fish taken in recent years has declined. The average weight of sea trout is about 4 pounds as compared to the Morrum's 8–9 pounds.

Permits to fish the Dalalven can be obtained in the village of Alvkarleby from the Fishing Office.

Indalsalven River The Indalsalven River offers some salmon fishing. A 55-pound fish was caught here in 1961. The season extends from April 1st through September, with the peak run in June. Accommodations can be found in Bergeforsen, Vardshusbacken, and in Sundsvall.

Sallsjon Lake Fishing in Lake Sallsjon and also in ponds and streams in the nearby mountains is available through Stafjo Turistgard, a country inn at Stavsjobruk. Fly-fishing for brown trout and char is the principal sport. Permits are obtainable at a low fee at the hotel. The season here is from July 1st–September 1st.

Grovel River Situated in the northwest part of Dalecarlia Province at the village of Grovelsjon near the Norwegian border, Lake Grovelsjon is a popular tourist attraction and is the source of the Grovel River. The fishing is for brown trout which occasionally reach a weight of 5 pounds. The average is much smaller. The season is from July 1st–September 1st. Fishing permits can be obtained at a low fee.

Osterdalalven River This river is very wide and shallow in parts, and can be fished either from a boat or by wading. There are mainly grayling, which can weigh up to 3 pounds, and brown trout. During August large brown trout migrate upstream from Lake Siljan, and these fish, which are usually caught by spinning, have been recorded to 19 pounds. The best fishing season depends on the level of the water. Normally it extends from the beginning of July until the middle of September. Fishing cards can be obtained for a small fee through Salens Hogfjalls Hotell, which also provides guides.

Ljungan River Ljungdalen is one of the most northwesterly of the villages of Harjedalen and is surrounded by magnificent mountain country. The Ljungan River has its source above the village. The fishing is mainly for brown trout. It also is possible to reach other lakes and streams on foot from here. In some of these small waters fairly large fish are caught. Fishing permits can be obtained at the hotel.

Lofsjon Lake Situated near Lofsdalen, one of the prettiest villages in Harjedalen Province, the lake has several good fishing waters in the vicinity. There is brown trout and grayling fishing available in Lofsan, Randaan, and other nearby streams. Browns weighing 2–3 pounds are sometimes taken in the Randaan, which offers good opportunities for dry fly-fishing. The season lasts from the beginning of July until September 1st. Accommodations are available in Lofsdalen.

Ljusnan River The Ljusnan River is near Tannas, a small village among the Harjedalen mountains, with a beautiful view of the Norwegian frontier. There is brown trout and grayling fishing in the Ljusnan and also in the Tannan and Myskelan rivers. Angling in these waters starts at about midsummer (June 23rd), and continues until September 1st. Trout up to 14 pounds have been caught in years past. The grayling seldom exceed 2 pounds. Fishing cards can be obtained for the Tannan and Myskelan. The Ljusnan River fishing is free. The only accommodation locally is in Tannas.

Skelleftealven River There is good brown trout and char fishing in this Lapland river between Lakes Vuoggatjalmejaure and Sadvajaure. In Lake Vuoggatjalmejaure there are very large brown trout, and it is possible in the course of a day to reach the upper part of the Ranekjokk River, which also holds big trout. The best time is from the middle or the end of July until the end of August according to the level of the water. Fishing permits must be obtained in advance from the Vasterbotten Tourist Association (Nygatan 25, 90247 Umea). The better accommodations are Hotell Malmia and the Stadsshotellet, both in Skelleftea.

Pitealven River There is excellent fishing in the Pitealven River at Vasterfjall above Lake Tjeggelvass, and also near Vildok higher up the river. The angling is for brown trout, char, and grayling. Very large grayling and also big brown trout have been taken with the fly. Waders are suggested.

Accommodations are available at the Miekak Camp in the form of 21 housekeeping cottages. This camp is modern and well planned. It is located near the Pitealven River headwaters and provides better than average fishing. It is reached by air from Arjeplog. All arrangements for transportation, cottage, and fishing licenses can be made through Turistflyg (Arjeplog AB, Drottninggatan 3).

Umealven River This outlet of Lapland's Lake Storuman offers a short stretch (2 miles) of strong, rocky river which is difficult to wade. The fish are principally brown trout. In August one can catch very large browns which migrate down the river from Lake Storuman. The water is owned by the Storuman Angling Club, which sells fishing cards at a low fee. The season lasts from the middle or end of July until September 1st, depending on the level of the water. Accommodations in Storuman.

Vindelalven River Usually fished from the resort town of Ammarnas, the best accommodation here is at the Ammarnasgarden. Angling is most productive in the

Vindelalven River above Ammarnas. There is good water also in the Tjulan River and in nearby small streams and lakes. The Vindelalven produces brown trout, char, and grayling. Big fish have been taken with the dry fly. The season is from the end of July to September 1st. Fishing permits must be obtained in advance from the Vasterbotten Tourist Association (Nygatan 25, 90247 Umea).

SALTWATER FISHING

Deep-sea angling of the head-boat variety is a popular form of fishing in Scandinavia. The chief quarry is cod, mackerel, plaice, ling, and skate. The main port in western Sweden is Varberg. The fishing grounds are at Fladen, which is a 20-square-mile oceanic reef. Daily trips are offered by Elbe-Produkter during the months of June through August and on weekends throughout the year. Elbe has a half-dozen well-equipped boats for what is usually an 11-hour trip including running time. Tackle can be hired. Hotel accommodations can be made by Elbe in Varberg.

Some sea trout are caught by boat-fishing in the fjords, particularly Abyfjorden, Koljefjorden, and Hakefjorden. Boat services are available in Mollosund, Sjallbacka, Grebbestad, and Lysekil. —A.J.McC.

SWIVEL A component of terminal tackle which basically consists of two metal eyes joined by a pin so that the unit can revolve freely. When connected between line and leader, or leader and lure, a swivel prevents to a greater or lesser degree the torsion produced by a rotating lure or bait, and thereby eliminates or decreases twist in the line. The greater the lure's resistance in the water, the more pressure is exerted on the swivel; thus its size, the number employed, and efficiency of the individual design are factors the angler must consider.

Three-Way Swivel

Swivels are used primarily in trolling, bait casting, spinning, surf casting, and with certain bottom fishing rigs (*see* fishfinder). The most common device is the snap

SWIVEL SPECIFICATIONS

Luxon Safety Snap Swivels

Size Number	4/0	3/0	1/0	1	3	5	7	10	12
Wire diameter (inches)	.070	.062	.056	.050	.045	.040	.033	.025	.021
Eye diameter (inches)	.250	.250	.210	.180	.150	.105	.091	.073	.056
Pound test	195	143	120	100	85	70	42	25	20

Kelux Interlock Snap Swivels

Size Number	4/0	2/0	1	3	5	7	10	12
Wire diameter (inches)	.080	.064	.051	.040	.040	.033	.026	.021
Eye diameter (inches)	.221	.191	.150	.136	.113	.098	.063	.060
Pound test	350	225	150	100	100	75	60	40

Kelux Lockfast Snap Swivels

Size Number	4/0	2/0	1	3	5	7	10
Wire diameter (inches)	.080	.064	.051	.040	.040	.033	.026
Eye diameter (inches)	.221	.191	.150	.136	.113	.098	.063
Pound test	350	225	150	100	100	75	60

Luxon Barrel Swivels

Size Number	5/0	4/0	3/0	1/0	1	3	5	7	10	12
Wire diameter (inches)	.080	.070	.062	.056	.050	.045	.040	.033	.025	.021
Eye diameter (inches)	.300	.250	.250	.210	.180	.150	.105	.091	.073	.056
Pound test	250	195	143	120	100	85	70	42	25	20

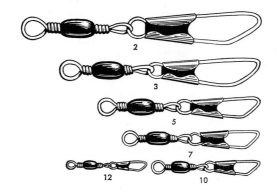

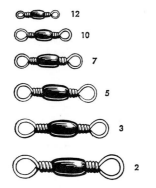

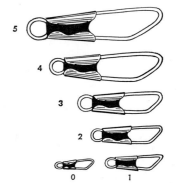

Safety Snap Swivels, Actual Size

swivel, which has the added feature of a metal snap that works on the same principle as a safety pin: when opened, the point of the snap can be slipped through the eye of a hook or lure, thus making it easy to change baits without cutting the line. A snap swivel is essential with all spinning lures, not only to facilitate lure removal, but to prevent line twist. Swivels and snaps are made of brass, stainless steel, nickel-plated stainless steel, and nickel-plated

Big Game Swivel with Snap

brass; black and tobacco brown finishes are suggested for schooling species, such as the mackerels which strike bright metal at any point in the terminal tackle, particularly when a fish has been hooked.

SWORDFISH *Xiphias gladius* A marine species of considerable importance to sport fishermen and commercial

men alike, it is also called broadbill or broadbill swordfish. Of worldwide distribution in temperate and tropical seas, the swordfish is readily identified by the long, flat sword, which is much longer than the rest of the head behind it, the absence of pelvic fins, the presence of but a single keel on each side of the caudal peduncle, and the absence of scales in adults.

The body of the swordfish is deepest just behind the head, beneath the dorsal fin, whence it tapers posteriorly to the tail, and the sides of the body are rounded rather than flat. The dorsal fin is high and sickle-shaped and lacks the low posterior portion that is characteristic of the related istiophorids (*see* Billfish). The anal fin is likewise sickle-shaped, and the second dorsal and anal fins are quite small. The spear, or sword, is long and flat, much longer than the rest of the head, and lacks prickles. There is only a single keel on each side of the caudal peduncle. The pectoral fins are moderately long, anal pelvic fins are missing entirely.

The color of the swordfish is quite variable, ranging from dark brown or bronzy to grayish-blue or black above, and whitish below. The extent of the dark color also varies. In some individuals, it extends no more than halfway down the sides, while in others almost the whole body may be colored, with only a little dirty white on the underside. The lower parts of the sides of the head are generally whitish, and all the fins are dark.

The usual size of swordfish taken commercially in the United States is probably not over 200–250 pounds, but some huge ones have been caught, weighing over 1,000 pounds. One specimen boated at Iquique, Chile, by Lou Marron, was 1,182 pounds.

HABITS

The swordfish is a summer spawner, and apparently the majority of the breeding activity takes place in tropical regions. Fish caught in the northern fisheries of both the Atlantic and Pacific have undeveloped reproductive organs, and the longline catches in the equatorial Pacific are dominated by small fish less than 3 feet long (not including the sword). All this points strongly to a tropical location for the major breeding areas. Another spawning ground is located near Messina, Sicily, in the Mediterranean Sea. Eggs, larvae, and juveniles are well-known from this region. The very young larvae have both the upper and lower jaw of about equal length, and the dorsal fin is long and fairly high. As growth and development progress, the upper jaw grows more rapidly than the lower, resulting in the long and characteristic sword. At the same time, the posterior part of the dorsal fin disappears, and body scales develop. The scales, however, are transitory and soon disappear. By the time the little fish is 2–3 inches long, it is quite readily recognizable as a young swordfish, and at a weight of 5 pounds it has all the characteristics of the adult.

Along the Atlantic Coast of North America, in the northcentral part of the Pacific Ocean, and doubtless in other parts of the world also, swordfish carry out seasonal north-south migrations. They appear off New England and further north in late June and early July, remaining in that area through the summer. After that, they disappear, moving south and offshore into deepwater with the onset of winter. Until very recently, their winter habitat was unknown, but in the fall and winter of 1962 good catches of swordfish were taken by longlining in deepwater along the edge of the Continental Shelf south of Block Island and Long Island.

In general, the adults seem to prefer cooler waters and, except for spawning, do not generally frequent the truly tropical parts of the ocean, at least in the surface strata. At any rate, commercial fishermen in the Pacific find that swordfish are only sporadically caught in tropical regions and that most of these are quite small. This combination of migratory and breeding characteristics suggests strongly that swordfish probably do not breed every year.

It is said that the swordfish may enter freshwater on occasion. If this is true, it is one of the few large marine forms that does so. There are reports from European areas of swordfish being taken as much as 30–40 miles from the mouths of rivers, presumably well beyond the influence of saltwater. Most of the reports are quite old, however, and it may be that they are completely unreliable. In any event, there are no indications that swordfish ever enter freshwater along the American coast.

Like its cousins, the marlins and sailfishes, the swordfish feeds extensively on smaller fish, squids, and almost anything edible that it can capture. When taking a single individual item of food, the swordfish simply opens its mouth and engulfs the food. But when feeding on compact schools of fish, the sword is brought into play, slashing and maiming the prey which are then picked up, one by one, at leisure. Such items as dolphin, menhaden, mackerel, bonito, bluefish, herring, whiting, squid, and others have been found in swordfish stomachs, not to mention a few deepsea fishes.

The swordfish is of virtually worldwide distribution in warm and temperate waters. In the Atlantic, authentic records show that it ranges from Newfoundland south at least as far as Cuba and the Rocks of St. Paul, and from Iceland, the Baltic Sea, and Scandinavia to the southern tip of Africa, as well as in the Mediterranean, the Sea of Marmora, and the Black Sea. In the Indo-Pacific, this species is known from California to Chile (slightly south of Caldera) in the eastern Pacific, and from Japan to New Zealand and Australia on the west side, as well as from numerous locations throughout the Pacific Ocean. In the Indian Ocean, records are more sparse, but Durban, South Africa, Mauritius, and Reunion are among the places where swordfish have been landed by fishermen. It is probable that swordfish are to be found throughout the Indian Ocean as well as in the Atlantic and Pacific oceans.

FISHING METHODS

This is an important food fish, and is the object of large commercial fisheries. Many are taken by harpooning, for they are prone to lie basking at the surface, with the dorsal fin and the upper lobe of the tail sticking out of the water. After the fish has been struck with the harpoon, it is usual to let it run free, dragging a buoy or marker of

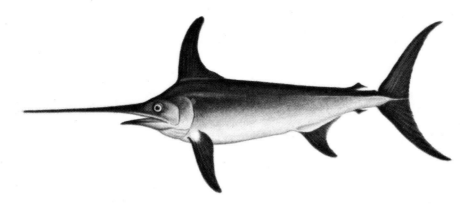

Swordfish

some kind attached to the harpoon line. When the fish is exhausted, the marker is picked up and the fish hauled in. Many swordfish are taken also by longlines, particularly in the Pacific. The longlines set especially for swordfish are usually fished at night, for night fishing with this type of gear brings much better returns than fishing during the day. In the Mediterranean, the swordfish is often caught in the tuna nets.

For anglers, trolling seems to be the most popular method of catching swordfish, although they may also be taken by still-fishing with live bait. Swordfish only rarely strike blind on a trolled bait. Generally, the fish is first seen on the surface. Then the trolled bait is presented carefully and as quietly as possible, for swordfish seem to be easily frightened by the approach of a boat. They seem also to be very finicky about taking a bait, and presentations may be made time after time before the fish either takes the bait or becomes alarmed and disappears.

—J.E.M.

BAITING THE BROADBILL

The method of baiting the broadbill is the same in all oceans. The squid, oceanic bonito, and small tuna are good baits. A double hookup is used. The forward hook is inserted below the gill, the second hook close to the tail. Large hooks, 14/0 or 16/0, are preferred. Off the west coast of South America 16/0 is better, since the fish run very heavy in these waters. The broadbill has a very soft mouth, and a big hook is needed so that it can hold better. Naturally, the big hook also gets a better bite in case of foul hooking whether it be in fin, body, or tail. The leader must be strong. The bill of this fish is a formidable weapon; therefore stainless-steel cable is essential. For general broadbill fishing the cable should have a breaking strength of 450 pounds, but if there are really big bruisers in the water, such as one finds in the Peru Current, a 900-pound-test is better. Thirty feet of cable is the preferred length, due to the tendency of the fish to wrap itself around the leader.

When stalking the broadbill one or two men stand in the crow's nest as lookouts. The boat cruises faster than at trolling speed since the bait is seldom tossed into the water until a fish is spotted. Most anglers prefer this method of stalking fish to blind trolling since it permits a rapid coverage of the area. The broadbill is fairly easy to spot because the fin and tail stand high out of the water and can be seen at a considerable distance. If it is definitely known that broadbill are in the area then it is wise to troll, often as deep as 400 feet, at which time the boat should proceed at a snail's pace while everybody aboard searches the area for a fin. The general procedure, however, is watchful cruising with the rod kept ready in the rod holder, bait and leader attached for immediate use. At the electric moment when a broadbill is spotted the angler picks up the rod and jumps into the chair, quickly attaching his harness. He now tosses the bait into the sea and proceeds to peel off about 200 feet of line. The bait should troll a good distance behind the boat. The mate stands in the stern and holds the line at approximately the 200-foot mark, between his thumb and first finger. The angler peels off another 75 feet of line which drags in the water forming a loop between the tip of the rod and the angler's finger. At the strike this loop permits a slow and uninterrupted dropback.

The boat should move at a very slow speed. The bait is kept approximately two feet under the surface and at no time is permitted to make a disturbance or a wake. The boat is maneuvered so that the bait is presented to the fish within 20–25 feet of its bill. Since the swordfish has a tendency to run in circles, it often turns away from the bait. When this happens the boat must maneuver repeatedly, until the fish dives for the bait. Any disturbance, such as the wake or motor vibrations, has a tendency to cause the fish to sound. The captain must use great precaution at this point; for instance, if the boat moves too fast or closes in precipitously the fish will sound. This does not necessarily mean it is gone forever. It may remain in the vicinity. The boat usually idles or slowly cruises the area, while everyone aboard is on the alert. This happened when the 1,182-pound record broadbill off Chile was spotted. The fish sounded, the area had to be stalked at least ½ hour before it reappeared. Drifting was necessary, and care was taken to cause no disturbance. After what seemed an eternity Eddie Wall, the guide, spotted the fish a little over a mile away.

HOOKING THE BROADBILL

The great moment comes when the fish spots the bait. The propulsion of its tail as it makes the dive is a never-to-be-forgotten thrill. The fish usually dives under and comes up to the bait. At this point the angler's attention is directed to the line on the spool of his reel. His fingers lie lightly on the spool to prevent a possible backlash as the reel is now in free spool. When the fish actually has the bait, there should be no disturbance or interference in the spilling out of line. Utmost caution and patience are necessary to hook the broadbill. The boat should be moving at about 3 knots, no more. The mate is tense with the line in his fingers. At the instant the fish smacks the bait, he lets go and shouts "strike." The boat is immediately thrown out of gear. Tense moments follow; the broadbill takes its time. The angler must sense the difference between the normal pulling out of the free-spool line by waves or tide and the usually slow but steady pull of the hooked broadbill. Occasionally a rapid pullout makes this a simple decision, but most often the hooked fish does not know it is hooked and the playout is slow and steady. When the angler is reasonably sure that the fish has taken the bait he signals the captain to go ahead. After the boat is in motion, the angler throws on the drag and strikes hard, again and again. The boat remains in motion until it is determined that the fish is hooked. From this point on fishing proceeds as usual with one exception. In the case of the broadbill, one never knows whether or not it is foul-hooked. That means that too tight a drag or a bad angle of the line or a jerky manipulation of the rod can tear the hook loose. More than ever the angler has to put up a steady tenacious fight.—L.E.M.

SWORDSPINE SNOOK *Centropomus ensiferus* This is the smallest and rarest of the snooks. It occurs in extreme southern Florida and southward throughout the American Atlantic tropics. Full-grown adults probably do not attain a total length of much more than 12 inches. The common and scientific name refer to the long, second anal spine. Two related species, *Centropomus armatus* and *C. robalito*, occur on the Pacific side of tropical America.

The swordspine snook has 49–59 lateral-line scales. Gillrakers 12–16 on lower limb of first arch, not including rudiments. Anal rays 6. Pectoral rays 14–16, usually 15. Second anal spine reaching beyond vertical from caudal base. Pectoral fin reaching to vertical from tip of pelvic. Pelvic fin reaching to or beyond anus. Maxillary not reaching beyond vertical from center of eye.

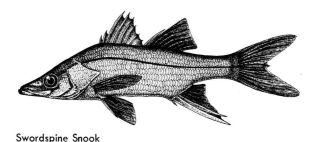

Swordspine Snook

In addition to its smaller size, this snook is distinguished from the other Atlantic species by the longer second anal spine and the fewer lateral-line scales.

ANGLING VALUE

This species occurs in estuaries and in the lower course of streams and canals. Despite its small size, the swordspine snook provides considerable sport when taken with light spinning or fly rod tackle. It will strike jigs, midget plugs, spoons, spinners, streamer flies, popping bugs, minnows, and live shrimp. The flesh is white, flaky, and of excellent flavor; it is small enough to be panfried. —L.R.

SYMBIOSIS The relationship of two dissimilar organisms that live together in close association. It may benefit one or both of the organisms; the association is called parasitic when it harms the host.

T

TACHOMETER Instrument used to measure the revolutions per minute made by the drive shaft.

TACKLE A collective term for all manufactured items of equipment used in connection with sport fishing. This includes rods, lines, reels, leaders, and lures. The two principal types of fishing tackle are *freshwater tackle* and *saltwater tackle*. These may be further identified according to function, such as *fly-casting tackle*, *spinning tackle*, *bait-casting tackle*, *big-game tackle*, or *surf-casting tackle*; or according to class, such as *ultralight-spinning tackle*, *medium bait-casting tackle*, or *heavy surf tackle*.

In boating, an assemblage of blocks and ropes used to obtain leverage in lifting or pulling. Among the various types of tackles used are the *gun tackle*, which consists of a pair of single blocks; the *luff* or *watch tackle*, which consists of a double and a single block with the weight to be moved attached to the latter; and the *single-whip tackle*, which has only a single block with the weight to be moved attached to the holding part of the rope.

TACKLE BOX A box usually made of metal or plastic, and sometimes of a hard wood such as mahogany, in which tackle can be stored. The box may be no more than a simple container with a lid or elaborately designed with

folding trays and compartments suitable for holding reels, lures, line spools, and other equipment. The best tackle boxes are waterproof, corrosion resistant, and have a high impact strength to prevent damage to the contents in travel. A small tackle box is more functional when fishing; large boxes are better suited to storing extra tackle at home or in camp. Metal boxes or metal parts, such as hinges and locks, should be oiled occasionally and hosed down if the box has been exposed to spray in saltwater fishing.

TADPOLE MADTOM *Noturus gyrinus* A small, yellowish-brown madtom with a tadpole-shaped body. No barbs on posterior edge of pectoral spine but with poison gland at its base. Lower jaw as long or nearly as long as upper. Caudal fin very rounded. Eye small. Adipose fin high but with no free lobe. The range of this madtom is from North Dakota to Quebec and south to Florida and Texas. Introduced into the Columbia River drainage.

Tadpole Madtom

LIFE HISTORY

The habitat of the tadpole madtom is stillwater of streams, lakes, marshes, and even springs. It is found hiding under stones and logs. Apparently mostly carnivorous, the tadpole madtom feeds on crustaceans, aquatic insect larvae, and some fish. This species spawns in early summer in the manner of others of the catfish family. The tadpole madtom seldom reaches a length of more than 4 inches.

ECONOMIC VALUE

Too small for value as food, the tadpole madtom is very tenacious of life when used for bait and is valued by bass fishermen. Its sting produces a sensation not unlike that of a bee sting. —R.A.J.

TAHOE SUCKER *Catostomus tahoensis* A large, dark-colored sucker with a large head. Color dark, with dusky fins. Mouth large. Lips moderate in size; upper pendant; the lower rather full. Scales small and crowded forward;

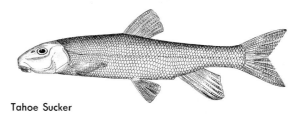

Tahoe Sucker

85–90 in the lateral line. Dorsal fin short and low with 10 rays. This species is native to the Lahontan system of Nevada and California.

LIFE HISTORY

The tahoe sucker is both lake- and stream-dwelling and appears to be the most abundant sucker within its range. Little is known of the food habits of this species. During the spring spawning season males develop a brassy coloration with a brilliant vermilion lateral stripe. One female is attended by as many as twenty-five males. Spawning occurs over a gravel nest amidst much thrashing and churning. The tahoe sucker reaches a length of 2 feet.

ECONOMIC VALUE

Although the flesh of this species is sweet and palatable, the amount of its use is unknown.　　—R.A.J.

TAILLIGHT SHINER *Notropis maculatus* The taillight shiner is a small, graceful, often reddish minnow seldom exceeding 2 inches in length, with a distinct large round spot at the base of the caudal fin. A small black spot also is present above and below the large caudal spot. The distinguishing characteristics of this minnow are a poorly developed lateral line which does not extend forward on the head; a lateral line scale count of 36–38 with 5 scale rows above and 3 below; not noticeably elevated lateral line scales; about 15 scales between back of head and the origin of the dorsal fin; 8 rays each in the anal and dorsal fins; and a pharyngeal tooth formula of 4-4. The head of the minnow is flattened above and the snout is rounded.

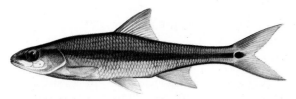

Taillight Shiner

The head is contained about 4½ times in the standard length and the eye is contained about 3½ times in the head. The mouth is small, terminal, and oblique. The body is slender, with the depth contained about 5 times in the standard length. The pelvic fins are abdominal in position. The color of the taillight shiner is pinkish-red above, paler below. There is a fairly prominent dark stripe from the tip of the snout to the base of the caudal fin, terminating in a distinct oval dark spot about the size of the eye. The posterior interradial membranes of the dorsal fin do not contain black pigment, and the lateral line scales have a black dot on each side of the lateral line pores.

LIFE HISTORY

The geographical range of the taillight shiner is from Missouri southward in the lowlands through Arkansas and southeastern Oklahoma to eastern Texas and Mississippi. On the Atlantic coast it is found from North Carolina southward to Florida. The taillight shiner is the most common shiner in the natural lakes of Florida. This minnow appears to prefer a hard sand-bottom habitat, with the water on the acid side. In North Carolina this fish prefers the deeper areas in the swift, blackwater streams, seldom being found in the shallow-stream areas.

The taillight shiner serves as forage for the largemouth bass, mud sunfish, warmouth, redfin pickerel, and redbreast sunfish. It is occasionally used as bait, but is not raised commercially.　　—D.E.L.

TAILRACE A river channel below a dam into which impounded waters are released. Tailrace fishing in the Southern United States is especially productive for brown and rainbow trout which thrive in the coldwaters below the hydroelectric dams in Arkansas, Missouri, Tennessee, and Kentucky.

TAIMEN *Hucho taimen* An Asian salmonid and a member of the same genus as the huchen (*which see*) but distributed from the Volga basin in the east to the Amur basin in the west. The taimen is fairly abundant in Siberian rivers and contributes to the inland commercial fishery of the U.S.S.R. The taimen resembles the huchen but differs in having a smaller number of gillrakers on the first arch (11–12). The taimen reaches a large size (over 150 pounds); it is not anadromous, living primarily in rivers where it feeds on other fishes.　　—A.J.McC.

TANGS Family Acanthuridae A large reef species, found throughout the world, which have little if any angling value. Some species are important food fish in Hawaii and Polynesia, such as the orangespot tang and the striped tang; however, the flesh of at least one is reportedly poisonous (the whiteline triggerfish). In Spanish-speaking countries, the tangs are known as *medico* and *barbero*, or doctor and barber, because of their razor-sharp caudal peduncle spines. When tangs are disturbed, the spines are erected and used in a slashing attack. These fish are characterized by their ovoid shape, which gives the appearance of looking the same in front or rear. *See* Blue Tang　　—A.J.McC.

TARAKIHI *Cheilodactylus macropterus* The tarakihi occurs throughout the coastal waters of New Zealand, but is most abundant in depths of between 40 and 100 fathoms. The main commercial catch comes from the east coast, especially from the southern half of the North Island and the northern half of the South Island. The tarakihi is also found off the southern half of the Australian coast and is known there as the jackass fish. It inhabits water over rocky, muddy, or sandy sea bottom, and it feeds on a variety of small bottom fauna. It grows to about 24 inches long.

The tarakihi has a compressed body and a roughly regularly curved outline. The greatest depth occurs a little behind the head and is rather less than half the length. The head is fairly small, with a slightly increased curvature where it joins the body. The mouth is small, and there are numerous rows of very small pointed teeth. The body is covered with large cycloid scales. The lateral line commences at the upper angle of the gill cover and follows the dorsal curvature of the body. The dorsal fin extends from just behind the head to the caudal peduncle and is composed of 18 spiny rays and 28 branched softrays. The caudal fin has 3 upper and 3 lower unbranched rays and 16 branched rays, and is deeply forked. The anal fin has 3 spines and 15 equal-length branched rays. The pectoral fins are roughly triangular and are large, the upper half being formed of 2 unbranched rays, with 7 branched rays below them, and the lower half by 6 unbranched rays, the uppermost of which is stouter and much longer than the others and extends back at least as far as the anus. The pelvic fins are midventral, commenc-

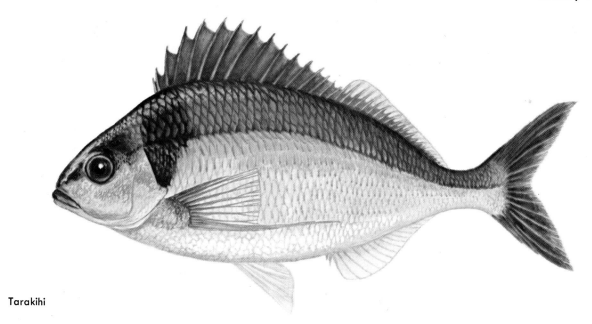

Tarakihi

ing in line about midway along the dorsal spiny rays. They have 1 fairly long spine and 5 branched rays, and reach back to the anus.

The names given to this fish both refer to the pectoral fin, the generic name to the long fin-ray and the specific name to the large size of the fin.

Coloring of the tarakihi is a light purplish-gray above the lateral line and silvery below it. There is a black saddle immediately behind the head extending down to the upper region of the gill cover. The fins may be slightly specked with dark pigment.

Another Australasian species, *Cheilodactylus douglasi*, known as the "porae" in New Zealand and as the "morwong" in Australia, is often confused with the tarakihi. It is generally found in warmer waters over the same types of sea bottom and grows to about the same size or rather larger. However, there are some readily distinguishable features. The porae has no dark saddle behind the head, and its color is greenish-silver flushed with yellow or pink above the lateral line, graduating to silver ventrally. The curvature of the body is more regular than that of the tarakihi; the lips are much thicker; and the long ray of the pectoral fin extends well beyond the anus. In New Zealand the commercial catch of porae is small compared with that of the tarakihi, and is included with the tarakihi for statistical records.

SPAWNING AND EARLY DEVELOPMENT

Spawning tarakihi have been trawled at depths of from 40-100 fathoms; the spawning grounds are usually near rocky coastlines where there are fairly strong currents and temperatures of between 15° and 18°C. Regions such as Cook Strait (between the North and South Islands of New Zealand) and off East Cape (midway along the east coast of the North Island) are two important spawning areas. The spawning season extends from March in the southern regions to early May in the more northern areas.

The female fish matures when it is about 4 years old and 10-11 inches long. The male fish may mature a year earlier when it is about 8 or 9 inches long, but most are 4

years old before they are ready for spawning. The sexes cannot be distinguished externally. The schools of fish are composed of both sexes of somewhat similar sizes in approximately equal numbers. Large numbers of small, colorless eggs are shed and fertilized in the water by the creamy-colored milt.

The early development is known only through experiments with artificially fertilized eggs. A very few juveniles of about 2 inches long have been netted in bays and harbors, and young fish of about 4 inches are caught only occasionally over the trawling grounds.

Eggs have been found down to a depth of 500 feet, but most have been taken between the surface and 150 feet deep. The egg is spherical, free-floating, and about 0.95 mm in diameter. The yolk, which contains a single oil globule, is colorless and almost fills the egg membrane. Embryonic development takes 2-3 days according to temperature—2 days at an average temperature of 17.5°C and 3 days at 14.5°C. On hatching the larva is about 3 mm long. All its organs except the paired fins are present in a rudimentary form, and the oval yolk sac (containing the anteriorly placed oil globule) reaches back to about half the total length of the larva. Distinctive pigment patches are also present, but at this stage the eyes are colorless.

The larva floats upside down near the surface for the first 12 hours, but later takes up the normal position and becomes an active swimmer. Its eyes are fully pigmented by the fourth day after hatching, and the pectoral fins become active a day later. The mouth opens on the fourth day and the gape rapidly widens. The yolk and oil globule are completely absorbed by the seventh or eighth day after hatching, and by this time the larva has grown to about 6 mm in length.

GROWTH RATE

As young specimens of tarakihi have rarely been caught, the growth rate during the first few years must be determined by some means other than by direct measurement. The scales, which form annual spawning or winter rings, are therefore used; and it is assumed that they grow proportionally with the increasing length of the fish. The largest and most clearly marked scales are found about ⅓ of the body length behind the head, and in this position they probably started to grow when the juvenile fish was about 1½ inches long. With the use of fish of known lengths and the measurement of the positions of the various rings from the point of origin of the scales and the scale lengths, the proportional growth rate can be calculated. These ratios can then be used to determine the length of the fish at the time of ring formation. (Taken into account is the initial juvenile length of 1½ inches before the scales commence to grow.) Calculations thus made agree closely with length measurements made of fish from the commercial catch, especially for fish up to a length of 13–14 inches. In the first year the fish grow to 4–5 inches, and thereafter they increase about 2 inches annually until they reach 10–12 inches; the rate of growth then becomes progressively slower and almost ceases by the time they reach a length of about 19 or 20 inches. A fish of 13–14 inches (the average commercial size) is usually about 6 or 7 years old.

FISH MOVEMENTS

A few observations on tagged fish have yielded limited information on the movements of tarakihi. However, some general trends have been noted. The fish apparently move in schools. There are seasonal inshore-offshore migrations, and during the two or three months before spawning, there is a marked movement toward the spawning grounds, which seem to be fairly clearly defined. Distance traveled apparently varies, but some fish have been found to travel at least 100 miles within a few months. After spawning there appears to be a return migration to the previous feeding grounds, but a considerable proportion continue along the coast in their pre-spawning direction.

LINE FISHING

Tarakihi are generally caught near reefs, but over fairly clear bottom in a depth of about 10–25 fathoms. They bite suddenly and vigorously. They play well on light tackle, but as the mouth is very soft, care must be taken not to strike too hard. Best fishing is at the turn of the tide. The fish make a brief squeak when being boated.

The line is usually made up with three traces, the highest one being about 6–9 feet above the sinker. The hooks must be small. Shellfish are the best bait, and chumming with fish or shellfish material also helps to attract them.

In shallow water the tarakihi are generally smaller than in deep water. In about 10–20 fathoms fish of about 8–12 inches are usual, but in deeper water the length of fish may be up to 18 or 20 inches or even bigger. A 10-inch fish weighs, on an average, about 10½ ounces; a 14-inch fish weighs about 1 pound, 10 ounces; and a 17½-inch fish weighs about 2 pounds, 10 ounces.

COMMERCIAL VALUE

This species occupies second place in the commercial catch in New Zealand (18.4 percent of the total weight in 1966 and 16.5 percent of the total value). It is caught almost exclusively by trawling. It is a popular species, is very palatable, and has a fairly high proportion of oil.

—M.K.McC.

TARPON *Megalops atlantica* Also called the tarpum, sabalo real, cuffum, silverfish, or silverking, this species belongs to a very primitive family (Elopidae) of bony fishes. Its nearest relative is the oxeye herring of the Indo-West Pacific. Like the ladyfish and the bonefish, it possesses an eel-like, leptocephalus larval stage. It occurs on both sides of the Atlantic; on the western side it has been taken as far north as Nova Scotia, although it does not regularly occur north of Cape Hatteras; it extends southward to at least Natal, Brazil. In the Eastern Atlantic it ranges from Senegal to the Congo.

The color is usually dark blue to greenish-black dorsally, shading to bright silver on the sides and belly. Specimens from inland waters sometimes display brownish or brassy colors.

Other distinguishing characters of the tarpon are body with almost vertical sides; dorsal outline of head nearly straight and horizontal, the back somewhat elevated; ventral outline strongly curved anteriorly; depth 3.4–4.3 in standard length. Scales large, firm with crenulate membranous border; 41–48 in lateral series. Lateral line complete, decurved anteriorly, the pores branched. Head moderately short and deep, its depth at middle of eye not quite twice its width at the same place; 3.2–4.7 in standard length. Eye 3.3–4.7 in head, much nearer to dorsal than to ventral profile. Mouth superior; mandible projecting far beyond the gape, entering dorsal profile in advance of mouth.

Dorsal fin high anteriorly with 13–15 softrays, the last ray greatly elongated; origin of fin about equidistant between base of caudal and anterior margin of eye. Caudal fin deeply forked, the lobes about equal in length, generally somewhat longer than head. Anal fin somewhat elevated anteriorly with 22–25 softrays, the last ray

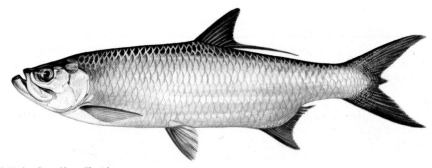

Tarpon, 94-pound Male, Pine Key, Florida

Tarpon, 145-pound Female, Loggerhead Key, Florida

elongated in adults, its base 4.6–5.6 in standard length. Pelvic fin rather large, inserted more than an eye's in advance of origin of dorsal and somewhat nearer to base of pectoral than to origin of anal. Pectoral fin rather long with 13–14 softrays, 1.2–1.4 in head. Axillary scale of pectoral rather small, only about a third of the fin length.

LIFE HISTORY

The tarpon is one of the most prolific of all fishes; a single large female may contain more than 12 million eggs. Spawning probably takes place in shallow, estuarine waters any time from May to September, at least in Florida. It is a very euryhaline species, often being found in purely fresh water. It seems to prefer the lower salinities of estuaries and the mouths of large rivers. It reaches a very large size; an individual over 8 feet long with an estimated weight of 350 pounds was taken from the Hillsborough River Inlet, Florida.

The tarpon's rate of growth is relatively slow. It probably does not attain sexual maturity until it is about 6 or 7 years old and attains a length of about 4 feet. Individuals weighing 100 pounds are probably 13–16 years of age. The young fish are common in small brackish or freshwater streams. As they grow larger they move into the larger streams and estuaries. They are carnivorous and are known to feed upon mullet, silversides, marine catfishes, and blue crabs. Tarpon are generally not eaten in the United States, but are highly esteemed for their food value in Central America. —J.C.B.

TACKLE FOR TARPON

The basic method of fishing for tarpon is to still-fish or drift with live or dead mullet, crabs, shrimp, or pinfish. However, trolling is more popular in many ports along the Gulf Coast. The standard charter-boat tackle for trolling is a 50-pound-test outfit with the terminal end protected by a No. 9 stainless-steel leader (104-pound test) to which are attached plugs, spoons, feathers, and various natural baits such as mullet, squid, and pinfish. Many skillful anglers troll with 20-pound-test gear and sometimes even lighter, depending on the size of the fish and the absence or presence of sharks. The usual trolling plugs are jointed or lipped swimmers in a 6-inch length and weighing 1½ ounces. Feathers and spoons, of course, are comparably large.

For the man who fishes simply for the enjoyment of jumping tarpon and the remoter possibility of boating one, either the bait-casting rod, spinning rod, or fly rod can be used. These should all be heavy-duty outfits designed for saltwater casting. The popular choice is a 6-foot plugging stick with a stiff tip and a service reel with 200 or more yards of 15-pound-test monofilament, or 18-pound-test braided line. A spinning rod of 6½–7 feet capable of working ⅝-ounce plugs and a reel that will spool 12-pound-test line is about right.

There are various ways of protecting the end of the line from chafing against the tarpon's rough body. The securest rig for the plug-caster is a short length of 100-pound-test cable leader (12–15 inches) spliced through a leader sleeve to 5 feet of 40–50-pound-test monofilament. The wire can take all the rasping of a giant tarpon's jaws while the heavy monofilament protects the casting line from its flanks. Some casters use a "shock" line by splicing 15 inches of 20-pound-test, 15 inches of 30-pound-test, and 30 inches of 40-pound-test monofilament to the end of a 14-pound-test monofilament casting line and eliminate the wire. But other terminal minimums and maximums are regionally popular, as there are many different situations and corresponding techniques depending on the size and location of the fish.

FLY-FISHING FOR TARPON

Fly-fishing for giant tarpon is considered the supreme thrill of angling by many veteran fishermen. The standard fly tackle is heavy. Tarpon in the 50–150-pound class require, first, a rod with a heavy tip and enough rigidity or backbone to drive a 3/0 or 5/0 hook into a seemingly concrete jaw. The rod must be able to recover or stand the force of 30 yards of G2AF or G3AF fly line plus 150 yards of 27-pound-test backing ripping through the water. Bear in mind that striking in this case means hitting a fish just as hard as you can, not once, but several times to drive the barb deep. Big tarpon sometimes run several miles, and they should be pulling against a strong drag. The standard fly reel for this fishing can be screwed down to a 6-pound drag, and this is applied almost constantly. Regardless of the inherent virtues of light tackle, the fact remains that a heavy rod is absolutely essential to meet the mechanics of the problem—striking the fish; water resistance against a heavy line; the necessary resist-

The acrobatic tarpon can leap as high as ten feet

ance of the reel drag itself, which places an additional burden on the rod; and the final "snubbing" of a 150-pounder as you position it for the jaw gaff for release. As a result, only the heaviest 9–9½-foot fiberglass fly rods are practical for these silver giants.

A favorite fly for tarpon fishing is a yellow-and-orange splayed-wing streamer. An all white or one with a touch of red has also proven to be most popular over the years, and next to that a yellow, or red-and-yellow. The splayed-wing tied with long, 3–5-inch hackle feathers is ideal because it produces a fluttering action at the slightest rod movement. Tarpon are prone to a slow retrieve and the "breathing" of the wings helps to animate the fly. A regular streamer is inclined to hang lifeless in the water unless it's moved rather quickly. Bucktail wings are more durable and when properly tied in large sizes are also effective. Hook size is very important; stock a variety from No. 2 to No. 5/0. As a rule, for small tarpon to 20 or 25 pounds, use a No. 2 to No. 2/0 fly with a 2½-to-3-inch wing; for giant tarpon use No. 3/0 to No. 5/0 with a 4-to-5-inch wing.

Although angling-club rules require a 12–15-pound-test tippet in tarpon competition, a short length (12 inches) of 80–100-pound-test is ordinarily added to absorb the abrasion in a tarpon's mouth. To achieve a lifelike action with big flies when using these shock tippets, some anglers prefer not to tie the heavy material in a knot directly to the eye of the fly. The alternate method is to secure a short loop in the filament which can be tightened with pliers, so that the fly "swings" freely (*see* Nail Knot Loop *under* Knots). A direct knot can cause the fly to look rigid in the water because of the weight of the heavy strand. Limp leader material is not satisfactory for this purpose. The entire tarpon leader should have a hard finish to prevent wear.

Large feather minnows and popping bugs are sometimes effective for tarpon. These lures seldom account for as many strikes as streamer flies except in milky or muddy water, but even under ideal conditions tarpon are much

more difficult to hook on floating baits, possibly because a buoyant lure is pushed away from the typical open-mouthed strike. Despite their unpredictable effectiveness, surface fly-rod lures draw exciting action.

In regions where baby to 20-pound tarpon are the rule, much lighter fly tackle can be employed. Any 8–8½-foot rod suitable for bass fishing is perfectly adequate. These small fish are extremely active, but they are not often encountered in habitats where long runs or deep sounding poses a problem. The leaders and flies may be comparably refined; baby tarpon can be very selective in ponds and canals, and the tendency here is to overcaliber the terminal gear. Streamers on Nos. 8, 10, and even 12 hooks are frequently successful on tarpon up to 5 pounds. It also pays to experiment with trout wet flies and panfish bugs.

BANKS AND FLATS

The technique of fishing in the Florida Keys is to sight fish on the banks and cast to them. The guide usually stakes out adjacent to a hole or channel and waits for the fish to come within range. Sometimes he'll see rolling tarpon or a cruising school and change locations to intercept them. Basically, however, it's a matter of knowing the paths favored by tarpon and waiting for shots. This method is seldom used elsewhere, as its success is unique to the vast mileage of shallow banks and an abundance of big fish. In May and June when 50–150-pound tarpon are most abundant, you may jump 5–10 fish or more in a day. Most of this fishing is done in 5–8 feet of water, and the silver king literally has no place to go but in the air. Yet for all its excitement, many tarpon anglers don't care about tackling the giants with light gear simply because the play can go on for hours, and the total number of fish jumped is therefore small. A 10–20-pound tarpon, on the other hand, is prime fly-rod fodder, and in productive locations, such as the Yucatán Peninsula in Mexico, vast schools of this size cruise and feed on the flats much like bonefish. Similar conditions can be found in Florida waters, but it is the exception rather than the rule. In the Yucatán the pace of the game is swifter, the fish more eager for the streamer or plug, and the number of tarpon jumped can go upwards of 30–60 on a good day. Although the giants are impressive when they get airborne, a steady flow of 20-pound acrobats hooked in 3–4 feet of water is high-voltage angling.

GULF FISHING

Another kind of tarpon fishing which has some of the elements of both the Keys banks and the Mexican flats is sight casting along Gulf Coast shores. Don't stake out here, as the fish lie along deep mangrove shores and the object is to find an area they are using; then pole or drift on a favorable wind until a tarpon is located. Sometimes you'll see a fish actively feeding, or rolling, or you'll spot a wake of bubbles, but most of these tarpon are simply "lying up." Your quarry may look like nothing more than a shadow or a log among dark reflections, and it's often difficult to make out which end to cast at. Experience and a good pair of Polaroid glasses help in this case. There is apt to be greater variety in the size of the tarpon sighted in the Gulf—20–100 pounds isn't unusual—and they can be difficult on light tackle because the shores are adjacent to deepwater. After a few jumps the fish may take off in an arm-wrenching 300–400-yard run, then sound. The angler who trolls deep banks and passes can get a lot more action out of medium to large tarpon because he can screw down on the fish and force them in the air. If a tarpon has more than 15 feet of depth handy, sooner or later he will quit jumping and slug it out where he has more space. Shallow water is a prerequisite to boating giants.

ROLLING TARPON

Tarpon have a lunglike gas bladder, and when "rolling" at the surface they take in atmosphere air. This enables them to survive in waters with a low-oxygen content. The angler frequently locates his fishing area by the appearance of rolling tarpon. However, such fish may or may not be feeding, and the latter condition is often the case. There is no universal solution to visible but nonfeeding targets. Sometimes you can catch tarpon on the bottom with a jig as they cavort topside. Or you can find tarpon in the same general vicinity which are not rolling but quite willing to strike. It all seems to boil down to the fact that rolling is a separate act from feeding, and whether the individual fish or the school responds is dependent on their desire to feed. At times nothing will arouse their appetites. When tarpon are actively foraging, particularly in shallow water, there is no mistaking their intent. The noise and splashing of a marauding school is nerve-wracking, especially when they work back under the mangroves—the very limbs shake as the water turns to foam.

HOW TO HOOK TARPON

If there is any trick in tarpon fishing, it's knowing how to hook them. Despite all the clichés about the savage strike of a tarpon, ordinarily it consists of nothing more than a bump or a stoppage of the lure. A tarpon does not take a plug or fly fiercely; in fact it is often such a casual affair that the inexperienced angler may never know he had a strike. Tarpon are frequently observed in clearwater to ease up behind a fly or a swimming plug and mouth it so gently that nothing except the visible disappearance of the lure would indicate a strike. The fish invariably comes from below in an arching roll, sucking the lure in on the upward half of its roll and clamping on it as it plunges downward. If you strike while its mouth is still open (and this is why so many fish are missed), you will simply feel a slight bump as the lure is pulled free. Baby tarpon or small ones up to 20 pounds are quicker in their movements, possibly because they occur in large schools and are more aggressive in their feeding. Nevertheless, the angler will only see the brief flash of a striking fish. Tarpon sometimes make a commotion, particularly when churning at surface baits, but it's important to separate the act from the actual contact with a lure. When casting into the sun or in dirty water, you may not even see the flash or movement of a really big fish. Although there can be some hesitation involved on the part of both fish and angler—tarpon must be struck forcefully.

HOW TO RELEASE TARPON

There have been several recorded instances of anglers being killed by tarpon, chiefly when attempting to bring a green fish aboard. Giant tarpon should be thoroughly played out before gaffing. This will become apparent when the fish slows down and begins "bubbling" at the surface. To release a big tarpon, slip a hand gaff in its lower jaw and remove the hooks with pliers while the fish is still in the water, or simply jerk the leader hard with a gloved hand and straighten the hooks out. Small tarpon can be landed in a net but they're bound to tangle a treble-hooked plug in the mesh, and it isn't worth all the bother. If the fish is very small, say up to 5 pounds, you can grab it behind the gills across the back while you get the hook free. Tarpon have little food value; so there's really no reason to kill them. Naturally, if it's a record fish or one that you want to keep for a mount, you'll have to use a billy to quiet it down.

FOOD VALUE

The flesh of the tarpon has very little food value. However, the roe is exceptionally good when pan sautéed or treated in the manner of shad roe. This is a popular food among the coastal people of Central America. *See also* Saltwater Fly-Fishing   —A.J.McC.

TARPON SNOOK *Centropomus pectinatus* In the United States, this species is confined to Florida, from the Caloosahatchee River southward. It occurs throughout the American Atlantic tropics. Although larger than the swordspine snook, the maximum known size attained is about 16 inches in total length. The common name refers to the upturned snout, reminiscent of the tarpon. A very close, nearly identical relative, *Centropomus grandoculatus*, occurs on the Pacific side of tropical America.

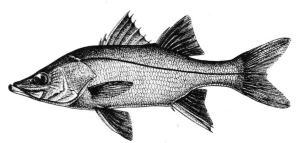

Tarpon Snook

The tarpon snook has 62–72 lateral scales. Gillrakers 15–18 on lower limb of first arch, not including rudiments. Anal rays 7. Pectoral rays 13–15, usually 14. Second anal spine not reaching beyond vertical from caudal base. Pectoral fin not reaching to vertical from tip of pelvic. Pelvic fin reaching beyond anus. Maxillary not reaching to vertical from center of eye.

The greater number of anal rays, fewer pectoral rays, and more upturned snout distinguish this species from the other Atlantic snooks. Also, the body is much more compressed.

ANGLING VALUE

This species occurs in bays, estuaries, and in the lower course of streams and canals. It takes live bait and artificial lures. Live shrimp and top-minnows are the best natural bait. Provides good sport when taken by spinning, fly-casting, or plug-casting. Good eating, especially if skinned and filleted.   —L.R.

TAUTOG *Tautoga onitis* Sometimes called blackfish, this is a fairly large member of the wrasse family Labridae. This Atlantic form, in comparison with other Atlantic members of the family, is distinguished by its plain coloration, lack of scales on the gill cover, and a blunt snout, with the dorsal profile markedly rounded. The cunner (*which see*) is also plain-colored but has a scaled gill cover, and the snout is more pointed. The body is plump yet elongate, and the long dorsal fin is about the same height throughout. It has thick lips, and the anterior canine teeth are well-developed in powerful jaws. The caudal fin is rounded, as are the tips of the soft dorsal and anal fins. It reaches nearly 25 pounds and 3 feet, although about 3 pounds is average.

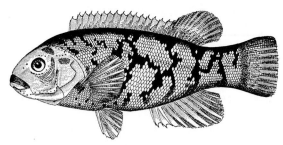

Tautog

The tautog is known from Nova Scotia to South Carolina, being most abundant between Cape Cod and Delaware Bay. It is a bottom species, and is largely restricted to the coastal environment, around rocky or sheltered areas or around mussel beds. But occasionally they are trawled from over smooth bottom. It is seldom found in more than 60 feet of water, the larger fish occurring in deeper water.

LIFE HISTORY

Spawning occurs in the summer, probably in deepwater. The eggs are floating and drift into shallow water, hatching and development occurring in transit. Young grow up in the shallow, protected nursery grounds where seaweed serves as shelter for them and for their food. Their color resembles the bright-green sea lettuce in which they hide. During the late fall, they move off into deepwater where they overwinter in a state of reduced activity. During the rest of the year, populations of tautog move about considerably within their own areas, but there is apparently little coastwise movement. Young tautog eat worms and small crustaceans, while the adults, well-adapted with their crushing teeth, eat barnacles, mussels, snails, hermit crabs, shrimps, and lobsters.

ANGLING VALUE

It is a popular fish with anglers and spearfishermen, and is taken to some extent in pots, traps, and trawls commercially. Its flesh is good, but it is not extensively eaten. —D.dS.

TAXIDERMY (FISH) Contrary to the popular opinion of most anglers, fish taxidermy is not difficult. The job of transforming an unusual catch into a permanent trophy can be accomplished with the aid of a few ordinary tools and supplies. The "do-it-yourself" angler does not have

to be a talented artist or technician. Any fisherman possessing enough dexterity to cast a line or wind a reel is capable of producing a good-looking fish mount that can be displayed proudly anywhere.

Taxidermy is an ancient art. Its origin can be traced back to the caveman's crude use of skins for ritual purposes when the skins were formed over mud and rock to resemble live animals. Centuries ago the Egyptians were the first to preserve human bodies from decay by embalming, and they embalmed animals as well. Peruvians preserved bird skins for ornamental purposes as early as A.D. 1200 and thus indulged in a type of taxidermy. As far as historians of taxidermy can ascertain, the first recorded attempt at preserving animal skins for purposes other than ritual occurred five centuries before Christ when Hanno, the Carthaginian navigator, collected gorilla hides which remained in good condition for generations. One of the earliest recorded efforts at preserving an entire animal hide in a lifelike aspect occurred in Italy; a rhinoceros skin was stuffed for the museum of Ulysses Aldrovandus in Bologna in the sixteenth century. Subsequently, the rhino was transferred to the Royal Museum of Vertebrates in Florence. From that point onward the taxidermy of birds and mammals has improved progressively; today, superb examples of modern taxidermy can be seen in many of our nation's great museums. Simultaneously, the bird and mammal creations of commercial taxidermists have improved tremendously, mostly because of the new methods invented by museum zoologists and technicians.

However, we cannot say the same for fish taxidermy. Although the steady improvement in bird and mammal work over the years can be traced fairly well, investigating the history of fish taxidermy proves to be a frustrating and fruitless task. Advances in fish taxidermy were not recorded in museum publications because there was no improvement to record. This condition existed, as it still does, because the preservation and old-fashioned stuffing of a fish skin is a discouraging and unrewarding task.

In contrast to bird and mammal taxidermy, the creation of a lifelike fish mount by using a skin is difficult. The anatomy of a mammal can be built up accurately by modeling in clay over the original bones before reproducing the hollow, thin-shell body over which the skin is placed permanently. A properly tanned mammal skin never cracks, and its true coloration is naturally retained. Similarly, with careful workmanship the head, wings, and legs of a mounted bird can be placed in correct anatomical position on the artificial body, and the specimen can easily be made to look respectable. Furthermore, feathers do not require painting, and they cover skin damage and discrepancies of anatomy in the artificial body which can be built with excelsior and thread.

A mounted fish skin, on the other hand, is never permanently satisfactory; it eventually cracks, and portions of it ooze grease regardless of how expertly the skin has been cleaned and degreased by various processes; the dried fins tear, the head is distorted by shrinkage, and rebuilding it is a painstaking job that does not reward the effort required.

The frustration of mounting fish which has plagued taxidermists for centuries and which remains highly apparent today was truthfully and amusingly depicted in 1892 by W. T. Hornaday, a well-known and respected scientist who was one of the first to deplore the lack of advancement in museum preparation techniques.

"Rays are the meanest of all subjects that vex the soul of the taxidermist. Shun them as you would the smallpox or the devil. Such abominable animated pancakes, with razor edges that taper out to infinite nothingness were never made to be mounted by any process known to mortal man . . . Once when I was young and innocent, I encountered an enormous ray . . . I mounted his vast, expansive skin over a clay manikin . . . He was lifelike and likewise was a great triumph. But almost the moment my back was turned he went back on me. He just got mad and tore himself to tatters. He became almost a total wreck, and to make my defeat a more genuine and unmitigated crusher, Professor Word sent word to me, all the way from Washington, that he would sell me that large ray for $5.00. I never forgave him for that."

The modern museum scientist, commonly referred to as a curator or preparator, is not a *taxidermist*. He does not manipulate, arrange, or stuff skins as the old Greek derivation of the word implies, nor does he mount the skins on artificial bodies carved from wood or styrofoam. (The word "taxidermist" is used in this discussion, however, because of its familiarity to sportsmen.) Instead, he makes a plaster mold of the fish from which is produced a cast constructed with a synthetic or plasticlike material. In effect the mold is the "negative," and the cast is the "positive." No part of the original fish is used in the cast or model, and yet the body form, scale definition, and fin structure are exact replicas of the fish's anatomy.

The prospective angler-taxidermist's first concern is to secure color photos or transparencies of the fish as soon as it is boated or beached. The camera should be used as soon as possible while the fish is still alive so that the true colors can be recorded. All fishes lose color as soon as they expire. However, the angler who is not a cameraman need not concern himself unduly; excellent color studies of all the popular sport fishes are usually in books and magazines. Color reproduction in such publications has improved greatly in recent years. Also, lack of artistic ability need not be a deterrent in the production of fish casts, as explained later.

The specimen should be wrapped in a wet cloth, towel, or sack, and if possible placed on ice or in a cool place away from the sun. The wet wrapping will prevent the skin and fins from drying as well as affording protection against damage. If the fish is to be frozen and held for future attention, the wet covering should remain when the fish is placed in the deep freeze. Place the specimen on newspaper; otherwise the wet wrapping will adhere to the freezer shelf. Also, be sure that the "showside" of the fish is up, and do not place other objects on the fish until it is frozen solid.

HOW TO MAKE THE MOLD

Grade A or No. 1 molding plaster (sometimes referred to as plaster of Paris) should be used in constructing the mold. The plaster is inexpensive. When mixing the water with plaster, always sift the plaster into the water, not vice-versa. The desired amount of water (varies with the size of the fish) is placed in a bowl or other suitable receptacle, and the plaster is spread evenly over the entire surface of the water until it is no longer absorbed and a thin layer of plaster remains on the surface. Now run your

hand slowly through the mixture until all the plaster on the surface disappears. Squeeze out all lumps that may form until the entire mixture is smooth and fluid.

A two-piece mold is usually made of any fish the size of a bass, perch, trout, salmon, bluefish, or striped bass. Before mixing the plaster the fish has to be prepared to receive the plaster. The pectoral and ventral fins can be folded against the body or they may be cut away and cast separately. Clean all foreign matter from the fish, and wipe off all slime. Vinegar in water helps to clean away slime. Commercial alcohol also works well.

Place the specimen on a table (on a piece of waxed paper). Wipe all moisture from the fish. Build a shelf of soil, sand, or wet, ground asbestos around the fish to the midline of the body. The shelf should extend about two inches around the entire fish. Be sure that the undersides of the dorsal, adipose, anal, and tail fins are in close contact with the shelf.

Flow the plaster over the fish and fins. Start at the head or tail end, and follow along the body until the entire fish and the shelf are covered. The plaster should be about ½ inch thick over the body of the fish and slightly thicker over the shelf. Add more plaster along the shelf for more strength if necessary.

When the mold is set (wait until the plaster warms up and then cools), turn it over and remove the soil, sand, or asbestos from it. Clean the shelf of the mold, and apply over it a separator such as vaseline, thin oil, or soap. Mix more plaster, and proceed to cover the exposed part of the fish and shelf the same way the other side was covered.

After the second half of the mold has set, insert a chisel between the halves and pry the mold apart. Set them aside to dry a day or two over a radiator, or 3–4 days in a warm room.

Before casting the fish, the mold halves are given three or four coats of shellac (thinned about 50-50 with alcohol), and a separator is applied so that the resin will not adhere to the mold. A good separator in this case is a pastelike mixture of wax, kerosene, and vaseline. The wax is scraped into the kerosene where it will dissolve overnight, and then the vaseline is added. A thin coat of the separator is rubbed into the mold (use your fingers).

The resin used for strengthening or repairing boat hulls can be used for casting the fish; it can be obtained at any dealer in boat supplies. Follow the instructions for mixing on the label of the can, and apply a layer of the resin to both halves of the mold and the impressions of the fins which are on the shelf of the molds. If the resin is too fluid, thicken it with whiting (obtained from hardware stores). It is not necessary to use both sides of the mold where the fins are concerned; use only that half of the mold which will produce the "showside" of the fish. When the first application in the body of the fish has set, add another layer over it reinforced with fiberglass. Then, mix a small batch of resin thickened to a pastelike consistency with whiting, and smear it along the seams or edges of the cast. When the mold is joined together the thickened resin binds the halves of the cast into one. Allow it to set overnight. Then pry the mold apart by inserting a chisel between the halves.

Water, as hot as possible, poured over the mold will help separate the cast from the mold. Sand the seams of the cast, fill in with plaster any imperfections, drill a hole for the eye socket, and secure the glass eye with a bit of resin. If a glass eye is not available, do not drill a hole; instead, paint directly over the eye area of the cast. The pupil of the eye is black, and the iris is silvery, stippled with a darker color. Drill small holes through the cast at the spots where the pectoral and anal fins are to be attached. The original pectoral and ventral fins can be spread until dried and inserted into the holes and permanently set with a thick mixture of resin and whiting. However, resin casts of the fins are superior. A two-piece mold is made. Place the fin on a piece of greased glass, so the plaster will not stick to it; flow plaster to a depth of about ¾ inch over the fin and about 2 inches all around it. When it sets, turn the mold over, dig out some plaster at the base of the fin (it will form an extension when cast), cut a couple of notches ("keys") into the shelf, apply a separator to the shelf, and flow plaster over it, as with the first half.

To cast the fins, simply apply thickened resin to both halves of the fin areas, and squeeze the mold halves together, not too tightly because it is better to have the cast fins slightly thicker than the originals. When the resin has set, pry the mold apart and remove the cast. Hot water run over the mold will soften them temporarily and thus facilitate removal of fins from the mold. Use a coping saw—fine-tooth blade—to cut away the extra resin from the edges around the fin. Insert the base of the fins into their proper places, and secure them with a heavy paste of resin.

PAINTING THE CAST

Before painting the cast remove all traces of separator that may have been transferred from the mold. Give the entire specimen a thin coating of shellac and then a spraying of silver. A choice of several methods may be used to paint the cast. An air brush and lacquer pigments are generally used professionally. However, excellent results can be obtained with brush and oil colors. Stylized color renditions are also effective. And an attractive collection of full mounts or half mounts (using only a one-half mold) can be produced by simply painting the cast silver, gold, or copper. The finished cast should be sprayed with clear enamel to protect it as well as to add a natural gloss. The fish can be attached with screws to a wooden plaque, but it looks better without it. Cut a rectangular hole in the back of the fish and hang it on a couple of small nails. (This should be done before the fins are attached.)

Although the resin cast produces the most permanent and accurate mounts, the fisherman can also make a fine fish trophy by casting in plaster (instead of resin) from a one-half mold—an easy method that costs but a few cents. He may still desire to use one of several methods of mounting the original skin, or he may want to record his big catch by burning its outline on a pine panel, or he may like to make a collection of preserved heads. —E.C.M.

PRESERVING FISH FOR STUDY

The student or biologist who wants to preserve wet fish specimens for school or museum collections may use alcohol or formaldehyde. The latter is much the easier to use in initial fixing and preservation and can be purchased in 1-pint bottles from almost any druggist. Formaldehyde, as purchased, is a solution of formaldehyde gas (CH_2O) in water; it is usually of 35–40 percent strength. One part of this commercial solution is diluted with nine parts of water for use as a preservative. This preservative is commonly called formalin. The only types of alcohol that are safe to use for preservatives are ethyl (CH_2H_5OH), otherwise known as "grain alcohol" or "spirits of wine," and isopropyl (C_3H_7OH). Either of these alcohols must be diluted with water for use as a preservative, since they are commonly sold at a strength of 95 percent (190 proof). Use of an alcoholmeter (spirit meter) is necessary to assure properly diluted solutions, but a satisfactory solution for preserving fishes may be made by mixing three parts by volume of 95 percent alcohol with one part of water.

Alcohol solutions weaken rapidly after specimens are placed in them and must be shaken up, tested, and strengthened by the addition of 95 percent every day for a period of a week, if the container is crowded. Formalin retains its strength much better, and specimens may usually be left indefinitely in the initial solution. However, a formalin solution once used to preserve a container full of specimens should not be drained off and re-used to preserve a new container full of specimens. It had best be discarded. The only difficulty with formalin is that prolonged immersion in it decalcifies the bones of specimens; six months should be a limit. Decalcification may be arrested by placing considerable household borax into the formalin to neutralize its free acid.

Field Processing Fish should be placed into preservative while still alive. Specimens dead before preservation are seldom in first-class condition. The collector should carry a bucket of preservative with him. Specimens over 6 inches in length should have the abdomen slit open on one side (not down the midventral line) to allow preservative to enter; this should be done no later than the evening of the day of collection. The incision should be deep enough to enter the abdominal cavity, but need not be long; a razor, a sharp scalpel, or small sharp scissors are useful for this. Specimens will harden within ½ hour; be sure none is bent or curled up. Straight specimens are much better. Specimens should harden in good preservative for at least two weeks before shipping. Scaled fishes over 12 inches and all fishes over 15 inches should have numerous cuts made into the deep muscles to permit preservative to enter.

Labeling Proper labeling is important to the collection. Each specimen should be accompanied by a label giving the minimum information of exact place and date of capture. The labels must be *with the specimens* and therefore of a material that will survive immersion in liquid. Most paper or cardboard will not survive. Use the best quality of bond letter paper or linen ledger paper, or parchment. Vegetable parchment is so impervious that either ink or pencil writing is liable to rub off and become illegible. Write *only* with ordinary medium-hard pencil, never with ordinary ink or with "indelible" pencil. "Eternal," India, or carbon ink may be used, if it is thoroughly dried by prolonged drying over heat before immersion. Fold the labels at least once, face in, before placing with specimens. Labels for large specimens may be tucked deep into the mouth, where they will not become dislodged. Labels for small lots are simply placed in the bottle or cloth wrapping with the specimens.

—A.J.McC.

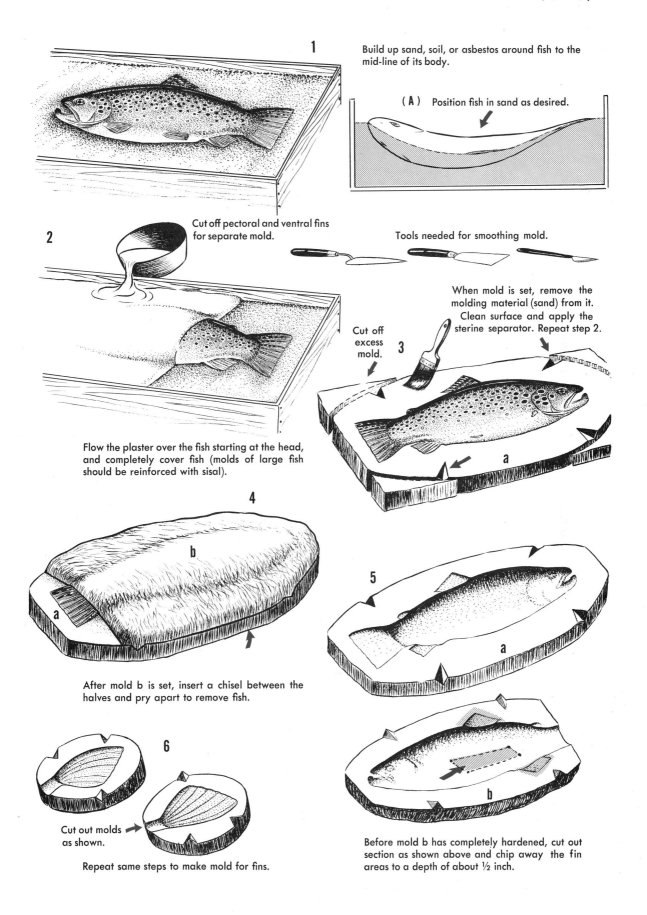

1 Build up sand, soil, or asbestos around fish to the mid-line of its body.

(A) Position fish in sand as desired.

2 Cut off pectoral and ventral fins for separate mold.

Tools needed for smoothing mold.

Flow the plaster over the fish starting at the head, and completely cover fish (molds of large fish should be reinforced with sisal).

When mold is set, remove the molding material (sand) from it. Clean surface and apply the sterine separator. Repeat step 2.

3 Cut off excess mold.

a

4 b

a

After mold b is set, insert a chisel between the halves and pry apart to remove fish.

5 a

b

6 Cut out molds as shown.

Repeat same steps to make mold for fins.

Before mold b has completely hardened, cut out section as shown above and chip away the fin areas to a depth of about ½ inch.

TENCH *Tinca tinca* A favorite of European anglers, Tench occur in nearly all eutrophic stillwaters and very sluggish rivers throughout Europe, being absent only from Scandinavia and Scotland. Although not indigenous to Ireland, the Irish Inland Fisheries Trust has built up stocks by introducing them into no less than fifty new waters since 1958.

Tench cannot be mistaken for any other European cyprinid. The scales are tiny, 95–100 in the lateral line, often glinting with a golden flash like sequins. The general ground color is a shade of olive or forest-green, becoming more yellow on the belly; this will vary from population to population, some being much darker. The fins are uniformly dark gray or green and rounded at the edges. The paired fins are shovel-shaped, the tail but little forked, the dorsal erect. The iris of the eye is always a bright orange-red.

A domestic xanthochroistic variety, the "golden tench" is frequently kept in aquaria but is very rare in the wild. This is an amber-yellow fish with pale, often coral fins. Sometimes very light, almost golden tench do occur in the wild, but they are confined to waters containing a great many suspended white particles, e.g., old chalk pits. In aquaria, tench often assume a smoky color, but this is temporary. In all variations the iris remains red.

Tench are a summer fish, feeding only at temperatures of 55°–80°F. During winter, they hibernate buried in the mud, and will aestivate in the same fashion should the pond dry up in summer. They have been dug out of their mud cocoons still alive several weeks after ponds have dried up. This tenacity is due to two properties—the body is coated with a coherent and slippery mucus, which blocks quite drastic attempts to dry the skin out; and the gill filaments are exceptionally finely divided to make more use of oxygen. The blood and tissues are very resistant to oxygen lack or excess carbon dioxide. In all, the tench is far more viable out of water than even the carp, and only the eel could be superior. This enables the tench to colonize small, ephemeral ponds, where it is characteristically the largest member of the fish fauna.

The tench shares the same habitats as the bream (*see* Bronze Bream), especially in the lower reaches of rivers. In lakes, it stays mostly within dense weed beds in the marginal shallows. In water less than 6 feet deep, it is rarely seen, as it makes its way along paths under the weed tops. Despite this preference for weed, there is no obvious adaptation; the body is not flattened in any way.

It does not specially prefer any particular kind of bottom but thrives on both mud and gravel. The diet is affected; on mud it lives off bottom animals and even scoops up black humus to extract nourishment from the organic matter. On gravel, it eats crustaceans, small mollusks, leeches, and epiphytic algae. On either bottom, it scavenges, taking carrion.

Its eyesight is probably poor, and it typically shuns strong light, but it sense of smell is acute, and it can search the bottom with sensory barbels on either side of the mouth, even in pitch darkness.

Tench of less than a pound are unusual to catch, the usual taken by anglers being from 1½–4 pounds. Anything over 5 pounds is a good fish, and over 6–7 pounds, noteworthy. The largest tench yet caught on rod and line run 8–10 pounds, but there is good reason to expect the existence of 12-pound fish.

LIFE HISTORY

Tench are unusual among European cyprinids in showing sexual dimorphism, the pelvic bones and fin rays of the male being larger and more massive. The purpose, presumably sexual, is not clear. Both sexes mature, depending on conditions, between their second and fourth years, males usually in advance of females.

They spawn in weedy shallows in June or July; it has been claimed that storms affect the onset of mating. No special breeding dress is developed. The female lays about 275,000 eggs of about one millimeter diameter per pound of her body weight when spawning is successful (on many waters it is not, and ova are carried until late in the year). The eggs hatch into small fry which hide in dense growths of weed away from predators. At the end of its first summer, the tenchling would be about 3 inches long; after the second, 6 inches; after the third and fourth, 8 and 10 inches, respectively. At this stage it would weigh about ¾ pound and be a completely mature tench.

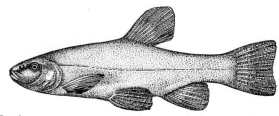

Tench

Spawning is gregarious, and the fry stay together in the same gregarious fashion. Throughout life, the tench is more or less a gregarious fish, though not formed into tight schools. The usual formation of tench is that of a cloud of small groups of two or three individuals each, making a large aggregate. The aggregate is not, however, the basic formation, which is in smaller groups.

In a given water, tench run very much to a size when taken on rod-and-reel, this being presumably due to infrequently successful spawnings and wide gaps between the year classes. Unlike other members of the carp family, the size is not dependent upon the size of water, very small ponds producing handsome fish. Except in unusual circumstances, competition with other species does not diminish the tench's growth rate; it is evident that it occupies an ecological niche which is as profitable as it is common.

In clearwater, it shows diurnal cycles of activity, feeding mostly in the early morning or late evening, or during the night. June dawns are traditional tench-fishers' times. If the water is turbid or weedy, however, it will feed into the day. One interesting phenomenon is that it is attracted by weed dragging (as distinct from cutting). Presumably this stirs up food and makes the water more turbid, inducing them to feed. Very large tench seem less shy of strong light and may bask in dense weed beds.

The scales are very small; so growth-rate measurements on wild fish (as given) are not common. Fish farmers using concentrated feeding methods can obtain 3-summer fish of a pound weight, a threefold increase on the average wild weight at that age. Under poor conditions such a fish would only be 3 inches long and weigh barely an ounce, so the latitude is very wide. Female tench put on 30 percent more weight than males; all the largest tench caught by anglers have been females. The life expectancy would be 20–30 years, with a usual life span of 10–15 years; such figures are typical for most members of the carp family.

ANGLING VALUE

Anglers are fond of the tench because it is widespread in most stillwaters and a very dogged fighter. Successful tench fishermen prepare their swims well in advance of fishing, sometimes for several weeks beforehand. Weeds are removed and groundbait mixtures compounded of meal and oxblood scattered into the water. Finally, the bottom is raked to cloud the water, can fishing begins at the first light of dawn.

Usual baits are bread or worms, lying either on the bottom or draped over weeds. The tench's poor eyesight will sometimes allow it to miss a stationary bait, so many tench-fishers move the bait every so often to catch its eye. A tench bite is slow and indecisive, taking a long time to warrant striking. Much of this is due to the energetic boring into the bottom the fish does near the bait, standing vertically on its head to do so; the fins are large in proportion and make considerable disturbance. Tench feeding in 4 feet of water can still roil the surface.

One of the surest signs of feeding tench is the appearance of fine bubbles in clusters forming a trail across the swim. This accompanies the fish boring into the pond mud, but the bubbles are not displaced methane directly from the bottom. The tench itself appears to emit them. What their purpose or origin is, is not known. Worms are the favored bait when this bubbling occurs.

Tench fishing is a popular sport, but it does require attention and preparation to be done well, and early rising for best results. For those reasons, it is not as popular as other branches of angling—many anglers find it demanding, though the tench as a fish is appreciated and admired.

ECONOMIC VALUE

In central Europe, tench are a much appreciated item of diet, rivaling only the carp as a favorite eating cyprinid. Germans regard baked tench as a particular delicacy. Its popularity is coupled with the ease with which it can be raised in inland ponds; it was probably reared for the table in this way before the carp displaced it.

Today, tench for the table are obtained either by traps and lines and sold locally; or else they are bred in ponds, when they may be transported live or frozen to markets all over Europe. They are not raised on their own, but as an adjunct to carp culture, which is economically more important. The food is almost the same as that of the carp, but fish farmers believe it makes better use of it; they argue that the tench burrows deeper and more thoroughly into the bottom than does the carp. This has not been borne out by recent experiments, but the tench is still used as a secondary crop in carp ponds. One tench to ten carp is the normal ratio used; with more apparently the carp growth suffers. Tench are also useful in raising a salable protein crop from ponds too overgrown for carp culture, but because they burrow in the mud, it can be time-consuming retrieving the crop.

Tench are also in demand as a fish for ornamental waters, especially the colored varieties; there is also a certain trade in small specimens among aquarists.

—D.M.

TENNESSEE There are several reasons why Tennessee is a leader in sport fishing. First, being the home of the "Great Lakes of the South," the state has more than a half-million acres of impounded waters in 22 large lakes; and it has an additional 8,000 miles of streams. Secondly, being located in the southeast, the winters tend to be mild, and the summers are long. Finally, Tennessee is fortunate in that most of the common gamefish, from bullheads to muskellunge, can be found within its borders. Fifty percent of the land is forested which, combined with an annual rainfall of about 49 inches, provides a continual supply of freshwater. The winters are generally mild with severe cold snaps lasting for only a few days at a time. This near optimum condition, coupled with an adequate forage-fish population, creates a generous growing season.

Tennessee has year-around fishing. A "run" of one species is hardly completed before another begins. In late winter and early spring, trout fishing dominates the scene in middle and east Tennessee. Spring also means crappie fishing to the panfish addict, and even before the "speck" season is over bass fishing begins. Following the spring bass action comes the summer catfish season. Fall brings the bass near the surface again, followed by trout runs in Doe Creek in east Tennessee. Winter is the time for sauger fishing. The colder and rougher the weather, the better the "jack" fishing becomes, especially in the tailwaters. It should be realized that there isn't a clear-cut distinction between these various seasons, but there is a peak period for all species. A skilled panfish angler will get results throughout most of the year, and the same is true of the bass or trout specialist.

Geographically speaking, Tennessee's fishing opportunities are varied. The eastern part of the state has numerous clear, cold mountain streams which provide some native trout fishing; in addition, the Game and Fish Commission carries out an extensive put-and-take trout stocking program. There are many large impoundments in this region, mostly TVA storage reservoirs, some of which are subject to severe drawdowns during summer. Moving westward across the state to the Cumberland plateau, here pollution from strip coal mining has plagued many streams. Furthermore, the sandy land has low fertility; many of the streams in this area lack the nutrients necessary for the growth of fish food. Paradoxically, it is in this region that the few muskellunge streams are located. Muskies are not a common gamefish in Tennessee waters. This is the southernmost limit of the fishery in the United States. Originally, muskellunge were more or less confined to the Cumberland plateau, in eight streams of the Tennessee River drainage and three streams in the Cumberland River drainage, totaling approximately 170 miles. The best streams are tributaries of the Emory River, including Daddy's Creek and some of the streams of the Catoosa Wildlife Management Area. The State Game and Fish Commission has greatly expanded the range of the muskie to include a number of major impoundments.

Situated on the western edge of the plateau are two of the most popular lakes, Center Hill on the Caney Fork and Dale Hollow on the Obey River, both U.S. Army Corps of Engineers impoundments. They provide excellent fishing, especially for smallmouth, largemouth, and white bass. However, a former North American record brown trout of 26 pounds, 2 ounces was also taken from the tailwater of Dale Hollow. Year-around trout fishing is found below both of these impoundments.

Middle Tennessee, or the Nashville Basin, is criss-crossed with streams most of which are marginal trout habitat but fine smallmouth-bass streams. The Elk, Duck, Buffalo, and Harpeth are very popular. The important lakes in the midstate area are Old Hickory and Cheatham on the Cumberland and Woods Reservoir on the Elk River, all U. S. Army Corps of Engineers impoundments. Most of the popular species may be taken from these lakes. Old Hickory produced a world-record walleye of 25 pounds.

Dividing middle and west Tennessee is the mammoth 158,000-acre Kentucky Lake, which crosses the entire state from north to south. This is a popular fishery, and, being the farthest downstream in the TVA chain, it is the most productive. Fertility in Kentucky Lake is most conducive to rapid fish growth. The major fishing waters of west Tennessee are sluggish, silt-laden rivers, and many of the fishermen go to Kentucky Lake, Reelfoot Lake, the Mississippi River, or a series of man-made lakes. Streams support very little of the fishing pressure in this area; however, upper stretches of these streams provide some good largemouth- and spotted-bass fishing.

TROUT FISHING

Trout fishermen are fortunate in that there are over 500 miles of trout streams in Tennessee, excluding those in the Smoky Mountain National Park. The Game and Fish Commission carries out an extensive trout-management program, and a year-round season is permitted on all streams and tailwaters except those on wildlife management areas where special restrictions still apply. Management includes protection, development of habitat, and stocking where the natural production cannot satisfy the fishing pressure. Rainbow are the most commonly used in stocking; however, some brown and brook trout are also released. A few mountain streams in east Tennessee maintain a population of native trout, but by and large the average fisherman will creel hatchery-reared trout. Additional fishing is provided in six wildlife management areas. These areas, all in the east Tennessee mountains, are Laurel Fork, Kettlefoot, Andrew Johnson, Unicoi, Ococee, and Tellico. The waters are stocked regularly through the summer, and beautiful "natives" may still be found in some of these streams. The Tellico area within the confines of the Cherokee National Forest is the most intensively fished. Special daily permits are necessary for all of these areas.

Marginal trout streams in the Cumberland Mountain area and middle Tennessee area afford some excellent fishing. Of course, all these streams are put-and-take trout waters. The average-size stocked rainbow is ¾–1 pound. These streams afford good fishing from the first of March until mid June when the waters become too warm to maintain trout.

Tailwater trout fishing, below some of the TVA and Army Corps of Engineers storage reservoirs, has really come into its own in recent years. Tailwaters flow through the dam from the bottom of the reservoirs and are very cold. Food is usually abundant, and trout grow to a large size in an amazingly short time. Good tailwater trout

fishing may be found below Watauga, Wilbur, Norris, Chilhowee, Fort Patrick Henry, Daniel Boone, Dale Hollow, and Center Hill reservoirs. Rainbows were also stocked in Watauga Lake, and now an annual run up Doe Creek, a tributary, takes place every late fall. Eight- and 10-pounders are not uncommon in Doe Creek. Trolling during the summer is the best bet for trout in Watauga.

BASS FISHING

The most universal fishing in Tennessee is probably bass fishing. There are few waters of the state which do not contain one or more species of bass. Three species of black bass are represented in Tennessee waters—the largemouth, smallmouth, and spotted. The largemouth is the most common and may be found in most lakes, ponds, and many streams. Reelfoot Lake in the northwest corner of the state has long been a famous largemouth area. Many of the more than 55,000 farm ponds provide large-mouth-bass and bream fishing. No one water can be selected as the outstanding bass lake. Any lake from a farm pond to mammoth Kentucky Lake might produce a record breaker. The best period for largemouth fishing is March through November.

Tennessee is famous for its smallmouth-bass fishing. Every season *Field & Stream* prizewinners in the 7–9-pound class are caught in the state; a world's record smallmouth of 11 pounds 15 ounces was taken from the

The Tellico River and its tributaries in Cherokee National Forest is one of the more popular trout waters

Dale Hollow Reservoir. Originally, the species was almost exclusively a streamfish, but with the impounding of rivers into lakes its distribution was extended to the new reservoirs. Today, the bronzeback is still found in many streams throughout the state. Most of the better waters, however, are in middle Tennessee. Some of the popular ones are the Elk River, Upper Duck, Caney Fork, Collins, Stones, Harpeth, and Buffalo rivers, as well as many of their tributaries. In east Tennessee, anglers favor the Powell and Clinch rivers above Norris Lake, the Holston River, Tellico, and Little River. The larger rivers of the Cumberland plateau also support smallmouth bass.

The spotted bass is less abundant than either the largemouth or smallmouth but may be found in most lakes and streams. Although sometimes associated with the smallmouth, it is common in the cleaner streams of west Tennessee, such as the headwaters of the Obion, Hatchie, Loosahatchie, and Wolf rivers. Harpeth River in middle Tennessee has large numbers of spotted bass. The heaviest spotted bass are usually taken from lakes.

REDHORSE AND STONEROLLER

To residents of the Volunteer State the redhorses and other species of suckers are seasonably more important than many gamefish. Almost all Tennessee streams contain suckers; however, the larger redhorse are found in the central and eastern part of the state. These fish weigh up to 15 pounds. They are taken by snatching with a gang of weighted hooks while the redhorse are on their spawning grounds, which is legal in Tennessee. This game reaches a peak on the Elk and Upper Duck rivers and their tributaries. A redhorse fisherman is just as dedicated to his sport as a dyed-in-the-wool bass fisherman. To many local people, a catch of redhorse is as necessary as a spring tonic. When the lookouts spread the word that the fish are on the shoals, all work including plowing ceases, and everybody heads for the river. The snatchers wade right in, and the fun begins. A 12-pounder on a twenty-foot cane pole requires considerable effort to subdue. The redhorse run begins in April and lasts for four weeks, depending on the weather.

Another rough fish which is highly esteemed by residents and is caught on rod-and-reel with worms or small wet flies is the stoneroller (*which see*). The stoneroller is a large minnow, up to 11 inches in length, and is also known as the hornyhead, steelback, or knottie. It is caught in large numbers from small streams during its spawning run. The stoneroller is a serious trout competitor, destroying their redds in waters where both species are present. However, the stoneroller is a sweetmeated delicacy when panfried, and angling pressure helps to hold their numbers in check. Although the species is common in clear streams east of Kentucky Lake, it is sought as a table fish mainly in northern Tennessee. It is caught during the early spring months, beginning in March, while on the spawning beds.

FARM-POND FISHING

Not to be overlooked by the angler are the more than 55,000 farm ponds scattered across the state. Averaging slightly more than one acre in size, the farm ponds have greatly increased the fishing waters available, especially in west Tennessee. The average farm pond is stocked with a combination of largemouth bass and bluegill. Since these ponds are private property, fishermen usually pay a small fee. Bluegill and bass fishing in these ponds is best during early spring and late fall.

IMPOUNDMENTS

Since the era of TVA and the U. S. Army Corps of Engineers lake-construction programs, Tennessee has become one of the most important fishing regions in the United States, ranking fourth in the sale of nonresident fishing licenses. There are twenty-two large impoundments open to public angling. The TVA lakes follow the Tennessee River drainage system beginning in the northeast corner of the state and moving southward across east Tennessee into Alabama and then north across the western part of the state. The Corps impoundments are all on the Cumberland River drainage system except Woods Reservoir which is located on the Elk River. Impoundments on the Cumberland drainage system are Dale Hollow on the Obey River, Center Hill on the Caney Fork, Old Hickory, Cheatham and Barkley, all on the Cumberland.

Dale Hollow Lake At full pool it contains 30,990 acres. Best known for its smallmouth bass fishing it also offers largemouth with peak periods in winter, spring, and fall. White bass runs occur early in the spring season. Muskellunge (record 28 pounds) are caught throughout the year. Tailwater trout fishing below the dam has produced some big browns.

Center Hill Lake At full pool it contains 23,060 acres. It has excellent white bass, walleye, largemouth and smallmouth bass, and crappie fishing. Bass fishing is productive in the winter, spring, and fall. There is trout fishing in the tailwater and tributary streams.

Old Hickory Lake Located just outside Nashville, at full pool it contains 22,500 acres. Old Hickory has produced walleyes to 25 pounds and is also popular for its largemouth bass, crappie, and bluegill. The Cumberland River above Old Hickory is famous for its early spring walleye run.

Cheatham Lake Located south of Nashville on the Cumberland River it covers approximately 7,450 acres at full pool. Due to a fluctuating water level Cheatham doesn't produce the same quality of fishing as other impoundments. However, anglers do take stringers of crappie, largemouth bass, catfish, and bluegill. Smallmouth bass fishing is good in Harpeth River and Turnbull Creek, which are tributaries to the lake.

South Holston Lake The northernmost of the TVA chain of lakes located near Bristol, this 7,500-acre lake is on the south fork of the Holston River. Fishing here consists mainly of largemouth and smallmouth bass, crappie, and sauger. There is a modest tailwater trout fishery also below Holston Dam.

Daniel Boone Lake The next impoundment to the south, also situated on the South Holston River, this 4,520-acre lake is best known for its largemouth bass and crappie fishing. It has trout in the tailwater. The peak bass fishing usually occurs in the winter season.

Watauga Lake A 6,430 acre lake, it is located on the Watauga River, which is also in the northeast section of the state. Watauga is better known for the rainbow runs up Doe Creek, a tributary, than for its lake fishing. This run normally takes place beginning in November and peaks at Christmas. Some rainbow may be taken in the lake throughout the year. Other fishing is for bass and crappie.

Wilbur Lake A small tailwater lake below Watauga, it is stocked heavily with trout.

Fort Patrick Henry On the south fork of the Holston River it contains only 893 acres of water. Fishing here is mainly for bass and also for bluegill. This is an old lake and is thus heavily sedimented.

Cherokee Lake On Holston River it has 30,200 acres of fishing water. Fishing activity here is primarily for largemouth, smallmouth, crappie, and white bass.

Davy Crockett A TVA-acquired lake it is small in size. The best fishing is for bass and bluegill.

Douglas Lake On the French Broad River it offers the angler 30,600 acres of water. The most popular species in Douglas are largemouth, crappie, catfish, and white bass.

Norris Lake On the Clinch River it is the oldest in the TVA chain, and was impounded in 1936. Norris has 34,200 acres of water and offers some fine walleye, smallmouth, largemouth, sauger, and white bass fishing.

Fort Loudon Lake At Knoxville, Fort Loudon is a 14,000-acre body of water on the Tennessee River, offering largemouth, crappie, white bass, and smallmouth fishing.

Watts Bar Lake Also on the Tennessee River it has 38,600 surface acres. Fishing here is mainly for largemouth, smallmouth, spotted bass, crappie, white bass, and sauger. Watts Bar is a very fine fishing lake.

Chickamauga Lake Just north of Chattanooga on the Tennessee River it contains 34,500 acres. Largemouth, smallmouth and spotted bass, crappie, and sauger are the most popular species in Chickamauga.

Ocoee Lake On the Ocoee River it contains 1,900 acres. The low fertility of Ocoee's water produces very little fishing, except for catfish, but there is fine skin-diving due to the clarity of the water.

Hales Bar Below Chattanooga on the Tennessee River it impounds 6,420 acres. The best fishing is for largemouth, crappie, and white bass.

The TVA chain of lakes continues on into Alabama, then re-enters Tennessee near Savannah. Pickwick is the next dam in Tennessee, but most of the water is in Alabama.

Pickwick Lake Offers some excellent largemouth and white bass and crappie fishing in spring and fall; the Pickwick is, however, best known for its tailwater fishing. It provides sauger in the winter; white bass, crappie, smallmouth, largemouth, and bream in the spring; and in summer the activity switches to blue catfish, many of which weigh in excess of 50 pounds. Fall sees the bass,

Reelfoot Lake is actually a vast submerged forest created by an earthquake. The shallow lake bed produces bass and panfish

crappie, and white bass fishing return; and winter brings back the ever-popular sauger. Pickwick tailwater is a year-round fishing location.

Kentucky Lake This is the farthest downstream in the TVA chain and impounds 158,000 acres at full pool. By being the last in the TVA chain, Kentucky Lake is also the richest in fertility. Just about all the native game-fish are found here, including the spotted, smallmouth and largemouth bass; sauger; crappie; and three species of catfish. Bass, crappie, and white bass fishing is best in early spring and fall; catfish year round; and sauger in the winter season.

Great Fall Lake Located on the Caney Fork River above Center Hill this is a TVA impoundment covering 2,270 acres. The best fishing is for largemouth bass, blue-gill, and crappie.

Reelfoot Lake In the northwest corner of the state Reelfoot is an earthquake-formed lake covering 12,000 acres. It has long been famous as a fisherman's paradise and a waterfowl haven in the wintertime. Fishing is for bass, bluegill, and crappie. In addition to fishing and waterfowl, Reelfoot is famous for its cypress trees and bird life. It is a major tourist attraction.

STATE LAKES

Thirteen state lakes are operated by the Game and Fish Commission for fishermen. Qualified resident managers are on duty ready to assist the angler at eight of these lakes. Year-round fishing is permitted, and the statewide creel limit applies except on catfish. The creel limit on channel catfish is 7.

Bedford Lake Located near Normandy it impounds 47 acres. Two bass weighing more than 13 pounds each have been taken from Bedford. Bluegill, redear sunfish, crappie, and largemouth bass are major species caught here.

Brown's Creek Lake In the Natchez Trace Forest it offers largemouth bass, crappie, bluegill, and redear sun-fish. It contains 167 acres of water.

Burgess Falls Lake On Falling River Water near Cookeville it impounds 400 acres. Largemouth bass, blue-gill, and crappie are the most common fish to be found.

Carroll Lake Near McKenzie it covers 100 acres, and offers bass, bluegill, catfish, and crappie fishing.

Herb Parsons Lake A 177-acre body of water near Memphis it offers bluegill and largemouth bass fishing.

Garrett Lake In Weakley County Garrett has 183 acres of water, and offers bass, bluegill, channel catfish, and chain pickerel fishing.

Humboldt An 87-acre lake near Humboldt it offers channel catfish, bluegill, and largemouth bass fishing.

Laurel Hill Its 327 acres near Lawrenceburg offer muskellunge, bass, bluegill, pickerel, and channel catfish.

Maples Creek Lake The 90 acres located in the Natchez Trace Forest have bass, bluegill, and crappie fishing.

Marrowbone Lake Its 60 acres off Highway 41A, between Nashville and Clarksville, have bass, bluegill, crappie, and channel catfish.

Whiteville Lake It is located east of Whiteville on U.S. Highway 64. Principal fish are bass, bluegill, crap-pie, and bullheads in this 158-acre lake.

Copperhill-Ducktown Lake 70 acres it is located north of Ducktown off U.S. Highway 68. Principal fish are bass, bluegill, and channel catfish.

VFW Lake 22 acres it is located 14 miles from Lawrenceburg, and has bass, bluegill, and channel catfish.
—E.C.

TEREDO Commonly called "shipworm," this marine woodborer destroys pilings, docks, and ship hulls. The Teredinidae have a life span of 2–10 months, during which time they grow to a length of 10–12 inches. Some

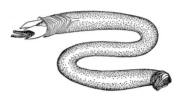

Teredo (*Teredo navalis*)

tropical species reach a length of 3 feet or more. The teredo is not a worm, but a wormlike mollusk which digs a cylindrical burrow in the wood. *See also* Gribble

TERELYNE A material used in the manufacture of fish-ing lines. Terelyne is a polyester based on polyethylene terphthlate. It is of some importance in the form of a fly line and displays qualities at the midpoint between Dacron and nylon. Terelyne does not sink as readily as the former, nor does it have the buoyancy of nylon; it approximates the silk fly line in specific gravity and weight per diameter. Terelyne is the registered trademark of Imperial Chemical Industries Ltd., Harrogate, England. *See also* Fly Line

TERMINAL TACKLE Used in a collective sense to indi-cate any items attached to the end of a fishing line such as the leader, hook, sinker, swivel, or lure. Terminal tackle varies according to the type of fishing practiced. *See also* Bait-Casting Tackle, Fly-Casting Tackle, Spin-ning Tackle, Surf-Casting

TESTES Male reproductive organs

TEXAS Freshwater resources are widely varied in Texas. Impoundment of rivers and streams has created over 200 reservoirs, from a few hundred to many thousands of acres in surface area. The state's 1.8 million acres of im-pounded water exceeds that of any other state; flowing waters total more than 80,000 miles. Approximately 2 dozen freshwater fish species provide good sport fishing for an estimated 3 million Texans. The 55 percent increase in fishermen during the 1965–1970 period, compared to a nationwide 2 percent decline, reflects the overall good quality of Texas sport fishing.

Most of the freshwater sport fishing in Texas is for largemouth bass, white bass, and crappie. Dams, erected across stream beds in various areas of the state to im-pound floodwaters, have created suitable habitats. There are no known smallmouth bass in Texas at present, but the Texas Parks and Wildlife Department plans in the near future to stock these fish in reservoirs and streams where high water temperatures are not a problem. The spotted bass is found in many streams and also has be-come established in many of the major reservoirs. In ranch "tanks" or ponds the warmouth (locally the goggle-eye) is also plentiful. But the species which has started the careers of most Texas anglers is the white bass.

How the white bass got from the Great Lakes area to Lake Caddo on the Texas-Louisiana border is not certain. One hypothesis is that the fish came down the Mississippi

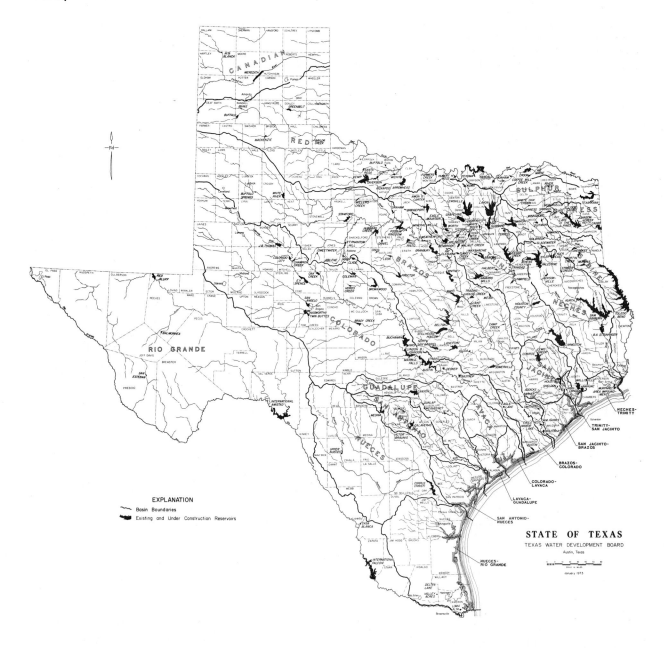

EXPLANATION

Basin Boundaries

Existing and Under Construction Reservoirs

STATE OF TEXAS

TEXAS WATER DEVELOPMENT BOARD
Austin, Texas

January 1973

and moved into the Red River during a flood period, and from there moved into Lake Caddo. Their widespread distribution through Texas began about 1930, when white bass were planted in Lake Dallas, then a small lake near Denton. From here the fish moved upstream to spawn in the Trinity River. Within a decade they became so numerous that the species was planted in all large impoundments. Today, the white bass is extremely abundant. When they are running or schooling, it is no trick for a fisherman to catch a hundred "sandies" in a few hours. Texoma, a reservoir on the Texas-Oklahoma border, provides these large catches frequently. The best period varies according to the lake and climate. It usually begins on south Texas lakes as early as February, continuing through March. In north Texas lakes the spawning migration starts around March, depending on the temperature.

Other pan species are plentiful in Texas. The crappie, for example, thrives in most lakes across Texas. In the eastern part of the state both black and white crappie are harvested. However, in western Texas, where salinities are high in freshwater lakes, only white crappie are present. Much of this fishing is done at night. Catfish are abundant too; they are a favorite of many Texas anglers. The channel and blue catfish are the principal species sought, but flathead catfish also occur.

The carp, carpsucker, and buffalo are problem fish in Texas. These species have virtually taken over many impoundments. As a result total chemical kills have been made on many lakes. In lieu of chemical treatments biological control of rough fish is being tried with introductions of striped bass, walleye, northern pike, flathead catfish, and marine species. However, carp and buffalo do furnish some limited sport to residents.

Many reservoirs have floating fishing docks—a huge sheet-metal building erected on pontoons off the shoreline of many lakes. Within these buildings the fisherman finds all the conveniences of home, often including air-conditioning and television. Many docks have lunch facilities and cold-drink bars for their customers. The surrounding lake bottom is baited to attract fish. These docks are ideal for crappie fishermen, although other species are caught also.

Texas is practically rimmed by rivers. The Red River cuts across the north, separating much of the state and Oklahoma. To the east there is the Sabine, which flows to the Gulf of Mexico. The dusty and romantic Rio Grande is the boundary between the United States and Mexico on the west and south. Through its middle Texas is slashed by a half-dozen rivers and scores of creeks. The watershed of each is characterized as a basin, and this provides a convenient way to locate and discuss the major fishing areas of the state.

CANADIAN RIVER BASIN

The Canadian River Basin occupies the northernmost part of the Texas Panhandle. Public access to the rivers and streams of the region is limited almost entirely to highway crossings. These waters provide very little public fishing. The most significant fisheries in the region are found at Lake Meredith. This 16,505-acre lake, 30 miles north of Amarillo, has an established walleye fishery. Largemouth bass, crappie, channel catfish, blue catfish, and flathead catfish have also been introduced into the lake.

RED RIVER BASIN

The Red River Basin begins in the Panhandle of Texas. The little, almost always dry creeks that make up the bulk of the Basin soon fit into the main body of the Red River at the southeast corner of the Panhandle where it borders Oklahoma. There are a number of smaller lakes within the headwaters of the Red River. Of these, Greenbelt Lake, a 1,990-acre body of water, 5 miles north of Clarendon, offers excellent fisheries. Northern pike, channel catfish, hybrid sunfish, blue catfish, largemouth bass, and crappie are there for the taking. Northern pike have grown to 13 pounds within four years after stocking. Near Denison there is a dam which impounds over 93,000 surface acres to create Lake Texoma. The impoundment lies both in Texas and Oklahoma. Texas has 29,300 acres and 152 miles of shoreline. An Oklahoma license is needed to fish in Oklahoma waters and a Texas license is needed in Texas waters. In the turbid waters of the upper lake the principal fish are channel catfish, white bass, and crappie. Largemouth bass enter the fishing picture as you go down the lake toward Denison Dam. Striped bass stocked by Oklahoma are also taken occasionally in the lake, as well as below the dam. Sauger, a cousin of the walleye, are being caught in increasing numbers below Denison Dam. Catching sauger is an experience that local anglers appreciate greatly.

SULPHUR RIVER BASIN

Lake Texarkana, a 20,300-acre impoundment completed in the early 1950's, deserves special mention because of its large variety of gamefish. Largemouth bass, white bass, black and white crappie, channel catfish, blue catfish, and flathead catfish are available to catch. However, fishermen should be careful of the numerous underwater hazards, such as stumps, logs, and other obstructions found in this lake.

CYPRESS RIVER BASIN

Perhaps the oldest and best-known lake in Texas is Caddo, which straddles the Texas-Louisiana boundary line with 40,000 surface acres of tree-filled, alligator-infested waters. The lake covers approximately 14,000 surface acres in Texas. Indian legend credits an earthquake as originally forming the lake in 1811. Another theory concludes a huge log jam in the Red River created the lake. It is a swamp-type of lake, with huge cypress trees, lily pads, and other aquatic vegetation. Caddo is noted for its large variety of fish species. Largemouth bass, black crappie, channel catfish, and various sunfish species provide good fishing. The chain pickerel, a species native to Caddo Lake, provides a bonus to bass fishermen during the winter months. Caddo has a heavy population of trash fish such as gar and carp. However, the main problem of biologists is controlling the spread of lily pads, duckweeds, and milfoil, which almost cover the lake in certain areas. Colorful names of lake areas such as Hogwallow, Eagle Nest, Old Folks Playground, Whistle-berry Slough, and many more add to the enchantment of Caddo Lake. Fishing regulations are simplified for Caddo anglers by a reciprocal license agreement for border waters of Texas and Louisiana.

Caddo is at the mouth of Cypress Creek, and a dozen or so miles upstream there is an impoundment, Lake O' the Pines. This lake contains 18,700 surface acres at water supply pool level. It provides good fishing for all native gamefish species, including largemouth bass, Kentucky spotted bass, crappie, and sunfish. Although only a limited channel catfish fishery exists in the reservoir, a good population of flathead catfish provides sport for the trotline fisherman.

SABINE RIVER BASIN

The Sabine watershed, which forms a large part of the eastern boundary of Texas, contains three lakes that merit special attention. One of these is Lake Murvaul. It is a 3,800-surface-acre reservoir located on Murvaul Bayou in Panola County. This lake has developed the reputation of being one of the best lakes in Texas for large bass. Many lunkers ranging from 8–10 pounds have been taken. January, February, and March are the favorite months for Murvaul bass fishermen.

Lake Tawakoni, a 36,500-acre lake located mostly in Hunt County, offers to the fisherman white crappie, channel catfish, largemouth bass, and yellow bass. The yellow bass is a relative of the white bass, but does not get as large. This vast, often wind-swept lake requires a good boat and motor for safe angling. There are several fully-equipped marinas around Tawakoni, as well as expert guide services.

The largest impoundment on the Sabine River watershed is Toledo Bend Reservoir (181,000 acres). Construction was completed in 1968, and the reservoir quickly filled to conservation pool level. Toledo Bend is one of the most popular bass lakes in the nation. In Texas and Louisiana, the reservoir contains over 1,200 miles of shoreline and the Texas portion lies in the Sabine National

Forest. The reciprocal fishing license agreement for border waters of Texas and Louisiana honors the license of either state.

NECHES RIVER BASIN

Lying in the Neches River Basin is a 114,500-acre body of water called Sam Rayburn reservoir. Angelina, Nacogdoches, San Augustine, Sabine, and Jasper counties each have land areas within the boundaries of this reservoir. Much of the upper portion of the lake and some areas of the lower portion have much inundated timber, which provides excellent largemouth bass fishing. Crappie, channel catfish, flathead catfish, and sunfish are also plentiful. Excellent camping, picnicking, and fishing facilities are available at numerous U.S. Forest Service and U.S. Corps of Engineer recreation areas.

TRINITY RIVER BASIN

The Trinity watershed also is vast in its scope. Most of the dam sites are in the general vicinity of Fort Worth and Dallas. Some of the lakes on the Trinity River are old and well known. They include Bridgeport, Eagle Mountain, Benbrook, Grapevine, Graza-Little Elm, Lavon, and others. They were built both for flood control and domestic water supply, with recreation as one criterion. These provide largemouth bass, crappie, white bass, channel catfish, flathead catfish, and sunfish for a large population area. The hottest largemouth bass fishing in this watershed, and possibly the whole state, is Livingston Reservoir. It lies within Polk, San Jacinto, Trinity, and Walker counties on the Trinity River, and covers an area of approximately 82,250 acres.

BRAZOS RIVER BASIN

The Brazos runs diagonally across Texas with a watershed of more than 40,000 square miles, and has several important lakes. Among these are Possum Kingdom, De Cordova Bend, and Buffalo Springs, although there are a number of other lakes that provide good fishing.

Possum Kingdom Lake is a scenic 19,800-acre lake in Palo Pinto County that has well-developed recreational facilities. White bass are caught throughout most of the year. Largemouth bass, channel catfish, flathead catfish, crappie, sunfish, carp, and buffalo are also taken regularly. The tailwaters from Possum Kingdom Dam support a successful fall and winter trout fishery. The first 4 miles of the Brazos below the dam is prime trout habitat; it also produces large sunfish as a bonus.

De Cordova Bend Lake, located 8 miles southeast of Granbury on the Brazos River, has a surface area of 8,500 acres. It has an active striped bass stocking program that will hopefully help to establish a new predator and sport fish for Texas.

Buffalo Springs is a small, 260-acre lake 5 miles from Lubbock. It has several types of trailer hookups and plenty of picnic areas. Hybrid redear and green sunfish up to 2 pounds have been harvested in this lake. This growth was attained within two years after stocking.

COLORADO RIVER BASIN

The Colorado rises at the New Mexico state line and runs diagonally across the state, spreading out in the center like a fan. It is a stream of many tributaries, most of which flow through semiarid country, but carry torrential floodwaters during the rainy season. Some of these tributaries are popular, such as the three branches of the Concho which converge near San Angelo. A lake of particular importance to fishermen here is E.V. Spence (Robert Lee). This is a 15,000-acre body of water completed in 1969. It provides good fishing for white and black bass, white crappie, channel and flathead catfish. Also the best striped bass population in Texas is found here. It is an interesting fact that the stripers are readily taken by trotlines. Another lake in this area that supports an exotic fish is San Angelo Reservoir. The reservoir covers 5,440 acres when full. It is a murky lake with a good population of walleye which have shown an appetite for small carp. Walleye have proven their worth in rough fish control in many west Texas lakes.

Further downstream the Llano River brings in additional water from the limestone and granite country of central west Texas. This spring-fed river is a favorite of many Texans. The waters abound with black bass and catfish.

The Colorado is famous also for its Highland Lake area, which begins at Austin, the capital city, and extends northward, with a half-dozen fine lakes in a 100-mile stretch. These lakes include Town Lake, almost at the foot of the state capital; Lake Austin, Lake Travis, Lake Marble Falls, Lyndon B. Johnson, Inks, and Buchanan. Buchanan is the largest (23,200 acres). Being located in central Texas these lakes draw tremendous numbers of recreationists from the larger population centers. This is especially true of lakes Travis and Lyndon B. Johnson. These lakes offer good fishing for largemouth bass, channel catfish, flathead catfish, and sunfish. Fishing for white bass and crappie is seasonally good.

GUADALUPE RIVER BASIN

The Guadalupe watershed includes only one major impoundment, Canyon Reservoir. This reservoir, 8,240 acres, provides good fishing for largemouth bass, channel catfish, flathead catfish, and sunfish. The Guadalupe River below Canyon Dam is a popular rainbow and brown trout fishery.

SAN ANTONIO RIVER BASIN

A body of water that has made a name for itself in Texas is the 5,575-acre Medina Lake. It is located 8 miles northwest of Riomedina on the Medina River, a tributary of the San Antonio River. The state record largemouth bass (13 pounds, 8 ounces) was caught here in January 1943. However, in comparison with some of the state's hot bass lakes, Medina is considered only fair for its bass fishing; but it is great for its flathead fishery.

Two other lakes in this watershed deserve special mention. Calaveras and Braunig near San Antonio have for many years been quality largemouth bass-fishing waters.

NUECES RIVER BASIN

The Nueces River Basin holds in its boundaries possibly the best channel and blue catfish trotline fishing lake in the state. This is Corpus Christi Lake, a 22,050-acre impoundment, that was constructed by the city of Corpus Christi on the lower Nueces River.

The watershed is also noted for its troutlike streams. These waters offer good largemouth bass, spotted bass, catfish, and sunfish fishing. Among the best known are the Atascosa River, Hondo Creek, Frio River, Sabinal River, and Nueces River. Many of these will go underground at points (upside-down streams) and run a mile or so before resurfacing again. Unfortunately, these beautiful streams for the most part are on private lands and, therefore, offer very little public fishing.

RIO GRANDE RIVER BASIN

The Rio Grande watershed has two important reservoirs, Falcon and Amistad. Both are located on the Rio Grande River between the United States and Mexico.

Falcon's dam is around 150 miles above the mouth of the Rio Grande. The lake has a maximum area of 115,600 surface acres at its highest elevation; and it has large crops of black bass, crappie, white bass, catfish, and sunfish. An empty stringer at the end of a day's fishing indicates that the fisherman either didn't bait his hook or left his lures at home. Excellent camping facilities are found at Falcon State Park. Fishermen should keep in mind that a Mexico fishing license is required of all persons fishing on the Mexican side, and a Texas license is needed on the Texas side of the lake.

Amistad Dam is located 12 miles northwest of Del Rio. The 85-mile-long, 67,000-acre reservoir was completed early in 1969. This project is an international recreational area effort administered by the National Park Service on the United States side. Fishing success has been excellent with largemouth bass, channel catfish, flathead catfish, blue catfish, crappie, and sunfish being available. Fishing on this lake requires a Mexico license in Mexican waters, and a Texas license in Texas waters.

Amistad Lake is one of the finest lakes in the Southwest.

Other impoundments are scattered all over the state. Practically every tributary to the principal streams has one or more dams, usually for flood control, but affording recreation possibilities.   —N.E.C.

SALTWATER FISHING

The 1,200 miles of Texas coastline bordering the northwestern Gulf of Mexico offers a variety of opportunity for the sports fisherman. The major part of this coastline is sheltered from the open Gulf by means of a chain of long, narrow, barrier islands and peninsulas. The main components of this chain are Galveston Island in the north, then the Matagorda Peninsula, Matagorda Island, St. Joseph Island, Mustang Island, and Padre Island. An 88-mile stretch of Padre Island is set aside as a National Seashore.

The broad, shallow lagoons and bays that lie between the barrier islands and the mainland are some of the most productive marine areas in the world. Hundreds of thousands of pounds of spotted seatrout, red and black drum, sheepshead, and southern flounder are taken commercially each year, and the sport fishermen's catch is almost as large. These vast inland waterways are particularly attractive for the small-boat fisherman since, for the most part, they are well-protected from the heavy seas of the open Gulf.

Sport fishing in the marine waters of Texas takes place in four distinct kinds of area, and, in general, each has its characteristic species of fish. In the lagoons and bays, the most numerous and sought-after game species is the spotted seatrout (locally speckled trout). Next is the red

drum (redfish), then such species as the southern flounder, black drum, sheepshead, Atlantic croaker, sand seatrout, southern kingfish, gafftopsail catfish, and sea catfish. Also, especially for the benefit of the young angler, there are millions of the smaller pinfish, pigfish, and spadefish.

Along the beaches on the Gulf side of the barrier islands there is fishing from the surf, piers, jetties, and from small boats that can be taken out when the weather is favorable. Many fishes tend to congregate about buoys and other floating objects, oil-rig platforms, wrecks, and artificial reefs. In recent years, sport fishing for big sharks with special heavy equipment has become quite popular. This usually takes place from the piers and jetties, and the catch consists of such species as the great hammerhead, finetooth, blacknose, blacktip, bull, lemon, tiger, sharpnose, and sand sharks. Also, large rays and sawfishes are occasionally taken.

The usual sport catch from the shallow Gulf and surf area will consist of such species as the ladyfish, snook, comb grouper, black grouper, pompano, permit, crevalle jack, red drum, Spanish mackerel, king mackerel, silver seatrout, tripletail, and cobia. Around the turn of the century, Port Aransas on Mustang Island was known as the tarpon capital of the world. Now, only a few tarpon are taken each year. The decline is probably due to a series of dry years that have raised the salinity of the inland waters which may effect some phase of the tarpon's life history.

Close to the edge of the shelf some 30–40 miles offshore is located a series of natural reefs that are locally known as the "Snapper Banks." Large party boats, especially built for the snapper-bank trade, carry fishermen out to these areas from such ports as Galveston, Corpus Christi, Aransas Pass, Port Aransas, and Port Isabel. On the banks, the most popular species is the red snapper, a highly valued food fish. Other species frequently taken are the Warsaw grouper, vermilion snapper, rock hind, red grouper, cubera snapper, yellowtail snapper, wenchman, saucereye porgy, and the smooth dogfish shark.

Offshore trolling in the bluewater areas for the big-game species is an important activity, particularly from the Corpus Christi-Port Aransas area south to Port Isabel. The Atlantic sailfish is the most frequently caught, but other species, such as the great barracuda, amberjack, wahoo, blackfin tuna, blue marlin, swordfish, dolphin, and bluefish, are common. Also taken are the big pelagic sharks, the thresher, silky, whitetip, and the white (maneater) shark.   —J.C.B.

THERMAL STRATIFICATION Water is separated into distinct horizontal temperature layers, typically three, during summer in deep or sheltered lakes in the temperate zone. Thermal stratification also occurs in the ocean, although the situation is complicated by salinity and other factors. Water temperatures are important in controlling fish activity and distribution at all seasons of the year, hence, they are of interest to fishermen.

TEMPERATURE CYCLE IN LAKES OF TEMPERATE ZONE

The striking annual temperature cycle in lakes of temperate regions is due to the relationship between water temperature and water density. The physical law involved is as follows: freshwater is at maximum density at a temperature of 39.2°F. (4°C.); at temperatures above or below this point, water becomes lighter, hence rises. The phenomenon of water becoming lighter between 39.2°F. and 32°F. instead of heavier has great biological implications, for it means that lakes freeze from the top down rather than the bottom up. If the latter situation prevailed, lakes in temperate and colder regions would freeze solid, and summer warmth would only bring about superficial melting to relatively shallow depths. Thus, the annual temperature cycle in a typical deep lake located in the temperate zone can be described by the vertical temperature series taken at four characteristic stages corresponding roughly to the four seasons—winter stagnation (inverse stratification), spring overturn, summer stratification, and fall overturn.

Winter Stagnation Under conditions of ice cover, a state of inverse stratification exists in which the lightest and coldest water lies immediately under the ice. The temperature rapidly increases from a low of 32°F. to or near to the maximum density temperature of 39.2°. The ice cover effectively cuts off major external disturbances, such as wind, so the state of inverse stratification is a relatively stable condition.

Spring Overturn With spring warmth and melting of the ice cover, the superficial cold stratum is rapidly warmed. Since the difference in density of water at 39.2°F. and 32°F. is relatively slight (1.00000 and 0.999868, respectively, for pure water), wind is an effective mixing agent in dispersing the ice-chilled waters with the relatively warmer waters below. The net influence of exposure to mixing and simultaneous warming is to bring all depths to maximum density. When the vertical temperatures are at or near 39.2°F., wind action can readily circulate the entire water mass. The period of homothermy and attendant mixing and circulation is of great biological importance because any depletion of oxygen that may have occurred in deeper waters is replenished and nutrient materials, such as phosphorus and nitrogen, are circulated into upper, more productive layers.

Summer Stratification As the air warms with the onset of spring, superficial water layers also rise in temperature and decrease in density. At first this is of no great apparent consequence, since difference in density is not sufficiently great to prevent mixing of the warmer, superficial layers. Soon a state is reached, however, where the thermally induced density differences become sufficiently divergent to resist mixing except in the most superficial layers. The development of this stage is, of course, gradual. Temporary states of stratification may exist during periods of weather that is relatively warm, only to be broken up by high winds or change in wind direction to quarters more favorable to mixing. In the transition period, vertical temperature series falls rapidly from maximum temperatures in the top feet into colder waters below.

True summer stratification produces three characteristic layers of water that remain identifiable throughout the summer and early autumn. The three layers are known as the epilimnion, the thermocline, and the hypolimnion. The epilimnion is a layer of warmwater that circulates freely with wind action and whose temperatures follow trends in air temperatures. The thickness of the epilimnion, and other thermal layers, is influenced, in addition to seasonal air temperature, by wind action, shape, size, and depth of the particular body of water, as well as latitude and the usual vagaries of weather.

The circulating layer grades rather abruptly into a zone of rapid temperature drop, known as the thermocline. Technically, it is defined as the area where water temperature decreases 1°C. for each meter increase in depth (English equivalent, 0.548°F. per foot).

The thermocline grades rapidly into the hypolimnion, and the temperatures here fall gradually to minimum readings. The minimum temperature is reasonably constant for any given body of water that is deep enough to stratify, and is determined by the composite effect of the

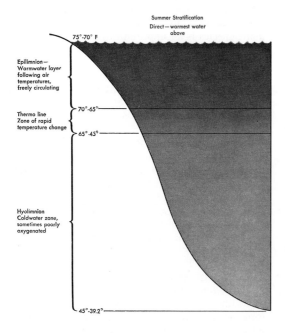

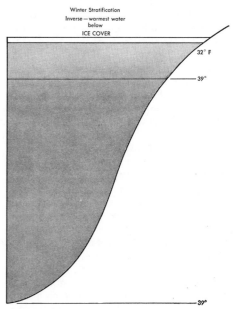

Thermal Stratification of a Lake

factors enumerated above. This minimum temperature may be at the maximum density of 39.2°F. but often will be in the 40°F. range. In lakes exhibiting depths of several hundred feet, the minimum temperature is slightly below 39.2°F. due to the depressing effect of the weight of the water above.

Some lakes may develop temporary stratification in early season, only to have it dissipated as the heat input increases with time. In general, the thickness of the epilimnion increases, and the thermocline narrows as summer progresses. Thus the thickness of the epilimnion in a large lake in early summer may be 30 feet, but by early autumn may be 70 feet. By contrast in a small, well-sheltered lake, the warm, superficial water layer might not exceed 10–15 feet throughout the season. And if the water had a dark stain typical of bog lakes, then the epilimnion might be only 3–5 feet in thickness because the heat rays are rapidly absorbed by the reddish-brown color of the water. In the latter case, water temperatures of the epilimnion might be 75°–85°F. on warm days, while a clearwater lake with otherwise similar characteristics might exhibit temperatures of 70°–75°F.

On the other side of the scale, the largest inland lakes, such as the upper Great Lakes, have sufficient volumes of coldwater and such an expanse exposed to wind action that summer stratification doesn't occur. Deep polar lakes may not get enough heat in the short Arctic summer to raise surface temperature much above 50°.

Influence of Wind Wind action can cause profound variations in the temperature picture in large lakes. Sometimes double thermoclines appear, but these are of temporary nature. Strong prevailing winds blowing along a favorable geographical axis cause water drift to windward, and a rise in water level is observable on this shore. The "piling up" of water results in a depression of the thermocline on the windward shore and an elevation to leeward, with increase or decrease in the thickness of the overlying warmwater stratum (epilimnion).

In the tendency to return to equilibrium, regular seesaw oscillations may be observed. In addition, subsurface currents are developed, running opposite to the surface current moving in the direction of the wind. This general phenomenon is called a *seiche*. Seiches may also be due to differences in atmospheric pressure or by a sudden influx of water in a localized area at opposite ends of a long lake.

Fall Overturn Cooler weather in autumn lowers the temperature of the epilimnion, water sinking to its own density level as it is cooled at the surface. Ultimately as maximum density (or the prevailing temperature of the hypolimnion) is reached, the lake circulates again, bringing renewing oxygen supplies to deeper water and a redistribution of nutrients. Surface waters approaching 39°F. will usually freeze quickly with any subsequent cold, calm weather, because of inverse stratification noted previously. Large, deep lakes freeze later than others because the "heat budget," the amount of heat stored in the water in summer, is greater. Thus the largest and deepest freshwater lakes of the temperate zone may freeze only rarely. Lakes that do not freeze in winter do not develop inverse stratification, and are circulated freely by the wind, hence are homothermous (same temperature) from surface to bottom throughout the winter. Temperatures continue to fall throughout the winter, and March temperatures of 34°–37°F. may be reached. Thus lakes that freeze present "warmer" winter climates than those that do not.

EFFECT ON FISH

The seasonal thermal changes have profound influences on the distribution of fishes, since coolwater species must move deeper as the water warms in late spring and as the thermocline is depressed by seasonal changes of weather. In productive lakes and many artificial reservoirs, the cold deepwater of the hypolimnion may become uninhabitable to fish if the oxygen endowment received during the spring or fall overturns is exhausted (mostly by decomposition of organic matter "raining" down from the well-lighted strata above). The thermocline usually contains sufficient oxygen to provide a habitat for coldwater species such as trout. Not all deep lakes and ponds develop an oxygen deficit in the hypolimnion in summer or winter. These lakes have sufficient volumes of deepwater to store up adequate oxygen, and, because of a lower productive level, dissolved oxygen does not fall to critical levels. In some smaller sheltered lakes, mixing may be incomplete or may not occur in some years if weather conditions are such that surface waters warm rapidly without mixing in early spring.   —D.A.W.

THERMOCLINE A biological and physical term to describe the intermediate layer of water in a lake where temperature changes rapidly. The thermocline begins at 15–25 feet below the surface. From its top to the beginning of the hypolimnion, the temperature drops 1.8°F. (minimum) every 3.28 feet in depth. *See also* Thermal Stratification

THORNBACK RAY *Raia clavata* This is one of the commonest and most typical of European rays. Skates and rays may be distinguished from each other by examining the snout. In rays the snout is less than half as long as it is broad; the thornback shows this feature well. Skates, on the other hand, have a longer snout.

The coloration of the thornback ray is rather variable, but usually the back is mottled brown, and in many young specimens the tail is banded. The underside or belly is plain white. Specimens may bear ocelli or dark spots on the "wings." These ocelli, when present, are pure black, perhaps with some white blotches *around* them. However, abnormally colored individuals are sometimes caught.

More diagnostic of *R. clavata* are the rows and patches of sharp spines (modified placoid scales as in other cartilage fishes) on the back. Most outstanding are the large thornlike spines on the central region of the back. Basically the pattern is of 2 or 3 rows running parallel to each other. There may be 4–6 spines in each row, and each spine has a large swollen base. The normal pattern is of 1 row along the midline, and 2 others parallel to it at some small distance away.

Further spines are found on the tail (used as a lashing weapon when boated), but these are also thornlike and never long daggers as in the stingrays (*Trygon* spp.).

Much smaller patches of fine spines are found at the base of the snout and near the eyes and the large prominent spiracles. In the male there are patches of smaller spines on the extremity of each "wing." Males can also be distinguished, as in other cartilage fishes, by the copulatory claspers on the pelvic fins (the wings are mostly pectoral fins). In abnormal specimens some larger spines may also sometimes be found on the underside.

Thornback rays are found in the Mediterranean and the Eastern Atlantic northward to the latitude of Norway. Other rays may overlap this range, and one must be careful to distinguish them in claiming fishing records.

One constant feature which will serve to distinguish thornbacks from other European rays is the markedly angular outline. Other European rays are much more rounded in shape. Thornbacks are also more common within their range; 37 percent of all rays landed in English Channel ports are thornbacks. The next most common, the cuckoo ray (*R. naevus*), only makes up 19 percent of landings.

Two other Atlantic European rays bear spines on the back:

(a) The Cuckoo Ray, which has a double row of spines along the midline of the back, the rows being close to each other, also has smaller spines extending *onto* the snout itself. It has a very rounded outline, and ocelli on the wings are marbled black and white.

(b) The Starry Ray (*R. Radiata*) is a more northern species, found mainly on the Scottish and Scandinavian coasts, and is much more "thorny" on the back than even the thornback.

The thornback lives at all depths and on nearly all bottoms in inshore European waters. It is said to prefer sand or gravel, and will come in close to shore within casting range of the beach. However, most anglers seek them from boats. According to marking experiments thornbacks tend to stay in the same general area the whole year round. The normal group met with is a male-female pair.

Though they may not move far, they are not sluggish. Thornbacks can in fact swim quite well in the usual skate or ray manner; that is, by wavelike motions of the pectoral wings. Fishermen have even observed them surface and chase pilchard shoals, though this is without doubt unusual behavior; they are normally bottom-dwellers.

It is here, on the bottom, that the food is found— mainly hermit crabs, ordinary crustaceans, small bottom fish, worms, and mollusks. The teeth are typically flat and crushing for this diet, especially in the female. The male is more piscivorous and has sharper teeth. Crushing jaws and teeth require powerful muscles, and in both sexes the jaw muscles form a large rounded mass marketed and eaten as "skate eyeballs."

Thornbacks grow to 40–50 pounds; but the usual weight is 3–15 pounds.

LIFE HISTORY

Breeding takes place in the areas in which thornbacks are found in the warmer months. As with other skates and rays fertilization is internal and is effected by the male's claspers. The eggs are laid in horny capsules or "mermaid's purses." A thornback "purse" is squat and rectangular, with a horn at each corner. Excluding horns, the main part of the case measures up to 3½ inches long and 2½ inches broad. Other identifying marks on the egg case are the keel and the profile, which is flat on one side and convex on the other. The convex side bears sticky filaments, and longer ones drape from the margin of the purse. These filaments are for anchoring the egg to weeds and other cover during development.

Development within the egg takes up to 5 months, ending in the hatching of a perfect miniature ray about 2½

inches across the wings, which swims off to assume the adult mode of life.

COMMERCIAL VALUE

The proportion of thornbacks in Channel catches has already been stated earlier; it will therefore be seen that thornback flesh must be much used in the fish trade. It is widely sold skinned, the delicacies being the wings and "eyeballs." Such cutlets may be offered for sale raw or ready-to-eat by the fried-fish trade. It is considered a delicacy in France, England, and elsewhere, where it is normally sold, like all ray meat, under the general name of "skate." The commercial catch is almost entirely by trawls and longlines.

ANGLING VALUE

Thornbacks are commonly sought by inshore anglers from dinghies, pier, and the shore. Along the eastern coast of England they are the premier summer fish, while cod take their place in winter. They are taken under many conditions, but a favorite time with anglers are the warm close nights of high summer, with a calm or slightly swelling sea.

The normal tackle has lines of between 15 and 30 pounds test, with hooks up to size 4/0. The bait is laid on the bottom, generally with a leger rig and free-running sinker. Fish strips are the most widely used baits; but shellfish, squid, and crab are also employed. The first indications of a bite should be left and a run waited for— off the spool of a multiplying reel with an audible check, for example. In summer they are paired for spawning, so a second thornback is often caught after the first.

The fight is much harder than that of most of their relatives, such as the skate; thornbacks have been known to leap clear of the water. Generally they "kite" against the tide, and may take some time to bring to the gaff.

—D.M.

THREADFIN JACK *Citula otrynter* Also called thread pompano and sometimes listed under the scientific name of *Citula dorsalis*, this eastern Pacific species may be identical to another species described from the central Pacific.

The body of the threadfin jack is less deep and less broad and the head less blunt than the Pacific threadfin. Only the first softray of the dorsal and anal fins is excessively elongated, and this becomes shorter in larger fish. The 7–8 spines in the first dorsal fin may be covered by skin in large fish, and the remainder of the fin contains one spine and 18–19 softrays. The two detached anal fin spines are covered by skin in large fish, and the remainder of the fin contains 1 spine and 15–17 softrays. The first gill

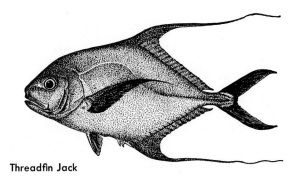

Threadfin Jack

arch has 5–7 gillrakers on the upper limb and 17–18 gill-rakers on the lower limb. There are about 48–56 weakly pointed scutes in the straight lateral line. The body and head may be slightly dark above, with most of the body silvery. The young have 5–6 body bars.

The threadfin jack is known from Peru to Topolobampo, Mexico, and at Conception Bay on the east coast of Baja California, and at the Galápagos Islands. The species may grow to 2 feet long.

LIFE HISTORY

The life history is not known. Specimens with developed gonads have been taken from Panama in April and from Mexican waters in June. The smallest known specimen, ½ inch long, was taken off Costa Rica in February.

ANGLING VALUE

The threadfin jack is taken by angling, and in Mexico, at least, it is sold commercially. *See also* Carangidae, Threadfins —F.H.B.

THREADFINS Three species of two genera of threadfins (*Alectis* and *Citula*) occur in American waters.

They are distinguished by very elongate lobes of the dorsal and anal fins in fish up to a foot or more in length (these become shorter at larger sizes); pointed scutes along the straight part of the lateral line; 7–8 spines in the first dorsal fin which are never greatly elongated at any size, and may be reduced in large fish. *See also* Carangidae —F.H.B.

THREADFIN SHAD *Dorosoma petenense* This species closely resembles the gizzard shad, *Dorosoma cepedianum*, from which it differs in the coloration of the back and the caudal fin, which are yellowish. The anal fin is shorter in the threadfin shad, there being 20–23 rays in the anal fin, while the gizzard shad has about 31 anal rays. The adult has a distinct spot on the shoulder which is usually not seen in the gizzard shad. The threadfin shad is generally smaller than the gizzard shad, the adult reaching only 6–8 inches.

It is found along the Gulf Coast from Florida to Texas, and northward into the Mississippi valley to Tennessee and southern Arkansas and Oklahoma. Taken as far south as British Honduras, this fish was recently introduced in California and Arizona as a forage fish for more desirable sport fishes.

ECONOMIC VALUE

Because of its smaller size, the threadfin shad remains available longer as forage for predators and thus is more desirable. Like the gizzard shad, it feeds on mud from which it extracts plant material and organic debris. It is used as bait for catfish, while the young are also used as bait for other gamefishes. —D.dS.

THREESPINE STICKLEBACK *Gasterosteus aculeatus* The numerous bony plates on the sides of this fish (28 or more), the convex outline of the tail, and the two large dorsal spines followed by a smaller, third spine identify this member of the family Gasterosteidae. Its color is dull olive above, with faint bars or blotches, to white or silvery on the belly. This color varies depending upon the breeding season, state of sexual maturity, and the habitat. It grows to about 4 inches long.

A widely ranging species, it is found from Labrador to Chesapeake Bay and from northern Norway and Iceland to the Mediterranean and Black seas. It also occurs in northern China, southern Japan, and Baja California, as well as the Hudson Bay region and Lake Ontario. It occurs in salt- or brackish water, apparently readily adapting to either mode of life. While coastal forms are largely restricted to estuaries, a few may drift off to sea in clumps of floating weed. A year-round resident, particularly where grass or weed can be found, it moves into somewhat deeper water during the winter.

LIFE HISTORY

Spawning occurs in brackish or freshwater, from May to July, and is accompanied by one of the most elaborate nest-building and egg-care patterns known among fishes. In about 6 weeks, the young have grown to a length of about ⅗ inch long, when they closely resemble the adults.

It is a pugnacious species, driving away other fishes from its territory with its sharp spines. Omnivorous in habits, small invertebrates, such as copepods, mysids, and young shrimp, and small fishes and fish eggs are eaten.

ANGLING VALUE

Although it has no apparent value to the angler, its peculiar nest-building habits render it important to science, and its abundance reflects a key role in the ecology of shallow coastal waters. —D.dS.

THRESHER SHARK *Alopias vulpinus* Easily recognized by its very long tail, this species cannot be confused with other Atlantic sharks except for the bigeye thresher (*which see*), from which it differs essentially in having a smaller eye. The tail is about as long as the body, and the pectoral fins are long and sickle-shaped, although they are relatively shorter than those of the bigeye thresher. The snout is blunt but pointed, and the smooth teeth lack cusps.

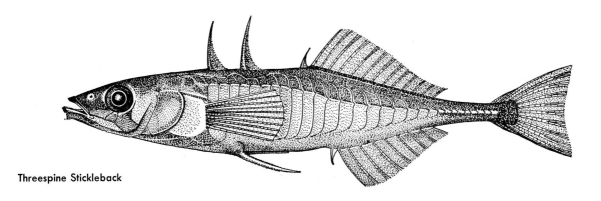

Threespine Stickleback

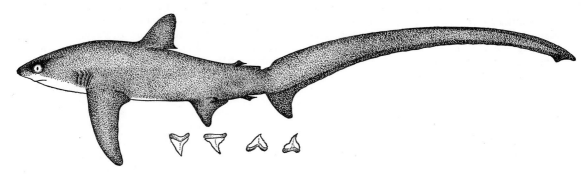

Thresher Shark (teeth upper jaw *left*, lower jaw *right*)

The coloration is nearly uniform on the sides and back, ranging from brown to blue-gray or black with metallic hues. The lower parts are white, occasionally with gray mottlings.

The thresher shark grows to 20 feet and a weight of perhaps 1,000 pounds. A 14½-foot fish weighs about 500 pounds. This shark is predominantly a dweller of the subtropics and warm temperate zone, and occurs from Nova Scotia to Argentina, and from Ireland to the Cape of Good Hope, and throughout the Mediterranean. In the Pacific it is known from Oregon to Chile, and Hawaii, Japan, and China to Arabia and Australia. It is not certain if these forms from the various areas are identical.

LIFE HISTORY

Found largely at or near the surface, it occurs predominantly in the open sea, and is found offshore during the cold months. It is seldom taken in the tropics, being a fish of cooler waters. It feeds on schooling fishes, such as bluefish, mackerel, and menhaden, using its long tail to herd and stun its prey. When its prey is extremely common, threshers occasionally congregate to the extent that they become a nuisance to commercial fishermen by tearing their nets.

DANGER TO MAN

There is no indication that threshers are ever dangerous to man. —D.dS.

TIBURON The Spanish name for certain sharks (*which see*)

TIDES Tides are created by the gravitational forces or "pull" of the sun and moon. Being closer to earth, the moon exerts more influence. Twice during each 24-hour period the tide pours out of bays and estuarine waters, running away from the coast, and then after a pause or "slack" period it flows back. How much the tide falls depends on the location. It may be just 2–3 feet in one place, and 6–7 feet just a few miles away. Oceanographers attribute the variation to bottom contours and oscillations. Generally speaking, the tidefall is less close to the Equator, and greater toward either the North Pole or the South Pole. But for most anglers in the United States, the rule of thumb is that the moon rises approximately 50 minutes later each day, which results in the tide being 50 minutes later in each 24-hour period. There are local variations, particularly in bays, which may cause a difference of 30 minutes or more. Fishermen generally figure the tide as one hour later each day.

This wouldn't work if you were fishing in Tahiti, for example, but there you'd never need a tide table. This is one of the exceptions to the rule. In Tahiti it is always high tide at noon and midnight, and always low tide at sunrise and sunset. This island is located near a nodal line where the effect of the moon is nonexistent. The sun creates a very slight tide, which is always the same day after day.

Tides are important to the angler because they are closely related to the movements of fish. For some species, such as the red drum, coho salmon, bonefish, chinook salmon, permit, tarpon, spotted seatrout, and snook, a knowledge of local tidal conditions is often essential to success. There is no single rule in relation to all bays, flats, inlets, and beaches, but there are some general factors which the angler can evaluate. High tides will put water in spots which are otherwise too shallow to hold gamefish at lowwater. This can be good, and it can be bad. For example, a flat which is exposed at lowwater may attract red drum on the flood and provide excellent fishing. On the other hand a mangrove-bordered river which holds snook can be absolutely worthless on the flood because the fish work right up under the roots to forage for crabs and baitfish; this is a common frustration, and all you can do is wait for the tide to ebb. Although the ebbing tide on the flat should still be as productive as the flood, this is not true everywhere. Some of the extremely large and shallow flats are vacated almost at once when the tide turns because they empty so fast. An ebb tide is usually ideal when fishing around inlets, because as the water of the bay level drops, baitfish, crabs, and shrimp are sucked out to the sea by the currents that are in effect.

In fishing terminology the tide is *flooding* on the way in to the coast. It is *half tide* three hours later. When it reaches its peak six hours later, it is said to be *highwater slack*. The tide is *ebbing* on the way out again and is at *lowwater slack* just before the tide turns and starts to flood back to the coast. How this affects fishing is often as follows: during a slack tide, the baitfish scatter and move in close to shore, under banks, and on the beaches where they can feed unmolested by predatory species. As the strong ebb and flood tides occur, these little baitfish are pulled along in the flow. This creates good fishing in and around inlets or at the mouths of estuaries, where the best period is usually in the first two hours of an ebbing tide or a flooding tide.

Dead water occurs at both high and low slacks, when the current stops flowing. There are exceptions to this where tides ebb from bays or lagoons through narrow inlets. Great volumes of water may rush through an inlet from an otherwise landlocked body of water long after the tide has turned. This can result in extremely choppy water where both currents meet head-on and is dangerous to small boats. However, it is seldom a favorable situation for gamefish either, and generally speaking "dead-water" periods are just that.

Spring tides, which occur when the sun and moon are in line with the earth (thus combining their forces), occur twice each month at full and new moons. These tides have no relation to the season and are abnormally high. If pushed by a strong wind they flood over docks and sea walls. When the Fisheries Research Board of Canada was investigating the migrations of Arctic char on the Sylvia Grinnel River in 1951, it was found that the mass movement of fish took place on the spring tides. At the mouth of the river, in saltwater, great numbers of fish were observed moving in with the tide, some jumping clear of the water, others breaking the surface with their backs as they headed toward the falls at the river mouth. When the tide turned, they reversed their direction and returned to the bay. The falls presented a barrier, and, not having the jumping ability of Atlantic salmon, the char had to take advantage of the highest tides to enter the river in even small numbers. When the spring tides occurred twice during the month, this was accompanied by a large-scale run of fish. This is not an isolated circumstance in the north country; many salmon, char, and sea-trout migrations coincide with spring tides, and it's the wise angler who takes them into account.

An extreme spring tide leaves a strange pattern in the powder-like sand around a Bahamian island

Neap tides, the counter condition to spring tides, are abnormally low. They also occur twice each month at the first- and third-quarter moon phases. The sun and moon form a right angle, with the earth as the center, which reduces their gravitational pull. Neap tides can spoil flats and banks fishing completely in some areas, simply because there's miles of mud or marl between you and the fish. But they can be a boon to the inlet angler because the narrow confines of its channel may be inundated with baitfish. Some exceptional mackerel, bluefish, and striper runs occur during neap tides.

INFLUENCE OF THE WIND

Tides are by no means the sole criteria in determining fishing success. This is particularly true in surf-fishing where the wind is an equally important factor. Winds provide the energy necessary to create a wave. The size of a wave depends on four things—the wind's velocity; the duration of the wind; its fetch, or the distance it blows without obstruction; and its consistency in direction. These conditions vary greatly and produce seas from 4 inches to a probable 40 feet (at 60 miles per hour over a distance of 900 miles). Actually, the sea itself is not moved very much by the wind in a horizontal direction. The water rolls in a circular path as each wave passes through it. However, when a wave reaches shallow water, the circular motion becomes flattened due to the proximity of the bottom, and this new shape causes the wave to become higher, and with the now increasing velocity it surges ahead, until, lacking support from below, it literally falls on itself. There is tremendous energy in a breaking wave, and stones, shells, mollusks, sandbugs, and even baitfish get tossed shoreward by its force. Large numbers of gamefish which usually occur further offshore may appear in shallow water following storms to take advantage of the food dislodged inshore. The first big storms of September mark the beginning of fast striped-bass and drum fishing along the Atlantic seaboard, and in October, when the surf is creased in leaden furrows, the beach caster gets good results. *See* Currents, Marine Ecology   —A.J.McC.

TIGERFISH *Hydrocyon lineatus* A gamefish endemic to Africa. The body of the tigerfish is elongate and compressed. The scales are moderately large; there is no scaly process at the base of the ventral fin. The dorsal fin has 10–11 rays, and is situated above the ventral fin, which has 13–18 rays. The mouth is large and has very strong, pointed, sharp-edged teeth, which are wide apart and form a single series. Dorsally, the tigerfish is a dull brown with a somewhat lighter snout and bluish-silvery reflections. The sides are yellowish-silvery, whitish near the ventral surface; their whole length with black points and dark blue-gray longitudinal markings. The iris is yellowish, suffused with dark gray above and anteriorly. The dorsal fin is a pale brown, edged with red; the adipose fin is black with a transparent base. The middle base of the caudal is dark, the upper lobe transparent brownish with a broad red margin and narrow terminal edge, and the lower lobe transparent gray, its margin vermilion. The pectoral, ventral, and anal fins are a transparent gray, with chrome-orange at the tips.

Tigerfish are distributed from the Lower Nile to the Blue Nile, Lakes Albert, Rudolf, Marguerita, the Senegal, Niger, Benue, Volta, and Offin rivers (Gold Coast), Lake Tanganyika, Upper Zambesi, Great Leteba, Olifants,

Tigerfish

Crocodile, and Komati rivers (Eastern Transvaal), Rivers Lomati, Black Mbuluzi, and Usutu (Swaziland), Limpopo, Lake Rukwa, and Lake Bangweulu.

ANGLING VALUE

A great gamefish. The tigerfish is very active when hooked. It has been recorded up to 30 pounds and may go very much bigger in Lakes Tanganyika and Albert, but a 10-pounder is powerful even on strong tackle. It jumps repeatedly.

Wire leaders must be used when fishing for tigerfish. The small ones will take any bright wet fly but will soon ruin them. They will strike any spoon or dead or live bait. They are found in fastwater, especially where it enters a quiet pool. —A.J.McC.

TIGER GROUPER *Mycteroperca tigris* A rather uncommon species occurring throughout the tropical American Atlantic but rarely taken. It is known to reach a total length of over 20 inches. The common and scientific names refer to the tigerlike crossbanded color pattern.

The tiger grouper has 11 dorsal spines, 16–17 dorsal rays, 10–11 anal rays, and usually 17 pectoral rays. Posterior nostril much larger than the anterior. Insertion of pelvic fin under lower end of pectoral base. Posterior margin of caudal fin straight or somewhat concave. Sides of body with several oblique, narrow, light bands.

The color pattern distinguishes this grouper from the others.

ANGLING VALUE

Not much is known about the habits of this species. It occurs on rocky bottom in waters of medium depth. Takes live or dead bait. A good fighter but not known to have been taken on artificial lures. The tiger grouper is edible, but not a food fish of commercial importance. —L.R.

TIGER MUSKELLUNGE *See* Muskellunge

TIGER ROCKFISH *Sebastodes nigrocinctus* This rockfish (*which see*) is abundant in Juan de Fuca and Johnstone straits. Its range is from California to southeastern Alaska.

The tiger rockfish is typified by high cranial ridges, more so than in any other rockfish, and prominent, spinous, median frontal ridges. Color, pink, gray, or pale rose background, with 5 vertical carmine bars; or background bright orange-red with 5 black vertical bars. The color pattern can be changed from one phase to another and back in less than one minute.

Many of the species were killed in the Ripple Rock demolition explosion in April, 1958, in Discovery Passage in British Columbia.

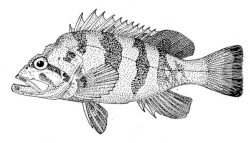

Tiger Rockfish

It has been caught in depths of 180–900 feet. —J.R.

TIGER SHARK *Galeocerdo cuvieri* This is a large, distinctively marked requiem shark of the tropics, which is characterized by a short, sharp-pointed snout, which is squarish when viewed from above. The dorsal fin is relatively far forward, and the second dorsal fin is long and low. The caudal fin is long and slender, and the lower lobe is large. A median keel is prominent along the caudal peduncle. The distinctive teeth are recurved and notched at their inner margins, with the tooth margins serrate. Young tiger sharks have characteristic bars and spots on the back and upper sides, but large adults are usually nearly plain-colored brownish-gray.

LIFE HISTORY

Maximum size of the tiger is 18 feet, but reports of 30-foot specimens persist. Weight ranges in tiger sharks of 13–14 feet are about 1,000–1,400 pounds, the weight depending largely on the fatness, sex, and the reproductive state of the female. This species occurs throughout the tropical and subtropical regions of the world, and although it is taken offshore, it seems to be more nearly a coastal species, occasionally entering very shallow waters.

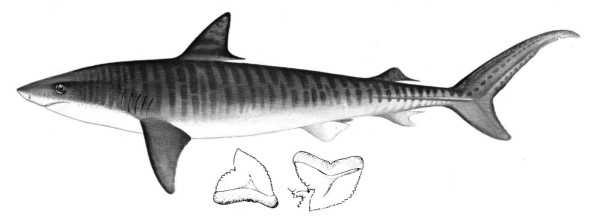

Tiger Shark (tooth lower jaw *left*, upper jaw *right*)

It is omnivorous on live and dead matter, eating fishes of all kinds, and crabs, whelks, lobsters, squid, turtles, and sea lions. Tigers are cannibalistic and eat other species of sharks as well. Their apparently impervious stomachs have yielded cans, bottles, sacks of coal, clothes and shoes, various bits of bird remains, dogs, and even parts of a crocodile.

Spawning apparently occurs throughout the year, and the young are born in shallow waters. Eggs are hatched within the mother, and the young are born ready to swim. From 10 to 82 young have been taken from females, and the young are about 18–19 inches long at birth. A sluggish species under normal conditions, it becomes voracious and strong-swimming in the presence of food.

DANGER TO MAN

Because of its size, efficient teeth, and proneness to enter shallow water, it is a potential danger to swimmers, and it has been responsible for a number of attacks on skindivers and bathers. It is occasionally taken by anglers. Commercially, its hide is first-class in the manufacture of leather.   —D.dS.

TIGER TROUT A trout hybrid produced from a female brown trout × male brook trout. The name is suggested by the body markings and the ferocity of feeding habits. *See also* Hybrid Trout *under* Fish Culture

TILAPIAS A large genus of the family Cichlidae distributed throughout the African continent from Egypt in the north to the Cape of Good Hope in the south. Tilapias also occur or have been introduced to Syria, Israel, Madagascar, southern Asia, the Philippines, Formosa, Ceylon, Malaya, Hawaii, Puerto Rico, the British West Indies, and Central and South America. The species vary from small ornamentals to fishes weighing in excess of 5 pounds. Although most tilapias inhabit freshwater, some occur in brackish and saltwater; considerable numbers have entered the commercial fishery along the Florida Gulf coast in recent years. All tilapias are characterized by their long continuous dorsal fin, the anterior portion of which consists of a varying number of spiny rays and the posterior portion of softrays. These cichlids are unique in having two incomplete lateral lines. Tilapias have been experimentally bred in the southern United States (Alabama and Florida) where they have been stocked and caught in public waters. They are also reared in Hawaii on the island of Maui where the fish was used as a bait supplement for the Pacific skipjack fishery.

LIFE HISTORY

One common species in the world distribution is the Java or Natal tilapia, *Tilapia mossambica*. The most important feature in distinguishing the tilapias is the number of gillrakers, which are the short, white, forwardly projecting teeth on the first gill arch. In the Java tilapia the number varies from 15–20 with the average at 18. There are 3 anal spines. The teeth are in bands, usually notched, not conical. Size, shape, and color are of little taxonomic value, as they vary with season and locality. In general, however, they are brownish or olive green on the back and silvery on the flanks, often with reddish tips to dorsal and anal fin rays in adults. There are three more-or-less distinct blotches on the sides. Male and female differ markedly in the shape of the head. The forehead of the male is concave and the mouth is wide and flattened dorsoventrally. The forehead of the female on the other hand is convex and the mouth is small. The young are silvery and very distinctly marked with dark cross bars. This species grows to 5 pounds.

Tilapias feed chiefly on algae. Their intestines are very long in adaptation to this food. Crustaceans, aquatic insects, and worms are a minor part of the diet of some species.

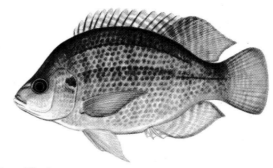

Java Tilapia

Tilapias are mouth breeders. A small saucer-shaped depression is prepared by the male with its mouth in the soft pond bottom. The female then enters the nest and deposits the eggs which are then fertilized. The eggs are picked up by the female and carried in her mouth for 10–14 days until the fry hatch and are large enough to care for themselves. During this period the eggs and fry are aerated by a continuous chewing movement. When the fry are free swimming they begin feeding on algae and plankton.

After the breeding season tilapia congregate in shoals and on warm calm days can be observed just below the surface of the water. At this time they are most readily caught using earthworms.

ANGLING VALUE

Similar to most panfish. However, few species of tilapia provide much sport for the angler using artificial lures. Their food value is only fair. One reason why tilapias are of interest to United States fish culturists is that they will control obnoxious algae such as *Pithophora* to some degree.   —A.J.McC.

TILEFISH *Lopholatilus chamaeleonticeps* It belongs to the family Branchiostegidae, a small group of fishes that are widespread in tropical and temperate waters. Most of the species occur in comparatively deep water. This species is found along the outer continental shelf and upper slope from northern Nova Scotia to southern Florida and the Gulf of Mexico.

A colorful fish with bluish to olive-green on the back and upper part of its sides, changing to yellow or rose on lower sides and belly, the latter with white midline. Head reddish on sides, white below. Back and sides above lateral line with many irregular yellow spots. Dorsal fin dusky with larger yellowish spots, its softrayed portion pale-edged; adipose flap greenish-yellow; anal fin pinkish with purple to blue iridescence; pectorals pale sooty-brown with purplish reflections.

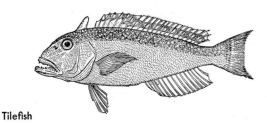

Tilefish

Other distinguishing characteristics of the tilefish are body stout, greatest depth 4 in total length at level of gill opening from which point the body tapers to caudal peduncle, somewhat compressed; caudal peduncle moderate; a triangular, thin, fleshy flap projects from the upper midline of the head in the nape region, its height 1½ times eye diameter. Head large, strongly convex in dorsal profile, nearly straight in ventral profile, 3½ in total length; mouth moderately large, lower jaw projecting, angle of mouth under front of eye, a small barbel-like projection on each side of lower jaw near the angle, canine teeth in both jaws followed by bands of smaller teeth. Eye 6½ in head.

Dorsal fin with 7 spines followed by 15 softrays, originating above gill opening and extending to caudal peduncle, nearly twice the length of the head; caudal fin moderate, lunate, lobes pointed; anal fin with 2 spines and 13 softrays, extending from under middle of dorsal fin to under end of dorsal; pectorals moderately large, pointed, ⅔ of head length, located immediately behind gill opening and low on sides; pelvics smaller than pectorals on ventral edge, base slightly in front of pectoral base. Lateral line present. Moderately large scales on body and head.

The tilefish is a benthic species, generally found between 45 and 170 fathoms. It prefers water temperatures of 47°–53°F. Its food is crabs, shrimp, squid, mollusks, marine worms, sea cucumbers, and other invertebrates. Sometimes small fishes are eaten. Spawning takes place in July. The eggs are about .05 inch in diameter and are believed to be pelagic. Tilefish grow to a weight of about 50 pounds.

The first commercial catch of tilefish was made in 1879 off the Nantucket Shoals Lightship. While draggers were still looking for the mother lode in 1882 an inexplicable mortality occurred in this species which resulted in 4,250 square miles of the Atlantic being covered with dead tilefish. It is generally believed that a drastic thermal change virtually erased this population. During the following five years not a single one could be found. Gradually the tilefish began to appear again, and today they are taken at the rate of 10 million pounds a year.

ANGLING VALUE

Due to the great depths which tilefish frequent, the sport fishery is limited. Partyboats operating out of New York and New Jersey ports catch tilefish on the slopes of the Hudson Canyon. A standard codfish outfit with a stiff rod and 4/0 reel spooled with 50-pound-test dacron or wire is necessary. Sinkers of 12–20 ounces are required according to the amount of current running, and the bait (usually squid or skimmer clams) is fished at depths from 50–70 fathoms.

FOOD VALUE

Tilefish have firmly textured flesh which is often compared to lobster or scallop meat. They can be prepared in a variety of ways including poaching, baking, smoking, and can be made into a chowder.   —J.C.B.

TINKER MACKEREL *See* Mackerels

TIP ACTION A type of rod action in which the flexion is limited to the upper third of the shaft. Because of its shorter working length in comparison to its total length, a tip-action rod is said to be "fast" and therefore more or less desirable according to its purpose. The action is achieved through the rod's tapers in building. *See also* The Theory of Rod Function in Casting *under* Rod Building

TOGUE A regional name in the Northeastern United States for the lake trout (*which see*)

TOMCOD *See* Atlantic Tomcod

TOMTATE *Haemulon aurolineatum* This is the most widely ranging species of grunt. It is found from Cape Cod to Brazil, including the Bahamas and the West Indies. Mature adults of this rather small species run 6 to 8½ inches in total length. It rarely reaches a much larger size. This grunt is distinguished from the others by the color pattern, which consists of a yellow or brown stripe from the opercle to a black blotch on the caudal-fin base.

The tomtate has 13 dorsal spines; 14–15 dorsal rays, usually 15; 9 anal rays; and 17–18 pectoral rays, usually 17. Pored lateral-line scales 50–52. Gillrakers 24–28. Its pectoral fin is naked.

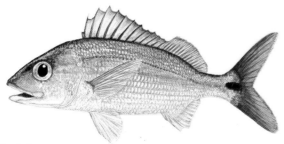

Tomtate

With the exception of the white grunt (*which see*), this species seems to be more tolerant of colder (extratropical) water than the others. The tomtate is a bottom feeder, abundant in shallow water from the shore to the outer reefs.

ANGLING VALUE

This species is too small to be considered a gamefish. It is easy to catch with cut bait. The tomtate is good eating but usually too small to be worth while cleaning and cooking. —L.R.

TONKIN CANE A bamboo used in rod building (*which see*). Prior to 1920, the bulk of all bamboo imported to the United States came from India. This species *Dendrocalamus strictus* was given the name "Calcutta" because all shipments were made from that port. The rods produced from this material had a low or sluggish response to casting. Calcutta canes quickly disappeared from the market with the discovery of Tonkin cane *Arundernaria amabilis* from China. Since that time, all bamboo imported and used in the United States has been the Tonkin variety. This bamboo is a cultivated crop which comes from an oval-shaped district approximately 25 miles in length in Kwangsi Province, near Canton, China. It is known in China as *Cha Kon Chuk* (tea-stick bamboo). When the culms are cut and harvested, they are selected for weight and diameter, wrapped in a mat of bamboo, and sent by water to Hong Kong. There it is given the trade name *Tsing-Li* canes by the export companies.

Tonkin, by virtue of its toughness, straightness, stiffness of its stems, and very small protrusion at the nodes or joints, is far superior to any of the 200 odd species of bamboo in either hemisphere for the making of bamboo rods. The author together with F. A. McClure, Research Associate, Department of Botany, at the Smithsonian Institution, tested various species for possible use in the manufacture of fishing rods and ski poles; none of the canes tested could economically serve because of the large nodes and great bulk of pith compared to the small percentage of cellulose fibers. The bamboo *Longispiculata* from Honduras has limited value; because of its long internodes it can be used for making lightweight rods of three-piece construction.

Tonkin has a greater percentage of the tough cellulose fibers which run parallel to the outer skin or enamel of culms. One can observe with a microscope that adjoining these fibers are egg-shaped cells connected by minute tubes. The inner surface is very soft and pithy, and this particular cell structure causes bamboo to be quite sensitive to moisture. It should be stored in as dry a place as possible. Canes of twenty years in storage have produced visible water while being heat-treated. The cell structure of bamboo allows for impregnation of dyes and water-soluble resins through osmosis.

There have not been any imports of Tonkin from China since the beginning of World War II. There is a good supply of 6-foot canes available, but good or excellent, 8-foot canes would be hard to obtain.

HOW TO SELECT TONKIN CANE

When selecting bamboo for fly, bait, and casting rods, 1½–1¾-inch canes are the most desirable. For use in the home workshop, one should order 6-foot canes of 1½–1¾ inches that weigh not less than 2¼ pounds. The best material for rod tips is provided by 1¼ inch canes, 6 feet in length and weighing not less than 2 pounds, because of the finer, resilient compact bundles of tough fibers contained in the upper section of culms. Canes that show blue or black discolorations at the nodes indicate long exposure to moisture and should be rejected for use.

—W.J.

TOOTH SQUEEZE *See in* Skin and Scuba Diving Dangers *under* First Aid

TOPE *Galeus vulgaris* Small members of the carcharidae or requim sharks, the family includes the much larger and more ferocious tiger and blue sharks and also the various soupfin sharks (*Galeorhinus zygopterus* and *G. australis*).

Tope are well known in European waters. They have many local names in Britain. Some are tope, toper, penny dog, miller's dog (when young), silver dog, white hound, and rig. In common with some dogfish it is sometimes called "sweet William"; and in Wales it is known as "ciglas," the blue dog. The commonest names, tope and toper, are said to be derived from its occasional practice of following longlines or nets as they are drawn to the surface and snapping fish from them—hence "topper" and so "toper" and "tope."

The tope shows its relationship to other requim sharks in its long streamlined and active shape. Like them it has an all-cartilage skeleton, a skin of backward-pointing and thorny "placoid" scales, and 5 small gill slits. The internal anatomy is exactly like other sharks and dogfish; for example, the ones commonly used in biology classes.

The snout is long and pointed, with an underslung crescentic mouth full of triangular and serrated teeth. The sensory nostrils are not joined to the mouth by grooves as in the smaller dogfishes. The eye may be covered by a nictitating membrane; small spiracles are present behind it.

Small tope could be mistaken for the spur dog (*squalius acanthius*), were it not for the fins, which are distinctive. Tope fins have no spines. The pectoral fins are large (nearly as long as the head) and sickle-shaped. The first of the two dorsal fins starts just behind the rear or posterior edge of these pectoral fins, and is distinctly square rather than triangular. The lower lobe of the caudal or tail fin is characteristically notched.

In color tope are a dull steel-gray to blue on the back, fading to a whitish-silver on the belly. This pattern is uniform and never spotted.

Tope are much smaller than their better-known and feared relatives, the ordinary weight range being 20–40 pounds. Individuals, however, may reach 70 or 80 pounds and a length of 6 or 7 feet.

Despite the suggested derivation of its name, tope are in fact largely bottom-feeders. The diet is mainly fish, with occasional echinoderms and crustaceans. Older authors have suggested that tope are shoal or pack fish, but angling experience seems to indicate the normal hunting group is composed of a pair or so of fish. Groups have been seen to enter areas of sand or sandy mud and sweep rapidly over them searching for food on the bottom. Finding none, they will move on rapidly.

Tope have been claimed to be cosmopolitan in distribution; in European waters they tend to be a southerly fish, coming up to the latitude of North Wales.

LIFE HISTORY

The winter and early spring is spent in deep waters up to 900 feet. In the rest of the year, from April until December, they will move closer inshore, frequenting deepish sandy bays and estuaries. It is at this time, when they are inshore, that breeding takes place. Mating itself is by copulation, as in other sharks, as male tope possess "claspers" on the pelvic fins. The females are larger than the males and are viviparous, producing up to 50 young from a full-grown specimen. Little direct observation, however, has been done on the breeding of tope.

The young, born alive as perfect miniature adults, spend their first winter inshore. Their parents, mating completed, migrate back to deeper water. During their first onshore winter the young tope grow to between 12 and 20 inches long; even at this age the sexes are distinguishable by well-developed male claspers.

Young tope migrate out to deeper waters at the onset of their second winter. As with most other sharks neither the life span nor the growth rate is accurately known.

COMMERCIAL VALUE

Though normally bottom feeders tope are occasionally taken in drift nets; less rarely they are caught by trawls. They normally come to the notice of commercial fishermen because of their habit of robbing—or even breaking—longlines. There is no real market for them even though they are said to be fair eating, and the fins can be made into Chinese-style soups like those of their relatives. The smell of the flesh is said to have given rise to the rather ironic name of "sweet William." Damaged fish taken by anglers are sometimes fed to pigs.   —D.M.

TORPEDO HEAD LINE   *See* Weight Forward Line
TOTUAVA *Cynoscion macdonaldi*   This member of the weakfish or corvina (*which see*) group is the largest of the genus, reaching 6 feet and 225 pounds. The totuava is called *totoaba* in Mexico. It is found only in the middle and upper Gulf of California and moves to the upper Gulf at spawning time. It seems to have definite movements at other times of the year, appearing in numbers at specific localities, as near the mouth of Willard Bay in October-December and from San Felipe to the head of the Gulf in January and February.

Adult totuava are blue on the back and silvery-gray on the sides and belly. Over-all is a glistening, coppery, iridescent sheen of changing color. Young fish have obscure spots on the back.

The soft dorsal-fin membrane is scaleless; stripes or bars absent on body; dorsal with 24–25 softrays; central ray of caudal fin longest; belly without a central ridge. The air bladder is of a special form, with large lateral horns.

LIFE HISTORY

In the first year of life, the totuava reaches a length of about 11 inches; in the second, 16 inches; and in the third, about 39 inches.

The young fish, which feed on shrimp and gobies, are to be found in shallow water, while the adults, which take anchovies for the most part and crustaceans and other fishes, frequent greater depths except at spawning time.

ANGLING VALUE

A large and active gamefish. A small corvina hooked through the back or a corvina belly strip is an effective bait. The totuava will also take trolled spoons. Lures must be fished at considerable depths.

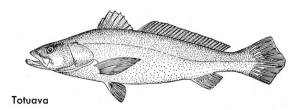

Totuava

The totuava is one of the best food fishes in its family. A demand for the air bladder by Orientals for use as a condiment in soups caused extensive depletion of the species in the first quarter of the twentieth century. As much as $5 per pound was paid for the bladders. The remainder of the fish was discarded. In 1924 the flesh was first exported, and shipments to the United States reached 1,838,000 pounds in 1928. Landings have been inversely proportional to the commercial shrimp catch because the fishermen prefer to pursue the crustacean when the market is favorable. In recent years the catch has averaged about 500,000 pounds annually. The species was felt to be well on the way to extinction in the early years of over-exploitation because the fish were captured in gravid condition at the spawning grounds in the head of the Gulf. They were exceedingly abundant and could be speared in shallow water. Recently a closed season for commercial fishing has been in effect from March to May. A protected area encompasses the upper Gulf.   —J.R.

TOURNAMENT CASTING   *See* American Casting Association
TRAHIRA *Hoplias malabaricus*   A predaceous freshwater fish, with a range from Mexico to northern Argentina. This is rather vicious and heavily toothed, and is an elongate, brownish, scaly fish found abundantly in sluggish tropical rivers, lakes, and swamps. It has the ability to traverse overland on marshy grounds. The *trahira*, while edible, is very bony and rather soft of flesh. It reaches a weight of several pounds and more than 20 inches. A vicious predator, this fish is readily taken on bait and on almost any kind of artificial lure which moves.—T.D.W.
TRAMMEL NET   A type of gillnet (*which see*) composed of three walls of netting attached to the same top and bottom line. The two outside walls have a large mesh while

the inner wall is of smaller size. When a fish strikes the net it passes through the large outer mesh usually with sufficient force to push through the second, smaller meshed wall, thus forming a pocket with the third wall in which it is trapped. A trammel may be run out from shore around the fishing grounds and drawn back in an irregular semicircle or it may be drifted with the current.

—A.J.McC.

TRANSOM The flat stern of a boat

TRANSOM CHINE That area of a boat where the bottom of the hull and bottom of the transom meet. *See also* Chine

TRANSOM DOOR An integral part of equipment on off-shore fishing boats. *For details see* Transom Door *under* Sportfisherman

TRAWLING A method of commercial fishing which generally consists of a boat dragging a large conical net or trawl along the sea bottom; the net is closed at the small end and held open mechanically at the mouth or large end by two "otter boards," which plane out to keep the trawl mouth opened. Trawls may also be floated and dragged at various depths between the surface and bottom (midwater trawling), and they may be operated by two boats in handling very large nets (paranzella). Bottom trawling is done primarily for ground fish such as the ocean perch, hake, flounders, whiting, and cod. Midwater trawling, which was not reliable until the introduction of asdic (sonar) and echo-sounding gear for locating schools of fish, has become more efficient for pelagic species, notably the herrings. Small specialized trawls are also used as sampling tools by marine research organizations.

—A.J.McC.

TREE-WALKING FISH *See* Skipping Goby

TREMATODE The common name for a parasitic worm of the class Trematoda, a fluke.

TRIGGERFISH Family Balistidae The triggerfishes are found in warm seas throughout the world. They are a distinctive group of fishes named for the interlocking arrangement of the bases of the first 3 dorsal spines such that the enlarged first spine can be fixed in the erect position. If the second spine is depressed with the finger the first spine is no longer locked in the vertical position. The fishes are already deep-bodied, so the elevation of the dorsal spine plus the additional depth from depression of the ventral flap ostensibly makes them less desirable to a predator. Also, these fishes use their extended first dorsal spine and ventral flap to wedge themselves into small holes in reefs in which they seek refuge.

Other characteristics of the family and the related filefishes are a tough skin with platelike scales that often bear spinules or tubercles, a single short but stout spine in place of pelvic fins, a short gill opening, a mouth which is small but bears powerful jaws with close-set projecting incisiform teeth. *See* Ocean Triggerfish, Queen Triggerfish

TRIM When a boat is floating on an even keel, she is described as being trimmed.

TRIPLETAIL Lobotes surinamensis Also called the buoy fish, buoy bass, blackfish, and chobie. This species has a broad distribution in the Atlantic, Indian, and western Pacific oceans. In the western Atlantic it is found from Bermuda and Massachusetts to Argentina (38° S.) and throughout the Gulf of Mexico. It has only one close relative, *L. pacificus*, found on the Pacific Coast from Petacalco Bay, Mexico, to Panama.

The tripletail is distinguished as follows: head 2.6–2.9 in standard length; depth 1.8–2.0; dorsal spines 12, rays 16; anal spines 3, rays 11; lateral scales 45; body deep, compressed; anterior profile concave; head small; snout short, 4.1–5.0 in head length; eye rather small, 4.0–6.0 in head; mouth moderate, oblique; the lower jaw projecting; maxillary barely reaching middle of eye, 2.6–3.0 in head; teeth small, pointed, with an irregular outer series and a band of minute teeth behind it; preopercular margin strongly serrate, the serrae at angle much enlarged; scales moderate, strongly serrate, wanting only on snout; dorsal spines strong, the median ones very slightly longer than the posterior ones, the soft part of fin much higher, stronger convex to slightly pointed; caudal fin rounded; soft part of anal fin similar to that of dorsal and opposite it; ventral fins long, pointed, exceeding length of head to preopercular margin; pectoral fins very short, 1.8–2.1 in head.

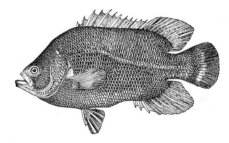

Tripletail

The color varies widely, but most specimens seen have been black, brown, or yellow. Sometimes the yellow and brown of a large, autumn leaf are perfectly imitated.

Although the adults seem to prefer a pelagic existence, the young are found close to shore, often in bays and estuaries. In such places, they are usually found floating on their sides at the surface. Both the movement and coloration of a dead leaf are imitated. This fish offers one of the best examples of protective mimicry in marine fishes.

ANGLING VALUE

The tripletail attains a length of 3 feet and a weight of 30–50 pounds. It is a good food fish and puts up a strong fight when hooked. Tripletail are usually sought around wrecks, buoys, and floating or sunken debris. Live baits, such as shrimp, clams, and mullet, are preferred, but jigs and spinning lures are successful at times. *See also* Tsuke Raft

TROLLING A method of angling whereby an artificial lure or natural bait is drawn behind a moving boat at any depth from the surface to the bottom and at varying speeds according to the species of fish being sought. Some gamefish in both fresh- and saltwater, such as the walleye, lake trout, sailfish, wahoo, marlins, and tunas, are ordinarily taken by trolling rather than by casting or still-fishing. This may be necessitated by the depth at which the fish are located or by the size of the bait (up to 6 pounds in some forms of big-game angling). Trolling is accomplished in all types of craft, from a canoe to a sportfisherman, and with many types of tackle, from a handline to heavy big-game gear. As a rule, motor power, either outboard or inboard, is used, but freshwater

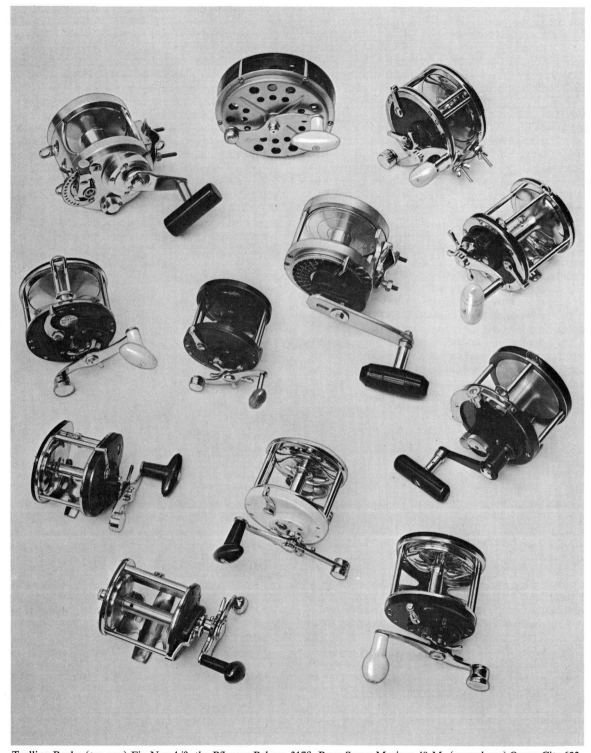

Trolling Reels: (*top row*) Fin-Nor 4/0, the Pflueger Pakron 3178, Penn Super-Mariner 49-M, (*second row*) Ocean City 603, Penn Special Senator 113H, Everol No. 2½-0, H-I Dolphin 425A, (*third row*) H-I Starfire 520B, Mitchell 606, Shakespeare Wonder-Troll, (*bottom*) Pflueger Bond 2004, Ocean City "Bay City" 112. *Reels Courtesy of Abercrombie & Fitch, Pflueger Corp., True Temper Corp., Harrocks-Ibbotson Co., Shakespeare Co.*

anglers often operate their craft manually with oars or paddle, and in some inland states motor power is prohibited by law. *See also* Atlantic Sailfish, Bahamas, Blue-fish, Bluefin Tuna, Chinook Salmon, Coho Salmon, King Mackerel, Sportfisherman, Summer Flounder, Swordfish, Virgin Islands, Wahoo, Wire Line   —A.J.McC.

TROOP A collective name for a number of dogfish: "a troop of dogfish"

TROPHOGENIC REGION The superficial layer of a lake in which organic production from mineral substances takes place on the basis of light energy.

TROPHOLYTIC The profundal zone of a lake, including the lake bottom in which food is utilized faster than it can be produced. *See also* Lake Zones *under* Freshwater Ecology

TROPHOLYTIC REGION The deep layer of a lake where organic dissimilation predominates because of light deficiency.

TROTLINE A heavy line usually extended across a stream from one bank to the other, or buoyed, or extended parallel to the shore, from which short lines or "stagings" are attached often at intervals of every 3 feet. Hooks are secured to the stagings. The trotline is primarily a commercial fishing method used for various species of catfish.

TROUT *See* Blueback Trout, Brook Trout, Brown Trout, Cutthroat Trout, Gila Trout, Golden Trout, Lake Trout, Rainbow Trout, Sand Seatrout, Sea Trout, Silver Seatrout, Spotted Seatrout, Sunapee Trout

TROUTPERCH *Percopsis omiscomaycus* Despite its name, this fish is neither a trout nor a true perch. It is easily recognized by a combination of an adipose fin on the back and spiny rays in the dorsal and anal fins. The scales are also rough or ctenoid. It is an olivaceous fish with lightish lower sides and underparts, and with a series of spots forming a broken line along the lateral line. Its back is also covered with less obvious and more diffuse spots. Most specimens are about 4 inches; and it seldom exceeds 6 inches.

Troutperch

The troutperch is widely distributed from the Yukon in the northwest and Hudson Bay, southeastward to the Lake Champlain region, and south to the Potomac River in the east. In the Midwest it is found from the Great Lakes region southward to West Virginia, Kentucky, and Kansas. In the northern part of its range it is generally found in lakes, but in the South it lives in silty streams. Throughout much of its range it is unusual to see it at any other time of the year than during the spawning season, and it is thought that it stays in deep water. A related species, the sand roller (*Columbia transmontanus*) occurs in the lower Columbia River drainage.

LIFE HISTORY

The troutperch is a spring spawner and may be found concentrated in tributaries of lakes and along lake shores, usually late in April and May. It feeds on small crustacea, insects, and other aquatic animals. —A.J.McC.

TROUT, UNLIMITED Incorporated as a nonprofit organization in 1959 for the sole purpose of the general improvement of trout fishing in the United States. Although Trout, Unlimited, was founded by fifteen anglers in Michigan, it now has chapters in many other states.

The organization recognizes that trout fishing can be provided in many waters in trout states and in some waters in nontrout states only by planting hatchery fish. But it advocates planting programs only in those lakes and streams where research and experience indicate the practice is practical and beneficial. Such fishing is not to be confused with the quality angling sought for the streams that over the generations have provided the sport of catching wild trout. In such streams, the organization is striving to preserve the trout fishing heritage.

Wherever new regulations, such as flies only and trophy fishing, have helped the trout resource and have increased the quality of the fishing, Trout, Unlimited, supports their adoption as management methods. Among specific objectives are the encouragement of research into winter mortality of trout, the practicality of building artificial spawning areas, the effect on the trout populations of night-fishing restrictions and the effect of "any-lure" regulations.

Another objective is to provide numerical and financial support to institutions, agencies, organizations, and individuals actively engaged in carrying out the aims and objectives of Trout, Unlimited. This is not a social or fraternal organization. Its members are not concerned primarily with their own welfare, but with the welfare of trout. They are engaged in a campaign to preserve what natural trout fishing remains and even to make it better.

Trout, Unlimited, encourages management methods that promote propagation and survival of wild trout rather than policies that would turn our trout streams into adjuncts of fish hatcheries. In line with this, it advocates increased emphasis on stream improvement, watershed rehabilitation, and lake reclamation. And it supports research into the basic biology and ecology of trout populations.

Because of the demonstrated success of flies-only and other artificial lure regulations coupled with higher size limits, the organization is vigorously promoting the extension of such regulations to all suitable waters—waters that have native trout and adequate natural food, shelter, and spawning facilities for those wild fish. It does not back willy-nilly the application of any restriction simply for the sake of the restriction. The intent is to create high quality fishing for wild trout.

Trout, Unlimited, encourages further experimentation with catch-and-release regulations (often referred to as fishing-for-fun projects), particularly in those states which do not have them. In many areas such regulations have produced a quality of fishing that previously could be expected only in remote regions. —A.C.N.

TRUITE The French name for trout and used specifically as *truite arc-en-ciel* (rainbow trout), or *truite brune* in Quebec or *truite commun* in France (brown trout). The word is not used in connection with chars; *omble chevalier* (Arctic char), *omble rouge du Québec* (Quebec red trout, a form of Arctic char), and *omble de fontaine* (brook trout) are the common names. The lake trout is identified as *touladi* or *truite gris* in Quebec.

TRUNCATE Cut off squarely. Refers to the shape of the caudal fin. *See also* Anatomy

TRUNKFISH *See* Cowfish

TSUKE RAFT A Japanese innovation to saltwater fishing, the tsuke raft is made of bundles of bamboo poles which are lashed together and anchored at sea, the purpose of which is to attract marine gamefish. Such species as dolphin, mackerel, and tuna congregate in the vicinity of the raft either because the floating object attracts small fish and other marine life or because it provides shade. United States Gulf Coast anglers have used the same system with floating brush mats for many years in catching cobia and tripletail. Flotsam of all kinds, such as logs, boxes, and weed occurring on the surface, will often attract gamefish; however, the anchored tsuke raft is a methodical attempt to exploit this behavior.

TUCUNARÉ A Brazilian-Indian name for a number of cichlids; in South America they are more widely known by the common name pavón (Spanish). *See also* Brazil, Butterfly Pavón, Colombia, Peacock Pavón, Venezuela

TULE PERCH *Hysterocarpus traski* This unique surfperch (*which see*) inhabits freshwater in central California from Lassen to San Luis Obispo counties. There are two pattern phases—one, a slender form, in Clear Lake, and the other, more robust, in rivers; the one with gray overlying a brassy color, dark gray dorsally thinning to white on belly; the other with about eight slate-gray bars which run across the body, fading just above the belly. The dorsal and anal fins are dusky, the pectorals and pelvics plain. Dorsal softrays 9–13; the unique count of 15–18 dorsal spines characterizes the genus. —J.R.

TUNA *See* Albacore, Bigeye Tuna, Blackfin Tuna, Bluefin Tuna, Little Tunas, Skipjack Tuna, Yellowfin Tuna

TUNA TOWER An integral part of equipment on offshore fishing boats. *For details see* Tuna Tower *under* Sportfisherman

TURBIDITY The amount of suspended matter in water, thought of as muddiness. *See also* Physical Characteristics of Water *under* Freshwater Ecology

TURBOT **(1)** A European flatfish with several related species along North American shores, the most common eastern member being the sand flounder found from Maine to South Carolina. There are also several species of turbot in tropical waters, notably the peacock flounder found in the West Indies. In Pacific waters the sanddab, curlfin turbot, diamond turbot, and sharpridge turbot comprise a small market. Highly esteemed by continental epicures because of its firm, delicate white flesh, the turbot is most abundant from the Black Sea through the Mediterranean and north to the Baltic.

(2) *Rhombus maximus* Synonymous with *Scophthalmus maximus*, turbot are much esteemed European marine food flatfishes. They are closely related to the brill (*which see*), but differ in a number of aspects. They both lie on their right side, but the turbot is larger, lacks scales, and yet is covered with blunt bony tubercles. In the northern part of its range the turbot may have tubercles on the blind left side as well as on the exposed right.

Turbot are markedly diamond-shaped in outline, as against the more oval brill. Turbot fin-ray counts are: dorsal 61–72, anal 45–56. When freshly caught the upper or left side is brownish-gray with speckles, the right side opaque white. This, however, may vary for two reasons:

(a) Like brill they rely on changing pigment cells to camouflage where necessary
(b) Aberrant specimens are sometimes found with coloration on both sides.

Other abnormalities are sometimes encountered, notably a forward-projecting dorsal fin and incomplete mouth migration.

Turbot normally live on sandy banks off estuaries in depths up to 500 feet, though most are taken commercially in water shallower than 300 feet. Its geographical range is southern, mainly Mediterranean and East Atlantic up to northern England.

Turbot are predatory, their normal tactics being to lie in wait while camouflaged to seize sand-eels (*Ammodytes* spp.) and other small fish. Some mollusks and worms are also taken, but the teeth are basically long and sharp for fish-catching. Despite their hunting habits, turbot can swim very well.

Average specimens grow up to 30 pounds, but 50 pounds is not unknown.

LIFE HISTORY

Turbot spawn in offshore waters in spring and early summer, females laying perhaps as many as 500,000 eggs per pound of body weight. The eggs themselves are about 1 mm in diameter with a wrinkled outer case and a single ochre-colored oil droplet. They float in the upper waters for dispersal like those of other flatfish. Hatching occurs in about a week, giving rise to a black-and-red-orange-colored larva about 2–3 mm long. They have large yolk sacs. Once they have absorbed their yolk sacs turbot fry are more heavily pigmented than those of other flatfish. At this stage they possess swimbladders, but these are lost when they sink to the bottom and change, or metamorphose, into the adult flatfish.

The active pelagic life in the upper waters (usually inshore over the shallows) is comparatively long in the turbot. It may be anything up to ⅘ths of an inch long when it metamorphoses. Once this process has started, the head is altered by the appearance of spines, especially over the eyes. The function of these spines is not known; they disappear after the initial flatfish stages. At a length of 2 inches the young turbot is fully a bottom dweller, though its active swimming means it may be taken at all levels. Male turbot mature at about 12 inches in length; the female usually at 15–20 inches.

COMMERCIAL VALUE

Turbot are a much prized "epicure" dish in European countries with seafood markets. They are taken in trawls

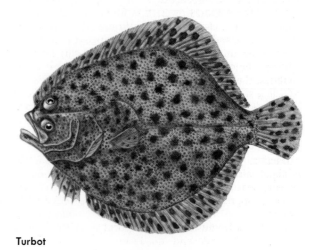

Turbot

and widely sold, but are not the most common of flatfish offered for sale.

ANGLING VALUE

Turbot (British rod-caught record 28 pounds) haunt steep banks of pulverized shell and sand in the vicinity of strong tide races, where they lie on the sea bed waiting to ambush sand-eels and other small fish swept along by the fast currents.

They are more esteemed for their culinary properties than their sporting qualities, and in the main, when hooked, merely offer passive resistance by arching their broad bodies to catch the tide. Nevertheless strong tackle is usually required to combat the tidal conditions where they are found. A powerful 7-foot boat rod and a large single-action reel containing at least 150 yards of 25-pound-test line is the most useful tackle combination.

Ground fishing using a single size 4/0 hook baited with a bunch of live sand-eels or a long strip of mackerel is the most popular method, although many fish are captured from a drifting boat by trailing the bait along the sea bed. In places where sand-eels are particularly abundant they can also be caught by jigging a flight of feather lures.

The most famous areas for turbot fishing off the English coast are the Varne, the Shambles, and the Skerries Banks in the English Channel. *See also* Diamond Turbot—D.M.
—P.G.

TURKEY Occupying the peninsula of Asia Minor across the Black Sea from Russia and bordering the Mediterranean, Turkey offers a limited amount of saltwater fishing; swordfish and tunas enter the sport catch on the Mediterranean side. Some freshwater fishing in Turkey exists in the Anatolian region, where warmwater species such as the walleye have been planted. Two of the most important fisheries exist at Lake Nicoax and Lake Egridir.

There is excellent brown trout fishing in the Tarsus Mountain region near Maras. This is difficult access for tourists; the nearest city of any size with accommodations is Adana about 4–5 hours away by road. The rugged mountain streams produce trout up to 10 pounds or more. There is at least one subspecies of brown trout in Turkey (*Salmo trutta abanticus*) as well as a subgenus *Salmo* (*Platysalmo*) *platysephalus* in the south central portion of the country. The main tourist center in southern Turkey is at Antalya, and the fishing is found north of the city.

TURKEYFISH *See* Zebrafish

TURKS AND CAICOS ISLANDS Until recently known only to stamp collectors and geography buffs, the Turks and Caicos Islands form an isolated British crown colony where a few thousand inhabitants raked salt and caught lobsters. Ignored by tourists because of the lack of facilities, the chief attraction was to small aircraft as a refueling stop and to yachtsmen for the best deep-water harbor (Cockburn Harbour) north of the Windward Passage. Geologically these islands are part of the Bahamas chain, but politically they are independent, a situation which European and American investors found attractive. The number of available hotel rooms is still minimal, although several new hotels and a real-estate development are in progress. The islands remain unspoiled, with miles of deserted beaches and literally virgin fishing.

The Turks Islands (Grand Turk and Salt Cay) lie east of the 22-mile-wide and 7,000-foot-deep Turks Island Passage. The Caicos Islands (South, East, North, West, and Middle Caicos, plus the island of Providenciales) lie to the west of the passage. Their total land area is about 166 square miles. Middle, sometimes called Grand Caicos, is the largest, being 25 miles long and 12 miles wide. The name Turks derives from a local cactus which resembles a fez; while Caicos is from *cayos*, the Spanish word for cay.

Warm sunny skies prevail throughout the year, with an average temperature of 77°F in the winter months and 83°F in summer. Rainfall averages only 26 inches annually. Low humidity and trade winds are fairly constant during winter and spring. The best fishing months are April, May, and June.

These islands remain unspoiled, with miles of deserted beaches and literally virgin fishing

INSHORE FISHING

The Caicos Islands are surrounded by extensive shallow bays and in many places by barrier reefs. Due to the size of the area involved and the lack of accommodations, and therefore minimal angling pressure, it will be several years before the potential of the area is fully known. The bonefish is the principal flat species, and small tarpon occur in tide holes at various points around the islands; tarpon are not abundant, however, and average 20–40 pounds. Bonefish are found along sandy shores and in the intricate network of marl-bottomed tidal creeks. There is no extreme rise and fall (2½ feet average) of water except during spring tides. Snappers, notably the yellowtail and mutton snappers, crevalle, various groupers, barracuda, and cero mackerel constitute the bulk of inshore fishing along the reefs and in tide holes.

OFFSHORE FISHING

There has been no concentrated effort made at offshore sport fishing in the Turks and Caicos Islands. The potential is primarily for sailfish, dolphin, and king mackerel. A few small white marlin have been caught.—A.J.McC.

TYEE A regional name for the chinook salmon (*which see*) in the Pacific Northwest. Tyee is the Siwash Indian word for "chief" and refers in this case to the size of the salmon. The Tyee Club at Campbell River (British Columbia) defines a tyee as any chinook salmon of over 30 pounds; this is the qualifying weight for a catch to become eligible for club recognition.   —A.J.McC.

U

UGANDA This landlocked East African state lying west of Kenya and east of the Congo has a total area of 91,134 square miles, of which about 16,400 square miles consist of lakes, rivers, and swamp. The northern half of Lake Victoria, the eastern portion of Lake Albert, and the northeastern corner of Lake Edward are Uganda territorial waters. The outlet of Lake Victoria is a powerful stream that passes through the Owen Falls Dam at Jimja and forms the source of the Nile River. The Victoria Nile enters Lake Kyoga, then emerges from its west arm following a steep gradient before passing through a cleft less than 20 feet wide at Murchison Falls and entering Lake Albert. The Albert Nile continues across Uganda and becomes the White Nile at the Sudan border. Scenic attractions include vast Lake Victoria, mighty waterfalls, and the misty "Mountains of the Moon" in the Ruwenzori Range that rises 16,794 feet above the perpetual snow line despite lying on the equator. The national parks are unexcelled for their opportunities to see wild game at close range.

Uganda has a higher mean annual rainfall than neighboring Kenya, with few areas receiving less than 40 inches per year. Generally speaking the wettest months are March through May and to a less extent October through November. Typical of equatorial countries, Uganda's temperatures vary with altitude, but over most of the country January and February are the hottest months and June through August the coolest. Most of the country lies at over 3,500 feet altitude so average temperatures range from 66°–80°F, providing comfortably warm days and cool nights.

THE FISHING

The principal freshwater gamefish in Uganda are the Nile perch and tigerfish. The former is most abundant in the Nile River below Murchison Falls and at Chobe (75 miles upstream). The fishing is done by casting from shore into very fast water using large plugs with heavy spinning or bait-casting tackle. At the Falls a 160-pound Nile perch was caught on 18-pound-test line, which is the present rod record for the Nile. Casting from the rocks immediately below the Falls into strong currents adds some spice to the angling. At Parra several fish exceeding 200 pounds have been taken on handlines. Chobe also has some good fishing locations, and the rod record here is 140 pounds. There is also excellent fishing for perch in Lake Albert, where fish of over 200 pounds are possible. In the broad slow-moving reaches of the Nile at Namasagali, where it opens into Lake Kioga, about 50 miles from Lake Victoria, fish of up to 150 pounds have been taken. Bear in mind that these are maximum weights. For any number of Nile perch, say a dozen or more in a day's fishing, an average of about 35 pounds is considered good when both small and large catches are collectively totaled.

Despite its great size the Nile perch is not a difficult or spectacular quarry in the sense of a tarpon, for example, with which it might be compared on the basis of weight and the tackle used. Small Nile perch (up to 50 pounds) are more active gamefish than the larger specimens, which are inclined to sulk on the bottom. Occasionally the smaller fish will jump out of the water when hooked, and big perch invariably shake their heads over the surface in an effort to break free; but it is mainly the size of the fish rather than its resistance that provides angling thrills. Any kind of fish of over 100 pounds is awkward to handle, especially when casting from the bank in a fast-flowing river.

By contrast the tigerfish doesn't compare to the Nile perch in size, but whatever it lacks in weight this remote relative of South America's dorado is a first-class gamester with acrobatics to spare. There are 5 species of tigerfish in Africa. The smallest of these is *Hydrocyon forskalii*, which rarely weighs more than 2 pounds, and the largest is *H. Goliath*, found only in the Congo River watershed and Lake Tanganyika, which grows to about 100 pounds. Between these extremes are *H. lineatus*, *H. brevis*, and *H. vitatus*. Only *H. forskalii* (locally called "ngassa") and *H. lineatus* (locally called "wagassa") occur in Uganda. The latter has been recorded to weights of 35 pounds, but the range of fish taken in Uganda ordinarily runs from 1–6 pounds. Tigerfish are found in the same waters as the Nile perch—in Lake Albert and the Nile and its tributaries downstream from Murchison Falls. They are most common along rocky shores and in weedy bays, but there is a seasonal variation in their distribution and numbers.

TACKLE

A medium-action bait-casting or spinning rod suitable for lures in the ½-ounce class is sporty equipment for tigerfish in Uganda. A 10- or 12-pound-test line is adequate for the average run of fish, but still offers a margin of safety.

Tigerfish will take any form of live bait or lure that represents a fish. Often an angler trolling for Nile perch with a 6-inch-long plug will find tigerfish striking at the lure; some good fish are taken this way. They are not easy to catch. They hit voraciously, but they are difficult to hook. Their mouths are extremely bony and have few places where a hook will penetrate. Further, their jaws are immensely strong and can clamp down on a spoon so firmly as to resist even a heavy strike. For this reason some anglers use the heaviest tackle.

Live bait, dead bait, plugs, spoons, various spinners, and even flies can be used with success for tigerfish; but a lure with plenty of flash and movement, such as a small bright wobbling spoon about 1¼ or 1½ inches is ideal. Really big tigerfish are exceptional in Uganda, and a spoon of this size is most effective.   —A.J.McC.

ULCERATIVE DERMAL NECROSIS (UDN) *See* Diseases and Parasites

ULCER DISEASE *See* Diseases and Parasites

ULTRALIGHT SPINNING A method of fishing with specialized spinning tackle, originated in France (*ultralancer léger*) during the 1930's and introduced to the United States in 1948. As the name implies, ultralight spinning is accomplished with refined tackle; lines of less than 3-pound-test and rods of less than 3 ounces (total weight) are usually employed. The value of ultralight is in the capture of small gamefish and panfish, but it also serves a definite tactical purpose. The art of "hairlining" is based on two fundamental premises: (1) certain fishing conditions, which more or less fall in a pattern, demand the use of tiny lures; and (2) tiny lures can only be cast with the lightest tackle. In general, the advantage of spooling lines in the .002–.005-inch diameters is that they will cast a $\frac{1}{16}$–$\frac{1}{20}$-ounce spinner 50–60 feet away with little or no splash and no disturbing shadows on the stream bottom. Of course, the lure itself is so small that a hungry game-fish is not apt to inspect it carefully. On streams that have been thumped daily with hardware, even cautious fish like the brown trout are attracted to baits no bigger than a collar button. With the higher ratio of strikes comes a greater number of breakoffs, and the beginner especially will not only need patience, but considerable dexterity to get the feel of it. The almost invisible line is hard to see and difficult to control, particularly in a wind. Hairline technique requires an absolute mastery of spinning tackle; some points which are only incidental to the use of standard gear can make the difference between success and failure.

FINGER CONTROL OF CAST

Due to the fact that much of the fishing is done facing upstream in very shallow water, even a small spinner or spoon sinks very quickly and snags in the bottom if you do not control the cast manually. When using an orthodox spinning reel your forefinger does three important jobs. It holds the line free of the spool preparatory to a cast; it retards the flight of the lure by touching or "feathering" the line as the loops spin off; and it stops the cast on target. Some casters shoot for the bullseye and don't bother to check the cast manually. For a delicate presentation, however, it's necessary to aim slightly beyond the target and stop the lure in flight to knock some of the momentum out of it. The hairline angler should get in the habit of checking each cast because when the lure is stopped by touching the forefinger against the spool, it's a simple matter to raise the rod and give the blade some initial forward motion before turning the handle to close the bail. With this technique the lure is moving ahead—not diving for the stones—while the bail is snapping down. Precious moments are lost if you finish your cast; then retrieve in the normal manner without bringing the rod up and back. The bail must gather slack before the spinner gets started. True, your trout or smallmouth may be hiding in a deep pocket behind a boulder, but in low summer water such stations are invariably surrounded by shingles of moist gravel. The crafty hairliner will place his lure on these bare spots and swim it back into the holes to minimize splash and shadow. By using initial finger control, he can glide the spinner through a wet dishpan.

USE OF THE DRAG

The reel must be first-class. A wispy line requires a sensitive drag. The dragbrake of most spinning reels is in principle an adjustable, frictional resistance against spool rotation. This works with a slipping clutch ordinarily composed of a pressure spring, a washer, a wingnut, and the spool. By tightening the wingnut, the spool is compressed between the seat and the washer, creating the friction that resists rotation of the spool. Mechanically, no friction-type brake is 100 percent efficient. On rare occasions a drag will "freeze." Trying to loosen the wingnut while a runaway fish stretches the monofilament requires considerable presence of mind. With a hairline you seldom get that chance; if the spool merely hesitates, the

line breaks. However, modern reels are generally more responsive than their anglers. The trick is to set the drag on the low side. You don't need any more than a *suggestion* of drag when casting a hairline. If you set the drag high, or close to the breaking strain of the line, everything from air temperature to the elasticity of the monofilament becomes a potentially adverse factor. Bear in mind that the force required to start the drag working is at right angles to the spool—over the roller mechanism—and all the impact strain is confined to a few inches of line. When hand-testing a drag you pull the monofilament off smoothly, but fish rarely hit and run with the same precision. Their response to the sting of a hook is wild head shaking and body rolling, which comes back to the reel in violent and jerky pulls. None of these forces is sustained enough to get a high drag setting started; yet they may exceed the strength of the line. For this reason, the great majority of breaks occur at the reel, and these can be minimized by using the drag sparingly.

LINE ELASTICITY IMPORTANT

Although many anglers feel that the kind of gear employed is too fragile for serious work, the fact of the matter is that with a little experience almost anybody can use it. By holding the rod high, keeping as much line as possible out of the water, and taking advantage of the full bend of the rod, you can finger the spool and make the stretch of the monofilament wear the fish to exhaustion. The elasticity of the line acts as a shock absorber. In fact, the more yardage the fish peels off, the easier you can control the situation. Line breaks often occur because the angler snubs a green fish just a rod's length away where sudden lunges or jumps can't be counteracted with the flexibility of the tackle. It's imperative to keep a reasonable distance between yourself and your quarry, applying finger pressure against the spool as needed and pumping with gentle upward sweeps of the rod to control the fish's direction. The antireverse should be in the "on" position until the fish has been brought to net. But don't attempt to land a lively gamefish with hairline until it's absolutely whipped.

TO AVOID LINE TWIST

It is axiomatic that when you crank a spinning reel against a dead weight, the line becomes twisted. Not that the fish is dead—but it does become an immovable object at various times and creates the same effect. The line, which is stretched against his weight and at right angles to the path of resistance, turns back on the spool in twists as it passes over the roller mechanism. When a heavy fish is played incorrectly, even with a standard spinning tackle, the line will become a tightly snarled mass of hoops the moment all tension is released. Of course, a small fish which swims directly back to the angler won't cause much trouble. But with hairline gear all fish are "big," and the angler must be particularly careful, as even minimum twisting is enough to pop a fragile monofilament. The correct way to regain line is by pumping. Actually, it is more of a stroking motion—a gentle upward sweep of the rod which prods the fish in your direction. When the fish shows signs of weakening, press your forefinger right against the spool and raise the rod slowly backward; then lower it quickly and reel in the slack. The slack will not twist. Never, under any circumstances, crank the reel when your quarry is stationary and unyielding. The fish must be continually prodded with gentle nudges of the rod. Even if you don't have visual contact, a hairline rod is so sensitive that it telegraphs the fish's movements precisely.

DEEP FISHING

Apart from casting in shallow streams, hairline fishing is a good method of taking trout out of deep spring holes in summer. The cobweb monofilament offers very little resistance to a $1/5$–$1/8$-ounce lure as it sinks to the bottom. Frequently, a jig or spinner dropped to the gravel and danced back with twitches and hops is sure-fire for big squaretails. Here, finger control of the spool is of no importance in presentation because the lure has 20–30 feet to sink before reaching paydirt. But don't make the mistake of leaving the bail open unless your finger is feathering line while the lure drops. Fish often strike a tiny bait as it flutters downward. Most line breaks in deep fishing occur in using too much drag. There is a temptation to put the pressure on and rush the play along. It's natural to get impatient when the line is vertical, right beside the boat, springing taut from the water to the tip-top. Even if you succeed in raising a gamefish near the surface, it will invariably dive and sound again. With a tight drag that might be the last you see of it. The safest way to handle a deep fish is to let it have its way for a few minutes at least; then, pressing against the spool with the forefinger, raise the rod slowly, but with enough pressure to make the fish come up a bit. After lowering the rod quickly, reel fast to spool any footage earned, and pump the fish again. If the fish makes a surge, simply lift your finger off and let the drag take over.

STREAM TACTICS

The correct rod for hairline casting will be $4\frac{1}{2}$–6 feet long and weigh in the neighborhood of $1\frac{1}{2}$–$2\frac{1}{2}$ ounces. It must have a very sensitive action, soft without excessive vibration, and flexing well down into the butt. A short, stiff rod is no good even if it's very light in weight. Many ultralight lures are in the $1/20$–$1/10$-ounce class, and in themselves they can hardly provide one flea power toward developing a rod's resistance to bend. These diminutive spoons and spinners don't have the feeling of an orthodox casting weight. It's there, but it's delicate and takes some practice for the caster to get the right touch.

Generally speaking, upstream casting is more effective than fishing in a downstream direction because you can approach the fish more closely. Game fish are easily alarmed at 40–50 feet in low-water, and in view of the fact that your casting range is somewhat limited with ultralight lures, it helps to take advantage of their head-to-the-current position. In working a typical stretch of river, use the longest cast practical, and select targets that are beyond the place where a fish is holding. If there's a deep pocket behind a log, for example, aim for a spot 10 or even 15 feet above it, and run the spinner back to draw the fish out. Ultralight lures have very little surface impact, but you will find that swimming the lure at the right depth and speed is very important, particularly when dealing with large brown trout. They are susceptible to ultra-

light baits, but the blade must be moving at the right speed. Although the size of the lure is deceptively natural, its aerial entrance invariably arouses suspicion. The same tactic applies to downstream casting. If you want to pass your spinner through an undercut or into a dark, gurgling pocket, aim your cast into the shallows well below it; the instant the lure touches the surface bring your rod up and back to get the lure in forward motion. With the whirling blade creating tension on the line, it's a simple matter to guide the bait into the lair. You can steer a lure left or right, and even under overhanging bank brush, by holding the tip low in the desired direction. Never aim at the fish—always try to find a natural entrance to its feeding station, and swim the spinner to it. This tactic is certain to increase strikes and eliminate those follow-ups. Frequently, one type of lure will be superior to another, but their relative effectiveness depends on how artfully each is presented.

ULTRALIGHT LURES

There is a tremendous variety of ultralight lures on the market today, encompassing spinners, spoons, jigs, and plugs. As in all methods of fishing, the smart angler will stock a selection of each. Although microscopic baits don't lose their effectiveness as readily as standard-size lures, the fact remains that a fish population can become almost immune to artificials of any kind if the stream or pond is worked intensively. On civilized waters, angler success drops sharply after opening day because the hatchery-reared fish have been cropped off, and the caster must deal with native trout or those who have survived one or more seasons in the wild. The same thing applies to bass even if they aren't of hatchery origin—they become conditioned to the sight and sound of hardware running through the water. Any angler who has fished for a few years is aware that the celebrated lure of yesterday can be a dud tomorrow. Consistent success in any kind of angling requires a change of pace, and one way to achieve that is by using different types of baits.

ULTRALIGHT IN SALTWATER

Although few ultralight casters seek large fish in saltwater, there is a great deal of sport in the variety of species that can be caught. As a general rule, a natural white nylon or polar bear hair jig of $1/10$ ounce will hook flounders, croakers, snappers, lookdown, sennet, pompano, whiting, scup, and many other small inshore species which do not readily strike artificials. In addition, ladyfish, Spanish mackerel, school stripers, weakfish, and other modest-sized gamesters, which are usually caught on tackle that is too heavy for maximum enjoyment, are important to the ultralight fan. Bottom-bouncing a little jig along channel edges and over shell beds is apt to produce a dozen different kinds of fish. Most of these are crustacean and mollusk feeders, and consequently the day's bag merely reflects the area being fished. The reason for the jig's attraction probably rests on the fact that many mollusks and crustaceans will "hop" when disturbed. Even a scallop can jump off the sand by jetting water through its valves and its motion is not unlike that of the erratic behavior of shrimp and sandbugs. So the hopping movement of a correctly fished jig may resemble food forms which plugs, spinners, and flies cannot emulate. Conventional spinning tackle does not lend itself to long casts with tiny jigs, but ultralight gear greatly extends your range and the fine line and sensitive rod of ultralight equipment is an ideal combination for bottom-bouncing. —A.J.McC.

UNDERWATER PHOTOGRAPHY *See under* Scuba Diving

UTAH Compared with other intermountain states, Utah has fewer miles of large trout streams, though it has 30 miles of lunker rainbow in Green River below Flaming Gorge Dam and streams on the Boulder Mountains, which are still producing 5–7-pound brook trout. The Great Basin sector, one-third of the state, has summer droughts, but the rest of Utah has relatively heavy precipitation and flood control can be a problem.

Utah harbors some of the West's best fishing and has also supplied many pounds of prize-winning brown trout to *Field & Stream's* annual fishing contests. Because of Utah's constantly increasing need for water, many dams have risen to plug her streams. Experts have estimated that 75 percent of the stream habitat has already been harmed. Pollution is also a serious problem.

On the positive side of the picture there are two major drainages in Utah (excluding a trickle out of northwestern Utah into the Columbia River system). The western half of the state drains into the Bonneville Basin, a closed circuit which is dominated by Great Salt Lake. Eastern Utah waters flow into the Colorado River Basin and, eventually, the Gulf of California. The major trout waters lie along a broad belt running north and south through the center of the state. In northcentral Utah this belt divides to the east to encompass the 150-mile length of the Uinta Mountains in northeastern Utah.

BEAR LAKE

Bear Lake is a big, natural lake lying high in the mountains northeast of Logan. Partially in Idaho, the lake is fished on a reciprocal-license basis by residents of both states.

A Utah game official once described Bear Lake as a fine fish hotel with no dining room. Experts are now refuting this statement, but something is wrong with Bear Lake; it remains a poor trout fishery despite stocking and some attempts at habitat improvement.

However, shortly after the spring ice breakup hardy anglers take big lake, rainbow, and cutthroat trout by wading out and casting spoons. Also, the lake produces an abundant supply of Bonneville cisco (*see* Cisco). This unique whitefish spawns along the eastern shores of the lake in January or February. Increasing numbers of frost-bitten dipnetters annually throng the spawning gravel to scoop up limits of these small but tasty fish.

There are the usual resort accommodations at Lakota and also at Fish Haven, or you may want to camp above the lake in the magnificent Cache National Forest.

UTAH LAKE

Utah Lake lies 150 miles south of Bear Lake, near Provo. In pioneer days cutthroat trout abounded here, but pollution, nets and land development destroyed them. Although the trout are gone, recent attempts at cleaning up this lake have resulted in excellent channel catfishing.

Late spring and early summer (although the lake is open year around) are the popular seasons for filling a stringer with husky cats. In addition, the state recently stocked white bass and the species has become established. Spinning lures, worked on a mild, winter day, will frequently fill a bass angler up in less than half an hour.

There is also a limited walleye fishery here, and some nice fish are taken every spring in the tributary Provo River.

Several boat liveries are on the lake, and excellent motel accommodations are available in the nearby metropolitan areas.

FISH LAKE

South of Utah Lake another 150 miles is Fish Lake. Cradled in the mountains above Richfield, Fish Lake is perhaps the loveliest large natural lake in the state of Utah. And many anglers regard its thick-bodied rainbows as the scrappiest in the state.

Opening days, week ends, and holidays are best avoided here, unless you like crowds. But week days, especially after Pioneer Day on July 24, are idyllic, and so is the fishing.

Evening fly-fishing along the lake's east shore is often superb. Some enjoy it from boats while others hike a bit, then wade out to watch for, and cast to, rising fish. Improbable patterns like the Jock Scott and Silver Doctor have won a following among some tippet poppers.

Lake trout in the 20-pound class are taken only occasionally by trollers who know, or are guided along, the lake's famous "mack runs." Some 5–15-pound browns are taken each year just after ice out and again in November.

A lodge located midway along the west shore has long been an angler's rendezvous and information center. In addition, there are other good camps at each end of the lake which can provide accommodations, boats, and guides. It's best to make reservations well in advance, especially during the busy part of the summer. There are also excellent, but somewhat limited, Forest Service campgrounds for those who prefer them.

UINTA MOUNTAIN LAKES

The remainder of Utah's natural lakes are too small or numerous to mention except by area. Undoubtedly, the best of them are in the Uinta Mountains of northeastern Utah. King's Peak towers above 13,000 feet to dominate this long, east-west range. This is big-sky and wool-shirt country and, some say, so lonely that the hoot owls make love to the pine hens. You could spend a summer in the Uintas and never fish the same lake twice. In fact, you wouldn't have time to fish the majority of them.

All of the lakes which will support fish are regularly stocked by airplane, and few of them go sour for more than a season or two. (Roadside lakes get the truck treatment and are flailed by the multitude.) The bulk of the plants are cutthroat and brook trout, but you can also find wonderful Arctic-grayling fishing as well as occasional rainbows and rare golden trout.

The western portion of the Uintas are designated a Primitive Area so it's shank's mare or the kind you straddle. Many of the better lakes are really too far for even the hardiest hikers. And this has helped the Mirror Lake area, east of Kamas, to become a center for guides, pack strings, and tinkling horse bells. However, there are other capable outfitters serving the northern and eastern sections of the range. The Department of Fish and Game will furnish a list of them on request.

Because the growing season is short, Uinta fish average 10–12 inches. Still, 2-pounders are possible, and lunkers of well over 5 pounds are sometimes landed.

Most of the lakes may be fished from rafts, but check before attaching a motor as they're prohibited on many of the smaller lakes. Besides plenty of bug dope, take both a fly rod and a spinning outfit. Many of the lakes' margins are too brushy for fly-casting, and sometimes flies don't produce. A pair of feather-weight waders can be helpful, but a lot of the lakes are too abruptly deep for effective wading. Most anglers cast from shore and do just fine.

Although the Uinta's portals are an easy half-day's drive from Salt Lake City, remember that beyond those portals lies a wilderness. Brief but vicious hail or even snow storms sweep through in July.

It's often a long way between the trail markers (although the main trails are excellently maintained), and someone is always getting lost—sometimes for several days. Finally, although that rented horse seems gentle, don't sit up there, as so many do, waiting to be launched into the nearest ravine when a deer jumps across the trail. Few mountain states can surpass Utah's Uinta fishing. No angler should spend his lifetime without sampling it at least once.

BOULDER MOUNTAIN LAKES

Far to the south of the Uintas are the lesser-numbered but equally productive Boulder Mountain Lakes. Sometimes called "Thousand Lake Mountain," this area is just as remote, but not quite so rugged, as Uintas. Most of the lakes can be reached by pickup or, better, jeep, plus a bit of hiking. The Boulder isn't as heavily fished as the more accessible sections of the Uintas are; hence, your catch will frequently weigh more. The state's biggest brook trout—with many taken to 7½ pounds in 1971–1973—were taken in Boulder Mountain creeks and ponds. If you forget your spin stick, a fly rod will do very nicely on the rainbow, brook, and cutthroat trout waiting here. Current information on this area is best obtained by asking locally at sporting goods or general stores in Richfield, Loa, or Bicknell. There is a state conservation officer and a fish hatchery at Loa. They'll also be able to advise you.

If you're a western-story as well as a scenery fan, you'll recall that the writer Zane Grey set some of his rip-snorters in this section of southeastern Utah.

THE MANTI

This high-country area in central Utah abounds in small but productive creeks, lakes, and reservoirs. Tackle, trout, and technique are the same as for the Boulder or Uintas.

Starting-off points (at last report there were no professional guides serving the area) are the little towns of Ephraim, Mayfield, Orangeville, or Manti. A road, the Skyline Drive, provides sigh-making scenery as well as access to all of the lakes on the southeastern slope of the

Manti. This area is also one of Utah's better deer-hunting territories; so, if you come in the fall, bring your rod and rifle.

STRAWBERRY RESERVOIR

From an angling standpoint, Utah's reservoirs are good to terrible, and either adjective may apply to any reservoir on any particular day. The average angler won't have consistent good luck on any of them. He will, however, have to have a boat license. Contact the State Parks and Recreation Commission, Salt Lake City, for complete (and voluminous) boating regulations.

The Strawberry Reservoir is one of Utah's oldest and largest. It's easily reached during an hour and a half drive east from Salt Lake City on U. S. 40. During the thirties and forties Strawberry was a four-star producer of giant cutthroat trout. Unfortunately, live bait was too often the lure, and the big pond became saturated with chubs, carp, and stunted yellow perch. Eventually, in the fall of 1961, the lake was chemically treated and subsequently restocked with cutthroat and rainbows. After giving the young trout a year in which to grow, the season was reopened successfully in 1963. Trophy anglers might well watch for a reblossoming of this particular Strawberry.

There are cabins, boats, and guides, but a weird land leasing system has made it inadvisable to invest in expensive cabins. The result has been an eruption of two disreputable shanty towns along the lake. Public camping facilities are available at lakeside, but they're almost as grim as the cabins. Instead, stay at one of the excellent motels in nearby Heber City or Provo, and commute, or use one of the attractive Forest Service camps in the adjacent hills.

In the past fly-fishermen stood in the bows of their boats while a companion rowed. Casting big flies long distances to the rises brought many a handsome fish aboard. Of course, many trolled hardware and did well too.

Bank-fishing has never been as productive as boat fishing. One spot is locally known as "Velveeta Point," which should be indicative of the angling techniques on the banks at Strawberry. However, knowledgeable bankside fly anglers produce rainbows and cutthroats, averaging from 3–8 pounds, by the thousands each year.

DEER CREEK RESERVOIR

South of Heber City, Deer Creek Reservoir is a big, fickle lake which has never rivaled nearby Strawberry as a trout producer. Big trout are occasionally boated, but, overall, the place rates no better than fair.

The reservoir has a huge population of runty, yellow perch, and many dads whet their sons' fishing appetites and skills by letting them catch a mess of eager but worthless perch.

SCOFIELD RESERVOIR

This large reservoir is near Price in eastcentral Utah. It once produced some giant trout, but trash fish outflanked, then outnumbered the gamefish. People avoided the place until the game department poisoned the chubs and restocked with rainbow trout and kokanee salmon. They claim, and there's no reason to doubt them, that the pounds of gamefish taken during the first season more than paid for the cost of the eradication project.

Since then Scofield has suffered from partial winterkills, but the fishing has remained good, especially for boaters. Most of the fish weigh ½–2 pounds and that's it—few lunkers have been reported. Public accommodations are meager (as is the scenery); so load the tent or hook on your camp trailer.

PINEVIEW RESERVOIR

A few minutes drive east of Ogden, Pineview has also been treated to remove trash fish. The first opening day after the treatment and restocking was a resounding success. Since then the lake has suffered from severe drawdowns, and all the other ills associated with reservoir management. Nevertheless it has continued to produce nice trout for both bank and boat anglers.

FLAMING GORGE AND GLEN CANYON RESERVOIRS

These enormous reservoirs are located on the Green and Colorado rivers respectively. Flaming Gorge inundated the old Green River bed and canyon in Utah and extends into Wyoming. The two states of Utah and Wyoming completed an extensive non-gamefish eradication program prior to the closing of the dam's gates. The lake was stocked with rainbow trout, which have displayed an exceptional rate of growth and now provide excellent angling.

The main access points are from Rock Springs, Wyoming, or Vernal, Utah. The two nearest towns are Dutch John and Manila, Utah. Manila hasn't changed much since the days when Butch Cassidy and Tom Horn rode in, but Dutch John caters to the tourist trade.

Glen Canyon Dam and its lake, Lake Powell, are on the Utah-Arizona border. Glen Canyon is an interesting tourist attraction, situated in the perpendicular, tawny-red canyon country on the Colorado River. Powell, with its 1,800 miles of broken shoreline, is red-hot largemouth water.

MINOR LAKES

Utah has many other reservoirs and a few lakes which can provide good angling. However, they aren't large enough or consistent enough to rate more than a mention.

Navajo Lake, east of Cedar City, is a handsome body of water which, unfortunately, is subject to frequent winter-kills (as are many of Utah's lakes and reservoirs). Strike it after a couple of favorable winters, and you'll enjoy good fishing.

Steinaker Reservoir (pronounced, "stan-a-kur") near Vernal is new and so far has produced better trout fishing than was anticipated.

Echo and Rockport reservoirs are near Coalville and Wanship respectively. The latter produced phenomenal trout fishing when it was first impounded, but has now settled down to being as tight-watered and unpredictable as the nearby Echo.

Koosharem Reservoir wasn't named after a sneeze, but don't sneeze at it if the June wind has driven your boat off the nearby and infinitely more beautiful Fish Lake. Otter Creek Reservoir, near Koosharem, also has its rare moments.

Minerville Reservoir, out of Beaver, might be a good spot to try while you are prospecting around in the more interesting mule-deer country there.

Locomotive Springs is in the desert at the northern tip of Great Salt Lake. The place is bleak, but its rehabilitated waters produce some excellent, late-winter rainbow fishing. Summer fishing may be good too, but the mosquitoes, which send their runts to Alaska, make finding out impossible. Locomotive is also a public waterfowl-hunting area, and, periodically, the shooting (ducks and geese) is better than the fishing.

Pelican Ponds, southwest of Logan, offer some of Utah's limited largemouth-bass fishing—and it's good in the spring. Salt Springs, located a few miles southeast of Wendover, Nevada, also grows bass and bluegill while being an erratic producer of fine duck shooting. Utah's other bass waters are limited and not worth mentioning except to residents who already know about them.

UTAH STREAMS

Anything moving and not in a bottle is called a river in Utah. The state's real "rivers" are the Green, San Juan, and Colorado. These streams are typified by heavy silt loads and no trout. Still, there is some good to indifferent channel-cat and black-bullhead fishing in all of them.

The Green once harbored a giant minnow, the Colorado squawfish (see Northern Squawfish), but intensive chemical treatment just prior to the construction of Flaming Gorge Dam eliminated it. The Green from the Dam into Dinosaur National Monument at the confluence of the Yampa is now excellent rainbow trout water. Fish up to 10 pounds have been taken, and 5-pound fish are not uncommon if the angler works the riffles carefully. The Green also yields browns and cutthroats of lunker size.

BEAR RIVER

The Bear River heads on the north slope of the Uinta Mountains, and, there, it affords good fishing. But once it leaves the mountains, to terminate eventually at the Bear River Migratory Bird Refuge, it is dammed, polluted, silted, and otherwise defiled until it is of little recreational value.

LOGAN RIVER

Logan Canyon, a beautiful, steep-sided, easterly slash through the Wasatch Mountains, shelters one of Utah's best trout streams. Even though a major highway (U. S. 89) parallels it, the Logan is a consistent producer of husky rainbows, cutthroats, and heavy brown trout. An attempt to build a new highway up the center of the stream was thwarted; so the Logan should continue to stay consistent.

Average trout are taken by average efforts. The angler who'll skip suppers to work a wet fly in late summer may read his name in *Field & Stream* as a winner in the brown-trout division.

The Logan produced the largest brown ever taken in North America (36 pounds, 12 ounces), although it is not in the record books since it was taken by snagging.

BLACKSMITH FORK RIVER

This oddly named stream is just south of the Logan River and east of the town of Hyrum. It offers fishing similar to the Logan's, plus a few rattlesnakes. Like many

Western streams with consistent flows, fishing on the Blacksmith gets better later in the season. The Blacksmith is an especially beautiful stream which yields many 2–4-pound browns.

There is also a winter season for mountain whitefish on this stream and the Logan. The fishing is good for folks who like chilblains and the not-too-gamey whitefish. A small yellow fly has been proclaimed as the absolute tops for winter whitefishing.

WEBER RIVER

The Weber (pronounced "wee-bur") heads in the western end of the Uinta Mountains and empties into the Ogden Bay Waterfowl Management Area on the shore of Great Salt Lake. The upper Weber River slips briskly down from the mountains and through a handsome, but heavily posted alpine valley east of Peoa. If you can get access, you'll find it a good fly stream that yields cutthroat, rainbow, and brown trout. At Peoa the river turns north, and there's good brown fishing along it until you reach Rockport and then Echo reservoirs. Some people fish below Echo, but the jaded-looking resorts in Weber Canyon are mute witnesses to the quality of the fishing.

PROVO RIVER

You'll find big, Provo River browns listed in *Field & Stream*'s catalog of prizewinners. At one time this river, which heads in the Uintas and tails in Utah Lake, was one of the best small trout streams in America. In many ways it's gone the way of the Weber. Still, if you are skilled at brown trout fishing, you can take heart-stoppers along the lower river in spectacular Provo Canyon. Rainbows are also heavily stocked in the Provo. There is moderately good fishing, in the undredged sections, above Deer Creek Reservoir all the way to the Uinta Mountains. Posting is an unsolved problem along many sections of the river, and some landowners charge a trespass fee.

Tackle shops in Provo or Heber City are good sources of last-minute dope on the river. There is also a regional office of the Department of Fish and Game in Provo which handles all sorts of fin and feather business.

DUCHESNE RIVER

Stemming from the high-lake basins on the southern slope of the Uinta Mountains, the Duchesne (Du-shane) has been a good trout and mountain-whitefish stream—north of the town of Duchesne. The river is also a good base for visiting the many other streams which wander enticingly out of these mountains.

FREMONT RIVER

In southcentral Utah, the Fremont has been guardedly described as the best fly stream in the state. Fishing pressure is lighter here than on streams in northern Utah.

The river crosses the main highway in places, but reaching much of it takes some walking or back-roading. This helps to explain why the browns and rainbows grow large and are relatively easier to hook. Recently, the Fremont has been open year 'round, and winter angling there has been excellent.

OTHER NATURAL STREAMS

Among the streams that originate in the Uinta Mountains are such excellent trout waters as Henry's Fork, on the north slope; Rock Creek, which has produced a 13-pound brown; Whiterocks, which runs without a dam, road, or artificialization of any kind for about 20 miles and produces natural cutthroats; Uinta, on the south slope which is credited with a 12½-pound brown; and Lake Fork, which has produced browns to 10½ pounds.

Two other south-central streams provide excellent fly-fishing waters: the Asay and Mammoth Creek, which is south of Panguitch.

JONES CREEK

This isolated creek is one of the best and also one of the few unviolated streams left in Utah. About 25 miles northeast of Vernal it's accessible only by jeep or horseback. The sporting goods store in Vernal can give you directions for reaching it.

Located in a deep canyon and partially in Dinosaur National Monument, the creek in Jones Hole is dream fodder. Many-riffled and deep-pooled, this 10-mile ribbon consistently produces browns of 5 pounds and more. The opening week end of the fishing season is about the only time it might be called crowded.

The water, from springs at its head, is seldom dirty or roily. It occasionally experiences flash floods, maybe one every five years. Look out for them, but mind your fishing even more; you've got to treat this stream cautiously because its clearwater doesn't tolerate clumsiness. Neither do the rattlers who live in the canyon walls.

Nearly every Utah hamlet has its fishing area. The game department offices in Price, Provo, Ogden, Cedar City, Vernal, or Salt Lake City will be glad to help you find them.
                                                            —F.C.

UTAH CHUB *Gila atraria*   A large minnow which can be a serious competitor of gamefishes. The original distribution of the Utah chub was in the drainage basin of Lake Bonneville and in the Snake River above Shoshone Falls. It has spread to other Western waters because it is widely used as a baitfish. The coloration of the Utah chub is variable but is frequently a dark green, blue, or black on the dorsal surface, shading to a silvery or even golden color. Some individuals have bright yellow or orange ventral parts. The origin of the dorsal fin is directly over the insertion of the pelvic fins. Usually 9 dorsal rays and 8 anal rays. The lateral line has 45–65 scales. The oblique mouth has two rows of pharyngeal teeth.

LIFE HISTORY

The Utah chub occurs in a variety of habitats and in a broad temperature range. In Yellowstone Lake it is found where water temperatures reach 88°F. An omnivorous feeder, this chub consumes higher water plants, algae, terrestrial and aquatic insects, snails, crustaceans, and small fish. It spawns from early to late summer and deposits its eggs at random over the bottom. It may attain a length over 20 inches and a weight of 3 pounds, but is more frequently 5–8 inches long.

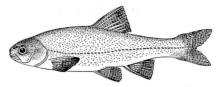

Utah Chub

ECONOMIC VALUE

Although used as bait, the Utah chub is felt to be destructive to other species, especially young trout. It has been the subject of chemical eradication. —R.A.J.

V

VARIANT A type of dry fly having oversize hackles but otherwise dressed as any standard pattern. *See also* Spider

VEER A nautical term to indicate a shift in the wind in a clockwise direction. If the wind shifts in a counterclockwise direction it is a *backing wind*. If the wind shifts from abeam to aft (whether clockwise or counterclockwise) it is described as *veering*. If it shifts from abeam to forward it is said to *haul*.

VENEZUELA Larger than the combined states of Texas and Minnesota, the 352,143 square miles of Venezuela are only sparsely populated. The tropical interior, which is dominated by the Orinoco watershed, has over 1,000 rivers which support such endemic species as the pavón, payara, cachama, dorado, brycon, piranha (locally *caribe*), and numerous catfishes. These constitute an immense fishery, which is largely utilized by the native peoples as food. Few anglers visit the Venezuelan jungle country. The coastal saltwater fishing, which is centered on blue marlin, white marlin, sailfish, and tarpon, is of unusual quality but organized to a very limited extent. There are excellent accommodations but few boats available for charter. An annual marlin tournament in September, which has resulted in some remarkable catches, is an invitational match for private craft.

The southern border of Venezuela runs to within 1 degree of the Equator but the country's climate is tropical, modified by elevation and prevailing winds. The hot zone, from sea level to about 3,000 feet, averages 85°F except where cooled by winds from the sea. The leeward or southern slopes of mountains, together with the Llanos, cut off from prevailing trade winds by the peaks of the coastal mountain range, are generally the hottest. The coast itself, though fanned by onshore breezes, is often oppressive because of high relative humidity.

Much of inland Venezuela, however, is above the hot zone in a moderate range from 3,000 to about 6,000 feet, where the annual mean temperature runs about 65°F. Here the warmest months are April and May, the coolest December and January. The wettest months are July and August; the driest is February. Because of the cooling effect of altitude probably the most pleasant climate in Venezuela is found fairly near the Equator—in the high jungle country south of the Orinoco.

Except for a few remote American oil camps, which are not available to the public, there are no facilities or resorts on the interior Venezuelan rivers catering to anglers. There is only limited road access across the Llanos, although some streams can be reached by four-wheel-drive vehicle. Essentially, however, this is for the more adventurous sportsman.

FRESHWATER FISHING

There are two seasons in the tropics—wet or *invierno* and dry or *verano*. The dry season in the Orinoco is generally from January into April, and on the Amazon to the south from late June to November. During the wet season these rivers rise 20–50 feet over their banks and flood the surrounding lands for 20 miles or more. Fishing is possible only in the dry season. High temperatures prevail in the lowland jungles and plains with daily maximums in the 90's and occasionally over 100°F, particularly toward the end of the dry season.

Peacock pavón of 12 and 13 pounds make for good fishing on the Ventuari River

All the important angling rivers in Venezuela are Orinoco tributaries. The mainstream itself is both large and for the most part muddy, and while it supports an active commercial fishery water conditions are seldom suitable for sport fishing. The third largest river system in South America, the Orinoco rises at 3,523 feet elevation in the Parima Mountains of southern Venezuela almost on the Brazilian border, and flows 1,281 miles before entering the Atlantic. Its drainage basin covers more than 360,000 square miles or roughly four-fifths of Venezuela and one-fifth of Colombia. Near its headwaters the river divides as it leaves the Great Plain or Gran Sabana, a part of its flow running northwest to form the Orinoco while a branch stream, the Casiquiare, turns southwest into the Rio Negro, which in turn joins the Amazon. The Equatorial jungle at this point is a vast green canopy—no pure forest in our North American sense but a region where Louis Agassiz once identified 17 different species of trees in an area only a half-mile square. This diversity of flora is comparable to the vast number of fishes inhabiting both the Amazon and the Orinoco. It has been estimated that nearly 2,000 species of fish occur in each of these watersheds.

Although the main rivers are muddy for the most part, the upper tributaries flow clear over sand and rock bottoms. In the brief months between rains their luminous beauty has no equal. The fishing, on a river such as the Ventuari (Territorio Amazonas, Venezuela) is without parallel. Catching 50 or even 100 pavón in one day, averaging 8 pounds or more, is the norm. Whether you use fly, plug, or spoon, many other gamefish such as the powerful and leaping payara, various brycons, pacu, trachira, pike-characins, and the acrobatic striped catfish will take the lure just as readily.

The outstanding and most widely distributed native gamefish is the pavón (*Cichla* spp.). Pavón occur in most rivers tributary to the Orinoco. There are at least 4 species found in Venezuela; among the largest is the peacock pavón (locally pavón cinchado), which has a probable maximum weight of 30 pounds with an average of 6 pounds. Equal in size is the spotted pavón (locally pavón truchas) the strongest and most spectacular cichlid in South America. The third species is the butterfly pavón (locally pavón mariposa), which averages 2½ pounds with a maximum weight of about 11 pounds. The butterfly inhabits slower water than the peacock and spotted pavón and is somewhat easier to catch. Comparable in size and found in fast-flowing sections of stream is the royal pavón (locally pavón real), which is common to the upper Orinoco tributaries in the vicinity of Puerto Páez.

Of comparable distribution and usually found in the same waters with the pavón is the payara. A payara has the vicious nature of a bluefish, the poise of a rainbow trout, and when hooked the jumping ability of a tarpon. Its mouth is nearly hook-proof. Equipped with sharp canines including 2 front teeth which fit in sockets on top of its head, the payara can chop through plastic lures and wire leaders quite easily. There are 3 species found in Venezuela. The most abundant is *Hydrolicus scomberoides*, which attains weights over 30 pounds. They will take literally any lure or bait and display a particular enthusiasm for topwater plugs. On light-casting tackle payara put up a terrific scrap, making powerful runs and frequent jumps.

In contrast the pacu (*Colossoma spp.*) looks more like an overgrown bluegill in shape. The pacu is one of the strongest fish in South American rivers—not a jumper but a determined body-shaking bottom plunger. Pacu weigh from a 5- or 6-pound average to 40 pounds or more. There appears to be two common species, the blue pacu (locally cachama azul) and the red pacu (locally cachama roja). Although this fish is primarily herbivorous it can be taken on artificial lures, particularly small spoons and spinners. Pacu inhabit swift-water streams as well as standing waters, and are often associated with dorado throughout their mutual range from Colombia south to northern Argentina.

Dorado have a more spotty distribution in Venezuela than the pavón. They do occur, however, in gravel-bottomed streams in the Barinas watershed, such as the

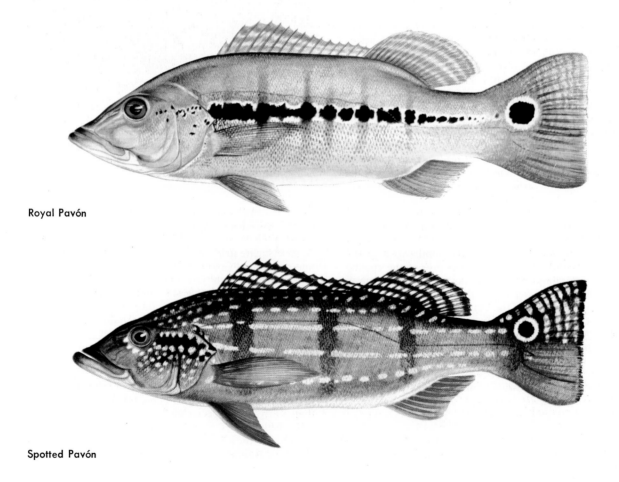

Royal Pavón

Spotted Pavón

Paguey and Canagua rivers. They are also found in rivers to the west as far as Barcelona and south to the Meta River on the Colombian border. This species of dorado (*Salminus hilarii*) is not as heavy as the dorado of Argentina, Paraguay, and Brazil. An 8- or 9-pound dorado is considered quite large in Venezuela.

The jungle and its wildlife is no small part of the enjoyment of a South American trip. Jaguar, puma, tapir, capybara, wild boar, and deer are sometimes seen along the riverbanks, and the green canopy of trees is often teeming with howler monkeys. It is a bird-watcher's paradise, where dusky skimmers do their surface-cleaving quadrille over the water while herons silently watch the performance. Native wild turkeys, bellbirds, and colorful warblers (which vie with the butterflies in brilliance) flush at the passing of a boat. There are piranha, cayman, crocodiles, electric eels, giant anaconda, and stingrays in all of the upper streams; and of these potentially dangerous creatures the stingray is most feared by the Indian. The freshwater ray is more potent than its marine counterpart, as it has two or more toxic barbs—one extending out to the tip of its tail. But caution is the keynote in an alien environment and few adventurers have returned with anything more harrowing than a mosquito bite.

TACKLE

There are no soft-mouthed gamefish in the Orinoco country, so the emphasis should be on fairly stiff, if not heavy, rods. A stout 5½-foot bait-casting rod equipped with 15-pound-test line, or a 6½-foot spinning rod and a minimum 10-pound-test mono is about right. Your fly-fishing equipment should be steelhead caliber. For lures you need heavy-hook streamer flies in a good range of sizes. Mostly you will use No. 2 to No. 2/0, with yellow or white wings predominating.

The best all-round lures for spinning and bait-casting are wooden plugs with heavy-gauge hooks. Big pavón have powerful jaws and toss their heads like fighting bulls, twisting out hardware and straightening ordinary hooks. They also bite through plastic lures. Payara are natural plug busters, with their long canine teeth. Dorado have relatively short but nevertheless sharp teeth. The pacu has molars like a horse—oversize grinding teeth with jaws like a vise. A 20-pound pacu can crush a plug to splinters if he grips it right. You will lose many plugs, so it's advisable to bring along a few dozen. Spoons designed for saltwater-casting are usually effective and not easily damaged. Bring plenty of wire leaders; 18-inch-long stainless steel coated with vinyl in 30-pound test provides ample protection.

SALTWATER FISHING

Venezuela has over 1,700 miles of coast, which is bathed on its north shore by the North Equatorial Current and along the east coast by the Guiana Current, which receives freshwater, especially in the rainy season, from the Amazon, Orinoco, and many lesser rivers. These river waters are rich in nutrients, which favor the growth of aquatic life on Venezuela's continental shelf and inshore areas.

Generally speaking, the season for white marlin is from July through September, but blue marlin are present all

year. The whites, which peak in September, are of large average size, with the majority of fish weighing over 60 pounds; the blue marlin average about 225 pounds, with 400–450-pound fish being the exception. Most of the marlin fishing is done 15 miles westnorthwest of the port of LaGuaira. Some sailfish are taken in this same area, but larger concentrations appear to exist near Isla de Margarita. Swordfish and bluefin tuna also occur off the Venezuelan coast notably around the island of La Blanquilla. Dolphin are common to all marlin grounds and run to a large size with 25–40-pound fish being the usual.

Venezuela offers sensational fishing for the high-jumping white marlin during September

Schools of tarpon appear along the coast during the summer months (July through September) and are often caught from small boats and in the surf. However, there is some tarpon fishing in bays, lagoons, and rivers at all times. Snook are very abundant in the surf as well as all brackish-water habitats. —A.J.McC.

VENT The external opening of the alimentary canal, also called anus. *See* Anatomy

VENTRAL The abdomen of the lower side of a fish.

VERMILION ROCKFISH Sebastodes miniatus The species is one of three leading rockfish (*which see*) in the California commercial markets. It ranges from northern Baja California to Vancouver Island. The vermilion rockfish is similar to the canary rockfish. Lower jaw rough to the touch; lower jaw slightly projecting, a knob on lower tip; small spines on top of head; peritoneum white. Color vermilion or brick-red above, shading to pink laterally with red belly; black dots on back and sides give a dusky appearance; three orange stripes across head radiating

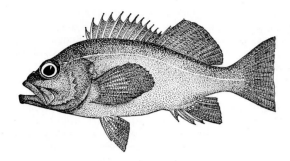

Vermilion Rockfish

from eye; dorsal fin gray at base, others vermilion; mouth lining and lips red; yellow on sides of some large specimens. Length to 36 inches.   —J.R.

VERMONT   The Green Mountain state is small (9,564 square miles), but it's sparsely populated, and because of an abundance of coldwaters, Vermont is one of the better trout fisheries in the northeast. Bordered by Lake Champlain on the west and the Connecticut River on the east, the state has hundreds of lakes and ponds of 20 acres or more and miles of streams rising along the spine of the Green Mountains. Vermont is rocky, yet heavily timbered, and relatively undeveloped. Civilization exists mainly along the stream valleys and at the borders of highways, where cows graze and a patch of land can be plowed. Miles of small headwater streams, tributary to creeks and rivers which run into Lake Champlain or the Connecticut River, spill off the mountains and afford angling which ranges from modest to excellent. Among these peaks (Mount Mansfield, 4,393 feet) are uncounted ponds and lakes. A third group of trout streams occurs in the northern watershed and runs into Lake Memphremagog, which lies partially in Quebec.

All of these streams were originally brook-trout habitat, and there are few cold headwater brooks which do not hold at least a token population of squaretails today. The larger rivers in the valleys have been stocked with brown and rainbow trout. Brook trout are stocked in many of the ponds, while lake trout and landlocked salmon are planted in the larger, deeper lakes. The "native" trout, however, remains foremost on the list of resident anglers.

Opening day of the trout season in towns near the better rivers is like the first day of deer season; every business is short-handed, and if you go into the general store you will be served by oldtimers who can no longer face the coldwater, wind, and freezing rain of early angling. Traditionally, the bait fisherman is king; and with the coming of lowwater in summer, local trout fishermen lay away their rods (except for occasional highwater periods after summer thunder storms) until the fall run of spawning brook trout brings them out again in September. This means plenty of elbow room for the expert fly-fisherman. The mountain streams along both slopes of the Green Mountains run almost bank full all summer and hold temperatures in the 60's even in July and August. Here, in streams above 1,000-feet elevation, brook, brown, and rainbow trout will take the fly beginning in May and ending with September.

Many experimental projects have been conducted by the Vermont Fish and Game Department in cooperation with the U.S. Fish and Wildlife Service and the Forest Service (which administers the Green Mountain National Forest) in research and management which are aimed at long-term improvement of the existing fisheries. Typical of these are the experimental stocking of lake trout behind the Harriman Dam on the Deerfield River; the development of a rainbow-trout fishery in Chittenden Reservoir near Rutland; the reclamation of small lakes and ponds, using rotenone and restocking after treatment. Pond culture of brook trout has been particularly successful in Vermont, whereas attempts to re-establish the squaretail in streams have been largely unsuccessful, as in other Northeastern states. Some of the most striking results of fish-planting work (for example, the almost unexploited bass fishing in Somerset Reservoir at the head of the Deerfield River) have received little publicity. Ponds in remote mountain areas not accessible by road or jeep trail will probably remain unvisited by fishermen for years.

BATTENKILL RIVER

The Battenkill, in the southwest corner of Vermont, is a productive trout river. Like all large streams in Vermont, the lower Battenkill is public water, and the farmers who own the forests and meadows of the upper reaches will usually open their pasture gates to any courteous angler who knocks at the farmhouse door.

Brown trout were stocked in the Battenkill at the turn of the century. It is one of the best natural brown-trout streams in New England. The records of the Vermont Fish and Game Department show that although occasional brown trout of over 5 pounds have been taken for many years (and most of the hatchery planting recently has emphasized brown trout) the Battenkill is, nevertheless, predominantly brook-trout water. Big browns lie behind almost every sunken snag and wherever there is food and cover. Brook trout of 7–10 inches are found in increasing numbers as you go up toward the Green Mountains along the valley from the New York State line.

Most of the Battenkill lies within a short walking distance from paved highways, and the trout in the river are well-educated. With summer lowwater, the hatches of mayflies are replaced by swarms of midges and other small insect life, and the dry-fly and nymph fishermen take over along these 15 miles of wide, tree-shaded river. An evening in summer on the Battenkill can be an event never to be forgotten by the fly-fisherman. He will observe rising fish in numbers. But unless he knows the river and has flies and nymphs tied on No. 18 and No. 20 hooks to match the insect life, he will not take many fish.

OTTER CREEK

Beginning at Emerald Lake only a few hundred feet from the source of the Battenkill to the south, Otter Creek runs north, roughly paralleling Route 7. This is the longest stream entirely within the state of Vermont. The Creek comes out of the little lake and flows through miles of beaver flats to a point abreast of Danby. There are big squaretails all through this swamp, but the bottom is soft, the stream cannot be safely waded on account of quicksands, and fallen snags and beaver rubbish make canoeing impossible. Farther north, at Wallingford, and downstream to Middlebury, there is a series of dams, or ruins of dam abutments. In the fastwater below there are big rainbows and browns, and the oxbow bends of the creeks in the meadows hold squaretails wherever there are springs, heavy shade, and undercut banks. In the past few years, warmwater species have come up Otter Creek from Lake Champlain, and the angler spinning for trout in any deep pool from Emerald Lake to the north is likely to be surprised by the lunging strike of a northern pike.

Beginning with Big Branch (opposite Danby) and all the way north, a number of tributary streams flow down from the high Green Mountains into Otter Creek. Much of this mountain country is a part of the Green Mountain National Forest. Several of these streams have established populations of rainbow trout. Furnace Brook at Pittsford, for example, is one of the few Eastern streams where rainbow trout have maintained themselves for years by natural spawning. Rainbows in these rushing mountain streams grow larger in the deeper pools and increase in average size as the fisherman comes down the mountain gorges.

CONNECTICUT RIVER

The upper Connecticut River was once the most productive Atlantic-salmon river on the continent. In colonial days, indentured servants insisted on a clause in their contracts which specified that salmon would not be served to them more than a few days of every week. Almost every big Vermont stream flowing into the Connecticut had its run of Atlantic salmon in addition to the brook-trout population. Then came the dams; industry in Massachusetts and Connecticut polluted the lower river, and the immense salmon runs passed into history. Today, of the tides of ocean fishes that once ran up into Vermont, only the shad are left, and these are barred by modern dams from reaching the Green Mountain State. The railroads of the 1800s brought industry (and pollution) to the Connecticut River valley. They also brought in the walleye and the black bass, and probably the northern pike. Today the waters of the Connecticut above White River Junction contain a population of bass and walleye almost undisturbed by fishermen. The whole upper Connecticut River offers a warmwater fishery, with 4–5-pound bass and walleyes and northern pike to 10 pounds or more. At the present time there are boat landings available at Brattleboro, Wilder, and Moore Dam, near lower Waterford. There are also some big rainbows in the river above Colebrook.

OTHER TROUT WATERS

Above Burlington, the Winooski has an excellent spring run of rainbows from Lake Champlain, and the headwaters of this flat valley river are all trout brooks. The Lamoille, crossing Route 7 near Milton, is one of the best rainbow streams in the East. As in other Vermont waters, the brook trout have retreated into the hills, but downstream stretches with cover and food hold big rainbows and browns.

Crossing Vermont from St. Albans along Route 105 east, through Newport to Bloomfield on the Connecticut River, you drive through one of the great fishing and hunting areas of the Northeastern United States. This is the Northeast Kingdom, with a network of streams and a series of lakes and ponds.

Big Lake Memphremagog, stretching north into Canada, provides landlocked salmon, rainbows, and some large browns, as well as the usual Northern lake population of big walleyes. There was once a run of big lake salmon into the Clyde at Newport. Dams on the river seem to have killed that run, but occasional salmon are still taken. In May, there are large walleyes to be had at the river's mouth, and 3–5-pound fish are common.

The Averill Lakes, Lake Seymour, and Salem Lake are the best landlocked salmon water in the state. Willoughby, Echo, and others hold rainbows and lakers, and Norton Lake has been reclaimed and now holds a growing rainbow population. Lake Willoughby, and the river below it, are famous rainbow waters.

Most of the streams from the Mississquoi, in the valley below Jay Peak, east to the upper Connecticut are good trout waters. The Black, the Barton, the Clyde (between ponds), and the Nulhegan, which flows into the Connecticut near Bloomfield, and the Connecticut itself from Colebrook north are all worth study by the fisherman.

Turning south again at Bloomfield and passing down the lovely Connecticut Valley on Route 5, you will cross a number of trout streams. Wells River and Wait's River, among others, furnish some fly-fishing for brown trout; their days as brook-trout water are nearing an end. The White River, with a number of good tributaries rising west of Randolph and Bethel, contains some really excellent rainbows and browns. The main river is big, wide, rough, and winding, with strong riffles and sweeping currents through white-sand and gravel-bottomed pools. Here in May or June, you can take big fish with spinning lures or streamer flies; and in summer lowwater, you can use dry fly or nymph.

Farther south, streams like the Black River, the Williams, Saxton's River, and the West River, which flows into the Connecticut at Brattleboro, are all trout waters when you get back into the hills, where there are spring brooks and forested slopes to shade the water and keep temperatures low in summer. The West River, above the Ball Mountain Dam at Jamaica, may hold as many big brown trout as any stream in Vermont.

LAKE CHAMPLAIN

Lake Champlain, with the blue line of the Adirondacks against the western horizon, contains as wide an assortment of freshwater fish as any lake in the United States. Northern pike, chain pickerel, walleye, large and smallmouth bass, whitefish, smelt, and an occasional muskellunge and landlocked salmon are supplemented by a large population of yellow perch, rock bass, and other panfish. Deep down under the immense expanse of wind-swept water are fish such as the bowfin, the lake sturgeon, and the ling or cusk, a freshwater cod left behind when the ocean receded.

Few resident Vermonters fish for bass, pike, or panfish. Ice fishing, however, is a well-established institution, and it flourishes on all the lakes mentioned above. Lake Champlain is perhaps the center of the ice fishing. At Chipman's Point, Shelburne, Mallette Bay, and Grand Isle, shanties, complete with stove, tackle, and a bucket of bright minnows, are furnished at a modest price. The reward, a big string of walleye of 3 pounds or better, is well worth the cost. In Champlain and in other lakes and ponds all through Vermont, pickerel, smelt, and yellow perch can be taken through the ice. With good down clothing, snowshoes, an ice chisel, a bucket of bait minnows or cut bait for smelt, ice fishing without a shanty is feasible in many places unknown to visitors. Exploration of the ice fisherman's world is equal to skiing as a winter sport, to those who love it. —G.B.G.

VERTEBRAE The segments of the back bone, whether these are bony or cartilaginous

VIRAL HEMORRHAGIC SEPTICEMIA *See* Diseases and Parasites

VIRGINIA In variety of gamefish and opportunities to fish for them, the Old Dominion is hard to beat. From her icy mountain waters, some of which find their way via West Virginia and Tennessee to the Gulf of Mexico rather than to the eastern seaboard, anglers take native brook, rainbow, and brown trout. In Tidewater Virginia largemouth bass, pickerel, and various members of the sunfish tribe compete with saltwater and anadromous species for the fishermen's attention. And in larger, coldwater streams, flowing through limestone valleys and across the Piedmont Plateau between mountains and seashore, smallmouth and spotted bass are established.

The state is divided naturally into four main physiographic sections or provinces. Bordering the Atlantic Ocean is the Coastal Plain, or Tidewater area, extending west to the Fall Line. The broad, gently rolling Piedmont Plateau lies between the Fall Line and the foothills of the Blue Ridge Mountains, whence the Valley and Ridge Province extends to the West Virginia state line. And finally the Appalachian Plateau, in the extreme southwestern part of the state, includes most of the territory bordering Tennessee, Kentucky, and the southern tip of West Virginia.

Eleven major river basins lie wholly or in part within the borders of Virginia, and two of the largest, the James and Potomac, traverse three of the four major physiographic provinces. Throughout the state, especially in the Piedmont and Tidewater sections, numerous large impoundments provide thousands of acres of public fishing water. Most of these impoundments are best suited to warmwater species of gamefish. One, however, contains a landlocked race of striped bass. Another produces large rainbow trout. Still others, in the mountain areas, yield good walleyes.

TIDEWATER FISHING

Tidewater land is both temperate and semitropical, hilly and flat, overpopulated and wild. In short, it is a land of contrasts, interspersing the old and the new, the exciting and the quiet.

To many largemouth-bass and bream fishermen, Tidewater country is Mecca. To the striped-bass enthusiast it is the land of high expectations. To the saltwater bottom fisherman it is the Chesapeake Bay and its great tidal estuaries, to which he returns again and again. To the solitary surfman, it is Cobb and Parramore and Assateague; and hours of patient waiting with occasional moments of bursting excitement as a channel bass picks up a baited hook and rushes out to sea.

Best time to fish varies according to species. For largemouth bass it's April and May, October and November. April and May are best for shad. White perch bite freely nearly all year. Striped bass (locally rockfish) start their runs in May and remain active until winter. Croakers show up in May and leave in early autumn. Weakfish or seatrout appear briefly in spring, then are present again from September until November. Red drum fishing usually is best in May and June. Cobia are summer fish in Chesapeake Bay. They seldom are caught other than in July and August. Marlin and tuna appear in the same months. Mackerel and blues arrive in June.

Tidewater extends up the Potomac River to above Washington, and here a vast horde of spawning fish attract thousands of anglers from Virginia, the District of Columbia, Maryland, and even Pennsylvania and West Virginia each spring. Any kind of tackle, even dipnets, will do. The bonanza usually starts the last week in March with a run of big white perch which lasts until about mid May. Herring and hickory shad follow in April, and soon after, when the water becomes reasonably clear, crappie begin to strike. The prized Potomac white shad and striped bass come along in May.

The Fall Line on the Rappahannock is at Fredericksburg. Tidewater on the James ends at Richmond. Shad and herring put on a spectacular spring spawning run at both points.

Farther down these and other tidal rivers, perch and striped bass come more into the picture, while on out the Chesapeake Bay bluefish, spot, croakers, and cobia share the limelight with the stripers.

From the eastern side of the Bay, known as the Eastern Shore, there is a choice of Chesapeake Bay or ocean fishing. Stripers and drum are taken from the surf, while the ocean bays and inlets are prime places to fish for blues, mackerel, and seatrout. Offshore shoals and banks produce catches of marlin and tuna.

The waters of Back Bay, southeast of Norfolk, are nearly fresh in the Virginia end of what North Carolina calls Currituck Sound. Here 25,000 acres of water provide unique largemouth-bass fishing. Spring and early summer months are usually best. If big lakes are desired, one would not go wrong in trying one of the beautiful, clearwater reservoirs that supply the cities of Norfolk and Suffolk with water—Lake Prince; Lake Kilby; Lake Meade; Lake Cahoon; or Lake Smith, from which more prizewinning largemouth bass have been taken than any other body of water in the state. Then there are Lee Hall, Harwood Mill Pond, and Burnt Mill Reservoirs of the Newport News waterworks, which boast excellent bass, crappie, and bluegill fishing.

One of the most popular of all bodies of impounded water is Chickahominy Lake, within 35 miles of Richmond. This lake was created when a dam was built across the river in 1942. Backed up for several miles, this body of stillwater accommodates hundreds of fishermen, but the fishing remains good year after year despite heavy angling pressure.

Some sportsmen prefer to fish flowing water rather than ponds and lakes, contending that the fish are more active and fight harder. For these there are plenty of big waters in the many tidal rivers of eastern Virginia. As a rule, however, fishing for such species as bass is not as good in the rivers themselves as in many of the creeks that flow into them.

Northwest River, the Blackwater, the Nottoway, and the Meherrin, in the southeastern region of the state, all furnish excellent fishing for the warmwater species, as do their many smaller tributaries. The lower Nottoway may surprise the lucky angler with smallmouth bass, walleyes, and rock bass, species usually found in waters farther west, well above the Coastal Plain.

The Chickahominy, a large river itself although a tributary of the James, is a famous bass stream throughout its length. Even at that it is hardly as celebrated as a number of creeks flowing into it such as Disacund, Gordon's, Yarmouth, and Morris creeks.

FISHING IN THE PIEDMONT

As well as occupying the largest geographic area of any region in the state, the Piedmont Plateau boasts the greatest quantity and variety of freshwater fishing. Almost all of the major game species—smallmouth bass, largemouth bass, trout, striped bass, rock bass, bluegill, and crappie—are to be found in the varied habitat offered by the flowing streams and the many impoundments of the Piedmont Plateau. Carp, catfish, fallfish, suckers, and eels also are abundant in some of these waters.

In the southern Piedmont, near Clarksville in Mecklenburg County, the often muddy Dan and Staunton rivers, which drain the heart of Virginia's flue-cured tobacco country, meet at Buggs Island Lake, or Kerr Reservoir, a 50,000-acre impoundment formed by the John H. Kerr Dam near Buggs Island on the Roanoke River. Before impoundment the Dan and Staunton rivers offered little for sport fishermen. Excessive silt interfered with gamefish reproduction and reduced food production. Carp, catfish, and suckers were the dominant species. With construction of the reservoir in 1952, and subsequent clearing of the water, gamefish began to thrive. Now, largemouth bass, crappie, and bluegill furnish excellent fishing. But the remarkable thing about Kerr is its landlocked striped bass. This anadromous species was introduced into the reservoir during the early 1950's. In 1957 yearling stripers showed up in the Roanoke River, evidence enough that successful spawning had been accomplished in the reservoir or tributary streams, since no striper fry had been released since 1955. This led to a series of studies which have convinced fishery biologists that the species is permanently established and that Kerr's striped-bass fishing can be perpetuated on a sustained-yield basis. Herring, gizzard shad, and threadfin shad have been introduced to provide additional forage for the expanding striper population. The landlocked stripers retain the instincts of their anadromous forebears and travel great distances upstream to spawn. The spring migration begins in late April when water temperatures rise to 58°–60°F. Greatest spawning activity takes place in the Staunton River, 37–43 miles above the reservoir near Brookneal, and in the Dan River near Paces. It appears that, barring construction of more hydroelectric installations upstream which would interfere with spawning run, the survival of Kerr's striped bass is assured.

Gaston Reservoir, a 20,000-acre power impoundment located on the Roanoke River near the North Carolina-Virginia line, below Kerr Reservoir, was filled in 1962. The northern pike, a species new to Virginia waters, has been introduced.

In Patrick, Franklin, and Henry counties lies Philpott Reservoir, a 2,800-acre flood-control and power development, which provides good fishing for largemouth bass, smallmouths, crappie, and bream plus such rough fish as catfish and carp. A record largemouth for Virginia, weighing 15 pounds 2 ounces, was taken at Philpott in 1962. Just as Kerr Reservoir has its unique striper population, Philpott has its big rainbows. These fish do not reproduce successfully in the lake, but they do put on a spectacular fall run as they attempt to spawn. Fish weighing up to 5 pounds are taken. The water is stocked annually with yearling rainbows, which grow at a phenomenal rate as they gorge on threadfin shad. The relationship here between rainbow trout and threadfin shad is an interesting facet of modern fish management. The threadfin is a particularly valuable forage fish in Philpott Lake precisely because it does not survive Virginia's winters and thus does not overpopulate the lake as many prolific forage species are prone to do. It is stocked each spring primarily as a food for the lake's warmwater gamefish. It spawns several times during the summer months, and the first one or two hatches produce mature fish which spawn. Fish weighing up to 5 pounds are taken. Threadfins have produced a bountiful food supply for predatory game species. Cold weather and hungry trout take care of the removal of the excess during late fall and winter.

The Philpott tailwater, for about 7 miles below the dam, is heavily stocked with trout throughout the summer. The Dan River near Kibler, in Patrick County, is similarly stocked.

Lake Brittle, a 75-acre impoundment located in the northwest section of the Piedmont near New Baltimore, Virginia, and 218-acre Burke Lake, near Fairfax, have been built by the State Game Commission. Because of their accessibility to the Washington-Alexandria area, they are fished heavily for largemouth bass, bluegill, and crappie. Intensive management of such lakes produces a sustained yield of 120–140 pounds of game- and panfish per acre of water, per year.

Other commission-owned impoundments in the Piedmont are Albemarle Lake in Albemarle County, Fluvanna Ruritan Lake in Fluvanna County, Brunswick Lake in Brunswick County, Lake Conner in Halifax County, Lake Gordon in Mecklenburg County, and Lake Burton in Pittsylvania County.

The Rappahannock River in Spotsylvania County ranks among the better smallmouth fishing streams in northern Piedmont. Most of the better water is inaccessible and lies between Remington and Fredericksburg. This stretch can be float-fished by expert canoeists. The Rapidan River, a tributary of the Rappahannock, which flows through Madison and between Culpeper and Orange counties, offers fair smallmouth, bluegill, crappie, carp, and catfish angling. In Albemarle and Fluvanna counties the Rivanna affords good fishing for smallmouth bass, sunfish, and catfish.

Virginia's largest river, the mighty James (the even larger Potomac is shared with Maryland), produces by far the most rewarding smallmouth-bass fishing in the Piedmont. From the city limits of Richmond west to Buchanan, smallmouth fishing on the James is excellent. No other river in the state except the Shenandoah can rival the James River in either the quality or the extent of its smallmouth water.

ANGLING IN THE BLUE RIDGE MOUNTAIN
AND VALLEY REGION

The mountain and valley region of the Old Dominion offers attractive and exciting waters for sport fishermen. Here is some of Virginia's most beautiful trout country, and here in the shadows of the Blue Ridge and high Alleghenies are some of the finest smallmouth-bass waters.

It is unfortunate but true that most Virginia trout streams do not have the productivity and year-round holding capacity to furnish good trout fishing through natural reproduction and survival. Trout fishing in this state, as it is practiced today, simply could not exist without the support of a vast hatchery and restocking program. Were it not for the spring release of hundreds of thousands of "keeper" trout in the larger streams, the pressure on the true native fish in the relatively few year-round headwater trout streams would be unendurable for fish and fishermen alike. About three-quarters of a million trout are released each year in some two hundred streams in Virginia. Ninety percent are yearlings, and the rest are 2-year-olds. Combining in-season stocking with preseason releases has proved successful in adding to the number of successful fishing days throughout the season, which opens the first Saturday in April and closes the end of December. Experiments with brown trout, which are not as easily caught on opening day as are hatchery-reared brooks and rainbows, promise a similar effect.

Shenandoah National Park, stretching from near Waynesboro on the south to near Front Royal on the north, contains good streams which support wild trout. These include Big Run and Broad Run on the west side and the Jordan, Rush, Thornton, Hughes, Robertson, the head of the Rapidan, the head of the forks of the Rivanna, and the head of the forks of Moormans River.

The Big Levels Game Refuge, George Washington National Forest, lies south of Stuart's Draft. It is drained by St. Mary's River, a good trout stream. St. Mary's River is accessible all summer, but refuge roads to the smaller streams are closed July 1. Spring Pond, the nearest thing to a true bog in Virginia, is found in the refuge. Sherando Lake, a George Washington National Forest recreational lake on upper Back Creek, is on the Waynesboro side of the refuge. This 22-acre mountain lake is stocked with trout, and supports a few warmwater game- and panfish as well.

The Tye River is a popular trout stream with wild trout abundant in the headwaters and tributaries. The same is true of the Rockfish and Piney nearby. Smallmouth bass and panfish are taken in the lowest stretches of the streams.

To the west of the Tye is the Pedlar, another favorite trout stream. In the same area are several other good streams—Irish Creek, North Folk Buffalo River, and Rocky Row Run. This area offers both wild and stocked trout.

Flowing through Lexington and entering the James near Glasgow is the North or Maury River. This stream produces some prize smallmouth bass plus panfish. Above Goshen it is called the Calfpasture.

The Cowpasture River rises in Highland County and flows to the James near Iron Gate. This is a popular smallmouth, pickerel, and panfish stream that can be floated with a light boat. A major tributary, the Bullpasture River, offers some of the best trout fishing in the state, and fine scenery, particularly in the gorge area near Williamsville in Bath County. Smallmouth and panfish are taken downstream. In the upper section of Highland County, Laurel Fork offers good wild-trout fishing in good wild country.

Near Clifton Forge is Douthat State Park, with Douthat Lake and its public fishing for bass and bream. Wilson Creek, which feeds Douthat Lake, is stocked with trout in its left prong. Just to the west is Smith Creek, which is stocked with trout.

The head of the James River is known as Jackson River from its origin in Highland County to the point where it meets the Cowpasture near Iron Gate. The upper section of the Jackson in Bath and Highland counties is stocked heavily with trout. Fishing is excellent, especially in the 13-mile stretch flowing through the game-commission-owned Gathright wildlife management area. The lower section offers smallmouth bass, chain pickerel, and panfish from about Bacova to Covington. This stream is heavily polluted for a considerable way below Covington.

Back Creek rises just over the ridge from the origin of the Jackson. It follows a parallel valley until it joins the Jackson near Bacova. The upper section of Back Creek is stocked with trout. The lower section, known as Big Back Creek, provides smallmouth bass, pickerel, and panfish. The fishing may be poor at times, but the scenery is always good.

The Shenandoah River offers Virginia anglers good smallmouth-bass fishing from Riverton to the West Virginia line. This rich limestone stream consists of deep eddies separated by long shallow riffles. Channel catfish are taken in large numbers—especially at night. The stream may be fished from the bank, by wading the riffles or by floating.

Many fishermen believe the best smallmouth-bass fishing in the state is found in the South Fork Shenandoah River from Port Republic to Riverton. Channel catfishing is good here also. The stream may be fished from the bank, by wading, or by light boat. Since the riffles are long and shallow, float fishermen should stick to light boats during dry seasons. The North, Middle, and South rivers, which make up the South Fork, offer considerable fishing for smallmouth, largemouth, and panfish. Although the South River supports some gamefish, it is heavily polluted.

The North Fork Shenandoah River offers trout fishing in its headwaters and tributaries around Bergton and smallmouth and panfish from below Fulks Run to its mouth at Riverton. In the Woodstock area several small dams change the nature of this stream, and many largemouth bass and crappie are taken. Float fishermen who are unfamiliar with the stream should check on the location of these dams.

Three major tributaries of the North Fork furnish trout fishing. Big Stony with its tributary, Little Stony, provides trout fishing from the Liberty Furnace area to its mouth at Edinburg. Upper Cedar Creek and its tributary, Paddy Run, are stocked with trout. Smallmouth bass and panfish with an occasional trout are taken in lower Cedar Creek. Passage Creek flows between the North Fork and the South Fork and enters the North Fork near Waterlick. This stream is stocked with trout in the two sections in the George Washington National Forest.

Lake Shenandoah, a 39-acre public fishing lake in Rockingham County, Virginia, is of special interest to Virginia anglers because of the "two-story" fish management techniques through which it has come to support both trout and warmwater species of game- and panfish. Originally constructed by the Game Commission as a trout lake, Lake Shenandoah soon developed two distinct layers of water—a layer of aerated-water on top and a layer of cold, stagnant water at the bottom with almost no dissolved oxygen. During July and August the surface water warmed, leaving insufficient water in the lake with both the right temperature and oxygen content for trout. By modifying the dam, biologists were able to draw off the stagnant water from the bottom and retain the aerated water of the upper layer. Now fresh coldwater from the feeder springs enters the lake and flows *between* the upper warm layer and the bottom stagnant water, mixing with neither. Bass and bluegill thrive in the warmer water near the surface, while trout find water to their liking at greater depth. Fishermen enjoy the added spice and variety provided by a lake that produces bass, bluegill, and trout fishing, although the warmwater species and the trout really do not occupy the "same" water at all.

FISH-FOR-FUN ON THE RAPIDAN

The fish-for-fun area on the headwaters of the Rapidan River, where fishermen use only artificial lures with single, barbless hooks and return all hooked fish to the water, is the first area of its kind established in Virginia. It has been operated by the Virginia Commission of Game and Inland Fisheries and the Shenandoah National Park since April 1, 1961.

The Rapidan River fork, which begins near Camp Hoover, is accessible by car for its entire length from either Criglersville (Route 231) or Wolftown (Route 230). There are over 5 miles of scenic and productive trout water on this branch with nearly 3 miles in the Ward-Rue management area and the remaining 2 miles, above and below this area, in the Shenandoah National Park. The other fork of the stream, called the Staunton River, provides another 1½ miles of fishing water, all in the park and accessible only by foot trails.

Fishing is a lot better in the fish-for-fun area, where all fish caught must be released, than on comparable put-and-take streams. Creel records show that on opening day each fisherman can expect to land between three and four times as many trout on the fish-for-fun streams as, for example, the angler who chooses nearby Garth Run or Moormans River. Both native brook and introduced rainbow trout thrive in these waters the year around, and there is natural reproduction of both species. Half of the rainbows landed are 14–18 inches in length. Empty-creel fishing has evoked many enthusiastic comments from dedicated trout fishermen who would much rather catch than kill their fish and who return time and again to the streams that never become depleted of trout.

WATERS OF SOUTHWEST VIRGINIA'S APPALACHIAN PLATEAU

The main streams of southwest Virginia's high country are the New River and the three forks of the Holston. Smallmouth bass, an occasional largemouth, spotted bass, channel catfish, white bass, walleyes, and huge flathead catfish are all taken from the New River. Claytor Lake, a 4,800-acre power impoundment near Radford on the New River, is an especially popular spot in this area where "big" water is uncommon. The largest walleyes in the state, up to 15 pounds, are taken here as well as trophy smallmouth and spotted bass.

South Holston Reservoir, one of the storage reservoirs in the TVA chain, lies on the Virginia-Tennessee border near Bristol and is another popular fishing spot. Unlike Claytor Lake, South Holston Reservoir produces a greater abundance of largemouth than of smallmouth and spotted bass. Scott-Wise Lake, a beautiful 50-acre body of water near Norton, furnishes fine bass, bluegill, and crappie.

The Pound and Levisa rivers offer fair trout fishing in their headwaters, and smallmouth and rock bass are found lower down. Runs of white bass and walleyes are common in the spring.

Big Tumbling and Little Tumbling creeks flowing through the publicly owned Clinch Mountain wildlife management area, are prime trout streams, as are some of their tiny, headwater, feeder streams. Probably the very best trout streams in the whole area, however, are Whitetop Laurel in Washington County, Big Stony in Giles, Big Wilson in Grayson, and South Holston River in Smyth County.

This is true mountain-fishing country. There are few large bodies of water and few large concentrations of fishermen, except perhaps on opening weekend of trout season. But the fisherman who likes to work the little meandering streams flowing through some of the most beautiful outdoor scenery in the world can find his private bonanza. Native trout, rock bass or redeye, and an occasional smallmouth provide most of the sport. The fish are seldom large, but for the angler who likes to fish the mountain and meadow streams there is ample opportunity in southwest Virginia, and a respectable string of redeyes and the occasional thrill of a native trout or smallmouth are enticement enough.   —R.M.
—J.F.McI.

VIRGIN ISLANDS The Virgin Islands offer a variety of marine environments. St. Thomas and St. John are part of a chain extending from Puerto Rico to the Anegada Pass. All these islands rise from a continuous, rather wide shelf, most of which is less than thirty fathoms deep. This shelf has extremely steep dropoffs, quickly reaching depths of over one thousand fathoms on both the northern and southern sides. St. Croix rises like a detached peak from equally great depths, but along its southern and northeastern coasts, it has narrow shelves with reefs which extend 10 miles to the eastward to form Lang Bank.

Thus St. Thomas and St. John are surrounded by a great deal of shallow water, with several reefs and small islands, which might be expected to produce quantities of the smaller gamefish. The deepwaters where one might expect the large fish are inconveniently distant on the north side and about ten miles from St. Thomas on the south side. Off the east end of St. John, however, the edge of the shelf is considerably closer. St. Croix has much less shallow shelf, and the water that is really deep is therefore much more accessible from this island. There are a few small flats and lagoons around St. Thomas and St. John which are suitable for bonefish. Much more extensive flats are found along the south coast of St. Croix. There are no real rivers in the Virgin Islands.

As the islands are in the Trade Winds zone, fresh easterly winds are the rule. There is, however, some fairly calm weather in the spring and from late August through October. Strong winds may be expected in the winter (December into early January). Surface water temperatures on the offshore grounds run 80°–85°F. in the spring, summer, and fall. The largest fish are found along the edges of the shelf or out in the deepwater. The Puerto Rican system of fishing seems well-suited for trolling these waters; 80-pound rigs are fished from the outriggers with large baits, and 50-pound rigs as flatlines with smaller baits. The Puerto Ricans use mullet and balao almost exclusively, but good results have been obtained locally with cero-mackerel, round robin, and needlefish. Strip baits are also effective. Large plugs are used successfully for yellowfin tuna, wahoo, and king mackerel. Some large tuna and wahoo have been hooked on feather

and nylon lures, but these are most effective for the small tunas and bonitos, which will occupy most of your time if lures of this type are used. Trolling speeds of 6–7 knots seem best. Lighter tackle would take most of the fish encountered, but there is always the chance of hooking a blue marlin or a large tuna. Water that is very deep (2 miles in depth in places) is not favorable for light-tackle fishing, and it seems impossible to predict what kind of fish will be hooked. A record 814-pound blue marlin was boated off St. Thomas in July of 1964.

The practical terminal tackle for trolling in the Virgin Islands is as follows:

On 80-pound and 130-pound-test-class tackle, when baiting with large mullet, use 25–30 feet of No. 15 wire or light cable with a 9/0 or 10/0 hook. The same length of No. 12 wire with an 8/0 hook is appropriate for balao and similar baits.

Many reef formations around the Virgin Islands hold all kinds of small gamefish suitable for light tackle casting

On 50-pound-test-class tackle, when baiting with large mullet, use 15 feet of No. 12 wire or light cable with a 9/0 hook. The same length of No. 12 wire with an 8/0 hook or the same length of No. 10 wire with a 7/0 hook will handle smaller baits.

On 20-pound- or 30-pound-test-class tackle, use 15 feet of No. 10 wire with a 7/0 hook.

The Puerto Ricans consider it most important to watch for birds at all times, and this is also the case off the Virgin Islands. Most of the large fish have been hooked around schools marked by wheeling and diving boobies and frigate birds. The core of these schools usually consists of oceanic bonito or blackfin tuna or a mixture of the two, but the larger fish are often found with them. Frigate birds circling slowly high in the sky usually indicate the presence of large fish, even if nothing is showing on the surface. Relatively few blind strikes occur, most of them near the edges of the deep. Generally, if fish cannot be located by sighting birds, the fastest action may occur by working along the edge of the shelf, zigzagging from the deep over the shelf and vice-versa. A good depth-finder is most important for this type of fishing. Anglers who seek only the largest fish, however, should stay slightly away from the edge or troll blind in the deepwater. The species encountered in the deepwater include those mentioned above, plus the white marlin, sailfish, dolphin, and blue marlin, except for the king mackerel, which is usually found on or near the shelf. Blue marlin are sometimes raised at the edge of the shelf south of Norman Island, just east of St. John. They are also raised, as are white marlin, along the north and west coasts of St. Croix. Sailfish have been caught in larger numbers, mostly in the winter months. Very small individuals have been reported. Most of the sailfish have been taken in the shallow waters north of St. Thomas, St. John, and Tortola in the British Virgins. Yellowfin tuna are found chiefly in the deepwater, although schools of them are often sighted on the shelf north of St. Thomas and Culebra. They are encountered off the edge of the shelf south of St. Thomas and St. John, and off the northern and western coasts of St. Croix. Wahoo have been taken in the same areas as the yellowfin, but seem especially large and abundant around St. Croix. Large dolphin are sometimes found in the deepwater in good numbers but are regarded as rather spotty in their occurrence. These larger offshore species appear to be most abundant from September or October to May or June, while the king mackerel and most of the inshore fish appear to be available during the entire year.

Species taken along the edge of the shelf or closer inshore include, besides the king mackerel, the little tuna, cero mackerel, blue runner, bar jack, the horse-eye jack, and, of course, the barracuda. The shore fisherman may find tarpon throughout the islands but mainly along the north coast of St. Thomas, bonefish chiefly on the flats on the south side of St. Croix, and, occasionally, snook and ladyfish. In addition, large snappers and various jacks are often taken from the shore. Bottom fishermen take groupers, big mutton snappers, and other reef fish, often with the aid of chum. Many yellowtail are caught by this method.

The fishing to which the Virgin Islands compare most favorably with other Atlantic grounds is the yellowfin tuna, the wahoo, and the king mackerel. The first two

A sportfisherman heads out for the shelf near Virgin Gorda. Big blue marlin appear here in the summer months

species are sometimes very abundant in the winter, while the latter is available all year round. Large individuals of all three species are common. Dolphin also run to a good size in the winter months, but they are regarded as more erratic in their occurrence. The tarpon on the north coast of St. Thomas probably offer the best inshore fishing. Blackfin tuna, oceanic bonito, and little tuna may be taken in good numbers by fast trolling with feather or nylon lures. Blue runners and bar jacks are sometimes exceedingly abundant around St. Thomas and St. John.

Many excellent accommodations exist throughout the Virgin Islands and charter boats as well as guides are available. Being a popular tourist area, it's advisable to make all your reservations well in advance.   —F.J.M.

VOMERINE TEETH Teeth in the middle of the roof of the mouth.

W

WADERS Waterproof footwear, generally divided into two types—boots, or hip waders, and chest-high waders. Both types are important in many kinds of freshwater and saltwater fishing. Although the foot portion of most waders is made of rubber the remainder or pants portion is usually made of a lightweight material such as rubberized cloth to allow greater freedom of movement.

HIP WADERS

Hip waders (hip boots) give ample waterproofing to wade small streams or shallow water. In warm weather they are more comfortable than chest-high waders and often the better choice for that reason. Quality lightweight hip waders with cushion insoles and nonslip, cleated rubber outsoles are standard equipment for the stream angler.

These should have reinforced toes and edges to prevent foot bruises when wading on rocks. Hip waders may also be obtained with felt outsoles, or felt sandals or spiked creepers may be slipped over the feet for greater security on moss-slippery stream beds.

Hip waders can be decidedly dangerous if the angler is not cautious and goes over their tops in swift deepwater. They will become extremely heavy and almost impossible to lift against the force of a current. Chest-high waders on the other hand have a greater safety factor, particularly when they are snugly secured at the top with a belt (the puckering string is inadequate). Contrary to the popular belief, a "spill" is not necessarily a serious affair—so long as the waders do not fill with water to drag you down. If snugly drawn at the top there will be enough air imprisoned actually to help float you. This knowledge should not encourage reckless wading, for common sense tells us that deep swiftwater can always be dangerous.

CHEST-HIGH WADERS

Chest-high waders permit wading in deeper water and are essential on all big streams. In the early season or during cold-weather periods they also provide more warmth. Chest-high waders are divided into two types—stocking-foot waders, which require the use of brogues or wading shoes, and boot-foot waders which are made with regular boot feet. Both types are popular, but the older stocking-foot wader is preferred by many experts. One advantage is that the lower leg, being small and of thin material, presents a minimum of resistance to the current when it is folded around the calf and held snugly at the ankle by the brogue. And the stocking wader, of thin, flexible material including the feet, can be easily turned inside out for drying. However, while the brogue is comfortable enough on the foot, it is rather heavy and clumsy, since it must be worn at least a size larger than your shoe size to permit wearing a pair of heavy, wool socks over the wader foot to protect the rubber from abrasion by sand and gravel. The feet will wear out comparatively quickly. If you prefer this type of wader, wear only felt or hobnailed brogues for safe footing. The felt may be had on a canvas shoe, much like the standard basketball shoe, which is a bit lighter than the standard wader brogue with its heavy leather sole, and is more easily dried out.

The boot-foot wader may be slightly heavier, but it also has advantages. You do not have to remove and dry the wading shoes after each trip. The semistiff boot leg comes about half way up the calf, where it is cemented to the lighter wader material, and it thus protects the shins during the many inevitable stumbles over logs and boulders. The heavier material of the lower leg also resists snagging on sharp underwater rocks and other hidden hazards. Some anglers think it difficult to dry out the boot-foot type when the inside is wet from perspiration, but this is easily accomplished by turning the tops down as far as possible, spreading the boot top, and either placing the waders out in the sun or hanging them upside down to catch the warm air rising from the stove or camp fire.

It is wise to always buy waders of a generous size. In cold weather you may want to wear extra underwear or trousers inside them, and it is better to have the legs wrinkled and crotch loose to permit unhampered climbing over fences and logs. Waders too tight will bind your every movement, and the strain will cause undue wear at the seams.

SOCKS

All outdoor footgear should of course be purchased large enough to allow for heavier socks and also to permit your feet to "work" and spread naturally without cramping. One blister, caused by tight shoes, can bring misery. Resulting infection might be serious.

Wear heavy, wool socks for the waders, of course, both for warmth and foot comfort. It is wise, when wading coldwater, to wear a pair of lightweight, wool socks inside a pair of heavy, knee-length ones, thus employing the principle of insulation afforded by the air space between.

If your rubber boots or waders are hard to pull off, with feet and wool socks damp from perspiration, just wear a pair of silk socks next to the skin, and these will enable your feet to slip out easily.   —C.M.K.

WAHOO *Acanthocybium solandri* A fish of the mackerel family, quite similar to the Spanish mackerel, it has a long and slender body. The snout is long and tubular, and the teeth are strong and flattened laterally. There are 21–27 spines in the dorsal fin, and gillrakers are absent.

Wahoo

Its sides are usually marked with narrow, vertical bars. Among the largest fish known is one caught off southern Florida, 6 feet 9 inches long and weighing 139 pounds.

Wahoo are found around the world in tropical and subtropical seas. Unlike most other mackerel-like fishes, they do not ordinarily occur in schools. Their food consists of fishes and squids. They may spawn over an extended period of time, and a single female may shed several million eggs.

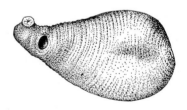

Giant Trematode Stomach Parasite

Large, leechlike trematode parasites are almost always found in the stomach.

Wahoo are excellent gamefish, usually caught by trolling. The flesh is white and tasty, though somewhat dry.
—B.B.C.
—R.H.G.

ANGLING METHODS

Wahoo are most commonly caught by fishermen who are seeking other species, such as sailfish, tuna, or marlin. In certain waters, such as Bermuda and Grand Cayman, where the wahoo is seasonally abundant, special methods and baits may be employed. The most common trolling bait is the balao (ballyhoo), but mullet and other small fishes are also successful. The majority of wahoo are caught on flatlines rather than on the outriggers, and at a fairly close distance to the boat; their strike is swift, and the automatic dropback of an outrigger bait does not help in setting the hook. Wahoo also hit artificials, particularly feathers in the 1/0–5/0 sizes. They are also taken by drift-fishing with live bait on hook sizes from 5/0–8/0. In common with the king mackerel, wahoo often strike a swivel or a light-reflecting leader wire, and breakoffs occur often when the fish are abundant.

Although wahoo do occasionally leap from the water when hooked, swift runs with sudden changes in direction are more typical of their play. The most popular tackle for wahoo fishing is the 20–30-pound-test class.

—A.J.McC.

WAKASAGI *Hypomesus transpacificus transpacificus* This smelt (*which see*) is found in the United States only in the brackish and freshwater portions of the lower Sacramento-San Joaquin River. A similar subspecies *Hypomesus t. nipponensis* is found in Japan. The wakasagi is distinguished by having 54–60 midlateral scales; a pneumatic duct attached to the anterior end of the air bladder; and 4–5 pyloric caeca. —J.R.

WALES The Principality of Wales is the mountainous area of Great Britain bounded in the south by the Bristol Channel, in the west by St. George's Channel and the Irish Sea, in the north by the estuary of the Dee, and in the east roughly by the line of the river Severn. As different from England as is Scotland, with its own language and its own traditions, Wales possesses some of the best fishing to be found in the British Isles.

The regulations, species of fish sought, and the methods of catching them are similar to those of England (*which see*). In the eastern part of Wales, particularly in the Wye and Severn, which both flow through the Principality before entering England, and in their tributaries, there is excellent coarse fishing for grayling, chub, roach, dace, and pike. This fishing is, however, mostly enjoyed by the English. The Welshman by and large is interested mostly in salmon, trout, and sea trout (locally called *sewin*).

The Severn, once a great salmon river, is, through wise management, rapidly regaining its stature. Its tributaries, both in Wales and along the border, provide excellent trout fishing. The Wye, accepted as the best salmon river south of Scotland, likewise affords excellent trouting in its upper waters and feeder streams such as the Lugg, Irfon, Ithon, Monnow, and Hondhu.

Pre-eminent among Welsh rivers is the Usk. Once the finest salmon river of its size in Europe, despite pollution at its mouth it still has a good run. It is also probably the best trout stream in Britain, holding a population of good-size fish and with prolific insect life to bring them on the feed. In some years it has a fair run of sea trout.

The Teifi and the Towy are both good salmon and trout streams and particularly good sea-trout rivers. The Cothi, a tributary of the Towy, is an outstanding, though very rough stream for the latter fish.

The Dovey and the Conway are splendid sea-trout rivers. Each season, large numbers of fish over 8 pounds are taken from both of them. Both hold salmon, and the Conway (and its tributary the Lledr) is the most improved river in Britain for these fish.

The Welsh Dee is a good salmon river; it holds a substantial population of trout and has a fair run of sewin. It also holds good grayling.

Besides these well-known rivers there are many other smaller streams which have a run of salmon, often a big run of sea trout, and which hold of course resident brown trout. Likewise there are many lakes, natural and man-made, which provide good trout fishing. *See also* Hotel Fishing in England and Wales *under* England

WALKING CATFISH Family Clariidae There are numerous species of clarid catfishes distributed from Africa and Madagascar over the whole of southern Asia to the Philippines and the Malay Archipelago. They are all elongate (sometimes eel-like) catfishes with broad, flat heads and 4 pairs of long barbels. Characteristic of the entire family is an accessory air-breathing organ either in the form of paired tubular blind sacs extending backward from the gill chamber or an aborescent accessory organ projecting into the gill chamber. These air-breathing organs permit clarids to live in poorly oxygenated water and to exist out of water for prolonged periods.

Walking Catfish

One species, *Clarias batrachus*, is known to occur in the United States. It was accidentally introduced to Florida from Bangkok in 1966 and is now found in a discontiguous range in the Tampa Bay area and from Lake Okeechobee south to Miami. Due to the fact that the walking catfish can migrate over land and thrive in brackish water its ultimate range is unknown. Only the lethal temperature zone (from 41°–48°F.) has kept the species from invading other states; this may change on the genetic basis of thermal history. Exposed to low temperatures for brief periods the survivors could become adapted. Chief predators are snook, bass, bluefish, and gar. It is often found on Florida roads after a rain. Nocturnal in habits and readily caught on scentbaits, particularly cheese, it is edible but the foul-smelling skin is difficult to remove. Use extreme caution in handling, as pectoral spines cause severe pain.

WALLEYE *Stizostedion vitreum vitreum* The walleye is the largest member of the perch family, attaining a weight of over 20 pounds. Its size, sporting qualities, and savory flesh make it one of the most important game species in North America. Though originally found primarily in the Northern states and Canada, widespread stocking has extended its range throughout the East and to all but a few of the states in the Far West and South. It is common to large bodies of water, seldom being found in streams or in lakes smaller than 50–100 acres. Its predaceous habits and its popularity with anglers make it a favored species for purposes of stocking and management by conservation officials in most states. The walleye is also relatively easy to hatch and rear artificially. Its habitat requirements include coolwater (summer temperatures

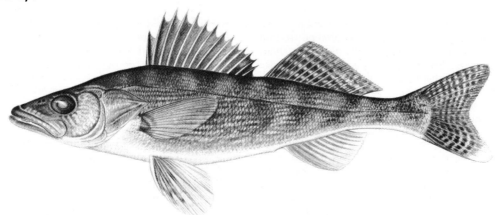

Walleye, 2½-pound Male, Delaware River, New York

preferably less than 85°F.), clear or unmuddied water, adequate food in the form of forage fish, extensive gravel or rubble areas on which to spawn, and plenty of lake area which is deeper than 10 feet.

The walleye has a round and elongate body, forked tail, spines on the first dorsal fin and the anal fin, sharp canine teeth on the jaws and palatine bones (roof of the mouth), and large eyes with a glassy cast which shine under light at night. The belly is light-colored, blending into olive-green or brassy-olive-buff on the sides and back. The back is crossed with 6–7 narrow dark bands. Markings on the tail and spinous dorsal fin serve to distinguish it from its close relative, the sauger. The tail of the walleye has a silver or milk-white tip on the lower lobe, which is absent in the sauger. Often, this silvery tip affords the first sighting of the fish when it is being brought in close to the boat or shore. The spinous dorsal fin of the walleye usually is streaked or blotched with dark pigment, but there are no regular or clearly defined rows of spots such as found in the sauger. One large dark spot or blotch is present near the base of the last 2–3 spines of the walleye but is absent in the sauger. An internal difference between the walleye and sauger is the size and number of the pyloric caecae. These are dead-end appendixlike projections attached to the intestinal tract just ahead of the stomach. They usually are buried in fat and are similar to the stomach or intestine in color and texture, though somewhat more firm. The walleye has 3 pyloric caecae, each about as long as or longer than the stomach. The sauger has 3–9 (usually 5), each one being considerably shorter than the stomach. The second dorsal fin of the walleye has 20–22 rays, usually 21–22; anal fin with 2 spiny and 12–13 softrays; 80–89 scales along the lateral line; and cheeks usually sparsely scaled.

The walleye is known by this name throughout most of North America. The term "walleyed pike" is sometimes used, although this truly is a misnomer since it is not a member of the pike family. In areas of Canada it may be called a number of names, including pike, jack, jackfish, and pickerel.

The size of the walleyes which end up on the stringer usually runs 1–3 pounds, depending upon where they are caught. A 6–8 pounder is one to be proud of, and anything over that is a trophy. In most states where walleyes are abundant, yearly records will run 12–16 pounds.

LIFE HISTORY

A walleye begins its life as one of 25,000–700,000 eggs. The number varies with the size of the fish, usually being 25,000–50,000 for each pound the female weighs. About the time the ice breaks on the lakes or streams and the water temperature reaches 45–50°F., the adult female will move to a spawning area where her arrival is awaited by the males. The spawning area may be a tributary stream, a shallow area of a river, or a desirable shoal area of a lake. In any case, it should be and usually is an area with clearwater 1–5 feet deep, and with the bottom covered with rubble or gravel. The area also is likely to have current, the result of either flowing water or the action of waves. If such conditions do not exist, the adult fish may spawn in other areas, but survival of the eggs and young will suffer.

The eggs are usually deposited at night. Several males will accompany a female across the spawning ground in erratic and thrashing movements, with eggs and milt being emitted simultaneously. Approximately 95 percent of the eggs will be fertilized and fall to the bottom. The individual egg will lodge in a rubble or gravel crevice where it will be protected and where water may circulate around it, keeping it clean and oxygenated. No protection is provided by the parents. Once they have completed spawning they leave the area.

Under the best of conditions 5–20 percent of the eggs will hatch in 12–18 days, depending upon the water temperature. Cold weather which delays hatching, extremely heavy winds or currents which might wash the eggs ashore, or dirty water which coats the egg with silt are prime factors which work to decrease the hatching odds.

Upon hatching, the walleye is about ½ inch long and paper-thin, making it difficult to spot with the naked eye. For several days it will drift about, absorbing the yolk sac and gaining strength. When the yolk sac is absorbed, the fry will begin feeding on microscopic animals (zooplankton), first the smallest of these and later the larger ones. By now, the walleye has made its way to deeper waters. By the time it has attained a length of several inches, fish have become its primary diet. Though spending most of the time in deeper waters, at night it may move into shore to feed on other small fish.

By the end of summer the walleye has attained a length of 4–12 inches, depending on latitude and the fertility of the water. Generally speaking, the farther south the longer the growing season and the larger the walleye will grow per year. As the water cools in the fall and winter, the walleye will eat less and less and will cease growing, eating only enough to maintain a very slow rate of metabolism.

The odds that a walleye has lived from spawning through this first year of life are about 1 in 10,000. From now on its odds each year are much better, perhaps as high as 1 in 2 or 1 in 3 (35–50 percent). If it is a fast-growing individual living in a fertile lake in the Central or Southern states, it may attain a length of 15–16 inches by the end of its second year. In this case it will reach adulthood and spawn during its third year of life. If it is living in the Northern states or Canada, it may take 4 or even 5 years for it to reach a length of 12–15 inches and take on the role of a parent. However, the fast-growing Southern fish seldom live longer than 6–7 years, while the slow-growing Northern populations often live 12–15 years.

Walleyes usually reach a pound when they are about 14 inches long, 2 pounds at 18 inches, and will add at least a pound in weight for each 2 inches thereafter. A 14 pounder should be about 36 inches long.

ANGLING VALUE

It is questionable whether any species has greater angling value than does the walleye. Wherever it is found in abundance it is the primary target of most anglers. Walleyes bite readily, are generally concentrated in schools, put up a dogged fight when hooked, attain a large size, and are unexcelled in eating qualities. Although many techniques have been developed to catch them, there are only a few basic facts which must be retained by the successful angler. (1) Walleyes tend to congregate in schools; when you catch one it is likely that there are others in the same spot or vicinity. (2) Except on rare occasions walleyes are found on the bottom of the lake or river, so the odds are with you if you keep your bait on or very near the bottom. (3) The primary food of walleyes is fish, and your bait should be, or closely resemble, a live fish. (4) Walleyes usually are found near or on a sandbar or other physical feature which provides a good feeding area in close proximity to deeper waters. (5) Walleyes usually are slow and methodical in taking food. Keep your bait still or, preferably, moving very slowly and give the walleye plenty of time to look it over. (6) Walleyes feed primarily during the evening and night hours so you can expect the best results after the sun goes down.

COMMERCIAL VALUE

The commercial value of the walleye is limited only by its availability to the commercial fishermen. The species demands top prices at the fish markets and in restaurants. However, its high angling value limits commercial fishermen to operating only in the largest waters or in remote areas where there is little or no competition with anglers. These waters occur primarily in Canada, the Great Lakes, and in a few of the large inland lakes in the Northern states. Gillnets are the primary method by which walleyes are taken by commercial fishermen.　　　　—J.T.S.

WALLEYE POLLOCK *Theragra chalcogrammus* This cod is sometimes known as whiting, and is distinguished from its other Pacific relatives by the projecting lower jaw, large eye, the placement of the anus midway between the first and second dorsal fins, and the reduced or absent barbel on the lower jaw, in contrast to the Pacific cod and Pacific tomcod (*which see*). The lateral line is arched somewhat higher than in these two species. As in other closely related forms, it is a heavy-bodied, large-mouthed species, with 3 dorsal fins and 2 anal fins. It is greenish to

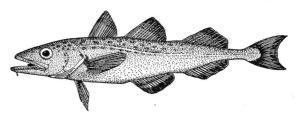

Walleye Pollock

olive on the back, with mottlings similar to the Atlantic tomcod (*which see*), and silver to white on the sides and belly. The fins are dark or dusky. The young are distinguished by two yellow, lateral stripes. It attains a length of 3 feet.

It occurs from northern California to northwestern Alaska and is abundant in waters of moderate depth, where it feeds on planktonic crustaceans. An excellent food fish, it is taken commercially by seines and trawls, and is of some importance locally as a sport fish.—D.dS.

WALLEYE SURFPERCH *Hyperprosopon argenteum* A handsome fish, steely-blue above and silver ventrally, with black-tipped pelvic and caudal fins and about five obscure dusky bars on the sides. No frenum between lower lip and symphysis of lower jaw; eye about one-third of head length; longest dorsal spine longer than softrays; closed mouth outline parallels lower edge of head. Length to 12 inches.

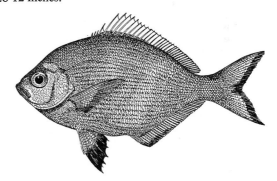

Walleye Surfperch

Life history, food, and angling value as other surfperch (*which see*).

COMMERCIAL VALUE

It is the second most important surfperch in California.
　　　　　　　　　　　　　　　　—J.R.

WALTON, ISAAC Walton's Christian name is sometimes given as *Isaac* instead of Izaak, and either form may be correct. He was christened at St. Mary's Church, Stafford, on the 21st of September. The register reads, "*1593. Septem. Baptiz. fuit Isaac filius Jervis Walton xxj die mensis et anni praedict.*" However, in later life Walton used both the *z* and the *k*, except on his wedding day when he signed the register with a *c*. The name as it appears on his tombstone in Winchester Cathedral reads "Mr. Isaac Walton." *See* Walton, Izaak

WALTON, IZAAK British (1593–1683) "The gentlest teacher and powerfullest preacher" of the art of angling and the science of conservation was the author of *The Compleat Angler*, first published in 1653 and issued in five editions within his lifetime. This "darling book," as it was called by its first American editor in 1847, appeared in 385 different editions or separate reissues in English by the end of the year 1967, and at the rate of between two and three a year since then, making its author one of the best-known and most loved figures of all English literature, and his name as much a synonym for an angler as Nimrod is for hunter.

The book's original appearance in the author's sixtieth year had brought him the friendship of Charles Cotton who, though thirty-seven years younger, was to outlive Walton by only four years. For the fifth edition, in 1676, Cotton wrote Part Two at Walton's invitation. This second part, devoted to fishing "fine and far off" for trout and grayling in a clear stream, has become an integral part of *The Compleat Angler*, and has been included in all but a very small minority of its subsequent editions, most of which have given equal billing to the two authors' names. As a handbook of practical utility to modern anglers, Cotton's part is vastly more pertinent today than

The window over Izaac Walton's tomb in Winchester Cathedral expresses philosophy of angling's patron saint

Walton's, since the younger man was an accomplished fly-fisherman, whereas his master, Walton, was primarily a bait fisher and had been obliged to rely heavily upon secondhand sources at best, with open acknowledgment, and third-hand material at worst, and without acknowledgment, for the fly-fishing portions of his original work. Thus, while Walton has remained for three centuries the patron saint of fishing in general, it is his disciple, Cotton, who has actually held that relationship to dedicated fly-fishermen.

But in literature quite the reverse has been the case, for there Cotton has been rescued from his otherwise obscure position as a minor Restoration poet only through his association with Izaak Walton as a universally renowned literary figure.

Walton was that great rarity of the days before the Industrial Revolution, a self-made man, whereas Cotton was a gentleman to the manner born, though plagued continually by pecuniary troubles. Yet it was "meek Walton," rather than the high-born Cotton, whose literary style made *The Compleat Angler* one of the most joyous pastorals ever composed in any language and a work that has been revered, over the centuries, less because of its subject than in spite of it. And although Charles Cotton, the squire of Beresford, knew his subject better at first hand than the Stafford yeoman, Walton, he was content to ape the latter's style, to the best of his ability, in contributing the second part to the "booke." More, he saw fit to include, wherever possible, adulatory references to "his father" Walton.

Most of the early editors and biographers of Izaak Walton were clergymen, beginning with Moses Browne in 1750, who at the suggestion of the great lexicographer Dr. Samuel Johnson reclaimed *The Compleat Angler* from the literary oblivion in which it had lain for seventy-four years, giving it a new edition that was issued at intervals until 1851. Both Reverend Browne and Reverend Thomas Zouch, another early biographer, stressed how good the book was in spite of its being about fishing. Throughout the eighteenth century this attitude prevailed pretty generally, and it was not until the latter part of the nineteenth century that Walton's editors were inclined to dismiss, as "irrelevant and garrulous," many of those highly moral and spiritual, discursive passages which were regarded as the book's chief ornament by its earliest admirers. The book has been praised by many literary figures, such as Wordsworth who wrote of "meek Walton's heavenly memory," Alexander Pope, Richard Brinsley Sheridan, Charles Lamb (who said, "it would sweeten a man's temper at any time to read it"), Washington Irving, James Russell Lowell, Richard le Gallienne, and Andrew Lang. But it is only the latter who, apart from being literary, enjoys stature in his own right in angling annals.

It is true that after the comparatively simple first-edition version of 1653 Walton becomes progressively long-winded and preachy, with the latter element of his style reaching its apex in the fifth edition of 1676 (when he was 83). Still nothing could destroy the spirit of innocent mirth with which he continued to invoke the rustic pleasures and honest enjoyments of the angler's life in an idyllic setting that has become synonymous, in our time, with Merrie England.

That the England of Walton's time was not so merry makes his work only the more remarkable, for in the pages of *The Compleat Angler* the England of that day now seems to us a land of sweet leisure all compact. But for Izaak Walton, an ardent Royalist, the time of Cromwell was a time of trouble, and Walton more than once risked his purse and his head by remaining true to his convictions.

Though born in Staffordshire in the Elizabethan era, Walton early made his fortune in London, where he became a member of the Ironmonger's Company. Early biographers were under the impression that he was a wholesale linen draper, but later researchers tended to render that assumption questionable, although without being able to substitute, with any exactness, any equally specific role for his activities in business. In any case, by the time he was fifty he had amassed enough in worldly goods to permit his retirement to the country, and for the last forty years of his life he was able to devote himself entirely to his writing and his fishing. There was the added advantage, for a Royalist, of being able to keep out of harm's way better in the country than in London, during the era of conflict between the Cavaliers and the Roundheads, and particularly during the long years of Cromwell's reign.

According to Anthony Wood, a contemporary, he left London "in 1643 (at which time he found it dangerous for honest men to be there) and lived sometimes at Stafford and elsewhere, but mostly in the families of the eminent clergymen of England, of whom he was much beloved." This retirement, like many other purported facts of his life, was disputed and debated by later biographers, notably Sir Harris Nicholas in his monumental edition of *The Compleat Angler* in 1836, but it is beyond question that after 1640, when his life of Dr. John Donne was first published, Walton was a man of letters first and leisure second, and no longer a man of business. Apart from *The Compleat Angler*, his literary output consisted almost entirely of biographies of such worthies as Sir Henry Wotton, Provost of Eton, the poet Herbert, and the Bishops Hooker and Sanderson. Without *The Compleat Angler* Walton would have been known to our time, if at all, only as a rather tediously pious Plutarch, and Cotton as a rather reprobate poet and parodist, and both would have been largely forgotten and almost entirely unread.

The remarkable durability of this sporting classic is best attested by the avidity with which its various editions are continually sought, not only by bibliophiles, but by anglers otherwise utterly uninterested in book collecting.

Of the various editions, after the original five which appeared in Walton's lifetime between 1653–1676, the following are the most noteworthy: the Moses Browne, which first appeared in 1750, and in four subsequent editions until 1851; the Hawkins, which appeared in fourteen editions between 1760 and 1826; the Major, which enjoyed fifty-six printings between 1823 and 1934; the Rennie, twenty printings between 1833 and 1851; the Nicolas, five editions between 1836 and 1913; the Bethune, which was the first American edition and was printed five times between 1847 and 1891; the Ephemera (Fitzgibbon) which had nine editions between 1853 and 1893; the Jesse, which also had nine, from 1856 to 1903; the Davies which had eleven between 1878 and 1930; the Marston, which made the hundredth of the various editions and appeared in four printings from 1888 to 1912; the Lang, which had twelve editions between 1896 and

1932; and the le Gallienne, which appeared six times between 1897 and 1931. All of these are sought by collectors.

There have also been numerous translations and one interesting novelty, a Japanese edition in English, but with introduction and notes both in English and Japanese, in the Kenkyusha English Classics series, published in Tokyo in 1926. There have been many limited editions, such as that of the Peter Pauper Press, and others illustrated by such artists and designers as Arthur Rackham and W. A. Dwiggins.

Among the modern editions, what was probably about the three hundredth appeared in 1953, on the tercentenary of Walton's first edition, sponsored by the Izaak Walton League, published by Stackpole, and revised and edited by Eugene Burns.

The exact number of editions, as of 1963, is difficult to determine, although it is certainly in the neighborhood of 350, with 5 in the seventeenth century, 10 in the eighteenth, 164 in the nineteenth, and all the rest since 1900. Those interested in the comparative details of all the editions published in English up to 1935 may find them described in *A New Chronicle of the Compleat Angler* by Peter Oliver, published in 1936 by The Paisley Press, Inc., New York, and Williams and Norgate, Ltd., London. Virtually all of the editions may be seen in the New York Public Library.

The famous Fifth Edition of 1676, which was the first to include Cotton's Part Two, was actually the sixth printing of the book by Marriott, the original publisher, having been preceded by those of 1653, 1655, 1661, 1664, and 1668. It also included, as Part Three, *The Experienced Angler*, by Colonel Robert Venables, another Marriott author and, although a veteran of Cromwell's armies, sufficiently rehabilitated in Restoration times to earn a flattering and friendly dedicatory letter from Izaak Walton. The book as a whole was entitled, for that one editon, *The Universal Angler*. Unlike Cotton's portion, the Venables work was not, apart from a later facsimile reprint, carried in subsequent editions of *The Compleat Angler*.

Just as Lindbergh was not the first to fly the Atlantic, although his subsequent fame led many to believe that he was, so Izaak Walton was by no means the first to write a book on fishing in English. That distinction is generally accorded to Dame Juliana Berners (*which see*), the prioress who contributed *A Treatyse of Fysshynge wyth an Angle* to the second edition of *The Book of St. Albans* in 1496. Other works to appear ahead of Walton's were *The Arte of Angling* (1577), *A Booke of Fishing with Hook and Line* by Leonard Mascall (1590), *The Secrets of Angling* by John Dennys (1613), *A Discourse of the General Art of Fishing with an Angle* by Gervase Markham (1614), and *The Art of Angling* by Thomas Barker (1651).

Walton openly acknowledged his own dependence on Barker's work, though saying that he was repeating Barker "with a little variation," but all of the above mentioned authors had leaned heavily upon Dame Juliana's original list of twelve artificial flies, and some, such as Markham, had simply cannibalized all preceding works on the subject. Walton followed Markham into some of his errors, as well as his borrowings. Walton was generally supposed, by most of his early editors, to have patterned his dialogue form on a number of the many books which had been written in this form in the preceding century, *Herebaschius' Husbandry* of 1577 and *A Treatise on the Nature of God* of 1599 being the two books cited as most closely resembling his. And, of course, the casting of discourses in dialogue form was as old as antiquity—dating back to the Socratic dialogues of Plato's time. Thus while the question of plagiarism was often raised in the earlier notices of Walton's work, chiefly because of the vicious attack on him for "plagiary" by Richard Franck in his *Northern Memoirs* (written in 1658 but not published until 1674), honest Izaak was never impugned with borrowings beyond those considered sanctioned by the very liberal literary practices of his day. But the question has regained currency in recent years, since Carl Otto von Kienbusch's discovery, in London in 1954, of the one known copy of the 1577 volume, *The Arte of Angling*. This little book, which had somehow escaped being recorded anywhere at all, is in general structure the exact prototype of the first edition of *The Compleat Angler*, being a series of episodes, in dialogue form, with two characters, Piscator and Viator, and with the former undertaking the instruction of the latter. After the first edition, Walton changed *his* Viator to Venator and added a third character, Coridon. Cotton, on the other hand, when he wrote Part Two for the fifth edition of *The Compleat Angler*, stayed with the original two characters of the first edition, Piscator and Viator.

Much has been made of the number of exactly parallel passages between *The Arte of Angling* and *The Compleat Angler*, and it would be fair to say that it does, in its general structure and outline, bear very nearly as much resemblance to the first edition of Walton's work as that simple little first edition itself bears to the greatly expanded fifth edition. To say that it bears the same relation to *The Compleat Angler* as a preliminary sketch might bear to a finished painting is another matter, for that would be to assume that it served Walton, wholly and simply, as a source book. In his introduction to the facsimile reproduction of *The Arte of Angling*, which he generously caused to be issued by the Princeton University Library in 1956, von Kienbusch does so characterize the earlier book's relation to Walton's, and this opinion is shared by its editor, Gerald Eades Bentley, in his preface.

That Walton was widely read is evident on almost every page of *The Compleat Angler*, and that he was willing to give credit where he knew it to be due is almost equally evident. He gives the name Jo Davors as the poet who wrote *The Secrets of Angling*, though Dennys later came to be known as the angler's "glorious John," but the orthography of the time made many names hard to untangle. In any case, he did not try to palm off the quoted verses as his own. He even quoted foreign sources with acknowledgment, such as Rondelet and Gesner, who wrote in France and in Germany a century before him. He need not have worried about them, as he might have about a contemporary like Thomas Barker, that they would be around to plague him if he quoted them without credit.

Even if it were conceded that he had *The Arte of Angling* propped up before him as a source book when he sat down to write *The Compleat Angler*, it could still not account for more than some of the more rudimentary elements of his work. Since the one copy of *The Arte of*

Angling lacked its prefatory matter, its authorship will presumably remain unknown, although T.P. Harrison, in *Notes and Queries*, October 1960, quite persuasively attributed it to William Samuel, vicar of Godmanchester in Huntingtonshire (*d.* 1580). However, vicar or not, the author of *The Arte* is crude and blunt where Walton is subtle and sensitive, and although they both be "merry men," the earlier writer's humor comes in quick, short jibes, whereas Walton's flows on as gently and continually as, in his own words, "these silent silver streams which we now see glide so quietly by us." For his is, as John Buchan said of it, "about the best cheerful prose in our literature, prose which is all air and dew and light." If *The Arte of Angling* does, admittedly, whistle the selfsame tune that Walton picked up in *The Compleat Angler*, still it is his own orchestration of it, his weaving of it into a garland of imperishable beauties, that has given it its immortality. He gave angling not a how-to book of enduring utility, though even that could be said of Cotton's part, but the greatest literary idyll that any language has ever bestowed on any sport. In this respect it may still be said of him, as Andrew Lang said in the nineties, "He is not so much unrivalled as absolutely alone. Heaven meant him for the place he filled, as it meant the cowslip and the mayfly." *See also* Horne, Bernard S.

—A.G.

ANGLING IN WALTON'S DAY

"And before you begin to angle, cast to have the wind on your back, and the sun, if it shines, to be before you, and to fish down the stream; and carry the point or top of your rod downward, by which means the shadow of yourself, and rod too, will be the least offensive to the fish; for the sight of any shade amazes the fish, and spoils your sport, of which you must take a great care." This quaint, yet entirely modern, advice is one of the many practical observations made by Izaak Walton. Even though he breathed in an atmosphere of troubled times, his cut-crystal words have been ringing through the dimness of time for centuries. Most of the world still thought it was standing on a flat, immovable platform when the serious business of fly fishing began. This first text, *A Treatyse of Fysshynge wyth an Angle*, was credited to a woman in the year 1496. Dame Juliana Berners (*which see*) not only preceded Walton, but her technically detailed work stood the test of time and shaped much of Izaak's early learning. Whether she was the "Lady Prioress of Sopwell" or a mere fiction matters little, as the volume was a well-spring of information.

Heat treating and hollow-built rod construction were well known to Berners, and she set down very precise instructions for both. The hollow-built rod, however, had none of the serious implications of greater power for less weight, but existed solely as a means of disguising the rod, "so that no man will know the errand on which you are going." Angling was in her day a game of questionable amusement, and by hiding the rod sections inside a crop or walking stick one could look like anything but an angler in the received sense of the word. This explains the protracted maundering to herself over the sports of hunting, hawking, and fowling—the hunter must blow his lips to a blister, while the hawker's hawk pays no attention to him, and the fowler must be out in the coldest and most inclement weather. Even Walton had to reaffirm the virtues of being an angler by starting off his book with a few quick jabs at the three manly amusements. The difference between Berners and Walton, however, is that Izaak created a popular habit.

On any Saturday in the year 1653, holiday seekers funneled out of the city's maw to breathe in the hills and plains and the dying sunsets. Izaak Walton was, of course, one of the country-goers and he went from Fleet Street to the rivers around London, usually in partnership with a pastry cook by the name of Thomas Barker. The tackle they carried was far from crude. Their hazel and ash fly rods were long, carefully tapered, and light enough to be fished with one hand. Tom bought his rod at Charles Brandon's tackle shop, and Izaak used one made by John Margrave, whose store was at the sign of the three trout in St. Paul's churchyard. They were earthbound among a mass of quiet folk, and in the warm sun their faces shone with perspiration. It was twenty miles to the River Lea at Wareham. But the "May butter" was on the water—that great hatch of green drakes which fattens a trout to bursting. As the sun rose above the trees, Walton's rod threw a long shadow across the green paths ahead.

The house where Walton spent his last years and died at the age of 93 is at 7 Dome Alley in Winchester

New readers to *The Compleat Angler* are usually bewildered by the fact that his book is written in dialogue form. We expect a direct monologue in our angling works, but in Walton's day there was time to wet now-dried Elizabethan prose, and it is a pity really that words

are perishable. As the two men walked to their river, the tremendous secret of an honest life was unfolded. Izaak's literary harvest was merely the shreds of these conversations, for he was by nature a profoundly inquisitive man. Even in reading him as the practical fisherman we find none of the dull stuff chronicled by scholars in the years following. To this day, nobody has written a more finely detailed study in the art of using live baits. Walton's eloquence lagged only when the subject of fly fishing became too pressing, and here he turned to his friend, Charles Cotton.

Cotton would be on the River Dove that day, fishing with Captain Henry Jackson. Their fly rods came from Yorkshire and were made of eight sections of seasoned fir and willow. The fir was used in the first three butt pieces, and, lacking ferrules, the end of each section was beveled to fit the other and then wrapped around with silk thread. In winters, when they didn't go grayling fishing, the windings could be removed and the pieces stored in a dry place. But Cotton seldom put his rods away—he was casually lethal in his approach, a practiced hand of great skill. His companion would be sitting in the meadow grass with a bag of feathers and hairs, building copies of insects on hooks that he had armed the night before. Jackson was a keen fly tyer and he worked his miracles with blunt, seamy hands—camel's hair, bright bear hair, and the beard of a black cat were spun ever so carefully.

Their play has been told against a thousand backdrops and will be told against a thousand new ones before the curtain finally falls. A Green Drake settling to the water, a flash of gold, and then a trout dashing toward his shelter of weed before threshing against the pliant rod. Cotton knew how to keep a fish from this dangerous retreat, and even though he may have angled for reasons different from Walton's, his talents helped lubricate the machinery of Izaak's philosophy. The reader is left to bob impotently on a river of words if he looks to *The Compleat Angler* for supernatural aid in the capture of fishes. Yet, the fundamentals of angling are here. In a practical sense, tools used for fly fishing were productive of excellent results. The fly line of 1653 was made of horsehair and it was tapered. A horse's tail isn't long enough to make twelve or fifteen feet of line, so equal lengths of hair were twisted and then knotted together by using a Water Knot. Each one of these line sections was known as a link. Walton used a somewhat heavier line than Cotton because he angled differently. Cotton built a light front taper of two hairs for two links next to the hook, three hairs for the next three links, four hairs for the next three links, and so on up the line. He concluded that such a taper would fall much better and straighter and with greater accuracy. The horsehair line was so light that the angler was forced to sink part of it in order to keep the fly in the water when a strong wind blew. Cotton's taper shows us that fly fishing had become a great deal more sporty since Dame Berner's day. She advised the two-hair taper for perch and twelve hairs for trout. Walton's disciple was not given to idle boasting when he set down his mark of ability: "He that cannot kill a trout of twenty inches with two, deserves not the name of angler." A 20-inch trout is, of course, a good 3 pounds, and it would be no mean feat to subdue a brown trout of this size on two hairs.

The average tensile strength of horsehair is less than that of raw nylon monofilament. It is somewhat stiffer and has a greater elongation than nylon—stretching about 30 percent. Horsehair diameters range from .010 to .006, or 1X to 4X, with a tensile strength of 1.7 to 0.9 pounds. White, or "glass-colored," hair proved consistently stronger than dark-colored hairs. Charles Cotton probably fished with a tippet testing about 2½ pounds. Remember, the angler couldn't let his fish run, so a two-hair trout was no easy mark.

The real problem in line building was finding the right horse. Walton's ideal was a lock of round, clear, glass-colored hair without scabs or galls. The hairs had to be of equal diameter so that they would stretch at the same ratio and have an equal breaking strain. This parallels the problem of our modern line builder in getting a finish that stretches at the same ratio as the raw line inside. Unless the elongation is identical, the line simply stretches away from its outside protective cover and it cracks apart. But oil and plastic finishes weren't used in those days; finishing usually consisted of dyeing the line some color for purposes of camouflage. Berners in a truly feminine fashion believed there was a color for every situation and gave instructions for dyeing lines red, green, yellow, blue, brown, and whatnot. Walton decided that most of this was unnecessary and advised a nearly transparent line with just a slight greenish tinge. "And for dying your hairs, do it thus: Take a pint of strong ale, half a pound of soot, and a little quantity of the juice of Walnut-tree leaves, and an equal quantity of allum; put these together in a pot, pan, or pipkin, and boil them half an hour; and having so done, let it cool; and being cold, put your hair into it, and there let it lie; it will turn your hair to a kind of water or glass colour, or greenish, and the longer you let it lie, the deeper coloured it will be; you might be taught to make many other colours, but it is to little purpose; for doubtless the water colour, or glass coloured hair, is the most choice and most useful for an Angler; but let it not be too green." This agrees with the choice of many experts today.

Walton went through an evolution of rods, starting with simple, painted, two-piece sticks—many of which he made himself—to eight- and ten-piece rods built by more clever hands. As his friendship with Cotton sprung to mushroom intimacy—the young disciple providing a temple for his prophet in the Dove fishing cottage— Izaak became steeped in fly-fishing lore. In his first edition, Walton recommends Charles Brandon, Mr. Fletcher, or Dr. Nowel as suppliers; he next made a marginal note on the value of tackle in his second edition, and finally there appears on the reverse leaf of Cotton's part of the fifth edition in 1676, a memorandum to the effect that one may be fitted with the best fishing tackle by John Margrave. Before you suspect Walton of whimsy, realize that this change kept pace with his new interest.

Actually, the length of a fly rod was determined by the width of the river one fished. It had to be long enough to make a cast near midstream. The standard length for trout fishing was fifteen to eighteen feet, and if no wind was blowing, the angler would employ about half that length of line. When the wind blew, Walton and Cotton fished the quick fly, which required using a line as long as the rod, "wherein you are always to have your line flying before you up or down the river as the wind serves." One evening after a rain, Charles Cotton stood in a whistling wind and played his Green Drake over the surface, catching thirty-five very great trout. Five or six large fish broke off, even though he tried them on three hairs.

This same method of fly fishing occurs to almost every generation of anglers as a novel departure from orthodox casting, but actually it is the oldest way of getting a natural or artificial fly to feeding fish. Using a long fly rod, a short but light line, and a long leader, the modern angler turns his back to the wind and lets his bivisible flap in the breeze, lowering it to the surface where he thinks the trout might be. There is absolutely no drag and the fly dances like a live insect.

Cotton had a self-conscious elegance that led him directly through his narrative minus those touches of unexpected detail that marked Izaak Walton's style. Walton had never been yoked by the harness of royalty—his soul was unmarked by artifice as the face of his milkmaid was unmarked by modern paint. Not only did they write differently, but they fished differently. Without a wind, Walton and Cotton whipped their lines back and forth, but basically they had two different styles of angling. Walton was a short-line artist—"Now you must be sure not to cumber yourself with too long a line, as most do" —and he much preferred the rustic art of dibbling. Cotton was for his day a long-line caster—"to fish fine and far off, is the first and principal rule for trout angling"— and, indeed, with a fifteen-foot rod he was working thirty to thirty-five feet away from his quarry.

The sometimes-wealthy Cotton could afford such luxury, because the problem with a reelless rod and long line was in landing the fish. A gentleman angler would hire some rubber-handed fellow to take the line in for him. This is what he meant when he said in his discussion on line length, "Every one that can afford to angle for pleasure has somebody to do it for him." It also explains why the art work of that period frequently depicted an angler taking his fish with the help of an assistant. Landing nets were used a great deal, but even a long-handled one served very poorly when the angler couldn't release the line at the critical moment.

Dibbling with both the natural and the artificial fly was probably the most common method of catching trout, and the technique is as effective today as it was then. The dibbler usually works very close to his fish by crawling or knee-walking along the bank. At a place where he knows the trout are, or ought to be, such as an undercut, the pool below a footbridge, a weed bed, or boulder, he cautiously pokes his rod out over the water and drops his fly to the surface. A minimum of rod and line will show if the angler is crafty. Perhaps he'll watch the float of this fly, but the skilled dibbler plays by sound, keeping himself well out of sight. Of course, the fly will float beautifully, as there is no drag from the line and no more than an inch of leader will touch the river. Walton liked this method and well he should—country boys have taken billions of trout this way in the past 300 years.

You would be blessed to breathe the nights in that little stone house on the Dove, when copper mugs finished their rattling courses around the black marble table, and our two anglers waded into the bottomless pool of fly patterns. Walton described his "jury of flies likely to betray and condemn all the Trouts in the river" in his first edition, and they were almost exactly the same twelve patterns recommended by Dame Juliana Berners 157 years before. Fly fishing had changed very little in that period; less than a dozen other works on angling had been published. A feather or two had changed in some of the dressings, but the Dun, Stone, Moore, Shell, and Wasp flies, for instance, were still identical. In fact, Berners' descriptions of certain patterns give us the origin of the March Brown, Black Gnat, Alder, Stonefly, Whirling Dun, and the fly that was "discovered" in our Ozark Mountains, the Woolly Worm. Being a comparative neophyte in fly fishing, Walton allowed that there were other patterns that would kill as well, and promised to correct or add to his list in future editions. But on the Sow, the Tame, the Derwent, and the ever glorious Lea, these twelve simple flies served him well. Cotton brought such technical embellishments to fruition in the fifth edition, with his "Instructions how to Angle for a Trout or Grayling in a Clear Stream." Here we find the Cow-dung, Green Drake, Stonefly, and many others which are either new patterns or versions of old ones. It is notice-able that Cotton escaped from the use of wools in his fly bodies; almost all of these patterns require dubbed under fur. In his Blue Dun, for instance, he suggests that the angler "comb the neck of a black greyhound, and the down that sticks in the teeth will be the finest blue you ever saw." His two favorite flies were the Stonefly and the Green Drake, and he observed that "the trout never feeds fat, nor comes into his perfect season, till these flies come in." This, of course, is as true today as it was then.

Although Walton's instructions on fly tying were sketchy by modern standards, he had the professional tyer's approach in stressing the right proportion between material and hook size and strongly urged that his pupil see a fly made by "an artist in kind." Furthermore, he advised that the angler study aquatic insect life and carry a bag of tying materials at the streamside so that he could make imitations of whatever flies might be hatching. Cotton elaborated on this point and also advised that the angler open the trout's stomach to learn what the fish was feeding on. The beginning fly fisher of today can profit immeasurably by this same advice.

Hooks (*which see*) in the fifteenth century were made from needles. The smallest ones were made from em-broiderers' needles, while tailors' and shoemakers' needles were used for larger fish. Commercial hook making was established as a business in that period between Berners' and Walton's time, but many fly tyers continued to make their own hooks, as prescribed by Dame Juliana. "You must place the square headed needle in a red hot charcoal fire until it becomes the same color as the fire. Then take it out and let it cool and you will find that it will be tempered for filing. Then raise its barb with your knife and sharpen its point. Then temper it again or else it will break in the bending. When the hook is bent, beat the hind end flat and file it smooth for the purpose of bind-ing the line to it. Place it in the fire until it barely glows. Then quench it in water and it will become hard and strong."

Eyed hooks were unknown in Walton's day, so when making flies the tyer used a line of one, two, or three horsehairs to serve as a snell. This was secured to the hook first, and then the fly was dressed over it; whenever more than one hair was necessary, there was always some question whether they should be twisted or left untwisted. Cotton decided that the untwisted way was better "be-cause it makes less show in the water," but he wisely ob-served the twisted hairs to be stronger. Hair twisting was a semi-mechanical procedure, in that the angler used a stand having a perforated arm which held the hairs at the upper end, while a turning weight at the lower end made the necessary twists.

Although dry-fly fishing is considered by many students of angling history as a modern innovation, floating flies were used as much as sunken flies in Walton's era. Dry-fly fishing did not exist as a definitive method; the idea was to put the fly over a trout, "angling on top," and then either drift or retrieve it back, floating or wet. Al-though very few fly patterns other than the popular palmer-tied flies had hackles, most of them had dubbed fur bodies which were picked out, or "bearded," making the small steel needle hooks very buoyant. Walton was much more concerned with presentation, a point that is not nearly so well exploited today: "When you fish with a fly, if it be possible, let no part of your line touch the water, but your fly only; and be still moving your fly upon the water, or casting it into the water, you yourself being always on the move downstream." Walton preferred to fish with three hairs next to his hook for this reason: there was no line left to give to a large trout after he struck, as the fly dangled on the surface directly below his rod point. Not having a reel (contrary to the art work in many later editions), he was "forced to tug for't," and a strong link of hair meant the difference between success and failure. Only a few salmon fishermen of the seven-teenth century used reels, and these were crude wood cylinders that were much too heavy for trout fishing.

Walton admitted to throwing his rod in the river when he couldn't play a large fish, tactics which earned him a trout nearly one yard long and whose picture was traced and hung at Rickabie's place, the George, in Ware. Purist Cotton found this innocent directness uncomfortable in print and censored him thus: "I cannot consent to his way of throwing in his rod to an overgrown trout, and afterwards recovering his fish with his tackle. For though I am satisfied he has sometimes done it, because he says so, yet I have found it quite otherwise." Actually, fly fishers of the day fastened their lines to the rod tops with waxed silk and in Izaak's south country rivers there must have been a few large trout that demanded more than fifteen feet of line.   —A.J.McC.

WARMOUTH *Lepomis gulosus* A freshwater panfish of minor importance, sometimes called the goggle-eye or goggle-eyed perch. This thick-bodied sunfish superficially resembles the rock bass. It can be distinguished from the latter species by the 3 spines on the anal fin, teeth on the tongue, and the small spots on dorsal and anal fins. The color varies from olive to gray, with mottled markings on sides and back. The mouth is large, extending beyond the eye, and the eyes are reddish. Maximum length is about 11 inches.

This species is found from Minnesota east through the Great Lakes region to western Pennsylvania and south to Texas and Florida. It has also been introduced in the states of California, Washington, and Idaho.

The warmouth prefers dense weed beds and soft bot-toms, but if these conditions don't exist, they are found

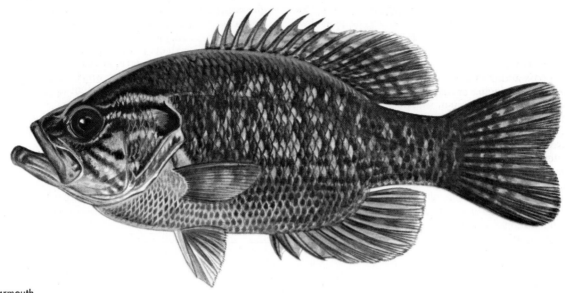

Warmouth

around stumps, hence the name stump-knocker. They have more tolerance for muddy water than most species.

The food of this sunfish is crayfish, aquatic insect larvae, and fishes. It has been found that most of the feeding is done early in the morning. By afternoon the feeding ceases.

LIFE HISTORY

The warmouth reaches sexual maturity at about 3–3½ inches. In Illinois it spawns from mid May to mid August. The male builds the nest in water from six inches to five feet deep, usually near some projecting object and on a bottom of loose stones containing silt and detritus. Ovaries of the females may contain as many as approximately 126,000 eggs. The year the young are hatched they may grow to 1½ inches. At the end of the seventh year the fish may be 8½ inches long.

ANGLING VALUE

The warmouth is small and has little food value, so angling for this species is usually incidental to the quest of some other game- or panfish. It will take a wide variety of live and artificial baits. —K.B.

WARP To move a boat from one place to another by means of a rope made fast to some fixed object or to an anchor. If the rope used for warping is bent to an anchor or kedge and the boat is pulled ahead in stages, it is called kedging. Kedging is frequently used to work a boat off a sandbar.

Also used to refer to the towing lines on a fish trawl, used commercially to capture fishes.

WARPAINT SHINER *Notropis coccogenis* A large colorful minnow, it sometimes reaches a total length of 5 inches. The geographical range of the warpaint shiner is from the Tennessee River uplands in Virginia and Kentucky southward to Georgia and Alabama. It is also found in the New and Catawba-Santee River systems in North Carolina.

The body of this minnow is long, compressed, the depth a little less than 0.25 the total length. The head is pointed and the mouth is large and oblique, with the lower jaw protruding. The eye is large, contained 3.5 times in the length of head. The lateral line scales usually number 42. The dorsal fin has 7 rays and the anal fin 9. The pharyngeal tooth formula is 2, 4-4, 2. The color of the warpaint shiner ranges from a light green on the back to silvery on the belly. During the breeding season the belly takes on a rosy coloration. The lateral scales have a dark edge; there is a faint lateral line; and a dusky band occurs on the shoulders. A scarlet vertical bar is located between the eye and gill opening. The upper muzzle and lip are red, and a red spot occurs on the body near the base of the pectoral. The lower half of the dorsal fin is yellow and the outer half is black. The pectoral fins are white.

LIFE HISTORY

This highly-colored minnow is found in medium to large clearwater streams having a moderately rapid current. Warpaint shiners are usually found over a rock, gravel, or sand bottom in the upper half of large deep pools. This fish is most active during daylight hours throughout the year. They mature at 2 years of age, at which time they have a mean total length of 77 mm. Spawning takes place in early June when the water temperatures are between 68° and 82°F. The warpaint shiner usually spawns over the nest of some other fish with the male holding a territory and driving off all other fishes. During spawning the fish head toward the current with the males in the upstream position and the females to the rear. Both settle to the bottom, vibrate, and spawn. After spawning, the fish leave the nest. The number of eggs (size 1.0–1.5 mm in diameter) spawned by the female numbers 300–1,636. An average growth rate of this minnow is 42, 61, 80.5, and 96.5 mm for age groups I through IV, respectively. The food of the warpaint shiner is chiefly insects, with Ephemeroptera being the choice food. During the spring aquatic organisms make up the main diet, whereas terrestrial forms are found in greater numbers in the stomachs during the summer and fall. Feeding takes place on the surface of the water.

The warpaint shiner serves as forage for the small-mouth bass and the redbreast sunfish.   —D.E.L.

WARPING   Swinging or turning a boat at the dock by either manual or engine power applied to a line or lines secured anywhere aboard the boat; or to move a boat, either forward or astern, by means of hauling on a line secured to an anchor which has been transported ahead or astern in a small boat and then carefully set, as may be found expedient in order to free a boat which is grounded.

WARSAW GROUPER *Epinephelus nigritus*   This is one of the largest of groupers, reaching a weight of several hundred pounds. It occurs in the tropical American Atlantic including southern Florida. Also erroneously called black grouper (*which see*) in reference to its color.

The warsaw grouper has 10 dorsal spines; 13–15 dorsal rays, usually 14; 9 anal rays; and 18–19 pectoral rays, usually 18. Posterior nostril equal to, or somewhat larger than the anterior. Insertion of pelvic fin in advance of upper end of pectoral base. Posterior margin of caudal fin convex. Coloration nearly uniformly dark, sometimes with a few scattered white spots.

This species is distinguished from the other Atlantic groupers by the number of dorsal spines. The others have 8, 9, or 11.

ANGLING VALUE

A bottom fish occurring in offshore waters of moderate depth, it takes live or dead bait and will occasionally strike artificial lures.

The large size attained makes this fish a spectacular catch. It is one of the best-fighting groupers. Since it does not occur close to shore, a boat is required. Small individuals can be broiled in chunks or fingers, and the larger fish can be chunked in making an excellent chowder. The flesh must be skinned.   —L.R.

WASHINGTON   A land of lakes, rushing rivers, and ocean shorelines, Washington is an angler's dream come true. In bewildering array, it offers to its citizens some of the nation's outstanding trout fishing. It is the center of the Steelhead Kingdom, ruled by the mighty ocean-going rainbow. Its Pacific Ocean beaches and its vast inland Puget Sound offers top fishing for two species of salmon, the husky chinook and the leaping coho. Washington is far from being a one-season angler's paradise. Here the sportsman can, every single day of the year, take some species of gamefish, whether he is angling in summer, spring, winter, or fall.

Within its confines, Washington exhibits a scenic background varying from the tallest mountain to the minus tides of the Pacific. One can explore the conifer-crammed peaks of the Olympics, scale the heights of Mount Rainier, or tramp the Pacific Crest Trail over the Cascades. And everywhere he will find trout water whether it be turbulent stream or mountain lake.

The angler can visit over 6,000 lakes in Washington with the promise of finding fish in virtually every one. More than one-third of these waters are high-country lakes, lying above the 2,500-foot mark. In the lowlands he can choose between the rain-drenched lakes of the Puget Sound country and the lush waters of the sagebrush lands east of the Cascades. The turbulent rivers flowing into the ocean all hold steelhead runs. He can fish for steelhead from December into April for the large winter fish. Then when spring comes and the rivers drop with the warming weather, he can try for the summer-run steelhead, using light tackle or regulation fly gear.

WASHINGTON GAMEFISH

Washington offers nearly all the species of gamefish to be found elsewhere in the United States. There are four native salmonids, including the rainbow, cutthroat, Dolly Varden, and kokanee; and four races of cutthroats: the sea-run or anadromous form, the Montana blackspotted, the Yellowstone, and the Crescenti—found only in Crescent Lake. The Beardsley, a form of rainbow, is also

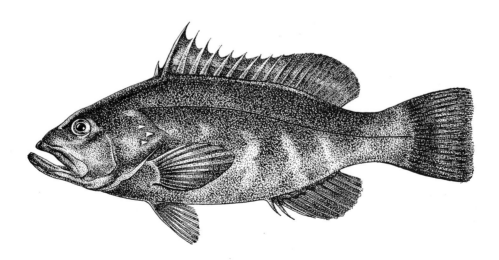

Warsaw Grouper

found only in Crescent. The introduced species include the brook, brown, lake, and golden trout and the grayling. However, the golden and the grayling are only found in a few remote lakes which require that the sport fisherman take a rugged mountain trip to reach them.

The most numerous and most popular gamefish in Washington is the rainbow. During the lowland lake season at least 75 percent of the trout that reach an angler's creel are rainbows. Most of the lake-caught trout will be in the 7–10-inch class. However, many of the rich waters in eastern Washington produce rainbows going 2–4 pounds. The cutthroat are not nearly as numerous as they were twenty years ago. But they are still planted in many lakes, and coastal rivers hold the sea-run variety. The Dolly Varden inhabits the same streams as the steelhead. It is also found in most of the larger lakes where it commonly grows to about 7 pounds. The kokanee prefers deep, clear lakes. They run 10–15 inches in length and afford fine sport from May into August. The brook trout is planted mainly in the mountain lakes and the small creeks and beaver ponds. It is not found here in the larger rivers. The lake trout has been introduced into the deep lakes, mostly in the northeast corner of Washington state. Many of these lake trout are in the 20-pound class.

Washington annually plants 20–30 million trout in its waters, both into the lakes and rivers. Its trout program is divided into two sections, one being the planting of legal-size trout to be caught on a put-and-take basis. About 3 million of these are released each spring just before the opening of the season, which normally falls on the third Sunday in April. These trout, going 7–10 inches in length, virtually all rainbow, are placed into the so-called mixed-species lakes, or waters holding several species of fish. Where these lakes are close to the centers of population, the trout may be harvested as early as within the month after the fishing season is opened.

The second part of the trout program is the planting of the "pure" trout lakes. These are waters that either have never held any species other than trout, or they are lakes that have been rehabilitated and then stocked. The small-fry plant averages about 15 million rainbow, between 1–2 million cutthroats, and about 2 million brook trout. Between 14–20 million small kokanee fry are also released. This program has proved very successful. Since the Game Department started the use of rotenone in eliminating undesirable fish, it has rehabilitated 295 lakes. These waters and the most popular and most intensively fished of all the lakes.

Returns to the angler's creel are as high as 80 percent. The fry are planted in late spring and remain in a lake for one year to enter the sport catch the next season. In most of the lakes in western Washington the trout in the rehabilitated waters will grow to 8–11 inches within the year. In some of the fertile lakes east of the Cascades the trout often grow to 12 inches or more the first year.

The Game Department has developed an ambitious steelhead program. Each winter it obtains about 3 million steelhead eggs from a stream that is used as a brood stock source. From this stock about 1 million steelhead are reared to migratory size (7–10 inches) and then released into the estuarine rivers. The returns of these hatchery plants have proved to be phenomenally successful. In many rivers a large portion of the angler's catch comes from these hatchery plants. The statewide catch of winter steelhead has averaged about 135,000 fish annually during the ten years from 1955–1965.

Salmon are propagated by the State Fisheries Department and planted in the tidal rivers. Because salmon are fished commercially, it is difficult to determine the harvest of the sport catch from such plants. However, the statewide sports catch of chinook and coho salmon totals well over a half million fish annually.

TROUT FISHING

Washington's trout waters fall into four classifications. On the west side are the put-and-take waters planted with legals and the rehabilitated lakes. Most of these waters will be fished out within the first 4–6 weeks after the season opens. A pick of the top pure or rehabilitated lakes in western Washington would include such stand-bys as Erie, Hart, Pass, McMurray, and Deer in the northwest corner embracing Skagit and Whatcom counties. Grandy Lake in the same area is a good cutthroat lake suitable for fly- or bait-fishing. Whatcom Lake turns out lunker cutthroat, many being in the 4–7-pound class. The 255-acre Green Lake, located in the center of the city of Seattle, offers fine rainbow fishing during the entire season. One end is reserved for juveniles. Other good waters in the Seattle area include Steel, Desire, Wilderness, all of them holding rainbow.

South of Seattle we find waters such as Clear Lake, Summit Lake, Lawrence Lake, American Lake, and Bay Lake, which are capable of producing trout by the tens of thousands on opening day. To the west is Merrill Lake, holding nice-sized rainbow and brook trout, and Merwin Lake for big rainbows and kokanee. Spirit Lake, reached by a paved highway, lies at the foot of Mount St. Helens in a spectacular setting. It provides excellent rainbow fishing during the summer months. Silver Lake, in the same section, is the best mixed-species lake in western Washington, producing fine full creels of bass, crappie, perch, and also the big rainbows.

Located in the Cascade Mountains northeast of Seattle is the Wenatchee River. It rises in Lake Wenatchee and flows 55 miles to its confluence with the Columbia River. The upper half of the Wenatchee runs through heavily forested mountainous country, while the lower portion is in rolling farm country. The principal gamefish here are whitefish and steelhead trout. Wenatchee Lake is one of few rearing areas for the sockeye salmon of the Columbia River drainage. Some Dolly Varden and cutthroat trout are also caught in the river and its tributary streams, such as Icicle Creek, Nason Creek, and Chiwawa River. On the Olympic Peninsula, Sutherland for big cutthroats and Spencer for rainbows are two of the better waters. The Olympic National Park holds many fine mountain lakes as well as creeks and rivers filled with trout.

Three reservoirs lying behind power dams provide excellent trout fishing. At Diablo, rainbow and large Dolly Varden are taken right into the summer months. Ross Lake, which does not open until July, holds some of the prettiest rainbows in the state, as well as cutthroats and Dolly Varden. Lake Cushman on the Olympic Peninsula is a spot noted for kokanee.

East of the Cascades below Grand Coulee Dam in the Columbia Basin, the newly created lakes offer some of the best rainbow fishing to be found along the Pacific

Coast. The so-called Seep Lakes, small bodies of water created by seepage out of irrigation canals and reservoirs, are so rich in food that planted rainbow trout attain tremendous size within a year or two. There are about 70 of these lakes which maintain carry-over rainbows in the 2–4-pounds class. They are bright, clean fish, full of fight. They hit bait or trolled lures and are fine fish to take on a fly. Most of the waters may be reached from the towns of Moses Lake or Othello, where motels are available. Virtually all of the Seep Lakes are without resorts, and the angler must bring his own boat. Camping areas are provided at many waters, all of which lie in dry sagebrush country. A sampling of the outstanding lakes for large rainbows includes Quincy, Burke, Warden, Corral, Heart, Blythe, Upper Hampton, Windmill, and Goldeneye.

The reservoirs in the Basin, large waters ranging up to 30,000 acres, are excellent warmwater fisheries. These include Banks Lake and the Potholes Reservoir, both holding bass and crappie, with Banks producing an occasional rainbow up to 12 pounds. Both Winchester Wasteway and Evergreen Reservoir are perch and crappie waters.

The lakes of northcentral Washington in Chelan and Okanogan counties constitute some of the most popular waters of the state. The trout may not grow as large as they do in the Basin, but fishing is more consistently good than in any other area of the state. The trout are mostly rainbow, with some cutthroats and a few brooks, running 10–14 inches, with most waters holding carry-overs. Many of the lakes lie in heavily forested areas, affording fine camping spots during the hot summer months.

In the Okanogan Valley, near Omak, the waters that always receive a heavy play include Spectacle, Aeneas, Fish, Conconully, Salmon, Wannacut, Green, and Bonaparte lakes. Aeneas is a fly-fishing-only lake with trout up to 3 pounds. Alta Lake out of Pateros is one of the better opening-day lakes in the district.

Jameson Lake in Douglas County, deep in Moses Coulee, is one of the top rainbow lakes of the state. It is a narrow lake, 1½ miles long, that holds fat rainbows ranging from 10 inches to 4 pounds. The fish are terrific fighters and may be taken on a fly or bait or by trolling.

The northeast corner of the state holds another series of lakes that offer top trout fishing throughout the summer season and into the fall months. The waters hold rainbows, cutthroats, and some fine brook trout. In the Spokane district are Clear, Silver, and West Medical, which are noted as rainbow lakes. The trout will go 1–3 pounds. Both Silver and West Medical are fly waters. Others include three top lakes in Ferry County. Curlew Lake puts out rainbows going 14–20 inches in both spring and fall months. It lies in the heart of the mule-deer country, where a combined hunting and fishing trip may be easily arranged. The two Twins, large pieces of water, are little fished, but produce rainbows of large size. Trout up to 8 pounds have been creeled here.

Deep and Pierre lakes in Stevens County are outstanding cutthroat waters, with both holding some very large brook trout. Browns Lake in Pend Oreille County, which holds cutthroats, is rated as one of the state's best fly-fishing-only waters.

The Olympics and the high Cascades are dotted with thousands of mountain lakes that can be fished from July into September. Most of the waters lie amid spectacular mountain scenery—snow-clad peaks, precipitous cliffs, and virgin forests. The lakes are little fished, and they promise really true wild fishing, unspoiled by litterbugs or the least touch of civilization. The ambitious angler can reach all of the waters by backpacking, with only a few of the waters not accessible by trail. Trails designed for horse travel have been built by the Forest Service or the Olympic or Rainier National Parks to reach many of the larger waters. Many of the best fishing spots can be reached by an overnight trip starting off from one of the three mountain passes—Snoqualmie, Stevens, or Chinook.

Washington's best trout fishing lies in its lakes and not in its rivers. Virtually all of the tidal rivers in western Washington are managed as steelhead or searun cutthroat waters. In eastern Washington a good share of the interior streams hold resident trout, and rivers such as the Yakima provide some top rainbow fishing for the angler from September into October.

In western Washington the smaller streams in the cutover back country and their beaver ponds are planted with rainbow, cutthroat, and brook trout.

STEELHEAD RIVERS

Steelheading makes a northwest angler's mouth water when he goes river fishing. When the season opens in December, about 150,000 fishermen who carry steelhead punchcards devote their entire outdoor leisure time to the taking of anadromous rainbows. The Game Department lists 162 rivers open during the winter steelhead season, which runs until March. New runs enter the rivers after every freshet. Fishing success depends mainly on river conditions, and the best catches are usually made after the rise in water has brought new fish out of the ocean. While most of the fishing is done from the bank, boat drifting becomes more popular every year. The lower sections of the larger rivers are all suitable to boat fishing. Guide service is provided on the Skagit River and on some of the ocean rivers of the Olympic Peninsula.

The Skagit is not only the state's top producer of steelhead, but year after year it turns out the largest number of trophy fish. However, the Olympic Peninsula rivers are quantitatively superior to others, but are followed by the Puget Sound streams with the Columbia River system in third place. For comparison, here is the listing of the top twenty-five of the steelhead rivers with a single season's total—Skagit 12,566; Green 8,449; Cowlitz 7,455; Skykomish 6,225; Snake 4,455; Columbia 4,350; Washougal 4,350; Puyallup 4,144; Snohomish 4,027; Humptulips 3,566; Lewis River 3,221; Chehalis 3,090; Dungeness 2,580; Nisqually 2,494; Samish 2,362; Toutle 2,193; Kalama 1,976; Snoqualmie 1,841; Pilchuck 1,744; Sol Duc 1,650; Stillaguamish 1,620; Hoh 1,545; Sammamish 1,436; Sauk 1,417; North Fork Stillaguamish 1,417.

In addition to the winter-run streams the Game Department lists thirty-eight rivers that contain summer-run fish. Many of these are tributaries of the Columbia. The summer fish usually start showing in late May or June, and the runs may continue into October. The summer-run steelhead is a spectacular trout and when taken on the fly affords some of the most exciting fishing to be found in the nation's rivers. The rivers that are rated as holding the best populations of summer fish include, from the Columbia River system, the Columbia itself and its tributaries, Grand Ronde, Kalama, Klickitat, Snake, Washougal, and Wind. Of these the Grand Ronde, Kalama, Washougal, and Wind as well as the Big One are considered fine fly streams.

The best Puget Sound summer rivers are Skykomish, Snoqualmie, Tolt, and the Stillaguamish system. The North Fork of the Stillaguamish is classed as a fly-fishing-only stream during the summer season.

The top Olympic streams would be the Queets, Quinault, and Sol Duc.

SALMON FISHING

Washington's salmon fishing is done mainly in salt-water, as many of the coastal rivers are closed to sport fishing for salmon. About 200,000 Washington residents search the salt chuck for two species of salmon. A large percentage of the anglers own outboard cruisers, which are hauled on trailers from one ocean feeding ground to another. The chinook (locally king salmon) season usually starts in early May and is at its peak in August. The coho salmon (locally silver salmon) come later than the kings with their peak from mid August into September.

The chinook is the heavyweight of the salmon family, many being in the 30–40-pound class, some weighing 50–60 pounds. They are tough, powerhouse fighters, hard to stop when they make their long, powerful runs.

The silvers, which normally weigh 8–15 pounds with a few in the 20-pound class, are the acrobats of the salt chuck. They will take off on the surface on long, smoking runs, leaping repeatedly. Silvers may be taken on light gear, and the sport of hooking them on regulation fly tackle is growing in popularity.

The top salmon spot in the Pacific Northwest is the fishing hamlet at Westport, situated at the entrance of Grays Harbor on the Olympic Peninsula. A large fleet of charter boats sallies out over the harbor bar onto the swells of the Pacific Ocean from mid April into September. The boats drift-troll (mooch) for salmon 2–15 miles off shore. Westport is the best place for a tourist effort, as the charter-boat skippers are thoroughly familiar with the fishing grounds and can supply gear, knowledge, and bait. The limit is three salmon a day. The charter boats accommodate 6–15 fishermen, and on good days many will obtain their limit by midafternoon. The angler's catch may be canned right at Westport, or it can be iced and shipped home to any place in the United States. In one summer a record sport catch at Westport consisted of 143,000 coho salmon and 50,000 chinooks.

Other prime salmon areas include Neah Bay and Sekiu in the Strait of Juan de Fuca. Here most of the fishing is done off outboard cruisers or smaller "kicker" boats. The fish are boated either off Cape Flattery and Tatoosh Island or inside the Strait. La Push off the Quillayute Indian Reservation provides fine summer fishing directly on the ocean feeding grounds. The mouth of the Columbia River, too, is one of the top salmon spots. In one season, 115,900 silvers and 29,000 kings were landed there.

Inside Puget Sound the chinook runs usually appear in August and the coho in September. Hope Island off the mouth of the Skagit River is noted for lunker kings. Puget Sound also provides fishing all winter long for young chinooks locally called "blackmouth." They normally weigh 3–10 pounds, but some will tip the scales up to 25 pounds. *See also* Chinook Salmon, Coho Salmon, Steelhead Fishing *under* Rainbow Trout   —E.B.

WATERDOG *Ambystoma tigrinum* The waterdog is not a fish but is the larval stage of the tiger salamander, the eggs of which are deposited in water and develop into "waterdogs." The larvae live a fishlike existence for several months and then generally transform into the terrestrial salamander. However, some waterdogs become sexually mature and breed before acquiring adult characteristics or seeking land. The waterdog superficially resembles a catfish, but it has three pairs of external gills and two pairs of legs instead of fins. It may reach a length of 9 inches.

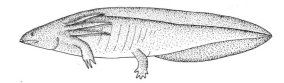

Waterdog

ANGLING VALUE

The waterdog is an important "baitfish" in Western and Southwestern United States bass waters.

WATERFLEAS Order Cladocera These are largely microscopic swimming crustaceans ranging from less than $1/100$ inch to $3/4$ inch in size. Waterfleas feed primarily on algae and diatoms. They often form a major portion of the zooplankton population and are a staple food of young fishes. *See also* Plankton *under* Freshwater Ecology, Habitats *under* Marine Ecology

WATERLINE A line painted on the hull showing the point to which a boat sinks in the water when properly trimmed with a normal load.

WATER SPOUT A storm at sea that corresponds to a land storm of cyclonic character, but in this case the funnel-like center actually draws on the surface of the water and may be of destructive force. In general appearance it is a funnel-shaped, whirling formation of cloud extending below low-lying clouds and reaching down to the surface of the water.

WATERWAY A navigable channel, or a whole navigable body of water.

WATERWAYS Fore and aft timbers found on either side of a boat joining the deck with the sides and with scuppers (*which see*) cut through them. In larger vessels these timbers are the last overly-heavy outboard planks in a wooden deck, and formed so as to lead water out through the scuppers.

WAVYBACK SKIPJACK *See* Bonito

WEAKFISH *Cynoscion regalis* A popular marine gamefish which generally resembles the spotted seatrout in appearance. The name "weakfish" refers to the delicate mouth structure from which a hook can easily tear free. It is also regionally called gray weakfish, squeteague, and yellowfin.

The weakfish is a slim, well-shaped fish, about four times as long as deep (to the base of the caudal fin). Its color along the dorsal surface is a dark olive or greenish or greenish-blue. The sides are burnished in tones of blue, green, purple, and lavender, and have a coppery or golden tinge. The back and upper sides are peppered with small, vaguely defined spots of black, dark green, and sometimes bronze. Some of these spots are confluent to form irregular lines which extend diagonally downward and forward. The spotting is confined mostly to the upper part of the body. The underside is white or silvery. The weakfish has a head (nearly one-third the body length) characterized by a large mouth, a somewhat pointed snout, and a lower jaw which projects beyond the upper. It has a well-developed tail with a slightly concave outer edge. This caudal fin is dusky or olive, sometimes with a yellow tinge on its lower edge. The shorter, higher first dorsal fin has 10 spines. The longer second dorsal is soft and has 26–29 rays. The dorsal fin color is dusky, usually with some yellow tinges. The ventral, pectoral, and anal fins are also tinged with yellow.

The extreme general range of weakfish is on the Atlantic Coast of the United States extending from Massachusetts southward to Florida's eastern seaboard, with stragglers wandering into more northerly New England waters and even beyond. The largest populations are concentrated between the Chesapeake Bay region and New Jersey and New York. Centers of abundance include Chesapeake Bay, Delaware Bay, coastal areas of New Jersey, and the Peconic Bay system of Long Island, New York.

Within their range, weakfish are found in the surf, and in sounds, inlets, bays, channels, and saltwater creeks. They also enter estuaries of rivers, but do not venture into freshwater. By nature they are schooling fish, with a marked preference for shallow, sand-bottom areas.

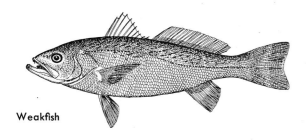

Weakfish

The average size of the weakfish has declined. Today the approximate length-weight range is 10–12 inches and ½–1 pounds up to about 21–23 inches and 3–4 pounds, with a possibility of 25–27-inch specimens in the 5–6-pound class in some areas. Once anglers caught early-autumn "tiderunners" which weighed up to 11–12 pounds. Oldtimers who fished the Peconic Bay region of Long Island, one of the greatest weakfishing areas of all, recall specimens up to 15 pounds in the heyday of that fishery; and there is a world record of 17½ pounds (Mullica River, New Jersey) on the books. But the era of those large weakfish appears to be over.

FEEDING HABITS

The food of weakfish includes sea worms, shrimp, squid, sand lance, crabs, mollusks, and small fishes such as silversides, killifish, butterfish, and young menhaden. Because of this varied diet, weakfish seek prey at different levels of the water. Frequently they feed right at the surface or close to it. This near-surface feeding can occur in shoal areas, such as over the sandflats of bays and other

places where killifish, silversides, and other forage species are available. It also can occur in estuarine creeks and in shallow, grassy areas where there is apt to be a supply of shrimp. Weakfish adapt themselves to local food conditions. When there is no food near the surface, they go deeper. Thus they may prowl at some intermediate level or go close to the bottom. Thus, they should be fished at three general levels—the top, some intermediate plane, and on the bottom. Accordingly, the angling methods are—top-fishing at anchor and trolling, bottom-fishing at anchor, and while drifting, jigging, and surf-angling.

CHUMMING FOR WEAKFISH

A favored method of surface weakfishing is done at anchor, using chum. The two requirements are an uninterrupted chum line and absolute quiet. The latter is essential in weakfishing because the fish tend to "spook" rather easily. The anchor should be lowered with a minimum of disturbance, and any unnecessary noise aboard the boat, particularly on smaller craft such as rowboats, should be avoided. As for a chum line, grass shrimp are among the most effective ingredients. Chumming can be so important to this kind of weakfishing that it merits special treatment.

A chum line should be established in a place where other boats cannot cut across it and disturb it. Boat traffic can impair and even destroy a chum line's effectiveness. It also is important to gauge the distribution of chum according to the current flow in the area fished. For a chum line to operate properly there should be some flow of current. Ideally, though, this should not be too swift. The shrimp are dropped overboard in clusters of 3–5 at a time, a foot or two between clusters. Frequency of distribution will depend upon current velocity. If it is fast, the shrimp clusters can be dropped overboard from the bow. With a slow current they should be distributed as close as possible to the baited rigs. (Under such conditions, squeezing or pinching the heads of the shrimp will keep them from scattering.) A good supply of chum is necessary. It is better to have too much than to run out just as the fish start to respond. At least 2–3 quarts are required for one or two anglers fishing one tide.

Although grass shrimp are about the best weakfish chum, other items can be substituted when these are scarce, such as the kind of shrimp sold in fish markets for one. Another is the pulp of ground-up menhaden. Others are clams, mussels, and fishes such as sardines, porgies, killies, and silversides. They should be chopped up or ground fine and should be used rather sparingly, because their pulp tends to sink rapidly, thereby detracting from its effectiveness and also drawing undesirable species. Enterprising substitutes for shrimp chum have included plain oatmeal, boiled rice, bread crumbs, and even finely broken egg shells. Those items also have been mixed with shrimp chum to make a small supply last longer.

TOP-FISHING RIG

The top-fishing rig consists of a single hook on a 2–3-foot leader of nylon monofilament. A barrel swivel between the line and leader is optional. Hook designs include the O'Shaughnessy, Sproat, and Carlisle. Sizes will vary to a certain extent according to weights of the fish currently running. A No. 1 may be needed for small weakfish. A 1/0 or 2/0 can handle fish up to 4–5 pounds.

For weakfish heavier than that, sizes range from 3/0 up to 6/0. In general these sizes can be used in all weakfishing methods.

Current speed and strength will determine whether or not a top-fishing rig must be equipped with small weights or a cork float. If a strong current forces the rig right to the surface, it may be necessary to put one or two small split shot on the leader, a foot or so ahead of the hook. If the current is sluggish, causing the rig to sink too deep or preventing it from drifting away from the boat properly, it may be necessary to add a small cork float to the terminal tackle. Too much weight or too large a float should not be used. The former can detract from the fish's fight. The latter interferes with setting the hook when light tackle is used.

Baits used in top-weakfishing include shrimp (favored) and a piece of sandworm or bloodworm, or just a plain hook baited with shrimp, but an effective lure sometimes is a small tin squid baited with shrimp or worm. Still another attractor, used in strong currents, is a small mackerel jig, its hook baited. No further weighting is needed.

A certain amount of experimentation is advised for the start of top-fishing. The rig should be allowed to drift out into the chum line—and held 100–200 feet away from the boat. If this doesn't produce a strike, the rig should be fished at various distances beyond the boat and weighted to ride at different levels. When the first weakfish is caught, the distance and depth are noted and the other rigs adjusted accordingly. Jigging the rig at intervals is also helpful. Weakfish often strike on a retrieve.

HIGH-LOW RIG

In bottom-angling for weakfish a popular hook arrangement is the high-low rig. Its specifications vary according to individual preference and areas fished, but basically it consists of a low hook, just above the sinker, and a high hook attached at a desired distance above that. Swivels usually are employed in attachment of hooks to line.

One procedure is to bait the low hook, of suitable size, for some local bottom species, such as porgy, in which case it can be tied into the line, without a leader, about 6–12 inches above the sinker. The high hook, on a 3–5-foot leader 3–6 feet above the sinker, is baited for weakfish. When both hooks are baited for weakfish they are attached to the line at similar distances above the sinker. The low hook is given a 2–3-foot leader of monofilament or gut; the high hook has a leader 4–5 feet long. An obvious advantage of this high-low rig is that it is ready for weakfish cruising at different levels above the bottom.

Bottom-fishing baits include shrimp, strip of squid, sandworm, bloodworm, live killy, piece of shedder crab or softshell crab, hard or soft clam, and strip baits cut from young "snapper" bluefish, porgy, herring, or even searobin. Combination baits on the same hook are also used, such as a strip of squid and a shrimp, a piece of clam and a live killy hooked through the lips, or perhaps a worm and shrimp, with the hook's point hidden by a piece of clam.

The sinker for a high-low rig should be heavy enough to hold bottom, yet not so heavy that it remains firmly planted in one spot or detracts from the fish's fight. Its weight will be dictated by current strength. A bank-type

sinker can be used, but a round or oval type with a built-in swivel is superior because it allows the rig to move with currents and so cover more ground.

A suggested bottom-fishing method is to lower the rig until its sinker touches bottom, then lift it slightly at intervals so that the current can move it along and impart some action to it. This is repeated until 100–200 feet of line is paid out. Sometimes a strike will not occur until the terminal rig has traveled quite a distance from the boat. If there is no response, the rig is retrieved by reeling slowly and repeatedly lifting it a little and allowing it to settle. If there is no strike, the entire pay-out-reel-in process is repeated.

DRIFT-FISHING

Drifting is a variation of bottom-fishing. The advantage claimed for it over bottom-fishing at anchor is that it covers more territory. One rig used in this technique consists of a single 1/0 or 2/0 hook on an 18–24-inch leader which is attached, with or without swivel, about 6 inches above the sinker. If desired, a second hook of similar size can be attached on a short leader about two feet above the first. For mobility the preferred type of sinker is a round one with built-in swivel. It should be only heavy enough to hold bottom.

Jigging can be done at anchor or while drifting. Terminal tackle calls for a small, shiny metal jig, armed with a hook of suitable size. The jig is attached to the line via a short monofilament leader, and its hook is left unbaited. For its real effectiveness jigging relies on the metal lure's motion, shine, and flash. Jigging consists of alternately raising and lowering it short distances spasmodically with the rod tip in a continuous process. Experimentation may be necessary to determine at which level jigging should be done.

TROLLING FOR WEAKFISH

Trolling is a weakfishing method employed in some areas, and it has been used effectively where schools congregate. It has an added advantage, apart from covering more ground, in that it also will account for schooling striped bass. The rig consists of an artificial lure on a short monofilament leader. Basic trolling lures are spinners, such as Willow Leaf, Cape Cod, and June Bug patterns baited with sandworm, small metal squids, bucktails, spoons, and plugs of the surface and diving types.

SURF-FISHING

Surf-angling for weakfish is divided into two techniques. One is bottom-fishing with a natural bait, such as sandworm, bloodworm, sand eel, shrimp, or a piece of squid, softshell crab, shedder crab, mullet, menhaden, or mackerel. Either of two rigs can be used. One is a standard surf-bottom rig—a swivel with three loops, to which are attached line, 14–24-inch leader and hook, and pyramid sinker. The other is the fishfinder (which see). Here the hook, on a leader up to 2–3 feet long, is attached to the line through a barrel swivel. Ahead of the swivel is a pyramid sinker equipped with a connector which allows the sinker to slide freely along the line up to the swivel. Purpose of this arrangement is to lend greater maneuverability to the rig without interfering with the cast. Force of the cast keeps the sinker as far down on the line as it will go, adding to the momentum which carries the rig out. Once on the bottom, the sinker keeps the rig where it belongs, yet the rig is free to move so that a striking weakfish can take the bait, unhampered by the sinker's weight. Another component of both rigs is a small cork float with a hole through its center so that it can be adjusted. This float is mounted on the leader, and its purpose is to keep the bait out of the reach of crabs.

SURF-CASTING FOR WEAKFISH

Many different kinds of artificial lures are productive of surf-run weakfish. The oldest is a shiny, block tin squid, notably one shaped like baitfish on which weakfish feed, with a fixed or movable hook. The lure is often enhanced by adding small bits of feather or bucktail around the hook, or a piece of pork rind to the hook itself. Some anglers paint their squids a color such as white or yellow. Chrome-plated squids are useful also; however they cannot be bent as easily as lead squids to resemble certain baitfishes, and the chrome can be damaged in rocky areas. Other good lures are small surface plugs which create a commotion when retrieved, small wobbling or darting plugs, and small spoons with a bright, flashy finish. These artificials are used on a 3–6-foot monofilament leader. A snap-swivel at the end of the leader facilitates changing of lures. If bluefish are thought to be in the area, each lure should be preceded by 6 inches of wire leader.

The success of artificials depends upon their action in the water. The lures which resemble and/or imitate the actions of bait on which weakfish feed are naturally the most effective. Action is imparted to the lure as it is retrieved. Depending upon the kind of lure, it may be retrieved slowly or fairly quickly, with the angler giving it extra action by motions of his rod tip. Some lures must be retrieved more quickly in clearwater. Similarly, a lure being swept toward the beach by breakers must have its retrieve hastened to prevent slack in the line. Conversely, a lure being pulled seaward by waves will have its retrieve slowed.

TACKLE

Weakfishing equipment can be almost as varied as the lures and methods. Both conventional-type and spinning tackle are used. In the former category, a light to medium rod, about 5½–6 feet overall, including butt, will do for surface-angling, bottom-fishing, jigging, drifting, trolling, and dockfishing. Whether you use glass or bamboo, the important thing is that the rod have strength combined with flexibility for maximum sport. This can be mounted with a 1/0 reel.

Casting in surf-angling necessitates a longer rod. A light conventional rod can measure 8–9 feet overall and will handle the lighter lures to about 2½ ounces and line to about 30-pound-test. Such a rod can be used in jetty-fishing, on a beach where distance is not a requisite, and when heavy terminal rigs are not involved. When casting distance is required, or when heavier lures or sinkers are used, a medium surf rod is indicated. The over-all length is about 8½–10 feet. It will handle lures to about 4 ounces, sinkers to about 5–6 ounces in bait-fishing, and lines in strengths up to about 36 pounds. Conventional surf reels have a star-drag, free-spool operation, and a rather wide spool with a gear ratio of 3:1 or 4:1 for fast retrieves. To match the lighter surf rods, a reel with a spool capacity of about 150 yards is used. For the medium rods a reel with a 200-yard capacity is suggested.

Spinning tackle has become increasingly popular in recent years because it is light and easier to operate than conventional gear. Spinning rods for jetty and oceanfront use are marketed in a variety of lengths and actions. Two general sizes can be used in surfing for weakfish. The lighter of the two is a "whippy" stick measuring about 7–9 feet long. On this can be secured one of the smaller saltwater spinning reels. The outfit will cast plugs, metal squids, jigs, and spoons up to 2 ounces. It is primarily tackle for use with small artificial lures. It is not, however, a satisfactory rod for bottom-fishing unless water and weather conditions are such that the fisherman can use light sinkers. A medium surf-spinning rod, 8–10 feet over-all, will cast the larger artificials up to about 3 ounces and can be used in bait-fishing when sinkers do not exceed approximately that same weight. A rod in this category is matched with one of the larger saltwater surf-spinning reels. Because it can handle up to 3–4 ounces, and therefore can be used in bait-fishing, a medium outfit is more versatile than a lighter one. This will take other surf species, such as bluefish and striped bass.

Lines used with conventional surf tackle include braided nylon and linen, and some anglers favor monofilament. The line's strength will be determined by the weight of the outfit and the size of the fish sought. The range is about 25–45-pound-test for the heavier outfits. Lines used with spinning tackle are monofilaments in one of the modern synthetics. Quantity of line needed will depend upon the size of the tackle, the casting distance required, and the general sizes of the fish sought. Generally speaking, minimum should be about 200 yards. If longer casts and/or larger fishes are involved, 250–300 yards are better.

FISHING TECHNIQUE

The approach of weakfish to a bait varies. Sometimes, particularly when surface-fishing it will be a hard, smashing jolt. The fish may hook itself, or the surprised angler will respond forcefully and tear the hook out of its fragile mouth. At other times the approach to a bait will be fairly gentle and leisurely, the fish moving away slowly with the offering and showing no force. Here is where a sensitive rod is valuable. On such occasions the angler must be patient, maintaining constant contact with his rig, paying out line slowly, and tightening it carefully at intervals to feel for the fish's weight. When the weakfish definitely has taken the bait—indicated by a steady pull on the line—the hook can be set by a short, upward movement of the rod tip. It is important not to set the hook before the fish has taken the bait into its mouth. Such premature action will only yank the bait away. Weakfish also take a bait slyly, nibbling on it but not swallowing it. Here again is a test of the angler's patience. Attempting to set the hook will only pull the bait away. Instead, let the line out slowly, a few feet at a time, so that current can impart action to the bait and entice the quarry into seizing it. Not until the fish's weight is felt on the line should the hook be set.

When a weakfish is hooked, its play consists of long runs or surges followed by a series of erratic dashes. These can be sudden, swift, and unpredictable. A weakfish will often run around the boat in a long arc, or streak away on a tangent, or even swing suddenly toward the angler, giving him the problem of taking up any slack in the line. These unpredictable antics, plus surprise maneuvers and the ever-present danger of the hook ripping loose, are the kinds of problems which make a weakfish tricky to catch.

The weakfish is subdued primarily with the rod, rather than with rod and reel. That is why a flexible but sturdy rod is good for this kind of fishing. Although the strike is often savage and the initial run long and swift, subsequent dashes do not match the first few for strength and distance. Nevertheless, a weakfish makes an angler earn his catch every inch of the way.

SEASONS AND LOCATIONS

The over-all sport-fishing season for weakfish, depending upon sections of the coast from South to North, is from about April into November. In the Chesapeake Bay area, for example, the season can get under way in April and last through October into November. In the New York-New Jersey region the run usually begins in May and lasts until October. Still farther north, when there are weakfish in southern New England waters, the run might not start until June, and it will be over in September. Regional water temperatures are a key factor. They, and weather conditions in general, also determine a run's duration.

The list of areas with weakfishing potential includes tide rips, sloughs, holes, saltwater creeks, shallow bays, channels, shelving beaches, and the surf. Sometimes at dusk and at night they can be caught in the vicinity of bridges and from docks and piers. In autumn, quiet creeks threading through salt marshes are potentially good for weakfishing.

In some areas weakfish tend to feed on a tide's ebb and flow, such as an hour before highwater and two hours after the tide has turned. But tides and winds, like weather and other local conditions, are variables. Their effect on weakfishing can change from place to place, and even from day to day within the same area. An angler should inquire about such factors in the area he intends to fish. A little experimentation with baits and techniques also will help.

FOOD VALUE

Weakfish are excellent eating. The meat is white and possesses delicious flavor. They are scaled or skinned and dressed, after which baking and broiling are two of the ways to prepare them. The bones can be lifted out easily with a fork after cooking. *See also* Saltwater Fly-Fishing, Surf-Fishing   —B.W.

WEBUG SUCKER *Catostomus fecundus* A large, slender-bodied sucker. Color, brown to black above and whitish below. Fins dark. Dorsal fin long and low with 12–13 rays. Lateral-line scales 64–75. The range of this sucker is confined to the Bonneville and the upper Snake River in Utah and Wyoming.

LIFE HISTORY

Abundant in the lakes and rivers within its range, the webug sucker in some areas is at home in waters well above 80°F. Spawning in June, this species is observed in large numbers in the tributary streams. It spawns in a manner similar to others of the sucker family in that two

males attend each female, and eggs are spread among the sand and gravel of the creek bed. The webug sucker is an omnivorous feeder, and is said to consume large numbers of trout eggs. A large sucker, the webug reaches a length of 25 inches and a weight of 12 pounds.

Webug Sucker

ECONOMIC VALUE

Although useful as food, it is doubtful that this value overrides its spawn-eating habits.   —R.A.J.

WEDGESPOT SHINER *Notropis greenei* This shiner receives its name from a characteristic wedge-shaped spot at the base of the tail which is detached from a lateral band; sometimes this spot may be indistinct. It is dusky on the back and pale below the mid-dorsal stripe. The dorsal fin is moderately long. The lining of the peritoneal cavity is heavily speckled with black. The pharyngeal tooth count is 2, 4–4, 2. The mouth extends obliquely from a point even with the center of the eye to a point below and even with the front of the eye or a little beyond.

Wedgespot Shiner

LIFE HISTORY

This is a small minnow which attains a length of about 2½ inches. Spawning takes place in July and August. It is found in the Ozarks of Missouri, Arkansas, and Oklahoma.   —C.A.P.

WEEVERFISH *Trachinus* spp. Two species, the greater weever, *Trachinus draco*, and the lesser weever, *Trachinus vipera*, are found in the eastern Atlantic. The greater weever, known from Norway, the British Isles, the Mediterranean, the Black Sea, and the North African coast, is the larger species, having a deep yellow body, varying to reddish-gray, with dark bandings and pale yellow lines on the scales. The head and body are compressed, and the mouth is comparatively large. Its elongate body gradually tapers to a square-edged caudal fin, and the anal and second dorsal fins are long and low, while the first dorsal is short and high. It has about 30 dorsal rays and about 31 anal rays. A deepwater species, it spawns in the summer. It eats small fishes and is itself delicious to eat. The lesser weever ranges from the North Sea to the Mediterranean. It differs from the greater weever in having a mouth which points more obliquely upward. Its back is gray, becoming paler below. The second dorsal fin has 21–24 rays, and the anal fin about 24 rays. This species has about the same habits, but it is found in predominantly shallow water, and spawning occurs from May to September.

DANGER TO MAN

Both species possess poison glands at the base of the fin. Five to 7 erect spines and the opercular spines can inflict injury. Toxin flows through the hollow spines from the poison glands. The effect is neurotoxic and hemotoxic, similar in effect to some snake venoms. Pain is instant and increases to the point of excruciation, and sometimes death results. No antidotes are known, and the treatment is symptomatic.

See also Dangerous, Poisonous, and Injurious Aquatic Life *under* First Aid —D.DS.

WEIGHT-FORWARD LINE A type of line used in fly-casting. Also called forward taper line, torpedo head, rocket taper, bass bug taper, and three-diameter line. *See also* Fly Line

WEST VIRGINIA The highest state east of the Mississippi, West Virginia has a variety of fishing water from mountain trout streams to large rivers. However, the Mountain State isn't blessed with an abundance of water. There are only 101 square miles of natural inland water surface in West Virginia. The state also has only one natural lake. Partially to overcome this scarcity of water and lack of natural lakes, West Virginia has pursued an energetic lake-building program in recent years. Several warmwater and trout impoundments have been built, and the State Department of Natural Resources estimates that in the next ten years at least 6 major impoundments and more than 30 smaller ones will be built.

West Virginia, one of the smaller states, with an area of 24,282 square miles, ranges in altitude from 240 feet at Harpers Ferry in the Eastern Panhandle to 4,860 feet at Spruce Knob in Pendleton County. Basically, the state is divided into two physiographic provinces by the Allegheny Front, a mountain range that extends along the eastern side of the state in a general north-south direction. Northern Pocahontas County contains the headwaters of most major streams in the state, including the South Branch, which flows eastward into the Potomac, and the Gauley, Elk, Cheat, Tygart, and Greenbrier rivers, all of which flow westward toward the Ohio.

Most of West Virginia's waterways are in the Ohio system. The three largest tributaries of the Ohio—the Monongahela, New, and Kanawha rivers—drain 21,000 square miles of the state. The North and South Branch rivers in northeastern West Virginia are the major tributaries of the Potomac drainage, which flows into the Chesapeake Bay.

Rivers play an important part in determining the boundaries of the state. The Ohio River forms the northwestern boundary between Ohio and West Virginia for 277 miles, and the Tug Fork and Big Sandy rivers form 99 miles of boundary between West Virginia and Kentucky in the southern and western sections of the state.

One of the popular gamefish in West Virginia is the smallmouth bass, which is found in most warmwater streams in the state. Four- and 5-pounders are caught occasionally in larger streams and reservoirs. Other species of gamefish found in the state include largemouth and spotted bass, rock bass, muskellunge, walleye, catfish, crappie, bluegill, and brook, brown, and rainbow trout.

Muskellunge are found in most streams in the Ohio drainage, including the Elk in the central part of the state, Coal and Poca rivers in southern West Virginia, Little Kanawha and Hughes rivers in the western section, and Middle Island Creek in the Northern Panhandle. Some smaller streams also hold muskies.

Trout fishing in West Virginia is confined mostly to the mountainous areas in the eastern half of the state, although some new trout water has been opened in Elk River below the Sutton Reservoir. Fishery biologists found that water flowing out of the reservoir was cooled sufficiently to support trout for several miles downriver. That section of the Elk River was added to the stocking list, and is open year round.

West Virginia's trout-stocking program is one of the best in the East. Four state and three federal hatcheries amply supply the mountain streams and impoundments with trout.

Warmwater fishing isn't confined to any one geographical area. The larger streams are well-distributed—New River in the south, Elk in the center, Little Kanawha in the west, Greenbrier in the southeast, and South Branch and Cacapon in the Eastern Panhandle.

Farm ponds are numerous in the state, and, although they do not constitute a major contribution to the available fishing water, a farm pond in Cabell County did produce a state record largemouth bass—an 8 pounder.

Any discussion of fishing in West Virginia would have to include some comments on coal pollution. West Virginia is one of the top coal-producing states in the country, and coal-washery wastes and acid mine drainage constitute serious pollution problems. Acid drainage, which is difficult to eliminate, is a particular menace.

The State Water Resources Board has made great strides in recent years in reducing the flow of coal-washery wastes into streams. An example is aptly named Coal River, which has its source in the middle of the coal-mining region of southern West Virginia. Vigilant attention to coal-washery facilities along the river and its tributaries has cleared Coal up to a great extent, and some gamefish are being caught again. The Tug Fork and Guyandot rivers in southern West Virginia have also been cleaned up considerably.

On the other hand, acid mine drainage has seriously hurt the West Fork and Monongahela rivers in the northern part of the state, and the lower reaches of the Cheat and Tygart have been affected. There are some acid-drainage problems on the Little Kanawha, one of the state's best smallmouth and muskie rivers.

Municipal and industrial wastes also contribute to stream pollution in West Virginia. The Kanawha Valley chemical complex—thirteen major plants and nine smaller ones in a thirty-mile area—has eliminated gamefishing on all but the upper part of the Kanawha River.

WARMWATER STREAMS

West Virginia fishermen often differ as to the best fishing streams in the state, but their list generally boils down to five—Greenbrier, New River, South Branch of the Potomac, Elk, and Little Kanawha.

The Greenbrier, 167 miles long from its source in the mountains of Pocahontas County to its junction with the New River at Hinton, is considered the "showcase" smallmouth stream in the state. Fishery biologists describe it as ideal smallmouth habitat because it has numerous ledges and boulders for cover, a minimum of high, muddy water, and good gradient. It is an excellent stream for float-fishing, although much of it can be fished by wading. The Greenbrier is estimated to have a smallmouth population of 30 percent of the total fish population in the river. It is also one of the best walleye streams in the state and offers the best rock-bass fishing. The big bass taken in the Greenbrier are generally caught at night on surface lures. This type of fishing is very effective in late summer and early fall when the water is low.

New River, which starts in the Blue Ridge Mountains, enters West Virginia near Glen Lyn, Virginia, and flows 87 miles to Gauley Bridge, where it connects with the Gauley River to form the Kanawha River. Wide and swift, New River cannot be fished well except from a boat. As a word of caution, boaters not familiar with the river should use extreme caution when floating over the shoals. They can be treacherous. New River is the top spot in the state to catch big walleyes, with 12–14 pounders taken occasionally. Walleye fishermen on New River stick mostly to the swiftwater on the head and foot of the rapids, fishing weighted spinners and other bottom-bumping lures. Trolling the deeper water produces on occasion. New River also has reasonably good smallmouth fishing and is the state's best stream for channel catfish, a sporty species that will often hit an artificial bait.

The South Branch of the Potomac starts in Virginia and heads in a northeasterly direction through West Virginia's Eastern Panhandle to join the North Branch and form the Potomac River. Many fishermen rate the South Branch the best smallmouth stream in the state, particularly the "Trough" section between Moorefield and Romney, a 7-mile run through an uninhabited gorge. The South Branch and neighboring Cacapon River are well-suited to float-fishing. A float-trip service is operated on both rivers. Another feature of the South Branch is its ice fishing for suckers in the winter months. Approximately 2,500 fish were caught in one eddy near Petersburg during a single winter season.

Elk is the longest river in the state which has its source and mouth entirely within the state borders, flowing 172 miles from western Pocahontas County to its meeting with the Kanawha River at Charleston, the state capital. The Shawnee Indians called the Elk "Tis-chil-waugh," or river of "plenty fat elk." It is the only river that has all four major species of gamefish found in the state—largemouth and smallmouth bass, muskellunge, and walleye. Largemouth and muskies, as well as spotted bass, can be taken in the eddies, and smallmouth and walleyes in the riffles. Smallmouth are caught less frequently in the Elk than in the Greenbrier or South Branch rivers, but Elk bass generally run bigger. Few walleyes are caught in the Elk except during the months of March and April, and again occasionally in late fall.

A state-record muskellunge, a 43½ pounder, was caught in the Elk at the mouth of Birch River in 1955. Every spring and fall several good muskies are taken from the Elk, an easily accessible stream that follows a major highway (West Virginia 4) from Sutton to Charleston, a distance of 85 miles. More muskellunge are caught on live bait—suckers or large chubs—but the state record was taken on a spinning lure. The Elk cannot be fished thoroughly except by boat.

The placid Little Kanawha, flowing westward from Upshur County to join the Ohio at Parkersburg, is another West Virginia stream that provides roadside musky fishing. Muskies are caught along the river from Burnsville to Grantsville and below, as are smallmouth, white perch, and catfish—sometimes very large catfish. In the spring of 1963, three fishermen hauled a 50-pounder out of the river. Natives along the Little Kanawha claim the fishing has declined in recent years, possibly due to local pollution problems.

WARMWATER IMPOUNDMENTS

There are five reservoirs in the state—Bluestone, Sutton, Cheat, Tygart, and Stony River, although only two of them—Bluestone and Sutton—provide serious fishing. Another reservoir under construction on the Gauley River at Summersville will have a recreation pool of 2,723 acres, dwarfing the others in size.

Bluestone, formed by a dam across New River at Hinton, contains largemouth and smallmouth bass, white bass, crappie, bluegills, and catfish, and some muskies have been caught below the dam as the result of a 1958 stocking of fingerlings in the reservoir. Bluestone has an average summer depth of less than 20 feet, providing better fishing conditions than deeper reservoirs. Smallmouth exceeding 7 pounds and crappie better than 2 pounds have been caught in Bluestone.

The Sutton Reservoir on Elk River in Braxton County, like Bluestone a U. S. Army Corps of Engineers flood-control project, has an average summer depth of about 42 feet. The best fishing there is in early spring, before the water is raised to summer pool stage, and in late fall, during water drawdown. The hot fishing usually occurs in April and October. Smallmouth are the prime attraction at Sutton, but bluegills are plentiful, and the reservoir has been stocked with largemouth and muskies. There are several boat-launching sites on the Sutton Reservoir—at Bee Run Recreation Area near the dam, at Kanawha Run on the Holly River arm, at Wolf Creek on the Centralia side of the reservoir, and at Bakers Run near Centralia on the upper end of the reservoir. There are two docks on the Bluestone Reservoir where boats, motors, and baits may be obtained, and these are available at the Bee Run dock on the Sutton Reservoir.

Other warmwater impoundments in West Virginia include 164-acre Lake Sherwood in Greenbrier County and 100-acre Plum Orchard Lake in Fayette County. Both are stocked with largemouth bass. Sherwood, 2,700 feet above sea level in the scenic Monongahela National Forest, is the largest lake built by the Department of Natural Resources. Free camping facilities are available.

TROUT STREAMS

West Virginia has many good trout streams in its Appalachian highlands, and they are liberally stocked each year with approximately one million trout. Streams and lakes are stocked weekly for a 2-month period, starting with the opening weekend of the season, and some of the larger streams receive a fall stocking prior to the opening of hunting season—a popular innovation.

Virtually all trout fishing in the state is the put-and-take variety, although there is some natural reproduction of brook trout in some tiny mountain streams, and rainbow trout are said to propagate in the headwaters of Turkey Creek in Monroe County.

Among the rainbow trout stocked in West Virginia is a yellow-colored mutation that has attracted nationwide attention. Approximately 40,000 "golden" rainbows were stocked in 1963.

The strain was started in 1955 at Petersburg Trout Hatchery when a yellow-colored fish was found among several thousand rainbow fingerlings. The fish, a female, produced 900 eggs the next year which were fertilized with milt from a normal-colored rainbow male. Nearly 300 of the hatch changed to the golden color at fingerling size, and within a few years the state had a stockable supply of "goldens."

Hundreds of streams are stocked with trout each year, but the three which receive the heaviest fishing pressure are the Cranberry, Williams, and Shavers Fork rivers.

Cranberry is a picture trout stream, forming in the Cranberry Glades of Pocahontas County and flowing westward through Webster and Nicholas counties. The Glades alone make a trip into this area worthwhile. They are located in a high spruce valley where the botanist can find arctic tundra, sphagnum moss, orchids, cranberries, and other plants normally found in more northern life zones. The Glades and upper Cranberry can be reached off West Virginia 39 between Richwood and Mill Point. About 14 miles of Cranberry runs through the "back-country" area of the Monongahela National Forest where vehicle travel is prohibited. Many trout fishermen walk in with backpacks; others ride bicycles or horses. Camping areas are located at the upper and lower gates on Cranberry, but expect to have plenty of company if you're there on the opening weekend of trout season.

Williams, across the mountain from Cranberry, is accessible by car along virtually its entire length, and is fished as heavily as Cranberry. It is stocked from the Webster County line upstream to Black Mountain Run. Both Williams and Cranberry are good fly-fishing streams, with wet flies effective early in the season and dry flies later when the water is lower and clearer.

Shavers Fork River is the longest trout stream in the state, heading in the Cheat Mountain range in Pocahontas County and flowing northward through Randolph County and into the Dry Fork River near Parsons, Tucker County. Several miles of the stream near its headwaters are stocked by taking the trout up the mountain on a railroad handcar. Fishermen going into this area can walk up the railroad track from Cheat Bridge on U. S. 250 near Durbin. The lower portion of the stream, near Elkins, is accessible from U. S. 33.

Other popular trout streams in West Virginia include Seneca Creek, which heads near Spruce Knob, the state's highest mountain; Anthony Creek in Greenbrier County; and Blackwater River in the scenic Canaan Valley of Tucker County.

TROUT IMPOUNDMENTS

Impoundments have become an important part of the trout-fishing picture in West Virginia and have made trout fishing a family recreation. Impoundments operated by the Department of Natural Resources include lakes at Seneca and Coopers Rock State Forests in Pocahontas and Monongalia Counties, respectively; at French Creek Game Farm Pond in Upshur County; at Teter Creek Lake in Randolph County; at Edwards Run Pond in Hampshire County; and at Warden Lake in Hardy County.

National Forest trout impoundments include Spruce Knob Lake in Randolph County; Summit Lake in Greenbrier County; and Trout Pond in Hardy County. The latter is the state's only natural lake. —S.J.

WET FLY A sparsely dressed artificial fly which is somewhat flat in appearance. A wet fly is fished under the surface, and generally imitates a submerged insect. An ideal wet fly has "good entry" and sinks immediately upon contact with the water. Wet flies are used for a variety of freshwater species, but they are principally designed for trout and salmon; patterns used for the latter group are often large and fanciful rather than imitative. *See also Wet-Fly-Fishing* under Fly Fishing, *Wet-Fly-Fishing* under Atlantic Salmon, *How to Tie a Wet Fly* under Fly-Tying

WHALEBONE WHALE *See* Whales

WHALES Order Cetacea Whales belong to an order of mammals and are warm-blooded, possess a four-chambered heart (in contrast to a fish's two chambers), have large elastic lungs, and nurse their young. Like porpoises (*which see*) their streamlined bodies superficially resemble those of fishes.

Although fishes have always lived in the water, whales have secondarily evolved from land mammals, and their fishlike appearance has resulted, through evolution, from their aquatic ways of life. While fishes have gills and external gill openings, whales use lungs to breathe, and the nostrils are modified into a single or double blowhole which is connected by a passage to the lungs. The opening is closed by a series of valves when the animal is submerged, and whales can breathe with a large amount of the head submerged with only the blowhole in contact with the surface. The geyserlike stream of water spouted by whales is finely divided water droplets and oil which are associated with the functions of breathing and diving.

Most mammals possess hair, but in whales only a few bristles may be present on the head and snout, if at all. Beneath the skin is a thick layer of fatty blubber, important in insulating these warmblooded creatures against the cold.

The tail of fishes is vertical, but the flukes of whales are fleshy, horizontal extensions. A fleshy fin is usually present on the back of a whale and is triangular or sickle-shaped and somewhat resembles the dorsal fin of fishes. The forelimbs or flippers of whales resemble the pectoral fins of fishes, but the flippers contain all the bones found in the arms of land mammals, while the pectoral fins of fishes are merely simple, supporting rays.

Like other advanced mammals, whales bring forth living young which suckle. The mother has two teats in pocketlike grooves on the underside. The young whales can suckle without taking in water. Unlike land mammals, females can force milk out of mammary gland reservoirs to aid feeding.

SUBORDERS

Whales are divided into two suborders, the toothed whales and the whalebone whales. The toothed whales have teeth either in both jaws or in the lower jaw only. Unlike teeth of other mammals, which may be divided into different types, such as canines, molars, and cuspids, all whale teeth are conical, and there may be 1–50 teeth. In the beaked whales, the pair of teeth in the lower jaw of the female is usually largely covered by the gums. Toothed whales have a single blowhole and have a comparatively smaller mouth.

The sperm whales are well-known and have a large, squarish head which projects far past the lower jaw, which has functional teeth. Sperm whales grow to 60 feet and are 12–14 feet at birth. They are found throughout the world, in warm-and coldwater alike, but prefer warmer areas. They feed principally on large squids, but fishes are eaten as well. A related species is the pigmy sperm whale, which reaches 14 feet. Its head is less square than that of the sperm whale, and it has a small dorsal "fin" which the sperm whale lacks. Porpoises (*which see*), dolphins, narwhals, beaked whales, and killer whales also belong to this suborder.

Sperm Whale

The whalebone whales lack teeth in both jaws but possess whalebone or baleen in the upper jaw. Baleen is a series of five plates suspended from the roof of the mouth and used for filtering minute plankton organisms.

Small, planktonic, shrimplike animals, called "krill," are the principal food of whalebone whales, and are filtered through the baleen and ingested. Small fishes, such as herrings, are also eaten. Areas of heavy plankton concentration, such as regions of upwelling or areas of mixing of currents (*see* Currents), often support large whale populations which are the target of commercial whalers.

Whalebone whales are huge, and the blue whale, which is the largest of all living organisms, may reach 100 feet and a weight of well over 100 tons, being over 24 feet long at birth. It is found worldwide, and has been sought for commercially since about the middle of the eighteenth century. Other commercially important whalebone whales include the Greenland right whale, which reaches 60 feet, the black right whale, the rorqual, and the sei whale.

ECONOMIC VALUE

Whales are caught for their oil, which has been used for lamps, soap, leather preparation, paint manufacture, and lubrication. The meat is sometimes used for meal for cattle and poultry. Spermwhale teeth and the carvings made from them (scrimshaw) are popular souvenirs, and ambergris, derived from the stomachs of sperm whales, is used as a perfume base which, until its synthesis, brought a high market price. Whalebone is used for stuffing, brushes, and artificial feathers. Overfishing and lack of conservation practices have seriously depleted the world's whale stocks, but, hopefully, international conservation agreements will reduce further depletion.   —D.dS.

WHALE SHARK *Rhincodon typus* Exceeded in size only by some whales, this species is easily recognized by the terminal position of the mouth, the wide gill openings, and the dark gray to brown background, with white or yellow spots separated by thin, whitish crossbars. It is reported to reach over 70 feet long, and a 40-foot fish was estimated to be 13½ tons. Distributed throughout the tropical waters of the world, it is a sluggish, harmless shark, which is usually seen basking near the surface. Adults feed on small fishes and plankton with their specialized, comblike gillrakers, and they have been seen to stand vertically in the water to feed on schools of small fish. Small whale sharks eat small planktonic plants and animals and larval fishes. The young are hatched from egg capsules which are over 2 feet long.   —D.dS.

WHIP FINISH A type of knot used to finish off the head of a fly or the windings on a rod. It is formed by winding several turns over the end of the thread and pulling the end back through. *See also* Fly-tying

WHIRLING DISEASE *See* Diseases and Parasites

WHISTLING BUOY A buoy fitted with a whistle actuated by the movement of waves.

WHITEBAIT A seafood resembling a plate of fried minnows. Whitebait is considered a gourmet dish largely because of its scarcity. Correctly made, it requires five or six species of saltwater fish in the immature stage. Whitebait had its origin in England about 1780. The man credited with its invention was a Thames fisherman named Robert Cannon. In subsequent years, his heirs assumed the purveying of whitebait and during the ten-year reign of King George IV, they supplied the royal household every day of the season (from February through August). The esteem in which whitebait was once held is reflected in the annual Ministerial Whitebait Dinner which some observers believe helped formulate the British Constitution. Greenwich, Blackheath, Lovegrove, and Quartermain were great whitebait centers according to Victorian epicures. The dish consisted of very tiny herring, sand eels, smelts, sticklebacks, and pipefish being rolled whole in fine flour and deepfried to a crisp succulence. In America today young sardines, herring, anchovies, silversides, and Pacific surf smelts are all marketed as whitebait.   —A.J.McC.

WHITEBAIT SMELT *Allosmerus elongatus* This smelt (*which see*) is almost colorless, with a pale green cast and a silvery, very shiny band on the side. There is a single, large canine tooth on the middle of the vomer. It is normally found from the Straits of Juan de Fuca to San Francisco; a single specimen is recorded from southern California. Length to 9 inches.

COMMERCIAL VALUE

Although of minor commercial importance, it forms the major part of the whitebait fishery. Used as bait by commercial and sport fishermen, it is sometimes taken in the surf by sportsmen with small nets in the spring and summer. *See also* Smelt, Whitebait   —J.R.

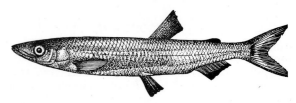

Whitebait Smelt

WHITE BASS *Morone chrysops* The white bass is a member of the Percichthyidae or temperate bass family, which includes the yellow bass, striped bass, and white perch. The eagerness of a white bass to bite, its schooling habits, and its fine flesh have caused it to gain increasing favor among the nation's anglers in the past twenty-five years. This popularity has led to a rapid increase in its distribution. At the turn of the century it was found scattered from the Great Lakes south to Arkansas, Kansas, and Missouri, and from the western slope of the Allegheny Mountains west to the Mississippi River system. Continual transplanting has consolidated its distribution and also has extended its range to the states along the Missouri River and most of the Southern and the Southwestern states. The white bass is found in large streams and rivers, but seems to prefer large lakes with water that is relatively clear. Rarely will the species maintain a population in a lake of less than three hundred acres. Extensive construction of reservoirs, especially in the South and Southwest, has greatly favored the white bass. In addition to expansive waters, habitat preferences include extensive areas of waters deeper than 10 feet, and gravel or rubble on which to spawn.

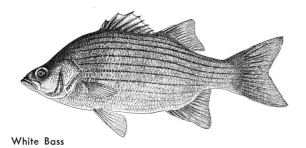

White Bass

The white bass has a moderately compressed body, forked tail, two separate dorsal fins, teeth on the base of the tongue, spines on the first dorsal fin, and three spines on the anal fin. It is a "clean-cut" looking fish of silvery color, tinged with yellow below. About 10 narrow, dark lines or stripes run the length of the body, with 5 of these stripes lying above the lateral line. The mouth is typically basslike, with the lower jaw projecting beyond the upper jaw. To distinguish it from the yellow bass, note the silvery color, unbroken stripes, protruding lower jaw, 11–12 soft anal-fin rays, and teeth on the base of the tongue. The separated dorsal fins and the stripes along the sides will serve adequately to distinguish it from all members of the sunfish family.

The usual size of white bass caught by anglers runs ½–2 pounds. A 3–4 pounder is a trophy, and anything over that approaches record size. Maximum size attained is about 6 pounds.

LIFE HISTORY

White bass spawn from late April to early June, depending on the latitude. The female may deposit from about 25,000–1,000,000 eggs. Fertilized by a male as it leaves the female, the egg settles to a gravel- or rock-strewn bottom in 6–7 feet of water. Favorable conditions, including current or wave action and steady temperatures (usually 58°–64°F.), will allow the egg to hatch in 2–3 days. However, conditions must be nearly perfect; this

is attested to by the fact that white bass usually have successful reproduction only once in 3–4 years. These successful years produce an abundance of the species, while in poor years only a few, if any, will survive. After hatching, the minute fry will join its kind in massive schools seeking food and protection. The survivors at this stage represent only a small percentage of the eggs which were spawned. Food in the form of minute zooplankton is taken at first, and as the weeks pass larger crustaceans and insects are eaten. Small fish, if available, also contribute heavily to the diet later in the summer. The white bass are not generally cannibalistic, however, and such species as perch, bluegills, crappies, and gizzard shad are most apt to be the victims of their hunger.

At summer's end the white bass will measure about 5 inches in Northern waters and 7½ inches in Southern waters. Growth for the year will terminate in September or October, when water temperatures drop below 55°–60°F. From then until the water warms again the following spring, only enough food will be taken to maintain a slow rate of metabolism.

It is difficult to establish the odds for survival from time of spawning to the end of the first year of life, but placing them at 1 in 25,000 is probably close to being accurate. In subsequent years the odds are considerably better, but even then no more than 20–40 percent can be expected to survive each year.

After the age of one, white bass continue to travel in large compact schools. They often retire to deeper waters during the day and invade the shallows at twilight. When feeding on small fish they often present a startling and spectacular sight. Their schools are so compact and their feeding so voracious that they sometimes cause the smaller fish to break the surface or swim up on shore. Small fish, usually of the species mentioned earlier, comprise the bulk of their food, supplemented primarily by insects and crustaceans. However, in the absence of a plentiful supply of fish, they will fare well on the smaller forms of life.

The life expectancy of a white bass is short. Few of them live more than 3–4 years in the South or 4–5 years in the North. Even in the North maximum age is 7–9 years, while in the South it is 6–7 years. Adulthood usually is attained during the third year of life but may be delayed a year in Northern waters or where growth conditions are poor. Average length attained in the North is about 5½, 10, 13, 14, 15, and 15½ inches at ages 1–6 respectively. In the South comparable lengths are about 7½, 12, 14½, 16, 17, and 18 inches.

White bass will weigh ½ pound at 10½ inches, 1 pound at 13 inches, 2 pounds at 16 inches, and 3 pounds at 17½ inches.

ANGLING VALUE

Although often disdained by anglers used to an abundance of northern pike, walleye, and large- or smallmouth bass, the white bass is earning ever-increasing esteem among the nation's fishermen. Anglers who seek and locate a school of feeding white bass can ask for no faster or sportier action, especially when using light tackle. Fishing for the species is more apt to run hot and cold than for other species, however. This is true not only from day to day but from year to year. The day-to-day luck is governed by the species' schooling and feeding habits, while the year-to-year luck is dependent upon reproductive success in the particular lake. The boom or bust type of reproduction leads to an abundant year class which will dominate the population for 2–3 years. When this age class disappears, it may take a year or two for the next strong year class to attain a size desirable to the angler. But these factors are both good and bad from the angler's point of view. And the fact that intensive efforts have been made in the past thirty years to increase the distribution of the species indicates that fishermen feel that the good points far outweigh the bad ones.

Maximum angling value of the species is found in the Southern and Southwestern states. For example, in recent years in Oklahoma the white bass has contributed about 2,500,000 pounds to the annual catch by anglers, which is about one-fifth of the total catch of all species. Liberal limits and seasons are offered by most of the states since it is next to impossible to overharvest white bass by angling.

Tips to white bass anglers should include: (1) use of light tackle for maximum enjoyment; (2) use of flies, spinners, small plugs, or minnows for bait; and (3) location of feeding schools which usually occur toward evening in shallow areas.

COMMERCIAL VALUE

Commercial fishing for white bass is limited primarily to some of the largest Northern waters, especially Lake Erie. Medium to good prices are brought at the fish markets and in restaurants. The high reproductive potential and short life expectancy of the species make it a suitable object for commercial fishing, since it can stand heavy harvest without endangering future abundance.

—J.T.S.

WHITEBONE PORGY *Calamus leucosteus* This probably is the most frequently encountered member of this large (some dozen species in all) and wide-ranging genus in the Southeastern United States. It is found in the Atlantic waters off the Carolinas, Georgia, and Florida, and also in the eastern Gulf of Mexico. Other members of the genus range from New England to the central Atlantic coast of South America. In the West Indies in particular, species of the genus *Calamus* are a primary food fish for human consumption, some species reaching nearly 3 feet. *C. leucosteus* may reach about 18 inches.

Members of this genus, including the whitebone porgy, have conical teeth in the front of the mouth, rather than incisors. The posterior nostril is slitlike.

The color of the whitebone porgy is silvery, with irregular, dark markings of varying intensity on the side of the body, more like splotches than spots. There may be a tendency for the side to bear darkish crossbars. There is no distinct axillary spot.

Most species of the genus *Calamus* occur in the western Atlantic, but the genus also is represented in the eastern Pacific on the mainland shores of southern North America, Central America, and northern South America, and in the Galápagos Islands.

LIFE HISTORY

Like other American sparids, *C. leucosteus* apparently spawns offshore in the late fall or winter.

Food habits of this species are poorly known, but inasmuch as they readily take a hook, it is presumed that they primarily are carnivorous. They provide considerable sport as a bottom dweller in places where such fishing is pursued.

—D.K.C.

WHITE CATFISH *Ictalurus catus* A bluish and silvery catfish, with a moderately forked tail. The white catfish has 19–23 rays in the anal fin. Lacking distinct spots, this catfish may give a bicolor appearance as there may be a sharp demarcation line between the darker color of lower sides and whitish ventral areas. Some specimens appear mottled with colors ranging from milky-gray to dark blue.

White Catfish

The natural distribution of the white catfish extends from the Chesapeake Bay region in coastal streams southward to Texas. It has been introduced widely on the West Coast and into the Northeast.

The white catfish, in its native range, inhabits the fresh- and slightly brackish water of streams, ponds, and bayous. Although it is tolerant of rather swiftly flowing streams, it prefers a more sluggish current than does the channel catfish. It appears to occupy a habitat rather intermediate between that of the channel cat and the bullheads. The white catfish is somewhat migratory in its spawning habit, although it is less so than the channel catfish. As with other members of its family, it is a nest-builder, and the male guards the young for some time after they hatch.

An omnivorous feeder, the white catfish subsists on nearly all aquatic forms, including fish and aquatic insects. Smaller than the channel catfish, this species runs 10–18 inches long and seldom exceeds 3 pounds.

ANGLING VALUE

An excellent food fish, the white catfish is prized for its firm, white flesh. This catfish is popular with "fish-for-pay" private-lake operators due to its desirable size and habit of biting freely. In some areas of the Northeast where the white catfish has been introduced, it has replaced the brown bullhead in popularity. This is due to its larger size, less nocturnal habits, and ability to withstand the predations of the largemouth bass. The white cat is easily taken on live bait.

—R.A.J.

WHITE CRAPPIE *Pomoxis annularis* A popular freshwater panfish in the United States, it may grow to a fairly large size in suitable environments. The white crappie is the only member of the sunfish family having 6 spines in the dorsal fin and 6 spines in the anal fin. This is one method of distinguishing it from the related black crappie which has 7–8 dorsal spines. Also, the spots on the sides of the white crappie are arranged into 7–9 vertical bars, while those of the black crappie are scattered. The sides of the white crappie are silvery-olive, shading into an olive-green on the back. The paired fins are plain while the median fins are mottled. The white is also more elongate, and the black has a high, arched back in comparison. Both fish range from silvery to yellowish, but while the white has 8–9 dark, vertical bands on its side, the black crappie has irregular, dark mottlings that suggest an old calico print. For this reason it is sometimes called calico bass. Because both have tender mouths, they are also called papermouths, and because the male guards the nest at spawning time, they are also called bachelor perch. Although the usual white crappie is 6–12 inches in length and weighs less than 1 pound, 2–3 pound fish are not uncommon, and individuals of over 5 pounds have been recorded.

The white crappie was originally distributed from Nebraska eastward to Lake Ontario, and southward through the Ohio and Mississippi rivers to Texas and Alabama, and northward from there along the coastal plain to North Carolina. It prefers silty rivers and lakes to clearwater and is common in Southern impoundments. The original habitat of the black crappie was from southern Canada south through the Great Lakes and Mississippi River to Texas and northern Florida. The black prefers clear, weedy lakes and rivers, but both species occur together frequently, as they have been widely transplanted from East to West. The first introduction of crappies to Western waters was made in Lake Cuyamaca in southern California, back in 1891. These fish were later planted in other parts of the state, but the white crappie only survived in the San Diego area and in the Colorado River drainage. The white crappie is not a bottom dweller and consequently can be found over both hard or soft bottom. It can tolerate more turbidity than the black crappie and does not need the cool clearwaters required by the latter species.

When small, this crappie feeds on aquatic insects and plankton, but when it grows larger, the major portion of its diet is fish.

LIFE HISTORY

Crappies are noticeably cyclic in their populations. They may be caught readily for 2–3 seasons, then practically disappear for the same length of time. There are probably several reasons for this fluctuation in abundance, but one factor advanced is that abundance is affected by a dominant year class. In a good year, when spawning and food conditions are right, the crappies will produce a large brood which survives. This is known as a dominant brood, and in subsequent years the dominant brood devours its own young as well as other fish. This periodic elimination of young continues until the original dominant is so reduced in number that the surviving members can no longer remove all the young spawned during that period. Then the cycle repeats. During part of the cycle the great majority of fish may be of catchable size, and this is followed by a period in which only 1–2 percent of the crappies are large fish. As with all pan species, overcrowding also affects the size of fish caught. Usually, in the early history of a lake, the crappies grow very large; 2–4 pounds is not uncommon, and unless they are cropped off, they become so dense that subsequent young gradually settle into a slower rate of growth. The crappie is short-lived, seldom reaching the age of 6.

The spawning habits of the white crappie are typical of the nest-building sunfish, with the exception that the nests are in deeper water, sometimes up to 8 feet deep. The females produce from about 2,900–14,800 eggs. It is a very prolific fish and tends to stunt because of overpopulation more quickly than black crappie. Because of its stunting characteristics in some environments, growth is quite variable. It will grow 1–4½ inches the first year, 2–9 inches the second year, and 6-year-old fish may be 6–12 inches long. Their food consists of all kinds of fish, mollusks, shrimp, plankton, crayfish, and insects. Fish, especially gizzard shad, form well over 50 percent of their diet in the South, although a larger amount of insects is eaten in northerly areas such as Iowa, Illinois, and Wisconsin.

ANGLING METHODS

The white crappie is one of the principal species taken in the early spring and in some areas furnishes the major fisheries in large impoundments and natural lakes. Slow trolling with small minnows in water up to 15 feet deep is one of the favorite methods of capturing these fish in early spring. The fly-fisherman can do best by fishing about an hour before sunset to dark. Spinners in com-

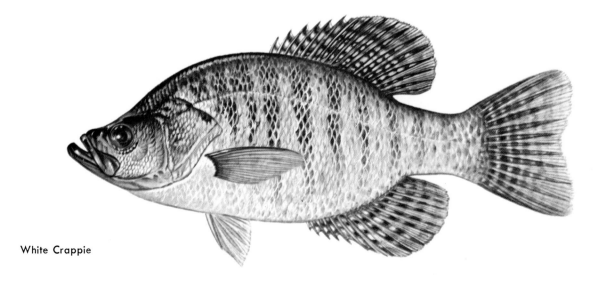

White Crappie

bination with flies, minnows, or other attractors are good baits. Streamers, wet flies, dry flies, and popping bugs can be effective.

The need for protective cover is instinctive in the crappie. Fallen trees, cut banks, pad beds, and even a few stalks of reeds give the crappie a place to hide. One of the most productive springtime methods on big Southern creeks is slow trolling the "buckbrush." This consists of throttling the outboard down until it just purrs and pushing along the creek edge trolling live minnows with two or more cane poles. Fish which are hiding under the banks are attracted to the moving baits. But the ideal home to a crappie is a pile of sunken brush, and, as anglers discovered long ago, if their lake doesn't have one, the best thing is to go out and build one. Just one man-made brush pile in Lake Chautauqua, Illinois, for instance (10 feet wide and 100 feet long), produced over 20,000 crappies in a single season.

In early summer, as a lake level drops and the marginal weed beds or bank brush can no longer hide minnows, the crappies move out to deepwater. Knowing where they went is obviously a great advantage, so specialists anchor large brush mats 50–100 yards from shore. The brush attracts myriads of minnows and fry, and the crappies naturally congregate with them. These mats consist of small trees, limbs, logs, or brush wired together and sunk on the lake bottom with stones or scrap metal. A good mat will cover several hundred square feet and be at least 4–5 feet high. Willow is favored in the Midwest because it will eventually root in the pond bottom. In storage reservoirs where farm lands have been flooded, you can usually find natural crappie "beds," and there's no need to build them.

Crappies will take about every kind of artificial lure—plugs, bass bugs, spoons, streamer flies, jigs, dry flies, and spinners of all sizes, but none of these baits is effective all the time. The only general rules that might be made are that speckled perch are not usually fond of surface lures, they are very susceptible to trolled lures, and any lure you use should be retrieved slowly but with plenty of action and close to the bottom. When crappies are schooling in Southern creeks, it is often possible to catch them on No. 8 and No. 10 bucktails. The flies can be worked along the bank brush without getting hung. But when the fish are out in the lake over a brush heap, you have to work straight down on them with a midget jig or live minnow. If you don't know where the schools are located, slow trolling with a thumbnail-sized spinner and a strip of pork rind will find them. The most consistent lure. in Northern waters has been a fly-and-spinner combination, preferably a nickel spinner with a white or red fly. Hairwing wet flies are also useful, especially patterns with flared wings like the Badger Spider made famous on Gerber Reservoir in Oregon. There are dozens of small wobblers and spinners designed for the spinning rod that will take fish some of the time, but even those are not infallible. *See also* Black Crappie, Panfish —A.J.McC.

WHITEFIN SHINER *Notropis niveus* A small minnow, it seldom exceeds 2½ inches in total length. The geographical range of the whitefin shiner is from southern Virginia southward to South Carolina in streams east of the Appalachian Mountains. The body of this minnow is regularly fusiform with the dorsal region more arched than the ventral. The distinguishing characteristics of the

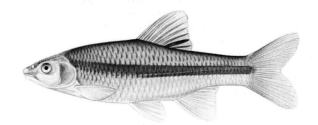

Whitefin Shiner

whitefin shiner are a body depth of 0.2 the total standard length; a conical-shaped head, with its length contained 4.5 times in the total body length; obtuse muzzle, with the mouth nearly terminal and a non-fleshy snout; an eye equal to the snout length, contained 3–3.5 times in the total length of the head; 35–39 scales in the lateral line with the number of scales preceeding the dorsal fin numbering 15 or 16; a decurved lateral line; a dorsal and anal ray count of 8 and 8 or 9, respectively; slightly hooked pharyngeal teeth in two rows 1,4–4,1 with grinding surfaces. The color of this small minnow is pale, with a narrow, bluish, lateral band ending in a faint spot on the caudal base. There is an interradial pigmented spot located slightly anterior to the sixth principal ray on the dorsal fin. The dorsal and caudal fins are creamy to yellow in color, and the tips of the fins, as well as the entire anal fin, are charged with a milky-white pigment.

LIFE HISTORY

The whitefin shiner is usually found in isolated populations rather than being distributed throughout a watershed. This species prefers a pH range of 6.2–6.9. It is usually found in streams having a sand, gravel, or muck bottom. It feeds primarily on zooplankton and small aquatic insects. Very little life history data is known about this species.

The whitetail shiner serves as forage for the largemouth bass, bluegill, redbreast sunfish, green sunfish, warmouth, and black crappie. —D.E.L.

WHITEFISH *See* Lake Whitefish, Mountain Whitefish, Round Whitefish

WHITE GRUNT *Haemulon plumieri* This is probably the most common species of grunt. Its range is also wider than that of the others and extends from Chesapeake Bay southward to Brazil. Mature adults average about 10 inches in total length, but they may grow larger. The white grunt is distinguished from all the others by the color pattern, which consists of numerous blue and yellow stripes on the sides of the head and body. The inside of the mouth is red. The white grunt has 12 dorsal spines; 15–17 dorsal rays, usually 16; 8–9 anal rays, usually 9;

White Grunt

and 17 pectoral rays. Pored lateral-line scales 48 to 51, usually 50–51; 21–27 gillrakers, usually 25. Its pectoral fins are not scaled.

The white grunt appears to be more tolerant of colder (extratropical) waters than the others, with the exception of the tomtate (*which see*). A bottom feeder, it is abundant in shallow water from the shore to the outer reefs.

ANGLING VALUE

This species is easy to catch on natural bait, such as cut mullet, cut pilchard, and dead shrimp. It fights well on very light tackle. The white grunt is excellent eating. A panfish much appreciated in the Florida Keys, it is a commercial fish of importance in the Caribbean area, where it is nearly always seen in the markets.   —L.R.

WHITE MARGATE *Haemulon album*   This is the largest of the grunts. Mature adults average 2 feet in total length, and larger individuals are not uncommon. In addition to the Florida Keys and the Bahamas, the range of this

White Margate

species extends southward throughout the West Indies to Brazil. The margate is distinguished from other grunts by the combination of characters comprising the number of pectoral rays, anal rays, and gillrakers, in addition to its larger size. It is plain colored or with dark brown stripes. The margate has 12 dorsal spines; 16–17 dorsal rays, rarely 17; 7–8 anal rays, usually 8; and 18–19 pectoral rays. Pored lateral-line scales 49–52. Its pectoral fins are naked.

This grunt is apparently not common in Florida where it prefers clearwater about offshore reefs. It is much more abundant in the Bahamas where it occurs in inshore waters as well as the outer reefs. It feeds on or near the bottom.

ANGLING VALUE

Large individuals put up a very good fight on light tackle, especially in deepwater. Like other grunts, it may be taken on cut bait. It is good eating, and large specimens may be filleted or baked whole. It is a market fish of importance in the Bahamas and the West Indies.

—L.R.

WHITE MARLIN *Tetrapturus albidus*   A marine species confined to the Atlantic Ocean, this game fish is very popular with American anglers. The white marlin differs from all other members of the family in that the tips of the dorsal and anal fins are rounded, rather than sharply pointed. The pectoral fin is long, and rounded at its tip. Its body is slender, the sides rather flat, and the lateral line is single and fairly prominent. The vent is placed close to the base of the anal fin. The spear is moderately long, the upper jaw being noticeably longer than (about twice as long as) the lower jaw. The anterior peak of the dorsal fin is as high as or higher than the greatest depth of the body, while the posterior part of the dorsal fin is much lower.

This species commonly shows more green than do other marlins. The upper part of the body is brilliant greenish blue, which changes abruptly to silvery white at about the lateral line. The belly is white. Along the sides of the body are a varying number of light blue or lavender vertical bars, which usually fade out and disappear soon after death. The dorsal fin is bright blue, usually spotted or blotched with black or purple, and with white marks on the basal part of the fin. The anal fin may be similarly marked. All fin rays are dark. The pectoral fins are long, about one-fifth the length of the body, and their tips are rounded.

The white marlin does not reach great size, although it is larger than the spearfishes. The maximum recorded weight for white marlin taken on rod and reel is 161 pounds, but the usual weight for fish taken in this manner runs 50–60 pounds.

HABITS

Spawning habits of the white marlin are poorly known, nor have its free-floating eggs been identified. Spent fish are often taken off Ocean City, Maryland, in July and August, suggesting that these fish probably spawn in late spring or early summer.

White Marlin, 120-pound Female, La Guiara, Venezuela

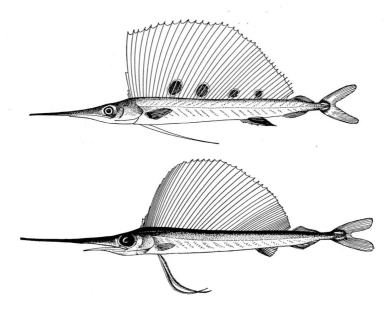

Postlarval sailfish (*bottom*) and white marlin are separated by relative bill length and dorsal fin spots

A number of white marlin have been tagged by anglers at various fishing centers along the east coast of the United States, but as yet the results are inconclusive. However, the times at which concentrations of fish occur in places like Ocean City, Maryland, and Montauk Point, New York, suggest that the fish make coast-wise migrations each year, moving north in the spring and south in the fall. These may well be post-spawning migrations, or equally well they may merely be the result of these large, carnivorous fish following their food northward and remaining in areas where plenty of food is available. Or perhaps a combination of both factors is responsible. At any rate, several thousand fish are taken each year at such places as Ocean City, Maryland, the majority of them being released.

Like all the other istiophorids, the white marlin is mainly piscivorous in its diet. Its favorite foods along the middle Atlantic coast are the round herring, *Etrumeus sadina*, and squid, *Loligo pealei*, but it will also eat anything it can capture, such as anchovies and jacks.

The white marlin has been found all the way from Nova Scotia in the north to Brazil in the south. The normal northward limit to the range, however, seems to be south of Cape Cod, and the Nova Scotian records probably represent strays that wandered further to the north in unusually warm summers. The species ranges eastward in the South Atlantic to St. Helena Island, and has been taken at Walvis Bay and off Capetown, South Africa. In the North Atlantic, white marlin have been found in the Azores, Madeira, along the coasts of France and Portugal, and in the Mediterranean Sea.

ANGLING VALUE

Most white marlin are taken by angling from power boats. They will strike at almost any kind of a lure, including spoons, feathers, whole fish, and strip baits.

White marlin strike hard and run fast with repetitive jumps. They average somewhat larger than the Atlantic sailfish in size and are regarded as a stronger gamefish. This billfish is considered by many veteran anglers as the top light tackle offshore quarry. One of the largest concentrations of whites in the western Atlantic occurs each September off the coast of Venezuela (*which see*). Here thirty-five strikes per boat per day is not unusual. The fish are located by the activity of birds and whales working in the bait schools. These fishing grounds are close to the port of La Guiara.

—J.E.M.

The white marlin is a spectacular gamefish when it is caught on suitable light tackle

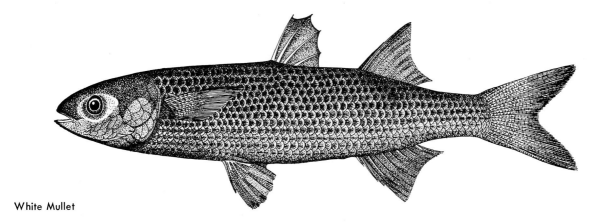

White Mullet

WHITE MULLET *Mugil curema* The white or silver mullet is known on the Atlantic Coast from Cape Cod to South America and on the Pacific Coast from about Chile to the Gulf of California. Along the Atlantic Coast of the United States it is caught in commercially significant quantities only in Florida, where it constitutes about 5 percent of the total mullet landings. Two other mullets, *M. trichodon* (fantail mullet) and *M. gaimardiana* (redeye mullet) are combined with *M. curema* in the fishery statistics; they, however, only contribute a very small percentage of the total white mullet landings.

LIFE HISTORY

In contrast with the striped mullet, which spawn during late fall or winter when water temperatures are falling, the white mullet begins spawning in early spring when water temperatures are rising over the Continental Shelf. The young of this mullet (and the other mullets) spend the first several weeks of their lives in the open ocean. At a length of about ¾–1 inch the larvae move inshore where they thrive in estuarine habitats until they have reached lengths of up to 5 inches. These juveniles apparently move from the estuary areas to the outer beaches. In the fall they school and migrate south.

ANGLING VALUE

After their first year, white mullet are seldom caught north of Florida.

WHITE PERCH *Morone americana* A popular panfish which is caught in fresh-, brackish, and saltwater, it does not resemble the yellow perch (*which see*). The white perch is a member of the Percichthyidae, and in small sizes there is a general similarity between it and the striped bass. But the perch is about 2½–3 times as long as it is deep (not counting the tail) and is more flattened, which gives it a chunky appearance. There is no space between its two dorsal fins, although they are separated by a notch. The white perch has about 48 rows of scales between the gill cover and the base of its tail, whereas there are 60 or more in the striped bass. The first dorsal fin of the white perch has 9 spines and the second dorsal fin has 1 spine and 12 rays. The anal fin originates under the second dorsal, and the ventrals, which are armed with one stout spine on the forward margin, are located slightly behind the pectorals.

The most apparent difference between the two species is coloration; when very small a white perch may have pale, longitudinal stripes similar to the striped bass, but ordinarily, and at the size perch are usually caught, no stripes are present. Its back or dorsal surface varies from olive to a dark blackish-green, shading to a paler silvery-green on the sides and a silvery-white on the belly. White perch taken in saltwater or brackish-water ponds are apt to be lighter in color.

LIFE HISTORY

The average white perch is 8–10 inches long and weighs 1 pound or less. In the more fertile New England ponds fish up to 15 inches in length weighing about 2 pounds are not uncommon. Perch of over 2½ pounds are rare, although 3 pounders are occasionally reported. But the fish is active for its size, and wherever it occurs the white perch is numerically abundant. Catches of 50–60 in an afternoon are not unique. Perch populations have cycles, but their abundance cannot be changed by angling. The annual production from a single pair of large white perch can more than replace all that are caught by fishermen. State of Maine fishery personnel have literally netted tons of perch from small lakes year after year without affecting the standing crop. This rabbitlike characteristic can create problems when a population is on the upswing, resulting in many small and stunted fish. Ironically, the white perch is a careless spawner. The schools migrate into tributary streams, and without pairing off, the females release thousands of tiny eggs (about 150,000 in the case of a 1-pound fish) which adhere to anything they touch, and immediately afterward the males release millions of sperm cells. This haphazard fertility rite is one of the most prolific nature has devised because the ratio of hatched eggs is enormous in comparison to other fishes. The only critical factor is a temperature change of 4–5°F.; however, the fry ordinarily hatch within a few days instead of within the fifty-odd days it might require to produce a trout, for example. Furthermore, white perch have a long life span. Fish of 12 years old are common, and Maine has recorded at least one in its seventeenth year. So everything works in favor of the white perch, including their sometimes whimsical attitude toward the angler.

White perch inhabit salt-, brackish, and freshwater from Nova Scotia to North Carolina. They occur inland as far as the Great Lakes. Actually, their range has increased in recent years due to environmental changes made by man. The seaward distribution of the white

White Perch, 10-inch Male,
West Grand Lake, Maine

perch is more restricted than that of the striped bass; although they are caught in pure saltwater at various locations sometimes as deep as 20 fathoms, they are much more plentiful in ponds connected to the sea and in brackish bays and estuaries. Even though schools of perch in saltwater wander about in the search of food, they are resident populations in any area they inhabit. During the winter the fish congregate in the deeper parts of bays and creeks where they either hibernate or endure the cold weather in a dormant state. In the spring and early summer the saltwater perch which migrate into rivers from Massachusetts south to Chesapeake Bay constitute an important sport fishery. However, the strictly landlocked perch populations are becoming more numerous.

FEEDING HABITS

The state of Maine did a comprehensive study on the feeding habits of white perch, and their findings more or less parallel what has been learned about the species elsewhere in its range.

The white perch, like most fish, will eat whatever food is available in large quantities, and their diet varies according to the season. For example, in winter and early spring the fish grub larvae out of the pond bottoms (mostly midge). As the weather warms and large burrowing mayflies emerge from the mud, they gorge on nymphs. During the summer months crustaceans and waterfleas become abundant, as do small fish of many kinds; so the perch schools change their diet once again. By fall, any young fish present in most lakes are now too large for the perch to eat; so they concentrate on insects and crustaceans once more. White perch seldom venture into shallow water where minnows would be abundant. But the pattern of their feeding usually consists of the schools' remaining in water that is comparatively deep by day and moving close to shore at sundown. In marine habitats white perch forage on small fish of all kinds, as well as squid, crabs, and shrimp. Here they bite freely on any natural bait and are readily caught with spinning lures or streamer flies.

ANGLING TECHNIQUES

The standard technique of catching white perch is first to locate a school. Perch grounds can be identified by asking a local resident, looking for a collection of boats, or the hit-and-miss method of trying various locations. However, it's fun prospecting, and you can begin by checking areas which are 15–30 feet deep with a firm mud bottom (where burrowing mayflies and midge larvae are most abundant). Drop anchor; then lower a worm or minnow to the bottom. If you don't get a nibble within a few minutes, then raise the bait 4–5 feet higher until you've checked all levels. Sometimes the perch will be very close to the surface over deepwater. If this location doesn't produce after a reasonable trial, move to a new spot 50–100 yards away, and repeat the procedure. Once you find a school the action will be fast. However, it can also stop abruptly as the school wanders off to another area. You can also troll with a small spinner and worm until the fish are located; then drop anchor and still-fish. If it's a windy day, just let the boat drift as you work the spinner close to the mud. In the evening, a trolled streamer fly is often productive, as are small wet flies with or without spinners attached. On rare occasions, a jig will excite white perch, but this probably happens when a school is particularly dense and ravenous. A spinner, however, is invariably effective, but you don't want to use a blade more than 1 inch long. Regardless of its shape, it must be thin enough to spin at the slightest pull. With a fly rod or spinning rod, this should be cast and left to sink to the bottom, then it should be moved very gently to surface in slow, short strokes.

FLY-FISHING FOR WHITE PERCH

The pinnacle of perch fishing usually occurs in the evening when the fish come to the surface to feed on insects. White perch will hit a small bass bug now and then and at times you can catch them with very small poppers from No. 8–10. But nymphs and dry flies which represent the naturals are usually far more effective because perch can be quite shy. As a rule of thumb, floating patterns like the Light and Dark Cahill, Black Gnat, Black Ant, and McGinty are greedily accepted. Almost any brown, black, or straw-colored nymph will work and, like the dry flies, should be dressed on a No. 10 or No. 12 hook. Of course, there's no problem in locating surface-feeding perch, as they'll dimple the water over a large area. The rise generally begins at sundown and continues until dark. However, during those periods when ants, bees, and other terrestrial insects are abundant you may get a good rise during the bright daylight hours.

As with all panfish, the white perch lacks a capacity for prolonged struggle. But when caught on very light tackle there is a patent of nobility about the perch. A large fish will get the leader over its shoulder and do the familiar bucking and circling which slab-sided species adopt as their tactic. After scampering in circles, a perch may try boring straight for the bottom. The search, the strike, and the final ceremony of putting the perch in the pan make it a worthy sport.

FOOD VALUE

There is no finer fish to eat than the white perch. It has firm white meat and makes a delectable fish chowder. They can be fried in the usual way by coating the fillets with corn meal, bread crumbs, or just plain flour. An excellent method is to cut the perch fillets in 2–3-inch "fingers" and dip these in a tempura batter. *See also* Fish Cookery, Panfish   —A.J.McC.

WHITE SEABASS *Cynoscion nobilis* This species is one of the weakfishes or corvinas (*which see*) and not a true seabass. It is closely related to the totuava and the shortfin seabass of northern Mexican waters. The white seabass is known as white corvina in Mexico. It is found from Alaska to Chile but is uncommon north of San Francisco. Although the white seabass reaches 80 pounds and 4 feet, weights over 40 pounds are rare.

The dorsal fins of the white seabass are at least in contact; the pectoral fin more than half of head length; caudal fin yellow; second dorsal base longer than base of anal fin; no enlarged canine teeth in upper jaw; lower jaw protrudes slightly; belly with a raised ridge from vent to pelvic fin base.

White Seabass

The body color is gray to blue on back, silvery on sides, white on belly; pectoral with inner basal dusky spot; 3–6 crossbars in young fish.

LIFE HISTORY

Found near kelp beds. Spawns in spring and summer and is most numerous from May to September in California. Males spawn at about 24 inches in length, females at about 27 inches. The species feed on other fishes, crustaceans, and squid.

ANGLING VALUE

In 1960 the party-boat catch was 15,111 fish in California waters. Assuming an average weight of 15 pounds, the total weight would be 226,665 pounds. In the same year commercial fishermen took 1,236,198 pounds valued at $311,714. Although much live-bait still-fishing is done for white seabass, they are also taken by trolling and surf-casting with feathers, underwater plugs, spoons, and metal squids. Night fishing is often most productive. White seabass are reluctant to strike fast-moving lures; they should be worked slowly and near the bottom—J.R.

WHITE SEAPERCH *Phanerodon furcatus* An important sport fish, it ranges from northern Baja California to Vancouver Island along sandy coasts.

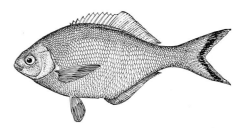

White Seaperch

It is silver; darker dorsally; anal often has dusky anterior spot; ventrals plain; dusky caudal fin margin; a continuous dorsal margin; last spine of dorsal as long or nearly as long as first softray; deeply forked tail; peduncle slender; posterior groove of lower lip interrupted by a frenum; 4–5 rows of large scales between lower edge of scale sheath at junction of spiny and soft portions of dorsal fin and lateral line (one small scale may be present above larger ones). Length to about 12 inches.

Life history, food, angling as with surfperch (*which see*) in general.

COMMERCIAL VALUE

In California, it is the most important of the family, while elsewhere it is taken in lesser amounts.   —J.R.

WHITE SHARK *Carcharodon carcharias* This is also known as the maneater or great white shark and is recognized by its streamlined shape, the pointed snout, the triangular, serrated teeth, and the crescent-shaped caudal fin, with the dorsal lobe only slightly longer than the lower. It resembles the mako (*which see*), but can be told from this by the anal fin, which is nearly completely behind the second dorsal in the white shark. The tips of the dorsal and pectoral fins are more rounded in the mako, and the mako's snout is more pointed. And the body of the white shark is much deeper and less elongate than the mako. The smooth teeth of the mako are more slender and curved inward and protrude from the mouth. The color is grayish-brown grading to slate-blue or gray, with dirty-white below. In the young, there is a black spot above the pectoral fin which is lacking in large specimens. Large white sharks are leaden-white.

The largest white shark ever measured was 36½ feet. This is a robust shark, for a specimen measuring about 8 feet long weighed 600 pounds, while one about 13 feet weighed over 2,100 pounds. There is great variation in the

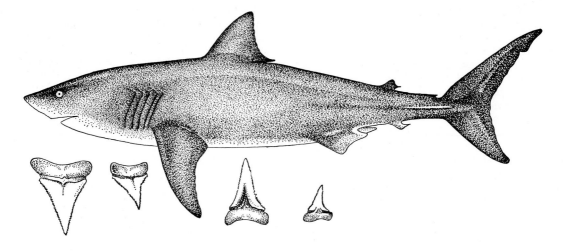

White Shark (teeth upper jaw *left*, lower jaw *right*)

weight at a given length, depending on the condition of breeding and food intake.

It is an oceanic species which roams the tropical and temperate waters of the world. It is nowhere common but apparently is less common in the tropics than in warm-temperate regions.

DANGER TO MAN

Fortunately for bathers, this active swimmer usually stays well offshore and also appears to prefer somewhat cooler waters, so that it is not as abundant in the summer months, at least on the Atlantic Coast. However, it may enter very shallow water in populated areas, and it has been definitely implicated in several attacks on humans. And its teeth have more than once been removed from boats which it has attacked. Its large size makes it a very real potential danger.

It eats a variety of large animals, and other sharks 4–7 feet long have been taken from stomachs. Sea lions, seals, sturgeon, tuna, sea turtles, chimaeras, and squids are also regularly taken. It is also a scavenger on dead flesh and refuse.   —D.dS.

WHITE STURGEON *Acipenser transmontanus* This is the largest fish found in inland waters of the United States. It is identified as a sturgeon by its elongated snout, with a sucking mouth below, and by five rows of bony, shield-like plates on its body. The upper lobe of the tail is longer than the lower, and its skeleton is cartilaginous. This species can be differentiated by its short, broad snout with four barbels, located much further forward than those of other sturgeons, and by its gray color. The toothless mouth is small with thick lips, and is directed downward.

The white sturgeon is found along the Pacific Coast from Alaska south to Monterey, California.

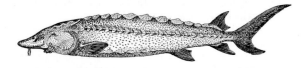

White Sturgeon

LIFE HISTORY

Many white sturgeon spend part of their lives in the ocean and ascend the larger rivers along the Pacific Coast to spawn. In some headwaters, such as the upper Columbia River, they are entirely landlocked. Adults make a winter or spring migration to spawn in the spring over upstream gravel beds and return downstream in summer. It does not care for the eggs or young. It averages 19 inches long the second year and 40 inches the seventh and matures at about 12 years when 50–53 inches at weights of 35–50 pounds. Ages of the very large fish reported have not been determined, but growth rates of 2.1–2.6 inches per year after fast initial growth the first 8 years indicate that 14–16-foot fish are 60–75 years old.

In freshwater it takes crustaceans, mollusks, insect larvae, and other bottom organisms which it sucks up as it works along the bottom.

The roe of an 800-pound sturgeon weighs 50 pounds and is valued for caviar (*which see*). The largest reported taken weighed 1,800 pounds. It is prized as a food fish. These trophy fish have been overfished in the past, and careful regulation of harvests has been necessary to ensure maintenance of a fishable population.   —C.A.P.

WHITE SUCKER *Catostomus commersoni* An olive-brown, cylindrical sucker, with 55–85 scales along the lateral line. The rounded snout projects only slightly or not at all beyond the tip of the upper lip. The dorsal fin contains 10–13 rays. The sucker family, sometimes confused with some minnows, is easily distinguished by the position of the anal fin. If the distance from the anal to the tail fin is contained more than 2½ times in the distance from the snout to the anal fin, the fish is a sucker. Excepted are carp and goldfish, which have a dorsal spine not found on suckers. The commonest of all suckers, the white sucker, ranges from northern Canada south to Florida and west to Montana.

LIFE HISTORY

The white sucker is quite tolerant of a great variety of conditions. It apparently prefers large streams and the deeper water of impoundments. It is found in fastwaters and sluggish streams and in association with dense weed beds. It is tolerant of large amounts of pollution, siltation, and turbidity and is able to survive in waters low in oxygen.

White suckers feed on a variety of foods, including aquatic insect larvae, crustaceans, mollusks, and algae, particularly those forms found in bottom ooze.

Normally migrating into streams of all gradients and all sizes at night to spawn, the white sucker deposits its slightly adhesive eggs in shallow water. The vigorous spawning act serves to cover the eggs lightly. These suckers are also known to spawn in the shoal areas of lakes. Radical changes in color of these fish, especially the male, take place during the spawning act. The back becomes olive-colored with a bright lavender sheen, and there is a lateral band of pink or red along the side.

White Sucker

The white sucker usually runs 10–20 inches in length, and commercial fishermen have reported their weight to be as high as 8 pounds.

ECONOMIC VALUE

A soft and bony fish, the white sucker is not highly valued for food. During the spring spawning run, however, the flesh is firm and palatable. Large numbers are taken by spears. They are of some commercial value, and are caught in a variety of nets. White suckers are often accused of preying on the spawn of more desirable species, but this theory is not well-founded. The role of the young sucker in providing forage for predator species undoubtedly outweighs any harm done by its possible spawn eating. —R.A.J.

WHITETAIL SHINER *Notropis galacturus* The whitetail shiner is found from the eastern slopes of the Ozarks in Missouri and Arkansas through the Tennessee Valley to South Carolina and Mississippi. This large minnow sometimes reaches a maximum length of 6 inches.

Whitetail Shiner

Its distinguishing characteristics are its body is elongate, fusiform, slightly compressed, and the depth is a little less than 0.25 the total length; its mouth is large, with the lower jaw being included within the upper; the eye is small; the somewhat decurved lateral line has 41 scales; the dorsal and anal rays number 8 each; and the pharyngeal teeth are in two rows 1, 4-4, 1. The coloration of the males is steel blue (females olivaceous) above and silvery below. The dorsal fin has a posterior interradial membrane which is black, and the caudal fins are creamy yellow at the base. During the breeding season the dorsal, anal, and caudal fins of the males are charged with a milk-white pigment, and sometimes the anal and caudal fins are reddish in color.

LIFE HISTORY

The whitetail shiners, either individually or in schools, are usually found in the upper half of small to medium-sized mountain streams having fairly clear water and a moderate current. This fish is associated with riffle areas having a bottom of rubble, bedrock, and gravel. The species is most active during daylight hours throughout the year. The whitetail shiner reaches maturity during its second year of growth at which time it has a mean total length of 71 mm.

Spawning activity begins when the water temperature reaches 75°F. The time of day chosen for spawning is between 11:00 A.M. and 4:00 P.M. Prior to spawning, the males select and guard a territory around a gravel nest from which they drive away all other males. Once the female is selected, the male and female turn on their sides upward and toward each other several times, each time releasing eggs and sperm. After spawning, the female leaves the nest and the male takes over the task of guarding the eggs. Inasmuch as the eggs are adhesive they adhere to rocks, fallen tree branches, or the first object they come in contact with. When the eggs hatch, the young embryos measure about 5.5 mm in total length. An average growth rate for this short-lived species is about 54, 67, and 79 mm for the years I through III, respectively; however, few of them live to age III. The whitetail shiner feeds on material that drifts along with the current, principally aquatic and terrestrial insects, depending on availability. This minnow is carnivorous.

The whitetail shiner serves as forage for smallmouth bass, largemouth bass, redbreast sunfish, and others. It is sometimes used as bait, but is seldom sold commercially. —D.E.L.

WHITETIP SHARK *Carcharhinus longimanus* This is a distinctively marked tropical shark which can be recognized by its short, broadly rounded snout and rounded first dorsal and pectoral fins. Further, it has a large, high dorsal fin, and the lower lobe of the caudal is convex at its posterior margin. The body is short and relatively chunky, and the free rear tip of the second dorsal fin nearly reaches the caudal pit. The upper teeth are triangular and serrated, while the lower ones are erect and have a broad base, and only the tips of the teeth possess fine cusps. It varies from light gray or pale brown to slaty-blue above to yellowish-brown to dirty-white beneath. Usually the pectoral, pelvic, and first dorsal fins and the lobes of the caudal fin are light or white-tipped in the adult, and the newborn may have black tips which, in medium-sized specimens, may show as irregular, black spots. A few reach 13 feet, but most are 7–10 feet long.

LIFE HISTORY

The whitetip is entirely a pelagic species, occurring far out at sea in the tropical and subtropical parts of the western Atlantic and the eastern Pacific. It is also reported

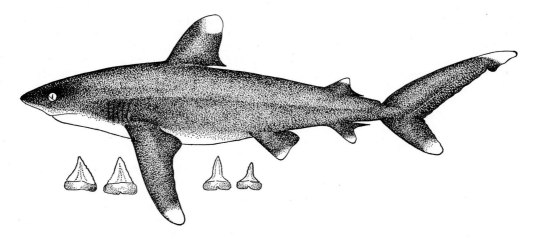

Whitetip Shark (teeth upper jaw *left*, lower jaw *right*)

from Madeira. In the western Atlantic it is known from off Long Island to Barbados and throughout the Gulf of Mexico. Almost without exception, it is restricted to waters of greater than 100 fathoms. It travels singly or in packs, being the commonest of the pelagic sharks of the tropical parts of the North Atlantic. Although it is ordinarily a sluggish species in its search for food, it can capture squids and tunalike fishes. The sexes segregate during parts of the year, as do many other pelagic sharks. Mating occurs in late spring or early summer, and the young are born after a gestation period of about a year. Two–9 young are born at a time, depending on the mother's size.

ANGLING VALUE

Adults are occasionally caught by anglers, but whitetips are too sluggish to provide good sport. But they are persistent in their pursuit of prey, and they cause great damage to commercially caught tuna.　　—D.dS.

WHITE TROUT *See* Sand Seatrout
WHITE ULUA *See* Pacific Threadfin
WHITINGS *Menticirrhus* **spp.** Four species of whitings frequent the Atlantic and Gulf coasts of the United States. The southern kingfish, *M. americanus*, ranges all the way from New York to Argentina and to the northern Gulf of Mexico. The Gulf kingfish, *M. littoralis*, extends from Virginia to Florida and throughout the Gulf of Mexico. The northern kingfish, *M. saxatilis*, is found only on the Atlantic Coast from Maine to Florida. The mink-fish, *M. focaliger*, is confined to the Gulf of Mexico.

The whitings are small shore fishes usually found over a sandy bottom. The group is characterized by having a

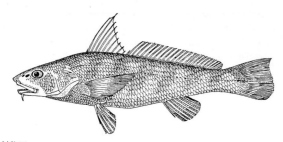

Whiting

small, subterminal mouth; teeth in bands in both jaws; a single barbel on chin; short gillrakers; 10–11 rather high, slender dorsal spines; anal fin with a single, sharp spine; asymmetrical caudal fin, the upper lobe sharp, the lower rounded; and no air bladder.

KEY TO THE ATLANTIC SPECIES OF MENTICIRRHUS

A. Gillrakers slender; upper body a uniform silvery-gray without markings　　　　*littoralis*
AA. Gillrakers stout; upper body with dark bands or bars.
　B. Lateral scales 89–104　　　　　*saxatilis*
　BB. Lateral scales 75–90.
　　C. Anal softrays 8; body very dark　*focaliger*
　　CC. Anal softrays 7; body rather light　*americanus*

Along the Texas coast, the southern kingfish and the Gulf kingfish are the two most common species. The former is most common in the bays, although they migrate out to deepwater during the coldest weather, and the latter mainly inhabits the surf. Both species are bottom feeders, existing on such items as crabs, shrimp, and various mollusks. Spawning takes place anytime from spring to early fall.

ANGLING VALUE

The whitings are of minor importance to the sport fisherman mainly because the adults are small, seldom reaching over a foot in length. However, they are good eating, and are fished commercially in the Chesapeake Bay area.　　—J.C.B.

WICHITA SPOTTED BASS *Micropterus punctulatus wichitae* A subspecies of the spotted bass occurring in the Wichita Mountains of Oklahoma. *See also* Black Bass, Spotted Bass

WINCH A hoisting engine secured to the deck, used to haul lines and wire ropes by turns around a horizontally turning drum. It may be gasoline-powered on larger boats, operated by electrical power in small pleasure craft, and many are manually operated while providing for mechanical advantage. A manual winch is mounted on most boat trailers accommodating larger-size outboards, although power winches operated off your car's battery are also in use.

WINDOWPANE *Scophthalmus aquosus* Also called the brill or spotted flounder, this distinctive flatfish is the only member of its genus. The windowpane is found in the coastal waters of eastern North America from the Gulf of St. Lawrence to South Carolina.

Its color is reddish to grayish-brown with many brown spots, each made up of several sections; dark mottling on dorsal, anal, and caudal fins; the right side usually white, occasionally with some dark blotches.

Other distinguishing characteristics of the windowpane are body broadly ovate, lying on right side, much compressed; greatest width scarcely 2 in total length at tip of pectoral fins. Head 4½ in total length; mouth large oblique, its angle under front edge of pupil, 1 row of teeth in each jaw. Eyes 4 in head, moderately spaced.

Dorsal fin with 63–73 softrays, the first 12–15 free and branched at their tips, beginning slightly in front of right eye and ending on base of caudal peduncle; caudal rounded; anal fin with 46–54 softrays, originating directly under preopercle and terminating on caudal peduncle under end of dorsal; pectorals large, ⅔ length of head, inserted on sides behind gill opening, fin on blind side smaller; pelvics dissimilar. Lateral line arched above pectoral. Scales smooth, covering body and posterior part of head.

LIFE HISTORY

The windowpane lives in comparatively shallow water on sandy bottoms. On the Georges Bank it has been taken as deep as 40 fathoms. There is apparently no regular migratory movement. Spawning is in the late spring or early summer. The eggs are spherical, about ¹⁄₂₀ of an inch in diameter, with a small oil globule. They float in seawater. Incubation requires 8 days at 51°–56°F.

The growth of this species has been studied in Long Island Sound. There, 2-year-old fishes averaged 4½ inches in length, 4-year-old fishes averaged 9½ inches, and 7-year-olds 12 inches. Mysids appear to be the preferred food of the young, but individuals over 11 inches long eat sand shrimp and small fishes in about equal amounts. The young fishes eaten are tomcod, smelt, lake, pollock, striped bass, and herring. The maximum length of adults is about 18 inches.

FOOD VALUE

Edible but an extremely thin flounder (the body transmits light when held to the sun, hence the name windowpane) it has no commercial value. —J.C.B.

WINTER FLOUNDER *Pseudopleuronectes americanus* One of the best-known flounders to anglers, this important species is a "right-handed" fish, although a few specimens turn up with pigment on the left side, and occasionally on both sides. It is also known regionally as flatfish, blackback, blueback, black flounder, and mud dab. It has a small mouth like the yellowtail flounder, from which it differs in its straight lateral line, with no arch over the pectoral fin, the thicker body, and the widely spaced eyes. The color varies from reddish-brown to dark slate, occasionally with hues of dark green. During the brown phase, small, dark spots are usually visible.

It occurs from Labrador to Georgia, commonly from the Gulf of St. Lawrence to Chesapeake Bay. This is a shallow-water flounder, found from well up into the high-tide mark to depths of at least about 400 feet. Generally, smaller fish are to be found in shallow water and large fish in deeper water, although large fish will enter water less than a foot deep. They prefer muddy sand but may occur on sand, clay, or fine gravel. Offshore, they may be

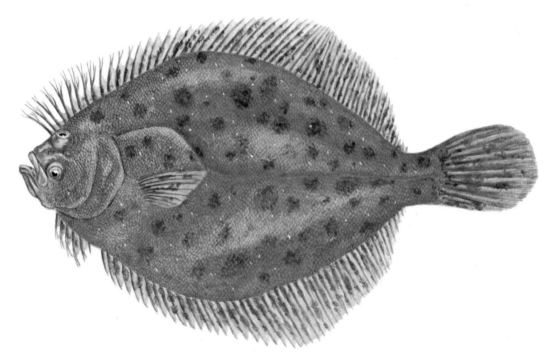

Windowpane

Winter Flounder

found on hard bottom as well as soft. They enter mouths of estuaries, and occasionally are taken in water that is nearly fresh.

LIFE HISTORY

Spawning occurs usually from January to May, with a peak of from March to April over sandy bottom. The spawning depth is 1–40 fathoms, and the eggs, unlike other flatfishes, sink to the bottom and stick together. Metamorphosis is very rapid, during which one eye migrates to the right side of the head. Pigmentation is complete when the fish is only about $\frac{1}{3}$ inch long, this growth requiring $2\frac{1}{2}$–$3\frac{1}{2}$ months. Growth is rather slow, the flounder reaching an average length of 6 inches at the end of its first year. The young feed on small plants and crustaceans, then switch to worms, crabs, and shrimps. Because of its small mouth, only small invertebrates and larval or small fishes can be eaten. This common species moves about considerably in search of food, but does not generally migrate far from its home territory. There is a distinct movement from deepwater toward shallow water during the fall, and an offshore movement in the spring.

The distribution of the winter flounder extends along the Atlantic Coast of North America from Newfoundland and the Gulf of St. Lawrence southward to Chesapeake Bay. Some have been reported as far north as Labrador and as far south as the Carolinas and Georgia. Throughout this range they can be found in shallow bays and inshore coastal zones out to the deeper, offshore ocean grounds. The centers of abundance include the coastal waters of Massachusetts, Rhode Island, and Connecticut, Long Island Sound, both shores and the eastern reaches of Long Island, New York, and bays and coastal areas of New Jersey.

The size of the winter flounder is generally 12–15 inches and 1–2 pounds, sometimes reaching 20 inches and 5 pounds. The larger fish are sometimes called "sea flounders" to distinguish them from the smaller bay fish.

In waters off Montauk Point, New York, and around Block Island, Rhode Island, there exist populations of extra-large flounders, locally known as "snowshoes" because of their shape and size. These fish can weigh up to 6 pounds, and a winter flounder of 8 pounds has been caught. The Montauk-Block Island region is unique on the Atlantic seaboard in that it is one of very few yielding large flounders. Much farther north, Georges Bank has produced flounders weighing 6–8 pounds, but these are caught commercially.

For most anglers the bulk of the catch consists of flounders weighing about $\frac{1}{2}$–$1\frac{1}{2}$ pounds, with occasional specimens of 2–$2\frac{1}{2}$ pounds. During a run of sea flounders, such as occurs in the spring in the Peconic Bay system of New York, sizes consistently go into the 2–$3\frac{1}{2}$-pound bracket.

TACKLE FOR FLOUNDERS

One reason for the flounder's great popularity is that the simplest kind of tackle will suffice for the fishing. Flounders can be caught on just a handline with a hook and sinker, although this method furnishes no real sport. The flounder is pre-eminently a light-tackle fish. Heavy gear not only takes the fun out of the game, but it costs appreciable numbers of fish. Flounders bite rather lightly, and an overcalibered rod will not transmit the nibbling signal to the angler. A flounder can steal a bait and escape almost unnoticed.

Both spinning tackle and the conventional "bay" outfit are used for flounder fishing. Perhaps the ideal is a spinning rod of 6–$6\frac{1}{2}$ feet with a medium to light action. A standard freshwater spinning reel or a light saltwater model is perfectly satisfactory. This can be spooled with line up to about 8-pound test, which is quite adequate. Monofilament is very popular, but many anglers prefer Dacron or use braided nylon. Bear in mind that 50 yards of line is all you really need for these shallow-water fish. One potential drawback of light spinning gear, however, is that bottom-fishing demands a sinker of sufficient weight to keep the terminal rig on the bay or ocean floor. In some regions tidal currents can be quite strong, requiring a fairly heavy sinker, which, in the drag of a strong current, is often too much for a light tip to hold. For this reason, mediumweight spinning tackle or conventional bay tackle is sometimes preferred.

HOOKS FOR FLOUNDERS

Flounders have small mouths. To be on the safe side, a flounder angler might better have hooks which are a bit too small than some that are slightly too large. A flounder cannot mouth an oversized hook. Generally speaking, and allowing for variations among different hook designs, sizes ranging from about a No. 9 to a No. 6 will suffice. A No. 9 or No. 8 will take the small fish to a pound or so. A No. 6 will handle the heavier flounders. For the so-called snowshoes, largest of the species, hooks somewhat larger than No. 6 can be used. Hook patterns are a matter of personal preference; there are several good designs such as the Sproat, O'Shaughnessy, and Carlisle. A type which long has been popular with flounder fishermen is the Chestertown. This design is favored because it has a long shank. Flounders tend to gulp bait deep in their throat, and the Chestertown's long shank facilitates its removal.

FLOUNDER RIGS

There is a choice of rigs, but all are designed for the same requirement. Hooks must be kept as close as possible to the bottom—the zone to which flounders restrict themselves. For this reason no leaders are used, since they would tend to lift the hooks up and out of the flounder's reach. The only exception is a multipurpose rig used in the Montauk-Block Island area for snowshoes, cod, and pollock. Flounder hooks are sold with an attached gut snell about 6–8 inches long. These suffice to secure the rig.

The simplest terminal tackle for flounders is a single hook, tied into the line by its snell immediately above the sinker (already attached to the line). A three-way swivel is not necessary in attaching the hook and sinker, but to a certain extent it helps prevent the snell from becoming twisted around the line. The sinker is tied to the swivel's bottom eye; its middle eye receives the hook; and the top eye is for the line.

Two-Hook Rig Two-hook rigs are the most popular in flounder angling. With them, during a good run, it often is possible to catch two fish at a time. For best service from a two-hook rig a simple device known as a spreader is used. This consists of a slightly curved piece of wire with a loop at each outer end and a swivel in the middle with an eye on top and another underneath. A hook is attached by its snell to each outer loop. The line is tied to the center swivel's top eye, and the sinker is tied below the spreader, to the swivel's lower eye. The purpose of the spreader is to keep the two hooks from tangling with each other.

A simpler version of the two-hook rig is to tie one hook to the line, either directly by its snell or via a swivel, right above the sinker; then a second hook is added in similar fashion an inch or so above that. But this is inferior to the spreader rig because the two hooks tend to foul each other.

Another two-hook rig arrangement has been adapted for drifting for flounders. It also is used in some locales when flounders and blackfish (tautog) are in the same area. Here one hook is tied into the line immediately above the sinker as before, with or without swivel. The other hook is tied to the snell of the first, usually at about the midpoint. An advantage claimed for this rig over the spreader is that it is less likely to get caught on obstructions when drifting.

Multipurpose Rig There is a multipurpose rig which is used for snowshoe flounders, cod, and pollock in the Montauk-Block Island area. Because water that is fairly deep, heavy sinkers, and larger fish are involved, its use demands heavier tackle and stronger line. Here are the basics of a variation of this terminal tackle: a pair of three-way swivels is used. One swivel is tied to the line. To one of its remaining eyes is attached a 4-foot leader carrying a pollock hook. To the swivel's third eye is tied a 5-foot leader, on which is the second three-way swivel. The sinker is tied to this swivel. A cod hook on tarred line about 12–16 inches long is attached to the remaining eye. Tied and taped to the middle of that tarred line is a 12–16-inch length of gut, and on this goes the hook for snowshoe flounders. A sea clam or "skimmer" is used to bait all three hooks. One piece from the center of the clam's body is used for the pollock hook; a piece cut from the end baits the cod hook; and the tough "lips" of the clam go on the shoe hook.

A sinker completes any flounder rig. The bank type is the most popular. Weight of the sinker required to keep a rig on the bottom varies and depends upon depth and current strength in the area fished. Shoal, calm localities may demand only 2–3 ounces. In deeper waters, or where tidal currents are stronger, it may be necessary to use 5 ounces or more. It is important to use only enough lead to hold bottom. Excess weight will detract from the fish's fight. Whether or not enough lead is being used can be determined by trying to bounce the sinker on the bottom. If successful, the bouncing will be felt. If the sinker feels as though it is being thrust outward away from the bottom, a heavier one is needed.

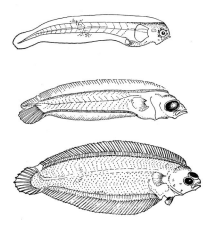

Eye Migration in Winter Flounder—(*top*) Larva 4.5 mm. long, (*middle*) Larva 8.2 mm. long, (*bottom*) Larva 9.3 mm. long

BAITS AND CHUMMING

Bloodworms, sandworms, clams, and mussels are the most widely used flounder baits. Bloodworms and sandworms are favored particularly. There are times when the flatfish exhibit a preference for clams or mussels, rather than worms, and wise anglers allow for that variation by carrying some of the bivalves in addition to worms. Also effective at times is a combination bait consisting of one piece each of bloodworm or sandworm and clam or mussel on the same hook. Often it pays to experiment on a double-hook rig with different kinds of baits, noting which takes the most fish, then changing the bait on the other hook accordingly. Whatever bait is used must be in small pieces because of the flounder's little mouth. A piece to cover the hook's point and part of its bend is sufficient. Somewhat larger pieces can be used for the bigger snowshoes.

Flounders may be feeding only a few yards from where a boat is anchored, yet not approach the hooks. Chumming frequently overcomes this reluctance. Chumming is the distribution of some item of natural diet, other than bait, to lure fish to the angler's vicinity. Mussels and clams are effective flounder chum, and are most commonly used. Oysters and scallops are also effective.

The mollusks can be used in either of two ways. In one method the shells are cracked, and they are dropped overboard, a few at a time, directly alongside the anchored boat. In the other technique the mussels or clams are cracked and placed in a coarse-meshed bag to which a length of cord has been tied so that it can be lowered to the bottom and "bounced" at intervals.

For the same reason that chumming is effective, flounder fishing in the vicinity of a clam digger or an oyster dredge can be productive. Such operations disturb the bottom, dislodging tiny shellfish and other tidbits which attract flounders. An angler can achieve similar results on a smaller scale in shallow water by periodically agitating the bottom underneath his craft with an oar, anchor, or boathook.

FISHING TECHNIQUE

Large numbers of flounders are caught from rowboats and larger craft at anchor. Drifting produces in some areas. The fish are also caught from piers, docks, banks of canals and saltwater creeks, and around the mouths of inlets. Bays, harbors, sounds, inlets, estuaries, and inshore ocean zones all contain areas with flounder-action potential. But the fish must be located. Certain areas may be literally "paved" with fish, while others nearby are quite barren. Flounder grounds include those with soft, rich, black mud, especially if there are crustaceans and mollusks on which the flounders feed. Grayish, slimy, foul-smelling mud usually is barren of flounders. Checking the composition of a mud bottom by hauling up the anchor will pay dividends: best spots are a combination of sand and mud bottom with patches of eelgrass; clean white sand and a pebbly floor, inshore or in a bay; and deeper holes in creeks, channels, and estuaries, especially at low tide. With a drop in tide, flounders tend to seek deeper water, particularly in shoal areas which can be heated or chilled too much for them. They are found over sandflats and mud bottom at high tide. They often feed more actively at high tide than at low. Channel areas include the center at low tide, and areas between center and banks at highwater; a creek bank or bend in a channel where there are deep spots or where currents have eroded sloughs in the bottom; and inside mouths of inlets. Inlets often are most productive toward the end of a run, when flounders gather to move out through the inlet to escape temperature extremes.

Flounder angling demands patience. Each place should be given a reasonable chance to yield fish, with chumming if necessary. If that location fails to produce, the angler should try another spot. Several shifts may be required to contact fish. Periodically the terminal rig should be reeled in to make sure its hooks are baited. Crabs and other bait stealers, such as blowfish (puffer), searobins, bergalls (cunner), and sculpins can strip a hook of bait.

Flounders bite lightly. Theirs is not the smashing strike of bluefish and other larger gamefish. Flounders tend to nip at the bait and release it. They do not toy with an offering very long. The hook should be set as quickly as possible. A short, smart, upward lift of the rod tip will do it. Sensitive contact with the terminal rig should be kept at all times. Some flounders approach a bait so daintily as to be scarcely felt. Then it may be necessary to feed the fish a few inches of line, tightening it carefully to feel for the fish's weight. Once that weight is felt, a short, steady pull—rather than a vigorous jerk—usually will set the hook.

Double-headers on a spreader rig are not uncommon during a good run. Two fish may bite almost simultaneously. Or, if the angler is patient, he sometimes can induce a second fish to bite when one already is hooked. His first fish securely on, the fisherman leaves his rig on the bottom briefly. A second flounder may join the first.

Flounders resist vigorously when hooked. Theirs is not a dramatic battle, but they dart for short distances and provide lively action on light tackle. During a good run catches follow one another quickly.

MOVEMENTS

These are influenced strongly by water temperatures. Flounders cannot endure excessive chilling or heating of the water. They desert shallow areas for deeper water to escape freezing in winter, then move back into shoal areas in the spring. When these waters become warm with the approach of summer, they find deeper spots, such as channels and inshore zones, then return in the fall. When waters get too cold for them in autumn they again seek deeper (warmer) places.

In such regions there are two bay runs of the fish annually. The first starts as spring approaches. Depending upon how quickly local waters warm, flounders can begin to appear in late February or the first half of March. A spring run generally reaches its zenith in April and May, then tapers off as the fish move to deeper, cooler waters. In summer they usually are scarce in shallow bays, but the deeper areas of channels, sounds, and inlets may harbor them well into summer, or even throughout that season.

A second run occurs in the fall, when flounders return to enclosed, shallow bodies of water from deeper spots. Initiation of this run, like its predecessor, depends upon water temperatures, the fish waiting until their autumn areas lose some of their summer warmth. Their fall run can last deep into November, with the fish finally shifting to deeper waters to escape fatal freezing in the shallows.

FOOD VALUE

The flounder is an excellent table fish. It has white, firm, delicately flavored meat. The only criticism is that it has numerous bones. After the smaller flounders are cooked, most of their bones can be lifted out intact with a fork during eating. The larger fish should be filleted. This requires a sharp knife and a little practice. The flounder is placed, eye side up, on a cutting board. The first cut is made through to the spine, just behind the gill cover and at right angles to the long axis of the fish. A second cut is made from the tail to the head, close alongside the fin and in at an angle. Next, this lengthwise incision is deepened, working carefully so as not to gouge meat from the fillet. Working from the head toward the tail, the fillet is lifted and carefully cut away from the fish. Finally, the fillet is skinned. This is accomplished by placing the fillet with its skin side down, grasping it by the tail end, and cutting the meat free by working as close to the skin as possible. Dressed or filleted, flounders can be fried, baked, or broiled. *See also* Fish Cookery   —D.dS.
                  —B.W.

WINTER-KILL A term used to describe a chain of events that sometimes takes place during the winter months which kills fish by suffocation. When a lake or pond freezes over, it can no longer absorb oxygen from the air. But if the ice remains clear, green water plants will produce enough oxygen to keep the fish alive.

If the ice will not permit sunlight to penetrate, however, such as when there is a heavy snow cover, the plants may die and, instead of producing oxygen, will use up the oxygen as they decompose. In this situation, the fish suffocate due to a lack of oxygen.

Ponds with less than 10 feet of water and with high fish populations are in danger of fish kills. The results of winter-kill sometimes aren't seen since the dead fish may decompose before the ice cover leaves. A winter-kill can, in some instances, be beneficial; in overpopulated waters where there is no adequate food supply and the fish are stunted, a winter-kill reduces that population, and the remaining fish may achieve good growth temporarily. *See also* Coldkill   —A.J.McC.

WINTER SKATE *Raja ocellata* This species closely resembles the little skate (*which see*), from which it differs essentially in having two large, whitish spots near the rear angles of the upper part of the disk. But these spots are sometimes absent, and the large number of teeth in the upper jaw of the winter skate (at least 80 and usually 90–100) separates it from the little skate, which has less

than 66, and usually less than 54. The upper parts are light brown, with numerous black dots which vary in size and number. It grows to about 3½ feet long and about 10–12 pounds. Specimens have been reported from Nova Scotia to North Carolina, but its center of abundance is between southern New England and New Jersey.

LIFE HISTORY

Seldom common anywhere, the winter skate occurs over hard bottoms of sand or gravel from shallow water to 50–60 fathoms. It prefers waters of salinities slightly lower than those of ocean water. In addition, it exhibits a tendency to undergo extensive migrations. There is a shoreward movement in the fall coincident with cooling water temperatures, with an offshore movement in the late spring in response to warmwaters. Like the barn-door skate (*which see*) this species breeds throughout its range, the eggs being laid in late summer and early fall in the North but throughout the year in the South. It eats about the same food as the little skate, such as crabs, squid, worms, clams, and small fishes, including smaller skates. Anglers take it often on hook and line, and it enters fish traps and weirs.

FOOD VALUE

It has some value as food and for fishmeal. —D.dS.

WIRE LINE A metal line made of stainless steel, bronze, copper, or Monel (nickel alloy), designed for deep trolling. The basic problem in many kinds of trolling is to get a lure to extreme depths. Neither a heavy drail nor a bulky planer is often desirable for this purpose, but a wire line will sink unencumbered, and, being inelastic, it allows the fisherman to impart movement to his lure by jigging the rod. Wire lines are made in a wide range of sizes, and the most popular for general saltwater and freshwater fishing are 15–45-pound test.

The disadvantage of all wire lines is the fact that they are not easy for the beginner to handle. Wire kinks very easily, and the angler must be careful when paying out and spooling the line back. Most kinks are caused by letting the line spin out too fast behind a moving boat. Never, under any circumstances, throw the reel into free spool without engaging the click or placing the thumb firmly on the spool to prevent an overrun.

WIRE-LINE TACKLE

The reel is an important component of wire-line fishing. The best type is a saltwater star-drag model with a fairly wide, shallow spool. Deep, narrow-spooled reels have been designed for wire-line fishing, but it's easier to pick a backlash out of a wide spool than a narrow one. The spool should never be completely filled but have a clearance of at least ¼ inch between the line and the crossbars. When retrieving wire line, always level-wind it across the spool from side to side; never let it pile up at one point. This greatly reduces the chance of backlashing.

It is not necessary to fill the reel with wire line. Most of the reel can be spooled to about two-thirds capacity with a Dacron or monofilament line, and the appropriate amounts of wire is spliced to it. For general purposes 300 feet of solid Monel is often sufficient in saltwater; yet on the Great Lakes solid Monel lines of 600 yards are used on rods and reels especially made for trolling the lake trout at water depths exceeding 500 feet. The braided

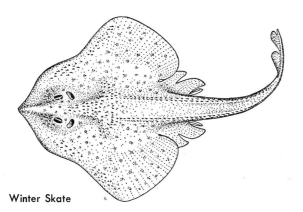

Winter Skate

and twisted Monel lines, being especially suitable for lesser depths, do not ordinarily require more than 300–450 feet, but they do require more yardage than the solid Monel lines to go down to equal depths. This is the important point to consider when substituting braided and twisted lines for solid Monel. The boat speed and lure weight, as well as the sinking coefficient of the wire itself, are highly variable factors (a 300-foot length of solid Monel line will seldom attain more than a 50-foot depth at an average trolling pace). It is useful therefore to mark the wire line at 50–100-foot intervals with nail polish, adhesive tape, or masking tape to determine just how much line should be dropped back in fishing specific areas. Experience counts in this type of angling.

Wire line has no elasticity; so therefore a suitable rod is one with some flexibility in the tip. Quick-taper, 6-foot fiberglass trolling rods with a fairly stiff butt are ideal for this purpose. To minimize the tendency of wire to cut through the guides, select Carboloy rings or roller guides.

WIRE-LINE SPLICE

To attach a wire line to a backing line, tie a short loop in the end of the Dacron or monofilament; then tie a single becket bend into the loop of soft line with the end of the wire. Draw the bend tight with your pliers. Finish off the splice by "marrying" or twisting the tag end of wire back onto the main part and make three or four close, smooth finishing turns before cutting and crimping down the end of the wire.

To guard against a sharp, finger-cutting end on the twist, allow an inch or more of wire to extend beyond the last finishing turn. Hold the finishing turns in the tip of the pliers and work this stub of wire up and down with the fingers. If the pliers have been properly applied the wire will break off smoothly at the last turn. *See also* Trolling —A.J.McC.

WISCONSIN Wisconsin is located near the northern boundary of the United States and is about one-third of the way from the Atlantic to the Pacific Ocean. The state is some 320 miles long and 295 miles broad at its widest point, and is named for the major river that flows through it, the Wisconsin River. This aquatic highway received its name from the Chippewa Indians who called it *Meskousing*, "the gathering of the waters." The French took this as *Ouisconsin*, from which came the English version, Wisconsin. The state is literally surrounded by world-renowned waters, the Mississippi on the west and the two largest Great Lakes to the north and the east. Rivers in Wisconsin either flow north and east into the St. Lawrence Waterway or west and south to the Mississippi. Countless inland lakes dot the state while thousands of miles of spring-fed streams and rivers bisect the area. It is difficult to drive more than a few miles without crossing a stream or sighting a lake.

Wisconsin's climate is temperate. The surrounding Great Lakes moderate the winter's cold and summer heat in much of the state. Rain and snow are abundant enough throughout the year so that all but the smallest streams have water in them the year round. The altitude of the state is 700–800 feet in the southeast to 1,600–1,800 feet in the north. The landscape of Wisconsin is one of its greatest assets because of the contrast of vegetation climaxes of northern conifers, prairie, and maple-beech forests. Glaciers were very important in shaping the terrain over most of the state. Old and worn mountain ranges were leveled, ridges were formed, flat, glacial lake beds were left, and between the edges of two glacial tongues the scenic Kettle Moraine area was created. The glaciers were responsible for several lake districts in the state. Glacial action scoured the land surface, leaving lake depressions, and transported part of the land so that upon melting, gravel ridges and deposits prevented drainage which impounded the water to form thousands of lakes. Gravel deposits left by glacial action formed underground water reservoirs that collect rain and snowmelt and release it gradually in the form of springs. Huge blocks of ice were buried in the glacial debris and upon melting left kettle-shaped depressions in many areas to become lakes. Many of these were named for their beautiful appearance, and names such as Crystal, Mirror, Green, Spring, and Silver are common.

HISTORICAL ASPECT

The coasts and large rivers were important in the history of the state. The famous Fox-Wisconsin Waterway from Lake Michigan to the Mississippi and the Gulf of Mexico was explored by Marquette and Joliet in 1673, and later by Father Hennepin and Perrot. Another route from the Great Lakes to the Mississippi was traveled by Duluth via the Brule River and the St. Croix River in northwest Wisconsin. The St. Louis River and the Chequamegon Bay area of Lake Superior were first explored after Nicolet explored the Green Bay region in 1634. In 1658 Radisson and Groseillers built the first white man's dwelling known in Wisconsin on the west shore of Chequamegon Bay.

These explorations, the route of fur traders, missionaries, and soldiers, followed the Indian highways, the rivers, coasts, and lakes of Wisconsin, which may still be followed today. As a result, many lakes and streams carry Indian and French names such as Minocqua, Namekagon, Waupaca, Ojibwa, Winnebago, Lac Court Oreilles, Butte des Morts, Lac du Flambeau, Dubois, Lac Vieux Desert, and St. Croix.

GREAT LAKES FISHING

The coast of Wisconsin is some 600 miles long and contains some of the prettiest scenery in the state. There are two large peninsulas each forming a great bay and each with an archipelago of islands. The Door peninsula, with Washington and adjacent islands in Lake Michigan, forms Green Bay and strongly resembles parts of the rugged North Atlantic sea coast. The rugged Lake Superior coast is broken by the Bayfield peninsula, surrounded by the Apostle Islands and forming Chequamegon Bay. The shoreline here in many places consists of red sandstone cliffs with many wave-formed arches and caverns.

Fishing is a major attraction of these areas, beginning with the smelt run in early spring. These slender, silvery fish are taken with seines and dip nets in the lower reaches of tributary streams and along the beaches of Lakes Michigan and Superior. It is great sport for families or groups to dip washtubs full of fine-eating smelt at night while a bonfire or lantern dimly lights the shoreline and reflects a catch of shimmering silver. Smelt dippers line the shores from the metropolitan complex of Milwaukee, Racine, and Kenosha to the historical Green Bay shores of Lake Michigan and later to the sandy beaches of Lake Superior. Although smelt are an important commercial species, the majority of dippers and seiners are sport fishermen eager to start the spring fishing season and also fill the home and neighborhood frying pans with this abundant silvery resource.

Following Michigan's lead in its coho salmon-stocking program, Wisconsin began a similar project in 1968 in both Lakes Michigan and Superior. This has resulted in phenomenal angling, notably in the Door and Kewaunee County areas from April well into July for a mixed bag including brown trout, steelhead, lake trout, coaster brook trout, coho and chinook salmon. Top spots in April are on the Green Bay side at Egg Harbor, Fish Creek, and Sister Bay. In May and June the east side of the peninsula is best, especially for hog-proportioned brown trout in the 10–12-pound class in the area around Bailey's Harbor. There is good pier fishing at Kewaunee and Algoma, but boat anglers score at Bailey's Harbor and Cave Point. The chief factor here in getting results is the water temperature. A strong west wind in this area can drop the surface waters by 20°F in a 24-hour period. Normally, you count on fishing right at the surface through June, but recurrent winds can generate good fishing until July 20th at least.

Northern pike and walleyes reach large sizes and are popular in the Great Lakes area. Smallmouth-bass fishing is excellent, particularly in the scenic Door peninsula area. These spectacular fighters may be taken alongside steep limestone bluffs in deepwater or in the reedy shallows with fly rods and poppers. Jumbo yellow perch are all-season favorites off the Door "thumb" and during the warmer months along the entire Lake Michigan shoreline, especially off the breakwaters in the shadows of large metropolitan areas. Here, numerous perch fishermen escape the city for cool lake breezes and long stringers of brightly colored perch.

Commercial fishing is an important industry in both Great Lakes. The picturesque fishing tugs, typical of these waters, are found in almost every small port. Since the decline of the lake trout which, prior to the sea-lamprey invasion, were taken in quantities over 3,000,000 pounds annually, the commercial catch is dependent on lake chubs (deepwater cisco), lake herring (shallow-water cisco), whitefish, smelt, and perch.

LAKE STURGEON IN THE LAKE WINNEBAGO SYSTEM

Lake Winnebago, the Wolf, and Upper Fox River form one of the state's largest sport-fishing areas. On the Wolf River it is possible to travel over 125 miles by boat and not encounter a single dam. Shortly after the walleye run, the largest freshwater fish in Wisconsin, the lake sturgeon (*which see*), swims the distance from its home in Lake Winnebago and adjacent Lakes Poygan, Winneconne, and Butte des Morts to spawn in the rapids as far as 125 miles upstream. These fish are known to reach over 300 pounds and over 7 feet long. And although there is no legal angling for sturgeon because of their great vulnerability, their spawning habits make them visible to hundreds of viewers at several spawning sites. However, a unique spearing season is held each February when some 2,000 spearing shanties or "dark houses" are erected on 215-square-mile Lake Winnebago. There, spearmen poise over a 3 x 5-foot hole in the ice floor of their shanty and

wait for the huge fish, which average close to 50 pounds, to swim by. Often they see only a shadow in 15–20 feet of water due to the abundant microscopic plant and animal organisms that enrich and cloud the water. Carefully balanced spears are aimed and thrown, and then, if the fish is hit, a lively tug of war begins. Sturgeon as large as 180 pounds have been taken, and 100-pounders are not uncommon. This lake provides the largest known sport fishery for lake sturgeon in North America, and more than 1,500 have been taken in one season. Although hook-and-line fishing may seem more sporting, the lake sturgeon is rarely taken on a line due to its habit of feeding on tiny insect forms on the lake bottom. Spearing sturgeon in Wisconsin is a tradition taught to the white men by the Indians. Early settlers wrote accounts of their spearing methods, which have changed very little except for the shanties in use today, which are more modern and comfortable. The sturgeon spearing season ends about March 1 and brings to a close most of the winter fishing activities, which also include a lively walleye, sauger, and northern pike "tip-up" fishery on these frozen waters.

STREAM TROUT FISHING

Wisconsin has some 1,400 trout streams with over 8,000 miles of trout habitat. These streams are generally found in six areas of the state. Those in the unglaciated, rugged hill country of southwestern Wisconsin flow from springs in the deep valleys to the Mississippi directly or by way of tributary rivers. Streams along the coast of Lake Michigan flow from the many spring heads in the kettle moraine forests to the lake coast. In the eastcentral part of the state, some of the finest spring-fed streams originate in the sand counties and flow into the Wolf and Fox rivers system or to the Wisconsin River. In the northeastern forested sector are located a concentration of swift trout waters that flow to Green Bay. Tributary streams of the St. Croix and Chippewa rivers in the northwest form another important group of trout streams. Historically, and traditionally, the most famous river is the Brule.

The "Bois Brule" was an important water highway known to the Indians and early explorers who used it as a route to the Mississippi by portaging from its headwaters to Upper St. Croix Lake and thence down the St. Croix River. The Brule's trout fishing was known to several presidents and other notable persons. Before the introduction of rainbows and brown trout, catches of 300 brook trout a day were regularly reported by the early fishermen. The Brule has two personalities—the quiet, upper river, with its wide spread and bubbling springs, and the lower river, a swift stream containing a number of whitewater rapids that took 10 days for early fur traders to transverse to the upper Brule. The stream is now surrounded by a state forest and is also well-known to canoe enthusiasts.

Today a special early season begins around the first of April for the large Lake Superior rainbow trout (steelheads) that move upstream to spawn in these streams. In addition, large brown trout that spawned the previous fall linger in the streams on their way back to Lake Superior. These streams are also open for a special fall season that lasts until the middle of November when browns move into the stream to spawn along with many early steelhead migrants which breed in late winter and early spring. Scenery along the Brule in the fall is an added bonus to the spectacular fishing.

During the first half of May the general stream-trout season opens, which to thousands of fly-rod-wielding fishermen is the only season that counts. The trout-stream resources of the state contain large numbers of native brook trout besides the introduced rainbows and browns. The smaller streams across the northern part of the state, particularly in northeast and northwest Wisconsin, are mostly brook-trout waters and are located in forested areas. The larger streams in these areas are also excellent for brown and rainbow trout. In the east-central sand counties is a belt of some of the state's finest waters. Many flow through hay meadows and are a fly-fisherman's paradise, especially when the abundant mayfly hatches occur. These streams usually contain brook trout in their headwaters, brown trout in the downstream areas where deeper water is common, and rainbows in some of the rapid water. The streams in western and southwestern Wisconsin are found in the hill country in steep-sided, picturesque hollows and valleys. Brown trout predominate in these streams. Of special interest are two well-known streams that have been set aside as "fly-fishing-only" waters. These are sections of the Upper Wolf and the Peshtigo rivers in northeast Wisconsin. Besides limiting the fishing to artificial flies, a bag limit of 5 fish per day with a minimum size of 12 inches is established. These restrictions are popular among many of the dyed-in-the-wool fly-fishermen. The effects of these regulations and their general acceptance are closely followed by the Conservation Department at these streams and at the Lawrence Creek trout research center.

WISCONSIN LAKE REGIONS

The more than 8,000 of the lakes in Wisconsin are found in four general regions. In the southern and eastern sections are found scattered moderate- to large-size lakes in several types of landscapes—agricultural, the broad leaf forests of the kettle moraine, and the oak-pine sand country. Another is the highland of northern Wisconsin, which is covered with mixed conifers and hardwoods that surround a great concentration of lakes. In one three-county area of this highland the lakes are so numerous that the land area appears as a series of peninsulas, islands, and isthmuses. Few parts of the world are known where so large a portion of the land is occupied by lakes. In northwest Wisconsin a third concentration of lakes is found in the forested area of five counties. These waters are very similar to the group in the highland regions. The hundreds of flood-plain lakes in the wide Mississippi River valley, plus Lake Pepin and St. Croix Lake on the western border of the state, make up the fourth group.

The Mississippi River is now a series of navigation pools which maintain innumerable backwater lakes of all sizes and shapes, many that rarely see an angler because of the vast area they cover and the comparatively light fishing pressure they receive. In these backwater lakes one may find exceptional largemouth, northern pike, and panfish angling. Fishing in the river channel, especially below the navigation dams and at the many wing dams, is often very productive for walleyes and saugers. Catfish are abundant in the channel, and setline (trotline) or bank pole-fishing is popular for this species.

SPRING FISHING

The general spring fishing season for gamefish, such as walleyes and northern pike, and for panfish, such as bluegills, sunfish, crappies, yellow perch, white bass, rock bass, and bullheads, gets under way in May. Although there is no closed season for panfish, spring fishing is dependent on weather. By early May, the shallower bays and shorelines of lakes warm up enough to attract the panfish that build nests in shallow water. Taking panfish at this time in the shallows with fly rod or cane pole while either wading or boating is one of the most satisfying types of angling in Wisconsin. The panfish are often termed the "bread and butter" fish, not only because of their abundance and eagerness to take a hook but because they are excellent table fare.

About the time the smelt are running, some of the finest early walleye fishing begins in a number of Wisconsin rivers and their tributaries, such as the Wisconsin, the Rock, the Upper Fox, and the famous Wolf River. The walleye is one of the state's most abundant and popular gamefish. Almost all waters of moderate size contain walleye populations, but the most productive are those larger lakes connected or fed by rivers. Lake Winnebago, virtually an inland sea, harbors a vast population of walleyes that migrates almost 100 miles up the Wolf River in order to spawn. To thousands of Wisconsin anglers "ice out" on the Wolf River announces spring. For 50 miles of river one can spot anchored boats along the river channel, and at night many of the river bends are lit up by the all-night fishing shanties. As the season progresses to summer, angling skill, knowledge of the water being fished, and fishing during the right time of day (usually early morning and evening) are more important elements for successful walleye fishing.

Northern pike are common in most lakes and larger rivers. This voracious fish provides many thrills as it strikes most lures with abandon, and can be taken without the skill often necessary for taking walleyes. The species is most abundant in lakes containing lush growths of aquatic vegetation and those with marshy shorelines or connections to marshes that flood during the early spring spawning period. Most northerns caught are in the 2–4-pound class, but fish of 10–20 pounds are not uncommon, and occasionally a fish approaching 30 pounds is taken.

THE WISCONSIN MUSKELLUNGE

The official state fish is the muskellunge, the tiger of Wisconsin's northern waters and the species for which the state is most widely known. The two northern lake districts seem to be the center of this species' range in North America. There may be certain physical characteristics about these concentrated lake areas and natural flowages that maintain the species because its abundance has not spread to other regions even though it has been extensively stocked. It is also found in the Great Lakes waters but only to a limited extent. Muskellunge are solitary fish with a temperament different from the northern pike. They commonly slash at and take surface lures, which is seldom true of pike. A musky may often follow a lure or remain in sight of the angler's boat, though all efforts fail to excite it enough to take the lure. Nevertheless, the annual catch of Wisconsin muskellunge is considerable. In 1963, 101 camps and resorts in the northwestern part of the state recorded a catch of 2,022 legal fish, totaling more than 10 tons. The largest fish was a 54-inch muskellunge, but 11.4 percent measured over 40 inches. The highest harvest per acre reported was 3.9 pounds, or one legal muskellunge for every 2½ acres of water. As to the fishing techniques used, three types of baits accounted for 75 percent of all fish caught; surface plugs accounted for 29.4 percent; bucktail baits (mostly with spinners attached) 27.3 percent; while live bait produced 18.5 percent.

Besides the many northern lakes noted for muskellunge, several flowages are popular, particularly the well-known Chippewa and Flambeau flowages. These sprawling waters are each over 17,000 acres in area and originally consisted of a number of lakes that were joined together by impounding. They are located in forested wilderness, dotted with many islands, and have very irregular shorelines. A number of other smaller flowages are found across the northern part of the state. These picturesque flowages and some of the larger rivers are also excellent musky waters.

SUMMER AND AUTUMN FISHING

Summer fishing is one of the most popular recreational pursuits in Wisconsin. The resort industry of the state is to a large extent built around the sport-fishery resource. Facilities are available for all types of anglers from family groups interested in quiet relaxation to dyed-in-the-wool musky fishermen or dry-fly addicts who go at their sport as perfectionists. The habits of some species of fish change in summer. Walleyes and northern pike are often taken in deeper water; panfishing is often more rewarding when trolling is tried; evening and night fishing are recommended for largemouth-bass action; and white bass can most easily be taken by locating surface-feeding schools in the openwater areas and then simply casting streamer flies into their midst.

When the autumn season begins in Wisconsin, fishing is far from over. Walleyes again frequent shallow-water areas, often simulating the spring spawning run. Muskies are often most active at this time, and a serious musky fisherman takes advantage of this habit to view some of the finest scenery of the year when maple and birch leaves put on their colorful displays. Also during the fall in the state's largest rivers (not including the Winnebago system), anglers seek the largest freshwater fish in the state, the lake sturgeon. Heavy tackle is used for these monsters, and at least one fish weighing over 100 pounds was taken in recent years on rod-and-reel. Some of the rivers where sturgeon are found are the Wisconsin, the Menominee, the St. Croix, the Chippewa, and the Manitowish rivers. Baits such as minnows and night crawlers are soaked in a likely deep-river pool.

Just prior to ice formation in November hardy dippers and seiners come forth to seek the silver-sided, deepwater whitefish and ciscos that are found in many of the state's cold lakes. Provisions are made to permit harvest of the whitefish with seines and dipnets, as these species are difficult to harvest with hook and line. In this sport as well as the smelt dipping which begins just as the ice leaves Wisconsin lakes, seining and dipping are done after dark. It's also a group sport as plenty of hands are needed to help pull the seine or row the boat for the dipnetter.

TROUT LAKES

Besides stream trout fishing many of Wisconsin's lakes are cool and clear enough to support and provide conditions for excellent trout growth. These lakes are annually stocked, as most of them do not have tributary streams that provide trout spawning grounds. Rainbows put on excellent growth and soon resemble lake-run steelheads in coloration and spectacular fighting qualities. Rainbow trout are the predominant species stocked, although brook trout and brown trout, and more recently splake (*which see*), are being stocked. The temperate climate, especially in northern Wisconsin, aids in maintaining cool summer temperatures in a large share of the lakes. Trout in these lakes compete well with many warmwater species, such as bass and panfish, so that many are two-story lakes—trout in the open deepwater and warmwater species in the near-surface and shoreline areas. Lake trout are found in several of the state's large and deep lakes. An intensive management program on 230-foot-deep Green Lake has provided some outstanding lake-trout fishing winter and summer. Trout Lake in the northern highland region is known for its scenic islands and shoreline besides lake trout and large walleyes. The splake, a trout hybrid, grows rapidly in several lakes in this northern lake country that now contain them.

WINTER FISHING

Once the ice has formed well enough to walk on, the ice-fishing season begins. The ice fisherman dons his insulated clothing, picks up his tip-ups for walleyes and northern pike, and brings his sensitive, short "jig poles" for panfish that are more timorous in coldwater. Later he may drive his auto on the ice and pull a heated shanty out to his favorite fishing spot, often among a village of shanties. He can comfortably fish in shirt sleeves through the floor of his shanty or watch for "tip-up" flags through the windows of his heated shelter. Although ice fishing for walleyes and northern pike is popular in many lakes, panfish, such as bluegills, yellow perch, and crappies, are more often sought. Fishing success is usually much better through the ice than in the summer, which undoubtedly is responsible for its increasing popularity. Large catches of bluegills, crappies, and yellow perch are made in many waters. Catches of over 100 bluegills a day are common in the Mississippi River backwaters, and limit catches of the jumbo yellow perch are taken from Lake Mendota, which bounds the north side of the state capital in Madison. This 10,000-acre lake has been estimated to produce 40 pounds of jumbo perch per acre just during the ice-fishing season. In fact, it is suspected that this harvest maintains the fast growth of these fish by keeping them thinned down.

FISH RESEARCH PROGRAM

A number of Wisconsin waters are being used as outdoor laboratories for fish research by the Wisconsin Conservation Department. In such places as Murphy Flowage in the northwest, the "Five Lakes" in the northern highland, plus Yellowstone and Cox Hollow lakes in the southwest, anglers' catches are examined the year around to measure fish production, the effects of regulations, and to evaluate experimental techniques designed to improve angling success. In many of these and other experimental waters no closed seasons, bag, or size limits have been established to evaluate the effects of liberalized angling regulations. Based on fishery research, many liberal regulations have been established throughout the state. Similar research is being conducted on trout streams, among which Lawrence Creek in central Wisconsin is most intensively studied. Anglers' creels are examined, trout production in the stream is estimated, and various experimental management techniques are being evaluated by observing the trends or changes in the anglers' catch. Less intensive trout research is being conducted on a number of other waters located in each major trout-stream area of the state.

The University of Wisconsin has an outstanding hydrobiology program in which a number of state waters are used as outdoor laboratories, especially Lake Mendota in the south and Trout Lake and surrounding waters of the north. The science of limnology is synonymous with Wisconsin in scientific circles due to the pioneering research conducted by E. A. Birge and his co-workers, notably Chancey Juday. This work is continuing today, and, in addition, freshwater ecology (*which see*), fish behavior, production of trout in bog lakes, and algae nuisance problems are examples of university studies being conducted at present.

FISHERY CONSERVATION PROGRAMS

Although Wisconsin has experienced an increase in fishing pressure, there is still plenty of elbow room in the state's abundant waters for fishermen and other recreation seekers. The future of Wisconsin's abundant recreational waters is bright. The state constitution provides that all waters are to be held in trust for the public; therefore there are no private lakes unless they are completely constructed artificially on privately owned land. All navigable streams are public, which includes most streams that provide fishing. There are some waters inaccessible over land due to private ownership of shorelines, but there is fine public access to the majority of waters. Further, an outstanding land-acquisition program being conducted by the Conservation Department is adding more public access sites every year. A program designed to classify all waters in the state according to use was established in recent years. This program will enable a reasonable and logical direction of water use to ease the conflict that is expected to increase as recreation seekers increase. Through an additional 1-cent-a-pack tax on cigarettes, some 50,000,000 dollars is to be spent to purchase or insure conservation use through easements during the first "acquisition phase" of the program. This popular program established through legislation is expected to add materially to the recreational resources of the state.

Wisconsin is recognized as one of the nation's top fishing states, and has licensed more nonresident fishermen than any other state during the last decade. A vigorous fish management program is conducted by the Conservation Department. The program is aimed at perpetuation of the abundant water resources and the development of new management methods to increase further abundant angling opportunities. *See also* Ice Fishing, Muskellunge, Northern Pike —T.L.W.

WITCH FLOUNDER *Glyptocephalus cynoglossus* Also called the gray sole, Craig fluke, and pole flounder, this species, which is related to the rex sole on the Pacific coast, occurs in moderately deep water on both sides of the North Atlantic. Adults have been taken from the Gulf of St. Lawrence and the southern Grand Bank southward as far as Cape Hatteras. On the European side it is found at Iceland and from northern Norway to the west coast of France.

Its color is grayish-brown, sometimes darker, with transverse bars; dorsal and anal fins occasionally spotted and tinged with violet; membrane of pectoral fin on eyed side dusky to black; blind side grayish-white, with minute dark points scattered throughout.

Other distinguishing characteristics of the witch flounder are body elongate-oblong, lying on left side, much compressed, greatest depth 2¾ in total length a short distance behind tip of pectoral. Head relatively small, about 6 in total length; mouth very small, its angle well in front of eyes; a single series of incisorlike teeth in each jaw; blind side of head deeply sculptured, with about 12 mucous pits.

Dorsal fin with 100–115 softrays, beginning over middle of left eye and extending to base of caudal peduncle; caudal rounded, relatively small; anal fin with 87–100 softrays, preceded by a short preanal spine, beginning under base of pectoral and ending on caudal peduncle under end of dorsal; pectorals inserted on sides behind gill opening, ⅔ length of head; pelvics inserted on ventral edge slightly in front of base of pectorals, smaller than pectorals. Lateral line almost straight. Scales small and smooth covering body and most of head.

LIFE HISTORY

The witch flounder is found primarily in depths of 25–150 fathoms, but it has been taken as deep as 858 fathoms. It prefers a mud or sand bottom where the temperature may vary from 30°–50°F. Spawning takes place in late spring to summer. The pelagic eggs are spherical and about $\frac{1}{20}$–$\frac{1}{25}$ of an inch in diameter. At temperatures of 46°–49°F, hatching occurs in 7–8 days. Growth is slow and young of 7–8 inches in length have been calculated to be 3 years old. Adults reach up to 25 inches in length and a weight of a little over 4 pounds.

This species prefers to feed on small shrimp, amphipods, marine worms, and small mollusks. Although its body is thin the flesh has a fine flavor, so it supports a considerable commercial fishery. Most are taken by means of the Danish seine and the otter trawl.

—J.C.B.

WOLFFISH See Atlantic Wolffish, Spotted Wolffish

WOODS HOLE OCEANOGRAPHIC INSTITUTION A private, nonprofit, scientific organization established in 1930 for the purpose of conducting basic research into all matters dealing with the ocean, the air above, and the bottom below. The institution is located in the village of Woods Hole on the southwestern tip of Cape Cod, Massachusetts.

The institution's research staff of more than one hundred includes scientists representing the basic disciplines of physics, chemistry, biology, geology, geophysics, meteorology, mathematics, and electronics. With a large supporting group of scientific assistants, technicians, maritime personnel, administrators, and clerks, the total year-round employment of the institution numbers around 550.

The work of the instituion is divided into six major departments—Applied Oceanography, Biology, Chemistry and Geology, Geophysics, Physical Oceanography, and Theoretical Oceanography and Meteorology.

Policy for the institution is set by a board of trustees elected from the members of the corporation.

Although the institution is not directly associated with a university, close contact is maintained with a number of educational institutions. Some members of the Woods Hole research staff hold parttime teaching assignments in a number of universities; and many teachers of the marine sciences come to Woods Hole to conduct investigations, particularly in the summer.

Currently, around 150 fellowship holders, students, visiting investigators, and parttime employees are added to the institution's year-round personnel each summer. There are formal courses for advanced students during the summer, which include sea-going instruction as well as classroom work.

The purpose of the Woods Hole Oceanographic Institution is basic research into all aspects of the world's oceans. For example, in 1962, staff members published ninety-six scientific papers covering the entire spectrum of the marine sciences.

One area of research that has been of particular interest to sport fishermen, and one that has had their direct cooperation, is a continuing study into the growth and distribution patterns of large pelagic fish, including tuna, marlin, and swordfish. Sport fishermen have been of assistance in this program by tagging and releasing fish, which, when recaught, add to the data on their migratory habits. In 1962 there were 49 returns from 2,766 releases, including recovery in Norwegian waters of three giant bluefins tagged in the Florida Straits.

Another recent result of this program was the accumulation of information of the general autumnal distribution of the broadbill swordfish along the Continental Slope and apparent differences in its habitat according to size and sex. This species was taken in quantity throughout the fall of 1962 by longline fishing at night in the vicinity of the five hundred-fathom curve from Georges Bank to the Hudson Canyon.

The above mentioned project is just one of dozens of scientific investigations conducted at the institution. In the field of physical oceanography, scientists are seeking to identify the currents in the ocean, discover how they behave, and calculate their future courses. The Marine meteorologists are exploring the complex physics of convection, condensation, and cloud formation, as well as the exchange of energy and matter across the sea surface.

Geophysicists are interested in the composition and origin of the ocean sediments, as well as the depth and composition of the crustal layers beneath the sediments. Chemists are analyzing the sediments and attempting to isolate the very dilute organic compounds in seawater. Marine biologists are working to understand the environmental conditions which determine and control the size of all types of populations, ranging from bacteria to whales.

The above are just a few of the many projects and directions of the complete scientific program. The physical facilities of the institution include three large laboratories ashore along with a number of smaller auxiliary buildings.

The institution has its own dock behind its main buildings on Great Harbor, Woods Hole, where it maintains its fleet of five sea-going ships, "Atlantis," "Atlantis II," "Chain," "Crawford," and "Gosnold," and several smaller craft for work in nearby waters. The institution also operates two aircraft, a four-engine C54Q equipped primarily for meteorological observations, and a Helio-Courier for shorter flights. A deep-diving, two-man submarine, *Alvin*, is also a part of the program.

The institution has no public exhibit area, nor does it conduct tours for the general public. For general information about the institution, letters should be addressed to the Public Affairs Office, Woods Hole Oceanographic Institution, Woods Hole, Massachusetts.   —H.V.R.P.

WRASSES Family Labridae Saltwater fishes comprising about 450 species. Although chiefly found in tropical seas, some species also occur in the temperate zone, such as the tautog, cunner, hogfish, and California sheephead. All labroid fishes are distinguished by their heavy pharyngeal or "throat" teeth which they use to crush their food. *See also* Bluehead Wrasse, California Sheephead, Cunner, Hogfish, Señorita, Slippery Dick, Tautog

WRECK BUOY A buoy painted with red and black horizontal stripes and marking a wreck. Such a buoy often reveals the location of a good fishing ground because species such as grouper, barracuda, snappers, sea bass, and tautog find cover and food among the debris. *See also* Buoy

WRYMOUTH *Cryptacanthodes maculatus* Also known as the ghostfish or spotted wrymouth, it belongs to a family of northern blennys called the Stichaeidae. This is a group of elongate fishes with poorly developed lateral lines; they are often called pricklebacks because the long dorsal fin is supported entirely by spines. This species is found along the Atlantic coast of North America from southern Labrador and the Grand Bank to New Jersey.

Its background color may be various shades of brown or reddish-brown; belly grayish-white; upper part of body with three irregular rows of small dark brown spots running from the head to the tail; top of head thickly spotted; dorsal and anal fins with smaller brown spots. Albino specimens have been seen.

Other distinguishing characters of the wrymouth are body very elongate, eel-like, greatest depth 14 in total length, much compressed. Head 7 in total length, flat-topped, snout very blunt, mouth terminal, oblique, lower jaw projecting markedly, angle of mouth under posterior edge of eye; stout, conical teeth in jaws and on vomer and palatines; conspicuous mucous secreting pits on sides of head; eye small, 14 in head.

The first dorsal fin with 73–77 spines, all stout and somewhat hidden by skin, fin begins over middle of pectoral, extends full length of back and is continuous with caudal; caudal small, oval-shaped, and pointed; anal fin with 47–50 softrays, beginning under 20th spine of dorsal, extending to and continuous with caudal; pectorals small, longest rays 3½ in head, located low on sides behind gill opening; pelvics absent. Lateral line not evident. Body naked.

The wrymouth lives on soft bottom where it burrows in mud, sometimes building an extensive branching system of tunnels. It occurs in shallow water and up to 60 fathoms. It is known to feed on amphipods and shrimps and, under captive conditions, will eat pieces of fish. The presence of small fry in early spring suggests winter spawning. It grows to a length of about 3 feet.—J.C.B.

WYOMING Wyoming is located at the headwaters of three of the nation's major river drainages—the Colorado, Missouri, and Columbia. Associated with these drainages is some of the best natural trout habitat to be found in the United States today.

Twenty thousand miles of fishing streams flow in every direction across Wyoming. They tumble down precipitous mountain slopes, wander through narrow canyons, and glide away in placid runs and rippling riffles across grassy meadows. Nearly 5,000 crystalline lakes dot the lowlands and nestle among the crags of the Rockies. Lodgepole pine stands in dark masses against the far distant ranges, climbing to the snows of timberline. Wyoming typifies the West. And few other states can boast of quality trout fishing as it exists here today.

Excellent cutthroat trout fishing exists in the remote waters of the Grand Canyon of the Snake

Wyoming's low population (330,000 in 1960) is a major contributing factor to the state's excellent natural trout fisheries. The rapid growth of population which results in the loss of natural fish habitat, and already felt greatly in most states, has not been experienced in Wyoming. Perhaps some day Wyoming will have these "growing pains" which have seriously damaged or destroyed top-notch fishing in many states. But at present, outstanding trout fishing is still available, and careful management continues to assure that it will be enjoyed for years to come.

One of the main programs in Wyoming is the state's propagation and stocking program. While large numbers of fish are planted each season little stocking is done strictly on a put-and-take basis. Most of the fish planted

are of subcatchable size. They are liberated with the objective that they will provide natural spawning stock in years to come.

Projects designed to improve and protect fish habitat, create new fishing waters, and manipulate fish populations in favor of desired fish species are also in continuous operation. Since 1950, more than seventy-five waters across Wyoming have been converted from havens for coarse fish and overpopulations of small panfish to excellent habitat for trout and other gamefish.

Another program, perhaps the most important one, through which Wyoming is working toward perpetuation of its fishing resource, is sponsorship of free fisherman access to important fishing waters across the state. Wyoming carries on a program of purchase of fishing easements on key waters from private landowners. For example, easements have been purchased on the North Platte River and the Salt River in western Wyoming. At present there is not a major problem of fishermen access to private lands. Furthermore, there are numerous dude ranches, crossroads villages and towns, and even working ranches and farms along the rivers, which welcome tourists. Many ranchers, in particular, are equipped to take a visitor on a one-day or a month-long pack trip high in the mountains to waters where trout seldom if ever see an artificial fly.

All types of fishing are available in Wyoming, and it is impossible to say which method is most popular or produces the best results. Fly-fishing, casting, trolling, and ice fishing are all enjoyed at different times of year in various localities. Eighty-nine fish varieties are found in Wyoming's waters. Of this number, twenty-one are considered gamefish by law. Most popular are the state's six trout species—the cutthroat, rainbow, brook, brown, lake (locally mackinaw), and the golden. The kokanee (*which see*) is one of the resident anglers' favorites. Walleye, whitefish, grayling, ling, largemouth bass, and channel catfish are important in various localities. Other popular species include the sauger, yellow perch, green sunfish, black crappie, rock bass, and black bullhead.

NORTHEASTERN AREA

This area takes in five counties—Crook, Weston, Campbell, Sheridan, and Johnson counties. Quality trout fishing, as found in some areas of the state, is limited in Crook, Weston, and Campbell counties. A number of top-rate fishing waters are found in Sheridan and Johnson counties, however.

Sand Creek Undoubtedly the top fishing water in Crook County, Sand Creek is located northeast of the town of Sundance. About 5¾ miles of this excellent trout stream are either leased or owned by the state. Additional fishing is available on the Belle Fourche Club property for a small fee. The stream contains an abundance of brown trout, and catchable-size rainbow and brook trout have been stocked. The best fishing is enjoyed from April through September. Facilities include picnic tables, garbage cans, fireplaces, toilets, and good access roads. Motel accommodations are available in nearby towns.

Cook Lake Located west of the small town of Beulah in Crook County, this lake yields rainbow trout up to 19 inches, but usually averaging 10 inches. Good fishing is enjoyed from late June through October. The lake is located in the Black Hills National Forest. Picnic tables, fireplaces, garbage cans, and toilets are available at the lake, and living accommodations are found in nearby towns.

Keyhole Reservoir Near the town of Moorcroft in Crook County, Keyhole is a 6,500-acre Bureau of Reclamation reservoir. Good gravel roads and camping facilities and fair boat-launching facilities are available. Fishing is fair for walleye, pike, and channel catfish during the spring and early summer.

Lak Reservoir Located near the city of Newcastle in Weston County, Lak is located on private land with free public access allowed. It has good fishing for rainbow trout averaging 12 inches. Good roads and boat-launching facilities are available. Stockade-Beaver Creek, the inlet to Lak offers good fishing for small rainbow trout and some brookies in the upper reaches. The creek is located on private land, but there is no access problem.

Gillette Fishing Lake It is located east of the city of Gillette in Campbell County. Heavy fishing pressure is experienced on the lake, and it is managed strictly on a put-and-take basis. Camping facilities are available.

Powder River The Powder River proper provides little top-notch fishing, but three forks, the North Fork, Middle Fork, and Red Fork, near the town of Kaycee in Johnson County, provide good to very good fishing. The North Fork has 30 miles of angling for small cutthroat, a few browns and rainbows, from the small town of Mayoworth to its headwaters. Access to the North Fork is good in most areas except the canyon section. The Middle Fork provides very good fishing from the mouth of Buffalo Creek to its headwaters. Brown and rainbow, averaging 12 inches, are taken in the canyon section, and small brookies are available at the headwaters. Access is fairly good except in the canyon section. The Red Fork provides about 10 miles of good fishing for brown and rainbow averaging 10 inches. All of the Red Fork is located on private property, and landowners charge a small trespass fee in the lower portion.

Lake DeSmet A 2,000-acre lake north of the city of Buffalo in Johnson County. Lake DeSmet has long been noted as one of the state's prime fishing waters. Rainbow fishing is excellent, and some lunker browns are also taken occasionally. Perch and rock bass abound, and no creel limit is placed on either species. Two resorts at the lake offer boats, cabins, and meals. Camping areas and boat-launching facilities are available around the lake shore.

Seven Brothers Lakes, Lake Angeline, Florence Lake All these lakes are located in the Big Horn National Forest west of Buffalo. Seven Brothers is a series of seven lakes, six of which provide good fishing for rainbow and mackinaw averaging 15 inches. Lake Angeline has an excellent population of good-size cutthroat and some smaller rainbow trout. Florence Lake produces cutthroat trout averaging ½ pound. All the lakes are located at nearly 11,000 feet and are accessible by horse trail and foot only.

Clear Creek and Drainage Clear Creek, from a point 5 miles below the city of Buffalo to the junction of the Middle Forks of Clear Creek, provides very good fishing for small rainbows, browns, and brookies. Remote sections of the drainage provide the only access problems. Camping facilities are available.

Piney Creek and Drainage Piney Creek and its tributaries flow through northwestern Johnson and southern Sheridan counties. About 10 miles of Piney Creek, below the junction of its north and south forks, offer good fishing for small rainbow and brown trout. Three excellent fishing lakes are found on South Piney. Frying Pan Lake provides fishing for cutthroat and Flat Iron Lake for rainbow and cutthroat. The big producer is Cloud Peak Reservoir, a 171-acre lake, which yields rainbow and cutthroat averaging 3 pounds. Rainbow up to 9 pounds have been taken from Cloud Peak. Access is good to canyon sections of North and South Piney, but most water is on private land.

Kearney Lake Located on Kearney Creek, a tributary to South Piney Creek, the lake produces good rainbow and mackinaw fishing. Occasionally, "macks" go over 20 pounds. Horses may be rented in the towns of Buffalo and Story.

Tongue River The river provides 15 miles of very good fishing upstream from the town of Ranchester in Sheridan County, mostly on private land. Good fishing for whitefish, averaging 14 inches, and for rainbow and browns, about 12-inch average. The North Tongue River parallels State Highway 14 for most of its length and provides about 25 miles of very good fishing for rainbow, cutthroat, and brown trout. The South Fork provides about 15 miles of top-notch fishing from its junction with the Tongue to its east and west forks. Small brook trout and rainbows and browns averaging 12 inches are the rule.

EAST CENTRAL WYOMING

This area takes in portions of Carbon, Natrona, Converse, Platte, and Goshen counties. Much of the fishing in this area is provided by Bureau of Reclamation reservoirs on the North Platte River. The North Platte has more dams than any other river in the state, and most of the reservoirs backed up by these dams have long been among the top fish producers in Wyoming. All of the reservoirs are open year round.

Boat-launching facilities are available at all the reservoirs except Kortes. Camping facilities are limited, and generally food and lodging are available only at the nearest town to the particular reservoir.

Seminoe Reservoir This reservoir, with about 20,000 surface acres of water, is located northeast of Rawlins in Carbon County. Large rainbow and brown trout, averaging 12–20 inches, are available to anglers, and fishing is good both in summer and winter. The reservoir's fluctuation is slow and gradual and doesn't affect fisherman success a great deal. The best boat-launching facilities are located on the west shore. The nearest food and lodging are found in Rawlins.

Kortes Reservoir One of the smaller North Platte reservoirs, Kortes is located just downstream from Seminoe. Access is very poor since the reservoir's shoreline is located for the most part in an inaccessible canyon. The only access, and it is poor, is located immediately below Seminoe Reservoir. Shore fishing is impossible. Fishing success is only fair for rainbow, brown, and a few mackinaw, but the fish are of good size. The North Platte River below Kortes to the backwaters of Pathfinder Reservoir provides very good fishing from time to time for large rainbow and brown trout with the best brown fishing in the fall of the year. The water level fluctuates a great deal in this section of the river, and fishing varies accordingly. The nearest lodging is at Rawlins or Casper, both about 65 miles away, and the nearest gas and groceries are available at Alcova, which is about 35 miles from Kortes.

Pathfinder Reservoir It is located on the border of Carbon and Natrona counties. The nearest gas and groceries are at Alcova, 12 miles away, and the nearest lodging in Casper, 40 miles to the north. Fishing varies because of extreme fluctuation in water level. Rainbow trout running 16–20 inches are taken from Pathfinder.

Alcova Reservoir Located about 30 miles southwest of Casper in Natrona County, its fishing is primarily for rainbow trout, although some large brown trout are taken. An oiled road leads to the lake, and excellent boat-launching ramps are available. Food and gas are available at the lake, and lodging is in Casper. Boat trips up the Alcova Canyon are available, and this is undoubtedly one of Wyoming's most scenic areas that can be viewed without the expense of pack trips. Boaters and water skiers affect fishing during midsummer. The best fishing is enjoyed in spring and early summer and early fall.

Glendo Reservoir This reservoir, containing about 12,000 surface acres, has been one of the state's top trout producers in recent years. The reservoir is located only 2 miles from the town of Glendo in Platte County, and food and lodging are readily available. Glendo is primarily a rainbow-trout water, with fish usually 10–15 inches. Good boat-launching facilities are available. The North Platte River downstream from Glendo Dam for a distance of about one mile provides some of the best rainbow fishing in the state. The rest of the river downstream to Guernsey Reservoir also produces good angling. Fishing is poor in Guernsey Reservoir because of extreme drawdown.

The North Platte River from Guernsey Dam to the Nebraska state line is subject to heavy fluctuation because of irrigation demands in the summer. This section of river is presently maintained on a put-and-take basis. Some private lands adjacent to the river in this area are closed to trespass.

SOUTHEASTERN WYOMING

This area includes waters in Laramie, Goshen, Platte, Albany, and Carbon counties.

Cheyenne, Wyoming's capital city, is located in Laramie County, the most populous in the state. Top-rate fishing is fairly limited in Laramie County and the portion of Goshen County in this section. Some of the state's better angling areas are found in Carbon and Albany counties, however.

Granite and Crystal Reservoirs These two reservoirs are located west of Cheyenne and take up a great deal of the fishing pressure from the capital city. The reservoirs, while heavily fished, have an abundance of rainbow trout averaging 10 inches. Public fishing is allowed, and both reservoirs are easily reached by good dirt roads. Boat permits must be obtained from the city of Cheyenne. Boats are easily launched from the shoreline of either reservoir.

Lodgepole Creek An important local fishing water in the Cheyenne area, the creek provides fishing for small brookies and rainbows, and is reached by good graded roads.

Hawk Springs Reservoir and Packer's Lake Hawk Springs Reservoir is located a few miles west of the small town of Hawk Springs in Goshen County, and Packer's Lake is just northeast of the town. Both waters provide fishing for walleye averaging 14 inches. Small bass were stocked in Packer's some time ago. Both lakes are accessible by dirt roads.

Lake Hattie A man-made lake west of the city of Laramie in Albany County, the lake contains 2,240 surface acres of water, and access is good by dirt or paved roads. The lake is open to public fishing, and good boat-launching facilities are available. Rainbow and brown trout averaging 15 inches are available in excellent numbers, and some real lunkers are reported every year. Perch are also available in great numbers, and no limit is placed on the species. This lake is undoubtedly one of the top producers in the southeastern area.

Sodergreen Lake, Carroll Lake, Big Gelatt Lake, Leazenby Lake These are four of the top producers of the great number of small lakes in the Laramie area. All are easily reached by good paved or dirt roads. There is good fishing for brook, brown, and rainbow trout, usually 10–14 inches. Sodergreen and Leazenby are public fishing lakes, but permission must be obtained from private landowners to fish most other lakes.

Saratoga Fishing Lake A public fishing lake near the town of Saratoga in Carbon County, it is primarily a producer of 12-inch brown, brook, and rainbow trout. It has a good dirt access road.

Snowy Range Area This area is one of the most scenic in Wyoming. The majestic mountain range stretches for about 60 miles from Laramie to Saratoga and provides countless lakes and streams which provide good fishing throughout the summer. Many lakes and streams, next to State Highway 130 which crosses the range, provide very good fishing for small trout. If an angler wants larger fish, he must be willing to walk a few miles from the main highway. Overnight campgrounds are abundant throughout the area. Information on individual lakes and streams may be obtained from the Game and Fish Department's fisheries management crew in Laramie.

Big Laramie River The river flows from southwestern Albany County through the city of Laramie. It provides very good fishing for about 15 miles in its upper reaches, and is considered an important trout water through most of the rest of its drainage. Public fishing is available on state land above Woods Landing Junction, and some fishing is allowed on private lands between Woods Landing and Laramie. Brown and rainbow trout run 10–12 inches. It is accessible by paved road.

Little Laramie River Located west of Laramie, the river and its tributaries provide very good fishing in its upper reaches. Fishing is allowed by some landowners, and all ranches are accessible by graded roads.

Rock Creek It provides 23 miles of excellent trout fishing from the town of McFadden in Carbon County, south into the Medicine Bow National Forest in Albany County. Access is by dirt roads in the upper areas.

North Platte River This stretch of the North Platte, from the U. S. Highway 30 bridge at Fort Steele in Carbon County upstream to the Colorado state line, provides 65 miles of the finest fishing found in Wyoming. Brown and rainbow run 12–14 inches, but many larger fish are taken each summer. Public fishing areas on state-leased or -owned lands are located in the Saratoga area. The river is easily floated, and the popular stretch is from the Baldwin access downstream to Saratoga. This is fished with live bait and spinners in the early season, but provides good fly fishing from mid-July into September.

Douglas Creek There are 25 miles of very good fishing for small rainbow and brook trout, mostly in the Medicine Bow National Forest in Albany and Carbon counties. Most areas are easily reached by car, but the more remote areas must be hiked into. A state access area is provided on the lower portion of the stream where it enters the North Platte.

Encampment River Excellent trout fishing occurs on 13 miles of the river in the Medicine Bow National Forest, from the Colorado state line to within a few miles of the town of Encampment in Carbon County. Access is by dirt road.

The upper Green River north of Pinedale is a popular area for brook and rainbow trout and small grayling

SOUTHWESTERN WYOMING

This area includes Sublette, Sweetwater, and Uinta counties and a portion of Lincoln County.

Sublette County with its innumerable lakes and streams is without a doubt one of the outstanding fishing areas in Wyoming and probably the nation. Only a partial list of waters available in Sublette County may be listed here. Most of these are located within the boundaries of the Bridger National Forest and Wilderness Area, where fishing streams and lakes are available in almost unbelievable abundance. In addition, this area is one of the most scenic and rugged in the state. Many waters, not listed here, are located off the beaten track, and fishermen unfamiliar with the country should consider the services of a qualified guide.

Fishing is also good in several areas of southern Lincoln County, but quality angling is fairly limited in Sweetwater and Uinta counties.

Green River The upper Green River in Sublette County is rated as one of Wyoming's prime trout-fishing streams. From its junction with the New Fork River east of the town of Big Piney, upstream to the Green River lakes, it provides 105 miles of excellent fly fishing for rainbow trout with some cutthroat, brook, and the occasional brown trout present in various parts of the stream. The fish are of large average size, with 1½–2-pounders fairly common. The entire upper section is easily reached, and accommodations are readily available. From the junction with the New Fork downstream to the town of Green River in Sweetwater County, the Green River is considered important, but not on a par with its upper areas. The best period for fly fishing here, as elsewhere in Wyoming, is from mid-July into the fall season. Flaming Gorge Reservoir, shared with Utah (*which see*), also produces excellent trout angling.

East Fork River Flowing into the New Fork River, the East Fork provides excellent trout fishing for 21 miles in its upper reaches. A paved road from the small town of Boulder crosses the river at one point.

Green River Lakes Located north of the town of Pinedale in Sublette County the upper lake contains 320 acres and provides fishing for rainbow and cutthroat. It is accessible by well-marked horse and foot trails. The lower lake provides fishing for trout averaging 14 inches. Forest camps and dude-ranch accommodations are available at the lower lake which is reached by fair graveled road. Boat-launching facilities are also to be found at the lower lake.

New Fork Lakes These two lakes are considered as one body of water with about 1,100 surface acres. The lakes are up to 200 feet deep in spots and provide top-rate fishing for rainbow usually of 10–15 inches and mackinaw between 15–20 inches. Shoreline forest camps are available. The lakes are readily accessible by fair gravel roads from dude ranches and motels in the area. There is access for boat launching.

Willow Lake It contains about 2,000 surface acres, with depths to 230 feet. Rainbow, cutthroat, and mackinaw, 10–20 inches, occur here. Lake shore camps are available, and the lake is easily reached by fair gravel roads from nearby dude ranches and motels.

Soda Lake It provides fishing for brook trout of 10–15 inches. Soda is a landlocked, highly alkaline lake. It is readily accessible by fair graveled roads. No motor-powered boats are allowed.

Fremont Lake One of Wyoming's real lunker producers, Fremont contains 5,000 surface acres with depths up to 600 feet. Mackinaw are usually 15–25 inches and rainbow 15 inches. Good kokanee-salmon angling is also enjoyed. Lakeside resort and shoreline camping facilities are available, as is access for boat launching.

Long Lake A 480-acre mountain lake, it has large cutthroat trout available in good numbers. Access by good foot trail is from the head of Fremont Lake or steep horse and foot trail from the head of the Skyline Drive road.

Half Moon Lake Rainbow and brook trout average 10–15 inches. Forest camping areas and resort facilities are available, as well as boat-launching access. Pole

Creek, above Half Moon Lake, provides 12 miles of excellent trout fishing.

Burnt Lake A 1,000-acre lake, Burnt Lake contains rainbow trout usually of 10–15 inches. Roads are rough, but access is possible to the lake from dude ranches and motels in the area. Small boat-launching access is available.

Cook Lakes Two adjacent mountain lakes with acreages of 150 and 75 acres, it contains brook trout running 6–10 inches. A record golden trout, weighing 11 pounds 4 ounces, was taken from one of these lakes. However, the water has since become overpopulated with small brook trout and the golden fishery is no longer evident.

Johnson Lake A small mountain meadow lake, it has grayling usually of 10–15 inches. A rough road provides access.

Middle Piney Lake A mountain lake of about 150 acres, its mackinaw average 17 inches. Brook and rainbow trout are also available. A fair road leads to the lake from the town of Big Piney, and lakeside forest camps are available. Boat-launching access is available, but no motor-powered boats are allowed.

North Piney Lake A 50-acre lake, it provides good cutthroat angling. It is accessible by several miles of trails from roads on North and Middle Piney creeks.

Middle Piney Creek and South Piney Creek The upper reaches of these two streams provide very good fishing for small rainbow and brook trout. North Piney Creek provides fair trout fishing.

LaBarge Creek and Drainage LaBarge Creek flows southeast across southern Lincoln County to the town of LaBarge where it empties into the Green River. The stream is a good fishery for brook and rainbow trout. It has easy automobile access.

Fontenelle Creek and Drainage Fontenelle Creek parallels LaBarge Creek and flows into the Green River below the town of LaBarge. It is considered a very good fishery in its upper reaches, and has easy access.

Ham's Fork and Drainage Ham's Fork from the city of Kemmerer upstream provides 62 miles of very good rainbow- and brook-trout fishing. Forest camps are located throughout the area, and access is through Kemmerer. Ham's Fork Reservoir provides fishing for rainbow running about 10–15 inches.

Smith's Fork and Drainage It is considered an important water in the Cokeville area of Lincoln County. Streams in this drainage provide fishing for brook and cutthroat trout. Lake Alice, located on Smith's Fork, provides fishing for cutthroat, 10–15 inches. Access to the upper areas is good, but a rough road leads to forest camps about 1½ miles from Lake Alice. This last leg must be hiked or traveled by horseback.

Bear River It provides 18 miles of very good fishing from the Utah state line into Uinta County. The remainder of the stream is considered as an important water on the district level.

CENTRAL WYOMING

This area includes Fremont County, one of Wyoming's largest counties, both in population and area. Fremont County has long been noted as one of the top fish-producing areas of the state. The best fishing is found in the northwestern and southwestern parts of the county, but good fishing definitely isn't limited to those areas. All waters within the Wind River Indian Reservation in Fremont and Hot Springs Counties require a $5.00 fishing license from the Indian Service in addition to a regular Wyoming fishing license. The special license may be obtained from Indian Service Headquarters in the town of Fort Washakie.

Sweetwater River The river south of historic South Pass City and above U. S. Highway 287 is a good bet for large rainbow, and is considered an important water on the district level. The river in its lower reaches is a low producer. The East Fork of the Sweetwater, northwest of State Highway 28, is easily fished with a fly rod. Brown, rainbow, and brook trout are available in good numbers. The East Fork is reached by dirt roads, but driving caution is necessary.

Little Popo Agie River Located southeast of the city of Lander, the Little Popo Agie is a good trout producer from State Highway 28 upstream. A public fishing area has been developed about one mile upstream from Highway 28. Brook and rainbow trout are found in the upper reaches and browns and rainbows in the lower areas. The Middle Fork of the Popo Agie near Lander provides very good angling for 22 miles above the Sinks Canyon area into the Shoshone National Forest.

South Fork of the Little Wind River West of Dickinson Park and accessible only by Forest Service trail, the South Fork has a very good population of California golden and rainbow trout. Although the fish are small, excellent fly-fishing is offered. The setting is one of the most scenic in Wyoming.

Christina, Tomahawk, and Atlantic Lakes These are all in the Shoshone National Forest. Christina is at the head of the Little Popo Agie River and is best for mackinaw trout in late spring and early summer. It is reached only by four-wheel-drive vehicles. Atlantic is 2 miles above Christina and offers cutthroat- and brook-trout fishing. It is reached only by Forest Service trail. Tomahawk is in the same general area and offers fair cutthroat and brook-trout fishing. It is accessible by Forest Service trail from the Fiddler's Lake picnic area.

Shoshone Lake Brook-trout fishing is generally good from July through August when Shoshone Lake, Lost Cabin Reservoirs, and Shoshone Creek all close to fishing. The lake is reached by walking or use of a four-wheel-drive vehicle from Dickinson Park. Use of the jeep route necessitates receiving permission in crossing private lands at the foot of the mountain.

Valentine, Washakie, Grave, Deep Creek, and Lonesome Lakes All these lakes lie generally west of Dickinson Park. Accessible only by horse or foot trail, Valentine, Washakie, and Deep Creek are all a good bet for golden trout. Grave Lake provides fishing for mackinaw, and Lonesome Lake has cutthroat trout.

Ocean Lake Located a few miles northwest of the city of Riverton, its crappie fishing is unbeatable throughout the summer. Bluegill, sunfish, and largemouth bass are all present in the lake. Largemouth angling is best in May and June. This is a public fishing area with picnic and boat-launching facilities available. Commercial boat-launching facilities are also available.

Lake Cameahwait Northwest of the town of Shoshoni, it is one of Wyoming's top largemouth bass producers.

The North Fork of the Shoshone River produces fair cutthroat and rainbow trout fishing amid typical Wyoming scenery

Boysen Reservoir Boysen, in the Riverton-Shoshoni area, is one of the state's most versatile fishing waters. Rainbow- and brown-trout, walleye, perch, and sauger fishing is good during spring and fall.

Ocean, Ring, Trail, and Torrey Lakes and Pilot Butte Reservoir Some of these waters have been mentioned earlier, and some will be mentioned later, but an extra note is added here concerning winter ling fishing. These are the only waters of the state open for a special winter setline ling fishing season, with the season lasting through December, January, and February. The ling, a true freshwater codfish, isn't usually thought of as a fish of the Rocky Mountains, but in Wyoming it provides good winter sport plus excellent eating fare.

Torrey Creek Public Fishing Area The area includes Torrey, Ring, and Trail lakes, plus about 3 miles of Torrey Creek. Game and Fish Department signs mark the

area about 4 miles from the town of Dubois. Ring provides fishing for rainbow plus some mackinaw and whitefish. Trail furnishes good fishing for rainbow and some lunker mackinaw. Torrey Creek is stocked regularly with rainbow and brook trout. Camping and boat-launching facilities are available, and access is good.

Ross Lake, Upper Ross Lake, and Hidden Lake These are all in the Torrey Creek drainage. Ross Lake is noted for its large rainbow, and Upper Ross has a good population of small cutthroat trout. Hidden Lake provides very good fishing for rainbow and cutthroat.

Jakey's Fork Near the town of Dubois, this stream is readily accessible by automobile. Brook, brown, and rainbow trout are abundant, and good fishing is found in the section of stream within the State Fish Hatchery boundaries. Simpson, Soapstone, and Blanket lakes, all in this drainage, offer good brook-trout fishing.

Wind River Lakes and Brook's Lake Located northeast of Dubois, near the Teton County line on U. S. Highway 287, it is easily reached by automobile. Fishing is for rainbow and mackinaw trout. Warm Springs Creek, Sheridan Creek, and Brook's Lake Creek, all in this general area, provide good rainbow fishing. Accessible by auto, it has camping sites available.

Wind River From the Wind River Indian Reservation border upstream for a distance of about 45 miles, the Wind provides some excellent whitefish and trout angling. The DuNoir River, a tributary to the Wind, is considered an important fishing water. Whitefish take readily to a fly in this area and provide as much sport on light tackle as some trout species.

NORTHWESTERN WYOMING

This area includes Teton County and northern Lincoln County. Undoubtedly one of Wyoming's most famous and scenic areas, northwestern Wyoming has some of the state's prime fishing waters. Many of the waters in this area are located within the borders of Grand Teton National Park. A Wyoming fishing license is required in the park, and general Wyoming fishing regulations apply, but there are some exceptions.

The exceptions include: (1) A boat permit (no fee) is required for use of boats on any park water and may be obtained from any ranger station. (2) Motor-propelled boats or rafts are prohibited in some waters. Information on these waters is available from park headquarters, and is furnished with each boat permit. (3) Fishing from all boat docks and bridges in the park is prohibited. (4) The use of fish eggs or live fish for bait is prohibited. Dead fish on the shore of Jackson Lake may be used as bait, and authorized dealers also have fish for bait.

It is suggested that fishermen contact the Grand Teton Park headquarters for more detailed information.

Snake River About 65 miles of this river are classified as one of the state's outstanding fishing waters. About 16 miles of the river, from the Yellowstone border to the head of Jackson Lake and 48 miles from the town of Moran on the southern end of the lake southward into Lincoln County and to the Idaho state line, are considered prime trout-fishing waters. The river ranges from slowwater with numerous side channels to fastwater in rugged canyons. Cutthroat run 14–16 inches, and are found throughout the river's length. The entire river is bordered by paved highway, and dude ranches, motels, and camping facilities are available throughout its length. Guided float trips are also available.

Gros Ventre River A tributary to the Snake, the Gros Ventre is another excellent producer of large cutthroat. The best fishing is found from Highway 187 upstream for about 50 miles. The lower part of the river has cutthroat and brown, averaging 15 inches, while the upper portion has cutthroat, 12–14 inches. The river has many deep pools and is crystal clear, so must be fished with care. Unimproved camping facilities are available in the Teton National Forest, and the town of Jackson is quite nearby.

Hoback River Another tributary to the Snake River, it provides about 17 miles of fair cutthroat fishing from its mouth to Dell Creek. Fish run 10–14 inches. Most of the river is bordered by paved road, with dude ranches and camping available on its banks.

Buffalo Fork and Drainage This river drains a large portion of the Teton Wilderness area. Most of the area is accessible by pack trip only. The North Fork, South Fork, and Soda Creek in the river's upper area provide very good angling. Several small lakes in the area contain cutthroat, brook, and golden trout averaging 12 inches.

Jackson Lake Containing about 26,000 surface acres, the lake produces mackinaw, cutthroat, and brown trout averaging 18 inches. Accessible by paved road, it has lake-shore camps and lodging. Rental boats and guide service are also available.

Jenny Lake and Leigh Lake Leigh Lake is located just south of Jackson Lake. It provides good fishing for cutthroat averaging 16 inches and mackinaw usually of 20–25 inches. Leigh is accessible by foot or horse trail about one mile from paved road. Camping and dude-ranch accommodations are nearby, and rental boats are available. Jenny Lake, located just below Leigh, is accessible by paved road. Cutthroat, brook, rainbow, and mackinaw, the latter averaging 16 inches, are found in Jenny Lake. Camping and dude-ranch facilities are located near both lakes, and rental boats are available.

Grassy Lake A 350-acre lake north of Jackson Lake, it provides cutthroat and rainbow fishing. It may be reached by a fair dirt road. Cabin accommodations are available.

Lower Slide Lake Located in the Gros Ventre River area, it is a 1,100-acre lake providing fishing for cutthroat, mackinaw, and rainbow trout. Fair access by graveled road, with camping permitted on improved camp sites.

Salt River There are about 60 miles of excellent fishing water in Lincoln County. A number of fishing easements have been purchased by the state of Wyoming on the Salt. The easements are located from Alpine Junction to the town of Afton. These public fishing areas are clearly marked on main travel routes. Some of the river is on private land, and permission must be obtained on all except the public fishing areas. The Salt is a meandering meadow stream, with numerous small tributaries throughout its length. Fly fishing is very good for cutthroat, brown, brook, and rainbow trout. It has easy access with accommodations at Afton and Thayne.

Grey's River An extensive mountain drainage, it provides about 53 miles of excellent cutthroat fishing in Lincoln County. Access is by fair gravel road, with forest camps available.

NORTHCENTRAL WYOMING

This area takes in Park, Big Horn, and Washakie counties. This is a large, picturesque region, with fishing provided in a wide variety of waters.

North Fork of the Shoshone River This river is considered one of Wyoming's prime trout-fishing waters. From the Yellowstone Park border to Buffalo Bill Reservoir in Park County, the North Fork provides 33 miles of fishing for cutthroat generally 10–15 inches. An occasional brown and brook trout is also taken. Flies, lures, and bait all produce well at different times throughout the season. This mountain river is paralleled by oiled highway from the city of Cody to the east gate of Yellowstone. Plenty of living facilities are available along the stream.

Shoshone River From Buffalo Bill Dam to Cody provides about 7 miles of very good fishing for cutthroat.

The rest of the river northward is considered an important fishing water on the district level. The South Fork of the Shoshone, flowing into the south arm of Buffalo Bill Reservoir, is also considered an important local water.

Buffalo Bill Reservoir This is a 7,000-acre man-made reservoir at the junction of the North and South forks of the Shoshone River, 8 miles west of Cody. Rainbow, cutthroat, and brown trout average 14 inches, with mackinaw averaging 18 inches. Mackinaw weighing up to 20 pounds are reported occasionally. Good oil and gravel roads lead to all shores of the lake. Camp sites are available around most of the lake shore with boat launching, boat rentals, and eating accommodations available.

Bridger Lake A fisherman's paradise in the high-mountain wilderness area called the "Thorofare," the lake is located an hour's drive southwest of Cody and about ten hours ride by horseback from the road. Forest camps are available along access trails and along the lake's shoreline. The lake provides fishing for cutthroat usually of 15–18 inches.

Beartooth Lake A 120-acre lake accessible by U.S. Highway 12 near the Montana state line in Park County, it has tourist accommodations, boat-rental, and private boat-launching facilities. There is fishing for rainbow, cutthroat and brook trout.

"T" Lake This is an easy two-hour hike from U.S. Highway 12. Small brook trout abound, and there is no number limit. Ten pounds is the only creel limit. Several other small lakes are within a few minutes walk of "T." Accommodations are within easy reach of the lake.

Deep Lake South of Highway 12 by about 4–5 miles of rough dirt road and a steep hike of about 1 mile, its cutthroat trout run 11–12 inches. Forest camps are accessible by auto.

Upper Clay Butte Lake A small lake north of U.S. Highway 12 near the Montana line, it has fishing for grayling averaging 12–14 inches. Accessible by two miles of poor foot or horse trail, it has forest camps, dude ranches, and camping sites available.

Sunshine Reservoir Access by oiled and dirt road is about 15 miles west of the town of Meeteetse in Park County. This 600-acre lake provides fishing for cutthroat, running 16–24 inches. No accommodations are available in the immediate area. Boats may be launched at several points around the lake. Trolling produces the best results.

Wardell Reservoir Located east of the town of Basin in Big Horn County, it is accessible by dirt roads from the town of Otto in Big Horn County. Walleye usually of 16–20 inches and black bullheads up to ¾ pound are taken. No accommodations are available at the lake, but it is a short drive from other towns in the area. The lake's water level affects boat launching.

Shell Creek The creek, east of the town of Shell in Big Horn County, produces about 16 miles of very good fishing for brown, rainbow, and brook trout. The rest of the stream is a poor producer. Dude ranches and motels are available in the lower stream area, and forest camps along the upper areas. Shell Reservoir near the head of Shell Creek provides good fishing for brook trout, generally of 10–13 inches. Access is by poor auto trail. Boats may be launched, but it is difficult to get them to the reservoir. Forest camps are found in the Big Horn National Forest.

Tensleep Creek This comprises 22 miles of very good rainbow- and brown-trout fishing waters in Washa-

kie County. All of the stream is reached by U.S. Highway 16. Accommodations are readily available.

Meadowlark Lake Located east of the town of Ten Sleep in Washakie County, it has an oiled highway around the lake on two sides. Fishing occurs for rainbow of 11–13 inches. Boats may be launched or rented at the lake, and living accommodations are available.

Lake Solitude A high-mountain lake, it is an easy day's horse ride from several forest-service roads. Brook trout running 8–10 inches abound, and the only creel limit is 10 pounds a day. Forest Service camps are available. Several other good fishing lakes are also available within easy riding distance.

Lost Twin Lake No. 2 A half-day's horseback ride or hike from a rough forest service road north of U. S. Highway 16, it has excellent fishing, providing occasionally for golden trout of 15–16 inches. Success varies, however. Forest camps are available along the route or at the lake. —A.L.R.

X (1) The letter symbol used to indicate leader diameters in natural silkworm gut and synthetics. Although the X designation is not wholly satisfactory due to the variation in size which often exists, it does put meaning in figures such as 2X, 4X, or 6X for the average angler, largely as a basis for comparison. Beginning with 0X and progressing to 8X, the diameter of the leader material becomes one size smaller. Thus we know that while 2X is reasonably heavy (for certain kinds of fishing), a 6X or 7X is extremely light. Although each size has a precise numerical equivalent in thousandths of an inch, the figures are difficult to remember.

THE REASON FOR SYMBOLS

The popularity of X as a diameter symbol is over two hundred years old. When watchmakers and jewelers made their own draw-plates, there were three mathematical systems in use—the metric, linear, and Swiss ligne. To resolve their differences, the holes of draw-plates were marked in an X progression, so a 5X watch part would be the same in Switzerland as it was in France or anywhere else. A century later, silkworm gut was drawn on these same plates by literally sharpening the end of a strand, then pulling it through a mounted jewel bored to the desired diameter. This requires skill and poses certain material problems. Caterpillars, from which gut comes, are not prone to assembly-line production. The raw material is extruded in different lengths and thicknesses. If the strand is .003 inch larger than the size desired, then it has to be passed through successive holes and gradually shaved to the correct diameter. From this we get the symbol —/5 which we use for all sizes greater than 0X. This is a basic draw-plate measurement (or point of reference) in that it is half X or half-drawn; thus a ⅕ strand (.020 inch) is twice the diameter of an 0X strand. Drawing removes the outer surface of the gut, leaving it round and smaller in diameter; carried to its theoretical end, a natural .020 inch strand (which is about the caterpillar's maximum) could be reduced eventually by progressive drawing to a

.001 inch strand or a 10X point. It was half-drawn in progression at the 10/5, or .011-inch size. This system of measurement is not only complicated but impractical. On the Continent, which is one source of synthetic leader materials, manufacturers express diameters in hundredths of a millimeter (from $^{12}/_{100}$ to $^{50}/_{100}$). The United States system is in one-thousandths of an inch. Here again there is no accurate conversion even after multiplying the European size by .0003937 ($^1/_{100}$ millimeter) as there is no exact metric equivalent. *See also* Fly Leader   —A.J.McC.
(2) The letter symbol used to indicate wire diameter of hooks (*which see*).
XANTHO A combining form meaning yellow, as in xananthochroistic variety of fish, such as the golden tench. *See under* Tench
XUREL DE CASTILLA The Spanish (Mexico) name for the Pacific bumper, *Chloroscombrus chrysurus*. A similar species is the Atlantic bumper (*which see*). *See also* Carangidae, Jacks

Y

YAQUI CATFISH *Ictalurus pricei* Found from northern Mexico into southern Arizona, little is known of its life history, as the species is seldom identified by commercial or sport anglers. It's easily confused with a channel catfish. However, the body lacks spots and the caudal fin is not deeply forked. The base of the anal fin is shorter than the head length. The anterior part of its dorsal fin is conspicuously higher than the posterior part.
—A.J.McC.

Yaqui Catfish

YAW To steer badly, zigzagging back and forth across the intended course, frequently caused by following seas.
YELLOW-AND-BLACK ROCK BEAUTY *See* Queen Angelfish
YELLOW BASS *Morone mississippiensis* A freshwater panfish, regionally known as barfish, brassy bass, stripe, striped bass (erroneously), and streaker, the species is a temperate bass, found only in freshwater, as is its close relative, the white bass. The two species exhibit rather similar life-history characteristics, and both are eagerly sought by fishermen. The yellow bass has a very restricted range, however, and thus is familiar to anglers only in the central portions of the country. Beginning in southern Minnesota, Wisconsin, and Michigan, the yellow bass ranges southward to the Tennessee River drainage in Alabama and to Louisiana and eastern Texas. In this limited area it is found in selected lakes and the larger rivers. Efforts to transplant the species

into new waters both within and outside the boundaries of this natural range have met with little success. Attempts to propagate the yellow bass artifically have also been unsuccessful. One of the primary habitat requirements of these fish apparently is extensive areas of shallow gravel and rock reefs.

The yellow bass closely resembles the white bass, having a moderately compressed body, forked tail, 2 dorsal fins, spines on the first dorsal fin, and 3 spines on the anal fin. Its clean-cut body is dark olive-green above, with silvery to bright golden-yellow sides and a white belly. Six or 7 dark, longitudinal stripes run the length of the body, 3 of which are above the lateral line. The stripes lying below the lateral line are broken or interrupted toward the tail. These broken stripes, the yellowish coloration of the sides, the absence of teeth on the base of the tongue, and the even length of the upper and lower jaws are characteristics which serve to distinguish it from the white bass. There are 51–55 scales along the lateral line and 10 softrays in the anal fin.

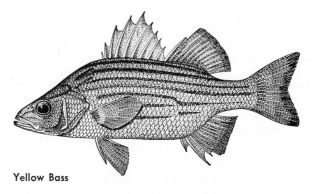

Yellow Bass

The size of the yellow bass usually caught by anglers is 8–11 inches, or ¼–¾ pound. Anything over 1 pound is considered unusually large. Records of exceedingly large yellow bass are absent from the literature, but it is likely that maximum size is 2–3 pounds.

LIFE HISTORY

The life of a yellow bass begins in May or early June, when adults spawn over gravel or rock reefs in water only a few feet deep. Water temperature is in the high 60's. The eggs are extremely tiny, and each adult female may lay from about 250,000 to 1,000,000 eggs. The eggs are left unprotected, and under favorable conditions will hatch in a few days. The percentage of eggs which hatch usually is low as is the case with most species which produce such an abundance of eggs. The minute fry swarm in schools once they have absorbed their yolk sacs and can swim freely. These schools of fry remain in the shallows where they feed on minute zooplankton. At this time they are very vulnerable to predation. Small yellow bass provide excellent forage for many species of fish, including larger yellow bass. As the weeks progress the fry grow to fingerling size and will gradually begin to take larger zooplankton, such as crustaceans and insect larvae. By September or October, when the water cools, they have attained their year's growth and will be 2½–5 inches long. If all conditions have been favorable, there will be an abundance of these young yellow bass. However, such conditions usually occur only about one year in three, with the result that the population of the species is very erratic.

The following year these young bass will begin growing again in late May or early June. Their food will continue to be comprised primarily of crustaceans, insects, and insect larvae, but by late summer they will be large enough to begin supplementing this diet with small fish. They continue to travel in schools, but now they will roam into the deeper waters and come into the shallows primarily to feed. By summer's end they should measure about 7 inches. If conditions have been average, 20–40 percent will survive this second year.

At age 3 most of the yellow bass reach adulthood. Another important change occurring is that their diet changes almost entirely to fish. They still eat crustaceans and insects on occasion. The schools tend to stay in deepwater, coming into the shallows in the evening and very early morning to feed. These basic habits will continue for the remaining years of life.

The life expectancy of a yellow bass is short. Few live more than 3–4 years, and 7 years is about maximum. Annual survival after the first year of life is about 20–40 percent. Average size varies with latitude and food conditions but approximates 4, 7, 9, 10, and 11 inches at the end of years 1 through 5 respectively.

Yellow bass weigh ¼ pound at 7½ inches, ½ pound at 9½ inches, and ¾ pound at about 11 inches. They become attractive to fishermen when they reach a weight of about ¼ pound, which usually is late in the summer of their second year or early in their third year of life.

ANGLING VALUE

Yellow bass are a favorite among panfish anglers in the central United States. They are active fighters for their size and provide good sport on light tackle. They may be taken on a variety of baits, including worms, minnows, flies, spinners, spoons, and small plugs. They sometimes feed on the surface, but usually are caught in middepths or near the bottom. Schools often are located by trolling, but once a school is found it is customary to stop and fish the area intensively.

The flesh of the yellow bass often is compared to that of the yellow perch, being white, firm, flaky, and delicious. It usually is considered superior to the flesh of the white bass.

The primary limiting factors in the angling value of the yellow bass are its confined distribution and the fact that population levels are apt to fluctuate radically from year to year.

COMMERCIAL VALUE

Little or no commercial value is associated with the yellow bass. This is due to its limited distribution, the relatively small size of the species, and its favor among sport fishermen. —J.T.S.

YELLOWBELLY SUNFISH A regional name for the redbreast sunfish (*which see*)

YELLOW BULLHEAD *Ictalurus natalis* A yellowish catfish with rounded tail and light barbels. Dorsally it is yellow-olive to slaty-black, depending on habitat. The sides are lighter and more yellowish. The lower surface of head and body is bright yellow, yellow-white, or milk-white. Anal fin with 23–27 rays. Rear edges of pectoral spines with sharp teeth or serrations. It is separated from the brown and black bullheads by white or light barbels, the absence of spots on the body, and more anal rays, and distinguished from the blue, white, and channel catfish by the rounded or square tail. The range of the yellow bullhead is from North Dakota to the Hudson River and southward to Florida.

Yellow Bullhead

HABITS

The yellow bullhead appears to be most abundant in sluggish streams and shallow portions of lakes and of streams and ponds over soft bottoms. Spawning in a manner similar to others of its family, the yellow bullhead deposits its eggs in a nest or burrow in May and June. The nest may be under a stone or log, or it may be an excavated burrow little larger than the fish itself. Both sexes participate in the nest building. The male guards the yellowish-white, adhesive eggs and the young fish for some time after they leave the nest.

The yellow bullhead is a scavenger in its food habits and consumes almost anything found in the water, minnows, crawfish, insect larvae, and snails by preference. Plant material is also found in their diet.

This catfish attains a length of 18 inches and weight of 3 pounds.

ECONOMIC VALUE

Because few anglers distinguish the yellow from the brown bullhead it is difficult to ascertain its value. Cyclic in abundance, the yellow bullhead enters the southern United States commercial fishery to some extent when populations are at a peak. The cream-colored flesh has good food value, but this bullhead should be iced soon after capture or it is inclined to have a mushy texture. —R.A.J.

YELLOWEDGE GROUPER *Epinephelus flavolimbatus* This deepwater grouper occurs in the tropical American Atlantic including southern Florida. The common name refers to the yellow margin of the dorsal fin, which is a distinguishing mark for the species.

The yellowedge grouper has 11 dorsal spines; 13–15 dorsal rays, rarely 15; 9 anal rays; and usually 18 pectoral rays. Posterior nostril about as large as the anterior. Insertion of pelvic fin under, or in advance of upper end of pectoral base. Posterior margin of caudal fin convex (young), and straight or slightly concave (adult). Sides of body with white spots in longitudinal and vertical rows (young). Top of caudal peduncle with a black saddlelike blotch (young). These color marks gradually disappear with age and are absent in specimens over 15 inches in total length.

The yellow margin of the dorsal fin distinguishes this grouper from the others. The white body spots and the caudal-peduncle blotch also occur in the young of the snowy grouper (*which see*), but in the latter, the posterior nostril is much enlarged.

HABITS

Although juveniles and young occur in shallower water, the adults, especially large specimens, are taken on rocky bottom along the edge of shelves (80–120 fathoms).

ANGLING VALUE

This grouper has little angling value since it occurs mostly in deepwater. However, it is fun to catch on a wire line with live or cut bait. It is taken on handlines by the West Indian fishermen.

FOOD VALUE

In the Caribbean area, this grouper is a food fish, but it is rarely seen in the markets.   —L.R.

YELLOWEYE ROCKFISH *Sebastodes ruberrimus* This high-quality rockfish (*which see*) is found from Alaska to southern California, commonly at depths of 180–750 feet. The yelloweye rockfish has rough, spiny cranial ridges, which, in large specimens, become broken off into short spines. The third preopercular spine is split and the peritoneum is white. The body color is crimson above, paler on belly; a whitish streak on lateral line and at the end of the pectoral fin. Length to 36 inches.

A female weighing 19½ pounds was found to be bearing approximately 2,700,000 eggs according to Dr. J. L. Hart of the Fisheries Research Board of Canada.   —J.R.

YELLOWFIN GROUPER *Mycteroperca venenosa* This medium-sized grouper is fairly common in southern Florida and throughout the tropical American Atlantic. The usual size is 3 feet or less in total length. The common name refers to the yellow margin of the pectoral fin.

The yellowfin grouper has 11 dorsal spines; usually 16 dorsal rays; usually 11 anal rays; and usually 17 pectoral rays. Posterior nostril larger than the anterior. Insertion of pelvic fin under or somewhat behind lower end of pectoral base. Posterior margin of caudal fin concave. Head and body with red spots and irregular longitudinal rows of rounded or quadrangular dark blotches. Outer third of pectoral fin yellow.

The color pattern, especially the yellow margin of the pectoral fin, distinguishes this grouper from the others.

ANGLING VALUE

This grouper occurs on rocky bottom in shallow to medium-depth water. It is frequently taken around coral heads with live or dead bait or artificial lures. A very good fighter but habitually dives among rocks as soon as hooked. The yellowfin grouper will strike a plug, spinner, or spoon.

FOOD VALUE

Excellent eating, but the flesh is considered occasionally poisonous in some of the West Indies. *See also* Ciguatera   —L.R.

YELLOWFINNED CORVINA *See* Orangemouth Corvina
YELLOWFIN SOLE *Limanda aspera* A Pacific flatfish, it is identified by a well-marked arch of the lateral line over the pectoral fin, a narrow black line along the bases

of the dorsal and anal fins, and the orange-yellow color of the fins. The yellowfin sole is decidedly oval in shape. This righteyed species has moderately large eyes and the teeth chiefly on the blind side. It is light brown, with white on the blind side, occasionally with yellow tinges. Reaching a length of 15 inches, it is found from northern British Columbia to northwestern Alaska. Some of its food includes worms, hydroids, mollusks, and brittlestars.

ANGLING VALUE

Common in otter trawls, it is fairly important as a market fish, the flesh being sold as fillets. It is of limited interest to anglers.   —D.dS.

YELLOWFIN TUNA *Thunnus albacares* The yellowfin tuna is a fish of the mackerel family. It is difficult to distinguish from some of the other four species of tunas in American waters, especially the blackfin and bigeye tunas. The length of its pectoral fin is greater than 80 percent of the head length, the finlets behind the second dorsal and anal fins are yellow with black margins, and there is no white margin on the caudal fin. In large individuals the second dorsal and anal fins become very long, and such individuals cannot be mistaken for any other species. There are 25–34 gillrakers, and the ventral surface of the liver has no striations.

The yellowfin is the most brilliantly colored of the tunas, with a poorly defined stripe of golden-yellow on its upper sides and much bright yellow in most of the fins. The lower sides commonly have white spots and vertical streaks, even in quite large fish.

Yellowfin Tuna

The Atlantic and Pacific forms of yellowfin have been called separate species, but all yellowfins are now considered to be a single species, found in tropical and subtropical waters around the world. Individuals with exceptionally long second dorsal and anal fins have been called Allison tuna, but these are merely variations.

Yellowfin tuna grow to a fairly large size. Most fish caught weigh 20–120 pounds, but the largest yellowfin ever taken with rod-and-reel, caught in Hawaii, was 6 feet 10½ inches long and weighed 266½ pounds. The species may possibly reach 400 pounds.

DISTRIBUTION

Yellowfin tuna are found in tropical and subtropical waters around the world. In the western Atlantic, they are found regularly as far north as New Jersey, where the Gulf Stream makes its influence felt, especially in late summer and fall. Exploratory fishing has shown them to be found in the Gulf Stream throughout the year. Very rarely is a yellowfin caught inshore in the New

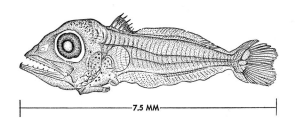

Yellowfin Tuna Larva

England states and Canada, unlike the bluefin tuna, which becomes common there during the summer and early fall.

Tagging of yellowfins indicates that they do not travel great distances as do the bluefin and albacore. Much remains to be learned, however, about their actual movements.

SPAWNING AND GROWTH

Atlantic yellowfins have been little studied. Most of the information on yellowfin biology comes from the Pacific. Spawning takes place throughout much of the year in tropical waters but tends to be restricted to late spring and summer in subtropical regions. Each female is believed to spawn at least two batches of one to several million eggs each year. The young grow rapidly, averaging 7.5 pounds at 18 months of age. Four-year-old fish weigh about 140 pounds.

Yellowfins seem to be nonselective in their feeding habits, and a great variety of fishes, crustaceans, and squids has been found in their stomachs. The abundance of organisms in a given area determines what the yellowfins eat.

COMMERCIAL VALUE

Yellowfin tuna are taken commercially in great abundance in all tropical regions of the world. The species is the mainstay of the California-based tuna fleet. Japanese fishermen are now operating over virtually the entire world range of yellowfin tuna and deliver their catch to the market or to canneries in North and South America as well as Europe, Africa, and Asia. Of the world catch of about 800,000 tons of mackerel-like fishes in 1960, over 250,000 tons were yellowfin.

Live-bait-fishing, using feathered jigs or baited hooks attached by short lines to bamboo poles, accounts for the capture of most yellowfins. In recent years, most American fishermen have switched from live bait to purse seine, and most of the eastern Pacific catch is made by this method. The longline technique is also used to a considerable extent, particularly by the Japanese high seas fishery.

The flesh of yellowfin tunas is light, neither so dark as that of the bluefin nor so white as that of albacore.

ANGLING VALUE

Yellowfins are commonly caught by sport fishermen in the West Indies and Gulf of Mexico and as far north as Maryland and New Jersey. On the American Pacific Coast, they are caught in small numbers in California, but most are caught south of that area.   —B.B.C.
—R.H.G.

YELLOW GOATFISH *Mulloidichthys martinicus* This species might better be named the yellow-banded goatfish, for it is not entirely yellow (like one tropical Pacific goatfish) but has a lengthwise, bright yellow band along the side of the body on an otherwise pale background. The fins, however, are yellowish, especially the tail. Like other goatfishes, *M. martinicus* is elongate, has two dorsal fins, a forked tail, and the characteristic pair of long barbels on the chin.

The yellow goatfish is the only representative of the genus *Mulloidichthys* in the western Atlantic (*M. samoensis*, also with a yellow band, is a close relative from the Indo-Pacific region). *Mulloidichthys* lacks teeth on the vomer and palatine bones in the roof of the mouth, and is thus distinguished from the other American goatfish genera *Pseudupeneus* and *Upeneus*. The spotted goatfish (*P. maculatus*) is the only other common mullid found in shallow tropic seas with the yellow goatfish. It is readily separated not only by having teeth on the vomer and palatine bones but also in having fewer scales in lateral series (30–32, whereas *M. martinicus* has 37–40), and by color. Instead of a yellow band, the spotted goatfish has a series of three or four large, dark spots more or less following the lateral line.

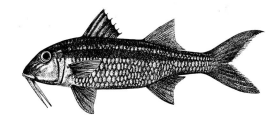

Yellow Goatfish

As its scientific name implies, the yellow goatfish was described from Martinique. It is known from the West Indian region, including Florida and Bermuda, and is commonly seen in small schools. Although feeding primarily in sandy areas, it usually does not stray far from coral reefs.

The barbels of goatfishes are evidently supplied with chemoreceptor organs, for these fishes seem to taste their way to their food with them. Goatfishes may be seen during the day plunging their heads into the sand almost to their eyes in search of food. The barbels are thrust into the sand before the mouth. A great variety of small food organisms has been found in stomachs of yellow goatfishes from the Virgin Islands. These include polychaete worms, brittlestars, clams, snails, chitons, crabs, snapping shrimps and other types of shrimps, isopods, amphipods, ostracods, and sipunculid worms. The fish ingest sand with their food but manage to eject most of it through their gill openings. *See also* Spotted Goatfish

FOOD VALUE

The yellow goatfish reaches a length of about 1 foot and is a moderately good food fish. It is not hardy and dies soon after removal from the water.   —J.E.R.

YELLOW JACK *Caranx bartholomaei* Also called *cibi amarillo*, at times, it has been mistakenly called bar

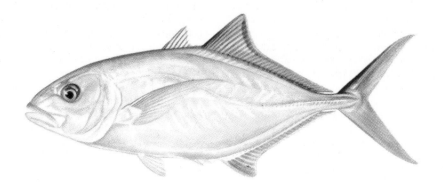

Yellow Jack

jack, and undoubtedly had been confused with that species (*Caranx ruber*). This is an endemic western Atlantic species.

The second dorsal fin has one spine and 25–28 softrays. The anal fin has two detached spines, followed by one spine and 21–24 softrays. On the first gill arch there are 18–21 gillrakers on the lower limb and 6–9 on the upper limb.

The body is moderately deep. The dorsal- and anal-fin lobes are only slightly produced. The scutes in the straight lateral line number about 22–28. The straight lateral line is as long as or only slightly longer than the curved part. The coloration is light bluish-green on the back, and silvery sides with a golden yellow tint. The fins are chiefly yellow. Particularly after death this fish has a yellowish cast to which it owes its name. The pigmentation changes in small juveniles are unique. Like most jack crevalles, the yellow jack develops vertical body bars, usually 5 (rarely 4–6), plus one on the nape and a prominent nuchal band through the eye. These develop at a length of about ¾ inch. Then in a very compressed length interval, several changes occur. At about 1 inch long the upper and lower parts of the posterior 3–4 bars bend backward; by 1⅛ inches all of the bars have become distorted or wavy; and by 1⅜ inches all the bars have broken into a mottled or spotted pattern that persists to about 4½ inches in length or larger.

The yellow jack has been recorded from Maceió, Brazil, to Woods Hole, Massachusetts, and in the West Indies. It seems to be fairly common in the Bahamas and around Cuba. A maximum size of about 39 inches has been recorded. A specimen from Puerto Rico was 35¼ inches long and weighed 16 pounds 11 ounces.

LIFE HISTORY

The life-history knowledge is meager. Spawning off the United States is rare, and is probably concentrated to the south, extending from about February to September, and occurring principally in offshore waters. The young are frequently found in association with jellyfish and floating sargassum. This seems to be more of a bottom fish at larger sizes than the bar jack (*Caranx ruber*), which it resembles. A dozen or more yellow jacks have been observed swimming in almost single file a few inches from the bottom.

ANGLING VALUE

It is usually taken trolling, occasionally still-fishing, and is a strong light-tackle sport fish. It is fished and sold commercially in the West Indies, and its flavor is considered fair to good. At one time when this species and the bar jack were thought to be unsafe for food and their sale prohibited in the Havana market, a number of small specimens of both species were seen on sale there. *See also* Carangidae, Jacks —F.H.B.

YELLOWMOUTH GROUPER *Mycteroperca interstitialis* A fairly common grouper in southern Florida and throughout the tropical American Atlantic, its usual size is less than 20 inches in total length.

The yellowmouth grouper has 11 dorsal spines; 16–17 dorsal rays, usually 17; usually 11 anal rays; and usually 16 pectoral rays. Posterior nostril much larger than the anterior. Insertion of pelvic fin usually somewhat behind lower end of pectoral base. Posterior margin of caudal fin concave. Coloration uniform dark brown or with light lines forming reticulations enclosing small dark spots.

The color pattern distinguishes this grouper from the others.

HABITS

Occurs in shallow to water that is moderately deep. Takes live or dead bait and artificial lures.

ANGLING VALUE

Fights well, especially when caught by trolling with artificial lures or natural bait.

FOOD VALUE

Good eating, it is a fish of some commercial importance in the West Indies. —L.R.

YELLOW PERCH *Perca flavescens* This is the most widely distributed member of the Percidae. It is regionally known as ringed perch, striped perch, coon perch, and jack perch. The yellow perch is generally classified as a panfish, and though lacking the sporting qualities of its larger relatives, the walleye and sauger, it provides fine fishing for the multitudes of anglers seeking fast action and good eating. The yellow perch is found in the southern portions of westcentral and eastern Canada, south to Kansas, Missouri, Illinois, Indiana, and Ohio. In the Atlantic drainage it is present from Nova Scotia to South Carolina. Its natural range has been greatly enlarged through widespread stocking, and it is now present in many of the Far Western states. The perch is at home in small and large lakes alike, and though found in rivers it is considered primarily a lake fish. Cool cleanwater with ample amounts of sandy or rocky bottom make the better perch lakes.

The perch has a moderately elongate body which is slightly compressed, giving it a somewhat humpbacked appearance. The two dorsal fins are separated, and the tail is moderately forked. Spines are present on the first dorsal fin, the anal fin, and the pectoral fins. The mouth contains many tiny teeth but no canine teeth. The opercle or gill cover is strongly serrated and contains one or more sharp spines. Coloration may vary but usually is olivaceous on the back blending into a golden-yellow on the sides and white on the belly. Six to 8 dark bands extend from the back to below the lateral line. It has 12–13 softrays in the dorsal fin and 7–8 in the anal fin; 57–62 scales along the lateral line; and 8–10 rows of scales on the cheeks.

The angler's catch of perch usually consists of fish weighing ¼–¾ pound. However, some lakes occasionally will produce a crop of jumbos weighing from 1–2 pounds. Such lakes are sure to attract an army of anglers. Maximum size attained is about 4 pounds.

LIFE HISTORY

Imbedded in a sticky, gelatinous mass strung over weeds or brush, a perch begins its life as one egg among 10,000–75,000 which are spawned in a ribbonlike string by an adult female. The gelatinous mass absorbs water rapidly as it is emitted by the female, and may swell to the size of two handfuls. The eggs are fertilized by one or more males who are at the side of the female as she emits the spawn. The spawning act usually occurs at night in weedy or brushy areas several feet deep when the water temperature is about 45°–50°F. In relative terms, this is about a week after walleye spawning.

Fertility of the eggs is ordinarily very high, and under good conditions one-fourth to one-half of the eggs will hatch into minute fry in 2–3 weeks. No protection is provided by the parents. After hatching, however, the life of a perch is extremely hazardous. Being a slow swimmer and traveling in large schools, it affords excellent food for predaceous fishes, especially the walleye. The young perch seek the protection of weeds and brush and feed on small zooplankters and insect larvae. The slow growth of the perch, usually 2–4 inches the first year, keeps it within the size range of prime forage for practically all gamefish throughout its first year of life and even into its later years. Thus the odds for survival are very low (perhaps 1 in 5,000) during this first year.

Yellow Perch, 3½-inch Juvenile

Notwithstanding the extreme hazards of the life of a perch, the species manages to produce and maintain itself in abundance wherever habitat is suitable. In fact, overpopulation of perch is a definite problem in many lakes. Where such overpopulations occur, the fish become stunted and thin and provide poor-quality fishing. Corrective measures may include drastic thinning of the perch population by mechanical or chemical means, along with attempts to increase the population of predaceous species. Sometimes it is best to rid the lake of all fish and restock. Seldom, however, will the addition of predaceous species be effective unless it is in conjunction with a drastic reduction in the stunted perch population.

Yellow Perch, 13-inch Male, Georgian Bay, Ontario

GROWTH RATE

Growth of perch under normal conditions will average three inches the first year, three inches the second, two inches the third, and about one inch each year thereafter. These growth rates will, of course, vary with latitude and with habitat conditions. Maximum age in the far north is about 11 years, while in the southern end of its range 5–6 years is maximum. A ¼-pound perch will measure about 8 inches, ½ pounder 10 inches, ¾ pounder 12 inches, and a pound perch will be 13 to 14 inches long.

In its second and third years of life the yellow perch continues to provide good forage for other fish, since it will range in size from about 3–6 inches during its second year and 5–8 inches during its third year. During these years the hazards of life will account for as high as 60–80 percent of the population each year. Thereafter, the usual annual loss may be in the range of 50–70 percent. Adulthood usually is attained at the age of 3–4 years, at which time the hardiest and most fortunate few survivors take on the task of filling the voids created by mortalities from disease, parasites, and predaceous fish.

The food of the yellow perch after it has reached a size of several inches will gradually change to larger zooplankters, insects, young crayfish, snails, and small fish, including the young of its own species. Continuing to travel in schools throughout its life, it roams throughout the lake, often staying in the deeper areas during the day and moving closer to the shallows toward evening. There is some evidence that at times the males and females will travel in separate schools. Schools also may consist primarily of perch of the same age class and size.

ANGLING VALUE

It is unlikely that one can overestimate the angling value of the yellow perch. Wherever the perch is found it provides hours of fun and pounds of delicious food for fishermen of all types and angling proficiency in all seasons of the year. Whether fishing from shore or a dock with a handline and a worm or from a boat with a trolling rig and a minnow, the perch will provide fast action. Not renowned for its fighting qualities, the perch makes up for this in numbers and appetite. Almost any natural bait will be accepted by a hungry perch, and even some of the artificial lures, especially flies and small spinners.

Perch usually bite best during the daylight hours, especially around noon and again toward evening. The bait should be fished a foot or two off the bottom. In the winter, fishing through the ice with small minnows or grubs usually is rewarding.

COMMERCIAL VALUE

The commercial value of the yellow perch is limited primarily by its small size. However, in some of the larger northern lakes, where it attains a size of ½ pound and larger, it serves to supplement the income of commercial fishermen. The larger fish demand excellent prices on the commercial market. *See also* Fish Cookery, Panfish —J.T.S.

YELLOW STINGRAY *Urolophus jamaicensis* It has a nearly circular disk and a thick tail which is about as long as the disk length, and near the tip of the tail is a well-developed, serrated spine. The distinctive, rounded caudal fin curves around the tip of the tail and is longer on the lower surface. Except for a well-developed patch of thorns along the midsection of the back, the skin is smooth. A distinctively beautiful color pattern characterizes this little stingray. The upper surfaces are often covered with wormlike markings of greenish-pinkish or brown on a lighter background. These markings vary and may be broken up into a series of small, yellowish dots on the background color. But the pattern varies considerably, with intermediate patterns between the spotted and wormlike patterns occurring. The lower sides grade from yellow to greenish to brownish-white, with dark mottlings on the tail. It grows to about 26 inches long and about a foot wide.

LIFE HISTORY

The yellow stingray is recorded from Trinidad to Florida, with strays occurring to North Carolina, but it is essentially a tropical species limited to the confines of the Caribbean. A shallow-water species, it occurs in quiet waters, where it prefers sand bottom. In the Bahamas it is fairly common in quiet lagoons, where it forages for food, occasionally in some numbers, over the vast expanse of sand bottom. The young are born alive, and three or four are produced at a time. Spawning evidently occurs at least in spring and summer.

DANGER TO MAN

Like most other stingrays, this species carries a potent weapon on its tail. It is capable of inflicting a severe wound, which is accompanied by excruciating pain. As in the case of the round stingray (*which see*), the treatment for the wound should be as soon as possible.

—D.dS.

YELLOWTAIL *See* California Yellowtail, Yellowtail Snapper

YELLOWTAIL FLOUNDER *Limanda ferruginea* Also known as the rusty dab, this right-handed flounder is characterized by its small mouth, pointed snout, and thin body, which has a definite arch in the lateral line over the pectoral fin. The top of the head is slightly concave, and the general body shape is nearly oval, its depth being about half of its length. It varies from grayish-olive-green to reddish-brown, with large, irregular rusty spots. The tail fin and the edge of the dorsal and anal fins are yellow.

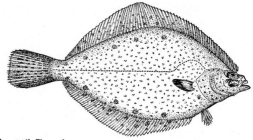

Yellowtail Flounder

Yellow markings are also seen on the caudal peduncle on the blind side, the rest of which is white. A medium-sized species, its maximum size is about 22 inches and a little over 2 pounds.

Found along the Atlantic Coast from Labrador to Virginia, it is most common in the northern part of its range. It occurs at about 30–300 feet, although occasionally it is in shoaler water, and has been taken in nearly 600 feet of water. It shows a preference for sand or sand-mud bottom. Small crustaceans such as shrimps, amphipods, and mysids are eaten, as are small shellfish and worms. Apparently it does not feed during the spawning period.

LIFE HISTORY

Spawning occurs from late March to August, and the pelagic eggs have been taken in the Gulf of Maine between the 20–50-fathom curves. The eggs hatch in approximately five days. The young assume a bottom existence when they reach a little over ½ inch long. From tagging studies, it has been shown that this species moves about considerably. Formerly of little commercial value, it is now one of the most important flatfishes.

ANGLING VALUE

It is taken commercially in otter trawls and occasionally by anglers drift-fishing from party boats. —D.dS.

YELLOWTAIL ROCKFISH *Sebastodes flavidus* This rockfish (*which see*) reaches a length of 26 inches. It is found from Vancouver Island into Baja California. It is one of six or seven leading species on the California markets.

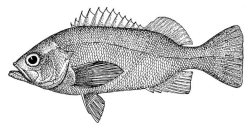

Yellowtail Rockfish

On the yellowtail rockfish the interorbital space is highly convex; lower jaw projecting, with knob on underside of tip; anal fin with 8 sometimes 7 softrays; white peritoneum; membranes of the spinous portion of the dorsal fin are deeply incised. Color, grayish above, washed with dark green, shading to white ventrally; yellow on tip of tail, dusky yellow on other fins. —J.R.

YELLOWTAIL SNAPPER *Ocyurus chrysurus* A rather small, fairly common snapper occurring around southern Florida and throughout the tropical American Atlantic, it seldom reaches a weight of over 5–6 pounds, and most of the individuals seen weigh less than 2 pounds.

The yellowtail snapper is distinguished by its 10 dorsal spines, 13 dorsal rays, and 9 anal rays. Pectoral rays normally 16. Gillrakers 19–21 on lower limb of first arch, not counting rudiments. Rows of scales around caudal peduncle 25–26. Cheek scales in 5–6 rows. Upper jaw reaching to or somewhat beyond vertical from anterior margin of orbit. Pectoral fin not reaching beyond vertical from origin of anal fin. Anal fin broadly rounded, not angulate posteriorly. General coloration pale olivaceous with yellow spots above, paler and tinged with violet below. A yellow stripe from snout to caudal fin which is deep yellow. Dorsal, pectoral, and anal fins yellow.

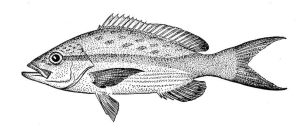

Yellowtail Snapper

Pelvic fin colorless. Black spot on sides of body absent. Eye red.

The more numerous gillrakers and the number of dorsal rays, combined with the characteristic color pattern, distinguish this snapper from the others.

ANGLING VALUE

This snapper usually occurs offshore in schools and seems to feed better at night. Cut bait (pilchard) is a favorite bait for this species. A good catch can be obtained by chumming. The yellowtail snapper fights well but has a small mouth; the hook size must be selected accordingly. It is for this reason that this species is not caught more frequently by anglers trying for snappers in offshore grounds.

FOOD VALUE

Excellent eating. A highly valued food fish in Florida and in the Caribbean. —L.R.

YOUNG, PAUL H. American (1888–1960) Rod-maker and fly-tier who came originally from Arkansas and started making fishing tackle in Duluth in 1914, Paul Young moved to Detroit in 1921 to open a shop that was at first devoted primarily to taxidermy. He was venerated in the last decade of his life as "the Stradivari of the Midge Rod," and died enjoying near-legendary status as a cult figure. Never a fanatic on the subject of light tackle, he developed the Midge rod at 6¼ feet and an average weight of 1¾ ounces for use with HEH (No. 4) line, 5X and 6X leaders, and size 18–24 flies purely as an answer to what he regarded as the highly specialized needs of the sophisticated fly fishermen of the limestone streams of Pennsylvania. He offered it first in the early 1950's as only one of a dozen different designs of fly rods that he made spanning a wide range of lengths and weights, and was surprised and frankly incredulous when he first heard of its use as a salmon rod.

He rather grudgingly acknowledged its bestseller status in his line of rods; for his own use he greatly preferred the Parabolic 16, an "all purpose" rod of 8 feet and 3¾ ounce weight, and regarded the use of a "toothpick" like his Midge for long casts and large fish as something of a perversion of its natural purpose. He testily refused either to claim, or even to acknowledge, that he had pioneered the small-rod craze, pointing out that the H.L. Leonard line had featured a Baby Catskill rod, at 6 feet and ¹⁵/₁₆ ounce, several years before he made his first Midge, and that Wm. Mills and Sons had even advertised it as "the world's smallest fly rod." Admitting that his Midge was clearly out of the "baby rod" class, which he considered "about as practical as a wet noodle," he still contended that it was being put to uses for which he neither intended it nor considered it suitable; and he was both amused and puzzled when he saw the term "midge rod" come into generic use as categorizing all split-cane rods with light mountings, measuring under 7 feet and weighing 2 ounces or less, and thus outgrow its original application to a specific model in his line.

Other Paul Young light rods are the Driggs, at 7 feet 2 inches length and 2⅞ ounces weight, a much stouter stick than the Midge; the Perfectionist at 7½ feet and 2½ ounces (really a Midge at extended length); and the Martha Marie (named for his wife) of 7½ feet and 3.05 ounces when supplied with featherweight fittings. The other Young rods ranged up to the Texas General at 8½ feet and 5½ ounces and the Bobby Doerr at 9 feet and 6 ounces.

Paul Young didn't live to see the momentary craze for a still smaller category, the Bantam rods, which were turned out by a number of makers in the mid-60's at 4 feet 4 inches and weighing exactly 1 ounce. As made by Hardy and Orvis, and even in a couple of instances by Payne, these are treasured by light-tackle devotees, but are now generally no longer made except on special order.

What Paul Young is best remembered by, aside from his monument, the Midge rod, is his unique creation, the Strawman nymph, an impression via clipped deer hair of the rather shaggy look of the straw housing of the caddis nymph at one stage in the process of becoming a fly.

The Paul Young Company's business locations in the Detroit area ran afoul of highway developments in the suburbs so often in the years following his death that it was finally moved to Traverse City, where his younger son, John, of whom Paul always said that "he was the one born with bamboo in his blood," carries on as the family rodmaker.

The outstanding attribute of the Young light rod, as exemplified most notably in the Midge and its longer mate the Perfectionist, is the attainment of backbone and power to permit the vigorous use of the double-line-haul for long casts without sacrifice of the "slender ankle" effect of the last foot of the delicate tip, affording accuracy and finesse in fishing "fine and far-off." It is the exploitation of the first of these two qualities, by its use for grilse and salmon, and the ignoring of the second, which can only be brought into play in the upper reaches of trouting, that went against the artistic grain of the rod's maker, and made him such a reluctant exponent, less royal than his courtiers, of the craze for ever-bigger fish on ever-lighter tackle of which he was at one time regarded as the king.   —A.G.

YUGOSLAVIA Embracing the western half of the Balkan Peninsula and bordered by Austria, Italy, Hungary, Rumania, Bulgaria, Greece, and Albania, this small (98,766 square miles) European country has such a variety of landscapes, from Alpine peaks to rolling hills and a spectacularly precipitous coast spilling into the sea, that it refers to itself as a traveler's "compact." There are more than 1,000 islands off its Dalmatian Coast, of which about a hundred are permanently inhabited. The annual array of cultural and sporting events attracts tourists in such numbers that from mid-June to September Yugoslavia is literally overrun with visitors. The fact that fishing exists at all is almost anticlimactic, and while the overall picture is modest, no angling education is complete until you've sampled a beautiful river like the

Sava-Bohinjka or puzzled over Yugoslavia's exotic salmonids. Almost the entire country is based on limestone (every street and every building in the fabulous old city of Dubrovnik is made of limestone), a geological endowment that is the hallmark of fertile trout streams. By the same token its seawater is so clear that plankton and marine plant life is minimal along the Adriatic shore, and saltwater fishing is limited to a small number of reef species—although it is a paradise for the skin or scuba diver.

May and June are the best months for Yugoslavian trout fishing. Average daily temperatures will range from 63°–68°F, and rainfall during this period averages about 15 days out of each month. The summer season can be very hot, with a mean in July of 75°F but daily maximums running to 85°F or more. Good fishing can be obtained in high altitude streams during summer months.

Yugoslavian freshwater fishing is primarily for brown and rainbow trout. The brown is native to Yugoslavia and the rainbow was introduced from California. Grayling are also native to the country. However, rivers draining into the Adriatic contain postglacial species which, with the possible exception of the Ohrid trout (*Salmo letnica*), do not occur elsewhere. A similar relict species, the Lake Garda trout (*Salmo carpio*), exists on the Italian side of the Adriatic. In addition to the Ohrid trout Yugoslavian angling may produce marble trout (*Salmo mormoratus*), which grows to very large sizes exceeding 40 pounds, and the softmouth trout (*Salmo obtusirostris*), which weighs up to 10 pounds. Another primitive genus of salmonine fishes is *Hucho*, a strictly Eurasian freshwater group composed of 4 species and commonly known to most Europeans as huchen. A large, landlocked salmonid (one species *Hucho taimen*, which occurs in Russian Arctic rivers from the Pechora River east, attains a recorded weight of 176 pounds, although the Yugoslavian species *Hucho hucho* is known to exceed 80 pounds) the huchen is highly regarded by anglers. Huchen are caught primarily by casting spoons, spinners, and plugs. The fight consists of long hard runs at great speed. It is a strong fish and fairly heavy spinning tackle is favored. Huchen are essentially a riverine species usually found at the bottom of deep pools near fast water.

Yugoslavia consists of six separate Socialist republics: Slovenia, Bosnia and Herzegovina, Croatia, Macedonia, Serbia, and Montenegro. Each has its own system of licensing which can confuse the visitor. When in doubt your hotel or the local tourist office will direct you to the correct office. Basically, you need a separate permit for each river, which averages about $4 per day. Yugoslavia has a very active staff of game protectors, so don't get a lapse of memory about which stream you are on or whether the permit covers that particular day. Size and bag limits are strictly enforced, and also vary according to the waters fished; this information will appear on your permit.

SAVA-BOHINJKA RIVER

Located in Slovenia, the Sava-Bohinjka is a crystal-clear, gravel-bottomed stream that rises in Lake Bohinjka which nestles among the Julian Alps. Although the highest peak, Triglav (9,393 feet), is of modest stature when compared to other mountain ranges, the heavily glaciated limestone and granite walls are remarkably beautiful.

The river offers many miles of first-class fly-fishing for rainbows, browns, and grayling. The fish in this stream are plump and colorful, with an average of about ¾ pound and the occasional 2- or 3-pounder. Dry flies and nymphs are most effective. The river is easy to wade. Look for the larger trout along undercut banks and willows.

Literally situated in a corner opposite Austria and Italy, the resort city of Bled offers every amenity to the traveler, from casinos to sauna baths and a variety of lakefront hotels. A fishing license can be obtained from Zavod za ribistvo (the Fishing Institute) in Ljubljana, Zupanciceva 9, which manages these waters; the Tourist Society of Bled; the travel agency Kompas at Bled; Ribogojstvo (the fish-hatchery) Bohinj at Bohinjska Bistrica; and from the Tourist Society Bohinj in the Tourist Office at Lake Bohinj.

KRKA RIVER

The Krka River (pronounced Kur-ka with a rolled *r*) is not far from the city of Ljubljana. Except for the farmhouses with their red-tile roofs the countryside is very similar to the Catskill Mountain region around the Beaverkill River. However, the rivers are distinctly different. The Krka is mainly a slow-flowing stream with long, deep stretches that flow between steep hills; comparatively little of the trout water between its source and the village of Zuzemberk is wadable. About every quarter mile or so the Krka flows over shallow limestone ledges of several hundred yards in length which offer access to the river. Despite this limited wading area numbers of fine trout can be caught, especially during the frequent mayfly hatches. The average size is about 1 pound, although the river holds very large browns and rainbows and 5–6-pounders are not uncommon. The lower river, from

The Sava-Bohinjka is a swift, clear-flowing mountain stream. Easily reached from the city of Bled, it produces excellent angling

Zuzemberk to Novo Mesto, is primarily grayling and huchen water. The Krka is noted for its large huchen, which average about 15 pounds. From Novo Mesto downstream the river becomes broader and slow-moving; northern pike and pikeperch are common here.

For the Krka you can find accommodations at an old castle situated on an island in the river at the village of Otocec (pronounced Aw-toe-shots). Actually, it doesn't put you any closer to the fishing, because you'll still have to drive almost halfway back to Ljubljana to reach the better trout water, so it's just as easy to stay in the city where the food and amenities are first class.

GACKA RIVER

The Gacka River (pronounced Gots-ga) in Croatia is one of the most fertile chalk streams in central Europe. At one time it produced very large brown and rainbow trout (to 20 pounds), and although occasional big fish are still caught, their numbers have declined and the stream average is about 1½ pounds. The Gacka is intensively fished, particularly in the prime season from May through June, after which the angling tapers off with some fair catches being made on evening rises. However, due to a great abundance of aquatic foods the fish are highly selective and the angling is not easy. Long a favorite of German and Italian tourists, the Gacka gets plenty of rod pressure, even in summer months. There are no good accommodations near the river. The choice is to stay in Otocec, which has a lower than B-Category hotel but is within 5 miles of the river, or at the A-Category Hotel located in the National Park 25 miles from the Gacka at Plitvice. The drive from Plitvice to the Gacka takes 1 hour and is about 25 miles in large part over switchback road.

Big brown trout inhabit the Neretva River. This is a tricky stream to wade because of its fluctuating water level

NERETVA RIVER

The Neretva River is one of the largest in Yugoslavia, and is usually fished from the town of Konjic or Mostar. This broad, slightly turbid river has a daily fluctuating water level due to a hydroelectric impoundment near its headwaters. The level may increase from 2–4 feet depending on demand, with the stream at its low stage in the morning hours and rising by midday. Any wading must be done very cautiously. However, the Neretva contains a variety of salmonids including brown, rainbow, softmouth, and marble trout. It also produces some exceptional huchen in the 50-pound-plus class. Chiefly, this is a stream for the spinning rod, as it is almost all bank-casting; over much of its length the Neretva is about a quarter-mile wide. Ideally, you should fish the Neretva early in the morning while the water is low, then drive to the Buna River for an afternoon of trout fishing. Accommodations can be found in Mostar.

BUNA RIVER

The Buna River, a tributary of the Neretva, is located near the city of Mostar. This charming stream has many good riffles and pools, and produces rainbow, brown, and softmouth trout. The popular fishing area is from the riverside restaurant at its source (the Buna emerges from a great spring in a cave at the foot of a mountain) to about 5 miles downstream. Although this upstream section is productive, with an average of about ¾ pound, any of the lower beats are preferable.

UNA RIVER

One of the most scenic rivers in Yugoslavia, the Una has a great number of waterfalls (at the rate of about one every 1½ miles in its 133-mile course), which creates the impression of a chain of narrow lakes rather than a river. The Una and its tributaries—the Unac, Klokot, Krusnica, Bastra, and Sana rivers—are principally grayling and brown trout streams, although large huchen occur in the Una from the waterfall at Kosteli downstream; a popular 12½-mile stretch is at Bosanska Krupa. The main fishing center for the Una is at Martin Brod.

UNICA RIVER

Overlooked in the official guide books, but about an hour's drive south of Ljubljana near the town of Postojna, the Unica is one of the best if not *the* best grayling stream in Yugoslavia. A narrow, meandering river, it is quite easy to fish with a fly. You can headquarter either in Ljubljana and drive, or stay in Postojna. The road from Ljubljana is the main artery into Trieste and points south on the Adriatic. There are many switchbacks on the highway, with heavy commercial traffic. To reach the best fishing on the Unica, take the road from Planina toward Rakek. After a half-mile turn left at the bridge. Continue a quarter-mile until you see an unlikely track sloping down into the field on the left. Follow this until you arrive at a big loop in the river. Good fly water here; and 60–80 grayling in a day would not be unusual. Fish average about ¾ pound with the occasional 2-pounder.

MORACA RIVER

The Moraca flows through Titograd in Montenegro and is one of the better marble trout streams in Yugoslavia. A 46½-pound marble trout was caught here in 1968 (this species is known locally as *glavatica*). The

Moraca also contains large brown and rainbow trout. A road parallels the river for almost 50 miles, so the water is accessible. Like the huchen, marble trout tend to stay in deep places (the Moraca has many steep gorges) and make strong runs when hooked, but rarely jump. Spinners, spoons, and plugs are favored for these large trout.

Two other streams worth exploring in this area are the Cijevna and Zeta rivers. Accommodations can be found in Titograd or in the village of Niksic.

TACKLE

Any standard trout fly rod according to preference can be used. Most Yugoslavian waters can be fished with fairly light tackle; however, as a second rod bring along a 9-footer with a No. 8 line if you plan to fish a weedy river like the Gacka. It takes a stout rod to hold big trout out of the cress beds. Too, the Gacka flows through open country where winds are a problem. All the usual trout patterns in dry and wet flies will take fish, but nymphs are often most effective; make sure to stock a supply in cream, grays, and browns. Much of this fishing is in crystal-clear water, so long fine leaders (9–12 feet and from 3X–6X) are a must. Spinning or bait-casting tackle for the huchen should be calibered at 12-pound-test minimum; wobbling spoons, spinners, and small plugs are effective. —A.J.McC.

YUKON TERRITORY This 207,000-square-mile triangle of northwestern Canada is one of the least exploited wilderness areas on the North American Continent. It has only two major towns—Whitehorse, near the lake district, and Dawson City, on the Yukon River just upstream from Eagle, Alaska. The topography varies from rolling highlands in the central part of the territory to the rugged St. Elias Range where Canada's highest peak, Mt. Logan (19,850 feet), is located in the southwest. There are two major watersheds. The central Yukon River complex includes such rivers as the White, the Teslin, the Donjek, the Kluane, and the Pelly. The extreme northern part of the territory drains into the Mackenzie River in the western Northwest Territories via the Ogilvie, Hart, and Bonnet Plume rivers, which all join to form the large Peel River. Oddly enough, the southeastern district also drains eventually into the Mackenzie River through the Liard, which has its headquarters draining the Watson Lake region. Important and accessible tributaries in this system are the Meister, Frances, Coal, and Rancheria rivers.

As one would expect with such a large area, there is a great variety of fishable waters. Some of the major streams that run north from the St. Elias Range are rough, brawling, and treacherous glacial torrents, while others are deep and slower, offering an exceptional challenge and adventure to the angler with a small boat. The lakes range in size and character from the long and narrow Teslin Lake, which cuts an eighty-mile swath across the Yukon-British Columbia border and harbors lake trout to forty pounds or more, to countless small tundra and muskeg pothole lakes which contain northern pike.

The principal gamefish of the Yukon are much the same as they are in Alaska—grayling, northern pike, lake trout, rainbow trout, burbot, inconnu, Dolly Varden, Arctic char, whitefish, silver salmon, chinook (king) salmon, and chum (dog) salmon. The last two species of

salmon are of particular interest. The chinook salmon reach Nisutlin Lake on their annual migration up the Yukon from the Pacific and the Bering Sea, a distance of about 2,000 miles. The chum salmon are known to penetrate the waters of Teslin Lake 1,753 miles from tidewater.

THE ALASKA HIGHWAY

The Alaska-bound motorist is in an excellent position to enjoy some of the finest water in the Yukon with very little effort and expenditure, if he is willing to take his time and travel slowly. The Alaska Highway traverses the lake district for many miles and sends off branches which connect with other important lakes. As it winds through some of North America's most beautiful scenery, it follows mile after mile of small grayling streams.

One of the largest fish in the Yukon is the lake trout. At least eleven major lakes containing this huge predator can be reached by road, with four of these bordered by the main Alaska Highway and the remainder only a short drive from the highway by good road. The four most accessible are, in order as you drive northwards, Teslin, Little Atlin, Marsh, and Kluane. Local guides are available for hire and may be located in such small villages as Teslin, Johnson's Crossing, M'Clintock, Kluane, Burwash Landing, and Destruction Bay. Although guides are not necessary, they are highly recommended, as they have a good knowledge of their areas and because of the extreme length of unbroken waters involved where sudden winds can create treacherous waves for the smallboat man.

The light-tackle shore fisherman is not apt to fare exceptionally well during the summer months, but just after the ice goes out the lake trout feed voraciously near the surface and in some of the shallow bays, providing an excellent opportunity for the shorebound angler.

Grayling and whitefish may be encountered near the mouths of some of the creeks and small rivers that feed into the lakes. In a few of the larger and weedier bays trophy-sized pike lie unmolested by everyone except the occasional nomadic Indian and the rare angler who has taken the effort to find these fish. Notable for its pike is the outlet of the Nisutlin River into Nisutlin Bay on Teslin Lake. This is easily reached by small boat and motor, as the highway crosses the mouth of this bay on the first large bridge in the Teslin area.

Kluane Lake deserves special mention if for no other reason than its wild and desolate beauty. Lying to the southwest is a federal game range, and one can often see such wildlife as the magnificent Dall sheep from the road that borders the lake. Because this body of water is in generally open tundra the wind poses a particular problem, but those who venture against it are often rewarded with beautiful lake trout.

Lake Aishihik, which may be reached by turning north at the village of Canyon, is fast becoming famous for producing large mackinaws. Another interesting lake, Quiet Lake, may be found by turning north at Johnson's Crossing on the Canol Road. This road is occasionally in poor shape, so it is best to check conditions at the village before proceeding. The road originally lead to Norman Wells on the banks of the Mackenzie River, but is now maintained only to Ross River, at which point the

The remote rivers of the Yukon offer excellent angling for trout, American grayling, and whitefish

lack of a bridge blocks the motorized sportsman. An intriguing float-trip may be started from the vicinity of Quiet Lake, as the road parallels the Nisutlin River for several miles. A kayak or life raft launched here would eventually bring you back into Teslin's Nisutlin Bay, from which you can paddle or motor back to the town of Teslin on the highway.

The motorist crosses, follows, and recrosses many small rivers that are very inviting to the grayling enthusiast. Because the average tourist is always hurrying to get to Alaska or back home again, these rivers receive surprisingly light fishing pressure. However, to enjoy them at their best, the angler should try to follow them back away from the road for a mile or so, in order that he can be completely assured of solitude while in pursuit of the grayling. These streams vary in size and character. A typical one is the Rancheria River which lies just over the British Columbia border. This is a small stream with many nice pools, and is ideally suited to very light fly-fishing. There is a good place to pull off to camp on the south side of the road near the bridge. Dolly Vardens as well as medium-sized grayling may be caught in the bridge pool. The best fishing is out of sight of the road. Just slightly further up the highway, the road follows the Swift River, which is another fascinating grayling stream. This picturesque creek contains Dolly Vardens (locally called mountain trout) and eating-sized grayling that delight the dry-fly enthusiast by hitting a No. 12 Black Gnat with alarming gusto. Although the stream parallels the road, people seldom stop to catch their supper, so the few tourists who are not in a rush find their fishing not only accessible, but uncrowded—a rarity along southern highways.

Further on toward the Alaska border, in the Kluane region, the picture is not so promising for the stream fisherman as most of the rivers are glacial in origin. Besides being full of milky silt, they are much too precipitous and treacherous for any sort of fishing. Here it is necessary to make local inquiries or hire a professional guide. The chances are that they will try to discourage the stream fisherman and tempt him with the joys of Lake Kluane itself.

NORTHERN WILDERNESS

For the man with his own float plane, or the where-with-all to hire a bushpilot, the vast empty lands north of the Alaska Highway offer the promise of completely untouched lakes and rivers. Although the discovery of major ore deposits is rapidly changing this picture, the northern sectors of the Yukon are virtually untouched by the fisherman. Stories have filtered back to civilization about the spawning runs of huge Arctic char in the streams that drain into the Beaufort Sea. The shee fishing of the northern Yukon Territory is almost completely unassessed, but the species ranges all through northern and Mackenzie drainages. Sheefish should be found in the Peel, Ogilivie, Hart, and Bonnet Plume watersheds. Sheefish can also be found in the Yukon River tributaries and in Teslin Lake, which is the southern limit of this magnificent whitefish with a tarpon complex. Here, however, it is largely unappreciated.

TRAVEL SUGGESTIONS

As in all the states and provinces, the nonresident needs a fishing license, but this can hardly be considered a financial burden as the out-of-state permit is nominal. It can be had by stopping at any of the small settlements along the highway, at the sporting goods stores of the larger towns, or by writing the Department of Fisheries in Whitehorse. Tackle should include a very lightweight fly rod, a medium-weight spinning rod, and, if you are going to seek the mackinaws during the midsummer or early fall, a light- to mediumweight freshwater trolling outfit. It is advantageous to bring your own small boat and motor, but not necessary, since boats may be rented at most of the small settlements on the lakes. For those who will have their own craft—a warning: the larger lakes allow the wind to have a tremendous fetch, and sealike waves can kick up very suddenly. Venture forth cautiously, and always wear a life jacket.

For the summer traveler, it should be realized that, in spite of popular legends, the snow and ice do disappear for several months and warm weather prevails. Warm sweaters should be carried for evening fishing (which is a generous pastime as the sub-Arctic evening is stretched out well toward midnight during the early summer). Another important piece of apparel is the headnet to discourage the mosquitoes and black flies that can at certain times cloud around the fisherman's head.   —R.S.L.

Z

ZAPATERO The Spanish name for the leatherjacket (*which see*)

ZEBRA *Diplodus cervinus* A South African species, the zebra has a typical porgy profile. It is silvery, with dark vertical crossbands, the first through the eye, and the sixth, which is sometimes faint or absent, across the caudal peduncle. The snout is black, and the dorsal, anal, and ventral fins are dark. The lips of the zebra are very thick and fleshy. There are 12 oblique incisor teeth in the upper jaw and 8 in the lower. There are two series of small molars in both jaws. Although the zebra generally weighs 2–4 pounds, individuals of 8–10 pounds are sometimes caught.

ANGLING VALUE

The zebra is considered a sporting fish when taken on light tackle. Ordinarily it is caught by bottom-fishing with a worm bait.

FOOD VALUE

In South Africa the zebra is considered very delicate eating.   —A.J.McC.

ZEBRAFISH *Pterois volitans* Also known as lionfish, tigerfish, and turkeyfish, this member of the scorpionfish family (Scorpaenidae) has an elongate, compressed body, a large head covered with stubby spines, and short, fleshy appendages. Its mouth is large, with fine teeth in the jaws. The general appearance of this species is one of plumage, for the feathery fin spines undulate gracefully with the water's movement. The spinous dorsal fin is very high and contains 12–13 sharp, slender spines tipped with feathery connections, which are connected by a membrane only at their base. The soft dorsal and anal fins are smaller, rounded, and identically shaped, and the caudal and pelvic fins are also broadly rounded. Its pectoral fins are very large, and, like the spinous dorsal fin, are composed of long, slender spines connected by a basal membrane, the spines sometimes reaching to or past the caudal fin. Its coloration is rich and gaudy, with hues of reddish-brown bands over a background of yellowish-brown to orange-brown or light pink. Numerous bands cover the body in varying widths, while irregular, broken bands cover the rays and spines of the fins. The species grows to about 10 inches long.

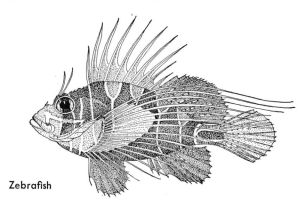

Zebrafish

LIFE HISTORY

Zebrafish are Indo-Pacific forms, found from the Hawaiian Islands to Australia, South Africa, and the Red Sea and throughout the coral islands of the western Pacific and the Indian Ocean. Their relatives are largely coldwater forms inhabiting deepwater, but zebrafish are coral-reef dwellers. Young occur in shallow tidepools, while adults may occur about estuaries. They can be seen resting gracefully in crevices or casually moving over small coral patches in shallow water. A related species, *P. macrurus*, is found in deeper water, up to 150 fathoms.

DANGER TO MAN

Usually a peaceful species, the zebrafish will occasionally become aggressive and stab at an object with its dorsal spines. Its gaudy coloration warns swimmers to avoid it, for there is a poison gland at the base of each spine, and poison flows along the front of the shallow spine groove into the victim. Each groove possesses a venom gland within it, which is covered by a thin sheath. Zebrafish definitely should be handled delicately (*see* Dangerous, Injurious, and Poisonous Organisms *under* First Aid).

ECONOMIC VALUE

Like their relatives, the scorpionfishes, zebrafish are edible but are neither large enough nor common enough to be of commercial value. Their chief importance is in their popularity to aquarists, for the beauty and grace of the zebrafish ranks it high as a thing of beauty in a collector's tank.   —D.dS.

ZEBRA TROUT *See* Trout Hybrids *under* Fish Culture

ZIPOLA *Sebastodes ovalis* A common name for the speckled rockfish. See Rockfish

ZOANTHIDS Members of the coelenterate subclass Zoantharia. Zoanthids include the strong corals and sea anemones. They are frequently found encrusted on the exteriors of other animals, such as on other corals and sponges. Often of large size, they have tentacles and may secrete a strong or horny skeleton, as in the black corals.

ZOOGEOGRAPHY A study or description of the geographical distribution of animals or fishes, especially the determination of the land and marine areas characterized by special groups or species and the study of the causes and significance of such groups or species. *See* Zoogeography of the Lake Trout *under* Lake Trout

ZOOPLANKTON Protozoa and other animal microorganisms living unattached in water. These include small crustacea such as daphnia and cyclops. *See also* Freshwater Ecology, Marine Ecology, Plankton

About the Author

A. J. McClane, a native New Yorker, fished the Beaverkill and Neversink of his home state as a boy. Now, as Executive Editor of *Field & Stream,* he fishes with notables the world over from the Arctic Circle to Tierra del Fuego. The author joined the staff of *Field & Stream* as Fishing Editor in 1947. His training in fish culture and fisheries research and his wide fishing experiences enable him to provide readers of his magazine columns with down-to-earth practical information.

A resident of Palm Beach, Florida, Mr. McClane literally commutes around the globe. He has written outstanding books on his subject: *The Practical Fly Fisherman, Spinning for Fresh and Salt Water Fish of North America,* and *The American Angler,* as well as the first edition of his monumental *Standard Fishing Encyclopedia.* He has also served as angling historian for the *Encyclopaedia Britannica.*

About the Artists

Richard Evans Younger came to Florida about twenty years ago, and his move to the state stimulated his earlier interest in fishing. Born in Marshall, Missouri, Mr. Younger was a student at the Kansas City Art Institute and a pupil of the late Remington Schuyler. He has always been interested in nature and wildlife subjects, and before working on *McClane's Standard* and *New Standard Fishing Encylopedias,* he painted primarily for private collections.

Frances McKittrick Watkins came to Florida from New York State in 1965, after earning a Ph.D. at Cornell University, where she also began her career as a scientific illustrator. Her family has produced artists for several generations, and she has done many pen-and-ink drawings for scientific journals and books. Her fisherman husband has been instrumental in helping her develop a technique for posing and photographing specimens so as to produce images of the highest quality.

The paintings done for this book were drawn from live or frozen specimens caught by the author and artists or by far-away fishermen who were asked to obtain specific hard-to-get specimens. The preliminary sketches and finished drawings for this book number in the thousands and many years went into their completion.

Bibliography

GENERAL LITERATURE Often an angler will wish to obtain additional information on his catch. Unfortunately, the scientific world has not been able to learn enough about most fishes to keep up with the angler's often insatiable desire to know something about the name, food habits, spawning cycle, and general habits and life history of the fish he catches. Most books on fishes deal with "keys" to identification: methods for identifying the specimen on hand. Most keys are technical, but with a little practice an angler can often learn to identify a fish where no picture book exists. Since there are perhaps 20,000 species, only a fraction of which can be treated in any one book, the angler will undoubtedly be confronted with puzzling catches. The books listed in the following sections may be of assistance, but, unfortunately, there are few adequate, inexpensive guidebooks, especially in color, which the angler can take along on his fishing trip. In the interim, until handy guidebooks are produced, and as an adjunct to the present volume, which can only hope to cover the more common species, the serious angler is referred to the books listed below. Although some of these are out of print, one may consult them through the permission of public, university, state, federal, or state fish and game libraries. As a rough rule, most books on fishes printed more than 10–20 years ago are out of print.

The following abbreviations are used:

N—essentially nontechnical
T—essentially technical
S—saltwater
F—freshwater

The geographical categories are listed here as convenient *general* guides only. Because fishes recognize no political boundaries, the reader should also check the reference suggested for adjacent geographical regions. For example, Bigelow and Schroeder (1948-1953) are listed as a reference under "Fishes, Atlantic Coast, . . ." but this reference is also valuable for identifying specimens from the Caribbean and Central and South America. Similarly, several books on freshwater fishes of Europe or Africa may be used where the species occur in a common drainage system. See also Oceanography, Marine Biology, Diving, and related fields.

FISHES—GENERAL STUDY

Berg, Lev S.   1947–T
Classification of Fishes, Both Recent and Fossil. J. W. Edwards, Ann Arbor, Michigan, 517 pp.

Bertin, Léon   1975–N
Eels, a Biological Study. Philosophical Library, New York, 192 pp.

Boulenger, Edward G.   1931–N
Fishes. Chapman & Hall, Ltd., London, England, 174 pp.

Boulenger, George A.   1895–T
Catalogue of the Fishes in the British Museum. British Museum, London, England, 2nd ed., several volumes.

Bridge, Thomas W., and
  George A. Boulenger   1904–T
Fishes. In The Cambridge Natural History. Vol. 7. The Macmillan Co., New York; Reprint edition, 1958, Hafner Publishing Co., Inc., New York, New York.

Brown, Margaret E., editor   1957–T
The Physiology of Fishes. Vol 1: "Metabolism," 447 pp., Vol 2: "Behavior," 526 pp. Academic Press, Inc., New York.

Constantin-Weyer, Maurice   1956–N
The Private Life of Fishes. Translated by Ray Turrell. G. P. Putnam's Sons, New York, 150 pp.

Coppleson, Victor M.   1958–N
Shark Attack. Angus & Robertson, Sydney, Australia. 266 pp.

Curtis, Brian   1962–N
The Life Story of the Fish; His Morals and Manners. Dover, New York, 293 pp.

Dean, Bashford   1895–T
Fishes, Living and Fossil; an Outline of Their Forms and Probable Relationships. The Macmillan Co., New York, 300 pp.

                                                                1917-1923–T
A Bibliography of Fishes. Vol. 1, 718 pp.; Vol. 2, 702 pp.; Vol. 3, 707 pp. Reprinted, 1962, by Russell and Russell, Inc., New York.

Fichter, George S.   1963–N
Fishes. The Golden Bookshelf of Natural History, Golden Press, New York, 104 pp.

Frost, W. E., and M. E. Brown   1967–F-T
The Trout. Collins, London, England, 286 pp.

Gilbert, Perry W., editor   1963–T
Sharks and Survival. D. C. Heath Co., Boston, Massachusetts, 578 pp.

Goode, George B., editor   1884-1887–T
The Fisheries and Fishery Industries of the United States. U. S. Government Printing Office, Washington, D. C., 6 volumes.

Grassé, P. P., editor   1958–T
Traité de Zoologie. Agnathes et Poissons. Anatomie, Ethologie, Systématique. Vol. 13. Masson et Cie., Paris, France, 3 volumes, 2758 pp.

Günther, Albert C. L. G.   1880—T
An Introduction to the Study of Fishes. Adam &
Charles Black, London, England, 720 pp.
Helm, Thomas   1961—N
Shark. Dodd, Mead & Co., New York, 260 pp.
Hoar, W. S., and D. J. Randall, editors   1969—FS-T
*Fish Physiology, Volume III—Reproduction and
Growth. Bioluminescense, Pigments, and Poisons.*
Academic Press, Inc., New York, 485 pp.
Jensen, Al   1973—S-T
The Cod. Thomas Y. Crowell Co., New York.
Jordan, David S.   1905—T
A Guide to the Study of Fishes. Holt, Rinehart and
Winston, Inc., New York, Vol. 1: 599 pp., Vol. 2:
624 pp.

                                      1925—T
Fishes. D. Appleton & Co., New York, 773 pp.
Kyle, Harry M.   1926—T
The Biology of Fishes. The Macmillan Co., New
York, 396 pp.
Lagler, Karl F., John E. Bardach, and
Robert R. Miller   1962—T
Ichthyology. John Wiley & Sons, Inc., New York,
545 pp.
La Gorce, John Oliver, editor   1961—N
The Book of Fishes. National Geographic Society,
Washington, D. C., 339 pp.
La Monte, Francesca R.   1952—N
Marine Game Fishes of the World. Doubleday &
Co., Garden City, New York, 190 pp.
Lanham, Url   1962—N
The Fishes. Columbia University Press, New York
and London, 116 pp.
Le Danois, Edouard, and others   1957—N
Fishes of the World. George G. Harrap & Co.,
London, England, 190 pp.
Lineaweaver, Thomas H., III, and
Richard H. Backus   1970—S-N
The Natural History of Sharks. J. B. Lippincott
Co., Philadelphia and New York, 256 pp.
McCormick, Harold W., Tom Allen, and
William E. Young   1963—N
Shadows in the Sea. Chilton Co., Philadelphia,
Pennsylvania, 415 pp.
Meek, Alexander   1916—T
The Migrations of Fish. Edward Arnold, London,
England, 427 pp.
Nikol'skii, Georgi V.   1954—T
Special Ichthyology. State Printer "Sovyetskaya
Nauk," Moscow, U.S.S.R., 538 pp. (In Russian).
Translated for the National Science Foundation
and available from the Office of Technical Ser-
vices, United States Department of Commerce,
Washington, D. C.

                                      1962—T
Ecology of Fishes. Academic Press, Inc., New
York, 352 pp.
Norman, John R.   1934—T
A Systematic Monograph of the Flatfishes. Vol. 1.
British Museum (National History), London,
England, 459 pp.

                                      1958—T
A History of Fishes. E. Benn, London, England,
463 pp.

Ommanney, Francis D., and the editors of
Life Magazine   1963—N
The Fishes. Life Nature Library, Time, Inc., New
York, 192 pp.
Pincher, Chapman   1948—N
A Study of Fish. Duell, Sloan & Pearce, Inc., New
York, 343 pp.
Roule, Louis   1933—N
Fishes, Their Journeys and Migrations. W. W.
Norton & Co., Inc., New York, 270 pp. Trans-
lated by Conrad Elphinstone.

                                      1935—N
Fishes and Their Ways of Life. W. W. Norton &
Co., Inc., New York, 312 pp. Translated by Con-
rad Elphinstone.
Schultz, Leonard P. and Ernest A. Lachner   1962—T
*Directions for Collecting, Preserving, and Ship-
ping Fishes to the U. S. National Museum.* Smith-
sonian Institution, United States National Museum,
Washington, D. C., 7 pp.
Schultz, Leonard P. and Edith M. Stern   1948—N
The Ways of Fishes. Van Nostrand Co., Inc., New
York, 264 pp.
Smith, J. L. B.   1956—N
Old Fourlegs, the Story of the Coelacanth. Long-
mans Green and Co., London, England, 260 pp.
                                      1956—N
*The Search Beneath the Sea, the Story of the Coe-
lacanth.* Holt, Rinehart and Winston, Inc., New
York, 260 pp.
Smithsonian Scientific Series   1930—T
*Fishes, Amphibians and Reptiles, Cold-blooded
Vertebrates.* Pt. 1. *Fishes* by S. F. Hildebrand, Pts.
2 and 3. *Amphibians and Reptiles* by C. W. Gil-
more & D. M. Cochran. Vol. 8. Smithsonian Insti-
tution Series, New York, 383 pp.
Walford, Lionel A., editor   1947—N
Fishery Resources of the United States. Public Af-
fairs Press, Washington, D. C., 134 pp.
Whitley, G. P. and J. Allan   1958—N
The Sea-horse and Its Relatives. Georgian House,
Melbourne, Australia, 84 pp.
Young, J. Z.   1962—T
The Life of Vertebrates. Clarendon Press, Oxford,
England, 820 pp.
Young, William E.   1933—N
Shark! Shark! Gotham House, New York, 287 pp.

FISHES—GENERAL IDENTIFICATION

Coates, Christopher W. and J. Atz   1954—FS-N
Fishes of the World. In The Animal Kingdom,
Vol. 3, Book 4. Greystone, New York.
Cuvier, Georges and
Achille Valenciennes   1830-1849—FS-T
Historie Naturelle des Poissons. Levrault, Paris,
France, Vols. 1-22.
De Buen, Fernando   1952—FS-T
Las Familias de Peces de Importancia Económica.
Food & Agricultural Organization, United Na-
tions, Santiago, Chile, 311 pp.
Goode, George B. and T. H. Bean   1895—S-T
Oceanic Ichthyology. Washington, D. C., 2 vols.,

553 pp. + atlas. (Also Smithsonian Institution Publications, 981, 982).

Herald, Earl S.   1961—FS-N
Living Fishes of the World. Doubleday and Co., Inc., Garden City, New York, 303 pp.

McPhail, J. D.   1961—F-T
A Systematic Study of the Salvelinus alpinus *Complex in North America.* Journal Fisheries Research Board of Canada, Vol. 18, No. 5, pp. 793-816.

1963—F-T
Geographic Variation in North American Nine-spine Sticklebacks, Pungitius pungitius. Journal Fisheries Research Board of Canada, Vol. 20, No. 1, pp. 27-44.

1963—F-T
The Post-glacial Dispersal of Freshwater Fishes in Northern North America (manuscript). Department of Zoology, Ph. D. Thesis, McGill University, Montreal, Canada, 167 pp.

Morton, W. M., and R. R. Miller   1954—F-T
Systematic Position of the Lake Trout, Salvelinus namaycush. *Copeia,* No. 2, pp. 116-124.

Norden, C.R.   1961—F-T
Comparative Osteology of Representative Salmonid Fishes, with particular reference to the grayling (Thymallus arcticus) *and its phylogeny.* Journal Fisheries Research Board of Canada, Vol. 18, No. 5, pp. 679-791.

Norman, John R. and F. C. Fraser   1938—S-N
Giant Fishes, Whales and Dolphins. W. W. Norton & Co., Inc., New York, 361 pp.

1949—S-N
Field Book of Giant Fishes. G. P. Putnam's Sons, New York, 375 pp.

Schindler, Otto   1957—F-N
Freshwater Fishes. Thames and Hudson, London, England, 243 pp. Translated and edited by P. A. Orkin.

Sterba, Günther   1959—F-T
Süsswasserfische aus aller Welt. Zimmer U. Herzog, Berchtesgaden, Germany. Translated by Denys W. Tucker as *Freshwater Fishes of the World.* Vista Books, London, 878 pp.

Vesey-Fitzgerald, Brian and
Francesca La Monte, editors   1949—FS-N
Game Fish of the World. Harper and Brothers, New York, 446 pp.

Zim, Herbert S. and
Hurst H. Shoemaker   1956—FS-N
Fishes, a Guide to Fresh- and Saltwater Species. Simon and Schuster, Inc., New York, 160 pp.

FISHES—AQUARIUM

Axelrod, Herbert R.   1952—F-N
Tropical Fish as a Hobby, a Guide to Selection, Care and Breeding. McGraw-Hill Book Co., New York, 264 pp.

Axelrod, Herbert R. and L. P. Schultz   1955—FS-N
Handbook of Tropical Aquarium Fishes. McGraw-Hill Book Co., New York, 718 pp.

Innes, William T.   1939—F-N
The Modern Aquarium. William Innes Co., Philadelphia, Pennsylvania, 64 pp.

1956—F-N
Exotic Aquarium Fishes. Innes Publishing Co., Philadelphia, Pennsylvania, 19th edition, 525 pp.

Ladiges, Werner   1956—S-N
Tropische Meeresfische. Arten, Lebensweise und Haltung. Alfred Kernan Verlag, Stuttgart, Germany, 112 pp.

McInerny, Derek and Geoffrey Gerard   1958—F-N
All About Tropical Fishes. The Macmillan Co., New York, 480 pp.

O'Connell, Robert F.   1969—S-N
The Marine Aquarium for the Home Aquarist. The Great Outdoors Publishing Co., St. Petersburg, Florida, 158 pp.

Straughan, Robert P. L.   1963—S-N
The Salt-water Aquarium in the Home. A. S. Barnes & Co., New York, 256 pp.

FISHES, UNITED STATES—GENERAL

Bailey, Reeve M., and others   1960—FS-T
A List of Common and Scientific Names of Fishes from the United States and Canada. American Fisheries Society, Ann Arbor, Michigan, Special Publication, No. 2, 102 pp.

Jordan, David S. and
Barton W. Evermann   1896-1900—FS-T
The Fishes of North and Middle America. A descriptive catalogue of the species of fish-like vertebrates found in the waters of North America, north of the Isthmus of Panama. Bulletin United States National Museum, Washington, D. C. 3313 pp. + 392 plates (4 volumes).

1941—FS-N
American Food and Game Fishes. Doubleday & Co., Inc., Garden City, New York, 574 pp.

Jordan, David S., Barton
W. Evermann, and
Howard W. Clark   1930—FS-T
Check-list of the Fishes and Fishlike Vertebrates of North and Middle America, North of the Northern Boundary of Venezuela and Colombia. Report United States Commission of Fisheries, 1928 (1930), Part II, 670 pp. Reprinted 1962 by Eric Lundberg, Ashton, Maryland.

La Monte, Francesca R.   1950—FS-N
North American Game Fishes. Doubleday & Co., Inc., Garden City, New York, 202 pp.

UNITED STATES—ATLANTIC COAST, INCLUDING NORTHERN GULF OF MEXICO

Bean, Tarleton H.   1903—FS-T
Catalogue of the Fishes of New York, Bulletin New York State Museum, Albany, New York, No. 60, Zoology 9:784 pp.

Bigelow, Henry B. and
W. C. Schroeder   1948-1953—S-T
Fishes of the Western North Atlantic. Memoir,

No. 1, Part 1, *Cyclostomes and Sharks;* Part 2, *Sawfishes, Guitarfishes, Skates, Rays and Chimaeroids.* Sears Foundation for Marine Research, Yale University, New Haven, Connecticut, 2 volumes.

1953—S-T
Fishes of the Gulf of Maine. Fishery Bulletin the Fish and Wildlife Service, Washington, D.C., Vol. 53, No. 74, 577 pp.

Bigelow, Henry B., and others   1964—S-T
Fishes of the Western North Atlantic. Part 4, *Softrayed Bony Fishes. Order Isospondyli* (part). *Suborder Argentinoidea. Suborder Stomatoidea. Suborder Esocidea. Suborder Bathylaconoidea. Order Giganturoidei.* Memoir, Sears Foundation for Marine Research, Yale University, New Haven, Connecticut, No. 1, 599 pp.

1963—S-T
Fishes of the Western North Atlantic. Part 3, *Softrayed Bony Fishes.* Memoir, Sears Foundation for Marine Research, Yale Universiy, New Haven, Connecticut, No. 1, 630 pp.

Boyle, Robert H.   1969—FS-N
The Hudson River, A Natural and Unnatural History. W. W. Norton, New York, 304 pp.

Breder, Charles M., Jr.   1948—S-T
Field Book of Marine Fishes of the Atlantic Coast, from Labrador to Texas, Being a Short Description of Their Characteristics and Habits with Keys for Their Identification. G. P. Putnam's Sons, New York, 332 pp.

Fowler, Henry W.   1906—FS-T
The Fishes of New Jersey. Part 2. Annual Report of the New Jersey State Museum for 1905, pp. 35-477.

1945—FS-T
A Study of the Fishes of the Southern Piedmont and Coastal Plain. Monograph, Academy of Natural Sciences, Philadelphia, Pennsylvania, No. 7, 408 pp.

Gordon, Bernard L.   1960—S-T
The Marine Fishes of Rhode Island. The Book & Tackle Shop, Watch Hill, Rhode Island, 136 pp.

Greeley, J. R., and S. C. Bishop   1933—F-T
Fishes of the Upper Hudson Watershed, with annotated list, in *A Biological Survey of the Upper Hudson Watershed.* New York State Conservation Department, Supplement 22, Annual Report, 1932, pp. 64-101.

Hildebrand, Samuel F. and
W. C. Schroeder   1928—FS-T
Fishes of Chesapeake Bay. Bulletin of the United States Bureau of Fisheries, Washington, D. C., Vol. 43, 388 pp.

Kendall, William C.   1914-1935—FS-T
The Fishes of New England, The Salmon Family; Part 1, *The Trout or Charrs,* Vol. 8, 1914; Part 2, *The Salmons, loc. cit.,* Vol. 9, 1935. Memoirs, Boston Society of Natural History, Boston, Massachusetts.

King, Willis   1947—FS-N
Important Food and Game Fishes of North Carolina. The Department of Conservation and Development, Raleigh, North Carolina, 54 pp.

Migdalski, Edward   1958—S-N
Angler's Guide to the Salt Water Game Fishes. The Ronald Press Company, New York, 506 pp.

Nichols, John T., C. M. Breder, Jr.   1927—S-T
The Marine Fishes of New York and Southern New England, Zoologica, New York, Vol. 9, No. 1, 192 pp.

Perlmutter, Alfred   1961—S-T
Guide to Marine Fishes. New York University Press, New York, 431 pp.

Smith, Hugh M.   1907—FS-T
The Fishes of North Carolina. North Carolina Geological and Economic Survey, Vol. 2, E. M. Uzzell & Co., Raleigh, North Carolina, 453 pp.

Taylor, Harden F.   1951—S-T
Survey of Marine Fisheries of North Carolina. University of North Carolina Press, Chapel Hill, North Carolina, 555 pp.

UNITED STATES—PACIFIC COAST

Barnhart, Percy S.   1936—S-T
Marine Fishes of Southern California. University of California Press, Berkeley, California, 209 pp.

Clemens, W. A. and G. V. Wiley   1961—S-T
Fishes of the Pacific Coast of Canada. Bulletin of the Fisheries Research Board of Canada, Ottawa, Canada, No. 58, 2nd edition, 443 pp.

Roedel, Phil M.   1953—S-T
Common Ocean Fishes of California. California Department Fish and Game, Fish Bulletin No. 91, 184 pp.

Schultz, Leonard Peter   1936—FS-T
Keys to the Fishes of Washington, Oregon and Closely Adjoining Regions. University of Washington Publication in *Biology,* Vol. 2, No. 4, pp. 103-228.

Walford, Lionel A.   1937—S-T
Marine Game Fishes of the Pacific Coast, from Alaska to the Equator. University of California Press, Berkeley, California, 205 pp.

UNITED STATES—FRESHWATER

Adams, C. C. and T. L. Hankinson   1928—F-T
The Ecology and Economics of Oneida Lake Fish. Roosevelt Wild Life Annals, Syracuse, New York, Vol. 1, Nos. 3 and 4, 548 pp.

Baxter, George T. and James R. Simon   1970—F-T
Wyoming Fishes Bulletin No. 4, revised. Wyoming Game and Fish Department, Cheyenne, Wyoming, 168 pp.

Blair, W. Frank, Albert P. Blair,
Pierce Brodkorb, Fred R. Cagle,
and George A. Moore   1957—FS-T
Vertebrates of the United States. McGraw-Hill Book Co., New York, 819 pp.

Caine, Lou S.   1949—F-N
North American Fresh Water Sport Fish, Description and Habits, Fishing Tackle and Methods. A. S. Barnes & Co., New York, 212 pp.

Carpenter, Ralph G. and
Hilbert R. Siegler   1947—FS-T
A Sportsman's Guide to the Fishes of New Hampshire. New Hampshire Fish and Game Commission, Concord, New Hampshire, 87 pp.

Churchill, Edward P. and William H. Over   1933—F-T
Fishes of South Dakota. South Dakota Department Game and Fish, Pierre, South Dakota, 87 pp.

Clay, William M.   1962—F-T
A Field Manual of Kentucky Fishes. Kentucky Department Fish and Wildlife Resources, Frankfort, Kentucky, 147 pp.

Cook, Fannye A.   1959—F-T
Freshwater Fishes in Mississippi. Mississippi Game and Fish Commission, Jackson, Mississippi, 239 pp.

Eddy, Samuel   1957—F-N
How to Know the Freshwater Fishes. William C. Brown Co., Dubuque, Iowa, 253 pp.

Eddy, Samuel and Thaddeus Surber   1947—F-T
Northern Fishes, with Special Reference to the Upper Mississippi Valley. University of Minnesota Press, Minneapolis, Minnesota, Revised edition, 276 pp.

Eschmeyer, P. H.   1957—F-T
The Near Extinction of Lake Trout in Lake Michigan. Transactions, American Fisheries Society, Vol. 85 (1955), pp. 102-119.

Evermann, Barton W. and
Howard W. Clark   1920—F-T
Lake Maxinkuckee, a Physical and Biological Survey. Indiana State Department of Conservation, Indianapolis, Indiana, Vol. 1, 660 pp.

Forbes, S. A. and R. E. Richardson   1909—F-T
The Fishes of Illinois. Natural History Survey of Illinois, Illinois Printing Co., Danville, Illinois, 357 pp. + atlas.

Gerking, Shelby D.   1945—F-T
The Distribution of the Fishes of Indiana. Investigations of Indiana Lakes and Streams, Bloomington, Indiana, Vol. 3, No. 1, 137 pp.

Gowanloch, James N.   1933—FS-T
Fishes and Fishing in Louisiana. State of Louisiana Department of Conservation, Baton Rouge, Louisiana, Bulletin No. 23, 638 pp.

Greene, C. Willard   1935—F-T
The Distribution of Wisconsin Fishes. Conservation Commission, State of Wisconsin, Madison, Wisconsin, 235 pp.

Harlan, J. R. and E. B. Speaker   1951—F-T
Iowa Fish and Fishing. State Conservation Commission, Des Moines, Iowa, 2nd edition, 237 pp.

Harper, F.   1961—F-T
Field and Historical Notes on Fresh-water Fishes of the Ungava Peninsula and on Certain Marine Fishes of the North Shore of the Gulf of St. Lawrence. J. Elisha Mitchell Scientific Society, Vol. 77, No. 2, pp. 312-342.

Henshall, J. A.   1907—F-T
Culture of the Montana Grayling. Report, United States Commission of Fisheries for 1906, Document 628, Washington. D. C., 7 pp.

Hubbs, Carl L. and R. M. Bailey   1938—F-T
The Small-mouthed Bass. Cranbrook Institute of Science, Bloomfield Hills, Michigan, Bulletin No. 10, 89 pp.

Hubbs, Carl L. and G. P. Cooper   1936—F-T
Minnows of Michigan. Cranbrook Institute of Science, Bloomfield Hills, Michigan, Bulletin No. 8, 84 pp.

Hubbs, Carl L. and Karl F. Lagler   1958—F-T
Fishes of the Great Lakes Region. Cranbrook Institute of Science, Bloomfield Hills, Michigan, Bulletin No. 26, Revised edition, 213 pp.

Koster, W. J.   1957—F-T
Guide to the Fishes of New Mexico. University of New Mexico Press in co-operation with the New Mexico Department of Game and Fish, Albuquerque, New Mexico, 116 pp.

Kuhne, Eugene R.   1939—F-T
A Guide to the Fishes of Tennessee and the Mid-South. Tennessee Department of Conservation, Nashville, Tennessee, 124 pp.

Loftus, K. H.   1958—F-T
Studies on River-spawning Populations of Lake Trout in Eastern Lake Superior. Transcript, American Fisheries Society, Vol. 87 (1957), pp. 259-277.

Miller, Robert R.   1952—F-T
Bait Fishes of the Lower Colorado River from Lake Mead, Nevada, to Yuma, Arizona, with a Key for Their Identification. California Fish and Game, Sacramento, California, Vol. 38, No. 1, pp. 7-42.

Rounsefell, G. A.   1958—F-T
Anadromy in North American Salmonidae. United States Fish and Wildlife Service, *Fishery Bulletin*, Washington, D. C., Vol. 58, No. 131, pp. 171-185.

    1962—F-T
Relationships Among North American Salmonidae. United States Fish and Wildlife Service, *Fishery Bulletin*, Washington, D. C., Vol. 62, No. 209, pp. 235-270.

    1951—F-T
Breeding Habits of Lake Trout in New York. United States Fish and Wildlife Service, *Fishery Bulletin*, Washington, D. C., Vol. 52, No. 59, pp. 59-76.

Schrenkeisen, Raymond   1938—F-T
Field Book of Fresh-water Fishes of North America North of Mexico. G. P. Putnam's Sons, New York, 312 pp.

Schultz, Leonard P.   1941—F-T
Fishes of Glacier National Park, Montana. United States Department of the Interior Conservation Bulletin, Washington, D. C., No. 22, 42 pp.

Sigler, William F., and Robert Rush Miller   1963—F-T
Fishes of Utah. Utah State Department of Fish and Game, 203 pp.

Simon, James R.   1939—F-T
Yellowstone Fishes. Yellowstone Library and Museum Association, Yellowstone Park, Wyoming, 39 pp.

Smith-Vaniz, William F.   1968—F-T
Freshwater Fishes of Alabama. Auburn Univer-

sity Agricultural Experiment Station, Auburn, Alabama, 211 pp.

Trautman, Milton B.   1957—F-T
The Fishes of Ohio. Ohio State University Press, Columbus, Ohio, 683 pp.

Vladykov, V. D.   1954—F-T
Taxonomic Characters of the North American Chars (Salvelinus and Cristivomer). Journal of the Fisheries Research Board of Canada, Ottawa, Canada, Vol. 11, No. 6, pp. 904-932.

Webster, Dwight A.   1942—F-T
The Life Histories of Some Connecticut Fishes. In A Fishery Survey of Important Connecticut Lakes. Connecticut State Geological and Natural History Survey, Hartford, Connecticut, Bulletin No. 63, pp. 122-227.

Weed, A. C.   1934—F-N
Notes on the Sea Trouts of Labrador. Copeia, No. 3, p. 127.

Wickliff, Edward L. and
  Milton B. Trautman   1947—F-T
Some Food and Game Fishes of Ohio. Ohio Division of Conservation and Natural Resources, Columbus, Ohio.

Wigley, R. L.   1959—F-T
Life History of the Sea Lamprey of Cayuga Lake, New York. United States Fish and Wildlife Service, *Fishery Bulletin,* Washington, D. C., Vol. 54, No. 154, pp. 561-617.

CANADA AND ALASKA

Carl, G. Clifford and W. A. Clemens   1948—F-T
The Freshwater Fishes of British Columbia. British Columbia Provincial Museum, Handbook No. 5, Victoria, British Columbia, 132 pp.

Carl, G. Clifford, W. A. Clemens, and
  C. C. Lindsey   1959—F-T
The Fresh-water Fishes of British Columbia. British Columbia Provincial Museum, Handbook No. 5, 3rd Edition, 192 pp.

Clemens, W. A., R. V. Houghton, and
  J. A. Rattenbury   1945—F-T
A Preliminary Report on a Fishery Survey of Teslin Lake, British Columbia. Report, British Columbia Department of Fisheries for 1944, pp. 70-75.

Cuerrier, J. P.   1954—F-T
The History of Lake Minnewanka with Reference to the Reaction of Lake Trout to Artificial Changes in Environment. Canadian Fish Culturest, Vol. 15, pp. 1-9.

Dufresne, Frank   1946—FS-N
Alaska's Animals and Fishes. Binfords and Mort, Portland, Oregon. 297 pp.

Dymond, John R.   1928—F-T
The Game Fishes of Canada. Canadian Pacific Railway Co., Montreal, Canada.

                                        1928—F-T
Some Factors Affecting the Production of Lake Trout (Cristivomer namaycush) in Lake Ontario. University of Toronto Studies, Biological Series, No. 31, Ontario Fish Research Laboratory, No. 33, pp. 27-41.

                                        1947—F-T
A List of the Freshwater Fishes of Canada. Royal Ontario Museum of Zoology, Miscellaneous Publication No. 1, Toronto, Ontario, Canada, 36 pp.

Ellis, D. V.   1962—F-N
Observations on the Distribution and Ecology of Some Arctic Fish. Arctic, Vol. 15, No. 3, pp. 179-189.

Greenbank, J.   1954—F-T
Sports Fisheries Survey, Katmai National Monument. Administration Report, United States Department of the Interior, National Parks Service, Washington, D. C., 31 pp.

Evermann, B. W. and
  Edmund L. Goldsborough   1907—FS-T
The Fishes of Alaska. Bulletin United States Bureau of Fisheries for 1906, Washington, D. C., Vol. 26, pp. 219-360.

Hinks, David   1943—F-T
The Fishes of Manitoba. Manitoba Department Mines and Natural Resources, Winnipeg, Canada, 102 pp.

Lindsey, C. C.   1963—F-T
Sympatric Occurrence of Two Species of Humpback Whitefish in Squanga Lake, Yukon Territory. Journal Fisheries Research Board of Canada, Vol. 20, No. 3, pp. 749-767.

Livingston, D. A.   1951—F-T
The Fresh Water Fishes of Nova Scotia. Proc., Nova Scotian Institute of Science, Vol. 23, No. 1, pp. 1-90.

MacDonald, W. H.   1951—F-N
Fishing in Alberta. Alberta Travel Bureau, Department of Economic Affairs, A. Shnitka, Edmonton, Alberta, Canada, 36 pp.

Manning, T. H.   1943—F-N
Notes on Some Fish of the Eastern Canadian Arctic. Canadian Field-Naturalist for 1942, Vol. 56, pp. 128-129.

                                        1953—F-N
Notes on the Fish of Banks Island, Arctic, Vol. 6, No. 4, pp. 276-277.

McAllister, D. E. and C. C. Lindsey   1961—F-T
Systematics of the Freshwater Sculpins (Cottus) of British Columbia. Bulletin, Natural Museum of Canada, No. 172, pp. 66-89.

Radforth, Isobel   1944—F-T
Some Consideration on the Distribution of Fishes in Ontario. Contribution Royal Ontario Museum Zoology, Toronto, Canada, No. 25, 116 pp.

Rawson, D. S.   1951—F-T
Studies of the Fish of Great Slave Lake. Journal of the Fisheries Research Board of Canada, Vol. 8, No. 4, pp. 207-240.

                                        1961—F-T
The Lake Trout of Lac la Ronge, Saskatchewan. Journal of the Fisheries Research Board of Canada, Vol. 18, No. 3, pp. 423-462.

Scott, William B.   1954—F-T
Freshwater Fishes of Eastern Canada. University of Toronto Press, Toronto, Canada, 128 pp.

Scott, William B. and E. J. Crossman   1959—F-T
The Freshwater Fishes of New Brunswick: A Checklist with Distributional Data. Contribution,

Royal Ontario Museum, Division of Zoological Paleontology, No. 31, 37 pp.

1964—F-T

Fishes Occurring in the Fresh Waters of Insular Newfoundland. Queens Printer, Ottawa, Canada, 124 pp.

Stefansson, V.   1913—F-N

My Life with the Eskimo. "Report on the Natural History Collections of the Expedition" by R. M. Anderson, *Fishes,* pp. 450-455. The Macmillan Co., Inc., New York.

Townsend, C. H.   1887—F-T

"Notes on the Natural History and Ethnology of Northern Alaska," *in Report of the Cruise of the Revenue Marine Steamer* Corwin *in the Arctic Ocean in the year 1885* by Captain W. A. Healy. House Executive Document 153, 49th Congress, 1st Session, Vol. 32, pp. 81-102.

Walters, V.   1953—F-T

The Fishes Collected by the Canadian Arctic Expedition, 1913-18, with Additional Notes on the Ichthyofauna of Western Arctic Canada, Bulletin, National Museum of Canada, Vol. 128, pp. 257-274.

1955—F-T

Fishes of Western Arctic America and Eastern Arctic Siberia. Bulletin, American Museum of Natural History, New York, Vol. 106, No. 5, pp. 255-368.

Wynne-Edwards, V. C.   1947—F-T

North West Canadian Fisheries Surveys in 1944-1945. The Yukon Territory, pp. 6-30, Bulletin, Fisheries Research Board of Canada, No. 72.

1952—F-T

Freshwater Vertebrates of the Arctic and Subarctic. Bulletin, Fisheries Research Board of Canada, No. 94, 22 pp.

CENTRAL AMERICA—GENERAL

Hubbs, Carl L.   1936—F-T

Fishes of the Yucatán Peninsula. Carnegie Institution of Washington, Washington, D. C., Publication No. 456, pp. 157-287.

Regan, C. Tate   1908—FS-T

Biologia Centrali-Americana. Pisces. Taylor and Francis, London, England, 293 pp.

CENTRAL AMERICA—SALTWATER

Berdegue, Julio   1956—S-T

Peces de Importancia Comercial en la Costa Noroccidentale de México. Secretaria de Marina, Comisión para el Fomento de la Piscicultura Rural, México, 345 pp.

Gilbert, Charles H. and Edwin C. Starks   1904—S-T

The Fishes of Panama Bay. Memoir, California Academy of Sciences, San Francisco, California, No. 4, 304 pp.

Hiyama, Yoshio   1937—S-T

Marine Fishes of the Pacific Coast of Mexico. Nissan Fisheries Institute and Co., Ltd., Tokyo, Japan, 75 pp.

Meek, Seth Eugene and
S. F. Hildebrand   1923-1925—S-T

The Marine Fishes of Panama. Publication Field Museum of Natural History, Chicago, Zoological Series, Chicago, Illinois, *15,* parts 1-3, pp. 1-1065.

Walford, Lionel A.   1937—S-T

Marine Game Fishes of the Pacific Coast from Alaska to the Equator. University of California Press, Berkeley, California, 205 pp.

CENTRAL AMERICA—FRESHWATER

Alvarez, José   1950—F-T

Claves para la Determinación de Especies en los Peces de las Aguas Continentales Mexicanas. Secretario de Marina, Dirección General de Pesca Industries, Conexas, México, pp. 3-136.

Meek, Seth Eugene   1902—F-T

A Contribution to the Ichthyology of Mexico. Field Columbian Museum, Chicago, Publication 65, Zoological Series, Vol. 3, No. 6, 128 pp.

1904—F-T

The Fresh-water Fishes of Mexico North of the Isthmus of Tehuantepec. Field Columbian Museum, Chicago, Publication 93, Zoological Series, Vol. 5, 252 pp.

Meek, S. E. and S. F. Hildebrand   1916—F-T

The Fishes of the Fresh Waters of Panama. Field Museum of Natural History, Chicago, Publication No. 191, Zoological Series, Vol. 10, No. 15, pp. 217-394.

CARIBBEAN AND ADJACENT COUNTRIES

Beebe, William   1933—S-T

Field Book of the Shore Fishes of Bermuda. G. P. Putnam's Sons, New York, 337 pp.

Beebe, William and John Tee-Van   1928—S-T

The Fishes of Port-au-Prince, Haiti. Zoologica, New York, Vol. 10, No. 1, pp. 1-279.

Böhlke, James E. and
Charles C. G. Chaplin   1968—S-T

Fishes of the Bahamas and Adjacent Tropical Waters. Livingston Publishing Co., Narberth, Pennsylvania, 771 pp.

Evermann, B. W. and H. C. Marsh   1900—S-T

The Fishes of Porto Rico. Bulletin United States Fish Commission for 1900, Vol. 20, Part 1, pp. 51-350.

Gunter, Gordon   1945—S-T

Studies on Marine Fishes of Texas. Publication Institute of Marine Science, University of Texas, Austin, Texas, Vol. 1, No. 1, 190 pp.

Jaen, Ruben   1960—S-N

Pesca Mayor en el Caribe. Editorial Arte, Caracas, Venezuela, 239 pp.

Kaplan, Moise N.   1937—S-N

Big Game Angler's Paradise. Department of Agriculture, State of Florida, 400 pp.

Longley, W. H. and S. F. Hildebrand   1941—S-T

Systematic Catalogue of the Fishes of Tortugas, Florida. Papers Tortugas Laboratory, Vol. 34, 1931, Carnegie Institution of Washington, Washington, D. C., Publication No. 535, 331 pp., 34 plates.

Metzelaar, Jan   1919–S-T
Over Tropisch Atlantische Visschen. Part I, West Indian Fishes, A. H. Kruyt, Amsterdam, Holland, pp. 1-179. (In English.)

Nichols, John T.   1929-1930–S-T
Scientific Survey of Porto Rico and the Virgin Islands. Vol. 10, Part 2, The Fishes of Porto Rico and the Virgin Islands. Branchiostomidae to Sciaenidae, pp. 161-295; Part 3. Pomacentridae to Ogcocephalidae, pp. 299-399.

Parr, Albert E.   1930–S-T
Teleostean Shore and Shallow-water Fishes from the Bahamas and Turk Island (3rd Oceanographic Expedition. "Pawnee" 1927). Bulletin Bingham Oceanographic Collection, New Haven, Connecticut, Vol. 3 (Article 4), 148 pp.

Poey, Felipe   1858–S-T
Poissons de Cuba, Espèces Nouvelles. Memorias sobre la Historia Natural de la Isla de Cuba, . . . Imprenta de la Viuda de Barcina, Havana, Cuba, Vol. 2, pp. 115-441.

                                                  1868–S-T
Synopsis Piscium Cubensium. Repertorio físconatural de la Isla de Cuba, Havana, Cuba, Vol. 2, pp. 279-468.

Randall, John E.   1968–S-T
Caribbean Reef Fishes. T. F. H. Publications, Inc., Jersey City, New Jersey, 318 pp.

Röhl, Eduardo   1942–SF-T
Fauna Descriptiva de Venezuela. Caracas, Venezuela, Peces, pp. 353-413.

Schúltz, L. P.   1949–FS-T
A Further Contribution to the Ichthyology of Venezuela. Proceedings, United States National Museum, Washington, D. C., Vol. 99, No. 3225, pp. 1-211.

Vincent, H.   1910–S-N
The Sea Fish of Trinidad. I. J. Little, Inc., New York, 97 pp.

SOUTH AMERICA—GENERAL

Evermann, B. W. and L. Radcliffe   1917–FS-T
The Fishes of the West Coast of Peru and Titicaca Basin. Bulletin of the United States National Museum, Washington, D. C., No. 95, 157 pp.

Mago, Francisco L.   1970–FS-T
Lista de los Peces de Venezuela, Ministerio de Agricultura y Cria, Oficina Nacional de Pesca, Caracas, Venezuela, 283 pp.

Ribeiro, Alipio de Miranda   1907-1915–FS-T
Fauna Braziliense, Peixes. Arquivios do Museu Nacional, Rio de Janeiro, Brazil, Vols. 14-16 (1907, Vol. 14, No. 1, pp. 25-128; No. 2, pp. 129-212; 1909, iv, 504 pp., 144 figs.; 1915, Vol. 17, No. 5, 600 pp.)

SOUTH AMERICA, EAST COAST—SALTWATER

Fowler, Henry W.   1942–S-T
A List of the Fishes Known from the Coast of Brazil. Arquivios do Zoologia do Estado de São Paulo, Sao Paulo, Brazil, Vol. 3, Article 6, pp. 115-184.

SOUTH AMERICA, WEST COAST—SALTWATER

Fowler, Henry W.   1941-1943–FS-T
Fishes of Chile, Systematic Catalogue. Revista Chilena Historia Natural, Santiago, Chile, No. 45 (1941), No. 46 (1942), No. 47 (1943), 171 pp.

Hildebrand, S. F.   1946–S-T
A Descriptive Catalogue of the Shore Fishes of Peru. Bulletin United States National Museum, Washington, D. C., No. 189, 530 pp.

Mann, Guillermo   1954–S-T
Vida de Los Peces en Aguas Chilenas. Ministerio de Agricultura and Universidad de Chile, Santiago, Chile, 342 pp.

SOUTH AMERICA—FRESHWATER

Eigenmann, Carl H.   1912–F-T
The Freshwater Fishes of British Guiana, Including a Study of the Ecological Grouping of Species and the Relation of the Fauna of the Plateau to that of the Lowlands. Memoir, Carnegie Museum, Pittsburgh, Pennsylvania, Vol. 5, 578 pp.

                                                  1924–F-T
The Fishes of Western South America. Part I, Memoir, Carnegie Museum, Pittsburgh, Pennsylvania, Vol. 9, pp. 1-277.

Eigenmann, Carl H.
  and William Ray Allen   1942–F-T
Fishes of Western South America. University of Kentucky Press, Lexington, Kentucky, 494 pp.

Fowler, H. W.   1948-1954–F-T
Os Peixes des Agua Doce do Brasil. Arquivios do Zoologia do Estado de Sao Paula, Sao Paulo, Brazil, Vol. 6, 204 pp.; Vol. 9, 400 pp.

MacDonagh, E. J.   1938–FS-T
Contribución a la Sistemática y Ecología de las Peces Fluviateles Argentinos. Revista del Museo La Plata, La Plata, Argentina, Vol. 1 (Serie Zoología), pp. 119-208.

Magalhaes, Agenor Couto de   1931–F-T
Monographia Brazileira de Peixes Fluviaes. "Graphicars" Romiti, Lanzara & Zanin, Sao Paulo, Brazil, 262 pp.

Miles, Cecil   1947–F-T
Los Peces del Rió Magdalena. Economia Nacional, Sección Piscicultura, Pesca y Caza, Bogotá, Colombia, 214 pp.

EUROPE—GENERAL

Andersson, K. A.   1942–FS-N
Fiskar och Fiske i Norden. Bokförlaget Natur och Kultur, Stockholm, Sweden, 2 vols., 1016 pp.

Couch, Jonathan   1863-1865–FS-N
A History of the Fishes of the British Islands. Groombridge & Sons, London, 4 vols.

Cunningham, J. T.   1896–FS-T

The Natural History of the Marketable Fishes of the British Islands. The Macmillan Co., New York, 375 pp.

Curry-Lindahl, K.   1957—FS-N
Fiskarna i färg. Almqvist and Wiksell, Stockholm, Sweden, 189 pp.

Day, F.   1880-1884—FS-T
The Fishes of Great Britain and Ireland. Williams & Norgate, Edinburgh, Scotland, 2 vols., text and atlas, 179 pls.

Jenkins, J. Travis   1942—FS-T
The Fishes of the British Isles, Both Freshwater and Salt. Frederick Warne & Co., Ltd., London, New York, 2nd edition, 408 pp.

Lozano y Rey, Luis   1952—FS-T
Peces Fisoclistos. Memorias de la Real Academia de Ciencias Exactas, Físicas y Naturales de Madrid, Madrid, Spain, Vol. 14, 2 pts., 703 pp.

Macan, T.T.   1970—F-T
Biological Studies of the English Lakes. American Elsevier Publishing Co., Inc., New York, 260 pp.

Smitt, F. A.   1892—FS-T
A History of Scandinavian Fishes. P. A. Norstedt & Söner, Stockholm, Sweden, 3 vols., 1240 pp. + atlas.

Yarrell, William   1841—FS-T
A History of British Fishes. John van Voorst, London. Vol. 1, 464 pp.; Vol. 2, 628 pp.

EUROPE—SALTWATER

Bougis, Paul   1959—S-T
Atlas des poissons. Poissons marins. Editions N. Boubée et Cie, Paris, France, Vol. 1, 201 pp., Vol. 2, 234 pp.

Fries, B. F., C. U. Ekstrom, and
   C. J. Sundevall   1893-1895—FS-T
A History of Scandinavian Fishes (with colored plates and text illustrations). 2nd edition revised by F. A. Smitt, 2 parts, Stockholm and London, 1240 pp. Translated by D. L. Morgan.

Joubin, L. and E. Danois   1925—S-T
Catalogue illustré des animaux marins comestibles des côtes de France et des mers limitrophes avec leurs noms communs français et étrangers. Seconde partie, Poissons Cartilagineaux, Mollusques, Crustacés, etc. Mémoirs, Office Scientifique et Technique Pêches Maritimes, Paris, France, Spec. Series 2, 77 pp.

Joubin, L., E. Danois and G. Belloc   1928—S-T
Catalogue illustré des animaux marins comestibles des côtes de France et des mers limitrophes avec leurs noms communs français et étrangers. Mémoirs, Office Scientifique et Technique de Pêches Maritimes, Paris, France, Spec. Series, No. 8, pp. 7-133.

Lozano Rey, Luis   1928—FS-T
Fauna Ibérica. Peces (Generalidades, Ciclostomi y Elasmobranchi). Museum Nacional de Ciencias Naturales, Madrid, Spain, Vol. 1, 692 pp.
                                           1947—FS-T
Peces Ganoideos y Fisostomos. Memorias Academia Ciencias, Madrid, Spain, Vol. 2, 893 pp.

McIntosh, W. C. and A. T. Mastermann   1897—S-T
The Life-histories of the British Marine Food Fishes. C. J. Clay & Co., London, England, 516 pp.

Nobre, Augusto   1935—FS-T
Fauna Marinha de Portugal. Descriçao dos Peixas de Portugal, Lisbon, Portugal, Vol. 1, No. 3, 574 pp.

Poll, Max   1947—S-T
Faune de Belgique. Poissons marins. Musée Royal d'Histoire Naturelle de Belgique, Brussels, Belgium, 452 pp.

Saemundsson, B.   1949—FS-T
The Zoology of Iceland. Marine fishes, Reykjavik, Iceland, Vol. 4, No. 72, 150 pp.

EUROPE—FRESHWATER

Griffini, A.   1903—F-T
Ittiologia Italiana, Descrizione dei Pesci de D'acqua Dolce. Ulrico Hoepli, Milano, Italy, 475 pp.

Grote, W., C. Vogt and B. Hofer   1909—F-T
Die Süsswasserfische von Mittel-Europa. Werner & Winter, Frankfurt, Germany, 558 pp.

Heckel, Johann Jakob and Rudolf Kner   1858—F-T
Die Süsswasserfische der Osterreichischen Monarchie mit Rücksicht auf die Angrenzänder Länder. Leipzig, Germany, 388 pp.

Maxwell, Herbert   1904—F-T
British Fresh-water Fishes. Hutchinson & Co., London, England, 316 pp.

Rasmussen, K., editor   1937—F-T
Report of the Fifth Thule Expedition, Copenhagen. "Fishes" by J. R. Pfaff, Vol. 2, No. 1, pp. 1-19.

Regan, C. Tate   1911—F-T
The Fresh-water Fishes of the British Isles. Methuen & Co., Ltd., London, England, 287 pp.

Seely, H. G.   1886—F-T
The Fresh-water Fishes of Europe. Cassell & Co., Ltd., London, England, 444 pp.

Steinmann, Paul   1948—F-T
Schweizerische Fischkunde. H. R. Sauerländer & Co., Aarau, Switzerland, 222 pp.

MEDITERRANEAN SEA AND BLACK SEA

Conseil Général des Peches
Pour La Méditerranée   1960—S-T
Catalogue des Noms de Poissons ayant une Importance Commerciale en Méditerranée. Food and Agricultural Organization of the United Nations, Rome, Italy, 250 pp.

Palombi, A. and M. Santarelli   1953—S-T
Gli Animali Commestibili dei Mari d'Italia. Ulrico Hoepli, Milano, Italy, 349 pp.

Slastenenko, E. P.   1938—S-T
Catalogue of the Fishes of the Black and of the Azov Seas. Trudy V. M. Arnoldi Biological Station Novorossisk, U.S.S.R., Vol. 2, pp. 109-149.

Soljan, T.   1948—S-T
Fishes of the Adriatic: Fauna and Flora of the Adriatic. Vol. 1. Nakladni Zavod Hrvatske, Za-

greb, Yugoslavia, 437 pp. Translated for the National Science Foundation and available from Office of Technical Services, United States Department of Commerce, Washington, D. C.

Tortonese, Enrico   1956–S-T
Leptocardia, Ciclostomata, Selachii. Fauna Italia, Edizioni Calderini, Bologna, Italy, 334 pp.

AFRICA—GENERAL

Barnard, K. H.   1949–FS-T
A Pictorial Guide to South African Fishes, Marine and Fresh-water. Maskew Miller, Ltd., Cape Town, South Africa, 226 pp.

Boulenger, G. A.   1901–FS-T
Les Poissons du Bassin du Congo. Etat Indépendent du Congo, Brussels, Belgium, 532 pp.

Copley, H.   1952–FS-N
The Game Fishes of Africa. Witherby, London, England, 276 pp.

AFRICA, WEST—SALTWATER

Belloc, Girard   1934–S-T
Catalogue des Poissons Comestibles du Maroc et de la Côte Occidentale d'Afrique. Première Partie. Poissons Cartilagineaux. Revue des Travaux de l'Office des Pêches Maritimes, Paris, France, Vol. 7, No. 2, pp. 117-193.

Cadenat, J.   1950–S-T
Poissons de Mer du Sénégal. Institut Francaise d'Afrique Noire, Initiations Africaines, Dakar, Sénégal, Vol. 3, 345 pp.

Fowler, H. W.   1936–S-T
The Marine Fishes of West Africa. Bulletin of the American Museum of Natural History, New York, Vol. 70, Parts 1 and 2, 1493 pp.

Irvine, Frederick R.   1947–S-T
The Fishes and Fisheries of the Gold Coast. The Crown Agents for the Colonies, London, England, 352 pp.

Pfeffer, Georg   1896–SF-T
Die Fische Ost-Afrikas. In K. Möbius, Deutsch-Ost-Afrika, Berlin, Germany, Vol. 3, Part 5, pp. 1-72.

AFRICA, SOUTH—SALTWATER

Barnard, K. H.   1925-1927–S-T
A Monograph of the Marine Fishes of South Africa. Annals South Africa Museum, Cape Town, South Africa, Vol. 21, pp. 1-1065.

Roux, Charles   1957–S-T
Poissons Marins. Part 1. *In* Collignon, J., M. Rossignol, and Charles Roux, *Mollusques, Crustacés, Poissons Marins de Côtes d'A.E.F. en Collection au Centre d'Océanographie de l'Institut d'Etudes Centrafricaines de Pointe-Noire.* Office de la Recherche Scientifique et Technique Outre-Mer, Paris, France, pp. 137-368.

Smith, J. L. B.   1961–S
The Sea Fishes of Southern Africa. Central News Agency, Ltd., Grahamstown, South Africa, 550 pp.

AFRICA, EAST—SALTWATER

Fowler, H. W.   1956–S-T
Fishes of the Red Sea and Southern Arabia. Vol. 1, Branchiostomida to Polynemida. The Weitzmann Science Press of Israel, Jerusalem, Israel, 240 pp.

Playfair, R. Lambert and
   A. C. L. G. Günther   1866–S-T
The Fishes of Zanzibar. John van Voorst, London, England, 153 pp.

Poisson, Henri   1953–S-T
Contribution à l'Etude des Poissons de Mer de Madagascar. Société Amis Parc Botanique et Zoologique Tananarive, Madagascar, Section d'Océanographie, Part 5, pp. 1-80.

Sauvage, M. H.   1891–SF-T
The Fishes of Madagascar. L'Imprimerie Nationale, Paris, France, 543 pp.

AFRICA—FRESHWATER

Boulenger, G. A.   1907–F-T
Zoology of Egypt. The Fishes of the Nile. 2 vols., B. Quaritch, London, England, 578 pp.

Daget, J.   1954–FS-T
Les Poissons du Niger Supérieur. Mémoir Institut Française d'Afrique Noir, Dakar, Sénégal, No. 36, 391 pp.

Fowler, Henry W.   1936–F-T
Zoological Results of the George Vanderbilt African Expedition, 1934. Part III. The Freshwater Fishes. Proceedings Academy of Natural Sciences, Philadelphia, Pennsylvania, Vol. 88, pp. 243-335.

Gilchrist, J. D. F. and W. W. Thompson   1913–F-T
The Freshwater Fishes of South Africa. Annals South African Museum, Capetown, South Africa, Vol. 11, Part 5, pp. 321-464; Part 6, pp. 465-575.

Nichols, J. T. and Ludlow Griscom   1917–F-T
Fresh-water Fishes of the Congo Basin Obtained by the American Museum Congo Expedition, 1909-1915. Bulletin American Museum of Natural History, New York, Vol. 37, pp. 653-756.

Pellegrin, J.   1923–F-T
Les Poissons des Eaux Douces de l'Afrique Occidentale (du Sénégal au Niger). Générale l'Afrique Occidentale Française, Publication Commission d'Etudes Histoire Scientifique, Paris, France, Vol. 8, 373 pp.

Poll, Max   1957–F-T
Les Genres des Poissons d'Eau Douce de l'Afrique. Royaume de Belgique, Ministers des Colonies, Brussels, Belgium, 191 pp.

INDO-PACIFIC AND INDIAN OCEAN—GENERAL

Fowler, H. W.   1928-1949–S-T
The Fishes of Oceania, Memoirs of the Bernice P. Bishop. Vol. 10 plus 3 supplements, B. P. Bishop Museum, Honolulu, Hawaii.

1944—S-T

Results of the Fifth George Vanderbilt Expedition (1941), the Fishes. Monograph Academy of Natural Sciences, Philadelphia, Pennsylvania, No. 6, 529 pp.

1959—S-T

Fishes of Fiji. Government of Fiji, Suva, 670 pp.

Günther, A. C. L. G.   1877—S-T

Andrew Garrett's Fische der Südsee, . . . J. Museum Godeffroy, Hamburg, Germany, 3 vols.

Herre, A. W. C. T.   1936—S-T

Fishes of the Crane Pacific Expedition. Publication Field Museum of Natural History, Chicago, Illinois, No. 353, Zoological Series, Vol. 21, 427 pp.

Jordan, David S. and Alvin Seale   1905—S-T

The Fishes of Samoa; Description of the Species Found in the Archipelago (with a provisional check list of fishes of Oceania). Bulletin United States Bureau of Fisheries, Washington, D. C., Vol. 25, pp. 173-488.

Munro, Ian S. R.   1958—S-T

The Fishes of the New Guinea Region (a checklist of the fishes of New Guinea incorporating new records of species collected by the Fisheries Survey vessel *Fairwind* during the years 1948 to 1950). The Papua and New Guina Agricultural Journal, Port Moresby, New Guinea, Vol. 10, No. 4, pp. 97-369.

Nichols, John T. and Paul Bartsch   1945—S-N

Fishes and Shells of the Pacific World. The Macmillan Co., New York, 201 pp.

Rofen, R. R.   1963—S-T

Handbook of the Food Fishes of the Gulf of Thailand. Scripps Institute of Oceanography, La Jolla, California, Ref. No. 63-18, 236 pp.

Schultz, L. P.   1943—S-T

Fishes of the Phoenix and Samoan Islands, Collected in 1939 during the Expedition of the U.S.S. Bushnell. Bulletin, United States National Museum, Washington, D. C., No. 180, 316 pp.

Schultz, L. P., and others   1953-1960—S-T

Fishes of the Marshall and Marianas Islands. Bulletin, United States National Museum, Washington, D. C., No. 202, Vols. 1 and 2.

Smith, J. L. B., and
  Margaret Mary Smith   1963—S-T

The Fishes of Seychelles. Rhodes University, Grahamstown, South Africa, 215 pp.

Weber, M., and L. F. de Beaufort   1911-1953—S-T

The Fishes of the Indo-Australian Archipelago. E. J. Brill, Leiden, Holland, 10 vols.

U.S.S.R.—GENERAL

Borisov, P. G., and N. S. Ovsyannikov   1954—FS-T

Identification of the Commerical Fishes of the USSR. Pishchepromizdat, Moscow, U.S.S.R., 260 pp. (In Russian.)

Rass, T. S., and others   1957—FS-N

Fisheries Resources of the U.S.S.R. All-Union Scientific Research Institute for Marine Fisheries

and Oceanography (VNIRO). Many colored plates, Moscow, U.S.S.R. Unpaged.

Svetovidov, A. N.   1948—FS-T

Fishes. Gadiformes [cods], Fauna of the USSR, Vol. 9, No. 4, Zoologicheskii Institut Akademii Nauk S.S.S.R. Moscow, U.S.S.R., New series No. 34, 221 pp. (In Russian.) Also available in English translation from Office of Technical Services, United States Department of Commerce, Washington, D. C.

1952—F-S

Fishes. Clupeidae [herrings]. Fauna of the USSR, Vol. 2, No. 1, Zoologicheskii Institut Akademii Nauk S.S.S.R., Moscow, U.S.S.R., New Series No. 48, 331 pp. (In Russian.)

U.S.S.R. AND ASIA MINOR—SALTWATER

Andriyashev, A. P.   1954—F-T

Fishes of the Northern Seas of the USSR. Determination of the Fauna of the U.S.S.R., Zoologicheskii Institut Akademii Nauk S.S.S.R., Moscow and Leningrad, U.S.S.R., 566 pp. (In Russian.)

Shmidt, P. Iu.   1950—S-T

Fishes of the Okhotsk Sea. Transactions of the Pacific Ocean Committee, No. 6, Printed by the Academy of Sciences of the USSR, Moscow and Leningrad, U.S.S.R., 370 pp. (In Russian.)

Soldatov, V. K., and G. U. Lindberg   1930—S-T

A Review of the Fishes of the Seas of the Far East. Bulletin, Pacific Scientific Fisheries Institute, Vladivostok, U.S.S.R., Vol. 5, pp. 1-567. (In Russian.)

U.S.S.R. AND ASIA MINOR—FRESHWATER

Berg, L. S.   1948—F-T

Freshwater Fishes of the USSR and Adjacent Countries. Printed by the Academy of Sciences of the USSR, Moscow and Leningrad, 3 vols., 1382 pp. (In Russian.) Vol. 1 translated for the National Science Foundation and available through the Office of Technical Services, United States Department of Commerce, Washington, D. C.

Chevey, P., and J. Lemasson   1937—F-T

Contribution à l'Etude de Poissons des Eaux Douces Tonkinoises. Notes Institut Océanographique, Indochine, Saigon, Indochina, Vol. 33, 183 pp.

Heckel, Johann Jakob   1843—F-T

Abbildungen und Beschreibungen der Fische Syriens. Stuttgart, Germany, 258 pp.

Nichols, J. T.   1943—F-T

A Provisional Check-List of the Fresh-Water Fishes of China (Central Asiatic Expedition). Natural History Central Asia, Vol. 9, XXXVI + 322 pp., Publications of the Asiatic Expeditions of the American Museum of Natural History, New York, Contribution No. 83.

Nikol'skii, G. V.   1956—F-T

Fishes of the Amur Basin. Academy of Sciences, Moscow, U.S.S.R., 551 pp. (In Russian.)

Pellegrin, J. 1928—F-T
Les Poissons des Eaux Douces d'Asie-Mineure.
Voyage Zoologique d'Henri Godeau de Kerville en
Asie-Mineure. Paris, France, Vol. 2, pp. 1-131.

INDIA AND SOUTHEAST ASIA—MAINLAND

Blegvad, H. 1944—S-T
Fishes of the Iranian Gulf. Einar Munksgaard,
Copenhagen, Denmark, 247 pp.
Day, Francis 1875-1878—SF-T
The Fishes of India, . . . Bernard Quaritch, Lon-
don, England, 2 Vols., 778 pp. + atlas.
1889—FS-T
Fishes. In W. T. Blanford (editor) *The Fauna of
British India, including Ceylon and Burma,* Lon-
don, England, 2 Vols.
1915—S-T
The Fishes of Malabar. Bernard Quaritch, Lon-
don, England, 293 pp.
Deraniyagala, P. E. P. 1952—S-T
*A Colored Atlas of Some Vertebrates from Cey-
lon.* Vol. 1, Fishes, The Ceylon Government Press,
Colombo, Ceylon, 149 pp.
Lane, W. H. 1917—S-T
The Game Fishes of the Persian Gulf. Journal,
Bombay Natural History Society, Bombay, India,
Vol. 25, pp. 121-135.
Masya, Chitrakarn, Luang and
Chote Suvatti 1951—SF-T
Drawings of Thai-Fishes. Department of Fish-
eries, Bangkok, Thailand, 150 pp.
Maxwell, C. N. 1921—SF-T
Malayan Fishes. Methodist Publishing House,
Singapore, 104 pp. + 72 plates.
Munro, I. S. R. 1955—FS-T
The Marine and Freshwater Fishes of Ceylon.
Australian Department of External Affairs, Can-
berra, Australia, 351 pp.
Scott, J. S. 1959—S-T
An Introduction to the Sea Fishes of Malaya. Gov-
ernment Press, Kuala Lumpur, Malaya, 180 pp.
Shaw, E. E. and E. O. Shelbeare 1937-F-T
The Fishes of Northern Bengal. Journal Royal
Asiatic Society Bengal, Science, Calcutta, India,
Vol. 3, 137 pp.
Smith, H. M. 1945—F-T
The Fresh-water Fishes of Siam, or Thailand. Bul-
letin, United States National Museum, Smithso-
nian Institution, Washington, D. C., No. 188, 622
pp.

AUSTRALIA AND NEW ZEALAND

Graham, D. H. 1932—S-N
A Treasury of New Zealand Fishes. A. H. & A. W.
Reed, Wellington, New Zealand, No. 2, 404 pp.
Ogilby, J. D. 1893—S-T
*Edible Fishes and Crustaceans of New South
Wales.* Charles Potter, Sydney, Australia, 212 pp.
Roughley, T. C. 1951—SF-T

Fish and Fisheries of Australia. 2nd edition, An-
gus & Robertson, Sydney and London, 343 pp.
Stokell, G. 1955—F-T
Fresh-water Fishes of New Zealand. Simpson and
Williams, Christchurch, New Zealand, 145 pp.
Waite, E. R. 1923—S-T
The Fishes of South Australia. Government Print-
er, Adelaide, Australia, 240 pp.
Whitley, G. P. 1940—S-T
The Fishes of Australia. Part I, The Sharks, Rays,
Devil-fish, and Other Primitive Fishes of Australia
and New Zealand. Royal Zoological Society of
New South Wales, Sydney, Australia, 280 pp.

JAPAN

Kamohara, Toshiji 1955—SF-T
Coloured Illustrations of the Fishes of Japan. Hoi-
kusha, Osaka, Japan, 135 pp.
Okada, Yaichiro 1955—SF-T
Fishes of Japan. Maruzen Co., Ltd., Tokyo, Japan,
434 pp. + index.
Tanaka, Chigeho 1912-1914—SF-T
Figures and Descriptions of the Fishes of Japan.
Tokyo, Japan, Nos. 5-15, pp. 71-262.

HAWAII

Gosline, William A., and
Vernon E. Brock 1960—S-T
Handbook of Hawaiian Fishes. University of
Hawaii Press, Honolulu, Hawaii, 372 pp.
Jordan, David S., and
Barton W. Evermann 1905—S-T
The Shore Fishes of the Hawaiian Islands (with a
general account of the fish fauna). Bulletin of the
United States Fish Commission for 1903, Wash-
ington, D. C., Vol. 23, 574 pp.
Tinker, Spencer W. 1944—S-T
*Hawaiian Fishes, a Handbook of the Fishes Found
Among the Islands of the Central Pacific Ocean.*
Tongg Publishing Co., Honolulu, Hawaii, 404 pp.

FISHERIES

Bird, Esteban A. 1956—N
Fishing off Puerto Rico. A. S. Barnes & Co., New
York, 111 pp.
Borgstrom, George, and
Arthur J. Heighway 1961—T
Atlantic Ocean Fisheries. Fishing News (Books),
London, England, 336 pp.
Graham, Michael, editor 1956—T
*Sea Fisheries, Their Investigation in the United
Kingdom.* Edward Arnold, London, England, 487
pp.
Hampton, John F. 1947—T
*Modern Angling Bibliography, Books Published on
Angling, Fisheries, Fish Culture, from 1881 to
1945.* Jenkins, London, England, 99 pp.
Hela, Ilmo and Taivo Laevastu 1961—T
Fisheries Hydrography, How Oceanography and

Meteorology Can and Do Serve Fisheries. Fishing News (Books), London, England, 137 pp.

Rounsefell, George A., and
W. Harry Everhart   1953—T
Fishery Science, Its Methods and Applications. John Wiley & Sons, Inc., New York, 444 pp.

Walford, Lionel A.   1947—N
Fishery Resources of the United States. Public Affairs Press, Washington, D. C., 134 pp.

        1958—N
Living Resources of the Sea, Opportunity for Research and Expansion. Ronald Press, New York, 321 pp.

FRESHWATER BIOLOGY

Carlander, Kenneth D.   1950—T
Handbook of Freshwater Fishery Biology. Wm. C. Brown Co., Dubuque, Iowa, 281 pp.

Clegg, John   1959—T
The Freshwater Life of the British Isles; a Guide to the Plants and Invertebrates of Ponds, Lakes, Streams and Rivers, with an Additional Chapter on the Vertebrates (2nd edition). Frederick Warne & Co., Ltd., London and New York, 352 pp.

Hutchinson, G. Evelyn   1957—T
A Treatise on Limnology. Vol. 1, Geography, Physics and Chemistry. John Wiley & Sons, Inc., New York, 1015 pp.

Lagler, Karl F.   1956—T
Freshwater Fishery Biology. Wm. C. Brown Co., Dubuque, Iowa, 2nd edition, 421 pp.

Muenscher, Walter Conrad   1944—T
Aquatic Plants of the United States. Comstock Publishing Co., Inc., Ithaca, New York, 374 pp.

Needham, James G., and J. T. Lloyd   1937—T
The Life of Inland Waters, an Elementary Textbook of Fresh-water Biology for Students. Comstock Publishing Co., Inc., Ithaca, New York, 3rd edition, 438 pp.

Needham, James G., and
Paul R. Needham   1962—T
A Guide to the Study of Fresh-water Biology. Comstock Publishing Co., Inc., San Francisco, Calif., 5th edition, 88 pp.

Needham, Paul R.   1938—T
Trout Streams, Conditions that Determine Their Productivity and Suggestions for Stream and Lake Management. Comstock Publishing Co. Inc., Ithaca, New York, 233 pp.

Pratt, H. S.   1948—T
A Manual of the Common Invertebrate Animals (exclusive of insects). Blakiston Co., Philadelphia, Pennsylvania, 854 pp.

Smith, Gilbert M.   1950—T
The Fresh-water Algae of the United States. McGraw-Hill Book Co., New York, 2nd edition, 719 pp.

Ward, Henry B., and George C. Whipple   1959—T
Fresh-water Biology. John Wiley & Sons, Inc., New York, 2nd edition, edited by W. T. Edmondson, 1248 pp.

Welch, Paul S.   1948—T
Limnological Methods. Blakiston Co., Philadelphia, Pennsylvania, 381 pp.

        1952—T
Limnology. McGraw-Hill Book Co., New York, 2nd edition, 538 pp.

ZOOGEOGRAPHY—NORTH AMERICA

Antevs, E.   1953—F-T
Geochronology of the Deglacial and Neothermal Ages. Journal of Geology, Vol. 61, pp. 195-230.

Borns, H. W.   1963—F-T
Preliminary Report on the Age and Distribution of the Late Pleistocene Ice in North Central Maine. American Journal of Science, Vol. 261, No. 8, pp. 738-740.

Deevey, E. S.   1949—F-T
Pleistocene Research. Section 3, Biogeography of the Pleistocene, Part I, Europe and North American, *Bulletin,* Geological Society of America, Vol. 60, No. 9, pp. 1315-1416.

Ferrians, O. J., and H. R. Schmoll   1957—F-T
Extensive Preglacial Lake of Wisconsin-Age in the Copper River Basin, Alaska (abstract). *Bulletin,* Geological Society of America, Vol. 68, p. 1726.

Flint, R. F.   1945—F-T
Glacial Map of North America (2 halves). Special Paper 60, Part I. Geological Society of America.

Heusser, C. J.   1956—F-T
Postglacial Environments in the Canadian Rocky Mountains. Ecological Monograph, Vol. 26, pp. 263-302.

        1960—F-T
Late-Pleistocene Environments of North Pacific North America. Special Publication 35, American Geographical Society, 308 pp.

Hopkins, D. M.   1959—F-T
Cenozoic History of the Bering Land Bridge. Science, Vol. 129, No. 3362, pp. 1519-1528.

Hussakof, L.   1916—F-T
Discovery of the Great Lake Trout, Cristivomer namaycush, *in the Pleistocene of Wisconsin. Journal of Geology,* Vol. 24, pp. 685-689.

Karlstrom, T. V.   1961—F-T
Pleistocene Physical and Biological Environments of Pacific South-Central and Southwestern Alaska (abstract). Vol. 2, p. 895, *In* G. O. Raasch (editor), *Geology of the Arctic.* Alberta Society of Petroleum Geologists, International Symposium, No. 1, University of Toronto Press, Toronto, Canada.

Sachs, V. N., and S. A. Streleov   1961—F-T
Mesozoic and Cenozoic of the Soviet Arctic. Vol. 1, pp. 48-67. *In* G. O. Raasch (editor) *Geology of the Arctic,* Alberta Society of Petroleum Geologists, International Symposium No. 1, University of Toronto Press, Toronto, Canada.

Taylor, R. S.   1960—F-T
Some Pleistocene Lakes of Northern Alberta and Adjacent Areas (revised). *Journal,* Alberta Society of Petroleum Geologists, Vol. 8, No. 6, pp. 167-185.

Wilson, J. T., chairman   1958—F-N
Glacial Map of Canada. Geological Association of Canada, Ottawa, Canada.

JOURNALS—ICHTHYOLOGY, FISHERIES, AND RELATED FIELDS

Biological Abstracts. Philadelphia, Pennsylvania. T
Bulletin of the Bingham Oceanographic Collection, Yale University, New Haven, Connecticut. T
Bulletin of Marine Science. University of Miami, Miami, Florida.   T
Bulletin of the Sport Fishing Institute. Bond Building, Washington, D. C.   N
California Fish and Game. Division of Fish and Game of California, Sacramento, California.   T
Journal du Conseil, Conseil Permanent International pour l'Exploration de la Mer, Copenhagen, Denmark.   T
Rapports et Proces-Verbaux. Conseil Permanent International pour l'Exploration de la Mer, Copenhagen, Denmark.   T
Copeia. American Society of Ichthyologists and Herpetologists, Northridge, California.   T
Deep Sea Research. Pergamon Press, London, England.   T
Ecology. The Ecological Society, Durham, North Carolina.   T
Fish Bulletin. Division of Fish and Game of California, Sacramento, California.   T
Fish Survey Reports. Maine Department of Inland Fisheries and Game, Augusta, Maine.   T
Fishery Circulars. United States Fish and Wildlife Service, Washington, D. C.   T
Fishing Gazette. 461 Eighth Avenue, New York, New York.   N
Illinois Natural History Survey Bulletin. Urbana, Illinois.   T
Japanese Journal of Ichthyology. Tokyo, Japan. T
Journal of Marine Research. Yale University, New Haven, Connecticut.   T
Journal of the Fisheries Research Board of Canada. Publications of the Fisheries Research Board of Canada, Ottawa, Canada.   T
The Journal of Wildlife Management. Wildlife Society, Lawrence, Kansas.   T
Limnology and Oceanography. American Society of Limnology and Oceanography, Lawrence, Kansas.   T
Michigan Academy of Science, Arts and Letters.

Ann Arbor, Michigan.   T
New Hampshire Fish and Game Department, The Survey Reports. Concord, New Hampshire.   T
New York Fish and Game Journal. Albany, New York.   T
New York State Conservationist. Albany, New York.   N
Oceanus. Woods Hole Oceanographic Institution, Woods Hole, Massachusetts.   N
Proceedings of the Gulf and Carribbean Fisheries Institute. University of Miami, Miami, Florida. T
Proceedings of the International Game Fish Conference. International Oceanographic Foundation, 1 Rickenbacker Causeway, Miami, Florida.   N
Publications of the Institute of Marine Research. University of Texas, Port Aransas, Texas.   T
Report of the Reelfoot Lake Biological Station. Published by Tennessee Academy of Science, Nashville, Tennessee   T
Scientific American. Scientific American Publishing Co., New York, New York.   N
Sea Frontiers. International Oceanographic Foundation, 1 Rickenbacker Causeway, Miami, Florida.   N
Special Scientific Report: Fisheries. United States Fish and Wildlife Service, Washington, D. C.   T
Stanford Ichthyological Bulletin. Stanford University, Palo Alto, California.   T
The Aquarium. Innes Publishing Co., Philadelphia, Pennsylvania.   N
The Aquarium Journal. Steinhart Aquarium, California Academy of Science, San Francisco, California.   N
The Conservation Volunteer. Minneapolis, Minnesota.   N
The Fish Culturist. Pennsylvania Fish Culturists' Association, Academy of Natural Science, Philadelphia, Pennsylvania.   T
The Progressive Fish Culturist. Government Printing Office, Washington, D. C.   T
Transactions of the American Fisheries Society, Washington, D. C.   T
Transactions of the North American Wildlife Conference. American Wildlife Institute, Washington, D. C.   T
Undersea Technology. Sheffield Publishing Co., Washington, D. C.   T
Zoologica. New York Zoological Society, New York, New York.   T
Zoological Record. Zoological Society of London, London, England.   T

**OCEANOGRAPHY, MARINE BIOLOGY, DIVING AND RE-
LATED FIELDS** A selected list of titles of general interest
may introduce the reader to the general subject of the
science of the sea and its inhabitants. The list is subjec-
tive and necessarily incomplete, and can merely introduce the reader to a very large field, but pertinent
references can be found in most books for the person
who wishes to explore the field further.

The books have been indexed roughly as technical
(T) or nontechnical (N), but there's is no hard and fast
dividing line between the two. Most books in the list are
available directly from the publisher, but most of those
still in print can also be obtained from the International
Oceanographic Foundation (*which see*).

Abbott, R. Tucker   1954–N
American Seashells. Van Nostrand, New York,
New York, 541 pp.

                                                        1955–N
*Introducing Seashells; a Colorful Guide for the
Beginning Collector.* Van Nostrand, New York,
New York, 70 pp.

                                                        1961–N
How to Know the American Marine Shells. New
American Library of World Literature, Inc., New
York, New York, 222 pp.

Abbott, R. Tucker, and Herbert S. Zim   1962–N
*Sea Shells of the World, a Guide to the Better-
known Species.* Golden Press, New York, New
York, 160 pp.

Alexander, Wilfrid   1954–N
Birds of the Ocean, a Handbook for Voyagers.
G. P. Putnam's Sons, New York, New York, 306
pp. Revised edition.

Allan, Joyce   1956–N
Cowry Shells of World Seas. Georgian House,
Melbourne, Australia, 170 pp.

Alpers, Antony   1961–N
Dolphins, the Myth and the Mammal. Houghton
Mifflin, Boston, Massachusetts, 268 pp.

Arnold, Augusta Foote   1901–N
*The Sea-beach at Ebb-tide, a Guide to the Study of
the Seaweeds and the Lower Animal Life Found
Between Tide-marks.* The Century Co., New York,
New York, 490 pp.

Barnes, H.   1959–T
*Oceanography and Marine Biology, a Book of
Techniques.* George Allen & Unwin, Ltd., Lon-
don, England, 218 pp.

Barrett, John H., and C. M. Yonge   1958–N
Collins Pocket Guide to the Sea Shore. William
Collins' Sons, London, England, 272 pp.

Bates, Marston, and D. P. Abbott   1958–N
Coral Island, Portrait of an Atoll. Charles Scribner & Sons, New York, New York, 245 pp.

Beebe, William   1926–N
The Arcturus Adventure. G. P. Putnam's Sons,
New York, New York, 439 pp.

                                                        1928–N
*Beneath Tropic Seas, a Record of Diving Among
the Coral Reefs of Haiti.* G. P. Putnam's Sons,
New York, New York, 234 pp.

                                                        1934–N
Half Mile Down. Harcourt, New York, New York,
334 pp.

Berrill, N. J., and Pacquelyn Berrill   1957–N
The Living Tide. Dodd, Mead & Co., New York,
New York, 256 pp.

Berrill, N. J., and Jacquelyn Berrill   1957–N
1001 Questions Answered About the Seashore.
Dodd, Mead & Co., New York, New York, 305 pp.

Bigelow, H. B.   1931–T
*Oceanography, Its Scope, Problems, and Econom-
ic Importance.* Houghton Mifflin, Boston, Massachusetts, 263 pp.

Bigelow, H. B., and W. T. Edmondson   1947–T
Wind Waves at Sea, Breakers and Surf. United
States Navy Hydrographic Office, Washington,
D. C., Publication No. 602, 177 pp.

Bonde, Cecil von   1956–N
So Great Thy Sea, a Study of the Oceans. A. A.
Balkema, Amsterdam-Capetown, 214 pp.

Boulenger, Edward G.   1936–N
A Natural History of the Seas. D. Appleton-Century Co., New York, New York, 215 pp.

Bowditch, Nathaniel   1958–T
American Practical Navigator. United States Hy-
drographic Office, Washington, D. C., Publication
No. 9, 1524 pp.

Brightwell, Leonard R.   1948–N
Sea-shore Life of Britain. B. T. Batsford, Ltd.,
London, England, 116 pp.

Brindze, Ruth   1945–N
The Gulf Stream. Vanguard, New York, New
York, 63 pp.

                                                        1960–N
All About Underseas Exploration. Random
House, New York, New York, 145 pp.

Bruun, Anton F.   1956–N
The Galathea Deep Sea Expedition, 1950-1952.
The Macmillan Co., New York, New York, 296
pp.

Buchsbaum, Ralph   1950–N
Animals Without Backbones. University of Chicago Press, Chicago, Illinois, 405 pp.

                                                        1954–T
The Life in the Sea. (Condon Lectures.) Oregon
State System of Higher Education, Eugene, Ore-
gon, 101 pp.

Burton, Maurice   1954–N
Margins of the Sea. Frederick Muller, Ltd., London, England, 210 pp.

                                                        1962–N
Under the Sea. Watts, New York, New York, 256
pp.

Buzzati-Traverso, A. A., editor   1956–T
Perspectives in Marine Biology. University of California Press, Berkeley, California, 621 pp.

Carr, Marion Bergner   1959–N
*The Golden Picture Book of Sea and Shore, Tide
Pools, Shells, Small Animals, the Big and Little
Creatures of the Ocean, Tides, Currents, Islands
and Other Wonders of the Sea.* Golden Press, New
York, New York, 57 pp.

Carrington, Richard   1960–N
*A Biography of the Sea, The Story of the World
Ocean, Its Animal and Plant Populations, and Its
Influence on Human History.* Basic Books, New
York, New York, 285 pp.

Carson, Rachel L. 1941—N
Under the Sea-wind, a Naturalist's Picture of Ocean Life, Simon and Schuster, New York, New York, 314 pp.

1951—N
The Sea Around Us. Oxford University Press, New York, New York, 237 pp. Revised edition, 1961.

1955—N
The Edge of the Sea. Houghton Mifflin, Boston, Massachusetts, 276 pp.

1958—N
The Sea Around Us. A special edition for young readers, adapted by Anne Terry White. Simon and Schuster, New York, New York, 165 pp.

1961—N
The Sea Around Us. Oxford University Press, New York, New York, 237 pp.

Catala, René 1964—N
Carnival Under the Sea. R. Sicard, Paris, France, 141 pp.

Challenger Society 1928—N
Science of the Sea, an Elementary Handbook of Practical Oceanography for Travellers, Sailors and Yachtsmen (prepared by the Challenger Society for the promotion of the study of oceanography, originally edited by G. Herbert Fowler). Clarendon Press, Oxford, England, 2nd edition, 502 pp.

Chapin, Henry, and F. G. Walton Smith 1952—N
The Ocean River. Charles Scribner's Sons, New York, New York, 325 pp.

Chapman, Valentine J. 1950—T
Seaweeds and Their Uses. Methuen & Co., Ltd., London, England, 287 pp.

Cheney, Cora, and Ben Partridge 1961—N
Underseas, the Challenger of the Deep Frontier. Coward-McCann, New York, New York, 125 pp.

Ciampi, Elgin 1960—N
Skin Diver. Ronald Press, New York, New York, 315 pp.

Clark, Eugenie 1953—N
Lady with a Spear. Harper and Brothers, New York, New York, 243 pp.

Clark, John R., and Roberta I. Clark, editors 1964—T
Sea-water Systems for Experimental Aquariums (a collection of papers). Circular, United States Fish and Wildlife Service, Washington, D. C., Research Report No. 63, 190 pp.

Clarke, Arthur C. 1960—N
The Challenge of the Sea. Holt, Rinehart and Winston, Inc., New York, New York, 167 pp.

Clarke, William D. 1961—N
The Young Pathfinder's Book of Oceans, Streams, and Glaciers. Hart Publishing Co., New York, New York, 128 pp.

Coker, Robert E. 1962—N
The Great and Wide Sea, an Introduction to Oceanography and Marine Biology. Harper and Brothers, New York, New York, 325 pp.

Colman, John S. 1950—N
The Sea and Its Mysteries. W. W. Norton & Co., Inc., New York, New York, 285 pp.

Constance, Arthur 1958—N

The Impenetrable Sea. Oldbourne, London, England, 279 pp.

Cousteau, Jacques-Yves, and James Dugan 1963—N
The Living Sea. Harper and Brothers, New York, New York, 325 pp.

Cousteau, Jacques-Yves, and Frederic Dumas, assisted by James Dugan 1953—N
The Silent World. Harper and Brothers, New York, New York, 266 pp.

Cowen, Robert C. 1960—N
Frontiers of the Sea, the Story of Oceanographic Exploration. Doubleday & Co., Inc., Garden City, New York, 307 pp.

Cromie, William J. 1962—N
Exploring the Secrets of the Sea. Prentice-Hall, Englewood Cliffs, New Jersey, 300 pp.

Crompton, John 1957—N
The Living Sea. Doubleday & Co., Inc., Garden City, New York, 233 pp.

Daglish, Eric Fitch 1954—N
The Seaside Nature Book. J. M. Dent & Sons, Ltd., London, England, 231 pp.

Dakin, William J., Isobel Bennett, and Elizabeth Pope 1953—T
Australian Seashores. Halstead Press, Sydney, Australia, 372 pp.

Daly, Reginald A. 1942—T
The Floor of the Ocean, New Light on Old Mysteries. University of North Carolina Press, Chapel Hill, North Carolina, 177 pp.

Davis, Charles C. 1955—T
The Marine and Fresh-water Plankton. Michigan State University Press, East Lansing, Michigan, 562 pp.

Dawson, E. Yale 1956—T
How to Know the Seaweeds, an Illustrated Manual for Identifying the More Common Marine Algae of Both Our Atlantic and Pacific Coasts with Numerous Aids for Their Study. William C. Brown Co., Dubuque, Iowa, 197 pp.

Deacon, G. E. R. 1962—N
Seas, Maps, and Men. Doubleday & Co., Inc., Garden City, New York, 297 pp.

Defant, Albert 1960—T
Ebb and Flow, the Tides of Earth, Air and Water. University of Michigan Press, Ann Arbor, Michigan, 121 pp.

1961—T
Physical Oceanography. Pergamon Press, New York, New York, 2 vols.

Dietrich, Günter 1963—T
General Oceanography, an Introduction. Feodor Ostapoff, translator. Interscience Publishers, Division John Wiley & Sons, New York, New York, 588 pp.

Douglas, John S. 1952—N
The Story of the Oceans. Dodd, Mead & Co., New York, New York, 315 pp.

Douglas, T. S. 1946—N
The Wealth of the Sea. John Gifford, Ltd., London, England, 144 pp.

Doukan, Gilbert 1957—N
The World Beneath the Waves. John DeGraff,

Inc., New York, New York, 356 pp. Translated by A. and R. M. Case.

Dugan, James   1963–N
Man Under the Sea. Collier Books, New York, New York, 332 pp.

Edmondson, Charles H.   1949–N
Seashore Treasures. Pacific Books, Palo Alto, California, 144 pp.

Ekman, Sven   1953–T
Zoogeography of the Sea. Sidgwick & Jackson, Ltd., London, England, 417 pp. Translated by E. Palmer.

Engel, Leonard   1961–N
The Sea. Life Nature Library, Time, Inc., New York, New York, 190 pp.

Fisher, James   1957–N
The Wonderful World of the Sea. Garden City Books, Garden City, New York, 68 pp.

Flattely, Frederick W., and C. L. Walton   1947–T
· *The Biology of the Sea-shore.* The Macmillan Co., New York, New York, 336 pp.

Fraser, James   1962–N
Nature Adrift, the Story of Marine Plankton. Dufour Editions, Chester Springs, Pennsylvania, 178 pp.

Galtsoff, Paul S., editor   1954–T
Gulf of Mexico, Its Origin, Waters, and Marine Life. United States Fish and Wildlife Service, Fishery Bulletin No. 89, 604 pp.

Gillett, Keith and Frank McNeill   1962–N
The Great Barrier Reef and Adjacent Isles. Coral Press, Sydney, Australia, 194 pp. revised edition.

Graham, Michael, editor   1956–T
Sea Fisheries, Their Investigation in the United Kingdom. Edward Arnold & Co., London, England, 487 pp.

Green, James   1961–T
A Biology of Crustacea. Quadrangle Books, Inc., Chicago, Illinois, 180 pp.

Guilcher, André   1958–T
Coastal and Submarine Morphology. John Wiley and Sons, Inc., New York, New York, 274 pp.

Günther, Klaus, and Kurt Deckert   1956–N
Creatures of the Deep Sea. Charles Scribner's Sons, New York, New York, 222 pp. Translated by E. W. Dickes.

Hahn, Jan   1961–N
A Reader's Guide to Oceanography. Woods Hole Oceanographic Institution. Woods Hole, Massachusetts, 10 pp.

     1954–N
1001 Question Answered about the Oceans. Dodd, Mead & Co., New York, New York.

Halstead, Bruce W.   1959–T
Dangerous Marine Animals. Cornell Maritime Press, Cambridge, Maryland, 146 pp.

Halstead, Bruce W., and
Courville, Donovan A.   1965, 1967–T
Poisonous and Venomous Marine Animals of the World. Volume One–Invertebrates, 994 pp.; Volume Two–Vertebrates, 1070 pp.; Volume Three –in preparation; U. S. Government Printing Office, Washington, D. C.

Hardy, Alister C.   1957–N
The Open Sea, Its Natural History. Part 1, The World of Plankton. Houghton Mifflin, Boston, Massachusetts, 335 pp.

     1959–N
The Open Sea, Its Natural History. Part 2, Fish and Fisheries (with chapters on whales, turtles, and animals of the sea floor). Houghton Mifflin, Boston, Massachusetts, 322 pp.

Harvey, H. W.   1955–T
Chemistry and Fertility of Sea-water. Cambridge University Press, New York, New York, 244 pp.

Hatfield, H. Stafford   1951–N
The Sea and Its Living Things. Evans Brothers, Ltd., London, England, 149 pp.

Hedgpeth, Joel W., and
Harry S. Ladd, editors   1957–T
Treatise on Marine Ecology and Paleontology. Vol. 1, Geological Society of America, Memoir No. 67, 1296 pp.

Herdman, Sir William A.   1923–N
Founders of Oceanography and Their Work, an Introduction to the Science of the Sea. Edward Arnold, London, England, 340 pp.

Heyerdahl, Thor   1950–N
Kon-Tiki, Rand McNally, Chicago, Illinois, 304 pp.

Hill, M. N., and others   1962–T
The Sea, Ideas and Observations. Vol. 1, Physical Oceanography. John Wiley and Sons, New York, New York, 664 pp.

Huxley, Anthony   1962–N
Standard Encyclopedia of the World's Oceans and Islands. G. P. Putnam's Sons, New York, New York, 383 pp.

Idyll, C. P.   1964–N
Abyss, the Deep Sea and the Creatures that Live in It. T. Y. Crowell, New York, New York, 396 pp.

International Oceanographic Foundation   1964–N
Training and Careers in Marine Science. Parker, Coral Gables, Florida, 13 pp.

Jägersten, Gösta, and Lennart Nilsson   1964–N
Life in the Sea. Basic Books, New York, New York, 184 pp.

Jenkins, J. T.   1921–N
A History of the Whale Fisheries, from the Basque Fisheries of the Tenth Century to the Hunting of the Finner Whale at the Present Date. H. F. & G. Witherby, London, England, 336 pp.

Johnson, Myrtle E., and Harry J. Snook   1927–N
Seashore Animals of the Pacific Coast. The Macmillan Co., New York, New York, 657 pp.

Johnstone, James   1928–T
An Introduction to Oceanography, with Special Reference to Geography and Geophysics. University Press, Liverpool, England, 2nd Edition, 368 pp.

Johnstone, James, Andrew Scott, and
Herbert C. Chadwick   1934–T
The Marine Plankton, with Special Reference to Investigations Made at Port Erin, Isle of Man, during 1907-1914, A Handbook for Students and Am-

ateur Workers. University Press, Liverpool, England, 194 pp.

Keep, Josiah   1935–N
West Coast Shells, a Description in Familiar Terms of the Principal Marine, Fresh-water, and Land Mollusks of the United States, British Columbia, and Alaska, Found West of the Sierra. Stanford University Press, Stanford, California, Revised by J. L. Baily, Jr., 350 pp.

Kellogg, Winthrop N.   1961–N
Porpoises and Sonar. University of Chicago Press, Chicago, Illinois, 177 pp.

King, Cuchlaine A. M.   1963–T
Ocean Geography for Oceanographers. St. Martin's Press, New York, New York, 336 pp.

Klingel, Gilbert C.   1961–N
The Ocean Island (Inagua). Doubleday-Anchor, Garden City, New York, 415 pp.

Kuenen, Ph. H.   1950–T
Marine Geology. John Wiley and Sons, Inc., New York, New York, 568 pp.

                                                1955–T
Realms of Water, Some Aspects of Its Cycle in Nature. John Wiley and Sons, Inc., New York, New York, 327 pp.

Kunz, George F., and Charles H. Stevenson   1908–N
The Book of the Pearl. Century, New York, New York, 548 pp.

Lane, Ferdinand C.   1947–N
The Mysterious Sea. Doubleday & Co., Inc., Garden City, New York, 345 pp.

                                                1953–N
All About the Sea. Random House, New York, New York, 148 pp.

Lane, Frank W.   1962–N
Kingdom of the Octopus, the Life History of the Cephalopoda. Pyramid Publishing, New York, New York, 287 pp.

Latil, Pierre de   1955–N
The Underwater Naturalist. Houghton Mifflin, Boston, Massachusetts, 275 pp. Translated by E. Fitzgerald.

Latil, Pierre de, and Jean Rivoire   1956–N
Man and the Underwater World. G. P. Putnam's Sons, New York, New York, 400 pp. Translated by E. Fitzgerald.

Levring, Tore, Heinz A. Hoppe, and
  Otto J. Schmid   1969–S-T
Marine Algae: A Survey of Research and Utilization. Cram, De Gruyter & Co., Hamburg, Germany, 421 pp.

Lilly, John C.   1961–N
Man and Dolphin. Doubleday & Co., Inc., Garden City, New York, 312 pp.

Llano, George A., and
  I. Eugene Wallen, editors   1971–S-T
Biology of the Antarctic Seas IV. American Geophysical Union, Washington, D.C., 362 pp.

MacGinitie, George E., and
  Nettie MacGinitie   1949-T
Natural History of Marine Animals. McGraw-Hill Book Co., Inc., New York, New York, 473 pp.

Malkus, Alida   1956–N

The Sea and Its Rivers. Doubleday & Co., Inc., Garden City, New York, 221 pp.

Marmer, Harry A.   1926–T
The Tide. D. Appleton & Co., New York, New York, 282 pp.

                                                1930–T
The Sea. D. Appleton & Co., New York, New York, 312 pp.

Marshall, N. B.   1954–T
Aspects of Deep Sea Biology. Hutchinson's Scientific & Technical Publications, London, England, and Philosophical Library, New York, New York, 380 pp.

Miner, Roy Waldo   1950–T
Field Book of Seashore Life. G. P. Putnam's Sons, New York, New York, 888 pp.

Moore, Hilary B.   1958–T
Marine Ecology. John Wiley & Sons, Inc., New York, New York, 493 pp.

Morgan, Elizabeth   1962–N
In the Deep Blue Sea. Prentice-Hall, Englewood Cliffs, New Jersey, 72 pp.

Morris, Percy A.   1951–N
A Field Guide to the Shells of our Atlantic and Gulf Coasts. (Revised Edition) Houghton Mifflin, Boston, Massachusetts, 236 pp.

                                                1952–N
A Field Guide to the Shells of the Pacific Coast and Hawaii. Houghton Mifflin, Boston, Massachusetts, 220 pp.

Murray, Sir John, and Johan Hjort   1912–T
The Depths of the Ocean, a General Account of the Modern Science of Oceanography Based Largely on the Scientific Researches of the Norwegian Steamer Michael Sars *in the North Atlantic.* Macmillan Co., Ltd., London, England, 821 pp.

Nicol, J. A. C.   1960–T
The Biology of Marine Animals. Interscience, New York, New York, 707 pp.

Odum, Eugene P., and Howard T. Odum   1959–T
Fundamentals of Ecology. W. B. Saunders Co., Philadelphia, Pennsylvania, 546 pp.

Oldroyd, Ida S.   1927–T
The Marine Shells of the West Coast of North America. Stanford University Press, Stanford, California, 297 pp.

Ommanney, Francis D.   1949–N
The Ocean. Oxford University Press, New York, New York, 245 pp.

Pérès, Jean Marie   1961–T
Océanographie Biologique et Biologie Marine. Vol. 1. La Vie Benthique. Presses Universitares de France, Paris, France, 538 pp.

Pérès, Jean Marie, and L. Devèze   1963–T
Océanographie Biologique et Biologie Marine. Vol. 2. La Vie pélagique. Presses Universitares de France, Paris, France, 514 pp.

Perry, Louise M., and
  Jeanne S. Schwengel   1955–T
Marine Shells of the Western Coast of Florida. Paleontological Research Institution, Ithaca, New York, 318 pp.

Petersson, Hans   1953—N
Westward Ho with the Albatross. Dutton, New York, New York, 218 pp.

       1954—T
The Ocean Floor. Yale University Press, New Haven, Connecticut, 181 pp.

Piccard, Jacques, and Richard S. Dietz   1961—N
Seven Miles Down, the Story of the Bathyscaph Trieste, C. P. Putnam's Sons, New York, New York, 256 pp.

Pincus, Howard J.   1960—N
Secrets of the Sea, Oceanography for Young Scientists. American Educational Publishers, Columbus, Ohio, 31 pp.

Potter, John S.   1960—N
The Treasure Diver's Guide. Doubleday & Co., Inc., Garden City, New York, 501 pp.

Pough, Richard   1952—N
Audubon Water Bird Guide. Doubleday & Co., Inc., Garden City, New York, 352 pp.

Pratt, H. S.   1948—T
A Manual of the Common Invertebrate Animals (exclusive of insects). Blakiston Co., Philadelphia, Pennsylvania, 854 pp.

Quilici, Folco   1954—N
The Blue Continent. Rinehart & Co., New York, New York, 246 pp.

Ray, Carleton, and Elgin Ciampi   1956—N
The Underwater Guide to Marine Life. A. S. Barnes & Co., New York, New York, 338 pp.

Raymont, John E. G.   1963—T
Plankton and Productivity in the Oceans. The Macmillan Co., New York, New York, 660 pp.

Rebikoff, Dimitri, and Paul Cherney   1955—T
A Guide to Underwater Photography. Greenberg, New York, New York, 2nd Edition, 113 pp.

Redfield, Alfred C.   1960—T
Education and Recruitment of Oceanographers in the United States, a Report by the Committee on Education and Recruitment. The American Society of Limnology & Oceanography, Inc.; Supp. Limnology & Oceanography, Ann Arbor, Michigan, 23 pp.

Reid, George K.   1961—T
Ecology of Inland Waters and Estuaries. Reinhold Publishing Co., New York, New York, 375 pp.

Richards, Horace G.   1938—N
Animals of the Seashore. Bruce Humphries, Inc., Boston, Massachusetts, 273 pp.

Ricketts, Edward F., and Jack Calvin   1952—T
Between Pacific Tides. Stanford University Press, Stanford, California, 3rd Edition, Revised by J. W. Hedgpeth, 502 pp.

Roberts, Fred M.   1960—T
Basic Scuba, Self-contained Underwater Breathing Apparatus. Van Nostrand, Princeton, New Jersey, 386 pp.

Rogers, Julia E.   1951—N
The Shell Book, a Popular Guide to Knowledge of the Families of Living Mollusks and an Aid to the Identification of Shells Native and Foreign. C. T. Branford, Boston, Massachusetts, Revised Edition, 503 pp.

Roughley, T. C.   1952—N
Wonders of the Great Barrier Reef. Angus & Robertson, London, England, 279 pp.

Russell, F. S., and C. M. Yonge   1936—T
The Seas, Our Knowledge of Life in the Sea and How It is Gained. Frederick Warne & Co., Ltd., New York, New York, 2nd Edition, 379 pp.

Russell, R. C. H., and D. H. Macmillan   1953—T
Waves and Tides. Philosophical Library, New York, New York, 348 pp.

Scheffer, Victor B.   1958—T
Seals, Sea Lions and Walruses, & Review of the Pinnipedia. Stanford University Press, Stanford, California, 179 pp.

Schenck, H. Van N., and H. W. Kendall   1957—T
Underwater Photography. Cornell Maritime Press, Cambridge, Maryland, 126 pp.

Sears, Mary, editor   1961—T
Oceanography (invited lectures presented at the International Oceanographic Congress). American Association for the Advancement of Science, Washington, D. C., No. 67, 645 pp.

Shepard, Francis P.   1948—T
Submarine Geology. Harper and Brothers, New York, New York, 348 pp.

       1959—N
The Earth Beneath the Sea. Johns Hopkins Press, Baltimore, Maryland, 275 pp.

Sindermann, Carl J.   1970—S-T
Principal Diseases of Marine Fish and Shellfish. Academic Press, Inc., New York, New York, 369 pp.

Slijper, E. J.   1962—N
Whales. Basic Books, New York, New York, 475 pp.

Smith, B. Webster   1940—N
The World Under the Sea, a Concise Account of the Marine World. D. Appleton-Century Co., New York, New York, 230 pp.

Smith, F. G. Walton   1948—N
Atlantic Reef Corals, a Handbook of the Common Reef and Shallow-water Corals of Bermuda, Florida, the West Indies and Brazil. Farrar, Strauss, New York, New York, 112 pp.

Smith, F. G. Walton, and Henry Chapin   1954—N
The Sun, the Sea, and Tomorrow, Potential Sources of Food, Energy and Minerals from the Sea. Charles Scribner's Sons, New York, New York, 210 pp.

Smith, Gilbert M.   1944—T
Marine Algae of the Monterey Peninsula, California. Stanford University Press, Stanford, California, 622 pp.

       1951—T
Manual of Phycology, an Introduction to the Algae and Their Biology. Chronica Botanica Co., Waltham, Massachusetts, 375 pp.

Smith, Maxwell   1940—N
World-wide Sea Shells. Tropical Photographic Laboratory, Lantana, Florida, 139 pp.

Spilhaus, Athelstan F.   1959—N
Turn to the Sea. National Academy of Science-

National Research Council, Washington, D. C., 44 pp.

Stambler, Irwin 1962—N
The Wonders of Underwater Exploration. G. P. Putnam's Sons, New York, New York, 128 pp.

Step, Edward 1954—N
Shell Life, an Introduction to the British Mollusca. Frederick Warne & Co., Ltd., London, England, 2nd Edition, Revised by A. L. Wells, 443 pp.

Stephens, William M. 1962—N
Our World Underwater. Lantern Press, New York, New York, 254 pp.

Stephenson, E. M. 1951—N
The Naturalist on the Seashore. Adam and Charles Black, Ltd., London, England, 96 pp.

Stewart, Harris B., Jr. 1963—N
The Global Sea. Van Nostrand, Princeton, New Jersey, 128 pp.

Stewart, John Q. 1945—T
Coasts, Waves and Weather for Navigators. Ginn & Co., Boston and New York, 348 pp.

Stommel, Henry 1945—T
Science of the Seven Seas. Cornell Maritime Press, New York, New York, 208 pp.

1958—T
The Gulf Stream, a Physical and Dynamical Description. University of California Press, Berkeley, California, 202 pp.

Street, Philip 1953—N
Between the Tides. Philosophical Library, New York, New York, 175 pp.

Sverdrup, H. U., Martin W. Johnson, and
Richard H. Fleming 1949—T
The Oceans, Their Physics, Chemistry, and General Biology. Prentice-Hall, Englewood Cliffs, New Jersey, 1087 pp.

Taylor, William R. 1957—T
Marine Algae of the Northeastern Coast of North America. University of Michigan Studies, Scientific Series 12, Ann Arbor, Michigan, 2nd Revised Edition, 509 pp.

Thomas, Sir Charles W. 1873—N
The Depths of the Sea. Macmillan & Co., London, England, 527 pp.

Tiffany, Lewis H. 1958—N
Algae, the Grass of Many Waters (2nd edition). Charles C. Thomas, Springfield, Illinois, 216 pp.

Tinker, Spencer W. 1952—N
Pacific Sea Shells, a Handbook of Common Marine Mollusks of Hawaii and the South Seas. Mercantile Printing Co., Honolulu, Hawaii, 323 + (7) pp.

Troebst, Cord-Christian 1962—N
Conquest of the Sea. Harper and Brothers, New York, New York, 269 pp.

United States Department of the Navy 1961—N
Your Future in Oceanography, with the United States Navy Hydrographic Office and other Federal Establishments (Revised edition). United States Civil Service Commission, Washington, D. C., 22 pp.

1963—T
Diving Manual. Government Printing Office, Washington, D. C., 456 pp.

United States Interagency Committee
on Oceanography 1962—T
University Curricula in Oceanography, Academic Year 1962-63. ICO pamphlet No. 6, Washington, D. C., 111 pp.

Verrill, A. Hyatt 1936—N
Strange Sea Shells and Their Stories. L. C. Page & Co., Boston, Massachusetts, 206 pp.

1950—N
Shell Collector's Handbook. G. P. Putnam's Sons, New York, New York, 228 pp.

1955—N
Strange Creatures of the Sea. Grossett & Dunlap, New York, New York, 233 pp.

Vevers, H. G. 1954—N
The British Seashore. Routledge & Kegan Paul, Ltd., London, England, 160 pp.

Walford, Lionel A. 1958—N
Living Resources of the Sea, Opportunities for Research and Expansion. Ronald Press, New York, New York, 321 pp. + maps.

Webb, Walter F. 1942—N
United States Mollusca, a Descriptive Manual of Many of the Marine, Land and Fresh Water Shells of North America, North of Mexico. Walter Freeman Webb, Rochester, New York, 220 pp.

1948—N
Handbook for Shell Collectors (8th edition). Walter Freeman Webb, St. Petersburg, Florida, 236 pp.

Williams, Jerome 1962—T
Oceanography, an Introduction to the Marine Sciences. Little, Brown Co., Boston, Massachusetts, 242 pp.

Wilson, Douglas P. 1951—N
Life of the Shore and Shallow Sea (2nd edition). Nicholson & Watson, London, England, 213 pp.

Wimpenny, R. S. 1966—S-T
The Plankton of the Sea. American Elsevier Publishing Co., Inc., New York, New York, 426 pp.

Yonge, C. M. 1930—N
A Year on the Great Barrier Reef, the Story of Corals and of the Greatest of Their Creations. G. P. Putnam's Sons, New York, New York, 246 pp.

1949—N
The Sea Shore. William Collins' Sons, London, England, 311 pp.

Zenkevitch, L. 1963—T
Biology of the Seas of the U.S.S.R. Interscience Publishers, New York, New York, 955 pp. Volume translated from the original Russian language text by S. Botcharskaya.

Zim, Herbert S., and Lester Ingle 1955—N
Seashores, a Guide to Animals and Plants Along the Beaches. Simon and Schuster, New York, New York, 160 pp.

—D.d.S.